MACMILLAN
COMPENDIUM

EVERYDAY LIFE: AMERICAN SOCIAL HISTORY

MACMILLAN
COMPENDIUM

EVERYDAY LIFE:
AMERICAN SOCIAL HISTORY

SELECTIONS FROM THE
THREE-VOLUME
Encyclopedia of American Social History

MACMILLAN LIBRARY REFERENCE USA

Simon & Schuster Macmillan
New York

Prentice Hall International
London Mexico City New Delhi Singapore Sydney Toronto

Cover Image: *July 4th—The Family Portrait,* by John Falter © The Curtis Publishing Company/Christie's Images.
Photo credits can be found on p. 1011.

Designed by Kevin Hanek

Macmillan Library Reference USA
Simon & Schuster Macmillan
1633 Broadway, 5th Floor
New York, NY 10019

Manufactured in the United States of America.

printing number
1 2 3 4 5 6 7 8 9 10

Library of Congress Cataloging-in-Publication Data

Everyday life : American social history.
p. cm. — (Macmillan compendium)
"Selections from the three-volume Encyclopedia of American social history."
Includes bibliographical references and index.
ISBN 0-02-864976-1 (alk. paper)
1. United States—Social conditions—Encyclopedias. 2. United States—Social life and customs—Encyclopedias. 3. Social history—Encyclopedias. I. Encyclopedia of American social history. Selections. II. Series.
HN57.E93 1998
306′.0973—dc21 98-35920
CIP

This paper meets the requirements of ANSI/NISO Z39.48-1992 (Permanence of Paper).

Everyday Life

Table of Contents

S

T

U

V

W

Everyday Life

Synoptic Table of Contents

Preface

ORIGINS

Social history has been variously defined as: "history from the bottom up"; the history of everyday life; or the history of groups and the power relationships between them. History from the bottom up immediately brings to mind images of the working class, black slaves, and the poor. The history of everyday life chronicles change over time in the fabric of ordinary existence—sometimes minute and subtle, occasionally rapid and momentous. Social historians explore the relationships between diverse groups, but they also examine how people develop the cultures and ideologies that bind them together or set them at odds (from the Preface to the *Encyclopedia of American Social History*, 1993).

Those curious about American social history have learned to rely on the distinguished three-volume *Encyclopedia of American Social History* published by Charles Scribner's Sons Reference. Since its publication in 1993, library patrons, historians, and students have expressed an interest in a single-volume version of this prestigious work, especially one that focuses on the ways in which groups of Americans lead their lives. The *Compendium of Everyday Life: American Social History* is designed to fulfill that need.

Grand in scope, *The Compendium of Everyday Life* is organized in an A-to-Z format. Fascinating articles explore physical space (farms, small towns, cities, and suburbs) and their impact on social life and structure; patterns of everyday life, centering on topics such as food, clothing, and housing; the impact of science and technology on American life; as well as the influence of work and labor. Work then yields to leisure, with essays on recreation and popular culture. Other articles consider aspects of social life according to the phases of the life cycle, with a stress on age and gender.

In preparing this one-volume version of the *Encyclopedia of American Social History*, it was agreed that articles would be excerpted in their entirety and presented in a manner we hope readers will consult first. Blind entries, appearing throughout the work, and cross references at the end of each article will assist readers as they explore the compendium. A comprehensive index will provide further assistance.

FEATURES

To add visual appeal and enhance the usefulness of the volume, the page format was designed to include the following helpful features.

- Call-out Quotations: These relevant, provocative quotations are highlighted to promote exploration and add visual appeal to the page.
- Cross References: Appearing at the end of each article, cross references will encourage further research.
- Photographs: Chosen to complement the text, the photo program is designed to further engage the reader.
- Index: A thorough index provides thousands of additional points of entry into the work.
- Alternate Tables of Contents: Two tables of contents are provided at the beginning of the compendium. An alphabetical list corresponds directly to the order of presentation in the work while a synoptic table of contents presents articles thematically as they are organized in the parent set.

ACKNOWLEDGMENTS

The *Compendium of Everyday Life* contains over one hundred illustrations. Acknowledgments of sources for illustrations can be found on page 1011.

The articles herein were written for the *Encyclopedia of American Social History* (the parent set of this volume) by leading authorities at work in the field of social history. Mary Kupeac Cayton, Elliott J. Gorn, and Peter W. Williams of the Department of American Studies at Miami University (Oxford, Ohio) served as Co-Editors for the original set.

This book would not have been possible without the hard work and creativity of our staff. We offer our deepest thanks to all who helped create this marvelous work.

Macmillan Library Reference

A

ADOLESCENCE

Historical inquiry into American adolescence has been marked by a lively debate, kindled in the 1970s when several scholars took the position that adolescence did not exist, as a formal concept or stage of life, prior to the twentieth century. According to John and Virginia Demos and Joseph Kett, the terms "adolescence" and "adolescent" were rarely used before the 1890s. These words entered the popular lexicon only as Americans acknowledged the peculiar difficulties of coming of age in an urban industrial society: unlike colonial or early-nineteenth-century youths, "adolescents" lived in a world of rapidly changing ideals and expectations. Twentieth-century America measured the success of adults by their ability to perform in complex technological and bureaucratic settings; thus, "adolescents" endured prolonged dependency as they prepared for adulthood in extrafamilial educational institutions. "Adolescents" clashed with their elders, evincing such acute "storm and stress" that the older generation turned to experts in psychology, sexology, and medicine to explain the character and course of adolescent development. Finally, "adolescents" created their own subcultures, interacting with consumer industries that alternately invented and catered to their desires and spending habits.

Certainly, the experience of young people in colonial or antebellum America could not have mirrored that of modern adolescents. Nonetheless, the singular characteristics of twentieth-century adolescence should not prevent our recognizing the similarities between young people approaching adulthood in this century and those doing so in earlier times. Though they called this stage "youth" rather than "adolescence," Americans in the seventeenth, eighteenth, and nineteenth centuries acknowledged that young people in their teens and twenties were no longer children in mind, body, or capability. Parents demanded that their maturing offspring prepare deliberately for adulthood yet denied them full independence. Young people communicated the difficulties of growing up through antisocial conduct, indecision, and crises of identity. In turn, youths' struggles and rebellion provoked adults to devise a wide variety of coping strategies.

Adolescence has been a transitional and problematic stage of life in America throughout the past four centuries. Over time, adolescence has changed in response to transformations in the family, economy, and culture. Gender, race, region, ethnicity, and class have shaped the lives of adolescents, ruling out a single or inclusive definition of adolescence that holds for any particular time period.

The Colonial Period

Divergent patterns of development in New England and the Chesapeake created wide regional disparities in the experiences of seventeenth-century adolescents. The Puritans sailed from their homeland in family groups, hoping to create godly communities in the wilderness. Settling on the North Atlantic coast, they established productive agricultural villages and a patriarchal family system in which fathers directed the spiritual and worldly activities of wives, children, and servants. Puritans prized paternal guidance and filial obedience, yet perhaps because of their intense religiosity and strict behavioral expectations, they also knew the meaning of youthful uncertainty, crisis, and rebellion.

Although Puritan society was not rigidly age-graded, seventeenth-century New Englanders recognized the years from puberty to the twenties as a stage of earnest training for adult roles and of religious conversion. Young men and women were still dependents, required by law and custom to follow the dictates of their elders and excluded from marriage and from the economic and political roles appropriate to adults of their sex and social rank. Nonetheless, occupational choice and generational conflict were not entirely absent from their lives.

Most Puritan parents placed their offspring in the homes of other families during adolescence, hoping both to provide youths with necessary training and to undercut rebellious tendencies. Puritan girls were "placed out" as household servants in their early teens; they could not choose their future occupation and learned to become housewives like their mothers. Boys also were placed out to learn a trade or attend school, but for them occupational choice was an important step toward manhood. The Puritans believed that young men must choose a "calling," using their talents to serve God and society. Although fathers guided sons in discerning a calling, some boys were apprenticed to masters in several different trades before settling down.

If seventeenth-century fathers and sons sometimes worked together to overcome the quandaries of adolescence, in other instances Puritan youths actively questioned or repudiated the expectations of their elders. Unable to suppress their intense feelings of lust and willfulness as Puritan doctrine demanded, many young men and women experienced years of religious doubt, punctuated by periods of "exquisite anguish and inner torment," before surrendering unconditionally to God (Phillip Greven, *Protestant Temperament*, p. 95). Others attained adulthood without seeking conversion or church membership, prompting New England's religious leaders to devise the halfway covenant, establish church-sponsored young men's societies, and issue innumerable jeremiads denouncing youths' waning piety. The halfway covenant permitted adults who had never experienced "saving faith" to have their offspring baptized if they themselves had been baptized as children; however, "halfway" members of the church were denied communion and voting privileges.

Adolescent rebellion was social as well as religious, collective as well as individual. Roger Thompson's work on seventeenth-century Middlesex County, Massachusetts, shows that adolescents violated community norms through vandalism, drinking, theft, and premarital sexual experimentation. The participants were male and female; they were the sons and daughters of both elite and lower-class parents; and they were residents of college towns and farming villages. Although the youths were not highly organized, Thompson believes their activity shows that the "beginnings of . . . a distinct [youth] culture" may be traced "back to the middle of the seventeenth century" ("Adolescent Culture in Colonial Massachusetts," p. 141).

Although marriage marked Puritan youths' entry into adulthood, courting couples were frequently reminded of their abiding dependence on the patriarchal family. Males could not marry before inheriting land from their fathers, thus obtaining the means to establish an independent household. Most men married in their mid or late twenties; their wives were typically a few years younger. Financial negotiations between the parents of young couples were central to Puritan marital arrangements, and courtship took place for the most part in public, under the watchful eye of the community. Still, New Englanders did permit young couples to engage in "bundling"—sleeping together while heavily clothed and separated by a wooden board. This traditional English custom gave young adults an opportunity to test their affection in a controlled setting; it was especially important to young women, who otherwise were passive in courtship.

In contrast with New England, where adolescence was shaped by the weighty presence of church and family, young people in the early Chesapeake came of age in a society notable for the light hold of these two institutions. Virginia and Maryland were more commercial than religious ventures, and most of the Chesapeake's initial migrants were unmarried Englishmen in their teens and twenties who came as indentured laborers to cultivate tobacco. They arrived without family ties and found it difficult to form them, encountering few female settlers. Moreover, disease ravaged the early Chesapeake, forcing it to depend on further immigration for population growth. The region's unbalanced sex ratio and high mortality rates undermined reproductive increase and family stability, preventing patriarchal authority from taking root until the eighteenth century.

Whether male or female, the status of young migrants in the early Chesapeake was uncertain, marginal, and paradoxical: they were not adults, but neither were they protected adolescents. The colonies' unmarried male laborers were free of parental intervention but deprived of parental aid. They looked after themselves, yet long terms of indenture and an unequal sex ratio prevented them from marrying and attaining independent status until their late twenties or thirties.

Young female migrants looked forward to a wide choice of marriage partners and an advantageous union. Because family and church were weak, females were able to engage in premarital sex without loss of reputation: more than one-third of the Chesapeake's immigrant women were pregnant at the time they wed. But, outnumbered by men and living as servants on plantations scattered about the countryside, young women were extremely vulnerable to rape. Moreover, the birth of an illegitimate child, whether the issue of forced or consensual sex, usually resulted in a heavy fine or a lengthening of the term of indenture.

The Chesapeake's first generation of native-born youths grew up within family settings, yet they, too, knew the meaning of an ill-defined and unprotected adolescence. Parental death was so commonplace in the early Chesapeake that most native-born children and youths lived in impermanent households, amid a succession of stepparents and stepsiblings. Erratic supervision and abuse were commonplace, and educational opportunities were meager.

Darrett and Anita Rutman contend that the Chesapeake's high rates of parental death undercut the emotional content of family life, forcing youths to mature early; young people passed into adulthood without experiencing adolescent turmoil or engaging in adolescent rebellion. But this interpretation assumes that adolescence exists only in a protective or watchful family setting. In contrast, Lorena Walsh argues that seventeenth-century Maryland's familial instability actually provoked an "adolescent crisis," at least for boys. Responding to the confusion in their homes, boys spent their inheritances unwisely, argued with their elders, avoided work, ran away, took up with dissolute companions, and got into scrapes with the law.

Over the course of the eighteenth century, the Chesapeake's mortality rate declined and its sex ratio reached a point of balance, permitting stable patriarchal families to assume a pivotal role in society. Yet even as the patriarchal family emerged in the Chesapeake and remained important in New England, diverse societal developments challenged its singular preeminence, altering the meaning of adolescence.

For white males of both British American and non-English parentage, adolescence became a stage of life associated both with widening opportunities for autonomous behavior and with heightened tension and ambiguity. Unmarried immigrant and native-born young men flocked to burgeoning commercial cities, seeking employment as storekeepers, clerks, insurance brokers, innkeepers, merchants, and laborers. They eschewed traditional apprenticeships, and the moral component of the master-apprentice relationship began to dissolve. Youthful rural-to-urban migration occurred even in New England as population growth outstripped the availability of inheritable lands, depriving Puritan fathers of the ability to secure their sons' futures.

Adolescent males faced the prospect, both exhilarating and frightening, of engineering their economic futures without paternal aid or direction; they might achieve prosperity or fall into the expanding ranks of the urban poor. Young men, Puritans especially, faced the additional challenge of weighing urban secular values against the competing ideals of their parents. City life exposed them to diverse cultures, to Enlightenment ideals emphasizing individual happiness, and to recreational drinking, gambling, and prostitution.

Fearing that the decline of patriarchal authority would produce a generation of dissolute young men, the colonies began to assign extrafamilial institutions more responsibility for managing and socializing adolescents. Elite parents and educators in New Jersey, New York, and Pennsylvania established colleges to provide the discipline and direction that families no longer offered. The select churchmen of Charleston, South Carolina, attempted to curtail youthful disorder by levying taxes to support foster homes, schools, and apprenticeships for the poor, and New England enacted strict laws against youthful disobedience.

Similarly, Puritan ministers condemned the wanton behavior of young men—night revels, filthy songs, tippling, and fornication—and urged youths to convert before encountering the temptations of secular society. Perhaps frustrated with the difficulties of achieving success in secular terms, many young men responded enthusiastically to calls for renewed religiosity; during the Great Awakening (1739–1744) the age of conversion for men dropped from the late twenties and thirties into the teens and early twenties.

Families also responded to the changing character of male adolescence, modifying their methods of parenting. As fathers acknowledged their diminishing authority and as Enlightenment values penetrated the home, parents placed new emphasis on affection, moderation, and liberty. Maturity was to be achieved not by forcing the male child or youth to submit to his parents, but by encouraging the development of self-control and autonomy. In addition, as independence and strength of will became prerequisites to male adulthood, parents began to accentuate gender differences, making sharp distinctions between appropriate "masculine" and "feminine" traits of character.

Knowing that their fate—whether sorrowful or happy—lay in the hands of their prospective husbands, girls sought the advice of parents when choosing a spouse.

Discouraged from seeking "masculine" autonomy, adolescent girls nonetheless drew some benefit from the shift toward moderate parenting and greater gender-role differentiation. Eighteenth-century mothers perfected moderate parenting techniques, cultivating "egalitarian friendships" with their adolescent daughters. "Femininity"—tenderness, purity, and piety—was the crux of these friendships, their "invariable point of reference" (Norton, *Liberty's Daughters*, [1980] pp. 102, 111).

At the same time, however, the new trends exacerbated adolescent girls' apprehension about marriage, sharpening their awareness of the socially induced differences in temperament, role, and power that distinguished women from men. Increasingly, eighteenth-century society countenanced male sexual adventurism, provoking "good" women to protect themselves from unwelcome advances by claiming to be passionless. And while ambitious young men might carve out a future in the marketplace and the fledgling professions, young women looked to a future defined by marriage and legal subordination. Knowing that their fate—whether sorrowful or happy—lay in the hands of their prospective husbands, girls sought the advice of parents when choosing a spouse. They also turned to the church; young women's notable piety during the Great Awakening developed in response to anxieties about marriage and childbirth.

Yet if white males and females came of age in an era of diminished or moderated patriarchalism, the same cannot be said of African American youths. Patriarchal authority was central to the development of slavery; sentimentality may have obscured its operation within the white slaveholding family, but slaves felt its full force.

It was generally during adolescence that slaves began to experience and thoroughly comprehend the harsh reality of enslavement. White male slaveholders demanded more and more work of slaves as they reached physical maturity. By the age of sixteen most females and males worked from dawn to dusk in the fields; only a small minority were trained as house servants or craftsmen. The ability to assume a full workload frequently coincided with slaves' sale and forced separation from family; it was also during adolescence that slaves first felt the sting of the whip, usually for failing to complete a task satisfactorily. Finally, as they reached adolescence, slave girls became increasingly vulnerable to sexual harassment and rape by their white masters and overseers.

The slave community and family sustained and succored African American youths as they confronted the trials of adolescence. By the early eighteenth century slaves were reproducing in sufficient numbers to form families and resilient kin networks, especially on large plantations. The slave family taught youths how to resist and to cope with bondage. It also established clear patterns of normative behavior, discouraging promiscuous premarital sex and directing young men and women toward marriage, sexual fidelity, and church membership.

The New Nation

The political and ideological ferment of the American Revolution injected a new degree of self-awareness and self-assertion into the lives of American youths. Black slaves of both sexes and all ages used the war as an opportunity to escape servitude. White males began to employ the language of republicanism to challenge parents' intervention in courtship.

Young white women and girls also demonstrated their identification with republican ideology, revising the conventional script for women's coming of age. In the decades after the war, some young females repudiated marriage and embraced "blessed singleness." Others displayed a new assertiveness in courtship, demanding that suitors treat them as equals and that parents respect their right to choose a partner without interference. Teenage girls also rejected an adolescence devoted entirely to domestic endeavors. Reflecting the nation's growing interest in female education, and hoping to learn how republican values might be incorporated into their future work as wives and mothers, America's "daughters of liberty" began to enroll in female academies in significant numbers.

These young men "on the make" championed a rough-and-tumble democracy, joining nonhierarchical mechanics' clubs, fraternal organizations, and fire-fighting companies.

Late-eighteenth-century parents tolerated, even applauded, their offspring's assertiveness, seeing in it the budding virtues of a republican citizenry. In contrast, by the 1830s and 1840s, Americans widely condemned male youths' contempt for authority, perceiving it as a grave threat to the public weal. College students rioted and rebelled against traditional rules of comportment. A much larger population of urban youths flouted authority and convention in their work and social relations. These young males "on the make" changed commercial and industrial employers frequently, taking years to settle into a trade or profession. They championed a rough-and-tumble democracy, joining nonhierarchical mechanics' clubs, fraternal organizations, and fire-fighting companies. More troubling still, most urban youths roomed in hotels or boarding houses and were completely free of adult supervision during nonworking hours. Devoting their leisure time to theater performances, gambling, and womanizing, they created a subculture that shunned sincerity and moral restraint.

America's disorderly young men were a frightening sign of fathers' declining ability to orchestrate their sons' transition to adulthood. Moreover, to traditionalists and critics of Jacksonian democracy, male youths were an apt symbol of national decline, of democracy gone awry. Their opportunism and disregard for virtue proved that the nation erred grievously in permitting mass politics, rampant economic speculation, the factory system, and urbanization to take root in republican terrain.

Significantly, the antebellum denunciation of urban males aroused Americans to deliberate analysis of youth as a life stage. Writing for the popular press, moral reformers and educators attempted to balance criticism with inquiry into the emotional, physiological, and mental characteristics of the young as they passed between childhood and adulthood. The emerging middle class rejected Calvinist notions about childhood; instead of seeing children as inherently sinful, parents viewed children as innocents who were responsive to systematic moral nurture. Set against this vision of purity, antebellum authors depicted youth as a stage of moral dilemma. Susceptible to passion, overstimulation, and mental confusion, youths nonetheless faced a season of pivotal decision making; the course chosen in the teens and twenties determined the character of adult life.

Thus, in this view, urban males' uncontrolled individualism and sexual indulgence set them on a course toward moral depravity, poverty, disease, and possible insanity. In contrast, the thousands of young men who heeded the impassioned preaching of the Second Great Awakening in the early nineteenth century were destined for lives of robust health, prosperity, and moral rectitude. Both groups were susceptible to high emotion; according to purity reformers and educators, the critical distinction between them was their differing degree of exposure to principled adult instruction.

Not surprisingly, antebellum ideas about youth produced new extrafamilial strategies for socializing adolescent males and assuaging older Americans' anxieties about the new democratic and industrial order. Primary schools, secondary schools, and Sunday schools proliferated as Americans proclaimed a growing need for educational institutions to prepare young people, mentally and morally, for adulthood. Moral reformers founded houses of refuge and reform schools for impoverished and delinquent juveniles, both male and female. College administrators replaced old rules of student conduct with new procedures for judging academic performance, and thereby encouraged good behavior and self-control. Employers and managers urged young workers to develop more conscientious and productive habits. Finally, the Cadets of Temperance reinforced adolescent males' moral and religious sensibilities; and fraternal orders, including the Odd Fellows and Freemasons, promoted their identification with the competitive demands of the workplace.

Simultaneously, middle-class families adopted new methods for rearing their adolescent offspring. The urban "youth crisis" heightened parents' class consciousness, and families with means invested growing sums of money in education so that sons might develop skills and attitudes that would distance them from the "lower classes." Urban parents also prolonged adolescence, insisting that sons reside at home during their teens and early twenties to take advantage of educational opportunities and to avoid the temptations and pitfalls of working-class culture.

Most important, middle-class families promoted intense emotional and psychological bonding between mothers and sons, hoping that sentimental attachments would inspire youths to internalize an ethic of benevolent morality and self-restraint. As proponents of the nineteenth-century ideology of separate spheres, middle-class mothers emphasized the social value of gender difference, urging their sons to strive for "manly independence" while daughters aspired to "moral purity" and "true womanhood." But "manliness" need not conflict with virtue or devotion to the family, and young men were advised to look to their mothers rather than to their male peers for a moral standard of conduct. Maternal influence was especially critical to young men's sexual development; by offering their sons a compelling model of sexual purity, mothers hoped to convince them that sexual indulgence degraded women, the family, and the human spirit.

Whatever Americans may have gained by devising new strategies to manage adolescent males, they neither erased opportunities for youthful autonomy nor eliminated the tension between young men and their middle-class elders. The most carefully bred boy might rebel against a confining domesticity, dash his parents' expectations, break his mother's heart. Laboring-class and immigrant youths who encountered middle-class values only occasionally—in charity workers, employers, and fraternal associations—were even less likely to pass through adolescence without moral taint. A youthful working-class subculture continued to thrive in nineteenth-century cities, unconstrained by genteel ideals or pretensions.

Young women excited less public anxiety in antebellum America than did young men, being seen as less openly contemptuous of traditional values and authority. Nonetheless, the outpouring of advice literature on girls' manners, morals, and physical health suggests that middle-class Americans worried about young women's ability to travel the road to "true womanhood" without encountering dangerous obstructions or delays.

Middle-class girls confronted the problem of reconciling opportunities for education and employment with the antebellum emphasis on gender difference and female domesticity. In the decades prior to the Civil War, female academies multiplied rapidly, offering adolescent girls sex-segregated education at the secondary level. Simultaneously, the teaching profession opened its doors to young unmarried women with a secondary education, and textile mills offered jobs to adolescent girls from New England's farm families.

Certainly it was possible to fit these developments into the framework of domesticity. Middle-class parents, educators, and reformers generally supported secondary education for teenage girls, believing that it prepared them to be better wives and mothers. They also defended young women's temporary employment as teachers or mill workers, deeming these occupations to be fully consonant with feminine capabilities and domestic interests. But the real experience of young females defied formulaic evaluations. Even as education and teaching encouraged young women to refine their skills in nurture and moral guardianship, they also taught them the value of self-esteem, mental stimulation, and independence.

Indeed, growing numbers of young women hesitated to give up the liberty gained through education and employment for marriage and a narrow home life. Of course, the vast majority of middle-class young women eventually married, knowing that they would be socially anomalous and economically insecure if they remained single. Nevertheless, they reluctantly withdrew from close circles of female friends and wondered whether marital happiness was possible in a society that required men and women to cultivate disparate mental, emotional, and behavioral traits.

African Americans found it difficult to shelter girls from sexual molestation; young women who resisted rape or abuse of a white master or overseer did so at great risk of punishment or sale.

Although working-class girls were less burdened by domestic ideology than were middle-class girls, they were also denied the opportunities for education and satisfying employment that their privileged sisters enjoyed. Many working-class girls spent their adolescence as subordinates in the "outwork" system, manufacturing clothing or other consumer products at home under the supervision of older relatives. Other working-class girls found employment as live-in domestic servants.

The constraints of subordinate status and familial obligation did not prevent working-class young women from carving narrow avenues of assertion into their overburdened lives. Discovering openings for unskilled hands in factories and workshops, native-born girls quit domestic service in droves, leaving this field of work to immigrants. The latter, knowing that the demand for servants was always greater than the supply, guarded their independence by moving on to new jobs whenever their mistresses became too demanding or judgmental. In New York City, growing numbers of wage-earning young women broke away from expected patterns of filial obedience and dependence, leaving their parents' homes to live with peers in boardinghouses and tenements. These girls became members of a working-class youth culture that flourished along the Bowery; seeking a rough equality with their male peers, they used casual sex and prostitution to finance autonomy, fancy clothes, and recreation.

Of course, working girls' self-assertion was neither unlimited nor free of danger. Whatever independence they found in adolescence, most young women confronted a future defined by severe economic constraints and marital dependency. Moreover, in boldly rejecting both working- and middle-class notions of female respectability, New York's Bowery girls risked family ostracism, rape, arrest, and placement in an industrial school for delinquent girls.

More than any other group of antebellum female adolescents, young women in slavery were deprived of social autonomy, education, and satisfying employment. In addition, they directly confronted the underside of domesticity: nineteenth-century Americans honored the "pure" woman by setting up the "fallen" or "impure" woman as her foil. In the Northeast, female reformers tried to shorten the distance between the two classes of women, blaming lustful men for "innocent" women's "fall." By contrast, patriarchal planters in the slave South drove the two groups of women apart to excuse and camouflage their own sexual license; on the one hand, planters' rhetoric and rule stressed white women's "purity" and vulnerability; on the other hand, it emphasized the libidinous nature of slave "wenches."

Distressed and angered by the treatment they received from whites, slave girls struggled to preserve their integrity and well-being. From adult slave women, female adolescents learned to escape overwork by feigning illness, breaking tools, or disobeying orders. Just as important, the slave community's religious activities and courtship practices provided adolescent girls with a field of action outside the humiliating master-slave relationship, thereby boosting their self-esteem. But African Americans found it difficult to shelter girls from sexual molestation; young women who resisted the rape or abuse of a white master or overseer did so at great risk of punishment or sale.

Urban Industrial America

During the late nineteenth and early twentieth centuries, American society reeled from the effects of change: the collapse of slavery and the rise of Jim Crow laws, urban growth, industrial consolidation and technological development, high rates of immigration, and the settlement of the West. The nation grew more heterogeneous and embattled than ever before, filled with the acrimonious debate of competing class, ethnic, race, and gender interests. The privileged fought to protect and enhance their status in the name of democracy; so, too, as partisans of democracy, the marginalized and dispossessed struggled to resist violence, deprivation, and discrimination. Amid this period of painful adjustment, adolescence acquired new experiential and cultural meaning. For young people of all backgrounds, adolescence emerged as an increasingly distinct stage of life; at the same time, class, race, ethnicity, and gender marked and fractured adolescence in significant ways.

Families of all kinds responded to the exigencies of urban industrial living by sharpening youths' dependency and sense of filial obligation. Realizing that young men could not become well-paid bureaucrats or professionals without acquiring specialized skills, growing numbers of middle-class parents sent their boys to high schools, professional schools, and colleges for training and formal certification. The child-centered Victorian family intensified the dependence of its adolescent girls in a different manner, keeping daughters at home to protect them from the perceived hazards of girlhood in late-nineteenth-century life: premarital romance and seduction, marketplace exploitation, and mental overstimulation.

In another pattern, impoverished immigrant and native-born white families sent millions of adolescents of both sexes into the industrial work force. Although these youngsters bore a heavy burden of responsibility for the welfare of their parents and siblings, they were not treated as adults; they were dependents, required to respond obediently to the dictates of their elders. And African American families in the urban South struggled to keep adolescent sons and daughters in school and out of a discriminatory job market, believing that education was the only authentic route to upward mobility.

Yet even as families sought to accentuate adolescents' dependency, young people elaborated distinctive forms of autonomy. Young unmarried black men and women migrated to northern cities, determined to lead their families out of the Jim Crow South. Although primarily in search of economic opportunity, these teenagers and young adults were also drawn to the excitement and cultural sophistication of northern city life.

The wage-earning sons and daughters of immigrants developed a subculture that pitted the autonomy and pleasure of the young against familial responsibilities. As champions of consumerism, adventurous heterosexuality, and self-assertion, they spent the wages needed at home on stylish clothes or commercial amusements, and indulged in heterosexual experimentation with their unmarried peers.

Similarly, male college students challenged their status as dependents, engaging in rowdiness and ritualized violence that offended the sensibilities of parents and violated the paternalistic rule of college administrators. White middle-class females also found ways to spurn the protective embrace of their families. Some gave voice to their discontent in self-destructive patterns, refusing food or cultivating physical fragility; others resisted dependency by pushing their way into higher education and the professions.

Southern black families responded to the migration of their young sons and daughters with pride, hope, and trepidation. Immigrant parents reacted to their adolescents' growing assertiveness with varying degrees of tolerance and moral outrage. White middle-class parents and their allies in Progressive reform criticized the "immoral" amusements of lower-class immigrant youths, worried that their own offspring would follow suit. In addition, they agonized over the meager ambition of their sons and the excessive ambition of their daughters, fearing that these developments signaled social collapse—that is, the collapse of the Victorian gender system and the demise of the Christian middle-class family.

Indeed, middle-class anxieties contributed directly to the formation of a modern ideology of adolescence. Anxious about the future of their children, middle-class Americans sought a "scientific" understanding of youth. G. Stanley Hall, president and senior professor of psychology at Clark University, responded to their call, synthesizing the research of dozens of physicians and psychologists and drawing on the theoretical models of Darwin and Freud to offer a systematic analysis of adolescence.

According to Hall's early-twentieth-century writings, the development of the individual from childhood to adulthood "recapitulated" the biological and cultural evolution of the human race. Much like "primitive" peoples who struggled to find a place for moral values amid the pressing demands of daily survival, adolescents experienced profound "storm and stress" as "old moorings were broken and a higher level attained" (G. Stanley Hall, *Adolescence*, vol. 1, p. xiii). Significantly, the conditions of modern life exacerbated adolescent stress by exposing immature minds and bodies to social and sexual disorder. Hall emphasized the importance of protective environments that discouraged "precocity," the assumption of adult behaviors and responsibilities; most important, adolescence should be a stage of idealism in which budding sexual impulses were sublimated in moral, athletic, academic, and artistic endeavors.

Hall's work provided inspiration and direction to a generation of middle-class parents and Progressive activists eager to reorganize adolescent life. Formal education became an important component of the adolescent experience within both the working and middle classes as state laws were passed that prohibited the employment of children below specified ages. New state legislation also extended the age of compulsory full-time school attendance and required part-time attendance of working adolescents at continuation schools. Educators created age-graded vocational and comprehensive high schools for adolescents of disparate class and racial backgrounds. The high schools prepared adolescents for college, white-collar, and skilled industrial occupations; between 1890 and 1920 the number of adolescents attending public high schools rose from two hundred thousand to more than two million.

Simultaneously, adult-sponsored youth organizations including Boy Scouts, Girl Scouts, 4-H Clubs, settlement-house clubs, and the YMCA, YWCA, and YMHA offered structured athletic, social, and cultural programs to American youths in cities, towns, and urban villages around the country. Reformers, social workers, and psychiatrists developed special courts, probation programs, child guidance clinics, and state reformatories for juvenile offenders; they claimed that youthful delinquents acted in response to age-specific environmental stresses and mental conflicts that could be resolved with expert assistance in age-segregated settings.

Although Progressive Era reforms reduced the role of the family in the socialization process, they increased adolescents' dependency, enlarging the authority of unrelated professionals who provided instruction or supervision to adolescents and judged them on their performance and progress. Progressive reforms also prolonged adolescence: they discouraged early wage earning, made high school attendance a prerequisite to upward mobility, and restricted adolescents' informal social interaction with adults.

The institutional developments of the Progressive Era did not, however, eliminate modern youths' desire for or access to autonomy. Indeed, high schools provided fruitful ground for the further development of semi-autonomous peer cultures. School administrators promoted extracurricular activities, hoping to foster greater homogeneity in culturally diverse student bodies, but discovered that high school peer groups were less malleable than desired: many peer groups developed normative patterns that subverted adult authority.

Certainly, high school peer cultures were not necessarily openly rebellious or contemptuous of adult values. According to Reed Ueda, the peer culture that developed in Somerville, Massachusetts, between 1890 and 1910 encouraged loyalty to the genteel culture of the students' Yankee parents. At the same time, however, by "transfer[ring] emotional ties from the family to the peer group," high schools prompted youths to express "independence from the codes of adults" (*Avenues to Adulthood*, p. 132). In suburban Somerville, students indulged in relatively superficial forms of rebellion: boys smoked in public, girls came to school without wearing hats, the student paper published cartoons that mocked social convention and propriety. In contrast, as William Graebner has shown, the student secret societies, cliques, and gangs that formed in inner-city working-class high schools developed rituals and codes of conduct that posed a serious challenge to school officials' authority.

Moreover, American adolescents continued to patronize the expand-

American parents in the early 20th century believed that adolescent life should be structured. Boy scouts, shown here doing calisthenics at a summer camp in 1925, offered athletic, social, and cultural programs to youths across the country.

ing world of consumer fashions and cheap amusements. They socialized in amusement parks, dance halls, and movie theaters, and tested the moral boundaries of their communities by smoking and drinking, wearing cosmetics and sophisticated clothing, and engaging in open heterosexual flirtation. Initially, immigrant working-class youths were far more engrossed in such activities than were adolescents from the white middle class, but by the 1910s white community leaders began to note the early signs of a sexual revolution among their own sons and daughters.

Just as early-twentieth-century adolescence was characterized by growing tension between dependency and autonomy, so adolescents felt the pressure of forces that both unified and divided them. Psychologists, settlement workers, and youth workers laid emphasis on the universal patterns in adolescents' emotional, psychological, and sexual development, and high schools brought adolescents of varied backgrounds into a common social and educational environment. In addition, the fashion and entertainment industries shaped the tastes and aspirations of adolescents whether they were rich or poor, black or white, immigrant or native-born. Nonetheless, adolescents' experience continued to be determined by race, class, gender, and ethnicity.

Expected to become the next generation's high-status professionals and community leaders, white middle-class boys took high school course work that prepared them for a business career or college study. The YWCA and the Boys Scouts encouraged these privileged young men to cultivate character and "go-ahead masculinity." By contrast, adolescent girls and boys from working-class, immigrant, and nonwhite homes were commonly viewed by teachers and reformers as inferior students and potential delinquents or dependents. The public high schools generally steered these youngsters into vocational rather than academic courses, training them for "respectable" but low-ranking positions in the industrial, clerical, or domestic sectors.

Similarly, inner-city youth organizations focused on delinquency prevention, emphasizing social control rather than youthful creativity or ingenuity. And, unlike their middle-class counterparts, adolescents from working-class and immigrant districts faced the real possibility of legal sanctions for offending the moral sensibilities of parents, teachers, police officers, and community social workers. Adolescent girls were vulnerable to arrest and institutionalization for incorrigibility, promiscuity, and prostitution; boys were vulnerable to arrest for minor property damage or petty theft.

White middle-class young women's experience of adolescence reflected both the privileged ambitions of their class and race and the disadvantages of their gender. During the late nineteenth century, white middle-class girls fought for access to higher education, struggling against social and scientific critics who denied their capacity to withstand the rigors of college education and condemned their aspirations for an intellectual or professional life. Many young women who completed college experienced a crisis afterward as parents tried to engineer their reimmersion in domestic life and the elite professions barred them entry or advancement. By the first two decades of the twentieth century, the debate over higher education for women was dying down, but adolescent girls faced a new crisis about their identity and behavior: educators and psychiatrists fretted about the latent lesbianism in young women's friendships with one another, and they suggested that career ambitions might be further evidence of psychosexual perversion or deviance.

Modern America

During the 1920s, middle-class adults watched in astonishment as their sons and daughters threw off the shackles of Victorian sexual control en masse, flaunting heterosexual desire and defying the moral authority of their elders. Astonishment quickly hardened into opinion voiced in the pages of newspapers, popular journals, and advice books. "Progressives" applauded modern youths' vitality and rejection of "false standards," while "traditionalists" argued that the youth rebellion must be put down before it destroyed the social order.

Historians agree that changes in the middle-class family lay at the heart of adolescents' unconventional conduct. The middle-class family defined itself increasingly as a "companionate" rather than as a hierarchical unit. Husband and wife embraced an ideal of mutuality and sexual fulfillment in their relations with one another. Similarly, parents put new emphasis on the happiness and emotional security of their offspring; they willingly funded adolescents' prolonged economic dependence but withdrew from directing youths' educational performance or vocational choices. Instead, parents left these matters to the high schools and colleges and focused on cultivating affectional bonds with their children—not realizing, perhaps, that they would have to compete with the bonds their offspring formed with each other.

Modern parents did not expect strict obedience from their adolescents. Still, they wanted to guide their sons' and daughters' social development and were unprepared for the youth rebellion of the 1920s, a rebellion that grew out of adolescents' unique degree of segregation from their parents and other adults. Schools and the new youth-oriented sector of the consumer market heightened adolescents' sense of separation from the adult world; students turned their backs on adults, celebrating the sensuality, the idealism, the style, and the daring of their peers. At the same time, prolonged residential and economic dependence on parents and long years of schooling sharpened adolescents' sense of indeterminacy, promoting anxiety about social and sexual identity and a keen desire for adult status.

Experts in family social work and psychology attempted to convince middle-class parents that America's "flaming youth" were less rebellious than they imagined. Indeed, historians have noted that adolescents'

Schools and the new youth-oriented sector of the consumer market heightened adolescents' sense of separation from the adult world; students turned their backs on adults, celebrating the sensuality and the daring of their peers.

subculture, although resistant to adult rule, effectively socialized youths for modern adulthood. Peer groups enforced gender-appropriate behavior, heterosexuality, competitiveness, conformity to organizational demands, and consumerism. Their dating system recognized female sexuality and permitted necking and petting, but it established marriage rather than promiscuity as youth's goal. Far from upsetting the conventional inequality of the sexes, the dating system accentuated the social and economic prerogatives of men and the subordination of women.

Of course, not all adolescents participated equally in the youth culture of the 1920s. Working-class adolescents were active in urban youth subcultures at school and on neighborhood streets, but they lacked the clothes, cars, and cash required for full participation in the dating system. Small-town and rural adolescents participated in school-based subcultures, but they had little access to commercial amusements and were subject to closer community surveillance than were their urban counterparts. Black youths from middle-class and upwardly striving families were held to strict moral codes by parents who wanted to differentiate their offspring from those of the impoverished masses.

Despite adolescents' varying degrees of participation in youthful rebellion, the 1920s witnessed the emergence of a mass youth culture. Adolescents proclaimed a loyalty to values and a social identity all their own. Within their peer groups, adolescents offered each other protection from adult expectations; at the same time, as a mass youth culture took shape, generational conflict became an institutionalized and prominent feature of modern American culture.

The Great Depression temporarily interrupted American anxieties about youth. It placed severe financial constraints on middle-class families, and adolescents were denied the clothing, cars, and money for entertainment that made their distinctive life-style possible. The dating system continued, but on a straitened budget, and adolescent dependency deepened in both middle- and working-class homes. Adolescents stayed in school longer, lived at home without employment after leaving high school, and postponed marriage.

World War II abruptly ended America's protracted encounter with the Great Depression, promoting a decisive increase in adolescents' autonomy and new freedom from economic constraints. Millions of young men left their parents' homes and joined the armed services; young women migrated to cities and found employment, lodging, and opportunities for socializing with their peers. Undoubtedly the war encouraged casual heterosexual experimentation among adolescents. Attracted to men in uniform and feeling a sense of high adventure, many adolescent girls engaged in promiscuous sex with GIs. Equally important, by drawing large numbers of young men and women into sex-segregated, nonfamilial environments, the war promoted the development of a distinct gay identity and gay subculture.

The sharp breakdown of community and familial controls during the war led to growing anxiety about adolescent immorality and delinquency. These sentiments intensified during the postwar era even as adolescents from both middle- and working-class homes demonstrated their adherence to the 1950s ideal of domesticity by endorsing steady dates and early marriage.

Middle-class parents believed that the practice of "going steady" would lead to premarital intercourse and to hasty marriages. More important, parents, members of Congress, and the U.S. Children's Bureau worried that a peer culture spread by comic books, television, radio, and the movies obstructed generational communication, promoting "lower-class" tastes, delinquency, and a disregard for family values. Just as the cold warriors of the 1950s tested the loyalty of government officials, so parents, politicians, and educators tested youths' loyalty to the values of white middle-class America. In both cases, the investigators declared themselves unhappy with their findings, having discovered substantial evidence of subversion and rebellion.

The widespread political and cultural activism drew its support and momentum from the baby boom generation; indeed, the countercultural revolution of the 1960s was in large part an adolescent rebellion more profound than any that had preceded it. Adolescents of the 1960s were determined to engineer (and often to delay) their own transition to adulthood. College students called themselves an oppressed group; they rejected as false their parents' and teachers' loyalty to a society that accepted the cold war but refused to acknowledge persistent inequalities of race, class, and age. Black and white adolescents proclaimed themselves committed to a new vision of peace, prosperity, and equality; by the end of the decade, many young people added tolerance for sexual diversity and gender equality to their list of revolutionary goals.

Rebellious adolescents encountered adversity and opposition in a variety of forms. The mass consumer market distracted them from political activism even as it helped to solidify their counter-cultural identity and supplied them with distinctive music, clothing, movies, and drugs. More significant, a conservative backlash developed, proclaiming itself loyal to traditional forms of parental rule and opposed to government programs designed to redistribute opportunity, power, or wealth. Furthermore, by the late 1960s and early 1970s young people were splintered and distrustful of each other. They wanted to solve problems that defied easy resolution; their organizations were wracked by internal divisions and weakened by government infiltration. The rebellion of the 1960s injected new racial, sexual, familial, and gender values into American life, but it also provoked bitter opposition. Adolescents in the 1970s, 1980s, and 1990s have lived with the consequences of both of these developments.

Looking Ahead

In researching the years from 1920 through the 1960s, historians have amassed evidence of modern adolescents' distinctive agency, that is, their ability to be self-directing. Denied full independence, adolescents nonetheless acted as innovators. Taking advantage of their protected status and exclusion from adult responsibilities, they engineered the transition to adulthood on terms that were largely of their own choosing. But historians have only begun to study the meaning of adolescence from the 1970s to the early 1990s; their assessment of adolescents' agency may require modification as they analyze the impact of a declining capitalist economy on youths of all races from both middle-class and working-class homes. Our understanding of adolescents' identity and autonomy may also change as scholars investigate how adolescents have been affected both by feminist changes in the family and by rising resistance to a nontraditional gender system.

Young adolescents in the late twentieth century are still segregated from adults, and they continue to socialize within self-conscious semiautonomous subcultures. Undoubtedly many middle-class adolescents continue to demonstrate significant self-direction in making the transition to adulthood. However, high rates of divorce, a weak economy, and a faltering social welfare system have surely increased adolescents' exposure to adult worries and responsibilities, affecting their perceptions and options. Similarly, state efforts to restrict adolescents' access to abortion may have significantly eroded young girls' ability to postpone the obligations of parenthood. Finally, adolescents' increasing vulnerability to poverty, drugs, AIDS, and suicide, and their growing involvement in gangs and violent crime, point to growing indeterminacy and despair, declining idealism and hope. As historians study adolescence in the last decade of the twentieth century, they may need to take into account the mounting burdens of this life stage, the growing evidence of violence, distress, and chaos in youthful lives.

[See also Childhood and Children; Family Structures; Labor: Great Depression through 1990; Life Stages; Public Education; Rock Music; Sexual Behavior and Morality.]

BIBLIOGRAPHY

General Works

D'Emilio, John, and Estelle B. Freedman. *Intimate Matters: A History of Sexuality in America* (1988).

Demos, John, and Virginia Demos. "Adolescence in Historical Perspective." *Journal of Marriage and the Family* 31 (November 1969): 632–638.

Fox, Vivian C. "Is Adolescence a Phenomenon of Modern Times?" *Journal of Psychohistory* 5, no. 2 (1977): 271–290.

Gutman, Herbert G. *The Black Family in Slavery and Freedom, 1750–1925* (1976).

Hawes, Joseph M. "The Strange History of Female Adolescence in the United States." *Journal of Psychohistory* 13, no. 1 (1985): 51–63.

Hawes, Joseph M., and N. Ray Hiner, eds. *American Childhood: A Research Guide and Historical Handbook* (1985).

Horowitz, Helen Lefkowitz. *Campus Life: Undergraduate Cultures from the End of the Eighteenth Century to the Present* (1987).

Jones, Jacqueline. *Labor of Love, Labor of Sorrow: Black Women, Work, and the Family from Slavery to the Present* (1985).

Kett, Joseph F. *Rites of Passage: Adolescence in America 1790 to the Present* (1977).

Mintz, Steven, and Susan Kellogg. *Domestic Revolutions: A Social History of American Family Life* (1988).

The Colonial Period

Beales, Ross W., Jr. "In Search of the Historical Child: Miniature Adulthood and Youth in Colonial New England." *American Quarterly* 27, no. 4 (1975): 379–398.

Greven, Philip. *The Protestant Temperament: Patterns of Child-rearing, Religious Experience, and the Self in Early America* (1977).
Hiner, N. Ray. "Adolescence in Eighteenth-Century America." *History of Childhood Quarterly* 3, no. 2 (1975): 253–280.
Morgan, Edmund S. *The Puritan Family: Religion and Domestic Relations in Seventeenth-Century New England* (rev. ed., 1966).
Norton, Mary Beth. *Liberty's Daughters: The Revolutionary Experience of American Women, 1750–1800.* (1980).
Norton, Mary Beth. "The Evolution of White Women's Experience in Early America." *American Historical Review* 89, no. 3 (1984): 593–619.
Rutman, Darrett B., and Anita H. Rutman. " 'Now-Wives and Sons-in-Law': Parental Death in a Seventeenth-Century Virginia County." In *The Chesapeake in the Seventeenth Century: Essays on Anglo-American Society*, edited by Thad W. Tate and David L. Ammerman (1977).
Shumsky, Neil L. "Parents, Children, and the Selection of Mates in Colonial Virginia." *Eighteenth-Century Life* 2, no. 4 (1975–1976): 83–88.
Smith, Daniel Blake. *Inside the Great House: Planter Family Life in Eighteenth-Century Chesapeake Society* (1980).
Thompson, Roger. "Adolescent Culture in Colonial Massachusetts." *Journal of Family History* 9, no. 2 (Summer 1984): 127–144.
Walsh, Lorena S. " 'Till Death Us Do Part': Marriage and Family in Seventeenth Century Maryland." In *The Chesapeake in the Seventeenth Century: Essays on Anglo-American Society*, edited by Thad W. Tate and David L. Ammerman (1977).

The New Nation

Cott, Nancy. *The Bonds of Womanhood: "Woman's Sphere" in New England, 1780–1835* (1977).
Diner, Hasia R. *Erin's Daughters in America: Irish Immigrant Women in the Nineteenth Century* (1983).
Halttunen, Karen. *Confidence Men and Painted Women: A Study of Middle-Class Culture in America, 1830–1870* (1982).
Hawes, Joseph M. *Children in an Urban Society: Juvenile Delinquency in Nineteenth-Century America* (1971).
Norton, Mary Beth. *Liberty's Daughters: The Revolutionary Experience of American Women, 1750–1800* (1980).
Novak, Steven J. *The Rights of Youth: American Colleges and Student Revolt, 1798–1815* (1977).
Ryan, Mary P. *Cradle of the Middle Class: The Family in Oneida County, New York, 1790–1865* (1981).
Smith-Rosenberg, Carroll. "Sex as Symbol in Victorian Purity: An Ethnohistorical Analysis of Jacksonian America." In *Turning Points: Historical and Sociological Essays on the Family*, edited by John Demos and Sarane Spence Boocock (1978).
Stansell, Christine. *City of Women: Sex and Class in New York, 1789–1860* (1986).
Stott, Richard Briggs. *Workers in the Metropolis: Class, Ethnicity, and Youth in Antebellum New York City* (1990).
White, Deborah Gray. *Ar'n't I a Woman?: Female Slaves in the Plantation South* (1985).

Urban Industrial America

Brenzel, Barbara. *Daughters of the State: A Social Portrait of the First Reform School for Girls in North America, 1856–1905* (1983).
Brumberg, Joan Jacobs. *Fasting Girls: The Emergence of Anorexia Nervosa as a Modern Disease* (1988).
Chapman, Paul Davis. "Schools as Sorters: Testing and Tracking in California, 1910–25." *Journal of Social History* 14, no. 4 (Summer 1981): 708–718.
Gordon, Linda. "Incest and Resistance: Patterns of Father-Daughter Incest, 1880–1930." *Social Problems* 33, no. 4 (1986): 253–257.
Graebner, William. "Outlawing Teenage Populism: The Campaign Against Secret Societies in the American High School, 1900–1960." *Journal of American History* 74, no. 2 (1987): 411–435.
Hall, G. Stanley. *Adolescence: Its Psychology.* Vol. 1 (1905).
Macleod, David I. *Building Character in the American Boy: The Boy Scouts, YMCA, and Their Forerunners, 1870–1920* (1983).
Norwood, Stephen H. *Labor's Flaming Youth: Telephone Operators and Worker Militancy, 1878–1923* (1990).
Peiss, Kathy. *Cheap Amusements: Working Women and Leisure in Turn-of-the-Century New York* (1986).
Platt, Anthony. *The Child Savers: The Invention of Delinquency* (1969).
Schlossman, Steven, and Stephanie Wallach. "The Crime of Precocious Sexuality: Female Juvenile Delinquency in the Progressive Era." *Harvard Educational Review* 48, no. 1 (1978): 65–94.
Ueda, Reed. *Avenues to Adulthood: The Origins of High School and Social Mobility in an American Suburb* (1987).

Modern America

Bailey, Beth L. *From Front Porch to Back Seat: Courtship in Twentieth-Century America* (1988).
Evans, Sara. *Personal Politics: The Roots of Women's Liberation in the Civil Rights Movement and the New Left* (1979).
Fass, Paula. *The Damned and the Beautiful: American Youth in the 1920's* (1977).
Gilbert, James Burkhart. *A Cycle of Outrage: America's Reaction to the Juvenile Delinquent of the 1950s* (1986).
Graebner, William. *Coming of Age in Buffalo: Youth and Authority in the Postwar Era* (1990).
Modell, John. *Into One's Own: From Youth to Adulthood in the United States, 1920–1975* (1989).

— RUTH M. ALEXANDER

AFRICAN AMERICAN MUSIC

The most popular and influential music in the late twentieth century is African American music. This music, which reflects the continuing creative vitality of a deep-rooted tradition, derives its dynamism from its African roots and illustrates both the persistence of fundamental African musical beliefs and practices and their ongoing transformation in the New World African diaspora. In colonial North America and later in the United States, particularly from the nineteenth century on, these patterns of persistence and of transformation have spawned a variety of genres and offshoots.

The contemporary significance of African American music is evident in its tremendous worldwide appeal and influence. Its historical significance encompasses the window it provides into the hearts and minds of African Americans; the focus here is the insight it offers into the historical development of distinctive forms of African American culture. The history of African American music has reflected, especially in the twentieth century, the tension between revitalization and assimilation as well as that between communalism and individualism. In each case, over time, the tension has become more, rather than less, complex. This situation, in turn, has further complicated the meaning of African American music in how it might illuminate African American identity, vision, and struggle. African American music is a critical arena of ongoing creative expression and cultural struggle. In our time, this music remains an important marker of African American ethnic/racial and cultural distinctiveness, in spite of assimilation, commercialization, and a notable measure of African American success in the mainstream music business.

Recognition of the importance of African American music has grown dramatically in the twentieth century, notably after World War II. While the judgments of musicians, ethnomusicologists, and critics have helped enhance this recognition, the cultural politics unleashed by the growing black assertiveness of the civil rights and black power movements has been equally pivotal. Not only did these movements deeply influence culture and music, but the music itself revealed its irreducibly social essence by seeking more openly and directly to influence the struggle.

Why is unraveling this interpenetration between culture and politics so vital to an understanding of African American musical history? First, the African American musical tradition is a central ingredient in the development of modern American culture and music. Second, the meanings and functions of African American music depend heavily upon historical context. Third, a major reason for the tremendous influence of this music has been its openness and adaptability, its ability to integrate outside influences. Finally, worldwide United States cultural dominance and the commercialization and appropriation of African American music have added to its influence.

This historical analysis of how, why, and to what effect African American music has become so dominant is principally a close look at its origins and development. Examining the period between 1619 and 1865, the first section of this article discusses the social origins and functions of the music. The emergence of a distinctive African American musical idiom is the key issue in this period. Following the Civil War and emancipation, African American music has become far more complex, with important innovations unfolding, sometimes at a rapid pace. The article's second section emphasizes the creation of new forms and approaches, the vital role of innovators, the dialogue between tradition and change, and the factors of secularization and commercialization.

The explanatory model followed here for African American music's popularity and significance builds upon several interrelated themes. Broadly speaking, the music's impact emerges from the creative tension deriving from the syncretism of the various musical traditions informing its development, notably the African roots. This syncretic process enhances the music's organic and affirmative qualities. More narrowly, the music's resonance grows out of its profound conceptual and philosophical bases, which go far deeper than issues of specific aspects of African, European, or New World music making that contribute to the construction of African American music.

In other words, the music is much more than the sum of its primary components. Its power is based on the persistence of a traditional African orientation toward music as an inseparable and pervasive component of a social and cultural whole. While transformed in complicated ways among African peoples throughout the African diaspora, this conceptual structure can be seen in the United States in at least three interwoven ideas: music as affective; music as reflective of a spiritual or sacred worldview; and music as a multidimensional experience necessarily embracing cultural forms such as dance and poetry and, on a more elaborate level, ritual and ceremony.

"How I Got Over": African American Music Before 1865

In 1619, when the first twenty Africans set foot on the soil at Jamestown, they entered a new cultural milieu. It was literally a new world where the two Old World cultures—African and European—underwent an ongoing process of change and adaptation as they interacted with one another and with the culture of Native Americans. Over time, the nature and degree of these patterns of cultural contact and change have had enormous consequences for all involved. For each group, the result has been a complicated cultural history in that part of colonial North America which eventually became the United States; more specifically, for Africans it has meant the elaboration of syncretic African American cultures with significant commonalities and differences.

The emergence of African American music signified an integral development within the broader matrix of African American culture. Approximately four hundred thousand Africans, largely from a variety of West African states and ethnic groups, were brought here as slaves between the seventeenth and early nineteenth centuries. As involuntary migrants, typically forbidden and unable to re-create their lost political and economic worlds, they relied heavily on refashioning former beliefs and practices to fit the exigencies of their slave lives. Notwithstanding important cultural differences in language, kinship arrangements, and religion among enslaved Africans, they had many cultural traits in common. In addition, the unifying character of shared experiences over time facilitated the creation of a distinct African American identity incorporating a sacred worldview, a cyclical view of time, and a communal social ethos. Further, these preliterate Africans came from oral cultures that placed great emphasis upon the verbal arts, including song and storytelling. This traditional emphasis was echoed in aspects of both the European and the Native American cultures with which newly arrived Africans interacted, and reinforced the commonalities among the groups.

The dialectic between slavery and resistance broadly defined the situation of African Americans before 1865 and influenced the evolving culture, especially the music. Not a great deal of evidence about African American music in the seventeenth and eighteenth centuries has been uncovered. Enough exists, however, to document clearly the coexistence of traditional African music, European music and instruments played by Africans, and the evolving outlines of a distinctive African American music. Certain defining characteristics set African music, whether traditional or hybrid, apart from European music. Continental and diasporan African music featured a basic complexity structured around one or more of the following: (1) antiphony, or call-and-response (responsorial exchanges within the music itself and among musicians, singers, and other participants in the music-making process); (2) cross rhythms and polyrhythms providing an intricate pattern of beats and meter; (3) a communal or group basis; (4) improvisation; (5) functionality; (6) an integral association with dance and body language or movement; and (7) an emotive, at times ecstatic, mood.

Whereas European music emphasized melody, African music emphasized rhythm. In terms of singing style, in the African tradition this quality contributed to a percussive, as opposed to a lyrical, feel: singing emphasized intensity, emotional immediacy, and accents such as shouting, slurring, offbeat phrasing, falsetto, guttural tones, and trills (vibratory effects). Hand clapping, heel stomping, thigh slapping, "patting juba" (an intricate and rhythmic alternation of hand clapping and thigh slapping), head bobbing, and body weaving exemplified this percussive style and the relationship between music and body motion. Likewise, percussion often dominated instrumental music.

The overwhelming preponderance of the information about early African music in the colonies comes from Europeans who typically neither understood nor appreciated what they heard. Some did, however, recognize something extraordinary about slave music. Much of this music making, though, took place among the slaves themselves when whites were absent or few in number. In this context, slaves were far more comfortable and appeared to favor the traditional in music making. Even on those occasions when whites and blacks made music together, descriptions by whites make it clear that in important ways Africans and Europeans came from different cultures. Nonetheless, this situation did not seem to prevent Africans from musical expression in traditional modes.

While often ethnocentric, the white accounts are revealing. Variously described by many whites as uncivilized, uncouth, disgusting, sinful, and unharmonious, African American music clearly hit a nerve, epitomizing for innumerable whites an inferior people lacking culture—defined as Western and European. Even among those like Thomas Jefferson, who thought that blacks were musically gifted or that certain features of African American music were estimable, racist attitudes toward African Americans persisted.

Regardless of how whites viewed African American music in the early period, for blacks it represented a central feature of the cultural world they created to sustain themselves. Exactly how African American music originated is unclear. There is written evidence of slaves in the colonies singing in various African languages and in mixtures of African and European languages. Much of this singing struck many white observers as unintelligible, ludicrous, or noise at best. Nevertheless, this melding of musical influences undergirded the transculturation process and enhanced the development of a shared musical idiom. Furthermore, early on instruments such as the drum, played in similar ways, functioned as a kind of common language or, more precisely, a common grammar. As musicians from diverse backgrounds played together, they simultaneously enhanced the development of a common language and culture.

Hand clapping, heel stomping, thigh slapping, head bobbing, and body weaving exemplified this percussive style and the relationship between music and body motion.

The concept of "drum language" or "talking drums" is common in African music, going far beyond the idea of drums as instruments to send signals and codes. Skillful players can achieve a sound that vividly captures the meaning of spoken language. Because many African languages tend to be tonal, linguistic meaning can be created and varied within a piece of drum music through the deft use of pitch and similar inflections. Such a drumming style plainly illustrates that the instrument was played melodically and rhythmically. This highly advanced drumming sensibility was evident throughout the African diaspora and served to unify disparate African peoples and cultures.

Still, the question of how the music developed persists. Several intriguing bits of evidence provide tantalizing clues. The innumerable and often-harrowing sounds of captured Africans during the traumatic process of enslavement revealed what European and some African observers described as an eerie musical quality. Indeed, beyond those exclamations which might be called "songs," shrieks, groans, moans, screams, and phrases welled up out of a consciousness in which spirited vocalizing was part of the traditional musical vocabulary. The awful experience of enslavement gave this vocalizing and singing added meaning. These demonstrative modes, drawing upon deep cultural wellsprings, would persist in various New World transformations, such as field hollers and street cries.

Likewise, there is significant evidence that on board slave ships African music was not at all unusual. Many slave captains indulged in a practice, sometimes referred to as "dancing the slaves," in which the ship's human cargo was ordered to dance and play drums and other instruments. Obviously they did so in African ways. This custom reinforced shared and compelling elements among the diverse musical traditions. Those Africans who survived the dreadful "Middle Passage" from Africa to the New World (the journey from Africa to the West Indies, the second leg in the so-called Triangle Trade) continued to experience enormous, often disorienting, changes. The continuation of a traditional worldview emphasizing a holistic and sacred social ethos might ease the pain of adjustment. Music typically played an essential role in the adjustment process.

Africans brought to the New World as slaves revitalized the spirit and memory of African music. In the early nineteenth century, however, when the formal prohibition against importing slaves into the United States took effect, this direct invigoration dwindled significantly. Even during the previous century, when the importation of African slaves reached its peak, the music and culture were becoming increasingly a blend of New World influences with Old World African sensibilities. As more and more African descendants were born into slavery, that blending proceeded more rapidly. With fewer Africans arriving to reinvigorate the original spark of the culture, African Americans increasingly relied on memory to recapture the spirit.

A primary manifestation of early African American music was the use of a variety of instruments of African, European, and shared origins. Early on, the drum was the basic instrument, but European Americans were afraid of its power and its potential for promoting slave unity. Many slave owners were explicitly concerned that the drums might be used to assist in slave insurrection, a fear derived in part from the general white fear of slaves congregating for diversion, where music making and dancing predominated. Throughout the late seventeenth and eighteenth centuries, numerous laws sought to end these assemblies and to ban drums and other loud instruments that might be employed to plot resistance. The banning of the drum was most successful wherever whites took seriously the challenge of slave control. For those areas with large numbers of slaves, especially where blacks outnumbered whites (for instance, the coastal lowlands of South Carolina and Georgia), this challenge assumed a special urgency. Only in Louisiana, apparently, did open drumming persist to a significant extent. Elsewhere suppression appeared to be effective. Drum banning sent the practice underground. It also accelerated both the use of other percussion instruments—tambourines, sticks, and bones—and the intensified percussive use of other instruments, notably banjos and horns, as well as the body and the voice. It deflected without deterring the emphasis on rhythmic complexity.

Drums aside, the banjo was the most common African instrument in the New World. Other popular instruments included rattles, bells, pipes, iron gonggongs, castanets, keyboards (thumb pianos), horns, and small flutes and clarinets. In light of their familiarity with a wide variety of instruments, it is not surprising that Africans quickly became proficient on the European instruments most often encountered: violins, horns, and flutes. Because of the fundamental adaptability of African music, the cross-cultural impact of shared instrumental traditions proved enriching. African Americans learned to play European classical and folk music quite well, performing in elite and popular settings. Slave masters typically placed a high value on good slave musicians who entertained the whites at their dances, balls, and impromptu social gatherings. Similarly, slave musicians played trumpets, fifes, and drums in militia bands. Here again the music was principally European, but often African influenced.

Musicians who garnered favor among whites by skillfully playing European music often achieved notable status among blacks as well. Those who were proficient in African American musical idioms frequently achieved a higher status among the slaves. Skill in both musical traditions greatly enhanced a slave musician's status. An interesting index of the value slave masters placed on slave musicians is that newspaper descriptions seeking runaway slaves often mentioned their musical talent.

The integral relation between African music and dance continued in the New World. Many experts see the continuities between Old World and New World dance as among the most pronounced examples of African influence on African American and American culture. African dance featured flexibility, spontaneity, rhythm, gliding and dragging steps, smooth movements, pelvic action, little if any body contact among dancers, and animal imitations. European dance, however, emphasized more formal postures and approaches. Even when Africans took up European dances like jigs, fandangos, and Virginia breakdowns, they often reworked them in African idioms.

Intimately interwoven, African music and dance literally conflate. This inseparability between sound and motion—music and dance—is evident from patting juba and work songs in the early period to the contemporary explosive performance style of soul music innovator James Brown. Indeed, the practice of music as a social performance builds upon the interwoven quality of music and dance. The ultimate incarnations of this practice are the various cultural events—rituals, ceremonies, and festivals—at which African Americans utilize the expressive arts to affirm a sense of identity and to celebrate life and death. Music is an indispensable element of these events.

There are fascinating and revealing examples throughout the colonial and early national period of African American holidays and celebrations that include music and dance. These reveal the fundamental affective, spiritual, and multidimensional aspects of the music. Even in New England, where the percentage of African Americans in the population typically registered in low single digits, African Americans came together and celebrated in ostensibly African-derived ways. Two noteworthy examples were Election Day and Pinkster Day.

Election Day was a special holiday on which blacks elected their own leaders as part of a grand celebration. Taking place roughly between 1750 and 1850 and in May or June, the event often lasted several days. The highlights were a parade featuring the slaves in their best attire, the formal elections, and the subsequent series of parties. Surviving descriptions make it clear that the best singers, dancers, and musicians put on a spectacular show as African Americans celebrated in a rousing African-inspired mode.

Similarly, Pinkster Day, or Pentecost Sunday, celebrations featured serious merrymaking highlighted by vigorous singing, drumming, and dancing. Typically described as saturnalian, with African music and dance, these events attracted large numbers of participants and onlookers. At times, festivities lasted as much as a week after Pentecost Sunday. These celebrations were officially forbidden, and declined in the early nineteenth century.

Similar examples abound from the South. In areas of eastern North Carolina, African Americans observed the John Canoe festival from the eighteenth century until around 1900. As in similar Caribbean and West African observances, it included a series of informal festivities and stylized celebrations with ritual significance held during the Christmas-New Year holiday season and featuring elaborate masks and costumes. Playing a variety of instruments, singing, and dancing, the celebrants in one part of the event went from house to house seeking gifts. When a household was not generous, the singers responded with satirical improvised verse.

In the exceptionally diverse milieu of New Orleans, African cultural traditions thrived. Creolization proceeded in this setting in countless and untold ways. Still, the Africanness of African American culture here was extraordinary. Blacks, for example, danced and made music—most notably they drummed—in very African styles well into the nineteenth century. Long before the Civil War, there had been a tradition among the slaves of Sunday dancing, accompanied by thunderous drumming, in what was called Place Congo (now Louis Armstrong Park). Not surprisingly, large crowds, flocked to participate and to observe these stirring performances, which went on for several hours. Similar events had been prohibited and suppressed in other areas of the South in the previous century; in 1834 authorities outlawed Sunday dancing among African Americans in Place Congo. Nevertheless, this and similarly strong traditions of rhythmic music and dance persisted in less public contexts and strongly influenced the cultural history of New Orleans.

The inseparability between sound and motion in African music is evident from patting juba and work songs in the early period to the contemporary explosive performance style of soul music innovator James Brown.

Scholars often point to New Orleans as well as the South Carolina and Georgia Sea Islands as the two most striking sites of African influence on African American culture in the United States. Whereas cross-cultural contact and cultural intermixture helped to shape African American music in New Orleans, the relative isolation of the Sea Islands gave music there the most vividly African flavor of any variety of African American music in the United States. The African cultural aesthetic thrived in this overwhelmingly black area where whites meddled comparatively little in black community life. The distinctive and demonstrably African-derived culture of this group, commonly referred to as Gullah after its unique language, fascinated outsiders, black and white. While the sacred and secular music of this region struck early observers as uniquely African and non-Christian, much of what survives today in the records is religious music that draws upon nineteenth-century African American Christianity. Nineteenth-century white collectors of black music typically found this religious music more compatible with their own tastes and outlooks. African Americans, especially the slaves, were ever wary of white motives and tended both to feed the collectors what they wanted and to prefer to sing religious music for them.

Spirituals were common in the early nineteenth century and proliferated in the revivals, in church services, in less formal worship settings, and even in ostensibly secular contexts. Many religious events brought together whites and blacks in an intensely soul-searching experience, especially during the waves of nineteenth-century antebellum religious revivalism often termed the Second Great Awakening. It was during this period that a significant proportion of the slave population combined traditional African religious beliefs with Christianity to create a distinctive slave religion and a distinctive African American Christianity. Unlike the Christianity of free urban blacks, slave Christianity reflected a more clearly African-inspired sensibility. After emancipation, this kind of difference would enhance the complexity of African American music.

The importance of the spirituals cannot be overstated. In many ways this music accurately captures the essence of traditional black culture, especially its sacred core, and vividly reflects its affective, spiritual, and multidimensional qualities. That spirituals represent the bulk of the surviving musical record from the nineteenth century strongly suggests that blacks have treasured them. The spirituals have survived so well also because they so pointedly symbolize the black freedom struggle and the black quest for self-definition. In the spirituals, as in other vital modes of cultural expression, communal values—notably unity—dominate.

Lyrically the spirituals draw heavily upon traditional psalms, hymns, and vivid biblical and moral imagery.

Spirituals symbolize the black freedom struggle and the black quest for self-definition. They signify hope, confidence and transcendence in the face of seemingly insurmountable obstacles.

African American spirituals, as distinguished from white spirituals, however, transformed the texts, reworking various elements in a communal act of improvisational revitalization. Evolving out of a spontaneous, emotional, often ecstatic process of group composition and musical re-creation, African American spirituals fervently display their Africanness: antiphony, rhythmic complexity, repeat phrasing, uninhibited vocals, and bodily movements. Rather than functioning as written texts to be followed precisely, the spirituals emphasize the folk process in which the group aurally re-creates a text within a flexible narrative musical format. This textual openness was crucial for a people most of whom could neither read nor write, but for whom verbal artistry, social interaction, and religion were central.

The spirituals signify hope, confidence, and transcendence, even in the face of seemingly insurmountable obstacles. Through this sacred music and the ethos it gives meaning to, the slaves identified strongly with the Children of Israel and their travail as God's chosen people. Indeed they envisioned the Israelites' deliverance from slavery through God's handiwork as emblematic of their own impending liberation. Likewise, they personalized their relationship to God and heroic religious figures, often referring to them in fictive kin terms. These songs were similar to white spirituals in revealing ways, including common origins in standard Protestant hymns sung in churches and camp meetings attended by whites and blacks. Common themes encompassed community, the eternal bliss of the heavenly afterlife, and martial imagery. Even more revealing, however, are the striking differences, including the African spiritual and musical imprints, more vivid biblical imagery, and the compelling sense of identification with God's chosen people. The slave spirituals were clearly a unique music which spoke profoundly to the slaves' experiences and needs.

Improvised, functional, and multipurpose, field hollers, whoops, or water calls could range from a commentary on loneliness, to a plea for help, to a rhythmic work accompaniment.

African Americans, slave and free, preferred to worship apart from whites. When whites demanded that slaves attend joint services run by whites, slaves went and may even have been moved. Nevertheless, there persisted a vibrant tradition of separate—often surreptitious—slave worship services in secluded praise houses. In these secret meetings of the "slave church"—as opposed to the master's church—the spirit could reign unchecked. Shouting, weeping, moaning, even spirit possession were not uncommon. In this setting, the spirituals flourished, as did the ring shout (a religious dance performed in a counterclockwise-moving circle with a shuffling gait, picking up in vigor as the spirit intensified). In continental and diasporan African contexts, this kind of dance was a primary part of important rituals and celebrations.

Similarly, funeral customs often featured African forms of ritual celebration. Unlike the somber rites typical of many European American burials, those of African American slaves were frequently joyous, possibly featuring song and dance as well as libations, animal sacrifices, and grave decorations. Highlighting the cultural importance attached to the afterlife and the ancestors, these customs vividly reflected the slaves' sacred worldview and social holism. The music ranged from the mournful to the ecstatic, but the context emphasized a positive spirit.

A remarkably similar spirit characterized antebellum African American secular music. In fact, the traditional worldview of African slaves in a sense recognized the sacred and the secular as more singular than dual. This relatively undifferentiated boundary between sacred and secular in the traditional ethos became more differentiated after emancipation as the freed people grew more literate and educated. As modernity—notably individualism, secularism, and urbanization—increasingly challenged tradition in African American culture, the tension between the spiritual and the worldly intensified. Similarly, the number and percentage of Africans born in the United States grew and as cross-cultural exchanges expanded, creolization increased. Growing Christianization added another layer of complexity to African Americanization. Emancipation enabled free and freed African Americans to accelerate the process of bridging their cultural differences with other Americans. Nevertheless, within the folk culture, especially the music, important unifying commonalities persisted.

One of these unifying cultural traditions is secular music. While relatively little antebellum African American secular music has been preserved, enough accounts exist to show that this music was far more extensive and significant than the slender written record suggests. Drawing upon an African cultural framework in which music and work were interwoven, the secular music tradition was, not surprisingly, revitalized in America. It especially helped to define the various social affairs dedicated to leisure and entertainment.

Work songs, including industrial, domestic, and field work songs, are a particularly prominent element in the extant evidence. Tunes often accompanied maritime jobs such as roustabout and stevedore, and were sung as blacks worked the inland and coastal waters. Black watermen not only developed distinctive kinds of music but also played a vital role, notably in the antebellum period, in the dissemination of regional varieties of African American music. One of the most important factors serving to integrate such differences in the twentieth century is growing geographic mobility; in the antebellum era, however, mobility was quite restricted, particularly for slaves. Nevertheless, similar work song patterns evolved.

Field hollers, whoops, or water calls, in addition to city street cries, constitute an important yet neglected vocal musical tradition. The former are rare in the antebellum literature. Clearly improvised, functional, and multipurpose, they could range from a commentary on loneliness, to a plea for help, to a rhythmic work accompaniment. This mode of expression—notable for its variety, flexibility, mundane essence, and improvisational flair—is basic to African American music. Similarly, the street cries were extemporaneous and wide-ranging, yet direct. Originating with itinerant laborers seeking jobs and vendors hawking goods, they also influenced the developing musical tradition.

Although over time the distinction between sacred and secular music became more important, in the traditional antebellum world evidence of interpenetration abounds: the sharing of phrases, texts, tunes, and structures; the use of sacred songs in secular contexts; and the African-inspired musical aesthetic suffusing both.

Clearly music has been a vital element in the complex of cultural strategies African Americans have devised to endure and to rise above the hardships they have confronted. Beyond its function as a coping or adaptive mechanism, music has served in many ways to witness and to promote protest, even insurrection. For example, the many references in the spirituals to the liberation of the Hebrews as God's chosen people spoke plainly yet powerfully to the liberation quests of both slave and free African Americans. That songs like "Steal Away to Jesus" and "Follow the Drinking Gourd" functioned as a means of communication among runaway slaves within the Underground Railroad is likewise instructive. That music inspired and united revolutionaries such as Nat Turner and his followers is provocative. (Turner, a slave preacher, led an uprising in Virginia in 1831.) From the standpoint of the history of African American music, however, the primary point is the centrality of music to the culture. African American music helped African Americans make sense of their often difficult lives, offering a sense of autonomy within an oppressive and restricted world.

"Soul Deep": African American Music 1865 to the Present

Emancipation appeared to offer much to African Americans. The fragile euphoria of the Civil War, emancipation, and Reconstruction years (1861 to 1877), however, gave way to the institutionalization of Jim Crow (discrimination against African Americans sanctioned by law or tradition) throughout the South at the turn of the twentieth century. Dashed hopes and dreams became more common as peonage increasingly ensnared massive numbers of blacks, although a modest African American urban middle class developed, primarily providing goods and services for their segregated communities. Given the persistent social, political, and economic gulf separating blacks and whites, it is not surprising that black culture and black music retained their distinctiveness.

Freedom, notwithstanding its contradictions, represented expanded cultural and musical horizons for African Americans. The "invisible institution" of the slave church came above ground, functioning as a spiritual and musical hothouse. Similarly, secular music found more public spaces in which to develop. Antebellum holiday celebrations had included (besides those previously mentioned) Christmas, New Year's Day, and, in the North, West Indian Emancipation Day (begun in 1834). After emancipation in the United States, that event itself was often the focus of a major celebration, as in the Juneteenth commemoration among black Texans.

A constellation of forces complicated the development of black music in the late nineteenth and early twentieth centuries. First, secularization accelerated the tension between the spiritual and secular realms. Second, rising rates of literacy and formal education meant intensified interaction between the traditional oral and modern literate aspects of the culture. Third, urbanization, particularly in the twentieth century, augmented the culture's parameters and directions, with a heightening of the interpenetration between the rural and the urban. Fourth, a growing measure of class differentiation resulting from a degree of African American social mobility enhanced the creative tensions between the folk culture and black middle-class culture. Fifth, in spite of racism and segregation, ongoing creolization enhanced cross-cultural musical influence.

Another factor—the expanding commercialization of American culture and African American cultural productions since the late nineteenth century—has had tremendous consequences for African American music. With the seemingly ever-expanding marketing of the music throughout the twentieth century, its hybrid qualities have become increasingly significant. As African American musicians have sought to broaden the music's scope and audience, the African taproot has grown deeper in some ways, less potent in others. Cross-pollination has enriched American music greatly, even though many underestimate and misconstrue this fact for a variety of reasons, including racism, ethnocentrism, and cultural nationalism.

White racial privilege has warped the inevitable process of cross-cultural musical influence, making the white appropriation of black music especially lucrative. Countless whites have preferred other whites performing assimilated black music, at best, and gross caricatures of black music, at worst, to blacks performing black music. In the late twentieth century, moreover, musical genres and styles have blurred in some instances to the point where African American music itself is no longer the special preserve of African American artists.

In a world of equality and freedom, this would be a positive achievement. In our own real world of racial exploitation, though, where black music fuels significant white corporate wealth and many white musical careers, the white appropriation of black music is problematic.

Two nineteenth-century developments in particular heralded the expanding cultural complexity wrought by the phenomenal growth of black music. To begin with, even in the slave South, African Americans had created an impressive body of music. In the post-emancipation world, drawing upon that rich musical vocabulary, African Americans fashioned new and, in many cases, equally impressive musical languages. The importance of a musical tradition deeply rooted in social life and cultural practice cannot be overestimated; it constituted the essential building blocks for subsequent musical innovation.

Second, the place of nineteenth-century black music in the period's racial politics played a key role in shaping the music's development. The exceedingly complex patterns of ambivalence and ambiguity distinguishing race relations between whites and blacks have been both cultural and social. These patterns have proceeded in often unanticipated, ironic, and multifaceted ways. White power and privilege have remained substantial, but so have black endurance and transcendence. As whites controlled the political and economic high ground, blacks controlled the moral and spiritual high ground. On one level, in terms of a national culture, this dynamic has favored white tastes, styles, and productions over black ones. On a deeper level, it has given African American culture a broad and compelling impact.

Blackface minstrelsy vividly exemplifies the complicated quality of race in the nineteenth century. Beginning around the 1830s and 1840s, it grew out of white efforts to mimic and make fun of blacks for entertainment and for profit; it became the most popular form of mass entertainment in the nineteenth century. Minstrel tunes were a music of caricature and flattery, of ambivalent and tangled white feelings about blacks and their music. The supreme irony, of course, came when blacks appropriated this idiom and reinterpreted it. While white minstrelsy gave countless whites a racist white interpretation of black culture, the effect of black minstrelsy—given the inherent limitations of the minstrel form—was often no more enlightening or sensitive. Black performers could neither alleviate nor overcome the deeply disturbing racial politics of minstrelsy. Despite its popularity, blackface minstrelsy did not represent a central musical tradition. The more important musical forms came directly out of authentic African American worldviews and communities.

Following the brief gestational period of the immediate post-emancipation years, a series of innovations occurred within African American music that led to the maturation of distinctive yet inextricably interwoven genres. This creative outburst would help to shape twentieth-century American music and the burgeoning twentieth-century worldwide market for popular music. Gospel, blues, jazz, and rhythm and blues are the primary and most influential genres. The fundamental similarities among them reflect a common cultural aesthetic whose bedrock sensibility remains African. Two thematic clusters dominate: discontent and alienation, on the one hand, and struggle and affirmation, on the other. The best of these twentieth-century forms and their offshoots brilliantly capture the affective, spiritual, and multidimensional qualities so vital to the culture.

While the spirituals remained popular with African Americans in the new century, many—notably upwardly mobile assimilationists—saw them as quaint and embarrassing relics of the past. Middle-class blacks, including aspirants and supporters, typically displayed defensiveness and ambivalence about any aspects of the folk culture—like the spirituals—that might not throw what they saw as the best light on African Americans and their progress since slavery. Similarly, as the outside world increasingly intruded upon African American consciousness, the sacred worldview that had given meaning and direction to African American life slowly came under attack.

Gospel music—"good news" or jubilee music—arose in the late nineteenth century among whites as well as blacks as a revivalist and evangelical response to the perception of rising immorality. This music stressed the joy of Christian salvation in the here and now as well as the benefits of a sanctified life-style. It was not simply fixated on the glories of the heavenly afterlife, as so many of its critics assumed. Among African Americans, gospel took root most firmly in the Church of Christ, Holiness, Pentecostal, and Church of God in Christ faiths with their strict evangelicalism and fervent religiosity. An awesome emotional intensity deeply influenced the maturation of black gospel, which was far livelier than white gospel during the early period. Black gospel took literally the biblical injunction to serve God with a "joyful noise." As rural southern blacks migrated north, they carried their music, especially gospel, with them. The countless northern storefront churches steeped in the evangelical tradition, as well as Baptist and Methodist citadels, furthered the spread and development of gospel music, especially in the 1920s and 1930s. By 1930 it had surpassed the spiritual as the major African American religious music. By 1950 it had entered what some have regarded as its golden era (roughly 1945 to 1960).

Gospel music flowered in a spontaneous and expressive context comparable with that which had often served as the seedbed for the spiritual. Growing out of a process of group improvisation often featuring antiphonal give-and-take between the group and leaders, gospel music also featured holy dancing and shouting reminiscent of the ring about, especially in the rural South. The truly sanctified spoke in tongues (glossolalia), achieved spirit possession, and during Communion washed feet (as an act of humility). This multilayered and participatory worship experience enhanced the fiery depth of gospel music. Like the spiritual, early gospel music was typically sung a cappella. Soon, however, instruments were incorporated, augmenting the music's visceral power. Tambourines, pianos, organs, and guitars were common by mid century. Drawing extensively from other forms, notably jazz and blues, gospel music had also quickly added other instruments, such as horns and drums.

Lyrically, gospel music initially drew heavily upon a common stock of religious songs. Pioneer composers like Charles Albert Tindley (1856–1933) reworked these often raw rural expressions into texts. Within the gospel tradition, however, the text remains a malleable framework to be recast in accordance with the demands of the Holy Spirit. Still, the growing popularity of gospel music beyond the more evangelical faiths to the dominant Baptist and Methodist churches depended heavily upon the efforts of composers and popularizers like Thomas A. Dorsey (b. 1899). Personifying the cross-pollination between secular and religious music,

An awesome emotional intensity deeply influenced the maturation of black gospel music, which took literally the biblical injunction to serve God with a "joyful noise."

Dorsey initially wrote gospel and blues tunes. An accomplished musician, he first achieved notoriety in the blues field as "Georgia Tom," the pianist for Gertrude "Ma" Rainey, a blues-singing sensation in the 1920s. He also had a four-year partnership with blues singer Tampa Red during this period that led to the writing and recording of the highly successful tune "It's Tight Like That." Not until the early 1930s did he succeed in the gospel vein. In addition to penning the classic gospel number "Precious Lord, Take My Hand," he became an important publisher and the composer of over four hundred gospel songs, a gospel publicist, and, with Sallie Martin (a pioneering and influential gospel singer in her own right), a cofounder of the National [Black] Convention of Gospel Choirs and Choruses.

Gospel's growing popularity also derived from its variety of formats and formidable vocal talent. There were male quartets early in the century; by the 1930s their numbers were growing dramatically. Among the most notable organized prior to 1940 were the Dixie Hummingbirds, the Soul Stirrers, and the Swan Silvertones. During the 1940s, women's groups achieved prominence, notably the Sallie Martin Singers, the Ward Trio, and the Angelic Gospel Singers. Among the outstanding soloists was Sister Rosetta Tharpe, who mixed blues-based guitar and sanctified music to gain a national following by mid century. She excelled as a rousing performer, taking the music to Carnegie Hall, jazz venues, or wherever it led. In addition, her records, such as her bluesy interpretation of Dorsey's gospel tune "Rock Me," sold well.

The most influential soloist of this period was Mahalia Jackson. Artfully combining a variety of early influences—Baptist hymns, gospel songs, spirituals, blues, and jazz—she created a contralto style notable for its fire, dignity, and rare beauty. A charismatic performer, she had an electrifying vocal and performance style that captivated audiences worldwide and inspired generations of admirers and followers. Jackson's 1947 recording of "Move on up a Little Higher" sold over a million copies—the first gospel million seller. In 1950 the National [Black] Baptist Convention selected her its official soloist. She was indeed the "Queen of Gospel." Her rising recognition among whites enabled her to achieve unparalleled fame for a gospel singer, including a recording contract with Columbia Records and appearances on television talk and variety shows.

Above all else, gospel is a performance-based, live, social music. Whether in the church or the concert hall, the gospel performer participates in a musical incantation aimed at praising the Lord and promoting spiritual ecstasy, typically highlighted by shouting, hand clapping, oral antiphony ("Sing it!"; "Amen!"; "Praise Jesus!"), humming, moaning, body weaving, foot tapping, and head bobbing. Vocal pyrotechnics—melisma (stretching words and syllables across several notes), full-throated and lyrical textures; scintillating runs among low and high notes, bending notes, and screams, cries, and whispers—are common. Ultimately, if the musical ritual works, audience and performer become one, exemplifying the communal consciousness basic to African American music and traditional African American religious worship styles.

The famous gospel extravaganzas of the 1950s and 1960s featured a variety of performers—male quartets, women's groups, soloists, choirs—each vying to outperform the others. Success was judged by how well one captured and elevated the spirit. From the dress—fancy robes, gowns, and suits—to the dramatic touches—marching and swaying choirs, dropping to one's knees, shouting, intense facial expressions, stirring monologues and dialogues, and the like—the goal was to deliver a spine-tingling and memorable performance. "Church wrecking" or "house wrecking"—achieving an incandescent spiritual peak throughout the audience or congregation—solidified the reputations of performers like Mahalia Jackson, the Sensational Nightingales, the Dixie Hummingbirds, Bessie Griffin, and Professor Alex Bradford. Particularly effective at church wrecking were the singing preachers, practitioners of the chanted or "performed" sermon, such as the Reverend C. L. Franklin.

In a sense, gospel music is the modern spiritual. The distinctive spiritual genre evolved from a rural, folk, preliterate sensibility, with an Old Testament bias. Gospel, which began as a transitional music signifying post-emancipation hope and affirmation, evolved in a context of movement away from the folk sensibility of the spirituals toward a more urban and polished sensibility, with a New Testament bias. Still, the emotional depth unifying spirituals and gospel blurs their differences.

Disagreement persists between those favoring a more or less rigid distinction between sacred and secular African American music. While the very strong disapproval within the gospel community of what was often called "the devil's music" has softened a bit with time, it continues to this day in many quarters. For many the problem is simple: the boundary between spiritual and secular pleasure has to be both maintained and solidified. In reality, however, this boundary blurs and proves permeable: musicians consciously and unconsciously cross it, often with provocative results. Sister Rosetta Tharpe's 1939 recording of Dorsey's gospel number "Rock Me," for example, featured Lucky Millinder's blues band in the background and became a pop smash. Many found this objectionable. Nevertheless, a measure of gospel's vitality, like that of other genres, flows from an openness to borrowing outside elements and reshaping them along gospel lines.

Many have characterized the blues in particular as secular spirituals. In fact, many secular music artists, blues musicians included, began their musical immersion in the church. Much of the cross-referencing and cross-fertilization between the sacred and the secular, then, has strong religious roots. Ultimately, their mutual dependency has led to a fascinating paradox. This bond has both reinforced and blurred the distinction between them.

The blues vividly exemplifies this paradox. Indeed, compared with gospel artists, secular artists have appeared far less anxious about this issue, especially over time. Having been musically nourished in a tradition with a broad reservoir of forms and elements visible in both sacred and secular music, countless blues and jazz musicians have reveled in the resulting artistic possibilities. Many have consciously drawn upon the sacred musical grammar and vocabulary, included sacred music in their repertoire, and performed and recorded religious tunes. This same creative eclecticism has enriched later developments, notably 1960s soul music and post-1960s "progressive gospel."

Even more than those of gospel, the origins of the blues are hard to pinpoint. They clearly date at least as far back as the post-emancipation world of the late nineteenth century. The primary sources for this music are amazingly diverse. On the secular front, they include work songs, field hollers, urban cries, ballads, minstrel songs, ragtime tunes, and maritime music. Spirituals and revival hymns were the most influential religious music sources. Inspired, like gospel, by freedom and spatial mobility, the blues began as folk music. Throughout its history, it has maintained folk roots and forms even as many observers have lamented what they have interpreted as a decline in the blues as a folk music.

As a distinctive musical genre, the blues emerged as a personalized expression of the day-to-day experiences of ordinary folk. While still intimately wedded to a social ethos, the perspective is typically that of the self. Exploring the range of human emotions and feelings, the blues can be didactic, but above all else, they are a celebration of the human spirit: entertainment or "good time" music. The common mistake of confusing the popular definition of the word "blue(s)" as sad and mournful with the musical genre of the blues has thus been unfortunate and misleading. Although there are sad and mournful blues, they constitute only a slice of an emotionally rich pie. The blues run the emotional gamut from high to low, sometimes incorporating both in a single tune. This candid baring of the soul underscores the music's intrinsic realism and honesty.

Preeminently an aural and performance-based music, the blues evolved early on as improvisations building upon a common pool of lyrics and phrases. Improvisation took place largely as variations on a fundamental base: a twelve-bar form with a three-line verse and rhyming words. This flexible structure has yielded countless permutations. There are melodic and percussive styles. Essentially vocal music, the blues cull from the panoply of techniques typical of African American folk vocalizing, including moans, shrieks, cries, grunts, bends, slides, and dips; various textures and shadings, like vibrato and falsetto; and, most distinctive in the blues, falling pitches to express emotion. Early blues musicians favored a wide variety of accompanying instruments. While the guitar emerged as the favorite, the list encompassed the banjo, fiddle, piano, harmonica, washboard, jug, and kazoo.

The blues incubated in a variety of contexts: front porches, street corners, parties, juke joints, medicine shows, tent shows, vaudeville shows, clubs, taverns, red-light districts, and steamboats. Throughout southern and border states, in rural and urban areas, in places public and private, the blues gained players and supporters, as this singular yet diverse music came to speak so clearly and deeply to its hearers. The sundry themes—ranging from love to anger, from problem naming to problem solving, from accommodation to resistance—are universal. Several observers have cogently argued that feel and nuance are more important than lyrical integrity. A moving evocation of a mood, a place, an emotion—this is the stuff of the blues.

Many argue that Robert Johnson, of "Terraplane Blues" and "Hellbound on My Trail" fame, was the greatest bluesman not only of his generation but in the music's recorded history.

Given the diverse origins and wide—primarily southern—territorial domain of the blues, the early emergence of unique blues styles and varieties is not surprising. Most blues experts recognize three major types: down-home, rural, or country blues; classic blues of the 1920s, principally a black woman's genre; and urban blues. In the late 1920s and early 1930s, the most influential of the early down-home blues singers was "Blind" Lemon Jefferson out of Texas. His high voice and spare tone typified Texas blues. The most important regional variety of the down-home blues, however, came from the Mississippi Delta. Here a gritty approach prevailed, distinguished by a heavy rasping vocal quality, although there were high-voiced singers as well. Charley Patton, Eddie "Son" House, and Tommy Johnson epitomized this earthy style.

The most influential Mississippi Delta blues-man of this period, however, came on the scene a little later and met a violent death in 1938. Many argue that Robert Johnson, of "Terraplane Blues" and "Hellhound on My Trail" fame, was the greatest bluesman not only of his generation but in the music's recorded history. Legend and his superb yet limited recorded output reveal a compelling vocal and guitar talent whose disciples have included Muddy Waters and Elmore James. During his rediscovery in the 1960s, Johnson influenced many, including black folk singer Taj Mahal and white rock performers such as the Rolling Stones, and guitarist and vocalist Eric Clapton. His vocal and instrumental technique reflected a variety of influences transformed into a mesmerizing style. A self-assured player, he used falsetto howls, dramatic vocals, rapid bottleneck runs on the guitar, strong beat, lyrical detail, and aggressive delivery to create a gripping, if small, body of work. He skillfully presented powerhouse down-home blues while anticipating the urban, modern music still in the making.

In part, the impact of Johnson and other blues legends owes much to the tremendous growth of the "race records" market aimed at African American consumers. The extraordinary success of Mamie Smith's 1920 recording of "Crazy Blues" greatly advanced the commercialization of black music. The profits and wealth from this development, however, remained largely in the hands of white-owned record companies. Not until the postwar period, with the establishment of major black-owned record companies like Vee-Jay, Motown, and Philadelphia International, did this imbalance begin to shift measurably: Nevertheless, in the 1920s, records quickly outpaced traveling productions such as vaudeville shows as the principal method for the music's dissemination among blacks. Furthermore, records were far more important in this regard than published blues sheet music, like that of W. C. Handy. In addition, records gradually increased the popularity, among whites as well as blacks, of other kinds of African American music.

A significant result of the scramble among white-owned record companies to get into the race records market was the recording of a number of blues divas. The two most important were the "Mother of the Blues," "Ma" Rainey, and the "Empress of the Blues," Bessie Smith. While both got their start within the minstrel-vaudeville context; both soon emerged as overpowering solo artists in their own right. "Ma" Rainey's vocals tended in the folk direction, while Smith's went toward jazz. Smith rapidly became a huge success, eclipsing Rainey, whose records did not do justice to her strong and expressive voice. Smith's ability to combine blues intensity with jazz phrasing enabled her to handle jazz and blues material equally well. Among her stellar recorded performances are a 1925 duet with Louis Armstrong of "You've Been a Good Old Wagon" and her 1927 effort, "Back Water Blues." The proud and assertive posture of Smith and Rainey was an important contribution in the ongoing struggle of black women to speak for themselves from their own cultural world.

The blues necessarily encompassed much musical territory. This terrain incorporated early jug, string, and washboard bands; professional bands like Lucky Millinder's; and piano blues, most notably the irrepressible boogie-woogie with its firm left-hand rhythms and agile right-hand melodic and rhythmic lines. As with gospel, however, the end of the Great Depression, the entrance of the United States into World War II, and the growing militancy of the continuing black liberation struggle from the 1940s on, dramatically altered the blues. For one thing, urban blues became increasingly distinctive, with Chicago leading the way. Figures like blues harmonica pioneer John Lee "Sonny Boy" Williamson and the popular blues guitarist Big Bill Broonzy personified this trend.

The migration of hundreds of thousands of blacks out of the South during World War I, seeking jobs in northern cities like New York and Chicago, profoundly influenced African American culture and music. Similarly, during World War II blacks migrated in search of wartime jobs with corresponding cultural and musical results. This time hundreds of thousands headed west as well as north. Consequently, since 1945 African American music has witnessed a series of very rapid developments. Nowhere is this more evident than in jazz.

Like gospel and blues, jazz has a complicated and most likely irrecoverable prerecording history. Its origins go back at least to various kinds of music played around the turn of the century, including blues, brass band music, dance orchestra music, syncopated dance music, and ragtime. A unique piano music style in its own right, ragtime was not an early jazz form. Rather, it—like other related but autonomous styles—contributed to jazz's early evolution. With its infectious steady left-hand beat and syncopated right-hand melody, ragtime spawned several important composers, most notably Scott Joplin, whose "Maple Leaf Rag" sold over a million copies in 1899 alone. Associated in the public mind at the time with the cakewalk, a turn-of-the-century dance craze based on moves first observed among slaves and popularized by minstrels, ragtime was a composed rather than improvised music. As such, while it led in directions that had influence in jazz, notably the stride piano style (so called because of the "striding" left hand that alternated between a chord on the off beat and a single note on the on beat) of Eubie Blake and James P. Johnson (also known as Harlem stride), it is best seen as a limited but distinctive form which served in addition as a tributary in jazz's early history.

Consistent with its diverse sources, jazz took root and flourished in various environments, especially that great musical polyglot New Orleans. The music sprouted in places throughout the urban South and Midwest—particularly Chicago, Memphis, and Kansas City—as well as New York City and points on the West Coast. Still, out of New Orleans came the acknowledged initial masters: the elusive cornetist Charles "Buddy" Bolden; Jelly Roll Morton, the first great jazz composer; and Louis Armstrong, the first great innovative soloist.

Not enough reliable information on Bolden remains to verify his turn-of-the-century reputation, but Morton left a solid recording legacy, notably his work with the Red Hot Peppers band (1926) and his fifty-two-record set made at the Library of Congress (1938). While considerable controversy has whirled around his flamboyant life-style, personality, and musical claims, his considerable jazz achievements have been well documented. First, his music is a unique and coherent blend of a variety of elements—blues, ragtime, and brass band music, with operatic touches. In fact, he effectively combined the heavily European-influenced music of the French Creoles of color with the more African-based music of the darker-complexioned uptown African American community. This he accomplished notwithstanding his own prejudice against African Americans darker than himself. Second, he convincingly met one of the central challenges of jazz: the integration of improvisation and composition. Third, his work demonstrates complexity on numerous levels, such as his successful negotiation of another major jazz challenge: blending solo and ensemble into a coherent whole. His musical legacy lives on through the numerous important works he contributed to the jazz repertoire, including "Black Bottom Stomp," Smoke House Blues," and "King Porter Stomp."

The two most important blues divas—"Ma" Rainey and Bessie Smith—both got their start within the minstrel-vaudeville context, and both soon emerged as overpowering solo artists in their own right.

Growing up poor and surrounded by music in his native New Orleans, Louis Armstrong (1900–1971) sang for small change alongside other children on the streets. After picking up the trumpet in 1914 during a stay at the (Colored) Waifs Home for Boys, he began a period of rapid musical study and growth. By the time he electrified the burgeoning jazz scene in Chicago and New York in the 1920s, he had imbibed a great deal from the extraordinary musical scene in New Orleans, especially from the honky-tonks of the notorious Storyville red-light district. Drawing upon a great trumpet tradition which included Buddy Bolden, Bunk Johnson, and King Oliver (an important early mentor as well), he soon developed his own unique style. Armstrong's greatness as a trumpeter resided in a complex of factors: superb technique (especially his marvelous tonal range), his innovative brilliance, bluesy passion, keen musical logic, and unparalleled ability to swing. And most of all, he was a wonderful entertainer. His musical contributions, as a result, are numerous and significant. Two of the most striking were his melodic creativity and his rhythmic artistry. Indeed those were crucial to his mastery of the swing aesthetic. The latter is notoriously difficult to explain, but it revolves around exploration of the myriad subtleties of rhythm. Much of subsequent jazz history has been deeply influenced by his melodic paraphrasing and his uncanny sense of swing. While his recording, performance, and show business careers stretched into the 1960s, he created his most innovative and influential work in the late 1920s and early 1930s. These pieces include "Potato Head Blues" (1927), "West End Blues" (1928), and "Weather Bird" (1928). Armstrong is widely acknowledged to have been one of the greatest musicians of this century.

Edward Kennedy "Duke" Ellington (1899–1974) grew up in middle-class surroundings in his native Washington, D.C., and by his high school years had demonstrated considerable artistic and musical talent. After leading several local bands as a teenager, in the 1920s he relocated in New York City where he honed his piano and band-leading skills, absorbing the rich influences of some of Harlem's most notable composers, arrangers, and musicians. A 1927 engagement at the Cotton Club launched him and his band on an extraordinary career. Ellington set the inventive standard for orchestra or big band jazz in much the same way that Armstrong did for solo jazz. There had been several notable bands prior to Ellington's, including King Oliver's Creole Jazz Band and Fletcher Henderson and His Orchestra. Both featured Armstrong for periods in the early to mid 1920s. Henderson and his early arranger Don Redman had pioneered the standard big band format, deftly mixing written parts, improvised solos, and call-and-response exchanges between sections of the orchestra. Ellington's greatness grew out of his innovative exploration of the central challenges in ensemble jazz that Morton negotiated so well. Going far beyond Morton, Fletcher Henderson, and his contemporaries, Ellington resolved the problems of integrating improvisation with composition, on the one hand, and the soloist with the band, on the other, through various creative blends and juxtapositions. These combinations relied heavily upon collaboration with first-rate band members, building upon their individual talents. This careful attention to the band's sonorous reservoir enabled Ellington to compose music with extraordinary harmonic range and beauty, and equally extraordinary color and texture. A prolific and talented composer and an indefatigable performer, Ellington (and his orchestra) contributed enormously to the popularity of 1930s big band jazz or swing jazz.

A prolific and talented composer and performer, Duke Ellington and his orchestra contributed enormously to the popularity of big band jazz or swing jazz.

Another aspect of Ellington's achievement was his ability to combine vernacular and elite forms and sensibilities. This is clear from his astounding body of around fifteen hundred works encompassing popular tunes like "Sophisticated Lady," "Satin Doll," and "Mood Indigo"; jazz orchestra works like "Harlem Airshaft" and "Ko-ko"; extended concert pieces like "Suite Thursday"; and operas, film scores, and ballets. Ellington was truly a creative giant and possibly the greatest composer America has ever produced.

Ellington's amazing achievements cannot diminish the outstanding contributions of many contemporary artists. Among the other great bands of the period, Count Basie's, coming out of Kansas City, merits special mention for bringing together the best of the midwestern variants of blues, boogie woogie, and dance music. More squarely in the Henderson big band mold, Basie's aggregation distinguished itself with its exceptional swing capability, its bluesy boldness, and its strong solo tradition, personified by the legendary work of tenor saxophonist Lester Young. The preeminent jazz vocalist of the 1930s was Billie Holiday, whose work spanned the 1930s, 1940s, and 1950s. Typically surrounded by superb supporting musicians like Young, she excelled at creating and sustaining an intense musical moment, much like her acknowledged musical influences, Bessie Smith and Louis Armstrong. Her vocal artistry has been lavishly praised and she has influenced many, notably Sarah Vaughn and Dinah Washington. Particularly noteworthy were her melodic and rhythmic inventiveness, her ability to personalize a song, and her arresting emotional poignancy.

The 1920s and 1930s witnessed tremendous strides in jazz even as African American musicians and their efforts, like African Americans generally, remained subject to prejudice and discrimination. Jazz, in fact, initially often met serious opposition from some middle-class blacks who, like many whites, labeled the music sensual and barbaric. Even within the Harlem Renaissance (largely a literary and visual arts movement) of the 1920s, few realized the importance and potential of jazz. Nevertheless, the swing music craze of the 1930s greatly enhanced jazz's popularity. With whites, bands like Paul Whiteman's and Benny Goodman's were critical to this popular acclaim. Even black artists like Armstrong and Ellington found a growing measure of support among whites. Radio broadcasts, dances, concerts, and the overall development of the entertainment media in which jazz played a role—as well as jazz records—helped to expand the music's popularity. Depression America found a measure of release and joy in jazz.

The war years witnessed trends, most notably the intensifying black civil rights and black power struggles, that would seriously influence African American music. The rapidly growing black liberation struggle enhanced the move toward greater freedom of expression and experimentation throughout African American culture, especially within its music. This setting also fed the rise in black-owned music businesses, most notably record companies like Motown and Philadelphia International, aimed primarily at bringing black music to a larger audience. These efforts greatly expanded the impact of blacks throughout the music industry at all levels, from artists to executives, by skillfully exploiting the popularity and clout of African American music. Projecting themselves as both successful ethnic/race enterprises and authentic creators and purveyors of the music, these companies have reaped great success. In turn, the major white-owned record companies have effectively redoubled their efforts to dominate the market in African American music. The effects of this freedom, growth, and competition on the music can be traced in developments in the music, especially jazz and blues, since around 1945.

Gospel began to change most noticeably after the late 1960s when artists like the Hawkinses—Edwin, Walter, and Tramaine—and Andrae Crouch began to draw more confidently and openly upon secular music. This conscious and well-conceived blending of gospel and secular music is often referred to as "progressive" gospel, to distinguish it from traditional gospel. In the late 1980s one of the most popular gospel groups was Take 6, with its a cappella renditions steeped in jazz and gospel. Such cross-fertilization has revitalized interest in gospel among many and has generated countless new admirers in the United States and abroad.

The changes in the blues between the 1940s and the 1990s ranged from the minor to the cataclysmic. In 1949 the music industry via *Billboard*, its trade publication, changed the designation of popular music aimed at black audiences from "race music" to "rhythm and blues." This music encompassed a broad array of blues styles; its most characteristic features were its increased use of amplification and its steady beat. While country blues continued to be sung and played in rural areas, the rural blues became urbanized as blacks increasingly migrated to cities. Chicago artists like former Mississippi Delta bluesmen Muddy Waters, Howlin' Wolf, and John Lee Hooker blazed this trail, bringing the country to the city with a stirring intensity.

In the blues band tradition, Louis Jordan's Tympani Five built upon its leader's jazz background to forge a highly popular and influential dance and "good time" music known as "jump." Guitarist T-Bone Walker proved influential as a bandleader, vocalist, and performer. His dazzling electric guitar work and show-stopping antics influenced artists such as B. B. King. Indeed, for countless fans in the 1990s, B. B. King still personifies the urban blues tradition, with its thrilling guitar runs and emotional immediacy.

As urban blues continued a distinctive line of development, other blues offshoots emerged in the 1950s from within the rhythm and blues rubric that spoke more plainly to both the changing status of African

Americans and the emerging youth culture. Soul, as well as rock and roll, frequently crossed both musical lines and categorical boundaries such as age, race, class, and national origin. By the early 1990s, the most popular and influential music in the world was music that had grown out of this blues or rhythm and blues matrix. As styles and forms increasingly mixed, the creole quality of the music also grew, this hybrid flavor greatly contributing to its worldwide impact.

Rock and roll emerged as a 1950s expression of rhythm and blues aimed initially at adolescent white audiences. While a number of the pioneering artists were black—Little Richard, Chuck Berry, and Bo Diddley—the breakthrough artist was Elvis Presley, a white Mississippian who combined blues and country music influences into a "rockabilly" mix and whose important work brought heavily black-influenced music to an ever-increasing white American and worldwide audience in the late 1950s and early 1960s. As the civil rights movement gained momentum, racial barriers fell, and blacks and whites did more soul searching, more and more black artists had crossover appeal. This diminished the practice of white artists' covering black tunes, releasing denatured versions aimed at allegedly more refined white tastes. Interestingly enough, in the late 1960s, electric-guitar virtuoso Jimi Hendrix (1942–1970) forged a blues-based brand of high-voltage, flamboyant, and very influential rock and roll, which creatively explored the illusory yet resonant boundary between "black" rhythm and blues and "white" rock. Both, as his music shows, clearly derive from the blues tradition.

As "the Godfather of Soul" and "the Queen of Soul," James Brown and Aretha Franklin used their music to tap into a revitalized black consciousness.

In light of the similarities among blues varieties, often the very idea of boundaries among them was dubious. Within the African American musical tradition, nevertheless, the rhythm and blues idiom spawned several innovations beginning in the 1950s. Chief among these were soul, which reigned supreme from around 1960 to the early 1970s, 1970s and 1980s funk and disco, and 1980s hip hop and rap. Soul music features hard-driving rhythm and blues with a heavy gospel background. Its intensity draws heavily upon the deep emotional reservoir of both of these sources. Major innovators in this tradition have penetrated the interrelatedness between African American sacred and secular music traditions in highly influential ways. In the 1950s Ray Charles openly and effectively mixed traditional gospel melodic and lyrical frameworks with secular concerns and found a large white and black audience, notwithstanding the alarm of many who felt the mix was sacrilegious. Charles, a consummate artist, has also produced important work perceptively exploring the links between rhythm and blues and jazz, country and western, rock and roll, and mainstream popular song. He has truly stretched the idea of boundaries in African American and American music and culture.

The music of James Brown and Aretha Franklin brilliantly captured the growing assertiveness and self-confidence of African Americans during the civil rights—black power years. As the "Godfather of Soul" and "the Queen of Soul," these singers, in their music, tapped into a revitalized black consciousness. When Brown sang "Say It Loud, I'm Black and I'm Proud," he contributed to a groundswell in black pride. When Franklin sang "To Be Young, Gifted, and Black," a stirring anthem by the "High Priestess of Soul," Nina Simone, people took notice.

Brown's work as a superb dancer, powerful vocalist, leader of a cutting-edge band, arresting conceptual artist, and legendary performer has exerted enormous influence on African American music. His driving rhythms and heavy bass line were basic to disco—the popular, more lightweight dance music typically structured around less complex rhythms—and funk—the raw and hard-driving rhythmically based idiom he literally created. Furthermore, rap music draws liberally from his extensive body of work. Creole inventiveness at its finest, rap music employs the latest electronic musical technology to appropriate disparate musical riffs and phrases as a means of creating a unique musical mosaic. Highly developed and highly stylized verbal artistry in which rhyming lyrics are rhythmically delivered over music dominated by a pulsating beat characterizes this music.

Franklin's musical significance lies in her extraordinary vocal blending of the intense emotionality of both gospel and rhythm and blues. She imbibed the gospel tradition in the church of her father, the Reverend C. L. Franklin, and her best work in the soul idiom, like her classic first Atlantic album, *I Never Loved a Man the Way I Love You*, is heavily gospel-laced. In addition, she personifies the tradition of black women vocalists who have greatly enriched African American music. The search for black women's contributions to modern African American music must encompass this diverse and potent vocal music tradition. Here, at least, the sexist and racist constraints they have endured in a male-dominated music industry appear to have been less restrictive, than, say, in the instrumental tradition. Stretching across musical boundaries and reflecting diverse points of view, the tradition of black women vocalists includes the likes of Bessie Smith, Mahalia Jackson, and Aretha Franklin. Most important, this wide-ranging tradition provides a most revealing window onto their private/personal world as well as their relationship to others both within and outside the African American community.

In jazz, the shifts and changes since the early 1940s have been especially dizzying. The two most significant developments have been 1940s bebop and 1960s free jazz. Once again, both of the musics reveal a critical shift in African American consciousness and aesthetic values reflecting the accelerating black liberation struggle. In both movements, the artists approached their music with a seriousness that rejected popular notions of jazz as merely dance music or simple entertainment. Catering to their own creative muses rather than the dictates of popular taste, leaders in both movements forged music with uncompromising substance and impact, enhancing the popular conception of jazz as art music.

Bebop favored smaller groups over big bands and emphasized an aggressive and complex rhythmic charge fueling extraordinary harmonic imagination and melodic inventiveness. Alto saxophonist Charlie Parker, trumpeter John "Dizzy" Gillespie, pianists Thelonious Monk and Earl "Bud" Powell, and drummers Max Roach and Kenny Clarke were among those who pioneered bebop. In particular Parker's improvisational brilliance in melody, harmony, and rhythm mesmerized musicians and audiences alike. His best solos have been highly praised for their conceptual structure, technical acuity, and breathtaking execution. For many, including nonmusicians, who were alienated from mainstream American culture, he became a hero because of his iconoclastic personal and artistic style.

As bebop flowered out of innovations forged by artists such as Armstrong and Young, so free jazz evolved out of the harmonic innovations of bebop as well as the challenging work of musicians like pianist Cecil Taylor and bassist-composer Charles Mingus. The essence of the new jazz was radical harmonic freedom, best exemplified in the work of alto saxophonist Ornette Coleman, the late 1950s and early 1960s work of trumpeter Miles Davis, and the work of tenor saxophonist John Coltrane. Notwithstanding the enormous influence of the music of Davis and Coltrane, Coleman's innovations have proved to be even more compelling. In his albums and his performances, he surrounds himself with superbly supportive musicians. As a result, he has pioneered a music that has given each player unparalleled license to explore his own vision within a common musical ideal, beyond constraints of rhythm, key, and chord structure. At bottom, Coleman's music is a probing exploration of the social and collective possibilities of improvisation, typically using African American musical traditions as the launching pad.

In the 1990s, the lure of money and crossover success appear to threaten African American musical creativity, but there are hopeful signs. Beyond the extraordinary international success of popular music icons like Prince and Michael Jackson, both of whom draw heavily upon African American musical tradition, there are hip hop and rap, both evolving out of urban African American vernacular culture. In addition, young jazz players, like the exceptional trumpeter Wynton Marsalis, are helping to restore popular interest in the whole of jazz's musical history, not just its most recent and often less significant popular expressions. Similarly, the continuing improvisational brilliance of veteran artists like tenor saxophonist Sonny Rollins and vocalist Betty Carter augurs well for the future. Finally—whether labeled sacred or secular, classic or progressive, new or old, jazz, gospel, or blues—the music of contemporary groups like the World Saxophone Quartet, the Art Ensemble of Chicago, and Sun Ra's latest aggregation confirm that the powerful African American musical tradition endures.

[See also Folk Song and Folk Music; The Plantation; Popular Music before 1950; Theater and Musical Theater; Slavery.]

BIBLIOGRAPHY

General and Interpretive

Cone, James H. *The Spirituals and the Blues: An Interpretation* (1972).

Ellison, Mary. *Lyrical Protest: Black Music's Struggle Against Discrimination* (1989).

Ellison, Ralph. *Shadow and Act* (1964).

Epstein, Dena J. *Sinful Tunes and Spirituals: Black Folk Music to the Civil War* (1977).

Haydon, Geoffrey, and Dennis Marks, eds. *Repercussions: A Celebration of African-American Music* (1985).

Jackson, Irene V., ed. *More Than Dancing: Essays on Afro-American Music and Musicians* (1985).

Jones, LeRoi. *Blues People: Negro Music in White America* (1963).

Levine, Lawrence W. *Black Culture and Black Consciousness: Afro-American Folk Thought from Slavery to Freedom* (1977).

Oliver, Paul. *Songsters and Saints: Vocal Traditions on Race Records* (1984).

Oliver, Paul, Max Harrison, and William Bolcom. *The New Grove Dictionary of Music and Musicians: Gospel, Blues, and Jazz, with Spirituals and* Ragtime (1980; 2d ed. 1986).

Sidran, Ben. *Black Talk* (1971).

Small, Christopher. *Music of the Common Tongue: Survival and Celebration in Afro-American Music* (1987).

Southern, Eileen. *The Music of Black Americans: A History* (1971; 2d ed. 1983).

Stuckey, Sterling. *Slave Culture: Nationalist Theory and the Foundations of Black America* (1987).

African Music

Chernoff, John Miller. *African Rhythm and African Sensibility: Aesthetics and Social Action in African Musical Idioms* (1979).
Nketia, J. H. Kwabena. *The Music of Africa* (1974).

Spirituals and Gospel

Heilbut, Tony. *The Gospel Sound: Good News and Bad Times* (1971; 2d ed. 1985).
Spencer, Jon Michael. *Protest and Praise: Sacred Music of Black Religion* (1990).

Blues

Barlow, William. *Looking up at Down: The Emergence of Blues Culture* (1989).
Charters, Samuel B. *The Country Blues* (1959; 2d ed. 1975).
Ferris, William R. *Blues from the Delta* (1978).
Keil, Charles. *Urban Blues* (1966).
Murray, Albert. *Stomping the Blues* (1976).
Oliver, Paul. *The Meaning of the Blues* (1960).
Oliver, Paul. *Songsters and Saints: Vocal Traditions on Race Records* (1984).
Palmer, Robert. *Deep Blues* (1981).
Titon, Jeff Todd. *Early Downhome Blues: A Musical and Cultural Analysis* (1977).

Jazz

Gitler, Ira. *Swing to Bop: An Oral History of the Transition in Jazz in the 1940s* (1985).
Kofsky, Frank. *Black Nationalism and the Revolution in Music* (1970).
Litweiler, John. *The Freedom Principle: Jazz After 1958* (1984).
Schuller, Gunther. *Early Jazz: Its Roots and Musical Development* (1968; repr. 1986).
Schuller, Gunther. *The Swing Era: The Development of Jazz, 1930–1945* (1989).
Spellman, A. B. *Four Lives in the Bebop Business* (1966; repr. 1985).
Stearns, Marshall. *The Story of Jazz* (1956; 2d ed. 1970).

Rhythm and Blues, Rock and Roll, Soul, Rap, and Hip Hop

Garland, Phyl. *The Sound of Soul* (1969).
George, Nelson. *The Death of Rhythm and Blues* (1988).
Gillett, Charlie. *The Sound of the City: The Rise of Rock and Roll* (1970; 2d ed. 1983).
Guralnick, Peter. *Sweet Soul Music: Rhythm and Blues and the Southern Dream of Freedom* (1986).
Haralambos, Michael. *Right On: From Blues to Soul in Black America* (1974; repr. 1979).
Hirshey, Gerri. *Nowhere to Run: The Story of Soul Music* (1984).
Shaw, Arnold. *Honkers and Shouters: The Golden Years of Rhythm and Blues* (1978).
Toop, David. *The Rap Attack: African Jive to New York Hip Hop* (1984).

— WALDO E. MARTIN, JR.

AGRICULTURE

The European invasion of North America grew out of the social dislocation wrought by the transition from feudalism to capitalism in seventeenth- and eighteenth-century European, especially English, society. Land enclosure drove people from the countryside into the cities and left those remaining on the land in a state of impoverishment. The commercialization of agriculture in the English countryside was paralleled in the cities by an emerging bourgeoisie and a growing class of paupers. English society in the seventeenth century was increasingly characterized by class conflict and religious and political strife. The settlement of North America originated in this caldron of privilege and dispossession. Many who came to the colonies sought to escape the ravages of capitalism while benefiting from its successes. Thus the history of early American agrarian life was shaped by contradictory actions as the settlers sought to reap the rewards offered by the Atlantic economy while avoiding some of its harsher aspects.

When the first English settlers arrived in Jamestown, Virginia, they began a process of conquest that would take three centuries to complete. When it was over, the boundaries of the United States would stretch across the Pacific to Hawaii, reach toward the Arctic as far as Alaska, and south into the islands of the Caribbean. Whether carried out by the southern slave-owner, the sturdy pioneer family, the gold rusher, or the rancher or cattleman, the conquest of this vast territory brought with it genocide, slavery, indentured servitude, and peonage. It was a process marked by violence and greed coupled with hope for a better life, and it brought into sharp conflict different notions of property, liberty, and individualism.

The free labor society that had emerged in seventeenth-century England was not immediately transplanted to the New World. Instead, as Eugene Genovese has argued, the transition from feudalism to capitalism and the rise of free labor in Western Europe led, ironically, to the creation of various forms of unfree labor in the New World. With the exception of the early New England Puritans, the majority of those who came to America in the seventeenth and eighteenth centuries came as indentured servants, redemptioners, convicts, or slaves. And as the settlers moved farther west, they encountered the labor systems of an earlier conquest—the Spanish haciendas that employed various forms of tribute, peonage, and slavery.

Thus the history of American agriculture reflects less the traditional story, chronicled in school textbooks, of a free people conquering a wilderness and liberating primitive natives from their backward cultures and economies. Instead, the development of American agriculture must be understood within the context of the emergence of Western capitalism and the process of making a nation-state. Its history was embedded in the expansion of a world-market economy, even though many regions retained noncapitalist forms of production until after the Civil War. The rise of American capitalism, then, was not a unilinear process but involved the transformation of different kinds of subsistence and labor systems that spanned the hunter and gatherer societies of Native Americans as far north as Alaska, the haciendas of the Southwest, the southern slave plantations, and the partially subsistence households of the northern colonies and the southern backcountry. It was a process marked by resistance and at times by violence.

One of the first problems encountered by the colonists was the hundreds of thousands, probably millions, of native peoples, who had inhabited North America for over ten thousand years. The numerous tribes that peopled the coasts of North America practiced various forms of subsistence agriculture or lived as hunters and gatherers. During the early years, colonists in all regions traded and often maintained good terms with the many tribes. However, as the demand for reliable labor increased, many Europeans, especially in the southern colonies, turned to the enslavement of the native peoples. The attempts at enslavement were not generally successful, though South Carolinians managed a rather profitable Indian slave trade with the Caribbean.

The invasion of America had disastrous consequences for the Indians. Disease killed thousands while others perished in the many wars that characterized the first decades. And the intrusion of the Atlantic economy, especially the trade in furs, hides, guns, and liquor, undermined the subsistence economy of the preconquest years. As the Indians came to realize that the settlers intended not only to stay but to occupy most of the land, they increased their opposition to what was no longer an invasion but a conquest.

The extermination of the native peoples was crucial to the growth of the colonial economy, for without land the northern family farms and the southern plantations could not survive. Indeed, as events in Virginia revealed, the lack of land could lead to major class conflict. During the seventeenth century, Virginia had developed a staple-crop economy based on tobacco and worked by indentured servants. By the 1660s, the number of servants completing their contracts increased. Plantation owners, faced with a labor shortage, illegally extended the terms of their laborers' contracts and worked them as hard as slaves. Freedom became an equally difficult struggle for those who managed to survive the terms of their indenture. Physically worn out from their years as field laborers and often deprived of their legal claim to land, money, and tools, most became landless and poverty-stricken.

By the late seventeenth century, Virginia experienced increasing class conflict as a growing group of landless white men demanded land and opportunity. However, their aspirations were stymied in the east by plantation owners who did not welcome small landowners, and in the west by Indians. These growing class tensions erupted in Bacon's Rebellion in 1676, when property owners on the frontier defeated the Indians and opened up new lands for the landless. Virginia, like other southern colonies, was characterized by a slave economy bordered by a backcountry yeomanry. The cost of yeomen's freedom, then, was borne by the enslavement of Africans and the extermination of the Indians.

On the eve of the American Revolution, the colonies had developed into regional economies that were defined as much by the labor employed as by the crops produced. The New England and Middle Atlantic colonies consisted of small family farms that produced grains and livestock. In sharp contrast, the Hudson River valley estates employed a mixture of tenants, indentured servants, hired hands, and slaves, while in the South, a staple-crop economy emerged that was based on African slavery.

The republican ideology of the Revolution gave meaning to farmers' struggles, as Thomas Jefferson and others argued that democracy rested on small producers' ability to control their property and the means of production.

During the late eighteenth century, these regional economies experienced dramatic growth. Population increases in the new nation and in Europe during the 1790s created a demand for foodstuffs both at home and abroad. In the northern colonies, rural society was increasingly transformed by an expanding market that reached into the rural households, and in the southern colonies, the invention of the cotton gin, combined with a growing market for cotton, breathed new life into a flagging slave economy. The growing commercialization of the northern agrarian society and the expansion of the southern slave economy led to increasing class conflict over questions of land and its relationship to the broader issues of political and economic rights. Whether it was the Regulators of the Carolinas, the anti-rent rioters in the Hudson Valley, or participants in Shays's Rebellion in western and central Massachusetts, at issue was the right of small-scale producers to have access to land and protection from the vagaries of the market. Yeomen's struggles to retain control over their property and production would continue in the North until the Civil War, and in the South and West until the late nineteenth century. Rural capitalism was met in the countryside with ambivalence as households sought the benefits of the market without the exploitation. The republican ideology of the Revolution gave meaning to their struggles, as Thomas Jefferson and others argued that democracy rested on the ability of small producers to control their property and the means of production.

Thus, the petty commodity producers of rural America entered the nineteenth century armed with an ideology that encouraged them to participate in commercial production while warning them against debt and the vagaries of the market. However, few households could survive without the commodities that the market offered. Their struggles to balance their household economy with capitalist penetration defined the lives of rural families until 1860. In the North, a rapidly expanding industrial order shaped the response of households, while in the plantation South, yeomen found themselves hedged in by a slave economy. Thus the stages and ways in which small farmers entered the market were contoured by the dominant productive relations of the societies in which they lived.

Most antebellum northern farmers sought to maintain some degree of autonomy over a household economy that was based on a local exchange of mutuality and reciprocity. Neighboring households traded their labor and their produce for needed goods or services. Within the household itself, the division of labor was along gender lines. The men were responsible for the cultivation of the crops while women maintained the home and cared for the children. Yet both often shared in making candles, soap, and textiles, and either might tend the barn or the garden, usually with the help of their children. The survival of the household depended in part on the ability of children to inherit land.

The farms that dotted the northern countryside were embedded in a growing industrial capitalist market that increasingly undermined the autonomy of the households. By the 1820s, declining fertility rates and land shortages, combined with an expanding textile industry in the towns, led to a growth in rural wage labor and an increase in household manufacturing. Farm women participated directly in a larger market as they traded their handmade textiles to local merchants for household commodities and luxury items. On one level, the penetration of industrial capitalism into the countryside allowed women to earn wages that sustained the household and prevented family members from having to migrate to the factories or to the West. Yet on another level, the outwork system undermined the old ways of subsistence and barter. Thus, the rise of industrial capitalism transformed the countryside by incorporating it into the wage labor and consumer markets. In turn, household labor played a crucial role in the rise of northern industry.

An emerging capitalist North based on free labor and political democracy contrasted sharply with the southern slave economy that vested property rights in both land and humans. As Eugene Genovese has argued, after 1820 a mature slave-owning class had developed that rejected the principles of economic and political liberalism. It was a society that was decidedly noncapitalist, participating in a national and global market while maintaining a world based on slave labor.

The slave economy had major implications for the yeomen who lived on the periphery of the plantations. Unlike their northern counterparts, southern yeomen had more limited access to a market economy. Planters refused to provide the internal improvements necessary to link the plantations with the backcountry subsistence farms. Thus, in contrast with Europe and the North, yeomen were limited in their ability to participate as small commodity producers in a regional commercial economy. Instead, they existed as semi-subsistence farmers until the consequences of the Civil War forced them into an emerging capitalist economy.

Both the free labor North and the slave South depended upon the vast lands of the western territories for the survival of their economies. Northern farmers escaping the encroachments of a capitalist market joined southern backcountrymen and aspiring slave owners in search of more and better land. The Louisiana Purchase in 1803 and the defeat of Native Americans following the War of 1812 opened the Missouri and Ohio territories, with slave owners generally moving into the region south of Missouri and the small landowners taking the lands in what became Illinois and Indiana. Settlement in the West, however, was laden with ideological significance, for the millions of acres of public domain held the key to the nation's economic and political survival.

The settlement of the western territories was connected to the national policies of the newly created American republic. For Thomas Jefferson and his successors, an abundance of land made possible the realization of a citizenry of independent small property owners unimpeded by the class divisions of the Old World. Without the shackles of servitude or wage labor, these small commodity producers would sustain the republican virtues of independence and hard work. Thus, the national land policies from the Northwest Ordinance of 1787 to the Homestead Act of 1862 sought in principle to provide cheap land to family farmers. However, the reality of land distribution and labor relations on the frontier often fell short of this democratic vision.

The settlement of the ever-extending frontier in the nineteenth century must be understood within the context of the emergence of capitalism in the Northeast. With the rise of factories and towns came a demand for agricultural products, and by the eve of the Civil War, a network of roads, railways, and canals had connected the hinterlands to the northeastern markets. Thus, the first generation of settlers lived initially as subsistence households. But by the 1840s, agrarian life on the frontier increasingly resembled the harsher realities of the commercial world many had sought to escape.

What kinds of communities did the pioneers create during the antebellum years? The answer to this question depended upon time and place. For example, the initial settlements in Illinois differed from those in the Southwest, California, or Hawaii. Access to land and the market depended upon the kinds of labor and tenure relations encountered in the different regions.

Sugar Creek, a community in central Illinois that was settled in 1818 by families from the southern upcountry, represented one kind of frontier community. Unable to plow the hard sod, most families cleared the trees and planted where the soil was softer. Family labor and neighborly reciprocity sustained Sugar Creek until the 1850s, for most lacked income to hire wage labor. However, as in New England, households could not survive completely outside of the market. It took money to move west, and many had to borrow from loan sharks at exorbitant rates. Farm improvements also required money, as did necessities such as gunpowder, crockery, and coffee. Farmers searched for ways to obtain cash by trying to sell hogs and garden products. However, Sugar Creek was isolated from the roads that fed into the expanding area of Springfield, Illinois. Farm women, as they had in New England, earned much of the money for the household by selling their eggs, butter, and textiles to local merchants.

Family farm owners were only half of the population in Sugar Creek. The other part of the community consisted of squatters who built log cabins on unclaimed lands, grazed their livestock on the commons, and hooked timber from the Congress lands. During the 1830s and 1840s, however, these squatters were displaced as the expansion of the eastern market through railways and roads brought land speculators. Inspired by technological innovations such as the steel plow, horse-powered corn planters, mowers, reapers, and machine threshers, speculators carved up the common lands and sold them to local farmers looking to expand their operations or to newly arrived settlers. With the destruction of public lands for woodcutting and the abolition of a commons for grazing, the squatters lost any chance of becoming landowners.

By 1850, Sugar Creek had become a community divided along class lines as the landowners extended their holdings and hired the former squatters as wage hands or tenants. Thus farmers now became landlords and employers, while the squatters lost any rights to the land and became wage workers or tenants. Subsistence households, whether of squatters or of freeholders, represented the transitional form of agricultural society until the expanding northeastern economy pulled the outlying regions into its orbit.

By 1860 the prairie cornbelt had been established and integrated into the spreading market economy. And, if

Farm women in the mid to late 19th century earned household money by selling eggs, butter, and textiles to local merchants. These two children feed the chickens in a barnyard near Echo, Minnesota.

Sugar Creek was any example, only a few families prospered. Most either moved farther west, onto the Great Plains, or followed the Overland Trail into Oregon and California. Still others became hired laborers or tenants with little hope of obtaining land of their own. The Jeffersonian vision of a nation based on an independent yeomanry removed from debt and oppression was not often the reality of the frontier.

The yeoman's dream certainly floundered in the Southwest, where settlers encountered the Spanish land system that dated back to the sixteenth-century conquest. In southwest Texas, Mexican hacendados used peon labor to raise cattle in a system that resembled the paternalistic slave-owning South. Property existed not for individual ownership but for the inheritance and continuation of lineages. The livestock was raised not for the market but to sustain the hacienda. In 1836, the hacendados were defeated when the Republic of Texas was created. Entailed notions of property were quickly replaced by those of private property when the republic declared all Mexican livestock public property. With the help of the Texas Rangers and cowboys, ranches were raided and the landowners were forced through violence and intimidation to sell or abandon their lands. However, the Texas conquest did not go unchallenged. In 1859–1860, Juan Cortina led many displaced peons in raids against the Texans and briefly held the Rangers at bay. In the end, the Anglos prevailed, attached themselves to the Mexican hierarchy through intermarriage, and continued as ranchers.

The Mexican-American War brought in additional domains that stretched from Texas to California. Within these new territories were landowning elites who employed various forms of unfree labor. For example, in New Mexico the *partidaro* system existed, whereby a patron loaned land and sheep to the head of a household, who owed payment in the form of ewes. Under this system, over twenty families controlled the economy of New Mexico in the nineteenth century. As late as 1900, one patron had access to over twenty-seven thousand ewes through the *partidaro.*

When the gold rushers and land seekers reached the coast of California, they encountered a Spanish tenure arrangement that included haciendas and missions that employed Indian labor to raise cattle. After 1848, California entered a period of transformation, especially after the 1860s when railroads connected the region with markets in the East. However, California did not produce a land of yeomen farmers; rather, the large Spanish estates were transferred to the American owners, who used vagrancy laws to impress Indian labor. By the 1850s, the agricultural economy was characterized by bonanza farms that produced wheat and other cereals until the Civil War. However, labor continued to be a problem, and many migrants from the South argued for the adoption of African slavery. When that possibility was lost, landowners turned to Chinese contract labor until the 1880s. The roots of the large-scale agribusiness economy that dominated California in the late nineteenth and twentieth centuries were planted in the early years of conquest.

Historians have traditionally discussed the American West within the context of expansion to California. However, there were two other quite different regions that would eventually become states. In Alaska, the Aleutian peoples lived as hunters and fishermen, while across the Pacific, native Hawaiians worked plots of land under various chiefdoms. Both societies differed considerably from that of Sugar Creek.

The first American sugar planters arrived in Hawaii in the 1830s. They justified their invasion by arguing that they were emancipating a backward people from an oppressive chiefdom. Instead, native peoples lost their land and were turned into plantation wage laborers who were paid in scrip. Landowners never had enough labor, however, because the majority of native peoples had been killed by diseases introduced by explorers and traders in the late eighteenth and early nineteenth centuries. And of those who remained, few were willing to work on the terms established by their new conquerors. Consequently, the planters were forced to recruit Chinese contract laborers who worked the processing mills while natives sweated in the sugar fields.

The sugar plantation economy accelerated in 1848–1850, when land tenure laws were changed to allow non-natives to purchase property. In addition, the California gold rush created a market not only for sugar but also for vegetables, turkeys, and swine. Near the end of the century, five American companies controlled the political economy of the islands.

By the time of the Civil War, the rapidly expanding capitalist economy of the Northern states had reached as far as Hawaii to encompass many different land and labor systems that produced a wide variety of products. This growth was fueled by state policies that subsidized railroads and land speculators, and privileged commercial production over other forms of agriculture. Technological changes also contributed to the commercialization of agriculture and to further concentration of land and capital as fewer farmers had the money to purchase additional land or to mechanize.

While the territorial limits of the continental United States were established by 1860, the actual incorporation of these regions and their peoples into a nation remained to be accomplished. The defeat of the slave South paved the way for the final expansion of capitalism and the creation of a nation-state based on the principles of economic and political liberalism. Yet the incorporation of regional elites and labor systems entailed new definitions of liberty, property, and citizenship that clashed with views rooted in republican notions of free labor or, in the case of Native Americans, in a communal vision of property. In any case, the expansion of capitalist agriculture in the late nineteenth century brought in its wake violence and social dislocation. Its triumph was not without challenge.

The American Civil War destroyed the noncapitalist slave South and emancipated more than three million slaves. However, the meaning of that newly won freedom was a contested issue that was not settled for decades. Nor could the struggle over the meaning of freedom for the freed men and women be understood outside the context of the white yeomen or the former slave owners. Above all, the destruction of slavery required new definitions of property and citizenship. The postbellum South was shaped by constant class conflict as planters, freedmen, and yeomen clashed over the issues surrounding landownership and labor. At issue were the rights of the freedmen to have access to land and to control their own labor. This notion of freedom collided with that of the former masters who sought to retain a dependent labor force, at first through coercion and force, then through the legal power of the state.

As soon as Yankee troops liberated portions of the plantation South, former slaves asserted their independence. Initial efforts of northern planters and missionaries to discipline the freedmen as free workers encountered tremendous resistance. Nor did freedmen heed their former masters' orders to work on what they considered unfair terms. They challenged planter efforts to impose gang labor and other forms of coercion by withdrawing women and children from the fields, by joining Union League Clubs, by boycotting and striking for decent working conditions, and by disputing crop settlements. Planters responded to such militancy by passing vagrancy and apprentice laws and other forms of coercion designed to force freedmen back to work on landowners' terms.

The postbellum South was shaped by constant class conflict as planters, freedmen, and yeomen clashed over issues surrounding landownership and labor.

The struggle over land and labor in the postbellum South centered on different notions of freedom and property. During slavery, many slaves had insisted on and secured the right to maintain their own gardens and livestock, to fish and to hunt. After the war, they avoided working for the planters by continuing these subsistence activities. By the 1870s, planters employed the legal instruments of the state to control their labor force. Through fishing, game, and fence laws, freedmen lost access to their subsistence and were left with no alternative but to work on the plantations in what had emerged as the system of sharecropping. Growing out of the refusal of blacks to work as gang laborers, sharecropping allowed freedmen to retain limited access to the land. As Harold Woodman has shown, it was a form of wage labor whereby the worker received his wages in the form of a share of the crop—usually one-half or one-fourth. The planter provided housing, food, clothing, tools, and the means of production. Credit was issued at the commissary, where workers had to purchase all of their necessities at high prices and an interest rate that was as high as 20 percent. After the harvest, accounts were settled and the cropper families almost always came out deeper in debt. In its most extreme form, the new plantation economy led to debt peonage.

While freedmen fought over rights to the land and their labor, the up-country yeomen struggled to retain their semi-subsistence households that were based on local exchange, reciprocity, and common rights to the land. After the war, railroads and merchants moved into the upper piedmont and backcountry hills, bringing with them the cotton economy. The rapidly expanding market, combined with fencing and game laws, transformed the subsistence farmers into cotton producers who relied heavily on merchant credit. Poor harvests and the crop-lien system drove many into bankruptcy and tenancy. Yeomen and freedmen alike learned the meaning of freedom in the emerging capitalist order. For both it spelled dispossession and powerlessness.

The freedmen's struggles over landownership and decent wages, the transformation of the yeomanry, and the expansion of the market economy led to the southern agrarian movements of the late nineteenth century. The National Farmers' Alliance and Industrial Union, or the Southern Farmers Alliance, was formed in the late 1870s in the Cross Timbers section of Texas to combat the economic woes of southern farmers. The southern alliance was one of three such alliances. A "northern" alliance was organized in 1880 in Chicago as the National Farmers' Alliance and gained considerable support in the Midwest. A third, the Colored Farmers' National Alliance, was formed in 1886 in Texas as the segregated counterpart to the southern alliance. Of these, the southern alliance was the largest and played the most significant role in what would become the Populist party in the 1890s. The Alliance movement embodied the republican ideology of small semi-subsistence farmers who believed that democracy rested in the right of small producers to control the fruits of their own labor. Their demands for a subtreasury system and public ownership of railroads and telegraph companies, represented their efforts to democratize the growing centralization of economic and political power. As Steven Hahn has argued, they sought the creation of a "cooperative commonwealth" similar to the vision advocated by the Knights of Labor and the Greenback Labor party.

In the Populist party's challenge, small producers waged a rearguard battle against the encroachments of capitalism, seeking to democratize both the polity and the economy.

The Alliance movement swept into the Midwest as well, where farmers were caught in a web of indebtedness, rising rates of tenancy, and exploitation by middlemen, bankers, and railroads. In spite of the Homestead Act of 1862, farmers found it difficult to secure 160 acres of good land, for most of the public domain had been parceled out to railroads and mining companies. While midwestern farmers did not have to compete with a plantation system, they had a similar problem with the large bonanza corn farms in Illinois and Indiana, and the wheat estates in the Red River valley of North Dakota. These concerns were run like modern businesses with managers, accountants, and wage labor.

In the Populist challenge, small producers waged a rearguard battle against the encroachments of capitalism. Drawing from a republican heritage that stressed a society of small farmers, artisans, and businessmen, the Populists sought to democratize both the polity and the economy. The subtreasury system, the nationalization of railroads and telegraph companies, the direct primary, and many other of their reforms aimed to return government and the economy to the world of the petty producers. The Republican party's victory in the 1896 presidential election signaled the triumph of the corporate order and removed a large number of Americans from the political arena.

The Populists failed in part because of limitations within the movement. Their base consisted of classes of farmers whose interests were not always compatible. By stressing the credit and marketing side of farming, leaders avoided confronting the issue of land distribution and the related question of tenancy, sharecropping, and casual labor. Both large and small landowners and their tenants suffered the ravages of the market and middlemen, and thus could rally around a platform that called for their regulation. But to call into question the actual productive relations in the countryside would have focused attention on other aspects of class conflict that landowners sought to avoid.

Thus, that wing of populism which belonged mainly to the larger landowners and town businessmen saw its goals accomplished during the Progressive Era. Congress provided funds for cooperatives, agricultural credit, and the establish-merit of the Agricultural Extension Service and an expansion of funding for the land-grant colleges. These reforms combined with the highest farm prices in American history to create boom times for American farmers until World War I.

However, these good times were not shared by all. In the South, for example, the defeat of populism resolved the struggle over the meaning of freedom that was raised with the abolition of slavery. The plantation economy actually expanded in the first two decades of the twentieth century and was undergirded by segregation and disfranchisement. In the Arkansas and Mississippi deltas there emerged large-scale business plantations that were often owned by corporations from the North and England; were run by professional managers and accountants; and were advised by county agents who stressed scientific farming. Thousands of black sharecroppers and wage hands labored under close supervision, often working in gangs. Anti-enticement laws that prohibited the recruitment of labor by employers outside the country, peonage, and planter control of the local authorities ensured that few would find other employment. Not until the great migration of World War I would southern African Americans find genuine alternative opportunities.

Plantation agriculture was only part of the modern southern economy. In the older cotton and tobacco regions, small farmers and tenants eked out an existence amid a declining world market, the boll weevil, and soil erosion. The twentieth-century rural South, with its large-scale plantations and an impoverished class of sharecroppers and tenant farmers, resembled the underdeveloped regions of a colonial world. Its wrenching poverty was manifested in high rates of illiteracy and death from preventable diseases combined with the lowest standard of living in the country—a condition that bore testimony to the success of the capitalist revolution initiated by the Civil War.

The rise of business agriculture in the South and Midwest following the Civil War mirrored developments in the Southwest and the West as the expansion of capitalist agriculture led to a growing concentration of land and capital coupled with a rise in indebtedness and tenancy. As in the South, the incorporation of the West involved resolving questions of land and labor.

The development of the West involved far more than the trek of pioneers and corporations, for in defeating the slave South, radical Republicans had raised the issue of citizenship and had vested it with promises of education, political participation, and landownership. While southerners of all classes and races struggled throughout the late nineteenth century over the questions surrounding citizenship and landownership, a similar conflict occurred in the West over the status of Native Americans. Federal policymakers joined northeastern reformers, land-hungry settlers, and corporations in a battle over the future of the Indians, When it was over, Native Americans found themselves in much the same situation as southern blacks—segregated and disfranchised. Reservations were not plantations, but the power relations that governed their creation and operation were not very different.

As the growing number of homesteaders realized that most of the public lands had been taken by larger business concerns, they turned to the Indian lands for relief. Corporations also had their eyes on those lands, for some of them contained rich sources of minerals and others blocked the expansion of railroad lines. Thus, by the 1870s the "Indian problem" became a major issue for American policymakers, who linked the question of Indian citizenship and landownership to economic expansion. Strengthened by scientific theory, reformers, intellectuals, and politicians argued that Indian lands stood in the way of progress and the march of civilization. No people, they insisted, had the right to live on undeveloped property. And according to leading anthropologists, the only salvation for native peoples lay in displacing them from the tribal lands which they held sacred and which were connected to "primitive" rituals. If Indians were settled on individual farms, their ties to their sacred land and rituals would be severed. Whether couched in the lofty terms of uplift and reform or the language of corporate self-interest, the federal policies as they related to Indians had the same effect—displacement and further impoverishment.

The solution devised incorporated notions of citizenship with economic expansion. Indians would be civilized through ownership of small plots and through education. Once they had been integrated into a booming economy, their success would be reward enough for the loss of their lands. Reformers assumed that the engine propelling civilization was private property. Their views found expression in the passage of the Dawes General Allotment Act in 1887, which provided for individual allotments giving citizenship to all Indians who took an allotment as well as to those who moved off reservations. Once Indians had proven their ability to manage their own farms, they would be granted citizenship. The surplus lands were to be sold to the public with tribal consent.

The allotment plan failed to meet the demands for more land. By the turn of the century, the population and economy of the western states had rapidly expanded as railroads united agricultural markets in the Midwest with the Pacific Coast. Urbanization placed further demands on agricultural production. In the face of increasing demands for acreage, most tribes refused to sell their surplus lands, especially when they were not offered the market price for them. Frustrated by this obstinacy, politicians and businessmen appealed to the Supreme Court to gain access to tribal holdings. The Court granted their wish by allowing Congress to negate treaties and to sell Indian lands without tribal approval. The first decades of the twentieth century saw the seizure and sale of millions of tribal acres. In addition, Congress used the funds from these sales to launch massive irrigation projects on the reservations. Since the concept of beneficial use governed access to water, any Indians who did not farm their irrigated lands stood to lose them to their more aggressive white neighbors who obtained government leases. Thousands of acres of tribal lands were leased to mining and corporate agricultural interests. As Frederick E. Hoxie has shown, by the twentieth century, a campaign to assimilate the Indians as citizens had turned into one to integrate their natural resources into the national economy, with the Indians taking the hindmost.

Corporate agriculture also swept across southwest Texas, transforming the cattle haciendas of the border region and the cowboy culture of the Panhandle. The removal of the Apaches and Comanches in the 1870s opened up new lands in the central and northern plains of Texas. Initially independent ranchers and cowboys grazed their livestock on the open range. However, in the 1880s, English, Scottish, and northeastern capital moved into the region, formed cattlemen's associations to fight the homesteaders and cowboys, and enclosed the range. The fence wars of the 1880s represented the last struggle of homesteaders and independent ranchers to survive in the Panhandle, for they viewed their access to open ranges and water supplies as a common right. At issue was a redefinition of property rights that shifted the balance of power from small producers to corporate operators.

The development of the Texas frontier, then, consisted of claiming land, livestock, and water as private property. Thus, the world of the independent rancher and cowboy gave way to the corporate holdings such as the famous King Ranch. Consisting in 1885 of 500,000 acres, Richard King's ranch operated like a Mississippi Delta plantation with its own commissary, homes for five hundred workers, wagon sheds, blacksmith shops, and stables. By 1932, it had grown to encompass almost 1.25 million acres. The Texas cattle industry could match any industrial concern in the East with its millions of acres of cattle supervised by cowboys who lived in bunkhouses and worked as wage laborers. And cowboys often behaved like the proletariat they had become by engaging in strikes for better wages and working conditions.

Farther south, along the Mexican border, the expansion of capitalist agriculture destroyed the remnants of a cattle hacienda system, replacing it with large-scale vegetable and cotton farms worked by Mexican migrant labor. By 1900 the ranch societies of both the border and parts of central Texas gave way to commercial farming. Overgrazing, northern quarantine laws, and world overproduction, combined with the development of refrigerated cars and the refinement of irrigation technology, made vegetable and cotton production a profitable business. In addition, the rapid exhaustion of free lands in the plains led farmers from that region into Texas in search of greater profits. However, the invading capitalists did not always acquire their lands through the most ethical means, often using violence and intimidation to obtain the property of reluctant Mexican American landowners.

Capitalist penetration of the border regions did not go unchallenged. As David Montejano has shown, the Mexican American peons and small ranchers, who were displaced when the hacendados left, fought their decline into wage labor. Social tensions culminated in 1915–1916 in the Plan de San Diego when bands of displaced peons and rancheros raided farms, burned bridges, derailed trains, and sabotaged irrigation pumps. For five months they held the landowners in captive fear. In the end, they were defeated by the Texas Rangers, who used the rebellion as an excuse to invade Mexican American communities, murdering innocent people and forcing others to sign over their lands. By the 1920s, the agricultural economy of southwest Texas had developed into a class system that placed Anglos in control of production while Mexican Americans were relegated to the status of wage laborers.

Of all the regional agricultural economies that emerged after the Civil War, California stood as the most spectacular symbol of corporate agriculture. The expansion of the transcontinental railroads created markets for California fruits and vegetables throughout the country. Improvements in irrigation technology allowed the cultivation of thousands of acres of semiarid lands.

A persistent concern of the California growers centered on the issue of labor. Citrus and vegetable crops required large quantities of unskilled labor during the harvest. Thus, landowners sought to secure the cheapest seasonal wage workers. After the Chinese Exclusion Act (1882) was passed, they turned to Japanese workers. However, the Japanese proved far too independent for the corporate farmers. Using their own contractors, they bargained for lower wages and thereby became the dominant labor pool. Then they withheld their labor until owners paid them decent wages. Even worse, their goal was to become landowners. Their success in achieving this end resulted in 1910 in legislation restricting their rights to own land. Growers did not tolerate any competition, even that of small commodity producers like the Japanese.

From 1910 until the eve of World War I, California growers relied on a predominantly white labor force as people were driven back to the land during the economic hard times that preceded the war. These years also saw the first efforts to organize California agricultural workers; both the conservative American Federation of Labor and the radical Industrial Workers of the World (IWW) launched unsuccessful organizing campaigns. Not until the 1930s would farmworkers mount a major challenge to the landowners' power.

After World War I, California growers turned to a predominantly Mexican migrant labor force. Like southern plantation owners, the fruit and citrus companies of California exercised unparalleled control over their workers. Remembering the influence of the IWW during the war, landowners in the 1920s established cooperative labor bureaus in conjunction with the Farm Bureau Federation, the chambers of commerce, and the farm employers' associations. Utilizing local law-enforcement officials, the labor bureaus enforced wage agreements and eliminated competition for workers. Above all, these measures made labor organizing more difficult, for no longer could workers strike on a single farm. Instead, they would have to organize an entire region. Thus, as Cletus Daniel has argued, as industry in the 1920s saw the rise of welfare capitalism, in the fields of California, corporate farmers sought to cut costs by further reducing their laborers' standard of living.

As in industry, the development of agriculture in the United States from the end of the Civil War until World War I was marked by growing consolidation and specialization. The formation of growers' associations in California, Texas, Hawaii, and the South revealed that large-scale producers viewed themselves as part of the emerging corporate world. Their connections to the research wings of the U.S. Agricultural Extension Service and the state agricultural universities placed them in the forefront of scientific knowledge as it related to agricultural modernization and efficiency.

The agrarian unrest of the late nineteenth and early twentieth centuries, then, must be understood within the context of the rise of corporate agriculture. Whether it was in the form of the Southern Alliance members, Grangers, Populists, or the strikers on the sugar plantations of Hawaii, the ranches of Texas, and the Delta cotton fields, or in the form of bloody Indian wars, at issue were the rights of small producers to land and of wage workers to decent working conditions. The social upheavals of these years made it clear that farmers were not an undifferentiated mass united by their ties to the soil. Rather, the violence and human misery that accompanied the advance of capitalism in the countryside revealed that class divisions distinguished agrarian life, as they did that in the factories.

The violence and human misery that accompanied capitalism's advance in the countryside at the turn of the century revealed that class divisions distinguished agrarian life, just as they did in the factories.

In the late nineteenth and early twentieth centuries, regional agricultural elites solved the land and labor problems. In the South, after the defeat of populism, segregation and disfranchisement assured a plantation labor force of poor and unskilled blacks, whereas most whites were confined to tenancy. In the Southwest and in California, corporate agriculture depended on a cheap, controllable, and powerless labor force of Mexican and Chicano labor. And throughout the West, Native Americans lost their lands and were confined to marginal areas that were called reservations. Like African Americans, Chicanos, and Mexicans, they were removed from the realm of citizenship and thus lacked the power to challenge their plight successfully.

Agrarian unrest did not end with populism, for as tenancy continued to rise in the southwestern states, the antimonopoly wing of the Populists in that region merged with the Socialist party to form renters' unions. And along the border in Texas, small farmers, renters, and migrant workers formed the Mexican Protective Association in opposition to the large-scale agriculture that had emerged there. And still farther west, the IWW organized the harvest stiffs in the wheat fields of the Midwest and the migrant workers on the Pacific Coast. In short, the failure of the populist movement did not end dissent. Rather, rural people continued to struggle against the large-scale interests that were destroying their lives.

The antimonopoly strain of populism reached its fullest expression in the Midwest, where it emerged as a significant component of progressivism. One of the major political movements of the twentieth century developed in North Dakota and Minnesota with the creation of the Farmer-Labor party. From its inception, the movement was torn by internal ideological disputes that reflected the different approaches to agricultural problems in the first decades of the twentieth century.

Farmers in the Midwest were surrounded by an industrial world of agricultural processing corporations that deprived producers of a fair share of their crops. A reformist wing, drawing from the Populists, sought to regulate the grain elevators, railroads, warehouses, and banks. These farmers organized into the Equity Cooperative Exchange, which became a model for cooperatives in the twentieth century. As supporters of Theodore Roosevelt's Bull Moose party, they sought enactment of legislation to provide federal support for agricultural credit and cooperatives. During Woodrow Wilson's administration, many of their objectives were realized in the Federal Farm Loan Act (1916). Eventually the cooperatives of the Midwest competed with large companies like Pillsbury and General Mills.

Another wing of the farmer-labor movement grew out of the North Dakota Socialist party. Known as the Nonpartisan League, it sought to form an alliance with labor and to nationalize the banks, railroads, and grain elevators. Its strategy centered on seizing the Republican party and enacting a social democratic platform through the party machinery. The Nonpartisan League achieved success in South Dakota, where in 1919 the legislature created a state-owned bank and flour mill. However, because many of its members opposed America's entry into World War I, the League suffered from wartime anti-radical hysteria. Nevertheless, in 1918 the Farmer-Labor party was created and remained a force in midwestern politics until the 1940s (even later in Minnesota), electing several governors, congressmen, and senators.

By far the most important farmers' organization in the twentieth century was the American Farm Bureau Federation. Created in 1920 from a network of local bureaus, it became the major lobbying group for commercial farmers, particularly those in the Midwest and the South. The Farm Bureau stressed the business side of agriculture and sought legislation to secure better farm prices and to improve marketing, transportation, and credit facilities. Another major organization, the Farmers' Union (1927), invested its efforts in forming cooperatives.

All of these farm organizations entered the debates over production and prices that sharpened after 1920 as the wartime boom years gave way to the bust period of the 1920s and 1930s. American agriculture entered a depression as declining world markets led to low prices, the collapse of the rural credit structure, increasing indebtedness, and foreclosures. Following the dictates of the Agricultural Extension Service, farmers had purchased tractors and farm implements, thus increasing their indebtedness. Nor did farm income keep up with costs, for by 1933 farm prices had dropped 63 percent while the costs of implements and motor vehicles had declined only 6 and 16 percent, respectively. Thus, many commercial growers supported the McNary-Haugen Bill (1928), which called upon the federal government to bring farm prices into parity with those of industry.

Households came to measure themselves against the ads they saw in the Sears Roebuck catalog: Pictures of shining kitchens with all the modern conveniences contrasted sharply with homes in which kerosene was burned for light and clothes were scrubbed on washboards.

Not all sectors of the agricultural economy experienced the depression equally. For example, the plantation South saw the complete collapse of its economy as cotton fell to six cents a pound. Em-battled by floods, drought, soil erosion, and the boll weevil, planters reduced the meager earnings of their workers even more. In contrast, large-scale enterprises specializing in vegetables and fruits expanded in the 1920s. Spurred by increasing urbanization, mechanization, better varieties of seeds, and improved irrigation, intensive truck farming increased in the North Atlantic and Pacific Coast states and in the Carolinas, Florida, Texas, and the Great Lakes region.

Thus, the economic crisis of the 1920s did not fall evenly on everyone. Southern sharecroppers and tenant farmers watched as their access to credit and food dwindled and their children died from preventable diseases. And as the Great Depression. came, thousands of southern families followed those from other parts of the country into the migrant labor stream, driving out the Mexican Americans, thousands of whom were illegally deported by the federal government. Refugees from federal policies, mechanization, and the Dust Bowl, these black and white families drove west in worn-out cars and trucks in search of work in the giant fields of California. None of the farmers' organizations addressed the desperation of these people.

When the American economy collapsed in the early 1930s, many rural peoples hardly noticed a difference. However, as the Depression deepened, grass-roots agrarian movements emerged all over the nation as workers sought to defend themselves against increasing exploitation resulting from the economic hard times. Still others found themselves worse off due to New Deal reforms. Thus, structural changes combined with federal policies in the 1930s to create massive agrarian unrest.

Federal policymakers held conflicting views about how best to solve the agrarian problem. One group, headed by the American Farm Bureau Federation and the Federal Extension Service, saw the solution in production control and parity payments. For these people, the problem with farming centered on its inability to keep up with the modernizing pace of industry. Others saw farming as a way of life deserving of preservation. For these experts, like Rexford Tugwell, rural society must be reformed to save the small family farmer while elevating the sharecroppers and tenant farmers to the status of landowners.

These opposing views derived from different visions of the role of agrarian life in a democracy. The first saw agriculture as a business and sought to equalize its competitive edge with other sectors of the industrial economy. The second drew from the long-standing republican vision that stressed the importance of small-scale farming to the survival of democracy. They reflected the different directions that American agriculture had followed since the opening of the frontier, and both battled for power in the administration of Franklin Roosevelt.

New Deal agricultural policies reflected these polar ideas. The centerpiece of Roosevelt's agricultural program, the Agricultural Adjustment Administration (AAA), embodied the goals of the Farm Bureau and businessmen. Concerned with boosting prices, the AAA paid farmers to plow under one-third of their crops and to slaughter one-third of their pigs. It favored large-scale producers over smaller ones and actually displaced sharecroppers and tenant farmers. Yet Tugwell and the social planners secured support for their programs in

The Farm Security Administration was created in the 1930s to help croppers and tenants purchase their own farms with low-interest loans. This FSA Client, on his Florida farm in 1942, was one of the few that benefited from the program.

the creation of the Resettlement Administration in 1935 and of the Farm Security Administration (FSA) in 1937, both of which sought to address the needs of small farmers, tenants, and croppers. Under the FSA, farmers were resettled on marginal lands that they purchased at low interest rates. Others lived in cooperatives that combined industrial with agricultural work. The FSA also sought to aid migrants by building government camps for families.

Other New Deal programs sought to integrate rural life into the national economy and society. In a sense, the agrarian problem of the 1930s centered on definitions of modernity and progress. Much of rural America in the early twentieth century had become an eyesore in a nation that was characterized by suburbs, automobiles, department stores, and a vast array of consumer goods and gadgets, radios, and the talking movies. Households and communities came to measure themselves against the ads they saw in magazines or the Sears Roebuck catalog. Pictures of shining kitchens with all of the modern conveniences contrasted sharply with homes that still drew their water from a well, burned kerosene for light, cooked on wood stoves, and scrubbed clothes on washboards.

Thus, many government programs aimed at equalizing rural society with urban, industrial America. Federal agencies built a massive dam system that brought rural electrification and possibilities for future economic development. Public health programs sought to eradicate hookworm, pellagra, typhoid, malaria, and many other diseases that plagued the countryside. Credit was extended to allow farm improvements as well as home ownership. Soil conservation became a major aspect of agricultural policy as reforestation and grasslands bills sought to replenish the worn-out soils and to prevent future droughts and the Dust Bowl tragedy.

Yet major New Deal measures that granted industrial workers Social Security, a minimum wage, maximum hours, collective bargaining, and the right to organize denied those benefits to the agrarian working class. Indeed, some measures actually worsened their plight. As a result, the 1930s witnessed massive grass-roots mobilization in the countryside. From the southern plantations to the citrus and vegetable fields of California, hundreds of thousands of sharecroppers, tenant farmers, migrants, and wage hands called upon the federal government to grant them economic and political rights. Unfortunately, policymakers turned their ears to the voices of the large landowners.

Some of the most violent strikes in the 1930s occurred in the fields of California, where workers saw their wages reduced drastically. Filipino vegetable and fruit workers and Mexican cotton-pickers organized major strikes in the early 1930s that were met with evictions and violence. California growers, backed by local officials and chambers of commerce, refused to negotiate and gained a reputation for brutal repression. Despite the blatant violation of civil liberties and some murders, the federal government refused to grant a minimum wage to the workers. Not until the 1960s, with the rise of César Chávez and his United Farm Workers Union, would migrant laborers obtain a minimum wage, abolition of child labor, and rights to decent housing and health conditions.

In the plantation South, the AAA displaced thousands of sharecroppers as landowners plowed under their tenants' land and stole their parity checks. In the Arkansas Delta the Southern Tenant Farmers' Union (STFU) was organized in 1934 to obtain the workers' share of the agricultural program. Planters employed the state and local authorities to evict some union members, and to beat and murder others. The terror that swept across the Delta revealed the complete lack of protection for southern rural blacks, as well as many whites, and made it clear just how far outside the realm of citizenship they were.

The STFU forced a debate within the AAA and the Department of Agriculture over how to deal with southern poverty. Chester Davis, the head of the AAA and a close ally of the plantation owners, argued that conditions were not as bad as the union had presented them. President Roosevelt, fearful of losing his southern support in Congress, sided with Davis and the planters. Thus, the major agricultural legislation of the administration actually worsened rather than relieved the plight of the plantation workers. Those sympathetic to the poor secured the creation of the Farm Security Administration to help croppers and tenants purchase their own farms with low-interest government loans. However, planter opposition, underfunding, and restrictions within the agency meant that few benefited from the FSA.

The 1930s, then, witnessed the collapse of the plantation system of sharecropping and tenant farming as New Deal programs initiated crop diversification, land consolidation, and mechanization. By the 1960s, the agricultural South had made the transition from a labor-intensive to a capital-intensive economy. However, the human costs were high, as thousands were driven from the land, including small family farmers who could not afford to mechanize or who could not compete with the increasingly large estates.

In the long run, the policies underlying the AAA prevailed over those of the social planners. Indeed, the Farm Bureau and its partners on the West Coast lobbied to restrict funding for the FSA and succeeded in destroying it during World War II. Parity and production control remained the essence of agricultural policy for the rest of the twentieth century. After the 1930s, agriculture consolidated into larger concerns, branched out to include processing and marketing in the citrus and poultry businesses, and was based more than ever on scientific management and efficiency. These developments, combined with federal policies that encouraged farmers to invest more in technology, led to the demise of the family farmer.

By the end of the twentieth century, the chicken or beef one purchased in a grocery store more likely came from a subsidiary of Gulf and Western than from a family farm. The business side of agriculture had finally defeated the agrarian vision of farming as a way of life. Thus, family operators of the late twentieth century shared many of the burdens of their ancestors: indebtedness, competition from corporations, and exploitation by middlemen, often in the form of cooperatives supposedly designed to protect their interests. The only difference was that the family farmers, who had played so central a role in American ideology since its inception, were rapidly disappearing, destined to take their place next to the McCormick reaper and the southern sharecroppers in the museums.

[See also Foodways; The Frontier; Geographical Mobility; Labor: Colonial Times through 1820; The Plantation; Rural Life in the North; Rural Life in the South; Rural Life in the West; Slavery.]

BIBLIOGRAPHY

Barron, Hal. *Those Who Stayed Behind: Rural Society in Nineteenth-Century New England* (1984).

Chan, Sucheng. *This Bittersweet Soil: The Chinese in California Agriculture, 1860–1910* (1986).

Clark, Christopher. *The Roots of Rural Capitalism: Western Massachusetts, 1780–1860* (1990).

Cronon, William. *Changes in the Land: Indians, Colonists, and the Ecology of New England* (1983).

Danhof, Clarence H. *Change in Agriculture: The Northern United States, 1820–1870* (1969).

Daniel, Cletus. *Bitter Harvest: A History of California Farmworkers, 1870–1941* (1981).

Daniel, Pete. *Breaking the Land The Transformation of Cotton, Tobacco, and Rice Cultures Since 1880* (1985).

Faragher, John Mack. *Sugar Creek: Life on the Illinois Prairie* (1986).

Fields, Barbara Jeanne. "The Nineteenth-Century American South: History and Theory." *Plantation Society in the Americas* (April 1983).

Fields, Barbara Jeanne. *Slavery and Freedom on the Middle Ground: Maryland During the Nineteenth Century* (1985).

Fite, Gilbert. *American Farmers: The New Minority* (1981).

Foner, Eric. *Nothing but Freedom: Emancipation and Its Legacy* (1983).

Fox-Genovese, Elizabeth, and Eugene D. Genovese. *The Fruits of Merchant Capital: Slavery and Bourgeois Property in the Rise and Expansion of Capitalism* (1983).

Gates, Paul. *The Farmers Age: Agriculture, 1815–1860* (1960).

Genovese, Eugene D. *The Political Economy of Slavery: Studies in the Economy and Society of the Slave South* (1965).

Genovese, Eugene D. *Roll, Jordan, Roll: The World the Slaves Made* (1974).

Gjerde, Jon. *From Peasants to Farmers: The Migration from Balestrand, Norway, to the Upper Midwest* (1985).

Grubbs, Donald H. *Cry from Cotton: The Southern Tenant Farmers' Union and the New Deal* (1971).

Hahn, Steven. *The Roots of Southern Populism: Yeoman Farmers and the Transformation of the Georgia Upcountry, 1850–1890* (1983).

Hahn, Steven, and Jonathan Prude, eds. *The Countryside in the Age of Capitalist Transformation: Essays in the Social History of Rural America* (1985).

Hicks, John D. *The Populist Revolt: A History of the Farmers' Alliance and the People's Party* (1931).

Hoxie, Frederick E. *A Final Promise: The Campaign to Assimilate the Indians, 1880–1920* (1984).

Jamieson, Stuart. *Labor Unionism in American Agriculture* (1946).

Jensen, Joan. *Loosening the Bonds: Mid-Atlantic Farm Women, 1750–1850* (1986).

Kelley, Robin D. G. *Hammer and Hoe: Alabama Communists During the Great Depression* (1990).

Kirby, Jack Temple. *Rural Worlds Lost: The American South, 1920–1960* (1987).

Kulikoff, Allan. "The Transition to Capitalism in Rural America." *William and Mary Quarterly* 3rd ser., vol. XVI, no. 1 (January 1989): 120–142.

Montejano, David. *Anglos and Mexicans in the Making of Texas, 1836–1986* (1987).

Morgan, Edmund S. *American Slavery, American Freedom: The Ordeal of Colonial Virginia* (1975).

Takaki, Ronald. *Pau Hana: Plantation Life and Labor in Hawaii, 1835–1920* (1983).

Webb, Walter Prescott. *The Great Plains* (1931).

Woodman, Harold D. "Post-Civil War Southern Agriculture and the Law." *Agricultural History* 53, no. 1 (January 1979): 319–337.

Woodman, Harold D. "Postbelium Social Change and Its Effects on Marketing the South's Cotton Crop." *Agricultural History* 56, no. 1 (January 1982): 215–230.

Woodruff, Nan Elizabeth. *As Rare as Rain: Federal Relief in the Great Southern Drought of 1930–31* (1985).

Woodward, C. Vann. *Origins of the New South, 1877–1913* (1951).

Worster, Donald. *Dust Bowl: The Southern Plains in the 1930s* (1979).

— NAN ELIZABETH WOODRUFF

ALTERNATIVE FORMS OF EDUCATION

While study of American education has focused largely on the public school and other traditional forms, the history of alternative education is important in several respects. The magnitude of such activities throughout American history gives them a major significance. Since at least the beginning of the nineteenth century most Americans have been exposed to some form of alternative education. Today, few people above infancy are not the beneficiaries of such education. A complete understanding of the development of American social institutions and their impact on the nation is impossible without a knowledge of alternative education.

The study of alternative modes of teaching and learning provides a variety of prisms through which to view American life and culture at particular points in time, or to look at the history of particular subpopulations. Examination of alternative kinds of education not only helps us to describe these eras or groups; it also illuminates various aspects of their values and cultures. This is especially true because alternative education serves constituencies outside the educational mainstream. Some of these are traditional in most respects but belong to religious and ethnic groups seeking to transmit cultures other than that of the mainstream who dominate public education. Extensive networks of religious schools are examples of such alternative education.

Other constituencies are more marginal. Throughout American history, educational opportunities have been less available to women than to men. Ethnic groups such as blacks and Indians have been severely limited in both the scope and the quality of educational resources offered them. Less dramatically, workers, those below and above traditional ages for school attendance, and those unwilling or unable to matriculate in traditional institutions have found themselves outside the mainstream of traditional education.

The institutions that serve these groups of individuals arose to meet specific demands. They have tended, as a result, to be somewhat more responsive to their particular constituencies than have more traditional forms of education with their massive bureaucracies. Thus, study of the agencies themselves is helpful in understanding the women and men they served. The formation, growth, and decline of such modes of education mirror changes within specific populations. The examination of alternative educational arrangements becomes important for its illumination of such groups, who frequently are among the least studied in American society.

The Colonial Period

CHILDREN'S EDUCATION. During the colonial era, the majority of formal education in America was under religious sponsorship. Seen as an extension of the church's teaching role, schools were used to transmit the culture of the sponsoring community, including its religious aspects. Only with the firm establishment of the common-school movement in the years surrounding the Civil War did secular publicly supported education come to predominate.

In colonial America, early educational activities were carried on by French and Spanish Catholic missionaries in upper Maine and New York, New Orleans, Florida and the Spanish Southwest. Some of the institutions these Jesuits, Franciscans and Dominicans founded were for the maintenance of the colonizing culture among the children of settlers. Schools for Indians represented an extension of the culture of the colonizing power.

In the English-speaking South, schools were conducted by the Anglican Society for the Propagation of the Gospel in Foreign Parts, founded in London in 1701. While this organization was initially created to provide schooling for marginalized groups such as blacks and Indians, its missionaries quickly found that schooling opportunities for whites were virtually nonexistent. Schools were also founded by Roman Catholics, Quakers, and Presbyterians, although these were few in number, mirroring the relatively smaller numbers of adherents to these churches. The literacy rate in the South, therefore, was notably lower than those in the other colonies. While some of this can be traced to the difficulty of providing schooling for the dispersed agricultural settlements that characterized the region, the strong belief in education as a private rather than a social good and the consequent lack of public involvement were also important factors.

New England's extensive educational network, in contrast, was denominationally controlled but publicly sponsored. Massachusetts Bay, the largest colony in the region, led the way in educational development. Fueled by Puritan insistence on universal basic literacy sufficient for reading the Bible, the General Court passed legislation in 1642 mandating the establishment of schools. The "Old Deluder Satan" Act of 1647 provided a detailed plan for creating schools to counter the devil and Romanism. These acts implicitly were rooted in the belief that education is a social good, and that the community itself bears responsibility for its maintenance and oversight. Their provisions became the basis for legislation throughout the region.

Besides more conventional schools, basic literacy was promoted by the dame schools. These home schools in which women gathered local children and taught them basic reading while going about their household chores were the institutions in which many youngsters received their first formal education.

In the middle colonies, the ethnic and religious heterogeneity of the population discouraged a single network of schools. Early education in New York was under the direction of the Reformed church, and therefore emphasized Dutch language and religion. With the accession of the British, English-speaking schools propagated Anglican religious culture.

In New Jersey and Pennsylvania, education was sponsored by a wide array of religious groups, including Lutherans, Presbyterians, Huguenots, German pietists, Catholics, and Jews. The presence of non-English-speaking immigrants motivated groups like the Germans in Pennsylvania and the Dutch in New Jersey to sponsor schools in which both religion and language were important. Quakers were especially prominent in education in Pennsylvania. Unlike the schools run by virtually every other religious group, Quaker institutions served students of both genders, as well as blacks and Indians.

> *Aimed at an audience aspiring to upward social mobility, the popularity of colonial etiquette literature testifies to the eagerness of middle-class Americans, especially women, for self-improvement.*

Formal schools run for profit were found throughout the colonies. During the era, much of the elementary and secondary schooling was carried on by schoolmasters who set up institutions on a for-profit basis. These varied widely in quality, and taught whatever subjects the local community was willing to pay for.

In all three colonial regions, schooling was utilized to maintain the culture of the sponsoring community. Only in New England were large numbers of the poor and women given basic literacy education. For the most part, colonial education was a white, upper- and middle-class, male phenomenon.

School curricula virtually always included reading and writing skills. More advanced institutions taught mathematics and classical languages. Some specialized schools provided instruction in modern languages, surveying, and other practical skills, but these were in the minority. The dominant focus was on basic literacy.

EVENING SCHOOLS. The first evening schools were founded in New Netherland in the 1660s to provide apprentices and others with basic reading, writing, and mathematics, as well as more advanced subjects such as bookkeeping and navigation. By the eighteenth century, they offered instruction in both practical and classical subjects determined by the schoolmaster or local demand.

SELF-EDUCATION. Given the enduring themes of self-improvement and upward mobility that have permeated the American consciousness since earliest times, it is not surprising that self-education has always occupied an important place in alternative education. One form such education took was self-help literature. That one of its earliest authors should be the quintessential self-made American, Benjamin Franklin, is unsurprising. Beginning with the brief essay "The Way to Wealth," in *Poor Richard's Almanack* (1732), he championed the cause of self-betterment. Franklin was also among the first promoters of the study group as a vehicle for self-improvement. The Junto, a men's literary and discussion group, founded by him in 1727, became the most famous example of this educational agency in colonial America.

Franklin helped to create what in the nineteenth century would become a deluge of literature on etiquette. His *Reflections on Courtship and Marriage* (1746) followed earlier works like Cotton Mather's *Ornaments for the Daughters of Zion* (1692). For the most part, however, colonial etiquette literature was a British import. William Kenrick's *The Whole Duty of Woman* went through ten American editions between 1761 and 1797, and W. H. Dilworth's *The Complete Letter-Writer* ran to thirteen editions during the same period. Aimed at an audience aspiring to upward social mobility, the popularity of these works testifies to the eagerness of middle-class Americans, especially women, for self-improvement.

Libraries came into existence during this period, providing resources for self-education. America's first publicly accessible library began with a 1655 gift by Robert Keayne to Boston that became part of a library opened in the town hall in 1673. In 1731, Benjamin Franklin started a subscription library in Philadelphia, and by 1780, there were fifty such libraries in New England alone.

The Nineteenth Century

A number of factors in nineteenth-century America encouraged the development of alternative education. Massive immigration, beginning in the second quarter of the century and continuing until its end, fueled the establishment of alternative institutions in several ways. The desire to maintain ethnic culture, including its religion and language, encouraged the development of separate institutions and agencies to socialize the young. In addition, the poverty that characterized many immigrant groups discouraged attendance at traditional schools because of embarrassment and the need to have as many family members as possible in the labor market. Alternative means of education were frequently the only ones available to such people.

The great industrial growth of the post–Civil War period created new pressure for education to meet the demands of new workplaces. Alternative vehicles for education were created to deal with these new tasks. In addition, the desire for upward social mobility encouraged individuals to seek out various sorts of nontraditional education.

CATHOLIC SCHOOLS. While formal educational activities were begun by Spanish and French missionaries in the territories under their nations' rule, and English Jesuit schoolmasters labored in Maryland and Pennsylvania, Catholic parochial schooling was largely the product of the massive increase in immigration of the nineteenth and early twentieth centuries. The Catholic population increased from 318,000 in 1830 to twenty million a century later.

Initially, hierarchs attempted to co-opt the nascent public school systems. Because the notion of a religiously neutral or secularized common school became fixed only in the period following the Civil War, bishops were quick to seek the sort of state funding for their educational activities that was given to Protestant groups. In a few states like Ohio, they were initially successful in their efforts, but more typically they found themselves rebuffed. A good example of this latter result was the futile attempt by Bishop John Hughes in New York to obtain public funding for Catholic schools in the 1840s.

Disillusioned bishops turned to separate schools to maintain Catholic and ethnic culture. Their success was especially notable in certain urban centers. Cincinnati, for example, with a large population of Irish and German Catholics, had a parochial school enrollment of around fifteen thousand by 1866, representing thirty-seven percent of the city's school attenders. However, the pattern differed from diocese to diocese. Successful attempts by Irish Catholics in Boston to co-opt public schools lessened the desire for parochial education. By 1915, most members of the Boston School Committee were Catholics, as were a majority of the assistant superintendents, one of whom was the sister of the Jesuit dean of Boston College's School of Education. With a large force of Irish teachers in the common schools, as well as a cohort of Catholic administrators, public education became a de facto Catholic enterprise. As a result, in 1880 only 10 percent of the city's schoolchildren attended Catholic schools, compared with 22 percent in Chicago.

Catholic parochial education was designed to meet important needs in the transmission of ethnic cultures. While common schooling emphasized the Anglo-Saxon evangelical Protestant character of the dominant American culture, Catholic schools were able to stress the religious, linguistic, and ethnic heritages of the groups who supported them. The goal of such schools, staffed almost exclusively by religious teachers, was to provide a total religious and ethnic environment unavailable in the public schools.

The establishment of Catholic schools was heavily promoted after the Civil War. Communities of teaching sisters and brothers were recruited from Europe or the United States or, in some instances, founded to meet specific local or ethnic needs. Support by their constituencies differed depending on ethnic origins. Germans and Poles were quick to found Catholic schools and provide for their support, while the Italians tended to be more lackadaisical.

In most Catholic communities, parochial schools functioned as an alternative common-school system. Charging little or no tuition, they were open to all who wished to attend. Thus, they served poor constituencies as well as wealthy ones. In poorer communities, they were viable only because of the willingness of religious teachers to work for subsistence wages and the decision to tolerate large classes and substandard physical plants.

PROTESTANT SCHOOLS. Protestant schooling, like Catholic schooling, has been motivated largely by the desire to maintain religious and ethnic culture. Among the most notable proponents were German Lutherans. The Missouri Synod by 1872 had founded 446 schools in 472 congregations as agencies to propagate conservative Lutheran doctrine, as well as German language and culture. By the 1960s, over 150,000 students were enrolled in its schools and those of the fiercely conservative Wisconsin Synod.

Calvinist education in America was promoted by Dutch immigrants who settled in western Michigan in 1847. Since the 1850s, these schools have moved from strictly parochial status (controlled by local parishes and clergy) to that of private religious schools with lay boards, which draw enrollment from broader constituencies.

The Protestant groups most involved in education have tended to be those with distinctive conservative theologies and strong ethnic roots. Their perception, similar to that of Catholics, has been that their needs will be better met by schools in which their religious and ethnic heritage can be freely propagated. In many instances, these schools have been sponsored by local parishes. Within the Lutheran Church, Missouri Synod, the presence of an explicitly defined teaching ministry provided a source of educational labor similar to religious sisters and brothers in their motivation. The same economic factors (e.g., hierarchical organization, personnel willing to work for subsistence wages) that tended to make Catholic education possible, however, worked against most Protestant day schools.

Protestant schools were also established for the evangelization of blacks and Native Americans. The American Missionary Association, a largely Congregationalist organization, founded a number of schools in the South after the Civil War, the most famous of which was the Hampton Institute (1868). The establishment of the Office of Indian Affairs in 1819 led to the policy by which federal funds were given to Protestant missionary groups to establish and operate schools. With the development of the reservation system after the Civil War, individual Indian reservations were assigned to various religious groups which then became responsible for the formation of schools, though these were funded by the federal government.

PART-TIME RELIGIOUS EDUCATION. Part-time religious instruction flourished during the nineteenth century. Following the model developed by the British newspaper publisher Robert Raikes, the first American Sunday school was founded at Philadelphia in 1790. Less oriented toward the lower classes than its British antecedents, it promoted middle-class respectability through the incalcation of such virtues as hard work and thrift.

After the Civil War, Evangelicals like Dwight Moody enlisted the support of entrepreneurs like John Wanamaker and H. J. Heinz to produce a religiously efficient system of schools that reached its peak with the 1872 introduction of a standardized seven-year cycle of Scripture topics for each Sunday. By 1900, three million students were studying these lessons.

Similar religious activities have also been carried out by the Young Men's Christian Association (YMCA), imported from England in 1851, and the Young Women's Christian Association (YWCA), founded in 1855. Both groups, in addition to a wide range of secular educational activities and cultural and academic subjects, have taught courses in various aspects of Christianity to hundreds of thousands of young people.

Among American Jews, most educational activity has been on a part-time basis. The foundation of the Polonies Talmud Torah in New York in 1808 set the pattern of the Jewish school as a supplement to secular education. While the Jewish community in colonial America had been relatively homogeneous, consisting mainly of Jews of German origin, the disintegration of its cohesiveness caused by the massive nineteenth-century immigrations from eastern Europe promoted the part-time religious school as an instrument for the preservation of Jewish religion and culture. Talmud Torahs and the Young Men's and Young Women's Hebrew Associations (YMHA, YWHA), as well as the socialist and Zionist Shalom Aleichem schools and the Arbeiter Ring (Workers' Circle) schools of radical workers, advanced the cause of traditional Jewish culture and religion, as well as new political movements such as socialism and Zionism.

EVENING SCHOOLS. As common schooling became more established in the middle of the nineteenth century, so did evening education. Both the number and the age of students increased throughout the remainder of the nineteenth and early twentieth centuries. In Cleveland, Ohio, for example, the 135 students in 1851 had become 11,383 by 1915. In Saint Louis, the average age went from sixteen between 1884 and 1909 to eighteen between 1908 and 1910. The curriculum broadened to include Americanization classes for immigrants, high school and vocational subjects, and the beginnings of adult education. While numbers have decreased in the latter half of the twentieth century as the result of other educational options and the continual rise in the minimum school-leaving age, such schools still serve recent immigrants and school dropouts.

CORRESPONDENCE STUDY. The first significant use of correspondence study was as part of the Chautauqua movement in 1878. Within a few years, the idea was taken up by commercial interests. In the 1880s, Thomas J. Foster, editor of the Shenandoah, Pennsylvania, *Mining Herald*, developed a course in coal mining to improve mine safety. This developed into the international Correspondence Schools of Scranton, Pennsylvania, in 1891. By the 1920s, this single school had a cumulative enrollment of over 2.2 million students. William Rainey Harper, founding president of the University of Chicago, took the correspondence study idea from his tenure at Chautauqua, and established an extension division at the university in 1894. By 1913, thirty-two colleges and universities sponsored correspondence courses with a total enrollment of approximately 20,000 students. Since the early part of the twentieth century, both commercial and higher educational organizations have participated in this form of alternative education.

PROPRIETARY SCHOOLS. Even after the advent of public education, proprietary schools (privately owned and operated for profit) continued to teach subjects of a more practical nature, as well as to provide basic education where common schooling had not yet developed. The academy, the most common secondary institution until the late nineteenth century, was frequently a proprietary school.

Few generalizations can be made about the academy. In some cases, the level of education equaled that of a college, while in others the standard was barely that of an elementary school. Curricula were determined by local demand. In many instances, academies stressed the classical studies seen as normative by most educators. In others, however, the teaching of applied mathematics, modern languages, and history marked the institution as more innovative and pragmatic.

The clientele of academies tended to be white and male. There were, however, exceptions. From the early nineteenth century on, female academies and seminaries provided virtually the only post-elementary education available for most women. Specializing in humanistic and practical studies that were thought appropriate to middle-class women, they also served as a training ground for "women's true profession," teaching. By 1839, nearly five hundred former students at Zilpah Grant Banister's Ipswich Academy had become teachers.

A small number of academies served minority populations. Before the Civil War, Colonel Richard Johnson's Choctaw Academy had an Indian student body, and in Florida, the Orange Park Normal and Industrial School for Negroes served a black clientele.

The late nineteenth and early twentieth centuries witnessed a tremendous growth in institutions to teach technical and commercial subjects, a result of the rapid development of American business and industry following the Civil War. The New York Trade School (1881) and the Williamson Free School of Mechanical Trades in Delaware, Pennsylvania (1891), were among the first, teaching skills such as plastering, tailoring, printing, and carpentry. At the same time, proprietary institutions to teach skills such as stenography, typewriting, and bookkeeping came into existence. Most of these latter were short-lived, in part because the lack of any form of regulation encouraged profiteering.

CORPORATE EDUCATION. Corporate education arose in the early nineteenth century to educate workers for specific tasks and functions in the developing factory system, as well as to provide general education. Attempts were made in places like Lowell, Massachusetts, to provide lectures and literary evenings for mill girls who lived in company boardinghouses.

Formal corporation schools began at least as early as the 1870s, providing combinations of full-time instruction, work-study, and study at outside institutions. Classes involved technical education, basic cultural education, and training for upper-level occupations in the corporation. The goal was greater efficiency in the workplace, a characteristic concern of America's industrially oriented Gilded Age society. By 1916, sixty thousand students were attending corporate classes.

WORKERS' EDUCATION. Institutions for the education of workers outside the workplace were the product of American industrialization in the early nineteenth century. These were modeled on the schools established by George Birkbeck and others from 1800 to 1804 in Britain. The earliest was the New York Scientific and Mechanical Institution founded by the General Society of Mechanics and Tradesmen in 1822. This was followed by the Franklin Institute of Philadelphia (1824), the Ohio Mechanics' Institute in Cincinnati (1828), the Lowell Institute in Boston (1836), and Cooper Union in New York (1859).

Serving the new skilled labor force, such workers' institutes concentrated on two forms of education. By stressing science and technology, they hoped to produce a cohort of highly skilled workers that would give America the lead in technological advances. At the same time, by providing opportunities for education in the humanistic disciplines, they sought to provide skilled workers with the sort of education thought to be the mark of genuinely cultured individuals.

SELF-DIRECTED EDUCATION. The self-help literature that had begun in the colonial era continued and expanded during the nineteenth century. This was due both to an increase in the volume of printed material, reflecting a growing literacy rate, and to the aspirations of the growing middle class.

One common theme of such literature was economic success. The venerable English tradition of uniting God and mammon was continued on this side of the Atlantic by divines like John Todd, the author of *The Young Man* (1844) and *Nuts for Boys to Crack* (1866), and Matthew Hale Smith in *Twenty Years Among the Bulls and Bears of Wall Street* (1870) and *Successful Folks* (1878).

If clergy were strong in their insistence on the relationship between Christianity and wealth, the same theme was evident in the writings of successful American entrepreneurs. John D. Rockefeller's *Random Reminiscences of Men and Events* (1909) and Andrew Carnegie's *The Gospel of Wealth* (1889) and *Autobiography* (1920) emphasized similar themes, as did works by the showman P. T. Barnum. Educators like Horace Mann and Henry Barnard also entered this arena with success. So did their colleague William A. Alcott, whose *The Young Man's Guide* (1833) went through sixteen editions in eleven years.

Besides the guides to fame and fortune, there was a considerable market for books on etiquette and letter writing. Typical of these were *The Art of Good Behavior; and Letter Writer on Love, Courtship, and Marriage* (1846) and Francis Lieber's *The Character of the Gentleman* (1846). The numerous American editions of Lord Chesterfield's *Letters to His Son* after 1774 also testify to the concern of the upwardly mobile about proper behavior. At the same time, the increasing market for uniquely American etiquette books pointed out the increasing differences between cultural norms in Britain and the United States. Dealing with topics as varied as courtship, the hiring of servants, and style of dress, the growing number of works by American authors signaled the social aspirations, especially of women, even in the midst of republican rhetoric.

Increased literacy and the inadequacy of educational opportunities for women created a popular form of self-education, the women's study group or discussion club.

Increased literacy, coupled with the inadequacy of educational opportunities for women, helped to create one of the most popular forms of self-education, the women's study group or discussion club. They sprang up in the 1860s and reached their peak in the 1890s. Usually meeting for two hours on a biweekly basis, these groups of middle-class women were centers of personal growth and support. Before their decline in the twentieth century, the General Federation of Women's Clubs listed five thousand such organizations in 1906, and these probably represented only five to ten percent of the clubs in existence.

In many respects, the antecedent of such study clubs was the lyceum. The lyceum involved individuals studying together and teaching each other, generally in weekly meetings. Lectures and exhibitions were common activities, as were such service functions as providing books for a library. The universal goal was self-improvement. In 1826, Josiah Holbrook described a plan for the organization of an educational society that would reach every part of the United States, and had organized eleven lyceums in Massachusetts within the next two years. By 1835, according to one estimate, there were about three thousand town lyceums, over one hundred county ones, and more than fifteen at the state level.

National organization of the movement was never successful: lyceums tended to be independent local organizations. By the end of the Civil War, they had begun to decline, replaced by women's clubs, popular lecture series, and other groups. Only in New England, with its venerable tradition of individualism and self-education, did they continue to be a significant force. Their legacy has, however, remained. They became one of the most potent forces urging the establishment of public schooling. More directly, the lyceums developed educational techniques that were later utilized by Chautauqua, university extension, the Great Books Program, and public forum movements.

Another of nineteenth-century America's innovative vehicles for alternative education was Chautauqua, founded by John Heyl Vincent, a future Methodist bishop, and Lewis Miller, a self-educated rural teacher, inventor, and entrepreneur. Begun in 1874 as a Sunday school teachers' assembly, it quickly broadened its scope and became largely oriented toward secular subjects.

Chautauqua's main focus was on lectures, discussion groups, and dramatic and musical programs at its lakeside site in upstate New York. Besides these activities, Chautauqua soon became involved in other educational programming. Extension work was carried on for a time, and the institution was briefly incorporated as Chautauqua University (1883). The most important of the experiments, however, was the establishment in 1878 of the Chautauqua Literary and Scientific Circle. This consisted of home reading groups engaged in an organized program of personal study leading to an examination and certificate presented at the annual meeting at Chautauqua. Initial membership in the program was four thousand, and four years later, Vincent awarded diplomas to the eight hundred who finished. By the 1890s, however, this part of the program had begun to decline as a result of the wider availability of books and book clubs, and later, as a result of the growing influence of radio.

The founding of libraries that had begun in the late colonial era continued in the nineteenth century, but with added sources of support. Initially, subscription libraries were the most popular form, outnumbering public libraries two to one by the end of the Civil War. However, the public library soon came to predominate.

The greatest boost to free libraries came from Andrew Carnegie, who between 1881 and 1917 gave more than $40 million to build libraries, provided that the local community guarantee 10 percent of the building costs for annual upkeep.

Its roots lie in grants given by states to communities for library development and in the passage of laws allowing taxation for libraries after the mid nineteenth century. The first real free town library was founded in Peterborough, New Hampshire, in 1833. The greatest boost was given by Andrew Carnegie, who between 1881 and 1917 gave over forty-one million dollars to finance the building of libraries, provided the local community would guarantee ten percent of the building costs for annual upkeep. By 1917, Carnegie had financed 1,679 such libraries. Although Carnegie's interest later waned, public libraries became a fixture on the American scene. Even small communities sought to create them, if for no other reason than their perceived value as a signal of a town's high cultural standards.

Technical libraries came into existence, spurred by the same forces that promoted mechanics' institutes. The earliest of these were libraries established for apprentices in New York, Boston, Portland, Salem, and and Philadelphia in 1820. These soon multiplied, and were found in most of the nation's major cities by the time of the Civil War.

The nineteenth century was also the period when many of America's greatest museums were founded. Most American museums founded before the middle of the century were oriented toward natural history. These included the New York Academy of Sciences (1817) and the Academy of Natural Sciences in Philadelphia (1812). This development mirrored the growing fascination of the nation with all forms of natural science.

Only a few of the earliest museums—the Pennsylvania Academy of Fine Arts (1805) and several university collections—were art museums. The foundation of museums like the Boston Museum of Fine Arts (1871), the Philadelphia Museum of Art (1876), and Chicago's Art Institute (1879) signaled a new aesthetic emphasis in museums. Their development reflected both a growing American interest in fine arts and the willingness of the nation's new capitalists to finance their foundation and expansion.

The Twentieth Century

Changes in American society during the twentieth century helped to bring about shifts in alternative education. The growth of American business and industry encouraged the development of technical and commercial education. The growing strength of American corporations, moreover, encouraged many of them to become directly involved in worker education.

New patterns of immigration also had their effects. The curtailing of immigration after the 1920s helped to change the focus of Catholic education, and eventually contributed to its decline. At the same time, however, the influx of new immigrants in the forty years following World War II hastened the development of such institutions as the part-time ethnic school.

Institutions for self-education, such as libraries and museums, continued their traditional roles but expanded into new forms of education and developed new constituencies. Such activities were the results of development in their understandings of their scope, and of increased competition for funding.

CATHOLIC SCHOOLS. The years between the end of World War I and the 1960s were ones of significant expansion for Catholic parochial schools. In the period between 1950 and 1960, Catholic elementary school attendance grew by 171 percent, compared with a 142 percent growth rate for public schools. This is attributable to both the higher birthrate immediately following World War II and the growing Catholic affluence that made schools more viable. After 1957, the situation changed drastically. Fueled by the increasing assimilation of Catholics into the more secularized American mainstream, economic shifts resulting from a decreasing supply of religious sisters and brothers, and the end of the post-World War II "baby boom," parochial education reached a plateau and then declined. While the demise that some predicted has not materialized, the parochial school remains in a problematic state, both economically and ideologically.

PROTESTANT AND JEWISH SCHOOLS. Changes in the landscape of Protestant education have reflected shifts within American Protestantism. Newer denominations have developed their own educational networks. Adventist education, for example, began with the founding of a school at Battle Creek, Michigan, in 1872. By the early 1980s, the Seventh-day Adventist church operated 1,106 elementary and eighty-one high schools in the United States, with a total enrollment of 68,575.

The most striking new religious educational phenomenon is the rise of the Christian day school. While only 150 such schools were founded between 1920 and 1960, between 9,000 and 11,000 have been established since 1960, with an estimated enrollment of one million. Their growth has been a result of dissatisfaction with the mainstream American culture propagated in the public schools. Issues such as the teaching of evolution, sex education, and nontraditional interpretations of history have encouraged conservative American Protestants, especially those belonging to nondenominational churches, to establish alternative networks of schools to transmit their own culture.

While Jewish day schooling began with the 1731 founding of Yeshibat Minhat Areb in New York City, it remained a minor phenomenon through most of the nineteenth and twentieth centuries, despite the massive immigrations from Germany and eastern Europe that made the United States home to 30 percent of world Jewry by 1920. The post-World War II prosperity of American Jews, coupled with the general surge of religious sentiment, the events of the Holocaust and establishment of Israel, concern over a declining birthrate, and increased attention to ethnic identity have contributed to a significant growth in Jewish schooling. Most of the present 360 schools, largely under Orthodox or Conservative auspices, have been founded since the 1940s. For the most part, they serve a middle-class constituency.

PART-TIME RELIGIOUS EDUCATION. Many of the forces influencing developments in religious day schooling have affected part-time religious education. The twentieth century has seen the decline of some institutions as well as the consolidation and strengthening of others.

The religious education of Catholic children who attend public school has become more sophisticated during the twentieth century. Organized Catholic efforts began with the Confraternity of Christian Doctrine founded in 1902. Now, as a result of the increased affluence and stature of the Catholic community and the fact that most Catholics send their children to public school, the arrangements for part-time religious education are strong. Catholic children from kindergarten to twelfth grade are entitled to released-time and after-school classes. For teenagers, the Catholic Youth Organization, along with other clubs and parish programs, provides both formal and informal educational activities.

Mainstream Protestant education has declined in the twentieth century. After what seemed to be a golden age in the first years of the twentieth century, the Sunday school fell

Catholic elementary school attendance grew dramatically between the end of World War I and 1960. Growing catholic affluence and a higher birthrate transformed the Catholic classroom.

victim to a number of social forces. Tension developed between the volunteers who had traditionally administered and staffed Sunday schools and the new professional religious educators who decried their efforts as old-fashioned. By the 1930s, Sunday school attendance in mainline Protestant denominations was down, whereas activity has increased among conservative Protestants, in some cases dramatically.

The American Jewish revival after World War II that motivated the foundation of day schools also promoted part-time Jewish education. By the late 1950s, over eighty percent of Jewish children attended some form of religious school. By the mid 1980s, Jewish community centers, camps, and YMHAs and YWHAs enrolled nearly one million members in various activities, testifying to the continued vitality of this form of ethnic and religious education.

ETHNIC SCHOOLS. Ethnic education multiplied during the great immigrations of the nineteenth century, especially as groups became settled and prosperous enough to support it. Immigration since World War II has encouraged the formation of a wide variety of such institutions; by the 1960s, over two thousand were in existence. Generally they have taken the form of weekday afternoon programs meeting two or more times a week, or of weekend schools. Only a small number have operated on a daily basis.

Somewhat different in structure were the folk high schools established by Scandinavian groups in the late nineteenth and early twentieth centuries. Institutions such as the Ashland Folk School, founded in 1882 by H. J. Pedersen near Grant, Michigan, taught the ethnic group's language, religion, and culture as well as English and the civic subjects required for citizenship. These schools catered to a varied clientele, including youth and recent immigrants. The Danes alone founded ten of them in the United States by the early twentieth century. Although all eventually ceased operation as a result of declining interest, they exercised a significant influence on the development of folk schools for native-born Americans.

FOLK SCHOOLS. Inspired by the Danish folk schools, individuals concerned with the problems of working people and the poor moved to create comparable American institutions. The John C. Campbell Folk School was founded in 1925 by Marguerite Butler and Olive Dame Campbell, near Brasstown, North Carolina, to assist in the preservation of folk culture and to aid economic development. In 1927, Ashland College in Michigan was created to teach a mixture of academic and craft subjects to local students. Initially, both teachers and students paid their own expenses at this institution.

Arguably the most famous of the folk schools was the Highlander Folk School, founded in 1932 at Monteagle, Tennessee, by Myles Horton, a disciple of Reinhold Niebuhr at Union Theological Seminary in New York City. Influenced by Hull House in Chicago and the Danish folk schools, he developed a program emphasizing psychology, cultural geography, revolutionary literature, and social and economic problems.

By the time of World War II, Highlander had begun to develop a commitment to racial justice. During the postwar era, the song of the civil rights movement, "We Shall Overcome," was written there. Highlander's involvement in integration put it on a collision course with the state of Tennessee. After numerous accusations of communism and prosecution, the state seized the school's property and revoked its charter in 1959. It was later reorganized as Highlander Research and Education Center and moved to Knoxville. Since 1964, it has again made Appalachia the center of its efforts.

The folk schools combined an interest in the preservation of local culture with a concern for economic betterment. They supplied unique resources, especially in rural areas.

WORKERS' COLLEGES. More closely resembling folk schools than the nineteenth-century mechanics' institutes, workers' colleges developed in conjunction with the growth of labor radicalism in the late nineteenth and early twentieth centuries. In 1895 residential Avalon College, later renamed Ruskin College, was established as a labor school in Trenton, Missouri. Similar institutions included the Bread Winners' College, founded at New York City in 1898 to disseminate the classics to workers, and the Rand School of Social Science (1906). In Minneapolis, the Work People's College developed in 1907 out of a Finnish folk high school. Two of the most prominent schools of the post-World War I era were Brookwood Labor College (1921) at Katonah, New York, and Commonwealth College (1925) at Mena, Arkansas.

Rooted in social discontent and dissatisfaction with organized labor as well as with public education, these schools sought to develop leaders for American labor. Their curricula ranged from basic Americanization classes to labor history, drama, and journalism. Courses lasted from a few weeks to three years. Rarely did any have over one hundred students, most of whom had completed only the eighth grade.

The radical character of such schools was ultimately responsible for their demise. Work People's College, having allied itself with the Industrial Workers of the World, fell afoul of public reaction to this organization's opposition to World War I. By 1920, the college's appeal had begun to decline, and it closed in 1940. Brookwood was denounced as Communist in 1928 by the American Federation of Labor as a result of its radical stance, and eventually closed. Commonwealth was investigated on several occasions by the state legislature and was forced to close in 1941 after continuing accusations of communism. The work of these schools has been carried on in folk schools and, more recently, in the education programs developed by individual unions and larger labor organizations such as the Southern Labor School, the Rocky Mountain Labor School, and the Union Leadership Academy.

CORPORATE EDUCATION. While the 1920s saw a growth in corporate education because of a resurgence of interest in the employee as a human resource, the greatest growth occurred after World War II. By 1956 General Electric was offering 1,500 courses to 32,000 students at a cost of $35–40 million, and nearly 85 percent of American companies offered some sort of training program.

By the 1980s, about 400 business sites had some form of educational center, utilizing outside resources or, more commonly, their own educators. The most common programs have been orientation courses, followed by subjects like managerial development, human relations, technical and professional education, and general education.

The level of study ranges from basic skills to graduate education. In 1923, General Electric began a three-year basic engineering course leading to a certificate. Subsequently, over eighteen corporations developed bachelor's and master's degree programs, and a few now offer the doctorate.

PROPRIETARY SCHOOLS. While corporations increasingly began to be involved in education, the proprietary sector was also growing; by the end of World War I, such schools had become big business. In 1925, the fees paid by students in such institutions totaled around seven million dollars. About eighty percent of the institutions have typically been owned or controlled by private companies, with the remainder owned by partnerships or stock companies. The passage of the Servicemen's Readjustment Act (GI Bill of Rights) in 1944 gave an impetus to such schools, since it allowed returning military personnel to use their educational benefits in them.

The proprietary sector in American education continues to grow. Technical and commercial schools have blossomed, with several operating campuses across the nation. Devry Institute of Technology, a subsidiary of another proprietary, the Keller Graduate School of Management, was founded in 1931 as the DeForest Training School. At present, it enrolls twenty-three thousand students on nine campuses in the United States and two in Canada. Proprietary colleges and universities such as Golden Gate University in San Francisco and the American Graduate School of International Management, Thunderbird Campus in Glendale, Arizona, are a newer element on the proprietary school landscape.

SELF-EDUCATION. The twentieth century has witnessed the decline of some forms of self-education and the growth of others. New modes of self-teaching have also developed during this period.

The market for self-help literature has continued to blossom. With the massive exodus of Americans to the suburbs after World War II, a new literature involved with home repair came into print, as did books on family life and child raising, such as the many editions of Dr. Benjamin Spock's *The Common Sense Book of Baby and Child Care* (1946). The growing availability of leisure, together with the development of introspective cultures in recent decades, has spawned an emerging personal growth literature. The traditional linkage of religion and economic prosperity has continued with bestselling writings like Norman Vincent Peale's *The Power of Positive Thinking* (1952) and Robert Schuller's *Self-Esteem* (1982).

After World War II, a new literature involved with home repair came into print, as did books on family life and child raising, such as Dr. Benjamin Spock's The Common Sense Book of Baby and Child Care.

While the quest for self-improvement is most visible in the success of explicit self-help literature, participation in other kinds of literary activity offers testimony to the desire to become more educated. The number of books published in the United States from 1880 to 1900 was three times as great as that before the Civil War. During the 1870s and 1880s there was a great increase in the selling of books by subscription. With the 1919 publication of Charles W. Eliot's "Five Foot Shelf of Books," later known as the Harvard Classics, the notion that information could be used to mold personality rose to prominence.

The Literary Guild, created by Samuel W. Craig in 1921, was the largest book club until World War II, after which it was overtaken by the Book-of-the-Month Club. This organization, created by New York advertising executive Harry Scherman in 1926, had more than 60,000 members within its first year, and over 100,000 by 1929. Indeed, except for the worst part of the Great Depression, the club has grown each year, evidence of the strength of self-education.

The proliferation of similar ventures is further testimony to the continuing viability of this form of self-education. Clubs specializing in history, romance, cooking, and mystery fiction, to cite only a few examples, offer more specific forms of self-education, as does the series sold by *Time-Life* books on topics as diverse as home repair and World War II.

More focused were the "Great Books" discussion groups. Developing from roots in the 1921 General Honors course begun at Columbia University and brought to the University of Chicago by Mortimer J. Adler, the concept was expanded to include nonuniversity audiences. In 1947, the Great Books Foundation was organized, and within a year, over 43,000 people were attending its seminars in 300 cities. The movement flourished in the 1950s and 1960s, then declined. Such study clubs, however, are still found under school, community, and religious sponsorship, with a membership that remains primarily female.

Libraries have undergone considerable change during the twentieth century. Although Carnegie's interest waned after 1917, as a result of a study he commissioned that showed local communities were far more interested in getting free money than in building libraries, library development continued at a rapid pace. Libraries began to lend records (1923) and films (1929), to develop mobile library services with trailers (1937), and to deal with a broadened constituency that included children, shut-ins, and the elderly. In 1924, the American Library Association created a commission to deal explicitly with adult education, thus signaling the movement of libraries from a passive to an active role in the education of adults. By the 1950s, libraries were involved with classes and other forms of adult education, as well as literacy programs for children.

Museums, too, underwent considerable change. Institutions dedicated to science and technology began to appear in the early twentieth century, testimonies to America's love affair with industrialization. Like libraries, museums became more active in their educational ventures. After the Depression, they found themselves comparatively more dependent on the public and less on wealthy patrons for support. As a result of this shift, as well as of increasing interest in adult education, the "curriculum" offered by museums broadened considerably. This trend continued through the 1980s and broadened into formal educational programs for children.

Chautauqua, on the other hand, has declined. Although enrollment in the summer program at Chautauqua decreased during the Depression, the organization maintained fiscal solvency and continued. After World War II, interest declined somewhat because of shifts in American culture. Highly structured programs tended to be supplanted by more informal ones, and the advent of television sped the decline of the lecture as entertainment. By the 1970s, Chautauqua found itself with three distinct constituencies: those who came for single or special events, perennial attenders, and an inner circle made up of owners of cottages on the property. While Chautauqua's constituency has been middle-class since its inception, recent years have enhanced its character as politically conservative, Republican, white, and Protestant. For several generations of middle-class Americans interested in self-improvement, it provided peer support and organized direction for their efforts.

An Assessment

Since colonial times, Americans have utilized a wide range of alternative arrangements to promote their education. In many instances, these have involved formal institutions supported by sources other than public revenues. Before the development of common schooling in the early nineteenth century, the vast majority of Americans were educated in such institutions, and these have retained constituencies down to the present day.

Nontraditional institutions have served special educational needs throughout most of American history. These have concentrated on particular populations, such as working people and those unable to attend regular classes, or have been designed to meet highly specific needs. Examples of this latter group are proprietary schools and corporate education.

Finally, a wide variety of self-educative agencies have provided the resources for individuals to meet their desires for personal growth. Some, like lyceums and libraries, have had directly educative missions, while others, such as religious groups and service clubs, have included educational activities among their goals.

The population served by such institutions, with a few exceptions, has not been typical of American society. For the most part, private schooling, both religious and secular, has catered to publics desiring to hold themselves out of the mainstream.

For groups like women, blacks, and Indians, the story has been different in one important respect. For them, the development of separate educational vehicles was frequently the result not so much of choice as of necessity. Though they may have wished to be part of the mainstream, their rejection by it necessitated the development of alternative arrangements.

Opportunities for both informal and formal learning have been seized by groups and individuals more interested in education than the population at large. Because most such arrangements have not been compulsory, involvement has been the result of personal choice. The majority of working people in the nineteenth century, for example, did not choose to attend night or labor schools, and even today corporate education serves only a portion of industrial employees. The same is even more true of opportunities for self-directed educational activity: Benjamin Franklin was unique precisely because of his intense interest in self-improvement.

As a result, participants in such activities have come disproportionately from the middle class or from those aspiring to join it. Conversely, an overwhelming majority of schools, programs, activities, and resources have been directed toward this segment of the population.

None of this ought to be surprising, given the ideology of upward mobility and personal growth through individual effort that has characterized American culture since colonial times. Whether seen in the myth of rags to riches or the conviction that democratic persons can accomplish any task to which they set their minds, the persistence of this belief is evident. When coupled with the myth of education's efficacy, it has encouraged the development of alternative educational arrangements to meet specific needs of particular groups. Thus, alternative education has served both as a useful vehicle for individual development in America and as a potent symbol of deep-rooted societal values.

At the same time, the examination of alternative ways of teaching and learning facilitates an understanding of the clienteles served. More immediately responsive to particular needs than the massive bureaucracies that have come to characterize traditional education, alternative agencies are more immediately shaped by their environment. An understanding of them illuminates our awareness of their constituencies, women and men who by choice or necessity stood outside the mainstream. The history of alternative education in America thus becomes a significant element in the alternative history of America itself.

[See also Collegiate Education; Literacy; Public Education; The Research University; Urban Cultural Institutions.]

BIBLIOGRAPHY

Aresty, Esther B. *The Best Behavior* (1970).

Bennett, Charles Alpheus. *History of Manual and Industrial Education up to 1870* (1926).

Boylan, Anne M. *Sunday School: The Formation of an American Institution, 1790–1880* (1988).

Cayton, Mary Kupiec. "The Making of an American Prophet: Emerson, His Audiences, and the Rise of the Culture Industry in Nineteenth-Century America." *American Historical Review* 92, no. 3 (1987): 597–620.

Dickson, Paul. *The Library in America: A Celebration in Words and Pictures* (1986).

Eurich, Nell P. *Corporate Classrooms: The Learning Business* (1985).

Fisher, Berenice M. *Industrial Education: American Ideals and Institutions* (1967).

Fishman, Joshua A., and Vladimir C. Nahirny. "The Ethnic Group School and Mother Tongue Maintenance in the United States." *Sociology of Education* 37, no. 4 (1964): 306–317.

Glen, John M. *Highlander, No Ordinary School, 1932–1962* (1988).

Knowles, Malcolm S. *The Adult Education Movement in the United States* (1962; rev. ed. 1977).

Lynn, Robert W., and Elliott Wright. *The Big Little School: Sunday Child of American Protestantism* (1971).

Macdonald, Dwight. *Against the American Grain* (1962).

Martin, Theodora Penny. *The Sound of Our Own Voices: Women's Study Clubs, 1860–1910* (1987).

Morrison, Theodore. *Chautauqua: A Center for Education, Religion, and the Arts in America* (1974).

Paulston, Rolland G., comp. *Other Dreams, Other Schools: Folk Colleges in Social and Ethnic Movements* (1980).

Perko, F. Michael. "Religious Education." In *Encyclopedia of the American Religious Experience.* Vol. 3 (1988).

Rubin, Joan Shelley. "Self, Culture, and Self-Culture in Modern America: The Early History of the Book-of-the-Month Club." *Journal of American History* 71 (1985).

Seybolt, Robert Francis. *The Evening School in Colonial America* (1925).

Stone, Elizabeth W. *Historical Approach to American Library Development: A Chronological Chart* (1967).

Wyllie, Irvin G. *The Self-made Man in America: The Myth of Rags to Riches* (1954).

— F. MICHAEL PERKO, S.J.

ALTERNATIVE MEDICINE

The concept of "alternative" medicine draws attention to the fact that healing is a profoundly cultural activity. Labeling a disease, diagnosing its cause, and prescribing treatment express a healer's commitment to a particular set of assumptions about the forces that govern reality. Thus, to speak of an "alternative" medicine is to imply that a healing system utilizes conceptions about reality that are not widely accepted by the culture's established medical authorities. For this reason it makes little sense to speak of alternative medicine in the United States prior to the late eighteenth century, when the practitioners of "regular" medicine gradually gained dominance and aligned medical orthodoxy with the general worldview spawned by the Western scientific tradition. Prior to this time the American colonies lacked a social system that was sufficiently structured to support an organized medical profession. As a consequence diverse medical systems existed alongside one another throughout the colonial period with no one group able to establish philosophical or economic dominance. Since the beginning of the nineteenth century, however, medical systems that operate outside the credentialing mechanisms of the officially sanctioned medical profession have found themselves relegated to an alternative or unorthodox cultural status. This, of course, is not necessarily to imply that they are less effective as curative agents. It does, however, indicate that these alternative medical systems have social roots and social functions that differ from those of the officially sanctioned medical profession, and for this reason they constitute an interesting chapter of American cultural history.

The Colonial Period

Various folk-medical traditions flourished both before and during the colonial era. The healing practices of Native Americans, for example, operated out of worldviews that varied considerably from the Western scientific heritage. It is difficult to offer simple generalizations concerning the medical practices of the many North American Indian tribal cultures. Using as many as 550 distinct languages, Amerindian tribes had their own unique social structures and religiocultural traditions. Theories of disease and medical treatment were interwoven with these social, religious, and cultural traditions. For Amerindians, the world was suffused with sacred powers and nonhuman spirits. Social customs and taboos reflected their belief that well-being depends upon preserving harmonious relationships with the spirits who dwell within nature as well as preserving the tribal or kinship bonds that connect humans with the sacred. Nearly any action that violates a tribal taboo might offend a particular spirit and thereby prompt it to afflict sickness upon the offending individual. The function of the medicine man or healer was thus to serve as an intermediary between the world of humans and the world of spirits. The healer's duty was to communicate with offended spirits and to discern what actions might propitiate them and cause them to cease their malevolent actions toward the afflicted person. The medicine man relied upon incantations, prayers, ritual dancing, and often hallucinogenic drugs to commune with the spirit responsible for the sickness and to divine the appropriate conciliatory actions. Such appeasement might require ritualistic action to flatter the offended spirit, the intervention of a friendly spirit, or the promise of the afflicted person to change his or her behavior so as to abide more strictly with social and religious custom.

Native American healers were also well acquainted with plants of medical value and made frequent use of botanicals in helping to restore harmony between individuals and the natural, social, and spiritual worlds they inhabited. Although each tribe used only a small number of botanical drugs, Amerindian tribes collectively used over 150 indigenous plants that have subsequently been deemed to have some therapeutic value. Indian drugs did not so much cure diseases as relieve symptoms. These botanical substances proved effective at controlling fevers and serving as emetics, purgatives, diuretics, or coagulants. Many Indian healers shared their botanical knowledge with early white settlers and in this way contributed to medical treatment during the colonial era (which depended greatly on homegrown or homemade remedies). Amerindian healers were also successful in treating most injuries. They developed techniques for treating fractured bones, stopping bleeding, and washing out open wounds with clean water or botanic drugs. Native American medicine, then, was relatively adequate to the needs of the population and compared favorably with European medical practices of the sixteenth or seventeenth centuries.

Prior to the arrival of Europeans, Amerindians were a relatively healthy population. All evidence suggests that North American Indians were exempt from such infectious diseases as malaria, typhoid, smallpox, diphtheria, venereal diseases, scarlet fever, and measles. The arrival of European settlers, however, drastically affected the health of Amerindians, whose lack of immunological defenses made them tragically vulnerable to the infectious diseases listed above, particularly smallpox. Whether they came into contact with white settlers for trade or for war, sickness and death were the inevitable consequences. The inability of Amerindian medicine to treat these diseases undermined confidence in its techniques. What remained of Amerindian culture after extensive European settlement was soon confined within isolated reservations, and thus native medical systems were effectively displaced from the arena of mainstream American medicine. The principal concept of preserving harmony between individuals and their wider environments that was central to Amerindian medicine has, however, been self-consciously championed by many of those drawn to holistic and New Age medical systems in the late twentieth century.

The folk-medical traditions of the four hundred thousand African slaves transported to the United States between 1619 and 1808 represent another strand of alternative medicine that, while nearly eclipsed by the nation's dominant medical system, nonetheless continues in many African American communities throughout the United States. The African medical heritage carried to America by the first groups of slaves recognized that disease was, in part, due to physical causes and employed various herbal medicines to treat sickness.

Medicinal roots, herbs, and leaves were all part of the pharmacological arsenal employed by early African American healers. Yet such medicines were rarely thought to be sufficient. In the African worldview, sickness results from discordant relations between an individual and the natural, social, and spiritual worlds in which he or she lives. African religious beliefs depict nature as permeated by a variety of spirits who are capable of influencing human health or sickness in very real ways. To preserve or restore health, traditional African medicine utilizes the powers of priests, diviners, and mediums who are skilled in various methods of propitiating spirits and mediating their divine power for the purpose of effecting cures and warding off evil influences. Fundamental to this heritage is the use of special charms to protect oneself from evil influence and "conjures" that evoke the power of charms to harm or even kill one's enemies (making the conjured person dependent upon the therapeutic powers of a healer adept at the conjuring process and capable of reversing the effects of this negative spiritual influence). These overtly supernaturalistic forms of medicine persist in the United States in both urban and rural areas, particularly among recent immigrants from the Caribbean, where voodoo (or vodun) and *santería* have kept these African traditions fairly intact.

The faith-healing services of Protestant Christianity and traditional African medicine both interpret life as primarily personal and regard relationships with other persons (divine and human) as the ultimate cause of health and sickness.

Such reliance upon charms, conjuring, and mediumistic communication with spirits receded to the background, but did not disappear, as the majority of African Americans converted to Protestant Christianity. The use of herbalism, conjure, and spiritualism combines with the more widespread participation of black Americans in Protestant, pentecostal-inspired faith-healing services in ways that meet needs not addressed by medical orthodoxy. The faith-healing services of Protestant Christianity and traditional African medicine both interpret life as primarily personal and regard human relationships with other persons (divine and human) as the ultimate cause of health and sickness. For this reason they enable healers to articulate and reinforce shared social and moral values as part of the therapeutic process. Because many other forms of social and political leadership have been closed to black Americans, faith-healing ministries have provided an effective vehicle for the expression of religious, social, and political leadership. In sum, black Americans have historically relied upon various forms of alternative medicine out of necessity because they have had limited access to the more costly methods of scientific medicine. Yet the continued presence of both traditional African medical practices and biblically oriented faith healing can also be explained by their evocation of worldviews that better address the individual's relationship with the community's moral and religious values.

Anglo-Americans of the colonial period were likewise "medical pluralists" in that they were almost equally likely to avail themselves of the advice of a minister-physician, the herbal remedies of a folk healer, or the skills of either a midwife or a barber-surgeon. Since even the best European physicians of the period could neither prevent nor cure most illnesses, it is not surprising that the colonial public often did not know which way to turn for sound medical treatment and selected healers as their level of desperation demanded. It was only after the Revolution that American communities became large enough to support professional medical institutions such as medical schools and training hospitals, and to enact licensure laws. The emerging corps of "regular physicians" agreed upon little other than their common scorn for belief in the healing powers of nature. Regular medicine was thus allopathic—that is, it sought to counteract or even combat the patient's physiological system. The regular physicians' weaponry of alcohol, opium, mercury, arsenic, and strychnine—let alone the continual use of violent purgatives and bloodletting—eventually earned them the apt designation as practitioners of "heroic" medicine. Doctors literally assaulted their patients with these techniques in an effort to stimulate and reinvigorate their constitutions. Those hardy and heroic patients who did not die in the course of these largely futile endeavors were at the very least weakened by the ordeal. Popular resentment lingered concerning the emerging medical establishment's inability to cure the vast majority of human ailments, despite continuing progress in anatomical science that enabled regular physicians to improve their medical practice.

Thomsonian Medicine

Even as state and local medical societies were growing, licensing laws were being enacted, and medical schools were being standardized, the first real challenge to the orthodoxy of regular medicine appeared in the form of Thomsonianism. Samuel Thomson (1769–1843) came from a poor farming family in rural New Hampshire. In early adulthood he saw his mother die from the excessive doses of mercury and opium prescribed by a regular physician. A few years later, when his wife fell ill and barely survived the bleedings and mercurial drugs forced upon her by a physician, he called upon two local "root and herb" doctors, who used botanical compounds to restore her health. This experience led him to the study of the medicinal value of herbs, and in 1805 he struck out on his own as an itinerant botanical healer. The premise of the Thomsonian healing system was that there was only one cause of diseases, cold, and one cure, heat. Combining steam baths with botanics such as cayenne pepper, Thomson was able to restore "heat" to his patients' systems and thus assure them that they were getting well. Thomsonianism, therefore, did not utilize harsh bleedings or mecurial drugs, as did regular medicine. Nor did it entail much cost to the patient and economic dependence on physicians who cloaked themselves in an aura of cultural superiority. In 1832 Thomson published a book entitled *New Guide to Health; or, Botanic Family Physician* and commissioned agents to help him sell it at twenty dollars per copy. The purchase price entitled the buyer to practice this "entirely new" system of botanic medicine within his or her own family. Thomson claimed to have sold about one hundred thousand copies of this book throughout the Northeast, Midwest, and South. His followers organized into local Friendly Botanic Societies to help promote his healing philosophy, and began publishing several periodicals that provided a forum for glowing testimonials and continued elaboration of Thomson's philosophy.

The Thomsonian system appealed to Americans in the first few decades of the nineteenth century for a number of reasons. First, it was easily understood and could be practiced inexpensively by family members. In this way Thomsonianism reinforced the principal roles of parents, especially mothers, in an age witnessing the early stages of professionalization and specialization in the United States. Second, it gave succinct popular expression to the fierce democratizing spirit of Jacksonian America. Adherents were zealous in their advocacy of a system that would help to seize medicine from the rich and powerful and return it to the private citizen. As one of the movement's magazines declared, Thomsonianism intended "to make every man his own physician." And, finally, Thomsonianism fit in with the period's moral and religious climate, which stressed human perfectibility and encouraged individuals to take responsibility for overcoming all personal shortcomings and restoring their rightful relationship to the providential powers God had placed in nature.

Homeopathy

A second form of "sectarian" medicine, homeopathy, began to emerge more or less concurrently with the public's gradual loss of enthusiasm for the Thomsonian system. The homeopathic system of medicine was the creation of the German physician Samuel Hahnemann (1755–1843), who grew increasingly critical of the indiscriminate prescription of drugs by his contemporaries. Believing that much more needed to be learned about the effects of each individual drug, he began taking doses of the purest samples of various drugs in order to observe their physiological effects. When he swallowed a dose of cinchona, a bark commonly used to combat fever, he broke out in a fever. Hahnemann deduced from this that a drug which causes an illness in a healthy person will cure that same illness in a sick person. This principle, which he termed *similia similibus curantur* (like is cured by like), became the cornerstone of homeopathic doctrine. Hahnemann's investigations led him to enunciate a second fundamental principle of homeopathic medicine, which came to be known as the doctrine of infinitesimals. It was his conviction that the greatest therapeutic benefit was to be obtained by administering diluted doses of a drug. He claimed, for example, that even 1/500,000 or 1/1,000,000 of a gram was in actuality more potent than a larger dose. Ironically, although the homeopathic physicians' use of infinitesimal doses undoubtedly negated any therapeutic value their drugs might have had, at least these small doses had the virtue of not assaulting the patient's own recuperative powers, as did the regular physicians' use of bleeding and poisonous drugs. It is thus not surprising that so many ailing persons found homeopathy a viable alternative to orthodox medicine.

Homeopathy spread rapidly in the United States. It was first introduced by Hans Gram, who opened an office in New York after studying the homeopathic system in Europe. By 1833 a homeopathic college had been formed, and a national association of homeopathic physicians soon followed. Throughout the 1800s approximately 10 percent of the country's medical schools and medical school graduates were adherents of homeopathy. Indeed, homeopathy's success in recruiting both clients and new physicians was a major factor in the formation of the American Medical Association (1847), as economic motives joined with scientific ones to rally regular physicians in opposition to their irregular competitors. It might be noted that in many instances, homeopathy provided a new outlet for those whose enthusiasm had previously been aroused by the Friendly Botanic Societies. Yet whereas the clients of Thomsonianism tended to be rural and poor, homeopathy thrived among the urban upper classes. One possible reason for this difference in clientele is that homeopathy insisted upon formal medical education for its practitioners. And Hahnemann's description of the "spiritlike" activity of the small doses he prescribed encouraged progressive thinkers to envision homeopathy as having discovered the means of inducing a subtle form of interaction between the material and spiritual dimensions of life. Many adherents of homeopathy were attracted to such mystical philosophies as Swedenborgianism, transcendentalism, and mesmerism, which fostered their belief that homeopathic techniques in some way helped humans to become receptive to infusions of a higher spiritual power.

Hydropathy, Graham, Seventh-Day Adventists

Faith in the power of water to restore the body's purity goes back to the native Indian belief in the curative properties of mineral springs; by the 1660s numerous mineral-water sites were commonly used by the early European settlers. It was not until the mid 1840s, however, that the healing practices of Vincent Priessnitz made their way across the Atlantic from his native Austria and that a fully articulated system of hydropathy, or water cure, made its appearance in the United States. The first major American spokesmen for the hydropathic cause, Joel Shew and Russell Trall, opened a water-cure institute in Lebanon Springs, New York, in 1845 and soon began publishing *The Water-Cure Manual* to promote their belief in the therapeutic powers of water. Whether taken internally by drinking or applied externally through baths, showers, or wrapping the body in a wet sheet, it was said that water removes various impurities from the body and replaces them with the most wholesome, clean fluid on earth. The philosophy of water cure, then, was based not so much on combating illness as on enhancing the natural vitality intrinsic to living organisms. American water curists advocated eclectic approaches to health and advised their clientele to combine the therapeutic benefits from external applications of water with the curative powers of fresh air, exercise, diet, sleep, and proper clothing. Such a comprehensive hydropathic regimen was advertised as a certain cure for fever, hiccups, cholera, constipation, malaria, bladder infections, obesity, and even excessive sexual desire.

The water-cure movement conveyed a message that was clearly moral in tone. As one unnamed hydropathist put it,

> We regard Man, in his primitive and natural condition as the most perfect work of God, and consider his present degenerated physical state as only the natural and inevitable result of thousands of years of debauchery and excess, of constant and wilful perversions of his better nature, and the simple penalty of outraged physical law, which is as just and more severe than any other. (*Water-cure World* 1 [April 1860]: p. 5)

Disregard of the laws of healthful living was thus to be equated with sinful defiance of God's will. In the hydropathic vision, then, systematic efforts to promote healthful living were not only the means to personal well-being but also the key to human progress and the spiritual renovation of the earth. This underlying perfectionist philosophy attracted a number of the period's moral and religious reformers to the hydropathic cause, William Andrus Alcott, Lucy Stone, Amelia Bloomer, Susan B. Anthony, and Horace Greeley all frequented the major hydropathic retreat centers and there circulated reformist agendas ranging from vegetarianism to utopian socialism. Hydropathy, like many alternative medical systems throughout American history, resonated with the period's feminist thought. Because alternative medicines tend to be critical of the alleged superiority of official authorities, they often provide a vehicle for those seeking to redress faulty social and political institutions. Hydropathy identified nature rather than officially sanctioned male medical authorities as the source of healing, and thus provided a natural medium for the expression of feminist visions of the path to personal and cultural well-being.

Closely linked with the causes promoted by hydropathy was Sylvester Graham (1794–1851), who was without question the era's leading health reformer. An ordained Presbyterian minister and itinerant evangelist, Graham believed that humans have an important role in effecting their own salvation-especially by diligently obeying the laws of physical health that God bestowed upon creation. In addition to advocating abstinence from alcohol and from overstimulation of the sexual organs, Graham launched a dietary crusade that equated healthful eating with moral and religious holiness. The coarse bread he advocated as a dietary staple, later produced in the form of a cracker, carries his name to this day. Graham's dietary principles were among the most widely circulated of all the nineteenth-century health philosophies. Perhaps the most intriguing extension of Grahamism is its embodiment in the second largest religious denomination ever to originate in the United States, the Seventh-day Adventists. The prophetess and founder of Seventh-day Adventism, Ellen Gould White (1827–1915), was an occasional visitor at a major hydropathic resort in Dansville, New York, where she was exposed to Graham's dietary gospel. Several years later White had a mystical vision in which God revealed to her that his hygienic laws were to be kept as faithfully as the Ten Commandments. Thereafter all of those who joined her in awaiting the Second Coming were admonished to keep the body temple holy through adherence to Grahamite principles. To this day Seventh-day Adventists support a number of health sanitariums and hospital complexes, and combine their evangelical religious faith with a strong emphasis upon abstinence from foods and activities that prevent conformity with the God-given laws of physical health.

Mesmerism, New Thought, Christian Science

In the late 1830s yet another European healing system was introduced to the American public. Franz Anton Mesmer's "science of animal magnetism" had already attracted the attention of European intellectuals and popular audiences alike. Mesmer (ca. 1734–1815), a Viennese physician, believed that he had detected the existence of a superfine substance or fluid that had previously eluded scientific notice. He maintained that this invisible fluid, which he named animal magnetism, was evenly distributed throughout the healthy human body. His theory postulated that if an individual's supply of animal magnetism was thrown out of equilibrium, one or more bodily organs would be deprived of sufficient amounts of this vital force and eventually begin to falter. Mesmer proclaimed that "there is only one illness and one healing." Since any and all illnesses could ultimately be traced back to a disturbance in the body's supply of animal magnetism, medical science could be reduced to a simple set of procedures aimed at supercharging a patient's nervous system with this mysterious life-giving energy.

In the early part of his career, Mesmer passed his hands—sometimes while holding a magnet—over his patients' heads and along their spinal columns in an effort to transmit some of his own abundant supply of animal magnetism to the patient. Over time Mesmer's pupils discovered that this technique would put their patients into a trance that was thought to make them especially receptive to the inflow of animal magnetism. "Mesmerized" patients felt inwardly transformed. They reported feeling prickly sensations running up and down their bodies that they interpreted to be animal magnetism flowing into their bodies. Upon awaking from their sleeplike trance, they invariably reported relief from such disorders as rheumatism, digestive problems, nervousness, liver ailments, epilepsy, stammering, insomnia, and the abuse of coffee, tea, and alcohol. Some patients fell into even deeper states of trance and allegedly performed feats of telepathy, clairvoyance, and precognition. Still other mesmerized individuals gained the ability to diagnose other people's diseases clairvoyantly and to prescribe appropriate remedies.

These claims concerning mesmerism's ability to activate otherwise latent paranormal powers of the human psyche contributed as much (or even more) to its growing popularity as its reputed healing powers. Hundreds of individuals throughout New England became practitioners of the science of animal magnetism; some opened offices in their hometowns, while others became itinerant lecturers who specialized in giving staged demonstrations of this novel medical system's mysterious powers. Interestingly, most of mesmerism's practitioners and clients were drawn from those middle- and upper-class Americans who styled themselves progressive thinkers and who dabbled in the many "metaphysical" philosophies such as transcendentalism and Swedenborgianism which taught that the material world is directly connected with higher spiritual worlds with which people may make inner contact. Mesmerism's healing feats were taken as empirical proof of humanity's inner connection with higher realms from which powerful and sanative energies might be obtained.

The American mesmerists were to have a long-lasting influence upon the continuing presence of alternative medicine in America. For example, mesmerism unwittingly gave rise to America's nineteenth-century fascination with spiritualism when some mesmerized subjects began to report making contact with souls of the deceased. Nineteenth-century spiritualists, like the "trance channelers" who became famous in the late twentieth century, frequently assisted their clientele with their illnesses by gaining advice from spirits concerning the true cause (often moral, dietary, or pertaining to interpersonal relationships) of their ailments and an appropriate course of treatment.

The Viennese physician Franz Anton Mesmer believed he had detected a superfine invisible fluid called animal magnetism, which, if thrown out of equilibrium in the body, would result in the inability of one or more organs to function.

Mesmerism gave rise to the "power of positive thinking" movement in America that has direct connections with many themes found in today's holistic medicine advocates. The famed nineteenth-century mesmerist Phineas P. Quimby (1802–1866) trained several disciples who together gave rise to what was known as the

Mind Cure or New Thought movement which taught Americans that their thoughts can be real forces contributing to their sickness or health. The New Thoughters popularized the notion that physical health, spiritual composure, and even economic well-being flow automatically from possession of a mental attitude that fosters harmony with the cosmos. In so doing the New Thoughters drew public attention to the role of mental and emotional factors in the cure of disease long before orthodox medicine followed suit. No doubt the New Thoughters' popularity owed much to the changing socioeconomic structures of American life. Urbanization, industrialization, and immigration combined to disorient the white middle class. Unable to make sense of the complicated public sphere, Americans found it more convenient to embrace strategies aimed at reorganizing their private or psychological sphere in ways that promised them greater control over their lives. The kind of popular psychology advocated by the New Thoughters effectively adapted Americans' optimistic, success-oriented individualism to the kinds of self-healing required of an advanced industrial society.

During the 1960s growing dissatisfaction with in-hospital care and with the seeming insensitivity of the male medical establishment led to a resurgence of interest in home births and midwifery.

Mesmerism was instrumental in the formation of one of the five largest native-born American religious denominations, Christian Science. Mary Baker Patterson (later Mary Baker Eddy, 1821–1910) arrived at Quimby's doorstep in 1862 as a physical and emotional wreck. The mesmeric healer cured her afflicted body and gave her an entirely new outlook on life based upon the principle that our thoughts determine whether we are inwardly open—or closed—to the activity of a subtle healing energy (animal magnetism). Soon after Quimby's death, Mary Baker Eddy transformed the lessons she had learned from her mesmeric mentor into the foundations of Christian Science. Her principal text, *Science and Health with Key to the Scriptures*, made clear her intention to shift the science of mental healing away from mesmerist categories to ones that bore more resemblance to Christian scripture. In brief, Christian Science asserts that God creates all that is, and that all which God creates is good. From this theological postulate it follows that such things as sickness, pain, or evil are not creations of God and therefore do not exist in any real sense. They are instead only the delusional appearance of an erring, mortal mind that has lost sight of the fact that only that which is created by God has true ontological existence.

Christian Science views health as primarily a spiritual rather than a physical condition. Christian Science healers, known as practitioners, are consequently dedicated to the task of assisting individuals to elevate their minds and mental attitudes above the delusions of the senses and instead to center their thoughts solely on the higher laws of God's spiritual presence. The conditions that create spiritual and physical well-being are fostered by a combination of prayer, the reading of the Bible or Christian Science materials, and moral resolve. This approach to health has understandably placed Christian Scientists in direct opposition to prevailing American conceptions of medicine and is partly responsible for the numerous legal difficulties and court cases (in such matters as their refusal to take vaccinations and their right to practice "medicine") that Christian Science has faced over the years. In the late 1800s, Christian Scientists defended themselves not by appealing to the constitutional protection of religion, but on the right of Americans to choose their own healers. Over the years, however, and owing partly to the courts' increased regulation of medical practice, Christian Scientists have tended to defend their practices on the grounds of religious freedom. Although no formal membership statistics are available, Christian Science probably attained a membership as high as four hundred thousand in the early twentieth century before witnessing a decline in membership in the second half of the twentieth century. Approximately two-thirds of its members in the late nineteenth and early twentieth centuries were women. Most were urban. In an era in which urban women were affected first and worst by the strains of modern living, they were undoubtedly most likely to find Christian Science's message both physically and spiritually therapeutic. And in an age in which women had few avenues of leadership open to them, the clergyless Christian Science organization offered women positions of responsibility in carrying out its healing ministry and weekly worship services.

The Twentieth Century

By the early twentieth century, regular physicians redoubled their efforts to rid the medical. scene of their "irregular" counterparts. The American Medical Association gradually emerged as a powerful national organization and succeeded in its efforts to enact strict licensing regulations and to restrict hospital privileges to physicians who had graduated from AMA-accredited medical schools. As a consequence, practitioners of alternative medical systems found themselves increasingly at the far periphery of the nation's medical marketplace. One such casualty was midwifery. While midwives were never as popular in the United States as in other parts of the world, lay midwives nonetheless provided the only obstetrical assistance available to many women until early in the twentieth century. As obstetrics became a recognized medical specialty primarily under the control of male physicians, hospitals equipped with surgical facilities supplanted the home as the usual site for giving birth. Midwifery came increasingly to serve only those who could not afford hospital births and generally fell into disrepute as an outmoded form of medical assistance. During the 1960s growing dissatisfaction with in-hospital care and with the seeming insensitivity of the male medical establishment led to a resurgence of interest in home births and midwifery. By the 1990s more than a dozen universities offered certification programs for nurse-midwives who were care providers at about 2 percent of all deliveries in the United States.

OSTEOPATHY AND CHIROPRACTIC. Two noteworthy examples of medical systems that have managed to compete successfully with the American Medical Association during the twentieth century are chiropractic and osteopathic medicine. Osteopathic medicine, which is practiced by more than twenty-four thousand physicians who collectively treat at least twenty million patients per year, originated in the healing philosophy of Andrew Taylor Still (1828–1917). A former spiritualist and mesmeric healer, Still developed techniques for manipulating vertebrae in ways that he thought removed any obstructions to the free flow of "the life-giving current" that promotes health throughout the body. Although Still's early osteopathic (from two Greek words meaning "suffering of the bones") had overt metaphysical overtones, his followers insisted that osteopathic medical education be grounded in anatomy and scientific physiology. By the 1950s so few differences existed in the training or practice of osteopaths and medical doctors that their two national organizations agreed to cease the overt rivalries that had existed for several decades and to cooperate in such matters as access to hospitals, residency programs, and professional recognition.

Chiropractic medicine was developed by Daniel David Palmer (1845–1913), a mesmerism-inspired magnetic healer in Iowa. Palmer, who knew of Still's osteopathic techniques, discovered that he could restore the flow of a spiritual life force throughout the body by making appropriate manual adjustments to the spine. Daniel Palmer and his son, B. J. Palmer, operated a chiropractic (from two Greek words, meaning "performed by hand") college that trained individuals in the art and science of curing individuals by adjusting the spine in ways that permit a more perfect flow of this life force, to which the Palmers referred as Innate Intelligence. Over the years chiropractic physicians began downplaying the movement's metaphysical origins and emphasizing instead their scientific approach to the treatment of musculoskeletal disorders. Chiropractic, particularly in the first half of the twentieth century, attracted patients from the lower half of the socioeconomic spectrum. This was due in part to the fact that blue-collar workers were more prone to the musculoskeletal problems for which chiropractic techniques were well suited and because of chiropractors' comparatively lower fees. Perhaps more important for chiropractic's continued growth in stature within the American medical system is the fact that it took seriously a range of ailments that were at the margins of the concern and interest of medical doctors, whose medical training is not especially oriented to the treatment of musculoskeletal disorders. Chiropractic physicians' sustained attention to this lacuna in the orthodox medical system gradually helped them to achieve a viable niche in the medical marketplace, as is evidenced by the fact that there were over nineteen thousand chiropractic physicians who treated more than three million patients annually in the 1990s.

ETHNIC MEDICINE. The last few decades of the twentieth century witnessed a remarkable resurgence of popular interest in medical systems whose techniques and philosophies differ dramatically from those of the American Medical Association. One expression of contemporary alternative medicine is the continuing viability of folk-medicine traditions. American folk medicine covers a very large and diverse assortment of health practices that vary by region and ethnicity. For example, the rural Pennsylvania Germans ("Dutch") still practice variations of "powpow," an eclectic tradition using charms, prayers, and rituals both to prevent and to cure disease. A similar therapeutic system, *curanderismo*, flourishes among Mexican American communities in the Southwest, and immigration from the Caribbean has rekindled folk medical traditions peculiar to the African American heritage. Immigration from Southeast Asia has given rise to new ethnic communities utilizing such Hindu or Buddhist medical practices as Ayurvedic medicine based on ancient Hindu metaphysics and ritualized prayers to the heavenly bodhisattvas who reward the faithful with their healing powers. Immigration from the Far East has likewise brought dedicated practitioners of such religiomedical systems as t'ai chi ch'uan (based on a series of body movements that are intended to unite body and mind), shiatsu (a traditional form of Japanese finger-pressure massage), and Chinese acu-

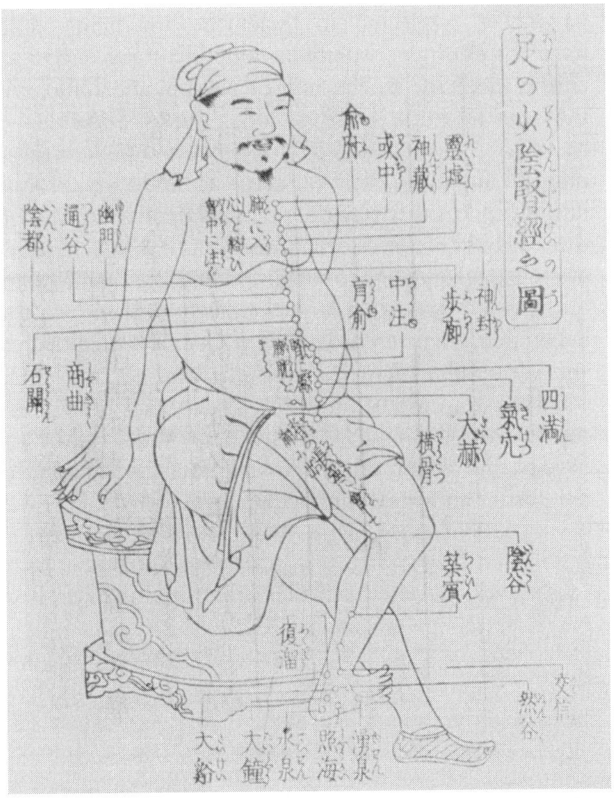

This medical illustration illustrates the acupuncture points on a human body. American popular interest in ethnic medicine of the Far East has surged over the past few decades.

puncture. It is not clear whether such continued use of the medical traditions belonging to one's ethnic heritage represents a form of preserving one's distinct cultural identity, economic disenfranchisement from the nation's more expensive established medical system, or the seeds of a new era of genuine medical pluralism in which many different, but equally effective, healing systems exist side by side. The sustained viability of these medical systems does, however, make clear that medicine is a profoundly cultural activity and that conceptions of disease and cure necessarily have social dimensions.

THE NEW AGE. The explosion of interest in what is commonly referred to as the New Age movement provides a second perspective on contemporary alternative medicine. The various religious and medical groups that make up the New Age movement all endorse an approach to health and medicine that is said to be holistic and that envisions every human being as a unique, interdependent relationship of body, mind, emotions, and spirit. New Agers are for this reason especially drawn to those Eastern religious and medical systems which teach that humans can potentially open up the inner recesses of their psyches to the inflow of a higher spiritual energy (variously referred to as *ch'i, prana, kundalini,* animal magnetism, or divine white light) capable of restoring harmony in the physical and emotional systems. Yoga, t'ai chi ch'uan, Ayurvedic medicine, shiatsu, acupuncture, and various oriental massage systems are eclectically embraced for their advocacy of attitudes and life-styles geared to the renovation of personal and collective consciousness. Believing that the entire universe is a manifestation of the "pure white light" of divine spirit, New Age medical systems embrace techniques that can open up inner receptivity to this higher spiritual reality. The therapeutic use of crystals, for example, is predicated upon the assumption that humans possess seven spiritual centers, or *chakras,* that are able to receive this divine energy and transmit it throughout the body in ways that promote physical and emotional health. Crystal healing—like various forms of psychic healing, Eastern meditational systems, color healing, and healing with the aid of trance channeling—seeks to open up receptivity to higher metaphysical levels of reality and thereby restore individuals to their rightful condition of harmonious interaction with the physical, natural, social, and spiritual environments they inhabit.

New Age adherents are thus not so much rejecting the therapeutic efficacy of established medical science (though they do condemn what they perceive to be an overreliance on drugs and invasive surgical techniques) as the secularist and materialistic worldview upon which it is based. The medical techniques they advocate rely upon conceptions of the universe that stress the importance of finding personal harmony with nature, fellow human beings, and higher spiritual forces. Such an approach to well-being is especially attractive to those persons who are sensitive to the excesses of the hierarchical, exploitative, and overly male institutions that have historically dominated Western culture. Those who are attracted to New Age ideas and healing techniques are thus seeking to create a counterculture that provides a remedy for the increasing mechanization, secularization, and de-personalization of modern life (and modern medicine). Those who espouse New Age concepts are characteristically white, middle or upper-middle class, well educated, and either urban or suburban. Most view their advocacy of alternative medical systems to be directly connected with their concern for giving contemporary Americans a new metaphysical outlook that makes spirituality central to understandings of physical or emotional well-being. New Age healing concepts, as with New Age ideas generally, have spread among contemporary Americans in ways that circumvent conventional political, religious, and social boundaries. Literature describing its many healing techniques can be found in the bookstores in almost every shopping mall in the country, in displays located at health-food stores, and in advertisements placed in sundry "human potential" publications. And while it is probably a small percentage of Americans who rely primarily upon New Age healing practices, a good many others drawn from all regions of the country and all religious denominations have been influenced by the movement's insistence upon the interdependence of humanity's physical, emotional, and spiritual natures.

Summary

The social history of alternative medicine in America is, as we have seen, varied and diverse. Simple generalizations should be avoided because they obscure the very real differences that exist among the many medical systems which are outside a given historical period's medical establishment. It would be just as mistaken to conclude that all alternative medical systems represent a prescientific, superstitious approach to healing as to extol them for preserving a long-forgotten or neglected healing wisdom that is far superior to modern medicine's reliance upon drugs and invasive surgical techniques. Any effort to make comprehensive assessments of alternative medical systems must bear firmly in mind that they vary a great deal in terms of social origin, the socioeconomic status of practitioners or clients, and the principal routes by which their ideas and techniques have been disseminated throughout society.

It can, however, be safely concluded that although alternative medical systems are characteristically labeled improper or even fraudulent by the nation's dominant group of medical practitioners, they have for the most part performed vital social and medical functions. And they have hardly been as much on the social fringe as might appear to be the case. Americans are far more medically pluralistic than is ordinarily assumed. Individuals operate with a range of well-differentiated preferences and tendencies for medical treatment. The same individual who might consult an orthodox medical physician to receive a prescription for an antibiotic during one kind of illness might consult a chiropractor for a back injury, utilize folk remedies for a common cold (such as intercessory prayer, hot water baths, or large doses of vitamin C), attend a seminar on positive thinking, and utilize conventional prayer or a New Age meditational system to find harmony with the healing power of God.

On the whole, "alternative" medical systems have provided Americans with balanced and thoughtful approaches to healing by drawing attention to attitudinal, interpersonal, and philosophical or religious issues that have been neglected in "scientific" medicine. They have, for example, usually been more attentive than scientific medicine to the role of psychological and even moral factors in disposing one to illness. Second, they have stressed the body's own recuperative powers rather than relying exclusively on drugs or surgery to combat illness (and in this way they reinforce the decidedly optimistic bent of American culture). And third, they have offered developed theoretical systems that understand human well-being in a larger philosophical context that helps individuals comprehend what full health really is and what values it will enable them to affirm. In this way they draw attention to the larger social and cultural contexts in which we label "sickness" and "health" and have permitted Americans to seek new ways of defining the nature and meaning of their lives.

[See also Health Care; The Medical Profession; Public Health.]

BIBLIOGRAPHY

Cayleff, Susan. *"Wash and Be Healed": The Water-Cure Movement and Women's Health* (1987).

Fuller, Robert C. *Alternative Medicine and American Religious Life* (1989).

Gevitz, Norman. *The D.O.s: Osteopathic Medicine in America* (1982).

Gevitz, Norman, ed. *The Other Healers: Unorthodox Medicine in America* (1988).

Gottschalk, Stephen. *The Emergence of Christian Science in American Religious Life* (1973).

Hufford, David J. "Contemporary Folk Medicine." In *The Other Healers*, edited by Norman Gevitz (1988).

Kaufman, Martin. *Homeopathy in America: The Rise and Fall of a Medical Heresy* (1971).

McGuire, Meredith. *Ritual Healing in Suburban America* (1988).

Nissenbaum, Stephen. *Sex, Diet, and Debility in Jacksonian America: Sylvester Graham and Health Reform* (1980).

Numbers, Ronald L. *Prophetess of Health: A Study of Ellen G. White* (1976).

Numbers, Ronald L., and Darrel W. Amundsen, eds. *Caring and Curing: Essays on Health, Medicine, and the Faith Traditions* (1986).

Raboteau, Albert. "The Afro-American Traditions." In *Caring and Curing*, edited by Ronald L. Numbers and Darrel W. Amundsen (1986).

Vogel, Virgil J. *American Indian Medicine* (1970).

Young, James. *The Medical Messiahs: A Social History of Health Quackery in Twentieth-Century America* (1967).

— ROBERT C. FULLER

AMUSEMENT AND THEME PARKS

According to the social historian John F. Kasson, the phenomenon of the amusement park and its offshoots, in addition to symbolizing a displacement of genteel culture with a new mass culture, represented a "cultural accommodation to the developing urban-industrial society in a tighter integration of work and leisure than ever before." Ultimately, parks such as Coney Island led to a "passive acceptance of the cycle of production and consumption" and, as is certainly true today with the major theme parks, even the early amusement parks fostered an egalitarian spirit that led to a blurring of class differences and distinctions within American society.

Until the 1970s it was easy to distinguish an amusement park from a theme park, and a traveling carnival from each of these. Coney island in its heyday was an amusement park, or rather a complex of three amusement parks, built in one location with a wide array of attractions, rides, games, and shows. Disney World and Six Flags over Texas were constructed as theme parks and were designed around one unifying theme or idea, or a series of related concepts. A carnival was a traveling amalgam of riding devices, shows or exhibits, and concessions, often providing, as they still do, the midway entertainment for small fairs, though some of the larger state fairs (like that of Texas) boast elaborate permanent midways that operate during the off-season as traditional amusement parks. According to the Outdoor Amusement Business Association, today there are still some five hundred carnivals in North America, employing fifty thousand individuals. In contrast to the nomadic existence of the carnival, the outdoor amusement park evolved as a permanent collection of rides, shows, and concessions.

Today it is more difficult to distinguish between theme and traditional amusement parks, once called iron or steel parks for the construction of their rides, always the main attraction. Early in the twentieth century, prior to the theme idea, traditional amusement parks existed in nearly every American city; they transported patrons into eclectic and exotic fantasylands. The International Association of Amusement Parks and Attractions argues that in the 1990s every entertainment facility in the United States has some aspect of a theme park; thus in quoting a figure of approximately 600 active amusement parks in the United States in 1991 (compared with 1,500 in 1919), the only criterion used by the association is that of fixed-site amusement rides.

All profit-making outdoor entertainment forms operated as business ventures by professionals (as opposed to trade or agriculture fairs and expositions designed to demonstrate products and goods) have the same roots and ancestry. Elements of the American amusement park can be traced back to antiquity; its obvious precursors include various European traditions—the medieval fair and carnival (quite different from the later American version) and the seventeenth-century pleasure garden, common to England and France. Several similar gardens appeared on the East Coast in provincial cities prior to the American Revolution, providing patrons simple pleasures—food, drink, music, and some free variety, acts, fireworks, or balloon ascensions.

Genteel amusements for a largely rural culture in a pastoral setting, however, gave way in the late nineteenth century to forms of amusement that mirrored the new urban, industrial age. Enterprising entrepreneurs—including hotel and resort operators,

The World's Columbian Exposition of 1893 in Chicago is often cited as fostering the Amusement Park. Here visitors stroll through the Midway Plaisance with the giant Ferris Wheel in the background.

railway and trolley car executives, and brewers, who supplied the major refreshments to amusement venues—were quick to see the potential for profit. By mid century seaside resorts along the upper Eastern Seaboard, from the Jersey Coast to Maine, began to appear. At first catering to a wealthy and elitist clientele, their status changed rapidly as public transportation reached areas like Coney Island and Atlantic City in the 1850s.

The Amusement Park

The stimulus of the World's Columbian Exposition of 1893 in Chicago (with the Vienna World's Fair of 1873 as inspiration) and its Midway Plaisance and the development from 1895 of the Coney Island amusement parks are often cited as fostering the modern amusement park. As Richard W. Flint clearly demonstrates in "Meet Me in Dreamland," however, other entertainment precursors can be identified. Mechanical rides in this country, for example, date back to 1800 and were fairly common by the 1870s; many added excitement to otherwise tranquil picnic groves. The carousel or merry-go-round and the Ferris wheel, as well as the "switchback railway," an early, tame version of a roller coaster, were in limited circulation by the 1880s. Resort areas, such as those on Lake Ontario serving Rochester, New York, were beginning to exploit a new working-class patron. By the turn of the century there were seaside resorts or picnic groves at Lake Compounce Park in Bristol, Connecticut (1846); Rocky Point, Rhode Island (1847); Jantzen Beach, Portland, Maine; Revere Beach outside Boston; and Gravesend Beach on Long Island, among others. Most of these could be reached only by the new trolley, and "trolley parks" developed by street-railway companies and seaside entrepreneurs extended the profit margin of the trolley by providing public transportation to these resorts in late afternoons and weekends.

CONEY ISLAND. Regardless of the number of pre-Coney Island attempts to establish an amusement park tradition, all are prosaic in comparison to the City of Fire, which was called by one religious leader, in a typical Coney Island-style overstatement, "a suburb of Sodom." From its beginning as a beach resort area in the 1870s (where it has been suggested the hot dog, or a version of the frankfurter, was invented in 1871 and the first United States antecedent of a roller coaster was built in 1884) up to its heyday before World War I, Coney Island set the example and pattern for the great twentieth-century versions of the amusement park. As John E Kasson so vividly illustrates in his important social history, of Coney Island, the development of this phenomenon marked the emergence of a new period in American history, one marked by changing economic and social conditions that contributed to a new mass culture. "Its purest expression at this time," writes Kasson, "lay in the realm of commercial amusements, which were creating symbols of the new cultural order, helping to knit a heterogeneous audience into a cohesive whole. Nowhere were these symbols and their relationship to the new mass audience more clearly revealed than at turn-of-the-century Coney Island" (*Amusing the Million*, pp. 3–4).

Coney Island owed much to both the 1876 Philadelphia Centennial Exposition and the Columbian Exposition of 1893. From the former came the Sawyer Observatory, a 300-foot (90-meter) observation tower with steam-powered elevators; it was moved to Coney Island, where it became the first mechanical amusement device on the island, standing until destroyed by fire in 1911. From the Chicago's World Fair came the idea of a midway and the demonstration of George Washington Gale Ferris's (1859–1896) famous wheel. Though similar devices had been built as early as 1872, this giant version (thirty-six pendulum cars, each with a sixty-passenger capacity, within a 300-foot-high and 30-foot-wide structure) once and for all established the phenomenal drawing power of mechanical rides, which Coney island so imaginatively exploited.

From its beginning as a beach resort (where the hot dog was said to have been invented in 1871 and the first U.S. antecedent of the roller coaster built in 1884) up to its heyday before World War I, Coney Island set the pattern for the great twentieth-century amusement park.

Three amusement parks were created at Coney Island between 1895 and 1903. A pioneer but largely unsuccessful effort called Sea Lion Park built by Paul Boynton in 1895 was followed two years later by George C. Tilyou's (1862–1914) "Steeple-chase Park" with its mechanical horses that sped passengers along a curving half-mile track in a half-minute. Then, in 1903, Elmer "Skip" Dundy and Frederic Thompson bought Boynton's faltering Sea Lion Park and rebuilt it at a cost of $1 million into a lavish version of Chicago's Midway Plaisance: Luna Park, a "blazing architectural jumble" with a widely eclectic environment of attractions, was considered by many to be the epitome of an amusement enterprise. Dreamland, built by real-estate speculator William H. Reynolds for $3.5 million, followed within a year across the street from Luna; it burned to the ground seven years later. While it lasted, Dreamland, illuminated by one million incandescent lights, offered everything from a recreation of The Fall of Pompeii to three hundred midgets, girly shows, Venetian canals, a representation of hell, a leapfrog railroad, and a view of the first incubator, complete with babies.

Coney Island attracted one million patrons on one day in 1914. But soon Coney Island would begin its decline; before World War I, Dreamland burned down, Luna Park went bankrupt, and Tilyou died. By World War II, Coney Island's slide gained momentum, with the middle-class moving to the suburbs and fewer patrons making the subway trip from Brooklyn to the island. Today, the one remaining park, Astroland, part of a scant two-by-twelve-block entertainment area, is a gritty slum by the sea, fighting the ravages of poverty, crime, and blight.

POST-CONEY ISLAND PARKS. Nevertheless, while it lasted, the Coney Island model inspired countless other Luna Parks and Dreamlands all over America. The period following the Saint Louis World's Fair of 1904 marks the era of the greatest contribution of railroad, traction, and trolley car companies in building amusement parks. Ohio's Lakeshore Electric Railway, for instance, earned much of its revenue from fares to Cedar Point, which became a full-fledged amusement park in 1905; the Northern Ohio Transit and Light Company owned at least ten parks in Ohio.

With the 1920s came a tremendous upsurge in the development of mechanical rides, followed in the 1930s by the Great Depression and the introduction of parks to new patrons seeking inexpensive entertainment and brief escapes from their dreary existences. The final decline of the traditional amusement park dates from World War II when materials used by parks were needed for the war effort and patrons were growing bored with aging attractions. Natural disasters, vandalism, and other less tangible factors also contributed to the decline. Beginning in the late 1950s, a postwar baby boom brought a resurgence of interest in the amusement park business. Nevertheless, such historic parks as Palisades Park in New Jersey, Chicago's Riverview, Cleveland's Euclid Beach, and Massachusetts's Lincoln Park have closed since the 1960s and other urban parks are struggling to survive. In the 1970s and 1980s conflicting reports announced an upswing in amusement park business, the reaching of a saturation point, concern over the safety of rides, and the ultimate demise of amusement parks.

THE ROLLER COASTER AND CAROUSEL. In the early 1990s, voices of doom seem premature. Thrill rides, for example, have never been more popular. Roller coaster aficionados demonstrated the insatiable attraction of coasters by establishing in the late 1970s an organization called American Coaster Enthusiasts with its own publication, *RollerCoaster!* Choosing to place oneself on the edge of disaster has great appeal to lovers of thrill rides (although their danger is actually quite minimal). Amusement park entrepreneurs constantly rise to the challenge, creating new and more unbelievable thrill rides, especially roller coasters. A few 1991 examples will illustrate: "Mean Streak" ($7.5 million coaster) at Cedar Point in Sandusky, Ohio, claims to be the world's tallest and fastest wooden roller coaster (coaster addicts debate the advantages of old-style wooden coasters versus steel monsters) with a 160-foot (48-meter) hill, a 155-foot (46-meter) first drop, and a speed of 65 miles (104 kilometers) per hour; the $5 million "Anaconda" at Kings Dominion near Richmond, Virginia, boasts a 126-foot (37.8-meter) underwater tunnel; Kings Island near Cincinnati has added "Adventure Express," a special-effects coaster to its offerings; "Steel Phantom" at Kenneywood near Pittsburgh claims the fastest steel coaster (80 miles [128 kilometers] per hour top speed); "The Viper" at Six Flags Magic Mountain, Valencia, California, is the largest looping coaster with seven loops. A new coaster is being developed that functions like a jet airplane with endless rolls in a pipeline construction. It is estimated that since 1985 some $135 million has been spent on thirty-seven new coasters.

In vivid contrast to the roller coaster, the traditional carousel has been the salvation for other sites. While the coaster serves as a dazzling reminder of modern technology and controlled violence, the merry-go-round remains an icon of a more relaxed, quaint, and remote past. Carousel animals today are valued collector items, some costing thousands of dollars. Some complete carousels have been declared landmarks; local groups have battled land developers and local governments to save amusement areas or at least to enshrine a number of the beautifully constructed older carousels still in existence. The number of hand-carved wooden carousels has dwindled from about 5,000 in the late nineteenth century to some 160 today.

The Theme Park

The savior of the outdoor amusement business has been the theme park, a dynamic example of Madison Avenue advertising packaging at its most persuasive and often an astonishing example of organizational know-how. Conceived first by Walt Disney (1901–1966) in the

1950s, the concept of organizing amusement areas around one or several themes was a revolutionary idea, providing new methods of exploiting the amusement industry. Not all theme parks were successful (and some still are not), as the collapse of such early examples as Beanyland in Santa Monica, California, Freedomland in New York City, Magic Mountain near Denver, and Circus World in Barnum City, Florida, indicates. The World of Sid and Marty Krofft, in Atlanta, Georgia, one of the first attempts at an indoor amusement park, closed in 1976, only months after its opening.

However, since the 1955 opening of Disneyland in Anaheim, California, built by Walt Disney in his own backyard of Southern California on a fifty-five-acre tract with a $17 million investment, the theme park idea has spread throughout the United States and into other parts of the world, with major Disney parks in Paris and Tokyo. Ironically, Disney, who chose a crowded urban setting for Disneyland, had no idea of the tremendous growth of this aspect of his empire. In the 1990s, in fact, plans to expand Disneyland in Anaheim have been restricted due to the lack of readily accessible land and expansion is planned elsewhere. Still considered by many to be the best amusement park in the world, in part because it was Disney's personal project, reflecting his taste, imagination, and style, Disneyland is organized around a central hub with the idea that the patron leaves the world of today and enters the worlds of yesterday, tomorrow, and fantasy (via seven themed areas: Main Street, Tomorrow, and Fantasyland, Frontierland, New Orleans Square, Adventureland, and Critter Country).

The Disney empire has now grown into a diversified corporation with interests in film and television production, hotels (the designs of which have attracted some of the world's great architects, such as the postmodern architect Michael Graves), and extensive merchandising of the Disneyana. Even during difficult economic times (fiscal 1983–1987) Disney's annual revenues more than doubled, to $2.9 billion, with profits that nearly quintupled to $444.7 million. New schemes continue to be projected by the Disney team, from a new Disneyland in South America to an American theme-park based on the workplace as well as EuroDisney, which opened near Paris in 1992.

Although originally scoffed at, the idea of the theme park began to catch on by the 1970s; it attracted large corporations and businesspeople in contrast to the old-time showmen of the early amusement park era. Disney imitations appeared throughout the country: Astroworld in Houston; Cedar Point in Ohio; Hersheypark in Pennsylvania; Kings Island in Ohio; a revamped Knott's Berry Farm in Buena Park, California; Magic Mountain in Valencia, California; Opryland, U.S.A. in Nashville; the Six Flags circuit in Texas, Georgia, and Missouri (and later in New Jersey and Illinois); and, finally, in 1971, the giant of them all, Walt Disney World Resort in Orlando, Florida. Built on a site of over 27,000 acres (10,800 hectares) it has never ceased its expansion, adding to the original Magic Kingdom, EPCOT Center, Disney-MGM Studios theme park, and a complex of hotels, golf courses, and other service and entertainment components. From an initial 700 employees, Disney World now employs 33,000 and on its property includes shops (where everything from trash cans to trams are constructed), a production department for live performances, warehouses, its own training school, called Disney University, and a separate company (Disney Development) responsible for hotels and service components outside of the amusement park areas proper. It all works with incredible precision and care, with no detail ignored or slighted. And, despite the uniformity demanded of all employees (including grooming and appearance regulations), Disney personnel appear surprisingly pleased with their positions, the operational procedures, and the Disney corporate image.

Clustered along Highway 441 through Pigeon Forge, Tennessee, are such ventures as Magic World, Treasure Ship Golf Course, Parkway Speedway, Wild Wheels & Waterbugs, Smoky Mountain Car Museum, Rockin' Raceway & Arcade, Hillbilly Village, Dixie Stampede, Museum of Reptiles, and dozens of other tourist attractions.

In many ways Disneyland and Walt Disney World illustrate how different the modern theme park is from the traditional amusement park. Other than having fixed rides, the theme park is often the antithesis of the older parks (though many of the survivors have been transformed into theme parks). For many patrons, the theme park is all they have known and its extremely conservative, homogenized, hygienic ambience and the youthful, clean-cut appearance of the typical employee are taken for granted. In contrast, the older amusement parks were run with traditional showmanship, included gaming operations and pitchmen, and were often a bit seedy with their worn attractions. Many amusement parks grew with no preplanning or organizational scheme; theme parks revel in the designed plotting of their amusement areas, often with open spaces and generous landscaping added to create an aesthetically pleasing ambience.

Other than cleanliness, the greatest single difference between the two types of parks is location. Traditional amusement parks moved closer and closer to urban centers and attracted a fairly circumscribed clientele. Theme parks have sought isolation, though proximity to a major highway, an area devoted to tourism, or even an urban area is desirable. By the 1980s theme parks were often part of a larger leisure area. For example, north of the Smoky, Mountain National Park in Pigeon Forge and Gatlinburg, Tennessee, a staggering array of commercialized leisure businesses can be found. The centerpiece is Dollywood, country singer Dolly Parton's park built around the theme of "Smokies Spirit" and country music, with forty-five musical performances each day. Clustered along Highway 441 through Pigeon Forge are such venues as Magic World, Treasure Ship Golf Course, Parkway Speedway, Wild Wheels & Waterbugs, Smoky Mountain Car Museum, Rockin' Raceway & Arcade, Hillbilly Village, Dixie Stampede, Museum of Reptiles, and dozens of additional attractions catering to tourists. A few miles away in Gatlinburg, once a small, quaint mountain hamlet, the main street is cluttered with such commercial attractions as Ober Gatlinburg, Mysterious Mansion, World of Illusions, the American Historical Wax Museum, Ripley's Believe It or Not, Haunted House, and the Guinness Hall of World Records. Just across the mountain range, Ghost Town in the Sky is located in Maggie Valley, North Carolina, and Santa's Land (with its Rudicoaster), billed as a fun park and zoo, is situated on the outskirts of Cherokee, North Carolina. Six Flags over Texas, in Arlington, Texas, between Dallas and Fort Worth, is situated in an area that also includes Arlington Stadium, home of the Texas Rangers baseball team, The Palace of Wax and Ripley's Believe It or Not, Wet 'n Wild (one of a growing number of water parks, totaling some 270 in the United States by 1991), and International Wildlife Park (a number of parks, such as Busch Gardens in Tampa, Florida, are theme parks with the veneer of animal preserves). Central Florida, with Disney World as its centerpiece, has spawned an enormous variety of entertainment venues, from Sea World (there are four Sea Worlds nationwide, each part of the Busch Entertainment Corporation) to Universal Studios, and a host of smaller leisure businesses scattered through the area.

If the theme park prefers isolation to an urban location (and there are exceptions—Busch Gardens in Tampa, Florida, and Disneyland, whose growth was curtailed because of its urban setting), the more successful parks draw on a national or even international patronage rather than the local clientele of the traditional amusement park. Even the smaller theme parks depend on regional rather than local business. And big business it is. In 1990 it is estimated that there were 243 million visits to amusement parks. Even related outdoor venues, such as miniature golf courses and water parks, did a large volume of business. The former attracted 120 million visits, while 49 million visits were made to water parks. Unlike the traditional amusement park, most theme parks have an entry fee or pass, costing in 1991, at Disney World, as much as $111 for a four-day adult "passport" and $88 for a child (ages 3 to 9). In 1991, a four-day/three-night visit, without airfare, could easily cost over $1,500 for a family of four.

When Disney World opened the EPCOT (Experimental Prototype Community of Tomorrow) Center in 1982, the theme park moved closer in intent to that of the world's fair or international exposition. Disney propaganda heralds:

> Journey through time and space, across the continents of the earth and beyond your wildest dreams in two dazzling and different worlds. At Future World you'll get an inspiring look at space-age technology and what lies ahead, while World Showcase will present you with the fascinating traditions and cultures of people from around the world.

Indeed, not unlike the New York World's Fair of 1939–1940, EPCOT attempts, as Andrea Dennett notes, "to challenge the patron to reinvestigate past achievements in order to grasp a better comprehension of future technological inventions." But Disney World, Six Flags, and other theme parks that claim to reflect history or to teach painlessly science and technology never lose sight that their first goal is to entertain a patron, usually a family unit, with plenty of money to spend. Consequently, history, science, and technology are handled in a way palatable for mass consumption and packaged in a fashion that will amuse and mesmerize as well as instruct. Indeed, the end result is often a kind of invented historical or scientific fantasy. In the realm of historical reenactment or representation, the product is rarely a realistic depiction but rather a utopian re-creation (sometimes with automata) that reflects history based on a selectivity of detail, most frequently positive in attitude, politically conservative, and underscoring a belief in the efficacy of power and the correctness of capitalism. Marginalized groups, when represented, are idealized; all threats to existence are virtually ignored.

INDOOR FAMILY ENTERTAINMENT CENTERS. The most recent development in the amusement industry, and arguably the newest amusement park mutation, is the Indoor Family Entertainment Center (FEC). Some limited areas set aside for amusement, usually with a few kiddie rides or a penny arcade, have existed in shopping centers and malls for decades. However, with the completion in 1985 of the West Edmonton Mall in Alberta, Canada, claiming as one component of its complex the world's largest indoor amusement park, the potential of the Indoor Family Entertainment Centers was realized, prompting other enterprising entrepreneurs to get on the bandwagon. Enclosed within the West Edmonton Mall, a shopping and entertainment complex covering 483,600 square meters, an area equivalent to 115 football fields, is Fantasyland, a full-sized amusement park complete with roller coaster. Although harking back to early trade fairs and expositions in large indoor halls or specially built structures, such as the Crystal Palace constructed for London's Great Exhibition of 1851, the FEC is very much a contemporary phenomenon, made possible by current technology and building techniques that allow for highly automated attractions and rides to be constructed within massive covered indoor spaces. It is the amusement industry's response to what they see as an increasingly family-oriented marketplace. For years entertainment venues, such as bowling alleys, video arcades, theaters, ice- and roller-skating rinks, have been tenants at shopping centers but have not been considered major or anchor tenants. However, in the 1990s the FEC has begun to be seen as a "developer-produced and operated signature space." In what is seen as a soft market for retail nationwide, the FEC is one way to diversify market appeal, extend the stay of the customer, and even attract tenants during the initial leasing period.

The obvious advantage of an indoor amusement park is the protective environment, especially during inclement weather or in colder climes. And, the mail-related center has the added possibility of drawing business from other attractions in the complex. Unlike most theme parks, admission to the center is free, with the patron paying for individual games, attractions, and rides. Larger Indoor Family Entertainment Centers, either attached to other commercial areas or freestanding warehouse-like operations, are becoming major tourist attractions. The West Edmonton Mall, for example, draws fifteen million visitors a year from Canada, the United States, and abroad. In the United States it is estimated that 97 million visits to Indoor Family Entertainments Centers took place in 1990.

To date, the United States' most prominent example of an FEC is Camp Snoopy (scheduled to open in 1992), as of this writing under construction by the Knott's Berry Farm organization at the future Mail of America in Bloomington, Minnesota (a cold climate similar to Alberta's). Within the center of this 4.2 million-square-foot (378,000-square-meter) facility will be a seven-acre FEC, its theme and contents similar to Knott's outdoor Camp Snoopy in California. Sixteen rides are proposed for this FEC, including a "Tivoli-style" steel roller coaster and a long flume twisting through a 70-foot (21-meter) high mountain. Illustrating the problem of definition of amusement and theme parks, Camp Snoopy is really an indoor theme park, as are most FECs. In this case it is the North Woods that creates the ambience, mirroring in an idealized fashion the Minnesota outdoors. The roof of the Minnesota mall is 100 feet (30 meters) high, 65 percent of which is glass, providing the interior of the complex with over 1.2 square miles (3 square kilometers) of sky light. With so much space available, Camp Snoopy will include a full acre covered in live landscaping, including trees 40 to 50 feet (12 to 15 meters) high.

Like the earliest amusement parks and carnivals, as well as theme parks such as Disney's EPCOT Center (built around an artificial lagoon), Camp Snoopy and virtually all FECs are arranged in a loop design that keeps traffic moving in a circular pattern, avoiding dead ends and guaranteeing that patrons pass all attractions, while allowing them to arrange their own programs in the environment.

Few FECs currently fall into the category of a Fantasyland or Camp Snoopy with a complete indoor amusement park. Most range in size from 20,000 to 150,000 square feet (1,800 to 13,500 square meters) with indoor ride- and show-based entertainment and participatory attractions, sports and food (and other merchandising facilities). These range from Neptune's Kingdom on the Santa Cruz, California, Beach Boardwalk—a $5.2 million indoor adventure entertainment center in a large building resembling an airplane hangar—to Fame City in Houston, a complex of hundreds of arcade games and kiddie rides combined with ten other major activities (roller-skating rink, bowling center, miniature golf, fun house, a laser maze, cinema); 49th Street Galleria, a 125,000-square-foot (11,250-square-meter) two-level complex in the Franklin Mills Mall (Northeast Philadelphia) and a 145,000-square-foot (13,050-square-meter) development in Salt Lake City, Utah (with more Gallerias planned); or "Celebration Station" in Baton Rouge, Louisiana, an FEC that caters to all ages, with redemption and video games, three types of go-carts, coin-operated mechanical animal rides for small children, and a 54-hole miniature golf course and nine batting cages for the sports-minded.

The amusement park industry, whose death, like that of the Broadway theater, is often predicted, has followed a natural course from trolley park and picnic grove to urban amusement park and the technologically superior theme park, including the current trend toward indoor family centers. It has grown prosperous along with America's increasing propensity for conspicuous consumption. Its current association with indoor malls is no coincidence. The new Mall of America in Minnesota, for example, expects to attract 40 million visitors annually by 1996, more than Disney World, and anticipates sales of $1 billion by that year. With home-entertainment centers ever more elaborate, the MTV generation will likely demand more sophisticated and spectacular attractions from the parks. Universal Studios in Florida, for example, in order to attract its clientele, has deemphasized its theme park identification and attempted to package itself more like a film and television facility, throwing the patron into a fantasized reality world, a center of special effects, and offering them a glimpse of a "hot" set, one that's ready to be filmed. It seems likely, therefore, that creative initiative, and stronger appeal to adults as well as children, will assure the industry's continuance well into the future.

[See also Nightlife; Popular Entertainment before the Civil War; Travel and Vacations.]

BIBLIOGRAPHY

Adams, Judith A. *The American Amusement Park Industry: A History of Technology and Thrills* (1991).

Beard, Richard R. *Walt Disney's EPCOT Center: Creating the New World of Tomorrow* (1982).

Cartmell, Robert. *The Incredible Scream Machine: A History of the Roller Coaster* (1987).

Davis, Tracy C. "Theatrical Antecedents of the Mall That Ate Downtown." *Journal of Popular Culture* 24, no. 4 (1991).

Dennett, Andrea Stulman. "A Postmodern Look at EPCOT's American Adventure." *Journal of American Culture* 12, no. 1 (1989).

Flint, Richard W. "Meet Me in Dreamland: The Early Development of Amusement Parks in America." In *Victorian Resorts and Hotels: Essays from a Victorian Society Autumn Symposium*, edited by Richard Guy Wilson (1982).

Francis, David W, and Diane DeMali Francis. *Cedar Point, the Queen of American Watering Places* (1988).

Fried, Frederick A. *Pictorial History of the Carousel* (1964).

Funnell, Charles E. *By the Beautiful Sea: The Rise and High Times of That Great American Resort, Atlantic City* (1975).

Kasson, John F. *Amusing the Million: Coney Island at the Turn of the Century* (1978).

Kyriazi, Gary. *The Great American Amusement Parks: A Pictorial History* (1976).

Onosko, Tim. *Funland U.S.A.* (1978).

Rydell, Robert W. *All the World's a Fair: Visions of Empire at American International Expositions, 1876–1916* (1984).

Schickel, Richard. *The Disney Version: The Life, Times, Art, and Commerce of Walt Disney.* Rev. ed. (1985).

Wallace, Mike. "Mickey Mouse History: Portraying the Past at Disney World." *Radical History Review 32* (1985).

Weedon, Geoff, and Richard Ward. *Fairground Art: The Art Forms of Traveling Fairs, Carousels, and Carnival Midways* (1981).

Wilmeth, Don B. *Variety Entertainment and Outdoor Amusements: A Reference Guide* (1982).

— DON BURTON WILMETH

ARCHITECTURE, COMMERCIAL

See COMMERCIAL ARCHITECTURE

ARCHITECTURE, PUBLIC

See PUBLIC ARCHITECTURE

THE ARISTOCRACY OF INHERITED WEALTH

While seventeenth-century Virginia and Maryland have sometimes seemed the antithesis of Puritan New England, the availability of productive land and the rise of a strong European tobacco market initially produced significant equality of circumstance and opportunity in the Chesapeake area, similar to that in New England. This was partly because many people vital to the colonies—royal administrators, London creditors, and shippers—lived in England, not America; partly because Chesapeake life in this age of primitive accumulation was so grim that large landholders often worked as hard and lived as sparsely as those of lower economic status, mostly because a planter working alone could profitably produce a thousand pounds of tobacco from three acres of land. Those who could buy large acreage and indentured servants predominated, to be sure. In the mid seventeenth century the median wealth of the top fifth of the white Chesapeake population was forty times that of the bottom fifth, and many in the top fifth came from English gentry or merchant families. But a factor of forty between top and bottom is actually low for the modern world, and most landholders were not well born. Similarly, although officeholding, despite a rudimentary system of representation, was the monopoly of the propertied, one-third of new mid-seventeenth-century officeholders were either illiterate or former indentured servants, and a truculent factionalism inhibited the evolution of these and other politicians into a cohesive ruling elite.

Several factors increased the living standards of the rich and the distance between rich and poor in the late seventeenth and early eighteenth centuries. One was the acquisition of large tracts of land beyond the tidewater; another was chronically low tobacco prices, which rewarded economies of scale. Most important was the introduction of African slaves. Slaves were more permanent and productive farm laborers than indentured servants—meaning that slave ownership would bring a decisive competitive advantage, especially in clearing and working the large tracts. And slaves cost more—meaning that ownership was likely to be concentrated among the better-off. By the early eighteenth century, wealthy planters owned two-thirds of all Chesapeake slaves, thus putting real distance between themselves and those below, who now possessed property worth less than a hundredth of the property of the top fifth. With significant wealth in land and slaves, moreover, came easily transmissible estates and hence a hereditary planter elite capable of consolidating itself through intermarriage and political alliances and of establishing an upper-class standard of living centering on the country estate, the county seat, and the colonial assembly. As the eighteenth century progressed, holdings in land and slaves brought access to English credit and cultural amenities and preferment for imperial appointments and naval contracts, all reinforcing the system of hereditary privilege wrought ultimately by slavery.

Puritan New England sought to combat the materialism and economic conflict of the seventeenth century by constructing "Christian commonwealths" centering on church life and such humble occupations as subsistence farming and traditional crafts. Initial land distributions were remarkably even, and colony officials frequently imposed either wage or price controls to prevent sudden accumulations from conditions of scarcity or glut. For this reason and also because New England provided few ways to amass wealth compared with England or the early Chesapeake, and therefore attracted fewer people determined to gain wealth at any cost, the distance between rich and poor was generally smaller during the first two generations of settlement—on the order of five to one—than for any other private property system of the modern era. Both the church and the town polity were broadly participatory, moreover, and most landowners could expect to hold at least local office at one time or another.

A five-to-one ratio is not equality, however. A more or less permanent "standing order" of ministers and better-off landholders existed from the start; they were gradually joined by thriving coastal merchants. Initially, religious fervor assured ministers predominance of place in this elite. But ministers could neither bequeath their pulpits nor prevent the diversity and secularism that weakened the role of the church. They therefore relinquished their place to the merchants, who benefited from colonial growth and could bequeath their wealth easily and in highly flexible form. During the eighteenth century this mercantile ascendance intensified as a result of expanding opportunities for imperial trade and preferment, a seaboard population boom that multiplied urban land values, and strategic marital alliances that preserved capital and connections. Except in its rarefied imperial reaches, commerce remained easier to enter than plantation agriculture, particularly for prosperous craftsmen and others familiar with trade. Nevertheless, in the commercial towns the proportion of wealth owned by the top tenth of the population rose steadily from 40 percent in the late seventeenth century to over 50 percent in the 1770s; the wealth of the top 5 percent—the imperial mercantile establishment—rose from 25 percent to 40 percent. Ministers capitalized on their status to become in-laws to and spokesmen for the merchants, intertwining with them socially but losing autonomy. Farmers, scattered and isolated save for a few big timber suppliers, remained a part of the standing order only by virtue of the votes they still mustered in the colonial assemblies, which continued to draw members from a broader socioeconomic net than in Maryland and Virginia.

The largest middle colonies followed divergent paths. In New York the Dutch and later the first English governors bestowed vast Hudson River estates on favored families. During the eighteenth century, tenants gradually occupied this land on long leases. Some used the profits from fur trapping and wheat production to purchase their farms outright. Most, however, remained tenants, leaving to their landlords not only the profit from milling and marketing the grain but also the capital gains and rents from owning the land. Landowners therefore remained an important element of the New York elite in a way that New England landowners did not. But neither was this the Chesapeake. The Hudson River funneled all production through the harbor of New York City, which became a notable shipping town and, eventually, a major port of settler debarkation. As the city grew, so did its merchant community, which cemented its position through intermarriage and joint investments with the great landowners. While New York's elite included Huguenots and Dutch Reformed families, the Anglican attachment was very strong, as was the connection to England and English institutions generally. Perhaps reflecting the manorial tradition, wealthy New Yorkers owned more African slaves than did other northern elites.

Pennsylvania, too, had a manorial presence—the Penn family not only owned the colony initially but also retained ownership of all undistributed land throughout the colonial era. Most grants went outright to actual settlers, however, so that eighteenth-century Pennsylvania, blessedly fertile, consisted chiefly of freehold family farms producing grain and other commodities for Atlantic markets rather than great holdings on the New York pattern; as late as 1760 the upper tenth of wealthy farmers and middlemen controlled just 30 percent of rural wealth. The only significant Pennsylvania elite was therefore in Philadelphia, where an aggressive merchant community made itself the chief colonial carrier and merchandiser of the British empire. This merchant elite had two wings. The smaller was Anglican in the New York fashion, with strong attachments to England (from which it drew credit) and extensive involvement in politics (from which it gained contracts and protection). The larger was, like the Penns, Quaker. Apolitical by creed, self-reliant by choice, Quaker merchants relied heavily on the transatlantic Friends network for commercial contacts and credit, and on the social life of the Quaker meetings to shape the marriages of their children in ways that consolidated wealth. By 1770 some 150 Quaker and Anglican merchants controlled 70 percent of Philadelphia's trade, while the top tenth of the population, with interests in shipbuilding, distilling, and real estate as well as commerce, owned 65 percent of the city's wealth.

In 1860 the top 10 percent of white families owned half of the South's property and two-thirds of its slaves, and possessed, as it had a century earlier, more than a hundred times as much property as the bottom 40 percent.

The Federal and National Periods

The withdrawal of British authority affected elite formation in several ways. Most immediately, it shook the pro-British Tory establishment that most relied on imperial connections and protection, and opened the way, particularly in the North, to men eager to raid British shipping, supply the Continental Army, open nonimperial markets, and develop alternative commodities. Many prominent Boston, New York, and Philadelphia families trace their "arrival" to this crucial period. Second, since the conflict with Britain disrupted British financing, there was both a need and an opportunity to develop domestic sources of credit. Alexander Hamilton's promotion of a national bank and a national debt were responses to this need, but more serviceable were the elite-sponsored, state-chartered banking and property insurance corporations that arose in every region, together with a swarm of savings banks, life insurance companies, investment banking firms, and stock markets, all working to convert accumulated funds into venture capital. Third, independence focused attention on the North American continent as well as on the Atlantic Ocean. This led on the one hand to efforts, eventually successful, to erect protective tariffs against manufactured goods, and on the other to the creation, chiefly by federal and state governments at the instigation of the northern elite, of a rudimentary wagon and water transportation system reaching not only from state to state but also far into the trans-Appalachian West.

Historians once assumed that the development of economic infrastructure within the context of territorial expansion and democratic government must have produced a churning and leveling that shattered the seaboard elites. This appears not to have happened. While certain southerners, especially in Virginia, dissipated their fortunes by clinging to public service and worn-out land, most wealthy planters benefited from westward expansion by, if they were mobile, purchasing and clearing the richest Gulf cotton lands or, if they were not mobile, selling slaves to those who were. As cotton and slave prices rose, so did the wealth of the old planters as well as of the new ones. In 1860 the top 10 percent of white families owned half of the South's property and two-thirds of its slaves, and possessed, as it had a century earlier, more than a hundred times as much property as the bottom 40 percent.

Northern elites, too, adapted well. The landed wing of elite New York State was badly damaged by the British departure. The commercial wing did better, in part because New York City's strategic location, enhanced by the opening of the Erie Canal in 1825, enabled merchants to remain merchants. Commercial profits accumulated so rapidly that by mid century New York was a major financial center as well, providing capital for the expansion of the cotton kingdom and the early canal and railroad system. Merchant capital from Boston flowed into textiles, railroads, and insurance; profit from these ventures then flowed into rudimentary trust companies and cultural institutions designed to combine and preserve family fortunes. Philadelphians invested in coal, iron, chemicals, and machine-tool production as well as banking and railroads. In all locales there was a shift in professional careers from the ministry to medicine and especially to law, a crucial new adjunct to success in a nation of "laws, not men." Partly for these reasons, the maldistribution of northern wealth increased steadily, particularly in urban areas. In the seaboard cities a tenth of the population owned three-fourths of all property by 1860; the top 1 percent owned nearly half.

Despite these patterns, prior to the Civil War the various regional elites did not resolve themselves into a Hamiltonian national upper class, able to reap the benefits of continental hegemony while remaining insulated from democratic control. There were two principal reasons for this. First and more important, the issue of slave labor versus free labor opened a vast chasm between the southern elite, whose prosperity rested on huge investments in forced agricultural labor, and their northern counterparts, who prospered by investing in labor-saving industrial machinery. National financial and cultural institutions of genuine power might have bridged this division for a while. In the event, the Civil War destroyed the basis of the division by destroying the slave wealth and political power of the great planters, and therefore their relevance to the process of national elite formation.

Besides this fundamental regional schism, the older seaboard elites, while they persisted well enough, found it difficult to absorb and control the decentralizing forces thrown up by the new order—the railroad boomers and commodity traders of the West, the lawyers and politicians spawned by electoral politics, particularly in the cities and the Midwest; and the swarming parvenu manufacturers and retailers of the early industrial era. Fewer wealthy Americans were self-made than was once thought, but they were more numerous than ever before. In the upper Mississippi Valley, where these trends converged during the 1850s, property ownership tended to be egalitarian, politics middle-class, loyalties fragmented. Fortunately for the easterners—like Stephen Douglas and Long John Wentworth—midwestern politicians were promoters, not redistributionists, and midwestern businessmen—like Cyrus McCormick and Charles Ogden—though autonomous, generally emulated and cooperated with eastern institutions instead of assailing them. Northern politics and manners acquired a decidedly western hue; northern economic and cultural life, somewhat less so.

After the Civil War

The next major phase of elite development coincided with the emergence between 1870 and 1930 of a mature industrial economy built around transcontinental railroads and urban transit systems, large-scale extractive industries and electric-power generation, and mass-produced, mass-distributed industrial and consumer goods and services from steel to telegrams to newspapers to automobiles. Industrialization produced a very high rate of economic growth and therefore both higher average family income and more opportunities for new business activity, especially in the industrial heartland. Yet the key to this new industrial order proved to be its immense physical and organizational scale—physical because the bigger the factories and rail systems, the more productive they were; organizational because such vast enterprises necessitated both huge capitalization and complex managerial controls. As it turned out, the readiest tool for capitalizing and controlling such ventures was the giant corporation, a form of business organization that also facilitated the consolidation of firms vertically, in order to control materials, and horizontally, in order to control markets. And whereas industrialization per se brought income and opportunity to many Americans, the industrial corporation brought a more extreme concentration of ownership, even after antitrust legislation broke up some monopolies, than had existed in American business since the mid eighteenth century. The same is true of family wealth. The tenth of the population that had owned over half of everything in 1860 owned 65 percent by the early twentieth century, and drew a third of the national income as well. At the apex, just 1 percent of American families owned two-fifths of America's wealth, including all its federal bonds; 70 percent of its corporate stock; and an astonishing one-fifth of its real estate. The distance between the top and bottom of society, once a serviceable comparative measure, was now all but infinite.

The tenth of the population that had owned over half of everything in 1860 owned 65 percent by the early twentieth century, and drew a third of the national income as well.

There were significant centrifugal forces within this corporate elite. Many new industries not only were located outside the East but also were run by aggressive, contentious men whose loyalties ran as much to locale and industry as to big business generally. Chicago meat packing is one example; Detroit automobiles, Minneapolis flour milling, and Ohio rubber are others. In contrast with earlier periods, moreover, some leading capitalists were Catholic—like Thomas Fortune Ryan and William Grace—rather than Protestant, or Jewish—like James Loeb and Felix Warburg—rather than Christian. There was no fissure comparable with the slaverynonslavery division because the basic patterns of investment and accumulation were everywhere the same. But the captains of industry controlled powerful, almost feudal, enterprises. Subsurface tensions over corporate behavior or political attitudes could therefore become debilitating rifts between regions or individuals or, more likely, industrial combinations, as eventually happened in Germany.

Developments in three areas of elite life—society, finance, and culture—pushed the new order in the direction of a national business class rather than of warring industrial fiefdoms. Of these, society was perhaps the most noticeable if the least significant. A striking feature of this industrial elite was its unprecedented conspicuous consumption: bejeweled attire, palatial residences, travel by private train or fleets of luxury automobiles, culture (art collections and opera houses), and sport (yachting, polo, and golf). The object of such expenditure, besides coarse pleasure and the mimicry of Europe, was to demonstrate success in accumulation and social standing. Every newspaper had its society columnist, every community its society leader, every city its *Social Register* of those who had "made it." The charity ball, a spectacular example of carefully chronicled conspicuous display, became the main social event of the year, followed closely by the debutante ball signaling the marriage availability of upper-class daughters. High society thus organized had divisive features because it rested in part on envy and exclusion. But by inducing new money to emulate and chase old money, it united as well. It also united because New York, with more millionaires than elsewhere and more nouveaux riches, captured society's center stage, thus setting trends that other elites, particularly in the Midwest, soon imitated.

In finance the chief figures were the investment bankers, most notably J. P. Morgan, who grew concerned about "cutthroat competition" that might bring industrial collapse and speculative excesses that might shatter credit. Morgan's solution to the problem of competition was to create European-style cartels either by forming quasi monopolies, as with the steel industry in 1900, or by influencing firms through financial leverage and interlocking directorates, as occurred by 1915 with over a hundred giant corporations, including American Telephone, Westinghouse, and Standard Oil as well as several rail systems and big commercial banks. His solution to the problem of speculation was to demand sound practices from the companies he dealt with and to conduct himself with visible integrity and restraint. Other combinations arose to challenge the Morgan interests, and the founding of the Federal Reserve System in 1913 partly undercut the influence of investment banking.

Financiers like J. P. Morgan pushed the new order in the direction of a national business class rather than warring industrial fiefdoms. Morgan's solution to "cutthroat competition" was to create European-style cartels.

Finance capitalism was in any case not adequate to handle the enormous imbalances that led finally to the Great Depression. But Morgan and the financiers who followed his lead in the proper uses of capital did induce greater cooperation among industrialists. Since Morgan's home, New York, was the nation's chief financial center, this, too, worked to pull the business system back into an eastern orbit.

Society and finance had more short-term than long-term impact. The reverse was true of culture. A kind of cultural curriculum emerged at the turn of the century consisting of the experience to be gained by passing through a constellation of exclusive institutions. The Episcopal church, which became the denomination of choice for successful people (including some erstwhile Catholics and Jews) was a part of this curriculum, as were resorts such as Newport, Rhode Island, and Bar Harbor, Maine. So were the right schools (chiefly a cluster of New England boarding schools with a half-dozen Episcopal schools at their core), the right colleges (chiefly the Ivy League institutions centering on Harvard, Yale, and Princeton), and the right clubs (chiefly downtown establishments with yacht and country clubs at the periphery). The curriculum provided a means of absorbing wealthy parvenus and their children into elite ranks, and of providing elite youth generally with a body of common knowledge, some useful career training, proper role models, and, it was hoped, suitable marriage partners, badges of affiliation, and business contacts. Elite Boston, though still economically robust, contributed to upper-class formation principally through the New England elements of the curriculum.

The new class had three other features of note. First, in politics the class operated largely as a Republican party patriciate, occasionally holding office but more commonly influencing politicians through co-optation, party organizations through campaign contributions, and governments by filling top judicial and administrative posts. Second, in occupational terms the sheer size of the great industrial firms meant that management was a more important career alternative than in the nineteenth century. While in theory this rewarded ability instead of wealth, and thus diminished the ability of the rich to guarantee positions (instead of mere money) to their children, in practice managers of this era came chiefly from those with connections to capital or with the right college credentials, thus enhancing the career prospects of elite children. The Forbses of Boston, the Welds of Boston and New York, and the Aldriches of New York and Providence exemplify this change. Third, the class was intensely tribal, particularly in the East—wholly exclusionary as to race, partially exclusionary as to religion and gender. Jews, though prominent in business and the elite colleges, were not admitted to key schools, clubs, and resorts or to certain industries, including commercial banking and oil. Upper-class women could spend and marry money but not make it. Jews developed Jewish schools, resorts, and clubs in part because they were excluded from those of the Christian upper class. Women developed women's schools, colleges, and social organizations because the upper class was male dominated, if not misogynist.

The Twentieth Century

In the late twentieth century, the elite evolved in new directions. Within the corporate economy, the new prominence of petrochemicals, aerospace industries, electronics, and consumer services, much of it driven by an enlarged federal government, shifted economic initiative from older industrial areas to the Sunbelt regions of Florida, California, and the Southwest, producing large numbers of new elite families, including some Asian Americans, as well as arriviste corporate managers, many of them from state universities or provincial versions of the upper-class cultural curriculum. Partially offsetting these trends was a long wave of mergers, conglomerations, takeovers, and buy-outs that, in the manner of a century earlier, further concentrated corporate ownership and control and also increased the influence of the New York investment bankers who financed the deals and the Washington regulators who favored them. But since many of the investment bankers and regulators were themselves new men, many of them from Irish, Italian, and Jewish backgrounds, it is not clear that the eastern establishment reasserted its authority in quite the earlier fashion. Nationwide, a third of the five hundred richest families of the 1980s did not inherit substantial wealth, while two-thirds of top corporate managers were of middle-class origins. Upper white-collar professional and managerial families in Boston and Philadelphia may have skidded into lower socioeconomic categories more than they had a hundred years earlier; many leading lawyers, managers, and financiers in these cities were in fact transplants from the Midwest.

On the other hand, the combination of new trust devices to preserve family fortunes and the effective working of the cultural curriculum meant that most members of the national upper white-collar class persisted across generations. Moreover, 80 percent of the one hundred richest families inherited great wealth, while 70 percent of key individuals holding four or more corporate directorships and 60 percent of the directors of major banks were members of the upper class. A chief distinguishing feature of the contemporary upper class, besides its modest ethnic and religious diversity, may be that it includes more top corporate executives (most of them large company stockholders) than at the turn of the century. It seems also, as befits a government-driven bicoastal-Sunbelt economy, to be less local and more national in orientation. In 1976 local *Social Registers* were consolidated into a single national volume. "Society" itself, based initially on exclusivity and formality, is now celebrity oriented, attaching itself to a remarkable degree to personalities from sports, the arts, and especially television. The handful of upper-class African American families have come predominantly from these areas, especially television, as have a few of the small number of autonomous corporate women.

The rise of television, a politically effective but enormously expensive medium, has meant that those with money are more dominant, particularly in national elections, than they were even during the patrician era at the turn of the century. Partly for this reason, federal policy since the 1970s has favored the corporate rich in numerous ways: regressive taxation, decreased corporate regulation, high military spending, large-scale, high-interest deficit financing. By the end of the 1980s, income and wealth had reached their highest concentration ever. The top 10 percent of the population, which had owned 60 percent of all wealth in 1860 and 65 percent in 1910, now owned 70 percent; the top 1 percent owned 45 percent of total wealth. There were now 1,300,000 American millionaires; there were 50 billionaires. The 400,000 wealthiest households owned 27 percent of net American worth; the 500 richest families owned 170 billion dollars of net business worth and thus controlled 40 percent of all nonresidential private capital. Income from rents, dividends, and interest surpassed income from wages and salaries for the first time, with the result that the top 20 percent of the population—the broad managerial and professional elite—made 45 percent of all after-tax American income, or 50 percent if capital gains are included. The top 1 percent—the corporate upper class—made 11 percent of all after-tax income, or 15 percent including capital gains.

A final notable development is the internationalization of wealth in the late twentieth century. American corporations have greatly increased their investment abroad, so that overseas operations now contribute substantially and disproportionately to overall corporate earnings. American branch managers abroad are often members of the host country's elite if they reside there long enough. Yet the U.S. share of world output has fallen almost to its pre-1914 level of 25 percent, while its total national assets have fallen behind Japan's by a sizable amount. Foreign, especially English and Japanese, companies have invested heavily in the United States and have purchased government bonds in order to take advantage of high American interest rates. Multinational corporations also have multinational management more than ever before. It is nonetheless suggestive that of the twenty-five richest men in the world as of 1989, nine were Japanese and seven were west European. Four were from the United States.

[See also Business Culture; The Culture of Consumption]

BIBLIOGRAPHY

Aldrich, Nelson W., Jr. *Old Money: The Mythology of America's Upper Class* (1988).

Bailyn, Bernard. *The New England Merchants in the Seventeenth Century* (1964).

Baltzell, E. Digby. *Philadelphia Gentlemen: The Making of a National Upper Class* (1958).

Benjamin, Philip. *The Philadelphia Quakers in the Industrial Age, 1865–1920* (1976).

Chandler, Alfred, Jr., and Richard S. Tedlow, eds. *The Coming of Managerial Capitalism: A Casebook on the History of American Economic Institutions* (1985).

Domhoff, G. William. *Who Rules America Now? A View for the '80s* (1983).

Gilbert, Dennis, and Joseph A. Kahl. *The American Class Structure: A New Synthesis* (1982).

Hall, Peter D. *The Organization of American Culture, 1700–1900: Private Institutions, Elites, and the Origins of American Nationality* (1982).

Henretta, James A., and Gregory H. Nobles. *Evolution and Revolution* (1987).

Jaher, Frederic C. *The Urban Establishment: Upper Strata in Boston, New York, Charleston, Chicago, and Los Angeles* (1982).

Miller, Elinor, and Eugene D. Genovese, eds. *Plantation, Town, and Country: Essays on the Local History of American Slave Society* (1974).

Morgan, Edmund. *American Slavery, American Freedom: The Ordeal of Colonial Virginia* (1975).

Pessen, Edward. *Riches, Class, and Power Before the Civil War* (1973).

Phillips, Kevin. *The Politics of Rich and Poor: Wealth and the American Electorate in the Reagan Aftermath* (1990).

Rutman, Darrett B., and Anita H. Rutman. *A Place in Time: Middlesex County, Virginia, 1650–1750* (1984).

Thernstrom, Stephan. *The Other Bostonians: Poverty and Progress in the American Metropolis, 1880–1970* (1973).

Thernstrom, Stephan, and Richard Sennett, eds. *Nineteenth-Century Cities: Essays in the New Urban History* (1969).

— RONALD STORY

B

BUSINESS CULTURE

John Locke blamed it all on money. In the beginning, in America, as in a state of nature, the "want of people and money gave men no temptation to enlarge their possessions." Individuals enjoyed liberty and formed governments without fear of injustice or tyranny. But money fostered accumulation and stimulated greed, while "ambition and luxury . . . taught princes to have distinct and separate interests from their people" (*Second Treatise on Government*, sections 108, 111). The result was corruption, born of wealth and the freedom to pursue it.

Colonists in British North America thought they saw themselves in Locke's treatise on government, because they lived in something like a state of nature. Freely they entered into compacts to govern themselves; freely they made their own livings. Then, just as Locke predicted, corrupt princes, their hands filled with money, conspired from a distance to enslave them. With great righteousness, Americans took up the work of rebellion, determined to eliminate corruption while protecting wealth and freedom.

From this peculiar starting point, self-creating Americans fashioned a business culture in the nineteenth century that liberated private ambition, celebrated innovation, and helped usher in a worldwide capitalist revolution. Practical entrepreneurs in a mercantilist world, they rejected imperial frameworks and adopted limited republican governments. Because they found the origins of corruption in government, early Americans held their princes at bay and expected developing markets to sort out inevitable clashes of interests. At first their approach fostered freedom of enterprise, but eventually competition gave rise to new princes in the form of giant monopolistic enterprises. After a century of liberation, Americans found themselves possessed of a rich but distorted economy, and no less worried about freedom and riches than the founders of the republic had been. Another century made them masters of a global economy—and yet more fretful than ever about the maintenance of their prosperity.

The Business Environment in 1800

In 1800, Americans were farmers. Only 6 percent of the 5.3 million population resided in thirty-three "urban" places. Cities sheltered the majority of merchants, artisans, and laborers—figures most often associated with the business world. Everyone else lived on farms and plantations, or in small towns where the rhythms of agricultural life established community values. The overwhelmingly rural character of this economy seems almost to preclude discussion of a business culture at the beginning of the nineteenth century. But in 1800, the business of Americans was agriculture.

AGRICULTURE. The great staple-crop planters dominated agriculture in the southern United States. With few tenants to farm their land, large and small planters decided for themselves which crops to plant, how best to employ vacant land, when and where to sell commodities, and what to take in exchange. If they were slaveowners, they assumed the additional responsibility of managing the lives of their laborers. Their pose as gentry notwithstanding, American planters worked hard to manage their complex enterprises.

A much larger number of American husbandmen worked smaller family farms. Best characterized as semisubsistence farmers, these landowners met most of their immediate needs directly or by trading goods and services with their neighbors. Middling farmers commonly planted patches of tobacco, wheat, barley, rye, flax, or hemp, intended for sale in commercial markets. Farm families located near urban centers also specialized in dairy products, vegetables, fruits, and meat. Many farms raised sheep for wool, from which the women of the household produced their family's clothing. How much farmers produced expressly for the market depended largely on their distance from centers of exchange, although individual customs, ambitions, and the availability of credit also played a part.

At the bottom of the agricultural social pyramid, a class of farm laborers worked for some kind of "wage." The adolescent sons of white farm owners fell into this category. White females might be employed in the farmhouse or dairy until they married. Inevitably some individuals labored all their lives on other people's farms. Genuine subsistence farmers infringed as squatters on frontier land, scraping out livings for their families but never accumulating tangible wealth. Most of the one million African American slaves labored in their masters' businesses, with no real economic freedom. Free blacks found their opportunities almost as closely circumscribed.

THE MANUFACTURING TRADES. Ancillary to the agricultural economy, artisans and tradesmen often lived in rural communities, where their work became embedded in the agrarian cultural framework. Truly urban places in early America, however, exhibited artisanal cultures reminiscent of the European craft tradition. The standard unit of enterprise for skilled artisans in America was the independent workshop. Owned (and usually occupied) by the master craftsman, the independent shop employed one or more journeymen working for wages as well as apprentices bound for a term of years in exchange for room and board and initiation into the mysteries of the trade. Together this group of laborers produced finished goods from raw materials, usually without power equipment. Craftsmen sold their products directly to consumers, purchased their materials directly from suppliers, and supervised all aspects of their enterprises. In such shops, the master worked *and* managed the work of others; customarily he was the most skillful artisan in the establishment.

Certain preindustrial trades required larger and more specialized facilities and locations. Tanning yards often were banished to suburban fringes because of the filth and smell they created. Mills of all kinds necessarily stood where falling water offered a power source. Heat-using industries (liquor, turpentine, candies, glass, iron) required large equipment or fuel supplies that influenced their location and organization. Iron "plantations," for example, typically were built in hardwood forests where the furnace's appetite for charcoal could be met. Yet even in these relatively capital-intensive enterprises, working masters directed the activity and trained the apprentices while simultaneously tending their accounts.

Much of what Americans owned and used in 1800 was produced in the home. Sometimes homemade furniture, flatware, candles, and shoes substituted for fancier products a farm family could not afford. Other items, such as textiles, issued primarily from the household. Farm women produced most clothing and bed and table linens, using hand carders, spinning wheels, and hand looms. Some specialists, both men and women, wove coverlets at home, and where the markets sustained them, skillful weavers might work full time in the "putting out" system, producing cloth for yarn manufacturers.

American communities suffered from chronic shortages of skilled labor, and market conditions fostered high wages, easy mobility, and a fair degree of instability within the artisan community. Apprentices abandoned their obligations with impunity, and masters just as casually ignored their obligations to nurture and educate their charges. Half-trained journeymen found employment in rapidly growing cities long before they perfected their skills. While the cultural values of the traditional artisans—cooperative work, honor to the trade, and a competence for all practitioners—found ready expression in America, the foundations of that culture were compromised from a very early date.

MERCHANTS AND SHOPKEEPERS. The markets to which both farmers and artisans directed their productive ambitions were tended in 1800 by a small class of merchants and shopkeepers. At the bottom end of this network, nearest the great majority of farmers and consumers, stood the small town or country storekeeper. A general-purpose merchant offering all kinds of hardware, soft goods, and imported "groceries" (spirits, coffee, tea), the country storekeeper bought his stock from a mercantile house in the city. He retailed goods on credit (keeping his own detailed books); received farm produce in trade; brokered goods, services, debts, and credits among his customers; exported the accumulated surplus of his neighborhood; and hoped in the end to make a profit for himself.

In port cities, both large and small merchants engaged in a high-stakes speculative game of import-export trade. The size and organization of mercantile operations depended on each merchant's capital stock and strategy for making money. Some tied up huge sums in shipping, then scrambled to gather cargoes to keep their vessels filled. Others leased space for discrete "adventures," hoping to profit from buying cheap and selling dear. Some merchants specialized in a few transactions at which they became acknowledged experts; others played all markets promiscuously. Some sold on credit to the network of interior retailers, while others dumped their goods at dockside auctions in order to return their capital immediately to the Atlantic trade. One thing united these merchants in a community of business: they played a risky game filled with uncontrollable variables, in which lucky newcomers often got rich and wealthy veterans sometimes went broke with the turning of the evening tide.

Credit tied the whole system together. Long denied the right to coin their own money, colonists early learned to substitute merchant paper, book credits, and simple barter as their media of commercial exchange. Rural residents traded goods and services with each other, often documenting debts with paper notes or entries on the storekeeper's ledgers. Storekeepers purchased stocks of goods on long credits which they hoped to extinguish with what little cash and surplus produce they collected from their customers. Urban wholesalers extended credit to their buyers while accepting credit from their sellers, hoping that the markup and quick sales would cover all debts and yield a profit. Importers bought on credit from their overseas connections, who demanded payment in cash or good bills of exchange, usually acquired in unrelated export transactions.

Supporting this pyramid of debt, the output of American land and labor increased so that American business probably was solvent (if highly illiquid) even while it teetered on the brink of disaster. Lacking uniform systems of banking, insurance, collections, and exchange, merchants depended on their own confidence and the good faith of others. Lapses of either produced sudden panics, which ruined certain players (usually the weak) and profoundly restructured the game. Country storekeepers protected themselves to some extent by owning land and keeping a hand in the local rural economy; urban merchants invested in real estate and consumer durables as a hedge against uncertainties in trade—and as proof of their success.

WAS IT CAPITALISM?. Was business in 1800 already a modern capitalist game? Historians disagree sharply on the answer to this question. Clearly, most

Because Americans in 1800 responded primarily to perceived family or community needs, rather than to some analytical goal of profit maximization, they appear to some historians to have been guided by a sense of "moral economy."

Americans at that time depended on themselves and their local communities for most of their daily needs. Relatively few worked for cash wages, and few employers followed strictly rational calculations. Rural Americans engaged in market transactions at least occasionally, yet they did not depend on markets for survival, nor did they surrender their sense of values to iron laws of supply and demand.

Because these early Americans responded primarily to perceived family or community needs, rather than to some analytical goal of profit maximization, they appear to some historians to have been guided by a sense of "moral economy." Other scholars (and insightful contemporaries) have pointed to widespread competitive behavior and a tendency to embrace (or repel) changes according to selfish interest as proof of a modern, liberal, capitalistic outlook in the founding generation. However motivated, this first generation of Americans did not impede the rise of complicated markets. Neither did their rhetoric and understanding condemn the economic liberty from which capitalist principles evolved. As colonists, Americans had grown up in a mercantilist network closely bounded (in theory) by government structures and regulations. While this large imperial framework protected and even promoted colonial enterprises, Americans more often noticed barriers to innovation and private gain. Strong competitive forces, stemming from abundant land, scarce labor, and unsatisfied colonial consumer demand, frustrated mercantilist theory and influenced American economic ambitions, even among the most traditionally minded farmers and artisans. Lacking a scholarly explanation for their economic system, Americans tended to describe what they wanted as freedom from outside control.

Whether Americans consciously embraced mercantilist orthodoxy or the radical liberal doctrines published in Adam Smith's *Wealth of Nations* (1776), the world in which they lived exhibited elements of both ideals. Some principles belonging to the past they took for granted and preserved; novel tenets of liberal capitalism they often seized as rights in tradition or natural law. The business culture they created never perfectly reflected any single system.

The Revolutionary Legacy

The American Revolution redefined the business culture of the early United States, but that was not its expressed intention. Conceived in political terms of "republicanism," the Revolution promised freedom and equality to people who supplied their own shades of meaning to these powerful concepts. Therefore, while revolutionary republicanism did not dictate the rise of capitalism in America, the promise of the Revolution empowered and encouraged individuals to pursue wealth and innovation in ways which fostered that result.

REVOLUTIONARY IDEOLOGY. American radicals diagnosed a sickness—"Old Corruption"—in eighteenth-century English society, against which they mounted their rebellion. New money, gained in speculative trade, had greased the wheels of English politics, bathed aristocrats in decadent luxury, and subverted the landed basis of the English constitution—or so complained the English "country" Whigs. This old-fashioned critique ill suited American elites, who were themselves really entrepreneurs; but it helped justify American frustrations with the imperial regime, and it laid the foundations for revolutionary republicanism.

Republicanism appealed to American elites because it promised relief from the prerogatives of alien governors. In a republic, only the people at home—not some distant ruling class—could control the governing agenda. Provincial societies seemed uniquely made up of "common" people. Widespread landownership qualified most Americans as independent citizens. With the largest number of dependent laborers encapsulated within the system of black slavery, revolutionary enthusiasts could imagine the "whole people" of the colonies as independent householders sharing common interests in property, security, and personal liberty.

Republicanism appealed to the "lower orders" in America because it promised relief from the pretensions of elites whose claims to power and respect had never been proved. Freed from restraint by privileged classes in England or at home, ordinary Americans could imagine an open political culture that more nearly matched the open environment in which they lived. Thus the rhetoric engendered different postwar images in the minds of urban artisans, who followed the class-based radicalism of Thomas Paine; in the minds of country farmers, for whom self-government often meant a return to rural tradition; and in the minds of lesser planters, merchants, and manufacturers, who wished to share the prerogatives of power with their "betters."

If revolutionary republicanism failed to harmonize these visions of the new republic, it nevertheless mobilized whole communities to throw off the British yoke and embark upon the experiment. As soon as independence was secured by the Treaty of Paris (1783), however, American politics unraveled. It was then that revolutionaries discovered the irretrievable force of the promises they had made: liberty and equality, once tendered, were not easily abridged within the framework of republican ideals. In post-Revolution America, the future belonged to those who called for freedom. In business and economic matters, the result was a culture that increasingly favored innovation and development at the expense of traditional rights.

LAW AND THE ROLE OF GOVERNMENT. The decline of tradition in the face of restless ambition can be seen in the changing uses of law and government in the early United States. European traditions placed responsibility for prosperity and welfare squarely in the hands of government; and although in America controls over prices, wages, and market transactions never operated effectively, new governments still set out to guide economic behavior. Republican theory obligated government to protect and promote the "general welfare." Exploiting this language in the federal Constitution, Treasury Secretary Alexander Hamilton laid down fiscal and banking policies in the 1790s that quickly revived the public credit and facilitated national commerce. Given control over money and trade, the new national government practically guaranteed that economic policies would be uniform (and probably congenial) for commercial and developmental interests.

Hamilton's program sparked political opposition, especially in Virginia and the South, but this reflected local fears of federal power and a preference for agriculture more than popular doubts about the wisdom of economic legislation. State governments in all regions passed their own laws to improve transportation, create banks and issue currency, stimulate commerce, control product quality, fix weights and measures, open up new land, and encourage capital development. Municipalities retained time-honored powers to regulate prices and wages—although they usually found them inexpedient to use. Ordinary citizens habitually turned to their governments to protect their livelihoods, adjudicate their conflicts, and enhance the environment for seeking wealth.

What changed at first, then, was not the traditional role of government in the economy but the effects of such intervention. American courts, for example, gradually enlarged the freedom of entrepreneurs by favoring innovation over tradition in cases of conflicting property rights. In 1805 (*Palmer* v. *Mulligan*), the New York Supreme Court upheld a mill builder's interference with the rights of downstream proprietors, even though he proved no prior common law right. Gradually, American courts began rejecting as "obstructionist" the claims of vested interests who resisted change. Such a legal bias fed on itself, undermining ancient habits whenever ambition challenged the status quo. Before long, judges found themselves forced to rule in favor of new claimants against parties who, once favored, now sought protection from further innovation. In 1837 (*Charles River Bridge* v. *Warren Bridge*), the U.S. Supreme Court embraced the doctrine of "creative destruction," systematically favoring growth over vested rights. More to the point, judges increasingly looked to market forces, not the rule of law, to allocate society's resources.

Legislators discovered similar limits to their capacity for making economic laws. The evolution of business corporations illustrates a steady retreat from regulatory tradition by lawmakers faced with ever-more popular electoral demands. Early corporate charters established a unique relationship between the government and private "incorporators," who were engaged to provide a public benefit in exchange for special privileges. Traditionally limited to charitable trusts, hospitals, schools, and asylums, such charters were adapted in the early United States to establish bridges, turnpikes, banks, and occasionally industrial concerns. Conceived in traditional terms, to accomplish a public good with private resources, these early American corporations proved useful for capitalizing large, expensive enterprises—especially capital-intensive public works like canals and, later, railroads. Legislators found themselves besieged with applications. To escape the unenviable task of bestowing privileges on some while denying others, democratic lawmakers adopted general incorporation laws, first in New York (1811) and then throughout the nation as markets developed. Thereafter corporations lost much of their special policy orientation and became simply business instruments.

LIBERATION AND IMPROVEMENT. Neither entrepreneurs nor lawmakers began the nineteenth century determined to eliminate the role of the state or establish the doctrine of laissez-faire as the centerpiece of American policy. It was their shared desire, however, to foster prosperity, encourage innovation, eliminate arbitrary preferments, knock down barriers, open up opportunities, and cultivate the "better sort" of private ambitions. All these objectives were thought of as "improvement," and improvement—whether private gain or the advancement of humankind—seemed to many early Americans to be the very proof of the virtue of liberty.

How did improvement relate to enterprise? At a rhetorical level, the terms often seemed to be synonymous; in practice, however, Americans often disagreed about the "improvement" accomplished by particular examples of enterprise. Innovations usually displaced earlier systems in which some persons sought their livings. Bridges destroyed ferry operators; new roads routed traffic away from the establishments of tavern keepers; improvements in rivers eliminated the need for haulers and warehouse operators who lived off breaks in traffic. Later, steamboats injured keelboats, railroads hurt canals, and steam engines threatened waterpower. In industry, machines displaced skilled workers; in farming, new lands outproduced old; on the plantation, the cotton gin inexorably tightened the noose of slavery around the necks of African American laborers.

Within the framework of American liberty, these problems of distributive justice took on heightened importance in the first decades of the nineteenth century. Originally, the elite founders of the new nation confidently believed they could design and direct improvements for the benefit of the whole people. But competing interests and insistent demands, from the middling and lower classes, to participate on their own behalf rendered it increasingly hazardous for men in office to take firm, positive action. Many entrepreneurs—especially visionary advocates of canals, railways, and large factories—clung to government preferment and endorsement, but an emerging majority of people embraced freedom *from* public policy as more likely to suit their needs. Thus in 1825, when President John Quincy Adams challenged Congress to seize boldly the task of improvement, the lawmakers demurred. Were they "palsied by the will of their constituents," he asked. They answered, proudly, Yes.

Liberation, promised in a revolution set forth in republican terms, produced democracy and entrepreneurial freedom in the new United States. What emerged as liberal, capitalist America over the course of the nineteenth century was not the design of the founding elites. Neither was it the product of sinister forces at work subverting the republican experiment. The American business culture resulted from the activities of individuals who were already entrepreneurs (in custom if not in self-concept), in a field of abundant resources, under a political regime that could not justify erecting barriers to private ambitions.

Traditionally limited to charitable trusts, hospitals, schools, and asylums, corporate charters were adapted in the early United States to establish bridges, turnpikes, banks, and occasionally industrial concerns.

Expansion of Antebellum Markets

Armed with a culture of liberation, American entrepreneurs in the nineteenth century remodeled a continent and revolutionized everything about the means of production. The first step required expanding and perfecting the market as the primary institution of resource allocation and economic exchange over a fast-growing geographic field that soon stretched from sea to sea. The annihilation of spatial and temporal distances, the rationalization of work, and the triumph of cash transactions took place within a single generation and sprang from such indigenous American roots that the most strident critics found the transformation practically irresistible.

TRANSPORTATION AND COMMUNICATION. Simple distance and the difficulty of getting around in the new United States kept markets local and oriented to the Atlantic trade. Port cities communicated more readily with London and Le Havre than with their own hinterlands. Members of the new federal Congress complained bitterly about traveling to sessions in New York and Philadelphia, and news traveled so poorly that during sessions they made little effort to stay in touch with constituents back home.

To address this communications problem, investors in the port cities as well as leaders in state and national governments quickly turned to public works of transportation improvement. Beginning in the 1790s, turnpikes improved main routes between cities or into urban hinterlands. Canals promised greater improvements, but they posed much greater technical and financial challenges. Only in the 1820s and 1830s were important works such as the Erie, the Chesapeake and Ohio, the Wabash and Erie, and the Dismal Swamp Canal opened for traffic.

Steamships introduced a fundamentally different category of change based on fossil fuel energy. After 1807, when Robert Fulton demonstrated the *Clermont* on the Hudson River, steamboats quickly mastered two-way navigation on America's rivers. By 1830, steam navigation on the Mississippi and Ohio rivers, the Great Lakes, and the coastal waterways offered steadily improving access to the trans-Appalachian frontier. New roads and canals—many built or projected by states as public works—augmented the river system. In the states of the Old Northwest, great schemes of internal improvement collapsed in the Panic of 1837 and the depression years that followed. Nevertheless, by mid century this network of highways, rivers, and three thousand miles (4,800 kilometers) of canals had brought a regional population of about eleven million into the market.

No sooner had the steamboat capped this impressive waterborne network than the railroad appeared to overwhelm it. Experimental lines such as Baltimore and Ohio, the Boston and Providence, and the Camden and Amboy proved successful in the early 1830s; rapid technical evolution during the next decade placed increasingly powerful locomotives on heavy "T" rails, pulling eight-wheeled cars and coaches at unbelievable speeds (over 30 miles, or 48 kilometers, per hour) just as the capital market righted itself for a mid-1840s burst of expansion. By the outbreak of the Civil War, American railroads had laid some thirty thousand miles (48,000 kilometers) of track.

The railroad's unique contribution was speed. Ten times faster than canal boats and wagons, railroads set new standards of impatience for a generation that soon craved instantaneous communications. Postal railroad cars, introduced in 1837, cut delivery time for many letters from days to hours. The same year, Samuel F. B. Morse invented the electric telegraph and the fantasy came true. Virtually instantaneous communication of news, orders, prices, and inventories awaited only the erection of transmission lines. Railroads quickly adopted the telegraph for their own traffic control, sharing rights-of-way to string the wires.

The magnitude of these changes in transportation and communication rendered old environments practically incomparable with the new. Average freight rates fell by nine tenths, but this misses the point: the vast majority of freight hauled in 1850 would not have entered the market without these

This steamboat is an example of a nineteenth century "improvement" which displaced existing systems (in this case, the keelboat) thus angering the average American.

improvements. The same was true of the circulation of news and information. Of course, not every place received equal treatment in the emerging networks, and earlier systems of transportation and communication played important (and profitable) roles long after shiny innovations appeared.

DOMESTIC MARKETING NETWORKS. Important social consequences attended the creation of interregional markets. After 1820 the development of export markets, particularly for grain and cotton, lured new settlers into the West in record numbers. Within a year or two of relocation, most pioneer farmers found new markets for their produce; after 1850, railroads actually overtook the westering settlers and began purposefully colonizing new lands. Federal land sales boomed; twenty new states entered the Union by 1860; exports of cotton, grain, and other farm produce approached $1 billion.

To pay remittances to exporting farmers, streams of manufactured goods flowed into the countryside, tended by merchants and carriers whose number, scale of operations, and sophistication steadily increased. Cities such as Cincinnati and Saint Louis took shape as exporting centers, then quickly acquired processing industries (pork packing, distilling, milling) and manufacturing trades. As transportation improved, competition between local producers and more distant vendors drove down consumer prices and rewarded more efficient suppliers. The increasing volume of trade allowed merchants to specialize in cotton, wheat, hardware, groceries, insurance, or forwarding services. New agents called "jobbers" helped local merchants navigate among large specialty houses by breaking down large lots into smaller retail stocks. Such specialization and expertise enhanced the efficiency of market transactions.

Gifted with excellent natural waterways, New York State was plunged into debt in 1817 when Manhattan merchants initiated the building of the spectacular Erie Canal, which served to reorganize the country's commerce.

The extension of complex markets across half a continent brought most Americans into more regular dependency on the money economy. Barter economies survived on the frontier as temporary expedients, not as alternatives to the larger commercial networks. Once in place, markets fostered their own elaboration. Innovative merchants and manufacturers bought goods in larger lots, built more efficient steamboats, invented machines, adopted telegraphic communication, extended credit in novel ways (or exploited credit extended to them), incorporated railroad companies and banks, lobbied governments, occasionally lied and cheated each other—all seeking competitive advantages in this burgeoning market economy.

The spiraling velocity of transactions required constant infusions of new "money," for which antebellum entrepreneurs turned to federal and state governments, private and incorporated banks, canals, railroads, insurance companies, cotton warehouses, merchant paper, personal promissory notes—anything to circulate as currency in impersonal, long-distance transactions. Although the Second Bank of the United States, established in 1816, foundered in 1833 on the rocks of political opposition, lesser banks and private networks of credit (assisted after 1850 by the credit reporting services of the Brad-street Agency and later R. G. Dun and Company) kept the money supply buoyant, if not always safe. Panics shook financial markets in 1819, 1837, and 1857, ruining the overextended and reminding everyone how unpredictable the game could be.

Nobody could cling for long to the old pace of life—or business—in these rapidly developing markets, and the relentlessness of these changes disappointed individuals who pinned their hopes on the status quo. Farmers in Michigan in the 1830s, for example, gained high-speed access to markets but had to fence their pastures to keep livestock off the tracks. Forwarding merchants and local middlemen everywhere found their markets invaded by better-heeled distant competitors. In the 1830s, Hudson River farmers complained that the Erie Canal brought unfair competition from wheat farmers in the Genesee Valley; two decades later Genesee Valley farmers complained that railroads brought the same from Michigan and Illinois. Bankers and debtors found their notes appearing for payment more quickly. Confidence men and speculators watched their "float," the delay of information, disappear. A generation of Americans confronted, for the first time, the bewildering complex of reinforcing changes they chose to call "progress."

Nowhere was the potential for cumulative change more clearly realized than in New York City. Gifted with excellent natural waterways, New York merchants plunged their state into debt in 1817 to build the spectacular Erie Canal, which served to reorganize the commerce of the country. New York merchants pioneered sailing on schedule to England; organized coastal service to the cotton ports; perfected the system of dockside auctions; and multiplied banking, insurance, investment, information, and credit facilities until they offered the quickest and cheapest services, the freshest news, the latest prices, and the widest selection of buyers, sellers, and merchandise of any city on the continent. They gained such dominance over American markets that even the railroads, which ignored existing patterns of trade in so many places, confirmed the rise of the port of New York.

THE TRANSFORMATION OF WORKSHOPS. Expanding and quickening markets revolutionized the structure of American manufacturing in the first half of the nineteenth century. New factories filled with big machines impressed everyone with the abruptness of their novelty, but far subtler changes in artisans' workshops started the making of an American working class. To meet rising demand or seize novel opportunities, master craftsmen experimented with systems of production that tended to enlarge the shop, capitalize techniques, subdivide tasks, routinize work, and return to the master a larger share of the fruits of labor. In this way, the vast majority of American workers, who before 1850 never entered a factory, joined the ranks of people who worked all their lives for wages.

The deterioration of workshop traditions stands out in the experience of booming canal towns such as Rochester, New York. In 1823, when the Erie Canal arrived, this sleepy country town virtually exploded with entrepreneurial changes. Giant flour mills on the Genesee River anchored an export trade that canal transportation made possible. Farmers turned to growing wheat for export and consuming more "store-bought" goods, which local merchants and artisans scrambled to provide. To meet the extraordinary demand for barrels, coopers subdivided their craft, hiring farmers to cut rough staves which journeymen finished into barrels in the shop. Shoemakers rationalized the cutting and fitting of shoes, then hired women at piece rates to sew the uppers and soles together. Apprentices became runners, delivering pieces and collecting finished articles but learning nothing about the craft. Journeymen, lured by ready employment, found wages but not "positions" in Rochester.

Market forces thus altered economic and social relations without the influence of big machines. Innovative masters invested more in tools, materials, and facilities, and then sought to reduce the wage bill. Alternatively, merchant investors with cash and credit gained control of markets and supplies, and then dictated new conditions in the workplace. Collegiality within the shops disappeared, and profits for the owner no longer implied upward mobility for apprentices and journeymen. Rochester's successful manufacturers moved into new homes in different parts of town, leaving their employees to neighborhoods (and aspirations) that could not share in their proprietary values. Terms of employment once appropriate to the temporary status of the journeyman did not provide a living for workers with families—yet such were the wages the market offered. Frustration, jealousy, and alienation mounted as workers watched the innovations of their masters undermine the quality of life to which they thought they, as free men and women, were entitled.

The degradation of the artisans' culture produced political as well as social tensions. In New York City, rapidly becoming the nation's premier manufacturing center, workingmen's parties and trade union movements tried repeatedly to discipline the masters, block the influence of merchant investors, and preserve the rights of labor within the Painite republican tradition. All over America, however, a strategic dilemma pitted artisans who would resist the progress of capitalization against those who aimed more narrowly at better wages and shorter hours within the framework of class employment.

DARK SATANIC MILLS. Nothing evoked more American pity and scorn at the end of the eighteenth century than the abject poverty and hopeless dependency of Europe's industrial classes. In 1791, Treasury Secretary Alexander Hamilton had tried to promote industrial growth in his *Report on the Subject of Manufactures;* but negative voices silenced Hamilton, and most Americans seemed content to leave factories (and factory workers) in Europe. Yet at precisely the same moment, American industrialization began at a small water-powered mill in Rhode Island.

In 1789, an English textile mechanic named Samuel Slater teamed up with Providence merchant Moses Brown to build the first American spinning mill. Slater's first mill (1791), and the dozens like it that quickly followed, exploited small sources of waterpower in southern New England to drive carding and spinning machines that spewed miles of cotton yarn into easily glutted markets. Confined primarily to rural settings by the location of the streams, employing the surplus labor of women and children while men worked at technical jobs (or farmed nearby company land), and limited in size by the power available and the number of neighborhood hand-loom weavers recruited to fashion the yarn into cloth, Slater-style mills at first seemed to complement the rural economy by generating incomes for poor families. As a result, the textile revolution was well established in America before many people acknowledged the importance of the factory system.

It was Francis Cabot Lowell's large-scale, fully integrated textile factory that drew all the attention in 1814, when the Boston Manufacturing Company first produced cotton cloth. Lowell combined in a single building all the processes from "picking" raw cotton to weaving finished cloth (and later dyeing and printing as well), integrating the machinery for efficiency, subdividing work into simple (and repetitive) tasks, capturing transaction costs and economies of scale lost to Slater-style firms, and turning out yard after yard of cheap cloth especially suited to clothing the southern planters' slaves.

A corporate charter sustained Lowell's first industrial venture, and by 1822 the dividends encouraged the same investors to develop a huge source of waterpower on the Merrimack River. At this site, named Lowell, Massachusetts, over the next twenty years the Merrimack Manufacturing Company developed five enormous cotton mills worth $5 million, employing 1,800 workers and producing 250,000 yards of cloth per week. Eight additional corporations, owned largely by the same investors, compounded operations at Lowell into the nation's largest industrial complex. Sensitive to the alien appearance of their giant enterprise, Lowell and his followers had stressed the public service that their corporations performed by stimulating the regional economy and creating employment for young unmarried women. Model boardinghouse environments theoretically protected Lowell operatives from the evils that degraded European workers; besides, according to the owners, Lowell "girls" saw factory work as a temporary prelude to a traditional domestic life. But market forces soon replaced such talk of social benefits with concern for efficiency, competition, and the profit margin.

This phenomenal success notwithstanding, few American manufacturers before the Civil War copied the system of the Lowell corporations. Even in textiles, where all the largest firms appeared, most companies remained private concerns or partnerships. After 1828 the use of steam power in factories freed manufacturers to locate anywhere they pleased, but this did not produce dramatic concentrations of capital. Textile magnates such as Samuel Slater multiplied their holdings by adding firms or joining complex webs of partnerships. Most industrialists managed their businesses as separate proprietary firms, and few fully mastered systems of cost accounting or managed to dominate their primary markets. Nobody sought the social experimentation suggested by the Lowell boardinghouses.

FREE LABOR IDEOLOGY. Between the gradual transformation of traditional workshops and the radical alternatives of cotton mill employment, most antebellum workers found that the world in which they worked kept changing. Technological innovations embedded more capabilities in machines that required less talent or experience to operate. The "American system of manufacturing" with interchangeable parts, developed by Eli Whitney, Samuel Colt, and other manufacturers of small machines, further removed the artistry of the maker from the utility of the product. Social perquisites long respected on the job—drams of liquor or impromptu suspensions of work to attend the circus, toast a birthday, or engage in political debates—fell before the rational calculations of employers who now paid wages by the hour and measured productivity in marketable output.

Because these changes in the world of work came at the hands of thousands of autonomous employers, they did not generate the kind of sympathy that might have followed the sudden spread of English-style "dark satanic mills" (the phrase is William Blake's). As long as most white Americans still owned farms, as long as skilled artisans nursed proprietary hopes, as long as most wage earners still knew "the boss" face to face and "mill girls" returned to hearth and home, the progress of capitalization seemed indistinct. Articulating a "free labor ideal" by mid century, middle-class people in the North insisted that as long as they were free from government corruption and class rule, their independence would survive in the marketplace. Objective measures did not entirely justify their confidence; but because the strident critics of free labor ideology—labor radicals and southern slave-holders—clearly spoke a language of class interest, most Americans entered the Civil War era believing that independence, free markets, and democratic politics still guaranteed personal liberty.

Rise of Big Business

Americans' delight in freedom of the marketplace reflected their belief that governments, not businesses, distorted the results of competition. John Locke had implied, and Adam Smith clearly had written, that no player in the game of capitalism could long sustain an unfair advantage, except through artificial preferment. Although many antebellum artisans found reason to wonder if the marketplace really "played fair," it was after the Civil War that the rise of big business introduced truly shocking contradictions to the liberal ideal. Under certain circumstances, free markets rewarded efficiency by favoring enormous enterprises that could sustain their productive advantages only by controlling or suppressing competition. This phenomenon surprised businessmen as much as consumers, and the rise of big business in America is best seen as both a problem *for* business and a problem *about* business in society.

BUREAUCRACY AND THE RAILROADS. The key to operating very large businesses lay in bureaucratic systems of management, and these techniques emerged as antebellum railroads struggled to control complex operations. From the beginning, railroads developed as technologically integrated systems, with one enterprise owning the roadway, selecting the equipment, operating trains, and handling the freight. Monopolistic operations worked even better when railroads integrated service over long lines or complex networks. Accordingly, after 1850, railroads began to combine into systems such as the Erie, New York Central, and Pennsylvania railroads, which managed about five hundred miles (800 kilometers) each and influenced policies on hundreds more, stretching from the Atlantic to Chicago and beyond.

Twenty times more expensive than the largest cotton mills, these trunkline railroads by 1860 employed more workers and engaged in more complicated transactions over a vastly larger geographical field than any other business in the country. In a cotton mill, everybody worked in a single complex of buildings, and almost nobody handled money. But train crews moved across the landscape, station hands worked in isolated spots, machinists repaired equipment, track gangs fixed the roadway, and conductors, agents, and paymasters handled money. No enterprise before had tried to coordinate so many different activities over great distances with exacting accuracy.

After 1850, railroads began to combine into monopolistic systems like the Pennsylvanian railroad which each managed about five hundred miles and influenced policies on hundreds more.

To control this complex business, managers on the Baltimore and Ohio, the Western Railroad, the Erie, and the Pennsylvania pioneered line-and-staff command structures; separated finance and business strategy from traffic and operations; further divided operations, maintenance, and machinery; and broke their lines into divisions of approximately fifty miles (80 kilometers). Statistical records made it possible to check the performance of one division against that of another. Auditors tracked down income and disbursements, guaranteeing faithful service from a legion of "middle managers" (who carried out transactions for entrepreneurs but earned wages themselves). Superintendents assumed operating responsibility for their divisions as if they were independent railroads; however, their performance was judged—and their salaries set—not by the market but by upper management.

Bureaucratic structures made it possible for American railroads to deliver relatively convenient and efficient services across a network that after 1869 spanned the continent. Capitalization for major lines reached into the hundreds of millions while total system mileage approached two hundred thousand (320,000 kilometers) at century's end. Easily expanded or subdivided, bureaucratic management techniques functioned roughly like machines in a workshop: they fixed the nature and dimensions of each task and required of the servant only the faithful execution of routine operations.

Bureaucratic complexity and rapidly changing markets taught railroad managers to discourage competition wherever possible. Driven to run full trains every day, in order to minimize the burden of high fixed costs, competing railroads often took business at less-than-profitable rates. They recovered any lost revenue through higher charges on noncompeting service, presenting consumers with a wildly distorted market in which identical goods might travel on the same train to the same destination, at rates that differed by a factor of ten. Railroad owners blamed distortions on cutthroat competition, which resulted when consumers forced the carriers to bid against each other. To eliminate such hurtful competition, railroads leased or purchased competitors' lines, formed pools to divide the traffic, and—like sovereign nations—forged strategic alliances to maintain peace and prosperity. Consumers denounced these efforts to restrain free trade.

ECONOMIES OF SCALE. As the nation's first big businesses, railroads introduced the problems of cutthroat competition and monopolistic influence into the American marketplace. Their success as big businesses made it possible for certain manufacturing and distribution industries to pursue strategies of giantism. In the 1870s and 1880s, economies of scale, rooted in technological advantages, prohibitive capital requirements, transportation discounts, or perhaps secret (and dishonorable) deals, catapulted certain firms into commanding positions from which they proceeded, like the railroads, to manipulate the game of competition.

Technology drove Andrew Carnegie's conquest of the steel industry. By quickly adopting the Bessemer process in the early 1870s, running his mills at maximum output, cutting costs, and selling steel as cheaply as possible, Carnegie seized a spiral of advantages. Quality and price gave him an edge with which he forced competitors to sell out; greater capacity improved his leverage in coal, iron ore, and labor markets; lower costs yielded cheaper steel, a larger share of the market, more takeovers, and greater control over the cost of materials and labor. Carnegie's furnaces burned out faster than those of more careful producers, but new equipment incorporated the latest innovations.

Oil baron John D. Rockefeller started with a secret railroad contract that lowered his transport costs and paid him kickbacks on competitors' shipments as well. Rockefeller undersold his Cleveland competition and took over the regional business. With volume under his control, he demanded greater transportation concessions, took over pipelines, forced down crude oil prices, built efficient new refineries, made his own tin cans, and pinched every penny in the process. His aptly named "Standard" brand of kerosene became practically the only one on the shelves.

Wholesale and retail merchants captured economies of scale by combining larger markets (reached by the railroads) with volume discounts. Manufacturers of clothing, housewares, tools, furniture, toys, and other mass consumer products gladly discounted large lots (and the railroads discounted shipping) to vendors, such as Marshall Field in Chicago, who opened huge retail department stores designed for "one-stop shopping" and customer satisfaction. Economies of scale allowed these giant merchants to beat local outlets on price, quality, and selection. Once established, these firms always commanded special terms and sometimes developed exclusive product lines, invested in manufacturing, and extended networks of branch stores. Marshall Field and Company's huge capital base supported money-back guarantees that would easily bankrupt a small shopkeeper trading with only his own capital.

According to classical theory, monopolists sold shoddy goods at artificially high prices, yet here were Carnegie, Rockefeller, and Field selling first-rate products at bargain prices. Vertical integration (controlling processes from raw material to retail sale) and horizontal combination (buying out the competition) explained their ability to do this. Railroads provided the expanding mass markets; bureaucratic systems made such firms manageable; consumer benefits kept them appealing to the great body of private customers. But interlocking economies of scale allowed a few players to dominate the market, while vast sums of capital tied up in plant, equipment, and inventories encouraged these high-stakes gamblers to protect themselves from competition. The giant firms of the Gilded Age were built by vigorous entrepreneurs, but a system of oligopoly was curtailing natural market forces. More alarming, a small number of very rich men held interlocking investments in giant firms that potentially controlled the economy of the country.

A NATIONAL CAPITAL MARKET. Andrew Carnegie built a $480 million empire by investing retained earnings from companies he owned alone or with selected partners. His was the exception to the rule, however, for most Gilded Age capitalists took advantage of new corporate structures and a rapidly developing securities market to marshal the capital of many investors behind the efforts of a few entrepreneurs. Once again, railroads led the way. First organized as franchise corporations, railroads sold shares to raise money but quickly pioneered the use of corporate mortgage bonds that borrowed funds against a pledge of future earnings and the value of the capital plant being built. When railroads paid off, which they did handsomely during and after the Civil War, passive investors often found these securities more attractive than risky enterprise or public debt. Limited liability, which after 1860 protected most corporate stockholders from individual responsibility for the debts of the firm, rendered passive investment even more attractive.

Stocks and bonds generated capital only if convenient markets traded them. Big-city stock exchanges filled the need, dominated from the 1870s by the New York Stock Exchange. First railroad securities, then in the 1890s industrial stocks and bonds, flooded Wall Street; brokers, investment bankers, and corporation lawyers appeared (as if by magic) to assist this new business of financing business. These instruments of capital formation separated ownership from entrepreneurship. Corporate leaders played with other people's money, not just their own; investors piled up wealth not from productive work but from securities manipulation. As a result, ambitious entrepreneurs such as Rockefeller wielded much more financial power than their private fortunes implied (especially early in their careers), while quick profits from stock operations introduced speculation as a separate career.

Corporations generated capital and structured these giant new firms, but booming capital markets exaggerated problems of cutthroat competition as mass markets approached saturation. Fabulous profits born of economies of scale lured more investors than the railroads and other center industries could support. Price-cutting strategies destroyed the weak, but too much competition took the profit out of everybody's business. Integration and combination removed some of the danger for innovative firms, but what could stop ruinous competition among the handful of giant survivors? The custodians of large corporations, originally owners but increasingly professional managers responding to boards of directors, seized every opportunity to protect their masters' capital by controlling costs and wages, binding customers with special terms, securing favorable government policies, incorporating technological advantages, and suppressing price competition.

In this manner what Alfred D. Chandler has called the "visible hand of management" challenged the invisible hand of Adam Smith's markets for control of America's economic resources. Railroads tried pooling—formal agreements that set rates between competing cities and divided the proceeds according to agreed-upon market shares. In 1882 John D. Rockefeller invented the "trust," in which leading shareholders surrendered control of competing firms to trustees who then managed the whole industry on cooperative terms. Still other enterprises joined trade associations designed to fix prices, limit production, manipulate labor, or discourage new entrants into crowded fields. All these solutions met with angry opposition from the American people, who wondered in increasing numbers if corporations were corrupting their free markets.

ANTITRUST AND THE PROBLEM OF MONOPOLY. The antitrust critique of American business always reflected a fundamentally liberal or Smithian foundation. Free markets were supposed to work best, and combinations to restrain competition by definition were ruled out of order. Since the 1850s, when the eastern railroads first manipulated their rates to accommodate trunkline competition, local businesses had bitterly condemned pricing policies that built up or destroyed whole communities without regard for their economic right to exist. Railroad managers insisted that if they gave up rate-making power, they would become mere public utilities. To compete as businesses—and therefore deliver cheap and efficient transportation according to Smithian principles—railroads demanded economic freedoms that significantly compromised the freedom of others.

This dilemma existed because large railroad systems now controlled the networks in which other businesses found their markets. Competition among carriers dictated one set of strategies while competition between shippers and carriers encouraged others. Building on common law traditions that recognized the capacity for common carriers to distort commodities markets, Gilded Age shippers begged their governments for relief from railroad oppression. State legislatures responded sympathetically, especially in the Midwest during the 1870s Granger Movement; but interstate corporations sought refuge from rate regulation under the "equal protection" clause of the Fourteenth Amendment. Industry leaders proposed that legalized pooling or cartelization might generate more uniform and stable rates, but skeptical voters and lawmakers clung to their faith in competition. The 1887 Interstate Commerce Act outlawed pooling as well as discriminatory rates. As a result, railroad companies merged into larger systems, labored vigorously to frustrate the enforcement of the law, and tried to find a niche between ruinous competition and illegal collusion.

As giant firms appeared in steel, oil, sewing machines, farm equipment, beef, jute bags, and other industries, popular agitation against monopoly spread. Congress responded in 1890 with the Sherman Antitrust Act, which outlawed all "restraints of trade" but left the prosecutors and judges considerable room to interpret the principle in practice. Sensitive to the economic power of the corporations (major sources of bribes and campaign contributions), neither the executive branch nor the courts rushed to impose the Sherman ideal. With unmeasured cynicism, American justices in the 1890s could find serious restraints of trade only in the activities of organized labor.

Corporate leaders played with other people's money, not just their own; in short, quick profits from stock operations introduced speculation as a career in itself.

Antitrust legislation did little to dismantle America's big businesses at the end of the nineteenth century, but it did restate in clarion terms that century's confidence in free markets and the liberal ideal. Antitrust advocates seldom addressed the fact that many of their foes performed more efficiently than smaller firms. In fact, most anti-monopoly rhetoric issued from injured interest groups—small merchants and manufacturers, rural middlemen, and organized labor. At issue, they insisted, were not current prices, wages, or rates but accumulations of power that threatened the fundamental liberty of all entrepreneurs. Not yet ready to adjust theory to changing realities, most Americans still hoped that conspirators could be punished and the automatic system of competition restored to its natural glory.

What antitrust legislation did accomplish in American business was another tremendous round of consolidations, known to historians as the "great merger movement." Federal proscriptions on all forms of collusion forced closely allied firms into outright consolidation. Over two thousand individual firms disappeared in corporate mergers between 1895 and 1904. Unbelievable giants, such as the $1.4 billion United States Steel, concentrated power in American industry more narrowly than ever before. Investment bankers such as J. P. Morgan played crucial roles in arranging these mergers and placed themselves on the new boards of directors. Thus, because of antitrust pronouncements designed to restore entrepreneurial liberty, control of America's center economy shifted further away from the entrepreneurs.

Heroic or Monopolistic Enterprise?

Wholly unprepared for the rise of big business, Gilded Age Americans celebrated the progress of industrialization, with its consumer benefits and rising living standard, at the same time denouncing their betrayal by cynical monopolists and "bloodless" corporations. Nothing in their views on civil liberty or economics explained the triumph of monopolistic firms, and nothing preoccupied the culture quite like the problem of economic justice in the age of the business titans. On the one hand, self-made captains of industry fulfilled the grandest American myth; on the other hand, their networks of corporate power seemed to block the aspirations of all who would follow in their steps. In a search for self-understanding that formed a bridge to the coming century, this generation struggled to reconceive the revolutionary promise of liberty in a harsh new corporate world.

TRIUMPHANT CAPITALIST VALUES. Despite the rise of the "visible hand" in the Gilded Age business community, traditional liberal values absolutely dominated the thinking of the business culture. Even while they struggled to control market forces, businessmen (and they were almost exclusively men) praised the "natural selection" process that gave them wealth and power. Charles Elliott Perkins, president of the Chicago, Burlington, and Quincy Railroad, for example, pontificated endlessly on the folly of lawmakers bending the laws of trade, never admitting that half his days were consumed in trying to do the same. After bribing politicians, corrupting the courts, falsifying records, swindling investors, and breaking competitors through all manner of extortions, the robber barons never tired of praising natural markets, individual liberty, and freedom of enterprise.

Business values received academic sanction at the hands of social Darwinists such as William Graham Sumner, who explained "scientifically" why some grew rich while many drifted toward poverty. Only the fittest survived, according to a tautological formula in which fitness was measured in well- or ill-gotten wealth. By such a standard, no social failures could be blamed on the business classes. No capitalist could threaten the public interest, because business success defined appropriate social results. Trapped in a cruel parody of earlier values, American entrepreneurs in the Gilded Age found liberal principles turned against them until it seemed that mass dependency and abject poverty were the natural results of a free society.

For those who found sociological justification a bit too harsh, Christian clergymen such as Russell Conwell explained business triumph as the work of the Lord. "To make money honestly is to preach the gospel," proclaimed this Philadelphia Baptist. Furthermore, "ninety-

The Vanderbilt family's summer cottage, called The Breakers, was just one example of conspicuous consumption by millionaires of the Gilded Age.

eight out of one hundred of the rich men in America are honest. That is why they are rich" ("Acres of Diamonds," quoted in Ray Ginger, *Age of Excess*, p. 281). Some extraordinary characters sincerely believed in this gospel of wealth; Carnegie wrote books on the theme and poured much of his fortune into philanthropies that alone, he argued, justified riches. Yet the most pious of the moguls stubbornly ignored the parts they played in creating conditions of squalor about them.

For lighter diversion, Horatio Alger cranked out over one hundred popular novels in which heroes like "Ragged Dick" propelled themselves from "rags to riches." These remarkable celebrations of the self-made man invariably keyed the heroes' success to benevolent sponsorship or outrageous good fortune—a plot device that mimicked reality all too accurately. Astonishingly, considering the ambivalence with which Americans beheld their business leaders, Alger's readers seemed not to recognize the irony in stories that elevated one (and only one) lucky boy to the top of the heap.

CLASS AND CONSPICUOUS CONSUMPTION. In reality, neither natural selection nor pluck and luck determined who got rich and who did not in late-nineteenth-century business. Except for Andrew Carnegie (always the exception), the very rich of the Gilded Age came mostly from a preexisting class of elites who enjoyed family connections, capital assets, education, and leisure reaching back to the Civil War. Rockefeller and certain railroad schemers, such as Jay Gould and Jim Fisk, multiplied their original, modest, assets through dishonest (or dishonorable) gambits. Most business leaders, however, hurried to cultivate respectable appearances. The unfortunate Gould, who seemed particularly nasty, found himself ostracized by peers who sacrificed him to the sharks of popular criticism.

Criticism mounted, too, as millionaires flashed their money. Ideologically prepared to doubt the honesty of railroad magnates and industrial monopolists, Americans watched in amazement as the superrich built extraordinary town houses in New York, bought extravagant furniture and clothing, threw lavish parties, served outrageous delicacies, and built fabulous summer "cottages" by the shore. Multimillion-dollar dwellings lined the sea walk at Newport, Rhode Island, the "castles" of the Vanderbilts, Rockefellers, and others of this new American royalty.

In 1899, Thorstein Veblen blasted such "conspicuous consumption," and the entire business culture, in his *The Theory of the Leisure Class.* His was not the first critical voice, by any means: for a generation of activists and essayists—Henry George, Eugene V. Debs, and Henry Demarest Lloyd, to name just three—had been denouncing the excesses of "wealth against commonwealth." Veblen, however, broke free of contemporary rhetoric, stripping bare his subjects with anthropological detachment, driving home a functional analysis of the economic system and the class structure that echoed John Locke's appreciation for the state of nature.

Veblen's writings punctured the capitalists' self-satisfaction and exposed the distortions of language and perception that inhibited cultural criticism. Yet nothing seemed to change as a result. Established economists and sociologists rushed to minimize the damage, and businessmen simply ignored Veblen. Political radicals continued to hope that sheer numbers in a democratic culture would eventually bring power to the people. The middle classes beheld the spectacle of Gilded Age capitalism with a mixture of envy and admiration. As long as liberal values survived in the minds of middling proprietors, the glitter of Newport and uptown Manhattan kept petty capitalists in the game.

Thorstein Veblen's Theory of the Leisure Class, *written with an anthropologist's detachment, provided a functional analysis of America's capitalist system and class structure that echoed John Locke's appreciation for the state of nature.*

HOW NARROW THE PORTAL? In retrospect we can see that the window of opportunity in American business grew narrower throughout the nineteenth century. By the exercise of liberty and innovation in relatively unrestricted markets, individuals accumulated property and power, which brought others into increased dependency. At times such gains were illegitimate, even by the standards of the day, and once ahead, people often cheated to protect their positions; but much of the economic hierarchy resulted from successful competition in the marketplace. When giant firms in the Gilded Age began to prey upon the business class itself, critics inside the business culture began to ask if the age of enterprise was passing. If so, was the experiment of liberty endangered?

Women, blacks, and American Indians no doubt could see the question coming, because the promise of liberty never had extended fully to these dependent, "inferior" classes. Women had entered the story as "surplus labor" in Alexander Hamilton's *Report on the Subject of Manufactures*, and while many individual women played business roles and whole troops of women labored in the work force, women never gained equal rights as entrepreneurs. African Americans found entrepreneurial opportunities strictly limited by universal race discrimination. Black entrepreneurs often thrived in special industries or sectors that catered to the black community, but always the frontiers of opportunity were bounded by the interests of the dominant culture. As wards of the federal government under the reservation system, most American Indians were "protected" (read "excluded") from the enterprise system. The 1887 Dawes Act, intended to integrate them into the commercial economy as proprietors, cruelly exposed new Indian landholders to unscrupulous white speculators.

American Jews participated more successfully in business, yet Anglo-Saxon capitalists never failed to stereotype their character. Some of the most successful New York bankers endured personal insults and social exclusion because they were Jews. In the final decades of the nineteenth century, when eastern European Jews poured in through the gates of immigration, anti-Semitism grew significantly more ugly. In fact, Americans harbored prejudices against a wide variety of ethnic groups. In *How the Other Half Lives* (1890), Jacob Riis, himself a Scandinavian immigrant and a reformer out to improve the lot of New York's urban poor, nevertheless published nasty caricatures of "Shylock" Jews, drunken Irishmen, and passionate, knife-wielding Italians.

Even white Anglo-Saxon Protestants paused to wonder, by 1900, if opportunities were declining. Main Street entrepreneurs felt besieged by huge suppliers, carriers, and competitors who dictated the terms of business. Middle managers by the thousands carried out millions of transactions on behalf of corporate directors who seemed increasingly powerful and few in number. Even consumers, whose preference for cheap, plentiful goods had helped "elect" the new captains of industry, found that once established, monopolistic firms could disregard their interest in quality, style, or price. The people still elected their governors, but business orthodoxy admitted no legitimate role for government in business. If business set the terms of most people's lives, and if the visible hand of management took over business systems, how could liberty—or even enterprise—prevail?

Epilogue: The American Century

How could liberty and enterprise prevail? This question stalked Americans relentlessly in the second century of national existence. In the twentieth century Americans perfected a consumer economy and a widespread popular mythology that, by the 1950s, offered the "American Dream" as the very definition of human freedom. Three themes illustrate the evolution of the American business culture in the twentieth century. First, to tame the business cycle, politicians and private bankers gradually developed systems of monetary and fiscal policy designed to mediate the forces of the marketplace. Second, in pursuit of profits, individual firms grew large and bureaucratic, diversified their lines, expanded overseas, and articulated professional management systems. Third, to make a living, more and more Americans surrendered their farms, small shops, and domestic duties in favor of wage or salaried positions, swelling the "labor" pool to include middle- and upper-class men and women. What bound this nation of employees together was not so much the earning as the spending of money. In the popular mind, capitalism became of system of buying goods and services. By the end of another century of business evolution, Americans found themselves unbelievably affluent by world standards, yet frustrated by inequalities, dangerously unsure of how their economic system functioned, disappointed in the performance of both government and business, and profoundly insecure.

TAMING THE BUSINESS CYCLE. The first achievement of the twentieth century, that redounded to everybody's benefit, was the relative taming of the business cycle. Throughout the nineteenth century, financial panics sparked by crises in the monetary system had pitched the economy into serious depressions. Uncertain how to create an elastic but sound form of currency, American bankers and entrepreneurs clung to the gold standard and weathered storms that produced more social misery with each repetition. By 1907 private bankers such as J. Pierpont Morgan had found that they could prop up the financial pyramid during moments of business anxiety, and in 1913 Congress created the Federal Reserve System to do the same. This network of twelve regional bankers' banks created a common reserve currency that could be loaned to member banks to stem emergencies. Part fiscal agency, part central bank, the new "Fed" acquired in the course of a generation both the power and expertise to manage the American money supply, but not without some painful failures along the way.

The Fed was too new, or too perversely wedded to "hard money" doctrines, to prevent the 1929 crash of American—and world—capitalism. For years Wall Street's bull market vacuumed up investment cash and bank credits, drawing even country banks and small town investors into high-risk speculative purchases. When confidence collapsed, the value of securities evaporated and the downward spiral drained the banking system of money—most painfully the savings accounts of frugal, hardworking people. Contrary to everyone's expectations, the Great Depression grew more severe for three full years. Unemployment rose to a high of 25 percent, the quoted value of all Wall Street stocks plummeted 83 percent, stores and factories closed or cut their hours; yet no automatic mechanism checked the unfolding disaster. Beginning in 1933, President Franklin D. Roosevelt's New Deal measures—the Bank "Holiday," the Federal Deposit Insurance Corporation, the Gold Reserve Act, the Securities and Exchange Commission, all kinds of relief and public works programs, and finally the Social Security Act—dramatically (if often accidentally) expanded the money supply and rekindled confidence among business and household consumers. Strong recovery marked the years 1933–1937, but so great was the damage that full confidence in economic growth did not return until the mobilization for World War II.

The lessons of mobilization during two world wars, together with the experience of interwar boom and bust and the fear of renewed stagnation, convinced postwar American politicians that the automatic workings of the gold standard, the business cycle, and even free competition did not guarantee acceptable levels of social welfare. Postwar demobilization programs, such as the G.I. Bill of Rights, aimed at reconverting the wartime economy without shocks to domestic prosperity. Partial remobilization for the cold war kept the federal government in the marketplace as an enormously important consumer, while the Truman and Eisenhower administrations cautiously manipulated social security benefits and taxes for countercyclical purposes. Beginning with the 1964 Kennedy Tax Cut and Lyndon Johnson's Great Society programs, the hand of government boldly maneuvered money and credit policies, public works, entitlements and transfers, taxes, and all kinds of subsidies and incentives, always seeking to stimulate growth, relieve inequities, encourage enterprise, preserve consumer and investor confidence, improve the quality of life, and protect Americans from enemies (real and imagined) at home and abroad.

Contrary to expectations, the Great Depression grew more severe between 1929 and 1932: Unemployment rose to a high of 25 percent, the value of Wall Street stocks fell by 83 percent, and stores and factories closed or cut their hours.

The results of these countercyclical government policies proved frustrating, especially as the cold war arms race, a shooting war in Vietnam, and external shocks such as the 1973 Arab oil embargo inflated the costs of these experiments without achieving the desired effects. A popular backlash, encouraged in the 1980s by President Ronald Reagan, brought significant deregulation to the banking system, airlines, telecommunications, and other businesses, as well as a natiowide taxpayers' revolt. Most recently, corrupt practices on Wall Street, savings and loan bankruptcies, rising unemployment, and consumer malaise have reminded Americans how much they depend on regulatory agencies, federal deposit insurance, and other modern tools of economic management for their confidence in the capitalist system.

BUREAUCRACY AND THE MODERN FIRM. Corporate strategies, a second theme illustrating major trends in twentieth-century business, favored more growth and bureaucratization to handle complex operations. Besides practicing the vertical integration and the horizontal combination perfected during the Gilded Age, center firms in the new century began to diversify into new product lines that exploited similar processes, materials, or technologies. Highly efficient new management structures, pioneered in the 1920s at DuPont and General Motors, decentralized operations among nearly autonomous divisions, while top management kept control of finance and strategic planning. Elaborate statistical controls made it possible for cost accountants to measure the efficiency of every step in a complex manufacturing process, while decentralized command identified those to hold accountable among hundreds of corporate servants.

Diversified companies triggered no antitrust watchdogs because they did not monopolize any one line of products; still, giant multidivisional, multifunctional corporations gained internal control over many transactions that would have taken place in open markets, thereby suppressing competition where it mattered most. Full-time research and development laboratories fed new product and process ideas into such companies, while increasingly professional (and effective) advertising analyzed and stimulated markets for finished products. By the 1950s, experts in finance and organization began building huge conglomerates out of companies with almost nothing in common. Beatrice, for example, a Nebraska creamery that in the 1890s pioneered brand name butter, eventually diversified into eight thousand product lines! Of course the leaders of such corporations knew more about stocks, bonds, and bank loans than they knew about butter (or any product). Finance capitalism, a game of speculative harvest invented by Gilded Age titans such as Jay Gould, and played so disastrously in the Roaring Twenties, experienced glorious reincarnation during the merger mania of the late 1960s, and the junk bond scams of the 1980s.

Overseas expansion of American business followed naturally from the growth of the firm, the decentralization of management, and the rise of American influence in the markets of the world. The earliest multinational firms (Singer Sewing Machine, Standard Oil) moved overseas to better serve distribution, sales, and service of their products. In the twentieth century, American companies invested overseas to help finance expanding sales, to rebuild war-torn trading partners, to develop resources such as oil, rubber, or fruits, and to exploit populations of low-paid workers. American companies invested most heavily in industrialized Canada and Europe, and in nearby Latin America; but with the decline of formal empires after World War II, American firms moved quickly into Middle Eastern, African, Indian, and Asian markets. Liberal economists such as Walt W. Rostow (whose *The Stages of Economic Growth: A Non-Communist Manifesto* first appeared in 1960) declared a new capitalist millennium, that promised to place "third world" peoples on the sure road to modernization and prosperity.

Unfortunately, the potential for corruption in foreign investment proved enormous, especially when undemocratic regimes eagerly traded valuable franchises, unique resources, or the welfare of their people for American dollars and military hardware. Cold war competition between Marxist and capitalist countries and the rising tide of post-colonial revolutions encouraged the United States government to support and protect business investments that secured friendly relations, protected strategic resources, or thwarted the enemy's influence around the globe. Thus cloaked in patriotic rhetoric, terribly exploitative deals were struck in the name of democracy and the "free world." Government and business alike deflected criticism of their unholy collaborations in Guatemala, Iran, or Venezuela (to name three) as "communist propaganda." By 1970, however, even scholars at the Harvard Business School had begun to question the character of multinational enterprise, and some abuses had been exposed.

If business seemed to be running the world, it became less clear in the twentieth century who was running American business. Back in the Gilded Age, everybody knew the names of leading business tycoons; but by the 1930s a class of professional managers—men (rarely women) who did not own the firm or even necessarily understand the business, but who managed the assets for salaries—had taken control of corporate boardrooms. Herbert Hoover early noticed that public corporations technically were owned by thousands of individual shareholders, a "democratic" tendency he celebrated in a 1922 booklet entitled *American Individualism.* In 1932, more critical analysts Adolf A. Berle and Gardiner C. Means published a detailed study, *The Modern Corporation and Private Property,* that documented the separation of ownership and control. Passive shareholders increasingly left managerial decisions to salaried executives and became mere constituents, like consumers of products, to be satisfied with quarterly dividends. Such an arrangement encouraged executives to favor security over risk and to adopt strategies that paid high salaries and dividends regardless of market conditions. Today, critics as diverse as junk-bond wizard Michael Milken, billionaire entrepreneur H. Ross Perot, and management specialist W. Edwards Deming all charge that American executives have paid themselves millions to mismanage other people's property and destroyed American competitiveness in the process.

WORKING FOR A LIVING. If there has been a decline of entrepreneurship among American business leaders, it has been more than matched by the transformation of almost everybody into employees. In 1900, about half the American work force worked for pay; the other half owned their own businesses (mostly farms). By 1970, 85 percent of the entire work force (93 percent of the nonfarm sector) turned up on somebody's payroll! Americans in the twentieth century increasingly faced the marketplace not as capitalists but as workers. Yet this nation of workers did not develop a working-class view of the world or the business system. Even organized labor, which gained a powerful bargaining position during and after World War II, never seriously attacked the capitalist system. Although twentieth-century Americans no longer owned the means of production, they continued to think like proprietors, and they sought through income the security and comfort they used to enjoy as entrepreneurs.

Ethnic and racial diversity contributed in part to this bourgeois outlook. Before 1920, the worst cutthroat competition for jobs took place inside urban immigrant communities while native-born Americans still owned farms or practiced skilled trades. The flood of new immigrants, averaging about one million per year from 1905 to 1914, frightened the natives and sparked restrictive legislation in the 1920s that abruptly reduced this flow. At the same time, up to two million persons annually left farms for America's cities, adding new black and white workers with varying skills to the burgeoning urban workforce. Better education, English language skills, and racial discrimination generally lifted Anglo-Saxon whites to the top of labor markets, while prejudicial attitudes and settlement patterns sharply divided communities of workers into hostile competitive subgroups. Spurred by civic reformers to seek respectability in frugal habits and property, successful laborers bought homes and quickly attached (or transferred) proprietary values to this new form of family estate. Almost nothing in this process of individual striving fostered a culture of solidarity or alternative working-class values.

Mechanization, automation, and the evolution of wholly new industries spelled opportunity for these ambitious, urbanizing masses (even while it dislodged established workers from skilled or semiskilled positions). Average real income of employees increased steadily after 1900, and in the 1920s wage-earners gained another 30 percent, while consumer prices remained essentially static. Not everybody enjoyed average income, of course, and a great proportion of profits remained in the hands of the capitalists; but for a majority of workers before the Great Depression, prospects had improved and promised to continue. Not surprisingly, union membership actually dropped after 1920 and remained unchanged until the rise of industrial unions in the middle 1930s.

As America's middle class swelled within suburbia, so did enclosed malls, where major department stores, smaller shops, restaurants, and movie theaters beckoned customers to enjoy shopping in air-conditioned comfort.

The Great Depression blasted the high hopes of American workers and called into question the capacity of business to provide jobs for the population. National unemployment figures masked disastrous conditions in major industrial cities: unemployment in Toledo, Ohio, topped out at 80 percent! Angry workers denounced the capitalists whose recklessness had produced such misery, and labor organizers encountered their most receptive American audience in a generation. Local governments and New Deal programs distributed millions in relief; but President Roosevelt (like most conservative businessmen) hated doling out money, and federal legislation tried to focus on getting people back to work. Section 7a of the National Industrial Recovery Act (1933) encouraged the formation of industrial unions powerful enough to bargain with organized capital, and the Wagner Act (1935), creating the National Labor Relations Board, admitted big labor to the national policy table. Between 1937 and 1939, Congress of Industrial Organization (CIO) affiliates won recognition for steel workers, miners, and auto workers—most dramatically in sit-down strikes at General Motors, violently at Ford Motor Company and Republic Steel. Overall, union membership doubled between 1935 and 1937, then doubled again by 1953, to an all-time high of 25 percent of the labor force.

The success of big labor during and after World War II, coupled with rising progressive income taxes and social security transfers affected a slight redistribution of wealth from the top to the middle classes of American society—not as great as wounded conservatives in the 1950s pretended, but enough to help reestablish middle-class aspirations among the majority of American workers. The real bonus came from unprecedented economic growth: from 1945 to 1970, the American gross national product doubled, as did average household consumption (despite a 46 percent increase in population). American business seemed miraculously cured of whatever ailed it in the 1930s. Important causes of the postwar boom could be found in defense outlays (rising to 9 percent of GNP) and government welfare spending (almost 15 percent of GNP by 1970) for housing, education, medical care, job training, and family income support. Nobody fully understood this complex economy, but as long as it grew and tried to include the lower classes, not very many complained.

Rising expectations more than matched rising incomes as postwar families swelled the American middle class. Buying and trading homes, buying and trading cars, and shopping for goods and furnishings became favorite pastimes in themselves. Enclosed malls sprang up near suburban subdivisions, where major retail department stores together with dozens of shops, restaurants, boutiques, and movie theaters beckoned customers to enjoy evening and Sunday shopping, in air-conditioned comfort, with acres of free parking. This latest consumer revolution stimulated both construction and retail service sectors in nearly every local economy (often ruining downtown business districts in the process). A new generation, the "baby boomers," knew nothing of the Great Depression but came of age at a time when jobs seemed secure, incomes *always* rose, and spending came too easily. Such was the American way of life at the height of the cold war, and unless attacked by maniacal Russian communists, American business seemed capable of perpetuating the fun indefinitely.

AFFLUENCE AND INSECURITY. In the 1960s, women staged a feminist revolt, demanding equal pay and equal access to careers traditionally pursued by men; blacks turned up the heat of their attack on racial segregation; and college students mounted angry assaults on business and government for involvement in the Vietnam War. Besieged with contradictory demands, the federal government under presidents Kennedy and Johnson tried to finance guns *and* butter out of economic growth. After 1965, the resulting inflation began to erode prosperity; but the feminist movement brought millions of women into paid employment in time for their earnings to help counteract downward pressures on many people's standard of living. Single-income households, working mothers with children, unskilled or marginal workers (among whom blacks and minorities were represented disproportionately) suffered steady degradation. Unemployment (except during certain war years) persisted throughout the postwar expansion at between 4 and 7 percent, and this stubborn level of joblessness excluded a subclass of chronically unemployed persons no longer looking for work. Everyone ignored the frustrating hardships of the working poor—upwards of fifty million people in what Michael Harrington as early as 1962 called "the other America." In a modern nation of employees, a rising number of individuals and families not only held no property, but they could not find a job.

According to Harrington, poverty in modern America was more pernicious for being "invisible." Because of the postwar boom, America's masses no longer were poor, and it became easier for business, government, and ordinary taxpayers to blame the victims of chronic poverty. Economist John Kenneth Galbraith once warned in *The Affluent Society* (1958) that economic theories designed around classic conditions of scarcity might ill-serve an age of abundance; however, it remained unclear by the 1990s whether economic thought or abundance itself had failed to sustain the American Dream. A decade of "Reaganomics"—recycled versions of supply-side policies first recommended to President Kennedy—had not produced desired levels of real growth or retired the national debt. If the collapse of worldwide communism yielded a "peace dividend" at home, it remained to be seen where and how to redeploy those resources. Confronting public debts in the trillions of dollars, burdened with consumer charges, frustrated by the cruel failure of antipoverty and welfare programs, staggered by health care inflation, frightened by a rising underclass at home and stiff competition from abroad (especially Japan), and bombarded by shrill voices of criticism at every gesture, Americans slipped into a blue mood as they contemplated the end of the "American century."

Advice abounded from all perspectives. In *Workforce 2000*, published by the conservative Hudson Institute (1987), William B. Johnson and Arnold H. Packer predicted a steady deindustrialization of the economy, with a corresponding rise in service jobs, presistent unemployment for the unskilled and a graying and increasingly female work force. Productivity gains in service industries, they argued, were the key to future growth. For the liberal Brookings Institution, Robert Z. Lawrence asked *Can America Compete?* (1984). His answer was yet, because America was *not* deindustrializing. Reduce the federal deficit to correct trade imbalances, he argues, and growth would follow. W. Edwards Deming, in *Out of the Crisis* (1986), blamed the American management system for demoralizing workers, rewarding inept bureaucrats, and corrupting corporate executives. Where these and other prophets, armed with alternative histories and theories, would lead American business in the twenty-first century cannot yet be discerned. Our historical commitment to liberty and enterprise seemed likely to endure, yet in their affluence Americans remained not happy but insecure.

[See also The Aristocracy of Inherited Wealth; The Culture of Consumption; Technology and Social Change.]

BIBLIOGRAPHY

General Works

Blackford, Mansel G., and K. Austin Kerr. *Business Enterprise in American History*, 2d ed. (1990).

Chandler, Alfred D., Jr. *The Visible Hand: The Managerial Revolution in American Business* (1977).

Hall, Kermit L. *The Magic Mirror: Law in American History* (1989).

Hounshell, David A. *From the American System to Mass Production, 1800–1932* (1984).

Hurst, James Willard. *Law and Markets in United States History: Different Modes of Bargaining Among Interests* (1982).

Laurie, Bruce. *Artisans into Workers: Labor in Nineteenth-Century America* (1989).

Scheiber, Harry N. "Federalism and the American Economic Order, 1789–1910." *Law and Society Review* 10 (1975): 57–118.

Business in 1800

Clark, Christopher. "Household Economy, Market Exchange and the Rise of Capitalism in the Connecticut Valley, 1800–1860." *Journal of Social History* 13 (1979):169–189.

Doerflinger, Thomas M. *A Vigorous Spirit of Enterprise: Merchants and Economic Development in Revolutionary Philadelphia* (1986).

Jensen, Joan. *Loosening the Bonds: Mid-Atlantic Farm Women, 1750–1850* (1986).

Mitchell, Robert D. *Commercialism and Frontier: Perspectives on the Early Shenandoah Valley* (1977).

Tryon, Rolla M. *Household Manufactures in the United States, 1640–1860* (1917).

Ulrich, Laura Thatcher. *A Midwifes Tale: The Life of Martha Ballard, Based on Her Diary, 1785–1812* (1990).

Revolutionary Ideology

McCoy, Drew R. *The Elusive Republic: Political Economy in Jeffersonian America* (1980).
McDonald, Forrest. *Novus Ordo Seclorum: The Intellectual Origins of the Constitution* (1985).
Matson, Cathy D., and Peter S. Onuf. *A Union of Interests: Political and Economic Thought in Revolutionary America* (1990).
Nelson, John R., Jr. *Liberty and Property: Political Economy and Policymaking in the New Nation, 1789–1812* (1987).

Antebellum Business

Albion, Robert Greenhalgh. *The Rise of New York Port, 1815–1869* (1939; repr. 1961).
Blewett, Mary H. *Men, Women, and Work: Class, Gender, and Protest in the New England Shoe Industry, 1780–1910* (1988).
Clark, Christopher. *The Roots of Rural Capitalism: Western Massachusetts, 1780–1860* (1990).
Cochran, Thomas C. *Frontiers of Change: Early Industrialism in America* (1981).
Faragher, John Mack. *Sugar Creek: Life on the Illinois Prairie* (1986).
Hammond, Bray. *Banks and Politics in America, from the Revolution to the Civil War* (1957).
Handlin, Oscar, and Mary Flug Handlin. *Commonwealth: A Study of the Role of Government in the American Economy: Massachusetts, 1774–1861.* (Rev. ed. 1969).
Johnson, Paul E. *A Shopkeeper's Millennium: Society and Revivals in Rochester, New York, 1815–1837* (1978).
Scranton, Philip. *Proprietary Capitalism: The Textile Manufacture at Philadelphia, 1800–1885* (1983).
Stansell, Christine. *City of Women: Sex and Class in New York, 1789–1860* (1986).
Tucker, Barbara M. *Samuel Slater and the Origins of the American Textile Industry, 1790–1860* (1984).
Wilentz, Sean. *Chants Democratic: New York and the Rise of the American Working Class, 1788–1850* (1984).

Era of Big Business

Fine, Sidney. *Laissez-Faire and the General Welfare State* (1964).
Ginger, Ray. *The Age of Excess: The United States from 1877 to 1914.* 2d ed. (1975).
Kirkland, Edward C. *Dream and Thought in the Business Community, 1860–1900* (1956).
Lamoreaux, Naomi. *The Great Merger Movement in American Business, 1895–1904* (1985).
Larson, John Lauritz. *Bonds of Enterprise: John Murray Forbes and Western Development in America's Railway Age* (1984).
Livesay, Harold C. *Andrew Carnegie and the Rise of Big Business* (1975).
McCraw, Thomas K. *Prophets of Regulation* (1984).
Porter, Glenn. *The Rise of Big Business, 1860–1910* (1973).
Sklar, Martin J. *The Corporate Reconstruction of American Capitalism, 1890–1916* (1988).
Thomas, John L. *Alternative America: Henry George, Edward Bellamy, Henry Demarest Lloyd and the Adversary Tradition* (1983).

Twentieth Century

Barnet, Richard J., and Romand E. Müller. *Global Reach: The Power of the Multinational Corporations* (1974).
Berle, Adolph A., and Gardiner C. Means. *The Modern Corporation and Private Property* (1933; rev. ed., 1968).
Bernstein, Michael A. *The Great Depression: Delayed Recovery and Economic Change in America, 1929–1939* (1987).
Boesky, Ivan. *Merger Mania: Arbitrage, Wall Street's Best Kept Money-making Secret* (1985).
Chandler, Alfred D., Jr. *Strategy and Structure: Chapters in the History of the American Industrial Enterprise* (1962).
Collins, Robert M. *The Business Response to Keynes, 1929–1964* (1981).
Deming, W. Edwards. *Out of the Crisis* (1986).
Dengen, Robert A. *The American Monetary System: A Concise Survey of Its Evolution Since 1896* (1987).
Galbraith, John Kenneth. *The Affluent Society* (1958; rev. ed. 1984).
Harrington, Michael. *The Other America: Poverty in the United States* (1962; rev. ed. 1981).
Kindleberger, Charles R. *Multinational Excursions* (1984).
Rostow, Walt W. *The Stages of Economic Growth: A Non-Communist Manifesto* (1960; 2d ed. 1971).
Schwartz, John E. *America's Hidden Success: A Reassessment of Public Policy from Kennedy to Reagan* (1988).
Vernon, Raymond. *Sovereignty at Bay: The Multinational Spread of U.S. Enterprises* (1971).

— JOHN LAURITZ LARSON

C

CHILDHOOD AND CHILDREN

Children's experience over the course of American history evolved in response to changes in the family and to new ideas about childhood as a stage of life. It also varied according to geographic location, gender, class, race, and ethnicity. While the current cultural category of childhood, with its assumptions about children's vulnerability, malleability, and dependence on parental love, is believed by many to be an invention of the early-nineteenth-century bourgeois family, throughout American history the experience of those younger than age twelve has always differed from that of other age groups.

The Colonial Era

Settlers of seventeenth-century New England towns recognized childhood as a separate stage of life. Preacher Gilbert Tennent noted four stages of life in a 1741 sermon: "old and aged Persons"; "middle-ag'd People, of thirty Years old and upwards"; "my younger Brethren, of fourteen years and upwards," and "little children, of six Years old and upwards," leaving out children under age six. In the seventeenth and eighteenth centuries, early childhood was brief, and historians find evidence of its end in changing patterns of dress: boys and girls, who had dressed in similar long robes that opened down the front, by age six or eight began to dress much like their parents.

Infant mortality rates varied by region in the seventeenth-century colonies. In the healthiest areas of New England, only one child in ten died before its first birthday, whereas in the Chesapeake region the rate was one infant in four. In the malaria-prone parts of the middle and southern colonies, as many as one child in three died in the first year of life.

In contrast, the likelihood of the death of an infant or the early death of a parent was a frightening dimension of seventeenth-century family life in the Chesapeake. The norm in the region was that one or both of their parents would die before the children were old enough to care for themselves. The death of one parent often led to remarriage by the surviving spouse, resulting in complex relationships between children and stepparents and stepbrothers and -sisters. Fear of infant mortality and early parental death created some emotional detachment, especially among parents in the South, where premature death was more common, but it did not prevent the emergence of the typical strong and loving bond between parent and child throughout the colonies during the seventeenth and eighteenth centuries.

In all of the colonies, most mothers breast-fed their infants for the first twelve to eighteen months. While very young, babies often slept in their parents' bed; later, they were transferred to their own cradle or to a trundle bed shared with siblings. New England Puritan families were quite large, with an average of eight children, and surrounding the infant with warmth and comfort. After the tranquility of the first year of life, the baby's existence was disrupted by two events: weaning and the arrival of a new sibling. Weaning is said to have been done quite abruptly after the infant's first year. Sometimes the mother applied a bitter substance to her breast to curb the infant's desire to suck; other mothers left the household entirely for several days in order to stop nursing. Then, by the time the infant was two, a new baby generally arrived, further shifting the mother's attention from the child.

Literature on Puritan child rearing emphasized the importance of curbing the child's will from roughly the second year of life. This process related to the centrality of ideas of original sin—the belief that newborn infants embodied sin and depravity—in the Puritan mind. Confronting a child's self-assertions and aggression was a crucial parental duty necessary to winning God's grace and achieving salvation for the child. This beating down of the child's early efforts at autonomy instilled a lasting sense of shame and doubt that left its imprint on the adult Puritan community. Less harshness is evident in the scant sources on childrearing in the South, where parents tended to indulge their young children, delighting in their play and lavishing them with affection. White children in the South moved freely on the plantation and enjoyed the companionship of neighboring children; all efforts were geared toward nurturing autonomous, self-reliant children.

Donning adult clothing between the ages of six and eight symbolized a new status for the child—the end of early childhood and the beginning of childhood proper. Though some historians contend that this transition marked the end of childhood and the initiation into "miniature adulthood," rich evidence suggests that childhood lasted until the stage of youth referred to by

Tennant, when at age twelve or fourteen the child was prepared to leave home. The years from age six to the early teens were, however, less sheltered than childhood today, since children began to assume productive roles within the self-sufficient household economy by age six or seven. Boys learned farming and fence making from their fathers, and girls learned cooking, spinning, and cloth making from their mothers. Parents provided whatever academic training children received in these years, with special emphasis on instruction in religion. Society's recognition of the immaturity of children roughly below the age of fourteen is indicated by the fact that it was highly unusual for pre-teenage children to experience a religious conversion signifying God's grace through personal faith. However, by age fourteen, or sometimes younger, children were "bound out" as apprentices to other families.

Changes in society in the eighteenth century led to important transformations in the experience of children. In New England, the strictly hierarchical Puritan social order gave way as population growth placed pressure on available land. This forced sons either to leave home to find land elsewhere or to enter the emerging commercial economy. These situations separated children from parents, both geographically and psychologically, weakening parental authority.

In addition, by the mid eighteenth century the philosophers of the European Enlightenment promoted new ideas about the nature of children and childhood influencing parents throughout the colonies. In particular, notions of infant depravity gave way to ideas of the unique needs and impulses of children. Both John Locke's concept of the child's mind as a blank slate and Jean-Jacques Rousseau's celebration of childhood innocence emphasized the child's malleability. These ideas led parents to use the childhood years as preparation for responsible adulthood by developing their children's conscience and capacity for self-reliance.

The special children's toys and literature that appeared in the late eighteenth century reflected this new recognition of childhood as a distinctive stage of life. The use of pastel colors in furniture and pictures designed for children, with fantasy animals and images from nursery rhymes, all reflect the new concept of childhood as a time of play and innocence.

Childhood for Native American and African American children in the seventeenth and eighteenth centuries differed from the experience of colonial white children. When the English settlers arrived in North America in the seventeenth century, there were between 850,000 and two million Native Americans living throughout the continent. Most Indian families were small because of high infant and child death rates and because the practice of breast-feeding babies for two or more years suppressed fertility. While the significance of other practices is disputed, some indicate the variety of Native American attitudes toward children: for example, in some tribes children were born in a special birth hut, located some distance from the family's home. Often, newborns were rubbed with animal oil or dipped in cold water. Infants of several months were initiated into their tribe in a special ceremony at which they were given their name. Some tribes also had rituals that included piercing the child's nose or earlobes.

In some Indian tribes, child rearing was the exclusive responsibility of mothers or grandmothers; in others, uncles, grandfathers, and other male relatives had a critical role as mentors and disciplinarians. Indians disciplined their children by praising and publicly rewarding good behavior and shaming and ridiculing children for misbehavior. They believed these methods produced

Young Indian boys learned to fish, hunt game, and gather fruits, berries, and nuts, while girls learned to sew by making doll clothes and to farm by raising corn and beans in miniature plots.

independent, self-reliant adults and rarely used corporal punishment, which they felt created timid children. Indian children may have participated in work earlier than white children, since their play was modeled on their parents' work; very young boys learned to fish, hunt game, and gather fruits, berries, and nuts, while girls learned to sew by making doll clothes and to farm by raising corn and beans in miniature plots.

The growing-up process for both Indian girls and Indian boys was marked by puberty rites. At the time of their first menstruation, young girls were isolated for periods of time ranging from several weeks to a year, during which they were cared for by older women and instructed in the duties of adult womanhood. Boys underwent a more extensive series of initiation rites, marking their first tooth, first steps, and first game kill. In many tribes, when a young Indian boy approached puberty, he went alone to a mountaintop or into a forest to fast and seek a vision from a guardian spirit. When the boy returned to the community, he assumed adult status. Maturity for Native American children involved the acquisition of economic skills, cultural heritage, and spiritual awareness; and while these things were understood in ways that differ radically from a non-Indian conception, they nevertheless engendered self-reliance and courage.

The early eighteenth century witnessed the importation of huge numbers of black slaves to the colonies. While in 1675 there were only 4,000 black slaves in the colonies, by 1780, 550,000 Africans had been forcibly brought to the mainland colonies. Improved health and an increasing proportion of female slaves enabled the black population to maintain itself through reproduction by the middle of the eighteenth century. Although slave marriage was not recognized by law, African Americans created a distinctive kinship system under slavery. Slaves conducted their own marriage rituals, and parents named children after themselves, grandparents, or other kin, passing down traditional African family names to their children. These naming patterns reinforced family bonds.

Black mothers in the eighteenth and nineteenth centuries spaced their children closely together and breastfed their infants for at least one year. Newborn slave children were the center of attention and concern, attended by their mother and sometimes by a midwife and visited by their father, the parents' friends, and relatives in the slave community. The plantation overseer and mistress also immediately came to see the new infant, but in their case the visit was to view the plantation owner's new property. Slave mothers generally were granted from two weeks to one month "lying-in time," when they were free from plantation work and able to devote themselves entirely to the new baby. After the lying-in, mothers were permitted to return from the fields several times a day to suckle their infants. Children were nursed for at least a year. Once weaned, young children were cared for by female relatives while parents worked or, in many cases, in communal nurseries. Although in most nurseries children were left to their own devices, on one large Florida plantation an energetic woman ran the nursery like the kindergarten of today, telling stories and inventing imaginative games. At the end of the day, children joined their parents in their cabin and helped prepare the evening meal. In the evening they did chores such as washing, repairing furniture, gardening, sewing, and spinning.

According to some slave narratives, children were protected from the reality of slavery while they were young and often remembered the years before their induction into the master's work force as the happiest time in their lives. "As a barefoot boy," J. Vance Lewis recalled, "my stay upon the farm had been pleasant. I played among the wild flowers and wandered in high glee over hill and hollow, . . . and knew not that I was a slave and the son of a slave." The shelter of childhood ended when, youngsters of age five or six assumed responsibility for infant care; later, between the ages of ten and fourteen, slave children were forced to begin work in the fields. On some plantations, younger children were given lighter tasks advancing from "quarter-hands" to "half-hands" until they were grown and able-bodied and became "full-hands."

Still, slavery imposed serious stresses on the lives of slave children: squalid plantation living quarters often forced slaves to live with nonrelatives, and some children were moved to cabins separate from their parents at anywhere from age seven to ten. Families lived under the constant threat of breakup through sale, and children were frequently sold away from parents. Moreover, slavery undermined the authority of parents: children were forbidden to call their natural mother "mother," forcing them to call the plantation mistress by that title instead. When slave children were punished or abused by slaveholders, parents were unable to help them. In spite of this, parents managed to transmit a sense of family bonds to their children and endeavored to give their children the strength necessary to endure slavery.

The Nineteenth Century

In the North, a sharp drop in marital fertility rates in the early part of the nineteenth century profoundly changed the experience of white children. Several factors converged to create this trend toward fewer births. First, as the population grew, parents no longer had sufficient land to pass on to the next generation, creating an incentive for parents to limit the number of children they had. At the same time, economic life became more specialized, families no longer functioned as economically self-sufficient units, and productive work increasingly occurred in shops and factories outside the home. This meant that children ceased to be economic assets in the agricultural home economy and became increasingly costly to raise. While a typical white woman in 1800 bore seven or eight children, by 1860 she bore only five or six. This decline in fertility continued until the end of the nineteenth century, when the average number of children born to white women declined to three or four. Overall, fertility in the United States declined by one-half between 1800 and 1900.

Smaller size families fit well with new ideas about the nature of childhood; the notion of childhood as a special, malleable stage of life encouraged greater attention to the proper care and development of the individual child. Having fewer children made it easier to nurture each one. With fewer births and the removal of much of domestic production from the home to the factory, women were now free to devote most of their time to rearing their children. Indeed, after 1800, when a father's labor shifted outside the home, the role of the paternal disciplinarian was replaced by that of the maternal nurturer, and child rearing emerged as married women's primary responsibility. The role of mother was glorified by the idea of "republican motherhood," created during the American Revolution, which charged mothers with the vital task of raising capable citizens—especially sons—for the new republic.

These shifts also freed northern white children from their household labors and led children to remain in their parents' homes until their teens and even early twenties. Childhood emerged as a time of leisure and prolonged financial and emotional dependence, devoted specifically to preparation for adulthood. In the model of nurturance that emerged by the 1830s, each mother manipulated the emotional bond between herself and her child to ensure proper behavior in the child. Her chief methods were maternal martyrdom and withdrawal of love. One mother explained to her three-year-old daughter the countless sacrifices she had made on the child's behalf, all the while "caressing her affectionately." Another mother, in an article in *Mother's Magazine* in 1833, described the effectiveness of withdrawal of love in curbing her son's disobedience. When she told her son, "I would not smile upon you, I should not receive your flowers, but should have to separate you from my company," her son responded, I could not be happy if you did not love me." In each case, obedience was ensured by provoking guilt in the child. According to advice written for mothers, moral nurturance demanded constant vigilance and supervision to be effective, as if to ensure that child rearing would take all of the mother's available time. Every aspect of the child's behavior was monitored by the mother, with the goal of lovingly shaping the child's conscience, instilling the preeminent middle-class values of honesty, industry, frugality, and self-control deep within the child's personality.

With children at home under their mother's care and productive labor generally accomplished outside the family, children were socialized into the more sharply defined gender roles that began to characterize society. Daughters were prepared for marriage and the responsibilities of motherhood; they were reared to be chaste, delicate, loving, and emotional and to become self-reliant, nurturing, efficient caretakers. Girls attended school along with boys but grew up in a specifically female world of intense friendship and emotional intimacy. Boys, on the other hand, were raised to be aggressive and assertive in the public sphere but to exhibit gentlemanly self-control and self-restraint within the family.

By the 1840s schools emerged as a setting for socialization, especially into adult occupational roles, mediating between the world of the family and the adult world of work. The need for this kind of socialization was particularly acute for boys. While prior to the 1830s and 1840s, rural boys and girls attended local "winter schools," leaving them free for field work in summer, by the 1840s public elementary schools emerged in Massachusetts, New York, Philadelphia, and the Midwest. Such early schooling was erratic, and by the 1830s reformers were calling for systematic education for all children between the ages of five and sixteen. By mid century, the majority of northern white children between those ages were enrolled in schools.

By the 1850s, schools for younger children had become increasingly formal settings for the inculcation of disciplined habits. Age-graded classes were introduced by mid century, and routines of rote learning were imposed on each age group so that entire classrooms of children stood together as they chanted their lessons. Regimented classes permitted greater behavioral scrutiny and fostered conformity. Carefully graded lessons at school reinforced the mother's moral nurturance at home, and both were designed to enforce the "semi-mechanical" virtues of industry and regularity in middle- and working-class northern children.

The effect of such bourgeois socialization techniques was hardly uniform, and poor children living in northern cities in the 1850s missed its influence entirely. Such children never experienced the emotional world of the protected, private family with its intense maternal attention. Poor children at mid century lived in the public world of the streets, where they gained independence and economic responsibility as young as the age of six or seven; they were sent there by their parents to earn part of their keep and to contribute to the household economy.

The youngest of these children worked as scavengers, gathering salable trash such as cinders, coal, rope, metal, bottles, paper, and even kitchen grease and bad meat. These children learned how to use castoffs to "make something out of nothing" and either brought them home, sold them to neighbors, or peddled them to junk dealers. Older children worked at street peddling or huckstering, selling everything from tea cakes and sweet potatoes to matchsticks, scrub brushes, strings, and pins. Several low-paying trades were specially reserved for children; girls, for example, would sweep street crossings, and for boys it would be running errands, bootblacking, horse holding, and newspaper selling.

Children who worked in the streets far from adult supervision often strayed into illicit pursuits, such as petty theft and prostitution. Such shady activity drew concern from respectable parents who needed the income from their children's work and from reformers who disapproved of the habits of poor families. Street life became crowded and appeared increasingly depraved and dangerous to reformers, since the large influx of Irish and German immigrants in the 1840s made the poor a more visible presence in large cities. The presence of unsupervised children in cities—whether huckster boys whose taste of freedom led them to run away from home, orphans, or gangs of mischievous youth—rubbed sharply against the grain of middle-class notions of domesticity and a sheltered childhood. These children elicited a critique of working-class family life from social reformers, who endeavored to abolish poverty by teaching the poor the virtues of middle-class family life as a means to self-improvement. Charity workers viewed the poor homes they visited with disdain: "Homes . . . if it is not a mockery to give that hallowed name to the dark, filthy hovels where many of them dwell."

Reformers such as Charles Loring Brace, who established the Children's Aid Society in 1853, pioneered new institutional arrangements for dependent and delinquent children. So severe was the middle-class indictment of poor urban childhood that reformers con-

Poor children at mid century lived in the public world of the streets, where they gained independence and economic responsibility as young as the age of six or seven.

sidered the removal of a poor child from its parents to be in the child's best interest. In the 1850s, a new system of foster care placed urban children in rural homes, where they were supposed to not only learn the virtues of hard work by providing labor on the farm but also receive the morally strengthening influence of country life. This placing-out system was used where possible for orphans and juvenile offenders. Institutions that housed delinquents and orphans also underwent changes by mid century. Large houses of refuge established in the 1820s that used corporal punishment to reform youthful criminals were replaced by institutions that attempted to replicate family life through small residential cottages and an emphasis on education and hard work to reshape and reform the delinquent's character.

Another aspect of the late-century reformers' investigation of poor family life was an effort to protect children against family violence. While family violence was not restricted to the poorer classes, wealthier families were able to escape community attention, and in the late nineteenth century violence against wives and children was identified with poorer and immigrant families. Formal efforts at child protection began with the establishment of the first Society for the Protection of Cruelty to Children in New York City in 1874, with similar agencies opening in ten other cities by 1880. The society was created in response to both benevolent desires to protect children and fears among the wealthy, urban elite of social disorder brought about by poverty, drunkenness, and crime. In spite of the society's claim that it placed the protection of children above the preservation of families, parents were rarely prosecuted, and agents often upheld a father's authority by asserting that the "child deserved a beating." The SPCC did intervene in threatening situations and removed a significant number of children from abusive families. Although the agency's establishment represents an important step on behalf of the protection of children, efforts to identify and prosecute child abuse continued to be hampered because of strong cultural beliefs about paternal authority and the privacy of the family.

While middle-class families continued to try to insulate their children from the threatening and disorderly elements of urban life in the second half of the nineteenth century, the experience of children varied in newly settled regions of the country and among the different immigrant groups who brought their distinctive values and traditions to this country. In frontier towns, for example, childhood was hardly sheltered. Youngsters in these new settlements mingled freely among the adults in their midst, many of whom were single and transient, lusting after immediate gratification and seeking their fortunes in the West. The youngest boys and girls—sometimes as young as six—began to work panning gold or selling their mother's pies. Even on the frontier, as children got a little older, tasks were rigidly differentiated according to gender. Young girls began to work at the traditional domestic tasks of cooking, cleaning, and making clothes, whereas boys' work took them away from the household. By the age of twelve or thirteen, boys did the more menial work in mining towns, such as feeding pack mules and pounding out drills in a blacksmith shop, but sometimes even took charge of businesses in the absence of the adult owner.

Work beginning at a young age, frequent contact between young and old, exposure to the seamier side of frontier life, and the difficulty of maintaining adult supervision all meant that frontier children grew up amid disturbing if not corrupting circumstances. In light of this, many parents worked hard to instill in their children habits and values similar to those of children living in the Northeast. Children were given moral and religious instruction in secular and sabbath schools, and parents, as soon they could afford it, pressed for formal education, libraries, and bookstores. In addition, many adults without families took an active interest in the education and upbringing of neglected children. Childhood in frontier towns was an imprecise blending of the realities of the roughness of life in these new communities and efforts both to live up to contemporary notions of child nurturance and to maintain some continuity with older moral lessons that parents had learned in their own youth.

Children of the immigrant groups who came to the United States in the late nineteenth century—Italians, Irish, Slavs, and Jews—were raised according to values and practices brought over from the old country, while both parents and children endeavored to adjust to the conditions of life in their new culture. Ethnic groups varied in birthrates, material circumstances, gender values, attitudes toward education and child labor, and the strength of parental authority over children. In general, first-generation immigrant families tended to have more children than did native-born parents but experienced higher infant mortality, due to inadequate diet and poor sanitary conditions. Decisions on whether to keep children in school or to send them out to work reflected the varying values and the financial circumstances of the immigrants as they adapted to this country. First-generation Italians, for example, made the overall well-being of the family their chief priority. In their struggle for financial security, parents saw children as wage earners rather than as students; thus, rather than keeping their children in school, the offspring were sent to work in their early teens, and married women were not usually permitted to work. This pattern made sense at the turn of the century, when high rates of fertility and infant mortality among Italian families made it unreasonable to invest resources in individual children. By the 1930s, however, lowered infant mortality rates encouraged fewer births and made it possible for Italian parents to make greater investments in individual children, encouraging them to remain in school.

Several low-paying trades were reserved for poor children of the 19th century. Boys sold newspapers and ran errands.

Jewish families, by contrast, were often better off financially in the first generation than were Italian families and thus could afford to forgo the earnings of their children, enabling them to remain in school. Like Italians, Slavic families depended on their children's wages and urged sons and daughters to acquire job skills rather than stay in school. For these children, contributing to family well-being took precedence over their individual success. Later on, in the mid twentieth century, children of Chinese immigrants followed a pattern of high achievement in school similar to that of Eastern European Jews. Chinese families valued education and saw it as a route to upward mobility, keeping their children in school in spite of family poverty.

The Twentieth Century

Around the turn of the twentieth century, the rapid pace of social change gave rise to child saving, new public responses to children. Large-scale population growth, urbanization, and massive economic transformations such as the growth of heavy industry and corporate capitalism all created a desire for control and order and an anxiety about the future, encompassing concern about the well-being of children. These social and economic changes conjured fearful images of social dislocations, such as broken and inadequate families, poverty, dependency and neglect, crime, and immorality, each of which would affect children. The child-saving movement sought both to protect children from such threatening social transformations and to provide them with the benefits of recent discoveries in medicine and the social sciences. The resulting public reforms ranged from compulsory schooling laws, child labor laws, widows' pensions, and the creation of juvenile courts to the establishment of child health clinics, nursery schools, kindergartens, and playgrounds. These reforms combined two strategies—the Progressive tactic of addressing issues of class and urban life through community-wide efforts at broad social improvement and the implementation of programs nurturing individual differences.

The new system of juvenile justice that emerged in the late nineteenth century was designed to separate youthful from adult criminals and to treat young offenders on an individual basis. The first juvenile court was established in Chicago in 1899, although Massachusetts required separate hearings for children's cases as early as the 1870s. By 1920, all but three states had juvenile courts. The new penology that emerged from the juvenile court movement was designed to keep children out of institutions and to educate, treat, and rehabilitate young offenders. Courtroom procedures were informal and designed for "diagnosis" of the causes of criminal activity and the prevention of future crime. Age-segregated detention facilities were provided, and penal sanctions were imposed on neglectful or malicious adults.

Rehabilitative treatment, through the new probation system, centered on the child's home or family. Probation was designed to be educational and tutelary, and the instruction extended to the youth's family on the premise that the rehabilitation of the delinquent depended on the reeducation of the parents. In 1909, a psychiatric clinic was attached to the original Cook County juvenile court with the goal of using psychiatric and psychological insights into human behavior to prevent juvenile crime by investigating the causes of individual delinquency. While the new system of juvenile justice was a landmark achievement of the Progressive movement of the early twentieth century, juvenile crime persisted as a social problem.

With the passage of compulsory schooling laws, after the turn of the century nearly all children attended elementary school from age five to fourteen, and increasing numbers of children remained in school longer. By 1920, 61.2 percent of those age fourteen to seventeen were enrolled in school, and by 1930 the figure had risen to 73.1 percent. An even higher percentage of younger children was enrolled in elementary school. Progressive reforms of public schools accomplished by the 1930s included the use of uniform curricula, structured and expanded extracurricular activities, the decline of rote recitation, the introduction of attractive textbooks, flexible student groupings, and the hiring of better trained teachers. Public schooling emerged as a mechanism through which to fit individuals into the economy; educators believed that teaching specific skills and behavior patterns would create efficient workers and good citizens. Many scholars emphasize that urban school reform was imposed from above by business classes and directed at controlling poor and minority children in order to maintain their lower-class position in the industrial order. But in many communities, labor and immigrant groups played their own hands in school reforms and used education to enhance the economic welfare of their children.

Federal efforts on behalf of children after the turn of the century included the White House Conference on Care of Dependent Children of 1909, which led to the creation of the Federal Children's Bureau in 1912. The Children's Bureau began with a focus on child labor legislation and broad issues of child health. The bureau's efforts culminated in the passage of the Sheppard-Towner Act in 1921. This landmark legislation extended the state's responsibility in matters of social welfare by providing federal funds for infant and maternal health care.

The child health movement of the 1920s, funded privately but promoted by the Children's Bureau, created local child health clinics that offered to children examinations and vaccinations and provided advice to mothers on caring for their children's health. Child guidance clinics emerged in the 1920s, as an outgrowth of the first court-affiliated psychiatric clinic. Child guidance clinics were initially designed to prevent mental illness by offering psychiatric and psychological examinations, but after the 1930s they became community facilities offering short-term psychotherapeutic treatment for normal children who exhibited mild behavioral or emotional problems. Taken together, all of these efforts significantly extended the authority of the state in the protection of children; they buttressed the role of the family as the proper place for the care and, if necessary, the rehabilitation of children, and they established novel institutions designed exclusively to meet the needs of individual children.

Within the family, fewer births and the infusion of new "scientific" child rearing advice changed childhood and relations between parents and children. In 1890, more than half of families in all occupational groups had three or more children, although people in the professions and in business had fewer children than members of the other classes. By 1910, very large families were less common for every group, with small families of from one to three children most common among the middle class. This decline in the birth rate also meant a decline in the proportion of children in the population. The proportion of the total population that was under fifteen dropped from 34.4 percent in 1900 to 29.3 percent in 1930. Smaller families, fewer children and more adults per child in the general population paved the way for even more attention to be focused on the individual child. For most families, the distinctive features of early-twentieth-century childhood was that children lived at home longer and attended school longer. Childhood experience was increasingly uniform among children of the same age group—increasingly leisured, sheltered from adult life, and focused on preparation for adulthood.

After the turn of the century, new reactions to child death and campaigns to exclude children from the labor market indicated new attitudes toward children. Children were "sacralized," that is, invested with new religious and sentimental meaning, as they were set above financial considerations. While over the course of the nineteenth century the death of a child became the most painful and tragic of all deaths, tremendous public outcry at the accidental killings of children by automobiles and streetcars after the turn of the century indicated children's new sentimental value. Likewise, child labor laws after the turn of the century removed children from the market, in part because it became more efficient to educate children than to employ them but also because of new cultural definitions of legitimate and illegitimate forms of work for children. Acceptable work for children was now instructional rather than instrumental, and even poor parents were expected to subsidize their children's expenses by providing them with an allowance. The value of the new economically "useless" child was then measured in strictly emotional terms, in the parents' joy in a child's smile or goodnight kiss.

Consistent with the emotionally priceless child, relations between parents and children in these smaller families became more democratic. The formerly rigid roles that defined the interaction between parents and children were relaxed, giving way to more spontaneous expressions of emotion and affection throughout the family. The decline in the number of children per family and the focus on emotional satisfaction and nurturance made hierarchically defined relationships between parents and children both unnecessary and undesirable.

The behavior of some parents at the time was influenced by new scientific advice on child rearing offered by behavioral psychologist John B. Watson. Watson and other child study researchers accumulated data on "normal" child development and made popular a behavioral model of child rearing in the 1920s that offered the appeal of scientific approaches to parents anxious about raising children equipped to deal with modern life. Watson argued that the key to psychology was stimulus and response and believed he had found evidence that children were born without definite instincts and that human nature at birth was more or less plastic. Thus, he asserted, the child's personality was shaped through systematic habit training early in life.

> *After the turn of the century children came to be "sacralized"—invested with new religious and sentimental meaning as they were set above the household's financial considerations.*

John Watson was the most severe of the behaviorists, asserting that families overindulged their children and that affection was responsible for social maladaptation. He counseled parents to curb their displays of affection, to shake their children's hands rather than to kiss and hug them, and never to let their children sit on their laps. Mothers were instructed to enforce a strict regimen of habit training and to resist their emotional responses to the child. While Watson's harshness limited his popularity, overall the behavioral emphasis on rigid adherence to "scientific" rules and schedules in feeding, toilet training, and discipline influenced the behavior of middle-class parents in the 1920s and early 1930s.

The economic stringency of the Great Depression forced many children to take on productive tasks both within and outside the household, reversing the trend of a childhood sheltered from adult responsibility. One important development of the Depression was that the shrinking size of the labor market increased the proportion of children remaining in school through high school graduation. Still, according to a sample of families from one community, children from both lower- and middle-class families faced with unemployment were often forced to take on new responsibilities at home or to find some kind of work to supplement family income.

Where possible, these tasks were assigned according to conventional gender definitions of acceptable "child work." Thus, girls took on housework and child-care responsibilities or earned wages by babysitting or working in neighborhood businesses. Boys were messengers, delivery boys, or dishwashers. In more economically comfortable families, children kept their wages for personal school expenses, clothing, and social activities, while in families facing the greatest hardship, some of the children's earnings went to basic household expenditures. The experience of boys working outside the home inculcated an early sense of independence, dependability, and mature judgment about money, while girls who took on new household roles were reinforced in their domestic responsibilities and family obligations. Thus, the Depression placed children in responsible positions at younger ages and interrupted the pattern of complete dependence on parents; it also changed the parents' central focus, which had been responding to the needs of their children.

While public responsibility for poor and needy children has chronically fallen short of the mark in the United States, some concern for the welfare of children in the 1930s was manifest in the federal relief agenda of the New Deal. Limited federal daycare programs were established through the Works Progress Administration (WPA) in the 1930s and expanded significantly during World War II. The WPA also provided local school hot lunch programs and built playgrounds, swimming pools, and athletic fields, enhancing recreation facilities for children. The largest public maternity program in the United States to that time was the wartime Emergency Maternal and Infant Care Program, and the 1935 Social Security Act provided aid for rural, disabled and dependent children (ADC). The Federal Emergency Relief Administration (1933) worked on the assumption that poverty alone was not a sufficient reason to separate a child from his or her family and provided relief to enable poor families to remain together. In spite of these important precedents, American society's deeply held notions of the privacy of the family and the sanctity of motherhood have persistently interfered with the full assumption of public responsibility for child welfare.

The economic stringency and absence of fathers during World War II created unique conditions for children growing up in the 1940s. The wartime labor shortage led both servicemen's wives and young people to find jobs. This resulted in a relaxation of child labor and school attendance laws, enabling youths to assume adult responsibilities by age thirteen or fourteen. The scarcity of school personnel shortened school days and forced school closings in many communities, leading many young people to leave school. Women who headed their families while their husbands were overseas often moved in with their parents, resulting in further social dislocation for children and a dilution of parental authority.

The war shortened the sheltered childhood of many youths; it left children unsupervised and families stressed by separations, deaths, and financial constraint. Wartime anxiety over the neglect and premature independence of children was prompted by the disruption of the ideal of the nuclear family and sheltered childhood created by women's wartime participation in the labor force. The inadequacies of individual women, rather than society's failure to take responsibility for the trauma created by the war or the lack of public responsibility for child welfare, were improperly held to blame for the stresses on childhood in the 1940s.

Child-rearing literature in the 1940s continued to address the middle-class mother, at home full-time. This writing returned to an emphasis on affection and emotional expression and on the importance of responding to the child's needs. Arnold Gesell's influential *Infant and Child in the Culture Today*, first published in 1943, avoided the entire issue of discipline and urged parents to follow rather than "force" the child's development. Parents were urged to recognize and respond warmly to their children's needs, on the theory that a satisfied child was a secure child. This renewed emphasis on affection and responsiveness to the child's needs may have been subtly geared to reinforcing an ideology that urged women to return to full-time mothering after their wartime participation in the labor force.

This indulgent advice to parents set the stage for the care of the postwar baby boom generation. The birthrate in the United States, which had steadily declined since 1800, made a dramatic turnaround after 1946. The birthrate went from a low of 18 per 1,000 population in the period 1930 to 1940 to a peak of 25 per 1,000 population in 1957, so that in the eighteen years after World War II (from 1946 to 1964) the nation's population increased more than it had in the fifty years before 1946. Perhaps the most important causes of the baby boom were a revitalization of family values after the war and a particular glorification of motherhood as women's proper social role, although postwar economic prosperity was another important cause.

Advice to parents set out in Benjamin Spock's *The Common Sense Book of Baby and Child Care*, first published in 1946, provided the underpinnings of the permissive child-rearing style in the postwar child-centered family. Spock endeavored to relieve anxious mothers by urging them to feel confident about their natural maternal responses to the child. He advised mothers to monitor their child's growth and development carefully and to offer the praise and encouragement that would enable the child to reach his or her full potential. *Baby and Child Care* as Spock's book was called in its many later editions, stressed a cheerful and congenial mother and a gentle and flexible intervention that would enable her to avoid conflict with her child. Feminists now claim that Spock undermined rather than affirmed a mother's confidence in her child-rearing ability by engendering guilt and suggesting consultations with child-care experts when problems emerged. His advice, however, was the template for the emerging 1950s ideal of the full-time, suburban, middle-class mother devoted exclusively to her children.

Postwar prosperity led to rapid housing construction that created new suburban communities, while government subsidies increased the rate of home ownership by 50 percent between 1940 and 1960. Suburban life was "child centered" in the 1950s, creating for some families a unique stage in the history of children. The most common reason given by one surveyed group of adults for moving from the city to the suburbs was "for the sake of the children." New suburbs promised children more space, fresh air, less traffic, and no neighbors in the same building. The suburbs offered parents child-centered organizations such as the Parent-Teacher Association (PTA), Girl Scouts and Boy Scouts, and the Little League. The needs of children dominated the life of the suburban family; postwar parents were ready to give their children "everything," which for some parents meant exclusively material indulgence; for others, the benefits of education; and for still others, thought and concern for their children's development and emotional well-being.

The carefree "Father Knows Best" suburban childhood of the 1950s was more a historical aberration than a long-standing pattern. Demographically, marriage and birth rates were exceptionally high, while the divorce rate was unusually low, making family life in the 1950s exceptionally stable. Families had more children than at any other time in the century, and more women devoted themselves exclusively to child rearing. Postwar prosperity and full-time mothering, combined with Dr. Spock's advice, led to children showered with maternal attention. Single-family homes gave families more privacy and allowed more permissive treatment of children. The conveniences of washing machines and diaper services permitted later and more relaxed toilet training. Central heating in homes made infants less dependent on heavy clothing for warmth, allowing them greater freedom of physical movement. The strong ideological emphasis on gender differences in the 1950s was translated into child-rearing practices, with particular concern that the child develop a firm sexual identity by identifying with the parent of the same sex. Working-class parents placed greater emphasis on traditional gender roles than did middle-class parents of the 1950s, and they tended to be stricter in the treatment of their children.

The baby boom also challenged public schools to meet the demands of their swelling enrollment. Spending on public elementary and secondary education went from $5.8 billion in 1950 to $15.6 billion in 1960. Reforms in the public school curriculum in the 1950s were in part spurred by cold war political anxieties, which claimed that this nation's schools were inferior to those of the Soviet Union, leading to significant innovation in mathematics and science curricula. In addition, the 1954 Supreme Court decision *Brown* v. *Board of Education of Topeka* (Kansas) mandated racial desegregation of public schools, making schools an instrument to end racial discrimination.

Isolated in developments of single-family homes, suburban parents structured their children's leisure time so that children's lives were filled with endlessly scheduled lessons, sports teams, and clubs. All of these activities were supervised by adults, and children often had to be brought from home to school to after-school activities and home again by car. While parents encouraged these activities to foster the child's development, suburban childhood was more heavily supervised and scheduled than childhood had been in the cities a decade before. The safe and clean suburbs allowed children to ride bicycles to school, parks, and around their homes, but children were unable to explore beyond their residential neighborhoods without an adult, thus losing the opportunity for independent movement while they were young.

Medical advances of the 1950s improved the health of children. The most notable was the development by Dr. Jonas Salk of a vaccine against polio, which was approved by the federal government in 1955. While children of the 1950s have been called the healthiest, best-fed, best-clothed, and best-housed generation in this nation's history, some children—notably poor and especially poor black children living in inner cities or in rural areas—were left out of the suburban dream entirely. While postwar housing growth created lower-class and working-class suburbs with neighborhoods populated by Irish, Italian, and Jewish families, restrictive covenants kept black families out of suburbs.

While postwar prosperity expanded the size of the middle class and actually reduced the percentage of poor in the population, the distribution of wealth in the postwar boom meant that the impoverished received an ever smaller share of the nation's resources. Government health care was poorly distributed after the war, to the detriment of the poorest families, and while overall infant mortality rates went down in the 1940s, for nonwhite infants the rate actually went up from 1950 to 1960. In the late 1980s, the United States ranked nineteenth among industrial nations in its rate of infant mortality. Moreover, children have been the slowest group to move out of poverty, since federal relief programs, notably Aid to Families with Dependent Children (AFDC), have been less effective in helping children than other groups. This is because American society views the care of poor children as primarily the responsibility of their parents. It is reluctant to support poor parents, since it represents "pauperizing" them. Thus, it limits its responsibility to poor children, creating a cycle of poverty that has been particularly devastating to children.

Recent History of Childhood

The type of sheltered childhood enjoyed by many privileged children who grew up in the 1950s and 1960s changed when a combination of feminism and the end of the postwar economic boom caused a series of transformations in the family. First, the birthrate fell from the late 1950s peak of 3.8 children per family to less than 2 in the late 1980s. Second, the divorce rate rose sharply: the number of divorces in 1988 was twice as high as in 1966 and three times higher than in 1950; by 1988 one-third of all marriages ended in divorce. This led to an increase in the number of single-parent households, and the number of female-headed households doubled between 1966 and 1988. Finally, married women entered the labor force in unprecedented numbers; in 1980, middle-income families were likely to have mothers in the labor force, and in 1988 more than half of all mothers with children in their first year were employed. Thus, by the late 1980s only 15 percent of households were composed of a breadwinner father, a full-time housewife mother, and children, the pattern that described 70 percent of all households in 1960.

The fact that most mothers with young children now work full time and that many of these women are single heads of households have dramatically changed the experience of children. They have reduced the amount of time children spend with their mothers, though in some cases the father's involvement in child rearing has increased. While the issue of child care was previously identified only with poor families, increased labor force participation of mothers later linked it to families across the economic spectrum for the first time and challenged definitions of what constitutes quality child care and who should provide it. The traditional assumption that mothers alone can provide care that is essential for the well-being of young children was replaced by a widely held belief that what children need is responsible, responsive adult care that includes a relationship with at least one adult based on love and long-term commitment. This loving, responsible adult need not be the mother or any relative; the important point was the quality of the relationship between the adult and child.

Still holding to the notion that child care was primarily the private responsibility of parents, American society had yet to provide adequate public child care to meet the needs of dual-earning parents and single parents. This created stresses for both children and parents, especially for working mothers. Only in the most exceptional families with working mothers were family roles realigned so that both parents shared equally in child care and in household responsibilities. In such cases, children learned new gender roles—fathers who shared in nurturance and the expression of emotions and mothers who were equal contributors to the family economy. More typically, working mothers shouldered double obligations of family and job responsibilities, and both the quality and quantity of time children spend with parents were limited.

Children came to grow up in what are called "new families," which included families where both parents work full-time, single-parent families, families with unwed parents, families with gay or lesbian parents, and families in which remarriage created a series of step relations. The process of divorce and the reconstituting of families had a range of effects on children. Children often blamed themselves for the breakup of their parents' marriage; they worried about the separation and their continued relationship to each parent and became anxious as they anticipated the new set of relationships that came with parental remarriage. Many children experienced temporary depression or anxiety or exhibited antisocial behavior, but the trauma of divorce and remarriage in many cases were mitigated by sustained and loving relationships with parents who were responsive

Marriages in the 1950s and birth rates were exceptionally high, while the divorce rate was unusually low, making family life during the decade remarkably stable.

to the child's needs, so that children emerged well adjusted after their parents' divorce.

The care children received in these newly configured families varied, but in general, children in new families experienced greater responsibility and independence at an earlier age than did children in conventional nuclear families. Some developed close relationships with several different adults and benefited from the variety of role models. Increased household responsibilities, when assigned with sensitivity to the child's developmental stage and needs, often strengthened the child; children derived self-esteem from the real contributions they made to the family and developed an enhanced sense of self-reliance and autonomy. Children who grew up in single-parent families may have been given even greater household responsibilities to relieve their overburdened parent. In these families there were risks that childhood may be foreshortened if children took on too much household responsibility or if the child became the emotional support and confidant of the single parent.

Those who grew up in female-headed households were often subject to special stresses since these families were frequently poor. One year after divorce, women and children experienced, on average, a 73 percent drop in the standard of living, while men experience a 43 percent improvement. The feminization of poverty was due in part to fathers' noncompliance with child support awards after divorce and in general to the sex-segregated workplace in which women earn less than men.

The late 1980s and 1990s were a period of transition in gender roles and family composition that has changed the experience of children. The feminist movement, which led women into the labor market seeking equality in both the family and in society, also pressed for quality care for all children. Much of the progress in securing day care, maternity and paternity leaves, and part-time and flextime work were political achievements of the women's movement. The provision of adequate health care and quality day care for all children depends on society's willingness to take public responsibility for the well-being of all its children.

Throughout American history the stage of childhood has been sensitive to economic changes and to changes in the roles of women. The image of a childhood utterly sheltered from the adult world and under a mother's exclusive care has been idealized in our society. It was in fact rarer than is commonly assumed and was always associated with affluence; many theoreticians now question whether it is best for the child. Social anxiety over the quality of childhood has recurred frequently through our history; the current tension reflects a conflict between changes in women's roles and society's unwillingness to make child welfare a public responsibility, rather than a direct concern for the well-being of children. American society has yet to achieve what is best for all its children.

[See also Adolescence; Family Structures; Household Labor; Life Stages; Public Education; Public Health.]

BIBLIOGRAPHY

Seventeenth and Eighteenth Centuries

Beales, Ross W., Jr. "In Search of the Historical Child: Miniature Adulthood and Youth in Colonial New England." *American Quarterly* 27 (1975).

Bremner, Robert, et al. *Children and Youth in America: A Documentary History.* 3 vols. (1971–1974).

Demos, John. *A Little Commonwealth: Family Life in Plymouth Colony* (1970).

Greven, Philip J., Jr. *Four Generations: Population, Land, and Family in Colonial Andover, Massachusetts* (1970).

Greven, Philip J., Jr. *The Protestant Temperament: Patterns of Child Rearing, Religious Experience, and the Self in Early America* (1977).

Gutman, Herbert G. *The Black Family in Slavery and Freedom, 1750–1925* (1976).

Kerber, Linda K. *Women of the Republic: Intellect and Ideology in Revolutionary America* (1980).

Mintz, Steven, and Susan Kellogg. *Domestic Revolutions: A Social History of American Family Life* (1988).

Nineteenth Century

Bodnar, John E. "Socialization and Adaption: Immigrant Families in Scranton, 1880–1890." *Pennsylvania History* 43 (1976).

Ryan, Mary P. *Cradle of the Middle Class: The Family in Oneida County, New York, 1790–1865* (1981).

Schlossman, Steven. *Love and the American Delinquent: The Theory and Practice of "Progressive" Juvenile Justice, 1825–1920* (1981).

Stansell, Christine. "Women, Children, and the Uses of the Streets: Class and Gender Conflict in New York City, 1850–1860." *Feminist Studies* 2 (1982).

West, Elliott. "Heathens and Angels: Childhood in the Rocky Mountain Mining Towns." *Western Historical Quarterly* 14 (1983).

Twentieth Century

Cohen, Miriam. "Changing Education Strategies among Immigrant Generations: New York Italians in Comparative Perspective." *Journal of Social History* 15 (1982).

Elder, Glen. *Children of the Great Depression: Social Change in the Life Experience* (1974).

Fass, Paula. *The Damned and the Beautiful: American Youth in the 1920s* (1977).

Gesell, Arnold L., et al. *Infant and Child in the Culture of Today* (1943; rev. ed. 1974).

Gordon, Linda. *Heroes of Their Own Lives: The Politics and History of Family Violence, 1880–1960* (1988).

Grubb, W. Norton, and Marvin Lazerson. *Broken Promises: How Americans Fail Their Children* (1982).

Horn, Margo. *Before It's Too Late: The Child Guidance Movement in the United States, 1922–1945* (1989).

Modell, John. *Into One's Own: From Youth to Adulthood in the United States, 1920–1975* (1989).
Schlossman, Steven. "Before Home Start: Notes Toward a History of Parent Education in America, 1897–1929." *Harvard Educational Review* 46 (1976).
Spock, Benjamin. *Baby and Child Care* (1946; rev. ed. 1985).
Tyack, David B. *The One Best System: A History of American Urban Education* (1974).
Tyack, David B., and Elisabeth Hansot. *Learning Together: A History of Coeducation in American Schools* (1990).
Watson, John B. *Psychological Care of the Infant and Child* (1928).
Zelizer, Viviana A. *Pricing the Priceless Child: The Changing Social Value of Children* (1985).
Zuckerman, Michael. "Dr. Spock: The Confidence Man." In *The Family in History*, edited by Charles E. Rosenberg (1975).

Collections

Graff, Harvey J., ed. *Growing Up in America: Historical Experiences* (1987).
Hawes, Joseph M., and N. Ray Hiner, eds. *American Childhood: A Research Guide and Historical Handbook* (1985).
Hawes, Joseph M., and N. Ray Hiner, eds. *Growing Up in America: Children in Historical Perspective* (1985).

— MARGO HORN

THE CITY

From the earliest days of colonization to the present, American cities have been central places, providing a focal point for economic development, local government, culture, social reform, and technological innovation, and a site where newcomers clustered and became acculturated. A city is a site with at least twenty-five hundred residents that performs various specialized functions for itself and surrounding smaller communities and supports a cosmopolitan life-style. Organic entities that change over time, cities are composed of three major elements: physical structures (spatial dimensions, demographics, economy, and technology); organizational structures (class, ethnic, and racial groups, social institutions, and government); and value systems (attitudes, ideologies, and behavior). Their evolution can be categorized into four eras: the early American city (1630–1820), which comprised about 5 percent of the population; the walking city (1820–1870), which existed when urbanization occurred at its fastest rate and cities began to provide essential services; the industrialized radial city (1870–1950s), an entity of imposing physical dimensions inhabited by immense populations, a product of industrialization, immigration, and cheap mass transit; and the suburban metropolis (1945–1990s), characterized by the dominance of suburbia, the decline of the urban core, and the emergence of the Sunbelt.

The Early American City

The first colonial cities, starting with Spanish Saint Augustine, Florida (1565), were clusters of concentrated populations, vanguards of settlement located on bodies of water, whose functions included defense, government, trade, and the support of religion and culture. Their importance transcended population. They were the most dynamic colonial places, and loci of an urbane and cosmopolitan life-style, and sites of key colonial institutions ranging from governments to churches. Their weak and often oligarchic governments provided few public services unconnected to commerce, relying instead on private initiative. Later cities learned from their experience, copying physical layouts, social organizations, and privatism.

Boston was the first English colonial city, founded in 1630 by the Puritans as a model settlement of Visible Saints who shared the same values and beliefs. Boston was an exceptionally homogeneous city, although the Puritan community weakened as the second and third generations were less likely to have a saving experience. By 1690 Boston had a population of seven thousand, which made it the fourth largest city in the British Empire. Philadelphia, New York, Newport, and Charleston, all compact ports, were the other major colonial cities. They were originally overwhelmingly English except for Charleston, which by 1680 had become a haven for French Huguenots, who had first come to South Carolina in 1670, and New York, the cosmopolitan former Dutch colony of New Amsterdam, where eighteen languages were spoken. The early residents of the latter included Sephardic Jews.

Cities became more heterogeneous following Queen Anne's War (1702–1713), as indentured Germans and Scotch-Irish migrated to New York and especially to Philadelphia. After the French and Indian War (1754–1763), there was a substantial immigration of Irish and Scotch-Irish that temporarily halted during the Revolution and resumed afterward. The immigrants shied away from Boston because of its historic intolerance and limited economic opportunities for newcomers.

The colonial cities all had substantial black populations. In the early 1700s, Charleston's black and white populations were equal, and blacks comprised one-fourth of New York and one-sixth of Boston. As late as 1771, 15 percent of New York's adult male work force were slaves.

Colonial cities had a multilayered social structure. Ministers were at the apex of Boston's social structure until they were supplanted in the late seventeenth century by professionals and wealthy merchants who had the biggest homes and the most prominent church pews. Boston's merchants then controlled 40 percent of colonial shipping, but by the mid eighteenth century they had lost their leadership because of an unproductive backcountry and the maturation of aggressive challengers, primarily Philadelphians who shipped wheat from the hinterland to Caribbean and transatlantic markets. Newport emphasized the slave trade; Charleston, rice; and New York, wheat and livestock.

The "better sort" enjoyed a high standard of living and dominated society and public affairs. In 1687 Boston's richest 5 percent controlled 25 percent of the city's taxable wealth, a figure that increased to 44 percent in 1771, about the same ratio as in other cities. The upper class was an open elite, and there were rags-to-riches stories, especially in New York, where 33 to 40 percent of the merchants in 1775 were self-made men. The rich owned elegantly furnished brick homes, rode in carriages, wore expensive clothing and powdered wigs, socialized at the finest coffeehouses, belonged to restrictive voluntary organizations like Philadelphia's Schuylkill Fishing Colony (1732), and married within the elite circle.

The "middling sort" composed about 70 percent of society. They had smaller homes, less property, and cheaper clothes. One-fifth of urban male workers were shopkeepers or other low-level nonmanual workers, and about half were self-employed or highly paid artisans who had a strong self-image as hard working, frugal, and competent.

Three-fifths of all colonial cities were unincorporated, especially in New England, where town meetings gave freemen the power to enact laws, levy taxes, settle disputes, and elect selectmen to run affairs between meetings.

At the bottom of the social ladder were the impoverished "inferior sorts": unskilled workers, indentured servants, and slaves, comprising 20–30 percent of urbanites in 1770. No permanent white proletariat existed because of opportunities to advance or move on, but the gap between rich and poor was growing. In 1687, 14 percent of Bostonians had no property; the figure had doubled to 29 percent in 1771. The poor mainly lived on the periphery in crowded housing and were increasingly insecure, disaffected, and less deferential.

Municipal governments had limited authority to tax or spend, and outside of New England were regarded as exclusive, elitist, tight-fisted, and insensitive to changing conditions. Their primary duty was to promote commerce rather than to provide essential services or social conformity. Three-fifths of all colonial cities were unincorporated, especially in New England, where they had considerable autonomy. Power there resided in the town meeting, where freemen (only 16 percent at mid century) enacted laws, levied taxes, settled disputes, and elected selectmen to run affairs between meetings. Under the British, New York was originally a royally chartered municipal borough run by a mayor and council dominated by merchants appointed by the governor, but charter reform in 1731 made it an open corporation with annual elections that forced the notables to be more responsive to the growing electorate. Political factions emerged over economic issues and conflicts between rival elite families. Philadelphia, whose government was one of only three closed corporations in the colonies, was run by an oligarchy with long terms, the prerogative to appoint successors, and, except for taxation, other wide-ranging powers. Charleston had no municipal government at all until 1715, when the provincial assembly appointed insensitive commissioners to supervise specific tasks.

Most new laws concerned economic matters because commerce was the cornerstone of urban economies. Municipalities regulated and supervised sites of mercantile activity like the wharfs and markets, and by 1690 all but Boston had a regulated market with standards of quality, weights, and measures. In Boston, however, economic laws comprised a mere 9 percent of all edicts. Bostonians believed that open markets provided opportunities for smaller purveyors and thus did not have a permanent public market until Faneuil Hall was built in 1742.

Cities did a poor job of coping with such public problems as morality, health, poverty, safety, and streets. Homogeneous Boston was the best-governed and most communally responsible city. Its earliest laws included fire-prevention measures, bans on garbage dumping, and penalties for Sabbath breaking and adultery. In 1701 over half of its ordinances dealt with public safety, order, and peace. Public services were paid for by license fees, fines, tariffs, lotteries, rents from public markets and wharves, and, later in the century, by property or poll taxes. There was also heavy reliance on private initiative. Streets received considerable attention because they were essential for commerce, created health hazards by draining poorly, and were dangerous for pedestrians and children at play. Boston had excellent paved streets and sewers, but it took other cities as long as forty years to catch up, mostly through relying on private efforts. Boston had some of the strictest fire regulations and best fire-fighting equipment in the world, yet there were severe fires in 1676, 1679, and 1711, after which the first volunteer fire company was established. The model for the future, however, was Philadelphia's elite Union Fire Company, formed in 1736 by Benjamin Franklin to fight fires and prevent looting.

Chronic poverty, particularly among women and children, materialized by the 1700s and was a major concern by mid century. In Charleston between 1751 and 1774, over 80 percent of people receiving aid were women and children. Impoverishment was frequently caused by the economic dislocations and bloodshed resulting from colonial wars. Thirteen percent of Boston's adult women were widows following King George's War (1744–1748), many of them left without any means of support or marketable skills other than sewing. Assistance to the deserving poor comprised a major portion of municipal expenditures, rising in New York from £250 in 1698 to £5000 in 1770, supplemented by private aid from philanthropists, churches, and voluntary associations. Most assistance was outdoor relief (money, food, clothing, and fuel) rather than indoor relief (institutionalization in almshouses).

Crime was less widespread and less severely punished in the colonies than in England. Homogeneous Puritan communities tried to prevent deviance through social pressure and regulation of public houses, but when necessary they relied on harsher methods such as banishment (the "antinomian" Anne Hutchinson), whipping, and even execution (Quakeress Mary Dyer). As cities became more heterogeneous through the influx of outsiders like sailors, blacks, escaped felons, and runaway servants, the crime rate increased. The rise was accounted for primarily by morals violations, punished by fines and whippings. Policing was originally done by privately organized patrols—as late as 1690 New York was the only city with a paid watch—but by 1720 all the cities had copied the European system of municipally paid daytime constables and night watches to apprehend offenders, report fires, and maintain order against occasional riots caused by such lower-class grievances as impressment and soaring bread prices. Charleston and New York had the added special problem of potential slave insurrections. New York had a slave riot in 1712, and in 1741, when nearly one-fourth of the labor force were bondsmen, rumors of a slave revolt resulted in thirty-one executions.

Little was accomplished in the area of public health. Cities were hard-pressed to cope with the garbage dumped in the streets that attracted hogs and stray animals. Boston had the cleanest streets, yet in 1711 the garbage on the streets caught fire. Infectious diseases were deadly threats, although port officials inspected and quarantined entering ships. Smallpox was particularly dreaded, and there were three outbreaks in Boston between 1666 and 1702. After a fourth episode in 1721 that infected almost 6,000 and killed about 850, Cotton Mather and Dr. Zabdiel Boylston encouraged inoculation. The procedure gained acceptance only slowly, however, and was not widely applied until the 1760s.

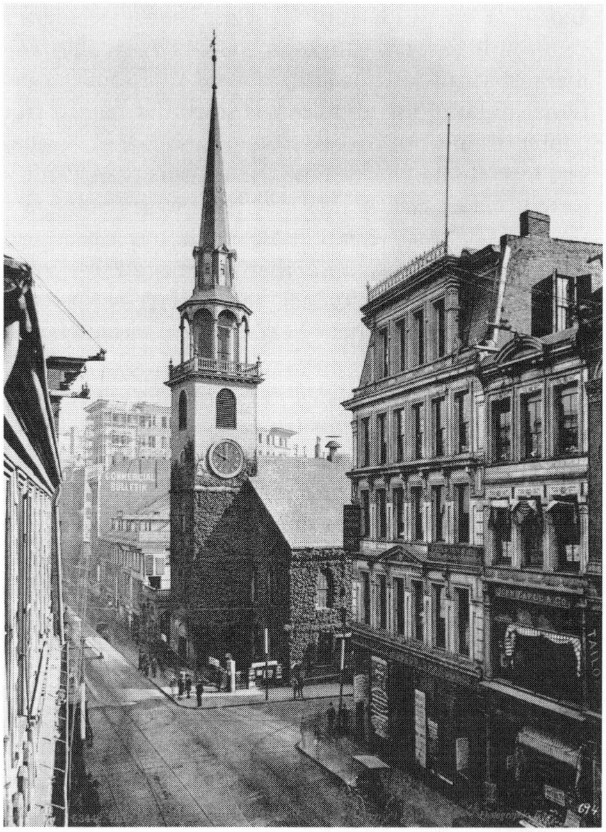
A 1900 view of Boston's Old South Meeting House, built in 1729, was a symbol of revolutionary Boston. Cities like Boston were instrumental in the American Revolution.

Religion was the most important semipublic institution, and a church was usually the city's most prominent physical structure. Religion promoted morality and discipline, a message that became less salient with increased secularization, the worship of money and status, and the popularity of taverns, drinking, gambling, and blood sport. By 1737 Boston had 177 innkeepers and liquor retailers, one for every twenty-five adult males. Religious life was reinvigorated in the 1730s and 1740s by the Great Awakening, which promoted evangelical Protestantism and made thousands of converts. The revival led to higher moral standards and the formation of new churches, denominations, and seminaries that fragmented urban society.

Colonial cities were centers of a cosmopolitan lifestyle. In Puritan Boston children attended school to learn to read the Bible; future clergymen studied at the publicly supported Boston Public Latin School (1635) and went on to Harvard College (1636). By the mid eighteenth century, education was largely secularized, a mark of status for classically trained elite sons or vocational training for middle-class sons that ranged from apprenticeships to baccalaureate training at the College of Philadelphia (1755, now the University of Pennsylvania). Cities had weekly newspapers, beginning with the *Boston News-Letter* (1704), public and subscription libraries, bookshops, and other institutions like coffeehouses, mechanics' societies, and Philadelphia's American Philosophical Society (1743) that encouraged enlightened discourse.

Cities were instrumental in the coming of the American Revolution because they were the scenes of the greatest oppression and because they had the human resources and communication facilities (inns, coffeehouses, and print shops) to plan and implement resistance. Merchants led the opposition to George III's reassertion of royal authority, particularly following the Stamp Act (1765), to protect their rights as Englishmen. To secure repeal, leading Bostonians drew up petitions, organized boycotts and nonimportation agreements, established committees of correspondence, and allied with other social groups who staged organized riots. The Sons of Liberty subsequently led the opposition to the Townshend Acts (1767) and the Tea Tax (1770), culminating in the Boston Tea Party (16 December 1773). The Coercive (Intolerable) Acts then closed the port of Boston and revoked the charter of Massachusetts, thereby throttling commerce and liberty. Boston's Committee of Correspondence responded by appealing to other cities to organize a continental congress to coordinate collective action against the Crown. After independence and the defeat of the British, urbanites became the leading supporters of a strong national government to facilitate trade and promote economic stability. In 1787, when only 5 percent of Americans lived in cities, twenty of the fifty-five delegates to the Constitutional Convention were urbanites, and these cosmopolites saw the Constitution through to ratification.

The urban population over the next four decades remained at about 5 percent, although the number of cities with over ten thousand residents increased from five in 1790 to twenty-three in 1830. Twenty-five cities obtained more democratic charters, the franchise was liberalized, and most closed corporations like that of Philadelphia (1796) were replaced. An urban frontier emerged on the fringe of a rising national urban network, copying the methods older cities had employed to plat their sites and deal with emerging problems. Towns like Pittsburgh, Louisville, and Cincinnati promoted economic growth at transfer points along navigable waterways like the Ohio River by centralizing and distributing goods and services. These cities also brought the accoutrements of civilization, including institutions of higher learning like Transylvania College (now University) in Lexington, Kentucky.

The Walking City

The era of most rapid urbanization occurred between 1820 and 1870, when the urban proportion of the national population reached 25 percent, a product of economic growth, the transportation revolution, and immigration. In the period 1830–1860 the number of cities with a population in excess of ten thousand quadrupled from 23 to 101. New York was the largest in 1860, with 813,600 residents, and eight others surpassed 100,000. These physically small cities seldom extended more than two miles in any direction, and consequently walking was the main form of locomotion. They were still primarily centers of commerce in which land uses were very mixed, although their populations became heterogeneous, divided into ethnic and class subcommunities. Municipal government grew increasingly powerful, often under the control of professional politicians, and began to provide essential public services.

The biggest cities were densely populated, led by New York's 135.6 persons per acre in 1850, and land was extremely valuable, not only in Manhattan (where property values tripled between 1819 and 1836) but also in newer cities like Chicago.

The core of the walking city was the waterfront with its docks, warehouses, business offices, factories, and homes. The economic elite lived nearby in choice locations, particularly the healthier high land, while the poor resided in back lots, alleys, or shanties at the outskirts of town. The biggest cities were densely populated, led by New York with 135.6 persons per acre in 1850; slums were even more packed. Land was extremely valuable, not only in Manhattan, where property tripled in value between 1819 and 1836, but also in instant cities like Chicago. Growth and development were promoted primarily by speculators, businessmen, and politicians who stood to directly profit.

The transportation revolution had a huge impact on urban commerce. New York's emergence as the leading trade center after the War of 1812 was achieved through such innovations as the American Black Ball Line, a regular packet service to Liverpool (1818) that facilitated planning, auctions that cut out middlemen, steamship service via the Atlantic all the way to New Orleans, and the Erie Canal (1825). The city became the nation's financial and communications center, and the home of the finest lawyers, accountants, and other professionals. By 1841 New York controlled 59.1 percent of American foreign trade and dominated the hinterland.

The Erie Canal's success promoted a canal-building mania culminating with the Illinois and Michigan Canal (1848), which connected Chicago to the Mississippi River. Canals were soon surpassed, however, by railroads, introduced by aggressive Baltimoreans who established the Baltimore & Ohio Railroad (1828) to expand the city's nodal zone. Railroads carried freight and passengers rapidly, year-round, and wherever workers could lay tracks. Trackage rose from 2,800 miles in 1840 to 30,600 miles in 1860. The railroad was especially the key to western development. Chicago's emergence as a railroad hub in the 1850s enabled it to overtake conservative Saint Louis as the West's leading city.

The introduction of mass transit in the largest cities encouraged physical expansion by enabling residents to travel longer distances in the same amount of time. In 1827 the omnibus, a large, twelve-passenger vehicle drawn by two horses, was introduced in New York. The slow (three to four miles per hour), uncomfortable ride over fixed routes cost one shilling (12.5 cents), a sum limiting ridership to the middle and upper classes. Nonetheless, by 1853 New York had 683 licensed omnibuses transporting 120,000 riders. The omnibus accustomed people to ride to work, and led to the emergence of the commuter.

In 1832 the superior horse-drawn streetcar was introduced in New York. The forty-passenger vehicles rode on rails, resulting in faster (six miles per hour), cheaper, smoother, and safer rides. They operated under municipal franchises that specified terms of service in return for the right to lay tracks on public streets and long-term contracts. The streetcars were an enormous success, making journeys fast and predictable, and fit in well with a time-driven society. By 1860 at least nine cities had street railroads, led by Philadelphia with 155 miles of track. Philadelphia took advantage of the transportation revolution to annex its surrounding communities in 1854, thereby growing in size from 2 to 129 square miles.

The urban social structure became increasingly unequal. In 1833, Boston's top 4 percent had 59 percent of the city's wealth, and 64 percent in 1848, figures typical of major cities. A few made it from rags to riches, typically in new or smaller industrial cities whose economies were growing rapidly and where there was no entrenched elite. The rich segregated themselves by joining prestigious churches and restricted voluntary associations like the Union Club or a yacht club, and moving toward the periphery, into large mansions with such conveniences as indoor plumbing.

The middle class, 40 percent of the work force, were predominantly white-collar workers who had wide social contacts and belonged to voluntary associations; advocated such values as hard work, self-discipline, and domestic tranquillity; and limited leisure time to useful, moral recreations like baseball. They earned more than blue-collar workers and worked in clean and quiet settings. Under 10 percent were salaried clerks, salesmen, or bookkeepers—typically young men who could realistically expect substantially higher future incomes. The middle class lived in good neighborhoods near their jobs, in nicely furnished and carpeted homes with four to six rooms that provided privacy. Their wives shopped at specialty shops until mid century, when an important shift in merchandising occurred with the rise of large department stores with elegant interiors and huge inventories, like A. T. Stewart's in New York, which had two thousand salesclerks.

Blue-collar workers' standard of living declined as wages fell between 1830 and 1850, and it became harder to achieve a competency. Boston's propertyless rose from 44.6 percent in 1830 to 57.3 percent in 1860. At mid century, when the minimum budget for the average New York family of five was nearly $540, tradesmen earned only $300 a year, and wives and children had to work. One-third to one-half of the middle and lower classes were vertically mobile, accumulating property and advancing into better jobs. However, these gains were shaky because of boom-and-bust cycles, and required enormous familial sacrifices. Urbanites, especially young clerks and blue-collar workers, were geographically highly mobile, seeking better opportunities. Only one-third to two-fifths of urban residents remained in the same city for a decade between 1830 and 1860.

Cities were the locus of an emerging working-class community with a shared consciousness of interests, residential propinquity, and a common life-style. Manual workers unaccustomed to time-work discipline maintained an oppositional pre-modern culture largely expressed by leisure-time activities over which, unlike work, they exercised considerable control. These members of the male bachelor subculture enjoyed violent, socially dysfunctional, time-wasting participatory pleasures at gambling dens, groggeries, brothels, cockpits, boxing rings, and raucous theaters.

Manufacturing was mainly small scale in artisan-owned shops, but the rise of a national market at mid century encouraged entrepreneurs to increase production by employing the American system of manufacturing. The earliest factories, in small New England towns like Waltham (1813) and Lowell, Massachusetts (1822), harnessed the energy from fast-running rivers to operate machinery. The textile mills employed single farm girls sixteen to twenty-five years old who lived in a highly regulated and paternalistic community until, in the 1840s, they were replaced by unskilled Irish immigrants. The introduction of steam power enabled industrialists to locate in major cities near cheap labor, transportation, large markets, and sources of credit, information, and technological innovation. However, the urban occupational structure kept a preindustrial flavor because small-scale production lingered on, and many factories did not feature extreme division of labor. New York became the leading manufacturing center, but most plants had fewer than twenty workers. The great industrial boom came during the Civil War, to fulfill military requirements for munitions, food, and clothing.

Privatism slowly gave way to public efforts to deal effectively with urban problems beyond the scope of individual efforts. The movement for municipally sponsored services was advocated by boosters, businessmen, social reformers, and professional politicians. By mid century, state legislatures revised charters to empower municipalities to levy taxes and provide essential services. As local governments gained power, politics became a career for upwardly mobile men who belonged to emerging political machines like Tammany Hall that supported municipalization of services, which meant patronage.

Improved security was a prime requirement. The propertied classes were apprehensive about robberies, assaults, vice, labor unrest, and riots (there were thirty-seven in 1835 alone), which they attributed to lower-class Irishmen unable to cope with urban life; demands grew for deterrence, apprehension, and punishment. Municipalities responded by organizing professional police departments loosely modeled on the London Metropolitan Police (1829). Boston organized the first professional force in the United States (1838), but the prototype was New York's, established in 1844. The police were salaried, appointed and promoted by political connections, worked regular beats, exercised considerable discretion, and by the mid 1850s were armed and uniformed.

Fire protection was originally provided by middle-class volunteer fire companies, but by the 1830s they had become lower-class fraternal and athletic clubs, centers of ethnic, occupational, or neighborhood gangs more interested in racing or in fighting than in quenching fires. Businessmen and fire insurance underwriters lobbied for tougher fire codes, advanced technology, and professionalized fire departments in order to improve fire-fighting capabilities. Most cities established professional fire departments by the 1860s, including Chicago (1858) and New York (1865)—usually following a disastrous fire.

Physicians, journalists, and health faddists pressured municipalities to take greater responsibility for public health. Key problems included potable water; epidemics (cholera killed 10 percent of the population of Saint Louis in 1849); infant mortality, which surpassed 50 percent in New York at mid century; and clean streets. The first major action occurred in Philadelphia. The city had a history of yellow fever, and in 1798 established its own water system. New York followed suit in 1842, yet as late as 1860, one-fourth of major cities still relied on private water companies that inadequately serviced poor neighborhoods. Cities dealt ineptly with sewers and streets. As late as the 1850s, New York and Chicago still used pigs as scavengers, and only around 1860 were private street cleaning companies hired. Chicago dealt with the sewage problem in the late 1850s by raising street levels so the refuse would flow into Lake Michigan, the source of its water supply. At mid century, one-fourth of city budgets went to paving and cleaning streets, principally major commercial avenues, yet by 1880 only one-half of streets were paved, making street sweeping difficult. Seventy percent of cities had public street cleaning in 1880, but only one-fourth had municipal garbage collection.

As working-class communities began to emerge in the cities, manual laborers unaccustomed to time-work discipline enjoyed violent, time wasting pleasures in their leisure-time.

The public health movement further advocated that cities provide breathing spaces for moral and health purposes. These needs were first fulfilled by private romantic cemeteries like Cambridge's Mount Auburn (1831), which had landscaped gardens, tree-lined walks, and lakes that provided picnickers an escape from urban hustle and bustle. A municipal park movement emerged in the 1840s to secure fresh air and sites for exercise to make workers healthier, develop choice new neighborhoods, and promote the reputation of cities. New York's secluded 840-acre Central Park (1858), designed by Frederick Law Olmsted and Calvert Vaux with rustic areas and formal gardens, became the model for future suburban parks.

Moral reform was largely in the hands of middle-class voluntary societies motivated by Christian morality and fears about the urban milieu. They advocated public education to promote order by indoctrinating immigrant children with traditional values and behavior and training them for jobs. Boston was the first major city to have a public education system (1818), followed by New York (1832) and Philadelphia (1836), and such systems were commonplace outside the South by 1860. The Children's Aid Society (1853) publicized the plight of homeless children and sent them to rural foster homes where they would have a good family environment, learn the work ethic, and become healthier. The temperance movement sought to curtail drinking, the reputed root of poverty, unreliable workers, and crime. Penal reformers promoted asylumlike penitentiaries to rehabilitate deviants by separating them from a bad environment and indoctrinating them with Christian morality, a work ethic, and respect for authority. Charity was limited to the deserving poor of high moral character. Thus pregnant women lacking proof of good moral character were turned away from New York's Asylum for Lying-in Women.

Reformers admired the home as the locus of female domesticity and a sanctuary from an increasingly dangerous outside world. Urban families were nuclear and smaller than in the past, but were frequently extended to include unmarried relatives, servants, or boarders. Women were expected to be exclusively homemakers, but poorer wives could not be, and at mid century about one-tenth held jobs, primarily as domestics. They comprised one-fourth of manufacturing workers. Schoolteaching, an extension of the domestic domain, was the only appropriate profession for middle-class young women. In 1860, they comprised nearly four-fifths of teachers in heavily urban Massachusetts. Middle-class women's activities outside the home were largely limited to shopping, often at massive new department stores like A. T Stewart's in New York, with their elegant interiors and huge inventories; to services at evangelical churches, where they comprised a majority; and to reformist voluntary organizations through which they extended their domestic role.

Cities were major destinations for Irish and German immigrants who came to America at mid century to escape poverty and persecution. More than two-fifths of New Orleans; over half of New York, Boston, and San Francisco; and over three-fifths of Saint Louis, Chicago, and Milwaukee were foreign born. The Irish settled mainly in eastern cities and the Germans in the Midwest, both groups in ethnic villages that helped to ease culture shock. Germans were geographically highly concentrated—in 1860, 83 percent in Milwaukee lived with their own kind, compared with 47 percent of the Irish and 53 percent of the native born. Their neighborhoods provided a full range of Old World institutions, including beer gardens, delicatessens, and turnvereins. Germans arrived with skills, literacy and some capital, and fared far better than the poor, uneducated, and unskilled Irish, who got the lowest-level jobs. At mid century over half of New York's day laborers were Irishmen, and three-fourths of Irishwomen were domestics. They endured deadly riots and other hostility from nativists because of anti-Catholicism, job competition, and political rivalries between native-born Whigs and Know-Nothings and Irish machine Democrats.

Antebellum blacks were the least urban ethnic group. There were sizable free African American communities in southern cities in the 1820s whose residents were relatively more skilled and dispersed than in the North. Three-fourths of free black Charlestonians in 1860 were artisans, primarily barbers, carpenters, and caterers, comprising 16 percent of the city's skilled workers. Northern blacks were overwhelmingly urban, encountered severe prejudice—they could seldom vote or serve on juries, were subject to race riots, and even expulsion—and lived in highly concentrated neighborhoods where segregation encouraged the establishment of a wide-reaching community including churches and mutual aid, educational, and fraternal societies seldom seen in the South except in New Orleans. About one-tenth of slaves lived in cities where they worked as servants, craftsmen, and factory laborers. They comprised over half of the work force in Charleston and Richmond, where feared contacts with freedmen and whites resulted in stringent restrictive laws and, after 1840, a stable slave population.

The Industrial Radial City

The United States emerged as an urban country in 1920, with over half the population (51.4 percent) residing in cities. The national culture was shaped by urban values, attitudes, and behavior, and cities became a focus of the federal government. Sixty-eight cities had over 100,000 residents, led by New York with 5.6 million. The post-Civil War city differed dramatically from the walking city because it was much bigger, had a larger and more heterogeneous population, enjoyed cheap mass transit, and had highly specialized land uses and industry-based economies. Radial cities were the locus of powerful political machines, impoverished slums, and ethnic villages that encouraged the rise of the Progressive movement to promote political democracy, social justice, economic opportunity, and moral order. These cities promised a better life for poor immigrants, rural dwellers fleeing boring small town society, and African Americans escaping Jim Crow laws.

Urban spatial relationships were reshaped by the emergence of cheap, rapid mass transit. The geographic distribution of businesses, industries, and homes was altered by soaring land costs in the old urban core and expansion toward the periphery made possible by improved transportation. By the mid 1880s, horse-drawn streetcars were used in three hundred cities, supplemented in fourteen major cities by cable cars. In 1888 fast (ten to twelve miles per hour), reliable electric trolleys were introduced, in Richmond, Virginia, and two years later there were 1,260 miles of electrified tracks, compared with 500 miles of cable car tracks and 5,700 miles served by horse-drawn vehicles. In 1902, 22,000 miles of urban tracks were electrified, including elevated routes over crowded downtown streets. Even more advanced were subways, built in Boston (1897), Philadelphia (1908), and especially New York (1904), which had a one-hundred-mile system by 1920. Traction lines required large capital investments for expensive equipment and consolidations, and great political clout (or bribes) to secure necessary franchises and rights of way; nevertheless, they generated substantial profits from millions of five-cent rides. Traction lines enhanced real estate values along their routes and facilitated urban sprawl, streetcar suburbs, annexations (Chicago in 1889 grew from 35 to 185 square miles and added 200,000 residents), and consolidations like the merger of Brooklyn and New York in 1898.

Streetcar traffic increased steadily until about 1923, when it began to encounter strong competition from automobiles. Several major cities, particularly Los Angeles and Detroit, dropped plans for subways, opting for better roads instead. By 1930, more than 50 percent of nonfarm families owned a car, typically the cheap Model T, and that ownership had an enormous impact on urban life. Riders traveled independently of fixed streetcar routes and schedules, could live in suburbia, and had greater leisure options, ranging from picnics to necking in the back seat. Furthermore, hundreds of thousands of jobs were created in production, repair, and related industries, and trucks greatly lowered freight costs.

The enhanced mass transit and skyrocketing realty values combined to create central business districts. In Chicago, for example, downtown property values rose by 700 percent between 1877 and 1891, making the old urban core too expensive for housing or factories. The central business district became the locus of administrative, financial, and commercial activities, cultural institutions, and light industry. Suburbanites worked in its office buildings, tourists and business travelers stayed at its hotels, and housewives shopped at its specialty shops and department stores. High land-costs encouraged construction of taller structures, originally built with thick brick or masonry walls limiting interior space. An important improvement was the modern skyscraper. Chicago's ten-story Home Life Insurance Building (1885) was the first, employing a lightweight steel skeleton frame. Tenants of skyscrapers were independent professionals and major companies that centralized large bureaucracies in monumental structures erected for self-advertising, exemplified by Manhattan's fifty-five-story Woolworth Building (1913). New York was the site of nearly half of all American skyscrapers. Its skyline symbolized the city's stature, topped off in the early 1930s by the 102-story Empire State Building.

The central business district was surrounded by concentric rings of residential housing beginning with the slums—impoverished, densely populated, heterogeneous residential areas. Slums had inadequate municipal services and high rates of poverty, substandard housing, infant mortality, communicable diseases, and crime.

By 1930, more than 50 percent of America's nonfarm families owned a car, typically the cheap Model T, and that ownership had an enormous impact on urban life.

Housing stock included cellars, shacks, lofts, subdivided warehouses and former mansions, and six-to-eight-story tenements constructed after the Civil War that housed up to 150 individuals—with a single water tap per floor, no ventilation, little light, and outdoor privies. Eighty percent of inner-city families had both parents present and were nuclear, although 20 percent included lodgers to help pay the rent.

Outside the slums were lower-middle and upper-lower-class residential neighborhoods, comprised mainly of modest single-family homes purchased with short-term mortgages from savings and loan associations. Residents included native-born craftsmen and second-generation blue-collar Germans and Irishmen. These urbanites worried about protecting what they had earned and feared the encroachment of slum dwellers into their communities. In the 1920s, they became prime candidates for Ku Klux Klan recruiters. Half of Klan members lived in cities of over fifty thousand, especially in the South and Midwest.

The final concentric ring was the suburban periphery. It was a safe, homogeneous, middle-class WASP area of large single-family homes with enclosed yards. Residents employed mass transit to travel to work, play, or shopping. Middle-class folk also lived in modest new apartments constructed along major streetcar routes. They were modeled on the luxury apartments of the rich located near the central business district in such exclusive neighborhoods as Chicago's Gold Coast. The rich also had other housing options, ranging from Fifth Avenue mansions to suburban estates.

Industry drove the economy of northeastern and midwestern cities, employing the American system of manufacturing and taking advantage of cheap labor, capital, consumer demand, and support services. Factories relocated to the outskirts or satellite suburbs like Gary, Indiana, where land was cheap, taxes were low, and bosses could exercise more control over their work force, particularly in company towns like Pullman, Illinois. By the 1910s several individual factories, including General Electric (Schenectady), International Harvester (Chicago), and U.S. Steel (Gary) had over fifteen thousand workers, and in the 1920s, sixty-eight thousand worked at Ford's River Rouge plant (Dearborn), the largest in the world.

The huge demand for low-paid unskilled and semi skilled workers was filled by immigrants who earned less than a family of four's minimal needs (fifteen dollars a week), and the entire family had to work at dehumanizing, dangerous, and boring jobs. Wives earned about half as much as their husbands, and children earned one-fourth. Advancement in the late nineteenth century was unlikely. Only one-fifth to one-sixth of manual workers, mainly native-born whites, were vertically mobile. Workers progressed by establishing a savings account and acquiring property. Urbanites were geographically mobile, especially the native-born who moved to better themselves. One in four urban residents moved each year, and the ten-year persistence rate was typically around 50 percent.

The industrial city was a metropolis of immigrants and their children. In 1910, 41 percent of urbanites were foreign-born. Three-fourths of immigrants lived in cities, led by Russian Jews (89 percent), Irish (87 percent), Italians (84 percent), and Poles (80 percent). Milwaukee was nearly 90 percent first- or second-generation immigrant; New York and Chicago, 80 percent. The new immigrants came from traditional societies and were mostly uneducated, unskilled, and indigent, unprepared for urban America. Their goal was not to surpass their fathers but to get a manly job, support their family, and purchase a home as insurance for old age. Jewish migrants were different because they had no homeland, were seldom formerly peasants, were more educated or at least respected scholarship, and had skills (tailoring) and an entrepreneurial tradition. Consequently, they were about two and a half times more likely to end up with a white-collar job than were other new immigrants.

The new immigrants lived in ethnic villages in slum neighborhoods where they reestablished old institutions like churches, maintained high rates of endogamy, and started mutual aid societies, social and athletic clubs, foreign-language newspapers, and parochial schools. Twenty to forty percent of school-children in major immigrant cities attended Catholic schools. Children attended public school briefly because they were uncomfortable, parents feared Americanization, and their labor was needed. Immigrants were marginal people with one foot in each of two different worlds. Daughters were closely supervised but boys were not, and they often grew up tough and street smart. They frequently joined street gangs, hungry for recognition, excitement, money, and a sense of belonging. The gangs provided good training for future boxers and hoodlums.

On the other hand, African Americans, 90 percent of whom resided in the South, were the least urban group. In 1900 only 17 percent of black southerners were urbanites. The great migration north began in 1916, caused by the boll weevil's devastation of cotton fields, the availability of factory work, and aspirations for a safer and better life. Within five years the number of black men in major industrial cities more than doubled, but usually they worked in low-level, dead-end jobs; black women were predominantly domestics. They lived in slums that became ghettos because of white flight, discrimination, blockbusting, and violence against blacks who tried to move into white neighborhoods. African Americans had legal access to schools and public accommodations but encountered prejudice, embarrassment, lower-quality facilities, and brutality if they contested traditional exclusionary customs. Discrimination and ghettoization created opportunities for blacks to service their community's financial, cultural, recreational, and cosmetic needs, resulting in the emergence of such institutions as black insurance firms, newspapers, and baseball leagues. The concentration of black voters increased black political power, and in 1928 Chicago Republican Oscar De Priest became the first northern African American elected to Congress.

Political corruption, urban pathology, growing anomie, and the need for improved public services encouraged the rise of urban reform in the late nineteenth century.

The city was the locus of a vibrant culture. A major city was expected to have several newspapers and such institutions of high culture as museums, a symphony, a public library, and universities. Popular recreation was cheap and accessible, enjoyed at such public sites as streets, parks, and beaches; semipublic facilities like amusement parks, arenas, ballparks, racetracks, dance halls, saloons, and vaudeville and movie theaters; and private social and athletic clubs. Urban recreation was largely class based until the 1920s, when higher wages and a shorter workweek democratized leisure. Until Prohibition, the saloon served as the poor man's club; workingmen also favored indoor sports like boxing, bowling, and billiards, and accessible resorts like Coney Island. Thereafter they could afford commercialized spectator sports and had greater access to municipal parks. In the 1920s crowds surpassing fifty thousand attended professional baseball and college football games, boxing championships, horse races, and the Indianapolis 500. However, the most popular entertainment was the movies, which had emerged from inner city nickelodeons in the early 1900s into luxurious, large downtown theaters a decade later.

Lord Bryce (*The American Commonwealth,* 1888) and other early social critics described city government, run by corrupt, self-serving politicians, as the worst American institution. From the 1880s to 1914 nearly 80 percent of the largest cities had machine-run governments, at least for a brief period. They grew stronger over time; in the largest cities during the 1930s, one-third had been in power for over two decades. The boss usually operated from behind the scenes, but a few were also long-term mayors, like Martin Behrman of New Orleans (1900–1920, 1925–1926) and Frank Hague of Jersey City (1917–1947). Machines were not ideologically oriented but cranked out the vote with precision by providing patronage and other services to inner city constituents, or by fixing elections through payoffs or intimidation.

Bosses dispensed personalized government, providing help to people who could turn to no one else, ranging from fixing a traffic ticket to food, relief, and jobs. They sponsored outings, secured preferential treatment from the municipality for business allies, awarded utility franchises and valuable contracts to politically connected entrepreneurs, and gave organized crime a free hand. Boss Richard Croker of New York (1886–1895, 1898–1902) grew rich on "honest" graft, using inside information to make astute investments or securing stock and contracts from firms seeking city business. His colleague George Washington Plunkitt distinguished this from "dishonest" graft, which was stealing from the city or taking payoffs to protect criminal activity.

Bosses centralized power and decision making, modernized city politics, and promoted urban development, building the urban infrastructure, albeit inefficiently and at a great cost. They were not omnipotent, however, as commonly believed. Tammany Hall, for instance, did not have complete control over New York's Democratic party until 1886, when a disciplined coalition of ward bosses was established on the basis of patronage and election victories. And even under Croker, Tammany did not win every major election, often because of scandals resulting from police corruption.

Furthermore, as David Hammack has pointed out, power in New York was so diffused because of ethnic, religious, and philosophical differences that neither machines nor urban elites could unilaterally postulate a coherent policy, much less act decisively. Finally, rural Republican control of state legislatures made it difficult for machine liberals such as Al Smith and Robert Wagner to repeal restrictive blue laws or enact such reforms as factory regulations or housing codes to improve conditions for their constituents.

Political corruption, urban pathology, growing anomie, and the need for improved public services encouraged the rise of urban reform in the late nineteenth century under the leadership of upper-class mugwumps, investigative journalists, Social Gospelers, the new professionals, and settlement workers. The reform impulse culminated in the Progressive movement (ca. 1900-ca. 1916), which sought to ameliorate life in impersonal-ized, segmented cities by promoting efficiency, social justice, political democracy, and economic opportunity.

In the 1880s, businessmen seeking efficient and honest government inaugurated the civic reform movement to investigate corruption, elect and promote "the best men," restructure government so as to weaken political machines, and improve sanitation, police, and fire services. They established local good government groups that affiliated into the National Municipal League (1894), which had moderate success electing reform candidates. Certain reform mayors, most notably Hazen Pingree of Detroit (1890–1897), did achieve major accomplishments. Pingree employed business principles to efficiently build parks and schools, reduce utility rates, and cut corruption while making no effort to impose Yankee norms on the new urban folk. Pingree's example was duplicated in the Progressive era by Samuel M. ("Golden Rule")Jones (1897–1904) and Brand Whitlock (1905–1913) in Toledo and Jim Loftin Johnson (1901–1909) in Cleveland.

Since a few good men could not clean up corruption, reformers advocated structural changes including greater home rule, secret ballots, nonpartisan, at-large elections, and stronger administrative schemes, such as the city manager and the commission system in which experts administered urban agencies. Midwestern and western cities secured greater home rule under new charters that took power from councilmen elected from readily corruptible wards and gave greater authority to mayors. The commission system had its first major test in 1900 in Galveston, Texas, following a devastating flood that killed over 7,200 people. It was a success, and by 1917 had been adopted in nearly five hundred mostly small cities. The city manager system was first employed in Staunton, Virginia, in 1908, and within fifteen years 270 largely suburban cities had adopted it.

Settlement workers were among the most liberal Progressives. The first American settlement house was New York's Neighborhood Guild (1886); there were over four hundred by 1910, located in slums and staffed by idealistic middle-class men and women. Volunteers sought to identify neighborhood problems and then arrive at solutions. Settlements offered classes in English, civics, crafts, and job skills; employment bureaus; and recreational facilities ranging from gymnasiums to theaters. In addition, the workers promoted reforms in juvenile justice, playgrounds, housing, public health, and morality.

WASP reformers like Anthony Comstock of the Society for the Suppression of Vice (1873) tried to impose traditional middle-class behavior upon urbanites by fighting immorality. Crusaders expanded temperance into a prohibition movement against the ubiquitous workingman's saloon (New York had seven thousand in 1880), a reputed cause of poverty and broken families, and center of crime and political corruption. Ironically, the Eighteenth Amendment generated a boom in organized crime that had originated in late-nineteenth-century politically protected Irish crime syndicates involved in gambling and prostitution. Vice was rampant in urban slums and red light districts like Chicago's Levee district, where gambling and prostitution operated freely. Occasional crackdowns followed investigations of police corrupted by gamblers and madams, and hysteric episodes over white slavery. Chicago closed its vice district in 1911, and about one hundred cities followed suit during World War I, most notably New Orleans (Storyville). However, vice soon reemerged in the slums and in working-class suburbs.

Progressive professionals advocated urban planning to address the quality of urban life while creating the efficient city. It began as the City Beautiful Movement that sought to enhance urban life by improving civic design, the impetus coming from Chicago's Columbian Exposition (1893), which influenced public architecture, municipal art, and planning. Fair coordinator Daniel Burnham's comprehensive Chicago Plan of 1909 marked a transition to the City Efficient Movement, directing environmental reform through spatial policies. Planners coordinated mass transit with planned land uses like garden cities, and employed zoning regulations for rational separation of incompatible land uses or buildings and protection of existing areas. New York in 1916 was the first city to introduce comprehensive zoning by establishing specific land use areas, limiting building heights, and restricting lot use to prevent the garment district from expanding toward Fifth Avenue. Ten years later, 591 cities had zoning codes.

The federal government first became deeply involved in the problems of cities during the Great Depression, when urban unemployment skyrocketed from 3.2 percent in 1929 to 15.9 percent in 1931 and 24.9 percent in 1933. In 1932, for instance, 1 million New Yorkers (30 percent), six hundred thousand Chicagoans (40 percent), and far greater proportions in industrial and mining cities (90 percent in Gary, Indiana) were out of work. By the end of 1930, the seventy-five largest municipalities appropriated $420 million for public works. Detroit's relief expenditures rose from $2.4 million in 1929 to $14.9 million in 1931. Cities tried to cope by borrowing, introducing sales taxes, and printing scrip to pay municipal workers. Little assistance came from the Hoover administration, save $300 million from the Reconstruction Finance Corporation.

Urbanites provided the backbone of Franklin Roosevelt's constituency, and the New Deal immediately responded with relief, recovery, and reform programs. Jobs were the biggest problem. The Federal Emergency Relief Administration distributed $500 million, mainly for work relief. In the winter of 1933–1934 about 8 million families received federal assistance, half from Civil Works Administration minimum-wage projects. The Public Works Administration (1933) promoted recovery through planned public works, especially in New York, where Robert Moses secured one-seventh of its allocations. The majority of Works Progress Administration (1935) grants went to the fifty largest cities, providing work relief (1936–1941) for nearly one-fifth of the work force in public construction projects and in programs like the Writers' Project that supported the arts.

Housing was another major problem. Hundreds of thousands had lost their homes (in 1933 there were one thousand home foreclosures a day), and the construction industry was moribund. The New Deal promoted recovery by establishing the Home Owners' Loan Corporation (1933) to stabilize the mortgage business, and the Federal Housing Administration (1934) to refinance private loans at 4 percent for up to thirty years. The Public Works Administration financed slum clearance and public housing, and the U.S. Housing Authority (1937) helped the neediest with $500 million for loans and grants for slum clearance, and 47,500 new low-cost rental units.

The New Deal instilled public confidence in Washington's ability to cope with major problems and shape the direction of urban development. The federal government provided services once supplied by machines but did not supplant the bosses, who became brokers between Washington and their constituents, doling out jobs, relief, and construction projects.

Urban America in the Suburban Age

The postwar metropolis was the locus of enormous change, much of it fostered by federal programs. The most important developments were suburbanization, the expansion of inner city ghettos, the decline of the northeastern and midwestern Rustbelt, and the emergence of the Sunbelt. The postwar city was an exciting and dynamic site of opportunity with industry prospering because of pent-up demand, the needs of baby boomers (consumer goods purchases tripled in fifteen years), and housing shortages. Hundreds of thousands of white veterans moved their growing families to suburbs using their government benefits, while central cities became increasingly black ghettos. By the 1960s, as the economy shifted into a postindustrial phase, the promise of the old industrial cities began to fade as problems mounted with the loss of jobs, fleeing taxpayers, growing impoverishment, spiraling disorder and violence, increasing needs for expensive public services, and an aging infrastructure. Thereafter the most dynamic areas were the suburbs and Sunbelt cities that became the desirable places to live.

As late as 1950, only one of the ten largest cities was located outside the Northeast and Midwest, but by 1980 half were in the booming Sunbelt. New York and Chicago had fewer residents in 1970 than twenty years before, and Saint Louis in 1980 had declined to the level of 1890! Columbus, Ohio, was the only major northern city to grow in the 1970s. The decline in the Rustbelt was tied to white flight to suburbia and the loss of industrial jobs through automation and factory relocation to suburbs and the Sunbelt—and abroad by the 1970s. In the latter decade the number of jobs in the Sunbelt rose by 40 percent, compared with 12.4 percent in the North. New York and Philadelphia alone lost 16 percent of their jobs between 1960 and 1972. The Sunbelt first boomed because of the need during the cold war for military bases and defense-related high-tech industries. It soon attracted an aging population who retired to warm climates (especially after the introduction of air conditioning), and lured industrialists, real estate developers, and entrepreneurs in leisure businesses because of weak unions, low taxes, cheap land, and improved roads and jet travel.

As late as 1950, only one of the ten largest cities was located outside the Northeast and Midwest, but by 1980 half were in the booming Sunbelt.

Thirty million Americans lived in suburbia in 1950 and seventy-six million by 1970, when the suburbs surpassed central cities in population (37.6 to 31.4 percent). These were mainly bedroom suburbs made accessible by such federal programs as G.I. loans, FHA mortgage insurance, and highway funding acts (1947, 1956), and by the low cost of cars and gasoline. Mass transit ridership peaked shortly after the war, but the automobile became so ubiquitous that by 1958 ridership on public transportation fell below the rate in 1900. Families left cities for privacy, lower taxes, escape from declining neighborhoods and rising crime, and a higher quality of life that included better schools, parks, and other public services. The new suburbs included totally planned communities like Levittown, New York, and Park Forest, Illinois, where mortgages cost less than rent. Among the fastest growing was Anaheim, California, located at an exit on the Santa Ana Freeway and home to Disneyland, which increased from 17,267 residents in 1952 to 91,100 seven years later.

Urban leaders after World War II encouraged development and the protection of assets by improving highways, ports, and airports, and revitalizing central business districts. Physical expansion was impossible in eastern and midwestern cities because there was no room outside their old boundaries. Pittsburgh and Philadelphia provided a model by employing insurance company capital to refurbish the central business district through cleaning and brightening it up, and enhancing accessibility with buses and underground parking. Pro-development businessmen worked with like-minded politicians, including reformers like DeLesseps Morrison in New Orleans, bosses like Richard Daley of Chicago, and professional politicians like Robert Wagner of New York, who hired able administrators and secured revenue for capital improvements.

There was far less cooperation from conservative, self-interested business leaders, especially in Sunbelt cities like Dallas, Houston, and Los Angeles, who used their power in publishing, banking, and insurance to shape major policy decisions according to their personal interests. These cities had considerable space available for expansion, mainly through annexation (Phoenix thereby grew from 17 to 187 square miles), that promised greater efficiency and prestige. Consolidations, on the other hand, were quite rare, most notably the Miami/Dade County metropolitan federation (1957), established to avoid duplication of governmental services.

Civic leaders usually focused on the central business district, giving less attention to the needs of residential neighborhoods. One-fifth of urban homes were substandard after the war, and cities began to rely on Washington for assistance. The Housing Act of 1949 sought to eliminate substandard areas and provide decent homes and environments through slum clearance, public housing, and an expansion of FHA mortgage insurance. However, FHA hurt working-class neighborhoods by recommending that developers build homogeneous tracts and redlining inner city areas by refusing to guarantee loans in localities that had older homes or were likely to experience black encroachment. Stable lower-class areas were ruined because mortgages became unavailable, homeowners could not get loans for home improvements, and merchants had a hard time getting affordable insurance.

Cities like Los Angeles had considerable space available for expansion after World War II. Business leaders used their influence to shape major policy decisions like development according to their personal interests.

Developers were expected mainly to construct low-cost public housing on the cleared sites, but frequently they evaded the spirit of the law by building luxury apartments, parking lots, shopping malls, or even factories that urban boosters applauded, anticipating an enhanced tax base and revitalization of decaying areas. It was expected to take six years to build 810,000 new units, but it took twenty. Meanwhile, about three times as many units were abandoned or razed for highways or urban renewal. The new public housing failed to promote communities as originally planned, and became places to hide the urban poor. Huge multistory developments like Chicago's Robert Taylor Homes, built in the early 1960s, became dangerous places where residents were intimidated by gangs and afraid to leave their apartments.

Working-class communities got another jolt in 1954 when Washington changed its emphasis from redevelopment to urban renewal. The new goal was to fix up decaying neighborhoods to attract more affluent residents, revitalize investment opportunities, and protect the central business district. Neighborhoods that residents considered alive and worth protecting, like Boston's West End, were bulldozed for urban renewal or highways with little concern for dislodged residents. Viable or potentially viable communities were replaced by public or semipublic institutions such as university campuses (University of Illinois on Chicago's Near West Side), baseball parks (Dodger Stadium in Los Angeles's Chavez Ravine), convention centers, and hotels. Displaced residents and small businessmen seldom received adequate assistance.

Major development plans after the 1960s continued to focus on the central business district in hopes of encouraging confidence, investment, resettlement, and tourism. Municipalities improved public transportation with downtown bus malls in Portland and Minneapolis, and subways in San Francisco (1972) and Washington (1976); constructed major symbols of progress like arches, domed stadiums, convention centers, and malls; and supported private restorations of historic but rundown waterfronts like Baltimore's Harborplace and dilapidated markets like Seattle's Pike Place Market. Local governments also supported refurbishment of older inner city housing to attract affluent youthful taxpayers seeking exciting, safe, and convenient neighborhoods. Gentrification began in the 1960s at Philadelphia's Society Hill and Washington's Capitol Hill, and thereafter spread to most major cities, improving their tax base but showing little consideration for those displaced.

The combination of declining industrial employment and the migration of the middle class to suburbia resulted in a major shift in urban demographics and social structure. This was exemplified in the 1970s by the first decline of median family income among urban core residents. The flight of the middle class was crucial because they paid the taxes; supported businesses, cultural institutions, and schools; and promoted social and political reform. Public school demography dramatized the changes: two-thirds of New York's public school students were white in 1957; 14 percent were white in 1987. People had lost their confidence in the city and no longer believed that its problems could be solved. Cities tried to raise taxes to make up for lost revenues and to defer maintenance and services, which encouraged more businesses to leave. New York's infrastructure began to collapse in the late 1960s: buildings were abandoned, and one out of eight residents were on welfare. The outcome was financial collapse in 1975, and a bailout by Washington.

The people left behind and the new in-migrants were increasingly poor people of color. A second great black migration had occurred during World War II, and it continued after the war. By 1970 three-fourths of African Americans lived in cities, comprising the majority in Washington, D.C. (71.1 percent), Newark, Gary, and Atlanta. One decade later, they were a majority in Detroit, Baltimore, New Orleans, and Birmingham as well. Nearly all of the increase between 1950 and 1966 (86 percent) occurred in central cities at a time when 70 percent of white increase was in suburbia. There was also a postwar boom in Spanish-speaking urban populations. New York's Puerto Rican population rose from 61,000 in 1940 to 613,000 in 1960. Ten years later the city was 10 percent Puerto Rican. Substantial Puerto Rican communities have also been established in midsized industrial cities in the metropolitan New York region and in Philadelphia, Cleveland, and Chicago. By the late 1980s Miami had a Hispanic majority. It has elected Puerto Rican and Cuban mayors, and the social climate is set by its Cuban immigrants, who have made it the economic capital of the Caribbean. On the West Coast, one-third of Los Angeles in 1980 was Hispanic, and one-tenth Asian.

These newcomers generally ended up in ghettos like New York's Bedford-Stuyvesant, Chicago's West Side, or Los Angeles's Watts, whose populations greatly increased and whose boundaries expanded. White residents in zones of emergence used various methods to prevent integration, including neighborhood improvement associations that promoted solidarity and political pressure on elected officials, restrictive covenants (illegal since 1947), zoning laws to encourage stability, and violence. The ghetto residents lived in decayed, overcrowded housing, had substandard educational and health facilities, high unemployment, few well-paying jobs with advancement opportunities, and high rates of crime.

Widespread frustrations, epitomized by the black power movement, provided the underpinnings for the eruption of racial hostilities in the summers of 1964 through 1968, when there were about seventy-five "commodity riots." These involved the destruction of neighborhood shops and property, largely white-owned, whereas race riots encompassed interracial conflict over contested turf. About 10 percent of local residents looted white-owned neighborhood stores that symbolized oppression and the unfulfilled expectations of the civil rights movement. The worst violence occurred in Detroit in 1967; forty-three died and two thousand were injured. The riots drew national attention to the problems of the black ghettos and led to increased federal assistance to the inner city.

The black power movement energized the community into grassroots political activity ranging from New York's local school district elections to campaigning for mayors. The first African American mayor of a major city was Carl B. Stokes of Cleveland (1967), who promoted public housing and urban services. By 1970 there were black mayors in fifty cities, primarily those with large African American populations, and by 1990 African Americans had been elected mayor in New York, Chicago, and most of the largest cities, generally because of exceptionally strong black turnouts at the polls.

The riots were an important reason that cities in the 1960s received renewed positive attention from Washington under Democratic administrations already influenced by the "discovery" of poverty in Michael Harrington's *The Other America* (1962). Lyndon Johnson's $390 million Great Society program comprised a variety of initiatives to fight the War on Poverty. In 1964 the Office of Economic Opportunity established such programs as the Job Corps, Head Start, and the community action programs that empowered neighborhood service agencies. Johnson expanded food stamp and urban housing programs and established the Model Cities program (1966), which targeted federal funds for thirty-six neighborhoods, relying on local involvement to coordinate programs to enhance education, housing, health, and jobs. By 1969, total federal expenditures for cities soared to $14 billion, and the number of Americans below the poverty line was cut nearly in half. Under the Nixon administration funds nearly doubled by 1974, but the administration sought to reduce Washington's role in local affairs, first by cutting allocations and reducing or eliminating programs, and later by New Federalism (1972), which gave local governments policy planning responsibilities.

While the federal share of local budgets rose from 15 percent in 1960 to 25 percent in 1975, revenue sharing ended up mainly benefiting suburbia. Ghetto conditions seem to have gotten worse rather than better. African American males have a hard time finding employment (black teenagers' unemployment nearly doubled between 1965 and 1980, to 46.9 percent, reflecting their poor education and lack of access to jobs), and black female-headed households are nearly the norm, rising from about 20 percent in 1960 to 43 percent in 1988. The result is pervasive hopelessness and gang violence among a young and seemingly permanent underclass.

POPULATION OF LEADING U.S. CITIES

1690		1800	
1. Boston	7,000	Philadelphia	69,000
2. Philadelphia	4,000	New York	60,000
3. New York	3,900	Baltimore	26,000
4. Newport	2,600	Boston	25,000
5. Charleston	1,100	Charleston	20,000
1850		**1900**	
1. New York	515,500	New York	3,437,202
2. Philadelphia	340,000	Chicago	1,698,575
3. Baltimore	169,600	Philadelphia	1,293,697
4. Boston	136,880	Saint Louis	575,238
5. New Orleans	116,375	Boston	560,892
6. Cincinnati	115,435	Baltimore	508,957
7. Brooklyn	96,838	Cleveland	381,768
8. Saint Louis	77,860	Buffalo	352,367
9. Albany	50,763	San Francisco	342,782
10. Pittsburgh	46,601	Cincinnati	325,902
11. Louisville	43,194	Pittsburgh	321,616
12. Buffalo	42,260	New Orleans	287,104
13. Providence	41,573	Detroit	285,704
14. Washington	40,001	Milwaukee	285,315
15. Newark	38,890	Washington	278,718
16. Rochester	36,403	Newark	246,070
17. San Francisco	34,776	Louisville	204,731
18. Chicago	29,963	Minneapolis	202,718
19. Detroit	21,019	Indianapolis	169,164
20. Milwaukee	20,061	Kansas City	163,752
1950		**1988**	
1. New York	7,891,957	New York	7,352,700
2. Chicago	3,620,962	Los Angeles	3,352,710
3. Philadelphia	2,071,605	Chicago	2,977,520
4. Los Angeles	1,970,358	Houston	1,698,090
5. Detroit	1,849,568	Philadelphia	1,647,000
6. Baltimore	949,708	San Diego	1,070,310
7. Cleveland	914,808	Detroit	1,035,920
8. Saint Louis	856,796	Dallas	987,360
9. Washington	802,178	San Antonio	941,150
10. Boston	801,444	Phoenix	923,750
11. San Francisco	775,357	Baltimore	751,400
12. Pittsburgh	676,806	San Jose	738,420
13. Milwaukee	637,392	San Francisco	731,600
14. Houston	596,163	Indianapolis	727,130
15. Buffalo	580,132	Memphis	645,190
16. New Orleans	570,445	Jacksonville	635,430
17. Minneapolis	521,718	Washington	617,000
18. Cincinnati	503,998	Milwaukee	599,380
19. Seattle	467,591	Boston	577,830
20. Kansas City	456,622	Columbus	569,750

SOURCES: Carl Bridenbaugh, *Cities in the Wilderness: The First Century of Urban Life in America, 1625–1742* (1964), 143; Marshall A. Smelser, *The Democratic Republic, 1801–1815* (1968), 22; Howard P. Chudacoff, *The Evolution of American Urban Society* (1975), 56; *World Almanac and Book of Facts, 1989*, 538–539; *Information Please Almanac, 1991*, 787.

The Future of the City

Cities are likely to remain the focal point of economics, government, culture, and innovation for residents of metropolitan districts. Institutions like corporate offices and sports arenas may move to greener pastures, but museums, libraries, and universities are less mobile. Long-term efforts to sustain historic institutions and enterprises by protecting and rebuilding the central business district remain important. Cities will also have to attend to their infrastructure before highways and bridges begin to crumble. These are difficult tasks as revenue sources dry up, historically powerless and voiceless people with their own agendas gain political power, and the gap between the haves and have-nots broadens. Low levels of academic achievement, rising crime rates, and growing proportions of female-headed households provide the potential for a frightening future. Scholars and planners believe there needs to be a balanced metropolitan vision for the future based on a pluralistic symbiotic model with greater shared responsibilities. Yet even more basic is the enormous need for jobs and development in the urban ghettos before conditions become so intolerable and unacceptable that anarchy emerges.

[See also Business Culture; Commercial Architecture; Housing; Public Architecture; Urban Cultural Institutions; Urban Parks.]

BIBLIOGRAPHY

General Works

Chudacoff, Howard P., and Judith E. Smith. *The Evolution of American Urban Society.* 3d ed. (1988).

Goldfield, David R., and Blaine A. Brownell. *Urban America: A History.* 2d ed. (1990).

The Early American City

Bridenbaugh, Carl. *Cities in the Wilderness: The First Century of Urban Life in America, 1625–1742* (1938).

Bridenbaugh, Carl. *Cities in Revolt: Urban Life in America, 1743–1776* (1955).

Lebsock, Suzanne. *The Free Women of Petersburg: Status and Culture in a Southern Town, 1784–1860* (1984).

Nash, Gary B. *The Urban Crucible: Social Change, Political Consciousness, and the Origins of the American Revolution* (1979).

The Walking City

Blumin, Stuart M. *The Emergence of the Middle Class: Social Experience in the American City, 1760–1900* (1989). Also invaluable on the early American city.

Boyer, Paul S. *Urban Masses and Moral Order in America, 1820–1920* (1978). Also excellent on the industrial city.

Dawley, Alan. *Class and Community: The Industrial Revolution in Lynn* (1976).

Stansell, Christine. *City of Women: Sex and Class in New York, 1789–1860* (1986).

Thernstrom, Stephan. *Poverty and Progress: Social Mobility in a Nineteenth-Century City* (1964).

Wade, Richard C. *The Urban Frontier: The Rise of Western Cities, 1790–1830* (1959).

Wade, Richard C. *Slavery in the Cities: The South, 1820–1860* (1964).

Wilentz, Sean. *Chants Democratic: New York City and the Rise of the American Working Class, 1788–1850* (1984).

The Industrial Radial City

Barrett, James R. *Work and Community in the Jungle: Chicago's Packinghouse Workers, 1894–1922* (1987).

Barth, Gunther Paul. *City People: The Rise of Modern City Culture in Nineteenth-Century America* (1980).

Cohen, Lizabeth. *Making a New Deal: Industrial Workers in Chicago, 1919–1939* (1990).

Grossman, James R. *Land of Hope: Chicago, Black Southerners and the Great Migration* (1989).

Hammack, David C. *Power and Society: Greater New York at the Turn of the Century* (1982).

Kantowicz, Edward R. *Polish-American Politics in Chicago, 1888–1940* (1975).

Kasson, John F. *Amusing the Millions: Coney Island at the Turn of the Century* (1978).

Mohl, Raymond A. *The New City: Urban America in the Industrial Age, 1860–1920* (1985).

Nelli, Humbert S. *Italians in Chicago, 1890–1930: A Study in Ethnic Mobility* (1970).

Philpott, Thomas Lee. *The Slum and the Ghetto: Neighborhood Deterioration and Middle-Class Reform. Chicago, 1880–1930* (1978).

Rabinowitz, Howard. *Race Relations in the Urban South, 1865–1890* (1978).

Riess, Steven A. *City Games: The Evolution of American Urban Society and the Rise of Sports* (1989).

Spear, Allan H. *Black Chicago: The Making of a Negro Ghetto, 1890–1920* (1967).

Thernstrom, Stephan. *The Other Bostonians: Poverty and Progress in the American Metropolis, 1880–1970* (1973).

Warner, Sam Bass, Jr. *Streetcar Suburbs: The Process of Growth in Boston, 1870–1900* (1962).

The City in the Metropolitan Era, 1945–1990

Abbott, Carl. *Urban America in the Modern Age, 1920 to the Present* (1987).

Caro, Robert. *The Power Broker: Robert Moses and the Fall of New York* (1974).

Fox, Kenneth. *Metropolitan America: Urban Life and Urban Policy in the United States, 1940–1980* (1986).

Gluck, Peter R., and Richard J. Meister. *Cities in Transition: Social Changes and Institutional Responses in Urban Development* (1979).

Hirsch, Arnold. *Making the Second Ghetto: Race and Housing in Chicago, 1940–1960* (1983).

— STEVEN A. RIESS

THE CLERGY

The ministry in early colonial America was a public office marked by long tenure in a single congregation, public leadership in the local community, and frequent close links to local and colonial governments. By the early nineteenth century, it had become a profession marked by leadership of voluntary congregations and detached from its earlier symbolic and financial linkage to the state. But more than the other professions, it felt the democratizing impulses that flowed from the American Revolution. These kept the clergy close to the people, but they also created enduring tensions over clerical roles and standards.

Colonial Office

No one knows how many priests and preachers labored in seventeenth-century America, but by 1680 at least 270 ministers, mostly Puritans, had led congregations in New England, and 119 more, mostly clergy comfortable with the rites of the Church of England, had worked in Virginia. Maryland provided a place for at least forty-five clerics, most of them Catholic missionaries, and the Delaware Valley served as home for at least twelve, half of them Swedish Lutherans. Forty-six Protestants, mostly Dutch Reformed and Presbyterian, and fifteen French Catholic missionaries served in New Netherland and New York, and at least 142 additional Catholic missionaries, including 116 Jesuits, worked in the settlements of New France. Numerous Franciscans, Dominicans, and Jesuits spent their energies in Florida and New Mexico. At least 218 Franciscans labored in Florida alone: in 1634 around thirty-five of them maintained the forty-four missions there; in 1630 fifty Franciscan priests worked in the twenty-five missions of New Mexico.

Between 1607 and 1776 more than 4,714 clergymen became settled ministers in congregations formed by colonists. Thirty-five percent were Congregationalists, clustered in New England; 25 percent were Episcopalians in the middle and southern colonies; 12 percent led Baptist congregations; 10 percent were Presbyterians; 6 percent came from other Reformed churches; 3 percent were Lutherans; 2 percent were Moravians; and 2 percent were Roman Catholics. The remaining 5 percent were divided among an array of smaller groups (Weis, p. 17).

Several of the earliest ministers were men on the margins of European and English elite culture. The New England Puritans were alienated from English culture for ideological reasons, and some of the Anglican ministers in the early southern colonies were reputed to be men of mediocre abilities and modest social backgrounds. But no easy generalization can encompass the range of social settings from which the clergy came. Information on social background is available for 36 of 72 seventeenth-century New England ministers listed in Sprague's *Annals*: nineteen had clergymen as fathers; four, merchants; four, yeomen; two, lawyers; two, owners of large estates; two, mayors; one, a "gentleman"; and two, "poor" workers. In other regions the data are too sketchy to generalize. By the early eighteenth century 63 percent of the Harvard graduates who became Congregational ministers were the sons of relatively affluent merchants, physicians, innkeepers, and clergymen (Youngs, p. 12).

Subject far more than their European counterparts to the whims of local congregations, the clergy expressed anxiety about their status throughout the colonial era. The abler ministers, however, stood near the apex of cultural influence. They occupied a revered public office: the state officially recognized and supported them, and local custom elevated the office even when the people found individual occupants to be deficient. In 1650 almost 80 percent of the clergy received support from public taxation or trading companies. By 1750 that percentage had declined by half, but eighteenth-century clergy still benefited from the laws of establishment.

By 1650 the colonists had formed at least 112 religious congregations; by 1750, at least 1,711; by 1780, about 3,234. (The increase reflected not only population growth but also accelerating denominational competition.) As the presiding officers of these congregations, the ministers directed the only small public groups in the colonies that included men, women, and children, imposed discipline for moral infractions, and provided weekly commentary and information. Until the mid eighteenth century many towns and villages had only one minister, who oversaw not merely the church but also the moral and religious ethos of the community. The minister was a public figure.

Often that public role entailed political responsibility. In New England the clergy held no governmental positions, but they served as advisers to the general courts and expected governors to heed their counsel. John Cotton (1584–1652) helped draft the Massachusetts Bay legal code; Thomas Hooker (1586[?]–1647) shaped legislation in Connecticut in 1639; and after the Glorious Revolution of 1688 Increase Mather (1639–1723) secured the new charter creating the royal province of Massachusetts. Annual sermons to colonial assemblies symbolized the subtle political influence of the established clergy. Outside New England, ministers sometimes occupied seats of political power, as when James Blair (1655–1743) served for over forty years as a member of the Governor's Council in Virginia. By the time of the Revolution, therefore, it seemed natural for the clergy to express themselves on political topics, and they were active in debates over revolutionary politics. Some, like the Catholic priest John Carroll (1735–1815) undertook political and diplomatic duties for the revolutionary cause.

As a literate elite, the colonial clergy issued public commentary about a multitude of themes. Cotton Mather wrote about the history of Massachusetts Bay, education, and science.

They were respected partly because they were more educated than most other colonists. Ninety percent of the one thousand preachers in colonial Massachusetts were college graduates, and in the seventeenth century 50 percent of Harvard's graduates became ministers. At least 60 percent—and probably up to 80 percent—of the 489 Anglican ministers in colonial Virginia had received college training. The governor of Maryland was amazed in 1714 when he found some "illiterate men . . . in holy orders." The ministry was a learned calling, and until the 1740s only a few "hot-gospelers," Quakers, and other eccentrics questioned that. As a result, clerical libraries were among the largest in the colonies; the clergy often provided the only legal advice and medical care available in the villages, and ministers were frequently the educators of colonial children.

Most of the presidents of the nine colonial colleges were clergymen. Other clergy founded parish and private grammar schools and classical academies, often serving as the village schoolmaster. By the eighteenth century they had begun to write some of the texts used in those schools and colleges—such as the physics manuscripts of the Puritan Charles Morton 1626/27–1698), which were read at Harvard for almost forty years; or the *Accidence to the English Tongue* (1724), the first colonial grammar in English, by the Virginia Anglican Hugh Jones (ca. 1670–1760); or the *Elementa Philosophica* (1752), the first philosophy text published in America, by the Anglican Samuel Johnson (1690–1772), who presided over King's College (now Columbia University) in New York from 1754 to 1763 and served a parish in Connecticut.

By no means did all the clergy distinguish themselves by publishing. In the seventeenth century, for instance, most clerical publications originated in New England, and even there 66 percent of the clergy never published anything and only 5 percent managed to publish ten or more tracts or treatises. The publishing clergy mainly produced short works—only 8 percent exceeded one hundred pages—designed for polemical or devotional purposes. Sixty-nine percent of their publications were sermons (Selement, "Publication and the Puritan Minister," 1980, pp. 219–241).

Yet no other colonial group equaled the clergy as writers, and they wrote on manifold topics. Such New England divines as Thomas Shepard (1605–1649), Samuel Hopkins (1721–1803), and Nathaniel Emmons (1745–1840) produced intricate theological treatises; John Witherspoon (1723–1794) at Princeton wrote philosophy; Jonathan Edwards (1703–1758) at Northampton, Massachusetts, combined philosophical and theological interests. Scores of other ministers wrote and published poetry. Some, like the Puritan Michael Wigglesworth (1631–1705), achieved popular success; others, like Edward Taylor (ca. 1645–1729) of Westfield, Massachusetts, attained a genuine aesthetic subtlety. Clergymen wrote several of the discovery narratives and promotional treatises that attracted settlers and investors. As early as 1540 the *Relation* of the Franciscan Marcos de Niza brought Spaniards looking for the legendary golden Seven Cities of Cibola; the Jesuit Andrew White (1579–1656) promoted settlement in Maryland; Francis Higginson's *New-Englands Plantation* (1630) lured settlers to the Massachusetts Bay Colony. They also furnished their share of colonial historians: Increase Mather (1639–1723), William Hubbard (1621–1704), and Cotton Mather (1662/3–1727/8) wrote on Massachusetts Bay; James Blair (1655–1743), Hugh Jones (1670–1760), William Stith (1707–1755) on Virginia; and Jeremy Belknap (1744–1798) on New Hampshire. Still others wrote on scientific topics. John Clayton (ca. 1685–1773?) and John Banister (1650–1692) in Virginia prepared botanical reports, while Samuel Danforth (1626–1674) published astronomical observations and Jared Eliot (1685–1763) wrote on iron and on field husbandry in New England. As a literate elite, the clergy issued public commentary on a multitude of themes.

Their writing amplified the cultural significance of their encounters with the Native American population. Missionaries often proved to be the colonial era's most accomplished observers of the indigenous peoples. The *Relations* written by the Jesuits in New France contained detailed descriptions of Iroquois and Huron cultures, and although cultural biases marred clerical descriptions of Native American religious and burial practices, they gave English and European readers a new awareness of radical American cultural diversity. The missionaries also provided the first grammars and dictionaries that deciphered for Europeans the Native American languages: Andrew White in Maryland, for instance, prepared an Algonkian grammar, and Benjamin Ingraham wrote one for the Creek language.

Despite their accomplishments, the clergy discovered from the outset that the laity in their local churches expected to hire their own ministers and set their own policies. This local lay assertiveness troubled some ministers, who complained that churches treated them as "hirelings," withheld salaries, and made the decisions about ministerial tenure. By the late seventeenth century, ministers and congregations in New England often negotiated detailed contracts; by the early eighteenth, Anglican clergy in Virginia were embroiled in litigation and political disputes over salaries and status. Eventually the colonial ministers organized themselves in presbyteries, synods, coetuses, ministeriums, and associations that attained greater authority over local congregations, but the tradition of local lay control never fully disappeared.

Professionals and Populists

In the early nineteenth century, ministers moved around more than they ever had. This increased mobility signaled three new developments: the first was a new tendency to treat the ministry as a professional career; the second was a proliferation of itinerant preachers who disdained any suggestion that the ministry was a learned profession; and the third was the accelerating immigration from Europe (including Ireland).

By 1830 the Protestant ministry was becoming a career in the modern sense: in New England, for example, clergy no longer served a lifetime in one community but moved upward through a sequence of local positions toward increasingly influential assignments with larger churches. Many of them served four or five congregations during their ministry, with the top tier attaining high prestige and salaries while others languished in lesser posts. Some moved into translocal agencies, ranging from mission and reform societies to editorships. The growing number of journals and associations intended exclusively for the clergy enhanced the sense of the ministry as a professional class (Scott, pp. 148–151).

Outside New England and New York, the enduring change in the Protestant ministry resulted from the upsurge in the number of zealous laity who entered clerical ranks without bothering to acquire either the traditional degrees or the customary learning. In 1775 America had around 1,800 Christian ministers; by 1850 the census found 26,842, though denominational statistics, which included farmer-preachers and other part-time clergy, suggested far more. The vast majority served in popular denominations—especially Methodist and Baptist churches—that did not require formal education. Such populist preachers as the revivalist Lorenzo Dow (1777–1834) both reflected and promoted a cultural style that encouraged colorful colloquial speech, fervent appeal to the emotions, earthy and pointed polemics, disdain for formal learning, and democratic confidence in the common people (Hatch, pp. 3–66).

In 1775 America had around 1,800 Christian ministers; by 1850 the census found 26,842, although denominational statistics, which included farmer-preachers and other part-time clergy, suggested far more.

This democratizing impulse, which drew on the ideals and rhetoric of the American Revolution, opened the ministerial vocation to groups previously excluded: a score of women, like Nancy Towle and Jarena Lee (1783–c. 1850), claimed a divine call. In 1853 a Congregational church ordained Antoinette Brown Blackwell (1825–1921) as the first regular woman minister in a mainline denomination. In far greater numbers, hundreds of black preachers exhorted the slaves on the plantations and served many of the 931 separate black congregations founded during the antebellum era (Sobel, p. 222). Such prominent black clergy as Henry Highland Garnet (1815–1882) in the North and Morris Brown (1770–1849) and Andrew Marshall (?–1856) in the South exemplified the public leadership that would make the minister the most prominent figure in the black community throughout the nineteenth century.

Similar cultural tensions, though with a distinctive ethnic character, appeared in the Catholic and Jewish traditions. The Catholic church had a predominantly immigrant clergy: even at the Second Plenary Council of Baltimore in 1866, 10 of the 45 bishops had been born in France; out of the total of 3,505 Catholic priests in the United States in 1869, one-third were either natives of Germany or German speakers; as late as 1870 only 6 of 88 priests in the diocese of Detroit were native-born Americans. In the early nineteenth century the dominance of the French clergy, cultured and well-educated, generated conflict between them and the growing numbers of Irish priests, who had a greater sense of cultural isolation in America. Similar tensions soon divided the Irish, Germans, and Poles (Ellis, pp. 17–28).

The Jewish rabbi found the American environment especially forbidding. American Jews had no regularly ordained rabbi until 1840, when Abraham Rice immigrated from Bavaria to Baltimore. The early Jewish clergy were not scholarly, ordained rabbis, learned in the Talmud, but enterprising innovators, like the American-born Gershom Mendes Seixas (1746–1814) in New York and the German immigrant Isaac Leeser (1806–1868) in Philadelphia, who functioned more like Protestant ministers. They flourished by meeting the expectations of largely uneducated congregations, but the traditionalist Rice resigned his position in 1849 and opened a dry goods store (Jick, pp. 3–78).

Even in the populist denominations, however, substantial numbers of ministers aspired to a measure of learning and gentility, with the result that the educated antebellum clergy often became cultural mediators, interpreters at boundaries where one cultural sphere touched another. Missionaries, for instance, not only transmitted American values to other cultures but also interpreted exotic cultures to the American majority, whether by pleading their cause, as Samuel Austin Worcester (1798–1859) did on behalf of the Cherokees in Georgia, or by propagating information about them, as in the writings of Adoniram Judson (1788–1850) on Burma, of Titus Coan (1801–1882) on Hawaii, and of William Griffis (1843–1928) on Japan. Such scholarly ministers as James Freeman Clarke (1810–1888), Samuel Johnson (1822–1882), and Lawrence Mills (1837–1918) published or translated the first serious studies of Asian religious traditions to appear in America.

The clerical elite helped to mediate the new forms of literary and academic culture, usually European in origin, to a broad middle-class laity. Often this mediation was indirect, as when scholars like Moses Stuart (1780–1852) and Theodore Parker (1810–1860) transmitted to other clergy the methods and presuppositions of German scientific biblical criticism. Nineteenth-century clergy continued to occupy chairs of philosophical instruction in American colleges, and such figures as James McCosh (1811–1894) at Princeton and Laurens Hickok (1798–1888) at Union College used their textbooks and teaching to introduce American students to German and Scottish philosophy and psychology. Still other clergymen promoted the nurturing of a literary sensibility: by 1865 ministers edited roughly 350 periodicals. Most were narrowly religious, but the clergy also provided editorial leadership for such literary journals as the *North American Review.*

Early-nineteenth-century clerics wrote much of the popular literature that graced Victorian coffee tables. All but two of the seventeen members of the Transcendental Club had ministerial careers lasting ten years or more, and Ralph Waldo Emerson spent three years as a pastor (Hutchinson, p. vi). Ministers wrote poetry and fiction—ranging from the historical romances of William Ware to A. B. Longstreet's humorous *Georgia Scenes* (1835)—along with travel narratives, popular historical studies, literary criticism, geographies, rhetorical texts, hymns, and devotional manuals. A select few produced a considerable body of technical theology. To embody the ideal of gentility required that one at least display an interest in literary culture, and the educated minister was expected to be a cultured gentleman.

The ministerial elite occupied a comfortable station in society. In 1860 the average wealth of the urban Protestant and Jewish clergy in fifty towns and cities was $5,782, with the southern urban clergy, many of whom were slave owners, holding an average of $10,177. This placed the clergy far below the wealth of urban lawyers, who had average holdings of $22,610, and of urban physicians, who held an average of $11,263, but it elevated them considerably above the national average of $2,580 for free white adult males (Holifield, "The Penurious Preacher?" pp. 17–36).

Such elite ministers as Lyman Beecher (1775–1863) in New England and Gardiner Spring (1785–1873) in New York were prominent in the "benevolent empire" of antebellum reform societies. They served as officers of the national movements to abolish slavery, promote temperance, distribute tracts, end wars, circulate the Bible, rescue fallen women, educate children, and maintain the Sabbath. The northern clergy furnished much of the leadership in the abolition movement; southern ministers responded by publishing proslavery treatises. The Civil War and Reconstruction promoted new forms of clerical social activism, ranging from military chaplaincy and leadership in such wartime agencies as the Sanitary Commission to political leadership in Reconstruction legislatures on the part of such black preachers as Richard Cain (1825–1887) in South Carolina and Henry M. Turner (1834–1915) in Georgia.

The social involvement continued after the Civil War, especially among the small group of clergy who assumed leadership in the Social Gospel movement. The Congregationalist Washington Gladden (1836–1918) in Columbus, Ohio, not only preached and wrote on social issues but also led the opposition to local monopolies and gave his support to labor unions. Sympathy with factory workers was especially visible among the Catholic clergy, and James Cardinal Gibbons (1834–1921), archbishop of Baltimore, lobbied in Rome to prevent papal condemnation of the Knights of Labor, whose secrecy violated Vatican policy.

Such elite ministers as Lyman Beecher in New England and Gardiner Spring in New York served as officers of national movements to abolish slavery, promote temperance, end wars, and rescue fallen women.

The dominant trend of the late nineteenth century, however, was the continued democratization of the ministry. The evangelist Billy Sunday (1862–1935), for example, had no difficulty—and saw no need for professional training—when he moved in 1891 from professional baseball to the pulpit. By 1890 the census found 84,531 ministers in America; the denominations claimed to have 111,036. But the percentage of college students who entered the ministry declined: in the mid seventeenth century 66 percent of graduates had become ministers; by the late eighteenth century the figure was 23 percent; by 1890 only 12 percent of college graduates entered the clerical ranks. Although enrollment in seminaries increased, the ratio of seminary students to active clergy remained small: in 1850 it was 1:20; in 1890, 1:12 (or 1:15 if we use the denominational tally of clergy). Jewish leaders worried about unqualified rabbis who advertised their services in local newspapers. Catholics and Eastern Orthodox Christians maintained more successful scrutiny over their candidates for priesthood, but the result was that they still had to depend on an immigrant ministry (May and Shuttleworth, 2:24–36, 4:45–46).

In the South the black clergy had an especially prominent role in the black community. One study of seventy-eight elite black ministers between 1865 and 1902 found that fifty-two of them had college or seminary training and fifty-nine were leaders of colleges, secondary schools, fraternal societies, or newspapers. But they also shared the poverty of their communities: forty-one had been slaves; fifty-three had to hold a job outside the church in order to support themselves (Wheeler, pp. 17–21, Appendix).

By 1890 observers noted that clerical success among Protestants depended not on scholarly attainment or even sermonic profundity but, rather, on winsomeness and zeal. A small nationwide poll in 1905 revealed that 61 percent of churchgoers wanted their ministers to be sympathetic, benevolent, fatherly, and kind, while 40 percent gave the highest rating to clergy who were manly and strong, and possessed good business instincts; both groups agreed that a minister should be a man of imposing physique, stately bearing, and winsome personality (Hill, pp. 16–18). The embodiment of such ideals was the flamboyant Henry Ward Beecher (1813–1887) at Plymouth Congregational Church in the borough of Brooklyn, New York, whose topical, witty, and sentimental sermons carried the democratic style into an urban middle-class setting. Beecher was preeminent among the "Princes of the Pulpit" who attracted overflow audiences to large downtown churches.

Such ministers could be authoritative within their local congregations. But the clergy were losing some of the positions of authority that they had once held in the larger culture. In the earlier nineteenth century they had presided over most of the nation's colleges, but Harvard had its last ordained president in 1869, Yale in 1899, Princeton in 1902. Other elite schools followed their example. In the nineteenth century the clergy had furnished the colleges with their trustees, but at fifteen typical private colleges, clerical trustees declined from 39 percent in 1860 to 23 percent in 1900 (Hutchinson, ed., pp. 56–57).

In some regions the clergy remained active as educators. In the frontier West they established secondary school systems and served as the superintendents of education. Parochial schools founded under Bishop Jean-Baptiste Lamy (1814–1888) became the foundation for the public schools of New Mexico and Arizona. Colleges founded by clergymen formed the basis for at least half a dozen of the western state universities—including the University of Kansas, the University of Tulsa, and the University of South Dakota—and denominational colleges under clerical leadership still proliferated throughout the nation (Szasz, pp. 58–165). The didactic schoolbooks of William Holmes McGuffey (1800–1873), moreover, helped to form more than one generation of American schoolchildren.

A clerical elite continued the traditions of scholarly and literary productivity that had distinguished the antebellum ministers. Philip Schaff's *History of the Christian Church* (1882–1892), J. D. G. Shea's *History of the Catholic Church in the United States* (1886–1892), Charles W. Upham's *Salem Witchcraft* (1867), G. W. Williams's *History of the Negro Race in America* (1883), and Edward Eggleston's *The Transit of Civilization* (1901) represented important contributions to nineteenth-century historiography. Eggleston's novels of the middle border inspired a regional genre of American writing; Charles Sheldon's Social Gospel novel *In His Steps* was the best-seller of 1897; and Edward Everett Hale's (1822–1909) fiction, oratory, and historical writing made his name recognized throughout the country. But the majority of clergy continued to think of their responsibilities as local.

Specialists and Generalists

In the twentieth century most ministers were still leaders of local congregations. While other professions established national associations that determined common standards of competence and regulated entry into professional ranks, the clergy relied on local congregations or on denominational boards that remained attuned to local lay expectations. Because of denominational divisions, the profession had no way of enforcing a common standard of preparation or performance. As a result of the democratizing traditions, any zealous convert could, in some denominations and communities, become a minister without any rigorous preparation.

By 1920 the census counted 127,270 ministers. They were divided between a small elite, educated in select schools, and a far larger number of populist preachers. In 1926 only 24 percent of the clergy in the nineteen largest predominantly white Protestant denominations had graduated from both a college and a seminary; 46 percent had graduated from neither. In the largest black denominations only 7 percent of the ministers had both a college and a seminary education; 86 percent had neither. Catholic educational levels were higher: 68 percent of Catholic clergy had graduated from both college and seminary and only 7 percent had no higher education. Catholic reformers, however, lamented the absence of intellectual rigor and curiosity in clerical education. Jews had been more successful at creating selective training schools and formal rabbinic organizations that maintained common standards. But this still meant that more than half of the American clergy had neither a college nor a seminary degree (May and Shuttleworth, 2:14).

An intensive study of sixty-three Protestant seminaries published in 1934 revealed that most of their seminarians came from low-income families in small communities. Their parents had, on average, two years of high school education. A second study, published in 1935, found that almost half of the Protestant clergy came from smaller rural communities, and that 31 percent said their parents had been poor, while only 4 percent represented them as affluent (Douglass and Brunner, pp. 110–111). Catholic clergy were far more likely to have grown up in larger cities; only 18 percent of them came from rural areas. But almost a third of them came from immigrant households (Fichter, p. 70). In Conservative and Orthodox Judaism, most seminary graduates were still European-born even though they had graduated from American universities. Few of the clergy in the early twentieth century came from families or communities of high economic or social status.

The democratizing impulse generated reactions that stimulated renewed efforts to set uniform standards. In Judaism such institutions as the Central Conference of American Rabbis (1889), the Rabbinical Assembly (1919), and the Rabbinical Council of America (1923) began to establish common expectations. In Protestantism the report *The Education of American Ministers* (1934) encouraged the formation in 1936 of the American Association of Theological Schools as an accrediting agency to develop stricter admission policies and higher levels of faculty expertise. Catholic seminaries tightened their standards during the 1940s, when they began seeking accreditation from regional and national secular organizations.

Between 1930 and 1954 several denominations slowly elevated their educational requirements for new clergy, with the result that the number of seminary students increased from roughly 9,000 to 28,760, representing a 1:6 ratio of divinity students to active clergy. The same period saw a fourfold increase in the number of accredited seminaries that admitted only college graduates, and a 62 percent increase in the number of their faculty with Ph.D. degrees or the equivalents. (Niebuhr, Williams, Gustafson, pp. 1–26). By the 1950s the average minister in a mainline denomination had received more years of schooling than had the clerical elite in the previous century, but many religious groups—and local congregations—still required only faith and zeal. The democratic impulse held on in popular American religion.

The clergy maintained relatively high social status. Ten social scientific studies of professional status between 1936 and 1963 found that Americans consistently ranked ministers high in occupational prestige and usefulness to society (Glasse, pp. 105–107). During the 1940s such prominent clerics as the liberal Harry Emerson Fosdick at Riverside Church in New York and the conservative radio preacher Charles E. Fuller attracted popular adulation; during the 1950s such masters of the media as the Catholic Bishop Fulton J. Sheen and the revivalist Billy Graham ranked high on the lists of most admired Americans. More scholarly ministers like H. Richard Niebuhr and Reinhold Niebuhr brought religious issues into intellectual and political discourse.

By the mid twentieth century the ministry was in transition. One sign of change was a growing division between generalists, who labored in local parishes, and specialists, who concentrated their energies on academic scholarship, college or university teaching, social reform, chaplaincy, counseling, or administration within religious bureaucracies. The division of labor often led to tensions, since parish ministers still had to meet local lay criteria of effectiveness and faith while specialists strove to meet the standards of scholarly guilds, schools, health agencies, and professional associations. The division of labor meant, for example, that parish ministers no longer published scholarly essays in theology, as they often had done in the nineteenth century. A study of 558 theologians in 1978 found that only fourteen held nonacademic positions (Hall, *Systematic Theology Today*, 38). By the end of the 1950s, moreover, Protestants had created at least eighty-four centers staffed by pastors who specialized in counseling, and by the 1970s substantial numbers of pastoral counselors had begun to go into private practice. Some churches began to worry about the recruitment of clergy willing to serve in local parishes: while a few denominations, like the Episcopal church, had a surplus of trained clergy, others faced shortages. The Catholic church, shaken by debates over clerical celibacy and authority, witnessed a steady decline of both parish priests and seminarians in the two decades after 1967.

> *During the 1950s such masters of the media as the Catholic Bishop Fulton J. Sheen and the revivalist Billy Graham ranked high on lists of most-admired Americans.*

A second sign of transition was the growing number of women in the ministry, a trend accelerated by the feminist movement and paralleled by similar patterns in other professions. By 1986, 84 out of the 166 larger American denominations ordained women, and women increasingly sought ordination. In 1977 they constituted about 4 percent of the total number of clergy; by 1986, 20,730 women clergy formed 8 percent of the total. The change evoked divisive controversy in several denominations. Despite vigorous internal debate, the Catholic church still forbade the ordination of women as priests; the Southern Baptist Convention also condemned ordination, though individual congregations could disregard that prohibition. In the Episcopal church an "irregular" ordination in 1974 led to a decision by the General Convention in 1976 to permit the regular ordination of women priests.

Increasing immigration from Spanish-speaking regions produced a third change in American clerical ranks, especially in the Catholic church. In 1972 Latino Catholic clergy instituted a national pastoral congress to examine the pastoral care of Hispanic Catholics and the role of Spanish-speaking clergy in the church. The attention to leadership led to political change: In 1970 the Catholic church had only one Latino bishop; by 1985 it had seventeen, with increasing numbers of Hispanic clergy. The Hispanic immigration has now begun to create change in Protestant denominations. By 1990 the Los Angeles area alone had more than six hundred Hispanic Protestant congregations, almost all led by Latino preachers.

Whatever the transitions, the clergy retained an influential place in American cultural and political movements. They occupied both ends of the political spectrum. During the 1930s Father Charles Coughlin used the radio to excoriate Roosevelt, while Reinhold Niebuhr supported the New Deal and the labor movement and excoriated isolationism (a poll of 21,606 ministers in 1936 revealed that 70 percent of them opposed the New Deal). By the 1960s, however, sociological surveys found the clergy far more inclined than their parishioners toward political liberalism. William Sloane Coffin, the chaplain at Yale, along with the radical Catholic priests Philip and Daniel Berrigan, represented an activist liberal minority, probably about 5 percent of the clergy, who took to the streets to protest the Vietnam War. The fundamentalist Carl McIntire represented the equally small minority who loudly protested against the liberal protesters. Pollsters during the late 1960s found that a slight majority of ministers opposed United States military policy in Vietnam.

Such traditions of clerical activism formed the background for the resurgence of a religious rightwing political movement led by such television evangelists as Jerry Falwell and Pat Robertson during the 1980s. The presidential campaign of yet another minister, the Baptist Jesse Jackson, dramatized the opposition to the conservative trend. Those campaigns evoked the longer history of clerical leadership in social movements.

No social movement elicited greater clerical involvement than the struggle for civil rights by black Americans. With impressive regularity the leaders of the movement emerged from the ranks of the black clergy, and such leaders as Ralph Abernathy, Andrew Young, and Martin Luther King, Jr., introduced into American political life the rhetorical style of the black church. The march on behalf of black voting rights in Selma, Alabama, in 1965 demonstrated the extent to which prominent white clergy—Protestant, Catholic, and Jewish—had begun to rally to King's leadership. In 1965 only 7 percent of the Protestant clergy, compared with 44 percent of the adult Protestant population, expressed disapproval of the civil rights movement.

Social commentators have periodically reported the demise of clerical influence in American society, but their reports have invariably proven to be premature. The patterns of social and political influence have varied, with politically liberal clergy from mainline denominations more publicly visible between 1945 and 1979, and politically conservative ministers more prominent in the subsequent decade. But little evidence exists for any claim that ministers have disappeared from the public arena. One reason for the continuing clerical presence in cultural debate has been the leadership of ministers within grass-roots communities—religious congregations—in which fully 40 percent of Americans gather each week. Not even the mass appeal of such television evangelists as Robert Schuller and Jerry Falwell can equal the more subtle forms of influence exercised by the clergy in the more than 345,000 local churches and synagogues throughout America. The democratizing tradition has, for better or worse, linked most of the American clergy to the standards and expectations of the people in those congregations, and the linkage has been the source of both their limitation and their strength as leaders in the society.

[See also The Professions.]

BIBLIOGRAPHY

Annals of the American Academy of Political and Social Science 387 (January 1970). An issue devoted to "The Sixties: Radical Change in American Religion."

Brunner, Edmund de S. *Church Life in the Rural South* (1923).

Dolan, Jay P., ed. *The American Catholic Parish: A History from 1850 to the Present.* 2 vols. (1987).

Douglass, H. Paul, and Edmund de S. Brunner. *The Protestant Church as a Social Institution* (1935).

Ellis, John Tracy, ed. *The Catholic Priest in the United States. Historical Investigations* (1971).

Fichter, Joseph H. *Religion as an Occupation: A Study in the Sociology of Professions* (1961).

Fichter, Joseph H. "Catholic Church Professionals." *Annals of the American Academy of Political and Social Science* 387 (January 1970).

Gaustad, Edwin S. *Historical Atlas of Religion in America* (1962).

Glasse, James D. *Profession: Minister* (1968).

Hall, David. *The Faithful Shepherd: A History of the New England Ministry in the Seventeenth Century* (1972).

Hall, Thor. *The State of the Arts in North America: Systematic Theology Today* Part 1, (1978).

Hatch, Nathan O. *The Democratization of American Christianity* (1989).

Hill, David Spence. *The Education and Problems of the Protestant Ministry* (1908).

Holifield, E. Brooks. *A History of Pastoral Care in America: From Salvation to Self-Realization* (1983).

Holifield, E. Brooks. "The Penurious Preacher? Nineteenth-Century Clerical Wealth: North and South." *Journal of the American Academy of Religion* 58 (Spring 1990): 17–35.

Hutchinson, William R. *The Transcendentalist Ministers: Church Reform in the New England Renaissance* (1959).

Hutchinson, William R., ed. *Between the Times: The Travail of the Protestant Establishment in America, 1900–1960* (1989).

Jick, Leon A. *The Americanization of the Synagogue, 1820–1870* (1976).

Luecke, Richard Henry. "Protestant Clergy: New Forms of Ministry, New Forms of Training." *Annals of the American Academy of Political and Social Science* 387 (January 1970).

May, Mark A., and Frank Shuttleworth. *The Education of American Ministers.* 4 vols. (1934).

Niebuhr, H. Richard, Daniel Day Williams, and James Gustafson. *The Advancement of Theological Education* (1957).

Sarna, Jonathan D., ed. *American Jewish Archives* 35, no. 2 (1983). Special issue on the American rabbinate.

Scott, Donald M. *From Office to Profession: The New England Ministry, 1750–1850* (1978).

Selement, George. "Publication and the Puritan Minister." *William and Mary Quarterly*, 3rd ser., 37, no. 2 (1980): 219–241.

Sobel, Mechal. *Trabelin' On: The Slave Journey to an Afro-Baptist Faith* (1979).

Sprague, William, ed. *Annals of the American Pulpit* (1857–1869).

Szasz, Ferenc M. *The Protestant Clergy in the Great Plains and Mountain West, 1865–1915* (1988).

Weis, Frederick Lewis. *The Colonial Churches and the Colonial Clergy of the Middle and Southern Colonies, 1607–1776* (1938).

Wheeler, Edward L. *Uplifting the Race: The Black Minister in the New South, 1865–1902* (1986).

Youngs, J. William T. *God's Messengers* (1976).

— E. BROOKS HOLIFIELD

CLOTHING AND PERSONAL ADORNMENT

Clothing and personal adornment are the most immediate means human beings have of communicating personal identity and social position, and the study of dress and appearance leads inevitably to a consideration of the complex and changing relationships of gender, class, and power. Attitudes toward men and women, work and leisure, success and failure, youth and age, health and sickness, beauty and sexuality, are all reflected in America's concern with personal appearance. This concern has from colonial days supported a fashion industry that, in advising us how to acquire the right hair, face, body, and clothes, claims to tell us not only who we can be, but who we ought to be.

Native Americans

When Europeans visited America in the sixteenth and seventeenth centuries, they sent back accounts of a myriad of native peoples with varying customs in dress and adornment. In many regions, Native Americans made clothing from well-dressed skins, but some groups also used woven textiles made from wild cotton (in the Southwest), cedar and spruce bark fiber (in the Northwest), grass, or animal hair. Typical garments included breech-clouts (or, for women, short skirts), belts and leggings, moccasins, and robes or mantles, but how much was worn depended on weather and occasion. While utilitarian clothing might be left plain, many garments were elaborately decorated with painted figures, quillwork, feathers, copper disks, beads, or fringe, according to local custom. Some tribes oiled, painted, or tattooed their bodies. Head hair was greased and blackened with charcoal, and, among men, varied widely in cut and style. Body hair was pulled out. Both men and women wore necklaces, earrings, headbands, and other adornments, ornamented with wampum, feathers, animal claws and teeth, turquoise (in the Southwest), or pearls.

European settlers appreciated the comfort and practicality of Indian snowshoes and moccasins, and moccasins became a permanent feature of American dress, not just where other shoes were unavailable but as house slippers, carriage boots, and, in altered form, modern leisure shoes. In a similar vein, the Indians admired European wool and linen textiles, and as their traditional hunting lands were lost, they added more and more woven garments to their wardrobe. But these were integrated into Indian patterns of dress rather than being worn in European style. Blankets (their barter price in beaver skins woven as stripes along the selvage) were used as mantles, for example, and shirts were belted and worn over breechclouts and leggings rather than tucked into trousers. Trade beads were assimilated into traditional Indian ornamentation. Even when the basic garb is European, as it appears in many mid-nineteenth-century photographs, Indian men and women maintained a distinctive culture by adding the blanket mantle and traditional necklaces and headgear.

The Seventeenth Century

Information about the clothing of colonial Americans is thin compared with the wealth of data available on clothing worn after 1800. We do know what styles were fashionable in England, and it is fair to assume that American dress was similar, since most textiles and many made-up garments were imported from the mother country. Contemporary American portraits (especially of women) provide but equivocal evidence since many sitters were depicted in ambiguous draperies. Where clothing is distinct, there is seldom proof that the sitters were painted in their own clothes. Little actual clothing survives from the colonial period. We have a few accessories owned by seventeenth-century Americans, but nothing like a complete outfit. A number of eighteenth-century dresses and suits exist, but the majority are made of rich materials and have been altered several times. Given the ambiguity of portraits and the scarcity of surviving clothing, scholars interested in early American dress must depend heavily on the written word.

Inventories tell us that the basic garments for seventeenth-century women were (1) the shift (a knee-length white linen undergarment with high or low neck and long or elbow-length sleeves); (2) the skirt (known as a petticoat or "cote"), of which several might be worn, the upper one often tucked up to show another of contrasting color beneath; and (3) a fitted bodice (usually called a doublet or waistcoat), boned when intended for formal wear. With these were worn stockings, garters, and shoes, a cap to cover the hair, and a cloak for warmth. Women of greater means might also own one or more gowns (a one-piece dress). To this basic wardrobe were added white linen neckerchiefs, collars and cuffs, gloves, fans, ribbons to trim the sleeves, masks to protect the complexion from the sun, silk hoods, and jewelry, including rings, necklaces, and earrings.

The typical man's wardrobe consisted of (1) the shirt (a linen undergarment corresponding to a woman's shift); (2) breeches (knee-length pants cut in many variations of fullness but never very tight); and (3) coats, jackets, waistcoats, and doublets (upper-body garments that are difficult to distinguish but that seem to have been worn in layers and that sometimes matched the breeches). To complete the outfit, a man wore stockings with garters, leather shoes or boots, a collar, cuffs, a hat, gloves, and sometimes a muff, cane, and rings.

Except for the linen shirt and shift, the most common material used for clothing was wool of varying weight and quality. Summer garments were sometimes made of linen. For common clothes, solid colors were typical, but utilitarian striped and checked patterns were also used. Printed textiles, however, were still very rare. In more prosperous families, the outer clothing was made of better quality wool or of silk, the latter sometimes woven with complex multicolored designs. Good fabrics were trimmed with gold, silver, or silk braid and ribbon loops and bows. Collars and cuffs of fine linen were trimmed with lace. The wealthiest might own a jeweled hatband. Military men frequently wore hard-wearing doublets of buff leather, which afforded some protection in battle.

Seventeenth-century Americans wore fabrics of every color, and in the clothing of the well-to-do, glittering braids and lace-edged linens created dramatic contrasts. While the Puritan settlers of Massachusetts disapproved of excess in dress, it is not true that they dressed primarily in black and gray. Tans and browns were probably the most common colors, being practical in a period when outer clothes were seldom washed, but red petticoats, green stockings, and green or blue aprons were a common sight among women of all classes. The "sad" colors often mentioned in inventories do not imply melancholy or gloom. "Sad" is etymologically related to "sated" and signifies being fully saturated with dye, resulting in a dark shade rather than a light one. But a sad (dark) color can be of any hue, and green, purple, orange, and various shades of brown are specifically mentioned.

What diversity there was in colonial dress arose more from class than from region, since Americans everywhere continued to import most of their fabrics and garments from England. Mice Morse Earle does mention a visitor to New York in 1704 who noted that middle-class Dutch women, unlike the English, tended to "go loose," that is, without corsets, and that they liked earrings and wore a different style of cap. Otherwise the differences were chiefly economic.

Surviving correspondence proves that Americans took a lively interest in fashion, but in New England the picture was complicated by Puritan religious principles. Like all seventeenth-century Americans, the Puritans who settled New England brought with them the assumption that fine clothing was an appropriate way of displaying rank and wealth. But for them dress was also a visible sign that revealed the spiritual health of both individual and community. Since the division between rich and poor was part of God's plan, the classes ought to be distinguished by their dress, but since everyone, rich or poor, was supposed to be working toward the good of the community as a whole rather than his own self-aggrandizement, it was not appropriate to compete to see how many luxuries could be acquired nor to spend an inappropriate proportion of one's income on clothing. New fashions were objectionable because they made the old ones unwearable before they were worn out and encouraged competition in wasteful luxury. It was also inappropriate to use clothing as a means of sexual display. Thus the first laws regulating dress, passed in 1634 and 1636, little more than a decade after the first Puritan settlement, targeted "new and immodest fashions" and any garment judged to be "uncomely [meaning inappropriate rather than unattractive] or prejudicial to the common good."

Inappropriate fashions included certain items made with silver, gold, silk, lace, or needlework, and garments that wasted material by being cut with unnecessarily full sleeves or by being slashed. Slashing was a decorative technique in which a garment was slit to allow puffs of the linen shirt or shift beneath to be pulled through the gap. The Puritans tolerated moderate slashing roughly equivalent to leaving a sleeve or bodice seam open. But sometimes fabrics were entirely covered with a pattern of tiny slits. Such fabrics must have ripped and worn out quickly and been difficult to reuse, making them a particularly wasteful example of conspicuous consumption.

The lack of contemporary references to cosmetics or face patches suggests that these European vanities were little known in America. The immodest fashions most often mentioned were women's low necklines and sleeves that left the arm bare below the elbow. Bare arms apparently possessed the erotic attraction that any customarily covered body part may acquire when newly exposed. Female modesty was enjoined by the Bible and felt to be necessary under the Calvinist principle that men and women were predisposed to sin and therefore needed restraints. Modern readers should not confuse this with prudery. In a century when husband, wife, and children all slept together in the same bed, with servants of both sexes in the same room, prudery could hardly exist, while prudence might welcome the support of modesty.

Men were the targets of sumptuary law chiefly in the matter of long hair, which the Bible branded as "shameful." The dislike of long hair extended to the very long and elaborately curled men's wigs that came into widespread use in the 1660s and 1670s. Seventeenth-century preachers racked their brains for words strong enough to express their disapproval (John Eliot called the periwig a "luxurious feminine protexity"), but the fashion gradually spread until wigs were a necessary part of any respectable man's appearance.

In 1651, a new Massachusetts law acknowledged that excess in dress was still a problem, "especially amongst people of mean condition, to the dishonor of God, the scandal of their profession, the consumption of estates, and altogether unsuitable to their poverty." The solution was to forbid silk hoods, thigh-high boots, gold and silver, and other luxuries to any family whose estate was less than £200. Anyone who held public office, who was well educated, or who had been well off in the past was exempt from the ban. Where the earlier laws had touched both rich and poor and been enforced by the churches, this law regulated only the poor and was enforced by the town constables—the temporal authorities were enforcing the privileges of the upper class.

By the middle of the seventeenth century, Puritan society had begun to show signs of change. The rigors of the early years had eased, and increasing prosperity allowed people to acquire more than the bare necessities. The great exodus of Puritans from England had ceased when the Civil War (1642–1652) gave them a cause to fight at home, and the younger generation had difficulty duplicating the same depth and intensity of religious experience known by its parents. Under these conditions, people found it more difficult to accept restrictions in dress. Hannah Lyman of Northampton, Massachusetts, not only wore a forbidden silk hood, but she brassily wore it into court when she was presented to the judge. The last sumptuary laws appeared during the Indian war of the 1670s, an upheaval perceived as divine punishment for a spiritual decay visibly symbolized by the inclination toward luxurious dress. But in spite of bare arms and silk hoods, ribbons and wigs, the Indian threat was turned back, and after the middle 1680s the laws seem no longer to have been enforced.

The Eighteenth Century

In the seventeenth century, rich and elaborate clothing had often appeared in startling contrast to the relatively primitive living conditions. But in the growing culture of consumption in the eighteenth century, fine clothing found a more fitting setting in fine houses with elaborate furnishings, and the importance of being in fashion became a recurring theme in American social life. The Puritan paradigm whereby both rich and poor dressed with restraint but according to their condition had been replaced in the later seventeenth century by the older and simpler idea that costly dress was a privilege vested only in people of wealth and rank. After 1700, that privilege began to be perceived as an obligation to dress well. Taking pains with one's dress (and suffering them too) was a way both of showing respect and of receiving it.

The importance of clothing and fashion in eighteenth-century society resonates throughout the personal diary of Samuel Sewall. In 1720, his third wife having died, Sewall (then aged sixty-eight) began to court a wealthy widow, Madam Winthrop. On 12 October, he found her barricaded behind a piece of black needlework, but when at last it was taken away, "I got my Chair in place, had some converse, . . . [and] Ask'd her to acquit me of Rudeness if I drew off her glove. Enquiring the reason, I told her 'twas great odds between handling a dead goat, and a living Lady. Got it off." It is hard not to smile at Sewall's note of triumph, but Madam Winthrop wore gloves indoors not primarily to keep suitors at a distance but to prove that she could afford servants to do all but the most refined and unnecessary needlework. On another visit Sewall was pleased to receive courteous treatment but noted that Madam Winthrop was "not in Clean Linen as sometimes." The implication is that she had not taken any special care in her dress to please or impress him—not a good sign. Madam Winthrop was apparently embarrassed by Sewall's personal appearance: "she spake somthing of my needing a Wigg." Sewall abominated wigs and told her that since God, his "best and greatest Friend," had given him the hair he had, he had no heart to go to some lesser person for a wig. Madam Winthrop, countering with an argument from a book Sewall himself had given her, "quoted him saying 'twas inconvenient keeping out of a Fashion commonly used." Few of Madam Winthrop's contemporaries would have considered her point of view inappropriate or frivolous—even "Col. Townsend spake to me of my Hood: Should get a Wigg." Sewall continued to visit Madam Winthrop for a time, but by 7 November "I did not bid her draw off her glove as sometime I had done. Her Dress was not so clean as somtime it had been." And with these eloquent messages in the language of costume, Samuel Sewall's courtship came to an end.

Wigs in a myriad of styles were worn by every man with any pretense to fashion or respectability until late in the eighteenth century; by the 1780s many men merely powdered and curled their hair to make it look like a wig.

Wigs in a myriad of styles were worn by every man with any pretense to fashion or respectability until late in the century. The voluminous wig of Sewall's day diminished only slowly. By the 1780s, many men merely powdered and curled their own hair to make it look like a wig, and in the next decade powder was gradually abandoned; but some conservative men wore wigs into the nineteenth century. Women's hair was relatively simple until about 1770, when elaborately built-up styles came into fashion. Anna Green Winslow described hers in her diary for May 1773: "I had my HEDDUS roll on, Aunt Storer said it ought to be made less, Aunt Deming said it ought not to be made at all. It makes my head itch, & ach, & burn like anything." This "head roll" was made of cow tail, horsehair, and human hair carded together and formed into a cushion. Anna's natural hair was combed up over it, pomaded, and probably powdered and augmented with extra curls. From hairline to the top of her cap, twelve-year-old Anna's hairstyle measured an inch longer than her face. In Europe, elaborate powdered hairstyles appeared above faces enameled with dangerous white lead paints and cheeks flaming with rouge. This extreme of artificiality was probably rare in America, but rouge, pearl powder, and patches were known.

The adoption of wigs in the later seventeenth century coincided with a broader change in men's clothing. The doublet disappeared, and the ancestor of the modern three-piece suit—breeches, coat, and vest (waistcoat)—came into use. As the century passed, the knee-length vest shortened, the coat became slimmer, and the breeches tighter. The formal coat was cut so as to require a very straight posture, with shoulders drawn back. For less formal occasions, the looser and more comfortable frock coat was worn, and for private moments at home, coat and wig could be replaced by a loose dressing gown and cap. Farmers protected their clothing with a large, shirtlike linen or wool coverall (also called a frock), while laborers doffed their coats and waistcoats in hot weather.

Women's clothing also changed around 1700. Over the linen shift, a woman now put on separate boned stays that created a stiff, cone-shaped torso. One or more petticoats were worn, the top one meant to show, and for most of the century, fashion required that these be supported by a hoop. Over these garments, the fashionable woman wore an unboned gown open down the center front from neck to hem and made so that the front edges did not meet. The gap was filled at the bottom by the petticoat, and at the top by the stomacher, a triangular piece of material, often elaborately decorated. Working women omitted both hoop and gown and instead wore a hip- or thigh-length, front-opening bodice. Some were form fitting and were worn over stays. Others, called bed gowns or short gowns, were cut loose enough to require no stays, allowing the freedom of movement necessary for heavy work.

The chief materials continued to be linen for undergarments and wool or silk for suits and gowns. Where summers were hot, people wore unlined linen, and as the century progressed, printed cottons were increasingly fashionable for gowns. Silk weaving reached high levels of sophistication in the eighteenth century, and fine silk dresses were so highly prized that they were remade and passed down for generations. Men's suits for special occasions were beautifully embroidered in colored silks, and the buttonholes were outlined with metallic braid. None of these stylish materials were made in America. Northern colonial communities did raise sheep and cultivate flax, producing woolens and linens suitable for sheets, towels, blankets, and common clothing. Virginia cloth, a southern-made cotton fabric, was used to clothe slaves. But silk, fine linen, broadcloth, and other quality wools had to be imported.

Along with imported fabrics came imported fashions. Some Americans kept their measurements with London agents, but most depended on local tailors and dressmakers to keep them in the mode. Imported shoes, silk stockings, hats, gloves, fans, and laces rounded out the American wardrobe. The desire to be in fashion was an entirely respectable concern for both sexes. Since men took care of business and were more likely to travel to London or correspond with London agents, they were often the ones who selected fabrics and accessories for their families. When shopping was done by proxy, personal taste was difficult to consult, and Americans tended instead to stipulate that whatever was purchased be in the latest fashion. This, coupled perhaps with the fear of appearing provincial, resulted in Americans' dressing even more elaborately than their counterparts abroad, a fact noted by many travelers. In 1784 Abigail Adams wrote from London, "I am not a little surprised to find dress, unless on public occasions, so little regarded here. The gentlemen are very plainly dressed, the ladies much less so than with us. . . . There is not that neatness in their appearance which you see in our ladies" (quoted in Earle, *Two Centuries of Costume*, p. 733).

Americans recognized their dependency on foreign manufactures as a weakness, especially when England began to tax them. From the 1760s through the 1780s, it became patriotic to spin and wear homespun rather than enrich England by wearing imported fabrics. Anne Hollingsworth Wharton's 1897 biography of Martha Washington mentions visitors to Mrs. Washington in 1777 who "felt rebuked by the plainness of her apparel and her example of persistent industry, while we were extravagantly dressed idlers, a name not very creditable in these perilous times" (p. 117).

The eighteenth-century day was divided into morning and afternoon. Relatively informal and comfortable clothing was permitted until dinner, but genteel folk dressed formally for the afternoon. The midday change of clothes is recorded by a London merchant who, visiting Mount Vernon in 1785, found George Washington coming from his farm in morning "undress" (plain blue coat, white cassimere waistcoat, black breeches, and boots). After chatting, the General excused himself. He returned dressed for his three o'clock dinner wearing a clean shirt, a drab coat (probably a good deal tighter than his blue one), a white waistcoat, white silk stockings, and powdered hair. Another Mount Vernon story related by Wharton describes some visiting young girls who neglected to dress for this midday meal, only to be surprised by the arrival of several young French officers. Hastily requesting leave to go up and dress properly, they were mortified to be told by Mrs. Washington to "remain as you are, what is good enough for General Washington is good enough for any guest of his." The girls' morning dress was probably loose and cool (it may not even have required a corset), while to dress formally meant to look attractive but feel uncomfortable, a combination that signified both self-respect and a desire to please others. To eyes accustomed to the rigidly controlled body shapes of corseted women, the loose look appeared slatternly and undisciplined. Thomas Jefferson wrote to his daughter Patsy on 22 December 1783:

> Some ladies think they may under the privileges of the dishabille be loose and negligent of their dress in the morning. But be you from the moment you rise till you go to bed as cleanly and properly dressed as at the hours of dinner or tea. A lady who has been seen as a sloven or slut in the morning will never efface the impression she then made with all the dress and pageantry, she can afterwards involve herself in.

CHILDREN'S CLOTHING. Children's clothing underwent a number of changes during the eighteenth century. In the seventeenth century, infants were swaddled for the first four to six weeks and thereafter were dressed very much like their mothers until age five or six, when boys changed their skirts for breeches. Beginning in the early eighteenth century, however, swaddling was replaced with diapers and dresses made too long to be kicked off. These were shortened when the baby began to walk. At two or three, children were put in adult clothing, but, as before, there was no distinction of gender until the boys were breeched. Even little children's dresses had stiffened bodices or were worn over stays. Padded caps called puddings protected the head from falls, and leading strings attached to the shoulders kept little ones from straying.

The influence of Jean-Jacques Rousseau's *Émile* (1762) brought a gradual relaxation in the style of children's clothing. Young children were allowed loose muslin dresses sashed at the waist, a style that was eventually extended to older girls as well. Boys old enough to be breeched were put in "skeleton suits," consisting of a tight jacket with two rows of buttons on the front rising over the shoulders and a pair of ankle-length pants.

The Nineteenth Century

The early nineteenth century saw significant changes in both men's and women's dress. For men the most visible were the replacement of knee breeches by trousers and the loss of ornamentation and color. Black gradually replaced other dark and neutral colors until, by 1860, all business and formal coats and trousers were black wool and waistcoats were limited to black and white.

> *By 1800 women's dress permitted a new degree of naturalness and comfort: Silk-covered hoops were discarded, stiff stays were replaced with lighter corseting, and softly gathered white cotton dresses were chosen to reveal the moving body beneath.*

The monotony was relieved somewhat by the new casual sack suits, made of pronounced checks and plaids in the 1850s and 1860s and of tan and brown tweeds toward the end of the century. Nineteenth-century masculine models included two opposing figures. The first was the businessman (a gaunt Yankee early on, later a portly entrepreneur), whose conservative clothes reflected his success through expensive materials and tailoring, and his obsession with work in their avoidance of color and ornament. The second was the dandy or masher, who specialized in conspicuous and time-consuming dressing and other behaviors redolent of idleness. The desirable male look was clean-shaven except for sideburns in the early nineteenth century, but by the 1860s beards and moustaches were becoming indispensable, suggesting that the ideal had shifted toward older men.

Women's clothing about 1800 permitted a new degree of naturalness and comfort inspired by classical models. Whereas eighteenth-century dress had imposed a highly artificial shape on the body, now the body gave its shape to the clothes. Hoops were discarded, along with the large-scale floral silks that had spread over them. Stiff stays were replaced with lighter corseting, and softly gathered white cotton dresses revealed the moving body beneath. High-heeled buckled shoes gave way to flat sandals, and hairstyles so diminished that some women cropped their hair. The new fashions required little material and less trimming, so they were available to nearly all classes. Some Americans deplored the new styles as immodest, others criticized any emulation of foreign fashions as unbefitting a free nation, but these skimpy, high-waisted dresses were nevertheless universally worn and are the first garments that commonly survive with American documentation and minimal alteration.

The freedom of classical styles did not last very long. Shortly after 1820, the waistline dropped, tight lacing returned, and skirts became fuller. Over the succeeding decades fashionable dresses managed to restrict movement through every possible means: sleeves or skirts too wide for doorways and hats to match, armholes cut so that one could not raise the arms, sleeves too tight to bend the arms, sleeves that dragged in the soup, bonnet brims so deep one could see only straight ahead, layers of heavy petticoats, bulky trains that swept the streets, tied-back skirts in which it was difficult to take a normal step, bodices so heavily boned and tightly fitted that they became second corsets.

Burdensome fashions persisted in ironic contrast to the improvement in women's condition in other areas. By century's end, many women enjoyed the benefits of secondary and college education, and the traditional occupations of domestic service and needlework had expanded to include teaching, factory and clerical work, social work, and nursing. Women had increasing impact on public life through their participation in the abolition, temperance, and women's rights movements, community social work, and women's clubs. But most women clung doggedly to the latest fashion, no matter how uncomfortable. In 1851 feminist leaders introduced the bloomer, a kind of Turkish trouser worn under a matching dress of ordinary, style except for being knee-length. It provoked a storm of abuse, as if women in trousers were ready to expropriate the entire male domain, leaving emasculated men home with squalling babies. The bloomer was soon abandoned for public wear, but it continued a covert existence in the health dress worn at spas and the gym suits girls wore for single-sex sports. Later reformers advocated lightening or discarding corsets, redesigning underwear, and reducing the oppressive weight of clothing. "Aesthetic dress" advocates rejected the fashionable stiff bodice and draped skirt in favor of softly gathered classical dresses with Pre-Raphaelite details.

Most women did not benefit from these new ideas until the twentieth century, but other changes did find widespread acceptance. The thin footwear of the early nineteenth century gave way to more substantial leather boots after 1860. In the 1890s young women adopted the shirtwaist, a white, tailored blouse worn with a simple skirt and optional tailored jacket, which allowed greater freedom of movement than the heavily boned fashionable bodice. This style, based on men's suits, was associated with "The Gibson Girl," a new and distinctive American type with freer manners and a more active life-style than her mother. Shirtwaist suits were worn on the street, by clerical workers at the office, and while participating in the new fads for tennis, golf, and bicycling.

Fashionable dress in the mid to late nineteenth century restricted movement in every way. The layers of heavy petticoats, full sleeves and tight waistline of this 19th century dress severely hindered mobility.

The nineteenth century continued to observe the division between tight-fitting public and more comfortable private forms of dress. Women wore loose wrappers at breakfast, while doing housework in the morning, and in their own rooms (a refuge women often sought in the summer heat); and from the 1880s a tighter version called a tea gown could be worn at home in the afternoon. But a corset and fitted bodice were required when receiving visitors or appearing in public, for loose clothing out of its limited sphere suggested immorality, slovenliness, or lack of self-respect. As the century progressed, etiquette became even more complex, and different activities required different clothes. The latest canvas shoes, chic at Newport, had no place on the street in New York, and attention to such distinctions were as much a symbol of wealth and leisure as were more ostentatious kinds of display. Dressing well, which in the eighteenth century had been an upper-class obligation, now became a female obligation, partly because men's clothing had become so dull.

Middle-class women were also strongly admonished by etiquette books and popular magazines to take pains with their dress. Clean, well-fitting, becoming, and above all appropriate clothing was an important part of female attractiveness, and being attractive was the source of a woman's power (or "influence," as it was called in the nineteenth century). Only beauty could draw men, inclined by nature to "baser passions," into a domestic circle where they could be "influenced" by wives and mothers stronger than they in moral sensibility and religious sentiment. According to the magazine *Demorest's* in 1883, "many a man's heart has been kept from wandering by the bow on his wife's slipper." Beauty was duty, and the lesson was taught from earliest childhood. Jefferson had warned his six-year-old daughter Maria "not to go out without your bonnet because it will make you very ugly and then we should not love you so much" (20 September 1785). Pale skin, considered beautiful and ladylike everywhere, acquired additional importance in the South, where children of mixed blood lived on every plantation. Obvious rouging of the cheeks ended soon after 1800, but the English traveler Frances Trollope noted in *Domestic Manners of the Americans* (1832) that in the late 1820s the ladies of Cincinnati "powder themselves immoderately, face, neck, and arms, with pulverised starch; the effect is indescribably disagreeable by day-light, and not very favourable at any time" (1949 ed., p. 300). Later in the century, skin washes and lotions were used, but other cosmetics were supposed to be unobtrusive.

There was little regional variation in women's dress within the United States, partly because all new fashions emanated from one source—Paris. If anything, this fixation on Paris intensified through the century with the rise of highly publicized designers like Charles Worth and Jacques Doucet, to whom rich American style-setters went for their clothes. Conformity to fashion was encouraged by a growing system of transatlantic and coastal packet ships and a network of canals and railroads that sped new textiles, accessories, and fashion information to increasingly remote areas. Beginning with *Godey's Lady's Book* in 1830, American magazines began to include fashion plates (copies of French designs, not indigenous American styles), and their wide circulation helped bring all classes into the fashion mainstream.

The great exception, of course, was field slaves, who were provided coarse cotton clothing of extremely simple cut. House slaves, being more visible in public, tended to be better dressed and were more likely to receive castoff clothing as gifts. Some slaves were able to buy bright accessories to help individualize their holiday dress. Among free people, what deviation there was from mainstream fashion was found chiefly among sects like the Quakers, Shakers, and Mennonites, who dressed "plain" on religious principle. People in California and other parts of the Southwest that were under Spanish or Mexican rule also wore distinctive styles until those regions were overrun by American culture in the 1840s. Otherwise most differences reflected economic class and, to some degree, climate. Immigrants, encouraged to adopt American customs as quickly as possible to speed their assimilation, rarely retained elements of national dress beyond the first generation.

The sewing machine transformed the ready-made clothing industry in the 1850s; it was widely used by dressmakers and in homes in the 1860s and was also the first step in mechanizing the shoe industry.

Only very close-knit groups such as the Hasidic Jews kept distinctive garments in daily wear.

Although the United States continued to look to Europe for new fashions, it became increasingly independent in its manufactures. The cotton gin (1793) made southern cotton profitable, encouraged slavery, and supplied the New England textile mills founded after the Revolution. Some mills specialized in coarse "Negro cloth" to clothe field slaves, and most emphasized quantity rather than quality. Not until April 1863 did *Godey's Lady's Book* note that "in previous seasons [Lowell calicoes] have been very nice, common, cheap goods, not remarkable for beauty. But this season they are equal to any English prints." Repeated attempts to establish silk culture were unsuccessful, and silk weaving took hold only after heavy duties were levied on imported silks during the Civil War.

The sewing machine transformed the early ready-made clothing industry in the 1850s and was widely used by dressmakers and in homes by the 1860s. It was also the first step in mechanizing the shoe industry, which by century's end not only provided this continent with footwear of every grade but was a significant exporter as well. Pattern drafting systems simplified and standardized the art of cutting out clothing and made paper patterns in graduated sizes available to the general public by the late 1870s. By 1900 most American men were wearing ready-made clothes. Women could buy ready-made cloaks, underwear, wrappers, and accessories, but because fashion required an exact fit in the bodice, most dresses were still custom-made.

CHILDREN'S CLOTHING. Nineteenth-century children did not wear fully adult styles until their teens, suggesting it was now desirable to prolong childhood. Little boys were given suits with skirts, and older ones wore suits with knee pants before graduating to adult trousers. Girls' dresses were gradually made longer as the wearer approached maturity.

The Twentieth Century

The acceptance of loose, unstructured clothing in the 1910s permitted the success of ready-made dresses and made the private dressmaker obsolete. The new styles also eliminated the traditional division of the day into private and public times according to whether loose or tight clothing was worn. Evening wear was signaled instead by fabric, decoration, décolleté, or archaic elements such as long skirts that were no longer found in daytime clothing.

The twentieth century was the first to see the development of a specifically American style, emphasizing sportswear. It grew out of an increasingly informal lifestyle and found its models in the movies. In the 1930s, New York stores began to recognize and feature American designers (who had been working incognito for years), a development given further impetus when World War II cut New York off from its fashion sources in Paris. The century was also noteworthy for the use of artificial fibers and materials. Rayon came into wide use by the 1930s, and nylon stockings became a staple at the end of World War II. These were followed by acrylics, polyesters and related fibers, tubular jerseys, bonded knits, and permanent-press fabrics. In spite of domestic technological advances, many textile and apparel industries were lost to foreign countries with less expensive labor.

Regional differences in dress, never very distinct, were further discouraged in the twentieth century by the explosion of nationally distributed images in movies, television, and magazines and by the mobility of the population. The clearest exception occurs in the western hats, boots, and fancy belt buckles men wear in Texas and the Southwest, but there are also subtle differences in taste elsewhere in the country. These have less to do with cut than with what styles are chosen for what occasions. Life in New York and Washington requires more formal clothing than in Boston. Like Boston, California is informal, but it is far more flamboyant and experimental in color and style.

Men's business and formal suits changed only in detail in the twentieth century, gaining minimal variety through the use of wide or narrow trousers with or without cuffs, double- or single-breasted coats with wide or narrow lapels, and more or less shoulder padding. Richard Martin and Harold Koda suggest that while men's basic garments are not subject to dramatic seasonal style changes, there are persistent stylistic types that fall into twelve categories (including jock, nerd, businessman, and rebel). Although reinterpreted over time, these types remain recognizable from decade to decade.

More important than changes in cut has been the creeping informality in dress. As early as 1900, women's magazines inveighed against the "shirt-sleeve habit" indulged in by men who went coatless at home and even on the street, looking slovenly beside their corseted wives. By century's end, many businesses that once would have expected their male employees to appear in three-piece suits now required only trousers, buttoned shirt, and tie. Non-matching coats and trousers became acceptable and vests were increasingly omitted altogether. Sportswear cut loose from traditional khakis and tweeds and was made in every bright color, a trend echoed faintly in formal clothes as well. Early in the century and into the 1920s, men wore knickers and knee socks (often bright tartans) for sports, with perhaps a sweater replacing the vest. Informal shirts were often colored and patterned, and the collar gradually became lower and softer. Beginning in the 1930s, men began to wear swimsuits without tops, shorts that bared the leg, and short-sleeved, knitted "sport shirts." From the knit sport shirt, the next step was the "T-shirt," which by the 1960s was made in colors and by the 1970s and 1980s was printed with mottoes and pictures so that it looked less like underwear.

Not only did women enjoy greater informality in the twentieth century, they saw the basic cut of their clothing change radically as well. The first steps were to loosen the bodice and to shorten the skirt to the knee. Once a skintight fit was abandoned, corsets became less necessary for creating the fashionable line. The introduction of pantyhose gave the coup de grace to the gartered foundation garment and made possible the miniskirts of the 1960s. These changes allowed real freedom of movement but were offset by the persistent fashion for extremely high heels. Women's hats, a necessary component of decency for two centuries, fell out of use in the 1960s except for functional headgear. In the 1930s, pants and shorts came into common use, at first for sports and loungewear but gradually for more occasions, until they went nearly everywhere by 1975. The wearing of trousers, so controversial in the nineteenth century, simply seemed practical after two world wars in which women had worn them while employed in war industries. The 1970s and 1980s saw revivals of 1920s and 1930s styles, with a growing emphasis on broad shoulders and narrow hips that was interpreted by some as an attempt to minimize the waist, by others as an attempt to ape masculine body lines. The "dress for success" books for businesswomen of the period recommended masculine-style jackets worn with skirts and heels to establish the wearer's gender, suggesting that symbolism in dress was still far more important than practicality.

When women bobbed their hair in the 1920s, they symbolically discarded the burden of traditional femininity in favor of boyish freedom. But our culture is not nearly so disturbed by women borrowing masculine traits as by men taking on feminine qualities. Thus when young men adopted long hair in the 1960s, middle America was outraged. In that same decade many black Americans stopped straightening their hair and wore it in natural "Afro" styles. These styles were widely imitated by whites in the 1970s, reflecting the new acceptance by both races that "black is beautiful."

Aside from the tendency toward informality and the adoption by women of men's garments, the most important long-term trend in the twentieth century is the fashion emphasis on body rather than clothes. The roots of this development are complex. The moral superiority claimed for women in the nineteenth century had justified many advances in women's position, but it also required eschewing personal indulgence and putting family (or substitutes like schoolchildren or the urban poor) before self. As middle-class women spent less time immured at home and more time in the world, such restraints perhaps came to seem unfair. At any rate, moral superiority was rarely claimed or conceded by the 1920s. This allowed women greater freedom in a climate of self-indulgence, but it also left personal attractiveness as the chief criterion of female distinction. Whereas in the nineteenth century the essential female grace lay in the inner character, and careful grooming and dress were recommended chiefly as means of attracting men to the benign domestic sphere of female moral influence, now physical attractiveness was an end in itself. The cultivation of beauty became for women a means of personal aggrandizement, and the acquisition of beautiful women became for men a symbol of status and wealth. The growing prevalence of divorce may well have put pressure on women to preserve a youthful and attractive appearance.

An attractive appearance came to be defined less in terms of clothing than of the body itself. This was encouraged by the tendency toward informality in dress and the relaxation of etiquette, so that clothes simply became less important, and also by the tendency to wear fewer and scantier clothes for many occasions. As short skirts, sleeveless and backless dresses, and increasingly brief bathing suits revealed more and more of the body, the body itself inevitably became the focus of attention. Beauty parlors had already become common by the 1890s, specializing not only in hair care but in manicures, wrinkle removal, massages, face peeling, and even rudimentary plastic surgery. Makeup began to come out of the closet soon after 1900, and by the 1920s lipstick and powder were applied in public. With the popularity of short skirts, sheer stockings, and sleeveless dresses, women of the 1920s routinely began to shave leg and underarm hair.

After 1900, a new generation of women's magazines, including *Vogue* at the couture end and *Ladies' Home Journal* for the middle class, depended for their survival more on advertising than on subscriptions, and at present women's magazine advertising is dominated by perfumes and skin- and hair-care products. This change grows partly out of the emphasis on beautiful bodies, but it also reflects the fact that makeup, unlike clothing, is not really essential, so that manufacturers must market not only the product but the need for it. Doing this requires massive advertising. Thus a symbiotic relationship developed between women's magazines and beauty product manufacturers that conspired to teach women that unembellished looks were ugly and that "natural" beauty is possible only with the aid of art. During this same period, photographs gradually replaced drawings in both fashion articles and advertising. At first the new images of real bodies with their ordinary waistlines and big feet clashed with the idealized drawings. This conflict was solved not by moderating the ideal but by idealizing the models. Real women, chosen for their height and slenderness, carefully posed, and cleverly photographed, create an exemplar more powerful than any drawing because they prove that the ideal can actually be attained and thus impose on women the obligation to attain it.

Feminists have protested the exploitation of women in advertising as in pornography, but Rita Freedman in *Beauty Bound* suggests that by teaching personal control through assertive behavior, feminism may have encouraged women to reshape their lives by reshaping their bodies. Certainly by the 1980s, the traditional emphasis on dieting had expanded to include physical fitness, and women are now expected to develop their muscles like men. This change is often described as a liberation from traditional models of dependent femininity, but the implication that natural female bodies are unacceptable still entraps all too many young women in masochistic behaviors such as anorexia and compulsive fitness training.

Men have not escaped this growing emphasis on the beautiful body, although it has taken longer to show pernicious effects. Twentieth-century models of male attractiveness have in general been more athletic than those fashionable in previous centuries. Portliness went out in the 1890s, and now a slim, athletic build implies health and strength. Transient models such as the hippie radical or the sensitive male of the 1960s and 1970s did not counter the general expectation of physical fitness in men. By the 1980s, a barrage of images of heavily muscled cartoon heroes, movie stars, and athletes created such pressure for a powerful body that young men felt obligated to spend hours working out with weights, and many took drugs to build their muscles artificially, a kind of self-destructive behavior formerly associated with women. The pressure on both sexes to have lean and muscular bodies has inflated the market for diet programs, special foods, expensive equipment, and special clothing for exercise. As a result, "attractively fit" bodies have become a status symbol, along with overdesigned, high-priced athletic shoes and tight exercise leotards and bicycling pants whose elastic materials allow freedom of movement and yet reveal every nuance of muscle.

CHILDREN'S CLOTHING. Children's clothing has also changed dramatically in the twentieth century, reflecting the prevailing trend toward increased informality. In the early twentieth century, rompers became available to toddlers of both sexes, and dresses were abandoned by boys out of infancy. In the last several decades, children's dress has become increasingly gender-specific. For fancy occasions, even tiny boys wear suits and girls dresses. Everyday clothes differ less in cut, but a rigid color code, beginning with pink for girls and blue for boys, was established by 1950. In spite of the interest in unisex dress in the 1970s, children's clothing clearly reflects contemporary concern with establishing gender identity from a very early age.

[See also The Culture of Consumption; Gender Roles and Relations; Manners and Etiquette.]

BIBLIOGRAPHY

General Works

Banner, Lois. *American Beauty* (1983).

Corson, Richard. *Fashions in Hair: The First Five Thousand Years* (1965).

Corson, Richard. *Fashions in Makeup: From Ancient to Modern Times* (1972).

Cunnington, Phillis, and Anne Buck. *Children's Costume in England from the Fourteenth to the End of the Nineteenth Century* (1965).

Earle, Alice Morse. *Two Centuries of Costume in America, 1620–1820* (1903; repr. 1974).

Kidwell, Claudia Brush. *Suiting Everyone* (1978).

Kidwell, Claudia, and Valerie Steele. *Men and Women: Dressing the Part* (1989). Essays on gender symbols in dress, including children's.

McClellan, Elisabeth. *History of American Costume, 1607–1870* (1937; repr. 1977). Outdated but not yet superseded.

Montgomery, Florence. *Textiles in America, 1650–1870* (1984).

Waugh, Norah. *The Cut of Men's Clothes, 1600–1900* (1964).

Waugh, Norah. *The Cut of Women's Clothes, 1600–1930* (1968).

Native Americans

Conn, Richard. *Robes of White Shell and Sunrise: Personal Decorative Arts of the Native American* (1974).

Maxwell, James A. *America's Fascinating Indian Heritage* (1978).

Seventeenth Century

Trautman, Patricia. "When Gentlemen Wore Lace: Sumptuary Legislation and Dress in Seventeenth-Century New England." *Journal of Regional Cultures* 3, no 2 (1983).

Trautman, Patricia. "Dress in Seventeenth-Century Cambridge, Massachusetts: An Inventory-based Reconstruction." *Dublin Seminar for New England Folklife: Annual Proceedings* (1987).

Eighteenth Century

Baumgarten, Linda. *Eighteenth-Century Clothing at Williamsburg* (1986).

Los Angeles County Museum of Art. *An Elegant Art: Fashion and Fantasy in the Eighteenth Century* (1983).

Wright, Merideth. *Put On Thy Beautiful Garments: Rural New England Clothing, 1783–1800* (1990).

Nineteenth Century

Blum, Stella, ed. *Victorian Fashions and Costumes from "Harper's Bazar,"* 1867–1898 (1974).

Cunnington, C. Willett, and Phillis Cunnington. *Handbook of English Costume in the Nineteenth Century* (1959). Good coverage of men's clothing.

Gernsheim, Alison. *Victorian and Edwardian Fashion: A Photographic Survey* (1982).

Majer, Michele. "American Women and French Fashion." *The Age of Napoleon: Costume from Revolution to Empire, 1789–1815* (1989).

Rexford, Nancy. *Shoes.* Vol. 1 of *Women's Clothing in America, 1795–1930* (1992). Social history, etiquette, and dating/identification.

Severa, Joan. *Dressed for the Photographer: Ordinary Americans and Fashion, 1840–1900* (1992).

Twentieth Century

Blum, Stella. *Everyday Fashions of the Thirties, as Pictured in Sears Catalogs* (1986).

Blum, Stella, ed. *Everyday Fashions of the Twenties, as Pictured in Sears and Other Catalogs* (1981).

Ewing, Elizabeth. *History of Twentieth-Century Fashion* (1986).

Freedman, Rita. *Beauty Bound* (1986).

Martin, Richard, and Harold Koda. *Jocks and Nerds: Men's Style in the Twentieth Century* (1989).

Milbank, Caroline Rennolds. *New York Fashion: The Evolution of American Style* (1989). Also includes a short chapter on the nineteenth century.

O'Donnol, Shirley. *American Costume, 1915–1970: A Source Book for the Stage Costumer* (1982).

— NANCY REXFORD

COLLEGIATE EDUCATION

Introduction

A much larger percentage of Americans have, from the eighteenth century on, attended college than have done so in any other country. Similarly, the United States has outpaced other nations in both the number and the diversity of collegiate institutions—schools sharing the title "college" but having widely different missions and curricula. Because of this broad accessibility and institutional variety—which, as we shall see, are closely interrelated phenomena—collegiate education in America has served as a widely accepted mechanism for distributing power, prestige, and privilege in a nation that, due to successive waves of immigrants, lacked the fixed, traditional social hierarchies that normally regulate that distribution.

Before 1900, especially, America was a relatively unstructured society that continually renewed itself as it repeatedly seized and developed new lands to the west, and as populations from all over the world streamed in to take advantage of the cheap land and need for labor. In more traditional societies, parents' social standing largely determined their children's place in that society, but because of Americans' constant movement—from Europe to America, from the East to the Midwest and then to the West, from farm to town, from town to city, from city to suburb—neither family lineage nor wealth could effectively determine the place an individual would take in society. In a sense, ever-changing American communities had to establish the social ranking among their people anew, in each generation. New kinds of credentials had to be found that would confer social standing in evolving communities.

College attendance became one of the most important of these credentials. A college education signified that a person possessed the knowledge and skills to take a leading role in building the economy and culture of a new community. Before 1900 colleges emphasized recitation, declamation, and other oral forms of instruction that helped students to prepare for leadership in a culture where the forms of politics and persuasion were still largely face-to-face and oral. As twentieth-century America came to rely more on expert knowledge, colleges moved away from general education to offer dozens of different specialized curricula to prepare students to hold important positions in the economy and society. Throughout American history, a college credential served to enhance its holder's prestige and access to capital and well-paid employment.

"Collegiate education" as used here includes any formal education that occurred after people had completed "common school" or what later came to be called "high school." The distinction here is between attending the local and (usually) fully tax-supported public school—which the majority of young people were expected to do—and attending an institution of learning, often outside the community; comparatively few were expected to attend the latter, and those who did paid some form of tuition. Whereas attending the local public school was customary, attending college or its equivalent was unusual, requiring extra effort of the students (and sometimes parents), who had to decide what to do with their lives, what kind of career or social standing they sought, and how much educational time and money they wished to invest in their future. We can define "collegiate education," then, as that formal education which students explicitly sought out, and for which they were willing to pay.

Defined thus, "college" includes a great variety of institutions—today as well as in the 1830s or 1880s or 1920s. There are traditional four-year, privately funded liberal-arts colleges and universities; state-funded four-year colleges and universities; privately and publicly funded junior and community colleges; non-degree-granting, proprietary occupational schools; religious and Bible colleges representing almost every faith; colleges exclusively or primarily for women or for African Americans, Native Americans, and other racial or ethnic groups; military schools; and other types. Community colleges joined the mixture in the twentieth century, but all the other kinds of college existed well back into the nineteenth century; and two other kinds of institution—the normal school and the academy—provided college opportunities to large numbers of students in the nineteenth century.

The great variety of collegiate institutions has made it difficult for historians to determine exactly how many students attended and who they were. Historical statistics, especially nineteenth-century statistics, sometimes exclude students in occupational, technical, and teacher-training schools; they usually express enrollment as the percentage of a certain age group attending college, but because that age group varies across time and region, comparisons are somewhat unreliable. Nevertheless, the statistics clearly demonstrate that the American system of collegiate education was far more open and accessible than any other system of higher education in the developed world. Historians have estimated that while 1 percent of white males aged eighteen to twenty-one in the United States attended a formally designated collegiate institution in 1800, less than one-quarter of 1 percent of those aged twenty to twenty-four were doing so in England or Germany. By 1900, 5 percent of white men and women aged eighteen to twenty-one attended college in the United States, compared to less than 1 percent of twenty-to-twenty-four-year-olds in England or Germany; by 1930 more than 15 percent of white Americans aged eighteen to twenty-one were enrolled, while no Western European country exceeded 3 percent. By the late 1980s about 47 percent of Americans aged eighteen to twenty-four (over 57 percent of high-school graduates) were in college; Japan, Canada, and Sweden enrolled a little over 30 percent, and the remaining developed countries even less.

How representative of the population were American college students? Although American collegiate institutions were significantly more open than those in other nations, access was not equally available across social classes and racial or ethnic groups. The well-to-do and white males were over-represented in the college population; people from the lower middle class and below, women until the 1980s, and African Americans were greatly under-represented. Who were the Americans who took advantage of the openness of American collegiate institutions? Not until the twentieth century was it "normal" for students to proceed first to elementary and then to secondary school, and thence, for the increasing numbers who did advance, to college and then to graduate or professional school. Before 1900 most colleges admitted students who had not completed high school; students could enter medical or law school with as few as two years of high-school education. Moreover, before 1900 many "colleges" offered only secondary-level work; because colleges in many areas were built before secondary schools, their "preparatory divisions," as their remedial departments were called, often filled up even as the college-level courses their catalogs listed found no takers. Conversely, many institutions called "academies" (one predecessor of the public high school) offered a course of study more advanced and rigorous than did most colleges.

Before 1900, students were not expected to secure their collegiate education before they began their careers. In the early nineteenth century, institutions calling themselves "colleges" enrolled students ranging in age from twelve to thirty. Large numbers of students entered college in their mid and late twenties, after spending several years working. The age range served by colleges narrowed toward the end of the nineteenth century and into the twentieth. This stemmed in part from college administrators' hopes that a student population of a more limited age range would be easier to discipline; and it was fueled by a growing conviction among parents and those who advised them that college offered a particularly appropriate atmosphere in which late adolescents could mature, as well as a growing perception that access to professional and managerial careers was available only to those who began work with a college diploma already in hand. By the 1920s, although many older students pursued collegiate education, educators and society had settled on eighteen to twenty-four as the proper age for attending college; those who fell outside that range—almost all of them twenty-five and older, since high schools were by then widely available and high-school graduation had become an almost universal college-admission requirement—were considered exceptions, identified as "nontraditional" or "adult" students. This shift in nomenclature obscures the nature of the twentieth-century collegiate population. Even among institutions calling themselves "colleges" (excluding proprietary occupational and technical schools), enrollment of "adults" seems never to have fallen below 20 percent since 1900 but had risen as high as 42 percent by 1985.

By the 1920s, although many older students pursued collegiate education, educators and society had settled on eighteen to twenty-four as the proper age for attending college.

James McLachlan has suggested a model of college development that illuminates how institutional diversity and open access have worked together to create a distinctive American pattern of collegiate education. Whatever the motivation of its founding group, a typical college in fact began as a local institution—"local" meaning anything from a town to a city to a region of a state—and enrolled from its immediate environs a student body that reflected the social and ethnic variety of that locale. A new college needed to create a paying student body quickly, but it would not have a reputation that would attract students from any distance; consequently, it would admit all comers from the local area.

As the college gained financial stability, a more professionalized faculty, and a wider reputation, its ties with the founding locality would gradually loosen, and its connection to a more national academic, intellectual, and collegiate culture would grow stronger. As it became more "cosmopolitan," the college would seek students willing to travel greater distances to partake of its specialized offering—whether that was a religious atmosphere, an orientation toward engineering, or an easy degree. Such students, able and willing to travel farther from home and reasonably well informed about the choices among colleges, would tend to be more sophisticated and more well-to-do than the students who had originally attended the college because it was closest to home. However, while this college was growing away from its local roots, most often another college was being founded nearby, which would become the "local" college for the region—until it too grew more cosmopolitan and a third "local" college was born, and so on. The chronological survey that follows shall discuss each of these waves of college foundings in turn starting with the nine colonial colleges begun as local alternatives for students unable to return to England for higher education, moving on to the public and private denominational colleges founded in the first half of the nineteenth century as alternatives to the increasingly nationalized colonial foundations, and then turning to their replacement as local institutions—first by the land grant and state normal schools and then by the community colleges. What should be noted before we turn to the chronology is this pattern's implications in terms of social class: new clients for collegiate education in America tended to come from backgrounds that were less affluent and less established than were the backgrounds of those who had traditionally attended college; and they were accommodated largely through the development of new institutions rather than being taken into already established ones. Thus individual colleges tended to be relatively homogeneous in terms of social class—another aspect of institutional distinctiveness among American colleges.

A survey of collegiate education in America can best be divided at the Civil War. Before 1860, colleges were established, supported, and administered by nongovernmental entities. Colonial and state governments usually offered some form of encouragement to these colleges—through tax exemptions, a share of state lottery revenues, ferry or bridge tolls, income derived from the sale of government land, or the exclusive right to offer higher education in a specified area—as a way of stimulating nongovernmental or "private" groups to perform a function that the government thought important—providing higher education. After 1860, state and municipal governments began to take much more direct responsibility for providing higher education, and even as "private" colleges continued to play an important if ever-diminishing role, the late nineteenth and the twentieth centuries were dominated by the growth (in numbers of students and in institutions) of public higher education.

Early Trends in Collegiate Education

The American colonists established nine colleges; at the time of the Revolution America had more separate colleges than England, despite the latter's much larger population. Harvard, founded in 1636 outside of Boston, was the first; the second, William and Mary, in Williamsburg, Virginia, was not chartered until 1693. Seven more followed in the eighteenth century: each of the remaining major northern seaports founded a college during that century—Providence (the College of Rhode Island, later Brown, 1764), New Haven (the Collegiate School, later Yale, 1701), New York (Kings College, later Columbia College, 1754), and Philadelphia (the Philadelphia Academy, later the University of Pennsylvania, 1751)—and others grew out of the sectarian squabbling provoked by the Great Awakening in the 1740s (the College of New Jersey, later Princeton, 1746; Queens College, later Rutgers, 1766; Dartmouth 1769).

The period from the Revolution to the Civil War saw a great surge in college founding, with nearly five hundred established, perhaps four hundred of which existed long enough to have some impact on enrollment. (Many colleges were "founded," in that they received governmental charters, but never opened their doors or quickly changed from collegiate to high-school status.)

MOTIVATIONS FOR FOUNDING COLLEGES. This surge in college founding, which far outstripped the need for higher education in the sparsely populated country, came about because groups of people with similar aspirations and needs believed that establishing a college would further their shared goals. Before the Civil War, these purposes were primarily religious, civic, and economic. Confessional groups came together to found many colleges, as in 1701, when twelve Congregational ministers founded what was to become Yale College to provide an advanced education based on distinctly more conservative religious principles than those employed at the more liberal Harvard. (Groups of coreligionists have gotten together to found new or revitalize existing colleges ever since.) Such sectarian colleges helped the group to fulfill their faith and to maintain their membership, a responsibility made necessary by the disestablishment of religion in the United States. And they did so: first, by providing a "safe" place where parents could send their children without fearing that they would lose, or change, their faith, and second, by training the ministers needed to propagate that sect's beliefs throughout the nation. (Because sectarian colleges sought to provide a general education, they differed greatly from the seminaries built by each faith to provide theological and occupational training for priests, rabbis, and ministers.) Protestant sects were the first to build their own colleges to preserve and expand their faith, but Catholic groups soon followed, starting with Georgetown in the 1790s and St. Mary's just after the turn of the century. There were fourteen permanent Catholic colleges at the beginning of the Civil War.

Various groups were also motivated by civic pride to build colleges in order to enhance their region by providing, close to home, suitable training for the community's future leaders in the fields of law, medicine, government, education, business, and cultural affairs. They believed further that a local college would also enhance a city or town's reputation, certifying that it was large, wealthy, and sophisticated enough to have a cultural institution as distinguished as a college.

Interest in bolstering their town's or region's economic vitality also inspired groups to come together to found a college. Especially after 1820 it was widely acknowledged that college students and faculty would spend money in the town (many colleges did not initially build dormitories in part to force students to pay townspeople directly for room and board); construction and maintenance would provide jobs for townspeople; and a college would make a town and region more attractive to prosperous settlers. This perceived relation between colleges and economic growth persists into the present, with the added argument emerging after 1950 that colleges and universities would attract industry to their locale because of their capacity to provide research and to train specialized workers.

In truth, most colleges founded between 1636 and 1860 grew out of a mixture of the three motives; although each had a particular religious affiliation, their purpose was much wider than simply propagating the faith. Because Harvard's founders cited the training of a learned ministry for the colony as one of the reasons for starting a college soon after the colony began, Harvard and the other colonial colleges have often been regarded primarily as training grounds for the clergy. This view is too narrow: in reality each of them was founded to provide the colonies with educated leaders in business, government, and the professions, as well as in religion. The need for an educated leadership could not be met through England's institutions, for only the wealthiest and most ambitious young Americans could afford to travel there. The colleges were also founded as a means of symbolizing the colonists' commitment to civilization and to culture, of proving that although they lived far from the seats of European learning and culture, they were committed to and capable of preserving and indeed expanding that culture on the frontier.

Harvard, founded in 1635 outside of Boston, was the first college established by the American colonists. This view, rendered in 1795, shows Hollis, Harvard, and Massachusetts Halls around Harvard Yard.

THE STRUCTURE OF COLLEGES. The same motivations spurred the surge of college foundings following the Revolution. Although these colleges were usually associated with a particular religious denomination and played some part in the churches' struggle to attract and maintain stable constituencies, they were founded primarily as local colleges, catering to all young men (and very occasionally to young women), without regard to denominational commitment, who lived within a fifty-to-sixty-mile radius of the college. Like their colonial predecessors, these colleges, most often built in recently settled sections by European peoples as they migrated toward the Pacific Ocean, symbolized for the migrants their continued connection to the civilization they had left. Some of the colleges got underway long before there were enough people living in their area to provide pupils. Their existence was very tenuous, for they were short of students, of endowment, and of qualified faculty willing to work for poor wages. Their curricula were rudimentary, largely devoted to subjects that could be taught inexpensively—classical languages, philosophy, mathematics. Recent studies indicate that of college-age white males, 1.5 percent enrolled in these colleges in 1820 and over 3 percent by 1860.

Students in colonial and antebellum colleges ranged widely in age, typically from fourteen to twenty-five; it was enormously difficult to control groups that included students at such different maturational levels.

Nearly all of the hundreds of colleges started before 1860 followed the English model, in which students moved away from home in order to attend college. This "residential" model required colleges to shoulder many responsibilities beyond classroom instruction, most notably housing, feeding, exercising, and disciplining groups of boys and young men removed, usually for the first time, from the discipline and support provided by home and family. Residential colleges were committed to educating the whole person, to helping their charges not only to learn Latin and mathematics but also to mature into responsible, civic-minded young adults. Their commitment was high, but their record of success was mixed at best. Tensions ran high in eighteenth- and early-nineteenth-century colleges, where faculty members sought to play the role of parents by closely supervising the students' personal lives—when they went to bed, how they dressed for chapel, who they met when allowed to leave campus, how they spent their money—while the students fought this oppressive supervision in order to claim more adult roles commensurate with their age (most young men of their age who were not at college had already moved away from home, and many had wives and children). The students in the colonial and antebellum colleges ranged widely in age, typically from fourteen to twenty-five. It was enormously difficult to control groups that included students at such different maturational levels—oversight appropriate for the sixteen-year-old was galling to the twenty-four-year-old.

The faculty charged with responsibility for providing discipline were not always well suited to the task. Prior to the Civil War, and after it in many cases, the qualifications for teaching college amounted to a college degree and a willingness to work with boys for relatively low (and often unpredictable) pay. Colleges were led by a president, usually a minister or other learned professional, who often was the only truly adult person on the campus. The rest of the faculty—it would be a quite successful college that had as many as ten—consisted most often of a mixture of recent college graduates (sometimes younger than the students they were supposed to discipline) who were waiting for their real careers to begin, ministers between churches, and other professionals somehow down on their luck. Recitation was the basis for almost all instruction: students took turns reciting assigned passages from memory or giving their translations of passages from classical texts. The instructor followed along from his text, making appropriate corrections and noting students' mistakes in the grade book. Such pedagogy required the instructor to know little about the subject at hand; in the small colleges, a single instructor often heard recitations in all the subjects the college taught. Instruction seldom varied (the lecture was a pedagogical innovation of the 1820s); some students were lucky enough to study with working scientists—such as Benjamin Silliman at Yale or Asa Gray at Harvard—who lectured and conducted experiments or demonstrations in class. Only in the course in moral philosophy, usually conducted as a discussion by the college president in the senior year, were students encouraged to talk in class about their own interpretations and applications of the material being read.

THE COLLEGIATE EXPERIENCE. The tensions between faculty and students sometimes boiled over into riots; more often, though, they simply created a seldom-bridged gulf between adults and students on campus. On their side of the divide students began to construct their own social institutions, most often against the wishes of the college faculty. In the mid eighteenth century students began to form debating clubs and literary societies (they are first recorded at Yale in 1753); these societies provided opportunities for the students elected to them to discuss (and, in their literary magazines, to write about) the issues of the day—especially political issues—which were ignored in curricula based largely on the study of Latin and Greek (and some Hebrew) and the important texts in logic, rhetoric, ethics, metaphysics, natural philosophy, and mathematics written in those classical languages. Literary societies began to collect books so that their members could read contemporary works not available in the college libraries; the resulting society libraries were often larger and more accessible than those of the colleges.

Beginning in the 1820s and 1830s, students developed the Greek-letter fraternities and similar social clubs—all with their own housing and eating facilities—to provide students who were chosen to join them with a social life almost completely separate from that sponsored by the faculty. Clubs and fraternities grew increasingly powerful as students used them to replicate on the college campus the social stratifications of the larger society. Those with the highest financial and/or social standing joined the "best" fraternities (and later sororities), those with somewhat less joined the next best, and so on. In most instances, clubs and fraternities included only a minority of a college's students.

Athletics was another area where student desires predominated. Inspired by German interest in gymnastics in the 1820s, students formed clubs where they could learn and perform exercises (and through which they could pressure the colleges into building and maintaining of athletic facilities). After mid century, students created teams—first in crew and then in rugby/football—to compete with similar club teams from other colleges (the first intercollegiate "football" game pitted Princeton against Rutgers in 1869). These unsupervised events often led to violence. At first, colleges sought to abolish student-developed intercollegiate athletics; when those efforts failed, colleges set out to regulate the competition.

With the triumph of the Greek system and intercollegiate athletics by the end of the nineteenth century, students had succeeded in shaping the residential college in ways unexpected and unwelcomed by college administrators. But the colleges gradually stopped opposing student initiatives and learned to manage and regulate them; indeed, by the twentieth century colleges began hiring specialized professionals to direct "student life" and athletics. Colleges adopted this new strategy in part because the tensions between faculty and students at residential colleges eased as the nineteenth century progressed. As the age range of resident students narrowed, it was easier to treat them all alike and appropriately at the same time; pedagogy improved with the widespread use of the lecture and the seminar; faculty members, who gradually grew more specialized (a luxury that larger colleges allowed) and professionalized (the master's and later the Ph.D. degree became the de facto license for college teaching), became more fully engaged in active teaching. But the colleges also adopted the new strategy because they found that their acceptance of and support for these student-developed activities contributed greatly to the maintenance of order on campus, to students' enjoyment of their collegiate experience, and to alumni loyalty to the college.

Post-Civil War Trends in Collegiate Education

From the tension between faculty and students in the colonial and antebellum colleges grew the institutional arrangements that have since become standard in residential college life. These arrangements—which were adopted in almost all of the public colleges after the Civil War—consisted of a college housing or dormitory system with attendant food services, an alternative room-and-board arrangement through a fraternity/sorority system open only to those students with high social standing, an indomitable emphasis on intercollegiate athletics, and an extracurriculum that engaged students in activities ranging from journalism to cultural performances to community service. In most cases these arrangements were completely isolated from the colleges' instructional activities—a situation apparently preferred by the students and perhaps by the faculty. Popular writing about higher education has tended to identify these characteristics of the residential college as the essence of "collegiate education"; certainly the majority of the students who participated in these nonacademic activities, and probably many of those who did not, also saw them as the core of the college experience. But it is well for the social historian to remember that most college students did not participate in these activities; indeed, in the twentieth century, less than half of all students were enrolled in residential colleges.

AN EMERGING DIVERSITY. In the half century after the Civil War most of the colleges founded before 1860 gradually severed their close alliances with their founding locales to become more "cosmopolitan." This process took many forms. A local college originally supported both by denominational and by local funds might switch to drawing all its support from the religious denomination and become an avowedly sectarian institution catering to a national audience of students (and parents) highly committed to that denomination. In most cases (with Catholic colleges being the clear exception) the movement took the opposite direction. Protestant colleges that had firmly identified with a specific denomination came to understand that they could not attract and keep enough students to sustain the college if they restricted admission to members of that faith. To make themselves more attractive, they first adopted an inoffensive form of generalized Protestantism and, by the second decade of the twentieth century, dropped their religious identity completely. As the public colleges grew stronger and larger, the "private" colleges eagerly emphasized their uniqueness—that they remained small enough for each student to receive personal attention; that their curricula emphasized liberal arts, not occupational training; and that their more rigorous entrance requirements and their high cost ensured a relatively elite student body. A few of the pre–Civil War foundations—especially colonial colleges such as Harvard, Columbia, Yale, Princeton, and Pennsylvania—increased greatly in size, identified research as a principal function, and recruited the most able students from the upper middle and upper classes to their undergraduate colleges.

Although, after the Civil War, growth in public higher education dominated developments, private college founding continued at a rapid pace for the rest of the century. Although the rate of college founding by confessional groups slowed significantly in the twentieth century, the process still continued—as at Oral Roberts University (founded in 1963 as one of several collegiate offshoots of nationwide televised ministries) or at the MidAmerica Nazarene College (founded in 1966). The highest rate of growth in confessional-college establishment occurred among Catholics, who rapidly expanded their limited pre–Civil War activities in an effort to serve the children of Catholic immigrants from Ireland and from southern and eastern Europe, who came to America in increasing numbers after 1840. By 1900, sixty-three permanent Catholic colleges had been started; there were 126 by 1930.

Business was probably the most prolific developer of specialized occupational schools by the turn of the century; the increase in firm sizes and the growing rationalization of business practices created a need for new white-collar skills that could not be learned on the job.

After the Civil War, groups often established colleges to promote a certain profession or occupation by systematizing and making more rigorous the training of its incoming members. Some private medical schools and law schools had been founded, either as separate institutions (medicine at the College of Philadelphia in 1765, and Judge Tapping Reeve's law school in Litchfield, Connecticut, in 1784) or as parts of already functioning colleges (the medical department at Kings College in 1767 and the law school at Harvard in 1817). Younger professions created training institutions—like engineering between 1847 and 1870 or journalism between 1910 and 1930—in order to claim the prestige associated with requiring practitioners to hold a collegiate credential. What was true of professions also held to some degree for occupations. The late nineteenth and early twentieth centuries, especially, saw the founding of a great number of institutions, few of them actually called "colleges" but most offering specialized training for a specific occupation beyond the high-school level. Probably the most prolific developer of specialized occupational schools was the field of business, which found by the turn of the twentieth century that the increase in firm size and the growing rationalization of business practices created a need for new white-collar skills that could not be learned efficiently on the job. Hundreds of schools sprang up to provide such training in business and other white-collar fields. Before 1920 these institutions served as an alternative path to a career credential; since 1920, though, most of these institutions specializing in business-office training have died away as their functions and sometimes the schools themselves were absorbed into the ever more rationalized collegiate system. Many of the late-twentieth-century specialized college curricula—areas such as business, communications, theater, nursing, dentistry—first appeared in these separate institutions; the established colleges added these innovative efforts to provide occupation-specific preparation as part of their effort to widen access and serve a broader population.

WOMEN'S AND MINORITY COLLEGES. Race and gender have also been a basis for the founding of distinctive colleges when the needs of such groups have been systematically neglected in more heterogeneous institutions. After the Civil War, while blacks were excluded—first by custom and then by law—from attending any college attended by white students, special colleges for blacks were founded in each of the southern states. Among the most famous and successful were Atlanta (1865) and Fisk (1866) universities, modeled on liberal-arts colleges, and Hampton (1868) and Tuskegee (1881) institutes, industrial schools emphasizing skill-building in manual trades. Although originally established to separate blacks from whites, these colleges have become a source of great pride for the black community. By the end of the nineteenth century, they were attracting ambitious black students throughout the nation who came to prepare to be professionals and community leaders while continuing to live in a supportive, prideful atmosphere.

As more and more of these colleges came under black leadership, they provided one avenue of advancement for the growing black professional class. Until World War II, these separate southern institutions—some state supported and some privately funded—offered most of the collegiate opportunities available to blacks (they granted 86 percent of the undergraduate degrees earned by black Americans between 1914 and 1936). Since then almost all collegiate institutions have opened their doors to black students—some voluntarily, some involuntarily, when required to do so by federal courts during the great civil rights battles of the 1950s and 1960s. In 1988, more than 80 percent of black college students attended traditionally white institutions. However, the approximately one hundred historically black institutions—which, according to the same laws that opened traditionally white institutions to blacks, are now open to white students—continue to play an important role in educating black students in an especially supportive environment. Currently, Native Americans are developing collegiate institutions—most notably a nationwide network of community colleges—where their children can master the skills necessary for success in modern American society while acquiring a greater understanding of and affinity with their traditional cultures.

Before the Civil War, collegiate education with few exceptions was restricted to males. Prevailing opinion held that higher education was unnecessary for women, who, after all, were going to devote their lives to their families and their homes; furthermore, it was widely believed that higher education's intellectual demands would overtax women's delicate constitutions and thus make them unfit for their primary tasks of childbirth and family nurturance. Throughout most of the nineteenth century even in the institutions that professed coeducation—first Oberlin in 1833 and then most of the midwestern state universities in the 1840s and 1850s—women often could not attend classes with men, could study only certain "appropriate" subjects, and had to follow an oppressively restrictive social regimen that effectively isolated them from campus life. In reaction to this exclusion and restriction, and as a direct challenge to the prevailing notion of women's circumscribed roles and frail constitutions, a number of women's colleges were founded after 1850. None that opened before the Civil War survived very long, but stronger ones appeared after the war: Vassar in 1865, Wellesley and Smith in 1875, Bryn Mawr and Goucher in 1884. Three female seminaries—Mills, Rockford, and Mount Holyoke, the last founded as a seminary as early as 1837—were rechartered as colleges in the 1880s. In 1870, 12 percent of American colleges admitted only women, 59 percent were restricted to males, and 29 percent were coeducational. In 1890 the number of colleges accepting only women peaked at 20 percent, while 47 percent were coeducational. Coeducation was clearly to be the wave of the future: by 1981, 92 percent of American colleges were coeducational. Yet even in 1986, 102 exclusively female colleges remained, stoutly defended as superior places for young women to receive their collegiate education because of the supportive atmosphere that an all-female environment offered.

These groups faced a dilemma regarding the advisability of maintaining separate institutions for their members. On the one hand, they sought for their children a supportive atmosphere that would also preserve the traditions of their culture or group; on the other, they wanted to overcome the very exclusivity in society and higher education that had originally kept their children from attending traditional colleges. Thus, even as they were maintaining—indeed celebrating—their ethnic- or gender-exclusive institutions, these groups were fighting valiantly, and successfully, to end exclusive practices in regular institutions. But while opening the doors of virtually all institutions of higher education in America to blacks, women, and Native Americans, these battles have not been as successful in getting those institutions to provide the kind of supportive atmosphere for those groups that more distinctive institutions can.

THE EMERGENCE OF PUBLIC COLLEGES. The idea that there is a public responsibility for providing higher education was not, as we have seen, new in 1860. Colonies and states had supported "private" colleges to some degree; several founded state universities in the antebellum period, but they were weak and relied much more on tuition dollars and gifts than on state revenues. They offered no real alternative to the private colleges. The first clear distinction between the public and private sectors of collegiate education came about with the Morrill Federal Land Grant Act of 1862, which deeded federal land to each the states, the proceeds of which were to be used to establish a new kind of institution. In the words of the legislation, the "land-grant" colleges were "to promote the liberal and practical education of the industrial classes in the several pursuits and professions of life." They were to direct their attention to practical education for future farmers and skilled workers ("mechanics" in the terminology of that era), to eschew classical languages and abstruse mathematics in favor of German and French (the languages of modern science), mensuration, animal husbandry, chemistry, horticulture, engineering, mechanical drawing, and the like.

Although the Morrill Act prescribed equal emphasis on agriculture and engineering, the early land-grant supporters focused their hopes on these institutions' ability to teach future farmers the practical skills and scientific applications needed to make American agriculture more productive. Initially the land grants did not fulfill this promise very successfully. Youngsters from farms and small towns most often enrolled in the land-grant colleges in order to escape from farming and small-town life. Even had they wished to become scientific farmers, what little was then known about the science of agriculture was not well codified for instructional purposes, and there were only a handful of people qualified to offer instruction in that subject. Indeed, in these early years the land-grant colleges behaved very much like other colleges, attracting the same sorts of students to the same sort of curriculum. By 1900, however, scientific agriculture had advanced to the point that the land-grant colleges could effectively offer a distinctive curriculum for those planning to make their careers in growing and processing foods and fibers.

"Land-grant" colleges were intended "to promote the liberal and practical education of the industrial classes in the several pursuits and professions of life."

This distinctive curriculum, though, attracted relatively few of the increasing number of students enrolled in those colleges. The significance of the land-grant movement lay elsewhere. First, in states that combined their land-grant college with their state university, the federal money provided the financial stability to enable the university to set a course of steady growth; this was true of Wisconsin and Minnesota, whose state universities (founded in 1848 and 1851, respectively) assumed the responsibility for agricultural and mechanical education in 1862. In states with separate land grants, on the other hand, the federal funding for the agricultural college tended to encourage governors and legislators to find similar amounts of financial support for the state university; this was true of Texas Agricultural and Mechanical College (1862), Ohio State University (1864), and the Virginia Polytechnic Institute (1872). Second, the land-grant legislation clearly stated—and began to implement—the principle that all taxpayers should subsidize the higher education of a relatively few students in order to further the public good. Third, the land-grant movement signaled the beginning of a growing vocational orientation in college education.

The continuing expansion of collegiate opportunities required greater justification than the antebellum appeal for educated leaders. Those who were asked to support college education through either contributions or attendance wanted a clearer understanding of what "good" it would do. That it would recruit and prepare young people for the increasingly sophisticated jobs society needed—whether in animal husbandry, teaching high-school science, or computer programming—became an increasingly popular reason thereafter for expanding college opportunities.

NORMAL SCHOOLS. Normal (teacher-training) schools were a pre-Civil War innovation that would have major repercussions in collegiate education only after the war. The first public normal school, opened in 1839 at Lexington, Massachusetts, offered a one-year course in elementary and grammar-school pedagogy for women; New York and Pennsylvania opened state normal schools in the 1840s. (Although later normal schools were open to men as well, women predominated at most—in part because of the growing conviction that women's affectionate natures made them ideal guides for young children, and in part because of the need to staff the rapidly expanding public schools as cheaply as possible.) The movement experienced its greatest expansion in the 1850s and 1860s, spurred by the desire—which also had fueled the land-grant movement—to provide public financial support of collegiate training for jobs.

Normal schools represent another of those nineteenth-century institutions whose exact categorization as high school or college is difficult to determine. Most began as one- or two-year training courses designed for young women without high-school diplomas who wished to become elementary-school teachers. Rather quickly most of them sought a more collegiate character—by adding somewhat advanced coursework in high-school subjects, recruiting more men and promising to prepare them for both high-school teaching and school-administration posts, and even suggesting that graduates could ultimately enter college and receive some credit for their coursework. This expanding sense of mission led the normal schools, by the turn of the century, to claim collegiate rank as state teachers' colleges. In time, the teachers' colleges became general state colleges; and in the surge of enrollment that followed World War II, many bid successfully to become regional universities by adopting the research orientation and comprehensive curricula of the leading state universities.

Normal schools have played an important but little-studied role in American history. As publicly supported colleges catering mostly to women, they offered an affordable avenue for advancement to those women not well served by any other institutions except the mostly distant and expensive private women's colleges. Further, because they were so prolific (there were nearly two hundred in 1928), young women from sparsely populated rural areas—and as these schools grew more collegiate, young men—did not need to travel far or risk being "corrupted" by living in larger communities that housed the more distant state universities or land-grant colleges. Finally, because they were closely associated with preparation for a practical employment considered suitable for women, these colleges were attractive to parents who did not want their daughters to aspire beyond a woman's place and thereby disqualify themselves for marriage by attending a liberal-arts college. As such, the normal schools probably provided thousands of young women, especially those from rural areas, with some taste of the learning and independence that their parents and communities would not otherwise have tolerated.

Like the land-grant colleges, normal schools were committed to practical education and thus were attractive to the sons and daughters of the artisan and agricultural classes: evidence indicates that in the mid nineteenth century between 60 and 70 percent of normal-school students in Massachusetts came from blue-collar families. Unlike the agricultural colleges, which had much trouble defining a practical education and attracting students to it, normal schools were widely successful in defining their purpose and recruiting students. Indeed, throughout the nineteenth century and well into the twentieth, preparing schoolteachers was the bread and butter of every kind of American college. For every other occupation, colleges had to overcome the widespread belief that "book learning" would retard a person's success in that field; however, there was an almost universal commitment to the desirability of having better-educated (although not necessarily better-paid) teachers. As public education reached greater numbers of young people, the demand for trained teachers grew constantly. This dependable demand for those who had attended college was the major cause of the expansion of collegiate education in the nineteenth century.

COLLEGIATE EDUCATION AND BUSINESS. In the twentieth century, the demand for college-educated workers grew in almost every field. Most dramatically, the world of business relinquished its dominant philosophy, which held that those who started at the bottom, as office boys or clerks, would rise through the ranks to become heads of firms; instead, it increasingly relied on hiring young men (usually) who had acquired the verbal and numerical skills and the social polish associated with college attendance. With the rationalization of business after 1890, managerial functions grew more abstract, depending more on the review of figures and the exchange of memos than on face-to-face encounters; therefore managers needed better-developed verbal and numerical skills—just the skills that colleges could claim to develop. In addition, the standardization and mechanization of manufacturing processes created less need for skilled laborers but more need for technically proficient managers and supervisors—again a need that colleges could claim a special role in filling. However, the real scope of business's need for individuals trained at the college level is not so clear. To some extent business appears to have used the colleges as a screening device: companies found it efficient to recruit only the college-trained for management positions, apparently assuming that those who aspired to get ahead by attending college and had the academic capacity to do so would usually be better employees than those without such aspirations and capacity.

Because the number of business positions absolutely dwarfed the number of jobs in any other field, even teaching, this shift in business-recruiting practices had an enormous effect on colleges. Enrollments soared when it became clear that white-collar jobs in business would come much more readily to college graduates. Even if a young person were not looking toward business, attending college made more and more sense. By 1920, entrance to virtually all training programs in law and medicine required an undergraduate degree. The growth of collegiate education itself created a growing demand for college teachers, who, of course, had themselves to have graduated from college, if not graduate school. New fields such as social work and pharmacy, as well as already established fields like engineering and the civil service, began to require college credentials. Enrollments soared in absolute numbers and in terms of percentage of the available age group. In 1870 approximately 2.3 percent of white males and females aged eighteen to twenty-one (62,000 people) attended college (including normal and professional schools); in 1900 that percentage had risen to 5 percent (256,000); in 1920, 9 percent (598,000); and on the eve of the Great Depression, 15 percent (1,174,000). These numbers do not include the thousands of young people preparing for business and professional careers in the hundreds of proprietary schools that filled the burgeoning cities of the era.

THE JUNIOR COLLEGE. The early decades of the twentieth century also saw the creation of an entirely new publicly supported institution of higher education, the junior college. In California, Michigan, and Illinois, especially, university presidents sought to build an alternative institution for the huge influx of new students interested only in introductory work, and thereby to maintain the status of the "senior" colleges, which concentrated on developing graduate and professional work. The first junior college opened in 1901, an extension of the high-school system in Joliet, Illinois. A few more followed before 1920, and dozens more in the 1920s and 1930s. Initially these institutions sought indeed to be "junior" colleges, preparing their students to transfer to four-year institutions by offering courses like those at the state universities. These alternative institutions had several advantages beyond protecting universities from unwanted students. Their appearance in population centers otherwise lacking in colleges enabled many students to save money by living at home while completing the first two years of college. Because junior colleges emerged as a part of the public-school system, instructional costs were lower than they would have been had those students been taught by college instructors. And because they were smaller than the statewide four-year schools, students new to college work could secure more personalized attention and a more comfortable atmosphere in which to mature. However, by the 1930s leaders of the junior colleges, which had begun to call themselves "community colleges," sought to replace the almost exclusive concern with transfer education with a commitment to train young people for what they began to call the "semiprofessions," occupational roles above the level of skilled worker but requiring an academic training less rigorous than that offered by four-year colleges. These reformers wanted community colleges to offer "terminal" education for potential practitioners of these occupations, rather than to encourage students to expect to transfer to regular colleges and compete for real professional jobs. By 1970, the number of students enrolled in such terminal programs rose slowly—much too slowly, according to the reformers—to one-third of the total community-college enrollment; by 1979, though, it had exploded to over one-half.

Post-World War II Trends in Collegiate Education

The four decades following World War II saw a massive growth in the number and percentage of young people enrolling in both two-and four-year colleges. Enrollment grew from 7.5 percent of the eighteen-to-twenty-four-year-old population in 1930 to almost 47 percent by 1986, from 1.1 million to 12.5 million. Attendance at all institutions grew, but most markedly at public institutions (from 1.2 million in 1950 to 9.5 million in 1985–1986) and spectacularly in the community colleges (from 217,572 in 1950 to 4.5 million in 1985–1986). By 1965, half of the graduates of American high schools (and nearly 60 percent by 1986) moved on to attend some recognized collegiate institution. More than 50 percent began their college careers in community colleges. These latter institutions also served increasingly as the avenue through which adults, many of whom had never before attended college, were entering or re-entering college to update or gain skills that would enable them to compete in a job market demanding higher numerical and verbal competency.

This surge in enrollment occurred in part because of the infusion of massive amounts of federal student aid. Modest scholarship programs had existed since the seventeenth century in the form of special gifts from in-

The almost four million veterans who attended college on the GI Bill comprised the first surge in post-World War II enrollment: This unprecedented participation level helped Americans form the habit of attending college.

dividuals or organizations: for example, a wealthy merchant endowed a fund to support the education of a "poor but deserving" boy from his hometown, or the Society for the Propagation of the Gospel in Foreign Parts donated funds to support young men who agreed to become foreign missionaries upon finishing college.

The federal government first offered substantial financial aid when demobilized World War II soldiers received up to four years of college tuition and living allowances through the GI Bill of Rights. The almost four million veterans who attended college on the GI Bill comprised the first surge in postwar enrollment. This unprecedented level of participation in collegiate education helped Americans form the habit of attending college. Probably 75 percent of those who took advantage of the GI Bill would not have gone to college without it; having attended college themselves, they were more likely to send their own children to college a decade or so later. Veterans of both the Korean and Vietnam wars received similar educational benefits, although their participation was dwarfed by the ever-expanding nonveteran college population. More important in the long run were the student-aid entitlements first instituted in the Higher Education Act of 1965 (with some precursors in the National Defense Education Act of 1958). The 1965 act and its successors established a grant program for low-income students that covered a portion of tuition and living expenses while the student attended college, community college, or proprietary school, as well as a loan program whereby middle-income students could borrow money for tuition and living expenses at low interest rates subsidized by the federal government. These programs enabled hundreds of thousands of students to attend college: in 1985–1986 students received nearly five million federal grants, loans, and work-study assignments. They also contributed the bulk of federal support for higher education after 1970. Because students received that aid to spend at any institution they chose, the massive aid program (amounting to over $8 billion in 1986) supported the continuation of the pattern of distinctiveness among collegiate institutions. Student choice, not government directives, dictated which institutions would receive aid.

Because most postwar students attended college to prepare directly for employment, vocational preparation came increasingly to dominate curricula. This change issued less from a shift in curricular focus at individual institutions than from the fact that the public and urban colleges that had always emphasized vocational training grew much more rapidly than did the privately supported liberal-arts colleges. At the same time, all colleges moved to ensure that their graduates received some liberal training along with their vocational preparation. "General education" or "distribution" requirements meant that all students completed introductory coursework within each of the great fields of knowledge—science, mathematics, social science, and the humanities. Where students in an earlier era intent on becoming, say, pharmacists or electrical engineers would have devoted all their coursework to those subjects, after 1945 they were more likely to begin their college career with a series of liberal-arts courses before devoting the last two years of college to their vocationally oriented major.

COMPETITION AND FAIRNESS IN ADMISSIONS. The period after 1945 also saw increasing debate as to whether educational opportunities at the collegiate level were being distributed equitably. Although this question had been a source of friction since at least the 1920s, the debate was greatly exacerbated by the massive increases in enrollment in the post-1950 era and the concern for social justice triggered in large part by the civil-rights movement. Beginning around 1920, when the increasing limitation of business positions to the college-educated swung public opinion decisively toward viewing collegiate education as the surest way for ambitious young people to advance, more students wanted to attend college, especially the more established ones, than there was space for them. The problem grew more serious after World War II. To meet this problem, almost all existing colleges expanded, and new colleges were rapidly founded: from 1950 from 1980 the number of four-year institutions rose by 75 percent, and the number of community colleges more than doubled. But that was not enough. Many colleges, especially the more established ones, abandoned the essentially open admissions policies prevalent in the nineteenth century, when anyone capable of meeting a college's very minimal requirements could study there. Before 1920 higher education was a buyers' market with more places for students than there were students to fill them, but with the surge of enrollments thereafter, many colleges had to become more selective.

Colleges that selectively admitted students needed to do so in a manner that was, or at least appeared to be, fair. Finding fair selection methods became an increasingly contentious issue, especially after 1950. Social discrimination in colleges first became controversial after 1900, when elite colleges in the Northeast and near large cities throughout the country established various policies to restrict the number of Jewish students admitted. They argued that gentiles would not attend a college that admitted too many Jews, and therefore turned away many qualified Jewish applicants in order to maintain a diverse student body and the loyalty and financial support of alumni who were overwhelmingly Protestant. This same line of argument was also used against working-class and immigrant students, but because these groups did not seek entrance to high-quality schools in the same numbers as did Jews, the discrimination was less noted.

In these colleges social background was more important in the selection process than academic capability. After 1945, colleges worked to change this balance. Cold-war fears of American vulnerability stemming from shortages of highly skilled scientists and engineers encouraged colleges to search out and train the best and the brightest, whatever their social background. Further, because faculties at research universities—and increasingly college faculty members who had been trained at research universities—wanted to teach the intellectually talented, they pressured university and college admissions officers to recruit the academically able rather than the socially connected. Colleges usually resorted to "objective" testing to determine academic or intellectual merit. The College Entrance Examination

Board began a national testing program for college-bound high-school seniors as early as 1901. Use of the Scholastic Aptitude Test became popular in the 1920s and widespread after 1950. This test, and others like it, promised colleges an objective, nationally consistent means of selecting the most academically meritorious students for admission to their colleges.

Objective tests promised to eliminate social background as a criterion for college admissions and access to the benefits that accompanied it, but these tests of academic merit favored those who attended private preparatory schools and wealthy suburban high schools—the very schools that applicants from the social elites attended. Therefore, objective measures of academic merit, adopted to guarantee greater accessibility to collegiate education, continued to favor those who came from well-to-do, well-educated families. The civil-rights movement highlighted this problem when a renewed sense of social justice and court-mandated integration of public schools encouraged (and sometimes forced) colleges across the country first to open their doors to and later to seek out black applicants. Generally, black applicants did not place highly on the usual criteria of academic merit that had come to prevail in colleges by 1960. Coming predominantly from underfunded southern or urban high schools, these applicants did not have strong test scores or well-developed academic skills. Many were profoundly ambivalent about leaving their communities to compete in a white academic world, and many were not particularly eager to learn about the cultural and scientific heritage of western European white males which the college professoriate was equipped to teach. But because colleges had become so important in controlling access to social and economic success, social justice demanded that they accommodate the needs of young black people so that they too could have the opportunities open only to college graduates.

These efforts provoked in the colleges a fundamental reexamination of what is meant by academic merit and of what materials and perspectives should comprise the fundamental building blocks of curricula appropriate to a diverse and globally-oriented nation. Although it was the crisis stemming from the need to bring black students into the colleges that provoked this reexamination, the process has become a many-sided conversation involving women, Native Americans, Asian Americans, Hispanic Americans, gay men and lesbians, the handicapped, and other minority groups.

This debate over fairness, over what constitutes merit—in students and in the curriculum—can best be viewed as a continuation of an American tendency to keep broadening the definition of collegiate education and widening people's access to it. Exclusivity has never characterized collegiate education in the United States for very long. Although it is true that children of the well-to-do are found disproportionately in the most prestigious institutions and children of the poor and of minority background disproportionately in institutions of lesser rank, a larger and larger number of children from less favored backgrounds have attended college as the nation has grown. Over time more people from all backgrounds have recognized that a college education provides a useful credential, and many set out to obtain one. And it has been increasingly easy for them to do so. Collegiate institutions have grown more plentiful and widely dispersed; they have developed an increasing number of relatively inexpensive paths to the degree. They have also geared their programs to the level of the student: if the region was without high schools, the college offered preparatory work for its students, and if the high schools failed to teach their graduates to read, the college offered remedial classes in reading. In effect, they have rejected almost none.

As more and more people sought college credentials, philanthropists and then the states and finally the federal government saw to it that there were enough institutions to accommodate their desires. These institutions have been of many distinctive kinds and many distinct levels of quality—a variety far greater than is found in any other nation—but each has come to represent both the culmination of some group's efforts to embody its beliefs and culture for the benefit of the next generation and an open invitation to individuals to establish their own place in the social structure through their own educational efforts.

BIBLIOGRAPHY

Allmendinger, David F., Jr. *Paupers and Scholars: The Transformation of Student Life in Nineteenth-Century New England* (1975).

Anderson, James D. *The Education of Blacks in the South, 1860–1935* (1988).

Angelo, Richard. "The Social Transformation of American Higher Education." In *The Transformation of Higher Learning, 1860–1930: Expansion, Diversification, Social Opening, and Professionalization in England, Germany, Russia, and the United States*, edited by Konrad H. Jarausch (1983).

Bledstein, Burton. *The Culture of Professionalism: The Middle Class and the Development of Higher Education in America* (1978).

Bowles, Samuel, and Herbert Gintis. *Schooling in Capitalist America: Educational Reform and the Contradictions of Economic Life* (1976).

Brint, Steven, and Jerome Karabel. *The Diverted Dream: Community Colleges and the Promise of Educational Opportunity in America, 1900–1985* (1989).

Brubacher, John S., and Willis Rudy. *Higher Education in Transition: A History of American Colleges and Universities.* 3d rev. ed. (1976).

Burke, Colin B. *American Collegiate Populations: A Test of the Traditional View. Education and Socialization in American History* series (1982).
Burke, Colin B. "The Expansion of American Higher Education." In *The Transformation of Higher Learning, 1860–1930: Expansion, Diversification, Social Opening, and Professionalization in England, German, Russia, and the United States*, edited by Konrad H. Jarausch (1983).
Eddy, Edward Danforth, Jr. *Colleges for Our Land and Time: The Land-Grant Idea in American Education* (1957).
Fields, Ralph R. *The Community College Movement* (1962).
Gladieux, Lawrence E., and Thomas R. Wolanin. *Congress and the Colleges: The National Politics of Higher Education* (1976).
Greeley, Andrew M. *From Backwater to Mainstream: A Profile of Catholic Higher Education* (1969).
Herbst, Jurgen. *And Sadly Teach: Teacher Education and Professionalization in American Culture* (1989).
Horowitz, Helen Lefkowitz. *Campus Life: Undergraduate Cultures from the End of the Eighteenth Century to the Present* (1987).
Jencks, Christopher, and David Riesman. *The Academic Revolution* (1968).
Kett, Joseph F. *Rites of Passage: Adolescence in America, 1790 to the Present* (1977).
Levine, David O. *The American College and the Culture of Aspiration, 1915–1940* (1986).
McLachlan, James. "The American College in the Nineteenth Century: Toward a Reappraisal." *Teachers College Record* 80, no. 2 (1978).
Novak, Steven J. *Rights of Youth: American Colleges and Student Revolt, 1798–1815* (1977).
Rudolph, Frederick. *The American College and University: A History* (1962).
Rudolph, Frederick. *Curriculum: A History of the American Undergraduate Course of Study Since 1636* (1977).
Solomon, Barbara Miller. *In the Company of Educated Women: A History of Women and Higher Education in America* (1985).
Synnott, Marcia Graham. *The Half-Opened Door: Discrimination and Admissions at Harvard, Yale, and Princeton, 1900–1970* (1979).
Veysey, Laurence R. *The Emergence of the American University* (1965).
Wechsler, Harold S. *The Qualified Student: A History of Selective College Admission in America* (1977).

— ROBERT L. CHURCH

COMMERCIAL ARCHITECTURE

The history of commercial and industrial architecture in the United States is integrally connected with the emergence and development of the most characteristic attitudes, values, and ideals of middle-class Americans. While important facets of the national psyche are reflected in American civic and residential architecture, it is in commercial and industrial building that the most cherished precepts concerning the relationship between private and public enterprise have been dynamically interwoven and expressed.

The Atlantic colonies were established in large part for mercantile purposes. Although many inhabitants had other reasons for settling in the New World, the mercantile impulse was germane to the culture and politics of the new land. Although in 1789 government was constitutionally separated from religion, its fertile relationship to private enterprise, cultivated from the outset of the colonial period, was affirmed. This relationship has remained so vital that in the twentieth century, commercial architecture emphatically represents such national cultural ideals as individualism, ambition, wealth, success, and personal power, as well as social and economic power, the growth of urbanization, and the rise of a market economy.

Freedom, pragmatism, ingenuity, functionalism, and technological progressiveness are among the obvious qualities associated with American commercial and industrial architecture; however, these qualities only began to generate an identifiable architectural expression in the early nineteenth century. Prior to that they had borrowed forms and images from both the civic and residential spheres. Early colonial commercial architecture reflected a mixture of medieval traditions and more urbane seventeenth-century English and continental architectural taste. Retail and small commercial ventures were often managed as family businesses and installed in residences or buildings of residential character, such as the Paul Revere House (1677) in Boston. Trade restrictions imposed by Britain inhibited the development of mill or industrial building, although European visitors often found American applications of wind- and waterpower in smaller projects to be ingenious and more frequent than in Europe.

Colonial versions of European high-style architecture, based in large part on pattern books, available materials, and incidental local craft, were first introduced in governmental, religious, and residential structures. These eventually lent larger cities such as Boston and Philadelphia a character similar to contemporary London. As the familiar vocabulary was adapted for the agencies of finance and commerce, a uniquely American urban character began to evolve.

One of the earliest examples of such an adaptation is Faneuil Hall (1740), given by Peter Faneuil to the city of Boston to enclose and improve the farmers' market on Dock Square. The plans were prepared by the portrait painter John Smibert (1688–1751), which indicates the absence of professional architects in mid-eighteenth-century America. It was constructed of red brick with an arcade around the first-floor market space and sash windows admitting light to the second-story public meeting hall, an arrangement generally derived from European models. The whole block was covered by a gabled roof surmounted by a cupola and loosely resembled the familiar New England meetinghouse. The adjacency of market and meeting room reinforced the fact that Faneuil Hall was a popular forum where town worthies informally exchanged opinions on public matters while shopping.

In 1760, land in Newport, Rhode Island, was dedicated to the construction of a market building which, like Faneuil Hall, had an open trading area on the first floor surmounted by two stories of flexible space used for storage, offices, and shops. The Brick Market (1772) was designed by Peter Harrison (1716–1775), a British-born merchant whose intense interest in architecture had caused him to collect the largest library of treatises and pattern books in the country. His scheme was based on a design by Inigo Jones, who had introduced Italian classicism to England in the late sixteenth century and whose work had been in revival since the early eighteenth century in England.

Although Harrison was no more than a gifted amateur, professional architecture was encouraged and supported by the country's other great amateur, Thomas Jefferson, as a mark of sophistication and wise planning. Commercial architecture began to profit from professional architectural services upon the immigration of Benjamin Henry Latrobe (1764–1820) from England in 1796. The Bank of Pennsylvania (1798–1800; razed 1860s) in Philadelphia is a distinguished example of his early work. It exhibited masonry construction, including interior vaulting for both structure and architectural effect. Temple porticos fronted both ends of a block supporting a low pantheonic dome, beneath which was located the banking room, generously illuminated by daylight. The design established a standard of elegance and efficiency that was followed in banking and commercial buildings throughout the country.

William Strickland (c. 1787–1854), who was a talented designer and Latrobe's pupil, won a competition in 1818 for the Second Bank of the United States (1819–1824) in Philadelphia. Faced with Pennsylvania marble, this was the first public building to derive from the Parthenon and signaled the advent of the Greek Revival, the style with which Americans identified nationally after the War of 1812. The Greek Revival style was also employed by Strickland in his design for the Merchants' Exchange (1832) in Philadelphia that converted irregularities of the city plan to advantage. The wedge-shaped site was terminated at its narrower end by a semicircular Corinthian portico surmounted by a lantern modeled on the choragic Monument of Lysicrates of late classical Athens. A similar dependence on classical models characterized the Merchants' Exchange (1836–1842) in New York by Isaiah Rogers (1800–1869). Its exterior Ionic colonnade on a high podium screened a brick-vaulted exchange room 80 feet (24 meters) in diameter.

Such references were certainly signs of sophisticated architectural taste and erudition on the part of designers; but they also directly reinforced popular sentiments about the manifest destiny of the United States as the modern descendant of ancient democratic Greece. This was particularly important during the period of Jacksonian expansionism when the drive westward was envisioned as bringing civilization to the wilderness as well as taking advantage of the limitless natural resources of the Great Plains and western mountains. Towns founded during this period often took Greek names as symbols of this spirit: Athens, Syracuse, Sparta, Utica, Ithaca, Arcadia, Alexandria, Delphos, Troy, Memphis, Corinth. Commercial architecture along the principal streets of these and similar towns was often of a reduced neoclassicism, thus serving as an understated context for more prominent civic, religious, and residential structures in Greek Revival style.

The Greek Revival style and similar classical models that emerged in America after 1812 directly reinforced popular sentiments about the manifest destiny of the United States as the modern descendent of ancient democratic Greece.

With British restrictions on manufacturing removed by the Revolution, the United States sought to achieve economic independence through the development of industry. In the late eighteenth century, structures based on existing sawmills in New England began to house waterpowered machinery for producing textiles. The earliest mills employed traditional materials and structural techniques, amplified around the turn of the century with the malleability, permanence, and strength of cast iron.

Probably the first building to be planned and constructed as a textile mill was the 1793 spinning mill designed by Samuel Slater (1768–1835) in Pawtucket, Rhode Island. Based on his experience and familiarity with English textile production, the machinery was housed in a frame structure whose proportions and noble simplicity were consonant with the residential context. The main requirements—large, continuous interior spaces in a two-story block, adequate daylighting, and a structural system rigid enough to stabilize the building against vibrations from the power mechanism and machinery—were all satisfied functionally without sacrificing basic architectural principles or pleasing design. Such a successful integration of social, commercial, and architectural values by manufacturers allayed the fears of many agrarian-minded citizens that industrialization would contaminate the morality of the nation.

The rapid growth of manufacturing in the period between 1810 and 1820 began to alter the size and form of mill buildings. Mills became larger in all dimensions and were increasingly constructed in stone or brick masonry for rigidity and fire protection. They acquired clerestory-light monitors to make their attic spaces more useful, as in the Lippitt Mill (1809–1810) in West Warwick, Rhode Island. With cupolas holding bells to call the workers to their jobs, mills became increasingly important as the focus of community life, especially in small towns.

In the first four decades of the nineteenth century, manufacturing moved beyond the limits of local capital and mechanical skills. To increase output capacity, the textile industry was gradually transformed by an investment and managerial structure geared to efficient production and the organization of a large labor force. Mill buildings evolved to meet new safety needs and production realities. Large lateral towers added for circulation, fire containment, and vertical mechanical runs separated the mill from the meetinghouse typologically, as in the woolen mill by Zachariah Allen (1822; enlarged 1839) in Allendale, Rhode Island. Landscape design, reliance on neoclassical architectural principles to govern a complex of buildings, and a concern for appropriate living quarters for single men and women as well as for families transformed factories from isolated objects into planned communities, sometimes of compelling visual appeal. In the Crown and Eagle mills (1825, 1829, respectively) by Learned Scott in North Uxbridge, Massachusetts, boardinghouses, dormitory structures, and row housing, along with the factory buildings, began to reshape the urban fabric in conjunction with waterways and green areas.

While manufacturing before the Civil War frequently remained rural due to the necessity of locating mills and factories where waterpower could best be harnessed, retail architecture was decidedly urban and more directly responsive to changing technology and economics as well as fashion. The shopping arcade or *passage*, inaugurated in France in 1790, appeared in the United States in Philadelphia (1827) and Providence, Rhode Island (1828–1829). Designed by John Haviland (1792–1852), the Philadelphia Arcade had street-front arcades while the Providence Arcade, designed by Russell Warren (1783–1860) and James C. Bucklin (1801–1890), had a glass-roofed interior.

The Gothic Revival, a romantic phenomenon that followed on the heels of the Greek Revival, produced a few retail buildings, for example, the step-gabled and pinnacled Oak Hall on North Street in Boston, a frame structure of mid-century date. The use of wood for such highly detailed ornamental buildings was actually facilitated by the invention of the jigsaw during this period, a by-product of the industrial revolution.

In the end, neither the Greek nor the Gothic Revival lent themselves to the economic or spatial exigencies of retail building. Rather, in the late 1840s the Palazzo style began to dominate retail and office buildings, where rows of arched windows separated by engaged columns in the manner of sixteenth-century Venetian palaces defined the stories. Stewart's Downtown Store in New York (1845), executed in white marble, was the first to apply this generalized Renaissance style whose main advantage was its ability to be extended both horizontally and vertically over a large commercial facade.

The rapid spread of the Palazzo style in the 1850s and 1860s was encouraged by the development of cast iron as a finish material as well as a structural component. Pioneered in the United States by James Bogardus (1800–1874), an inventor and foundry owner, iron appeared in the Baltimore Sun Building (1848), which he designed in collaboration with R. G. Hatfield, and in his design for the Harper Brothers Building in New York (1854). The Sun Building had two iron fronts that had been cast in sections at the Bogardus foundry, shipped to the site, and assembled with bolts as a prefabricated building skin. Iron thus made the repetition of facade units entirely practical as well as far cheaper than building in conventional materials and methods. Cast iron was normally rendered in forms that imitated stone and, because it needed to be painted to protect against weathering, it could be given any color the architect or patron desired. Flexible, practical, and cheap, the popularity of cast-iron components spread rapidly from urban centers to towns and villages to become the first identifiable commercial vernacular architecture.

Perhaps more important, Bogardus used iron as a system of cast columns and wrought beams in the Sun Building. The slender columns, which eliminated the need for heavy masonry-bearing walls, afforded unprecedented interior space as well as lightness and rapid construction by semi-skilled labor. Iron also lent itself to other building components such as stairways and railings. It thus set the stage for the concept of a structural cage in which loads could be carried on continuous columns from top story to foundation. This system was utilized already in the A. T. Stewart Store in New York (1862) by John Kellum, one of the largest cast-iron buildings anywhere. Its central rotunda was surrounded by galleries beneath a skylight and contained a pipe organ for the entertainment of the customers.

Bogardus pushed his system further when he constructed a shot tower for the McCullough Shot and Lead Company of New York (1855). A metal frame served as the structure of the tower with brickwork used merely as infill, thus adumbrating the emergence of the steel skeletal frame in Chicago and New York some thirty years later. In addition to the employment of cast iron, the Haughwout Building (1856) in New York by John P. Gaynor and Daniel Badger incorporated the first passenger elevator. Invented by Elisha Otis, the elevator became the second stimulant of vastly increased height in commercial buildings throughout the country.

Skyrocketing urban land values demanded that technology address higher density and concentration in commercial buildings; this powerful combination of profit and prestige drove the motivation for ever-taller buildings.

Cast iron was also used widely in other commercial-building types. The Crystal Palace (1853) in Bryant Park by Carstensen and Gildemeister brought both the materials and the concept of the London Exposition and its Crystal Palace of 1851 to New York. A twenty-minute fire that destroyed the gossamer exposition building in 1858 proved that the major disadvantage of iron was its low melting point. The train shed of the first Grand Central Station (1871) in New York by John B. Snook used a metal skeleton carrying glass panels, as did many other railroad stations. These were superseded by less-combustible steel structures after about 1875 due to the spread of the Bessemer steel process, invented simultaneously in England by Henry Bessemer and in Kentucky by William Kelly in 1856.

Rapid commercial growth after the Civil War produced the most important developments in commercial and industrial architecture. Skyrocketing land values in urban centers demanded that technology address higher density and concentration in commercial buildings. The powerful combination of profit and prestige became the driving motivation for ever-taller buildings. Never before had the largest, tallest, and most dominant buildings in an urban skyline represented the private power of the commercial, financial, and industrial enterprises of a society rather than the power and authority of its religious or governmental institutions.

In New York, the Tribune Building by Richard M. Hunt and the Western Union Building by George B. Post (both built from 1873 to 1875) announced the success of private investment in mass communication. Yet by extending their Victorian masses upward through picturesque clock towers without giving up traditional bearing-wall masonry, they remained only on the cusp of stylistic and technological change. But in the frantic effort to rebuild Chicago after the disastrous fire of 1871, the technological and engineering advances begun by James Bogardus and others came to fruition. Large quantities of concentrated office space were needed to house the growing legions of white-collar workers and secretarial staffs required by the administrations of the vastly expanding business enterprises there. The advantages of metal and glass radically altered the engineering and design of the new fireproof buildings that mushroomed in the Loop to meet the demand.

The first Leiter Building (1879) by William Le Baron Jenney (1832–1907) used cast-iron columns for both interior and peripheral loads, situated columns next to the brick envelope of the facade, and substituted huge plate-glass windows for bearing-walls. Jenney, who had been trained as a civil engineer in France, took the next step towards skeletal engineering in the Home Insurance Company Building (1883–1885), which is considered the first skyscraper. Although some bearing masonry continued to support peripheral load in the first two stories, a combination of cast-iron columns and wrought-iron girders established a true skeletal frame for the upper eight stories.

Unfortunately, Jenney's engineering genius far surpassed his abilities in architectural design, where he remained bound to historical precedent and uninspired eclecticism. The question of an appropriate expression for the shell, an expression of contemporary social, economic, and cultural conditions, was taken up by other firms. That Chicago architects were dissatisfied with the initial expression of the new technology in a cloak of revivalist styles is partially attributable to the tradition of practical thinking that began with Thomas Jefferson, Charles Bulfinch, and Benjamin Henry Latrobe, manifesting itself in mill and factory design. It continued under the impulse of sculptor and critic Horatio Greenough who in his writings had called for an organic relationship between the form of a building and its internal realities.

Among those who took up the search for appropriate expression was the firm of Burnham and Root. Although he was in command of the technology at his disposal, John Wellborn Root (1850–1891) was equally concerned with the functional and aesthetic accomplishments of his buildings. The Rookery Building (1885–1886), framed in steel with masonry outer walls, addressed several practical problems by introducing a hollow core in its block-square volume. The resulting light-well permitted the handsome lobby to be brightly illuminated through skylights and insured that all offices on the inside of the upper stories would have the benefit of adequate light and ventilation. The exterior composition was additive and eclectic, a manner that Root rejected in the unornamented Monadnock Building (1889–1891), the first tall building to be treated as a slab in one continuous upward sweep. The steel cage of the Reliance Building (1894–1895) was protected against fire with terra-cotta cladding using Gothic motifs; but its vast expanses of plate glass "Chicago windows" projected the impression that its exterior was truly an expression of the frame and the interior space.

Contemporaneous with the Rookery, Henry Hobson Richardson (1838–1886), one of the foremost architects on the East Coast, designed the Marshall Field Wholesale Store (1885–1887) in Chicago. The structure consisted of a mix of terra-cotta-clad, cast-iron columns on the first three floors and wood-framing typical of New England mill buildings on the floors above. The understated exterior, however, made an enormous impact on Chicago architects who saw in it an appropriate solution to the form of a modern commercial building. In his religious, civic, and private commissions, Richardson had popularized an energetic neo-Romanesque style. For the Field Wholesale Store, he abandoned all romantic qualities of the revival mode in favor of a severe treatment that projected unity, integrity, economy, and rationality.

Among those most influenced by Richardson were Dankmar Adler and Louis Sullivan (1856–1924) who designed the mixed-use Auditorium Theatre Hotel (1887–1889), an important turning point in their work. Retaining their characteristic finish, ornament, and detail, especially on the interior, in their final scheme they incorporated numerous qualities of the Field Store design, including its solidity, its understatement, and its reliance on the arch as an organizing device. Sullivan developed a personal philosophy about balancing the engineering aspects of the skyscraper with the poetry of ornament derived from geometry and plants. In a series of structures for Saint Louis, Missouri (Wainwright Building, 1890–1891), Buffalo, New York (Guaranty [now Prudential] Building, 1895), and Chicago (Gage Group, 1898–1899) he envisioned tripartite vertical compositions articulated by organic ornament. Perhaps his most notable accomplishment was the Schlesinger and Mayer (now Carson Pirie Scott) Store in Chicago (1899–1904), a celebration of the social aspects of shopping, in which he enclosed the steel cage with a subtle terra-cotta skin that contrasted with an elaborate two-story band of florid wrought-iron ornament enframing the display windows and entrances at pedestrian level. After this tour de force, Sullivan spent his late career designing small banks and thrift institutions as essays in organic ornament for midwestern towns such as Grinnell, Iowa, Owatonna, Minnesota, and Sidney, Ohio.

In 1893, the World's Columbian Exposition opened in Chicago. Planned by Daniel H. Burnham (1846–1912) and landscape architect Frederick Law Olmsted (1822–1903), the Exposition was envisioned as a symbol of American industrial, commercial, and social progress four centuries after the arrival of Columbus. McKim, Mead, and White, Richard Morris Hunt, and other architects from the East Coast were invited to join stylistically conservative Chicago designers such as Burnham to create a complex of classical-revival buildings in the manner of the École des Beaux-Arts in Paris, all in an artificial setting replete with Venetian canals and a lagoon on the lakefront. They succeeded in raising consciousness about architectural and urban-design values, especially among midwesterners of limited background, who saw in the "White City" a model of urbanity. Yet they also sent a powerful message about the venerability of historical revival architecture derived from Europe—in contrast to the emerging Chicago School of commercial building—as the appropriate vehicle to express commercial, industrial, and social progress as well as national identity.

The impact of the Columbian Exposition can be measured in the spread of the City Beautiful movement, a trend toward improved urban design related to Burnham's master plan for Chicago (1909), and in the continued dominance of revival styles for commercial as well as civic architecture throughout the country. In New York, the technology of steel framing reinforced rising land prices and led to ever higher buildings and more conservative design. When it was erected, the impressive Woolworth Building by Cass Gilbert (1910–1913) in Lower Manhattan was the tallest in the world at 792 feet (238 meters). Its terra-cotta cladding was cast as Gothic ornament, which inspired the nickname "cathedral of commerce" for the corporate headquarters of Frank Woolworth's chain of variety stores.

By contrast, Sullivan's protégé, Frank Lloyd Wright (1867–1959), had designed an innovative office building for the Larkin Soap Company administration in Buffalo, New York (1903). Avoiding historical references altogether, Wright produced an environment derived not only from the utilitarian realities of the building and the formal precedents of Chicago commercial architecture but also from the need for programming the tasks and duties of a large secretarial staff and managerial team, for social interaction, and for a sense of dignity in the workplace. Nevertheless, apart from the circle of Sullivan and Wright, functionally based architecture without historical ornament remained limited in large part to industrial structures where it could be justified as an expression of economy and efficiency.

Perhaps the clearest indication of this dichotomy is in the architecture produced for the automobile industry. Having experimented with several alternatives to conventional mill construction in the design of factories for automotive production, the Detroit architect Albert Kahn (1869–1942) began to employ reinforced concrete as a structural system in 1905. Commissioned by Henry Ford in 1909, Kahn designed a huge assembly plant in Highland Park, Michigan, in which concrete stabs and steel-girder beams afforded not only strength, safety, and permanence but adequate clearspan space for production. In 1912–1915, the plant incorporated a continuously moving assembly line, the basis of most factory production ever since.

Kahn continued to improve the architecture of factories, creating dramatic forms based on clearly analyzed functional relationships. Vast expanses of glass in industrial framing, jagged roof lines, rows of columnar smokestacks rising out of power plants, and complex truss systems for clearspan space became his trademarks, especially in huge complexes such as the Ford River Rouge Plant in Dearborn, Michigan, begun in 1916. Yet when General Motors commissioned him to design its headquarters in Detroit, Kahn turned out an impressive structure based on classical revivalism.

The General Motors Building (1922) is an early example of the expression of a corporate culture, rather than the expression of the taste and power of an entrepreneurial individual or family. Rising from an arcade of show windows to display its products at street level, separate tower-like elements are connected to a slab at the back, the whole crowned by a classical colonnade at the top. The location of executive offices at the top level and the general composition of the structure metaphorically suggest the gathering of the five automotive companies into one corporate body. Research and development was housed in a lower block just behind the main building, reflecting its supportive but less prominent character.

The extent to which eclectic architectural vocabularies continued to connote grandeur and magnanimity in the minds of patrons can be judged by the Chicago Tribune Tower competition of 1922 in which a neo-Gothic design by John Mead Howells and Raymond Hood took first place over a group of some two hundred entries. Yet the second-place entry by Eliel Saarinen, a tower dynamically telescoping itself skyward with a limited amount of abstract ornamental detail, made its impact on countless office buildings throughout the United States and Canada, even influencing Hood and Howells in their subsequent design work, and paved the way for the important changes in skyscraper design.

In his design for the Larkin Soap Company in Buffalo, Frank Lloyd Wright created an environment that encouraged social interaction and provided a sense of dignity in the workplace.

The first of those changes was the Art Deco style, which reconciled the continuing taste for ornament and traditional materials with the growing interest in new industrial metals, in technology as a form of power, and in air transportation, electricity, and radio waves as symbols of progress. Art Deco also exploited architecture as a form of advertising, partly in pure verticality and partly in the identifiability of a building profile in the urban skyline. The Union Trust Building by Smith, Hinchman, and Grylls in Detroit (1929) and the Chrysler Building by William Van Alen in New York (1930) both used night illumination to enhance their presence; and the Empire State Building (1931) by Shreve, Lamb, and Harmon in New York relied on its 101-story height to dominate most of midtown Manhattan. These qualities began to disappear as the impact of the Great Depression cautioned corporation presidents and boards of directors to seek ways of representing fiscal responsibility in architectural form.

The Philadelphia Saving Fund Society building (1933) by George Howe and William Lescaze was the first corporate tower to draw on contemporary German functionalist design in order to make the structure as maintenance-free as possible and to prevent shareholders from suspecting unnecessary expenditure. During the 1930s and 1940s, the Moderne style, a softer version of functionalism influenced by French sources, was especially popular in retail and smaller commercial buildings. In gasoline stations, grocery markets, drugstores, barber shops, beauty salons, and variety stores,

A view of the Chrysler Building in the year it was completed (1930). Art Deco style reconciled the continuing taste for ornament and traditional materials with a growing interest in technology as a form of power.

it implied an architectural connection with the culture of large-scale business enterprise.

In reaction to European functionalism and the Moderne, Frank Lloyd Wright offered his own solution to the office building and corporate headquarters in the Johnson Wax Administration Building (1939) in Racine, Wisconsin. Its smooth brick surfaces rest on reinforced concrete platforms resembling lilypads and its fenestration consists exclusively of glass tubing held in place by steel spacers. As in the Larkin Building, Wright designed not only the architecture but also the furnishings. The final effect of the whole building was to inspire the work force into a stronger sense of social cohesion.

In an effort to generate electric power, raise living standards in rural areas, provide jobs during the Depression, and implement a policy of long-range regional planning, the federal government initiated a series of hydroelectric dam projects during the 1930s. The most extensive of these, the Tennessee Valley Authority (TVA), begun in 1933, consisted of eight dams along a seven hundred-mile waterway between the Appalachians and the Ohio River. It was echoed in other projects in the Pacific Northwest, the West, and the Southwest. The architecture of the TVA was cast into the Moderne style and was considered important enough by the Museum of Modern Art in New York to deserve a special exhibit in 1938.

Meanwhile, the rise of the automobile after World War I brought countless other changes to commercial architecture. In the 1930s, freeways had already begun to change the face of Los Angeles. Cross-country travel and truck transport was facilitated and encouraged by a growing system of state and federal highways, along which service stations and tourist cabins sprang up. The motor lodge or motel was geared to travelers on the move in private vehicles. Motels were accompanied by an entirely new culture of culinary establishments offering low- to medium-priced fare for people of modest means who were in transit. Diners, sometimes literally converted from railroad cars, connoted both the convenience and transitory quality of eating on the road and inadvertently acknowledged the demise of rail transportation that was in decline after 1914. Public transportation was supplied by the development of bus lines that installed terminals in towns and cities but relied on service stations and stores as stopping places in rural areas. The mobile home also emerged at this time as a kind of updated Conestoga wagon that permitted owners to pull their shelter on the road after them.

The impact of the automobile and the general rise of consumer culture between the world wars was documented by the Chicago World Fair of 1933 and the New York World Fair of 1939. In contrast to the Columbian Exposition of 1893, exhibits representing transportation, electrical power, industry, communication, consumer products, and entertainment at both the 1933 and 1939 fairs were contextualized in architectural environments designed with the collective intention of looking stunningly futuristic. This was accomplished in large part by the use of dramatic lighting and water displays and, at the New York fair, by elevated walkways and curvilinear buildings, imparting a sense of free movement. Although the fair buildings were no more than imaginative variations on the Moderne and functionalist styles, they popularized the equation of technology with progress and confirmed the notion of architecture as a vehicle of public relations and advertising.

One of the most important effects of the automobile during this period was its implementation of suburban development. Liberated from having to live near their workplaces, Americans began to move from central cities to newly subdivided neighborhood developments at the edge of or outside city limits. Flourishing central business districts began to be eroded, imperceptibly at first, by decentralized commercial strips and shopping districts. The Country Club Plaza in Kansas City, Missouri, developed by J. C. Nichols and designed by Edward Beuhler Delk (1922–1925), offered a master-planned commercial quarter that responded to the rapid growth of the city southward and set a standard for similar developments elsewhere. The use of a neo-Spanish colonial architectural idiom, the concentration of parking in designed areas, and tight controls placed on signage, lighting, and future development, not only preserved the image Nichols planned but made environmental control serve private enterprise in a way that had rarely been seen before.

Suburban shopping strips of less pretension in the 1920s, 1930s, and 1940s offered convenience to motorists who could easily park their cars while doing light shopping. The success of strips eventually led to the development of the supermarket as well as several other concepts, including the drive-in restaurant, drive-in movie theater, and drive-through store. It also led to the shopping center, a concept first articulated in the 1950s by Victor Gruen, an immigrant Austrian architect who saw in it a way to bring a desirable quality of public interaction to the highly decentralized life of the American suburb. Early examples such as Northland Center (1954) in Southfield, Michigan, were treated as elaborate complexes of retail establishments connected by covered sidewalks, interspersed with parklike elements such as fountains, benches, and plantings, and surrounded by parking lots. They thus drew on the imagery of urban and civic life while remaining totally private developments. Their popularity even had the reflexive impact of causing towns such as Richmond, Indiana, and countless others to eliminate automobile traffic from their principal commercial streets and convert them into pedestrian zones in hopes of revitalizing their commercial districts. The enclosure of Southdale Center (1956) in Edina, Minnesota, to avoid inclement weather created the first self-contained shopping concourse.

After World War II, a wave of Modernist influence swept through American business and commercial architecture, due in part to the immigration of several leading European architect-educators to the United States in the late 1930s: Ludwig Mies van der Rohe, Walter Gropius, and Marcel Breuer. Their influence brought about a strong school of commercial building represented by pace-setting structures such as the Lever House by Skidmore, Owings, and Merrill (1952) and the Seagram Building by Mies van der Rohe with Philip Johnson (1957) in New York City. These understated minimalist slabs expressed corporate identity through machine precision and the elegance of tinted glass in a light curtain-wall skin that has no support value and serves only as an insulating envelope. In contrast to earlier complexes such as Rockefeller Center (1931–1933 and later) in New York in which a group of buildings was organized around a public plaza where outdoor activities could be centered, these buildings were conceived as objects isolated by set-back plazas, a concept related to the Modernist urban-planning principle of functional separation and zoning.

Understated minimalist slabs such as Mies van der Rohe and Philip Johnson's Seagram Building expressed corporate identity through machine precision and the elegant effect of a light, tinted, curtain-wall glass serving only as an insulating envelope.

Modernist concepts likewise dominated such other areas of commercial architecture as transportation. In the Lambert Air Terminal (1956) in Saint Louis, Missouri, Minoru Yamasaki covered large waiting rooms with thin concrete shells whose lightness and curvilinearity for the first time metaphorically suggested aerodynamic forces. Similarly Eero Saarinen engaged the air terminal as a serious architectural problem in his reinforced concrete sculptural design for the Trans World Airlines Terminal at Kennedy Airport (1962) in New York. By contrast, the United Airlines Terminal (1988) by Helmut Jahn at Chicago's O'Hare Airport contextualizes the high technology of air transportation in reminiscences of the rail transportation buildings of the nineteenth century.

In the early 1960s, the main concourse of Grand Central Terminal (1913) by Reed and Stem with Warren and Wetmore in New York nearly faced demolition when the Pan Am Building (1963) by Emery Roth,

Pietro Belluschi, and Walter Gropius was proposed to replace it. The struggle to save Grand Central and the failure to preserve New York's Pennsylvania Station (1910; demolished 1963) by McKim Mead and White were early signs of the conflicts that would continue to emerge in the 1960s and later over the preservation of historic buildings in American cities. In some cases, preservation activities were directed against developers who sought to redevelop the potentially lucrative sites of historic buildings more densely; in others, preservationists fought for historic buildings as the last vestige of history and stability in decaying urban centers.

The preservation movement began just as the sociopolitical base of architectural Modernism came under attack during the postmodern revolution. Postmodernism is associated with broader cultural changes in the United States during the 1960s and 1970s that are also coincidental with the rise of consumerism and late capitalism. In some cases, it fosters the revival of historical styles; in others, it manipulates Modernist architectural language for commercial purposes. The commercial typologies of this period include signature office buildings—whether corporate or speculative—atrium hotels, regional and urban shopping malls, and festival marketplaces: buildings that frequently project the image of public domain but are completely controlled by private interests. They are often generated by public/private partnerships in which market success and architectural imagery ambiguously mix with political values.

The earliest example of a postmodern signature office building is the AT&T Building (1976) by Philip Johnson in New York; it sent shocks of reaction through both architectural and business communities when it was announced. Long the champion of architectural Modernism, Johnson offered AT&T a revivalist granite-clad slab topped by a pediment. In his design for the Humana Building (1985) in Louisville, Kentucky, the winner of a national competition, Michael Graves explored his interest in abstraction fused with classicism through sensuous color and traditional materials. Ironically, the luxurious building denotes health care as a successful business just at the time that health care was in crisis nationally. In these and other cases, the name of the architect and his personal style have become as important an asset as the real estate itself.

The burgeoning suburbs eventually attracted another typology: the office building built on speculation. Found usually along main thoroughfares and often at the exits of interstate freeways, suburban office complexes are predominantly horizontal rather than vertical, often include atrium courts, and are always accompanied by parking decks or surrounded by parking lots. They usually lease space to small businesses, sales personnel, and professional firms, offering them the convenience of suburban location along with an image derived from the signature tower.

The evolution of the regional shopping mall, especially from the late 1960s on, exploited the ambiguity of a private domain open to the public. Excluding whomever its owners wished and eliminating truly civic interaction, malls became paradises of consumerism in contrast to the increasingly empty, and dangerous urban centers. Fairlane Town Center (1976) in Dearborn, Michigan, developed by the Taubman Company, is a consummate example of the interiorization of commercial architecture around atrium courts with corridors of shops strung between large anchor stores. It is also an example of design that alters the users' perceptions of space, time, and movement as retail strategy. Festival marketplaces, an outgrowth of regional malls and open markets, have been developed by James Rouse in Baltimore, New York, Boston, Miami, and many other cities. Usually directed toward leisure activities, these marketplaces often incorporate outdoor dining and entertainment, and are frequently sited on rivers, shores, or harbors.

Commercial architecture had already lent its image to other building types during the twentieth century. The Nebraska State Capitol (1916–1928) in Lincoln by Bertram Grosvenor Goodhue replaced the prevailing classical dome with a vertical tower in the manner of a skyscraper. The Shrine of the Little Flower (1929–1936), a large Roman Catholic church by Henry J. McGill and Talbot F. Hamlin in Royal Oak, Michigan, reflected Art Deco commercial architecture in Detroit and New York. Even more radically, however, the State of Illinois Center in Chicago (1988), a state-office building designed by Helmut Jahn, incorporates a mall into its atrium lobby and encloses it in a curtain-wall structure that rejects all conventional civic imagery and substitutes for it the commercial marketplace. The most public part of the building, the hearing chamber, is buried under the sidewalk near the entrance. Similarly, Philip Johnson's design for the Garden Grove Community Church, the "Crystal Cathedral" (1987), in Garden Grove, California, adopts the reflective-glass skin of nearby suburban office buildings to cover its surfaces.

Historically, the dominant institutions of any culture have determined an architectural language that has been assumed by related or subordinant institutions. On that basis, it may be argued that by the end of the twentieth century, capitalism in the United States is embodied in a variety of related building types possessing a vocabulary that has been assimilated by other sectors of the culture that were formerly considered dominant, especially the religious and the civic. Apparently, this vocabulary stimulates and bears enough meaning, power, and authority that it is an acceptable vehicle to express the values of contemporary religious and political institutions for a large number of citizens of the late capitalist social order. At the least, commercial and industrial architecture have established the visual appearance of American cities and suburbs in the twentieth century; and by the last decade, they have also determined the shape and character of the buildings and spaces in which American public life is formed, ordered, and takes place.

[See also The City; Mass Culture and Its Critics; Public Architecture; The Suburbs; Urban Parks; Village and Town.]

BIBLIOGRAPHY

Andrews, Wayne. *Architecture, Ambition, and Americans: A Social History of American Architecture* (1964).

Condit, Carl W. *The Chicago School of Architecture: A History of Commercial and Public Building in the Chicago Area, 1875–1925* (1964).

Fitch, James Marston. *American Building: The Historical Forces That Shaped It* (1966; 2d ed. 1973).

Gayle, Margot. *Cast-Iron Architecture in New York: A Photographic Survey* (1974).

Gifford, Don, ed. *The Literature of Architecture* (1966). An invaluable anthology of writings on the evolution of architectural theory and practice in nineteenth-century America, drawn from many sources, and made accessible through excellent annotations.

Hamlin, Talbot F. *Greek Revival Architecture in America: Being an Account of Important Trends in American Architecture and American Life . . .* (1944; repr. 1964). This book remains the standard work on the Greek Revival.

Hildebrand, Grant. *Designing for Industry: The Architecture of Albert Kahn* (1974).

Hitchcock, Henry-Russell. *The Architecture of H. H. Richardson and His Times* (1936; rev. ed. 1966). This is neither the first nor the only book on Richardson, but it is scholarly, completely reliable, and probably still the best.

Jencks, Charles. *Late Modern Architecture and Other Essays* (1980).

Jencks, Charles. *The Language of Post-Modern Architecture.* 3d rev. enl. ed. (1981). This work is as good an introduction to the subject of postmodernism as any, but no work that is completely clear or unproblematic in its interpretation has appeared yet.

Jordy, William H. *American Buildings and Their Architects.* Vol. 3, *Progressive and Academic Ideals at the Turn of the Twentieth Century* (1972). This series is collectively and individually the finest single study of American architecture that has been published. One volume remains uncompleted, but the quality of scholarship and the authenticity of viewpoint represented by the authors of the other four volumes is extraordinary. See also Pierson titles in this series below.

Jordy, William H. *American Buildings and Their Architects.* Vol. 4, *The Impact of European Modernism in the Mid-Twentieth Century* (1972).

Kaufmann, Edgar, Jr. *The Rise of an American Architecture* (1970).

Kirker, Harold and James Kirker. *Bulfinch's Boston, 1787–1817* (1964).

Pierson, William H., Jr. *American Buildings and Their Architects.* Vol. 1, *The Colonial and Neo-classical Styles* (1970).

Pierson, William H., Jr. "Part I: The Corporate and the Early Gothic Styles," In *American Buildings and Their Architects.* Vol. 2, *The Corporate and Early Gothic Styles* (1970).

Twombly, Robert C. *Louis Sullivan: His Life and Work* (1986). Of the many studies of Sullivan, this is the most up-to-date and reliable.

Whiffen, Marcus, and Frederick Koeper. *American Architecture, 1607–1976.* 2 vols. (1981).

— ROBERT ALAN BENSON

COMMUNICATIONS AND INFORMATION PROCESSING

Of all the forces that have shaped American society in the past four centuries, few have had a more palpable influence on the pattern of everyday life than the remarkable transformation in the means of communication. But until quite recently, few historians devoted much attention to just what this transformation entailed. Eponymous inventors like Samuel Morse, of course, received detailed treatment, as did major inventions like the telegraph. Yet most historians regarded these developments as little more than disconnected bits of information, mostly of the "famous first" variety, that bore little relationship to the critical turning points in the making of the modern world.

In the past few years, all this has begun to change. For a growing number of scholars—whose ranks include not just historians, but also historically inclined political scientists and sociologists—the means of communication has become a historical actor in its own right. While no synthesis of this literature has yet appeared, four recent books can be taken as representative of the main lines of inquiry. Ian K. Steele's *English Atlantic* (1986); Richard D. Brown's *Knowledge Is Power* (1989); William J. Gilmore's *Reading Becomes a Necessity of Life* (1989); and James R. Beniger's *The Control Revolution* (1986). Steele explores the pattern of communications in the British Empire in the eight decades following the Restoration (1660), with implications far broader than its title might suggest; Brown and Gilmore analyze the epochal "communications revolution" that occurred between the American Revolution and the Civil War; while Beniger furnishes a stimulating, if highly speculative, survey of technological innovations in communications between the coming of the railroad and the present day.

These four books share the premise that the history of communications is best understood not as a chronicle of famous firsts but as a social process involving the relationship between ordinary people and the large-scale institutions that have come to play such a prominent role in their everyday lives. Thus far, there is no general agreement as to just what this process ought to be called.

For Steele, the preferred term is "circulation"; for Brown, "diffusion"; for Gilmore, "dissemination"; for Beniger, "control." That each has adopted a slightly different terminology is hardly surprising. Each has chosen a term that aptly describes this process in the particular historical epoch with which he is primarily concerned.

This matter of definition is of no small moment since concepts have a way of carrying their etymologies with them forever. For the purposes of this essay, the most semantically neutral term for this process is "transmission." Alternatives include "processing" or even "access." None of these terms, of course, is entirely free from multiple associations. Nonetheless, they do serve to highlight the shared concern of communications historians with the pattern of collective behavior in language capacious enough to embrace the whole sweep of the American past.

Contexts for the Study of Communications History

COMMUNICATIONS, MODERNIZATION, AND THE STATE. Perhaps the most distinctive feature of recent scholarship in communications history is its preoccupation with questions of *process* and *scale.* Like the practitioners of the new social history, communications historians use theoretical models borrowed from social science to link the recorded experience of large numbers of people to patterns of collective behavior. Above all, they seek to answer a number of rather specific questions about how information was transmitted at specific points in the past: How geographically extensive was the process? How far did it penetrate into the social order? Whom did it exclude? What were the major trends over time? Indeed, just as the new social history has come to be distinguished from the more purely descriptive old social history, so too the new communications history might well be distinguished from an old communications history that chronicled the life and times of inventors and inventions.

The similarities between the new communications history and the new social history extend beyond their shared commitment to social science. Both draw on models of social change associated with modernization theory—that is, with the large body of sociological literature that seeks to chart the transition from tradition to modernity in terms general enough to embrace the United States, western Europe, Japan, and the postcolonial nations of the Third World.

That communications historians should draw on modernization theory is hardly surprising. Few models of social change assign communications a more fundamental role in the making of the modern world. Ever since 1953, when Karl Deutsch published his *Nationalism and Social Communication,* modernization theorists have stressed the role of communications technology in the social-psychological transformation that hastened the shift from tradition to modernity. According to Deutsch, the global penetration of communications technologies such as newspapers, radio, and television would encourage the spread and eventual worldwide triumph of the cosmopolitan mind-set that, or so Deutsch believed, had already gained ascendancy in the West.

Such conclusions are hardly implausible. Yet it is worth noting that today most social scientists would question Deutsch's interpretation of the relationship between technology and culture. Few would reject out of hand the proposition that changes in communications technologies have cognitive consequences. Yet none would assume that these technologies *necessarily* promote the ascendancy of the cosmopolitan mind-set that Deutsch so obviously admired. Indeed, the recent rise of Islamic fundamentalism in the Middle East suggests a rather different scenario. In a world in which the followers of the Ayatollah Khomeini smuggled back to Iran tape-recorded messages that their leader prepared while exiled in Paris, the cognitive consequences of new communications technologies have come to seem, at least to most Western observers, far more unpredictable and far less benign.

The limitations of modernization theory are by no means confined to its oversimplified account of the relationship between technology and culture. An even more basic limitation is its implicit premise that, in accounting for social change, socioeconomic processes are, in some subtle yet ineluctable way, more fundamental than processes set in motion by public policy. Or put somewhat more abstractly, that *society* is more fundamental than the *state.*

The limitations of such a society-centered perspective—and the possibilities of an alternative, state-centered perspective—are especially evident in the historical study of communications. The state has almost always fixed the boundaries of the prevailing pattern of information transmission, while most new communications technologies—from the postal system to the computer—have either been sponsored outright by the state or powerfully shaped by its influence. It is thus one of the principal contentions of this essay that, however refurbished, modernization theory—and, by implication, the society-centered explanatory strategies favored by the new social historians—provides too limiting a conceptual framework for historians intent on exploring the role of communications in shaping the pattern of the past.

THE NEW COMMUNICATIONS HISTORY AND THE TORONTO SCHOOL. While historians of communications have drawn extensively on modernization theory, they have thus far mostly neglected the contributions of the so-called Toronto school of media theorists, whose most prominent members include Harold A. Innis, Marshall McLuhan, and Walter J. Ong. In 1975, Harry S. Stout observed that, for historians interested in communications, the insights of the Toronto school provide "vast opportunities for integrative studies of social change" ("Culture, Structure, and the 'New' History," p. 223). Yet in the ensuing years, surprisingly few historians have chosen to follow Stout's lead.

Innis, McLuhan, and Ong are best known for their provocative, wide-ranging, and unfailingly stimulating ruminations on the relationship between communications technology and culture. Unlike modernization theorists such as Deutsch, the Toronto school focuses less on the content of a given communication than on its form. For McLuhan, the act of silently scanning a printed page is far more consequential than the ostensible information its author sought to convey. It is precisely this preoccupation with the form, or medium, of communication rather than with its content, or message, that inspired McLuhan's famous adage "the medium is the message."

Among the more provocative of the Toronto school's contributions is its expansive conception of the role of communications technology as an agent of change. Following Innis, McLuhan and Ong go so far as to periodize the whole course of human history around technological transformations in the means of communications. For Ong, these technologies include writing (the "most momentous" technology of all), the printing press, and the computer; for McLuhan, the telegraph, Sputnik, and television. According to Innis, who has done the most to work out the implications of this perspective, each communications technology—whether it be the newspaper, radio, and stone tablet, or the human voice—exerts a palpable influence, or "bias" on the political order. Newspapers and radio are easily transmitted over long distances; as a consequence, they promote the establishment of large, territorially bounded empires. Stone tables and the human voice are far more difficult to transport; as a consequence, they discourage the establishment of political units larger than the city-state.

The Toronto School's preoccupation with the role of communications technology in the historical process often verges on the baldest kind of technological determinism. It is almost as if, like the tin soldiers in *The Nutcracker*, the famous firsts in communications history have suddenly sprung to life. Especially problematic in this regard is McLuhan's cursory understanding of the process by which information got transmitted from place to place. Mechanical contrivances like the printing press command McLuhan's attention; yet he dismisses the postal system, a key element in the communications infrastructure, as little more than a "charming relic of the hardware age."

These limitations notwithstanding, the Toronto school does offer historians a host of valuable insights on the relationship between technology and culture. And in at least one regard, it offers a useful corrective to the new communications history. With few exceptions, the new communications history has devoted far more attention to the consumption of information than the production of knowledge. The Toronto School, if anything, errs in precisely the opposite direction. McLuhan may be rather vague about precisely how information gets transmitted yet, like Innis and Ong, he has quite definite notions about where all this information is coming from. For McLuhan and Ong, the source is ultimately religious, or, more precisely, Christian: in the beginning was the Word, and the Word was with God. For Innis, the source is more likely to be rooted in the political order.

The Toronto school may well have come up with the wrong answers—few historians, after all, are likely to embrace the avowedly theological, quasi-millennial ruminations of McLuhan and Ong—yet its members have asked fresh and imaginative questions, and historians would do well to follow their lead. It may, in short, be time to pay more attention not merely to who is getting the message, but to who is spreading the word, and perhaps even to why it is being sent.

Communications and Empire

Until quite recently, few American historians would challenge the assertion that, in the pre-electronic era transatlantic communication was slow, infrequent, and hazardous. Or that it was, in a word, bad. Recent scholarship on the pattern of information transmission in the colonial period, however, points in an altogether different direction. In this period, as Ian Steele has observed, the Atlantic Ocean was anything but a "vast social moat" separating the New World from the Old. If anything, it functioned instead as a convenient thoroughfare for an immense multitude of people, goods, and information.

How could historians have gotten the story wrong for so long? The answer lies partly in the assumption that maritime empires are somehow "unnatural." For the period before the nineteenth-century revolution in land transportation, this assumption is dubious at best. The Dutch, the Florentines, the Venetians—and, for that matter, the Greeks and the Romans—had all established far-flung domains that were organized primarily, if not exclusively, around water rather than on land. So too had the English.

This new perspective has prompted a new way of thinking about the prevailing patterns of information transmission. These patterns fall into three main phases: 1607 to 1660, 1660 to 1763, and 1763 to 1781. In the first phase, which stretched roughly from the first permanent European settlement at Jamestown in 1607 to the restoration of the Stuarts, the settlers found themselves largely cut off from the main currents of European civilization. For a period of time, at least, America was truly a strange new world.

Yet even during these early decades, the settlers' isolation is easily exaggerated. Consider the case of Puritan New England, the most demographically self-contained of all the settlements. Despite the Puritans' many quarrels with English society, they retained an abiding interest in English politics, about which they managed to stay exceedingly well-informed, and maintained an extensive correspondence with their friends and relations back home. A similar pattern prevailed in the Chesapeake, the other principal area of settlement. At no point did the settlers completely lose contact with the European world from which they had come. As David D. Hall has remarked, America was "*never* really a frontier society with culture radically dispersed into local units; the technology . . . was derived from a metropolitan tradition, and most of the books . . . had originated in centers such as London, Edinburgh, Boston, or New York" (*On Native Ground*, p. 322).

This point is worth stressing since, in the 1970s, several prominent historians questioned the importance of long-distance communications in the colonial past. Drawing on the scholarship of the cultural anthropologist Clifford Geertz, these historians posited that, in the colonial period, community life was "primordial"—which is to say, that it more closely resembled the world of the nonliterate Balinese villagers that Geertz had so evocatively described than the technologically sophisticated world of the present.

In the 1980s, a reaction set in. While historians have by no means abandoned their interest in the small-scale communities of the colonial past, they have become far more sensitive to the differences between the inhabitants of colonial America and the villagers of Bali. In particular, they have come to distinguish rather sharply between what Ong terms the "primary orality" of nonliterate peoples like the Balinese and the "high oral residue" of the white settlers of colonial America. The mental universe of even illiterate colonists, it is now assumed, had been so fundamentally transformed by their intimate familiarity with the ways of the literate world that it may best be described as "verbal" rather than "oral." As Ong observes: "It takes only a moderate degree of literacy to make a tremendous difference in thought processes" (*Orality and Literacy*, p. 50).

However isolated the colonists may have been during the opening decades of the seventeenth century, with the restoration of the Stuarts this first phase of colonial communications came to a close. The second phase owed its impetus to the crown: like the financial revolution of the 1690s, it was part of the crown's broader effort to consolidate its authority over its far-flung imperial domain.

Since the 1980s, historians have come to distinguish rather sharply between what Walter J. Ong terms the "primary orality" of nonliterate peoples like the Balinese and the "high oral residue" of the white settlers of colonial America.

This effort succeeded, at least for a time. In the century between the Restoration in 1660 and the Treaty of Paris in 1763, the prevailing pattern of information transmission reinforced—and, indeed, helped to forge—the links between the inhabitants of British North America and Great Britain. The colonists were becoming, as it were, not "Americanized," but "Anglicized." As this process went forward, it became increasingly plausible for them to conceive of themselves as the inhabitants of a single, transatlantic society, whose boundaries were defined not by the largely inaccessible, and still mostly unexplored, North American continent, but by the oft-traveled and familiar English Atlantic. To the extent that the settlers' identity was informed—or, as Innis would say, biased—by the prevailing pattern of information transmission, then, in this period, its trajectory was decidedly imperial.

Of the various crown ventures that helped to institutionalize this new pattern, the most notable included the reorganization of the imperial postal system in 1711—which, for the first time, brought the postal network in British North America under direct crown control—and the permanent establishment, under government supervision, of the colonial newspaper press, beginning with the *Boston News-Letter* in 1704. Both of these institutions were designed primarily to facilitate communications between Great Britain and British North America. The imperial orientation of the postal system was especially marked. As late as 1761,

Benjamin Franklin, the crown-appointed deputy postmaster general for British North America, could state matter-of-factly that the inhabitants of Amboy and Burlington, New Jersey, should not be expected to send many letters through their respective post offices since they engaged in "little or no foreign trade." The newspapers displayed a similar orientation. To the eternal frustration of colonial historians, who have assidiously searched their pages for information about local life, these newspapers were overwhelmingly preoccupied with European affairs. Rather than the distillation of local gossip, newspapers in this period were, in Steele's apt phrase, "paper windows on the world."

To be sure, in the eighteenth century the scope of these institutions remained quite limited. Only in the nineteenth century would the postal system and the press come to exert a palpable influence on the pattern of everyday life. As late as the 1760s, probably no more than 5 percent of the population had more than the most incidental contact with either institution, though thus far too little work has been done on this topic to say for certain. Most of these individuals were public officers, merchants, or ministers living in the port cities on the Atlantic seaboard. And, needless to say, almost all were white men.

To highlight these limitations is not to suggest that the situation was markedly different in Great Britain. Indeed, the expansion of the postal system and newspaper press in both places is probably best regarded as part of a single, integrated process. The newspaper press in British North America resembled quite closely its provincial counterpart in Great Britain. Much the same could be said for the postal system: in 1765, there were roughly as many post offices per capita in British North America as in England and Wales.

Perhaps the most remarkable feature of communications in this period, at least from a twentieth-century standpoint, is the extremely limited nature of the demand for translocal information. The diffusion pattern was strictly top-down: that is, information from overseas typically came first to the provincial gentry, who would then pass it along on a "need to know" basis. Members of this gentry, such as Boston merchant Samuel Sewall (1652–1730), rarely shared information with members of the lower orders. If one word were to describe this process, it might well be circulation. Within the charmed circle of the gentry, information traveled freely. Only rarely did it travel downward to the common people, a circumstance that might have been expected to generate at least a modicum of concern. Yet it apparently did not. Outside of the gentry, no one really seems much to have cared.

Following Great Britain's victory over France in the Seven Years' War, which was formalized by the Treaty of Paris in 1763, the prevailing pattern of information transmission entered a third distinct phase. For the first time, large numbers of provincial Americans began to embrace the momentous proposition that the widest possible circulation of information ought to be regarded, in and of itself, as a public good.

Despite the enormous outpouring of scholarship on the coming of the War of Independence, this pivotal transformation in prevailing assumptions regarding the proper role of communications in the political culture remains obscure. A number of questions suggest themselves. Precisely why did this transformation emerge at this time? How did it affect the prevailing pattern of information transmission? Could it have contributed to the emergence of an organized opposition to the crown?

One hypothesis points to the role of imperial legislation like the Stamp Act (1765) in galvanizing the provincial gentry to reconsider the traditional relationship of knowledge and power. This legislation inspired an unprecedented flurry of pamphlets and newspaper articles, including the impassioned attack upon all monopolies of knowledge that Massachusetts lawyer John Adams penned in 1765, and which would later become known as the "Dissertation on the Canon and Feudal Law."

An alternative hypothesis fixes the spotlight on the mid-century religious revivals, the Great Awakening. According to Harry S. Stout, the extemporaneous, emotionally charged sermons of itinerant evangelicals like George Whitefield (1714–1770) inspired thousands of ordinary people to secure for themselves the kind of scriptural knowledge that Whitefield had so impressively displayed. In the language of Walter J. Ong, Whitefield had interiorized the Bible, providing his audience with a compelling example of how direct access to print could challenge the status quo. It was this impulse, Stout contends, that created the social world that would render plausible the "typographic ideology" of the revolutionary-era pamphleteers.

The role of novel preaching styles in the coming break with Great Britain remains hotly contested. One obvious problem with Stout's hypothesis is the question of timing. The revivals had mostly petered out by the end of the 1740s; the revolutionary movement did not get underway until 1765. According to Jon Butler, the true significance of George Whitefield lay in neither his message nor his medium. Rather, it lay in his utilization of recent improvements in the communications and transportation infrastructure, which greatly facilitated his ability to travel about the countryside and his followers' ability to participate in the revival meetings that he so elaborately staged. In either scenario, one conclusion seems clear: poor communications did not bring on the war.

Communications in the New Republic

Following the defeat of the British at Yorktown in 1781, the successful revolutionaries sought to institute a communications policy for the newly established republic. The policy they devised was far more expansive than anything that had ever been attempted by the crown. Despite the crown's support for the postal system and the press, it had retained tight control of constraints on the transmission of public information. Following the ratification of the Constitution, all this would change. Under the leadership of the Federalists, who included most of the framers of the Constitution, a government was instituted that was explicitly committed to broadcasting news of its ongoing activities throughout the land.

The Federalists justified their communications policy on two principal grounds. First, following President George Washington, they contended that the widest possible diffusion of information regarding the operations of government would counterbalance the centrifugal forces that might tear the republic apart. Nowhere was the importance of such a policy more obvious than in the far-flung transappalachian West. Washington feared especially that the paucity of certain information regarding the newly established central government might encourage malcontents to circulate wild rumors that could undermine its legitimacy. By making public information easily accessible, Washington hoped, as the editor of the official government newspaper, the *United States Gazette*, made plain, not only to enable the citizenry to monitor its activities, but also to "tranquilize" the public mind.

The second rationale was articulated most forcefully by the Philadelphia physician Benjamin Rush (1745–1813). If Washington intended the government to *diffuse* authoritative information, Rush hoped it would *disseminate* practical knowledge. Rush's vision, like Washington's, was basically political. By disseminating knowledge—through newspapers, public schools, and, or so Rush hoped, a national university—the government would promote the creation of a virtuous, public-spirited citizenry that would protect the republic from internal decline and external assault.

Rush's bold agenda for the future is often contrasted with his later disillusionment over his failure to get this agenda translated into law. With respect to communications, this juxtaposition is misleading. For much of Rush's communications policy—and, in particular, his commitment to the widest possible circulation of political newspapers, those "centinels of our liberties"—would become institutionalized in the 1790s, with far-reaching consequences for the future course of American history. Indeed, it may not be too much to suggest, as would James Madison—a leader of the Republican opposition, as well as a major architect of the Constitution—that in the new nation this policy worked powerfully to consolidate the authority of "public opinion" as a political force.

The Federalists' communications policy was, quite literally, unprecedented in the history of the world. Never before had popular access to information regarding the ongoing activities of government been presumed to be not a privilege but a right. Never before had a government been founded on the premise that an informed citizenry was fundamental to its very survival. For the first time in world history, a politics of vigilance has supplanted a politics of trust.

The creation of an informed citizenry was by no means identical with the task of informing the population-at-large. Excluded from the citizenry were Indians, slaves, and women, as were those men who failed to meet the various property requirements established by the individual states. Even so, the task of keeping the propertied, white male population informed posed an enormous challenge for the fledgling administrative apparatus of the new republic.

To meet this challenge, Congress moved quickly to upgrade the major elements in the communications infrastructure: the postal system and the press. The upgrading of the postal system—the principal pre-electronic long-distance communications technology—

By making public information easily accessible, President George Washington hoped, as the editor of the United States Gazette *made plain, not only to enable the citizenry to monitor its activities but also to "tranquilize" the public mind.*

was accomplished with the passage of the Post Office Act of 1792. This act had two main features. First, it required postal officers to admit newspapers into the mails at rates far below their actual cost of delivery. Second, it mandated that henceforth the postal system would expand into the hinterland virtually without regard for the possible impact of this policy on postal finance. Both of these policies had major consequences for the press. The former guaranteed it a market; the latter ensured that this market would expand with the population. The consequences of this policy were little short of astounding. In 1792, the postal system consisted of some 250 offices; in 1800, 903; in 1860, 28,498.

Press coverage of public affairs expanded in a parallel fashion. It may be something of an exaggeration to declare, as the historian J. R. Pole does, that, during the whole course of the colonial period, "nowhere and at no time . . . did any newspaper or magazine report one single assembly debate." Yet it remains undeniable that, in the period prior to the ratification of the Constitution, press coverage of public affairs was distinctly limited. In the 1790s, this coverage would expand enormously, thanks to a variety of public policies that included, in addition to those already mentioned, generous press subsidies, the opening of Congress to the public, and, perhaps most importantly, the constitutional guarantee of a free press.

The Communications Revolution

The communications policy established by the Federalists exerted an enormous influence on the subsequent history of the United States. Indeed, it may not be too audacious to suggest that it marked the opening chapter in the communications revolution that has proceeded more or less without interruption from the 1790s to the present day.

At no time were these changes more dramatic than in the half-century following the ratification of the Constitution. Of the numerous changes that occurred in this period, perhaps the most notable was the extraordinarily rapid increase in the volume of books, religious publications, public documents, and newspapers. In the book trade, the period marked the crucial transition from a world of scarcity to a world of abundance. A parallel shift occurred in religious publishing. By the 1820s, the American Bible Society (founded 1816) and the American Tract Society (founded 1825) were distributing so many publications that they have been aptly described as having created the first American mass media. Equally impressive, though often overlooked, was the enormous expansion in the publication of public documents. Taken together, the federal and state governments constituted by far the largest publisher in the United States. In 1830, these two sources accounted for 30 percent of *all* the imprints in the United States.

Nowhere was this incredible expansion in the volume of printed matter more obvious than in the newspaper press. In 1790, there were 92 newspapers in the United States; in 1800, 242; in 1860, 3,725. Beginning in 1833 with Benjamin Day's New York *Sun*, the cheap "penny dailies" would take advantage of the steam press to expand enormously not only the potential audience for newspapers but also their coverage of urban news—and, perhaps above all, of crime. For what may have been the first time in the history of the republic, a publisher had flatly rejected Rush's hortatory mission and had put out a newspaper purely to entertain.

The social consequences of this communications revolution remain highly uncertain. Did the explosion in printed matter democratize knowledge by destroying existing monopolies over the transmission of information? Or did it merely make possible new controls on popular thought? What other consequences might this process have entailed?

The communications revolution encouraged thousands if not millions of Americans to believe that knowledge is power: that is, that improvement in popular access to information translated readily into the democratization of knowledge.

For the moment, answers to these questions must necessarily be tentative. Part of the problem is empirical. Only recently have historians begun systematically to gather data on the influence of printed matter on the pattern of everyday life. More fundamental still are the methodological questions that arise once the data are assembled.

Thus far, as discussed above, the principal theoretical model that historians have drawn upon is derived from modernization theory. Like the social theorist Karl Deutsch, they have tended to focus above all on the consequences of the communications revolution for social psychology. For Richard D. Brown and William J. Gilmore, the communications revolution represents a net gain for the common man—and, in particular, for the propertied, white male citizenry whom the Federalists' communication policy was intended to reach. For Brown, the communications revolution fostered a commitment to the discernibly "modern" values of competition, pluralism, and individual choice. No less importantly, it encouraged thousands if not millions of Americans to believe that knowledge is power: that is, that improvement in popular access to information translated readily into the democratization of knowledge. For Gilmore, the communications revolution ushered in an age of reading in which, for the first time in world history, lifelong reading became, at least for the farmers of northern New England, a cherished ideal.

The consequences of the communications revolution for groups on the periphery—for women, children, and slaves—were far more ambiguous. The emergence of periodicals like *Godey's Lady Book* that were aimed specifically at the burgeoning market of middle-class women introduced their female readership to the cosmopolitan world of fashion and genteel deportment even as they accentuated their exclusion from the male-dominated world of politics and commerce. Children lucky enough to have access to books designed specifically for their use—the children's book was largely a nineteenth-century innovation—were encouraged to embark upon imaginative journeys to worlds far removed from the everyday affairs of their parents. Slaves took advantage of improvements in transportation to devise remarkably elaborate communications networks linking far-flung plantations, yet as all but a tiny minority were illiterate, the communications revolution increasingly left them behind.

The consequences of the communications revolution extended far beyond their impact on individuals. For the white men who were its primary beneficiaries, the physical act of reading a newspaper served not merely to encourage a heightened sense of individualism, but also to encourage a new vision of community. It is this vision that the French traveler Alexis de Tocqueville so brilliantly analyzed in his *Democracy in America* (1835; 1840) and that the genre painter Richard Caton Woodville so evocatively depicted in his *War News from Mexico* (1848). In Woodville's painting, the citizenry of the village—all white, all male—are assembled at the local post office to discuss the affairs of the day. On the fringes of the scene, a woman and a free black listen in. Yet it is clearly the men who are at center stage. For these men, newspaper-reading serves less as a means of generating knowledge than as a ritual that reinforces a distinctive, emphatically fraternal, vision of community.

The role of newspapers and other forms of political discourse in creating new visions of community was extremely complex. Often it worked less to foster consensus, as George Washington might have hoped, than to encourage dialogue. Sometimes this dialogue was heated and acrimonious. Still, the very fact that it was taking place at all worked, at least in the short run, to promote a vision of community that extended beyond the locality and the state to embrace the entire nation.

This national vision was, of course, imagined. It existed not in a specific place, like a New England town, but rather in the minds of large numbers of people, most of whom would never meet. Yet it was very real for those many people who thought of themselves not just as members of a specific region, or religion, or class, or race, or gender, but as Americans.

The creation of this national community inevitably involved a complex process of exclusion and inclusion. The extension of citizenship to virtually all white men hastened the stigmatization of non-citizens and especially of Indians and blacks. This process, in turn, was powerfully reinforced by the virulently racist, and typically Democratic, mass-circulation newspapers and magazines that flourished, beginning in the 1830s, in the urban centers of the North.

The process of creating a national community met with opposition even from some of the groups it was supposed to embrace. Beginning in 1810, male Evangelicals, joined behind the scenes by women, opposed a government policy that required the delivery of the mails and the opening of the post offices on the Sabbath. In the 1830s, northern anti-abolitionist mobs destroyed abolitionist presses and murdered the antislavery printer Elijah P. Lovejoy. In the same decade, white southerners took a variety of legal and extralegal steps to prevent the distribution of abolitionist literature. In July 1835, a mob backed by former South Carolina governor John Lyde Wilson ransacked the Charleston, South Carolina, post office and publicly burned in the town square a bundle of abolitionist tracts that the New York–based American Antislavery Society had attempted to send through the mails.

Yet what is perhaps most remarkable about this process of community creation is the extent to which it has since come to be regarded as perfectly natural and indeed almost foreordained. In the half-century following the ratification of the Constitution, an imperial community spanning the English Atlantic had been transformed into a national community that more or less coincided with the middle-third of the North American continent. This transformation was neither predictable nor inevitable. Indeed, as the recent history of the post-colonial third world makes plain, it may well be the exception rather than the rule. Yet its consequences were profound. For by creating a vision of a national community, it may well have provided the impetus for those many thousands of northerners, women as well as men, black as well as white, who, in 1861, when the South chose to secede, dedicated themselves to saving the union by winning the war.

The Information Society

From the perspective of the late twentieth century, what is perhaps most striking about the nineteenth-century communications revolution is the extent to which it marked, for contemporaries no less than for historians, a genuine democratization not merely of information but also of knowledge. It is almost as if Benjamin Rush's republic of knowledge had reached its apotheosis in Tocqueville's America.

Today the relationship between information and knowledge is far more complex. The rise of the professions, the modern corporation, the government agency, and the whole panoply of organizations that make up what has come to be known as the information society have enormously widened the gap between the information conveyed by news or entertainment and the knowledge necessary to command the levers of power. In an age in which the management of public relations has become a major industry, it is by no means clear that the simple act of reading a newspaper, or of watching the news, bears any obvious relationship to the exercise of power or authority in government, business, or everyday life. In short, it is no longer plausible to conflate the *consumption* of information with the *production* of knowledge.

The origins of the information society date back to the second half of the nineteenth century. It was during these decades that, for the first time in the history of American business, information processing became a key element in corporate strategy. The catalyst for this striking development, as James R. Beniger explains, was the "crisis of control" occasioned by the general speeding-up in the processing of goods and services that began in the 1850s with the expansion of the railroad into the transappalachian West. The crisis was resolved when corporate managers devised new accounting techniques and related communications technologies to coordinate the myriad activities of geographically extended enterprises like the Pennsylvania Railroad. If there were one word to describe this process, it might be control.

Of these new technologies, by far the most important was the electric telegraph. Following the establishment of the first line between Washington and Baltimore by Samuel Morse in 1844, the electric telegraph was quickly extended throughout the United States, reaching New Orleans by 1851 and San Francisco in 1861. Funding for the Washington-Baltimore line had been provided by Congress, which, for almost three years, left open the possibility that it might purchase Morse's patents outright and place the industry under the authority of the postmaster general. Despite Morse's fervent commitment to government ownership, his lobbying efforts failed, and the industry went private. By 1866, a single firm—Western Union—would come to dominate the industry. Capitalized at over forty million dollars, Western Union was not only the largest firm in the industry, but the largest single business enterprise in the United States.

Samuel Morse established the first electric telegraph line between Washington and Baltimore in 1844. The telegraph allowed corporate managers to coordinate the activities of geographically diverse enterprises.

The patrons of the electric telegraph were largely, if not almost exclusively, merchants, newspaper editors, and corporate managers. Corporate managers came to rely on it to coordinate their increasingly far-flung operations. Newspaper editors used it to obtain the nonlocal, time-specific information about politics and commerce that is commonly called news. And merchants took advantage of its capacity to provide them with the most up-to-date information regarding the often volatile international markets for agricultural commodities such as cotton and wheat. Most other Americans, including virtually all women, would continue to rely on the postal system as their principal long-distance communications technology and would continue to do so until well into the twentieth century, when it would become supplemented—but never entirely replaced—by the telephone.

From the standpoint of everyone other than the commercial and editorial elite, the electric telegraph marked far less of a turning point in the history of communications than the postal reform act of 1845. In this landmark piece of legislation, Congress for the first time reduced the rate of letter postage to a level that eliminated the cost of the postage as a major constraint. Henceforth, letter writing was no longer confined merely to politicians (who under federal law could send and receive most of their letters without charge) and the well-to-do. Indeed, it was the postal system—more than any other institution, and certainly more than the electric telegraph—that created the technological preconditions that would make possible the extended friendships by letter between family and friends—and, perhaps above all, among women—that were such a prominent feature of popular culture in Victorian America.

In the twentieth century, information processing has become, if anything, even more central to American business. Rapid improvements in telecommunications have rendered nineteenth-century technologies such as the electric telegraph virtually obsolete. Of these new technologies, perhaps the most ubiquitous was the telephone. Invented in the 1870s, the telephone system was extended from New York to Boston by 1884, and coast-to-coast by 1915. By that year, the industry had become dominated by a single firm and a single individual. The firm was American Telephone and Telegraph (AT&T) and the individual was Theodore M. Vail. As the president of AT&T, Vail, a former superintendent of the railway mail service, dedicated the firm to the attainment of "One System, One Policy, Universal Service," a motto that reflected Vail's familiarity with postal policy. This goal would soon help to make the telephone almost as common a feature of daily life as the posted letter.

To attain his objective, Vail committed AT&T to the deliberate strategy of using long-distance communications to subsidize local service. While this strategy reduced somewhat the firm's short-term profitability, it increased considerably its base of popular support within Congress and the electorate and, in this way, protected itself against the possibility of hostile government legislation in the future. Vail's strategy kept long-distance rates high and, therefore, mostly confined to business until well after the Second World War (much as postage had been in the period before 1845). Local service, however, was subject to no such constraint and expanded accordingly. In 1891, fewer than one American in a hundred had a telephone; by 1921, that number had expanded to almost thirteen per one hundred. By 1925, AT&T would emerge as the largest corporation in the United States, just as Western Union had been in 1866.

If the telephone was the most ubiquitous of the new technologies, then the most far-reaching in its political and economic implications was the digital computer. The first computers were invented during the Second World War as the product of a notable collaboration between government, business, and the university. Like so many communications technologies—including the postal system and the electric telegraph—it was, at least initially, less the product of market forces than of political fiat.

In the post-Second World War period, the computer has revolutionized the storage, retrieval, and analysis of data. In certain instances, it has facilitated the performance of tasks that antedated its invention, such as the taking of a business inventory or the compilation of the federal census. In other instances, it has made it possible to embark on unprecedented new ventures such as high-energy physics and space travel. By the 1980s, even small businesses had come to rely upon sophisticated computing and telecommunications technologies in conducting their routine operations. For the multinational corporations that have increasingly come to dominate the world economy, telecommunications have made it possible for them to conduct their operations on a truly global scale. For these firms, the principal theater of operations is no longer the nation-state, nor even the industrialized West, but the world.

In 1891, fewer than one American in a hundred had a telephone; by 1921, that number had expanded to almost thirteen per hundred; and by 1925, AT&T had emerged as the largest corporation in the United States.

The impact of the computer upon ordinary Americans, however, is more ambiguous. As corporate managers have increasingly turned to computers to monitor the production process, the size of the semi-skilled blue-collar work force has decreased, undermining the influence of the traditional blue-collar unions. In addition, the proliferation of public and private data banks containing detailed financial and medical information about millions of ordinary Americans has raised troubling questions about confidentiality and the potential for abuse.

Few communications innovations better illustrate the complex relationship between private enterprise and public policy than commercial radio. The origins of the industry date to the 1910s, when radio buffs began to experiment with homemade receivers. By the end of the decade, however, the buffs found themselves outmaneuvered by the military and a number of major corporations, which began to consolidate their control over the all-important wavelength. In the 1920s, thanks in part to this corporate sponsorship, a radio boom began: in 1922 there were 30 broadcast stations; in 1923, 556. By 1933, a radio could be found in fully two-thirds of all homes in America.

Throughout the 1920s, public officials remained deeply ambivalent about the prospect of permitting the radio industry, like the newspaper, to be financed out of advertising revenue. It is "inconceivable," declared Secretary of Commerce Herbert Hoover in 1922, that "we should allow so great a possibility for service to be drowned in advertising chatter." The establishment of two major radio networks—NBC in 1926 and CBS in 1927–doomed Hoover's hopes.

Now that radio commanded a national audience, advertisers redoubled their efforts to reach this vast new market. Before long, they would largely succeed. With the exception of unusual ventures such as National Public Radio, which receives partial funding from the federal government, most radio programming since the 1920s has been funded neither by the government nor by the locally oriented ethnic, religious, labor, and public groups that had flourished briefly before the rise of the networks, but rather by the national—and, increasingly, multinational—corporations that had the financial resources to foot the bill.

The early history of television followed a similar pattern. The first public television program dated from 1947; the television boom began in 1949. By 1953, television had found its way into twenty million American homes. Once again, advertisers saw their opportunity and, once again, neither the federal government nor local groups proved either able or willing to check their rise. By 1970, 97 percent of all American households had at least one television. Like radio, the new technology was overwhelmingly dominated by its corporate sponsors—whose advertisements, in turn, encouraged lavish and often wasteful patterns of mass consumption that hastened, at least in the minds of some of its more radical critics, the "commodification" of desire.

The regulatory regime that emerged with radio and television was hardly inevitable. In other countries, different arrangements prevailed. Radio could conceivably have remained in the public sector or, alternatively, it might well have been obliged to provide greater popular access to the airwaves. Television, similarly, might have been encouraged to feature more special-interest broadcasting, just as has occurred since the 1980s with the emergence of cable television. Yet few Americans seem aware of the possible alternatives, at least partly because broadcasters so repeatedly invoke the myth that the industry is controlled ultimately by its audience rather than by the major corporations—or, as it were, by the consumers of information rather than by the producers of knowledge.

Corporate control of the mass media ought not to obscure the fact that its influence on ordinary Americans can be extraordinarily complex. Sometimes, as in the nineteenth century, the mass media could reinforce an attachment to the national community. More recently, its influence has often been more divisive. Ethnic and religious groups routinely use the mass media to promote their distinctive agendas. Often these agendas work to fragment the national community into diverse and often antagonistic camps. In Chicago during the 1920s, the impact of mass culture—radio, movies, and records—upon the mostly immigrant, working-class audience worked less to promote cultural homogeneity, as social scientists have often assumed, than to reinforce a sense of shared class or ethnic identity. Italian immigrants who listened to the records featuring the great Italian tenor Enrico Caruso or to the radio broadcasts prepared especially for their benefit by the Italian dictator Benito Mussolini, might well take away from the experience a heightened sense of their own distinctiveness. Given the extraordinary, heterogenity of the American people, such outcomes are to be expected. What is perhaps more notable is the extent to which, two centuries after the founding of the American republic, the vision of a national community continues to retain its undeniable allure.

Conclusion

Over the course of the past four centuries, the means of communications have had an enormous influence on the pattern of everyday life. Nowhere has this influence been more far-reaching than in the ever-changing relationship between state and society. In the period between 1660 and 1765, communications strengthened ties between Britain's North American colonies and the crown. Following the ratification of the Constitution, it helped to create a national community. In the twentieth century, it has simultaneously hastened the internationalization of business and the revitalization of intranational conflicts rooted in ethnicity and religion. Each of these processes has occurred over an extended territory whose boundaries have been shaped less by social circumstances than by political fiat. Thus, they can best be understood by adopting a national—or, more precisely, transnational—perspective that is sensitive to the role of state-formation in the making of the modern world.

[See also Business Culture; Journalism; Mass Culture and Its Critics; Radio; Technology and Social Change; Television.]

BIBLIOGRAPHY

General and Theoretical

Carey, James W. *Communication as Culture: Essays on Media and Society* (1989). Includes a critique of the literature on mass communications.

Czitrom, Daniel J. *Media and the American Mind: From Morse to McLuhan* (1982).

Hench, John B., ed. *Three Hundred Years of the American Newspaper* (1991). Reprinted from the *Proceedings of the American Antiquarian Society* 100, pt. 2 (1990).

Innis, Harold A. *The Bias of Communication* (1951). Idiosyncratic yet illuminating; deserves to be better known.

John, Richard R. "Remembering McLuhan." *Reviews in American History* 18, no. 3 (1990). Touches on McLuhan's impact on American historiography.

Ong, Walter J. *Orality and Literacy: The Technologizing of the Word* (1982). The best introduction to the Toronto school.

Shils, Edward. *The Constitution of Society* (1982).

Skocpol, Theda. "Bringing the State Back In: Strategies of Analysis in Current Research." In *Bringing the State Back In*, edited by Peter B. Evans, Dietrich Rueschemeyer, and Theda Skocpol (1985). A lucid introduction to the state-centered tradition in historical sociology.

Stout, Harry S. "Culture, Structure, and the 'New' History: A Critique and an Agenda." *Computers and the Humanities* 9, no. 5 (1975). Includes an extensive bibliography.

The Seventeenth Century

Cressy, David. *Coming Over: Migration and Communication Between England and New England in the Seventeenth Century* (1987).

Hall, David D. "On Native Ground: From the History of Printing to the History of the Book." *Proceedings of the American Antiquarian Society* 93, pt. 2 (1984).

Steele, Ian K. *The English Atlantic, 1675–1740: An Exploration of Communication and Community* (1986).

The Eighteenth Century

Brown, Richard D. *Knowledge Is Power: The Diffusion of Information in Early America, 1700–1865* (1989).

Butler, Jon. "Enthusiasm Described and Decried: The Great Awakening as Interpretive Fiction." *Journal of American History* 69, no. 2 (1982). Critical of Stout.

Pole, J. R. *The Gift of Government: Political Responsibility from the English Restoration to American Independence* (1983).

Stout, Harry S. "Religion, Communications, and the Ideological Origins of the American Revolution." *William and Mary Quarterly* 34, no. 4 (1977).

Warner, Michael. *The Letters of the Republic: Publication and the Public Sphere in Eighteenth-Century America* (1990). Highly theoretical.

The Nineteenth Century

Gilmore, William J. *Reading Becomes a Necessity of Life: Material and Cultural Life in Rural New England, 1780–1835* (1989). Wide-ranging and extremely detailed.

John, Richard R. "Taking Sabbatarianism Seriously: The Postal System, the Sabbath, and the Transformation of American Political Culture." *Journal of the Early Republic* 10, no. 4 (1990).

Nord, David Paul. "The Evangelical Origins of Mass Media in America, 1815–1835." *Journalism Monographs* 88 (1984).

Saxton, Alexander. *The Rise and Fall of the White Republic: Class Politics and Mass Culture in Nineteenth-Century America* (1990).

Yates, JoAnne. *Control Through Communication: The Rise of System in American Management* (1989).

The Twentieth Century

Beniger, James R. *The Control Revolution: Technological and Economic Origins of the Information Society* (1986). Extremely ambitious, often reductionist, yet suggestive.

Cohen, Lizabeth. *Making a New Deal: Industrial Workers in Chicago, 1919–1939* (1990). Includes a chapter on the impact of movies and radio on the ethnic communities of Chicago.

Douglas, Susan J. *Inventing American Broadcasting, 1899–1922* (1987).

John, Richard R. "Out of Control." *Isis* 79, no. 4 (1988). A review essay on Beniger's *Control Revolution.*

Meyerowitz, Joshua. *No Sense of Place: The Impact of Electronic Media on Social Behavior* (1985). Provocative, though highly speculative; draws fruitfully on the Toronto school.

— RICHARD R. JOHN

CONCERT MUSIC

The history of American concert music is a story of interactions between "cultivated" and "vernacular" traditions. These interactions often suggest a variety of comparisons: between, for example, the music of the concert hall and opera house, on the one hand, and more indigenous folk musics (including jazz), on the other; between the established styles of European composers and performers, and the unproven talents of American musical artists; and between the idea of music as an art and as an accompaniment to work, religious expression, or celebration.

These comparisons were often the source of tension between arbiters of "good taste," who advocated continuing or imitating European models in order to create good American music, and those who searched for an authentic American idiom in the music of everyday life. For most critics prior to World War II, American concert music lay at the margins of artistic respectability, and the tendency of American composers to interpolate the vernacular traditions of their own country into pieces written for the concert hall only exacerbated the tendency to view our music as something less than serious. Since World War II, the increasing internationalization of musical culture has blurred many of the national and class lines upon which these distinctions relied; in this period American concert music has achieved distinction in its own right.

The earliest music heard in North America was likely not considered art at all but an integral part of religion,

(with the support of local businessmen who were eager to promote their city as the new cultural capital of the nation), and the Philadelphia Orchestra in 1900. With the exception of the New York Philharmonic Society, which was founded as a cooperative, symphony orchestras were supported by men of new wealth, whose ability to purchase culture quickly made them pillars of local society. American orchestras performed to please their patrons, and concert programming was characterized by a predominance of tried and true European "classical" compositions. Music by American composers rarely found its way into such programs, except perhaps as a novelty.

During the last third of the nineteenth century, as the United States assumed a more prominent role in the world, the nation took many opportunities to celebrate its democratic past and promising future. From 15 to 19 June 1869, Boston bandmaster Patrick Sarsfield Gilmore (1829–1892) staged the National Peace Jubilee and Music Festival "in Honor of the Restoration of Peace and Union Throughout the Land." The festival, with its orchestra and chorus of five hundred performers each, attracted most notably President Ulysses S. Grant. Among its innovations were the use of synchronized church bells and fifty cannons firing live ammunition triggered by an electrical switch installed in the conductor's stand. Gilmore staged another peace jubilee in 1872 to commemorate the end of the Franco-Prussian War. In keeping with the cultural assumptions of the day, the music he chose came from the pens of European rather than American composers.

American accomplishment was the theme of the Philadelphia Centennial Exhibition of 1876, which featured the five-thousand-horsepower Corliss Engine and Alexander Graham Bell's telephone. Music for the exhibition included the "Centennial Hymn" composed by John Knowles Paine (1839–1906), the first professor of music at Harvard University and the most respected American concert-music composer of the late nineteenth century at that time. Church-music composer Dudley Buck (1839–1909) wrote the music for Sidney Lanier's cantata, "Centennial Meditation of Columbia." But the exhibition's Women's Committee, which sponsored the musical events, sought to engage the services of a famous European composer to create the musical showpiece of the summer. As a result, it was Richard Wagner, rather than an American composer, who was commissioned to write the "Centennial March" to celebrate the hundredth anniversary of the Declaration of Independence.

The four-hundredth anniversary of Christopher Columbus's voyage occasioned another celebration, the World's Columbian Exposition in Chicago in 1893, whose theme was the industrial and commercial progress of the United States. Conductor Theodore Thomas, who was famous for his orchestral performances of the music of Richard Wagner, was again engaged to plan the concert programs and conduct the orchestra, as he had done for the Philadelphia Centennial. Paine composed the "Columbus March and Hymn" especially for the Chicago exposition. Several concerts featured music by American composers, including Paine, Arthur H. Bird (1856–1923), Charles C. Converse (1823–1918), Arthur Foote (1853–1937), Edward MacDowell (1860–1908), and Margaret Ruthven Lang (1867–1972); but the audience for these American composers was small and elite compared with the thousands who toured the midway in search of more popular entertainments. At the end of the nineteenth century, concert music remained the preserve of the wealthy who could subsidize orchestras and pay to hear the best European standard repertoire; and the country's major orchestras and opera companies were still dominated by European performing and conducting talent. To be accepted, an American composer had to compose music that sounded as though it had been written in Vienna or Berlin.

In the early twentieth century, new ideas about the nature of art rapidly produced new approaches to creating music—so rapidly that composer Edgard Varèse was prompted in the mid 1920s to describe music as nothing more or less than "organized sound." But the end of the nineteenth century did not signal a leap into modernity in American concert music; rather, the challenge to nineteenth-century musical traditions took many forms as American composers joined in the search for new ways to organize sound.

American versions of the European art song, the marches and arrangements of European symphonic pieces by John Philip Sousa and a generation of bandmasters who brought middlebrow American music to hometown audiences, and music for the vaudeville stage and musical theater were integral to the life of middle- and working-class white audiences. African American music had distinctly rural and urban flavors, from southern work songs, hollers, and spirituals to the urban blues of northern cities, which were sung to the accompaniment of the trumpet, piano, and other instruments of European origin. In New Orleans, black marching bands performed for funerals and festivals the syncopated rhythms that would soon become familiar as early jazz. Scott Joplin (1868–1917) and Charles Lamb wrote piano pieces for indoor performance, and the cakewalk, a dance performed in music in "ragged time" became the rage in black urban enclaves. White and black popular musical traditions coexisted without influencing each other or American concert music to any great extent.

Nevertheless, early in the century, a small group of American concert music composers looked to popular music specifically to express a national identity in their symphonic music. Henry F. B. Gilbert (1868–1928), Arthur Farwell (1872–1952), John Powell (1882–1963), and others used Native American melodic fragments, African American rhythms and familiar tunes, and the ballads of rural southern whites. Edward MacDowell's "Indian" Suite (1897) is typical of this approach to musical nationalism. It uses a brief horn call and a few fragments from music of the Iowa and Kiowa tribes in a symphonic musical context.

At about the same time, Charles Ives (1874–1954) quoted popular hymns, patriotic songs, and music by other composers. Unlike his contemporaries, however, Ives placed his familiar quotations in a polytonal and/or a polyrhythmic context in which they often sound both modern and American. Ives was not embarrassed to bring the most mundane musical images, such as small-town marching bands and church choirs, into the concert hall. Only late in his life, long after he had stopped composing, was Ives's music recognized as significant to the development of modern American music. Ives was unique in his willingness to experiment with a variety of musical sounds and textures. His goal was to evoke scenes from the New England of his youth. In doing so, he often created dissonant, modern-sounding music.

When, in the first decades of the twentieth century, many African Americans migrated from agricultural to urban, industrial regions of the north, the outdoor bands came with them. The locus of jazz activity shifted from New Orleans to Chicago, Kansas City, and New York; as performances moved indoors, jazz ensembles modified their instrumentation to include a piano rather than a tuba and stationary percussion rather than a portable bass and snare drum. Groups such as Jelly Roll Morton's Red Hot Peppers and King Oliver's Creole Jazz Band (including the young Louis Armstrong), recorded in a style that featured "hot" solos and simultaneous improvisation. After World War I, Armstrong (1898?–1971) recorded a number of pieces in this early Chicago style with a group called the Hot Fives and, later, the Hot Seven.

In elite musical circles and in the press, the rise of anti-German sentiment precipitated by World War I prompted a debate over the importance of culture and its relation to patriotism. For many critics, high culture was presumed to have German origins—*Kultur*—and some feared that the demand for "100 percent Americanism" would result in the elimination of most if not all of the repertories that concert and opera audiences paid to hear. A furor over the Boston Symphony Orchestra's refusal to play "The Star-Spangled Banner" at a concert in Providence, Rhode Island, in 1917 contributed to a severe criticism of German *Kultur.* BSO conductor Karl Muck was arrested, interned, and eventually deported on suspicion of disloyalty—partly due to his insistence on separating art and politics and partly because he haughtily denigrated the quality of the American song (which became the national anthem in 1931).

In effect, the war forced orchestras to expand their concert repertories. In place of the romantic symphonic music by German, Austrian, or Hungarian composers, the mainstay of most concert programs became music by modern French, Russian, and even American composers, who often were receiving their first hearing. For a brief period, orchestra audiences heard more music by American composers (they even saw the employment of the first American-born concertmaster in Boston); but with the end of hostilities, these same elite audiences were quick to demand music by German, Austrian, and Hungarian composers.

Although the American composer's move into the American concert mainstream was short-lived, after the war many young American composers sailed for Europe. There was nothing unique about the presence of Americans in European studios and conservatories, but now some were traveling to study new techniques with Arnold Schönberg (1874–1951) and other nontonal composers in Vienna, while others—notably Aaron Copland (1900–1991) and Virgil Thomson (1896–1989)—went to study with Nadia Boulanger at the American Academy at Fountainebleau in Paris. The war had seen the arrival of American jazz and dance in France when James Reese Europe's orchestra performed with dancers Vernon and Irene Castle. In the 1920s, inspired by American jazz, a number of French, Russian

---

George Gershwin's "Rhapsody in Blue," "An American in Paris," and " 'I Got Rhythm' Variations" foreshadowed the jazz idioms used by Aaron Copland in the 1930s and Leonard Bernstein in the 1950s.

---

and German composers—including Darius Milhaud (1892–1974), Erik Satie (1866–1925), Igor Stravinsky (1882–1971), and Adolph Weiss (1891–1971)—wrote modern compositions employing sounds recognizable to devotees of American popular music.

By the mid 1920s, concert music composers in America as well were beginning to explore ways to synthesize jazz and symphonic music. In 1924, for example, the Paul Whiteman Orchestra performed George Gershwin's "Rhapsody in Blue," orchestrated by Ferde Grofé. That piece—an example of symphonic jazz in which the influence of the composer's early years as a Tin Pan Alley song plugger (a pianist who performed the latest songs seated in a store window in order to sell more sheet music) was apparent—as well as his "An American in Paris" and " 'I Got Rhythm' Variations" foreshadowed the use of jazz idioms by Aaron Copland in the 1930s and Leonard Bernstein (1918–1990) in the 1950s. The popularity of all three composers attests to the significance of bringing jazz into the concert hall to create an American symphonic style.

Starting in the 1920s, the development of radio technology brought American music into American homes; audiences could hear bluegrass and country music, symphonic and operatic performances of standard works (performed by Arturo Toscanini's [1867–1957] NBC Symphony and the Metropolitan Opera Company), and popular dance orchestras. Radio leveled many of the class distinctions of the concert hall: anyone who could afford a radio set could bring European high culture—along with dance band music, country songs, and the World Series—into his or her home.

This democratizing trend was dealt a blow by the Great Depression, which brought hard times for American musicians and American music. Public schools ran out of money for music curricula, performers had fewer opportunities, and composers—rarely able to support themselves on their creativity, in any case—now found themselves facing even bleaker prospects. The Federal Music Project of the Works Progress Administration, however, created useful work in the form of concerts and teaching projects, as well as by sponsoring the cataloging of American folk music and the copying of many new works to prepare the parts for performance.

During the depths of the Depression, many American concert music composers and songwriters developed an interest in the history, ethnic diversity, and current plight of the American people. Singers Woody Guthrie (1912–1967) and Hudie Ledbetter ("Leadbelly" [1885–1949]) created songs from both white and black folk traditions, and composers such as Copland and Elie Siegmeister (b. 1909) incorporated everyday music into symphonic works; of these efforts, Copland's

Leonard Bernstein (1918–1990) used many jazz idioms in his composition, helping to create what is known as an American Symphonic style.

"Billy the Kid" (1938), "Rodeo" (1942), and "Appalachian Spring" (1943–1944) are the best known.

In the late 1930s, the music of working people and the cultural history of labor struggles inspired members of the Composers' Collective in New York, which included Charles Seeger (1886–1979), Earl Robinson (b. 1910), Copland, Siegmeister, and Marc Blitzstein (1905–1964). They wrote songs and rounds for two *Workers Song Books* (1934, 1935) and debated the most appropriate form of workers' music in *New Masses* and *Modern Music,* the journal of the League of Composers.

In this time of growing consciousness of race prejudice. African American performers and composers achieved success beyond the traditional realm of black American music. White audiences had long applauded the musically "correct" arrangements both of spirituals set by Harry T. Burleigh (1866–1949) and those sung by such groups as the Fisk Jubilee Singers. In the 1930s, Paul Robeson (1898–1976) was popular not only as a performer of spirituals but as an actor and singer in several languages. When Marian Anderson (b. 1902) was denied permission to sing in Washington's Constitution Hall by the Daughters of the American Revolution, her performance to an audience of more than seventy-five thousand on the steps of the Lincoln Memorial in the spring of 1939 brought the interrelation of race and high culture to the American public. In 1955, Anderson made her belated Metropolitan Opera debut. However, it was only in the decades after World War II that African Americans crossed the high-culture barrier as successful singers and symphonic performers in significant numbers.

Concert music audiences were no less patriotic during World War II than they had been in the previous world war, but the issue of American nationalism had receded considerably—one could listen to music by German composers and still remain loyal to the United States and its war aims. By this time, European refugee composers, including Béla Bartók (who taught at Columbia) and Paul Hindemith (at Yale), had influenced the development of modern American music. Once again, audiences heard first performances of compositions by Americans, but the composers' names were far from obscure, and the likelihood of subsequent performances of new American works was much greater than it had been in 1917–1918.

After World War II, American composers again joined in the search for new musical effects. Like their European counterparts who experimented with *musique concrète* and electronically produced sounds, American composers benefited from the technology that had given radio and television to the larger culture. At first, their efforts were isolated in universities and special centers for new music, as the postwar realization of Varèse's "organized sound" did not sound anything like music to most audiences. Harry Partch (1901–1974) found it necessary to invent his own instruments to create sounds that diverged from the Western tempered scale. John Cage (b. 1912) organized notes and rhythms randomly, and even created a silent piece. Electronic music composers Mario Davidovsky (b. 1934) and Vladimir Ussachevsky (b. 1911) generated sounds mechanically and made the stopwatch and tape recorder integral to their musical performances.

Although the first synthesizers of electronic sound occupied entire rooms and were used exclusively for composition, synthesized sound generated by portable computerized instruments had by now become commonplace, especially in the commercial and popular music realms. The same public that disdained electronic music as too esoteric and too far removed from understandable melody and rhythm now hears electronically synthesized music every day, albeit in catchy and singable melodies not common to more experimental modern music.

In popular music, swing held sway during and after World War II, but in the early 1940s a group of young black musicians struck out on their own to create a musical style that was less tied to the convention of the twelve-bar blues or the thirty-two-bar popular song. The result was "be-bop," a challenging musical style based on the creative art of the soloist, which Charlie Parker (1920–1955), Dizzy Gillespie (b. 1917), Max Roach (b. 1924), and Curly Russell made popular. The small size of bop groups created opportunities for extended flights of soloist virtuosity, and bop musicians often pushed their instruments and voices to the limits of their capabilities. Bop was "hot"; it demanded attention and could not be considered background or dance music. It was most popular with young people who felt that swing band music had become tired. The early 1950s saw a creative reaction to the intensity of be-bop in the form of "cool" jazz; this style, pioneered by Miles Davis (1926–1991), Thelonious Monk (1917–1982), and Lenny Tristano (1919–1978), was no less creative or intense, but it was quieter. Early bop and cool jazz performers were analogous to the creators of electronic and modern music, in that they all experimented for its own sake and cared little for audience acceptance.

After World War II, American musicians saw this country's major cities, especially New York, as major cultural centers on par with the capitals of Europe. As an important locus of the new television industry, New York was the site of innovative broadcasting by the New York Philharmonic under Leonard Bernstein's direction. Young People's concerts and special programs narrated by the conductor were broadcast to millions of homes all over the country. Orchestral music and, later, opera were made accessible to citizens who otherwise might never have attended a concert because of their distance from a concert hall or lack of resources. High culture was, in a sense, democratized; and the advent of public television in the early 1960s expanded these opportunities for concerts broadcast live and simultaneously on radio (a "simulcast").

By the late 1960s, rock musicians, influenced by blues, jazz, and music from all over the world were creating eclectic works that were inappropriate because of their length or their verbal content for standard AM radio play. A 1966 ruling by the Federal Communications Commission created large blocks of FM airtime, which was quickly filled with albums and songs that were too long or too sexually or politically explicit for the AM band. While the FCC's goal had been to free the FM band from the dominance of "sister" AM stations, the effect was to create more room for college and independent stations to play music that appealed to young, affluent audiences. FM radio quickly became the medium through which young people heard the latest music. This so-called album-oriented radio (AOR) continues to provide a venue for unconventional styles (fusion, crossover, and experimental); and FM radio continues to be the medium of choice for most classical music broadcasting.

The 1970s and 1980s saw the emergence of musical minimalism, a style that relies extensively on repetition of rhythmic patterns and chord structures. Philip Glass (b. 1937) and Steve Reich (b. 1936) are often cited as exponents of this style, which, in its relative simplicity, bears some resemblance to some rock music. Glass, Reich, performance artist Laurie Anderson (b. 1947), and the underground rock band Sonic Youth have all recorded pieces that blur generic boundaries and bear the "crossover" label. A variety of crossover neoromanticism is apparent in New Age music, some of which includes instruments and tonal effects of non-Western—particularly Tibetan and Japanese—cultures. The New Age phenomenon has offered a successful multicultural synthesis of Western concert instruments and musical forms with melodic ideas and inspiration from non-Western cultures.

In concert music, the latter decades of the twentieth century saw debates among composers over the continued viability of varieties of modernist musical thought. Composers for whom melody has remained more important than rhythmic invention continue to create accessible modern music, which is sometimes labeled "neoromantic." David Diamond (b. 1915) integrated neoclassic and romantic musical sounds into some of his compositions, as did William Schuman (b. 1910), composer of symphonies and an opera, "The Mighty Casey," based on the popular poem. Elie Siegmeister composed "I Have a Dream" a cantata based on the life of Martin Luther King, Jr., and Ned Rorem (b. 1923) set to music the work of American poets as diverse as Walt Whitman and Sylvia Plath. Elliott Carter (b. 1908) and Leonard Bernstein have been strong propagandists for American music, Carter in an academic context and Bernstein in his many books, lectures, and television appearances. Although composing and conducting have long been the province of men, the work of countless women composers, including Louise Talma (b. 1906) and Miriam Gideon (b. 1906), and such famous conductors as Sarah Caldwell (b. 1924) has contributed to the development of American concert music for a broader public.

American music is not confined to a set of national tunes, myths that inspire great symphonies, or a single folk music tradition. It reaches small avant-garde audiences in the academy, millions of fans through concerts and recordings, and almost everyone in the form of more or less ambient music piped into public and private architectural spaces. Indeed, in the last decades of the twentieth century, Virgil Thomson's assertion that American music is simply music written by Americans is being realized through the variety of the American musical product itself. Earlier cries for a higher standard of European culture in the music we hear in this country have given way to a plethora of approaches to composition that rely on no national label. In its diversity and availability through electronic media, concert music in the United States has assumed a place in the mainstream of American culture.

[See also Popular Entertainment before the Civil War; Theater and Musical Theater; Urban Cultural Institutions.]

BIBLIOGRAPHY

Barzun, Jacques. *Music in American Life* (1956).

Chase, Gilbert. *America's Music: From the Pilgrims to the Present* (1955; rev. ed. 1987).

Copland, Aaron, and Vivian Perlis. *Copland: 1900 Through 1942* (1984).

Elson, Louis C. *The History of American Music* (1901).

Hughes, Rupert. *Contemporary American Composers* (1900).

Jones, LeRoi (Imamu Amiri Baraka). *Blues People* (1963).

Lang, Paul Henry. *One Hundred Years of Music in America* (1961).

Lawrence, Vera Brodsky. *Strong on Music: The New York Music Scene in the Days of George Templeton Strong, 1836–1875* (1988).

Levine, Lawrence. *Highbrow/Lowbrow: The Emergence of Cultural Hierarchy in America* (1988).

Levy, Alan Howard. *Musical Nationalism: American Composers' Search for Identity* (1983).

Levy, Alan Howard, and Barbara L. Tischler. "Into the Cultural Mainstream: The Growth of American Music Scholarship." *American Quarterly* 42, no. 1 (March 1990): 57–73.

Mason, Daniel Gregory. *The Appreciation of Music.* Vol. 4, *Music in America* (1915).

Rockwell, John. *All American Music: Composition in the Late Twentieth Century* (1983).

Tischler, Barbara L. *An American Music: The Search for an American Musical Identity* (1986).

Zuck, Barbara Ann. *A History of Musical Americanism* (1980).

— BARBARA L. TISCHLER

COUNTRY AND WESTERN MUSIC

In forty years of rapid modernization after 1920, much of the southern-eastern United States was transformed from a rural, agricultural society to an urban, industrial one. During this time the region also endured a severe economic depression, contributed heavily to a world war, and accommodated new government programs designed to commercialize agriculture, import new economic systems, and improve home life. One by-product of these changes was a dramatic increase in migration throughout the region and subsequent economic displacement, divorce, and social disruption among families. This situation was congenial to the rise of a popular music focusing on personal hardship or invoking nostalgia for a more orderly way of life imagined as the region's rural past.

Dramatic social change was common in southern society during the early twentieth century. In Appalachia, where a novel form of rustic musical entertainment was invented in this period, nineteenth-century family farming was made obsolete by industrial urbanization and agricultural modernization. First came timber cutting, then coal mining, textile mills, commercial manufacturing towns, railroads, highways, land acquisition for national parks, tourism, and government flood-control and hydroelectric projects. So much Appalachian land was removed from private ownership by these incursions that during the downside of boom-and-bust cycles government welfare programs were required by almost half the mountain population before World War II. A similar displacement occurred throughout the South. Between 1920 and 1960 sharp increases in mechanized farming and related changes in southern agricultural regions had unprecedented demographic effects. Jack Temple Kirby estimates that if each 1920 southern farm household consisted of five persons, in the forty years before 1960 nearly eight million people migrated from farms and nine million people left the region altogether. This extraordinary migration precipitated both urban and nationwide markets for country and western music.

During the same forty years that southerners were displaced from rural environments, complex institutions to promote popular entertainment were built in the South. New technologies were essential to this process. Radio broadcasting, phonograph recording, and electrical amplification equipment used in concerts made it possible for large numbers of people to hear intricate levels of nuance in singing and instrument playing. Paved highways, automobiles, and bus transportation allowed enterprising performers to be booked in concerts throughout the region and beyond. Concerts became both a source of major income and an important setting where entertainers could build emotional relationships with their fans by singing of personal hardship or pain, love traumas, memories of family and kin. Movies, television, music festivals, and concert tours spread this musical subculture widely in the 1950s and 1960s. Combining a fortunate location in the middle South with business entrepreneurship and investment capital, Nashville, Tennessee, became a major center for the nationwide marketing of country and western entertainment by 1960.

An Emerging Star System

In the early 1920s recording-company entrepreneurs began packaging mountain string music into rustic formats with market appeal. A style that would later come to be known as "hillbilly" music began in June 1922 when Alexander Campbell "Eck" Robertson and Henry Gilliland, old-time fiddlers from Texas and Oklahoma, were recorded at Victor studios in New York City. Radio broadcasting quickly embraced rusticity. On 24 January 1923 station WBAP in Fort Worth, Texas, aired the first radio program of hillbilly string music to an extremely receptive audience that responded with telephone calls and telegrams of praise. Successful radio barn-dance programs were soon begun in Chicago, Atlanta, Nashville, and other cities.

Recording companies responded to radio's success with string-band music by offering an alternative—solo vocalists. Marion T. Slaughter is often cited as the most important of these. A graduate of the Dallas Conservatory of Music and a figure of the New York light opera stage, Slaughter was an ironic candidate for success as a hillbilly; he had also recorded songs in black dialect for the "race" market. In 1924 he began making records in New York City under the pseudonym Vernon Dalhart—a recording persona constructed from the names of towns in Texas where he had once worked as a cowboy. His 1924 version of "The Prisoner's Song," the first hillbilly vocal to sell a million records, was a guitar- and viola-accompanied ballad about loneliness and separation from a lover. Slaughter followed his hit record with numerous releases having sentimental themes.

Hillbilly records were made in several cities in the 1920s. Although New York City was the earliest recording site, formative events that would lead to a popular-music industry took place in Tennessee. In the summer of 1927 Ralph Peer, a young entrepreneur working with the Victor Talking Machine Company, went to Bristol, Tennessee, to make field recordings. He was searching for hillbilly entertainment that would boost record sales for Victor. An arrangement would soon emerge that would allow his music publishing company to receive royalties on songs copyrighted and performed by the artists he selected; this would encourage Peer to give much attention to his stars.

Peer advertised for local musicians; he would record their work for fifty dollars per song plus royalties. Spread by a newspaper story, this offer attracted much notice. According to Charles Wolfe, in about two weeks at Bristol, Peer made over seventy recordings of pop and vaudeville, fiddle, banjo, and gospel music (*Bristol Sessions,* vol. 1, liner notes). Among the many acts responding to Peer were two that would become the earliest national stars in country and western music: the Carter Family and Jimmie Rodgers.

THE CARTER FAMILY. This trio had a pervasive influence on subsequent performing styles. Probably most important for the formation of country music instrumental styling was Maybelle Addington Carter, a creative guitarist and alto singer. A. P. (Alvin Pleasant) Carter, Maybelle's brother-in-law, sang bass and managed the act. A. P. Carter and Ralph Peer may have initiated the practice of copyrighting and recording songs that were collected from many sources and adapted to a particular group's playing style. Sara Dougherty Carter, A. P.'s wife, sang lead and played the Autoharp in an unusual way, picking an instrument designed for strumming a rhythmic accompaniment.

Signature innovations of the Carter Family in the late 1920s were crucial to their commercial success and influence. Maybelle Carter perfected a distinct guitar style by playing melody on bass strings with her thumb while chording rhythm on treble strings. A. P. Carter's song arrangements reduced complicated traditional melodies and accompaniments to standard vocal lines sung in a repetitive fashion against a regular rhythm of basic chords. These two innovations may have been developed partly under the influence of Leslie Riddles, a black guitarist and songwriter from Kingsport, Tennessee. Riddles's periodic travels with A. P. Carter influenced the latter's method of song collecting.

Carter Family music is marketable popular music featuring lyrics with broad appeal for a changing society. While the trio adapted many kinds of music to their format, a main theme was personal hardship and emotional responses to it. In their first six songs recorded at Bristol, a daughter sentimentalizes her mother's Bible reading, a young woman pines for unrequited love, a mother longs for her wandering boy, lovers pledge loyalty in a lament over pending separation, blessings are asked for poor orphan children, and a bride complains of constraints in married life. The lives of Carter Family members suggest that such themes may have been derived from personal experience. Always maintaining jobs other than music in order to make a living, they were frequently separated because family members worked as far away from their Scott County, Virginia, homes as Detroit or Washington, D.C. Marital life was problematic: in 1933 A. P. and Sara separated; in 1939 they were divorced, and Sara married A. P.'s cousin in Texas. Yet despite personal problems they recorded consistently between 1927 and 1941, releasing more than three hundred songs.

Carter performing style was readily distinguished from that of previous hillbilly artists—it was precise in execution, emotionally exciting, and repetitive—and could be imitated or elaborated upon by other musicians. The Carters got important airplay during the three years they spent in San Antonio and Del Rio, Texas, in the late 1930s making transcriptions for radio stations licensed in Mexico as XEG, XENT, and XERA. These border radio stations were built beyond the reach of American law by colorful figures who had violated American radio regulations and power limits by zealously promoting a startling array of money-making schemes. The Carters' promoters recognized the audience appeal of rustic music and used it heavily; consequently, the Carter Family received nationwide exposure virtually every evening at a time when radio listening was America's novel form of popular entertainment.

With both radio and record exposure the Carter Family was able to create enduring music that both inspired future entertainers and nurtured a popular market for them. Although the family act disbanded in 1943, Maybelle Carter remained an influential musician well into the 1970s. The Carter name remained prominent through the marriage of Maybelle's daughter, June, with Johnny Cash, as well as through the Carters' touring with Cash's show.

In the Carter Family's first recorded songs, a daughter sentimentalizes her mother's Bible reading, a woman pines for unrequited love, and a bride bemoans the constraints of married life.

JIMMIE RODGERS. Jimmie Rodgers The brief recording career of Jimmie Rodgers also began in Bristol, Tennessee—he first performed for Peer two days after the Carter Family. Rodgers was the first major success story of Peer's promotional arrangement with Victor. The attention Peer accorded Rodgers (and all his stars) gave him reason to remain loyal to Peer. Rodgers was an enduring role model for male stardom and a symbol of individual wealth and popular acclaim, and his performance innovations helped to define a "western" musical genre.

In 1927 Rodgers, an itinerant railroader from Mississippi, was working as a part-time cab driver and as a deputy for the Asheville, North Carolina, police. Recently diagnosed with tuberculosis and wanting to leave the railroad, Rodgers was sleeping in an Asheville firehouse and singing with a hillbilly band at a local radio station. He discovered the Peer recording sessions accidentally during a visit to Bristol. Just before recording for Peer, Rodgers split with his band in a billing dispute and chose to sing solo. Peer recorded two of Rodgers's songs; he performed each in a slow tempo and sang them from a woman's point of view. "The Soldier's Sweetheart" was a popular World War I song, a lament about a lover lost in battle. "Sleep, Baby, Sleep" was a mother's soothing lullaby to an infant. It included a novelty, item—a variation on the Swiss yodel that had been a stage feature of vaudeville. Peer detected commercial possibilities in Rodgers's yodel and soon recorded him at Victor studios in Camden, New Jersey.

In a contribution analogous to the Carter Family's innovations in rhythm and instrumentation, Rodgers combined the yodel with the blues to create his signature "blue yodel." Rodgers had learned blues from black workers during his fourteen years on the railroad, beginning as a teenage water boy. When he brought together the yodel and blues traditions, Rodgers was able to express personal emotion, particularly the pain of vagabond living or turbulent love relationships, in a novel way. The blue-yodel phenomenon was popular in an era that also produced jazz, and it had financial results that impressed aspiring musicians. In 1928 "Blue Yodel" ("T for Texas") became the first hit record of modern country music.

Jimmie Rodgers died of tuberculosis complications at age thirty-five in 1933. In only six years of recording he had become the first pop superstar of country and western music. His signature blue yodel appeared a dozen times among 111 recorded titles. He also recorded sentimental ballads, popular and novelty, songs, jazz, blues, Hawaiian music, and songs with, variously, an orchestra, a jug band, a whistler, and a musical saw. He was one of the first white performers to record with black artists. Despite this varied repertoire Rodgers had a memorable styling that greatly influenced the tone of later country and western music. Nolan Porterfield reports that Rodgers, instructing his musicians at a rehearsal to play in a distinctive manner, said, "It's gotta have pathos. Make folks feel it—like we do, but we gotta have the feelin' ourselves first. This is supposed to be pathetic" (*Jimmie Rodgers*, pp. 75–76). Rodgers pressed this point so far as to record songs about his own terminal illness, such as "T. B. Blues" and "Jimmie Rodgers' Last Blue Yodel." His emphasis on pathos tapped much popular feeling during the Great Depression years; by the year of his death he had sold almost twenty million records.

The blue yodel and pathetic themes cannot, however, fully account for Rodgers's success. In another innovation he modeled a stage demeanor that would be elaborated upon by later singers who understood that the emerging star system required performers to provide stage entertainment well beyond singing. In his apprenticeship Rodgers worked medicine shows, minstrel shows, tent shows, schoolhouses, beer joints, and street corners, perfecting a personal style that touched his listeners' emotions. His mature stage manner was extremely relaxed and unaffected, and his usual stage attire and props were informal; he often appeared alone with his guitar. Rodgers lengthened or shortened words for emotional expression, and during performance he carried on a stream of verbal comments to encourage other players or to enliven his audience—more adaptations from blues stylists. Rodgers's vivacity was memorable. He became the first country and western star to have a fan club operated entirely by his followers, and in 1961 he was the first performer voted into the newly formed Country Music Hall of Fame.

After the example of Jimmie Rodgers the performance style of many country and western stars favored individual singing, guitar playing, informal interaction with fellow musicians and the audience, expressive voice innovations, emotional styling, and lyrical themes invoking pathos about the hardships of life and love. While some entertainers copied virtually everything Rodgers did, including his novelty sounds, most used his example to establish their own innovations. Depictions of the American West that had long been a staple of American popular culture were partly responsible for the emergence of western music, but Rodgers influenced the genre as well.

At the height of his popularity Rodgers built a home in Texas. He had posed for photographs in cowboy garb and used western themes in his music. Looking for a signature style and inspired by Rodgers, Gene Autry found it in a yodeling cowboy persona. Between 1929 and 1933 Autry recorded twenty-four Rodgers titles, launching his own rise to record and movie stardom and substantially advancing western imagery. Other male stars affiliated with western music have paid tribute to Rodgers. In 1932 Ernest Tubb (The Texas Troubadour) began a half-century career that after Rodgers's death earned the blessing of Rodgers's widow and the gift of Jimmie's guitar.

The *Grand Ole Opry*, Radio, and the Music Business

Jimmie Rodgers never appeared on the *Grand Ole Opry*, yet during his lifetime this vaudeville show developed from a "radio barn dance" by an entrepreneurial newspaper reporter was already becoming a major institution. Today the *Grand Ole Opry* is America's longest-running radio program; its stage is a shrine for country and western fans, a focus of aspiration for many performers, and the centerpiece of impressive commercial activity reaching into tourism, cable television, and other aspects of American popular culture.

In 1923 George D. Hay, a reporter and radio editor for the *Memphis Commercial Appeal*, began broadcasting over the newspaper's radio station. The following year he moved to Chicago, where he began the *National Barn Dance* on station WLS and won a national poll naming him the most popular radio announcer in America. In 1925 the National Life and Accident Insurance Company opened a thousand-watt radio station in Nashville, designated WSM for the insurance company's sales slogan, "We Shield Millions." Hay joined WSM that year to host a new barn dance from studios in the insurance building.

Hay had a shrewd grasp of the emerging radio audience for sentimentalized rural experience in an era when rural life was being permanently transformed. He readily moved to Nashville, which was well located for his promising market, and from the beginning of his work at WSM, he positioned his entertainers carefully. Hay sought performers who could project primitive rural images and material with nostalgic themes. He appeared to favor performers of advancing age who could impart wisdom and a feel for tradition. Although only thirty, Hay presented his own *Opry* persona as the "Solemn Old Judge." With marketing wit he renamed his barn dance the *Grand Ole Opry* to contrast with a symphonic music program broadcast just ahead of it—music he said was far from earthy realism because it was taken from grand opera.

Many of Hay's early performers were staged as rustics or curiosities. The first to perform on the evening Hay christened his *Grand Ole Opry* program was DeFord Bailey, a black man who played blues harmonica through a megaphone and was called by Hay the "Harmonica Wizard." Bailey was an elevator operator in the insurance company's building who became quite popular and was kept with the program until the early 1940s. Another act reflecting Hay's early emphasis was a musical physician from the county just north of Nashville who headed Dr. Humphrey Bate and His Augmented Orchestra. Hay dressed Bate's group in exaggerated rural garb and named it The Possum Hunters. Other acts were similarly styled as the Fruit Jar Drinkers or the Gully Jumpers to project rural nostalgia.

The first solo singing star of the *Grand Ole Opry*, Uncle Dave Macon, was a symbol of age and tradition. A vaudeville performer, banjo player, and gospel singer, Macon joined the *Opry* in 1926 at the age of fifty-six, then toured and performed regularly until three weeks before his death at age eighty-two. A fully modern *Opry* star, clearly influenced by both Jimmie Rodgers's stage manner and Carter Family musical styling, first appeared in 1938. A former semiprofessional baseball player who had learned to play fiddle while recovering from sunstroke, Roy Acuff came to the *Opry* with his band, The Crazy Tennesseans, to fill in for a canceled act. Acuff's nostalgic and rhythmically precise gospel rendition of "The Great Speckled Bird" received an outpouring of adoring mail, and his version of the Carter Family's famous railroad song, "Wabash Cannonball," brought him national attention as the *Opry* audience

Today the Grand Ole Opry *is America's longest-running radio program; its stage is a shrine for country and western fans, a focus of aspiration for many performers, and the centerpiece of impressive commercial activity.*

expanded with the advent of radio broadcasting networks. Billed as the "King of Country Music," Roy Acuff was still singing Jimmie Rodgers's blues on the *Opry* in the 1990s.

The *Opry* has featured a long series of vaudeville-style comedians who portray zany images of rural life. In the minstrel tradition country comics focus on the foibles of country people, especially their alleged inability to cope with modernity or their naive observations about it. Comics have had an important influence on country and western stage shows. Most prominent among them has been Sarah Ophelia Colley Cannon, whose character Minnie Pearl first appeared in 1940, when Colley was twenty-eight years old. A graduate of Ward-Belmont College in Nashville, she studied stage technique; after Colley's family lost their Tennessee lumber business in the Depression, she taught drama and dance until she joined the *Opry*. She based Minnie Pearl on a rural woman she met in north Alabama. *Opry* insiders feared that this act might be disliked as a negative image of rural life, yet the first airing drew hundreds of positive cards and letters. After more than fifty years in entertainment, in the early 1990s Sarah Cannon was still personally answering fan mail; she believes that comic performers serve country and western fans by providing relief from the music's main focus on unhappiness.

Minnie Pearl was elected to the Country Music Hall of Fame in 1975.

George D. Hay's radio formula of rural rusticity, string-band music, country singing stars, vaudeville comedians, and aging images of tradition had a strong audience appeal that commercial advertisers found attractive. The National Life and Accident Insurance Company saw the value of its insurance policies quadruple between 1925 and 1940. The R. J. Reynolds Tobacco Company, Pet Milk, Royal Crown Cola, Coca-Cola, Rudy's Farm Country Sausage, and the Standard Candy Company (makers of an item whose name invokes imagery of unrestrained infants seeking treats, the Goo Goo Cluster) have been prominently associated with the *Opry.* Between 1945 and 1949 Martha White Flour expanded its sponsorship of WSM programs from one P.M. to eight P.M., and its unit sales for that period tripled. In 1945 each sponsored musical program was estimated to increase flour sales for that year by 152,062 units. Commercial advertising has been so intrinsic to this musical subculture that many stage acts have been named for products that sponsored them.

Tuned to prospects for building a new music business, WSM and radio broadcasters helped establish country and western music's other basic institutions. In 1934 WSM created the Artist Service Bureau to help stars book lucrative personal appearances and tours. In 1939 a dispute over license fees charged to radio stations as a way of collecting royalties for songwriters resulted in broadcasters' forming their own licensing agency; Broadcast Music, Inc. (BMI), was set up—in competition with the American Society of Composers, Authors and Publishers (ASCAP)—to support country, western, blues, and jazz songwriters. Bill Ivey, director of the Country Music Foundation, regards the creation of BMI as the event most important to the professionalization and commercial success of the country and western music business. After broadcasters had assured a fiscal foundation for the new music, record companies moved south. In 1946 Nashville's first permanent studio, Castle Recording Company, opened. Soon studios of major record labels such as Capitol, RCA, and Decca were established in Nashville.

Since World War II, Nashville and country music have emerged as a notable financial and cultural force. In 1960, for example, Nashville studios produced singles that hit number one on *Billboard* magazine's top hits chart for twenty-eight out of fifty-one weeks. Two years earlier the Country Music Association had been formed to promote country and western music at a time when rock and roll—a derivation that many regarded as heresy—threatened its popularity. In another response to rock and roll, innovative producers like Chet Atkins at RCA Victor Studio B developed the Nashville sound as smoother country pop stylings aimed at new listener markets. By the 1980s, at the height of its popularity, country and western music grossed over $500 million annually—about 15 percent of the $3.8 billion market for all popular music then recorded in the United States. It was also being played full-time on more than twenty-two hundred radio stations. Since that time, the business has increasingly emphasized restoration of traditional styling in the promotion of its stars.

The solid position of country and western music in American popular culture since the 1980s is indicated by its continuing impact in urban radio markets, where it competes well with easy-listening music and frequently surpasses in popularity other established genres such as rock, blues, and jazz. The culture associated with country music has spawned clothing fashions, music palaces, bars, hotels, theme parks, trade publications, movies, novels, and museums, and it has been the subject of both popular and scholarly writing. Its most vivid contemporary symbol is an elaborate theme park fittingly named Opryland U.S.A. A showcase of American popular music, this vast tourist attraction occupies four hundred acres adjoining a Nashville outer freeway loop and the Cumberland River, where the park operates a 285-foot riverboat, the *General Jackson.* Opryland, which had an attendance of 2.35 million in 1989, features a 1,070-room resort hotel, syndicated cable television on The Nashville Network (reaching more than twenty million homes), and an array of tourist attractions. One of these, an annual event called Fan Fair, attracts almost twenty-five thousand people to the Tennessee State Fairgrounds each June, where they may see thirty-four hours of stage shows and visit booths where the stars provide personal thanks to their supporters. Replacing the Ryman Auditorium to become the sixth official home of country and western music since the 1920s, a fifteen-million-dollar Grand Old Opry House opened at Opryland in 1974 with a guest piano performance by President Richard Nixon. (Nixon was the first of several American presidents, including Jimmy Carter, Ronald Reagan, and George Bush, to publicly affiliate their politics with country and western music and its fans.) In 1983 the Opryland complex was sold for $270 million to a national media company based in Oklahoma.

Major Trends and Stars

Since the 1950s country and western music has become a sophisticated commercial enterprise. Yet it has continued to emphasize themes of personal hardship and emotional trauma consistent with its social origins. As a musical tradition it, like the blues, has evolved distinct conventions. To become a star, a performer must devise a novel way to address traditional themes and musical styling—through voice innovations, creative instrumental motifs or special dexterity, elaborations on stage manner and performing style, or modification of existing genres to create a new one. Country and western musicians are highly conscious of one another, and the work of a successful performer influences that of aspiring ones. These relationships and conventions are illustrated in the careers of six artists whose achievements suggest notable trends in the music.

WESTERN SWING: BOB WILLS. Early southwestern swing music modified by popular dancehall bands and broadcast nationally by radio networks in the late 1930s and early 1940s came to be known as western swing. Bob Wills was among its most significant innovators. As a child in migrant labor camps Wills, the son of a country fiddler from Texas, listened to blues musicians and other ethnic performers. As an adult he admired Bessie Smith as well as the dance orchestras of Tommy Dorsey, Count Basie, Bob Crosby, and Glenn Miller. Famous for a signature blues fiddling with a string band that yielded a jazzy swing, Wills added woodwinds, horns, and drums so that his Texas Playboys could perform numbers ranging from Jimmie Rodgers's blues to popular dance-band and jazz renditions to Rossini's "William Tell Overture." By 1938 Wills's band could play almost thirty-six hundred pieces, yet despite this crossover virtuosity he retained a strong interest in western themes and in the 1940s appeared in many western movies. After World War II he moved his operation to the West Coast, where a potential audience among southwestern migrants was growing; although his national popularity declined, he remained influential into the 1960s.

Merle Haggard, who describes his own distinct sound out of California as a form of jazz, has called Bob Wills a national hero and honors him often in performance. Wills fused several pop traditions into the country and western idiom, and in turn he influenced country pop styling as well as other popular music. Bing Crosby recorded his "New San Antonio Rose" in 1941; it became a gold record, selling 1.5 million copies. Wills was voted into the Country Music Hall of Fame in 1968.

HONKY-TONK: HANK WILLIAMS. A country and western subgenre, honky-tonk music is especially characterized by themes of turbulent love, romantic anguish, and excessive drinking. Hiram "Hank" Williams greatly extended the popularity of this music after World War II. A gifted songwriter, he used an approach directly in the Jimmie Rodgers tradition—his signature songs spoke with great emotion of the hardships of life, and he had a charismatic stage manner. The son of a lumber company railroader from rural south Alabama, Williams learned music from Cade Durham, an old-time fiddler who worked in a local shoe shop, and from Rufe "Tee Tot" Payne, a black street singer who probably introduced him to whiskey as well as to the blues when he was a teenager in the mid 1930s. After an apprenticeship in Alabama honky-tonks, in 1946 Williams came to Nashville, where his songwriting impressed Fred Rose of Acuff-Rose Publishing, and he was signed to a contract. Williams appeared on the radio barn dance *Louisiana Hayride* at Shreveport in 1948. By the spring of 1949 his records became so popular that he was invited to appear on the *Opry.* In a repeat of Rodgers's instant success story, at the end of the 1940s and into the early 1950s Williams's hits dominated both country and pop charts, selling millions of records.

But success pressed Williams severely. Alcohol and drugs, phobias, and the effects of painkillers for spina bifida affected his work. A dramatic divorce followed. He soon became an erratic performer and was fired by the *Opry* in August 1952. That year Minnie Pearl described him as a "pathetic, emaciated, haunted-looking tragic figure" (Koon, *Hank Williams,* p. 45). The date of Williams's death has become a matter of considerable investigation. Either on the last day of 1952 or the first of 1953, Williams died of a heart attack in the back seat of his Cadillac while being driven to a concert in Canton, Ohio. Public response to his death was reminiscent of the death of Jimmie Rodgers—he was so widely memorialized that his legend greatly extended his lifetime fame.

With his charismatic stage manner and signature songs speaking with great emotion of the hardships of life, Hank Williams greatly extended the popularity of honky-tonk music after World War II.

Williams's influence on other male singers was important. In an impressive vocal career George Jones, in particular, has kept Hank Williams's examples of honky-tonk singing (and personal behavior) alive. In the early 1990s popular young male singers are creating innovative stage personas in the honky-tonk genre: Clint Black, Garth Brooks, Alan Jackson, George Strait, Randy Travis, Dwight Yoakam.

Bill Monroe, shown here with his mandolin, created a modern style of string-band playing and vocal harmonizing known as bluegrass music.

BLUEGRASS: BILL MONROE. Bill Monroe created a modern style of string-band playing and vocal harmonizing that has attracted numerous followers to an elaborate country and western subgenre known as bluegrass music. As a boy Bill Monroe worked on his father's 655-acre farm in Kentucky, where he witnessed timber cutting, sawmilling, and coal mining. A loner with poor eyesight, he gravitated toward the music played by his older brothers. His uncle, Pendleton Vandiver, taught him rhythm and timing through old-time fiddle playing, and a black fiddler and guitarist, Arnold Shultz, taught him the blues. Monroe's later stylistic innovations were in part a blending of these traditions.

At age eighteen Monroe migrated to Indiana, where he began working in an oil refinery near Chicago. There he collected hillbilly string-band records, listened to radio barn dances, and performed with his brothers, Birch and Charlie, for an audience of Appalachian migrants. The Monroe Brothers had a Gary, Indiana, radio show by 1934; turned professional to perform full-time in Iowa and Nebraska; moved to the Carolinas in 1935; and made best-selling records during the next two years. In 1938, in Atlanta, Monroe formed the Blue Grass Boys; this band gave its name to a new type of string-band music and trained many of the musicians who spread it. Monroe's bluegrass used five instruments: mandolin (played with great dexterity by Monroe), fiddle (played in a jazzy and soulful manner), banjo (played in a charismatic picking mode introduced to this audience by Earl Scruggs), guitar, and bass. By 1939 Monroe was on the *Grand Ole Opry*, where his first performance was an adaptation of Jimmie Rodgers's blue yodel "Mule Skinner Blues."

Bluegrass is a distinct style within country and western music. Its rhythms stress offbeats, tempos are usually quite fast, vocal harmonizing is intricate and high-pitched, and instrumental virtuosity is prominent. Lyrics are conventional, focusing on home, family, love, hard times, work, and religion. Bluegrass invokes a potent tone of nostalgia for the rural past. In the late 1950s and early 1960s national magazines promoted bluegrass; during the "folk" movement Monroe played college campuses, and in 1963 he headlined the Newport Folk Festival.

There were more than a hundred bluegrass festivals by 1975, as well as record companies and magazines catering to an avid audience. Young *Opry* stars such as Ricky Skaggs and comedian Mike Snider, as well as the syndicated television program *Hee Haw,* actively promote rustic imagery and bluegrass music. A patriarch in his eightieth year, who in 1991 still performed as "The Father of Bluegrass Music," Bill Monroe was elected to the Country Music Hall of Fame in 1970—the same year as the Carter Family.

COUNTRY POP: PATSY CLINE, LORETTA LYNN, DOLLY PARTON. After World War II, many significant country and western music stars sought a broad audience by adopting variations of a country pop sound and image. Patsy Cline, Loretta Lynn, and Dolly Parton are important female stars who exemplify this phenomenon. None came from privileged circumstances, all were devoted to a successful professional career, and each promoted a signature identity related to changing gender roles in America. They provided an important artistic precedent for many younger women singers.

Patsy Cline was born Virginia Patterson Hensley near Winchester, Virginia, in 1932. Her parents separated when she was fifteen. By then Cline was a radio singer; at sixteen she dropped out of school to work by day and sing in clubs at night. In 1954 she got a recording contract, and three years later won national attention on a network television show, *Arthur Godfrey's Talent Scouts.* Intensely ambitious and an admirer of female pop singing stars as well as of Hank Williams, Patsy Cline devised a sound produced by Owen Bradley that was close to mainstream popular music and a precursor of the Nashville sound. This came at a time when, as an antidote to rock and roll, Nashville was recruiting an audience of American pop music lovers. Meanwhile, divorce rates were rising and a mystique praising faithful women in nuclear families was evident in popular culture. Despite Cline's own reportedly audacious personality, her musical signature was slow-tempo songs about the painfulness of unquestioning and compliant femininity, done in renditions richly backed by harmonic vocals and strings. Cline was an emerging *Grand Ole Opry* star with several hit songs lamenting male behavior in romantic relationships when she died in a plane crash in 1963. Paul Kingsbury quotes Robert K. Oermann's description of her as "the first great country torch singer" (p. 330) who influenced many later female artists. In 1973 she was the first woman solo artist voted into the Country Music Hall of Fame.

Loretta Lynn was the second of eight children in a coal miner's family of Butcher Holler, Johnson County, Kentucky. Born in the mid 1930s (she won't say when), married at fourteen, and eventually mother of six, Lynn began singing in bars near Custer, Washington, where her husband had migrated to find work in the timber industry. In the early 1960s she won a talent contest in Tacoma hosted by Buck Owens, made a hit record, moved to Nashville, and appeared on television as well as the *Grand Ole Opry.* Lynn's musical signature may have responded more to Patsy Cline's personal life than to Cline's singing; Lynn wrote and sang of women who openly object to men who cheat romantically. With a soulful voice featuring a tearful quality and singing titles such as "You Ain't Woman Enough to Take My Man," "Your Squaw Is on the Warpath," "Fist City," and "The Pill," Lynn built an image as an assertive, noncompliant female whose behavior defends traditional family values.

This formula was highly attractive in American popular culture of the early 1970s. In 1972 Lynn became the first woman named Entertainer of the Year by the Country Music Association, and in 1973 she received honorable mention in a Gallup poll of the world's ten most admired women. By the mid 1970s she had over one hundred music awards, and in 1988 she was elected to the Country Music Hall of Fame. Her life story was told in a movie intended as an accurate depiction that would personalize the country music business; *Coal Miner's Daughter* (1980) includes several actual stars playing themselves in places where life events occurred. Lynn and her husband own a chain of western clothing stores, the nation's largest rodeo, three publishing companies, and a 1,450-acre ranch and theme park near Nashville. This park pays nostalgic homage to Lynn's youth, featuring a replica of her childhood home.

Dolly Parton is a precocious product of Holiness church-singing as well as the offspring of a musical mother and a grandmother who played harmonica. Born in 1946 into a family of twelve children at Locust Ridge, Tennessee, Parton appeared on a television variety and radio show in Knoxville by the age of ten and on the *Grand Ole Opry* at fifteen. She moved to Nashville immediately after completing high school and formed a recording partnership with *Opry* star Porter Wagoner. They won the Country Music Association Vocal Duo of the Year award in 1968, 1970, and 1971.

In a variation on Loretta Lynn's gender themes, Dolly Parton's stage persona exaggerates her ample feminine characteristics to attract audience attention while singing songs that invoke conventional values; music critic Ken Tucker has described the effect of Parton's wig, bustline, and high heels as a deliberate cartoon sex symbol. Her signature titles about the hard times of her family—"Coat of Many Colors," "My Tennessee Mountain Home," and "The Bargain Store"—reinforce the image of a poor girl whose cultivated femininity can be marketed to improve her economic and social status. With a vivacious stage presence, a soprano voice capable of virtuoso coyness, and a powerful imagination that has produced over thirty solo albums with hundreds of her own compositions, Parton has become one of popular music's most commercially successful artists.

Named CMA Entertainer of the Year in 1978, Parton has starred in a television variety show, had important roles in five movies, and earned six-figure salaries in Las Vegas. In 1986 she opened a multimillion-dollar theme park named Dollywood in Pigeon Forge, Tennessee. A candid proponent of gender imagery, Parton achieved ultimate crossover status when Gloria Steinem honored her in *Ms.* magazine as a woman who "has turned all the devalued symbols of womanliness to her own ends" (p. 66).

Country and Western Music and Social History

Country and western music emerged in the late 1920s partly as a reaction to modernization—it provided musical images of rural rusticity on radio programs and promoted recording stars who expressed emotions typical of the personal hardships and romantic traumas evident during social change. It also took advantage of technological innovations in electronics, communication, and travel to build a national music subculture radiating from Nashville, Tennessee. This hastened regional modernization through the financial success of a modern music business, its stars, and its commercial sponsors. The themes of country songs, however, remained close to the impulses that initiated them; in its first six decades of growth to a multimillion-dollar enterprise, country and western music has offered traditional agrarian values to an audience for whom rural life probably functions more as nostalgia than as lived experience.

Perhaps partly because of this, the country and western subculture is usually associated with the white majority in America, and most of its major stars have been white males. Yet many of its important instrumental and vocal innovations were inspired by the art of minority musicians. By adopting blues and jazz motifs such as persistent rhythms, improvisational instrumental features, and emotionally expressive vocal renditions, country and western musicians played a role in bringing musical motifs associated with nonwhite Americans to the general popular culture, and influenced the early era of rock and roll.

Country and western music has illustrated but not embraced the changing roles of women in America since World War II. It has typically rewarded female stars who, in their art, may elaborate upon but not deviate fundamentally from conventional gender expectations. While a few women singers challenged gender boundaries during the 1980s and 1990s as a nationwide women's movement gained strength, and important female artists have achieved much popularity since the 1960s, the masculine perspective has dominated this musical subculture. Of sixty-one members elected to the Country Music Hall of Fame between 1961 and 1991, only seven were women—and three of these were solo artists. One was a comedian whose famous character, Minnie Pearl, nicely satirizes but does not threaten accepted roles.

There is no lack, however, of certain sexual themes. Lovers of this music praise its plain speaking—usually called "sincerity—because so many songs speak convincingly of emotions arising from fragmented or failed love relationships. A study by Jimmie N. Rogers of the four hundred most popular country and western songs from 1960 to 1987 found that 75 percent of them were love songs. Most of those were about unhappy, hurting, or lost loves; next most frequent were songs about cheating situations; and least frequent were songs of happy love. Dorothy Horstman found country and western songwriting to be a complex literature "full of death, sadness, and self-pity." This persistent pathos of wasted love complements themes of fading rusticity and nostalgia for lost rural life.

Rustic imagery, adaptations of jazz and blues motifs, conventional gender roles, and pathetic themes of broken hearts are central features of country and western music. They resonate with a tacit assumption: the proper way to confront hardships in a difficult world is to live in a monogamous marriage with traditional family life and conventional religion. Even though country and western stars are often unable to meet this standard themselves, they persistently elaborate upon an art that celebrates it. Fans know this. Perhaps they admire in their stars this elusive striving for a stability not characteristic of their historical experience. Regarded this way, despite its modernity, country and western music in American life amounts to a conservative critique of modern society and a very human resistance to social change.

[See also Folk Song and Folk Music; Rural Life in the South.]

BIBLIOGRAPHY

Books and Articles

Cantwell, Robert. *Bluegrass Breakdown: The Making of the Old Southern Sound* (1984). Cultural implications of bluegrass music.

Country Music Foundation. *The Country Music Hall of Fame and Museum* (1990). Official guide for the nation's most extensive museum devoted to a form of popular music; information on fifty-eight elected members of the Country Music Hall of Fame in Nashville.

Eller, Ronald D. *Miners, Millbanks, and Mountaineers: Industrialization of the Appalachian, South, 1880–1930* (1982). Results of economic transformation.

Fowler, Gene, and Bill Crawford. *Border Radio: Quacks, Yodelers, Pitchmen, Psychics, and Other Amazing Broadcasters of the American Airwaves* (1987; repr. 1990). One way country and western music was first heard across America.

Green, Douglas B. *Country Roots: The Origins of Country Music* (1976). Has a chapter describing country comedians.

Haggard, Merle, with Peggy Russell. *Sing Me Back Home: My Story* (1981).

Horstman, Dorothy, comp. *Sing Your Heart Out, Country Boy* (1975; rev. ed. 1986). What country and western song lyrics mean.

Kingsbury, Paul, ed. *Country, the Music and the Musicians: Pickets, Slickers, Cheatin' Hearts and Superstars* (1988). The best introduction, it includes photographs, essays by sixteen authors, vignettes, discography, and bibliography.

Kirby, Jack Temple. *Rural Worlds Lost: The American South, 1920–1960* (1987). Agricultural modernization and its vivid effects in an American region.

Koon, George William. *Hank Williams: A Bio-Bibliography* (1983). Best scholarly biography; it has a song study, bibliographical essay, and discography.

Lomax, John III. *Nashville: Music City USA* (1985). How the music business developed and how it operates in Nashville; good visual material.

Lynn, Loretta, with George Vecsey. *Coal Miner's Daughter* (1976). Autobiography and movie source.

Malone, Bill C. *Country Music U.S.A.: A Fifty-Year History* (1968; rev. ed. 1985). The most detailed and scholarly history of country and western music.

Malone, Bill C. *Southern Music/American Music* (1979). Interactions of ethnic music forms in the South and their exportation to the nation.

Malone, Bill C., and Judith McCullough, eds. *Stars of Country Music: Uncle Dave Macon to Johnny Rodriguez* (1975). Biographical essays, including important accounts of the Carter Family by John Atkins; of Jimmie Rodgers by Chris Comber and Mike Paris; of Bob Wills by Charles R. Townsend; of Bill Monroe by Ralph Rinzler; and of Loretta Lynn by Dorothy A. Horstman.

Nash, Alanna. *Dolly* (1978). Life of Dolly Parton.

Nassour, Ellis. *Patsy Cline* (1981; rev. ed. 1985).
Porterfield, Nolan. *Jimmie Rodgers: The Life and Times of America's Blue Yodeler* (1979). Best scholarly biography; includes detailed discography.
Rogers, Jimmie N. *The Country Music Message: Revisited* (1989). Content analysis of lyrics in the four hundred most popular country and western songs from 1960 to 1987.
Rosenberg, Neil V. *Bluegrass: A History* (1985). Definitive scholarly study of bluegrass music and its elaborations.
Schlappi, Elizabeth. *Roy Acuff: The Smoky Mountain Boy* (1978).
Stambler, Irwin, and Grelun Landon. *The Encyclopedia of Folk, Country and Western Music* (1969; rev. eds. 1982, 1984).
Steinem, Gloria. "Dolly Parton." *Ms.* 15 (January 1987). Reviews gender issues.
Strobel, Jerry, ed. *Grand Ole Opry: WSM Picture-History Book* (1984). Official *Grand Ole Opry* book; has biographies of sixty-one acts plus information on Opryland, The Nashville Network, WSM, *Hee Haw,* and *Opry* history.
Tassin, Myron, and Jerry Henderson. *Fifty Years at the Grand Ole Opry* (1975).
Townsend, Charles R. *San Antonio Rose: The Life and Music of Bob Wills* (1976). Best scholarly biography; includes discography.
Whisnant, David E. *All That Is Native and Fine: The Politics of Culture in an American Region* (1983). Cultural politics and music in Appalachia.
Williams, Roger M. *Sing a Sad Song: The Life of Hank Williams* (1970).
Wilson, Charles Reagan, and William Ferris, eds. *Encyclopedia of Southern Culture* (1989). An exploration of regional culture by many writers; includes numerous items on country and western music.
Wolfe, Charles K. *The Grand Ole Opry: The Early Years, 1925–1935* (1975). Detailed history of the Opry's early days.
Wolfe, Charles K. *Tennessee Strings: The Story of Country Music in Tennessee* (1977).
Wolfe, Charles K. *Kentucky Country: Folk and Country Music of Kentucky* (1982). Detailed study focused on a state.

Recordings

The Bristol Sessions: Historic Recordings from Bristol, Tennessee. Country Music Foundation CMF-011-C. Selection of earliest recordings by the Carter Family, Jimmie Rodgers, and twenty-one others from 1927 sessions with Ralph Peer. two tapes, notes by Charles K. Wolfe.
The Carter Family on Border Radio. John Edwards Memorial Foundation JEMF 101. Reissue of Carter Family music from electrical transcriptions made between 1939 and 1942 for Mexican border stations; history, annotation, and bibliography by Archie Green, William H. Koon, and Norm Cohen. One record, twenty-three songs plus music and discographies.
Classic Country Music: A Smithsonian Collection. Smithsonian Institution RD 042-1-4; RC 042CD DMK4-0914. One hundred country and western songs illustrating the history of country and western music; four volumes selected and annotated by Bill C. Malone, with brief history and bibliography.
Country Music Hall of Fame 20th Anniversary Collection. Country Music Foundation CMF-SP1/SE4-10684. Forty-five selections on three tapes.
Sixty Years of Country Music. RCA CPK 2-4351. Historic overview includes twenty-four artists; one tape.
Sixty Years of Grand Ole Opry. RCA CPK 2-9507. Thirty-six selections from the history of the Grand Ole Opry; two tapes.

— CURTIS W. ELLISON

COURTSHIP, MARRIAGE, SEPARATION, AND DIVORCE

There are no universally accepted definitions of the terms "courtship," "marriage," "separation," and "divorce," but working definitions can be established in the context of American history and tradition. Courtship is the process of identifying and testing potential marriage partners and of selecting the best candidate. Marriage is the alliance of a man and a woman, of them and the state, and of two sets of kin in a socially and legally legitimized union. This union regularizes a couple's sexual relationship and childbearing, and it creates an economic unit that will support the married pair and any children they produce. Marriage usually begins with a public announcement, some sort of ceremony, and a legal document, all of which assume a degree of permanence in the marriage. Often, marriage confers adult status on the new spouses in their own eyes, and those of their families and of society.

Separation and divorce are processes that dissolve and dismantle the legal and emotional ties a married couple create. Although a marriage remains legally intact during separation and is totally nullified in divorce, both processes must provide for division of joint property, care of children, support of a financially dependent spouse, and financial arrangements in case of illness, disability, and retirement. In addition, separation and divorce must address the dissolution of kin ties—for example, grandparents' right of access to their grandchildren.

During the course of American history, these institutions have modified in several significant ways. Today the most noticeable trends are an increase in the number of people who contract several marriages of limited duration and an increase in the number of people who resort to divorce as a solution to marital problems. Most Americans think of their ancestors as people who formed enduring, stable families, but serial marriage and widespread divorce were present early in the nation's history.

Colonial America, 1607–1776

American Indian customs and laws were diverse and well established when the first permanent European settlers arrived in 1607. Native practices included patriarchal and matriarchal families; patrilineal and matrilineal descent; patrilocal and matrilocal residences; polygamy; and relative ease of divorce. Anthropologists estimate that perhaps as many as one-third of Indian tribes were matriarchal, matrilineal, and matrilocal; polygamy and ease of divorce appear to have been more widespread.

Early settlers, who of course brought their own beliefs and practices with them, frequently commented upon and criticized these native customs. Most Europeans believed that all marriages and families should be patriarchal, patrilineal, and patrilocal. They expected marriage to involve one man and one woman, bonded by a religious sacrament into a lifetime union. Some Europeans, however, accepted the idea of separation in cases of physical abuse and divorce in cases of adultery or other serious violations of the marriage compact.

Puritan settlers in what became the Massachusetts colony were the first to break with some of these accepted ideas regarding marriage. Because they had adopted Martin Luther's and John Calvin's belief that marriage was a civil rather than a religious concern, Plymouth officials formally declared in 1620 that marriage was a civil matter. As the colony's second governor, William Bradford, explained, marriage was to be "performed by the magistrate, as being a civil thing." Puritan leaders in other colonies also adopted this philosophy. By removing marriage from the jurisdiction of the church, they hoped to create strong, state-regulated families that would serve as the keystone of their society. They expected well-ordered, religiously oriented, patriarchal families to bring about their dream of a harmonious community in the wilderness.

Because effective mate selection was crucial to stable marriages, courtship was a public affair that involved not only the courting couple but their families and neighbors as well. Romantic love was not a high priority. Rather, a couple was to be well matched in abilities, ambitions, backgrounds, and beliefs. Once they married, established a productive economic unit, and produced children, conjugal love would develop.

But family members, friends, ministers, and officials could not always oversee courting couples. Sometimes necessity dictated that they be left alone while others worked, worshiped, or slept. At bedtime, a young woman's family might bundle her and her swain, both fully dressed, into the same bed. Often a board was placed between them. The rest of the family could then bank the fire and retire for the night. The custom of bundling was not a Puritan invention; it had roots in cultures all over the world, including the British Isles and American Indian civilizations. But it was controversial. Its supporters maintained that it was an innocent practice, while its critics argued that it led to fornication and pregnancy before marriage. Certainly, court records indicate that a significant number of Puritan marriages were contracted as the result of fornication which led to pregnancy. In the New Haven colony (later part of Connecticut), the sin of fornication could lead to marriage even if no pregnancy occurred.

Like courtship, marriage was a public concern regulated by social expectations, church rules, and community law. Both men and women were expected to marry Typically, men married between the ages of twenty-five and twenty-eight. Young men who delayed marriage, or were unable to find a mate due to the high ratio of men to women, often were subject to a bachelor tax levied by their townships. During the seventeenth century, the greater number of men than women put pressure on women to marry while in their teens. During the eighteenth century, however, women customarily married between the ages of twenty and twenty-two. In 1692, Puritan minister Cotton Mather declared in *Ornaments for the Daughters of Zion*, "For a woman to be praised, is for her to be married." It is little wonder that nine out of ten women married at least once in their lifetime. Women who did not marry lived with their nearest male relatives, performed child-care duties, and did spinning—and as a result were usually known as spinsters.

Despite their rejection of marriage as a religious concern, Puritans, like other European settlers, favored the patriarchal family form in which the husband was the head of the family. He was to make decisions for his wife and children as well as to direct and oversee their behavior. He also owned any wages they earned. But a husband also faced certain restrictions. He was, for example, liable for his wife's support, responsible for her crimes and debts, and required to leave at least one-third of his land and one-third of his movable property to her in his will. He was also supposed to be faithful sexually to his wife, to live with her in peace and harmony, and to avoid abusing her.

Puritans considered a wife the "weaker vessel" who owed submission to her husband. Guidebooks titled *A Good Wife, God's Gift* and *Marriage Duties*, both published in 1620, spelled out a married woman's duties. Although before marriage she might hold the legal status of *feme sole*, which allowed her to manage her own affairs and even establish a business, after marriage she shifted to *feme covert*, which made her part of her husband's legal and political identity and prohibited her from conducting her own affairs. This change in status derived from the civil death concept early settlers brought from England. Civil death, summarized in Sir William Blackstone's *Commentaries on the Laws of England* (1765–1769), prescribed that a married woman had no legal, political, or social identity apart from her husband. She could not sign contracts, had no right to her own earnings, was not able to own property, could not vote on civil or religious matters, and lost her children in case of separation or divorce. In actual practice, however, many wives were partners in family businesses, ran their own enterprises, or took over a husband's business in case of his absence, illness, or death.

As with courtship, not all Puritans obeyed the rules concerning marriage. New England church records indicate that wayward spouses were regularly brought to trial and punished. Puritan ministers usually rebuked the erring mate and ordered troubled couples to reconcile, but many feared that forcing embattled couples to remain together would undermine the social harmony they hoped to achieve. They especially feared adultery, which minister John Robinson called a "foul and filthy sin." Adultery also threatened property rights, for if a man impregnated another man's wife, the other husband's property might go to a child not his own.

As a result, New England officials sometimes followed the English practice of granting "divorces of bed and board," or legal separations. In this arrangement, a couple remained married but lived separately. The husband was expected to support his wife, and both were barred from remarriage. This solution was usually unsatisfactory because husbands often missed payments, while wives, because they were still married women, could not start their own businesses or marry men who could better support them.

In certain cases, divorce seemed a far better solution than forcing spouses to remain legally wed. After divorce, women returned to *feme sole* status or could remarry. Consequently, in 1639 the Massachusetts Bay Court of Assistants granted the first divorce in America to a woman who claimed her husband was a bigamist. The second divorce occurred in 1643, when Anne Clarke charged her husband with living with another woman. As these cases suggest, divorce involved a court trial in which one party sued the other. The plaintiff had to prove fault on the part of the defendant. Property, support, and child custody awards were made by the court, which typically favored the injured party. As a result, a woman who could prove her husband's sins had a far better chance of a favorable settlement than a woman whose husband proved her guilty of a marital misdeed. It is little wonder that by the early 1700s, more women than men sued for divorce in America, a situation that has continued to the present day.

Surviving court records indicate that Massachusetts magistrates had granted nearly one hundred divorces by the time of the American Revolution, a rather high number for a society dedicated to the family and in an early stage of experimentation with divorce. Also, these figures omitted nonwhite people. American Indians were left to tend to their own marital disputes, and African Americans seldom sought, or were granted, white legal sanctions. A rare African American case occurred in 1758 when free black Lucy Purnan successfully charged her husband with extreme cruelty, including kidnapping and selling her as a slave.

Other New England and middle colonies experimented with separation and divorce. Each jurisdiction defined its own grounds for divorce, which included adultery, bigamy, willful desertion, extended absence, and nonsupport. Divorces might be granted by local courts or the governor of the colony. Some officials condoned physical and even mental cruelty as a substantiating charge, thus laying the basis for later generations' acceptance of cruelty as a ground for divorce. Of these colonies, only Connecticut appears to have surpassed Massachusetts in the number of divorces granted relative to the size of its population.

In the southern colonies, marriage and divorce differed slightly from other regions. Marriage was patriarchal, while law and custom restrained husbands from abusing their power. Such early guidebooks as *A Godly Form of Household Government* admonished husbands to "seldom reprove" and "never smite" their wives. Wives were supposed to be agreeable and obedient mates, capable and energetic household managers, and prolific and loving mothers.

Personal letters, family and court records, and similar documents indicate that numerous southern couples enjoyed devoted relationships, while others destroyed their unions with arguments and abusive behavior. But, unlike the situation in New England and in some of the middle colonies, estranged couples could only seek separations. In the colonial South, every government maintained a belief in the long-standing Anglican practice of granting only divorces of bed and board. But implementing such divorces was problematic because the southern colonies lacked the ecclesiastical courts necessary to give such decrees. Consequently, courts of chancery (courts of equity rather than common law) filled the void by giving separate maintenance orders to disgruntled spouses. Following English ecclesiastical court procedure, chancellors ordered husbands to continue to support wives who were to live on their own. They also prohibited both parties from remarrying.

Women initiated virtually all separate maintenance requests. Such orders brought desperately needed financial support to women who had absent, cruel, adulterous, and bigamous husbands. Aggrieved husbands had little to gain through such orders because they could separate from their wives without paying anything, or paying only what they thought sufficient.

The legal system of marriage and separation in the southern colonies excluded African American slaves. Slave owners usually decreed whether slaves could marry or part, and frequently ordered them to do so. In other cases, slaves turned to their churches or communities for approval of their matings and partings. The one notable law regulating African Americans' marital behavior—whether they were slave or free—were miscegenation provisions prohibiting black women and men from marrying white mates. Such laws had their roots in color prejudice and fear of "race suicide." Soon local prohibitions were enacted into colonial codes of law. Although these laws, which persisted in some states until the 1960s, were not always observed, essentially two systems of marriage developed in the colonial South, one white and one black.

The New Nation, 1776–1861

By the time the American colonies declared independence from Great Britain in 1776, a wide range of social and economic factors had modified the institution of marriage. Certainly the emergence of a market economy, new forms of production, and technology had already begun to alter the family's role as the basic unit of production. As early as the mid 1770s, the economic partnership of spouses in producing agricultural and other goods began to decline. In addition, the growing mobility of Americans and the gradual development of a trend toward western migration placed severe stresses on marriages and families. During the 1760s and 1770s, existing social and economic stresses were exacerbated by an expanding rhetoric of individualism, a philosophy which argued that liberty, justice, and the pursuit of happiness were American rights—both politically and personally. Then the Revolutionary War itself created temptations for spouses at home or at the front, encouraged people to marry without forethought, and called into question women's usual roles within the family.

When leaders in the new states hastened to write constitutions and enact codes of laws, they had to decide how each of the thirteen new states would regulate and order the marital status of citizens under their jurisdiction. At first, most simply integrated existing practices and laws into their constitutions and laws, but in the years following the Revolution, states began to change and expand the rules. As a result, the thirteen states developed thirteen different sets of rules governing marriage.

When the United States Constitution created a federal government, which went into effect in 1789, the diverse legal patterns might have been standardized if the Constitution had given the new government the power to regulate the marital status of Americans. But each colony had controlled the marital status of its own citizens since the beginning of settlement in 1607, and the new states resisted losing this, or any other, power. Thus, individual states retained the right to regulate marital status within their boundaries. In 1792 the U.S. Congress tried to bring harmony to the situation by passing a "full faith and credit" bill reinforcing a statement in the Constitution that each state was required to give full faith and credit to the acts of other states. In the matter of marital status, however, this was a practical impossibility because states still refused to relinquish their sovereignty in this matter; it was eventually adjudicated by the Supreme Court.

Marriage was further complicated by the fact that Americans exhibited all three of the basic forms of family structure. The nuclear family consisting of two parents and their children gradually became the idealized form in the new nation. But some people chose the extended family in which two or more nuclear families were affiliated by parent-child relationships, or the polygamous family in which two or more nuclear families were affiliated by plural marriage, usually one husband and several wives. The extended family was often used in cases of scarce resources. For instance, western settlers lived together to pool goods and services. Polygamy was a preferred form for a number of practical and religious reasons among Mormons, who moved westward during the mid nineteenth century, first to Nauvoo, Illinois, and then to Utah.

Although the nuclear family gradually became the nation's idealized form, some chose the extended family, or the polygamous family.

Diversity occurred in other ways as well. In Philadelphia and Boston, New York and Virginia, during the 1780s and 1790s, for example, close kin marriages were commonly used to solidify family wealth and power. And while such northeastern states as Massachusetts and Connecticut refused to give wives a measure of protection from husbandly abuse or mismanagement by recognizing a married woman's right to hold property, southern states did so through prenuptial agreements. Such contracts usually stipulated that the property of a bride-to-be would be held in trusteeship for her exclusive use and that she could not be held liable for her husband's debts. One example was an 1824 agreement between Henry M. Armistead and Mary Robinson of Virginia, stipulating that the bride-to-be's "considerable" land, slaves, and other personal property would be held by a trustee for her sole use throughout her lifetime. Although such agreements were usually negotiated by wealthy families, they were widely used in some areas of the South. For instance, in Louisiana, people of many backgrounds, races, and ethnic origins signed them. During the early 1830s in Louisiana, an Irish widow protected her plantation and slaves with a contract, and two free African Americans, who held 7 acres (2.8 hectares) between them, made their marks on a premarital agreement.

During the post-Revolution period, American marriage altered in yet another way. The traditional view of patriarchal marriage was increasingly under attack. An emerging ideal of companionate marriage—a partnership of equals and companions who would respect each other in a reciprocal, loving manner—challenged the customary idea of male-headed, male-dominated unions. Articles, essays, speeches, and sermons spoke of the need for spouses to give each other respect, reciprocity, and romance during both courtship and marriage.

Wives, who had long been taught to respect their husbands, especially began to ask for more consideration. As early as 1776, political wife and farm manager Abigail Adams argued that wives should be helpmeets rather than slaves and should be free from husbandly "tyranny." The wife-slave analogy was a popular one during these years. But in 1831, an essay in *Godey's Lady's Book* informed readers that tyranny was now "out of fashion" because men were becoming "more enlightened and more rational."

Women's rights' advocates especially called for respect in marriage. Abolitionist and feminist Sarah Grimké claimed in *Letters on the Equality of the Sexes* (1838) that God intended wives as "companions, equals, and helpers" rather than as servile housekeepers. In 1843 and 1845 transcendentalist Margaret Fuller argued that wives should be companions and equal members of "household partnerships."

Reciprocity was another key ingredient to successful marriage. In 1874 popular novelist Timothy Shay Arthur explained that marital "felicity" meant that spouses tried to please each other whenever possible. And when reformer Robert Dale Owen married Mary Jane Robinson in 1832, he released a statement on reciprocity in marriage. In it, he repudiated his "unjust rights" that "an iniquitous law tacitly give over the person and property of another," and he labeled a husband's legal right the "barbarous relics of a feudal, despotic system." Later a few other couples, such as reformers Lucy Stone and Henry Blackwell, attempted to create equal marriages by issuing similar statements.

The third component of marriage was heightened romantic love. Letters of courting couples from this period clearly exhibit an intensified interest in romance rather than in practical matters. Many mentioned that they had the right to reject parental advice regarding their choice of mate, for how could another person judge the presence of true love?

The theme of romantic love also appeared in thousands of essays, stories, and novels. In 1785 an essay in *Boston Magazine* encouraged unmarried people to resist parental advice. Instead, they were to "avoid sacrificing a life of happiness" by bending to their parents' will. T. S. Arthur also advised couples to marry for love. In *The Stolen Wife* (1843), he told the story of a woman whose true love carried her off half an hour before she was to wed the man her parents had chosen.

Of course, the three r's—respect, reciprocity, and romance—did not immediately eclipse longstanding beliefs regarding courtship and marriage. Writers of innumerable guidebooks, such as *The Young Wife*, which was popular between 1800 and 1860, argued that wives must be submissive, pure, and domestic. The home was, after all, wives' "proper sphere." Husbands were the center of women's lives, for women lived best in "the regions of sentiments and imagination." Women's sphere also included motherhood. A growing idealization of republican motherhood—mothers who raised virtuous citizens for the new republic—reinforced the customary view that motherhood was the be-all and end-all of women's lives. In 1842, Margaret Coxe unequivocally stated that motherhood was the "most important channel through which woman was to direct her special moral agency" (*Claims of the Country on American Females*, p. 37).

This dual system of values bewildered many people. Was marriage to be patriarchal or was it to be companionate? How could a person select a suitable mate in this situation? In 1850 novelist Nathaniel Hawthorne described the confusion that reigned in many romantic relationships. In *The Scarlet Letter*, distressed women come to Hester for advice about marriage, but she can only soothe them by predicting that love and marriage will be easier in the future: "At some brighter period. . . . a new truth would be revealed, in order to establish the whole relation between man and woman on a surer ground of mutual happiness."

Other observers of the situation took a far different stance. Some reformers argued that marriage itself was the culprit. As early as 1826, Frances Wright's utopian community, Nashoba, Tennessee, rejected the concept of marriage entirely. Wright and her supporters argued that love and respect, rather than legal ties, should bind couples. When love and respect disappeared, couples could simply separate. As a consequence, public outrage rose against Wright; her critics accused her of being a free-love advocate. On July 4—Independence Day—of that same year, Robert Dale Owen declared that no one should be trapped in a distressing marriage. In his view, only marriages that resulted in equality and companionship ought to continue.

Other utopian communities also experimented with marriage. Under the leadership of Ann Lee, Shakers established their first socialistic Christian community at Watervliet, New York, during the mid 1770s. In hopes of hastening the millennium, Shakers advocated and practiced total celibacy. As Shaker communities multiplied, problems arose when one spouse wanted to join the Shakers and the other did not. Shaker leaders were afraid their communities would become havens for runaway husbands and wives. Accordingly, they refused to accept a married person without his or her spouse unless they were legally separated or divorced.

Also in New York, the Oneida Community, founded by John Humphrey Noyes in 1848, followed the practice of "complex" marriage in which every woman in the community was married to every man, and every man to every woman. The goal of complex marriage was to eliminate competition, jealousy, and inequality between men and women. Noyes hoped mates would no longer feel "ownership" of their spouses, so the need for divorce would disappear. In 1850 an Oneida tract described marriage as "contrary to natural liberty," as "a cruel and oppressive method of uniting the sexes," and as a "huge Bastille of spiritual tyranny where men and women have the power to debar each other from their rights . . . " (Oneida Community, *Slavery and Marriage: A Dialogue* [1850], pp. 7–13).

Most Americans rejected these and other criticisms of traditional, white, middle- and upper-class marriage. Religious leaders, notably Episcopalians and Catholics, spoke in favor of marriage as a lifetime religious sacrament. By the 1820s and 1830s, when European immigration began to increase significantly, immigrants who brought their strong religious and family beliefs with them reinforced the conservative position. But definite changes were occurring as well, especially concerning women's legal position in marriage. In 1839 the state of Mississippi passed the first Married Women's Property Act, allowing wives to own and control property. In 1848 the New York legislature adopted a similar bill; Pennsylvania and several other states soon followed suit.

As the American debate regarding the future of marriage accelerated, cases of marital dissatisfaction also multiplied. Apparently the new, freer, romantic courtship was failing to help people select partners they could love for a lifetime. Moreover, Americans' rising expectations of marriage were complicating an already difficult situation at the same time that industrialization was placing unthought-of demands on marriages. Among the middle and upper classes, women remained at home while their husbands spent long days at offices in town. Among the working classes, both spouses often went to work, but at different workplaces. Working women usually were still expected to take care of domestic chores and arrange for child care. Consequently, numbers of separations and divorces rose. When the Frenchman Michel Chevalier toured the young nation during the early 1830s, he commented that marital connections were far more easily dissolved in America than in Europe. The most noticeable change had occurred in the South, where legislatures, except in South Carolina, radically revised their divorce policies beginning in 1790. The first divorce in the South was granted by members of the Maryland General Assembly in 1790 after John Sewall proved his wife had borne a mulatto child. By the mid 1830s the Maryland legislature was granting over thirty divorces each year. But in 1842, legislators passed a bill placing primary jurisdiction for divorce in the courts. The legislators felt overburdened by the volume of divorce petitions and distracted from their other work. In 1852 the Maryland constitution prohibited legislative divorce entirely. For better or worse, divorce was now in the hands of the courts.

As the mid-eighteenth-century debate about the future of marriage accelerated, people apparently found that the newer, freer romantic courtship was failing to help them select partners they could love for a lifetime.

A similar process occurred in other southern states. As states ended their confusing dual systems of divorce by lodging jurisdiction in courts only, divorce began to expand and become easier to obtain. Divorces of bed and board were still available, but growing numbers of people sought the finality of divorce instead. In so doing, they brought a plethora of causes, complaints, and requests to judges who gradually extended the number of acceptable causes—or urged the state legislature to do so—and made a wide variety of decisions concerning alimony, property, and child custody. In particular, judicial pliancy led to a broader definition of the ground of cruelty.

As divorce developed in the Northeast—the former New England and middle colonies—similar patterns emerged. One was the gradual abolition of legislative divorce, and another, a steady expansion of lists of grounds for divorce. Of the northeastern states, Connecticut created the most comprehensive divorce laws. In 1843 legislators added habitual intemperance and intolerable cruelty to an already generous list of grounds. In 1849 they added life imprisonment, committing an infamous crime, and the omnibus provision citing "any such misconduct as permanently destroys the happiness of the petitioner and defeats the purpose of the marriage relation."

During these years, new western states and territories tended to copy existing practices and laws, often adding refinements of their own. Divorce became more flexible and easier to obtain than in the East. For instance, in 1825, Illinois lawmakers restrained a guilty party from remarriage for two years rather than for life, allowed either wife or husband to obtain a divorce of bed and board for cruelty or intemperance, and efficiently divorced two couples (rather than one) with one legislative bill. In this land of mobility and haste, residency requirements for divorce were sometimes as low as ninety days, a situation that soon made western regions attractive divorce meccas for those who could afford temporary relocation.

Unfortunately, from divorcing women's point of view, little was done during these years to regulate and stabilize alimony, property, and child custody decisions. Most states referred such matters to judicial discretion, making settlements a lottery at best. Still, the effect of divorce upon early American women is unclear. While there is some evidence that New York and Louisiana provisions made it difficult for women to obtain divorces, the growing number of female petitioners in such states as Connecticut and Tennessee dispute the contention that divorce was punitive to women and difficult for them to obtain. American women of the early 1800s did have more recourse than their mothers and grandmothers.

At the time, Americans disagreed on the subject of divorce. Congregational minister Benjamin Trumbull in 1788 expressed his outrage when he learned that 390 couples had divorced in Connecticut during the preceding half-century. But in 1795, Judge Zephaniah Swift complimented Connecticut policymakers on their "temperate" divorce policies, which were conducive to "the virtue and happiness of mankind." Opponents of divorce believed the spread of divorce indicated decay and evil in society as well as breakdown in the family. They feared for the future of the nation and its people. Supporters argued that divorce dissolved dysfunctional marriages and released spouses to make better matches. They also believed freedom and happiness were rights of all people living in a democratic country.

Civil War to World War I, 1861–1914

Like all wars, the Civil War encouraged couples to marry in haste before men left for the battlefront. The war also created distances that heightened people's sense of romance. One young northern soldier claimed that only thoughts of his wife sustained him through battle, while a southern officer wrote to a friend that he avoided the pain of war by dreaming of the "fair and gentle wife" he would pursue once war ended.

During the postwar period, romance retained its hold on courting couples, but the nature of courtship itself gradually changed. Growing numbers of young women and men leaving home for college, young working women who lived in boardinghouses on their own or with other women, and finally the invention of the automobile caused the demise of the custom of men "paying calls" upon women. By the end of the nineteenth century, few women still had the power to decide if a man could come to her home and meet her family. Instead, he tendered the offer of a date, took her away from the safety of her home, paid for the date, and often expected at least a kiss in return. As the historian Beth Bailey put it, courtship was in the process of moving from the front porch of a woman's home to the backseat of a man's automobile.

The post–Civil War era brought a number of significant modifications in American marriage as well. For one thing, the emancipation of African American slaves beginning in 1863 created an opportunity for newly freed slaves to register their marriages with legal authorities. Despite the widespread belief that slaves cared little about marriage, large numbers of freed blacks reported their marriages, and others searched for mates taken from them by sale. By the 1880s, African American marriages showed the same proportion of husbands present—approximately four out of five—as did those of white Americans of the same social classes and occupational categories.

Prejudice and discriminatory laws, attitudes, and practices, however, continued to discourage, or legally prohibit, black-white marriages. Both blacks and whites argued against interracial marriage because they feared the demise of the autonomy and integrity of their own race. But others argued for marriage between the races as a way of solving differences; blend black and white into one, and prejudice would disappear.

Marriage among whites was also a source of controversy and debate during the postwar years. By the late 1880s and 1890s, a rash of self-help books and marriage manuals appeared that revealed the pressing concerns of the day. Typical advice told people to marry for love rather than wealth or status, to pick someone with compatible interests, to avoid marrying someone to save him or her, and to institute mutual decision making and open communication in marriage. In 1909, Anna B. Rogers warned potential husbands and wives to avoid "the latter-day cult of individualism; the worship of the brazen calf of Self." She especially counseled women to remember that marriage was "their work," and to get "the germ of divorce"—selfishness and individualism—out of their veins (*Why American Marriages Fail* [1909], pp. 6–7, 16).

Novelists and essayists also dissected marriage, often supporting the traditional view. In 1880, Nathan Allen maintained in the *North American Review* that American individualism was destroying marriage, for it was a "supreme selfishness" that drove mates apart ("Divorces in New England" [June 1880], pp. 558–59). In 1902, *The Outlook* decried the breakdown of marriages because of the havoc wreaked on children who, through no fault of their own, were torn away from their mother or father and lacked any redress or rights to offset their suffering ("Children's Side of Divorce" [February 1902], pp. 478–80).

During the late 1800s and early 1900s, religious leaders joined the fray. Episcopal Bishop William C. Doane of Albany, New York, helped organize an Inter-Church Conference on Marriage and Divorce that met in 1903. At this conference, representatives from twenty-five religious denominations supported the ideal of lifetime marriage. Early in 1905, the Inter-Church Conference sent representatives to plead with President Theodore Roosevelt for help. In January of that year, President Roosevelt assured the committee that "questions like the tariff and the currency are of literally no consequence whatsoever when compared with the vital question of having the unit of our social life, the home, preserved." He proclaimed that "one of the most unpleasant and dangerous features of our American life is the diminishing birth rate, the loosening of the marital tie among the old native American families." Roosevelt declared that "no material prosperity, no business growth, no artistic or scientific development will count if the race commits suicide" (quoted in U.S. Department of Labor, *Marriage and Divorce*, 1861–1906 [repr. 1978], vol. 1, p. 4).

Certainly, Americans continued to believe in marriage. Even women who hoped to pursue a career now thought it was possible to be married as well. Although earlier generations of career women, such as Frances Willard, had eschewed marriage because of its demands and limitations, her successors married in greater numbers, worked toward companionate relationships, and continued to work. These college-educated women, however, bore no children or limited their childbearing.

In fact, after the Civil War the birthrate in general had begun to show signs of decline, especially in urban areas and among native-born women. Among immigrant women, first-generation women tended to produce large numbers of children, but second-generation women reduced their childbearing. Both birth control devices and abortion were responsible for the decline.

In 1873, the Comstock Law, which grew out of the American Medical Association's and the Young Men's Christian Association's campaign for the "suppression of vice," attacked both birth control and abortion. The Comstock Law prohibited "trade in, and circulation of, obscene literature and articles of immoral use." This included mail-order pessaries that women used to avoid conception. The act additionally banned "any article or thing designed or intended for the prevention of conception or procuring of abortion." Because the birthrate failed to rise after its passage, it is likely that the Comstock Law did little more than anger many people and drive birth control and abortion underground.

At the same time, other people worried far more about the divorce rate than the birthrate as the inexorable forces of industrialization, urbanization, changing gender roles, and rising expectations of marriage continued to disrupt American marriages. In 1860, 1.2 of every 1,000 marriages ended in divorce; in 1864, 1.4 did so; and in 1866, 1.8 did so. Undoubtedly, the Civil War was partially responsible for this increase, but figures later collected by the U.S. Census Bureau showed that the number of divorces continued to increase even after the war ended. Between 1872 and 1876, divorces rose 17.9 percent over the late 1860s, and between 1877 and 1881, they rose 30.3 percent over the early 1870s.

During the post–Civil War period, Horace Greeley's *New York Tribune* aired a long-running divorce debate, women's rights' leader Elizabeth Cady Stanton spoke on behalf of divorce and free love, and the McFarland-Richardson divorce case of 1867 stunned the nation with its sex, intrigue, and blood. In 1872, esteemed minister Henry Ward Beecher was implicated in one of the most sensational divorce trials in American history. And during the 1880s and 1890s, South Dakota, North

Dakota, and Oklahoma Territory spent fleeting moments in the limelight as divorce mills.

In 1881 the New England Divorce Reform League was organized; it soon became the National Divorce Reform League, and in 1896 the Family Protective League. Under the leadership of Congregational minister Samuel W. Dike, the league urged Congress to collect marriage and divorce statistics so the extent of the problem would be clear. The resulting statistics did nothing to calm people's minds. They showed plateaus in the divorce rate, but they also showed an overall upward trend. Many reformers believed a uniform national divorce law would at least stop migratory divorce and lower the divorce rate somewhat. Although Dike had doubts about how much migratory divorces contributed to the total, he worked for this cause until his death in 1913. Others carried on the campaign until 1947, but the states were unable to agree on a uniform set of laws and unwilling to give up their power to the federal government. In addition, women's rights' leaders, divorce reformers, and social scientists argued for divorce as a protective device for wives and as a citizen's right in a free society.

By 1910 a "new" morality seemed to be sweeping America: Socialist reformer Emma Goldman argued insistently for equality and free love, branded marriage obsolete, and advocated birth control six years before Margaret Sanger began her campaign.

By 1910 a wave of "new" morality, seemed to be sweeping America. Progressives and feminists called for freedom of choice in entering and leaving marriages. Socialist reformer Emma Goldman argued insistently for equality and free love, branded marriage obsolete, and advocated birth control six years before Margaret Sanger began her campaign. And in 1913, a middle-class woman named Sara Bard Field left her husband to live with attorney and reformer Charles Erskine Scott Wood without benefit of marriage.

By this time, Nevada had gained public attention by combining lax divorce laws, leisure pursuits, a pleasant climate, a six-month residency requirement (reduced to six weeks in 1931), and a long list of grounds for divorce. The city of Reno especially gained notoriety as a divorce mill. Eastern lawyers established branch offices there and advertised widely. The rich and famous—as well as average couples—responded, providing fodder for every journalist and reformer in the nation.

World War I Through World War II, 1914–1945

By the time World War I erupted in 1914, further alterations were in the offing for American courtship and marriage. Social scientists began to argue that love and mate selection were at the mercy of such factors as propinquity, membership in ethnic and racial groups, and prospective mates' educational levels. Psychologists began to maintain that personality played a larger role in courtship than previously thought. In their view, if a person could reestablish the personality dynamics of his or her own home and parents with another person, they were likely to select that person despite his or her overall suitability as a mate. It seemed, then, that underlying forces directed the course of courtship and married love in the United States.

But the nature of courtship and marriage was altered far more by the birth control revolution than by scientific studies. In 1916, public health nurse Margaret Sanger founded the first birth control clinic in the nation. Although her opponents argued that birth control would lead to "race suicide," increased promiscuity, and lessened respect for motherhood, in 1921 Sanger organized the American Birth Control League to disseminate birth control information. By 1930, fifty-five birth control clinics existed in fifteen states. And by 1937, all states except Massachusetts and Connecticut permitted doctors to dispense birth control information to their patients. If they wished, married couples could now legally attempt to regulate family size.

America's entry into the war in 1917 fostered yet other revolutions in family life. Before men left for the front, many couples married in haste. And with so many men leaving the labor force, the federal government urged women—whether single or married—to take jobs, especially in war-related industries. By 1918 many women workers felt confident enough to seek better-paying positions, join labor unions, and participate in strikes and other militant actions.

When the war ended, conflict was inevitable. Because returning veterans wanted their jobs back, women workers experienced mass layoffs. While many women stayed in the labor pool by taking lower-paying jobs, others returned home, often grudgingly. During the 1920s, an emphasis on consumerism that raised people's expectations regarding standards of living and the material goods marriage should involve helped further erode marital satisfaction. By 1929 approximately one out of every six marriages ended in divorce, an all-time high.

Many Americans believed that people's increasing affluence and mobility, coupled with the availability of easy divorce in certain jurisdictions, contributed to the breakdown of marriages. Social scientists, psychologists, statisticians, social commentators, and novelists suggested other root causes of marital breakdown, including rising expectations of marriage, industrialization, decline in economic functions of the family, weakening of religious tenets, and the decreased stigma of divorce. Women's changing roles were especially blamed for divorce. Supposedly the leading culprits were woman suffrage, women's employment, the rising number of working mothers with small children, and the growing availability of birth control devices.

Statisticians attempted to test these hypotheses, but the figures proved fickle. Arranged one way, divorce statistics supported one assumption; arranged another way, they proved the validity of a different cause. The erratic collection of statistics also hampered analysis. Although government officials hoped to collect marriage and divorce statistics every ten years, the nation's entry into World War I in 1917 coincided with, and disrupted, the next scheduled survey. Data collection remained erratic until 1958, when the U.S. Census Bureau established divorce registration areas to facilitate the process.

Following World War II, the average American family produced two to four children, thus creating the "baby boom."

After World War II, 1945–1991

After World War II, courtship and marriage took on a staid and traditional tone for over two decades. The back-to-the-home movement for women and a return to a belief in customary gender roles served as a buffer against a world marred by memories of the Great Depression and world war, by fear of nuclear weapons, and by anticommunist hysteria. To many Americans, stable family life, located in suburban sprawl and characterized by stay-at-home wives, seemed to be a hedge against the disintegration of the modern world.

During these postwar decades, more Americans married than in previous ones: single people accounted for 31 percent of the population in 1940, a figure that dropped to 23 percent in 1950, and to 21 percent in 1960. In both courtship and marriage, men were dominant figures; they proposed dates and marriage, earned and controlled money, and made a couple's larger decisions. Despite the increasing availability of birth control devices, the average American family produced two to four children, thus creating a "baby boom."

But when the "boomers" reached young adulthood, they questioned, and often rejected, their parents' beliefs and practices. By 1970 these young women and men, who, unlike their parents, had grown up in stable financial and political times, created and engaged in a plethora of protest activities, including the feminist movement. The baby-boom generation soon changed the face of courtship and marriage. For instance, women took some of the initiative in the courting process. During the late 1960s, American women began to go out in groups or alone, go to bars without male escorts, and join singles' groups. By the early 1990s, more women than men placed personal advertisements for dates and mates in newspapers and utilized dating services. Women's growing dedication to jobs and careers, and the resulting increase in their work hours, suggest that this trend will continue as they actively look for companionship through a quick and safe means.

Many Americans "courted" by living together before marriage. In 1988 the Census Bureau estimated that the number of unmarried couples living together, which included never-married, divorced, and widowed people, had reached 2.3 million. Seven hundred thousand of these couples were raising children. Another 1.5 million same-sex couples were cohabiting, 92,000 of them with children.

Despite these changes in courtship, mate selection during the 1980s and early 1990s failed to be any more effective than in earlier times. Studies demonstrated that cohabiting couples tended to divorce sooner than couples who had not lived together before marriage. In

1989 a University of Wisconsin study indicated that 38 percent of cohabiting couples divorced within ten years, while only 27 percent of noncohabiting couples did so.

Psychologists argued that courtship had to take a different direction if it was to be effective, a direction that relied less on romance and more on common sense. In *The New Male-Female Relationship* (1984), psychologist Herb Goldberg recommended man-woman relationships based upon "authentic friendship, companionship, and sexuality" rather than "the romantic, illusion-filled approach to courtship and marriage" that dominated American culture.

Despite this advice, love continued to be the byword in marriage during the postwar period. Spouses valued each other's personal qualities above all other considerations. Once married, they often found themselves embroiled in arguments, but these were different arguments than their parents and grandparents had had. Two-earner families argued over division of household tasks and child care, duties that in an earlier era would have fallen automatically in the woman's realm. Many wives expected to participate in financial decisions and planning, and demanded a voice in frequency and quality of sexual relations. In return, they expected their husbands to participate in disciplining and playing with children.

At the same time, effective and fairly reliable birth control, notably contraceptive pills, allowed couples to eliminate or to limit childbearing if they chose. For the first time in history, sexual relations and conception were separated into two functions, each with its own norms and expectations. In addition, by the late 1970s and early 1980s, women especially began to believe they

By the late 1970s and for the first time in American history, sexual relations and conception were separated into two functions, each with its own norms and expectations.

did not need husbands to have children. Significant numbers of both poor, lower-class women *and* educated, middle-class women had babies without getting married. One-person and single-parent households mushroomed. By 1970, 17.1 percent of all American households consisted of only one person; by 1985, this figure reached 23 percent. In addition, single-parent families more than doubled. In 1985, single-parent families included 893,000 custodial fathers.

A growing tolerance for interracial marriages brought further diversity to the American family. In 1967 the U.S. Supreme Court struck down the last remaining miscegenation law in the United States, thus allowing black and white people to marry legally anywhere in the nation. Marriages that were mixed in terms of religion, ages, and other factors also increased and gained some acceptance. By the early 1990s, mixed marriages still exhibited a higher degree of stress and breakdown than homogamous matches, while the pattern and stability of homogamous marriage differed from group to group. Among Hispanics in the southwestern United States, for example, nearly 78 percent of Hispanic women between thirty-five and forty-four had a husband present, compared with approximately 68 percent among African Americans.

Americans tended to be far less tolerant of lesbian and gay couples who began to demand their right to legal marriage during the 1980s. Opponents called same-sex marriages outrageous and immoral, while supporters pointed out that Americans should be able to marry whomever they wished. In 1990 a special feature in *Newsweek* magazine noted that numerous same-sex couples were raising children without benefit of marriage. These children had been born in previous marriages, conceived by artificial insemination, conceived with a third person, or adopted. Clearly, the number of gay and lesbian couples who "married" during the early 1990s and the legal tangles surrounding their children would soon demand adjudication and perhaps an adjustment in legal codes.

Many significant changes occurred in divorce after the end of World War II. In 1949 South Carolina ended its prohibition of divorce. In 1966 New York expanded its list of grounds for divorce from only adultery by adding cruelty, abandonment, confinement in prison, and living apart for two years. Separation also became a precondition for divorce in many states. Even conservative South Carolina accepted a couple's separation for two years as a ground for divorce.

In 1970 California implemented no-fault divorce. No longer was divorce to be an adversary procedure in which the plaintiff had to blacken the reputation of the defendant. Other states soon followed California's lead. In 1971 Iowa became the second state to adopt no-fault divorce. By late 1977, only three states retained adversary divorce: Illinois, Pennsylvania, and South Dakota. Fifteen states had established irretrievable breakdown of a marriage as the sole ground for divorce, and sixteen had added irretrievable breakdown to existing grounds. By 1985, only South Dakota had fault divorce.

No-fault divorce changed divorce from the punishment of an offending spouse to a remedy for unendurable situations, made collusion between spouses unnecessary because one no longer had to "sue" the other, and provided relief to dissatisfied spouses on nonjudgmental grounds. Still, it was not the nirvana that reformers hoped it would be. In 1986 an article in the *New York Times Book Review* declared "no-fault" was "no fair." Its author reviewed several books that revealed the destructive effects of no-fault divorce on women and children, wives' lack of redress for a husband's adultery and defection from the marriage, and the failure of judges to offset women's low earnings with proportional alimony and property awards.

During the 1980s, experts tried to determine how legislators had adopted no-fault divorce without a searching analysis of what it might mean to women and children. Sociologist Lenore Weitzman explained that in the feminist flush of the late 1960s, legislators had envisioned wives as full economic partners. In practice, however, few wives earn as much as their husbands; many earn no cash income at all. The tragic result of no-fault divorce has been a contribution to the growing poverty of women and their children in the United States.

One of the most revealing symptoms of these changing attitudes toward marriage and divorce was the growing self-help literature. In 1945, marriage manuals were common and divorce books were few. Typically, marriage manuals of the 1940s described marriage as a lifetime undertaking and advised wives to cater to their husbands to keep their marriages intact. Authors who did address the issue of divorce did so in dismal terms. They referred to divorce as the nation's "number one social problem" and declared that women who allowed it to happen to them would be shunned by family and friends. The postwar back-to-the home movement, the teachings of Dr. Benjamin Spock, and such popular magazines as *Life* reinforced the view that women were meant to be wives and mothers; any other choice would bring them only despair and disdain.

By the 1960s, however, such traditional ideas were under attack. In 1961 President John F. Kennedy created the President's Commission on the Status of Women, and in 1963 Betty Friedan's *The Feminine Mystique* exposed the frustrations women felt regarding domestic life. Self-help literature responded accordingly. Although women's emancipation was linked to the divorce rate during the 1920s, writers now sharply indicted women as culprits. Working wives were too aggressive, unable to combine work and marriage, and ready to dispute their husbands' every word. Should they divorce, however, that same aggressiveness would stand them in good stead, for they could expect to receive satisfactions from their work that other women derived from marriage.

During the 1970s, conventional wisdom concerning marriage and divorce expanded even more. Responding to the feminist call for marriage based on equality and communication, self-help authors urged wives and mothers to become independent beings who deserved respect and reciprocity in marriage. A host of books such as Jerry Greenwald's *Creative Intimacy* (1975) instructed readers, who were primarily women, how to achieve the ideal marriage. From self-counseling to biofeedback, from no-fault marriage to creative aggression, self-help manuals offered ways to avoid divorce.

By the mid 1970s and early 1980s, a huge number of divorce manuals had appeared. They carefully shunned the word "failure" and emphasized a practical approach to divorce instead. Because no-fault, community property, and other recent developments had complicated divorce, they explained its intricacies and included charts, worksheets, checklists, and time schedules. Still others specialized in emotional advice. Written largely by marriage counselors and psychotherapists, the books offered approaches developed through counseling patients and leading workshops. They stressed personal growth through divorce and the ability to find happiness as divorced people. Another new line was the emphasis on getting professional help—lawyers, accountants, and counselors. Marriage and divorce were no longer matters to be handled by the individual. Nor was divorce any longer a matter of embarrassment and shame.

The 1990s and Beyond

During the early 1990s, the great American debate concerning marriage and divorce continued. Some studies claimed that the marriage rate was rising—that marriage was back in style—while others predicted the end of marriage in the twenty-first century. At the same time, some studies maintained that the divorce rate continued to rise, while others argued that it was receding somewhat. Due to the variations and difficulties in methods of computation, statisticians were unable to agree upon one position or the other. Even after the U.S. Bureau of the Census established divorce registration areas in 1958 as a way of collecting necessary data, statistics remained erratic due to state inconsistencies in reporting and the common practice of including annulments and separations in divorce statistics. And as improved collection methods and computer analysis developed, it was soon clear that every means of computing the divorce rate had its weak point. For instance, comparing the number of divorces with the number of marriages in a given year ignores the fact that most divorces are of marriages contracted in previous years. And if the number of marriages in a given year is unusually low, the divorce rate will appear high. Or if the number of divorces is compared with the population in a given area and the population contains a large number of children under marriageable age, the divorce rate will appear low. In other words, there is no such thing as a valid, conclusive divorce rate.

But what is clear, despite the method of computation, is that the overwhelming majority of Americans marry—and remarry—and remarry yet again. Marriage rates have held steady between 8 and 10 per 1,000 each year. Although the marriage rate drops during times of economic depression, it hovers around 10 per 1,000 during stable periods. The censuses of 1980 and 1990 indicated that the rate had held stable at around 9 to 10 per 1,000.

In 1990, "Mister Rogers," longtime host of a widely aired children's television program, commented "If someone told me twenty years ago that I was going to produce a whole week on divorce, I would never have believed them."

It was also clear that the overall trend in the divorce rate is upward. The rate rose after World War I, dropped somewhat during the Great Depression (although the number of desertions may very well have increased), rose after World War II, settled on a plateau between 1955 and 1963, and then began to rise again. Figures also show that since the end of World War II in 1945, urban areas continue to have more divorce than rural areas; African Americans divorce more frequently than other racial groups (although the divorce rate of Mexican Americans and Asians is rising); growing numbers of women employed outside the home seek divorces; an increasing number of families with children dissolve; and the West has the highest rate of divorce, the South is second, and the Northeast third.

If the divorce rate continues to rise, family relationships will become incredibly complicated. Statistics show that the more frequently a person divorces, the shorter the duration of his or her next marriage. In 1983 the average duration of marriage for all divorcing couples was 9.6 years; for the once-married, 10.8 years; for the twice-married, 7.0 years; and for the thrice-married, 4.9 years for women and 5.1 years for men. It may eventually become mandatory for remarriers to negotiate and sign prenuptial agreements to protect property and children.

Divorce has become more acceptable than ever before; it is commonplace in the media and in daily life. In 1990, "Mister Rogers" commented on the effect of the growth of divorce on his widely aired children's television program: "If someone told me twenty years ago that I was going to produce a whole week on divorce, I never would have believed them."

By 1990, another attitudinal change was evident. Although religious and other groups continued to support lifetime marriage and to oppose divorce, the numbers of divorces convinced them to recognize and attempt to deal with its existence. Most Catholic parishes, for example, required extensive premarital counseling, offered marital counseling and marital enrichment workshops, and organized workshops and other programs for separated and divorced Catholics.

Today, approximately one marriage out of two will end in divorce. Of course, this statistic neglects multiple remarriers and divorcers. It also overlooks the fact that people live far longer than they did during the nineteenth century; thus, divorce terminates a marriage that would have ended in the death of one spouse in earlier eras. It might also be speculated that given the modern system of computers, social security numbers, and other identification, it is more difficult for a spouse to desert than formerly. Perhaps a number of potential desertions become divorces instead.

This summary of courtship, marriage, separation, and divorce might well be interpreted as a distressing picture of the American family, one that seems to portend destruction and despair. Or it might be seen as a hopeful scenario. Because old norms are being challenged and changed does not necessarily indicate decline and social ills. It is far more likely that American society is in a transition phase—an evolution to new forms and mores. After all, in other contexts, Americans are fond of calling rapid change and lack of permanence by the name of progress.

Rather than bemoaning these changes, it is more helpful in the long run to devise constructive coping strategies. Courtship could be improved by counseling and education so that it functions as effective mate selection. Marriage and remarriage would benefit from increased community support, such services as child care, and extensive counseling resources. Separation could be used as an exploration and counseling period rather than as a road to divorce. And divorce could be accepted as a long-term historical trend, an integral part of American life that can be made into a more positive, healing institution than it is now. The old and continuing problems of support for a dependent spouse, division of property, and custody and care of children must be addressed more thoroughly and dealt with more effectively.

During the next few decades, diversity in American marriage and dissolution practices will surely continue. Many Mexican Americans, for example, are likely to cling to more traditional ideas, while Hollywood stars and other public figures will continue to engage in multiple marriages and divorces. American society may also find itself creating and accepting new forms of marriage and dissolution. Some couples have tried open marriage and cooperative marriage in recent decades. Many have tried no-fault divorce with a wide range of results. During the twenty-first century, however, contract marriage may become commonplace. And at time of divorce, one court may grant a dissolution while another may decide custody and financial arrangements. Premarital and post-divorce counseling may become mandatory.

Despite the potential changes, the historical record indicates that the American family will survive. Marriages may be short in duration, long-distance, two-career, or gay or lesbian, but Americans will continue to court, marry, and remarry in huge numbers. Perhaps it is fallacious to judge marital success by the length of a marriage. In coming years, marriage may increasingly be judged by the success it achieved while in force, the fulfillment of mates' expectations, and the harmony and positive nature of its dissolution, should it end.

[See also Family Structures; Gender Roles and Relations; Manners and Etiquette; Reproduction and Parenthood; Sexual Behavior and Morality.]

BIBLIOGRAPHY

Courtship

Bailey, Beth L. *From Front Porch to Back Seat: Courtship in Twentieth-Century America* (1988).

Cancian, Francesca. *Love in America: Gender and Self-Development* (1987).

Lystra, Karen. *Searching the Heart: Women, Men, and Romantic Love in Nineteenth-Century America* (1989).

Rothman, Ellen K. *Hands and Hearts: A History of Courtship in America* (1984).

Seidman, Steven. *Romantic Longings: Love in America, 1830–1980* (1991).

Whyte, Martin King. *Dating, Mating, and Marriage* (1990).

Marriage

Basch, Norma. *In the Eyes of the Law: Women, Marriage, and Property in Nineteenth-Century New York* (1982).

Butler, Edgar W. *Traditional Marriage and Emerging Alternatives* (1979).

Davis, Kingsley, and Amyra Grossbard-Shechtman, eds. *Contemporary Marriage: Comparative Perspectives on a Changing Institution* (1985).

Degler, Carl N. *At Odds: Women and the Family in America from the Revolution to the Present* (1980).

D'Emilio, John, and Estelle B. Freedman. *Intimate Matters: A History of Sexuality in America* (1988).

Demos, John. *A Little Commonwealth: Family Life in Plymouth Colony* (1970).

Ehrenreich, Barbara, and Deidre English. *For Her Own Good: 150 Years of the Experts' Advice to Women* (1978).

Gordon, Linda. *Heroes of Their Own Lives: The Politics and History of Family Violence, Boston, 1880–1960* (1988).

Grossberg, Michael. *Governing the Hearth: Law and the Family in Nineteenth-Century America* (1985).

Kern, Louis J. *An Ordered Love: Sex Roles and Sexuality, in Victorian Utopias-The Shakers, the Mormons, and the Oneida Community* (1981).

May, Elaine Tyler. *Homeward Bound. American Families in the Cold War Era* (1988).

Mintz, Steven. *A Prison of Expectations: The Family in Victorian Culture* (1983).

Mintz, Steven, and Susan Kellogg. *Domestic Revolutions: A Social History of American Family Life* (1988).

Oneida Community, *Slavery and Marriage: A Dialogue* (1850).

Pleck, Elizabeth H. *Domestic Tyranny: The Making of Social Policy Against Family Violence from Colonial Times to the Present* (1987).

Salmon, Marylynn. *Women and the Law of Property in Early America* (1986).

Scarf, Maggie. *Intimate Partners: Patterns in Love and Marriage* (1987).

Spurlock, John C. *Free Love: Marriage and Middle-Class Radicalism in America, 1825–1860* (1988).

Swerdlow, Amy, Renate Bridenthal, Joan Kelly, and Phyllis Vine. *Household and Kin: Families in Flux* (1981).

Separation and Divorce

Griswold, Robert L. *Family and Divorce in California, 1850–1890: Victorian Illusions and Everyday Realities* (1982).

Halem, Lynne Carol. *Divorce Reform: Changing Legal and Social Perspectives* (1980).

Jacob, Herbert. *Silent Revolution: The Transformation of Divorce Law in the United States* (1988).

Lantz, Herman R. *Marital Incompatibility and Social Change in Early America* (1976).

May, Elaine Tyler. *Great Expectations. Marriage and Divorce in Post-Victorian America* (1980).

Phillips, Roderick. *Putting Asunder. A History of Divorce in Western Society* (1988).

Riley, Glenda. *Divorce: An American Tradition* (1991).

Weitzman, Lenore J. *The Divorce Revolution: The Unexpected Social and Economic Consequences for Women and Children in America* (1985).

— GLENDA RILEY

CULTURAL INSTITUTIONS

See URBAN CULTURAL INSTITUTIONS

THE CULTURE OF CONSUMPTION

During the early stages of industrialization, the provision of basic necessities absorbed most of the nation's productive capacity. Railroads, iron and steel, foundries and machine shops, lumber, textiles, and meat packing ranked among the leading industries in 1900. By the middle of the twentieth century, however, the shift from heavy industry to consumer goods—automobiles, household appliances, radios and television sets, ready-made clothing, prepared food—was unmistakable. At the height of the postwar boom, consumer debt (excluding real estate loans) increased from $27.4 billion to $41.7 billion (52 percent) in the four years from 1952 to 1956 alone. Half of the families in the middle-income range carried installment payments.

Their ancestors had been taught that "he that goes a borrowing goes a sorrowing," in the saying of Benjamin Franklin's Poor Richard. In the "affluent society," as John Kenneth Galbraith called it in 1958, this homespun philosophy seemed as archaic as homespun clothing. The morality of thrift, it seemed, was hopelessly misplaced in an economy based on immediate gratification. "Buy now, pay later" sounded like a more appropriate axiom. Who could object to a little everyday extravagance when it helped to sustain unprecedented prosperity, an outpouring of goods? In supermarkets, shoppers chose from "thousands of items on the high-piled shelves," according to an excited report in *Life* magazine, "until their carts became cornucopias filled with an abundance that no other country in the world has ever known."

The growing acceptance of indebtedness provides one measure of the degree to which a culture of consumption has come to shape Americans' habits and expectations. The consumption of goods and services that do not contribute to the bare maintenance of life goes on in every society, of course, and as soon as a society accumulates a surplus beyond subsistence, consumption often assumes riotous proportions. In the book of Revelation (18:12–13), we read of ancient Babylon with its "merchandise of gold, and silver, and precious stones, and of pearls, and fine linen, and purple, and silk, and scarlet, and all thyine wood, and all manner vessels of ivory, and all manner vessels of most precious wood, and of brass, and iron, and marble, and cinnamon, and odours, and ointments, and frankincense, and wine, and oil, and fine flour, and wheat, and beasts, and sheep, and horses, and chariots, and slaves, and souls of men." As this recital reminds us, however, a luxurious way of living usually rests on the back of a degraded laboring class, servile in condition if not always in law. It is only when the masses become consumers in their own right, entitled, as they see it, to the comforts formerly monopolized by the few—entitled even to an occasional taste of genuine luxury—that we can properly speak of a whole culture pervaded by the ideal of consumption.

Theories of Consumption

In the United States, a mass market in consumer goods began to take shape in the 1920s, collapsed in the Great Depression, and finally became the dominant fact of economic life in the 1940s and 1950s, thanks to the combined effects of government spending and the improvements in workers' standard of living achieved by labor unions. But the hope that mass consumption would generate economic growth and prosperity on an unprecedented scale had a much longer history. It figured prominently in the political economy of the eighteenth century, especially in the writings of Bernard Mandeville, David Hume, and Adam Smith. Mandeville (1670–1733) disputed the long-accepted idea that luxury led to corruption and civic decline. Hume (1711–1776) insisted that a refinement of taste, even when it led to sensual gratification, was a mark not of decadence but of social and economic progress. According to Smith (1723–1790), the "effort of every man to better his condition" was the "principle from which public and national, as well as private opulence is originally derived" (*Wealth of Nations*, vol. 1, p. 348). Smith admitted that ordinary people had an exaggerated respect for wealth and for the "vain and empty distinctions of greatness"; but even if worldly goods could not buy happiness or peace of mind, it was "well that nature imposes upon us in this manner," he thought (*Theory of Moral Sentiments*, pp. 182–183). Ambitious men and women worked harder, as long as they had some prospect of success, than those who lacked the acquisitive impulse.

Insatiable desire, formerly condemned as a source of social instability and spiritual corruption, thus acquired the sanction of economic theory. The appetite for better things, once these things were placed within reach of the common people, would lead to the indefinite expansion of the productive forces necessary to satisfy it. In the United States, a country blessed with an abundance of land and a shortage of labor that made for high wages, the democratic implications of the new political economy were spelled out by reformers who identified social improvement with a revolution of rising expectations. "Improvement" rested on a general expansion of the taste not just for material comforts but for amenities and refinements of every kind, moral and mental as well as material. The Unitarian clergyman Theodore Parker (1810–1860), by way of contrasting slavery with free labor, argued that "every farmer and day-laborer" in Connecticut was a "consumer" of "tea, coffee, sugar, rice, molasses, salt, and spices; of cotton, woolen, and silk goods, ribbons and bonnets; of shoes and hats; of beds and other furniture; of hardware, tinware, and cutlery; of crockery and glassware; of clocks and jewelry; of books, paper, and the like." The effects of this consumption stimulated the "mechanic and the merchant" to improve production and distribution; their efforts stimulated the farmer and laborer "in return, all grow up together; each has a market . . . continually enlarging and giving vent to superior wares" ("A Letter on Slavery," p. 65).

In the flush times following the Civil War, the equation of improvement with democracy no longer appeared as plausible as it had to antebellum reformers like Parker. The rich set a high, some would have said an obscene, standard of consumption; but it was no longer clear that hard-pressed farmers and wage earners were in any position to follow their example or to aspire to anything, indeed, beyond sheer survival. In a nation polarized between extremes of wealth and poverty, social theorists began to argue that progress and poverty went hand in hand. Henry George (1839–1897) took the position that the accumulation of wealth widened the gap between the rulers and the ruled; that advanced civilizations had to devote more and more of their resources to the maintenance of an idle ruling class; and that they finally collapsed, top-heavy, of their own weight. Thorstein Veblen's (1857–1929) attack on the leisure class could be cited in support of the same conclusions. Defenders of American capitalism, meanwhile, retreated from the claim that economic growth would benefit everyone in the long run. Instead they justified inequality on the grounds that it represented the "survival of the fittest." Increasingly worried about overproduction, they despaired of expanding the domestic market. Overseas expansion, they believed, was the only way to absorb the American economy's excess capacity. Charles A. Conant (1861–1915), a leading imperialist, estimated that the "creation of new demands at home" would continue "as long as human desires continue expansible," but he pointed out, rather gloomily, that "there has never been a time before when the proportion of capital to be absorbed was so great in proportion to possible new demands" ("The Economic Basis of 'Imperialism,'" p. 337).

The Case for Consumption

Faced on the one hand with agitation for a radical redistribution of wealth and on the other with an aggressive imperialism (which invoked the same Darwinian ideology that was used to justify inequality at home), spokesmen for what came to be known as the Progressive movement revived the argument, in a bolder and more sweeping form, that the only hope for democracy lay in mass consumption. Some of these Progressives harked back to Adam Smith, whose economic theory contained a democratic undercurrent, according to the sociologist Albion Small (1854–1926), that was usually overlooked by his latter-day disciples. If Smith had lived until the end of the nineteenth century, Small maintained, he would have welcomed democratic reforms that increased the demand for goods and led to a general improvement in the standard of living. Simon Patten (1852–1922), a leading economist, attempted to refute pessimists like Henry George by arguing that consumer spending annulled the "ancient tragic model" of growth and decay, progress and poverty. "Those who would predict to-morrow's economic states from a study of the economic states of Rome or Venice," according to Patten, overlooked the unprecedented abundance made possible by the modern productive system, which placed civilization on a "new basis" (*The New Basis of Civilization*, pp. 9, 14). Walter Weyl, one of the editors of the influential weekly *The New Republic*, invoked Patten's "brilliant" analysis of the "transition from a pain economy to a pleasure economy" in support of the contention that abundance, which generated a growing demand for a "full life for all members of society," represented the best "hope of a full democracy" (*The New Democracy*, pp. 191, 197). Another admirer and protégé of Patten, the political scientist Rexford Tugwell, later a member of Franklin D. Roosevelt's brain trust, likewise identified democracy with higher wages, more leisure, and better recreation. But it was left to John Maynard Keynes (1883–1946), whose theory of deficit spending guided the economic policies of the New Deal, Harry Truman's Fair Deal, John F. Kennedy's New Frontier, and Lyndon Johnson's Great Society, to work out the most sophisticated rationale for mass consumption as the key to full employment and economic growth. Orthodox economists had exaggerated the value of abstinence and thrift, Keynes argued. The expectation of profits, not abstinence, was the engine that drove economic enterprise, and profits in turn presupposed a rising standard of living in the population as a whole and a general desire for a more abundant existence.

Social and economic theories that tied democracy to abundance and consumption not only influenced public policy—chiefly by making full employment, high wages, and the management of consumer demand important priorities—but also helped to undermine the weight of moral traditions that condemned extravagance and self-indulgence. Both the biblical and the republican tradition saw nothing but trouble in the excess of wants over needs. Theorists of consumption, on the other hand, celebrated this same excess as a "superlative machine," in Patten's words, " . . . for the quickening of progress" (p. 55). This is not to say that economic theory alone was enough to discredit the austere ethic of plain living and high thinking or that a culture of consumption was the outcome envisioned by all those who condemned the old "puritanical" morality of scarcity. In the years immediately preceding World War I, inherited moral traditions came under attack from a variety of critics advancing quite different and often incompatible programs.

Some of these critics wanted to replace religion with a new religion of art. Others took their cue from science—a more reliable guide to the conduct of life, in their view, than moral precepts founded on religion. Avant-garde intellectuals, sometimes appealing to the authority of Freud, proclaimed the liberation of personality from repression. Feminists proclaimed the emancipation of women. Professional healers began to articulate a therapeutic ethic that was more concerned to make people healthy than to make them wise or good. Social workers questioned the value of self-reliance in a complex, interdependent society in which people had to rely on others. In general, the expansion of professional authority had the effect of discouraging people from relying on their own resources—on their local communities, their neighborhoods, and their churches. The churches themselves, influenced by liberal theology and the Social Gospel, redefined their mission as a form of therapy designed to assure peace of mind, not to activate a slumbering sense of sin.

The Celebration of Waste

All these developments tended to weaken moral traditions that stressed the value of hard work and self-command, cautioned against extravagant expectations of a trouble-free existence, and held individuals strictly accountable for their actions. In the 1920s, permissive moralities spread from elites to the masses. The postwar "revolution in manners and morals," much discussed at the time, in retrospect can be understood as the flowering of a consumer culture. The advertising industry, which first achieved prominence in the 1920s, allied itself with movements of cultural liberation or at least exploited liberationist ideologies for its own purposes. Edward Bernays, one of the founders of modern advertising and public relations, boasted of having broken the taboo that kept women from smoking in public. Seizing on cigarettes as "torches of freedom" and invoking the memory of prewar parades for woman suffrage, he persuaded a contingent of women to join New York's Easter parade in 1929, ostentatiously smoking "as a protest against women's inequality," as he put it (Stuart Ewen, *Captains of Consciousness*, pp. 160–161). The flapper, who personified both the emancipation of women and the revolt of youth, appealed to advertisers as the personification of consumption as well. She embodied the spirit of change, the restless craving for novelty and excitement recognized by advertisers as the most important stimulus to consumption. Since young people were presumably more receptive to change than adults, advertising psychologists stressed the importance of introducing inno vations by addressing

This 1914 Model T sold for $550 with equipment. Henry Ford hated extravagance and froze the design of the Model A believing that Ford owners would prefer to buy one car to last a lifetime.

them to the young. The rapid pace of change made even children more knowledgeable about the new world of commodities than their parents. "Were it not for the children, some of you parents would not know even now what a tremendous change for the better Paramount has [made] in motion pictures" (Ewen, p. 148). Such advertisements had the effect of elevating the young to arbiters of taste, whose consumer preferences had to be respected by adults struggling to keep up with the changing times.

Advertisers made no secret of their intention to promote novelty for its own sake, in the hope that consumers would exchange perfectly serviceable goods for goods that conformed to the latest fashions. Earnest Elmo Calkins (1868–1964), one of the first to grasp the principle of "artificial obsolescence," distinguished between goods "we use" and "those we *use up*." It was the second category that fascinated advertisers and the manufacturers who followed their lead. "Artificial obsolescence," Calkins explained, meant the continual redesign of products, "entirely apart from any mechanical improvement, to make them markedly new, and encourage new buying, exactly as the fashion designers make shirts longer so you can no longer be happy with your short ones." The taste for "better things," as William L. Day pointed out, required an "ideal of beauty that happens to be current." "The world depends on obsolescence and new merchandise," said the industrial designer John Vassos (Jeffrey L. Meikle, *Twentieth-Century Limited*, pp. 16, 70, 83).

RESISTANCE TO CREATIVE WASTE. This open celebration of waste, so obviously incompatible with the ideals of thrift and saving in which most Americans had been raised, met with a good deal of initial resistance in the business world. Henry Ford (1863–1947), a pioneer in the technology of mass production, took an unfashionably narrow view of consumption. In 1926, he declared that Ford owners represented the "vast majority[who] cling to the old-fashioned idea of living within their incomes." A year later, he brought out the Model A and immediately froze its design, to the dismay of the advertising industry. His intention, he said, was to manufacture a car "so strong and so well-made that no one ought ever to have to buy a second one." But Ford's rival Alfred P. Sloan (1875–1966) had already pointed the way to the future by introducing annual model changes at General Motors. By 1927, his Chevrolet was outselling the Model T; the introduction of the Model A, notwithstanding Ford's hatred of extravagance, was itself a concession to the principle of "creative waste," as the advertising consultant Christine Frederick called it (Roland Marchand, *Advertising the American Dream*, pp. 157–159). Eventually Ford capitulated to fashion and allowed his designers to introduce new models every year, like his increasingly successful competitors.

The Great Depression forced millions of Americans to spend less freely than before, but it did not revive respect for the simple life. Walter B. Pitkin (1878–1953), a Columbia professor, warned advertisers that hard times might encourage a "return to the primitive, a back-to-the-soil type of living" (Marchand, pp. 300–301). Instead of deploring such a prospect, a handful of prominent figures actually welcomed it. Senator John H. Bankhead (1872–1946) of Alabama called for an agrarian revival, a "restoration of that small yeoman class which has been the backbone of every great civilization." Ford himself, still unreconciled to the culture of consumption, launched an abortive movement back to the land in 1932: "The land! That is where our roots are. No unemployment insurance can be compared to an alliance between a man and a plot of land" (Schlesinger, *The Age of Roosevelt: The Coming of the New Deal*, pp. 361–363).

Beginning in the 1920s, advertisers made no secret of their intention to promote novelty for its own sake, in the hope that consumers would exchange perfectly serviceable goods for goods that conformed to the latest fashions.

SPENDING FOR PROSPERITY. But nothing came of these appeals. Those who set the terms of public discussion argued that spending, not saving, held out the best hope of prosperity. Advertisements and motion pictures continued to admire the rich, dwelling in loving detail on their pearls, yachts, and luxurious mansions. Advertisements designed to exploit the "whole ground of feminine longing and feminine envy," as the Hoover Company explained to its salesmen, encouraged middle- and working-class women to aspire to opulence and ease. "You see her wearing a plain little house dress, but she sees herself someday in velvet and ermine." In the meantime, she used a vacuum cleaner "that the richest woman in the world can't outdo her in." The idea behind its advertising campaign, Hoover pointed out, was to picture the "woman of wealth and the woman of little means," to "contrast their situation" and reveal the "gulf" between them, and then to "bridge that gulf" by showing that both owned a Hoover. A trade journal, *Advertising and Selling*, held up the Hoover campaign as the epitome of psychological insight. "Ordinary folks are always pleased to know they can have the products good enough for Vanderbilts, Astors, Huttons, Mellons, and Fords" (quoted in Marchand, pp. 292–295).

World War II, in spite of shortages and rationing, did nothing to reduce the social prestige of goods or the appeal of consumption. On the contrary, wartime propaganda explained the war essentially as a defense of the high standard of living Americans were privileged to enjoy. The "American way of life" was now identified so closely with the American standard of living, and freedom with a wide choice of competing consumer goods, that appeals to any larger war aims seemed almost superfluous—unlikely to succeed in any case. The postwar migration to the suburbs, even more clearly than the war effort, indicated how completely the consumerist ideal had eclipsed older conceptions of the American dream. Any lingering sense of a common civic identity was unlikely to flourish in communities populated by rootless, transient individuals and organized around the pursuit of private pleasures. Single-family dwellings and private motorcars, not to mention the absence of civic amenities, made this commitment to privacy unmistakable. Physically removed from the workplace, suburbs were devoted to leisure by definition, and the vast housing tracts that grew up on their fringes, pushing farther and farther into the countryside, announced in every detail of their design that leisure was to be enjoyed in private—more often than not, in front of a television set.

In 1946, only six thousand television sets were manufactured in the United States. By 1953, the figure had risen to seven million. The number of sets in use rose from seventeen thousand in 1946 to ninety million in 1971. This seductive new medium promoted consumption not merely in advertising but in programs that typically showed suburban families surrounded by their possessions. Its imagery of abundance, however fantastic and dreamlike, had a firm basis in fact. In the 1950s, the number of Americans owning their dwellings surpassed the number of renters for the first time in the twentieth century. By 1960, a quarter of those dwellings had been built during the previous decade—striking evidence of the postwar housing boom. Only 12 percent of them lacked a bathtub or shower, as compared to 39 percent in 1940. Ninety-eight percent had a refrigerator. Thirteen percent had air conditioning, and by 1968 this figure had risen to 37 percent.

In the 1920s, most industrial workers still enjoyed neither paid holidays nor vacations. By 1963, eight holidays and a two-week vacation were the norm. Leisure spending accounted for 15 percent of the gross national product by 1950. The emergence of a youth market further testified to the shift from a production to a consumption ethic. In 1963 American adolescents spent $22 billion—an amount, as William E. Leuchtenburg points out, that was double the gross national product of Austria (*A Troubled Feast*, p. 65).

It was no wonder that America was now admired when it was not hated or feared—less for its democratic institutions or its championship of democratic revolutions abroad, as in the old days, than for its vast and seemingly inexhaustible wealth. A lavish display of American products in a Swiss department store, accompanied by the injunction to "live like an American," left no doubt about the meaning of that slogan. When Vice President Richard M. Nixon and Soviet Premier Nikita Khrushchev debated the merits of capitalism and communism at the American National Exhibition in Moscow in 1959, it was entirely fitting that their argument took place in a model kitchen full of laborsaving appliances. What Nixon and Khrushchev said on that occasion was of no importance; the goods spoke for themselves.

THE AFFLUENT SOCIETY. Consumer goods spoke so loudly, in fact, that social critics began to fear that the voice of moderation and sobriety was in danger of being completely submerged in the clamorous invitation to buy, to borrow, and to spend without a second thought, and to indulge every whim as quickly as it came to mind. When Dwight Eisenhower engaged an advertising firm to promote his campaign for the presidency in 1952, many commentators objected to this packaging of a candidate by Madison Avenue—a practice that threatened to replace political discourse with advertising slogans. Mass promotion, it was now clear, would not stop with the marketing of washing machines and refrigerators. In *The Image* (1962), Daniel Boorstin pointed out that images of reality threatened to replace reality itself, so that politics came to revolve not around events but around "pseudo-events" staged for the benefit of the mass media. Paul Goodman argued that American youth were "growing up absurd," unable to look forward to useful, honorable work that made some lasting contribution to society instead of producing goods no one really needed. Galbraith's *Affluent Society* (1958) called attention to the contrast between "private affluence and public squalor." According to Galbraith, neither economists nor politicians and administrators admitted the "diminishing urgency of wants" in the age of abundance. Instead they sought to engineer a constantly rising level of private consumption, while public services and amenities were allowed to decay.

> The family which takes its mauve and cerise, air-conditioned, power-steered, and power-braked automobile out for a tour passes through cities that are badly paved, made hideous by litter, blighted buildings, billboards, and posts for wires that should long since have been put underground. They pass on into a countryside that has been rendered largely invisible by commercial art. . . . They picnic on exquisitely packaged food from a portable icebox by a polluted stream and go on to spend the night at a park which is a menace to public health and morals. . . . Is this, indeed, the American genius? (Galbraith, pp. 146, 253)

Critics of Consumption

In the 1960s, criticism of consumption figured prominently in the rhetoric of the New Left. The 1962 Port Huron Statement, founding charter of the Students for a Democratic Society, condemned marketing techniques intended to "create pseudo-needs in consumers" and to make "wasteful 'planned obsolescence" a permanent feature of business strategy" (Miller, "*Democracy Is in the Streets*," p. 339). This was a familiar line of criticism by that time; but spokesmen for the New Left soon began to elaborate it into a more sweeping condemnation of American society. Not content merely to repeat the indictment already drawn up by liberals like Boorstin and Galbraith, they maintained that mass consumption was part of a larger strategy of "social control" deliberately designed to tranquilize the public and to prevent discontent from finding political expression. The "new authoritarianism," as Herbert Marcuse called it, provided "satisfaction in a way which generates submission and weakens the rationality of protest." Instead of using forcible repression to keep people in line, it relied on "repressive desublimation" and "repressive tolerance." Theodore Roszak, building on Marcuse's work, explained: "The strategy chosen is not harsh repression, but rather the *Playboy* version of total permissiveness. . . . The business of inventing and flourishing treacherous parodies of freedom, joy, and fulfillment becomes an indispensable form of social control" (*Making of a Counter Culture*, pp. 14–15). Radical theorists of the sixties turned criticism of affluence on its head. In their view, "symbolic sexual stimulation" and other "attenuated forms" of pleasure, in Philip Slater's words, served to maintain the illusion of scarcity in the midst of abundance. "Our society has become so affluent," Slater wrote, "that it threatens to give the show away—to disclose the absurdity of the scarcity assumptions in which it is based." Capitalist production could now maintain itself only by getting people "to substitute products for real satisfactions"—by "generating esoteric erotic itches that cannot be scratched outside the world of fantasy, but lend themselves well to marketing" (*The Pursuit of Loneliness*, pp. 90–92). Americans did not really think of themselves as an affluent society at all; if they did, they would come to see that they already had everything they needed in the way of material goods.

CONSUMPTION AS SOCIAL CONTROL. Consumption thus came to be understood by the New Left as a system of total control, more insidious than harsher forms of totalitarianism because it rested not on violence but on the semblance of hedonism and self-indulgence. If totalitarian states terrorized their subjects into submission, the culture of consumption allegedly achieved the same result by gentler methods. Advertising was a more sophisticated and therefore more effective method of thought control than torture, by means of which totalitarian regimes brainwashed political prisoners into confessions of political nonconformity. In America, conformity was assured by a type of brainwashing unrecognizable as such (except to those equipped with theoretical insight into its operation), since consumers were supposedly free to make their own decisions. In reality, their capacity for independent judgment, according to theorists of the New Left, was systematically destroyed by the propaganda of commodities.

This indictment contained a core of truth, which could not be dismissed on the grounds that consumers seldom buy mindlessly what they are told to buy. Those who replied to the New Left by questioning the efficacy of advertising, often citing spectacular marketing failures like the Edsel or the Nehru suit, never managed to counter the more important point that advertising serves not just to promote a given product but to promote consumption as a way of life. The importance of advertising is not that it invariably succeeds in its im-

New Left spokesmen of the early 1960s charged that mass consumption was part of a larger strategy of "social control" designed to tranquilize the public and prevent discontent from finding political expression.

mediate purpose, much less that it lobotomizes the consumer into a state of passive acquiescence, but simply that it surrounds people with images of the good life in which happiness depends on consumption. The ubiquity of such images leaves little space for competing conceptions of the good life. A society in which the market is the central institution, moreover, is quite different from a society that restricts the operation of the market to ascertainable limits—for example, by regulating wages and prices, by setting aside certain lands or facilities for common use, by passing sumptuary laws and other impediments to consumption, or simply by declaring that some things are not for sale. Such restrictions are by no means unknown even today, but they seem destined to wither away as the market inexorably expands.

THE COMMERCIALIZATION OF LIFE. Mass markets do not easily coexist with institutions that operate according to principles antithetical to the market—schools and universities, newspapers and magazines, charities, families. Sooner or later, it tends to absorb them all. It puts an almost irresistible pressure on every activity to justify itself in the only terms recognized by the market—to become a business proposition, to pay its own way, to show black ink on the bottom line. It turns news into entertainment, scholarship into professional careerism, social work into the scientific management of poverty. Even the family, widely regarded as the last bastion of spontaneous fellow feeling, comes to be modeled on the market. It becomes a little factory for turning out a distinctive product, the well-adjusted child. Parents are encouraged to consume great quantities of expert advice in order to improve the product. Professional helpers advise and intimidate them, correct their mistakes, or replace them altogether when the occasion seems to warrant this ultimate form of interference. The child-care industry itself competes for control of the child with the mass media and the advertisers, who regard children not as products but as consumers, endlessly demanding and entitled to immediate gratification.

The impact of mass communications on the world of ideas provides another example of the expansion of the market at the expense of activities initially resistant to commercialization. Improved technologies of communication would seem to make it possible for artists and intellectuals to reach a wider audience than they ever dreamed of. By transforming the certification of literary and artistic excellence, however, the new media turn ideas into commodities. Their appetite for novelty (that is, for old formulas in new packages), their reliance on immediate recognition of the product, and their need for ideological revolutions at regular intervals make "visibility" the overriding test of intellectual merit. The first judgment of a book or an idea becomes the last; a book either becomes a best-seller or drops out of sight; and the book in any case takes a back seat to the article or interview it occasions. Here, as elsewhere, journalism no longer reports events; it creates them. It refers less and less to actual events and more and more to a circular and self-validating process of publicity. It no longer presupposes a world that exists independently of the images made about it.

The self-referential character of mass media usually defeats attempts to hold them up to high standards of objectivity, for example by enforcing "truth in advertising." Movements intended to protect consumers against false or misleading advertisements, to organize consumers' lobbies, or to exploit collective buying power for constructive political ends once seemed to hold out some promise. Collective action by consumers, however, has proved almost impossible to achieve. Consumers have no interests in common, except perhaps for a common stake in truthful communication; and the campaign against flagrant falsehood does not confront the real difficulty. The mass media seldom traffic in outright lies. Their effect is more subtle: to obliterate the very distinction between truth and falsehood. They conjure up a world in which it is hard to tell the difference between fantasy and actual events—a world that bears a certain resemblance to the world of everyday experience but resists moral or epistemological judgment. The only mode of judgment that seems appropriate to the mass media is aesthetic—whether an advertisement or a news program is sufficiently dramatic, amusing, or otherwise appealing to compel attention and to get high ratings from the agencies that monitor audience response.

> *The self-referential character of the mass media usually defeats attempts to hold their members up to high standards of objectivity—for example, by enforcing "truth in advertising."*

For the same reasons, the influence of consumerism on politics is not confined to the packaging of candidates. The mass media gradually replace political parties as the agents of political education. The media define the issues, select the candidates, and announce the outcome of elections in advance by continually polling the electorate. Opinion surveys help to shape opinion instead of merely recording it. Indeed they make the concept of public opinion increasingly anachronistic by destroying collective memory, by replacing accountable authorities with media-selected "spokesmen" and political celebrities, and by treating all ideas, all programs, all controversies and disagreements, as equally newsworthy, equally deserving of fitful attention, and therefore equally inconsequential and forgettable. In a culture of consumption, political life ceases to be guided by controversies about the common good and becomes another exercise in mass promotion. The citizen disappears into the consumer of political imagery, and the pressure to please and entertain the electorate makes it increasingly unlikely that political leaders will speak truthfully, make hard choices, or call for sacrifices in the general interest.

The Revisionist Defense of Consumption

Historical studies of the culture of consumption have not always distinguished very carefully between the erosion of citizenship and public culture, on the one hand, and the allegedly totalitarian implications of consumption on the other. The first studies, which began to appear in the 1970s, were heavily influenced by the New Left and specifically by Herbert Marcuse (1898–1979) and other members of the Frankfurt school of social theory. The works of Stuart Ewen, for example, leave the impression that consumption is part of an all-embracing, quasi-conspiratorial system of control, which eliminates every form of autonomous activity and renders the consumer incapable of independent judgment. Such at least is the standard criticism of Ewen's and other early interpretations, which have been challenged in several ways by a growing body of revisionist scholarship. A number of studies have objected to the passivity these interpretations attribute to consumers.

According to the new way of thinking, consumers should be understood as active participants in the culture of consumption, choosing the goods they please and endowing them with significance not always anticipated by those who sell them. Charles F. McGovern, Daniel Miller, Elizabeth Wilson, Michael Denning, and George Lipsitz, among others, have claimed that consumers' ability to "recontextualize" commodities makes it impossible to regard consumption as a monolithic system of exploitation and domination. Often drawing on literary theories associated with "postmodernism" (which displace attention from the author to the reader and see the reader as a creator of meanings unintended by the author), these historians insist that consumers arrive at "negotiated" or even "subversive" readings of commodities and mass culture. In this way they allegedly escape the control of their would-be controllers.

A second line of revisionism takes issue with the contention that consumption is exploitive or oppressive even in the intention of its promoters. Warren Susman was one of the first historians to claim that consumerism often has a liberating intent and certainly that it has liberating effects. Many other scholars have followed him in arguing that the culture of consumption generates a new sense of possibility, encourages subject populations to demand their share of good things, and thus leads just as easily to a radical politics of redistribution as to a politics of acquiescence. The emancipatory potential of consumerism is emphasized, in varying ways and degrees, by Fredric Jameson, Andrew Ross, Richard King, Roy Rosenzweig, Kathy Peiss, John Kasson, Ronald Edsforth, and William R. Leach.

A third strategy of revision alters the chronology of consumer culture by extending it backward in time. Whereas earlier interpretations treated it strictly as a twentieth-century phenomenon, Colin Campbell traces its roots to nineteenth-century romanticism, while Neil McKendrick goes back to the expansion of consumption in eighteenth-century England. Chandra Mukerji insists that the origins of consumer culture can be traced all the way back to the sixteenth century, when the English nobility began to cultivate a taste for luxuries and refinements unimagined by their ancestors. Like other revisionists, Mukerji emphasizes the symbolic and communicative aspect of objects. The goods so eagerly consumed by the nobility, she argues, carried with them a new appreciation of the art of living and prompted a search for a more efficient system of production. Consumption, formerly seen as a byproduct of capitalism (of late capitalism at that), thus comes to be understood as one of its principal causes.

This is not the place to comment on the strengths and weaknesses of these revisionist interpretations of consumption. One point needs to be made in conclusion, however. By depicting the culture of consumption in a genial light and by vastly extending its chronological scope, revisionism makes it seem more inescapable than ever critics of consumption in the 1960s and 1970s, even though they probably exaggerated the "cultural hegemony" of those who controlled and directed it, wrote in hopes that it might eventually give way to a more satisfying way of life to a participatory democracy as opposed to a democracy of consumption. As these hopes recede, consumption takes on a certain air of inevitability. If we believe the revisionism, a culture of consumption has been with us for a long time and shows no sign of disappearing. Consumption is now experienced, by historians no less than by the general public, as the "very element in which we all breathe," in Michael Denning's words (Agnew, "Coming Up for Air," p. 12). These words testify, if nothing else, to its powerful grip on the contemporary imagination.

[See also Business Culture; Communications and Information Processing; Mass Culture and Its Critics; Print and Publishing; The Suburbs; Technology and Social Change; Television.]

BIBLIOGRAPHY

Primary Materials Cited

Boorstin, Daniel J. *The Image: The Guide to Pseudo-Events in America* (rev. ed. 1972).

Conant, Charles A. "The Economic Basis of 'Imperialism.'" *North American Review* 167 (1898).

Galbraith, John Kenneth. *The Affluent Society* (1958).

Miller, James. *"Democracy Is in the Streets": From Port Huron to the Siege of Chicago* (1987). Contains the complete text of the Port Huron Statement.

Parker, Theodore. "A Letter on Slavery" (1847). *In The Slave Power,* edited by James K. Hosmer (n.d.).

Patten, Simon. *The New Basis of Civilization* (1907; repr. 1968).

Roszak, Theodore. *The Making of a Counter Culture: Reflections on the Technocratic Society and Its Youthful Opposition* (1969).

Schlesinger, Arthur M., Jr. *The Age of Roosevelt: The Coming of the New Deal* (1959). Contains material on back-to-the-land movements in the 1930s.

Slater, Philip. *The Pursuit of Loneliness: American Culture at the Breaking Point* (1970).

Smith, Adam. *The Theory of Moral Sentiments* (1759). Edited by D. D. Raphael and A. L. Macfie (1976).

Smith, Adam. *The Wealth of Nations* (1776). Edited by Belfort Bax. 2 vols. (1908).

Weyl, Walter. *The New Democracy* (1912).

Historical Studies of Consumption

Agnew, Jean-Christophe. "Coming Up for Air: Consumer Culture in Historical Perspective." *Intellectual History Newsletter* 12 (1990).

Bronner, Simon J., ed. *Consuming Visions* (1989).

Campbell, Colin. *The Romantic Ethic and the Spirit of Modern Consumerism* (1987).

Denning, Michael. *Mechanic Accents: Dime Novels and Working-Class Culture in America* (1987).

Edsforth, Ronald. *Class Conflict and Cultural Consensus: The Making of a Mass Consumer Society in Flint, Michigan* (1987).

Ewen, Stuart. *Captains of Consciousness: Advertising and the Social Roots of the Consumer Culture* (1976).

Horowitz, Daniel. *The Morality of Spending: Attitudes Toward the Consumer Society in America, 1875–1940* (1985).

Jameson, Fredric. "Reification and Utopia in Mass Culture." *Social Text* 1 (1979).

Kasson, John. *Amusing the Million: Coney Island at the Turn of the Century* (1978).

King, Richard. *The Party of Eros: Radical Social Thought and the Realm of Freedom* (1972).

Leach, William R. "Transformations in a Culture of Consumption: Women and Department Stores, 1890–1925." *Journal of American History* 71 (1984).

Lears, T. J. Jackson, and Richard Wightman Fox, eds. *The Culture of Consumption: Critical Essays in American History, 1880–1980* (1983).

Leuchtenburg, William E. *A Troubled Feast: American Society Since 1945* (rev. ed. 1979).

Lipsitz, George. *Time Passages: Collective Memory and Popular Culture* (1989).

McCracken, Grant. *Culture and Consumption: New Approaches to the Symbolic Character of Consumer Goods and Activities* (1988).

McKendrick, Neil, John Brewer, and J. H. Plumb. *The Birth of a Consumer Society: The Commercialization of Eighteenth-Century, England* (1982).

Marchand, Roland. *Advertising the American Dream: Making Way for Modernity, 1920–1940* (1985).

Meikle, Jeffrey L. *Twentieth-Century Limited: Industrial Design in America, 1925–1939* (1979).

Miller, Daniel. *Material Culture and Mass Consumption* (1987).

Mukerji, Chandra. *From Graven Images: Patterns of Modern Materialism* (1983).

Peiss, Kathy. *Cheap Amusements: Working Women and Leisure in Turn-of-the-Century New York* (1986).

Rosenzweig, Roy. *"Eight Hours for What We Will": Workers and Leisure in an Industrial City, 1870–1920* (1983).

Ross, Andrew. No *Respect: Intellectuals and Popular Culture* (1989).

Susman, Warren. *Culture as History: The Transformation of American Society in the Twentieth Century* (1984).

Wilson, Elizabeth. *Adorned in Dreams: Fashion and Modernity* (1987).

— CHRISTOPHER LASCH

CULTURE AND ITS CRITICS

See MASS CULTURE AND ITS CRITICS

D

DEATH

Historical interest in death and dying has grown considerably since the 1960s. Both demographic and cultural studies of death and dying in the past have enriched the understanding of American social history and have provided a useful perspective for dealing with these issues in the present. Most of the studies of death and dying have been focused on colonial and nineteenth-century America with much less attention to developments in the twentieth century. Moreover, the monographic studies of death and dying are often appear in obscure and hard-to-find publications so that it is difficult for the general reader to access them. As a result, despite the considerable expansion of literature on this topic, much of it has not been thoroughly integrated into the broader syntheses of American social development.

Colonial America

Earlier historians such as Oscar Handlin (1959) argued that death rates were high throughout colonial America and that this made stable family life nearly impossible. For their information on mortality rates, these scholars relied almost exclusively upon contemporary literary accounts, which reported high death rates in both the North and the South. According to these historians, the high death rates meant that few parents could expect to survive long enough to raise their own children. Coupled with the other disruptions of coming to the New World, the early settlers therefore created institutions such as churches and schools in order to overcome the problems created by the disruption of family life in the American wilderness.

More recent demographic studies of early America, including those by John Demos, Philip Greven, and Kenneth Lockridge, provide a very different picture—especially for New England. Using lists of births, deaths, and marriages and employing the technique of family reconstitution, demographic historians have provided much more accurate estimates of colonial mortality. Infant and child mortality rates were quite high in New England, but adult death rates in rural areas were surprisingly low. In colonial Andover or Plymouth, Massachusetts, for example, twenty-year-olds could expect to live more than another forty years. While adult death rates in larger towns such as Boston or Salem were considerably higher than in the countryside, more than 95 percent of the population lived in the smaller towns. As a result, family life in New England was much more stable demographically than previously suggested and most children even had the opportunity to know and interact with their grandparents.

Some analysts contend that female life expectancy in New England was considerably lower than that of males because of the dangers of childbearing. Certainly some women did die giving birth, but the overall evidence suggests that the extent of maternal mortality has been exaggerated. Nevertheless, colonial women greatly dreaded the dangers of childbearing, since death under those circumstances was particularly gruesome and painful. Moreover, Puritan ministers, in urging pregnant women to acknowledge and repent their sins, often reminded them that they were likely to die during childbirth—thereby reinforcing the impression that maternal mortality was very high in early America.

Even if adult mortality rates in colonial New England were lower than had been suggested, infant and child mortality remained high. Since most families had large numbers of children, high infant and child mortality meant that most families experienced the loss of at least one member of the household during the childbearing years. Moreover, periodic epidemics in both rural and urban areas contributed to the sense that life was short and unpredictable. In 1721, for example, during an outbreak of smallpox in Boston, about 10 percent of the entire population died. Puritan religion also placed great emphasis on death and dying and reinforced the notion that death was always imminent for both children and adults. Consequently, most adults in early New England underestimated their actual life expectancy and thought that they were likely to die at any moment—even though most of them survived for many more years.

Initially, Puritans did not devote much attention or resources to burying their dead. The dying person was cared for at home and given a simple funeral. (Puritans buried their dead in both cemeteries and churchyards.) Over time, however, funerals became more elaborate and expensive. The practice of distributing gifts of gloves, rings, or scarves at funerals became so widespread that colonial legislatures tried unsuccessfully to curtail it. Funeral sermons, which earlier had been either avoided altogether or kept very simple, now became common and expected. The simple, wooden gravemarkers of the early seventeenth century were replaced by elaborately carved gravestones with symbolic illustrations of death. The image on many of the early gravestones was the death's-head, while on later ones angel's heads and weeping willows predominated. While historians are still debating the exact meaning or the significance of the changes of the symbols on New England gravestones, there is little doubt that by the eighteenth century the nature of the Puritan funeral had changed dramatically.

If adult death rates in rural New England were lower than earlier scholars had guessed, those in the South were as high as had been first suggested. Based upon extensive demographic studies of the Chesapeake region, it appears that because of the unhealthy climate, death rates in the seventeenth-century South were very high, for both children and adults. The life expectancy of twenty-year-olds in the Chesapeake was only another twenty to twenty-five years—about half that of their rural counterparts in New England. High mortality rates, combined with a great excess of males over females, made family stability difficult in the South. In seventeenth-century Middlesex County, Virginia, only 46 percent of children age thirteen had both of their parents alive and that figure dropped to 31 percent by age eighteen. While mortality rates appear to have improved in the second half of the seventeenth century, they continued to be much higher than in New England.

Given the high mortality and family instability in the Chesapeake, settlers looked for alternative ways to care for orphaned children. Unlike the situation in New England, most of the early settlers to the Chesapeake did not come with any kin who might take care of their orphans in an emergency. High adult mortality rates also meant that few children had any living grandparents to care for them if their parents died. Instead, the roles of godparents were expanded as they were expected to look after the orphans. In addition, special courts were set up to protect the estates of young children who had lost their parents.

The high adult mortality in the Chesapeake also discouraged the early planters from importing African slaves; it was more economical to bring short-term white indentured servants who were less expensive and therefore presented a smaller loss to the planter if they died. Once mortality conditions in the Chesapeake improved, however, it became profitable to import African slaves; even though the initial costs of an African slave were considerably higher than that of an indentured servant, the slaves worked for the planter for the rest of their lives and their children remained the property of the master. Partly as a result of the improvements in mortality rates in the South, the proportion of African slaves in the population increased rapidly in the late seventeenth and early eighteenth centuries.

Throughout colonial America, widows found it difficult to survive unless their husbands had left them an unusually large estate. Therefore most widows with young children tried to remarry as quickly as possible in order to support their families. Remarriage was much easier in the South because of the greater shortage of women there than in the North. Older women and those with young children found it more difficult to remarry than younger widows with no children. Widows who were unable to remarry had to support themselves by working or receiving assistance from their relatives or neighbors. Those who were unable to sustain themselves were forced to rely upon the very limited and inadequate local town or county poor relief. Despite continued public professions about the importance and value of families, colonial Americans often were willing to separate indigent widows from their children if this reduced the welfare burden on the rest of the community.

Nineteenth-Century America

There is considerable disagreement on the course of mortality in nineteenth-century America. Some scholars think that mortality increased in the antebellum period as the United States became more urbanized and industrialized while others maintain that it decreased as per capita incomes rose. Much of the disagreement stems from the use of inadequate and faulty eighteenth- and nineteenth-century life tables (actuarial tables based on age-specific mortality statistics). The most commonly used life tables of the period, the Wigglesworth Life Table of 1789 or the Jacobson Life Table of 1850, are methodologically seriously flawed and misleading. Moreover, most of the existing life tables are based only upon Massachusetts, which was more urbanized than the rest of the nation and therefore not representative of the country as a whole. Several recent studies, however, have provided more accurate life tables for that period. For the New England area, for which the best evidence exists, mortality rates seem to have been fairly stable from the late eighteenth century to the Civil War. After the Civil War there appears to have been a gradual improvement in life expectancy.

Despite the worsening of environmental conditions in some American cities owing to population concentration and the negative health effects of early industrial development, public health measures such as the introduction of sewage disposal and the improvement of the drinking water helped contain or even reduce mortality levels. Concerns about high rates of infant mortality also led to efforts to sanitize the milk supply—though most of these public health improvements came only after 1900. It is clear that by the 1890s mortality was declining in both rural and urban areas throughout most of the United States.

Antebellum Americans were concerned and fascinated with death, but their images of death became softened and muted over time, as people became more optimistic that they might be among the saved and would go to heaven when they died. Dying people continued to be cared for at home and most of the funeral preparations were carried out by friends and neighbors. Only in the larger cities after the Civil War did funeral directors emerge as a specialized profession to help to dispose of the dead.

A great deal of attention was paid to how one died. The ideal ritual occurred at home with the dying person saying goodbye to family and friends. He or she was also expected to reflect calmly on past deeds and express confidence of soon entering heaven. When the idealized death rituals were followed, the survivors sometimes published these accounts as a guide for others. Pressure was placed on the dying person to suppress any fears or anxieties about the future and to acknowledge the supremacy and wisdom of God. When the dying person did not follow the prescribed steps, however, those present were usually confused and embarrassed. Compared to the early colonial period, nineteenth-century clergymen played a more active role in officiating at both the bedside of the dying person as well as at the grave.

Having a proper funeral was deemed especially important. A great fear of many, especially members of the lower classes, was that they might die alone and unattended or be buried as a pauper. Special programs were set up to provide for burial insurance, some by the many fraternal lodges, especially those for immigrants and members of the working-class. While some efforts were made to purchase life insurance to support the widow and surviving children, most nineteenth-century Americans either were not interested in such policies or could not afford them.

Whereas cemeteries in colonial America had not attracted much attention or care, in the nineteenth-century much more effort was made to landscape and maintain a rustic burial site. A few widely publicized rural cemeteries, like Mount Auburn (established in 1831) just outside Cambridge, Massachusetts, were established, which permitted the living and the dead to share pleasant surroundings. These rural cemeteries captured the imagination of contemporaries and historians have devoted considerable attention to them. Yet most people continued to be buried in more traditional and less expensive cemeteries, while the poor and minorities were often still relegated to an ignominious burial in a potter's field.

There is considerable debate over how emotionally upset colonial and nineteenth-century Americans were over the deaths of very young children. Some scholars have maintained that given the high infant mortality of the period, parents did not immediately invest emotionally in their newborn children and therefore did not grieve very much if their children died young. Although grieving parents were often restrained by religious and societal conventions from expressing themselves fully, there is considerable evidence to suggest that most parents deeply mourned the loss of even young infants.

Fears of dying in childbirth continued into the nineteenth century, but the social context of that experience was altered. Increasingly in northern cities, male doctors replaced midwives in superintending the birthing process. Gradually the male doctors tried to eliminate the female friends and relatives from the scene so that pregnant women now had to face this ordeal isolated from their traditional sources of emotional support and comfort. Yet it was only in the early twentieth century, as children were increasingly delivered in a hospital, that male doctors finally gained full control over the birthing process and eliminated the presence of close female friends and family. While the health care professionals who replaced the friends and family provided better medical treatment, they were not as attentive to the emotional needs of the expectant mother.

Widowhood continued to be difficult for most women in nineteenth-century America. Poverty and the difficulties of raising children by themselves led most widows to remarry if possible. Widows who could no longer provide for their young children were likely to enter an almshouse or have their children placed in an orphanage. According to a study of Petersburg, Virginia, during the period 1784 to 1860, wealthier widows who could maintain themselves economically were reluctant to remarry as reentering matrimony meant giving up some of their new freedoms from male dominance.

Historians have often minimized the role of wars in affecting the life course of Americans. Indeed, social historians specializing in the nineteenth century have almost entirely ignored the importance of the Civil War, even though the number of men who died in that conflict alone (nearly 620,000) is almost larger than the combined total number who died in all other American wars. Compare the approximately 50,000 American troops who died in the Vietnam War or the 400,000 killed in World War II. The relative devastation of the Civil War becomes even more apparent when death rates are compared: while there were approximately 2 deaths per 10,000 population in the Vietnam War and 30 deaths per 10,000 population in World War II, there were 180 deaths per 10,000 in the Civil War. Nearly 10 percent of the white military-age population in 1860 died in the Civil War. The losses were particularly high in the South, where almost one out of every five white Southern males between thirteen and forty-three in 1860 died. While relatively few African Americans were allowed to fight for their freedom in the Civil War, for those who did were more likely to die than their white counterparts in the Northern armies.

The impact of the war not only decimated the male population, but it also left large numbers of widows. One estimate is that in 1890 there were about 195,000 Civil War widows—or about 10 percent of all widows at that time. Special orphanages were often created by states to care for the surviving children and an elaborate and expensive pension system was devised for Union widows. An analysis of rural and urban widows in Massachusetts and Michigan suggests that those receiving federal pensions were less likely to be compelled to join the labor force than those who were ineligible for such assistance. Since federal pension benefits were revoked if the widow remarried, the system may have also encouraged some of them to remain single. Overall, the federal pension system to surviving Union veterans or their widows was a very large and expensive program. In 1893, for example, more than 40 percent of the entire federal budget went for pensions for Union veterans or their widows. Although a few Southern states in the late nineteenth century provided some pensions, most Confederate widows did not receive any pensions (and those who did received only a small amount). Only in 1958 were federal benefits made available to Confederate soldiers and their survivors.

Antebellum Americans were concerned and fascinated with death, but their images of death became softened and muted over time, as people became more optimistic that they might be among the saved and would go to heaven when they died.

Not only did the Civil War affect America demographically, it also may have had a profound effect on the ways in which Americans viewed death. Before the Civil War, they were comfortable and open in their discussions, but the great loss of men during the war made it more difficult for many Americans to deal forthrightly with death. As a result, a preliminary study of mentions of death in short stories in popular magazines revealed a dramatic drop during the Civil War; afterwards, the total number of mentions of deaths in the short stories never recovered to pre–Civil War levels. Moreover, when there were mentions of death in the short stories after the Civil War, they were less explicit and direct; usually they referred to death and dying only euphemistically.

Twentieth-Century America

Compared to the mortality data for the seventeenth, eighteenth, and nineteenth centuries, the information for the twentieth century is much more plentiful (though the data for the early twentieth century are not as reliable as those for the mid twentieth century). Therefore, it is possible to document the rapid improvements in mortality rates during the past ninety years.

There was a great improvement—indeed, a great revolution—in life expectancy at birth. In 1900 the average child born could expect to live 47.3 years; that figure jumped to 59.7 years by 1930 and to 69.7 years by 1960. In 1986 the average life expectancy at birth was 74.8 years—or 27.5 years more than in 1900.

Most of the increase in life expectancy at birth was due to the great reductions in infant and child mortality. In 1915 the infant mortality rate was 99.9 deaths per 1,000 live births; in 1930 the rate dropped to 64.6 deaths and in 1960 the rate was down to 26.0 deaths. In 1987 the rate of infant mortality is only 10.1 deaths per 1,000 live births. While the United States continues to have a higher rate of infant mortality than most other advanced nations, there has been a tremendous improvement since the turn of the century.

Improvements in life expectancy at older ages have not been as dramatic as at younger ages. For example, in 1900 the average white male at age twenty could expect to live another 42.2 years, while in 1986 he could look forward to another 53.4 years. Similarly, in 1900 the average white male at age sixty could expect to live another 14.4 years, while in 1986 his remaining life expectancy was 18.2 years.

Race and gender differences in life expectancy continued in the twentieth century. In 1900 the life expectancy at birth of African Americans was 33.0 years (against 47.6 years for whites). By 1986 the life expectancy of African Americans had risen to 69.4 years (against 75.4 years for whites). Thus, while there continued to be differences between the races, the size of the gap in life expectancy at birth narrowed from 14.6 years in 1900 to 6.0 years in 1986. Concern about the differences in mortality continued into the 1990s, with particular attention to the higher rates of mortality among African American infants and the growing number of homicides among African American young males.

While the gap in life expectancy between whites and African Americans has been declining, the differential between women and men has been actually increasing, for both African Americans and whites. In 1900 female life expectancy at birth was 48.3 years (against 46.3 years for males). In 1986 female life expectancy at birth had risen to 78.3 years (against 71.3 years for males). In other words, while females at birth could expect to live two years longer than their male counterparts in 1900, that differential increased to seven years by 1986.

Notably, maternal mortality has declined. In 1915 there were 60.8 maternal deaths per 10,000 live births; in 1930 that figure had risen to 67.3 deaths, but dropped to only 3.7 deaths in 1960 and a relatively rare 0.7 per 10,000 births in 1986. While maternal mortality rates for African Americans continued to be twice as high as for whites in the 1990s, for neither group was the likelihood of dying in childbirth as large or as frightening as it had been in colonial and nineteenth-century America.

While the gap in life expectancy between whites and African Americans has been declining over the past hundred years, the differential between American women and men has actually been increasing, for both African Americans and whites.

The explanations for this revolution in mortality are complex, but fundamentally Americans experienced an epidemiologic revolution during the twentieth century. In 1900 the leading causes of death were pneumonia-influenza-bronchitis, tuberculosis, and diarrhea and enteritis. Today, degenerative and man-made diseases are the major causes of death with heart disease, cancer, and stroke leading the field.

Not only was there a great decrease in death rates during the century, but birth rates fell as well. The combination has had a great impact on the likelihood of children experiencing the loss of a family member. Peter Uhlenberg has calculated that the likelihood of children experiencing the loss of one or both parents before age fifteen dropped from 24 percent in 1900 to 5 percent in 1976 ("Death in the Family," pp. 313–320). Moreover, the probability of that same child experiencing the loss of a nuclear family member (parent or sibling) decreased dramatically from 50 percent in 1900 to 10 percent in 1976. Finally, the changes in mortality have also affected the likelihood of having grandparents. In 1900 less than one out of five children at age fifteen had three or more grandparents alive, whereas in the 1990s that figure had risen to 55 percent. Thus, whereas death was a common and integral part of growing up in the early twentieth century, it has become much less salient for most children in the late twentieth century.

The decrease in death rates also greatly affected single-parent households. In the past, most single-parent households were the result of the death of either the father or the mother. Even as late as 1970, 18.5 percent of children living in a single-parent household resided in ones created by the death of a father. Yet in 1986 only 1.4 percent of all children under eighteen lived in a single-parent household headed by a widow; and of all children living in single-parent households, only 6.7 percent of them were due to the death of one of the parents. In other words, whereas single parenting in the past resulted mainly from the death of one of the spouses, in the 1990s death accounted for only a tiny fraction of single-parent households.

The provision for the care of widows and orphans has also changed greatly in the twentieth century. In colonial and nineteenth-century America, widows were expected to take care of themselves and their children. If they could not support themselves, they risked being sent to a poorhouse or having their family broken up, with their children sent to an orphanage or apprenticed to some employer. In the late nineteenth and early twentieth centuries, however, there was a concerted movement to keep dependent children in their own homes rather than sending them to any institution. As a result of this new emphasis on the importance of home care, efforts were made to find alternative ways of helping widows with children.

One very popular and innovative program was the development of mothers' pensions. Illinois passed the first state mothers' pension program in 1911, which provided assistance for widowed, deserted, and never-married mothers with children. The mothers' pension programs were quickly adopted by many other states. Reactions against the provision of assistance for divorced and never-married mothers meant that the bulk of the money went to widows, who made up 82 percent of all those receiving assistance in 1931. African American widows were eligible for these benefits, but they were less likely to receive them than their white counterparts. While in theory the mothers' pensions were intended to allow women to stay at home with their children, in practice most widows were expected to enter the labor force and contribute to the family income. Nevertheless, despite the small amounts of money available and the continued discrimination against certain categories of needy mothers, the state mothers' pension programs were an improvement over the colonial and nineteenth-century forms of welfare assistance.

With the collapse of the funding for many of the state programs during the Great Depression, the federal government stepped in to assist poor mothers and their children under the Social Security Act of 1935. The Aid to Dependent Children portion of this legislation was modeled on the state mothers' pension programs and explicitly provided financial assistance for children of widows as well as for those of divorced, separated, and never-married mothers. The number of families receiving such assistance doubled within two years compared with those who had received aid through the state mothers' pension programs. While the Social Security Act of 1935 provided for equal treatment of children regardless of the status of the mother, the revision in 1939 reversed this policy and privileged the children of widows.

Children of widows in the 1990s continued to enjoy a significant differential in income compared to other single-parent families. In 1982 the total cash income of widows was $17,799 in mother-only white families, while their counterparts in divorced ($13,845), separated ($10,122), and never-married ($7,812) families had much lower income. In large part this disparity was due to the fact that benefits provided through the Survivors' Insurance were much higher than those available through the Aid to Families with Dependent Children (AFDC).

If the demography and economics of death and dying have changed in the twentieth century, so have the institutional and cultural settings. In colonial and nineteenth-century America, most people died in their own homes or those of a friend. In the late twentieth century, however, most people died in some institution. In 1949, 49.5 percent of deaths took place in an institution; in 1958 that figure increased to 60.9 percent, and in 1968 it rose to 68.1 percent. Moreover, in urban areas like New York City the percentage of deaths occurring in an institution were even higher. As the scene of dying shifted from a home to an institution, the dying person was isolated from friends and relatives. Professionals replaced close acquaintances in the last moments and the separation of the dying from the rest of society made it easier for people to deny the existence of death. Whereas deathbed scenes were central to the ritual of dying in colonial and nineteenth-century America, today many Americans die without any last-minute interactions with their loved ones.

Although funeral directors came into being in some urban areas in the second half of the nineteenth century, it was only in the twentieth century that they came virtually to monopolize the disposal of the dead in the United States. While many view the role of funeral directors as comforting and helpful, others have denounced them as unnecessary and exploitive. Jessica Mitford's best-selling *The American Way of Death* caused a sensation in 1963 by ridiculing how Ameri-

The Civil War decimated the male population and left large numbers of widows. Rows of white grave markers fill a large Civil War cemetery, shown here, in Alexandria, Virginia.

cans buried their dead and attacking the funeral directors for taking advantage of people during their period of grief. While her overall analysis of the American way of death was more anecdotal than analytic and based upon an inadequate understanding of the history of American practices, her calls for reforming the funeral industry were heeded by the Federal Trade Commission.

In other societies burials are not always the preferred way of disposing of the dead. In Japan, for example, over 90 percent of those who die are cremated. While cremation was advocated by some American reformers in the late nineteenth century, it has not attracted a sizable following in this country-though there is a slight increase in its popularity today. In 1976 about 7 percent of Americans who died were cremated, while by 1985 the figure had risen to almost 13 percent. Nevertheless, more Americans were trying to reduce the costs of their burials by joining memorial societies, which provide consumer education and alternatives to traditional funerals. During the 1960s and 1970s memorial societies grew rapidly in the United States and it is estimated that in 1983 there were approximately 175 such societies, with a total membership of about 500,000.

American concerns with death and funerals in the twentieth century were not confined to human beings. A surprising number of Americans are concerned about the disposal of their pets. The oldest pet cemetery in the United States, the Hartsdale Canine Cemetery, was established in 1896 in New York, and today there are over five hundred pet cemeteries in operation.

During most of the twentieth century, Americans were reluctant to discuss or even acknowledge the presence of death and dying. Since the 1960s, however, there has been much more public and scholarly attention given to dying people, much of it due to the efforts of Elisabeth Kübler-Ross, who popularized the idea that people should interact with the dying rather than trying to pretend that they do not exist.

Her best-selling book, *On Death and Dying*, argued that dying patients went through five stages: denial and isolation, anger, bargaining, depression, and acceptance. While her pioneering work did much to encourage people to treat the dying person as a human being, she may have unwittingly created a twentieth-century model of the "good" death that is at times counterproductive. Although Kübler-Ross claimed that her five-stage model was based upon careful, scientific clinical work with dying patients, closer scrutiny suggests that her research was inadequate and impressionistic. Critics of Kübler-Ross have pointed out that many dying patients do not experience the five stages or go through them in the sequence suggested by her model. The danger is that some health practitioners have accepted Kübler-Ross's stages as not only descriptive but also prescriptive. Dying patients who do not follow the prescribed model are sometimes castigated by health professionals as being deviant and forced into adjusting their behavior to the Kübler-Ross model. As a result, just as the nineteenth-century rituals of dying were both a source of comfort and difficulty for the dying person, so Kübler-Ross's twentieth-century model proved to be both helpful and problematic.

Despite the growing awareness of death and dying in the 1990s, many Americans still found it difficult to discuss or even acknowledge the presence of death. Moreover, while there were some significant improvements in the clinical understanding of the bereavement process, American society as a whole was not very emotionally supportive of those who have lost a loved one. As a result, Americans still did not handle bereavement as well as their colonial and nineteenth-century ancestors, who regarded death as an inevitable and natural part of life.

[See also Alternative Medicine; Health Care; Life Stages; Old Age; Public Health.]

BIBLIOGRAPHY

General Works

Ariès, Philippe. *The Hour of Our Death.* Translated by Helen Weaver (1981).

Gerhan, David R., and Robert V. Wells. *A Retrospective Bibliography of American Demographic History from Colonial Times to 1983* (1989).

Habenstein, Robert W., and William M. Lamers. *The History of American Funeral Directing.* rev. ed. (1962).

Sloane, David Charles. *The Last Great Necessity: Cemeteries in American History* (1991).

Stannard, David E., ed. *Death in America* (1975).

Uhlenberg, Peter. "Death and the Family." *Journal of Family History* 5 (1980).

Vinovskis, Maris A. "Death and Family Life in the Past." *Human Nature* 1, no. 2 (1990).

Vinovskis, Maris A., ed. *Studies in American Historical Demography* (1979).

Colonial America

Benes, Peter. *The Masks of Orthodoxy: Folk Gravestone Carving in Plymouth County, Massachusetts, 1689–1805* (1977).

Geddes, Gordon E. *Welcome Joy: Death in Puritan New England* (1981).

Ludwig, Allen I. *Graven Images: New England Stonecarving and Its Symbols, 1650–1815* (1966).

Moran, Gerald E, and Maris A. Vinovskis. *Religion, Family, and the Life Course: Explorations in the Social History of Early America* (forthcoming).

Stannard, David E. *The Puritan Way of Death: A Study in Religion, Culture, and Social Change* (1977).

Nineteenth-Century America

Farrell, James J. *Inventing the American Way of Death, 1830–1920* (1980).

Lane, Roger. *Violent Death in the City: Suicide, Accident, and Murder in Nineteenth-Centuty, Philadelphia* (1979).

Linden-Ward, Blanche. *Silent City on a Hill: Landscapes of Memory and Boston's Mount Auburn Cemetery* (1989).

Rosenblatt, Paul C. *Bitter, Bitter Tears: Nineteenth-Century Diarists and Twentieth-Century Grief Theories* (1983).

Vinovskis, Maris A., ed. *Toward a Social History of the American Civil War: Exploratory Essays* (1990).

Zelizer, Viviana A. Rotman. *Morals and Markets: The Development of Life Insurance in the United States* (1979).

Twentieth-Century America

Becker, Ernest. *The Denial of Death* (1973).

Kamerman, Jack B. *Death in the Midst of Life: Social and Cultural Influences on Death, Grief, and Mourning* (1988).

Kübler-Ross, Elisabeth. *On Death and Dying* (1969).

Mitford, Jessica. *The American Way of Death* (1963).

Osterweis, Marian, et al. *Bereavement: Reactions, Consequences, and Care* (1984).

Pine, Vanderlyn R. *Caretaker of the Dead: The American Funeral Director* (1975).

Sudnow, David. *Passing On: The Social Organization of Dying* (1967).

Vinovskis, Maris A. "Kübler-Ross and the Five Stages of Dying: Some Methodological and Conceptual Reservations." *Proceedings of the World Conference on Records* (1981), vol. 3, ser. 328.

— MARIS A. VINOVSKIS

DIVORCE

See COURTSHIP, MARRIAGE, SEPARATION, AND DIVORCE

E

EDUCATION, ALTERNATIVE

See ALTERNATIVE EDUCATION

EDUCATION, COLLEGIATE

See COLLEGIATE EDUCATION

ENTERTAINMENT, POPULAR

See POPULAR ENTERTAINMENT BEFORE THE CIVIL WAR

ETIQUETTE

See MANNERS AND ETIQUETTE

F

FAMILY STRUCTURES

In recent years, no area of American social history has attracted as much interest, or been subject to such drastic revision, as the history of the family. By applying new methods, such as "family reconstitution" and "cohort analysis"; by using new concepts, such as "life course" and "family cycle"; and by tapping new sources of data, family historians have debunked many myths about families in the past and corrected many misconceptions about the nature of familial change. Among the topics that have drawn the attention of family historians are subjects as diverse as domestic violence, courtship practices, family law, inheritance customs, child rearing, and birth control.

As the result of sifting through census schedules, church records, family papers, paintings, house plans, marriage contracts, and other sources, and applying the analytical tools of demography, social anthropology, family sociology, and developmental psychology, the "new" family history has challenged social scientists to reconsider many traditional notions about the historical evolution of the family. It has shown that diversity, and not uniformity, has been the defining characteristic of American family life since the beginnings of colonization. It has challenged the older view that industrialization produced a shift from an extended family system to the modern nuclear family. It has demonstrated that despite the recent increase in the divorce rate, the rate of family dissolution—by death, desertion, or divorce—is no greater today than it was a century ago, and has rebutted the notion that the high incidence of single-parent, female-headed households among African Americans today is a legacy of slavery. Most important of all, family historians have shown that the family, far from being an institution in decline, is instead highly flexible, resilient, and adaptive.

After tracing the growth of interest in family history and discussing the different methodological and conceptual frameworks that family historians have employed, this essay will describe changes over time in family composition and structure in colonial British America and the United States. It will use both demographic and descriptive data to illuminate the character of family membership in various regions and eras and the factors that contributed to family change over time. Special emphasis will be placed on the differences that race, class, religion, and ethnic and regional origins have made in family composition and family structure. This essay will also discuss nontraditional family structures and situations, such as utopian communitarian settlements, boardinghouses, and "Boston marriages," that provided an alternative to traditional structures or active resistance to them. And finally, this essay will examine how changes in the nature of the family are tied to broader transformations in religion, economy, and the state.

The Growth of Interest in Family History

Research into the history of the family began in the mid nineteenth century, when pioneering anthropologists, legal historians, and sociologists, recognizing that family organization varies across time and cultures, attempted to explain the family's origins and evolution. Frédéric Le Play constructed a typology of families ranging from the stem family to the nuclear family and argued that industrialization was creating "unstable" families. Friedrich Engels drew upon the anthropologist Lewis Henry Morgan's studies of kinship terminology to argue that the development of a conception of private property transformed the family from a matriarchal to a patriarchal unit. Sir Henry Maine's research into the law of marriage, property, and inheritance led him to construct a family model in which relations based on status gradually gave way to relations based on contract.

Around the turn of the twentieth century, the first important histories of the American family appeared. Alice Morse Earle's studies of the lives of well-to-do women and children in colonial America explored child-rearing practices, parent-child relationships, and women's economic roles. George E. Howard's *History of Matrimonial Institutions* (1904) traced the development of domestic relations law in Britain and the United States. The most comprehensive and influential early survey was Arthur W. Calhoun's three-volume *Social History of the American Family* (1945—1946). Based upon a largely unsystematic, impressionistic reading of newspapers, court records, sermons, novels, letters, and diaries, Calhoun's study described a shift from a large, extended family in colonial America to a smaller nuclear unit in the early twentieth century Calhoun's volumes helped to create a series of influential myths about the early American family that later family historians would revise: that family life was very similar in all the colonies; that colonial families contained several generations and a number of siblings and their spouses; that marriage took place at very young ages; that fertility and infant mortality rates were very high; and that maternal death as a result of childbirth was extremely common.

Apart from the works of Earle, Howard, and Calhoun, only a handful of truly significant books on American family history appeared before the 1960s, of which Edmund Morgan's *The Puritan Family* (1944) and *Virginians at Home* (1952) were the most important. The declining interest in family history was part of a broad shift in the social sciences away from evolutionary thought and toward more static synchronic forms of analysis, and away from broad theorizing and toward more carefully focused empirical studies. In the field of family studies, evolutionary theories were supplanted by functionalist and interactionist studies.

Despite a professed lack of interest in the historical evolution of the family, functionalists and interactionists did hold certain assumptions about the long-term direction of change in family structures. Functionalist studies emphasized how both the structures of and role relations within families form part of a larger whole, i.e., society. Interactionist perspectives emphasized socialization, personality formation, and interpersonal dynamics within families. According to the view popularized by the sociologist William F. Ogburn, the family, under the pressures of urbanization and industrialization, was stripped of many of its traditional functions until its only remaining functions were psychological: to socialize children and to provide emotional sustenance and support for family members.

After World War II, Talcott Parsons played a central role in defining the issues that informed the study of the family. He treated the family as a small group that served basic functions for the larger society, including reproduction, regulation of sexual behavior, socialization into adult roles, and emotional support. He argued that small, isolated nuclear families in which men specialized in instrumental, goal-oriented activities and women specialized in expressive, relationship-oriented activities were particularly well adapted to the demands of an urban, industrial society. Parsonian structural-functionalism was profoundly ahistorical, and discouraged historical analysis of the family. It treated the family as a static unit that could be studied apart from a broader social context.

During the 1950s and early 1960s, the groundwork was laid for renewed interest in family history French and English historical demography played a particularly important role in stimulating interest in family history. Louis Henry, a French historical demographer, developed a method known as "family reconstitution" that permitted historians to reconstruct the demographic history of individual families from birth, baptismal, marriage, and death records. The family reconstruction technique allowed historians to calculate changes over time in family size and composition, life expectancy, mobility and migration patterns, fertility and nuptiality rates, spacing of children, and the developmental cycle (changes in household composition over its members' life span).

The most startling finding to emerge from the early research using the family reconstitution method was that in the eighteenth century, well before the onset of large-scale industrialization, many French families adopted effective methods of contraception. This finding inspired other scholars to apply quantitative analysis to other sources of data. Interest in demographic analysis received added impetus from the work of the Cambridge Group for the History of Population and Social Structure, directed by Peter Laslett. The Cambridge Group found that from the seventeenth century on, western European families had a distinctive pattern characterized by a late average age of marriage for men and women (around twenty-seven or twenty-eight for men and twenty-five or twenty-six for women) and a relatively low birthrate (of between 5 and 6.5 children per married woman). Most controversially, Laslett and his associates rejected the idea that prior to industrialization, large and complex households, containing grandparents, aunts and uncles, cousins, and nieces and nephews had been common and that industrialization had brought about a shift from an extended-family system to a nuclear-family system. The Cambridge Group argued that census materials showed that small nuclear families predominated in England centuries before the industrial revolution.

Laslett's findings provoked a great deal of controversy and helped to stimulate further research in family history. Among the criticisms that were leveled against the Cambridge Group's research was that it assumed England was typical of other countries; that it failed to take into account kinship relationships among households; and that it paid no attention to the developmental cycle of households—the fact that households were more likely to take in kin and non-kin at distinct points in the family cycle. Above all, further research demonstrated that while extended kin did not usually live in households in the past, nonrelatives—such as servants, apprentices, and boarders and lodgers—often did.

Apart from historical demography, another early influence upon the study of the family came from the French cultural historian Philippe Ariès's classic *Centuries of Childhood* (1962), which argued that the modern, tightly knit, private, child-centered nuclear family is a relatively recent historical development. Using house plans, paintings, and popular novels, poems, and plays to trace changes in public ideologies of the family, Ariès argued that, beginning in the seventeenth century, the child-centered, emotionally intense nuclear family replaced a more open form of family life, devoid of privacy, in which children were ignored until they were old enough to be treated as little adults.

In sharp contrast with the quantitative historians, who focused on changes in the family's demographic structure and form, cultural historians who built upon Ariès's pioneering work dwelt on changes in the emotional texture of family life. By drawing upon diaries, letters, folklore, naming practices, marriage contracts, sermons, divorce suits, prescriptive literature, and literary sources, they studied changes in child-rearing practices, sexual behavior, spousal and parent-child relationships, gender roles, courtship and marriage decisions, and rituals surrounding death. In their work these scholars traced the gradual emergence, beginning in the sixteenth century, of a conception of marriage emphasizing mutual affection and companionship between spouses; a view of children as special creatures needing attention, love, and time to mature; and a growing emphasis on privacy within the home.

Another major influence on family history came from the field of social anthropology. Long before the rise of social history, social anthropologists developed a rich body of research and theory on kinship structures and relationships, inheritance practices, the life cycle, and the interaction of the family and an economic context. Unlike cultural historians of the family, who have explained shifts in the family's interior life in terms of the impact of new religious or philosophical ideals (such as the rise of new notions of equality, individual autonomy, and personal privacy), family historians influenced by social anthropology have emphasized changes in the social relations of production. These historians have focused their attention on the "strategies" families use to earn income or acquire property, transmit land, sustain or improve a standard of living, or strengthen and preserve kinship ties. Migration, child labor, and the adoption of specific inheritance practices are viewed as strategies that families employ to achieve specific ends.

The Language of Family History

Students of the family have developed a technical terminology and idiom that are useful in describing the structure and organization of family types. When used by specialists, such words as "family," "household," and "kinship" have technical meanings that differ from their popular usage.

In popular parlance, the word "family" is used broadly and loosely. It can refer to any group of persons of a common ancestry, to any group of individuals residing under one roof, and to a unit composed of one or more adults living together and cooperating in the care and rearing of their own or adopted children. In an effort to give the term a more rigorous and formal meaning, social scientists have tried to disentangle its diverse definitions. "Family" is defined as a kinship and legal unit based on affinal or biological relatedness (that is, relationships based on marriage or parent-child linkages), while "household" refers to a residential unit, the group of kin and non-kin who share a common residence.

Students of the family draw further distinctions based on the family's organizational structure. The nuclear or conjugal family is the unit composed of a husband, a wife, and their dependent children living in an independent household. Other types of families include

The word "family" is used broadly and loosely: It can refer to a group of persons of common ancestry, to individuals residing under one roof, and to a unit composed of one or more adults living together and cooperating in the care and rearing of their own or adopted children.

the consanguineous family, which is a unit made up of a single parent and children, and various kinds of "complex" families, units based on generational ties (such as three-generation households) and lateral ties (such as households containing two married siblings, their spouses, and children).

By "kinship," social scientists refer to consanguineous relations or relationships, such as adoption, modeled on consanguinity. In small-scale societies, including most Native American societies, kinship ties structure ownership and inheritance of property, land-use rights, succession to political or religious office, and even whom one may marry. The term "descent group" refers to social groups whose identity is based on kinship relations. In patrilineal societies membership in the group flows through the father. In matrilineal societies group membership is determined by the mother's family's identity. In cognate societies group membership is based on ties through either the father or the mother. In modern industrial societies like the United States many functions traditionally assigned to kinship groups are taken over by impersonal public institutions, such as schools and insurance companies. Nevertheless, extended family ties remain important. "Kindred"—relatives on a person's mother's or father's side—help fellow kin carry out a variety of tasks and often provide assistance in times of emergency.

Over time, the size, composition, and organizational structure of a family or a household unit vary. A household's size and membership change as children are born or leave home, or as boarders and lodgers come and go. To understand variation in household and family structure over family members' lifetimes, family historians have used the concept of a "family cycle," which describes the stages through which families go from the time they are formed to the time they are dissolved.

Another analytical construct that has proven useful is the "life course," which describes the movement of an individual through various family roles. The life course perspective focuses on the timing of major transitions in individual lives, such as age at marriage, duration of schooling, age at leaving home, and timing of childbearing during marriage. Family historians have discovered that the timing of key life-course transitions is shaped by a particular historical and cultural context, which helps define the proper age for marriage or bearing children or joining the labor force.

The Transformation of American Families

Since the seventeenth century American families have undergone far-reaching transformations in their functions, roles, emotional dynamics, demographic characteristics, and organizational structure. The American family has been transformed from a public institution whose main functions were economic—to carry on farming and domestic manufacturing and to transmit property and craft skills—into a private institution whose major roles are emotional and psychological, to socializing children and providing emotional support for its members.

SEVENTEENTH-CENTURY FAMILY FUNCTIONS, IDEALS, AND ROLES. In structure, role, and conception, seventeenth-century families differed profoundly from their twentieth-century counterparts. Then, the household's functions were broad and diffuse, and its boundaries elastic. Not only were seventeenth-century families the economic center of production, they were also responsible for religious instruction, transferring occupational skills to the next generation, and caring for the elderly and infirm. They were flexible units which took in orphans, the destitute, and the elderly, and housed servants and apprentices. In New England, as many as a third of all households contained servants or other distant kin or non-kin at any one time.

Seventeenth-century Americans conceived of the family as a hierarchical institution in which the father was endowed with patriarchal authority. Law and custom made the father the undisputed head of his household. He led his family in prayer and Scripture reading, represented his family in politics, and had the power to give or deny his consent to his children's marriages. Under the legal doctrine of coverture, a wife's legal identity was subordinated to that of her husband. All property she brought to marriage belonged to him unless they had signed a prenuptial agreement.

Paternal authority ultimately rested on a father's control over property and inheritance. Since seventeenth-century fathers were permitted wide discretion in how they would distribute property, children who wanted to marry and set up an independent household had to show deference to their father's wishes. The timing and manner in which fathers conveyed property to the next generation helped determine when and whom his children married.

Seventeenth-century Americans regarded marriage simply not as an emotional bond but as an economic partnership. Love was not necessarily considered a prerequisite for marriage. Ministers told the young to choose a spouse on grounds of property, religion, and family interest, not on the basis of physical attraction or romantic love. Love, it was assumed, would follow marriage. Marriage was a union to which both husband and wife were expected to bring skills and resources. A prospective bride was expected to contribute a dowry (usually in the form of money or household goods) worth about half the value of the property the bridegroom brought to the marriage. Within marriage, wives had important responsibilities for the family's well-being: not only cooking and caring for children but also tending gardens, brewing beer, raising chickens, making clothes, and helping to plant and harvest crops.

The social experience of childhood differed markedly from childhood today. One difference was that children were much more likely to die in infancy or to be orphaned. Even in New England, which had a relatively healthful climate, one infant in ten died in healthy areas and three in ten died in less healthy climes. In certain respects, children were treated casually. Newborn infants of well-to-do families were sometimes "put out" to wet nurses who were responsible for breast-feeding, thus freeing the mothers for household duties. As in Europe, a child might sometimes receive the same name as a recently deceased sibling.

In the more intensely evangelical families, infants were viewed as embodiments of sin and corruption, and child rearing was conceived in terms of breaking a child's sinful will by physical punishment or fierce psychological pressure. Evangelical techniques of child discipline included whipping, physical isolation, and threats of death and damnation.

If childhood is defined as a protected state, a carefree period of freedom from adult responsibilities, then a seventeenth-century childhood was quite brief. Around the age of seven, children in New England adopted adult clothing (earlier, both boys and girls wore frocks or petticoats) and assumed work responsibilities. Young boys weeded fields, combed wool, and wove garters and suspenders on small looms. Young girls hoed gardens, spun flax and cotton, tended orchards, cared for domestic animals, and made clothing, lye, soap, and candles.

While childhood ended early and abruptly, adulthood did not begin right away. Between the ages of seven and fourteen, children entered a prolonged intermediate stage of semidependency, shifting back and forth between work experiences inside and outside their parents' home. During their teens, many children spent much of their time under the tutelage of adults other than their parents. They were "fostered out" as indentured servants or apprentices or, in rare instances, sent to boarding school.

VARIATIONS IN SEVENTEENTH-CENTURY FAMILY STRUCTURE. Diversity was the hallmark of family life in seventeenth-century America. Climatic variations, the prevalence of disease, and migratory patterns all contributed to fundamental regional differences in family patterns. Seventeenth-century, New Englanders enjoyed longer and healthier lives than their counterparts in the Chesapeake colonies of Maryland and Virginia. The severe New England winters helped reduce the incidence of diseases like malaria and yellow fever. Most men lived into their late sixties, and even though almost half of New England women died from causes associated with childbirth, most lived into their early or mid sixties.

Long life spans contributed to lengthy marriages and large and stable families. New England men typically married in their mid twenties, after they had received an inheritance or property from their father; their wives were usually two or three years younger. During a typical twenty-four-year marriage, a couple had between eight and ten children, and 70 to 80 percent of their offspring survived until adulthood. The long life spans meant that many grandparents lived to see their grandchildren.

More than any other colonists, New Englanders emphasized nuclear-family ties. Adult sons and their aging parents often inhabited neighboring households, a pattern that has been described as a "modified extended family structure." Compared with other settlers, New Englanders were more likely to name eldest children for the parents, less likely to take in servants, and much less likely to bequeath property to cousins or other extended kin.

Death rates were much higher in the Chesapeake colonies than in New England, due to the prevalence of malaria, typhoid fever, and dysentery and poisoning from brackish drinking water. Before 1640, migrants to the Chesapeake had no more than a 50 percent chance of surviving their first year in America. Even after the high death rates of the early years of settlement passed, life expectancy remained much lower than in New England or western Europe. Few men lived past their early forties, and few women past their late thirties.

The high death rate had profound consequences for family life. Marriages were usually short-lived, averaging seven years before one of the spouses died. High mortality, also meant that Chesapeake women bore fewer children than their New England counterparts, averaging four or five, two or three of whom reached maturity. Parent-child ties were extraordinarily fragile. In Middlesex Country, Virginia, two-thirds of all surviving children lost one parent by the age of eighteen, and one-third lost both. Parents' short life span meant that children often received inheritances by their late teens, much earlier than in New England.

Seventeenth-century New England men typically married in their mid twenties; their wives were usually two to three years younger; and during a typical two-decade marriage, a couple had between eight and ten children.

The high death rate contributed to very complicated family structures. Chesapeake households were much more likely than New England households to contain stepchildren, wards, and servants. Because of high rates of remarriage, some households contained children from three or four different marriages. To protect children from abusive stepparents, localities established special Orphans' Courts.

The high death rate did not necessarily mean that emotional bonds among family members were weak.

Husbands in the Chesapeake were more willing than their New England counterparts to trust their wives to manage their estates after their death. And although generational ties between parents and children were fragile, emotional ties among siblings, cousins, and half siblings appear to have been strong.

In addition to experiencing a high death rate, the settlers of the Chesapeake also confronted a severely skewed sex ratio. Whereas New Englanders crossed the Atlantic in family groups, most migrants to the Chesapeake were young, unmarried, male indentured servants. Before 1640, only one woman migrated to the Chesapeake for every six men; and as late as 1700, males outnumbered females by a ratio of more than three to two.

The skewed sex ratio meant that many Chesapeake men never had an opportunity to marry. Because female servants were prohibited from marrying until they had served their term of indenture, most did not marry until their mid twenties, which limited the number of children they could bear. Native-born women married at much younger ages, usually in their late teens.

The skewed sex ratio and the high proportion of women who were servants contributed to high rates of illegitimacy. One-fifth of Maryland's indentured females faced charges of bastardy. Native-born women with parents alive were less likely to bear children out of wedlock, but the illegitimacy rate remained high among young women whose parents were dead.

At the end of the seventeenth century, family life in the Chesapeake stabilized. The death rate fell, life expectancy rose, and the imbalance between the sexes eased. Marriages lasted longer, fewer children died in infancy, families grew larger, and the birthrate rose sharply.

EIGHTEENTH-CENTURY PATTERNS OF CHANGE. During the eighteenth century, family life underwent far-reaching changes. In the northern, middle, and southern colonies, a new style of family life began to emerge, one emphasizing romantic love, domestic intimacy, and the care and nurture of children.

Quaker families inhabiting the Delaware Valley of eastern Pennsylvania, West Jersey, and northern Delaware and adjacent areas of northeastern Maryland were at the forefront of change. From the beginnings of large-scale Quaker migration in 1675, the sect conceived of the family in less hierarchical terms than did many other colonists. Rather than regarding it as a patriarchal institution, Quakers viewed the family as a union of individuals bound together by love. Compared with other colonists, they attached much more importance to the idea that love was the only proper basis of marriage, that men and women were spiritual equals, that child rearing was the family's primary function, and that restraining sexual activity within marriage was desirable.

Quaker beliefs about marriage, gender, and sexuality had profound implications for personal behavior. Quaker marriages were subject to an unusual degree of communal supervision, usually requiring not only parental consent but also approval by a Quaker meeting. Not only were first-cousin marriages prohibited, which was the general practice in New England, but second-cousin marriages were discouraged as well. The stress that the Quakers placed upon love in marriage may have contributed to the fact that Quaker women were somewhat less likely to marry than other colonial women. About 84 percent of Quaker women married, compared with 95 to 98 percent of women in New England and Virginia. The emphasis on sexual restraint in marriage may help to account for the fact that the Quakers were the first colonial Americans to control fertility within marriage. As early as the mid eighteenth century, Quakers consciously limited births in marriage. Extended sexual abstinence seems to have been a major method of birth control. Quaker families were also unusual in the egalitarianism of their inheritance practices, the attention they gave to child rearing, the moderation with which they used corporal punishment, and the emphasis they placed on keeping children at home until adulthood.

During the eighteenth century, New England families increasingly resembled their Quaker counterparts as the ideal of patriarchal authority eroded and the conception of marriage as an economic partnership between two families based on property considerations declined. During the eighteenth century, parents' ability to control the timing of a child's marriage or to influence the choice of a partner decreased, reflecting a significant erosion of fathers' control over property. Expanding opportunities for nonagricultural employment allowed children to live farther away from their parents, to engage in premarital sex, and to marry early if pregnancy should result. At the same time, many fathers showed a greater willingness to grant their sons economic independence by conveying property to them at an earlier age.

Rapid population growth was a major factor contributing to the decline of paternal authority. Some communities grew by 5 or 6 percent annually, and the number of surviving sons proved to be greater than the resources necessary to establish viable farms. Parents adopted a number of strategies to cope with the growing shortage of land. Some fathers willed their estate to the oldest or youngest son and encouraged their other sons to migrate to newer communities where land was available, or converted inheritances into some form other than real estate, such as formal education or a gift of money. In other instances, whole families moved to areas with abundant land. Still other parents adopted a "stem family" pattern, willing one son the bulk of the father's property and requiring him to pay money or provide goods to younger children.

The declining ability of fathers to transmit land to their sons undermined the traditional basis of paternal authority. A symptom of the decline in paternal control was a sudden upsurge, in the mid eighteenth century, in the illegitimacy rate and the proportion of brides pregnant at marriage. During the seventeenth century, the proportion of women who were pregnant at the time of their wedding was below 10 percent. By the middle of the eighteenth century, it had shot up to over 40 percent. Another indicator of a decline in paternal authority was an increase in children's discretion in deciding whom and when to marry. Children began to marry earlier than in the seventeenth century, and an increasing number of daughters married out of birth order.

The weakening of paternal authority was accompanied by the emergence of a "companionate" conception of marriage: as an emotional bond involving "mutual esteem, mutual friendship, [and] mutual confidence." Within marriage, couples displayed affection more openly. Instead of referring to each other in their correspondence as "Madam" or "Sir," spouses used first names or such terms as "dear" or "honey." At the same time, parental interest in child development grew markedly. Increasingly children were seen as special creatures with unique needs—a view made evident in a profusion of books, games, toys, and furniture specifically for children. Child-rearing ideals shifted away from suppressing children's willfulness through physical punishment to instilling a capacity for self-government through such techniques as evoking guilt and withdrawing love.

During the second half of the eighteenth century, family patterns in the Chesapeake increasingly came to resemble those found in the northern colonies. Planters' children became more likely to select marriage partners without parental interference. Instead of asserting ties to a broad network of kin and friends, planter families began to focus their emotional affection on their immediate families. Open expressions of affection between spouses and between parents and children became more common, and mothers devoted more time to the nurture of their children.

NINETEENTH-CENTURY TRANSFORMATIONS. By the 1830s, a new kind of middle-class family had emerged. It was characterized by new marital ideals based primarily on companionship and affection; a new domestic division of labor, in which the husband was expected to be the family breadwinner and the wife to care full-time for children and the home; a new conception of childhood that looked at children as distinct individuals with unique needs; and growing acceptance of birth control. In sharp contrast to the seventeenth-century family, which was conceived as a microcosm of the larger society, the middle-class family was now viewed as essentially private, a shelter and refuge from the materialistic corruptions of the outside world.

The emergence of this new conception of the family was closely tied to larger economic transformations that deprived married women of earlier "productive" roles and transformed them into housewives; created the demographic transition which reduced family's birthrates; and prolonged the length of childhood and produced a new stage of life called "adolescence." During the first decades of the nineteenth century, the expansion of a market-oriented economy separated work from the home and gradually extinguished the domestic industries—such as weaving and spinning—which had employed all family members. Instead of participating in domestic industries, the middle-class wife was expected to devote herself full-time to keeping house and raising children. Psychologically the daily lives of men and women became more separate and specialized. For a growing number of men, the place of work shifted away from the farm or household to the countinghouse, the mill, the factory, the shop, or the office, where work was defined by wages and a clearly demarcated working day. Women's work, in contrast, was unpaid, unsupervised, and task-oriented. Wage work and family life came to be viewed as two distinct and separate endeavors.

The weakening of parental authority in the mid eighteenth century was accompanied by the emergence of a "companionate" conception of marriage: as an emotional bond involving "mutual esteem, mutual friendship, [and] mutual confidence."

The displacement of economic partnership from the matrix of middle-class family life contributed to a fundamental demographic change: a marked lowering of the birthrate. Until 1800, marriage was followed by a repeated cycle of pregnancy and childbirth. A woman might bear her first child at the age of twenty-three and continue to bear children at two-year intervals until she was in her early forties. This twenty-year span of childbearing typically consumed more than half of a woman's married life, since her husband usually died when the wife was in her mid-forties.

Between 1800 and 1860, a dramatically different pattern of family life emerged as women lengthened the interval between births. Instead of bearing seven or eight children, most women had five or six. By the end of the nineteenth century, women had further reduced the number of children to three or four, spaced them closer together, and ceased childbearing at an earlier age.

The sharp decline in the birthrate is a phenomenon easier to describe than to explain. It was not the result of improvements in contraceptive devices. The basic birth control techniques used before the Civil War—such as abstinence, *coitus interruptus* (withdrawal), douching, and condoms—were known earlier but had been employed haphazardly and ineffectively. Nor was the decline in the birthrate a result of urbanization. Although fertility fell earliest and most rapidly in the urban Northeast, the decline in fertility occurred in all parts of the country, in rural as well as urban areas and in the South and West as well as the Northeast.

In part, the reduction in fertility reflected the growing realization that in an increasingly commercial and industrial society, children were no longer economic assets who could be productively employed in household industries or bound out as apprentices or servants. Instead, children required significant investment, in the form of education, to prepare them for respectable careers. The shrinking size of families was not, however, simply a matter of economics; it also reflected women's growing desire to assert control over their lives, as well as changing relationships between husbands and wives and a growing concern with child development. So long as husbands regarded their wives as little more than chattels, they had little incentive to reduce the number of births. But when husbands took an increasing interest in their wives' welfare, a reduction in fertility seemed desirable. Smaller families also permitted parents to improve the quality of their children's upbringing by allowing them to invest more time and energy, as well as more financial resources, in each child.

By the middle of the nineteenth century, the realities of middle-class childhood differed drastically from those prevalent a century before. Instead of shifting back and forth between their parents' home and work experiences as members of other households, a growing proportion of older children continued to live with their parents into their late teens or twenties. One justification for this new practice of keeping children at home longer was the growing belief that adolescence was a particularly unsettled phase of life during which children were greatly in need of parental protection and supervision.

Prolonged residence of children in their parents' home was part of a broader middle-class emphasis on domesticity and family privacy. During the early nineteenth century, an increasing number of apprentices and paid laborers moved out of rooms in their masters' homes and into boardinghouses in distinct working-class neighborhoods. While many middle-class families expelled non-kin, an increasing number of middle-class families supported dependent extended relatives, usually the parents or siblings of the husband or wife. The proportion of families taking in extended kin doubled between 1750 and the late nineteenth century, climbing to about 20 percent of households; the proportion was greatest among families in the highest economic strata. The heightened emphasis on family ties was apparent not only in residence patterns but also in the rise of a series of family-oriented celebrations, such as the birthday party, (after the Civil War), Thanksgiving (during the Civil War), and decorating the Christmas tree (a custom brought to the United States by German immigrants in the 1840s and 1850s).

Alternatives to the Middle-Class Family

The middle-class family was only one of a number of distinctive family patterns that coexisted in nineteenth-century America. Hundreds of early-nineteenth-century utopian communities explicitly rejected the tenets of middle-class family life. Within the institution of slavery, African Americans forged their own unique family and kinship system which helped them to survive the physical and psychological hardships of life in bondage. Industrial immigrants also developed their own distinct family and kinship patterns which helped them adapt to new working and living conditions.

UTOPIAN EXPERIMENTS. During the 1820s, 1830s, and 1840s, literally hundreds of religious and secular communities in Massachusetts, New York, Ohio, Indiana, Tennessee, and Texas experimented with alternative familial and sexual practices. While some of these experimental communal societies were inspired by a religious faith that Christ's second coming was imminent and others were the product of an Enlightenment faith in reason, all were united by a belief that the nuclear family posed a threat to a harmonious society. Utopian critics of the middle-class family argued that conventional sex roles stultified women's intellect and constricted their development; that monogamous marriage distracted individuals from broader social obligations; and that children needed to have contact with more than two adults and to take part in the world of work.

Many communities tried to emancipate women from traditional household and child-rearing responsibilities and to elevate them to positions of equality with men. Each Shaker "family" was presided over by an elder and an eldress, reflecting the bisexual nature of the Shaker godhead. A number of experimental societies, such as the Shakers, the Rappites, and (for a time) the Separatists at Zoar, Ohio, practiced celibacy. Other communities retained "traditional" families while adopting liberal divorce practices and communal child rearing. A third type of group experimented with more communal forms of marriage and sexuality, such as polygamy, complex marriage, eugenics, and free love. All of these utopian communities were united by a desire to extend the intimacy of the family to a wider range of social relationships.

The most notorious utopian experiment was John Humphrey Noyes's Oneida Community. Noyes, a lawyer who studied theology at Andover Theological Seminary and Yale Divinity, School, became convinced that the final millennium would occur only when people strove to become perfect through an "immediate and total cessation from sin." At Putney, Vermont, in 1839, and at Oneida, New York, in 1848, he established perfectionist communities that practiced communal ownership of property and "complex marriage." Exclusive emotional and sexual relationships were forbidden, and the latter were arranged through an intermediary in order to protect a woman's individuality. Men were required to practice coitus interruptus as a method of birth control, and after the Civil War the community conducted experiments in eugenics. Another notable feature of the community was communal child rearing. Oneida flourished in its original form until 1880.

The most revolutionary early-nineteenth-century experiment in restructuring family life was Mormon polygamy. Mormons practiced polygamy for half a century before Mormon policy changed in 1890. The Mormon church justified the practice theologically as an effort to reestablish the patriarchal Old Testament family. Polygamy also served an important social function by absorbing single or widowed women into Mormon communities. Critics denounced polygamy as "a slavery which debases and degrades womanhood, motherhood and family." Contrary to popular belief, it was not widely practiced. Altogether, only 10 to 20 percent of Mormon families were polygamous; nearly two-thirds of such families involved a man and two wives.

During the nineteenth century, most Americans lived in families or family-like settings. Only about 3 percent of the population lived alone. The proportion of women forgoing marriage increased markedly during the nineteenth century and was particularly large among college-educated women. These unmarried women sometimes lived in a partnership called "Boston marriage."

The most striking example of early-nineteenth-century experiments in restructuring family life would be Mormon Polygamy. A Mormon family of this type included two wives and many children.

Young unmarried men and women often resided as boarders or lodgers. Most lodgers took a room in a private house; usually this was a room that had been vacated after an older couple's children had left home. Other lodgers resided in boardinghouses; but even these institutions resembled family households, both in architectural design and in the fact that lodgers dined together.

SLAVE FAMILIES. No area of family history has aroused more controversy or provoked more sweeping revision than the study of slave families. Until the late

1960s, it was widely assumed that slavery destroyed the African family and kinship system, emasculated slave fathers, and forced slave families into a matriarchal structure in which women played the dominant role in the household. The classic statement of this argument is found in E. Franklin Frazier's influential 1939 book *The Negro Family in the United States*, which links the high incidence of female-headed households and out-of-wedlock births among contemporary black families to the strong role of women and the disruption of two-parent, nuclear families under slavery.

This viewpoint, it is now clear, is entirely incorrect. Although slave marriages and family ties lacked legal sanction, and owners were free to sell husbands away from wives and parents away from children, most African Americans married and lived in two-parent households both before and after emancipation. Fathers played a larger familial role than previously thought. The nuclear family received support from an involved network of kin. Indeed, the kinship system forged under slavery would continue to function in twentieth-century rural and urban communities as a source of mutual assistance and cultural continuity.

During the seventeenth century, slaves had little opportunity to establish family units. Newly imported African slaves were often kept in sex-segregated quarters. In the Chesapeake colonies and the Carolinas, most slaves lived on plantations with fewer than ten slaves. These units were so small and so widely dispersed, and the sex ratio was so skewed (two women for three men) that it was difficult for slave men and women to find a spouse of roughly the same age. A high death rate compounded the difficulties slaves faced in forming families, since many slaves did not live long enough to marry or, if they did, their marriages were brief.

At the end of the seventeenth century, the number of imported Africans and the slave fertility rate increased sharply. These demographic developments gradually eased the imbalance of the sex ratio and permitted a growing proportion of slaves to marry. During the 1720s, the African American population became the first slave population in the New World to reproduce itself by natural increase.

By the 1770s, slaves had succeeded in creating a distinctive African American system of family and kinship. To sustain a sense of family identity, slave children were often named for a parent or other blood kin or given a traditional African name. The strength of the slave family is nowhere more evident than in the advertisements eighteenth-century slave owners posted for runaway slaves. The advertisements reveal that one of the major reasons why slaves fled their masters' plantations was to visit spouses, children, siblings, aunts, uncles, and grandparents. In Virginia, advertisements indicate that over one-third of all fugitives were attempting to visit relatives; in Maryland, the advertisements show that nearly half were seeking to visit family members.

The kinship system that slaves developed was not an imitation of patterns typical of southern white families. The distinctiveness of slave family practices is apparent in the slaves' perpetuation of West African taboos against marrying cousins or other near relatives. The taboo against first-cousin marriages was one indication of the importance that slaves, even in the eighteenth century, attached to the extended kinship group. The extended kinship network played a particularly important role in helping slaves adapt to family breakup. Whenever children were sold to neighboring plantations, grandparents, aunts, uncles, and cousins often took on the functions of parents. When blood relatives were not present, strangers cared for and protected children. Slave parents taught their children to call all adult slaves "aunt" or "uncle," and to refer to younger slaves as "sister" or "brother." In this way slave culture taught young people that they were members of a broader community in which all slaves, whether related or not, had mutual obligations.

Two decades of intensive research has established the demographic contours of slave family life. During the decades before the Civil War, most slaves lived in nuclear households consisting of two parents and their children. In 1850, approximately 64 percent of all slaves lived in two-parent families and 25 percent in single-parent families. Another 10 percent lived outside of a family unit, either alone or with others of the same sex. Family breakup, however, was apparently very common. Although many lasted twenty years or more, slave marriages were very vulnerable to breakup by sale. Interviews with former slaves indicate that one-third of all single-parent households were the result of the sale of a husband or wife. Even when marriages were not broken by sale, slave husbands and wives often resided on separate farms or plantations and were owned by different

The Mormon church justified polygamy theologically as an effort to reestablish the patriarchal Old Testament family; the practice was also important as a way to absorb single or widowed women into Mormon communities.

individuals. On large plantations one man in three had a different owner than his wife and could visit his family only at his master's discretion. On smaller holdings, divided ownership was even more common.

Other obstacles stood in the way of an independent family life. Many slaves had to share their single-room cabins with relatives and others who were not related to them. On larger plantations food was cooked in a common kitchen, and young children were cared for in a communal nursery while their parents worked in the fields. On larger plantations, children were taken from their parents between the ages of seven and ten and sent to live in sex-segregated barracks.

Compared to white Americans, African American slaves experienced much higher rates of miscarriage and infant and child mortality, and had a much shorter life expectancy. Poor nutrition and high rates of infant and child mortality contributed to a short average life span—just twenty-one or twenty-two years—compared with forty to forty-three years for whites. Plantation records reveal that over half of all slave babies died during the first year of life—a rate twice that of white infants. Although slave children's death rate declined after the first year, it remained twice the white rate. Poor nutrition may account for the facts that slave women suffered very high rates of spontaneous abortions and stillbirths, and that over half of all slave infants weighed under 5.5 pounds at birth, a dangerously low weight that makes newborns particularly vulnerable to diarrhea, dysentery, whooping cough, respiratory diseases, and worms.

Slave fertility and marriage patterns varied widely, depending on the size of the plantation or farm and the type of crop produced. Slave women on small farms typically married younger, had longer childbearing periods, and were less likely to remain childless than women on large plantations. Similarly, slave women on tobacco farms were more likely to marry than women on cotton, rice, or sugar plantations, and also married earlier and continued childbearing over a longer period.

The strength of black family and kinship ties was revealed clearly after the abolition of slavery. At the end of the Civil War, Union forces did not find the huge numbers of abandoned mothers and orphaned children they had expected but, rather, a vital kinship network through which, as one white minister put it, "all indigent or helpless people are supported by relatives, parents or friends." After emancipation, thousands of freemen roamed the South, struggling desperately to reunite families that had been separated by sale. Many couples, forbidden formal marriage during slavery, took the opportunity to formalize their unions.

During Reconstruction, slavery was replaced by new systems of labor, the most common of which was sharecropping. Instead of cultivating land in gangs supervised by overseers, landowners divided plantations into twenty- to fifty-acre plots suitable for farming by a single family. Former slaves preferred sharecropping to gang labor because it allowed them to have an independent family life. Black wives and daughters sharply reduced their labor in the fields and instead devoted more time to child care and housework. For the first time, black families could divide their time in accordance with their own priorities.

NINETEENTH-CENTURY IMMIGRANT AND WORKING-CLASS FAMILIES. During the nineteenth century, household structure and size varied sharply according to ethnicity and social class. Most families, regardless of class or ethnic background, were nuclear in structure; between 1 and 3 percent of households contained a solitary resident, and between 9 and 12 percent of households contained extended families. But these aggregate statistics should not obscure important socioeconomic differences. Families from higher occupational strata were more likely to take in extended relatives (today, in contrast, the poor are more likely to reside in extended families); immigrant and working-class families were more likely to take in non-kin as boarders and lodgers.

The available demographic evidence suggests that a higher proportion of urban African American and Mexican Americans than immigrant or native-born whites lived in female-headed households. In a variety of urban settings (including Atlanta, Mobile, Natchez, Philadelphia, Richmond, and several cities along the Ohio River), between 1850 and 1880, between 26 and 31 percent of African American families were headed by women—generally two to three times the rate among immigrant or native-born whites. This differential appears to be due not to higher rates of divorce, desertion, or illegitimacy, but rather to sharply skewed black sex ratios in urban areas and to very high levels of adult black male mortality.

Nineteenth-century Mexican Americans, like nineteenth-century African Americans, were more likely than Anglo-Americans to reside in female-headed households. In Los Angeles, San Antonio, Santa Fe, and Tucson in the period 1850 to 1880, between 25 and 38 percent of all Spanish-surnamed households were headed by women (compared with 4 to 9 percent of Anglo-American households), reflecting, in part, a Mexican American adult male death rate, in the 20 to 40 year age group, twice that of females. Mid-nineteenth-century Mexican Americans in the urban Southwest were much less likely than Anglo-Americans to live as lodgers and more likely to reside in extended-family units. In 1850, for example, 13 percent of Mexican

American households in the urban Southwest consisted of extended families, compared with 5.7 percent of Anglo-American households. Mexican American families were more likely than Anglo-American families to take in displaced children.

For nineteenth-century immigrants and the working class, families functioned as cooperative economic units. All household members were expected to contribute to the material support of the family and subordinated their personal wishes to larger family considerations. At a time when most middle-class families had only one breadwinner, relatively few working-class families could support themselves without the economic contributions of other family members, including children.

Typically, a male laborer earned two-thirds of his family's income. The other third was earned by his wife and children. Many married women contributed to the working-class family economy by performing work that could be done in the home, such as embroidering, tailoring, or doing laundry, or caring for boarders or lodgers. The wages of children were particularly critical for a working-class family's standard of living. Children under the age of fifteen contributed 20 percent of the income of many working-class families. Among many ethnic groups, it was common for daughters to leave school at an early age and go to work so that sons could continue their education. It was also customary for a daughter to remain unmarried so that she could care for younger siblings or her parents in their old age. The concept of the "family economy" describes this pattern,

Mid-nineteenth-century Mexican Americans in the urban Southwest were much less likely to live as lodgers and more likely to reside in extended-family units than were Anglo-Americans; they were also more likely to take in displaced children.

in which decision making was a by-product of collective needs rather than of individual preferences.

One strategy that many working-class families used to supplement their income was to take in boarders or lodgers. By the 1990s, fewer than one family in twenty shared its home with a boarder. During the nineteenth century, in contrast, 20 to 30 percent of urban households took in lodgers or boarders, usually unmarried men or women between the ages of twenty and thirty-five who were of the same ethnic background as the household's head. Working-class households were particularly likely to take in boarders or lodgers after their children had left home.

In their allocation of family roles, their internal dynamics, their housing arrangements, their attitudes toward female and child labor, and their kinship patterns, families of various ethnic and class backgrounds differed profoundly. Immigrant families had higher birthrates than native-born whites or blacks; they were also more likely to own their own house and to put their children to work.

Each ethnic group adapted to the circumstances of American life in its own distinct way. Jewish families tended to rent larger apartments and share their residence with lodgers. Italian families, in contrast, resided in smaller and cheaper single-family apartments, while urban blacks often rented space in another family's household. Ethnic families also varied greatly in their attitudes toward female and child labor. Some immigrant groups, such as the Irish and Slavs, were willing to forgo their children's education rather than send married women into the work force. Other groups, particularly Jews and blacks, tended to keep their children in school despite the lost earnings. Italian families, more than almost any other ethnic group, discouraged women from working outside the home. Italian girls were rarely permitted to work unsupervised by relatives or friends, and Italian mothers tended to work outside the home only intermittently, when required by family illness or emergency. When Italian mothers did work for wages, they preferred homework to factory work.

Rejecting the older view that migration to urban areas, poverty, and integration into an industrial economy weakened family ties and undermined the extended kinship networks of immigrants, family historians have found that family and kinship relationships played a critical role in easing the stresses of migration and facilitating adjustment to an urban and industrial way of life. Family connections were a basic resource in effecting the immigrants' transition to their new environment. Most immigrants made use of kin and friends in traveling and settled in neighborhoods already populated by people from the same home village or community, who provided information about urban life, offered temporary housing, and assisted in finding work. During critical life situations, such as illness, unemployment, injury, or old age, kinship networks provided assistance with child care, loans, or a place to live.

During the early twentieth century, ethnic and working-class families began to show a superficial resemblance to middle-class families. As a result of rising real wages and greater job security due to the seniority systems instituted as a result of labor union pressures, a higher proportion of working-class families were able to withdraw wives and children from the labor force. Ethnic differences in fertility rates declined; rates of intermarriage among ethnic and religious groups rose; and home-ownership rates jumped sharply. Whereas only a third of families owned their own home at the beginning of the century, by mid century the figure had climbed to two-thirds. As early as the late 1920s, social commentators increasingly spoke of a "typical" American family, transcending class and ethnic lines, characterized by a firm division of labor between a breadwinner husband and a homemaker wife and an intense child-centered orientation.

Twentieth-Century Patterns of Change

At the end of the nineteenth century, many Americans feared that the family was disintegrating. Three developments contributed to a sense of crisis: a declining birthrate, a rising divorce rate, and efforts of a growing number of women to break out of their separate sphere of domesticity by obtaining a higher education, joining women's organizations, and taking jobs outside the home.

Many educators, legal scholars, and social workers responded to these developments by popularizing a new ideal of family life, termed the "companionate family," that emphasized equal rights, sexual attraction, and companionship. According to this new ideal, spouses would be "friends and lovers," and parents and children would be "pals." To achieve this ideal, influential groups recommended liberalized divorce laws, marriage counseling, sex education, easier access to birth control information, and permissive child-rearing practices that would stress physical affection and self-expression over impulse control.

The impact of this new ideal was delayed by the Great Depression and World War II, only to resurface dramatically after the war. During the Depression, unemployment, reduced pay, and the demands of needy relatives tore at the fabric of family life, forcing many families to share living quarters with relatives, delay marriages, and put off having children. The divorce rate fell because fewer people could afford one, but rates of desertion and separation soared. By 1940, over 1.5 million married women were living apart from their husbands.

Families sought to cope with the crisis by pooling incomes and planting gardens, canning food, and making clothing. Many children took part-time jobs, and many wives earned supplementary income by taking in sewing or laundry, setting up parlor groceries, and housing lodgers.

World War II subjected the nation's families to severe strain. During the war, one-sixth of the nation's families suffered prolonged separation from sons or fathers. Five million "war widows" had to cook, clean, launder, and care for children alone. Wartime migration added to familial strain, as more than fifteen million civilians moved in search of new jobs. Wartime families faced a severe shortage of adequate housing and a lack of child-care facilities. These stresses contributed to a dramatic upsurge in the postwar divorce rate and to severe problems of child welfare, including tens of thousands of unsupervised "latchkey" children and high rates of juvenile delinquency, venereal disease, and truancy.

The next decade witnessed a sharp reaction to the stresses of the Depression and the war. The wartime housing shortage was relieved by extensive construction, and millions of families moved to new single-family homes in the suburbs. During the 1950s, young adults married in record numbers, and they married earlier than other twentieth-century. Americans. At the same time, the rate of increase in divorces during the 1950s was slower than in other decades of the century.

THE 1950S AS THE GREAT EXCEPTION. To many Americans, the 1950s represent a sort of "golden age" of the family, a reference point against which recent changes in family life can be measured. In fact, the pattern of family life characteristic of the late 1940s and 1950s differed dramatically from that observed earlier in the twentieth century and since. The high marriage rate, low age at marriage, high birthrate, and relatively stable divorce rate of the 1950s were all sharply out of line with long-term demographic trends. Throughout the nineteenth century, the proportion of Americans marrying remained relatively stable. During World War II and the immediate postwar period, however, that proportion shot up. By the end of World War II, there were 2.5 million fewer single women than in 1940, and by the end of the 1950s, 70 percent of all women were married by the age of twenty-four, compared with 42 percent in 1940 and 50 percent in 1990. Since 1972, the marriage rate (defined as the number of marriages per thousand women over fourteen) has fallen to its lowest levels since the Depression.

During the 1950s, the age at marriage fell to a record low. Since the late nineteenth century, men have tended to marry in their mid to late twenties and women have wed in their early or mid twenties. In 1890 the median age at first marriage for men was 26.1 years and 22 years for women. The median age at first marriage gradually fell until 1955, when it stood at 22.6 years for men and 20.2 years for women. Since the mid 1950s, the median age at first marriage has risen. Although it is often said that young people today are delaying marriage to unusually late ages, in fact the average age at marriage is in line with historical averages. It was the young men and women of the 1950s, reacting against the hardships and upheavals of the Depression and war, who married unusually early.

Families of the 1950s were distinctive in their increasing size. Since the beginning of the nineteenth century, American birthrates had fallen fairly steadily. During the 1950s, however, this pattern reversed itself as women of childbearing age bore more children, spaced them closer together, and had them earlier and faster than their mothers had. The fertility rate rose 50 percent between 1940 and 1957; the birthrate doubled for third children and tripled for fourth children.

And, finally, the relatively stable divorce rate of the 1950s was out of line with long-term trends. From the Civil War to World War II, divorce rates rose fairly steadily, then shot upward immediately after World War II, when hundreds of thousands of wartime marriages were dissolved. During the 1950s, divorce rates stabilized; at the end of the decade, rates were no higher than in 1947. During the mid 1960s and 1970s, divorce rates rose very rapidly, peaking at 22.8 divorces per 1,000 married couples in 1979. Since the late 1970s, divorce rates have stabilized again. Rates of remarriage following divorce or a spouse's death increased from the early 1930s until World War II, declined during the late 1940s and 1950s, rose rapidly during the early and mid 1960s and early 1970s, and then began to decline again.

LATE-TWENTIETH-CENTURY CHANGES IN FAMILY STRUCTURE. During the 1950s, the Cleavers on the television show *Leave It to Beaver* epitomized the American family. In 1960 over 70 percent of all American households were like the Cleavers: made up of a breadwinner father, a housewife mother, and their children. Thirty years later, "traditional" families with a go-to-work father, a stay-at-home mother, and one or more children made up less than 15 percent of the nation's households. As America's families changed, the image of the family on television changed accordingly. In the 1990s television families ran the gamut from two-career couples like the Huxtables on *The Cosby Show* to two single mothers and their children on *Kate and Allie* and an unmarried couple (a male housekeeper and his employer) who cohabit in the same house on *Who's the Boss?*

Americans in the 1990s were much more likely than their counterparts in the 1950s to postpone or forgo marriage, to live alone outside a family unit, to engage in sexual intercourse prior to marriage, end a marriage in divorce, to sanction the employment of mothers of young children outside the home, and to accept children living in families headed by a mother, with no husband present. The term "family" has gradually been redefined to apply to any group of people living together, including single mothers and children, unmarried couples, and gay couples.

Profound demographic transformations have reshaped American family life. Between 1965 and 1975, the divorce rate doubled. The number of divorces in 1990 was twice as high as in 1966 and three times higher than in 1950. The rising divorce rate contributed to a sharp increase in the number of single-parent households—what used to be known as broken homes. The number of households consisting of a single woman and her children doubled since 1960. Climbing divorce rates also contributed to a sharp increase in the number of stepfamilies—what came to be called "reconstituted" or "blended" families. In 1991 there were 11 million families in which at least one spouse had been married before, an increase from 8.9 million in 1970.

In 1960, over 70 percent of American households resembled the fictional Cleaver family on television's Leave It to Beaver; *by 1990, such "traditional" families with a go-to-work father, a stay-at-home mother, and one or more children made up less than 15 percent of the nation's households.*

While the divorce rate rose, the marriage rate fell as a growing number of young people delayed marriage. In 1960, only one man in four and one woman in ten had never married by the age of twenty-six. By 1987, half of the men and over 40 percent of the women had not married by that age. The birthrate also declined, from an average of nearly 3.5 children per mother to 1.8, below the natural replacement level.

Living arrangements changed drastically. The number of people living alone grew by 60 percent during the 1970s, and by 1980, nearly a quarter of all American households consisted of one person. At the same time, the number of couples cohabiting outside of wedlock climbed steeply. Between 1970 and 1990, the number of unmarried couples living together quadrupled. Nearly half of all Americans who married between 1980 and 1984 had cohabited with a member of the opposite sex while they were single, compared with just over 10 percent of Americans married between 1965 and 1974.

American sexual behavior also changed radically. In 1960 nearly half of all women waited until marriage to become sexually active; by the 1990s the proportion had declined to one in five. Meanwhile, the proportion of births among unmarried women more than quadrupled. In 1965 just 5 percent of births were out of wedlock; by 1986 the figure had climbed to 23 percent—suggesting that out-of-wedlock births would soon overtake divorce as the primary cause of families headed by single mothers.

EXPLANATIONS FOR CHANGES IN FAMILY STRUCTURE. What are the causes of the dramatic transformations that have taken place in American family life since the late 1950s? The driving force behind these transformations lies in a far-reaching shift in values. In the 1960s, an overwhelming majority of Americans endorsed marriage as a prerequisite of well-being, social adjustment, and maturity. Men and women who failed to marry were denigrated as "sick," "neurotic," or "immoral," and couples who did not have children were deemed "selfish." A large majority of the public believed that an unhappily married couple should stay together for the sake of their children; that a woman should not work if she had a husband who could support her; that premarital sex was always wrong; and that an unmarried couple should get married if they were expecting a baby.

During the 1960s and 1970s, popular attitudes toward marriage, sex, and divorce underwent a dramatic change. Cultural biases against divorce, working mothers, premarital sex, and out-of-wedlock births eroded, encouraged by a sexual revolution, expanding job opportunities for women, women's liberation, and the growing popularity of psychological therapies stressing "growth," "self-realization," and "fulfillment."

Economic affluence played a major role in the emergence of a new outlook. Individuals who came of age during the 1960s and 1970s spent their childhoods during an era of unprecedented affluence. Between 1950 and 1970, median family income tripled. Increased affluence brought greater opportunities for education, travel, and leisure, all of which helped to heighten expectations for fulfillment and personal happiness.

Another factor reshaping family life has been a massive influx of mothers into the work force. In 1950, 25 percent of married women living with their husbands worked outside the home;, in the late 1980s, the figure had climbed to nearly 60 percent. The increase in the number of working mothers was particularly rapid among women with young children. By 1988 more than half of all mothers of school-age children held a job. The major forces that propelled women into the work force included a rising cost of living, which spurred many families to seek a second source of income; increased control over fertility through contraception and abortion, which allowed women to work without interruption; and rising educational levels, which led many women to seek employment for intellectual stimulation and fulfillment.

As wives assumed a larger role in the family's financial support, there was a greater need for husbands to perform a larger share of child care and housework. At the same time, fewer children had a stay-at-home mother and an increasing number were cared for during the day by adults other than their mother. In 1990, over two-thirds of all three-to-five-year-olds were enrolled in a day-care, nursery school, or prekindergarten program, compared with one-fifth in 1970.

As wives assume a larger role in the family's financial support, an increasing number of children are cared for in a day-care, nursery school or pre-kindergarten program.

Feminism has been another major force that has transformed American family life. The women's liberation movement attacked the societal expectation that women would defer to the needs or wants of spouses and children as part of their roles as wives and mothers. Militant feminist activists like Ti-Grace Atkinson denounced marriage as "slavery" and "legalized rape." The larger mainstream of the women's movement articulated a powerful critique of the idea that child care and housework were the apex of a woman's accomplishments or her sole means of fulfillment. As a result of feminism, a substantial majority of women now believe that both husband and wife should have a job, do housework, and take care of children.

Demographic and economic factors also contributed to changes in family patterns. Slow economic growth, declining average earnings, and an increase in premarital sexual activity may have discouraged early marriage during the 1970s and 1980s. In addition, many women in the 1970s faced a "marriage squeeze." Born in the last years of the baby boom, these young women substantially outnumbered eligible prospective grooms, which forced many to postpone or forgo marriage. Meanwhile, increases in social security payments allowed an increasing share of the elderly to live independently. Over half of all Americans living alone, outside of family units, are fifty-four years old or older; about two-fifths are widowed.

FAMILIES IN POVERTY. Divorce rates, single parenthood, and out-of-wedlock births have risen among all segments of American society since 1960, but have posed particular problems for poorer African American communities, where rates of divorce and desertion historically have been higher than among other groups. In 1990, over half of all black children lived in single-parent homes (compared with 20 percent in 1960); over 60 percent of black children were born to an unmarried mother (compared with 25 percent in 1960); and 25 percent of all black babies were born to teenage mothers, most of them unmarried. In contrast, 16 percent of white children and 27 percent of Hispanic children lived in single family homes; 17 percent of white children were born to teenage mothers; and 17 percent of white children were born to unmarried mothers.

Conservative social analysts such as Charles Murray took the position that state and federal welfare policies encouraged family dissolution and out-of-wedlock births. The belief that government welfare expenditures caused family breakdown rests on the close chronological correlation between rising welfare spending and dramatic increases in female-headed households and illegitimacy among the poor.

Did the expansion of state services contribute to rising rates of illegitimacy and single-parent families? The answer appears to be no. Scholars have found no correlations between the level of welfare payments and the incidence of out-of-wedlock births (although states with higher welfare benefits do tend to have slightly higher divorce rates and lower rates of remarriage). Between 1972 and 1980, the number of black children in single-parent families jumped 20 percent, even though the number of black children receiving welfare payments declined. And even though welfare benefits fell in real terms during the 1970s, the number of black female-headed families continued to climb.

An alternative explanation of the growing number of single-parent families in central cities emphasizes structural changes in the American economy. Sociologist William Julius Wilson argues that increases in joblessness among black men made marriage a less attractive option for poor black women. He contends that the number of marriageable black men capable of supporting a family fell after 1970, as the number of jobs in central cities requiring less than a high school education decreased. In 1960, there were seventy employed black men ages twenty to twenty-four for every one hundred black women in the same age group. By the early 1980s, the proportion of employed black men had fallen to less than fifty.

Is male joblessness the primary cause of high rates of single parenthood in poor black communities? The answer is uncertain. The marriage rate among employed black men has fallen nearly as much as the rate among all black men, suggesting that noneconomic factors contribute significantly to the decline in black marriage rates.

ASSESSING RECENT CHANGES IN FAMILY STRUCTURE. When viewed from a comparative perspective, contemporary American family life presents a paradox. No other industrialized nation shows a stronger commitment to marriage or invests the family with more responsibility for social welfare. At the same time, in no other advanced country are family ties as precarious or family forms more diverse. The United States has at once among the highest marriage and remarriage rates in the industrialized West and the highest divorce rate—roughly twice as high as in other advanced societies. In certain respects the United States is staunchly traditionalist—notably in the relatively high proportion of religious weddings and the high value that American culture attaches to family loyalty and identity. But in other respects the United States appears to have departed farther than other nations from a commitment to the "traditional" family. It has the industrialized

West's highest rate of single parenthood and one of the highest rates of illegitimacy.

While American family patterns have undergone far-reaching changes in recent years, it would be a mistake to conclude that the American family is in danger of imminent collapse. Despite the declining birthrate and rising divorce and illegitimacy rates, commitment to familial relationships remains strong, though family ties are defined in increasingly flexible ways.

Birthrates have fallen dramatically, to be sure, but rather than reflecting an increase in the proportion of couples wanting no children, this decline reflects a sharp reduction in the number of unwanted births and in the number of families with four or more children. A reduction in unwanted births, as a result of improved methods of contraception and easier access to abortion, accounts for roughly 40 percent of the fertility drop between 1961 and 1982.

Cohabitation outside of wedlock has increased, but rather than becoming an alternative to marriage, unmarried cohabitation appears, in most cases, to be a temporary stage prior to marriage or remarriage. Although growing numbers of young men and women have postponed marriage into their late twenties or thirties, commitment to marriage has not eroded. The overwhelming majority of Americans marry at some point in their life; approximately nineteen out of every twenty Americans marry before they reach middle age. This rate is higher than the late-nineteenth-century marriage rate.

Although the family is often considered to be the social institution most resistant to change, in fact it is as embedded in the historical process as any other institution. Since the seventeenth century, diversity and change—not uniformity and continuity—have been the norm. Recent changes in family roles and structure represent simply the latest stage in an ongoing process of change and adaptation.

[See also Adolescence; Childhood and Children; Courtship, Marriage, Separation, and Divorce; Gender Roles and Relations; Life Stages; Old Age; Reproduction and Parenthood; Sexual Behavior and Morality.]

BIBLIOGRAPHY

Surveys and Overviews

Coontz, Stephanie. *The Social Origins of Private Life: A History of American Families, 1600–1900* (1988).

Degler, Carl N. *At Odds: Women and the Family in America from the Revolution to the Present* (1980).

Gordon, Michael. *The American Family: Past, Present and Future* (1978).

Mintz, Steven, and Susan Kellogg. *Domestic Revolutions: A Social History of American Family Life* (1988).

Concepts, Methods, Analytic Frameworks

Anderson, Michael. *Approaches to the History of the Western Family, 1500–1914* (1980).

Degler, Carl N. "Women and the Family." In *The Past Before Us: Contemporary Historical Writing in the United States,* edited by Michael Kammen (1980).

Vinovskis, Maris. "The Historian and the Life Course." *Life-Span Development and Behavior* 8 (1986): 33–59.

Demographic Characteristics

Ruggles, Steven. *Prolonged Connections: The Rise of the Extended Family in Nineteenth-Century England and America* (1987).

Seward, Rudy Ray. *The American Family: A Demographic History* (1978).

Sweet, James A., and Larry L. Bumpass. *American Families and Households* (1987).

Wells, Robert V. *Revolutions in Americans' Lives: A Demographic Perspective on the History of Americans, Their Families, and Their Society* (1982).

Wells, Robert V. *Uncle Sam's Family: Issues in and Perspectives on American Demographic History* (1985).

Colonial New England

Demos, John. *A Little Commonwealth: Family Life in Plymouth Colony* (1970).

Greven, Philip J., Jr. *Four Generations: Population, Land, and Family in Colonial Andover, Massachusetts* (1970).

Lockridge, Kenneth A. *A New England Town: The First Hundred Years, Dedham, Massachusetts, 1636–1736* (1970).

Morgan, Edmund S. *The Puritan Family: Religion and Domestic Relations in Seventeenth-Century New England.* rev. and enl. (1966).

Middle Colonies

Fischer, David Hackett. *Albion's Seed: Four British Folkways in America* (1989).

Levy, Barry. *Quakers and the American Family: British Settlement in the Delaware Valley* (1988).

Zuckerman, Michael, ed. *Friends and Neighbors: Group Life in America's First Plural Society* (1982).

Colonial South

Lewis, Jan. *The Pursuit of Happiness: Family and Values in Jefferson's Virginia* (1983).

Smith, Daniel Blake. *Inside the Great House: Planter Family Life in Eighteenth-Century Chesapeake Society* (1980).

Tate, Thad W., and David L. Ammerman, eds. *The Chesapeake in the Seventeenth Century: Essays on Anglo-American Society* (1979).

Nineteenth-Century Middle-class Families

Johnson, Paul. *A Shopkeeper's Millennium: Society and Revivals in Rochester, New York, 1815–1837* (1978).

Mintz, Steven. *A Prison of Expectations: The Family in Victorian Culture* (1983).

Rothman, Ellen. *Hands and Hearts: A History of Courtship in America* (1984).

Ryan, Mary P. *Cradle of the Middle Class: The Family in Oneida County, New York, 1790–1865* (1981).

Nineteenth-Century Southern White Families

Censer, Jane T. *North Carolina Planters and Their Children, 1800–1860* (1984).

Lebsock, Suzanne. *The Free Women of Petersburg: Status and Culture in a Southern Town, 1784–1860* (1984).

Black Families

Borchert, James. *Alley Life in Washington: Family, Community, Religion, and Folklife in the City, 1850–1970* (1980).

Fogel, Robert W. *Without Consent or Contract: The Rise and Fall of American Slavery* (1989).

Gutman, Herbert. *The Black Family in Slavery and Freedom, 1750–1925* (1976).

Horton, James O., and Lois E. Horton. *Black Bostonians: Family Life and Community Struggle in the Antebellum North* (1979).

Kulikoff, Allan. *Tobacco and Slaves: The Development of Southern Cultures in the Chesapeake, 1680–1800* (1986).

Pleck, Elizabeth. *Black Migration and Poverty: Boston, 1865–1900* (1979).

Nineteenth-Century Working-class Families

Ehrlich, Richard L., ed. *Immigrants in Industrial America, 1850–1920* (1977).

Griswold Del Castillo, Richard. *La Familia: Chicano Families in the Urban Southwest, 1848 to the Present* (1984).

Hareven, Tamara K. *Transitions: The Family and the Life Course in Historical Perspective* (1978).

Hareven, Tamara K. *Family Time and Industrial Time: The Relationship Between the Family and Work in a New England Industrial Community* (1982).

Hareven, Tamara K, ed. *Family and Kin in Urban Communities, 1700–1930* (1977).

Hershberg, Theodore, ed. *Philadelphia: Work, Space, Family, and Group Experience in the Nineteenth Century* (1981).

Katz, Michael B. *The People of Hamilton, Canada West: Family and Class in a Mid-Nineteenth-Century City* (1975).

Smith, Judith E. *Family Connections: A History of Italian and Jewish Immigrant Lives in Providence, Rhode Island, 1900–1940* (1985).

Yans-McLaughlin, Virginia. *Family and Community: Italian Immigrants in Buffalo, 1880–1930* (1977).

Utopian Alternatives

Fellman, Michael. *The Unbounded Frame: Freedom and Community in Nineteenth-Century American Utopianism* (1973).

Foster, Lawrence. *Religion and Sexuality: Three American Communal Experiments of the Nineteenth Century* (1981).

Muncy, Raymond Lee. *Sex and Marriage in Utopian Communities: Nineteenth-Century America* (1973).

Farming and Frontier Families

Barron, Hal S. *Those Who Stayed Behind: Rural Society in Nineteenth-Century New England* (1984).

Faragher, John Mack. *Women and Men on the Overland Trail* (1979).

Faragher, John Mack. *Sugar Creek: Life on the Illinois Prairie* (1986).

Jeffrey, Julie Roy. *Frontier Women: The Trans-Mississippi West, 1840–1880* (1979).

McNall, Scott G., and Sally A. McNall. *Plains Families: Exploring Sociology Through Social History* (1983).

Turn of the Century

May, Elaine Tyler. *Great Expectations: Marriage and Divorce in Post-Victorian America* (1980).

Great Depression

Scharf, Lois. *To Work and to Wed: Female Employment, Feminism and the Great Depression* (1980).

Ware, Susan. *Holding Their Own: American Women in the 1930s* (1982).

World War II

Anderson, Karen. *Wartime Women: Sex Roles, Family Relations, and the Status of Women During World War II* (1981).

Campbell, D'Ann. *Women at War with America: Private Lives in a Patriotic Era* (1984).

Hartmann, Susan M. *The Homefront and Beyond: American Women in the 1940s* (1982).

The 1950s

Cherlin, Andrew J. *Marriage, Divorce, Remarriage* (1981).

May, Elaine Tyler. *Homeward Bound: American Families in the Cold War Era* (1988).

Recent Transformations

Bane, Mary Jo. *Here to Stay: American Families in the Twentieth Century* (1976).

Fuchs, Victor R. *How We Live* (1983).

Levitan, Sar A., et al. *What's Happening to the American Family? Tensions, Hopes, Realities*, rev. ed. (1988).

Popenoe, David. *Disturbing the Nest: Family Change and Decline in Modern Societies* (1988).

— SUSAN KELLOGG AND STEVEN MINTZ

FILM

In 1872, Leland Stanford, a former California governor, wagered $25,000 that a galloping horse lifted all four legs from the ground simultaneously and hired Eadweard Muybridge to shoot an experimental set of photographs to prove his point. The first experiment failed, but five years later, the two men tried again. At a Sacramento racetrack in 1877, they set up a track equipped with trip wires connected to twenty-four cameras, so that the horses set off the cameras' shutters as they galloped past, momentarily airborne.

The Invention of the Movies

The resulting set of photographs—which looked much like the minutely changing still frames on a strip of twentieth-century celluloid movie film—won Stanford's bet for him. Stanford's experiment with Muybridge also, inadvertently, proved to be a major innovation in the scientific study of motion and the development of the motion-picture camera. Muybridge's series of still photographs created an illusion of motion that impressed the French scientist and inventor

Étienne-Jules Marey. Marey had previously worked with photography to re-create action, but never with Muybridge's success. It was Marey who made the technical breakthroughs that gave rise to the motion-picture camera in 1882.

The American inventor Thomas A. Edison pushed the new inventions further toward an entertainment medium. Working with his assistant, William K. L. Dickson (an often-unacknowledged contributor to the cinematic inventions attributed to Edison), the famous inventor attempted to devise a means of projecting the film sequences that captured an illusion of motion. Interestingly, Edison's first experiments with motion pictures were attempts to coordinate moving images with sound as a visual accompaniment for his new invention of the phonograph. The synchronization of the aural with the visual was quickly abandoned, however, as a futile effort, and Dickson's endeavors turned toward perfecting silent motion pictures. It took approximately thirty more years—until 1927—for sound to accompany the moving pictures.

In 1891, Dickson discovered how to make motion-picture film by perforating the celluloid so that it moved through the camera. Later that same year, he invented a boxlike machine through which the images could be projected. Looking through an opening in the top of the machine, an individual viewer could see the pictures move. By 1891, Edison had been granted a patent for both Dickson's camera, the kinetograph, and his projecting device, the kinetoscope.

What emerged in the 1890s, as inventors in several countries competed to perfect the motion-picture camera, was a primitive entertainment device. The first "movies" were projected in peep shows, not on the large screens associated with the cinema today. In April 1894, Edison first demonstrated the kinetoscope on Broadway in New York for the relatively high price of twenty-five cents. There, peering through a binocularlike lens, a single spectator could see tiny figures juggling balls or ocean waves washing toward the shore. It was an instant success with audiences who waited eagerly to see the tiny living pictures.

But Edison's greatest ambition was a more realistic projection of moving pictures on a human scale. Unlike the inventor-scientist Marey, Edison was a shrewd businessman and self-promoter who turned the new discovery into profitable entertainment for the masses. Edison's earliest films were simple, nonnarrative documentations of the fact that motion could be preserved on film. In 1903, *Electrocuting an Elephant* illustrated the death of a circus elephant that had gone berserk. One of the first uses of trick photography in film was in a short titled *The Execution of Mary, Queen of Scots* (1895), in which an actress was filmed walking to the block. A dummy was then substituted for the beheading, and the resulting footage spliced together. Such early films were already purveyors of sensationalist entertainment.

In films usually running under ninety seconds, the earliest motion pictures thus simply entertained vaudeville theater audiences with the magic of the new invention. Dickson began shooting short segments of the era's variety-show acts, such as Annie Oakley, Buffalo Bill Cody, and the dancer Ruth St. Denis. Other film promoters shot prizefights as a means of making the new medium popular and profitable in peep shows.

It was in Paris in 1895, however, that motion pictures were first projected to a large audience who paid for the entertainment. The brothers Auguste and Louis Lumière had experimented with motion-picture equipment in France; they expanded on Dickson's kinescope and kinetograph, developing a projector they called the *cinématographe*. It is in this term that the current word "cinema"—from the Greek for "motion"—has its origins. The cinématographe was capable of projecting film on a screen, allowing many people to view motion pictures at once.

The invention of what we currently know as "the movies" is thus the product of many inventors. Once both the camera and the projection equipment had been invented, entrepreneurs quickly scrambled for a way to make the new motion pictures profitable. Edison, rapidly working from the ideas of the Lumière brothers, developed his own projector, called the vitascope. In the spring of 1896, he premiered his invention at Koster and Bial's Music Hall in New York. The showing included short films of women dancing, a comic portrayal of a boxing match, and—most popular of all—scenes of high waves breaking dramatically on a shore.

Soon, motion pictures were running on the bill of vaudeville programs, where they followed comedy acts or song-and-dance skits. Such films typically ran at the end of live vaudeville shows, becoming known as "chasers"—the act that signaled it was time to leave.

It was not long before audiences grew tired of the novelty of watching simple pictures move. The next step forward in the development of the entertainment medium was its evolution as a narrative form. When, around the turn of the century, films began to tell stories, another important development in the evolution of the motion picture occurred: theaters rose that devoted their bills solely to film.

Called nickelodeons, after the five-cent price of admission, the new storefront theaters sprang up in cities all over the country. By 1905, neighborhood theaters were finding increasingly enthusiastic audiences, pushing their coins across box office windows to watch an entire bill of short, often one-reel, films. It was not long before thousands of nickelodeons existed throughout the United States; in 1907, one estimate figured that five thousand of the theaters were in operation, drawing primarily working-class audiences.

The First Narrative Films and the First Studios

One of the most sophisticated motion pictures of this period is *The Great Train Robbery,* directed by Edwin S. Porter in 1903. In his use of close-ups and parallel editing, Porter created a visual sense of suspense and action that made his film a popular success. Using many shots of both interior and exterior scenes, the film raced quickly from one action to the next, following the railroad bandits through the countryside with heightening drama. While Porter's techniques brought new life to the cinema, his themes also captured an important element of America—the legend of the West in all its violent lawlessness.

Porter's development of film techniques, especially the sophistication of his editing, provided important building blocks for the new art form. At the time of Porter's greatest success, Hollywood had not yet been born as the location of America's "dream machine." Several factors created the West Coast mecca for the movies: it had an ideal climate and it offered raw, dramatic scenery unavailable at the studios on the East Coast. Most important, however, the Hollywood site, with its distance from the East Coast and its proximity to Mexico, offered independent film companies some modicum of protection from Edison's Motion Picture Patents Company (MPPC), commonly known as the Trust.

In 1908, Edison had formed a group of nine film-producing companies and one importer, all agreeing to share the patents that each company held. In an effort to dominate the industry, the ten companies made an agreement with Eastman Kodak (the nation's only manufacturer of raw film stock) that the Kodak product would be sold only to MPPC members. To further consolidate their control, the Trust companies licensed only select distributors and exhibitors for their films. They thus threatened both to outlaw all other companies and to prevent new ones from forming. Edison's shrewd business tactics paid off handsomely; his annual profits skyrocketed after the formation of the Trust.

Several renegade film companies fled to the West Coast and set up business in the inviting climate of southern California. It proved to be a lucrative move for the independents. The competition between the independents and the Trust, however, had several positive results for the film industry. In order to compete with the MPPC, the independent companies took risks and experimented in ways that the conservative Trust members did not need to. Independents such as Carl Laemmle, with his Independent Motion Picture Company (1909), invested in the quality of their films, so that by 1915, when the MPPC was broken up after the Supreme Court's *Mutual Film Corporation v. Industrial Commission of Ohio* decision, the Independent motion pictures were generally of better quality than the lower-budget, short MPPC pictures.

In 1909, Laemmle tried one of the most enterprising tactics of all when he initiated a phenomenon that later film audiences would take for granted—the star system. Prior to the rise of the star system, the actors and actresses in early silent films remained uncredited, and the anonymous stars were identified by fans simply by titles such as the "Girl with the Curls" or as "Little Mary," the character often played by the actress who would later become famous as Mary Pickford. Recognizing the curiosity that audiences had for the anonymous early film "stars," Laemmle made the unprecedented move of releasing personal information about the actress Florence Lawrence. The shrewd film producer first gave false information to the press about the actress, claiming that she had been killed in an accident. The resulting outcry from fans proved Lawrence's box office appeal. Laemmle quickly retracted the information, and brought Lawrence before a new set of adoring, curious fans. When Lawrence had worked for Biograph Pictures and then with Laemmle's Independent Motion Pictures, she was known only as the "Biograph Girl" or the "IMP Girl."

In The Great Train Robbery *(1903), one of the era's most sophisticated pictures, director Edwin S. Porter created a visual sense of suspense and action with his use of close-ups, parallel editing, and many shots of both interior and exterior scenes.*

Following the release of Florence Lawrence's name, the surge of public interest in the actress made the identification of featured actors and actresses commonplace—and launched the star system. The new celebrities provided audiences with fantasy figures, and it was not long before fan magazines and posters catered to the curiosity of moviegoers. As the American public looked to the larger-than-life figures on the screen for their ideals of human perfection and romantic fantasies, the stars became valuable commodities. Salaries of actors and actresses quickly skyrocketed to as much as $10,000 a week for Charlie Chaplin in 1916. As their power increased within the industry, actors and actresses even began to form their own companies, the biggest being United Artists, established in 1919 by Mary Pickford, Charlie Chaplin, Douglas Fairbanks, and D. W. Griffith.

One of the most important outcomes of the competition brought on by the Trust was the creation of the feature film. In order to draw more middle-class audiences and to secure respect for the often-criticized new entertainment form, independent filmmakers began to experiment with longer motion pictures. During the Progressive Era, feature films, such as those made by IMP, slowly began to rival the MPPC's one-reelers and bill of shorts with a single movie attraction.

THE BIRTH OF A NATION *and* THE BIRTH OF A RACE. One of the most famous and technically influential early features was David Wark Griffith's controversial *The Birth of a Nation,* released in 1915. New York City was the original base for Griffith, one of the most important directors in the history of the medium. He came to the filmmaking business in 1907, leaving behind his acting career in the New York theater in an effort to make more money. At Biograph Studios, Griffith experimented with cinematic technique in a way that would later influence directors all over the world, particularly the Russian filmmaker Sergei Eisenstein. Griffith's films, *The Birth of a Nation* (1915) and *Intolerance* (1916), provided glimpses of the technical achievements possible for the new medium. The rapid cross-cutting of parallel editing so that two narrative events could be presented simultaneously heightened the suspense of Griffith's films. The extreme close-ups he used in *The Musketeers of Pig Alley* (1912) brought a new, gritty realism to the urban characters and conflicts of the film.

It is ironic that *The Birth of a Nation,* one of the greatest early motion pictures, should be so progressive technically, yet so thematically retrogressive. A Kentuckian by birth, Griffith wanted to extol the ideals of the Old South and its concept of white racial supremacy. Based on *The Clansman* (1905) by Thomas Dixon, Jr., Griffith's melodramatic epic reveals the origin of the Ku Klux Klan as if its leaders were heroic saviors of the white women of the South during the Reconstruction era. Except for those loyal to the white families, former slaves are depicted as demonic creatures going berserk with their new freedom. Yet Griffith told the saga of the Deep South so dramatically that many audiences found its visual images emotionally compelling, despite what was, for the era, an extraordinarily long running time of over two and a half hours. It was, stated Woodrow Wilson after he saw *The Birth of a Nation* in a private screening at the White House in 1915, "like writing history

United Artists was formed by (l-r) actor Douglas Fairbanks, producer Samuel Goldwyn, actress Mary Pickford, and actor Charlie Chaplin. This photograph was taken in 1935 as Alexander Korda (far right) joins the Board of Directors.

with lightning": such was the power of the cinema to blend propaganda with historical fact and make it appear to be objective truth. The rapid building of suspense and tension played on the emotions, even discouraging analytical thought.

Not everyone, of course, was so favorably impressed with *The Birth of a Nation* as Woodrow Wilson—though many were emotionally affected. In protest of the showing of the racist film, riots broke out in Boston. It was, perhaps, the first time that the visceral power of the motion picture was so publicly recognized. (Griffith was appalled at what he deemed the misunderstanding of his intention. [He had felt that his cinematic portrayal of loyal former slaves was respectful.] In response to the protests, he immediately began making *Intolerance*, a lengthy historical film in four parts that campaigned against intolerance in any form throughout history.)

A lesser-known film than Griffith's famous Southern epic is the black cinematic response to it. Booker T. Washington and his assistant, Emmett J. Scott, felt that the best protest would be for a black motion-picture company to make a film that would be a counterpoint to *The Birth of a Nation.* After many months of fund-raising and organizing (during which Washington died), *The Birth of a Race* was released in 1918. Its makers were a panoply of filmmaking interests including the white Selig Polyscope Company and Daniel Frohman, a vaudeville producer. Unfortunately, neither the film company nor its final product were what Booker T. Washington had originally hoped to achieve. The makers were not the all-black company he and Scott had worked so hard to establish. The result was virtually two films—shot independently by both Selig and Frohman—and was blasted by critics who thought the two halves haphazardly pasted together.

While *The Birth of a Race* was a critical failure, it succeeded in one important area: it inspired black filmmakers to work all the harder to secure a powerful cinematic voice. In 1915, the Lincoln Motion Picture Company had been formed by the African American actor Noble Johnson, who, with his brother George, began to make films that bolstered the position of blacks in society. Lincoln's first film, *The Realization of a Negro's Ambition* showed an Alabama farm boy graduating from Tuskegee Institute and then heading west to work in the oil business. He is first denied a job because of his race, but he heroically saves the boss's daughter from an accident and is hired. Soon, he is prospecting for oil, and by the film's end, he has found wealth and happiness with the girl of his dreams. In 1916, the Lincoln Company released *The Trooper of Troop K,* which portrayed a black soldier who rises in society by performing heroic military acts. Essentially, many of the films made by the black companies urged black audiences to aspire to membership in the rising bourgeoisie in America; the films' typically happy endings told moviegoers that such aspirations would be amply rewarded.

Thus, during the Progressive Era, many films designed for black audiences celebrated hope and perseverance—and the heroism that seemed the only path out of the blacks' oppressed circumstances. Since many of the early nickelodeons were segregated under the nation's Jim Crow laws, films such as *The Realization of a Negro's Ambition or The Trooper of Troop K* played in theaters catering to black audiences. The films are testimony to the power of the cinema to speak to the needs of a community. This was especially important during a time when white film companies usually showed blacks in positions of comic servitude—if they portrayed black people at all.

MELODRAMAS OF REAL LIFE. When the black companies were formed in the early Progressive Era, however, white audiences often saw another portrayal of what it meant to be a struggling American. Countless melodramas explored what life was like in urban tenements or in sweatshops or mining communities. Often, what the films concluded was that a surrender to "destiny" was the protagonist's only recourse.

Chief among the creators of this sort of film was Griffith. During his early years Griffith influenced cinematic themes as well as techniques. When he began work as a director at the Biograph Company in 1908, Griffith walked the streets of New York looking for subject matter for the one-reelers he might typically shoot in a week's time. What he found—alcoholism, poor tenement conditions, child labor, unemployment, disease, sweatshops, police corruption—all became themes in his melodramas.

One of Griffith's best early films, *The Musketeers of Pig Alley* (1912), was shot on the streets of New York, with close-ups and unusual camera angles to heighten the dramatic tension, as well as extraordinary depth of focus. The story centers on a working-class couple played by Lillian Gish and Walter Miller, who struggle to survive in the corrupt ghetto; it ends with a gesture that indicates that the police are as corrupt as the street gang that victimizes the couple.

While the silent-film era is often stereotyped as a period of clowns, vamps, or mustache-twirling villains, the movies of the Progressive Era reflected the nation's controversies just after the turn of the century. In numerous melodramas and comedies, socialism, female suffragism, temperance, and even the push to legalize birth control, were explored and turned into sources for both entertainment and political persuasion.

This was an era in which women were often able to find work as directors and editors in Hollywood. Directors such as Lois Weber made countless acclaimed films during the silent era, especially prior to the 1920s. Weber even made films that crusaded for the cause of the legalization of birth control, *Where Are My Children?* (1916) and *The Hand That Rocks the Cradle* (1917). The latter film was based on the trials of Margaret Sanger, the famous nurse and birth-control activist whose jail sentences for releasing information about birth control had put her in the public spotlight.

Dorothy Gish, already famous as an actress, occasionally directed her own films—including a woman suffrage comedy called *The Suffragette Minstrels*, in which dancing women use their short skirts and shapely legs to persuade men to give them the vote. Earlier, in 1912, Anita Loos was already writing the humorous scripts that would make her famous in the twenties. Her comedy, *A Cure for Suffragettes* (1913), ended with the title card "Even a suffragette can be a mother."

During the period, such "crusading" films— masquerading as popular entertainment—were not unusual. Leading woman suffragists such as Emmeline Pankhurst, Elizabeth Cady Stanton, and Jane Addams collaborated with Hollywood filmmakers to turn out melodramas that would also serve as propaganda for their cause. Such films as *Votes for Women* (1912) and *What Eighty Million Women Want—?* (1913) circulated through the nation's movie houses much as ordinary film releases did.

At a time when the film industry was still shaping itself, it is not surprising that special-interest groups sought access to the new medium to promulgate their causes. The cinema was not seen as a closed-off, inaccessible force. Perhaps in a way akin to the current uses of the home-video camera, some Americans saw the motion pictures as a form that they, too, could use for their own concerns.

Since the early films drew audiences of primarily working- or lower-middle-class people, at least one frightened critic worried that the films would actually teach anarchists and revolutionaries how to overthrow the government. At the time, film was a new invention with potential repercussions that were feared by would-be guardians of society. The new entertainment form might become "the daily press of . . . Socialism, syndicalism, and radical opinion," warned Frederic Howe, in an article in *The Outlook* on 20 June 1914. The attempts at censorship of the new medium revealed the tensions in American society, as a controversy raged about the immorality and socialism shown in motion pictures—especially to working class audiences who might be most vulnerable to their message.

For instance, a 1913 drama called *Why?* shocked many people with its scenes of Manhattan workers pleading to their boss, who sat next to a sack of gold, and children laboring—literally—on treadmills. The film ended with the protesters burning down the Woolworth Building, in hand-painted red flames. *Why?* suggested that there was no easy solution for the discontent of many workers, and it refused a "happy ending." These were the films that roused concern among those who would censor the motion picture. Films, believed such reformers, should educate and "uplift," in the spirit of the Progressive Era.

The crusade of state censors was given further credibility, in 1915, when the Supreme Court ruled in its *Mutual* decision that film censorship was permitted under the First Amendment. The Court found that motion pictures were "a business, pure and simple," to which free speech was not guaranteed. The result was that states, on an individual basis, continued to establish which scenes might be viewed by film audiences.

Yet, for every social problem film that championed the liberal causes that many censors feared, such as labor unionism or birth control, another melodrama suggested the evils of such movements. Many comedies satirized the idea of the votes-for-women movement or portrayed melodramatic heroes defeating striking miners. While most films remained simply escapist, many motion pictures offered a cinematic forum for the social and cultural issues of the time. Entertainment helped negotiate the cultural changes of the Progressive Era by bringing volatile issues into a public forum and resolving them within the conventions of melodrama or comedy.

During that period, Charlie Chaplin shuffled his way into the hearts of American moviegoers with his famous character, the Little Tramp. Chaplin's famous character was an everyman, an often-bullied, long-suffering hero whose large spirit and dogged determination became his way of survival in the cold, mechanized world in which he found himself. Chaplin's own liberal political sensitivities made their way into his films. In the 1917 comedy *Easy Street*, the Little Tramp demonstrated sympathy for a large working-class family, which obviously suffered the consequences of the era's laws making birth control a crime. Later, the comedian directed and starred in important cinematic statements against industrial mechanization and fascism with his films *Modern Times* (1936) and *The Great Dictator* (1940).

The Studio System and the Ritual of Moviegoing

During the early years of Chaplin's career, the film industry underwent changes that slowly turned moviegoing into the familiar ritual we know today. Motion pictures were becoming longer, generally running from an hour to ninety minutes—closer to the feature length that we now associate with the average running time of the movie. Most films were shown on a double bill, replacing the old bill of shorts in a run-down neighborhood nickelodeon. In 1914 the Strand Theater on New York's Broadway opened as the first movie "palace," elevating the moviegoing experience into a grand fantasy that took place not only on the screen but in the immediate surroundings as well. Soon movie houses were constructed in cities across the nation as luxurious, mammoth halls, resplendent with colorful ushers, plush carpeting and seats, and ornate decor with Greek or Oriental motifs. During the Great Depression, such fantastic movie halls took on even more special importance, allowing audiences to escape the drudgery of everyday life.

In the 1917 comedy Easy Street, *Charlie Chaplin's Little Tramp demonstrated sympathy for a large working-class family, which obviously suffered the consequences of the era's laws making birth control a crime.*

The rise of the feature film and the film "palace" revolutionized the filmgoing experience and drew increasing audiences from the middle and upper classes—audiences that helped make the cinema a more "respectable" form of entertainment. Films were made with higher budgets, and a new generation of film directors began to experiment with the medium.

Entrepreneurs also began to experiment with the industry. With the coming of World War I, the film industry underwent significant changes. The structure of the industry began to shift in ways that would alter the entire face of Hollywood for decades by giving rise to the studio system. In 1914 a leading Hollywood mogul, Adolph Zukor, initiated the "vertical integration" of the industry—a system through which film manufacturers also distributed and exhibited the films they made. This created a monopoly within the film industry, as film companies not only produced motion pictures, but also had power over their national distribution and their exhibition in local theaters.

Between 1919 and 1921, Zukor oversaw the control of at least three hundred theaters across America for the exhibition of Paramount films. Thus was born the theater designed to show only a certain company's films—of which the neighborhood "Paramount Theater" is one typical example. Zukor's concentration of power in the hands of film producers was the beginning of Hollywood's studio system. Later, in the 1930s, the major studios—Warner Bros., Paramount, RKO (Radio-Keith-Orpheum), Metro-Goldwyn-Mayer, and Twentieth Century–Fox—consolidated their control over distribution and exhibition. With power over most of the nation's first-run movie houses, the big studios set the trends for the kind of motion pictures produced in America. Individual moguls such as Zukor, Sam Goldwyn, David O. Selznick, Louis B. Mayer, Jack Warner, and Irving Thalberg wielded tremendous power over the films that moviegoers saw. It is perhaps noteworthy that many of Hollywood's most successful producers were Jewish immigrants who personified the "American Dream."

This monopoly of the big studio was to continue for decades, until the Supreme Court decided that such vertical integration constituted an unfair economic monopoly with the *United States* v. *Paramount* decision in 1948. Under the studio system, Hollywood's "classic" period lasted from about 1930 through the 1950s, when the system's dismantling finally began in earnest.

THE WESTERN. As the studio system began, film genres evolved into more sophisticated fare. By the 1920s, the Western was a popular draw at the box office. (*The Great Train Robbery*, had proven as early as 1903 that the genre held a popular appeal for film audiences.) In 1917, a young Irish-American director named John Ford had made his first film, and, by the 1920s, he was finding his métier in formulating various versions of the Western genre. Later, with such classics as *Stagecoach* (1939), *My Darling Clementine* (1946), *She Wore a Yellow Ribbon* (1949), and *The Searchers* (1956), Ford established a career as an "auteur" director of Western films. (After World War II, French critics developed the notion of the director as "author" of the motion picture to indicate that films may be seen as artistic visions of a single creative spirit.) Ford also helped to establish the career of a premier "auteur actor"—John Wayne, who starred in many of Ford's Westerns.

The Western was rich in contradictions that held the potential for social commentary. "Good" versus "bad" might be represented as "civilization" versus "savagery," "white" versus "Indian," "farm or garden" versus "wilderness or desert," and "community" versus the "individual."

Yet, in the early Westerns, the freewheeling independence of a young nation giddy with its own rapid economic development is present; so is the violence of the frontier. In the classic Westerns of the 1930s and 1940s, much of the concern lies with settlement of the frontier, set largely in the period from 1870 to 1890, when the major Indian wars were fought and the territories were still open. In general, the hero is presented as an unambiguous good guy, fighting to preserve both the rights of the community and his own individualism. In a classic Western such as Ford's *Stagecoach*, for instance, all the elements of the struggle between settlement and lawlessness are present—and are resolved in a fashion that offers an unambivalent closure to the conflicts.

Later, in the 1950s, the Western hero became increasingly complex, and sometimes likely to have neurotic characteristics. In 1956, with *The Searchers*, Ford presents John Wayne's character as a man fanatically obsessed for years with finding his niece, captured by the Indians. Once his mission is completed and he has reunited his family, he turns his back on the community and leaves, again for the frontier. The hero was less a one-dimensional, white-hatted "good guy" and more an increasingly disturbed protagonist who revealed the dark side of his character.

In the 1950s, the Western also came to serve as an analogy for the terrible clashes that ruptured the nation during the McCarthyite red scare. In the films *High Noon* (1952) and *Johnny Guitar* (1954), for instance, the directors Fred Zinnemann and Nicholas Ray found covert ways to make political statements about the hysteria in American society. As a traditional American genre celebrating deep values of individualism and freedom, the Western lent itself well as a vehicle for subversive statements about the loss of freedoms during the decade. At about the same time, with Delmer Daves's *Broken Arrow* (1950), Robert Aldrichs *Apache* (1954), Sam Fuller's *Run of the Arrow* (1957), and, later, Ford's *Cheyenne Autumn* (1964) and Kevin Costner's *Dances with Wolves* (1990), Hollywood films began to portray the Indian as the "good guy."

Along with the more positive portrayal of the Indian, Westerns revealed more psychological complexities in their white "heroes," as Wayne's character in *The Searchers* had indicated in 1956. Issues of individualism came to represent, at times, America's role in the world. For instance, an intrepid hero who knew that "a man's gotta do what a man's gotta do" reflected America's image of itself as the post–World War II leader of the free world. Later, however, the Western hero in Sam Peckinpah's Vietnam-era film *The Wild Bunch* (1969) was a member of a self-serving, greedy band of entrepreneurs whose morality could not be taken for granted. The unquestioningly good, individualistic hero was already in decline, however: in 1960, John Sturges's extremely popular film, *The Magnificent Seven*, depicted a hired gang of gunslingers with as much interest in the pay they received for their skills as in keeping order. In the 1970s, as the Western became more self-conscious as a genre, the conventional contradictions became a source of nostalgia, as in Don Siegel's *The Shootist* (1976).

SOPHISTICATES AND CENSORS. During the 1920s, however, the Western was not yet so complex a genre. The Roaring Twenties was a period when other motion-picture genres, such as the melodrama and the slapstick comedy, were causing would-be censors to rise up in protest that the sexuality and violence on the screen would corrupt the nation's morals. This was an age when Clara Bow emerged as the " 'It' Girl," in all her unbridled, jazz-age hedonism; even "America's sweetheart," Mary Pickford, cut her adolescent golden ringlets in the early 1920s to star in Rosita (1923), directed by Ernst Lubitsch.

Hollywood in the 1920s saw the influx of foreign film directors, notably Lubitsch and Erich von Stroheim, who brought with them more sophisticated, European social values. Lubitsch's *The Marriage Circle* (1924) and *Lady Windermere's Fan* (1925) contained the comic celebrations of free-wheeling hedonism present in his later sound pictures. The confusion and uncertainty of his characters' feelings often leave simple resolution impossible. With his European elegance and wit, Lubitsch transcended the Victorian melodramatics that had so thoroughly suffused many Hollywood films. In a somewhat similar vein, the films of Stroheim, such as *Foolish Wives* (1922) and *Greed* (1925), portrayed characters with more complicated psyches than were seen in the usual Hollywood fare of the period.

By the 1950s, the Western hero started to become complex: In John Ford's The Searchers *(1956), John Wayne's character is less a one-dimensional, white-hatted "good guy" and more an increasingly disturbed man with a dark side to his personality.*

In the early 1920s, a Hollywood scandal involving the comedian Roscoe "Fatty" Arbuckle had helped to create a popular suspicion of Hollywood as a scene of moral debauchery. In 1921 the rotund Arbuckle was accused of raping and then causing the death of the young actress Virginia Rappe in a San Francisco hotel.

Along with other negative publicity, the resulting uproar and a drop in movie attendance so frightened filmmakers that they inaugurated their own internal "watchdog" organization. In 1922, the Motion Picture Producers and Distributors Association was formed. To further legitimate the MPPDA, Will Hays, a former postmaster general of the United States, was signed on to serve as the promoter of "right" values and mores in Hollywood film. Hays, acting as a sort of public-relations specialist, initiated a list of "Don'ts and Be Carefuls"—including sexuality and controversial political issues—which he circulated among the film community. At the same time, Hays crusaded against more formal, outside censorship of the movies.

As disturbing as censorship was, however, it was not the biggest challenge faced by the film industry in the 1920s. In October 1927, Warner Bros. released an innovative film called *The Jazz Singer*, starring Al Jolson. What made the film unusual was its use of sound. Warners' gamble paid off richly: *The Jazz Singer* was an immediate success with audiences in New York, and soon moviegoers across the country were demanding talking films. The experiment thrust Warner Bros. into the forefront of the film industry.

The coming of "talkies" thoroughly revolutionized the industry. Once the popularity of the sound films was established, the change within the industry was rapid and irrevocable. Though sound was an innovation that would destroy the careers of some actors and actresses, the film industry in general went through a renaissance. It was not long before Depression-era moviegoers flocked to see Warners' spectacular Busby Berkeley musicals such as *Forty-second Street* (directed by Lloyd Bacon) and *Gold Diggers of 1933* (directed by Mervyn LeRoy). Movies had become a genre virtually unthinkable without sound.

The outcries of the Roman Catholic church's Legion of Decency—formed in 1934 to protest "immoral" entertainment—had become so vociferous that Will Hays capitulated to their growing power. He joined with the Legion to establish the Production Code Administration in 1929. The resulting Production Code (1930) established a rigid, eight-page set of conventions for American films, stating that family values must be upheld at all times and forbidding the showing of detailed violence or sexuality.

The earlier suggestions of the Hays office had failed to curtail the sexual suggestiveness of many of the era's films. At the time, melodramas (sometimes called "women's weepies," made largely for female audiences) depicted their heroines in situations that often compromised the dominant ideals of marriage and the family. For instance, in 1932 the earliest version of Fannie Hurst's classic melodrama *Back Street* (directed by John M. Stahl) revealed the heroine engaged in a lifelong affair with a married man. While the protagonist of such melodramas typically paid dearly for her choices, she was nevertheless presented as a sympathetic and understandable character.

Mae West also titillated audiences with her witticisms and sexual allusions. In 1933, *I'm No Angel* and *She Done Him Wrong* were filled with her bawdy humor and salty one-liners. At the same time, W C. Fields's acerbic wit and the anarchic play of the Marx Brothers challenged the censorial push for obedience to rules and order.

Other motion pictures of the early 1930s also tested the tolerance of many religious and community groups. The gangster film's violence celebrated the criminal as a new American antihero. In Mervyn LeRoy's *Little Caesar* (1930), William Wellman's *The Public Enemy* (1931), and Howard Hawks's *Scarface* (1932), American audiences saw a sordid underside of life in America, in which gangsters often seemed to be a product of the chaotic world around them. Such films increased the movement toward censorship. In 1934, after protests and threats of boycotts from religious groups across the country, the Production Code's restrictions were, finally, fully enacted. In that year, Hays put Joseph Breen, a prominent Catholic layman, in charge of administering the Production Code's rules. Motion pictures had to pass the code's standards before they were released to public audiences. By 1934, even married couples could not be shown in the same bed.

The taming of Mae West's screen persona ended her best film performances. And the genre of the gangster film underwent a modification of its most overt violence. One response to the Production Code was the rise of the G-man film, which championed the government law official as its hero. In William Keighley's *G-Men* (1935), James Cagney leaves the underworld of organized crime to join the FBI; one year later, in Keighley's *Bullets or Ballots*, Edward G. Robinson played a policeman who breaks up a mob ring. The gangster-hero deplored by the Breen code was replaced, in part, by a series of films celebrating the law-enforcement official.

SCREWBALL COMEDIES. In the field of comedy, an ingenious response to the Production Code appeared: the screwball comedy. While avoiding overt sexuality, the screwball comedy typically portrayed an upper-class woman in a romantic liaison with a working-class man (and, often, vice versa). Frank Capra's *It Happened One Night* (1934) starred Clark Gable and Claudette Colbert in a very successful comedy (it was the first film to win all five major Oscars) that also spoke to the economic crisis of the time. By bringing together a couple from radically different class backgrounds, the comedy suggested that the nation itself could perhaps heal the wounds of class conflict, and that American democracy could survive despite the decade's economic calamities. Screwball comedies also offered audiences sexual suggestiveness without actual breaking of the code; in so doing, they freed women from the bedroom, and put them in newspaper offices and corporate boardrooms. The genre often depicted women as assertive, independent heroines, such as Rosalind Russell in Howard Hawks's *His Girl Friday* (1940) and Ruth Hussey in George Cukor's *The Philadelphia Story* (1940). Katharine Hepburn was at her feisty best, for instance, in Hawks's *Bringing Up Baby* (1938), and opposite Spencer Tracy in later screwball comedies such as George Stevens's *Woman of the Year* (1942).

The Depression

The film industry itself weathered the Depression only after terrific struggles to win back the audiences that had flocked to the movies soon after the coming of sound in 1927. Declining attendance plagued theaters in 1931 and 1932. In response, theaters offered double bills, "Depression glass" favors, and more emphasis on the escapism offered by the elaborate movie palace. By 1934, the economic crisis had largely been survived, despite the additional threat of the Production Code. Americans still needed the movies. Even former President Herbert Hoover suggested that the unemployed should be given movie tickets as a sort of "dole," so that potential unrest might be kept to a minimum. At the time, however, several motion pictures were made to portray the plights of the unemployed or the victimized.

In 1932, Mervyn LeRoy's *I Am a Fugitive from a Chain Gang* starred Paul Muni as a hero whose life was completely out of his own control. Through false implication in a robbery, the hero is imprisoned and his parole repeatedly denied. By the end of the grim tale, he has escaped and stands wild-eyed in the darkness, telling his former lover that he must survive by stealing. Such films suggested the powerlessness of the individual, and the terrible abuse of authority taking place in America's legal system.

ANIMATED FILMS. While such films offered audiences realistic fare, Depression-era moviegoers could also readily find escapist entertainment at their local theaters. The 1930s was a decade of innovations made in the most fantastic cinema of all—animation. With the development of Betty Boop, the Fleischer brothers—Dave and Max—created one of the most popular cartoon characters of the period. At the Fleischer studio, animation achieved new, complicated heights with surrealistic portrayals of Betty Boop in *Snow White*, complete with a jazzy soundtrack provided by Cab Calloway's band. Such sophisticated cartoons were intended more for adults than children, and were a success with audiences.

At the same time that the Fleischer brothers were making cartoons with an anarchistic spirit, the Walt Disney Studio was perfecting the art of animation with a painstaking attention to detail. Mickey Mouse evolved from a rodentlike creature in his second film, *Steamboat Willie* (1928) (in his first, *Plane Crazy*, he had appeared under the name Mortimer) to a more human, lovable character during the 1930s, and became the first Disney "star." Disney's typically sweet characters and moral tales captured the hearts of moviegoers.

With the use of color and sound, the Disney cartoons grew more sophisticated through the decade, though the content remained that of idealized fantasy. In contrast to the anything-goes Fleischer cartoons, the Disney films were often morality tales in which the world had rules that must be obeyed. In the late 1920s, censorship was still such a strong force that Disney was ordered to remove the udders from an animated cow, and—while the late 1920s cartoons were wilder and more primitive—during the 1930s, the Disney cartoons became increasingly mild and inoffensive portrayals of conservative American values. Even in the depictions of dark fairy tales and the evil that threatened Snow White or Bambi, the protagonists never lost their innocence or purity—and the films remain largely sentimental.

HORROR FILMS. Audiences who attended the cartoons of the 1930s escaped to the mild fantasies offered in animation. In the era's horror films, however, audiences escaped the realities of the Depression to a very different fantastic landscape—one that was filled with nightmarish images of a world gone hopelessly awry, in which strange forces had been set loose. In Tod Browning's *Dracula* (1931), the horror came not from the known, "civilized" world of London, but from the mysterious, vampire-inhabited realm of Transylvania. In a world in which little seemed to be under human control, the films allowed audiences to see their terrors in physical form. In 1933, audiences paid to see a berserk giant ape terrorize Manhattan in *King Kong*. Part of the film's message warned of the danger in tampering with the unknown, in bringing "monsters" to civilization from the wild islands of the Pacific.

Other horror films of the decade emphasized a similar moral: scientific experimentation could lead to threats to the human race. Such was the message of the film that made Boris Karloff a star—James Whale's *Frankenstein* (1931). Despite censorship problems over a scene in which the monster throws a little girl into a lake, *Frankenstein* was Universal's biggest box-office success in 1932. (The excised scenes were restored in 1987.) One of the most unusual of the decade's horror films was Tod Browning's *Freaks* (1932), set in a circus and cast with actual sideshow performers. The film portrayed the deformed characters as a community of survivors who band together to rid themselves of an evil interloper. The Depression-era horror films allowed audiences to see their worst fears expressed, and, finally, contained in a way that reassured them that society would survive and humankind ultimately prevail.

The Promise of the Forties

By the end of the thirties, of course, not only had the movies survived, but new genres and brilliant directors had emerged from Hollywood. Many European film talents, such as Michael Curtiz, William Dieterle, William Wyler, and Lubitsch, had found a new creative home in Hollywood. Their films carried the innovations of Europe and of German Expressionism to California.

Such directors were integrated into the studio system, and by the late 1930s the big studios determined the fate of their countless stars such as Joan Crawford and Bette Davis, as well as new directors. David O. Selznick, Samuel Goldwyn, and Louis B. Mayer, for instance, were tycoons who controlled their studios with a sometimes tyrannical hand. When Selznick began the production of his mammoth *Gone with the Wind* (1939), it was with an absolute control over decision-making that he wielded until the film was finally wrapped. *Gone with the Wind* was already practically a legend by the time its world premiere was held in Atlanta, largely because of the fame of Margaret Mitchell's novel and the publicity over Selznick's meticulous attention to the details of his epic production, particularly his search for the perfect Scarlett O'Hara. Despite the enormous success of the film, however, it would be the last of such huge cinematic enterprises until after World War II.

> Gone with the Wind *was already somewhat of a legend by the time of its 1939 premiere in Atlanta, partly because of the publicity surrounding David O. Selznick's meticulous attention to the details of epic production and his search for the perfect Scarlett O'Hara.*

The war years were a time of internal turmoil and also technical experimentation for Hollywood. With budgets drastically cut for the war effort, directors were forced to find inexpensive means of making cinematic innovations. Creative minds found a way to reach beyond the funding cuts—using actual streets or buildings instead of elaborate sets. Working in black-and-white, many film-makers made use of unusual camera angles and lighting to attract the eye. Often, oblique angles fractured the scene and created a sense of restlessness. Heightening the uneasiness might also be shadows that obscured a character's face while the light illuminated inanimate objects.

It was a foreboding, even ominous, film style that French critics, seeing the Hollywood films for the first time after the war had ended, dubbed *film noir* (black film). The term alluded both to the black-and-white quality of the films and their dark dramatic themes. Often inspired by the hard-boiled detective novels made popular by writers such as Dashiell Hammett and James M. Cain (and later Mickey Spillane), the films delved into the perverse side of human nature, exploring violence, greed, and existential loneliness. Such films as Edgar Ulmer's *Detour* (1945), Billy Wilder's masterpiece *Double Indemnity* (1944), and Howard Hawks's *The Big Sleep* (1946) epitomized the *noir* style of film-making. Orson Welles's classic *Citizen Kane* (1941) used striking *noir*-like lighting techniques and camera angles that helped to convey the greed and paranoia of its rags-to-riches American hero, based on William Randolph Hearst.

Many elements of German Expressionism also shaped the making of that body of films characterized as *film noir*, such as the sense of bleak, fatalistic despair and shadowy, sinister dramas.

Film noir was, perhaps, a reflection of the wartime disorientation and confusion about what the future held for the nation, though it was not limited to the wartime necessity imposed by limited budgets. The dark films continued into the early 1950s, growing even bleaker with their portraits of human despair and evil. In 1955, Robert Aldrich's adaptation of a Mickey Spillane novel, *Kiss Me Deadly*, contained a frightening vision of a society in which nuclear power is bandied about in a black box. Aldrich's Mike Hammer is one of the darkest protagonists of the era. Other heroes or heroines bordered on the psychotic as the later cinema of *film noir* explored the dark undercurrents in the human psyche. Nicholas Ray's *In a Lonely Place* (1950) captures the hero's inner turmoil and self-destruction. (His *Rebel Without a Cause* [1955], though not an example of *film noir*, cynically portrayed the underside of the American family through James Dean's confused adolescent hero.) Many of the fears of the era—atomic warfare, the cold war, and the paranoid grip that the McCarthyite red scare had upon the nation during the 1950s—were brought to the screen in the form of *film noir*. The *noir* techniques, born of wartime hardships, survive to influence filmmaking and television in the 1990s.

The war effort made its demands on Hollywood in other ways as well. Frank Capra, who established his career in the 1930s and 1940s with homespun populism in *Mr. Deeds Goes to Town* (1936), *Mr. Smith Goes to Washington* (1939), *Meet John Doe* (1941), and his widely seen Christmas classic *It's a Wonderful Life* (1946), set to work for the government. His *Why We Fight* series (1942–1945) comprised a number of influential propaganda films.

Inquisition and Blacklist

Internally, wartime Hollywood was shaken by the technical workers' efforts to unionize. It was a community divided by conservative forces such as Walt Disney and Jack Warner, who created the Motion Picture Alliance for the Preservation of American Ideals (MPA). One of the chief purposes of this group was to defend the Hollywood filmmaking community against infiltration by Communists. Men like Disney and Warner were deeply threatened by the liberalism they saw in the development of trade unionism and by the ensuing empowerment of the workers within the industry. The film community that survived the traumas of the Great Depression had new forces tearing at it during the 1940s.

Not the least of these elements came from Washington. In 1940 the head of the then-temporary House Committee on Un-American Activities (HUAC), Martin Dies, journeyed to Hollywood to make the first of what would become a wave of inquisitions into liaisons between the film industry and the Communist party. At that time, he found a Hollywood united against his efforts. For the most part, producers refused to listen to his accusations that the Screen Writers Guild and Screen Directors Guild were primarily Communist fronts, and the first investigation thus failed.

Several years later, however, the existence of the MPA gave the HUAC investigation a vehicle into conservative Hollywood. Hollywood trade unionism had divided the entertainment community with strikes, and when Rep. J. Parnell Thomas called the first "friendly witnesses" before the committee in 1948, the witnesses—among them Ronald Reagan, Gary Cooper, Louis B. Mayer, Jack Warner, and Walt Disney—were willing to "name names" of those suspected of being Communist sympathizers.

The hysteria began in earnest, as both the famous and the relatively obscure were brought before the committee and questioned about their membership in the Communist party. During the 1930s, when communism had been seen by some as a viable alternative to both the fascism rising in Europe and the failure of capitalism in the West, there had been a lively interest

Walt Disney as he testifies before the House Un-American Activities Committee on October 24, 1947.

in the party among some members of the Hollywood community. In the 1950s, when the horrors of Stalinism had been revealed and the cold war was in deadly earnest, they paid dearly for their past interest. When the group known as the "Hollywood Ten" were called before the committee, they refused to testify on the grounds of both self-incrimination and free speech. Convicted of contempt of Congress, the ten—mostly directors and screenwriters such as Ring Lardner, Jr., Edward Dmytryk, Herbert Biberman—were all sentenced to serve prison time. Ironically, Lardner served time with J. Parnell Thomas in a minimum security prison in Danbury, Connecticut. Thomas, who had tried to appear so loyal to American causes as he led the inquisition, had been accepting kickbacks from the members of his staff.

The effects of the HUAC inquisition on Hollywood during the 1950s were devastating. The hysteria from Washington left a divided, suspicious community, with many of its most-talented members blacklisted. Hollywood lost some of its greatest talents. Charlie Chaplin grew disgusted with American conservatism (and high taxes) and, in 1952, left for Switzerland, never to work in America again. (His last two films, *A King in New York* [1957] and *A Countess from Hong Kong* [1967] were made in Great Britain.)

The HUAC's investigations of Hollywood figures during the 1950s had devastating effects: The hysteria from Washington left a divided, suspicious community, with many of the film world's most talented members blacklisted.

The censorship of free speech put some filmmakers in the position of making films that became covert statements against the mentality of paranoia and hysteria in the country. In 1952, Fred Zinnemann's *High Noon* (written by the later-blacklisted Carl Foreman) poignantly depicted a sheriff (Gary Cooper) who could not win the support of the townspeople in fighting off returning criminals. The film was a subtle allegory about the nature of betrayal and deception and the loss of integrity. Such pictures were the only vehicle for safely expressing protest against the prevailing mood. Even in allegory, however, artists were not always safe in making criticisms of the political climate. Upon his release from prison, Herbert Biberman directed *Salt of the Earth* (1953), a film about striking miners in New Mexico which was financed by a miners' union. The film was blacklisted and shown in only one American theater, though it received critical success in Europe. Over ten years later, in 1965, *Salt of the Earth* was finally distributed in the United States. Even Arthur Miller's historical play, *The Crucible* (1953) caused him to be called before the committee for investigation.

The Threat of Television

In addition to the HUAC investigations, Hollywood faced other challenges during the 1950s. The advent of television threatened motion pictures as American families found its accessibility attractive. In the age of the postwar "baby boom," television quickly became a popular entertainment form. The film industry responded in various ways. To enhance the appeal of the movies, color began to be used increasingly, with a number of cheap new processes eventually supplanting the expensive original Technicolor. Various wide-screen systems, such as Cinerama and CinemaScope, three-dimensional effects, and stereophonic sound were developed to emphasize the theatrical experience. In addition, drive-in theaters began to spring up across the country to compete against television. They were an invitation to families to bring children to the cinema in the privacy of their cars, or to young couples to use moviegoing as part of a courting ritual.

Metro-Goldwyn-Mayer began to turn out elaborate musicals to win audiences away from their television sets. After sponsoring an audience survey, the studio discovered that American moviegoers wanted to see musical comedies more than any other genre. In the late 1940s, Vincente Minnelli's lavish *The Pirate* (1948) had proved that musicals could be exhilarating escapism for audiences, and the survey respondents indicated that they wanted more of the same.

MGM was quick to react to the findings. Musicals such as Stanley Donen and Gene Kelly's *Singin' in the Rain* (1952) became huge popular hits. In 1953, Fred Astaire starred in Minnelli's *The Band Wagon*, continuing his screen persona that had evoked wonder from the days of such Depression-era musicals as *Swing Time* (1936). Astaire's fantastic dancing gave a sense that the physical world could be surmounted and even transcended in joyous play of body and spirit. The musicals presented a kind of utopian society in which characters might break into song and dance at any minute, rupturing the mundane world of the taken-for-granted. Like the Warner Bros.' musicals of the 1930s, these lavish musicals offered a happy face for America—fantasies in which troubles could be forgotten and innocence regained.

In the 1950s, the melodramas of Douglas Sirk also pushed the genre of the "woman's film" to a new level of sophisticated social commentary. With films such as *All That Heaven Allows* (1956), *Written on the Wind* (1956), and *Imitation of Life* (1959), Sirk presented an unsettling portrait of the American family, and particularly of the narrow-minded ideals and values that restrict independence for women. Just as Fred Zinnemann used the Western genre as a means of conveying a larger statement about American culture in *High Noon*, so Sirk exposed the underside of American traditions and family values through the melodrama.

The era's horror films also reveal the underside of the prosperous 1950s. While the horror films of the 1930s typically portrayed a monster coming from outside America—from a shadowy landscape in Transylvania or South Sea islands—in Don Siegel's *Invasion of the Body Snatchers* (1956), the monster came mysteriously in the form of giant seed-pods. As the pods evolved into humanoids who resembled the inhabitants of the town of Santa Mira, it was the average American who became the "monster." The film was a warning against the peril of communism and the vulnerability of even small towns to its insidious takeover. Yet *Invasion of the Body Snatchers* can also be interpreted in an opposite way—as a protest against mass hysteria and conformism.

By the decade's end, Alfred Hitchcock signaled the coming of a new age in horror films with *Psycho* (1960). The "monster" no longer comes from outside America, or outside us. Rather, it resides in the very structure of our family, and in the madness the family generates in the human psyche.

Changes in the Sixties

By the 1960s, several factors were changing the shape of the film industry. Censorship restrictions had begun to lift during the 1950s, so that by the 1960s, partial nudity and violence became more prevalent. In 1966, the Motion Picture Association of America selected Jack Valenti, a former aide to President Lyndon Johnson, as its head. Valenti's first job was to initiate a ratings system to guide audiences about the nature of the less-restricted film content. Originally, there were four categories: G for general, M for mature, R for restricted, and X for no one admitted under age eighteen. Though Valenti's rating system has gone through many revisions—and the content of films that warrant certain ratings has changed drastically—the system's basic concept has remained in place.

In addition, the old studios declined as vertical integration was thoroughly dismantled. According to the Supreme Court *Paramount* decision of 1948, the unification of production, distribution, and exhibition was finally outlawed. The result was that the film companies were taken over by corporate empires, an action that put the ultimate power over filmmaking decisions in the hands of business executives who primarily understood only the profit-making end of the industry. TransAmerica bought United Artists; Gulf and Western bought Paramount, and Kinney took over Warner Bros.

The big corporations, however, inherited the financial problems that the studios had suffered during the previous decade. As profits at the box office fell during the 1960s, the emphasis was increasingly placed on the blockbuster hit. Epics such as Joseph L. Mankiewicz's elaborate *Cleopatra* (1963) and musicals such as Robert Wise's *The Sound of Music* (1965) were high-stakes gambles at winning the jackpot at the box office, and one outcome of the emphasis on big-budget films was that smaller, independent films were neglected by the large corporate interests.

One important producer of low-budget films during the sixties was American Independent Pictures. AIP provided experimental vehicles for young directors and actors. Among those directors was Roger Corman, who went on to form his own studio and distributorship, New World Pictures, in 1970. Many of Hollywood's best talents of the 1980s and 1990s—among them Jack Nicholson, Martin Scorsese, Robert De Niro, and Jonathan Demme—got their starts with AIP and New World in the 1960s and 1970s. Corman had made a name for himself with extremely low-budget films such as *A Bucket of Blood* (1959) and *The Little Shop of Horrors* (1961), which was shot in two days. Though both films have the plots of horror movies, they are also quirky social satire—and even parody the horror film genre.

In part because of Corman's low-budget successes, the cult film began to burgeon by the late 1960s. George Romero's *Night of the Living Dead* (1968) and Jim Sharman's British-made *The Rocky Horror Picture Show* (1975) captivated American audiences, who went to see the films time and again, often at midnight showings.

Another important event in the 1960s was the rise of film studies as a serious area of scholarship in the nation's universities. In college towns and cities across the country, "art" movie houses that exhibited foreign or independent films flourished, exposing young people to the cinema of foreign directors like Ingmar Bergman, Federico Fellini, and the French New Wave directors such as François Truffaut and Jean-Luc Godard.

A further consequence of the establishment of university film studies was that many current directors received their training not on Hollywood studio lots but in film schools. Young directors of the 1970s, among them Steven Spielberg, George Lucas, Francis Ford Coppola, Brian De Palma, and Martin Scorsese, attended such film production schools as the University of Southern California, New York University, and the University of California–Los Angeles. The late 1960s were a time of transition as the older, studio-educated filmmakers saw the rise of a generation of directors just out of film school. Increasingly, it is the film school that provided the aspiring director's entry into professional work in Hollywood.

The Counterculture and After

Late in the tumultuous decade of the 1960s, several successful films, among them Arthur Penn's *Bonnie and Clyde* (1967) and Mike Nichols's *The Graduate* (1967), reflected the confusion and alienation of many young people. In 1969, Dennis Hopper's *Easy Rider* proved that lower-budget films about the era's counterculture could be smash hits, and also demonstrated the economic power of what was called "the youth generation" at the box office. Attendance at theaters began to rise substantially; the "youth market" had been successfully tapped.

In 1969, Dennis Hopper's Easy Rider *proved that lower-budget films about the era's counterculture could be smash hits, and also demonstrated the economic power of what was called "the youth generation" at the box office.*

The phenomenonal success of the younger directors carried over into the seventies, as Robert Altman's *M*A*S*H* (1970), Coppola's *The Godfather* (1972) and Lucas's nostalgic *American Graffiti* (1973) brought critical raves as well as solid revenues. But it was Lucas's *Star Wars* (1977) and Steven Spielberg's *Jaws* (1975) and *Close Encounters of the Third Kind* (1977) that focused attention on the special-effects blockbuster. While such films cost a great deal to produce, they also paid off handsomely.

By the end of the 1970s, successful films spawned not only imitators, but, increasingly, sequels. In 1976, John Avildsen's *Rocky* starred Sylvester Stallone as a model of a simple American hero rising to fame and wealth in his career as a boxer, and established a formula for the subsequent *Rocky* films. Stallone's model of an uncomplicated super-hero carried over into his portrayal of *Rambo*, the machine-gun–toting warrior-soldier who promised to resurrect the pre-Vietnam era values of militaristic glory. The success of the first *Rocky* led to five more movie versions of the boxer's attempts at championships. The Stallone films, however, were not the ultimate representative of the sequel phenomenon—that unlikely distinction fell to the horror series, *Friday the 13th*, which, by 1988, had seven versions. The film found most of its audience among young adolescents willing to return time and again to witness the latest horrors of Jason. Similarly, *A Nightmare on Elm Street* (six versions by 1991) had young fans returning to watch Freddy Krueger, the villain who invades young people's minds.

At the same time, Hollywood finally began to come to terms with the Vietnam War, with such films as Michael Cimino's *The Deer Hunter* (1978), Hal Ashby's *Coming Home* (1978), and Coppola's *Apocalypse Now* (1979). Instead of the heroics of World War II dramas, these films portrayed the complexity and darkness of war and its aftermath at home. In the following decade, the Vietnam conflict would become the focus of many motion pictures, most of which portrayed the horror of war rather than the glory of battle.

The emphasis on megabucks films continued into the 1980s, to the extent that smaller films were seen as a greater risk. By the end of the 1980s, several successful directors felt the impact of Hollywood's skittishness about smaller motion pictures. Robert Altman, who received financial backing from Twentieth Century–Fox for such "small" films as *Three Women* (1977) and *A Wedding* (1978), by 1990 had to rely on European funding to make his *Vincent and Theo*, based on the life of Van Gogh.

In the late 1980s, Spike Lee proved that a film made by a black director could be a lively, controversial—and lucrative—statement on American culture. With *Do the Right Thing* (1989), alluding to the actual killing of a black man by a white police officer in Brooklyn, he created a cinema that both white and black audiences found visually compelling as well as provocative. Released in 1990, Charles Burnett's *To Sleep with Anger*—a compelling portrait of a black family in south-central Los Angeles—received less promotion, and, consequently, less critical attention and box-office revenues. Burnett's film, however, is a powerful, sometimes comic, portrait of what happens in a black family when a relative arrives from Louisiana, with all the folklore and superstitions of that region. Such quieter films, however, are often overlooked as producers and distributors concentrate on blockbusters.

A phenomenon that began in the 1970s permanently changed the film industry in the 1980s: the video revolution. More Americans enjoyed the convenience of watching movies at home with the entire family as the videocassette recorder became a household item. The rise of the demand for videotaped movies provided another market for films, which might slowly make most of their profits from video rentals.

Regardless of the inroads made by video, the early 1990s saw both the continuation of the Hollywood blockbuster and the circulation of independent films that speak to quieter subjects and smaller audiences. Lucrative Hollywood motion pictures continued to generate imitators—the phenomenon of the sequel attested to the avoidance of risk taking by big producers. Many of the most inventive films, however, are produced outside the mainstream, from independent producers and directors. Whether mainstream or independent, however, the cinema has proven itself throughout the decades of American film history to be both a vital reflector of cultural values and a creator of national trends.

During the twentieth century, America became a nation of moviegoers who, even through the crises of the Great Depression and the advent of television in the 1950s, never lost their devotion to the cinema. It was on the big screen that the latest fashions and romantic role models were discovered. While the ritual of moviegoing has shifted through the decades, from the early era's multiple shorts and the later double bill—when one might enter the film in mid-screening and stay through to the next showing—its function as an element of courtship and a social rite has remained virtually unchanged for audiences attending contemporary feature films. It is in the nation's moviehouses that modern audiences, like their early counterparts, find themselves entertained with their deepest hopes and horrors.

[See also Humor and Comedy; Radio; Television; Theater and Musical Theater.]

BIBLIOGRAPHY

Balio, Tino, ed. *The American Film Industry* (1976).
Barnouw, Erik. *Documentary: A History of the Non-Fiction Film* (1974).
Bergman, Andrew. *We're in the Money: Depression America and Its Films* (1971).
Bowser, Eileen. *The Transformation of Cinema: 1907–1915* (1990).
Brownlow, Kevin. *The Parade's Gone By* (1968).
Brownlow, Kevin. *The War, the West, and the Wilderness* (1979).
Ceplair, Larry, and Steven Englund. *The Inquisition in Hollywood: Politics in the Film Community, 1930–1960* (1980).
Cook, David A. *A History of Narrative Film* (1981).
Cripps, Thomas. *Slow Fade to Black: The Negro in American Film: 1900–1942* (1977).
Deming, Barbara. *Running Away from Myself: A Dream Portrait of America Drawn from the Films of the Forties* (1969).
Everson, William K. *American Silent Film* (1978).
Fielding, Raymond, comp. *A Technological History of Motion Pictures and Television* (1967).
Hampton, Benjamin. *A History of the American Film Industry from Its Beginnings to 1931* (1970).
Jacobs, Lewis. *The Rise of the American Film* (1939).
Jowett, Garth. *Film: The Democratic Art* (1976).
Kaminsky, Stuart M. *American Film Genres: Approaches to a Critical Theory of Popular Film* (1985).
Kay, Karyn, and Gerald Peary, eds. *Women and the Cinema* (1977).
Koszarski, Richard. *An Evening's Entertainment: The Age of the Silent Feature Picture, 1915–1928* (1990).
McClure, Arthur F., ed. *The Movies: An American Idiom* (1971).
Mast, Gerald. *A Short History of the Movies.* 3d ed. (1981).
Musser, Charles. *The Emergence of Cinema: The American Screen to 1907* (1991).
Navasky, Victor S. *Naming Names* (1980).
O'Connor, John E., and Martin A. Jackson, eds. *American History/ American Film: Interpreting the Hollywood Image* (1979).
Ray, Robert B. *A Certain Tendency of the Hollywood Cinema, 1930–1980* (1985).
Schatz, Thomas. *Hollywood Genres: Formulas, Filmmaking, and the Studio System* (1981).
Schickel, Richard. *Movies: the History of an Art and an Institution* (1964).
Sklar, Robert. *Movie-made America: A Social History of American Movies* (1975).
Sloan, Kay. *The Loud Silents: Origins of the Social Problem Film* (1988).
Stanley, Robert H. *The Celluloid Empire: A History of the American Movie Industry* (1978).
Taylor, John Russell. *Strangers in Paradise: The Hollywood Émigrés, 1933–1950* (1983).
Thomson, David. *America in the Dark: The Impact of Hollywood Films on American Culture* (1979).
Wood, Robin. *Hollywood from Vietnam to Reagan* (1986).

— KAY SLOAN

FOLK SONG AND FOLK MUSIC

Folk Song as a Representation of American Culture

Folk song and folk music are constantly changing as ever-varying cultural representations of the society in which they are performed and perpetuated. Political boundaries do not necessarily delineate a cohesive culture, so it is not surprising that folk song and folk music in the United States has always consisted of a wide variety of styles and forms. Only since the latter half of the twentieth century has there been an interest in the entire spectrum of folk music, most of which had been ignored previously in favor of the more highly valued Anglo-American tradition. Consequently, although this essay is restricted to the study of folk song that originated in the British Isles and has been perpetuated in American English, the reader should keep in mind that the United States always has included diverse folk song cultures: Latino, African American, Cajun, and French-Canadian, to name but a few. Every group that has come to America has brought its own music, songs, dances, and instruments, and these unique musical heritages were continually refashioned by the American experience. That experience not only altered the various types of imported folk songs, it also forged new folk groups that developed their own ever-changing repertoires. American workers—such as miners, sailors, lumbermen, and cowboys—sang folk songs that reflected their work experience. Because categories of women's work gained validation only recently, most studies and recordings of workers' songs have focused on men rather than women.

Folk songs tell us about how various social, economic, religious, and political issues were perceived by the people who sang them. Such issues have always been topics of folk songs either directly or indirectly. Songs about orphans, young girls who went wrong only to be murdered by their sweethearts, or noble Indian maidens who took their own lives, all of which abound in this country's repertoire, tell us as much about our social history as do songs concerning presidential assassinations, railroad disasters, shipwrecks, or cowboy heroes.

Assumptions Behind Folk Song Studies in America

Until the second half of the twentieth century, most people assumed that the "genuine" folk traditions of the United States were Anglo-American, despite the fact that numerous indigenous peoples already were living on this continent when Europeans first settled here. It is incorrect to think that the complex of cultures that make up the United States has been influenced mainly by Anglo-American settlers. The monolithic view of American culture was perpetrated by those who held power, themselves products of a generalized European worldview and a part of an Anglo-Celtic tradition.

American folk song scholarship had its roots, just as did early anthropology, psychology, and sociology, in the social Darwinism that dominated Europe and the British Isles at the end of the nineteenth century. This theory of culture postulated that all societies developed through a series of stages, and that northern European and British cultures were deemed superior to all others. By the end of the 1800s, American scholars who were self-conscious about the nation's lack of historical tradition simply assumed that the Anglo tradition was America's authentic one. Such a view identified this country with "superior" cultures and effaced the unsophisticated image of the United States.

Genres of American Folk Song

THE CHILD BALLADS AND OTHER BALLADS. The folk songs that first drew the attention of scholars in this country were those now known as the Child ballads, named after Francis James Child, the Harvard University, professor who compiled and systematized them. Child's most important work was the multivolume *English and Scottish Popular Ballads,* which was published between 1882 and 1898. Child's criteria for inclusion of a song in his work were closely linked to the social Darwinism of the day. He included narrative songs that he believed had an oral tradition in either England or Scotland.

Child organized by number what he judged to be distinct ballad narratives, clustering the versions that he believed were related and publishing them under the title and number of the version that he felt was the oldest. In all he found 305 basic ballad stories. When field collectors of folk song in the United States later came across versions of these ballads, they listed them in their own collections using Child's numbering system. For example, "The Wife of Usher's Well," a representative example of the ballad genre, became known as Child no. 79:

1 *There lived a wife at Usher's Well,*
And a wealthy wife was she;
She had three stout and stalwart sons,
And sent them oer the sea.

2 *They hadna been a week from her,*
A week but barely ane [one],
Whan word came to the carline wife
That her three sons were gane.

3 *They hadna been a week from her,*
A week but barely three,
Whan word came to the carlin wife
That her sons she'd never see.

4 *'I wish the wind may never cease,*
Nor fashes [fishes] in the flood,
Till my three sons come hame to me,
In earthly flesh and blood.'

5 *It fell about the Martinmass,*
When nights are lang and mirk,
The carlin wife's three sons came hame,
And their hats were o the birk.

About half of the 305 distinct ballads to which Child gave numbers crossed the ocean and gained currency in the English-language tradition of American folksingers. For almost three quarters of a century following the publication of *The English and Scottish Popular Ballads,* collectors combed the United States looking for versions and remnants of Child ballads, often ignoring other vital types of folk song that surrounded them. These songs were interpreted as poems by Child and the many others who studied Anglo-American ballads through the 1950s. Attention was paid to the poetic devices by which the lyrics developed the story. Not until the publication of Bertrand Bronson's *The Traditional Tunes of the Child Ballads* (1959–1972) was this neglect of the music partially redressed. Today we recognize that ballad texts are inseparably bound to the tunes to which they are performed.

The study of English and Scottish ballads became the earliest and, until recently, the most enduring type of folk song scholarship in America. Among the poetic devices that were valued by scholars in folk ballads were a specific stanzaic form (4-3-4-3 with a-b-c-b rhyme); understatement; leaping and lingering (on only the most important elements of plot); the advancement of narrative through dialogue; repetition; focus on the most important elements of plot; beginning the story in the midst of the action; the use of commonplace word groups and stanzas (that appear in other ballads), and the lack of a personal narrator (an "I" who editorialized).

Today numerous ballad traditions are studied in addition to the Child canon. Students now analyze the folk song narratives of occupational, ethnic, and regional groups, and study outlaw ballads, war ballads, and other specific types of folk songs. Malcolm Laws, in his work *Native American Balladry*, offers a classification system for "ballads which have originated in the United States and the Maritime Provinces of Canada" (Laws 1964: 9).

BROADSIDES. A broadside is a sheet of paper that has a message usually printed on one side. The broadside song, dating from the earliest days of movable type, usually contained only text. Quite often the text was accompanied by a graphic woodcut, not necessarily related to the contents of the song itself, which helped sell the broadside much as covers on books do today. The title of the song was usually followed by the name of a well-known tune to which it could be sung. These songs were hawked by street vendors who often established small stalls on which they displayed the ballad sheets. Sometimes the printers varied the color of the paper, printed two songs on a single sheet, changed the size of the paper, hand-colored the accompanying woodcuts, or added elaborate borders to the texts.

On one bright summer's morning,
the weather being clear,
I strolled for recreation down by
the river fair.
I overheard a damsel most
gracious-like complain
All for an absent lover who
plowed the raging main.

(Laws, 1957:221; Laws N 36,
"John (George) Riley I")

Even though the broadsides were often described as "ballads," many of these songs did not tell a story. They could have been lyric songs, nonsense songs, or other non-narrative texts. Many of the broadsides did tell stories, however, and they often were the source of information about the latest scandal, disaster, strange occurrence, or other community news. During slow news times, broadside writers would recast the stories of the folk ballads currently in oral circulation. The printed word and the tradition of oral transmission were intertwined.

Broadsides were a tradition in numerous countries and cultures. Great Britain had a thriving broadside press, as did the United States. Philadelphia, New York, and Boston were early centers where broadsides could be bought, and they continued to be well into the twentieth century. Rural America also had its own broadside writers, performers, and hawkers. Small books called "songsters," which could fit into one's pocket, were an offshoot of the need for both news and song texts. With the rise in literacy the personal songbook, printed, handwritten, and perhaps pasted with clippings of songs from publications, became popular as a handy reference for individual singers.

The textual style of the broadside ballad is different from that of the sparse Child ballad. The rhyme schemes, usually a-b-c-b or a-a-b-b, were followed with such strictness that forced rhymes often resulted. The texts told the listener how to feel about the events and, unlike the Child ballads, were presented using the first person as narrator. Some broadsides are called "Come All Ye"s, since those words were part of the first line of the text, sung by the hawker to attract an audience of prospective customers.

Broadsides tell us much about American culture, since many of them either were gleaned from folk tradition or entered (and reentered) the oral tradition. They had a great influence on all of American folk song tradition.

LYRICAL SONG. The lyric folk song has no narrative but instead presents a feeling or mood, much like the blues. There is no system of classification or exhaustive study of Anglo-American lyrics in the United States, probably because these songs have extremely malleable texts. For example, a song that could express high-spirited courting humor as a dance song could also be sung in a different mood by the same singer to indicate that life is a dreary and tragic existence. Both renditions are lyrics in the sense that they express emotions while they lack a narrative thread, but they vary greatly in mood. Most lyrics that have been collected in the United States express sadness, usually over a loss.

Although the lyric does not have a narrative, the listener often thinks that a story has been told, because the lyrics imply a narrative. These songs often contain stanzas that begin "If I were . . . " or "When we were . . . ," thus implying, but not telling, of past or future events. "Floating stanzas" are added or removed as the singer wishes. Variations of the following two stanzas, for example, are found in many Anglo-American lyric songs:

Dig my grave both wide and deep;
Put a tombstone at my feet,
And on my heart carve a turtle dove
To tell the world I died for love.

If I had wings like a turtle dove,
I'd fly away to the one I love.
I would fly away to the one so dear
And talk to him while she is near.

If I had the wings of a turtle dove
I would fly away to the one I love,
I would fly to the one I love so dear
And talk to him while she is near.

(Belden: 479)

I wish that I had never been born
Or died when I was young
And never lived to wet my cheeks with tears,
Oh, for the love of another woman's son.

(Belden: 482)

Singers of lyric songs have a vast repertoire of these floating stanzas that they can alter and insert while singing so as to better express the emotion they wish to convey.

The lyric folk song, unlike the Child ballad, makes wide use of metaphor, similes, tropes, and other symbolic devices, although their stanzaic form is much like that of the Child ballad. The lyric aims to create a mood, even if, at times, the tune may be one usually associated with a contrary feeling, like the fast dance tune sung as a lament.

Entire stanzas that are sung to a particular tune one day may be replaced the next with floating stanzas or lines that the singer prefers to sing on that day. The determination of what is "the song" is thus rendered "subjective" in terms of the singer, and is almost always a subjective call on the part of the collector who does not ask the singer about the identity of the song sung. Most collectors did not ask for titles, but rather gave titles to lyric songs as they transcribed them.

DIALOGUE SONG. The dialogue song develops its mood or story entirely through the use of dialogue. The "action" usually takes place in a dramatic dialogue between speakers who usually alternate verses, and the story is revealed retrospectively through the dialogue. If there is a digression from the alternating voices, it usually comes in the introductory verse that sets the scene.

'O where ha you been, Lord Randal, my son?
And where ha you been, my handsome young man?'
'I ha been at the greenwood; mother, mak my bed soon,
For I'm wearied wi hunting, and fain wad lie down.'

'An wha met ye there, Lord Randal, my son?
And wha met you there, my handsome young man?'
'O I met wi my true-love; mother, mak my bed soon,
For I'm wearied wi huntin, and fain wad lie down.'

Some of the "ballads" that Child collected fall into this category, although he might have felt that they were narratives in time. His rationale for labeling them as ballads might well have been based in the belief that oral tradition had eroded the rest of the story line, leaving only the dialogue. Be that as it may, certainly "Lord Randal" (Child no. 12) and "Edward" (Child no. 13) are such songs, as are the Anglo-American songs "Paper of Pins" and "Oh No John." Dialogue is an important device that advances the action of ballad narratives, and so it is possible that some dialogue songs are related to earlier ballads. It is also probable that many dialogue songs were composed by a singer to be just that, dialogue songs.

WORK SONG. While songs have been identified as belonging to certain "genres" or types by their textual characteristics, scholars have also defined genres by the function that they served or by the groups that sang them. There are numerous folk songs whose subject matter and use were at the heart of people's livelihoods. The most collected of these songs were those of work groups who both lived and worked together.

Come, butter, come!
De King an' de Queen
Is er-standin' at de gate,
Er-waitin' for some butter.
An' a cake.
Oh, come, butter, come!

(Scarborough, 215. Woman's butter-churning song; one of the few examples of women's work songs found in American collections of the early twentieth century.)

There were three kinds of work song. First there were the songs in the worker's general repertoire that were not specifically about the singer's work experience. These were usually sung at general gatherings when there was no work to do. The second type, sung mostly for entertainment in the same context, were songs about the work itself. This group might include songs about disasters, heroes, or humorous incidents on the job. Among the third type were those songs that literally helped the workers with the task at hand. Most often these were songs that had a set rhythm and allowed a group of workers to coordinate effort—to hoist a sail, to coordinate blows of hammers, or to hoe a field in unison. (Vocal expressions that border between song and speech were used by groups to communicate important information, such as the call to "mark twain" on riverboats or the calls that cowboys used to soothe cattle at night.)

Some of these work songs originated in the United States, while others owe traits, themes, and even entire texts and tunes to foreign song traditions. American lumbering songs have ties to both the Australian folk song tradition and to Irish folk music. Cowboy ballads show a range of influences as wide as the vastly eclectic mix of persons who became cowboys, "from the folk-song repertoires of African Americans or Latinos working the range, to those of the popular-song tradition of the day" (Thorp: 20, 23). Sailor's songs, both from the Great Lakes and the oceangoing ships, reflect the lumbering, farming, and immigrant traditions.

As the concept of work has changed since the 1970s books have begun to appear that address the wider question of how an occupation can be seen reflected in the folk songs both of workers and of other groups. The extensive folk song tradition of coal miners in the United States has been studied by Archie Green, and Norm Cohen has shown the major significance of railroading in both American life and song.

TOPICAL SONG. Topical songs are those that deal with issues of immediate importance to a group. The tradition of writing topical songs is at least as old as the earliest broadsides of the fifteenth century. They concern themselves with social, economic, and political issues such as disasters (storms, shipwrecks, floods, earthquakes), movements (temperance, abolition), wars, local community issues (including murders and scandals), or labor strife. There are a few reasons why a topical song could persist as part of the folk song tradition long after the particular incident upon which it has been based has occurred. The issue that the song addresses may still remain unresolved and of importance to the group; the song might be regarded as a historical song (such as songs about past presidents and their assassinations); or the song may have been changed or reinterpreted so that it has become meaningful in a context different from that in which it originated.

Come, listen, fellow-workingmen, my story,
I'll relate,
How, workers in the coal-mines fare in
Pennsylvania State;
Come, hear a sad survivor, from beside his
children's graves,
And learn how free Americans are treated
now as slaves.

They robbed us of our pay,
They starved us day by day,
They shot us down on the hillside brown,
And swore our lives away.

(Foner: 202)

The topical song is of ideological importance to the singer and listener. Its goal is to enact change or allow catharsis. Many topical songs are written by those who have suffered harm or feel they are in jeopardy. Thus, while topical songs may be considered folk songs, they are perhaps the only folk songs that have as a goal their own demise, since they seek the elimination of the causes for which they are written and sung. In this sense, songs urging women's suffrage became obsolete after women were granted the vote.

The words to topical songs are written by persons familiar with the immediate situation, and the tune is often one commonly known by both singer and audience. Either popular or folk tunes are used. This flexibility in the use of different melodies is also characteristic of religious folk songs, as is the attempt to create change or intensify feelings relating to group identity (social, religious, political, and so forth). In fact, Joe

Hill, the famous songwriter and organizer of the IWW (Industrial Workers of the World, whose members were known as "Wobblies"), often used hymn tunes for his topical songs. And it was not infrequently that the Wobblies found themselves singing their songs on a city street corner within distance of competing religious groups such as the Salvation Army.

The words of topical songs that are set to borrowed tunes are often similar to the lyrics of the original song, a fact that makes these songs parodies of a sort, since they rely on a referent text for their impact and often for their humor. At times the use of familiar tunes and texts allows for "sing-along" topical songs. Such songs could inspire a group to act. At other times a topical song might be sung to impart a story. However, not all topical songs are built on other folk songs. Some are original compositions that serve the group's needs. When labor began to organize in this country toward the end of the nineteenth and the beginning of the twentieth centuries, repertoires of topical labor folk songs developed with it. Groups both adapted existing folk song texts for their own use and created new songs to carry their message and help with the activities of the labor movement.

"It Isn't Nice" is an example of a song that inspired action, sitdowns, and other peaceful resistance, first in the 1960s in the San Francisco area and in many other places thereafter. This song was sung widely in the 1960s. Judy Collins and others have recorded it, including its writer and composer, Malvina Reynolds.

> [Verse 2]
> *It isn't nice to carry banners*
> *Or to sit in on the floor,*
> *Or to shout our cry of Freedom*
> *At the hotel and the store,*
> *It isn't nice, it isn't nice,*
> *You told us once, you told us twice,*
> *But if that is Freedom's price,*
> *We don't mind.*
>
> [Verse 5]
> *It isn't nice to go to jail,*
> *There are nicer ways to do it*
> *But the nice ways always fail.*
> *It isn't nice, it isn't nice,*
> *But thanks for your advice,*
> *Cause if that is Freedom's price,*
> *We don't mind.*

As with any repertoire of songs, topical folk songs developed a set of commonplaces, terms that had a shortcut meaning for the listener. Calling someone a "brave young comrade" in a song about the mining troubles in Harlan County, Kentucky, in the 1930s was a way of saying that the person in question was a fighter for the people and a martyr. One can often date topical songs by their commonplaces.

At times it is the context that defines a topical song. During the civil rights movement of the 1960s, the religious folk song "We Shall Overcome" was used by marchers to express their feelings. Although the song's text was little changed from what was sung in church, the singing of it during a civil rights march provided a context in which it became a protest song. Thus, any song, if sung in the right cultural context, is a potential protest song. Likewise, it can be said that a topical song, once it has lived past its historic and social contexts, can become popular with a different group of singers than those intended by the original writer or singers. This occurred with Woody Guthrie's "This Land Is Your Land."

In her history of topical songs in this country in the 1930s through the 1950s, Robbie Lieberman points out that "This Land Is Your Land" "was written as a [left-wing] parody of Irving Berlin's "God Bless America" (the first version was "God Blessed America for Me"). [Today] schoolchildren do not learn the more militant verses, such as this one:

> *Was a big high wall there that tried to stop me*
> *A sign was painted said: Private Property*
> *But on the back side, it didn't say nother—*
> *This land was made for you and me.*
>
> (Lieberman: 163)

In other words, Guthrie literally meant that we, not just monied and politically powerful people, should own the United States. Lieberman's insightful work is very much beholden to the pioneering scholarship of Richard Reuss, who began the trend toward careful study of the interrelationship of twentieth-century American left-wing politics and topical song.

SENTIMENTAL SONG. It is not a great step from the style of the broadside to the style of the sentimental or "parlor" song. Both are transmitted through the complex interaction of print and oral tradition. The sentimental song, a product of the lower- and middle-class parlors of the nineteenth century, used commonplaces that were the clichés of the time. These songs employed the imagery of Victorian moralism and described events and their consequences with a heavy hand. Because the aesthetic of such songs was associated with the lower classes, people who regarded their tastes as more refined were reluctant to pay attention to them.

Scholars considered them subliterature and not worthy of study.

"Young Charlotte" is an example of a widely sung sentimental ballad. It warns young women against vanity, dancing, not heeding parents, and the frivolities of youth.

Young Charlotte lived by the mountain side
In a wild and dreary spot
With no other dwelling for miles around
Except her father's cot[tage].

On many a cold and wintery night
Young swains would gather there;
Her father kept a social board,
And she was young and fair.

[On a bitterly cold Christmas Eve she wants to go to a nearby dance.]

. . . .

When dashing up to the cottage door
Young Charles in his sleigh appeared.

[Mother warns daughter to wrap in blankets in sleigh.]

"Oh, no, no," the daughter said,
And she laughed like a gypsy queen.
"To ride in blankets all muffled up
I never will be seen."

[She freezes to death as they drive, but Charles realizes it only as they reach the dance.]

He bore her out into the sleigh
And with her he drove home;
And when he reached the cottage door
Oh, how her parents mourned!

They mourned the loss of a daughter dear,
And Charles mourned o'er his doom,
He mourned until his heart did break—
They slumber in one tomb.

(Belden: 309–310)

But despite this historical social stigma, these songs about gray-haired mothers being led to the poorhouse, of orphaned and blind children, of dying nuns, and of loyal Indian maidens held as honored a place in the repertoires of traditional singers as did the older imports from the British Isles. A few early collectors such as H. M. Belden and Vance Randolph recognized that sentimental songs were as much a part of America's folk song tradition as were the Child ballads, and they included them in their collections.

RELIGIOUS SONG. Religious folk songs are identified as those sung during the services of groups that practice folk religion, or as songs that have religious events or stories as their central theme. During colonial times both psalms and hymns were sung by congregations through the technique of lining out. The preacher would sing a line and the congregation would repeat that line after him. This technique was especially helpful where books were scarce or where the congregation was not able to read.

During the Great Awakening in the mid 1700s spiritual songs appeared in congregations that wished to incorporate group singing into the church service. These new songs often took current secular folk tunes and combined them with new words to make religious texts. With the advent of camp meetings in about 1800, large numbers of people traveled great distances to set up "camp" in order to hold church services over a period of days or weeks. These meetings produced a simpler spiritual song, one whose words and stanzaic form allowed for greater group participation than occurred during the Great Awakening. The camp meetings were part of the religious movement known as the Second Awakening, during which the religion preached was far more personalized than that of the earlier period. The Second Awakening was primarily a rural phenomenon, and its activities were scorned by urban populations, because of the unlettered who participated and the ecstatic states to which they rose.

As the urban centers swelled after the Civil War and toward the end of the nineteenth century, the social gospel developed in the cities. This religious movement preached the "City of God on Earth," where material rewards can be had in this rather than the afterlife, which had been the focus during the Great Awakening. Religious folk songs consequently changed with the times, taking on the trappings of the urban popular music that had been forged through a mixture of many different cultural influences. The result was the gospel song, a modification of the earlier camp meeting songs in an urban context. The gospel song incorporated the developing ragtime sound, an upbeat rhythm, and words that depicted a far more intimate relationship to God or Christ than did earlier religious folk songs.

With each turn in this country's religious history, new instruments and folk instrumental styles found their way into church services and church music. With the development of string bands and the country music industry in the early twentieth century, religious songs were sung in hillbilly, bluegrass, and other singing styles. Folk groups such as the Carter Family were welcomed by the commercial recording and music industry.

The Carter Family was a southern mountain family singing group. They were one of the most popular commercial country music groups from the late 1920s through the early 1940s, whose records and regular radio appearances were very popular. They sang both religious and secular songs, and wrote many of their own pieces, and came to represent the American family and pristine morals (Malone: 63–65).

OTHER GENRES OF AMERICAN FOLK SONG. Genres of American folk song are not delineated just by textual form or by function. Some kinds of American folk song have been accepted as genres simply because there has been a good deal of scholarship or public attention devoted to them. Because of this inclusiveness, the list of American folk song genres could be long. Various other types of folk song in the United States might include children's songs, game and play-party, songs, dance songs, bawdy songs, nonsense songs, dialect songs, and patriotic songs.

Performed Folk Song

Folk song is a complex of elements far beyond simple text. In the same manner that a movie is not only its screenplay, or a stage play is not only its text, folk song must be seen as a total performance. Each element of that performance is learned traditionally, and each is judged by a traditional aesthetic. Every folk group has a folk aesthetic by which it judges text, music, and style of performance. What one culture values is not necessarily what another one will. Only when we examine folk songs in terms of these elements can we begin to understand the folk songs of a culture.

TEXT. Cultures recognize certain arrangements of words as texts to given genres of folk song. Texts have various characteristics, most of which are derived from the study of written poetry. A text can be analyzed, for example, in terms of its meter, stanzaic form, rhyme scheme, point of view, or themes. In order for a song to be considered good, all of its textual elements must meet aesthetic criteria learned traditionally within the group that perpetuates it.

MUSIC. A folk song's music, like its text, contains elements that are immediately recognizable to its composers, players, and audience. There is a culturally learned musical vocabulary used with each genre, and the performer must know the limits of individual choice and creativity when choosing and performing a song. For example, southern mountain traditional singers seldom used instrumental accompaniment to sing the old ballads. They often sang them without a "regular" rhythm and strove for a high, tense pitch, sometimes called a "high, lonesome sound." This music seems understated to current urban American audiences, especially since this traditional musical aesthetic emphasizes limited use of dynamics (loudness and softness).

STYLE OF PRESENTATION. When referring to style of presentation, we should be aware that there are separate styles for texts and for music. What is meant here by style of presentation is the way in which different types of songs are performed in different manners. Style of presentation is essentially what is done by the voice, the body, and the instruments that makes a song performance a definite "type" of song. There are vocal and instrumental techniques as well as appropriate gestures (or lack thereof) that good traditional singers learn and master and that can be varied within culturally condoned limits. There are folk standards of good and bad folk performance just as there are of popular and classical performances.

There were two distinct styles of a cappella folksinging presentation brought to this country from the British Isles. One was a generally plain, unornamented vocal style that had virtually no vibrato, used no dynamics, and had a varying rhythm. The sound was produced by a nasal or throat effect. This style is primarily English. The second style was an ornamented one, often with a set rhythm, which featured a glottal vibrato without pitch alteration, and dynamics often unrelated to the text. This style is primarily derived from the Scottish and Irish tradition. In addition, there were definite instrumental styles that were brought to America and further developed here.

Southern mountain traditional singers seldom used instrumental accompaniment to sing the old ballads: They often sang them without a "regular" rhythm and strove for a high, tense pitch, sometimes called a "high, lonesome sound."

Two of the best-known European American instrumental styles to develop in this country are the string-band musical styles of bluegrass and "old timey" (a precursor of bluegrass). Instruments such as the Autoharp, the five-string banjo, and the southern mountain dulcimer were Americanizations of instruments brought to this continent from Europe, Africa, and Scandinavia. For the most part, however, the Americanization of music had more to do with the manner in which instruments were played than the development of entirely new instruments. Fiddle-playing in Texas in the 1800s sounded very different from the violin playing of "classical" musicians in Boston of the same period, even if each performer was playing a physically identical instrument.

FUNCTION. In a given culture, singers learn what songs to sing, when, where, and why to sing them, and with whom or to whom they can be performed. This knowledge is a vital part of folk song; it constitutes the function of the song or music. To know these particulars means that a singer has an understanding of the proper context in which a song may be sung or must be altered. A judicious choice of a song or a sequence of songs can be as creative an act as a remarkable performance.

Once a folk song is learned, each singer makes changes that best suit her or his aesthetic and the situation in which the song is to be sung. The folksinger can change any aspect of the song as long as the audience will tolerate the change. Considering the potentials for variation in all the elements of a folk song, the folksinger in the United States has extensive opportunities for creativity.

Governmental Institutions and Folk Song Study

Early academic interest in folk song began in America in the last half of the nineteenth century. It was centered in the Northeast, with Francis James Child, his student George Lyman Kittredge, and Phillips Barry as the major proponents. At Harvard, where Child and Kittredge worked, many of this country's folklore and folk song scholars began their careers. Although neither Child nor Kittredge did any fieldwork, and although neither showed an interest in the performance of folk song, they were responsible in part for later folk song scholars who were.

One of Kittredge's students was John A. Lomax, who traveled to the western United States in order to record cowboy songs. In 1910 he published *Cowboy Songs and Other Frontier Ballads*, one of the earliest and most popular firsthand collections of what lie believed were genuine American folk songs.

John Lomax was accompanied in much of his fieldwork by his son Alan Lomax who took up his father's vision of presenting to the United States its own folk song legacy. To a large extent through publications of commercial collections such as his *Folk Songs of North America* (1960), his extensive issuing of field recordings for labels such as Columbia and Atlantic, and through academically affiliated projects such as that which forms the core of his work on folk song style, Alan Lomax has been one of the most influential persons in the twentieth century to spur the development of both academic and popular interest in American folk song.

Among the recordings that were used by city singers to learn new songs during the folk song revival of the 1960s were the field recordings that are still issued commercially by the Archive of Folk Song in the Library of Congress. This archive was established in 1928, and scholars such as John A. Lomax, Benjamin A. Botkin, and Alan Lomax were among its first directors. Today that archive is known as the Archive of Folk Culture. In 1976 it was placed under the umbrella organization of the congressionally established American Folklife Center. This organization remains located in the Library of Congress. The Library of Congress, along with the National Endowment of the Arts' Folklife Programs and the Smithsonian Institution's Folklife Program, are the central governmental organizations devoted to ongoing research and presentation of American folk life.

The primary forum for both scholars and nonscholars of folklore is the American Folklore Society, founded in 1888, whose periodical, the *Journal of American Folklore*, has continuously published for over a century. In addition, numerous regional folklore societies and publications flourish throughout the country.

Major universities in the United States offer advanced degrees in the study of folklore. A doctorate in this field is offered by Indiana University, UCLA, the University of Texas at Austin, and the University of Pennsylvania. These universities and numerous others offering master's degrees in folklore often cooperate in projects with the governmental institutions. In addition, governmental organizations also help fund regional and state folklife centers, which have flourished throughout the country since the 1970s. Local historical societies and arts boards, privately funded, state run, or supported by the National Endowments of the Arts and Humanities, also employ folklorists and encourage the study and presentation of American folklife and folk song.

Commercialization of Folk Song and the Folk Song Revival

The earliest commercialization of folk music undoubtedly occurred through whatever early institutions were considered the mass media of the time. European and British troubadours, as well as the broadside press, certainly spread folk songs. There is a constant interaction among potentially fixed aspects of song performance (those that can be spread by mass media and recorded in some manner, such as the text of a tune) and elements of folk song that are passed on through the performance itself. A pure oral tradition probably never existed during the time humans made written records. The extent

Leadbelly, photograph 1966, and his music came to the attention of the 1930s and '40s urban audiences at political rallies, union meetings, and at hootenannies.

to which a folk song has been "commercialized" is not a measure of whether or not the song is a folk song in any given context. The transmission of a song (all four elements) within a group, without reference to a fixed source for continual correction, constitutes a folk song.

It is only recently that the concepts of "commercial" and "folk" have seemed contradictory. In the early days of professional entertainment in the United States, the vaudeville stage, traveling tent shows, medicine shows, and minstrel shows all contributed to and received from general popular tradition. From the beginning, radio broadcasts used local talent. Right before the Great Depression, the recording industry, then in a slump and sensing the threat of the new radio technology, sent scouts to the southern mountains to seek out local musicians. In the 1920s Ralph Peer, talent scout and recording director for a number of record companies, introduced to the commercial recording industry both African American and Anglo-American folksingers. He discovered Mamie Smith and Fiddlin' John Carson among others, and he was a key player in establishing the commercial country and western music industry. This industry catered to an underclass that longed for music from "back home."

In the 1930s and 1940s folk songs were brought to the attention of urban middle-class audiences through the federal government's Works Progress Administration (WPA) and by left-wing political groups who felt that "people's songs" were most appropriate as a vehicle for political ideology. For left-oriented urban singers of folk songs, the "folk" meant the "people" or the working classes (farmers and the industrial workers), Folk songs and folklike songs were sung at political rallies, union meetings, and at hootenannies. The urban "hoot" of the mid twentieth century was usually an advertised event with featured artists who espoused left-wing causes. They would perform from a stage-like area and sing songs with clear political messages, many of which were selected (and written) so that the audience could join in the singing.

Were it not for the political left wing of the 1930s and 1940s, urban middle-class America might never have known Woody Guthrie, Leadbelly, Sarah Ogan Gunning, and other traditional folksingers. And if it were not for the persistence of urban singers who believed in the principals of the left-wing ideology of the day, such as Alan Lomax, Peggy Seeger, Burl Ives, Pete Seeger, Will Geer, and Ronnie Gilbert, American mass media and popular culture never would have seen many major talents.

In the 1950s there was a burgeoning interest in folk song outside of political circles. Some performers, such as Pete Seeger and the group in which he sang, the Weavers, felt the need to carry their political messages to new audiences, especially those that were developing on college campuses. Seeger's and the Weavers' brilliance as musicians and performers allowed them a wide range of expression, and their audience was extensive. In their commercial recordings they presented an apolitical repertoire; by the early 1950s they had numerous hit records such as "Good Night, Irene," "On Top of Old Smoky," and "The Midnight Special," and they had performed at Carnegie Hall. However, blacklisting during the anticommunist McCarthy era removed the Weavers, collectively and individually, from public media.

To understand the urban folk song world of the 1940s, 1950s, and 1960s, one needs to make a distinction between traditional folksingers and singers of folk songs. The former includes those singers who learned all elements of folk song from traditional sources, while the latter encompasses those musicians whose repertoires relied on regional folk song collections. The texts and tunes that singers of folk songs performed originated with traditional groups. These singers performed for urban audiences in a recast style of presentation and with a function particular to their urban needs. Eventually some of these singers and others would begin to write their own texts and tunes based on a folklike model.

In 1958 the folksinging Kingston Trio hit the charts with "Tom Dooley," a song they learned from the recording of a traditional folksinger. For almost twenty years thereafter popular song would be heavily and directly influenced by Anglo-American and African American folk song. It was this introduction of various aspects of folk song into the mainstream of American popular music that allowed for the drastic shift in the popular aesthetic that occurred by the 1970s and had blossomed earlier with Bob Dylan and other singers and songwriters of his generation, such as Joan Baez, Judy Collins, and Tom Paxton.

The folk song revival flourished throughout the decade of the 1960s. Basically four kinds of singers emerged during this period, some of whom found more in common with the currents of preceding decades and some of whom foreshadowed the sound and style of the decades to come.

The first kind of singer that formed the basis of the folk song revival of the 1960s was the "traditional" performer or "folksinger" who had learned all four elements of folk song through the culture in which he or she was raised. Such performers were invited to sing at folk festivals, on college campuses, and in coffeehouses. Before the 1960s, urban audiences had not been prepared to hear their style of presentation. The major folk song element that each of them had to alter in his or her performance, which seriously distorted their art, was the function. It was virtually impossible to present accurately in an urban setting songs that originally had been performed in an entirely different context. This affected texts, tunes, and style of performance. Many traditional singers began to "urbanize" their performances, increasing the tempo of the songs that they sang for urban audiences, adding accompaniment to their previously a cappella traditional performance style, and dropping local references from their texts. Nevertheless, the difference between what they presented and what their audiences were accustomed to hearing was startling. It raised basic questions in the minds of urban audiences about what standards should be used to judge "good" songs and performances. Typical of this kind of singer were Sarah Ogan Gunning, Mississippi John Hurt, and Glenn Ohrlin.

In the 1950s, performers such as Pete Seeger and the Weavers, the group in which he sang, felt the need to carry their political messages to new audiences, especially those that were developing on college campuses.

It is interesting to note that the two kinds of traditional folksingers who were in demand in urban America at this time were poor white southerners and poor rural African Americans. These were the same groups sought by the early recording industry. One seldom heard other groups in the urban revival, despite the fact that audiences were rarely composed of poor whites or African Americans. The audience of the urban folk song revival in the 1960s was primarily white middle-class youth from urban suburbs.

The second type of performer in the 1960s urban folk song revival was the emulator. These performers were, like their audiences, mostly white middle-class suburban or urban young people who chose to immerse themselves in both the music and culture of the traditional singers. The emulators found profound meaning in both the traditional texts and music, as well as in the style of presentation. Many of the performers became so versatile at emulating a traditional folk song style that they were accepted as traditional by the cultures that they sought to emulate. Some of them were not only able to imitate, they were able to create. The one element that they found most difficult to master, however, was function. Among those of this type were the New Lost City, Ramblers, Dave Van Ronk, the Greenbriar Boys, and the Jim Kweskin String Band.

The third kind of singer in the urban revival was the utilizer. These performers were singers of folk song who took traditional texts and music and set them to a style which, in the early 1960s, was acceptable to the established aesthetic of mainstream urban audiences. These singers appealed to the urban "pop" sound (the music of the Kingston Trio, for example), and the urban "art" sound (represented by those such as Alfred Deller and Richard Dyer-Bennet).

The fourth kind of folksinger in the 1960s urban folk song revival was the singer who personified the new revival aesthetic. These singers differed from utilizers in that they did not remold the material in terms of an aesthetic that already existed. This group of singers attempted to blend traditional and urban aesthetics in their performance. They developed a new way of accommodating the inevitable tensions that existed among various song styles in nonurban and urban cultures. They and their audiences synthesized new aesthetic criteria for all four elements of folk song. The sound of this group was one that blended folk, classical, jazz, and pop styles. Almost all of the revival aesthetic singers performed with accompaniment. They crafted ways to harmonize the modal traditional tunes, and they created what at the time was a new effect in their performances.

It was this sound of the revival aesthetic that became the sound of the urban folk song revival of the 1960s. It was Joan Baez, Peter, Paul, and Mary; and Bob Dylan. The days of the popular crooner who had reigned during the 1940s and 1950s was replaced by the sounds of these new singers and their derivatives. Pete Seeger, one of the most gifted arrangers, creators, and performers of this revival aesthetic, was a leading influence in developing a new popular music in the United States. With the urban folk song revival, mass media developed a commercially successful new sound of the 1960s. It was one that would influence generations to come. Popular taste was dramatically altered, and listening skills were expanded.

The opening of aesthetic choices in the 1960s led the way to a new diversity: and inclusiveness in popular music suited for the coming age of global communications. It also gave many singers in urban centers a new repertoire and a new folksinging tradition. This urban tradition has yet to be studied with the enthusiasm of America's earlier rural traditions, although it presents just as rich an area of cultural expression. Folksinging is now recognized as a viable form of expression in modern urban America, for which we are indebted to both commercial interests as well as to the scholars of the multifaceted American folk song.

[See also African American Music; Country and Western Music; Popular Music before 1950; Rock Music; Rural Life in the South.]

BIBLIOGRAPHY

General Works

American Folklore Society. *Folklore/Folklife* (1984).

Barry, Phillips. "Communal Re-Creation." *Bulletin of the Folk Song Society of the Northeast*, no. 5 (1933): 4–6. Pioneering work by a folk song and folk music scholar.

Ives, Edward D. *Joe Scott: The Woodsman-Songmaker* (1978).

Journal of American Folklore: The Centennial Index, edited by Bruce Jackson et al. (1988). A comprehensive index to one of the most important publications on folklore in the United States.

Genres Other Than Ballad and Lyric

Herrera-Sobek, Maria. *The Mexican Corrido: A Feminist Analysis* (1990). A study of a Latino folk song form popular in the American Southwest.

Knapp, Mary, and Herbert Knapp. *One Potato, Two Potato . . . : The Secret Education of American Children* (1976).

Malone, Bill C. *Country Music, U.S.A.* Rev. ed. (1985). See esp. chap. 1, "The Folk Background Before Commercialism," chap. 2, "The Early Period of Commercial Hillbilly Music," and the bibliographical essays.

Newell, William W. *Games and Songs of American Children, Collected and Compared* (1883; rpr. 1963).

Music

Bronson, Bertrand Harris. *The Traditional Tunes of the Child Ballads: With Their Texts, According to the Extant Records of Great Britain and America.* 4 vols. (1959–1972).

Ballad and Lyric Genres

Abrahams, Roger, and George Foss. *Anglo-American Folksong Style* (1968).

Child, Francis James, ed. *The English and Scottish Popular Ballads.* 5 vols. (1882–1898; repr. 1965).

Coffin, Tristram P. *The British Traditional Ballad in North America.* Rev. ed., with a supplement by Roger deV. Renwick (1977).

Laws, George Malcolm. *American Balladry from British Broadsides: A Guide for Students and Collectors of Traditional Song. Publications of the American Folklore Society. Bibliographical and Special Series.* Vol. 8 (1957).

Laws, George Malcolm. *Native American Balladry: A Descriptive Study and a Bibliographical Syllabus.* Rev. ed. *Publications of the American Folklore Society. Bibliographical and Special Series.* Vol. 1 (1964; repr. 1975).

Wilgus, Donald Knight. *Anglo-American Folksong Scholarship Since 1898* (1959).

Style

Lomax, Alan. "Folk Song Style." *American Anthropologist* 61, no. 6 (1959): 927–955.

Rosenberg, Neil V. *Bluegrass: A History*, (1985).

Spottswood, Richard K. *Ethnic Music on Records: A Discography of Ethnic Recordings Produced in the United States, 1893–1942.* 7 vols. (1990).

Topical Song and the 1960s Folk Song Revival

Klein, Joe. *Woody Guthrie: A Life* (1980).

Lieberman, Robbie. *My Song Is My Weapon: People's Songs, American Communism, and the Politics of Culture, 1930–1950* (1989).

Reuss, Richard A. "American Folklore and Left-Wing Politics: 1927–1957." Ph.D. diss., Indiana University, 1971.

Stekert, Ellen J. "Cents and Nonsense in the Urban Folksong Movement: 1930'1966." In *Folklore and Society: Essays in Honor of Benjamin A. Botkin*, edited by Bruce Jackson (1966). This essay will be reprinted in the forthcoming study of the folk song revival *Transforming Tradition: Folk Music Revivals Examined*, edited by Neil Rosenberg.

Work and Labor

Cohen, Norm. *Long Steel Rail: The Railroad in American Folksong* (1981).

Doerflinger, William Main. *Shantymen and Shantyboys: Songs of the Sailor and Lumberman* (1951).

Foner, Philip N. *American Labor Songs of the Nineteenth Century*, (1975).

Green, Archie. *Only a Miner: Studies in Recorded Coal-Mining Songs* (1972).

Lomax, John A. *Cowboy Songs and Other Frontier Ballads* (1910).

Reynolds, Malvina. *The Malvina Reynolds Songbook* (1984).
Thorp, N. Howard. *Songs of the Cowboy* (1908; rev. ed. 1966).

Religious

Downey, James C. "Revivalism, the Gospel Songs and Social Reform." *Ethnomusicology* 9 (May 1965):115–125.
Jackson, George Pullen. *White Spirituals in the Southern Uplands: The Story of the Fasola Folk, Their Songs, Singings, and "Buckwheat Notes"* (1933; rpr. 1965).
Jackson, George Pullen. *Down-East Spirituals and Others* (1939).
Jackson, George Pullen. *The Story of the Sacred Harp, 1844–1944* (1944).
Jackson, George Pullen. *Another Sheaf of White Spirituals* (1952).
Yoder, Don. *Pennsylvania Spirituals.* (1961).

Regional, Occupational, and General Collections

Ancelet, Barry Jean. *Cajun Music: Its Origins and Development. Louisiana Life* series, no. 2 (1989).
Belden, Henry Marvin, ed. *Ballads and Songs Collected by the Missouri Folk-Lore Society,* (1940; rpr. 1955).
Lomax, Alan. *The Folk Songs of North America in the English Language* (1960).
Lomax, John A., Alan Lomax et al. *Folk, Song U.S.A.: The 111 Best American Ballads* (1947).
Randolph, Vance, et al. *Ozark Folksongs.* 4 vols. (1946–1950).
Scarborough, Dorothy. *On the Trail of Negro Folk-Songs* (1925; repr. 1963).
Sharp, Cecil J., comp. *English Folk Songs from the Southern Appalachians.* Edited by Maud Karpeles. 2 vols. (1917).

— ELLEN J. STEKERT

FOODWAYS

Arugula, big macs, barbecue, C rations, caviar, chitterlings, chop suey, Gerber's strained peaches, jambalaya, johnnycakes, kielbasa, Moon Pies, pemmican, sauerkraut, and Weight Watchers frozen pizzas are all food items that have been consumed at one time or another in the United States of America. Though some foods, such as the humble but omnipresent hamburger, transcend lines of age, class, and geography, preferences for others clearly correlate with historical period, region, social class, gender, age, occupation, race, and ethnicity. Foodways—the manner in which groups of people select, prepare, and ingest edibles—are thus a valuable source of information about the character of the various social groupings of the United States and their interrelations at any given time. Although the term is most commonly used by ethnologists and ethnologically influenced students of folklore and folklife in examining "folk" societies and subcultures, the following essay will focus on the role of food in American society more broadly.

The Columbian Exchange

The story of North American foodways begins with the "Columbian exchange," the process that began in 1492 with the European arrival in the New World, through which the natural and human ecologies of the two broad cultural zones began to become inextricably intertwined. European newcomers were faced with the absence of indigenous sources of food—such as wheat bread—to which they had been accustomed. The English "Pilgrims," near starvation after their arrival at Plymouth on coastal New England in 1620, were happy enough to incorporate the maize (corn), beans, and squash offered by the native peoples into their diets, together with the wild turkey, venison, and abundant seafood that the new land offered. The Spanish also reluctantly learned to make do with manioc or cassava as substitutes for wheat in Central and South America until more familiar patterns could be reestablished.

Prior to the coming of the Europeans, the diet of the indigenous North American peoples had varied by region, but was broadly based on locally available fish and game and the three vegetable staples of maize, beans, and squash, together with nuts and berries. As a result of the Columbian exchange this diet also was altered, as were the broader life patterns of the native peoples, who became employed in the cultivation of bananas, sugarcane, rice, and coffee—all of them Old World imports, though now for centuries associated intimately with the Americas. In addition, the Spanish introduced Iberian staples such as wheat, olives, and wine grapes into those areas where they could be successfully cultivated. (Junípero Serra and the Franciscans who organized the California Indians into mission colonies in the late eighteenth century attempted to Europeanize their charges in part through the cultivation of these crops.) A major result of this importation of European food plants and animals and their rapid flourishing was the creation of a living environment both materially and culturally hospitable to succeeding waves of Old World colonists.

Where pre-Columbian native peoples had raised little livestock other than poultry for food, they accepted the introduction of pigs and cattle much more readily than they did most European food plants. Native peoples living near the northern edge of New Spain in what is now the southwestern United States—the Navajo, Pueblo, and Apache—eagerly turned to cattle raising. The horse, previously unknown in the New World, was used more in the raising of cattle and other food animals than for food itself. Its introduction revolutionized the cultures of the Plains peoples through its usefulness for transportation and warfare as well as pursuit of the bison and wild cattle. In the longer run, Spanish cattle and horses paved the way for a western culture featuring latter-day vaqueros (cowboys—sometimes a role ironically played by Indians under the Spanish) and a fierce

American appetite for beef. The overall result, according to biohistorian Alfred W. Crosby, Jr., was "so successful . . . that . . . [it was] probably the greatest biological revolution in the Americas since the end of the Pleistocene era" (*The Columbian Exchange*, p. 66).

Anglo-American Colonial Patterns

English-speaking colonists began early in the seventeenth century to fashion their own sets of foodways, which combined regional English patterns of cooking and eating successively with locally available foodstuffs, foods transplanted from England, and, eventually, imports from a wide variety of foreign locales. Borrowings from Native American and other neighbors, together, in some cases, with religious and ideological considerations, further influenced Anglo-American patterns. William Bradford describes the earliest patterns of interaction and adaptation in *Of Plymouth Plantation* for the year 1621:

> [In April] they began to plant their corn, in which service Squanto stood them in great stead, showing them both the manner how to set it, and after how to dress and tend it. Also he told them except they got fish and set with it (in these old grounds) it would come to nothing. . . . Some English seed they sowed, as wheat and peas, but it came not to good, either by the badness of the seed, or lateness of the season, or both. . . .
>
> They began now [in September] to gather in the small harvest they had. . . . Others were exercised in fishing, about cod, and bass, and other fish, of which they took good store, of which every family had their portion. All the summer there was no want. And now began to come in store of fowl, as winter approached, of which this place did abound when they came first (but afterward decreased by degrees). And besides water fowl, there was great store of wild turkeys, of which they took many, besides venison, etc. Besides they had about a peck of meal a week to a person, or now since harvest, Indian corn to that proportion. Which made many afterwards write so largely of their plenty here to their friends in England, which were not feigned, but true reports.

The alternating abundance and want that characterized these and subsequent years in New England gave rise to days both of thanksgiving and of fasting and repentance, the only occasions other than the Sabbath that constituted Puritan collective ritual observance for many decades.

THE NEW ENGLAND DIET. Cattle from England had been introduced into the Plymouth Colony by 1624, thus reducing the necessity for hunting, an occupation or recreation alien to the British "middling" classes. (John Winthrop, the leader of the much larger 1630 settlement of the Massachusetts Bay Colony, was not averse to an occasional expedition with his fowling piece, though.) Wheat and rye supplemented the indigenous maize, and chicken, hogs, and fruit trees were also introduced into New England before long. The Puritan "plain style"—a cultural aesthetic based on a religious objection to overelaborateness, whether in preaching, clothing, or cooking—combined with circumstance to produce what David Hackett Fischer has called "one of the most austere foodways in the Western world" (*Albion's Seed*, p. 135).

The resultant cuisine has endured as part of the New England diet to the present day. After they had overcome their initial aversion to the giant lobsters that abounded in coastal waters, New Englanders appropriated the aboriginal custom of holding clambakes, in which clams, other shellfish, and later accompaniments were cooked while buried in sand with heated rocks. Such affairs were easily turned into communal and, eventually, commercial ventures. Succotash, a mixture of beans and Indian corn, derived both its name and its character from Algonkian usage. Cornmeal yielded various edible products such as samp, a coarse hominy now sold by the Vermont Country Store as a semiexotic, seminostalgic regional item; johnnycake (journey cake), a baked or fried kind of cornbread suitable for taking along on travels; and Indian pudding, made with milk and molasses, and now served at restaurants featuring regional cuisine such as Boston's Durgin Park.

After colonial New Englanders had overcome their initial aversion to the giant lobsters that abounded in coastal waters, they appropriated the aboriginal custom of holding clambakes, in which clams and other shellfish were cooked while buried in sand with heated rocks.

Other aspects of the New England diet that arose from necessity and were later regarded as embodiments of frugal virtue were baked beans, described by Lucy Larcom in the nineteenth century as the "canonical dish of our Forefathers" (Fischer, p. 136), and prepared in advance to avoid cooking on the strictly observed Sabbath; the New England boiled dinner, based on carrots, potatoes, cabbage, and corned beef, that is, meat "corned" with salt as a preservative, then boiled in unseasoned water; and codfish balls or cakes, made from the ubiquitous fish enshrined in a six-foot model at the Massachusetts State House as the "Sacred Cod" in tribute to its role as provider of both food and commercial value. The expansion of trade with Britain, the West Indian colonies, and other ports that did so much to create many coastal mercantile fortunes also enriched the regional diet with molasses, rum, and citrus fruits from the West Indies; tea, coffee, chocolate, spices, and sugar from the East Indies; tapioca from Latin America; dates from the Middle East; wine, brandy, and raisins from the Mediterranean; ginger from China; and rice and corn from the southern colonies. Farther north, those intrepid settlers attempting to eke out a living in the mountains of what would become Vermont and New Hampshire found domestic uses as well as external markets for maple sugar, and a confluence of cultural patterns with nearby French Canada led to other regional adaptations. Pies, an English institution and ubiquitous to all parts of New England, were sometimes fried in Vermont. (Part of Yankee folklore, or perhaps "fakelore," has it that a Yankee is simply anyone who eats pie for breakfast.)

Patterns of food preparation in New England were derived primarily from East Anglia, the region of origin of the majority of the earliest English settlers. Dark English beer was the beverage of choice in the seventeenth century, and was later augmented by fermented apple cider and the universally popular rum, some of it home-brewed from cherries. Pork and beef were the preferred meats. (An abundance of meat and dairy products distinguished the diet of the "middling" classes from their poorer neighbors, and imported products such as tea were at least at first a mark of luxury.) Boiling and baking were the most common means of food preparation. The latter operation could be done in iron kettles or, as circumstances began to permit, in the more elaborate brick ovens that soon became common. Food preparation was strictly gender-typed, and women managed domestic gardens and chicken coops in addition to buying food and preparing meals.

OTHER BRITISH COLONIAL FOODWAYS. New England's culture has received extensive scholarly attention, and provides a useful example of the social and ecological complexities involved in foodways. There were, of course, other sorts of British colonial societies in North America. Virginians also continued English foodways, but more according to the customs of southwestern England. The great planters were the closest thing the colonies produced to an aristocracy, and their ample means and conservative tastes produced the closest the era came to a haute cuisine. "Dining," observed the eminent historian Edmund Morgan, "was a fine art in Virginia," and dinners offered by the plantation elite were major social occasions (*Virginians at Home*, p. 75). In such grand households, kitchens were separate from the main building, and meals were prepared there by slaves or servants. Humbler Virginians had to be content with one-dish "messes" of greens and salt meat seasoned with wild herbs, and ample doses of cornmeal mush. Unlike their more austere New England cousins, Virginians of all classes enjoyed ample seasonings in their foods.

David Hackett Fischer, in *Albion's Seed*, argues that two other cultural zones emerged in the English-speaking colonies that reflected as well the foodways, as well as other folkways, of still other parts of Britain from which they were originally settled. The Delaware Valley Quakers, who hailed primarily from the North Midlands and Wales, were as similar to the New England Puritans in their pragmatic and rigorously antisensual approach to cuisine as they were in their "work ethic." Boiling was the preferred cooking technique, with dumplings and puddings as regional favorites. Sugar came to be shunned, since it was produced by slave labor, a practice abhorrent to Friends' humanitarian principles. Some interchange also developed with the nearby "Pennsylvania Germans" (or, incorrectly, "Dutch") as both groups produced versions of scrappie, a fried mixture of cornmeal and finely chopped miscellaneous parts of the pig or cow.

A more widely spread and perhaps even more enduring approach to food preparation was that of the "backcountry." This was the piedmont and mountain region west of the original coastal zones of settlement, populated originally and primarily by emigrants from the northern British borderlands, many of whom came to be categorized as Scotch-Irish (that is, Scottish lowlanders or transplants in Ulster). These people came culturally prepared to be frontier settlers. Their culinary staples included oats, which in the New World yielded to maize in the form of hominy grits; pigs, which similarly replaced the Old World sheep; potatoes, accepted in Britain only as the fare of simple people; clabber, made from sour milk, curds, and whey; and various sorts of unleavened fiat cakes cooked on a griddle. Whiskey—first Scotch, then bourbon—was the backcountry beverage of choice. Vegetables indigenous to North America rounded out the regional diet. It is clear enough how many of these elements combined in various ways to form the bases of a generic southern regional style.

Regional Developments in the Nineteenth Century

The social and economic polarization of the South was reflected in its foodways as they took shape during the early nineteenth century. Thomas Jefferson was widely known as one of America's first gourmets, a distinction which earned him Patrick Henry's denunciation for unrepublican culinary elitism. Jefferson acquired a first-hand knowledge of continental European foods and techniques for their preparation during his sojourns abroad. A widower at an early age, he employed his daughters, granddaughters, and slaves in the elaborate process of food selection and preparation at Monticello, and utilized inventions of his own such as dumbwaiters to minimize eavesdropping by servants at his frequent elaborate dinners for highly placed guests. His introduction of French chefs and their fare into the White House and the enormous "bar bill" for French wines and champagne—five hundred bottles a year of the latter—generated in the course of official entertaining placed an enormous strain on his resources. Jefferson's largess reflected not only his own expansive temperament but also the tradition of southern hospitality that had originated among the planter class as a means of entertainment among widely scattered plantations, a service to travelers, and a visible means of demonstrating status through conspicuous consumption.

SLAVE FARE AND ITS INFLUENCE. The other side of the southern social spectrum was reflected in the fare of slaves, who frequently subsisted on the three M's—meat (sow belly), meal (corn), and molasses. Several African foodstuffs and descriptive words entered the regional repertoire. Okra (Ashanti, *nkru*; in other West African languages, *nkru, nku, ruma*, or *nkruma*) is a pod containing seeds and a thick, gluey substance eaten fried or in gumbo (Bantu, *ngombo*), a synonym for okra also used in Louisiana Creole and Cajun cuisine to describe a variety of soups or stews thickened with okra or *filé* (French for "threads") powder made from dried sassafras leaves. Goober (Kongo, *nguba*) remains a regional synonym for peanut, transplanted from South America to Africa and then back to the North American colonies. Corn (maize) and yams (a word of mixed African origins) also played a major role in southern black fare; like the goober, yams were also introduced from South America to Africa in the sixteenth century by Portuguese traders. The experience many slaves acquired in food preparation facilitated entry into the broader economy after the Civil War; among the few niches in the work force open to them for many decades were jobs as cooks, waiters, and, in the armed forces through World War II, mess stewards. Aunt Jemima and Uncle Ben persist to this day as commercial emblems of nurturing slaves associated with bountiful food service. Interestingly, the Nation of Islam (called Black Muslims), which became influential in many urban black ghettos in the 1950s and 1960s, adopted a dietary code very loosely based on that of traditional Islam, which banned on religious grounds most items associated with soul food; instead, they promoted—ironically, given their ideology—a diet favoring foods characteristic of the white middle-class norm.

The sorts of foods eaten by slaves and, later, sharecroppers were by no means restricted to blacks; rather, a diet based on pork, corn, and such other vegetables as sweet potatoes and cowpeas emerged early as characteristic of the South as a whole, and has persisted with a staying power far in excess of that of most other parts of the country. The earliest stages of settlement saw a heavy reliance on game—deer and bear, as well as smaller animals such as squirrels, opossums (from Virginia Algonkian, *apasum*) and raccoons (Algonkian, *arahkun*). Indian corn rapidly established itself as a primary food, giving rise to innumerable popular derivatives such as hominy (Algonkian, *rockahominie* or *rokahamen*), produced by treating ripe corn with lye; grits (or hominy grits), made of finely ground hominy; cornmeal mush; hush puppies, fried balls of cornmeal and, sometimes, onions; and hoecake and other forms of cornbread. (Wheat bread was eventually introduced into the region, but never displaced cornbread in popularity.) Cowpeas and greens—collard, turnip, and others—were boiled (with frying, a favorite form of preparation) and eaten, with the remaining pot likker (liquor) relished for sopping as well. Chicken was a favored food for special occasions among the poorer classes, while pork was the standby. Little of the pig was wasted, with even such parts as the chitterlings or chitlins (intestines) entering the repertory of blacks in particular. Beef and lamb were not disdained, but the expense, particularly of the latter, relegated them to the

> *Indian corn rapidly established itself as a primary food among American slaves; it gave rise to innumerable popular derivatives, including hominy (made by treating ripe corn with lye), grits (made of finely ground hominy), cornmeal mush, hush puppies (fried balls of cornmeal), and hoecake.*

wealthier classes. Catfish—fried and served with hush puppies and cole slaw—remains a favorite among southerners of all sorts and conditions.

SOUTHERN FOODWAYS. Although these foods have remained popular throughout the South, other foods were abundant more locally and helped to shape a more restrictedly regional cuisine. Seafood was plentiful in coastal areas, and attained a special place in the closely related cuisines of the Creoles (American-born descendants of Europeans or, locally, any residents of New Orleans) and Cajuns (displaced French-speaking Acadians from Nova Scotia who settled amid the bayous of southern Louisiana). New Orleans was particularly a cultural and culinary melting pot, with French, Spanish, African, and Native American elements enhancing its complexity and giving rise to a mixture of spices unacceptable to most Yankees. (Gumbo, mentioned earlier, was built around celery, tomatoes, and bell peppers, with andouille [ANN-dooey] sausage, chicken, or seafood sometimes added.) Cajun foodways built on abundant seafood such as crawfish and redfish; in the 1980s, this hitherto obscure regional culture received national attention through the work of the New Orleans chef Paul Prudhomme, and blackened redfish—as well as blackened almost everything else—began to grace fashionable restaurant menus across the country. (Zydeco music, a similar regional cultural blend, also attained a national following in this period.)

Following the Civil War, the gradual entrance of the South into a national market economy led to mixed consequences. Once antebellum agriculture had become established, according to Joseph R. Conlin, slaves on the better plantations consumed over four thousand calories a day. After the war, though, as Joe Gray Taylor notes, heavily milled corn and fatback (fat meat from the back of the hog) from the Midwest rather than bacon undermined the nutritional value of the diet of rural people. A similar decline in the quantity of fruits and vegetables they consumed further made them vulnerable to malnutrition-related diseases such as pellagra and hookworm. The resultant endemic poor health nurtured the image of a "lazy South" filled with "tobacco roads" of poor, illiterate, disease-ridden sharecroppers.

Though this stereotype was not entirely baseless, reflecting economic circumstances more than character, southerners have expressed a typical ambivalence toward their past in their enshrinement of regional foodways, even as they began to participate fully in a national culture and economy. Coca-Cola (regionally pronounced Koh-KOH-lah) originated in Atlanta in 1886, and ultimately became an international symbol of American national culture and mass marketing. ("Cocacolonization" has emerged as a synonym for such commercial hegemony.) RC Cola is a more localized taste and is linked with the Moon Pie, a marshmallow sandwich invented in Chattanooga around 1918. Another favorite regional confection is the Goo Goo Cluster (Nashville, 1912). Ice(d) tea is the drink preferred in genteel circles, while corn likker—originally a convenient way of transporting corn in highly condensed and remunerative fashion—is a beverage reflecting another side of regional taste (together with its more sophisticated counterparts, Jack Daniels and Rebel Yell sour mash whiskeys).

National franchising elevated Colonel Sanders' Kentucky Fried Chicken to transregional eminence, making that staple of fine southern cooking an attenuated regional counterpart of the aregional McDonald's and Burger Chef. (Harland Sanders opened his first stand in Corbin, Kentucky, in 1956, but was later bought out by a national syndicate.) Other chains such as Stuckey's, Po' Folks, and Cracker Barrel now market regional cuisine of greater or lesser authenticity along interstate highways within and beyond the South itself, each capitalizing on a "countrified" image in the manner of the Grand Ole Opry and the television program *Hee Haw.* Traditional southern cooking, whether perpetuated through family oral tradition or "yuppified" à la *Southern Living* magazine, retains its hold on the indigenous populace more perhaps than in any other extended cultural region in the United States to this day.

THE GREAT AMERICAN STEAK RELIGION. The crude, pork- and corn-based food habits of the frontier South were also characteristic of the broader frontier of the earlier nineteenth century. European travelers viewed with alarm the monotonous diet of heavy, greasy foods consumed by the locals and offered to these sojourners as well, and noted that dyspepsia—a severe, chronic form of indigestion no longer common—was a widespread problem. (Modern-day truckstops offer similar fare, making it clearer why fast-food franchises have become so popular.) Once family farms had become established, the diet of countryfolk became more varied and salubrious, but continued to be heavy and abundant to generate the energy necessary for strenuous outdoor work. John Mack Faragher, in his *Women and Men on the Overland Trail,* describes a typical midwestern farm family's daily provender at mid century as including two kinds of meat, eggs, cheese, butter, cream, corn, bread, several vegetables, jellies, preserves, relishes, cake, pie, milk, coffee, and tea (p. 52; cited by Conlin, p. 8). Conlin estimates that Americans at the time consumed an average of four thousand calories per day, a startlingly large amount compared with a late-twentieth-century average of about half that, or with the barren diet of contemporary British and Continental laborers and peasants. (Many of the poor, however, consumed far less, often from foods of dubious nutritive value, and malnutrition and its related diseases were scarcely unknown in both rural and urban areas.)

Though corn and pork remained popular especially in the South, it was midwestern beef and wheat that began to rival and eventually surpass them as national dietary staples, especially as the railroads and new agricultural technology made their growth and distribution rapid and economical. The preference for beef, more plentiful in the United States than in any part of the world except perhaps Argentina, would persist as a distinctive character of an emergent national taste, and would later be characterized by food reformer Frances Moore Lappé (*Diet for a Small Planet*, 1971) as the "great American steak religion." The *Statistical Abstract of the United States* (1980) indicated that approximate daily consumption of beef by Americans rose from 2.4 ounces (67 grams) in 1910 to 4.2 ounces (118 grams) in 1976, which accounted in part for a 28 percent increase in fat consumption during that period. (Pork consumption declined slightly from 2.7 to 2.6 ounces [76 to 73 grams] during the same period.) A similar preference for white over whole-grain bread was also in this period emerging as a not entirely wholesome dietary preference. Diurnal alcohol consumption also yielded during the early nineteenth century to coffee and tea, stimulants conducive to the disciplined effort that a nascent national market economy demanded.

FOOD REFORMERS. This seemingly relentless progress toward a heavy, calorie-laden diet, whether based on pork and corn or beef and wheat, was not without its challengers. A Puritan reformist strain was manifest in the urgings of Catharine Beecher, in *A Treatise on Domestic Economy* (1841), toward a temperate regimen eaten deliberately. She cited physical as well as spiritual health as primary rationales. Beecher's contemporaries also denounced excessive seasonings and fried foods with a similar mixture of motives. One of the most influential reformers of the era was the Presbyterian minister Sylvester Graham (1794–1851), whose name has ever since been connected intimately with the cracker made from the unbolted flour he promoted. Utopian experiments, ranging from Bronson Alcott's vegetarian Fruitlands (1844–1845) to the herb-loving celibate Shaker communities, similarly practiced variations on the theme of a simple, natural diet that contributed physically to a life-style harmonious with higher laws. (Thoreau's primitive urge to devour a woodchuck raw was only an apparent exception to this tendency.) Religious motives were also prominent in the Seventh-day Adventist movement, which arose out of the Great Disappointment over William Miller's unfulfilled millenarian prophecies in the mid 1840s. Influenced by Graham as well as the Adventists, both John Harvey Kellogg (1852–1943) and C. W. Post (1854–1914) contributed to the quest for a salubrious, natural, precooked food in their respective development of the cornflake and the grape nut. The heavily sugared cold cereals favored by children in the later twentieth century were a far less healthful variation on the Post-Kellogg theme characteristic of the child-oriented consumer culture promoted especially by television commercials.

Immigration and Ethnic Foodways

The quest for a better diet was a primary motive for the vast immigration that altered American society so dramatically during the entire nineteenth century. The potato, another example of the Colombian exchange, was first exported from the highlands of South America to Europe in the sixteenth century, but was originally categorized as an aphrodisiac, a cause of leprosy, and the fare of peasants. Though it eventually became a staple, especially of eastern European folk society, its introduction into Ireland during the later years of the 1500s transformed the diet of that nation and promoted an extraordinary growth in population in the ensuing centuries. This growth came to an abrupt halt in the 1840s, when a devastating blight on the potato crop combined with other political, economic, and demographic factors to result in massive famine and emigration, primarily to the northeastern coastal cities of the United States. (The typical Irish diet had consisted of up to 10 pounds [4.5 kilograms] of potatoes per day, often with little else but milk.) The rapid assimilation of the initially despised but English-speaking Irish militated against the perpetuation of a fare that was basically a variant on a broader northern European peasant theme. Though corned beef and cabbage remains an ethnic favorite on Saint Patrick's Day, this is a residual reminiscence of a vanished folk culture characteristic of many deracinated ethnic groups attached more in nostalgia than in everyday behavior to their ancestral past. (Jiggs's attachment to the dish in the comic strip "Bringing Up Father," however, was a sign of his passive resistance to the hectoring Maggie's attempts at assimilation and social climbing.)

The heavy diet of the German immigrants who streamed into first the middle colonies and then Ohio and other parts of the Old Northwest in the days of the early republic was similarly characteristic of the agrarian folkways of northern Europe. Like the Poles and other Slavs who swelled the ranks of America's newcomers during the latter decades of the century, Germans consumed prodigious quantities of pork together with potatoes, beets, cabbage, and other vegetables that kept well without refrigeration. This fare, which has never gained culinary esteem because of its lack of variety and seasoning (apart from salt, sugar, and vinegar), was developed to its fullest among the misnamed Pennsylvania Dutch. These sturdy people were in fact German Anabaptists drawn to southeastern Pennsylvania through the appeals of their pacifist counterparts, the Quakers, beginning in the late 1600s. Abundance rather than subtlety characterizes this regional cuisine exemplified in such traditional dishes as shoofly pie, chicken corn soup, schnitz (seasoned ham) and apples, scrapple, and the variety of preserved fruits and vegetables that make up the proverbial "seven sweets and seven sours."

NEW IMMIGRANT FOODS. The "New Immigration" of the decades from the 1870s through the outbreak of World War I enriched the American diet in a number of ways. Central and eastern European fare, again, did not gain a wide audience outside of a few highly spiced items such as kielbasa (Polish sausage) and Hungarian *gulyas* (goulash). Much more influential beyond the limits of particular ethnic communities was Italian pasta- and tomato-based fare such as spaghetti, lasagna, and, of course, the pizza that has become omnipresent in the mass culture of the later twentieth century. (Tomatoes were also introduced into Europe as a result of the Columbian exchange, but were grown in Britain until the nineteenth century only as an ornamental plant. These "love apples" were feared as poisonous in some places until the turn of the twentieth century.) Ironically in retrospect, many New Immigrants were derided as "garlic eaters" by native-born Americans unaccustomed to highly seasoned foods.

As Evan Jones has pointed out, the presence of Italians in California from the time of the gold rush launched their cuisine into American life through their cultivation of plants and vineyards characteristic of their traditional foodways and also through their involvement in the restaurant business. The durum wheat from which Italian pasta was made began to be grown in Kansas on a large scale through Department of Agriculture encouragement, and the shutting off of European imports by World War I gave further impetus to domestic cultivation. The introduction of the pizza to the United States is a topic of contention perhaps second only to the discovery of America in some circles, but many favor the hypothesis that Wooster Square, New Haven—the old center of that city's strong Italian population—deserves the honor. (Nearby Louie's Lunch is sometimes credited with the introduction of the hamburger as well; other schools of thought give it a German origin, imported via the English Salisbury steak and popularized at the Saint Louis World's Fair in 1904.) The dramatic popularity gained by what was originally known as the "pizza pie" following World War II is a prime example—together with the hamburger, fried chicken, and tacos—of the assimilation of selected items of ethnic diet into the mainstream of popular culture through mass production, franchising, and aggressive advertising and merchandising.

The Greek immigrants who constituted another major wave of the New Immigration have been particularly distinguished as restaurateurs, originally gaining an economic niche through proriding food to urban workers seeking a quick lunch on their breaks from the office and factory work that dominated the new economic order of the early twentieth century. Greek proprietors later capitalized on a growing demand for a more distinctive cuisine, providing moussaka, *pastitsio*, and a variety of lamb dishes from the old country in Greektown restaurants and the diners that proliferated in the urban Northeast. A distinctive Greek-American contribution is Cincinnati "five-way" chili, made from ground beef and a complex combination of flavorings (including cumin, allspice, and unsweetened chocolate), served over pasta with grated cheese, kidney beans, and onions. Developed locally in the 1920s, this culinary hybrid later began to encroach on the broader popularity of the Tex-Mex chilis that themselves represent an adaptation and indigenization of Mexican traditions. Though Greek Americans, like most groups of New Immigration provenance, have become increasingly assimilated into the middle-American culinary and broader cultural mainstream, events such as the annual *panegyri* held at many Greek Orthodox churches feature traditional foods—together with music, dancing, and folk costumes—as occasions in which traditional folkways are still honored, if only in the breach.

The Jews who emigrated from the ghettos and shtetls of central and eastern Europe during these tumultuous decades illustrate the complex relationship between ethnicity, cultural adaptation, and religion in their foodways as well as in other aspects of their lives. What has come to be known as Jewish cooking—that characteristic of urban delis—is a variation on the foods of Germany, Romania, Hungary, and the Slavic-speaking countries in which Jewish culture flourished prior to the devastation of the Holocaust, and includes pastrami, corned beef, latkes (potato pancakes), and borscht. Other foods, like matzoh (flat, crisp unleavened bread), are used especially on ritual occasions, and are uniquely Jewish. Also governing the foodways of observant Jews are the kosher (ritually clean) laws, which among other things prohibit the consumption of pork and the mixing of milk and meat products. The maintenance of these customs has been a major issue between Orthodox or Conservative Jews who have chosen to be faithful to tradition, and Reform or secular Jews who reject such practices as obsolete. Roman Catholics, among whom were many Irish, Italian, German, and eastern European immigrants, maintained a similar distance from the dominant American Protestant and secular cultures through their observance of "fish on Fridays," a practice made optional (except during Lent) after the Second Vatican Council of the early 1960s.

Another set of foodways is that of Spanish-speaking peoples—who, in fact, are a wide variety of different groups united mainly by variants on a common language. West Indian (Cuban and Puerto Rican) cuisine varies considerably from that of Mexican Americans, whose poverty, language, and frequent illegal status have helped to preserve traditional foodways longer than those of immediately European origin. In the barrios of southern California and Texas, the tortilla—the traditional flat maize cake—is still a dietary staple, together with salsas (sauces) made from tomatoes and chilis, all reminders of the pre-Columbian regimen. Variations on these themes have led not only to the simplifications purveyed by Taco Bell and other fast-food chains, but also to the hominy-based *posole* of New Mexico and the barbecue (from West Indian, *barbacoa*) that characterized pre-Anglo California and, in endless varieties, Texas and the South.

What has come to be known as Jewish cooking is a variation on the foods of Germany, Romania, Hungary, and the Slavic-speaking countries in which Jewish culture flourished prior to the Holocaust: it includes pastrami, corned beef, latkes (potato pancakes) and borscht.

Forces of Standardization

In striking contrast with the diversity of ethnic foodways in the history of American food patterns was the simultaneously emergent force of standardization. A major factor in the growing homogenization of national foodways that began to take shape during the middle decades of the nineteenth century was technology. Beginning in the 1830s, expanding railroad networks provided rapid transportation of goods between city and country, with each being gradually transformed as a result. The availability of a wider and less expensive variety of foodstuffs in urban kitchens and dining rooms was particularly accelerated by the development of the refrigerator car, which permitted the slaughter and processing of animals near where they had been raised and their subsequent distribution virtually anywhere in the world. Large-scale fortunes were made beginning in the 1880s by industrialists such as Gustavus Franklin Swift and Philip Danforth Armour, whose names later attained a nearly generic status as synonymous with meats. Refrigeration also made possible the development of large-scale cultivation of a wide range of vegetables and citrus fruits in Florida and California that had until then played only a limited role in the general American diet, but could now be easily brought to distant markets.

Another technical innovation of long-range importance was quick-freezing. Early in the twentieth century, Clarence Birdseye—better known today as a brand name than as an inventive and eponymous individual—developed a technique for preserving foods through rapid freezing, which precluded decay by not generating the large ice crystals that could destroy cellular walls. Such freezing was the culmination of a whole series of innovations over the course of a century or so, which began with improved canning techniques and continued through Gail Borden's perfection of a condensed form of milk shortly before the Civil War. Corresponding developments in domestic technology, including the refrigerator, the home freezer, and the microwave oven, which permitted rapid defrosting, made possible the widespread use of these preservation techniques from the farm to the kitchen.

By the 1920s, "scientific" advertising had united with aggressive new marketing strategies and techniques of mass distribution to alter national patterns of food selection dramatically. Brand names such as Swift, Birds Eye, and Betty Crocker—a fictional personage whose image is periodically updated—became fixed in shoppers' imaginations as synonymous with uniform, dependable, and reasonably priced products. The supermarket, exemplified by the Great Atlantic and Pacific Tea Company (A&P), began during the 1930s to displace locally owned stores—sometimes by incorporating them into national chains—with new, seemingly giant emporiums featuring self-service and a vast variety of fresh and processed foods and other household goods.

Fast-food chains were a variation on the theme. Their symbiotic relationship with other modernizing forces was exemplified in the monopoly obtained by Howard Johnson's for food service on the Pennsylvania Turnpike, which in 1940 opened as the nation's first inter-

Ray Kroc, founder of the McDonald's Corporation, developed a successful formula: a recognizable brand (golden arches) and clean, strategically located franchise outlets that served a limited but popular menu.

state highway. HoJo's, as the orange-roofed purveyor of updated versions of traditional New England fare later came to be known, had been founded in 1925; in the 1970s it began to yield to newer, still more efficient chains, such as Ray Kroc's dramatically successful McDonald's. Kroc, the son of a Bohemian immigrant, who rivaled Henry Ford as an archetypal American rags-to-riches entrepreneur, took over a local California drive-in in the 1950s and developed an inordinately successful formula: the easily recognizable golden arches trademark; a national chain of clean, standardized franchised outlets; headquarters at Hamburger Central in Oak Brook, Illinois; a restricted, unsubtle range of products, broadly based in appeal; minimum-wage employees, mainly teenagers; aggressive advertising and public relations campaigns; sophisticated but easily operated standardized equipment; and strategic locations designed to attract travelers, teenagers (since the 1950s, possessed of vast discretionary income), and inner-city dwellers. By the 1990s, ecological and nutritional concerns were successfully prevailing upon McDonald's and other fast-food chains to minimize nonbiodegradable packaging and to decrease the fat content of their usually flied products. The introduction of salad bars at such establishments was also indicative of heightened consumer health consciousness.

THE INFLUENCE OF GOVERNMENT. In counterpoint with business and technology as agents of standardization were government, science, and education. The distrust of fresh vegetables and milk that was commonplace through the early decades of the nineteenth century gradually yielded to advances in bacteriology and new processing techniques such as pasteurization. These enabled children especially to take advantage of these vital sources of nutrients, vitamins, and minerals without risk of acquiring mortal diseases spread through improper sanitation. Outrage over widespread unsanitary conditions in food processing was epitomized in the public outcry that followed the publication of Upton Sinclair's The *Jungle* in 1906. The Pure Food and Drugs Act passed by Congress the same year was the first of a long series of measures through which the government sought to regulate the condition of the public diet. This law brought to the federal level the movement among state and local governments to ensure a supply of pure milk that had been in progress since the 1880s. Larger producers, who were in these same years banding together into trade associations, tended to welcome such regulation as enhancing their own efforts to rationalize their industries and squeeze out smaller competitors.

Other governmental involvements played major roles in the standardization of the national diet as well. Just as the Civil War had accelerated the phenomenon of mass production in its demand for rifles with interchangeable parts, it also stimulated demand for vast quantities of edible, palatable, and nutritious foods in standardized form. Gall Borden capitalized on this demand by creating a network of licensed plants throughout the country to provide the Union forces with the condensed milk he had recently perfected. The usual soldier's ration of salt beef or pork and hardtack—a baked mixture of flour and water—was neither appetizing nor salubrious, however. Plentiful coffee was a more popular staple of the military diet. Unpleasant as the regimen of the Union troops may have been, the scarcity of any food at all among their opponents doubtless hastened the collapse of the Confederacy. Growing nutritional knowledge, the "embalmed beef" scandal of the Spanish-American War, and new techniques of food preservation led in subsequent wars to a better and more varied diet, including the C and K rations of World War II, and the once universally reviled Spam, a canned pork product improved in later years.

In addition to war, poverty was a potent factor in mobilizing a variety of institutional forces toward the transformation, the improvement, and, as a byproduct, the standardization of the national diet. The muckraking interests that had galvanized public interest in the purity of foods also called attention to the miserable nutritional condition of the poor, especially urban immigrants and the rural native-born, and more especially their children. The Great Depression of the 1930s was a further spur to federal extension and educational work by a number of agencies in promoting better knowledge of preventive nutrition and wholesome techniques of food preparation.

SCIENTIFIC HOUSEKEEPING. Still another source of standardization was the "scientific housekeeping" movement that arose among middle-class women in the late nineteenth century. Laura Shapiro, though deploring its bland culinary consequences, interprets it as an attempt by women to attain a new professional dignity and sense of usefulness, while not simultaneously appearing radical. This they attempted by elevating a traditional woman's sphere to a more exalted status. Manifestations of this were the "home economics" movement—the name was first adopted in 1899—which placed many women in university positions, and the cooking schools exemplified by the Boston Cooking School of 1879. The latter, originally aimed at providing working-class girls with commercially and domestically useful skills, soon grew popular with middle-class women as well.

The most distinguished graduate and later director of the Boston Cooking School was Fanny Farmer, whose *Boston Cooking School Cook Book* of 1896 had sold over a third of a million copies by the time of her death in 1915. Although recipe books had been in circulation since the colonial era, Farmer's was the first to approach food preparation with an enthusiastic but no-nonsense practical attitude, utilizing, for example, standardized spoon-and-cup measures that had recently become available commercially. (Farmer's work foreshadowed many later variants, such as Irma S. Rombauer's prodigiously successful *The Joy of Cooking* of 1931.) The overall effect of this movement was the promotion of a nationally standardized cuisine prepared from identical recipes with identical equipment, a development that probably advanced nutrition while certainly abetting the success of brand-name foods and related products in a national market system.

In the decades following World War II, outdoor patio living saw new uses for the previously regional barbecue, an adaptation symptomatic of the prestige that California customs now began to exert across the nation.

Postwar Transformations

The prosperity that many Americans enjoyed during the decades following World War II made possible suburban life-styles whose followers sought appropriate culinary expression. Outdoor patio living saw new uses for the previously regional barbecue, an adaptation symptomatic of the prestige that California customs now began to exert across the nation. The popularity of the hibachi, a small grill, and of rumaki, an hors d'oeuvre consisting of chicken livers, water chestnuts, and bacon, testified to the new influence of Japanese culture mediated in various ways to North American shores. "Gourmet" cooking, however, was largely synonymous with the culinary Francophilia of a tradition-minded elite, and "American" restaurants tended toward the chophouse, the supper club, the neighborhood family establishment, and the corner bar and grill.

THE POLITICS OF FOOD. The social, cultural, and political ferment that swept the nation beginning with the civil rights and antiwar movements of the 1960s had complex ramifications in the realm of foodways. The alarm over the contamination of foods by pesticides sounded by Rachel Carson in her 1962 *Silent Spring* not only led to growing pressure for increased government regulation of agribusiness; it also helped promote a new enthusiasm for organically grown food among counterculturalists and other, more mainstream middle-class Americans concerned with the purity of their diet. For the more radical, the purity of food was not simply rooted in a concern with physical health, but became as well a metaphor for a broader preoccupation with social, political, and spiritual integrity. Macrobiotics, a dietary regimen based on whole grains, beans, and vegetables, attracted many followers, especially in avant-garde enclaves in academic communities and on either coast.

Later twentieth-century food reform, usually based on a call to simplicity of diet, had its roots in the reform movements of the pre–Civil War era. Beginning in the late 1960s, food also became associated with political causes. The feminist movement helped focus attention on both the physical and psychological dimensions of women's health, and promoted a growing awareness among adolescent and younger women in particular of eating disorders such as anorexia—eliberate self-starving in an attempt to attain a fashionably though unhealthily thin figure—and bulimia, consisting of bingeing followed by bouts of self-induced vomiting. A less excessive dieting that found continuing favor among both genders was motivated by a desire to be physically attractive; the irrepressibly American cult of youthfulness as an escape from the ravages of mortality; and a more sensible desire to promote health and longevity through the avoidance of excessive strain on the heart and other organs. Feminism for some has become associated with a vegetarianism based on animal rights, a linkage expounded in Carol J. Adams's *The Sexual Politics of Meat* in 1989. Still other political issues involving food were boycotts of grapes, lettuce, and other crops harvested by migrant workers striving to achieve better pay and working conditions; protests against the sale of infant formula in third-world countries by American firms; and the adequacy of nutrition supplied by school-lunch and other programs in inner-city neighborhoods.

THE EXPANSION OF GOURMET DINING. The social and political concerns that focused on food use during these years were paralleled by other developments of somewhat different import. It was this same period that witnessed the transformation of "gourmet" dining from the preoccupation of a small, well-to-do elite into a much broader middle-class phenomenon. Since Lorenzo Delmonico's founding of his celebrated establishment in New York around 1830, French cuisine had enjoyed—with other aspects of that culture—a place of honor among the cognoscenti. *Gourmet* magazine (1941) was the first of what would later become a proliferation of glossy magazines devoted to food and its preparation; it and Julia Child, the Cambridge-based "French Chef" of television fame, helped introduce home preparation of food in the approved manner to growing audiences.

By the early 1970s, something of a revolution had begun to take place in the social functions of food as a mark of status, as well as in its acceptable modes of preparation. Food columns, such as Craig Claiborne's in the *New York Times*, now appeared in life-style rather than women's sections and advocated a wide variety of cooking styles. The introduction of a variety of Chinese regional cuisines, especially those of Szechuan and Hunan provinces, began to displace the primacy of the blander Cantonese and Chinese American dishes that had been the staples of chop suey joints for the previous century, begun originally by Chinese employed to feed logging and railroad crews. Other cuisines—*nouvelle* French, north Italian, regional Mexican, Vietnamese, Cajun—proliferated bewilderingly as trendy foods among a new consumer culture of "yuppies" eager for novelty and the prestige of seeming to be in on the latest trends. Restaurants, including many formula-following, modish "fern bars," flourished in an industry known for rapid changes of fashion and a correspondingly brief life expectancy for new establishments.

Both regional magazines, such as *Southern Living*, and less sedate rivals of the long-established *Gourmet*—*Bon Appetit, Food and Wine, Cook's* magazine—aimed at an audience of aspiring upper-middle-class clientele desiring sophistication in the purchase, preparation, and consumption of food as an entree into a breathless new social world. Such glossies aimed at an audience of men as well as women. Formerly associated with professional chefs and gay men, cooking skills now became a necessity both for fathers of young children expected by working wives to share in domestic duties, and for both married and single men wishing to flaunt this newly prestigious social skill. New cooking equipment such as the food processor filled kitchens as well as shops and mail-order catalogs designed for an upscale audience. A cultivated taste for wine—California-produced as well as the traditional French—was an important adjunct to this quest for sensual experience and enhanced status.

An American Diet?

American foodways have often been cited as a particularly good example of the melting pot metaphor once hailed as the essence of American society and culture. The long procession of foods discussed above indicates that this image is not groundless; many Americans today consume regularly a wide variety of edibles reflecting a similarly wide variety of cultures in both their modes of preparation and their ultimate sources. However, some nuances must be added for a more accurate picture.

The food consumption patterns of most Americans in the latter part of the twentieth century reflect a linear progression from the regional British foodways imported during the colonial period to the patterns of mass production and distribution and standardized preparation exemplified in today's supermarkets and fast-food restaurants. In continual tension with this axis have been the variant ethnic, regional, and class-associated foodways that, beginning with the basic crops and game of the aboriginal Native Americans, have interacted with and modified the transition from early modern Britain to the postindustrial United States. Americans today do not so much partake of a common diet as eat within a common matrix, in which certain choices favored by the middle classes are easier to make but others are available as well, though with greater effort or expense. Beef is still plentiful and popular, and the fast-food chains have promoted the consumption of beef, cheese, and wheat flour for hamburger rolls and pizza dough as well as bread. Tea and especially coffee continue as favored daytime beverages suitable to a competitive work force, and their popularity remains strong to the point of addiction. Fresh fruit and vegetables are a still-increasing part of the diet of a health-conscious middle class in which women strongly influence patterns of food selection and preparation.

As the food critic Raymond Sokolov laments, regional foodways are going, but are fortunately not yet gone. Social class and income level push some Americans toward "gourmet" restaurants and others toward government surplus commodities. "Real men" may prefer steak to quiche, and women may choose the salad bar over red meat. Middle-class blacks may occasionally pine for soul food at homecomings, as Italian Americans long for pasta with traditional "gravy" at *feste* and family gatherings. Handmade tortillas may still be the everyday fare of Mexicans isolated in the barrios of southwestern cities. Few, however, are immune to the lure of the hamburger and the pizza. American foodways, in sum, are neither unilinear nor immutable; they are, however, as recognizable as the blue jeans and rock music by which non-Americans, for better or worse, see ours as a distinctive culture.

[See also Agriculture; Public Health.]

BIBLIOGRAPHY

Bibliographies and Research Guides

Anderson, Jay Allan. "The Study of Contemporary Foodways in American Folklife Research." *Keystone Folklore Quarterly* 16, no. 4 (Special Food Issue; 1971).

Camp, Charles. "Food in American Culture: A Bibliographic Essay." *Journal of American Culture* 2, no. 3 (1979).

Camp, Charles. "Foodways in Everyday Life." *American Quarterly* 34, no. 3 (1982).

Camp, Charles. *American Foodways: What, When, Why, and How We Eat in America* (1989). Introduction to study of foodways, with most comprehensive bibliography.

Camp, Charles. "Foodways." In *Handbook of American Popular Culture*, edited by Thomas M. Inge (1989).

Mariani, John F. *The Dictionary of American Food and Drink* (1983).

Surveys and Historically Oriented Cookbooks

The American Heritage Cookbook and Illustrated History of American Eating and Drinking (1964). Popular, well-illustrated topical essays with recipes.

Beard, James. *James Beard's American Cookery* (1972). Primarily a cookbook, but with interesting running commentary.

Cummings, Richard Osborn. *The American and His Food: A History of Food Habits in the United States* (1940). Old, but never superseded on some topics.

Hooker, Richard J. *Food and Drink in the United States: A History* (1981). Popular overview.

Jones, Evan. *American Food: The Gastronomic Story* (1975). Popular, but still best historical survey.

Regional and Period Studies

Benes, Peter, ed. *Foodways in the Northeast* (1984). Valuable scholarly essays from Dublin Folklife symposium.

Booth, Sally Smith. *Hung, Strung, and Potted: A History of Eating in Colonial America* (1971).

Carson, Barbara G. *Ambitious Appetites: Dining, Behavior, and Patterns of Consumption in Federal Washington* (1990). Exhibit catalog.

Conlin, Joseph R. *Bacon, Beans, and Galantines: Food and Foodways on the Western Mining Frontier* (1986). Provides background beyond rather narrow title topic.

Egerton, John. *Southern Food: At Home, on the Road, in History* (1987). Informal and anecdotal.

Faragher, John Mack. *Women and Men on the Overland Trail* (1979). Occasional discussion of foodways.

Feintuch, Burt. "Foodways, Geography of"; Joe Gray Taylor, "Foodways"; and shorter articles by various authors on foodways topics (e.g., "Moon Pies"). In *Encyclopedia of Southern Culture*, edited by Charles Reagan Wilson and William Ferris (1989).

Fischer, David Hackett. *Albion's Seed: Four British Folkways in America* (1989). Brief, well-annotated foodways sections.

Hillard, Sam. *Hog Meat and Hoecake: Food Supply in the Old South, 1840–1860* (1972).

Kimball, Marie. *Thomas Jefferson's Cook Book* (1976).

Leonard, Jonathan Norton. *American Cooking: New England* (1970), and other volumes in the Time-Life Foods of the World series. Lushly illustrated; scholarly value of texts varies among volumes.

Low, W Augustus, and Virgil A. Clift. "Cuisine." In *Encyclopedia of Black America* (1981).

Morgan, Edmund S. *Virginians at Home: Family Life in the Eighteenth Century* (1952).

Taylor, Joe Gray, *Eating Drinking and Visiting in the South* (1982).

Weaver, William Woys, ed. *A Quaker Woman's Cookbook: The Domestic Cookery of Elizabeth Ellicott Lea* (1982).

Ethnological and Folkways Studies

Brown, Linda Keller, and Kay Mussell, eds. *Ethnic and Regional Foodways in the United States* (1984). Essays from a variety of disciplinary viewpoints; primarily folkways/ethnological.

Crosby, Alfred W, Jr. *The Columbian Exchange: Biological and Cultural Consequences of 1492* (1972).

"Focus on American Food and Foodways" section in *Journal of American Culture* 2, no. 3 (1979). Variety of articles, stressing fast food and popular culture.

Humphrey, Theodore C., and Lin T. Humphrey, eds. *"We Gather Together": Food and Festival in American Life* (1988).

Jones, Michael Owen, et al., eds. *Foodways and Eating Habits: Directions for Research* (1983).

Sokolov, Raymond. *Fading Feast: A Compendium of Disappearing American Regional Foods* (1981).

Sokolov, Raymond. *Why We Eat What We Eat* (1991).

Mass and Popular Culture

Boas, Max, and Steve Chain. *Big Mac: The Unauthorized Story of McDonald's* (1976). Journalistic but well-informed and perceptive.

Boorstin, Daniel J. *The Americans: The Democratic Experience* (1973). Chapters 35 to 37 on the technology of food processing and distribution since the Civil War.

Dickson, Paul. *Chow: A Cook's Tour of Military Food* (1978).

Green, Harvey. *Fit for America: Health, Fitness, Sport, and American Society* (1986). Discussion of diet reform movements.

Gustafson, Donna, et al. *Art What Thou Eat: Images of Food in American Art* (1991). Exhibit catalogue.

Hitshorn, Paul, and Steven Izenour. *White Towers* (1979). Photographic essay on fast-food architecture.

Langdon, Philip. *Orange Roofs, Golden Arches: The Architecture of American Chain Restaurants* (1986).

Shapiro, Laura. *Perfection Salad: Women and Cooking at the Turn of the Century* (1986). Journalistic but solid treatment of "scientific nutrition" movement.

Stern, Jane, and Michael Stern. *Goodfood* (1983); *Real American Food* (1986); *Square Meals* (1984). Informal explorations of popular diet.

— PETER W. WILLIAMS

FRATERNAL ORGANIZATIONS

In late-nineteenth-century United States, fraternal orders such as the Masons and Odd Fellows grew to enormous size and influence. Paralleling them was an array of mutual benefit associations which sought to offer both financial security and group identity to members of immigrant communities and to black Americans. Moreover, fraternalism was a widely used form for the organization of trade unions, agricultural associations, and nativist and racist groups. Despite its ubiquity in the social, cultural, and political life of American communities, it is only recently that scholars have made a concerted effort to explain fraternalism's popularity through a recognition of its specific appeal.

The term "fraternal" commonly refers to those organizations which approximate the Masonic model of a secret society with elaborate rituals and degrees or levels of membership. More broadly, fraternalism may designate any organization that organizes the practice of mutual aid around the metaphor of kinship. Mutual benefit societies were found throughout the population, while Masonic fraternalism was, in general, most influential among native-born populations of British and northern European descent, and among African Americans, where secret societies were a fundamental part of community life.

As fictive kinship groups, fraternal orders used ritual to effect bonding, and presented family as metaphor for relations of mutual support and unselfish concern. Additionally, fraternalism implies a brotherhood, a society of men. Most, though not all, lodges have excluded women, but they vary in the extent to which the articulation of masculinity is symbolically central, the more highly ritualized Masonic tradition being most adamant about its all-male character. By 1900 most fraternal orders had parallel or auxiliary organizations of women attached to them. These women's groups, like the Order of the Eastern Star and the Daughters of Rebekah, are most properly designated fraternal auxiliaries rather than sororal organizations, since they functioned primarily within the framework of the male fraternal world rather than within the broader sisterhood of nineteenth- and early-twentieth-century women's organizations. Since the 1940s the fraternal world has been in decline in both size and prestige, but during the late nineteenth and early twentieth centuries, fraternal associations were the largest national secular membership organizations.

From Colonial Era to Civil War

The principal fraternal organizations of this period, the Masons and the Odd Fellows, both originated in Britain. Of these, Freemasonry is particularly important, not only because the Masonic institution was itself large, well-known, and long-lived but also because Masonic fraternalism functioned as the implicit model for so many subsequent organizations. The Masonic model may be defined in terms of three characteristics. First, its ritual is organized around degrees or levels of membership, which are ascended one by one, in separate initiation ceremonies. For example, the neophyte Mason begins as an Entered Apprentice, then becomes a Fellow Craft, and a Master Mason, with numerous higher degrees, up to thirty-two in Scottish Rite Masonry, as a further option. Second, orders operating within this model all adhere to the Masonic concept of the order as a moral system directed toward the edification of the individual member. Finally, quasi-Masonic organizations claim to disregard "worldly" identity, stating that occupation and class position, like religious and political views, are irrelevant to the brotherly bonds of the lodge.

Freemasonry originated in the seventeenth century, when British gentlemen began to request admission into the lodges of practicing stone masons, and then to adapt and refashion the traditional rituals of operative masons in their own autonomous or "accepted" lodges. In the American colonies, it began as an organization of the elite, composed primarily of wealthy merchants and professionals. By the time of the Revolution, the membership base had broadened, prompted by a schismatic dispute between rival factions of Ancients and Moderns in which the newer and more inclusive Ancients recruited significant numbers of the era's upwardly mobile, newly assertive artisans. The first black fraternal order also was founded during the revolutionary war when Prince Hall, a minister, and fourteen other African American residents of Boston were initiated as Masons by British soldiers. Their Masonic credentials were thus completely regular, recognized as such by the Grand Lodge of England, despite their rejection by the white Masons of Massachusetts.

Masonry emerged from the revolutionary war with enormous prestige, derived in part from its association with Washington and other Revolutionary heroes. At the same time Masonry provoked hostility and suspicion because of its secrecy, its elite pretensions, and belief that Masons favored each other in business and politics. The order also drew opposition from Evangelicals and Calvinists, who disliked Masonic optimism and worldliness, and from women, who may have seen its claims of masculine moral sufficiency as an attack upon the emerging canons of domesticity. Thus in 1826, when William Morgan of Batavia, New York, sought to publish an exposé of Masonic secrets, his kidnapping and alleged murder by Masons, coupled with an attempted cover-up by sympathetic local authorities, crystallized earlier suspicions and led to the emergence of Anti-Masonry as a major political and social movement.

The social base of Anti-Masonry remains unclear. Earlier scholars portrayed it as the reaction of economically and socially marginal farmers to modernizing trends. More recent research suggests the opposite: that Anti-Masonic activism drew its support from flourishing commercial centers that were also centers of evangelical religion and civic voluntarism. What is uncontested is the effect of the Anti-Masonic movement in decimating the fraternity. In New York, for example, membership plummeted from between twenty thousand and thirty thousand to 1 to 15 percent of that figure (sources conflict); in Vermont and Illinois all lodges ceased operation for a time. While Anti-Masonry as a political movement was ineffective by 1834, its condemnation of Freemasonrv continued to have a social impact; in most regions normal Masonic activities were resumed only in the 1840s.

The Masons were a multiclass organization which transformed artisanal rites and customs into a highly elaborated system of rituals articulating moral ends. In contrast, the Odd Fellows began as a convivial society, much closer to the traditional journeyman's society than to the Masonic model. Yet by the 1840s, white American Odd Fellowship had been transformed into something much closer to Masonry—a multiclass organization espousing morality and the promotion of individual self-improvement. At the same time (1843), the Grand United Order of Odd Fellows received its charter of origin from one of the English Odd Fellows' organizations, thus establishing Odd Fellowship among African Americans.

During the 1820s, educated, middle-class reformers began to join the white Odd Fellows. Their attack on conviviality, or drinking in the lodge room, was accompanied by restrictions on fraternal mutual aid practices and, most important, by revision and expansion of the ritual. The new rituals invested the order with a sense of decorum and moralism that was intended to attract higher-status members while promoting in the "industrial classes," its traditional base, an ethos of discipline and self-improvement.

The Golden Age: Fraternalism After the Civil War

The Civil War represents a watershed in the history of American fraternalism. Before the war, fraternal growth meant primarily the expansion of the Masons and Odd Fellows, the organizations that largely defined the boundaries of social fraternalism. After the war their membership increased, not just steadily but exponentially. In the state of Missouri, for example, membership of white Odd Fellows grew from 4,000 in 1866 to 93,000 in 1914. By 1907 national membership of the white Masons and Odd Fellows reached over one million each, while black Odd Fellows numbered 270,000 and black Masons 100,000.

Equally important, however, was the creation of many new fraternal organizations. The *Cyclopaedia of Fraternities* (1907), a directory of fraternal secret societies, identified some three hundred fraternal organizations. The years from 1864 to 1884 were the crucial period when the Knights of Pythias (1864), the Benevolent and Protective Order of Elks (1868), the Ancient Order of United Workmen (1868), the Ancient Arabic Order of the Nobles of the Mystic Shrine (or Shriners, 1867–1872, variously), the Knights of Honor (1873), the Royal Arcanum (1877), the Knights of the Maccabees (1878), and the Modern Woodmen of America (1883) were among the major orders established. The new orders spread rapidly, so that a town of fifteen thousand, like Belleville, Illinois, which had only Masons and Odd Fellows' lodges in 1868, was home to thirty-five lodges of sixteen different national organizations by 1884. By 1900, contemporary observers estimated that from 20 to 40 percent of the adult male population belonged to at least one lodge; if that is correct, then an even larger proportion must have belonged at some point in their lives, making the fraternal order a truly massive presence in late-nineteenth-century popular culture and community life.

The fraternal world became not only larger but also more variegated. The founding of the Ancient Order of United Workmen in 1868 marked the creation of the first insurance fraternity, which offered a death benefit to members along with a ritual experience. Many new organizations of this period were insurance fraternities, and some older orders felt compelled by the competition to offer an insurance option to members. The offering of insurance extended fraternalism's practical side by transforming the traditional death and sick benefits into something more substantial and rationalized.

Two other fraternal innovations, the playground lodge and the military branch, sought to elaborate the pageantry and ritualism of the lodge movement. The quintessential playground lodge was the Ancient Arabic Order of the Nobles of the Mystic Shrine, an organization whose membership is restricted to Masons of the highest degree. Shriners became known for their comically exaggerated titles, lavish parades, and red fezzes; because they are today the most visible remnant of the fraternal movement, they are often mistakenly seen as representative of what fraternalism means. The idea of the military branch was much more successfully disseminated through the nineteenth-century fraternal movement. Military branches were parade units, drill teams elaborately costumed and trained to march with military precision. Yet they represented something more than pure spectacle, for they were quasi-military organizations. Military branches surely drew upon nostalgia for the Civil War, but it seems equally significant that they emerged during an era of intensified nativism and unprecedented labor unrest.

Women's auxiliaries, including the Order of the Eastern Star, the Daughters of Rebekah, and the Pythian Sisterhood emerged during these decades. Important black orders like the Independent Order of St. Luke were established, while the Prince Hall Masons and the Grand United Order of Odd Fellows experienced significant growth, facilitated by the ending of slavery and the consequent greater ability of southern blacks to engage in civic and community activities. The Patrons of Husbandry, commonly known as the Grange, was organized in 1867 as a social, political, and self-help association for farmers, and the Knights of Labor was created in 1869 to advance the interests of workers. They, like many other political and labor organizations, made intentional use of fraternal ritual to create solidarity among their members.

Inclusion and Exclusion

CLASS COMPOSITION. The fraternal world, if we can talk about one world, reflected and reinforced divisions of class, race, and gender.

In terms of class composition, fraternal orders were somewhat heterogeneous. Some scholars have characterized mainstream fraternal orders as middle class in composition and ethos, while others have seen them as working-class institutions contributing to class solidarity. Analysis of the membership of lodges in a variety of locales consistently finds that they were mixed-class organizations. The Masons, always the most selective group, tended to be primarily middle class, but even Masonic lodges typically contained an identifiable minority of blue-collar workers. Other orders, such as the Odd Fellows and Knights of Pythias, contained many more working-class members than the Masons. Individual lodges were often skewed in their composition, but core membership was drawn from the ranks of small proprietors and skilled workers, with significant representation among professionals, clerks, salesmen, and factory operatives as well. Most significantly, even the most class-homogeneous local lodge was symbolically a part of a heterogeneous national organization whose members were united in ritual brotherhood. Indeed, the irrelevance of class was a central tenet of fraternal ideology: "Every good citizen, be he laborer in the streets, or a judge, a farmer, mechanic, or capitalist, stands on a footing of exact equality in the Modern Woodmen of America" (Clawson, *Constructing Brotherhood*, p. 176).

ETHNICITY. It is generally assumed that the white Masonic-type fraternal orders were ethnically as well as racially homogeneous, composed almost wholly of native-born white Protestant men of British or northern European descent. Groups like the white Masons and Odd Fellows often appeared to be strongholds of nativist sentiment; there is, for example, evidence that Masonic lodges served as recruiting grounds for the Ku Klux Klan during the 1920s. Yet evidence from an earlier period suggests a more complex history, with significant variation in fraternal policies toward immigrants.

From the 1860s through the 1880s, most orders not only accepted immigrants as members but also allowed local lodges to operate in languages other than English and even provided foreign-language versions of their rituals. German immigrants were undoubtedly the most numerous beneficiaries of such policies; almost every town with any significant German population had German-language lodges of Masons, Odd Fellows, and Pythians. During the 1880s a nativist upsurge, coinciding with the beginnings of large-scale immigration from southern and eastern Europe, led to the abolition of foreign-language lodges. While none of the major orders enacted policies of outright ethnic exclusion, the changing character of immigration, the increasing articulation of nativist sentiments, and the polarization created by the interaction of fraternal anti-Catholicism and Catholic antifraternalism resulted in the abandonment of whatever degree of cultural pluralism had characterized earlier years.

Immigrant groups formed two sorts of fraternal associations. Local mutual benefit societies organized on the basis of province, region, or city of origin were common among southern Italians, Poles, Russian and Polish Jews, and Czechs, who brought their European associational experience to the United States. These small, localized benefit societies were not usually ritualized secret societies, but they were fraternal in their adherence to the principle of mutual aid and their conception of themselves as a logical extension of kin-based networks of exchange governed by norms of reciprocity, rather than by notions of charity or benevolence. To traditions of self-help and mutuality brought from their societies of origin was added a sense of ethnic identity, a sense that in organizing for their own survival, immigrants were acting to preserve a cultural heritage.

In addition, most immigrant groups formed national fraternal organizations, such as the Ancient Order of

Hibernians (1836) and the Order of Sons of Italy (1905). Some of these organizations followed in the benefit tradition by offering insurance to members; others engaged in charity fund-raising. Often, as secret societies with initiation rituals, they resembled Masonic fraternalism. They differed from the localized benefit societies in their concern to articulate a sense of nationality or national ethnic identity—but as an ethnic group *in America*, whereby ethnicity began to be seen as a form of Americanism. In this sense the decline of local ethnic benefit societies and the growth of these national ethnic organizations in the 1920s and 1930s indicates a growing assimilationism.

One obstacle to the incorporation of immigrants into the Masonically oriented fraternal movement was its proscription by the Roman Catholic church. As early as 1738 the church had condemned Freemasonry as a type of natural religion which denied that divine grace and revelation are necessary to lead a good and moral life. Furthermore, the church opposed the possibility that Catholics could join with non-Catholics in secret

The Masons, always the most selective group, tended to be primarily middle class, but even Masonic lodges typically contained an identifiable minority of blue-collar workers.

societies. In the late nineteenth century, papal condemnation was extended to the Odd Fellows and Knights of Pythias, and American bishops frequently wrote and preached against Catholic participation. These admonitions, coupled with anecdotal evidence in lodge records and numerous attempts to create Catholic fraternal societies, suggests that Catholic participation in proscribed orders was common and regarded by the church as a serious problem. This Catholic ethnic presence probably diminished in the early twentieth century in response to increased nativism and the creation of visible Catholic alternatives.

The Knights of Columbus, established in 1882, became the preeminent Catholic fraternal order, including members from all ethnic groups. Although the organization was created by a priest and consistently sought ecclesiastical approval, a few bishops disapproved of it in the early years because of its parallels with Masonry. Indeed, the intent of the organization, with its signs, passwords, and ritual of three degrees, was to offer Catholics a fraternal alternative. What is most striking about the Knights of Columbus is its assimilationism, a movement away from ethnic identity toward a religious one, and the articulation of that religious identity as a form of Americanism within a pluralistic society.

RACE. Masonic fraternalism was inconsistent in its approach to ethnic and religious difference; alternative ethnic and religious brotherhoods emerged in response to its openness as much as to its policies of exclusion. About race there was much more consistency; indeed, racial exclusion was a hallmark of mainstream American fraternalism from its inception. The enforcement of white racial purity was accomplished not simply on a de facto basis, which could have been done through the blackball, but by formally requiring that prospective members be white and by denigrating black orders. This was particularly true of the white Masons, who persisted in viewing Prince Hall Masonry as an irregular or "clandestine" body that was not "genuinely" Masonic—despite its "regular" origins and recognition by the Grand Lodge of England.

Challenges to the all-white character of orders, usually from the position that it violated claims of fraternal universalism and brotherhood, surfaced periodically in fraternal debate. National policies mandating white racial status as a prerequisite for membership allowed such challenges to be quickly and summarily suppressed. Fraternal orders existed in and reflected the values of a racist society. The public commitment of the national organizations to racial hierarchy worked to suppress oppositional tendencies by making loss of fraternal legitimacy the price for any attempt, however minimal, to breach or weaken the color line. The national groups thus worked not only to reflect but also to enforce racial boundaries, to serve as one institutional resource, however small, for the organized defense of a segregated society. Black fraternal orders consistently rejected these values even as many sought to use the cultural apparatus of white fraternalism to build their own communities.

Fraternal societies have been extraordinarily important in African American communities, perhaps even more so than in white ones. Earlier generations of white scholars tended to devalue black lodges as largely expressive in function, giving otherwise powerless people the opportunity to enact hierarchical relations that severed them from the larger community and reinforced acceptance of the status quo. It is clear that black people, like their white counterparts, delighted in the enactment of fantastical ritual dramas that may seem bizarre or laughable today; these may have carried an especially powerful symbolic charge to individuals who were denied so many public roles.

Organizations that placed themselves directly within the traditions of white Masonic fraternalism were the largest and oldest black fraternal orders. They attracted a membership of largely middle- and upper-working-class men, and provided their members with the pleasures of ritual, fellowship, and mutuality. Black Masons, Odd Fellows, Knights of Pythias, and Elks used the same rituals but were not recognized by the white-only orders. This replication of the rituals and practices of organizations that were flagrantly racist might seem like a bizarre act of identification with the oppressor. Yet if the exclusion of blacks sought to convey that adult manhood, as defined and ratified by fraternalism, was not available to black males in American society, then the organization of such parallel groups may have represented one way of denying this claim, through the assertion of a right that white groups sought to deny.

Black orders displayed a self-conscious concern for the welfare of the race, which they articulated through increasingly politicized actions. In 1926 the Improved Benevolent and Protective Order of Elks established a Civil Liberties Department, which engaged in litigation against racial segregation. The Prince Hall Masons pursued similar ends through a policy of contributing to the National Organization of Colored People. Thus their allegiance to the forms of a racially exclusive institution was coupled with an explicit rejection of its racist tenets.

Through practices of mutual aid, fraternal associations in black communities, like those in white communities, contributed to the marshaling of collective resources needed for everyday survival and improvement among the economically marginal. Moreover, benefit societies and fraternal orders provided their participants with leadership roles and experience in managing money, speaking in public, directing meetings, and engaging in concerted collective action. A study of postbellum Richmond, Virginia, finds that virtually every black political and union activist had a history as an officer of multiple lodges and benefit societies. "These societies provided the necessary social foundation to address black issues collectively" (Rachleff, *Black Labor in Richmond*, p. 33).

Black local mutual benefit societies in many ways paralleled the ethnic benefit societies described earlier, but differed in that female societies were more common. This was true as well of national benefit societies; such organizations as the Grand United Order of Galilean

Black Fraternal Orders, like the Black Masons shown here in 1897, were formed in response to the racially exclusive mainstream of American fraternalism. They used the same rituals but were not recognized by the white-only orders.

Fishermen (1856), the International Order of Twelve Knights and Daughters of Tabor (1872), and the United Brothers of Friendship (1861) and the Sisters of the Mysterious Ten (1878) were established as both-sex organizations or as parallel but closely related men's and women's groups. These groups, several of which included up to one hundred thousand people by 1900, were created within the black community. They had internally generated traditions, some of which may have had African antecedents, incorporated into the fraternal vocabulary that was so current throughout nineteenth-century America.

WOMEN'S ORDERS. The emergence of fraternal women's auxiliaries as organized entities occurred in the last third of the nineteenth century, a period that saw the development of many mass women's organizations, including suffrage groups, the Woman's Christian Temperance Union, and the women's club movement. In contrast with these autonomous women's organizations, which barred or discouraged male participation, women's fraternal auxiliaries were defined by their connection to existing male societies. To join the Order of the Eastern Star, for example, a woman had to be the wife, mother, sister, or daughter of a Master Mason. Though women were excluded from the ceremonies and lodges of Masons and Odd Fellows, men could become members of the women's organizations; indeed, the Eastern Star and Daughters of Rebekah (now the International Association of Rebekah Assemblies) required male participation, with certain offices reserved for men. With their rituals focusing on the feminine virtues of fidelity, purity, and domesticity, these organizations might seem to have been created by men to placate their women relatives at a time when women were increasingly demanding participation in public life. Yet, as with black orders, such an analysis of women's auxiliaries is too simple, for it ignores both the depth of male opposition and the commitment to feminine advance that characterized their proponents.

Black fraternal orders displayed a self-conscious concern for the welfare of the race, which they articulated through increasingly politicized actions.

Degrees for wives had been suggested within the Masons and established by the Odd Fellows before the Civil War. These degrees, however, were envisioned by their creators as honorary titles, awarded as a device to reduce feminine antipathy to the all-male lodge by symbolically incorporating women into it. They were not intended to establish separate women's organizations, which developed and grew from the initiative of women, frequently against the opposition of men. When women recipients of the Daughters of Rebekah degree, for example, began to form their own lodges, the Odd Fellows' Grand Lodge initially tried to suppress them. But women continued defiantly to hold meetings until 1867, when they were incorporated into the order. Subsequently, women in Rebekah lodges sought to expand their autonomy, gradually gaining the right to hold meetings without men present, to head local lodges and preside over meetings, and to be represented at the state level of the male organization.

Similarly, women in the Order of the Eastern Star, the organization for women relatives of Masons, sought to transfer power from the Grand Patron, who was necessarily a man and a Master Mason, to the Grand Matron, the highest woman officer, who was originally placed in the role of an assistant. The Grand Matron eventually became the executive officer of the lodge, but the Grand Patron remained the central ritual figure, in whom resided the sole right to confer degrees. Eastern Star lodges thus based their identity on Masonic involvement, even as membership was predicated upon a willingness to acknowledge the legitimacy of women's exclusion from Masonry.

Masculine opposition to the auxiliaries was, in the nineteenth century, widespread and persistent. The Knights of Pythias, for example, did not recognize the Order of Pythian Sisters as an official Pythian organization until 1904, twenty-seven years after it was first proposed. The Masons have never officially acknowledged the Order of the Eastern Star as Masonic in character, despite its hundred-year existence. Yet the twentieth century witnessed an accommodation in which the male orders increasingly accepted the energy and support of the auxiliaries while guarding their symbolic separation.

Why Fraternalism?

The immense popularity of fraternal organizations, like other types of voluntary associations, was the product of massive economic and social changes transforming the postbellum world: the growth of commerce and manufacturing, the increasing urbanization of the population. Urbanization was particularly important in facilitating mass fraternal participation, for rural people could not easily be active in organizations that met weekly, usually in the evenings. Time was as much a factor as was proximity. Fraternal participation assumed the regular availability of "free time" and, for those who had such time at their disposal, a diverting way to use it.

BENEFITS. Lodges offered a range of practical social and economic benefits to members. The society's high rates of geographic mobility made membership in a national organization advantageous, for an Odd Fellow or Pythian could arrive in a strange community and be guaranteed access to the local lodge with the opportunities for acquaintanceship it represented. Many must have hoped that fraternal membership carried with it not only social recognition but also the possibility of preferment in business and politics.

Lodges also offered material benefits through the practice of mutual aid. Traditionally these were relatively modest sums, distributed by the local lodge on the occasion of a member's death or disability. Societies like the Ancient Order of United Workmen and the Modern Woodmen of America extended the idea of fraternal mutuality to the dispensing of life insurance, paying out larger, predetermined sums derived from assessments levied on the entire state or national membership rather than on the local lodge. Access to insurance could be a valuable service, and even the smaller disbursements of traditional lodge practice often represented important aid to needy members or their survivors. Yet the value of such economic benefits does not explain why they were so often obtained through the medium of a ritualized fraternal organization. This requires consideration of the social and cultural meanings that were at the heart of fraternalism's popularity.

FRATERNALISM AS RELIGIOUS EXPRESSION. The ritual practices and moral claims of fraternal orders must have been experienced by members and interpreted by outsiders as religious in character. This was especially so when lodges claimed responsibility for public ceremonies like funerals, which were traditionally the province of religious authority. As contemporary scholars have begun to recognize fraternalism as a mode of religious expression, a variety of interpretations have been advanced. Tony Fels (1985) characterizes Masonry as the bearer of popular Enlightenment traditions of religious rationalism and an ameliorism that located virtue in individual character-building and benevolence toward needy brethren. Lynn Dumenil (1984) sees Masonry as a nonsectarian extension of American Protestantism, dominated by the tenets of religious liberalism but encompassing a range of theological views. In contrast, Mark Carnes (1989) argues that fraternalism articulated an implicit critique of both rationalist and evangelical Protestantism, with the eerie displays of skulls and skeletons, ubiquitous in fraternal ritual, portraying an ominous God and a depraved and mortal humanity. Most important in this view, the lodge, as an exclusively male institution, represented a masculine response to the feminized theology and social milieu of the era's Protestant churches.

FRATERNALISM AS ENTERTAINMENT. If fraternal ritual partook of the sacred, it also served as entertainment. The initiation rite is in essence a drama, a miniplay in which the initiate takes on a role, undergoes a test of courage, and demonstrates that he is worthy of acceptance into the brotherhood. In the highest Pythian degree, for example, the initiate braves skeletons, snakes, a black-clad Pluto, and the demand that he prove his courage by jumping onto a bed of nails. Participation in such a drama worked to generate "an emotional response not unlike the visceral excitement teenagers find so compelling in horror movies" (Carnes, p. 55). Fraternal leaders consciously used ritual to attract members, changing it at will if it proved ineffective or unappealing. Almost every order went through some revisions: the Odd Fellows in 1835, 1845, and 1880; the Knights of Pythias in 1866, 1882, and 1892; the Elks "several times" from 1866 to 1895. Lodge officials sought interesting effects and catchy themes, and hoped to attract attention through the creation of elaborately costumed parade units, thus extending fraternal theatricality into the public sphere of the street and the civic event. In the increasingly competitive environment of late-nineteenth-century fraternalism, both an appealing ritual and a colorful public image were deemed essential in the contest for members.

The nineteenth-century lodge bears a marked resemblance to more traditional forms of popular culture in that it was a vehicle through which members made their own entertainment, participating as actors rather than spectators in the ritual performance. At the same time, it was a highly standardized entertainment, specified to the last detail of words and costume by the national order. In this sense, it anticipated twentieth-century mass media entertainment. The national fraternal organization was a social technology that made possible the marketing and consumption of a standardized entertainment product through organizational rather than electronic means.

RESPONSE TO CAPITALIST TRANSFORMATIONS. The popularity of fraternalism has been explained as a traditionalist response that asserted the value of kinlike relations in opposition to the impersonality of the market and the dislocations of capitalist development. Mutual benefit societies sought to guarantee their members protection against the threats of death and illness, functioning as a type of insurance. Yet mutual benefit societies differed symbolically from commercial life insurance, which was widely rejected because it transformed relations of trust and solidarity into market relations and subjected the worth of human life to a strictly financial calculus. Fraternal insurance dealt with this moral dilemma by defining insurance provision as a system of mutual aid based in quasi-kin relations rather than in commodity exchange. As a result, it was immensely popular, outselling the offerings of commercial life insurance companies in the 1890s despite the greater security the latter offered. In its use of kin-based imagery, fraternalism invoked the moral community of the family, proposing; a model of social life that was noncontractual and anti-individualist, that resisted the subordination of human relations to market mechanisms.

Yet fraternalism did not represent a simple rejection of capitalist development in the name of tradition; rather, its symbolic structures combined accommodation and resistance, legitimation and critique. Masonic ritual, and others inspired by it, affirmed the worth of economic productivity, using artisans' tools to symbolize morality and imbue members with the virtues of industriousness and self-discipline. Systems of degrees or levels of membership presented members with an idealized model of class structure, to be ascended over time. They thus maintained that upward mobility was available to all industrious men who cared to seek it.

Fraternalism defined the lodge as a cross-class institution that bound men together, regardless of who they were. By constructing bonds of loyalty across class lines, it argued for the irrelevance of class as a social identity and envisioned a social order founded on harmonious class relations. Yet fraternal membership was itself a commodity, a form of modern leisure marketed aggressively but available only to those who could afford to pay for it.

Mutual benefit societies differed symbolically from commercial life insurance, which in the late eighteenth century was widely rejected because it subjected the worth of human life to a strictly financial calculus.

While the degree structure proclaimed the inevitability of success for all, fraternal mutuality, the obligation to assist needy brothers, implicitly conceded that some would fail. Fraternalism thus recognized the social dislocations precipitated by individualistic, market-oriented relations and proposed voluntary association, the construction of a compensatory moral community outside the sphere of production, as the means to alleviate the costs of change.

FRATERNALISM AND MASCULINITY. Fraternalism was centrally "about" the articulation of masculine identity. Its rituals idealized relations of brotherhood between men and established the lodge room as an exclusively masculine space. As a cultural institution that maintained solidarity among white men, Masonically oriented fraternalism offered gender, along with race, as a central category for the organization of collective identity A variety of reasons may be adduced to explain its appeal.

Fraternal initiation rituals may have offered a means for young middle-class men to attain a problematic masculinity, to reconcile themselves with a paternal authority that was increasingly distant in the nineteenth century, as child rearing became more feminized and adult men more remote, more embedded in an economic sphere separate from the home. Alternatively, fraternal ritual could serve to proclaim the moral self-sufficiency of men, and masculine social organization, in an era that emphasized the spirituality of women and men's moral dependence upon them. Fraternalism could also represent a response to perceived attacks on spheres of male camaraderie or masculine control of public social space. To those who experienced the church as a feminine realm, the fraternal order offered a ritual sphere that belonged to men alone. But lodges could also serve as more casual, but no less important, institutions of male sociability. This was especially significant for men who were answerable to the moral suasion and social pressures of the temperance crusade, and thus deprived of the tavern as a sex-segregated, male-only social space. Finally, for many men the benefit and insurance features of lodge membership promised security for their families and helped to consolidate their view of themselves as good providers, able to live up to the era's dominant masculine ideal.

The Decline of American Fraternalism

By the late twentieth century, the fraternal movement was for most people only a memory. Membership declined steadily in the post–World War II era and precipitously from the 1960s on. Well before this, however, in the early twentieth century, informed observers had noted a loss of momentum, a declining commitment, as the fraternal ideal was replaced by other models of social life.

By the 1920s and 1930s, commercial life insurance easily outsold fraternal insurance, even in those ethnic communities which had been its last stronghold. Government provision of benefits beginning in the 1930s dealt a further blow, as did growing assimilation within ethnic communities. Among middle-class men, cross-class social fraternalism was weakened by the vogue of service clubs such as Rotary and Kiwanis, organizations that restricted their membership to proprietors and professionals. While the creation of service clubs did not lead immediately to a wholesale exodus of businessmen from fraternal orders, it offered a new and prestigious rival for their energy and commitment.

Changes in social relations between men and women also reduced the appeal of the male-only fraternal order.

The ideal of companionate marriage was accompanied by new expectations of a more gender-integrated social life, beginning with dating and courtship and continuing throughout married life. These expectations posed a challenge to the fraternal orders' defense of masculine camaraderie. The orders that experienced the greatest growth in the twentieth century were those like the Elks, which deemphasized ritual and offered a more couple-oriented sociability to their members.

Finally, the lure of new forms of commercialized recreation, such as movies, radio, and television, greatly reduced the entertainment value of the lodge. The drama of fraternal ritual could not hope to compete with the technical sophistication and thematic variation of the new mass media products, which would, moreover, become central to the conduct of the twentieth century's more gender-integrated social life, in which new rituals of courtship and family life were organized around new diversions available to both women and men.

In their rediscovery of fraternalism, scholars have interpreted it in strikingly varied ways. It has been seen as religious expression, popular entertainment, an early form of trade union organization or life insurance provision, a means of constructing masculine identity or racial and ethnic solidarity, a vehicle for sociability, self-improvement, or self-aggrandizement. Fraternalism offered the metaphor of kinship as a way of conceiving and thus creating social solidarity. Like "family," "fraternity" was an elastic concept, capable of containing and reconciling contradictory elements into a highly resonant whole.

[See also Family Structures; Urban Culture Institutions; Village and Town.]

BIBLIOGRAPHY

Bullock, Steven C. "The Revolutionary Transformation of American Freemasonry. 1752–1792." *William and Mary Quarterly* 3rd ser., 47, no. 3 (1990).

Carnes, Mark C. *Secret Ritual and Manhood in Victorian America* (1989).

Clawson, Mary Ann. *Constructing Brotherhood: Class, Gender, and Fraternalism* (1989).

Dumenil, Lynn. *Freemasonry and American Culture, 1880–1930* (1984).

Fels, Tony. "Religious Assimilation in a Fraternal Organization: Jews and Free-masonry, in Gilded-Age San Francisco." *American Jewish History* 74, no. 4 (1985).

Greenberg, Brian. *Worker and Community: Response to Industrialization in a Nineteenth-Century American City, Albany, New York, 1850–1884* (1985).

Huss, Wayne A. *The Master Builders: A History of the Grand Lodge of Free and Accepted Masons of Pennsylvania, 1731–1873.* Vol. 1 (1986).

Kauffman, Christopher J. *Faith and Fraternalism: The History of the Knights of Columbus 1882–1982* (1982).

Kutolowski, Kathleen Smith. "Freemasonry and Community in the Early Republic: The Case for Antimasonic Anxieties." *American Quarterly* 34, no. 5 (1982).

Kutolowski, Kathleen Smith. "Antimasonry Examined: Social Bases of the Grass-Roots Party." *Journal of American History* 71, no. 2 (1984).

Kuyk, Betty M. "The African Derivation of Black Fraternal Orders in the United States." *Comparative Studies in Society and History* 25, no. 4 (1983).

Muraskin, William A. *Middle-Class Blacks in a White Society: Prince Hall Freemasonry in America* (1975).

Rachleff, Peter. *Black Labor in the South: Richmond, Virginia, 1865–1890* (1984).

Schmidt, Alvin J. *Fraternal Organizations* (1980).

Smith, Judith E. *Family Connections: A History of Italian and Jewish Immigrant Lives in Providence, Rhode Island, 1900–1940* (1985).

Stevens, Albert C. *The Cyclopaedia of Fraternities* (1907; repr. 1966).

Thelen, David. *Paths of Resistance: Tradition and Dignity in Industrializing Missouri* (1986).

Zelizer, Viviana Rotman. *Morals and Markets: The Development of Life Insurance in the United States* (1979).

— MARY ANN CLAWSON

THE FRONTIER

"The Frontier" is a troublesome term for historians. On the one hand, it evokes one of the most important processes in American history, the movement of European peoples across the American continent. It encompasses exploits of heroic exploration and violent warfare and, though less dramatic but no less significant, the spread of settlements and social relations. Unfortunately, the notion of the frontier has become encumbered with many misleading images based on assumptions of racial and national superiority. Above all, the dislocation and destruction of native tribes in the face of European American advance has often been taken for granted as an inevitable, even necessary, step in American history, the price of "progress." The bias built into the story of the frontier has been regularly reinforced, not just in popular fiction and film but also in the work of professional historians.

The foremost, if not the first, historian to focus scholarly attention on the American frontier was Frederick Jackson Turner. While still a young professor at the University of Wisconsin, he wrote a path-breaking essay, "The Significance of the Frontier in American History" (1893), that became a classic work in American historical writing. Indeed, over the course of the next half-century, Turner and the disciples of his "frontier thesis" formed one of the most prominent schools of historical thought in the United States. Turner identified the frontier as a "fertile field for investigation," a distinct conceptual category that could "be isolated and studied as a factor in American history of the highest importance." More to the point, he argued that "American history has been in a large degree the history of the colonization of the Great West. The existence of an area of free land, its continuous recession, and the advance of American settlement westward, explain American development" ("Significance of the Frontier," p. 1). The frontier was, in short, the most important element in the evolution of the United States, the critical factor that made the American people culturally unique. From the earliest days of colonial settlement, westward movement to successive frontiers promoted the "steady movement away from the influence of Europe" and thus helped Americans develop new standards of democracy and equality. As long as people had the prospect of moving west to free lands, they could "escape from the bondage of the past" and "escape to the free conditions of the frontier." Unfortunately, Turner argued, that prospect had dimmed by the end of the nineteenth century: "the frontier has gone, and with its going has closed the first period in American history" ("The Significance of the Frontier," p. 38).

Turner was a remarkably creative and insightful historian, but his "frontier thesis" was seriously flawed. Throughout the first half of the twentieth century, and especially in the 1930s and 1940s, other scholars refined or rejected his argument, challenging both his scholarship and his historical vision. According to Turner's critics, he overstated the effect of the frontier environment on the development of democracy and individualism, and he offered rather loose and imprecise definitions of those terms. He took little or no account of the impact of urbanization and industrialization on American society. Moreover, his emphasis on American exceptionalism overlooked or obscured the continuing significance of European influence on American culture. In general, by the 1950s, Turner's "frontier thesis" had become if not a ruin, then certainly a relic. It still stood as an impressive monument to an important academic achievement, but it no longer formed a stable foundation for future scholarship.

One issue that was not resolved by the scholarly debate over Turner's frontier thesis was the very idea of "the frontier" itself. Both Turner and his critics used the term freely, sometimes arguing about its precise definition but seldom questioning its inherent assumptions. Yet it is important to note that "the frontier" is an ethnocentric notion that has meaning primarily from the standpoint of Europeans or European Americans, but not from that of Native Americans, the people Europeans called Indians. Turner, for instance, described the frontier as "the outer edge of the wave—the meeting point between savagery and civilization" ("Significance of the Frontier," p. 3). Even when stripped of its most obvious cultural bias—the distinction between Indian "savagery" and European "civilization"—the description of the frontier as "the outer edge of the wave" still adopts the point of view of the advancing (or, indeed, invading) culture. For those native inhabitants resisting or retreating before that advance, the idea of the frontier had a very different meaning—or, more accurately, no meaning at all.

For that reason, recent historians have attempted to develop alternative terminology or at least to take a more multicultural approach to the study of the frontier. Rather than describing the frontier as a line or an edge of cultural division, many scholars prefer to talk of "contact zones" of intercultural exchange. In this sense, the emphasis is on the plurality of frontier regions in North America, and not just on the Anglo-American wave of westward expansion. More important, the emphasis is not so much on place as on process, the patterns of interaction between different peoples. Again, plurality is important; there was no single, predictably repeated process of frontier interaction. Historians now seek to understand the varieties of interaction among different groups at different times in different places. Indians and Europeans frequently engaged in warfare and violent conflict, but they also cooperated as allies and trading partners. Whatever the case, neither group remained unchanged by extended contact with the other. The recognition of the two-way relationship helps break down the distinction between "savage" and "civilized," and offers a more complex and ultimately more compelling history of human interaction on the North American continent.

The Colonial Frontiers

The early period of intercultural contact makes one point clear: just as one cannot talk of a single frontier, much less a single frontier experience, neither can one talk of "Europeans" and "Indians" as single, monolithic entities. Both groups included people who exhibited significant differences in language, identity, and interest.

On the eve of European colonization, the native population of North America was both large and diverse. Descended from nomadic groups that crossed the Bering Strait from Asia over thirty thousand years before, Indian people had been well established in North America for thousands of years. Thus they, rather than Europeans, were not only the original discoverers of America but also the first settlers. Indeed, some North American Indians, like the Hopewell culture of the Ohio Valley or the Mississippian culture, had developed complex and sophisticated societies and then, long before the advent of Europeans, had begun to decline. Population estimates for the area north of Mexico in the pre-European period vary widely, ranging from a low of around one million to a higher (and more recent) figure of over ten million.

The Indians of North America comprised hundreds of linguistic and societal groups. Some, like the Siouan peoples of the Great Plains, were primarily nomadic hunters, but far more were comparatively settled agriculturists. In the desert Southwest, for instance, the Hopi and Zuni cultures had developed elaborate irrigation systems to facilitate farming in their arid region. Moreover, their villages of substantial, multiroom, apartment-like houses (called *pueblos* by the Spanish) stood as monuments to the people's persistence. To the east, especially along the Atlantic seaboard and in the interior piedmont region, people of the Muskogean, Algonkian, and Iroquoian language groups combined hunting, gathering, fishing, and farming.

Numbering about half a million and divided into dozens of kinship networks, chiefdoms, and confederacies, Indians of the eastern woodlands lived in villages within distinct tribal territories. Unlike Europeans, they did not emphasize individualism or private property but tended to share land and other natural resources communally among members of the village or tribe. Men and women shared a greater degree of equality than was common in European culture. Like Europeans, however, eastern woodland tribes had sometimes cordial but often conflicted relations with groups outside their own. They traded extensively with each other, but they also fought ferociously to avenge violations of tribal territory or honor. Indeed, long-standing antagonisms between some tribal groups mirrored the traditional rivalries of the European powers and contributed to the complex military and diplomatic alliances of the early North American frontier.

The major European colonizers of North America—the Spanish, French, Dutch, and English—shared a common goal of extracting wealth from the New World, and the pursuit of that goal led them into fierce competition. Indeed, they fought against each other as much as against the Indians; their New World settlements became imperial outposts in a broader struggle for economic and military supremacy on both sides of the Atlantic. Even their maps of the New World were designed to reflect not so much geographical accuracy as imperial policy. Cartographers often claimed much more territory than military men could hope to acquire, and the maps of the major European colonizers almost always showed competing claims to vast expanses of the North American interior. Moreover, when Europeans actually settled on the land, their respective modes of colonization revealed strikingly different strategies of social and economic development. Those strategies had long-term implications not only for the continuing competition among the European powers but also for their relationships with the natives of North America.

The Spanish, for instance, did not make a significant attempt to establish large-scale, well-populated settlements inhabited by emigrants from their own country. Rather, they sought to continue along the path of plunder that had taken them through South and Central America, extracting the riches of the New World to send back to Spain. Lured northward by their lust for gold and silver, sixteenth-century Spanish explorers laid claim to large parts of what is now the southern United States, from Florida and the Gulf of Mexico to the coast of California. One conquistador, Francisco Vásquez de Coronado, pushed as far north as present-day Kansas in his search for the fabled Seven Cities of Cibola. He never found the gold he sought, nor did the other Spaniards in North America. Still, by the end of the sixteenth century, they had set up numerous small military garrisons and Catholic missions, from which they managed to impose considerable control over the economic and religious lives of the native peoples. Moreover, they used these outposts as bases of military operations against other European powers. Although their numbers were never very large, the Spanish played an important role in North America well into the nineteenth century.

Similarly, the Dutch and French established a significant presence in North America without sending over large numbers of settlers. Both nations developed an extensive fur trade with native tribes, and during the first half of the seventeenth century they did a lively and lucrative business in beaver pelts. From their main settlement at New Amsterdam (present-day New York City), the Dutch dominated trade in the Hudson, Connecticut, and Delaware river valleys. In the third quarter of the seventeenth century, however, a series of wars between the Dutch and the English resulted in the loss of Dutch territory and trade on the North American mainland.

The French, by comparison, maintained control of an increasingly extensive North American trade network. They established fishing operations along the northern Atlantic coast in the sixteenth century, and beginning in 1534, the explorer Jacques Cartier led expeditions up the Saint Lawrence River. The Saint Lawrence soon became the first major area of French influence in North America. In 1608, Samuel de Champlain established a small settlement at Quebec, and by the 1620s French traders had ventured into the North American interior as far as the Great Lakes. In the 1670s and 1680s other French explorers—most notably Louis Jolliet, Father Jacques Marquette, and René Robert de La Salle—pushed west well beyond the Missouri River and south to the mouth of the Mississippi River. By the end of the seventeenth century, then, the French claimed a huge expanse of territory that reached from southern Canada to the Gulf of Mexico and covered roughly the middle third of what is now the United States. Like the Spanish, they reinforced their claim by creating a network of trading posts, military garrisons, and Catholic missions. Still, the number of French colonists in North America in 1700 totaled little more than ten thousand.

The English adopted a much different strategy for North American colonization. They were comparative latecomers to New World exploration and settlement, and they did not establish a permanent foothold on the North American mainland until 1607, with the creation of Jamestown in Virginia. Like the other European colonizers, the English sought to extract the abundant riches of the New World—fish, furs, and, if they were fortunate, gold and silver—but they did more than set up forts and trading posts. They planted permanent agricultural communities populated by English and other European emigrants. From the staple-producing plantations in the South to the quasi-communal farming villages of New England, these colonists quickly spread over the landscape in their quest for land.

By the 1750s, England's North American colonies reached from present-day Maine to Georgia and as far west as the Appalachian mountain chain. Although this area was quite small compared with the vast territories claimed by Spain and France, it held a comparatively large population of nearly a million and a half English subjects. This approach to colonization had important implications for the future of the Anglo-American frontier: unlike the Spanish and French, the English sought not only to subdue the native tribes but also to remove them.

This process of removal had begun in the first period of contact. Everywhere they went, Europeans carried with them diseases—especially smallpox, diphtheria, and measles—against which North American natives had no natural or acquired immunity. Long before the main force of European colonizers arrived in North America, imported illnesses had swept the native peoples, devastating tribes in every region and depopulating some by as much as 90 percent. Especially along the eastern seaboard of North America, in the region ultimately dominated by the English, Indians suffered a demographic catastrophe that greatly undermined their ability to resist European invasion. Thus the early colonizers accomplished more through this unwitting germ warfare than they could ever have achieved through force of arms.

Frontier Warfare before 1800

Force of arms did, of course, play a critical role in the longer history of the North American frontier. Warfare on the frontier was seldom a clear-cut contest between European invaders and Indian resisters. The European colonizing powers fought among themselves, and so did native tribes. Both Europeans and Indians took advantage of the other's animosities, creating complex intercultural alliances out of overlapping layers of long-standing hostility. They used those alliances to further their own diplomatic and military ends, and when making new alliances served their purposes, they did so.

In the seventeenth and eighteenth centuries, the imperial wars of the European powers brought Indian-European diplomacy into play on a broad scale. Although the contest in the colonies was essentially a sideshow to the larger, long-lasting Old World conflict, the American frontier increasingly became both battleground and prize in the struggle among the European powers.

For instance, in the major imperial struggle of the colonial era, the Seven Years' War—or the French and Indian War, as it was called in the British American colonies—Great Britain established dominance over a huge expanse of territory on the American frontier. This conflict began with a series of clashes on the Pennsylvania frontier in 1754 and spread throughout North America, from Canada to the West Indies. Within a few years, almost thirty thousand British regulars joined colonial militia units to combat a much smaller French force aided by a substantial number of Indian allies.

Everywhere they went, Europeans carried with them diseases—especially smallpox, diphtheria, and measles—against which North American natives had no acquired immunity.

Both the British and the French attempted to gain Indian support. In the early years of the conflict, a few hundred Mohawk and Cherokee warriors fought briefly for the British as mercenaries, but they were hardly loyal or long-standing allies. The Iroquois confederacy, of which the Mohawk were a part, chose for the most part to adopt a position of neutrality, letting the Europeans fight between themselves while accepting gifts from both. Only when the military situation began to shift in favor of the Anglo-Americans—especially after their victories over the French at Louisbourg in 1758 and at

Joseph Brant (1742–1807), Mohawk leader who supported the British in the French and Indian War and the American Revolution.

Quebec in 1759—did the Iroquois tilt toward the British side.

In the South, the Cherokee turned toward the French after their limited alliance with the British turned sour, and after 1758 they posed a serious threat to Anglo-American settlers in the southern backcountry. They attempted to bring the powerful Creek into the war against the Anglo-Americans in a multitribal alliance with other southern Indians. But the Creek, like the Iroquois, played one European side against the other for favorable trade concessions. In the end, this position of neutrality proved beneficial. The Iroquois and Creek emerged from the European conflict with their trade relations and tribal lands intact; the Cherokee suffered because of the loss of French trade goods, and they had to accept territorial boundaries imposed by the victorious British.

By 1763, at the end of the war, the British had greatly expanded their North American territories. Above all, the removal of the French presence from the trans-Appalachian interior promised new opportunities for Anglo-American expansion, and thousands of land-hungry settlers looked forward to moving west.

But almost immediately two obstacles rose to stop them, or at least impede them. In 1763, a chief of the Ottawa tribe, Pontiac, led the tribes of the Great Lakes region in a resistance movement to stop Anglo-American encroachment. Pontiac's forces attacked and destroyed several British garrisons, and they threatened to drive the British army out of the area. By 1764, war-weary British regular troops, just returned from fighting the French in the West Indies, managed to break up Pontiac's forces and maintain a presence in the Northwest. Still, the volatile situation in the region led British policymakers to try to prevent further conflict between Indians and Anglo-Americans by keeping white settlers out of Indian territory. While Pontiac's uprising was still in progress, the government in London imposed the Proclamation of 1763, which prohibited settlers from moving west of the Appalachian Mountains. The British army was too sparsely stationed to enforce the policy effectively, and thousands of whites simply ignored the ban and moved west anyway. Nonetheless, the policy seemed oppressive to many potential migrants, and the government's attempt to restrict access to the trans-Appalachian West was one of the many tensions contributing to the antagonism between Britain and its American colonies.

The American War for Independence had important implications for the future of the frontier. It created a new North American nation that took over not only the territory formerly held by the British but also the lands of native tribes. As was the case in the Seven Years' War, Indians were considered valuable allies in frontier fighting, and both the British and their rebellious colonists sought to recruit them. In the North, tribes of the Iroquois confederacy fought on both sides, sometimes attacking each other and often suffering devastating losses. Once the war was over, the Iroquois confederacy was weakened almost beyond repair, and its leaders were forced to concede a large area of western land to the victorious United States in the Treaty of Fort Stanwix (1784). In the South, the Cherokee fought for the British—or, more properly, against American expansion. Like the Iroquois, they suffered greatly from retaliatory expeditions, and at war's end they, too, had to surrender territory to the new American republic.

The Struggle for Order on the American Frontier

The acquisition of western land both from the native tribes and from the British fueled expansionist fever among white Americans. Having been legally limited by the Proclamation of 1763, settlers and speculators now eagerly sought to take advantage of the opening of new lands in the Old Northwest. One of the main tasks (and few successes) of the American government under the Articles of Confederation was the organization of orderly settlement in that region. Beginning in 1785, government surveyors divided the territory into a grid-work of townships, each six miles square with thirty-six one-mile-square sections of 640 acres, which could be subdivided into smaller lots and sold. (In fact, this straight-line design became the model for the government's land policy of the west throughout the nineteenth century.) The assumption was that, once populated with productive settlers, these western territories would enter the Union as new states, thereby adding to the size and strength of the new nation.

But the imposition of an orderly plan on the western territories did not guarantee control. Although the British were required by the Treaty of Paris (1783) to relinquish their military garrisons in the Northwest, they did so very slowly. The United States government, with its army demobilized and somewhat demoralized at the war's end, could do nothing to hurry the British on their way. The Spanish likewise caused trouble in the West. They held New Orleans, which they had acquired at the end of the Seven Years' War, and thus controlled the outlet from the Mississippi River to the Gulf of Mexico. In 1784 they closed New Orleans to American shipping, denying frontier farmers access to foreign markets and discouraging the commercial development of the trans-Appalachian interior. To make matters worse, Spanish agents were reported to be encouraging western settlers to break away from the United States and ally themselves with Spain. At the same time, native tribes throughout the trans-Appalachian region, from the Ohio country to Georgia, resisted further white expansion and attacked settlers who encroached on tribal lands.

By the time the first federal government under George Washington took office in 1789, the western frontier of the United States was a vast but extremely vulnerable appendage to the original thirteen states. Foreign intrigues and Indian unrest made the region a source of national insecurity, and the government's claims to control rang hollow. Washington himself—who had had extensive experience in the western country as a military leader and who still held a sizable financial interest there as a land speculator—made securing the frontier one of the main items on his political agenda. There was little he could do militarily to oppose Britain and Spain, but he could take action against North American inhabitants.

Washington committed a large armed force to combat native tribes in the Northwest Territory, and in 1794, at the Battle of Fallen Timbers in northern Ohio, United States troops under Major General Anthony Wayne gained a decisive victory against a combined force of Shawnee, Ottawa, Ojibwa, and Pottawatomi warriors. In the same year, Washington sent (and for a while personally led) a huge military expedition into western Pennsylvania to suppress the Whiskey Rebellion, an uprising of local farmers opposed to the Washington administration's excise tax on whiskey, a marketable commodity crucial to the local economy. The rebellion broke up before Washington's army arrived, so there was no climactic battle like that against the Indians. Still, by dispatching federal troops to assert governmental authority, Washington made clear his resolve to put down frontier unrest, whether it came from Indians or whites.

The Whiskey Rebellion points to a phenomenon that had long been part of Anglo-American frontier relations: intracultural, as well as intercultural, conflict. That is, Anglo-Americans not only fought against Indians and other Europeans for control of the frontier, they also fought among themselves. This conflict manifested itself dramatically in a series of armed insurrections, the most notable of which were Bacon's Rebellion in Virginia (1676), the Land Riots in New York (1766), the Regulator movement in North Carolina (1766–1771), and the Regulator movement, or Shays's Rebellion, in Massachusetts (1786–1787), and then the Whiskey Rebellion. In each case backcountry settlers felt themselves economically and politically oppressed by their fellow countrymen, both the elite in their own frontier regions and the merchants and officials in the more established regions to the east. When their pleas and petitions to the established authorities brought no positive result, they rose up in arms to seek redress of their grievances. Even though these frontier insurrections were usually suppressed by the superior military might of the government, they still represented a recurring threat to the established order of Anglo-American authorities.

On a lower, less dramatic scale, frontier folk frequently lived in tension with those lawmakers and landowners who sought to impose their notions of spatial, social, and economic order on the process of settlement. Elite proprietors of back-country tracts hoped to populate the frontier with sturdy, stable, hardworking farmers who would improve the land (and land values) and produce a marketable commodity. They also wanted settlers who would pay proper respect to the landowning elite. For this reason proprietors often tried to attract German and Swiss immigrants, ethnic groups that were thought to fit the profile of the productive settler.

Yet large landowners often found that the people who actually settled (and sometimes squatted) on their land were not the people they had planned for. The early American backcountry attracted an ethnically diverse group of settlers, not only sturdy Germans but, more often, Scotch-Irish immigrants who had been driven out of Ireland and were hardly more popular in the

American colonies. The Scotch-Irish made up a sizable proportion of the emigrants who swept down the Shenandoah Valley of Virginia in the middle of the eighteenth century. Members of the Virginia gentry found these new inhabitants of the western lands to be hardly the decent and deferential sort they had expected. Instead, these newcomers tended to be independent-minded people who had their own ideas and expectations about making their way in the wilderness. Rather than making the kinds of permanent improvements needed for commercial development, these settlers lived off the natural bounty of the environment. Rather than engaging in such gentlemanly forms of competition as horse racing, dancing, and dueling, they took sport in cockfights and brutal gouging matches. Rather than accepting the orderly religion of the Anglican church, they lived according to the spiritual, almost supernatural, intensity of enthusiastic, evangelical religion.

Bound together by mutual need and mystical belief, people in the Virginia backcountry and elsewhere on the American frontier formed their own communities that existed outside of, and even in defiance of, the control of elite landowners. Accordingly, those landowners increasingly came to scorn these settlers as disorderly, slothful people who, according to the common complaint, lived like Indians. In fact, the term "white Indians" became a common slur cast against these settlers by members of the Anglo-American elite. In their eyes, these "white Indians" represented obstacles to orderly development, and therefore they, no less than "red" Indians, had to be subdued or removed.

National Expansion and Military Conquest

In the first half of the nineteenth century, the United States government pursued an aggressive policy of territorial expansion, acquiring huge tracts of land by both peaceful and violent means. The first and most dramatic step came with President Thomas Jefferson's purchase of the Louisiana Territory from France in 1803. Although he acted without proper constitutional authority, Jefferson bought over eight hundred thousand square miles of land that reached from the Gulf of Mexico as far north as the headwaters of the Mississippi River and as far west as the Rocky Mountains—for less than two dollars a square mile. In addition to being a remarkable bargain, the Louisiana Purchase created great opportunities for future frontier farmers. Indeed, the expansion of an agrarian republic was one of the main motivations behind Jefferson's move to acquire the Louisiana Territory.

Expansion would first require exploration, and Jefferson acted quickly to send expeditions into the newly acquired territory. In 1804, a team of explorers led by Meriwether Lewis and William Clark left Saint Louis, on the Mississippi River, to begin a two-year trek northwest across the northern Plains and the Rocky Mountains to the Oregon Territory and the Pacific coast—far beyond the bounds of the Louisiana Purchase. While Lewis and Clark were heading northwest, the government sent Zebulon Pike to explore other regions of the American frontier. In 1805, Pike led an expedition northward from Saint Louis along the Mississippi River to what is now Minnesota. In 1806, Pike set out on a second trip westward to the southern Rocky Mountains and south into Mexico before returning to Louisiana. In the years following these early exploratory expeditions, the United States government established a handful of military outposts west of the Mississippi River. In the first two decades of the nineteenth century, then, the path had clearly been prepared for the massive migration of white settlers into the western frontier.

In the 1820s, several thousand of these settlers moved out of the United States into Texas, a Mexican possession. Mexico, which had gained its independence from Spain in 1821, encouraged settlement of its northern borderlands by offering generous inducements to immigrants. Farmers from the American South, many of whom were slave owners, responded eagerly to this opportunity to acquire new lands for cotton production. By the end of the decade, settlers from the United States far outnumbered Mexicans in the Texas Territory. At that point, the Mexican government attempted to curtail their influence in the region by outlawing slavery and blocking additional immigration from the United States. The resulting tension between the Mexican government and the North American emigrants developed into armed conflict in 1835–1836, during which rebellious settlers defeated a Mexican army and declared Texas an independent republic. For nine years thereafter, expansionist political leaders in the United States government pushed for the annexation of Texas, and finally, in 1845, Texas entered the Union.

Bound together by mutual need and mystical belief, people in colonial Virginia's backcountry and elsewhere on the American frontier formed their own communities that existed outside of, and even in defiance of, the control of elite landowners.

The annexation of Texas accelerated the engines of expansion. Claiming that the nation had a divine mission, or "manifest destiny," to control the whole continent, expansionist politicians and their allies in the press promoted a final push to the Pacific. In 1844 the Democratic party had made acquisition of the Oregon Territory a major plank in its platform, and the Democrats took a very aggressive stance toward Great Britain, which disputed the United States' territorial claims. In 1846 James K. Polk, the Democratic president, negotiated a treaty with Great Britain that compromised American territorial demands but nonetheless gave the United States its first foothold on the Pacific. In the same year, lingering tensions over Texas brought the United States into war with Mexico, and the American victory two years later forced the Mexican government to cede a huge expanse of land stretching from Texas to California.

In less than half a century, the results of expansionist policy proved dramatic. Between 1803 and 1848, the United States had tripled its original territory and, in the minds of many of its citizens, had fulfilled its manifest destiny to reach from the Atlantic to the Pacific. Moreover, warfare and diplomacy had reduced the power and presence of Spain, Britain, and Mexico in North America, and the United States faced no foreign competition for its continued conquest of the continent.

Foreign powers were not, of course, the greatest obstacle to national expansion. Native tribes had occupied much of the North American interior for hundreds, even thousands, of years, and they would not easily accede to the more recent claims of the United States. Indeed, in the earliest years of nationhood, the federal government adopted an official policy of recognizing traditional tribal lands as legitimate territorial possessions that could be acquired only through treaties. At the same time, however, the young agrarian nation's demands for new land increasingly led political and military leaders to exact territorial concessions from Indian tribes through warfare rather than diplomacy.

In the years after the Battle of Fallen Timbers, for instance, the United States government continued to push for land cessions from tribes in the Old Northwest, especially in the Indiana and Michigan territories. In response to this growing pressure from whites, two Shawnee leaders, Tecumseh and his brother Tenskwatawa ("the Prophet"), began to organize widespread resistance among Indian people, and established a sizable confederation of tribes in the region. In response to the Indians' threat to white expansion, the territorial governor of Indiana, William Henry Harrison, sent an armed force against Tecumseh's warriors. In two decisive engagements, the Battle of Tippecanoe (1811) and the Battle of the Thames (1813), Harrison defeated the tribal confederacy and killed Tecumseh. The destruction of the confederacy reduced Indian resistance in the Midwest and opened the Indiana and Michigan territories to rapid white settlement. Harrison's victories also provided him with a claim to military fame as a frontier fighter that proved useful in his campaign for the presidency in 1840.

In the South, a similar pattern of conquest was played out in the first four decades of the nineteenth century. The Creek tribe, which inhabited much of present-day Georgia and Alabama, sought to stop white encroachment onto tribal lands. Beginning in 1813, they carried out a series of devastating raids on recent settlers. Whites reacted with horror and hostility, and another future president, Andrew Jackson, organized a punitive expedition of militiamen from Kentucky and Tennessee and Indian warriors from tribes hostile to the Creek. Over the spring and summer of 1814, Jackson won decisive victories, most notably at the Battle of Horseshoe Bend in Alabama. Then, having subdued the Creek militarily, Jackson demanded land cessions of more than twenty million acres in the Southeast. Like William Henry Harrison, Andrew Jackson built his political career on a foundation of his fame as a frontier Indian fighter—a new kind of American hero.

Even those tribes which chose not to resist forcibly suffered eventual defeat. The Cherokee, who had supplied fighters for Jackson's campaign against the Creek, attempted to maintain friendly relations with the United States. During the first three decades of the nineteenth century, they even developed a society which mirrored that of the whites, with settled farms, African slaves, a written alphabet, and, in 1827, a tribal constitution modeled on the state constitutions of their white neighbors.

But nothing appealed to whites so much as Cherokee land. During the 1820s, several southern states, most notably Georgia, began to push the federal government to remove Indians to lands west of the Mississippi River. Moreover, in response to the framing of the Cherokee constitution, the Georgia legislature declared it invalid and laid claim to all Cherokee land within state boundaries. The Cherokee were to be considered nothing more than "tenants at will," with no legal right to call the land their own. Playing by the white man's rules, the Cherokee challenged Georgia's action in the United States Supreme Court, which ruled in favor of the Cherokee in *Worcester* v. *Georgia* (1832).

But Andrew Jackson, the former Indian fighter who had been elected president in 1828, had little regard for either the Cherokee or the Supreme Court, and he refused to enforce the Court's ruling. Indeed, Jackson had already promoted the Indian Removal Act (1830) in Congress, giving the federal government the power to force the Cherokee and other tribes to exchange their tribal lands for territory in the West. Between 1831 and 1839, thousands of Chickasaw, Choctaw, Creek, Seminole, and Cherokee people were forced to move to reservations in what is now Oklahoma—an area of vast plains that scarcely resembled the eastern woodlands they had known. The Cherokee's forced migration along the "Trail of Tears," which claimed the lives of nearly a fourth of the tribe, underscores one of the most unfortunate features of frontier history: like whites, Indians also moved west, but seldom of their own accord and almost never with the prospects of a better future.

The Emigrants' Experience

The westward migration of white Americans did not result in the same degree of cultural dislocation as that of the native Americans, but it was not without its share of social, familial, and individual crises. There was, in fact, no single pattern of "frontier life" for whites moving west, but a complex and often conflicted interplay of expectation and experience.

Throughout the first half of the nineteenth century, the image of the West took on a decidedly romantic tinge in the minds of many Easterners. Popular writers—most notably James Fenimore Cooper, but also scores of other novelists and journalists—depicted the frontier as a region of danger, drama, and heroic deeds. Similarly, in the era before photography, prominent painters such as George Catlin and Albert Bierstadt offered eastern audiences vivid eyewitness views of the West and its native inhabitants. The result was that people setting out for the West often began their journey with a great sense of anticipation and adventure.

Along the way, however, the trail exacted its toll on settlers' spirits, and the romanticism of the East eventually faded in the face of the realities of the West. The trip west proved a difficult test of endurance, both for individuals and for the social units they formed. Most emigrants traveled in groups, and their caravans became short-term communities of necessity, mobile models of the established social order. At least at the outset, the social organization of migrant trains tended to reinforce the standard gender roles and power relationships of the white American family. Even the decision to move west reflected different perceptions. What might have seemed to men an opportunity for a new life often seemed to women the loss of an old life, a separation from the relationships of kinship and community left behind. Once under way, migrant communities generally replicated the division of labor according to customary notions of "separate spheres." Men took primary responsibility for driving and defending the wagon train, while women cooked, cared for the children and the sick, and generally provided the emotional support that kept the family—and the migrant community—together.

As the trip wore on, internal conflict often threatened to drive the migrant community apart. The arduousness of the journey caused roles to change and relationships to become strained. Men argued among themselves about who should determine the route and pace of migration; sometimes these disagreements boiled over into open power struggles that ultimately resulted in the division of the migrant community into two separate caravans, each going its own way. Within individual families, necessity caused women to assume new roles and take on tasks that had formerly been the exclusive responsibility of men. In the end, the long, difficult trip not only tarnished people's expectations about the adventure of moving west, it also challenged some of their basic assumptions about fundamental human relationships.

Once they reached their destination, migrant groups generally sought to re-create the familiar patterns of community life they had known before. In the early nineteenth century, for instance, towns on the farming frontier of Ohio, Indiana, and Illinois often took the names of the towns from which the majority of the initial inhabitants had come. Especially in new communities settled by New Englanders, government and church reflected the form and even the composition of the town of origin, and leaders in each tended to be a preselected, self-perpetuating local elite. The re-creation of the established social order thus resulted in the reinforcement of social inequality. The more prosperous first settlers had a distinct advantage in being able to acquire land and set down permanent roots. Their poorer counterparts, not to mention those who came

The Cherokee's forced migration along the "Trail of Tears," which killed nearly one-fourth of the tribe, underscores one of the saddest aspects of frontier history.

later, often stayed only a comparatively short while and then moved on, looking for land and better prospects elsewhere. While the towns on the midwestern frontier included some people in their strong ties of community, they excluded others—as had been the case in the New England towns from which they originated.

In the settlements farther west, the familiar social patterns were more fluid and fragile. For instance, in the wake of the discovery of gold in California in 1848, thousands of migrants swarmed west, most of them young, single, and eager to get rich. Almost overnight, they created dozens of little mining camps inhabited largely by prospectors and prostitutes. With men outnumbering women sometimes by more than ten to one, life in these new communities tended to be volatile and violent, and there were few churches, schools, or other institutions of moral guidance and social control. In time, however, with the growth of commercial centers such as San Francisco and Portland, the cities of the West began to offer at least a pale—or sometimes quite gaudy—reflection of the genteel life of the urban East.

The western replication of eastern society and culture was not simply a matter of popular preference, it was also an important question in national politics. Throughout the second quarter of the nineteenth century, westward expansion heightened the conflict between two competing models of eastern society: the free labor system of the North and the slave labor system of the South. Both northerners and southerners came to believe that the expansion of their particular way of life was crucial to the future of their respective regions, and therefore the future of the frontier became especially crucial to both. From the acceptance of slavery in Missouri in 1820 to its rejection in California in 1850, political leaders had attempted to reach a compromise on the issue in the new states created out of the western territories. Compromise, rather than offering a complete resolution of the controversy, increased tensions over the future of the territories.

That tension turned to open violence in 1854, soon after Congress passed the Kansas-Nebraska Act, which had been sponsored by Senator Stephen A. Douglas of Illinois. Douglas's original intent had been primarily to promote a northern route for a proposed transcontinental railroad, not to add more fuel to the debate over slavery. But to gain southern support, he agreed to open the question of slavery in the Kansas and Nebraska territories to the doctrine of "popular sovereignty," the notion that the inhabitants of the territories, and not Congress, should have the right to decide on slavery for themselves before entering the Union. When the Kansas-Nebraska Act passed, thousands of pro-slavery and anti-slavery settlers rushed into Kansas, each faction intent on shaping this rich farming region according to its particular social system. The conflict quickly turned to armed struggle, and "Bleeding Kansas" became the scene of small-scale but brutal civil war. Indeed, the violence on the farming frontier foreshadowed—and, to some degree, triggered—the larger, bloodier struggle that would engulf the whole nation in 1861.

Integrating the Western Frontier into Industrial Society

While the North and South were locked in civil war, the United States government adopted two policies that would have a profound effect on the future of the West. First, Congress passed the Homestead Act in May 1862, to encourage settlement and development of the western frontier. Any settler could get 160 acres of land essentially for free, on the condition that he cultivate it and live on it for at least five years. Although unscrupulous speculators succeeded in turning the law to their own advantage, thousands of actual settlers were lured west by the promise of free land.

Two months after Congress passed the Homestead Act, it authorized massive land grants and other benefits to railroad companies to promote the construction of a transcontinental railroad. Two companies started working toward each other, the Union Pacific moving west across the plains from Omaha, Nebraska, and the Central Pacific heading east through the Sierra Nevada. After years of back-breaking and often deadly labor by ethnically distinct work forces—the Irish of the Union Pacific and the Chinese of the Central Pacific—the two lines of track met at Promontory Point, Utah, in May 1869. Technology and human toil had finally forged an iron link between the Atlantic and the Pacific. Thus, in the post–Civil War era, uniting the rapidly growing West with the industrializing East became as important a process as reuniting the North and the South.

The combination of cheap land and easy transportation spurred a remarkable surge of settlers to the West. A trip that once took up to six or seven months by wagon train now took six or seven days. Those who came west on the railroad, like those who built it, added greatly to the ethnic diversity of the region. Recent immigrants from almost all parts of northern and eastern Europe—England, Ireland, Scandinavia, Germany, Poland, Russia—joined native-born settlers in the search for new farmland. Often they formed distinct ethnic communities, and in some territories, like Minnesota and Wisconsin, the concentration of Scandinavians and Germans created an immigrant culture that shaped the future of the states.

No matter where they settled, or with whom, the new immigrants faced a difficult struggle to secure a living from the soil. Although the land of the Great Plains was generally fertile, it was also quite dry and bare. Such discouraging environmental conditions challenged even the most committed and courageous farm family. Sometimes living in miserable huts made of prairie sod and always contending with violent weather and voracious insects, many families soon gave up in one place and moved on to another. In some midwestern regions, the rate of persistence from one decade to the next was well below 50 percent, and in some cases was even below 30 percent.

Those who stayed, however, eventually managed to make a decent if sometimes precarious living. Building modest yet handsome frame houses, schools, and churches, they made the Midwest the mythical as well as the geographical center of the nation, America's heartland. Moreover, using new agricultural technology developed in the middle of the nineteenth century—more efficient plows and harrows, large, horse-drawn reapers and threshers—grain farmers made the Midwest one of the most productive agricultural regions of the nation, America's breadbasket. The high cost of modern farm equipment encouraged most farmers to specialize in one main crop, usually corn or wheat, that had a high market value. Connected to large milling operations by the railroads, frontier farms in the newly opened parts of the West soon provided a significant part of the foodstuffs needed to feed an increasingly industrialized East.

So, too, did western cattle ranches. Although cattle ranchers and farmers were usually bitter enemies in the competition for access to prairie lands, they played a similar role in the national economy. Cowboys drove huge herds to new stockyards adjoining railroads in Kansas, and from there the cattle were shipped to slaughterhouses, the largest and most technologically advanced of which were in Chicago. After the cattle had been killed and sent through a "disassembly line," the meat could be shipped in refrigerated railroad cars to eastern cities. About half the beef consumed in the United States originated on the western cattle ranches. Here again, the inhabitants of the West—including the cowboy, the highly romanticized but very hardworking and low-paid laborer in the cattle industry—helped feed those who worked in the offices and factories of the East.

Along with cattle and grain, the third critical contribution the West made to the economic development of the industrializing nation was its vast mineral resources. Mining operations extracted gold, silver, copper, lead, zinc, and other valuable minerals from the high plateau west of the Great Plains. Rich discoveries in the Rocky Mountains and the Sierra Nevada created new gold and silver rushes to rival that of the 1848 California boom. As had been the case earlier, some of the rough, rapidly growing, and predominantly male mining camps soon turned into sizable—and surprisingly civilized—towns, complete with elegant hotels, restaurants, and theaters. They did so, in part, because of the increasing concentration of wealth in the hands of a few mine owners. Individual prospectors usually sold their claims to large entrepreneurs, and mining became part of industrial capitalism, with high-priced machinery and low-paid workers.

Native Resistance to National Integration

Throughout the post–Civil War era, the settlement, development, and national integration of the western frontier may have seemed an inexorable process, but it did not go unopposed. Despite the extensive claims of the United States government, the trans-Mississippi West was still home to more than three hundred thousand Indians, dozens of tribal groups that inhabited the region from the Great Plains to the desert Southwest to the coastal Northwest. These native inhabitants of the West lived in a variety of ways—some farmed, some fished, some followed the buffalo—but despite their diversity, all eventually faced the common fate of encountering the huge influx of white settlers. As had been the case more than two centuries before, in the first period of Indian-white contact on the eastern coast of North America, new diseases decimated the Indian peoples of the trans-Mississippi regions. Some tribes were repeatedly devastated by the sicknesses brought by white settlers, and they were virtually helpless to resist the steady encroachment of white society. Other tribes resisted forcefully and, for a while, successfully. Eventually, however, even the most warlike tribes were reduced by disease and military defeat, and had to accept being limited to life on government-controlled reservations. The struggle and ultimate subjugation of the western

By the latter 1800s rich discoveries in the Rockies and Sierras created new gold and silver rushes that rivaled the one of 1848.

Indians in the second half of the nineteenth century remains one of the most dramatic and tragic chapters in the history of the American frontier.

The majority of these western Indians lived on the Great Plains, and there the buffalo became the source, or certainly the symbol, of the conflict between Indians and whites. For over three centuries—ever since the Spanish had introduced horses to North America—Plains Indians had been skilled, wide-ranging hunters who depended on the buffalo for their survival. They used the meat for food, the hide for clothing and shelter, and virtually all parts of the animal for some purpose, including ceremonial dress and religious symbols. In the post–Civil War era, whites developed an apparent need for the buffalo, but more for show than for survival. Seeking skins for blankets and heads for trophies, whites hunted the buffalo for sport and profit. So extensive was the hunting by the end of the 1870s that the once-vast herds were near extinction, the number of buffalo having dropped from the tens of millions to only a few thousand in the space of less than two decades. The decline of the buffalo spelled the decline of the Indian as well.

The native inhabitants of the Great Plains faced not only a devastating decline in the buffalo population but an equally threatening increase in the white population as well. The United States government's policy of promoting orderly settlement and economic development in the West did not allow Indians their accustomed access to the land. Rather, Indians were to be restricted to reservations, far removed from the railroad routes and new farming communities, where they could be regulated by the government's Bureau of Indian Affairs and reformed by Christian missionaries. Some Indian tribes accepted removal to reservations without open resistance. Others, however, refused to accommodate themselves to the demands of the white man, and they fought back in a bitter warfare. From the Apache in the Southwest to the Nez Percé in the northern Rockies to the Sioux, Cheyenne, Comanche, and other tribes on the Great Plains, Indians' resistance made white expansion a costly and deadly process.

The Sioux played the most dramatic role in this war for the West. Although several western Sioux tribes in the Dakota, Montana, and Wyoming territories of the Upper Midwest and the northern Rocky Mountain region had been assigned to a reservation by the Treaty of Fort Laramie (1868), many Sioux refused to be limited to the reservation. Moreover, the discovery of gold in the Black Hills of South Dakota, which was part of the Sioux reservation, prompted a rush of white prospectors into Indian territory. To push the Sioux onto the reservation and thereby to promote settlement by white miners and farmers, the United States government sent a military expedition to the region in 1875. Government troops led by a flamboyant young general, George Armstrong Custer, suffered a crushing defeat at the hands of the Sioux leader Sitting Bull at the Little Bighorn River in the Montana Territory in June 1876. The massacre of Custer's force frightened white Americans and encouraged Native Americans, but it proved to be the exception rather than the rule in the war between the Sioux and the United States. Over the next five years, the United States Army stalked and eventually subdued the Sioux, forcing them not only to return to their reservation but also to cede about a third of their land to the government.

In 1889, however, the Sioux once again rose up in resistance. Reservation-bound Indians began to practice a new ritual, the Ghost Dance, which reinvigorated their sense of their culture and created a new sense of defiance. Concerned federal officials saw the implications inherent in this ritual of resurgence, and they used armed force to put an end to the Ghost Dance movement. The results were disastrous for the Sioux. The government's attempt to take Sitting Bull into custody ended in his being shot and killed. Two weeks later, on 29 December, a detachment of the Seventh Cavalry—Custer's old regiment—rounded up some 350 Sioux at Wounded Knee, South Dakota; and when someone fired a shot, the soldiers massacred about 300 Indians in a matter of minutes.

The slaughter at Wounded Knee was not the last step in the suppression of Indians—some tribes still engaged in armed struggle against the United States government well into the twentieth century—but it did signal the end to Sioux resistance. Moreover, it symbolized a more widespread defeat for Indian peoples throughout the West. By 1890, the reservation had become virtually their only recourse. The superintendent of the 1890 census declared that the process of white settlement had spread so completely across the continent that "there can hardly be said to be a frontier line." That simple bureaucratic pronouncement inspired the historian Frederick Jackson Turner to see the "closing of a great historic movement" ("Significance of the Frontier," p. 1). Indeed, the "closing" of the American frontier led to the opening of a new area of interest in the writing of American history.

The Enduring Significance of the American Frontier

It is difficult for historians to declare the frontier truly closed. The frontier is, as noted at the outset, an ambiguous, often deceptive, concept. Yet the notion of the frontier has become so deeply embedded in American culture that it cannot be dismissed no matter how inaccurate or anachronistic it may be. From the fiction of James Fenimore Cooper and other popular novelists to nineteenth-century "Wild West" shows and twentieth-century "westerns," the frontier has been a powerful mythic symbol of unfettered individualism, a place where a person could live, perhaps thrive, without the standard constraints of society. In a word, the frontier represented freedom.

For many people, the promise proved to be true, at least to a degree. Not only white men but black men as well rode the ranges as cowboys. African Americans could never fully throw off the burden of prejudice in American society, but in the West they could escape the institutionalized racism that prevailed in the South (and often in the North). Similarly, women could not completely overcome the legal and cultural restrictions imposed on them, but in some western states they gained the right to vote almost fifty years before woman suffrage became the law of the land. Moreover, in an era when it is no longer easy, as Huck Finn put it, to "light out for the territory," many people in twentieth-century America still long to escape "civilized" society by going to the "wilderness," whether in the vast spaces of Alaska, in the relatively confined and well-designed recreational areas of national and state parks, or in the even greater comfort of a motor home.

But as the experience of Indian peoples made clear, the history of the frontier is not a chronicle of openness and opportunity for all. Indeed, whatever freedom most Americans gained as a result of national expansion came at the expense of the freedom, even the very existence, of Native Americans. The remnants of tribes restricted to reservations in the twentieth century now struggle to preserve a culture that once covered the continent.

The fate of Indian peoples mirrors that of the land itself. The ever-expanding resource demands of industrial capitalism have led to the exploitation and near-extinction of the wilderness. Beginning in the nineteenth century, nature writers began to express concern for the future of the American wilderness, and at the turn of the century the naturalist John Muir issued a clear call for the preservation of the natural beauty and grandeur of the western landscape. Accordingly, state and federal governments began setting aside parks and nature preserves in the nineteenth century, and today there are still vast wilderness areas that remain essentially undeveloped. But even these are not safe from the nation's increasing need for timber products, minerals, and water. Alaska, for instance, is now connected to the "Lower Forty-eight" by a lengthy oil pipeline, a controversial project that has brought both economic benefits and environmental disaster to the "last American wilderness."

The debate over the Alaska Pipeline is merely the latest, and certainly not the last, chapter in a history of human and environmental interaction that began on the North American continent thousands of years ago. The experience of the past, with all its promise and pitfalls, is still the best guide to the proper path to whatever frontier may yet exist in America's future.

[See also Agriculture; Geographical Mobility; Landscapes; National Parks and Preservation; Rural Life in the West; The West.]

BIBLIOGRAPHY

General Works

Billington, Ray Allen. *America's Frontier Heritage* (1966; repr. 1974).

Limerick, Patricia Nelson. *The Legacy of Conquest: The Unbroken Past of the American West* (1987).

Turner, Frederick Jackson. "The Significance of the Frontier in American History." In *The Frontier in History* (1920).

Historiographical Works

Hofstadter, Richard, and Seymour Martin Lipset, eds. *Turner and the Sociology of the Frontier* (1968).

Nash, Gerald D. *Creating the West: Historical Interpretations 1890–1990* (1991).

Nobles, Gregory H. "Breaking into the Backcountry: New Approaches to the Early American Frontier, 1750–1800." *William and Mary Quarterly*, 3d Ser., 46, no. 3 (1989).

Native Americans

Hoxie, Frederick E. *A Final Promise: The Campaign to Assimilate the Indians, 1880–1920* (1984).

Jennings, Francis. *The Invasion of America: Indians, Colonialism, and the Cant of Conquest* (1975).

Prucha, Francis Paul. *The Great Father: The United States Government and the American Indian.* 2 vols. (1984).

Utley, Robert M. *The Indian Frontier of the American West, 1846–1890* (1984).

European-American Expansion

Faragher, John Mack. *Women and Men on the Overland Trail* (1979).

Jeffrey, Julie Roy. *Frontier Women: The Trans-Mississippi West, 1840–1880* (1979).

Kolodny, Annette. *The Land Before Her: Fantasy and Experience of the American Frontiers, 1630–1860* (1984).

Nash, Roderick. *Wilderness and the American Mind* (1973; 3d ed. 1982).

Paul, Rodman Wilson. *Mining Frontiers of the Far West, 1848–1880* (1963).

Robinson, Walter Stitt. *The Southern Colonial Frontier, 1607–1763* (1979).

Slotkin, Richard. *Regeneration Through Violence: The Mythology of the American Frontier, 1600–1860* (1973).

Slotkin, Richard. *The Fatal Environment: The Myth of the Frontier in the Age of Industrialization, 1800–1890* (1985).

— GREGORY H. NOBLES

G

GENDER ROLES AND RELATIONS

In several respects gender roles in the modern American family resemble those that existed during British settlement in the 1600s. Caring for young children, maintaining the family's home, and preparing food remain largely the woman's job, while the role of family breadwinner and protector is still central to the man. Since gender roles of the past are recognizable even today, it is easy to assume that they are immutable and inevitable. Yet gender roles are flexible and ever-changing. They vary across time and place and from one social group to another. Economic circumstances and demographic configurations alter gender roles, as do new ideas and political currents.

Certain biological facts are constant. Not all women menstruate, become pregnant, or breast-feed, but only women do so. Only a man can impregnate a woman, although not all men do. Chromosomal makeup, hormonal composition, and internal or external sex organs determine sex in a biological sense, and an infant is assigned that gender label at birth. By contrast, gender role encompasses the non-biological or social and cultural elements that give meaning to the terms "male" and "female," the expectations and cultural rules that govern male and female behavior, and the assignment of different tasks, routines, and responsibilities according to gender.

Gender is one of the most common ways of dividing labor, and although differences between the sexes in physical strength, pregnancy, breast-feeding, and child rearing responsibilities have played a part, the criteria for such division has a strong basis in cultural attitudes. Children learn gender roles at an early age from their families and friends; early learning at home, cultural images, the division of productive work and leisure by gender, and the operation of social institutions (schools, the church, and the courts) contribute to adult gender role beliefs and practices.

With the exception of some Indian tribes, Americans have always divided gender roles into two categories, male and female. Many Indian groups recognize a third gender, a "half-man, half woman" a male who dresses, acts as a female, and takes the passive role in sexual intercourse with another male. The Mojave have four gender groups: males; females; boys who adopt female roles; and girls who adopt adult male roles. In Western culture, it has often been assumed that the assignment of certain tasks and responsibilities to males and females inevitably results from biological differences. Given this assumption, departures from traditional roles are often viewed as unnatural and threatening, not just to individuals but to the social order.

As members of the human race, males and females are more alike than different. And, the family has often been a shared project of men and women. Yet gender roles, assume that men and women should, even must act differently, according to rules appropriate to their gender alone. The prescriptions for the appropriate behavior of one gender imply cultural rules for the other gender as well. If a man is supposed to be a provider, it also follows that a woman should not be one. Indeed, it is seen as unmanly or unwomanly for one gender to take the role of the other except in unusual circumstances or on a temporary basis.

Throughout American history, experts from various walks of life have enunciated societal ideals of gender. In the colonial era ministers' sermons conveyed the dominant views. In the nineteenth century, men and women turned to ladies' magazines and advice books; a century later, they took their cue from doctors, television, film, and newspaper advice columns. Human behavior, more various in practice than precept, has always diverged from the social ideal. Yet gender ideals have molded behavior and defined the standard against which deviance is measured.

There have been four major ideals about gender roles in the American family over the course of four centuries: patriarchy in the colonial era; separate spheres in the nineteenth century; companionate marriage from the 1920s to the 1950s; and quasi-egalitarian roles beginning in the 1960s. These ideals have implications for the roles of sister and brother, and mother and father, although the major emphasis has been on the roles of wife and mother, and husband and father. The nature of these ideals and the reasons for their emergence will be explored here. Instead of viewing changes in ideals as four distinct domestic revolutions, it is best to think of family change as a process of adding new layers, without ever totally replacing older ones.

The promoters and foremost adherents of these four ideals belonged to the socially dominant, propertied classes of white society. The gender role ideals of other social groups were considered different and inferior.

Skilled workers, immigrants, and nonwhites have found some elements of these ideals appealing, especially as they have gained a foothold in the middle class. But missionaries, teachers, and reformers often forcibly imposed the prevailing gender role ideals to encourage assimilation, conversion to Christianity, or to demonstrate racial and class superiority.

Historical writing about gender roles in the family gave initial attention to the dominant cultural ideals of society, and later to the discrepancy between cultural ideals and domestic realities. More recently, scholars have investigated a wider range of social experience among various ethnic and racial groups, and the working class. Nonetheless, the historical research upon which this essay relies has given more attention to the female than the male role, and more attention to white native-born middle-class than to the experience of racial minorities or the working class.

Patriarchy in the Colonial Era

Indian gender roles varied greatly from tribe to tribe. Great Plains tribes, which depended primarily on hunting and fishing for their food, were patriarchal and patrilineal. In a patriarchal family, the father controlled all the economic resources and held the primary authority over all members of the family and household. Kinship in patrilineal tribes was traced through the male line. Men killed deer, moose, beaver, and buffalo; women processed the skins and hides, making clothing, tepees, and moccasins from the skins. Women in these tribes carried the family's belongings on their back on frequent moves to new hunting grounds, freeing the men to clear the trail and defend the tribe from animal or enemy attack. In tribes farther south, men hunted and fished, while women, using a short hoe and working in all-female work groups, cultivated corn, squash, and beans and picked wild berries, nuts, and fruits. Southern tribes were usually matriarchal and matrilineal. In matrilineal tribes, members traced their descent through a common female ancestor. Children inherited property and were subject to discipline by the mother's eldest brother. Mothers arranged the marriages of their children; newlyweds went to live with the bride's clan.

Scholars remain uncertain as to why matrilineal kinship was so well suited to Indian agricultural societies, and patrilineal kinship to Indian hunting societies. The absence of men for months at a time—hunting, trading, or making war—while women remained in the villages planting crops and caring for children may have made it advantageous for groups of related women to live together on a permanent basis. Whatever the reasons for the prevalence of matrilineal kinship, the result was that the status of women in such tribes was high. Women in matrilineal tribes were able to exercise substantial economic and political power far greater than that of white women in patrilineal societies. In many such tribes women elders designated a man who could speak for them in council, the decision-making body of the tribe. Seneca clan mothers, for instance, elected civilian leaders and deposed those who were corrupt or incompetent. Cherokee war women controlled the fate of war captives. Because of women's economic and political power, the pattern of residing with female kin, and the support women could depend on from female relatives, divorce was easy to accomplish. John Heckewelder, a missionary to the Delawares, for instance, noted in 1819 that both parties understood that they "are not to live together any longer than they shall be pleased with each other."

European missionaries justified their need to Christianize Indians based on these gender roles. Europeans, who usually encountered Indian men in villages during respites from hunting, fishing, and trapping, castigated them for their laziness and pitied Indian women as drudges. Their own women, they claimed, carried a lighter load. In making these observations, missionaries sought to prove the superiority of white civilization and to refute the commonly held English and European belief that the New World was too harsh an environment for white women.

Indian gender roles were gradually transformed as Indians came into greater contact with whites. The fur trade between Indians and whites, beginning around the 1600s, introduced the first of many alterations in Indian gender roles. Indian men trapped beaver or deer, and traveled to trading posts to exchange pelts and skins for needles, pots, beads—and liquor. Because the Indian man contributed trading goods to his clan, his role as economic provider was enhanced. The fur trade appears to have had both positive and negative effects on the role of Indian women. They welcomed the needles and metal cooking pots the men distributed among the tribe. The fur trade, insofar as it absented men from their villages, may also have enhanced women's responsibility for and power over the tribe's daily affairs. Alcohol sometimes led Indian husbands and fathers to ill-treat their wives and children, damage the property of neighbors and kinspeople, and avoid their responsibilities to the tribe.

The English Colonies of North America

North American colonists brought English expectations about gender roles to the new continent. Among the most important of these was that women be fruitful and multiply, and that the wife and children obey the husband's commands. In the colonial family a father was the primary authority in the household. He also served as the family's representative in political and legal affairs. Disobedience could be punished by "moderate correction" of a child or a servant, although two New England colonies outlawed wife-beating.

Protestant religious beliefs and the common law of England reinforced the patriarchal attitudes of English settlers. Most colonists in the New World, especially those who came to New England and the mid-Atlantic region, were devout Protestants, who believed the properly ordered patriarchal family to be the most godly. Except by special prenuptial agreement, a married woman was civilly dead; she could not own property, sue or be sued, draft a will, buy or sell property, or keep any wages she earned. By law all property the couple acquired during the marriage belonged to the husband. At her husband's death the widow customarily was bequeathed a lifetime interest in a third of marital property, not the full amount. The other two-thirds belonged to the children. If they were minors, the mother or a court-appointed guardian managed their property until they came of age.

The two major regions of initial English settlement were New England and the colonies of Maryland and Virginia that arose along the banks of Chesapeake Bay. New England colonists found it easier to realize patriarchal ideals than settlers in the Chesapeake, while the family practice of immigrants to the mid-Atlantic colonies of New York, New Jersey, Delaware, and Pennsylvania fell somewhere between these two extremes. Several reasons account for the differences between New England and Chesapeake family structures. The New England colonists migrated in family groups, rather than as individuals. Two-thirds of the English Puritans who founded Plymouth Colony in 1620 and the larger, contiguous Massachusetts Bay Colony ten years later, traveled to the New World in family groups. Moreover, New England colonists could expect to lead reasonably long and healthy lives. Although New England winters were harsh, water was fresh and fowl plentiful. The death rate was relatively low. Marriages were often long-lasting, and few children were orphaned. Women were usually widowed only later in life and unlikely to remarry. Fathers lived long enough so that they could rule their children's lives into adulthood, and exercise veto power over a child's potential mate.

The husband in the colonial New England family was spiritual guide and head of the household, but both marital partners were obliged to live together harmoniously. A husband was expected to be a good and faithful provider, instructor and guide to his children and servants, and a responsible member of his community. The New England woman, like her English counterpart, was supposed to excel in housekeeping, childbearing, and child rearing, to be a good Christian and neighbor, and a sexual partner and companion to her husband. The bad wife let her pigs roam in her neighbor's yard, spread malicious gossip, scolded her husband, and did not keep her home and yard clean. The bad husband beat his wife, children, or servants without cause, did not tend properly to his fields, and failed to provide proper religious instruction for the members of his household. It was believed that women did not require formal education. A woman might be driven to insanity by excess reading. A bookish man, by contrast, was considered intelligent. A man or woman who departed too much from the conventional path might find the neighborhood minister visiting them to pray for "family harmony" or subjecting them to disciplinary warning at church.

The New England woman was to excel in housekeeping, childbearing, and child rearing, and to be a good Christian, neighbor, and sexual partner and companion to her husband.

Throughout the original thirteen colonies most settlers lived on farms, where every able-bodied laborer was needed because only a small number of slaves were imported. Most farm labor was done by family members, supplemented by an occasional domestic servant or hired hand with various tasks performed according to sex and age. Men and older boys worked in the fields and around the barn and other farm buildings; women and children were responsible for the house, dairy, and garden. With the help of sons, servants, or hired hands, men cleared the land, chopped wood, built fences, planted, plowed, harvested, hunted wild game, slaughtered and butchered meat, and built and maintained farm buildings and tools. Women cooked, baked, made beer and cider, washed the clothes, sewed, spun yarn, tended a vegetable garden, raised poultry, milked the cows, salted meat, and made soap, candles, and herbal medicines.

In a husband's absence, a wife might take on some of his responsibilities, keeping the books, planting the corn, or running the tavern; however, when the husband returned, she resumed the tasks properly assigned a wife and mother. The large range of activity that colonial wives often assumed and the flexibility in women's roles have led historians to consider colonial New England women's status as being rather high and relatively free of constraints imposed by gender norms. Yet the colonial woman was dependent, a social subordinate. The concept of a wife as a "deputy husband" explains how a woman could perform men's work without upsetting the patriarchal order.

Parental responsibilities for child rearing were divided according to the child's age. Mothers breastfed their infants and provided most of the care for them. With relatively large families—on average about six to eight surviving children per couple—older children often cared for younger siblings. A mother instructed her daughters in household routines, and a father took responsibility for training his sons. He provided discipline and instruction for both sons and daughters and often taught them the rudiments of reading and writing. He was expected to supply reason and discipline to counterbalance a mother's excessive fondness and indulgence. Because rationality was more valued than emotion, courts granted fathers custody of their minor children in cases of separation or divorce.

White colonists of Maryland and Virginia believed in the patriarchal family but were often unable to realize fully its ideals. Most immigrants to these colonies were young men who sought wealth rather than spiritual communion or family stability. Although they were nominal members of the Church of England, they were not devout. The economy of the two Chesapeake colonies was based on the tobacco crop, and for the first three quarters of the seventeenth century, Englishmen, young and poor, met the region's demand for labor to cultivate it. Most immigrants could not afford to pay their passage from England and instead chose to serve a term of four to seven years as an indentured servant in exchange for their passage, room and board while in service, and some seeds, tools, and clothing when they finished their term.

Women, white or black, were not thought capable of doing a full day's field work. After brief, unsuccessful attempts to employ Indians as field laborers, the Chesapeake colonists concluded that they did not make suitable workers. Those few white women who were imported were generally brought as domestic servants, although some ended up in the fields planting and hoeing tobacco. Because servant women had to complete their terms before marrying, they married later, and as a consequence, bore fewer children. White women of the Chesapeake were frequently widowed, and after a short period remarried.

Most male immigrants to the South did not live long enough to realize their dream of returning to England or buying a Chesapeake plantation. In the damp, humid climate of the Chesapeake, malaria, typhoid, and dysentery ran rampant. In the first decades of settlement, life expectancy was twenty years shorter in Virginia and Maryland than in New England. But the harsh conditions and absence of family migration from England gave Chesapeake white women some unusual freedoms. A young woman, working as an indentured servant, often made her own decision about whom to marry, since she did not have a father whose preferences she had to accommodate. Because so many mothers of minors were widowed, husbands in the Chesapeake, fearing the interventions of an avaricious stepfather, usually made their wives the executor of the will, the guardians of minor children, and the recipients of the entire estate, rather than the customary third. By the end of the seventeenth century, however, death from epidemics had fallen off, and there were almost as many women as men. A stable white family life began to emerge. The younger generation of Chesapeake white women had somewhat less freedom—although a more comfortable existence—than their mothers. As the sex ratio evened out, women had fewer choices in the marriage market. They married earlier and had longer lasting marriages. Because husbands were less concerned about the fate of a surviving wife with minor children to raise, women were less likely to be granted sole control of property as widows.

Like the colonists farther to the north, the whites of the Chesapeake were mainly farmers, who divided the labor of the home according to gender and race. Women were responsible for garden and dairy, as well as house; men did the heavy farm labor. Female slaves performed household chores, although planters preferred to use male and female slaves in the fields, expecting their wives to handle most of the household work. The more slaves a family had, the greater the role of the mistress in feeding, clothing, and nursing them. Since most early plantations had only a few slaves, the master often worked alongside his slaves and white hired hands.

With the waning of white immigration to the Chesapeake in the third quarter of the seventeenth century, large numbers of Africans, most of them male, were imported as field laborers. Although a few Africans, like whites, were originally indentured servants, most were considered slaves, the lifetime property of their owners, by the 1680s. Africans came from both matrilineal and patrilineal societies. The institution of slavery with its imbalance of males to females thwarted the ability of men and women to marry. African men usually lived isolated existences on white homesteads where there were too few women to accommodate all the slave men who wished to marry, leading men to find a wife on another plantation. A few men continued the African practice of polygamy, although this was impossible for most because of the skewed sex ratio. More commonly, a slave father lived on a neighboring plantation and was permitted by his owner to visit his family perhaps once per week. Slave husbands, if deprived of visiting privileges, often ran away to see their families. Since the slave husband and father often did not reside with his family, his wife had the major responsibility for raising the children. She taught her children how to work in the fields, and showed them how to get along with the master. In Maryland by around 1720, the rise in birthrates led to a slave population with a more equal sex ratio of male to female. Courtship and marriage became possible and more slave families included a resident father.

If kinship was the central organizing feature of African life, it retained much of its power on the American continent. But, in being transplanted onto the North American continent, Africans lost their puberty rites and initiation ceremonies. They no longer resided in compounds with co-resident adult siblings. Elders did not arrange marriages as alliances between families. Slave men and women could not give kinship and child rearing their highest priority, because masters put them to work to produce wealth for the Big House, rather than for the slave family. Africans were never fully able to transfer their traditional family ideals and practices to North America. Slavery did not destroy the African family, but it took centuries for settled family life on plantations to emerge. When it did, it was an amalgamation of response to circumstance, the influence of white ideals, and remnants of African heritage.

The nineteenth-century American home was supposed to be a refuge from the outside world, a "home, sweet home" where the "empire of the mother" held sway.

British settlers to North America varied in their success in transplanting English gender role ideals to North America. The hardest years were the first ones. By the eighteenth century, more farmers had risen above subsistence level. Families purchased teapots, glassware, and china, the embellishments of every English home. Women could spend more time outfitting their household through the domestic manufacture of cloth, candles, and soap. In prosperous families a mother could devote herself to child care, since house servants performed most of the household chores. Ministers in their sermons began to praise devout mothers for providing children with religious and moral instruction and lavishing a child with undivided attention. The ideal of the family remained the patriarchal household, albeit a slightly more private, prosperous, and mother-oriented one.

The Middle-Class Family and Cultural Variations

The idea of man as ruler of the home, and the home's representative to the world persisted as the gender role ideal among many American groups of diverse economic circumstances, regions, and racial and ethnic identities. These included southern planters, Hispanics, many immigrant groups from Europe, Mexico, and Asia, and some Indian tribes, such as the Plains Indians. In all these groups, the extended family, more than the conjugal unit, served as the building block for community life and as the source for distributing resources.

One major social group to adhere to a new ideal of family power was the middle class. Between the 1820s and 1840s a new ideal of gender and the family emerged. The family hierarchy of the colonists, in which father ruled the home, with his wife as his chief deputy, was replaced by the view that the home was primarily a woman's world. The new ideal of home was not simply an alternative to the patriarchal beliefs of so many other social groups but a new, dominant ideal against which all other family forms were measured and found wanting. The nineteenth-century home was supposed to be a refuge from the outside world, a "home, sweet, home" where the "empire of the mother" held sway. A man's role as family provider was still valued, but breadwinning was now seen as a distinct and separate activity engaged in by a man on behalf of his family.

SEPARATE SPHERES. The home functioned as a place of repose for the husband at the end of his workday. The home and the world were seen as two separate spheres of activity. The husband moved from one to the other; the woman's sphere remained the home. She was expected to devote herself to home and children. This new view of family and gender roles, promoted especially by women authors and magazine editors, has been referred to variously as the cult of domesticity or the doctrine of separate spheres.

Historians have identified multiple roots for the doctrine of separate spheres. In the national spirit invoked by the American Revolution, the husband and father became a citizen of the new nation and, if propertied, a voter. The wife of an American citizen, although excluded from suffrage, was called upon to play a special role in nation-building. As a "Republican mother," she was expected to raise moral, responsible sons and daughters who could become virtuous citizens of the new nation. Enlightenment philosophers argued that the child's character was formed in the early years. Since mothers were the principal caretakers of young children, it fell to them to shape the child's personality for good or ill.

A second American revolution was economic rather than political. The urban middle-class home was no longer the family workshop. The woman at home did not make her own candles or soap; she bought bolts of textile at the store, rather than weaving cloth on the loom. Time spared from production was devoted instead to giving greater attention to each child, to higher standards of homemaking, and to participation in church or community affairs. At the same time, as the pace of business and commercial enterprise quickened, a husband turned his attention from domestic matters to the task of making a profit or speculating in land.

Ladies' magazines that extolled the virtues of the "angelic mother" were published in Philadelphia and Boston but reached farmer's wives and wagon trains of settlers headed West. The doctrine of separate spheres resulted in enormous changes in family practice. The mother became the primary, parent, a moral guardian of the home who had more say over child discipline. Government by affection, or milder punishment, such as spanking, rather than hitting a child with a stick or a rod, characterized a woman's regime in the urban middle-class home. The father functioned as a court of last resort in family matters. Sons turned to their mothers, rather than fathers, for affection and guidance. In the colonial period, most sons corresponded with their fathers, adding as an afterthought a greeting for their mothers. Victorian sons who were away from home usually wrote to their mothers rather than to their fathers. Whereas in an earlier period a father was credited or blamed for a child's behavior, now it was the mother who was regarded as the responsible parent. American law tended to follow these new social attitudes toward motherhood. By the 1860s many state courts held that a mother was the proper custodial parent of minor children.

The doctrine of separate spheres was also one of several reasons why fertility declined in the nineteenth century. The average birthrate of white women fell from 7.04 children in 1800 to 3.56 in 1900. Lacking methods of reliable birth control, such as the diaphragm or birth control pill, American couples chose to limit conception for a variety of reasons, one of which was the change in the mother's role. Only by curtailing family size could mothers devote more time to the rearing of each child. Historians suspect that the Victorians employed a variety of birth control methods, including condoms and abortion, although voluntary abstinence and withdrawal of the penis from the vagina prior to ejaculation seem to have been the most common means.

The doctrine of separate spheres promised women greater respect in family matters, though it restricted the scope of their activity to the home. Immigrants, especially in the second and third generations, also welcomed the romanticized ideal of a new family order that promised a cozy cottage and well-scrubbed children attending to their schoolwork. However, in the hands of urban reformers to the poor and missionaries to the Chinese, Indians, and Mexicans, the doctrine of separate spheres became a tool for destroying cultures, and blaming poor mothers for failing to keep their children in school. To protect Chinese prostitutes, for example, Presbyterian women missionaries refused to allow them to leave the rescue home without an escort. Bureau of Indian agents taught Hopi girls to make cakes and pies, only to find that their families rejected them for not serving traditional fare.

Missionaries and government agents, hoping to save Indians east of the Mississippi from losing their land and being forcibly resettled, preached the value of assimilation, the importance of individual land ownership, and the white culture's ideals of gender roles. During the American Revolution most eastern Indian tribes, although initially neutral, sided with the British. In retaliation, American troops burned Indian villages, orchards, and crops. After the Revolution white settlers steadily encroached on Indian land, and tribes east of the Mississippi had to choose between extermination and assimilation. Quaker missionaries to the Seneca Indians of New York, for example, urged Indian men to take up the plow and Indian women to abandon communal agriculture in favor of sewing and weaving for their family. They wanted the Seneca to give up the traditional longhouse for a log cabin, inhabited by husband, wife, and children. Indian response to these suggested changes was mixed. Indian women welcomed cotton clothing because it was easier to clean than deerskins. Young girls at mission schools came to regard their own traditions as heathen and enjoyed learning how to read and write. But older women, who among all women enjoyed the greatest power in traditional native culture, were most antagonistic to the proposed changes. Despite several decades of missionary influence, however, Seneca kinship remained matrilineal at the end of the nineteenth century and frequent divorce and remarriage, a traditional Seneca practice, persisted. Similarly, Presbyterian and Congregationalist missionaries to the Cherokees wanted to turn the women into housewives and the men into farmers, and frowned upon the practice of polygamy. Cherokee kinship remained matrilineal, although the residential unit was composed of the married couple and unmarried children.

The doctrine of separate spheres became the ideal of home-as-retreat from a viperous world and the rationale for transforming the lives of the poor. Middle-class women, who saw themselves as the guardians of the home, began investigating conditions of the urban poor by the 1830s. Working-class and poor women did not adhere to the doctrine of separate spheres; these women were guardians of the neighborhood as well as the home. Family privacy was not respected or valued. Immigrant boys and girls were often sent to the street to peddle, pick up bits of coal, shine shoes, or sell newspapers. Girls turned to occasional prostitution and children of both sexes sometimes picked pockets. Since it was believed that mothers were the primary moral influence in the home, and since the fathers were largely absentee, it was mothers who were blamed for neglecting their children, failing to keep them in school, or provide the proper moral supervision. Some reformers believed the best policy was to remove "neglected" children from their homes and place them in asylums, foster homes, or with Protestant families in rural areas; others favored reforming families of the poor by teaching daughters and mothers the domestic arts, so that the laboring poor could replicate the homes of the middle class. Boys and men received vocational training to help them become family breadwinners.

The planter family of the South was patriarchal: The master ruled over his wife, his children, and his slaves, and the plantation did not have two clearly separated spheres but was the site of home and work for master, mistress, and slaves.

Skilled workingmen subscribed to the belief that a mother should not leave the home to work and that a man should be the sole family breadwinner. Indeed, a man whose wife worked for wages was considered a poor provider. Beginning in the 1820s and 1830s, trade unionists advocated a "family wage" sufficient for a husband to support the family without relying on the labor of his wife. By the last half of the nineteenth century, union men wanted pay sufficient so that a man's children as well as his wife would not have to work. The effect of the family wage was to take women and children out of economic competition with men. For most workingmen, the notion of the family wage was not the reality. Very few families could subsist without income from a lodger, child labor, or a mother's income from outwork. Among poorer families, the contribution of children's scavenging or a daughter's occasional prostitution was necessary.

In contrast to the separate spheres of the northern middle class, the planter family of the South was patriarchal. The master ruled over his wife and children, and his slaves. Moreover, the plantation did not have two clearly separated spheres; it was the location of home and work for master, mistress, and slaves. The white mistress of the southern plantation differed from the "true woman" of the North. The belief of northerners in woman's purity, superficially resembled southern reverence for female chastity. The purity of the northern woman, however, was an emblem of *her* character; chastity in the southern woman was a certificate of racial purity and a husband's prestige.

The planter's role varied according to how many slaves he owned. Planters were expected to be providers and rulers of their family and slaves. The majority of southern slaveholders who owned fewer than ten slaves worked alongside them in the field: they cleared the land, plowed, planted and hoed. Large planters, however, supervised labor, bought and sold slaves and farmland, took their crops to market, acquired supplies, and engaged in a variety of financial transactions. Some dabbled in politics or worked as lawyers or store owners on the side.

The mistress of the slave household, like the northern farmer's wife, was responsible for the care of home, children, and gardens. The wives and daughters of small slaveholders planted and tended vegetable gardens, helped at harvest, milked the cows, looked after the smokehouse, cooked, and sewed. The mistress supervised servants who did the laundry, housework, and child care. Her special responsibilities included the care of the slaves—cutting and sewing their clothing, and nursing the sick and elderly among them. Many mistresses felt obligated to inculcate Christian religious principles in the slaves. Legendary southern hospitality required the mistress of a large plantation to be a model hostess to guests who stayed for days or dozens of visitors who came for breakfast and remained for the noonday meal. In the absence of her husband, the mistress also kept the plantation accounts.

Masters created the gender division of labor among slaves, since they assigned tasks to slave men, women, and children. Black men cleared the land, planted, plowed, weeded crops, harvested, repaired fences, and barns, dug ditches, fattened and killed hogs, picked cotton, and gathered corn. A few on larger plantations were also skilled craftsmen: blacksmiths, coopers, carpenters, stonemasons, weavers, mechanics, and millers. Slave women were not restricted to home and garden as were white women, but neither did they perform all the tasks of black men. Falling into a middle category, slave women were neither treated as women, to be protected from field labor, nor regarded as men. The women hoed, planted and picked cotton, dug potatoes, and planted rice in fields with water up to their knees. Slave women plowed, but less often than men. They did not do artisanal labor or serve as overseers and drivers. Slave women were laborers, but they had an added value in being able to produce slave children.

Slave fathers tried to be providers for their families as best they could. A father living on the neighboring plantation might bring his children sweet potatoes or some sugar. Fathers comforted their children when they were sick. Some men tried to protect their wives and children from physical or sexual abuse. A father had a responsibility for his wife and children, but the greatest bond in the slave family was between mother and child. She was less likely than her husband to be sold or to live on a neighboring plantation away from her children. The relationship between mother to child was assumed to be close, warm, and affectionate. Nonetheless, the mother-child bond was only one of several significant relationships within the slave family since African heritage recognized obligations between extended kin. In fact, American slaves were forced to depend on relatives and fictive kin for help if they tried to run away. Sisters, grandmothers, aunts, and other female relatives and quasi kin often mothered children.

The gender roles of slaves have been mistakenly regarded as egalitarian. It is true that the slave woman, like her male counterpart, might toil under the sun fourteen hours per day, six days a week. But the slave women actually worked a double day, putting in as many hours as men in the fields as well as doing family labor after dusk. Moreover, the idea of equality usually connotes a relationship freely chosen. The slaves had no choice in their work roles: these were assigned them by the master.

In leisure moments and on holidays, slaves demonstrated their own preference for North American gender roles. A slave husband sought to be the family provider by hunting, fishing, growing vegetables in a small plot, whittling furniture, or making tools. He tended to be a stern disciplinarian of children. Slave men believed that child care, cooking, and sewing were women's work, unsuitable for men. Masters sometimes punished black men by making them engage in female work, such as doing the laundry.

After emancipation, former slaves still living in the South aspired to adopt conventional American gender roles denied them during slavery. Sharecropper husbands negotiated the year's labor contract with a landlord and went to town for supplies. With their husbands' approval, black women in large numbers withdrew from field labor in order to care for home and children. But many families found that they could not subsist without a woman's contribution to field labor or family income, and eventually many sharecropper wives reluctantly took up the hoe. Moreover, black men sought to protect wives and daughters from physical and sexual attack by whites.

Africans came to America because they were forced to do so. Before emancipation, slave parents, no matter how strong the bonds of affection, could not pass along to children the gift of freedom. Immigrants, by contrast, chose to move to the New World. The decades between 1880 and 1920 comprised the high point of foreign immigration; most came from southern and eastern Europe, from rural areas and peasant cultures where patriarchy was the rule. Because immigrants were predominantly single men, family formation was delayed.

Many immigrant families did not contain the first requirement of patriarchy, a present, involved father. In some families the mother acted as dominant authority and in others the father ruled. When the husband was present, leisure and religious activities were generally segregated according to gender. For most immigrants, the husband and wife occupied separate worlds and shared very few activities in common. Orthodox Jewish women worshiped in a separate section of the synagogue. Some American Catholic parishes included an all-men's mass, while women formed the majority of worshipers at other masses. Husbands and wives often arrived at a party separately, and did not leave together.

The immigrant father was rarely the sole support of the family. His wages were not high enough and he was often out of work or sick. In order to survive, the household usually depended upon several sources of income, including the wages of one or more children. Immigrant families often took in boarders for whom the woman of the house usually cooked, cleaned, and sewed. After clearing the dishes, a mother might set to work with her children making artificial flowers, finishing cloaks, or doing laundry. The extent of this labor participation varied, depending on the family's economic need and the work opportunities available to mothers and children. Wage-earning Italian mothers preferred homework to factory jobs or domestic service. Black, Irish, and Scandinavian women frequently became servants or laundresses. Jewish women, rarely found in domestic service, often sewed garments by the piece at home or in small sweatshops; many opened their own shops or worked as shopkeepers with other family members.

Immigrant parents often took their daughters and sons out of school to help support the family. Exposed to American culture and more fluent in English than their parents, immigrant children served as interpreters of the new culture. Although they were family breadwinners, immigrant children still had to submit to the restrictions imposed by the family's patriarch. Sons were given more freedom than daughters; daughters were often expected to turn over their entire wages to their family as well as to conform to parental rules. Demands for greater freedom by unmarried daughters often provoked angry response from their Old World parents.

The immigrant woman's world was her home, the apartments of her neighbors, and the streets outside the family's living quarters. The domestic routines, obligations, and identity of these women left them isolated from American life. The immigrant mother was the least likely member of the family to speak or write English. She had received little formal instruction in the country of her birth. In America she usually lived in an ethnic neighborhood where she could rely on her native language and was not forced to learn English. The Irish woman was the exception to this general rule of woman's isolation. She was frequently employed as a domestic servant in a Yankee home prior to marrying, or as a laundress afterwards. Since her husband usually worked with other Irishmen and might have had minimal contact with Americans, the woman was more likely than the man to be the agent of Americanization.

The fact that immigrant mothers remained unassimilated offered proof that the group had not lost its cultural moorings. Native-born Americans also favored the idea that mothers should not work outside the home, but they did not approve of making the home into a family workshop or of taking children out of school to put them to work. In the twentieth century, as immigrant families entered the middle class, they generally adopted gender roles, fertility behavior, and child-rearing norms of the dominant society.

As in immigrant families, the father was rarely the sole breadwinner among blacks. The majority of black mothers did *not* earn wages outside the home until the 1960s. However, the mother's employment in the nineteenth century and most of the twentieth was invariably higher among blacks than among white immigrants for two reasons. Black husbands, predominantly employed as domestic servants and unskilled laborers, earned low wages and were often unemployed. Consequently, black women took jobs for pay. They preferred doing laundry in the home or taking in boarders, since these activities could be combined with child care without having to leave home. Black families were also less likely than immigrants to depend

After Emancipation, many former slave families found that they could not subsist without a woman's income. This Negro laundress is working on a Florida Plantation.

on child labor. Because of high mortality, rates among children and an effort to limit family size, there were fewer children to send to work. Moreover, black adolescents left home to find work, usually as field laborers or domestic servants, and generally kept a larger share of their wages for themselves. Because racial discrimination limited their factory and shop labor opportunities, black women usually became domestic servants in white homes where they confronted sexual harassment and racial condescension. Nevertheless, black women took pride in earning wages and being able to contribute to the family, and women who headed households were even more likely to be employed than those whose husbands were present.

Black husbands and fathers had greater difficulties in attaining the role of breadwinner as exemplified by males in the dominant society. They sometimes considered themselves failures *as men* because they were not able to provide adequately for their families. Black wives and mothers felt called upon to salvage male egos at the same time that they carried the double burden of combining outside work with domestic responsibilities. As women who earned a goodly share of family income, black wives and mothers had a great deal of influence over family decision making, spending, and child rearing. Poverty and racial discrimination forced this economic arrangement upon black families, and many tensions and conflicts in black marriages resulted.

Black husbands and fathers had greater difficulties in attaining the role of breadwinner: They sometimes considered themselves failures as men *because they were not able to provide adequately for their families.*

Companionate Marriage

Economic survival and opportunities for work shaped the choices confronting immigrant and black families. The American middle-class family, cushioned from the daily struggle for bread, still required a more modern updating of gender roles. The young woman of the 1920s, who bobbed her hair and smoked in public, did not want to suffer the restrictions of the "true woman." Growth in their educational and employment opportunities and the sexual revolution prompted young women to challenge some of the gender restrictions their mothers had tolerated, or even helped to put in place. Social scientists and commentators worried about the falling birthrate among the middle class and the rise in divorce. Juvenile court judge Ben Lindsey, in a book entitled *Companionate Marriage* (1927), called for lifting restrictions on divorce (especially for childless couples), the legalization of birth control, and sex education for youth.

The new woman wanted home and family, but a more modern marriage. Husband and wife should be soulmates and lovers, and as parents they should become the "pals" and playmates of their children. Although child rearing in such families was still important, the advice-givers tended to elevate to special importance the couple's sexual compatibility, an aspect of marriage neglected during the era of Victorian sexual repression. Anything that stood in the way of the couple's romantic and sexual intimacy threatened the marriage. Adultery was still feared, but the experts also railed against feminism, careers for women, remaining single, and sexual frigidity. Same-sex relationships in adolescence, once considered harmless adolescent crushes, were now regarded as deviant. In the new view, homosexuality in adults represented a pathological failure to find happiness in marital sexuality, a condition that might be cured through psychological counseling.

The new ideal of the companionate marriage, like the older doctrine of separate spheres, had little to say about the actual division of labor in the household. It was still assumed that the husband remained the breadwinner and the wife a full-time homemaker. But the companionate husband was expected to help out by doing the dishes and some of the housework and by allowing his wife access to money without having to ask for it. The father—now referred to as "dad" or the more affectionate, "Daddy"—was a recreational companion to his children, especially his sons. He taught them how to catch a ball, cast a fly, or pitch a tent.

The 1930s and 1940s thwarted the ability to achieve the companionate ideal, without in any way dampening its basic appeal. During the Depression many men failed to be good providers, let alone support the family solely by their efforts. Children had to quit school to go to work, many couples moved in with relatives, and others delayed childbearing. The birthrate fell during the Depression, as did the divorce rate. Housewives took in laundry or boarders to earn extra income, economized by gardening, canning, bargain hunting, making their own clothes, and by reviving women's traditional skills, such as baking bread, knitting, and sewing. Some poverty-stricken women turned to prostitution to make extra money. When other strategies failed wives took in homework, or wives and teenage boys worked outside the home.

It is often believed that World War II marked a revolution in gender roles, since many American women took on men's jobs, becoming welders, riveters, and full-time workers in the war industry. World War II did mark one important watershed in American history: The typical woman worker who, until that time had been young and single, was now married. Still, Rosie the Riveter was little more than the modern equivalent of the deputy husband, expected to fill job vacancies during her spouse's absence, then to resume her customary role as homemaker when he returned. A War Department brochure reminded female workers that "a woman is a substitute, like plastic instead of metal."

Despite women's participation in the war effort and the armed forces, the public still disapproved of married women leaving home to go to work. Such attitudes were reflected in the scanty government funding for child-care centers. Only one out of every ten children of women defense workers could find a slot in a federally funded child-care center. Children of mothers who could not find or afford babysitters often had to fend for themselves until their mother returned from work. Some women left their youngsters in a parked, locked car while they entered the plant.

Americans During and After World War II

Wartime relocation compressed into a few years' changes in Japanese American gender roles that might otherwise have taken a generation. Suspected of being enemy sympathizers or saboteurs, over one hundred thousand Japanese Americans, two-thirds of them born in the United States, were relocated from their homes in Pacific Coast states to internment camps in the western desert. At the camps families were housed in military barracks, subdivided into cramped family apartments. Some families tried to eat meals together, but for the most part the tradition of family dining broke down. Strict parental control of children dissolved. When some of the American-born Japanese were allowed to leave the camps to work in wartime industry, parents reluctantly agreed. The Japanese tradition of arranged marriage evaporated; young couples fell in love and married, with or without parental permission. Since men and women, parents and children were paid the same wages for doing camp labor, a father's authority as the family breadwinner broke down. As was true among Native Americans who experienced change in gender roles imposed by white missionaries and government agents, the older generation found their traditional values trampled upon, and had the hardest time adjusting. They frequently suffered from psychological depression after they were released from these camps.

THE MIDDLE-CLASS HOME. The return of prosperity after war's end, the building of suburban ranch houses and Cape Cods, and the importance of leisure for domestic life encouraged couples, especially from a broad range of the middle class, to live up to the ideal of bourgeois domesticity. Many women set aside their hopes for career to marry and have children. The marriage rate soared, couples married at younger ages, and they had more children. The fertility rate in the United States rose fifty percent from 1940 to 1957.

The ideal of manhood and womanhood in the 1950s blended some elements of the doctrine of separate spheres with the companionate marital ideal. American advertising in that decade portrayed the housewife as a dedicated consumer, who made most of the family's purchasing decisions. The "true woman" was not an inveterate shopper like her 1920s counterpart. But like the ideal woman from that earlier generation, the 1950s housewife was expected to keep romance alive in her marriage and worry if sexual passions cooled. In its emphasis on "occupation: housewife" and the importance of the mother in raising happy, well-adjusted children, the gender ideals of the 1950s functioned as the modern bearer of Victorian tradition.

Nothing was more important in rearing a child than mother love. Dr. Benjamin Spock's highly popular *Baby and Child Care* (1946) urged mothers to meet a child's needs for love, attention, and proper care. In so doing a mother in turn would find fulfillment. The ideal father was expected to be committed to the family, and urged to become involved in child care as an appropriate "sex role model." Psychological experts, studying fathers' absence during World War II, concluded that it caused innumerable social adjustment problems in children, especially sons. Some claimed that boys who did not have proper male role models became juvenile delinquents, violent criminals, or homosexuals. A father, although an appropriate sex role model, was not expected to perform too many domestic chores because it might confuse sons and daughters about proper sex-role identity.

All was not happy in the middle-class home of the 1950s. In receiving a college education, the middle-class woman's individual aspirations had been stirred. Pouring her productive energies into child rearing and home care did not provide fulfillment. A mother often lived vicariously through a child's good report card or a husband's promotions. Isolated and trapped, the housewife received too little credit for her sacrifices on behalf of home and children.

Reality in the 1950s was more various than the gender role dramas of such popular television situation comedies as *The Honeymooners*, *Father Knows Best*, or *I Love Lucy*. In fact the proportion of married women at work continued to climb. Much of the increase came from women over 35, and women whose children were already in school. Moreover, black families never did fit the model of husband as breadwinner, wife as mother at home. For many black women, and other women employed in arduous, low-paying work, a retreat to domesticity represented a welcome vacation from the double day of work and family responsibilities.

Working-class husbands in the 1950s, as in decades before, were expected to be "sturdy oaks," men who did not disclose their true feelings or reveal their vulnerability. Only a weak man, it was believed, asked for help or sympathy. They did not expect extensive conversation with a mate. A husband retained his male friends, with whom he socialized after work or on a boys' night out. When the marital relationship faltered, these men tended to withdraw. Instead of the ideal of marital equality, working-class men often believed that wives and children should be obedient and that the father should make the major decisions for the family. Wives did not expect husbands to help with the housework. Sympathetic commentators explained that the working-class man threw his weight around at home because he did not have the chance to do so in the larger world.

Studying the absence of fathers from families after World War I, some psychologists claimed that boys lacking proper male role models became juvenile delinquents, violent criminals or homosexuals.

THE QUASI-EGALITARIAN IDEAL. Expressions of domestic discontent first came from middle-class women—and later from their daughters. In 1963 Betty Friedan's *Feminine Mystique* announced that the family home, complete with stove, kitchen, blender, and two-car garage, was actually a velvet concentration camp. She considered women's investment in home and children, at the expense of education, employment, and involvement in public life, a bad bargain. Friedan's book was one of the several sparks that lit the fire of the women's liberation movement in the 1960s. Friedan wanted to reshape marriage and child rearing and send women into the work force, at least part-time. Some younger women influenced by the counterculture of the 1960s favored overthrow of the nuclear family. Others preferred lesbian to heterosexual relationships. A future was foreseen in which babies were bred in test tubes. Most feminists preferred reform of marriage rather than a radical attack on it. But there was general agreement that motherhood was not the true calling for all women, that a child could be raised well without constant attention from the biological mother, and that men as well as women were suited to be caretakers of young children.

The women's movement was the result, as well as the cause, of changes in gender roles. The political activism of the 1960s and the growth of college education for women created a feminist constituency. But more than any other social trend, the women's movement resulted from the growing numbers of women entering the labor force, and among these, especially college-educated and professional women. In 1955, thirty-five percent of mothers with school-age children were employed; by 1987 the comparable figure was seventy-one percent (Cynthia Taeuber, ed., *Statistical Handbook on Women in America*, p. 108). Women's employment outside the home had been advancing since the 1890s, but the slope in the curve turned sharply upward after World War II. Service and clerical jobs had become stereotyped as female work. These sectors of the economy were growing and hiring women workers. Barriers to the employment of married women in many jobs such as teaching fell, and more employers offered scheduled, part-time work, which made it easier for mothers to take a paying job and still arrive home before children returned from school.

Mothers of the 1950s often withdrew from paid work once their children were born, and did not return until their children entered school. By the 1970s inflation had whittled down the purchasing power of wages and a mother's job became an important means of maintaining a middle-class standard of living. The proportion of employed mothers with a child under age six rose from sixteen percent in 1955 to fifty-seven percent in 1987 (Taeuber, p. 108). Social attitudes toward the employment of mothers reversed themselves. A 1937 poll showed that eighty-two percent of the public opposed the employment of a married woman, if her husband could support the family. By 1972, sixty-eight percent of those queried favored married women working.

In the new quasi-egalitarian marital ideal, both husband and wife held paying jobs and assumed important responsibilities as parents. The new mother kissed her children goodbye and picked up her briefcase to go to the office. The new father, portrayed in film and advertising, helped his wife with deep breathing during labor, changed diapers, cooked evening meals, picked up his child at day care, and coached his daughter's soccer team. But even in the ideal, the woman did not do the same jobs as the man of the family. The husband was expected to be more involved in his work than his wife, and the wife was expected to take major responsibility for home and children. By the 1970s the working-class family had adopted many more middle-class elements. The boys' night out had all but disappeared. Husbands were more likely to stay at home in the evening watching television or doing home repairs. Working-class women wanted intimacy, sharing, and companionship in marriage, not simply a stable relationship with a man who turned over his paycheck and didn't drink or act violently.

In 1965–1966 National Time Diary Study, the 1975–1976 Study of Time Use, and the 1977 Quality of Employment Survey reported that husbands did a substantial amount of the housework and child care although considerably less than half (Joseph Pleck, *Working Wives, Working Husbands*, p. 30). Women in two-earner families still carried the heaviest burden of caring for home and children, while also contributing to family income. The wife made the dentist appointments and stayed home when the children were sick. She managed and coordinated domestic tasks and child care. The husband functioned as a "deputy wife" who assumed a variety of tasks his wife might delegate to him. Most often she had to ask for help, rather than expect fifty/fifty sharing as a matter of course. But the woman's "double day" was eased somewhat by the purchase of goods and services (child care, baby-sitters, and take-out food), a relaxed standard for home care, as well as an increase in the husband's responsibility for housework and child care. According to national surveys, a husband's share of total housework and child care rose from 20 percent in 1965 to 30 percent in 1981.

The new family ideal was not without its critics. The American family had undergone wrenching, dramatic changes since the 1960s—rising divorce rates, accompanied by more children being raised in fatherless homes; dramatic increases in teen sexuality, having as its consequence more teen pregnancy and higher rates of abortion; and the growth in the number of employed mothers, especially among women with young children. Homosexual couples were demanding to be recognized as families, too. A Gallup poll in 1977 found that half of the American public believed that the family was in trouble, if not in danger of extinction. Some women, disillusioned by the promise of personal fulfillment through career, abandoned high-paying jobs to become homemakers and mothers. Others blamed the woman's movement for encouraging mothers to leave the home, when children needed full-time attention. Political and social conservatives, along with religious opponents of abortion, asserted that they stood for "family values" against a tide of narcissism. They accused feminists of encouraging the sexual revolution, abortion, divorce, the devaluation of homemakers, and the growth of employment among mothers. The family could not survive, they argued, unless women sacrificed themselves for the sake of their children.

The proper roles for women and men were now subject to political debate. Putting rhetoric aside, however, one could see that the two-job family had become the dominant American family form by the 1960s. Families, consisting of a husband, a wife who was a full-time homemaker and children, had not disappeared but were a minority of American households. In 1988 about 20 percent of the adult population lived alone (Taeuber, *Statistical Handbook of Women in America*, p. 247). Many marriages were "blended," consisting of remarried couples, often with children from prior marriages. Some couples were "empty nesters" whose children had grown and left home. Others provided rooms for adult children, unable to afford housing on their own. About 2 percent were homosexual men or women who lived in diverse family arrangements (Robert E. Fay, Charles F. Turner, Albert D. Klassen, and John H. Gagnon, "Prevalence and Patterns of Same-Gender Sexual Contact Among Men," *Science* 243 [January 20, 1989]: 338–348).

As a result of the rising divorce rate and the birth of children to unwed mothers, the number of single-parent households, usually headed by a mother, rose. In 1988 13 percent of white households, 23 percent of Hispanic households, and 44 percent of black households were headed by single parents. The majority of black children were raised in mother-only households. Most such headed households were the outgrowth of divorce, and second, of the increase in childbearing among unmarried women. Because women's standard of living fell after divorce, and because many mother-only households had not received child support or the support they received was inadequate, these households were the most likely family form to fall below the poverty line.

In contrast to the "good dad" of advertising and television there were the "bad dads" who refused to financially support their children. Was the male role changing for better, or for worse? Most mothers who were awarded child support were receiving it, but they and their children were paying a "divorce penalty" since the award the courts handed down was not adequate to live on. Most "derelict dads" like their counterparts one hundred or two hundred years ago, were poor, unskilled, and ill-educated. Some claimed that men were refusing to honor their breadwinning obligations because they were no longer receiving the privileges of deference and domestic service from women. After all, feminists rejected the idea that a husband must carry the sole burden of family support. Did some men take their argument one step further, and abandon the idea of carrying *any* burden of family support? No doubt this was true for some men. At the same time, the largest group of men paying no child support were teen fathers who had little or no income.

Conclusion

Although American families have continued to divide productive labor by gender, men and women have come to share the work of the home. The growth of women's employment, which accelerated after World War II, has continued to have the most far-reaching consequences for the reordering of gender roles within the American family. Married women have become permanent participants in the paid labor force. The majority of employed wives in the early 1990s are full-time, not part-time, workers. Women's attachment to the world of work is still not the same as men's, but the gap is closing. Men's commitment to the home has increased as well, but it does not match that of women. Most, but by no means all, men take their responsibilities as family breadwinners seriously. Far more than his predecessors, the contemporary American husband has been sharing the domestic work.

Personal, cultural, economic, and institutional barriers have impeded Americans from a 50/50 sharing of the work of the home. Many husbands and wives have preferred a traditional gender division of labor. Many of the wives who wanted more equitable sharing of homework and childcare have not wanted to force the issue, fearing marital tension, and the prospect of divorce. Government and employers have offered only small incentives and limited options to ease the conflict between work and family obligations. Finally, all of the demands for change have faltered in confronting the economic fact that on average, men still earned more than women. A few "supermen" have shared at home and carried a full work load. But most men have sacrificed family for the sake of commitment to paid work. To do otherwise was to jeopardize the family's economic well-being. In sum, while many men have been committed to the ideal of equality in the abstract, the daily realities of existence have encouraged men to devote more time to work than to family, so that the mortgage and car payments could be met.

Few still believed that the husband was the "boss" of the family, the head of the household. The ideal of marriage as a more equal partnership has begun to emerge, shaped by economic realities and the ideological imperatives of the women's movement. But for most it is an ideal, not reality. Most Americans still believe that the husband has the greatest, if no longer the sole, responsibility for providing family income, and that he must act to protect the family from harm.

While a woman's place is no longer only the home, the home is still a woman's place. Changes in the overall status of women and their participation in the workforce have not radically altered some of the most salient features of the earlier doctrine of separate spheres. Consider the following statement: "The family and home are female concerns, and the mother-child bond is the most important family relationship." This statement could have been written in the 1830s, when the doctrine of separate spheres emerged, yet it is used by Theodore Caplow and his coauthors to describe family life in Muncie, Indiana, in the early 1980s. Despite all the evidence of changing gender roles since the 1960s, for better or worse, the association of women with home, child rearing, and family feeling, which emerged in the 1820s, remains the cornerstone of American domestic ideals. As had always been true, reality was more various than paeans to motherhood. Still the gender mainly responsible for family life—both its work and its rituals—was female.

[See also Family Structures; Household Labor; Reproduction and Parenthood; Sexual Behavior and Morality; Women and Work.]

BIBLIOGRAPHY

Overviews of Sexuality, Women's History, and Gender Roles in the Family

Degler, Carl N. *At Odds: Women and the Family in America from the Revolution to the Present* (1980).

D'Emilio, John, and Estelle B. Freedman. *Intimate Matters: A History of Sexuality in America* (1988).

Demos, John. *Past, Present, and Personal: The Family and the Life Course in American History* (1986).

Evans, Sara M. *Born for Liberty: A History of Women in America* (1989).

Mintz, Steven, and Susan Kellogg. *Domestic Revolutions: A Social History of American Family Life* (1988).

Women's Roles During the Colonial and Revolutionary Eras

Carr, Lois, and Lorena Walsh. "The Planter's Wife: The Experience of White Women in 17th-Century Maryland. "In *A Heritage of Her Own: Toward a New Social History of American Women*, edited by Nancy Cott and Elizabeth H. Pleck (1979).

Kerber, Linda K. *Women of the Republic: Intellect and Ideology in Revolutionary America* (1980).

Norton, Mary Beth. *Liberty's Daughters: The Revolutionary Experience of American Women, 1750–1800* (1980).
Norton, Mary Beth. "The Evolution of White Women's Experience in Early America." *American Historical Review* 89 (June 1984): 593–619.
Ulrich, Laurel Thatcher. *Good Wives: Image and Reality in the Lives of Women in Northern New England, 1650–1750* (1982).

Nineteenth-Century Studies

Fargaher, John Mack. *Women and Men on the Overland Trail* (1979).
Grossberg, Michael. *Governing the Hearth: Law and the Family in Nineteenth-Century America* (1985).
Rothman, Ellen K. *Hands and Hearts: A History of Courtship in America* (1984).
Ryan, Mary P. *Cradle of the Middle Class: The Family in Oneida County, New York, 1790–1865* (1981).
Stansell, Christine. *City of Women: Sex and Class in New York, 1798–1860* (1986).
Welter, Barbara. "The Cult of True Womanhood: 1820–1860." *American Quarterly* 18, no. 2 (1966): 151–174.

Women's Work

Goldin, Claudia Dale. *Understanding the Gender Gap: An Economic History of American Women* (1990).
Jones, Jacqueline. *Labor of Love, Labor of Sorrow: Black Women, Work, and the Family from Slavery to the Present* (1985).
Kessler-Harris, Alice. *Out to Work: A History of Wage-earning Women in the United States* (1982).
Strasser, Susan. *Never Done: A History of American Housework* (1982).

Racial and Ethnic Minorities

Del Castillo, R. Griswold. "La Familia Chicana: Social Changes in the Chicano Family of Los Angeles 1850–1880." *Journal of Ethnic Studies* 3, no. 1 (1975): 41–58.
Diner, Hasia R. Erin's *Daughters in America: Irish Immigrant Women in the Nineteenth Century* (1983).
Horton, James Oliver. "Freedom's Yoke: Gender Conventions Among Antebellum Free Blacks." *Feminist Studies* 12, no. 1 (Spring 1986): 51–76.
Jensen, Joan M. "Native American Women and Agriculture: A Seneca Case Study." *Sex Roles* 3, no. 5 (1977): 423–440.
Kulikoff, Allan. "The Beginnings of the Afro-American Family in Maryland." In *The American Family in Socio-Historical Perspective*, edited by Michael Gordon (1978).
Matsumoto, Valerie. "Japanese American Women During World War II." In Ellen Carol DuBois and Vicki L. Ruiz, *Unequal Sisters: A Multicultural Reader in U.S. Women's History* (1990).
Perdue, Theda. "Southern Indians and the Cult of True Womanhood." In *The Web of Southern Social Relations: Women, Family, and Education*, edited by Walter J. Fraser, Jr., R. Frank Saunders, Jr., and Jon L. Wakelyn (1985).
Young, Mary E. "Women, Civilization and the Indian Question." In *Women's America: Refocusing the Past*, edited by Linda Kerber and Jane De Hart-Mathews. (1982).

Male Roles in the Family

Pleck, Joseph H. "American Fathering in Historical Perspective." In *Changing Men: New Directions in Research on Men and Masculinity*, edited by Michael S. Kimmel (1987).
Rotundo, E. Anthony. "American Fatherhood: A Historical Perspective." *American Behavioral Scientist* 29, no. 1 (1985): 7–23.

Gender Roles in the Family from 1920 to the Present

Anderson, Karen. *Wartime Women: Sex Roles, Family Relations, and the Status of Women During World War II* (1981).
Caplow, Theodore, et al. *Middletown Families: Fifty Years of Change and Continuity* (1982).
Ehrenreich, Barbara. *The Hearts of Men: American Dreams and the Flight from Commitment* (1983).
May, Elaine Tyler. *Homeward Bound: American Families in the Cold War Era* (1988).
Pleck, Joseph H. *Working Wives, Working Husbands* (1985).
Wandersee, Winifred D. *Women's Work and Family Values, 1920–1940* (1981).

— ELIZABETH H. PLECK

GEOGRAPHICAL MOBILITY

Americans have been a highly mobile people. Their geographical mobility has shaped the history and development of the United States. They have moved to the frontier to take advantage of the country's abundant land and natural resources, and they have moved to the cities to work in expanding industries and factories. Both of these migration streams exemplify how available opportunities attract migrants trying to better themselves through their movement.

Theories of geographical mobility have at least implicitly considered conditions thrusting movers away from an area and the opportunities attracting them to a destination: the "push" and "pull" factors. Furthermore, much of past research has suggested that migrants respond primarily to economic conditions. According to this labor mobility model, labor flows from areas with few economic opportunities to areas with surplus opportunities as a means of establishing equilibrium between available jobs and available workers. Yet, just as not all areas have equal resources, so not all workers have equal abilities to take advantage of an opportunity. To understand mobility fully, therefore, it is necessary to consider how the patterns of movement differ for specific groups within the population. For example, mobility patterns differ by age and socioeconomic status, and these differences have varied over time.

Geographical mobility involves a change in an individual's usual place of residence. Measuring this change in residence has been somewhat problematic. Typically, place of residence is compared at two points in time. If the locations differ, the individual is assumed to have moved once. Of course, frequently the individual has moved more than once. The possibility also exists that an individual who has moved more than once may not be counted as mobile at all if the second move is back to the original residence.

An additional issue involved with this measure is how different the location must be before mobility is assumed to have occurred. Movement across the country is different from movement across town. Considering any change of residence, no matter how short the distance involved, as mobility, as is done in the United States, will produce much higher mobility rates than if only those moves crossing some specified boundary are considered. In fact, the Census Bureau does distinguish between mobility (any move) and migration (crossing a county line), and finds many more people who are mobile than who are migrants.

Historical Trends

COLONIAL PERIOD. Much of what is known about geographical mobility during the early history of this country comes from studies of persistence within a community. These studies attempt to follow individuals over time by using records available for a community at two or more points in time. Several types of records have been used for these studies, including tax rolls, militia registers, and city directories. If an individual is recorded at both points in time, he or she is considered not to have moved away from the community. Persistence rates, the percent of the population still in the area at the second time, calculated from these sources are not completely accurate. Some people could have not been enumerated at the second time even if they had not moved. For example, rather than moving, the person could have died. Furthermore, enumeration was probably more complete for higher-status individuals. Given the limitations of record linkage, results from these studies should be viewed with caution.

In spite of their limitations, studies determining persistence rates do provide some information about geographical mobility. They suggest that commercial cities on the East Coast, like Boston, had lower persistence rates than smaller farming towns in the interior, like Andover and Dedham, Massachusetts. Such a difference should not be surprising. The coastal cities frequently served as ports of entry for immigrants who were pulled to the interior by better opportunities. As long as they had land, those living in the interior villages did not need to seek opportunities elsewhere.

Some of the mobility that occurred in the smaller towns was within the town limits, as in Andover, where many of the original settlers moved from the town center to the periphery for better farmland. The original settlers also were able to limit movement of their children through their control of the community's land—movement that has been learned about through the use of record linking as well as of wills and property records. First-generation fathers in Andover restricted the movement of their sons, especially the eldest, by withholding land from them until the sons were older, thus causing the sons to marry relatively late in life. Often along with the inheritance would come an obligation to care for the father's widow, a duty that further restricted the son's mobility. Parents also controlled their daughters' mobility through both inheritances and marriages. If a woman married a man from another town, she typically moved to his town.

Movement into the interior of the continent was restricted by the Appalachians. These mountains served as a formidable physical barrier to migrants and also marked the line beyond which the British attempted to restrict settlement. A royal proclamation of 1763 forbade surveys beyond the Appalachians although this policy was altered over the next several years to open new lands in the Ohio region.

Natural barriers forced those leaving the Middle Atlantic region to move south. This stream was dominated by Scotch-Irish but also included smaller groups with other ethnic backgrounds who settled throughout the Southeast. One such group was the German Lutherans, whose descendants can still be found scattered throughout the predominantly Baptist-Methodist South today.

Pennsylvania, Maryland, and Virginia appear to have been losing young men through out-migration before the American Revolution. They were pushed from older, densely settled coastal regions in search of open spaces for new settlements. Many of these migrants moved to the Carolinas. Another stream flowed northward into upstate New York and parts of New England; it originated mostly north of Pennsylvania and contributed to the high in-migration to New York and New Hampshire.

ADVANCING THE FRONTIER. The first census of the United States, taken in 1790, provided a reasonable count of the nearly four million citizens of the new country. It did not, however, provide any information on previous places of residence from which mobility patterns could be ascertained. Not until the 1850 census was even place of birth asked. After the 1800 census, it was possible to compare records for two time periods, thereby providing an additional source for record linkage to determine migration.

Many studies using record linkage have found higher persistence rates—lower rates of geographical mobility—among higher-status individuals. Again, these results may reflect weaknesses of the method. Higher-status individuals were more likely to be recorded. It is not too surprising that the unskilled, the propertyless, and the poor would find a need to move during the nineteenth century. The costs of mobility were relatively low, and the benefits of settling in a new area could be great.

Almost 95 percent of the population in 1790 lived east of the Appalachians. In fact, most of the 1790 population lived on or near the coast in the Northeast and Middle Atlantic regions. Thus the geographical center of the population was about 23 miles (37 kilometers) east of Baltimore—the farthest east it would ever be.

The barrier of the mountains was soon overcome. Led by frontiersmen like Daniel Boone, whose exploits have become an important part of the frontier culture, settlers followed the Wilderness Road, which Boone had helped to cut in 1775. Many of these pioneers were children of the settlers who had moved into Virginia from Pennsylvania a generation earlier and now were pulled to new frontiers opening farther west.

Some of these settlers and their families continued into Indiana and Illinois (Abraham Lincoln's family was among them). Interestingly, much of the movement was almost directly westward. Some Virginians, as well as newer Kentuckians and Tennesseeans, began to push up into Ohio and other East North Central states. The Middle Atlantic states also sent settlers to the Ohio basin who took with them their beliefs and practices.

Northerners, particularly New Yorkers and southern New Englanders, were attracted to the opportunities in the Midwest at latitudes similar to those of their origins; they settled in upper Ohio, southern Michigan, and Wisconsin before pushing even farther into the middle western plains. The opening of the Erie Canal in 1825 provided a new water route, and many took advantage of improved transportation to move to the interior. This new means of transportation facilitated the movement of goods as well as people. By 1800 over fifty thousand people were living in what are now the states of Ohio, Indiana, Illinois, Wisconsin, and Michigan, the majority of them in Ohio.

New Englanders played a more significant role than their numbers might suggest. In both the first and the second decades of the nineteenth century, the New England region experienced net out-migration: 1 percent in the first decade and 2 percent between 1810 and 1820. New Englanders took with them their educational system as well as their business skills. Regional origins were identifiable when people moved into the Midwest, but a new culture blended the traits of the various regional groups.

Also important in expanding the country were the Louisiana Purchase in 1803 and the reduction of tensions between the United States and Britain at about the same time. Gaining the Louisiana Territory further opened the area west of the Mississippi. Between 1810 and 1820, Louisiana almost doubled its population from about 77,000 to over 153,000. Then Texas declared its independence from Mexico on 2 March 1836. Mexico had consistently tried to limit the number of American settlers in the Southwest. The settlers, over thirty thousand when the fighting began, wanted to Americanize Texas and led the fighting against Mexico. Texas quickly won its independence, thereby increasing its attractiveness to those from the United States. With the granting of statehood at the end of 1845, Texans finally won what they had sought since moving to the region. Five years later the first federal census of the state found that it had almost 213,000 people.

The gold-seeking Forty-niners rapidly increased the population of California from fewer than one thousand Americans in 1846 to 93,000 in 1850; other important gold strikes included one near Pike's Peak (1858), which attracted perhaps 100,000.

During the 1820s and 1830s a few hundred traders followed the Santa Fe Trail to New Mexico. The Mexican government permitted this movement, probably not overly concerned because of the small number of people involved. As in many areas of the West, the early settlers established a foothold and laid the groundwork for further movement to the Southwest.

A similar foothold was established in the Pacific Northwest. Methodists established a mission in Oregon in the early 1830s, and they spread the word about favorable conditions in the region. By the 1840s, hundreds of pioneers were traveling the Oregon Trail, passing through Missouri and Wyoming, and eventually reaching Oregon. By the middle of the decade about five thousand Americans were settled in the region.

THE GOLD RUSH. Traders and other explorers blazed the trails that later were followed by the wagon trains. The discovery of gold created an economic pull for miners seeking a quick fortune. The Forty-niners rapidly increased the population of California from fewer than a thousand Americans in 1846 to 93,000 in 1850. Other important gold strikes included one near Pike's Peak (1858), which attracted perhaps one hundred thousand in search of wealth that many did not find. The last important strike occurred at Cripple Creek, Colorado, in the early 1890s.

Many of these miners did not strike it rich by discovering gold, but some did contribute to the belief that social mobility could result from physical mobility. Yet for every successful gold mining settlement, there is probably at least one ghost town where the gold quickly ran out. Those settlements which survived and prospered frequently had more resources than just gold. They had favorable environments allowing residents to engage in activities other than mining. Perhaps they were at the intersection of transportation lines, as was Sacramento, founded at the junction of the Sacramento and American rivers. Many people who originally went west in search of gold became successful after they switched from mining to other activities. They opened stores, or more likely trading posts, and provided other services to the miners and settlers who followed. Eventually a stable community grew to replace the boisterous mining settlement.

The discovery of gold was a stimulus for movement to California and contributed to the territory's growth. California also attracted migrants because of the importance of its ports. Ships from the East Coast called regularly. In addition, individuals of Spanish descent were settling in California, thereby contributing to its distinctive Spanish flavor. By 1860 the state had grown to a population of almost four hundred thousand, about four times its size in 1850.

THE MORMONS. At about the same time that adventurers were seeking their fortune in the gold rush, others were searching for an area where they could pursue another type of reward: fulfilling the promises of their religion. The Mormon religious movement had begun in the early 1830s in upstate New York. Pushed out of New York because of conflict over their beliefs, the Mormons, in a continued search for a homeland free from religious persecution, moved to Ohio, Missouri, Illinois, and finally Utah.

Following the death of their founder, Joseph Smith, in 1844, Brigham Young took over the leadership of the Mormons. Young left Illinois in 1846 with a small, well-prepared group, much better organized and equipped than most groups moving west at the time. By 1847 these migrants had arrived at the Great Salt Lake, an area that proved to be an ideal home for the Mormons. It was isolated enough for them to practice their religion without interference and was protected from attack by natural features; yet it was close enough to the Oregon Trail for trade with passing settlers. The area was rather barren, but to the Mormons it provided opportunities. Working together under the leadership of church authorities, they survived and prospered.

These towns also had as strong a religious influence as colonial New England towns had often had. Mormons carefully planned their towns in the New England style, in contrast with the isolated homestead patterns characteristic of much of the rest of the region. Mormons established an irrigation system permitting agricultural development. As they became secure and prosperous, they spread throughout what was to become Utah, taking with them their religiously based social system and their form of community organization. The Utah Territory almost quadrupled in size between 1850 and 1860, at which time it had over forty thousand residents, most of whom were Mormon.

MANIFEST DESTINY. One of the biggest challenges in settling the frontier came from Native Americans, who did not leave easily or peacefully as they continued to be pushed westward. The conflicts between the settlers and the natives played an important part in the history of the West, a role that has been documented by both the academic community and in popular entertainment media. Certainly these battles played a significant role in shaping the culture that emerged around the old West. Children today play cowhands and Indians, imitating their favorite figures from this earlier time. Furthermore, a large number of books portray the settling of this region. The Western movie may even have helped Ronald Reagan to become president—he became well known through his appearances in films and television programs about the western experience.

Citizens of the United States came to see it as their manifest destiny to fill the continent—at least the part which they felt Canada could not reasonably claim. In fact, filling the frontier became almost an all-encompassing passion of the country. The land beckoned with opportunities attracting settlers. The people drawn by these opportunities were the restless ones who saw the chance to better themselves. They worked to create a new life for themselves while creating the institutions and organizations of a new community.

Frontier values spread and became incorporated into American culture. The frontier was a place of opportunities for those willing to work hard and to take a chance. With hard work an individual could survive and prosper. The frontier was also a land of plenty contributing to the wasteful overconsumption characteristic of American culture. But perhaps the overriding value emerging from the frontier was optimism. The United States became the land of opportunity both for those already here and for millions of immigrants. Opportunities for geographical mobility were readily available, and geographical mobility was perceived by many to lead to social mobility. All was possible for the individual in a democratic society.

As the Civil War approached, there was increased concern about geographical mobility. In 1850, for the first time, the census asked about place of birth. Almost one-fourth of the native-born population reported living in a state other than the one in which they were born. Further evidence of increased concern about mobility is the fact that a census conducted in New York State asked respondents how long they had lived in their community.

These studies demonstrated a mobile population; in addition, they showed a population moving westward in search of opportunities. By the Civil War almost half of the population lived west of the Appalachians. Americans were already following Horace Greeley's suggestion that they go west. The geographic center had moved west to 20 miles (32 kilometers) southeast of Chillicothe, Ohio. Mountains obviously were no longer a barrier to migration. Trails had been cut through the mountain valleys and passes, and water routes carried migrants westward. Even though a significant proportion of the population was no longer living on the East Coast, the United States had not yet fulfilled its manifest destiny. Most of the West was still wide open, waiting for the coming of the railroad to transport settlers and goods to the region.

AFTER THE CIVIL WAR. The Civil War marks an important turning point in the history of the United States. A number of changes in the mobility patterns of the country began about this time. Many southerners, both black and white, were displaced by the war and its aftermath. Some of these southerners pushed west; others moved to the industrializing cities of the North.

The South also attracted significant migration during Reconstruction. Carpetbaggers, Republican northerners moving to the South, are probably the best-known of these migrants. While the number of Carpetbaggers was not great, their influence on the region and its history is significant. In addition, other northerners who were neither Republican nor politically active settled in the South.

The total number moving into the South was small. In 1870 only about 133,000 of the 6.5 million counted in the census South (a Census Bureau region that includes more states than were in the Confederacy) were born in New England or the Middle Atlantic region. Some of these individuals moved south before the war. Including those born in East-North Central states doubles the number of "northern" born, who still were only a small percent of the total number of southerners.

Many moving to the South saw the region as a land of economic opportunities—an image that many southern states tried to cultivate. This image further demonstrates the historical importance of the labor mobility model for explaining geographical mobility. During this period southern states actively tried to recruit new residents. Many states had agencies to advertise their opportunities. They even sent representatives to Europe to recruit immigrants.

Some in-migrants during Reconstruction were Union soldiers who had fought in the region and had been attracted by the southern environment. Others moved to the South because they felt they could help rebuild the region. Many of this latter group saw the potential for personal profit and advancement, but others had more altruistic motives for their movement, such as helping to educate the freedmen.

CLOSING THE FRONTIER. Southerners who could no longer support themselves in the South left the region. They sought new lands in the West, in the Midwest, and in the border states. They joined others seeking their fortunes in newly opened lands. Poor farmers and laborers felt they could be more successful by moving. They saw the opportunity to own their land, to be their own boss. Between 1870 and 1900, more new land was settled than had been settled in the history of the country. Over 430 million acres (172 million hectares) were opened, much of which went into agricultural production.

Increased population pressure contributed to the development of new areas, as did increased industrialization and improvements in transportation. In addition, more reliable information coming from the West about the types and amounts of land available provided a better picture of the opportunities. Many Americans, gaining their information from geography texts published during the first half of the nineteenth century, had an image of the great American West as the great American desert. As traders and settlers moved across the region, more accurate information filtered back to the East.

Many of the pioneers moving to the Great Plains were pushed by dissatisfaction with their home or by perceived overcrowding. During the 1870s most of the states bordering the Mississippi, with the exception of Arkansas, experienced net out-migration. Tennessee, for example, is estimated to have had 91,800 more people move out than move in. Texas, Kansas, Nebraska, and the Dakotas were all gaining people. Texas added over 308,500 more than it lost, Kansas 366,800, Nebraska 204,400, and the Dakotas 86,800. These territories attracted both rural and urban dwellers, and new cities grew to provide services. A hierarchy of cities emerged, each higher order serving an increasingly larger hinterland (as principles of central place theory would suggest).

The agriculturalists developing the rural areas faced many problems. The environment often was harsh. In years of favorable weather, settlements increased, only to decline in years with poorer conditions. For example, the grasshopper invasion of the mid 1870s forced many pioneers to reconsider their decisions to settle the prairie and to seek other places of residence.

Those who stayed had to develop new methods of farming and ranching. The wide-open spaces of the Great Plains required fencing to contain cattle in a given area, leading to the invention of barbed wire as an inexpensive means of fencing the prairie. Lack of trees and water led to innovations such as sod houses. Windmills were developed to help pump water, and dry farming techniques were employed to conserve limited water supplies.

Another technological development that made possible the settling of the Great Plains was the railroad. One of the most significant events in the history of the West was the joining of the Union Pacific and the Central Pacific at Promontory Point, Utah, in 1869. In addition to transporting settlers to the West, the railroad provided a means for shipping the goods they produced to the markets in the East.

Railroads contributed to closing the frontier in other ways. They were large property holders, having been granted extensive rights-of-way along the tracks. They went to considerable effort to advertise and to sell this land. Selling their land helped to create settlements, which in turn created demand for the railroads to carry freight that would help the companies meet their expenses. In Wyoming, for example, towns such as Cheyenne and Laramie were laid out along the railroad right-of-way, although they remained sparsely settled for years.

One of the important events in the history of the West was the joining of the Union Pacific and Central Pacific railroads; aside from transporting settlers to the West, the railroad provided a means for shipping the goods they produced to the markets in the East.

The passing of the homestead acts, one in 1862 and another in 1866, further contributed to settlement of the Great Plains. Many industrialists opposed passing these acts because opening up new lands would decrease the supply of labor for their factories.

The Homestead Act of 1862 had some success. Any citizen could pay a ten-dollar filing fee and claim 160 acres (64 hectares) of public domain in the West. After five years of residence, the claimant would receive title to the land. The 1862 act was not a complete success, however. Much of the best land was claimed by speculators who hoped to sell it at a profit. They prevented many farmers and laborers from being able to move by keeping land prices high. Farmers and laborers could not afford enough land for profitable farms if they also had to cover the cost of moving.

The Homestead Act passed in 1866 was primarily directed toward providing land in the Southwest for the freed slaves. As with many programs to help African Americans, this one was a failure. Some blacks did join the movement west, however. Many followed Henry Adams and Benjamin "Pap" Singleton in the Kansas Exodus of 1879. Pushed by social and economic discrimination in the South, these blacks were attracted to a promised land free from racial intolerance. Estimates of the number of blacks involved vary. Between 1870 and 1880 the Census Bureau reported an increase in the black population of Kansas from 17,000 to 43,000.

Probably the most famous land rush occurred in 1889, when Oklahoma was opened for settlement. The federal government negotiated with Native Americans to free the Oklahoma Territory for white settlement. When the horns were sounded, signaling the opening of the territory, thousands rushed to stake their claims. In many cases they found "sooners" already there. These sooners had entered the territory early to grab the best land. By the time Oklahoma became a state in 1907, more than a half a million inhabitants had been attracted.

When Oklahoma became a state, the frontier was closing, at least in the minds of many. In 1890, about the time that Frederick Jackson Turner was declaring the significance of the frontier in American history, the superintendent of the census was declaring the frontier closed. Over one-fourth of the population of the United States lived west of the Mississippi. There remained open spaces in the West, as well as in the East, but no line could be drawn to mark the frontier. Settlements across the country served as bases for further movement into the remaining open spaces and allowed the country to turn its attention away from the frontier to other types of settlement.

URBANIZATION. Movement to the frontier constituted one major migration stream throughout the history of the United States. A second major stream was the movement to urban areas. In fact, in many ways the city served just as much as a safety valve for a rapidly growing population as did the frontier. Cities began with the colonization of the continent, and they played an important role in American development. The majority of growth throughout the nineteenth century was in cities, not at the frontier. But city growth, and more generally growth in urban areas, increased dramatically during the latter part of the nineteenth century, about the time the frontier began to close. However, rapid urbanization was due to more than the closing of the frontier.

Immigrants made a major contribution to urban growth, and immigration increased during the late nineteenth and early twentieth centuries. Immigrants were most important for cities in the Northeast and Midwest. Rural-to-urban migration increased during this time period, being especially significant for the growth of southern and western cities. Rural migrants were both pushed from the countryside and pulled to the cities. Increasingly mechanized agriculture required larger farms, but fewer people, for greater efficiency. Smaller farmers such as southern sharecroppers could not compete. Southern farmers also were losing the fight against the boll weevil, and were forced to leave their farms for cities. By 1880 less than half of the labor force was employed in agriculture.

The implements being introduced on the farms were produced in urban industries. Northern cities began to industrialize first, but not long after the Civil War, southern cities followed. Birmingham, Alabama, for example, built steel mills, and Greenville, South Carolina, attracted textile mills. As opportunities became limited in rural areas and new opportunities were created in urban areas for unskilled laborers, rural dwellers moved to take advantage of the opportunities.

Young people, both male and female, white and black, left their parents' homes to seek jobs in the new factories, both to improve their life chances and to establish their independence. Men found jobs in factories and in emerging service industries that were developing to meet the needs of an increasingly larger population. Women also worked in factories, particularly textile mills in New England and later in the South. Furthermore, many women found jobs as domestics. For young women, working outside the home usually lasted until they married, at which time they quit their paid job. Not until World War II did a large percentage of married women living in cities work outside the home.

Movement away from home did not break family ties completely. Young people sent money home to help support their families and returned to visit. In addition, they received support from relatives living in the cities, typically the relatives who had provided information about the urban opportunities in the first place. Households in the cities took in both related and unrelated boarders and lodgers, providing a homelike atmosphere for first-generation city dwellers. With marriage, these boarders established their own households.

Young men and women wanted jobs in industrializing cities, but the bright lights and excitement of city living also attracted them. Some of the literature of the day discussed the dullness of rural life and the freshness of the city, though not all scholars presented the city in a positive light. Many of the early American sociologists, particularly those at the University of Chicago, were concerned with the social problems that faced rapidly growing industrial cities such as Chicago. They longed for the

The Homestead Acts of 1862 and 1866 tended to benefit white settlers like this Nebraska family and speculators who hoped to sell the land for a profit.

idyllic experience, the gemeinschaft, of smaller settlements. Many city dwellers had that same longing and moved back to the rural areas they had left. Poor southern textile workers were noted for their frequent movement between factories and farms.

Cities continued to grow and to spread their influence. By 1920 only the South, of the four major census regions, had more people living in rural than in urban areas. It is difficult to underestimate the importance of industrialization for movement to urban areas. There were, however, other technological innovations that contributed to movement. Improvement in transportation greatly increased the size of a city's hinterlands, making it possible to move goods over greater distances. The railroad, for example, played a major role in the growth of midwestern cities such as Chicago. More recently, growth in air transportation has contributed to Atlanta's emergence as a regional center. Furthermore, the invention of the elevator allowed for expansion upward and for greater spatial concentration. Only with extensive automobile ownership were cities able to spread out to create the urban sprawl familiar today.

John Steinbeck's 1939 novel, The Grapes of Wrath, *followed a poor Oklahoma migrant family's trek to California, showing the often hostile conditions they faced and how their movement led to a period of struggle for basic necessities.*

BLACK MIGRATION. Blacks tend to move less than whites, and they tend to move over shorter distances. Before emancipation, blacks had been limited in their ability to move, and their movement was largely forced on them by their owners. Those who gained their freedom before the Civil War often sought refuge through the Underground Railroad in the North. By moving to the North, blacks felt they could escape the racial intolerance of the South and find opportunities for paid employment.

With emancipation, blacks as a whole gained more freedom to choose their place of residence, although their movement was still restricted by economic and social conditions. As noted before, some blacks were attracted to Kansas. Other freed blacks chose cities in both the South and the North. The few who moved to the North during the nineteenth century blazed the trails for later generations of blacks. They established both support networks and information networks to ease the burdens on future migrants. Family members and friends followed these pioneers to the same northern cities.

During the two world wars, large numbers of blacks moved north to cities. The 1920 census found that the North had gained about 695,000 southern-born blacks through domestic migration. Between 1940 and 1950, New York State alone gained almost 244,000 blacks born in another state. Illinois added 180,000 during this period and Michigan 163,000, reflecting the flow of black migration into New York, Chicago, and Detroit. Demand for labor for the wartime industries was high. The traditional sources of labor were low. White males were fighting the war. Immigration was restricted, especially during World War I, leaving positions available for any able-bodied individual, including blacks.

Black movement was influenced by economic conditions, and thus it experienced a significant decline during the Great Depression between the Wars. Social conditions also strongly influenced black movement. Blacks desired to escape the castelike southern system and perceived more equal treatment in the North—which, of course, was not always the case. Still, the desire for greater equality contributed to black movement to northern cities into the 1950s and 1960s.

OKIES AND HILLBILLIES. During the Depression, general residential mobility declined. Nevertheless, some of the most enduring images of internal migration come from this period—images of poor, displaced farmers moving from Oklahoma and the surrounding Dust Bowl to the bountiful West. As many as one hundred thousand Oklahomans moved to California during the 1930s, accompanied by another quarter of a million moving from the surrounding states to the West.

The strongest of these images, perhaps, comes from John Steinbeck's *The Grapes of Wrath* (1939). His descriptions brought the Okies to the country's attention. Steinbeck showed that migrants often faced hostile conditions. Their movement did not necessarily produce immediate benefits but frequently led to a period of struggle for basic necessities. As Steinbeck suggested, many of the Okies, who included migrants from Texas, Arkansas, and Missouri in addition to those from Oklahoma, had to live in their cars or in tents or shacks. The term "Okie" was not one of endearment; it was used by natives to denigrate migrants. Internal migrants were seen in a negative light, not as rugged pioneers changing residences for upward social mobility but as poor, homeless families with little hope for the future.

A negative image of migrants also can be seen in the treatment of those who left Appalachia during the 1930s and 1940s, and even among those moving more recently. Poor whites left the hills of Kentucky, Tennessee, and West Virginia to seek a better life in the cities of the Midwest. By 1930 over 390,000 people born in these three states lived in Ohio. These "hillbillies," a term with connotations much like those of "Okies," did not totally leave their old communities behind. They maintained close family ties and communication links both back to the hills and with their fellow migrants. Like the Okies, this group was not always appreciated or admired in its new residences. In midwestern cities such as Cincinnati, the "hillbilly" neighborhoods can still be seen.

SUBURBANIZATION. Recognizing the interdependence between a city and its surrounding counties, the Census Bureau in 1950 created the Standard Metropolitan Area, later replaced by the Standard Metropolitan Statistical Area and still later by the Metropolitan Statistical Area. Metropolitan areas included the central city and the surrounding counties that were socially and economically integrated with the city. The Census Bureau was somewhat late in recognizing the existence of such areas. Growth around cities—suburbanization—had started much earlier.

During the first half of the twentieth century, growth in suburban areas accounted for about half of "metropolitan" growth. As the central cities filled, urban dwellers began to move to the open space surrounding cities. This trend accelerated during the 1950s. Approximately 80 percent of the metropolitan growth during this decade was suburban.

The post–World War II baby boom contributed to suburbanization. Newly formed families with young children sought residences with enough land for a yard in which the children could play, but they wanted to be close enough to the city to take advantage of its social and economic opportunities.

Suburbs provided the ideal compromise, especially since the government was building a system of limited-access highways making movement between the cities and the suburbs easier. The government also began to provide low-interest home loans through the Federal Housing Administration and the Veterans Administration. The 1950s were characterized by economic expansion. Stable jobs meant that people could afford to buy their dream homes in the suburbs. The development of mass home-building techniques made these homes more affordable, but the middle class remained most likely to take advantage of these opportunities.

Up to 1970, suburbs were almost totally white as blacks became increasingly concentrated in central cities. More recently diversity has increased significantly in the suburbs. Suburbs have continued to attract whites trying to escape the buildup of central cities, and since the 1970s more blacks, especially middle-class blacks, have been moving to the suburbs. Suburban neighborhoods remain highly racially segregated, as do central-city neighborhoods; but suburbs in general contain rising numbers of minorities.

Recent Trends

GENTRIFICATION. While the twentieth century witnessed large-scale migration from central cities, a small yet significant movement into central cities began in the mid 1960s. Cities throughout the country experienced this gentrification, although only a limited number of people were involved in each city. Middle- and upper-middle-class whites moved into older areas to revitalize dilapidated buildings. These people, most of them young and either single or married with no children, desired a city lifestyle and rejected suburban living. Many moved from apartments in the city to their first house elsewhere in the same city.

Aesthetic and economic benefits, such as an increased inner-city tax base, resulted from gentrification. It had negative consequences as well. Many of the residents of the areas being revitalized were displaced as multifamily dwellings were restored to their original single-family use. Most of the displaced were minorities, frequently elderly, and had no other source of low-cost housing.

NONMETROPOLITAN MOVEMENT. During the 1970s, nonmetropolitan areas grew faster than metropolitan areas, a surprising turnaround in migration patterns. At first, movement to nonmetro areas was thought to be a continuation of suburban growth, with people moving to nonmetro counties adjacent to metropolitan areas. But nonadjacent counties grew as fast as, and in many cases faster than, adjacent ones. Furthermore, this growth was evident in all regions of the country, with about 80 percent of the nonmetropolitan counties gaining population. The average annual growth rate of all nonmetropolitan counties during the 1970s was 1.34 percent. Between 1970 and 1975, the years of most rapid nonmetropolitan growth, 2.3 million more people moved into these counties than left.

Social science surveys have long noted a preference among Americans for living in uncongested, open areas such as those in nonmetropolitan places. During the 1970s movement reflected these preferences. As improvements in transportation had contributed to suburbanization, so further improvements contributed to this movement. In addition, technological innovations in communications and the infrastructure in general made non-metropolitan living more attractive.

Nonmetropolitan movement was not a return to the soil. The percentage of the population engaged in agricultural pursuits continued a long-term decline. Industries and services moved out of the cities, taking advantage of better transportation and communications technology. Furthermore, an increased retirement-age population had moved to these areas. In spite of the attention paid to this nonmetropolitan growth by the media, or perhaps because of it, this growth was rather short-lived. By 1975 growth rates had peaked, and by 1980 traditional migration patterns to the metropolitan areas were evident. In fact, during the 1980s most large metropolitan areas experienced substantial growth.

SUNBELT MIGRATION. For the first half of the twentieth century, the South experienced net out-migration of both blacks and whites. These losses were not uniform throughout the region. Rural areas lost more as southern farms mechanized and jobs became available in industrializing cities. During the century's second half, the dominant direction of migration changed. The South's first gains from migration were between 1955 and 1960, when it attracted three hundred thousand more migrants than it lost.

Led by Florida, which had positive net in-migration as early as the 1920s, every state in the census South had more net in-migration than out-migration of both blacks and whites at some point during the 1970s. California, at the western end of the Sunbelt, also had a long history of attracting migrants, as illustrated by the gold rush and the Okies. Virginia, Texas, and Arizona are other Sunbelt states that have experienced substantial in-migration. Growth rates for states between the censuses of 1950 and 1990 were phenomenal: Florida grew by 366 percent, Arizona by 388 percent, California by 181 percent, Texas by 120 percent, and Virginia by 86 percent, as compared with 64 percent growth in the United States as a whole.

Numerous factors have been suggested to account for this turnaround. One of the most important technological innovations was probably central air-conditioning, which greatly improved living conditions. Northerners moved to escape the harsh winters, and now a way had been found to make the hot summers more tolerable. It is somewhat ironic that a means of modifying the climate contributed to movement, since the climate itself had attracted many. For example, the buildup of military establishments throughout the South during World War II occurred because training could take place year round. In addition to the climate, other environmental conditions contributed to the South's growth. Plentiful supplies of clean water attracted industries, as did timber for lumber and paper manufacturing. Industries also were drawn by the lower cost of doing business. Labor costs were low, and southern opposition to labor unions, it was thought, would help to keep them that way.

The Sunbelt also attracted retirees. Again, Florida, California, and Arizona led the way. In fact, about 20 percent of the migrants to Florida in recent years have been age sixty-five or older. Other elderly migrants wanted a more moderate climate, such as that found in the mountains of Arkansas.

Every migration stream has some impact on its destination. Transplanted northerners are no exception. The South has a long history as a distinct region at least somewhat in opposition to the North; after all, it had fought a war against the North. What impact will all these Yankees have on southern culture? The final answer to this question cannot be determined. Northerners in the South do have views distinct from those of southerners. They tend to be more Republican than natives, and the South has recently experienced the growth of a two-party system. While northerners cannot take all the credit, or blame, for this development, they have assumed leadership roles reflecting the traditionally high rates of political participation characteristic of members of higher social classes. These migrants also have more conservative economic views than do natives. They even tend to be less supportive of labor unions—most likely reflecting their white-collar occupational status. Furthermore, transplants have more liberal views on social issues than do native southerners, suggesting the potential for changes in southern culture. The distinct South should not be written off too quickly, however. it has survived greater threats than that posed by a few million migrants.

Future Trends

Americans have spread across the continent, settling the frontier and filling the cities. They have developed technologies and facilities to overcome all the obstacles in their path. Railroads increased accessibility to the West; automobiles made suburbanization possible; and satellite dishes improved communications in remote nonmetropolitan areas. These technologies may indirectly contribute to the next mass movement in this country—movement away from coastal areas that may become necessary if global warming occurs as a result of the predicted greenhouse effect.

In recent years the typical American has moved about once every five years. There are reasons to suspect, however, that mobility may slow down. Young people just starting a career are the most mobile segment of the population. The number and percentage of young people in the American population is decreasing as the baby boom generation ages; thus the number of highly mobile persons in the population is declining.

Another change within American society reducing mobility is the increase in two-career families. With both spouses working, especially where they have similar occupations and incomes, geographical mobility becomes increasingly problematic. Migration rates tend to be lower for these families because two new jobs are necessary in order for the family to relocate. When these families do move, they are more likely to move short distances than are other families.

The presence of two-worker families has increased the number of "commuter marriages" in which each spouse has a job and a residence in a separate place. A growing number of professional couples live in different parts of the country. These couples move frequently between two different residences, creating a new type of mobility.

Historically, migration has played an important role in relieving labor imbalances between areas and in providing a way for individuals and families to improve their standard of living. Today, economic causes of mobility are still important; but as economic conditions become more similar throughout the country, other factors take on more importance. The South, the region that had lagged behind in economic development, is now one of the fastest-growing regions, with new residents attracted by its warm climate and its economic opportunities. Movement by the elderly also exemplifies the decreased importance of economic conditions. Retirees, not being dependent on where a job is located, often base their selection of an area on life-style considerations. With further economic standardization in the twenty-first century, noneconomic opportunities will exert even more influence on migration. It also seems that there will be an increase in movement between similar types of areas. Instead of rural-to-urban or city-to-suburb, for example, there will probably be more urban-to-urban movement—a trend that has already begun.

[See also Agriculture; The Frontier; Landscapes; National Parks and Preservation; Transportation and Mobility; The West.]

BIBLIOGRAPHY

Allen, James P. "Changes in the American Propensity to Migrate." *Annals of the Association of American Geographers* 67, no. 4 (1977).

Biggar, Jeanne C. "The Sunning of America: Migration to the Sunbelt." *Population Bulletin* 34, no. 1 (1979).

Frey, William H. "Metropolitan America: Beyond the Transition." *Population Bulletin* 45, no. 2 (1990).

Gerhan, David R., and Robert V. Wells, comps. *A Retrospective Bibliography of American Demographic History from Colonial Times to 1983* (1989).

Hudson, John C. "North American Origins of Middlewestern Frontier Populations." *Annals of the Association of American Geographers* 78, no. 3 (1988).

Johnson, Daniel M., and Rex R. Campbell. *Black Migration in America: A Social Demographic History* (1981).

Kirby, Jack Temple. "The Southern Exodus, 1910–1960: A Primer for Historians." *Journal of Southern History* 49, no. 4 (1983).

Kirby, Jack Temple. *Rural Worlds Lost: The American South, 1920–1960* (1987).

Kuznets, Simon Smith, and Dorothy Swaine Thomas, eds. *Population Redistribution and Economic Growth: United States, 1870–1950.* 3 vols. (1957–1964).

Lebergott, Stanley. "Migration Within the U.S., 1800–1960: Some New Estimates." *Journal of Economic History* 30, no. 4 (1970).

Lee, Everett S. "A Theory of Migration." *Demography* 3, no. 1 (1966).

Long, Larry. *Migration and Residential Mobility in the United States* (1988).

Parkerson, Donald H. "How Mobile Were Nineteenth-Century Americans?" *Historical Methods* 15, no. 3 (1982).

Ritchey, P. Neal. "Explanations of Migration." *Annual Review of Sociology* 2 (1976).

Sharpless, John. "Population Redistribution in the American Past: Empirical Generalizations and Theoretical Perspectives." *Social Science Quarterly* 61, nos. 3 and 4 (1980).

Thernstrom, Stephan. *Progress and Poverty: Social Mobility in a Nineteenth-Century City* (1964).

Tindall, George Brown. *America: A Narrative History (1984).*

Turner, Frederick Jackson. *Frontier and Section: Selected Essays of Frederick Jackson Turner* (1961).

United States Bureau of the Census. *Historical Statistics of the United States, Colonial Times to 1970. Bicentennial Edition* (1975). Also published in other years.

Vinovskis, Maris A. "Recent Trends in American Historical Demography: Some Methodological and Conceptual Considerations." *Annual Review of Sociology* 4 (1978).

Wilkie, Jane Riblett. "The United States Population by Race and Urban-Rural Residence 1790–1860: Reference Tables." *Demography* 13, no. 1 (1976).

— ROBERT HOWARD FREYMEYER

H

HEALTH CARE

The history of America's health system is deeply intertwined with the social and political history of the nation. America's hospitals are an amalgam of institutions whose function and sponsorship reflect the diversity of the country's ethnic, religious, political, and racial groups. Similarly, American financing of health services is a mixture of public and private sources, organized through state and local regulatory agencies and nonprofit and for-profit insurance companies. Like its hospital system, which reflects the idiosyncratic histories of the nation's diverse populations, the health care financing system reflects the varieties of local political and economic circumstances of the country's regions and populations. For the past two hundred years, the health care system has adapted to enormous changes in the social, economic, political, and medical landscape, and its heterogeneity in organization, mission, and patient base reflects the diversity of the communities and interests it serves. Here we explore the historical culture in which hospitals, physicians, the insurance industry, and governmental regulatory functions have developed, however inadequate their responses may sometimes be to the changing needs of society's dependent and sick.

Those familiar with American history need little reminding that for most of the country's history life revolved around small communities and narrow personal contacts. The wide variety of groups that made up the city, while close to each other, nevertheless lived in highly structured communities separated by culture, ethnicity, and language. Until after the Civil War the vast majority of health services was provided through informal networks of caretakers, families, and friends whose views of what constituted health care reflected local customs, social practices, and beliefs. Care for society's dependent was provided in the home, the community, or not at all.

During much of the nineteenth century it was widely recognized that medical knowledge was inexact at best; professionals often engaged in bitter and highly publicized disagreements about the causes of disease or its proper management. Consequently, the treatment chosen was often a reflection of the customs and medical beliefs of a particular community or group of practitioners rather than of a standardized professional or scientific consensus. The medicine practiced in one section of the country or by a particular group of practitioners was often quite different in form and theory from that of another area or group. In much of rural America, lay people combined local folk customs with information gleaned from medical dictionaries and popular medical texts to arrive at their own idiosyncratic body of therapeutic practices. Similarly, doctors, who were not yet an elite professional group, were generally trained locally through a combination of formal medical school preparation and apprenticeship. The many medical schools were generally proprietary institutions organized to profit local practitioners in which students, often from lower middle class or lower class backgrounds, paid to attend lectures of dubious worth. Formal medical education, largely unregulated and nonstandardized, could vary in length, content, and structure and was, from 1847 when the American Medical Association was formed, criticized for its lack of standardization of practice.

Few during the nineteenth century could agree on what might constitute appropriate practice among the myriad individuals who ascribed to the wide variety of schools of medicine. Furthermore, most practitioners and educated laymen of the period were skeptical of those who sought to unify practitioners under any one therapeutic umbrella. Throughout much of the nineteenth century, the disparate demands of different groups in various areas of the country created a diverse body of therapeutic knowledge and practice. Accordingly, medical training differed for rural and urban practitioners, homeopaths, allopaths, eclectics, Thomsonians, and a host of other practitioners of the art of medicine. Even those treating different classes and ethnic groups within the population were forced by the realities of the medical marketplace to adjust their practices.

This disparity between the educational requirements of various schools was reflected as well in differences between medical nosologies, views, and theoretical positions. Different groups of practitioners generally identified with their own schools or "sects" of medicine.

Unlike today, when patients have little meaningful control over or choice of the types of therapies used, patients in nineteenth-century America could choose from among a host of practitioners and a fairly wide variety of therapies. By and large, doctors were family or community practitioners who were engaged in general medicine. Although a small number of doctors specialized in surgery, ophthalmology, or other areas, specialization was largely tangential to the practices of most physicians.

Family practitioners, who made up the bulk of the profession, generally lived within the communities where they practiced, providing health services either at the homes of their patients or in the doctors' offices, which were generally located in their own houses. They served a patient population that typically lived within a neighborhood and were often members with their patients of the same church or other local community clubs and organizations. The family doctor would preside at the significant events in peoples' lives. He would be fetched for births and deaths and saw it as his role to comfort the family; it was not unusual for him to move into a patient's house for the duration of an illness.

The relationship between doctor and patient was not necessarily the product of a deep-seated intellectual or professional belief in democracy nor in the importance of trust and understanding in the therapeutic process. Rather it was in large measure an outgrowth of a professional environment wherein practitioners working in an era of significant medical uncertainty with regard to procedures and outcomes were in severe competition with each other for clients. An abundance of doctors turned out by a large number of loosely organized and unregulated medical schools combined with loose licensure requirements uncontrolled by the state or the profession to produce a surfeit of practitioners. Without the options now available of research positions in universities, hospitals, and institutes, and before the era of highly specialized forms of practice, doctors depended on the goodwill of their patients for their economic survival. The competition among practitioners for patients that was fierce by the end of the century made familiarity, dress, demeanor, courtesy, cultivation, and common understanding essential qualities for the successful practitioner. What might have been lacking in scientific rigor and detailed knowledge was made up for by the intimacy of the practice itself. The authority of the practitioner rested as much on his social relationship to his patient as upon the consistency or scientific base of his therapeutics.

In the decades surrounding the turn of the century a significant reform movement arose within medicine that held as its guiding principles the need to standardize medical education. Underlying this reform effort lay a notion that, by standardizing the training of physicians and by controlling entrance into the profession through specific licensure procedures, medical practice would become more uniform. This movement culminated in the now-classic 1910 Carnegie Foundation bulletin known as the Flexner Report, which called for the reorganization of the medical school curriculum. The Flexner Report, named for its primary author, Abraham Flexner, was the end product of a long, involved process among medical educators, predominantly within the American Medical Association's Council on Medical Education, to standardize American medicine. But it was successful only in certain narrow respects. Although medical practice remained a field filled with uncertainty and nonstandardized procedures performed by individual practitioners, the standardization of the social background of medical practitioners was achieved. By the end of the nineteenth century, the eclectic nature of the practice of medicine and the largely unregulated environment in which medicine had developed had created a large, diverse set of educational institutions catering to women, blacks, and poorer students. By 1900 there were sixteen women's medical schools and ten black medical colleges, primarily in the southern states. The majority of medical students attending the various proprietary medical colleges was of a lower or lower middle class social background. By 1916, however, only one female women's college and two black schools remained, and many of the proprietary institutions that had once catered to part-time and working students had gone out of existence.

Reformers saw little need for protecting these poorly endowed institutions, in part because of their belief that a future era of scientific medicine would make social diversity within the ranks of those in medicine unimportant. If the physician of the future was to become a scientist treating patients irrespective of their social class, then there was little practical justification for protecting certain groups in medicine. Doctors were to treat organs rather than people and were to cure diseases irrespective of the social, racial, and class characteristics of the bodies the diseases attacked. In Flexner's model for the new science of medicine it mattered little who the practitioner was as long as he trained in modern scientific institutions. If what was seen to be the best also turned out to be white, upper middle class, and male, so much the better, for the general social position of medical practitioners would then be enhanced as well. Flexner's discussion of the future roles of the "poor boy," women, and negroes in medicine showed a simple and, from today's perspective, naive belief in the ability of medical science to solve the issues of equity and equality that became the central concerns of health planners and professionals in the 1960s and 1970s.

The Growth of Institutional Care

Before the Civil War, only a handful of hospitals existed. Philadelphia's Pennsylvania Hospital (1751), New York

Hospital (founded 1791), and Boston's Massachusetts General Hospital (1811) were the oldest nongovernmental institutions in the nation. They were generally governed by lay trustees many of whom were descendants of the earliest Dutch and English settlers. Bellevue Hospital in New York City, the largest of the public facilities, evolved as an adjunct to an eighteenth-century almshouse. The few pre–Civil War facilities were large institutions that often served as long-term-care establishments for the city's dependent poor, travelers, and the mentally ill. Others, such as Kings County Hospital in Brooklyn, were municipal institutions.

After the 1870s, hospitals began to be built in large numbers throughout the growing cities of the Northeast and Midwest. Generally, these institutions were diverse and served a wide variety of social and medical needs. Very often the elite of a community, generally its merchants, local businessmen, and members of the clergy, would initiate and sponsor the formation of what were known as charity hospitals to serve the working class and the dependent poor. Such hospitals generally differed in their religious and ethnic orientations, sources of financial support, size, medical orientation, and the types of services they provided. Most of these hospitals reflected the particular nature of the community they served. Specific hospitals catered to different groups of Jews, Catholics, Italians, Germans, and blacks. Children's hospitals arose to care for orphaned children. Maternity hospitals, often located in working class neighborhoods, were as much shelters for unwed mothers as they were maternity medical services. In communities with a significant number of elderly and dependent persons, local merchants often organized a home or hospital for supposedly incurables or for the chronically ill.

Most of the health-care institutions that developed around the turn of the century were small, locally sponsored charity facilities serving working class and poor patients almost exclusively. Because they reflected the social diversity of their ethnic and religious sponsors and working class patients, no "typical" hospital can be said to have existed. Many in fact looked and functioned like homes or churches and were therefore not readily distinguishable from other establishments and organizations within the community.

The hospitals that developed during the early period of growth before the 1920s were organized around various notions of purpose and function. For one thing, there was little interest or concern with establishing a standardized institution. In fact, most of the hospitals were tiny in comparison to even the smallest of today's institutions and were established in a seemingly haphazard manner. Many institutions exhibited a degree of spontaneous organization characteristic of the fluidity of nineteenth-century social organization. Small hospitals of fifty beds or fewer showed an average life span of little more than five years, often being organized and disbanded with a frequency that would shock modern observers.

The small late-nineteenth-century institutions were not only liable to closure at any moment but were also in danger of immediate eviction. During the late nineteenth century, the typical East Coast city underwent fundamental changes in economic and social organization that placed tremendous pressures on charitable institutions, not only forcing them to adjust to new demands for services

An operation at Bellevue Hospital in the 1870s. New York's Bellevue is the largest public institution built before the Civil War.

but also making them relocate and adjust to changing uses of land and space. As older, pedestrian-oriented communities gave way to new industrial and commercial centers, the land upon which many institutions sat often became more valuable. Streets were widened, electric trolley lines laid down in many cities, elevated train lines introduced, and new means of personal transportation such as the bicycle and later the automobile brought in that forced city governments to pave and clean their streets. Once-sleepy commercial shopping districts that had aimed to serve local neighborhood clientele suddenly emerged as busy, bustling downtowns with large department stores, massive traffic jams, and crowded streets. Pressure for space arose from newly established stores, warehouses, and government establishments in growing downtown commercial areas. Older communities were destroyed as people moved out to new "streetcar suburbs" that began to develop on the peripheries of central-city neighborhoods. As the new economically segregated city arose, its institutions adopted class-specific identities that tended to undercut their older ethnic identifications.

The relative variability in the nature of the nineteenth-century hospital might seem a sign of weakness or instability, but this would be only partially accurate. While individual institutions were subject to tremendous social, demographic, and economic pressures that often forced them to move or go out of existence, the system as a whole flourished. Charity hospitals increased in number throughout the period, and the system continued to experiment with form and function. The tremendous variety of institutions that served the dependent poor in nineteenth-century America gave the system as a whole a dynamism and stability that is remarkable.

The turn-of-the-century institutions under discussion were not solely medical facilities. Rather they were institutions that provided shelter, food, and care to those in need. Because upper-class community leaders and the middle class were generally cared for in their own homes, hospitals treated the working class residents who were forced to become dependent on the larger society during times of hardship. The forms that this hardship took varied significantly from one segment of the working class community to another. Sometimes dependence was created by illness, but often it was social circumstances that caused the growing dependence of a class of the population. The urban hospital can in fact be understood to have its origins in the variety of forms that dependence—not illness—took in the later nineteenth century.

Within this context the nineteenth-century institution played a varied, ambiguous role. It functioned simultaneously as a health-care facility, a social service provider, and an agent of social control. Admission to one of numerous hospitals depended less on a patient's medical situation than on a determination by wealthy patrons that the patient's physical and social circumstances made him or her an appropriate candidate for admission to it.

In many ways nineteenth-century hospitals reflected the diversity of the communities that sponsored, organized, and populated them. Often the values of the trustees, patients, and workers were incorporated into the very order of an institution. Assumptions regarding the meaning of dependence and disease, their moral context, and their relationship to poverty or a patient's occupation were active factors in shaping the diverse institutions that addressed the special needs of particular neighborhoods, religious groups, occupations, and races. In short, institutions differed from each other in much the same way as the diverse communities that founded them differed.

The moral and political objectives of these diverse nineteenth-century institutions had a profound impact on their internal order and organization. In general, the use of large, undifferentiated wards with many beds, which was the usual form of housing in the nineteenth-century hospital, met the needs of an institution trying to supervise and control patients confined there for long periods of time. Having the ward's beds lined up along its walls allowed nurses or attendants to watch many patients simultaneously and guaranteed strict supervision of potentially disruptive or untrustworthy poorer "inmates." Such a ward arrangement also allowed patients to socialize in an institution that in practice substituted for a home. And ambulatory patients could learn good work habits by serving as orderlies or nurses and by helping nearby patients who were incapable of helping themselves. By performing assigned and necessary tasks, patients made the administration of the hospital less complex and in effect paid for their stay. At the same time, they learned the value of work by performing vital tasks for their fellow patients.

The only social characteristics used to separate patients in wards were their sex, age, and medical condition. Although the institutions of the period were often administered by particular religious or sectarian orders, most trustees believed in a moral obligation to admit poorer patients regardless of race or religion. In fact, with their strong missionary zeal many trustees understood the inclusion of a wide range of religious, racial, and ethnic groups to be an important indication of the usefulness of the institution. Furthermore, the missionary function of some facilities dictated that the hospital not merely accept poor patients who presented themselves but also seek out and welcome such people. The annual reports of the various hospitals of the time remarked regularly on the wide variety of races, religions, and nationalities of those who appeared in their beds. Even the architectural detail of many such institutions reflected an overriding concern with social and moral objectives, as many of these facilities were built to resemble churches, mansions, and homes rather than prisons, schools, or factories.

The organizational changes that overtook city hospitals during the early years of this century profoundly affected the relationships between trustees and their medical staffs. In part the new relationships were forced on all concerned by the changing social conditions under which both medical and hospital care now functioned. And the changing internal economy of these institutions altered the pattern of traditional paternalistic control that trustees had exerted over their institutions. While it is sometimes said that the voluntary hospital has become a workshop for the physician, closer inspection of the history of trustee-physician relationships shows that the modern professional and administrative structure of the hospital is the product of a series of profound compromises and adjustments in the running of the facility.

To understand the changing relationships between trustees and their medical and administrative staffs it is necessary to review briefly some of the central elements of the crisis in hospital financing that overtook American hospitals in the late nineteenth century. For most of that period, the country's charity hospitals were inexpensive institutions that could run on relatively small sums of money per year. In New York in the 1890s, for example, nearly all of the voluntary charitable institutions in the city spent less than $30,000 each to provide care. Partly because they were small institutions, rarely having more than 150 beds, partly because patients provided much of the labor, and finally because medical care then was a decidedly low-tech enterprise, these institutions generally spent less than $1.50 per patient per day. Funded by the institutions' benefactors, by a variety of state and local government sources, and by minimal patient payments, these institutions ran at modest deficits every year, which were generally covered by trustee contributions.

Throughout the nineteenth century, the number of charity hospitals grew, and the tremendous variety of institutions that served the dependant poor gave the system a remarkable dynamism and stability.

By the end of the century, however, costs for patient care began to increase substantially as advances in medical technology and changing standards of cleanliness began to affect the care provided. Also, philanthropists who had formerly supported hospitals now faced competing demands from other agencies, and as the number of poor increased substantially, hospitals found themselves strapped for funds. Increasingly, as hospital trustees were forced to make hard choices about the futures of their charitable enterprises they began to turn to new, untested sources of income: private middle-class patients. In order to attract paying patients into charity hospitals, however, their trustees needed to change both the types of services and the administrative structure of their facilities. They needed to bring into their facilities private community practitioners who had previously been excluded, for it was they who largely controlled the loyalties of paying patients. Without the private practitioner there was no mechanism to attract the patient who could afford to pay for his or her own care. Along with this, hospitals had to underplay their traditional image as facilities for the poor. Furthermore, they had to introduce the new services and amenities that would be expected by a wealthier clientele. During the decades before the Great Depression, many hospital trustees faced wrenching decisions about whether or not to fundamentally restructure their facilities.

For many institutions the introduction of private practitioners into their voluntary institutions was the most troubling aspect of the restructuring. Before this period, hospitals' trustees had previously run very closely controlled institutions in which most of the workers, patients, administrators, and even "house staff" physicians lived together in a closed environment. Within the older closed "house" in which a limited number of physicians were younger "house staff" who depended upon the paternalistic authority of the trustees, the institutions' leaders generally didn't hesitate to reprimand, limit, and even dismiss rebellious doctors. For example, as late as the 1890s, protests by physicians in Brooklyn over living and working conditions resulted in the dismissal of the entire staff. In another facility, doctors who protested their treatment at the hands of the head nurse and who demanded her dismissal were themselves dismissed by indignant trustees. As late as 1900, hospital trustees believed that the efficient functioning of an institution depended more on its nursing staff than its medical staff. In institution after institution, trustees reluctantly and slowly opened up their facilities to practitioners from the private community.

For many trustees facing the challenge of private practice in their previously closed houses, the answer lay in organizing two parallel systems of health services. The trustees sought to protect traditional charitable institutions from entrepreneurial private practitioners by giving local doctors only visiting privileges rather than staff appointments in their institutions. By keeping local practitioners outside the formal structure of their facilities, trustees believed they could shield charitable hospitals for the deserving poor from the commercial aspect of private care. Thus, trustees organized private wings, wards, and rooms within their institutions as much to shelter charity patients from the commercialization of medical care that paying patients, private practitioners, and private services represented as for reasons of care. As part of this process, care became structured around the patients' social class, with the poor or uninsured being served in wards by ward staff and paying patients being served by attending or visiting physicians in private or semi-private rooms.

The tensions that plagued hospital administrators reflected larger pressures affecting the very leadership of such institutions. After World War II, trustees lost sight of their earlier commitment to charity and community, as traditionally defined. The growing involvement of the federal government in financing research, construction, and medical education altered the relationships between institutions and their local communities. Furthermore, the long, historical evolution of private practice medicine into the hospital and out of the private office significantly changed the internal culture of health-care institutions as their trustees lost their role and legitimacy as guardians of the poor, the dependent, and the sick. As the social-class makeup of these institutions changed, their commitment to traditional religious, ethnic, and economic constituencies slowly lessened. In their place a newer commitment to communities of professionals—most notably of doctors—developed. With such new communities came abandonment of older, traditional rationales of social service and the development of new, if vaguer, definitions of success. Medical definitions of disease came to replace the older social definitions of dependence as the reason for the existence of the institution, and less specific community needs took a back seat to medically defined priorities. Institutions now relied less and less on the decisions of trustees who understood little about medical technology and medical decision making. Trustees became solely concerned with the finances of their institutions.

The very idea of community was significantly altered in the aftermath of World War II. While earlier generations of trustees and patients often shared certain religious or moral assumptions, the development of highly stratified communities divided along lines of class or race made the whole concept of community more nebulous. As the interstate highway system spurred the growth of wealthy suburbs and then hastened the economic decline of the inner cities, health facilities' trustees found themselves more and more removed, socially and physically, from the communities of the poor they ostensibly served. The social origins of patients in hospitals became mere abstractions amid larger efforts by trustees and administrators to maintain the economic integrity of institutions dedicated to medical care rather than social service. By the mid 1960s, as hospitals responded to calls for unionization, the notion of health care institutions being closely connected to their communities seemed like romantic remnants from a prescientific era. Health planners and activists alike began to call for community-based services as the very institutions that had once appeared to be central to community life now appeared ever more remote. Federal programs through the Office of Economic Opportunity were organized under the rubric that health was a "community affair" which demanded the creation of neighborhood health centers to respond to locally defined needs. At the very time there was a rebirth of interest in locally based health services, hospital leaders seemed increasingly distant, perhaps even antagonistic, to such efforts. In some communities, such as New York City's South Bronx, Bedford-Stuyvesant in Brooklyn, and elsewhere, the hospitals that had once been the cornerstones of community social service were perceived as the enemy and on occasion even occupied in demonstrations. The growing distance between community leaders and hospital trustees spoke to the tremendous historical journey that community hospitals have set out upon during the twentieth century. Along with hospitals' abandonment of community came the growth of national standards to measure progress and success.

After World War II, medical definitions of disease came to replace the older definitions of dependence as the reason for the institution's existence, and less specific community needs took a back seat to medically defined priorities.

Women in the Changing Twentieth-Century Hospital

Throughout the late nineteenth and early twentieth centuries, when most hospitals were considered part of the extensive network of charity institutions, most hospital administrators were women. Especially in the numerous smaller charity institutions scattered throughout the nation many nurses, nuns, or laywomen who functioned as caretakers within the facilities rose through the ranks to assume major roles as ward or institutional managers. Until as recently as 1929, women made up nearly 40 percent of all chief hospital administrators. A 1929 survey of superintendents of 7,610 health institutions in the United States and Canada by Michael M. Davis reported that 20 percent were nurses, 8 percent were sisters, and 11 percent were laywomen. Of the 61 percent remaining, 37 percent were male physicians, 10 percent were laymen, and the remaining 14 percent were unspecified.

The significant role that women have played in shaping modern health administration has hardly been recognized. In the years when the health system was growing dramatically, the administration of the hospital and the clinic was seen as the natural preserve of largely single middle-class women whose social role was to maintain the harmony, stability, and cohesiveness of their communities. Just as married woman ran households, single women—who were often sisters in Catholic institutions or nurses and laywomen in smaller ethnic facilities—were thought appropriate candidates to run the community's voluntary institutions. In these generally smaller institutions, such women were responsible both for providing care and for managing the business functions of their facilities. For a large part of the first third of this century, caregiving and financial management abilities were seen as coequal qualities considered necessary in hospital administrators. Therefore, women, with their claim on the running of the household and on the emotional lives of the community, made excellent candidates for administrative positions and shaped institutions' goals as their administrators. The importance of women in the administration of many early-twentieth-century health institutions grew out of the unique blend of moral, religious, medical, and social services hospitals were expected to provide. While sickness was one major form of dependence that increased the demand for health care, it was the social surroundings of a community's life that made these institutions the appropriate centers to care for the poor or for immigrants. In such a setting, women's traditional role as caretaker could merge with their career aspirations to create career paths that were unavailable in the male-dominated outside world. Women, locked out of many of the professions, government service, and business, found a relatively welcoming field in hospital administration.

Women's traditional role as the protectors of the moral life of the nation added a degree of legitimacy to their positions as hospital administrators. In late nineteenth and early twentieth century urban society, where dependence, poverty, and illness were often interpreted as interlocking indications of the general morality or immorality of patients, medical care was seen as intimately linked to the success of moral reform within the health-care institution. Hence the administrator, as the person responsible for the total life of the institution, largely controlled the program designed to teach patients acceptable standards of moral behavior.

Internally, the institution's facilities reflected the underlying moral goals of the program's originators and of the head administrator. The superintendent was responsible for the daily running of the institution, and he or she functioned as a patriarch or matriarch of the extended family that the hospital was supposed to resemble. The entire structure of the administration of the facility was modeled on the ideal of the middle-class family of late nineteenth- and early twentieth-century America. The superintendent or matron served as mother or father. Nurses, sisters, long-term patients, and young house-staff physicians played the roles of older children who had varying degrees of responsibility for the housekeeping chores needing to be done in the institution. Newly admitted patients not yet socialized into the life of the institution were in effect infants, in need of constant guidance and supervision by parents and siblings. Only the trustees, the institution's spiritual leaders, escaped the confining environment of the "house," as it was called.

Women's role as administrators augmented their other positions in hospitals, most notably as nurses. From the very earliest moments of hospital history, nurses were central to the care of patients. Yet because their role was so defined by the mission of caregiving, women were placed in ambiguous and ambivalent positions within the institution's hierarchy. The origin of nursing in the traditions of charity and volunteer work has led to a significant undervaluing of nurses' role and status. Despite repeated historical attempts to professionalize nursing fundamentally, nurses have continually found themselves caught between one image as the handmaiden to physicians and another as professionals with skills, status, and an identity of their own.

Despite the fact that schools particularly for nursing were opened in the late nineteenth century, the system of nursing education was fractured and multilayered. More often than not, nurses were seen as a source of unskilled labor by hospital trustees eager to keep costs low and to maintain the charitable aura of the institution. The nursing schools associated with hospitals were built to produce an inexpensive labor force, not to create a cadre of skilled professionals. Similarly, physicians, whose role in the hospital expanded greatly during this period, rarely allowed nurses autonomy, thereby reinforcing their image as adjuncts to the male-dominated medical profession. Drives by institutions to lower costs and a concomitant increase in hospital-based nursing schools then created an oversupply of nurses that also served to fragment the profession.

Throughout the twentieth century, tension has existed within the nursing field. Those interested in autonomy have striven to decrease the output of nursing programs, thereby creating a nursing shortage, and have sought to professionalize the field by increasing the skill levels to those associated with highly trained professionals. Yet the ideology of professionalism has come into conflict with the division of labor within medicine that gives authority and responsibility to a medical profession that lacks interest in ceding control to a new group of professionals.

The Rise of Private Health Insurance

While caregivers and hospitals have been central components in the health system of this country, it seems fair to say that the system for financing health services is probably its single most problematic aspect in the minds of millions of poorly insured or uninsured Americans. A chronic issue that affects nearly everyone at one time or another, the system of health insurance has throughout the twentieth century led to repeated calls for governmental involvement. Yet despite the unhappiness of millions with existing private, nongovernmental health financing, calls for national or compulsory health insurance programs have been regularly sidetracked or delayed. For instance, in the early twentieth century a movement for the creation of statewide plans to finance health care, modeled along the lines of workers' compensation, was defeated. In the middle years of the Great Depression, health insurance was specifically left out of the Social Security Act. In the 1940s and 1950s, despite apparent presidential support, attempts to pass national health insurance legislation were defeated. Only in the 1960s did Congress pass Medicare and Medicaid, two programs to fund care for the elderly, the disabled, and the desperately poor.

To comprehend the ability of a widely criticized insurance industry to withstand these pressures for change and even grow in the midst of ongoing public discontent demands understanding on both the political and the cultural levels. To do so it is necessary to appreciate the traditional resistance that has existed to governmental involvement in the provision of health insurance and also American laborers' traditional interest in self-help, the ideal of establishing programs, services, and benefits through voluntary or nongovernmental forms. Furthermore, it is critical to understand the long-held distrust of both management and government control over these programs by many elements in the labor movement.

After wages and hours, the provision of health and welfare benefits has always been central to the struggles of labor and management to control the workplace. Throughout the nineteenth and twentieth centuries, both management and organized labor have sought to sponsor programs aimed at providing health and welfare benefits to workers. In the early nineteenth century, paternalistic textile mill owners in Lowell, Massachusetts, initiated what became known as the Lowell Plan. Late in the century, railroads, logging, and mining companies began to contract with physicians to provide minimal health services to workers. Into the 1920s, welfare capitalists at U.S. Steel, International Harvester, and other such companies developed welfare plans. Throughout, labor has distrusted employee benefit plans that were not under their own control.

While the various health and welfare programs were portrayed by management as paternalistic responses to the felt needs of the work force, most union representatives saw them as a means of undermining worker-

Despite apparent presidential support, attempts to pass national health insurance legislation were defeated in the 1940s and 1950s, and it was not until the 1960s that Congress passed Medicare and Medicaid, programs to fund care for the elderly, the disabled, and the poor.

and union-based initiatives to improve working conditions. These management-initiated programs were seen as attempts to make workers dependent upon the goodwill of the company, thereby creating a nonmilitant, acquiescent labor force. The programs were thought to be inadequate and temporary at best. At worst they were perceived as tools in management's attempts to cover up the dangers of the workplace and to hide deaths or disabilities caused by unsafe, unclean working environments. Because of the general lack of availability even of management programs and in light of dismal experiences and widespread distrust of management's motivations, workers and unions organized their own health and benefit societies, self-insurance and disability compensation programs, old-age pensions, and even clinics and hospitals. In the late eighteenth and early nineteenth centuries, many workers organized mutual aid and benevolent societies. By the mid twentieth century, there were well over two hundred group health plans in the country. Among the more important employee-sponsored plans were the hospital and medical care program of the United Mine Workers of America's welfare and retirement fund, the Union Health Center, the International Ladies Garment Workers Union, and the Sidney Hillman Medical Center of the Male Apparel Industry of Philadelphia of the Amalgamated Clothing and Textile Workers, members of the CIO.

The 1930s are a critical period for understanding labor's changing attitude toward what labor leaders considered their long support for voluntary (union initiated) health and welfare programs. During this time, under the financial pressures of the Depression, the development of the New Deal administration in Washington, and the impact of specific pieces of pro-labor legislation such as the 1935 National Labor Relations (Wagner Act), and because of splits within the labor movement itself, labor showed a willingness to consider new models to provide health and welfare services to their members.

During the Depression, organized labor faced innumerable problems as millions of its workers found themselves unemployed and dependent. Also in that era the longstanding supremacy of the American Federation of Labor was challenged by organizing drives in heavy industry that were spurred by the Committee for Industrial Organization (later the Congress of Industrial Organizations). With the development of the CIO in the second half of the 1930s, organized labor faced not only an internal schism in its ranks but also a split over its long-held belief in self-help. Many of the new CIO unions saw themselves as in close alliance with New Deal government politicians and administrators, especially in the years following the passage of the Wagner Act. In fact, many unionizing drives used the image of a pro-labor president and sympathetic congressmen in their organizing literature. For the first time in labor history, significant sectors of organized labor looked to the national government for support, protection, and sometimes even advice. In the context of the Depression, as the new CIO became deeply involved in organizing millions of workers, significant portions of the labor movement supported governmental programs in the areas of social welfare, protective legislation, and even working hours and wages. Walter Reuther and the United Auto Workers, along with other leaders of the CIO, even went so far as to endorse various calls for national health insurance.

This was a dramatic break with the traditions of the American Federation of Labor regarding self-reliance and voluntarism in the development of critical labor programs. Here for the first time labor accepted the notion of third-party intervention. This change proved important in the more conservative postwar years, when Blue Cross emerged as a viable, nongovernmental, and nonmanagement-oriented insurance alternative.

One important factor affecting labor was the previously mentioned passage in 1935 of the National Labor Relations Act, specifically its mandate for management and labor to engage in collective bargaining. Collective bargaining had always existed in industrial and labor relations, but this act greatly expanded the number of industries that could now reach agreement on any number of management-labor issues. The development of nonpartisan or third-party insurance schemes at the same time collective bargaining was spreading gave tremendous impetus to both labor's and management's interest in this new approach. During World War II, wage raises were restricted and many unions thus turned to expanding their members' fringe benefits. The years following World War II saw the rapid expansion of third-party health insurance systems, most notably the Blue Cross program, which grew by the infusion of funds into welfare and health programs established through collective bargaining agreements.

For most of this century, voluntary institutions such as hospitals and nongovernmental insurance companies have dominated the health system. But the end of the century is a critical time for health care because now, for the first time in many decades, the field has become increasingly responsive to forces outside the traditional nexus of care providers, patients, politicians, and institutions. Today corporations and consulting firms control vital elements of the health care system. Others are organizing what are termed "preferred provider organizations" or "health maintenance organizations" for corporations. In these new settings it remains unclear whether the culture of health services, with its focus on profit rather than care, will be capable of withstanding the growing political and popular impatience with a system that is a central factor in determining a health professional's identity. Fifty years from now, we may look back at this period and note how it was a period of change when the basic contours of health care were altered by demands for new services from the elderly,

AIDS patients, an increasingly dependent population of sick, poor people, and an insurance system that could not meet even the most basic needs of the population.

[See also Alternative Medicine; The Medical Profession; Public Health, Reproduction, and Parenthood; Women and Work.]

BIBLIOGRAPHY

Drachman, Virginia G. *Hospital with a Heart: Women Doctors and the Paradox of Separatism at the New England Hospital, 1862–1969* (1984).

Duffy, John. *The Healers: The Rise of the Medical Establishment* (1976).

Fox, Daniel M. *Health Policies, Health Politics: The British and American Experience, 1911–1965* (1986).

Gamble, Vanessa. "The Negro Hospital Renaissance: The Black Hospital Movement, 1920–1945." In *The American General Hospital: Communities and Social Contexts*, edited by Diana Long Hall and Janet Golden (1989).

Ludmerer, Kenneth M. *Learning to Heal: The Development of American Medical Education* (1985).

Melosh, Barbara. *"The Physician's Hand": Work Culture and Conflict in American Nursing* (1982).

Reverby, Susan. *Ordered to Care: The Dilemma of American Nursing, 1850–1945* (1987).

Reverby, Susan, and David Rosner, eds. *Health Care in America: Essays in Social History* (1979).

Risse, Guenter B., R. S. Numbers, and J. W. Leavitt, eds. *Medicine Without Doctors, Home Health Care in American History* (1977).

Rosen, George. *The Specialization of Medicine with Particular Reference to Ophthalmology* (1944).

Rosen, George. *The Structure of American Medical Practice, 1875–1941.* (1983).

Rosenberg, Charles E. *The Care of Strangers: The Rise of America's Hospital System* (1987).

Rosner, David. *A Once Charitable Enterprise: Hospitals and Health Care in Brooklyn and New York, 1885–1915* (1982).

Rosner, David, and Gerald Markowitz. *Deadly Dust: Silicosis and the Politics of Occupational Disease in Twentieth-Century America* (1991).

Rosner, David, and Gerald Markowitz, eds. *Dying for Work: Workers' Safety and Health in Twentieth Century America* (1987).

Rothstein, William G. *American Physicians in the Nineteenth Century: From Sects to Science* (1972).

Starr, Paul. *The Social Transformation of American Medicine* (1982).

Stevens, Rosemary. *In Sickness and in Wealth: American Hospitals in the Twentieth Century* (1990).

Vogel, Morris. *The Invention of the Modern Hospital, Boston, 1870–1930* (1980).

Walsh, Mary Roth. *"Doctors Wanted. No Women Need Apply": Sexual Barriers in the Medical Profession, 1835–1975* (1977).

Warner, John Harley. *The Therapeutic Perspective: Medical Practice, Knowledge, and Identity in America, 1820–1885* (1986).

— DAVID ROSNER

HEALTH, PUBLIC

See PUBLIC HEALTH

HOLIDAYS

See PARADES, HOLIDAYS AND PUBLIC RITUALS

HOUSEHOLD LABOR

Ever since the first settlements in the seventeenth century, the vast majority of women in this country have performed household tasks on a regular basis throughout their adult lives. Indeed, housework is perhaps the single most common work experience shared by women around the world. Yet household labor has become a significant topic of research and analysis only in the last few decades. Before women's history achieved legitimacy within the historical profession, most historians considered the lives of ordinary women and the unpaid work they did at home unworthy of scholarly inquiry. Those who did undertake such research discovered that, although household tasks appear commonplace and routine, the study of housework is complex. In the United States it involves examining cultural ideals about the home and family, ethnic and gender ideologies about the division of household labor, beliefs about paid and unpaid work in a capitalist economy, and the dependence of household processes on larger economic and social systems, such as energy sources and municipal services. The tools people use to perform household tasks, generally referred to as "household technology," further link the study of housework to larger industrial systems and to manufacturers' strategies in producing, advertising, and distributing new appliances and products. Understanding the relationship of household labor to the larger economy also involves looking at the home as a workplace, for paid domestic service has been an important source of income for generations of immigrant, working-class, and African American women.

Moreover, unlike many other historical topics, the question of who does the housework is a widely discussed and debated issue today. The increasingly large number of working mothers with small children has created a "second shift" for wage-earning women across the economic spectrum and shaken old assumptions in many families and among government policymakers about who should provide child care and other housekeeping services. And ever since the women's movement of the 1970s raised issues about equity for men and women in all areas of life, including housekeeping and child rearing, decisions about who cooks dinner and who diapers the baby have taken on political overtones, especially in two-career families. Whether or not historians personally wrestle with such dilemmas, they are aware of the public debate. Historical studies on household labor invariably throw light on the current discussion about the allocation of domestic tasks today. The study of housework, then, involves not only documenting and interpreting the changes and continuities in household labor over time, but also in understanding the ideas and attitudes, deeply embedded in the culture, about how it should be done and who should do it.

Preindustrial Households

Seventeenth-century New Englanders did not use the term "housework" to describe the tasks they performed to maintain the household. Instead the word "housewifery" differentiated the tasks women did from those done by men. In the rural preindustrial conditions that characterized the early colonies, every family member worked around and in the house to produce most of the products and perform many of the services necessary for the family's survival. The family's level of self-sufficiency varied depending on whether it lived on the frontier or close to a settled area, but some generalizations can nevertheless be made. Women were responsible for a wide range of duties that began at sunrise and ended after nightfall. To the repetition of tasks that filled each day—preparing and cooking meals, caring for young children, managing the hearth, hauling water, spinning, tending livestock, cleaning utensils—was added the weekly or monthly chores of laundering, brewing hard cider and beer, mending clothing, churning butter, and making candles. The changing of the seasons engaged women in still another round of activities: pickling and preserving fruits, vegetables, and meats; planting gardens; making lye and soap; and weaving linen and sewing new clothes for the coming season to replace those garments worn or outgrown in the previous year. Of all these tasks, spinning required the most complex skills and filled many of the extra minutes in a woman's day, for it could be done with one eye on small children and another on the hearth. Women also performed the tasks that contributed to the community's health and wellbeing. They concocted medicines from herbs, cared for the sick and aged, assisted each other at childbirth, and prepared the dead for burial.

Men and boys carried out essential steps in many of the labor processes that culminated with women's efforts. Males of the household felled trees and split wood for the hearth; they cultivated crops and cared for livestock; and they, as well as women, hauled water for cleaning and laundering. Men took grain to the mills for grinding, and usually made regular trips to the nearby town for tools and foodstuffs that the family could not produce itself. They hunted for animals and fished to add variety to the family table. Women spun and sewed cloth, but men worked leather for shoes and whittled wood into kitchen implements or made furniture.

A common household inventory would have included a loom, a butter churn, a wooden bucket for hauling water, a spinning wheel, mortars, pestles, candle molds, salt barrels, iron kettles, quilts, assorted wooden implements for cooking, and wooden trenchers for eating. To acquire many of these tools, a relatively self-reliant household had to be connected to a larger market economy that provided products made by skilled artisans, such as iron pots, axes, or guns, and to have surplus food or other objects to barter or sell. As probate records show, whether household utensils were bought or homemade, they were very valuable and often bequeathed to the next generation.

The gender-segregated, but mutually dependent, division of labor that characterized the New England colonies was nearly universal. The proper and expert use of household tools and the acquisition of craft skills required the mastery of complicated processes. Young girls and boys acquired the skills necessary for adult life by imitating their mothers or fathers or through apprenticeship with a relative or adult of the same sex. In times of illness or the absence of her husband, a wife could step in and take over a man's chores and was then called a "deputy husband," but in normal circumstances men and women infrequently exchanged roles. Historians disagree over how rigid the sexual division of labor was or whether there was rhyme or reason to who did what task, but the decision of who would cook dinner or care for the baby was less a personal one than a traditionally prescribed role.

Both men and women acquired their senses of self-identity and self-worth from this clear delineation of roles. Yet, although the work was reciprocal, it was not equally valued. New England families existed in a patriarchal society in which the law and religious doctrine upheld the father's position as head of the household and as the family's public representative. The economic value of women's work did not increase their autonomy or authority within the family or their status in the community. Husbands controlled the family's resources, and in most cases even the possessions their wives brought into the marriage. Men and women knew that they could not easily maintain a household without the special skills of the other, but larger cultural and religious ideas about women's "nature" and their subordinate and dependent status lessened the value placed on women's domestic tasks.

In the seventeenth-century Chesapeake Bay colonies of Maryland, Virginia, and the Carolinas, an initial scarcity of women in the early years of settlement meant that men were forced to do some domestic chores and women to work in the fields to help produce the cash crops that justified their indentured status. When stable nuclear families became the norm in the late 1600s, more rigidly defined sex roles developed and women took over responsibility for household chores. Slaves or indentured servants might help lighten some women's work by providing an extra pair of hands and female companionship, but more often such women worked in the fields, leaving the domestic tasks to their mistress. She tended the garden, the livestock, and the dairy; prepared food and clothing, raised her children, and cared for the sick. As the economy expanded and the number of plantations grew, affluent women increasingly supervised and managed the domestic work of slaves within their households, but the vast majority still clothed and nursed all the members of their households, including slaves. Without denying the benefit and privilege that white women derived from owning slaves, historians have shown that all women in the early colonies worked long and hard at domestic tasks to sustain their largely self-sufficient households.

The Rise of the Domestic Ideal

Women's routine domestic activities took on political significance during the colonies' struggle for independence from Great Britain. Without women's refusal to buy imported goods and their willingness to increase their production of homespun, the economic boycott against British products might have failed. But instead of acquiring for them the full rights of citizenship after the war, women's patriotism was rewarded with only a heightened appreciation of their roles as mothers. In this function, women were the most important educators of their young children and could best serve their new nation by dedicating themselves to teaching republican virtues to the next generation. Historian Linda Kerber has called the new image that emerged the "Republican Mother." Instead of exercising the rights of citizenship themselves by voting or holding political office, the republican mother would raise virtuous, responsible male citizens who would govern the nation in the future. Although there were benefits to the title and the role—both strengthened the argument for the expansion of women's education, for example—in general the redefinition of women as primarily mothers subordinated their role as housewives.

In the northeastern part of the United States, these new ideas about the importance of motherhood coincided with the growth of cities and industry at the end of the eighteenth and the beginning of the nineteenth centuries and helped to rationalize and give meaning to the changing nature of women's household work. The new market economy that began to develop by the mid eighteenth century made manufactured products such as textiles, clothing, baked goods, and other foodstuffs readily available to families living in urban areas. As the family produced fewer of the necessities of daily life, the need for both female and male labor to maintain the household diminished. Young daughters and sons, unmarried sisters, and husbands left the household to work in factories, mills, and offices for the wages the family needed to buy the new consumer goods. About the same time, family size began to diminish. More widespread use of birth control methods, combined with the realization that children were not economic assets in an urban environment, had, by 1850, reduced the average family size to four or five children, compared to seven or eight a century earlier.

These economic and demographic changes contributed to a new ideology about the home. In popular magazines and literature, religious sermons, advice books, and manuals, the household was transformed into a private refuge. It became a haven from the dangerous, competitive world of the capitalist marketplace. Left behind in the home when others went "out to work," the wife and mother preserved what some remembered as the virtues and morality of an older era.

As the mid-1800s family produced fewer of the necessities of daily life, daughters and sons, unmarried sisters and husbands left the household economy to work in factories, mills, and offices for wages that the family needed to buy the new consumer goods.

The woman presumedly did not "work," for in an economy that defined value by wages she was not paid for the activities she performed within the privacy of her home. Instead, popular images showed the ideal housewife creating a pleasant and cultured environment for her family, educating her children in Christian and republican principles, entertaining graciously, and easing the emotional cares and worries of her work-weary husband. The home had become women's special sphere and she a "lady" within it. Some historians have labeled this vision of the domestic, pious, and submissive female the cult of true womanhood, and have used the ideology of gender spheres to designate the nineteenth-century notion that men's natural place was in the public world of wage labor and politics, women's within the sanctuary of the home.

Most women, whether they were wealthy or poor, immigrant or African American, were affected by the cultural expectation that they should strive to become ladies. Class distinctions throughout the nineteenth and early twentieth centuries make generalizations difficult, but overall, the reality of most women's lives made achieving the ideal a virtual impossibility. Although more prosperous women might have hired help to assist them, the majority of middle- and working-class women continued to perform arduous, demanding household tasks, as had their mothers and grandmothers before them. Housework was as vital to the well-being of the family as it had ever been, but in the popular culture its importance was ignored, if not denied. Advertisements for the new household products that were beginning to appear in abundance at the turn of the century pictured servants, not the mistress of the house, performing most of the hard physical labor in the home. For the women from poor and working-class families who could not even dream of hiring servants, cooking, cleaning, and laundering had not disappeared from their daily routine, but were now devalued as menial chores. Moreover, by pronouncing women's true place to be at home, the doctrine of gender spheres rendered wage work inappropriate for women. Those women forced to leave their homes to work as laundresses, domestic servants, vendors, or even prostitutes to help their families survive could never hope to achieve the American middle-class ideal of womanhood.

Southern Plantation Society

Southern households differed from northern ones mainly in that they existed in a rural, slave society that remained largely self-sufficient for a longer time than the commercial, urbanizing northeast. With less access to larger economic markets than women in the north, southern women and their slaves produced more of the necessities of daily living. They spun and wove cloth for most of the plantation's needs; grew, preserved, baked, stored, and cooked almost all their food throughout the year; tended gardens and livestock; and nursed the sick.

Slaves relieved slaveholding women of many of their daily housekeeping chores, but not of the major tasks of managing the house servants, storing and inventorying supplies that were purchased in bulk, supervising and participating in fall and spring cleaning and, on smaller plantations, repairing and sewing clothes for their own families and their slaves. Some plantation mistresses also cared for sick slaves and assisted them at childbirth.

Depending on the size of the plantation, a slave might be assigned specific tasks, but generally slave women who worked within the plantation house did the full range of domestic chores. They cleaned, hauled water, cooked, laundered, ironed, cared for children, tended the garden and livestock, and helped the mistress cure, salt, and preserve the family's meats and other foods. Many also prepared herbal remedies to cure illnesses and nursed the sick. Slave women sewed for the white household and for themselves, but rarely alongside their mistresses.

While in the North the hearth was the center of the kitchen and the home, in the South the kitchen and the heat it produced in summer were separated from the house and presided over mostly by slave women. These women apparently took pride in their cooking skills, and good cooks were respected by both African Americans and whites.

Early in the morning or late at night, slave women performed a second set of domestic chores in their slave quarters. On some plantations slaves ate in communal kitchens, but most slave women cooked meals for their own families. They supplemented their daily rations of food with vegetables grown in small garden plots, food pilfered from their mistresses' kitchen, or with fish or game their husbands brought to the table. Both slave men and women possessed skills, passed on from the community's elders, that made them as resourceful and self-reliant as colonial families had been. Slave men, for example, chopped wood for fires, constructed and repaired furniture and other wooden implements, and sewed leather items for clothing and household use.

The gender division of labor that existed during slavery endured as freedmen- and -women reconstituted their families after the Civil War. Domestic duties then fell to women; the men worked in the fields, with the women joining them when needed in the harvest or planting seasons. Most historians conclude that if many African American women seemed eager to embrace the duties of housewife and mother after slavery, this may have been because they found it a relief to devote their energies and domestic skills solely to the well-being of their own families after generations of working in white women's households.

Professionalizing Housework

In the late nineteenth century, the home economics or domestic science movement attempted to regain society's respect for women's domestic labor and to relieve the unrelenting drudgery of housework by introducing notions of professionalism, order, and efficiency into the home. Catharine Beecher, a precursor of the home economics movement and an early advocate of the idea that housewives required training in proper household management, published *A Treatise on Domestic Economy, For the Use of Young Ladies at Home, and at School* in 1841 and a second edition of the book in 1869 coauthored with her sister, Harriet Beecher Stowe, entitled, *The*

American Woman's Home, or, Principles of Domestic Science; being a guide to the formation and maintenance of economical, healthful, beautiful, and Christian homes. In encyclopedic fashion, both volumes instructed women in the care of their homes and families, including chapters on home decoration, exercise, care of babies and the disciplining of children, baking, cooking, and nutrition, consumer advice, and suggestions for the most efficient arrangement of kitchens and the best designs for toilets. The Beechers' intent was to recapture for the American housewife the place she lost in the economy when she ceased to produce the necessities of daily life for her family. The Beechers were steeped in the domestic ideal, however, and their goals were to make women better housewives, not relieve them of their domestic chores. Nevertheless, their efforts later helped initiate domestic science classes in women's colleges and state universities in the Midwest and West. Cooking schools and privately owned training institutions in northern cities offered similar instruction in housekeeping to employers of domestic servants, those servants themselves, and to young women embarking on marriage or work in settlement houses where such skills were needed. During the Progressive Era (1870–1900), urban reformers also advocated offering courses in home economics in the elementary and high schools, arguing that girls prepared to do sewing, cooking, and cleaning would later find respectable employment in middle- and upper-class homes and acquire useful habits of industry. Teaching housekeeping skills seemed a particularly effective way to indoctrinate immigrant girls with the American values of thrift, order, cleanliness, and efficiency. Reformers who saw the participation of immigrant women in the labor force as the cause of many urban problems believed that training them in the "domestic arts" would keep them at home or working in the homes of other women and out of the industrial marketplace.

Early in the morning or late at night, slave women performed a second set of domestic chores in their slave quarters: On some plantations slaves ate in communal kitchens, but most slave women cooked meals for their own families.

Those middle-class women who worked to redefine housework as a professional, scientific occupation formed the Home Economics Association in Lake Placid, New York, in 1899. This association emphasized the importance of a sanitary, healthful, well-managed home environment and urged homemakers to accept the advice of "experts" on nutrition, time management, budgeting, and consumption to ensure the physical and moral well-being of their families. Although formal training in homemaking skills justified the expansion of higher education for women, the association's goals were to make women content to remain in the home by equating domesticity with challenging professional work outside. Home economists reached housewives around the country through women's magazines, housekeeping manuals, and cookbooks and by endorsing household products that purportedly saved time and energy. The experts set ideal standards for the home, frustratingly elusive even for those middle-class women who could afford to hire help. In evaluating the influence of the home economics movement, some historians believe that the association's emphasis on time-budgeting activities and its reliance on experts undermined women's traditional ways of sharing information and support across generations and within neighborhood communities.

Charlotte Perkins Gilman, like Catharine Beecher an important theorist in rethinking women's work in the home, promoted communal alternatives to the image of the ideal household. Writing in 1898 in *Women and Economics* and later in 1903 in a book called simply *The Home: Its Work and Influence*, Gilman equated the solitary woman laboring to maintain her own household with a primitive stage in the evolution of work. She proposed a more progressive vision that included industrialized kitchens and collective child care. But Gilman and women like her, such as Melusina Fay Pierce, who founded the Cambridge Cooperative Housekeeping Society in 1869 to organize a cooperative bakery, store, and laundry for housewives, were in the minority in their desire to reform America's households. When they wrote at the turn of the century, most women were still full-time housewives. The demand for commercially prepared meals, group child care, and other household services would not arise until more women with children entered the labor force in the 1960s and 1970s.

Paid Household Help

In the seventeenth century, one-third of colonial households included domestic help. Often they were young immigrant women and men who arrived in the New England colonies as indentured servants, bound or indebted to a family for five to seven years in exchange for passage to the New World and room, board, and clothing. Generally, female servants performed the same tasks as their mistresses, cleaning, tending the garden and the animals, and spinning, weaving, and sewing. Young girls from poorer families might also join a household as apprentices, learning more complicated household chores such as spinning or weaving from their mistresses in exchange for labor of all kinds. So acceptable and widespread was the practice of young women living and working in households other than their own that no stigma was attached to the position. These forms of domestic service continued until after the American Revolution.

By the 1830s, however, the expanding urban middle class was buying many of the household commodities it needed and no longer required young women to help it prepare textiles, butter, cheese, or other products for the family or to sell in a nearby town. City families wanted women primarily to do housework. By then a pool of predominantly immigrant women was available, as native-born women began to earn wages in newly opened factories, shops, and offices. Many Irish, Scandinavian, German, and Slavic women came to the United States to work as domestic servants rather than do brutally hard farm work in their native lands. For the most part, domestic servants continued to live in the homes of their employers, but they now received wages as well as room and board. According to historian Faye Dudden, by mid-century approximately 15 to 30 percent of all urban households had live-in domestic help, and by 1870, the first year the U.S. Census documented women's employment, nearly one-half of all women who worked for wages were domestic servants. Whether in their own homes or in those of others, women's most important occupation in the nineteenth century was household labor.

Live-in servants in cities usually did not work alongside their mistresses as servants had done in self-sufficient colonial households, but their chores were similar to those all housewives did. As nurse-maids, laundresses, cooks, cleaning women, waitresses, and seamstresses, domestic servants often worked ten to twelve hours per day, seven days a week. Many relationships between domestics and their mistresses were amicable. Still, the imbalance of power between employer and employee was frequently made even more difficult by the prejudice that grew out of different ethnic, religious, or racial backgrounds between the two women. Employers complained about their "unwashed Irish immigrant servants" who were ignorant of the most rudimentary cleaning processes and if left unsupervised might debase the family's children with their Roman Catholicism. Domestics complained of loneliness and isolation, long hours, low pay, back-breaking chores, lack of privacy,

In the nineteenth century, African-American women of the South began to migrate North in large numbers and became the dominant source of paid household labor in urban areas.

unreasonable and exploitative employers, and the stigma of having a menial, low-status job. Proponents of domestic service for working-class and immigrant girls argued that, compared to factory employment, domestics worked in an environment that would protect their health and morals and would prepare them for their future roles as mothers and wives. And for some immigrant women, doing housework in middle-class homes may have quickened the pace of acculturation, for they thus learned English rapidly and were exposed to an American way of life they could teach their own children.

Whether they liked domestic service or not, for many women it was the only wage work they could find. Not until the decades just prior to the twentieth century, and only in some areas of the country, did alternative employment opportunities begin to appear. Then even immigrant women had more options and the paucity of domestics created what popular women's magazines referred to as "the servant problem," or a scarcity of "good help." At the same time, African American women began to migrate northward to become the dominant source of paid household labor in urban areas. These women preferred day work, which allowed them the flexibility to care for their own families and households in the evenings and on weekends. Day workers had largely replaced live-in help in most cities around the country by as early as 1920. Sufficient numbers of African American women remained as domestic workers in the South, however, that southern white women did not experience a scarcity of help until the 1940s and 1950s, when a second large migration of African Americans to northern cities occurred.

In 1900, African American women made up one-third of the servant population in the United States; by 1930 they constituted half of all servants. By then few worked full-time for a single employer. Usually they were hired on a weekly basis for only a day or two to do a specific task. During World War II, many African American women found higher-paying jobs in war-related industries, but after the demobilization most were forced to return to domestic work. In 1950, domestic workers constituted 41 percent of all wage-earning African American women. During the first half of the twentieth century, racial discrimination often combined with a lack of education to prevent African American women from finding work other than as domestic workers or laundresses. Unlike many white women, African American women remained in that occupation most of their lives.

Household Technology

The only household innovations that eased women's work in the nineteenth century, according to historian Susan Strasser, were the eggbeater, which replaced the fork for beating egg whites, and the coal or wood stove, which eliminated the hours women spent every day tending the hearth. With these two exceptions, food preparation took virtually the same amount of time and effort for a granddaughter as it had for her grandmother. Then in the four decades that spanned the turn of the twentieth century, a number of household machines and products changed the nature of housework, at least for the women who could afford them. Gas and electric stoves, vacuum cleaners, washing machines, irons, and prepared foods were mass produced and distributed and dramatically reduced the heavy, hard labor women had heretofore expended in housework. But before women could replace their manual labor with mechanical power, they had to have access to gas and electricity.

Utilities such as gas and electricity, water and sewerage, garbage collection, and central heating all required municipal expenditures. The uneven distribution of these services within a city or to outlying areas illustrated the political as well as economic nature of urban planning. Piped household water was generally available in wealthy homes by the end of the nineteenth century, but hot and cold running water were not found in many middle-class homes until the beginning of the 1930s. Rural and poor urban families continued to haul their water until after World War I, and some families had to wait for tap water until after World War II, when rural electrification and municipal water systems were fully developed. Most people did not have indoor plumbing until the 1930s.

Rural and poor urban families continued to haul their water until after World War I, and some had to wait for tap water until after World War II, when rural electrification and municipal water systems were fully developed.

Having indoor running water ended the back-breaking chore of lugging water, sometimes up several flights of stairs, heating it, hauling it to where the work was to be done, and eventually disposing of it. With tap water came higher standards of domestic and personal hygiene and an unexpected change in the most onerous household chore, doing laundry. Coupled with the washing machine, plumbing brought the family's dirty laundry back into the home.

Women had always dreaded washday and had found alternatives whenever possible to doing the laundry themselves, either by hiring washerwomen or using commercial laundries. Before 1920, almost all upper-class and many urban middle-class families, as well as a substantial percentage of working-class families, sent their laundry out to be done. Only three thousand washing machines were manufactured in 1909; by 1919 more than half a million were produced, and by 1925 that number had grown to 880,000. As washing machines appeared in more households, commercial laundries began to disappear, and for the first time in almost a century middle-class women became their own laundresses again.

Electricity produced the most dramatic changes in women's lives during the 1920s and 1930s. Electric current was available in many urban areas by the 1880s and by 1925 more than half the homes in America had access to it. By 1900, women could own electric irons and vacuum cleaners; but they had to wait until the 1920s and 1930s for other small appliances, such as toasters and coffee makers. The invention and widespread distribution of electric refrigerators did not occur until almost 1940. Before then the icebox, an insulated container for storing ice and food, was the norm for most families.

The story of the development of home refrigerators illustrates the complex interconnections between housework and larger economic factors. Historian Ruth Schwartz Cowan in *More Work for Mother* (1983) documents the support that electric utility companies gave major manufacturers of compression refrigerators, such as General Electric, by promoting both refrigerators and the idea of mechanical refrigeration to their customers. Smaller companies that sold gas absorption refrigerators eventually disappeared from the marketplace, because they could not compete with the aggressive marketing and national distribution capabilities of giants such as GE, General Motors, Kelvinator, and Westinghouse. Cowan offers other examples of alternative household appliances that never reached the stores—even though they were superior to existing products—because the companies that produced them believed they could not make a profit on their manufacture and sale. Even those who produced labor-saving devices, she notes, did not have saving the labor of housewives as their number-one concern.

Electricity removed some of the hard physical labor from household chores, but did not eliminate it. Electric irons, for example, replaced heavy, stove-heated flatirons but failed to change the process of ironing. Portable vacuum cleaners left cleaner carpets but required a greater expenditure of energy to operate than a carpet sweeper. Advertisements for electrically powered household equipment assured women that they need not lament the lack of hired help; with their "electrical servants" they could do all the work themselves. After World War I most advertisements for household products depicted housewives doing their own work; domestic servants had literally disappeared from the picture.

Even more than the availability of new energy sources and appliances, the packaging and preparation of foodstuffs outside the home eased women's household chores. National companies such as Van Camp, Campbell, and Heinz were offering canned foods for sale by the latter half of the nineteenth century. By 1910, even the urban working class relied on packaged baked goods. The purchase of canned goods rose with income levels, and as the century wore on consumers increasingly bought more of their food from stores rather than growing or making it themselves. Frozen foods were available as early as the 1930s, but it was not until after World War II, with the expansion of electrical service and the improvement of refrigerators, that frozen foods became commonplace in many American homes. In 1954 "TV dinners" appeared on the market, and two decades later the first meal packaged for the microwave oven was in the supermarket freezer ready for sale.

Technological innovations and unevenly distributed city services accentuated class and regional divisions among women. Poor immigrant women caring for their families in the tenements and basement flats of large cities in the early twentieth century struggled against dirt and squalor without running water or indoor toilets. If running water was available, several families often shared the tap, which meant that someone, usually the housewife, carried water in buckets for the family's needs a considerable distance. A large percentage of families used communal toilets located in the cellar or yard. Overcrowding and the presence of boarders to bring in extra money added to the clutter and noise and ultimately to the work. Middle-class social workers attributed slovenly housekeeping habits and incompetent child-rearing practices to immigrant women, often without understanding the difficult circumstances under which these women labored to feed, shelter, and clothe their families. Urban reformers urged foreign-born women to adopt "American" standards of nutrition, cleanliness, and infant care, demeaning the methods and beliefs immigrants had learned from their mothers and grandmothers. Without adequate living space, sufficient income, running water, garbage collection, and central heating, such advice only helped to increase the distance between the two groups of women.

The industrialization of the home, as some historians have described the changes brought about by new household technologies and products, eased the most onerous aspects of women's domestic chores but did not shorten the time housework took. Time-budget studies conducted from 1900 to 1930 showed that housework remained a full-time job in spite of new energy sources and mechanical aids. In 1930, as it had been in 1900, the average work week for housewives was over forty-five hours, with rural women spending more time in laundering, cleaning, and meal preparation than urban women. By 1930 women of all classes used similar equipment and utilities and strove to achieve the same standards of efficient housework. By 1970 the number of hours per week that women spent on housework had risen to fifty-five, but if the women also worked outside the home that number was reduced to twenty-six. How could this be? How could labor-saving machines not save labor?

A shift in the standard of living, and above all in cultural expectations about cleanliness, nutrition, and the activities women performed in the home helps explain why the new labor-saving machines did not reduce the time spent in housework. For some middle-class women a decline in the servant population meant they were doing their own housework. For those with a rising standard of living, this meant that a family had moved into larger living quarters and the housewife had more rooms to clean. Some women used the time they saved on washing clothes by hand to spend with or on beautifying their homes. But in general the American family now had higher standards and greater expectations about the finished product that resulted from all these new machines in the home. Vacuum cleaners meant carpets could be gotten cleaner and cleaned more frequently; washing machines meant people could change their clothes more often and expect to wear cleaner clothes than scrub boards alone could produce.

Two of the major shapers of these new expectations were the household products and appliances industries. Using guilt, shame, fear, and even competition with other housewives, manufacturers worked to reshape the image of the ideal wife and mother in order to sell their products. In their advertisements, manufacturers sold a message about homemaking along with their merchandise. The measure of the good American housewife, the companies declared, was brighter wash, cleaner floors, tastier meals, lighter cakes, and better-nourished children than her neighbor's. By the second decade of the twentieth century, women's magazines such as *Ladies Home Journal* and *McCall's* were filled with ads for labor-saving devices and products that would help housewives do everything better, quicker, and easier. By the 1920s the number of ads had doubled, as had the range of electrical goods and prepared foods on the market. The mass-circulation magazines helped spread the idea in the 1920s, and again in the 1950s, that home and marriage were a woman's highest calling and that her choosing among the myriad of consumer goods available expressed her judgment and creativity as a homemaker. Whatever time and energy a woman spent preparing meals, cleaning the bathroom, and decorating her home was an investment in her family's physical and emotional well-being.

Some historians argue that technology, rather than improving women's lives, increased their domestic responsibilities and impoverished their community interactions. Appliances, they say, were designed so that women could do all the household chores themselves without the assistance of other family members or hired help. Isolated and confined to their homes with their electric washing machines, refrigerators, stoves, and irons, women traded what historian Susan Strasser calls "craft satisfaction, intimacy, and community" for the illusion that in choosing consumer goods they were exercising autonomy and individualism.

During the Depression and the war years, many households took on some of the qualities of self-reliance they had abandoned decades earlier. To cope with unemployment and diminished household resources during the 1930s, families resorted to making what they might previously have bought. Many women revived old skills of knitting, canning, baking, and sewing, while others supplemented their family's income by dressmaking, cleaning, or taking in laundry. During World War II, food rationing encouraged women's gardening skills and the pickling and preserving of home-grown foods. Women learned to repair broken appliances or to substitute manual labor for mechanical energy. As riveters, welders, and workers in war industries women proved they could be both housewives and wage laborers. Nevertheless, for most young married women and mothers, the new role of wage earner was only temporary. When the war was over, traditional cultural stereotypes of women's proper place reemerged. The majority of women who remained in the labor force after the war were older, many of whom had been working before the war began. Dismissed from their wartime positions, most found low-status, low-paying jobs in traditionally female-dominated occupations. And the domestic ideal reasserted itself in new guises.

The New Domesticity

Often referred to as the decade of the new Victorian domesticity or the decade of the family, the 1950s were filled with contradictions. The popular media portrayed the ideal woman as a happy blend of "Supermom" and "Mrs. Consumer," spending her days in suburbia, shopping and chauffeuring her children from one activity to another. The portrait of the ideal family invariably showed dad cooking over a barbecue in the backyard while room, wearing heels, skirt, and sweater, pearls and an apron, stood smiling at the doorway of their one-family home as their 2.5 children played with their pet cocker spaniel. Women seemed to delight in maintaining the family's emotional equilibrium while submerging their own individuality for the good of their children and husbands. As in the nineteenth-century family image, the actual labor of cleaning, cooking, laundering, and running the household seemed to have been cropped from the picture.

Studies showed, in actuality, that in spite of new household technologies and growing affluence, women of all classes spent an average of four hours a day doing housework and an additional three and a half hours a day caring for children. Housework remained a full-time job even for women who worked for wages outside their homes. And in spite of the celebration of full-time motherhood and suburban living, increasing numbers of women were leaving home to work for wages outside it. Twenty-nine percent of the total work force was female in 1950, but by the late 1960s women's participation in the labor force was considered essential for working-class families to enter the middle class and for middle-class families to retain their comfortable standard of living. By the end of the 1960s, for the first time in American history women who did not work for wages were in the minority. In 1965, women represented 33 percent of the work force and by 1975 they accounted for 40 percent.

During the women's movement of the 1970s, housework became a prime target for feminists demanding changes in the nuclear family. In one widely read article, "The Politics of Housework," Pat Minardi wrote, "[Men] recognize the essential fact of housework right from the beginning. Which is that it stinks." Feminist Margaret Benston advocated communal kitchens, child care, and laundries, arguing as Charlotte Perkins Gilman had, at the beginning of the century, that only when the private work of housekeeping became public labor would women achieve equality with men. Some groups of individuals did form cooperative buying clubs or lived communally with equitable housekeeping arrangements for a while, but with the exception of cooperative child care few such efforts survived for long. For a brief time, an organization called Wages for Housework advocated paying women for the work they did at home, but the movement received little support from the majority of feminists. Although feminists raised fundamental questions about the division of labor in the family, virtually no major structural or institutional changes occurred in the society to support those changes. With the exception of the Displaced Homemakers' Bill (1977), which created training centers to help divorced or widowed women acquire skills to enter the job market, and the law's acknowledgment that a woman's past homemaking services had monetary value in arriving at a divorce settlement, housekeeping remained the most invisible and unappreciated labor of American women. The women's movement eventually focused its efforts on securing political and economic gains for women, and the New Right stepped in to champion, not to change, the traditional nuclear family and women's role as housewife within it.

The 1950s were filled with contradictions like the media's idealization of the "Supermom," a woman in heels, skirt, pearls, and an apron, either smiling at the doorway of her suburban home or chauffeuring her 2.5 children from one activity to the next.

In recent years, however, changes in the economy and in the makeup of American families have transformed many women's lives. By 1980, about 51 percent of all adult women worked outside the home, and by 1985 about 53 percent of women with preschool children were in the labor force. There also have been increases in the divorce rate, the number of women in poverty, the number of households without a husband or male living in them, and the creation of single-person households and single-child families. The large number of mothers in the work force has rendered old fashioned the ideal of the full-time homemaker and made many nonwage-earning women apologetic about being "just a housewife." In spite of these changes, women's roles in the home seem to have remained virtually intact. In the late 1980s, sociologist Arlie Hochschild surveyed two-income families across the economic spectrum and learned that women were still responsible for the home, as they had been for the last three centuries. Housework by men had barely increased, despite women's increasing wage-work. Studies even showed that women living without men did less housework, with and without children; the presence of men in the household seemed to create about eight hours of additional housework for a woman each week.

The explanations, like the study of housework itself, are complex. Some historians believe the housewife's role, although unremunerated and often unacknowledged, is crucial to the success of a capitalist economy. Capitalism depends on women's work in the home, they say, to reproduce the labor force in both the literal sense of bearing and rearing children and in the sense of feeding, clothing, and providing decent living quarters for wage laborers. Historically, employers offered men what they called "a family wage," and cultural norms—the persistence of the separate spheres ideology—reinforced the notion that husbands should be the sole supporters of their families. In the past, this cultural image that women belonged at home affected the kinds of jobs available to them when they did go out to work. Segregated in low-status, low-paying, female-dominated occupations such as clerical work, teaching, nursing, and sales, women continued to think of their wage work as only temporary and as a supplement to a husband's salary. Women defined themselves foremost as wives and mothers, and secondarily as workers. These historians believe that the inequities women encounter in the paid labor force are a result of their role as housewives. Some historians add the uneven power relations between men and women to this explanation, arguing that men's superior earning power in the marketplace and the cultural image that women should be subservient reinforces the gender division of labor in the home.

Others have disputed the notion that patriarchy and capitalism alone account for the persistence of traditional family life and the idea that women should be primarily responsible for work done in the home. Instead, they point to deeply engrained cultural values that lead individuals to choose privacy and autonomy above collective living arrangements or commercial solutions to household tasks. Women, they say, prefer to do their own housework and care for their children themselves, because they believe that doing so best contributes to the well-being of their families. Although the proponents of this theory concede that the allocation of housework to women is a social convention, they argue that, because new household technologies or women's participation in the wage labor force have not dramatically changed assumptions about who does what at home, only a conscious effort to equitably share housework on the part of individual families will make a difference.

Regardless of whether one accepts an economic or a cultural explanation for current beliefs about who does what in the household, the historical record offers useful insights for devising strategies for change. Contrary to the nineteenth-century ideal of the home as a haven from the capitalist marketplace, the record shows a continuous and increasing interconnection between the two spheres. Whether through the creation of new products and appliances, alternative employment options for immigrant and African American domestic servants, or the establishment of ideal standards of housekeeping, American economic interests have affected the work women do at home since the early nineteenth century. Images of the ideal housewife and American family that have been portrayed in the popular media and promulgated by advertisers of consumer products continue to influence contemporary beliefs about housework. This link between the home and the larger economy has led some historians to believe that until housework is acknowledged not as a service to family members or others but as a contribution to the well-being of society in general, those who do it will continue to be undervalued and under-compensated.

[See also The Aristocracy of Inherited Wealth; Clothing and Personal Adornment; Family Structures; Foodways; Gender Roles and Relations; Housing; Labor: Colonial Times through 1820; Labor: The Jacksonian Era through Reconstruction; Labor: The Gilded Age through the 1920s; Labor: The Great Depression to the 1990s; Minorities and Work; Women and Work.]

BIBLIOGRAPHY

Boydston, Jeanne. *Home and Work: Housework, Wages, and the Ideology of Labor in the Early Republic* (1990).

Cowan, Ruth Schwartz. *More Work for Mother: The Ironies of Household Technology from the Open Hearth to the Microwave* (1983).

Dudden, Faye E. *Serving Women: Household Service in Nineteenth-Century America* (1983).

Hartmann, Heidi. "Capitalism and Women's Work in the Home, 1900–1930." Ph.D. dissertation (1974).

Hayden, Dolores. *The Grand Domestic Revolution: A History of Feminist Designs for American Homes, Neighborhoods, and Cities* (1981).

Hochschild, Arlie. *The Second Shift: Working Parents and the Revolution at Home* (1989).

Jensen, Joan M. *Loosening the Bonds: Mid-Atlantic Farm Women, 1750–1850* (1986).

Katzman, David M. *Seven Days a Week: Women and Domestic Service in Industrializing America* (1981).

Matthews, Glenna. *"Just a Housewife": The Rise and Fall of Domesticity in America* (1987).

Ogden, Annegret. *The Great American Housewife: From Helpmate to Wage Earner, 1776–1986* (1986).

Palmer, Phyllis. *Domesticity and Dirt: Housewives and Domestic Servants in the United States, 1920–1945* (1989).

Strasser, Susan. *Never Done: A History of American Housework* (1982).

Ulrich, Laurel Thatcher. *Good Wives: Image and Reality in the Lives of Women in Northern New England, 1650–1750* (1980).

Vanek, Joann. "Household Technology and Social Status: Rising Living Standards and Status and Residence Difference in Housework." *Technology and Culture* 19 (Jan. 1978): 361–375. See table 3, p. 374.

— JUDITH BABBITTS

HOUSING

Americans' need for housing has been satisfied by an impressive diversity of house forms. This essay will identify some characteristic configurations of housing, consider what kinds of households used particular kinds of dwellings, and look at the ways that climate, materials, designers, builders, and construction methods created these houses. The diversity of ethnic heritages, the range of resources available for building, the historical moment, and the class position of dwellers all have affected the form of American housing.

This overview of American housing is organized chronologically. The first section, on seventeenth- and eighteenth-century houses, emphasizes regional differences, since both climate and European settlement patterns strongly influenced the shape of early houses. The second section, on the nineteenth century, focuses on new national trends, emerging class demarcations, and the effects of industrialization on house forms. The twentieth-century section considers the diversity of house forms within each income level, and closes with some indications of future directions in housing.

The Colonial Period

The future United States was colonized independently by several European nations in the late sixteenth and seventeenth centuries. Spanish, French, Dutch, and English colonists were sent to the New World to secure parts of North America for their home countries' economic benefit. They arrived to find a landscape inhabited by Native Americans speaking a wide variety of languages, living in a variety of structures, and with unfamiliar community organizations.

New England and the Chesapeake region were the focus of English colonization. The shelters the colonists made upon first arrival were rude constructions: tree branches, twigs, and bark created a wigwam; a hollow in the earth protected new arrivals from the weather. Colonial efforts at creating housing depended primarily on settlers' knowledge of house types, room arrangements, and building practices brought with them from their countries of origin, combined with the building materials available on New World sites. When woodworking skills and tools imported from England combined with a ready supply of wood in New England, timber-framed houses sheathed in overlapping clapboards and roofed in shingles resulted.

Many one-room houses were erected in New England and the Chesapeake by and for ordinary farmers and townspeople. A common type had wood posts planted directly in the ground—called earth-fast construction—supporting a pegged-together timber frame. Sheathed and roofed in wood, unpainted, often with a clay-covered wooden chimney, such houses could easily last for at least a decade or two. Owners of such structures may have planned to move on when agricultural opportunities called them elsewhere, or to return to the mother country after improving their fortunes. Such dwellings constituted the largest number of Anglo dwellings in the seventeenth and eighteenth centuries.

A one-room house had to contain all the persons and activities of the household that required shelter. When feasible, some activities were pushed outdoors. For example, a cooking fire with a tripod-suspended pot served as outdoor kitchen. Sleeping, socializing, and work spaces all could occupy a single room, activities changing with times of day. A one-room house might have extra space under the roof—a rough attic reached by a ladder served many people as a bedroom. For the poorest, one-room structures continued to provide housing through the nineteenth century both on the traditionally understood frontier, and in urban settings where poverty allowed no other choice.

New Englanders intending to create permanent towns built wooden houses on stone footings to protect the wood from decay; they constructed stone or brick fireplaces and chimneys to secure the wood structure from fire. They carefully cut mortises, tenons, and a variety of other timber joints to create a lasting structure, and added onto the house as family size and resources expanded. The hall-parlor plan represents a well-known organization of the main spaces in a seventeenth-century New England house. The main floor was divided into two rooms set left and right of a front door. The hall was the all-purpose room in which cooking and daily meals, spinning, and small-scale household production took place. Furniture was sparse, and tables and benches could be pushed against the walls to allow multiple activities to take place. The parlor was reserved for the finer household goods, special meals, visiting, and the parent's bed.

The exterior of the New England hall-parlor house reflected its internal organization. A massive chimney rose through the middle of the roof, signaling the presence of one chimney core opening into fireplaces in the hall, in the parlor, and perhaps toward the rear if there was a kitchen across the back of the house. Such a kitchen was often the first addition made by a growing family, and the extended roof that covered it gave New England houses their characteristic saltbox profile. On the floor above the hall and parlor might be additional rooms, named "hall chamber" and "parlor chamber" for their location, and used both as sleeping spaces for the children and servants or apprentices living in the household and for storage.

The middle states of New York, New Jersey, and Pennsylvania were early homes for German and Dutch settlers as well as the English. Dutch settlers occupied New York's Hudson Valley, and nearby New Jersey and Long Island in the mid seventeenth century. Houses were constructed of wood, framed with heavy timber anchor-beams visible on the interior. These knee-braced beams supported the high ceilings of rooms often arranged in linear fashion, each room having its own front door. Limestone or brick sheathed the exterior; dates, initials, or geometric patterns were sometimes introduced into the brick courses. Increasing prosperity allowed the Dutch to expand originally one- or two-room houses into multiroom long bar, L shape, or square plans.

In Pennsylvania, German immigrants arrived in the later seventeenth and eighteenth centuries. They built freestanding houses in farmstead settings. The preferred exterior wall materials for German house builders were stone or exposed timber framing with clay or masonry infill. The characteristic house form had as its principal ground-floor rooms the kitchen with a cooking fireplace and the *stube,* or entertaining room, with a heating stove and built-in seats along the walls. Like the early Anglo houses, German houses had exposed ceiling beams. Second-floor chambers complemented one or two ground-floor bedrooms. Stone cellars contained insulated storage rooms for food, and sometimes, a spring. In the eighteenth century, German settlers migrated south into Maryland, the Valley of Virginia, and North Carolina, where they continued to build stone and half-timbered houses.

Settlers in Maryland and Virginia built houses to suit a warmer climate. While the earliest established planters erected large houses with many rooms, by the eighteenth century it was common for a prosperous planter to construct multiple buildings clustered together instead of a single house. These forms were influenced by the southern commitment to an agricultural economy based on slave and indentured labor. One building provided a home for the planter and his immediate family. Slaves and servants had separate outbuildings in which to sleep. The kitchen, with its overheated atmosphere and hazardous sparks, occupied a building of its own. Additional storage and utility buildings dotted the near landscape, such that travelers described the planter's house as looking like a little village.

The houses erected for slaves in the South tended to provide minimum space for each household group—usually a single room for a family. The slaves built their housing with materials that were inexpensively acquired; sometimes leftovers from a more important piece of construction were handed along to them. A slave house might contain two or more households, each with one room on the main floor and an attic space above, the several households separated by partitions. A small window or two let in light; a door could create cross-ventilation; the fields served as privy. The slaves' scanty possessions were sometimes secreted in storage holes in the earthen floor.

Slave houses were located close to the work sites; a small cluster would be built near the fields where the slaves worked, creating a quarter apart from the owner's house. Sometimes slave houses were lined along a drive near the master's house, contributing to the townlike appearance of the planter's domain. If near the main house, slave dwellings were likely to have a coat of paint or other exterior finish, to give visual appeal to the planter's home grounds. If located at a greater distance, slave houses were made weatherproof but otherwise left unfinished on the exterior.

Ambitious families built houses in brick on both rural and town sites in Maryland, Virginia, and the Carolinas. They created symmetrical structures of two or three stories, sometimes extended laterally with wings or dependencies. The wealthiest looked to England for stylistic potential, adapting late Renaissance classical details for exterior door and window ornament, and for interior mantelpieces, moldings, door and window frames, elaborated staircases, and paneling. But they still relied on the aggregation of mostly wooden buildings to contain all the functions of the agricultural year, as did the majority of less prosperous planter households.

The French settlers arrived on the eastern shores of Canada and moved westward to the Great Lakes in the seventeenth century. Settlements followed the path of the Mississippi River; two of the original French foundations are the modern cities of Detroit and Saint Louis. Driven from Canada, French-speaking Acadians became Cajuns in the New Orleans-Delta region of Louisiana.

The French building traditions brought to America include the tall roof of northern Europe, the exterior veranda used for circulation, exterior staircases to the second story, and timber building methods such as *poteaux sur solle*—squared-off logs standing on a horizontal sill of wood. The spaces between the vertical logs were filled with clay and a binder such as hair or straw, or stones and mortar.

In the warm and wet Delta region, the raised creole cottage provided a convenient ground floor for services, relatively crudely finished, able to withstand an occasional flood, and a principal floor one level above ground where finely crafted woodwork would stay dry. A surrounding veranda that served the principal rooms was reached by a broad flight of steps in the country or smaller exterior stairs in urban settings.

Spanish settlers first colonized Florida in the late sixteenth century, then California, New Mexico, and the rest of the Southwest. Houses set flush with the street helped to create an urban clarity of definition for plazas and rectilinear street grids—features of the Spanish town plan prescribed by guidelines for the creation of colonial towns, the 1873 Laws of the Indies. In Florida, simple houses of two rooms, expanded by adding rooms in single file, were built of wattle and daub or boards and roofed in thatch. More sophisticated builders used coquina, a local stone made up of compacted seashells, or "tabby," a kind of cement mixture of shells, sand, lime, and water. Favored building materials in the Southwest were adobe (sun-dried brick) combined with local wood for ceiling beams, door and window frames, and veranda framing. In a dry climate, adobe was long-lasting, cheap to build with, and easily repaired with a periodic coat of clay to seal the surface.

The Spanish house was often a single range of rooms wrapped around a courtyard, sometimes with a second story. Extended roofs sheltered verandas and patios, characteristic of hot-climate architecture; outdoor courtyards and indoor rooms were equally essential in providing for the household's space needs. Elaborated wooden screens and grilles allowed Florida builders to encourage the passage of breezes through houses. The Spanish tradition of tile as a surfacing material gave color to the more expensive houses.

Climate played an important role in forming the configurations of colonial-era houses. In warm-climate areas, greater use was made of outdoor spaces than in the colder regions. Thus outdoor kitchens in separate buildings were used by French builders in the lower Mississippi Valley, Spanish settlers in Florida, and Anglo settlers in Virginia. Hispanic houses of the Southwest and Florida displayed a similar attitude to outdoor spaces with their second-story porches and courtyards. Outdoor passages from one part of the home grounds to another were common; one walked outdoors from the planter's main house to a subsidiary library or schoolhouse, often with bedrooms above; or one went onto the veranda of a creole cottage to get to the next room instead of using an interior hallway. Colder-climate architecture tended toward steep roofs, small window areas, and entranceways that faced south. Additional space in the attic above the parlor and hall was used as a sleeping area for household members and for storage.

Favored building materials in the Southwest were sun-dried bricks known as adobe combined with local wood for ceiling beams, door and window frames, and veranda framing.

The Nineteenth Century: Immigration and Industrialization

The coastal settlements of the early period expanded as a growing population moved inland, after the 1785 survey of western lands, to find new farmland, to found new towns, and to exploit new resources. The original settlers were joined by immigrants from Germany, Scandinavia, Ireland, Russia, and elsewhere. Land made available to settlers by the United States government through the Homestead Act of 1862 and other legislation drew new arrivals west of the Appalachians and across the Mississippi.

Well established before the nineteenth century, the single-family house continued to serve American households. For new arrivals on the frontier, migrant or immigrant, one-room houses satisfied the need for speedily erected and economical shelter, just as they had for seventeenth- and eighteenth-century settlers. In the longer-settled areas, prosperous planters, farmers, and merchants built showplace single-family houses with many rooms.

Houses were directly affected by industrialization, which added many new possibilities to the nineteenth-century repertoire of house ideas. New materials were mass-produced and shipped around the country by rail; these included sawn lumber, nails, ornament in wood or cast iron, and prefabricated dwellings. New town forms developed with characteristic new housing types: the company town added tenements and boardinghouses, communitarian utopias developed collective dwellings, and commuter suburbs served the burgeoning middle class with variations on the single-family home at all prices.

A long-mythologized house form of this period was the log house, associated with the self-reliant economy of the frontier. The log construction method was indeed widely used during the period of western migration as a conveniently and quickly erected, inexpensive house that made use of on-site materials. It afforded housing to rural people with small resources. While an individual, casually built log house might not last more than a generation, the tradition of building them persisted for many generations in rural areas. Small, one-room log houses could be assembled quickly with round logs, the gaps between them chinked with mud and straw.

By the early nineteenth century, water-powered mills were turning out mass-produced sawn lumber, nails, textiles, and other goods; mill workers settled near these workplaces, creating new towns and giving rise to new housing needs. One such new form was the company town. Housing produced by companies to house their workers ran from single-family cottages to two- and three-story houses for managers and tenements for single workers or for poorer families. Management-owned housing was rented to workers, and sometimes the rent was subtracted from the paycheck before payday.

At Lowell, Massachusetts, in the 1820s, the cotton company built boardinghouses where single women workers lived communally, sharing bedrooms and eating centrally prepared meals in group dining rooms; there was a housemother to guarantee propriety. Next to the cotton mills in Baltimore's Jones Valley, mill workers could live in company-sponsored two-family houses; each household had two rooms on each floor of a two-story house located within a block or two of the mill.

The elaborate and much-publicized company town of Pullman, Illinois, built in the 1880s, provided single-family, two-family, and four-family houses, tenements, boardinghouses, and a hotel. Workers at the vast Pullman railroad car plant lived in these many housing types, according to their means, across the street from the factory buildings in a nicely landscaped town with public market buildings, church, stables, and a park. Exorbitant rents caused the state to divest George Pullman of his interest in the town. The houses remain in good condition and are still inhabited. The town, now part of Chicago, is a historic site.

In cities of the industrial era, multifamily housing rather than houses for single families became the norm. At the turn of the nineteenth century, older houses that had been built for single families "filtered down" and were subdivided for renters at rates affordable to workers. The demolition and rebuilding that characterized urban centers in the 1830s and 1840s decreased this housing stock, leaving poor families in need of specially designed cheap rental quarters—tenements. The name "tenement" was applied to any house in which three or more households shared a common roof but lived in separate quarters. As urban housing after about 1830 took on distinctive class differences, "tenement" came to refer to a building for working-class, immigrant, or poor tenants; the term "apartment" came into use as the name for a middle-class family unit in a multifamily dwelling.

In the second and third quarters of the nineteenth century, thousands of tenement dwelling units were erected in New York, Philadelphia, and other growing cities. The physical form of early tenements was varied. Often built of wood, some resembled private houses, while others reminded contemporaries of huge barracks. Tenement landlords rarely supplied their tenants with pure water or sanitary facilities. Wood construction made tenement living a fire hazard, one not alleviated by the tendency to make fire escapes out of wood. High death rates in tenement districts drew attention to the health problems created by their unsanitary conditions, leading to legislative efforts to control their design in the 1850s, 1860s, and 1870s.

A poor family living in a one-room tenement apartment, ca. 1920. Parents, children, and boarders all slept in proximity to each other.

A typical tenement built for profit in the last quarter of the nineteenth century in New York was sited on a lot 25 feet by 100 feet (7.5 by 30 meters). It was called a dumbbell tenement after the shape of the plan: the plan narrowed in the center to create a light well, while at the front and back it spread to the full-lot width. Each tenement house had five floors with four units on each floor. Family units in such buildings usually had no more than three rooms—a living room used for cooking, eating, washing, income-producing work, and socializing, and two bedrooms, used for sleeping but also for income-producing piecework. Families frequently took in unrelated boarders to help pay the rent, so parents, children, and boarders all slept in proximity to each other—a lack of privacy that early social workers found threatening to morality. When there were indoor toilet facilities, they were limited to water closets in the public halls; bathtubs were not supplied in tenements. However, for those who wanted to bathe, public baths were common in larger cities after 1900.

Only two or three apartments per floor rather than the standard four was a variant of the tenement for tenants who could afford higher rents. Fewer units per floor meant that each family gained square footage. Two apartments per floor in a 25-foot-wide (7.5-meter) building each ran from front to back in a long string of rooms. When these apartments had no interior hallways, a space-saving device, they were called railroad flats because one walked from room to room as if going through the cars on a train.

Charitable organizations and individual philanthropists participated in the building of workers' housing. Alfred Tredway White promoted "5% philanthropy," the idea that public-spirited investors could put their money into progressively conceived workers' housing projects and still make a modest 5 percent return on the investment. White assembled large plots of land the size of an entire city block, and built model tenements such as the Tower and Riverside buildings, in Brooklyn, which provided three- or four-room units in two-room-deep perimeter-type buildings. These structures were built to wrap around the edge of the lot, leaving the land inside free to be used for recreation, laundry, and children's play. Every apartment had cross-ventilation and ample sunshine from both the street and courtyard sides. Unlike privately sponsored tenements, whose owners were bent on saving money, philanthropic housing often included bathtubs in the basement and private water closets within each household space.

The mid nineteenth century saw the definition of an American middle class with boundaries in part articulated by housing form. Farmers, the backbone of the American economy, built improved farmhouses with the aid of advice in agricultural journals. The modern farm included a house with heating and cooking stoves, a pump drawing running water into the kitchen sink, and many rooms to differentiate receiving company from work-related tasks or from the family's sitting and sleeping rooms. The activities of the farm, and therefore the specific spaces of the farmhouse and its linked, work-related buildings, were often divided by gender between husband and wife, their male and female children, and their farmhands. The women's sphere included the kitchen, the dooryard, and adjunct spaces for readying butter and eggs for market; the men's sphere was the barn, the barnyard, and adjunct spaces for tending to farm animals and crops.

Some farm families built larger and more refined log structures with several rooms. Building techniques such as finely cut corner notching, found throughout the Midwest and the South, exhibit highly developed building skills exercised with elaborate tool kits. In the upland South a double-pen log house (the dogtrot form) comprised two one-room log structures separated by an open passage and joined under a single roof. The open-air passage served as circulation (that is, the path of movement for residents), as an outdoor protected sitting area, and for the ventilation needed in hot southern summers. Nineteenth-century "improvements" led to sheathing log houses in clapboards or some other modern finish and enclosing the open-air passage, creating a center hall, often with stairs to an added second story. Such alterations sometimes made the log house look like a framed central-passage house.

In the northern Midwest, immigrant Finns, Swedes, and Norwegians brought northern European, refined corner-notching techniques to build houses of one and two stories with logs. As their farms prospered, their houses grew to several rooms, with interior walls notched into the exterior log structure. Often a porch was part of the basic plan. Logs for these houses were carefully squared off and the bark removed before the corner joints were cut. The logs were closely fitted and the internal walls plastered for a smooth finish.

Another new housing idea of the nineteenth century emerged from the flourishing utopian and religious communities in which the believers often lived in large collective dwellings rather than single-family houses. The Shaker community at Hancock, Massachusetts, created a large, collective dwelling form, the Brothers' and Sisters' House, which contained rooms for all the males and rooms for all the females of the group, spatially segregated from each other. The Shaker dwelling house included sophisticated built-in cupboards and drawers to accommodate the residents' need for storage and to free the floor from extra pieces of furniture. At Salem, North Carolina, a settlement of Moravians created large, gender-segregated collective dwellings for their single members, constructed using German half-timbering with brick infill. Married church members moved into single-family houses for raising families, and ultimately went to their final rest in gender-segregated cemeteries.

More middle-class families took up living in suburbs from the 1850s on. The first suburbs arose with the first transportation lines. Railroads and ferry boats linked urban downtowns with new residential districts created as bedroom communities for middle- and upper-middle-income households. Commuting husbands went to city, workplaces while homemaking women and children spent the day in the healthy fresh air and greenery of the suburb. A profusion of illustrated architectural books from the 1840s on promoted ornamental cottages in landscaped settings as the American single-family ideal.

By the 1880s trolley lines reached out from many American downtowns to open up new residential areas for middling families whose budgets might allow them to live in half of a two-family house or one floor of a triple (three-flat) house in a "streetcar suburb." The wide availability of factory-cut lumber gave rise to a proliferation of moderately priced wooden houses for members of the emerging middle class in towns and suburbs.

By the 1880s trolley lines reached out from many American downtowns to open up new residential areas for middling families in "streetcar suburbs."

Apartment houses for middle-class tenants provided another version of the collective dwelling in mid-nineteenth-century cities. This type first appeared under the name "hotel" in Boston about 1860. The conveniences provided by a hotel, including meals, maid service, central heating, gas or electric light, and security, tempted the well-to-do to renounce private houses and turn to apartment living. First called "flats," "French flats," or "Parisian dwellings," because they reminded early observers of the apartment-house tradition of middle-class Parisians, apartment houses designed expressly to preserve family privacy yet provide the pleasant services vices of a hotel were under construction in the late 1860s in New York, and in the 1870s in Washington, Chicago, and elsewhere.

Apartment houses for the middle class developed first as smaller buildings not too different in external appearance from large private houses. Inside, each floor was built to be a separate family unit. Early (1870–1880) apartment house designs of four or five stories made use of staircases rather than elevators. Servants slept on the topmost floor, and rents were adjusted so that those who had to climb the most stairs paid the least.

Much larger apartment houses of eight to ten stories appeared in the 1880s along with elevators, elaborate lobbies, doormen, and other service staff. Tall apartment houses in Chicago, Washington, Boston, and New York presented a new architectural image to passersby—one poised among the architectural conventions for a private house, a hotel, and an office building of the period. These buildings were constructed using new steel-cage engineering techniques, and were decorated on the exterior with stylish historical ornament in stone and terra-cotta.

The interior planning of an apartment unit was grounded in middle-class standards of family privacy and the sociable display of consumer goods. A formal parlor provided the space for receiving guests and placing the best furniture. Apartments for the wealthy, such as the 1883 Central Park Apartments in New York, had additional reception rooms—a library, a drawing room, and even a billiard room. Dining rooms were standard for all middle-class apartments. Family bedrooms ranged from one or two to eight or more; in addition there were always servants' rooms, either within the family unit or in attic or basement spaces. Apartment buildings set the standard for central heating, gas and electric lighting, telephones, refrigerators, and other technological household advances in the 1890s.

Private houses of the wealthy in the early-nineteenth-century city were often four or five stories high, with a basement half aboveground. In the basement were a kitchen and family dining room. It was important for the kitchen to have immediate access to the backyard, where a cistern or pump was located and where garbage could be dumped. On the first floor, raised somewhat above sidewalk level by a flight of steps, were the reception rooms—a front and back parlor, and perhaps a formal dining room. The upper floors contained bedrooms and family sitting rooms. At the top, in the attic, were servants' rooms, storage, and workrooms.

Some early houses also contained a "counting room" or office in which the male head of the household conducted business. However, one aspect of improvement in house design of the nineteenth century was purging the house of explicit business and income-producing activities, so the counting room did not persist. Of course, the house served to enhance a family's income-producing potential because it secured extended family and social connections so necessary for the successful conduct of business, certified the social rank of the inhabitants, and itself increased in value.

At the same time, the home was increasingly mythologized as a refuge completely separated from work. A middle-class woman was told—in household magazines, manners manuals, and fiction—that her primary role was to be the moral force in the household, educator of her children, and example to her husband. She represented honorable values untainted by the commerce that weakened the moral fiber of the working world beyond the home. This framing of women mystified the real work that went on inside the household and the cash relations that underpinned the existence of servants and housewives.

Wealthy families continued to live in private houses in the cities of the later nineteenth century, but often possessed at least one country house as well. Philadelphians built summer homes on the Atlantic coast of New Jersey in towns such as Elberon; a winter home in Manhattan was complemented by a summer home at Newport, Rhode Island, or Asheville, North Carolina. Country houses for the well-to-do displayed familiarity with European architectural styles, which were inventively interpreted in wood, brick, or stone. Popular styles were the Greek revival in the 1830s and 1840s, Italianate and Gothic revival in the 1840s and 1850s, French Second Empire in the 1860s and 1870s, Victorian in the 1870s, and Queen Anne in the 1880s. Information on up-to-date architectural styles was available to architects, clients, and builders in mass-distributed books—another influence of industrialization. All these styles allowed American builders to display ornamental vocabularies, both inside and outside, adjusting the use of lavish materials to suit the wealth of the patron.

The spaces provided for a wealthy family in a country house of the later nineteenth century included several reception rooms—drawing room, library, parlor, sitting room, billiard room, boudoir; a dining room and perhaps a separate breakfast room; family bedrooms, typically grouped together on the second floor; a service suite of rooms including the kitchen, several pantries, food storage rooms, laundry rooms, servants' dining room, servants' bedrooms; several bathrooms, located separately for family members and for servants; and additional services located in the basement, stable, and carriage house.

The kinds of activities and meanings the American house had to support changed with time, climate, ethnicity, gender, and economics. Such changes were evident even on the simple level of function. For example, the late-nineteenth-century middle-class urban dwelling, whether in a single-family or multifamily configuration, tended to include a kitchen and a bathroom, and to exclude the income-producing work site. In a Virginia farmhouse of the early nineteenth century, the reverse was the case: separate kitchens were in independent back buildings, frequent baths were not part of people's behavior, and income was produced by work done in the house and its immediate landscape.

Twentieth-Century Dwellings

The twentieth century continued to use many of the nineteenth century's innovations—apartment houses, suburbs, and multiroom single-family houses. The automobile affected both the location of houses and their design: garages became part of the home. Most influential was the increased role of the state in housing production and distribution, seen in areas as diverse as zoning law, publicly subsidized housing for the poor, and federal mortgage insurance. The state's negligence was also visible in the rise of homeless individuals and families.

Regional and climate characteristics so evident in houses of the eighteenth century continually diminished in the wake of industrialization. Modern building materials such as steel and concrete were used in every region, and inventions such as air-conditioning made climate-specific design solutions unnecessary. Manufactured housing increased rapidly since the 1970s, providing already-built houses that were trucked to sites all over the country and priced for households with very modest incomes. Such houses were designed for generic buyers; only after installing them were climate-specific adjustments made.

The twentieth century saw the distribution and incorporation of utilities into houses on a scale never before experienced. Most Americans since World War II lived in dwellings that had electricity for lighting and appliances, gas for cooking, stoves or furnaces for heating, indoor plumbing and sanitary facilities, and hot and cold running water. Before 1850 many of these conveniences were unavailable; some could be had only by the wealthiest households. Middle- and upper-class households that once had servants to light fires and lamps, cook meals, and empty slops now had plumbing and heating systems, power tools, and appliances to accomplish these housekeeping tasks. These same systems, tools, and appliances came to be a normal part of low-cost housing.

As immigrant populations moved into American cities, older generations, now Americanized, sought new homes, either in apartments or in single-family houses built for low-income households. Small houses priced to meet low-to-middling budgets and sized for the economy of servantless housekeeping were offered in diverse markets. In the first decade of the twentieth century, a house could be contracted for with a builder, or purchased already built from a developer. Mail-order houses such as Sears, Roebuck's could be purchased either as a set of plans and specifications that a local builder would follow, or as a complete house shipped as precut parts with instructions, to be erected on the site of one's choice, perhaps with one's own labor. Small, one-story houses with four rooms, called bungalows, were built nationwide, popularized by specialized magazines and even in songs. A living room, a kitchen, a bathroom, and one or two bedrooms provided lower-income families with homes of their own. Financing assisted those without savings to achieve independence. Manufacturers or developers offered special rates and installment payments at the turn of the century, a financial support system taken up later by banks and other thrift institutions, and subsidized by the federal government.

Early-twentieth-century housing also included multifamily alternatives located away from the center of the city in peripheral or suburban settings. Garden apartments emerged as a popular form of low-rise, three-to-five-story housing, set back from the street in landscaped grounds. Generous courtyards provided residents with recreational and even gardening possibilities. Apartment units were placed so that every one had generous light and cross ventilation; occupants of several units shared laundry equipment, garages, and storage rooms. Such apartment developments were sponsored by businesses that wanted sound investments, such as insurance companies, or by organizations working to improve the lot of their membership, such as labor unions.

Downtown housing accommodated households that did not fit the standard American family model. Single people, both male and female, found city housing to their taste in hotels or single-room-occupancy, apartments. One or two rooms with a private bath located close to cultural attractions and downtown workplaces satisfied those who had no need for larger apartments and who rejected the life-style of the suburbs. At the turn of the century many "bachelor flats" were built for this group, whose special needs were not much acknowledged at the end of the century.

Company towns sponsored by corporations and erected for their workers continued in the twentieth century. Companies located away from population centers had to make special provisions for bringing workers to the job site; a new town near the site was an obvious solution. An example is Copperton, Utah, built in the 1920s by a copper mining company next to a vast open mine. The town of several square blocks contained schools and playgrounds, public meeting spaces, and single-family houses built according to five different plans. Exterior gables, porches, and window details combined with varied colors and material finishes to give the houses a good deal of individuality. Four-car garages at the rear corners of four contiguous lots were the only collective features; each house had its own front and back yards, clothesline, and driveway.

Suburban homes were widely believed to be superior places to bring up children for both physical and moral health reasons. The outer edges of cities were built up as automobile-era suburbs in the 1920s and 1930s, each house with its own garage, front yard, and back yard. The model suburban town of Radburn, New Jersey, was built in 1929 to demonstrate the latest in planning theory for the automobile era. A commuter suburb, the town was located near railroad lines but was also structured around the private car. Modest three-bedroom houses were finished in brick, wood, and stucco using half-timbered and other historical motifs. Houses faced onto two circulation systems: the back of the house and its garage faced an automobile street; the front of the house and its entrance faced a paved pedestrian route. Car traffic near houses used cul-de-sac streets with a low speed limit; larger collector streets took traffic through town and linked it to highways. All the pedestrian paths crossed automobile paths by means of bridges and underpasses, to protect pedestrians (especially children) from accidents. Every house was linked by a network of walking paths to the school and to a small shopping district.

Beginning early in this century, mail-order houses could be purchased either as a set of plans that a local builder would follow or as a complete house shipped in parts with instructions.

The expansion in population after World War II gave rise to a demand for more single-family housing subsidized by federal loan programs. Huge numbers of houses were erected by developers such as the Levitt brothers, whose Levittowns in New York, Pennsylvania, and New Jersey became synonymous with repetitive and homogeneous suburban housing developments. Their houses, built by the thousands using traditional masonry and carpentry techniques, had minimum square footage, maximized the appliances and services that made for modern housekeeping, and were intended for future expansion. The company provided ideas to transform carports into garages, and garages and attics into bedrooms.

In the 1930s public housing began to redress problems created by the Great Depression. Poor but employed families were preferred as the tenants in federally produced row houses and low-rise apartments built all over the country. The best of these included playgrounds and landscaping; family unit sizes were kept to the minimum, and low-rise configurations meant that districts of subsidized housing did not reach the high densities that more prosperous neighborhoods found threatening.

After World War II, migrations of formerly rural Americans, especially southern African Americans, into cities pointed up the need for increased modern urban housing. Decades of suburban housing production had taken attention away from inner-city conditions. There, tenement buildings that had been constructed in the 1870s and 1880s still served poorer families in densely spaced, ethnically homogeneous enclaves. Houses once built for single families after the Civil War continued to serve as inner-city housing, subdivided to create two, three, or more apartments. Such housing lacked up-to-date plumbing and wiring and was often in serious disrepair. Neighborhoods, once identified as slums, were not thought worthy of the investment necessary for upgrading. The oldest, most decayed housing had always been inherited by those least able to pay; to city administrators and urban planners of the 1950s, this old housing looked too decayed to serve anyone. "Urban renewal" policies were formulated to demolish and replace it, rebuilding center-city neighborhoods with the most up-to-date dwelling units equipped with modern plumbing, heating, lighting, and other services. The tower form was preferred because it used less land and initially appeared to be cheaper to build.

The replacement housing planned in these years was government-sponsored, but the state had never been widely supported as a housing initiator. Many critics still felt that housing was the rightful province of private enterprise, and in the absence of full commitment, public moneys did not achieve the amount of replacement housing originally intended. Building costs far exceeded estimates, and high-rise housing turned out to be far more costly than the low-rise units developed in the 1930s. Such small row and single-family houses continued to be erected in rural and suburban settings under federal programs, such as the 1950s and 1960s housing found on Indian reservations.

An example of public housing erected in this era is the 1958 Pruitt-Igoe redevelopment neighborhood in Saint Louis. Dwelling units were organized in thirty-three towers, each eleven stories high. Family units included large windows, several rooms, and fully equipped kitchens and bathrooms. Apartments were reached by elevators which stopped on every third floor.

Houses once built for single families after the Civil War continued to serve the inner city, subdivided to create, two, three, or more apartments that often lacked up-to-date plumbing and wiring and usually were in serious disrepair.

The fresh paint and services seemed to create the atmosphere for successful home life, but the project as a whole was ill managed.

Housing such as Pruitt-Igoe concentrated large numbers of poor households in too limited an area rather than mixing varied income households or dispersing smaller housing projects for the poor in several neighborhoods. So many people without resources could not keep their dwelling units in good repair, and city officials did not invest in the necessary maintenance of the public spaces—halls and elevators, parking lots and playgrounds—that should have been their responsibility. Pruitt-Igoe was finally demolished in 1972 after it proved unrepairable. In many cities, tower public housing has been closed awaiting reuse plans or has been sold to middle-class buyers as condominiums; some projects are being reduced in height to create more domestically scaled environments.

Housing for the wealthy in the twentieth century has few characteristics besides size and location that differentiate it from that of the middle-income and the poor. A full array of services has been a feature of expensive housing since 1900, but has been available to middling and poor households as well since World War II. Since the 1930s, architect-designed modernist houses of one story with an open plan and walls of glass have satisfied wealthy clients willing to take an artistic risk. Suburban houses in historical styles, popular in the nineteenth century, have remained the most popular in well-to-do, exclusive suburbs outside many American cities. Zoning laws have been used to require very large lot sizes and costly houses in neighborhoods allocated to the wealthy. The phenomenon called gentrification characterized efforts to reclaim inner-city buildings for housing in the 1970s and 1980s. The historic preservation movement, having raised appreciation of historic architecture among the upwardly mobile, provided a counter to urban renewal by demolition. Late-nineteenth-and early-twentieth-century houses were sold to willing renovators who treasured the urbanity and historic character of aging city neighborhoods. Preserved blocks of such houses, now inhabited by wealthier owners, drove up real estate prices in areas previously deemed slums. In urban downtowns housing commanding high rents or sale prices has been created from underutilized older office and factory buildings, and sometimes even philanthropic tenements have been converted to high-priced condominiums.

High-rise towers have also been used for expensive apartments across the country, located in urban neighborhoods associated with social success. The sizes of household units for the wealthy can be much larger than units in middle-class or publicly subsidized apartment towers, and the material finishes are finer; the construction techniques and utilities and service systems use the same technologies. As in the nineteenth century, well-to-do people often possess more than one home, and a small urban apartment often suits their needs when combined with a large country house. The cost of renting or owning even a small apartment, however, depends significantly on location. Two rooms in the "best" building may cost as much as a dozen rooms in a less desirable place.

Since the 1970s some shifts in house form have suggested that developers and legislators acknowledge that household form is more diverse than the single-family standard. Municipalities recognized the need for families to incorporate an elderly parent into the household by structuring zoning laws to allow "mother-in-law" apartments attached to single-family houses. Apartment buildings were designed to allow two unrelated individuals to share one unit while each maintained a separate social life. Both bore the costs of rent on a shared kitchen and living room, services and utilities, and each had a personal bedroom and bathroom. Recognizing that many families were headed by a single parent, some multifamily dwellings were organized around collective day care for children. Housing forms were needed that recognize the many alternatives to a standard family that comprised households.

Near the end of the twentieth century, striking similarities between house forms for all classes and regions pointed up the triumph of modern construction techniques and services over ethnic and regional variants. Tall apartment towers served all income levels; they were just erected in different neighborhoods to serve different classes. The costliness and quality of materials and the square footage distinguished a single-family suburban house for a wealthy client from one for a poor client, but both were likely to have paved roads and driveway, gas and electric power, appliances, heat, cooking equipment, and indoor plumbing.

What Americans lacked was equal access to these house forms and to the comfortable and secure life they promise. Regional imbalances in price led to mansion price tags on four-room bungalows in some areas. Young middle-class or poor people could never expect to amass a down payment to buy their own house in inflated real estate markets. Low-income families who could only afford to be tenants found that income tax breaks were given to those who buy housing but not to those who rent. Racial discrimination in housing, although illegal, still prevented some from living in the district or the building of choice. The success of constructing and servicing houses must be followed up by economic and social structures that give everyone access to housing.

[See also The City; Family Structures; Public Architecture; The Suburbs; Village and Town.]

BIBLIOGRAPHY

General Histories

Bishir, Catherine W., Charlotte V. Brown, Carl R. Lounsbury, and Ernest H. Wood III. *Architects and Builders in North Carolina: A History of the Practice of Building* (1990).

Blackmar, Elizabeth S. *Manhattan for Rent, 1785–1850* (1989).

Clark, Clifford E., Jr. *The American Family Home 1800–1960* (1986).

Cromley, Elizabeth. *Alone Together: A History of New York's Early Apartments* (1990).

Cummings, Abbott Lowell. *The Framed Houses of Massachusetts Bay, 1625–1725* (1979).

Glassie, Henry. *Folk Housing in Middle Virginia: A Structural Analysis of Historic Artifacts* (1975).

Gottfried, Herbert, and Jan Jennings. *American Vernacular Design, 1870–1940: An Illustrated Glossary* (1988).

Hayden, Dolores. *Seven American Utopias: The Architecture of Communitarian Socialism, 1790–1975* (1976).

Hubka, Thomas C. *Big House, Little House, Back House, Barn: The Connected Farm Buildings of New England* (1984).

Larkin, Jack. *The Reshaping of Everyday Life, 1790–1840* (1988).

McMurry, Sally. *Families and Farmhouses in Nineteenth-Century America: Vernacular Design and Social Change.* (1988).

Nabokov, Peter, and Robert Easton. *Native American Architecture* (1989).

Plunz, Richard. *A History of Housing in New York City* (1990).

Upton, Dell, ed. *America's Architectural Roots: Ethnic Groups That Built America* (1986).

Upton, Dell, and John Michael Vlach, eds. *Common Places: Readings in American Vernacular Architecture* (1986).

Welfeld, Irving. *Where We Live: A Social History of American Housing* (1988).
Wright, Gwendolyn. *Moralism and the Model Home: Domestic Architecture and Cultural Conflict in Chicago, 1873–1913* (1980).
———. *Building the Dream: A Social History of Housing in America* (1981).

Housing Policies and the Future

Davis, Sam, ed. *The Form of Housing* (1977).
Franck, Karen A., and Sherry Ahrentzen, eds. *New Households, New Housing* (1989).
Goetze, Rolf. *Rescuing the American Dream: Public Policies and the Crisis in Housing* (1983).
Hayden, Dolores. *Redesigning the American Dream: The Future of Housing, Work, and Family Life* (1984).
Nutt-Powell, Thomas E. *Manufactured Homes: Making Sense of a Housing Opportunity* (1982).
Sternlieb, George, James Hughes, and Robert Burchell, eds. *America's Housing: Prospects and Problems* (1980).

— ELIZABETH COLLINS CROMLEY

HUMOR AND COMEDY

What is so funny about American humor? How have its forms evolved? Does American comedy fairly articulate American humor? Does American humor afford a measure of the nation's true character? Can we, in this pluralistic society, even define humor and comedy as American, or should we consider the nation's diverse communities of laughter separately?

The problem with such questions is that humor resists investigation, as do a number of its sources. Humor evaporates in the heat of critical examination, vanishing altogether whenever its thrusts cease to be timely or friendly. Example and analysis must contend in dramatic tension to uphold the context for laughter to erupt. Race, gender, age, ethnicity, and social role and status prescribe the commonplace categories of America's humor. Language, folklore, family life, religion, and politics establish its convenient frames of reference and modalities of communication. No form of native expression covers the spectrum of popular utterances and tastes more thoroughly. American humor spans the conceivable possibilities from crude and vulgar outbursts to elite literature and dramatic comedy. Native Americans, European colonists, indentured servants, African slaves, immigrants, and contract laborers all contributed to folkloric humor and to humor and comedy in the popular culture. Although not all Americans were originally Englishmen and American humor was not necessarily English humor, the styles and usages of literary humor had deep roots in British culture, as Mark Twain observed, undergoing major transformations in the New World environment. Today's humor reflects the social changes of our times. Its contents and purpose have been shaped by mass media, which have overwhelmed the original characteristics of American humor.

History and theory help to explain. Pressures of class, sex, race, ethnicity, religion, politics, and role have shaped popular humor over time into divergent modes of expression, and bequeathed disparate styles to subsequent generations.

Early Wit

In colonial America, there was laughter of course, earlier than studies of humor can demonstrate or explain. Children gleefully mimicked adults. Europeans mocked the Indians, who retaliated in kind. Englishmen burlesqued Dutchmen, the Dutch ridiculed the English. Slaves raked their masters. In Georgia, people took care not to be overheard giggling at the proprietor's funny name, General Oglethorpe. Older settlers tried out tall tales on newcomers, and both understandably laughed at their plight. Frontier struggles gave birth to native traditions of American humor. Hopes and dreams could break against harsh realities in the wilderness, but laughter afforded a sure avenue away from despair. Humorous storytelling grew out of real experiences. A proclivity for hilarious exaggeration rang true enough by 1670 to make its way, along with astronomical, navigational, astrological, and calendrical data, into New England's proliferating almanacs.

Homely, coarse, often earthy, embodying a peasant shrewdness, the colonial almanacs imported the tradition and styles of English country humor, thereby enriching the indigenous propensity for wit. Almanac humor profiled village and rural life: the distinctive but mutually dependent roles of man and woman, the power and majesty of the law offended by the plague of lawyers, the farmer and his animals, the youth and his damsel, the clergymen bewitched by a seductive widow. Scatological humor frequently appeared, and bawdy jingles competed for the reader's attention, as in Daniel and Titan Leeds's almanac of 1714: "Dick on the hay doth tumble Nell/ Whereby her Belly comes to Swell." The quality of almanac humor scarcely improved over the years, except in the output of the Ames and Franklin families. Dr. Nathaniel Ames of Dedham, Massachusetts, and his namesake son, likewise a physician, wrote elegantly humorous essays. James S. Franklin launched Poor Robin's *Rhode-Island Almanack* several years before his younger brother Benjamin's *Poor Richard's Almanack* (1732–1758) appeared in Philadelphia. Poor Robin's philosophy ("Some tell us Money is a curse. So 'tis, but want of Money's worse.") anticipated Poor Richard's copybook maxims to encourage enterprise, diligence, and thrift. Ben Franklin helped to invent America's longest-lasting comic figure as a fount of common sense—the homespun, uneducated, artless provincial, the teller of tall tales, and somehow our most enduring joke about that type. Franklin's Poor Richard satirized authority, false piety, and deceitfulness, expounding wittily about adultery, prostitution, excretion, and such unsavory subjects in a foreshadowing of black humor. William Cobbett, an outspoken Tory turncoat, castigated him as a deist, quack, fornicator, and infidel. Unchastened by such attacks, Franklin comforted himself that "there's more old drunkards than old doctors." Franklin's style of humor spread north, south, and west.

Since American humor was at once old and new, literary humorists and storytellers strove to strike the right note between colonial import and native local color, between personal idiosyncrasy and national significance. The Connecticut Wits, a loosely linked ring of poets active in the late eighteenth and early nineteenth centuries, aimed satirical epics at dissenters or backsliders from New England's upright standards of liberty and morality. The examples set by its members John Trumbull (M'Fingal), Joel Barlow, Timothy Dwight, David Humphreys, and Lemuel Hopkins reappeared in Washington Irving's *Knickerbocker's History of New York*, "Rip Van Winkle," and "The Legend of Sleepy Hollow," and still later in Oliver Wendell Holmes's wonderfully ironic "The Deacon's Masterpiece" about the "one-hoss-shay" and James Russell Lowell's acerbic *Biglow Papers*. Diedrich Knickerbocker's *History of New York* (1809), a purportedly serious account of Dutch life in New Netherlands, stands out as both a burlesque of history and a satire of the politics of Washington Irving's time and place. Knickerbocker's *New York* forecast great humor to come. Laughter would serve the white, male, upwardly aspiring forces of democracy as an avenging sword in the youthful republic, where ambition and pretension far outdistanced achievements. Laughter combined that same hostility toward intellect with a blessing for uneducated common sense that the almanacs had featured. Simon Suggs's judgment (1840) prevailed: "Booklarnin spoils a man if he's got motherwit, and if he ain't got that it don't do him no good." The people themselves and the wilderness confronting them abundantly supplied the comic materials for humorists. Writers and lecturers, usually eccentric literary figures and traveling showmen, jollied their audiences while fostering their own careers. More often than not, when geographical differences and telltale accents still distinguished one part of society from another, they relied on dialect humor for surefire laughter. Through the regional and ethnic speech patterns of rural New England and the frontiers of the West and Southwest, augmented in published form by bizarre typographical devices and spelling grotesqueries, they could depend on everyday incongruities to stimulate laughter.

Democracy's Voices

Mark Twain's Library of American Humor (1888), a guidebook for our purposes, compiled selections from forty-six authors. "Smack of whom it would," William Dean Howells enthused, "it has always been so racy of the soil that the native flavor prevails throughout, and whether Yankee, Knickerbocker, Southern California, refined or broad, prose, verse, or newspaper, it was and is always American" (*Twains Library*, p. x). In 1906, however, Samuel Clemens (Mark Twain) concluded that his anthology was by then nothing but "a cemetery," though he seemed self-satisfied at the durability of his own output against the literary demise of most of his contemporaries. Twain's favorite ploys—understatement, black dialect, hyperbole, burlesque, incongruity, straight-faced vernacular, and others—had been employed by humorists before him. Concentrating on politics at first, their slyly derisive commentaries pointed out one direction to follow, while the grotesquely exaggerated exploits of their tall tales indicated another. Twain endured because he surpassed his competitors in all of their specialties. Masterfully he blended and shaped their techniques into an oral-sounding style that raised him into the highest rank of prose writers. He mixed his somber moods so subtly with folk wisdom that he educated generations of comic writers about humor's profoundest possibilities. But the scandal-ridden officeholders of the Gilded Age overwhelmed his relish for political humor: "If I could keep my faculty for humor uppermost, I'd laugh the dogs out of the country. But I can't. I get too mad" (Dunne, Philip, eds. *Mr. Dooley Remembers*, 1963, p. 260). Fortunately, other humorists persisted. Gleeful mockery of politicians' pretensions articulated the democracy's doubting voices.

Since 1830, when Seba Smith of Portland, Maine, founded his *Courier*, the first daily newspaper in Maine, and published letters he himself was writing (purportedly from Jack Downing, an innocent rustic), a beguiling political humor began to appear on a regular basis. Downing blundered into the legislature and, in his quaint vernacular, commenced writing to his friends back home of the strange doings there. Smith's plan proved highly successful. His scope widened. "Major" Jack Downing in Washington became a confidential adviser to presidents from Andrew Jackson to Franklin Pierce. Soon newspapers everywhere were imitating Jack Downing's bizarre depictions of public affairs. Even Downing's character was appropriated by other writers. The *Letters of Jack Downing, Major*, written by

Charles Augustus Davis for the New York *Advertiser*, gained wide acclaim for a time, owing to the sharp bite of their satire. The immortal Sam Patch (1807?-1829) postulated that "some things can be done as well as others," while Jack Downing himself knew there was "an *outside* as well as an inside to everything," politics included.

There was much more. Comic tellers of local-color stories flourished. Foremost were the makers of the Davy Crockett myth. David Crockett's real self is lost in legend, but his prodigious reputation as a Tennessee frontiersman, three-time member of Congress, tall-story teller, and martyred hero of the Alamo perpetuated itself in popular history. Davy's motto, "Be sure you're right and then go ahead," caught the spirit of the times. The coonskin humor in the Crockett anecdotal books and almanacs most likely emanated from an array of unsung authors exploiting his fame. Whoever wrote his "Coon Story;" captured the flavor of frontier electioneering. Campaigning for Congress, Colonel Crockett grins the bark clean off a large knot on a tree branch to demonstrate to onlookers that his smiling opponent might likewise, if they were unwary, grin them out of their sound judgment on election day.

The Crockett myth played upon credulity, as Carroll Smith-Rosenberg points out in "Davy Crockett as Trickster." The mythic tale was actually a joke. Jokes and myths alike distort their subjects to conjure up illusions of truth. By inversion or comic reversal, the Crockett tales challenged middle-class respectability by opposing a wild West to the East that was too terrifying to abide. The Crockett depictions of women, for example, parody gentility, as with the young woman boldly disrobing herself except for a petticoat woven of brier bushes. "I could not come near her without getting stung most ridiculous," Crockett related. "I would as soon as have embraced a hedgehog." Panicked, he fled, leaving his coonskin cap behind.

Bemused or amused at safe distances, eastern readers devoured the comic works of nineteenth-century western storytellers: Augustus Baldwin Longstreet, Thomas Bangs Thorpe, Phillip B. January (Obe Oilstone), William Tappan Thompson, Johnson Jones Hooper John S. Robb, and Joseph G. Baldwin stand out. They all imparted an exuberance to their descriptions of regional life. Long-street's *Georgia Scenes* (1835), his earliest and most influential book, related true episodes modified to suit his narrative purposes into "fanciful *combinations* of real incidents and characters." Thorpe's masterful tall tale "The Big Bear of Arkansas" (1841), about a futile hunt for a creation bear, an "unhuntable bear," who died "when his time came," is spun by Jim Doggett aboard a Mississippi River steamboat before "a plentiful sprinkling of the half-horse and half-alligator species of men, . . . who appear to gain a livelihood simply by going up and down the river." January, a contributor to *The Spirit of the Times*, a magazine of indigenous humor, repeatedly demonstrated that the events of a tale mattered less than the manner of its telling. Thompson is remembered for his Georgia cracker dialect stories collected in several volumes, including *Major Jones's Courtship* (1843) and *Major Jones's Chronicles of Pineville* (1843). Hooper's Simon Suggs, a comic rogue ("It is good to be shifty in a new country."), resembles James Russell Lowell's Birdofredum Sawin and foreshadows W. C. Fields's roles as a confidence man.

Meanwhile John S. Robb (Solitaire), in Philadelphia, the author of "Swallowing an Oyster Alive" (1845) and Streaks from *Squatter Life, and Far-West Scenes* (1847), caricatured the westward movement as continuous hilarity. Robb depicted Old Sugar, "the standing candidate" in 1844 for elective office in Missouri's Niauga County, as brilliantly comic but never ludicrous, luring "sniggers" from his whiskey-drinking clientele. Robb's outlines of character were soft, wilderness crudity blending into urbane civilization. Like Andrew Jackson, Old Sugar lifted his glass to national unity: "Here is to the string that binds the states; may it never be bit apart by political rats!" Somewhere, perhaps, Old Sugar keeps a watchful, if bloodshot, eye on the American people. "Whar politicians congregate," quoth he, "I'm always thar at any rate." Baldwin's Ovid Bolus, Esquire, a lawyer like himself, in *The Flush Times of Alabama and Mississippi* (1853) elevated lying ("The truth was too small for him.") to the art form Mark Twain would make his own—for instance, characterizing Markiss as such a compulsive liar that his mendacious reputation obliged a coroner's jury to discredit his handwritten suicide note and enter a verdict of death by foul play at unknown hands.

Some humorists escaped both local-color and western categories. James Russell Lowell, a Massachusetts blueblood penning comic verses in parallel vein, was one such exception. His antislavery convictions led him to oppose westward expansion. In Lowell's *The Biglow Papers* (collected 1848), the principals are Hosea Biglow and his father, both ordinary but sensible farmers; Birdofredum Sawin, a volunteer soldier fighting in Mexico, the twisted incarnation of Manifest Destiny; and Homer Wilbur, an elderly clergyman epitomizing New England's cautious facets of personality and pedantry "with an infinite capacity of sermonizing muscularized by long practice." Lowell's satires suffered from excessive zeal. His humor, unlike Downing's, betrayed his lack of sympathy for its targets, an all-important element in democracy's laughter. George Washington Harris's *Sut Lovingood Yarns* (1867) featured a loud-mouthed, sex-driven Tennessee mountaineer, a brutal practical joker, a prototype scatologist and pornographer, a specialist in hell-raising. George Washington Cable, in the New Orleans dialects of his *Old Creole Days* (1879), captured the incongruities between the city's culture of French and Spanish whites and the state's Protestant Anglo-Saxons, which, ironically, irritated both the Creoles and Cajuns but won him admirers in the North and East.

Midway To Maturity

Charles Farrar Browne, influenced by Jack Downing, created Artemus Ward, a traveling showman and writer of comic tales. Showman Ward paraded his "moral wax figgers" and certain "sagashus beasts" before crowds of gaping rustics with comically mixed results. Couched in the semiliterate prattle of small-town America, Artemus Ward's sketches of his experiences appeared in

Like Mark Twain, who learned from him the tricks of the lecturing trade, Artemus Ward's appearance was difficult to capture in print.

Vanity Fair, "the grate komick paper" launched to compete with London's *Punch.* Lincoln read to his cabinet Ward's "High-Handed Outrage at Utica," a wildly plausible report of an indignant citizen's seizing of the show's effigy of Judas Iscariot. On the platform, Ward's humorous disquisitions depended on his masterful timing punctuated by shattering anticlimaxes. Like Mark Twain, who learned from him the tricks of the lecturing trade, Ward's appearance of personal distress and ignorance, his electrifying flashes of interest stalled by recurrent despair, his deadpan earnestness, and his meandering vagueness could not be duplicated in print. Unlike Downing, Ward devoted only part of his talent to politics, where he could be cunningly neutral. His classic shilly-shally compels conviction: "My perlitical sentiments agree with yourn exactly. I know they do, becaws I never saw a man whose didn't." In his celebrated "Interview with President Lincoln," Artemus Ward avowed: "I have no politics. Nary a one. I'm not in the bizniss . . . I'm in a far more respectful bizniss nor what pollertics is." Yet the secret of success was the same everywhere. Once, in heralding his traveling show, he played his high card. "You scratch my back," he proposed, "& Ile scratch your back."

In fact, the humorists of the Civil War and Reconstruction era scratched a lot of backs. Georgia's Charles Henry Smith (Bill Arp) blended genial humor, forceful satire, and common sense in his "rebellious" letters to "Mr. Abe Linkhorn": "I'm a good Union man—'so-called'—but I'll bet on Dixie as long as I've got a dollar." Arp backed up his convictions: "I joined the army and succeeded in killing about as many of them as they of me." In the Confederacy's darkest days, it was said, he kept southern hearts from breaking.

David Ross Locke (Petroleum Vesuvius Nasby), editor of the *Findlay* (Ohio) *Hancock Jeffersonian,* wrote serialized letters presenting diverse views, opinions, and prophecies of Nasby, who claimed to be the late pastor of the Church of the New Dispensation, the chaplain to the president, and postmaster at "Confederit X Roads which is in the State uv Kentucky." Petroleum Vesuvius Nasby's initial success lay in recognizing the widespread fear among northern workingmen that any emancipation of the South's slaves would release a flood of unwanted African American immigrants into the North. With deadly irony, Nasby contrived to "support" a petition to keep blacks out of Ohio, and leading journals throughout the country soon were reprinting his views. And in 1866, while "swingin' round the cirkle" with Andrew Johnson, a Unionist Democrat electioneering for favored congressional candidates, Nasby caricatured the president's supporters as sporting "a large proportion uv red noses and hats with the tops off." Nasby loved his party for its right, through election, to distribute the spoils of office. President Johnson could buy Nasby and his tattered ilk on easy terms, but he would have to furnish their ammunition. "Will he do it?" worried Nasby, who wanted a postmastership for himself. "That's the question a hundred thousand hungry soles, who hanker even ez I do, are daily askin'."

Joel Chandler Harris was, according to Lawrence Levine, "the most effective single force" to popularize the humor of African American culture. "All over the South, the stories of Br'er Rabbit are told," Octave Thanet (Alice French) noted in 1892. "Everywhere not only ideas and plots are repeated, but the words often are the same; one gets a new vision of the power of oral tradition." In his early volumes particularly, Harris, a Georgian, faithfully transcribed themes and speech from the humorous animal tales, songs, and folk traditions he heard recounted by former slaves. If in centering too much on Br'er Rabbit's comic misadventures Harris overemphasized the trickster tale, he nonetheless celebrated the victory of the weak over the strong. Decades would have to pass, however, before white men and women of the civil rights generation could appreciate the profound nature and functions of the laughter bubbling up from the repressed minority of blacks in their midst.

Not all Gilded Age humorists were memorable. The reputation of Robert Henry Newell (Orpheus C. Kerr), once ranked with Downing, Ward, and Arp, rests on his Civil War "papers," but his punning on "office seeker" was the funniest product of his wit. Henry Wheeler Shaw (Josh Billings) tried several careers before turning into a comic essayist and lecturer. Charles Farrar Browne persuaded his publisher to collect Billings's pieces in *Josh Billings, His Sayings* (1865), which led to nine more compilations and prompted Abraham Lincoln to rate Billings's aphorisms second only to Shakespeare's. Charles Heber Clark (Max Adeler), a Philadelphia local-color journalist who lightened the gloom of an odd corner in "My First Political Speech," sketched the dilemma of stolen thunder for those speakers unlucky enough to appear last on a program. Edgar Wilson Nye's political humor followed the pattern set by Downing, Ward, and Nasby, and later by Will Rogers, who would be compared with him. "Bill" Nye's letter accepting the postmastership at Laramie, Wyoming Territory, "a great triumph of eternal truth" published in the *Laramie Boomerang*, brought him widespread acclaim. Nye often lectured with the Hoosier poet James Whitcomb Riley, against whose bathos his humor shone. Riley's way of retelling old favorites was superb platform art. His rendition of "The Old Soldier's Story" was "about the funniest thing I ever listened to," Mark Twain recalled.

The problem is that Twain's *Adventures of Huckleberry Finn* (1885) overshadows all else, not only his other works but also his contemporaries' works and his appraisals of them. Southwestern humorous fiction furthered the literary context for many of Twain's writings, as did local colorists and rural humorists. In time, their reliance on back-country, speech, folkways, and local idiosyncrasies rendered them inaccessible to cosmopolitan readers; Twain escaped such constraints by mastering the main currents of American literature.

The Assault of Laughter

At this stage, humor and comedy underwent significant transformations. Southern blacks and waves of immigrants from Europe, including masses of Jews from eastern Europe, moved into the cities of the Northeast, carrying in their cultural baggage their own forms and usages of humor. Nasby's bigoted neighbors moved into urban complexes. So did the smug, onetime small-town elites Mark Twain vilified in "The Man That Corrupted Hadleyburg" (1900) and the pretenders to godliness he uncovered in "The Mysterious Stranger" (1916) as well as in "To the Person Sitting in Darkness" (1901). Alienated, self-detached humor had always been around, but its normal genialities fast became outweighed by newly belligerent absurdities expressed in racial, ethnic, sexual, religious, or political terms for urban readers and audiences. Filled with skepticism, derogation, and cruelty yet aloof from serious protests or revolutionary manifestos, humor's new strain afforded, in Jesse Bier's mind, "a means of perspective between exaltation and destruction." It explains Robert Benchley's insistence that "Sheer madness is, of course, the highest possible brow in humor." Will Rogers would be a significant exception.

A formidable critic of the arts, Henry L. Mencken lampooned popular politics and personalities in the Baltimore Sun *for nearly half a century, often labeling his fellow critics dubs, oafs, yahoos, galoots, wowsers, trimmers, stoneheads, and boob-bumpers.*

Often humorists were journalists or columnists at odds with governmental excrescences, hypocritical moralizing, patriotic pieties, and warfare. Ambrose Bierce (1842–1914?), the most bitter of them all, self-schooled in the dark recesses of Poe, was a twice-wounded veteran of the Civil War. In *The Cynic's Word Book* (1881–1906), renamed The *Devil's Dictionary* (1911), and his *Fantastic Fables* (1899), Bierce's satanic mordancy and misanthropy outdid Twain's final efforts. To appreciate his definitions required a special sort of sanity. Thus: "BELLADONNA, *n.* In Italian, a beautiful lady; in English, a deadly poison. A striking example of the essential identity of the two tongues." And "PATRIOT, *n.* One to whom the interests of a part seem superior to those of the whole. The dupe of statesmen and the tool of conquerors."

Mr. Martin Dooley, Chicago columnist Finley Peter Dunne's immortal saloonkeeper and public oracle, exuded an immigrant aura all his own. Dooley dispensed a satirically rich, jocose, and waggish humor in an amalgam of all the brogues of Ireland. Dooley's Irishness supplied an insider's insight into urban machine politicking and an underdog's perspective of American society with its democratic pretensions and nativist contradictions. At first, Dooley's opinions centered on local politics, as had Seba Smith's Downing letters, but soon he was capturing the excitements of the days of Cleveland, Bryan, McKinley, and the war with Spain. Merrily he discoursed on "Raypublicans," "Dimmycrats," and Populists, on the relationship of marriage and drink to politics, Christian Science, the Supreme Court ("th' supreme coort follows th' illiction returns"), and the vice presidency ("it isn't a crime exactly"). Politics was a great game, though never critical. "If ye don't win fair, ye may win foul," Dooley averred. "If ye don't win ye may tie an' get the money in the confusion."

From Chicago westward, in the 1890s whimsy and Bierce-like savagery flourished, paced by (Frank) Gelett Burgess, Eugene Field, and George Ade. In San Francisco, Burgess and his collaborators launched *The Lark*, a forerunner of the little magazines of the 1920s (including the comic *Life*, *Judge*, *College Humor*, *Captain Billy's Whiz-Bang*) and the zany *Mad* and *National Lampoon* of the present. In the first issue, Burgess published "The Purple Cow":

I never saw a Purple Cow
I never hope to see One
But I can tell you, anyhow
I'd rather see than be One.

Before winning renown for sentimental poems, Field composed mock Old English ballads, destroyed actors and plays in caustic one-line drama reviews for various newspapers, and contributed ghoulish burlesques of children's primers to the *Denver Tribune*. "This is a Cock Roach," wrote Field. "He is Big, Black, and Ugly. He is Crawling over the Pillow. Do not Say a Word, but lie still and Keep your Mouth open. He will Crawl into Your Mouth and You can Bite him in Two. This will Teach him to be Discreet in the Future." Ade's fables in slang were both gentle and corrosive. Ade implied sarcasm while jumping back and forth from sympathy to vituperation. Like Dunne, whom he greatly admired, he invariably concluded with a note of absurdity. His sixteen "Stories of Benevolent Assimilation" (1899) derided the intentions of Americans to transform the Filipinos into Asiatic reproductions of themselves as almost too ridiculous for words. "Give the people what they think they want," he sneered—and, for all his equivocations, Ade did just that.

Henry L. Mencken (1860–1956), the sage of Baltimore, lampooned popular politics and personalities in the *Baltimore Sun* for nearly half a century. A formidable critic of the arts and lexicographer (like Bierce, whom he admired extravagantly), Mencken bombarded his readers with well-chosen words. He excoriated President Harding's inaugural address as the worst example of English writing he knew. He assailed his fellow citizens as mediocrities: the dubs, oafs, yahoos, galoots, wowsers, trimmers, stoneheads, plus the booboisie's storied boobs, boob-bumpers, boob-squeezers, and other feeders at the public trough. Although puritanism—"the haunting fear that someone, somewhere may be happy"—had poisoned the soil ages ago, the nation's fundamental problem was democracy. Fact and theory, in Mencken's judgment, disputed Jefferson's tenet that wisdom lay in an electoral majority. Might one hope for improvement by urging men to seek office? Definitely not, Mencken thundered. This made no more sense to him than trying to halt prostitution by filling bawdy houses with virgins. In Mencken's jaundiced view, the man of culture was suffocating between the moneygrubber and the peasant. Not surprisingly, Mencken was both hated and adored.

Ethnoracial Subversion and Survival

New technological innovations began to carry humor and comedy to mass audiences: newspaper comic strips, motion pictures, radio, and television. If comedy can be defined as tragedy that happens to somebody else, this definition nowhere fit more neatly than the movies and the standardized formulas of radio and television humor such as the situation comedy or "sitcom." Much of the explanation lay in ethnicity. During the twentieth century, with the lingering exception of the comic strips, humor by Jews and blacks exerted profound influences on American popular culture.

People more than likely have always ridiculed those unlike themselves. In America, ethnic humor first expressed feelings of superiority by well-favored English-speaking, Protestant whites toward newer immigrants, especially if they were Roman Catholic Germans, Irish, Italians, or Poles, and against black slaves and freedmen, Hispanics, their children and their childrens children. Ironically, derisive stereotypes became adopted by their victims in self-mockery, then, in revenge, were turned against the tormentors. Economic and social distinctions perpetuated the joking form of slurs to reveal the dynamite underlying agonizing differences within America's increasingly pluralistic society. Certain roots and characteristics of ethnic humor were imported long ago from far away. European Jewish immigrants introduced centuries-old habits of humor, while the humor of blacks, with identifiable African folklore ingredients, matured in resistance to slavery and racist suppression.

The Jewish Purim play annually featured irreverent humor and raucous buffoonery. Droll figures—the schnorrers (moochers), schlemiels (simpletons), and luftmenshen (luckless dreamers), Yiddish-tongued precursors of countless stand-up comedians—fled among the throngs migrating from east European ghettos. Humorously and invariably, these fools—indignant, righteous, and victimized—won out in the end. Already, to the barbs of older stock Americans (Why is the wheelbarrow the greatest invention ever made? It taught a few Irishmen to walk on their hind legs.), Irish comedians were retaliating in kind. Likewise Jewish ethnic humor, taking advantage of vaudeville and burlesque stages, built on its origins. (*Priest*: When will you give up those silly dietary laws? *Rabbi*: At your wedding, excellency.) Minstrelsy was a case in point: even Jews donned burned cork, their blackened faces guaranteeing immunity from customary restraints. Sophie Tucker, Al Jolson, George Jessel, and Eddie Cantor were minstrel stars who later triumphed on radio and the silver screen. The Marx Brothers carried comic Jewish dialogues into vaudeville, brandishing madcap nihilism against established institutions. Jewish entrepreneur's operated many theaters, so Jewish comics flocked onto the stages to test their talents and chutzpah. Analysts Sigmund Freud and Theodor Reik emphasized the historic tendency of Jews toward skepticism and self-criticism, the springing of mirthless wit at a flash of subjective truth or profound insight.

Defiant in their survival after the Holocaust, Jewish humorists and comedians broke loose from their cultural bonds to inject massive doses of their ethnocentric wisdom into all corners of American life. The best included radio stars Jack Benny and George Burns, as well as Sid Caesar, Milton Berle, Mort Sahl, Mel Brooks, and novelist Philip Roth. Never again would American humor be the same.

Blacks responded differently. Skin color and the terrible heritage of slavery set them apart. James Weldon Johnson, black novelist and poet, recalled his stint as a teacher among his people in backwoods Georgia: "Their deep genuine laughter often puzzled and irritated me. Why did they laugh so? How could they laugh so?" Black poet Claude McKay agreed: "How can they consent to joy and mirth/who live beneath a world of eternal ban?" Blacks shared with Jews, women and others despised, the humor of the oppressed. Blacks retaliated against their fate with laughter. Inwardly their laughter could mock themselves. Outwardly their humor both attacked and concealed. Black comedians were aggressive, even acrimonious: cursing ironically, relying on double meanings, ethnic put-downs, and trickster ploys. Often blacks' humor and gallows humor were one and the same.

Springing from sub-Saharan sources, African American humor rode its vehicles for laughter along two major avenues. Externally it functioned, and functions, as a mechanism for accommodation to a hostile white society. The John-Master slave stories, an oral tradition, humorously and in coded language vented helpless anger. John ridiculed his owner if he felt like doing so, which was only when the master was up at the big house and John was laboring down in the field. In the animal trickster tales—parodies of white society in Lawrence Levine's verdict—rabbit masked the slave, yet rabbit also displayed the slave driver's tyranny. White minstrels in blackface makeup stole this style of humor to convulse white audiences with their blatant stereotypes of Jim Dandy, an effeminate hustler, and Jim Crow and Sambo, who were slow-witted buffoons. To perform before whites, black comedians had to caricature themselves. Bert Williams presented separate routines to white and black audiences. Either way, "Jonah Man" Williams, helped by "Nobody," drew his laughter from his people's sorrow. Stepin Fetchit (Lincoln Perry) and Rochester (Eddie Anderson) prolonged the time-honored accommodating character for movies and radio, respectively.

Out of the civil rights movement and the urban turmoil of the 1960s and 1970s, black stand-up comics and writers joined Jewish and other ethnic laughmakers to jar and delight white middle-class audiences with their folk commentaries fortified by anthropological insight. Dick Gregory, from the back of his segregated bus, hit especially hard. (*Restaurateur*: "We don't serve Nigras!" *Gregory*: "That's cool. I don't eat them.") "Do you realize," Godfrey Cambridge inquired, "the amount of havoc a Negro couple can cause just by walking down the street on a Sunday morning with a copy of the *New York Times* real estate section under the man's arm?" Scourging Sambo, Redd Foxx confided that "Boss" spelled backward meant "double S.O.B." Comedienne, writer, and film producer Jackie "Moms" Mabley, and later screen actor Richard Pryor, revisited folk sources for earthy soul food to nourish laughter in those most weary and heavy laden. The phenomenally popular Bill Cosby, on the other hand, virtually deracialized the characters in his situation comedies into a utopian, if incredible, harmony with their white neighbors.

Mass Media and the Masses

Throughout the silent film era and the talking pictures of the 1930s and 1940s, American-made comedy films swept to mass popularity. The movies rejuvenated traditional jesting and clowning and, as the carnivals, circuses, medicine shows, minstrel acts, theatricals, and burlesque shows had done, comedy films journeyed up and down the land, even crossing the oceans. Knockabout improvisations came first, followed by Mack Sennett's introduction (1912) of his satirically sharp, slapstick counterculture. Sennett introduced the Keystone Cops, bevies of bathing beauties, Fatty Arbuckle, cross-eyed Ben Turpin, Louise Fazenda, Harry Langdon, Marie Dressler, Charley Chase, Buster Keaton, and, briefly, Charlie Chaplin and Harold Lloyd. Chaplin left Sennett to launch his own company, developing his Little Tramp into the folk hero of the world. Chaplin and Keaton were alike in that both were at odds, the one with society and its defenders, the police, the other with his amazing props or the absurdity of life itself. Lloyd's "glass character," ill equipped for life, and his "human fly" stunts won him tremendous acclaim. Eventually, in catering to increasingly sophisticated theatergoers, Hal Roach outpaced Sennett by strengthening story lines and structures over and beyond visual gags.

Many performers with different styles were just as funny. The Micawber-like W. C. Fields, a longtime comic juggler on stage, repeatedly demonstrated man's helplessness in a world where inanimate objects, children, and dogs thwart one's innocent intentions. In *The Bank Dick* (1940) and other successes, Fields moved warily through life, protected by his flamboyant braggadocio, until he ran afoul of superior forces and invariably became obsequious or hostile to all who got in his way. Stan Laurel and Oliver Hardy—"two fools of God," Marcel Marceau called them—portrayed a physical contrariety that placed them beyond normal restraints. Laurel's forays into magic, such as igniting his thumb into a cigarette lighter, would lift him momentarily to leadership. Otherwise Hardy's "You after me Stanley" syndrome, abetted by his necktie twiddle and soul-deep resignation, pronounced his simpleminded conviction of his own superiority. Their derby hats inevitably switched themselves, expanding the confusion.

Again technology transformed the popular medium for humor and comedy. Motion picture theaters added animated cartoon comedies featuring "Silly Symphonies," "Betty Boop," "Looney Toons," and Walt Disney's incomparable Mickey Mouse to their short subjects. Although many vocally deficient comedians of the silent screen found themselves sidelined, Hal Roach sailed ahead into all-talking pictures with Laurel and Hardy, Charley Chase, and the rough-and-ready boys and girls of Our Gang. Likewise, for other producers, W. C. Fields, Charlie Chaplin, the madcap Marx Brothers, slow-burning Edgar Kennedy, Wallace Beery and Marie Dressler of *Tugboat Annie* fame, big-mouthed Joe E. Brown, sizzling Mae West, and Will Rogers made the transition.

Stan Laurel and Oliver Hardy performed a style of recognizable, physical comedy and contrariety that kept audiences laughing through many successful movies.

Audiences also loved screwball comedies—fast-action, romantic farces featuring witty dialogue by the leading characters, who were often drawn from disparate social classes but overcame their initial antipathy to fall magically in love. Frank Capra's *It Happened One Night* (1934), starring Claudette Colbert and Clark Gable, launched the genre, which went on to include *The Thin Man, Theodora Goes Wild, My Man Godfrey, Mr. Deeds Goes to Town, The Awful Truth, Nothing Sacred, Holiday, You Can't Take It with You, His Girl Friday,* and *The Philadelphia Story.* Screwball comedies suited the escapist spirit of the Great

Depression, then subsided with World War II. For home amusement, the radio networks introduced weekly comedy shows starring, among others, Eddie Cantor, Jack Benny, Fred Allen, Fanny Brice, Joe Penner, and Bob Hope. Commercial sponsors fed faithful listeners a weekday diet of fifteen-minute episodic comedies led by *Lum and Abner*, *Vic and Sade*, and others. Enormously popular, *Amos 'n' Andy* commanded prime time nightly for the misadventures of their blackface Fresh Air Taxicab Company, though most blacks were not amused.

Will Rogers, beloved cowboy humorist, mastered all of the media. He dispensed folksy commentaries on the news, especially on politics, while performing rope tricks in the *Ziegfeld Follies*, and later as a columnist for the *New York Times* syndicate and as a Sunday evening radio network broadcaster. In films, he starred as a fatherly problem solver humorously upholding the homely virtues in screwball comedies. Rogers was never sharper than when discoursing on the Great Depression. He patriotically offered his services for the campaign to restore confidence. "But you will have to give me some idea where 'Confidence' is," he insisted, "and just what you want it restored to." Of President Hoover's Valley Forge appeal for patience, Rogers commented: "He found somebody that was worse off than we are, but he had to go back 150 years in history to do it." And in 1931 he summed up the situation: "We got more wheat, more corn, more food, more cotton, more money in the banks, more everything in the world than any nation that ever lived ever had, yet we are starving to death. We are the first nation in the history of the world to go to the poor house in an automobile."

The beloved cowboy humorist Will Rogers on the Great Depression and its campaign to restore confidence: "You will have to give me some idea where 'Confidence' is and just what you want it restored to."

After Rogers's untimely death in 1935, there were only Mencken's twilight essays, Westbrook Pegler's rare mellow moments, and Langston Hughes's sensitive cameos about blacks through his Dooley-like characterization of Jesse B. Simple. In time, hopes for a successor to Rogers as the nation's court jester concentrated on television's promise. It was claimed that televised programs could be distributed for repeated enjoyment as easily as humorous lectures and radio broadcasts. Not until television and the VCR became commonplace did this dream come true.

Until then, *The New Yorker* magazine, abetted by big-city newspaper columnists, films, and stage comedies, dominated America's output of humor. Harold W. Ross, an unlikely genius, launched *The New Yorker* in 1925, "not for the old lady in Dubuque" but for sophisticated Manhattanites. A number of the Algonquin Hotel's Round Table wits lent their names as advisory editors and contributed scattered bits, but Ross soon learned that Dorothy Parker was the only member of that group on whom he could rely. He therefore recruited self-conscious urbanites who ranged along a lunatic fringe from Don Marquis, the creator of Archy, a lower-case, free-verse cockroach, and Mehitabel, an amoral cat, to Franklin P. Adams of "The Conning Tower," to the flippant, surreal Ring Lardner. Their Freudian denominator was a reliance on abnormal traits of personality, which Adams spoofed but Marquis and Lardner wholeheartedly accepted. The cartoonists were deliciously neurotic. Helen Hokinson's silly club women became fixtures, as did Peter Arno's voluptuously dizzy blondes and lecherous magnates. Otto Soglow and Mary Petty joined them, as later did Whitney Darrow, Sam Cobean, Charles Addams, George Price, and Saul Steinberg, and still later George Booth, Edward Koren, and William Hamilton. Alexander Woollcott condescended to write "Shouts and Murmurs" as a regular feature. Ogden Nash penned nonsense verses. Frank Sullivan invented the wonderful Mr. Arbuthnot, the cliché expert. And Clarence Day's stories accumulated into *Life with Father*. E. B. White, James Thurber, Robert Benchley, and S. J. Perelman completed *The New Yorker's* madhouse. Thurber was the funniest madman of them all.

Humor from all sides

After 1945, radio and film comedies continued to make their enormous audiences laugh, and so did musical comedies. But the longtime training schools for comedians, burlesque and vaudeville, with the exception of the Jewish Borscht Belt (Catskill Mountains) resorts or offbeat night clubs in Chicago and San Francisco, gave way to television. Radio and film stars had led the way into the electronic medium: Fred Allen, Jack Benny, Bob Hope, Amos and Andy, Abbott and Costello, and Groucho Marx. Yet these luminaries soon found themselves overshadowed by television's comic geniuses, including Sid Caesar and Imogene Coca, Ernie Kovacs, and Steve Allen. Television proved too visual for radio-style, imaginative comedy, and too demanding for stage or film actors and producers to keep up. Only Bob Elliott and Ray Goulding, who on radio for forty years hilariously parodied radio as though it were made for them, hung on to the microphone to get drivers through dense traffic, students ready for exams, and all listeners through long weekends. Who can forget Wally Ballou reporting a parade while facing the wrong way?

In contrast, Sid Caesar's timid sponsors sidelined him for lampooning sacred cows, while the hypercautious unities of the 1950s red scare squelched the tradition of jesting at the nation's leaders. Even Adlai E. Stevenson, Jr., the Democrats' presidential nominee, drew criticism for joking at public concerns. Thurber blamed the frightful hazards of living in the nuclear age—next door to catastrophe "on the brink of Was," he put it. Mort Sahl worried that he could not be certain if the unidentified aircraft approaching would "drop a hydrogen bomb or spell out Pepsi Cola in skywriting." "It is not expected that we will soon recover," Thurber went on about the witch-hunting of Senator Joseph McCarthy, "and contribute to a new and brave world literature of comedy." Satire, he judged, in words that raised protests from dairymen and threats to investigate his loyalty from congressmen, had declined until it reminded him of a drink of milk: "It won't hurt anybody, but who likes it?"

Humor recovered mightily in the civil rights struggles of the 1960s and the ensuing women's movement. Segregation's absurdities came to the surface through underlying veins of despair and moral indignation. Standup comedians assailed the hollow rhetoric, the principles betrayed, the meanness, the ignobility, and crass pieties. Laughter once again began to succeed where other weapons were failing. Ethnic comics counterattacked where their forebears—blacks, immigrant Jews, Italians, and Poles—once served as laughter's scapegoats. Dick Gregory ridiculed segregation. Mort Sahl hoped there were no groups he had not offended, trampling them all "anyway onward." Together they pressed their case against the waspish, prudish, stand-pat Americanism in their way. Knowingly or unknowingly, they were following the examples of Twain, Bierce, Mencken, Lardner, Thurber, Benchley, and Hughes. Lenny Bruce, the new era's heroic antihero, defined his fellow citizens in Jewish idiom as "schmucks." A schmuck, as Bruce saw him, believed in Uncle Tom and Santa Claus and labored in vain to sing "The Star-Spangled Banner," and brought up his hapless children to do likewise. Imported from Britain, on stage and screen, the anti-establishment mockeries of Peter Cook's *Beyond the Fringe*, Benny Hill's music hall vulgarity, and *Monty Python's Flying Circus* intensified the bedlam.

Sexuality in contemporary humor (other than the timeworn format for dirty jokes) was a product of the new feminism of the women's movement. Sex is to women's role in society as skin color and racist repression are to black personality. Feminist humor by women comedians supplied a fresh fount of laughter wherever there was an audience willing to listen. In films and nightclubs, Joan Rivers, Phyllis Diller, and Lily Tomlin became nationally known. Fran Lebowitz brilliantly and somewhat acidly analyzed womanhood in a male-dominated society. Erma Bombeck, the leading specialist on the funny side of motherhood, wrote a syndicated column, "At Wit's End," ultimately carried by several hundred newspapers. However, most feminist comics dressed like cartoon characters and quarreled aggressively on stage with the shortcomings of their own bodies and the men or women in their lives. To monologues on menstruation, intercourse, gynecologists, masturbation, toxic waste, and bureaucracy, they brought a grotesque carnival aura. Their humor was frightening, and it was meant to be.

> *In the hypercautious 1950s,* New Yorker *humorist James Thurber warned of satire's risk of becoming like a drink of milk: "It won't hurt anybody, but who likes it?"*

To explain such public manifestations, anthropologist Mahadev L. Apte reminds us that for the greater part humor is culture-based, and that the humor of a people can supply vital insights toward understanding them. In the United States, as Apte observes, humor is a big business, pervading every walk of the nation's life. Film comedies playing at theaters are advertised as "howlingly funny," "sidesplitting," "wacky," "whimsical," and "hilarious." Television programming is dominated by comedy shows, especially situation comedies, such as *Cheers* and *The Bill Cosby Show. M*A*S*H*, about a behind-the-lines hospital in the Korean War, and *Hogan's Heroes*, about Allied soldiers in a German prison camp, cleverly made light of grisly situations. The sitcoms give way around midnight to talk shows starring wisecracking hosts such as Johnny Carson, David Letterman, and Arsenio Hall. There are also the once-a-week skits of *Saturday Night Live*, which most memorably starred Chevy Chase.

Newspapers feature dozens of syndicated comic strips, which, over almost a century since the introduction of Richard Felton Outcault's "The Yellow Kid," have come to include both "funnies" and adventure dramas. Seldom bound by time's constraints, comic strips rely on theatrical conventions including dialogue, dramatic gesture, scene or backdrop, a rectangular frame, and props or stage devices. The comics, moreover, anticipated numerous film techniques, such as montage, angle views, panning, cutting, framing, and close-ups. Favorites like "Blondie," "Peanuts," "Beetle Bailey," and "Garfield" appear in about two thousand papers. Foreign-language adaptions travel around the world. The intellectually ironic "Peanuts" by Charles M. Schulz succeeded Walt Kelly's "Pogo" to captivate the 1960s. Gary Trudeau's "Doonesbury," with its counterculture philosophy, topped the 1970s. The leading comics of the 1980s and 1990s, except for the fantasy of Bill Watterson's "Calvin and Hobbes," Berke Breathed's "Bloom County," and Gary Larson's "Far Side," chronicle real-life problems and affronts, as Cathy Guisewite does for her perplexed, mistreated, and humiliated "Cathy." Images of comic strip characters as well as humorous maxims adorn shirts, household and recreational wares, toys, bumper stickers, watch dials, stationery, and many other products.

Newspapers also feature sharp editorial cartoons and witty columnists. Masters of the one-note message, the cartoonists upholding the satirical tradition of London's James Gillray (1757–1815) and Thomas Nast (1840–1902) of *Harper's Weekly* are Herblock, Paul Conrad, Jeff McNelly, Mike Peters, Tony Auth, Doug Marlette, Pat Oliphant, Don Wright, and Jules Feiffer. Art Buchwald, whose talent for punch lines resembled Mr. Dooley's, and Russell Baker lead the humorous columnists. Technology has widened distribution. Copy machines and facsimile networks speed jokes, clippings, and graphic humor to all accessible points on a round-the-clock basis.

Humor and comedy bubble up everywhere. Stand-up comedy, long the backbone of vaudeville, burlesque, and the variety theater—for example, Earl Carroll's *Vanities*—has spawned an industry of its own in hundreds of comedy clubs. The comedy clubs present a lengthy bill of comedians and would-be comedians who briefly, through exclusive control of the microphone, carry on the hallowed ritual of public joking, trying to make their audiences laugh. The social context and the procedures followed are as important as the text of the joke itself. Nevertheless, the laughter shared by a comedian and the crowd celebrates their agreement on whatever it is that merits mutual ridicule or sustains their common beliefs and behavior. The appeal of comedy clubs is tribal in composition and ritualistic in nature. A more familiar style of gently funny storytelling flourishes as well. Beginning in 1974, Garrison Keillor, a champion of small pleasures, broadcast his radio show, *A Prairie Home Companion* before live audiences. His anecdotes brought to life a comically fascinating array of the folks of Lake Wobegon, Minnesota, an authentic fictional village, "where all the women are strong, the men are good looking, and all the children are above average." Keillor's collected essays, many of them having appeared previously in *The New Yorker*, remind readers of Mark Twain, George Ade, Ring Lardner, and Peter DeVries. More than most humorists, Keillor's comic light, though truthful, is soft and compassionate.

The best American comic fiction since the 1950s has come from Vladimir Nabokov, Joseph Heller, Philip Roth, Kurt Vonnegut, Jr., and Peter DeVries. Nabokov, a Russian-born novelist, poet, playwright, and critic, displayed his astonishing verbal facility, seasoned by exquisite dashes of irony, in his highly acclaimed *Lolita* (1955) and *Pale Fire* (1962). Joseph Heller's weird and poignantly funny novel *Catch-22* relates the imaginative efforts of Captain John Yossarian to survive World War II, to outwit somehow the merciless logic of a regulation that stays one step ahead of his schemes. Philip Roth wrote *Goodbye, Columbus, and Five Short Stories, Portnoy's Complaint, Our Gang* (an outcry of rage against Nixon's Watergate), and the autobiographical Zuckerman trilogy. Roth, a Jew, has been castigated by Jewish spokesmen as anti-Semitic, while various critics have denounced him as a pornographer and traitor. Both Portnoy and Zuckerman, Roth's alter ego, star in comedies of entrapment—burlesques of psychic processes wherein irreverence and explicitness shock the pieties that protect inner sensitivities against unwanted turmoil.

Kurt Vonnegut, Jr., who as a prisoner of war experienced the firebombing of Dresden, has frequently combined science fiction with hilarious comedy in the satirical fashion of Aldous Huxley and Evelyn Waugh, sometimes as pure slapstick and sometimes for belly laughs, yet invariably to attack social ills. In *Player Piano, Cat's Cradle, Slaughterhouse Five*, and *Breakfast of Champions*, Vonnegut moved from wildly absurd frameworks to sanitary outcomes. His visions were so horrific that indignation could provide a basis for rejection, except for the laughter that for the moment allows one to manage. Peter DeVries, in terms of high-level productivity and sustained achievement, was for a time the greatest American comic novelist. Renowned as a punster with tongue firmly in cheek while acidly satirizing his fellow citizens, his triumphs numbered *The Tunnel of Love, The Blood of the Lamb, Let Me Count the Ways*, and *Mrs. Wallace.* The comic novels of Kingsley Amis, David Lodge, and Tom Sharpe, imported from Britain, enriched readers' amusement.

More visible in filmmaking, television, and stage productions, though outstanding as comic writers themselves, were Woody Allen, Mel Brooks, and Neil Simon. Woody Allen's collected humor, his stories, his screenplays, and his own acting performances demonstrated his comic talent. He is best known for his movies *Annie Hall, Sleeper, Radio Days, Love and Death, Hannah and Her Sisters, Broadway Danny Rose*, and *The Purple Rose of Cairo.* In a short story, "The Kugelmass Episode," Allen transports his hero into the pages of Flaubert's *Madame Bovary*, where he conducts a lively affair with Emma, to the confusion of readers and scholars everywhere. Mel Brooks (Melvin Kaminsky), comedian, writer, actor, and film director and producer, created such acclaimed films as *The Producers* and *Blazing Saddles.* A onetime social director at Catskills resorts who was inspired by the stand-up comedians he encountered, Brooks later wrote television skits for Sid Caesar's *Your Show of Shows.* The public learned to expect riotous comedy from him. Brooks and straight man Carl Reiner created that living witness to the history of mankind, the Two-Thousand-Year-Old-Man, a hilariously opinionated medical miracle. Neil Simon, a onetime comedy writer in succession for Goodman Ace, Phil Silvers, Garry Moore, Jackie Gleason, Red Buttons, and Sid Caesar, went on to write a string of popular comedies and musicals. His successes are legendary: *Barefoot in the Park, The Odd Couple, Sweet Charity, Promises, Promises, Last of the Red Hot Lovers, The Sunshine Boys, Plaza Suite, California Suite, Brighton Beach Memoirs, Biloxi Blues*, and *Broadway Bound.* Simon once defined his goal as "to make a whole audience fall onto the floor, writhing and laughing so hard that some of them pass out." He has often come close.

With the Watergate scandal over President Nixon's countenancing burglary, his obstruction of justice, and finally his resignation in disgrace, all restraints ended for political humorists. Jokes and tall tales abounded, affording comedians an undreamed-of opportunity. Even "Nixon's the One," the slogan used to reelect him, came to indict the faltering champion. Stand-up commentator Mark Russell hoped that the Watergate affair would never end. "If it does, I'll have to go back to writing my own material. Now I just tear it off the news service wires." And John Kenneth Galbraith decided that "We've passed from the age of the common man to the age of the common crook." With more than a touch of anger, presidents Ford, Carter, Reagan, and Bush, along with other public figures, were mocked unsparingly.

"Throughout our history," former President Gerald R. Ford, the only chief executive to put together a book on humor, wrote in *Humor and the Presidency* (1987), "humor and the laughter it brings has [*sic*] carried us over many different obstacles and through many difficult times." Ford, who often made himself the butt of his own jokes, recalled such an occasion: "I gave a speech in Omaha. After the speech, I went to a reception elsewhere in town. A sweet, little old lady came up to me, put her gloved hand in mine, and said, 'I hear you spoke here tonight.' 'Oh, it was nothing,' I replied modestly. 'Yes,' the little, old lady nodded, 'that's what I heard.' "'

All humor studies should begin and end with the problem set forth ages ago in Ecclesiastes 2: "I said of laughter, 'It is mad,' and of mirth, 'Of what use is it?' "

[See also Film; Popular Entertainment before the Civil War; Popular Literature; Radio; Television; Theater and Musical Theater.]

BIBLIOGRAPHY

Anthologies

Blackbeard, Bill, and Martin William, eds. *The Smithsonian Collection of Newspaper Comics* (1977).

Blair, Walter, and Raven I. McDavid, Jr., eds. *The Mirth of a Nation: America's Great Dialect Humor* (1983).

Clemens, Samuel Langhorne, William Dean Howells, and Charles Hopkins Clark, eds. *Mark Twain's Library of Humor* (1888; repr. 1969).

Dodge, Robert K., comp. *Early American Almanac Humor* (1987).

Dorson, Richard M., ed. *Handbook of American Folklore* (1983).

Dudden, Arthur Power, ed. *Pardon Us, Mr. President! American Humor on Politics* (1975).

Esar, Evan. *Esar's Comic Dictionary.* 4th ed., rev. and enl. (1983).

Hill, Leon. *O, for the Life of a Preacher!* (1975).

Lynn, Kenneth S., ed. *The Comic Tradition in America* (1958).

Muir, Frank, ed. *The Oxford Book of Humorous Prose from William Caxton to P G. Wodehouse* (1990).

Novak, William, and Moshe Waldoks. *The Big Book of Jewish Humor* (1981).

———. *The Big Book of New American Humor* (1990).

Randolph, Vance. *Pissing in the Snow and Other Ozark Folktales* (1976).

Reisner, Robert, and Lorraine Wechsler. *Encyclopedia of Graffiti* (1974).

Scherr, George H., ed. *The Best of "The Journal of Irreproducible Results"* (1983).

Untermeyer, Louis, ed. *A Treasury of Laughter* (1946).

White, E. B., and Katharine S. White, eds. *A Subtreasury of American Humor* (1941).

History and Criticism

Apte, Mahadev L. *Humor and Laughter: An Anthropological Approach* (1985).

Baring-Gould, William S. *The Lure of the Limerick* (1967).

Bergson, Henri. *Laughter: An Essay on the Meaning of the Comic.* Translated by Cloudesley Brereton and Fred Rothwell (1911).
Bier, Jesse. *The Rise and Fall of American Humor* (1968).
Blair, Walter, and Hamlin Hill. *America's Humor from Poor Richard to Doonesbury* (1978).
Boskin, Joseph. *Sambo: The Rise & Demise of an American Jester* (1986).
Cohen, Sarah Blacher, ed. *Jewish Wry: Essays on Jewish Humor* (1987).
Dorson, Richard M. *America in Legend: Folklore from the Colonial Period to the Present* (1973).
Dudden, Arthur Power, ed. *American Humor* (1987).
Freud, Sigmund. *Jokes and Their Relation to the Unconscious.* Translated and edited by James Strachey (1963).
Griffith, Richard, and Arthur Mayer. *The Movies* (1957).
Inge, M. Thomas, ed. *The Frontier Humorists: Critical Views* (1975).
Levine, Lawrence W. *Black Culture and Black Consciousness* (1977).
Murrell, William. *A History of American Graphic Humor.* 2 vols. (1933–1938).
Nelson, T. G. A. *Comedy: An Introduction to the Theory of Comedy in Literature, Drama, and Cinema* (1990).
Reik, Theodore. *Jewish Wit* (1962).
Rourke, Constance. *American Humor: A Study of the National Character* (1931).
Rubin, Louis, ed. *The Comic Imagination in American Literature* (1973).
Settel, Irving. *A Pictorial History of Radio* (1967).
Smith-Rosenberg, Carroll. *Disorderly Conduct: Visions of Gender in Victorian America* (1985).
Walker, Nancy. *A Very Serious Thing: Women's Humor and American Culture* (1988).

— ARTHUR POWER DUDDEN

I

INCOME DISTRIBUTION

See WEALTH AND INCOME DISTRIBUTION

INFORMATION PROCESSING

See COMMUNICATION AND INFORMATION PROCESSING

INHERITED WEALTH

See THE ARISTOCRARY OF INHERITED WEALTH

INTELLECTUALS AND THE INTELLIGENTSIA

For three centuries, the social history of American intellectual life has been characterized as a fall from wholeness to fragmentation. In the 1680s, Cotton Mather lamented that Puritans had abandoned the theological community of the founders for the pursuit of private gain. In the 1980s, Russell Jacoby complained that New Left intellectuals had fled from the wide-ranging commentary of their forebears to the narrow specializations of the academy. Such jeremiad, with its narrative of fragmented unity, has framed accounts of American intellectual life for several hundred years.

Popular historical metaphors, even when they are empirically inexact, often resonate with widespread memories, fantasies, and perceptions. In this case, the framework of fragmentation may reveal more than the preoccupations of the historical actors themselves. The French noun "*intellectual*" and its Russian precursor "*Intelligentsia*" were coined only in the last century and a half, the product of a splintering in those societies; both referred to a social group distinguished by its dedication to the life of the mind and by its critical opposition to the current régime. *Intellectuels* were first identified in Paris during the Dreyfus affair (1894–1906), as defenders of Alfred Dreyfus (a Jewish army captain accused falsely of treason) and opponents of the institutions—the church, the army, the aristocracy—that were persecuting him. American wisdom held it that the reactionary anti-Drefuysard virus had no place to fester in this free country; William James was not so sure. In 1899 James used the Dreyfusard term for the first time in the American context when he warned, "we 'intellectuels' in America must all work to keep our precious birthright of individualism, and freedom from these institutions [i.e., the ones that had whipped up militaristic and anti-Semitic fervor against Dreyfus]. *Every* great institution is perforce a means of corruption—whatever good it may also do. Only in the free personal relation is full ideality to be found." It would be hard to find a more forthright invocation of what has become a familiar picture of the intellectual—a free-floating critic of *every* established institution, spun off from any nurturing contact with the social body by his own centrifugal will to "full ideality." The intellectual, from this view, was a product of social fragmentation—made necessary by the emergence of the menacing new institutions of the bureaucratic nation-state.

The ideal of the free-floating intellectual would have puzzled Benjamin Franklin and Thomas Jefferson, not to mention Mather: the idea that serious and reflective people should disdain contact with "*every* great institution" would have stopped them in their tracks. In the American colonies and the early republic, intellectual life was conducted in the corridors of power as well as in the scholar's study, by thinkers who considered themselves men of affairs as well as men of letters and ideas. Indeed, any separation between "letters" and "ideas" would have been alien to them; the distinction was itself a sign of fragmentation, a movement away from a time when *scientia* meant knowledge as a whole, and toward a time when thought could be compartmentalized in individual "departments."

The man of letters and the intellectual share the same psychic history—the same sense of marginality in an activist society, the same masculine fear that marginality meant effeteness, the same desire to overcome that effeteness and to reconnect with the world of men. For many intellectuals, these feelings would tempt them to ignore James's warning and embrace the illusion of power in the "real world" by abandoning the only serious power they possessed: the power of independent, critical thought.

Intellectuals' longings for effectuality were rooted in their problems earning a living. Throughout the nineteenth century, they confronted transformations in the conditions of their livelihood, changes that can be traced to the seismic shift from a mercantile republic to an entrepreneurial democracy: the commercialization of patronage and the diminished opportunities for intellect to shine in religion or politics. In the earliest years of the republic, the men of ideas had abundant chances to participate in religious or political debate—both of which were arenas for resolving fundamental public questions. Belles lettres, too, were sanctioned if they contributed to the spiritual or ethical health of the community (for example, Puritan devotional poetry, or patriotic odes like Joel Barlow's lumbering "Columbiad" of 1807). Even allegedly bizarre bohemians like Charles Brockden Brown (1771–1810) were fired with public zeal. For a generation after the Revolution, there was little separation between intellect and institutions.

But economic, political, and religious changes gradually recast the social role of ideas. As new forms of market exchange spilled over traditional boundaries, as politics became less bound by deferential norms, and as religious conviction became less a matter of theological argument than of emotional fervor, cultivated men found fewer opportunities to shape public discourse. In the developing market society, work and leisure were more systematically sundered; the whole realm of culture became stigmatized as effeminate, a refuge for alsorans in the race of life. Victorian gender roles allotted practical efficacy to men, "the finer things of life" to women. Anti-intellectual assumptions began to pervade business, politics, and religion; the basis of patronage for the writer or speaker was transformed from the small local elite to the broader marketplace—more volatile Evangelical congregations, more heterogeneous political constituencies, less predictable literary audiences.

At about the same time that unruly popular tastes began to penetrate public discourse, new institutions arose to establish more secular and bureaucratic idioms of cultural authority. The whole range of sorting and categorizing institutions that has been studied so effectively by Michel Foucault—prisons, poorhouses, asylums, public schools, universities, professional societies—began to appear in the United States during the antebellum decades and came to full development after the Civil War. Intellectuals were both attracted to and repelled by these organizations: they felt the Dreyfusard reflex, the impulse to resist the socializing role of institutions in the service of the nation-state, but they also felt a seductive pull as well—the emergent apparatus offered a new entry into the world of men, a chance to fondle the phallic "lever of power" discussed admiringly by Henry Adams in *Democracy* (1880).

The mandarins who bid for the new forms of authority viewed the mind as an objective instrument for controlling the natural or social environment; that outlook rendered them less subject to charges of effete ineffectuality. This gendering of intellect was an ancient exercise, but it became more pronounced and systematic during the nineteenth and twentieth centuries as the development of market discipline and economic rationality encouraged a conventional wisdom that attributed empathetic intuition to women, instrumental reason to men. This Victorian (and post-Victorian) formula made it difficult for women to be taken seriously as intellectuals, except grudgingly in the field of literature. At the same time, the tendency to toss empathy into the dustbin of effeminacy led to all sorts of masculine posturing among intellectuals, from bohemians whose main victims were their wives, lovers, and children, to assimilated bureaucrats whose "tough-minded realism" consigned whole populations to oblivion.

The modern remarriage of knowledge and power made for strange bedfellows. Gradually during the twentieth century, defenders of humane values began to be housed with servants of state policy in the same institution—the university. During the mid twentieth century, the university became the chief site for intellectual life in our society. One can see in the emergence of the university-based intellectual the institutionalization of a new kind of hegemonic intelligentsia, held together not by loyalty to place or philosophy but by adherence to a particular style of academic discourse. That was certainly the view of functionalist sociology during the 1950s and 1960s: intellectuals had a large part in the script of Talcott Parsons's "social system."

The problem with this view is that it overlooks the variety of discourse still available on university campuses. The modern American university systematically fragmented intellect; this was its shame but also its glory. Fragmentation encouraged all the ills that specialists are heir to, but it also meant that campuses might provide havens for dissident intellectuals as well as for "policy scientists." By the second half of the twentieth century, the most traditional part of the curriculum, the liberal arts, became the most likely to nourish critiques of a dominant culture given over to the worship of technique. Along with alienation, then, fragmentation may have also fostered freedom.

Gradually during the twentieth century, defenders of human values began to be housed with servants of state policy in the same situation—the university.

Maybe this claim merely makes a virtue of necessity. In any case, this essay will trace the ambiguous relationships between intellect and institutions in American society, and suggest that the framework of fragmentation still has some vitality but that its larger meanings may have been misconstrued. The Foucauldian narrative recounting the merger of power and knowledge tells only part of the story, The rest requires attention to the ways that the pursuit of knowledge could be charged with religious and erotic longing; the importance of gender anxieties in shaping the intellectual's conception of his role (for it is almost always *his*); and the persistence of independent thought despite the pressure to make "realistic" compromises with established authority.

Intellectual as Vocation: Antebellum New England

In early American history, intellect endowed its proud possessors with political, cultural, and sometimes even spiritual power. This was clearest in colonial New England, as Moses Coit Tyler wrote in his classic *History of American Literature*, 1607–1765. "In its inception, New England was not an agricultural community, nor a manufacturing community, nor a trading community: it was a thinking community; an arena and mart for ideas, its characteristic organ being not the hand, nor the heart, nor the pocket, but the brain," Tyler observed (1949, p. 85). "Probably no other community of pioneers ever so honored study, so reverenced the symbols and instruments of learning. Theirs was a social structure with its corner-stone resting on a book" (p. 86). And the book was not only the Hebrew Bible but Aristotle and Thucydides as well, Horace and Tacitus. This commitment to both secular and sacred learning helped establish New England as the intellectual leader of the nation until the late nineteenth century.

But the sacred side of the equation played a more important role in promoting New England's regional cultural hegemony. The South and the Middle Colonies had their own impressive stocks of educated men, but—apart from the apocalyptic political debate of the revolutionary era, and the scientific work of a Franklin or a Jefferson—intellectual life in those regions was a provincial imitation of English coffeehouse amusements, conducted in salons for the pleasure of cultivated gentlemen. In New England it was a different matter: thought in the New England tradition carried a kind of erotic charge, and the serious cultivation of intellect was part of a religious calling. Despite Puritan divines' admiration for classical authors (and later interest in Newtonian science), theology remained central to their enterprise. The Puritan passion for learning was infused with longing to know a supposedly unknowable deity. Though Calvinist doctrine decreed otherwise, the belief that one could reason one's way to God had persisted from medieval times. The project involved the mix of piety and play that Richard Hofstadter once argued was a defining characteristic of the American intellectual. On the one hand, theology was the single-minded pursuit of Truth, with the worthiest of motives and the highest of stakes; on the other, it was a devotion to argument that expressed the quintessential spirit of the speculative intellect by continually turning answers into questions.

This driven theological quest was far less pervasive in the Middle Colonies, and almost altogether absent in the South. In New England it survived even the conflagration induced by revivalism, which most historians assume was uniformly anti-intellectual. From Cane Ridge, Kentucky, to Utica, New York, revivalists replaced reason with rant; in New England, at least in the early years of the nineteenth century, they suffused intellect with passion. The postrevolutionary generation of New Divinity men, often inspired by the preaching of Jonathan Edwards (1703–1758), sought like him to meld doctrine and devotion. Following the prescriptions of Samuel Hopkins (1721–1803), they emphasized conversion as a quiet and isolating mental experience that could often be evoked by reading a particular scriptural text. When Deacon John Phillips (1760–1865) of Sturbridge, Massachusetts, "came to read that passage 'it is finished,' [John 19:30] his burden left him.—He thinks he then met with a saving change," his eulogist reported, "and his sins were pardoned." The bloodless rationality of this report could be misleading. Even their critics admitted that the New Divinity men could reveal a remarkable radiance: "Under their hard, and, as some would say, stolid faces," recalled the liberal theologian Horace Bushnell of the elders in his childhood meetinghouse, "great thoughts are brewing, and these keep them warm. Free-will, fixed fate, foreknowledge absolute, trinity, redemption, special grace, eternity—give them anything high enough, and the tough muscle of their inward man will be climbing sturdily into it, and if they go away having something to think about, they have had a good day" (quoted in Richard Rabinowitz, *The Spiritual Self*, p. 36). One could hardly find a better description of the erotic charge that theology could give to thought.

But by the 1810s and 1820s, even New England could no longer withstand the anti-intellectual currents of the Second Great Awakening. As Rabinowitz has shown, two challenges began to confront the tradition of intellectual striving; both indicted the New Divinity men for elevating thought over true religious feeling. One critique was rooted in the concern that introspection would immobilize the motor of moral action, the other in the fear that excessive thought (or action) would block the soul's spontaneous growth toward likeness with God. One pointed toward organized moral reform societies—movements for temperance, sabbatarianism, prison hygiene, and the abolition of slavery; the other toward spiritual revery and private exploration of the soul's terrain. Although one used the language of character, the other of personality, both moralist and devotionalist discourses were inflected by idioms of romantic literary convention, and both would shape the social history of intellectuals for decades to come.

Moralists ranged in their theological views from the Calvinist Right to the Unitarian Left. One of the more conservative was Lyman Beecher (1775–1863), who sounded remarkably Wordsworthian as he warned his children against the killing frost of self-consciousness: " 'Some people,' " he would say, 'keep their magnifying-glass ready, and the minute a religious emotion puts out its head, they catch it and kill it, to look at it through their microscope, and see if it is of the right kind. Do you not know, my friends, that you can not love, and be examining your love at the same time?' " (quoted in Rabinowitz, p. 20). To moralists like Beecher, faith had become a mode of acting rather than thinking. Oversubtle thought could be paralyzing; the way out was effective work in the world.

The devotionalist critique, in contrast, charged intellect not with disabling the will but with chilling the springs of emotion. "I conceive that our devional performances are too often the language of the understanding, rather than of the heart," wrote the Reverend Edward T. Payson of Portland, Maine, in 1817 (quoted in Rabinowitz, p. 160). Whether or not Payson had ever read a line of Coleridge, it was a characteristically Coleridgean utterance: Coleridge spent much of his career devaluing the power of ordinary rationality and logic, which he called the Understanding and counterposed to Reason—the intuitive grasp of fundamental cosmic truths. Emerson and other American romantics would pick up the distinction and use it in a variety of contexts, but Evangelical ministers like Payson used it as well—albeit for religious rather than secular purposes. Payson's whole ministry was devoted to upending the New Divinity men's emphasis on the understanding as the key to salvation. Prayers came not from the "cold and spiritless" understanding but from the heart: "From the fulness of a heart overflowing with holy affections, as from a copious fountain, we should pour forth a torrent of pious, humble, and ardently affectionate feelings while our understandings only shape the channel, and teach the gushing streams of emotion where to flow, and when to stop" (quoted in Rabinowitz, p. 161). From this view, true religious feeling was neither a distraction from the serious contemplation of salvation, nor a prelude to reforming the besotted sabbath-breaker; it was a delight for its own sake.

Moralism was the activist masculine version of a nascent cult of immediate experience, reinforcing dedication to the practical, unexamined life; devotionalism was the feminine version, sanctioning sentimental withdrawal from the corruptions of "the world." The most immediate impact of both these tendencies was that they made the ministry a less attractive haven for men of ideas. Their long-term implications were more momentous. Both promoted the assumption that serious reflection required rejection of practical life; moralism provided the rationale for engagement, devotionalism for withdrawal. Throughout the nineteenth and twentieth centuries, American intellectuals would orchestrate the tension between those alternatives with a variety of religious and secular idioms.

At about the same time that the ministry was losing its theological dimension, anti-intellectual currents were divesting political life of possibilities as well. The career of John Quincy Adams (1767–1848) offers a case in point: as a young man Adams had been the very model of the gentleman scholar—Boylston Professor of Rhetoric and Oratory at Harvard and an occasional contributor to the Federalist literary magazine, *Portfolio.* But he felt the need of preserving his literary anonymity because, he wrote (privately) in 1801, "there is no small number of very worthy citizens among us irrevocably convinced that it is impossible to be at once a man of business and a man of rhyme, and who, if they know me for the author of the two pieces inclosed, would need no other proof that I ought immediately to be impeached for incapacity as a public servant." Some years later his suspicions were borne out in the presidential campaign of 1828. It was characterized by one wag as a contest between

John Quincy Adams who can write
And Andrew Jackson who can fight.

Adams could be stigmatized as the candidate of New England, and of Europe; he even had the temerity to suggest that European autocracies had done more for the advancement of learning than had the American democracy.

Against this cosmopolitanism, Jacksonian democrats could counterpose the rugged unschooled brilliance of their romantic hero. "Behold, then, the unlettered man of the West, the nursling of the wilds, the farmer of the hermitage, little versed in books, unconnected by science with the traditions of the past, raised by the will of the people to the highest pinnacle of honour, to the central post in the civilization of republican freedom," George Bancroft proclaimed. Jacksonian rhetoric was a compound of romantic nationalism and republican producerism; both idioms were hostile to intellect. To the romantic nationalist, the oversubtle mind was a barrier to intuiting the mystical will of the people; to the republican producerist, people who thought for a living looked suspiciously like the parasites—lawyers, bankers, middlemen of all kinds—who "produced" nothing substantial, who wore swallowtail coats instead of leather aprons, and who threatened to suck the lifeblood from the body politic. In politics as in the ministry, devotees of intellect depended on the patronage of a population more heterogenous and unpredictable than any they had faced before.

A similar problem affected the arena of belles lettres. Patterns of patronage were transformed in the transition toward a modern literary marketplace. Older aristocratic notions had presented the author as a well-bred amateur who sought fame but avoided publicity; he either exhibited his talent to his social equals without depending on it for a living or accepted the patronage of his social superiors while remaining independent of commercial sales. During the half century after the Revolution, the amateur ideal persisted in certain literary practices. Joel Barlow, would-be poet laureate of the young United States, and Ralph Waldo Emerson, would-be sage of Boston, both courted coterie audiences early in their careers. James Fenimore Cooper, Washington Irving, and Henry Wadsworth Longfellow all shunned the public eye when they were just starting out.

By the 1820s, though, the situation was changing. The growth of urban trading centers and the improvements in transportation brought by turnpikes, canals, and, later, railroads meant not only the beginnings of a national market economy but also the emergence of writing as a business. Cooper and Irving were transitional figures. They had independent incomes but they also made money from writing; they could finance their own books, take the risks themselves, and remain less dependent on success in an uncertain marketplace.

Even for Cooper and Irving, though, the pursuit of a writing career posed psychological if not economic dilemmas. In a society where culture was increasingly the preserve of women, the man of letters seemed little more than an effete refugee from practical life. Acceptance of this role promoted feelings of isolation and self-deprecation bordering on self-hatred. Cooper chose what became a characteristic defensive strategy by retreating into a pseudo-aristocratic posture of disdain for the mob.

Irving, on the other hand, gave the game away: he worked in what Ann Douglas has identified as the characteristic genre of male self-deprecation—the sketch. Tossed off lighlty with no pretensions to craftsmanship or seriousness, sketches risked little and claimed to be little more than ephemeral "jottings." They seemed an appropriate form for a culture that relegated writing to an allegedly nonproductive feminine sphere. In *Tales of a Traveller* (1824), Irving's narrator, Buckthorne, confesses to literary aspirations, only to comment, "that is to say I have always been an idle fellow and prone to play the vagabond." He is disinherited by his father on the grounds that poetry is "cursed sneaking household employment, the bane of all true manhood," and regains his legacy only by renouncing "the sin of authorship." "The Stout Gentleman" reinforced the notion that the literary man is an impotent spectator at the drama of life. The narrator becomes more and more curious about a portly gentleman who occupies an inn with him. But he fiddles around, never approaches the man directly, and the sketch closes abruptly with the gentleman getting into his coach, his backside thrust firmly in the narrator's face. From this view, the man of letters is passive, ineffectual, and altogether marginal to the serious business of life, or as Irving put it: "Unqualified for business in a nation where everyone is busy; devoted to literary leisure is confounded with idleness, the man of letters is almost an insulated being, with few to understand, less to value, and scarcely any to encourage his pursuits."

Irving's anxieties embodied broader social tendencies. By the 1830s, the pursuit of ideas in the United States was becoming a more problematic vocation, one that had to be pursued in the interstices of existing institutions rather than within the institutions themselves. The devotee of intellect who longed to float freely in the eddies of cultural life often found himself stuck between a rock and a hard place—at least if he had to make his own living.

In New England, though, the economic basis for an intelligentsia was beginning to form. The men who made fortunes in the clipper-ship trade with China or in the canals and railroads of the early republic were often the ancestors or in-laws of major figures in nineteenth-century American intellectual life. The flowering of New England was rooted in the compost of a *rentier* class: living off one's investments, or those of one's wife or parents, was a common practice of cultivated New Englanders from Ralph Waldo Emerson and Charles Eliot Norton to Henry Adams and William James.

The beneficiaries of Boston captial came to constitute what Lewis Simpson (b. 1916), using Coleridge's term for a body of educated men who claim responsibility for the cultural well-being of the entire society, has called "the New England clerisy." As Simpson observes, "Coleridge's notion of a clerisy is an aspect of his effort to grapple with the leading problem of his age: the bear-

Henry Wadsworth Longfellow (1807–1882), along with his fellow cultivated New Englanders, fulfilled the role of socially responsible intellectual elite.

ing of intellect on society when religious authority has lost its assimilating power over the primary civilizing agency in society, the use of letters." The vision of a socially responsible intellectual elite was fulfilled in the generation that came of age in the 1830s—men such as Richard Henry Dana and Francis Parkman, Henry Wadsworth Longfellow, Oliver Wendell Holmes and James Russell Lowell, Emerson, Thoreau, and Hawthorne.

No other region developed a clerisy comparable to New England's. New York remained more devoted to commercial than to cultural life, while southern thinkers suffered from a sense of deep isolation which they covered with a cult of Romantic genius. In 1845, the South Carolina writer William Gilmore Simms recalled his own youth in language that could have applied to most of his contemporaries: "Suddenly in the compass of a country village," he wrote,

> a boy springs into sight who claims to be in possession of a secret. He claims to have endowments which are not of ordinary acquisition. His ways are not like those of other boys. He engages in none of their sports. He goes apart from them, loves to muse in secret places and gloats over a book as one suddenly in the possession of a secret treasure. . . . The very sacrifice of the usual pleasures of boyhood—the fact that he is shy when they are frank; sad and thoughtful when they are uproarious; solitary when they crowd together, these, alone, should suffice to indicate to any but the wilful blind, the imperious exigencies of a peculiar moral constitution, from which the possessor, still striving, still reluctant, is himself unable to get free.

Trapped in the "peculiar moral constitution" of romantic genius, the southern man of mind was sometimes reduced to absurdity: the hysterical James Hammond, for example, continually claimed to be at death's door though he was becoming too fat to get through it. Hammond's hypochondria was the sort of "female complaint" one might expect from an emasculated male in a patriarchal society, and indeed Hammond admitted that "it is really much easier to cut a figure among women."

Despite their marginality, southern thinkers insisted on the utility of mind. George Frederick Holmes, who became president of the University of Mississippi in 1848, argued to his activist friends that learning could "furnish the Statesman and the combatant in the arena of politics with the brightest and keenest weapon in his armoury." The coming sectional crisis provided men like Holmes with their opportunity to test that proposition: they narrowed their energies into proslavery apologetics, and much of their force was lost in a flood of provincial defensiveness.

New England thinkers were far more fortunate. Inheriting some of the old Puritan sense of intellectual mission, the New England clerisy came to exercise a regionally based hegemony over much of American cultural life during the latter two-thirds of the nineteenth century. They managed to equate their particular section's interests and values with those of American society as a whole.

The strength of this hegemonic influence depended paradoxically on the clerisy's sense of detachment from the productive strife of the world. This feeling varied in accordance with each individual thinker's circumstances. It was reinforced by the romantic and Victorian differentiation of culture and society, which sanctioned the survival of the central rhetorical convention in Puritan and republican tradition—the jeremiad. It was easy for cultivated New Englanders (as for cultivated southerners) to lament the decline of the righteous community into commercial corruption. They confronted the spread of a market society dominated by entrepreneurial buccaneers who disdained "booklarnin'" and celebrated self-manhood (whether or not they embodied it). It was easy to believe that the world outside the study was a brutal or at best a boring place, and that the pursuit of intellect was a secular ministry with little direct reward. From this view, the clerisy were embodiments of the Protestant paradox, in the world but not of it, devoted to the betterment of the dominant culture but separate from its cruder manifestations. Inhabitants of a "feminized" sphere remote from productive economic life, they neverthless succeeded in making New England the metaphorical center of American culture.

Despite New Englanders' desire to elevate themselves above the sordid realm of money-making, their *rentier* status often shaped the character of their thought in subtle ways. Separated from production while they benefited from its proceeds, they yearned for manly engagement with immediate, demanding experience even as they recoiled from the practical realm of business. The sense that they were parasites in a society of producers intensified their fascination with power—and also their fear of it.

One way to exercise a kind of power was to take the apparent marginality of intellectual life in the early republic and redefine it as *heroic* marginality, nonconformity, masculinity. That was the key rhetorical move in the New Englanders' trek toward cultural hegemony, and it was perfected by Emerson—a representative man (as he might have said) whose life illuminates some perennial problems in the social history of American intellectuals. During the most fruitful period of his career

No other region developed a clerisy comparable to New England's: New York remained more devoted to commercial than to cultural life, while southern thinkers suffered from a sense of deep isolation, which they covered with a cult of Romantic genius.

he was torn between his impulse toward engagement with the bustling business of nineteenth-century America and his desire for withdrawal to the solitude of the scholar's study. It was the characteristic conflict of gender identity experience by Victorian intellectuals and by their twentieth-century successors. At some fundamental level of his being, Emerson oscillated between exuberant autonomous activity and depressive dependent passivity. The tension between these two modes of life affected his thought in profound ways. Ultimately it helped to explain why this shy recluse became the most popular moralist of the nineteenth century.

Emerson was born in 1803, one of five surviving children raised by a Congregational minister's widow. His early life was characterized by genteel poverty, provincial education, and religious orthodoxy. He attended Harvard, graduated in the middle of his class, and was ordained as a Unitarian minister at the age of twenty-six. When his first wife, Ellen, died two years later, Emerson withdrew into introspection. After a prolonged period of inner doubt, he resigned his ministry in 1832 in protest over what seemed to him the mummified formalism of Unitarian practices—especially the rituals of the Lord's Supper and the practice of public prayer. For the next few years, he lived on income inherited from his first wife and on the investments of his second wife, Lydia Jackson, whom he married in 1835. He also derived a little income from lecturing, but he was hardly self-supporting—hardly engaged in the manly strife of the business world.

In 1836 Emerson published "Nature," a transcendentalist manifesto that was also a straw in the wind of his turbulent psyche. Man was a god in ruins, he proclaimed: to reconstruct his stature he must penetrate nature (Coleridge's Understanding) to experience Nature (Coleridge's Reason). He must become a "transparent eyeball" and live in boundless union with the cosmos. On the one hand, this was Emerson's assertion of imperial self-hood; on the other, it was his recognition of his own dependence upon the underlying Unity of all living things. "Nature" expressed Emerson's ambivalence in philosophical terms.

Yet Emerson often reflected more directly on the problems faced by the thinker in an activist society. He sought to break out of his isolation in 1837, when he addressed the Phi Beta Kappa Society at Cambridge on the subject of "the American Scholar." He was eager to throw off the popular image of the scholar as a pathetic bookworm, meekly accepting his ideas from the authorities of the past: "We have listened too long to the courtly muses of Europe," he cried, urging his listeners to "give me insight into to-day, and you may have the antique and future worlds." It was the prototypical statement of what was to become a near-religion among American intellectuals—a reverential regard for the verities inherent in immediate lived experience. (Indeed the words "experience" and "life" assumed a talismanic significance for Emerson as they did for many of his intellectual descendants.) "What would we really know the meaning of?" Emerson asked. "The meal in the firkin; the milk in the pan; the ballad in the street; the news of the boat; the glance of the eye; the form and gait of the body," he answered. Emerson's scholar would not only be more American but also more egalitarian than any scholar had been before.

He would also be more active and more manly:

> The so-called "practical men" sneer at speculative men, as if, because they speculate or see, they could do nothing. I have heard it said that the clergy,—who are always, more universally than any other class, the scholars of their day,—are addressed as women; that the rough, spontaneous conversation of men they do not hear, but only a mincing and diluted speech. They are often virtually disfranchised; and indeed there are advocates for their celibacy. As far as this is true for the studious classes, it is not just and wise. Action is with the scholar subordinate, but it is essential. Without it he is not yet man.

Concern about the womanish role of intellect might be related to Emerson's anxiety about his own failure to live up to the Victorian male role. "The study of letters," he concluded hopefully, "shall no longer be a name for pity, for doubt, and for sensual indulgence." Dependence on his wives' income may well have reinforced his defiant stance of activism. "The one thing in the world, of value," he announced, "is the active soul." Emerson's celebration of action and manliness, his suspicion of book-learning and his near deification of "experience" all suggest that we are in the presence of that curious American paradox—the anti-intellectual intellectual.

Yet "The American Scholar" also contained evidence of mistrust of the vulgar herd and the longing for withdrawal into solitude. This was consistent with romantic and transcendentalist philosophical assumptions. Common things and common people were valuable only as entryways into the universal realm of Nature (or Reason); on the everyday level, they represented merely the world of nature (or Understanding). The scholar's duty, Emerson asserted, was "to feel all confidence in himself, and to defer never to the popular cry. He and he only knows the world." Such a statement, if uttered today, would call down the wrath of the righteous, hurling accusations of "elitism." Despite its apparent arrogance, though, Emerson's elevation of intellectual autonomy was more than a ridiculous bit of self-inflation; it had a more complex cultural significance. It was embedded in romantic epistemology and a healthy distrust of conventional wisdom, as the next sentences suggest:

> The world of any moment is the merest appearance. Some great decorum, some fetish of a govenment, some ephemeral trade, or war, or man, is cried up by half mankind and cried down by the other half, as if all depended on this particular up or down. The odds are that the whole question is not worth the poorest thought which the scholar has lost in listening to the controversy. Let him not quit his belief that a popgun is a popgun, though the ancient and honorable of the earth affirm it to be the crack of doom.

In a world where portentous commentary can conflate Saddam Hussein with Hitler, where political reputations can be created or destroyed in a week's time, Emerson's advice seems more emancipatory than elitist.

So Emerson resisted the temptation to define his own intellect out of existence, refused to defer so completely to the authority of common experience. His resistance was rooted in a romantic notion of defiant individual subjectivity, but also in social prejudices epidemic among the New England *rentier* intelligentsia.

Ralph Waldo Emerson oscillated between exuberant autonomous activity and depressive dependent passivity, and the tension between these two modes affected his thought in profound ways.

Throughout the late 1830s, Emerson's tendency toward withdrawal deepened as he brooded on the meaning of mass politics. "Men are become of no account. Men in history, men in the world of to-day, are bugs, are spawn, and are called 'the mass' and 'the herd,' " he observed in "The American Scholar." In an insight that would be elaborated by twentieth-century thinkers from Erich Fromm to Hannah Arendt, Emerson went on to note that the members of the herd imagined their will to be embodied in a powerful leader. One can see the allusions to Andrew Jackson in almost every line: "What a testimony, full of grandeur, full of pity, is borne to the demands of his own nature, by the poor clansman, the poor partisan, who rejoices in the glory of his chief," Emerson said. "The poor and the low . . . cast the dignity of man from their downtrod selves upon the shoulders of a hero, and will perish to add one drop of blood to make that great heart beat, those giant sinews combat and conquer. He lives for us, and we live in him." The subtlety of this observation was lost in his letters and journals, which often displayed mere contempt for ordinary folk.

This was especially clear in Emerson's reaction to the stock market crash of 1837 and the long depression that followed. Thousands lost their jobs and their savings as factories closed and banks failed. Emerson was unmoved by the plight of the poor and jobless: true to the tradition of the jeremiad, he saw the depression as fit punishment for the vulgar materialism of a Jacksonian middle class on the make. It was the reaction of a Boston patrician living on inherited wealth. New England had not enjoyed the wildcat prosperity of the early and mid 1830s and suffered much less than the rest of the country when the bubble burst. In 1838, at the bottom of the depression, Emerson wrote that he owned a house, $22,000 worth of stocks earning 6 percent, and had an income from lectures ranging from $400–800 per year. Yet during the depression he became more and more bitter toward the American passion for material wealth, and identified it increasingly with democracy. It was not the established leaders of the business class who aroused his ire; it was the small fry, who tended to be Democrats from the South and West. In 1838 the ardent Jacksonian George Bancroft visited him and bragged that the *Washington Globe*, the Democratic party organ, reached three hundred thousand readers. "I ought to have said what utter nonsense to name in my ear this number," Emerson complained to his journal, "as if it were anything. Three million such people as can read the *Globe* with interest are as yet in too crude a state of nonage as to deserve any regard."

Against this distrust of the Jacksonian mob, it is easier to see the larger social significance of "The American Scholar." Its audience, the Phi Beta Kappa Society at Harvard, were Boston gentlemen who, like Emerson, lived on their investments and were disgusted by the vulgarity of parvenu plutocrats. The address was a call to these men to reaffirm their manhood and reassert their cultural dominance by embracing an activist role.

From 1837 to 1841, Emerson was more and more disposed to withdraw from society, even as he reasserted the claims of the individual self and cut himself off from traditional Christianity. But a profound difficulty bedeviled this whole strategy of withdrawal: solitude could bring a sense of boundless mystical union with the cosmos—but what if the cosmos was a moral void? What if pure Being, which he exalted in the Divinity School Address and elsewhere, was actually just another word for Nothingness?

Emerson was too much a man of his time, too much a Victorian, to abandon faith that the universe had moral meaning. He could not rest content with the antinomian mysticism of the transparent eyeball. He had to cling to some of framework of moral government for the universe, but he had rejected the traditional comforts of supernaturalism. After his four-year-old son died in 1842, Emerson faced the real possibility of total despair: the universe threatened to become a bleak void in which his son's death had no meaning.

The way out lay in the doctrine of compensation—the belief that evil would be punished and good rewarded in *this* world. Emerson first presented it in his Divinity School Address and amplified it in his later essays. The radical potential of Emerson's antinomian revolt was smothered ultimately by his insistence that, in the end, everything would work out for the best. Fate was subject to moral law, evil "merely privative," an evanescent illusion. "Let us build altars to the beautiful necessity," he proclaimed in "Fate" (1852), accepting a deterministic universe as an inevitably beneficent reflection of pure Being—like Jonathan Edwards's idea of the universe as an "emanation and remanation of the Deity" but with all the tragedy left out. Personal need made Emerson an apostle of progress, and his cosmic optimism fit perfectly with the dominant national creed. He became a spokesman for the populace he had once despised, his language the coinage of positive thinkers from Mary Baker Eddy to Norman Vincent Peale.

For other New England writers popularity was more problematic. They spent their careers trying to establish a psychologically satisfying relationship with a society that seemed hostile to their deepest longings. In *Walden, or Life in the Woods* (1854), for example, Henry David Thoreau created a literary version of the simple life that, because it *was* literary, could be lived anywhere. The pattern was consistent with transcendentalist ethics: the quest for Emersonian "self-reliance"—for transcendence over the dependent impulses in oneself—was wholly mental; nature and the material world were only important for their symbolic inner meanings. So *Walden*, which begins with a ringing critique of alienated labor, can nevertheless end with Thoreau returning to Concord to work in his father's pencil factory.

Nathaniel Hawthorne had fewer transcendental resources than Thoreau, but (as Jane Tompkins has shown in *Sensational Designs* of 1985) more support from the established members of the New England clerisy. The growth of Hawthorne's literary reputation demonstrated the ways a regional elite could begin to establish national cultural hegemony, dissolving class, sectional, and gender rivalries in a universalist rhetoric of quality. Longfellow's *North American Review* piece on the second edition of *Twice-Told Tales* (1842) was a key document in this process. Longfellow observed that "Mr.

Hawthorne's . . . writings have now become so well known, and are so justly appreciated, by all discerning minds, that they do not need our commendation. He is not an author to create a sensation, or have a tumultuous popularity. His works are not stimulating or impassioned, and they minister nothing to a feverish love of excitement. Their tranquil beauty, and softened tints, which do not win the notice of the restless many, only endear them the more to the thoughtful few." Longfellow's invocation of "all discerning minds" helped to create the foundations of Hawthorne's canonical stature and to marginalize the work of writers outside the select community of northeastern men. We can assume that, in Longfellow's view, there were few "discerning minds" west of the Hudson, and none at all among the "damn'd mob of scribbling women" that so excited Hawthorne's animosity.

Scribbling women were a threat to male authors not only because they were professional rivals but because their success seemed to vindicate the sneers of practical men—the contemptuous dismissals of culture as a refuge for the effeminate and ineffectual. The desire to demonstrate engagement with "real life" and serious issues led men to exclude even distinguished female authors such as Harriet Beecher Stowe from the ranks of the clerisy. At the same time, a woman with intellectual aspirations as strong as those of Margaret Fuller (1810–1850) felt obliged to reject fiction and embrace the realm of "fact." Fuller's involvement with the fortunes of the Italian republic and her turn from transcendental musings to historical journalism were a flight from the cloistered role prescribed for the life of the mind in an activist society. Like many intellectuals in the twentieth century, she sought to escape feelings of isolation by immersing herself in what she felt were the most progressive political currents of her time. To be a free-floating intellectual, despite Emerson's brave pronouncements, was for her and for others merely to be outside those currents, washed up on the beach.

Intellectuals and Institutions

But for men of ideas who sought engagement with the world, a new set of alternatives was already in the making. During the antebellum decades there were powerful countercurrents at work that would create new institutions requiring the services of intellect, and a new social role for the intellectual to play. The vast apparatus of sorting and categorizing mechanisms that Burton Bledstein has called "the culture of professionalism" began to appear as early as the 1840s. Professionalism hastened the specialization and fragmentation of knowledge, the growing rift between the "expert" and the "man of letters." The expert would offer an increasingly appealing resolution to the conflict between intellect and practicality. The convergence of power and knowledge in large bureaucratic institutions marked the emergence of a new mode of domination—blank, impersonal, routinized—one that the expert administered and legitimated. Michel Foucault was the master analyst of this mode, and in *Discipline and Punish* (1977) he put his finger on its quintessential architectural expression: the panopticon designed by Jeremy Bentham to facilitate complete surveillance of prison inmates. This was only the most extreme expression of a broadly based effort to survey, count, and classify the general population more systematically than ever before.

The motives behind this effort were many. In the United States the classifying impulse was rooted in Protestant reform movements that sought to transform the dissolute through the creation of sabbatarian legislation, temperance societies, and the like. But there were soon secular offshoots of these movements, still charged with a mission to institutionalize self-control, but working directly through government administration rather than lobbying to change laws. The most striking of these developments occurred in the movements for prison reform and public education: both helped to create institutions where intellectual elites could serve the state as agents of socialization. In penology, reformers of the 1820s and 1830s sought systematically to gather information on inmates' families and personal backgrounds; this was gathered in documents like the Annual Reports of the Auburn (New York) penitentiary and used to promote the remaking of the prisoner into a useful member of society. The process required the services of a new breed of administrative intellectual, prototypes of the twentieth-century "policy scientist." In education, reformers like Horace Mann (1796–1859) stated plainly in their annual reports to the state school boards that public schooling was not a sentimental humanitarian movement; it was a necessary tool

Henry David Thoreau created a literary version of the simple life: the quest for "self-reliance" was wholly mental; nature and the material world were only important for their symbolic inner meanings.

in the civilizing of a working-class multitude that was ever more restless and alienated from bourgeois Protestant culture. School administrators, too, could demonstrate the importance of expertise in implementing new structures of social hierarchy to organize the untutored masses.

The coming of the Civil War brought new opportunities for Northern intellectuals to place themselves at the service of dominant institutions. A central figure in the assimilation of intellect to the state was Henry Bellows, minister of the main Unitarian church in New York City and later head of the United States Sanitary Commission, which systematized the response to suffering during the war. In 1859 Bellows gave in effect what was his own divinity school address, a response to the anti-institutional implications of Emerson's. "Would that I could develop here," Bellows said, "at a time so forgetful of the dependence of society on organization, *the doctrine of institutions*, the only instruments, except literature and the blood, by which the riches of ages, the experience and wisdom of humanity, are handed down . . . the only constant and adequate teachers of the masses. . . . " As George Fredrickson in his *The Inner Civil War* (1965) has shown, Bellows had his chance to implement "the doctrine of institutions" in his administration of the sanitary commission. He and other cultivated men sought to prune the commission of any sloppy womanish sentiment, to harness humanitarian aid to principles of efficiency and productivity, to make the relief of soldiers' suffering primarily a service to the state. The war provided the opportunity for men of mind to become "tough-minded," to escape the curse of effeteness.

To be sure, some continued to employ the old personal and moralistic idioms, resorting to the rhetoric of the jeremiad at what might seem to be the least opportune moments. Some comfortable bystanders positively gloried in the prospects of long-term suffering. Even as the staggering casualty figures came in from Shiloh, Charles Eliot Norton wrote a friend, "I can hardly help wishing that the war might go on and on till it has brought suffering and sorrow enough to quicken our consciences and cleanse our hearts." More commonly the vestiges of moralism slipped away; during and after the war, Northern intellectuals increasingly spoke the language of expertise and institutions, emphasizing the need to subordinate the unruly individual to the interests of the whole nation. And of course, those interests would be defined by people like themselves.

The immediate postwar years proved to be disillusioning. The ideal of government by the competent dictated an agenda of civil service reform. But as cultivated northeastern men attached themselves to that cause, they discovered that not everyone had been converted to the ideology of expertise. Opponents of civil service reform declared that competitive examinations would discriminate against veterans who had been risking their lives while the more privileged but less patriotic youth had been capering about college campuses. These same critics insisted on the distinction between formal education and practical intelligence; as Senator Matthew H. Carpenter of Wisconsin put it:

> The dunce who has been crammed up to a diploma at Yale, and comes fresh from his cramming, will be preferred in all civil appointments to the ablest, most successful, and most upright business man of the country, who either did not enjoy the benefit of early education, or from whose mind, long engrossed in practical pursuits, the details and niceties of academic knowledge have faded away as the headlands disappear when the mariner bids his native land goodnight.

As if to complete the ritual of anti-intellectual invective, critics of the reformers also resorted to crude sexual imagery. George William Curtis, the highly educated editor of *Harper's Weekly* and a leading civil service reformer, was denounced by Senator Roscoe Conkling of New York as one of "the man-milliners, the dilettanti, and carpet knights of politics"—the term "man-milliners" being a reference to the fashion articles in Curtis's magazine as well as a thinly veiled allusion to homosexuality. Another senator, Thomas Platt, referred in his memoirs to "a smart boy named Curtis, who parted his hair in the middle like a girl." However "tough-minded" their intentions, men of intellect could not escape the implication that they themselves were less than manly.

Gradually, though, cultural and institutional changes worked together during the years after the Civil War to promote the assimilation of the expert. The growing prestige of a positivistic science of society provided a theoretical rationale for the involvement of intellect in public policy; the emergence of the modern research university provided the locale. The last three decades of the nineteenth century saw the application of the Prussian model of graduate education to new universities like Stanford and Johns Hopkins as well as to older ones like Harvard and Yale. Colleges became more than seminaries, or holding pens for ruling-class bullies; more systematically than their antebellum predecessors, universities offered a sense of purpose to the devotee of intellect. As the economist Richard Ely wrote in 1902, universities should be preparing to "train experts for every branch of the public service." In just a few decades, the intellectual had shed his moralism and provincialism, his crippling effeteness, and emerged with a new tone of self-assurance. Ely repeatedly asserted that "government is a profession, not a business," implying that policy professionals rather than businessmen should rule; and indeed he did not shirk from the will to power embedded in his thought: "*We must have a class of officeholders,*" he announced. The impersonal, universalist language of "social science" was beginning to replace the old gentility. The implications for intellectuals were tremendous. From his university base, the academic expert could do more than catalogue the eternal verities or write impressionistic literary "appreciations"; he could also diagnose the maladies of the existing social order.

The favorite diagnosis was "cultural lag," a term in use among turn-of-the-century social theorists as various as Thorstein Veblen and Edward A. Ross. Notions of cultural lag were loosely based on Darwinian models of social evolution: conflict was a sign of inadequate "adaptation" to social change. The only "Darwinian" aspect of this thinking was the emphasis on ceaseless transformation, epitomized by the almost talismanic use of the word "evolutionary." ("Why Is Economics Not an Evolutionary Science?" Veblen complained in a title of 1900.) Cultural values were always trying to catch up to social realities, just as legal doctrines (to cite Oliver Wendell Holmes, Jr.) were constantly being remade to meet "the felt necessities of the time." The Darwinian script included a role for the expert: he was to promote social integration—or to use the more suggestive term coined by Ross in 1901, "social control." How? By "laying hold of the sacred ark of the permanent" (in John Dewey's phrase), revealing the relativity of all allegedly eternal cultural forms—by promulgating the new values and easing pragmatic adaptation to them.

As the staggering casualties came in from the battle at Shiloh, Charles Eliot Norton wrote a friend, "I can hardly help wishing that the war might go on and on till it has brought suffering and sorrow enough to quicken our consciences and cleanse our hearts."

The Darwinian coin of adaptation was converted into the sociological currency of "adjustment." As a strategy for achieving social control, the pursuit of adjustment seemed far superior to the old and ineffectual moralism of "thou shalt not." As Newton D. Baker observed, the new approach was based on the realization that "if you wanted to get a firebrand out of the hand of a child, the way to do it was neither to club the child nor to grab the firebrand, but to offer in exchange for it a stick of candy!" New visions of a malleable mass population encouraged intellectuals to think they might have something to learn from the "psychology of influence" perfected by the advertising industry. As Ellen Richards observed in *Euthenics* (1910), "perhaps the sword of Damocles must be visualized by such exhibits as the going out of an electric light every time a man dies, by the ghastly microbe in the moving picture, by the highly colored print or by a vivid reproduction of crowded quarters." Like the advertiser, social engineers could learn "how to apply the right stimulus at the right time in order to arouse the desired interest"; the difference was that they would be promoting the public welfare rather than a narrow commercial need.

Christopher Lasch has dissected the profoundly antidemocratic implications of these doctrines of adjustment, and has shown how Ross, one of their most vigorous advocates, was also aware of their darker dimensions. Ross foresaw the emerging educational apparatus as part of the larger oppressive structure of the modern state: "The coalescence of physical and spiritual forces in the modern state may well inspire certain misgivings," Ross wrote in 1901.

> When we note the enormous resources and high centralization of a first-class educational system; when we consider that it takes forcible possession of the child for half the time during its best years, and submits the little creature to a curriculum devised more and more with reference to its own aims and less and less with reference to the wishes of the parent; when we consider that the democratic control of this formidable engine affords no guarantee that it will not be used for empire over minds—we may well be apprehensive of future developments.

Rather than creating an empire of minds, intellectuals might well be collaborating in the creation of empire over minds. Ross warned that "the art of domesticating human beings may succeed only too well," as he contemplated the specter of mass society: "the great agencies of Law, Public Opinion, Education, Religion, and Literature speeded to their utmost to fit ignoble and paltry natures to bear the moral strains of our civilization, and perhaps by the very success of their work canceling the natural advantage of the noble over the base, and thereby slowing up the development of the most

The career of William Dean Howells (1837–1920) illustrated a crucial transition in American intellectual life from the complacent gentility of the Boston clerisy, entrepreneurial, socially conscious spirit of New York City.

splendid qualities of human nature." The Darwinian model of adjustment might be merely a prescription for mediocrity. The only alternative to this prospect lay in Ross's vague hope that "other spiritual associations lying over against the state" might provide some counter-strain to its imperatives.

The phrase "spiritual associations" suggested that Ross had in mind an ethical or philosophical rather than an institutional alternative. Maybe Ross was thinking of the romantic counterpoint to expertise, the notion of the intellectual as a free-floating critic, a nay-sayer to complacency and concentrated power. This vision of intellectual life resurfaced as well toward the end of the nineteenth century, nearly the same time that experts were gloating over the new career prospects in universities and government service. William Dean How-ells offered one model of critical independence, William James another.

The career of William Dean Howells (1837–1920) illustrates a crucial transition in American literary and intellectual life: from *rentier* to entrepreneur as the dominant style of livelihood, from New England to New York City as the dominant regional force. Howells always had to earn his way; no man with a trust fund could have written "The Man of Letters as a Man of Business," which is really about the writer as working stiff, selling his labor power in the marketplace like any other artisan. Yet it is also about the inability of the writer to make contact with ordinary workers, even to become visible to them. It is, in short, about Howells's own ambiguous vocation as a man of letters, occupying the noman's-land between bourgeoisie and proletariat, waiting for the society that would be governed by "that human equality of which the instinct has been planted in the human soul." By the time he wrote "The Man of Letters," Howells had traveled very far from his literary beginnings in Boston—his celebrated admission into the inner sanctum of the New England clerisy when he met Holmes and Lowell, and Holmes said, "well, James, this is something like the apostolic succession; this is the laying on of hands." Howells ascended to a position of high responsibility within the clerisy when he took over the editorship of the *Atlantic Monthly*; but he gradually came to doubt the place of Boston as the capital of the republic of letters. His move to New York in 1890 merely put the seal on a process that had been underway for a long time. He had come to question the complacent gentility of the Boston intellectual world, especially as he began grappling with his own social conscience in the wake of the Haymarket affair of 1886. A policeman had been killed during a labor demonstration; four anarchists who had been on the scene were accused of the murder. Defending their right to a fair trial, Howells alienated some of his comfortable friends and began to confront his own sense of public responsibility. But he never really overcame the tension between his ethical commitments and his class position as a well-paid tribune of the dominant culture—a tension he brilliantly expressed through the character of Basil March in *A Hazard of New Fortunes* (1890). March has come to New York from Boston to edit a new magazine called *Every Other Week*, which is published by a sharp-eyed literary promoter named Fulkerson. March is torn between his desire to identify with the city's poor and his aesthete's tendency to place their poverty in the framework of the picturesque. Fulkerson, meanwhile, recognizes that sensational stories of any kind sell magazines—whether they sympathize with the poor or merely aestheticize them.

Howells's career indicated one path for intellectuals in the late nineteenth century: a place somewhere in commercial publishing (on the fringes if necessary), writing literary journalism and fiction. The character of Fulkerson was aptly drawn; he represented a new social type, the literary promoter, participant in the "magazine revolution" that produced dozens of cheap new periodicals dependent less on subscriptions than on advertising. Promoters like Fulkerson helped to create new vehicles and new institutional homes, however temporary, for unattached authors. The trick was sustaining one's independent judgment in the midst of conflicting aesthetic, commercial, and ethical demands. The scrupulous Howells was never satisfied that he had.

William James enacted an alternative for the intellectual who sought to preserve his critical stance: His career suggests that universities could do more than replicate elites; they could also create and sustain the tradition of intellectuals.

William James enacted an alternative scenario for the intellectual who sought to preserve his critical stance. His career suggests that universities could do more than replicate elites; they could also create and sustain the tradition of *intellectuels.* The Dreyfus case was a key moment for thinkers on both sides of the Atlantic; it signified the emergence of intellectuals as the sworn enemies of any effort to suppress free debate in the name of "national resolve." In a 1907 address, "The Social Value of the College Bred," James claimed the chief value of a college education was that it "should help you know a good man when you see one"—in other words, that it should foster critical discrimination. "We ought to have our own class-consciousness. 'Les Intellectuels'! What prouder club-name could there be than this one, used ironically by the party of 'red blood,' the party of every stupid prejudice and passion, during the anti-Dreyfus craze, to satirize the men in France who still retained some critical sense and judgment!" James echoed Emerson's "American Scholar" in rallying his cultivated audience to a more active social role; if they did not warm to the task, he concluded, they might soon be eclipsed as educators by the "ten-cent magazines." University-trained educators, from this prescient view, were locked in rivalry with the developing mass media.

The Triumph of the Expert

The coming of World War I marked the subordination of the *intellectuel* to the expert, as universities and mass media overcame their rivalries and joined in service to the state. In general, the war served as an ideal laboratory for the state to explore the Foucauldian uses of intellect. George Creel's Committee on Public Information provided an opportunity for the government to use the "psychology of influence," as Ellen Richards had recommended, to promote adjustments to broad national goals. University administrators and most professors, along with nearly all the rest of the American intellectual community, abandoned any pretense at critical detachment and produced a variety of hard-boiled apologetics for repressive state policy. New forms of expertise were put to use, most notably in the sorting and categorizing of army recruits through intelligence tests. When war fever had finally subsided, even the editors of the *New Republic,* chief among the "realistic" voices for war, began to feel embarrassed. "If I had it to do all over again, I would take the other side," Walter Lippmann said. "We supplied the Battalion of Death with too much ammunition."

With only a few exceptions, antiwar protests were stronger among the untutored populace than among the intelligentsia. "In the opinion of Missourians," Senator Champ Clark announced, "there is no difference between a conscript and a convict." Populist antiauthoritarianism promoted a distrust of professional experts. Senator Lawrence Sherman of Illinois focused on the new prominence of psychologists in government:

> Psychologists with X-ray vision drop different colored handkerchiefs on a table, spill half a pint of navy beans, ask you in a sepulchral tone what disease Walter Raleigh died of, and demand the number of legumes without counting. Your memory, perceptive faculties, concentration, and other mental giblets are tagged and you are pigeonholed for future reference. I have seen these psychologists in my time and I have dealt with them. If they were put out in a forest or in a potato patch, they have not sense enough to kill a rabbit or dig a potato to save themselves from the pangs of starvation. This is a government by professors and intellectuals. I repeat, intellectuals are good enough in their places, but a country run by professors is ultimately destined to Bolshevism and an explosion.

The senator veered off into the traditional anti-intellectual theme of impracticality and the newer one of Bolshevism; his tirade has been noted and dismissed as a typical fulmination from an ignorant troglodyte. Yet, given the subsequent relationships between expertise and foreign policy in the twentieth-century United States, one has to give the troglodytes their due. The expert was no Bolshevik, far from it; but he was indeed a menace to democracy.

Amid the triumph of expertise, the most honorable heir to the critical intellectuals' tradition was Randolph Bourne. A founder of *Seven Arts* magazine and a model for the serious independent journalist, Bourne was a tireless opponent of the thoughtless "realism" that passed for policy debate then and now. "This realistic boast is so loud and sonorous that one wonders whether realism is always a stern and intelligent grappling with realities," he wrote in 1917. "May it not be sometimes a mere surrender to the actual, an abdication of the ideal through a sheer fatigue from intellectual suspense?" The difficulty lay in the devotion to adjustment: "The defect of any philosophy of 'adaptation' or 'adjustment' . . . is that there is no provision for thought or experience getting beyond itself. If your ideal is to be adjustment to your situation, in radiant co-operation with reality, then your success is likely to be just that and no more. You never transcend anything." Eager for transcendence, Bourne, better than any of his contemporaries, approximated the Jamesian ideal of independent intellect fostered among "free personal relations." Critical of the capitulation involved in the cult of adjustment, Bourne affirmed an alternative that today would be called "multicultural." In "Trans-national America" (1916), he observed that

> "America is already the world-federation in miniature" and . . . the country could conceivably foster "an intellectual internationalism which goes far beyond the mere exchange of scientific ideas and discoveries and the cold recording of facts. It will be an intellectual sympathy which is not satisfied until it has got at the heart of the different cultural expressions, and felt as they feel. It may have immense preferences, but it will make understanding and not indignation its end."

This viewpoint celebrated the demise of New England Anglo-Saxons' cultural dominance and looked forward to the coming decades when Jews and other immigrants, along with southerners white and black, would come to play a major part in creating a more cosmopolitan intellectual life.

Later in the century, intellectuals from a variety of regional and ethnic backgrounds carried on Bourne's tradition; Dwight MacDonald, Edmund Wilson, Alfred Kazin, Mary McCarthy, Allen Tate, James Baldwin, and Irving Howe, for example, all operated on the fringes of the academy. But the university was the place where "the role of the intellectuals" was most often defined and debated. The chief division was between professional expertise, on the one hand, and speculative, critical, or creative intellect, on the other. As the state relied increasingly on the services of scholarly technicians, nineteenth-century stereotypes were reversed: the humanities were more likely to encourage challenges to established authority than were the sciences (or social sciences). The most vigorous intellectual life continued to come from the free-floaters on the fringes.

Opportunities for institutional support increased with the coming of the New Deal. Roosevelt's Brain Trust even gave a few of them—Rexford Tugwell, Raymond Moley—a brief celebrity. Who could blame these hitherto obscure professors if they began to feel a bit pumped up with self-importance? "What would *you* do," H. L. Mencken asked in 1936, "if you were hauled suddenly out of a bare, smelly school room, wherein the razzberries of sophomores had been your only music, and thrown into a place of power and glory almost befitting Caligula, Napoleon I, or J. Pierpont Morgan, with whole herds of Washington correspondents crowding up to take down your every wheeze, and the first pages of their newspapers thrown open to your complete metaphysic?" Mencken was indulging in his characteristic hyperbole, but if one substitutes Henry Kissinger for Tugwell or Moley, one can see the ultimate implications of the expert-as-celebrity.

Government work was not the only way for intellectuals to grasp the ring of reality in the 1930s. The sentimental culture of the Popular Front encouraged them to venerate the gritty "real life" of the working class, and to embrace a more authentic vocation than effete aestheticism by committing themselves to the workers' cause. This outlook could produce an exalted meditation like James Agee's *Let Us Now Praise Famous Men* (1941), but more commonly it encouraged the pedestrian genre of proleterian literature. On the right wing of the Popular Front mentality was a pseudo-populist nationalism, a creed that specialized in filiopietistic history and tub-thumping hosannas to democracy; Van Wyck Brooks (in middle age) and Archibald MacLeish were two of its chief exponents. By 1940 they were excoriating literary intellectuals as "the irresponsibles" who had encouraged Hitler's success by refusing to confront the enormity of his evil. The confrontation they had in mind was mostly cultural; it involved the promotion of "primary literature" rather than "coterie literature"—of healthy upbeat portrayals of everyday American life (one thinks of Thornton Wilder's *Our Town* [1938]) rather than the brooding European pessimism of a Jean-Paul Sartre or a Ignazio Silone.

With the coming of World War II, the temptations to abandon what Bourne had called "skeptical creativity" began to multiply. For communists, loyalty to the party line required not only a strong stomach for a literary diet of proletarian mush, but also a capacity to perform intellectual and ethical gymnastics in accordance with every twist and turn of Stalin's policy. For mainstream liberals, especially after 7 December 1941, the pressure to abandon independent thought and embrace national policy became overwhelming. If any war could be justified, it was assumed, surely it was this one.

Yet the cultural implications of the move toward war continued to trouble some intellectuals. Brooks and MacLeish had defined the war from the outset as a cultural conflict, an effort to defend American values against goose-stepping Germans and treacherous Japanese. Anthropologists like Margaret Mead reinforced this framework by popularizing the "culture concept" and the idea of national character; both notions deemphasized social conflict and assumed that Americans were unified by a holistic, classless set of common values. This creation of a collective national identity—an "American way of life"—met the longings for security bred by depression and war, but its bland vision of consensus left little room for the critical intellectual.

But during the late 1930s a group of intellectuals came together to try to preserve the ideal of independent thought against the blandishments of communism, Americanism, or the professionals' cult of technique. The attempt became a legendary story (at least to the participants themselves); it led to the founding of the *Partisan Review. PR* editors and contributors wanted to heal the split in twentieth-century culture between a political radicalism dedicated to material progress and a "modernist" cultural radicalism that looked beyond the pleasure principle of the liberal or socialist imagination, toward the attainment of a kind of spiritual heroism. They aimed to avoid the philistinism of Mike Gold, the elitism of T. S. Eliot. They wanted, in other words, to create a radical stance that was also sensitive to intellectual and spiritual values. That was a difficult task, especially with the coming of World War II.

Apart from a few dissenters like MacDonald and Paul Goodman, the trajectory of the main *PR* group (represented by the founding editors William Phillips and Philip Rahv) was symptomatic of the general movement within the U.S. intellectual community. Reacting against the philistinism and moral idiocy of Stalinism, radical intellectuals backed into an uncritical acceptance of the American way of life. The stress of war was key: it ended the brief *PR* alliance between political and cultural radicalism. The *PR* intellectuals began by rejecting the celebration of material progress and the subordination of culture to politics in proletarian realism (or Brooks's "primary literature"). Shaken by the horrific events in Europe, they sought to cultivate a new awareness of the tragic conflicts in the human condition, to bridge the gap between the profoundest literature (Dostoyevski, Yeats, Eliot) and the drive for social justice. In the end the bridge fell: vague rumblings about "life's tragic complexities" became the excuse for abandoning all social hope. The war reinforced the tragic sense, but also the acceptance of America, warts and all, as the only conceivable alternative to the totalitarianism of the Left or Right. Under pressures of war, the independent radicalism of the late 1930s became the "realistic" cold war liberalism of the 1950s. Lionel Trilling's *The Middle of the Journey* (1947) presented a portrait of a Left intellectual in midpassage, caught between sentimental progessivism and cold war orthodoxy. For most "realistic" liberals the choice was not hard to make: they attacked as "sentimental" all critiques of a militarist foreign policy, indeed all pleas for social justice. For many intellectuals, tough-minded realism concealed their acceptance of the status quo and their abandonment of their critical role.

Institutional changes hastened these developments. After the war, the bureaucratization and professionalization of intellect accelerated with the growth of the national security state and the "knowledge industry." Government agencies, publishing houses, foundations, universities—all meant more jobs for intellectuals, more economic security. And in Trilling's view these developments also meant more influence for intellectuals on a once-indifferent business civilization. "Wealth," he wrote in 1950, "now shows a tendency to submit itself to the rule of mind and imagination, to apologize for its existence by showing taste and sensitivity." The irony, once again, was that in their quest for the feeling of power, intellectuals lost the actual power of independent thought. The institutionalization of intellect in the spreading doctoral system tended to turn out glib techniques rather than genuine critical thinkers. The professionals' cult of technique reinforced their desire to flee from engagement with historical circumstances; what emerged was a bag of tricks that could be used to sell oneself in the academic marketplace. Irving Howe observed in 1954 that "criticism seems to resemble

In the conflict between sentimental progressivism and cold war orthodoxy, most "realistic" liberals chose to attack as "sentimental" all critiques of a militarist foreign policy—indeed, all pleas for foreign policy.

Macy's on bargain day: First floor, symbols; second floor, myths (rituals to the rear on your right); third floor, ambiguities and paradoxes; fourth floor, word-counting; fifth floor, Miss Harrison's antiquities; attic, Marxist remnants; basement, Freud; subbasement, Jung. Watch your step, please."

Howe's consumerist metaphor suggests a major preoccupation of intellectuals in the 1950s (though not of Howe himself)—a concern with taste and style, epitomized in the popularity of a mass-culture criticism that ignored structures of power and focused on the pap allegedly demanded by the multitude. The fetishism of style kept much cultural commentary on a superficial plane; as perceptive a critic as Paul Goodman, for example, could complain that Eisenhower invited Fred Waring and the Pennsylvanians to the White House while ignoring Ike's more significant errors—such as, for example, his installation of a CIA-backed regime in Guatemala. By the late 1950s, intellectuals were openly complaining of boredom; in more apocalyptic moods they worried about being engulfed by what MacDonald called "the spreading ooze" of middlebrow culture.

Fears of cultural asphyxiation produced longings for regeneration. The stage was set for Camelot, where John F. Kennedy promised salvation through style, and invited Pablo Casals, rather than Fred Waring, to the White House. Kennedy was not only stylish, he was quick, decisive, manly—all those traits that made Norman Mailer pant with admiration, and that resonated with the anxiety, the secret self-contempt, at the heart of the male intellectual's psyche since the early republic.

The disaster of the Vietnam War freed some intellectuals from the Kennedy imprisonment and revitalized public discourse on university campuses. Fundamental cultural, ethical, and political issues were addressed as they had not been for decades. The split between technocrats and humanists widened into an abyss; both groups could be seduced by style, could embrace the anti-intellectualism of the intellectuals. But while the humanists may have sometimes uncritically celebrated countercultural protest, the technocrats created mountains of bad faith by adopting the pose of neutral values.

Since the Vietnam era, the most promising development is the rise of a serious assault on that stance of objectivity. The emergence of feminist, ecological, and poststructuralist critiques of Cartesian dualism, the attempt to lay bare the masculine anxieties behind Western traditions of science and rationality—these developments pose a fundamental philosophical challenge to the ethos of tough-minded realism. They even suggest a way out of the endless, repetitive cycles of American intellectual life, where each generation has seemed determined to be cooler and more pragmatic than its sentimental predecessors. It may be time to break the circuit.

[See also The Aristocracy of Inherited Wealth; Gender; Mass Culture and Its Critics; The Professions; The Research University; Roles and Relations; Urban Cultural Institutions.]

BIBLIOGRAPHY

Blake, Casey. *Beloved Community: The Cultural Criticism of Randolph Bourne, Van Wyck Brooks, Waldo Frank, and Lewis Mumford* (1990). Excellent introduction to an important set of figures.

Bledstein, Burton. *The Culture of Professionalism* (1976).

Charvat, William. *The Profession of Authorship in America, 1800–1870* (1961). Pioneering essays in the social history of literature.

Douglas, Ann. *The Feminization of American Culture* (1977).

Ellis, Joseph. *After the Revolution: Profiles of Early American Culture* (1979). Good on the shift from republican to romantic sensibility.

Faust, Drew Gilpin. *A Sacred Circle: The Dilemma of the Intellectual in the Old South, 1840–1860* (1977). Sensitive, probing.

Foucault, Michel. *The Archaeology of Knowledge.* (1972).

———. *The Birth of the Clinic: An Archaeology of Medical Perception* (1973).

———. *Discipline and Punish: Birth of the Prison* (1977).

———. *Power/Knowledge: Selected Interviews and Other Writings, 1972–1977* (1980).

Fredrickson, George. *The Inner Civil War: Northern Intellectuals and the Crisis of the Union* (1965).

Gilbert, James. *Writers and Partisans: A History of Literary Radicalism in America* (1968).

Graebner, William. *The Engineering of Consent: Democracy and Authority in Twentieth-Century America* (1987). Brilliantly dissects the seductions of "democratic social engineering."

Hofstadter, Richard. *Anti-Intellectualism in American Life* (1963). A lively account, a little too easy on the experts and hard on the "ignorant masses."

Jacoby, Russell. *The Last Intellectuals: American Culture in the Age of Academe* (1987).

Lasch, Christopher. *The New Radicalism in America: The Intellectual as a Social Type, 1889–1963* (1965). A classic in a class by itself.

Rabinowitz, Richard. *The Spiritual Self in Everyday Life: The Transformation of Personal Religious Experience in Nineteenth-Century New England* (1989).

Shils, Edward. *The Intellectuals and the Powers, and Other Essays* (1972). A blend of functionalist sociology and neoconservative apologetics.

Simpson, Lewis. *The Man of Letters in New England and the South: Essays on the History of the Literary Vocation in America* (1973).

Singal, Daniel. *The War Within: From Victorian to Modernist Thought in the South, 1919–1945* (1982).

Tompkins, Jane. *Sensational Designs: The Cultural Works of American Fiction, 1790–1860* (1985).

Tyler, Moses Coit. *A History of American Literature, 1607–1765* (1949).

Wald, Alan. *The New York Intellectuals: The Rise and Decline of the Anti-Stalinist Left from the 1930s to the 1980s* (1988).

Wilson, Christopher P. *The Labor of Words: Literary Professionalism in the Progressive Era* (1985). Superb synthesis of social history and literary criticism.

— T. J.JACKSON LEARS

J

JOURNALISM

The first printing establishment in the North American colonies was set up in Cambridge, Massachusetts, in 1639. Printing there and elsewhere in the seventeenth century was devoted largely to religious works along with job printing for business, legal, and governmental purposes. Journalism, if by that we mean the regular, periodic publication of information about contemporary affairs, did not exist until the very end of the seventeenth century.

Not until the beginning of the nineteenth century did daily newspaper publication make journalism a part of everyday life even for urban Americans. Not until the middle of that century did newspapers hire their own reporters and begin to establish journalism as an occupation or profession. Not until the twentieth century did the First Amendment protection of press freedom become a living tradition in the courts. Yet from its earliest days, American journalism has been an important institution for expressing democratic ideals and for embodying communal sentiment. Even in the late nineteenth century, when metropolitan daily newspapers became industrial giants, with leadership linked to money and power, another journalism flourished in the literary underbrush closely connected to ethnic communities and social movements. As a political institution and as a cultural form and forum, journalism has long been a key part of American life.

The Colonial Press

The first American newspaper was printed at Boston in 1690 by a bookseller and publisher, Benjamin Harris. *Publick Occurrences Both Forreign and Domestick* indicated in its first issue its modest ambition to publish once a month (oftener only if "any Glut of Occurrences happen") a faithful account of those "considerable things as have arrived unto our Notice." For the next seventy-five years, this would be the scope of news reporting in the American press—no affirmative gathering of news, only the making available of newspaper columns for what might fall into the printer's lap.

Because Harris failed to obtain permission from the governor and council of the Massachusetts Bay Colony, his paper died after one issue. The next paper, and the first successful one in the colonies, was the *Boston News-Letter*, begun by John Campbell in 1704. Campbell took news to be "recent history" and tried to keep his news printed in chronological order. However, because he had so little space to reprint news he received from London newspapers and occasional correspondents, he fell further and further behind. He caught up by printing more often but, even at that, he had little sense of urgency. In May 1719 he claimed that he was printing news from Britain up to the first week of March and other European news only as recent as October 1718.

The notion that news should be as timely as possible was not well established in the early eighteenth century. Even the notion that the newspaper should be devoted to accounts of recent events was not self-evident. Samuel Keimer, a Philadelphia printer, began publishing *The Universal Instructor in All Arts and Sciences: and Pennsylvania Gazette* in 1728. He saw the newspaper as an instrument of instruction and enlightenment and so chose to print serially Ephraim Chambers's *Cyclopaedia*, A through Z. In 1729, however, while Keimer was still working through the A's, Benjamin Franklin bought the paper and discontinued the encyclopedia project. He introduced a mode of journalism more literary and satirical on the one hand and more engaged in civic affairs on the other, something he learned not only from English literary models but also from his own experience in Boston as an apprentice at his brother James Franklin's *New England Courant.* James Franklin had begun his paper in 1721, despite the counsel of friends who said they thought the paper not likely to succeed, "one newspaper being in their judgment enough for America."

All this suggests that the first colonial newspapers were a motley group in their aims and directions and that the history of journalism in the United States must take up the development of the cultural category of "news" as well as the story of its institutional embodiment in weekly and daily newspaper publication (and later radio and television broadcasting).

The format of colonial papers as four-page weeklies was relatively standard and their contents, after a time, tended toward a common model. Newspapers presented readers an assortment of local advertising, occasional small paragraphs of local hearsay, and larger chunks of European political and economic intelligence. Much of this news, concerning, for instance, disputes between central European monarchs, would seem very far removed from the interests of the colonists.

What this model meant is obscure. Stephen Botein suggests that the newspapers may have been providing a kind of global mapping of Protestantism versus Rome, but he confesses that this is a highly speculative observation. More likely, he concludes, the printers operated by an economic rather than a political or ideological strategy: wanting to avoid offending their readers, they sought out remote foreign news that mattered little to people and would arouse no controversy, a practice known in journalism as Afghanistanism.

If this is so, much of what early colonial papers printed fit neither the criterion of timeliness nor that of interest or utility to readers. Local political news and political news of other colonies rarely appeared. Though the printer of the *New-York Weekly Journal*, John Peter Zenger, was tried for sedition for his paper's attacks on the royal governor and found not guilty by a jury in 1735, he was thereafter a tame journalist. Even though it set no legal precedent, the Zenger verdict gave support to popular sentiment in favor of liberty generally and liberty of the press specifically; but printers seemed impressed more by Zenger's harassment than by his exoneration. Zenger had been prudent to attack the governor rather than the legislature: throughout the colonial period, the legislatures, in defense of parliamentary privilege, were more likely than the governors or courts to suppress free expression, written or spoken. Even after licensing requirements for newspaper publication were withdrawn, colonial assemblies took publication of their votes or proceedings to be a breach of privilege. There is not much to suggest that many newspaper proprietors in the first part of the eighteenth century were strongly motivated to print political news and views; when they were, there were major constraints to doing so.

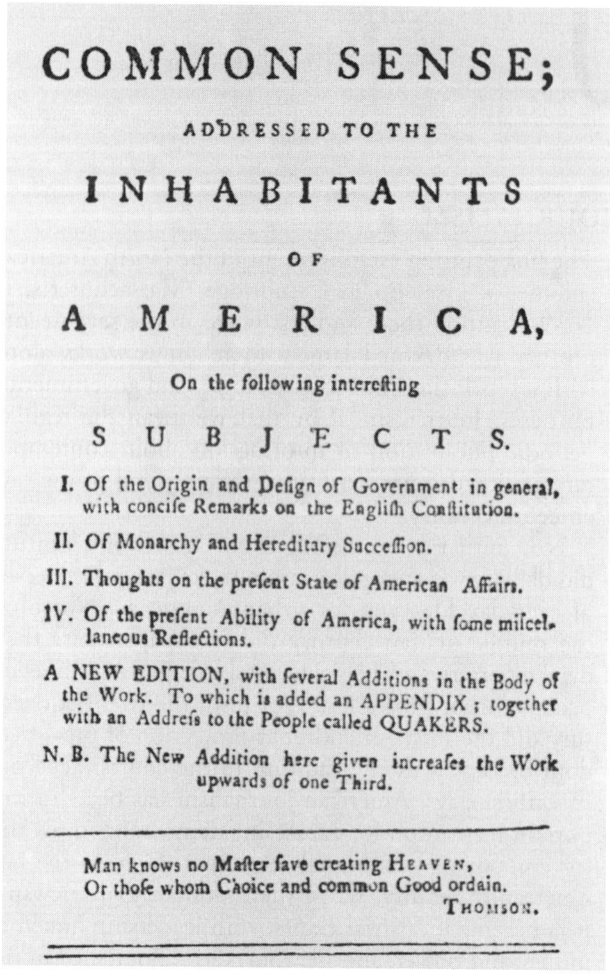
COMMON SENSE;

ADDRESSED TO THE

INHABITANTS

OF

AMERICA,

On the following interefting

SUBJECTS.

I. Of the Origin and Defign of Government in general, with concife Remarks on the Englifh Conftitution.

II. Of Monarchy and Hereditary Succeffion.

III. Thoughts on the prefent State of American Affairs.

IV. Of the prefent Ability of America, with fome mifcellaneous Reflections.

A NEW EDITION, with feveral Additions in the Body of the Work. To which is added an APPENDIX; together with an Addrefs to the People called QUAKERS.

N. B. The New Addition here given increafes the Work upwards of one Third.

Man knows no Mafter fave creating HEAVEN,
Or thofe whom Choice and common Good ordain.
THOMSON.

Pamphleteering, a popular form of political journalism, reached its heyday with the publication of Thomas Paine's Common Sense *in 1776.*

As economic enterprises, colonial papers were generally family affairs. Benjamin Franklin apprenticed with his older brother. Elizabeth Timothy, who became the country's first woman publisher by taking on the management of Charleston's *South Carolina Gazette* in 1738, was the first of at least fourteen women who ran colonial print shops, usually after the deaths of their husbands. The newspapers were not self-sustaining. Most printers of newspapers also conducted job-printing businesses that accounted for the larger share of their income.

While newspapers grew in number and importance, there was little magazine journalism in the colonial period. The first magazines in the colonies were *American Magazine*, issued by the Philadelphia printer Andrew Bradford, and *General Magazine*, issued by Benjamin Franklin, both begun in 1741. (The ubiquitous Franklin also began the colonies' first foreign-language paper, the *Philadelphische Zeitung*, which lasted only two issues.) But none of the eighteen magazines published before the end of the revolutionary war survived to see the founding of the new nation; only a few lasted as long as a year. Their content tended toward coverage of contemporary political or religious affairs, and they did not leave much of a mark on their times.

The political orientation of the press began to change in the 1760s. With the colonies on the brink of breaking with England after the Stamp Act controversy of 1765, colonial printers were compelled to choose sides. Reluctantly they did so, and modest print shops became hives of political activity. In the late seventeenth century and early eighteenth century, colonial politics had been a relatively private matter. The press generally avoided politics, and when an occasional pamphlet did take up a political issue, it was addressed to the colonial assembly, not to the general population. But pamphleteers became more active in political campaigning by the 1740s in the major colonial cities of New York, Philadelphia, and Boston. Although many conservative leaders objected to pamphleteering, they found themselves obliged to resort to it. The pamphleteers reached their height of influence with Thomas Paine's publication of *Common Sense* in 1776. At that time, the newspapers of largest circulation sold no more than two thousand copies of a weekly issue. The typical pamphlet was printed once or twice in editions of just a few thousand copies. *Common Sense* was reprinted twenty-five times in 1776 alone, and altogether it sold an estimated 150,000 copies. Paine, like other professional pamphleteers of his generation, addressed the general populace, but he extended and perfected the practice. He dropped esoteric classical references for familiar biblical ones, seeking a language the general population understood. His style, his own lowly social origins, and his political republicanism combined to make him the leading political pamphleteer of his day.

Newspapers took on a more and more active political role in the years leading up to the Revolution. John Dickinson's *Letters from a Farmer in Pennsylvania*, beginning in 1767, were among the articles attacking British legislation that appeared in newspapers and helped prepare for the break with England. Patriot journals began to print news, and rumor, of the offenses of British soldiers. The colonists advanced their economic boycotts of British goods by having the names of violators published in the newspapers.

Newspapers remained small in size (the four-page format was unvarying), few in number, and precarious in rates of survival. Of thirty-five papers in existence when the Revolution began in 1775, only twenty survived to the war's end in 1783, although thirty-five new ones were established in the same period. Print technology did nothing to further newspaper development; the technology of the wooden flatbed press was essentially unchanged since Gutenberg.

The Political Press in the Early Republic

The press in the new nation grew rapidly. *The Federalist Papers*, a series of political essays written by Alexander Hamilton, John Jay, and James Madison to persuade New York to ratify the Constitution, were published serially in several New York newspapers and widely reprinted in other parts of the country (without, as it happens, winning the hearts and minds of the New York legislature). The first daily newspaper, the *Pennsylvania Evening Post and Daily Advertiser* of Philadelphia, appeared in 1783. Although it did not survive long, by 1800 Philadelphia had six dailies, New York had five, Baltimore had three, and Charleston had two; altogether, there were 241 newspapers in the United States, 24 of them dailies. Noah Webster's *American Minerva* boasted in 1793, "In no other country on earth, not even in Great-Britain, are Newspapers so generally circulated among the body of the people, as in America." This was certainly true. *Porcupine's Gazette*, a Philadelphia daily, had a circulation of two thousand in 1799, as large a circulation as any newspaper in England. Foreign visitors—Crèvecoeur, Tocqueville, Trollope, and others—were repeatedly astonished in the next half-century by the widespread habit of reading, especially newspaper reading, in America. Edward Dicey, an English journalist visiting during the Civil War, claimed that the American might well be defined as "a newspaper reading animal." The two hundred papers of 1800 had become by 1830 more than seven hundred, including sixty-five dailies. By 1850 there were over two thousand newspapers, more than two hundred of them dailies. Not all European visitors found the spread of newspaper reading that these numbers reflected a good thing. One visitor, Thomas Hamilton, observed unhappily that newspapers "penetrate to every crevice of the Union." Since even the lower classes could afford papers, he observed, the newspapers catered to them and so grew "indifferent to refinement either of language or reasoning."

The Federalist Papers—*political essays by Alexander Hamilton, John Jay, and James Madison to persuade New York to ratify the Constitution—were published serially in several New York papers and widely reprinted in other parts of the country.*

In the first decades of the new nation, newspapers were identified with the editorial voice. Intensely partisan, they were frequently founded as weapons for party or faction, like Alexander Hamilton's *New York Evening Post*, begun in 1801 to recoup Federalist power after the loss of the presidency to Thomas Jefferson. Reporting of news was incidental, unorganized, and obviously subordinated to editorial partisanship. John Fenno, in the *Gazette of the United States*, spoke semiofficially for the Federalists and traded barbs with Philip Freneau at the *National Gazette*, the voice of the Jeffersonians, during the brief flourishing of that paper in the early 1790s. Journalistic vituperation was chilled by the Alien and Sedition Acts of 1798. The Sedition Act made it a criminal offense to print "any false, scandalous and malicious writing . . . against the Government of the United States." While there were relatively few prosecutions under the act, it was a partisan bone of contention and expired after Jefferson came to power in 1801.

Politicians objected to the other party's papers but still held a favorable attitude toward the press in general. The Postal Acts of 1792 and 1794 are instructive: all parties assumed that newspapers should have preferential mailing rates. While it cost six cents to mail a one-page letter up to sixty miles, a newspaper could be mailed up to a hundred miles for a penny. Publishers could use the mails free to exchange copies of their papers with other newspaper establishments. Subsidy of the press, like federal support for the building of roads and canals, seemed taken for granted, as both leading parties favored nationalization. Washington and Jefferson agreed that postal rates should be low. Jefferson, in his first annual message, even advocated abolishing newspaper postage "to facilitate the progress of information." Newspaper circulation, especially beyond an immediate locale where private news distributors could be employed, relied on the postal service. Thus from the republic's earliest days, the press was the beneficiary of federal laws intended to ease or to enlarge the newspaper business.

Thomas Jefferson, well known for his statement that he would prefer newspapers without a government to a government without newspapers (1787), was a prime target for the vituperation of the Federalist press. It is not surprising that, despite his vigorous defense of the role of the press in a democratic society, he also said in 1807, "The man who never looks into a newspaper is better informed than he who reads them, inasmuch as he who knows nothing is nearer the truth than he whose mind is filled with falsehoods and errors." Editors attacked one another as viciously as they attacked politicians, and sometimes carried rivalries into fistfights and duels in the street.

But by the 1820s newspaper competition began to express itself in less primitive fashion. Several New York papers began to send small boats out to incoming ships to get the news from London faster than their rivals. This was indicative of a turn toward reportage in newspaper work. The War of 1812 had precipitated a gradual shift to domestic news, although foreign intelligence still predominated. Some technological changes also began to affect the work of printers. Iron presses began to replace wooden ones at the turn of the century. The Fourdrinier papermaking machine, patented in 1799, significantly improved the production of paper. Hand-powered presses began to give way to steam-powered ones, and flatbed presses to the much faster cylinder presses. The first steam-powered cylinder press was used to print the *London Times* in 1814, turning out sheets at about four times the rate of the best flatbed hand press. However, it took much greater skill to use, the quality of the printing produced was low, and its productivity outstripped the needs of most printers.

By 1833 the American newspaper was well established as a vehicle for political parties and a bulletin board for the business community. Advertising was abundant: papers devoted half or more of their space to advertisements, including most or all of what we think of as the front page. (There is evidence that editors of the day judged the outside pages as a kind of cover, less important than the inside pages, notably the editorial column that ordinarily appeared on page 2.) Still, efforts to attract advertising were haphazard. Circulation grew, but even in 1833 the largest paper had a circulation of only 4,500—more than double the typical city paper's circulation. The newspaper was barely distinguishable in many cases as an independent venture. While the newspaper was by 1830 differentiated from the post office and distinguishable from the print shop—at least in some cases—it was not easily separable from the party, faction, church, or organization that it served. Journalism was certainly not yet an identifiable occupational path. Few papers hired reporters; what was called a correspondent was just that, a friend or acquaintance of the editor, an unpaid amateur who would write an occasional letter to the paper. Newspaper proprietors were publishers, editors, and editorial staff at once. Often they regarded their posts as stepping-stones to political office or at least the political largess of government advertising when their party came to power.

From 1780 to 1830, newspapers were not alone as a source of current information and views. Broadsides—any item printed on one side of a single sheet—were important, representing about 20 or 25 percent of all imprints before 1800. New England records suggest that before 1830 the broadsides most often concerned politics, music, secular ballads, reports of strange or supernatural happenings, and literature. The broadsides typically circulated locally and were published in runs of five hundred to fifteen hundred copies (and rarely went through more than two runs). Treated very much like newspapers, judging from the fact that they were only occasionally saved in family libraries, they seem to have been superseded by the increasingly successful newspapers early in the nineteenth century.

Magazines flourished in the early national period, too, despite the fact that the Post Office Act of 1792 provided very low rates for newspapers but not for magazines. In 1794 there were five magazines, twelve in

1800, and nearly a hundred by 1825, both weeklies and monthlies. The most important general magazine was Philadelphia's *Port Folio,* devoted to both politics and literary criticism, known for the lively wit of its editor, and gathering contributions from leading (Federalist) figures of the day. This period saw the beginning of the first specialized periodicals in the country, including the New York *Medical Repository,* a medical journal that lasted from 1797 to 1824. Magazines flourished more readily after Congress lowered postage rates for periodicals in 1825. The largest circulation magazine before the Civil War was *Godey's Lady's Book,* founded in 1830 by Louis Godey (as *Lady's Book*) and edited from 1837 to 1877 by Sarah Josepha Hale. Its circulation reached 150,000 by 1860 and may have come close to 500,000 at its height in 1869. While often remembered as an influential advocate of domesticity and a supporter of a "separate sphere" for women, *Godey's* was at the same time a strong voice for the support of women's education both in formal institutions and at home.

A New Breed of Papers

Journalism participated in the major social changes in American life of the Jacksonian era. As property qualifications for voting were repealed in the states, as lawyers came under attack as a kind of "aristocracy" and the examination and certification requirements for admission to the bar in many states were repealed, as reform movements for the abolition of slavery, for women's rights, and for rights of the working man flourished, journalism, too, experienced a democratic revolution. Beginning with the *New York Sun,* edited by the printer Benjamin Day and first published in 1833, a new breed of newspaper sought commercial success and a mass readership.

Between 1833 and 1835, in New York, Boston, Baltimore, and Philadelphia, venturesome entrepreneurs began "penny papers" selling for a penny an issue rather than the six cents at which papers were commonly priced. Moreover, the new penny papers were hawked on the streets by newsboys instead of being available exclusively by subscription, although it is likely that subscription remained the predominant form of distribution. The penny papers were typically more aggressive than their six-penny rivals in seeking out local news, assigning reporters to the courts, and even covering "society." They aggressively solicited advertising at the same time that they engaged in vigorous competition to get the "latest" news as fast as they could. For instance, James Gordon Bennett's *New York Herald* hired horse express riders who beat those of the most aggressive mercantile papers, the *Courier and Enquirer* and the *Journal of Commerce,* in getting Andrew Jackson's annual message to New York from Washington in 1835. Bennett also jumped into the newsboat competition that had developed in the 1820s and hired several newsboats to go out to sea to meet incoming European ships, get their newspapers, and bring them back to port ahead of the ships. By 1840 he organized an express service from Washington that was faster than the mails, and by 1844 another express service that met British mail boats in Boston and brought their news to New York ahead of regular mail delivery.

The great circulation gains of the penny papers were made possible not only by low price and aggressive distribution and marketing but also by aggressive use of recently developed technologies. The *Sun* began the penny-press revolution with a traditional hand-run flatbed press. Within a few months, however, Day bought a cylinder press that made a thousand, rather than two hundred, impressions an hour. In 1835, when it was already selling twenty thousand copies a day, the *Sun* became the first newspaper in the country to purchase a steam-driven press. The penny papers were also the most aggressive papers in making use of the telegraph. The *Baltimore Sun* made early use of telegraphic communication, and its example helped encourage both press and public acceptance of the invention. During

The New York Sun *began the penny-press revolution with a traditional hand-run flatbed press; within a few months, however, the paper acquired a cylinder press that made a thousand, rather than two hundred, impressions an hour.*

the war with Mexico in 1846, penny papers in New York and Philadelphia made the first and fullest use of the telegraph. The two-cylinder Hoe press, which became standard for much of the nineteenth century, was first used by a penny paper, the *Philadelphia Public Ledger,* in 1847. Technology was available, but it took the peculiar disposition of the competitive, news-hungry, circulation-building penny papers to make quick use of it.

The *New York Herald* was the penny paper with the most sustained commercial success. The editor, James Gordon Bennett, was a portent of changing times: unlike Day and most newspaper proprietors of the times, he had never worked as a printer. Educated for the Roman Catholic priesthood in his native Scotland, he emigrated first to Canada, where he worked as a schoolteacher, and then to the United States, where he was a clerk in a publishing and printing establishment in Boston; then a proofreader in New York, then an editorial assistant for the *Charleston* (South Carolina) *Courier*, where he translated foreign news from Spanish and French; then a free-lance writer for the *New York Enquirer* and other papers; and then as an associate editor for the *Enquirer*, writing on politics and society from Washington, Albany, and Saratoga Springs. After several years at the *Enquirer*, he bounced from one party newspaper to another before establishing the *Herald* in 1835, sympathetic to the Democrats but without personal ties or allegiances to any party. The penny papers typically proclaimed their independence from party—prematurely, one might add—but they proved to be the beginning of a modern press for which economic goals supersede political loyalties.

While the leading edge of journalistic innovation, commercial vigor, and competitive news-gathering was the penny press, the most widely circulated sorts of papers before the Civil War were country weeklies or other nondailies with local or regional circulations. These papers, with generally small circulations, nonetheless could have sizable readerships because a copy of one paper could have ten to twenty readers. The country press, whatever its political predilections, was invariably a booster of economic development in its own towns and regions.

Horace Greeley, like many other journalists of his day, began work on one such small weekly, the *Northern Spectator* of East Poultney, Vermont. He moved from his printing apprenticeship there to Erie, Pennsylvania, and to New York in 1831, looking for the main chance. If it is misleading to take New York journalism as representative of all journalism, it is nevertheless hard to exaggerate its influence as the radiating center of American communications. In New York, Greeley found himself in a world of journalistic ferment and change. Setting up his own printing business within a few years, by 1834 he began issuing the *New-Yorker*, a magazine of literature, reviews, and politics with a circulation that reached nine thousand. In 1840 he ran the Whig campaign paper, the *Log Cabin*, for William Henry Harrison (with a circulation of up to eighty thousand for its brief run) and in 1841 began his own penny paper, the *New York Tribune*. Quickly reaching a circulation in excess of ten thousand, this Whig paper was strongly antislavery and clearly showed itself a journal of ideas, reporting on women's rights and socialist experiments. Not an advocate of women's rights, Greeley nonetheless hired Margaret Fuller in 1844 as the first woman to be a regular staff employee on a major American newspaper. He hired Karl Marx as a European correspondent. The paper never rivaled the *Herald* in circulation, but the *Weekly Tribune* Greeley established to circulate outside the city was lucrative and for decades was widely known in rural communities throughout New York, New England, and the West. (The *Tribune* in 1924 bought the *Herald* and the merged *Herald Tribune* remained a leading paper until its demise in 1966, survived only by the Paris-based *International Herald Tribune*.)

THE ETHNIC PRESS. The pluralism of American society in the 1830s, spurred by renewed immigration, particularly from Germany and, in the 1840s, from Ireland, was reflected in the newspapers. In 1834 the Jacksonian New York *Staats-Zeitung* was founded, a paper that survived well into the twentieth century. Other German papers, mostly Democratic, emerged as immigration grew in the 1850s (by 1860 the 1.3 million German-born represented more than a quarter of all foreign-born citizens). In 1828, the *Cherokee Phoenix* was the first Native American newspaper, published in English and Cherokee. The African American press began with *Freedom's Journal*, published by John Brown Russwurm and Samuel E. Cornish in New York from 1827 to 1829, and later the *Colored American*, a New York paper that ran from 1837 to 1841. Frederick Douglass began the *North Star* in Rochester in 1847, changing the paper's name in 1850 to *Frederick Douglass' Paper*. The African American-run papers before the Civil War were a part of the abolitionist movement, whose most famous journalistic leader (apart from Douglass) was William Lloyd Garrison and his Boston-based *Liberator*, first published in 1831. The abolitionist press not only reached its own adherents with news and argument but also sought to propagandize others. In 1835 the American Anti-Slavery Society launched a major propaganda effort, shipping out more than a million pieces of abolitionist literature, directed especially to the South. Postmasters refused delivery and mobs burned sacks of mail in hysterical reaction. The onslaught of print convinced proslavery forces North and South that the abolitionist cause, still a very small and poorly funded set of political groups, was a vast and threatening mass movement.

News Gathering and News Agencies

Newsgathering was growing as the central function of the newspaper, but political reporting in the early nineteenth century was at first anything but taken for granted. The Senate did not make its proceedings public until 1795. Only two state constitutions made legislative sessions public. Congress did not officially keep its own records until the 1820s, nor did any newspaper outside Washington regularly cover Congress until this period. The *National Intelligencer*, founded in 1800, provided the best Washington news, especially after gaining the right to take notes on the floor of Congress in 1802. Reporting suffered from inadequate stenographic skills—only the *Intelligencer*'s Samuel Harrison Smith apparently had the requisite skills, and when he (frequently) left the city for reasons of health, government news essentially stopped. What did get reported, as Washington reporting became more competitive in the 1820s, did not necessarily resemble what was actually said in the Congress. Reporters and politicians developed a cooperative relationship which took for granted that the journalists would rewrite and improve upon what was originally said. There was not much regard for what one journalist called "unfeeling accuracy."

As late as 1846, only Baltimore and Washington papers assigned special correspondents to cover Congress. But as politics heated up in the 1850s, more than fifty papers hired Washington correspondents. State capitals also began to receive greater coverage. Still, most Washington correspondents wrote for half a dozen or more papers and earned further salary as clerks for congressional committees or as speechwriters for politicians. The occupational world of journalism was narrowly differentiated from politics.

A new journalistic enterprise, the wire service, began in the mid nineteenth century when New York newspapers joined in 1848 to establish the New York Associated Press (later the Associated Press) as a way to make better, and cheaper, use of new telegraphic services. The AP was a cooperative and gathered news for member newspapers with its own correspondents and part-time stringers. For hundreds of American newspapers with limited resources for their own newsgathering, most national and international news still comes from wire services in the 1990s. During the Civil War, Associated Press clients in the Midwest began to resent the control of the organization by the New York press. A subsidiary organization, the Western Associated Press, sought independent access to European news sources but quickly returned to the fold. The rival United Press began in 1882 but died in 1897. Publisher E. W. Scripps sought to create a rival wire service in 1907 with a new United Press, and William Randolph Hearst organized his own International News Service in 1909. The new services merged under Scripps-Howard ownership in 1958 as United Press International. By the 1980s UPI was struggling to survive and filed Chapter 11 bankruptcy before reviving, precariously, under new ownership.

Despite the proud independence of the penny papers, the intimate link between journalism and political parties, established in the early 1800s as electoral competition between Federalists and Jeffersonians, dominated through mid century. It was taken for granted that journals were political, that they were financially and literarily supported by one side or another, and that their task was more one of rousing the party faithful than of reporting the news. Not only parties had newspapers, so did factions of parties and so, sometimes, did individual politicians. But the connection between paper and party began to weaken late in the nineteenth century. The penny papers' economic success was the first sign of change, followed by new institutions self-consciously dedicated more to making profits than to promoting policies or politicians. In 1861, Abraham Lincoln began using the AP rather than an official or semiofficial newspaper as administration spokesman. This followed the establishment in 1860 of the Government Printing Office, whose existence cut away at the official status of the press and the patronage link between government and newspaper.

After the Civil War, development away from a political press accelerated. Newspapers rapidly expanded as profitable businesses, the biggest of them larger than all but a few other kinds of industrial operations. By 1870, every major daily in New York had at least one hundred employees. Competition over news grew more intense, the war having stimulated consumer expectations and demand for news. In the 1870s and 1880s, liberal reformers, first in the Republican party and then in the Democratic party began to criticize the notion of party loyalty. These reformers promoted new forms of electoral campaigning, urging an "educational" rather than a participatory or "spectacular" campaign, moving from parades to pamphlets, and arguing that the exercise of the franchise be the making of a rational choice among candidates, parties, and policies rather than a demonstration of emotional and traditional al-

The wire service began in the mid nineteenth century when New York newspapers established the New York Associated Press (later the Associated Press) as a way to make better use of new telegraphic services.

legiance to a party label. Newspapers at the same time became more willing to take an independent stance. Horace Greeley's and Whitelaw Reid's *New York Tribune*, and the *New York Evening Post*, the *Springfield Republican*, the *Chicago Tribune*, the *Cincinnati Commercial*, E. L. Godkin's *Nation* (founded 1865), and George William Curtis's *Harper's Weekly* (founded 1857) dared to dissent from party loyalty and helped direct the reform effort. By 1890, a quarter of daily newspapers in northern states, where the reform movement was most advanced, claimed independence of party. The largest papers were especially likely to be independent—nineteen of twenty-eight papers with circulations over fifty thousand.

Big-Business Newspapers and Syndicates: The Mass Audience

Newspapers in the last two decades of the nineteenth century saw a great increase in the size of their circulations. The development of wood pulp, rather than rags, as a paper source after the Civil War helped push the price of paper down from eight cents to two cents a pound in the course of a generation and encouraged newspapers to be more generous with white space and to use larger type sizes. The development of curved stereotype plates made it possible for papers to abandon the column rules that held type in place on the press and kept headlines, pictures, and ads from extending beyond one column. Typesetting was no more efficient in 1880 than it had been for Gutenberg, but Ottmar Mergenthaler's invention of mechanical typesetting in Baltimore in 1884 increased the speed of typesetting four or five times. Photoengraving of line drawings replaced and greatly improved upon wood engraving in the late nineteenth century. *The New York Daily Graphic*, begun in 1873, was the first heavily illustrated daily in the world and a pioneer in halftone photoengraving. Illustrations grew larger and more numerous in many papers, advertisements began to use display type, headlines became bigger and more informative; by 1900 technological improvements brought halftone photographs into the daily newspaper. Papers initiated campaigns to promote circulation and aggressively courted new audiences (particularly women). The newspapers were major enterprises in a rapidly industrializing nation. Advertising became a more central source of income. Between 1880 and 1900 the ratio of editorial matter to advertising shifted from about 70:30 to 50:50 or lower. Advertising income represented a growing proportion of total revenue. Paradoxically, this increased rather than diminished the importance of circulation for revenue because circulation became the measure of a newspaper's competitive standing. Circulation became less a private source of income and more a public (and audited) indicator of the newspaper's serviceability to potential advertisers. The department store became a major source of advertising income; as cities became integrated economically and knit together by new forms of public transportation, the newspapers became more indispensable than ever. As the mass medium with the widest coverage, they remained the likeliest source for advertising of nationally branded products as an integrated, national market in consumer goods expanded.

A key figure in the developing big-business model of the newspaper was Joseph Pulitzer, an Austrio-Hungarian Jewish immigrant who came to the United States in 1864. Though admitted to the bar in Missouri, his limited facility in English was a factor in keeping him from practice, so instead he became a reporter for a German-language newspaper in Saint Louis, the *Westliche Post*. He bought the *St. Louis Post* in 1878 and merged it with the *Dispatch*, serving as publisher, editor, and business manager. He made the crusade a constant feature of the paper. In 1883, he bought the failing *New York World*, which then had a circulation of fifteen thousand. By 1887 its circulation was more than 250,000. By 1895 the *World* was the biggest paper in the country with twelve hundred employees in circulation, production, editorial, advertising, and accounting departments. While some dailies retained the old four-page format, the *World* was normally twelve to sixteen pages on weekdays and three or four times larger on Sundays.

Pulitzer's success can be attributed to both business and editorial innovations. On the business side, he lowered the *World's* price to a penny (and forced other papers to lower their prices to stay competitive), sold advertising space on the basis of actual circulation, and in other ways rationalized the relations between newspapers and advertisers. He helped open the way to advertisers who wanted display ads using illustrations or breaking column rules. Before Pulitzer, newspapers regarded such advertising skeptically. James Gordon Bennett had laid down the law that advertisers should gain from what they said, not how their ads were printed or displayed. Charles Dana, editor of the *New York Sun*, the paper with the largest circulation in the city until Pulitzer came to the *World*, thought that advertising was a waste of space; as late as 1878 he hoped to do without it altogether. The new comradeship with advertising was marked by the establishment in 1887 of the American Newspaper Publishers Association, the main concern of which in its early years was to regulate commissions paid to advertising agencies and to standardize the ways in which advertising rates were calculated.

Editorially, Pulitzer brought his crusading Saint Louis journalism and an intensified attention to local news. What he added to these far from unique features was a variety of forms of self-advertisement for the newspaper. He used illustration, both sketches and political cartoons, lavishly. He played up any stories that the *World* had gained exclusively. Relatively simple words, content, and sentence structure, as well as the illustrations, helped reach the thousands of immigrants in New York. By 1880 New York had 479,000 foreign-born citizens and by 1890, 640,000, about 40 percent of the city's total population. If technological and economic changes made the new mass journalism possible, and the prospect of profit made it desirable, the changing habits and inhabitants of the cities made it necessary in the eyes of ambitious publishers.

Pulitzer intended his paper to be "a daily schoolhouse and a daily forum," as he put it; but it was also a daily carnival, incorporating a growing acceptance of the newspaper as a form of entertainment. In 1842 only one New Yorker in twenty-six bought a Sunday paper; in 1850, after heavy Irish immigration, it was one in nine. During the Civil War, more papers developed special Sunday editions with war news, which helped accustom people to the idea of a Sunday paper; but even by the early 1880s only a hundred newspapers nationwide published on Sunday. Pulitzer helped change that, introducing a Sunday paper brimming with entertainment features—for women, for young readers, for sports fans. By the end of the decade, half of New Yorkers bought a Sunday paper, nationally there were more than twice as many Sunday papers as there had been at the beginning of the 1880s, and there were more Sunday than daily newspaper readers. The Sunday papers, lavishly illustrated, were the first to adopt color comic strips and the first to develop special women's pages. The new mass-circulation papers promoted a consumerist orientation in the press and, no doubt, encouraged a consumer culture in the public as well.

If Pulitzer began this new-style mass journalism, it was his rival, William Randolph Hearst, who took it to its most notorious extreme. Like Pulitzer, Hearst was a businessman but not only a businessman. He, too, saw the press as a political agency and not just a lucrative business. Taking over his father's *San Francisco Examiner* in 1887, he bought the *New York Journal* in 1895, the *Chicago Evening American* in 1900, and the *Chicago Examiner* in 1902. At the *New York Journal*, he hired away many of Pulitzer's *Sunday World* writers and artists and the cartoonist Richard Outcault, whose "Hogan's Alley" featured a character known as the "Yellow Kid"—who, according to journalistic lore, gave "yellow journalism" its name. Within a year of buying the *Journal*, Hearst had added pages of comics, sensational news coverage, a self-promoting crusading spirit, and several hundred thousand readers. Battling the *World* for the biggest share of New York's mass readership, Hearst, followed somewhat more gingerly by Pulitzer, pushed for a war with Spain and sent correspondents to Cuba to cover the developing crisis. The war coverage was a high-water mark of sensationalism. Still, the popular view that yellow journalism "caused" American intervention owes a lot to Hearst's delight in taking credit for the war. Many other leading papers, including those with the greatest influence in elite circles, opposed American intervention.

Indeed, at the same time that Pulitzer and Hearst were competing for the largest number of newspaper readers, Adolph Ochs, a Knoxville printer's devil who rose to become publisher of the *Chattanooga Times*, bought the *New York Times*, a paper of fine pedigree but having a circulation of 9,000 at a time when the *World* sold 600,000, the *Journal* 430,000, and the *Herald* 140,000. In his famous declaration "to give the news impartially, without fear or favor, regardless of any party, sect or interest involved," Ochs set the paper on the path to its becoming the national paper of record and, perhaps, the finest newspaper in the world. Journalism in the 1890s and after was more differentiated than global references to an "era of yellow journalism" suggest. Newspapers were increasingly orienting themselves to market-defined rather than party-defined population segments. Advertising agents by the 1890s distinguished the "mass" from the "quality" audience. Newspaper competition for advertisers in both mass and quality papers led to the unsavory practice of "puffing," in which newspapers would present as news favorable information about the products of their advertisers. The independence that economic self-sufficiency brought to newspapers divorced from party threatened to become—and often enough did become—its own form of servitude.

Magazines addressed to a mass audience also flourished. *The National Police Gazette*, begun in 1845 in New York as a reporter of crime news, moved on to a special focus on sex crimes after the Civil War, diversified to include attention to theater and sports, and reached a circulation of 150,000 by the 1880s. The largest circulation success of the late nineteenth century, however, was *Youth's Companion*, founded in 1827—a magazine for young people that kept up its subscription list with aggressive campaigns offering premiums for both new and continuing subscribers.

Not all "mass" journalism, clearly, measured down to the sensationalist standards of Hearst. Hearst was not alone, of course, in a self-conscious insistence that newspapers could and should be entertaining as well as informative. Melville Stone, editor of the *Chicago Daily News,* insisted on three functions for the newspaper: to inform, to interpret, and to entertain. Pulitzer certainly offered a different model. So did E. W. Scripps, who developed newspapers aimed at working people in Cleveland, Cincinnati, Detroit, and Saint Louis in the 1880s. Scripps, who pioneered chain ownership of newspapers, held to an editorial policy sympathetic to labor and reform politics. His papers supported Theodore Roosevelt for president in 1912 and Robert La Follette in 1924.

Outside the mainstream

The world of journalism of the late nineteenth century and early twentieth century, like that of the antebellum period, was remarkably pluralistic. Besides the general commercial papers, newspapers flourished as agents of various special communities—religious groups, ethnic groups, political organizations, and social movements all fielded many newspapers. There were, for instance, hundreds of Populist weeklies. The *Topeka Advocate,* with a circulation of 80,000 in 1894, was the largest newspaper in Kansas. *Appeal to Reason,* a radical paper, reached a national circulation of 100,000 by 1900, and 450,000 a decade later.

There were, it is estimated, about 800 non-English-language newspapers in 1884 and close to 1,200 by 1910, reaching a high point of 1,300 by 1917. Thereafter, the number declined, especially the German papers—with 627 papers in 1910 but only 258 in 1920. The German papers' decline was not exclusively war-related; the number of German newspapers and magazines reached a high in the 1890s and began to drop off as immigration slowed and second-generation Germans switched to English. But the war put German Americans and their newspapers in a difficult position, and some readers avoided harassment by stopping their subscriptions. Moreover, the Trading with the Enemy Act (1917) required foreign-language newspapers to provide the Post Office with translations of any news concerning the war. Exemptions could be granted to papers that proved their loyalty, but this itself was a form of soft censorship. Some papers reduced their war coverage. Some went out of business. Most of the foreign-language papers were weekly or semiweekly. Non-English-language dailies reached a peak of 140 in 1914—a third of these were German-language papers; twelve each were French, Italian, and Polish; ten, Yiddish and Japanese; eight, Spanish and Bohemian. In ethnically concentrated areas, the influence of foreign-language newspapers could be significant. In the 1890s there were five or more German daily newspapers in Milwaukee, Chicago, Saint Louis, Cincinnati, Philadelphia, and New York. As late as 1940 there were four Yiddish dailies in New York (the last of them, *Forverts,* became a weekly in 1983).

Still, the opportunity for the mass-circulation English-language dailies was that many of the foreign-language papers were edited by European intellectuals whose ideas of journalism were modeled on European journals of politics and opinion. The foreign-language press proved most successful when it imitated the sensational or popular style of the English-language papers. Abraham Cahan, editor of the *Jewish Daily Forward,* pruned his Yiddish paper of difficult expressions, introduced English words his readers would be certain to have picked up, and tried to make the paper bright, simple, and interesting, as he had learned to do while working with Lincoln Steffens on the New York *Commercial Advertiser.*

The black press reached a high point of size and influence in the first half of the twentieth century. Black dailies attained large circulations, none larger than the *Pittsburgh Courier*'s (founded 1910) 300,000 in the 1940s. *The Chicago Defender,* a weekly founded in 1905, had a paid circulation of 230,000 by 1915, two-thirds of it outside Chicago. It was the first African American publication with a broad, national circulation. The editor, Robert S. Abbott, wrote regularly about the opportunities for blacks of living in northern cities; the *Defender* is credited with great influence in stimulating black migration north, not only in its editorial content but also in its efforts to help southern blacks form clubs to get group railroad rates. The black press during World War II urged on readers a "Double V" campaign—victory over the Axis abroad and victory over racism domestically. After the war, however, the black press was in decline as the mainstream press began to cover racial issues, the white-run media began to hire black journalists, advertising support weakened, and a

---

William Randolph Hearst's coverage of the Spanish-American War in his various newspapers was a high-water mark in sensationalism; still the popular view that yellow journalism "caused" American intervention owes a lot to Hearst's delight in taking credit for the war.

---

growing black middle class left the inner city and its newspapers.

After mid century there was a revival of the ethnic press, and by 1975 there were an estimated 960 non-English-language newspapers. Non-English-speaking broadcasting, with Spanish-language broadcasting the most notable, also appeared. Univision, the largest Spanish-language television network, had over four hundred affiliates in the 1990s, and thirty-one television stations broadcast entirely in Spanish. The black press survived, with nearly two hundred newspapers in 1986, only three of them dailies, and these had much smaller circulations than the black press had had a generation or two earlier. Magazines, however, were a different story, with *Ebony*, founded in 1945, gaining a circulation of more than a million and a half by the late 1980s. A religious press continued, and there were radio and cable television stations owned by evangelical and other Christian groups.

A small-town and rural press persisted alongside the urban papers. While in some cases aspiring to the news-centered model of the commercial urban press, most of these papers adopted a different view of what a newspaper should be, much more a kind of community cheerleader than a community tribune. Hometown boosterism has characterized this press, both past and present: local sports teams are cheered in the sports section, local real estate news is almost exclusively public relations rather than reporting. Local businessmen, in the boosterist press, are taken to be and are encouraged to be in business for the good of the community. The concept of news in the rural and small-town press, in the community press serving specific urban neighborhoods, and in much of the suburban press emphasizes building community as much as relaying information. The community press has typically emphasized good news over bad, has celebrated routine events (births, marriages, graduations, business openings, holiday pageants and celebrations), and has catered to community values of propriety and privacy. Politics in the small-town press, while typically an establishment politics, has especially in the twentieth century been a minor element in the papers. William Allen White, a celebrated editor of the *Emporia* (Kansas) *Gazette* from 1895 to the 1930s, wrote in his first editorial that his paper would be Republican and support Republican nominees "first, last, and all the time." But, he added, "politics is so little. Not one man in ten cares for politics more than two weeks in a year. In this paper, while the politics will be straight, it will not be obtrusive. It will be confined to the editorial page—where the gentle reader may venture at his peril" (William Allen White, *Autobiography*, p. 261).

Reporters and Muckrakers

Reporting was increasingly the center of newspaper life from the late nineteenth century on. Reporting became a self-conscious activity and reporters a self-conscious community in the larger cities with their own formal organizations and informal gathering spots and watering holes. While an occasional black journalist wrote for the mainstream press, newsrooms were effectively white. In Washington, reporters organized the socially exclusive Correspondents' Club in 1867 and another exclusive club, the Gridiron Club, in 1885; Washington journalists writing for African American papers set up their own organization, the Associated Correspondents of Race Newspapers, in 1890. In 1879, Washington correspondents formed the Standing Committee of Correspondents to control access to the congressional press galleries. The committee's rules sought to prevent journalists from acting as lobbyists. The rules also limited access to Congress to reporters whose salary came primarily from sending telegraphic dispatches to daily newspapers. This effectively eliminated black and women reporters, all of whom wrote for weeklies or sent dispatches by mail. Frederick Douglass, for instance, sat in the press galleries in the 1870s but no black reporter did so after him until 1947.

Reporters' status and income rose steadily in the 1880s and 1890s as reporting became more often a regular, full-time job and the custom of relying on free-lance reporters paid "on space" declined. Still, most newspapers paid their Washington correspondents only during months that Congress was in session, and it was common practice for reporters to supplement their newspaper income by working as clerks or secretaries in the Congress. Popular acclaim for dashing reporters—Elizabeth Cochrane Seaman (Nelly Bly) going around the world in eighty days, Henry Morton Stanley finding David Livingstone in Africa, the handsome Richard Harding Davis reporting on war and on football—added to the élan of the field.

The work of reporting became much more than stenography or observations and sketches. Reporters began to conduct interviews as a routine part of their work and to publish verbatim quotations or even whole question-and-answer stories. With only isolated exceptions, this was unheard-of before the Civil War and remained relatively uncommon into the 1880s. At that time, members of Congress were likely to refuse comment when questioned on the record by reporters; they had no special orientation toward the press for use in their own public relations. But increasingly the reporters pressed to do interviews, both with political leaders and with sports or entertainment celebrities. There was in this a spirit of enterprise and a sense of combative achievement in getting an interview or in tricking an interviewee into a surprising or embarrassing revelation. Foreign observers looked askance at the American interviewing habit, seeing it as crude, perhaps crudely egalitarian, and overemphasizing reporting at the expense of analysis and commentary. Interviewing spread more slowly among European journalists but was boosted by the prevalence of American reporters in Europe during World War I.

If interviewing was one sign of the new assertiveness of the reporter, muckraking was another. The rise of mass-circulation monthly magazines with national readerships and an appreciative middle-class audience in the 1890s helped the rise to prominence of muckraking. "Muckrakers" (so named by Theodore Roosevelt in a

The muckraking, crusading strain of journalism has been traced back to the eighteenth century, but certainly investigation, rather than polemical pronouncements or argumentation, was a rarity until the late nineteenth century.

sizzling attack on their negativism) investigated illegal and unsavory practices of capital, labor, and state and local government. The most celebrated of them worked for *McClure's Magazine*—Lincoln Steffens, Ida Tarbell, David Graham Phillips, Ray Stannard Baker—as well as for *Cosmopolitan and Munsey's*. These three journals cut the price of an issue to ten cents in 1893 and circulation zoomed upward, *Cosmopolitan's* growing from sixteen thousand to four hundred thousand in five years. The muckraking, crusading strain in journalism has been traced back to the eighteenth century, but certainly investigation, rather than polemical pronouncements or argumentation, was a rarity until the late nineteenth century. The *New York Times* pursued Tammany Hall with reportorial as well as editorial diligence in 1871, but the reportorial exposé became an art form, a circulation booster, and a routine political tool only after the 1880s.

Public relations developed apace in the early twentieth century, stimulated in part by muckraking attacks on business, in part by the general growth and rationalization of corporate enterprise. World War I was a major contributor to the advance of public relations after the war, as wartime propaganda provided a model for business and government public relations. Journalists complained in the 1920s that they were suddenly outnumbered by public relations agents, an entirely new occupation catering to the power of journalism. Where nineteenth-century reporters could naively believe that reporting consisted in gathering facts, now they could see that facts rained down on them not from "reality" but from interested parties. Two philosophers of democracy and public discourse, Walter Lippmann and John Dewey, pointed to the rise of public relations as the most significant change in the political life of the twentieth century.

Journalists' growing sense of the partiality, subjectivity, and manipulability of information, advanced by their awareness of public relations and their own experience in World War I as propagandists, led to important changes in journalism in the 1920s and 1930s. The most visible and important change was the institution of the political column. Until the 1920s, the only regular newspaper columnists were humorists and the occasional dispensers of gossip and advice. In the 1920s, David Lawrence, Mark Sullivan, Heywood Broun, Walter Lippmann, and others wrote regular political columns for leading newspapers; soon their columns were syndicated across the country. When Robert and Helen Lynd studied Muncie, Indiana, in 1925, the local papers carried two columnists; ten years later the morning paper had five columnists and the afternoon paper four.

There was a more subtle change in the same era in the writing of basic political news. While nineteenth-century coverage of political events could be, and usually was, highly partisan and highly colored, it could also be, and often was, highly routinized. For instance, newspapers that reported on important state papers or speeches generally would print the document verbatim. This is the way papers of various stripes reported the president's annual message (the State of the Union address) through much of the nineteenth century. Commentary was reserved for the editorial page. Only beginning in the early twentieth century did journalists highlight and summarize the main points of the presidential message in a news story. By the 1920s, correspondents not only summarized what they took to be the most important points of the presidential speech but also noted what the speech omitted or pointed to what it said "between the lines." This practice seemed to recognize and accept a need to interpret the complex world of national politics just as it accommodated the growing autonomy of reporters. In 1913 managers of the two main wire services, the Associated Press and the United Press, debated journalistic philosophy at a university symposium, the AP arguing for unbiased reporting and the UP claiming that there is no such thing.

Oddly enough, both views influenced journalism. By 1934, the UP view had convinced the American Society of Newspaper Editors to devote more space to "interpretive news." At the same time, an explicit faith in "objective" news reporting had become part of the toolkit of the journalist.

The recognition of interpretive news was sometimes taken to be a concession to readers overwhelmed by the world's complexity. It was also a type of marketing. Newspapers competed to make news more accessible to readers. *Time* magazine, begun in 1923, helped stimulate this competition. Newspapers began to concern themselves more with layout. They introduced news summaries. The *Baltimore Sun* was among the first to package news by putting related items together on a page rather than randomly scattering them through the paper.

This does not mean that journalism was fully institutionalized or professionalized, but certainly there were moves in those directions. Journalists in the nineteenth century had no formal training. Journalists in the twentieth century might be trained in one of the journalism schools or journalism or communications departments that emerged after World War I (a bequest in 1903 from Joseph Pulitzer established the most famous journalism school, at Columbia University, which opened in 1912) and developed on a large scale, particularly in the state universities of the South and Midwest, after World War II. But young people may enter journalism with bachelor's degrees in English or history as well as in journalism, and relatively few journalists have advanced degrees.

GOVERNMENT CENSORSHIP. One outcome of World War I was a new recognition of how manipulable information is. A related outcome was the recognition of—and in the courts, resistance to—the most overt and malicious forms of manipulation: censorship practiced by government. While the First Amendment, adopted as part of the Constitution in 1791, proclaimed that "Congress shall make no law . . . abridging the freedom . . . of the press," this had not prevented the Alien and Sedition Acts of 1798 from doing just that. Generally speaking, freedom of the press in the nineteenth century went unchallenged by government and little of a judicial tradition protecting press freedom developed until World War I and after. At that point, freedom of the press became a public issue. In 1917 Congress passed the Espionage Statute, which was used to suspend the mailing privileges of dozens of radical journals and resulted in the imprisonment of radical journalists. In 1918 the Sedition Act made prosecution of journalists easier still. Repression seriously damaged the American socialist movement, with many of its leaders in prison and many of its journals silenced. German-language publications, regardless of their politics, and black papers were intimidated. In the *Chicago Defender*, Robert Abbott vigorously attacked the segregation of and discrimination against black soldiers; he escaped imprisonment under the Espionage Statute only by consenting to promote the purchase of war bonds in the *Defender*.

While a "red scare" continued even after the war, several Supreme Court decisions established for the first time a tradition of defense of the First Amendment. The court, in *Abrams* v. *United States*, found against five New York radicals imprisoned for distributing pamphlets attacking American intervention in Russia, but Oliver Wendell Holmes, joined in dissent by Louis Brandeis, argued that "free trade in ideas" should be the guiding rule and that "the best test of truth is the power of the thought to get itself accepted in the competition of the market." In 1925, in the vital case of *Gitlow* v. *United States*, the court again upheld a conviction of radical pamphleteers, but acknowledged for the first time that First Amendment guarantees applied to the states under the Fourteenth Amendment. In 1931, *Near* v. *Minnesota* struck down a Minnesota "gag law" that permitted the suppression of malicious and scandalous publications. The *Near* decision held that prior restraint of publication was unlawful and suppression a greater danger than journalistic irresponsibility.

Corporate Journalism

Larger and larger corporate entities reaped the benefits of the press freedom that was often tested by lone individuals or small publications. Chain or group newspaper ownership, begun around the turn of the century by Scripps, Hearst, and others, grew enormously in the twentieth century. At its peak, in 1935, Hearst's empire included twenty-six daily newspapers with a seventh of the total circulation in the country and a quarter of Sunday circulation, as well as a fleet of magazines, radio stations, a features syndicate, and motion-picture companies. By 1980 two-thirds of 1,700 daily newspapers commanding three-fourths of total daily circulation were group-owned. City by city, newspaper competition fell off sharply, so that the number of cities with competing daily papers dropped from 181 in 1940 to 29 in 1986. The largest chain, Gannett, in 1982 founded a new national newspaper, *USA Today*, that by 1987 had a circulation of more than 1.5 million. It was a model of technological, if not journalistic, brilliance, printed at thirty-two different sites, produced by satellite transmission of copy, and making more use of color and attractive graphics than any other newspaper. Media critics might observe that some of the dailies which died were not paragons of journalistic virtue, and certainly many independent papers taken over by chains upgraded their product as a result. But the growing concentration of ownership in the media caused concern in a society in which the competitive marketplace is seen as a testing ground of truth.

Newspapers not only competed with new technologies but also used new technologies. Mechanical typesetting was replaced by cold type or photocomposition, and by the 1980s most newspapers used computerized systems in which reporters and editors could write and edit stories on word processors.

A major new influence on postwar journalism was television. Television borrowed personnel and style from radio for its journalism. Television news consisted of "talking heads" from its beginnings in the 1950s until the mid 1960s. On a separate track, documentaries and news-style programming, most notably the news shows of Edward R. Murrow, contributed to the shaping of American journalism. Maturation of television news presentation came with the expansion of the standard evening news program from fifteen to thirty minutes in 1963, a year in which the Roper poll found that, for the first time, more Americans claimed to rely on television than on newspapers as their primary source of news. (Whether their claims were true is open to some doubt. When asked what news source they actually examined the day before, more people said newspapers than television.) Three television networks produced national news programs beginning in the early 1960s. *60 Minutes*, an hour-long program of investigative journalism, began in 1968 and in the 1970s became the highest-rated program in the country. ABC began a late-night news program in 1980 called *Nightline*, and it became a regular part of the broadcast news diet.

The rise to prominence of television news was aided significantly by President Kennedy, who began holding live televised press conferences, and by the Vietnam War, during which television news coverage took on a symbolic centrality for both Washington elites and the public at large. Political campaigners measured their success as much by seconds on the evenings news as by polls; presidents, notably Lyndon B. Johnson and Richard M. Nixon, became obsessed with the television screen. Specific political events also promoted television as a news source. Walter Cronkite's personal interest in space exploration helped propel national news coverage of satellite (and later space shuttle) launchings. Cable News Network's growing international linkups during the late 1980s led to its eminence in covering the Persian Gulf War in 1991.

A family gathers in front of the television to watch the funeral of John F. Kennedy on November 25, 1963. Television unified the world during coverage of this event and its aftermath.

But, historically, nothing so established the symbolic centrality of television or its substantive national importance as the television coverage of the Kennedy assassination. Few people learned of the assassination first from television, but by the evening of 22 November 1963, millions of people were glued to their sets. They saw, on live television, Jack Ruby shoot Lee Harvey Oswald on 24 November, and they sat before their sets watching the Kennedy funeral procession, listening to the solemn beat of the drum, watching the riderless horse lead the way. The experience many people had in World War II of listening to Edward R. Murrow's live radio reports from London under aerial bombardment was amplified with the television coverage of the Kennedy funeral. It was the first media event to serve as a distinctively new form of modern, collective, participatory ritual, even if the participation is a kind of action at a distance.

Historically, nothing so established the symbolic centrality of television as the coverage of the John F. Kennedy assassination: Few people learned of the assassination from television, but by the evening of 22 November 1963, millions of people were glued to their sets.

Television news received some credit for stimulating the civil rights movement in the 1950s and 1960s. The civil rights movement occasioned a great benefit to journalism by giving rise to the case that transformed libel law by bringing all state libel laws under the restraints of the First Amendment. This was *New York Times* v. *Sullivan* (1964), in which an Alabama sheriff sued the *New York Times* for printing a political advertisement that he believed libeled him. The Supreme Court held that a public official, to show libel, must demonstrate that the news institution published something it knew to be false with "malice" or "reckless disregard" of its truth or falsity.

In 1970, the television networks had no competition—only 10 percent of American homes had cable systems. By 1989 the proportion had risen to 53 percent and the networks' share of total television viewership was in decline. Moreover, the cable industry began C-SPAN (in 1979) as a public-service gesture; while C-SPAN has a tiny audience, its presence in Congress has affected the conduct of public affairs, especially with live reports from the House (1979) and Senate (1986) floors. Cable News Network, begun in 1980 by the millionaire Atlanta businessman Ted Turner, provided news around the clock and quickly established a reputation for responsible reporting. In the Persian Gulf War in 1991, people who had never watched CNN tuned in to watch Peter Arnett, the last reporter for an American network in Baghdad. The Public Broadcasting System began the *MacNeil-Lehrer News Hour* in 1975. Radio, though never again the key source of news it was in pretelevision days, continued to be important. In 1970 National Public Radio was formed, launching *All Things Considered* in 1971. With only seven million listeners, NPR is small but much more than a headline service. NPR journalists are seen on television as well as heard on radio and command respect in their profession.

Journalism As A Political Issue

Increasingly in the 1970s and after, television became a political issue, not just a political observer. In reporting the war in Vietnam, the media ran increasingly into direct confrontation with the government. Presidents Kennedy and Johnson both objected to the *New York Times's* reporting of the war in Vietnam, and during the Johnson administration the press drew attention to what was called the "credibility gap," administration lies and half-truths about the war that reduced the believability of any government claims. During the presidency of Richard Nixon, all-out hostility emerged between the press and the president. Nixon came into office with a chip on his shoulder, regarding the media—particularly the eastern establishment media of the three networks, the *New York Times, Time, Newsweek,* and the *Washington Post*—as his enemy. He attacked television in particular for its "instant analyses" of presidential addresses in 1969. Proponents of the Vietnam war effort criticized what they saw as television bias against the war and, indeed, blamed the failed American war effort on demoralization caused by the onslaught of television scenes of bloodshed in Vietnam. While the research seems irrefutable that general public support for the war remained high until after the Tet offensive in 1968, that most television stories on the war remained more neutral or upbeat than critical until after Congress was much divided about the war, and that most stories on the war broadcast on television downplayed rather than emphasized the bloodshed, the network news programs became prominent public scapegoats.

Two moments in the early 1970s brought the press a new prominence, reporters a heightened status, and the *Washington Post* a new national position as the leading rival to the *New York Times* for national journalistic authority. In 1971, the *New York Times* published the first installment of the "Pentagon Papers," a classified Defense Department history of the Vietnam War that a one time Pentagon insider and Rand Corporation whiz kid, Daniel Ellsberg, copied and released to the newspaper. Nixon sought by court injunction to prevent further publication, but when an injunction succeeded against the *Times*, publication was taken up by the *Washington Post* and then the *Boston Globe*, the *Chicago Sun-Times*, and other papers. The Supreme Court found in favor of the newspapers, and the affair cemented the enmity between the press and Nixon.

It also made the aggressive new editor of the *Washington Post*, Benjamin C. Bradlee, feel intensely competitive with the *New York Times*. He had his opportunity to steal a march on his rival in 1972 with "Watergate," the collective term for the illegal campaign practices, burglaries, unauthorized wiretaps, use of intelligence agencies for domestic surveillance, use of the Internal Revenue Service to harass political opponents, and ultimately the lying, bribery, hush money, and perjury authorized by the president or his close associates to obstruct justice. Watergate was a milestone for the press. Though Watergate activities were uncovered by Congress, the courts, and federal administrative agencies, they were originally disclosed by the *Washington Post* and kept in the public eye by the *Post* and other news agencies. Investigative reporting was already rapidly expanding in leading newspapers, and even at the wire services, because of the growing distrust of government and other leading institutions in the Vietnam War years. Watergate served as the symbolic capstone to the newly aggressive journalism. Bob Woodward and Carl Bernstein, two *Post* reporters, became celebrities, and their account of Watergate became a popular film with Hollywood stars Robert Redford and Dustin Hoffman playing the brash, gutsy young reporters. In the 1980s, print reporters became celebrities of sorts, regularly appearing as panelists on television news talk shows, particularly in Washington. Enrollments in journalism and communications schools at colleges around the country had begun to grow rapidly in the mid 1960s, and the notoriety of Watergate may have kept enrollments high a little longer or at least given journalism courses a more focused identity (although enrollments in the advertising and public relations sections of these academic programs grew faster than enrollments in news and editorial).

At the same time, the ensuing convulsions in government and the resignation of Nixon were so traumatic that leaders of journalism almost instantly began to warn of too much investigative reporting. While Watergate stimulated a new interest in the muckraking tradition in American journalism and provoked a deeper skepticism in Congress about executive activities that led to new investigations and new scandals, government and media cooperation did not disappear by any means. Responding to the urging of CIA director William Colby in 1973 and 1974, investigative reporter Seymour Hersh sat on a story on the *Glomar Challenger* expedition (a secret operation to recover a sunken Soviet submarine), believing that revealing what he knew could put national security at risk. The *Washington Post* routinely provided CIA and other administrative spokesmen the opportunity to make a case that a given story threatened national security, leading to the delaying and modifying of news reports throughout the 1980s. Still, as government and media conflict over the reporting of the Grenada invasion (1983) and the Persian Gulf War (1991) indicated, tension between government and the fourth estate remained. Presidents continued to have "honeymoons" with the press. If the press was more self-confident and powerful as an institution, the executive was more savvy about the uses of the media.

Since the 1960s there has been a growing national consciousness about and nationalization of the news media. While various interest groups continue to spawn their own media, both print and broadcast, there has been a growing sense inside and outside mainstream journalism that the networks and leading newspapers have a public responsibility and should be answerable to public criticism. This sense of the public responsibility of the press has been most effectively demonstrated in the challenges women and minority groups have mounted to media coverage, media stereotyping, and media hiring practices. Before the 1960s, for instance, women journalists wrote about fashion and society and rarely anything else, although there were isolated exceptions of distinguished women foreign correspondents. The National Press Club admitted women only in 1971, and as late as the mid 1960s a *Newsweek* bureau chief turned down a woman reporter for a job, explaining, "What would you do if someone you were covering ducked into the men's room?" Women, and to a lesser extent minorities, are more numerous and more visible in journalism than they were, and their presence in newsrooms has made a real difference in what is covered and with what emphasis. And there is a sense, despite the status of media entities as private enterprises—often monopoly private enterprises—that the tradition of a free and independent press responsive to citizens as citizens, not just as consumers, is a tradition to which both journalists and critics of journalism as it is practiced today can legitimately appeal.

Within journalism, practitioners worry about improving coverage of minorities and improving representation of minorities in the newsroom. They worry about attracting more readers and point to alarming evidence that newspaper readership is especially low among young people, who are not adopting the newspaper-reading habits of their elders. They debate whether to emphasize investigative reporting or whether to err on the side of caution in patrolling the line between public and private life that investigative work sometimes challenges. Outside journalism, looking in, social groups from business leaders to religious, ethnic minorities or lesbians and gay men challenge what they see as inattention, inaccuracy, or ways of framing that belittle, marginalize, or trivialize their concerns. Media criticism is a small growth industry in universities. Despite the death of the critical journalism reviews that sprouted in the late 1960s, organized groups of media criticism like Accuracy in Media, on the right, and Fairness and Accuracy in Reporting, on the left, monitor political and cultural bias in the news. All this critical attention to journalism is the result in part of real growth in media power and prominence. It also owes much to the crisis of political legitimacy during the Vietnam War and particularly to efforts of the Nixon administration, which effectively painted "the media" as an autonomous source of power, and subversion, in American life. It is also a consequence of the rise of television news, which has stimulated new thinking about the meaning, function, and value of "news" in journalism, in cultural criticism, and in popular culture. This rethinking of the news media in the present encourages reconsideration of the role of journalism in the American past, too.

[See also The Culture of Consumption; Literacy; Mass Culture and Its Critics; Popular Literature; Print and Publishing; Radio; Technology and Social Change; Television.]

BIBLIOGRAPHY

Bibliographies

Caswell, Lucy Shelton, ed. and comp. *Guide to Sources in American Journalism History* (1989).

Cates, Jo A. *Journalism: A Guide to the Reference Literature* (1990).

Schwarzlose, Richard. *Newspapers: A Reference Guide* (1987).

Sloan, William David, comp. *American Journalism History: An Annotated Bibliography* (1989).

Surveys, Reference, and General Works

Barnouw, Erik. *A History of Broadcasting in the United States.* 3 vols. (1966–1970).

———. *Tube of Plenty: The Evolution of American Television* (1975; 2d rev. ed. 1990).

Bogart, Leo. *Press and Public: Who Reads What, When, Where, and Why in American Newspapers* (1981; 2d ed. 1989).

Emery, Edwin, and Michael Emery. *The Press and America.* 6th ed. (1988).

Hench, John, ed. *Three Hundred Years of the American Newspaper* (1991).

Miller, Sally M., ed. *The Ethnic Press in the United States: A Historical Analysis and Handbook* (1987).

Mott, Frank L. *A History of American Magazines.* 4 vols. (1930, 1968).

———. *American Journalism: A History, 1690–1960* (1962).

Sloan, William David, and James G. Stovall, eds. *The Media in America: A History* (1989).

Tebbel, John, and Mary Ellen Zuckerman. *The Magazine in America* (1991).

Other Works

Baughman, James L. *Henry R. Luce and the Rise of the American News Media* (1987).

Botein, Stephen. " 'Meer Mechanics' and an Open Press: The Business and Political Strategies of Colonial American Printers." *Perspectives in American History* 9 (1975).

Crouthamel, James. *Bennett's* New York Herald *and the Rise of the Popular Press* (1989).

Downing, John. *Radical Media: The Political Experience of Alternative Communication* (1984).

Gilmore, William J. *Reading Becomes a Necessity of Life: Material and Cultural Life in Rural New England, 1780–1835* (1989).

Griffith, Sally Foreman. *Home Town News: William Allen White and the* Emporia Gazette (1989).

Halberstam, David. *The Powers That Be* (1979).

Hallin, Daniel. *The "Uncensored War": The Media and Vietnam* (1986).

Kessler, Lauren. *The Dissident Press: Alternative Journalism in American History* (1984).

Kielbowicz, Richard B. *News in the Mail: The Press, Post Office, and Public Information, 1700–1860s* (1989).

Kluger, Richard. *The Paper: The Life and Death of the* New York Herald Tribune (1986).

Leonard, Thomas C. *The Power of the Press: The Birth of American Political Reporting* (1986).

McGerr, Michael. *The Decline of Popular Politics: The American North, 1865–1928* (1986).

Nord, David Paul. "Tocqueville, Garrison, and the Perfection of Journalism." *Journalism History* 13, no. 2 (1986).

Pollard, James E. *The Presidents and the Press* (1947).

Ritchie, Donald A. *Press Gallery: Congress and the Washington Correspondents* (1991).

Rosenberg, Norman L. *Protecting the Best Men: An Interpretive History of the Law of Libel* (1986).

Schilpp, Madelon G., and Sharon M. Murphy. *Great Women of the Press* (1983).

Schudson, Michael. *Discovering the News: A Social History of American Newspapers* (1978).

———. "The Politics of Narrative Form: The Emergence of News Conventions in Print and Television." *Daedalus* 111, no. 4 (1982).

———. "The Sociology of News Production." *Media, Culture and Society* 11, no. 3 (1989).

Shore, Elliott. *Talkin' Socialism: J. A. Wayland and the Role of the Press in American Radicalism, 1890–1912* (1988).

Smith, Sally Bedell. *In All His Glory: The Life of William S. Paley* (1990).

Steel, Ronald. *Walter Lippmann and the American Century* (1980).

Swanberg, W. A. *Citizen Hearst* (1961).

———. *Pulitzer* (1967).

Ungar, Sanford J. *The Papers and "The Papers": An Account of the Legal and Political Battle over the Pentagon Papers* (1972; repr. 1989).

White, William Allen. *Autobiography* (1946).

— MICHAEL SCHUDSON

L

LABOR, HOUSEHOLD

See HOUSEHOLD LABOR

LABOR: COLONIAL TIMES THROUGH 1820

Labor in early America is a topic that covers more than two hundred years and involves multiple economies and regional diversity. However, labor in all of the North American colonies shared two primary characteristics: the importance of the household and the scarcity of workers.

The household was the primary productive unit whether it was located in an urban or a rural setting, whether in the northern, southern, or middle colonies. A focus on the household not only provides a fuller understanding of the economy but also enables us to integrate the primary labor of women, housework, in order to assess its contribution to the economy, as well as its relationship to the emerging industrial order and to the production of surplus value and capital.

Scarcity describes labor everywhere. Until well into the eighteenth century, the supply of free laborers was both unreliable and expensive. Governor William Leete of Connecticut wrote in 1680, "there is seldom any want relief; because labor is deare" (Richard Morris, *Government and Labor in Early America*, p. 45). William Byrd II of Virginia echoed the lament. He abandoned a scheme to introduce the production of hemp in Virginia because "Labour being much dearer than in Muscovy, as well as Freight, we can make no Earnings of it" (Morris, p. 46). While one could argue with the rosy picture painted by these writers, the perceived labor scarcity was a problem to be reckoned with in each of the colonies. Whether the complaint came from tobacco producers in the Chesapeake or from craftsmen in the port cities, potential employers regularly complained about the chronic shortage of laborers.

The origins of labor scarcity are found in the nature of the imperial economy. The mother country, while rich in capital and labor, had very limited natural resources. The colonies, in contrast, were without capital and labor, but their natural resources were plentiful, especially land. No colonist needed to work for someone else when land was so readily available. In regions where staple crop production dominated, land was abundant and the demand for labor was particularly intense because it was the ability to control large numbers of laborers that separated the successful planter from the unsuccessful.

The port cities and agricultural regions of the northern and middle colonies solved some of the problems of labor scarcity by blending bound and free workers. Free labor continued to operate in a precapitalist mode. Most tradesmen, for example, until late in the eighteenth century paid their laborers with a combination of wages and goods. Merchant seaman were the only exception; they, by the early eighteenth century, were free and fully waged laborers. Unfree labor was best characterized by paternalism, a system that combined mutuality with the constant reminder that society was ordered vertically and masters controlled virtually all aspects of servants' lives.

Plantation owners of the southern and Chesapeake colonies responded to the shortage of workers by depending on unfree laborers to produce staple crops. Virginia and Maryland planters, for example, cultivated tobacco initially with white indentured servants, later replaced by black slaves. While Carolina planters also relied on unfree labor, slaves were present in the region from the beginning, and by the middle of the eighteenth century, the majority of workers were black.

Toward the end of the eighteenth century, labor systems diverged dramatically. In the cities and in the rural economies of New England and the middle colonies, the labor scarcity, which had created incentives for the use of unfree labor, was replaced by labor surplus, which began to render the system obsolete. Labor surplus was the result of a variety of factors. Most important, urban populations grew in the midst of unevenly developing economies. For the first time, substantial unemployment occurred that ushered in a new phase of labor relations. Employers turned less often to the labor of unfree workers, the paternalistic order disappeared, and a system of capitalist wage relations emerged. Staple crop producers, on the other hand, experienced no reduction in their needs for labor, nor did the middle of the eighteenth century usher in a period of labor surplus. Rather, they remained committed to slavery. Thus, in the northern and middle colonies unfree labor disappeared and free wage labor dominated, while in the Chesapeake and southern colonies, institutions of unfree labor became more firmly entrenched.

As a result of the relationship between production and labor, this essay focuses on three primary economic systems and their differing labor forms—agriculture, staple crop and mixed; the household, urban and rural; and the cities, skilled and unskilled. While it is uncontroversial to define labor in terms of production, I adopt a slightly amended, less traditional conception. In "Servants and Slaves" Richard Dunn defines the colonial laborer as any woman or man who performed manual labor for a head of a household either with or without wages: a slave, servant, apprentice, wage laborer, or dependent family worker. This excludes many manual workers who were independent or semi-independent producers: self-employed farmers, tenant farmers, or craftsmen; nevertheless, the men and women included constituted the majority of the population of early America.

This essay explores two primary aspects in the lives of laboring people in early America. Foremost, it investigates the nature of their tasks and the organization of their labors, and the impact of the various labor systems on workers' lives.

The Chesapeake

When the first ships touched shore at Jamestown in 1607, labor was not the central concern. Planners and immigrants assumed that American Indians would be molded into a labor force that would be compelled to do all manner of work. In addition, skilled craftsmen, recruited for the Virginia enterprise, would transform the region's natural resources into wealth. The majority of the colonists would be called upon to make key decisions and could spend their extensive leisure time counting their money.

The settlers' hopes for easy riches were dashed precipitously. Rather than wealth, the Jamestown settlers were greeted by the specter of death. In addition, American Indians refused to labor for Europeans; and even had the craftsmen survived the fevers of the Chesapeake, Virginia lacked the precious minerals like gold and silver that would either keep them busy or make them rich. The dismal picture brightened somewhat by 1612 when John Rolfe (1585–1622) discovered that the lands of Virginia were well suited for the cultivation of tobacco. Tobacco was used in England primarily for medicinal purposes until regular shipments arrived from the New World. As a result, the demand began to rise and people increasingly smoked for pleasure. The "jovial weed," while seeming to offer a solution to the colony's financial woes, had a hidden problem—its cultivation required intensive labor. Thus, the recruitment of labor became a critical issue.

In order to solve the problems caused by the shortage of workers, the Chesapeake colonists imported laborers. The Virginia Company of London, the joint stock company charged with promoting and developing Virginia, attempted to fill the immediate need for laborers by enticing young Englishmen to labor for them as indentured servants.

INDENTURED LABOR. Virginians used three primary forms of indentured labor. From the perspective of the laborer, sharecropping tenants were perhaps in the best position. They were transported to the colony by the Virginia Company and plantation owners, were assigned land to work, were supervised by company agents, and were entitled to half of what they produced. After seven years their tenancy ended and they received fifty acres of land. For each tenant whose transport he paid, a planter received a bonus of fifty acres.

Apprenticeship was the second form of unfree labor; from the individual's vantage point it was the worst extreme. The origins of apprenticeship are found in the Middle Ages, when the institution was devised by members of craft guilds to ensure proper training and to limit the numbers of individuals who could enter the trades. Apprentices contracted with masters for a specified number of years, to be trained in the "art and mystery of the craft" in exchange for clothing, food, and shelter. The Virginia variation only slightly resembled its English origins; it was fashioned less as a system of education than as a means to recruit agricultural laborers. Apprentices were transported to the colony and were bound for seven years to the planter who purchased them. At the end of the term, they became tenants for an additional seven years. If at any time during their service they were convicted of a crime, their term as a servant was to begin again for seven more years.

Indentured servitude, the final form, was a variation on contract labor, but the innovation in Virginia included the practice of selling servants. The first group of servants entered contract agreements with the Virginia Company of London. In exchange for transportation to Virginia, food, shelter, and clothing, they would labor for four to seven years and receive "shares in the venture's anticipated profits" (Warren Billings, "The Law of Servants and Slaves," p. 47). When the company's solvency became precarious, rather than continue to buy servants, it instituted a headright system that encouraged individuals to pay the costs of shipping servants to Virginia. For each servant brought into the colony, masters received fifty acres of land; servants were promised that at the end of their service, they too would be rewarded with land. By 1625, according to the first Virginia census, over 40 percent of the colony's residents were indentured servants, almost all of them from England.

Individuals became indentured servants in a number of ways. Most entered into servitude because they were too poor to pay their own passage to the colonies, and they were willing to exchange two to nine years of their labors for the hopes of more prosperous futures. Others were kidnapped. "Spirits" roamed the docks of seventeenth-century London, plying adults with alcohol and children with sweets to lure them onto ships bound for America. Although individual "spirits" claimed thousands of victims, their practices were short-lived and accounted for only a small proportion of the servants who emigrated. Still others were a part of "His Majesty's Seven Year Passengers," the mocking description for transported convicts or political prisoners exiled to do labor in America. Of as many as thirty thousand convict servants who were transported from British jails between 1718 and 1775, two-thirds went to Virginia and Maryland.

Although workdays in the New World plantations were from sunrise to sunset, during even the most intense growing seasons "field laborers were permitted five hours rest during the heat of the day, Saturday afternoon off, and the 'old Holidayes . . . observed' " (Lois G. Carr and Lorena S. Walsh, "Economic Diversification," p. 154). During the winter months, little was done except hunting and cutting firewood. The laws of Maryland and Virginia "required only that masters provide 'sufficient' food, clothing, and shelter; a Sunday free of hard labor; and moderation in correction" (Carr and Walsh, p. 155). To a very great extent, servants' lives depended most on the personalities of individual masters. If a master were humane, servitude might be tolerable; if not, life was a nightmare.

A legal system gradually developed to regularize the system of indentured labor. Some of the laws enacted by the Virginia legislature acknowledged how difficult it was to force servants to work. If a servant ran away, the law provided "added service, whippings, hair croppings, or, in the instance of habitual offenders, brandings" (Billings, p. 50). The laws also identified servants as chattel, and thus masters could handle them just as they did other forms of property like clothing or livestock. Finally, the laws licensed masters to use "reasonable" force to control their servants. The courts also provided recourse for those unlucky servants whose masters were cruel. Lois Carr and Lorena Walsh note, "servants might be forced to eat unfamiliar food, but they could not go unfed; they might be worked to exhaustion five or six days a week, but, on Sunday, they could rest" (p. 155).

Indentured servants in the Chesapeake were the human machines with which planters produced staple crops. In Virginia and Maryland, servants' labors were devoted primarily to the cultivation of tobacco. Tobacco was labor intensive—after seedlings were planted and thinned, the fields had to be weeded, and worms had to be removed continuously from the plants. Harvesting was also time consuming: the mature leaves were picked first, bundled, and transported for curing. As the smaller leaves grew, they were harvested. All of this work occurred in climates that varied from hot and steamy to steamy and unbearable.

Chesapeake planters appeared to have had such an insatiable appetite for servants that they enticed thousands of Englishmen to come to Virginia to grow tobacco for them. Over the course of the seventeenth century, improved techniques increased the amount of tobacco an individual could produce; and by putting more laborers into the fields, output grew even more rapidly: "About seventy-five thousand whites immigrated to the Chesapeake colonies from Britain between 1630 and 1680, and from half to three-quarters of them arrived as indentured servants" (Allan Kulikoff, *Tobacco and Slaves*, p. 32). Planters wanted men who could be put to work in the tobacco fields; not surprisingly, more than six times as many men as women served indentures.

In the last decades of the seventeenth century, the supply of English servants declined. More men and women were able to find jobs in England, and the push

Indentured servants in the Chesapeake were the human machines with which planters produced staple crops: In Virginia and Maryland, servants' labors were devoted primarily to the labor-intensive cultivation of tobacco.

to America lessened. In addition, with the founding of Pennsylvania and other colonies, English servants had a choice. In the early half of the seventeenth century, servants had only the option of remaining unemployed in England or risking their lives in the fever-ridden Chesapeake or West Indies. After 1682, the year Pennsylvania was founded, individuals who wanted to serve indentures in the New World could continue to fill the demand in the humid climates of Virginia and Maryland, Jamaica or Barbados, or sign on with a master who grew wheat or flax in Pennsylvania or made chairs or shoes in Philadelphia. Not surprisingly, fewer and fewer men and women were available to labor in the plantation colonies.

BLACK SLAVES. While the supply of servants declined, the demand for labor did not. According to Richard Dunn, "During the 1680s and 1690s in the Chesapeake, black slaves from West Africa began to replace English servants as the mainstay of the labor force" ("Servants and Slaves," p. 164). The shift from white servants to black slaves started slowly at the end of the seventeenth century. In 1660, there were at most seventeen hundred blacks residing in Virginia and Maryland; by 1680 this number had increased to four thousand. Slaves entered the colony in small numbers, primarily from the West Indies, and planters used them to supplement rather than replace their labor force. However, as white servants became difficult to obtain and a more regularized trade in slaves developed, planters began to purchase slaves in larger numbers.

The increasing supply of West African slaves for the English colonies was due to the opening of the slave trade. From 1663 to 1698, the exclusive rights to the English trade belonged to Adventures to Africa, a group that reorganized and rechartered its name in 1672 to Royal Africa Company. When its hold was broken, private slavers rushed into business, and for the first time a regular trade existed to supply North American planters with slaves. Between 1695 and 1700, three thousand Africans were enslaved, equal to the number in the previous twenty years. As a result, the racial composition of Chesapeake labor shifted, and by 1700 from two-thirds to three-quarters of the unfree laborers were black.

Other impulses besides timing highlight the switch from white to black unfree labor in the Chesapeake. Virginia and Maryland planters experienced a temporary supply shortage of servants during the English Civil War, but by the late seventeenth century the diminishing supply of English servants was permanent. In addition, mortality declined dramatically, thereby creating financial incentives to invest in slaves. For the first fifty years of the Virginia colony, the chances of anyone's surviving were extremely unlikely. Thus, owning a man for life was not a sound investment, especially since a slave cost twice as much as a servant. In his *American Slavery*, Edmund Morgan notes that "if the chances of a man's dying during his first five years in Virginia were better than fifty-fifty—and it seems apparent that they were—and if English servants could be made to work as hard as slaves, English servants for a five-year term were the better buy" (pp. 297–298). By the end of the seventeenth century, "the price of a lifetime slave became competitive with the price of a short-term servant" (Dunn, p. 164). Since slaves served for life, they became the cheapest form of labor.

Declining mortality contributed to an altered social constella-

Slaves were the cheapest form of labor in the seventeenth century and tobacco dominated production. Here, African-American slaves pack tobacco leaves into hogsheads.

tion in the Chesapeake that hastened the substitution of black slaves for white servants. Death during the first fifty years of settlement was indiscriminate—masters and servants died young. However, just as everyone began to live longer and increasing numbers of servants completed their terms, achieved freedom, and demanded land, the economic climate in Virginia worsened. Land became difficult to get and tobacco prices plummeted. As a result, tensions heated up and erupted, in 1676, in Bacon's Rebellion. Bacon's Rebellion defies a simple narrative. The fighting pitted white settlers against Indians, and white settlers against each other.

Bacon's Rebellion of 1676 defies a simple narrative, as the fighting pitted Virginia's white settlers against Indians, and white settlers against one another.

Of the hundreds who joined with Nathaniel Bacon to fight Indians, many were frustrated frontiersmen whose hopes for acquiring cheap lands were stymied by an agreement forged after the 1644 war, which prohibited white settlement north of the York River. Planters calculated that a move to a slave system would solve some of the labor problems because slaves served for life and thus would not become discontented freedmen.

Seventeenth-century planters were involved primarily in a transatlantic trade in tobacco; by the early eighteenth century, tobacco production ceased to dominate. As a result, labor was redirected as well. The origins of this shift are many. However, among the most important impulses were depressed tobacco prices after 1680, disruption in the trade as a result of the many colonial wars, increasing competition as more and more immigrants and newly freed servants entered the market, and soil exhaustion from too many tobacco crops.

The shift in production and the move from white to black unfree labor altered the character of the work system. Slaves were not protected by the laws of servitude that required masters to provide adequate food, clothing, or housing. Colonial lawmakers gradually chipped away at the vestiges of the slave's humanity. They began by distinguishing blacks from whites in the right to carry arms. Ultimately the status of black adults and their children was comparable with chattel, all rights stripped from them, including marriage, education, and, of course, freedom. The law gave masters the right to determine how much force was appropriate to punish various breaches of conduct. These laws assumed that no master would harm or injure his property without just cause.

As black slaves came to dominate unfree labor, work discipline changed for both servants and slaves. Saturday became a full workday, and there were only three holidays a year. In Virginia, by the 1730s only skilled servants who arrived under indenture retained a free Saturday afternoon. For slaves the work regimen was extremely constricted, and one day was very much like the next. They could not even depend on Sundays off. House slaves prepared meals for endless rounds of guests regardless of the day. Night-work was often added to field hands' chores: beating corn into meal or stripping tobacco leaves. Lois Carr and Lorena Walsh point out that in the 1770s, for example, Landon Carter had his slaves "tie up ninety tobacco plants into hands each night" (p. 159). Diversification also created additional work. Little had happened on a tobacco plantation during the months from December to February; this changed. More timber had to be cut and carted to meet the demands for more casks. Pastures were cleared and swamps were grubbed. Ultimately diversification worked to separate the labor of whites and blacks. Increasingly tasks requiring skills were reserved for white laborers while the cultivation of tobacco and corn fell to slaves.

Chesapeake labor altered dramatically over the course of two centuries. Initially it was organized to produce tobacco in exhange for European goods, and white indentured servants performed the bulk of the labor. Tobacco was grown into the nineteenth century, but now it was cultivated by black slaves and it no longer dominated production. Additional agricultural products and economic diversity changed work roles. Male and female slaves no longer worked together or performed the same jobs. Chesapeake labor had changed from white to black, from servant to slave.

CHANGE IN GENDER ROLES. Diversification in production altered gender roles of both white and black workers. From 1760 to 1820, as Virginia and Maryland planters abandoned tobacco cultivation in favor of wheat, other grains, and livestock, tasks became more varied and the gender division of labor became more marked. When tobacco was the primary crop, work routines for male and female slaves varied very little. The new tasks however, required a certain level of skill—"sowing and mowing grains, plowing, harrowing, carting, ditching, lumbering, fishing, and milling" (Carr and Walsh, p. 176)—jobs carried out primarily by men. Slave women continued to work in the fields, performing unskilled manual labor and separate from the men. They were assigned the less desirable chores: "building fences, grubbing swamps in the dead of winter, cleaning winnowed grain of weed seed, breaking up new ground too rough or weedy to plow, cleaning stables, and loading and spreading manure" (Carr and Walsh, p. 177).

The shift away from tobacco affected the labor of free men and women as well. The men and women with small holdings worked together to grow tobacco because labor was scarce and expensive. On the small number of wealthy plantations, the work roles of men and women diverged from the beginning. The men focused on the production and marketing of tobacco; the wives of planters were responsible for supervising household labor.

With diversification, men and women devoted their time to a larger range of activities and labor tasks separated more clearly along gender lines. Men continued to market crops, and "some planters began to raise a little wheat, rye, or beans and peas for variety in their diets" (Carr and Walsh, p. 145). Women had time for vegetable gardens; they made cheese and butter, preserved meat, and spun yarn. Home manufacturing increased, spurred in part by the nonimportation agreements during the Revolution. Planters' wives and daughters continued to card wool, hackle flax, spin, weave, knit, sew, mold candles, make cider, and salt meat. Wives and daughters of tenant farmers did piecework for planters and often made clothing for slaves.

Carolina

The economies of the Deep South were as dependent upon staple crop production and unfree labor as that of the Chesapeake, yet its original population and the development and nature of its labor systems differed greatly. In contrast with most of the American colonies that were populated by English, European, and African immigrants, Carolina's settlers came by way of the West Indies—planters and their slaves. Rather than an unfree labor system that evolved from white to black, black slaves were present in the colony from its inception.

The earliest Carolina population consisted of a mixture of Africans and Europeans who had been forced out of Barbados. These emigrants were either sons of lesser planters or small landowners. The sons of lesser planters had very little likelihood of inheriting any land; thus, they took their inheritance in the form of servants and slaves. The small landowners had been forced from their holdings. In terms of settlement and labor in the Carolinas, among the most important features of the push away from Barbados was that enslaved Africans were part of almost every outgoing contingent.

Thus in the earliest years of settlement (after 1670), the Carolina population was a mixture of black slaves and white planters. The proprietors, faced with virtually unlimited land supplies, sought a product or products that would bring them wealth and enable them to enter the transatlantic market. Livestock emerged as the first, if temporary, solution. With land abundant and settlement sparse, cattle could graze freely. In addition, the British West Indies provided a ready market because the settlers' obsession to grow sugar required that they import food. As a result, Carolina planters employed many of their slaves as cowboys—they moved with the herds into the remote interior of the colony, tending and protecting them. Carolina slaves often labored alone, beyond the view of overseers or bosses, and reappeared when the cattle were ready for market. Cattle production provided planters with a number of advantages: it enabled them to amass capital, it used relatively few laborers, and it made the larger part of the labor force available for the immense task of clearing the dense Carolina forests.

For the first two decades following the settlement of the colony, no labor form dominated, nor did any single economic activity occupy the work force. However, during the second generation, production shifted to rice, which altered labor relations. Although the English had known about rice since the seventeenth century, it was neither consumed nor traded with any regularity. However, southern Europeans had adopted rice as a dietary staple, and Carolina's proprietors recognized its trade potential. Early attempts to grow the grain failed, not because the soil and climate were unsuitable but because none of the planters knew exactly what they were doing. Rice production was successful in the Carolinas only after sufficient numbers of West Africans were present, because they were familiar with rice cultivation. Rice has shallower roots than tobacco, and the boggy soils of the Carolinas were ideal for it. Thus the labor organization of rice production in the Carolinas was not, as in other regions of staple crop production, a system imposed by Europeans on Africans. The style of planting and hoeing, the cooking, and the work songs that provided the rhythms of production were transported to the colony by West Africans. This is not to imply that slaves' playing an active role in determining the nature of production somehow mitigated the effects of slavery. Rather, ironically, as Peter Wood convincingly argued, rice cultivation was introduced by West Africans and "rice culture turned planters increasingly toward slave labor" (*Black Majority*, p. 37).

In addition to rice, Carolina settlers developed one other major export crop, indigo. Although indigo grew wild in some areas of the South, the most desirable variety, deep blue, came from the West Indies. During the 1740s, the war with France halted English importation of the West Indian variety, and Carolina planters began to develop the crop in earnest. Eliza Lucas

(Pinckney), a Caribbean immigrant, deserves much of the credit. She was born in Antigua where she learned indigo cultivation from her father. She was brought to South Carolina in 1738 and by 1741 was experimenting with West Indian indigo seeds. Lucas's initial crops were cultivated specifically to produce seed, which she distributed to local planters. West African skills contributed greatly to the success of indigo cultivation, since slaves working the fields used only slight variations on their rice techniques.

With the successful cultivation of rice and indigo, labor demand increased and planters sought laborers from a number of sources. As in the Chesapeake, American Indians were unwilling to work for them. Indentured servants were imported into the Carolinas, but the demand for them was so great that servants could contract for very short periods of time. More important, servants never came to the Carolinas in sufficient numbers to affect the size of the work force and, as in other regions of intensive agricultural production, indentured servants lacked sufficient incentives to work.

African labor provided the most reasonable alternative. A systematic slave trade had developed, which kept transportation costs lower than for white servants. Since a master owned slaves for their lifetime, slavery would solve some of the difficulties caused by servitude: short indentures and continual turnover. In addition, Africans were reputed to work more efficiently in the subtropical Carolinas.

Finally, West Africans did considerably more than provide labor. They brought with them to the New World the skills that contributed both to the adoption of rice as one of the region's staple crops and to a wide range of labors they performed. One critical problem confronting early Carolina settlers was clearing the forests. Slaves provided the labor and a three-stage technique: black men and adolescents felled and split the trees; slave women and children removed the brush and hauled the wood; and at night, the best time to avoid the winds, the slaves burned the fields.

Through the eighteenth century, blacks dominated labor in the Carolinas. The colony got off to a rocky start, and only after sufficient numbers of West African slaves were present did planters in the region produce sufficient quantities of rice and indigo for those crops to be profitable. These two export products, as well as the general economic health of the colony, owed much to the West African heritage of Carolina slaves.

The North

In the middle and New England colonies, the configuration of labor was different as a result of the nature of agricultural production and the existence of cities. No crops in these colonies required the intensive labor of tobacco or sugar, nor were there cities in the Chesapeake or the South that resembled the seaports of Boston, New York, and Philadelphia.

Rural production in the northeastern and middle colonies was characterized by mixed agriculture, in part as a result of the nature of settlement. Immigrants to New England organized into townships and divided lands among individual family units. New York settlement varied greatly, from the vast patroonships worked by tenants to smaller family holdings in newer areas. In Pennsylvania families joined together around churches and villages and farmed rich soil. Sizes of landholdings varied by social and economic status, but most founding families were given ample acreage and produced a wide range of crops, from grains and flax to apples and cherries. Most farmers sold or exchanged their surplus, but these transactions rarely involved cash.

The colonists who traveled from England to New England during the 1630s belonged for the most part to households that had been prosperous enough to own servants. They transported these servants to the New World in numbers far surpassing the proportion of families with servants in England—or, in fact, the proportion of families that would own bound labor in future generations. For example, about 13 percent of the households in England had servants, whereas more than 20 percent of emigrating families transported servants. These families had no illusions about the nature of the work required to found new settlements and, as Edward Johnson warned, it required "every one that can lift a hawe" (Daniel Vickers, "Working the Fields," p. 54).

However, once the servants who accompanied the earliest settlers were freed, they were not systematically replaced. Indentured labor never played a significant role in New England. Indeed, only 4 percent of the families in Essex County, Massachusetts, had servants. The owners of the largest estates, individuals like John Pynchon of Springfield, Massachusetts, continued to have servants. Pynchon, for example, employed his servants "to raise wheat, cattle and timber for shipment abroad" (Vickers, p. 54). Yet Samuel Symonds, who at his death owned seventeen hundred acres and was among the wealthiest landholders in seventeenth-century Massachusetts, had only two manservants in his home. Estimates suggest that only one-quarter of all Massachusetts families owned servants of either gender. New England farm families did need additional labor at various times—during harvesting, house building, and birthing—but they preferred, if possible, to use their own offspring. If their requirements for labor exceeded what their families could provide, they exchanged or hired labor for specific tasks or days.

Similarly, Pennsylvania's founding generation was well aware of the scarcity of labor in the colonies; the Free Society of Traders, the joint stock company in charge of promoting and organizing the colony, planned to import both servants and slaves. As in the colonies to the north, unfree labor was important for the founding generation, primarily in agriculture. However, Pennsylvanians continued to rely on unfree labor until well into the eighteenth century, primarily as an urban work force. Establishing farms required intensive labor, and as James Claypoole, the secretary of the Free Society of Traders revealed, he would use slaves "for cutting down trees, building, plowing or any sort of labor that is required in the first planting of a country" (Sharon V. Salinger, "To Serve Well and Faithfully," p. 22). While precise figures are unavailable, at least 271 individuals signed indentures to serve in Pennsylvania during the 1680s; estimates of the slave population in the early decades place it somewhere between four hundred and five hundred.

Like their counterparts in the Chesapeake, New Englanders and Pennsylvanians successfully put into place a gendered division of labor in which women had primary responsibility for the house, children, and garden while men worked in the fields. The exceptions to this were during peak labor demand. July in Pennsylvania, for example, was the time for the rye harvest. Farmers with sizeable acreage might hire a dozen or more day laborers to assist. However, most farmers hired one or two workers, and everyone in the family old enough to help did so. Women formed teams with the men and, using a slightly lighter scythe, helped reap and pile the grain. Haying followed. The scythes for this operation were heavier, so the women followed behind the men to spread the grass to dry. Afterward, everyone worked to load the hay onto the wagons.

Clearly the economic status of the household determined to a large extent the ways in which women spent their time: All were involved with the chores of the household, but, in addition, wives of middling households could trade or barter for items they needed.

Household economies in the seventeenth century were characterized by mixed enterprises in which the roles of men and women were interdependent. Household textile production provides a clear example of the many layers of family labor. Men "sowed, turned, and broke flax; the women weeded, pulled, combed, spun, reeled, boiled, spooled, warped, quilled, wove, bucked and bleached it" (Laurel Ulrich, "Martha Ballard and Her Girls," p. 75). For knitting and sewing, men's labor also provided the raw materials. Then the adult female and her daughters created a wide range of items including cotton wool, and linen hose, woolen "leggins" and "buskins," and shifts, skirts, aprons, and petticoats for the women, trousers and jackets for the men. However, men's coats and breeches and women's dresses were often made by the tailor or dressmaker.

Although women in all types of households had a comparable range of chores that needed to be accomplished, focusing for the most part on food preparation and child care, the economic status of the household dictated to a large extent the amount of time spent on various tasks. For example, women in middling families spent more time than their counterparts in other classes in food preparation and preservation. They had more equipment and a wider range of food available than poor women but, unlike wealthy women, they had no servants to supervise. Middling wives were required to do the work themselves or with the assistance of their daughters. Wives in poorer rural families lacked access to the varieties of food and equipment, and certainly had no servants to share the labor. They weeded gardens or gathered vegetables for others in exchange for food or a bit of money. Their city counterparts took in washing or sewing. Clearly the economic status of the household determined to a large extent the ways in which women spent their time. All were involved with the chores of the household. But in addition, wives of middling households could trade or barter for items they needed. Wealthy women were more likely to purchase these goods. Poorer women were involved in a complicated system of barter, labor, and scavenging.

Women also were responsible for milking cows, feeding the swine and chickens, and nursing sick animals. They were especially busy during slaughtering time, helping cut and salt, dealing with all of the parts—cleaning the tripe, dressing the calf's head or pig's feet, preparing sausage casings, and cooking organ meats. Their gardening chores occupied them from early spring, when the seeds were sown or seedlings transplanted, until late October, when the cabbages were stored in the root cellar and the seeds were gathered for next year's planting.

Besides the household tasks women performed, they participated in an often hidden but essential network of exchange of goods and services that rarely involved cash but contributed to surplus value and capital accumulation. Female neighborliness and social networks meant that women would help a sick neighbor or assist at a birth. They would meet to pull flax together or share recently caught fish. And the products women created were bartered in an informal economic network. Preserves might be exchanged for cheese, surplus cherries or cheese for candles.

During the seventeenth century, New England Puritans valued women's work highly and men acknowledged that their labors contributed greatly to the success of the household. In 1630, for example, the Massachusetts Court of Assistance allotted twenty shillings to each man whose family had not yet arrived from England. The money was to be used to hire the services ordinarily performed by their wives. In 1645, the Massachusetts Court of Elections reimbursed tavern keepers Richard Sherman and "ye wife of Richard Sherman" for the charges accrued by the colony's deputies and governor for room and board. Richard and his wife were paid separately and in different amounts. The court's payment made a distinction between male and female labor within the tavern and reflected, by assigning a monetary value to each, the economic legitimacy of both claims.

While women's work remained virtually unchanged throughout the eighteenth century and family production remained focused within households that continued to be primarily agricultural and not self-sufficient, the value of female labor eroded. This decline reflected not the nature or economic value of housework but the perception of housewifery. Many factors contributed to the devaluing of housework, but perhaps most critical was the gradual transformation of the economy during the eighteenth century into one in which men were the exclusive economic agents. In the colonial period, although women did not have equal social status with men, their position did not undermine their economic role in the household. However, as the role of money increased and market consciousness expanded, the economic realm became extra-household and the exclusive domain of men. And women, who continued to be relegated to the home and who realized no external cash value for their labors, were denied labor value. The emerging formulation of the economy as a complex of activities that could occur only outside the household made it impossible for women to "lay claim to the status of 'worker,' " and they ceased to be considered as part of the "real economy" (Jeanne Boydston, *Home and Work*, p. 21).

The value of women's work in the household experienced a brief resurgence during the American Revolution. American victory appears to have been dependent in part on women's home manufacturing. However, the effect was ephemeral, and at war's end the household once again lost much of its economic agency. In agricultural households, the growth of the market affected men and women differently. Women continued to spend most of their time converting raw materials into usable items, but the interdependence of male and female household labor ended. Rather than bringing their surplus or raw materials home, men were more likely to exchange them in the marketplace for cash. Women were not totally removed from the market, but their involvement increased as consumers rather than as producers. The political and economic orders in the new republic were based on the work performed by men, which increasingly was done outside the household. Domestic labor had become marginalized.

Urban Labor and Revolutionary Politics

Although Boston, Philadelphia, and New York contained only a small minority of the colonial population—never more than about 10 percent—these seaports played a far more important role in the social, economic, and political life of the colonies than their size would suggest. In addition, their changing labor relations portended the industrial order in nineteenth-century America. With Boston the oldest and Philadelphia the youngest, their growth and sizes remained relatively constant until the middle of the eighteenth century, when Philadelphia's population surpassed those of the other two. These cities were the hub in a system of maritime commerce, commercial interchange, and petty commodity production. Boston, Philadelphia, and New York provided entry to the huge numbers of immigrants—primarily English, European, and African—who arrived in an almost continuous stream throughout the colonial period. The urban laboring classes processed the products that linked the colonies to the international chain of labor and markets. The cities also served the populations of the hinterland—as markets for their agricultural produce and as places to procure manufactured goods from home and abroad.

The majority of urban laborers were employed in commerce and petty commodity production. They included the skilled and the unskilled, the unfree and the free. Unskilled laborers worked primarily as "porters, wood choppers, sawyers, scavengers, chimney sweeps, washerwomen, and waterside and construction workers who stowed and unloaded ship cargoes, excavated cellars, drained swamps, hauled materials, and the like" (Gary B. Nash, Billy G. Smith, and Dirk Hoerder, "Labor in the Era of the American Revolution," p. 416).

Merchant seamen belonged to this group, a reflection of their wage rates rather than of levels of skill.

Merchant seamen, or Jack Tars, were the largest group of free wage laborers in the eighteenth century, numbering somewhere between twenty-five thousand and forty thousand in the period from 1700 to 1750. They are important beyond the size of their group because their experiences provide a window on the emerging capitalist wage relations. Their labor task was to move cargo; their primary place of business, the docks and the ships that plied the Atlantic trade. The common seaman provided the labor that linked the colonies to the vast transatlantic world.

The ship has been described as a forerunner of the factory. On it, seamen were confined within an enclosed setting, had specific tasks, and were required to work cooperatively. Although mariners tended to stay with one ship only for the length of the voyage, the basic division of labor from ship to ship was the same; what may have varied was the size of the crew. Writing in *Between the Devil and the Deep Blue Sea* (1987), Marcus Rediker notes that each ship had "a master, a mate, a carpenter, a boatswain, a gunner, a quartermaster, perhaps a cook, and four or five able or ordinary seamen" (p. 83). A larger ship or one more heavily manned might include a "second mate, a carpenter's mate, and four or five more common tars." (Rediker [1987], p. 83).

Known also as tradesmen, mechanics, artificers, and leather apron men, artisans were the colonies' skilled craftsmen and accounted for "between one-third and one-half of all city taxpayers during the late colonial and revolutionary period."

Jack Tar performed a wide range of tasks that were determined primarily by whether the ship was in port or at sea. At sea, he worked the sails and rigging, repaired the ship's machinery, and performed navigational tasks. He learned to read the winds and weather. While rank dictated to a very large extent the tasks while in transit, the chores involved while docked were performed and known by everyone. Cargo required loading, maneuvering, and securing; and once the ship reached its destination, cargo had to be unloaded. It was a dangerous life. Merchant seamen suffered all of the ills of their contemporaries—yellow fever, typhus, skin diseases, and so on—but many of their afflictions were peculiar to their work. It was not unusual to lose a finger while rolling a cask, suffer a hernia while lifting a heavy load, or get a rope burn from the rigging. Shipboard life was dangerous, and men died from being swept overboard by high seas, from falling from the rigging, or from being struck by falling or shifting cargo.

Laborers and merchant seamen traditionally were on the lowest rung of the social and economic ladders in the cities. Economic necessity often forced them into these jobs, and while in them, their occupational and economic mobility was restricted. As a group they shared the lowest standard of living and status of any of the laboring classes of the port cities.

Artisans were the colonies' skilled craftsmen; while some tramped through the rural areas to ply their trades, most were concentrated in the cities. Artisans, known also as tradesmen, mechanics, artificers, and leather apron men, accounted for "between one-third and one-half of all city taxpayers during the late colonial and revolutionary period" (Steven Rosswurm, *Arms, Country and Class*, p. 14). They owned property that included their tools, skills, and produced commodities. Artisans occupied the middling and upper ranks of the laboring people. They ranged in status from the apprentice to the master, and in wealth from the tailors and shoemakers who clustered on the bottom of the economic heap to tanners and silversmiths, who often occupied the upper end.

Unlike England and Europe, in which the hierarchy of skills was adhered to fairly strictly, the crafts in the colonial cities were organized loosely, and within each craft there were gradations of status. Apprentices were the low extreme. They signed to serve a master for approximately seven to nine years in exchange for being taught the "art and mystery" of the trade. In the middle were journeymen. They had served an apprenticeship, owned their own tools, and hired themselves out. Masters were at the top. They were generally older and worked for themselves. In theory, serving an apprenticeship and a comparable amount of time as a journeyman assured the way to master.

Most of the seaports' trades were organized in this traditional way. In addition, Philadelphia's artisans, more than their counterparts in the other port cities, relied on unfree labor: indentured servants and slaves. They preferred servants but were willing to buy slaves when servants were unavailable. Most craftsmen produced "bespoke" work (items that were custom ordered) in small shops with five to ten workers, one or two of whom were unfree. The notable exceptions were shipyards and ropewalks, which often had up to twenty-five workers.

The work cycle depended on the vagaries of the weather and the seasons. When the port froze, shipping halted. In the winter of 1728–1729, for example, "36 ships lay frozen at dockside in Philadelphia; several decades later a visitor counted 117 ships icebound in the Delaware" (Gary B. Nash, *The Urban Crucible*, p. 10). A winter freeze not only put maritime laborers like stevedores and mariners out of work, it prevented the cooper from shaping the barrel staves outside, or the housewright from digging the cellar. Work time was in part controlled by the seasons, since most work could be done only by the light of day. The seasons affected wage rates as well. No standardized wage system existed in the eighteenth-century city; Philadelphia's master mechanics were paid both by the piece and by time. Often the newest journeyman in the shop received a piece rate until his productivity warranted payment by the day. However, master craftsmen used different pay schedules to their advantage to mitigate seasonal differences. In the 1790s, journeymen received a flat rate during the long days of summer, when production was higher, and a piece rate during the winter, when shorter days meant more limited production.

During most of the colonial period, craftsmen were aligned, regardless of status, on the basis of their craft and vague promises that they would rise through the ranks. Indeed, labor was fluid, and considerable mobility was possible both horizontally, from craft to craft, and vertically, from apprentice to master. Due to the scarcity of skilled labor in the colonies and an absence of guilds, craftsmen often developed many marketable skills: "The blacksmith was a toolmaker, a soap boiler, a tallow chandler" (Rediker [1982], p. 131) and although legislation was passed to prevent tanners from acting as curriers or shoemakers, they often did so. The Bostonian Paul Revere provides the classic example of the multitalented craftsman. He distinguished himself primarily as a silversmith, yet he engraved also copperplates, was "a dentist who set false 'fore-teeth,'" manufactured "clock faces for clockmakers," "branding irons for hatters," and "spatulas and probes for surgeons" (Rediker [1982], p. 132).

Labor relations in the early American port towns were relatively harmonious. However, after the Revolution, labor in the cities changed. "Merchant capitalists and master craftsmen restructured the social relations of production, [and] transformed wage labor into a market commodity" (Sean Wilentz, *Chants Democratic*, p. 5). This established a new set of labor relations and led to conflict. During the colonial period, craftsmen tended to make products on custom order and to rely mostly on household labor. As the size of the operation grew and the shop produced a surplus, the master might take on an apprentice, hire a journeyman, or buy the time of a servant or slave. In the period of the American Revolution, as free workers became more plentiful and less expensive, master craftsmen moved to the position of employers and merchant capitalists. Skilled laborers were hired and fired as economic necessity dictated.

The result was considerable labor unrest. In Philadelphia, for example, cracks appeared in the once cohesive community of work. In 1786, journeymen printers organized and went out on strike to protest a reduction in their wages. Carpenters were next. In 1791, journeymen united as employers attempted to cut wages. The cabinetmaking and chairmaking trades erupted next; beginning in 1794, the battle lines were drawn over prices and wages. Their quarrel spread, and they appealed to journeymen in a wide range of crafts, and to the public, in Philadelphia and in other cities. The journeymen won. Together with the masters, they agreed to guaranteed prices for all work. Labor conflict reached its peak with the city's shoemakers. The interests of masters and workmen began to diverge and in 1799 approximately one hundred journeymen walked out on strike to protest an attempted wage reduction. Although calm reigned for a short time, in 1805 journeymen demanded a wage increase. Masters rejected the raise, which propelled journeymen to strike once more; this time they stayed out of work for six weeks. The finale occurred with the 1806 Conspiracy Trial in which masters accused workmen of collusion. For masters, journeymen were simply one element in a complex system of costs that affected profit; journeymen pointed to the fortunes masters had made from their labors while they could barely put food on the table.

Capitalist wage relations usually associated with industrialization were in place in the mid-Atlantic and New England regions by the early national period. Population pressures on land supplies, especially in the older settlements of New England, forced men and women to seek work elsewhere, and they migrated to the cities in search of jobs. However, the urban economies were faltering. In Boston, by the mid eighteenth century, "it was no secret that for men of the laboring classes it was difficult to live as one's father" (Gary B. Nash, Billy G. Smith, and Dirk Hoerder, "Labor in the Era of the American Revolution," p. 422). Philadelphia's economy remained strong until about a decade and a half before the Revolution. Then, "wages of laborers and merchant seamen began in the early 1760s a decline which, interrupted only by a brief resurgence after 1765, continued until the outbreak of the Revolution" (Nash et al., p. 423). The urban laboring classes were accustomed to work interruptions caused by inclement weather. What was new were periods of unemployment brought by business slumps. Jobs, especially in the cities, became increasingly harder to find. Because of this labor surplus, men and women were forced to sell their labor cheaply. Thus, employers were provided with an inexpensive labor force which helped fuel the shift to the industrial order of the nineteenth century.

[See also Agriculture; Business Culture; Gender Roles and Relations; Geographic Mobility; Household Labor; The Plantation; Slavery; The South.]

BIBLIOGRAPHY

General

Dunn, Richard S. "Servants and Slaves: The Recruitment and Employment of Labor." In *Colonial British America: Essays in the New History of the Early Modern Era*, edited by Jack P. Greene and J. R. Pole (1984).

Morris, Richard. *Government and Labor in Early America* (1946).

Rediker, Marcus. "'Good Hands, Stout Heart, and Fast Feet': The History and Culture of Working People in Early America." *Labour/Le Travailleur* 10 (Autumn 1982): 123–144.

Thompson, E. P. "Eighteenth-Century English Society: Class Struggle Without Class?" *Social History* 3 (May 1978): 133–165.

The Chesapeake

Billings, Warren M. "The Law of Servants and Slaves in Seventeenth-Century Virginia." *Virginia Magazine of History and Biography* 99, no. 1 (1991): 45–62.

Carr, Lois Green, and Lorena S. Walsh. "Economic Diversification and Labor Organization in the Chesapeake, 1650–1820." In *Work and Labor in Early America*, edited by Stephen Innes (1988).

Kulikoff, Allan. *Tobacco and Slaves: The Development of Southern Cultures in the Chesapeake, 1680–1800* (1986).

Menard, Russell. "From Servants to Slaves: The Transformation of the Chesapeake Labor System." *Southern Studies* 16, no. 4 (1977): 355–390.

Morgan, Edmund S. *American Slavery, American Freedom: The Ordeal of Colonial Virginia* (1975).

Women and Labor

Boyalston, Jeanne. *Home and Work: Housework, Wages, and the Ideology of Labor in the Early Republic* (1990).

Jensen, Joan. *Loosening the Bonds: Mid-Atlantic Farm Women, 1750–1850* (1986).

Ulrich, Laurel Thatcher. "Martha Ballard and Her Girls: Women's Work in Eighteenth-Century Maine." In *Work and Labor in Early America*, edited by Stephen Innes (1988).

Unfree Labor

Dunn, Richard S. *Sugar and Slaves: The Rise of the Planter Class in the English West Indies, 1624–1713* (1972).

Galenson, David W. *White Servitude in Colonial America: An Economic Analysis* (1981).

Horn, James. "Servant Emigration to the Chesapeake in the Seventeenth Century." In *The Chesapeake in the Seventeenth Century: Essays on Anglo-American Society*, edited by Thad Tate and David L. Ammerman (1979).

Salinger, Sharon V. *"To Serve Well and Faithfully": Labor and Indentured Servants in Pennsylvania, 1682–1800* (1987).

Silver, Timothy. *A New Face on the Countryside: Indians, Colonists, and Slaves in South Atlantic Forests, 1500–1800* (1990).

Smith, Abbot Emerson. *Colonists in Bondage: White Servitude and Convict Labor in America, 1607–1776* (1947).

Ulrich, Laurel Thatcher. "Martha Ballard and Her Girls: Women's Work in Eighteenth-Century Maine." In *Work and Labor in Early America*, edited by Stephen Innes (1988).

Wood, Peter H. *Black Majority: Negroes in Colonial South Carolina from 1670 Through the Stono Rebellion (1974).*

Urban Labor and Revolutionary Politics

Lemisch, Jesse. "Jack Tar in the Streets: Merchant Seamen in the Politics of Revolutionary America." *William and Mary Quarterly* 3d ser., 25 (1968): 371–401.

Lynd, Staughton. "The Mechanics in New York Politics, 1774–1788." *Labor History* 5, no. 3 (1964): 225–246.

Nash, Gary B. *The Urban Crucible: Social Change, Political Consciousness, and the Origins of the American Revolution* (1979).

Nash, Gary B., Billy G. Smith, and Dirk Hoerder. "Labor in the Era of the American Revolution: An Exchange." *Labor History* 24 (Summer 1983): 414–439.

Olton, Charles S. *Artisans for Independence: Philadelphia Mechanics and the American Revolution* (1975).

Rediker, Marcus. *Between the Devil and the Deep Blue Sea* (1987).

Rock, Howard. *Artisans of the New Republic: The Tradesman of New York City in the Age of Jefferson* (1979).

Rosswurm, Steven. *Arms, Country, and Class: The Philadelphia Militia and the "Lower Sort" in the American Revolution, 1765–1783* (1987).

Smith, Billy G. "The Material Lives of Laboring Philadelphians, 1750 to 1800." *William and Mary Quarterly* 3rd ser., 38, no. 2 (1981): 163–202.

———. *The "Lower Sort": Philadelphia's Laboring People, 1750–1800* (1990).

Vickers, Daniel. "Working the Fields in a Developing Economy: Essex County, Massachusetts, 1630–1675." In *Work and Labor in Early America*, edited by Stephen Innes (1988).

Wilentz, Sean. *Chants Democratic: New York City and the Rise of the American Working Class, 1788–1850* (1984).

Young, Alfred. "The Mechanics and the Jeffersonians: New York, 1789–1801." *Labor History* 5, no. 3 (1964): 247–276.

— SHARON V. SALINGER

LABOR: THE JACKSONIAN ERA THROUGH RECONSTRUCTION

In 1820, free wageworkers were still a minority in a society where the dominant labor systems were slavery and independent family proprietorship (family farms, small craft-shops). Half a century later that minority had become a decisive majority. A society of independent farmers and craftsmen, slave-owners and slaves had become a society of employees and bosses. By 1870, two-thirds of all Americans earned their livings as manual wage earners. Some workers believed that abundant opportunities to climb the social ladder still existed, but a large majority would in fact remain wage earners all of their lives.

From morning to night, from birth to death, this new wage-earning majority lived differently from their grandparents. They rose to clocks, which had once been all but unknown except in church towers, village squares, or upper-class drawing rooms. They dressed (quickly) in store-bought clothes and donned machine-made shoes, quite different from their grandparents' homespun and homemade apparel. And then, quite unlike their grandparents who had worked at home (although even then in gender-specific tasks), the men left for the commercial world of factories, construction sites, or offices. Women, unless they were young and unmarried, or widowed or abandoned, remained home in their now-separate sphere of housekeeping, child rearing, and domestic production. Their grandparents had pondered the incomprehensible whims of a sometimes angry God who withheld rain or spread disease in unpredictable ways. To such mysteries now had been added new worries—the vagaries of a market that sometimes threatened employment just as unpredictably as the weather, and the all-too-comprehensible power of the boss upon whose whims that employment depended.

The relationship between employers and employees governed the lives of the majority of Americans directly and set the social and economic context for the rest. Farmers grew cash crops destined for urban markets. Merchants and shopkeepers sold the goods made by wage laborers. Bookkeepers recorded the sales and profits. Ministers and politicians praised the nobility of honest labor at the same time that, without any apparent sense of irony or contradiction, they also lauded the virtues of frugality and temperance as the sure path to upward mobility out of the wage class. A new economic class, a working class, had been formed in one lifetime, and the consequences of that event affected more Americans in more ways than any other event of the nineteenth century.

Working-class formation was so intertwined with a great many other social changes—agricultural improvements; virtual revolutions in transportation, communication, and finance; changing attitudes about work, family, gender, religion, and leisure; a new political party system; and technological innovations—that historians often subsume working-class formation under a larger process of societal transformation. For classical Marxists, working-class formation was the inexorable consequence of capitalist development: the history of class formation is essentially equivalent to the history of capitalism. For modernization theorists, proletarianization was merely one aspect of more fundamental processes of centralization, bureaucratization, and social differentiation. In retrospect, the dominance of capitalism in western Europe and North America, and the resulting European conquest of the rest of the globe, has made it seem almost inevitable that these changes took a capitalist form. But we need only to consider that capitalist hegemony in the United States was finally determined by the bloodiest war of the nineteenth century to recognize that economic development could have taken many forms. Over the last century and a half, working-class formation has taken place everywhere in the developed world, but always in different ways.

The particular way it happened in America has shaped American politics, culture, and institutions ever since. Three peculiarities of American working-class formation were especially important. First, the United States was the first democratic republic in which working-class formation took place. Elsewhere, workers' initial attempts to organize and improve conditions were mingled with struggles to abolish legally enshrined upper-class privileges, overturn sharply defined class boundaries, and establish political rights. In the United States, for most white males, such rights predated industrialization and working-class formation. American working people, in their initial industrial conflicts, were protesting usurpation of legally guaranteed equality rather than trying to overturn an Old Regime and establish a new political order.

Second, far more than in most countries, working-class formation in the United States was multiethnic, the result of the largest mass migration in human history. Between 1840 and 1930 close to forty million immigrants entered the United States, and the majority of them entered as workers. As a result, class conflict overlapped with ethnic, religious, and racial conflict. Bosses disproportionately tended to come from the culturally and politically dominant caste of white, native, Anglo-Saxon Protestants, while the majority of working people were outsiders—members of ethnic, racial, or religious minorities. While some immigration and interethnic conflict took place in nearly every industrializing country, American class relations mirrored those of a colonial regime to an extent unmatched in western Europe.

Third, the initial working-class formation took place in the United States at a time when the country was convulsed by the political conflict between free and slave labor. In that conflict, bosses and northern white workers found themselves on the same side: their differences seemed less important than their common struggle for freedom. However, once the supremacy of free labor was unequivocally established, both white employers and white working people were ambivalent about the status of the four million former slaves who outnumbered white non-agricultural manual workers in 1865. We still suffer from the consequences of that ambivalence.

The cumulative effects of republican traditions, ethnic diversity, and the heritage of slavery produced a particular pattern of class relations. Until well into the twentieth century the working class was so divided by ethnicity, race, religion, and regionalism that it is easier to talk about various working-class subcultures and ethnic fragments than about a common working-class culture. Nonetheless, American class relations were characterized by sustained conflict, bitterness, and often ferocious violence. Yet, despite the intensity of conflict, the dominant trends within the labor movement were usually reformist and ideologically moderate. Efforts were oriented more toward preventing the development of clear class boundaries, which threatened to undermine social and political equality, than toward sharpening those boundaries in order to mobilize workers for revolutionary reconstruction.

Paths to Proletarianization

Across the vast territory of antebellum America, people became workers in many ways. Each occupation changed at a different pace, and the same occupations developed differently in different places. Well into this period, the process of transition from earlier labor systems was still far from complete. The differences in how this change occurred are important for understanding the experiences and attitudes of each group of workers, but within the patchwork of variations we can identify three common paths, three ways that most people who became workers did so. Shoemakers, tailors, leather workers, printers, and hatters were among the many traditional craftsmen reduced from independent craftsmen to wage earners. Second, recruitment into new, large-scale, capital-intensive industries such as textile and paper mills, railroads, and iron foundries, swelled the ranks of workers. Finally, the numbers in such traditional occupations as domestic servants, laborers, wagon drivers, longshoremen, and sailors all grew as well.

REORGANIZATION OF THE CRAFTS. Despite the variations in the work cultures of individual crafts, nearly all functioned under a similar artisanal regime until the late eighteenth century. Production took place in small workshops organized by master craftsmen. Masters and journeymen performed the same tasks, and each made the entire product from start to finish. Craftsmen collectively maintained a monopoly over craft knowledge by limiting access to the craft to apprentices who completed training with existing craftsmen. Since journeymen were full parties to this control over craft knowledge, since they owned their own tools, and since the minimum capital entry requirements for proprietorship were modest, journeymen had considerable independence, and most journeymen could expect to become masters.

As merchant-capitalists and entrepreneurial masters slowly reorganized the crafts in the early nineteenth century, these businessmen increasingly departed from the artisanal model. They divided the production process into steps, with each worker performing only one task. While some tasks still required considerable skill, others could be performed by unskilled or semi-skilled labor. Simple hand-operated machinery—such as treadle sewing machines for sewing shoes and clothing, hand-operated presses for shaping materials to molds and patterns and so on—could be adapted to some of these tasks. The cost savings from division of labor drove down the prices of finished goods, undermining the competitive position of traditional craftsmen. Master craftsmen either adapted to the new system of labor and to technological innovations or were forced into the emerging class of wageworkers themselves. In the most radically transformed trades, even skilled workers now possessed full knowledge of only selected steps in production. Skilled labor was still crucial to nearly all of the craft-based industries, but the roles of skilled workers had changed. What had been the collective knowledge of all producers passed slowly to the newly emerging class of managers and bosses who now alone were capable of organizing production in its entirety.

As successfully reorganized firms expanded, the minimum firm size necessary for effective competition increased dramatically In Philadelphia in 1850, the mean industrial-firm size was 12.9 workers per firm, and 59 percent of all industrial workers worked in firms of twenty-six or more workers. This represented a dramatic change from only thirty years before, when 86 percent of the city's industrial workers worked in firms with less than ten employees and over 99 percent in firms with less than twenty workers. The Philadelphia pattern was typical of national trends: in virtually every place historians have studied, they have discovered similar changes in the old craft industries.

Increased firm size dramatically raised the capital requirements for proprietorship and cut journeymen off from access to the means of production even in those crafts that had not yet introduced any new machines. Workers now depended on bosses for employment and survival. The usual citywide price lists of the artisanal era, under which individual masters paid journeymen for each completed product a price that reflected both the market value of the product and traditional community norms of fair remuneration, gave way to unilaterally determined piece rates and daily wages. For craftsmen who were now paid wages, a term heretofore restricted to day laborers, the linguistic change reflected a profound psychological change. A journeyman cordwainer who was paid the established price for his shoe retained his republican sense of independence: he sold his product, not himself. A craftsman who was paid wages, even a well-paid craftsman like a shoe cutter, had sold himself for a day. A craft hierarchy characterized by common knowledge, in which each producer performed the same tasks and in which rank was a function of stage of life cycle, had evolved into a class system of employers and employees.

Increased firm size dramatically raised the capital requirements for proprietorship and cut journeymen off from access to the means of production even in those crafts that had not yet introduced any new machines.

In only a few of the reorganized craft industries did new machines or technology have a revolutionary influence, at least in their early stages of development. In such trades as shoe, hat, and saddle production, and clothing manufacture, machines sped up particular steps in the production process but did not alter the essential structure of production before the 1850s. Nor did the larger firm size usually offer decisive economies of scale beyond the minimum necessary for effective division of labor. The competitive advantage of reorganization stemmed from three critical factors: substitution of cheaper labor for more expensive labor, closer supervision of labor, and intensification of pace. Reorganization of the crafts was thus inherently an adversarial process. Employers gained competitive advantage primarily by undermining the skills of craft workers or pushing them to work harder, steadier, or faster.

Before the 1840s, women were by far the largest source of cheap labor for entrepreneurs who wanted to take advantage of new craft divisions of labor. In 1832, a third of the industrial workers in the Northeast (over 40 percent in Massachusetts, the most industrialized state) were women and girls. Gender barriers still restricted the use of female labor, even in some crafts where division of labor stimulated demand for low-cost unskilled labor. Cultural conceptions of appropriate gender roles were as important as economic forces in determining the sexual division of labor, but a gender-based division of labor provided the economic basis for most of the sweated crafts. Shoemaking and clothing manufacture are two examples: the predominance of subcontracting to small garret shop owners and of outwork—a system in which pieces precut in a shop are assembled by workers in their homes into finished pieces, which are returned to the shop—exerted a sharp downward pressure on wages. Most women who entered American industries before 1825 went to work in the new textile mills; after that time, with the expansion of crafts reorganized around a gender-based division of labor, more women entered craft industries. By 1850, the majority of female industrial workers in the United States worked in the reorganized crafts.

Closer supervision, which made acceleration of the work pace possible, complemented the cost advantages gained by division of labor. As Moses Brown, the Providence merchant-capitalist who helped finance the first successful cotton mill, established in 1790 by Samuel Slater, and who helped pioneer establishment of a variety of infant industries, explained, "one hundred looms in families will not weave so much cloth as thirty . . . constantly employed under the immediate inspection of a workman" (Gordon, Edwards, and Reich, p. 58).

Employers who sought to realize the advantages of Brown's insight faced a concerted struggle. While preindustrial artisans had always worked long hours, an intermittent work pattern with frequent breaks and holidays was deeply embedded in their work culture. Employers who demanded steadier work were thus forcing workers to abandon widespread traditions and expectations, expectations that not only made work less dreary and physically taxing but also had significance as symbols of republican independence. It is perhaps for this reason that manufacturers played crucial roles in antebellum moral-reform movements designed to alter public morality and increase individual restraint, such as temperance and sabbatarianism; manufacturers were also disproportionately overrepresented in evangelical Protestant revivalism, which usually emphasized attitudes and behavior conducive to good work habits.

THE INDUSTRIAL REVOLUTION: MILL HANDS AND FACTORY WORKERS. In the craft industries, proletarianization destroyed the independent status of the male artisan and expanded the roles of women as substitutes for more expensive male labor. By mid century, pockets of outworkers and craft manufactories were scattered throughout the rural economies of the Northeast, and the economies of large cities like New York, Philadelphia, and Cincinnati depended heavily on the reorganized crafts. In 1855, nearly half of New York City's labor force worked in these industries.

But in the Massachusetts towns of Lowell, Lawrence, Waltham, Fall River, and in dozens of lesser-known mill and factory towns, industrialization revolved around the large-scale, capital-intensive industries that captured the imagination of (and caused alarm among) contemporaries and subsequent scholars. Since the 1820s, new towns had sprung up as giant multistory brick mills lined fast-flowing New England streams, railroad repair shops mushroomed at unoccupied rail junctions, and mine shafts burrowed into Pennsylvania hillsides. Where farms and villages had recently dotted quiet landscapes, now the churning of waterwheels and the noises of leather belts, gearshifts, and power looms echoed over the roofs of boardinghouses and tightly packed alleys. Smoke from iron and glass furnaces or locomotive boilers darkened the skies. "When I went out at night," wrote a Lowell millhand in 1844 "the sound of the mill was in my ears, as of crickets, frogs, and jewsharps, all mingled together in strange discord. . . . You know that people learn to sleep with the thunder of Niagara in their ears, and a cotton mill is no worse, though you wonder that we do not have to hold our breath in such a noise" (as quoted in Bode, p. 33).

The size of such enterprises and their tight concentration around sources of waterpower, raw materials, and convenient transportation made them seem more economically important than they were. In 1850 agriculture still dominated the American economy: 55 percent of the labor force worked in agriculture. Within the industrial sector, the reorganized crafts and traditional unskilled occupations still employed a large majority of workers. There were more than twice as many tailors, milliners, seamstresses, and dressmakers (217,000) as cotton mill workers (92,000). There were twice as many carters, wagon drivers, and teamsters (39,700) as railroad workers (20,000). Cotton, iron, coal, metal fabricating, machine- and shipbuilding, railroads, glass, paper, and brewing together accounted for no more than 5 percent of the American labor force in 1850. But the immediate landscape-transforming power and the wider economic and cultural ripples of such industries seemed indeed to merit the term "Industrial Revolution." Nothing quite like it had happened before.

These industries had never been based on an artisanal model. They did not develop by reorganizing the work processes of an existing body of producers. The technological histories of these industries varied, belying any simplistic conceptions of a unified industrial revolution; but all used machinery, all operated on a larger scale than the artisanal crafts, all employed a variety of skilled and unskilled labor, all depended on the extensive division of labor precluding any artisanal sense of holistic responsibility for the final product, and all had always required a level of capitalization too high for even the most frugal and industrious craftsmen to raise without outside investors or government assistance.

The knowledge of skilled workers was critical to the success of these firms, but their recruitment and training, expected career paths, and relationships with both managers and unskilled workers were quite different from those of skilled workers in the craft-based industries. In the craft-based industries, most entrepreneurs had prior shop-floor experience. Outside investors who were attracted to the large-scale, capital-intensive industries because their mercantile experience alerted them to untapped potential markets often had no such knowledge about the industries in which they were investing. The Boston Associates who founded the cotton mills at Waltham and Lowell were all merchants. Given this lack of practical experience among managers and the costly consequences of mistakes in capital-intensive industries, skilled workers had considerable leverage. Mule spinners (textile thread machinists), glassblowers, and iron puddlers were among the most highly paid workers in America.

But workers learned their trades on the shop floor of enterprises they knew they had very little chance of ever owning. Training emphasized the day-to-day knowledge necessary to make production. Skilled workers trained their helpers and work crews; younger members of the work gang hoped gradually to work themselves up shop-floor promotional ladders based on the division of labor—from helper to gatherer to glassblower; or from railroad brakeman to fireman to engineer. Where factory crafts successfully maintained control over apprenticeship, apprenticeship had a different meaning than the prelude to proprietorship implicit in the craft shop. Iron puddlers' and glassblowers' struggles to control apprenticeship reflected the adversarial realities of the factory, where controlling access to skills helped protect craft power.

Nor did completion of apprenticeship necessarily carry with it the same life-cycle significance as in the craft shop. For the artisanal apprentice, apprenticeship marked graduation from unpaid to paid labor, entrance into the egalitarian fraternity of fellow mechanics, and accession to manhood. In the factory, the puddler's helper had been a paid member of a functioning work crew from the start, and completion of his apprenticeship did not guarantee a fundamental change in status. Opportunities to move into more highly paid tasks depended on turnover among the skilled workers or expansion of production.

All of the large-scale, capital-intensive industries employed both unskilled and skilled labor in multistage production processes that usually involved more complex division of labor than the reorganized craft industries. The artisanal crafts, the world of the craftsman before craft reorganization, had been a largely male world that sharply distinguished itself from the "lower orders" of laborers, dockhands, sailors, and servants. When reorganization brought women, untrained male immigrants, and country boys into the closely guarded preserve of the craftsmen, they were seen as threatening interlopers. Even in the eighteenth century, though, iron furnaces, glasshouses, shipyards, and paper mills had needed woodcutters to cut wood for charcoal furnaces, miners, rag sorters, wagon drivers, and a wide variety of helpers. The social, familial, and cultural relationships between the different kinds of workers necessary for these enterprises varied, but in no case were their worlds as clearly and self-consciously segregated as the mechanics were from the laborers of the preindustrial city.

In the textile mills, until the 1850s, gender marked the dividing line between skilled and unskilled labor. Men worked as overseers, mule spinners, carders, machinists and machine repairers, dyers, finishers, and skilled weavers (in woolens and worsteds)—all high-wage jobs that needed some combinations of physical strength, technical training, and mechanical experience. Women tended drawing frames and spinning machines and ran power looms and other machines that did not demand great strength or mechanical knowledge. Until the arrival of new waves of impoverished immigrants from Ireland in the mid 1840s (and a few years later from French Canada), gender barriers were sharp and distinct. Except for a few watchmen, virtually no adult males worked in jobs defined as unskilled, and even the most skilled women worked at tasks paid below the minimum for adult males. Gender segregation even extended, to some degree, into the tasks performed by children. While young boys and girls were equally divided among the "doffers" who replaced bobbins on spinning throstles as they filled with yarn (perhaps because the adults they worked with were all women), boys worked as piecers, tying up loose threads, for the male mule spinners. By their mid teens, girls and boys were consistently assigned gender-specific tasks.

Unskilled and skilled male workers worked together in many of the other large-scale industries. In the early and mid nineteenth century, in industries like glass, iron, and metal casting, where skilled blowers, puddlers, and molders directed work crews of helpers and assistants, work gangs were often based on kin and familial ties. The blowers, puddlers, and molders were middle-aged men; their crews included sons, nephews, neighbors, and children of friends. By the 1850s and 1860s, the hierarchy of such work crews also reflected the ethnic hierarchy of successive waves of immigration, but as each ethnic group attained footholds in the skilled ranks, it used its position to re-create kin and family work networks among relatives and fellow countrymen.

The Penobscot Cotton Mill in Tophsam, Maine. Gender marked the dividing line between skilled and unskilled labor in nineteenth century textile mills.

While there were many exceptions, the rapid expansion of large-scale, capital-intensive industries after 1825 generally represented a potential opportunity for many workers, a magnet that attracted willing recruits—in contrast to craft reorganization, which threatened the status and livelihood of a preexisting mechanic population. Life for early factory workers was heavy, hard, and hazardous, but for many workers, the life they had left behind was even worse.

EXPANSION OF PREINDUSTRIAL LABOR: LABORERS, SERVANTS, AND FARM HANDS. The term "industrialization" conjures up images of noisy steam engines, complicated machines, and "dark, satanic" mills, but the expansion of markets for industrial goods, the increasing pace of new transportation networks, mushrooming urban populations, and the commercialization of agriculture needed to feed city dwellers also created enormous new demands for very traditional forms of unskilled labor. Canals, railroads, factories, and tenements were built mainly with human muscle. In the genteel households of the new urban middle class, an emerging cult of female domesticity established new standards of cleanliness, order, and conspicuous consumption and declared for middle-class women new proprieties that could be fulfilled only with the help of domestic servants. Millions of acres of prairies had to be cleared away and sown with wheat, corn, and other crops to feed factory owners, millhands, and the burgeoning urban middle class and its servants.

While there were many exceptions, the rapid expansion of large-scale, capital-intensive industries after 1825 generally represented a potential opportunity for many workers, a magnet that attracted willing recruits.

The physical realities of shoveling dirt, scrubbing pots, or harvesting grain had not changed very much between the late eighteenth century and the mid nineteenth century. But the place of these occupations within the structure of American society, their social meaning and significance, had changed. In preindustrial society, the field labor that farmers had not done themselves, the domestic labor that wives and daughters had not done for their own households, and even much of the digging and lifting in the seaport cities or commercial villages had been performed either by people outside the polity—slaves, indentured servants, apprentices, free blacks, and other marginalized individuals—or by young people as part of preparation for marriage and setting up an independent household. Forced labor was not on a wage basis. Many of those who worked for wages did so intermittently, and few expected to do so all their lives. Their employers were often relatives, neighbors, or friends, and non-economic considerations of neighborliness, communal loyalty, and generational obligation influenced the relationship between employers and employees.

By 1850 most of the people who dug canals, laid railroad tracks, and cleaned houses earned wages paid by strangers; they had become a permanent segment of the emerging working class. An Irish construction laborer went from one canal or railroad to another or from the railroad to the mill. His daughter was not "help" for a neighboring farmer's wife but the live-in, full-time scullery maid for the wife of a merchant. When she left the merchant's household, it was most likely to run a tenement household where she would cook and clean for a laboring husband and several boarders.

The situation of free agricultural laborers in 1850, by far the largest group of traditional wage earners, was more ambiguous than that of urban laborers, canal boatmen, or servants. Many were young people still connected by non-economic bonds—family, kinship, and community—to the people who employed them. But many were now also immigrants, newcomers, or migrants. Nineteenth-century observers and generations of historians from Frederick Jackson Turner to recent economic historians have argued that most of these laborers were farmers in the making who worked for wages for a few years while either waiting to inherit the family farm or saving the relatively modest sum necessary to begin farming on the frontier. Such arguments, however, draw as much from the ideology and wishful thinking of latter-day Jeffersonians as from empirical investigation: despite the overwhelming evidence of persistent inequality in acquisition and ownership of land, social mobility via farm ownership has long been viewed as one of the bases of American democracy. More sophisticated versions of the Turner thesis do grant that there were serious impediments to a simple laborer-to-proprietor scenario. For many agricultural laborers in settled areas, a job in a nearby factory or on a railroad track gang seemed less risky and perhaps even more lucrative than migration to distant farming country where cheap land was available. For those willing to consider such moves, prime farmland was not easy to acquire, even in newly settled regions. The best lands and those most accessible to transportation went quickly, and thereafter newcomers had either to settle for more marginal lands or to pay premium prices. According to the estimate of an 1832 Illinois settler, even if a would-be farmer acquired government lands at the minimum price of $1.25 per acre, the costs of fencing, preparing the land for planting, building a house, and buying seed, livestock, and tools drove the start-up costs for a 160-acre farm up to $976 (Schob, *Hired Hands and Plowboys*, pp. 260–266). With annual wages for agricultural laborers no more than $150 per year in most eastern states, $976 was a large sum.

Optimistic scenarios that imagine sturdy and virtuous farmboys working for a few years before they assumed their Jeffersonian heritage as independent yeomen are certainly exaggerated. The optimistic scenario fits best for the first wave of settlers in newly settled areas. Early arrival did translate into greater opportunities; and while such frontier opportunities influenced migration patterns and helped to shape American culture, they hardly represent the situation of most mid-nineteenth-century rural laborers. Most people lived far from the frontier, and even in frontier regions, with each new arrival after the first cohort, the area came to be less and less a frontier.

The abundance of cheap land certainly provided opportunities for a great many nineteenth-century Americans. But with each decade, the westward march of settlement moved the sites of available land farther and farther from developed population centers, making them less accessible to the landless populations of long-established farming regions. As new areas were settled, they duplicated the dilemma that New England had faced by the late 1700s: too little land to allow all the increased population of the next generation to support themselves as farmers.

Abundant land helped American workers. Some laborers did become farmers; the pull of cheap land drove up the wages of the rest. But even a vast continent was not big enough to provide farms for everyone who might want one. Surplus rural populations would have to find work elsewhere. At mid century, with substantial portions of the Midwest still not fully settled, perhaps that was not completely clear. It would become so in the next generation.

Labor Organization and Working-Class Development

In the half-century from the 1820s to the 1870s, workers' efforts to organize were at the same time a story of recurring failure and of extraordinary success. From a purely bureaucratic or organizational point of view, most labor organization was temporary. Unions repeated a distressing cycle of initial success, expansion, optimistic hopes for dramatic improvement, and then virtual collapse after the next financial panic and depression. After a flurry of strikes (many victorious), some surprisingly successful forays into labor politics (including the world's first labor parties—the workingmen's parties, which appeared in several dozen cities at the end of the 1820s), the development of an impressive array of citywide labor federations of local craft unions and even embryonic national organization in the 1830s, nearly all labor organizations collapsed after the panic of 1837. Massive shorter-hours campaigns in the 1840s were followed by new and revived unions in the late 1840s and early 1850s, but many fell apart again after the panic of 1857. In the mid and late 1860s, several national unions finally seemed headed for permanence as national union membership reached several hundred thousand, but after the panic of 1873, most organizations disappeared once again. Fewer than ten national unions survived the mid-decade depression with even a skeleton crew intact, and stable labor organization seemed no closer than it had forty years before.

But the number of membership cards and the longevity of union charters are not the only measures of success. While labor activists between the 1820s and 1870s mostly failed to establish durable organizations or stable systems of collective bargaining, they succeeded at something as important: they convinced a substantial portion of their fellow workers to accept their critique of the emerging wage system and to accept their vision of a collective morality for coping with it. The language of labor, the symbolic collective embodiment of an emerging class, entered the vernacular. By the close of the era, every politician, regardless of what policies he actually advocated, proclaimed his sympathy for the rights of labor and asserted that his program was labor's only true salvation. Every worker knew what a strike was. Every craft had developed norms of appropriate output and acceptable work practices. And most Americans accepted the notion that the concept of liberty and justice for all was morally inconsistent with the lives of grinding poverty and underpaid toil so many of its citizens were now leading. Working-class activists could not yet provide convincing answers to the question of how to solve that problem, but few workers any longer had illusions that their situation was temporary, or that the problem would solve itself.

Immigrants

Before 1840 most workers had been native rural whites who migrated out of the countryside into nearby towns and cities. After 1840 immigration rates rose so quickly and immigrants concentrated so heavily in working-class occupations that they quickly exceeded the still considerable flow of native rural migrants. The Irish came in great numbers after the potato famine of the early 1840s. Less drastic but similar pressures began to affect the peasantry of the German-speaking regions of central Europe about the same time. By the 1850s an even larger flood of Germans followed on the heels of the Irish. Every city had its "Corktown" or "Little Germany." Boston's Irish outnumbered the population in every city in Ireland except Dublin. New York's Kleindeutschland was bigger than all but two or three German cities.

In scarcely more than a decade, foreign-born workers and their native-born children outnumbered workers of native rural origins in nearly every large American city or major mill town. Renowned as a destination for Yankee farm girls, Lowell, Massachusetts, had until almost mid century a working population that was mostly native Protestants. Only 3.7 percent of the work force of Lowell's Hamilton Manufacturing Company was foreign-born in July 1836. By August 1850, immigrants constituted 38.6 percent of the Hamilton workers; by June 1860, 61.8 percent. In Fall River in the 1820s, only 6 percent of local mill operatives named in two contemporary lists were foreign-born; by 1845, nearly half of the employees of a local iron works had Irish surnames, and in 1850, 59 percent of Fall River's factory workers and laborers were immigrants. In New York City in 1855, 70.4 percent of the workers in twenty leading blue-collar occupations were foreign-born. In Pittsburgh in 1850, 69.5 percent of the people in working-class occupations were immigrants.

Contrary to popular mythology, those who emigrated to America were rarely among the poorest or most oppressed in their own countries.

Contrary to popular mythology, those who emigrated to America were rarely among the poorest or most oppressed in their own countries. People pressured by economic changes were more likely to consider leaving farm or homeland and to seek new ways of making a living, but those who did were also responding to other motives. They were rarely compelled to leave out of sheer necessity.

The most obvious exception might be the post-famine Irish, but John Bodnar has noted that studies of Irish emigration show that "the poorest were not the first to leave" (*The Transplanted,* p. 6). The heaviest flow out of the Irish countryside in the famine years came from the wealthier and more developed eastern and central counties rather than from the poorest counties of the west with the highest proportion of landless residents. When the very poor did leave rural Ireland, they were more likely to be able to manage the passage to nearby England than to America. The Irish who did emigrate were much poorer than migrants from Yankee farms, but the preponderance of young, single people among the newcomers suggests that their motives for emigration may not have been so different from the motives of native migrants. For more than a generation before the famine, Irish young people had been leaving in increasing numbers. By the 1870s less than 16 percent of Irish immigrants to America were married. The rural young faced a more extreme version of the dilemma confronting developed agricultural regions in America. Because of dense rural populations, high and increasing land rents, evictions of tenants by modernizing landlords, very small family landholdings, and many children, rural Irish families could not provide the minimum livelihood their children would need before they could marry and establish their own families. For single adults faced with postponing marriage for many years, emigration may have looked appealing.

Among the other nationalities who emigrated to America in substantial numbers in the antebellum years, relatively few emigrants had been completely impoverished. Both British and German emigration came mainly from more developed and commercialized regions. In Scotland, for example, emigrants from the more urbanized and industrialized Lowlands outnumbered those from the Highlands by seventeen to one. Emigrants from both Britain and the German states came disproportionately from two groups adversely affected by capitalist development: traditional handcraft producers unable to compete with cheaper machine-made goods, and marginal agriculturalists who faced declining living standards because meager lands could not sustain more commercialized and competitive forms of agricultural production.

A substantial proportion of the immigrants did differ from native rural migrants in one crucial respect. Even those who had been artisans or small landholders had exhausted most of their resources to pay for the transatlantic passage. They arrived nearly penniless, and they had no nearby home or farm to return to if conditions in the city were worse than they had expected. A variety of immigrant aid societies organized by fellow countrymen tried to help them, but the enormous flood of immigrants into the major eastern ports after 1845 was so large that voluntary organizations could at best provide only token assistance to a fraction of the immigrants. Chain migration of kin and village cohorts helped ease the transition. Immigrants usually had a relative or former resident of the same village who had learned something about American ways to help them find work. But work they had to find, and quickly. They clustered in the most low-paying and unattractive jobs. Economic necessity may not have been essential to their decision to emigrate, but necessity shaped their job options once they arrived.

As they settled in, the initial networks of family, kin, and village acquaintances became the basis of organized ethnic communities. Because of their own preferences for association with people of their own language and background, on the one hand, and the hostility of natives, on the other, immigrant workers not only stuck together but raised their American-born children with clear ethnic identities. When unskilled construction workers organized into laborers' unions in New York in the 1850s, they did so quite consciously as Irish organizations. When German bakers, cigarmakers, and cabinetmakers met in newly organized craft unions in American cities in the 1850s and 1860s, they kept their minutes in German. Most union organizers professed interethnic unity, but for the most part their unions in these years were ethnically segmented nonetheless.

Where their native-born counterparts organized in the 1840s and 1850s, they often did so separately from the Irish and the Germans. Indeed, the movement that probably captured the most enthusiasm among native-born urban craftsmen of those decades was nativism. Using a populist and laboristic rhetoric that bore more than a superficial similarity to the language of 1830s labor organizers, nativist politicians denounced the immigrants as tools of the monopolistic corrupters of American liberty. Combining these appeals to the disgruntlement of hard-pressed craftsmen in the reorganized urban crafts with a heavy dose of anti-Catholicism, nativist politicians captured the mayorships of New York, Philadelphia, and Pittsburgh, and nativism emerged as a national political force in the 1856 presidential campaign of ex-President Millard Fillmore on the American ("Know-Nothing") party ticket.

With this heritage of ethnic identity and organized hostility among native workers, the American working class that emerged in the second half of the nineteenth century was something like a building with three massive columns. Native, Irish, and German workers each formed crucial segments of the industrial labor force, but segments separated from each other. Bridging the gaps between them would be a difficult problem for American labor organizers for several generations afterward.

Forced Labor

Early America was built by forced labor. At the time of the American Revolution, nearly one-quarter of the population of the thirteen colonies was African American; since all slaves except the very young worked, slaves represented a disproportionate part of the labor force. In addition, the majority of the whites who came to America before 1800 came in bondage as redemptioners: people who agreed to allow ship owners to auction them to the highest bidder for a period of years in payment for their ship's passage, as convicts who exchanged American bondage for a hangman's noose, or as debtors who traded servitude for debtors' prison.

At the end of the eighteenth and the beginning of the nineteenth centuries, a combination of economic and moral pressures seemed to be undermining servitude. In an increasingly commercialized economy, those who sought to buy labor recognized that hiring people on short-term wage contracts was often more flexible and less risky than assuming the large expense of purchasing a slave or a long-term indenture. The rapid expansion of waged labor gave those who sought opportunity in America a far more appealing alternative than indentured servitude. As improving transportation cut the time for transatlantic passage from months to weeks and, by the 1860s, to days even, the expense and danger fell correspondingly. Indentured servitude, already declining in the late 1700s, disappeared completely as the rising tide of free immigrants replaced the bonded labor of the previous century.

The idealism generated by the American Revolution also aroused serious opposition to black slavery. In all of the northern states, slavery was either outlawed or gradually abolished in the generation after the Revolution. Anti-slavery advocates at the Constitutional Convention were forced to compromise with slave-owners who threatened to torpedo American nationhood if slavery was outlawed, but they did win agreement for a clause prohibiting further importation of slaves into the United States starting twenty years after the Constitutional Convention. American slavery, never as profitable as in the sugar colonies of the West Indies or the plantations of Central and South America, looked like it might be slowly phased out.

Ironically, while the rise of the factory system sealed the final doom of other forms of servitude, it gave black slavery in the American South a rebirth. The explosive growth of the textile mills of New England and the English Midlands created a virtually insatiable demand for cotton. Before the cotton gin and mechanized production of cotton cloth, cotton had been a luxury good. Now it rivaled sugar as the world's great cash crop. Even though abolition of the American slave trade (in 1808) helped to drive up the price of slave labor, the cotton boom made slavery immensely profitable. After 1815, slave labor, high cotton prices, and the rich virgin bottomlands of the Gulf Coastal Plain turned American plantation cotton production into a great get-rich-quick scheme. The plantation elite, now unapologetic advocates for expanding the source of their wealth, was on a collision course with the equally enthusiastic advocates of capitalist commercial development in the North.

Only in these closing decades of the antebellum era did southern plantation slavery approach the *Gone With the Wind* stereotype of American popular culture. The majority of the last two generations of American slaves did work in the cotton fields of a few thousand wealthy planters and lived in the shadows of their mansions. Quantitative historians have squabbled about the exact composition of the plantation slave-labor force, but in the 1840s and 1850s, at least three-quarters—perhaps up to or over 90 percent—of American slaves worked as field hands. Most of the remainder were household servants or artisans such as carpenters, blacksmiths, or coopers. In the aftermath of slavery, most of the first small African American middle class—the initial cohort of ministers, teachers, professionals, and skilled workers—were the descendants of the house servants and artisans of the last slave generation.

The explosive growth of textile mills in New England and the English Midlands created an insatiable demand for cotton, which had been a luxury good before the cotton gin and the mechanized production of cotton cloth.

Those who had been field hands entered emancipation poorly equipped to compete in a wage-labor economy. Not only were most illiterate, but, equally important, they lacked essential experience in negotiation or handling money. They had no resources or marketable assets other than their capacity for physical labor.

Even those who did have skills, such as the former plantation artisans or the small numbers who had worked as slaves for hire in southern cities, encountered unremitting hostility from most white employers and white workers in both North and South. While some white workers had joined the abolitionist crusade on moral grounds, the majority of the northern public had been won to the anti-slavery cause because they had become convinced that the competition of slave labor threatened free labor. They did not look upon job competition from ex-slaves any more favorably than they had greeted competition with slavery.

This combination of white hostility and lack of marketable assets kept most of the ex-slaves out of the emerging industrial economy for two more generations. They remained in southern agriculture until the twentieth century. Yet given the constraints they faced, their, story is not one of total failure. Within a generation, the majority had escaped gang labor on their former plantations. They worked as small farmers, tenants, and sharecroppers—still for most a life of hard labor and poverty, but a life that allowed for far more independence and sense of achievement than had the lives of their parents.

Conclusion

The question of free versus slave labor had postponed a full reckoning with the contradictions of wage labor. But it was no coincidence that Boston machinist and labor organizer Ira Steward demanded, according to David Montgomery, at the end of 1865 that Radical Reconstruction be directed at the plight of wage workers as well as the former slaves: "So must our dinner tables be reconstructed, our dress, manners, education, morals, dwellings, and the whole Social System" (quoted in *Beyond Equality*, p. ix). No sooner had the question of free versus slave labor been settled than Americans were forced to recognize that they faced a new labor question: the relationship between labor and capital. Those who were slow to appreciate this fact had the point forcefully driven home to them in the summer of 1877. Just as Reconstruction symbolically ended with the withdrawal of the last federal occupying troops from the South, railroad workers, protesting wage cuts and increased workloads, virtually shut down the nation's entire transportation system. When hundreds of thousands of other working people in dozens of cities joined striking railroad workers in their battles with police, national guardsmen, and finally federal troops, they turned the 1877 railroad strike into the largest strike anywhere in the world in the entire nineteenth century.

In its aftermath followed mass-marketed popular exposés, a senatorial investigation into the conditions of labor and capital, sudden expansion of labor organization culminating in the explosive growth of the Knights of Labor in the middle of the next decade, and calls by nervous defenders of property for urban police reform, armory construction, and national guard reorganization. No one had a clear or convincing prescription for solving the central dilemma posed by this new labor problem: How to reconcile the democratic political culture that defined what it was to be an American with the social and economic hierarchies of capitalism. But for more than half a century thereafter, the labor problem and all of its ramifications persistently occupied center stage. The making of an American working class—even one so divided against itself by the cleavages of race, ethnicity, religion, region, and economic sector—had permanently and fundamentally altered American society.

[See also Agriculture; Business Culture; Household Labor; Minorities and Work; The Plantation; Slavery; Women and Work.]

BIBLIOGRAPHY

Bode, Carl. *American Life in the 1840s* (1967).

Bodnar, John. *The Transplanted: A History of Immigrants in Urban America* (1985).

Commons, John R., et al. *History of Labour in the United States.* Vol. 1 (1918).

Dawley, Alan. *Class and Community: The Industrial Revolution in Lynn* (1976).

Dublin, Thomas. *Women at Work: The Transformation of Work and Community in Lowell, Massachusetts, 1826–1860* (1979).

Dudden, Faye E. *Serving Women: Household Service in Nineteenth-Century America* (1983).

Faler, Paul G. *Mechanics and Manufacturers in the Early Industrial Revolution: Lynn, Massachusetts, 1780–1860* (1981).

Fogel, Robert W., and Stanley L. Engerman. *Time on the Cross: The Economics of American Negro Slavery* (1974).

Foner, Philip S. *History of the Labor Movement in the United States. Vol. 1, From Colonial Times to the Founding of the American Federation of Labor* (1947).

Gerber, David A. *The Making of an American Pluralism: Buffalo, New York, 1825–1860* (1989).

Gordon, David M., Richard Edwards, and Michael Reich. *Segmented Work, Divided Workers: The Historical Transformation of Labor in the United States* (1982).

Gutman, Herbert G. *Work, Culture, and Society in Industrializing America: Essays in American Working-Class History* (1976).

Handlin, Oscar. *Boston's Immigrants: A Study in Acculturation* (1941).

Hirsch, Susan E. *Roots of the American Working Class: The Industrialization of Crafts in Newark, 1800–1860* (1978).

Hugins, Walter. *Jacksonian Democracy and the Working Class: A Study of the New York Workingmen's Movement, 1829–1837* (1960).

Katz, Michael B., Michael J. Doucet, and Mark J. Stern. *The Social Organization of Early Industrial Capitalism* (1982).

Laurie, Bruce. *Working People of Philadelphia, 1800–1850* (1980).

Lebergott, Stanley. *Manpower in Economic Growth: The American Record Since 1800* (1964).

———. "Labor Force and Employment, 1800–1960." In *Output, Employment, and Productivity in the United States After 1800.* Vol. 30, *Studies in Income and Wealth* (1975).

Levine, Bruce, et al. *Who Built America?* (1992).

Licht, Walter. *Working for the Railroad: The Organization of Work in the Nineteenth Century* (1983).

McGaw, Judith A. *Most Wonderful Machine: Mechanization and Social Change in Berkshire Paper Making, 1801–1885* (1987).

Montgomery, David. *Beyond Equality: Labor and the Radical Republicans, 1862–1872* (1981).

———. *The Fall of the House of Labor: The Workplace, the State, and American Labor Activism, 1865–1925* (1987).

Pessen, Edward. *Most Uncommon Jacksonians: The Radical Leaders of the Early Labor Movement* (1967).

Prude, Jonathan. *The Coming of Industrial Order: Town and Factory Life in Rural Massachusetts, 1810–1860* (1983).

Ransom, Roger L, and Richard Sutch. *One Kind of Freedom: The Economic Consequences of Emancipation* (1977).

Ross, Stephen J. *Workers on the Edge: Work, Leisure, and Politics in Industrializing Cincinnati, 1788–1890* (1985).

Schob, David E. *Hired Hands and Plowboys: Farm Labor in the Midwest, 1815–1860* (1975).

Shelton, Cynthia J. *The Mills of Manayunk: Industrialization and Social Conflict in the Philadelphia Region, 1787–1837* (1986).

Stansell, Christine. *City of Women: Sex and Class in New York, 1789–1860* (1986).

Walkowitz, Daniel J. *Worker City, Company Town: Iron- and Cotton-Worker Protest in Troy and Cohoes, New York, 1855–1884* (1978).

Wallace, Anthony F. C. *Rockdale: The Growth of an American Village in the Early Industrial Revolution* (1980).

Ware, Norman. *The Industrial Worker, 1840–1860* (1924).

Wilentz, Sean. *Chants Democratic: New York City and the Rise of the American Working Class, 1788–1850* (1984).

— RICHARD OESTREICHER

LABOR: THE GILDED AGE THROUGH THE 1920S

The history of the American working class from the 1870s through the 1920s is characterized more by its disjunctures than its coherence. Radical and conservative labor organizations rose and fell. The greatest waves of immigration in American history redefined the American working class, and the entrance of women and blacks into the work force did the same. New industrial cities grew over the tops of hamlets and market towns along the Great Lakes and in the South. American corporate capitalism emerged in the 1890s out of the ruins of that decade's depression, the country's worst to date.

The new corporations of the early twentieth century made the assembly line the standard of the American factory, and they created a mass commercial culture that, particularly during the 1920s, reshaped the way American workers lived and thought about themselves. Growing bureaucracies in business and government created new kinds of white-collar labor, expanding the definition of work and the working class to include people such as telephone operators. Amidst the prosperity of the "roaring twenties," manufacturing workers reached their historically highest proportion of the American work force.

American politics changed almost as dramatically, shifting from an era of intense party competition in the Gilded Age, or the last third of the nineteenth century, to an era of Republican party dominance after 1896. Only Woodrow Wilson broke the Republican hold on the presidency between 1896 and Franklin D. Roosevelt's victory in 1932. In the first two decades of the twentieth century, a middle-class progressive reform movement provided an occasional ally for organized labor and positively reshaped the context of public opinion in which some labor issues were addressed. Yet the progressive movement declined in the 1920s along with the fortunes of labor. In the midst of all this social and economic change America fought the Spanish-American War in 1898 and entered the First World War in 1917. The country emerged from both as a world power with an empire and a foreign policy that was hostile to a Russian revolution that was made in the name of liberating the working classes of the world.

There were nonetheless patterns amidst the complexities and disjunctures. Some order was imposed from above by the changing American economy and political system. Workers struggled to define an order of their own from below, and their efforts shaped not only the American labor movement but also American society and culture. To understand the full dimensions of American labor history in these sixty years one needs to place the struggles of organized labor within the larger context of the history of the American working class, most of which was never incorporated within labor institutions. In turn, the history of the working class needs to be seen within the context of the phases of the American industrial revolution, the history of immigration, and the character of the political system of the late nineteenth and early twentieth centuries.

Gilded Age Workers and the Triumph of Corporate Capitalism

The last third of the nineteenth century was the classic period of American industrialization, when the country built its heavy industry and a national railroad system. Although the American industrial revolution had begun in the 1820s and 1830s, industrialization before the Civil War was restricted to a narrow sector of the economy—the production of light consumer goods such as cloth, boots and shoes, and clocks. In an overwhelmingly agricultural society the market for these goods was dependent on the prosperity of rural America. After the Civil War the growth of cities and the railroads helped create a market for industrial goods, such as iron and steel, that was not so dependent on a rural market. At the same time the railroad system gave access to a truly national market that stimulated the growth of all types of manufacturing.

Basic industry grew exponentially. The production of bituminous coal, the main energy source for smokestack America, expanded over ten times between 1870 and 1900. The production of rolled iron and steel grew over twelve times in the same period. The whole American economy developed with such rapidity that the gross national product in 1900 was approximately six times what it had been in 1869. By the turn of the century America was the preeminent industrial economy in the world with an output greater than its closest rivals combined.

The explosive growth of manufacturing capacity meant a similar expansion of the work force. The people employed in manufacturing jumped from over 2.6 million in 1870 to almost 7.2 million in 1900. Immigrant men filled much of the demand for industrial labor in America's cities, but women and children were also drawn into the work force in unprecedented numbers. In 1890, one-fifth of the children between the ages of ten and fifteen held jobs. By 1900 women made up one-quarter of the nonfarm work force, although they were not primarily in manufacturing. In Pittsburgh at the turn of the century less than one-quarter of employed women were in manufacturing; most were servants, waitresses, saleswomen, clerks, teachers, nurses, or midwives. Working-class families, especially those with unskilled breadwinners, needed income from women, and sometimes children, to survive; but wage labor was not the only source of income. Housewives took in boarders, for example, one of the many kinds of work they performed outside the wage economy. In a large sample of all types of Pennsylvania households in 1901, one-fifth of the families took in boarders.

The Gilded Age economy was unstable during this rapid expansion. America experienced two severe depressions in the mid 1870s and the mid 1890s, as well as sharp contractions in 1884 and 1888. Both the economy at large and people's everyday lives seemed out of control. Economic instability—in addition to inequality and the growth of big business—helps explain the appeal of mass protest movements in the 1880s, such as those led by the Populists and the Knights of Labor. Both tried to use politics and the government to define a new order controlled from below, based on local institutions such as cooperatives. The Populists and the Knights were mass movements with diverse constituencies that included substantial numbers of wage earners. The Populists were concentrated among farmers and farm workers in the rural West and South, while the core constituency of the Knights was among workers and small businessmen in cities and towns. The economic instability of the Gilded Age also helps explain why skilled workers—such as machinists, iron molders, carpenters, printers, and cabinetmakers—were attracted to unions in their crafts: these unions offered stability and concrete benefits in return for the high dues they charged. Craft unions provided another kind of control from below. Such unions were the backbone of the American Federation of Labor (AFL) founded in 1886.

Gilded Age workers lived with an almost constant threat of unemployment, and their organizations frequently disintegrated from insolvency and disinterest during depressions. The depression of the 1890s was the first one survived by a significant number of American trade unions, an organizational feat too seldom appreciated. It was, however, usually purchased at the price of limiting union membership to skilled workers who could pay their dues. This organizational achievement built on an unequal distribution of income within the American working class: on the average, America's skilled workers were better off than even their British counterparts, but America's unskilled workers were no better off than their British compatriots, and perhaps less so.

The distinction between the skilled and unskilled had even wider implications. In America unskilled workers were more likely to be recent immigrants, while the skilled were more typically immigrants of longer residence, the children of such immigrants, or Yankees—that is, the native-born of Anglo-American parents. As the European origins of immigrants to the United States shifted in the late nineteenth century, the craft workers were commonly from northwestern Europe, while the unskilled workers came from eastern, central, and southern Europe. The Yankees were especially prominent in the most skilled jobs in metal fabrication and in the best railroad occupations, such as train engineers. A typical Gilded Age production facility in heavy industry, a steel rolling mill, for example, had a work force with a sizable core of skilled northern European craft workers directing a larger group of laborers and helpers.

The depression of the 1890s was the first one survived by a significant number of American trade unions, an organizational feat too seldom appreciated; it was, however, usually purchased at the price of limiting union membership to skilled workers who would pay their dues.

The craft workers often acted as subcontractors within the plant, who reached agreements with management and hired laborers themselves to fulfill the tasks.

A long-term decline in prices lent a harsh and uncompromising character to the relations between capital and labor in the Gilded Age. The index of wholesale prices declined by 50 percent between 1870 and 1896, as new technologies increased productivity and lowered costs per unit. Businessmen also were able to lower costs by bringing previously unexploited, rich natural resources into the market for the first time, such as the iron ore of the Mesabi range in Minnesota. Often called the great depression before the cataclysm of the 1930s usurped the name, this price deflation was also caused by intense business competition. Businessmen constantly cut costs to outsell their competitors, and labor was frequently one of the costs they tried to cut.

The labor history of the late nineteenth century was punctuated by frequent, bitter, and often violent strikes in which neither side felt it could give much ground. From the railroad strike of 1877—America's first national strike—through the pitched battles of the Homestead strike in 1892 and the Pullman strike in 1894, conflicts between labor and capital took on a violent and volatile character. The larger conflicts spilled over into the wider community and usually involved state and national intervention by the courts and troops. Class conflict became a stark reality for Americans in the late nineteenth century. Declining profits also often became a stark reality for businessmen, who were frequently unable to cut labor costs due to working-class resistance. This resistance was usually led by the skilled workers who were also most able to form lasting unions.

The solution to the instability and declining prices of the Gilded Age economy came out of the private economy, not from the government, as the Populists and Knights of Labor had advocated. Leading the corporate merger movement between 1897 and 1904, investment bankers under the leadership of J. P. Morgan brought "fair" competition to industry by combining smaller companies into huge corporations which, if not monopolies, were large enough to shape the market in which they operated by influencing prices and dividing up market share. A notable achievement of the new corporate economy was a rising rate of prices. The wholesale price index increased by 50 percent between 1896 and 1913, just before the outbreak of World War I in Europe. These years were also marked by unprecedented prosperity and relatively mild swings in the business cycle. Led by investment bankers, American business had begun building a new order from above, a process that culminated in the 1920s.

Successful new corporations—and not all were successful—combined their increases in size and structure with new managerial techniques that provided greater control over their far-flung enterprises. Developed by the railroads in the late nineteenth century, modern management techniques meant creating departmentalized bureaucratic structures, usually broken down into functional units and coordinated by a strong central bureaucracy to which the middle managers regularly fed information. These middle managers were frequently innovators in their fields of responsibility, and they tried to increase their control by changing the ways workers performed their tasks. The subsequent struggles between managers and workers for control on the shop floor defined much of American working-class history in the early twentieth century. The main target of the new managers was the substantial power of skilled workers within the production process, a legacy of the Gilded Age. Also pitted against the new managers was a working class expanded by the "new" immigration of the Ellis Island era between the late 1890s and World War I. Immigrants often new to industrial work and urban life faced some of the most sophisticated and powerful business organizations in the world.

Applying mass production to heavy industry had occupied business in the previous era. The new corporations applied mass-production techniques in making consumer goods, such as cigarettes, electrical appliances, and cars. The new corporations also pioneered the application of electricity in the factory, so that it became the predominant industrial power source by the 1920s. So profound were these changes that some historians speak of a second industrial revolution, although it was, in fact, another stage in a process that had begun in the early nineteenth century. Changes in managerial structure and the application of new technologies produced huge increases in labor productivity—and corporate profits—in the 1920s. Between 1919 and 1929 labor productivity increased 2.2 percent annually, in contrast to 1.5 percent in the preceding decade.

New immigrants from such places as Austria-Hungary and Russia made the first ten years of the twentieth century the unparalleled immigrant decade in American history.

The mass production of consumer goods in the early twentieth century could only be sustained if the products were successfully marketed on a scale never before achieved. Advertising reached new levels of sophistication and influence in the 1920s. Business reached a wider public through electronic technologies, such as the radio; and advertisers helped define new images of everyday life in order to market everything from washing machines to cigarettes. American merchandisers and financial institutions also pioneered installment buying so that masses of Americans, including workers, could buy into a definition of the American dream through an unheard-of abundance of consumer goods. Installment buying was needed in part because the wages of American workers did not keep pace with increases in productivity or profits in the 1920s, although real wages did increase. This relatively slow increase in wages helped ensure that markets were inadequate for the flood of new consumer goods, one of the inner weaknesses of the American economy during the boom of the 1920s.

Immigrants, Blacks, and Organized Labor in the Progressive Era

Historians have usually distinguished the "old" immigration originating in northwestern Europe from the "new" immigration from eastern and southern Europe. The 1880s, when 5.2 million immigrants arrived, witnessed the historic pinnacle of the old immigration from Scandinavia, Germany, and the British Isles; but a rapid shift to the new immigration also began in the same decade. The numbers of new immigrants from places like Italy, Austria-Hungary, and Russia surpassed even the volume of the 1880s to make the first ten years of the twentieth century the unparalleled immigrant decade in American history. Over eight million entered the country, and Ellis Island became fixed in the American imagination as the gateway to a new life. Looking at these two decades separately obscures a larger fact, however: two-thirds of the thirty-three million immigrants who arrived in America between 1820 and 1920 entered the country after 1880. In one sense, the great majority of these immigrants did not enter America, they entered the American working class; and their arrival profoundly reshaped the hierarchies within it and its labor institutions.

Research by Peter R. Shergold sheds new light on the status divisions among American workers at the turn of the century. Comparing workers in Pittsburgh and Birmingham, England, Shergold found that, contrary to conventional wisdom, American workers did not necessarily have a higher standard of living. The main characteristic of the American working class was a sharp inequality between the skilled and unskilled. Divisions within Birmingham's working class were comparatively narrow. Pittsburgh's skilled craft workers were much better off than their Birmingham counterparts, earning in some cases up to twice as much. Pittsburgh's unskilled workers may have had slightly better wage rates, but their overall standard of living was hardly higher than their counterparts in Birmingham, in part because the community facilities available to Birmingham's unskilled workers were considerably better.

Skilled workers in Pittsburgh could live according to the "American standard" of which Samuel Gompers, president of the AFL, was so proud. They could purchase a small home, perhaps even with indoor plumbing, buy cigars, subscribe to a labor newspaper, and pay for tickets to watch professional baseball. This composite skilled worker in turn-of-the-century Pittsburgh would have found much in common with a German upholsterer in Chicago, described in a government report in 1884 (Illinois Bureau of Labor, *Third Biennial Report*):

> Family members 5—father, mother, and three children . . . The house they occupy contains four cozy rooms, all nicely carpeted. Family comparatively healthy. Wife quite intelligent, and children neat and well dressed. Father belongs to trades union, and carries some life insurance. He states that he has run in debt during the past year somewhat, but principally for groceries. Father works but about forty weeks during the year. . . . If he had work the entire year he would not now be in debt.

For breakfast they commonly had "coffee, meat, bread and butter," for supper "coffee, bread, potatoes and meat." The family's annual budget included expenditures for "books, and papers, etc." in addition to union dues and life insurance premiums.

The contrast with unskilled laborers was stark. Pittsburgh's common laborers at the turn of the century lived in rickety wooden tenements near the noise and stench of the blast furnaces where so many of them worked. Children played on unpaved streets, and leisure consisted of sleep and perhaps a drink at a local saloon. Particularly during the era of the new immigration, common laborers often came to America unaccompanied by families and lived in ramshackle boardinghouses near the plants where they worked or near railroad junctions from which they could more easily travel to their next job. The sharp contrast between the earning power and living standard of skilled and unskilled workers in America was compounded by ethnic and racial cleavages. In turn-of-the-century Pittsburgh, common laborers were typically Italians, Slavs, Poles, or Austro-Hungarians, whose cultural traits compounded the contrasting living standards of the skilled and unskilled. These new immigrants also had different agendas from the German, Scandinavian, British, and Irish skilled workers who occupied the upper echelons of the blue-collar work force. Recently arrived, the new immigrants commonly intended to save money in order to return home to their old villages as "rich" men. While hoarding what they could save from their meager wages, they lived in material squalor, which they hoped was temporary.

The Italians were a case in point. In the early twentieth century they replaced the Irish as America's typical unskilled construction laborers. Arriving as single men or without their families, Italian men worked in gangs of fellow countrymen, intending to go home when the opportunity arose. This helps explain why 3.8 million Italians arrived between 1899 and 1924, and 2.1 million left in the same period. And some of them returned to the United States a second or third time for the same reasons. When the new immigrants, such as Italian laborers, started to stay, bring their families over, and build urban neighborhoods, they started a new chapter in the social history of the American working class.

The new immigration ended abruptly with the beginning of World War I in 1914, and it did not resume in its prewar volume mainly because of the immigration quota laws passed in the early 1920s. In the absence of massive immigration, the increasing demand for labor that came with the wartime boom, and then with the prosperity of the 1920s, was met first by blacks and women. To an ever-greater extent Hispanics, especially Mexicans, also helped meet the need, since they were not covered by the immigration quota laws. Women occupied a special niche in the manufacturing economy, which will be discussed in the last section of this essay. Blacks from the South began to fill the ranks of common laborers, helpers, and unskilled machine tenders that had been the positions of the new immigrants. The racial hatred permeating American working-class life has obscured the extent to which the history of blacks in the American working class is analogous to that of the new immigrants.

Blacks were practically the only native-born Americans in the unskilled working class of Pittsburgh in the early twentieth century, and their numbers increased dramatically during World War I. Before the war the black American population was concentrated overwhelmingly in the rural South. Although there were pockets of black settlement in a few northern cities, dating in some cases to pre–Civil War times, there was no sustained migration from the South to northern cities. World War I changed the situation dramatically as corporations, led by the railroads, recruited thousands of black workers. Once the process began, blacks moved north on their own, as news of opportunities spread by word of mouth and through personal letters. The letters sent home by black laborers had an impact similar to the "immigrant letters" that were read in European peasant villages by family and friends.

With the black migration north during World War I a new era began in black American and working-class history. For the first time blacks made up substantial elements of the work forces of northern industries from steel and meatpacking to railroads and construction. They also started forming their own urban communities, reinforced in their size and homogeneity by racial prejudice that hindered black dispersal. The arrival of blacks in cities was marked by some of the largest race riots in American history. Racial prejudice also typified the reaction of organized labor, despite a few pronouncements from AFL leadership opposing provisions in union charters excluding people on the basis of race. Although there were some successful interracial organizing efforts, there were just as many cases where, understandably distrustful of unions, blacks served as strikebreakers. The history of such events is usually interpreted in the context of American race relations, but they also need to be seen in the light of the disparity between the different levels of the American working class and the impact that disparity had on organized labor.

The history of organized labor in the late nineteenth and early twentieth centuries had an almost schizophrenic character, typified on the one hand by conservative craft unionism incorporated into the AFL, and on the other by episodic flashes of militance embodied in massive strikes that often ended in violence and labor defeat. While the AFL moved cautiously in politics and kept its organizational efforts largely confined to craft workers, the Industrial Workers of the World (IWW) tried to organize one big union of all workers. The IWW led unskilled workers in dramatic and often violent strikes. Appropriately, the AFL was founded in the 1880s, a decade marked not only by massive labor unrest but also by the shift from the old to the new immigration. The AFL craft unions included in their membership, and were often founded and led by, immigrants from northwestern Europe. Samuel Gompers, founder and early president of the AFL, was of Dutch Jewish heritage, but he was raised in London, where he learned the ways of modern labor unions. The IWW was founded in Chicago in 1905 during the height of the new immigration. The IWW appealed to the lowest levels of the American working class, and it was particularly adept at organizing the single men who lived in the harsh and isolated logging camps and mining towns of the West.

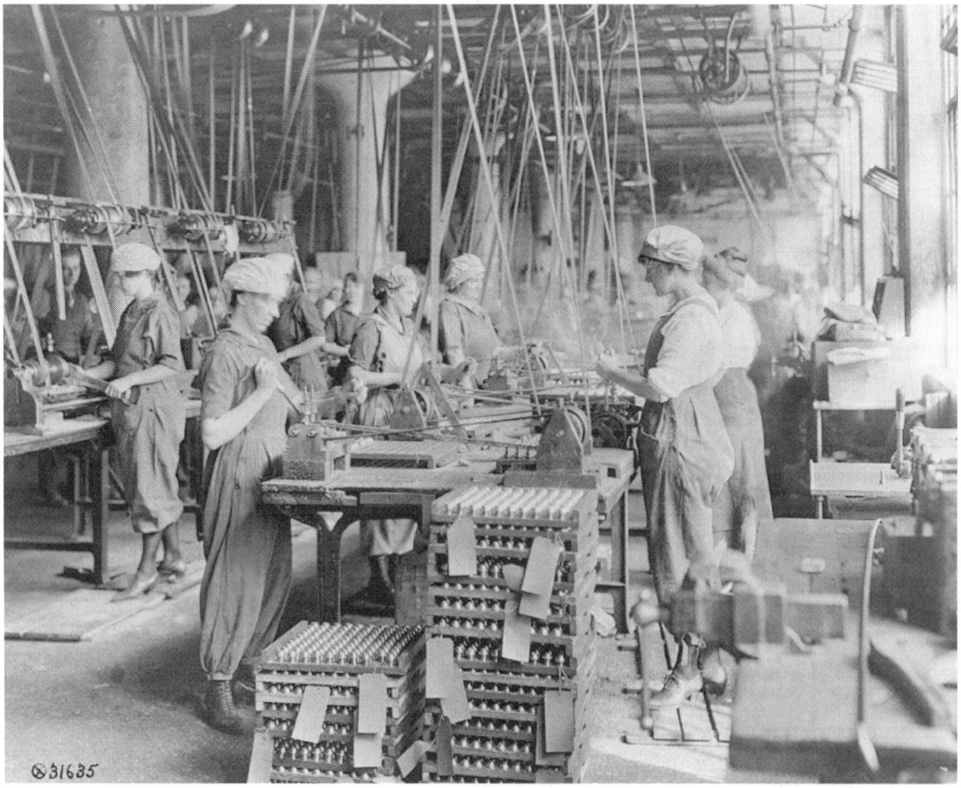

Female workers slot fuses at Gray & Davis Co. They were hired during World War I to help alleviate the manpower shortage produced ty Army recruitment.

This rooting of different types of labor organization in the differing strata of the working class is a necessary but insufficient explanation of the complex history of the organized American labor movement. The character of the national political system, for example, also profoundly shaped the history of organized labor, and not simply in its forays into electoral politics. A review of the history of organized labor can help illustrate the wider import of labor's social history and aid in defining questions and refining hypotheses about how social change influenced the subsequent history of the labor movement. In general, during the Progressive Era—the first two decades of the twentieth century—the most conservative elements of organized labor could extract modest gains from the political system, after extensive efforts. But these gains, such as the Clayton Antitrust Act, too often proved disappointing in their result for labor. The radical side of organized labor met with sustained hostility from business and government, and it was repressed during and after World War I.

In the 1890s, Gilded Age America seemed to be at a dead end of violence, disorder, and political ossification. Agrarian protest, represented by the Populists, shook the major parties, especially the Democrats in the South and West. Unemployed workers filled the streets of urban America. In the Pullman railroad strike of 1894, Grover Cleveland, a Democratic president, used federal troops against striking workers—just as a Republican president, Rutherford B. Hayes, had used them in the nationwide railroad strike of 1877. The class conflict of the 1890s was so extensive that it changed the thinking of important segments of American political and corporate leadership. Middle-class Progressives, such as Jane Addams, tried to make democracy meaningful to the immigrants crowding American industrial cities, cooperating with organized labor on issues like child-labor laws and factory inspection. Both middle-class reformers and enlightened conservatives in America's corporate business leadership also felt that a new and more productive way of managing the conflicts between capital and labor had to be developed. They formed the National Civic Federation to bring together representatives of business, labor, and the public, which usually meant urban middle-class reformers. Samuel Gompers participated actively in the organization, which promoted the use of arbitration in labor disputes, and generally worked to create a spirit of accommodation across the divide separating management and labor. Along with other reform groups, it helped create a more favorable public opinion on labor issues than had been the case in the Gilded Age.

Labor had new room to maneuver in the first two decades of the twentieth century, but this room was clearly circumscribed. During the anthracite coal strike of 1902, for example, Theodore Roosevelt—future candidate of the Progressive party in 1912—cajoled the mine owners into an arbitrated settlement with the United Mine Workers, instead of sending troops. Aided by the return of prosperity, a wide range of unions besides the miners gained significant organizational victories in the late 1890s and first few years of the century. In these years Chicago was probably the most unionized city in the world after London. By 1904 American unions had organized 20 percent of the workers in manufacturing, mining, transportation, and construction. This was an unparalleled union achievement, based in many cases on the cooperation on the local level between experienced labor leaders, who were usually old immigrants, and unskilled workers, who were frequently among the new immigrants. Hostility and misunderstanding were not the only relationships between the differing strata of the working class. In a huge 1904 strike, Chicago packinghouse workers of different income levels and ethnic backgrounds were able to work together because of their common experience on the shop floor and their cooperation with strong community organizations in nearby neighborhoods.

Gilded Age America seemed to be at a dead end of violence, disorder, and political ossification: Agrarian protest, represented by the Populists, shook the major parties, especially the Democrats in the South and West, and unemployed workers filled the streets of the larger cities.

The Progressive movement and the National Civil Federation notwithstanding, business greeted the union successes of the early twentieth century with an unprecedented, and largely successful, anti-union "open shop" drive that was aided by a recession in 1904. Despite cooperation between old and new immigrants in a major strike in the Chicago packinghouses during that year, the packinghouse owners won and the workers there remained unorganized. Business also attacked organized labor in the courts during the first decade of the century, and it was so successful that Gompers led the AFL out of its usual political passivity to make demands on the major political parties for legislation giving unions relief from the results of several Supreme Court decisions. Significant gains for labor had to wait, however, until Woodrow Wilson needed labor support to help secure his tenuous hold on the presidency.

Wilson owed his narrow victory in 1912 to Theodore Roosevelt's campaign as leader of the Progressive party, which drew votes from William Howard Taft, the Republican nominee. Further to the left of the Progressives, the Socialist Party of America, under the leadership of Eugene Victor Debs, polled an unprecedented 6 percent of the presidential vote, an achievement never again equaled. Wilson needed to appeal to these reform constituencies to stay in the White House for a second term, since he had won with only 41 percent of the popular vote in the election of 1912. In Wilson's first term there were several legislative victories for labor, the most significant being the Clayton Antitrust Act, which labor had advocated to limit the use of court injunctions against unions. The courts had been using the Sherman Antitrust Act (1890) to justify injunctions against strikes, calling them conspiracies in restraint of trade prohibited under the Sherman law. The Clayton Act amended the Sherman law to limit this use of the injunction as a measure to suppress strikes. As happened so frequently, however, this legislation—Gompers called it "labor's Magna Charta"—proved hollow because of its narrow interpretation by the courts.

World War I proved more beneficial to the conservative wing of organized labor than the programs of the first Wilson administration. Union membership increased substantially between 1914 and American entrance in the conflict in 1917, and it increased even more with American involvement in the war. During the war, membership in AFL unions reached an all-time high of about three million, up from about 1.6 million in 1910. The government needed labor's cooperation to maintain war production, which was threatened by a wave of strikes after America entered the war. The Wilson administration responded by including labor leaders and spokesmen in policy-making circles and granting most of labor's demands for wage increases and benefits. In return the administration demanded a no-strike pledge from labor. Never before had labor leaders been involved in the power circles of America, and Gompers became a member of the trusted inner circle of government policy. At the same time, the federal government cracked down on labor radicals, whom it accused of undermining the war effort. Since the Socialist party opposed the war, it suffered severely and Debs went to jail in 1919 for a violation of the Espionage Act. This crackdown on the Left foreshadowed what was to come.

When the war ended, so did government management of the economy that had given unions a new power in the American economic system. Workers, both organized and unorganized, sought to preserve their wartime gains against a determined effort by business to win back its old freedom of action. During 1919 more workers went on strike than in any year in American history. Major strikes in steel, bituminous coal, and among the Boston police set the pattern for a period of labor conflict—and labor retreat—that lasted through a sharp economic downturn in 1922. Government on all levels intervened against strikes, supported by a public mood aroused against radicalism and communism. Fears inspired by both the Russian Revolution and labor's postwar assertiveness produced America's red scare of 1919–1920. In 1919 and 1920 Attorney General A. Mitchell Palmer launched a wide-ranging and thorough attack on Left-leaning organizations. He decimated an American Left already weakened by internal divisions over how to respond to the Russian Revolution. Fears of foreign radicals also helped ensure the passage of immigration restriction laws in the early 1920s.

The red scare and union defeat began more than a decade of labor decline that did not end until the organizing drives of the Congress of Industrial Organizations (CIO) in the mid 1930s. Organized labor had gone from unparalleled success to a defeat that seemed permanent by the mid 1920s. The fact that its organizational and political successes in the second decade of the century depended on the unusual Democratic victory under Wilson and then on a world war had been obscured by the bright light of long-sought victories. With men like Calvin Coolidge and Herbert Hoover in the White House, corporate America claimed, with temporary credibility, to have the will and means to meet workers' needs for higher wages, job security, and greater benefits through what has come to be called "welfare capitalism." Corporations started providing a set of programs for their employees ranging from company sports teams through life insurance to profit sharing, all of which were designed to prove that unions were no longer needed. With unions weak or nonexistent, immigration a mere trickle, the Left practically impotent, and America awash in consumer goods, an era had ended in the history of the American working class. The death of Gompers in 1924 accentuated the point. Except for one year he had been president of the AFL since its founding in 1886.

For labor the 1920s marked a return to the "normalcy" of its hostile relation with the state. The formative years of the modern American labor movement took place at a time when achieving power in the political system seemed remote and other options for exercising power could easily appear more realistic. Seen in this light, the local cooperative communalism of the Knights, the conservative trade unionism of the AFL, and the revolutionary unionism of the IWW shared the common endeavor of founding a base for exercising power outside the established party system. Given this political environment, labor's organizational failures need less analysis than the working-class roots of its successes, and the limitations these roots carried with them.

Shaping Cities by Building Working-Class Neighborhoods

Both the successes and defeats of the labor movement have to be related to the distinctive character of working-class formation in the late nineteenth and early twentieth centuries, particularly to the urbanization of the working class and its reconstitution by immigration from Europe and migration from the South. For sixty critical years, as America became the world's preeminent industrial power, American workers were engaged in two fundamental projects—building urban communities and becoming Americans. The construction of labor institutions was part of, but subordinate to, these two primary endeavors.

The urbanization of the American working class was one of the most important developments in American history. Between 1870 and 1910 the urban industrial core of the nation expanded from the East to include the Old Northwest. New industrial cities emerged, such as Cleveland, Pittsburgh, and Detroit, each of which had at least 450,000 people by 1910. Chicago came to dominate the entire midwestern industrial region with a population in 1910 of over 2.1 million. Medium-sized industrial cities developed rapidly as well. In 1910 there were fifty-nine cities with populations between fifty thousand and one hundred thousand, and forty-two of them were in the industrial East and Midwest. Cities like Rockford, Illinois, South Bend, Indiana, Youngstown, Ohio, and Johnstown, Pennsylvania, formed part of the urban and industrial expansion of the country. They were also sites for the formation of its immigrant industrial working class, just like Chicago and New York.

Urbanization was part of the redistribution of economic and social resources that marked the industrial revolution. Urbanization, manufacturing growth, and gains in labor productivity moved in tandem; all three increased most rapidly in two decades of unusual prosperity, the 1880s and the first decade of the twentieth century. These decades also included the historic peaks of immigration to the United States. The immigrants of these decades settled disproportionately in American cities, and particularly in cities with rapidly expanding industrial economies—in the New England, mid-Atlantic, and midwestern states. In 1870 America's cities with at least twenty-five thousand residents averaged 34 percent foreign-born, although such cities in the South and West were consistently below this mean figure. The same regional distribution held true in 1910, when the average percentage of foreign-born in all large cities had declined somewhat to 29 percent, but the proportion of the urban population made up of the children of immigrants had increased considerably. Although these children were American-born, they were not yet part of the American mainstream. In the last quarter of the nineteenth century two-thirds or more of the populations of the cities in America's industrial core were composed of immigrants and their children. The fact that these urban immigrants were also overwhelmingly working-class is too frequently overlooked.

Foreign-born men, women, and children set about building a community life for themselves in American cities, and in the process they profoundly shaped the character of urban life. Numerous scholars have studied the formation of these ethnic working-class communities, documenting the strength and diversity of the institutions they created, from the churches, schools, and fraternal orders to singing societies, theater companies, and banks. The immense resources of time, energy, and money put into creating and maintaining these institutions can be understood by looking at any one of the massive churches that still mark the skylines of so many of the residential neighborhoods in America's midwestern industrial cities. The similar efforts of blacks to build urban communities in the North after World War I are too seldom compared to the construction of immigrant neighborhoods and social institutions. The building of black communities on Chicago's South Side and in New York's Harlem, for example, was part of the history of the American working class, as well as a critical chapter in the history of black America.

Before the depression of the 1890s, when the scale of so much American business was smaller, immigrant communities were often complemented by a substantial number of ethnic businesses capable of employing a significant portion of the immigrant work force. In fact, labor conflict often took on an intraethnic character, when German furniture workers struck the shops of German furniture manufacturers, or when east European Jewish workers struck Jewish-owned garment shops. The depression of the 1890s destroyed many ethnically owned businesses, and the corporate reorganization of the economy afterwards absorbed many others into larger corporations owned by native-born Americans. As the power and significance of ethnic businesses declined in the twentieth century, urban immigrant neighborhoods encompassed less of the lives of immigrant workers. The ability of labor organizers to use community pressure against employers declined as well.

Unions and political machines were two important parts of the building of working-class America. Both performed different mediating functions between workers and the larger society. Too often political machines are seen only as manipulators of their foreign-born constituents. In fact, immigrants were able to influence the machines to provide concrete benefits. Through political machines urban workers could have some say in directing public resources to themselves through jobs on public construction projects or through the paving of streets in working-class neighborhoods. The machines, of course, had their cost, and it was not simply

The creation of unions, benefit societies, mechanics institutes, socialist singing societies, and labor parties was part of the larger process of the formation of America's urban working class.

the corruption for which they were famous. Since the machines were the primary political vehicles for urban workers, they usurped a vote that unions, and especially Left political parties, claimed for themselves. Machines were especially sharp competitors for the political left, in part simply because they had integrated workers into American political life before parties of the Left were on the scene. Workers thus felt an allegiance to them, as well as receiving benefits and favors from them. The machines also co-opted working-class leaders with the jobs, money, and power at their disposal.

The creation of unions, benefit societies, mechanics institutes, socialist singing societies, and labor parties was part of this larger process of the formation of America's urban working class. Local unions after the Civil War were frequently analogous to fraternal orders, as well as to the craft associations from which so many derived. The Knights of Labor offer the best illustration of the use of fraternal ritual to build a labor institution. Uriah S. Stephens, the most important leader in the founding of the Knights in 1869, was a native-born Philadelphia tailor. The secret fraternal ritual he advocated helped the organization survive the depression of the 1870s, unlike most labor institutions; the fraternal ritual offered a wider basis for uniting workers of differing nationalities than the cultures of particular crafts.

Fraternalism, however, aroused the opposition of the Catholic church and limited the ability of the Knights to organize openly and effectively amidst the labor unrest of the late 1870s and 1880s. Terence V. Powderly, the son of Irish Catholic immigrants, took over as Grand Master Workman in 1879, ended the secrecy, and opened up the Knights to all working people. An ideology of radical republicanism with deep roots in the American Revolution replaced fraternalism as its unifying culture. The Knights became the most important labor organization of the 1880s by transcending their local and fraternal origins, while at the same time adopting a loose structure based on local and district assemblies that integrated a diverse multitude of local organizations into a larger whole. The Knights' complicated organizational structure sheds light on the tasks facing all labor institutions in the era: they had to draw on local institutions and separate national cultures while transcending their limitations. Yet the weak central authority of the Knights also limited their ability to control their own members and contributed to their demise.

The cigar makers offer a contrasting example. The Cigar Makers' International Union (CMIU) was the power base for Samuel Gompers and helped form the AFL in 1886. The AFL competed with and then supplanted the Knights in the late 1880s and early 1890s. When Gompers arrived in New York as a thirteen year old from London, the local cigar industry was based in small craft shops and dominated by central Europeans, primarily Germans and Bohemians. Gompers made his way as a leader in the cigar makers' union in alliance with Adolph Strasser, a German-speaking Hungarian immigrant. In the midst of the depression of the 1870s, they organized a local union on the basis of high dues, strong benefits, and abolition of special-language sections. They were not only trying to build on solid dues-paying members but also to form an organization to compete with the ethnic and fraternal groups that supplied their members with benefits and social activities. The German and Bohemian ethnic culture of New York's Lower East Side supplied Gompers and Strasser with organizational models, even when they worked to found unions that would compete with ethnic associations.

After a huge cigar makers' strike following the great railroad upheaval of 1877, Gompers and Strasser decided that their local in the CMIU had to have more centralized authority and more discipline, along with its high dues and benefits package, to survive and prosper. By the early 1880s they had achieved these organizational reforms, which provided models for other unions in the AFL. By then their main competitors among the cigar makers' union were immigrant socialists who disliked the limited goals of the union and wanted to appeal to a broader base of workers. Socialists remained a powerful force within the CMIU and the AFL into the twentieth century, despite the triumph of the policies of Gompers and Strasser. The price of the cigar makers' victory, however, was to limit their union to a narrow sector of their own industry. By the turn of the century their union organized primarily the makers of the most expensive cigars, while most workers in the industry, who were increasingly women, made cheap ones. The cigar makers refused to organize the women.

Although the organizational tactics of the CMIU had succeeded in creating a stable union, success cut it off from the vitality of American working-class life, which was deeply rooted in urban, ethnic, working-class neighborhoods, such as the Lower East Side in New York City where Gompers and Strasser had first organized. The strength and creativity of such communities was demonstrated again in 1909 and 1910 when the International Ladies' Garment Workers' Union (ILGWU) organized its industry on the Lower East Side. The industry was for the most part small-scale and immigrant owned, in contrast to the general trend in American industry toward large corporate organization. The ILGWU became one of America's few successful industrial unions, organizing all workers in an industry irrespective of skill. This union was as much a creation of the Jewish and Italian working-class communities on the Lower East Side as of the union movement. Community support helped give the striking garment workers, female and male, Jewish and Italian, a strength that invigorated the ILGWU and made it into one of America's strongest and most militant unions.

There are numerous examples of the strength and creativity of immigrant working-class neighborhoods.

New York City's immigrant enclaves would unite in crises, in opposition to temperance laws, or, for example, in response to such tragedies as the 1911 Triangle Shirtwaist Company fire—a fire that killed almost 150 young female garment workers, most of them Jewish.

Polish communities were the staunchest supporters of several coal strikes in the anthracite mining region of Pennsylvania. Neighborhoods of new immigrants united behind strikers in the Chicago packinghouse strike of 1904. Immigrant communities held out longest in the steel strike of 1919. Yet these local, usually ethnic, sources of support and solidarity also limited the formation of strong centralized labor institutions that could contest with the likes of U.S. Steel. At the same time unions drew on community support but had to compete with ethnic leaders and organizations that divided their members and claimed their resources. This tension between local working-class communities and the labor movement was inherent in the contemporary situation of American workers. The American industrial working class was still centrally engaged in building the local urban communities that would sustain it. The greatest wave of immigration in American history had only ended with the outbreak of World War I. The urbanization of the American working class, and the building of urban working-class communities, were still under way throughout the 1920s.

Shaping American Culture by Becoming Americans

Becoming Americans was the other major project of America's immigrant workers between the 1870s and the 1930s. The traditional image of assimilation pictured a process in which immigrants were acted upon by American society—a process in which they surrendered their original culture and received another one, along with at least a modicum of prosperity. A generation of social historians have struggled to show how assimilation was a two-way process in which accommodations were made on both sides. As they became Americans, immigrants helped redefine who Americans were, even while the dominant society struggled, with mixed success, to impose its definition upon them. The struggle to become American defined the culture of the working class, even when the struggles were not over questions that the labor movement considered critical to the interests of workers. Conflicts over temperance or religion in the schools were central to defining what it meant to be an American worker.

Immigrants—whether old or new—brought with them a variety of local and regional cultures, and usually dialects, which they used to build their communities. The Italian neighborhoods of a large city could encompass within them the folkways of Sicilian peasants and the anarchism of Italian industrial workers. The "little Germanies" of American cities were led by solid and conservative German-American businessmen—brewers, furniture manufacturers, clothing retailers—but they also included socialists exported in the 1880s as a result of Otto von Bismarck's antisocialist laws, and farm laborers from the landed estates east of the Elbe River. These immigrant enclaves could unite in crises, in opposition to temperance laws, for example, or in response to tragedies such as the 1911 fire at the Triangle Shirtwaist Company in New York City. That fire killed almost 150 young female garment workers, most of whom were first or second generation Jewish immigrants. The Triangle Shirtwaist fire galvanized the Lower East Side behind labor legislation in New York

State and was critical in the history of the ILGWU. In such ways these immigrant enclaves helped shape the urban political liberalism of twentieth-century America.

These same enclaves supported within them oppositional subcultures that shaped the way immigrant workers reacted to American industrial society. Peasants-turned-industrial workers not only found the discipline of routinized factory labor alienating—as many historians have documented—but they also brought with them concepts of a "just price" for food that could lead immigrant women to march on grocery stores in opposition to high bread prices. Immigrant socialists and anarchists, radicalized in the old country, founded political parties and radical unions, such as those that opposed Gompers and Strasser in New York City in the 1880s. The Chicago anarchists, made notorious by the Haymarket riot of 1886, represented the largest among several interrelated anarchist communities in American cities. People circulated among them, sometimes with traveling radical theater troupes, and the radical communities were bolstered by new recruits from European repressions. The German anarchists of Chicago were only a memory by the early twentieth century, but Italian anarchists revived the anarchist tradition, and the Sacco and Vanzetti trial of the 1920s showed again how radical politics could frighten the American public into supporting miscarriages of justice.

Before the depression of the 1890s these radical subcultures were sustained by enclaves of immigrant craftsmen in American factories. Still essential to the production process in the Gilded Age, these craftsmen were the workers most likely to regularly attend union meetings, subscribe to labor newspapers, and attend fundraising events, such as picnics. The craftsmen in factories complemented and helped sustain the ethnic enclaves of immigrant working-class communities in American cities. Even if they were not radicals, and most were not, such craftsmen helped create and maintain institutions and cultures that a wide range of native-born Americans considered alien and threatening. The Pledge of Allegiance was first published in a children's magazine in 1892, and school systems around the country rapidly adopted it as part of daily educational routine. Its popularity was stimulated by immigration and labor unrest such as the Pullman strike during America's worst depression until that time. The Pledge was clearly designed to indoctrinate at least the children of immigrants with American values, which too many of their parents apparently lacked. As the immigrant generation fought for its place in American society, it argued that its inherited culture was a legitimate part of America, protected by American constitutional freedoms. Necessity made the immigrants cultural pluralists, while the Pledge of Allegiance tried to integrate their children into a homogeneous political culture.

The children of immigrants are known for abandoning the culture of their parents and adopting American ways, but this is a stereotype that masks a more subtle reality. Members of the second generation enthusiastically adopted a particular segment of American culture—its popular urban variety—that they in turn helped to define, and which the established arbiters of American culture considered "low" and debasing. Herbert Gutman, one of America's premier labor historians, has asked (in *Power and Culture*, p. 387) what it meant for American culture, both popular and elite, when the children of immigrants became the largest group of American workers in the late nineteenth century: "What does the concept of 'assimilation' mean in the context of rapid capitalist development *and* the emergence of new popular urban culture?"

The easiest answer is that second generation immigrants participated in defining the terms of their assimilation by helping create the culture they adopted. They worked to redefine what it meant to be an American so that the new definition would encompass them. The prominence of second generation immigrants in creating popular music is one of the most obvious examples. Tin Pan Alley was dominated by second generation immigrants in twentieth century America. The same could be said of the movie industry. The creation of jazz, one of America's most distinctive art forms, by urban black America can be seen in a similar light. Blacks in the 1920s were engaged in building their own urban working-class communities after the great migration to the North had begun during World War I. Although blacks were not immigrants, they were new arrivals in urban America, and jazz was part of their effort to create black communities there. The cultural flowering of the Harlem Renaissance in the 1920s—a period marked by prohibition and a revival of the Ku Klux Klan—was not only an effort to create a new black culture but also to redefine American culture, to make it wide and supple enough to include black Americans, just as immigrants and their children were trying to define the terms of their assimilation. The results of both endeavors created a vital and powerful popular culture.

Corporate America also had its say about the character of the American working class and popular culture. As business tried to sell the flood of consumer goods it was producing, its sophisticated advertising redefined the American dream to include the availability of a cornucopia of commodities. Intellectuals reacted to the success of this new commercialism with cries against homogenization, but they were only half right. Before the advent of the television networks, the new radio stations in the 1920s were controlled to a surprising extent by local ethnic communities that used them to sustain their own cultures and institutions as well as to advertise the products created by America's second industrial revolution. The Chicago Federation of Labor even had its own station. Yet those who railed against homogenization were correct in seeing how commercialism was defining a new national standard for how Americans should live. This standard may have helped General Electric sell appliances, but it also helped unions argue that their immigrant members were satisfied with too little: Americans lived better than they dared demand. Popular commercial culture also built bonds between working Americans that were not based on ethnicity or craft. Similar bonds were being defined on the job, and a new culture in the workplace also contributed to defining what it meant to be a working-class American in the twentieth century.

Corporate America also systematically changed the process of production and the nature of work within it. New technologies were introduced that made the semi-skilled machine tender the most common type of factory worker, not the unskilled casual laborer. Although the work was routine, it required training and experience; and business discovered that the high rate of employee turnover that typified unskilled labor in the nineteenth century was too costly in the twentieth. Industry also discovered that women made good employees, precisely in such semi-skilled jobs. Women filled whole departments at General Electric and Westinghouse, producing coils for motors or light bulbs. Business showed even more preference for women in low-level white-collar jobs, and occupations such as secretary, bookkeeper, clerk, and telephone operator were almost completely feminized in the 1920s. The proportion of working-age women in the labor force rose from 20.6 percent in 1900 to 24.8 percent in 1930, with the greatest expansion in white-collar jobs. Not until well after World War II would the labor movement address the issues involved in organizing women in the white-collar work force. Women in the factories were harder for labor to avoid.

Scientific management techniques, usually identified with Frederick Winslow Taylor, became popular among businessmen around World War I as solutions to labor control, particularly for semi-skilled workers, whether male or female. Taylor's famous time and motion studies were used to define how tasks should be performed and at what speed. Taylorism also helped undermine the enclaves of craft labor that had been so critical to industrial production, and to the labor movement, in the Gilded Age. Taylorism was not as successful as its advocates had hoped it would be, but it was part of a thorough redefinition of work that made it more homogeneous—and under greater supervision—than it had been before. Both Taylorism and the benefits offered by welfare capitalism were efforts to keep and control semi-skilled workers. Scientific managers set production goals designed to maximize output through rewards to individuals. Workers were supposed to maximize their pay by surpassing their production goals, but they soon learned that the goals increased along with increased output.

Workers in departments informally joined together to limit production in a way that was more tolerable and did not induce higher production quotas. New workers were quickly educated by their fellows about what was expected and what punishments the group could inflict on those who violated workplace norms. A new shop-floor culture developed not based on craft or ethnicity but on workplace solidarities. As business hired more and more women in the 1920s to fill in for the immigrants excluded from the country by the new immigration restriction laws, solidarities among women supplemented the new workplace culture, just as rituals of masculinity played so prominent a place among men on the job. These new solidarities were more inclusive than the old ones of ethnicity and craft. They helped redefine who working-class Americans were, even as the institutions of the labor movement were in retreat.

The 1920s were an end and a beginning in American working-class history. The labor institutions created largely by the old immigrant generation in the Gilded Age and the Progressive Era were defeated or pushed to the periphery of the American economy. These institutions also never met the challenge posed by the entrance of women and blacks into the working class. At the same time, immigrants were rapidly becoming Americans, blacks were becoming urbanites, and women were becoming permanent wage earners. No homogeneous working class emerged from the 1920s, but a new generation of workers did emerge, one that held new ideas about what it meant to be both an American and a worker. These ideas were being shaped by the children and the grandchildren of immigrants, and by blacks from the South. These people were secure enough in their sense of being Americans to want to change American society rather than to build enclaves within it or accommodate themselves to it. Their day would come in the next decade.

[See also Agriculture; The Aristocracy of Inherited Wealth; Business Culture; The City; The Culture of Consumption; Geo-

graphic Mobility; Household Labor; Minorities and Work; The North; Transportation and Mobility; Women and Work.]

BIBLIOGRAPHY

General Works

Bodnar, John. *The Transplanted: A History of Immigrants in Urban America* (1985). Synthesizes contemporary scholarship on immigrants in urban America.

Brownlee, W. Elliot. *Dynamics of Ascent: A History of the American Economy.* 2d ed. (1988). An accessible introduction to American economic history.

Dulles, Foster Rhea, and Melvyn Dubofsky. *Labor in America: A History.* 2d rev. ed. (1984). Focuses on the organized labor movement.

Gordon, David M., Richard Edwards, and Michael Reich. *Segmented Work, Divided Workers: The Historical Transformation of Labor in the United States* (1982). Political economists place labor within the history of class relations and the economy.

Kessler-Harris, Alice. *Out to Work: A History of Wage-earning Women in the United States* (1982).

Montgomery, David. *The Fall of the House of Labor: The Workplace, the State, and American Labor Activism, 1865–1925* (1987). The best labor history of the whole era; interrelates the social, economic, and political dimensions of labor history.

Tomlins, Christopher L. *The State and the Unions: Labor Relations, Law, and the Organized Labor Movement in America, 1880–1960* (1985).

Ward, David. *Cities and Immigrants: A Geography of Change in Nineteenth-Century America* (1971).

Monographs and Essays on Labor History

Barrett, James R. *Work and Community in the Jungle: Chicago's Packinghouse Workers, 1894–1922* (1987). Particularly useful on the relations between the old and new immigrants in a major industry.

Bernstein, Irving. *The Lean Years: A History of the American Worker, 1920–1933* (1960).

Brody, David. *Steelworkers in America: The Nonunion Era* (1960). Good on the new immigrants in an industrial setting.

———. *Workers in Industrial America: Essays on the Twentieth-Century Struggle* (1980). Includes synthetic essays on major periods.

Cohen, Lizabeth. *Making a New Deal: Industrial Workers in Chicago, 1919–1939* (1990). Includes the best social history of workers in the 1920s.

Cooper, Patricia A. *Once a Cigar Maker: Men, Women, and Work Culture in American Cigar Factories, 1900–1919* (1987).

Fink, Leon. *Workingmen's Democracy: The Knights of Labor in American Politics* (1983).

Grossman, James R. *Land of Hope: Chicago, Black Southerners and the Great Migration* (1989).

Gutman, Herbert G. *Work, Culture, and Society in Industrializing America: Essays in American Working-Class and Social History* (1976). Includes essays that have redefined historians' views of Gilded Age America.

———. *Power & Culture: Essays on the American Working Class,* edited by Ira Berlin (1987). Path-breaking essays that complement those in the work cited above.

Hall, Jacquelyn D., et al. *Like a Family: The Making of a Southern Cotton Mill World* (1987). A case study of southern industry that is excellent on the role of women.

Hoerder, Dirk, ed. *"Struggle a Hard Battle": Essays on Working-Class Immigrants* (1986). Treats immigrant workers active in the labor movement by ethnic group.

Kaufman, Stuart Bruce. *Samuel Gompers and the Origins of the American Federation of Labor, 1848–1896* (1973).

Keil, Hartmut, and John B. Jentz. *German Workers in Chicago: A Documentary History of Working-Class Culture from 1850 to World War I* (1988). Translated documents illustrating the history of an immigrant working-class group, primarily in the Gilded Age.

Laslett, John H. M. *Labor and the Left: A Study of Socialist and Radical Influences in the American Labor Movement, 1881–1924* (1970).

Montgomery, David. *Workers' Control in America: Studies in the History of Work, Technology, and Labor Struggles* (1979). Includes essays that have shaped subsequent discussion about culture and politics in the workplace.

Moody, J. Carroll, and Alice Kessler-Harris. *Perspectives on American Labor History: The Problem of Synthesis* (1989). An introduction to the debate among labor historians about interpreting recent research in their field and linking it to other developments in American history.

Nelson, Bruce C. *Beyond the Martyrs: A Social History of Chicago's Anarchists, 1870–1900* (1988). Analyzes an oppositional labor subculture in Chicago.

Oestreicher, Richard Jules. *Solidarity and Fragmentation: Working People and Class Consciousness in Detroit, 1875–1900* (1986). Defines the idea of oppositional labor subculture and analyzes the phenomenon in Detroit.

Salvatore, Nick. *Eugene V. Debs: Citizen and Socialist* (1982). The best biography of America's most important socialist.

Schatz, Ronald W. *The Electrical Workers: A History of Labor at General Electric and Westinghouse, 1923–1960* (1983). An excellent study on workplace culture in the 1920s.

Schneirov, Richard, and Thomas J. Suhrbur. *Union Brotherhood, Union Town: The History of the Carpenters' Union of Chicago, 1863–1987* (1988). A social history of a local union movement, particularly strong on the interrelation of ethnic and class issues.

Shergold, Peter R. *Working-Class Life: The "American Standard" in Comparative Perspective, 1899–1913* (1982). A quantitative analysis of the living standards of workers in the United States and Great Britain.

Zunz, Olivier. *The Changing Face of Inequality: Urbanization, Industrial Development, and Immigrants in Detroit, 1880–1920* (1982). A social and urban history strong on the changing dimensions of class and ethnicity.

— JOHN B. JENTZ

LABOR: THE GREAT DEPRESSION TO THE 1990S

The six decades between 1930 and 1990 dramatically affected the lives of American workers in ways that varied according to race, ethnicity, gender, region, and occupation. Americans have had to redefine the nature and meaning of their work over this period in response to changing economic conditions, often outside their control. Despite numerous redefinitions, however, the primacy of work in American society has remained constant. As Robert and Helen Lynd wrote in their classic study of Muncie, Indiana, in 1935, "One's job is the watershed down which the rest of one's life tends to flow." During this period of labor history, community-based groups of workers united by race, ethnicity, and region, became a fragmented work force, identifying less with each other, and more as individuals living and working within a mass consumer culture.

Wearing collars of different hues—blue, white or pink—workers have tried to direct their work lives, individually and collectively throughout the period. Vying for control with a powerful corporate elite, Americans, whether members of trade unions or not, came to expect the federal government to be responsible for protecting their rights as employees. During the Great Depression, when workers exerted a new level of political power, protesting their conditions in ways that captured the attention of both government and business, protection came from the labor legislation of the New Deal. As the New Deal era gave way to war-generated prosperity, a growing numbers of Americans in the United States saw themselves as part of a labor force that shared a common work ethic, a political ideology grounded in freedom and individualism, and the promise of economic prosperity reflected in a high standard of living. As the nation's economic dominance waned in the 1970s, workers became more vulnerable to control by corporations. By the 1990s, wages were on the decline, jobs were scarce, the government was endorsing an antilabor platform, and economic security eluded a steadily increasing percentage of the labor force.

The Great Depression and the New Deal

Campaigning for the presidency in the autumn of 1928, Herbert Hoover proclaimed: "We are nearer today to the ideal of the abolition of poverty and fear from the lives of men and women than ever before in any land." One year later, the stock market came crashing down with ruinous effect, making a mockery of Hoover's words. Within three weeks, beginning in late October 1929, a total of $30 billion in paper value was lost in the collapse of the market and credit structure. The depression that followed devastated the nation, sowing poverty and despair.

Hoover's optimism, as misplaced as it appears in retrospect, was grounded in the growth of the nation's economy in the 1920s, years that witnessed record production levels. The steel, rubber, and glass industries boomed as Americans built new homes and purchased automobiles, small appliances, refrigerators, and telephones. High protective tariffs increased the demand for domestic goods over expensive imports, but despite sharp increases in production by American factories, the percentage of the U.S. labor force that was engaged in agriculture, mining, and manufacturing fell from 58 to 47 percent by 1930. Automation, heralded by corporations and scorned by workers, was taking its toll. The greatest increases in employment occurred in the white-collar sectors: clerical and service-industry jobs multiplied dramatically. Many of these new positions were filled by women, who made up a quarter of the nation's work force by 1930. Female employment grew by more than 27 percent during the decade (from 8.5 million in 1920 to 10.7 million by 1930). The flood of immigrant workers entering the country between 1890 and 1920 slowed to a trickle after restrictive quotas, the result of laws passed in 1921 and 1924, sharply curtailed entry. While African Americans continued their migration from southern farms to northern cities, racial and gender discrimination forged a segmented labor market.

Real wages, which had remained virtually constant from 1890 to 1915, increased by 40 percent from the beginning of World War I to 1929. But the bulk of this jump had occurred by 1923. When compared to the enormous increase in production, real wages had not kept pace. As the 1920s drew to a close, production was growing at a far greater pace than real wages, and overproduction plagued industries like textiles, garments, and small appliances. By 1929, unsold goods accumulated on stockroom shelves across the nation. Unemployment, which had generally remained below 5 percent of the work force throughout most of the decade, rose; by 1930 the figure had climbed to 8.9 percent.

In an economic climate newly dependent on consumer buying, unskilled and semi-skilled American workers found themselves easily replaceable and their job security more and more tenuous. After a record number of strikes in the years immediately following World War I, the 1920s witnessed a period of relative quiescence. This was not the result of contentment. The problems that had fostered labor unrest after the war remained. Union membership fell over the course of the 1920s, the American Federation of Labor (AFL) dropping from about 5 million members in 1919 to about 3 million in 1933. Industries that had burgeoned during the decade—auto, steel, electrical, glass—remained almost completely unorganized. Workers had few benefits, no means for voicing grievances, and no protection against unemployment. The once-militant United Mine Workers Union was quieted to an echo of labor's victories past. The industrial work force, divided along occupational, regional, racial, gender, and ethnic lines, could not speak in one voice. Dominated by white male craftworkers, the AFL could not command, and in fact shunned, this new industrial labor force.

At this point, the worst economic collapse in American history brought the economy to its knees. By the fall of 1930, unemployment had risen to 15 percent; it would hit almost 25 percent by 1933. Many workers saw their wages and/or hours cut. Each round of cuts diminished the nation's buying power and set off another round of cuts. Apple sellers and breadlines became the symbols of economic hard times. Many of the twelve million workers unemployed in 1932 hit the road, abandoning families and loved ones, but most stayed put. For many, the Depression forced a reliance on family. In an effort to weather the storm together, the most recent immigrants, especially those of southern and eastern European stock, drew on the same support systems they had used to sustain themselves when they first came to America.

Public relief was quickly overwhelmed by the severity of the situation. Hoover's philosophy of "rugged individualism" put the burden of assistance on state, and especially, local governments. The social consequences of this sharp economic downturn were widespread: malnutrition, high rates of infant mortality, increased rates of alcoholism and petty crime. Marriage and birthrates plunged as a generation of young Americans waited for prosperity to return.

In a society that stressed the values of hard work and thrift, many blamed themselves for being out of work. Others responded in angry protests against rapidly declining economic conditions. The Communist party organized Unemployed Councils in many major cities, staging protests and demonstrations. The "Ford Hunger March" in Dearborn, Michigan, in 1932 became the most infamous of these, when riots left four dead and dozens injured. Throughout the nation workers gathered for spontaneous anti-eviction protests and relief riots as demands for government intervention reached a frenzied pitch. Radicals hoped for the anticipated mass movement, but as the Depression worsened, none developed.

The single most dramatic mass political action came at the polls on 8 November 1932 when Hoover and the Republicans were soundly repudiated by working-class voters. Franklin Delano Roosevelt won the election by a landslide, winning all but seven states—not so much due to an articulated ideology or program, but more because Americans felt abandoned by Hoover. In the four "lame duck" months between FDR's election and inauguration the economy grew even worse: unemployment in industrial cities like Pittsburgh and Birmingham, Alabama reached 50 percent. Bank failures became commonplace, and breadlines and soup kitchens multiplied. Fear gripped American workers, those still employed, and those searching for a job.

The economic crisis reached its low watermark on Inauguration Day, March 1933 with a nationwide bank panic. President Roosevelt met it with the now-famous phrase from his inaugural address, "the only thing we have to fear is fear itself." He then proceeded to demand and be given unprecedented powers to change the monetary system and to create an army of federal agencies, which provided jobs for millions on government-sponsored projects. The New Deal president infused Americans with new hope. Banks had been failing at the rate of 921 per year since 1921. Nine days after his inauguration, and the Monday after the first of his Sunday evening "fireside chats" over the radio to the American people, banks across the country began to reopen. Over 75 percent of all banks were operating again by the end of March.

The Roosevelt administration also pushed for regulation of private industry, and on 16 June 1933, Congress passed the National Industrial Recovery Act, which established codes of fair competition to stabilize business and created the National Recovery Administration (NRA). Section 7a of the legislation guaranteed workers the right "to organize and bargain collectively through representatives of their own choosing," thereby advancing the legitimacy of unions. By linking the popularity of FDR to unionization, labor leaders counteracted the notion that unions represented radical, foreign ideologies, and urged workers to sign on with the slogan, "the President wants you to join the union." In reality, neither Roosevelt nor NRA head Hugh S. Johnson were pro-union. Nonetheless, Section 7a provided badly needed support for the labor movement in its darkest days. After Congress legalized collective bargaining, workers responded to union drives with unprecedented enthusiasm.

Banks had been failing at the rate of 921 per year since 1921, but nine days after Franklin Delano Roosevelt's first inauguration, banks across the country began to reopen, and by the end of March 1933 over 74 percent of America's banks were operating again.

That summer of 1933 the United Mine Workers (UMW), with John L. Lewis at the helm, launched a massive campaign among coal miners with great success. In the needle trades both the International Ladies Garment Workers Union (ILGWU) headed by David

Dubinsky and the Amalgamated Clothing Workers Union (ACWU) under Sidney Hillman also staged major recruiting drives. AFL unions signed on workers in industries as diverse as fruit picking and stage acting, claiming two million new members by 1934. These gains within the ranks of the AFL had the conflicting effects of strengthening the Federation while creating dissension within the organization. Significantly, many of the new members recruited after 1933 were in jobs classified as either semi-skilled or unskilled; thousands were women; many belonged to ethnic or racial minorities. This suddenly diverse membership actively challenged how the AFL was run, raised questions about the power held by the leadership, and advocated organizing workers on an industrywide basis without regard to trade, skill, or job classification.

At the AFL's 1935 convention, Lewis led the charge, fighting for more vigorous unionization of the mass-production industries. The AFL leadership, with William Green as president, resisted reform. The following month, on 9 November 1935, Lewis, together with Dubinsky, Hillman, and Charles Howard of the International Typographical Union (ITU), and four presidents of small AFL affiliates, formed the Committee for Industrial Organization (CIO). (In 1938 this CIO became the Congress of Industrial Organizations, also the CIO.) Green condemned the mavericks, but compromise was not in his repertoire. Once set in motion, the CIO approach to unionism could not be stopped.

Throughout the nation, workers in mass-production industries joined the CIO by the thousands. Steel, rubber, and auto workers who long had been ignored by the craft-oriented unionists in the AFL, flocked into newly organized locals from Pennsylvania to Georgia to Illinois. The CIO also broke new political ground in 1936 by making substantial contributions to FDR's reelection campaign. CIO-Political Action Committees helped the Democratic landslide that November, returning FDR to the White House, with the largest presidential vote cast up to that time. Scores of prolabor candidates also won federal, state and local offices.

The CIO victories continued into 1937 with an epic confrontation in Flint, Michigan, where the United Auto Workers sustained the first major sit-down strike: for several weeks they controlled Fisher Body Plant No. 2, turning back police, and facing down the National Guard to finally win recognition from General Motors on February 3. Autoworker solidarity was fueled by the Woman's Emergency Brigade, which marched outside the plants and got provisions through the police blockades to the strikers inside. Local citizens helped, and music composed and sung by strikers kept up morale. Victory over the corporate giant GM emboldened workers in other industries. For example, later in the same year, after months of Steel Worker Organizing Committee (SWOC) organizing in mills, U.S. Steel finally came to terms with the labor union. Victories in the auto and steel industries encouraged workers in industries and trades of all types to don CIO buttons and carry membership cards. By the end of 1937 over 200,000 had joined the UAW and over 300,000 came into the SWOC.

Industrial unionism gave workers new power in shops and plants across the nation. Voicing grievances, organizing nonunion workers, utilizing labor's political clout, unionism transformed the meaning of American labor. The CIO, unlike the AFL, was eager to recruit black workers. CIO leaders knew that success in many industries required across-the-industry organization. To this end they organized the kill floors of Chicago's meatpacking industry, the coke ovens in steel, the foundries in metalworking, all workplaces with large numbers of African American workers. CIO organizers stressed the importance of organizing black workers and sold the idea to white workers reluctant to belong to an interracial union by appealing to their pragmatism: bringing black workers into the union reduced the chance of their being used as strikebreakers. Many in the CIO endorsed the political left and the interracial ideology of socialists and communists. The CIO was willing to use political radicals, many of whom were experienced organizers whose expertise in the field was unparalleled. This made the CIO susceptible to the red-baiting that would plague it in the decade after 1938.

Workers in the 1930s militated against corporate giants in the nation's largest industries, and labor used its power as an effective political tool. Overall in the depressed 1930s, union membership tripled, growing from over 3 million in 1932 to almost 9 million in 1939. There were setbacks—Ford Motor Company remained unorganized, Little Steel proved elusive, and few government employees and other white-collar workers in the expanding clerical sector were organized. Nevertheless, the unparalleled success of industrial unionism permanently changed the American labor movement and the self-image of American workers. The idea of membership open to all workers, without regard to race, gender, or occupation, theoretically, although not always in practice, meant that workers, organized and unorganized, could see themselves moving from the margins of society into the economic and social mainstream of American life.

The New Deal played a decisive role in labor's ascendancy, creating a climate that protected workers' rights and encouraged union organization. The government's role worried many labor leaders who began to see the fate of labor tied too closely to Roosevelt's administration, federal legislation, and generally, forces outside their control. This concern intensified as the administration shifted its focus away from a singular emphasis on economic recovery toward preparation for war.

Returning Prosperity: The War Years

American war production began more than two years prior to the U.S. declaration of war. President Roosevelt started off the year of 1939 by recommending a $535 million defense program. Both Congress's authorization for rearmament and the demands for munitions by European countries at war with the Axis powers brought prosperity and growth to American manufacturers and industries. In the wake of this boom, unions continued to organize workers and push for higher wages, resulting in thousands of work stoppages between 1939 and 1941. Labor's effort to secure its share of the long-awaited economic recovery, recovery that New Deal programs had not fully accomplished, caused the government to prod the AFL and CIO unions to sign no-strike pledges once the nation entered the war.

In 1941, 2.3 million workers—70 percent of them CIO unionists—took part in over 4,200 work stoppages. Though less militant than earlier ones, this strike wave ranked among the most decisive in American labor history. One-and-a-half million American workers joined the union ranks between June 1940 and December 1941. Strong in numbers, unions were also now able to present a "solid front" in such industries as steel and autos, and that strengthened their hand in wage negotiations and contract provisions for favorable grievance procedures, benefits, seniority rights, and work rules. Protracted labor struggles threatened production timetables, so while the nation rushed to war overseas, employers sought to keep peace at home in order to win lucrative government and military contracts. The fervency of management's desire for prompt completion fed both the rapid growth of unions and the success of strikes during this relatively short period. Eventually, after the Japanese bombing of Pearl Harbor on 7 December 1941 catalyzed the nation to join the Allies, the AFL and CIO officially agreed to submit labor disputes to a federal mediation board, rather than to strike, for the duration of the war.

Meanwhile, successful labor organization intensified the battles between the AFL and CIO, and heated up the race to organize workers in the electrical, aircraft, paper, textiles, food-processing, and woodworking industries. Millions of Americans joined the armed forces, and unemployment, at record levels in the 1930s, finally diminished in the boom of industrial production. The influx of new workers into industry to replace men entering military service boosted union membership. To meet the increased demand for war materials, women became a larger portion of the work force, entering industrial production jobs previously held by men.

By 1945, nineteen million female laborers were part of a civilian work force of fifty-four million. Many of these women had been working before the war, but after 1940, as more industrial jobs became available, they moved from lower-paying positions, usually in the service or clerical sectors, into newly available higher paying industrial jobs. As the nation depended increasingly on women's labor, the government launched a media campaign in newspapers, magazines, and newsreels, urging women to serve their country as part of the "industrial army." These bulletins and advertisements always presumed the temporary nature of women's war work, stating pointedly that industrial jobs were really "men's work" to be filled by women only "for the duration." Millions of American women took advantage of the demand for their labor, moving into higher paying and full-time jobs, seeking specialized training to improve their chances of permanent industrial employment. Women comprised two-thirds of the twelve million workers who entered the labor force during the war; the majority of these women had been unemployed or under-employed prior to the war.

American women quickly proved themselves. They performed wartime jobs with all the diligence of their male counterparts and achieved the same levels of production and quality. Yet they were routinely paid less for the same work. Government directives opposed differential pay, but employers frequently manipulated job descriptions to suit their own ends to the disadvantage of female employees. Although female union membership increased dramatically during World War II, labor leaders were not really supportive either. In 1943, UAW president R. J. Thomas called differential wages for female workers "a women's problem." Unions, like governmental officials, the media, and most employers,

> *After 1940, women moved from lower-paying positions in the service or clerical sectors into newly available and higher-paying industrial jobs; by 1945, nineteen million female laborers were part of a civil work force of fifty-four million.*

considered women a temporary addition to the work force.

By the war's end, the government was waging a new propaganda campaign, this time one designed to get women out of the work force. Women industrial workers were reminded that they were "taking a man's place," and that he was about to return home having sacrificed for his country. Even though women held jobs across the traditional sexual division of labor, their entry into the job market during the war years was viewed by many as simply an extension of woman's role as helpmate. Regarded this way, their employment posed no threat to traditional gender roles. Meanwhile, government and industry turned a blind eye toward women's domestic responsibilities during the war, ignoring the crucial issues of adequate day care for children, and the increased burden of home and family duties borne by working women whose husbands, fathers, and brothers were overseas. Suddenly, women were being chastised, told that they were needed at home. Some government officials even implied that women workers were responsible for a perceived rise in juvenile delinquency. Increasingly, advertisements showed wives in the kitchen preparing meals for husbands returning home after a long day at work.

The notion that if women left the workplace men could have jobs did not match the reality of the immediate postwar economy in which manufacturing positions were being eliminated. With nine million servicemen returning from overseas, government officials feared another recession and consequently endorsed policies designed to avoid high unemployment. The G.I. Bill, for example, encouraged returning soldiers to go to school as a means of augmenting future employment prospects, rather than to look for a job immediately. Some industries reimposed Depression-era restrictions that had been lifted during the war, and once again mandated maximum age limits for female employees and the ban against hiring married women. Indeed, women lost their jobs at a rate 75 percent greater than that of their male counterparts. Even more significantly, as Ruth Milkman argues, the female-employment pattern set at that time established the paradigm for women's work that would continue for many decades after the war.

World War II also provided industrial opportunities for blacks as well as for white women, and they too fought against constant discrimination in the workplace. During the Depression, 50 percent of skilled blacks lost their jobs between 1930 and 1936. Even when the war upped the demand for workers, blacks were largely excluded from skilled jobs in the defense industry. Labor-starved plants in Connecticut, Maryland, and California imported whites from other parts of the country rather than hire local blacks for even unskilled work. The situation for African Americans grew so grim, with employers making public pronouncements they would consider blacks only for menial jobs, that A. Philip Randolph, president of the Brotherhood of Sleeping Car Porters, threatened President Roosevelt with a march of fifty thousand blacks on Washington, D.C., in 1941. When African Americans were first upgraded to skilled jobs in the auto industry, there were many wildcat strikes in defiance of union leaders and management alike. The worst eruption came after the influx of 300,000 southern whites and blacks into the area surrounding Detroit's war plants. Race riots exploded on 20 June 1941, with thirty-five killed and six hundred wounded, mostly blacks. At the end of two days, police had arrested fifteen hundred people; among them, less than three hundred were white.

The Detroit race riots, along with Randolph's threat, moved Roosevelt to ban employment discrimination by companies filing defense contracts, and later to create the Fair Employment Practices Commission (originally established as the Fair Employment Practice Committee on 25 June 1941) in order to enforce his executive order.

The percentage of black males in skilled jobs nearly doubled from 4.4 in 1940 to 7.3 in 1944, as they experienced more diversification in employment than they had in the previous seventy-five years. The number of black government employees, fifty thousand in 1937, had quadrupled by 1946. Nonetheless, as with women workers, the ideal and the reality of equality were two very different things. Blacks' greatest economic gains came between 1940 and 1950 as a result of world conflict, but the war at home of racial tensions flared, too. In many plants, whites refused to stay on the job with blacks, sometimes staging "hate" strikes. Many unions, including independent railroad brotherhoods, the International Association of Machinists, and the Boilermakers, continued to discriminate severely against black members or to bar them entirely. At war's end 95 percent of all professional jobs were held by whites.

Still, some gains were made. The median annual income for black full-time workers rose 45 percent between 1939 and 1955 (it rose 57 percent for white workers during the same period). Migrating north to escape marginal labor as sharecroppers and domestics, thousands of blacks settled in northern cities with available war production jobs. African Americans entered workplaces where there had been few if any minority employees previously. Industries organized by the CIO showed the greatest advances, if only because black workers had been virtually unheard of in these work forces before. In any case, black employment rose especially in steel, metals, and meat-packing, as well as in midwestern auto plants producing military vehicles, in California aircraft companies, and in shipbuilding southeastern coastal towns such as Norfolk and Newport News.

Full employment during the war years helped white women and African Americans in gaining better-paid manufacturing jobs which in turn enabled them to provide for their families and save for the future. Yet despite these new opportunities and higher wages, each year of war brought an increase in strikes: in 1942 there were 2,968 work stoppages involving 840,000 workers; in 1943 walkouts jumped to over 3,700 and involved almost 2 million workers, an upsurge due largely to a half-million UMW soft-coal miners walking off the job. In 1944, living costs rose nearly one-third, and by 1945 many of the nearly 3.5 million striking workers took action spontaneously in walkouts staged without the authority of union leadership. Wildcat strikes were only a gross measure of widespread worker discontent. Hiring novice workers, work speedups, fatigue from extended shifts, and unfamiliar machinery resulted in a marked increase in industrial accidents. Casualties from the war were both on the front lines and the production lines. The industrial army, just as soldiers in the war zones of Europe and Asia, grew weary of fighting. Rumors of massive wartime profits accruing to industrialists and entrepreneurs frustrated workers who were struggling to meet production on the shop floor. The high hourly wages so attractive to Depression-ravaged workers in 1939 and 1940 began to lose their appeal as wartime inflation, industrial accidents, and regular double shifts spent away from home and family made workers resentful and uneasy.

Migrating north to escape marginal labor as sharecroppers and domestics, thousands of blacks settled in northern cities with available war production jobs; thus African Americans entered workplaces where previously there had been few, if any, minority employees.

World War II was a major turning point in the history of American labor. Industrial workers, women, and African Americans gained some autonomy and power, foreshadowing major changes through the civil rights and women's liberation movements of the postwar era. But before those movements gained momentum in the 1950s and 1960s, the work force demobilized and in the process two things happened: white male workers, many of them war veterans, reestablished their hegemony over the workplace, and U.S. corporations, no longer hampered by full-employment levels, reasserted their control over American workers.

Labor in the Postwar Era

World War II gave new strength to American workers and to the labor movement. At war's end in 1945, more Americans than ever before had money in their pockets and a list of material goods they wanted to purchase. Industries converted as quickly as possible from war production to goods for personal consumption. The nation focused its attention on domestic issues. Concerns about jobs, wages, home, and family dominated the agendas of most American workers. Many feared another depression as returning servicemen flooded the job market and millions of workers looked to the labor movement for security and protection.

By 1945, union membership rose to an all-time high of almost fifteen million workers organized, over 35 percent of the nonagricultural labor force. The AFL maintained its dominance as the larger of the two federations with over 10 million members. Although relatively smaller with its 4.5 million members, the CIO controlled core industries such as auto and steel. After the war both the AFL and CIO had difficulty keeping their membership from participating in widespread strikes. In fact, 1946 was the most strike-ridden year in American history. Striking workers were no longer concerned about obtaining the right to collectively bargain under the union banner or about the existence of unions. Postwar workers walked out to protest layoffs and shortened hours.

Labor leaders, emboldened by the movement's new power, spoke up for more control over the industrial process, while industrialists attempted to reassert their authority in the workplace where they believed management had conceded too much control to workers in order to meet high production quotas during the war years. Union contracts negotiated in the war's immediate aftermath presaged the increasing control industry would exert in the succeeding decade. Some unions accepted the responsibility of disciplining members who defied contract agreements; many others, given little choice, bowed to terms set by employers seeking to circumscribe union power and contain the labor movement's role in industrial decision-making.

The limits of organized labor's power were further diminished by the Taft-Hartley Act. Impatient with the rash of strikes, a Republican-controlled Congress passed the law on 23 June 1947 over President Truman's veto. Revising the National Labor Relations Act (also known as the Wagner Act) of 1935, the Taft-Hartley Act established "unfair" labor practices, including secondary boycotts, jurisdictional strikes, refusal to bargain in good faith, and contributing to political campaigns. In addition, Taft-Hartley banned the closed shop, thereby allowing employers to hire nonunion workers. The law required newly hired workers to join the union in union shops, but it also permitted states to enact "right to work laws" that outlawed union shops. Taft-Hartley also required union leaders to sign affidavits stating that they were not Communists. It also changed the National Labor Relations Board (NLRB) from an advocate for labor into a neutral intermediary. Employers discovered they could drain a union's financial resources by engaging in lengthy NLRB proceedings.

United Mine Workers leader John L. Lewis and CIO and U.S. Steel Workers of America president Philip Murray refused to sign the anticommunist affidavits; but most union leaders could not afford to risk losing access to the NLRB by not signing. To combat Taft-Hartley, both the AFL and the CIO vigorously campaigned to elect a prolabor Congress. While during the 1930s and early 1940s some unionists envisioned a prolabor third party, by the late 1940s labor most often supported the Democratic party. In the 1948 election workers' votes and dollars returned Truman to the White House and restored a Democratic majority to both houses of Congress. Such effort brought limited benefits, however, for the new Congress failed even to revise the Taft-Hartley Act, let alone repeal it.

The reformist approach to politics that typified union political activity during the late 1940s was buttressed by the expulsion of a number of Communists from the CIO. Even though the Soviet Union had been an ally during World War II, American foreign policy became doggedly anti-Soviet, and suspicion about labor leaders and unions sympathetic to the left intensified. Red-baiting within unions resulted in the purging of radicals and the tempering of activism. More and more, labor leaders acquiesced to the general principles of capitalism, following the dictates of industrialists and the two-party political system. By 1950, although unions had established themselves as a fixture within the American political and economic system, their role in providing a counterbalance to industrial power was severely diminished.

For both organized and nonunion workers, the 1950s and 1960s were decades of seeming affluence. Real wages grew at an unprecedented pace. At first glance working men and women had joined the nation's burgeoning middle class. Enjoying the material benefits of postwar prosperity, more American families than ever before owned their own homes—60 percent by 1960. Working-class families sought their share of the American dream in the suburbs, moving from older neighborhoods in large industrial cities. The blue-collar work force was being assimilated into middle-class life; class distinctions, some said, were becoming blurred. Indeed, by 1956 white-collar workers had for the first time in United States history outnumbered blue-collar Americans—the first indicator that the nation was moving from an industrial to postindustrial economy.

During these years collective bargaining proved a potent tool for advancing wages for both white and black union members. Despite inflation, real earnings increased over 40 percent from the late 1940s through the 1960s. Union workers began to secure cost-of-living adjustments in their contracts, and automatic annual increases tied to rising productivity. Yet, workers failed to secure protection of their income against unexpected fluctuations in the economy. Employers successfully resisted the worker-management planning that many laborites advocated. Granted, unemployment compensation cushioned the blow of layoffs for many, but few enjoyed the kind of security won by UAW workers: supplementary employment benefits that, combined with government benefits, could provide up to 95 percent of an employee's weekly wages. Even under the UAW-negotiated provisions, supplementary unemployment benefits were paid only so long as the union's funds were solvent. As beneficial as these plans were, they did not engage the unions in production-planning.

In the 1950s and 1960s, in addition to bargaining for higher wages, workers sought "fringe" benefits. Pensions, health care, group insurance, vacations, and the like figured more prominently in the packages negotiated between labor and management. This created a mixed system of benefits with some—health care, for example—provided by industry, and others, such as social security, by the government. Forced to include these items in union contracts, many employers reversed their position on government spending for social security. In their minds, it was better for the government to pay the bill than the corporation. Critics noted that control of pension funds for investment was left in the hands of employers, not workers. These arrangements shifted labor-generated funds out of the hands of workers into the control of the banking establishment, in effect endorsing and buttressing the priorities of finance capitalism.

Some unions did direct their own pension funds and a few invested in cooperative housing projects, worker-managed industrial ventures, or other forms of innovative social investment. Others, the International Brotherhood of Teamsters under president James R. (Jimmy) Hoffa, for example, used pension funds in a number of highly questionable ventures. Benefit packages negotiated by unions also had the effect of accentuating the rift between the stronger unions in core industries, such as steel and auto, and those in the service sector and light manufacturing.

Nonunion workers often received improved wages and benefits as a result of successful collective bargaining by unionized workers within an industry. Keeping step with the unions was one way an employer could hope to remain free of unionization. Yet, although both unionized and unorganized workers made considerable gains in wages and other benefits as a result of collective bargaining, labor still had not gained entry into managerial decision-making. Workers sometimes did attempt to exert such control through slowdowns, wildcat strikes, and similar strategies. But overall, management maintained and even solidified its authority over production decision-making in the two decades after 1945.

The 1960s and 1970s: Years of Change and Reaction

During the 1930s the labor movement seemed to hold the potential for a profound transformation of American society. Militant workers called for radical changes in the political and economic system. During the 1960s, however, the majority of unions stayed away from the protest front. Taking labor's place on the front lines, the civil rights, antiwar, and women's liberation movements called for a reordering of social and economic priorities. To be sure, the boycotts against grapes, iceberg lettuce, and Gallo wines led by Cesar Chavez on behalf of Hispanic farm workers in California played a part in the protests of the 1960s. But generally, American workers did not support those demanding fundamental change. While many members of the Old Left were laborites advancing the cause of workers under the banner of the CIO, members of the New Left were seldom associated with unions. In fact, the long-standing support of American foreign policy by the AFL and CIO positioned them as but another facet of the American establishment, especially during the Vietnam War.

For example, George Meany, president of the AFL-CIO (which merged in 1955), publicly supported the war policy of the administration of President Lyndon B. Johnson, and criticized those unionists who argued against the war. At the 1967 AFL-CIO national convention, an antiwar resolution was defeated by a vote of

Apart from the Cesar Chavez-led boycotts against iceberg lettuce in California, American workers did not support fundamental change in the 1960s.

two thousand to six! And in 1972, the AFL-CIO's Executive Council refused to endorse Democratic candidate George McGovern for president because of his antiwar position, despite his prolabor record in Congress.

With respect to issues of race, too, the AFL-CIO failed to meet the challenges of the times. Only one African American, A. Philip Randolph, served on the twenty-seven member executive council even though 25 percent of the AFL-CIO's membership was black. In 1960 the Negro American Labor Council was formed to promote the interests of blacks in the unions. Although the AFL-CIO had long supported civil rights legislation, the leadership seemed unresponsive to blacks' demands for greater representation in leadership positions, and access to skilled jobs. Even in a traditionally progressive union like the UAW where African Americans comprised one-third of the membership, they held few leadership positions. Young militant blacks in a number of the auto plants in Detroit formed radical organizations to promote their interests, and while this movement was short-lived, involving only a small core within the UAW, it reflected a deep and widespread discontent.

For all African Americans there were both signs of gains and reasons for concern. Opportunities in public employment and federal benefits had improved family income for blacks from about 40 percent of that of whites in 1940 to over 64 percent in 1970. During the 1960s, as employment opportunities improved in the clerical sector and the computer and aerospace industries, the centers of employment shifted away from industrial urban areas, leaving many black workers isolated in urban ghettos. Poor educational opportunities kept blacks from obtaining the requisite training in new technologies. Even in the unions, where black workers had made great strides, continued occupational segregation kept black employees in lower grade jobs. Even the Equal Employment Opportunity Commission (EEOC), created to investigate complaints under the antibias mandate of Title VII of the Civil Rights Act of 1964, helped little, due to inadequate funding and slow procedures.

Meanwhile, women workers entered the labor force in unprecedented numbers. Passage of the Equal Pay Act (1963), Title VII of the Civil Rights Act (1964), and Executive Order 11246 (1964) led women to reassess their roles in the workplace and in their unions. The UAW's Women's Department and the Education and Social Action Department of the International Union of Electrical Workers (IUE) led the way by endorsing the elimination of discriminatory state laws, advocating job protection during maternity leaves as well as the establishment of child-care facilities. Workers' education programs in New York and Michigan began to offer seminars for union women, staff, leaders, and rank-and-file workers. Union women organized conferences to address issues of concern to female workers across the country: improving job conditions, gaining equal opportunity under the law, and increasing participation by women in their unions.

Female employment was a key factor in the material success of the American working class during the relatively affluent decades of the 1950s and 1960s. The twenty years between 1950 and 1970 witnessed unparalleled growth in the percentages of women in the work force—from roughly 31 percent in 1950 to 43 percent in 1970. During the entire half century from 1900–1950 it had increased only 10 percent. Significantly, the greatest increase occurred among married women. In 1940 only one out of seven married women worked outside the home; in 1950 this figure was one out of five, and by 1970 two out of five. Clearly, the prosperity and higher standard of living enjoyed by American workers was purchased in part with the wages of women.

In the postwar decades women were heavily recruited into the burgeoning service, clerical, and government employment, which comprised half the labor force by 1950. At the same time, mechanization in mining, agriculture, and factories kept the number of jobs relatively stable though production levels skyrocketed. The number of employees in mining and agriculture actually declined, from over 25 percent of the work force in 1940 to about 5 percent by 1970. For those remaining on the job, mechanization made the work ever more dull and monotonous. Whether on the assembly line or in the office, work failed to provide a sense of personal fulfillment. In the white-collar sector, the largest increase in positions was in sales and clerical work, jobs offering relatively low pay and little or no opportunity for autonomy or advancement.

Female employment was a key factor in the material success of the American working class during the relatively affluent 1950s and 1960s: The twenty years between 1950 and 1970 witnessed unparalleled growth in the percentages of women in the work force.

These changes in the work force had little effect on the distribution of wealth. In both 1950 and 1970, the top fifth of the population enjoyed over 40 percent of the nation's income while the bottom fifth received less than 5 percent. In 1970 a full 60 percent of American workers and their families fell below the U.S. Bureau of Labor Statistics own line for an "intermediate" standard of living ($10,700 in 1970).

In the early 1970s, women established two new organizations designed to improve the status of female employees. In 1973 the National Association of Working Women (known as Nine to Five) was formed to organize clerical workers, and six months later, the Coalition of Labor Union Women (CLUW). The latter, an umbrella organization of union women, explicitly sought to increase the number of women in trade-union leadership positions, to support legislation on women's concerns, to elect women to political office, and to organize the millions of nonunion female workers. Nine to Five created chapters across the country, gained a membership of over twelve thousand and made impressive gains in banks, offices, and insurance companies, while raising the consciousness of nonunion clerical workers across the nation. CLUW grew rapidly as well, constituting sixty-five chapters and fifteen thousand members by 1984. Paralleling the structure of most unions, CLUW established a convention format to pass resolutions and set policies to guide local chapters.

Though very different in their approach to organizing these two groups changed the labor movement's orientation toward female employees. Recognizing the importance of women within unions, the AFL-CIO endorsed the Equal Rights Amendment in 1973. During the next decade, many unions addressed "women's issues" such as affirmative action, child care, and pay equity. More women were elected to leadership positions, especially on the local level, and in 1980 CLUW president Joyce Miller was the first woman to sit on the AFL-CIO's Executive Council.

Despite the progress, relatively few women became national labor leaders, even in unions such as the Amalgamated Clothing and Textile Workers' Union or the Communication Workers of America, both with a majority of female members. Indeed, the dearth of female leaders is startling given the increased proportion of unionized women. As automation, deindustrialization, and overseas employment increased, eliminating manufacturing jobs, male union membership declined. Almost all of the labor movement gains of the 1970s derived from increases in female membership, as unions sought to offset the general decline in membership by targeting specific occupational groups: teachers, hospital personnel, and public-sector clerical and service workers.

In the years after the 1955 AFL-CIO merger, public employees comprised the one new area of unionization to emerge. President John E Kennedy gave it a boost when he issued Executive Order 10988 encouraging union membership among federal workers. Between 1955 and the early 1970s, the number of organized public employees increased tenfold, to over four million. In this period, the American Federation of State, County, and Municipal Employees (AFSCME), the American Federation of Teachers (AFT), the National Education Association (NEA), and unions of policemen, fire fighters, civil servants, nurses, and postal workers grew rapidly. By the early 1970s, AFSCME had become one of the AFL-CIO's largest affiliates.

Ironically enough, the success of organized labor's early radicalism contributed to its subsequent conservative image during the turbulent 1960s.

Ironically enough, the success of organized labor's early radicalism contributed to its subsequent conservative image during the turbulent 1960s. From a position of respectability, labor wielded considerable political power during the 1950s and 1960s. Democratic candidates were well aware of the importance of the labor vote, and liberal legislation, during the Kennedy and Johnson administrations, continued the work begun by the New Deal. But there were limits to what could be achieved by this marriage of organized labor and the Democratic party. Despite many attempts, the most hated elements within the Taft-Hartley Act were not repealed. Furthermore, when Richard M. Nixon narrowly defeated Hubert H. Humphrey in the 1968 presidential election, the death knell of labor's political influence was sounded.

Labor's political influence at the national level declined, but its role in state and local politics did not follow the same pattern. In fact, throughout the 1960s and 1970s and even into the decade of the 1980s and beyond, labor organizations operating at the grass-roots level exercised political influence by lending support to specific local issues, raising funds for political candidates, and fostering an informed electorate among their memberships.

Labor's enduring ability to wield power in local politics underscores the importance of rank-and-file commitment and raises the issue of participatory democracy within unions themselves. During the 1930s when workers struggled to gain recognition of their unions for collective bargaining, rank-and-file members actively participated in the fight. But with the entrenchment of unions in many industries during the postwar years, the relationship between leadership and membership changed. Contract negotiations with employers generally involved only a small cadre of union leaders. The decision to accept or reject what had been negotiated involved little more than a perfunctory vote by the rank and file, following the recommendations of their leaders. In some unions, such an atmosphere of disengagement bred negligence, nepotism, and corruption. Members tried to make leaders more responsive to their needs. Such a spirit of intra-union reform infused the Miners for Democracy movement, the Steelworkers Fight Back drive, and the Teamsters for Democratic Union. As the rank and file struggled to regain control over the decision-making process, management was figuring out ways to undermine labor's gains and make unions the scapegoat for America's economic problems.

Deindustrialization and American Labor

Throughout the 1970s, unionized manufacturing jobs declined, American industrial production was downscaled, and major industrial sites closed, most significantly in the iron, steel, automobile, rubber, and textile industries. At the same time in a nation where the majority of American workers held or aspired to white-collar jobs, lived in suburbs away from urban industrial centers, and participated in the educational boom of the 1960s by sending their children to college, there was dwindling public support for the labor movement.

The real economic growth that Americans enjoyed during the 1960s averaged over 4 percent per year; the nation's Gross National Product (GNP) expanded by 50 percent over the ten years; and the average American family had one-third more spendable income by the decade's end. The 1970s, however, told a different story. GNP growth slowed to 2.9 percent per year, and by 1980 American families had only 7 percent more real purchasing power than in 1970. Furthermore, all of this growth came between 1970 and 1973. After 1973 there was *no* real income increase. By the end of the 1970s the inflation rate, which had remained at a low 2.3 percent throughout the 1960s, averaged 12.5 percent. Unemployment, which hovered around 5 percent during the 1960s, averaged 7 percent of the labor force at the end of the 1970s. By 1980, the American standard of living, so touted in the 1960s, had dropped from first among the world's industrialized nations to tenth.

Moreover, during the 1970s the U.S. share of global manufactured exports fell from more than 25 percent (in the early 1960s) to less than 17 percent (in the early 1980s). Trade deficit figures soared during these years, and a close look at major exports reveals the fact that the United States, at least in comparison to Japan, has become an exporter of raw goods—soybeans, corn, and wheat—and an importer of cars, iron, steel, and electrical consumer goods.

The basic problem with the U.S. economy in the 1970s, 1980s, and on into the 1990s can be traced to deindustrialization. The impact on American workers and organized labor has been overwhelming. As economists Barry Bluestone and Bennett Harrison argue in *The Deindustrialization of America*, this process has involved the "widespread, systematic disinvestment in the nation's basic productive capacity." Capital has been "diverted from productive investment in our basic industries into unproductive speculation, mergers and acquisitions, and foreign investment." U.S. corporations have continued to invest their resources but not in the basic industries of the United States.

Examples of deindustrialization abound. Faced with aging equipment during the 1970s, U.S. Steel chose not to rebuild steel capacity but rather to spend five billion dollars to acquire Marathon Oil of Ohio. General Electric expanded its capital stock in the 1970s by investing outside the nation. GE's worldwide payroll increased by five thousand workers during the period—thirty-thousand foreign jobs were added while twenty-five thousand Americans lost their jobs. RCA Corporation and Ford Motor Company followed similar strategies, cutting U.S. employment, increasing their foreign work force, and spending their capital—in Ford's case more than 40 percent of its total budget—outside the country.

The impact of such capital mobility on organized labor has been profound. Beginning in the 1970s, the nation's core industries—auto, steel, and rubber—used the strategy of capital mobility, threatened or real, to demand smaller wage increases or actual wage rollbacks along with reductions in business taxes and cuts in community and social services. As Bluestone and Harrison argued, "corporate demands for wage concessions (give-backs) became the most prominent feature of industrial relations in the 1980s." By 1980, twenty states had passed "right-to-work" legislation that made paying union dues voluntary, undermining the financial strength of the unions.

During the 1970s, newly developed anti-union tactics continued to weaken the trade-union movement. A new generation of "union busters" sported gray-flannel suits and leather briefcases. They bore little resemblance to the company police, labor spies, or "goon squads" of earlier eras when physical violence characterized most labor-management conflicts, but they were no less effective. By the late 1970s, more than one thousand specialized consulting firms were advising corporations on how to keep union organizers and sympathizers out of the workplace, on how to defeat a union when elections could not be avoided, or, in cases where unions had won elections, on how to decertify them.

Paradoxically, while corporate deindustrialization strategies were demobilizing the labor movement, corporate officers managed to convince the public that American industry's problems stemmed not from executive decision making but from overpaid American workers protected by union contracts. Focusing on the gains that labor had made to secure a living wage deflected attention from the process of capital mobility and let labor stand as the scapegoat for the deindustrialization of the United States.

During the 1970s, the number of unfair labor practices recorded by the National Labor Relations Board against American businesses increased by 300 percent. The reason for this increase was that hundreds of companies, following the advice of anti-union consultants, found it more profitable to break the law and pay a small fine than to allow a union to organize their employees. The chances of a union winning a representation election fell by half between 1970 and 1978. At the same time, the number of annual decertifications multiplied from fewer than 240 to over 800. By 1978, unions were consistently losing elections—at a rate of three to one—in workplaces where there had been prior union victories.

Finally, the 1970s witnessed an assault on labor in the political arena. Trade unions, already confronted with capital mobility strategies, right-to-work legislation, sophisticated anti-union advisers, and blatant violations of fair labor practices had lost momentum. To deliver the knockout punch, American corporations formed nonprofit political action committees (PACs) designed to circumvent federal laws that prohibited private corporations from donating money directly to political candidates, and their growth was staggering. Corporate PACs proved effective in defeating labor law reform and maintaining the probusiness climate that enhanced profits and limited worker autonomy.

By the 1980s, new technology made the option of capital mobility from one region to another, or from one nation to another, a reality for most large U.S. corporations. Corporate access to wide-body jet transport, for shipping equipment and goods, to satellite-linked telecommunications systems, and to powerful computer networks for instantaneous coordination of worldwide operations shifted bargaining power in favor of capital to an unprecedented degree. Corporations used their enhanced power to demand more labor concessions within the United States. Their ability to move, to another community or another country, enabled corporations to make "take it or leave it" propositions to American workers, organized and unorganized. Interregional rivalry to attract capital intensified. American states and localities competed to provide businesses with incentive packages, including reduced corporate taxes and access to low-wage, nonunion labor. Clearly, there has been a close correlation between deindustrialization and deunionization.

But organized labor has not been the only target of corporate "reform" initiatives. By 1980 only one in four American workers belonged to a trade union. Consequently, changing the terms for organized workers alone would not be enough to bring about the significant, long-term decreases in labor costs that corporations were seeking. In order to achieve the level of worker "flexibility" they desired, corporations sought to hire nonunion labor, decertify existing unions, and dismantle the "safety net" that had protected American workers since the New Deal era. Increasingly throughout the 1970s and 1980s, private corporations made bold demands on state governments to foster low levels of workmen's compensation insurance, to reduce unemployment benefits per worker, and to set low minimum wages. States were encouraged to curtail programs that endorsed affirmative action and protected workers' health and safety. State laws providing income maintenance were also targeted as undesirable: food stamps, welfare, and job-training programs. Many of these programs were the result of past political victories by workers and their unions. These programs have served over the years to protect workers from the insecurity that comes from being totally dependent on the demands of capital. By 1980 it was clear that the labor movement's past gains were at risk. Moreover, collective bargaining proved an ineffective tool against capital mobility, for its case by case approach reaches few workers, and no amount of bargaining can provide for rebuilding a local economic base once a large corporation has pulled out of a particular community.

By the time Ronald Reagan entered the White House in 1981, the stage was set for another major shift in labor's political fortunes. Seven months into his first term, with significant budget and tax-cut victories to his credit, Reagan responded to a strike by the nation's air-traffic controllers with a forty-eight-hour ultimatum, followed by the massive firing of twelve thousand Professional Air Traffic Controllers Organization (PATCO) members. Briefing the press from beneath a portrait of Calvin Coolidge, whose election followed his ironfisted handling of the 1919 Boston police strike, Reagan insisted that "Dammit, the law is the law . . . if they strike, they quit their jobs." Refusing to negotiate while the strike continued, Reagan demanded that there be no amnesty for those who had walked out.

Organized labor reeled from the blow; the president's message to the labor movement was unmistakable. Furthermore, a majority of Americans, 57 percent, approved the president's abrupt action, believing that the air controllers, as public employees with a no-strike clause in their contract, were wrong to go on strike. Government action against PATCO, a union of relatively well-paid, white-collar supporters of Reagan in the 1980 election, did not stop with the firings. The FAA announced that disciplinary action would be taken, even against strikers who returned to work; the Justice Department prosecuted PATCO leaders; and a Federal judge penalized PATCO with staggering fines of $4.4 million for violation of a back-to-work order. Felony charges were filed against seventy-two PATCO leaders in twenty cities across the country. Robert E. Poli, PATCO president, threatened with a jail sentence and fined a thousand dollars per day for leading the strike, was stunned by the severity of the response and accused the administration of "brutal overkill." Not since the days of the Palmer raids in 1919 had the government waged such a massive assault against organized labor. Destroyed as a union, PATCO survives only as a new and powerful symbol of anti-union government policy.

During Reagan's first administration, union membership plummeted from 24.7 percent in 1980 to 18 percent in 1985. Never had there been such a steep decline in the number of workers belonging to a trade union. Moreover, the Reagan administration ordered

Without a fundamental redistribution of economic power, the working people of the 1990s would inherit a legacy of low-wage jobs, anti-union government policies, and an NLRB that ensures that almost every organizing drive and contract renegotiation turns into a lawsuit.

the Bureau of Labor Statistics to cease publishing data collected about union affiliation. Published government data on American unions were reduced from a range of categories that included types of unions and membership by gender and race to a single column that reported the number of "work stoppages" in a given year. However, unpublished data in the bureau's Washington office tell the story of the decimation of small unions, and the loss of hundreds of thousands of union members from the United Steel Workers, the United Automobile Workers, and the Teamsters, in the recession of the early 1980s. By Reagan's election in 1984, labor's political power seemed to have evaporated; unions appeared to have been relegated to the margins of public life.

In the mid 1980s, labor scholars and economists refocused attention on the positive political role that organized labor should play in a democratic society. Thomas B. Edsall's 1984 study, for example, finds that "the collapse of labor's legislation power facilitated the adoption of a set of economic policies highly beneficial to the corporate sector and to the affluent." He argues that the implications of labor's decline go far beyond the fate of the unions and their membership for "without a strong labor movement there is no broad-based institution in American society equipped to represent the interests of those in the working and lower-middle class in the formulation of economic policy." With the voice of labor effectively muted, corporate and business interests could continue to dominate the American political system unchallenged.

In this context, American workers face the daunting tasks of reorganizing workers, unifying an increasingly diversified American labor force, and attaining the political power required to influence, in fact to formulate, economic policy. The present leadership at the top levels of organized labor, labeled "the bald old men in Bal Harbour, Florida," by Thomas Geoghegan, resembles the AFL hierarchy of the late 1920s more than a dynamic, visionary cadre capable of leading American workers into a hopeful future. In 1990, just as in the early 1930s and the late 1940s, American workers stood at a crucial crossroads.

Without a fundamental redistribution of economic power, the working people of the 1990s would inherit a legacy of low-wage jobs, anti-union government policies, and an NLRB that ensures that almost every organizing drive and contract renegotiation turns into a lawsuit. American women and minorities, most of whom hold low-wage, service-sector jobs, will comprise a majority of the 1990s work force. Like the industrial workers of the Depression era, these Americans have few ways to voice their concerns. The community or factory-based labor forces of the 1920s and 1930s have given way to a fragmented work force divided against itself in a multiplicity of segments: blue- versus white-collar, African American versus white versus Hispanic, male versus female. This fragmentation works against the mobilization and political action of American workers.

Conclusion

In the 1930s Americans suffered from an economic collapse that spawned high unemployment and necessitated government intervention. The militancy of American labor in that decade, measured in part by a meteoric rise in union membership, reached a level unsurpassed in the twentieth century. Full economic recovery from the Depression came only with the nation's entry into World War II, a period when the scarcity of workers on the home front meant premium wages and powerful unions, but these were only for the war's duration. The need for wartime workers translated into a short-term redistribution of industrial jobs to women and African Americans previously excluded from the factory. The war's end changed the relationship between labor and management as both vied for power and control in postwar American society. Economic prosperity, fueled by consumer purchases and the demand for housing, raised hopes as well as real wages. Increasingly, American cultural life became consumer driven, and the desire for material well-being found more workers leaving traditional, urban blue-collar neighborhoods in favor of suburban comfort. Community changes reflected shifts in the labor force itself, for 1956 marked the first year a majority of American workers held white-collar jobs.

American workers faced years of change and reaction in the 1960s. African Americans sought equal rights in the voting booth and the workplace. Following the lead of black civil rights activists, American women laid claim to rights ranging from equal pay for equal work to gender-neutral hiring. White workers felt threatened by black militancy on the job and in white working-class suburbs where housing and school integration efforts were focused. Male workers felt threatened by the demands of working women and retaliated by reviving a domestic ideology reminiscent of that used to rationalize the displacement of female workers at the end of World War II.

As various groups contested their rights in the larger society and on the shop floor, industries such as textiles, shoes, and steel, continuing a quest for cheaper labor that dated from the late nineteenth century, shifted a greater percentage of their operations from older northeastern and midwestern plants to newly built facilities in the Southeast and Southwest, the region dubbed the "Sunbelt." This decentralization of American industry, which accelerated after the oil crisis of the early 1970s raised corporate costs and squeezed profits. Soon, Sunbelt perks—low-cost utilities, nonunion labor, and tax breaks—could not bridge the profit gap, and American companies looked overseas for workers willing to accept rates of pay far below those necessary for a living wage in the United States.

By the 1980s, widespread deindustrialization of American industry was under way, rapidly eliminating the number of high-wage, union-protected jobs. Recessions plagued the economy in 1970, 1973, 1979, and 1982; real wages declined; and workers struggled to make ends meet. Families became more dependent than ever on dual incomes as women moved into the work force in unprecedented numbers. By 1980 only 15 percent of American families resembled the 1950s ideal in which 70 percent of families claimed father as breadwinner and mother as homemaker.

As the 1990s began American workers faced increased vulnerability and difficulty in maintaining their standard of living. Unionization is one indicator of worker economic and political strength. By that measure, Americans have slipped badly in recent years. Organized labor claimed one out of seven nonagricultural workers at the end of the 1980s, basically the same percentage of the industrial work force that unions held in the late 1920s, before the great organization drives of the New Deal era. Thus, in the years between 1930 and 1990, American workers have come full circle (see Fig. 1), having survived the Depression-ridden economy of the 1930s, benefited from war-induced prosperity, and returned to an economically vulnerable position as the twentieth century draws to a close.

[See also Agriculture; The Aristocracy of Inherited Wealth; Business Culture; The City; Communications and Information Processing; Geographic Mobility; Minorities and Work; Technology and Social Change; Women and Work.]

BIBLIOGRAPHY

Historiographical Essays

Brody, David. "Labor History in the 1970s: Toward a History of the American Worker." In *The Past Before Us: Contemporary Historical Writing in the United States,* edited by Michael Kammen (1980).

Kimeldorf, Howard. "Bringing Unions Back in (Or Why We Need a New Old Labor History)." *Labor History* 32 (1991): 91–103; and responses by Michael Kazin, Alice Kessler-Harris, David Montgomery, Bruce Nelson, and Daniel Nelson. "The Limits of Union-Centered History: Responses to Howard Kimeldorf." *Labor History* 32 (1991): 104–127.

Montgomery, David. "To Study the People: The American Working Class." *Labor History* 21 (1980): 485–512.

Moody, J. Carroll, and Alice Kessler-Harris, eds. *Perspectives on American Labor History: The Problem of Synthesis* (1989).

Ozanne, Robert W. "Trends in American Labor History." *Labor History* 21 (1980): 513–521.

Zieger, Robert H. "Workers and Scholars: Recent Trends in American Labor Historiography." *Labor History* 13 (1972): 245–266.

General Works

Brody, David. *Workers in Industrial America: Essays on the Twentieth-Century Struggle* (1979).

Buhle, Paul, and Man Dawley, eds. *Working for Democracy: American Workers from the Revolution to the Present* (1985).

Davis, Mike. *Prisoners of the American Dream: Politics and Economy in the History of the U.S. Working Class* (1986).

Dubofsky, Melvyn. *American Labor Since the New Deal* (1971).

Filippelli, Ronald L. *Labor in the United States* (1984).

Fraser, Steve, and Gary Gerstle, eds. *The Rise and Fall of the New Deal Order, 1930–1980* (1989).

Gordon, David M., et al. *Segmented Work, Divided Workers: The Historical Transformation of Labor in the United States* (1982).

Green, James R. *The World of the Worker: Labor in Twentieth-Century America* (1978).

Green, James R., ed. *Workers' Struggles, Past and Present: A "Radical America" Reader* (1983).

Hall, Burton, ed. *Autocracy and Insurgency in Organized Labor* (1972).

Montgomery, David. *Workers' Control in America: Studies in the History of Work, Technology, and Labor Struggles* (1979).
Tomlins, Christopher L. *The State and the Unions: Labor Relations, Law, and the Organized Labor Movement in America, 1880–1960* (1985).
Zieger, Robert H. *American Workers, American Unions, 1920–1985* (1986).
———. *Organized Labor in the Twentieth-Century South* (1991).

Worker Culture

Aronowitz, Stanley. *False Promises: The Shaping of American Working-Class Consciousness* (1973).
Blauner, Robert. *Alienation and Freedom: The Factory Worker and His Industry* (1964).
Burger, Bennett. *Working-Class Suburbia: A Study of Auto Workers in Suburbia* (1960).
Chonoy, Eli. *Automobile Workers and the American Dream* (1955).
Frisch, Michael H., and Daniel J. Walkowitz, eds. *Working-Class America* (1983).
Gans, Herbert J. *The Levittowners: Ways of Life and Politics in a New Suburban Community* (1982).
Garson, Barbara. *All the Livelong Day: The Meaning and Demeaning of Routine Work* (1977).
Gerstle, Gary. *Working-Class Americanism: The Politics of Labor in a Textile City, 1914–1960* (1989).
Hall, Jacquelyn D., et al. *Like a Family: The Making of a Southern Cotton Mill World* (1987).
Halle, David. *America's Working Man: Work, Home, and Politics Among Blue-Collar Property Owners* (1984).
Howe, Irving, ed. *The World of the Blue-Collar Worker* (1973).
Howell, Joseph T. *Hard Living on Clay Street: Portraits of Blue-Collar Families* (1973).
Kirby, Jack T. *Rural Worlds Lost: The American South, 1920–1960* (1986).
Komarovsky, Mirra. *Blue-Collar Marriage* (1964).
Kornblum, William. *Blue-Collar Community* (1974).
Leggett, John C. *Class, Race, and Labor: Working-Class Consciousness in Detroit* (1968).
Levison, Andrew. *Working-Class Majority* (1974).
Levitan, Sar A., ed. *Blue-Collar Workers: A Symposium on Middle America* (1971).
May, Elaine T. *Homeward Bound: American Families in the Cold War Era* (1988).
Mills, Nicolaus, ed. *Culture in an Age of Money: The Legacy of the 1980s in America* (1990).
Rubin, Lillian B. *Worlds of Pain: Life in the Working-Class Family* (1976).
Sexton, Brendan, and Patricia C. Sexton. *Blue Collars and Hard Hats* (1971).
Shostak, Arthur B., and William Gomberg, eds. *Blue-Collar World* (1964).
Terkel, Studs. *Hard Times: An Oral History of the Great Depression* (1970).
———. *Working: People Talk About What They Do All Day and How They Feel About What They Do* (1972).
Widick, B. J., ed. *Auto Work and Its Discontents* (1976).
Whyte, William H., Jr. *The Organization Man* (1956).
Zweig, Ferdynand. *The Worker in an Affluent Society* (1962).

Gender, Race and Ethnicity

Baron, Ava, ed. *Work Engendered: Toward a New History of American Labor* (1991).
Benson, Susan P. *Counter Cultures: Saleswomen, Managers, and Customers in American Department Stores, 1890–1940* (1986).
Bracey, John H., August Meier, and Elliott Rudwick, eds. *Black Workers and Organized Labor* (1971).
Deutsch, Sarah. *No Separate Refuge: Culture, Class, and Gender on an Anglo-Hispanic Frontier in the American Southwest, 1880–1940* (1987).
Foner, Philip S. *Women and the American Labor Movement* (1980).
———. *Organized Labor and the Black Worker, 1619–1981* (1982).
Gabin, Nancy F. *Feminism in the Labor Movement: Women and the United Auto Workers, 1935–1975* (1990).
Goldin, Claudia. *Understanding the Gender Gap: An Economic History of American Women* (1989).
Groneman, Carol, and Mary Beth Norton, eds. *To Toil the Livelong Day: Americas Women at Work, 1780–1980* (1987).
Harris, William H. *The Harder We Run: Black Workers Since the Civil War* (1982).
Howe, Irving. *The World of Our Fathers* (1976).
Jacobson, Julius, ed. *The Negro and the American Labor Movement* (1968).
Jensen, Joan M., and Sue Davidson, eds. *A Needle, a Bobbin, a Strike: Women Needleworkers in America* (1984).
Kelley, Robin D. G. *Hammer and Hoe: Alabama Communists During the Great Depression* (1990).
Kenneally, James J. *Women and American Trade Unions* (1978).
Kessler-Harris, Alice. *Out to Work: A History of Wage-earning Women in the United States* (1982).
Kornbluh, Joyce L., and Mary Frederickson, eds. *Sisterhood and Solidarity: Workers' Education for Women, 1914–1984* (1984).
Meier, August, and Elliott Rudwick. *Black Detroit and the Rise of the UAW* (1979).
Melosh, Barbara. *The Physician's Hand: Work Culture and Conflict in American Nursing* (1982).
Milkman, Ruth, ed. *Women, Work and Protest: A Century of U.S. Women's Labor History* (1985).
O'Sullivan, Judith, and Rosemary Gallick. *Workers and Allies: Female Participation in the American Trade Union Movement, 1824–1976* (1975).
Van Raaphorst, Donna L. *Union Maids Not Wanted: Organizing Domestic Workers, 1870–1940* (1988).
Wertheimer, Barbara M. *We Were There: The Story of Working Women in America* (1977).

Biographies

Anderson, Jarvis. *A. Philip Randolf: A Biographical Portrait* (1973).
Barnard, John. *Walter Reuther and the Rise of the Autoworkers* (1983).
Dubofsky, Melvyn, and Warren Van Tine. *John L. Lewis: A Biography* (1977).
Fraser, Steve. *Labor Will Rule: Sidney Hillman and the Rise of American Labor* (1991).
Goulden, Joseph. *Meany* (1972).
———. *Jerry Wurf: Labor's Last Angry Man* (1982).
Larrowe, Charles P. *Harry Bridges: The Rise and Fall of Radical Labor in the United States* (1977).
Phelan, Craig. *William Green: Biography of a Labor Leader* (1988).
Robinson, Archie. *George Meany and His Times: A Biography* (1981).
Sloane, Arthur A. *Hoffa* (1991).
Velie, Lester. *Desperate Bargain: Why Jimmy Hoffa Had to Die* (1977).

Individual Industries, Unions, and Strikes

Billings, Richard N., and John Greenya. *Power to the Public Worker* (1974).

Braun, Robert J. *Teachers and Power: The Story of the American Federation of Teachers* (1972).
Brody, David. *Butcher Workmen: A Study of Unionization* (1964).
Brooks, Robert R. *As Steel Goes: Unionism in a Basic Industry* (1940; repr. 1970).
Brooks, Thomas R. *Communications Workers of America: The Story of a Union* (1977).
Clark, Paul F. *The Miners' Fight for Democracy* (1981).
Daniel, Cletus E. *Bitter Harvest: A History of California Farmworkers, 1870–1941* (1981).
Fine, Sidney. *The Automobile Under the Blue Eagle: Labor, Management, and the Automobile Manufacturing Code* (1963).
———. *Sit-Down: The General Motors Strike of 1936–1937* (1969).
Fink, Leon, and Brian Greenberg. *Upheaval in the Quiet Zone: A History of Hospital Workers' Union Local 1199* (1989).
Fitch, John A. *The Steel Workers* (1989).
Friedlander, Peter. *The Emergence of a UAW Local, 1936–1939: A Study in Class and Culture* (1975).
Gaventa, John. *Power and Powerlessness: Quiescence and Rebellion in an Appalachian Valley* (1980).
Herling, John. *Right to Challenge: People and Power in the Steelworkers Union* (1972).
Hume, Brit. *Death and the Mines: Rebellion and Murder in the United Mine Workers* (1971).
Leab, Daniel J. *A Union of Individuals: The Formation of the American Newspaper Guild, 1933–1936* (1970).
Schatz, Ronald W. *The Electrical Workers: A History of Labor at General Electric and Westinghouse, 1923–60* (1983).
Schwartz, Harvey. *The March Inland: Origins of the ILWU Warehouse Division, 1934–1938* (1978).
Zieger, Robert H. *Madison's Battery Workers, 1934–1952: A History of Federal Labor Union 19587* (1977).
———. *Rebuilding the Pulp and Paper Workers' Union, 1933–1941* (1984).

The Great Depression

Bernstein, Irving. *The Lean Years: A History of the American Worker, 1920–1933* (1960; repr. 1972).
———. *The Turbulent Years: A History of the American Worker, 1933–1941* (1969).
Galenson, Walter. *The CIO Challenge to the AFL: A History of the American Labor Movement, 1935–1941* (1960).
Morris, James O. *Conflict Within the AFL: A Study in Craft Versus Industrial Unionism, 1901–1938* (1958).
Preis, Art. *Labor's Giant Step: Twenty years of the CIO* (1964; 2d rev. ed. 1972).

World War II and Its Aftermath

Anderson, Karen. *Wartime Women: Sex Roles, Family Relations, and the Status of Women During World War II* (1981).
Foster, James C. *The Union Politic: The CIO Political Action Committee* (1975).
Glaberman, Martin. *Wartime Strikes* (1980).
Gluck, Sherna B. *Rosie the Riveter Revisited: Women, the War, and Social Change* (1988).
Gregory, Chester. *Women in Defense Work During World War II* (1974).
Gross, James A. *The Reshaping of the National Labor Relations Board: National Labor Policy in Transition, 1937–1947* (1982).
Harris, Howell J. *The Right to Manage: Industrial Relations Policies of American Business in the 1940s* (1982).
Lee, R. Alton. *Truman and Taft-Hartley: A Question of Mandate* (1966).
Levenstein, Harvey A. *Communism, Anti-Communism, and the CIO* (1981).
Lichtenstein, Nelson. *Labor's War at Home: The CIO in World War II* (1983).
Marcus, Maeva. *Truman and the Steel Seizure Case* (1977).
Oshinsky, David M. *Senator McCarthy and the American Labor Movement* (1976).
Seidman, Joel. *American Labor from Defense to Reconversion* (1953).

From the 1950s to the 1990s

Aronowitz, Stanley. *Working Class Hero: A New Strategy for Labor* (1983).
Bluestone, Barry, and Bennett Harrison. *The Deindustrialization of America: Plant Closings, Community Abandonment, and the Dismantling of Basic Industry* (1982).
Bowles, Samuel, David M. Gordon, and Thomas E. Weisskopf. *Beyond the Waste Land: A Democratic Alternative to Economic Decline* (1983).
Edsall, Thomas Byrne. *The New Politics of Inequality* (1984).
Ehrenreich, Barbara. *Fear of Falling: The Inner Life of the Middle Class* (1989).
———. *The Worst Years of Our Lives* (1990).
Freeman, Richard B., and James L. Medoff. *What Do Unions Do?* (1984).
Geoghegan, Thomas. *Which Side Are You on?: Trying to Be for Labor When It's Flat on Its Back* (1991).
Harrison, Bennett, and Barry Bluestone. *The Great U-Turn: Corporate Restructuring and the Polarizing of America* (1988).
Horowitz, Irving Louis, John C. Leggett, and Martin Oppenheimer, eds. *The American Working Class: Prospects for the 1980s* (1979).
Kuttner, Robert. *The Economic Illusion: False Choices Between Prosperity and Justice* (1984).
Lawrence, Robert Z. *Can America Compete?* (1984).
Levy, Frank. *Dollars and Dreams: The Changing American Income Distribution* (1987).
Thurow, Lester C. *The Zero-Sum Society: Distribution and the Possibilities for Economic Change* (1980).
Tolchin, Susan J., and Martin Tolchin. *Dismantling America: The Rush to Deregulate* (1983).

— MARY E. FREDERICKSON AND TIMOTHY P. LYNCH

LANDSCAPES

The landscapes of the United States are peculiarly American and decidedly unlike those of the nation's ancestral societies. Minimally constrained by the complexities of an Old World past, these man-made, or man-modified, ensembles of terrestrial objects are the purest expression anywhere in our contemporary world of the central dictates of capitalist economics, if modulated somewhat by the singularities of imported and commingled European cultures. In any event, the activities of European settlers and their progeny have transformed a vast territory into something radically different from the aboriginal scene.

Aboriginal Landscapes

The newcomers who began entering the future United States more than four centuries ago encountered a land already distinctly humanized over the millennia by some millions of Native Americans. Only locally, in portions of New Mexico and Arizona, were the inhabitants fully sedentary farmers. The great majority of aborigines subsisted by combining cropping systems with hunting, fishing, and gathering along the Pacific Coast and in Alaska; in the more thinly settled tracts west of the 100th meridian (running from the Dakotas to central Texas), they pursued only the latter.

The range and variety of cultural systems were considerable in pre-Columbian America, and the same was true for the resultant landscapes, although our knowledge of their actual appearance is quite fragmentary. House types and village patterns differed markedly from place to place, but most settlement was transient because of the prevailing system of shifting cultivation. The human impact on what appeared wild to the European pioneer was considerable. Substantial evidence indicates that repeated burning, for hunting and other purposes, had created the extensive grasslands of the central United States, while agricultural activity was responsible for the many openings punctuating the eastern forests, those "Indian old fields" that European farmers eagerly exploited. Furthermore, selective harvesting of various trees, shrubs, annuals, and other organisms certainly modified the biota of early America.

Perhaps the most crucial landscape-related factor in aboriginal life, as far as later dealings and misunderstandings with Caucasians were concerned, was a total absence of European concepts of private ownership of land or the precise delineation of property lines. Insofar as there was any thought of proprietorship, it was along communal lines; and boundaries between neighboring communities had always been vaguely defined or nonexistent. Be that as it may, the encounter between invader and aborigine was disastrous for the latter; among the unfortunate results was the near-total obliteration of antecedent landscapes as Native American populations were severely decimated and demoralized, shunted from place to place, and eventually confined to reservations where little of their material culture was left intact. Today perhaps the only remaining aboriginal landscapes with any semblance of authenticity are found in a few New Mexican localities.

The European Transformation

When the first wave of European settlers arrived—in the late sixteenth century in the Southwest, and along the Atlantic seaboard a few decades later—their automatic impulse may have been to re-create the traditional societies and landscapes of their homelands, but pioneer conditions in the New World seldom rendered such faithful transcription feasible. A spectacular abundance of usable land, virtually free for the taking, and the weakness of political and legal controls made it quite difficult to implement any sort of planning. In place of the orderly, compact, regularly aligned rural and urban settlements envisioned by the various grantees favored by the British, Spanish, Dutch, and French regimes, the actuality turned out to be much messier: scattered, often isolated farmsteads and a string of small seaports and even smaller inland trading centers with little pretense of regularity in layout or elegance in appearance. This statement applies equally well to New England, where, common myth to the contrary notwithstanding, clustered villages were the rare exception before the late eighteenth century. Approximations of European models, such as some of the Hispanic outposts in the Southwest, or New Orleans, Boston, Philadelphia, and Savannah, were few in number.

Building styles in early America tended to be generalized, simplified versions of Old World folk practice. Regional patterns did gradually emerge in the design of houses, barns, churches, cemeteries, and other visible features but, given the frequent mixing of peoples and influences from varied European localities and the impact of a novel environment, simple duplication of any specific Old World scene could hardly occur. Only much later, as wealth and sophistication grew, did individual homes and estates come to resemble what had become fashionable in Europe.

Many a foreign visitor recorded his or her impressions of the early American scene, including the frontier zone, and aside from occasional mild compliments for a major city or two and some of the older, more flourishing farming areas, they were uniformly taken aback by the pervasive physical crudities of town and countryside, a prodigal wastefulness in resource exploitation, and the jarring visual disharmonies in what they generally beheld. As David Lowenthal has noted, what struck them most was the vastness, wildness, and formlessness of a future-oriented land characterized by extravagant extremes. The passage of time has not canceled these early characteristics; indeed, just the reverse has happened in terms of formlessness and incongruous contrasts. As social disparities have widened, as the ranks of both the wealthy and the poor and underprivileged have grown substantially, we often find their two utterly irreconcilable landscapes existing side by side in some of our larger cities.

If the vestiges of aboriginal occupancy were negligible and if the shaping of the colonial and subsequent American scene has been essentially that of European peoples and ideas operating under new, unfamiliar circumstances, there remains one other set of influences, at least in the American South, that is still poorly understood: African influences. Cultural transfers from the Old World in African American church buildings and domestic architecture, yard treatment, agricultural and burial practices are quite plausible in light of the physical evidence despite the paucity of documentation.

The evolution of the American landscape from pioneer days to the present has been largely a matter of applying a series of ever more advanced technologies, along with the necessary investment of capital, to a varied set of places and resources, all in fulfillment of certain cultural and economic drives, as often as not unspoken and unwritten. The former set of forces—the technological and financial—may have altered greatly over the years, but the latter—those internalized imperatives which energize both individuals and the larger society—have remained remarkably consistent over time. As basic a principle as any is the supreme value of individualism and thus a vigorous, if not always productive, competition and the sacredness of private property. In landscape terms this article of faith finds expression in many ways, including the isolated farmstead, the detached, single-family urban or suburban home set on its own lot, the multitude of small burial plots in the countryside, the world's largest proliferation of church denominations and their buildings, weak or nonexistent control of commercial land use, and, consequently, that duplication and excess of facilities so fully embodied in the present-day commercial highway strip. It is the infrequent counterexample, most notably the Mormon communities of Utah with their compact, well-ordered, theocratic landscapes, that reminds us how extreme the general American case really is.

Allied to this powerful streak of individualism is a degree of mobility—obviously spatial, but social as well—that animates American life and landscape to a level no other country can rival. The acceptance—indeed, the celebration—of rapid change quite logically accompanies American individualism and mobility. The landscape results include endless turnover in land use and structures or their remodeling, frequent juxtaposition of building styles from different eras, a high incidence of abandoned farmland, derelict urban neighborhoods and ghost towns, a never-ending series of new highway projects or the relocation or improvement of existing roads, and, except during deepest economic depression, a great amount of construction at various stages of completion in favored localities.

Undergirding so fluid and seemingly anarchic a scene is the most basic principle of all: the sanctity of the profit motive for both individual and business firm. But if a creed common to all of modern Western society happens to be expressed most nakedly in a United States lacking the burden of ancient tradition, there is another facet of the American ethos (one possibly derived from the English cultural system) that is exceptional: an anti-urban bias. (The pastoral urges of Americans also find expression in another British heritage, the homeowner's passion for lawns.) Cities may be necessary evils in the furtherance of economic aims, but, unlike the situation in continental Europe, the American metropolis is, with few exceptions, an unloved creature. The results of such disaffection are visually obvious in the cities themselves, as well as in the extraordinary extent of suburbanization and exurbanization. A less direct but nonetheless genuine expression of this mind-set is the propensity to select smaller towns for state capitals and rural or small-town settings for colleges.

Among the environmental circumstances molding the American landscape, few are more noteworthy than the initial superabundance of trees in so much of the eastern half of the country and a good portion of the far West. It was both curse and blessing. Clearing a fifty- or one-hundred-acre (20-or 40-hectare) farm could mean an entire working lifetime of literally backbreaking labor for the homesteader, and the outcome for another generation or so might be unsightly, stump-filled fields and pastures. But the forest also provided absolute necessities: raw materials for house, barn, other outbuildings, fencing, furniture, vehicles, and tools, and, of course, fuel for warmth, cooking, and industrial processes. The fact that so many thousands of sawmills sprang up along the frontier illustrates the centrality of wood and lumber to American life. Rural and much of urban America, early and late, then, has been wood-dominated. Even today the woodlot remains on many farms.

Among the environmental circumstances molding the American landscape, few are more noteworthy than the initial superabundance of trees in so much of the eastern half of the country and a good portion of the far West.

In the past and to a surprising extent today, wood has been the preferred material for houses, churches, school buildings, shops, mills, bridges, and much else. In a land where labor has been dear and lumber cheap, the adoption of brick, stone, and other materials for construction has come about only gradually, locally, and incompletely. So deeply ingrained in the American psyche did the preference for wood become that when the settlement frontier entered the treeless Great Plains, other expedients, such as the sod house, were quite temporary; lumber, even entire prefabricated wooden buildings, were shipped in at considerable expense.

THE IMPACT OF TECHNOLOGY. In a country of such daunting size, the means for transporting people and goods have always been primary determinants of the material framework of American life and livelihood. The changes over time in the morphology of American cities clearly reflect this fact. For the first two hundred years or so of European settlement—certainly until the 1840s or 1850s—towns were relatively small, compact pedestrian places (with access to horse-drawn carriages limited to the more prosperous) that, with rare exceptions, were tied to waterborne commerce and thus oriented toward wharves and docks. They were also places with minimal spatial segregation of economic functions, classes, or ethnic groups.

The introduction of the steam railroad had a profound impact upon urban form and landscape and, eventually, on the countryside as well. Besides fostering vigorous growth in city size, commerce, and manufacturing, the new mode of transportation transformed the outward appearance of much of the city. There were new depots, freight houses, marshaling yards, maintenance facilities, associated hotels, bridges, and tunnels accompanied by the evisceration of much of the old urban fabric to provide space for tracks and all the other rail-related activities. New factory and warehouse districts arose at rail side, sometimes on a massive scale. By the close of the nineteenth century, the building of commuter and light-rail interurban lines enabled the city to sprawl outward in an unprecedented way, as did the installation of electric trolley service within the expanding metropolis.

Aside from the immediate physical stigmata—the many cuts and fills executed across all but the most subdued of surfaces, defoliation of rights-of-way, creation of parallel telegraph lines and signal systems, and the erection of innumerable small-town depots and ancillary structures—the indirect effects of inserting so many tens of thousands of miles of rail into the countryside were ultimately both visually and socially significant. The presence of an extended "metropolitan corridor" meant availability of city goods, information, and ideas in many formerly isolated villages and hamlets as well as the start of that gradual coalescence, or interdigitation, between town and countryside that has become so prominent an aspect of contemporary America. It is no coincidence that the onset of a standardized way of life became noticeable in the 1850s, just when the railroad began to monopolize long-distance transpor-

The introduction of the steam railroad had a profound impact upon urban form and landscape of the later nineteenth century.

tation. It was then that some magazines acquired nationwide readership, that a mass market developed for many types of mass-produced merchandise, and that fashions in house design and landscape architecture (including park cemeteries) showed signs of becoming uniform coast to coast thanks to widely circulated manuals and preachments such as those of Andrew Jackson Downing.

Dramatic and pervasive though the effects of the new railroad system may have been, there were many other innovations, less well publicized, that helped modify the American landscape during the latter half of the nineteenth century: barbed-wire fencing, cheap paint, indoor plumbing, mass production of portland cement, the mail-order catalog, the balloon-frame house, electric elevators, and streetlights. Equally important though less celebrated were advances in earth-moving devices and technology and, most especially, the invention and large-scale use of dynamite. In any event, remarkable alterations came about in the topography of American cities. Rough terrain was leveled (as happened in Manhattan), entire surfaces lifted (as in Chicago), dry land created out of swamps (as in Washington), and waterfronts remade (as in New Orleans). In many instances, as in Boston, the changes have been so thoroughgoing that if a seventeenth-century resident were to be resurrected, it is doubtful whether he or she would find any part of the metropolitan area or its harbor recognizable. No major American seaport, and few lake or river ports of consequence, have escaped extensive physical revamping.

Another crucial shaper of the landscape has been the automobile. The easy availability, since the early decades of the twentieth century, of personal vehicles to all but the very poorest, along with great numbers of trucks, buses, motorcycles, and other motorized conveyances as well as access to almost any point, have profoundly reordered the settlement structure and landscapes of America in ways that are still not fully appreciated. As far as the city is concerned, there has been a remarkable outward explosion of population, businesses, and traditional urban functions. In a number of cases, the old urban core has lost its dominance as suburbs, or even virtually autonomous "edge cities," have sprung up along the periphery. The feasibility of long-distance commuting and the new flexibility in delivering materials and information have facilitated the redistribution of enterprises and employees into what were once remote locations. The urbanization of the countryside is proceeding inexorably. One of the more visible aspects of the phenomenon has been the proliferation of second homes and seasonal housing in environmentally attractive locales within commuting range of major population centers—or, for the airborne affluent, almost anywhere in the country.

Within the more or less contiguous built-up area we still call a city, the imprint of the automobile is hard to ignore. Immense acreage is given over to paved streets and parking lots; multiple-lane, limited-access highways within and around the city with their massive interchanges, bridges, overpasses, and outsize signage and lighting have done more to revise the physiognomy of urban places than even the most imperious of railroad barons could have dreamed of doing. And the interstate highway system and similar projects, with their commercial clusters arising around every interchange, have transformed the face of much of rural America. Every self-respecting modern dwelling has a one- or two-car garage and an ample driveway; along every thriving commercial street we find not just filling stations, auto showrooms, parts dealers, repair facilities, and perhaps some motels but also an endless array of retail establishments geared to the drive-by and/or drive-in trade and a great swarm of often large, garish advertising signs designed to engage the attention and urges of the passing drivers. As symptomatic as anything of the new order is the profusion of auto-oriented shopping malls in city and suburb, a development that gives every indication of becoming the central social institution of our times.

Important as airborne passenger, mail, and freight traffic may have become, the landscape impact of the airplane has been much less profound than that of the automobile or truck. Nevertheless, one of the more striking localized features of present-day America is the airport complex on the outskirts of major metropolises with its mix of office, motel, and high-tech industrial facilities as well as the considerable acreage devoted to the airport proper.

THE IMPACT OF CULTURAL AUTHORITY. Ultimately rivaling the significance of technology as a shaper of the American landscape have been the workings of central authority, even though it was initially rather weak. A leading item on the agenda of the colonial proprietors and, later, the provincial, state, and national regimes was the rapid disposal of land to settlers through sale or other means. Until the early years of national independence, there was little regularity in the ways real estate was surveyed or bounded. The prevailing pattern throughout the original thirteen states is known as the metes-and-bounds systems, one that relied largely on natural features for designating property lines. The resulting highly irregular mosaic of parcels contrasts with the long-lot system used in areas of early French and some Spanish settlement, one in which long, narrow strips of property ran back at right angles from riverfront or road.

Such relatively casual modes of carving up the American land vanished in the late 1780s when the young republic adopted a rigidly rectangular survey system for the vast, as yet unsettled national domain to which it held title. Moving in advance of permanent settlers, federal surveyors laid out six-by-six-mile townships with straight-line boundaries oriented to the compass. Each township consisted of thirty-six sections, each containing 640 acres, or one square mile (256 hectares, or 2.6 square kilometers). Public roads and virtually all subsequent property lines and field boundaries within sections were aligned north, east, south, and west along or parallel with section lines, and most later urban street layouts followed suit. The result for the nearly 75 percent of American territory so marked off (not counting national parks and forests, early French and Spanish grants, and Indian reservations excluded from the system) is a remarkable geometric repetitiveness in the settlement fabric. It is a checkerboard regularity that can be discerned from the ground but appreciated fully only from the air. The federal example was emulated by several states that controlled unsettled lands not included in the national domain, notably Texas, Georgia, Pennsylvania, New York, and Maine, though their survey methods were not quite as rigorous as in the national case.

The rationale for such a relatively simple method for partitioning the American land was obvious enough: it made good business sense. Henceforth it would be easy to describe, advertise, sell, resell, subdivide, or combine parcels with a minimum of legal fuss and expense. But if the effects of the federal rectangular survey have been deep, widespread, and enduring, other visible evidence of the existence of a relatively underdeveloped central government was scarce during the first several decades of national existence. Perhaps the occasional fort, lighthouse, or customhouse was then the only visible token that some sort of national entity was ruling the land. The visible effects of state and local governments were even more difficult to detect.

The net balance of power and sentiment, as between government and the governed, and thus its landscape expression, began to shift substantially from the time of the Civil War onward, but certain deeply ingrained attitudes persist. Americans have always felt uneasy about centralized governance and the bureaucracy, or indeed any form of external interference with the exercise of property rights or the pursuit of wealth—thus the late, slow, reluctant acceptance of planning and zoning or other land-use regulations. But where controls have been effective, the contrasts between juxtaposed jurisdictions can be quite dramatic—for example, between the landscapes of the District of Columbia and those in its Maryland and Virginia suburbs or the differences between the roadsides of Vermont and those in adjacent states. But even though planners may enjoy their minor triumphs, the larger reality is that entrepreneurs, whether individual or corporate, have been the dominant creators of a landscape whose crevices the homeowner can modify only modestly. Perhaps nothing more vividly illustrates their hegemony than the ways they have contrived suburban housing developments and shopping centers.

However ambivalently Americans may regard control by distant government agencies, there is no escaping its necessity in a modern economy; and with the strengthened central regime a modern citizenry finds itself necessarily imbued with nationalist notions. Inevitably such collective loyalties and such concentrated political power take recognizable form in the landscape. Official architecture is the most obvious point of entry. Governmental edifices in Washington, especially from the 1850s on, and their facsimiles in various state capitals, not to mention the ubiquitous standardized post offices of the twentieth century, set standards that were copied not only by counties and municipalities but also by builders of commercial and residential structures. This is especially striking in the case of the long-lived popularity of various classical revival styles. And even without official sponsorship, nationalist sentiment shows up unmistakably in the persistence of colonial revival designs since the 1880s and all the many buildings reminiscent of Independence Hall.

The federal presence has manifested itself in many ways other than building styles. The American land is punctuated by a great many military installations, some of them quite extensive, and their inevitable offshoots: veterans' clubhouses, Veterans Administration hospitals, and military cemeteries—all readily recognizable. To a marked degree, the historical monuments that began to appear in the 1850s have been as nationalistic in tone as in other lands. But what makes the United States truly exceptional among modern nation-states is the unparalleled profusion of flag display, by private individuals and businesses as well as by official installations, along with a remarkable prevalence of eagles (the national totem) and the national colors (red, white, and blue) in every conceivable venue. A complete inventory of the impress of central authority would require more space than is available here, but certainly one cannot overlook the interstate highway system, the array of rather standardized national parks and forests, the countless accomplishments of the Army Corps of Engineers in their reordering of America's hydrology and much else, and the highly visible feats of the Tennessee Valley Authority and other federal dam projects, some of gargantuan magnitude. Since the New Deal era, we have had the many tangible deeds of the Works Progress Administration, Civilian Conservation Corps, and other agencies and the immediately identifiable federal housing projects in numerous cities.

If the power and prestige of the national regime have generated so many notable signs and symptoms on the American scene, another kind of centralized authority—that of the more successful national or regional business firms—has produced something of a parallel phenomenon. The earliest such expression may well have been the standardized facilities of the major railroad lines, but the trend has fully blossomed more recently with nationally uniform designs for filling stations, hotel and motel chains, and a great assortment of look-alike franchised eating and retail operations.

SALVAGE AND PRESERVATION. Although economic, technological, and political forces have been the prime determinants of America's humanized landscapes, certain counterforces have been in evidence. In large part they have been energized by the mistakes and excesses of the past. Exploitation of American soils, waters, forests, and mines for immediate gain was intense, rapid, and all too often totally heedless of ultimate cost or consequence. So thorough has been the assault upon the habitat that, taking plant cover as an example, the survival of any patch of original prairie is improbable, and genuine virgin stands of forest are exceedingly rare, as are streams in anything like their original condition. Virtually everything sylvan that seems wild is actually second- or third-growth forest at best. In some instances one can argue that human intervention may have improved conditions in both substance and appearance.

But the contrary situation is much easier to document, a notorious example being the cutover area of northern Michigan, Wisconsin, and Minnesota. The clear-cutting of the once splendid forest in the late nineteenth century, along with many subsequent fires, has yielded a scraggly semidesert of scrub vegetation with no prospect of regeneration for a good many decades.

It was only toward the close of the 1800s that an organized conservation movement was born. It was led by elite members of society who were primarily concerned over the future availability of resources (for both economic and recreational use) and only incidentally, if at all, with the visual aspects of the problem. The same statement applies to the soil conservation programs that began to be implemented seriously in the 1930s. In any event, the question of appearance, of the integrity of manmade or man-modified landscapes, has come to the fore slowly and gradually, in part as a result of the historic preservation movement. From a halting start in the mid nineteenth century with campaigns to safeguard especially memorable single buildings, the movement broadened to embrace entire early settlements and urban neighborhoods of a certain venerability and charm as well as the more significant American battlefields. No doubt sensibilities have been sharpened by such scathing jeremiads against uglification as those by Peter Blake and Ian Nairn, and issues involving both preservation and the look of the land and the works of man have gradually crept onto the political agenda.

Until the turn of the century, exploitation of American soils, waters, forests, and mines for immediate gain was intense, rapid, and all too often totally heedless of ultimate cost or consequence.

Serious problems remain unresolved. Is it possible or desirable to keep these places frozen in a state of suspended animation? Should these localities be museumized or (like Charleston's Historic District or New Orleans's Vieux Carrée) allowed to change ever so slowly? How is genuine authenticity to be attained? How does gentrification of older city neighborhoods fit into the preservation picture?

Another recent movement, the environmental, may have even greater long-term consequences for the American landscape. Pursuing as their most central objective the preservation or restoration of wilderness and various fragile ecosystems, since the 1950s and 1960s the leaders of the movement have gained much popular support and perhaps catalyzed what seems to be a mass conversion to "green," or organic, consciousness. The effect on the landscape is incidental but potentially important. In a parallel development, beautification projects are no longer uncommon in American municipalities, and some cities have gone out of their way to encourage public art.

We must reckon with still another set of forces, those which mold our collective mental landscape images and thus, indirectly but meaningfully, the ways in which we manipulate our environs. Through the media of fiction, verse, landscape painting, calendar art, photography, movies, and television, we have charted a constellation of ideal landscapes in the mind's eye. They include the New England village; the antebellum southern plantation; the idyllic yeoman farm; the Middle American Main Street (so cleverly miniaturized and embalmed in a sanitized Disneyland) with its elm-lined residential streets; the western ranch; the South Sea island paradise; and perhaps others. Much of today's commercial and residential design is a matter of life imitating art.

SCHOLARLY APPROACHES. If an awareness that landscapes or, more generally, the visual aspect of shared spaces are items of common concern were to dawn upon the general public quite belatedly, the academic community has been equally slow in recognizing the value of landscape study. Although for many years geographers in the United States and abroad have debated the definition of the term "landscape," or its equivalent in other languages—with meanings ranging from simple scenery or vista to such abstractions as entire regions—it is only recently that anything resembling a serious school of landscape analysis has emerged. Human geographers have been the most conspicuous members of this loose fraternity, one that also includes historians, landscape architects, and folklorists. The essential premise, eloquently expounded by Henry Glassie and Thomas Schlereth, is that the ensemble of material objects (the relevance of sounds and smells remains moot) we call the landscape represents a priceless archive, a deeply layered palimpsest, the richest sort of means for gaining a deep understanding of human societies past and present. It is interesting and important not just in and of itself but even more for its implicit messages. The contention is that the documentation furnished by the landscape, including the testimony of those large groups of humanity who leave no written records, offers a much more comprehensive view of human life, thought, and ideals than the paper trail traditionally exploited by historians.

If there has been any central figure in this enterprise, it is undoubtedly John Brinckerhoff Jackson, who through his essays has given the landscape school a certain philosophical coherence and who, through the journal *Landscape*, which he founded in 1951 and edited for many years, has provided practitioners a major forum. The agenda for geographers and other students of the American (and other) landscapes is enormous, a task involving both description, or inventory, and subsequent analysis. More often than not, they have barely begun taking up the challenge, but what has been achieved justifies the claims of the landscape advocates.

At this point one can only briefly sketch what has been done and the long list of future chores. Data and understanding are fullest when it comes to rural houses, farmsteads, barns, and bridges; students of them may have already passed the point of diminishing returns. There has been some progress in studying cemeteries, parks, fencing, roads, roadside architecture, lawns, and gardens, but a great deal remains to be learned. For a large number of other landscape components, our organized knowledge is quite skimpy or entirely lacking. The list includes vernacular church buildings, factories, office buildings and office parks, yard and porch ornaments, field patterns, hospital and school buildings, monuments, shopping malls and commercial structures in general, the entire array of items associated with sport and recreation, trailer parks, abandoned spaces, and, not least, refuse dumps.

Finally, beyond the task of assembling so much needed data there looms the challenge of adequate interpretation of finding and answering the many urgent questions embedded in the many material microworlds we have created or transformed. The potentials of such landscape exegesis appear in Banham's work on Los Angeles, Duncan's account of a Westchester County village, Zelinsky's treatment of the Pennsylvania town, or the essays on the historical geography of the American landscape edited by Michael Conzen.

Such publications suggest that landscape analysis may play an important, perhaps vital role in addressing the grander issues that have begun to engage social historians and social scientists—such as the meaning of community and the operations of power, class, ethnicity, and gender in American life. In any event, there is little prospect that even the most enterprising set of students can bring to closure any time during the foreseeable future an exciting, ever-expanding research agenda.

[See also Agriculture; The Frontier; Geographic Mobility; National Parks and Preservation; Technology and Social Change; Transportation and Mobility.]

BIBLIOGRAPHY

Banham, Reyner. *Los Angeles: The Architecture of Four Ecologies* (1971).

Blake, Peter. *God's Own Junkyard: The Planned Deterioration of America's Landscape* (1964).

Conzen, Michael P., ed. *The Making of the American Landscape* (1990).

Duncan, James S., Jr. "Landscape Taste as a Symbol of Group Identity: A Westchester County Village." *Geographical Review* 63, no. 3 (1973).

Francaviglia, Richard V. *The Mormon Landscape: Existence, Creation and Perception of a Unique Image in the American West* (1978).

Garreau, Joel. *Edge City: Life on the New Frontier* (1991).

Glassie, Henry. *Folk Housing in Middle Virginia: A Structural Analysis of Historic Artifacts* (1975).

Herbers, John. *The New Heartland: America's Flight Beyond the Suburbs and How It Is Changing Our Future* (1986).

Jackson, John Brinckerhoff. *The Necessity for Ruins, and Other Topics* (1980).

———. *Discovering the Vernacular Landscape* (1984).

Jackson, Kenneth T. *Crabgrass Frontier: The Suburbanization of the United States* (1985).

Johnson, Hildegard Binder. *Order upon the Land: The U.S. Rectangular Land Survey and the Upper Mississippi Country* (1976).

Liebs, Chester H. *Main Street to Miracle Mile: American Roadside Architecture* (1985).

Lowenthal, David. "The American Scene." *Geographical Review* 58, no. 1 (1968).

Marschner, Francis J. *Land Use and Its Patterns in the United States* (1959).

Marx, Leo. *The Machine in the Garden: Technology and the Pastoral Ideal in America* (1964).

Meinig, D. W., ed. *The Interpretation of Ordinary Landscapes: Geographical Essays* (1979).

Nairn, Ian. *The American Landscape: A Critical View* (1965).

Nash, Roderick. *Wilderness and the American Mind.* 3d ed. (1982).

Noble, Allen G. *Wood, Brick and Stone: The North American Settlement Landscape* (1984).

Schlereth, Thomas J. *Artifacts and the American Past: Techniques for the Teaching Historian* (1980).

Stilgoe, John R. *Common Landscape of America, 1580–1845* (1982).

———. *Metropolitan Corridor: Railroads and the American Scene* (1983).

Tunnard, Christopher, and Henry Hope Reed. *American Skyline: The Growth and Form of Our Cities and Towns* (1955).

Williams, Michael. *Americans and Their Forests: A Historical Geography* (1989).

Wood, Joseph S. "Village and Community in Early Colonial New England." *Journal of Historical Geography* 8, no. 4 (1982).

Zelinsky, Wilbur. "The Pennsylvania Town: An Overdue Geographical Account." *Geographical Review* 67, no. 2 (1977).

———. *Nation into State: The Shifting Symbolic Foundations of American Nationalism* (1988).

— WILBUR ZELINSKY

LIFE STAGES

In order to understand change over time in patterns of individual and family development, social historians have made extensive use of three important analytical constructs: the life stages, the family cycle, and the life course. The life stages—such as infancy, childhood, adolescence, adulthood, and old age—are developmental phases, each with its own biological, psychological, and social characteristics, through which individuals pass over the course of their lives. The family cycle (which social anthropologists call the "developmental cycle") refers to the stages through which families go as members age and family size expands and contracts. The life course refers to the passage of individuals through major life cycle transitions, such as leaving home, getting married, and entering and leaving school and the labor force.

Life-stages analysis has focused on the changing definition, demarcation, and social experience of the phases of individual development. It has shown that over the course of American history the definition of the life stages has grown more conceptually precise and more completely organized institutionally, and that the transition between stages has become more abrupt and disjunctive.

The family-cycle approach has concentrated on changes in the basic phases through which families go from the time they are formed to the time they are dissolved. It has revealed the impact of such important demographic developments as declining fertility rates, increasing life expectancy, prolonged residence of children in their parents' home, and the decline in the practice of boarding on the familial experience of individuals.

Life-course analysis has explored changes in the timing and sequencing of key life cycle transitions. It has found that since the eighteenth century the timing of major transitions has grown more rigid and uniform, and has increasingly come to reflect individual preferences rather than family needs. Taken together, the life-stages, family-cycle, and life-course approaches have underscored the fact that private life has undergone transformations at least as radical and far-reaching as those that have occurred in Americans' public institutions.

This essay will describe changes in the definition and demarcation of the life stages over time. It will examine the impact of such historical developments as the rise of the market and urbanization on the demarcation of the life stages and the timing of key life-cycle events and transitions, and the rituals surrounding them. It will also examine the changing significance of age in American culture and the shifting distribution of power among various age groups.

The Analysis of the Life Stages

The notion that human development passes through a series of stages is rooted in antiquity. Roman writers identified three to seven distinct ages of man, proceeding from conception to death. Medieval thinkers and artists formulated a variety of systems of age groups, dividing human life into three-, four-, five-, six-, seven-, ten-, and twelve-part schemata. Perhaps the best-known periodization of the human life cycle is found in William Shakespeare's play *As You Like It,* where he describes seven stages of human life, beginning with "puking" infancy and ending with "second childishness and mere oblivion, sans teeth, sans eyes, sans taste, sans everything."

Today, social scientists use the concept of the "life cycle" to refer to the division of individual lives into a series of sequential stages, such as infancy, childhood, adolescence, middle age, and old age. Each stage is defined in terms of three distinct conceptual components: biological, psychological, and social. The contemporary notion of adolescence, for example, consists of a biological component—involving pubertal physical changes, rapid physiological growth, and sexual maturation; a psychological component—involving drastic mood swings, inner turmoil, generational conflict, and a quest for identity; and a social component—which involves the shifting social experience, institutional treatment, and cultural definition of adolescence.

Each conceptual component of a particular life stage is affected by a changing historical and cultural context. This is true even in the case of biology. Recent scholarship has suggested that the age of first menstruation and the age at which young people attain full physical stature has declined since 1850. The age of menarche appears to have fallen from approximately fifteen or sixteen in 1850 to between twelve and thirteen in 1990, while the age of puberty for boys seems to have declined from around sixteen to thirteen or fourteen. Similarly, the age at which young men achieve full growth appears to have fallen from about twenty-five in the early nineteenth century to around twenty in the late twentieth century.

THE CHANGING CONTOURS OF THE LIFE STAGES. One of the most important conclusions to emerge from recent scholarship is that the life stages are historical constructs, shaped by the interaction of cultural, demographic, economic, and institutional factors. The definition, connotations, and experience of the life stages vary according to class, ethnicity, gender, and historical period.

The way that the life stages are periodized has undergone profound shifts over the course of American history. Seventeenth-century New Englanders usually identified four distinct life stages: childhood, youth, middle age, and old age. These categories were vaguely defined and were not rigidly linked to a specific age range.

Beginning in the late nineteenth century, the number of culturally identified life stages multiplied, as psychologists, sociologists, and other social commentators invented a variety of new age categories, beginning with adolescence, which acquired its modern connotations around the turn of the century. During World War II, the term "teenager" began to be used as an age category. In recent years, age categories have proliferated rapidly to include "preschoolers," "preadolescents," the "young old," and the "old old."

As the number of culturally delineated age stages increased, the boundaries demarcating the end of one life stage and the beginning of the next grew increasingly rigid and disjunctive. During the seventeenth and eighteenth centuries, generational lines were more blurred, and the transition from one life stage to another was less severe than in the nineteenth century. From an early age, colonial children worked alongside adults and dressed in adult clothing. In churches and other community activities and associations, the young and old participated together.

During the early nineteenth century, generational lines sharpened and the passage from childhood to youth and adulthood became more abrupt. In the late eighteenth and early nineteenth centuries, it was common for young men, and to a lesser extent for young women, to shift back and forth between their families and work experiences outside the home. By the middle of the nineteenth century, the living arrangements of young people had undergone a dramatic change, as an increasing number remained in the parental home, attended school, and postponed labor force participation until their late teens or twenties. The boundaries separating childhood, youth, and adulthood became more sharply demarcated.

SOCIAL AND CULTURAL CONSTRUCTION OF THE LIFE STAGES. The major differences between modern conceptions of the life stages and early notions of the "ages of man" are that contemporary conceptions of childhood, adolescence, middle age, and old age are much more age-specific and conceptually precise, and that the transition between stages has grown more disjunctive. A variety of factors have contributed to a more precise formulation of the life stages. These include scientific and medical discoveries that identify childhood, adolescence, and old age as biologically and psychologically distinct stages of life, with their own needs and characteristics; and such institutional developments as the emergence of age-graded schools, the enactment of laws prohibiting child labor, and the adoption of old-age pensions, which contribute to the segregation of age groups from one another.

The complex process by which a particular life stage was culturally and institutionally constructed can be seen in the eighteenth- and nineteenth-century "discovery of childhood." To speak of the "discovery of childhood" is not, of course, to imply that childhood was unknown to earlier Americans; they defined it, however, quite differently than later Americans did. Seventeenth-century New Englanders, for example, did not isolate children from the adult world. They did not establish special institutions for young children or set aside special rooms in their homes for them, nor did they assume that children had a unique psychology. Moreover, they did not dress children in distinctive clothing or represent them in art as special categories of beings.

Beginning in the eighteenth century, a new view of children gradually appeared. During a bitter mid-eighteenth-century theological debate over infant de-

To speak of the "discovery of childhood" in the eighteenth and nineteenth centuries is not to imply that childhood was unknown to earlier Americans; they defined it, however, quite differently than later Americans did.

pravity that deeply divided the New England churches, a new conception of childhood began to be articulated that viewed children not as little adults but as special creatures requiring attention, love, and time to mature. Religious liberals rejected older notions of original sin and upheld a new view of children as malleable creatures who embodied virtue, innocence, wholeness, and purity. The new focus on, and respect for, the child could be seen in the profusion of books and toys specifically for children; in the supplanting of the stiffly posed portraits of children in the seventeenth and early eighteenth century by more romantic depictions of childhood playfulness and innocence; and in the appearance of furniture specifically designed for children, painted in pastel colors, and decorated with pictures of animals or figures from nursery rhymes.

Early-nineteenth-century reformers and educators invoked the new images of childhood in their crusades for the creation of special age-segregated environments—such as Sunday schools, public schools, houses of refuge, and the Young Men's Christian Association—where youthful innocence could be protected and nurtured. By the second half of the nineteenth century, a growing sensitivity to children's unique needs and problems led physicians to establish a new branch of medicine—pediatrics—specifically devoted to infant and childhood diseases; inspired "child savers" to establish the first organizations in American history to protect children from neglect and abuse; and encouraged journalists to launch the first specialized children's magazines.

The term "adolescence," derived from the Latin *adolescere*, meaning to grow up, entered popular discourse in the late nineteenth century, denoting the distinct age range that extended from puberty to the end of the teen years. In contrast to the earlier concept of youth, which referred to a much wider age span (usually denoting those seven to thirty), adolescence carried much more clearly defined connotations and was much more rigidly set off from adult society. G. Stanley Hall (1844–1924), one of the nation's leading psychologists, helped to formulate and popularize the modern conception of adolescence as a period of "storm and stress" rooted in the physiological changes associated with puberty. Hall and numerous popularizers disseminated a conception of adolescence as a critical stage of life during which young people established their basic identity. Among the factors that contributed to a recognition of adolescents as a clearly defined age group were the systematization, bureaucratization, and prolongation of education and the classification of students by age; industrialization, which undermined apprenticeship systems and made occupations more specialized than in the past; and growing public concern over juvenile delinquency and child labor.

Adolescence as a distinct age group, with unique needs and problems, was institutionalized in the late nineteenth and early twentieth centuries. Educators, social workers, and other advocates of the young, convinced that adolescents needed time to develop the intellectual and emotional capacities to face the challenges of adult life, supported restrictions on child labor, and compulsory education laws, raised the school-leaving age, expanded the number of high schools, and created numerous adult-sponsored youth organizations, such as the Boy Scouts and the Girl Scouts. The separation of adolescence from adulthood was also embodied in the establishment of a separate juvenile court system and the emergence of a distinct youth market for leisure, evident in the rapid growth of dance halls and young men's clubs.

During the late nineteenth century, old age, like adolescence, began to be perceived in a new way: as a clearly delineated stage of life isolated from the rest of society. In colonial America, old age generally commanded authority and respect, but by the end of the nineteenth century, the status attached to age had declined, and old age was increasingly associated with such problems as dependency, physical disability, mental debility, and a host of character problems including depression, bitterness, hypochondria, and an inability to absorb new ideas. A number of factors contributed to this more negative perception of old age; these included the mounting economic dependency of the elderly in an increasingly urban and industrial society, the increasing incidence of chronic degenerative conditions among the elderly as medical advances reduced the number of deaths caused by infections and epidemic diseases, and a cult of youth, which regarded the elderly as inflexible, unadaptable, and out of step with the times, and as inefficient and unproductive workers.

Increasingly, social workers, government policymakers, and businessmen regarded old age as a social problem. Old-age homes began to appear at the end of the nineteenth century. During the Progressive Era, the first public commission on aging was established (in Massachusetts in 1909); the first federal old-age pension bill was introduced (also in 1909); the first survey of the economic conditions of the elderly was conducted (in Massachusetts in 1910); and the first noncontributory old-age pension system was enacted (in Arizona in 1914). Retirement was institutionalized during the early and mid twentieth century with the introduction of company pension plans, the enactment of mandatory retirement laws, and the adoption of the Social Security System.

Family Cycle

Just as individual lives pass through a sequence of developmental stages, so families go through a series of stages from the time they are formed until they are dissolved. Their size increases and contracts as children are born and older children leave home. Over the span of their members' lives, changes occur in family roles, in relationships between spouses and between parents and children, and in income and consumption patterns. Social scientists use the concept of the family or household cycle, or the developmental cycle, to refer to the sequence of changes through which families go from the formation of a union until a couple's deaths.

Social historians adopted the concept of the family cycle from family sociologists such as Evelyn Duvall and Reuben Hill, who defined the stages of the family cycle in terms of such characteristics as the presence or absence of children, the children's ages, and the employment status of the father. Hill developed a widely used nine-stage model of the family cycle:

1. Establishment (newly married, childless)
2. New parents (infant to three years)
3. Preschool family (child three to six, and possibly younger siblings)
4. School-age family (oldest child six to twelve, and possibly younger siblings)
5. Family with adolescent (oldest child thirteen to nineteen, and possibly younger siblings)
6. Family with young adult (oldest child twenty until first child leaves home)
7. Family as launching center (from departure of first to last child)
8. Postparental family, the middle years (after children have left home until father retires)
9. Aging family (after retirement of father)

A number of historians of the family have used the concept of the family cycle to better understand the economic functioning of the family. Historians of the colonial family have used the concept to examine indentured servitude and the transmission of property from one generation to the next. They have found that many poorer parents, lacking sufficient property to pass on a landed estate to their sons and daughters, often sent young children ranging in age from seven to fourteen to work as indentured servants in exchange for room and board.

More prosperous parents, eager to preserve the family estate, sometimes adopted a "stem family" pattern of inheritance. Aging parents would take a married son or son-in-law and his family to live with them, operate their farm, and inherit the property in return for assuming financial responsibility for the family's other children. Under the stem family arrangement, family composition alternated between a nuclear and an extended structure, depending on the stage of the family cycle. Some colonial families, toward the end of the family cycle, migrated to the frontier in order to provide land for their sons.

Historians of nineteenth-century working-class families have found that the economic well-being of the family depended on the stage of the family cycle. Working-class families faced particularly acute financial stress at the beginning and the end of the family cycle. During the early years of a marriage, when children were too young to work and contribute directly to the family's income, many working-class families lived with parents or boarded with another family. During the middle stages of the family cycle, when children could contribute to the family's income, economic well-being increased, only to decline at the end of the family cycle, after children had left home, since family income depended on the number of members in the work force. To maintain the family's standard of living, an older couple often took boarders or lodgers into their house.

While some social historians have used the family cycle to analyze the family's economic behavior, others have used the concept to understand changes in the family's demographic characteristics and patterns of development. Historians of the family have shown, for example, that the family cycle, like the life stages, has undergone far-reaching transformations over the course of American history. Changes in the definition of the stages of the family cycle are particularly striking. During the colonial period, the family cycle often began not with marriage but with cohabitation, especially in frontier regions. The high cost of a marriage license and a shortage of ministers or magistrates meant that many couples never formally married. The recent upsurge in premarital cohabitation (according to one late 1980s' estimate 53 percent of newly married couples cohabited prior to marriage) has produced a stage in the family cycle somewhat reminiscent of the earlier pattern.

As a result of changing fertility patterns and increased life expectancy, the family cycle has changed signifi-

The "empty nest" period of parenting now constitutes about one-third of a couple's married life; as a result of a growing sex differential in mortality, widowhood has increased in length and now averages nearly ten years.

cantly since the late nineteenth century. A reduction in the birthrate and closer spacing of children have meant that women spend a smaller portion of their lives raising young children. An eighteenth-century Quaker woman could expect to spend over seventeen years of a thirty-year marriage bearing children; for her, family life coincided with childbearing and child rearing. In contrast, a woman born during the 1920s spent only about ten years of a forty-four-year marriage bearing children; she and her husband could expect to live together for more than a decade after children had ceased to be responsibilities.

Increasing life spans have meant that husbands and wives spend more of their married lives without children. Over the course of the twentieth century, the number of years married couples spend together after children have left home has climbed from 1.6 years to 12.3 years. The "empty nest" now constitutes about one-third of a couples' married life. As a result of a

The number of years married couples spend together after children have left home has climbed from 1.6 to 12.3 years over the course of the twentieth century.

growing sex differential in mortality, widowhood has increased in length, and now averages nearly ten years.

Along with the shifts that have occurred in the periodization of the family cycle has come another important transformation: a marked decline in the earlier practice of taking kin and nonkin into the family at distinct points in the family cycle. During the nineteenth century, boarders and lodgers were an important fact of life; approximately 12 to 15 percent of urban households took in extended kin and 20 to 30 percent took in boarders and lodgers (compared with just 5 percent today). Middle-class families were particularly likely to take in extended kin, while working-class families were more likely to take in nonrelatives (who were usually members of their own ethnic group).

During the late nineteenth century, between half and two-thirds of all young people in urban areas left their parents' household, usually in their twenties, and lived temporarily as boarders or lodgers prior to marriage. Middle-aged and older persons—such as unmarried women, widows, and parents whose children had left home—supplemented their income by taking in young adults as boarders and lodgers. In contrast with the pattern common today, very few older or younger people lived by themselves; altogether, just 1 to 3 percent of all nineteenth-century households consisted of individuals living alone. Older people usually tried to keep their residence and have adult children or other relatives or unrelated lodgers move in with them. Except in remote western frontier communities, the overwhelming majority of Americans, regardless of age, lived in a family setting.

REGIONAL, ETHNIC, AND CLASS VARIATIONS IN FAMILY CYCLES. Social historians disagree about the usefulness of the family-cycle concept. The basic criticism is that it fails to capture the complexity of family life in the past. Critics note, for example, that the family-cycle concept is based on contemporary family patterns, which differ profoundly from those in the past. Earlier in American history, children were born over a longer time span than children are today, and shifted back and forth between the home and other residences frequently and irregularly. This pattern of leaving and returning home over a long time span does not fit readily into any sequential model of family stages.

In addition, critics charge that since the family cycle concept is based exclusively on intact, two-parent families, it tends to ignore the experience of single-parent families. Indeed, largely as a result of higher death rates, most American families in the past failed to complete all the stages of the family cycle. As recently as the beginning of the twentieth century, half of all parents experienced the death of a child (compared with 4 percent today), and a quarter of all children lost at least one parent before reaching the age of fifteen (against 5 percent today). At the start of the twentieth century, fewer than half of all American women experienced the "normative" female life cycle: marrying, bearing children, and surviving to age fifty with their marriage intact (long enough to see the youngest child leave home). Most women died early, never married, had no children, or had their marriages prematurely ended by death, divorce, or separation.

Today, as in the past, most families do not conform to any single, uniform family cycle. In recent years, rising rates of divorce and single parenthood have replaced mortality as primary sources of diversity in the family cycle. Recent estimates suggest that about half of all children (and 90 percent of black children) born in the 1980s will spend some time in a single-parent home, and over half of these children will spend six or more years with only one parent.

Yet despite the objections that have been raised, the family-cycle approach is useful in illuminating regional, ethnic, and class differences in patterns of family development. In seventeenth-century Maryland and Virginia, exceptionally high mortality rates made remarriage a regular part of the family cycle. In many instances, by the time the eldest children of a first marriage reached adulthood, they bore no blood relationship to the parents heading the household.

Nineteenth-century slave families had a family cycle very different from that of white Southerners. A significant minority of slave women bore a child prior to settling into a stable marital union; for these women, the family cycle started with premarital pregnancy rather than marriage. On many plantations, slave children, between the ages of seven and ten, were taken away from their parents and sent to live in separate cabins or barracks. Interviews with former slaves reveal that 30 percent of slave marriages were terminated by sale. Family disruption was an integral part of the family cycle under slavery.

Depending on their occupation and ethnic background, nineteenth-century working-class families developed distinctive family cycles. Among late-nineteenth-century coal mining families, relatively high wages early in the family cycle and an absence of employment opportunities for wives outside the home encouraged early marriage and frequent childbearing. Nineteenth-century urban black families, in contrast, facing chronic unemployment and high rates of poverty, tended to marry later and to have fewer children.

Obviously, it would be a mistake to try to impose a single, uniform model of sequential stages on families in the past. A challenge facing social historians is to devise alternative models of the family cycle that accurately reflect the experience of distinct cultural and socioeconomic groups in the past.

The Life Course

In their search for useful ways to analyze changing patterns of individual development, social historians have embraced the concept of the life course. Instead of identifying discrete stages of development, the life-course perspective focuses on major life-cycle transitions, such as marriage, schooling, and entry into and exit from the labor force. The life-course approach analyzes the way a particular historical context shapes the timing and sequencing of life-cycle transitions and pays particular attention to the way that large-scale social processes, such as a war or an economic depression, affect the life experiences of particular groups of individuals.

Like the life stages and the family cycle, life-course transitions are shaped by changing socioeconomic, cultural, and historical conditions. The cultural meaning, timing, and sequencing of key life events are influenced by such factors as class, gender, and ethnic identity.

CHANGES IN THE TIMING OF LIFE-CYCLE TRANSITIONS. Between the early seventeenth century and the mid twentieth century, the timing of major life-cycle transitions, such as entry into school, marriage, and participation in the labor force grew increasingly rigid and uniform. During the seventeenth and eighteenth centuries, the language of age tended to be vague and amorphous. The terms used to denote the life stages were extremely broad. The term "infancy" referred to any child still under a mother's care and was applied to children as old as six. The word "child" was also used broadly, referring to young people as old as sixteen. The term "youth" could refer to a person as young as seven or as old as thirty. Physical size and strength were more important than chronological age in describing individuals.

Even in the legal realm, age was a rather imprecise category. In seventeenth-century law, there was no single age of majority. The age at which the young might gain control over an inheritance ranged between fifteen and twenty-five; the age at which an orphan was permitted to choose a guardian varied between thirteen and sixteen; a person might receive the right to vote anywhere between twenty-one and forty.

One reason why age categories tended to be imprecise was that many key life experiences were not yet tied to distinct ages. Marriage customarily took place after a young man had achieved economic independence, which often occurred only after he had received an inheritance from his father. Women bore children until menopause. A woman might bear her first child around the age of twenty-three and not bear her last child until twenty years later. Consequently, the age range of children within families was much greater than it is now. In colonial New England, half of all children grew up in families with nine or more children and as a result, the term "child" included a spectrum of ages stretching from newborns to people in their twenties. Men and women retired only when they were incapable of working.

Underscoring the amorphousness of age categories was the wide age range of young people in academies and colleges. It was not uncommon, as late as the early nineteenth century, for school classrooms to contain students ranging in age from seven to twenty-five. Age differentiation in colleges tended to be limited. Colonial colleges contained students as young as thirteen or fourteen and as old as the mid twenties. Prior to 1850, nearly 60 percent of all deaths occurred among people fifteen or younger; another 20 percent of deaths took place among those between the ages of fifteen and forty-five. Today, in contrast, only about 10 percent of deaths occur among those younger than forty-five.

Although chronological age was a less important organizing principle in colonial society than it has since become, it would be a mistake to assume that age had no social meaning. There were a number of social and cultural rituals that marked an individual's progression through the life course. Around the age of six, colonial children stopped wearing shapeless smocks and began to wear breeches or skirts and petticoats. Between the ages of six and fourteen, many boys and, to a lesser extent, girls went to work in another household, as apprentices or servants. Full religious communion usually took place among individuals in their twenties or thirties.

Age norms and age consciousness were relatively weak but not nonexistent. Youths in colonial New England, for instance, developed a distinctive subculture characterized by such recreations as frolicking, dancing, and singing. Beginning in the early eighteenth century, youths set up their own religious and secular organizations.

Life-course transitions are shaped by changing socioeconomic, cultural, and historical conditions. The cultural meaning, timing, and sequencing of key life events are influenced by such factors as class, gender, and ethnic identity.

There were important regional differences in the demarcation of the life stages. In the Chesapeake colonies of Maryland and Virginia, a high mortality rate meant that many parents died young. As a result, sons generally received inheritances at an earlier age than their New England counterparts, giving them earlier autonomy in marriage decisions and choice of a career.

Over the course of the nineteenth century, Americans became increasingly sensitive to age. The growth of age consciousness was evident in the popularization of a number of age-specific religious rituals, such as Christian confirmation and the Jewish bar mitzvah; the increasingly regular celebration of birthdays; the appearance, beginning in the 1870s, of mass-produced birthday cards; and the first references to a "proper" age of marriage in late-nineteenth-century etiquette books. It was also apparent in the emergence of the late-nineteenth-century child study movement, which sought to identify the distinctive features of children's emotional, physiological, and psychological development at each age.

One factor that contributed to increasing age consciousness during the nineteenth century was a profound shift in the age structure of society. Prior to 1800, as a result of a very high birthrate and a relatively low death rate, America had one of the youngest populations in world history, with a median age around sixteen. After 1800 the birthrate fell sharply, and the median age of the population began to rise, reaching 18.9 years in 1850 and 24.1 years in 1910. As the population aged, the middle-aged and elderly made up a growing presence. Those over sixty increased from 4 to 6 percent of the seventeeth-century population to 15 percent in the late twentieth century. Another factor contributing to the growing awareness of age was the organization of public schools around a sequence of age-specific grades. As school attendance increased and schooling extended later into life, a growing number of young people were isolated in an age-graded environment apart from the rest of society.

Changes in the organization of the workplace also contributed to increasing consciousness of age. Between 1800 and the Civil War, apprenticeship declined and many teenage workers left the labor force or saw their status drop as they assumed unskilled jobs for "boy's wages." At the same time, many older workers, who were increasingly regarded as less productive than the middle-aged, retired or were forced out of the labor market. In the twentieth century, participation in the work force was further segmented by age as child labor laws and the first mandatory retirement rules (which appeared around 1910) defined entry into and exit from the labor force.

As a result of these shifts in employment, schooling, and the age structure of the population, the structure of the individual life course changed. During the early twentieth century, the timing and sequencing of major life course transitions—such as the age of leaving school, leaving home, beginning adult work, marrying, and establishing one's own household—became increasingly uniform and rigid; consequently, a growing number of individuals experienced these transitions at the same time as other people of their own age. Perhaps the most striking development was an increase in the duration of schooling and in the age at entry into the work force. Child labor dropped sharply; between 1910 and 1930, the proportion of employed fifteen-year-old boys fell from one in two to one in six; the proportion of employed fifteen-year-old girls declined from one in four to one in twelve. The decline in teenage employment was accompanied by a marked increase in the length of schooling; in 1870 just 2 percent of young people graduated from high school, but by 1930, the percentage had climbed to 28.8.

As high school attendance became more common, a new set of rituals marking a young person's progression through the life course, such as high school graduation, arose. As early as the mid 1910s, a new pattern of unchaperoned dating appeared among high school students. Other significant new age markers that gradually appeared included receiving a driver's license and entering military service.

In the 1980s and 1990s, the trend toward relatively rigid sequencing and timing of key life events eroded. The pattern of individuals progressing from schooling to work force participation became less dominant as an increasing number of high school students took after-school jobs. Similarly, the pattern in which couples progressed from engagement to marriage, cohabitation, and childbearing declined as increasing numbers of couples cohabited prior to marriage, a higher proportion of births occurred to unwed mothers, and more married couples waited several years before having children.

The trend away from rigid age norms was also apparent in increasing variation in the age of first marriage and the timing of college attendance. At the same time, certain institutionalized age categories, such as a twenty-one-year-old voting age and mandatory retirement at sixty-five, broke down. The Twenty-sixth Amendment reduced the voting age in federal elections to eighteen. In 1986, Congress amended the Age Discrimination in Employment Act of 1967 to strike down most maximum-age restrictions in the work force. The abolition of the peacetime military draft in 1973, which significantly reduced the proportion of adolescents entering military service, removed a major factor structuring the lives of young men.

CLASS, ETHNIC, AND GENDER DIFFERENCES IN LIFE-COURSE EXPERIENCES. During the seventeenth century, region and gender exerted a particularly strong influence on life-course experience. In the seventeenth-century Chesapeake colonies of Maryland and Virginia, a high mortality rate (due to typhoid fever, dysentery, and malaria), a severely skewed sex ratio, and a high proportion of individuals bound out as indentured servants produced life-course patterns fundamentally different from those found in New England. In New England, males and females who survived infancy were likely to live into their sixties or seventies; in the Chesapeake, men were unlikely to live beyond their late forties and women lived even shorter lives, since malaria caused a disproportionately higher death rate among pregnant women.

The fact that many immigrants were committed to long terms of service meant that many men never had an opportunity to marry and many marriages were delayed to relatively late ages. In Maryland, immigrant women were usually twenty-four or older at first marriage. Delayed marriage, combined with high levels of infant mortality—a quarter of all children died before their first birthday—helped limit the number of surviving children per family to an average of two or three, compared with seven or eight in New England. The short average life span meant that long marriages were extremely rare; the typical marriage lasted seven years. Other characteristics of the Chesapeake colonies in the seventeenth century included substantial numbers of orphans and bereaved parents, frequent remarriages, and a high illegitimacy rate. A third of immigrant women bore children out of wedlock, reflecting the dependent status of female servants.

During the nineteenth century, class differences in life-course patterns were pronounced, particularly during the teen years. The early phases of the industrial revolution accentuated demand for unskilled teenage laborers, prompting many working-class youths to enter the work force in their early teens. Meanwhile, a growing number of middle-class youths stayed in school during their mid teens. The divergence between prolonged formal education for the middle class and early entry into the work force for the working class grew even sharper in the late nineteenth century, as opportunities for professional training increased.

Gender differences in life-course patterns, particularly in employment patterns, were marked. During the nineteenth and early twentieth centuries, women's entry into and exit from the work force were closely linked to their stage in the life course. Large numbers of young, unmarried women worked upon leaving school, but upon marriage most ceased full-time work. Whether a woman remained in the work force following marriage was heavily influenced by her ethnic background. African American women and French-Canadian women were particularly likely to work after marriage, while other groups were much less likely to combine marriage and wage work.

Since World War II, differences between men's and women's life course patterns have narrowed somewhat as women's rates of labor force participation have risen. In 1940, 26 percent of American women were in the labor force. Most working women were young, single women, widows or women abandoned by their husbands, or impoverished immigrant or black wives. By 1980, 51 percent of all women sixteen and over were in the labor force, compared with 77 percent of all men, and included about half of all married women with children.

Racial differences in life-course experiences have been an important characteristic of American life throughout the twentieth century. In the early twentieth century, black children were consistently more likely than white children to be raised in a single-parent family, reflecting higher rates of premature death, divorce, separation, and out-of-wedlock births. The proportion of ever-married black women who were widowed, divorced, or separated was significantly higher than among white women (taking age distribution into account). In 1910, the dissolution rate (the proportion of widowed and divorced among women ever married) for marriages of native white women was 16 percent, 17 percent for foreign-born white women, and 29 percent for black women. Black mothers were also much more likely to be employed than white mothers; in 1890, 22 percent of married black women ages thirty-five to forty-four held jobs, compared with 3 percent of married white women.

In the early twentieth century, black children were consistently more likely than white children to be raised in a single-parent family, reflecting higher rates of premature death, divorce, separation, and out-of-wedlock births.

In recent years, racial differences in life course experience have persisted. Since 1960 there have been consistent differences in rates of marital disruption and single parenthood. Compared with non-Hispanic white women and Mexican American women, black women are twice as likely to be divorced or separated within ten years of marriage and less likely to remarry. About a third of black women remarry within ten years, compared with half of Mexican American women and two-thirds of non-Hispanic white women. As a result of higher rates of marital disruption and lower rates of marriage and remarriage, single-parent households are more common among blacks, and black children are more likely to spend part of their childhood in a single-parent household. Today, about five out of every six black children spend part of their childhood in a single-parent family, and this experience usually constitutes a majority of their childhood years.

THE TIMING OF LIFE-COURSE TRANSITIONS: FROM FAMILY NEEDS TO INDIVIDUAL PREFERENCE. Prior to the twentieth century, the timing of many key life decisions—such as the age of entering or leaving school, leaving home, marrying, or entering the work force—tended to be based on family needs rather than on individual preference. In many colonial families, and many nineteenth-century working-class, black, and immigrant families, individual family members were required to subordinate their personal wishes to larger family considerations. Social historians use the concept of "family strategies" to refer to the pattern in which the timing of major life-course transitions was a by-product of collective needs rather than of individual choices.

Economically, nineteenth-century working-class families functioned as a single entity; the desires of any particular individual often had to be sacrified for the good of the family. During the nineteenth century, many urban working-class children postponed marriage and continued to live in their parents' home, contributing their earnings to a collective "family economy." Among many ethnic groups, daughters were expected to drop out of school early so that their brothers could continue their education. It was also common for the youngest daughter to postpone marriage or fail to marry at all in order to care for aging parents. Family strategies involving the subordination of individual preferences to collective family needs in the timing of key life-course transitions allowed poorer families to overcome economic hardship.

During the twentieth century, life-course decisions have increasingly reflected individual choice or institutionalized age norms rather than family needs. The timing of marriage, attending school, leaving home, entering the work force, or retiring, rather than reflecting family pressures, has been determined by personal preference; by law, such as mandatory school attendance and retirement laws; and by norms disseminated by the peer group or the broader culture.

COHORT ANALYSIS. Major historical events, such as wars and economic depressions, exert a powerful influence on individual development. In order to assess the influence of historical events and trends on the individual life course, social historians compare and contrast the experiences of carefully defined groups of people, called cohorts, who move through the life course and experience historical events at approximately the same time.

To understand the impact of the Great Depression on the individual life course, Glen H. Elder, Jr., analyzed the lives of the cohorts born in the early 1920s, which experienced the Depression as preadolescents and adolescents. He found that girls in deprived families assumed a greater degree of responsibility for housework than those spared a sharp loss of income and status, and that they displayed a stronger commitment to motherhood and domesticity as adults. Boys from deprived households entered the adult work force at a young age, formed their career plans relatively early in life, and placed a high value on job security.

The varying size of age cohorts has been linked to individuals' life chances. Richard Easterlin contrasted the experience of the cohort born in the late 1920s and 1930s, a time when birthrates were depressed, with the baby boomers born in the 1950s. He found that the individuals born in the late 1920s and 1930s, who had been in their early childhood during the Depression, formed relatively modest material aspirations, faced little competition for jobs at maturity, and were financially secure enough to marry and have children at a relatively young age. Their children, in contrast, who grew up during the 1950s and 1960s, spent their childhood during an era of unprecedented affluence. Unlike their parents, they developed considerable expectations for their own material and emotional wellbeing. But because they were members of a large birth cohort, they encountered lower wages and poorer prospects for promotion because the supply of workers exceeded the demand.

One of the most striking conclusions to emerge from scholarship on the life course is that contemporary Americans are much more conscious of age than were their ancestors. Not only are contemporary Americans more likely to organize activities and social institutions around discrete age groupings, they also are more likely to associate distinct biological and psychological traits and behavioral norms with specific ages.

As historian Howard P. Chudacoff has persuasively argued, the growth of age consciousness and age grading is a product of diverse social processes, including the rise of new scientific and medical theories, which have linked certain physical and psychological characteristics and needs with specific ages; the creation of new social organizations, such as public schools and social welfare programs, which use age as an organizing principle; and the expansion of a consumer culture, which targets specific products and activities at discrete age groups and has helped to disseminate age norms. Earlier in American history, age categories tended to be broad and diffuse, and the timing of major life-cycle transitions tended to reflect family needs. Since the mid nineteenth century, age categories have become more narrowly defined and the timing of life-cycle transitions has increasingly reflected personal choice and institutionalized age norm.

[See also Adolescence; Childhood and Children; Courtship, Marriage, Separation, and Divorce; Death; Family Structures; Old Age; Reproduction and Parenthood.]

BIBLIOGRAPHY

Life-Course Histories

Chudacoff, Howard P. *How Old Are You? Age Consciousness in American Culture* (1989).

Demos, John. *Past, Present and Personal: The Family and the Life Course in American History* (1986).

Hareven, Tamara K. "Historical Changes in the Life Course and the Family: Policy Implications." In *Major Social Issues: A Multidisciplinary View*, edited by J. Milton Yinger and Stephen J. Cutler (1978).

Kett, Joseph F. "History of Age Grouping in America." In *Youth: Transition to Adulthood*, edited by J. S. Coleman, et al. (1974).

Vinovskis, Maris A. "From Household Size to the Life Course: Some Observations on Recent Trends in Family History." *American Behavioral Scientist* 21 (1977): 263–287.

———. "The Historian and the Life Course: Reflections on Recent Approaches to the Study of American Family Life in the Past." *Life-Span Development and Behavior* 8 (1986): 33–59.

Life-Cycle Transitions

Hareven, Tamara K., ed. *Transitions: The Family and the Life Course in Historical Perspective* (1978).

Hogan, Dennis. *Transitions and Social Change: The Early Lives of American Men* (1981).

Modell, John. *Into One's Own: From Youth to Adulthood in the United States, 1920–1975* (1989).

Wells, Robert V. *Revolutions in Americans' Lives: A Demographic Perspective on the History of Americans, Their Families, and Their Society* (1982).

Childhood

Graff, Harvey J., ed. *Growing Up in America: Historical Experiences* (1987).

Hawes, Joseph M., and N. Ray Hiner, eds. *American Childhood: A Research Guide and Historical Handbook* (1985).

Hiner, N. Ray, and Joseph M. Hawes, eds. *Growing Up in America: Children in Historical Perspective* (1985).

Adolescence

Graebner, William. *Coming of Age in Buffalo: Youth and Authority in the Post-war Era* (1990).

Kett, Joseph F. *Rites of Passage: Adolescence in America, 1790 to the Present* (1977).

Middle Age

Eichorn, Dorothy H., et al., eds. *Present and Past in Middle Life* (1981).

Waring, Joan. *The Middle Years: A Multidisciplinary View* (1978).

Old Age

Achenbaum, W. Andrew. *Old Age in the New Land: The American Experience Since 1790* (1978).

———. *Shades of Gray: Old Age, American Values, and Federal Policies Since 1920* (1983).

Fischer, David Hackett. *Growing Old in America* (1977).

Haber, Carole. *Beyond Sixty-five: The Dilemma of Old Age in America's Past* (1983).

Hareven, Tamara K., and Kathleen J. Adams, eds. *Aging and Life Course Transitions: An Interdisciplinary Perspective* (1982).

Class and Ethnic Differences

Hareven, Tamara K. *Family Time and Industrial Time: The Relationship Between the Family and Work in a New England Industrial Community* (1982).

Hareven, Tamara K., and John Modell. "Family Patterns." In *Harvard Encyclopedia of American Ethnic Groups*, edited by Stephan Thernstrom (1980).

Hareven, Tamara K., ed. *Family and Kin in Urban Communities, 1700–1930* (1977).

Hershberg, Theodore, ed. *Philadelphia: Work, Space, Family, and Group Experience in the Nineteenth Century* (1981).

Smith, Judith E. *Family Connections: A History of Italian and Jewish Immigrant Lives in Providence, Rhode Island, 1900–1940* (1985).

Sweet, James A., and Larry L. Bumpass. *American Families and Households* (1987).

Gender Differences

Faver, Catherine A. *Women in Transition: Career, Family, and Life Satisfaction in Three Cohorts* (1984).

Peiss, Kathy Lee. *Cheap Amusements: Working Women and Leisure in Turn-of-the-Century New York* (1986).

Tentler, Leslie Woodcock. *Wage-Earning Women: Industrial Work and Family Life in the United States, 1900–1930* (1979).

Theoretical and Methodological Issues

Clausen, John A. *The Life Course: A Sociological Perspective* (1986).

Easterlin, Richard A. *Birth and Fortune: The Impact of Numbers on Personal Welfare* (1980).

Elder, Glen H., Jr. *Children of the Great Depression: Social Change in Life Experience* (1974).

———. *Life Course Dynamics: Trajectories and Transitions, 1968–1980* (1985).

— STEVEN MINTZ

LITERACY

The Concept of Literacy

Literacy is a culture's method of reproducing itself. Because learning continues throughout life, the acquisition of literacy and the activities that accompany it comprise only one dimension of "functional literacy"—that is, literacy in use. Organized literacy training is nearly always intended to meet a set of culturally sanctioned goals. As culture changes, literacy training usually follows suit; the value of, and therefore the emphasis on, particular skills may change, and trainers may draw from new funds of accepted knowledge (information and opinion, beliefs and values). By fostering lifelong learning, a culture not only reproduces its most stable base of knowledge, but it also encourages growth and change. For this reason two structural elements of a culture have come to be viewed as essential to understanding the impact of literacy: educational opportunities and the diffusion of printed matter by communications networks.

The roots of American attention to literacy lie in English usage. Since the mid seventeenth century "illiteracy" has been an unfailingly pejorative term, freighted with notions of poverty, the lower orders, and ethnic and racial inferiority. Scholars increasingly discard "illiteracy" and analyze the more neutral research designation of "literacy," a term in American usage since the late eighteenth century. With Noah Webster's codification of usage in the early republic, *An American Dictionary of the English Language* (1828), "literate" came to denote "skillful," "lettered" (literally), trained, and disciplined. Webster stressed that learning letters to understand the meaning of words entailed instruction in "the representative of a sound." "As *sounds* are the audible, and communicate ideas to others by the ear," he wrote, "so *letters* are visible representatives of sounds, and communicate the thoughts of others by means of the eye." To read was to "utter or pronounce written or printed words"; to write was to extend speech by "forming letters and words," thereby preserving them.

As reading was "a recreation of the author's conversation," it was taught by building on experience in talking and listening, singing and chanting. Webster's pronouncing-form method likened reading to "talking from a book." Writing too was linked to speaking, as in the common copybook sentence: "A rapid and uniform handwriting is a speaking picture." Another of writing's critical uses was "to call one's self through the signature": because the self denoted "identity of person," the signature was a form of proof of one's identity.

Because literacy entails training and discipline as well as skills and knowledge, social agencies have regulated its inculcation. The family or household has been the core social agency for literacy training throughout American history, for that is where printed objects were purchased, subscribed to, or borrowed for use, where apprenticeship unfolded. The household was also the leading site for applying functional literacy to the tasks of everyday life; it was where intellectual privacy, the central root of individual freedom, germinated. The primary school, both public and private, was a second critical social agency for literacy acquisition, supplemented by the church and Sunday school. A third agency, offering institutional support, has been job training and adult education, including night school, lyceums, and discussion groups.

Social standing has strongly influenced the encouragement or restriction of literacy training. Constraints on literacy training and cultural participation by class, gender, and especially race have endured throughout American history. For example, because the Constitution excluded Native American groups from citizenship, they were denied access to the education required to become citizens until the twentieth century. The Constitution likewise excluded African American slaves from citizenship, and state statutes prohibited them from literacy training. Most free African Americans, also excluded from citizenship before adoption of the Fourteenth Amendment in 1868, were regularly segregated from local primary schools. Education opportunities for women lagged far behind those for men, with equality in female primary education emerging only after 1840.

The Emergence of Literacy Studies

To study American literacy is to study the dynamics of American society. For more than two centuries contemporary interpreters have linked American literacy levels and trends to various combinations of religious doctrine, education, communications systems, and government policy. Efforts to promote literacy have also been historically associated with America's fears of the wilderness, of being isolated from Europe, of having an insufficiently educated citizenry, of foreign influences on its people's lives, and of its own decline. Concern about rising illiteracy in the 1980s and 1990s is another phase in the perennial debate about the roles and uses of education and knowledge.

Literacy studies were first conducted in several states during the 1820s, culminating in 1840 with the federal government's decision to include its first literacy question in the United States census. Ideology informed a growing body of public opinion, which used the census results (ranging between 72 and 99 percent among the states) to confirm that mass literacy was a prime feature of American life, underpinning the nationalistic ideal of practicing Christians, contributing citizens, and the great divide between modern and premodern societies. These traits, complementing racially based analyses of societal advancement, were believed to distinguish European Americans from African Americans, Native Americans, and Americans of other ethnic origin. By the late nineteenth century mass literacy was widely assumed to be integral to modernization. Rising literacy marked the radical transition from a traditional and static society to a progressive and dynamic one.

Until the 1980s and 1990s two analytical approaches guided scholarship. Lawrence A. Cremin championed the view that literacy is an integral element of modernization. Another position, advocated by Harvey J. Graff, stresses literacy's limitations as an aspect of modernization. Graff's *Legacies of Literacy* emphasizes the tension between the "restrictions on human agency and choice" that accompany advances in literacy and literacy's inherent "liberating potentials."

The infusion of anthropology into the study of history has fundamentally altered literacy studies. Literacy draws the attention of historians when it is located in specific historical circumstances of society and culture. This trend has even changed the way historians define literacy. A narrower view, accenting the acquisition of initial skills, has given way to a conception of literacy as an interactive process in which skills and knowledge evolve through lifelong participation in cultural life.

Literacy studies remain controversial among historians partly because of problems with literacy's definitions, measures, and standards. It is agreed, however, that the signature/mark as indicator of some level of reading ability is the only broad standard available to trace systematic changes in literacy levels before 1840, although it is also agreed that signing is not a measure of further writing ability. The signature/mark standard is used to approximate functional reading based on evaluations of the site and sequence of skills training. Where reading instruction began at home and progressed toward fluency by means of classroom instruction, after which writing instruction commenced, signing levels approximate the share of functional readers.

E. Jennifer Monaghan suggests that signing underestimates the total number of readers because many early New England females, particularly "girls of modest social standing," while not learning to write, learned to read "to a limited degree," including "familiar material," especially Scripture and handwritten notes. Monaghan concludes that early New England female readership was probably closer to the calculated literacy rates for the region's males than for its females. That levels of writing instruction and schooling for women were extremely low before 1750 and yet female signing rates reached one-third of rural women and nearly two-fifths of Boston women before 1715 suggest that signing was learned—perhaps at home or alongside reading instruction at school as a badge of identity—but separated from writing instruction.

As literacy studies pay closer attention to the share of the total population being measured, earlier approaches which posit that literacy reached "universal" (or even approximately universal) levels have been discarded. No source from which researchers could calculate literacy rates for the entire population is available. For instance, marriage licenses, deeds, wills, and army enlistee forms offer the richest evidence of literacy yet discovered, but marriage licenses are rarely extant, and deeds, wills, and enlistee forms each target limited segments of the population.

Literacy studies in the 1980s and 1990s stress a long-term dynamic process affected by economic policy, political and legal currents, technological and communications strategies, social status and pressure, and religious mandates. Even immigration patterns both raised and lowered existing literacy levels. F. W. Grubb has outlined a three-stage process: high literacy levels among initial immigrants into some colonies were followed by a temporary, second-generation decline, recouped in the third generation.

Literacy and Cultural Participation to 1780

The most interesting finding in colonial literacy studies since the 1970s is that male and female literacy rates moved closer to parity by the Revolution than previous research had suggested. Newer estimates of male literacy have lowered earlier, extraordinarily high estimates, whereas estimates of female literacy have raised earlier, substantially lower estimates. Pioneering research into African American and Native American literacy trends has also been conducted.

The net result was that, by the Revolutionary decade, religious belief, governmental affairs, and economic activity had combined to provide a wide base of readers among literate former European males and females in each major region. Religious reading matter remained central to colonial household life. But as public policy issues garnered increasing attention, secular reading matter was disseminated ever more widely. No less than twenty-nine newspapers circulated weekly throughout the colonies in the 1770s, emanating from sixteen cities and large villages, evenly divided down the eastern seaboard (eleven in New England; ten in the middle colonies; and eight in the South). The American Revolution was the first reader's revolution in history.

Signatures and marks on wills have been the largest source of data concerning overall rates of male literacy in early New England. Kenneth Lockridge (1974) found that male literacy rates rose from 56 percent in 1660 to 67 percent by 1710 and then to about 80 percent by 1760. Lee Soltow and Edward Stevens found that by the late 1750s the highest male rates were in Boston and densely settled rural counties. Boston female literacy rates rose only slightly through 1715 (to 35 percent) but thereafter surged dramatically, nearly doubling by the 1760s (to 65 percent). Rural male literacy followed the same pattern, but rural female literacy expanded much more gradually into the 1760s, remaining between 30 and 40 percent. Whereas urban differences by gender narrowed, rural differences widened owing to a serious lag in schooling opportunities for rural females. As the number of rural schools increased, male literacy rates increased; female increases awaited their admittance, and this entailed continuing local community struggles. The struggle was waged in local town meetings. As late as 1788 in Northampton, Massachusetts, selectmen voted "not to be at any expense for schooling girls."

Where schooling opportunities in New England became more equal—first in urban locales—male and female rates converged (Lockridge, *Literacy in Colonial New England*). For instance, female signing rates in the large village of Windsor, Connecticut, rose from just over a quarter of those born between 1650 and 1669 to 90 percent for women born between 1740 and 1749 (Auwers, "Reading the Marks of the Past"). Female rates rose above 80 percent by the late 1770s in the largest village of rural Windsor County, Vermont, and remained level at 85 percent through 1830 (Gilmore, "Elementary Literacy"). In mountainous New England townships female signing rates fluctuated between 70 percent and 85 percent through 1830. Populationwide rates were probably at least 10 percent lower because those without real property were absent from the data.

Literacy also varied by social position. New England's laborers had the lowest rates; next were farmers. Literacy among artisans, reaching 85 percent by 1760, was considerably higher than in European societies. At the top of the scale were merchants, professionals, and the gentry (90 percent literacy by 1760). Wealth also shaped differences; rates among the poor rose only to about two-thirds by the Revolution. Because wills underrepresented women and the poor, populationwide rates were actually somewhat lower. Fragmentary evidence about active readers suggests that regular reading escalated with increased educational opportunities and expanding circulation of printed matter after 1720.

Less is known about the literacy of those outside New England, particularly women. Literacy levels for British colonists in the Middle Atlantic and southern regions rose more gradually than in New England. Levels were substantially higher among other groups, such as the residents of New Netherland (now New York and New Jersey), where limited data show literacy to have reached 75 percent by 1650 and 85 percent after 1700. These rates buttress Donna Merwick's contention that writing and maintaining archives were critical to Dutch identity. Rates among Pennsylvania German males reached three-quarters in the 1720s, stagnating thereafter. According to Alan Tully, general Pennsylvania literacy rates rose to 75 percent for males of populous Chester County who died in the 1730s (65 percent for less-populous Lancaster County) but then changed little through 1800. A 1795 petition weighted to poor tenants from Livingston, New York, revealed just 53 percent of signers literate according to Soltow and Stevens.

An early rise in literacy, mid-eighteenth-century stagnation, and great variety among counties marked literacy trends in the South. For male Virginians who died between 1705 and 1715 literacy rates reached three-fifths, dipping to 40 to 50 percent for those holding property worth less than a hundred pounds, but only rose to two-thirds by 1800. Kevin Kelly reported a 72 percent male literacy rate for taxpayers who signed a Virginia sheriff's voucher book in 1793. Soltow and Stevens reported an overall literacy rate of 80 percent for petition signers from Baltimore County, Maryland, in 1768 (but with variations between 50 and 99 percent). Literacy on six petitions printed in German and English was 89 percent. North Carolina oaths of allegiance to the colonies (1778) record an overall literacy rate of 90 percent (ranging from 48 to 98 percent).

Colonial-era literacy trends reveal great diversity among the population. Male and female literacy rates for former European New Englanders reached very high levels in the seaports by 1750; in long-settled, densely populated rural areas by the Revolution; and in more outlying rural areas by 1815. In the Middle Atlantic region male rates reached high levels in seaports and in long-settled, densely populated rural areas by 1750. In the South rates varied much more widely, particularly for the lower socioeconomic half of the population.

Kenneth Lockridge has provided the most elaborate explanation of literacy trends. As the central cause of colonial New England's rise to high literacy levels he cites a burning Protestantism seeking to infuse all with God's Word. This traditional religious aim of literacy instruction persisted into the Revolution, the harvest of a successful literacy campaign. Secondary causes include population concentration in long-settled townships, which enhanced the founding of schools, and the acceleration of commercial development, which raised school attendance. Female literacy trends are not related to the general pattern. In the absence of this combination—in England, Pennsylvania, and Virginia—literacy rates rose far more gradually. Lockridge's argument rebuts the view that Puritan literacy effectively served a liberating or modernizing function—that high literacy rates and an emphasis on schooling constituted an indigenous response to threatened disruption in familial values in a "wilderness" cultural situation.

Research suggests that differences among regions are best accounted for by New Englanders' heightened emphasis on education, beginning in the home and continuing at school and at the meetinghouse. Initially, access to most rural public schools was largely limited to boys. By 1800 parents had succeeded in extending the use of public funds to girls; girls attended more regularly, and male and female literacy rates converged. Adult female literacy training in New England also contributed to this end according to Gloria Main.

Evidence that indicates the quality of literacy is harder to come by. Colonial authorities, according to Lawrence Cremin and others, shared a trinity" of primary reasons for encouraging literacy that formed an American *paideia*: theology and maintaining a faith, reasons of state and administration, and trade and commerce. In line with Reformation assumptions that truth is found in the Word of God (the doctrine of *sola scriptura*), the central objective was to provide a proper foundation for lifelong Bible reading. Instruction proceeded from the hornbook and primer to the catechism, Psalter, and New Testament. Thereafter, David Hall reports, a distinctive print ideology blended two compound traditions of reading matter, one rooted in the Bible and related sacred texts, the other a torrid supplementary culture of almanacs, books of "wonder," execution sermons, captivity narratives, poetry and ballads, martyr and devil stories, and personal accounts of warfare against Satan. Melding an identity from what one colonial minister termed the "white heat of vital piety," these two sets of texts and ideas were diffused in a shared culture for half a century.

By the 1690s, however, the dominant New England vessel of shared religious belief began to lose its way, foundering on the shoals of the witchcraft hysteria at Salem. It sunk with the effective end, by 1720, of British and colonial laws requiring prior approval of all publications. Losing control over what could be printed, the clergy's power over the Word declined; consequently, functional literacy broke free of religious ideology. By the 1720s several developments altered uses of literacy. One was marked geographical expansion of printed matter. Cities and densely populated rural areas witnessed substantial increases in the volume and variety of imprints, which primarily consisted of secular and moral reading matter, especially the newspaper, the greatest American vehicle of lifelong learning before television. The newspaper's mainstay was knowledge about the world beyond one's community. Pamphleteers and newspaper essayists helped to broaden and make more republican the definitions of a public sphere of inquiry and controversy. Although applied primarily to bureaucratic, religious, and commercial pursuits after 1720, literacy gained new uses as the reading public expanded. Reading served colonists' almost carnal desire

Male and female literacy rates for former European New Englanders reached very high levels in the seaports by 1750; in long-settled, densely populated rural areas by the Revolution; and in more outlying rural areas by 1815.

to learn more about this world; it offered personal advancement, entertainment, and escape from earnestness and the monotony of everyday life.

As newspaper circulation expanded in the 1720s, regular channels for information about transatlantic events emerged in each region. Print centers (locations with facilities for printing, bookstore sales, and newspaper editing) in Boston, New York, Philadelphia, and, by 1728, Annapolis, Maryland, anchored sources of information distinct from official news filtered through British governors and their local appointees and allies. Variety in political intelligence marked a critical expansion in knowledge available to readers. The number of newspapers doubled during the 1730s; print-center production accelerated for other print media as well. While imports rose sharply, domestic book and pamphlet production doubled, from one hundred to two hundred imprints per year between 1720 and 1740, and almanac production expanded from an average of two to an average of five works per year during that period.

With centers in the Atlantic ports and their environs and in densely settled rural areas, the enriched communications system opened up new intellectual worlds by expanding choices for lifelong reading. Book and pamphlet production after 1763 doubled from 1740s levels, rising another third in the 1770s to 640 editions per year printed in three dozen communities. Almanac editions rose to fourteen editions per year for the 1760s and twenty during the 1770s, reaching more than a quarter of all households. Newspapers maintained their momentum; eighty-nine were printed in the fateful 1770s. A third of these newspapers survived more than five years in the leading towns of every colony except New Jersey and Delaware. America's was the first mass newspaper-reading revolution in history.

Issues of literacy in relation to African Americans and Native Americans are particularly complex. Two patterns of cultural interaction dominated: Native Americans' collaboration with English-speaking settlers to create and use written forms of their indigenous languages (no efforts with African Americans are known), and English acculturation of members of Native American and African American groups via literacy. Contact with the Massachusett, Wampanoag, and Nauset people in southeastern Massachusetts was continuous, and here the Reverend John Eliot (1604–1690) collaborated to create Massachusett (an eastern Algonkuian language) written-language forms. Promotion of Massachusett literacy was based in fourteen Christian Native American communities before King Philip's War (1675–1676), rising to more than fifty by 1700. Conversion to Christianity and subordination to the Massachusetts colony were the main aims of English-speaking language trainers; the Massachusett goal was to preserve land titles and other rights. A Massachusett-language New Testament appeared in 1661; devotional works and an "Indian Library" followed. First conducted by English teachers, language instruction soon shifted to Massachusett members, note Ives Goddard and Kathleen J. Bragdon. By the early eighteenth century nearly 30 percent of the Massachusett population were readers, just below the rate for local settlers in similar economic circumstances. This suggests the disturbing conclusion that greater English appreciation of social diversity was the missing ingredient to an early blossoming of cultural pluralism in North America.

In the half-century after King Philip's War, Massachusett-speaking groups lived in an English-supervised parallel universe of native township settlements. Many church and civic government officials were Native Americans, literate in their own language. Ives Goddard and Kathleen J. Bragdon note that, with time, Eliot's Bible and other works led to spelling changes from earlier Massachusett writing, an example of English-induced linguistic uniformity. But within a generation translations ceased as New Englanders abandoned their Christian literacy campaign, thereby cutting off literate tribal members from access to printing. In 1750 the Massachusett language was still widely spoken, but apparently this was not the case by the 1820s.

With the 1720 loss of control over what could be printed, the colonial clergy's power over the Word declined; consequently, functional literacy broke free of religious ideology.

The Catawba of South Carolina adopted an alternative literacy strategy, singling out one or a few members for direct English acculturation. James Merrell relates the complex tale of the William and Mary graduate, John Nettles. Through his knowledge, this "lone messenger across a cultural frontier" made it possible for the rest of his group to remain independent. The Catawba employed Nettles to interpret "the alien world." Carrying on this tradition, the group petitioned the South Carolina government in 1801 to have two or three young boys taught reading and writing.

Interaction between colonial New Englanders and African Americans established a portentous pattern. Colonists, William D. Piersen reports, were more comfortable providing literacy instruction to slaves than to free blacks. While many New England slaves were trained sufficiently for Bible reading and perhaps for simple numeracy, opportunities for schooling were few. New Englanders severely restricted literacy opportunities for free African Americans: adults were rarely allowed formal access to literacy training. Piersen uncovered few instances of free blacks attending school and just two charity schools. Intracommunity training became the major route to literacy for free African Americans.

An Age of Reading: Literacy and Lifelong Learning, 1780–1870

Literacy trends in the half-century following the Revolution continued to be shaped most directly by race, and then by gender, region, wealth, and occupation. With extensive geographical expansion—eleven new states in three decades—social evolution (city, village, hamlet, farmstead, and plantation) greatly influenced functional literacy. Each region experienced a feverish pace of migration and community building, which included post offices, printing facilities, and schools. By the early 1790s every state generated its own stable flow of information in printed form. But since the founding of local institutions, re-creating those existing in the communities from which settlers had left, took time, schooling opportunities lagged, primers, spellers, readers, and arithmetic books were not available in quantity, and lending libraries were slow to emerge. This often resulted in a temporary decline in and then a recovery of literacy rates in newly settled environs.

With literacy rates already exceptionally high for males and females in urban and long-settled rural communities, New England trends through 1830 were marked by increases in literacy rates for rural females generally and for males in recently (and in sparsely) settled townships. In rural northwestern New England, populated largely by emigrants from southern New England, William J. Gilmore reports that, by 1800, about 90 percent of all men and about 80 percent of all women had acquired literacy skills. Excepting sparsely settled areas, the Middle Atlantic region reached these levels by the 1820s. To the south and west, literacy spread more gradually, especially in farmstead environs away from villages and large hamlets. In every region literacy rates remained substantially lower among the poorest inhabitants of the early republic's largest cities and especially among African Americans.

By the 1780s the initial knowledge base acquired with literacy skills was changing. Training began at home and then proceeded either from a summer school to a winter school or directly to the latter. Primer and speller gave way at school to one and then several readers; as education continued an arithmetic, a geography, and a grammar were added. Lawrence Cremin described the knowledge base as a second popular *paideia* of "evangelical pieties, democratic hopes, and utilitarian strivings" wrapped in a fervent nationalism. An Americanized ideology emerged that stressed four reasons for a literate populace, two of which persisted from the colonial era. One was that literacy offered a means to salvation through Bible reading and, after 1815, through a Sunday school system and what David Nord described as a mass media of evangelical Protestantism adding moral reform to reading interests and involvements. The other was that reading encouraged the kind of good citizenship essential to the republic's preservation.

The newer, American ideology of literacy added two other reasons for mass literacy. Social and economic advancement was a conscious aim of functional literacy, as regular reading enhanced participation in commercial exchange through awareness of available products and services. Newspaper and pamphlet debates about state and federal development policies built a constituency for economic growth. By the 1830s intellectual currency, or keeping up with the latest events (in one's own region, in other regions, in the nation's capital, and abroad), added a final, wholly new justification of literacy. The nineteenth-century American ideology of literacy sought to hold in equilibrium a quest for a place in heaven and for material improvement and individual growth on earth.

National-level data, first available in the 1840 United States Census, offer a benchmark to observe the arrival of mass (not universal) literacy among dominant-culture males and females. Census enumerators asked: "How many white persons in your family over twenty years . . . ?" Combined adult literacy in 1840 ranged between 95 and 99 percent for the New England and Middle Atlantic states (excepting Delaware, which was at 82 percent); between 85 and 98 percent for the Midwest; between 88 and 94 percent in Louisiana, Maryland, Florida, and Mississippi; and between 72 (North Carolina) and 83 percent in other states. Mass literacy had become a leading characteristic among the male citizenry of most states and would arrive for dominant-culture females within a decade.

The boundaries of mass literacy between 1780 and 1880 are most apparent in studies of the predominance of the propertyless, the young, and the poor among U.S. Army enlistees. Nationwide, Soltow and Stevens report steadily expanding literacy rates from 58 percent between 1799 and 1819, to 65 percent in the 1840s, to 75 percent between 1850 and 1869, to 83 percent in the 1870s, and to 93 percent after 1880. By contrast,

African American literacy rates among beginning merchant seamen registered in Philadelphia ranged from 19 to 33 percent between 1798 and 1840. Variation by region was substantial. New England literacy rates among enlistees averaged 75 percent for the 1799–1829 decades and 88 percent thereafter, versus 60 and 81 percent, respectively, for the rest of the North. Rates in the South began at 50 percent between 1799 and 1829, climbing to 69 percent after 1830. Rates for foreign-born enlistees were slightly below southern rates, at 47 percent between 1799 and 1829, but rose to 75 percent thereafter.

Literacy rates also varied by social position and along regional lines. Laborers retained the lowest literacy rates among enlistees, at 46 percent before 1830; rates rose to 66 percent before the Civil War and to 82 percent after 1870. Rates for New England laborers already averaged 76 percent through 1830 (versus 46 percent in the rest of the North and 36 percent in the South) and rose to 82 percent for the rest of the century (versus 74 percent in the rest of the North and 64 percent in the South). Literacy rates for foreign-born laborers more than doubled during this same century. Literacy rates among the largest enlistee occupation—former farmers—also rose steadily, from just over half between 1799 and 1829, to three-quarters between 1850 and 1869 and five-sixths thereafter. New England again led the way. Literacy rates for skilled artisan-craftsmen rose to 85 percent after 1830, and the same regional pattern obtained. Schooling was again a key factor in literacy's advance, especially in closing the gap between New England and the rest of the country. Compulsory-education laws and then compulsory school-attendance laws further expanded literacy after the Civil War.

Undergirding the steady rise of mass literacy was the emergence nationwide, by the 1840s, of an "age of reading," an era in which functional literacy and lifelong reading moved to the center of cultural expression for a large majority of the citizenry and dominant-culture females. Anchored by the newspaper, this phenomenon followed the fault lines of eighteenth-century literacy expansion, spreading outward from New England and the central arteries of the Middle Atlantic states, where it was a reality of daily life by the late 1820s. A vibrant mass-communications system disseminated enormous quantities and a great diversity of sacred and secular reading matter: primers, spellers, schoolbooks and chapbooks for children, youth, and new readers; a steadily expanding flow of newspapers, almanacs, and periodicals; official proclamations, governmental actions, political pamphlets, and transcripts of speeches; the Bible and commentaries, denominational proceedings, sermons, devotional manuals, theological treatises, and hymnals; professional publications in law, medicine, and education; literary and historical works, books on travel, reprints of steady sellers, and clandestine literature.

From Vermont to North Carolina (opposite poles in literacy rates throughout the nineteenth century), multiple print-centers in every state disseminated scores of imprints each year. For instance, in the two decades after 1800 at least seventeen hundred imprints were issued from twenty-four Vermont communities and many times that number were imported into the state. As the magnitude of print diffusion raised the standards of functional literacy, the gulf widened between the literate and nonliterate. But in a country 96 percent rural in 1800 (80 percent as late as 1860), enormous variation in access to printed matter led to worlds of difference in the amount and types of imprints disseminated to various living situations.

Studies of the share of families retaining a private library reinforced belief that the country had entered an age of reading. More than three-fifths of all families in rural northwestern New England retained a private library by as early as 1800. In the more recently settled Midwest, Soltow and Stevens found that half of all families retained collections by the 1830s. Joseph Kett and Patricia McClung reached a similar conclusion for Virginia, studying inventories heavily weighted to the 1790–1830 decades, although variety in retention rates was greater (from 32 to 62 percent). Another group of households in each region—a conservative estimate is 10 percent—read regularly but did not retain private libraries.

More than three-fifths of all families in rural northwestern New England retained a private library by as early as 1800, and in the more recently settled Midwest, half of all families retained collections by the 1830s.

As America's age of reading became more evident beyond the Northeast between 1840 and the Civil War, regional differences in combined male and female literacy rates narrowed substantially. In 1860 they ranged from 95 percent in New England and the Middle Atlantic regions, to 92 percent in the north-central region (from Ohio to Missouri), to 85 percent across the South. While male literacy rates were slightly higher in each region for 1860, female levels were extraordinary: 95 percent in New England, 93 percent in the Middle Atlantic region, 91 percent in the north-central region, 82 percent in the south-Atlantic region, and 80 percent in the south-central region (outside the Northeast, up about 5 percent from 1850).

Functional literacy was also amplified by the common-school movement. Literacy campaigns aimed at transmitting a common-school education permeated both northern and southern states in the mid 1830s. Northern state legislatures implemented common schooling to manage commerce and industry. The southern campaign became fixated on a radically different agenda. School and society were to unite in creating an educational setting to purify southern life: eradicating outside evils and banning literacy instruction for African Americans.

The 1850 and 1860 United States censuses, asking schools and families the number of children (aged five to nineteen) in attendance, provide the first glimpse of the progress and boundaries of educational opportunities. Predictably, New England led the country, with 81 percent of its male and 76 percent of its female children attending school in 1850. Next came the Middle Atlantic region, with 66 percent of males and 60 percent of females in attendance, followed by the north-central region, with male rates of 61 percent and female rates of 56 percent. The two southern regions had considerably lower rates: 44 percent of males and 39 percent of females in the south-central region and 41 percent of males and 35 percent of females in the south-Atlantic region. Nationwide, combined school attendance rose substantially, from 38 to 59 percent in the dominant-culture group between 1840 and 1860; just under six in ten women attended school in 1860.

To scholars of literacy, a central question is how literacy has been constraining or liberating. At least 640 established newspapers (published for more than five years each) printed in three hundred cities and villages in 1830, reaching a majority of households in the Northeast and penetrating the variegated living situations in thousands of townships across the country, published articles of conformity and dissent. Increases in book, pamphlet, almanac, and periodical reading continued to outpace population growth. Literacy had a profound impact on political activity through connections between party newspaper circulation—especially during campaign years—and rising voting rates. After 1815 a second communications channel enriched conservative Protestant values with enormous numbers of religious tracts. Late in 1825 the *New Harmony Gazette* (published after 1829 as the *Free Enquirer*) of New York ushered in an exchange system that challenged many mainstream values. This exchange system—editors swapping newspapers—spread awareness of cultural dissent very widely as conventional editors excerpted writing endorsing more radical ideas, such as those expressed in the labor-advocating, utopian *New Harmony Gazette*. Reaction was swift and often violent: the perceived prominence of cultural dissenters stimulated outrage, vented at mass meetings and in mob activity. Antebellum reform received new force from this clash in uses of functional literacy.

Native American and African American encounters with mainstream culture remained complex. In late 1827 the most "civilized" of Native Americans, the Cherokee Nation, met in a constitutional convention and formed a second American republic. Their constitution included an editor to the nation (Elias Boudinot) who founded an official bilingual newspaper, the Cherokee *Phoenix*, in 1828. The *Phoenix* commenced with a side-by-side printing of the Cherokee Constitution in English and Cherokee, the latter made possible by Sequoya's Cherokee syllabary (1809–1821). Thus was inaugurated yet another indigenous group's experience with vernacular-written literacy. As with the Massachusett people, literacy rates in the indigenous language soon approached those of the surrounding population. The Cherokee had pursued a dual path to literacy. William G. McLoughlin reports that in an 1835 Cherokee census, 51 percent of households included at least one Cherokee literate in the vernacular language, as among the Massachusett people; and 17 percent of households contained at least one Cherokee who read English, as in most tribes seeking accommodation. There was also some overlap, overwhelmingly in households with at least some "mixed-blood" members. Raymond Yamachika discovered 147 Cherokee-language imprints before 1861. At least ten other Native American groups also inaugurated vernacular written script, leading to newspapers and periodicals (several bilingual) and distinct print communications networks before 1865.

The main complication to determining African American slave literacy is that in any crisis suspicion immediately indicted literate slaves. Sufficient evidence exists to show that, despite brutalizing retribution, African Americans were frequently successful at subverting slave codes. Janet Duitsman Cornelius has argued that W. E. B. Du Bois's estimate of 5-percent slave literacy by 1860 should be raised considerably. Charles W. Joyner confirms that, as in eighteenth-century New England, "many masters and more mistresses" taught Bible reading to slaves in antebellum South Carolina; indeed, some slaves were considered "bookish." Literate slaves' impact on Gullah speech—"de-Creolization"—caused it to resemble English more rapidly than would otherwise have occurred.

Despite segregation and restrictions—such as that, by federal statute, only free white persons could be employed in any aspect of mail delivery—knowledge flourished among the growing population of free blacks. In 1827 Samuel Cornish and John Russwurm's New York *Freedom's Journal* inaugurated a distinct African American communications network providing information about Africa, community life north and south, and important individuals, writings, speeches, and conventions. This printed tradition nurtured the "river" of protest Vincent Harding has delineated and fostered reading of biographies and autobiographies by former slaves and by non-slave African Americans, a major genre of American literature (275 editions printed before the Civil War). This access to information that furthered literacy among free blacks led them to produce a significant body of literature between 1847 and 1861 that well constitutes the first African American literary renaissance, primarily in the 1850s, paralleling that in mainstream culture.

The access to information that furthered literacy among free blacks led them to produce a significant body of literature between 1847 and 1861 that constitutes the first African American literary renaissance, primarily in the 1850s, paralleling that in mainstream culture.

The origins of active African American reading communities lay in the heroic but tenuous efforts of earlier intracommunity schooling efforts. Antebellum urban leaders denounced "ignorance" among African Americans while excluding them from public schooling. Despite this, Gary B. Nash reports 28 percent literacy rates for Philadelphia African American mariners during the War of 1812; 37 percent among slightly better-off male Bethel (Methodist) church members in 1807; and 61 percent among male communicants of Saint Thomas's (Episcopal) church in 1822. The 1850 United States Census provided the first estimates of the overall African American audience for print communications. Literacy rates by 1860 varied from nine to ten (up from 86 percent in 1850) in New England, the region with the smallest free black population; to more than seven in ten in the Middle-Atlantic and south-central regions (up from 69 percent and 59 percent, respectively, in 1850); to six and one-half in ten for the north-central region (59 percent in 1850); and to five in ten for the south-Atlantic region, with the largest free black population (47 percent in 1850). Literacy rates for women in African American communities were either equal to or at most a few points lower than rates for men. Schooling rates for African Americans varied widely among regions in 1860, from 48 percent in New England, to 34 percent in the Middle-Atlantic and north-central regions, to just 4 percent in the south-central and 3.5 percent in the south-Atlantic regions. Lest any of these rates deceive, one more statistic: nine in ten African Americans were slaves in 1860.

While there is wide scholarly acceptance of literacy's enormous amplification in the antebellum North, the substantial accomplishments and divergent results in the South await their historian. Radically different paths of functional literacy highlight cardinal fissures in the fabric of American society. To compare antebellum southern literacy not just with that in the North but with trends in European societies is to confront the progressive assumptions of modernization theory with a great shock: that the institution of slavery had advanced alongside modernization. The Civil War pitted against each other two of the most literate societies on earth, both committed to lifelong learning, each committed to a distinctive way of life, one officially prohibiting literacy instruction for a third of its population.

Functional Literacy in Metropolitan America Since 1870

Reports of 20 percent total African American literacy rates for the South in 1870, versus 88 percent in the dominant culture, suggest the largest unfinished agenda of literacy in metropolitan America. Burdened by segregation, African American literacy and schooling rates nevertheless rose, steadily through 1890 (to 39 percent literacy nationwide, 35 percent for the South, and 67 percent for the North and West) and dramatically after 1900. Literacy rates for 1910 reached 89 percent nationwide, dropped to 82 percent for 1930, returned to 89 percent in 1947, and rose to 93 percent in 1959 and 96 percent in 1969. Southern African American literacy rates reached 64 percent in 1910 and 78 percent in 1930; rates for the North and West reached 89 percent in 1910 and 95 percent by 1930. Elsewhere, literacy and schooling rates rose and fell within a fairly narrow range, with variations mainly owing to shifts in immigration rates.

Compulsory schooling laws, passed by every state legislature by the end of World War I and enforced with increasing diligence, expanded functional literacy. Differences by race, class, ethnicity, gender, and region declined slowly, but by the 1920s more than 90 percent of all American children aged seven through thirteen were reported as enrolled in a school. While schooling rates topped 95 percent by 1950 and were close to 99 percent by 1980, wide variation in educational quality persisted. Twentieth-century literacy campaigns aimed to make good on equal opportunity by creating what Lawrence Cremin termed a "metropolitan culture" and a truly pluralistic educational system.

Assuming that literacy was a direct outcome of schooling, the U.S. Bureau of the Census began in 1870 to use years of schooling as a surrogate for literacy. A fifth of the population ten and older had not achieved literacy in 1870 (defined as the ability to write in any language, not necessarily English), falling to less than an eighth by 1890, a twelfth by 1910, and a twentieth by 1930. Functional literacy was defined during World War II as the ability to read sufficiently to accomplish basic military tasks. After the war the standard employed was a fifth-grade education. Reported rates rose to 97 to 98 percent through 1960. The 1970 calculation was especially convoluted: 5 percent of the adult population (those fifteen and older were sampled) lacked a fifth-grade equivalency, but because four-fifths of these people could probably read, the bureau concluded, the literacy rate was 99 percent (and 99.5 percent in 1980). The duration of schooling was also rising. For every hundred pupils in fifth grade in 1972, ninety-six entered ninth grade, eighty-nine entered eleventh grade, and seventy-five graduated from high school in 1980. Years of schooling remained considerably lower for African, Hispanic, and Native American children than for Americans of European descent. Women, southerners, and people living in rural areas also attended school for fewer years than other Americans.

Cremin's view of the relationship between schooling and functional literacy was that ability to decode printed words and sentences increased proportionately with years of schooling. But he also noted, as have Harvey Graff and others, that as a metropolitan society emerged printed matter became more complex and difficult to master, raising minimum requirements for functional literacy. Cremin defined functional literacy as increasingly "liberating literacy," meaning reading "freely and widely," and he included reading for utility—advertisements, warning labels, and common business agreements—for job related activities, and for entertainment and escape.

In the 1970s, as the Census Bureau was reporting near "universal" literacy, the Educational Testing Service (established in 1947) surveyed national reading habits and reported that, while reading increased with rising socioeconomic level, almost three-quarters of all adults read a daily newspaper, nearly two-fifths read at least some parts of a magazine, and one-third read books. In 1982 the Census Bureau tested Americans aged twenty and older on common reading skills. Just over an eighth failed the test, administered at home, including a tenth of those whose native language was English (and 48 percent of those whose primary language was not English, many of whom were literate in their native language). Other surveys reported that literacy levels for Hispanic Americans, aged twenty-one to twenty-five, were significantly lower. Literacy and skills varied greatly among monolingual English, monolingual Spanish, and bilingual households, but Spanish-language background did not have a negative impact on English literacy levels among bilinguals. Variations were usually explained by levels of economic disadvantage.

By the mid 1960s television had emerged as a dominant medium, and as school and television competed, literacy training changed fundamentally. Most studies of this relationship concluded that television and other electronic media were altering both the content and variety of reading matter. Nonetheless, books, pamphlets, and magazines continued to thrive, and specialization of printed matter advanced. By contrast, newspaper reading declined—from nearly three in four daily readers in the 1970s to about two in three by the early 1980s. Critics of American education stressed the contradictions between school culture and television culture, shorthand terms used to describe two broad learning environments combining substance and form. Network television culture appeared to denigrate reflection. By the 1980s a phalanx of educational critics lamented a perceived decline in literacy standards and achievements. Both Left and Right attacked the schools, one side suggesting the mindlessness and boredom of contemporary literacy strategies and school environments, the other berating the absence of basic literacy training, traditional family values, and civics and citizenship skills.

Two major testing programs, the International Evaluation of Educational Achievement (IEEA) and the National Assessment of Educational Progress (NAEP), have assessed both knowledge and skills development between ages nine and seventeen. In cross-cultural comparisons first reported in 1977, the IEEA concluded that Americans achieved creditable knowledge levels in civics and literature, only fair knowledge in science, and extremely poor knowledge in mathematics and foreign languages. What is worse, according to the NAEP studies, achievement levels declined between the 1960s and the 1980s. Many explanations were offered by edu-

Literacy rates among African Americans rose steadily through the twentieth century but years of schooling remained considerably lower than for Americans of European descent.

cators—an increase in the number of high school electives, a decline of public attention to school environments, unstable family situations, reduced school budgets, and television viewing. These findings convinced many that America's educational decline had reached crisis proportions. Allan Bloom's *The Closing of the American Mind* and E. D. Hirsch, Jr.'s *Cultural Literacy*, both of which critiqued American education, achieved best-seller status in the late 1980s.

Another strand in the educational debate of the 1980s and 1990s involved an intense argument about the value of cultural literacy, a term which came into vogue with the 1987 publication of Hirsch's *Cultural Literacy*. Cultural literacy is best defined by Hirsch's subtitle: *What Every American Needs to Know*. Much of the subsequent dialogue has centered on the last third of the book, a "list" of approximately 4,500 items—"What Literate Americans Know." One of the most interesting collections of essays in response to Hirsch, titled, significantly, *Multi-Cultural Literacy* (1988), included its own list of nearly six hundred additional terms the editors suggest as equally essential.

The specificity of one or both of the lists has been seen by some commentators as a symbol of the current crisis in American education, turning knowledge into a trivia game. But profound issues concerning the nature of American society in relation to its educational system have also been discussed. The central theoretical questions have included whether shared information is a necessary background to true literacy; whether shared information should primarily focus on the heritage and lives of the dominant cultural group, former European Americans; and what is implied by a broader, pluralistic fund of knowledge encompassing the whole civilization. To date, the discussion has mainly emphasized the breadth of knowledge Americans should possess, rather than the depth of understanding. Few participants in the cultural argument have located the problem in terms beyond America and the perceived internal needs of its socially diverse population.

Not all commentators on culture and education have agreed, however. In a pair of significant studies Herbert H. Hyman and his collaborators surveyed adult men's and women's knowledge about sports, entertainment, public affairs, public figures, general academic information, and values. They found an enduring correlation between level of schooling completed and substantive knowledge possessed. While a "knowledge elite" drawn increasingly from the general population provides a large pool of talent for American business, government, agriculture, industry, and the professions, critics have maintained that these achievements have fallen far short of a truly educated citizenry.

Minority involvement in education has also been much discussed. On the positive side, Horace Mann Bond's *Black American Scholars* (1972) linked African American Ph.D. recipients with those communities which strengthened ties between family, church, and schooling and favored academic achievement and raised expectations. Critics have noted a decline of 23 percent in African American Ph.D. recipients between 1980 and 1990; the persistence of steep dropout rates from high school among urban African and Hispanic Americans; and the enormity of the social problems creating situations of intense competition in values and futures for all poor children and youth across America.

American society in the 1990s is rent with conflict over educational goals, levels of achievement, issues of merit and redress, and a perceived decline in quality education. Critics hold that American education suffers from ineffective literacy training, erosion of cultural literacy, and declining standards. Many see the cause of education as increasing pluralism in places of learning; finding this situation threatening, some conclude that education has deteriorated. Ironically, others hail several genuine advances, including a continued rise in African American high-school-retention rates and, until the early 1980s, a sharp increase in educational attainment levels; the beginnings of advance on each of these fronts for Hispanic Americans; increases in female college completion levels and in the share of female Ph.D. recipients; and landmark legislation to educate and integrate the disabled into regular community life. Into the 1980s two older, dysfunctional educational settings prevailed in education for the disabled: segregated facilities and "main-streaming," placement in a regular school but without adequate support services, and often in a segregated classroom. Inclusive education, pioneered by Lou Brown, has emphasized functional literacy for the disabled and has supported education in the regular classroom, leading to independent and interdependent adult living and work settings.

More relevant evaluations are essential to place the latest phase of the American secular jeremiad tradition of decline in a broader perspective. Many educators today advocate valid comparative measures for different nations, adjusted to the share of the population at the educational level being tested. The low priority given to foreign-language training in America presents a serious challenge to functional literacy in an increasingly multicultural world. Appropriate subject matter is also a complex problem. Replacing Western civilization with global civilizations as the basic building block of functional literacy in history is long overdue.

[See also Adolescence; Childhood and Children; Collegiate; Mass Culture and Its Critics; Popular Literature; Print and Publishing; Public Education; Radio; Television.]

BIBLIOGRAPHY

General Works

Cremin, Lawrence A. *American Education: The Colonial Experience, 1607–1783* (1972).

———. *American Education: The National Experience, 1783–1876* (1975).

———. *American Education: The Metropolitan Experience, 1876–1980* (1988).

Gilmore, William J. "Literacy, the Rise of an Age of Reading, and the Cultural Grammar of Print Communications in America, 1735–1850." *Communication* 11 (1988).

Graff, Harvey J. *Literacy in History: An Interdisciplinary Research Bibliography* (1981).

———. *The Labyrinths of Literacy: Reflections on Literacy, Past and Present* (1987).

———. *The Legacies of Literacy: Continuities and Contradictions in Western Society and Culture* (1987).

Hyman, Herbert H., and Charles R. Wright. *Education's Lasting Influence on Values* (1979).

Hyman, Herbert H., Charles R. Wright, and John Shelton Reed. *The Enduring Effects of Education* (1975).

Kaestle, Carl F. "The History of Literacy and the History of Readers." In *Review of Research in Education*. Vol. 12, edited by Edmund W. Gordon (1985). Excellent overview of recent literature.

Simonson, Rick, and Scott Walker, eds. *The Graywolf Annual Five: Multi-Cultural Literacy* (1988).

Soltow, Lee, and Edward Stevens. *The Rise of Literacy and the Common School in the United States: A Socioeconomic Analysis to 1870* (1981).

European Americans

Auwers, Linda. "Reading the Marks of the Past: Exploring Female Literacy in Colonial Windsor Connecticut." *Historical Methods Newsletter* 13 (1980).

Gilmore, William J. "Elementary Literacy on the Eve of the Industrial Revolution: Trends in Rural New England, 1760–1830." *Proceedings of the American Antiquarian Society* 92, pt. 1 (1982).

———. *Reading Becomes a Necessity of Life: Material and Cultural Life in Rural New England, 1780–1835* (1989).

Grubb, F. W. "Growth of Literacy in Colonial America: Longitudinal Patterns, Economic Models, and the Direction of Future Research." *Social Science History* 14, no. 4 (Winter 1990).

Hall, David D. *Worlds of Wonder, Days of Judgment: Popular Religious Belief in Early New England* (1989).

Kelly, Kevin P. Review of *Literacy in Colonial New England*, by Kenneth Lockridge. *William and Mary Quarterly* 3d ser., no. 32 (1975).

Kett, Joseph F., and Patricia A. McClung. "Book Culture in Post-Revolutionary Virginia." *Proceedings of the American Antiquarian Society* 94, pt. 1 (1984).

Lockridge, Kenneth A. *Literacy in Colonial New England: An Enquiry into the Social Context of Literacy in the Early Modern West* (1974).

Main, Gloria. "An Inquiry into When and Why Women Learned to Write in Colonial New England." *Journal of Social History* 24, no. 3 (1991).

Merwick, Donna. *Possessing Albany, 1630–1710: The Dutch and English Experiences* (1990).

Monaghan, E. Jennifer. "Literacy Instruction and Gender in Colonial New England." *American Quarterly* 40, no. 1 (1988).

Nord, David Paul. "The Evangelical Origins of Mass Media in America, 1815–1835." *Journalism Monographs* 88 (May 1984).

Perlmann, Joel, and Dennis Shirley. "When Did New England Women Acquire Literacy?" *William and Mary Quarterly* 48, no. 1 (1991).

Stevens, Edward W. *Literacy, Law, and Social Order* (1988).

Tully, Alan. "Literacy Levels and Educational Development in Rural Pennsylvania, 1729–1775." *Pennsylvania History* 39 (1972).

Vinovskis, Maris A., and Richard M. Bernard. "Beyond Catherine Beecher: Female Education in the Antebellum Period." *Signs* 3, no. 4 (Summer 1978).

African Americans, Native Americans, Hispanic Americans

Cornelius, Janet Duitsman. *When I Can Read My Title Clear: Literacy, Slavery, and Religion in the Antebellum South* (1991).

Goddard, Ives, and Kathleen J. Bragdon. *Native Writing in Massachusett.* 2 parts. *Memoirs of the American Philosophical Society* 185 (1988).

Harding, Vincent. *There Is a River: The Black Struggle for Freedom in America* (1983).

Joyner, Charles W. *Down by the Riverside: A South Carolina Slave Community* (1984).

McLoughlin, William G. "The Cherokee in Transition: A Statistical Analysis of the Federal Cherokee Census of 1835." *Journal of American History* 64, no. 3 (1977).

Merrell, James Hart. *The Indians' New World: Catawbas and Their Neighbors from European Contact Through the Era of Removal* (1989).

Monaghan, E. Jennifer. " 'She Loved to Read in Good Books': Literacy and the Indians of Martha's Vineyard." *History of Education Quarterly* 30, no. 4 (Winter 1990).

Nash, Gary B. *Forging Freedom: The Formation of Philadelphia's Black Community, 1720–1840* (1988).

Ortiz, Vilma. "Language Background and Literacy Among Hispanic Young Adults." *Social Problems* 36, no. 2 (1989).

Piersen, William Dillon. *Black Yankees: The Development of an Afro-American Subculture in Eighteenth-Century New England* (1988).

Webber, Thomas L. *Deep Like the Rivers: Education in the Slave Quarter Community, 1831–1865* (1978).

Yamachika, Raymond. *Cherokee Literature: Printing in the Sequoyan Syllabary Since 1828 with a Bibliography* (1961).

— WILLIAM J. GILMORE-LEHNE

LITERATURE, POPULAR

See POPULAR LITERATURE

M

MANNERS AND ETIQUETTE

To suggest the full significance of etiquette in American history, it is perhaps best to approach the subject obliquely, looking first to one of the central struggles in American history—the struggle over race. D. W. Griffith intended his epic film *The Birth of a Nation* to plead a case: the "birth" he envisioned was the reuniting of North and South, an Anglo-Saxon nation standing against the twin threat of blacks and immigrants. He meant to leave the white middle-class audiences of 1915 cheering as the white-robed Ku Klux Klan rode to the rescue of Anglo-Saxon civilization.

Griffith set up his argument carefully, with predictable scenes that portray black men sexually menacing white women. But Griffith also gave great weight to another scene, clearly intending it to raise the ire of proper audiences. The hero, a southern gentleman, walks along a sidewalk with a lady. They encounter the ambitious mulatto Silas Lynch, who not only does not relinquish the right of way to his "betters" but insists upon being "recognized" by them. While this scene lacks the raw racist charge of a black man sexually threatening a white woman, Griffith clearly intended it as a piece of emotional evidence. Lynch's claims were an egregious breach of etiquette—meant and understood as a challenge to social order. Modern audiences see the "Little Colonel" (the Civil War nickname for our gentleman hero) fuming over this affront and are vaguely puzzled. Audiences in 1915 saw the challenge as significant because they, like Griffith, lived within a system of etiquette that was closely tied to fears about social order and disorder.

The scene does not work with modern audiences partly because we do not know the rules Lynch is breaking. They have passed from our behavior; they have disappeared from the etiquette manuals. The middle-class man or woman today is thoroughly ignorant of the myriad rules of etiquette that would have defined his or her middle-class status fifty or one hundred years ago.

The term "etiquette" itself has fallen out of favor. It sounds quaint—like the system of manners it is most often used to describe. Etiquette, in contemporary American society, most often surfaces in rituals that lay some claim to formality, such as weddings, and in exhortations to politeness based on common good sense. But while the term remains attached to a tradition of rules and manners developed, elaborated, and overelaborated in the nineteenth century, we live within systems of etiquette no less complex and arcane.

Etiquette has played a complex and important role in American history. It is not just that, in Erving Goffman's words, "the gestures which we sometimes call empty are perhaps the fullest things of all" or, in the social historian John Kasson's words, that "the rituals of everyday behavior establish in important measure the structures by which individuals define one another and interact." Both points *are* important: a people's manners—the rituals of their everyday behavior—are full of meaning and of information. We can read manners as ritual and learn much.

But ritual is not the whole story, for manners and etiquette are not interchangeable terms. The term "manners" describes behavior, however unmannerly that behavior might be. Etiquette, on the other hand, is prescriptive. Etiquette is the code of manners, the set of rules, the definition of proper behavior. The relationship between manners and etiquette is complicated and often tense. It is in that tension, which prevents the perfect correspondence of manners and etiquette, that we often learn most.

Etiquette, in addition, is instrumental. In the course of American history, etiquette has often served as a tool—even as a weapon—in struggles over social change in America. Etiquette has often been concerned with drawing lines between people and boundaries between groups—most importantly, between social classes in the nineteenth century and between men and women in the twentieth century (the role of race remains complicated throughout). In observing etiquette, Americans enacted rituals of power and exclusion while claiming them to be natural manifestations of "taste" or of "breeding." But etiquette has also provided means to claim inclusion and served as a forum for testing conflicting claims about the nature and form of civility.

Many different systems of manners and of etiquette have existed in America. A modern high school might have an elaborate but local code of etiquette that, though unwritten, structures daily interactions. Immigrant groups brought the manners and etiquette of their home countries to the United States, and those systems changed through contact with other groups. The fine points of social usage differed between Charleston and

New York, Des Moines and Dallas. And in terms of etiquette, the past truly is another country.

Etiquette is a prescriptive system and never fully matches behavior. Even the most universally prescriptive system of etiquette is mediated by factors like religion, race, ethnicity, class, region, gender, and profession. Nonetheless, the observance of appropriate etiquette has been a precondition for participation in public life, and etiquette has worked both to determine social status and to structure relationships between individuals. Of course, what was "appropriate" etiquette was often contested.

While many have claimed otherwise, there is nothing timeless about etiquette—neither the behaviors prescribed and proscribed nor the definitions of the term. A nine-year-old boy in the mid 1960s declared: "I have good manners. I say good night and good morning. I say hello and goodbye, and when I see dead things lying around the house I bury them." His implicit definition and practical interpretation strain the bounds of credulity less than those of many older and better-known advisers. In the pages that follow, I will attempt to offer an overview of the changing definitions of etiquette and to analyze the significance and utility of etiquette in American history.

Early Codes

Those who journeyed to the New World carried with them, in addition to the supplies they thought would be useful in the unknown land, a vast store of cultural baggage. They brought to the new continents old ways of seeing, habits of behavior, and systems of manners: sets of assumptions so deeply rooted as to be unconscious and unremarked upon. The culture they transplanted did not flourish unchanged in new soil, but the manners and mores of these new Americans were marked as much by persistence as by change.

The development of American manners is not a story of creative synthesis through cultural contact: the colonists dismissed the aboriginal inhabitants of the new world as "barbarians," and the newly named "Indians," in other languages, thought pretty much the same of the settlers. The Europeans would never have survived in the new landscape without knowledge gained from the Indians, and contact with Europeans radically transformed the lives and culture of Native Americans. But the two groups came from very different worlds and assigned very different meanings to similar acts. What seemed to the Europeans to be trade, for example, was to the tribes of the eastern woodlands often gift-exchange, a ritualized system that served to create and maintain allegiances between tribes. Overall, Europeans tended to describe Native Americans as existing in a state of nature (meaning they were uncivilized), and Native Americans, though drawn into European trade networks and desiring firearms and other European goods, had no desire to wear European-style clothes, live in stuffy houses, or adopt the manners of "Christian people."

The British settlers of North America came from a highly rank-ordered society, and brought with them a belief in the naturalness of hierarchy. Such traditional forms did not serve the settlers of Jamestown well. In England, "gentleman" designated one who did not earn his living through manual labor, and in Jamestown the gentlemen refused to work until John Smith, Gent., subverted proper form and forced them.

In the New World, unlike the Old, a man without substantial fortune, education, or lineage might be addressed as a gentleman.

For the early settlers in Massachusetts Bay, rank and hierarchy were crucial. The colonists saw their settlements as small and fragile centers of Christian civilization clinging to the edge of a vast and menacing wilderness. The death rate was high, support from England not certain, winters harsh, and food scarce. Order was crucial, so that the community not succumb to chaos within. Order, to these seventeenth-century men and women, entailed hierarchy. John Winthrop, the governor of the colony and a gentleman, wrote in *A Modell of Christian Charity* (1630): "God Almighty in his most holy and wise providence hath so disposed of the condition of mankind as in all times some may be rich, some poor, some high and eminent in power and dignity, others mean and in subjection."

Many of the rules of etiquette transferred to the colonies were concerned with rank and status. The colonists dealt with the issue of hierarchy in ways that seem exceedingly direct to twentieth-century Americans, used to reading class and status in subtler signs. Titles designated status: "Mister" was reserved for gentlemen (a status determined not by behavior but by social position); the wives of gentlemen were addressed as "Madam." Those of commoner clay were called, as in England, "Goodman" and "Goodwife" (or less formally, "Goody"). In America, though, the title of gentleman lost some of its social significance, for a good-man might ascend to the "gentry" if he were elected captain by his peers in the local militia, or if he were chosen to hold a town office such as justice of the peace. In the New World, unlike the Old, a man without substantial fortune, education, or lineage might be addressed as a gentleman.

Rank was assumed as the most natural way of ordering a group of people. Students at Harvard and Yale were listed in order of family standing until 1772, when an alphabetical system was adopted. The change, significantly, seems to have stemmed less from a rise of democratic feelings than from increased difficulty in determining rank and the grumbling of parents who did not agree with the college's determination of their status.

Even in religious services colonists did not assemble as an undifferentiated community of worshipers. Pews were assigned according to community consensus on the social rank of each family, and services offered a ritual enactment of hierarchy and status. Still, rank-order was sometimes contested. Town records tell of shoving matches in the aisles, and of one Goody Elizabeth Randall who claimed the place she believed rightfully hers, pushing and scrambling her way over pews with backs four to five feet tall.

While the wealthiest colonists had begun to stock their homes with luxuries imported from Europe, most people lived very humbly.

The passing of sumptuary laws in the various colonies also testifies that the boundaries of rank and status were stretched in America. "One end of apparel," according to Urian Oakes (1631–1681), president of Harvard College, "is to distinguish and put a difference between persons according to their places and Condition." But the Massachusetts General Court felt it necessary to register its outrage "that men or women of mean condition, should take upon them the garb of Gentlemen," requiring that one must possess property equivalent to £200 in order to wear "gaudy apparel." The Virginia House of Burgesses had passed similar legislation in its first session. The law was violated, but offenders were rarely convicted.

The general manners of the people can be surmised from their surroundings. While the wealthiest colonists had begun to stock their homes with luxuries imported from Europe, most people lived very humbly. In the Chesapeake Bay area in the seventeenth century, for example, only one-third of the families had chairs or benches in their homes. Homes were small, with little separation of space or function. Few had real beds at first, but those who did kept them in the main room. Families slept together, welcoming travelers into the common bed. Privacy was seen neither as a good or necessary commodity, nor as a requisite for polite behavior.

To eat, common people gathered around a board laid on trestles. Hierarchy remained important: adults and guests sat "above the salt" (the salt cellar placed in the middle of the table) and servants and children below. They shared trenchers and cups, and freely dipped their hands into common serving bowls. European travelers were often appalled at the promiscuous sharing, as common cups became fouled with spit and grease, and bits of tobacco floated in the common drink. As late as 1827, Margaret Hunter Hall wrote home to England, "They are a nasty people, the Americans, at table; there is no denying that fact."

It was not only the common folk or lesser ranks whose concepts of privacy and proper deportment were shocking. The advice offered in the conduct or courtesy books popular in colonial America is telling. "Spit not in the room but in the corner, or rather go out and do it abroad," advises Eleazar Moody's *School of Good Manners*, the most popular of American courtesy books published in the eighteenth century. George Washington, at fifteen, copied out the following in his commonplace book: "Kill no Vermin as Fleas, lice ticks &c in the Sight of Others . . . " and "Being set at meat Scratch not neither Spit Cough or blow your Nose except there's a Necessity for it." Such rules were derived from conduct guides written for nobles at court in the fifteenth and sixteenth centuries; even here we see standards of proper behavior changing, for these versions had dropped proscriptions against "relieving" oneself before the doors of "court chambers"—this advice no longer had to be stated. Still, in colonial and early national America, it was deemed polite to blow one's nose not on the tablecloth but in one's fingers—as long as it was not the hand with which one was eating.

The South and the North

The manners of colonists differed by region—both because of the accidents of geography and because of the different traditions of polite behavior that served as models. Northern society looked to the moralist strand of English courtesy books, and, in revising them for American consumption, enhanced the religious component. Southerners looked to the landed gentry, reading works in the courtly tradition. Richard Allestree's *The Whole Duty of Man*, first published in London around 1660, was owned by both George Washington and Thomas Jefferson. Allestree presented a model of comportment based on the ideals of chivalry and hierarchy, emphasizing the criteria that made gentlemen. "Gentlemen," he insisted, "sweat only at the Engagement of their Sports," while the lesser ranks must live by the sweat of their brows.

Southern etiquette was based on a chivalric code of honor that was, as Bertram Wyatt-Brown argues in *Southern Honor*, "inseparable from hierarchy and entitlement, defense of family blood and community needs." The code of honor applied to all southern whites, though its proper manifestation differed depending on rank in society and upon gender. The southern code, though never so romantic or so "civilized" as it has been portrayed in retrospect, suffused southern life. In contrast, northern society, with its early emphasis on mercantile pursuits followed by its transformation into an urban-industrial society, developed an ethic and code of manners based on conscience and secular economic concerns.

Honor was enacted, in its most extreme form, through the highly ritualized performance of the duel (which one historian has described as men "killing each other according to strict rules of etiquette"). Dueling was introduced to America by French and British aristocrats serving (on different sides) during the Revolutionary War and was taken up in the ranks of America's military. But dueling became widespread in the postcolonial South, where, in spite of strong opposition, the *code duello* became a part of the gentleman's life.

Duels were fought in defense of honor. If one man insulted another's personal honor, custom and community opinion urged that the matter be resolved through a duel. Duels were governed by an etiquette, though many duelists were not clear on proper form; John Lyde Wilson, a former governor of South Carolina, compiled a "blue book" of dueling etiquette.

Dueling, in keeping with the hierarchical nature of the code of honor, was restricted to gentlemen; one did not challenge or accept a challenge from a social inferior. While a small percentage of southerners qualified as gentlemen in the strictest sense (for example, in 1860, 11,000 families, or 0.75 percent of the southern population, owned fifty or more slaves), a much larger number of white men laid claim to that status as officers in local militias. In a culture noted for its physical violence and hotheadedness, dueling may have served to mediate extremes of violence, for the proper duel offered cooling-off time as the rites of challenge and response were observed, and official intermediaries were sometimes able to settle matters with honor and without violence.

Southern etiquette was also tightly enmeshed with the South's peculiar institution. Deference was expected from slaves. In the physical embodiment of honor, according to Bertram Wyatt-Brown, southern culture linked honor to the body: "the eyes witnessed honor and looked down in deference or shame." Thus a slave who met the gaze of a white person was impudent. Travelers were sometimes confounded by the workings of hierarchy in the South. One young woman, overwhelmingly modest in her relations with white men, undressed freely in the presence of a male slave. His status rendered him unimportant—his race canceled the significance of his sex. The not-uncommon relations between white masters and slave women were also covered by the code of honor. The sexual union itself was no violation of honor or of etiquette, but if someone "violated good taste" and spoke of the liaison directly to any member of the man's family, the entire family was disgraced. In such matters, silence was polite.

While southern manners and etiquette remained rooted in the traditions of hierarchy and honor well into the nineteenth century, in the North both manners and the claims of etiquette had undergone a revolution. The sources of change are two: the rise of democratic sentiment in the wake of the American Revolution, and fundamental changes in the social and economic organization of the nation.

Much of our description of American manners comes from European travelers who were quick to attribute virtually everything to the effects of democracy. "Nothing does democracy more harm than its outward forms of behavior," wrote Alexis de Tocqueville (1805–1859) in a chapter called "Some Reflections on American Manners" in *Democracy in America*, for "many who could tolerate its vices cannot put up with its manners." It was the presumption of equality that rankled the most with Frances Trollope (1780–1863), who made herself very unpopular in America with the publication of her *Domestic Manners of the Americans* (1832). Mrs. Trollope experienced the friendliness of a Cincinnati neighbor as a "violent intimacy," and contact with members of the lower classes was infinitely uncomfortable. "I am very far from intending to advocate the system of slavery," she wrote. "I conceive it to be essentially wrong; but so far as my observation has extended, I think its influence is far less injurious to the manners and morals of the people than the fallacious ideas of equality, which are so fondly cherished by the working classes of the white population in America."

Some Americans rejected the European styles, as did a clergyman who argued that "we have already suffered much by too great an avidity for British customs and manners; it is now time to become independent in our maxims, principles of education, dress, and manners, as we are in our laws and government." Others made the point more directly, as did one Cincinnati lodging-house keeper, who turned Mrs. Trollope away because she did not want to take tea with the other lodgers. When she tried to apologize, explaining that she was not familiar with the manners of the country, he replied, "Our manners are very good manners, and we don't wish any changes from England." Still, travelers told tales of being fawned over by the members of local society, all of whom wanted reassurance that their manners, customs, furnishings, and entertainments matched those of Europe.

Foreign observers cast American etiquette as a drama of democracy, and to some extent it was. What was the proper role in a republic for a system of manners rooted in the chivalric tradition of European court life, of rules of behavior meant to maintain and reinforce hierarchy and fixed place? Formal systems of etiquette, however, did not decline in the face of democratic rhetoric and its limited reality. Instead, etiquette grew in importance as a means of control and a measure of stability in the often confusing and threatening urban-industrial-capitalist society that emerged in nineteenth-century America. An increasingly elaborate code of etiquette mediated the effects of the market economy and the relative mobility and anonymity felt keenly by our ancestors. This allowed newly useful boundaries to be drawn between the realms of public and private, and between people whose place was no longer fixed and whose status no longer secure.

Middle-Class Respectability

John Kasson, in his wonderful work *Rudeness and Civility*, argues that the redefinition of the term "genteel" in the nineteenth century "epitomizes enormous changes in economy and society," as the emerging urban-industrial-capitalist system replaced the rank-ordered society of colonial America. "Gentility," in colonial America, designated status; it referred to the well-born. By the 1830s, "genteel" referred to qualities of politeness and grace.

Central to the transformation of the concept of gentility—and to the crucial importance of etiquette in nineteenth-century American society—was the emergence of middle classes. As Kasson emphasizes, the emergence of the industrial-capitalist system did not create a more economically equal society, nor did it offer unlimited mobility. But the diminished importance of inherited rank, along with geographic mobility (especially the move to the rapidly growing cities), combined with the emerging system to offer new possibilities. The new economic system demanded new sorts of workers—clerks and managers, people who did a variety of white-collar work and who, no matter what the reality, defined themselves as upwardly mobile and who sought the trappings and manners of "respectability." While offering many the means to live in comfort, the new industrial-capitalist order left many in desperate poverty. It also created vast fortunes and intense jostling for social position, as money contested name for precedence.

In the ferment of change, all seemed possible. "It is not here, as in the old world," wrote one nineteenth-century adviser, "where one man is born with a silver spoon, and another with a pewter one, in his mouth. You may all have silver spoons, if you will." She was referring not solely to material wealth, but also to the outward signs of gentility. Any man might be a gentleman; any woman a lady "You may be whatever you will resolve to be," exhorted yet another adviser.

The redefinition of the term "genteel" in the nineteenth century "epitomizes enormous changes in economy and society," as the emerging urban-industrial-capitalist system replaced the rank-ordered society of colonial America.

In the flood of writing about society and manners, the "best society" was increasingly defined as middle class—and presented as attainable. "You have it in your power to fit yourselves by the cultivation of your minds, and the refinement of your manners, for intercourse, on equal terms, with the best society in the land," promised the influential writer Catharine Sedgwick (1789–1867). The manners that marked one as a gentleman or lady could be learned. One could master the rules and forms of etiquette and purchase the increasingly available accoutrements of gentility.

The flood of etiquette and advice books that appeared in the nineteenth century offered entree to the world of respectable middle-class behavior. In the 1830s, because of major developments in the technologies of printing and book publishing, books, magazines, and newspapers became much more widely available and much less expensive than before. Etiquette and advice books occupied a prominent place in the offerings of nineteenth-century publishers. According to Arthur Meier Schlesinger, an average of three new etiquette manuals appeared each year between 1830 and the decade of the Civil War, and from the 1870s through World War I, five to six new manuals appeared annually. This staggering number does not include reprints and new editions. Etiquette books were sold by sales agents who went door to door and in direct-mail advertisements in magazines and newspapers. Some were massive and expensive—encyclopedic in form—and others were short and inexpensive "dime books," designed for a mass market. While the forms of etiquette developed in the cities, they were copied by "respectable" folk in small towns and villages throughout the country. The majority of these works were American in authorship and addressed to the middle classes, broadly defined.

These works were very much "how-to" in spirit—self-improvement books—frequently with a heavy dose of moral exhortation. Readers were told, in precise detail, how to sit, how to stand, how to receive a guest, and how to decorate a parlor. No detail was too small for attention: "The general positions for the arms are about the level of the waist, never hanging down or being quite stiff, but being gently bent, the elbow a little raised, the fingers not stretched out stiffly, but also a little bent, and partially separated, or the hands half crossed one over the other, or placed in each other, &c.," offered a volume titled *A Manual of Politeness, Comprising the Principles of Etiquette, and Rules of Behavior in Genteel Society, for Persons of Both Sexes* (1837).

The promise of social mobility and the availability of such helpful advice made gentility, in Kasson's words, "increasingly available as a social desire and a purchasable style and commodity." By the second quarter of the nineteenth century, gentility seemed not so much a product of birth as the result of striving, of solid middle-class effort.

A knowledge of etiquette, no matter how arcane and complex, could serve as a tool for advancement in society. According to the best advisers, the effort involved was considerable, but it paid off. The rituals of etiquette, once mastered, were inclusive. They paved the way to an *attainable* middle-class gentility—and the phrase "middle-class gentility" did not seem contradictory. The importance of etiquette in the nineteenth century, in substantial measure, was a sign of the era's optimism. The rigors of etiquette were born of a sense of possibility.

But nineteenth-century American etiquette had mixed parentage: as it was inclusive, it also worked to exclude; as it grew from optimism, it was also an expression of profound social fears. Karen Halttunen, in her pathbreaking and sophisticated book *Confidence Men and Painted Women*, reads in nineteenth-century urban middle-class culture a "crisis of social identity faced by . . . men and women who were on the move both socially and geographically." As they aspired to gentility and to higher social status, they feared a world where other people were not what they seemed. Halttunen argues that such fears coalesced around the figures of the confidence man and the painted woman, hypocrites who "poisoned polite society with deception and betrayal by dressing extravagantly and practicing the empty forms of false etiquette."

Advice and etiquette books stressed sincerity as the heart of etiquette, insisting that the empty forms were meaningless—even destructive—but nonetheless furnishing detailed instructions on how to comply with those very forms. This paradox, Halttunen argues, was resolved through what she calls a "genteel performance," in which the complexities of etiquette were navigated and performed in a "sincere" manner. The genteel performance was a "polite fiction," presenting "the courtesy of those ladies and gentlemen who adhered to the hundreds of rules governing parlor conduct" as the result of "right feelings and not . . . of the painstaking study of etiquette manuals."

The fiction was fragile; its existence depended upon the collusion of those who participated. Thus its existence depended upon exclusion. Those who threatened the magic of the performance by recognizing it as performance must be excluded. Those who were insufficiently genteel to play their proper roles must be excluded. While a plethora of manuals told people how to be genteel—how to pass—many of the rules they were mastering detailed the art of "polite" exclusion. As Charles William Day's *Hints on Etiquette and the Usages of Society* (1844) explained:

> Etiquette is a barrier which society draws around itself as a protection against offences the "law" cannot touch; it is a shield against the intrusion of the impertinent, the improper, and the vulgar,—a guard against those obtuse persons who, having neither talent nor delicacy, would be continually thrusting themselves into the society of men to whom their presence might (from the difference of feeling and habit) be offensive, and even insupportable. (Halttunen, pp. 111–112)

The laws of etiquette provided a series of tests, or measures, of social acceptability. That someone could observe all the complex rules of etiquette and do so "sincerely," seemingly without effort, seemed to be a guarantee of "breeding" or, more accurately, class background, in a society that was both socially and geographically mobile.

In Victorian America, an etiquette of gentility came to be largely synonymous with an exceptional delicacy about matters physical or sexual. Frances Trollope wrote with disgust of American women's "ultra-refinement." Frederick Marryat, another traveler, claimed to have seen, in a seminary for young ladies, a piano with its legs—or limbs—covered by "modest little trousers, with frills at the bottom of them!" Hiram Powers's (1805–1873) statue *The Greek Slave* was dressed in calico blouse and flannel trousers for its exhibit in Cincinnati. Etiquette books advised ladies to avoid questions in polite conversation, for questions might lead to embarrassing subjects. One adviser rather breathlessly told of a lady who inquired of a gentleman what sort of medicine he practiced, only to discover that he was a doctor of "midwifery." This pretentious delicacy is comical in retrospect, but it is important to understand that, as Christopher Mulvey explains in *Transatlantic Manners*, this behavior was meant to demonstrate social status and good breeding as much as or more than to manifest an essential prudery. Refinement was the essential characteristic of respectability.

The formal dinner party was perhaps the greatest test—though of course one had to have passed as "acceptable" in order to be invited. While in the early nineteenth century Americans commonly ate with a two-prong iron or steel fork and a knife, using the rounded blade of the knife to carry food into one's mouth, by the 1830s eating had become a much more complicated business. In the 1830s, Andrew Jackson's White House dinners offered guests a choice of two forks, one silver, one steel. By the 1880s, successful silverware companies like Reed and Barton offered tableware in many patterns—most of which included specialized serving pieces, and up to ten different kinds of knives; twelve different kinds of forks (including those intended specifically for terrapin, for mango, for oyster, and for ice cream); and twenty different kinds of spoons. Knowing which fork to use was not so easy, and making one's way through a formal dinner with no breach of etiquette a formidable task. Washington society commonly noted which new congressmen from the provinces attempted to eat the doilies, and it was said that President Lincoln, when asked by a waiter at his first state dinner whether he would have white wine or red, replied, "I don't know. Which would you?"

"Calling" was the central act of the "genteel performance," and worked most directly to demonstrate social status and to test and reinforce social boundaries. The ritual of calling was controlled by women, who played important roles in advancing families' social status. Most middle- and upper-class women designated a specific day "at home" for receiving callers. Callers presented calling cards to the maid who answered the door, indicating their intentions by the ways the cards were folded. By bending the right-hand corner of the card, one indicated that he or she was only paying respects and did not ask to be received; by bending the whole right-hand side of the card, one asked to be received. The upper left-hand corner, when bent, signaled "congratulations," the lower left-hand corner "condolences." Gender played a role: a man was not to call on a woman without her express invitation. Thus young women had the sole right of initiative in courtship—for it was deemed most important that women be able to exclude unwanted attentions and unsuitable admirers.

Those seeking to be received were either ushered into the parlor or told that the lady of the house was "not at home." This might or might not be strictly true: she might not be receiving that day—or she might be signaling the social unacceptability of the caller. Etiquette books advised their readers to keep strict account of their calls—of whether or not calls were returned, of where they were received and where turned away. Such an accounting offered a clear statement of one's social status (or, in appropriate cases, one's romantic prospects). With characteristic overstatement, the influential writer Mrs. Sherwood (Mary Elizabeth Sherwood, 1826–1903) explained the importance of the calling system in nineteenth-century America: "The [calling] card may well be noted as belonging only to a high order of development. No monkey, no 'missing link,' no Zulu, no savage, carries a card. It is the tool of civilization, its 'field-mark and device.' "

While in the early nineteenth century Americans commonly ate with a two-prong iron or steel fork and a knife, using the rounded blade of the knife to carry food into one's mouth, by the 1830s eating had become a much more complicated business.

Part of the exclusionary nature of the system stemmed from the competitive struggle for social status. The middling classes meant to demonstrate respectability, but also to advance socially just as they advanced economically. At the same time, those in the upper reaches of society enacted a more stringent form of exclusivity. Caroline Astor, with her aide Ward McAllister, worked to hold the line of society against the claims of the nouveaux riches who flooded New York in the last half of the nineteenth century. Ward McAllister coined the term, "The Four Hundred," in trying to explain why only four hundred were invited to Mrs. Astor's annual Patriarch's Ball (the real reason was space limitation). "There are only about four hundred people in fashionable New York Society," he explained. "If you go outside that number you strike people who are not at ease in a ballroom or else make other people not at ease." Mrs. Astor's invitations determined who belonged to "society," and her insistence on proper form and ritual structured her particular brand of social exclusivity. Still, by the end of the century younger social leaders like Mrs. Stuyvesant Fish and her aide Harry Lehr mocked the strict forms of society, giving dinners that they called "vaudevilles" and that Mrs. Astor publicly called "undignified."

All this genteelly couched jostling for social position lay at the heart of Victorian etiquette. But at the less genteel gut of the system was a great sense of vulnerability. The genteel performance was enacted in controlled spaces—in middle-class parlors with doors kept by maids, in private dinners and balls and parties to which no one came without invitation. This protected world existed in tension with the new world of the industrial city, a city larger, more anonymous, more frightening than before. Money served to cushion existence; those who could afford it kept carriages and drivers, attempting to stretch the boundaries of the private to the public world. But the experience of walking down a city street, subject to the stares of strangers, the importunities of the ill bred, the insults of the common, the dirt and disorder and chaos—all contributed to the importance of etiquette as a system that stressed strict control of one's own body and emotions and of physical space, in an assertion of the importance of privacy and an emphasis on the ability to exclude the unsuitable.

Of course, the "unsuitable" had their own systems of etiquette. Immigrant groups carried the manners of their old countries, and though no etiquette manual seems directly addressed to immigrants, much of the material that was aimed at Americanization or assimilation dealt with points that might well be described as etiquette. And in the foreign language press, leaders and writers such as Abraham Cahan (1860–1951) of the Yiddish paper, the *Jewish Daily Forward* spoke of the significance of manners and mores. Black leaders advised others of their race on matters of character and etiquette, most notably in a manual called *The Negro in Etiquette: A Novelty* (1899). But while all African Americans were lumped together in common disdain by most whites, blacks were divided by class, by skin color, and by place of origin. Black society, epitomized in the late nineteenth century by the Society of the Sons of New York, guarded its gates against newcomers as carefully as did the originators of the Patriarch's Ball.

While the etiquette of Victorian America seems extremely rigid, changes in social organization continued to strain established forms. New technologies were often the impetus for change in social form. The telephone, for example, fit uneasily into the pattern of calling (the telephone was patented in 1876, and by 1900 approximately 1.5 million were in use in the United States). Advisers agreed that it was a greater assertion of intimacy to telephone than to arrive at the door and present a calling card. If "on a certain footing of intimacy," one explained in 1907, a man might telephone the lady of the house to see if it were all right to call that evening. Eventually, of course, the hierarchy of intimacy would reverse.

The automobile also would present new difficulties as the old system of etiquette tottered. Virginia Scharff argues in *Taking the Wheel* that "the cultural gap between social status and control of technology" caused great concern for the owners of the new machines. Men who drove their own automobiles were cautioned to differentiate themselves from professional drivers (chauffeurs) through dress and manner. Some worried about the amount of power and control vested in a chauffeur, especially when his passenger was a woman. (In French slang, the phrase *chauffer une femme* meant "to make hot love to a woman.") But at the same time, the automobile promised women privacy and protection from unwanted intrusions. The Detroit Electric Car was advertised so: "To the well-bred woman—the Detroit Electric has a particular appeal. In it she can preserve her toilet immaculate, her coiffure intact. She can drive it with all desired privacy, yet safely—in constant touch with traffic conditions around her."

The new technologies of American business also began to transform social etiquette. Typewriters, for example, introduced in the late 1800s, brought a flood of respectable young women into business offices. Women who typed were dubbed "typewriters" after the machines they operated. This label gave rise to the predictable joke ("Here I sit, my typewriter on my knee"), but the increasing presence of women in business complicated other traditional forms. What degree of deference based on gender did an employer owe a secretary? Did the forms of polite society transfer to business relations between the sexes? As more and more "respectable" women entered the public world, attending college, working in offices or stores, moving unchaperoned in public, the existing lines between men and women, public and private, genteel and unacceptable, were necessarily redrawn.

The etiquette of gentility broke down as the entire Victorian worldview, with its insistence on the absolute polarities of civilization and savagery, of good and evil, of men and women, began to crumble. More and more of those who came of age in the late nineteenth century felt stifled by the weight of gentility and the rigidness of form—some rebelling in profound ways and with profound results, others frivolously. But to a great extent, the breakdown of Victorian etiquette and the genteel performance came through those who were not afraid of the city, who found the intense *publicness* of the private world—attending dances with the same people, conducting polite conversations in genteelly appointed parlors—suffocating. They sought the privacy that the public world of the city offered in its anonymity. They sought the excitement of mixing with people of different conditions and backgrounds. And they sought a form of sexual freedom in the companionship of the opposite sex, exploring the new cabarets and restaurants, escaping into the world of the city that had so terrified their parents.

The Etiquette of Gender

If the etiquette of the nineteenth century centered on issues of class, the etiquette of the twentieth century coalesced on issues of sex and gender. The problem of defining relations between the sexes had, in many ways, replaced the problem of defining relations between the classes. Gender etiquette offered a means of controlling the relationships between men and women and of reinforcing the "natural" barriers between the sexes that seemed increasingly under siege in the twentieth century.

We see the shift from class to gender etiquette in the rise of the dating system and the elaboration of dating etiquette in the twentieth century. The calling system, as it operated in courtship, still centered upon class. As an invitation to call was an invitation into one's home, the calling system granted women and their parents the right of initiative, thus allowing them to screen out the unsuitable suitor. Dating transferred initiative to men and shifted the focus of etiquette from the barriers between classes as demonstrated in genteel performance to the roles of the sexes and the importance of gender politics.

The practice of dating originated in American cities in the last decade of the nineteenth century as young people of the working classes, pushed out of overcrowded tenement apartments and drawn to the new urban amusements that catered to them, took flirtations and courtship into the public realm. Their term "date" (which had referred to the temporal liaison with a prostitute) indicated the centrality of money in the relationship: the man paid for entertainment and the woman owed him something in return—flirtatious gaiety, quiet admiration, some degree of sexual intimacy. The practice of dating was taken up, in modified form, by the fast set of "society" youth who were drawn to the possibilities of the city, and filtered its way into middle-class conventionality by the mid 1910s to 1920s.

The new custom was confusing, as dating and calling coexisted for some years. A joke from the 1920s told of the young man who went to call on a young woman of his acquaintance only to find that "she had her hat on." The hat signaled that she expected to go out, and so he took her out, spending his scarce savings on their entertainment. Advisers in mass circulation magazines, such as Mrs. Burton Kingsland, who wrote the column "Good Manners and Good Form" for the *Ladies' Home Journal* in the early years of the twentieth century, attempted to make sense of the new system. The date, these advisers concurred, was an invitation into the man's world. The man was responsible for the expense, and thus claimed the right of initiative: only the man could ask for a date. The system of dating etiquette, as it developed, coalesced on the basic fact of men's money.

Whereas nineteenth-century manuals specified rules of chaperonage or simply assumed them, twentieth-century advisers more and more often discussed the etiquette of sexual relationships. In the 1930s, *Parents* magazine advised parents to deal with the issue of "petting" "dispassionately as being much more a matter of etiquette than of morals." A popular 1930s etiquette book for college women, *Coediquette*, offered information about how a girl should "conduct herself at a football game" and behave at a "rush tea." But the author's credentials were telling: traveling to forty-three universities, she had "dated college men and learned to know them by their lines." Another work linking etiquette and sex, Nina Farewell's *The Unfair Sex* (1953), begins, "Ever since the author's eighteenth birthday, when she surrendered her virginity because she was afraid to seem rude, she has felt a crying need for a handbook for girls—a manual on How to Cope with Men." Others

> *To a great extent, the breakdown of Victorian etiquette and the genteel performance came through those who were not afraid of the city, who found the intense* publicness *of the private world suffocating.*

offered very specific information about the etiquette of necking and petting: "for gallantry's sake a man is not in a position to withdraw from petting even should he very much want to," one adviser insisted. Women, according to the laws of etiquette and of nature, were to be the limit setters. Advisers differed in the etiquette of limit-setting: "Dear Abby," in the 1960s article "Blue Jean Biology," suggests a "stereophonic slap" to discourage a "mad lover"; a 1940s advice book suggested "excusing yourself from the room in a flustered way to adjust your hair with a 'Gracious, how I must look!' manner."

While etiquette played a role in the control of nonmarital sex, it was perhaps most important as it came to define qualities of masculinity and femininity. "Good etiquette, for a man, is whatever makes a woman feel more like a woman, without making her feel weak-minded. . . . Good etiquette, for a woman, is whatever makes a man feel more like a man, without making him feel more harassed and put upon than he normally does anyway," explained Peg Bracken in *I Try to Behave Myself* (1959). It was the barriers between the sexes that seemed most beleaguered by mid century, and scholarly journals and popular magazines alike were full of analyses of the problems of masculinity and femininity, both allegedly under threat of extinction in modern society. Masculinity and femininity seemed not things inherent, securely linked to one's physical sex, but a set of attributes to be achieved—largely through observing an elaborated and overelaborated gender etiquette.

Advice books, especially those for teenagers and young adults in the postwar years, were full of specific prescriptions, all pointing to the same end. Women, the system of rules made clear, were constantly to demonstrate their submission and need for protection, avoiding acts that they could perform perfectly well (like opening doors or ordering from menus) but that became "aggressive" and "competitive" in the company of a man. Men were to demonstrate control and dominance. As *Esquire Etiquette* declared in 1953: "When she's with you, etiquette renders her helpless. You're It." Not all young people, boys especially, conformed to the rules of etiquette—often much to the disappointment of teenage girls, who expected the conventionalized "perfect" date. But the newly developed teen magazines of the postwar years stressed etiquette (sometimes conflating it with "personality"), and teen advice books for girls spent a good deal of time offering strategies for "subtly" teaching their escorts proper behavior. A 1954 high school etiquette text reminded readers that the boy or man should walk on the outside, closest to the street. "Don't ignore the situation." If he walks on the inside, this book advised girls, "slip around" at the first opportunity.

The etiquette of masculinity and femininity did provide a comfortable script (in that the rules were clear) for a society in which dating was a central ritual that brought together strangers in a fairly intimate situation. The rules of etiquette offered protection, smoothing awkward encounters on those nights better spent washing one's hair, and turning others into the fairy tale stuff of teen magazines. But the etiquette of masculinity and femininity had greater significance than these uses suggest. It was born of deep-seated fears about changing relations between the sexes and served to reject—at least in the "private" world of ro-

The practice of dating was taken up by the fast set of "society" youth of the city and filtered down to middle-class conventionality by the 1920s.

mantic relationships—women's claims to greater roles in the public world. The etiquette of masculinity and femininity expressed social fears every bit as profound and conservative as the class-based fears that structured the genteel performance of the nineteenth century.

The shift from class to gender in the new etiquette books of the twentieth century does not mean that class lost all importance in American etiquette. The small points of etiquette still serve as signs of "breeding" and background and are easily read by those who seek to exclude others. But as Emily Post discovered from the response to her first etiquette book, published in 1922 under the unwieldy title *Etiquette in Society, in Business, in Politics, and at Home*, her readers were not interested in climbing the social ladder to challenge the ascendancy of the "Worldlys" and the "Wellborns." They were interested in more modest social mobility; they wanted not advice on the protocol of exclusive gentlemen's clubs and entertaining with a staff of twelve, but instead information about the rituals of middle-class inclusiveness—the luncheons and showers and dinners and weddings they intended to invest with grace and propriety.

There was still the threat of exclusion, and advertising played on fears of insufficiency. An advertisement for Doubleday's *Book of Etiquette* read: "Again She Orders—'A Chicken Salad, Please!' " (thus betraying to her date that she could not pronounce the French words that filled the menu). Many a suburban housewife pored over books of etiquette for the table setting that would convince her husband's boss that he had the right social stuff for a promotion. But much writing on etiquette, especially in the post–World War II era, aggressively assumed that America was a middle-class nation, and that all were subject to the same middle-class rules. And the new media taught etiquette in more pervasive fashion than etiquette manuals ever did: advertisements pictured the good life (and justified hiring female "admen" to make sure the ads showed correct table settings, for example); television shows like *Leave It to Beaver* portrayed the polite middle-class family dinner for all to watch and learn.

This middle-class inclusivity masked real barriers in American society, the most obvious, of course, being predicated on race. But the rhetoric of cultural inclusivity through participation in a common middle-class culture was strong, and the forms of etiquette were tightly bound up with this comforting vision. Thus when cultural rebels in the 1960s attacked the forms of politeness and civility, they had found a good target, partly because the etiquette of gender had become increasingly overelaborated and stifling. Proper etiquette also embodied a respect for authority that necessarily supported the status quo. Some of the prevailing forms of etiquette were tightly bound up with inequality, and some people violated these norms in attempts to create a more democratic society. Others simply rebelled against what they described as "uptight" behavior. However, to cultural conservatives, these attacks on civility seemed to be attacks on civilization itself.

The forms of etiquette have changed drastically in the past half-century. But despite the rejection of much of what passed for polite behavior in earlier decades, Americans have not abandoned the rules of etiquette. Society does require rules or codes, be they informal or formal, for its continued functioning, and many people seek some method of smoothing the travails of social interaction. The enormous popularity of Judith Martin, who writes as "Miss Manners" in a column syndicated in over three hundred newspapers and whose book *Miss Manners' Guide to Excruciatingly Correct Behavior* (1982) has become a classic, witnesses contemporary ambivalence about etiquette. Her authority lies in irony and wit, and while she may refer to "Dear Queen Victoria" her voice and her advice are firmly rooted in the late twentieth century. And, most importantly, her advice is taken seriously.

Prescriptive literature as a serious genre is three decades out of favor in America. But as Miss Manners's surprising success shows, a filter of irony can ease the rigors of etiquette into the modern age. Perhaps even more indicative of the advent of a new system of etiquette in the 1990s is the rise, most notably on college campuses, of whole new codes of civility, codes that are most directly concerned with race, gender, and sexual preference, and that are hotly debated. These codes take up many of the thorny problems of etiquette—the problems that underlie many of our historical systems of etiquette—and this time recognize the problems as political.

[See also Clothing and Personal Adornment; Courtship, Marriage, Separation, and Divorce; Gender Roles and Relations; Nightlife; Sexual Behavior and Morality; Women and Work.]

BIBLIOGRAPHY

Anderson, Jervis. *This Was Harlem: A Cultural Portrait, 1900–1950* (1988).

Bailey, Beth. *From Front Porch to Back Seat: Courtship in Twentieth-Century America* (1988). Gender etiquette.

Cable, Mary, and the editors of *American Heritage. American Manners and Morals: A Picture History of How We Behaved and Misbehaved* (1969). A popular survey.

Carson, Gerald. *The Polite Americans: A Wide-Angle View of Our More or Less Good Manners over 300 Years* (1966). A popular overview.

Cmiel, Kenneth. In *The Sixties: From Memory to History* edited by David Farber (1992).

Cowles, Virginia. *The Astors* (1979).
Elias, Norbert. *Power and Civility: The Civilizing Process.* Vol. 2. Translated by Edmund Jephcott (1982).
Erenberg, Lewis. *Steppin' Out: New York Nightlife and the Transformation of American Culture, 1890–1930* (1981).
Halttunen, Karen. *Confidence Men and Painted Women: A Study of Middle-Class Culture in America, 1830–1870* (1982).
Hawke, David Freeman. *Everyday Life in Early America* (1988).
Kasson, John. *Rudeness and Civility: Manners in Nineteenth-Century Urban America* (1990). Excellent analysis of nineteenth-century etiquette.
Levine, Lawrence. *Highbrow/Lowbrow: The Emergence of Cultural Hierarchy in America* (1988).
Marchand, Roland. *Advertising the American Dream: Making Way for Modernity, 1920–1940* (1985).
Mulvey, Christopher. *Transatlantic Manners: Social Patterns in Nineteenth-Century Anglo-American Travel Literature* (1990).
Scharff, Virginia. *Taking the Wheel: Women and the Coming of the Motor Age* (1991).
Schlesinger, Arthur Meier. *Learning How to Behave: A Historical Study of American Etiquette Books* (1968).
Wyatt-Brown, Bertram. *Southern Honor: Ethics and Behavior in the Old South* (1982).

— BETH BAILEY

MARRIAGE

See COURTSHIP, MARRIAGE, SEPARATION, AND DIVORCE

MASS CULTURE AND ITS CRITICS

Once upon a time, Left and Right met in their disdain for mass culture. Russell Kirk and Theodor Adorno engaged in a delicate pas de deux, denouncing the vapidity of comic books and cinema starlets. Now, though, that dance is over: it has become as fashionable to celebrate the emancipatory powers of sitcoms and soap operas as it once was to denounce their narcotic effects. Amid the upbeat uproar, there is a danger that older traditions of mass-culture criticism will be oversimplified and too easily dismissed. This essay will try to counter that danger by tracing the origins and development of mass-culture criticism in the United States since the early nineteenth century, charting major changes in the dominant discourse—down to and including the recent shift from critique to affirmation. The essay will conclude by suggesting an approach to the subject that tries to incorporate the insights of the newer scholarship without losing the critical edge of the older traditions.

Antecedents of Mass Culture

Men in the United States—at least the literate and generally affluent men who leave records for historians to read—have always been ambivalent about entertainment devised for the milling masses of people. In the classical republican tradition, the "people out of doors" were at once the scourge of tyrants and the strength of demagogues. This first aspect sanctioned the staging of popular political spectacles throughout the nineteenth century, the second promoted among the elite a recurrent brooding about mob rule. Pessimistic fears drew sustenance from republicans' cyclical theory of history: every republic had risen from barbarism only to slide into decadence, as "luxury" and "effeminacy" sapped manly civic virtue and the populace succumbed to the "vices of commerce," bartering their sacred constitutional rights for a mess of pottage. So, at any rate, it seemed to such students of history as John Adams and Thomas Jefferson.

It is difficult to understand the resilience of these republican ideas in American cultural history without tracing them to their Protestant origins. Calvinist and Pietist strains of Protestant Christianity came to dominate American public discourse by the mid eighteenth century, promoting ideals of sincerity and unified selfhood amid the snares and duplicities of the marketplace. The republican citizen was a political version of the unified Protestant self. He was honest, disciplined,

In Walden, Henry David Thoreau criticized mass culture within the Protestant-republican tradition.

and productive—resistant to the effeminizing allure of creature comforts as well as to the seductive persuasiveness of the demagogue. He was the embodiment of a profoundly masculine ego ideal.

Given the emphasis on masculinity, solidity, and straightforwardness in the republican construction of selfhood, it is not surprising that the American critique of mass culture has often drawn on a profoundly gendered discourse of authenticity. This discourse, though, could be inflected in various idioms. One was the utilitarianism of bourgeois moralists who decried popular amusements as ephemeral trash, distractions from the duties of work and citizenship: this sort of denunciation easily degenerated into the hysteria that European historians have noticed in nineteenth-century attacks on the carnival. The utilitarian idiom resurfaced as well in the twentieth-century Marxist assaults on mass culture as a promoter of "false consciousness." The significance of the critiques differed profoundly, depending on whether the critic identified the source of the problem as the depravity of popular taste or the imposition of ruling-class values. What the republican bourgeois and the Marxist had in common, though, was a productivist distrust of frivolity as well as a literalist conception of the real.

> What is the point? *Henry David Thoreau asked constantly in* Walden *when confronted with the "hurry and waste of life" around him—and much of the waste was spent on mass-marketed cultural products like the daily newspaper.*

But there was also a romantic idiom in the discourse of authenticity that could lead in different directions. It could promote a more capacious critique of mass culture—less fearful of fantasy, more attuned to the ways that emergent commercialized forms of amusement actually denied pleasure in the name of promoting it. Critics in this tradition recognized the fraudulence at the heart of much mass-marketed leisure, the compulsive busyness that linked play to work in cultures driven by the imperatives of "development." This was the viewpoint of the young Karl Marx, the Marx of *Economic and Philosophical Manuscripts* (1844), and of his American contemporary Henry David Thoreau.

Thoreau's *Walden* (1854) was by no means free of republican prejudices. He railed against fashion; he distrusted the opulent pleasures provided by modern publicans, warning that if the traveler "resigned himself to their tender mercies he would soon be completely emasculated" (Babcock, ed., 1966, p. 24). Like Nathaniel Hawthorne's famous complaint about the "damned mob of scribbling women," Thoreau's assaults on emergent mass culture often amounted to little more than misogynistic railings. And the philosophical basis of his critique was a hatred of modern "sham," grounded in a profound commitment to a realist epistemology. "Let us settle ourselves," he wrote,

> and work and wedge our feet downward through the mud and slush of opinion, and prejudice, and tradition, and delusion, and appearance, that alluvion which covers the globe, through Paris and London, through New York and Boston and Concord, through church and state, through poetry and philosophy and religion, till we come to a hard bottom and rocks in place, which we can call *reality*, and say, This is, and no mistake; and then begin, having a *point d'appui*, below freshet and frost and fire, a place where you might find a wall or a state, or set a lamppost safely, or perhaps a gauge, not a Nilometer, but a Realometer, that future ages might know how deep a freshet of shams and appearances had gathered from time to time. (p. 66)

This sort of peroration was squarely in the Protestant-republican tradition, the paean to a sense of solidity beneath the tissue of lying surfaces.

Yet the context of that peroration was a longer statement of determination to live deliberately, to ignore the incessant promptings to modern punctuality. "If the engine whistles, let it whistle till it is hoarse for its pains. If the bell rings, why should we run?" Thoreau asked. "We will consider what kind of music they are like" (p. 66). This was the deepest and most enduring undercurrent of Thoreau's *Walden*: an admonition to his readers (and himself) not to respond to the rhythms of industrial culture without considering what the music was like. *What is the point?* he asked constantly, when he was confronted with the "hurry and waste of life" around him. And much of the waste was spent on mass-marketed cultural products—the daily newspaper, for example.

> Hardly a man takes a half hour's nap after dinner, but when he wakes he holds up his head and asks, "What's the news?" as if the rest of mankind had stood his sentinels. . . . After a night's sleep the news is as indispensable as breakfast. "Pray tell me anything new that has happened to man any where on this globe,"—and

> he reads it over his coffee and rolls, that a man has had his eyes gouged out on the Wachito River; never dreaming the while that he lives in the dark unfathomed mammoth cave of this world, and has but the rudiment of an eye himself. (p. 63)

Elitism notwithstanding, this is an early version of an argument that became common in the discourse of authenticity—the argument that mass-produced descriptions of experience have become replacements for the real thing.

Thoreau's aphorisms captured themes that would resonate in the best mass-culture criticism of the century to come. "The mass of men lead lives of quiet desperation," he wrote (p. 5), and—recalling the young Marx on alienated labor—"men have become the tools of their tools" (p. 25). Under the regime of industrial rationality, the pace of manufactured leisure began to resemble that of manufacturing work; the problem was not pleasure but the marketing of factitious substitutes for it. Of course, if people really enjoyed those substitutes then the way is left open for a pseudopopulist response to Thoreau: Where does this old crank get off, pronouncing on what is or isn't real leisure? But to anyone who believes that cultural critics have an obligation to make discriminating judgments about the quality of everyday life, *Walden* represented a key move away from the utilitarian critique of popular amusements. Unlike the European bourgeois assault on vestiges of carnival, Thoreau's critique was not an attempt to suppress resistance to industrial routine; it was a rejection of that routine, and of the frenetic leisure that accommodated it, a protest against manufactured fun in the name of a more thoroughgoing hedonism. *Walden* suggested the range of possibilities in the romantic discourse of authenticity.

During the years after the Civil War, the *cri de coeur* against inauthenticity grew more intense. The passion for concrete actualities impelled Victorians to pack their parlors with wax daisies, ceramic collies, and stereoscopic views of dark continents. Whole industries were devoted to the mass production of simulacra—and yet the imitative aesthetic failed to satisfy longings for reality. Friedrich Nietzsche articulated a sentiment common on both sides of the Atlantic when he wrote that

> men of the seventies and eighties . . . were filled with a devouring hunger for reality, but they had the misfortune to confuse this with matter—which is but the hollow and deceptive wrapping of it. Thus they lived perpetually in a wretched, padded, puffed-out world of cotton-wool, cardboard, and tissue-paper.

There is more going on here than a male romantic idealist's distrust of the material world: the sense that culture could be purchased secondhand, through spectatorship or tourism as well as through mass consumption, posed a direct threat to Protestant and republican doctrines of coherent selfhood. Edwin Lawrence Godkin, editor of *The Nation*, made the connection clear in his diagnosis of "chromo-civilization" in 1874:

> The newspapers and other cheap periodicals, and the lyceum lectures and small colleges, have diffused through the community a kind of smattering of all sorts of knowledge, a taste for reading and for "art"—that is, a desire to see and own pictures—which, taken together, pass with a large body of slenderly equipped persons as "culture," . . . and raise them to a plane on which they see nothing higher, greater, or better than themselves. Now culture, in the only correct and safe sense of the term, is the result of a process of discipline, both mental and moral. It is not a thing that can be picked up, or that can be got by doing as one pleases. It cannot be acquired by desultory reading, for instance, or travelling in Europe. It comes of the protracted exercise of the faculties for given ends, under restraints of some kind, whether imposed by one's self or by other people. . . . In short, the man of culture is the man who has formed his ideals through labor and self-denial. To be real, therefore, culture ought to affect a man's whole character, and not merely stuff his memory with facts.

Contemporary historians tend to dismiss Godkin as a snob, but his critique of commodification involved more than an aristocrat's disdain for a tourist's definition of art. It was a late restatement of the Protestant-republican view that "real culture" and coherent selfhood were interdependent—a demanding construction of human subjectivity in which culture is the cement that holds the whole together. Godkin's obsession with "labor and self-denial" (not to mention with a "correct and safe" definition of culture) may seem narrowly puritanical, but it is difficult to dismiss his insistence that "culture ought to affect a man's whole character, and not merely stuff his memory with facts." This attack on a consumerist model of culture implies a parallel critique of education—one that resonates with pragmatism rather than puritanism. Godkin was more than a backward-looking snob.

Godkin's juxtaposition of "real culture" against "chromo-civilization" evokes a central conflict in mass-culture criticism that has persisted down to the present. The sense of inauthenticity has not gone away; indeed, it may even have intensified during the past century. Certainly the word "reality" has acquired an honorific quality in a society where six year olds (and up) tell their friends to "get real," where pundits advise politicians to embrace "the real world," and where advertisers claim their products are more "real" than those of their competitors. Yet, as these examples suggest, the discourse of authenticity has come to contain a variety of voices—variations on utilitarian and romantic themes. During the past century, it has been possible to locate "real culture" in a variety of embodiments other than Godkin's cultivated republican citizen: in the virtuous folk (the faith of the Popular Front as well as more sinister *volkiscb* ideologies—it was Germany's Oswald Spengler, not E. L. Godkin, who most notoriously popularized the antithesis between culture and civilization); in the functional rationality of a technocratic elite (the central myth of managerial liberalism); or in the heroic, autonomous artist (the romantic/modernist ego ideal). And, of course, there have been further variations on these major themes.

How one defines the real depends in part on how one defines the unreal. For some it was simply the new world of cheap goods and the apparatus used to promote them; for others the feeling of factitiousness was connected more broadly to conditions of everyday life in the modern world: the routinization of work, the isolation from nature, the evaporation of supernatural or religious frameworks of meaning, which had given gravity to ethical choice. The more capacious the critic's sense of modernity, the more nuanced the critique of mass culture was likely to be.

Among the least nuanced was the early ideology of aestheticism. The painter James McNeill Whistler provided its classic formulation in his "Ten O'Clock Lecture" (1885), which identified the agent of inauthenticity as the nineteenth-century bourgeoisie. "There never was an art-loving nation," Whistler asserted, but artists had been able to impose their superior taste on the mediocre multitude until the emergence of bourgeois hegemony.

> The world was flooded with all that was beautiful, until there arose a new class, who discovered the cheap, and foresaw fortune in the facture of the sham.
>
> Then sprang into existence the tawdry, the common, the gewgaw.
>
> The taste of the tradesman supplanted the science of the artist, and what was born of the million went back to them, and charmed them, for it was after their own heart; and the great and the small, the statesman and the slave, took to themselves the abomination that was tendered, and preferred it, and have lived with it ever since!
>
> And the artist's occupation was gone, and the manufacturer and the huckster took his place.

Here was the aesthete's characteristic tendency to ignore power relations, to trace the source of mass culture to the desires of the public rather than to the commercial purveyors' assumptions about what those desires were. Yet Whistler's diatribe was milder and more American than the ideology of aestheticism developed at about the same time by Oscar Wilde. For Whistler "the science of the artist" has been replaced by "the taste of the tradesman"; there is still some emphasis on the artist as the possessor of some definite knowledge or craft—in that sense, he is still a solid self and a bearer of authentic beauty. For Wilde, taste was all: the aesthete was both creator and connoisseur of fleeting impressions, elegant surfaces that shimmered and were gone. Ironic detachment distanced him from timeless ideals of beauty as well as from notions of unified selfhood. Not until the early 1960s, with the emergence of a "camp" sensibility in New York and other American cities, would Wilde's aesthetic of self-dramatization and surface effects take hold on this side of the Atlantic.

Critics Confront the New Culture

By the early twentieth century, though, some American thinkers were beginning to move beyond the aesthetic formulation typified by the "Ten O'Clock Lecture," beginning to realize that mass culture was more than a matter of proliferating gewgaws. What was being sold was often much less substantial than bric-a-brac: a developing leisure industry housed in amusement parks, sports stadiums, and picture palaces was vending vicarious intense experience (physical or emotional) to people who found it lacking in their daily lives. Projects that exploited a variety of sensations—erotic titillation, raw fright, delight in physical prowess and the tingle of danger, disgust at the horrific or deformed—these were being rationalized, turned gradually into more stable, predictable business ventures than similar projects had been in the era of P. T. Barnum (1810–1891). The invention of roller coasters and Ferris wheels, machines designed to do nothing but provide a few minutes' brush with feelings of mild elevation or danger, perfectly embodied the psychic agenda behind the leisure industry. The merchandising of thrills and chills—including the selling of imperial military adventures in the nascent tabloid press—was a major part of the emergent mass culture.

Confronting these developments, critics of mass culture began to refashion the idiom of utilitarian moralism in a managerial mold. Overt moralism faded, but male-centered productivism persisted. Thorstein Veblen's (1857–1929) work typified the emergent managerial critique, which leavened its pessimism about the frivolity of the folk with the hope that perhaps the pathetic creatures could be educated to better things by a technocratic elite. Veblen spent most of his career inveighing against the "irrationality" of consumption (and indeed of most other cultural rituals) and hoping the masses would develop revolutionary consciousness through "the discipline of the machine." A subtler version of this mentality appeared in the British Fabians' critique of mass culture—a critique that powerfully influenced Walter Lippmann (1889–1974) and other managerial liberals during the 1910s and 1920s.

One of the more engaging expressions of Fabian thought was H. G. Wells's novel *Tono-Bungay* (1908). Wells's recoil from the "fictitious values" of an advanced commodity civilization—the values that could be created out of whole cloth by advertising and promotion—

By the early twentieth century, projects that exploited a variety of sensations were being rationalized and gradually turned into more stable, predictable business ventures than similar projects had been in the era of P. T. Barnum.

was the mainspring of his plainspoken critique of mass culture. In his view, the hollowness at the heart of commodity civilization was paradoxically a source of its strength. Advertising intensified feelings of factitiousness but also promised release from them into a realm of intense, unmediated experience. Musing on the popularity of the patent medicine Tono-Bungay, one of Wells's characters (an artist named Ewart) says:

> Think of the little clerks and jaded women and overworked people. People overstrained with wanting to do, people overstrained with wanting to be. . . . People, in fact, overstrained. . . . The real trouble of life . . . isn't that we exist—that's a vulgar error; the real trouble is that we *don't* really exist and we want to. That's what this—in the highest sense—muck stands for! The hunger to be—for once—really alive to our fingertips! (1935, p. 156)

Patent medicines, Wells implied, reinforced this hunger even as they claimed to satisfy it. This was the cycle of deprivation and desire that accompanied commodity civilization and the mass-marketed culture that accompanied it.

The only way to escape from that cycle, in *Tono-Bungay*, is to find a reality more genuine than the advertised version. For George Ponderevo, nephew of the patent-medicine magnate and disillusioned manager of the company, the search for authentic experience leads him to "Science."

> She is reality, the one reality I have found in this strange disorder of existence. . . . You cannot change her by advertisement or clamour, nor stifle her in vulgarities. . . . I've never been in love with self-indulgence. That philosophy of the loose lip and the lax paunch is one for which I've always had instructive distrust. I like bare things, stripped things, plain austere and continent things, fine lines and cold colours. But in these plethoric times when there is too much coarse stuff for everybody and the struggle for life takes on the colour of competitive advertisement and the effort to fill your neighbour's eye, when there is no urgent demand either for personal courage, sound nerves or stark beauty, we find ourselves by accident. Always before these times the bulk of the people did not over-eat themselves, because they couldn't, whether they wanted to do so or not, and all but a few were kept "fit" by unavoidable exercise and personal danger. Now, if only he pitch his standard low enough and keep free from pride, almost any one can achieve a sort of excess. You can go through contemporary life fudging and evading, indulging and slacking, never really hungry nor frightened nor passionately stirred, your highest moment a mere sentimental orgasm, and your first contact with primary and elemental necessities the sweat of your death-bed. So I think it was with my uncle; so, very, nearly, it was with me. (pp. 282–283)

George is an aeronautical engineer, and is aloft in a glider while he reflects on the inauthenticity of modern life. The equation of applied science and reality links Wells, on the one hand, with modernist critics of mass culture—functionalist designers, for example, who like George were drawn to "bare things, stripped things, plain, austere and continent things"; on the other hand, it placed Wells amid a camp of positivist social engineers, men like the young Lippmann, who thought he saw the solution as well as the problem in the masses' yearnings for contact with elemental necessities. Indeed Lippmann quoted George's peroration in *A Preface to Politics* (1914), assimilating it to his own model of mass culture and using Wells's critique of aimlessness to justify social control by managerial-professional elites.

What if, instead of allowing the masses to satisfy their longings for intensity by watching ball games and indulging in other cheap amusements, elite policymakers could provide them "a life that shall be really interesting"? The impulses that lay behind mass culture could be channeled to more constructive ends. Lippmann presents this utilitarian plea as a liberating departure from old-fashioned moralism: the trick to managing social disorder is not to moralize against mass culture but to offer "positive" alternatives to it. Lippmann's fascination with the oxymoronic process of "democratic social engineering" links him to the pioneers in the emerging field of personnel management—the science that sought to make workers want to do what they had to do.

Managerial reformers constructed a vision of the mass audience that resonated with the views of fastidious aristocrats like José Ortega y Gasset and T. S. Eliot, as well as with those of corporate advertisers and other promoters of commercial entertainment. Whatever their differences, all emphasized the chasm that supposedly separated themselves from "the man in the street." (Indeed, that very phrase, which first appeared in the 1920s, suggested the marketers' determination to plumb the depths of the average.) Marketing professionals often seemed to be viewing "the masses" from the thirtieth story of a midtown Manhattan skyscraper—a vantage point that produced strikingly Eliotic visions of urban society. A contributor to the advertising trade journal *Printer's Ink* commented in 1908 on the great electric signs that had only recently transformed Broadway: "Flowers in natural colors stand out against the night sky. Garlands and drapery are traced in many-tinted furs. Delicate jewels of ruby, gold, and turquoise, wrought in tiny lamps, are suspended over dingy buildings in the sight of the hurrying ants called men." Just as mass culture brought novelty to the allegedly bleak cultural landscape of rural America, so its spokesmen also claimed to bring color to the supposedly drab routine that urban life had become.

The corporate vision of the modern consumer, if not quite Eliot's "young man carbuncular," was just as much a vacant-eyed straphanger, stupefied by monotonous work, craving instinctual release and a sense (however fleeting) of personal autonomy. The advertising copywriter John Starr Hewitt articulated the emerging conventional wisdom in 1925 thus:

> In spite of his seeming sophistication, the American citizen is naive, fresh, essentially childlike, full of generous enthusiasms and the capacity for wonderment. His everyday life is pretty dull. Get up–eat–go to work–eat–go to bed. But his mind is constantly reaching out beyond this routine. This is one of the reasons why the American is such a great fiction reader–movie goer–talking machine and radio fan. He compensates for the routine of to-day by the expectation of what his life is to be to-morrow.

The idea of consumption as compensation lies behind the "bread and circuses" notion of mass culture that links Lippmann and Hewitt with pessimists like Eliot. The differences are that while Eliot despaired of any redemption for the modern mass audience, Lippmann believed that professionals like himself could plan more nourishing bread and more elevating circuses, and Hewitt was convinced that the existing distractions were not only satisfactory but liberating.

But this liberation depended on the assumption that people were mired in "the rut of everyday existence," as a Paramount Pictures advertisement called it in 1930. Like the pleasures currently promoted by cigarette advertising, the fun in the ideology of mass consumption was a matter of moments snatched from a life depicted as relentlessly hectic or dreary. There was a symbiosis between managerial demands for personal efficiency and the temporary relief from them offered in advertisements. Corporate-sponsored hedonism legitimated the idea that everyday living must inevitably be gray. Without the dingy buildings and the hurrying ants as backdrop, those great electric signs would have lost some of their luster. There was a deep and symbiotic relationship between the glittering surfaces of mass culture and the developing structures of bureaucratic rationality—the "iron cage" glimpsed by Max Weber in the despairing conclusion to *The Protestant Ethic and the Spirit of Capitalism* (1904). The question was whether to accept the routine of rationality as inevitable and provide temporary release from it, as managerial reformers and promoters of mass culture alike tried to do, or whether to challenge the life of "quiet desperation" at its core—as Thoreau had done, and as numerous critics in the romantic and modernist traditions would continue to do during the late nineteenth and twentieth centuries.

When the romantic critique of mass culture resurfaced toward the turn of the century, it was sometimes still tinged with republican misogyny: in the United States as in Europe, men who remained committed to ideals of autonomous selfhood feared mass culture as a feminizing force. As Andreas Huyssen observes of the fin de siècle, the fear of mass culture "in this age of declining liberalism is always also a fear of woman, a fear of nature out of control, a fear of the unconscious, of sexuality, of the loss of identity and stable ego boundaries in the mass." Among male cultural critics, there was widespread concern about women crossing boundaries between private and public, entering (actively or passively) into commercial public life as voracious consumers—and actively seeking erotic pleasure, if only by appropriating "the agency of the look" in the darkness of the movie theater.

On the other hand, there were some mass-culture critics who were less tightly bound to conventional male ego ideals, who dropped their misogynist blinders and glimpsed the masculine will to technocratic domination behind the "feminized" surfaces of softness and pleasure. One was Henry Adams, whose emblem of modernity was not the moviehouse but the dynamo, and who juxtaposed the desiccated truths of instrumentalist rationality against the instinctual energy and religious faith embodied in the thirteenth-century worship of the virgin Mary. Two others were Waldo Frank (1889–1967), who combined Whitmanesque egalitarianism with antimodern vitalism, and Randolph Bourne (1886–1918), who understood better than any of his contemporaries the ways that new mechanisms of mass entertainment could become instruments of mass persuasion—who, during World War I, glimpsed the intimate relationship between new forms of corporate-sponsored culture and the mobilization of whole populations for modern, total war. All of these authors worked within the indigenous grain of Thoreau; they clung ambivalently to a concern for coherent selfhood while they searched for more flexible notions of personal authenticity than republican (or liberal) thought could provide.

Mass-culture critics such as Henry Adams and Waldo Frank dropped their misogynist blinders and glimpsed the masculine will to technocratic domination behind the "feminized" surfaces of softness and pleasure.

For some, especially Adams and Frank, that search led toward primitivism. By the 1920s the quest for authentic alternatives to mass culture had turned decisively toward the heart of darkness. Indigenous tribal cultures, American or African, enjoyed a vogue as avatars of authenticity; D. H. Lawrence typified the move in *The Plumed Serpent* (1926). African Americans, though, were closer to home and were more convenient embodiments of the palpitating vitality that seemed absent from the mass-produced "pep" of the regnant business civilization. The legendary assault on that civilization was led by Robert and Helen Lynd, Sinclair Lewis, and H. L. Mencken; their "attack on the village," according to conventional wisdom, was a critique of "puritanism" in the name of modernity. In fact, their cultural critique was more complicated: they assumed that puritanism was not only vestigial but resurgent, embedded in the business ethos that claimed to be its enemy. A fair number of the metropolitan cognoscenti, sharing that assumption, acted on it by trooping up to Harlem to boogie-woogie with the colored folk. Others, like Sherwood Anderson, went to the American South to sentimentalize Negro vitality.

For Anderson the celebration of Negritude was part of a prolonged assault on conventional definitions of the smart and up-to-date. As an advertising copywriter who was also a romantic primitivist, Anderson occupied the boundaries between mass culture and modernist sensibility. He was constantly seeking to slough off the evasions and compromises of business civilization, to recover some actual or imagined state of lost innocence and passion. "I am myself as I was when I was a boy," he wrote from Kentucky to a woman confidante in 1922; the trip South, which resulted in *Dark Laughter* (1925), was for him "a kind of pilgrimage back into the realities of life." in *Winesburg, Ohio* (1919), realities had been harder to find; the town was caught up in the standardizing patterns of corporate-sponsored culture. During his advertising career, Anderson had engaged that culture successfully if ambivalently; most of his literary career involved an effort to purge himself of the corruptions of commerce by drinking deeply from the modernist discourse of authenticity In *Winesburg* and other works he celebrated people who had been left behind by mass culture—"grotesques," he called them—juxtaposing their authentic experience against the standardized normality promoted by advertising.

By the 1930s, under the impact of the Great Depression, critics of inauthenticity found more overtly political vehicles to carry their cultural freight. Matthew Josephson, who had celebrated advertising and mass culture during the 1920s, posed the hypocrisy of "the gentlemen who spend their days and nights counterfeiting and misrepresenting, the copy-writers, the knights of press-agentry, the Junior Leaguers and the tennis champions who give lying testimonials" against the "true, simple human dignity" that could be found in "the most threadbare Soviet student or the grimiest of coal miners." Themes of plain speech and productiveness resurfaced: coal miners and sharecroppers (not to mention Soviet students) played starring roles in the morality play staged by the Popular Front; parasitic businessmen played the villains. Yet the theatrical metaphor is misleading: the Popular Front was more than a puppet show from Moscow. During the 1930s, a fascinated reverence for "the folk" gripped many Americans who had never been near a Communist party meeting. As Warren Susman has argued, when the bottom dropped out, middle-class Americans (that is, the ones who had something to lose) groped for emotional as well as economic security; they longed to belong to some collective community. Folkish ideology—right, left, or center—met that need by providing sustaining organicist visions. So it is not surprising that a more communitarian and egalitarian idiom began to reappear in the discourse of authenticity, or that many Americans sought the real in the actual or imagined culture of rural folk.

What was most important about the folkish version of classical republican themes—"communism is twentieth-century Americanism"—was not its most fervent formulations but the way it pervaded general culture. The process was promoted by corporate experts in marketing and communication, eager to roll back the ideological invasion of New Deal liberals who had captured the responsible centrist position in public debate. In advertising and mass media, managerial elites began to perform the shell game that has persisted down to the present: reselling the facsimile of "traditional values" to a population from whom they had been appropriated. By the end of World War II, in the visual and verbal rhetoric of Hollywood films and mass-circulation magazines, producerist authenticity was transformed into kitsch.

Small wonder that a small group of liberal and radical intellectuals began to develop a more rigorous and exclusive discourse of authenticity. The tale of the *Partisan Review* circle has often been told: the *PR* editors' break from the prison of orthodox Marxism, their rejection of the Popular Front—not only for its politics but also for its cultural style, their embrace of high modernism as an alternative to the philistinism of Left or Right. The story has been endowed with an almost epic significance by the participants themselves (who have retold it often) and by historians who accept the *PR* circle's estimation of its own intellectual importance, if not of its moral heroism. Whatever significance we assign the *PR* story, one thing is certain: the writers who clustered around *Partisan Review* during its first two decades of existence (1937–1957) played a major role in returning the discourse of authenticity to its individualist roots. The concept of totalitarianism provided mass-culture critics with a theoretical bridge between Nazi and Soviet kitsch—and with a spur line to American nationalism as well. When Van Wyck Brooks (1886–1963) and Archibald MacLeish (1892–1982) lashed literary intellectuals for their refusal to celebrate American democracy in the face of the fascist threat, Dwight Macdonald howled: "*Kulturbolschewismus* is here!" (that is, cultural bolshevism). The subordination of art to political propaganda was the nightmare vision of the age; in the face of Nazi, Soviet, or even Works Progress Administration murals, *PR* mass-culture critics held aloft the romantic-modernist ideal of autonomous art. The recoil from national socialist, socialist, or capitalist realism led to the deification of the difficult text, the fascination with rich ambiguity and dark truth. Writer Theodore Dreiser's stock fell sharply, as did that of all such earnest bumblers; the smart money was on ironists like Henry James, or on apocalypticians like Kafka and Orwell. The *PR* discourse of authenticity deemed the artist a hero of renunciation—he renounced the allure of cheap success, the temptation to curry favor with mass taste.

The artist or critic who wanted to maintain an independent spirit had to be tough. Indeed, if there was one kind of liberalism that still preserved a shred of honor in the post–World War II period it was "tough-minded liberalism." The deification of intellectual toughness, the relentless rejection of "secondhand" sentimentality, was rooted in understandable reaction against the sappier forms of folkish ideology; but that reaction allowed the discourse of authenticity to be stripped of its critical potential. This became clearest in the antics of individuals like Leslie A. Fiedler (b. 1917), who issued a series of farewells to the childish innocence of the Popular Front period—each more hard-boiled and disillusioned than the last. Before long, though, the cult of toughness showed up as well in the allegedly sentimental precincts of mass culture itself. Movies like *High Noon* and *Rebel Without a Cause* celebrated the stoic isolate in a social void, presenting images of authenticity that could easily be assimilated to dominant ideals of masculine identity and cold war politics. To be sure, there were constant efforts to create resistant alternative images of authentic (male) selfhood: not only the "White Negro" hipsters delineated by Norman Mailer—descendants of Sherwood Anderson who were parodied just as easily and who melded more easily with conventional power politics—but also the Beat poets, who at their best followed Allen Ginsberg and Gary Snyder beyond aesthetic complaints about mass culture into philosophical critiques of the instrumentalist mentality behind it. Yet overall, those who bobbed in the mainstream of public discourse robbed resistance to mass culture of any social or philosophical significance and reduced it to a stylized cult of masculine toughness.

The emphasis on style was characteristic of the historical moment. At a time when political choices seemed predetermined, questions of power were translated into matters of taste. Mass-culture criticism acquired some of the emotional charge that had previously infused debates over class struggle and social injustice. The results were often a little ludicrous, as in the uproar over middlebrow taste that convulsed contributors to *PR* and similar magazines like *Dissent* and *Commentary.* The mass marketing of high culture had become a cottage industry by the 1950s—epitomized by artifacts like RCA Red Seal recordings of Wagner's greatest hits and the *Saturday Evening Post's* "Adventures of the Mind" series, which featured full-page photographs of men with furrowed brows and five-page reflections on such topics as "The Decline of Greatness" (by Arthur Schlesinger, Jr., in the 1 November 1958 issue). The problem with this sort of enterprise, according to the *PR* circle, was not that it bowdlerized great originals but that it presented imitation profundity as if it were the real thing. The specter of high culture served up secondhand drove Dwight Macdonald (1906–1982) to resurrect the gendered metaphors of apocalypse favored by fin-de-siècle theorists of decadence like Gustave LeBon. Middlebrow culture, in Macdonald's view, was nature run amuck: "there is slowly emerging a tepid, flaccid Middlebrow Culture that threatens to engulf everything in its spreading ooze," he warned in 1953.

Despite the absurdity of this statement and other rhetorical excesses, Macdonald made an honorable effort to keep alive the Thoreauvian tradition of mass-culture criticism. He preserved its political edge in an era when most mainstream culture critics routinely transformed questions of power into matters of taste. Unlike so many of his contemporaries, Macdonald did not allow his distaste for Popular Front sentimentality to lead him into either tough-guy posturing or apologetics for the cold war.

Neither did the mass-culture critics associated with the Frankfurt school; those who survived the Nazi holocaust ended up in places like New York and Los Angeles, where they continued to develop arguments they had begun to elaborate in the 1930s. More than any other theorists, they underscored the symbiotic relationship between what they called "the culture industry" and the technocratic imperatives they recognized in fascism, Stalinism, and advanced capitalism. They often transcended the patriarchal, ascetic, and productivist tendencies that afflicted the utilitarian critique of mass culture—as well as the flat-footed functionalism of that critique. Theodor Adorno's essay on Thorstein Veblen, for example, recognized that *The Theory of the Leisure Class* (1899) was actually a sweeping "attack on culture" itself—since consumption and display were central to so much of the art and ritual that Veblen scorned. The totalitarian specter hovered over much of the Frankfurt school critique, darkening these theorists' views of ordinary human capacity: the chapter called "The Culture Industry: Enlightenment as Mass Deception" in Adorno and Max Horkheimer's *Dialectic of Enlightenment* (German, 1947; trans. 1972) did occasionally make the consumers of mass culture sound like passive and manipulable dolts. But the Frankfurt school provided the most challenging mid-twentieth-century critique of mass culture. They grasped the central insight of the American anarchist tradition—the desperate quality of leisure in a rationalizing society—but they rejected the puritanical functionalism of that tradition and brought to it a sophisticated Marxian understanding of the new kinds of cultural domination emerging in an era of imperialism and monopoly capital. They invigorated the American discourse of authenticity with an aesthetic dimension as well as a Marxist feel for power relations. Their influence, especially through the work of Herbert Marcuse, would play a major part in the resurgent critique of mass culture conducted under New Left and countercultural auspices during the 1960s.

After the Frankfurt School

During the 1950s the pessimism of the Frankfurt school and native critics like Macdonald was finally shunted aside by the pragmatic "center." For liberals like David Riesman and Arthur Schlesinger, Jr., the key move was to recognize the variety of social groups within the American population—to insist, in other words, that depressing European models of totalitarianism were inadequate to describe the rough-and-tumble pluralism of American society. For decades, in their trade journals, advertising executives had been discussing the need to tailor particular appeals to particular audiences—but this was mostly talk. The recognition of diversity had little impact in shaping mass-cultural forms. Where it really showed up was in the interpretation of those forms' significance, as cold war liberals groped for ways to affirm the exceptional qualities of American society.

The theoretical rationale was provided by Alexis de Tocqueville (1805–1859), who discovered the virus of anomic "individualism" but also identified its antidote—the "voluntary associations" he saw proliferating in the antebellum United States: churches, civic improvement leagues, fraternal societies, neighborhood clubs. These groups, according to Tocqueville, protected the citizen, prevented him from sliding into an abyss of social isolation where he might feel confined "within the solitude of his own heart" and vulnerable to the "tyranny of the majority." During the 1950s, defenders of mass culture discovered voluntary associations everywhere in American society; the alleged persistence and pervasiveness of these vital intermediate groups provided a bulwark against massification. So, at any rate, it seemed to observers like Schlesinger:

> The only answer to mass culture, of course, lies in the affirmation of America, not as a uniform society, but as a various and pluralistic society, made up of many groups with diverse interests. The immediate problem is to preserve cultural pluralism in the face of the threat of the mass media . . . [and its] policy of forcing the collective approach into the remotest corners of our intellectual life.

Yet the question of how cultural pluralism was to be preserved remained ambiguous—at least to intellectuals who assumed that their own tastes were more enlightened than those of less educated folk. For example, Riesman, though he innovatively emphasized consumers' capacity to reinterpret mass-mediated messages, also remained wedded to the managerial model of a society in which the untutored learned good taste from an elite. In 1950 he was encouraged to see the "the extremely rapid disavowal by Detroit auto workers of overstuffed, Grand Rapids furniture," observing hopefully that "many in the last several years have gone in for modern design." The preoccupation with taste afflicted even committed liberals like Schlesinger. By the end of the decade, he was complaining like all the rest about the blandness of the Eisenhower administration, and yearning for the regeneration that only a hard-nosed isolate could provide.

John F. Kennedy was perfectly cast for the role—or so it seemed to his celebrants. He was a pragmatist with style; he faced down Nikita Krushchev over Cuba and brought Pablo Casals to the White House. (His predecessor's preference had been Fred Waring and the Pennsylvanians.) Kennedy's New Frontier promised nothing less than release from imprisonment in flabbiness and fear, the return of masculine hardness after a decade of crooked quiz shows and children quavering under school desks. Acolytes of the Kennedy cult fell into unwitting parodies of Sartre and Camus, as they embraced the language of lonely choice and autonomous self-fashioning—the sort of language skewered by Donald Barthelme in "Robert Kennedy Saved from Drowning": "He experienced a night of dread" (in *Unspeakable Practices, Unnatural Acts* [1968]).

Despite Kennedy's style, it soon became apparent that he was enmeshed in the same power relations that had constrained his predecessors, and in the same ethos of technical rationality that underlay the standardization of blandness in mass culture. Kennedy's "telegenic" mastery of electronic media (not to mention his fondness for James Bond movies) highlighted the interdependence between mass-marketed entertainment and the hierarchical power structures of the imperial nation-state. By the early 1960s, the limits of pragmatic liberalism began to provoke a more politically sophisticated critique of inauthenticity.

In manifestoes like the Port Huron Statement—the founding document of Students for a Democratic Society (SDS)—a resurgent New Left mixed the native anarchist tradition with Frankfurt school Marxism, adding a dash of postwar existentialism. The attack on "dehumanization" in the Port Huron Statement echoed Camus as well as Thoreau and the young Marx. Mass culture, in this view, was merely a massive attempt to sustain "quiet desperation" by providing temporary escape from it. For those less inclined to start political organizations, Norman O. Brown had provided a parallel argument in *Life Against Death* (1959): he dismissed the busyness of modern civilization as merely a desperate effort to stave off thoughts of death and decay, a product of the repressive "genital organization" of sexuality under the reign of rationality; he offered instead a primitivist reversion to polymorphous perversity. A resurgent, hybrid discourse of authenticity powered a countercultural critique which focused on the phoniness of corporate-sponsored fun. That critique resonated among young, white middle- and upper-class Americans, many of whom had never read Brown (or Marx) and never heard of (much less joined) the SDS—but who instinctively recoiled from the boredom and anxiety of suburban life, the vapidity and emptiness of televisual standards of success. Many countercultural ventures during the late 1960s and early 1970s were part of a broad effort to create alternative ways of life that could not be assimilated to corporate-sponsored values.

Acolytes of the Kennedy cult fell into unwitting parodies of Jean-Paul Sartre and Albert Camus, as they embraced the language of lonely choice and autonomous self-fashioning.

Yet the countercultural discourse of authenticity always held the potential to dissolve into a search for alternative styles. Did this doom the seeker to accommodating the status quo? Not necessarily. Despite the confidence with which contemporary pundits counterpose "style" and "substance," the dualism does not hold neatly. This was especially true in the 1960s, a period that witnessed the resurfacing of Wildean aestheticism, with its provocative theatricality, its cult of irony, its rejection of the incessant search for meaning. "In place of a hermeneutics we need an erotics of art," Susan Sontag announced in *Against Interpretation* (1966), and the formulation provided a rationale for developments as diverse as the staging of artistic "happenings" and the emergence of camp sensibility from the chrysalis of gay culture into the larger society. Theatrical counterculturalism could be overtly political, as the Yippies demonstrated at the 1968 Democratic Convention when they mocked an effigy of Miss America alongside one of Hubert Humphrey—linking two icons of corporate-sponsored fraud. Theatrical gestures, in other words, could remain within the discourse of authenticity. But even when countercultural theatrics escaped that discourse altogether, into a Wildean celebration of aesthetic play, they remained an appealing alternative to a mass culture dominated by utilitarian "pragmatism" and compulsive male toughness.

The collapse of the New Left, and the descent of most countercultural impulses into faddish irrelevance, led to handwringing and diagnoses of death by "cooptation" at the hands of the mass media (as in Todd Gitlin's *The Whole World Is Watching* [1980]). By the late 1970s there was a resurgence of mass-culture criticism that emphasized the most pessimistic aspects of both the American and European traditions. Ann Douglas resurrected the idiom of puritan and republican moralism (along with some of its misogyny) in *The Feminization of American Culture* (1977); despite the limitations of that idiom, she produced a powerful critique of mass-marketed sentimentality as an evasion of the brutalities at the heart of an expanding capitalist economy. The most talented and controversial mass-culture critic of the 1970s was Christopher Lasch. His *Culture of Narcissism* (1978) was a bitter indictment of "the fake radicalism of the counterculture" as well as a sophisticated melding of Frankfurt school tradition with the native legacy of Thoreau and Macdonald. Lasch, like Douglas, was a defender of the classical, unified self—the republican or liberal citizen—against the forces making for its fragmentation.

Most readers overlooked the psychoanalytic complexities of Lasch's argument and boiled its social dimension down to this: the corporate media and their vast entertainment empires were instruments by which potentially subversive protest was turned into the harmless consumerism of "alternative lifestyles." This was the terrain where left- and right-wing critics of mass culture had always met—the vacuity of popular taste. Leftists (at their crudest) attributed it to the "false consciousness" engineered by the culture industry; rightists blamed the benightedness of the people themselves.

But by the 1970s, new challenges to this view were appearing. Many were related to the emergence of social history. Leftist historians in search of a usable past rejected the "elitism" allegedly inherent in the notion of false consciousness. Inspired by the work of E. P. Thompson and other British Marxists, they aimed to recover the activity of the people-as-subjects, to discover the ways working-class people actually used culture to meet their own needs and interests. This project worked well for the nineteenth century, as numerous historians uncovered a popular political culture of "labor republicanism" animating dime novel plots and fraternal rituals as well as labor organization and populist parties. But for the twentieth century the project became a little more difficult. After social historians sifted through the golden age of Eugene Debs–style socialism, the early years of the Congress of Industrial Organizations (CIO), and the very recent civil rights and antiwar movements, there was little clear evidence of an oppositional cultural tradition—except the native anarchist tradition of mass-culture criticism, which was now either ignored or subsumed under the umbrella of "Frankfurt school elitism."

Christopher Lasch's Culture of Narcissism *(1978) was a bitter indictment of "the fake radicalism of the counterculture" as well as a sophisticated melding of Frankfurt school tradition with the native legacy of Henry Thoreau and Dwight Macdonald.*

So it should come as no surprise that by the early 1980s more than a few scholars on the Left began to discover hitherto unnoticed virtues in mass culture. This reclamation project was guided by theoretical innovations as well as by political needs. Part of the rationale for a more sympathetic view came from the work of Mikhail Bakhtin (1895–1975), the Russian literary critic who never actually wrote about mass culture but who stressed the "dialogic" quality of every written or spoken utterance—that is, its multifaceted, contextual ambiguity. To Americans reading Bakhtin in translation, his formulations justified both a rejection of the Frankfurt school emphasis on the "monological"—totalizing, exclusive—character of mass-cultural texts, and a search for the gaps and fissures in those texts that allowed for dialogical engagement with an actual or implied audience. But Bakhtin was less important than an influence that came, as it had in social history, from the British Left. What Thompson did for the study of the nineteenth century, Stuart Hall and the Birmingham Centre for Cultural Studies did for the twentieth. Hall's key move was an emphasis on the consumer as an active interpreter of his own culture rather than a passive victim of media manipulation. Hall's American disciples, however, sometimes lost the edge of alienation that energized the Birmingham group's celebration of subcultural resistance. Sounding more like Edward Shils than Stuart Hall, some cultural historians discovered it was not only blues and bluegrass that expressed the pulsating heart of the people, but Tin Pan Alley tunes and even advertising jingles as well. This move involved more than leftists' discovery of new "resources for resistance"; it involved a redefinition of resistance as personal liberation. The new celebrants of mass culture drew unwittingly on the native anarchist tradition, with its concern for the quality of personal life, but they jettisoned its critique of corporate-sponsored modernity. The slogan "the personal is political" provided a clue to progressives in search of a usable past (and present): finding little evidence of oppositional culture, one could recast the notion of opposition to catch the minutiae of everyday life—a steelworker's passing notice of a TV show's flawed production when a cop car's wheels squeal on gravel and so on. Mass culture could be liberating if one limited the meaning of liberation; the people-as-subjects could express themselves through consumption as well as production. Since women were historically as well as folklorically associated with mass consumption, the discovery of mass culture's emancipatory potential had feminist resonances as well—especially if one overlooked the complicity of mass culture in legitimating the pervasively masculinist and technocratic nature of culture. Emancipatory manifestoes, by ignoring the nuances in Adorno's account of consumption, could dismiss the Frankfurt school as "patriarchal" as well as "puritanical." Leftist attitudes toward mass culture, like Virginia Slims smokers, had come a long way.

At the same time, the rightist assault on mass culture lost vigor and gradually fell silent. Organicist conservatives, scarce as hens' teeth in American society in the first place, became increasingly isolated and marginalized as Catholic intellectual circles (their principal refuge) moved toward an embrace of Kennedyesque "pragmatism" and a celebration of technological society. The career of the Canadian Marshall McLuhan (1911–1980), whose work was widely popularized in the United States, typified the pattern. Beginning his career in Catholic organicism during the 1940s, by the 1960s he had concocted a strange brew that mixed organicist longings for community with the sort of technological determinism that Americans seem to find so congenial. His focus was not on the texts generated by the emergent mass media but on the modes of perception allegedly inherent in the media themselves. Faced with the apparent omnipresence of mass culture, he snatched victory from the jaws of defeat through a clever rhetorical strategy: he declared that electronic information technology, far from destroying the organic community beloved by traditionalist conservatives, had reinstated that community in new forms by creating a "global village" through instant worldwide communication. Apart from a flurry of popular interest in the 1960s, McLuhan's ideas never enjoyed currency among more than a handful of technophiles who were so eager to jettison the sourbelly pessism of mass-culture critiques that they were willing to overlook their mentor's com-

The career of Canadian philosopher Marshall McLuhan (1911–1980) typified the marginalization of the right wing critique of mass culture.

plete inattention to the social, economic, and cultural conditions of the global village.

By the 1980s most of the avowed cultural conservatives left on the Right were either academic traditionalists like Allan Bloom whose agendas were mostly limited to curricular change, or evangelical Bible-thumpers whose commitments to "family" and "community" were compromised by their zeal for entrepreneurial capitalism. Despite lip service to "traditional" (bourgeois moralist) values, Ronald Reagan et al. represented the reign of let-'er-rip corporate capitalism in the cultural as well as the economic sphere. The 1980s were the era of blockbuster movies and seven-figure book advances, of top guns and smart-ass junior executives in starring roles, and of the return of "elegance" in personal style—which mostly meant hundred-dollar haircuts and stretch limousines.

The sensibility that accompanied these developments—one can only call it "postmodern"—threatened permanently to blur all familiar boundaries between the Left and Right. Devotees of the new sensibility declared the coherent, morally responsible self to be little more than a linguistic fiction: the essence of Western political thought in its classical liberal, Marxist, or social democratic forms was deemed a mere symptom of "essentialist" thinking. Life could be emptied of political or ethical content and devoted to aesthetic play. The aesthetes' creed of the late nineteenth century, having resurfaced in countercultural theatricality. and camp sensibility during the 1960s, became assimilated to the dominant culture of the 1980s as "the cultural logic of late capitalism" played itself out. The rejection of high seriousness and coherent selfhood, the conception of personal identity as merely a matter of surfaces to be manipulated—these notions could be imported from salon to shopping mall. Mass-produced goods, not merely fine objets d'art, could become counters in the game of self-fashioning.

The intellectual rationales for postmodernity were debated mostly among people who considered themselves of the Left, though that term had ceased to have much meaning in the cultural atmosphere of the 1980s. The rightist party-boys let the pinkos have the parlor pretty much to themselves. Apart from predictable potshots at the "humorless" antics of the "politically correct," conservative intellectuals failed to get into the postmodern spirit of surface glitter—failed, in short, to acknowledge the cultural consequences of the market economy they celebrated. Occasionally, conservative moralizers like George Will let on that they really *liked* hapless protagonists like Ferris Bueller (from the 1986 film *Ferris Bueller's Day Off*). But Left intellectuals developed an entire ontology of surfaces—most of which was articulated in poststructuralist literary theory. The poststructuralist rationale for defending mass culture turned Adorno et al. on their heads: So what if the self is fragmented? the argument went—that is a sign of freedom from frozen definitions of identity, not a mark of weakness and vulnerability to demagogues. Indeed, the whole point of poststructuralist epistemology was to melt those definitions by emphasizing the constructed, conventional character of apparently timeless categories of understanding: culture and nature, man and woman, subject and object. Poststructuralism posed a fundamental challenge to objectivist metaphysics and created a wonderfully rich atmosphere for venturesome interpretations of cultural texts. But when poststructural theory was used as a rationale for studying mass culture, it could also further sanction the implicit abandonment of a critical perspective. Evaluation and critique could fade in a fog of pseudopopulist slogans and "undecidability."

Given this convergence of intellectual tendencies, it is not surprising that contemporary observers like Michael Denning have spoken confidently of "the end of mass culture." The term has become a political embarrassment to Left intellectuals eager to show their solidarity with ordinary people's tastes (as other forms of solidarity become problematic), and a philosophical embarrassment to poststructuralist intellectuals eager to unmask the arbitrary conventions behind categories like "high culture" and "mass culture." Raymond Williams put the matter succinctly in his unwittingly poststructuralist comment: "There are no masses; there are only ways of seeing people as masses."

Yet Williams's observation does more than deconstruct the empirical base of "the masses"; it also suggests the continuing relevance of the term "mass culture." It focuses attention on the producers of mass culture, who have been "seeing people as masses" for nearly a century, and marketing cultural products in many of the same ways (and often in the same packages) that they use to market consumer goods. To be sure, in the last half-century there have been various gestures toward segmenting the market: consumers have been categorized in accordance with their age, income, region, ethnicity, and a proliferation of other subcategories; "focus groups" of potential buyers have been organized to provide market researchers with a more nuanced picture of consumer preference than they get from statistical data. But these are merely more sophisticated ways of carving up and packaging an audience for delivery to producers hungry for customers—an audience that is still seen as an anonymous mass, or as at best a set of submasses based on pop sociological categories. The obvious but often forgotten point is that popular magazine fiction,

Hollywood movies, network radio and television programs, and other mass-cultural products have been designed to be sold to the largest possible number of consumers; they have also been meant to enhance sales messages embedded within or placed alongside the cultural text itself.

In the conclusion of this essay, I shall sketch in an account of the rise of mass culture keeping these points in mind—recognizing the importance of the producers' intentions but remembering the ways the product can escape them.

Between Authenticity and Artifice

To understand American *mass* culture, it is helpful to recall some of the earliest manifestations of *popular* culture in this country: they were political and religious. A participatory republican politics based on pamphleteering and public ritual emerged at about the same time as a revivalistic religion: both had local roots but acquired national appeal. George Whitefield, the spellbinding revivalist preacher who toured major colonial cities in 1740, may have been the first celebrity "consumed" by a national audience. The flailing emotional style of Whitefield and later revivalists, as well as the frenzied enthusiasm they inspired in their audiences, ultimately spilled over into politics and commercial culture as well. By the early nineteenth century, theological conservatives' condemnations of camp meetings had begun to sound like later moralists' attacks on rock and roll. The connection is not fortuitous: both revivalism and rock and roll carried connotations of the carnivalesque.

The term 'carnivalesque' comes from Mikhail Bakhtin; the ideas that cluster around it, which he presents in *Rabelais and His World* (trans. 1968), are some of his most interesting and least-often used to illuminate mass culture. In traditional European society, carnivals marked the upending of established hierarchies, the elevation of flesh over spirit, low comedy over high seriousness. The wearing of masks sanctioned the slippage of social identity There were cultural as well as geographical connections between the carnival and the marketplace: the latter was very often where carnivals were staged, and both were a public space where one might experience chance encounters with strangers, where social masks might misrepresent motives and identities, where exotic goods might exude a carnivalesque aura of pleasure and danger. Yet the overall significance of the carnival was conservative: the temporary subversion of authority for the few days of carnivality reaffirmed its legitimacy during the rest of the year. A key to social order was the containment of the carnival in space and time—or so Bakhtin's work suggests, albeit far more subtly than this brief summary suggests.

Bakhtin does not discuss more contemporary instances of the carnivalesque, but one can extrapolate the following argument from his work. In modern Great Britain and the United States, after Protestant culture had eliminated the recurring rituals of the liturgical year and market exchange had spilled over traditional boundaries, carnivalesque impulses were scattered over space and time. In the United States, peddlers, strolling entertainers, revivalist preachers, and other itinerants gave off an aroma of the carnivalesque. It was no accident that patent-medicine salesmen adopted the tactics of the theatrical impresario as well as the oratorical style of the evangelical minister. Moreover, both minister and peddler promised magical self-transformation. In a market society more fluid and mobile than its European predecessors had been, that promise took on concrete actuality; it was not restricted to the ritualized expressions of carnival. At the same time, there was an underside to the promise—not only its potential subversion of established social hierarchies but also the possibility that the promise might be fraudulent. The scattering of carnivalesque impulses, no longer confined to a special time and place, meant the omnipresence of masked misrepresentation, the constant chance that social identities might be misapprehended.

The intellectual rationales for postmodernity were debated mostly among people who considered themselves of the Left, although that term had ceased to have much meaning in the cultural atmosphere of the 1980s.

Custodians of culture and morality, though, had never been willing to allow free play to these chaotic centrifugal forces. At about the same time that carnivalesque impulses began to seep over traditional barriers into everyday life, Protestant reformers were creating a new notion of selfhood, more unified and controlled by internalized norms than earlier ideals of selfhood had been. The unified self became the centerpiece of classical republicanism and bourgeois public life in general. It was as if the battle between carnival and Lent had been transformed from a liturgical ritual into a psychological drama. The conflict between self-indulgence and self-control had become a war within, a central dynamic in the psychic history of Anglo-American culture. So it was that evangelical Protestants promoted a host of repressive restraints to contain the boundless longings unleashed by revivalist preaching. So it was, as well, that business developed what Thomas Haskell has called "a norm of promise keeping" to counteract the misrepresentations of the marketplace, and that bourgeois moralists developed the ideal of a sincere self inhabiting a transparent social universe. Contractual mentalities and sincere moralities had epistemological as well as ethical interest (Haskell refers to a "cognitive style"): they promoted a discourse that contained carnivalesque subversions of commonsense reality. The developing bourgeois culture, at least in the Anglo-Protestant United States, was a complex balance of tensions between centrifugal markets and centripetal morals.

As cities grew in the nineteenth-century United States, popular cultural forms proliferated. Shakespearean drama, opera, purportedly "educational" museums like those run by P. T. Barnum—these sorts of entertainments mixed high and low in carnivalesque fashion. Yet even Barnum felt obliged to adopt the idiom of disciplined morality and unified selfhood in his autobiography and other promotional documents. A similar strategy of containing carnivality appeared in post–Civil War dime novels, which balanced sensationalism with labor republicanism, and retail advertising trade cards, which mixed sermons and sorcery.

Toward the end of the nineteenth century, though, with the rise to dominance of oligopolistic corporations, new patterns of institutional control as well as new idioms of cultural control began to appear. The older forms of popular amusement flourished, along with some new ones: vaudeville, nickelodeons, comic strips. But the emergence of the national corporation meant the mass marketing of cultural products as well as other consumer goods; new preoccupations with the rationalization of both production and distribution promoted the rise of a new managerial idiom that was positivistic rather than moralistic but still wedded to ideals of social transparency.

The shift from entrepreneurial to corporate control involved a change in form, from a carnivalesque exploration of performative language and playful imagery to a literalist, didactic narrative realism. One can see this clearly in the drift away from what film historians call "the cinema of attraction"—which was part of a vaudeville-style entertainment mix and which delighted in artifice for scopophilia's sake—toward the classical Hollywood cinema of extended "real-life" drama. One can see the same pattern in the syndication of comic strips, as the ferment of the turn of the century cooled and surrealist fantasy (such as Winsor McCay's "Little Nemo") gave way by the 1930s to wooden adventure stories. The rise of literalism afflicted advertising as well: rebuslike trade cards and exotic patent-medicine brochures yielded to the story-and-photo realism of J. Walter Thompson's "editorial style." Through the 1930s, at least, the rise of mass culture involved the standardization of popular cultural forms through the incorporation of transparent realist styles.

Standardization of aesthetic form was partly a consequence of economic concentration. The same logic that encouraged formulaic movies and magazine fiction reinforced the sameness of advertising art. Neither in advertising nor in other forms of mass culture was the predominance of realism a result of the industry executives "giving the people what they want." Despite market research (pioneered by J. Walter Thompson in 1903), nobody really knew what the people wanted, except that they wanted to be entertained; the trick, for advertisers as well as publishers and movie producers, was to keep profits predictable by entertaining as many as possible. As David Paul Nord has written, "formulas are, if anything, more likely to reflect producers' than audiences' values. . . . *The greater the market power a producer has (the greater the opportunity to control risk), the tighter and more standardized will be the formulas.*" Certainly this was true during the Depression, when the convergence of realistic forms embodied (at least in part) the common interest of image producers in an era when competition was declining and oligopolies were consolidating their market power.

The precondition for this convergence was the development of mass media's dependence on corporate advertising revenues during the early decades of the twentieth century. This dependence had gradually tightened the relationship between mass entertainment and the merchandising of goods. "There is still an illusion to the effect that a magazine is a periodical in which advertising is incidental," the advertising executive James Collins told a congressional committee in 1907. "But we don't look at it that way. A magazine is simply a device to induce people to read advertising. It is a large booklet with two departments—entertainment and business. The entertainment department finds stories, pictures, verses, etc. to interest the public. The business department makes the money." By the 1910s, the editorial matter, fiction, and illustrations in popular magazines like *Ladies' Home Journal* and *Saturday Evening Post* came to resemble closely the advertising. Network radio programs more directly served the interests of their corporate sponsors, who bought air time through their advertising agencies; the agencies then ensured a comfortable fit between the product and the entertainment. Writers recognized the need to tailor their scripts to sales criteria.

The case of Irna Phillips is instructive. Phillips was a successful soap opera writer from the 1930s through the 1960s. Her best-known show was *Today's Children*, sponsored in its early years (the 1930s) by General Foods and La France laundry products. Young and Rubicam was the agency representing those sponsors, and Phillips often proposed to Young and Rubicam specific story lines tied to the promotion of particular products. In soap operas, as in comedy and variety shows, the agency's aim was to erase the boundary between business and entertainment. The point of these examples is not to suggest some sort of corporate conspiracy but to underscore what is often forgotten by proponents of the emancipatory view of mass culture: in any form of commercial entertainment, it *does* matter who is paying the bills. Dependence on advertising revenues meant that advertisers could influence the entertainment offered to accompany the advertising.

Mass culture needed to incorporate the carnivalesque in order to retain any semblance of vitality. The history of rock and roll, for example, is a series of dialectical movements between corporate commodification and carnivalesque revitalization.

The situation was a little different in the world of cinema, where a looser symbiotic relation prevailed between mass culture and corporate marketing of consumer goods. "Motion pictures perform a service to American businesses which is greater than the millions in our direct purchases, greater than our buildings," the film industry czar Will Hays told a radio audience in 1930. "The motion picture carries to every American home, and to millions of potential purchasers abroad, the visual, vivid perception of American manufactured products." Sometimes the sales connection was obvious, as in star endorsements or the use of product "tie-ins," which began in earnest in the 1920s. By 1931, one reviewer was complaining that

> the Paramount picture "It Pays to Advertise" is nothing but a billboard of immense size. I have not been able to count all the nationally advertised articles that are spoken of by the characters, but some of them are the following: Boston Garters, Arrow Collars, Manhattan Shirts, Colgate Cream, Gillette Razors, B.V.D.'s, Hart, Schaffner, and Marx Clothes, Listerine, Victor phonographs, Murad cigarettes, Florsheim shoes, Dobbs hats, Forhans toothpaste, and others.

Since the movie was set in an advertising agency this list may have been longer than it usually was, but the use of tie-ins has continued down to the present and has especially flourished in recent years. More commonly, though, the Hollywood films propagandized indirectly for consumer goods by standardizing a taste for mass-produced elegance. The relationship between film and advertising remained indirect for many reasons, but one was no doubt the great distance—culturally and geographically—between Hollywood and Madison Avenue. Corporate advertising was a WASP enclave, whereas moviemakers were predominantly Jewish. After visting Hollywood, advertising copywriters commented privately on the antics of the "semitic tribes" and the vulgarity of their products. Even from the production side, mass culture was not monolithic. But its makers did share some elements of a common worldview, not only with each other but with the managers of the emergent national security state. They also shared management tools: the use of market research in the management of public opinion marked a major bridge between business and policy elites. By the end of World War II, the symbiotic relationship between mass culture and bureaucratic rationality had never been more apparent—in the United States as well as in the recently deceased fascist regimes. No wonder, then, that so many cultural critics saw nothing but uniformity and homogeneity.

Still, they missed a lot. The uniform sheen of mass culture's glittering surface blinded them to the vital ferment in more obscure corners of the society. Carnivalesque impulses, impulses toward libidinal release and the questioning of established authority, surfaced in a variety of areas, notably jazz and blues—this was one reason the seekers of authenticity so often headed uptown or down South. But the gap between "authentic" jazz or blues and "artificial" Tin Pan Alley was not as unbridgeable as it seemed to "White Negroes"; the career of Billie Holiday is a case in point. Indeed, one could argue that mass culture needed to incorporate doses of the carnivalesque in order to retain any semblance of vitality. The history of rock and roll, for example, is a series of dialectical movements between corporate commodification and carnivalesque revitalization.

At the same time, even within mass culture there were signs of life—idiosyncratic film directors, like John Ford, who survived amid the studio system, mad cartoonists like George Herriman, the creator of "Krazy Kat," who fortuitously enjoyed the patronage of William Randolph Hearst long after the media magnate had reduced poor Winsor McCay to bland illustration. Further, and perhaps most important, mass-cultural texts could almost always escape the intentions of their creators, let alone their sponsors. The textual approach encouraged by poststructuralism has enlivened the field, underscoring what the best cultural historians have known all along: that even the most apparently formulaic vehicles can carry a complex cargo of cultural freight. Despite the oversimplifications of Stuart Hall's Birmingham school by its American followers, their central insight retains its validity: audiences can derail those cultural vehicles, unpack their cargo, and repack it in interesting ways. The spread of this insight has enlivened the field. The study of mass culture has to be more than the study of the corporate marketing strategies embedded in mass-produced texts; the text can be a site of contested meanings, and to grasp the full range of those meanings we need to understand the audience not only as a set of social categories (the familiar litany of class, race, gender) but also as a disparate collection of individuals.

This returns us, albeit obliquely, to the discourse of authenticity. It is a position that invites poststructuralist scorn, but it is unavoidable. In spite of the constructed character of human subjectivity and the social definition of selfhood, there is a sense in which each of us experiences the world, including its mass-cultural products, as an individual. As Norman O. Brown and Martin Heidegger alike remind us, the crucial individuating experience is the prospect of death, which each of us must experience alone. Much of mass culture, Brown suggests, has been rooted in an effort to deny that prospect; but many mass-cultural artifacts contain materials individuals can use to make sense of their lives in an often senseless universe—to construct meaningful conceptions of their own experience. One task of the historian is to recover those constructions by investigating the audience (if possible) and interrogating the text. We do not need an essentialist concept of unified selfhood to acknowledge that in the analysis of mass culture, sweeping social categories must yield to the varieties and contrarieties of the irreducible individual consciousness.

[See also African American Music; Amusement and Theme Parks; The Culture of Consumption; Film; Gender Roles and Relations; Intellectuals and the Intelligentsia; Popular Entertainment before the Civil War; Popular Literature; Print and Publishing; Radio; Television.]

BIBLIOGRAPHY

Adams, Henry. *The Education of Henry Adams* (1907). An extraordinarily subtle attempt to link mass culture with broader features of modernity.

Adorno, Theodor. "Theses on the Sociology of Art" (1967). *Working Papers in Cultural Studies* (Spring 1972). A probing critique of the tendency to equate marketing and democracy.

———. "Transparencies on Film." *New German Critique* 24–25 (1981–1982). A forceful assault on the notion that "consumer-oriented art" is somehow democratic.

———. "Veblen's Attack on Culture." *Prisms* (1986). The first critique to zero in on Veblen's puritanical distrust of display.

Adorno, Theodor, and Max Horkheimer. *Dialectic of Enlightenment* (1947; trans. 1972). The chapter on "the culture industry" offers a cruder and more manipulative model than can be found in much of their other work.

Anderson, Sherwood. *Autobiography* (1969).

———. *Letters to Bab: Sherwood Anderson to Marietta Finley, 1916–33* (1985).

Bakhtin, Mikhail M. *The Dialogic Imagination.* Translated by Caryl Emerson and Michael Holquist (1981). Interesting and influential.

Barnum, P. T. *Struggles and Triumphs: Or, Forty Years' Recollections of P. T. Barnum, Written by Himself* (1869).

Bloom, Allan. *The Closing of the American Mind* (1987). Every right-thinking leftist's bête noire; his emphasis on establishing an erotic relation to knowledge deserves more than mere dismissal.

Bourne, Randolph. *War and the Intellectuals: Essays, 1915–1919* (1964). An eloquent voice, silenced too soon.

Brown, Norman O. *Life Against Death: The Psychoanalytic Meaning of History* (1959). A brilliant and challenging critique of modern culture, closer to Christian existentialism than its devotees in the 1960s realized.

Burke, Peter. *Popular Culture in Early Modern Europe* (1978). Packed with fascinating details.

Denning, Michael. "The End of Mass Culture." *International Labor and Working Class History* (1990).

Douglas, Ann. *The Feminization of American Culture* (1977).

Eliot, T. S. *The Waste Land* (1922).

Fiedler, Leslie A. *An End to Innocence: Essays on Culture and Politics* (1955). A caricature of the "tough-minded" cold war liberal—in a later incarnation, a caricature of the pop-culture maven.

Frank, Waldo. *The Re-discovery of America: An Introduction to a Philosophy of American Life* (1929).

Ginsberg, Allen. *Howl, and Other Poems* (1959).

Gitlin, Todd. *The Whole World Is Watching: Mass Media in the Making and Unmaking of the New Left* (1980). An intelligent media-centered analysis of the decline of the New Left.

Godkin, Edwin Lawrence. "Chromo-Civilization." *The Nation* (1874).

Hansen, Miriam. *Babel and Babylon: Spectatorship in American Silent Film* (1991). The best available synthesis of film theory and historical evidence—also the most creative attempt to grapple with the problem of film audience.

Haskell, Thomas. "Capitalism and the Origins of the Humanitarian Sensibility, Part I" *American Historical Review* 90, no. 2 (1985).

Huyssen, Andreas. *After the Great Divide: Modernism, Mass Culture, and Postmodernism* (1986). Probing and provocative essays.

Kirk, Russell. *The Conservative Mind* (1954). Wherein are revealed the difficulties of reconciling traditionalist conservatism with sympathy for American capitalism.

LaCapra, Dominick. "Bakhtin, Marxism, and the Carnivalesque." In his *Rethinking Intellectual History: Texts, Contexts, Language.* (1983). Enormously suggestive.
Lasch, Christopher. *The Culture of Narcissism: American Life in an Age of Diminishing Expectations* (1978). Cranky, controversial, and still worth grappling with.
Lawrence, D. H. *Studies in Classic American Literature* (1923). An illuminating glimpse into American male minds.
Lippmann, Walter. *A Preface to Politics* (1913).
———. *The Phantom Public* (1925).
Lynd, Robert S., and Helen Merrell Lynd. *Middletown: A Study in American Culture* (1925).
Macdonald, Dwight. *Against the American Grain* (1962).
McLuhan, Marshall. *The Gutenberg Galaxy: The Making of Typographic Man* (1962).
———. *Understanding Media: The Extensions of Man* (1964).
Mailer, Norman. "The White Negro." In *Advertisements for Myself* (1959).
Marcuse, Herbert. *Eros and Civilization: A Philosophical Inquiry into Freud* (1956).
———. *One-Dimensional Man: Studies in the Ideology of Advanced Industrial Society* (1964).
Mencken, H. L. *Prejudices: a Selection.* Edited by James T. Farrel (1956).
Nord, David Paul. "An Economic Perspective on Formula in Popular Culture." *Journal of American Culture* 3 (Spring 1980). A useful antidote to pseudopopulist celebration.
Ortega y Gasset, José. *The Revolt of the Masses.* Translated by Anthony Kerrigan and edited by Kenneth Moore. (1930; trans. 1985).
Riesman, David, et al. *The Lonely Crowd* (1950).
Sontag, Susan. *Against Interpretation, and Other Essays* (1962). Contains some classic critiques of the modernist ego ideal.
Susman, Warren. *Culture as History: The Transformation of American Society in the Twentieth Century* (1984). The introduction is a postmodern celebration of mass culture at odds with the critiques in the rest of the volume.
Stallybrass, Peter, and Allon White. *The Politics and Poetics of Transgression* (1986). Interesting appropriation and reinterpretation of the carnivalesque.
Tocqueville, Alexis de. *Democracy in America* (1835).
Thompson, E. P. *The Making of the English Working Class* (1963).
Thoreau, Henry David. *Walden.* Edited by C. Merton Babcock (1854; ed. 1966).
Veblen, Thorstein. *The Theory of the Leisure Class* (1899). Perhaps the single most overrated contribution to American social thought.
Weber, Max. *The Protestant Ethic and the Spirit of Capitalism.* Translated by Talcott Parsons (1904; trans., 1958).
Wells, H. G. *Tono-Bungay* (1909).
Whistler, James M. "The Ten O'Clock Lecture." In *Victorians on Literature and Art,* edited by Robert L. Peters (1961).
Williams, Raymond. *The Long Revolution* (1961).

Suggestions for Further Reading

Butsch, Richard, ed. *For Fun and Profit: The Transformation of Leisure into Consumption* (1990). Superb anthology of theoretical and historical essays.
Carey, James W., ed. *Culture as Communication: Essays on Media and Society* (1988). Key documents expressing the shift from behaviorism to hermeneutics within media theory.
Denning, Michael. *Mechanic Accents: Dime Novels and Working-Class Culture America* (1987). Interesting interpretation of nineteenth-century dime novels and their audience.
Ewen, Stuart. *All Consuming Images: The Politics of Style in Contemporary Culture* (1988). Sensitive to power relations as always, more sensitive to cultural nuance than his earlier work.
Hall, Stuart. "Notes on Deconstructing the Popular," In *People's History and Socialist Theory,* edited by Samuel Raphael (1981). Subtle and rewarding.
Hall, Stuart, and Tony Jefferson, eds. *Resistance Through Ritual: Youth Subcultures in Post War Britain* (1976). Enormously influential.
Hebdige, Dick. *Subculture: The Meaning of Style* (1979). Ditto.
Kasson, John. *Amusing the Million: Coney Island at the Turn of the Century* (1978). Illuminating.
Lazere, Daniel. *Mass Media and Society* (1987). High-quality collection of critical essays.
Peiss, Kathy. *Cheap Amusements: Working Women and Leisure in Turn-of-the-Century New York* (1987). Excellent account.
Radway, Janice. *Reading the Romance: Women, Patriarchy, and Popular Literature* (1984). Well-done.
Schatz, Thomas. *The Genius of the System: Hollywood Filmmaking in the Studio Era* (1988). A spirited defense of Hollywood during the "classic" era.
Slotkin, Richard. *Regeneration Through Violence: The Mythology of the American Frontier, 1600–1860* (1973). Despite its lumbering style and unpersuasive Jungian framework, a brilliant and pioneering effort to chart the emergence of an imperial mass culture.

— T. J. JACKSON LEARS

THE MEDICAL PROFESSION

The state of the American medical profession throughout its history has depended on three major factors: the body of clinical medical knowledge available to physicians, the nature of patient demand for physicians' services, and the types of institutions in which medicine is practiced.

The body of clinical medical knowledge has been important because it has distinguished physicians from other groups, such as religious and faith healers, apothecaries and nostrum vendors, and practitioners who use a distinctive treatment, like chiropractic, or set of drugs, such as botanicals. The medical profession's success since the 1890s has been due to the progress of clinical medicine, which has enabled physicians to treat patients more successfully than have other practitioners.

The demand for medical care affects both the amount and the nature of physicians' services. One determinant of demand has been the distribution and wealth of the population. Urbanization, with its denser population and higher standard of living, has been responsible for much of the growth of the medical profession. Another factor has been the health status of the population. Since the 1890s the steadily improving health of the American population has reduced the demand for some kinds of medical care while other factors, including the nation's greater wealth and the growing proportion of the elderly, have increased the demand for other kinds of care.

The third factor affecting the practice of medicine is the institutional structure for medical care, including medical schools; hospitals and ambulatory care facilities; the practice structure of physicians, such as solo, group, or salaried employment; and public and private health insurers. Changes in these institutions have had major impacts on the practice of medicine. For example, twentieth-century medical schools have structured their education to emphasize the medical and surgical specialties rather than family medicine, and the hospital rather than the home or office as a practice location. Hospitals and outpatient departments have expanded the provision of medical care by bureaucratic organizations rather than individuals. Health insurers have made more funding available for medical care and have affected the type of care provided through their methods and amounts of reimbursement.

This article will examine changes in these three factors throughout American history and relate them to changes in the practice of medicine. The analysis is based on the large and growing scholarly literature on the history of American medicine, an introduction to which is provided in the bibliography.

The Colonial Era

When the first settlers came to North America, little scientific knowledge existed in medicine. The causes and modes of transmission of practically all diseases were unknown, and the functioning of most organs was poorly understood. Diagnosis depended on signs and symptoms visible to the naked eye, and physicians lacked such rudimentary diagnostic tools as the thermometer and the stethoscope. The major treatments included cathartics and emetics to promote evacuations, whiskey and occasionally opium for pain, bloodletting for fevers and other conditions, and tonics to invigorate the patient. There were neither anesthetics nor methods of preventing surgical incisions from becoming infected, so surgery was limited to amputations, the setting of fractures, extraction of teeth, and the treatment of superficial wounds. Skilled lay healers were as competent as most physicians.

The colonists were in need of medical care because they confronted an inhospitable environment. Inadequate shelter, food, and clothing increased their susceptibility to disease, as did the hazards involved in clearing the wilderness and building settlements. Colonists and their children experienced a steady toll of injury and death and illness from influenza, pneumonia, and other infectious and gastrointestinal diseases. As the population grew, malaria, yellow fever, and smallpox became major problems.

Medical care was largely a family responsibility, especially in the rural areas where the great majority of the population lived. Those who could afford to do so imported drugs from Europe. The majority of the population grew garden plants brought from Europe that were believed to be of medicinal value, including dandelion, mustard, horseradish, sarsaparilla, and mints. They cultivated and gathered plants used for medicinal purposes by the Indians. The plants were prepared for medicinal use by drying them for use in teas; grinding them into powders that were dissolved in water, vinegar, wine, or brandy and boiled to a syrup; or cooking them with fats or oils for use as ointments. Recipes for medicines were published in almanacs and newspapers and passed from generation to generation. After about 1750 books on domestic medicine written by physicians for the lay public became popular. The best known was William Buchan's *Domestic Medicine; or the Family Physician*, which was first published in Edinburgh in 1769 and republished in dozens of American editions during the following century. John Gunn's *Domestic Medicine*, which went through numerous editions after its original publication in 1830, was an exceptionally successful example of the many American health guides oriented toward a regional audience (in this case the South).

Colonial medical practice was carried on by many different types of healers. The best educated were apprentice-trained physicians and a few physicians who emigrated from Europe. Many clergymen provided medical care to their congregations. The largest number of practitioners had no systematic training and included village elders, itinerant botanical healers such as "Indian doctors" and "root and herb doctors," and specialists like midwives and bonesetters.

The Late Eighteenth and Early Nineteenth Centuries

During the eighteenth and early nineteenth centuries some basic advances occurred in medical knowledge. Discoveries in anatomy, physiology, and pathology improved surgery, but the lack of anesthetics and means to prevent infection continued to limit its value and caused most physicians to shun it. In 1798 an English physician, Edward Jenner, published his findings that vaccination with cowpox prevented smallpox, which was promptly hailed as a momentous triumph against a dreadful scourge of mankind. Cinchona bark, which had been discovered in South America in the sixteenth century, was used with some success to relieve the symptoms of malaria. In the early nineteenth century quinine and morphine were extracted from cinchona bark and opium, respectively, and gradually became popular as they grew more inexpensive and available.

Little clinically useful medical knowledge existed, especially that needed to understand the infectious diseases which caused the most suffering and death. Physicians remained ignorant of etiological factors like bacteria and viruses; of the modes of transmission of diseases such as insect vectors, human contact, and impure water or milk; and of effective methods of diagnosis and treatment. They continued to depend on cathartics, emetics, bloodletting, and other dangerous or ineffective treatments. Few physicians trusted nature to restore the patient to health.

The growth of towns and cities created new health problems, which were aggravated by the waves of European immigrants beginning in the 1820s. Typhoid fever, tuberculosis, influenza, and other infectious diseases increased among the urban poor because of inadequate food and housing, polluted water, and open sewers. Urban children experienced high death rates from dysentery and diarrhea produced by adulterated milk and food. Foreigners arriving in port cities caused periodic epidemics of smallpox, yellow fever, and cholera.

Urbanization did improve opportunities for physicians. By 1800 many towns and cities had more than one physician per one thousand persons, and even rural areas began to have a regular supply of physicians. Despite their growing numbers, physicians were sufficiently diversified in their general education, professional training, clientele, and practice patterns that they did not yet constitute a unified profession. They competed with each other and a host of other practitioners in an era without legal regulations to restrict the practice of medicine.

Both urban and rural physicians spent their days visiting patients' homes as well as treating a few patients in offices in their own homes. Most medical practice consisted of preparing and dispensing drugs, but physicians also bled patients, bandaged wounds, set fractures, reduced dislocations, extracted teeth, lanced boils, and, increasingly, delivered babies. A few master surgeons regularly toured large regions amputating limbs, removing some kinds of tumors, and operating for cataracts. Most physicians shunned such dangerous operations.

Urbanization led to two new institutions to provide medical care, the hospital and the dispensary. Public hospitals began as extensions of almshouses for the poor. Important early public hospitals include the Philadelphia General Hospital (closed in 1977), which traced its origin to the Philadelphia Almshouse founded in 1713, and the Bellevue Hospital of New York City, which began as an almshouse in 1736. Voluntary hospitals were founded and operated by private citizens as charitable institutions to care for persons in need, including sick laborers, seamen, and travelers from other communities. Among the first in major cities were the Charity Hospital of New Orleans, which started operating in 1737 as a combined almshouse and hospital, the Pennsylvania Hospital of Philadelphia, opened in 1752, the New York Hospital, which first cared for civilian patients in 1791, and the Massachusetts General Hospital, which admitted its first patients in 1821. Governments frequently provided financial assistance to voluntary hospitals.

Until the twentieth century, hospitals provided only a small amount of health care, because they were expensive to operate and shunned by most patients; they functioned largely as convalescent homes, providing food, shelter, and nursing.

Until the twentieth century, hospitals provided only a small amount of health care, because they were expensive to operate and were shunned by most patients. They functioned largely as convalescent homes providing food, shelter, and nursing. The physicians on their medical staffs, who played a much less important role than modern hospital physicians, were unpaid but benefited from the prestige of their positions.

Dispensaries provided medical care and drugs for the bedridden poor in their own homes and for the ambulatory poor in the dispensary offices. They soon became the major source of medical care for the urban poor, because they were inexpensive to operate and popular with patients. Dispensaries provided salaried employment for many young physicians, who used them to gain experience and supplement their earnings.

A major development in medical care at the turn of the nineteenth century was the patent medicine industry. Patent medicines (nonprescription, trademarked drugs) were widely advertised, inexpensive, and readily obtainable, and became very popular. Many of them made fraudulent claims of curative or health-producing properties and contained opium, morphine, harsh purgatives, or other harmful ingredients that were not listed on their labels.

In rural areas, many physicians had little formal training and competed with botanical and other lay healers. Midwives delivered most babies there until well into the twentieth century. Lay healers were also important providers of medical care to slaves on southern plantations.

Local and state medical societies were organized as the number of physicians increased, although many were short-lived or had few members. Among the most active and influential early societies, together with their dates of founding, were the Massachusetts Medical Society (1781), the College of Physicians of Philadelphia (1787), the Connecticut State Medical Society (1792), the Medical Society of the State of New York (1806), and the Medical and Chirurgical Faculty of Maryland (1799). The major functions of medical societies were to enhance the reputations of their members by selective membership policies and to license apprentices, using the licensing powers granted to them by state legislatures. A medical license was largely honorific, because there were few penalties for practicing without one, and midwives and botanical practitioners were often exempt from the requirement to have one.

Medical societies also established what they called "fee bills," which listed charges for various professional services, and codes of ethics, which were actually rules of professional etiquette. Both were frequently violated in a highly contentious profession. Medical societies were supposed to undertake scientific investigations, but few actually did. Almost all important medical research before the twentieth century occurred in Europe.

Apprenticeship became the major method of medical training during the eighteenth century. Students sought out successful physicians or those who were good teachers and served a three-year apprenticeship for a fee of one hundred dollars per year. The apprentice acted as a nurse, traveled with the physician on his visits to homes, ground and prepared drugs, and performed chores around the physician's house. Apprenticeship training encouraged diversity in medical practice, because each preceptor taught his apprentice his own idiosyncratic medical practice.

The great value of apprenticeship training was that the apprentice participated in the care of patients and acquired much useful knowledge about illness, if not about treatment. He saw how patients lived and what they expected from their physicians. Its major disadvantage was the limited scientific knowledge of most preceptors.

To improve the training of students in the medical sciences, formal medical instruction was organized in the second half of the eighteenth century, at first in private classes and later in medical schools. Students flocked to medical schools because the degrees were prestigious and legally equivalent to a license, the admission requirements were low, and the theoretical and scientific subjects were taught by distinguished physicians. The number of degree-granting medical schools in operation grew from two in 1770 to twenty-two in 1830 and forty-seven in 1860. The number of graduates increased from about two hundred during the entire eighteenth century to almost fourteen hundred in the decade 1810–1819 and over seventeen thousand in the decade 1850–1859. Thousands of additional students attended medical school lectures but did not graduate.

Medical schools also succeeded because they were low-cost commercial enterprises. They were typically organized by four to seven physicians who obtained a state charter to grant degrees or established a nominal affiliation with a degree-granting college. The courses were taught in a single building with one or two lecture halls and a back room for dissection. Toward the middle of the nineteenth century, museums of anatomical specimens and chemistry laboratories were often added. Although admission requirements and student fees were low, the leading schools attracted enough students to be quite profitable to their faculty owners. Faculty positions were desirable because their prestige attracted patients, which led physicians in many towns and cities to organize medical schools.

A complete medical school education before the 1870s consisted of attendance at two identical courses of lectures of four to five months' duration, to learn the scientific and theoretical aspects of medicine, and a three-year apprenticeship with a preceptor of the student's choice, to learn the clinical aspects. The only laboratory instruction consisted of the dissection of cadavers, which was often hampered by public opposition.

Medical school graduates professionalized medicine. They organized new state and local medical societies and increased the membership of existing ones. They provided the medical staffs for hospitals and dispensaries. They subscribed to the growing number of medical journals. In 1847 the profession was large enough to support the formation of a national medical society, the American Medical Association. By 1850, almost forty-one thousand physicians (about eighteen physicians per ten thousand persons) were enumerated by the national census. Many, however, were not medical school graduates.

Medical schools standardized medical treatment by replacing the idiosyncratic teachings of hundreds of preceptors with those of a few textbooks and several dozen faculty members. The treatments advocated by faculty members were significantly harsher than those used previously. Drastic mineral cathartics and emetics, especially calomel (a compound of mercury), replaced botanical ones. Bloodletting was used to extreme in fevers, since it tended to lower the body temperature temporarily. These and other treatments became known as "heroic therapy."

The excesses of heroic therapy soon led to a popular rebellion against the medical profession. The major beneficiary was botanical medicine, especially in rural areas and on the frontier. The most successful botanical healer was Samuel Thomson (1769–1843), who in 1822 published a book on botanical domestic medicine, *New Guide to Health*, that described his theories of disease and gave recipes for many botanical remedies. Thomson employed salesmen nationwide to sell his book and drugs and to assist users in organizing Friendly Botanical Societies to help each other and avoid the need for physicians.

Professional botanical practitioners quickly gained control of Thomson's movement and split into several competing groups. The most important, called eclectic medicine, modeled itself after the regular medical profession. Eclectic physicians organized medical societies, journals, and medical schools with a curriculum similar to that of the regular medical schools. They gradually became an important source of medical care in the Midwest and rural areas, and survived well into the twentieth century.

In the towns and cities, other movements arose in opposition to heroic therapy. Several popular health and personal hygiene groups appealed to the working classes. The most successful movement was homeopathy, the creation of a German physician, Samuel Hahnemann (1755–1843). Hahnemann believed that patients should be given minuscule quantities of drugs that produced symptoms similar to those of their illnesses. The small, palatable doses of homeopathic drugs were in striking contrast to the drastic purgatives, emetics, and bloodletting of heroic therapy, and homeopathy attracted many physicians and educated laymen in both Europe and the United States.

A revolution in pharmacology occurred with the production of synthetic drugs, the most important of which were fever reducers developed from coal tar, with aspirin, introduced in 1899, being the most successful.

Homeopathy became the most successful competitor of regular medicine in the nineteenth century because of the wealth of its clientele. Homeopathic medical societies, medical journals, medical schools, and hospitals were established in many major cities. As scientific medicine advanced, the practices of homeopathic and regular physicians grew more similar and the two groups, together with most eclectic physicians, merged early in the twentieth century.

The Late Nineteenth and Early Twentieth Centuries

The underpinnings of scientific medicine were established in the second half of the nineteenth century. The major breakthroughs resulted from improvements in the microscope, which enabled scientists and physicians to study tissues, cells, and microorganisms like bacteria and protozoa and thereby discover the causes and modes of transmission of many diseases. By the turn of the century, great progress had occurred in diagnosis, such as the recognition of the contagious nature of many diseases, and in public health, especially safe water supplies, sanitary sewage-disposal systems, and pure milk.

The major advances in treatment occurred in surgery. The discovery of the anesthetic properties of ether and nitrous oxide in the late 1840s were the first major American contributions to clinical medicine and made surgery painless. While operations subsequently became more common and surgeons more skillful, the problems of infection, blood loss, and shock remained. The bacterial origin of wound infection was discovered by Joseph Lister, an English physician, in the late 1860s. By the end of the century surgeons had developed new techniques that prevented surgical incisions from becoming infected. Surgery became the most rapidly growing field of medicine.

Most illness and death continued to result from infectious diseases like tuberculosis, typhoid fever, influenza, and pneumonia. Infant and childhood mortality rates remained high because of infectious and gastrointestinal illnesses. Nevertheless, death rates from these categories of diseases declined substantially toward the end of the century as a result of better housing, higher standards of living, and public health measures.

A revolution in pharmacology occurred with the production of synthetic drugs, most of which were developed in Germany. The most important were antipyretics (drugs that reduce fever) developed from coal tar. The first were antipyrine and acetanilid, introduced in 1884 and 1886, respectively, but the most successful was aspirin, introduced in 1899. Other important new drugs included heroin (1898) and novocaine (1905). A few were great contributions to humanity, most notably diphtheria antitoxin (1894) and salvarsan, for syphilis

(1905), but the rest differed from those of a generation earlier primarily by being more palatable. The administration of drugs was also revolutionized by the invention of the hypodermic syringe in the early 1850s in Europe.

The new drugs affected medical practice by requiring greater skill on the part of the physician. Diphtheria antitoxin, one of medicine's greatest achievements, was effective only if the disease was diagnosed accurately and the drug administered in the proper dosage at a specific stage of the illness. Salvarsan was useful in the treatment of syphilis, but the dosage had to be regulated carefully to minimize the drug's toxic side effects.

Among the middle and upper classes, the patient's home continued to be the location for medical treatment, obstetrical care, and surgical operations. By the twentieth century, private duty nurses trained in the newly established hospital nursing schools were available to assist physicians in home care.

The urban poor and working classes received most of their medical care in dispensaries and used midwives to deliver their babies. At the end of the century many hospitals opened outpatient departments that soon replaced the independent dispensaries. The two differed in that hospital outpatients who required bed care were sent to the hospital wards, whereas bedridden dispensary patients were treated in their homes. Although outpatient departments were the hospitals' major contribution to the health of the community, they were understaffed and poorly equipped.

Hospital inpatient care continued to be shunned by most Americans, who believed that hospitals were places where people went to die. Most hospital patients were the sick poor and accident victims, who needed bed rest and nursing more than medical care. As a result, hospitals remained charitable institutions controlled by the lay public. Physicians did not assume a major role in them until the twentieth century.

The major improvement in hospital inpatient care at this time resulted from the development of professional nursing. Previously, hospital nurses had no medical training, and those in public hospitals were often convalescing patients. The first American hospital nursing school, which opened at the municipal Bellevue Hospital in New York City in 1873, was based on the model established in England by Florence Nightingale. In the next several decades, almost all large hospitals, and many smaller ones, opened nursing schools. These schools were successful in attracting students because they provided free room and board and paid the students a small stipend.

Hospitals used their nursing students as almost their total nursing labor force. Training programs consisted of a great deal of practical experience and a minimum of classroom education. Most schools employed few graduate nurses or other paid instructors and had no educational facilities.

Although nursing soon became a popular profession for women, the unwillingness of hospitals to employ graduate nurses left them with few career prospects. The great majority of these women were employed as private duty nurses in homes, and most of the others worked as public health or visiting nurses. Hospitals began to employ large numbers of graduate nurses in the 1930s.

Mental hospitals became more common at this time. Among the most important early voluntary mental hospitals, which admitted mostly paying patients, were, with the dates of their opening, the Friends Hospital of Philadelphia (1817), the MacLean Hospital near Boston (1818), the Bloomingdale Asylum in New York (1821), the Hartford Retreat in Connecticut (1824), and the Pennsylvania Hospital for the Insane in Philadelphia (1841). A few states opened small mental hospitals for those requiring care at public expense around the turn of the nineteenth century, but the Worcester, Massachusetts, state hospital (1832) initiated the model that became the standard for state mental hospitals until the 1960s. The demand for care in public mental hospitals rapidly surpassed the willingness of state governments to increase the number of beds and staff. Consequently, they soon degenerated into custodial institutions. Mental hospitals were also hampered by the paucity of useful treatments for the mentally ill.

The medical profession grew steadily during the century, reaching 132,000 physicians in 1900, about seventeen physicians per ten thousand persons. As it grew, it became stratified and specialized. At the top of the hierarchy were eminent general practitioners and surgeons, who monopolized the wealthy patients, the medical school faculty positions, and the prestigious hospital staff appointments.

Specialties were beginning to emerge at this time as a result of advances in surgery and medicine and of urbanization that provided enough patients to enable physicians to earn a livelihood in a specialty. Specialists changed and strengthened the institutional structure of the medical profession. They organized local and national specialty societies to disseminate knowledge and to provide evidence of their skills. The first national specialty societies were the American Ophthalmological Society (1864) and the American Otological Society (1866). Others followed in neurology (1875), dermatology and gynecology (1876), laryngology (1879), and surgery (1880). Specialists obtained staff appointments in hospitals and dispensaries to study patients with conditions treated by the specialty. They joined medical school faculties to teach their specialties. These activities also publicized their skills among other physicians and the public.

The bulk of the profession consisted of the general practitioners in the towns and cities. They were graduates of reputable medical schools who had acquired stable practices among middle- and working-class families. They were joined by young physicians who were establishing themselves in private practice and often worked in dispensaries for additional income. Both groups were employed by insurance companies to examine applicants for policies and by railroads and other firms to care for accident victims.

At the fringes of the profession were some graduates of disreputable medical schools, and charlatans. These groups gradually disappeared after states enacted medical licensing laws around the turn of the century.

Physicians assumed a greater role in their communities at this time. They constituted the boards of health that were regularly consulted by public officials and assumed more authority in hospitals. In addition, they were involved in public issues—for example, some physicians were among the leaders in the movement to restrict or outlaw abortions.

The growing stature of the medical profession was demonstrated by the strengthening of the American Medical Association (AMA). In 1901 it reorganized as a federation of state medical societies with the goal of becoming the voice of organized medicine. The AMA and its constituent state and local societies greatly expanded its membership and influence during the first half of the twentieth century.

In 1906 the AMA began to inspect and rank medical schools in order to raise the standards of medical education and reduce the supply of physicians. Its rankings were used by the state medical licensing boards to approve the medical education of applicants for licenses, which gave the AMA a dominant role in medical education. The AMA also participated in the famous 1910 (Abraham) Flexner Report, which allegedly forced the inferior medical schools to close and influenced the others to place greater emphasis on the basic sciences. Recent research has shown that these changes in fact antedated the report by many years.

The AMA also undertook programs to raise the scientific stature of the medical profession. The most effective was its attack on quack and dangerous patent medicines through legal action and an extensive public information campaign. The association also tested prescription drugs for decades until the federal government assumed this responsibility. On the other hand, the AMA and its constituent societies showed little interest in public health or medical care for the poor.

Medical education became extremely popular between 1880 and 1900; the number of medical students more than doubled and the number of medical schools increased from 100 to 160. The wealthiest medical schools adopted a three-year, and then a four-year, graded curriculum and added more laboratory and clinical teaching. The majority of schools adopted the new curriculum but lacked sufficient resources to implement the other changes fully.

About 1900 a series of crises brought about major changes in medical education. State medical licensing laws forced all schools to raise their entrance and graduation requirements, which reduced their enrollments and revenues substantially. The growing emphasis on laboratory instruction required the schools to procure expensive equipment and facilities and to employ full-time basic science instructors. The combination of lower revenues and higher costs forced more than half of all medical schools to close between 1900 and 1930. Most surviving schools affiliated with public or private universities to obtain a steady source of income. Some medical schools received private philanthropy, especially from the General Education Board supported by the Rockefeller family.

Medical schools improved their clinical instruction by affiliating with local hospitals or constructing their own university hospitals to enable students to observe the care of patients. The better schools, most conspicuously the new medical school at the Johns Hopkins University, introduced clinical clerkships whereby students participated in caring for patients in the hospital wards. Clerkships gave students actual experience in patient care, but they also required students to spend much time performing routine chores.

The end of the nineteenth century witnessed the entrance of women into the medical profession after decades of discrimination against them by many (but not all) medical schools. Although the great majority of women medical students attended coeducational medical schools, a few women physicians, together with some male ones, organized separate medical schools for women. In 1910 three were in operation, but only one, in Philadelphia, survived for any length of time. Women physicians also established a few hospitals and infirmaries.

Medical care was a major problem for blacks because of racial discrimination and segregation. Even though over 90 percent of the black population lived in the South, southern medical schools were closed to them. For this reason, southern black physicians opened at least seven medical schools to provide medical education for blacks. Only two of these—Howard (1868) and Meharry (1876)—survived for any length of time. Discrimination was also a problem in hospital care, because many northern and southern hospitals refused to admit black patients or permit black physicians to serve on their staffs. This led to the establishment of a number of private and a few public hospitals that were controlled by black physicians and administrators. Most of them were small institutions in southern towns, but others were located in Washington, D.C., Atlanta, Chicago, Philadelphia, Baltimore, and Kansas City, Missouri. In a few instances, most notably Harlem Hospital in New York City, public hospitals were put under black control due to the growth of the black population residing around them. These hospitals trained practically all the black nurses for many decades.

The First Half of the Twentieth Century

The early twentieth century saw an increasingly fruitful relationship between medical science and health care. Diseases like typhoid fever were reduced by improved water supplies and sewage systems. The role of insect and other vectors in disease was identified and used to combat yellow fever, malaria, and other diseases. Parasites were recognized as causes of disease, which led to an effective campaign to eradicate hookworm. The discovery of vitamins produced simple and effective methods of treating deficiency diseases like pellagra and rickets. Vaccines were developed against diphtheria, tetanus, and other diseases.

Major discoveries also occurred in drug therapy. Treatments for metabolism deficiencies were developed, most notably insulin injections for diabetes. Serums, used initially to treat diphtheria, were developed for pneumonia and some other diseases, but with much less success. In the 1930s, the sulfonamides became the first drugs to be effective against a variety of bacterial infections. Within a decade millions of Americans were being treated with them.

The first half of the twentieth century saw numerous advances that benefited surgery, including the discovery of blood types, which permitted transfusions; the discovery of methods for intravenous replenishment; and the development of X rays.

On the other hand, no effective drugs or treatments were available for viral and many other bacterial infections, or for other diseases of growing importance, such as heart disease and cancer. In many cases medical care changed little between the end of the nineteenth century and the middle of the twentieth.

Surgery benefited from numerous advances, including the discovery of blood types, which permitted blood transfusions; methods for the intravenous replenishment of salts, fluids, and nourishment; and the development of X rays. These and other innovations led to a vast increase in the number and variety of beneficial surgical operations but also to more faddish, useless, and harmful ones. The problem of inappropriate surgery was exacerbated by the unwillingness of hospitals to restrict their surgical privileges to properly qualified surgeons. Many surgeons were self-proclaimed specialists.

Fundamental changes in the demand for medical care resulted from higher standards of living and public health measures. The incidence of infectious diseases and diseases of infancy was greatly reduced, leading to longer life spans. As a result people contracted more degenerative and other diseases of old age, like cancer, heart disease, and stroke. They were also more likely to develop chronic diseases like hypertension and diabetes.

A number of important new diagnostic devices enabled physicians to detect diseases, even in asymptomatic patients. These included X rays, electrocardiograms, the sphygmomanometer, and chemical tests of blood, urine, and other body fluids. Improved methods of diagnosis encouraged periodic health examinations and the formation of a long-term relationship between physician and patient.

As physicians became better able to verify the presence or absence of specific organic diseases in patients, some persons with complaints that could not be verified by diagnostic tests sought out new kinds of healers. Unlike most alternative healers of the nineteenth century, these twentieth-century practitioners did not employ drugs. Rural patients patronized chiropractors and osteopaths, who used physical therapy and manipulation to relieve the aches and pains of rural life. Osteopathic medical schools later adopted the curriculum of regular medical schools and became accredited, and their graduates became regularly licensed physicians.

Patients in urban areas distressed by the strains of modern life turned elsewhere. Christian Scientists and other groups emphasized the value of faith in treating disease. Some physicians, originally called alienists and later psychiatrists, began to treat mental disorders in private patients. From the 1920s on, many psychiatrists adopted Sigmund Freud's psychoanalytic methods of treatment, or other techniques based on interaction between the patient and the therapist.

The early twentieth century was the turning point in the history of hospitals. Advances in medicine enabled

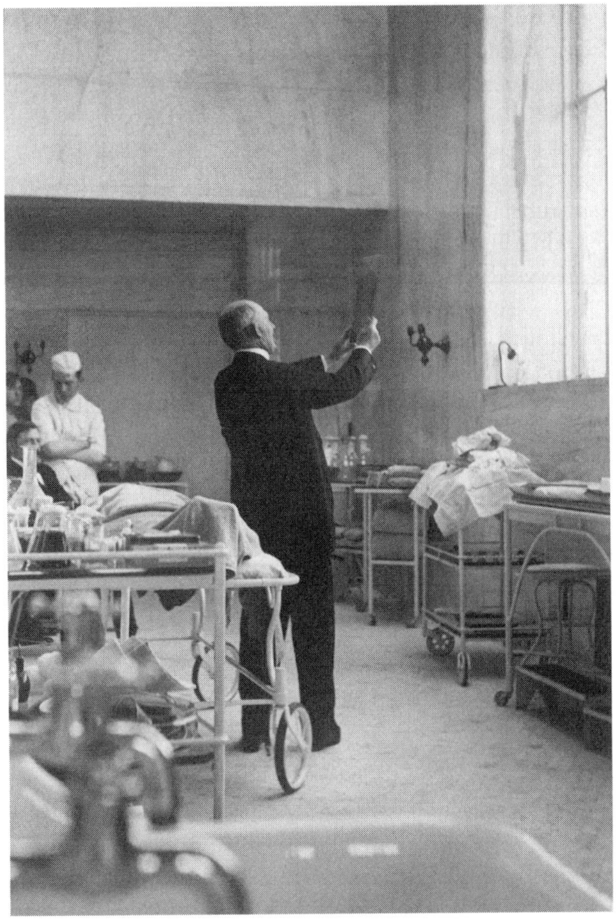

Dr. William S. Halsted examining an X ray at Johns Hopkins Medical School, 1905. The development of X rays led to an increase in the number and variety of beneficial surgical operations.

them to provide a level of care superior to that available in homes, especially for surgical and obstetrical patients. They also became diagnostic centers, because they had the equipment and personnel to perform X rays, electrocardiograms, and laboratory tests. The increasing demand for hospital care led to the expansion of existing hospitals and the construction of new ones in both urban and rural areas.

Voluntary hospitals attracted paying patients and began to function more like businesses and less like charities. They added private rooms, provided better food and nursing care, and reduced the amount of their charity care. To attract more paying patients, they opened their medical staffs to large numbers of community physicians and permitted them to receive fees from their hospitalized private patients. Hospital medical staffs gained power as hospitals increasingly depended on them for paying patients and medical expertise.

Public hospitals became more important as the demand for hospital care increased among patients who could not pay for the care provided in voluntary hospitals. The presence of large numbers of charity patients made public hospitals popular sites for medical school clinical teaching and for specialty training. Many public hospitals established affiliations with medical schools that permitted the faculty members to constitute the hospitals' medical staffs. While medical school affiliations improved their quality of care, public hospitals continued to suffer from inadequate facilities and funding.

A third type of hospital emerging at this time was the university hospital of a medical school. These hospitals also accepted many charity patients, but their primary focus was on teaching and research and on the care of patients with special or unusual problems.

As hospitals became more important providers of medical care, concern developed over the quality of that care. In 1918 the American College of Surgeons began to accredit hospitals, but it took many years for most hospitals to meet even the college's rudimentary standards.

The early decades of the twentieth century saw a drastic decrease in the supply of physicians, resulting from the great wave of medical school closings at the turn of the century. Even though total medical school enrollments rose after 1920, the number of physicians dropped to less than thirteen per ten thousand persons between the 1920s and the 1950s. They were scarcest in the rural areas, although the shortage was made less critical by the automobile and better roads, which enabled town physicians to visit rural patients and rural patients to come to physicians and hospitals in nearby towns. Another effect of the closings was to reduce the opportunities of many students from low-income families to attend medical school.

Medical education also changed in response to medicine's growing popularity and scientific nature. Greater competition for admission to medical school and higher admission standards improved the quality of medical students. The curriculum was divided into two years of basic science education, with a substantial laboratory component, and two years of clinical training, with considerable time spent on the hospital wards. The wealthiest medical schools employed some full-time faculty members, carried out medical research, and built impressive laboratories and research facilities. Most schools continued to rely on part-time teachers and offered less laboratory and clinical instruction.

As admission to medical school became a more competitive process, the criteria used by the schools to evaluate students became public issues. After World War I, large numbers of children of immigrants began to attend colleges and professional schools. Private medical schools, like many private colleges, responded by discriminating against them, especially Jews and Catholics of Italian heritage, the two largest recent immigrant groups. Because most immigrants and their children lived in the Northeast, which had few public medical schools, this became a major problem that was not addressed by government until after World War II.

The number of women attending medical school stabilized at about 5 percent of all medical students for most of this period, which equaled the proportion of women who applied to medical school. Opportunities for blacks to attend medical school in the South remained limited to medical schools operated by blacks, but improved elsewhere.

One major change in medical education occurred outside the medical school. The internship, a period of one to two years of essentially unpaid postgraduate training in a hospital, became universal. Internships were first offered by a small number of hospitals during the nineteenth century. Early in the twentieth century, the number of available internships multiplied as a result of the growing number and size of hospitals and the greater need of hospitals for the skills that interns possessed. By the 1920s all medical school graduates completed internships, partly because some states made completion of an internship a requirement for a license. Interns soon became indispensable to the effective functioning of hospitals.

Although the internship was supposed to provide meaningful postgraduate education, most hospitals, except some affiliated with medical schools, lacked the

By the 1920s, all medical school graduates completed internships, partly because some states made internships a requirement for a license; consequently, interns soon became indispensable to the effective functioning of hospitals.

staff and facilities to provide satisfactory educational programs. Interns spent most of their time in routine patient care and "scut work," the performance of simple chores. The most popular internships were those in the great public hospitals in the major cities, which had the largest number and most varied group of patients. After the mid 1920s, the number of internships available exceeded the number of medical school graduates, which forced hospitals to compete for the graduates. This did not include black medical school graduates, who found it extremely difficult to obtain internships, because of widespread discrimination.

Graduate medical education soon expanded to include the residency, a period of postinternship training in a specialty. Residencies were first offered by major medical school hospitals, which used faculty members to do the teaching. As the demand for specialty training increased, residency programs spread to hospitals that were less well equipped to provide such training.

The success of medicine at this time had a significant impact on lay healers, especially midwives, who delivered most babies in rural areas and many of those born to immigrants in cities. Physicians and public health officials criticized midwives for being poorly trained and unable to provide prenatal care, which was now recognized as indispensable to a safe delivery. They wanted to move obstetrical care to hospitals, which had better facilities and were staffed by physicians. Middle- and upper-class women espoused this viewpoint, and by mid century midwives were being used only in rural areas, particularly in the South.

The Second Half of the Twentieth Century

Medical research after mid century broke new ground in many fields. The major breakthrough was molecular biology, made possible by the electron microscope. The most dramatic molecular discoveries involved the nucleic acids, DNA and RNA, but molecular biology also affected most traditional research areas. Other types of medical research increased dramatically after the federal government committed itself to a policy of supporting medical research on a munificent scale.

The results of medical research have varied widely among fields. In public health, several new vaccines were produced, including ones for polio, measles, and rubella, but the major innovation was the "second epidemiological revolution," which resulted from findings demonstrating that personal behaviors and exposure to carcinogens and other disease-causing factors in the environment could produce disease.

The major development in drug therapy was the discovery of antibiotics, which revolutionized both medicine and pharmacology. Many diseases that had been untreatable or difficult to treat became curable, including venereal diseases and tuberculosis. Antibiotics permitted new types of surgery, such as open-heart surgery and organ transplants, that had been too dangerous previously, and practically eliminated the need for others, like tonsillectomies. Other new drugs that improved medical care included steroids, diuretics, antihistamines, and antifungal agents.

Psychopharmacology led to the development of tranquillizers and antidepressants that altered the mental states of patients without the sleep-inducing properties of earlier drugs. The new drugs enabled many patients in mental hospitals to return to the community and resulted in the widespread closing of these facilities. Deinstitutionalization and the community care of the mentally ill have been less successful than anticipated because of the inability of some patients to adapt to noninstitutional life. Tranquillizers have been widely used in general practice to such an extent that many physicians have been accused of prescribing them indiscriminately.

Another new drug that produced a significant change in social behavior was the birth control pill. Together with legalized abortions, it produced major changes in sexual behavior.

Some areas of medicine benefited less from new discoveries. Few effective treatments for viral infections accompanied the new vaccines. This was dramatically evident in the lack of treatments for acquired immune deficiency syndrome (AIDS) in the 1980s. The treatment of cancer continued to rely on surgery, radiation therapy, and chemotherapy of limited benefit. Better treatments became available for heart and vascular diseases and hypertension, but most of them served to stabilize the patient's condition rather than to treat the underlying problems.

The period after mid century produced the greatest increase in the demand for medical care in the nation's history, despite the continuing decline in the incidence of most infectious diseases. The rising standard of living enabled people to afford more medical care. The increased number of useful treatments led to greater expectations about the amount and quality of medical care. The proportion of the elderly in the population continued to increase, which was especially significant because the elderly have high rates of chronic and degenerative diseases.

The increased demand for medical care led to a major role for the federal government for the first time in the nation's history. The first major postwar federal legislation related to health care was the Hill-Burton Act of 1946. This act helped fund the construction of many hospitals, primarily in poorer states with inadequate hospital facilities. Hill-Burton funding also helped desegregate southern hospitals after Congress banned racial discrimination in hospitals constructed under the program.

The growing demand for additional federal health legislation was strongly resisted by most of the medical profession. Beginning about World War I, organized medicine, especially the American Medical Association and its constituent state and local medical societies, adopted policies that opposed federal government involvement in medical care, compulsory health insurance, and prepaid group health plans in which a number of physicians provided care to pre-enrolled patients who joined the plan for a monthly fee.

Organized medicine did accept private health insurance plans, largely because physicians were given considerable control over their operation. Blue Cross, which insures hospital care, traces its origin to a 1929 hospital prepayment plan provided to Dallas schoolteachers by Baylor University Hospital. Modern Blue Cross plans that give subscribers a choice of hospitals resulted from legislation enacted first in New York State in 1934 and later by other states. In 1939, California physicians developed the first Blue Shield plan, an insurance program for physicians' services. Commercial insurers soon offered comparable plans. Health insurance became widespread during and after World War II as part of collective bargaining agreements negotiated between unions and employers.

The poor and the growing number of the aged did not benefit from these employment-based programs. Efforts during the late 1950s and early 1960s to provide federally funded health programs for them were bitterly opposed by organized medicine. Finally, in 1965 Congress enacted Medicare, a federal health insurance program for the aged, and Medicaid, a joint federal-state health insurance program for the poor.

The popularity of Medicare and Medicaid made Congress realize that the public did not agree with organized medicine's opposition to federal health care programs. In the next decades, Congress enacted many laws involving health care. The Health Maintenance Organization Act of 1973 encouraged the development of HMOs, which provide comprehensive health care to groups of subscribers for fixed monthly premiums. A series of laws, particularly the Health Professions Educational Assistance Act of 1963 and the Health Manpower Training Act of 1971, provided funding to medical schools that increased their enrollments and thereby the supply of physicians.

Federal legislation was stimulated not only by the growing demand for health care but also by its escalating cost. The proportion of the gross national product spent for medical care grew from 5 percent in 1950 to over 11 percent in 1990. Beginning in the 1980s, the federal government began to regulate the growth in health care costs. The most important action has been Medicare's implementation in 1983 of Diagnosis Related Groups (DRGs). Hospitals are reimbursed a fixed sum for the care of each Medicare patient, based on the patient's assignment to a particular diagnostic category, regardless of actual expenditures incurred by the hospital. DRG payment systems are designed to encourage hospitals to reduce the length of stay of patients, eliminate unnecessary tests and procedures, and otherwise provide care in a cost-effective manner. They have been adopted by other health insurers as well.

The growing demand for medical care led to greater concern about the supply of physicians. Although a physician shortage was recognized as a serious problem well before mid century, most states and the federal government did not assume responsibility for medical education until the 1960s, partly because of opposition from organized medicine. For the next two decades, state governments built several dozen new medical schools and enlarged existing ones. The federal and some state governments also offered financial incentives to medical schools that expanded their enrollments. As a result of these programs, the supply of physicians per ten thousand persons increased from less than thirteen in 1950 to almost twenty in 1990. Since 1980 public attention has focused on adjusting imbalances in the geographic and specialty distributions of physicians rather than on increasing the overall supply.

The shortage of American-trained physicians has led many foreign medical graduates to immigrate to the United States. Unlike previous immigrant physicians, who were European trained, most of those entering the United States after the 1950s were educated in Asian medical schools. They became the major providers of health care in many public hospitals and underserved areas. More recently, many Americans who were not admitted to American medical schools have attended Mexican or Caribbean medical schools. The poor quality of most Asian and Latin American schools has been demonstrated by the high failure rates of their graduates on American medical licensing and other examinations.

The popularity of specialization among physicians has led to greater formalization of specialty training. These efforts began when groups of physicians organized specialty boards to examine and certify physicians in individual specialties. The first board, the American Board of Ophthalmology, was established in 1917. It was followed by the board in otolaryngology in 1924 and by eight other specialty boards in the 1930s. The requirements of the boards have come to include a period of education in an approved residency program and the passing of examinations given by the specialty boards. Board certification became popular after World War II because health insurance companies paid higher fees to board-certified specialists and hospitals preferred to have them on their staffs. The AMA and other medical societies then decided that every physician should be a specialist, which led to new specialty boards in fields like family medicine, and after 1970 to the replacement of the internship with a multiple-year residency in a specialty.

The office practice of medicine has steadily changed from solo to group practices. The more popular type of group practice consists of a number of physicians in the same specialty. The other type includes physicians in several specialties who collectively offer comprehensive care to patients. Many multispecialty group practices are employed by health maintenance organizations (HMOs) that provide comprehensive care to patients for a regular monthly premium.

Changes in medical practice have had a significant impact on the medical profession. The economic interests of physicians diverged as some of them became salaried employees of hospitals, clinics, and medical schools. The cohesiveness of the profession diminished as specialty medical societies grew at the expense of general ones like the American Medical Association. In order to regain its stature, the AMA reorganized in the 1970s to create closer ties with the specialty societies and medical schools, cooperate with government, and appeal to the growing number of physicians who were not members.

Because of the growing cost of hospital care, in the 1980s the federal government and state governments began to regulate hospitals more closely, especially with regard to inpatient care.

The increasing complexity of medical care has led to a steadily expanding role for hospitals. Because of the growing cost of hospital care, in the 1980s the federal and state governments began to regulate hospitals more closely, especially with regard to inpatient care. This has led hospitals to add new types of outpatient care, which has been their most rapidly growing activity since mid century.

The types of hospital inpatient care vary significantly among three broad groups of hospitals. The top tier consists of the leading teaching hospitals that are major affiliates of medical schools. These institutions have the elaborate equipment and skilled faculty members and residents to treat the most unusual and complex disorders.

The middle tier includes the nonprofit and proprietary community hospitals that treat the ordinary disorders of the private patients of community physicians as well as of patients with Medicare and Medicaid insurance. Community hospitals have steadily expanded the scope of their activities by offering treatments developed in the major teaching hospitals. Public hospitals in small communities function very much like voluntary hospitals.

The bottom tier consists of the municipal hospitals in the major cities that are open to all patients regardless of ability to pay. The shortage of American medical school graduates has forced most of these hospitals to use foreign medical graduates as residents and staff physicians. Many municipal hospitals have experienced a decline in utilization in recent years because insured patients have chosen to go to voluntary and proprietary hospitals. Some cities have sold or closed their municipal hospitals and contracted with other hospitals to care for uninsured patients. Most cities have continued to operate outpatient care facilities for their needy residents, either in municipal hospitals or in freestanding clinics.

The growth in hospital care has led to significant changes in the hospital labor force. As the skills required of registered nurses increased, community and four-year college educational programs replaced hospital training schools. Nursing became a stratified profession, with registered nurses at the top of the hierarchy and other grades below. New allied health occupations developed, partly to utilize the complex equipment essential to much hospital medical care. Relations between hospital workers and hospitals became more formalized, with workers often being represented by labor unions.

The institution that has changed most dramatically since mid century is the medical school, now usually called an academic health center. Each of its three major functions—teaching, research, and patient care—has expanded so greatly that medical schools now have the largest budgets in their universities, and many have become the largest providers of medical care in their communities.

The first significant change in medical schools occurred in the late 1950s and early 1960s with the great expansion of federal funding for medical research through the National Institutes of Health. Research funding enabled medical schools to replace their part-time clinical faculty members, who were local practitioners, with full-time specialists who carried out all of their teaching, research, and patient care in the medical school. Federal research grants enabled many basic medical science departments to expand and establish their own graduate programs. Funded basic science and clinical research have become major activities of medical schools and have been responsible for many major discoveries in biomedical science and medical care.

The second major change in medical schools occurred in the 1960s and 1970s as a result of state and federal funding that built new medical schools and enlarged existing ones. The number of four-year medical schools increased from 72 in 1950 to more than 125 in 1990, and the number of their graduates from about 5,500 to over 16,000 annually. Medical school hospitals also became the major centers for residency programs.

The need for more patients for their growing number of medical students, residents, and faculty members led medical schools to affiliate with additional hospitals. The hospitals were willing to affiliate because of their need for medical manpower and the preferences of residents for hospitals affiliated with medical schools. Currently, virtually every major hospital in the nation is affiliated to some degree with a medical school.

Concurrent with the growth in medical school enrollments was a growing interest in medical education among women. Since the 1960s, when women became interested in many traditionally male occupations, the proportion of women medical students has increased dramatically. In 1989 to 1990, they comprised 23,500 (36 percent) of the 65,000 undergraduate medical students.

The availability of medical education to traditionally underrepresented minorities, especially blacks, became a public concern in the 1960s. In recent decades many medical schools have made greater efforts to enroll more blacks and other minorities, but with less success than many had hoped for. In 1989 to 1990, 4,000 blacks and 3,500 Hispanics were enrolled among the 65,000 undergraduate medical students.

The expansion of the patient care function of medical schools received its greatest impetus from the enactment of Medicare and Medicaid in 1965, which compensated medical schools and their faculty members for the care of many charity patients whom they had previously treated at no charge as part of their educational activities. Medical school faculty members now offer their services to the community in competition with local hospitals and physicians. In recent decades most full-time clinical faculty members have obtained the bulk of their income from their patient care activities.

The new activities of medical schools have had a significant impact on the content of medical education. Specialization and research led medical schools to add elective courses in these subjects to the curriculum and to reduce the number of required hours in the basic sciences and general medicine. This has been criticized by those who believe that all physicians should receive thorough training in general medicine prior to specializing.

During the second half of the twentieth century the careers of physicians became more diverse. The largest group, the solo practitioners and members of single-specialty group practices, followed a traditional medical career. Another group became salaried physicians in multispecialty group practices, such as HMOs. Still others, such as medical school faculty members and hospital physicians providing direct patient care, were employed by large organizations.

The content of medical practice has changed. Concern over the growing cost of medical care has led government and other health insurers to intervene directly in the patient care activities of physicians. Major social, legal, and ethical issues have arisen over malpractice, abortion, the prolongation of life among the terminally and hopelessly ill of all ages, the rights of the poor to receive medical care, and the role of patient consent in the provision of medical care. Medical care is no longer a relationship between an individual physician and an individual patient or a family. It has become a basic social concern in which individual rights are inexorably intertwined with social needs, economic constraints, and ethical considerations. The result has been a fundamental transformation of the roles of physicians and health care institutions.

American Medicine in International Perspective

American medicine has differed from that in most other advanced nations in the twentieth century primarily because of the lesser role of government. Most European medical schools and hospitals have been public institutions, and European physicians have received most of their earnings from national health insurance accounts. This control has enabled European governments to determine the number of physicians trained, the admission standards for medical schools and the content of medical education, the number of physicians to become specialists, their relationship to hospitals, their earnings, and in some cases their practice locations. European governments have designated the number, location, and equipment of hospitals and other health care facilities and the types of patients each could admit.

In the United States, on the other hand, before mid century most aspects of medicine were part of the private and voluntary sectors of society. Most physicians were educated in private medical schools. They cared for patients who paid them directly or were covered by private health insurance. Physicians served on the staffs of voluntary and other hospitals that permitted them to receive fees from their private patients.

Since the 1950s, federal and state governments have increased their role in the American health system. Although government intervention has moved American medicine in the direction of the European systems, enormous differences remain. In the United States, governments have regulated and cooperated with rather than taken over the voluntary and private sectors, which continue to dominate the nation's health care system. For example, in most jurisdictions Medicare payments are disbursed through Blue Cross and Blue Shield plans. Public medical schools in the United States are indistinguishable from their private counterparts and are quite different from those in Europe. Private hospitals in the United States continue to dominate the health care system. The counterbalancing roles of the public, private, and voluntary sectors ensure that the American health care system will remain unique among advanced nations.

[See also Alternative Medicine; Life Stages; Death; Old Age; The Professions; Public Health; Science as a Profession; Technology and Social Change.]

BIBLIOGRAPHY

The major journals in the history of American medicine are the *Bulletin of the History of Medicine* and the *Journal of the History of Medicine and Allied Sciences.* The U.S. National Library of Medicine publishes the annual *Bibliography of the History of Medicine.*

Bowers, John Z., and Elizabeth F. Purcell, eds. *Advances in American Medicine: Essays at the Bicentennial.* 2 vols. (1976).

Buchan, William. *Domestic Medicine* (1769).

Bullough, Vern, and Bonnie Bullough. *The Care of the Sick: The Emergence of Modern Nursing* (1978).

Burrow, James G. *AMA: Voice of American Medicine* (1963).

Campion, Frank D. *The AMA and U.S. Health Policy Since 1940* (1984).

Commission on Hospital Care. *Hospital Care in the United States* (1947).

Dowling, Harry F. *Fighting Infection: Conquests of the Twentieth Century* (1977).

Duffy, John. *The Healers: A History of American Medicine* (1976; repr. 1979).

Fein, Rashi. *Medical Care, Medical Costs: The Search for a Health Insurance Policy* (1968).

Gamble, Vanessa N. *The Black Community Hospital* (1989).

Gevitz, Norman, ed. *Other Healers: Unorthodox Medicine in America* (1988).

Grob, Gerald N. *Mental Institutions in America: Social Policy to 1875* (1972).

———. *Mental Illness and American Society, 1875–1940* (1983).

Gunn, John. *Domestic Medicine* (1830).

Kalisch, Philip A., and Beatrice J. Kalisch. *The Advance of American Nursing.* 2d ed. (1986).

Kett, Joseph F. *The Formation of the American Medical Profession: The Role of Institutions, 1780–1860* (1968).

Leavitt, Judith W., ed. *Women and Health in America: Historical Readings* (1984).

Long, Diana E., and Janet Golden, eds. *The American General Hospital: Communities and Social Contexts* (1989).

Ludmerer, Kenneth M. *Learning to Heal: The Development of American Medical Education* (1985).

Mechanic, David, ed. *Handbook of Health, Health Care, and the Health Professions* (1983).

Numbers, Ronald L., ed. *The Education of American Physicians: Historical Essays* (1980).
Rosenberg, Charles E. *The Care of Strangers: The Rise of America's Hospital System* (1987).
Rothstein, William G. *American Physicians in the Nineteenth Century: From Sects to Science* (1972).
———. *American Medical Schools and the Practice of Medicine: A History* (1987).
Savitt, Todd. *Medicine and Slavery* (1978).
Starr, Paul. *The Social Transformation of American Medicine* (1982).
Stevens, Rosemary. *American Medicine and the Public Interest* (1971).
———. *In Sickness and in Wealth: American Hospitals in the Twentieth Century* (1989).
Whorton, James. *Crusaders for Fitness: The History of American Health Reformers* (1982).
Young, James Harvey. *The Toadstool Millionaires: A Social History of Patent Medicines in America Before Federal Regulation* (1961).

— WILLIAM G. ROTHSTEIN

MEDICINE, ALTERNATIVE

See ALTERNATIVE MEDICINE

MINORITIES AND WORK

From its colonial origins to the present, the United States labor market has been segmented along racial, ethnic, class, and gender lines. There has especially been a racial/ethnic hierarchy of labor, with people of color (Africans, Asians, Chicanos, and Latinos) clustered at the lower rungs in poorly paid, unskilled, and semiskilled positions, with little prospect of job mobility. Minority workers have often entered the labor market as "unfree" laborers, that is, as slaves, contract workers, or peons. They have performed the least desirable and lowest paying types of work, usually receiving less compensation for the same jobs held by whites under a dual-wage system.

Minority workers have been a reserve labor force, the last-hired and the first-fired, a buffer for employers during periods of expansion or contraction. They have also been used to discipline labor, to keep wages low, and to impede the organization of workers into labor unions. Minority workers supplied much of the hard labor that created the agricultural base and the transportation infrastructure for industrialization and modernization in the United States.

The labor market for most of the twentieth century has consisted of primary, secondary, and tertiary sectors. The primary labor market carries high wages, steady employment, and upward mobility. At the upper end, it is occupied by white-collar salaried or self-employed workers with high status, autonomy, and often supervisory duties. At the lower end are positions with high salaries but less autonomy. These are usually blue-collar skilled and unionized positions. The secondary labor market provides low wages, few or no benefits, little mobility, and unsteady employment. Work is often casual, that is, part-time, seasonal, and temporary. Until the 1970s a job in the primary sector generally yielded sufficient earnings to support a family. The secondary sector, however, where most minority workers were located, did not pay enough to sustain a family. The tertiary sector of the labor market includes the underground economy of crime, prostitution, gambling, and drug trafficking, as well as labor by undocumented workers and in sweatshops. This type of work is risky, often leading to incarceration or deportation. Because of limited opportunities in the primary and secondary sectors of the labor market, minority workers, especially in the barrios and ghettos, have found the underground economy a means of survival.

Table 1

DEFINITION OF LABOR MARKET SEGMENTS, 1980

UPPER-TIER PRIMARY:
—managerial and professional specialty occupations, except health assessment and treating
—supervisors and proprietors, sales occupations
—sales representatives, commodities, and finance
—farm operators and managers

LOWER-TIER PRIMARY:
—health assessment and treating
—technologists and technicians, except health
—protective service
—precision production, craft, and repair
—transportation occupations
—material moving equipment operators

UPPER-TIER SECONDARY:
—health technologists and technicians
—other sales
—administrative support occupations, including clerical
—machine operators and tenders
—fabricators, assemblers, inspectors

LOWER-TIER SECONDARY:
—private household occupations
—service occupations, except protective and household
—handlers, equipment cleaners, helpers, and laborers
—farming, forestry, and fishing, except farm operators and managers

Slavery

The colonists, who settled what later became the United States, initially relied on white indentured servants as a source of labor to clear the fields, tend livestock, and cultivate crops. The supply of white indentured servants was fairly abundant until the 1660s, when political and economic improvements in England reduced the number of individuals willing to risk the possibility of progress abroad in return for three to seven years of labor. Moreover, white landowners, particularly in the South, became concerned about potential disruption from the presence of a land-hungry class of white men. Bacon's Rebellion in 1676 confirmed their fears, when Nathanial Bacon, Jr. (1647–1676), a recent settler in Henrico County, Virginia, led a band of frontiersmen against the Indians, despite the disapproval of Governor William Berkeley. Bacon also sided with white settlers who complained about a restricted franchise, excessive taxation, inadequate protection against the Indians, and favoritism in the distribution of offices and tax exemptions. Although quickly suppressed after Bacon's death, the rebellion had a disquieting effect on the planters.

Slavery evolved gradually in the South after the mid seventeenth century and became entrenched by the beginning of the eighteenth century. Approximately a half million Africans were enslaved in the British colonies of North America; about 60 percent of them were imported between 1720 and 1780. During the seventeenth century, slaves were used to perform a variety of tasks from clearing the land, tending livestock, and planting crops to serving as skilled artisans. Large plantations were the exception during the eighteenth century, as most bondsmen worked on small farms with few slaves. Bondswomen generally did domestic work until harvest time, when all available hands were needed in the fields.

As plantations developed and grew larger, they became more complex and labor became more specialized. Plantations with thirty or more slaves had the greatest degree of specialization. A white overseer, employed by the planter to manage the labor force, usually relied on one slave as foreman and a few others as drivers to supervise the work of a gang of five or six slaves. On larger plantations, some slaves might devote full time to ditching, cultivating vegetables, tending livestock, driving wagons, and working as blacksmiths, carpenters, coopers, millers, sawyers, shoemakers, stonemasons, and weavers. Domestic slaves on larger plantations might be divided into butlers, coachmen, cooks, footmen, laundresses, maids, nurses, and seamstresses.

During the revolutionary war era, slavery stagnated as the colonies curtailed the slave trade and colonists, with the exception of those in the Carolinas and Georgia, enlisted slaves in the military with a promise of freedom. Slavery never took full root in the North, where there was a sufficient supply of European labor for most of the colonial period. Between 1780 and 1804, each northern state took measures to abolish slavery, and bondage virtually disappeared by the 1830s. Even some southerners, moved by the "Rights of Man" rhetoric of the period, manumitted slaves. Agricultural recessions in the 1780s and 1790s together with a shift in the Upper South from tobacco to wheat cultivation resulted in a slave surplus.

Several developments during the late eighteenth century, however, led to a renewed demand for slaves and the expansion of slavery into the Deep South. By 1780, there had been a revolution in cotton-cloth production in England due to several inventions and refinements, such as James Hargreaves's spinning jenny, Richard Arkwright's waterframe, and Samuel Crompton's mule. Population growth in Europe, which expanded by a third between 1750 and 1800, swelled demand for raw cotton. In 1793 Eli Whitney (1765–1825) improved the old roller gin to make separation of cotton lint from seed easier and cotton cultivation therefore more profitable. Improvements in cotton production coincided with similar changes in sugar refining. Moreover, refugees from the Haitian Revolution (1791) fled to Louisiana with their slaves and established sugar plantations. Although slaves cultivated a variety of crops, such as wheat and tobacco in Maryland and Virginia, tobacco in North Carolina and Kentucky, rice on the sea islands of South Carolina and Georgia, hemp in Kentucky, and foodstuffs like corn, sweet potatoes, and peas throughout the South, most slaves cultivated cotton.

The 1850 Federal Census reported 2.5 million slaves in southern agriculture, with 2 percent in hemp production, 5 percent in rice cultivation, 6 percent in sugar production, 14 percent in tobacco cultivation, and 73 percent in cotton production.

From 1790 to 1860, slaveholders resettled about one million blacks in the Deep South. Most slaves were taken in family units from the upper South. In the Deep South, they once again cleared the land, built homes, and prepared the area for settlement. In 1850, the Federal Census reported 2.5 million slaves in southern agriculture, with 2 percent in hemp production, 5 percent in rice cultivation, 6 percent in sugar production, 14 percent in tobacco cultivation, and 73 percent in cotton production. About one-fourth of the slaves belonged to owners with less than ten slaves, more than half lived in units of twenty slaves or more, and about one-fourth worked on plantations with more than fifty slaves.

Cotton was the United States' most important commercial crop and leading export, and slaves worked year round, from sunup to sundown, to bring in the crop. The cotton season began about March with plowing and sowing seed, as did planting corn and cultivating vegetables. By May, it was time to chop cotton and kill the weeds around the new shoots. This work continued throughout the summer until about September, when the cotton was picked, ginned, and pressed for shipment. From September to December, the slaves picked and shucked corn and harvested vegetables. With the start of the new year, there were hogs to be slaughtered and meat to be cured, wood to be cut and hauled, ditches cleaned, tools repaired, fences mended, and manure spread. There was always work to be done, in season and out.

More acres in the South were planted in corn than in cotton, because corn could be grown at little additional cost to cotton planters. About one-half of the corn crop was used for animal feed. In 1860, the South raised two-thirds of the nation's hogs. By 1860, the value of hogs and other butchered livestock was greater in the South than in the North. In those instances where slave-owners had extra hands, they hired them to work in the cities or in industry for short periods or for a year.

About 10 percent of the slave population—approximately 400,000 by 1860—lived in cities and towns. Slaves as well as free blacks worked in practically every skilled and unskilled occupation in the South. Blacks were more likely to enjoy skilled positions in the South than in the North. In 1860, there were about 250,000 free African Americans in the South and the same number in the North. Whether North or South, free African Americans faced segregation in transportation, accommodations, education, housing, and employment. Free blacks had a slight advantage in the North, where they could learn to read and write, form their own organizations, especially churches, and vote, although on the same basis as white men in only four states. While free African Americans possessed more rights in the North, they also had less occupational mobility and worked primarily as unskilled laborers or as servants. In the South, free blacks as well as slaves were likely to work as skilled artisans.

By the 1840s, about 5 percent of the slave population worked in industry, where they were either owned by companies or hired from the slave-owner. Slave labor was cheaper than wage labor and profitable to slaveholders, who received a return on investment equal to or greater than the average returns on other ventures. About four-fifths of industrial slaves were owned directly by industrial entrepreneurs. Slaves worked in textile mills, tobacco factories, and hemp manufacturing. They were barbers, blacksmiths, cabinetmakers, carpenters, coopers, sawyers, seamstresses, shoemakers, tailors, tanners, weavers, and wheelwrights. They worked in fisheries, gristmills, lumbering, quarries, sawmills, shipbuilding, and the turpentine industry. They built and repaired streets, turnpikes, and canals. Almost every railroad in the South was constructed in part with slave labor. Coal-mining and the iron industry made greater use of slaves over a longer period of time than any other business. Slaves were the chief labor force in Upper South ironworks. In 1861, the Tredegar Iron Company in Richmond, Virginia, employed nine hundred workers, half of them slaves. Tredegar was the South's leading iron mill, and it employed the third largest ironworking force in the United States. In total, about ten thousand slaves worked in southern ironworks before the Civil War.

By the 1840s, about 5 percent of the slave population worked in industry, where they were either owned by companies or hired from the slave-owner.

Industrial slaves worked from sunrise to sunset, six days a week, every week of the year, much like plantation slaves. They usually performed the hot, dirty, and hazardous work. Tobacco, hemp, and textile mills favored slave women and children for labor in which sprightliness and nimbleness were more important than strength. Slave labor in the main was as efficient as wage labor. Slaves were not used more widely in southern industry for fear they would undermine the institution of slavery. In cities and towns, they had examples of black men and women who were free, opportunities to become literate, and access to political news. The potential for disaffection, unrest, escape, and even rebellion was ever present under such circumstances.

Asians, Hispanics, Blacks: 1865–1915

While most African Americans toiled in agriculture, primarily cotton, even after the Civil War and emancipation, Chinese men entered the labor force as plantation workers in Hawaii, gold miners in California, and railroad construction workers in the West. A dramatic decline in Hawaii's indigenous population, from approximately 300,000 in 1778 to about 44,000 a century later, due to forced labor and European disease, caused planters to look elsewhere for labor.

In 1849, a major flood in southeastern China drove hundreds of thousands of Chinese men from their villages in search of work in China and overseas. Both Hawaiian and United States employers favored Chinese workers who, as single men or as married men without wives and children, were ideal for migrant farm labor, mining, and railroad construction. They could be housed inexpensively and transported easily to places where their labor was needed. Chinese workers first came to the United States in large numbers during the gold rush of the late 1840s. Two-thirds of the Chinese in the 1850s were miners. By 1860, they were 10 percent of California's population and 25 percent of its work force. Between 1850 and 1882, over 100,000 Chinese men entered the United States. They worked on the most dangerous segments of the transcontinental railroad as it was built through the Rocky Mountains. Ninety percent of the work force on the Central Pacific Railroad was Chinese in 1867. They cleared the trees, laid track, operated power drills, and handled explosives for boring tunnels. Thousands lost their lives.

Chinese men also worked in citrus and celery harvesting and in fisheries. After completion of the transcontinental railroad in 1869, most Chinese settled in California. Almost half the workers in San Francisco factories in 1872 were Chinese. Because of a shortage of women in the West, Chinese men were employed in domestic service, food service, and laundries. A dual-wage scale prevailed, especially in the garment industry where, in 1870, Chinese men averaged $300 to $400 per year, while white women earned $600 to $900 per year, and white men were paid $900 to $1,200.

Chinese men traveled to the United States as sojourners, with the intention of returning home after several years abroad. During the interval, they would send some of their wages to families back home and would seek to save enough to purchase land in China. Although more than 100,000 Chinese men immigrated to the United States between 1850 and 1882, only 8,848 Chinese women came during the same period. Family patriarchs assumed that by keeping wives and children in China, the men were more likely to send money home. The few Chinese women brought to the United States were usually purchased from destitute families in China for prostitution in the United States. By 1870, two-thirds of the Chinese women in San Francisco worked as prostitutes. When business was slack, they were forced to do subcontracted sewing work. For the most part, they labored under slavelike conditions.

As the Chinese appeared in the West, Chicanos—people of Indian and Spanish heritage—were no longer needed in the labor force and pushed off their lands into Mexico. After the Mexican American War in 1848, the United States acquired almost half of Mexico's territory, including the area that became the states of Arizona, California, Colorado, Nevada, New Mexico, and Utah. There were about 80,000 Spanish-speaking people and some quarter of a million Indians living on those lands. A combination of restrictive legislation, litigation, vigilantism, beatings, and murder forced many of them out; whites taking over the mines, the cattle boom of the 1860s, and railroad expansion in Texas drove others off their lands. By the late nineteenth century, the social, economic, political, and numerical dis-

Cotton was the United States' most important commercial crop in the nineteenth century and slaves worked year round to bring in the crop.

placement of Mexicans and Indians was evident. For example, in 1860, 30.5 percent of the Chicano population in San Diego worked as ranchers and farmers, 39.1 percent as skilled workers, and 15.9 percent as unskilled laborers. By 1880, less than 2 percent were involved in ranching, 4.8 percent held skilled jobs, and 80.9 percent were unskilled laborers.

After the Civil War, new labor arrangements replaced slavery. Many white planters did not believe that African Americans would work without coercion after emancipation. The planters required black workers to sign contracts that restricted their freedom of movement, required obedience to the landowner, and asserted the landowner's right to regulate their working hours. The freedmen preferred arrangements that gave them greater autonomy, removed them from the former slave quarters near the owner's home, and allowed them to work on their own rather than in gangs under the supervision of a driver, similar to slavery. Given the shortage of cash in the South after the war, planters were willing to try a system that did not depend on wages while offering incentive to the freedmen to work hard without strict supervision.

Planters and freedmen reached a mutual accommodation whereby the former slaves cultivated cotton for a share of the crop. By working for a share of the crop, the freedmen theoretically could earn more if they worked harder. They could also determine the extent to which family members would labor in the fields. Initially, women were withdrawn from the fields for domestic work as wives and mothers. However, at harvest time, the most labor-intensive point in the growing season, both women and children assisted in picking the cotton.

Two types of share arrangements developed in the South. If freedmen owned a mule, farm implements, and had sufficient capital until harvest, they became tenant farmers and paid the owner one-quarter of the crop for use of the land. If they did not have enough resources, landowners supplied everything except food and clothing in return for half the crop, and the freedmen became sharecroppers. To subsist until harvest, sharecroppers had to purchase goods on credit, with interest rates as high as 60 percent. Most sharecroppers ended the year in debt, and many tenant farmers became sharecroppers. Although cotton production doubled in the South from 1869 to 1889, the price fell by almost half due to competition from cotton grown abroad and a decline in global demand. Those circumstances made it even more difficult for sharecroppers to escape the burdens of debt peonage. Despite these obstacles, by 1880, one-fifth of black farmers owned their own land, although their farms, about 47.3 acres (18.9 hectares), were less than one-third the size of the average white farm.

To discipline black labor and to make black agricultural workers more pliant, white plantation owners recruited Chinese, Italian, and Mexican workers after emancipation. Chinese men who had worked constructing the Southern Pacific Railroad were brought into Louisiana and Mississippi during the 1870s. The largest group of Chinese in any southern state settled in the Delta region of Mississippi. Soon after their arrival, the Chinese left the cotton fields to become small grocers. They could not earn enough as sharecroppers to achieve their objective of saving money to retire in China. With a small amount of capital, the Chinese would rent a room to open a store and sell groceries. The Delta Chinese filled a niche left open by southern whites, who considered it demeaning to operate a store in a black neighborhood and to serve black patrons. Black men in the main were not able to fill that niche because they lacked the same access to credit as whites and Chinese. As outsiders, the Chinese were not concerned about their social status in the United States; they worried about saving enough money to secure their position in China.

To discipline black labor and to make black agricultural workers more pliant, white plantation owners recruited Chinese, Italian, and Mexican workers after emancipation.

The Chinese grocers did not have the same expectations placed on them for credit and special favors to friends as did black grocers. The Chinese could be more friendly toward their customers than whites in the racially hierarchical South. They offered greater services and were able to sell goods at lower prices because their family labor cut their costs. They did not require the deferential behavior demanded by whites, and their stores were often one of the few integrated public spaces in the South. As other Chinese entered the Delta, they worked first with relatives, where they learned enough English to survive and the fundamentals of business operation. With a combination of savings, loans from relatives, and credit from wholesalers, they opened stores in other areas. The Chinese maintained excellent credit. When a Chinese merchant defaulted on a debt, relatives usually made up the loss to keep their good credit standing.

After the fall of Radical Reconstruction and removal of African American men from politics, white planters saw no further need to import foreign labor. They preferred black laborers who worked harder, could be dismissed or disciplined with greater ease, and could be exploited economically with little fear of retribution or protest from a foreign government.

Often out of necessity, black women participated in the labor force at a much higher rate than any other racial or ethnic group. Black houseservants were usually young girls rather than older women. Once married and with a family, black women often switched to taking in laundry, allowing them to stay home with their children. In 1890, 85 percent of employed black men and 96 percent of employed black women worked in agriculture or domestic service. About one-quarter of married black women were in the labor force, eight times the proportion of U.S.–born married white women. By 1900, 44 percent of black women workers were in agriculture and 44 percent in private household service, mostly as servants and laundresses. Only 3 percent were in manufacturing and about 1 percent in professions, primarily as teachers. Although black women were one-third of southern female workers in 1890, they were only 3 percent of textile workers. The textile industry that emerged in the South after the Civil War was confined almost exclusively to white workers. In South Carolina, state law prohibited African Americans from working in the same room, using the same stairway, or even sharing the same factory window with white textile workers.

Although they did not have a foreign government to protect them, black workers did organize in the South to improve their condition. Black women in Atlanta formed the Washerwomen's Association in 1881 and struck for higher wages. About 3,000 women participated in the strike, which was put down by white landlords and the city government. Black agricultural workers in 1888 started the Colored Farmers' National Alliance and Cooperative Union. At its peak in 1891, the organization had 1.2 million members in twelve states. The group supported cooperatives, published newspapers, raised money for longer school terms for black children, and assisted members who faced hard times with their mortgages. The organization sponsored a cotton pickers' strike in 1891 that led to its demise. Cotton picking was grueling labor. To earn $1.20 per day, a cotton picker had to gather about two hundred pounds (90 kilograms) of cotton, working in the field from dawn to dusk, in excruciating heat. The strike for higher wages met brutal and successful opposition from the white cotton growers. Many black farmers joined the Populist party, formed in 1891, which for a time sought to unite black and white farm workers. Because it posed a threat to the status quo and brought black men more actively into politics, southern white landowners defeated the Populist party and barred black men from southern politics for more than half a century.

Although black men could vote for a time in the South, Chinese immigrants were denied that privilege until after World War II. The Naturalization Law of 1790 specified that naturalized citizenship was limited to "whites," a law that remained in effect until 1952. Moreover, according to the Cable Act of 1922, any American woman who married an alien ineligible for citizenship lost her own citizenship. Asians from the Indian subcontinent were generally classified as caucasian; however, the U.S. Supreme Court in 1923 ruled that Asian Indians were not "white," and therefore could not be naturalized as citizens. For a long time, the United States was a country whose citizens were almost exclusively of European ancestry.

Because of pressure from white workers, the U.S. Congress passed the Chinese Exclusion Act in 1882 that terminated Chinese immigration. Between 1850 and 1882, some 330,000 Chinese had entered the country. As they were pushed out of agricultural and factory work, the Chinese became laundry operators. In 1900, one-quarter of the employed Chinese males in the United States were laundrymen. Operating a laundry required little capital and little command of English. Similar to the Delta Chinese grocers, this was a niche left by others that the Chinese, especially on the West Coast, developed for themselves. After the Chinese Exclusion Act was renewed in 1892 and made indefinite in 1902, the Chinese population declined to about 62,000 by 1920. Approximately 47 percent of the Chinese who had immigrated to the United States returned to China.

After the Chinese Exclusion Act was passed, farm owners in the United States and Hawaii recruited Japanese workers. As contract workers, the Japanese could earn four to six times the wages paid in Japan. Between 1885 and 1924, 200,000 Japanese immigrated to Hawaii and about 180,000 immigrated to the United States. Almost 90 percent of the Japanese labored as agricultural or domestic workers. Like the Chinese, the Japanese came to the United States as sojourners. Japanese men outnumbered women by about twenty-five to one. In 1907, the so-called Gentlemen's Agreement between the United States and Japan barred the immigration of unskilled Japanese. Unlike the Chinese Exclusion Act, which prohibited the immigration of wives and relatives, the Gentlemen's Agreement permitted wives and relatives to join husbands who decided to remain in the states. Between 1909 and 1923, about 23,000 Japanese women entered the United States as "picture brides," whose marriages had been arranged by mail. After African American women, Japanese women had the highest labor force participation. Half of them worked in agriculture. By 1920, Japanese workers produced one-third of the truck crops in California.

Almost 70 percent of the Japanese population lived in California by 1930. Initially, they were migratory workers who labored on farms, railroads, and in canneries. During the fishing season, for example, they were shipped to Alaska and then back to California. Through ethnic solidarity and enterprise, the Japanese rose from field-workers to farmers. They formed credit-rotating associations, or *tanomoshi* to pool capital and to assist members in purchasing land and equipment. Through their farmers' organizations, they shared information about agricultural techniques and crop prices. Racist legislation impeded but failed to stop their progress. For example, California in 1913 passed a law denying land ownership to Japanese immigrants.

As Asian immigration declined owing to Congress's 1917 legislation that prohibited new immigration, the number of unskilled Mexican workers in the United States grew rapidly.

Twelve other states enacted similar legislation. Under the law, they could lease land for terms not longer than three years. To skirt the law, Japanese put land in the names of children or relatives born in the United States. The Japanese became farmers at a propitious moment, when industrialization and urbanization during the late nineteenth century created a demand for fresh produce in the cities. Irrigation projects in California, completion of the railroad, and introduction of refrigerator cars opened new markets for fruit distribution. Japanese farmers concentrated on short-term crops like berries and truck vegetables. By 1940, they grew almost 95 percent of California's snap beans and celery.

Almost as a form of ethnic succession, Koreans, Filipinos, Asian Indians, and Mexicans replaced the Chinese and Japanese as agricultural workers. Korean immigrants were more likely to come from urban areas and almost 40 percent were Christians. They assimilated more easily, but their numbers were small. Only about 8,000 Koreans immigrated to the United States between 1903 and 1920. Most Koreans were farm workers, although in the cities, they worked in restaurants and as gardeners, janitors, and domestic servants. Like the Japanese, they organized credit-rotating associations, or *kae* to help them purchase land. After Japan declared Korea a protectorate in 1905, it cut off Korean immigration to Hawaii and the United States.

With Japanese and Korean immigration restricted, Hawaiian sugar planters turned to the Philippines for cheap labor. By 1932, Filipinos were 70 percent of the plantation labor force in Hawaii. Almost 110,000 had settled in Hawaii and some 40,000 settled in the United States; they were nearly all male, and all but entirely confined to agricultural work and domestic service. Farm owners in the West held stereotypical views of Filipino men, who supposedly were well adapted to stoop labor because of their short stature. Nonetheless, the 1934 Independence Act halted Filipino immigration to the United States and the American Federation of Labor (AFL) sought legislation to pay Filipinos to return to the Philippines on condition that they would never return to the states. Under the Repatriation Act of 1935, about 20 percent of Filipinos returned home.

In 1907, Asian Indians began arriving on the West Coast. Only about 6,400 entered the United States; 99 percent of them were male. Families generally sent the second or youngest sons to earn money to pay off debts at home. Initially they worked on the railroads and in lumber mills but they were driven from those jobs by white workers and forced into agriculture. Most of the Asian Indians lived in California. In 1917, Congress enacted legislation that prohibited new immigration, and between 1920 and 1940, almost half the immigrants returned to India.

As Asian immigration declined, the number of unskilled Mexican workers in the United States grew rapidly. During the late nineteenth century, there was little difference economically between the United States and Mexico. By the beginning of the twentieth century, a gap developed that widened over time. By 1905, a Mexican family could make several times more money picking cotton in Texas than they could earn in Mexico. Mexican workers replaced Asian laborers on railroad construction and maintenance in southern California, New Mexico, and Nevada. They suffered from a differential pay scale under which Asian workers received $1.50 per day, Greeks $1.60 per day, but Mexicans only $1.25.

Mexicans became a critical labor force in the growth of agribusiness, which depended on a large mobile work force. By World War I, they were the most important ethnic group of agricultural workers in the Imperial Valley of California. A Mexican family might live in more than five places during the year as they followed the ripening crops. They picked tomatoes in Indiana, a job that required constant stooping and carrying heavy crates in the hot sun. Next, they might harvest sugar beets in Michigan, which was monotonous and difficult work with long hours, often in inclement weather. Large farmers considered Mexicans as particularly suited to drudgery in the fields and could exploit their labor because of worsening economic conditions in Mexico.

World War I–World War II

The United States experienced a severe labor shortage during World War I, as the nation restricted immigration from Europe and as large numbers of Europeans returned to protect their homelands during the war. The labor shortage provided an opportunity for minority workers in general and African Americans in particular to enter northern industry in large numbers for the first time. While the North needed workers, the South had a labor surplus due to boll weevil infestation and devastating floods in 1916 that wiped out crops in the Black Belt. In 1910, three-quarters of all African Americans lived in the South, where almost two-thirds worked in agriculture. Between 1910 and 1930, about 1.2 million African Americans migrated North, where they found employment in meat-packing, steel, automobiles, shipbuilding, and other areas of manufacturing.

African Americans were confined to so-called Negro jobs, positions that whites generally avoided, where the work was heavy, hot, dangerous, and dirty. Although the pay for the same jobs in plants was equal, black men were usually lumped into specific job categories with lower salaries. Black women were also barred from most good jobs. While women often refused to work beside black women and demanded separate eating and sanitary facilities; white customers objected to black saleswomen, receptionists, and secretaries. It was difficult for black women workers to secure employment in manufacturing, so that only 8 percent of them were in manufacturing by 1930, compared with 25 percent of black men. More than a third of black female industial workers were in the garment industry. Black women generally worked in factories, not as machine operatives but as service workers who cleaned factory buildings and equipment. The proportion of black women in domestic service grew from 44 percent in 1900 to 54 percent by 1930; it was one of the few areas of work open to them.

During World War I, black workers took over the unskilled positions that were previously held by European immigrants. Even unskilled jobs were attractive to black workers, who could earn three times as much in the North as in the South. Black workers were often introduced into northern industry as strikebreakers to discipline white labor. When white steelworkers in Pittsburgh went on strike in 1875, mill owners sought experienced workers to replace them and recruited black steelworkers from Richmond, Virginia. White steelworkers, similar to white workers in general, resisted the entry of black workers into the industry. In 1890, the Amalgamated Association of Iron, Steel, and Tin Workers in Pittsburgh went on strike to protest the presence of black workers. From 1881 to 1900, there were more than thirty strikes throughout the country against the employment of black workers in industry.

Initially, black workers in the iron and steel industry of western Pennsylvania occupied a range of positions from unskilled to white-collar jobs. During the late nineteenth century, race was not the barrier to job mobility it would later become. Immigrants from southern and eastern Europe at first trailed African Americans in skilled positions because of language barriers and limited industrial experience. In 1910, in western Pennsylvania, black steelworkers earned a weekly average of $14.98, while Slovak workers made $12.39, and Polish workers only $12.21.

At the time, black men made up about 3 percent of the work force in western Pennsylvania. They did not predominate in any department or critical area. Soon Germans gained control of the carpentry division, Poles the hammer shop, and Serbs the blooming mill at the Jones and Laughlin Steel plant in Pittsburgh. When black migrants arrived in large numbers between 1916 and 1930, they entered lower echelon jobs with limited opportunities for advancement, contrary to their earlier status. By 1920 in the Pittsburgh area, 13.6 percent of native-born whites held unskilled positions; 31.7 percent of the foreign-born whites and 54.4 percent of African Americans worked at unskilled jobs. Most black workers shunned unions because of hostile white labor. In western Pennsylvania, as in most parts of the country, they were barred from such craft unions as electrical workers, plumbers, and sheet metal workers. At the Homestead Steel Works, of 1,737 black workers, only 8 joined the steelworkers' union. During the strike of 1919, only one of them cooperated with the walkout. Steel companies in Illinois, Indiana, and Pennsylvania brought in about 30,000 black workers to break the strike. After the steel companies broke the strike, the number of black steelworkers dropped dramatically.

The introduction of black workers as strike-breakers in the metal industry in East Saint Louis, Illinois, in 1917 sparked labor unrest and major race riots. During the summer of 1919, race riots erupted in some twenty-five cities and towns across the country. Competition for jobs, housing, transportation, education, political power, and recreational facilities generated racial hostility and conflict. Racial tension continued during the 1920s as African Americans were confined to bulging ghettos of major American cities.

The prosperity of the 1920s eluded many African Americans who lost ground due to unionization and exclusion from skilled positions. Black labor force participation, which was higher than that for whites in 1910, declined by 1920 and became lower by 1930. The Great Depression struck the black population sooner, cut deeper, and lasted longer than for the rest of the country. During the early twentieth century, the number of black men in the building trades as carpenters and brickmasons dropped, while the number of white men in these occupations rose. From 1928 to 1949, the railroad unions prevented the hiring of black men as firemen, brakemen, trainmen, or yardmen. Prior to that time, most of the firemen and brakemen in the South were black.

During the Depression, African Americans lost a third of the positions they held in industry. White workers began to take jobs shunned before as "Negro work," especially in restaurants and service areas. White male railroad workers beat and even murdered black firemen to take over their jobs. By 1935, 30 percent of the black population depended on government relief for its survival. Other minority workers, particularly Chicanos, faced a similar situation. White workers replaced many Chicano field workers in California, and the United States government deported almost half a million people of Mexican origin during the 1930s, including tens of thousands who were U.S. citizens. Most New Deal legislation adversely affected minority workers. Payments to planters and large farm owners to plow under their crops and to reduce farm acreage pushed many sharecroppers and tenant farmers off the land. Landowners did not share federal payments with agricultural workers. Social security, workmen's compensation, and minimum-wage legislation did not cover agricultural workers, cooks, domestic servants, and yard workers. Minority workers were forced to rely more on the welfare programs of the New Deal than on job creation projects.

During the Depression and World War II years, black workers organized sharecropper unions, boycotted white businesses that did not hire them in the North, demonstrated against organized labor, and threatened a march on Washington against discrimination in defense industries. Their efforts produced improvements by 1945 for black workers in particular and for minority workers in general. After World War II, black workers achieved more progress in their labor status than at any other time, except the abolition of slavery. Labor demand during World War II, executive, legislative, and judicial action, as well as changes in racial attitudes in the fight against fascism led to dramatic improvements in the work status of black and other minority workers.

In New York and other northern cities, black boycotts led to employment as retail clerks, office workers, and bus drivers. Black workers in different parts of the country staged some twenty-two strikes against limited promotion opportunities, wage differentials based on race, and other forms of discrimination. The U.S. Supreme Court ruled in October 1940 that states could no longer use race as a basis for paying different salaries to black and white teachers. During the 1940s, more than 1.5 million African Americans migrated from the South to the North and West. More than half the black population lived in urban areas by 1950. Changes in the work force helped black women to escape domestic household service. The number of black female domestic workers declined as the number of black female manufacturing workers increased.

A. Philip Randolph (1889–1979), who organized the Brotherhood of Sleeping Car Porters in 1925 and won union recognition by 1937, announced in January 1941 that he would lead a march on Washington for fair employment in defense industries and desegregation of the armed services. To prevent a potentially embarrassing event as the United States mobilized for war, President Franklin D. Roosevelt issued Executive Order #8802 on June 25, 1941, in a successful effort to stop the demonstration, which was scheduled for July 1. Executive Order #8802 established a Fair Employment Practices Committee to encourage equal employment opportunities in companies with defense contracts. The establishment of the FEPC helped to improve the status of black workers through public hearings, publicity, and persuasion.

Black union membership increased tenfold during the 1930s, especially as the Congress of Industrial Organizations (CIO) conducted a massive unionizing campaign. The CIO organized industries as a whole rather than organizing individual crafts, as the AFL did. The CIO actively recruited black workers, who were important in organizing the automobile, meat-packing, and steel industries. Also, manpower shortages during World War II had the greatest effect in opening job opportunities for African Americans. In 1942, the CIO established the Committee to Abolish Racial Discrimination. Although the union helped to improve the general condition of black workers, it did little to change the status of black labor relative to white labor, especially in employment training and promotion.

Because of labor shortages on the mainland during World War II and depressed economic conditions on the island, large numbers of Puerto Ricans entered the labor force for the first time. About 81 percent of the U.S. Puerto Rican population lived in New York City. Puerto Rican men toiled in the garment industry, hotel and restaurant work, and in cigar manufacturing, while women generally did piecework at home, sewing and embroidering, and making lampshades, hats, and artificial flowers. Some Puerto Ricans came to the United States on temporary contracts to work on farms in New Jersey and New York.

Mexican workers during World War II received temporary visas to toil in the agricultural fields of the Southwest. Under the Bracero Program, the U.S. Farm Security Administration signed contracts with individual workers who agreed to labor in the United States for a specific time period in a certain occupation, such as farming. In return, the U.S. government provided transportation to and from the United States and guaranteed the prevailing wage, adequate housing, and medical services. Employers applied to the government to hire *braceros.* The program, which lasted from 1942 to 1964, aroused criticism on both sides of the border. The Catholic church in Mexico complained that the program broke up families and introduced Mexicans to immoral practices in the United States. Mexican employers denounced the program for depriving them of able workers. American labor charged that the program basically benefited agribusiness and kept wages low.

Because of labor shortages on the mainland during World War II and depressed economic conditions on the island, large numbers of Puerto Ricans entered the U.S. labor force for the first time.

Except for Japanese, Asians' status improved during World War II. In 1943, Congress repealed the Chinese Exclusion Act, provided for Chinese naturalization, and gave China a small annual immigration quota. Asian Indians were also granted naturalization rights. These changes occurred because of the strategic importance of China and India to the war effort. Executive Order #8802 opened industry to Filipino workers on the West Coast. During the war, the California attorney general reinterpreted the land laws to allow Filipinos who were not citizens to lease and to purchase land. After the Japanese attack on Pearl Harbor, President Franklin D. Roosevelt signed an executive order to evacuate 110,000 Japanese to internment camps. The Japanese Americans sent to the camps worked primarily in the agriculture fields established in the camps. They grew vegetable crops and raised poultry and cattle for their own consumption and for military posts, and earned one-third the wages that they would have been paid outside the camps. Japanese Americans lost almost $400 million in property because of their internment. Ironically, the Japanese in Hawaii, who were 37 percent of the population, with few exceptions, were not interned during the war. They were more critical to the island's economy than Japanese workers were to the economy of the West Coast.

From the 1950s to the 1990s

The civil rights movement of the late 1950s and early 1960s together with the Immigration Act of 1965 affected minority workers as profoundly as the changes during World War II. In 1961, President John F. Kennedy issued Executive Order #10925 requiring federal contractors to file periodic reports indicating compliance with nondiscrimination in employment and establishing the principle of affirmative action. Title VII of the 1964 Civil Rights Act set up the Equal Employment Opportunity Commission with power to seek legal remedy against discrimination by companies or unions.

With mechanization of farming and the growth of agribusiness, there was less demand for agricultural workers. Most minority workers by the 1960s were in clerical, manufacturing, and service positions. They started to move into the primary labor market, but at the lower end. At a time when greater opportunity existed for those minority workers able to find employment, their labor-force participation rates declined. In 1920, for example, 81.1 percent of African American men were in the labor force, but they comprised only 66.7 percent of the labor force by 1980. A similar decline occurred for Chinese and Filipino men who had labor-force participation rates of 87 percent and 96.5 percent respectively in 1920, but only 74.3 percent and 77.6 percent by 1980. While the labor force participation rates for minority males decreased, they increased for all women, especially white women. In 1920, 19.5 percent of white women were in the labor force, a figure that grew to 49.4 percent by 1980. Greater competition for jobs, especially with the entry of more women into the labor force, has led to a decline in minority labor force participation. Moreover, the loss of traditional unskilled and semi-skilled positions has also affected minorities in the labor force. The rate of labor force participation for African American women has continued to rise, but it has been outstripped by

Japanese, Chinese, and Filipino women, who bring higher educational qualifications to the market.

Minority workers since the 1960s have experienced contradictory trends. Between 1970 and 1986, the proportion of black families with incomes over $35,000 per year has grown but the percentage of black families with incomes under $10,000 per year has also increased. A man or a woman, regardless of race or ethnicity, with high-quality education or skills generally enjoys equal access at least to entry level and mid-range positions in the primary sector of the labor market. Many Asian immigrants after the 1965 Immigration Act, which eliminated racial and ethnic quotas, came from the professional class and immigrated as families.

Filipinos, who are now the largest Asian group in the United States, have the most highly educated women in the country. Forty-one percent of them have college or advanced degrees. They are heavily concentrated in the health-diagnosing and treatment occupations and work as doctors, dentists, pharmacists, and nurses. Filipino women also had the highest median income level of all women in 1980.

Forty-nine percent of recent Chinese immigrants, the second largest Asian group, have been managers, professionals, and technical workers. In 1980, a larger percentage of Chinese American men and women (44 percent and 30 percent) had college degrees than white men and women (21 percent and 13 percent).

Japanese are the third largest Asian group and have one of the highest family income levels, due primarily to the high labor force participation of Japanese women (exceeded only by Filipino women).

Vietnamese, the fourth largest Asian group, came to the United States in two waves. The first immigrants arrived in 1975, after the fall of South Vietnam. The earlier immigrants were generally well educated, could often speak English, were Christian, and they had worked closely with the Americans in South Vietnam during the war years. The second wave's were more diverse, many of them peasants and fishermen. They have been employed in the United States in agriculture, craft, operative, fishing, and service positions.

Koreans make up the fifth largest Asian group. They, too, have been highly educated at home and find themselves underemployed in the United States. Many Korean nurses and physicians have had to work as orderlies and medical assistants, while improving their language skills and studying to pass professional licensing examinations. According to a 1983 study, 78 percent of the Korean greengrocers in New York City had college degrees. They found a niche in the retail produce business, replacing older white merchants who retired or moved to the suburbs. In New York City, by 1980, Koreans owned three-quarters of the greengrocery stores. Most brought capital with them to start businesses or borrowed it from Korean American credit-rotating organizations.

Asian Indians, the sixth largest Asian group, increased their population in the United States from 10,000 in 1965 to more than half a million by 1985. The new Asian Indian immigrants come primarily from the professional class. Among Asian groups, they have the lowest percentage working in services and the highest percentage in professional and managerial positions. They have found a niche in the hospitality industry; in 1980, they owned almost a third of the hotels and motels in the United States.

Similar to African Americans, Asian American communities have become bipolar with a growing entrepreneurial-professional middle class and a stagnating underclass in the secondary and tertiary sectors of the labor market. In 1980, 51 percent of employed Chinese immigrants worked in menial service and low-skilled blue-collar jobs. They generally live in the Chinatowns of the big cities, where unemployment and impoverishment run high. In 1980, 25 percent of New York's Chinatown population lived in poverty. Although Filipinos have a high proportion of college graduates, Filipino-Americans have twice the high school dropout rate and lower enrollments in higher education than other Asian Americans.

A similar profile exists for the Latino population in the United States. Chicanos form the largest Latino group. They are concentrated primarily in the Southwest but also live in the Midwest. Because Chicanos move easily between the United States and Mexico, they have remained a reserve employment army. As Chicano agricultural laborers have organized unions to press for better pay and working conditions, growers have turned increasingly to Southeast Asian and Caribbean workers. Locked in the barrios of the Southwest, Chicanos in the main have become casual laborers, hired for part-time and seasonal work. Only about a third of Chicanos graduate from high school in the United States and less than 4 percent complete four years or more of college.

The second largest Latino group, Puerto Ricans, present a comparable picture. Perhaps because of their easy and frequent movement between the island and the mainland, they too have remained a reserve army of labor. While agriculture has diminished as the major employer, over half the island's work force is semi-skilled or unskilled. Most Puerto Ricans in the United States live in New York City, which had a Puerto Rican population of 1 million in 1983. They toil largely in the garment industry and as service workers. Over one-third of U.S. Puerto Rican families live in poverty, a higher rate than for any minority group. Next to Chicanos, they have the worst high school dropout rate.

The most prosperous Latinos, Cubans, are the third largest group. After the Cuban Revolution in 1958, approximately 10 percent of Cuba's population left the country. Professionals made up almost half the immigrants in the United States. Cuban immigrants to the United States after 1960 resembled western European immigrants more than Latinos. A disproportionately high number of businessmen, entrepreneurs, and professionals left Cuba. They were more urban than rural. Although about three-fifths of Cuba's population was considered white, almost 95 percent of the Cubans in the United States by 1970 classified themselves as white. By 1980, there were over 800,000 Cubans in the United States; Miami became the second largest Cuban city after Havana. In Miami, Cubans started numerous businesses, such as grocery stores, restaurants, banks, furniture manufacturing plants, garment plants, and cigar factories. The number of businesses owned by Cubans in Miami grew from 919 in 1967 to 18,000 by 1980. Cubans had the highest median family income of all Latinos and higher family incomes than African Americans. Initially Cubans came to the United States as sojourners, similar to Asian immigrants before World War II. Cubans left as families, however, not as single men. As of 1970, only 10 percent of Miami's Cubans were citizens, but by 1980, the figure rose to a third, with 86.4 percent of the noncitizens indicating that they planned to become citizens. Not all Cubans enjoyed prosperity; 17 percent of Cuban families were below the poverty line in 1980, with most impoverished Cubans living in the New York City area.

In Miami, Cuban immigrants started such businesses as grocery stores, restaurants, banks, furniture manufacturing plants, garment plants, and cigar factories. The number of businesses owned by Cubans in Miami grew from 919 in 1967 to 18,000 by 1980.

Chicanos, Puerto Ricans, and Cubans have been joined by Latinos from Central America, who came to the United States in large numbers only after 1950. Civil unrest and economic conditions increased immigration, both legal and illegal, of El Salvadoreans, Dominicans, Panamanians, Guatemalans, and Hondurans. By the mid 1980s, almost half a million Salvadoreans lived on the West Coast, primarily in Los Angeles. About half a million Dominicans resided on the East Coast, with 90 percent in New York City. Four-fifths of the Dominicans worked in semi-skilled and unskilled jobs in textile mills, as machine operators, in restaurants and hotels, and as janitors, domestic servants, and maintenance workers.

The relative prosperity of some minority workers and their entry into job categories previously closed to them might suggest the end of a labor market segmented along racial and ethnic lines. Los Angeles in 1940, for example, did not have a single Japanese American employed as a fireman, policeman, mailman, or public school teacher. Today, it is in the public sector that minority workers have found greatest access to employment. The shift of the United States economy from an industrial to a technological base has had as great an effect on minority workers as the change from an agricultural to an industrial economy. Unskilled and semiskilled minority workers have suffered from the exodus of big business to the suburbs. The central cities have become more dependent on a service economy that requires professional qualifications. Even with professional qualifications, however, race and ethnicity remain salient aspects of employment. Asian American men have joined the primary sector of the labor market but generally in mid-range and lower tier jobs. They hold more technical than managerial or executive positions. While white women are more likely to work as secretaries, women of color are more apt to be typists, keypunch operators, and file clerks.

African American male college graduates have higher unemployment rates and lower median incomes than their white counterparts. In 1989, the unemployment rate for college-educated black men aged twenty-five to sixty-four was about three times that of white men. Black male college graduates were also more likely to be underemployed than whites; almost a third of black men with college degrees were in occupations that do not require a college education compared with 14 percent of white men. Nearly half of white male professionals worked in higher paying primary jobs, while only a third of black male professionals held similar positions. The idea that the economic gap between blacks and whites is closing holds true more for women than for men, that is, when we compare black with white women. Part of the reason for such difference is that the labor market remains segmented along gender lines, with women, like men of color, holding lower

Table 2

DISTRIBUTION OF WORKERS ACROSS LABOR MARKET SEGMENTS, BY RACIAL-ETHNIC GROUP AND GENDER, 1980

	Upper-Tier Primary	Lower-Tier Primary	Total Primary	Upper-Tier Secondary	Lower-Tier Secondary	Total Secondary
WOMEN						
American Indian	18	8	26	45	28	73
Chicana	11	7	18	52	30	82
European American	23	8	31	51	18	69
African American	15	7	22	46	32	78
Japanese American	23	9	32	48	20	68
Chinese American	24	10	34	51	15	66
Filipina American	15	19	34	46	19	65
Island Puerto Rican	24	8	32	51	18	69
U.S. Puerto Rican	13	8	21	60	19	79
MEN						
American Indian	19	39	58	19	23	42
Chicano	12	33	45	24	31	55
European American	34	34	68	19	13	32
African American	14	32	46	26	28	54
Japanese American	41	25	66	16	17	33
Chinese American	43	17	60	16	25	41
Filipino American	24	25	49	26	24	50
Island Puerto Rican	24	33	57	22	21	43
U.S. Puerto Rican	14	28	42	33	25	58

Source: Teresa Amott and Julie Matthaei, *Race, Gender, and Work: A Multicultural Economist History of Women in the United States*, 1991, pp. 339, 340.

paying positions in the primary sector. All women are likely to face a dual-wage scale for work similar to that performed by all men. Black women in 1984, for example, earned 97 percent of the weekly wages of white women, 78 percent of those of black men, but only 53 percent of those of white men.

Since the mid 1970s, employment has shifted to industries in which minority participation, especially African American and Latino, has been and remains low. Additionally, businesses have moved to areas of the country, especially the Sunbelt, where wages are lower, fringe benefits are less, and unions are absent or weak. Black family median income, after rising from 54 percent of white family median income in the 1950s to 61.5 percent in 1975, fell to 57 percent by 1986. Latino family median income, 66.9 percent of white family median income in 1975 dropped to 65.2 percent by 1985.

For many African Americans and Latinos, the military has been an alternative to poor employment opportunities in civilian life. In 1986, 30 percent of the army, 20 percent of the Marines, 17 percent of the air force, and 14 percent of the navy was African American; 32 percent of the female enlistees in the army were African American. Black enlistees in the army had a higher educational level than whites and reenlisted more frequently. When recent veterans were asked to compare military and civilian life, African Americans rated the military more positively than whites. With the thawing of Cold War tensions, this employment option will probably become less viable for minority workers.

In 1988, 14 percent of all adults and 20 percent of all children under the age of seventeen were people of color. By the year 2000, one-third of all school-age American children and one-third of the net additions to the U.S. labor force will be people of color. The U.S. economy will become more dependent on minority workers in the primary sector of the labor market. The bipolarization of the minority work force into those with educational achievement and marketable skills and those with little education and few skills will pose as great a challenge to the labor market as its segmentation along racial, ethnic, and gender lines, which restricted occupational and economic mobility for most of the twentieth century.

[See also Agriculture; Business Culture; Geographic Mobility; Household Labor; Labor: Colonial Times through 1820; Labor: The Jacksonian Era through Reconstruction; Labor: The Gilded Age through the 1920s; Labor: The Great Depression to the 1990s; Literacy; The Plantation; Public Education; Public Health; Slavery; Women and Work.]

BIBLIOGRAPHY

Amott, Teresa, and Julie Matthaei. *Race, Gender, and Work: A Multicultural Economic History of Women in the United States* (1991).

Baron, Harold M. "The Demand for Black Labor: Historical Notes on the Political Economy of Racism." *Radical America* 5, no. 2 (1971): 1–46.

Boles, John B. *Black Southerners, 1619–1869* (1983).

Bonacich, Edna. "A Theory of Ethnic Antagonism: The Split Labor Market." *American Sociological Review* 37, no. 5 (1972): 547–559.

———. "Abolition, the Extension of Slavery, and the Position of Free Blacks: A Study of Split Labor Markets in the United States, 1830–1863." *American Journal of Sociology* 81, no. 3 (1975): 601–628.

———. "Advanced Capitalism and Black/White Race Relations in the United States: A Split Labor Market Interpretation." *American Sociological Review* 41, no. 1 (1976): 34–51.

Dickerson, Dennis C. *Out of the Crucible: Black Steelworkers in Western Pennsylvania, 1875–1980* (1986).

Gann, L. H., and Peter J. Duignan. *The Hispanics in the United States: A History* (1986).

Harris, William H. *The Harder We Run: Black Workers Since the Civil War* (1982).

Jaynes, Gerald David, and Robin M. Williams, Jr., eds. *A Common Destiny: Blacks and American Society* (1989).

Jones, Jacqueline. *Labor of Love, Labor of Sorrow: Black Women, Work, and the Family from Slavery to the Present* (1985).

Lewis, Ronald L. *Coal, Iron, and Slaves: Industrial Slavery in Maryland and Virginia, 1715–1865* (1979).

Loewen, James W. *The Mississippi Chinese: Between Black and White* (1971).

Loewenberg, Bert James. "Efforts of the South to Encourage Immigration, 1865–1900." *South Atlantic Quarterly* 33, no. 4 (1934): 363–385.

Meisenheimer, Joseph R., II. "Black College Graduates in the Labor Market, 1979 and 1989." *Monthly Labor Review* 113, no. 11 (1990).

Mirandé, Alfredo. *The Chicano Experience: An Alternative Perspective* (1985).

One Third of a Nation: A Report of the Commission on Minority Participation in Education and American Life (1988).

Stampp, Kenneth M. *The Peculiar Institution: Slavery in the Antebellum South* (1956).

Starobin, Robert S. *Industrial Slavery in the Old South* (1970).

Takaki, Ronald. *Strangers from a Different Shore: A History of Asian Americans* (1989).

Trotter, Joe William, Jr., ed. *The Great Migration in Historical Perspective: New Dimensions of Race, Class, and Gender* (1991).

Wade, Richard C. *Slavery in the Cities: The South, 1820–1860* (1964).

MORALITY

See *SEXUAL BEHAVIOR AND MORALITY*

MUSIC, AFRICAN-AMERICAN

See *AFRICAN-AMERICAN MUSIC*

MUSIC, CONCERT

See *CONCERT MUSIC*

MUSIC, COUNTRY

See *COUNTRY AND WESTERN MUSIC*

MUSIC, FOLK

See *FOLK SONG AND FOLK MUSIC*

MUSIC, ROCK

See *ROCK MUSIC*

MUSIC, POPULAR

See *POPULAR MUSIC BEFORE 1950*

MUSICAL THEATER

See *THEATER AND MUSICAL THEATER*

N

NATIONAL PARKS AND PRESERVATION

Contrary to popular understanding, the national parks of the United States do not exist solely to protect tracts of wild, unspoiled nature like Yellowstone and the Grand Canyon. While preservation of nature was an important historical reason for their establishment, national parks preserve not only wilderness areas but also significant cultural landscapes and historic sites, like industrial structures in Lowell, Massachusetts. These twin purposes—preservation of nature and conservation of heritage—have shaped the evolution of the idea of the national parks.

Originating in a nineteenth-century quest for a distinct American identity, the idea of national parks was transformed by twentieth-century interest in the country's ecological and cultural heritage. Initially, the national parks were designed to afford legal protection to areas considered significant for their scenic, patriotic, or recreational value. Recently, calculations about the utility of parks only to people have been supplemented by biocentric considerations of a park's contribution to ecological stability and continuity. Increasingly, national parks in the United States are seen as biological preserves and heritage landscapes as much as scenic playgrounds.

The Shifting Philosophy of Preservation

No grand design guided the growth of the national park system. It developed as a random collection of natural, historical, and recreational properties, and the American philosophy of preservation evolved similarly, in fits and starts.

The haphazard origins of the park idea are illustrated by the ambiguity of identifying the first national park in the United States. While Yellowstone National Park (1872) is usually accorded the distinction, federal action had previously established two other natural reserves. As early as 1832, the national government had set aside an Arkansas hot spring as a "reservation," chiefly for its medicinal value. And, in 1864, Congress ceded the Yosemite Valley and the nearby Mariposa Grove of giant redwoods to the state of California for permanent management as a state park, a public assertion of a national interest in scenic preservation.

In its original usage, the designation "national park" resulted from bureaucratic convenience rather than a federal commitment to nature preservation. The term was first applied to the Yellow-stone reserve created in the territories of Wyoming and Montana in 1872. Since no state government existed to which park administration might he shifted, as in the case of the Yosemite cession, responsibility devolved to the federal government for the preserve it carved from the territorial public domain. The burden was assumed rather grudgingly. At first no federal funds were allocated to administer the new national park, and, for its first forty-four years, the preserve was managed by the United States Army, until the National Park Service was created within the Department of the Interior in 1916.

Many people believe that national parks were created to protect wilderness. While this motive is a common rationale for national parks today, it was by no means the initial—and certainly not the only—reason for the American interest in nature preserves. Nationalistic pride, a new landscape aesthetic, the conservation movement, a recreational revolution, and ecological perspectives all shaped the evolving philosophy of nature protection. Preservation of historic and cultural resources followed a related but distinct route into the national parks.

PATRIOTISM AND AMERICAN IDENTITY. The impetus for national parks was rooted in the preoccupation of nineteenth-century Americans with their cultural identity as a nation. Originating shortly after the Revolution among intellectual and social elites, the search to define national distinctiveness became an exercise in patriotic virtue in the course of the century. To those drawing transatlantic comparisons, the United States lacked the traditional monuments of high culture from which European societies derived a sense of collective identity and history. But under the influence of European romanticism and American transcendentalism, cultural critics proclaimed natural scenery a source of American uniqueness and therefore pride. The timelessness of nature's monuments might compensate for the absence of civilization's antiquities.

As war and diplomacy extended the national boundaries to the Pacific by mid century, curiosity about the rugged geography of the Far West became a potent incentive for nature preservation. The dramatic topography of the Sierra Nevada and the Rockies fired the popular imagination. Thus, when Congress debated the Yosemite cession and the Yellowstone reserve in the

1860s and 1870s, interest focused on scenic marvels like the majestic drop of Yosemite's waterfalls and the thermal novelty of Yellowstone's geysers. Congressional proponents (and their railroad allies, anxious to stimulate tourist interest in the West) argued that such "natural curiosities" were national treasures to be protected for public enjoyment. Significantly, in terms of the development of a philosophy of preservation, the scenic—not the wild—qualities of the landscape were identified as worthy of national recognition.

The public domain of the West provided the means, as well as the inspiration, for the American invention of the national park. The sheer size of the public lands made possible nature preserves of remarkable scale, two million acres in the case of Yellowstone. Well into the twentieth century, the creation of a national park could involve a transfer of land from one federal agency to another, rather than an expensive real estate purchase.

In the creation of Yosemite National Park in 1890, a new and powerful rationale for preservation emerged: the idea that wilderness itself was useful and therefore worth protecting.

Outside the West, the absence of public lands retarded establishment of national parks, and, as a result, private philanthropy played a crucial role in the authorization of the first national parks in the East and the South. The first eastern park, Acadia on Maine's Mount Desert Island, was not established until 1919 and was a gift from wealthy summer residents of the Bar Harbor area. In the South, Great Smoky Mountains and Shenandoah parks were both authorized in 1926 and established in the 1930s. At Acadia, Great Smoky, and Shenandoah, the philanthropy of John D. Rockefeller, Jr. (1874—1960), augmented the campaigns for public subscriptions. Rockefeller continued to underwrite public (and even federal) efforts at park creation through the 1950s.

Curiosity and pride in the scenic and geological wonders of North America have provided the most consistent rationale for nature preservation in the United States. The appeal of visually spectacular topography animated the earliest proponents of the national park idea, and it has continued to inspire Americans to set aside mountain peaks like Hawaii Volcanoes (1916) and North Cascades (1968), gorges like Zion (1909) and Canyonlands (1964), and surrealistic landforms like Bryce Canyon (1923) and Badlands National Monument (1929).

A TASTE FOR WILDNESS. In the circumstances surrounding the creation of Yosemite National Park (1890), a new and powerful rationale for preservation emerged: the idea that wilderness itself was useful and therefore worth protecting. As much as anyone in his generation, the California naturalist John Muir (1838–1914), encouraged Americans to identify wild nature as a complement to civilization. Like transcendentalists earlier in the century, Muir found contact with nature rejuvenating to the body and enlightening for the soul. In contrast to most transcendentalist writing, however, Muir's nature essays were best-sellers. A "back to nature" impulse had seized many middle-class Americans by the turn of the century. The panoramic landscapes painted by Albert Bierstadt (1830—1902) and Thomas Moran (1837—1926) of the Rocky Mountain school, the new art of landscape photography pioneered by William Henry Jackson (1843—1942) and Carleton Watkins (1829—1916), and sundry works of exploration and nature fiction by John Wesley Powell (1834—1902) and Ernest Thompson Seton (1860—1946), among others, all testified to the discovery of wild nature in American popular culture.

Those who expressed enthusiasm for wildness did not face it from the perspective of the homesteader or lumberjack. They were people who could visit it voluntarily and temporarily and did not have to make a living there. As much as anything, it was the ability to contemplate wild nature from the safety and comfort of the city that diluted traditional animosities about wilderness. Rather than the antithesis of civilization and progress, raw nature became an antidote and complement to modern life. The taste for wildness was also rooted temporally, in nostalgia. The celebration of wild nature occurred as Americans contemplated the closing of the frontier, a historical and geographical boundary that many, including the historian Frederick Jackson Turner, had come to associate with the formation of the national character. Through nostalgic mists, preservation of the disappearing wilderness seemed to promise a living link with the pioneer past.

These emerging sensibilities offered receptive ground for John Muir's appeals for wilderness preservation. In 1890 Muir published a series of articles in *Century* magazine that urged protection of the Sierra Nevada high country beyond the previously reserved Yosemite Valley. The Yosemite National Park created in 1890 at Muir's urging was not the first national park in the country, nor even the first park in the Yosemite region, but it was the first park consciously designed to protect wilderness as a valuable quality in its own right.

The naturalist John Muir (1838–1914) encouraged Americans to identify wild nature as a complement to civilization. This photograph shows Muir with conservationist Theodore Roosevelt at Yosemite National Park.

In the late twentieth century, the Yosemite precedent culminated in three pieces of landmark legislation: the Wilderness Act (1964), which sought to protect undeveloped and roadless regions throughout the public domain; the Wild and Scenic Rivers Act (1968), which established a national system of free-flowing rivers; and the Alaska National Interest Lands Conservation Act (1980), which set aside 104 million acres of the Alaskan wilderness. The Alaska lands act alone doubled the size of the national park system and illustrated how preservation of wilderness had become an American priority by the eve of the centennial of Yosemite National Park.

THE CONSERVATION MOVEMENT. A major misconception about national parks is that they enjoy protection "forever"; in fact, the boundaries, acreage, and uses of national parks are transitory. This quality of impermanence is a legacy of the turn-of-the-century conservation movement and its utilitarian approach to natural resources.

The distinction between national parks and national forests is an important difference that illuminates much about the place of national parks within the history of conservation. While both are federal reserves, each is rooted in a separate resource philosophy: preservation of unaltered nature in the case of national parks, use of natural resources in the case of national forests. Unlike national parks, with their emphasis on outdoor recreation, national forests are "lands of many uses" that permit lumbering, mining, reclamation, and grazing, as well as recreation (including hunting, which is prohibited in national parks).

For turn-of-the-century conservationists like Theodore Roosevelt and his chief forester, Gifford Pinchot, national forests embodied the best of the utilitarian conservation idea: wise management of the public domain through the planned and efficient development of natural resources. Utilitarians operated within a materialist framework that viewed nature as a collection of commodities useful in production. While preservationists like John Muir spoke of forests as cathedrals where people went for spiritual insight and refreshment, utilitarians like Gifford Pinchot (1865—1946) regarded forests as factories that should produce lumber in an efficient and rational manner.

The national parks have been a bureaucratic entity separate from the national forests for some time, but the utilitarian doctrine nevertheless affected the politics of parks by tempering the tendency to absolute preservation. To meet the argument that productive land should not be locked up, advocates of national parks have been obliged to point out the economic marginality of the lands they sought to preserve. The complex compromises that preceded establishment of parks reflected this utilitarian perspective. Resource development clauses have been routinely inserted in the enabling legislation of major national parks to permit activities like mining, reclamation, forestry, grazing, railroads, or settlement, should it eventually be decided that such land use was in the national interest.

Perhaps the most celebrated instance of society redefining parklands occurred in 1913, when the federal government authorized a dam and reservoir in the Hetch Hetchy Valley of Yosemite National Park. Similar controversies have occurred in other parks in subsequent decades, as in a proposal in the 1960s to permit a reservoir to flood the Colorado River in the Grand Canyon. Despite the widespread public impression, preservation of nature in the United States has seldom represented permanent protection, even in the national parks.

OUTDOOR RECREATION AND AFFLUENCE. Closely tied to the nation's conservation battles and the emergence of a wilderness aesthetic were social changes that linked outdoor recreation with the good life. By the 1920s the growth in real wages, the invention of the annual vacation, and broadening automobile ownership permitted the middle class to appropriate the national parks. Heeding Theodore Roosevelt's exhortations about the utility of "the strenuous life" in an overcivilized world, hardy urbanites formed mountaineering groups, adventuresome youth joined the Boy Scouts, and countless others embraced the pleasures of tenting and automobile tourism.

The national parks themselves changed to accommodate the growing numbers of hikers, campers, and tourists. Initially nature tourism was the prerogative of the few, the rich, and the well-born, who traveled to stylish railroad hotels near the most notable scenic wonders. In contrast, middle-class visitors, who arrived in national parks by car, wanted good roads and convenient campgrounds.

The task of recreational development fell to the National Park Service. The Park Service had been created in 1916 to provide for the public in the parks, while also conserving the scenery. Some of the wild rawness of parks disappeared, as the Park Service fashioned highways and trails to provide safe and democratic access, erected interpretive facilities to educate and inform city folk, and built accommodations to feed and house the millions who eventually made the pilgrimage to parks each summer. In time, popular demands introduced tourist villages, complete with carnival amusements like bear feedings and the night illumination of scenic wonders.

While it has become commonplace today to point out that recreational development in parks has triumphed over sound biological management, it is important to remember that visitors provided a base of popular support and an economic rationale for the nascent national park system. The first director of the National Park Service, the influential Stephen Tyng Mather (1867—1930), was an enthusiastic advocate of mass recreation who worked assiduously to promote visitation and to cultivate a constituency for parks. When permission for automobiles to enter parks stirred debate in the 1910s and 1920s, Mather endorsed their use because cars got people to the parks and the entrance fees provided a source of government revenue. To accommodate wide-ranging public tastes, Mather encouraged private concessionaires to build hotels, stores, and transportation systems, as he championed the growth of a western tourist industry. The visitor, the automobile, and the concessionaire were democratizing forces that opened the national parks as never before.

But this legacy has been problematic. The modern paradox that Americans are loving the national parks to death reflects both the popularity of outdoor recreation in an affluent society and the institutional reluctance of the Park Service to ignore popular demands. The dilemma became especially acute following a period of recreational expansion in the 1950s and 1960s. Postwar affluence and population growth intensified demographic pressures on parks, and the Park Service responded with its traditional policy of accommodation, in the form of a massive ten-year construction program known as Mission 66. Completed in 1966 to mark the fiftieth anniversary of the National Park Service, the project attracted criticism for its enormous budgets, recreational overdevelopment, and even its abandonment of the rustic style popularized in park architecture by the Civilian Conservation Corps in the 1930s. By the 1970s and 1980s, many environmentalist critics had become convinced that parks-built-for-visitors threatened to uproot and replace parks-built-by-nature.

ECOLOGICAL PERSPECTIVES. The authorization of Everglades National Park in 1934 marked an important turning point in the history of the national parks. In the Florida Everglades, a national park was created primarily for reasons of biological preservation, to protect the wildlife and vegetation of a forty-mile-wide "river of grass." Habitat and animate scenery, rather than the physical endowments of visually striking landscapes, provided the pretext for preservation. Although land acquisition was slow in the new park and its borders never encompassed the entire watershed, Everglades suggested a fresh attitude toward nature preservation.

The idea of establishing national parks to protect ecological systems for their own sake has gained considerable currency in recent years. In debates over the future of the public lands of Alaska in the 1970s, for example, advocates of wilderness preserves argued that the proposed parks should have biological integrity. They lobbied for scientifically meaningful boundaries that would enclose whole watersheds and entire animal migration routes. The ecological perspective is also evident in discussions to reserve natural systems illustrative of all North American life zones. The prairies and plains of mid America, for instance, are preserved nowhere in the

The 1934 authorization of Florida's Everglades National Park was an important turning point. For the first time in U.S. history, a national park was created primarily for reasons of biological preservation.

national park system. That "representative" areas should be considered for national parks testifies to how far the philosophy of nature preservation has moved since nineteenth-century proponents made their case on the distinctive scenic qualities of Yosemite and Yellowstone.

Within existing parks, biocentric management has also attracted attention. As early as the 1930s biologists began pointing out that public recreation was compromising the protection of park wildlife, but the so-called Leopold Report of 1963 stirred the most discussion. The report urged a fundamental shift in thinking about parks, from a preoccupation with inanimate resources (like scenic vistas) to a program of managing ecological processes (through a proposal to restore the pre-European biology of major national parks). No such sweeping commitment was subsequently made to turn back the clock on four hundred years of environmental change, but incremental efforts at ecological restoration are evident in projects to reintroduce native species, as well as the current view of forest fires as a benign natural phenomenon that should not be suppressed in national parks. In these ways, the philosophy of preservation has been recently interpreted as a mandate for restoration.

CULTURAL PRESERVATION. Protection of unaltered nature was not the only form of preservation associated with the national parks. Heritage conservation—the preservation of historic and cultural resources—has been a responsibility of the national park system since the turn of the century. Today the role of the National Park Service in the field of historic preservation has broadened to include not only stewardship of the built environment of national parks but also administration of federal heritage programs unrelated to the parks, such as the National Register of Historic Places.

Federal involvement in cultural preservation evolved reluctantly, stimulated initially by patriotic pride and misgivings about vandalism on the public domain. In the 1890s, in response to pressure from veterans' groups, the War Department began efforts to set aside commemorative landscapes like Civil War battlefields and military cemeteries. Only slightly earlier, in 1889, Congress had authorized protection of a site in Arizona to protect its prehistoric ruins from looters.

Systematic federal protection of historic sites, though, began with passage of the Antiquities Act (1906) and establishment of Mesa Verde National Park (1906). As with the campaign on behalf of Yellowstone in the 1870s, the immediate stimulus for federal action was concern about private appropriation of what was seen as a valuable national treasure, in this case the recently discovered cliff dwellings and artifacts of precontact Indian societies in the Southwest. The Antiquities Act prohibited destruction of historic and prehistoric objects on the public lands and authorized the president to preserve archaeological, historic, and scientific sites as national monuments. By 1933, when a number of federal preserves were consolidated under the jurisdiction of the National Park Service, the historic properties in the national park system were largely commemorative sites associated with great deeds and famous men: revolutionary war and Civil War battlefields, military cemeteries and forts, presidential birthplaces, and memorials like Ford's Theatre and the Washington Monument.

Depression in the 1930s moved the federal government more vigorously into the field of historic preservation. New Deal legislation envisioned a significant federal responsibility for protecting the country's architectural heritage and authorized a number of labor-intensive projects to carry out this enlarged role. Through the Historic American Buildings Survey, for example, one thousand unemployed architects were hired for a nationwide inventory of vernacular and elite buildings. Similarly, the Civilian Conservation Corps employed hundreds of historians and technicians for its restoration projects at historical parks. Particularly significant was the Historic Sites Act of 1935, which defined an expanded mission in cultural preservation for the National Park Service, especially to survey, acquire, research, restore, and operate historic sites and structures. The act decisively shaped the historic preservation movement in the United States and conferred a leading role on the National Park Service.

The National Historic Preservation Act (1966) grew out of concern about the impact of urban renewal and the federal interstate highway program on American cities. While this far-reaching act did not focus on the national parks specifically, it did involve the National Park Service in new and significant ways in historic preservation, particularly through its administration of the National Register of Historic Places. As the nation's official list of cultural properties worthy of preservation, the register was to be a potent incentive for heritage conservation both nationally and locally. Amendments in 1980 to the National Historic Preservation Act called for a set of cultural parks within the national park system, an endorsement of a trend that began in the 1970s when a number of urban sites and cultural landscapes were set aside, such as in Lowell National Historical Park (1978) and Ebey's Landing National Historical Reserve (1978).

The Varieties of Parks

The role of parks in the stewardship of the nation's natural and cultural heritage broadened dramatically in the late twentieth century, transforming the conventional meaning of the national park idea. The traditional focus on wilderness areas and commemorative shrines linked to political and military events has expanded to include an array of cultural landscapes that seek to preserve the social and industrial heritage of the entire nation. As the philosophy of preservation has broadened, so, too, have the strategies and methods of protection. Reflecting both the fiscal constraints of tightening budgets and a desire to manage parks with a degree of local participation, the National Park Service has experimented with cooperative land use agreements, as it has eschewed acquisition and outright ownership of parklands.

The national park system is composed of almost four hundred natural, historical, and recreational units that run the gamut from parkways to an international peace garden, all arranged into a plethora of administrative categories that make subtle distinctions between a battlefield and a battlefield park, for example, or a park and a preserve. For a history of the national park idea, though, seven types of reserves under the jurisdiction of the National Park Service illustrate the most significant trends within the shifting preservation impulse: national parks, national monuments, historic sites, urban recreation areas, national historical parks, national historical reserves, and national heritage corridors.

NATIONAL PARKS. Traditionally, national parks have been areas afforded federal protection through an act of Congress, in recognition of their dramatic topography, wild character, or biological significance. The term "national park" was first used to designate the geysers and canyons of the Yellowstone region in 1872, and this reservation inspired the creation of large parks primarily in the American West for over a century. Today, about 90 percent of the acreage of the national park system is set aside as wilderness parks and preserves. Opportunities for creating nature reserves in the United States on the Yellowstone model began to recede in the 1980s, following the creation of Great Basin National Park (1986) in Nevada and the establishment in Alaska of twenty-five new wild and scenic rivers, twelve new national parks and preserves, and eleven new wildlife refuges.

NATIONAL MONUMENTS. The Antiquities Act of 1906 provided that national monuments could be designated by presidential proclamation to protect sites on federal lands with scientific or historical significance, as in the cases of the first two national monuments, Devil's Tower in Wyoming (1906) and Mesa Verde in Colorado (1906). Not until 1933 were all national monuments consolidated under the jurisdiction of the National Park Service. Generally, the designation "national monument" has been used to protect sites prior to their establishment by Congress as national parks. An unwritten sense of hierarchy distinguishes the two categories; thus, a national monument, like the Grand Canyon, set aside by Theodore Roosevelt in 1908, was "elevated" to national park status in 1919 by Congress. The most dramatic, recent use of the Antiquities Act occurred in 1978, at the height of the debate over the public lands of Alaska, when President Jimmy Carter reserved 56 million acres in seventeen new national monuments.

HISTORIC SITES. Large numbers of historic sites were first added to the national park system in the 1930s. Through presidential order in 1933, military sites administered by the War Department and national monuments managed by the Forest Service were transferred to the National Park Service, and the resulting properties were officially designated "the national park system." The addition of historic sites located predominantly in the eastern United States had two important consequences. First, it complemented the existing collection of western nature preserves, making the park system truly national in scope. Second, it emphasized the role of the National Park Service in preserving both the cultural and natural heritage of the United States. Today roughly half of all properties in the park system are sites preserved primarily for their historical significance.

URBAN RECREATION AREAS. Urban recreation areas go by a number of names: national lakeshore, national seashore, national recreation area. Although the first recreation area and seashore were authorized in the 1930s, most of the urban-based recreation areas in the national park system were established in the 1960s and 1970s. These include metropolitan open spaces like Indiana Dunes National Lakeshore (1966) near Chicago, Gateway National Recreation Area (1972) in New York and New Jersey, and the Cuyahoga Valley National Recreation Area (1974) near Cleveland. The idea of locating national recreation areas near cities sprang from congressional interest in urban reform and a desire to bring "the parks to the people," in response to the charge that national parks were remote and elitist preserves for the white middle class. The federal role in urban recreation has remained controversial, both for its redefinition of the national park idea and the hefty price tags associated with land acquisition. (Occasionally this expense has been minimized through land transfers, as in Golden Gate National Recreation Area [1972] in San Francisco.)

NATIONAL HISTORICAL PARKS. Some thirty or so national historical parks have been added to the national park system since establishment of the first at Morristown (1933), a revolutionary war site in New

Jersey. One of the most unusual national historical parks was authorized in 1978 within the city of Lowell, Massachusetts, to facilitate the preservation of the country's early industrial heritage. Through innovative public-private partnerships and cooperative agreements, the National Park Service and community groups have sought to adapt the national park idea in new directions designed to stimulate urban redevelopment through rehabilitation of heritage structures, while minimizing federal ownership. The Lowell model has become a much-studied example of how historic preservation can promote both economic revitalization and heritage tourism.

NATIONAL HISTORICAL RESERVES. One of the first national historical reserves was established by Congress at Whidbey Island, Washington, in 1978 to preserve the agricultural landscape associated with a nineteenth-century rural community. In a novel arrangement, the National Park Service will administer the Ebey's Landing National Historical Reserve only temporarily. When land-use restrictions have been developed, the reserve will be turned over to a unit of local government for management and administration. Most of the land in the reserve will remain as farmland, in private ownership.

NATIONAL HERITAGE CORRIDORS. The heritage corridor represents an effort to integrate preservation of significant cultural landscapes into regional planning and economic development, particularly along the nation's historically industrialized waterways. The first national heritage corridor was established in 1984 outside Chicago, along the Illinois-Michigan Canal. There, and in similar corridors elsewhere, a federally appointed commission seeks to coordinate the interests of landowners and local governments, while encouraging economic development that protects the region's historic and natural resources. As in the Lowell National Historical Park, on which the heritage corridor is modeled, the National Park Service chiefly provides technical assistance, with a minimum of ownership and long-term management.

Future Directions

If their history is any guide to future directions, national parks will continue to evolve, as society deems new aspects of its ecological and cultural heritage worthy of preservation. The idea of a national park has proved a flexible concept, and there is every reason to believe that Americans will continue to find it useful for enhancing the quality of modern life, as they add parcels of natural systems not yet represented in the park system, create international parks that transcend traditional political boundaries, or expand the definition of wilderness to include, perhaps, ocean environments.

[See also The Frontier; Landscapes; The Natural Environment: The North; The Natural Environment: The South; The Natural Environment: The West; Urban Parks.]

BIBLIOGRAPHY

Bartlett, Richard A. *Yellowstone: A Wilderness Besieged* (1985). A recent history of the first national park.

Davis, Richard C., comp. *North American Forest History: A Guide to Archives and Manuscripts in the United States and Canada* (1977).

Foresta, Ronald A. *America's National Parks and Their Keepers* (1984). History and critique of the National Park Service.

Fox, Stephen. *John Muir and His Legacy: The American Conservation Movement* (1981).

Huth, Hans. *Nature and the American: Three Centuries of Changing Attitudes* (1957).

Ise, John. *Our National Park Policy: A Critical History* (1961). Useful for early administrative history.

Murtagh, William J. *Keeping Time: The History and Theory of Historic Preservation in America* (1988). The National Park Service and heritage conservation.

Nash, Roderick. *Wilderness and the American Mind.* 3d ed. (1982). Definitive on parks and the wilderness movement.

National Parks (1919–). The bimonthly magazine of the National Parks and Conservation Association, Washington, D.C.

Newton, Norman T. *Design on the Land: The Development of Landscape Architecture* (1971).

Pomeroy, Earl. *In Search of the Golden West: The Tourist in Western America* (1957). Nature as a recreational attraction.

Runte, Alfred. *National Parks: The American Experience.* 2d ed. (1987). Best historical survey of the national park idea.

Sax, Joseph. *Mountains Without Handrails: Reflections on the National Parks* (1980). Provocative argument against development within national parks.

Schene, Michael G., ed. "The National Park Service and Historic Preservation." *The Public Historian* 9, no. 2 (1987).

Schmitt, Peter J. *Back to Nature: The Arcadian Myth in Urban America* (1969). Parks in the context of popular culture.

Sierra Club Guides to the National Parks. 5 vols. (1984—1986). Introduction to natural and human history of individual parks, regionally arranged.

U.S. Department of the Interior, National Park Service. *Preserving Historic Landscapes: An Annotated Bibliography* (1990).

— ROBERT R. WEYENETH

THE NATURAL ENVIRONMENT: THE NORTH

Over the past four centuries no part of the global environment has been changed more dramatically than the northern United States. What once was a vast forest and grassland inhabited by a native farming and hunting folk has been transformed into the world's largest industrial complex, supporting a dense population of more than one hundred million people linked in a network of sprawling megalopolises and satellite farms and towns. Bears once roamed across what is now the island of Manhattan, loons swam on the ponds of Connecticut, and dark, drifting herds of bison and elk grazed from Chicago to Pittsburgh. Now the only glimpse most northerners have of wild animals comes around the backyard birdfeeder or from a two-week vacation into the countryside. Nature is still a powerful force in their lives, but it has become more impersonal and distant to the point of invisibility: drought lowering the water level in a city reservoir, fungus attacking a corn crop, ice glazing a sidewalk. Nature has yielded an enormous wealth to Americans, but the cost of affluence has been a drastic impoverishment of the natural environment and a high degree of abstractness in human ecological relationships.

The region called the North is more a cultural than a natural entity, defined as it was by the Civil War, but there are some environmental unities to be found. Fronting the Atlantic Ocean in a myriad of bays, islands, and sandy beaches, the North stretches west all the way to the 98th meridian (which passes through the states of North and South Dakota, Nebraska, and Kansas), where the rainfall drops below 20 inches (500 millimeters), too low for European-style agriculture. The Ohio River suggests a southern boundary. Separating the North from Canada is that other "seacoast," the Saint Lawrence River-Great Lakes complex, the largest body of fresh water on earth, which once offered a rich fishery and an indispensable doorway into the continental interior.

Over the past million years this region has been repeatedly scoured by glaciers that penetrated as far south as Long Island in the east and the Missouri River in the west. Only a few areas like Pennsylvania escaped those grinding forces. As the glaciers retreated (the last did so about ten thousand years ago), they left behind a landscape of gravelly moraines, denuded mountains, potholes, and lakes, and a vast till sheet that was thin in New England but hundreds of feet thick in the Midwest. On this foundation both the native and immigrant peoples would build their civilizations.

The Impact of European Arrival

When the Europeans arrived, they found growing over much of this glaciated soil a luxuriant forest, one of the greatest in the world, as extensive as that of Brazil today. Ecologists divide the early forest into two broad provinces, more or less arranged in horizontal bands across the map: the northern or transition forest, comprising coniferous trees—hemlock, balsam fir, white pine—and such deciduous species as the sugar maple, American basswood, and yellow birch; and the mixed deciduous forest, populated by at least thirty major species, ranging from oaks, hickories, and maples to yellow poplar, white ash, chestnut, and black cherry. Accounts differ as to how thick those early forests were; some observers found them dark and gloomy, others open and parklike, a condition they attributed to Indian burning practices. Unquestionably, the natives fired them to encourage new grass growth and draw their prey closer to their habitations and to open up clearings of such cultivars as corn, beans, pumpkins, and tobacco. The northern environment supported hundreds of thousands of these first Americans, and at least one large city, Cahokia, in present-day Illinois, long before the white people came.

But despite these important human presences, the European newcomers were most impressed by the extent and grandeur, the power and richness, of the forest. They called it a "wilderness," meaning a nature beyond human control, inhabited by dangerous creatures; and in the minds of early Puritan clergymen, that howling wilderness became a common metaphor for an ungodly, unruly world needing Christian cultivation. Paradoxically, that same wilderness appealed to poor refugees from a Europe that had cleared away much of its own forest many centuries earlier. They found in the New World an endless supply of the most important natural resource, after soil, that they needed to create a prosperous life for themselves: wood. The forest provided plenty of fuel, and they cut immense woodpiles to keep themselves warm through the long northern winters. The forest also offered building materials for their houses, barns, churches, and fences, as well as for an overflowing cornucopia of the miscellaneous necessities of life—plows, rakes, bowls, ladles, wagons, gristmills, boats and ships, foodstuffs like game, sugar and nuts, pegs, caskets, bridges—even coins. The first promise of American abundance came from the forest, a promise that would take centuries of use to spoil and deplete.

Everywhere they went the European Americans tried to recreate the agricultural environment they had left behind in the Old World. They divided the country into estates of private property, irregularly shaped at first, following the contours of river and hill, but west of the Appalachians more regularized by federal surveyors, who imposed a rigid cadastral (property boundary) grid on the diverse lay of the land. To populate their properties the invading farmers introduced not only familiar crops and weeds but also a horde of domesticated animals, including sheep, cattle, pigs, and horses, all of which would radically alter the indigenous vegetation and fauna. They chopped down trees at a prodigious rate; before 1850 Americans cleared over 100 million acres (40 million hectares), and in the peak decade of clearance, 1850 to 1859, cleared almost 40 million acres (16 million hectares) more. These changes in the landscape, made with so little restraint, so little sense of what was being lost, added up to an ecological revolution. Whole species became extinct, such as the passenger pigeon, which once migrated in flocks as thick as clouds, as noisy as thunder, flocks numbering, by one reckoning, as many as four billion birds. Wild turkeys, beaver, wolves, mountain lions, wolverines, caribou, even deer disappeared. By the mid nineteenth century almost every acre in the state of Massachusetts had been cut over at least once, and men and women began to feel the pinch of scarcity. Wood, land, and game alike were harder and harder to come by cheaply.

Farther west the forest thinned naturally, making axes increasingly unnecessary, until eventually in Illinois, southern Minnesota, Iowa, northern Missouri, Kansas, Nebraska, and the Dakotas the landscape became the tall-grass prairie, almost devoid of trees. Away from the wooded river valleys the vegetation was dominated by big bluestem and Indian grass, both growing up to 8 feet high (2.5 meters), and by switchgrass. This was an environment that their European agricultural heritage did not prepare white farmers to settle or understand. Some wondered whether it offered a fertility equal to forest soils. Others argued that the grassland would have been covered with trees too if the Indians had not burned it, a view that held some truth but underestimated the role of a drier climate. Whatever the origin of the grassland, it posed a challenge to a society used to enjoying and exploiting a wealth of forests. Although the grassland would eventually offer its own kind of natural abundance, soils of far greater depth and humus content than those of the forest, settlers would take a while to discover that fact and turn it to their advantage. Had it not been for a continuing boom in Europe's population, forcing millions to look abroad for their living, that discovery might have been delayed indefinitely.

The Force of Industrial Capitalism

But a force beyond demography was pushing the white settlers forward in their relation to the land, the force of a rising and expanding industrial capitalism, which would profoundly alter people's use of nature in America and throughout the world. Its greatest achievement, and yet its most destructive, was to develop new sources of energy that could run factories, run railroads, and run the commodities of the land back and forth to consumers. The first such source was falling water, the second was anthracite coal. Together, they far overshadowed the old energy supply provided by the animal muscle power of humans and their beasts of burden, a form of energy that had always been severely limited by the quantity of food that could be raised in the growing season and stored for winter. That old source of energy remained as confining in North America, notwithstanding the abundance of wood, as it had been in other societies. Not until the nineteenth century did a rising group of engineers and entrepreneurs figure out how to escape the limits of muscle power, and thus remove all constraint on ambition. They did so by exploiting water and the fossil fuels, and as a consequence of that energy breakthrough the North left behind the old local, rural household economy of wood and soil and moved into a vastly more affluent life which drew its resources from the most distant corners of the continent and beyond.

The emergence of an industrial mode of production is conventionally dated to the mid 1830s, when northerners began to see for the first time a significant improvement in their per capita income. But during the preceding forty years they learned how to harness the power of rivers running from the mountains to the sea. Their most impressive achievements came along the Merrimack, which had its headwaters in the White Mountains of New Hampshire, where an abundance of rain and snow fell. In 1822 a group of Boston entrepreneurs came to the river's banks and began to construct the factory town of Lowell; within a few years they had managed to gain control of virtually the entire watershed, setting up on site after site their coordinated system of dams, canals, overshot waterwheels, multistoried factory buildings, and female laborers to manufacture cotton cloth. The system spread throughout the Northeast, and everywhere the outcome was devastating for anyone who depended on rivers in their natural state. The milldams stopped anadromous fish like salmon from migrating upstream to spawn, and they flooded the low-lying meadows used for fodder. With more and more people living and working along their banks, the rivers became increasingly polluted by sewage, forcing towns to look far and wide for fresh, safe water supplies. In order to exploit the kinetic energy of New England's rivers the early industrial capitalists had literally to take them apart and extract their power, a process they could not accomplish, given the technology at hand, without nearly killing them as ecosystems.

There were not many Merrimack Rivers around, however, and the potential of water power was soon exhausted. Every rivulet had its full complement of gristmills, and every large stream its factories for making cloth, shoes, wooden implements, or whatever. Move beyond the mountainous terrain into the Ohio and Mississippi River valleys, moreover, and the prospects of a new energy abundance become dimmer; the rivers there were too wide and flood-prone, too gradual in their fall, to harness. Fortunately for the advocates of economic growth, another energy breakthrough occurred that would make that flatter, more open country the heartland of modern industry.

The Coming of Coal

Americans had before them the model of Great Britain, which, after exhausting its own wood and water-power resources, had turned to burning coal, mined at great depths in the ground. Coal mining, it was said, produces manufacturing, and manufacturing produces railways, and railways produce money. If the equation worked in Britain, it ought to work in the United States too. The new nation had a great deal of coal, both hard anthracite and soft bituminous, formed in peat deposits 250 million years ago, but most of it tended to be found in rugged, inaccessible Appalachian mountain valleys, where the beds lay folded and pitched by geological processes. How to get that coal dug out and carried to markets was the challenge. The markets, moreover, were mainly limited to urban consumers in Philadelphia and Baltimore, who, unable to buy enough wood for home

The new nation had a great deal of coal, both hard anthracite and soft bituminous, but most of it tended to be found in rugged, inaccessible Appalachian mountain valleys, where the beds lay folded and pitched by geological processes.

heating, sought coal to burn in their Franklin stoves. Anthracite, though it burns long and hot, is very difficult to ignite, so householders were reluctant to turn to it as long as they could get soft coal from the riverbanks of Virginia. So if Americans wanted to follow the British model, they had to reverse the formula: they had to find capital to establish mines, develop transportation, encourage a market among iron foundries and manufacturers, and only then would the coal bring wealth and power. This was the challenge facing capitalists, and they soon appeared with solutions as they had in New England.

In the late 1820s and early 1830s the critical breakthrough to large-scale anthracite use occurred, and the North started down the road toward a fossil-fuel economy. Three major canals—the Pennsylvania Main Line, the Chesapeake and Ohio, and the Lehigh—were dug in those years, connecting the anthracite coalfields of eastern Pennsylvania with New York and Philadelphia, ports from which it was shipped up and down the seaboard. By 1837 the coal carried on those canals reached nearly 900,000 tons. Almost overnight an incredible source of energy had materialized for both household and industrial consumption, and at prices cheaper than wood, charcoal, or even that inferior Virginia bituminous. Great fortunes were waiting to be made, and coal towns like Scranton, Wilkes-Barre, Hazleton, Pottsville, and Shamokin began to appear on the map, representing an entirely new relationship with nature. From this point on people drew their energy from places they had never been and most likely would never see, and from a living world that had long ago died and been buried. Consumers depended on capitalists and their employees to extract that energy and bring it to them. All of them lived by mining, which is to say, by depleting. By 1859 other entrepreneurs had located a new fossil fuel called petroleum, or "rock oil." Together, these two black smelly substances, coal and oil, both erupting from the bowels of the Pennsylvania earth, would change the American landscape more profoundly than any force since the glaciers.

The fossil fuels helped towns and cities begin to grow at a phenomenal rate, but especially those engaged in manufacturing, which now had the energy to greatly expand their plants and hire more workers. By the early 1850s the factory had become largely an urban institution. Cities grew up around factories. They grew rapidly outward as coal allowed the mass production of iron, which in turn could be worked into railways and locomotives, streetcars and trams, the means of rapid transportation from suburb to downtown. Cities also began to grow upward as coal was used in the manufacture of steel, and inexpensive steel offered a wonderful new structural material for urban buildings, higher and stronger than wood or bricks could ever be. Coal became the very lifeblood of the northern metropolis as it was of the new economy.

By the middle of the nineteenth century, new metropolises were rising on the western side of the Appalachian mountain chain: Pittsburgh (which had its own ample supplies of coal), Cincinnati, Cleveland, and, above all, Chicago, the key city of the inland "coast" and the center (especially after it began to rebuild following the great fire of 1871) of an expanding commercial and industrial empire. Over all of them hung the polluted air of coal-burning chimneys and blast furnaces. Americans generally, from miners toiling deep in the tunnels to the conductors collecting tickets on the railroads, now had to endure smoke and coal dust penetrating their lungs and causing disease, as well as polluted water in their lakes and rivers. This new man-made environment was hardly healthy for the masses of people. By way of compensation they stood at the receiving end of a complex, far-flung system of food and raw-material production, one that seemed to be boundless in capacity. Cheap energy brought them corn and wheat from what had been the tall-grass prairie, meat and hides from as far away as Montana and Texas rangelands, oysters from Long Island Sound, whalebone from the Arctic, wine from France, sugar from Louisiana and Hawaii. The old giddy sense of living in the midst of extraordinary natural abundance began to give way to a fantasy of a technological horn of plenty, much more impressive, some thought, than any forest or prairie could be.

The Fate of the Forest

The fate of the northern forest in this new era of cheap, abundant fossil-fuel energy deserves particular notice. As coal began to replace wood as the primary source of energy—a point achieved by 1870—and iron began to replace wood in tools, machinery, and bridges, and as people began to live more and more in cities where the only trees they saw were the few that had been planted, the forest was no longer so prominent in the popular imagination. But, remarkably, the old deforestation continued apace, though now it was lumber companies doing much of the cutting, and the lumber was to construct housing for the masses.

Towering above all the other northern trees was the white pine, *Pinus strobus*, whose range extended from New Brunswick to Minnesota and down the Appalachians to Georgia. According to one estimate, there were over 100 billion commercially usable board feet of this tree standing in the primeval forest of Indian America. Over large areas it formed pure or nearly pure stands, and in the most favorable settings could reach over 200 feet (60 meters) tall. Its wood, especially in the more northern zones, was strong, light, durable, and easily worked—a good tree to go after—and here again capitalists were not reluctant. By 1837 there were, so Henry David Thoreau noted in *The Maine Woods* (1864), 250 sawmills on the Penobscot River north of Bangor, Maine, an area that became the cradle of the northern lumber industry. Their equipment was primitive—water-powered saws, human-powered axes, oxen teams, and the rivers themselves as a means of transportation—but it was effective. By 1860 the best stands of Maine pine trees had been cut, and the lumberjacks were forced to turn to spruce. Some simply picked up and went west to find virgin stands in New York State, then in Pennsylvania, and then in the extensive Great Lakes pineries, where they settled down for a few years to reduce the forests to shingles and boards.

The Saginaw Valley of Michigan had some of the best pine forests on the continent, and there were more such growths north of there all the way to the Upper Peninsula. Lumber crews arrived to do the cutting in winter, skidding the logs over the frozen ground to streamside; when spring arrived and the ice went out, they dumped the logs into the rivers and floated them down to saw mills on Lake Huron or Lake Michigan. Ships, and later railroads, carried the sawed lumber to Chicago and other cities and to farmsteads scattered across the land. Inevitably under such market demand, the supply of trees had to run out here too, and by 1900 the fabled North

By the middle of the nineteenth century, cities like Pittsburgh were shrouded in a haze of polluted air from coal-burning chimneys and blast furnaces.

Woods had become the Cutover—a wasteland of stumps, slash and debris, clogged rivers, and ready tinder waiting for fire. A slash fire broke out at Peshtigo, Wisconsin, in 1871 killing fifteen hundred people, and others followed in quick succession, until the Cutover had become in truth the Burntover.

As the forests were depleted, the lumber companies once more packed up to leave, some going to the Pacific Northwest, others to the South. The deforested land they abandoned was unfit for agriculture, unlike the cleared acres of Ohio, and it was left to regenerate itself as best it could. A full century later the primeval grandeur has still not come back to the country. Hardly anyone who had bought Great Lakes pine ever anticipated this lingering consequence; they seldom saw the men who cut the forest down, or the mess they left, or the fires they created. As consumers, they knew pine trees only as a pile of two-by-fours at the lumber yard, just as they knew wheat only as fine white flour purchased in a coarse cloth sack or a range cow as a restaurant steak. Without cheap fossil-fuel energy, that distancing of people from the land would have been impossible to achieve so completely. On the plus side, the new order of ecological relationships meant that daily life was easier in many ways and food and housing less expensive in labor or cash. But on the negative side, the growing distance between people and their natural environment left them more irresponsible and complacent about their impact.

The deforested North Woods that the lumber companies abandoned were unfit for agriculture, unlike the cleared acres of Ohio, and were left to regenerate itself as best it could.

The Automobile Age

By the 1870s large industrial corporations dominated the natural as they did the human environment. They alone could afford the new technology of production that sprang from the minds of inventors like Thomas Edison and George Westinghouse. As a result, they also came to own most of the country's resources. The corporation called Swift and Company, for example, founded by Gustavus Swift, a New England farm boy who became one of Chicago's greatest meatpackers, bought plains cattle by the millions and put them through a "disassembly line" that took their carcasses apart—and then bought ice-filled refrigerator cars that carried the meat to East Coast butcher shops. By 1900 such vertically integrated corporations were responsible for two-thirds of all the goods manufactured in the United States. As these economic institutions grew larger and larger (U.S. Steel started in 1901 with $1.4 billion of capital), they needed whole armies of workers. Thus began a vast influx of job-seekers, abandoning the rural countryside and swelling the size of the industrial cities. The population of New York City and its environs grew from less than 1 million in 1860 to more than 3 million in 1900. By 1920 a majority of Americans lived in urban areas of two thousand five hundred people or more.

After World War I the region entered the automobile age, both as manufacturer and consumer, and the implications for the natural world were profound. Detroit and its satellites became, after Henry Ford built his immense assembly plant at River Rouge, the mouth of an octopus that stretched its tentacles toward natural resources in every area of the continent and overseas—toward steel, wood, wool, rubber, copper, aluminum, plastic, even soybeans for making auto bodies. Putting society into private automobiles demanded more resources from the earth than any other technology in history. The coming of the automobile also led to the opening up of roads into the most remote areas, then paving and lining them with service stations, billboards, and hot-dog stands; down the roads came a flood of city dwellers looking for homes in the country. The products of the land began to move in the opposite lanes toward urban markets by means of an enormous fleet of trucks, all burning, as did the automobiles, great quantities of gasoline. Even the farms came to run essentially on this volatile fuel; by 1970, raising a single acre of corn in Illinois required the equivalent of 80 gallons (300 liters) of gasoline for plowing, cultivating, drying, harvesting, and shipping to the processor. So dependent were people on their cars, trucks, and tractors, so accustomed were they to expecting an abundance of energy in the form of coal-generated electricity as well as gasoline-driven transportation, that they became the world leaders in consuming fossil fuel. The consequences of that fact could be seen in the explosive growth of shopping malls, power lines, and refineries that spilled out of cities across the landscape.

The Effects of Pollution

Less obvious for a long time were the slowly accumulating effects of pollution on the atmosphere. Burning coal and gasoline put into the air a number of pollutants, such as sulfur and carbon, that might better have been left in the ground. The rain that fell over northern lakes and mountains became polluted with sulfur, forming sulfuric acid, which killed trees and aquatic life. The carbon in the fossil fuels turned into carbon dioxide, which began to increase significantly as an atmospheric gas, leading many scientists to warn of a "greenhouse effect" in which the sun's radiation would be trapped by the gas, warming the planet by three to five degrees centigrade, and causing a dangerous uncertainty in the climate. Nebraska might become another west Texas, and New York another Alabama, if profligate use of the fossil fuels continued.

By the end of the twentieth century the daily litany of insults to the natural environment reported in the news were overwhelming and amounted to a deadly critique of modern industrial society. Lake Erie was nearly dead from pollution, New York City had no place to dump its garbage, much of Iowa's groundwater was undrinkable because of nitrates from fertilizer, Pennsylvanians were worried about the radioactive effects of a near-meltdown of the nuclear power plant at Three Mile Island, and songbird populations were plummeting along the East Coast due to real estate development. Everywhere there were crowds of people trying to go in the same direction or use the same water: Massachusetts had, by 1985, more people per square mile than the Netherlands; New Jersey more than Japan or India; even Indiana had a higher population density than several Central American countries. As depressing as those facts might seem, they had to be confronted if the region was to understand fully what its history had been and what it had produced. Suddenly, it seemed to many observers, the very principles and institutions of an industrial capitalist society had to be questioned—notions of unlimited economic growth, liberal immigration, mass advertising to boost consumption, aggressive market freedom, and global trade.

All the news was not bad. Set over against the mounting evidence of environmental decline were a number of hopeful trends, chief among them the growth of an environmental concern that was as old and active as any in the world. The North had been a seedbed of such concern since the days of Henry David Thoreau (1817–1862) and George Perkins Marsh (1801–1882), a Vermont-born leader in conservation and the author of the path-breaking book, *Man and Nature*, published in 1864. What bothered them most at that early date was the heedless deforestation of New England, "breaking up the floor and wainscoting and doors and window frames of our dwelling," as Marsh put it, "for fuel to warm our bodies and seethe our pottage" (1965 ed., p. 52). Their warnings would be followed by those of John Muir (1838–1914), who left a pioneer farm in Wisconsin for California, where he founded the Sierra Club; by Frederick Law Olmsted (1822–1903) the designer of Central Park in New York and a major influence on the national park movement; by Gifford Pinchot (1865–1946) who as chief of the Division of Forestry in the Department of Agriculture from 1898 to 1910 put the national forest system together; by two environmentally active presidents, Theodore Roosevelt and Franklin Roosevelt; and by Aldo Leopold (1886–1948), an Iowan who did more than any other individual to create the new profession of wildlife management and who gave the country the idea of a "land ethic," which called on citizens to expand their moral horizons beyond society to include the preservation of the natural world, the diverse biological heritage that had been delivered into American hands. In 1962 this tradition of environmental reform took a disturbing new direction with the publication of *Silent Spring*, by Rachel Carson (1907–1964), a woman who had grown up in western Pennsylvania and was moved to write by reports of the harm that the pesticide DDT was causing to wildlife and people. Out of Brooklyn came the scientist-activist Barry Commoner, a critic of the pollution caused by profit-seeking corporations. All these regional voices contributed to a tradition of organized political action to achieve nature preservation and improve public health, and by the 1990s it had millions of supporters, some of them protesting toxic dumping in Buffalo's Love Canal, or sewage floating in Boston's harbor, or strip-mining of coal in West Virginia. Their common theme was that the natural environment is more limited, scarce, and vulnerable than a long history of easy abundance and industrial dependency had prepared Americans to see.

Inevitably, however, their message had to be a lament for what had been lost in the drive for power and prosperity and an urgent, often shrill sermon on ecological responsibility for a people whose very institutions had made freedom from responsibility a way of life.

What was surprising, and often difficult to keep in view, was how much of the original beauty and diversity of the natural environment survived—whether by public action or natural tenacity—the ravages of economic development. Unlike the tropical rainforests, the woods of the North did manage to return over large areas, and a state like Massachusetts, heavily populated though it was, could boast that two-thirds of its area had reverted to forest. One could stand on Fairhaven Cliff in Thoreau's Concord, look in all directions of the compass, and see hardly a rooftop among the sea of trees. With the return of the forest came black bears—over three hundred of them in that state in 1990—along with deer, beaver, even coyotes and a stray moose or two. The major reason for that regeneration was that agriculture had almost completely disappeared from the state; by the last decade of the century, Massachusetts was importing 85 percent of its food, much of it from what had been the grasslands. Yet, out there where the food was produced, little regeneration of nature was permitted; less than 1 percent of the tall-grass prairie is left today, and almost none of what is left is publicly protected.

Elsewhere, the federal government has used a small part of its gargantuan wealth to preserve remnants of the natural heritage in the form of parks, forests, and seashores. On the coast of Maine, for instance, Acadia National Park can provide a reasonably good sense of the pristine landscape that the French explorer Samuel de Champlain saw in 1604. On Isle Royale National Park in Lake Superior, the gray wolf still can be heard howling at the moon on crusty winter nights. The largest wilderness left in the region is the one set aside by New Yorkers in 1885, the Adirondack State Park, and a hundred years after its founding the state is still seeking to enlarge it for a growing population to experience a nature left to its own rhythms. Even near the dense metropolises of New York and Chicago one can find such natural areas as lakeshore dunes, riverine forests, and quaking bogs complete with frogs and muskrats. And the once-majestic Mississippi, dammed and locked and barge-laden though it is, still offers substantial stretches of quiet water, where eagles soar overhead, catfish rise to the surface, a mink prowls along the bank looking for dinner.

Nature may have moved to the edges of our predominantly urban imagination so that it is no longer the vivid, immediate force that confronted our ancestors; and as self-determining ecosystem or wild landscape, much of it may have disappeared under the heavy wheels of agricultural and industrial progress; but even after four hundred years of radical change it has not altogether vanished from our presence, our memory, or our fate.

[See also Agriculture; The Frontier; Landscape; National Parks and Preservation; Rural Life in the North; Technology and Social Change.]

BIBLIOGRAPHY

Cayton, Andrew R. L., and Peter S. Onuf. *The Midwest and the Nation* (1990).

Cronon, William. *Changes in the Land: Indians, Colonists, and the Ecology of New England* (1983).

Cronon, William. *Nature's Metropolis: Chicago and the West, 1848–1893* (1991).

Dunlap, Thomas R. *DDT: Scientists, Citizens, and Public Policy* (1981).

Dunlap, Thomas R. *Saving America's Wildlife* (1988).

Flader, Susan L., ed. *The Great Lakes Forest: An Environmental and Social History* (1983).

Hays, Samuel P. *Conservation and the Gospel of Efficiency: The Progressive Conservation Movement, 1890–1920* (1959).

Hays, Samuel P. *Beauty, Health, and Permanence: Environmental Politics in the United States, 1955–1985* (1987).

Johnson, Hildegard Binder. *Order upon the Land. The U.S. Rectangular Survey and the Upper Mississippi Country* (1976).

Melosi, Martin V. *Coping with Abundance: Energy and Environment in Industrial America* (1985).

Merchant, Carolyn. *Ecological Revolutions: Nature, Gender, and Science in New England* (1989).

Miller, Donald L., and Richard E. Sharpless. *The Kingdom of Coal: Work, Enterprise, and Ethnic Communities in the Mine Fields* (1985).

Nash, Roderick. *Wilderness and the American Mind* 3d ed. (1982).

Pyne, Stephen J. *Fire in America: A Cultural History of Wildland and Rural Fire* (1982).

Scarpino, Philip V. *Great River: An Environmental History of the Upper Mississippi, 1890–1950* (1985).

Steinberg, Theodore. *Nature Incorporated. Industrialization and the Waters of New England* (1991).

Vietor, Richard H. K. *Environmental Politics and the Coal Coalition* (1980).

Williams, Michael. *Americans and Their Forests: A Historical Geography* (1989).

— DONALD WORSTER

THE NATURAL ENVIRONMENT: THE SOUTH

The definition of the South as a region owes much more to culture than to geography. No natural feature or combination of features demarcate or bound the South as a distinctive environmental region. Quite the contrary, two of the distinguishing geographical features of the region, the Mississippi River and the Appalachian Mountains, link the South to other regions and repeat ecosystems found as far away as Canada. The southern climate in general has a distinctive cast, but a visitor can find New England winters in the Great Smoky Mountains and tropical summers in Florida. Though some features and characteristics of the natural environment of the South are unique to the region—the Mississippi Delta and the Okefenokee Swamp, for example, have no counterparts elsewhere in North America—culture, not nature, has determined the region's boundaries and distinctiveness.

People have usually used the land on a much more local than regional scale, and most modifications of the land—previous to the mid twentieth century—were discernible mainly on the local level. Southern society in the long duration has developed within certain broad contours, however, that have remained relatively unchanged. These physiographic traits have given structure and character to the larger history of the mutual development of culture and nature in the region.

Several features dominate the physical character of the South: a long coastline, backed by an extension of the continental shelf—the Coastal Plain—connects land and sea on the edge of the southeastern and lower South. The eastern and southeastern portion of this plain breaks at an ancient coastline—at the "fall line"—into a series of foothills, the Piedmont, where both soil and climate change. The Appalachian mountains create both relief and barrier in the topography of the region, and extend the range of montane conifers into a deciduous woodlands region. The Appalachians consist of three formations with different histories: the Blue Ridge, which is the backbone of the mountains and has the highest elevations; the "valley and ridge," a series of parallel flat, fertile valleys separated by sharp, folded ridges to the west of the Blue Ridge; and the Appalachian Plateau, the knobby hill country of West Virginia, Kentucky, Tennessee, and northern Alabama.

Mountains, piedmont, and plain are cut through and connected by several major rivers: the Roanoke, Shenandoah, Santee, Savannah, Altamaha, Chattahoochee, Alabama, and Tombigbee. Other important rivers connect the southern hinterland to the Mississippi: the Red, Arkansas, Missouri, Tennessee, Cumberland, and Yazoo. The Mississippi River and the alluvial valley it has created constitute yet another central feature. The Mississippi, because of both size and periodic floods, adds a waterfront and dynamic physical force to the region.

The western reaches of the South merge with the Central Lowlands of North America, which stretch from the Appalachians to the Rockies. The relief of the southern portion of this vast plain is cut through by the Mississippi and raised up by the Ozark and Ouachita mountains. For several cultural reasons, the Balcones Escarpment in central Texas, which marks the eastern boundary of the High Plains, has been regarded as the physiographic boundary between South and West.

The soils of the South vary with topography and locale, but have had several general characteristics. Though the Mason-Dixon line was not drawn to mark the southern advance of the glaciers, the soils south of the line are different from northern soils because they escaped the last glaciation. Southern soils do not have the topsoil of minerals ground mostly to dust by ice nor, like midwestern soils, the deep loess carried by wind from nearby glacial regions. They are old soils, in a region where high rainfall, humidity, and temperatures favor rapid decomposition of organic matter and leaching of soil minerals, and therefore tend to be acidic, low in humus content, and do not store water well. Within this general profile, many variations are prominent. Soils of the Coastal Plain, for example, often have higher proportions of sand—depositions from ancient advances of the sea—and lose organic material by leaching even more rapidly than Piedmont soils with their higher proportion of clay. The soils of the restless Mississippi River valley, by contrast, are constantly new, made up of layerings of sediments carried by water down the enormous watershed of the Mississippi.

The influential historian of the South, U. B. Phillips, claimed that it has been the weather that has made the South distinctive. The Southern climate has, indeed, been conducive to certain adaptations unique to the region. In general, summers are hot, winters are mild, and growing seasons range from an average of two hundred days in all but the higher elevations of the uplands, to two hundred and seventy days along the coast. Most of the South receives more than thirty inches (750 millimeters) of rainfall annually, but quantities vary in time and space.

The heat and humidity of a southern summer often impart the hazy quality to the vegetation of the region that W. J. Cash described in *The Mind of the South:* "blurring every outline and rending every object vague and problematical." The lush vegetation that has covered most of the region has been a changing mosaic with distinct boundaries, however, that can be clearly defined. Most of the South shares a dominant temperate deciduous vegetation with the rest of the eastern woodlands. The most widespread association in the deciduous forest in the South has been the oak-hickory, which dominates the forests along the Piedmont south into the Gulf Coast states, west to central Texas, and north to Minnesota. In the Piedmont the mature stands of oak and hickory have been and are sometimes very dense; in east Texas trees grade into grasslands.

Though the Mason-Dixon line was not drawn to mark the southern advance of the glaciers, the soils south of the line are different from northern soils because they escaped the last glaciation.

Species of oak and hickory are usually mixed with pine in the Piedmont and Gulf states. In the area that became Georgia, for example, the presettlement Piedmont forest probably consisted of thirty-five to forty percent hardwood stands—mainly oak and hickory—forty-five percent mixed pine-hardwood stands, and fifteen percent pine stands. Pine is particularly suited to the infertile, porous soil throughout the region, especially around and below the "fall line," and was also maintained by fires caused by lightning or people. Much of the Coastal Plain has been covered by a broad band of pine barrens that separated the maritime forests of the coast and the deciduous forests of the Piedmont. These pine forests have been remarkably uniform in composition, broken only by swampy areas and open savannas. On the other hand, the coastal forests—dominated by cypress, tupelo, and oak on the floodplains, and by magnolia, holly, laurel oak, and bay elsewhere—are unusually varied, because of the variety in moisture and nutrient conditions on the floodplains, in tidewater marshes and swamps, and on elevated hammocks and ridges throughout the coastal area. Other exceptional mixes of vegetation—for example, the subtropical forests of southern Florida and the temperate conifer forests of high altitudes in the Great Smokies—can be found in several parts of the South.

Environment and Society in the Precontact South

At the time Europeans came to this part of North America, Native Americans had been living in the river valleys and along the coast of the region for millennia. Most Indians in the region had an economy based firmly on horticulture, with maize, beans, and squash as the main crops, and supplemented by hunting, fishing, and gathering. All these practices shaped the land, sometimes profoundly, and created a unique landscape that reflected the settlement patterns and land use practices of the people of the oldest South.

Village sites and fields for growing crops required open spaces, and Indians created these by girdling trees and burning off underbrush and grasses. The combined effects of clearing and of gathering wood for fuel resulted in some deforestation. When Indians abandoned fields with declining fertility and took up new ones nearby, the old fields—called "tallahasees" by the Creeks—grew up in grasses, shrubs, and sun-loving species of young trees in the early stages of forest succession. Many Indian communities sometimes broadcast-burned the vicinity of the village to destroy vermin and weeds and to open up the landscape. This also favored mixed grasslands and young forests, and the deer, rabbits, turkey, grouse, and quail that live in such habitats. These animals remained wild, but Indians created a local environment that favored their survival within easy hunting distances. When the fields and firewood in a particular area played out, Indians moved their villages, usually not far from the earlier site. When Indians located their villages on the more fertile terraces along southern rivers they greatly extended the length of occupation, but used the surrounding forest land in the same ways. In the hands of the natives of the region, village locales became a hodgepodge of old fields, open spaces, shrublands, and young forests.

Indian-set fires thinned out some forest beyond recovery and extended the range of grasslands. The anomalous expanse of prairie in western Kentucky that was later colonized by European bluegrass, for example, was probably created by Indian burnings. The creation of prairies in turn created an environment for the bison, which moved from west of the region into the southeast during the late prehistoric period. Fires—many of them set by Indians—changed the vegetation composition of the forests to the extent that in some areas fire-tolerant species, such as longleaf, loblolly, and slash pine, became dominant. The pine forests, and the savannas and prairies that made up the "natural" landscape of the South when Europeans arrived, were largely a consequence of the Indian use of fire.

A parklike forest through which a man on horseback could gallop without impediment, partly created by Indian fires, greeted the first European explorers to the region. When disease microorganisms, packed to North America by explorers and colonists, killed natives who had no immunity to them, the natural environments of the area were opened up even more to the newcomers. They put the land to different uses and soon produced another landscape.

Colonization and Development of a Plantation Landscape

A variety of motives propelled Europeans to the New World, but the most common was the desire for profit. The Spanish in Florida sought to save Indian souls, but also wanted to consolidate a wealth-producing colony. The English who came to the South to trade and settle were even more determined to extract local resources and to produce valuable commodities. The climate made English-style farming difficult in the region, and colonists had to find new means for subsistence and profit. The market economy that was developing around the Atlantic drove them in this adventure and conditioned their perceptions of the environment they sought to inhabit and to exploit. Timber, furs, deerskins, and ginseng became valuable in whatever quantities they could be procured. Colonists justified by the same rationale the transformation of portions of the natural environment for the production of naval stores, livestock, tobacco, indigo, and rice.

The English also regarded "wild" environments as inferior landscapes, and sought to civilize them with "improvements." Buildings, roads, fences, and cultivated fields established in tangible form English conceptions of property, brought order to the environment, and mirrored the countryside at home. Moreover, the

English used the apparent failure of Indians to "improve" the land as a justification for appropriating it from them.

By the mid eighteenth century, the colonists had created a characteristic landscape of plantations, villages, small farms, and cowpens in Virginia, North Carolina, South Carolina, and Georgia. African slaves did most of the clearing and cultivating, girdling and firing trees much as Native Americans had. They herded cattle on the open range in South Carolina and Georgia, erected the hydraulic systems of banks, canals, and drains for tidewater rice plantations in the southeastern Atlantic tidewater, and planted, tended, harvested, and processed plantation crops throughout the colonies.

Staple-crop production expanded in the nineteenth century. Eli Whitney's invention of the cotton gin in 1793, and a market for cotton among British, and later, American textile manufacturers, rapidly made short-strand cotton the most important staple crop in the South, and assured the expansion of the plantation system. The spread of row-crop monoculture etched the plantation landscape into a larger proportion of the region, and the Cotton South took shape. By the 1820s and 1830s, production had become significant west of the Appalachians in the rich prairie lands—the black belt—of central Alabama and Mississippi, on alluvial river bottoms, and on uplands throughout the region, and this area became "southern" in character. Southern rivers—especially the Mississippi—were essential to this growth, linking cotton ports on the rivers to ocean ports. By 1860 three-fourths of the area's cotton was moving on the South's river system through Mobile, New Orleans, and the young Texas ports.

Plantation agriculture altered profoundly some parts of the natural environment. On cultivated lands, the removal of ground cover and monoculture made soils vulnerable to erosion. When planters had their slaves plow instead of using the hoe to prepare the ground, soils eroded even more quickly. Within a few short years after planters in the Chesapeake shifted from producing tobacco with hoe culture to growing wheat on plowed lands, for example, some streams were closed to navigation because of silting. Row-crop agriculture that "skimmed" the land also destroyed soil fertility, made floods and droughts more common, and modified the southern landscape by changing the relationships between ecosystems.

Large areas of the South remained uncultivated—nearly eighty percent of the region in 1860—and forests, wetlands, and savannahs were more common on the antebellum landscape than plantations, farms, and cultivated fields. Little of this land was unused, however. Small farmers and hill folk ranged cattle on wiregrass savannahs and in canebrakes, and hogs in mast-bearing deciduous woods. They hunted and gathered food in the untilled environment near their homes, and also burned the woods—in much of the South this was an early spring ritual—to destroy insects and improve forest understory and savannah browse for their cattle. Southerners also selectively used all kinds of woods from the region's forests for an array of purposes—cypress and cedars for shingles; hardwoods for staves and hoops, fences, and shipbuilding; and pine for scantling, tar, pitch, turpentine, and firewood—thereby modifying forest composition and extent.

Society and the Environment After the Civil War

Though the Civil War destroyed slavery and blasted much of the plantation landscape, Southerners remained committed to commodity-crop plantation agriculture. They often had little choice. The war and Emancipation left them capital-poor, and crop choice became hitched up to a chain of credit and market relationships that hinged on conditions outside the region. This "colonization" of the South was intensified by the development of extractive industries that were largely capitalized and commanded by northern investors. Southerners had few resources for economic development; like other undeveloped areas in a global capitalist economy, they experienced economic growth only by selling their labor and raw materials to outside investors at bargain prices. The consequence was the growth of an economy that did damage to the natural environment.

Cotton culture remained the dominant force in shaping the region's environment. By 1879, Southerners had returned cotton production to its prewar levels, and by 1900 they were producing three times the 1860 level. A combination of factors made cotton agriculture after the war even harder on the land than antebellum production had been. Since labor could no longer be as easily coerced, control of land and of credit became the means to control labor; landowners seldom developed fresh lands, but forced sharecroppers and tenants into debt and then required them to produce cotton year after year on the same land. Monoculture, as always, provided excellent habitats for population explosions of insects. In the early twentieth century the boll weevil, with devastating consequences, ate its way through cotton fields across the South from its point of entry in Texas. Crop rotation—even with corn, another heavy feeder—was seldom practiced. Cheap, easily available fertilizers created the illusion of fertility on soils that seldom had the structure to develop it, and allowed cotton-growers to continue to use poor soils. Erosion, gullying, and rapid runoff became a larger problem than it had been before the war.

In many places, but especially in the upper Coastal Plain and Piedmont, cotton production was expanded onto lands cleared by another major environment-shaping force of the period, industrial timbering. While other extractive industries, such as strip-mining in Appalachia and the petrochemical industry in Texas also caused massive damage to the environment, industrial logging cleaned off large blocks of the entire region. Northern lumbermen exhausted the timber resources of the Great Lake states then came south to clear another region's forests, spurred on by low acquisition costs, improved rail access, and unrestricted entry (after the repeal of the 1866 Southern Homestead Act, which limited land entries to eighty acres [32 hectares] in 1876). They were also supported enthusiastically by New South boosters who sought the development of industry. Northerners and Europeans bought up huge acreages of southern forests in the 1880s and used new industrial technology to strip them of timber.

The extensive longleaf forests of Georgia were the first to go, followed by the pine forests of Alabama and Mississippi. By the 1890s, Texas was the leading producer of lumber, and in 1900 Louisiana surged to the lead, producing 3.5 billion board feet. In the 1890s, lumbermen using a new pull-boat technology began extracting bald cypress from southern swamps and bayous—the hitherto worthless Yazoo lowlands in the lower Mississippi Valley and the Okefenokee Swamp, for example, now contained valuable resources—until unrelenting exploitation began to deplete the supply of cypress. Trunk rail lines penetrated some of the most rugged areas of the Appalachians and lumbermen there cleared out hardwood coves. By 1909 timbering and milling operations were producing nearly one hundred and forty million board feet per year, nearly half the total production for the United States. This high rate continued until the 1920s when the industry ran out of woods to cut.

Modernization, the Sunbelt, and the Environment

The 1930s were a watershed for the shaky Southern economy and the eroded, gullied, deforested landscape of the region. The already sagging economy hit bottom during the Great Depression, but New Deal relief programs provided the capital for southern planters to begin to modernize. New Deal capital, then the appearance of cheap petroleum agricultural chemicals, the out-migration of labor, higher cotton prices during World War II, and mechanization—the appearance of a mechanical cotton picker in 1941 was crucial—transformed southern agriculture and the agricultural landscape.

At the same time that yields and efficiency increased, the production of the traditional crops began to decrease. Cotton production declined in the western portion of the cotton South and disappeared from much of the eastern portion. Great areas of the Piedmont had become too eroded and gullied for agriculture and the small, hilly parcels of land there were unsuited for large-scale mechanized production. By the 1980s most of the cotton produced in the region was grown in the Mississippi Valley. Corn acreages also dropped by more than two-thirds between 1929 and 1982 and became concentrated on the South Atlantic coastal plain and parts of Kentucky and Tennessee. Tobacco, still a highly profitable crop, remained essential to the farm economy of North Carolina and Kentucky, but total acreages of this oldest of southern staple crops declined by more than half between 1930 and 1985.

Agriculture continued to be a transforming force in the southern environment, however, as new crops replaced the old and the cropland base shifted. By the 1980s, soybeans had become the leading crop in every southern state except Virginia, with over twenty-five million acres devoted to their production. Increased market demands, reduced labor supplies, and poor agricultural land converged to make soybeans profitable in the post-World War II years. Though rice did not carry the importance of soybeans as a crop, it rose in significance. The modern, heavily capitalized rice agriculture was based on the midwestern wheat technology, developed late in the nineteenth century, that changed the prairies of eastern Arkansas, Louisiana, and parts of east Texas.

The monoculture of cotton production provided excellent habitats for population explosions of insects: In the early twentieth century, the boll weevil ate its way through cotton fields across the South.

The decline of farming and a new silviculture together created new forests. Some practices favored the expansion of hardwood forests. The removal of the highest quality trees by timbermen meant that little old-growth forests remained, but where pines were selectively logged for mixed-species forests, hardwoods extended their cover. Federal and state fire-control programs largely eliminated natural fires and reduced fires set by small farmers to clear land or "green up" the range for cattle, and removed a major force that favored fire-adapted pine species at the expense of the more vulnerable hardwood species. Mixed deciduous hardwood forests still cover the more rugged slopes of the Appalachians and several forces worked toward the slow domination of hardwoods in mixed-species forests.

Other practices favored the expansion of pine forests. Abandoned croplands grew up largely in loblolly and shortleaf pines, often called old-field pine; these varieties also colonized land cut clear of longleaf pine. Modern forest-management practices, which shaped southern forests for commercial purposes, focused on increasing total forest fiber output by planting fast-growing species of pine. In addition, private forest companies created large plantations of pine that they plant and manage like crops—using controlled burning and herbicides. The result has been new pine forests with even less diversity of species than the barrens of the old ones.

Southern watersheds were also modified by large-scale calculated action, especially through the New Deal and other government programs. The most ambitious has been the New Deal's Tennessee Valley Authority, which engaged in the wholesale development of both land and water in an entire river basin. Through the TVA the federal government engaged in the management of nature on a grand scale, and established a model for future resource management programs in the South. By the late twentieth century, the South had more water management projects in place than any other region except California.

Disciplining the region's rivers—and especially the Mississippi—had long been the aim of Southerners who lived on them. On the Mississippi, two hundred years of levee building was completed in the 1890s by the Corps of Engineers and the Mississippi River Commission, and was apparently successful in controlling the often unpredictable pulses of the river. This controlled river abided the discipline of engineers most of the time, but was much more dangerous than the old when it did not. Because overflow areas were closed off and the channel was streamlined, the river moved much more quickly and was more dangerous when it topped or broke through the levees. Flood control also encouraged settlement on the floodplain. In 1927 the Mississippi escaped its embankments with disastrous consequences, flooding millions of acres and creating nearly seven hundred thousand refugees.

Federally sponsored Mississippi flood-control projects applied a new approach to flood control in the wake of the 1927 flood. These programs strengthened levees, deepened and straightened channels, developed floodways and storage reservoirs, and succeeded in establishing control along this largest of American alluvial valleys. Flood control has meant increased settlement along the river, and bottomland hardwood forests have become soybean fields. At the same time, however, flood control projects have channeled the sediments out from the Delta and into deep water, the river has ceased to build land on the Gulf Coast, and the Louisiana coastline is receding.

An African-American man, one of the seven hundred thousand refugees created by the Mississippi flood of 1927, awaits relocation.

As the southern economy modernized and was integrated into the larger national economy, the development of Sunbelt cities transformed large portions of the southern landscape and changed profoundly the natural environment. Cities remained small, developing later in the South, and took a different form than in other regions. The usual form of Sunbelt metropolitan development was the planned sprawl: urbanlike settlements stretching from one urban center to another. In 1960 the largest of these stretched from Pensacola to Houston and had a relatively low-density population of 3,400,000.

The appeal of the Sunbelt to migrants from other regions was greatly enhanced by changes in the disease environment. The long warm season of the region had perennially favored pathogens and vectors that seldom appeared in other regions. The South had been a land of fever since malaria became endemic in the early colonial era and yellow fever became a frequent visitor. After World War II the eradication of the vectors for the disease, the *Anopheles quadrimaculatus* and *Aëdes aegypti* mosquitoes, through the use of DDT and large-scale drainage projects, made the South a safer place, especially to newcomers who had no immunities. The progressive decline of hookworm and pellagra also contributed to the success of the new image of the South as a healthy Sunbelt.

The development of air-conditioning made southern summers less enervating and stimulated Sunbelt urban growth. By the late 1960s most public buildings and private homes were air-conditioned and designs for new office buildings, hotels, and enclosed shopping malls took this kind of climate control for granted. By the 1980s automobiles were also air-conditioned, and the average southerner—or migrant from elsewhere—could depend on an artificial climate to buffer the real one.

Rapid growth, changes in agriculture, reforestation, and the large-scale manipulation of watersheds caused dislocations for wildlife. Resilient species thrived: wild turkey, the ubiquitous opossums, and raccoons maintained large populations; white-tailed deer populations expanded enormously in old-field habitats. Some changes played to specific species; mechanical harvesting increased the grain supply in wheat and corn fields, for example, providing winter feed for the brown-headed cowbird and the common grackle. Other species that are adapted only to a specific habitat—wood storks, Florida panthers, the pitcher plant, for example—were put under pressure. Competitive newcomers in some places were much more successful than less adaptable natives. Most prominent of these was kudzu, an invasive vine introduced for erosion control and cattle food that has swallowed up enough of the southern landscapes—both in the countryside and on empty lots in cities—to have inspired its own folklore.

Sunbelt growth and prosperity did not come without a price. Both agricultural and industrial pollution increased. Because southern states have sought to attract American and foreign industry through reduced environmental standards and because the environmental movement was until recently weak in the South, industry was often free to contaminate air and water without penalty. Effluents from paper mills, toxic discharges from chemical plants, oil spills (especially in the newer oil belt that has developed just off the Gulf Shore), accidental spills of radioactive wastes from nuclear power plants, and less specific fertilizer, pesticide, and herbicide pollution all accompanied the Sunbelt's industrial development. Federal environmental quality standards and less-relaxed state standards later put a lid on many of the more serious pollution problems, but pollution still compromises the Sunbelt South's image as an attractive, healthy place to live and work.

In the last decades of the twentieth century, the relationship between human beings and the natural environment has been more seriously complicated by much larger by-products of an industrial economy and a consumer society. Acid rain, much of it originating in the highly industrialized Ohio Valley, may be reducing growth rates of southern forests at higher elevations. Ozone pollution produced in and around sprawling cities where automobiles are essential—and especially serious in the South's sunny, muggy summer climate—stunts the growth of both cultivated and natural vegetation. In the future, global warming because of the "greenhouse effect" could have several consequences, especially on agriculture in the area, if temperatures rise and precipitation patterns change. In the late twentieth century, environmental problems that are global in magnitude also affect the natural environment of the South and further weaken any claims of geographical distinctiveness. At the same time, the Sunbelt remains unique: a modern incarnation of regional distinctiveness and yet another creation of the changing relationship of culture and nature in the South.

[See also Agriculture; The Frontier; Landscapes; National Parks and Preservation; The Plantation; Rural Life in the South; Slavery; Technology and Social Change.]

BIBLIOGRAPHY

Arsenault, Raymond. "The End of the Long Hot Summer: The Air Conditioner and Southern Culture." *Journal of Southern History* 50, no. 4 (1984).

Brown, Ralph H. *Historical Geography of the United States* (1948).

Clark, Thomas D. *The Greening of the South: The Recovery of Land and Forest* (1984).

Cobb, James C. *The Selling of the South: The Southern Crusade for Industrial Development, 1936–1980* (1982).

Cowdrey, Albert E. *This Land, This South: An Environmental History* (1983).

Daniel, Pete. *Breaking the Land: The Transformation of Cotton, Tobacco, and Rice Cultures Since 1880* (1985).

Earle, Carville. "Regional Economic Development West of the Appalachians, 1815–1860." In *North America: The Historical Geography of a Changing Continent*, edited by Robert Mitchell and Paul Graves (1987).

Earle, Carville. "The Myth of the Southern Soil Miner: Macrohistory, Agricultural Innovation, and Environmental Change." In *The Ends of the Earth*, edited by Donald Worster (1988).

Fite, Gilbert C. *Cotton Fields No More: Southern Agriculture, 1865–1980* (1984).

Goldfield, David R. *Cotton Fields and Skyscrapers: Southern City and Region, 1607–1980* (1982).

Healy, Robert G. *Competition for Land in the American South: Agriculture, Human Settlement, and the Environment* (1985).

Hilliard, Sam Bowers. *Hog Meat and Hoecake: Food Supply in the Old South, 1840–1860* (1972).

Hilliard, Sam Bowers. *Atlas of Antebellum Southern Agriculture* (1984).
Hunt, Charles B. *Physiography of the United States* (1967).
Kirby, Jack Temple. *Rural Worlds Lost: The American South, 1920–1960* (1987).
Shelford, Victor E. *The Ecology of North America* (1963).
Silver, Timothy. *A New Face on the Countryside: Indians, Colonists, and Slaves in the South Atlantic Forests, 1500–1800* (1990).
Vance, Rupert. *Human Geography of the South* (1932).
Vankat, John L. *The Natural Vegetation of North America: An Introduction* (1979).
Williams, Michael. *Americans and Their Forests: A Historical Geography* (1989).

— MART A. STEWART

THE NATURAL ENVIRONMENT: THE WEST

The western United States contains a wide variety of physical environments. From the semi-arid Great Plains to the humid Pacific Northwest, flora and fauna vary as widely as does the topography. For all its diversity, much of the West beyond the hundredth meridian differs from the rest of the nation in its greater altitude and aridity. The deserts of the Great Basin and the Southwest and the peaks of the Rockies, Sierras, and Cascades are the most visible markers of the West's distinctiveness.

Human beings first came into the region over the Bering land bridge between 25,000 and 10,000 B.C. Archaeologists believe that these nomadic people were following large animal herds on which they depended for food and clothing. Climatic changes beginning in 8000 B.C., along with the possible overkill of large mammals, altered the subsistence opportunities for these early hunters.

Indians, Hispanics, Early Anglos

Small-game hunting and gathering practices intensified with the disappearance of the large herd animals. Ears of corn found in southwestern archaeological digs suggest that agriculture developed around 5000 or 4000 B.C., evidently through contact with MesoAmerican cultures. The possible predecessor to the Pueblo cultures, the Anasazi, began to practice communal agriculture around the time of Christ. By 1300, the Anasazi had developed large population centers at Mesa Verde, Colorado; Chaco Canyon, New Mexico; and Kayenta, Arizona. Their fate is a matter of uncertainty; probably at the end of the thirteenth century a combination of drought and attacks from nomadic raiders induced the Anasazi to leave their villages and settle along the more fertile Rio Grande Valley.

Along the Pacific coast and in the interior regions of the Great Basin and the northern Rockies, people held more closely to the hunter-gatherer tradition. Game was abundant, as were berries, seeds, and tubers. In the Pacific Northwest, salmon provided local people with a reliable source of protein. In villages along the west-to-east-running Plains rivers, farming added corn and beans to the supply of game and wild plants. In the arid Southwest, both floodplain and irrigation agriculture provided a significant portion of the diet, as well as the foundation for the rituals and beliefs of community life.

In many areas of the West, Indians practiced cyclical burning to improve certain areas as habitats for game and to encourage the proliferation of some plant species while reducing the numbers of less useful plants. With fire, hunting, gathering, and farming, Indian people had placed a human imprint on the land; what white Americans would later call pristine wilderness was in part a human creation. Just as important, native people had invested the landscape with social and religious meaning. Indian religions dealt in sacred places, pilgrimages, and codes of conduct for human behavior toward nature.

In 1540, Francisco Vásquez de Coronado led the first organized European expedition into the American West. His tour represented the arrival of behavior directed at transforming the land's resources into individual wealth. Nonetheless, in terms of minerals, New Mexico struck Coronado as a great disappointment. In a pattern common to colonization, his men might well have perished had they not seized Indian resources—food and clothing—for their own use. Spanish officials saw his journey as a failure and concentrated support on the silver mines of Zacatecas and Durango in what is now northern Mexico.

In 1598, Juan de Oñate brought permanent Hispanic settlers to New Mexico. Along with Christianity, missionaries introduced European livestock and crops. The Spanish presence strained the delicate balance that the Pueblos had created through irrigation of a limited amount of land. Spaniards devoured Pueblo corn, and took Pueblo people from their own fields to labor in settlers' fields. In 1680 the Pueblos joined in revolt and drove the Spaniards from New Mexico. Reconquered in the 1690s, New Mexico was a place of diminished economic ambition. Hispanic people settled in villages, relying on livestock and on small-scale agriculture supported by *acequias* (irrigation canals).

New Mexico was soon joined by Spanish colonies in Texas, Arizona, and California. Iberian cattle adapted readily to all these areas. And the horse, introduced by the Spanish, migrated northward and into the cultures of many tribes, turning hunter-gatherers into nomadic horsemen following the massive buffalo herds. Ironically, the horse provided nomadic natives in the Southwest with an unforeseen advantage: they could now raid

Hispanic cattle and sheep herds with relative impunity. In many ways, the propagation and distribution of livestock drew the lines of power and conflict in colonization.

Only one European import significantly protected Hispanic settlements from annihilation. Disease, especially smallpox and measles, provided the essential vehicle for conquest. No one will ever know the number of Indians killed by disease, but estimates range between a third and a half of the total population west of the Mississippi River. Moreover, disease did not require continual European presence; Indians fleeing from the horrifying effects of smallpox spread the disease all the way to Canada. Anglo-Americans exploring westward through the Great Plains and Rockies brought disease to the upper Missouri tribes. Smallpox came close to eliminating the once powerful Mandan and Arikara tribes. Before the arrival of white settlers in what they would call "wilderness," disease had brought enormous political, social, and religious changes. Disease wiped out chiefs, shamans, and other tribal leaders. Some tribes, remnants of formerly large cultural entities, were absorbed by other tribes. They had lost the right to determine their own tribal policies. In other areas new people assumed the role of chief or tribal leader.

Introduced by the Spanish, the horse ironically provided nomadic natives in the Southwest with the ability to raid Hispanic cattle and sheep herds in Texas, Arizona, and California with relative impunity.

Exploitation of the West Through the Great Depression

Along with disease, westward-moving Anglo-Americans brought a more exploitative environmental ideology. Unlike Indians and Hispanics, Americans took on the project of mastering the resources of the West with strong corporate and political backing. Viewing the West as an endlessly bountiful supplier of resources, individuals and institutions wanted a return on their investments of capital, energy, and faith. For decades to come, the pursuit of profit would dominate American environmental behavior in the West.

Preceded in a number of cases by French-Canadian and British fur traders, American fur trappers followed Meriwether Lewis and William Clark (1804–1806) into the West, hoping to trap the abundant beaver. Unlike the British Hudson's Bay Company, the American fur companies relied on European-American trappers, thereby elbowing Indian people out of their central role in the fur trade as both trappers and middlemen. Though traditionally portrayed as exemplars of rugged individualism, the American trappers of the 1820s and 1830s served as agents for eastern-based corporations. The trappers relied on companies for powder, lead, traps, and markets for their furs. The profitability of the fur trade led to intense competition between companies. Trappers raced each other to the richest beaver streams, reducing the animals to near extinction. From the fur trade on, the policy of exploiting western resources for eastern corporations became a standard practice in the West. A rapid shift from boom to bust characterized the fur trade, as well as the many extractive industries that followed it.

Other wildlife shared the same fate as the beaver. The arrival of steamboats on the Missouri River beginning in 1832 permitted the export of the otherwise difficult-to-transport buffalo hides. After the Civil War, the U.S. Army encouraged the slaughter of the buffalo in order to "pacify" the Plains Indians through the elimination of their food supply. The conquest of the Indians thus rested as heavily on environmental change as it did on military engagements.

With the removal of the buffalo, the grasslands of the Plains became a temporarily unoccupied ecological niche. Livestock drovers responded to that opportunity, replacing the herds of buffalo with herds of cattle and sheep. If not kept constantly moving, these animals ate the native grasses of the Plains to the roots. Once the original ground cover was destroyed, the soil became vulnerable to erosion by the intense winds of the area. With land too densely populated with cattle, the Plains' range cattle industry faced a near collapse in 1887, after a severe winter combined with overgrazing to kill off many of the malnourished animals.

Farmers, too, responded to the apparent opportunity of the Plains. In the years after the Civil War, a spell of abundant rainfall encouraged farmers to move onto the Plains. The return of more characteristic, sparse patterns of rainfall, as well as cycles of grasshopper infestation and periodic fires, broke the hopes of many farmers. For some, the technique of dry farming seemed to provide a solution. With the constant cultivation and packing of topsoil to trap a water reservoir, dry farming made it possible for crops to grow where conventional techniques were only wasted effort. In the long run, however, the plowing of the Plains contributed to one of the most dramatic environmental catastrophes on the continent; taking to the air during the droughts of the 1930s, Plains soil earned the region the grim name of the Dust Bowl.

In a pattern that seemed, superficially, to be very different from farming, the California gold rush of 1849 inaugurated a series of rushes to every territory in the West. Individual placer mining for precious metals quickly gave way to heavily capitalized industrial mining. Most gold and silver veins lay embedded in solid rock. Hydraulic mining washed away the economically useless bedrock and most of the hillsides in which the minerals lay buried. Stamp mills crushed the rock to expose the metals within, and smelters separated marketable metal from useless matter. Sold and transported out of the region, precious metals left behind a landscape dotted by abandoned mines and piles of tailings.

Precious metals were only a part of the mining story. Copper mining boomed in the late nineteenth century with the advent of electricity as a power source. In addition to creating a constant demand for copper wire, electricity provided a cheap source of power to run ore cars, air compressors, and pumps. In the late nineteenth and early twentieth centuries, coal mines proliferated in the Rocky Mountain states. Gold, silver, copper, or coal, the mines were generally industrial operations worked by wage employees hired by absentee owners.

Underground mining created a heavy demand for timber to support tunnels and drifts; viewed from a distance, mines in places like the Comstock Lode in Nevada would have looked like enterprises in which humans cut down local forests in order to bury them underground. Despite demands for mine timbers, for housing, and for fuel, the western timber industry remained a relatively small-scale operation until the end of the nineteenth century, with large-scale cutting instead in the Great Lakes region. At the turn of the century, however, the Weyerhaeuser Timber Company began purchasing large tracts in the Pacific Northwest. Mechanized sawmills and increased railroad connections enabled the western timber industry to boom. Tree removal led to erosion, loss of wildlife, and the silting of rivers.

Mining, farming, livestock grazing, and lumbering may have involved very different techniques and employed different labor forces, but they shared a pattern in common: an intensive extraction of raw materials until the resource became too expensive or too rare to exploit. By the dominant point of view of the nineteenth century, economic development counted as "improvement." But cutover lands, blasted mining sites, overgrazed ground cover, and eroded soil suggest destruction more than improvement.

The Conservation and Preservation Movements

The transformation of the forests through lumbering and grazing provided the impetus for both the preservation and the conservation movements of the late nineteenth and early twentieth centuries. John Muir, a Scottish immigrant in California, became the most visible and audible advocate of preservation, as he fought the intrusion of loggers and sheepherders into his beloved Sierra Nevadas. At the same time, the conservation movement, most commonly associated with Gifford Pinchot, appointed chief of the Division of Forestry in 1898, undertook to shift the gears of resource extraction from profligacy to "wise use." Frequently jumbled together under the shared label "conservation," Muir's preservation movement and Pinchot's conservation movement actually had very different motives and very different agendas for the management of western resources.

In 1872, the Yellowstone area became the first national park. Set aside for its distinctive geothermal features, the park came to exist be-

The lower basin of Mammoth Hot Springs in Yellowstone National Park. Created in 1872, Yellowstone became the first national park.

fore there was any philosophy, or even any institution, for the management of preserved lands. It was almost fifty years before Congress passed the act creating the National Park Service in 1916.

In California, Yosemite was a state park until 1890, when it became a national park. At Yosemite, the question of definition—both of the status of parks and of the differences between preservationists and conservationists—came into focus. The boundaries of Yosemite National Park included the Hetch Hetchy Valley, a smaller-scale version of Yosemite Valley's steep walls. Depending on one's point of view, Hetch Hetchy was either a valley of irreplaceable beauty or a naturally designed site for a reservoir. When planners and developers in San Francisco targeted the Hetch Hetchy Valley for a city reservoir, the battle was joined. John Muir and his allies fought for the sanctity of the national park and of the undammed canyon; the city of San Francisco, in company with its ally Gifford Pinchot, fought for the declared necessity of increased urban growth and water use. In 1913, the victory went to the city; Hetch Hetchy Valley has been a lake for most of the twentieth century. Defeated in battle, the preservationists had, however, learned how to fight; and John Muir's Sierra Club would be a power to reckon with in later struggles over western resources.

The arrangement of power on the federal side in these matters was by no means clear and consistent; power over public lands was divided among several agencies. Lodged in the Department of the Interior, the National Park Service was entirely separate from the Forest Service in the Department of Agriculture. The national forests originated in a law passed in 1891 that permitted the president to set aside forest reserves. Theodore Roosevelt especially made vigorous use of this power, finally installing his friend Pinchot as the ruler of this new bureaucratic domain. Forest Service policy required multiple use; lumbering, mining, grazing, and recreation were all to receive their due. Created in 1902 by the Newlands Reclamation Act, the Bureau of Reclamation, located within the Department of the Interior, pushed for the construction of large dams and the provision of water for agriculture and, increasingly, of electrical power for cities. In 1934, responding to the overuse of public lands, the Taylor Grazing Act created the Grazing Service, later named the Bureau of Land Management. Located in the Department of the Interior, the bureau was to supervise and allocate—by no means to eliminate—grazing rights on the remaining public domain.

By the mid twentieth century, Plains agriculture and ranching seemed to have gained a new lease on life as gasoline-powered pumps drew water from underground aquifers.

Each of these agencies—Park Service, Forest Service, Bureau of Reclamation, and Bureau of Land Management—had its own turf to defend, traditions to maintain, and appropriations to secure. Even though they squabbled among themselves for position and privilege, the rise to power of federal land management agencies nevertheless gave Westerners the impression that a monolithic power based in Washington, D.C., had taken over control of their natural resources. From time to time, western businessmen would launch campaigns, as much matters of rhetoric as of substance, to return the public lands to state control; as recently as the late 1970s, the so-called Sagebrush Rebels returned to this familiar demand. In fact, the very idea of "public lands" raised a fundamental issue of property and legitimacy. If the lands belonged permanently to the people of the entire United States, then local Westerners had no particular privileges of use or ownership over the federal lands in their vicinity.

With or without federal restrictions, western resource developers did not slow down in deference to any theoretical "end of the frontier" at the turn of the century. Already developed on a small scale in California (1893–1894), the western oil industry took off in 1901 with the discovery at Spindletop in Texas. Coal mines continued to expand, and experimental extractive industries, like the oil shale business on the Western Slope of Colorado, made tentative beginnings. The timber industry in the Pacific Northwest continued to grow. Often with federal sponsorship and subsidy, irrigation created farms on desert lands that had once seemed to be permanently and resolutely "useless." With water diverted from the Colorado River, California's Imperial Valley produced fruits and vegetables for growers who relied heavily on migrant labor. Homesteading continued on a large scale after 1890; fruit orchards went into production in the Pacific Northwest and in southern California; cotton moved out of the South and into the Southwest. By the mid twentieth century, Plains agriculture and ranching seemed to have gained a new lease on life as gasoline-powered pumps drew water from underground aquifers.

Perhaps most important, western cities expanded their populations and their resource demands. Towns and cities had, of course, been an important part of western expansion in the nineteenth century. Santa Fe governed the territory of New Mexico and served as an entry point for Americans trading in Mexico; San Francisco bankrolled a series of mineral rushes; Salt Lake City provided both a religious and a business center for the Mormons; Denver supplied miners with tools and capital; Los Angeles underwent a dramatic land boom in the 1880s. In the twentieth century, these cities attracted workers, investors, retirees, businessmen, and industrialists. Making the most of the region's wide-open spaces, western cities tended to expand horizontally rather than vertically, creating conditions that seemed to demand heavy use of automobiles. In many towns and cities, homeowners tried to replicate familiar landscapes from the eastern United States, planting lawns and gardens that required constant watering. As users of land, water, fuel, food, and electricity, western towns and cities became major players in the region's environmental history.

Exploitation of the West Since World War II

World War II acted as a major accelerator of western population growth. With the demands of the war's Pacific theater, the ports of Washington and California acquired new importance, and West Coast shipbuilding and airplane manufacturing prospered. Western aridity proved to have major value for defense operations; the dryness and remoteness of much western terrain, as well as its status as public land, gave the region the edge when it came to locating everything from air force bases to installations for the development of the atomic bomb. The military had played a vital part in the development of the region in the nineteenth century, and its role in land use in the twentieth century was just as, if not more, important. The opportunities presented by World War II inspired a population rush to the region that dwarfed the westward movement of the nineteenth century.

To the majority of Westerners, growth had long been a synonym for prosperity. Yet growth had always come with costs, even if the beneficiaries habitually dismissed them. Kicked into high gear by World War II, Los Angeles grew with a vengeance in the postwar years. Fumes from manufacturing facilities (especially synthetic rubber plants), carbon monoxide from millions of automobiles, water shortages, and an understandable reluctance to face up to these problems characterized Los Angeles and a number of other western cities. If the West had once promised opportunity, abundance, and a better way of life, it was, by the mid twentieth century, a promise obscured by smog and congestion. In the Southwest, especially Arizona, population boomed with the spread of air-conditioning. Even if it meant an enormous seasonal use of electrical power, technology seemed to have transcended the overwhelming summer heat that had previously limited the area's attractiveness for Anglo settlers.

Looking for refuge from the trials of urban areas, and joined by tourists from the eastern United States—indeed, from the whole planet—Westerners brought congestion to some rural areas as well. Cars jammed Yosemite National Park; parades of huge recreational vehicles lumbered through Yellowstone; backpackers bumped into each other on remote trails; those eager to raft down western rivers waited, for months, for permits and licenses. At the end of the nineteenth century, the aesthetic appreciation of nature and the attractions of outdoor places for recreation seemed to present a new, and entirely different, approach to the physical environment. But in the mid twentieth century, it began to seem possible that outdoors enthusiasts might, in fact, come to "love nature to death." With tourism and recreation emerging as crucial western industries, nature appreciation seemed to be another, temporarily disguised, form of commodity consciousness. Where previous generations of resource developers saw a piece of nature waiting to become a mine or a logging site, by another, only superficially different point of view, another kind of developer saw a site waiting to become a ski resort or a service station with a minimart.

The question of water use brings all these issues of growth and development into focus. Fifteen states now depend upon three major river systems for their water needs: the Colorado, the Columbia, and the Missouri rivers. The rivers have been dammed beyond recognition, yet they still fail to meet the demands of the thirsty West. The Colorado River provides the starkest case study of an over-allocated resource. In 1922, an interstate compact divided the estimated annual flow of the river between the upper basin states of Colorado, Wyoming, Utah, and New Mexico, and the lower basin states of Nevada, Arizona, and California. International agreements gave Mexico a share of the water as well.

Basing its estimate of annual flow on several well-watered years, the Colorado River Compact of 1922 turned out to have allocated more water than the river, in some years, contains. Playing water politics with enormous skill, the lower basin states got a head start in river development with the enormous project of Hoover Dam, completed in 1936. For Mexico, United States' use of the Colorado has meant a silty and salinized trickle of water arriving on the other side of the border, and long fights over both water quality and water quantity; for the western states, the development of the Colorado has triggered endless squabbles over who owns the rights to how much water, with the upper basin states striving to develop their claims to water that now benefits Arizona and California. Environmentalists clamor for an end to the disruption of free-flowing rivers by dams and reclamation projects; ranchers and farmers hope for more projects in their areas; urban users continue to water their lawns and depend heavily on electricity produced by waterpower. Through the middle of all these contests runs the legendary, overallocated river that carved the Grand Canyon.

An added variable in western water conflicts stems from the question of Indian water rights. In the *Winters v. the United States* decision of 1908, the Supreme Court ruled that the Indians on the Fort Belknap reservation deserved a share of the Milk River, which stockmen and settlers had diverted for irrigation projects. Since the creators and planners of reservations had intended Indians to farm, the justices reasoned, reservations have an assumed, reserved water right. Though the case has not yet significantly altered or improved Indian water projects, it has provided a valuable opportunity for Indian people to assert their rights; at the same time, the *Winters* doctrine sketches an unsettling prospect for non-Indian water-users.

As environmental historians have found in every part of the planet, the history of the physical environment and the history of human groups are not separable. Even if professional specialization has divided the turf, the fact that humans are biological beings makes social history and environmental history interdependent. In the American West, the last two centuries of environmental change have created a tangle of consequences, a direct inheritance from the people of the western past to the people of the western present.

Radioactivity is the most recent addition to that heritage. The development of the atomic bomb during World War II had its center of gravity in the New Mexican town of Los Alamos, chosen for its remoteness. Similarly, looking for a location for the production of plutonium, Leslie Groves and the planners of the Manhattan Project chose a site in eastern Washington with isolation and access to hydropower and cooling water from the Columbia River in its favor. The small town of Hanford, along with thriving orchards, was forced to yield ground to the new, and secret, Hanford Nuclear Reservation. The rush to produce plutonium led to careless handling of radioactive substances; before the war was over, Hanford had an almost casual system of waste disposal. Dumped into trenches in the ground, nuclear waste drained into the Columbia River and headed downstream to the major population centers of western Oregon, while the dominant west-to-east winds carried airborne radioactive material from Hanford to local towns and farms, as well as to the city of Spokane in western Washington.

In the cold war, nuclear development kept its western center of gravity. Within the United States, the major deposits of uranium proved to lie in the Black Hills of South Dakota and in the Colorado Plateau (where the states of Colorado, Utah, Arizona, and New Mexico meet). Uranium rushes had some of the same flair and energy as nineteenth-century mining rushes, even if the prospectors now carried Geiger counters. But mining and processing this resource involved a wholly new set of health risks; in the late twentieth century, the veterans of uranium production reported a high rate of illness and mortality. Seeking a continental site for nuclear testing, government planners made the usual choice in favor of western aridity and remoteness, and developed the Nevada Test Site, with above-ground testing through the 1950s and underground testing since then. In the same vein, when it came to sites for missiles and warheads, the West won most of the contests. Domestic use of nuclear power, as well as military use, made radioactive waste disposal an increasingly urgent question. Congress then had to choose a part of the United States to play permanent host to the nation's store of radioactive material. True to the pattern of previous atomic decision making, the West won again, with a controversial storage site planned near Carlsbad, New Mexico, and a much larger, permanent, and equally controversial, site slated for Yucca Mountain, Nevada.

Toward the Future

For nearly two centuries, when the Anglo-American mind met the enormity of western space, the result was a curious kind of optimism. By this faith, the western plains, mountains, and deserts were, in and of themselves, a solution to the problems of the eastern United States, a cure for the demographic, economic, and psychological congestion of the "older" region. Tested repeatedly, and not always successfully, this faith nonetheless had enormous staying power. The Dust Bowl of the 1930s was surely an enormous challenge, yet the clouds of blowing dirt produced little in the way of changed environmental attitudes. When the rains came back, optimism was their first crop. "The future is just opening up," one Plains resident put it. "Our future is all before us." This resilient faith in a second chance had important consequences in behavior, encouraging a resistance to regulation and restraint, a reluctance to look at the long-term costs and consequences of growth and development, and an unwillingness to face up to the actual limits of resources in the West, especially the finite supply of water. Tempered and moderated by the conservation movement, the commodification of western nature nonetheless remained the name of the game.

In 1893, the frontier historian Frederick Jackson Turner prematurely proclaimed the end of one era of western American history and the arrival of another. The frontier ended in 1890, Turner said, and his followers in the field of western American history stuck by this improbable article of faith, even as full-speed-ahead resource development continued in virtually every part of the West. And yet, in nearly all aspects of the human relationship to the physical environment, the last decades of the twentieth century suggest that a much more significant age of reckoning with environmental limits has come upon the region. On this count, Turner may have been right about a fundamental shift in the momentum of westward expansion; he simply missed the date by a century.

In the 1990s, examples of this reckoning are everywhere in the region. Abandoned mines drain toxic chemicals into western streams, and western states, in a time of strained budgets, struggle with the question of reclaiming and repairing these damaged sites. Environmentalists seek to restore wolves and other predator populations while ranchers oppose the reintroduction of any threat to their livestock. Dams on the Columbia River interfere with the migration and reproduction of salmon, a formerly abundant natural resource valued—and fought over—by Indian tribes, sport fishermen, and commercial fishermen. Irrigation produces not only crops but also increased salinity in the soil; meanwhile, the mounting federal deficit threatens to dry up the flow of federal cash that had underwritten the water empire of the West.

In a system called water ranching, western cities buy up agricultural water rights, a move applauded by some on the premise that irrigated farming had always been an inefficient and expensive use of water, and denounced by others who feel that a rural farm culture has its own legitimacy and rights to preservation. Pumps pull water from the Ogallala aquifer, the enormous deposit of underground water that supported much of Plains farming and ranching, depleting it faster than natural sources can replenish it.

A prolonged crisis of the farm economy also wore away at the underpinnings of rural life. As settlements on the Plains lost population, a courageous team of land-use analysts, Frank and Deborah Popper, argued that the heavy settlement of the area had been a mistake; that rural depopulation was a clear, established trend; and that social planners should aid in and ease the process. The Plains environment, the Poppers suggested, could reverse history and return to the ecological job it did best: supporting roaming herds of untamed herbivores. Restored as Buffalo Commons, the Plains would recover from its century-and-a-half-long interlude of error. Whether or not one embraced a vision of Omaha, Nebraska, as a jumping-off point for Plains safaris, the prospect of a regional future shaped by an awareness of limited water was hard to evade.

The sense of reckoning exemplified in these western crises was by no means unique in the nation or on the planet. But the West had for decades held onto its mythic standing as a place of abundant, even endless, resources, supplying Americans with infinite opportunities for second chances. The recognition of limits hit particularly hard in this region—hard enough, perhaps, to inspire a prudent and beneficial change in well-established habits of western resource use.

[See also Agriculture; The Frontier; Landscapes; National Parks and Preservation; Rural Life in the West; Technology and Social Change.]

BIBLIOGRAPHY

Abbe, Donald R. *Austin and the Reese River Mining District: Nevada's Forgotten Frontier* (1985).

Bartley, Paula. *Plains Women: Women in the American West* (1991).

Bean, Lee, Geraldine P. Mineau, and Douglas L. Anderton. *Fertility Change on the American Frontier: Adaptation and Innovation* (1990).

Beck, Warren A., and Ynez D. Haase. *Historical Atlas of the American West* (1989).

Billington, Ray Allen. *Westward Expansion: A History of the American Frontier.* 5th ed. (1982).

Brown, Dee Alexander. *Bury My Heart at Wounded Knee: An Indian History of the American West* (1970).

Carpenter, Allan. *The Encyclopedia of the Far West* (1991).

Chittenden, Hiram Martin. *The American Fur Trade of the Far West* (1935; repr. 1986).

Cochrane, Willard Wesley. *The Development of American Agriculture: A Historical Analysis* (1979).

Coe, Michael, Dean Snow, and Elizabeth Benson. *Atlas of Ancient America* (1986).

Cox, Thomas R. *Mills and Markets: A History of the Pacific Coast Lumber Industry to 1900* (1974).

Crosby, Alfred W. *The Columbian Exchange: Biological and Cultural Consequences of 1492* (1972).

Davis, James Edward. *Frontier America, 1800–1840: A Comparative Demographic Analysis of the Settlement Process* (1977).

Davis, Mike. *City of Quartz: Excavating the Future in Los Angeles* (1990).

Dawdy, Doris Ostrander. *Congress in Its Wisdom: The Bureau of Reclamation and the Public Interest* (1989).

Ebeling, Walter. *The Fruited Plain: The Story of American Agriculture* (1979).

Goetzmann, William H. *Exploration and Empire: The Explorer and the Scientist in the Winning of the American West* (1966; repr. 1978).

Gregory, James Noble. *American Exodus: The Dust Bowl Migration and Okie Culture in California* (1989).

Hazlett, Thomas W. *The California Coastal Commission and the Economics of Environmentalism* (1980).

Hurt, R. Douglas. *The Dust Bowl: An Agricultural and Social History* (1981).
Hyde, Anne Farrar. *An American Vision: Far Western Landscape and National Culture, 1820–1920* (1990).
Katz, William Loren. *The Black West* (3d rev. ed. 1987).
King, Philip B. *The Evolution of North America* (rev. ed. 1977).
Knoll, Tricia. *Becoming American: Asian Sojourners, Immigrants and Refugees in the Western United States* (1982).
Lamar, Howard R. *The Reader's Encyclopedia of the American West* (1977).
Lange, Dorothea. *An American Exodus: A Record of Human Erosion* (1939).
Lee, Lawrence Bacon. *Reclaiming the American West: An Historiography and Guide* (1980).
Limerick, Patricia Nelson. *The Legacy of Conquest: The Unbroken Past of the American West* (1987).
Lowitt, Richard. *The New Deal and the American West* (1984).
McCabe, James Dabney. *History of the Grange Movement: or, the Farmer's War Against Monopolies* (1874).
Malone, Michael P. *The American West: A Twentieth-Century History* (1989).
Mander, Jerry. *In the Absence of the Sacred: The Failure of Technology and the Survival of the Indian Nations* (1991).
Matson, R. G. *The Origins of Southwestern Agriculture* (1991).
Popper, Frank J., and Deborah E. Popper. "The Reinvention of the American Frontier." *Amicus Journal* (Summer 1991).
Reinhartz, Dennis, and Charles C. Colley, eds. *The Mapping of the American Southwest* (1987).
Robbins, William G. *Lumberjacks and Legislators: Political Economy of the US. Lumber Industry, 1890–1941* (1982).
Roosevelt, Theodore. *Good Hunting: In Pursuit of Big Game in the West* (1907).
Rosenberg, Bruce A. *The Code of the West* (1982).
Spence, Clark C. *Mining Engineers and the American West: The Lace-Boot Brigade, 1849–1933* (1970).
Steffen, Jerome O., ed. *The American West: New Perspectives, New Dimensions* (1979).
Turner, Frederick Jackson. *The Frontier in American History* (1962; repr. 1975).
Twain, Mark. *Roughing It* (1913).
White, G. Edward. *The Eastern Establishment and the Western Experience: The West of Frederic Remington, Theodore Roosevelt and Owen Wister* (1989).
White, Richard. *"It's Your Misfortune and None of My Own": A History of the American West* (1991).
Worster, Donald. *Rivers of Empire: Water, Aridity, and the Growth of the American West* (1985).
Worster, Donald. *Under Western Skies: Nature and History in the American West* (1992).

— PATRICIA NELSON LIMERICK, W. CLARK WHITEHORN

NIGHTLIFE

When the sun set and evening fell across late-nineteenth- and early-twentieth-century American cities, gas, and later electric, lights illuminated the alluring world of nighttime amusements. Many entertainment opportunities enticed the city dweller at night, including bars, cabarets and nightclubs, and dance halls. Each offered some combination of diversion and relaxation. These enterprises varied widely, depending on location, size, and nature of clientele. Music performance and dance, which were available in many of these venues, contributed to their sensory appeal. Alcohol often provided additional stimulation for the evening's fun.

Seeking recreation at night was a well-established pastime for many Americans throughout the nineteenth century. Before and after the Civil War, commercial spectator entertainment grew as people patronized theaters, circuses, minstrel shows, music halls, and institutions like P. T. Barnum's American Museum. Americans found time for these activities as industrial work discipline strictly divided their time between work and play. Leisure that offered a chance for physical or emotional relaxation might help one escape the dulling effects of routinized labor. Urban areas provided large enough markets for entrepreneurs to offer ever-increasing entertainment choices; in less populated areas Americans continued to rely more on their own devices for creating fun.

Although these diversions had potential appeal for any urbanite, many amusements were popular primarily with the working class, and entertainment choices often reflected ethnic preferences. Certain activities, such as sporting events, cockfights and ratbaiting, gambling, and prizefighting were part of a male-dominated subculture centered on the saloon. Elliott Gorn has noted that "Cliques of men created informal but stable brotherhoods in particular bars, where politics were argued, grievances aired, heroes toasted, sports discussed, legends told, songs sung, and friendships cemented" (*The Manly Art*, p. 133). Men were well aware that their participation in rough sports, prostitution, and saloon life challenged the dominant Victorian expectation that people would remain disciplined in work and play. Those who made all or part of their living by participating in sports, especially boxing, knew that the "very word 'sport' implied social deviance" (p. 139).

Eventually, those urban entertainment areas most associated with "sporting" activities became legally, or were, by custom, defined as vice districts. San Francisco's Barbary Coast, New York's Bowery, and New Orleans's Storyville became spatially distinct worlds promising sensual mysteries as well as seedy dangers. In them, many saloons, gambling houses, dance halls, and brothels operated. Because prostitutes sometimes lit red lamps to signal their location, these neighborhoods were called red-light districts; guidebooks advertising sexual services also directed patrons to houses of prostitution.

Those Americans who identified with Victorian strictures against "wasted" time frowned on any dissipation of energy and wages in the saloon or other amusement spots. Advocates of genteel values encouraged leisure-time pursuits that improved the mind and promoted "good" company. They valued self-control for themselves and encouraged it in others. By the turn of the century, however, bars, nightclubs, and dance halls attracted a new middle-class, and in some cases female, clientele that challenged Victorian strictures against immoral entertainment. Nighttime amusements continued to inspire considerable public debate and discussion, however, because reformers, law enforcement agencies, employers, and parents believed controlling leisure would ameliorate various social ills.

As the nineteenth century progressed, sophisticated mass-marketing strategies evolved to attract customers. Location, architecture, interior decor, and music helped set a nightclub or barroom apart from working life. The activities of bars, clubs, and dance halls were increasingly structured by the needs of entrepreneurs, as well as by zoning restrictions. For the price of a drink or the cost of the cover charge, patrons purchased entertainment as a commodity. Some opportunities for defining one's own free time always took place in these locations. One might dance, flirt, drink, gamble, or socialize. Except for establishment employees, people came for fun—an activity defined by the relaxation of physical and emotional restraints. Nightlife institutions also served an important function in helping successive generations of Americans define immigrant, ethnic, peer, and gender cultures. In some cases, the settings helped Americans break down class and racial boundaries.

Early-Twentieth-Century Nighttime Leisure

As industrialization and urbanization dramatically changed the nature and size of cities after the Civil War, saloon proprietors found that city dwellers were less likely to make their own alcoholic beverages. Previously, public consumption of alcohol took place primarily at inns or other establishments near major thoroughfares. Otherwise, citizens tended to drink at meals, on social occasions, and with friends in their homes.

By the late nineteenth century, Americans purchased beer or whiskey, as they did many other consumer products, from commercial manufacturers (through the saloonkeeper). Saloons offered the most common public setting for nighttime amusement, and they quickly became a ubiquitous feature of even the smallest towns. A few establishments catered to the wealthy elite, but most affluent drinkers joined private clubs. Consequently, the saloon tended to service working-class men.

Leisure and consumption patterns changed in tandem with the transformation of work. Beginning in the early nineteenth century, increasingly large and complex industrial manufacturing enterprises gradually replaced the artisan's shop and household-based production. In this process, employers were partially successful in keeping workers from consuming alcohol at the workplace. Previously, workers could correctly assume that drink would be a part of the daily regimen, especially when grog or some other alcoholic beverage was provided as part of the compensation.

But industrialization was accompanied by the growing influence of bourgeois values; employers encouraged sobriety because it would help workers exercise self-control at work and at home. Supervisors assumed this discipline encouraged greater productivity. Furthermore, since industrial manufacturing increasingly relied on machines that required workers to perform at a faster pace, the drink that might help one cope with the numbing effects of repetitive labor could also dull one's attention to potential workplace hazards. Drinking on the job could easily be perceived as both a moral and an occupational hazard by working-class Americans.

Industrial work discipline affected far more than the conditions of the shop floor, however; and when workers had increased leisure time, and in some cases greater discretionary income, the saloon proved an inviting location for sharing the joys and frustrations of the job. Away from the employer's gaze, a bar afforded some measure of privacy for workers who lived in densely populated urban neighborhoods. Since conversation during the production process declined with industrialization, the saloon offered a much-needed place to talk. Drinking rituals, such as buying successive rounds of drinks to treat one another, "embodied a resistance of sorts to the transformation of social relationships into'commodities'—a means of preserving reciprocal modes of social interaction within a capitalist world" (Rosenzweig, *Eight Hours for What We Will*, p. 60).

By buying one another successive rounds of drinks in saloons, American men were in a sense resisting "the transformations of social relationship into 'commodities' "; the habit constituted "a means of preserving reciprocal modes of social interaction within a capitalist world."

Saloons opened as early as 5:30 or 6:00 A.M. and closed late at night, thus providing workers with a location for drinking and socializing before and after work. In addition, patrons stopped in for the free lunch served in many establishments. Transients relied on the saloon not only for food and drink but also for sanitary facilities, warmth, and, in some cases, a place to sleep through the night. Saloonkeepers might cash checks, receive mail, or write letters for their patrons, and many provided free newspapers. Saloons also sold liquor, particularly beer poured into "growler" buckets, to be taken off the premises.

Patrons shaped a saloon culture within a context strongly influenced by brewers, distributors, and saloonkeepers. Seeking to maximize their market share, brewers designated particular saloons as outlets for their products. Some owned bars, or operated them, at or near their production facilities. Others rented fixtures, helped retailers pay licensing fees, and eventually paid the rent or mortgage. In the late nineteenth century, brewers, like other industrialists, competed in a volatile market where hundreds of saloons opened every year. Vertical integration of production and distribution facilities helped them manage their share of the market, and in the process they controlled many aspects of bar culture.

The taps, mirrors, and lighting rented or sold by the brewers were only one aspect of saloon decoration. Bars varied in size and quality of decor. Tables provided in the earliest saloons offered men an opportunity, for relaxed conversation, card games, and neighborhood camaraderie. Saloons located on major transportation routes were, by contrast, most likely to increase their standing room for commuting clientele. The largest venues might have a barroom in front and a room with tables, billiards, and (where legal) a dance floor in the back.

Other notable features included sawdust and drip mats on the floors, brass rails, spittoons, and pictures of sporting men (and women). Massive wooden bars, defining the location as a bar, dominated some saloons. The most elegant were made from expensive wood and were backed by ornate gilded mirrors. Prizefighter John L. Sullivan's portrait graced thousands of saloons—a legacy of earlier times, when saloons sponsored bare-knuckle fighting. The Anheuser-Busch Brewing Company distributed a popular print, *Custer's Last Fight*, which celebrated "military pugilism" on the frontier.

For recently arrived immigrants, the saloon could represent a reassuring connection with the Old World. Irish American drinking songs and rituals bore a strong resemblance to those in Dublin, for example. German Americans opened beer gardens and encouraged family-style saloons in their neighborhoods, and in many communities German brewers became prominent businessmen. Saloons also helped immigrants find out about jobs in their new neighborhoods, and the saloonkeepers might well speak one's native tongue. Since many bars were patronized almost exclusively by members of one ethnic group, the saloon became a cohesion-building social institution. Outsiders might receive a chilly reception.

Saloons in western cities developed in the earliest years of settlement, particularly where mining towns or cattle-drive depots dotted the mountains and prairies. Saloons survived when towns weathered boom-and-bust cycles. Like establishments in the East, the western saloon was multifunctional; it served as bank, post office, and hotel until other institutions took root.

Regardless of its geographical location, the

Saloons in western cities developed in mining towns or cattle-drive depots. They often served as bank, post office and hotel until other institutions took root.

saloon was a haven for working men; women patronized bars in much smaller numbers. One main reason for this gender segregation was the strong association of bars, especially the "low-class" dives and barrelhouses, with prostitution. Women who danced or offered other entertainment acts as part of barroom fare were typically labeled "scarlet women," and presumed to be guilty of lewd behavior. Even in cities where the activities of the bar or saloon were clearly restricted to the provision of drink, a risqué aura surrounded saloon life—particularly at night.

Women's employment patterns shaped their leisure choices. Women who worked in domestic service, or those tied to household chores for their own families, had far less freedom to patronize saloons than did men. Married women's leisure, according to historian Kathy Peiss, "tended to be segregated from the public realm and was not sharply differentiated from work, but was sinuously intertwined with the rhythms of household labor and the relations of kinship" (*Cheap Amusements*, p. 5). Women might "rush the growler" by buying a bucket of beer and carrying it home. Most female socializing—with or without male companionship—tended to take place at neighborhood social clubs, on street corners, or on house stoops. Occasional family excursions to the theater or an amusement park included women, but these adventures were luxuries for working-class families with tight budgets.

The saloon remained central to many working-class neighborhoods despite its limited accessibility for women. It served as a neighborhood communication center, which contributed to its importance as a location for political and, in some cases, union organizing activities. Politicians made the rounds of saloons to pitch their messages, often buying drinks for patrons. Nighttime entertainment became important for organizing and funding political life. Some saloonkeepers went on to become well-known political leaders—for example, "Bathhouse" John Coughlin and Michael "Hinky-Dink" Kenna in Chicago, and Tom Anderson in New Orleans.

The variety of services provided by the saloon did not change its primary function: it provided alcoholic beverages to men who could easily squander their paychecks and ruin their health behind the swinging doors. Temperance reformers lobbied against excessive alcohol consumption throughout the nineteenth and early twentieth centuries. Most temperance activists considered bars and their nightlife culture to be the scourge of stable and harmonious working-class life. The worker who exhausted his paycheck at the neighborhood bar might well deprive his family of food and shelter—a scenario vividly drawn when temperance literature and speeches portrayed drunken fathers as profligate spenders prone to domestic violence.

Even though prohibitionists were alarmed at drinking among all social classes, the public saloon was a more visible target than the private clubs of the elite. Saloon opponents were interested not only in the effects of alcohol on individuals and their families, they also felt the saloon fostered collective social ills, particularly prostitution, gambling, and political corruption.

The reputations of the worst saloons colored public opinion about many others. Vice raids did close down numerous saloons where illegal or violent activities had taken place. The most notorious dens of vice were "concert saloons," multiroom enterprises that featured separate rooms for gambling, dancing, drinking, and (often) prostitution. Bars figured prominently in campaigns against prostitution and gambling. Fears that young women were being lured into prostitution, or the "white slave trade," against their will proved well-grounded when a Chicago saloon operator and corrupt policemen were implicated in a prostitution ring. Such activities led to the Mann Act (1910), which made it a federal offense to transport females across state lines for immoral purposes.

All cities—even some young frontier towns—had temperance activists who fought for sobriety. National organizations like the Anti-Saloon League and the Women's Christian Temperance Union (WCTU) were joined by dozens of local groups. Their attempts to regulate the activities of the saloon often began with the use of moral persuasion through temperance lectures or religious sermons. Eventually, municipalities regulated saloon growth by limiting the number of licenses issued or by zoning restrictions on drinking establishments.

Critics resorted to other tactics to restrict the saloon, such as lobbying for municipal ordinances that abolished Sunday hours, reduced the number of licenses granted, or restricted activities like dancing on the saloon premises. When cities restricted the number of saloons, some brewers and saloon-keepers benefited because such ordinances favored established businesses. New suburbs sometimes incorporated as dry territories to set themselves off from their wet metropolitan neighbors, thus emphasizing the continued association of the inner city with salacious nightlife.

Settlement-house workers and other Progressive reformers tried to control working-class leisure, including saloon behavior, by providing alternatives to the services offered by the saloon. Some opened coffee houses or built facilities for hungry and weary urban dwellers. Numerous organizations, including the Young Men's and Young Women's Christian Associations, provided athletic facilities and reading rooms. Other reformers lobbied for improved parks and recreation. Settlement house leaders endorsed family outings as an antidote to destructive male drinking. Labor unions, sensitive to the accusations of vice lodged against the saloon, established their own lodges or halls where drinks might be provided.

But the regulation of bars and saloons could have unexpected consequences. For example, the licensing of liquor establishments eliminated many home-based "blind pigs" (a place where intoxicants are sold), a change that encouraged men to leave their families and drink with other men in saloons. In some places, fights over saloon regulation intensified class tensions. Workers defended the saloon as an example of their freedom to choose leisure-time activities—a realm of experience they did not feel outsiders should control. Saloon regulation did not necessarily reduce the amount of drinking that took place in public bars; it merely altered its social and economic context.

The saloon did not provide welcome leisure-time activity for all Americans; young people, especially young women, wanted alternatives. In the early twentieth century, young unmarried women increasingly sought nondomestic labor outside the home. When they found jobs as secretaries, clerks, or factory workers, more evening leisure time was available to them. Women tended to patronize new commercialized entertainment venues such as dance halls, amusement parks, and movie theaters—which were not perceived to be exclusively male worlds.

As Kathy Peiss has documented, young women considered these "frivolous" activities exciting. They could wear stylish clothes and escape the supervised and restrictive worlds of family and work in a dance hall or club. "A woman could forget rattling machinery or irritating customers in the nervous energy and freedom of the grizzly bear and turkey trot [popular dances]" (*Cheap Amusements*, p. 45). Like male co-workers in the saloon, women often based their leisure-time social networks on relationships developed at work. Some women used nights on the town as courtship opportunities. Women were acutely aware of their financial dependence on men, who generally earned higher salaries and wages, to treat them to a good time.

The treating that took place in saloons implied a mutual camaraderie for men, but treating for young women underscored hierarchical social divisions. As Peiss observes, "The culture of treating was reinforced in the workplace through women's interactions with employers, male workmates, and customers, particularly in service and sales jobs" (p. 54). Thus, although women sought entertainment as one way to create some autonomy in their lives—away from the control of families and bosses—they found their choices shaped by many situations in which male peers had more power than the women.

Beginning in the 1910s, many major cities across the nation reported a rapidly increasing number of dance halls that attracted young men and women: "In Chicago alone, in 1911, it was calculated that 86,000 young people attended dance-halls every evening—many more than attended movies or pursued any other forms of recreation" (Nye, "Saturday Night," p. 15). Observers in cities like New York, Cleveland, and Boston concurred. The smallest dance halls held only one or two hundred patrons, but lavish ballrooms, such as New York's Manhattan Casino held six thousand people. Like movie and vaudeville "palaces," the ballroom entrepreneurs sought to create an awe-inspiring alternative to boring daytime environments. Live music, in some cases at least two bands, provided a heady atmosphere. Commercial dance halls proved especially desirable for the young because they provided a relatively safe atmosphere in which to meet strangers away from the knowing eyes of chaperons.

In the early twentieth century, young working women tended to patronize new entertainment venues such as dance halls, amusement parks, and movie theaters—places that were not perceived to be exclusively male worlds.

Dance halls were not an entirely new institution in American communities; some saloons had spaces set aside for dancing, and many neighborhood and ethnic clubs held dances in rented halls. Sensitive to the associations of saloon dancing with prostitution, most twentieth-century dance halls posted rules and provided some supervision to ensure greater respectability. "Taxi-dance halls," where the sexual services of young women might be procured, still operated, but most of the new dance halls avoided any connection with prostitution.

Two other nighttime enterprises developed alongside the dance hall: cabarets and nightclubs. Building upon certain aspects of the saloon, such as the provision of alcohol and the use of elaborate decorations to shape patrons' leisure experiences, nightclubs were closely tied to commercial entertainment entrepreneurs who invested in them and sometimes acted as agents for performers. A nightclub or cabaret sold an entertainment experience for people who might be drawn from any part of town; it was not the neighborhood refuge typically offered by the bar or saloon.

Beginning in the late nineteenth century, restaurant entrepreneurs experimented with seating, floor design, and decorations that would attract upscale customers. Some of the earliest cabarets opened atop hotels or near theaters, places where middle-class patrons already felt comfortable. Restaurant owners, primarily motivated by financial considerations, transformed their businesses to attract more of these affluent customers. As long as dining remained the stated function of their enterprise, owners avoided theater licensing fees.

At the heart of the cabaret experience, entrepreneurs created what historian Lewis Erenberg described as "action environments." Diners were seated on the same level as musicians or the floor show; the proscenium stage and obstructive pillars of earlier, more formal decor were removed; and an intimate space was created that encouraged greater performer-audience interaction.

Increased participatory performance took place in several ways. Popular dancers Vernon and Irene Castle entered the floor from a table in the audience, for example, thus using their proximity to add excitement and informality to their dance routines. Comedians assimilated unsuspecting audience members into their acts. Singers, including many of the legendary blues women like Alberta Hunter, circulated among the tables to collect tips, thereby bringing the audience into greater contact with the performer.

The most ambitious cabaret owners drew on the examples of the music hall and theater by featuring Broadway revues and chorines in their clubs. Here, too, some kinds of intimacy could be staged, as when the "Balloon Girls" at Ziegfeld's Midnight Frolic moved among the tables, allowing men with cigars or cigarettes to pop the balloons attached to their costumes. Men and women generally attended the cabaret as couples, thus expanding the opportunities for public entertainment available to middle-class women. Reformers, suspicious of this gender-mixed audience, worried about women being exposed to "unrefined" amusements.

But even though the cabaret broke with the more formal decorum of an earlier era, interactions in these clubs were carefully staged and managed. Waiters brought people their drinks; a cabaret did not have the free-ranging ambience of a saloon. Since couples made up the majority of the clientele, unescorted women were often discouraged or barred from the premises. Tables brought patrons close to a dance floor or performance space, but they also provided barriers between patrons, thus obviating too much communal socializing.

Nightlife in the Jazz Age, the Depression, and World War II

Nighttime entertainment faced new restraints following World War I. Prohibitionists enjoyed a significant victory with the Volstead Act, which banned the manufacture and sale of beverages containing more than 0.5 percent alcohol and forced saloon owners to close their doors. The statute was ratified to enforce the Eighteenth Amendment in 1919. Many saloon owners had already experienced hardship because of state temperance laws, World War I rationing and hours restrictions, and increased competition from private home sales. German saloon operators and brewers were particularly hard hit in the war years because of anti-German sentiment.

Adaptable owners operated "speakeasies," so named because one might need a password to gain entrance. Many nightclubs had ties to members of organized crime; some of the decade's most notorious criminals, such as Chicago's Al Capone, amassed fortunes by supplying nighttime drinkers. Bars and saloons were relegitimated when the Twenty-first Amendment was ratified in 1933. In the meantime, prohibition did not discourage nightclub patronage—in fact, clubs multiplied during the 1920s.

Early cabarets appealed to a primarily middle-class clientele, but nightclubs diversified as their popularity grew. Some clubs continued to be located in hotels, but others opened underground or in similarly dark and womblike settings. Often the setting for new musical acts, smaller clubs had a bar and a dance floor, perhaps a short menu of food. Large, lavish clubs offered expensive fare and glamorous shows.

The name and decor of a nightclub helped establish it as a refuge or escape from daytime activities. Some clubs still had the aura of the tenderloin, and were called Bucket of Blood or Spider's Nest. Others pandered to fantasy or the interest in "exotica" by sporting names like Plantation, Dreamland, Pekin, and Elite. Club Alabam and Plantation Club suggested the Jim Crow South, and for potential black patrons the names proved accurate. Only the very lightest-skinned African Americans would be allowed inside—even though famous black band leaders like Duke Ellington and Cab Calloway graced the bandstand. "Black and tan" clubs, which tolerated a racially mixed clientele, challenged the racist limits of social respectability, and as a result became the targets of police harassment.

The Cotton Club, a premier entertainment haven in Harlem, was representative of the nightlife in 1920s nightclubs. Gangster Owney Madden opened it in 1923, and by building on the reputations of earlier clubs at the site, the Douglas Casino and Club Deluxe, created a new marvel. Designed to attract an affluent white audience to Harlem, the seven-hundred-seat Cotton Club featured an elegant interior with two tiers of seats around the performance space.

The Cotton Club built its floor show around Broadway-style revues. Musicians, tap and troupe dancers, comedians, and other acts were combined into one show. "Primitive" and "exotic" themes—which generally meant graphics depicting trees, drums, and scantily clad "African" natives—decorated the menus, walls, and stage props. Performers' costumes also reflected these ideas. Duke Ellington's accomplished jazz orchestra was reputed to play a "jungle sound," heavy with syncopated bass and drum accents.

In the 1920s, African American club owners opened their own establishments, some of which became popular after-hours spots for Broadway entertainers or those performing in whites-only Harlem clubs.

Few white revelers at the Cotton Club protested the exclusion of African American guests. Some undoubtedly agreed with Jimmy Durante's sentiments: "It isn't necessary to mix with colored people if you don't feel like it. You have your own party and keep to yourself. But it's worth seeing. How they step!" (Durante and Kofoed, *Nightclubs*, p. 114). Other white patrons believed the nightclub provided access to "liberating" African American culture that could serve as an antidote to the ills of overly regimented industrial society. When whites went slumming in black neighborhoods, they participated in what historian Nathan Huggins described as "a means of soft rebellion for those who rejected the Babbittry and sterility of their lives, yet could not find within their familiar culture the genius to redefine themselves in more human and vital terms" (*Harlem Renaissance*, p. 91). Unfortunately, when white visitors purchased illusionary nighttime visions of "exotic" black life, they failed to develop an accurate appreciation of the sobering daytime realities of African American life.

African American club owners opened their own establishments, some of which became popular after-hours spots for entertainers performing on Broadway or in whites-only Harlem clubs. Participants in the Harlem Renaissance patronized some of the clubs, using them as meeting and socializing centers. Nightclubs and fancy-dress balls also became part of the lesbian and gay subculture of Harlem, particularly as young homosexual migrants to the city sought to shape an entertainment world of their own.

Claude McKay depicted many of the conventional "primitive" motifs in his description of the Congo, a fictional Harlem nightclub: "Drum and saxophone were fighting out the wonderful drag 'blues' that was the favorite of all the low-down dance halls. In all the better places it was banned. Rumor said that it was a police ban. It was an old tune, so far as popular tunes go. But at the Congo it lived fresh and green as grass" (*Home to Harlem*, p. 36). McKay captures the participatory flavor of the music to convey the controversial reputation of the club. Other writers, such as Langston Hughes, found inspiration for their novels and poetry in blues and jazz, as well as cabaret dancers.

Ordinary nightclub patrons might hope to receive a whiff of the excitement associated with famous nightclub patrons, who brought some of the glamour of urban America's intellectual, sporting, and entertainment circles into the dusky club confines. The most exclusive nightclubs became places where one's reputation as a socialite could be legitimated. Many cities witnessed the arrival of these enticing opportunities: "Seattle, Salt Lake City, San Antonio, Cincinnati, Buffalo, Akron, Albany, Omaha, Miami, Syracuse, Baltimore, Pittsburgh, Cleveland and Denver experienced the expansion of vibrant nightclub entertainment with floor shows and bands" (Erenberg, "From New York to Middletown," p. 766). In Los Angeles, one might rub shoulders with stars from the film colony.

Nightclubs provided entertainment for patrons, but that was only one of their functions. Musicians and other employees experienced other aspects of these institutions. Unlike the saloons, in which the owner and saloonkeeper made many key decisions, a large nightclub brought together dozens of players. Owners, bartenders, cooks, performers, agents, doormen, and others put together the glitzy reality of the club. Some musicians felt that the ties to gangsters made 1920s nightclubs dangerous places to work. Jazz musician Earl "Fatha" Hines remembered that Al Capone was a frequent visitor to the Grand Terrace club in Chicago. Capone, Hines said, "liked to come into a club with his henchmen, order all the doors closed, and have the band play his requests" (Shapiro and Hentoff, *Hear Me Talkin' to Ya*, p. 130). In many cities, the capital provided by the men with connections to organized crime may have helped refurnish and improve nightclubs, however, and even raise salaries. Ronald Morris, who studied the relationships between gangsters and jazz, asserted that the underworld-influenced "cabaret owners of the 1920s transformed an otherwise lowly amusement palace into an occasionally lucrative business whose capabilities for self-promotion, in addition to showcasing jazz music, were far-reaching" (*Wait Until Dark*, p. 103). At the same time, the increasingly violent criminal activities associated with the gangsters continued to give an immoral reputation to nightclubs.

Jazz became the music most associated with the cabaret and nightclub in the 1920s. Large nightclubs showcased big bands with twelve- or fifteen-piece jazz ensembles, while smaller ones might host improvisational jam sessions. Intimate clubs allowed the audience to feel a part of the music being made, without any distracting staging. But in the next decade, economic pressures resulting from the Great Depression forced many club designers to eliminate the "facades and excesses of the architecture associated with failure" (Erenberg, "From New York to Middletown," p. 770). Jazz, especially swing, gained a wider following from the mid 1930s to World War II, when it became the preferred sound for many clubs, dance halls, and ballrooms.

Most dancing establishments were racially segregated, and black dancers were allowed in the predominantly white ballrooms only on specific nights—if at all. But because swing-style jazz was the most common music in the urban dance palaces, whites were exposed to African American musical culture even if they paid to see and hear predominantly white musicians. White jazz band-leader Benny Goodman, for example, was reputed to be unhappy unless "the floor was filled with activity. Dancers worked up to an ecstatic state in which, through a physical activity, they could leave this earth and fly through the air"; the combination of improvisational music and wild dance steps created the message that "ecstasy and personal freedom still existed in the modern world" (Erenberg, "Things to Come," p. 232).

African Americans were most welcome at the halls and ballrooms that opened in black neighborhoods. Musicians performing in the clubs catering to recent migrants from the South credited the dancers with helping to influence the style of music performed. Pianist Willie ("the Lion") Smith described how newcomers from the South Carolina Sea Islands helped shape the dance music: "The Gullahs would start out early in the evening dancing two-steps, waltzes, schottishes; but as the evening wore on and the liquor began to work, they would start improvising their own steps and that was when they wanted us to get-in-the-alley, real lowdown" (*Music on My Mind*, p. 66).

Recent migrants found clubs and ballrooms places in which to preserve some of the dancing traditions they had known in rural and small-town "jooks." As Katrina Hazzard-Gordon has documented, "Dances in the jooks included the Charleston, the shimmy, the snake hips, the funky butt, the twist, the slow drag, the buzzard lope, the black bottom, the itch, the fish tail, and the grind" (*Jookin'*, p. 83). Many white, as well as black, urban social dancers enjoyed later variations of these styles, which were based on vigorous physical abandon rather than the more restrained dancing of earlier generations.

Ballroom entertainers provided more than dancing music. Jazz cornetist Louis Armstrong remembered his ballroom gigs as a combination of dance music and comedy: "The Sunset had Charleston contests on Friday night, and you couldn't get in the place unless you got there early. We had a great show in those days with Buck'n' Bubbles, Rector and Cooper, Edith Spencer and Mae Alix, my favorite entertainer, and a gang of now famous stars" (*Hear Me Talkin' to Ya*, p. 111). Variety troupes toured ballroom circuits across the country in the 1930s and 1940s.

Some ballrooms acquired great fame. Chicago's Sunset and New York's Savoy, for example, created legendary environments that seemed to offer an almost sacred sanctuary from the outside world:

> The Lindy Hop reached its height of sophistication at the Savoy Ballroom in Harlem, the "Home of Happy Feet," which hired the best bands in the country and became something of a shrine. It was cavernous, a block-long structure with a half-lit, cathedral interior and two altar-like bandstands. Patrons coming in off the street for the first time discovered a sumptuous wonderland with its thick carpets, uniformed attendants, broad expanses of mirrored walls reflecting a large cut-glass chandelier, and an ornate, marble staircase leading to the crowded dance floor. (Leonard, *Jazz*, p. 167)

Malcolm Little (later Malcolm X) was one of the patrons impressed with the Savoy's ambience in the 1940s. He "went a couple of rounds on the floor with girls from the sidelines" while listening to Lionel Hampton and Dinah Washington (*Autobiography of Malcolm X*, p. 74).

The clientele of the Savoy changed its composition throughout the week. Malcolm X recalled that Thursday night was Kitchen Mechanics' Night at the Savoy. He wrote, "there were twice as many women as men in there, not only kitchen workers and maids, but also war wives and defense worker women, lonely and looking" (*Autobiography*, p. 74). The Savoy used a variety of ploys to attract dancers, including "bathing beauty contests, and a new car given away each Saturday night" (p. 82).

Depression-era migrants moving from the South across the Southwest and West brought an important dance institution with them. The "honky-tonk," a rural saloon much like the jook, was a common feature in many southwestern states. Country-western music historian Bill Malone described its intense appeal:

> Amidst the din and revelry there had to be, for both the dancer and the passive listener, a steady and insistent beat which could be felt even if the lyrics could not be heard. The music became louder: "Sock rhythm"—the playing of closed chords, or the striking of all six strings in unison in order to achieve a percussive effect—was applied to the guitar; the string bass became a fixture in the hillbilly band; and in rare cases drums were used. (*Country Music, U.S.A.*, pp. 163–164)

In Texas, the 1930s oil boom brought in many new workers who patronized these small joints, which often were located on the outskirts of town.

As these workers and other families migrated west, they took their taste for western swing and country music with them. Bands like the Light Crust Doughboys, Bob Wills's Texas Playboys, and Al Dexter and His Troopers became popular in dance clubs. Agricultural migrants in California considered honky-tonks one of the institutions, along with evangelical Christian churches, that connected them to the homes they had left behind. "Every San Joaquin Valley town had its Pioneer Club by the end of the 1930s," wrote James Gregory. "There the flipside of the Oakie population congregated: daring women, single men, married men with a taste for liquor and independence" (*American Exodus*, p. 222). The honky-tonk atmosphere became memorialized in hundreds of "cry in your beer" country-western songs that testified to broken love affairs.

By World War II, honky-tonk acts traveled an expansive dance club scene across the West, and country-western dance styles followed suit. In them, as in many others, ever-louder music was needed to reach large audiences. Electric guitars often replaced acoustic ones to meet the need.

Nightclubs and bars in the West had long promoted frontier themes in their decor, and the association of gambling with western nightlife intensified in the 1930s and 1940s after Nevada legalized casino gambling in 1931. Gambling was common in mining town and lumber camp saloons and brothels. Nevadans hoped that the legalization of gambling would attract people and capital in the midst of the Depression. Las Vegas grew quickly during World War II when investors, sometimes with ties to organized crime syndicates, funded the building of hotel-casinos.

The windowless casinos used artificial lighting, free food and drink, and many other amenities to create a world encouraging indulgent behavior. By the 1980s, casinos had added individual musical acts and revues, circuses, zoo animals, and spectacles like exploding volcanoes to their premises. Gambling resorts sold the pleasures of nighttime entertainment twenty-four hours per day.

Nightlife in Postwar America

Following World War II, more Americans than ever made drinking, dancing, and socializing central to their nighttime activities. The institutional structure as well as patron practices changed in several important ways. America shifted toward a managerial and service-oriented economy, and many Americans enjoyed unprecedented amounts of leisure time as the workweek shortened. A baby boom exploded following the war, and it produced a huge generation of young people who would define many entertainment trends between the 1950s and 1980s. Widespread ownership of phonographs, radios, television sets, and videocassette recorders provided mass-marketed music and entertainment that consumers could enjoy at home, which dramatically reduced the need to seek out public entertainment. Nighttime leisure reflected the tensions created when new generations of pleasure seekers questioned the homogenization and complacency that accompanied many of these postwar developments.

Bars and cocktail lounges became a common feature of American society, which every conceivable institution, including hotels and restaurants, laundromats, and airports, offering some sort of alcoholic fare. Corner pubs still served some functions of the saloon, especially where new groups of immigrants and urban migrants looked for places to congregate, watch television, shoot pool, and play video games. The bar continued to serve as an important location for individuals to meet friends or potential companions. Unescorted women were more welcome in bars after World War II, though bars often continued to be spaces in which men had considerably more freedom than women.

Agricultural migrants in California considered the "hony-tonk"—a rural saloon much like a jook—one of the institutions that connected them to the homes they had left behind.

Specialized bars served college and university populations, conventioneers in large hotels, and tourists. Bars became important meeting places for lesbians and gay men because they offered one of the few public places where homosexual socializing might be tolerated. In some cities, gay bars helped galvanize the early gay liberation movement, particularly the Stonewall Rebellion of June 1969, when working-class gay youth resisted a punitive police raid at the Stonewall Bar in New York City.

Rarely outlets for local beers, most late-twentieth-century bars featured mass-marketed products and national name brands. Some bars or bar-and-restaurant combinations were parts of regional or national chains. Bars continued to be criticized as environments encouraging inebriation and a lack of control, particularly when happy hours and other events featuring bargain drinks were promoted. The pervasiveness of the automobile in many cities added new urgency to the demands to control drinking. Many states raised the drinking age to twenty-one, and others passed stiff penalties for drunk driving.

In some cases, bar owners and bartenders found themselves legally liable for the behavior of drunken or abusive customers. Heightened public awareness of the costs of alcohol-related leisure activities led to new nighttime habits such as designated drivers and the creation of "dry" alternatives, especially for teens.

As the bar culture became more widely disseminated in the 1950s and 1960s, nightclubs and dancing establishments became more specifically focused on the young. Particular countercultural movements were associated with nightclubs, discotheques, and concert venues. In the late 1940s and early 1950s certain New York City nightclubs on West 52d Street became the center of avant-garde jazz, which broke away from the swing-band music of the 1930s. Bebop jazz, featuring the harmonic improvisation of musicians like Charlie Parker and Dizzy Gillespie, was performed in coffeehouses and small clubs. The music helped inspire iconoclastic poets like Allen Ginsberg, who read verse that railed against the regimentation and materialism of postwar America to small beatnik audiences.

Beginning in the 1950s, dance clubs increasingly responded to adolescent patrons' demands for rock and roll music, which had deep roots in both African American and working-class cultures. Like jazz in the 1920s, rock was attacked by adults who feared that its raucous sounds and values would harm young morals. Teenagers defiantly responded by embracing the music as a language voicing rebellion against restrictive authority figures, including their parents. Rejecting much of the social conformity promulgated during the cold war, teenagers danced to live and recorded music blasting with the raw sexual energy of performers like Elvis Presley, Chuck Berry, and Bill Haley and the Comets.

In addition, when young people became activists in the civil rights, antiwar, and women's liberation movements during these decades, music and dance helped convey their grievances. A growing commitment to bridging the distances between different racial, ethnic, and regional social groups was often articulated through folk, soul, and rock music. George Lipsitz points out that the music scene in Los Angeles was particularly representative of the growing merger of white, African American, and Chicano musical influences. Performers like Hannibal and the Headhunters, Ritchie Valens, and Johnny Otis represented young people who "identified themselves as a self-conscious and rebellious social group, they made music that reflected an unprecedented crossing of racial and class lines." As young Americans rejected the conformity and inequality, associated with the status quo, and formed an enthusiastic audience for the new music, they created a "calculated foolishness" that was "quite serious; its imagination and sense of play went a long way toward transforming American culture from the domain of a privileged elite into a 'land of a thousand dances' " (Lipsitz, "Land of a Thousand Dances," p. 267).

The pluralistic dancing Lipsitz described took place in increasingly large pavilions and ballrooms during the 1960s. Strongly associated with the hippie subculture, these venues witnessed evenings that combined sound-and-light shows, powerfully amplified hard rock music, and mind-altering drugs that underscored hedonistic pleasure. The Jefferson Airplane, the Jimi Hendrix Experience, and Janis Joplin played to wildly enthusiastic crowds. Some young people structured their lives around the concert tours of prominent groups like the Grateful Dead. For them, leisure dominated their lives; it was no longer a way to spend nonworking hours.

By the 1970s discotheques and nightclubs varied in accordance with patrons' tastes. For example, disco music in the 1970s, and hip hop and rap music in the 1980s, swept urban clubs. Each originated with black dance music, although disco clubs attracted a primarily white, and often male homosexual, crowd. The latter two dance and music phenomena drew on the leadership of disc jockeys, who spun the records at the clubs. Nightclubs continued to offer teenagers the opportunity to "play" with dress and behavior associated with music styles as diverse as heavy metal, punk, and top-40 pop hits. Prestigious clubs in New York and Los Angeles employed doormen, or bouncers, to screen patrons for dress deemed stylish. The lucky entrants enjoyed their upscale triumph at the expense of others waiting in line. Thus, the nightclub served as a vehicle for conspicuous consumption.

Conclusion

Nighttime entertainment trends resulted from a complex mixture of patron tastes and desires, the commercial aspirations of leisure entrepreneurs, and regulations set by local, state, and federal agencies. Many evening pastimes were determined by the changing nature of work. Shortened hours and workweeks made it possible to find more time for relaxation on weekends, and in some cases during the workday. The bar or dance hall ceased to offer a rare escape from alienating labor, particularly as activities like movies came to compete with live entertainment. Nighttime leisure lost much of its local flavor during the twentieth century as increased corporate control of bar, restaurant, and nightclub chains standardized entertainment experiences in many communities.

Still, young people often treated the dance floor or concert venue as a place where they could try to assert political and sexual autonomy from dominant adult values. Some bars and clubs continued to serve a clientele restricted on the basis of race, class, gender, or sexual preference; these patrons considered their entertainment spots reassuring havens in the face of an impersonal society. At the same time, jazz clubs, swing ballrooms, country-western honky-tonks, and rock and roll discotheques helped break down social and regional barriers. In addition, when youngsters mixed African American, white working-class and ethnic, and Hispanic music and dance styles, they nurtured pluralistic cultural trends in the face of increasing standardization of leisure through film, radio, and television.

By the late twentieth century, nightlife continued to appear as a clearly demarcated world, promising an exciting alternative to everyday experience. Americans continued to seek escape from the regimented aspects of their lives by finding places where they could raise an elbow at a brass rail or stamp their feet on a dance floor. Nightlife remained a process of negotiation in which revelers chose from a wide array of mass-media offerings, such as movies and television, and the continuing enticements of dance halls, ballrooms, nightclubs, gambling resorts, and music performance venues.

[See also African American Music; Amusement and Theme Parks; The City; Country and Western Music; Popular Entertainment before the Civil War; Popular Music before 1950; Rock Music; Urban Parks.]

BIBLIOGRAPHY

Allon, Natalie, and Diane Fishel. "Urban Courting Patterns in Singles Bars." In *Our Sociological Eye: Personal Essays on Society and Culture,* edited by Arthur B. Shostak (1977).

Butsch, Richard, ed. *For Fun and Profit: The Transformation of Leisure into Consumption* (1990). A useful introduction that helps put nightlife in its social context.

Daniels, Douglas Henry. *Pioneer Urbanites: A Social and Cultural History of Black San Francisco* (1980). An excellent description of African American nightlife in turn-of-the-century San Francisco.

Davis, Madeline D., and Elizabeth Lapovsky Kennedy. "Oral History and the Study of Sexuality in the Lesbian Community: Buffalo, New York, 1940–1960." In *Unequal Sisters: A Multicultural Reader in U.S. Women's History,* edited by Ellen Carol DuBois and Vicki L. Ruiz (1990). Analyzes the role of bar culture in shaping sexual identity as well as political organizing.

Deegan, Mary Jo. *American Ritual and Dramas: Social Rituals and Cultural Meanings.* (1989). Good introduction to dramaturgical analysis of leisure, including an important chapter on gendered bar rituals.

Duis, Perry R. *The Saloon: Public Drinking in Chicago and Boston, 1880–1920* (1983). A thorough comparative study.

Durante, Jimmy, and Jack Kofoed. *Nightclubs* (1931).

Erenberg, Lewis A. *Steppin' Out: New York Nightlife and the Transformation of American Culture, 1890–1930* (1981). The definitive study of nightclubs and cabarets in New York.

Erenberg, Lewis A. "From New York to Middletown: Repeal and the Legitimization of Nightlife in the Great Depression." *American Quarterly* 38, no. 5 (1986). Continues the analysis begun in *Steppin' Out.*

Erenberg, Lewis A. "Things to Come: Swing Bands, Bebop, and the Rise of a Postwar Jazz Scene." In *Recasting America: Culture and Politics in the Age of Cold War,* edited by Larry May (1989).

Fass, Paula. *The Damned and the Beautiful: American Youth in the 1920's* (1977).

Findlay, John M. *People of Chance: Gambling in American Society from Jamestown to Las Vegas* (1986). Excellent bibliography on gambling.

Frith, Simon. *Sound Effects: Youth, Leisure, and the Politics of Rock 'n' Roll* (1981).

Garber, Eric. "A Spectacle in Color: The Lesbian and Gay Subculture of Jazz Age Harlem." In *Hidden from History: Reclaiming the Gay and Lesbian Past,* edited by Martin Bauml Duberman, Martha Vicinus, and George Chauncey, Jr. (1989).

Gorn, Elliott J. *The Manly Art: Bare-Knuckle Prize Fighting in America* (1986). See especially chapters 4 and 6 for discussion of nineteenth-century nightlife.

Gregory, James N. *American Exodus: The Dust Bowl Migration and Okie Culture in California* (1989). Sensitive discussion of the role of nightlife in the establishment of an influential migrant subculture.

Haskins, Jim. *The Cotton Club* (1977). The best work on this influential nightclub.

Hazzard-Gordon, Katrina. *Jookin': The Rise of Social Dance Formations in African-American Culture* (1990). The most detailed study of the subject.

Heimann, Jim. *Out with the Stars: Hollywood Nightlife in the Golden Era* (1985).

Huggins, Nathan. *Harlem Renaissance* (1971).

Kingsdale, Jon M. "The 'Poor Man's Club': Social Functions of the Urban Working-Class Saloon." *American Quarterly* 25 (October 1973).

Kotarba, Joseph A., and Laura Wells. "Styles of Adolescent Participation in an All-Ages, Rock 'n' Roll Nightclub: An Ethnographic Analysis." *Youth and Society* 18 (June 1987).

Lender, Mark Edward, and James Kirby Martin. *Drinking in America: A History* (1982).

Leonard, Neil. *Jazz: Myth and Religion* (1987).

Lipsitz, George. "Land of a Thousand Dances: Youth, Minorities, and the Rise of Rock and Roll." In *Recasting America: Culture and Politics in the Age of Cold War,* edited by Larry May (1989).

Lipsitz, George. *Time Passages: Collective Memory and American Popular Culture* (1990).

McKay, Claude. *Home to Harlem* (1928).

Malcolm X, with Alex Haley. *The Autobiography of Malcolm X* (1964).

Malone, Bill C. *Country Music, U.S.A.: A Fifty-Year History* (1968). Detailed chronological explanation of the relationships among honky-tonks, clubs, music, and musicians.

Morris, Ronald. *Wait Until Dark: Jazz and the Underworld, 1880–1940* (1980).

Nye, Russell B. "Saturday Night at the Paradise Ballroom; or, Dance Halls in the Twenties." *Journal of Popular Culture* 7, no. 1 (1973).

Ogren, Kathy J. *The Jazz Revolution: Twenties America and the Meaning of Jazz* (1989).

Pearson, Anthony. "The Grateful Dead Phenomenon: An Ethnomethodological Approach." *Youth and Society* 18 (June 1987).

Peiss, Kathy. *Cheap Amusements: Working Women and Leisure in Turn-of-the-Century New York* (1986). Definitive study of white working-class women's leisure at the turn of the century.

Pielke, Robert. *You Say You Want a Revolution: Rock Music in American Culture* (1986).

Rosenzweig, Roy. *Eight Hours for What We Will: Workers and Leisure in an Industrial City, 1870–1920* (1983). A local study that thoroughly analyzes how workers sought to shape their leisure in Worcester, Massachusetts.

Shapiro, Nat, and Nat Hentoff, eds. *Hear Me Talkin' to Ya* (1955). Provides musicians' reminiscences of nightlife employment.

Smith, Willie "the Lion," with George Hoefer. *Music on My Mind: The Memoirs of an American Pianist* (1964).

Stearns, Marshall, and Jean Stearns. *Jazz Dance: The Story of American Vernacular Dance* (1968).

Sylvester, Robert. *No Cover Charge: A Backward Look at the Nightclubs* (1956).

Toop, David. *The Rap Attack: African Jive to New York Hip Hop* (1984). Establishes a useful context, accompanied by good photographs, for music and dancing in urban clubs.

West, Elliott. *The Saloon on the Rocky Mountain Mining Frontier* (1979). The most comprehensive study of the saloon in the West.

— KATHY OGREN

THE NUCLEAR AGE

The atom has had a powerful impact on every phase of American life in the years since World War II. The first atomic bomb, according to journalist Anne O'Hare McCormick writing in the *New York Times* on 8 August 1945, caused "an explosion in men's minds as shattering as the obliteration of Hiroshima," and in the decades that followed its dramatic appearance in 1945 the nation has operated within an altogether different framework in foreign and domestic affairs. The bomb has influenced military strategy and diplomacy, affected economic and political decisions, and conditioned the cultural climate of the United States. Throughout the atomic era scientists, policymakers, and social critics have engaged in a broadly-based triangular conversation aimed at reconciling fears of cataclysmic destruction with hopes for a bright nuclear future. Dominated by government leaders, that conversation has included a wide range of activists and involved groups, as it has defined the boundaries of both public policy and popular culture and so shaped the structure of the postwar years.

Building the Bomb

The bomb had its origins in the Manhattan Project, a huge undertaking that unfolded over a three-year period, cost more than two billion dollars, and included thirty-seven different facilities in the United States and Canada. Coordinated by the Army under the direction of Brigadier General Leslie R. Groves, the effort involved many of the nation's top scientists. In Chicago, Enrico Fermi, an Italian Nobel laureate then working in the United States, produced the first self-sustaining chain reaction on 2 December 1942, and boosted confidence that a nuclear explosion might be possible. In Los Alamos, in the New Mexico desert, J. Robert Oppenheimer, a brilliant University of California physicist with a talent for encouraging colleagues to work together, guided the attempt to amass fissionable material and shape it into a workable bomb.

The effort surpassed all expectations. In mid July 1945, at Alamogordo, a site two-hundred miles (320 kilometers) from Los Alamos, scientists tried out a first plutonium device. As the brilliant explosion of the Trinity test broke the predawn darkness, Oppenheimer was reminded of a passage from the Bhagavad Gita, the Hindu holy book, where the god Vishnu took on a fiery, multifaceted form and declared, "Now I am become Death, the destroyer of worlds." On 6 August an American B-29 bomber dropped "Little Boy," a uranium bomb, on Hiroshima, killing an estimated seventy thousand and injuring seventy thousand more. Three days after that first strike, another B-29 dropped "Fat Man," a plutonium bomb, on Nagasaki, this time killing about forty thousand and injuring another sixty thousand. Within days the Japanese accepted American terms and soon after signed a formal surrender document.

Why had the United States used these first atomic bombs? Other alternatives—a naval blockade, a demonstration, an invasion—were all considered and rejected by those commanding the war effort. A blockade might take too long; a demonstration might fail; an invasion might cost a million American lives. Even more important was the fact that most scientists and policymakers had always assumed that the new weapon would be dropped once it was ready. Although some scientists, particularly those working in Chicago, feared the impending success of their project and argued for wartime restraint, use of the bomb was a foregone conclusion. President Harry S. Truman would have been hard pressed to decide any other way. He inherited both advisers and policies from Franklin D. Roosevelt, who had intended to use the bomb. In office barely four months when the first nuclear weapons were ready, Truman would have had to exert tremendous force to overturn a decision that had effectively been made three years before. As Leslie Groves later observed, Truman's "decision was one of noninterference—basically a decision not to upset the existing plans."

The two bombs were as destructive as the scientists had feared. They devastated their Japanese targets, shattering buildings and incinerating people within two kilometers of the hypocenter. In both Hiroshima and Nagasaki some of the victims evaporated in the heat; others turned into charred corpses. Kimono patterns were occasionally burned onto remaining skin. Survivors in both cities, exposed to dangerously high levels of radiation, faced total chaos as they waded among swollen bodies cluttering streets and fields in search of nonexistent medical care.

Americans, unaware of the fearful devastation, greeted news of the bombs with a lighthearted excitement. Almost immediately after the first detonation, the Washington Press Club prepared an "atomic cocktail," made from a combination of Pernod and gin. Los Angeles burlesque houses featured "Atom Bomb Dancers." The music industry seized on a new subject for song. "When the Atom Bomb Fell," recorded in December 1945 by country and western singers Karl Davis and Harty Taylor, reflected a combination of awe and relief:

> Smoke and fire it did flow through the land of Tokyo.
> There was brimstone and dust everywhere.
> When it all cleared away, there the cruel Japs did lay.
> The answer to our fighting boys' prayer.

"Atomic Power," written the day after Hiroshima by cowboy singer Fred Kirby and recorded in its most popular version six months later by the Buchanan Brothers, asserted the divine origins of the bomb: "Atomic power, atomic power, was given by the mighty hand of God." Even before the second bomb fell on Nagasaki, the *New York Times* considered future civilian applications of nuclear power, including an atomic airplane.

Public Fears

Fears of atomic power surfaced as the public became more informed. Some religious leaders contended soon after Hiroshima that the new bomb was an unnecessary experiment with genocide, and their criticisms continued in the months that followed. Other Americans, coming from all social classes, tempered their gratitude that the war was over with a growing revulsion as they became aware of the consequences of the new weapon. Kept in the dark throughout the bomb's development, they learned about its impact on humans only gradually. The first accounts spared the most gruesome details. The earliest photographs were grainy images of smoke columns, with little reference to loss of life. *Life* magazine ran a lengthy spread two weeks after the Hiroshima bombing, but the photos showed landscape no different from that hit by conventional bombs. In a pretelevision age, before Americans came to expect grisly pictures on the nightly news, print journalism best conveyed the human suffering caused by the bomb. John Hersey, author of a number of popular wartime pieces, turned his attention to Hiroshima after the bomb fell. His account, published in the 31 August 1946 issue of the *New Yorker*, overwhelmed readers. Newspapers ran the entire text and radio stations read it aloud. The book version, *Hiroshima*, distributed free to many Book-of-the-Month Club members, became a best-seller and enjoyed a vast popular audience. Through dispassionate but detailed descriptions of six residents of Hiroshima, Hersey conveyed a vivid sense of the unprecedented crisis. As reviewer Charles Poore declared of the book in the *New York Times* on 10 November 1946, "It speaks for itself, and, in an unforgettable way, for humanity."

Meanwhile, many scientists were troubled by what they had done. Fears circulated after the war that larger bombs might ignite a cataclysmic chain reaction in the atmosphere, the earth, or the sea. Not until early 1946 did physicist Hans Bethe ease anxieties with calculations proving that such a reaction was impossible, but other fears proved more difficult to exorcise. "In the summer of 1945," biochemist Eugene Rabinowitch later recalled in "Five Years After," an article appearing in the *Bulletin of the Atomic Scientists*, "some of us walked the streets of Chicago vividly imagining the sky suddenly lit by a giant fireball, the steel skeletons of skyscrapers bending into grotesque shapes and their masonry raining into the streets below, until a great cloud of dust rose and settled over the crumbling city." Some scientists felt guilt; others, regret. Virtually all feared the future they had helped create. As Oppenheimer declared in the *Bulletin of the Atomic Scientists* a few years later, "In some sort of crude sense which no vulgarity, no humor, no over-statement can quite extinguish, the physicists have known sin, and this is a knowledge which they cannot lose."

At the war's end scientists descended on Washington, D.C., to persuade members of Congress of the importance of international control. When asked for specifics, they provided detailed information and ran a lecture series on nuclear physics for sixty congressmen. They established the Federation of Atomic Scientists (later the Federation of American Scientists) in November 1945 to focus their effort. They also founded the *Bulletin of the Atomic Scientists* to help convey the bomb's dangers and examine its social and political implications for scientists and nonscientists alike. Editor Eugene Rabinowitch was committed to "fight to prevent science from becoming an executioner of mankind." The doomsday clock, with hands approaching midnight, that first appeared on the cover of the journal in June 1947, became a haunting symbol of the nuclear age. Even Americans excited about nuclear prospects had to contend with the issues scientists were raising.

Scientists wanted the United States to share the secret of atomic energy and to establish a system of United Nations control. Although some administration members—departing Secretary of War Henry L. Stimson, incoming Secretary of War Robert P. Patterson, and Secretary of Commerce Henry A. Wallace among others—favored approaching the Soviet Union in an attempt at accommodation, others were vehemently opposed to such a course. Secretary of State James F. Byrnes hoped to rely on the bomb as a diplomatic bargaining chip. Military officials favored maintaining the American monopoly. A Gallup poll in September 1945 revealed that seventy-three percent of the respondents wanted the United States to retain control of the bomb, while only fourteen percent wanted to place it in the hands of the newly created United Nations. A survey of Congress showed even more resistance to a cooperative approach: thirty-nine Republicans and thirty-seven Democrats preferred to hold on to the secret, while only five Democrats were willing to turn it over to the United Nations.

Truman was clearly sympathetic to the majority stance. While he underscored the need for some form of international control in a message to Congress and sought to appear conciliatory, he understood the public mood and did not intend to give too much away. He had Secretary of State Byrnes appoint a committee, with Dean Acheson, second-ranking diplomatic official, as chair to look into the problem. Drawing on the expertise of such figures as David Lilienthal, chair of the Tennessee Valley Authority, and Oppenheimer, the committee drafted a proposal, known as the Acheson-Lilienthal report, that outlined a series of stages that would begin with a survey of materials and culminate with the surrender of weapons. Truman then appointed financier Bernard Baruch as ambassador to the new UN Atomic Energy Commission to present the plan. Arrogant and egocentric, Baruch altered the report to include firm penalties for violations and to specify that no Security Council veto was possible on questions of punishment. Despite apocalyptic rhetoric about making a choice "between the quick and the dead," he made no progress at the UN. The Soviets rejected the American proposal and offered one of their own that the United States refused to consider. At an impasse, the two nations went their individual ways and gave up on the prospect of international control at the time when it might have had its greatest chance for success. Despite the efforts of the scientific community, government leaders committed themselves to a more aggressive, and ultimately more dangerous, course.

The Arms Race

Instead of control, the United States and the Soviet Union embarked on what turned into a massive arms race. Locked into an escalating cold war in the years following World War II, they each jealously guarded their atomic secrets as they built bigger and better bombs. After the Soviet Union successfully detonated a nuclear weapon of its own in 1949, despite naive American expectations that such a step would take twenty years, paranoia grew more pronounced. Charges that secrets from Los Alamos had been transmitted to the Soviets by American spies culminated in the execution of Julius and Ethel Rosenberg for treason in 1953. At the same time the United States placed increasing reliance on its growing nuclear arsenal. Military planners were impressed by the results of tests conducted near Bikini Atoll in the Pacific in the summer of 1946 and suggested in a Joint Chiefs of Staff report in 1947 that "atomic bombs not only can nullify any nation's military effort, but can demolish its social and economic structures and prevent their reestablishment for long periods of time." Over the next several years the nation increased its supply of fissionable material and devised ways of using smaller amounts of plutonium to create powerful atomic explosions. By mid 1949, weapons had five or more times the explosive power they had in 1945, and the arsenal contained about two hundred bombs.

The arms race became even more deadly with the decision to create a new weapon—a hydrogen bomb. Simulating the fusion reaction taking place on the surface of the sun, a thermonuclear bomb promised to be far more powerful and thereby preserve the American lead in the now-joined nuclear race. Of the scientists who speculated about the possibility of creating such a weapon, Edward Teller, a refugee physicist from Hungary, was the most passionately interested. While working on the Manhattan Project, he devoted most of his attention to what was called "the Super." "I'm making an alarm clock," he said after the war, (according to Gregg Herken in *Counsels of War* [1985]), "one that will wake up the world." Persistent in his efforts to move the nation ahead, Teller found a more receptive audience after the explosion of the Russian bomb. Several members of the Atomic Energy Commission (AEC), created in 1946 when the United States decided to proceed alone in nuclear affairs, were sympathetic. Brien McMahon, chair of the Congress's Joint Committee on Atomic Energy, was another supporter. General Omar Bradley, chairman of the Joint Chiefs of Staff, concluded that if a thermonuclear bomb was possible, the Soviet Union should not be permitted to build it first. Industrialists who had been involved in the Manhattan Project were eager to maintain that association with the government and to continue to build bigger and better bombs.

Yet supporters faced formidable opposition. A number of scientists insisted as they had before that the United States should behave more responsibly in the nuclear arena. Oppenheimer, still the major spokesman for the scientific community, had been troubled by continuing atomic tests in the Pacific and at a new site in Nevada. He felt that a decision to develop the Super could spark an irreversible arms race and that only a decision to renounce such a development could offer real hope for world peace. Five of the six scientists on the AEC's General Advisory Committee agreed, as did three of the five AEC commissioners, including chair David Lilienthal.

The public was largely uninformed about the debate being waged within the government. A disclosure during a television interview with a member of the Joint Committee on Atomic Energy in the fall of 1949 hinted at the effort to create a far more powerful bomb, and stories in the *Washington Post* and *New York Times* elaborated on that revelation. But the public still had no voice in the deliberations, and the leak only made top officials eager to resolve the matter of whether to proceed with the new weapon as quickly as possible.

Despite a recommendation from the AEC's General Advisory Committee and then from the AEC itself not to push ahead, Truman only wanted to know, "Can the Russians do it?" When told that they could, his response was, "We have no choice. We'll go ahead," and he authorized a crash program to create a hydrogen bomb. Once again, as with the decision to drop the atomic bomb and the determination to forego further discussions about international control, top policymakers acted without the full support of the scientific community or the full knowledge of the public at large.

Once again the developmental effort was successful. The first test of a thermonuclear device—though not yet a workable bomb—occurred at Eniwetok in the Marshall Islands in the western Pacific in November 1952. A thousand times more potent than the first atomic bombs, it left a crater in the seabed one hundred seventy-five feet (fifty-two meters) deep and a mile (1.6 kilometers) wide and eliminated the island of Eleugelab. The next year, the Soviets successfully ignited a small amount of thermonuclear fuel with a large amount of fissionable material, and they too were on their way toward developing a hydrogen bomb. In March 1954, in the Bravo test, the United States exploded such a bomb, easily adaptable for aircraft delivery, and the Soviets followed suit a year later. In 1953, as the process unfolded, the editors of the *Bulletin of the Atomic Scientists* moved the minute hand of the signature clock further forward to two minutes before midnight.

As bombs became bigger and stronger, American strategists recognized that there was little chance of devising an effective defense against attack. They began to argue that the heretofore unthinkable destructiveness might make the bomb "a powerful inhibition to aggression," in the words of Bernard Brodie in *The Absolute Weapon*, and the notion of deterrence was born. In the 1950s, the superpowers recognized that a nuclear war could destroy them all and so spoke of a policy known as "mutually assured destruction," or MAD.

As bombs became bigger and bigger, American strategists began to argue that the heretofore unthinkable destructiveness might make the bomb "a powerful inhibition to aggression."

Fallout and Civil Defense

The development of the hydrogen bomb created problems with radioactive fallout that became the focus of bitter public debate. For years, researchers around the world had been aware of the dangers of radiation, although they had disagreed about the critical levels that had to be avoided. The Manhattan Project made the issue more pressing, as radiation lingered after the Trinity test and the detonations in Japan. Public concern mounted in response to the postwar American nuclear weapons testing program. In the Bikini tests particles of fallout—residual radioactive droplets of water or dust—contaminated everything they touched. Physician David Bradley, a member of the radiological monitoring team, warned in his book *No Place to Hide* of "the invisible poison of radioactivity" that lingered after a blast and noted its possible persistence for centuries to come.

The public became even more worried about fallout as a result of tests conducted at the Nevada site. One shot in mid 1953 blanketed residents of Saint George, Utah, with as much radiation as nuclear workers were allowed in a year. People in a town farther east became ill, and four thousand two hundred sheep grazing north of the test site died of mysterious causes. When ranchers claimed that fallout was responsible for the animals' deaths, an AEC investigation concluded that radiation was not at fault. In 1956 the government won a suit filed by the ranchers on the grounds that the sheep owners had not provided scientific testimony to support their claim. Still, adverse publicity from the episode caused continued anxiety about the tests themselves, and twenty-five years later critics were vindicated when a federal judge called for a new trial in ruling that the government had deliberately suppressed critical results and misrepresented the facts.

As criticism of domestic testing increased, an accident in the Pacific dramatized further the problems with fallout. In March 1954 the Bravo test of a first operational hydrogen bomb showered radioactive ash over crewmen of a Japanese fishing vessel, the *Fukuryu Maru* ("Lucky Dragon"), anchored well beyond the danger zone. Although the ship left the area quickly, crewmen began to complain of radiation-sickness symptoms—headache, fatigue, nausea, diarrhea—and suffered from skin irritation and loss of hair. Even after medical treatment on their arrival in Japan, many remained ill. Seven months after the explosion, Aikichi Kuboyama, the ship's radio operator, died of jaundice, complicated by heart trouble and inflammation of the lungs, and became the first known postwar victim of the nuclear age.

Some scientists in the 1950s were quick to highlight the growing dangers of radiation. The American testing program, they suggested, harmed present and future generations and created an unacceptable human risk. A. H. Sturtevant, a prominent geneticist at the California Institute of Technology, charged that radiation harmed both the exposed individual and his or her descendants. Chemist Linus Pauling, winner of a Nobel Prize, estimated in 1957 that ten thousand persons were either dead or dying of leukemia caused by nuclear tests and predicted that continued testing would lead to the birth of two hundred thousand physically or mentally defective children in each of the next twenty generations. Physicist Ralph Lapp, in the *Bulletin of the Atomic Scientists* in November 1954, declared that radiation from fallout "cannot be felt and possesses all the terror of the unknown. It is something which evokes revulsion and helplessness—like a bubonic plague."

Popular culture reflected the scientific critique. Science fiction stories described the horrible effects of fallout. Movies like *Them!*, which appeared in 1954, featured mutant ants the size of buses crawling out of a New Mexico atomic test site. The mutation, according to a scientist in the film, was "probably caused by lingering radiation from the first atomic bomb." Songwriter Tom Lehrer caricatured the domestic testing program better than anyone in "The Wild West Is Where I Want to Be" in 1953:

> Along the trail you'll find me lopin'
> Where the spaces are wide open,
> In the land of the old A.E.C.
> Where the scenery's attractive,
> And the air is radioactive,
> Oh, the wild west is where I want to be.

The editors of *Playboy* voiced serious concern about strontium-90, one of the radioactive elements in fallout, which threatened their version of the good life.

A Consumers Union study of strontium-90 reached an even larger audience. Applying its product-testing procedure to fallout, the organization surveyed milk samples in fifty different areas over a one-month period in 1958, and published the results in the March 1959 *Consumer Reports*. "The Milk We Drink" was restrained but still frightening and ended on a pessimistic note: "No doubt the Best Buy is milk without Sr-90, air without fallout, and adequate medical care without diagnostic X rays. But none of these solutions are to be had." The *Consumer Reports* study reached Americans otherwise oblivious to the nuclear danger. Despite their preoccupation with the pursuit of material gain, they too now had to consider the consequences of nuclear tests.

Fears were focused by the best-known protest group, SANE—the National Committee for a Sane Nuclear Policy (now known as SANE/FREEZE: Campaign for Global Security). Organized in mid 1957 by prominent figures like Norman Cousins, *Saturday Review* editor, and Clarence Pickett, secretary emeritus of the American Friends Service Committee, the organization attracted pacifists and nonpacifists alike in the effort, in psychologist Erika Fromm's phrase "to bring the voice of sanity to the people." It ran newspaper advertisements and TV spots publicizing the danger from both nuclear blast and fallout. One of the most effective was a full-page ad featuring world-famous pediatrician Benjamin Spock. Dressed in a suit with a vest, he looked down at a little girl with a frown on his face. "Dr. Spock is worried," the caption read. "I *am* worried," he said in the text that followed. "Not so much about the effect of past tests but at the prospect of endless future ones. As the tests multiply, so will the danger to children—here and around the world."

Another group carried the message still further. In 1961, five women who had been active in SANE grew restless at the male-led organization's stress on political lobbying rather than direct action. Meeting in the home of Dagmar Wilson, housewife, mother, and illustrator of children's books, they wanted to focus on "mothers' issues" like the radioactive contamination of milk. They called for women all over the United States to suspend normal activities for a day and strike for peace. On 1 November, an estimated fifty-thousand women marched and mobilized in sixty communities around the country, with slogans like Let the Children Grow and End the Arms Race—Not the Human Race. Although these groups may not have reflected the dominant mood of the time, they did reflect widespread popular sentiment and received considerable coverage in the press.

Faced with a growing public outcry, the AEC and the rest of the government fought back. Officials in Dwight D. Eisenhower's administration, committed to the President's "Atoms for Peace" program, argued, without apparent contradiction, first that fallout was harmless, then that any possible danger was offset by knowledge gained from the tests. They took on the promotional task of reassuring Americans that past and present detonations were safe while at the same time persuading them that there was nothing to fear from taking reasonable risks.

In the "Duck and Cover" campaign, three million schoolchildren nationwide were given comic books in which Bert the Turtle stressed the need to take cover from flying glass and other debris in case of an atomic raid.

Yet the public remained concerned, and anxiety over fallout led to renewed interest in civil defense that lasted through John F. Kennedy's tenure as president. In the immediate postwar years Americans recalled the successful efforts of the British to protect themselves from German bombs and sought similar ways to secure protection from an atomic blast. One possibility involved the dispersion of the nation's urban and industrial capacity by relocating plants in less-populated regions of the country. The *Bulletin of the Atomic Scientists* devoted an entire issue in 1951 to the prospects of such decentralization. A shelter program had some advocates, but the estimates of a cost of between $16 and $32 billion over a five-year period discouraged government leaders. Instead, they participated in a program of cajoling the public to learn how to cope with an atomic attack. The "Alert America" campaign sent three convoys of ten thirty-two foot trailers carrying portable exhibits to cities throughout the United States. They contained dioramas showing the possible impact of a bomb on a typical city and posters demonstrating how civil defense could help. *Survival,* a seven-part television series was shown on NBC in 1951. A film, *Survival Under Atomic Attack,* was made for civil defense authorities and produced under government direction with private money. The "Duck and Cover" campaign targeted school children. In three million comic books distributed nationwide, Bert the Turtle stressed the need to take cover from flying glass and other debris in case of a raid. One panel told young readers that in the face of danger "*BERT DUCKS* AND *COVERS.* HE'S SMART, BUT *HE* HAS HIS SHELTER ON HIS BACK. *YOU* MUST LEARN TO *FIND SHELTER.*" A subsequent panel advised, "OUTDOORS, DUCK BEHIND WALLS AND TREES. EVEN IN A HOLLOW IN THE GROUND. IN A BUS OR AUTO, DUCK DOWN BEHIND OR UNDER THE SEATS." A final one concluded, "*DO IT INSTANTLY.* . . . DON'T STAND AND LOOK. DUCK AND COVER!" Bert the Turtle also starred in an animated film that brought the same message to children who may have missed the comic.

The development of the hydrogen bomb undermined the early civil defense campaign. Val Peterson, head of the Federal Civil Defense Administration between 1953 and 1957, noted, "The alternatives are to dig, die, or get out; and certainly we don't want to die." Digging seemed far too costly in the face of more potent bombs, and so the new approach became one of evacuation if attacked. The orientation changed, according to The *Bulletin of the Atomic Scientists* "from 'Duck and Cover' to 'Run like Hell.' " But evacuation required an adequate system of roads. The 1956 act creating an interstate highway system provided easier automobile access to the suburbs and, at the same time, an expeditious means of exit from the cities in case of nuclear war.

The whole notion of evacuation suffered a real blow with the growing realization of the consequences of fallout. The creeping radioactive cloud that accompanied any nuclear blast minimized the value of running away, for the insidious dust remained deadly without some shield. While blast shelters were useless to safeguard people from a bomb's impact, less substantial and less

During the 1950's, anxiety about atomic bomb attack and fallout led to public safety and protection campaigns. These students demonstrate the "Duck and Cover" drill.

costly fallout shelters might nonetheless save them from the poisonous side effects of an attack.

The public became fascinated with fallout shelters. In the mid 1950s *Life* magazine featured an "H-Bomb Hideaway" for $3,000. At the end of the decade a Miami firm reported numerous inquiries about shelters that sold for between $1,795 and $3,895, depending on capacity, and planned 900 franchises. Interest became even more intense in the administration of President John F. Kennedy, particularly after his cold war confrontations with the Soviet Union over Berlin and Cuba. "At cocktail parties and P.T.A. meetings and family dinners, on buses and commuter trains and around office watercoolers," *Time* magazine noted on 20 October 1961 in "Civil Defense: The Sheltered Life," "talk turns to shelters." Men and women alike were concerned with the possible destruction of everything they knew and loved. For $30, AEC commissioner Willard Libby built a shelter out of railroad ties and bags of dirt. For $15,000, a California missile scientist and electronics manufacturer built a shelter that he stocked with food, water, and a 1925 edition of the *Encyclopaedia Britannica* to help in the reconstruction effort. Georgia senator Richard B. Russell summed up widespread popular sentiment when he declared (as quoted in the *New York Times*, 22 January 1971), "If we have to start over again with another Adam and Eve, then I want them to be Americans and not Russians, and I want them on this continent and not in Europe."

Yet none of those efforts was ever really effective. Opponents like SANE argued in "The Effects of Nuclear War" and "How Sane Are Fallout Shelters" that "fallout shelters are pitifully inadequate protection against nuclear attack" and proclaimed that they tended "to obscure the unprecedented catastrophe that nuclear war would bring, and the efforts that must be made to avoid it." Some critics demanded that the government and public explore serious questions of human purpose instead of becoming preoccupied with haphazard efforts to hide from the effects of nuclear attack. Others claimed that the very existence of a shelter program increased the likelihood of war by demonstrating that the nation thought it could survive such a conflict. Although a fair number of Americans were intrigued with the possibilities of protection, government officials were never willing to allocate the funds for a full-fledged program. Despite occasional revivals of interest in subsequent decades, civil defense waned as an issue of serious concern.

Commercial Nuclear Power

A more pressing public preoccupation was the question of atomic power. Soon after the first bombs fell in Japan, Americans dreamed of a nuclear utopia, with electricity generated at virtually no cost; with cars, planes, and ships fueled by an inexhaustible energy source; with isotopes readily available for industrial and medical use. Atomic energy could "usher in a new day of peace and plenty," according to University of Chicago chancellor Robert M. Hutchins in 1945. This wonderful new force, Walt Disney proclaimed a decade later in the animated film *Our Friend, the Atom,* could "be put to use for creation, for the welfare of mankind." AEC officials speculated about the glorious age that lay ahead and encouraged similar speculation in the country at large. The ubiquitous propaganda helped romanticize the atom and created a sense of expectation as scientists and engineers made the technical breakthroughs that led to increasing orders for reactors in the 1960s and 1970s.

The government played a major role in the promotion and development of nuclear power. The Atomic Energy Act of 1946 that established the AEC mandated a government monopoly over all nuclear materials, facilities, and experimental projects, and that policy effectively squelched private initiative in the first postwar years. Although an experimental reactor built by the government in 1951 became the first atomic power plant ever to produce small amounts of electricity, progress was slow until Eisenhower pushed successfully three years later for revision of the 1946 act to allow the AEC to issue licenses to private firms to build and operate commercial nuclear power plants.

Atomic power became a realistic possibility as a result of the efforts of navy captain Hyman G. Rickover. He had been interested in the problem of nuclear propulsion since 1946 and his single-minded effort to build a nuclear-powered submarine laid the groundwork for the creation of reactor-generated power on land. An ambitious, tireless administrator who refused to cut corners and demanded high standards from the contractors he employed, he forced both the navy and the AEC to accept his dream as a priority. In 1954 he achieved his goal as he oversaw the launch of the USS *Nautilus*, which operated with a small reactor in its hull. Because of his success in dealing with Westinghouse, the company most involved in building the *Nautilus*, the AEC asked Rickover to work with the firm in constructing the nation's first nuclear power plant for the Duquesne Light Company in Shippingport, Pennsylvania, in 1957. Using the same technology, Rickover succeeded in bringing the plant on-line at its full power rating just before the end of 1957. While the electricity it produced was expensive—sixty-four mills compared to six mills per kilowatt for conventional plants—the design and data derived from its construction were enormously valuable for future projects.

In the 1960s nuclear power came of age. Private firms became increasingly active in the field as they recognized the potential profits that beckoned. In 1963 General Electric and Westinghouse embarked on a series of "turnkey" projects in which they assumed all risks for building plants the utilities could take over. GE constructed a plant at Oyster Creek for the Jersey Central Power and Light Company and charged the utility an estimated thirty million dollars less than the unit cost, with the expectation that it would be a "loss leader" to demonstrate the feasibility of nuclear power to other customers. The strategy worked. In 1966 and 1967 utilities ordered about fifty plants. Between 1970 and 1974 they contracted for more than one-hundred.

A series of dramatic accidents gradually heightened concern about safety and eventually shattered the dream of a peaceful nuclear world once and for all. Accidents—in Idaho in 1961, in Michigan in 1966, in Alabama in 1975—had been troubling but paled against the 1979 mishap at Three Mile Island near Harrisburg, Pennsylvania, in 1979. Human error and mechanical malfunction led the reactor to overheat and almost caused a meltdown of the radioactive core. As reporters flocked to the region and covered the story for the world, nearly one hundred fifty thousand residents fled their homes. Although disaster was averted, the episode revealed serious flaws in the safety-monitoring system. *Mad* magazine's "Alfred E. Neuman" posed in front of the famous cooling towers and said, "Yes, me worry!" An even worse accident at a Soviet plant at Chernobyl in 1986 underscored still-smoldering American fears. Scientists and others began to ask whether even the most complex safety features could be trusted and to question whether nuclear power was worth the risk. Activists, drawing on the lessons of the civil rights movement, argued that catastrophes were not just possible but likely and launched direct-action protest campaigns to close down old plants and stop the building of new ones. Environmentalists, charging that nuclear power was a needless source of pollution, joined the fight. New orders for reactors dried up, construction of already-planned plants ceased, and a *Forbes* magazine cover story in 1985 called the nuclear industry "the largest managerial disaster in business history."

After the Three Mile Island accident in 1979, Mad *magazine's "Alfred E Neuman" posed in front of the reactor's famous cooling towers and said, "Yes, me worry!"*

Curbing the Arms Race

As Americans struggled with the question of nuclear power, they also sought to reduce the risks of nuclear war. Agitated over the danger of fallout, public opinion demanded a moratorium on testing and a concerted effort to control the arms race. Creative commentators, accustomed to giving their imagination free rein, played a major role in drawing attention to the possibility of holocaust. Some, such as poet Robert Lowell, offered sober warnings of impending disaster, as when he wrote in "Fall 1961":

> All autumn the chafe and jar
> of nuclear war;
> we have talked our extinction to death.

Others used satire to confront the problems more directly. Once again songwriter Tom Lehrer was a biting critic of American policy and its implications as he provided his own personal scenario for the next war in the 1965 song "So Long, Mom":

> So long, Mom
> I'm off to drop the bomb,
> So don't wait up for me,
> But while you swelter
> Down there in your shelter,
> You can see me
> On your TV
> While we're attacking frontally,
> Watch Brinkally and Huntally,
> Describing contrapuntally
> The cities we have lost.
> No need for you to miss a minute
> of the agonizing holocaust.

Artists, too, shared their anxiety about the nuclear threat. In 1980 Alex Grey painted *Nuclear Crucifixion*, which showed Jesus crucified in a mushroom cloud and conveyed a haunting message about the means of death. The following year Robert Morris created a huge, multimedia work called *Jornado del Muerto* ("Journey of Death") named after the New Mexico site of the Trinity test. Installed in the Hirshhorn Museum in Washington, D.C., it included a drawing of a Hiroshima bridge and photographs of Oppenheimer and Albert Einstein, father of the theory of relativity, juxtaposed with a photo of a badly burned boy. Far simpler was Erika Rothenberg's 1982 acrylic *Pushing the Right Buttons.* It pictured nothing but two circular buttons, the top one labeled "Launch" and the bottom one "Lunch," and dramatized fears caused by the casual conversation at the top levels of government about the possibility of nuclear war.

Equally engaging was the black humor of Stanley Kubrick's brilliant 1963 film *Dr. Strangelove; or, How I Learned to Stop Worrying and Love the Bomb.* It was a vivid and absurd tale of a world become prisoner to its monstrous machines, with outrageous characters like General Turgidson, General Jack D. Ripper, President Muffley, Premier Kissof, and Dr. Strangelove himself giving a wry, often ridiculous touch to unfolding scenes. The movie ended with the triumph of the Doomsday Machine—the ultimate but unsuccessful deterrent—as the camera panned across a series of mushroom clouds spreading through the sky.

Public pressure, generated by artists and authors on the one hand and citizens groups like SANE on the other, helped encourage the government to seek accommodation with the Soviet Union. In the spring of 1963, in a commencement address at American University in Washington, D.C., John Kennedy declared that in the nuclear age "total war makes no sense" and called for a treaty outlawing nuclear tests. The Limited Test Ban Treaty of 1963 was the result. It banned nuclear tests in the atmosphere, or in any environment where detectable radioactive debris might be spewed beyond territorial borders. While some scientists, such as Edward Teller, were outspoken in their opposition and a number of military officials and defense contractors were equally hostile to the agreement, it enjoyed overwhelming public support and secured the necessary Senate ratification. A decade later, in 1972, the SALT I Treaty, stemming from Strategic Arms Limitation Talks, limited the number of anti-ballistic missile systems the superpowers could construct and, in a five-year "interim agreement," specified ceilings on intercontinental and other ballistic missiles. A SALT II Treaty in 1979 capped the number of warheads that could be placed on missiles, limited the number of multiple-warhead missiles, and froze the number of delivery systems permitted, but it became tangled up with American opposition to a Soviet invasion of Afghanistan and was never ratified.

The dialogue that dominated the nuclear age continued into the 1980s. Scientists and their counterparts in the world of cultural affairs maintained their pressure on the government to take meaningful steps toward peace. They were particularly alarmed at positions voiced by Ronald Reagan, who assumed the presidency in 1981. Taking a militant approach toward the Soviet Union, which Reagan termed an "evil empire" in a casual reference to the popular film *Star Wars* (1977), the administration slowed efforts in the arms control arena and sought an unprecedented $1.5 trillion over a five-year period to support a massive military buildup. That spending, critics argued, promised to bring the world even closer to nuclear war.

Scientists and their counterparts in the world of cultural affairs were particularly alarmed at President Ronald Reagan, who took a militant approach to the Soviet Union, which he termed an "evil empire" in reference to the film Star Wars.

Scientists stepped up their attack. Some described the consequences of an atomic struggle in such journals as *Ambio.* Others, like astronomer Carl Sagan and four colleagues, speculated, both in a scientific paper and in the Sunday-supplement *Parade* magazine, about the prospect of a "nuclear winter," caused by dust and smoke from bombs exploding in the atmosphere, which could "generate an epoch of cold and dark" and possibly lead to the extinction of the human race.

Even more influential were writers who picked up on the arguments of worried scientists. By far the most compelling was Jonathan Schell who published an eloquent series of articles first in the *New Yorker*, then in book form in 1982 as *The Fate of the Earth*. Schell wrote about "A Republic of Insects and Grass," which might well result from a nuclear war. In terms a layman could understand, he began with the basic principles of radiation and summarized the immediate and long-range effects of a blast. "What happened at Hiroshima," he observed, "was less than a millionth part of a holocaust at present levels of world nuclear armament" (p. 45). He also contemplated "The Second Death," in which "every person on earth would die; but in addition to that, and distinct from it, . . . unborn generations would be prevented from ever existing" (p. 172).

The Disarmament Effort

A number of organizations focused the arguments of critics. Physicians for Social Responsibility, founded twenty years before by Bernard Lown, a Boston cardiologist and professor at Harvard University's School of Public Health, was revived in the 1980s after a period of hibernation. A 1980 symposium on "The Medical Consequences of Nuclear Weapons and Nuclear War," sponsored by the medical schools at Harvard and Tufts, gained widespread public attention. Numerous speakers described the devastation that would result from an atomic war. One principal participant, George Kistiakowsky, shared fears that stemmed from a lifetime of experience. Head of the Manhattan Project's explosives division, later scientific adviser to Presidents Eisenhower, Kennedy, and Johnson, and now a professor emeritus of chemistry at Harvard, he reluctantly assumed that atomic bombs would someday be used:

> I think that with the kind of political leaders we have in the world . . . nuclear weapons will proliferate. . . . I personally think that the likelihood for an initial use of nuclear warheads is really quite great between now and the end of this century, which is only twenty years hence. My own estimate, since I am almost eighty years old, [is that] I will probably die from some other cause. But looking around at all these young people, I am sorry to say that I think a lot of you may die from nuclear war. (Jonathan A. Leonard, "Danger: Nuclear War," in *Harvard Magazine*, November-December 1980, p. 22)

Other symposiums spread the same message, as membership in Physicians for Social Responsibility grew from three thousand in 1981 to sixteen thousand in 1982.

Another equally active group was the Union of Concerned Scientists. Henry W. Kendall, an MIT physicist and former consultant to the Defense Department, had founded the organization in 1969 to oppose the drift toward antiballistic missile systems. After winning that battle with the ratification of the SALT I Treaty, the group had concentrated on the dangers of nuclear power. Now it returned to the arms race. "There was Reagan talking about fighting and winning a limited nuclear war and handing out his laundry list of building up every conceivable nuclear weapon," Kendall declared in Fox Butler Field's article in the 11 July 1982 issue of the *New York Times Magazine*. "It brought out the latent anxiety" (p. 17). Capitalizing on public discontent, the Union of Concerned Scientists planned a series of teach-ins, like those held during the Vietnam War, at colleges on Veterans Day, 1981. Two dozen such assemblies were expected; one hundred fifty were held. The media publicized the protests and helped the movement along.

These groups supported the notion of a nuclear freeze. The idea came from Randall Forsberg, head of her own Institute for Defense and Disarmament Studies in Brookline, Massachusetts. When the superpowers failed to reach a comprehensive test ban settlement in the 1960s, she argued, experts simply accepted the concept of a permanent arms race and dedicated themselves to keeping things equal. "The buzz word," she said, "was stability." Then, as Reagan launched a massive military buildup, the United States seemed to reject even that limited goal. In response Forsberg proposed a mutual and verifiable freeze. It was a simple enough concept for the public to accept easily, and, if adopted, could limit the ever-increasing supply of nuclear arms. In early 1980 the Fellowship of Reconciliation organized a meeting of several dozen peace groups to consider the idea. Word reached Vermont, and as a result of the efforts of the American Friends Service Committee, the Forsberg proposal received a favorable hearing at town meetings throughout the state. Such discussions spread elsewhere and were soon occurring around the country. Ground Zero Week in the spring of that year provided further support as thousands of people in one hundred fifty cities and five hundred communities dramatized the devastating effects of a nuclear war. At a national political level, Senator Edward M. Kennedy, a Democrat from Massachusetts, and Senator Mark O. Hatfield, a Republican from Oregon, introduced a joint congressional resolution calling for a weapons freeze. Two dozen senators and more than one hundred fifty representatives signed their names as sponsors. Together they countered the Reagan administration's talk of a "window of vulnerability" which might prompt a Soviet attack with the assertion that there was, rather, a "window of opportunity" for arms control. They proposed, in short, to create a "firebreak" to circumscribe the arms race. In August 1982 the House of Representatives defeated the measure by a 204 to 202 vote, but later came back and passed it. While the proposal never became national policy, it clearly created pressure on the administration to consider more seriously the effort to control arms that culminated in Reagan's second term when an Intermediate-Range Nuclear Forces Treaty eliminated one entire category of nuclear weapons in American and Soviet arsenals. It also encouraged the Strategic Arms Reduction Talks (START) that continued into the 1980s and 1990s.

The protest effort, so much a part of American culture in the 1980s, dramatized concerns and mobilized opinion more effectively than ever before. Scientists and nonscientists alike were able to force institutional leaders to listen and to persuade a reluctant administration to resume the process of negotiation it had chosen to ignore. Results came slowly, to be sure. But, as Bernard Lown noted in the Eugene *Register-Guard* on 4 April 1986, after watching public concern develop over several decades, "It's like boiling water. Nothing happens, nothing happens, nothing happens, and then finally there's steam."

Conclusion

The nuclear age has been a period of painful struggle. Hopes for a dazzling nuclear future have been tempered by fears of an atomic holocaust, as Americans have grappled over the decades since 1945 with the same basic question: How to maintain an increasingly fragile national and international balance in the face of ever more powerful bombs? In the triangular conversation including scientists, social critics, and policymakers, the government leaders have long had the upper hand. The dialogue generated by opponents of nuclear development has been loud and articulate but has triggered no mechanism that might automatically force a response or alter the government's course. Critics have constantly found that those charged with making national decisions had priorities of their own. Bureaucratic inertia, coupled with a powerful and unchanging commitment to building bigger and better bombs, kept administration after administration on the course defined as the nuclear age began. The bomb, physicist Alvin C. Graves noted in 1952, "was a fact of life . . . [that] had to be lived with, like a heart condition." Government officials were willing to live with it, and to take modest ameliorative steps, but not to alter their fundamental approach.

Occasionally, though, protesters from a variety of camps have managed to shift America's nuclear approach. Once a decade the nation has gingerly backed away from the most truculent national positions and sought accommodation with adversaries in a joint effort to mute the global threat. At those points when critics were able to focus on prickly political problems and cause enough of a public scare, they managed to attract the attention of top officials. In response government policy shifted just a bit and for a time the world became a marginally safer place. A voluntary moratorium on testing in the late 1950s paved the way for the 1963 Limited Test Ban Treaty. Good-faith negotiating in the 1970s produced several more accords. Pressure in the 1980s generated still another agreement. Then interest waned, old positions revived, and the cycle of protest and counterprotest began anew.

Despite repeated discouragement, activists pressed on. "We are but transient passengers on the planet Earth," Bernard Lown told audiences in 1982. "It does not belong to us. We are not free to doom generations yet unborn. We are not at liberty to erase humanity's past or dim its future." That message provided a measure of hope in the continuing effort to come to terms with atomic energy and guarantee the survival of the human race.

[See also Childhood and Children; Death; Technology and Social Change; Television.]

BIBLIOGRAPHY

General Works

Boyer, Paul S. *By the Bomb's Early Light: American Thought and Culture at the Dawn of the Atomic Age* (1985). An outstanding account of the first years of the atomic age.

Bundy, McGeorge. *Danger and Survival: Choices About the Bomb in the First Fifty Years* (1988).

Clarfield, Gerard H., and William M. Wiecek. *Nuclear America: Military and Civilian Nuclear Power in the United States, 1940–1980* (1984).

Newhouse, John. *War and Peace in the Nuclear Age* (1989).

Weart, Spencer R. *Nuclear Fear: A History of Images* (1988).

Williams, Robert C., and Philip L. Cantelon, eds. *The American Atom: A Documentary History of Nuclear Policies from the Discovery of Fission to the Present, 1939–1984* (1984). The best documentary collection.

Studies of Arms Development and Use

Bernstein, Barton J., ed. *The Atomic Bomb: The Critical Issues* (1976).

Hersey, John. *Hiroshima* (1946).

Hewlett, Richard G., and Oscar E. Anderson, Jr. *The New World: A History of the United States Atomic Energy Commission. 1939–1946* (1976).

Jones, Vincent C. *Manhattan: The Army and the Atomic Bomb—United States Army in World War II, Special Studies* (1985).

Rhodes, Richard. *The Making of the Atomic Bomb* (1986). Winner of the Pulitzer Prize and the National Book Award.

Sherwin, Martin J. *A World Destroyed: The Atomic Bomb and the Grand Alliance* (1975). The best account of the decision to drop the atomic bomb.

York, Herbert F. *The Advisors: Oppenheimer, Teller, and the Superbomb* (1976).

Studies of National Security Policy

Gaddis, John Lewis. *Strategies of Containment: A Critical Appraisal of Postwar American National Security Policy* (1982).

Harvard Nuclear Study Group. *Living with Nuclear Weapons* (1983).

Herken, Gregg. *The Winning Weapon: The Atomic Bomb in the Cold War, 1945–1950* (1980).

Herken, Gregg. *Counsels of War* (1985).

Mandelbaum, Michael. *The Nuclear Question: The United States and Nuclear Weapons, 1946–1976* (1979).

Mandelbaum, Michael. *The Nuclear Revolution: International Politics Before and After Hiroshima* (1981).

Talbott, Strobe. *Deadly Gambits: The Reagan Administration and the Stalemate in Nuclear Arms Control* (1985).

Works Dealing with Nuclear Power

Del Sesto, Steven L. *Science, Politics, and Controversy: Civilian Nuclear Power in the United States, 1946–1974* (1979).

Hewlett, Richard G., and Jack M. Holl. *Atoms for Peace and War 1953–1961: Eisenhower and the Atomic Energy Commission* (1989).

Mazuzan, George T., and J. Samuel Walker. *Controlling the Atom: The Beginnings of Nuclear Regulation, 1946–1962* (1984). The most useful account of the first years of peaceful nuclear power.

Works Dealing with Protest

Divine, Robert A. *Blowing on the Wind: The Nuclear Test Ban Debate, 1954–1960* (1978).

Dyson, Freeman. *Weapons and Hope* (1984).

Schell, Jonathan. *The Fate of the Earth* (1982). A key work in helping generate protest in the 1980s.

Wittner, Lawrence S. *Rebels Against War: The American Peace Movement, 1941–1960* (1969).

— ALLAN M. WINKLER

O

OLD AGE

The meanings and experiences of growing older and being elderly in postindustrial America are both remarkably similar to and strikingly different from circumstances in the colonial period. To appreciate the novel dimensions of old age in the contemporary era, one first must understand why the universals of age matter greatly.

Universals of Aging

THE BIOLOGY OF SENESCENCE. For centuries people have acknowledged that senescence is in part a biological phenomenon. Elderly men and women are more likely than youth to have wrinkles and gray hair. The incidence of long-term disability and chronic disease increases with age. The last stage, demographers report, is characterized not so much by sickness as by frailty. People over sixty who fall are a hundred times more likely to suffer adverse physical consequences than those under sixty. Death ineluctably marks the end. Such realities have always colored images of the elderly.

Early in recorded history, adventurers and scholars sought the secret to prolonging life. Mesopotamian and Hindu legends hold that hags were transformed into damsels by bathing in oil-slick waters. Juan Ponce de León (1460–1521) searched for the Fountain of Youth. Charles E. Brown-Séquard (1817–1894), a French-American physician, regularly injected himself with an extract of ground dog testicles. None of these permanently effaced the marks of age.

Scientists have not discovered an elixir that rejuvenates the long-lived. Nor are they yet able to separate cause and effect in changes associated with aging. Many bodily functions decline with advancing age. Hardening of the arteries, however, does not cause senescence. Nor does digestive putrefaction or alterations in the endocrine system—though some American researchers around 1900 advanced theories of aging based on these symptoms. The mechanisms of senescence remain a mystery.

Recent biomedical discoveries have given rise to immune theories of human aging. Experiments show that human regulatory functions decline gradually, accelerating when normal aging processes are diseased. Yet lower forms of life, which lack specialized immune systems, also manifest functional declines at the cellular level. Immunological errors are associated with senescence, but they do not explain its developments.

Biological aging, according to the best research available, is partly played out at the genetic level. If all of one's biological parents and grandparents survive(d) past seventy, one's likelihood of living to a ripe old age is good. In addition, random degradations in DNA and at the cellular and organic levels affect basic processes. Decrements accumulate, impairing homeostasis.

Evolutionary advantages, moreover, go to species with comparatively large brains. Researchers believe that the capacity to learn, store, and retrieve information resides in brain neurons, which in humans are long-lived but finite. There is no indication that there has been any prolongation of the life span of neurons over time. This immutable biological limit helps to explain why there has been no change in maximum human life potential over several centuries.

"My spirit shall not abide in mortals forever, for they are flesh," says the Lord in Genesis (6:3), "but their days shall be one hundred and twenty years." That number approximates what scientists presume is the chronological limit to the human life span. Veterans' records and Social Security files do not challenge the figure. Nor do studies of centenarians. Life expectancy beyond age one hundred has increased by less than a year during the twentieth century.

Not only did Old Testament writers rightly understand that there is a natural boundary to human existence, but they also acknowledged physiological variations late in life. "The years of our life are threescore and ten, and even by reason of strength fourscore," observed the Psalmist (90:10). "Yet their span is but toil and trouble; they are soon gone, and we fly away."

Two points made in this verse apply directly to the American experience. First, most people do not survive to the maximum life span. The 1990 life expectancy for white infants was around seventy-five. Black infants could expect to live sixty-nine and a half years. These figures are close to the biblical seventy. Changes in life expectancy at birth, at forty, and at sixty, have altered the meanings and experiences of old age, particularly during the twentieth century. That said, the biblical notion of when one is old seems quite modern.

Second, the Psalmist stipulated that at least two physical states exist within old age. Mounting adversity sooner or later plagues the latter stage. This typology conforms to a distinction made since Elizabethan times between a "green old age" (which is healthful and vital) and "senectitude" or the "second childhood" (in which a person requires care). The twofold categorization remains salient. Gerontologists often distinguish between the young-old (people between the ages of fifty or fifty-five and seventy-five) and the old-old (those over seventy-five or eighty).

Throughout America's history, the chronological boundaries of old age have remained quite stable—and demarcated in a broadly similar fashion. There has never been a consensus in American culture about which birthday, if any, signals the onset of late life.

Invoking European traditions, colonial writers sometimes referred to 63 as the "grand climacteric," the magical product of multiplying 7 and 9, numbers fraught with symbolism. The 1935 Social Security Act, corporate pensions, and other public policies have made age sixty-five a trigger for entitlements in recent decades. The complementariness of such thresholds challenges the myths that once upon a time in America old age began at forty, and that it rose thereafter as life expectancies rose.

Yet age sixty-five is not the only benchmark for old age. Other birthdays have been proposed: fifty-five, sixty, sixty-two, sixty-four, sixty-seven, seventy, seventy-two, and seventy-five. Few have suggested a figure below fifty or over eighty, though Bernard Baruch in late life claimed that "old age is always fifteen years older than I am." Old age in the American experience might be said to begin at sixty-five, give or take fifteen years. This has always been the case.

THE SOCIAL CONSTRUCTION OF OLD AGE. Such looseness in defining chronological parameters suggests that senescence is not just biologically determined. Old age is also socially constructed. Many of the heterogeneous physical, mental, psychological, and social characteristics ascribed to the "old" in America today hark back to ancient roots. Competing conceptions of late life have long shaped norms and expectations affecting the elderly.

No single image captures the diversity of old age. Scripture, for instance, extols the elders' wisdom. Moses listened to Jethro, and Ruth took Naomi's advice; both grew wiser over time. But Noah and Lot acted foolishly in late life, when inebriated. Patriarchs were not always paragons of virtue. Nor were "hoary heads" always revered.

Although older men in the Bible were considered past their prime, they nonetheless contributed to the well-being of the community. Levites retired at fifty but still assisted in rituals. Octogenarians served as advisers. The early body Christians were led by "elders"—whose efforts were opposed by senior members of the Jewish ruling council.

Older women also played vital roles. Leviticus 27:1–7 indicates that, at every stage of life, women were valued less than men of the same age. Yet the differential narrowed past sixty. Some elderly women prophesied. The Israelites made special provisions for aged widows. In early Christian congregations, widows over sixty ministered to the sick and poor, and helped with religious ceremonies.

Greco-Roman culture provided the other major wellspring of ideas about old age and aging in America. Themes in modern-day jokes about dirty old men and constipated old women date back to motifs that fill Greek tragedy and Latin poetry. *Oedipus at Colonus* and the *Odyssey* reflect a wide range of intergenerational dynamics, universally shared. The myth of Tithonos—the comely prince granted long life but not eternal youth—inspired Juvenal, Jonathan Swift, Oscar Wilde, Aldous Huxley, Alfred Lord Tennyson, and contemporary science fiction writers. The nascent nineteenth-century American medical opinion that old age is a disease recalls Seneca's dictum, "Senectus morbidus est" (Old age is a disease).

Late-life experiences, which were as varied as images of old age in classical times, provide precedents for understanding how phenomena as diverse as senior power and elder abuse evolved in America. Older men with wealth often wielded considerable power. Militaristic Sparta was ruled by a *gerousia*, a council of twenty-eight elders. *Senex* was a term of respect for the *paterfamilias*. Emerson and Longfellow borrowed themes from Cicero's *De Senectute* in their paeans to old age. Yet the Romans also had a tradition of throwing off bridges those over seventy who had become burdens. Widows and old slaves, marginal in the best of times, suffered socioeconomic hardships.

Over the centuries positive and negative images of old age, as well as the contradictions and ambiguities ascribed to late life, were embellished. Venetian doges presided over a gerontocracy at roughly the same time Chaucer and Boccaccio mocked crones' lust and the cuckolds' plight. Medieval iconography, which stressed Father Time's associations with old age and death, later inspired American folk art depicting the stages of life. Shakespeare's characterization of Lear—complete with insights into insanity and power in impotence—has influenced portraits of late-life styles as different as those offered by Erik Erikson and May Sarton.

No single text transmitted all Western traditions concerning old age. But it is worth noting that in the colonial era John Bunyan's *Pilgrim's Progress* (1678–1684) was the most widely read tract on aging as a spiritual journey. True to its genre, the book is a treasure trove of ideas about age. It abounds in biblical allusions and references to Reformation ideals. Divided into two parts, it highlights basic differences between the ways men and women grow older. Christian makes his way alone to the Celestial City. Christiana, in contrast, takes her children along; she travels with a group following a less direct route. Such differences (instrumental/cooperative; solitary/nurturing) resonate in contemporary discussions of age and gender.

The social construction of old age in American history thus builds on centuries of motifs, folk wisdom, reinterpretations of classical texts, and "scientific" observation. It also reflects the fears, hopes, struggles, successes, failures, and adaptations that people through the ages have felt and experienced in growing older. Biological processes shape key parameters of late life. But the meanings and experiences of old age that have prevailed in any period of American history are malleable. They reflect and result from a concatenation of broader demographic, economic, political, social, and cultural forces in society at large.

There has never been a revolutionary shift in old-age history—no dramatic, sudden change in attitudes or behavior. Nor does modernization theory help much to explain significant shifts in how Americans perceived and experienced late life. Industrialization, declining fertility rates, and new political institutions all affected the lives of the aged, to be sure. And conceptions of older people's roles changed as society changed. But turning points in the history of old age in America do not dovetail neatly with watersheds in American economic and political history.

Demographic Patterns

FERTILITY, MORTALITY, AND MIGRATION. Population structures are shaped by three demographic factors: changing fertility and mortality rates, and shifts in (im)migration patterns. Of the three, rising and declining birthrates are the most important in determining the relative size of the elderly age group. Periods of high fertility produce a relatively youthful population. The proportion of elders rise as birthrates fall.

By this logic, the proportion of older people in the United States should have risen steadily throughout the national experience. Fertility rates had been high in the colonial period, reaching their peak in 1790. Since then, there has been a net decline in birth rates for white native-born women, particularly marked during wars, the Great Depression, and after 1964. Black fertility rates, higher than those of whites, have fallen strikingly since the 1870s. The same downward pattern obtains for women of various ethnic groups. Even so, there were not dramatic increases in the numbers of older people until the twentieth century.

Throughout the colonial period, proportions of the elderly remained quite stable. Based on extant town and county records, less than 2 percent were over sixty-five in 1790. A century later, the figure stood at 4 percent; the 1990 census reports that about 13 percent were over sixty-five. There was a 59 percent increase in the relative numbers of older men and women between 1870 and 1920, compared with a 115 percent increase between 1920 and 1970. During the 1970s and 1980s, the population over sixty-five grew three times faster than the group under sixty-five.

The social construction of old age in American history builds on centuries of motifs, folk wisdom, reinterpretations of classical texts, and "scientific" observation.

Comparable trends obtain if the "old" are defined as those over sixty. Older men and women constituted anywhere from 1.7 percent to 6.4 percent of the population according to scattered eighteenth-century records. It is unlikely that the proportion over sixty grew more than 1 percent between 1790 and 1830 (when the federal census first reported numbers of aged whites). The percentage over sixty rose from 4.1 percent in 1850, to 6.4 percent in 1900, to 10.4 percent in 1950. By 2050, the percentage is projected to soar to 27.7 percent.

The increasing proportion of older Americans has altered the distribution of children and elderly in the population. There were forty people under the age of eighteen for every four over sixty-five in 1900. By 1980, the ratio had fallen to twenty-eight to eleven. By 2050, demographers anticipate, there will be twenty-two senior citizens for every twenty-one children and youth.

The aging of the population has not affected the nation's dependency ratio—the proportion of people under nineteen *and* over sixty-five to the working-age population—as much as declining fertility rates have. There were 111 "dependents" for every 100 "prime age" Americans in 1870. The ratio fell to seventy by 1940. By 1970, it had risen to ninety-one. The ratio is not projected to reach pre-1900 levels until the middle of the twenty-first century.

Such data suggest that the aged have not been, and are not likely to be, burdens on society—as various media depict them. The young have typically been the nation's costly dependent class. But children have futures; the elderly are near the end of their lives. Perhaps it is the expected rate of return on outlays, and not the actual costs, that affects the calculus of the debate over generational equity.

Why did the growing numbers of older people not become more visible in the United States until the twentieth century? The answer lies in the dampening effect of mortality and (im)migration trends on falling birthrates. Both have made the population more youthful.

Demographers estimate that two-thirds of the improvement in longevity since prehistoric times has occurred since 1900. Most gains have improved life expectancy at younger ages. Children born in 1790, for instance, had as much likelihood of surviving to age one as children born in 1970 have of reaching age sixty-five. Babies born in 1900 could expect to live an average of forty-seven years; those born in 1985 are expected to live to be seventy-five.

Besides improvements in infants' and children's mortality rates, there have been notable gains in adult longevity. The average life expectancy of men aged forty in 1940 was only a year greater than for men aged forty in 1790. Forty-year-old women in 1940 on average could expect to live three years longer than forty-year-old women in 1790. Since then, thanks to better diets, reduced smoking, and medical interventions, there have been dramatic gains throughout the adult life course.

Americans who turned sixty-five in 1985 can expect to live another seventeen years, compared with the additional twelve that those who were sixty-five in 1900 on average might have enjoyed. Whereas the average sixty-five-year-old woman could expect to live only a few months longer than her male counterpart in 1900, there was a four-year differential in life expectancy by 1985. The gap has narrowed somewhat since then—in part because more adult women than men now smoke.

Mortality rates for blacks persistently have been, and remain, higher than those of whites. Blacks typically have had poorer diets, living conditions, and medical care.

Some gains in longevity mean that more people will live to old age. According to the life tables for 1949–1951, only two-thirds of all babies would live to age sixty-five; in 1990, almost 80 percent are expected to do so. As a result, there are more young and middle-aged people alive than might have been expected. This makes the American population younger, but more age conscious.

Similarly, (im)migration patterns tended to make America "young" in the 1800s. People are most likely to move between the ages of eighteen and forty-five. Successive waves of newcomers in the 1830s and 1840s, between 1880 and 1920, and after the mid 1960s rejuvenated the population. As the immigrants produced children, the percent of Americans in younger age groups grew proportionately

DIVERSITY AMONG THE ELDERLY. Besides influencing the relative size of the elderly population, the interplay of fertility, mortality, and (im)migration rates historically ensured considerable racial, ethnic, and regional variations within the ranks of the old.

There has always been a smaller proportion of all blacks than of all whites past the age of sixty-five. In 1890, 2.9 percent of all blacks were over sixty-five, compared with 3.9 percent of all whites. This disparity has widened since the 1920s. In 1985, the figures stood at 8 percent and 13 percent, respectively.

Differential fertility rates account for the black: white difference. Black rates, historically higher, have fallen more slowly than white rates since Reconstruction. Black immigration, minimal since the early nineteenth century, had no discernible effect on the age structure.

Mortality rates for blacks persistently have been, and remain, higher than those for whites. Blacks typically have had poorer diets, living conditions, and medical care. The mortality gap has been narrowing, however. From 1929 to 1931, there was roughly a thirteen-year difference in life expectancy at birth between whites and blacks; by 1983, the gap had narrowed to six years.

Whites generally live longer than blacks. In 1985, sixty-five-year-old blacks on average could expect to live another fifteen and a half years, about eighteen months less than whites. Those blacks who reached eighty-five, on the other hand, could expect to live another seven years, a year longer than whites of the same age. This reversal in life expectancy at advanced ages, some speculate, results from racial differences in diet and adjustment to old age.

The most interesting alterations in the foreign-born component of the elderly American population reflect variations in immigration patterns. Roughly a fifth of the older population was foreign-born in 1870. Most were of German and Irish descent, people who had come to America in the 1830s and 1840s. By 1900 the proportion of foreign-born aged exceeded 30 percent. This increase doubtless fueled nativist sentiments against old-age dependents, particularly in cities like Boston with large numbers of foreign-born residents. The percentage did not begin to fall below 25 percent until 1940. By then, older persons both in southern and eastern Europe were prominent in the ethnic pool—reflecting late-nineteenth-century immigration patterns.

The long-term effect of laws passed since the 1920s, which were designed to reduce and regulate the influx of foreign-born persons into the United States, has been to swell the proportion of all foreign-born people who are old. In 1920, 9.7 percent of all foreign-born whites were over sixty-five. The number soared to 33.5 percent by 1960.

The number of Hispanic elders will grow in the twenty-first century. Between 1970 and 1980, the Hispanic population grew by 61 percent, compared with a 7 percent increase for the non-Hispanic population. Although only 3 percent of the current aged population are Hispanic, in some places—notably southern California, Texas, Chicago, and New York City—aging Hispanics already exercise significant political and economic power.

REGIONAL DISTRIBUTIONS. Not surprisingly, states with the largest populations tend to have the largest concentrations of older people. Regional variations in the distribution of the elderly, however, also reflect differential fertility rates and internal migration patterns. The northeast section of the country has always had a high proportion of men and women over sixty-five due to comparatively low fertility and high out-migration rates. Frontier areas usually have lower percentages of senior citizens than do older settlements.

Even sparsely populated areas, like the Southwest, boast remarkable ethnic diversity. There, Hopi, Pueblo, Apache, and Navajo tribes, Mormons, descendants of Spanish-speaking explorers, Mexican émigrés, and easterners established their own cultural norms and social systems. Each ethnic group treated its old differently.

Because they are less likely than younger people to move, most older Americans have aged in place. As nineteenth-century youth moved to the cities, their elders stayed on the farms and in villages. As late as 1970, 27 percent of all aged Americans lived in small towns.

Since the 1930s, there has been a growing concentration of the old in established urban areas. Cities like Buffalo and Pittsburgh, which have experienced absolute declines in population, have larger elderly populations than "newer" cities like Houston and San Diego. Not until 1980 did more older people live in suburbs than in central cities. Even then, they resided in suburbs developed before 1914, places with lower average resident income levels, more rental housing, and lower home values than communities that attract yuppies.

Retirement communities are a relatively new phenomenon. Since World War II, large numbers of well-off elders have moved to temperate climates.

Although people in their twenties are six times more likely to move than those over sixty-five, Sun-belt states have experienced notable population aging. Especially since World War II, large numbers of well-off elders have moved to temperate climates. Florida is now the state that has the highest percent (18 percent) of people over sixty-five in its population; in absolute numbers, it ranks third in the nation. California, Texas, and Arizona also are favorite retirement destinations.

Before 1945, there was no such concept as "retirement community." The first housing development exclusively for senior citizens was called "Youngstown," completed in 1954. Its success inspired Del E. Webb to commit $2 million in 1959 to construct his first retirement housing project. By 1975, there were more than seven hundred mobile-home parks housing three hundred thousand senior citizens. Sun City, Arizona, and its imitators represent themselves as age-segregated communities that take pride in their recreational as well as their health care facilities. Sun City now houses more than 40,000 residents over 60.

THE SIGNIFICANCE OF SEX AND GENDER. Men and women grow older in such divergent ways that some scholars think two theories of human aging are required to take account of the range of experiences observed in later years. Some differences are sex-specific:

they are due to biochemical or reproductive factors. Others are gender-specific: they reflect different values and treatment in the marketplace or the private sphere. Unlike sex-related variations, these gender-specific manifestations vary over historical time. Still others—like smoking habits and thinking patterns—result from the interplay of both.

On average, women historically have lived longer than men. Although there are slightly more males at birth, three females for every male survive past seventy-five. Recent demographic trends have made older women more visible in America. Before 1870, there was little difference in the male-female ratio. A century later, only 8.5 percent of all men, compared with 11.2 percent of all women, were over sixty-five. The progressive effect of higher male death rates at each stage of life has widened the gender gap.

Despite a comparative advantage in longevity, women suffer a greater incidence of disease, which disables them for longer periods. Historical changes in chronic disabilities cannot be documented. Death records indicate, however, that women over forty have been less likely than men to succumb to coronaries and other fatal, acute maladies.

Divergent life expectancies have created differences in marital status. Older men have been more likely to be married than older women: in 1986, the figures were 77 percent and 40 percent. In the same year, half of all women over sixty-five were widows, five times greater than the number of widowers. As divorce has become more acceptable in the twentieth century, the percentage of divorced older persons has risen. Fewer reach old age nowadays never having married.

Living arrangements have changed over time. The husband-wife unit has long been the core of the American family, notwithstanding vicissitudes such as death, separation, illness, or accidents. In the 1890s more than 75 percent of all males over sixty-five were heads of household. With advancing age, the proportion of men reported living with a child, in-law, or sibling increased. Few went to an almshouse or a stranger's home.

Institutional statistics have changed surprisingly little over time. Never has more than 5 percent of the population over sixty-five been in institutions at any moment. An individual over sixty-five, however, has long had a 25 percent probability of entering an institution before death.

Older women's behavior historically differed from that of elderly men in two respects. The number of female heads of household increased as the number of "wives" decreased; the proportion never exceeded a third of the female population, however. Furthermore, women have been more likely than men (to be able) to turn to kin with advancing age.

Perhaps the most important trend has been the dramatic rise in the number of older people living alone. Roughly 40 percent of all women and 15 percent of all men over sixty-five lived alone in 1986. These figures represent a 68 percent increase since 1970, and nearly 300 percent since 1900. The decline in coresidency, however, does not necessarily signal a decline in intergenerational exchanges.

Social Patterns

DEFINING OLD AGE. Increasing numbers have made the elderly more visible. Demographics, however, have not been the sole force shaping images of old age. Far more important has been the historical interplay of social, economic, legal, cultural, and political currents.

Reinterpretations of the values and meanings of late life in America have tended to accentuate negative features of growing older. A deep strand of ageism has manifested itself in divergent ways over time. In recent decades, however, an effort has been under way to engineer positive ideas about late-life potential, building on earlier notions.

Antebellum Americans were not blind to the physical, psychological, and social liabilities of old age. Disparaging remarks often were made. Nonetheless, almanacs and magazines extolled the value of the aged in performing domestic duties, preserving the revolutionary spirit, and instilling appropriate values in the new nation.

Thomas Cole (1801–1848) portrayed old age as the ultimate stage of human existence in his painting *Voyage of Life* (1848). Though the vessel was battered and the scene gloomy, the old navigator at last had witnessed all there was to experience in this world and was prepared to meet his Maker. Sentimental images flourished in the antebellum period. Stephen Foster sold 130,000 copies of "Old Folks at Home" ("Swanee River") between 1851 and 1854. Currier and Ives's popular folio *Old Age* (1868) idealized the relationship between youth and age.

New ideas about age, associated with trends in commerce and science, gave rise after the Civil War to less flattering images. In the 1840s youthful politicians called themselves "Old Fogies" to signify a commitment to defending the wisdom of their elders. Later in the century the term referred to the obsolescence of age. Elders were not perceived to be at the cutting edge of progress. They suffered from "senile" disorders. "Geezer" and "fuddy-duddy" entered American speech in the latter quarter of the nineteenth century. Corporate managers, impressed by evidence suggesting that productivity began to wane after forty, selected sixty-five and seventy as ages appropriate for no-longer-efficient, but faithful, employees to receive pensions.

Around the turn of the century, old age came to be defined as a "problem." In some ways this reconception was a positive step, since it focused expert attention on "curing" or at least ameliorating difficulties ascribed to late life. I. L. Nascher published *Geriatrics* (1914), borrowing from the strategy physicians and caregivers had developed half a century earlier to make pediatrics a specialty. Social reformers began focusing on old-age dependency. G. Stanley Hall's *Senescence* (1922), a compendium of ideas about the vitality of people over fifty, set the stage for gerontology.

In due course, however, viewing old age as a problem itself became problematic: it unduly emphasized the negative. In the 1950s, a new set of euphemisms—senior citizen, golden-agers—came into vogue. These conceptions glossed over significant racial, class, and gender differences within the population. Images of age, to be faithful to late life's diversity, had to be ambiguous, subject to multiple and supple interpretations.

The law also shaped definitions of old age. In colonial times, men over sixty were typically exempted from military service and road repair work, though not from political office. Federal and state constitutions discriminated more against youth than against age in eligibility for voting and holding office. (Such provisions rarely acknowledged the status of older women. Large numbers of elders thus were rendered invisible.)

Statutes based on Elizabethan poor laws held family members responsible for kin who were infirm or dependent. Yet before 1914 no state made specific reference to aged relatives. There was little case law. Decisions in Colorado, Ohio, and Kentucky, which around 1900 made negligence of elders a criminal offense, set the foundations for elder law. Courts nowadays consider a wide range of cases, ranging from age discrimination and right-to-die appeals to elder abuse.

Charities and philanthropies have also shaped images of age. Early on, local elites contributed funds to provide institutional support and financial relief for certain segments of the aged population—spinsters, widows, or hitherto self-sufficient citizens down on their luck. Especially after 1865, Protestant denominations; Irish, German, Polish, and Italian parishes in the Roman Catholic church; and Jewish congregations built old-age homes for members of their communities. Religious groups operated more than 40 percent of all old-age social services in 1900.

Foundations underwrote research on aging. In Cleveland, Benjamin Rose left money for this purpose. The Josiah Macy, Jr., Foundation advanced biomedical research in the 1930s, and provided support that led officials in the Public Health Service to create a unit on gerontology. The Rockefeller and Ford foundations sponsored work in the social sciences, especially dealing with the economics of aging. The topic was increasingly timely as America became an advanced industrial country.

Economics of Aging

WEALTH AND POVERTY IN LATE LIFE. Generations of Americans have been inspired by the dream of rising from rags to riches. Until lately, most children could expect on average to enjoy a better standard of living than their parents. But against the promise of upward mobility lies the reality that few Americans of modest means have died rich in old age. Poverty has always threatened the old, especially women and minorities.

Tracing accumulations of wealth historically over the life course reveals that people tend to possess their greatest wealth in their fifties. People then begin to dissave, though on average they have more in their sixties than they had acquired by age thirty. Even so, around the Civil War, roughly a quarter of all elderly men left estates worth less than one hundred dollars. Most aged blacks died penniless. Nineteenth-century native-born elders tended to be better off than their foreign-born counterparts. Since Social Security, the extent of old-age poverty has declined, although improvements in the economic status of the aged vary by sex, race, and occupation.

Because of differences in marital status, working careers, and cultural norms, it is harder to generalize historically about women's wealth. Colonial inheritance laws varied, but by 1710, most widows could expect to receive a third of the estate for life. Prior to 1900, women were far less likely than men to have probated estates and wills. Such gender-specific differences made older women more economically vulnerable than older men. Higher rates of female old-age poverty persist today.

The magnitude of the threat of old-age poverty has long colored intergenerational relations. Coresidence, particularly among the poor and those who were economically vulnerable, often became an economic necessity. Since colonial times, fear of want has made older people fearful of yielding control of property. That choice has precipitated social advantages and psychological bruises.

Even today, issues surrounding presumed generational inequities make for good politics. Born of the Great Depression, the architects of the Social Security Act (1935) hoped to relieve hardships among the young and middle-aged by addressing the problems of the oldest members of society. (The omnibus legislation also provided aid to dependent children, expanded state-level unemployment compensation programs, assisted the blind, and augmented public-health services.) In addition, Social Security enabled workers to contribute to their own retirement pensions. Social Security has relieved adults of some of the responsibility of caring for their parents. For most Americans it is *the* major source of their old-age security. While financing provisions were amended during the 1980s, the system was never any more shaky than any other American retirement vehicle. Medicare has serious financing problems, but Social Security is not likely to go bankrupt.

Even so, yuppies who chafe under the program's high taxes deride their elders as "greedy geezers." There is genuine (if not well-founded) fear among those currently middle-aged that the system will not be there for them when they are old. Grandparents today give the young more than they receive—contrary to much of the rhetoric about intergenerational transfers. They have the wherewithal to assist with mortgages and tuitions. Yet in the absence of adequate insurance, nursing-home care and medical emergencies can still wipe out fortunes.

INVENTING RETIREMENT. The word "retirement" did not always have age-specific connotations in America. Colonial farmers "retired" from wintry storms. Youth in the early years of the Republic "retired" to their studies.

For two hundred fifty years, most men expected to work until they died. Farmers managed more and labored less with advancing years. Many older mechanics and journeymen disengaged in an equally informal manner. Occasionally they took a cut in pay and performed less taxing tasks. Annuities (sometimes called "tontine insurance") were sold in the nineteenth century. Prudent workers were more inclined to purchase disability or life insurance to cover the greater risk that they would be maimed or dead long before reaching sixty-five.

Retirement patterns of older women differed from those of men because of variations in their career histories. Women typically entered the labor force as youths and remained there only until they married. With widowhood, some reentered the labor force—taking in boarders and lodgers, working as clerks or nurses, tending bar, or doing some other service-related task—to make ends meet. Some ethnic groups frowned upon even this limited involvement outside the home.

In 1875 American Express permitted workers over sixty to receive some compensation for quitting work. The Baltimore and Ohio Railroad stipulated minimum age (sixty-five) and service (ten years) criteria in 1884. The pension movement grew slowly. Only 159 companies inaugurated programs before 1915. No more than 15 percent of the labor force qualified for old-age retirement plans by 1935. Fledgling labor unions concentrated on bread-and-butter issues for workers in their prime. In any case, the Great Depression wiped out most of these corporate plans.

Title II of the Social Security Act (1935), which established a retirement fund to which both employees and employers contributed, made it possible for more and more workers to provide for their old age. After the war, steel and auto unions demanded that pensions be included in collective bargaining. Coverage increased. By 1960, 30 percent of the labor force were covered by private plans; 80 percent of all workers were insured under Social Security.

Middle-aged yuppies who chafe under the Social Security program's high taxes deride their elders as "greedy geezers" and fear that the system will not be there for them when they themselves are old.

Virtually all workers now contribute to Social Security. The Employee Retirement Income Security Act (1974) was enacted to regulate private pensions. Roughly 70 percent of all full-time workers are covered by company retirement plans in addition to Social Security. With the expansion and liberalization of public and private plans, overall old-age poverty has fallen from 50 percent in 1935 to 33 percent in 1961 to 12.4 percent in 1986. More than ever before, older people can afford not to work if they so desire.

THE NEW OLD: ONE CLASS OR TWO? Labor force statistics indicate that the sharpest decline in older workers' participation in the marketplace has occurred since the 1940s. About 42 percent of all males over sixty-five were in the labor force in 1940, 29 percent in 1960, and 16 percent in 1986. Although the increase in gainful employment of females is one of the major trends of American history, older women remain less likely than men to be in the labor force. Never have more than 10 percent of all women over sixty-five been gainfully employed; 7 percent were in the labor force in 1986.

Researchers disagree about trends before 1935. Assuming that a significant number of all older men were disabled, probably no more than 75 to 80 percent of males over sixty-five were actually able to work. Some scholars claim that shifts in employment opportunities and ageism depressed labor-force percentages, possibly as early as the 1840s. By adjusting census data, others contend that opportunities probably opened up for older workers in the early phases of industrialization and commercialization. If so, the labor force participation rates of aged men may have risen slightly. Still others argue that there were merely fluctuations in older people's labor status until they were forced out of the marketplace. This occurred when Social Security was used by public officials and corporate managers as an instrument of social control.

In any case, whereas retirement was once a luxury, it is now perceived as a right. A 1978 survey reported that nearly two-thirds of all retirees had left work before sixty-five. Even so, 75 percent would like some kind of paid, part-time work after retirement; roughly a fifth of all retirees find such work within three years of collecting a pension. Trends point toward part-time, part-year "unretirement."

Healthier and more affluent than any cohort of old people in American history, many today take their senior-citizen discounts and head off to their retirement homes. Advertisers are noting their consumer patterns and leisure habits. Being old has begun to resemble a class distinction.

Not all elderly persons are so fortunate. More than a fifth were poor or near-poor in 1986. Economists estimate that without Social Security two-thirds of all senior citizens would have incomes less than 125 percent of the official poverty level. Older women are twice as likely as older men to be poor. A quarter of all who live alone or with nonrelatives are poor. That more than two-thirds of all black elderly women are poor suggests the baleful effects of racism, sexism, and ageism.

To the extent that smiling, white-haired couples in their kelly-green golf sweaters personified the new face of age in the 1980s, the stereotype hardly applied to a significant minority whose poor health, low income, and lack of basic amenities made their old age miserable. Old-age politics used to focus on old age as a problem. Now those who represent the interests of aging America have had to adjust to the paradox of being unable to grapple with economic and health-care needs that fester amid unprecedented affluence.

Old-Age Politics

FROM POOR LAWS TO OLD-AGE WELFARE. The federal government has dominated old-age politics since 1935—and vice versa. Many under fifty-five think of pork-barrel politics in terms of debates among silver-haired, golden-tongued senators. Some recall that it was two senior members of the Senate—Ernest Gruening and Wayne Morse—who cast the only two votes against the Gulf of Tonkin resolution that justified escalating the Vietnam War. At center stage in the 1980s was the oldest man to occupy the White House. Ronald Reagan may or may not have embodied the wisdom of age, but the septuagenarian's ability to survive an assassin's bullet and several operations affirmed the vigor of today's old.

More senior citizens are willing and able to serve in politics. Seniority gives advantages to incumbents. But this is not the first generation of older people to participate in politics. While we extol "the young men of the Revolution," it is worth remembering that the first five presidents of the United States were at least sixty-five when they left office. John Quincy Adams served in Congress after his presidency, dying on the House floor at age eighty-one. Older men filled various high-ranking city, county, and state posts.

Little is known about older women's leadership role in politics. Many of the most widely known took over their husbands' seats as widows or, like Eleanor Roosevelt (1884–1962), achieved worldwide recognition late in life by acting on deeply held convictions. Some like Lucretia Coffin Mott (1793–1880) and Martha Griffiths (1912-) remained active as reformers at advanced ages. Still others worked behind the scenes.

For most older Americans, government was less a source of employment than a resource for relief. Throughout most of American social history, local communities, counties, and states have paid for provisions that individuals, families, and friends could not pay for themselves. The elderly's safety net resembled a patchwork quilt. Institutional support and quality of care varied. Some elders were treated with respect in almshouses; many were committed to insane asylums because there was no alternative. Although private groups built old-age homes, it was not until 1903 that Homer Folks, commissioner of charities in New York City, converted a public facility for paupers in New York specifically into a home for the aged and infirm.

Ironically, although Congress rejected pleas that it address old-age dependency, the federal government did more for the elderly indirectly than any other agency managed to do directly. In 1818 it provided relief for Revolutionary veterans in need; most who were eligible were at least sixty-five.

Thereafter, each cohort of survivors could anticipate some delayed benefit for their military service. Union soldiers and their widows ultimately received eight billion dollars, twice as much as it cost the North to fight the war. (Some economic historians claim that the burden of caring for Confederate veterans through old age was one reason why the South took so long to modernize.) Veterans' benefits cost eight times as much as outlays for the Spanish-American War. Older people clearly benefited: in 1929, 82.3 percent of all beneficiaries of any private or public pension plan were recipients of veterans' benefits.

Since 1935, an impressive federal network to aid the aging has been created. The struggle for Social Security galvanized activities through the nation. States like California, Pennsylvania, and New York established commissions in the late 1940s. Massachusetts created a cabinet-level post in the 1970s. Michigan funded university research institutes and sponsors an annual senior-citizen rally on its capitol steps. The federal Administration on Aging was established in 1965, the same year that Medicare, Medicaid, and the Older Americans Act were enacted. As part of its Great Society initiatives, policymakers turned to the needs of older people after they had tackled problems of unemployment and training for minorities, the rural poor, and youth. The National Institute on Aging was chartered in 1974 to support basic research on aging. More than three hundred federal agencies now supervise programs that affect the lives of older Americans in one way or another.

THE GRAY LOBBY. When old age became perceived as a social problem, the elderly began to mobilize their efforts. Self-help social and educational groups emerged in the 1930s to "salvage" old age. In the Depression, Francis E. Townsend and Upton Sinclair capitalized on the fears and needs of the aged. Their radical politics affected the scope of federal and state old-age pension legislation, as did George McLain's movement to improve pensions in California a decade later. Early manifestations of a gray lobby tended to organize around a single issue under a charismatic leader.

The American Association of Retired Persons (AARP), founded in 1958, began similarly. It started as a modest effort by Ethel Percy Andrus, a retired Los Angeles principal. Now boasting more than thirty-six million members, it is the largest social group in America after the Roman Catholic church. Besides offering low-cost pharmacy services and travel discounts, AARP maintains an impressive network of policy analysts and activists in Washington and in each state. Local chapters disseminate information and mobilize members when necessary. To the extent that they join in activities and benefit from lobbying, AARP members (all over fifty) become more conscious of their power as an age group.

Whereas AARP mainly appeals to middle-class interests, the National Council of Senior Citizens has strong ties with labor. The National Council on the Aging was a product of the 1961 White House Conference on Aging. With initial support from the Ford Foundation, it is a federation of agencies helping the elderly. The Gray Panthers try to bridge the interests of young and old. Founded in 1970 by Maggie Kuhn, a sprightly woman now in her eighties, the Gray Panthers have been successful in capturing media attention with radical protests reminiscent of the Yippies. More than one hundred other national organizations cater to specialized needs within the elderly population.

Future Research

This article has emphasized the diversity of images and experiences associated with late life. It builds on interpretations published in the 1970s which offered overviews of major trends and modal tendencies. It complements subsequent work which has emphasized the significance of gender, race, and class.

This essay has stressed discontinuity in recent social patterns. Whereas pioneering studies highlighted revolutionary shifts in attributes between 1780 and 1820, or later in the nineteenth century, developments in the twentieth century attract the most attention here. This is because the aging of America's population has accelerated during this century. The most dramatic exodus of males from the labor force has occurred since the enactment of Social Security. Old-age welfare politics now raises the specter of generational rivalries at the federal level.

Besides offering low-cost pharmacy services and travel discounts, the AARP maintains an impressive network of policy analysts and activists in Washington, D.C., and in each state.

Subsequent reconstructions of the social history of old age in America will pay even greater attention to women. To what extent do males and females develop in separate spheres as they grow older? To what degree have matters of gender affected women's ways of aging independent of issues of class, race, or ethnicity? To raise such questions is to underscore the pluralist perspectives of the new social history. While we are only beginning to understand the history of all elderly subgroups, we are woefully ignorant about the feelings and experiences of Hispanics, blacks, southerners, people on the frontier, and the very old.

Although they were marginal for most of the nation's history, a case can be made for viewing our elders as pioneers, leading us into the postmodern era. The choices older Americans are making, and the constraints that shape their lives, provide an exhilarating if sobering glimpse at our future selves.

[See also Death; Family Structures; Health Care; Life Stages; Public Health.]

BIBLIOGRAPHY

General Works

Achenbaum, W. Andrew. *Old Age in the New Land. The American Experience Since 1790* (1978).

Achenbaum, W. Andrew. *Shades of Gray: Old Age, American Values, and Federal Policies Since 1920* (1983).

Achenbaum, W. Andrew, and Peggy A. Kusnerz. *Images of Old Age in America: 1790 to the Present* (1978).

Binstock, Robert H., and Linda K. George, eds. *Handbook of Aging and the Social Sciences.* 3d ed. (1990).

Calhoun, Richard B. *In Search of the New Old: Redefining Old Age in America, 1945–1970* (1978).

Chudacoff, Howard P. *How Old Are You? Age Consciousness in American Culture* (1989).

Cole, Thomas R. *The Voyage of Life.* Ph.D. diss. (1991).

Cole, Thomas R., and Sally Gadow, eds. *What Does It Mean to Grow Old? Reflections from the Humanities* (1986).

Fischer, David Hackett. *Growing Old in America* (1977).

Gratton, Brian. *Urban Elders: Family, Work, and Welfare Among Boston's Aged, 1890–1950* (1986).

Gruman, Gerald J. *A History of Ideas About the Prolongation of Life: The Evolution of Prolongevity Hypotheses to 1800* (1966).

Haber, Carole. *Beyond Sixty-five: The Dilemma of Old Age in America's Past* (1983).

Haber, Carole, and Brian Gratton. *Old Age in American History* (1992).

Pifer, Alan J., and D. Lydia Bronte, eds. *Our Aging Society* (1986).

Polisar, Donna, Larry Wygant, Thomas Cole, and Cielo Perdomo. *Where Do We Come From? What Are We? Where Are We Going?* (1988).

Spicker, Stuart F., Kathleen M. Woodward, and David D. Van Tassel, eds. *Aging and the Elderly: Humanistic Perspective in Gerontology* (1978).

U.S. Senate, Special Committee on Aging. *Developments in Aging* (1988).

Van Tassel, David D., ed. *Aging, Death, and the Completion of Being* (1979).

Van Tassel, David D., and Peter N. Stearns, eds. *Old Age in a Bureaucratic Society: The Elderly, the Experts, and the State in American History* (1986).

Comparative Analyses

Beauvoir, Simone de. *Coming of Age* (1972).

Dove, Mary. *The Perfect Age of Man's Life* (1986).

Hannah, Leslie. *Inventing Retirement: The Development of Occupational Pensions in Britain* (1986).

Laslett, Peter. *A Fresh Map of Life: The Emergence of the Third Age* (1989).

Quadagno, Jill. *Aging in Early Industrial Society: Work, Family, and Social Policy in Nineteenth-Century England* (1982).

Stearns, Peter N. *Old Age in European Society: The Case of France* (1976).

Stearns, Peter N., ed. *Old Age in Preindustrial Society* (1982).

Troyansky, David G. *Old Age in the Old Regime: Image and Experience in Eighteenth-Century France* (1989).

Diversity

Bass, Scott A., Elizabeth A. Kutza, and Fernando M. Torres-Gil, eds. *Diversity in Aging: Challenges Facing Planners and Policymakers in the 1990s* (1990).

Myerhoff, Barbara. *Number Our Days* (1978).

Premo, Terri L. *Winter Friends: Women Growing Old in the New Republic, 1785–1835* (1990).

Scadron, Arlene, ed. *On Their Own: Widows and Widowhood in the American Southwest, 1848–1939* (1988).

Work and Retirement

Achenbaum, W. Andrew. *Social Security: Visions and Revisions* (1986).

Graebner, William. *A History of Retirement: The Meaning and Function of an American Institution, 1885–1978* (1980).

Johnson, Paul, Christoph Conrad, and David Thomson, eds. *Workers Versus Pensioners: Intergenerational Justice in an Ageing World* (1989).

Myles, John. *Old Age in the Welfare State: The Political Economy of Public Pensions* (1984).

Quadagno, Jill. *The Transformation of Old Age Security: Class and Politics in the American Welfare State* (1988).

Shammas, Carole, Marylynn Salmon, and Michel Dahlin. *Inheritance in America: From Colonial Times to the Present* (1987).

Politics of Aging

Bolick, Clint, and Mary Chlopecki. *The Age Lobby: Mortgaging America's Future* (1990).

Neugarten, Bernice L., ed. *Age of Need? Public Policies for Older People* (1982).

Pratt, Henry J. *The Gray Lobby* (1976).

Weir, Margaret, Ann Shola Orloff, and Theda Skocpol, eds. *The Politics of Social Policy in the United States* (1988).

— W. A. ACHENBAUM

ORGANIZATIONS, FRATERNAL

See FRATERNAL ORGANIZATIONS

ORGANIZATIONS, WOMEN'S

See WOMEN'S ORGANIZATIONS

P

PARADES, HOLIDAYS, AND PUBLIC RITUALS

Introduction: Days Off

Holidays by definition are times out of time, when the familiar rhythms and practices of everyday life are temporarily suspended and replaced, often dramatically, by other possibilities, experiences, and sensations. Holidays of all sorts (official and unofficial, spontaneous and planned, secular and religious) are "days off" from the disciplines and demands of work, the usual relations among family members and friends, the familiar geography and ecology of everyday life, and even from what regularly passes as a person's normal self.

The variety of American holidays, from Memorial Day solemnities to the green-dyed hilarities of Saint Patrick's Day, have generally been interpreted as events of cohesion and integration. The great celebrations of civic life are viewed as the sacred liturgies of the nation's civil religion, while the festivals of immigrants are presented both as the way that the uprooted preserved and passed on their cultural traditions to their children and, at the same time, that both generations were connected (or connected themselves) to the national narrative. In a diverse, pluralistic society, according to these arguments, holidays and holy days have maintained the integrity of the different peoples of the United States as they have brought them together into one nation and a common civic culture.

But as countless reform-minded citizens have pointed out over the years, men and women do not behave on holidays the way they should (and normally do). Public festivals derive their peculiar energies from the tensions and conflicts between generations, classes, and cultures that surface in the absence of the restraints of routine. Popular rage and frustration with the discrepancies between the world as it is said to be and the world as it is experienced at work and at home have frequently erupted during civic and religious festivals. Furthermore, the institution of each major American public holiday was attended by social dissension—the controversies over whether or not to create a holiday in honor of Martin Luther King, Jr., are only the most recent example—adding to their complexities. The suspension of the ordinary makes holidays potentially very dangerous times.

From Calendar To Covenant

The men and women who risked the North Atlantic crossing in the mid seventeenth century to establish a pure church in a godly society on New England's shores had left behind them a world in which the passage of time was measured by holy days and saints' feasts, many of which had pre-Christian roots and were linked to the cycles of the agricultural year. The Puritans rejected this calendar and this way of being in time. They celebrated none of the old "popish" holidays, not even Christmas and Easter, both of which went scrupulously, almost ostentatiously, unobserved in New England. These were days like all others, which meant that God's will could be best served on them not by resting and merriment but by sharing the tasks of building the new world together in the wilderness.

New England's days-out-of-time reflected the Puritans' foundational commitment to the godly labor of the covenant. The special relevance of the word of God for New England was explicated by the clergy each week on the Sabbath, a day set aside by piety and law. Fast days were called by ministers and magistrates in response to troubles like war, epidemics, and internecine conflict that imperiled the very survival of the community and seemed to indicate divine displeasure; days of thanksgiving were proclaimed when God granted the covenanting people a reprieve. All work stopped on these days as the people gathered in their meetinghouses to fortify the bonds of the threatened covenant.

But the "grandest spectacles" of Puritan New England were public executions. The Puritans put to death murderers, adulterers, religious dissenters, witches, men accused of consorting with animals, and pirates in hugely attended public rituals. The "criminals" on the gallows (some of whom were hapless men and women snared in webs of godly suspicion and pettiness) had endangered the success of the New England way by their transgressions, and this demanded reparation and revenge before the eyes of the community. Tension mounted as the crowds strained to see if the condemned would repent. If he or she did, in a reenactment of every Puritan's inner passage from terror to something like assurance, then the assembled saints enjoyed the satisfactions of having their cosmology sanctioned by the scaffold, and printers did a brisk business in subsequent weeks hawking the spiritual capitulations of the doomed. But if the man or woman under the rope refused to play the part assigned, as some hardy and indignant souls did, then the crowds left troubled and uneasy, their world shaken a little by this unexpected and vexatious gallows obduracy.

A People Free And Enlightened

The first American secular holidays took shape amid deepening tensions with England in the 1750s and 1760s, when the dangerous hilarities of medieval and Elizabethan festival traditions fused with the intensity of colonial republican ideology to constitute brilliant and powerful public political theater. The Stamp Act, for example, passed by Parliament in 1765, unleashed a yearlong series of demonstrations. One of the first, in Boston, was organized with the assistance of the men responsible for the annual excitements of Guy Fawkes (or Pope's) Day. Realistic-looking effigies of stamp distributors were paraded in carts and then desecrated by crowds throughout the colonies; in subsequent years, patriots met together to commemorate this moment of resistance in further celebrations. In this way, by means of provocatively worded toasts, hanged effigies, public choral singing, and fireworks, the colonists celebrated themselves into revolution.

These political excitements were recalled but vastly outdone by the huge and brilliantly choreographed national parties that attended first the events of the war's end and then the ratification of the Constitution and Washington's inauguration in 1789. The festivities centered largely on Washington himself, whose two long journeys, homeward from the battlefields and later to New York and the presidency, became occasions for the outpouring of national sentiment (although some Americans protested what they saw as a monarchical or even "popish" quality to the proceedings).

The people were not so much celebrating their enthusiasm for the nation in these festivities as they were constituting it—"observing themselves," as Kenneth Silverman has written, "in the process of defining themselves." Men of diverse occupations and ranks marched side by side in ratification parades, carrying the tools of their trades (and sometimes stopping to demonstrate their skills to the crowds), with their feet making the case for civic republicanism.

Surprising Conversions

Washington's epochal journeys were anticipated almost half a century earlier by another itinerancy that generated almost as much excitement and enthusiasm. Evangelist George Whitefield's ride through the colonies on his second visit from England in 1739–1741 fanned the flames of a religious revival that had been flickering in New England and the Delaware Valley since the 1720s. The grandchildren of the founding generations, living in a more heterogeneous and fragmented society, were forced to find new idioms for religious experience and new sources of consolation; their response was protracted public gatherings in which neighbors moved from anxiety to reassurance—if not quite together, then at least side by side and within sight of each other. Revival meetings in this way resembled the earlier generations' public trials and executions, only now the mourners' bench replaced the scaffold as the site of the drama of conversion.

Revivals became one of the central instruments of American popular religion, shaping Protestant experience, identity, and participation, particularly in periods of internal migration. A second awakening, beginning at Cane Ridge, Kentucky, in 1801 (where more than fifteen thousand people assembled for six days of religious excitement) accompanied the expansion of the westward frontier; later in the century, eastern and mid-

In the eighteenth century, revivals became one of the central instruments of American popular religion, shaping Protestant experience, identity, and participation, particularly in periods of internal migration.

western evangelists organized similar gatherings in Texas and the Southwest.

Long and uproarious revival meetings, held outdoors under the trees either in the summer or at the end of the harvest season in the early fall, drew isolated farm and ranch families from miles around, offering them some sacred, and many more profane, encounters. Revivals were the early nation's most popular regional gatherings and the ancestors both of the state fairs of the late nineteenth century and of tourist attractions, like the Memphis Cotton Carnival and West Fargo, North Dakota's Pioneer Review Days, concocted by ingenious local boosters in the twentieth.

Outdoor religious meetings were also among the few occasions that African American slaves could come together apart from work and away from the scrutiny of their overseers. Initially ignored by white Protestants (and even forbidden conversion by their masters), slaves were swept up in the enthusiasms of the Great Awakenings. At camp meetings, which were segregated by race (and gender), slaves congregated behind the preacher's stand; but African Americans from different plantations often stole away at night to meet in hidden "hush harbors" where they forged a unique and powerful synthesis of revival Christianity and African religious sensibilities.

Storm-Tossed Celebrations

As the rift between the North and the South widened in the 1830s and 1840s, civic holidays which only a generation earlier had served as engines of national identity become spectacles of fear and regional hostility and mistrust. One of Georgia's representatives, Wiley Thompson, rose during the bitter and protracted congressional debate over how to celebrate the centenary of Washington's birth in 1832 to warn that the removal of the first president's remains to the capital would mean that in the event of secession, the great Virginian would repose "on a shore foreign to his native soil." Southern Fourth of July oratory in these years progressed inexorably from fulsome evocations of the national spirit to darkening predictions of conflict and heated apologiae for slavery, and finally to calls for secession, while in the North abolitionists turned the day into a forum for attacks on the peculiar institution. Not surprisingly, the popularity of this American holiday reached its nadir in the decade before the war.

Regional loyalties have always been important in determining the American calendar. For much of the nineteenth century, folks outside of New England resisted the celebration of a national thanksgiving, scorning it as a "Yankee" holiday and preferring instead locally rooted harvest home festivals. There are competing northern and southern versions of the origins of Memorial Day, and southern states continue to commemorate the heroes and events of the Confederacy. Indeed, there is, properly speaking, no truly "national" holiday in the United States, since congressional jurisdiction over the calendar is limited to the District of Columbia and federal employees, with each state retaining authority for its own cycle of holidays.

The Country And The City

In the years after the Civil War, millions of Americans, black and white, moved from farms and small towns to cities and factories, a vast internal migration with profound and lasting consequences for the texture of everyday life. People who were raised amid the smells, sounds, and rhythms of the countryside found themselves in the harsh, confusing, and competitive environment of the industrial city during the brutal heyday of American capitalism. The era's public gatherings and celebrations took shape in this break between worlds, as men and women struggled to keep body and soul together in daunting material circumstances. Dwight L. Moody's revivals at the end of the nineteenth century and Billy Sunday's in the early twentieth offered transplanted country folk the opportunity to reencounter the religious world of their childhoods until the summers, when they could make pilgrimages back to the old places for homecomings, family reunions, and church picnics. African American migrants came together in intimate Pentecostal congregations in small spaces just off the cold streets of northern cities, the urban equivalents of the hush harbors, where they could share powerful currents of feeling with people they greeted in the language of kinship.

The peculiar strains of this period on the transplanted urban middle classes, among whom desire and denial colluded to shape a culture of sentimentality, gave rise to a new holiday. In 1907, Anna Jarvis, a West Virginian who had migrated to Philadelphia, was moved by her mother's death back home two years earlier to begin a national campaign to celebrate the image of the old-fashioned mother. This appeal to nostalgia and innocence proved widely compelling at a time when many American mothers were staring for ten hours a day, in poorly ventilated and badly lit factories, at the pulsing needles of sewing machines or grinding through mounds of piecework at home, and others were seeking broader roles for themselves in public life. By 1912, Mother's Day was observed in every state. But the ultimate fate of sentimentality is cynicism, and the times quickly overwhelmed Jarvis's vision. She had wanted the day marked by church services, home-cooked meals, and small tokens of filial piety; by 1961, $875 million was being spent on the holiday, which had become a showcase for the powers of the advertising industry. Jarvis had disappeared from public awareness long before this; deeply disappointed by what had happened and defeated in her strenuous efforts to prevent it, she died alone and destitute.

More realistically, American workers managed to claim some time off for themselves (and their mothers) in the long stretch between the Fourth of July and Thanksgiving. The socialist New York Central Labor Union organized a parade and picnic in September 1882 to raise funds for a labor newspaper. More than ten thousand workers came out to march around Union Square and then up Fifth Avenue to Forty-second Street in a declaration of the power of unions. Labor Day was a legal holiday in all states but one by 1928.

Holidays Of The Huddled Masses

Immigrant celebrations also took place between worlds. Men and women from southern and eastern Europe,

Ireland, Mexico, and Asia brought the calendars of their homelands with them to these shores and continued to keep the special times of the old worlds, as much as the changed circumstances of their new lives and work would allow—and sometimes even when they would not. The premodern European calendar of holy days reappeared as the American Catholic population steadily increased during the nineteenth century, and Jewish immigrants brought an even more ancient cycle of days to the industrial city. In the familiar rituals of the Sabbath or a saint's feast day, immigrants could experience another kind of time than the regimented and closely monitored minutes of their workplaces.

The nation's cities, which seemed bizarre enough in these years to longer-established residents, became even more foreign and strange on important days in other calendars. Chinese immigrants in San Francisco and New York danced dragons in the streets to celebrate the start of their new year, and Jews threw breadcrumbs representing their sins into rivers shining with industrial effluvium on the first day of their year. In adjoining neighborhoods, Italian (or Portuguese, Puerto Rican, or Mexican) Catholics carried the statues of saints who had protected their crops, fishing boats, and villages in their home countries out into city traffic, dollar bills fluttering on their brocaded gowns.

All of this was a nightmare to the descendants of the Puritans, an almost unbelievable return of the repressed, and they fought back in kind. An organization grimly called the National Security League began promoting Constitution Day (17 September) in 1914 as a way of Americanizing immigrants, and the tricentennial of Forefathers' Day was celebrated in 1920 with particular enthusiasm. The old civic holidays were charged with a new agenda: in 1915, for example, the commissioner of immigration at the port of New York, Frederick Howe, asked that the Fourth of July be celebrated as Americanization Day.

These efforts to diminish the threat of the immigrants' otherness were welcomed by the ethnic middle classes, eager to find some connection to the society around them. Neighborhood doctors, lawyers, funeral directors, and high school teachers promoted holidays in honor of Pulaski, von Steuben, and Columbus as declarations of their own pride and achievement. The immigrant working classes could not always recognize themselves in these grandiloquent re-creations of what they were told was their history and culture—southern Italian immigrants, for example, knew more about the tax policies than the glories of Rome—so tensions over the right way to celebrate the tradition often erupted between classes within ethnic communities. The ethnic clergy often encouraged these middle-class "reforms" as a way of asserting church power over unruly popular devotions.

Ethnic holidays were not carried across the ocean like baggage. Instead, they became the occasion in this country for a troubled and anxious engagement with the difficult challenges of migration and for the enactment and experience of competing versions of the past and present between classes, men and women, insiders and outsiders, and generations. American-born children often found themselves forced to participate in these events by their parents and grandparents, who sought to secure through the discipline of family and community gatherings the younger generation's submission to an ethos it could not possibly share. Especially fierce hostilities centered on the daughters of immigrants, who during festivals risked what was ordinarily forbidden them—going out or talking to boys—which is why so many second-generation romances were begun on these days.

Festivals Of Collective Obscenity

Between January and May 1919, five black men were burned alive in separate incidents in Arkansas, Florida, Georgia, Mississippi, and Texas, before large and excited crowds. The lynching of African Americans and the desecration of their bodies became one of the central public spectacles of the South in this ugly year.

Lynch mob leaders used the language of holiday entertainments to describe the tortures they intended for the bodies of their victims; and when the crowds, which included men, women, and children of all social classes, had been sufficiently excited and amused by these promises, they torched the pyres. The noise of the flames competed with the crowds' roars of approval and shotguns fired in celebration. Afterward souvenir sellers picked through the smoking ashes for prizes, the most coveted of which were bits of rope and pieces of the victims' charred bodies.

Although these grim "holidays"—"festivals of collective obscenity" in Max Gluckman's phrase (quoted in Lincoln, *Discourse and the Construction of Society*)—were rooted in the pathologies of racism and the social organization of southern society in the early years of the twentieth century, they also recall the public executions of Puritan New England and the later colonial desecration of effigies, and in this way raise the broader issue of violence and American public celebrations. The Fourth of July has been a particularly gory feast: in 1908, to take just one year's statistics, more than six thousand people were killed or wounded during the "annual orgy of fire" (in the words of the National Fire Protection Association).

Each occasion of festival violence must be examined separately because these rituals of destruction and brutality, like other kinds of human performance, take on resonance and meaning in specific social and historical circumstances. The crowds scanning the faces of the condemned or rooting through the ashes of rope and flesh seem literally to have been looking for something, practicing a nervous divination. The social worlds around the scaffolds were under pressure from hidden

Each occasion of festival violence must be examined separately because these rituals of destruction and brutality, like other kinds of human performance, take on resonance and meaning in specific social and historical circumstances.

forces when these carnivals of desecration became an important feature of local popular culture; men and women could feel in their everyday experiences that what they called reality was cracking, and violence may have been the effort to articulate the old order of domination and seal it with the fixative of the blood of outsiders. The desecrated body of the victim represented, through ritual inversion, the fantasy of the social order restored.

But arguments like these, which are useful up to a point, ignore an essential feature of holiday violence: it was a source of pleasure, amusement, and satisfaction for many people. Fourth of July revelers went looking for bloodshed and took pleasure in the risk of gunpowder and brawls; in the more carefully sublimated domestic world of the middle classes, these thrills were found in antiquarian reconstructions of Wild West shoot-outs, Indian massacres, and Civil War battles that have been popular regional tourist attractions since the nineteenth century. The old paradigm of sacred liturgies and ritual integration was clearly off: holidays of all sorts have more often permitted men and women to experience the delights of violence as they performed their rage in the streets.

"Harlem Is Also A Parade Ground"

African Americans who migrated to the great black metropolis of the North found there a heterogeneous community of varied African American and African Caribbean classes, cultures, religious faiths, and political aspirations. But Harlem's many different peoples shared its streets in common, and these served as the theater of the community's richness and complexity, where people went to observe and be observed.

Harlem took its protests into the streets. In the summer of 1917, eight thousand Harlemites marched down Fifth Avenue in complete silence to the sounds of muffled drums to express their outrage and sorrow over the July massacres in East Saint Louis; in later summers, street protests against racism, police brutality, and economic exploitation took more violent forms. Harlem also took pride into the streets. On 17 February 1919 the 369th Infantry, Harlem's Hellfighters, which had fought with distinction under the French flag, returned in a glorious parade up Fifth Avenue to Harlem. And Harlem took its different and competing hopes into the streets: Marcus Garvey's followers paraded up Seventh Avenue in dress uniform in the early 1920s, and in the 1930s Father Divine's white-robed angels carried placards in processions to proclaim God resident in the community. On Sunday mornings, as James Baldwin remembers them in *Go Tell It on the Mountain* (1953), Christian men and women walked proudly past the shipwrecked survivors of Saturday night, making clear that there was another way to live than this. The young Baldwin knew, though, that Saturday night in Harlem (and around the country) had pleasures undreamed of (or denied) by Sunday folk, most of them on display, along Seventh Avenue.

The Movement For A Safe And Sane Fourth

The Fourth of July has always been a troubled holiday, if not for the dullness of its soporific oratory (which was already the butt of national ridicule by the 1830s) then for the intensity of its excitements, noise, and smoke. But in 1903 the *Journal of the American Medical Association* began publishing casualty counts for the day, and as these rose, so did national revulsion with the holiday. The Progressives set out to improve it.

The campaign for a "Safe and Sane Fourth" was initiated in 1909 by the Playground Association of America at its annual meeting in Pittsburgh. The enterprise was widely supported by fire and police departments (which began refusing permits for the sale of fireworks) and by medical doctors, who each year had to attend the horribly painful deaths of scores of adults and children from an affliction called "patriotic tetanus" or "Fourth of July tetanus," which developed in the infected wounds inflicted by fireworks. Reformers proposed in place of this annual patriotic firefight a "New Fourth," observed with civic pagents, alcohol-free picnics, and the revival of edifying oratory. In a widely reported and highly regarded model celebration at Springfield, Massachusetts, in 1908, people of Swedish,

In the 1930's Father Divine's white-robed angels carried placards in processions to proclaim God resident in the community through the streets of New York City.

English, Scottish, Irish, Greek, Italian, French, Chinese, Armenian, Syrian, Polish, and African American heritage marched in a parade of nations led by Buffalo Bill Cody's Wild West troupe.

But the motives of the reformers were not unmixed. They wanted the Fourth of July to be safer, more restful, and family-centered, but above all they wanted it to be quiet. Holidays articulate their discordant messages in many voices; in the case of the Fourth, the explosion of firecrackers eloquently tossed over the high fences surrounding the homes of factory owners delivered a clear enough greeting. As Roy Rosenzweig shows in his discussion of the holiday in Worcester, Massachusetts, at the turn of the century, the town's elite had become disturbed not only by the noise and violence of working-class festivities but also by their unmistakable political content. In the days of labor struggles the Fourth of July was threatening to become the nation's annual *charivari*, and when reformers called for a "safe" Fourth they meant safe for themselves as well as for other people's children.

"Sane" refers to something else. One of the sponsors of the campaign, Mrs. Isaac L. Rice, encouraged "those of us who know what the day means" to "endeavor to make it both memorable and illuminating to those who do not," by which she meant the children of "the poor and ignorant, of the distressed and disheartened alien within our gates" (quoted in Cohn, "Popular Culture and Social History," p. 177). A version of America's past and present, free of class struggle, racial hatreds, and regional hostilities, had to be constructed for these new Americans, although Mrs. Rice was not confident they would understand.

From Covenant To Consumption: Movable Sales

The United States had become an ambivalently, often anxiously, modern society by the third decade of the twentieth century, increasingly dedicated to an ethic of consumption that many feared was subverting the nation's traditional religious and cultural values. The story of American holidays in the twentieth century both reflects this development and serves as a counterpoint to it, because as everything solid was melting into air, some Americans used their days out of time to celebrate and test the possibilities of the new, others to exploit them, and still others to resist what they saw as the end of a Christian society.

The signs of a new national ethos were evident by the 1920s. Church activities which had once absorbed so much American time were competing, less and less successfully, with new and tantalizing secular opportunities for leisure such as movies and baseball, and the lure of Sunday outings in the family automobile seemed to spell the end of the traditional American Sabbath. Even the faithful who stayed behind could not help comparing their minister's all-too-familiar voice and well-worn morality with the mellifluous blandishments of radio preachers, peddlers, and crooners.

As Anna Jarvis discovered to her dismay, commercialism had come to dominate the seasonal round of American calendrical holidays. Beginning in the early 1920s, huge Thanksgiving Day parades sponsored by department stores like Macy's in New York and Hudson's in Detroit, consolidating their victories over smaller competitors, ushered in the frenzied Christmas retail season. The new advertising industry, wielding techniques of mass motivation perfected during the propaganda campaigns of World War I, transformed even relatively minor holidays like Valentine's Day into feasts of sales for the retailers of gifts and tokens.

Gradually, over the middle years of the century, consumption, and not commemoration or recollection, became the point of most American holidays. Patriotic pageantry diminished and civic parades were shortened or canceled as Americans took to the beaches, amusement parks, and, more recently, the malls rather than to their village greens, on their days off, a shift in holiday observance that reflects a broader trend in these years away from the public sphere and toward more private and domestic concerns and interests. Increasingly people wanted to spend their holidays in their own backyards, where they could watch holiday pageants or ball games on television; and the topography of the suburbs, which had no central meeting spaces other than stores, built this reorientation of the common life into the landscape.

Citizenship was being redefined as life-style; excitement and enthusiasm drained from the public square. The ebullient and hilarious partisanship that had once characterized the nominating conventions of the two major political parties and their subsequent campaigns were associated now with mass-marketed sporting events like the Super Bowl. And as the public meaning of holidays waned, the connection between specific dates and events in the nation's past (Lincoln's birthday, for example) and the holidays marking them was severed. Holidays are now routinely moved from their traditional locations on the calendar and reaffixed to convenient weekends to facilitate retail sales and private leisure activities, making all American civic celebrations into movable feasts.

Halloween was originally intended as a mockery of the pieties and spiritual comforts of the two days following it on the Christian calendar: All Saints Day (November 1) and the Day of the Dead (November 2).

Although these developments have permanently altered the character of American holidays, they did not proceed at the same pace around the country or go unchallenged. Several traditional holidays of the white South, like the birthday of Robert E. Lee and Confederate Memorial Day, retained strong historical and regional meanings. The African American festival Kwanzaa, which runs from 26 December to 1 January, was established in 1966 in part to provide black families with an opportunity to exchange gifts, enjoy family gatherings, celebrate their African heritage, and reaffirm community values in a less commercial atmosphere than that associated with Christmas. Ceremonies honoring local veterans, especially those who fought in the Vietnam War, became important events in small towns around the country during the 1980s, and there are signs that the patriotic Fourth has enjoyed a revival.

'Tis The Season . . .

Fierce public debates have erupted in the past several years over the place of Christmas in a secular and pluralistic society dedicated to the separation of church and state. That government offices and many schools and businesses are closed for two Christian holy days, Christmas and Good Friday, seems to be generally tolerable; but battle lines have been drawn over the issue of placing Christian holiday symbols in government spaces like post office lobbies or the corridors of city hall. Indeed, the appearance of civil liberties lawyers in court to argue against such displays has become almost as regular a feature of the American Yuletide as the descent of Santa Claus into shopping malls.

Some people have argued that the Christmas tree is a folkloric symbol drained of specific religious content that has become the common property of all Americans; others have attempted to balance Christian imagery in government spaces with holiday icons of other faiths, a gambit known as the "menorah defense"; a minority have defended the display of Christian symbols on the grounds that the United States is in ideals and history a Christian nation, however religiously diverse it has become. But civil libertarians and the nation's courts have found these arguments unpersuasive, and many religious citizens consider the arguments reductive of the integrity of their traditions. The debate over the appropriate place of religious imagery in a secular, tolerant society continues, however, making Christmas into an ongoing examination—and, obliquely, a celebration—of the First Amendment.

American diversity has more recently led to the reimaging of another popular holiday. Halloween was originally intended as a mockery of the pieties and spiritual comforts of the two days following it in the Christian calendar, All Saints (November 1) and the Day of the Dead, All Souls (November 2). In the United States it has always been mainly a children's festival, with only the faintest trace of the night's subversive possibilities lingering in its macabre costumes and in the rougher pranks of older children.

As Americans cut their ties to the public sphere and cities became more dangerous places, this holiday waned; parents were warned to inspect the candy their children had collected trick-or-treating for harmful objects inserted by unknown people out there in the empty and so threatening public square, and children were encouraged to limit their rounds to family and friends. But while the children's holiday shrank, another more adult and playfully subversive celebration appeared in its place. Halloween had already had an underground appeal as being one occasion when gay men and lesbians could publicly express and explore at costume parties the identities they otherwise had to guard. In the 1970s and 1980s, as gay and lesbian political activists pressed for recognition of their civil liberties and political rights, Halloween costume parades in New York and San Francisco became public celebrations of the nuances of gay identity and pride; more recently, the darker idioms available on Halloween have offered a way of expressing grief and mourning for friends and family lost to AIDS.

Recapitulations

The public spectacles of the 1950s and 1960s, some of which appeared strange and radical at the time, recalled many of the themes and traditions of earlier American festivals. The prurient fascination with the Rosenbergs' last moments, including the grisly details of Ethel Rosenberg's prolonged agony, offered an anxious nation the familiar satisfactions of revenging the betrayed covenant. The televised rituals of grief during the days after John F. Kennedy's assassination resembled the spontaneous outpourings of national sorrow at the deaths of Abraham Lincoln and Franklin Roosevelt. Even the bitter polarization of holidays like Memorial Day and Veterans Day during the Vietnam War was not new, as the history of the Fourth of July shows. The ritual-makers of the 1960s took these varied traditions and reassembled them into powerful and evocative forms; the improvisation of public rituals—sit-ins, teach-ins, "summers of love," and people's parks—became one of the decade's most accomplished arts. The greatest improvisations rose out of moral and political passions. The weary feet and rested souls of civil rights marchers, the angry demonstrations and riots in northern ghettos, and the street rallies of the Nation of Islam contributed to the beginnings of the remapping of relations between black and white, while the anti-Vietnam moratoriums and demonstrations helped end a war and a presidency.

What was truly new in this period was the technology of communications. The chant of protesters that "the whole world is watching" signaled a new age of public ritual. Millions looked on while cities burned and children ran from police dogs; now hundreds of millions watch football games and revolutions. Public spectacles have been transformed into global events.

Conclusions

Holidays exist in counterpoint to the world of work. The temporal rhythms of work, the impact of particular jobs on the postures of the body, and the psychological demands of different workplaces are fundamentally constitutive of the worlds of holidays, from harvesttime revivals to the sit-ins that freed students from exams. This is why such occasions seem endless, and why some people try to extend the oblivion with alcohol and drugs while others fling their bodies into unaccustomed excitements.

These liberated laborers then go to work on their worlds. The rituals and practices of holidays do not reflect or legitimize social practices and cultural styles; they create them. Worlds are made and unmade during holidays, and because the power of these days is so elemental, sex and violence in complex patterns of creation and destruction are inevitably a fundamental part of them.

Furthermore, holidays create and "decreate" worlds with many different tools, the least important of which, despite what all those sorry hours of oratory might suggest, are words. Protests, parades, homecomings, and saints' feasts are marked by particular smells, sounds, tastes, and textures. The power of these days works deeply in people, at the level of their senses, beneath their awareness: Americans abroad scour souks for cranberry sauce that they will not eat on Thanksgiving, and patriotism in the United States will always smell of the library paste that public school students used to make their collages of cherry trees, log cabins, and Pilgrims.

Finally, "public" does not adequately demarcate the terrain of such days and experiences. Revival meetings and ethnic festivals, for example, derive their power from the interplay between what happens in the tent and street and what happens at home. It is impossible to draw a clear line between public and private at such events; instead, they work their power in the interplay between the two spaces, just as they do between past and present, meaning and hope, desire and denial.

[See also Amusement and Theme Parks; The Culture of Consumption; Manners and Etiquette; Mass Culture and Its Critics; Nightlife; Popular Entertainment before the Civil War.]

BIBLIOGRAPHY

General Works

Anderson, Jervis. *This Was Harlem: A Cultural Portrait, 1900–1950* (1981).

Burning at Stake in the United States: A Record of the Public Burning by Mobs of Five Men, During the First Five Months of 1919, in

the States of Arkansas, Florida, Georgia, Mississippi, and Texas. (1919; repr. 1986).
Cohen, Hennig, and Tristram Potter Coffin, eds. *The Folklore of American Holidays* (1987).
Deems, Edward M., comp. *Holy-Days and Holidays* (1902).
Dolan, Jay P. *The American Catholic Experience: A History from Colonial Times to the Present* (1985).
Douglas, George William. *The American Book of Days* (1937).
Gitlin, Todd. *The Sixties: Years of Hope, Days of Rage* (1987).
Glassberg, David. *American Historical Pageantry: The Uses of Tradition in the Early Twentieth Century* (1990).
Johnson, James Weldon. *Black Manhattan* (1930).
Lincoln, Bruce. *Discourse and the Construction of Society,* (1989).
Linenthal, Edward Tabor. *Sacred Ground: Americans and Their Battlefields* (1991).
Shermanski, Frances. *A Guide to Fairs and Festivals in the United States* (1984).
Silverman, Kenneth. *A Cultural History of the American Revolution* (1976).
Smith, Sheldon. "The Re-establishment of Community: The Emerging Festival System of the American West." *Journal of American Culture* 8, no. 3 (1985).
Warner, William Lloyd. *American Life: Dream and Reality* (1953).
Zelinsky, Wilbur. *Nation into State: The Shifting Symbolic Foundations of American Nationalism* (1988).

Civic Holidays

Albanese, Catherine. "Requiem for Memorial Day: Dissent in the Redeemer Nation." *American Quarterly* 26, no. 4 (1974).
Cohn, William H. "A National Celebration: The Fourth of July in American History." *Cultures* 3, no. 1 (1976).
Cohn, William H. "Popular Culture and Social History." *Journal of Popular Culture* 11, no. 1 (1977).
Huff, A. V. "The Eagle and the Vulture: Changing Attitudes Towards Nationalism in Fourth of July Orations Delivered in Charleston, 1778–1860." *South Atlantic Quarterly* 73, no. 1 (1974).
Rosenzweig, Roy. *Eight Hours for What We Will: Workers and Leisure in an Industrial City,* 1870–1920 (1983).
Smilor, Raymond W. "Creating a National Festival: The Campaign for a Safe and Sane Fourth, 1903–1916." *Journal of American Culture* 2 (1980).
Watts, Theodore F. *The First Labor Day Parade, Tuesday, September 5, 1882: Media Mirrors to Labor's Icons* (1983).

Religious Celebrations

Bruce, Dickson D., Jr. *And They All Sang Hallelujah: Plain Folk Camp Meeting Religion, 1800–1845* (1974).
Hall, David D. *Worlds of Wonder, Days of Judgment: Popular Religious Belief in Early New England* (1989).
Neville, Gwen Kennedy. *Kinship and Pilgrimage: Rituals of Reunion in American Protestant Culture* (1987).
Orsi, Robert A. *The Madonna of 115th Street: Faith and Community in Italian Harlem, 1880–1950* (1985).
Schmidt, Leigh Eric. *Holy Fairs: Scottish Communions and American Revivals in the Early Modern Period* (1989).
Wilson, John Frederic. *Public Religion in American Culture* (1979).

— ROBERT A. ORSI

PARENTHOOD

See REPRODUCTION AND PARENTHOOD

PARKS, NATIONAL

See NATIONAL PARKS AND PRESERVATION

PARKS, URBAN

See URBAN PARKS

THE PLANTATION

Of all the characteristic components of the society and civilization of the Old South, by far the most important was the plantation. This institution largely influenced virtually every aspect of southern existence—political, judicial, social, cultural, economic, and religious. Southern planters (those with twenty or more slaves, the number that commonly qualified one as the proprietor of a plantation), while constituting little more than a tenth of the slaveholders in 1860 but owning over half the slaves, held most of the important political offices—local, state, and congressional—as well as the top judicial posts. They also established social and cultural mores for southern society in general and determined the economic posture of the antebellum South, with its commitment to large-scale agriculture and the considerable neglect of other aspects of the economy, such as industry, commerce, and banking. And with the exception of the backcountry, they were the leading members of most of the churches.

Neither small slaveholders (owning fewer than twenty slaves) nor nonslaveholding yeomen felt uncomfortable with the large measure of power and influence in the hands of the planters. They realized that the planter class, by producing the exportable surplus of southern staples, raised the living standard of all southerners. Less than 7 percent of the 1860 cotton crop in Mississippi, for example, was produced by free labor, with the major portion being grown by the big planters with fifty or more slaves. Slaveless farmers in Virginia produced only 5 percent of the tobacco crop. And hemp in Kentucky was characterized as a "nigger crop," with virtually the entire crop produced by slave labor.

The social structure of white southern society was relatively fluid, with small slave owners by dint of thriftiness, hard work, and a little luck very often able to move up to the planter group. Even a slaveless farmer could, by using a surplus bale or two of cotton, move up the economic stairway to first become a small slave owner and then possibly achieve the prized position of planter. By 1860 the number of landholdings qualifying as a plantation (in excess of 500 acres, 200 hectares) varied from only 2 percent in North Carolina to almost 9 percent in Mississippi and to more than 10 percent in South Carolina, which had the largest average-size landholding of any state in the United States.

A number of these plantations were held by self-made men. For example, a propertyless man in eastern North Carolina by great industry and thrift was able to acquire the farms of ten to twelve small owners and thus become the greatest landed proprietor in his area, living in style in an elaborate plantation house. Sometimes even overseers became plantation owners. President James K. Polk's overseer, Ephraim Beanland, accumulated enough land and slaves in Mississippi to elevate his family to a point where one son could become a physician and the others could achieve positions of standing in their communities.

Whether the southern landowner was slave-holder or nonslaveholder, planter or farmer, he achieved a great measure of self-respect and independence from being able to farm land that he could call his own. With the exception of South Carolina, where there was a virtual caste system—especially among the low-country chivalry of rice and the sea island cotton planters, where one's standing was based almost entirely on one's family affiliation and holdings in land and slaves—there was no common discrimination of slaveholders against nonslaveholders or planters against farmers in the antebellum South. Nor did any of these groups consider fieldwork degrading for white men. During emergencies even large slaveholders were sometimes forced to work in the fields, and their sons normally did so during college vacations. And in areas with few slaves, any farmer (slaveholder or not) could be elected to local offices, especially that of county sheriff.

Across the antebellum South planters committed themselves to a paternalistic ethos that was based on the concept of reciprocal responsibilities for master and bondsperson and the implicit recognition of the slave's humanity. Thus, the plantation provided a composite unit, where master and slaves could pool income and resources within the slaveholding household. Such a household always included the plantation house, outbuildings, fields, gardens, and slave quarters. The size, complexity, and comfort of the buildings varied considerably from one plantation to another, as did the size and variety of fields, gardens, pasture, orchard, and forest.

By gender the master assumed principal responsibility for the household, maintaining an appropriate balance between the care and safety of his dependents and the economic efficiency of the plantation. He determined what crops to plant and when, the work cycle on the plantation, the disciplining of field hands (especially male), the marketing of the crop, and any other responsibilities that tied the household to the market or to the outside world. Managing his black dependents—who were to him an extension of his family or in effect his own children—consumed the greater part of his time.

The plantation mistress, normally the planter's wife but sometimes his widow, mother, daughter, or sister, operated within the world of ruling lady, a position assigned to her by gender and class. She was the recognized superior of all other women of the household. The mistress oversaw the running of the plantation house, flower and vegetable gardens, and dairy. She carried, as a symbol of her status as supervisor of feeding and clothing members of the household, keys to the domestic buildings and the various plantation storehouses. She supervised the plantation infirmary and aided in childbirth. And should the master be absent from the plantation for any great length of time, the mistress assumed full control of the operation, although generally with some difficulty. Her training would have included little pertaining to the internal workings of the plantation or to its affiliation with the outside world. The male-dominated plantation hierarchy could never quite accept her as being anyone other than a delegate of the master and male authority.

Pooling of income and resources within the plantation household brought the slaves little opportunity to determine their own lives, relations, and culture. As property of the master, they could not legally hold property themselves. While they had some control over the composition of their subhouseholds, they had no legal rights there. Only in a marginal way could slaves affect the income that they received in way of food, clothing, and shelter. Most of their food came from crops and livestock they produced themselves. Much of the clothing was made by slave seamstresses. And slaves built their own cabins.

The relationship between master and slave was always one of give-and-take. Wise masters would accommodate a measure of slow work, pilfering, faked illness, or even running away. They also allowed the slaves to tend their own gardens and livestock and generally gave them Saturday afternoon and Sunday off to care for these. On the other hand, slaves had little say over the master's use of their labor or in how they should be compensated for it. Slaves justified their stealing from the plantation storehouses in terms of "taking" what should have been theirs already—in short, they were simply providing for a fairer distribution of the plantation's resources. While the slaves could never accept the master's justification for keeping them as permanent dependents, they realized that the success of the plantation determined the basic income and resources for themselves as well as for the planter's household. Thus, if the master were more prosperous, some of the prosperity might trickle down to them.

The Formative Period

The earliest antecedent of the southern plantation seems to have been the sugar estate of ancient India, characterized by extensive commercial acreage and a large labor force divided into clustered villages under centralized control. Arab traders introduced the Indian mode of operation to the eastern Mediterranean, especially the Levant, in the seventh century, whence it was carried to the western Mediterranean by the Crusaders of the eleventh and twelfth centuries. The Spanish and Portuguese imported black African slave labor to their plantations in the Iberian Peninsula and the Canary, Madeira, and Cape Verde islands in the 1400s and thence to their great sugar empires in the Caribbean and Central and South America the following century. Great Britain entered the overseas world of sizable sugar estates with massive slave forces in the 1640s in Barbados. By 1680 hundreds of Englishmen had developed virtually all the arable land of Barbados as sugar plantations, averaging 200 acres (80 hectares) of sugar fields with one hundred slaves who cultivated provision crops during the off-season of sugar.

The initial beginnings of the plantation in British North America were in the Chesapeake tobacco country of Virginia and Maryland. John Rolfe developed a sweet-smoking variety of tobacco at Jamestown in about 1612, and within a year or two tobacco was being shipped to England. Production of good-quality tobacco required painstaking care and mature judgment in performing a variety of operations; consequently, tobacco was generally produced on small units with a handful of highly skilled workers.

Indentured servants provided the principal labor force for the small tobacco plantations from the beginning; black Africans, although brought to Jamestown as early as 1619, numbered only about 2,500 as late as 1680. In the 1680s, however, with indentured servants becoming less and less available because of improved economic conditions in England and African slaves readily obtainable at affordable prices as a result of the saturation of the Atlantic slave trade, an increasing number of Chesapeake planters turned to slaves as a more dependable and economical means of labor. Nevertheless, the need for indentured servants who could perform skilled and managerial labor existed in the Chesapeake through the time of the American Revolution.

Out of the West Indian setting, however, a more mature plantation pattern was introduced to the American South. The saturation of sugar production in Barbados by 1680 prompted a number of the planters—at least 10 percent of the 175 wealthiest planters (with sixty or more slaves) and an even larger number of the lesser gentry (with twenty to fifty-nine slaves)—to seek large land-holdings in South Carolina. This semitropical locale, it was thought, would provide the advantages of Caribbean agriculture in the more wholesome environment of the North American mainland. Thus, these West Indian planters brought to South Carolina two things of major importance: the most extensively developed plantation system in British America and slavery on a massive scale.

However, it was not sugar that gave rise to the southern plantation but rice, although it proved to be exceptionally difficult to develop as a crop. While the Spanish in Central and South America, the Portuguese in Brazil, and the Dutch in the West Indies had all developed a highly successful rice culture, there is no evidence that any knowledge of rice planting was brought from any of these areas to South Carolina. Thus, rice production there, beginning about 1685, was largely through trial and error, even though 330 tons (2,000 to 2,200 barrels of 350 pounds [29.7 metric tons] each) were exported in 1700, according to Edward Randolph, surveyor of customs for North America from 1691. Recent scholarship has indicated that black African slaves from Madagascar and West Africa (a portion of which was called the Rice Coast) in the 1690s and early 1700s taught the white South Carolinians (whom they outnumbered by 1708) the techniques of rice growing as practiced in their homelands. With the application of irrigation to the rice plants by about 1724, half a century after the colony's founding, the rice industry needed only the successful development of suitable facilities for threshing and polishing the crop to reach full maturity.

Between 1685 and 1720, in conjunction with the rice industry, there had been a blending in coastal South Carolina of three factors essential to a plantation system: the land use system begun in the Levant and transplanted to the western hemisphere, a viable commercial crop suited to the plantation mode of production, and the development of a frontier colonizing project in conformity with the British concept of "plantation" as applied to their colonizing of Ireland in the sixteenth and early seventeenth centuries. In Ireland extensive landholdings had been granted by the British crown to English and Scottish settlers, and were manned by large labor forces (men of arms and their families brought over) committed to agriculture. Each family was assigned a "planting" (field), and a collection of these constituted a "plantation," sometimes as large as 12,000 acres (4,800 hectares).

The first half-century in South Carolina saw considerable use of both free and indentured labor and a limited use of native Indian slave labor, more than in any other English mainland colony. After 1720, however, the rice plantation complex necessitated large importation of black African slaves (especially those with experience in rice culture), to the extent that perhaps as many as 40 percent of the slaves brought to British North America entered through the port of Charleston. In addition, highly sophisticated techniques of plantation management (generally associated with plantations of the antebellum era) were developed; the plantations constituted literal "factories in the field," with few limitations in the way of economies of scale in either acreage or labor force.

After 1720, South Carolina's rice plantations necessitated large importation of African slaves, to the extent that perhaps as many as 40 percent of the slaves brought to British North America entered through Charleston.

The scarcity of shipping during the War of Jenkins's Ear (1739–1743) and King George's War (1744–1748) led to a glut in the Charleston rice market and a precipitous drop in rice prices—by 40 percent in the first conflict and down to 10 shillings per hundredweight by 1746, less than one-seventh of the peak prices of 1738. Among the alternatives open to the rice planters was the development of a second staple, more valuable for its size, to cope with the scarce shipping. Out of this circumstance indigo, grown on a small scale in the early years of the colony, was successfully developed as a crop by Eliza Lucas (Pinckney) in 1744 and produced in considerable quantities (spurred by a British bounty to compensate for loss of access to high-quality French West Indian indigo). It accounted for 10.39 percent of the value of the colony's exports by 1748 (compared with 54.78 for rice).

The period after 1750 (with peace restored and rice prices back up to 63 shillings per hundredweight) was one of exceptional prosperity for the rice planters. They now produced two staples, with each slave able to grow two acres (0.8 hectares) of indigo (produced on the higher areas of the plantation, in a work cycle that dovetailed well with that of rice) along with three acres (1.2 hectares) of rice (grown in the swamplands, which could be periodically flooded). A number of planters amassed enormous holdings of land and slaves. Henry Middleton and Gabriel Manigault accumulated 50,000 acres (20,000 hectares) of land each; Henry Laurens, 20,000 (8,000 hectares); and John Stuart, 15,000 acres (6,000 hectares). Middleton possessed 800 slaves; Laurens, 500; Manigault, 300; and Stuart, 200. Manigault and Laurens, as was common among the South Carolina aristocracy, were heavily involved in merchandising, to the extent that they were the two wealthiest men in the colony. Indeed, these four and a number of others were truly the elite of American plantation society, with their wealth based on the firmest footing anywhere in the British mainland colonies. In fact, these Carolina planters were virtually equal in prosperity and prominence with their Barbadian counterparts.

Rice culture spread from South Carolina northward to the Cape Fear River in North Carolina in the 1730s and southward to Georgia along the Savannah, Ogeechee, and Altamaha rivers in the 1750s. While rice never achieved much status in North Carolina, remaining throughout the colonial period as only an adjunct of the naval stores industry, along with indigo it achieved considerable proportions in Georgia, once the restrictions on landholding and slavery were removed in 1750. By the time of the American Revolution, a number of Georgia planters rivaled those of South Carolina in holdings of land and slaves.

On the eve of the revolutionary war tobacco plantations in Virginia and Maryland were much smaller than rice and indigo plantations in South Carolina and Georgia. The greatest planters—the Byrds, Carrolls, Carters, and Dulanys—who owned many thousands of acres of land and slaves by the hundreds, divided their operations into numerous "quarters" where the work force seldom exceeded a dozen or so laborers. This was necessitated by the closely supervised and highly regimented labor format used in tobacco culture. Robert Carter of Virginia, for example, dispersed his 500 slaves over eighteen widely scattered plantations, as opposed to Henry Middleton's 800 staves who were densely congregated along the Ashley River above Charleston.

Perhaps as much as 35 percent of the tobacco in the Chesapeake was produced on small farms employing no slave labor, whereas virtually all of the rice and indigo was produced on large units employing dozens of slaves. Thus, tobacco did not enjoy the economy of scale of rice and indigo in either acreage or work force. And while per capita tobacco exports from the Chesapeake by 1770 averaged about £3 for each free resident, the exports of rice and indigo from South Carolina brought £9 per white. Nine of the ten wealthiest men who died in the English mainland colonies in 1774 made their fortunes in South Carolina.

The post-Revolutionary era saw considerable change in the southern plantation system. Indigo, with the loss of the British bounty (essential to its profitability) and market (England now turned to the East Indies for its supply), and the invasion of the indigo fields by a destructive caterpillar in about 1780, virtually ceased to exist as a commercial crop. But it left behind a social structure and labor routine perfectly adaptable to the production of a new staple, sea island cotton, so called because it thrived best in the Sea Islands along the coastline of Georgia (to which it was introduced in 1786) and South Carolina.

The variety of cotton, with a silky fiber of from 1½ to 2 inches (37.5 to 50 millimeters), was used principally for the fine cambric and laces of the wealthy. Consequently it fetched premium prices, sometimes as much as $1.25 per pound but more commonly from 20 to 40 cents—two to three times the price of upland, short-staple cotton, of which the fiber was only an inch (25 millimeters) or less. The bulk yield of sea island cotton was about half that of the short-fiber, and it was considerably more difficult to produce and process for market. However, the higher prices and the suitability of sea island cotton as a replacement for indigo more than compensated for the difference. Profits were high, sometimes as much as 10 to 12 percent, with virtually the entire crop produced by large-scale slave labor.

The Cotton Kingdom stretched a thousand miles east to west, from South Carolina to Texas; it had a north-to-south breadth of some 200 miles in Carolina and Texas and 600 to 700 miles in the Mississippi Valley.

Whereas climate confined sea island cotton to the littoral of South Carolina and Georgia and middle Florida (where its production was developed in the 1850s), upland cotton, once Eli Whitney had perfected an inexpensive and workable gin in 1793, could be profitably produced anywhere the growing season was at least two hundred days and the annual rainfall 20 inches (500 millimeters)—on virtually any kind of soil, on flat or hilly land, and on a small scale by one-horse farmers or in massive amounts by large planters with dozens or hundreds of slaves.

The Antebellum Plantation

By the early 1800s, and especially after the War of 1812, Atlantic seaboard farmers and planters with badly worn soils and declining incomes—especially those of South Carolina and Virginia—moved west and southwest to the Black Belt of Alabama, to central Tennessee, to the lands along the Mississippi River from Arkansas and west Tennessee to the Gulf of Mexico, and eventually to east Texas in search of cheap, fertile lands—by then the price was $1.25 an acre (0.4 hectare) for government-owned land—and a new stake in life. With the insatiable British demand for cotton to fuel their booming textile industry keeping prices high, southern cotton production doubled about every ten years between the War of 1812 and the Civil War—from less than 150,000 bales (averaging about 450 pounds [202.5 kilograms] each) in 1814 to over 4,500,000 by 1860, the value of which amounted to 57 percent of the total exports from the United States.

Indeed, the Cotton Kingdom of the antebellum South stretched for a thousand miles (1,600 kilometers) from South Carolina westward to Texas, with a breadth from north to south of some two hundred miles (320 kilometers) in Carolina and Texas and 600 to 700 miles (960 to 1,120 kilometers) in the Mississippi Valley—a total of about 400,000 square miles (1,040,000 square kilometers). On the periphery the other great staples were produced—tobacco across the upper South (with more production west of the Appalachians by 1860 than east), hemp (used principally for cordage and bale cloth) in Kentucky and Missouri, sugar in Louisiana, and rice along the lower reaches of some seventeen tidal rivers on the South Atlantic coast from the Cape Fear River in southeastern North Carolina to the Saint Johns River in northern Florida.

But it was cotton—more than all the other staples put together—that dominated southern society, economy, and politics. Cotton could be produced with some profit by small independent farmers holding few, if any, slaves (more than half the landowners in the Cotton Kingdom owned no slaves at all); however, the greatest prosperity (especially in the 1850s) was enjoyed by the three thousand to four thousand big planters who owned most of the land and slaves and received as much as three-fourths of the annual cotton income.

Natchez, Mississippi, became the great mecca of cotton wealth, with perhaps a third of the millionaires in America in 1860 clustered there; and they made their great affluence visible in the hundred or so grand mansions that arose in and around the city. Individual landownerships and yields in the Natchez area were amazing. In 1859 (the crop year for the 1860 census) Levin R. Marshall, a Natchez banker who either owned or had a share in more than 25,000 acres (10,000 hectares) in Louisiana, Mississippi, and Arkansas, produced 4,000 bales; Stephen Duncan, with six cotton and two

The typical antebellum plantation house and grounds was colonnaded with Greek Revival porticoes and surrounded by lush gardens.

sugar plantations and 1,018 slaves (plus 23 at his residence near Natchez), 4,000 bales; John Routh, once called the "largest cotton planter in the world" but who by this time had settled much of his land on his children, 3,500 bales; and Frederick Stanton, with five large plantations in Louisiana and a small holding in Mississippi comprising 15,000 acres (6,000 hectares) and 444 slaves, 3,000 bales. Cotton sold in 1860 for 11 to 12 cents per pound. An average bale of 450 pounds (202.5 kilograms) would thus be worth about $50.

In Louisiana in 1859, Meredith Calhoun in Rapides Parish produced 3,800 bales on his plantation of 5,000 improved and 10,000 unimproved acres (the largest number of bales produced in the South on a single plantation), along with 531 hogsheads of sugar and 30,000 bushels of corn for the plantation's 700 slaves; Alfred Davis of Concordia Parish, 3,400 bales; and Joseph A. S. Acklen of West Feliciana Parish, 3,100 bales. Nine other Louisiana planters produced between 2,000 and 3,000 bales. In Georgia, Joseph Bond of Macon produced 2,199 bales in 1859, making him the largest producer in that state.

Among the producers of the other staples, only the great rice nabobs of South Carolina and the sugar magnates of Louisiana could rival the cotton lords in ownership and production. The rice princes were Nathaniel Heyward of Colleton District, largest of the rice planters, with 5,000 acres (2,000 hectares) of improved land and 30,000 unimproved acres (12,000 hectares) on seventeen plantations and over 2,000 slaves; Joshua John Ward in Georgetown District, with 3,000 improved and 7,000 unimproved acres (1,200 improved and 2,800 unimproved hectares) on seven plantations and 1,100 slaves; and William Aiken of Colleton District, with 700 slaves on his Jehossee Island plantation of 4,000 acres (1,600 hectares), 2,000 (800) of which were improved (Aiken and Meredith Calhoun of Louisiana were the only planters in the entire South in 1860 with as many as 700 slaves on a single plantation). The value of their crops rivaled or exceeded that of the largest cotton planters. The largest sugar holdings were those of John Burnside of Ascension and St. James parishes, comprising about 7,500 improved and 22,000 unimproved acres (3,000 improved and 8,800 unimproved hectares) on five plantations and 950 slaves. Samuel Hairston, with numerous plantations in both Virginia and North Carolina and 1,600 slaves, was the only tobacco planter of this magnitude.

Not only did these great planters build stately mansions adorned with colonnaded Greek Revival porticoes, finely furnished and surrounded by lush gardens, they also built or purchased expensive town houses in Charleston and New Orleans. Samuel Hairston beautified his plantation house and grounds with such lavish splendor that a neighboring minister described paradise as being "as beautiful as Mr. Hairston's."

As a result of the great holdings of these and lesser planters, the South in 1860 had 83 percent of the farms in the United States with 500 or more acres (200 or more hectares), fifty counties with populations of over 75 percent slaves, and the twelve richest counties in the country; Adams County, Mississippi (of which Natchez was the county seat) was the richest of all and had a slave population of more than 90 percent.

By 1850 the southern plantation system had reached maturity, with cotton plantations (those producing five or more bales) numbering 74,031; tobacco (raising 3,000 pounds [1,350 kilograms] or over), 15,745; hemp, 8,327; sugar, 2,681; and rice plantations (producing 20,000 pounds [9,000 kilograms] or more), 551. The fact that such a small quantity of production was needed to qualify a unit as a plantation doubtless means that many thousands of small cotton and tobacco farms with but one or two working hands were included in these numbers. One field hand could produce five bales of cotton, the normal yield from ten acres (4 hectares); two slaves could grow 3,000 pounds (1,350 kilograms) of tobacco, the average output of five acres (2 hectares); and two laborers could raise ten acres of rice, which should produce 20,000 pounds. Even including these many small units, there were only 101,335 plantations out of a total of 569,201 farms and plantations, slightly less than 18 percent.

With respect to the kind of staple produced, the number of slaves generally was inversely related to the number of plantations growing that kind of crop. The superintendent of the 1850 census estimated that 2.5 million slaves of all ages were directly engaged in agriculture: 60,000 in the production of hemp, 125,000 in rice, 150,000 in sugar, 350,000 in tobacco, and 1,815,000 in cotton. Thus, the rice plantations in 1850 would have 226 slaves per estate; sugar plantations, 55; hemp, 7; tobacco, 22; and cotton, 24.

What largely determined the physical size of the plantation was the walking distance from the slave quarters to the most distant field. Planters did not want this to exceed an hour or so; consequently, the middle-sized plantation consisted of 1,000 to 1,500 acres (400 to 600 hectares). While most planters used a portion of the improved land to produce provisions for their own use and that of the slave force, the principal function of the plantation was to produce a commercial crop for export. Thus, it was essential that it be located along a suitable transportation route (most often a river) and have fertile soil.

Planters in general were scientific farmers, as evidenced by their subscriptions to agricultural journals and the large number of articles written by planters for these journals. They practiced crop rotation to preserve soil fertility, and where practical and feasible they used fertilizing materials such as marl and guano and planted winter cover crops. Planters adapted agricultural procedures to their slave labor, using the latest techniques of planting and the most advanced machinery, tools, and implements. They were constantly striving to improve the quality of their seeds, draft animals, and livestock. And the planters wrestled with the problems of slave management, avidly reading the advice on such matters in the agricultural magazines and often writing responses.

The Culture of the Plantation

The antebellum plantation constituted a composite community. The bulk of the slave population consisted of field hands used directly in producing the commercial staple and the provision crops, such as corn (the most widely grown crop in the South), oats, peas, and potatoes. However, each plantation had another group of slaves employed in nonfield pursuits. They included animal raisers, baby keepers, barbers, blacksmiths, bricklayers, butchers, butlers, carpenters, coachmen, cobblers, cooks, coopers, engineers, gardeners, ginners, laundresses, maids, millers, nurses, seamstresses, shoemakers, tailors, tanners, valets, waiters, and weavers. Many of these skilled slaves were trained to perform two or more trades and could also double as field hands during critical labor periods such as the harvest. After accounting for the young, old, and infirm (who could do no more than a quarter to half the work that a prime hand could do), gender differences (women could do three-fourths as much as a prime hand), and days lost to illness (generally from one to two a month), the planter's slave numbers were reduced in prime worker equivalency to little more than half. Thus, a plantation with one hundred slaves of all ages could expect the work of only fifty to sixty prime hands.

The focal figure in administering the plantation was the overseer, who had complete charge of the plantation for the period of his contract (usually a document written in January for the calendar year). He was consequently responsible for the labor and well-being of the workers, the maintenance of the property, and, most important, the success of the crop, on which the renewal of the contract very often depended. Although in 1860 there were 46,274 slaveholders with enough slaves (20 or more) to justify the employment of an overseer, William K. Scarborough (in *The Overseer*) was able to find only about 25,958 overseers in the entire South at that time. Rice plantations, whose owners were away from the plantation during the malaria season (May to November), needed overseers, as did most of the large sugar plantations. Apparently many large cotton and tobacco planters, disgusted at bad experiences with overseers, who generally came from the small farmer or poor white classes, chose to administer their own plantation. Bennet Barrow of West Feliciana Parish in Louisiana, for example, supervised his plantation with two hundred slaves, using a slave foreman, or "driver," as assistant. Overseers were normally paid $500 to $700 annually, but those on large rice and sugar plantations often made $1,000 to $1,500; on his massive Jehossee Island rice plantation in South Carolina, with a slave force of seven hundred, Governor William Aiken paid $2,000. The tenure of an overseer was generally about three and a half years.

Below the overseer in the plantation hierarchy was the driver, who had direct responsibility for the day-to-day performance of the workers. The driver got the slaves to the fields in the mornings, organized the work gangs for the day, and excused them upon the satisfactory completion of the day's labor. He also generally administered plantation discipline. In addition, the driver was responsible for proper decorum in the slave quarters. He had certain perquisites: better food, clothing, and housing than was the lot of slaves in general;

freedom from physical toil; and the prestige and authority accompanying the position of supervisor. At the same time the driver operated under a number of handicaps. His workday was longer than that of other slaves; he often experienced considerable difficulty in being fully accepted by the other slaves in the quarters; and he was buffeted by demands from the owner and overseer above and the slaves below. Planters generally selected a driver for each fifty slaves and considered the services of a good driver more important than those of the overseer; consequently the tenure of the driver normally was much longer than that of the overseer.

The slaves on the plantation lived in simple quarters some distance from the plantation house, in single cabins or double houses of wooden boards or shingles with a chimney in the middle and occupied by two families. There was also a "sick house," where the plantation nurse cared for slaves suffering from various maladies and fevers (and occasionally from such deadly diseases as cholera). She administered the medicines prescribed by the doctor who looked after the health of the slaves on a number of plantations at once, normally under contract for $1.25 to $1.50 per year for each slave in his care.

Clothing was issued twice yearly to the slaves—in late April or early May for the summer season and in late November or early December for the winter. In addition, the winter issue included blankets. Rations, given out weekly, generally consisted of three and a half pounds of bacon and a peck (fourteen pounds) of cornmeal for each adult, with lesser amounts for children. The slave family was usually given a piece of land for a garden to supplement its diet and was allowed to raise its own chickens and pigs. The planter also attended to the religious welfare of his slaves by employing local ministers to preach and encouraging the holding of religious classes on the plantation, and by allowing them to attend churches of their faith, usually Baptist or Methodist, in the general neighborhood.

The labor system on most plantations was that of gang labor, with individual squads working under the supervision of the driver or a squad leader from sunup to sundown. The exception was on the rice plantations, where discipline would have been virtually impossible without the task system. Because the planter was gone from early May to the killing frosts of November, leaving only the overseer and slave drivers to control affairs, a labor format was needed in which the slaves could largely direct themselves. The task system provided for an assignment that the poorest worker could complete in eight to nine hours. In practice, however, most slaves finished their tasks by mid afternoon and could devote the rest of the day to working in their gardens, farming small tracts of rice of their own, looking after their livestock, or hunting or fishing. More than anything else, the task system kept lonely slaves on the isolated rice plantations from becoming restless and rebellious.

There was little interchange between rice slaves and those from the other plantations. Tobacco or cotton slaves would have difficulty acclimating to the isolated existence of the rice plantation and adjusting to the rice diet and the task system of labor. Thus, new hands on rice plantations were generally acquired from other rice plantations where sales were necessitated by the planter's overextension, by the breakup of the estates, or by slaves being too refractory to retain. The natural increase of slave numbers on rice plantations was normally about 5 percent. Conversely, rice slaves would not adapt very easily to the gang labor system of the cotton, tobacco, or sugar plantation.

Southern planters, with a considerable amount of fixed capital in their slaves, attempted to use their work force in the most efficient and profitable manner. Thus, they planted a much greater acreage in cash crops than in food crops (mainly cotton versus corn) and committed a larger share of the labor time of slave households to market production than was generally true for free families (mainly women doing fieldwork instead of housework). They could collectivize such household duties as food preparation and child care, thus freeing additional labor for fieldwork. The off-season of the commercial staple left ample time for the slaves to grow sufficient provisions; otherwise, as a fixed labor supply, they would have had little to do during much of the year.

As a result of these factors, slave labor was probably more efficient than free labor. The household economy of the plantation, with the work force able to produce great quantities of the staple, ample provisions, and most of the commodities needed on the plantation, doubtless contributed to the plantation's profitability. While most planters provided little more than bare subsistence in the way of food, clothing, and shelter for the slaves (as compared to what they took from the plantation profits for their households), there is ample evidence to demonstrate that planters well understood the correlation between fair treatment and the willingness of the slaves to work. In short, the masters who treated the slaves the best generally got the most efficient labor from them. Conversely, masters who were cruel to the slave force in the main found the slave labor output declining accordingly. Thus, the measure of treatment was a major factor in slave discipline on the plantation, generally of more effect than the constant threat of punishment. However, even the most generous master occasionally had to punish disobedient slaves to keep order among his work force.

While the plantation system brought high per capita incomes to individual planters (recent studies have demonstrated that plantation profitability was at least as much as the earnings of stocks and bonds in the North—6 to 8 percent—and sometimes considerably more), it ensured that the South, with its commitment to large-scale production of a few agricultural commodities in world demand, was dependent with respect to manufacturing (except for the household production on the plantations), merchandising, and banking. Southern planters showed little interest in internal improvements or in developing urban centers of manufacturing. However, while the South had only about twenty thousand manufacturing establishments in 1860, compared with one hundred thousand in the North, the gap is narrowed considerably when such facilities as cotton gins and rice and sugar mills on the plantations are considered in the South's overall manufacturing.

With respect to cultural matters, the southern planters put great stock in education to prepare their sons for public service and the professions. Accordingly, a large number of excellent academies sprang up throughout the southern states, and the area had the largest number of college students in the United States. At the same time, the planter elite saw little need to educate the masses, thus preventing much in the way of public schools. From the standpoint of religion, they supported the Episcopal church, whose ministers not only preached the gospel of slavocracy but often were slaveholders themselves (Leonidas Polk, the Episcopal bishop of Louisiana, owned four hundred). Some planters were Presbyterian or Roman Catholic (mostly in Louisiana), while the populace in general subscribed mainly to the Baptist and Methodist faiths.

The great planters buttressed their economic domination with political power. They produced great leaders such as John C. Calhoun, Robert Toombs, and Jefferson Davis, and exercised virtually total power at both the county and the state level (every governor in all the southern states in the 1850s was a slaveholding planter) and a large measure of control within national circles, especially in Congress and on the Supreme Court. At the same time, they drew together in support of such issues as the tariff and the westward expansion of slavery, developing the extreme doctrines of nullification and ultimately secession—a measure of how far the ultraconservative political views of South Carolinians had come to influence the section.

In alliance with the Old Northwest, the southern planters controlled the Democratic party from 1830 to 1860 and largely shaped the policies of the national government. They were able to force the lowering of the tariff in the nullification controversy of the 1830s and were in large part responsible for the Mexican War, fought to acquire new lands for the expansion of slavery and the plantation system westward to the Pacific. However, their insistence that all the newly acquired territory be open to slavery, and that Cuba and Central America were possible targets for annexation, alienated their western allies and ended their control of the party. The election of a Republican president committed to containment of slavery in 1860 made the threat of secession a reality, bringing on the Civil War.

The Plantation Legacy

Although the invading Union forces wreaked massive destruction upon the plantation facilities and the slaves were ultimately freed, the plantation system largely survived intact but with a vastly different labor format. Probably as many as half of the plantations changed hands over the following ten to fifteen turbulent years. The planters, labor lords before the war, were now landlords and thus forced to accommodate the demands of the emancipated blacks for more control of their lives and conditions of work. At first they tried to operate with a cash wage system, with the blacks living in their former slave cabins and subject to plantation discipline under the newly enacted black codes. However, this plan did not work well for either group. The planters could not force the blacks to work as hard as they had when they were slaves, nor could they be certain of how dependable the blacks would be to see the crop through. In addition, little capital was available to the planters, and where it was, the interest rates were prohibitive—2.5 to 3 percent a month. From the blacks' standpoint, the wage system resembled slavery too much and gave them little say in their own working lives.

Cotton and tobacco planters soon came up with a sharecropping system under which the blacks would be rented certain portions of the land (to which they would move, thus getting away from the distasteful slave quarters) and share in decision making with the owners. To the blacks the new system brought a large measure of independence; to the planters it brought a more dependable and cheaper labor supply. Generally, the planter furnished workers with land, seed, fertilizer, draft animals, and tools, and in exchange took half to two-thirds of the harvested crop.

Under this new organization the plantations survived with little change until the 1930s, but not without great difficulties. The cotton crop of 1875 equaled that of 1859 in amount but not in profits. A saturation of the world supply of cotton depressed prices (by the mid

1890s they were little more than a third of the inflated prices of the late 1850s), and the resulting economic hard times created as much havoc for cotton planters as the Civil War had. Indeed, the antebellum cotton planters would have fallen on hard times had there been no war nor emancipation of the slaves.

Other staples fared less well. The sugar crop in Louisiana was back to its prewar level by 1879, but the plantations is largely survived through outside capital, with about half of them owned by northerners.

Rice made the poorest recovery of all. The former slaves were not willing to go back into the snake- and mosquito-infested swamps, nor were they willing to do the "mud work" of cleaning out ditches and repairing banks. Outside capital was not available, and competition soon developed on uplands in Louisiana (led by Dr. Seaman A. Knapp, president of Iowa State College, and a group of midwestern grain farmers), with powered irrigation and harvesting machinery too heavy for the soggy swamplands of the Carolinas and Georgia. The new competition, coupled with a series of very destructive hurricanes around the turn of the century, spelled the death knell for the old rice coast. The plantations were converted to residential housing, resorts, and wildlife refuges, or allowed to return to their natural state.

While the plantation system brought high per capita incomes to individual planters, it ensured that the South, with its commitment to large-scale production of a few agricultural commodities, was dependent with respect to manufacturing, merchandising, and banking.

The New Deal of the 1930s dealt a sharp blow to the plantation system. What may be called an "American enclosure movement"—like the English movement of the 1500s that turned fields into sheep pastures, driving out agricultural workers—encouraged the displacement of sharecroppers and tenants (generally whites who had lost their small farms in the 1890s and early 1900s, and by now out-numbered the black sharecroppers), the expansion of home farms cultivated by family members rather than sharecroppers, and more reliance on hired labor. The concomitant development of mammoth farm machinery, including mechanical cotton pickers and tobacco harvesters, and the effective use of chemical herbicides and pesticides led to such a reduced need for labor that blacks and whites were forced to migrate in droves to the cities of the Northeast and Midwest to seek new employment. Thus, by the 1970s the plantation, the focal point in shaping southern life for three centuries, was little more than a memory, shrouded in such nostalgic distortions of the *Gone With the Wind* variety that it very often was difficult to separate the mythical from the real.

[See also African American Music; Agriculture; Business Culture; Family Structures; Household Labor; Labor: Colonial Times through 1820s; Labor: The Jacksonian Era through Reconstruction; Literacy; Minorities and Work; The Natural Environment: The South; Slavery.]

BIBLIOGRAPHY

General Works

Clinton, Catherine. *The Plantation Mistress: Woman's World in the Old South* (1982).

Eaton, Clement. *The Growth of Southern Civilization, 1790–1860* (1961).

Foner, Eric. *Reconstruction: America's Unfinished Revolution, 1863–1877* (1988). Excellent coverage of the plantations during the Reconstruction era.

Fox-Genovese, Elizabeth. *Within the Plantation Household: Black and White Women of the Old South* (1988).

Gaines, Francis P. *The Southern Plantation: A Study in the Development and Accuracy of a Tradition* (1924).

Genovese, Eugene D. *The Political Economy of Slavery: Studies in the Economy and Society of the Old South* (1965).

Genovese, Eugene D. *The World the Slaveholders Made* (1969). Marxist interpretations of the old South.

Kirby, Jack T. *Rural Worlds Lost: The American South, 1920–1960* (1987).

Oakes, James. *The Ruling Race: A History of American Slaveholders* (1982).

Phillips, Ulrich B. *Life and Labor in the Old South* (1929). Best introduction to the southern plantation.

Roark, James L. *Masters Without Slaves: Southern Planters in the Civil War and Reconstruction* (1977).

Scarborough, William K. *The Overseer: Plantation Management in the Old South* (1966).

Taylor, Rosser H. *Ante-Bellum South Carolina: A Social and Cultural History* (1942).

Thompson, Edgar T. *Plantation Societies, Race Relations, and the South* (1975). A sociological interpretation of the southern plantation.

Wright, Gavin. *Old South, New South: Revolutions in the Southern Economy Since the Civil War* (1986).

Cotton Plantations

Moore, John Hebron. *The Emergence of the Cotton Kingdom in the Old Southwest: Mississippi, 1770–1860* (1988).

Rosengarten, Theodore. *Tombee: Portrait of a Cotton Planter with the Journal of Thomas Chaplin (1822–1890)* (1986). The account of a sea island cotton planter.

Woodman, Harold D. *King Cotton and His Retainers: Financing and Marketing the Cotton Crop of the South, 1800–1925* (1968).

Hemp Plantations

Hopkins, James F. *History of the Hemp Industry in Kentucky* (1951).

Rice Plantations

Clifton, James M. *Life and Labor on Argyle Island: Letters and Documents of a Savannah River Rice Plantation, 1833–1867* (1978).
Dethloff, Henry C. *A History of the American Rice Industry, 1685–1985* (1988).
Heyward, Duncan C. *Seed from Madagascar* (1937).
Smith, Julia F. *Slavery and Rice Culture in Lowcountry Georgia, 1750–1860* (1985).

Sugar Plantations

Sitterson, Joseph Carlyle. *Sugar Country: The Cane Sugar Industry in the South, 1753–1950* (1953).

Tobacco Plantations

Kulikoff, Allan. *Tobacco and Slaves: The Development of Southern Cultures in the Chesapeake, 1680–1800* (1986).
Robert, Joseph C. *The Tobacco Kingdom: Plantation, Market, and Factory in Virginia and North Carolina, 1800–1860* (1938).

Slavery

Boles, John B. *Black Southerners, 1619–1869* (1984).
Genovese, Eugene D. *Roll, Jordan, Roll: The World the Slaves Made* (1974). A ground-breaking study of slavery from the vantage point of the slave.
Joyner, Charles. *Down by the Riverside: A South Carolina Slave Community* (1984). A superb study of a local slave community (on rice plantations on the Waccamaw River, probably the densest slave population in the South) from the interdisciplinary viewpoint.
Phillips, Ulrich B. *American Negro Slavery: A Survey of the Supply, Employment and Control of Negro Labor as Determined by the Plantation Regime* (1918).
Stampp, Kenneth M. *The Peculiar Institution: Slavery in the Ante-Bellum South* (1956).
Wood, Peter. *Black Majority: Negroes in Colonial South Carolina from 1670 Through the Stono Rebellion* (1974).

Agriculture

Daniel, Pete. *Breaking the Land: The Transformation of Cotton, Tobacco, and Rice Cultures Since 1880* (1985).
Gray, Lewis C. *History of Agriculture in the Southern United States to 1860.* 2 vols. (1933).

— JAMES M. CLIFTON

POPULAR ENTERTAINMENT BEFORE THE CIVIL WAR

The Evolution of the word "entertainment" between 1600 and 1860 suggests a broad outline for the social changes described in this essay. The verb "to entertain" was once closely allied to the verb "to maintain." It implied an obligation owed to a guest under one's roof and even extended to the legal responsibilities that came with the employment of domestic labor, as in "I entertained five ploughmen on my property." Over the course of the eighteenth century, however, this sense of personal obligation became muted, so that any form of social treating could be called an entertainment. Tavernkeepers now "entertained" their guests, even though the guests paid for the privilege. By the time of the Civil War, an entertainment could be any form of freestanding commercial amusement.

This change in the word's meaning reflects the rise of a popular market for leisure pursuits over the period, indeed a striking transformation; by the late nineteenth century, most entertainments were provided *for* families rather than *by* them. The change also suggests the transformation of early notions of duty and respectability into some fairly mercenary social practices. This moral reevaluation can be seen even more clearly in the parallel development of the concept of "amusement." "To amuse" once carried only negative connotations. It suggested planned trickery, as in a military general's sending out troops to amuse an enemy. Again, by 1860 Americans were using the term, almost with approval, to describe a whole range of popular recreations. Through amusement and entertainment, one might relieve the pressure of work or the anonymity of the city.

These shifts in meaning determine a dual agenda for those who wish to study the social history of American entertainment. One approach is to track the passage of leisure, however broadly defined, into an urban, commercial marketplace, noting the many new forms of amusement made available to an increasingly diverse and growing population. A second avenue is to highlight the problem of values, both moral and political, in this extension of popular entertainment. As various groups began to develop their own distinctive styles of amusement, there inevitably arose competing claims and doubts about the worth of these different forms of recreation in a single, virtuous republic. Far from being a neat linear description of ever-growing choice, the history of American recreation may appear as fractured and as problematic as the story of American political party formation. Without this second, evaluative task, the subject of recreation might remain inherently lighthearted, perhaps confirming G. R. Elton's remark that the social historian often appears as "second cousin to the tabloid journalist."

The Colonial and Early National Periods

The narrative must begin awkwardly, by questioning the very notion of "American" recreation in the colonial period. It is difficult to claim that before about 1840 the United States had a national cultural outlook as expressed by its amusements; most musical and theatrical life, for example, remained local in character until the 1820s. Americans' amusement customs reflected citizens' different ethnic and religious affiliations. In addition, the demands of regional farming and market patterns caused rural populations to have varying degrees of acquaintance with urban forms of pleasure. New England farmers tended to be more self-sufficient in meeting their needs for food than were their neighbors in the Middle Atlantic states and thus had less opportunity to come together in marketplaces that might have provided opportunities for popular amusements. In the South, the draconian demands of single-crop cultivation, especially of tobacco, severely limited the occasions for socializing and amusement for most residents.

Despite such variation, certain generalizations may be made about the place of entertainment in the overall fabric of colonial life. The most obvious point about early American society was that it was predominantly agricultural; indeed, the rural population increased as a percentage of the whole through most of the eighteenth century, and only 5 percent of the national population was urban as late as 1820. The leisure activities of most Americans during the colonial period and the early years of the republic revolved around the yearly cycle of agricultural work, with the traditional European celebrations of May Day, marking the arrival of spring, and Harvest Home (celebrating the gathering of the crops) being recast in local forms. In New England, the spring-training days for militias, despite their serious intent, took on the aspect of a "Maygame" (11th-century English phrase for "Mayday"), and the religious Thanksgiving celebration retained older images of abundance and sexual promise. The clearest case of a European seasonal festival surviving the passage to the New World intact is Louisiana's Mardi Gras, though New Orleans did not officially recognize the event until 1857.

Such holidays may have been traditional in the sense that the forms were ancient, but their social context in the infant society was new. Travelers observed that the most distinctive American entertainments were those connected to communal work. Because of the relative shortage of male labor in the early years of settlement, a premium was placed on cooperative effort, occasioning such "frolics" as cornhuskings and barn and house raisings. The social aspects of such work, especially the liberal treating to food and drink, were necessary for securing the labor of the villagers and added to the density of kinship and community ties upon which credit and livelihood depended. One of the more interesting aspects of these frolics is that they were viewed as such a necessary social ritual that even the most frugal farmers seldom registered the cost of these events in their account books. To refer back to the initial sense of the word, one's obligation to "entertain" still carried a sense of maintaining property and social standing. In addition to work-related frolics, families were also expected to treat the community on the occasion of births, baptisms, weddings, and, before the rise of the early-nineteenth-century vogue for protracted mourning, funerals as well.

Two other forms of amusement, though not strictly entertainments, were judged by both visitors and residents to have taken on distinctive qualities in the New World. The traditional field sport of hunting was immeasurably enhanced by the presence of plentiful and, for Europeans, unusual game. As James Fenimore Cooper recounted in the pigeon-shooting scene in *The Deerslayer* (1841), hunting soon became as much a form of recreation as a necessity, as settlers in all sections took to the woods and fields. The popularity of mass "coon" and squirrel hunts, turkey shoots, and deer draws (the use of horses to flush animals from cover) cannot be explained solely by the need to provide sustenance or to protect crops. The enthusiasm for hunting may have had much to do with the novel absence of aristocratic game laws and the greater availability of firearms among all social classes. As George Alsop, an indentured servant, observed in seventeenth-century Maryland, "Every Servant has a Gun, Powder and Shot allowed him, to sport with all on all Holidays and leasurable times."

The leisure activities of most Americans during the colonial period revolved around agricultural work, with the traditional European celebrations of May Day (marking the arrival of spring) and Harvest Home (celebrating the gathering of crops) being recast in local forms.

Quarterly training and annual election-day gatherings also drew the attention of travelers and the magistracy. Though both events were seen as central to the maintenance of colonial order, both also attracted their share of high jinks and drunkenness. Booths serving food and drink were often placed on the periphery of the marching ground at training sessions, and some seventeenth-century New England accounts record the presence of Native Americans as onlookers. (The interaction between the races in terms of amusements remains a remarkably unexplored subject.) Training days usually ended with informal target-shooting contests, wrestling matches, and footraces, as well as music and dance. Such festivities provided a welcome break from the rigors of work and offered a convenient occasion for young men to "keep company" with young women.

Frolics, bees, musters, and hunting were all later celebrated, especially in nineteenth-century genre painting, as occasions when American society was at ease with itself and most cohesive in character. Yet amusements could just as readily express the inequalities in the social structure. The most persistent fracture in the world of colonial recreation occurred along the lines of gender. Women's leisure remained tied to the domestic sphere, and despite the sewing parties, quilting bees, flax pullings and scrutchings, or celebrations organized around family rites of passage, women's recreations were probably more solitary and sparse than those of men. Laurel Thatcher Ulrich's wonderful account of New England women, *Good Wives* (1991), contains little about leisure, since domestic production remained paramount. Literature of the period suggested that women could not be both productive and ornamental at the same time, although during the eighteenth century thinking advanced to the point that it was conceded that a gentlewoman might take tea with her friends, polish the silver, and embroider lace. Recent studies of rural women have found that an increase in what might be termed women's discretionary time did not lead to a broadening of their social role; rather, it led to an increasingly ceremonial meaning of housekeeping, requiring further embellishment of the garden and the table.

Social class further regulated the access to, and the meaning of, entertainment. Most servants in early New England society were prevented by laws of indenture from visiting taverns and other places of resort, and since fully one-third of the men arriving in the northern colonies were under some form of servitude, their opportunities for regular recreation must have been fewer than those of free-holders. The class patterning of amusement was even more evident in the South. There large landowners adopted the ideals of the English gentry that linked the enjoyment of leisure with social prestige. The provision of entertainments to guests and workers conferred a sense of honor, and from the mid eighteenth century on, writers such as the indentured John Hammond promoted the South as a region given over to leisure and material abundance.

In hunting, the southern planter class differentiated itself from the commoners by emphasizing the chase rather than the kill and by preferring sports, especially horsemanship and fencing, associated with the aristocracy. The most glaring archaism was the popularity of ring tournaments, which referred back to the medieval pageantry of royal jousts. "Knights," often military cadets, had to scoop up with their lances rings suspended from posts, with the most skilled performer ending up as a "king." The gentry were certainly not above promoting and enjoying rougher sports; indeed, their position as judges and patrons of wrestling matches, cockfights, and eye-gouging contests further emphasized their social standing.

The class lines evident in patterns of amusement in the South were made much stronger by the presence of slavery, and most of the original work on American popular culture has been influenced by recent debates on the autonomy of slave religious and cultural practices. In contrast to the neo-abolitionist historians, who stressed the physical and psychological confinements of plantation slavery, most recent studies have documented the ways that slaves maintained both cultural identity and a sense of self-worth through family life, religion, and amusement. Even allowing for hyperbole among the later apologists and memorialists, many planters did "entertain" their slaves with a form of patriarchal benevolence. Most owners granted slaves the traditional Christian holidays and the sabbath, as well as Saturday afternoons and extra time after harvesting and planting. In addition, the provision of extra meat and drink for celebratory barbecues appears to have been customary. Historians Eugene Genovese and John Blassingame have detailed the ways in which slaves used this free time: securing passes to visit towns and other plantations, engaging in rural sports, and performing traditional African styles of music and dance, especially "patting juba." Disagreement arises, however, over the social and psychological consequences of such benevolence by slaveholders. From Frederick Douglass onward, many commentators have taken the provision of leisure to be little more than a cynical means of exercising social control. For Genovese, the granting of "entertainment" generated a curious double bind, characteristic of other aspects of master-slave (and, indeed, class) relationships. "Treating" permitted the masters to proclaim their benevolence as well as to allow slaves the social space to develop their own oppositional culture; on the other hand (and more problematic), the slaves' "acceptance" of entertainment tied them into their own domination.

After studies of the Old South, the recreational practices of Puritan New England have gained most scholarly attention, perhaps because the Calvinist emphasis on work spawned a debate about the danger of social pleasure that continues into the present. The role of amusements has also figured in the perennial debate over whether Puritan society suffered a decline, with a growth in hostility between sinners and saints, or whether it maintained its social cohesion at the local level, as manifested in relatively low rates of crime and of social deviance.

Puritanism in England emerged as a reformation in manners rather than as a distinct theological strain within Calvinism; the revelries associated with Guy Fawkes Day, Christmas, May Day, and Saint Valentine's Day were symptomatic of the popular culture that Puritans wished to escape in coming to America. Puritan society was also invested, to an unusual degree, in the adult and the patriarchal. All people—apprentices, children, servants, and wives—had to live within the firm government of the family. Sermons and conduct books contained long lists of prohibitions on the enjoyment of cards, dice, alehouses, and taverns.

Yet studies of New England towns have now shown that there was an embarrassing gap between rhetoric and practice and, moreover, that this gap widened during the eighteenth century. Folly and lewdness at harvest time continued despite the many warnings against such practices. As Roger Thompson has shown, though there was nothing quite like the "Abbeys of Misrule," a traditional opportunity for young folk to go on a spree, there was nevertheless a good deal of youthful revelry, usually at the festival times that Puritans formally abhorred. Young men who found a red ear of corn were allowed by custom (more American Indian than English) to kiss any women they chose, leading to predictable excesses and lawsuits. What is more surprising is that the magistracy displayed a certain degree of latitude in indictment and in sentencing, either because leniency is often the best way of maintaining hegemony or because Puritan theology contained a sophisticated conception of sin as a condition of the person, rather than as a proscribed set of behaviors.

Nathaniel Hawthorne was right about the problems of the maypole at Marymount—indeed, there was a riot in Middlesex when one was erected—but he was probably wrong about the gray joylessness that appeared in its place. We know that Puritans sang, danced, and drank and that ministers were tolerant of secular music and approving of man's dominion over fish and fowl as expressed in hunting. It was in fact a passionate society; the problem was that passion could so easily become lasciviousness.

Over the course of the eighteenth century, the practice of keeping "holy watchfulness" over neighbors' behavior eroded. Increasing geographical mobility militated against social control by patriarchs or community, and a number of studies have charted the changes brought on by a growing population, land shortages, and the search for new opportunities. New kinds of secular information and enjoyment were prized under such conditions. In addition, as historian William Rorabaugh has shown, plentiful supplies of both domestically produced grain spirit and imported rum affected both work and leisure pursuits.

In the towns, the mercantile elite threw off much of the productivist ethos that had bound its more religious forebears. By mid century, most cities held formal assemblies for the wealthy, and even Boston established regular social evenings for dancing and music after 1740. Charleston's Saint Cecilia Society founded the first subscription ball in 1762. The arrival of theatrical performances open to all sections of the public, however, formed the most distinctive change in entertainment in the towns. One Richard Hunter, sometime between 1699 and 1702, petitioned the corporation of the City of New York to permit him to stage a play, though there is little evidence that the show actually opened. Other bands of players occasionally performed in mid-Atlantic and southern towns throughout the early eighteenth century, but it was not until a troupe of actors led by Lewis Hallam arrived in New York in 1752 that any American city witnessed something that approached a full season of theatrical entertainment. New York gained its first permanent theater, on John Street, in 1767, and Philadelphia, on Chestnut Street, in 1794; Boston, in 1794, opened the Federal Street Theatre after a riotous crowd protested the closing of an unlicensed performance.

Despite New Yorkers' habit of calling the John Street Theatre "Old Drury," after London's major playhouse licensed by royal letters patent, or their briefly renaming lower Broadway "The Mall," in the hope of creating a formal promenade, the scale of refined urban entertainments was minute compared to those conducted under aristocratic patronage in European capitals. The John Street Theatre could contain only four hundred people at a time, and no American place of entertainment could accommodate more than one thousand people until 1810.

In response to the growing secularization of leisure in the towns, local ministers initiated moral-reform societies and pushed for formal "sabbatarian" legislation (no secular amusement on Sunday), raising the pitch of their anti-entertainment rhetoric. The reformation of psalmody in New England after 1720, for instance, has been seen as a central exercise in ministerial control over unruly congregational practices, and the Massachusetts General Court's 1750 act banning "public stage-plays, interludes, and other theatrical entertainments" was only a timely (and perhaps desperate) restatement of codes already on the books. Yet the greatest ideological challenge to the rise in secular entertainment came from less traditional sources of authority. The arrival of the English evangelist George Whitefield and the spread of the Great Awakening of the 1740s emphasized in a new way the emotional and personal side of salvation and called for a more active monitoring of personal pleasure; evangelicals resurrected the criticism of many amusements as representing a waste of time and a dissolution of self-control. Only by the beginning of the twentieth century would the notion of consuming pleasures or products come to mean anything other than the using up of resources that would be better saved for later.

On the other hand, it is possible to claim that evangelical revivalism accelerated the creation of a national, popular culture. Both amusement entrepreneurs and evangelicals stressed American innovation over European tradition, and competition over orthodoxy. Whitefield's use of advance publicity, paid puffs, and cheap pamphlets set new standards for the infant commercial culture. Since evangelicals did not allow one's standing as a Christian to rest on baptism only, a succession of public declarations of faith was required. Revivals were seldom spontaneous; they had to be—and were—worked up using the most modern forms of promotion available. By the time of revivalist Charles Grandison Finney's sweeps through New York in the late 1820s, the performative values of a protracted meeting, with its use of the anxious bench, certainly matched the melodramatic productions that were being staged in the new urban theaters. The rhetoric traded between ministers and amusement entrepreneurs was so hostile because both helped forge, and claimed as their own, the new American public of social actors who could be equally "recreated," regardless of class or background. When in the 1840s ways were found to link piety and commercial entertainment, as in showman P. T. Barnum's moral plays or moralist Timothy Shay Arthur's temperance tales, a profitable and enduring amalgam was created that survives to the present.

The vogue for panoramas and dioramas after 1790 answered the call for innovative, virtuous ways to blend instruction and amusement. Some cultural leaders even believed that public virtue might well deserve public funding.

Through the revolutionary and early national periods, evangelical piety combined with notions of republican simplicity and virtue to steady the growth in commercial amusement. Suspicious of the theater's historical association with European courtly corruption and wary of the practical fact that the British officer class and monarchists were the theater's avid devotees, the Continental Congress banned troops from attending staged performances throughout the War for Independence. Local revolutionary assemblies were more direct; Philadelphia's patriotic leaders, for instance, issued edicts against the theater, card playing, and dancing assemblies. One positive result of this republican fervor was a general movement, as in the promotion of shape-note musical notation (a simplified notation that was readily comprehended), to make cultural learning less arcane and more available to the average citizen. Physician Benjamin Rush suggested that republican citizens should be directly educated through the eyes rather than by the classical learning of the past, leading artist Charles Willson Peale to experiment with "moving picture" and transparencies at his Philadelphia museum. The vogue for panoramas and dioramas after 1790 also answered the call for innovative, virtuous ways to blend instruction and amusement. Some cultural leaders even believed that public virtue might well deserve public funding. Merchant and philanthropist John Pintard petitioned the New York legislature to turn an old almshouse building into an institution encompassing the Tammany and Historical societies, an art gallery, studio space, and a music school. New York theatrical manager William Dunlap dreamed of a time when the theater, under state ownership and control, might be turned into an "engine" of virtue, and Boston's Joseph Haliburton presented a plan for an enormous octagonal superdome that would provide space for public functions such as Harvard commencements as well as a place where indigent women could sew clothes.

Despite these modest efforts to hitch cultural forms to the bandwagon of internal improvements, almost no state sponsorship of recreation occurred, except for the movement to establish city parks, until the Progressive Era. To an unusual degree, considering religious and political concern about unproductive activities, the free market was left to provide for all forms of recreation with hardly any legal intervention; for example, New York City possessed no formal system of theater licensing until 1823.

The Rise of Commercial Entertainment

Between 1800 and 1850 the customary patterns of leisure for most Americans underwent a transformation within a dynamic and unregulated commercial setting; the impact of a tremendous increase in population and improved transportation, as well as the complex of social changes that accompanied urbanization, came together to forge a new amusement culture. The change was more than just a matter of scale and involved a decided and perhaps irreversible change in vector. Everywhere amusement for profit grew at the expense of customary pastimes and introduced a division of leisure activities by social grouping as marked as that of labor.

Although the innovation in recreational forms began in the cities, social change, and awareness of change, must have been most dramatic in rural society. The new turnpikes brought many more itinerant troupes of performers and sundry shows to farming regions, making their people's acquaintance with commercial amusement something more than just a seasonal experience. By 1829, according to Philip Jordan, the National Road was carrying several good-sized caravans of living animals and skilled performers, and the Mississippi and Allegheny rivers had flatboat theaters in operation before that date. Scott Martin has found that even in the communities of deepest rural Pennsylvania, entertainments were being provided after 1820. Harvest festivals, for instance, began to incorporate point-to-point horse racing with organized betting, in violation of a state ban on such equestrian contests. The arrival of planned agricultural fairs may offer the best way to date local changes in amusement practices. Promoter and agriculturalist Elkanah Watson organized the first formal fair for Massachusetts in 1810, which, though it professed an educational mission, immediately attracted a range of booths offering liquor, performances, and food. Most counties in the Northeast and Middle Atlantic regions had regularly scheduled fairs by the late 1820s, and the South developed its state fairs through the 1830s. These developments meant that itinerant showmen could now plan on having routes, audiences, and profits.

While there continued to be communitywide activities, a host of voluntary associations and orders now provided organized amusement specifically for their membership. The number of Masonic lodges multiplied tenfold between 1780 and 1820, and after 1820 the vogue for incorporating literary, singing, and philosophical societies brought new kinds of cultural knowledge to the countryside while at the same time further eroding whatever commonality of leisure existed.

The meaning of such changes for rural society remains to be charted. Studies of popular amusement beyond the cities are still few and far between, though there exists a wealth of information to be mined in the many county histories published at the turn of the last century. There is no general work on popular recreation for the antebellum period equivalent in its range and seriousness to Robert Malcolmson's study of leisure activities in England. Nevertheless, it is clear that the commercialization of recreation helped to differentiate the world of work from the pursuit of leisure. Though frolics and bees continued well into the nineteenth century, especially among the poor, the arrival of commercial amusement at the taverns and the fairs no doubt lessened their appeal and adjusted their frame of meaning. Recreation no longer oscillated within the rhythms of work but was to gain its own place in the commercial setting. Further, the same movement that lifted much entertainment out of its earlier community setting also allowed for a privatization of leisure pursuits. The advent of mass-produced musical instruments and sheet music allowed people to narrow their social sphere of entertainment rather than take their pleasures at increasingly anonymous sites of public performance. Parlor theatricals became popular within middle-class households after 1830, at the same time that the commercial theater gained a large working-class patronage.

The transformation in the scale and vector of commercial culture in the towns is most evident in the theater. As late as 1820, New York had only one theater, the Park, which was opened in 1798 by Lewis Hallam and John Hodgkinson to replace the John Street Theatre. In 1850, New York possessed six legitimate theaters operating during the winter season, four summer gardens, and at least sixty other places of minor amusement. Even Pittsburgh, which still had a population under fifty thousand at mid century, claimed eleven places of commercially staged entertainment, as well as nine bookstores and four music shops. Chicago gained its first theater in 1847, with eight more opening before 1860. Whatever index is examined, the increase in commercial staged amusement outpaced the growth rates in urban population.

Moreover, the cost of access to the expanding world of popular entertainment decreased as the century progressed. In 1820, admission to major American theaters usually cost one dollar for the boxes, seventy-five cents for the pit, and fifty cents for the upper gallery, prices that excluded all those below the ranks of regularly employed skilled artisans. By 1850, admission prices had been generally cut by half, despite inflation. All theaters, except for those offering opera and other costly spectaculars, then held to a scale of "fifty cents top." Entrance to the minor forms of minstrelsy, pantomime, and variety could be gained for as little as five pennies. High volume and low admission prices became the surest formula for success; elaborate subscription plans, which had supported America's first theaters, gave way to cash taken at the door or at ticket outlets distributed throughout the cities. The era of the common man, at leisure and in politics, had arrived.

This impressive expansion in the market for what was, by the Civil War, termed "the show business" was also dependent upon an ever-broadening range of amusements offered. As with other forms of commercial enterprise, curious divisions of labor and specializations occurred within the entertainment field. The late-eighteenth-century stage had hosted all manner of performance: tragedy, comedy, vocal and dance acts, sleight of hand, and equestrian dramas and other animal acts. All these were performed before a socially heterogeneous audience distributed within the auditorium according to rank and degree; the wealthy families occupied the boxes, younger elite men sat on benches in the pit, and the common folk crowded into the inexpensive upper galleries. During the summer, when the indoor theaters closed because of the heat, a similar mixture of performance and audience could be found in the summer gardens. By 1800, New York possessed two such gardens specializing in musical performances, fireworks, and transparencies.

Between 1820 and 1850, admission prices to American theaters had generally been cut by half, so that all theaters aside from those offering opera and other costly spectaculars held to a scale of "fifty cents top."

In both theaters and gardens, the irregular performance values issuing from the stage were matched by the untidy behavior of all sections of the audience. Before about 1830, a "long run" seldom lasted more than a few days, and it was not unusual for stock actors to perform in six different plays over a week. An evening at the theater included a "double bill" of a tragedy and a comedy separated by an entr'acte of a vocal or choreographic nature. Though performances rarely ended much before midnight, customers seldom felt it necessary to sit through the entire evening's presentation, as the house bars were open all evening and one could also secure a pass to visit neighboring hostelries. A constant shuffling among the audience, together with the ad-libbing of the actors, audible prompts from the wings, and outright disasters, such as might occur when an elephant urinated into the orchestra pit, added to the excitement. Since the performers themselves hardly presented a finished piece, the audience felt free to add its own interpolations of original wit and local allusion. It also felt entitled to close the performance down altogether by hissing and throwing oranges, chairs, and other projectiles if the management departed from customary practice or if the featured actor made unpatriotic statements. At least five British actors had their American tours terminated by such interference between 1825 and 1850. Under these conditions one can understand why actors deferred to the audience as their patrons and masters.

After about 1825, however, as the towns began to sustain more than one permanent theater, both sides of this audience/performance equation changed. In New York, which has always possessed the most active market in commercial recreation, the new Bowery Theatre, opened in 1826, began to specialize in lively melodramatic plays, in contrast to those presented at the Park, which continued to stage Shakespeare and genteel British comedy. By 1830 the Bowery had become known not only for its distinctive staging, which incorporated all the latest technology, but also for the raucous artisanal audiences who flocked to its presentations. Observers invariably tagged the most active section of the Bowery crowd as "Byronic" because of its appreciation of the daring, manly feats on stage and its overtly republican interjections. In its new popular form, melodrama presented a general social radicalism owing little to its "music and mime" origins in eighteenth-century France. No matter what the setting—gothic castles, republican Rome, or secluded forests—melodrama always specialized in male heroes who overcame the forces of nature, the state, or sheer evil. Most of the new American plays, including John Augustus Stone's *Metamora* (1829) and Henry M. Milner's *Mazeppa* (1831), featured a recognizably Jacksonian lead character who stumbled, drenched in blood, toward a magical resolution of injustice and inequality. By mid century, melodrama had become a byword for the merely popular, a theatrical form that pandered in its blood-and-thunder routines to the lowliest newsboy and mechanic. Foreign visitors were advised to avoid theaters other than the Park, and by 1840 most elite New Yorkers had relinquished their patronage of any staged drama.

As noted, there was nothing new about social distinction and exclusivity in the exercise of leisure, even in republican America. The gentry and mercantile elite had always spent their discretionary time in ways different from the common folk; indeed, only the elite possessed leisure of a nominally elevating kind, since others were bound to the world of daily work. Yet there are two aspects to the exercise of cultural distinction in the Jacksonian period that are strikingly novel. First, class separation in entertainment practices acquired a spatial reality in the growing cities. In New York, for instance, almost all of the new popular forms of amusement first appeared on the Bowery, in a narrow strip adjacent to the largest concentration of working-class housing. More-refined amusements followed their wealthy patrons out of the heavily congested commercial downtown into what then constituted the suburbs. Though this may be taken as a simple matter of real estate markets, a degree of planning was involved. For instance, the Astor family on occasion "seeded" its residential developments with low-cost leases for high cultural institutions to improve the social tone of the locale.

New forms of entertainment were also developed beyond the suburbs. Improved transportation led to a reconceptualization of the benefits of "nature," or rather allowed the temporary pursuit of older values celebrating the rural life. Wealthier New Yorkers, for example, developed and patronized a number of local resorts after 1810, especially Hoboken and the Rockaways, as Bostonians were to do at Nahant. Though such extraurban resorts initially attempted to offer relaxation in a pastoral setting, commerce soon moved in. By mid century Hoboken offered horse racing, ox roasts, fortune telling, and any number of spectaculars, such as a buffalo hunt staged by Barnum. As in the case of the theater, the wealthy largely abandoned these sites in the face of such popularization. By 1830 it was practical, and socially advantageous, to summer in the Berkshire hills in Massachusetts or in Newport, where one might hobnob with other regional elites or, in the case of Saratoga, with southern gentry as well. It has been estimated that upward of fifty thousand southerners vacationed annually at northern spa resorts in the decade before the Civil War, and the Yankee elite returned the flow by popularizing White Sulphur Springs, in West Virginia. As part of this discovery of extramural enjoyment, the seaside vacation was invented. Seawater had first been recommended by doctors for its therapeutic properties as a drink, but following aristocratic fashion, in which the nobility had followed the Prince Regent (later George IV) down to Brighton, polite Americans took to the surf. By the second decade of the nineteenth century, Far Rockaway, New York, and later Long Branch, New Jersey, featured bathing machines and other technologies for pleasurable paddling, such as devices to hide women's legs as they descend into the surf. The middle classes did not patronize coastal resorts much until after the Civil War.

Added to this spatial separation of recreation was the advent of new ethical and aesthetic claims for refined entertainments at the same time that the plebeians were gaining increasing access to all forms of dramatic and literary production. This movement to establish an ethical hierarchy in forms of entertainment was most marked in musical activity. Before about 1830, no American city had managed to sustain a permanent site for secular concert performances; the only regularly scheduled concerts featured sacred works, usually with a large choral component. In 1840, however, the Boston Academy of Music dispensed with its chorus and set about winning the support of the public for the classical secular canon centered on Beethoven. Behind this change in programming lay two assumptions about the nature of the Academy's public. First, the Academy could count on subscription support, for the first time, from a large sector of Boston's mercantile elite, including the Appletons, the Lawrences, and the Stoddards. Second, it claimed that the public attending the concerts possessed a certain discriminating taste. "Taste" indeed became a key word, shifting in meaning from an instant sensation, as in a taste of food, to an aesthetic understanding resident in a person. Concert music, claimed Samuel Eliot, the Academy's president, was no longer mere entertainment, something to be tasted occasionally; rather, music possessed a transcendent value that reached into the very soul of the listener and remained as part of that person's moral character. In one sense, since Eliot had trained to be a Unitarian minister, music became a necessary adjunct to formal religious experience.

Similar claims, redolent of German idealism, also issued from critics writing in the newly specialized musical and literary journals. Certain forms of music, poetry, and fiction apparently had an ethic of moral gravity, in contrast to the levity of the overtly popular amusements. In New York much ideological work was devoted to raising the opera out of the plane of amusement and into this sacralized sphere. Four attempts to found a permanent site for the opera after the notable arrival of the García troupe in 1825 failed until the opening of the Astor Place Opera House, with Astor family support, in 1847. The *New York Herald* noted that this opera house was the "first authentic organization of the upper classes . . . of the city." Yet, for those involved in the enterprise, the elite character of the patronage was not as important as their claim that opera, unfettered by a literal understanding, could ascend to a plane of moral purity untouched by the topicality of local theater.

Enthusiastic critics of music and opera claimed to be in tune with Jacksonian democracy to the extent that the common man was supposedly amenable to taste and cultivation, something eighteenth-century gentry might not have acknowledged or thought desirable. However, in practice the price of entry into the world of refined taste was high, and the social distance between self-consciously artistic performances and the popular stage broadened over the second quarter of the century. Opera houses and concert halls were the first performance spaces to introduce numbered seating and uniformed ushers and to demand a sense of decorum among the audience. Male patrons were expected to remove their hats (by 1830), refrain from eating, and withhold their applause until the end of the act. Music and opera, as well as Shakespearean tragedies, required an aesthetic sanctity and coherence that could not be violated by audience members shifting or gesticulating in their seats—behavior in which all social classes had engaged before 1830. Some critics, such as Walt Whitman, continued to dream of a genuinely popular operatic and concert life in America, yet by the Civil War most cultural nationalists had relinquished their fond hopes for a progressive elevation of taste through such forms. Taste might indeed improve, yet it was thought unlikely to reach deep down into the mass of society. Instead, the career of taste gravitated toward formal education, as American colleges after 1840 began to incorporate musical instruction and the study of contemporary literature into classical notions of humanistic education, taking what had been undergraduate enthusiasms and making them part of a broader understanding of cultivated character. Indeed, by the Civil War, the word "culture" was vying in popularity with "virtue" to describe the central principle of a civilized society.

Urban Popular Culture

While new notions of high cultural attainment were being developed in the domestic parlors and concert and opera houses of the urban elite, the vernacular, urban amusements were also being cut loose from their traditional moorings. Inexpensive places of public resort, especially saloons, increased dramatically after 1820. Bars and hotels set aside spaces for an ever-changing mix of music, dance, fantoccini (a form of puppet show), legerdemain, and ventriloquism. At the same time, genres that had been floating within the mixed offerings of the late-eighteenth-century stage also won their own dedicated sites. An inexpensive menagerie and hippodrome opened on the Bowery in 1833 for animal acts, and two halls to display dramatic panoramas opened a year later. There was little innovation in this embryonic variety entertainment, however, until the depression of 1837, during which the older tradition of the "free and easy," in which the landlord supplied free modest entertainment in hopes of increasing the bar trade, became reenergized and gave rise to new forms. Patrons were now invited to give their own renditions of native songs, to try their hand at feats of skill, or to provide other impromptu performances. In New York, for the 1841 season at the once-genteel Vauxhall Garden, an energetic manager named P. T. Barnum advertised "Grand Trials of Skill at Negro Dancing" and asked the public to witness enactments of such city types as "The Fireman," "The Fulton Market Roarer," and "The Catherine Market Screamer." Prizes for amateur slack-rope-walking and beauty contests rounded out the bill. Barnum and others thus began to appro-

An inexpensive menagerie and hippodrome opened on the Bowery in 1833 for animal acts, and two halls to display dramatic panoramas opened a year later.

priate, at very low cost, entertainments that had previously had their life in the streets and markets of the cities. Through the 1840s, various ethnic and local acts such as "Dutch" (German), Irish, and Bowery b'hoy sketches were transferred onto the commercial stage.

The most notable innovation of the period, however, was the rise of "negro" characterizations. Dressing up in blackface was not new to the antebellum era; indeed, the slave lyric had been a feature of sentimental drama in England during the late eighteenth century. After about 1820, however, at the same time that melodrama was becoming the dominant tragic mode in popular theater, a new kind of blackface appeared as a comic entr'acte in which subversive dandy figures—Zip Coon, Jim Crow, and Dandy Jim—poked fun at the enthusiasms of the day. In the hands of gifted actors like Thomas D. Rice these occasional sketches were extended into small-scale operettas such as *Oh, Hush!* (1833) and *Bone Squash* (1835). Finally, during the 1837 panic, as theater prices plummeted, minstrelsy proper arrived, in the form of multipart olio entertainment usually performed by at least four actors; credit for the first true minstrel troupe is usually given to the Christy's Minstrels' act at New York's Branch Hotel in 1843. By 1846, an old Bowery free and easy named the Melodeon became the first specialized "Ethiopian opera house," and through the Civil War blackface minstrelsy remained the most popular urban staged entertainment.

The dimensions of minstrelsy's popularity are, however, easier to chart than its meaning. Scholars have argued over whether the form was simply racist at its

Minstrelsy became a popular form of entertainment during the mid to late nineteenth century. White entertainers dressed up in blackface and poked fun at enthusiasms of the day.

root or stood in opposition of mainstream culture as a form of commercial charivari in which social hierarchy was turned on its head. In addition, there are varied opinions on what blackface owed to an authentic urban black culture, by way of dance forms and vocalizations, or how the predominantly white male audiences may have understood the portrayals of boisterous, sexually charged "black" figures.

Eric Lott's recent work promises to bring these diverging emphases into better and more sophisticated alignment. On the one hand, much of the fun of minstrelsy undoubtedly came from viewing the buffoonery of "inferior" people; the audience laughed "at" black people, and the performers certainly played up the distance between themselves and the personae they characterized. Yet overlaid onto this social distancing were attempts by the black characters to ape and critique the pretensions of white gentlefolk. Minstrel routines specialized in mock lectures on phrenology and lampoons of operatic stagings; in this frame of reference audiences laughed "with" the blackface performers at the claims of the cultivated tradition. Minstrelsy was a curious admixture of sympathy and distortion; it worked within a series of confusions that contributed to its continuing popularity.

The difficulties in recovering the meaning of popular forms such as minstrelsy will no doubt occupy scholars for years to come, especially since these entertainments gained their "life" only in the course of a performance before an audience that will never return. The best one can do is to emphasize their place within an expanding landscape of popular amusements and how they attracted or expressed the sentiments of a particular sector of the population. For while so much of respectable culture, especially as it unfolded in a host of polite monthlies after 1840, specialized in the domestic, the pious, and the literal, much of the popular stage worked with the aggressive, the transgressive, and the metaphorical.

Along with melodrama and minstrelsy, a third popular stage genre, travesty, was largely supported by working-class audiences. By 1850 almost all cities had a theatrical house that regularly offered "burlesques" and "extravaganzas." As the name suggests, travesty worked by violating and mocking theatrical convention. For instance, in John Brougham's *Hamlet* (1843) the tragic hero had to contend with a blue fly buzzing around his head while he asked the question, "A bee, or not a bee?" Any genre or enthusiasm could be cut down to size: Gaetano Donizetti's opera appeared as *Lucy Did Lamm Her Moor*, and Fanny Elssler's balletic *La Tarantule* ended up as *La Mosquito*. The results were so laughable that their effect hardly depended upon any exacting familiarity with the original. Nevertheless, like minstrelsy, travesty had to appeal to a certain sense of cultural entitlement and knowledge among the working classes. Travesty stood the revised cultivated tradition on its head and returned it to the popular audience; it continued the vitality of the stock company's relationship to a vigorous audience at the same time that high cultural production demanded a new decorum.

One further feature of travesty indicates that more than just class referents played a part in the making of this new popular culture. All female lead characters were played by men, and even a deadly serious figure such as Lady Macbeth found herself speaking in double entendres and innuendo (indeed, her unruliness was hinted to have issued from a lack of sexual relations with the king). Thus, as in other areas of American society, the rhetoric of gender had a central role in framing popular amusement. The culture of the Bowery and other popular entertainment zones was overwhelmingly male in character, whereas much of the monthly press and the lecture circuits placed the "woman's influence" at the center of moral value. Popular stage culture was so insistently masculine in its themes that it is tempting to see it as the mirror image to "the feminatization of American culture" as outlined by Ann Douglas.

Demography and geography partly account for this male modality. It has been estimated that from 1840 to 1860, at least 30 percent of male, urban workers lived outside regular family arrangements in northeastern cities and that this work force was unusually young compared to a standard distribution across age groups. The wards adjacent to the Bowery contained the largest concentration of boardinghouses in the city. The new spaces for working-class leisure—bars, theaters, and billiard halls—provided informality and conviviality for those with modest means and were firmly linked with older forms of masculine sociability. The Bowery Theatre, for instance, maintained its own militia company and band, and at least four New York volunteer fire companies had portraits of theaters and actors gracing their engines.

Fire-company antics, staged fistic duels, minstrel quarrels, and "fireladdy" plays all stressed physical prowess to such an extent that a demographic account seems hardly sufficient. The area around the Bowery produced a version of the upper-class "sporting life," though with a distinctly plebeian caste. Almost all of the traditional rural sports, save fox hunting, were incorporated into the urban scene. Mass pigeon shooting, rabbit coursing, gander pulling, cockfighting, and ratting, though banned in many cities through the 1830s, gained new commercial life. At least three animal pits in the backrooms of bars in lower Manhattan were in regular operation throughout the 1840s, untouched by police interference. It was the proliferation of these rough sports in urban settings that led to the formation of the ASPCA, with its own independent police powers of enforcement, in 1866.

Minstrel routines specialized in mock lectures on phrenology and lampoons of operatic stagings; in this frame of reference, audiences laughed "with" the blackface performers at the claims of the cultivated tradition.

Some scholars have seen this urban extension of rural sports as a form of compensation for a sense of power lost through the immiserization, or, the deskilling of artisanal work. Yet many leading figures on the sporting scene were drawn from regulated public trades, notably butchering, that had not experienced the introduction of machine technology or the breakdown of the apprenticeship system. Rough sports, dares, and physical prowess proved an effective way of claiming and appropriating public power and of rubbing shoulders with upper-class aficionados.

One of the most noted, though unexamined, features of the period is the way in which mass party politics and the popular amusement industry emerged in lockstep, often sharing the same personnel, constituencies, and routines. Part of the genius of early Jacksonian democracy was the way in which it absorbed traditional festivities such as the barbecue and recast them as techniques for securing loyalty and as demonstrations of popular support. In their "log cabin and hard cider" campaign of 1840, the Whigs outdistanced the Democrats in appropriating older communal customs; throughout the country, Whigs encouraged their supporters to raise an emblematic "barn" and to treat participants and onlookers to cider. Though these scenes referred to ideas of community, their significance was now totally changed, as ironically noted in William Sidney Mount's genre picture "Cider Making the Old-Fashioned Way." Such jubilees no longer celebrated community effort but rather partisan support; indeed, the lineaments of party affiliation reached deep into those areas of public life once known for neighborliness and cohesion as rural taverns declared allegiance and urban parades, illuminated arches, and liberty poles became rallying points for the faithful. Scott Martin has found that the party organization of leisure occurred within even the rural Pennsylvania German population.

Popular politics shared personnel as well as routines with the infant entertainment industry. In 1836, the famous American actor Edwin Forrest was asked by the New York "loco foco" wing of the Jacksonian Democrats to run for the Senate. That he declined the nomination is of less importance than the notion that an actor was this early seen as a "natural" for high political office. Both actors and politicians had begun to see their road to success not in patronage but in popular acclaim; both worked the crowd and possessed a vision of a career that moved on to larger and larger "stages." In New York the "platform" performances in Tammany Hall were judged to be so similar to the melodramatic stage that it was easy to move between the promotion of politics and the arena of amusement. At least three figures who had been free-and-easy proprietors on the Bowery during the same time as Barnum—Tom Maguire, David Broderick, and George Wilkes—later went on to have successful, if tortuous, careers as politicians and promoters in California.

Entertaining the Middle Class

While this account has so far stressed a bifurcation in commercial entertainment between the growing vernacular tradition and the cultivated tradition—between what was later termed "high" and "low"—in retrospect, the development of a middle ground of leisure activities, neither overly refined nor rowdy, is the perhaps most significant development in entertainment over the antebellum period. For every elite opera attendee or raucous Bowery b'hoy, there must have been many more who assented to Horace Greeley's pleas in the *Tribune* for earnest self-improvement. By 1850 almost every town with over ten thousand people possessed a mechanics' institute or lyceum, and most of these lecture sites were integrated into circuits, allowing intellectual luminaries such as Ralph Waldo Emerson to garner over ten thousand dollars per annum in fees. Lesser "professors" circulated promotional materials that promised illustrated talks on every subject from foreign travel to the reproduction of bees. On average, New York City offered five lectures every week night at mid century, in halls whose total capacity matched that of the commercial theaters. The centrality of the lecture in the formation of American culture has yet to gain the appropriate attention of scholars, despite the fact that writers, no matter their field, were able to gain more cash from lecturing than from book publication and often, like Mark Twain, viewed the former as a way of achieving the latter.

The social parameters of this middle ground of popular entertainment can be expressed in a simple formula: the absence of alcohol and the presence of families. The temperance movement, which possessed a much broader social base than abolitionism, profoundly shaped popular culture through the 1840s and after. Unlike earlier moral-reform and temperance societies, which were led by the established clergy, the Washington Temperance Society, which was active after 1840, promised a reconciliation of social advocacy with popular cultural forms. The Washingtonians did not demand an instant conversion in Christ or rely on the distribution of pamphlets and home visits but rather enticed potential pledges through torchlight parades, song recitals, and highly dramatic testimonial lectures, such as those offered by temperance lecturer John Gough. They realized, in other words, that the new commercial culture centered on saloons and cheap theaters had to be reformed by militantly public means. Most towns possessed a temperance hotel and an ice cream salon by 1850, and at least two genres—the temperance play and the singing "happy" family such as the Hutchinsons (1843)—became viable forms in their own right on the regular stage. W. H. Smith's *The Drunkard* (1844, revived in 1850) was the first play in America to achieve a run of one hundred consecutive performances. In the field of literature, both Walt Whitman and Timothy Shay Arthur gained reputations as temperance storytellers, although they had no formal connection to any temperance organization.

No career better illustrates this conscious fusing of domestic piety; temperance, and popular entertainment into a successful amalgam than that of P T. Barnum. After offering distinctly lowbrow entertainment, plus drink, at the Vauxhall Gardens, in 1842 Barnum moved downtown, buying the old Scudder's American Museum at a Depression price and turning it into arguably the most active site for amusement in the United States. In terms of style and audience, some of the Bowery traveled with him to this respectable location. Barnum festooned the front of the museum with glaring transparencies illustrating its permanent attractions. He placed a powerful Drummond (lime-burning) light on the roof, thereby dividing New York, according to guidebooks, into "above" and "below" Barnum's. He also employed a wind and brass ensemble to play on the balcony in hopes of luring customers inside. No building had so insistently imposed itself on an American city before.

Inside, Barnum employed a series of "transient attractions" such as the Feegee Mermaid, General Tom Thumb, and bearded ladies the likes of which had been the mainstay of itinerant showmen for decades. Now, however, they were bound to a "museum" complex that also claimed to educate citizens in the wonders of natural creation. The Linnean classifications that had informed American museum arrangements from Peale's museum onward were punctuated with a host of oddities, so that the typical oscillated with the idiosyncratic.

These changes produced almost a travesty of the museum form, yet Barnum's efforts were also directed at the creation of a moral environment in which all people, regardless of gender or class, could feel at home. In 1844 he opened a "lecture room" intended for "all those who disapprove of the dissipations, debaucheries, profanity, vulgarity, and other abominations, which characterize our modern theatres." into this hall he imported the proven vehicles of the temperance cause, such as singing families (eleven in all) and Smith's *The Drunkard*; he also allowed Shakespeare and minstrelsy "shorn of their objectionable features." The most remarkable innovation lay not in the forms but in their mode of presentation; in 1846 he invented the idea of the continuous performance to attract a new public, which he tagged "the family audience." The terms of entry into this new public were generous, yet exact: no alcohol or profanity were to be allowed.

Barnum's unending search for the largest, though respectable, audience found its greatest success in his management of Jenny Lind's tour in 1850–1852. Many European stars had traveled to the United States in search of cash before, yet almost all had fallen prey, in an era of heightened cultural nationalism, to their Old World, and potentially corrupt, origins. Dancer Fanny Elssler (1840) was criticized for her "aristocratic" sexual relations; violinist Ole Bull (1845) apparently pandered to the elite; and tragedian William Charles Macready was driven from the country by the Astor Place riot of 1849 for making antirepublican statements. In Lind, however, Barnum found a perfect object for his promotional genius, for though she possessed a fine operatic voice, she had developed a reputation for piety, charity, and republican sentiments made all the greater in Barnum's advance publicity. After her arrival, he carefully steered his valuable property to all the important New York institutions in a conscious orchestration of the city's competing cultures. He restricted the elite's access to her while allowing fire companies to parade before her hotel, and to further forestall accusations of favoritism he came up with the idea of auctioning the tickets to the concerts (of course, he also sold tickets to the auction).

By the standards of the time, the Lind tour was a great success, producing over half a million dollars in revenue for Barnum alone. Above all, it proved that mammoth productions need neither offend the respectable nor pander to the rowdy. Lind's image and her repertoire remained constant throughout her tour. She brought assured standards of production and moral value to a host of local stages. Lind carried an almost religious aura that demanded the use of an older religious word—"celebrity." The advent of such international celebrities, together with touring musical virtuosos such as Ole Bull and Henri Vieuxtemps, set new professional standards for entertainment for the whole nation. By the Civil War, localisms had become merely a mark of the vernacular, and ethnic acts appeared not as the product of genuine immigrant cultures but as a way of recycling cultural differences for national market returns.

By 1860, then, most American cities possessed some form of commercial entertainment that would be recognizable to us today—large stages with long runs, concerts for the masses, multiple sites for variety acts—while rural areas experienced increasing acquaintance with all forms of commercial pleasure, usually shaped by the standards and tastes of the eastern cities. The creation of this amusement landscape was a matter of some self-congratulation. Hawthorne observed in his *Passages from the French and Italian Notebooks* (1871) that in contrast to Europe, where amusements were staged by the aristocracy to blind people to the nobility's exercise of power, Americans crowding to their entertainments reflected the true spirit of democracy in action. This coupling of entertainment and democracy provided the dominant, positive story of American popular culture as documented by the American-studies movement after World War II.

However, the expansion of commercial amusement was not the simple unfolding of the promissory note of democracy. At every level, entertainment reflected and informed the tensions of race, gender, and class as the United States moved into the industrial age. Doubt could also be raised about the extent to which such developments were restricted to America, offering another case of American exceptionalism, for there was little in the popular forms themselves that was uniquely native. At least 80 percent of the staged dramas followed European scripts, and as late as 1850, 30 percent of "American" actors were British-born. Even something as apparently homegrown as minstrel and Yankee acts were quickly incorporated into a transatlantic repertoire of popular culture. Thomas D. Rice returned triumphant and wealthy from an 1837 display of "breakdown" dancing in London, the Hutchinson family claimed to have netted $30,000 from a European tour in 1845, and P. T. Barnum was the only entertainment figure to have secured three private audiences with an amused Queen Victoria. Laments about the current American hegemony over popular culture in the world have to be tempered by the observation that the appetite for any national novelty was there from the beginning.

The American case does appear exceptional, however, in that the domain of the "popular" spread out in an unusually free market. Much commercial amusement in England and France, because of the active power of the state, was thrown at its inception into the arms of working-class dissent. Lacking established institutions of cultural certification and state censorship, American popular culture has been left to draw its own boundaries between the respectable and the prurient, in a constant series of negotiations and contests as to what falls within such categories. Perhaps the very lack of state authority, rather than the informing presence of old Puritan traditions, accounts for the continued energy Americans expend on issues raised by the morality of popular amusement. The early nineteenth century left an especially strong legacy of linkage between respectability and the domestic sphere of feminine and family influence. No matter how free the market, issues of sexual representation therefore still remain matters of enduring public, and occasionally state, concern.

[See also African American Music; The City; Concert Music; Humor and Comedy; Mass Culture and Its Critics; Nightlife; Parades, Holidays and Public Rituals; Popular Literature; Popular Music before 1950; Print and Publishing; Theater and Musical Theater; Urban Cultural Institutions; Urban Parks.]

BIBLIOGRAPHY

General Works

Bode, Carl. *The Anatomy of American Popular Culture, 1840–1861* (1959). Path-breaking study.

Cunningham, Hugh. *Lecture in the Industrial Revolution* (1980). On Britain.

Dulles, Foster Rhea. *A History of Recreation: America Learns to Play* (1965). Useful survey.

Malcolmson, Robert. *Popular Recreations in English Society, 1700–1850* (1973). Though about England, it contains many useful ideas about general changes in patterns of recreation.

Rader, Benjamin. *American Sports: From the Age of Folk Games to the Age of Televised Sports.* 2d ed. (1990).

Colonial and Early National Periods

Breen, T. H. "Horses and Gentlemen: The Cultural Significance of Gambling Among the Gentry of Virginia." *William and Mary Quarterly*, 34 (1977).

Breen, T. H., and Stephen Foster. "Social Cohesion in Seventeenth-Century New England." *Journal of American History* 60 (1973–1974).

Hall, David D. "The Mental World of Samuel Sewall." In *Saints and Revolutionaries: Essays on Early American History*, edited by David D. Hall, John M. Murrin, and Thad W. Tate (1984).

Isaac, Rhys. *The Transformation of Virginia* (1982).

Jable, J. Thomas. "Pennsylvania's Early Blue Laws: A Quaker Experiment in the Suppression of Sport and Amusement, 1682–1740." *Sports History* 1 (1974).

Selement, George. "The Meeting of Elite and Popular Minds at Cambridge, New England, 1638–1645." *William and Mary Quarterly* 41 (1984).

Silverman, Kenneth. *A Cultural History of the American Revolution: Painting, Music, Literature, and the Theatre in the Colonies and the United States from the Treaty of Paris to the Inauguration of George Washington, 1763–1789.* 2d ed. (1987).

Smith, Billy Gordon. *The "Lower Sort": Philadelphia's Laboring People, 1750–1800* (1990).

Thompson, Roger. *Sex in Middlesex: Popular Mores in a Massachusetts County, 1649–1699* (1986).

Ulrich, Laurel Thatcher. *Good Wives: Image and Reality in the Lives of Women in Northern New England, 1650–1750* (1991).

The Nineteenth Century

Adelman, Melvin L. *A Sporting Time: New York City and the Rise of Modern Athletics, 1820–1870* (1986).

Buckley, Peter G. "To the Opera House: Culture and Society in New York City, 1820–1860." Ph.D. diss., State University of New York at Stony Brook, 1984.

Click, Patricia. "Leisure in the Upper South in the Nineteenth Century: A Study of Trends in Baltimore, Norfolk, and Richmond." Ph.D. diss., University of Virginia, 1980.

Danforth, Brian J. "Hoboken and the Affluent New Yorker's Search for Recreation, 1820–1860." *New Jersey History* 95 (1977).

Davis, Susan G. *Parades and Power: Street Theatre in Nineteenth-Century Philadelphia* (1986).

Douglas, Ann. *The Feminization of American Culture* (1977).

Faler, Paul. "Cultural Aspects of the Industrial Revolution: Lynn, Mass., Shoe-makers and Industrial Morality, 1826–1860." *Labor History 15* (1976).

Goodman, Paul. *Toward a Christian Republic: Antimasonry and the Great Transition in New England, 1826–1836* (1988).

Grimsted, David. *Melodrama Unveiled: American Theater and Culture, 1800–1850* (1968).

Jordan, Philip D. *The National Road* (1948).

Levine, Lawrence W. *Highbrow/Lowbrow: The Emergence of Cultural Hierarchy in America* (1988).

Lott, Eric. "The Seeming Counterfeit: Racial Politics and Early Blackface Minstrelsy," *American Quarterly* 43 (1991).

Martin, Scott, "Leisure in Southwestern Pennsylvania, 1800–1850." Ph.D. diss., University of Pittsburgh, 1990.

Wiggins, David K. "Good Times on the Old Plantation: Popular Recreations of the Black Slave in the Antebellum South, 1810–1860."*Sports History* 4 (1977).

— PETER G. BUCKLEY

POPULAR LITERATURE

The concept of "popular literature" as one half of a bifurcated literary universe emerged in the United States in the second half of the nineteenth century and became widely acknowledged in the twentieth. In this view "popular literature" designates the reading tastes of the common reader, "the masses," in contrast with the "serious" literature of an educated, cultured elite. Popular literature under this rubric is mass entertainment; serious or elite literature is art. Popular literature is distinguished from literary art both quantitatively (its greater audience) and qualitatively (its dependence on formula, on sensationalism, on stereotype, on accessibility); from the standpoint of sociology, it reaches a significantly wider range of social and economic classes. So considered, popular literature is the product of a culture industry; elite literature is the product of genius. Through the 1960s this division was accepted by most cultural historians across the political spectrum; they disagreed not in describing "popular literature" but in interpreting its uses. Conservatives damned popular literature for its degradation of taste; leftists, particularly those involved with or influenced by the Frankfurt school, damned it as an element in a manipulative, hegemonic "mass culture"; liberals celebrated it for contributing to a democratic culture within which individuals chose from a range of options according to their personal tastes.

Complications of the simple division between high and low, popular and elite, have often been noted: the popular writing that is granted literary merit (Mark Twain's fiction is the classic case in the United States) or the literary novel that becomes a best-seller (John Updike's novels are recent examples). But the division itself has become increasingly problematic, as literary scholars and historians have shifted their attention from aesthetics to the material conditions of book production and to the experience of reading. "Popular literature" has come to signify less a body of writing to be studied than a cluster of issues to be investigated: the complex relationships through history among authors, publishers, texts, readers, and the modes of production, distribution, and marketing. In order to reflect its current status as a field of study, "popular literature" ought perhaps to be written as "popular literature?" or, better yet, " 'popular'? 'literature'?"—the terms themselves often being the subject of investigation. On the one hand, to call into question the concept "literature" is to ask what distinguishes supposed literary texts from other kinds of writing—from daily journalism, private letters, personal journals, oral narratives. Such questioning challenges the distinction between "literature" and "popular fiction," with its assumption that writers of genius are somehow exempt from the pressures of the marketplace and the prevailing modes of production. It also challenges the privileged status of "literature" more generally, to the extent that some scholars have insisted that the study of popular literature ought to include not only best-selling novels and genre fiction but also posters, graffiti, T-shirt slogans, campaign buttons, billboards, the backs of cereal boxes—the entire universe of print that confronts us daily.

To call into question the concept of the "popular," on the other hand, is to raise the issue of whether literature is a popular medium at all. Through most of its history literature in whatever form has been relatively expensive, available, for economic reasons, to varyingly small portions of the population. Reading necessarily depends on literacy, which until the beginning of the nineteenth century, was largely restricted to an educated, prosperous, predominantly male elite. Most recently the supplanting of print by the electronic media as source of both entertainment and information has relegated literature increasingly to the margins of American culture.

Nonetheless, if understood as a relative rather than as an absolute term, popular literature has a long and important social history in the United States as the literature "of the people," in both the demographic and the political senses of that term. In its production popular literature has most fundamentally been "cheap" literature; in its consumption popular literature has usually served to entertain and to inform rather than to provide moral instruction or to elicit aesthetic appreciation (the primary criteria by which "serious" literature has been distinguished from "popular"). And in content it has been primarily fiction. A tradition of popular poetry can be traced from such writers as Lydia Sigourney and Henry Wadsworth Longfellow in the early to mid nineteenth century, through the newspaper poets (James Whitcomb Riley, Ella Wheeler Wilcox, Edgar Guest) in the late nineteenth and early twentieth centuries, to Rod McKuen and Judith Viorst most recently. But popular poets have been popular only in relation to other poets; even at its most popular, poetry's audience has been a fraction of that for fiction. Popular literature also includes a varied tradition in nonfiction ranging from devotional tracts and Indian captivity narratives in the colonial period, to political tracts before and during the Revolution, true-crime stories and populist economic treatises in the nineteenth century, celebrity biographies and self-help manuals in the twentieth. Nonfiction books have periodically outsold the fiction from the same period. The largest-selling book ever, next to the Bible, is Dr. Benjamin Spock's *Baby and Child* Care (thirty-nine million copies in print by 1989). In the early nineteenth century the *New England Primer* and Noah Webster's *American Spelling Book* were the greatest best-sellers after the Bible. Nonetheless, the hunger of "the masses" for fiction, which as recently as the late nineteenth century was a cause for intellectuals' condemnation, is basic to a historical understanding of the popular.

This essay, then, will focus chiefly on popular fiction. Its history in the United States entails not just a history of taste but also histories of printing and print technology, of literacy, of distribution and marketing, of postal and copyright laws, of permissiveness and censorship, of the profession of authorship, of reading and readers. Within these contexts the nature and most basic meaning of "popular literature" has changed over time. In the United States the period from the 1830s to the 1950s marks what might be considered the golden age of American popular literature, the time when printed fiction reached the broadest audience and figured most prominently in American lives. The period from the seventeenth century through the early national period marks a long prehistory, to this golden age; the decades following the 1950s have seen, paradoxically, the triumph of the "blockbuster" novel at a time when print has declined as a popular medium.

The Age of Scarcity: 1607–1830

The popular culture of early modern Europe, as documented by social historians, consisted of rural sports and urban amusements in which the common folk sought their private and public pleasures. "Popular" culture in this sense is virtually equivalent to "folk" culture;

Title page to Benjamin Banneker's Almanac, 1795. Almanacs, a popular form of literature in the colonial period, provided practical advice, calendars, proverbs, jokes and popular science.

that is, it was created by the people themselves for their own uses. To speak of the "popular literature" of early modern Europe is more problematic. While anyone could dance around a maypole, only a relative few wrote broadsides and chapbooks, and fewer yet printed them; more, yet still a small minority, could read them. Insofar as there was a "popular literature" in early modern Europe, it was a literature listened to in groups rather than read individually.

Within major constraints (Puritan restrictions in New England, reduced free time during periods of economic scarcity, the many necessities inherent in taming a wilderness), European popular culture crossed the Atlantic with the settlers of Massachusetts and Virginia in the seventeenth century. Faced with more pressing material needs, they brought few books with them; those they did bring were primarily religious or practical. That some of the founders brought as many as they did, and immediately began to import more, are the surprising facts. When John Harvard donated his personal library in 1636 to the college named for him in 1638, his collection numbered four hundred titles. Although the first printing press in the colonies was also established remarkably early, also in 1638, the majority of books read by Americans continued to be imported from England throughout the colonial period. But a vigorous colonial press nonetheless thrived. The first work printed in what is now the United States was a broadside, "The Freeman's Oath" (1639). The second was *An Almanacke for New England for the Year 1639.* In 1640 the first book was published, *The Whole Booke of Psalmes,* more commonly known as *The Bay Psalm Book* (sometimes identified as the first American best-seller). The literary production of the colonial press, in addition to such almanacs, broadsides, and religious tracts, included newspapers, medical handbooks, practical manuals of various kinds, "ready reckoners" (for computation), primers, hymnals, sermons, and chapbooks. Of these, almanacs, broadsides, and chapbooks can be considered, in relative terms, colonial America's popular literature. They were much cheaper than bound books, they were ephemeral (literally "read to pieces," as numerous commentators have noted), and they were the most widely read or listened to.

Almanacs and broadsides were local and topical, produced by a printer with a press and distributed, usually by peddlers, throughout the more or less immediate region. Almanacs, originally single sheets with eight pages to a side, began as practical guides—calendars and projections of the weather—but beginning in 1687 with the almanacs of John Tulley, they increasingly provided entertainment as well. Popular science and remarkable events, proverbs, and jokes, all copiously illustrated, were thrown together with useful facts to blur the distinction between information and entertainment. Broadsides (printed on one side of a single page) and broadsheets (printed on both sides) were abundantly produced in the colonies from the middle of the seventeenth century until the end of the eighteenth, when newspapers assumed their function. As a medium for information, broadsides carried official announcements, advertised the printer's inventory, recorded colonial laws, and commented on local events. After 1760 and through the Revolution, they became a primary source of information on political debates and major events. As entertainment, broadsides provided gossip, commentary on fashions, funeral eulogies, and news of more sensational sorts: slanderous attacks on various figures, confessions of criminals on the eve of execution, as well as lurid accounts of crimes, natural and unnatural disasters, and monstrosities. A small portion of the broadsides were written in verse, "literature" in the more conventional sense.

Chapbooks, finally—small (3.5 inches by 6 inches), paper-covered pamphlets, usually sixteen or thirty-two pages long, printed on coarse rag paper, often with crude woodcuts—were widely printed from the early eighteenth to the early nineteenth century. Chapbooks were the cheap books of the period and, as such, the forerunners of dime novels and inexpensive paperbacks. In content they ranged from devotional tracts to cookbooks and household manuals, to melodramatic tales of pirates and highwaymen. Songs, riddles, jokes, fortune-telling, and abridged versions of chivalric romances and the popular English novels of the day were printed in chapbooks. Because they were longer than almanacs and broadsides, and thus posed greater economic risk to the printer, the majority of chapbooks were imported from England up to the Revolution. But at least one native type, the Indian captivity narrative, was prominent among the colonial printers' offerings. In the case of both broadsides and chapbooks, even when the content was lurid or sensational, most of this writing remained essentially religious: captivity narratives, criminals' confessions, and descriptions of prodigies and portents were invariably presented as the workings of Providence.

Information on the culture and commerce of colonial printing is meager, and scarcer yet on ephemeral forms such as almanacs, broadsides, and chapbooks. Few copies exist today; titles often are known only through the surviving inventories and advertisements of a handful of printers. But it is nonetheless possible to sketch out the place of this popular literature in colonial and early national America, relative to the books that were available only to the most prosperous classes. It appears that about half of the males in New England were minimally literate (able to sign their name) in the middle of the seventeenth century, and nearly all by the end of the eighteenth; literacy was lower outside New England and among women. Given the possibility that the ability to read preceded the ability to write, these estimates may have to be revised upward, and the inability to read did not preclude access to print material transmitted orally. But whatever the precise figures, compared with the generations after 1830, reading played no large part in most colonial Americans' lives.

Access to print was limited. Although considerably less centralized than it would become after the triumph of industrialization, printing was more concentrated in New England than in the South, in major cities such as Boston, Philadelphia, and New York than in villages and the countryside. Imported books and pamphlets also were unevenly available. Distribution of books—chiefly through bookshops and peddlers (hawkers or chapmen)—was largely local, at best regional. Social libraries (with use of books restricted to members) began in the 1730s and circulating libraries (with books rented to the larger public) in the 1760s, but the first were prohibitively expensive for the majority, and both served chiefly the urban population in a nation that by the end of the eighteenth century was still 95 percent rural. The public library, did not become a significant institution until the 1830s.

And print was costly. According to Cynthia Z. and Gregory A. Stiverson, in mid-eighteenth-century Virginia an inexpensively bound book cost twice the daily wage of a common laborer. A shortage of rags for making paper continued to be a major problem well into the nineteenth century. Before the development of steam presses, rotary presses, and other mechanical improvements, printing was slow. Until the invention of stereotyping and electrotyping in the first half of the nineteenth century, later printings of books or pamphlets that sold well had to be completely recomposed and proofed again. All these factors contributed to the expense of books.

The high cost, small quantity, and limited access to print meant a popular culture that, according to Rhys Isaac (p. 233), was predominantly oral yet "contained within a book-defined cosmology"—that is, the information in books, preeminently the Bible, was available to common folk and shaped their consciousness. Even by the end of the eighteenth century, few families owned more than a few books: a Bible, an almanac, and perhaps a speller (Noah Webster's, most likely) or a devotional tract. Only 8 percent of the family libraries in a study of rural New England contained more than fourteen books. Thus the relative popularity of almanacs, broadsides, and chapbooks must be viewed within this context of scarcity. The so-called best-sellers of colonial America—primarily religious in orientation and probably printed as inexpensive chapbooks—can be characterized as "steady sellers," as opposed to the almanacs and broadsides that were more instantly popular and local in circulation, but short-lived. Lawrence C. Wroth notes (p. 40) that in 1766 Benjamin Franklin's press, assumed to be typical, printed books in editions of four hundred to five hundred copies, and broadsides in editions of two thousand to twenty-five hundred. Printings of almanacs ranged from ten thousand to sixty thousand.

Popular fiction began to reach a significant segment of the reading public only in the final quarter of the eighteenth century. The rise of popular fiction was tied to the emergence of a literate, largely urban, to some degree secularized middle class; diffusion of popular fiction throughout American society had to await the development of mass-production and mass-distribution technologies. As novels began to dominate popular reading taste, they were repeatedly attacked in intellectual journals as immoral, fallacious, and frivolous—the perennial disdain of the popular. By the beginning of the nineteenth century, reading remained the activity of an elite, but within these narrow limits a "popular" novel-reading public was emerging as the percentage of readers expanded. The rise of novel reading during this period meant less a transformation of popular literature, however, than a preview of the transformation that was to come.

The Age of Cheap Fiction: The 1830s to the 1950s

In the first half of the nineteenth century, the technology of printing was transformed, making this the most remarkable period in the entire history of print after the initial revolution of the fifteenth century. The building of an iron press in England in 1795 marked the beginning; American versions were developed over the first quarter of the new century. Steam-powered presses appeared in the 1820s, cylinder presses shortly after. Stereotyping was introduced in the United States in 1811, electrotyping in 1841—the major processes by which impressions were made from set type, so that subsequent editions could be made from the original plates. The first papermaking machine was patented in England in 1799; the first book printed on American machine-made paper appeared in 1820. The shortage of linen and rags for papermaking, which led to experiments with as many as five hundred alternative substances, was finally solved and put into practice around 1860 by the development of effective processes for making paper from wood pulp, of which American forests offered a seemingly limitless supply.

The best- and steady sellers of colonial America were primarily religious texts and probably printed as inexpensive chapbooks, in contrast to the almanacs and broadsides, which were more instantly popular but short-lived.

Thus was laid the industrial foundation for a massive proliferation of print beginning in the 1830s, and the centralization of publishing in a handful of northern cities. Nearly universal white literacy, the growth of a mercantile middle class and an upward-aspiring working class with tastes for entertaining fiction, the expansion of public schooling, and development of public libraries created vast audiences for the print that now could be produced more cheaply and abundantly. The United States remained a predominantly rural nation, 93 percent in 1830, 85 percent in 1850. And the local printer remained the chief source of print for small towns and the surrounding farms until mid century. But new technology, coupled with new social forces, led to the first mass-produced American popular literature in the 1830s and gave rise to the first large publishing companies, concentrated in New York, Boston, and Philadelphia. Beginning in the 1860s, comparable developments in transportation and distribution completed the creation of a truly national popular readership.

STORY PAPERS AND DIME NOVELS. Popular literature can be either widely read types of literature or widely read individual titles; this is the distinction today, for example, between Harlequin Books' romances and the latest best-seller by Stephen King or Judith Krantz. The print revolution in antebellum America produced popular literature of both kinds as the broadsides and chapbooks of the colonial period became the story papers and cheap novels of the nineteenth century.

This revolution began with the penny press in the 1830s, not just a cheaper newspaper but a new kind of newspaper: one aimed at the expanding urban middle classes. The penny papers commercialized journalism and to some degree democratized it, reaching an audience until then outside the universe of print. Among the new cheap papers were literary weeklies that capitalized on the lower postal rates for newspapers than for magazines (until the completion of a railroad system in the 1860s, distribution of print was dependent on the mails). Such papers as the Philadelphia *Saturday Courier*, the *New World*, and *Brother Jonathan* copied fiction from competitors, pirated English novels, and eventually developed a source of native material, creating both the first generation of professional American authors and the first "mass" audience. These literary weeklies quickly evolved to eight-page, nearly all-fiction story papers (with bits of humor, advice, correspondence, and editorials). The papers with the largest national circulations emerged in the 1850s: first Robert Bonner's *New York Ledger*, transformed in 1855 from a merchants' paper to a fiction weekly, then Street and Smith's *New York Weekly* in 1859. The story papers both created and thrived on star authors (for the *Ledger*, Fanny Fern, Sylvanus S. Cobb, and Mrs. E.D.E.N. Southworth; for the Weekly, T. S. Arthur, Horatio Alger, "Ned Buntline" [E. Z. C. Judson], and Mary J. Holmes). Exclusive contracts with such writers were immensely profitable to both publishers and authors (ten thousand dollars annually for Southworth, for example, and eventually more than two hundred thousand dollars annually for Bonner). Writers for the story papers, and later for the dime novels, were the least respected yet most financially successful authors in America. They were also the most prolific: Sylvanus Cobb wrote 122 novels or "long stories" for Bonner over a 30-year career; Southworth's output was comparable. Between 1839 and 1901, more than fifty different weekly story papers were published; the circulation of the *Ledger* reached four hundred thousand by 1860 but, more important, numerous lesser story papers far exceeded one hundred thousand in circulation. Collectively the papers reached their zenith in the 1870s, just before their sudden decline in the 1880s.

The story papers thus introduced the mass-produced, widely distributed cheap fiction that was continued by dime novels from 1860 to the 1890s, by pulp magazines from the 1890s through World War II, and by inexpensive paperbacks in the 1940s and 1950s. Dime novels both succeeded and competed with the weekly story papers for the late-nineteenth-century cheap-fiction market. Dime novels were latter-day chapbooks: originally 4-inch-by-6¼-inch pamphlets of about one hundred pages, in yellow covers, printed on pulp paper, selling for a dime; later 8½-inch-by-12-inch newsprint magazines selling for as little as a nickel. In all, more than 130 dime novel series appeared between 1860 and 1912, with circulations of a handful of the most successful ones approaching one million. They contained complete novels rather than serials and were aimed more toward juvenile readers than families. They were both a little more sensational and a little less respectable than the story papers, but their variation in content was in fact minimal, and prolific hacks of the day such as "Ned Buntline" wrote similar stories for both markets.

The most important fact about all of these forms of popular fiction was their cost. The six cents for a weekly story paper, the dime (or nickel) for a dime novel, later the ten or fifteen or twenty cents for a pulp magazine and the quarter for the early paperbacks made them affordable to readers otherwise excluded from the literary marketplace. This inexpensive fiction was also readily available: it was the publishers of story papers and dime novels—Robert Bonner, then the Beadle brothers and Frank Tousey and Street and Smith—who developed the marketing strategies and methods of distribution that revolutionized the commerce of literature. In ways that now seem crude they advertised their publications and accepted paid advertising within them. They pioneered in national distribution through the American News Company with its network of newsstands (the ANC held a virtual monopoly on periodical distribution from its creation in 1864 until 1904). The cheap-fiction publishers also developed techniques for building circulations: scholarships for top salespersons, premiums for subscriptions and renewals.

To emphasize the economics of cheap fiction is not to ignore the fact that the publishers were also the innovators of popular literature in matters of form and content. What we recognize today as the conventional genres and formulas of popular fiction were adapted in the story papers and dime novels from European models and then refined and augmented, particularly in the pulps. Gothic and sentimental romances, sins-of-the-city melodramas, work-and-win success stories, and heroic tales of the noble laborer or working girl dominated the story papers. To these the dime novelists added the

The audience for popular literature in America has always been, in a loosely defined way, "middle class," but the range of that middle-class audience was greatest for the cheap fiction available from the 1830s to the 1950s.

Western and the detective story. All of these were simply variations of either melodramatic adventure or sentimental romance: the perennial literary motifs of heroism and villainy, disguise and hidden identity, predicament and rescue, repeatedly adapted to the concerns of a highly unstable industrializing and urbanizing society, and simplified and intensified for an expanding, minimally literate, relatively undiscriminating audience.

The audience for cheap fiction in the nineteenth century included both the working class and the expanding middle class, between which there was considerable mobility and no clear demarcation. Whether it included the lowest economic group is uncertain. The audience for popular literature in the United States at any period has always been, in a loosely defined way, "middle class," but the range of that middle-class audience was greatest for the cheap fiction available from the 1830s to the 1950s. The effects of this popular fiction on readers, its cultural uses, have been widely and loudly debated, the extreme positions claiming that popular literature has functioned as social control (the "containment" model) or as social liberation (the "subversion" model).

Popular fiction has always been rooted in formula: the patterns of plot and character that are conventional within a culture and thus familiar to readers. Variation and innovation are essential, but only within the framework of the recognizable formula. And cheap fiction has always been more rigidly formulaic than other kinds of popular literature, the best-selling novels and fiction in upper-middle-class magazines to be discussed shortly. Yet story papers and dime novels were also less observant of Victorian propriety and social convention than were these more respectable literary forms. In *Adventure, Mystery, and Romance,* John G. Cawelti asserts that at the heart of American formulaic fiction in both the nineteenth and the twentieth centuries has been a conflict between what might be considered conventional values and subversive desires. Thus, a typical conflict in a woman's romance: the heroine's choice between marriage and family, on the one hand, and erotic abandon or self-serving career, on the other. Thus also, a typical conflict in a Western: the violence of the lone male versus the domestic stability his violence makes possible. The resolution of such conflicts is inevitably an affirmation of conventional values—thus formulaic narratives' political conservatism, their possible "containment" of disruptive or utopian desires. But cheap fiction, as a mark of its lower cultural status, also has always explored more openly the boundaries of the forbidden—thus its "subversive" or liberating potential.

The models of both containment and subversion are text centered; how actual readers have read and responded to formulaic fiction is largely unknown. If answers are elusive, however, issues of ideology remain important. It is significant that class and gender are considerably less stable and narrowly defined in nineteenth-century cheap fiction than in the more respectable literature of the period. While the resolution of the stories with working-class heroes, for example, invariably was conservative—the poor but noble sewing-machine girl marries her employer, the honorable laborer is handsomely rewarded for solving a crime or rescuing his benefactor's child—the realities of class, and the attendant antagonisms and discontents of social inequality, are nonetheless acknowledged in these narratives. Whatever "containment" of class resentments resulted from reading such stories must have been partial at best; whatever "liberation" for readers, equally incomplete. While the actual power of such narratives is uncertain, their value as a social record is undeniable.

MAGAZINES AND BEST-SELLERS. It is essential to recognize a plurality of popular reading publics rather than a single mass audience. Story papers and dime novels represent only one aspect of popular literature in the late nineteenth century. The story papers can be viewed as one end of the spectrum of the era's periodical literature, for which there was a range of audiences (as there were varied reading publics for the story papers themselves). Like literature generally, magazine reading had been largely restricted to an educated, prosperous elite from the appearance of the first American magazine in 1741 until the second quarter of the nineteenth century. The publication of the first fiction weeklies in the 1830s and 1840s coincided with a dramatic expansion in the circulation of general-interest magazines. *Godey's Lady's Book, Graham's Magazine,* and *Ladies' National Magazine* (renamed *Peterson's Magazine* in 1848) all thrived in the antebellum period as major sources of belles lettres for the expanding middle classes. In the 1850s *Harper's New Monthly Magazine* (1850), followed by *Putnam's* (1853) and *Atlantic* (1857), emerged as the first great general-interest monthlies, joined after the Civil War by *Scribner's, Century, Lippincott's,* and *Galaxy Harper's Weekly* and *Frank Leslie's Illustrated Newspaper* were the great general-interest weeklies of the period. Women's magazines (*Godey's* and *Peterson's* maintaining their popularity, to be joined and soon surpassed by *Woman's Home Companion* and *Ladies' Home Journal*), men's sporting journals (from *Spirit of the Times* to *National Police Gazette*), children's magazines (chiefly *Youth's Companion,* followed later by *St. Nicholas*), and a wide range of specialized magazines (of which the agricultural journals were the greatest sellers) also had large circulations. The age of cheap fiction was also an age of periodical literature more generally.

While the contents of these magazines varied, most included at least some fiction and can be said to have contributed to the popular literature of the period. The magazines differed in price, in circulation, and in level of sophistication, each a factor in determining their audience. As a group the weeklies were the cheapest and had the largest circulations and least sophistication; they were followed by the monthlies and then the much more exclusive quarterly reviews. Among the weeklies the story papers were cheaper, more widely circulated, and less sophisticated than the major general-interest magazines; among the monthlies the editors of *Atlantic* strove for a more literate, less popular audience than the readers of, say, *Leslie's Popular Monthly.* In the 1870s and 1880s the largest circulations were those of mail-order weeklies such as *People's Literary Companion,* whose editors claimed half a million subscribers by 1871. The large number and variety of periodicals with circulations of at least one hundred thousand suggests most concretely a multilayered popular audience.

Within this proliferation of periodicals, the democratization of the general-interest magazines—their increasing availability to a wider economic range of readers—was perhaps the most significant development for popular literature. At a typical price of thirty-five cents in the 1860s and 1870s, the major general monthlies—*Harper's, Atlantic, Century,* and so on—excluded readers below the upper middle classes. In the 1880s and 1890s, however, the prices of these magazines dropped to twenty-five, twenty, fifteen, even ten cents, in order to compete with a new generation of cheap monthlies led by *McClure's, Munsey's, Everybody's,* and *Cosmopolitan.* When *Saturday Evening Post* appeared as a newly redesigned family weekly in 1899, it sold for a nickel, the cost of *New York Ledger* and *New York Weekly* a generation earlier. Postal acts of 1874 and 1885 reduced the rates at which magazines could be mailed; new cheap techniques of photoengraving dramatically reduced production costs for illustrated magazines. But the most important factor was the replacement of copy price by advertising as the primary source of revenue. By 1900 magazines were becoming a primary medium of advertisement for emerging national brands of consumer goods. The printing of advertisements on the same page with stories and serials also created a new environment for the reading, or consumption, of popular literature.

The fiction in nineteenth-century magazines ranged from the extreme sentimentalism and melodrama of the story papers to the subtler sentimentalism and nascent realism of the literary monthlies, all part of the era's popular literature with its overlapping reading publics. The major novelists and short-story writers of the era—Henry James and William Dean Howells; Bret Harte, Sarah Orne Jewett, Mary Eleanor Wilkins Freeman, George Washington Cable, Kate Chopin, and the rest of the local-color school—supported themselves as writers by routinely publishing their fiction in magazines before it appeared in book form. The boundary between the "popular" and the "literary" has often been blurred in the United States, but particularly in this golden age of general-interest magazines.

A comparable range, with comparably overlapping audiences, is apparent in the popular books of the period. The paper-covered dime novels, at a nickel or a dime, reached a far wider readership than cloth-bound books selling for one dollar and a dollar and fifty cents (half the cost of books in the late eighteenth century, yet still equal to the average worker's daily wage). Among the relatively costly books, with their narrower, more educated, and more prosperous readership, it is necessary further to distinguish expensively bound volumes from cheaper reprints, in either cloth or paper, often in the publishers' "libraries" that became widespread in the second half of the century. In such editions appeared pirated novels by the most popular English writers, the serialized fiction from the story papers, and cheap reprints of native best-sellers. The best-sellers tended to be exceptionally pious and conventional, the story-paper serials more wildly melodramatic. The fact that reprints of both appeared in the cheap libraries suggests once more the overlapping of popular reading publics. The best-seller appeared at mid century: first Susan Warner's *The Wide, Wide World (1850),* followed by such spectacular successes as Harriet Beecher Stowe's *Uncle Tom's Cabin* (1852), Maria S. Cummins's *The Lamplighter* (1854), and Augusta J. Evans's *Beulah* (1859). Before 1850 there had been popular novels: gothic and sentimental romances and picaresque tales beginning in the late eighteenth century, the historical romances of James Fenimore Cooper and others beginning in the 1820s, preeminently the popular English novels that thrived until the Copyright Act of 1891 brought the United States into compliance with the Berne Convention and removed the financial advantages of publishing them. But the 1850s saw a spectacular leap in sales of native-authored novels of a certain type: the extraordinarily popular domestic romances that marked the decade for early social historians as the "feminine fifties."

For literary critics, the 1850s became known as the high point of an "American Renaissance"—the age of Nathaniel Hawthorne's Scarlet Letter, *Herman Melville's* Moby-Dick, *Henry David Thoreau's* Walden, *and Walt Whitman's* Leaves of Grass.

For literary critics, on the other hand, the 1850s became known as the high point of an "American Renaissance"—the age not of *The Wide, Wide World* and *The Lamplighter* but of *The Scarlet Letter, Moby-Dick, Walden,* and *Leaves of Grass.* Nathaniel Hawthorne's famous complaint to his editor, William Davis Ticknor, about the "damned mob of scribbling women" whose sales dwarfed his own, has been repeatedly quoted as a sign of the literary artist's newly heightened estrangement from a marketplace now dominated by trivializing popular fiction. In another much-quoted document in the brief against popular trash, Herman Melville complained to his friend Hawthorne, "What I feel most moved to write, that is banned,—it will not pay. Yet, altogether, write the *other* way I cannot. So the product is a final hash, and all my books are botches."

Although Hawthorne and Melville correctly perceived the consequences of marketplace conditions for American literature, what was different in the 1850s was not the commercial failure of serious literature but the dramatic success of popular books. From its rise in the eighteenth century, the novel had always been a "popular" genre in the sense that it provided entertainment for the newly emergent middle class. The mid nineteenth century marks the period in the United States not when a new kind of popular novel appeared but when the audience for popular novels significantly expanded, at the same time that certain writers, acknowledging the novel's preeminence among literary genres, attempted to transform what had been essentially a popular genre into art.

Before 1850 the only commercially successful American writer of belles lettres was James Fenimore Cooper. Beginning in the second half of the nineteenth century, more authors with literary ambitions became able to support themselves with their writing (usually through serialization of their novels in popular magazines). But with the rise of authorship as vocation rather than avocation, such writers as Henry James felt more keenly the tensions between art and the marketplace. Antebellum reviewers had made two primary demands on the novel: that it entertain and that it morally instruct. Not until the 1870s and 1880s did such writers as James and William Dean Howells begin articulating a theory of the novel as art. In the 1850s, then, Warner's *Wide, Wide World* and Hawthorne's *Scarlet Letter* were held to the same standard: judged for their fidelity to life, the typicality of their characters, their morality, their narrative interest and power. Middle-class readers found *The Wide, Wide World* more satisfying on these grounds.

And publishers found an expanded market for popular novels. The best-sellers of the second half of the nineteenth century were predominantly sentimental domestic tales, historical romances, instructive stories with either religious or secular messages. Together with the most respectable magazines of the era, they were fundamentally conservative, their general narrative strategy to reaffirm or consolidate traditional values in the face of troubling challenges. In contrast with the broad range of readers of cheap fiction, their presumed audience was more narrowly "respectable" and primarily female—the latter a fact with which male authors had to contend. A masculinist revolt in the 1890s and early twentieth century produced a "strenuous age" in American writing, in which novels of Western and international adventure competed for popularity with romances of business and nostalgic novels of simple rural life—a cacophony of responses to a rapidly modernizing world.

PULPS AND SLICKS IN THE TWENTIETH CENTURY. In the decades following the 1830s, then, there emerged a vast world of print within which "popular literature" signifies not a single body of writing but possibilities within a range of print media including books, magazines, and newspapers. This range, and the varied forms within this range, continued into the twentieth century. The appearance of the cheaper general-interest monthlies created a greatly expanded audience of magazine readers at the turn of the century. In 1885 there were only four general monthlies with circulations greater than one hundred thousand; at twenty-five to thirty-five cents a copy, their aggregate circulation was six hundred thousand. In 1905 twenty such monthlies had circulations over one hundred thousand; at ten to fifteen cents a copy, their aggregate circulation exceeded five and a half million. The new leaders emphasized journalism over belles lettres, but short stories and serialized novels remained a staple. A new generation of popular weeklies, led by the revived *Saturday Evening Post* and later by *Collier's*, continued to feature fiction by favorite writers.

The content of popular magazine fiction in the nineteenth century had been governed to a considerable degree by the literary and moral tastes of editors and publishers; in the twentieth century, as the magazines' "popular" readership expanded to become a "mass" audience (the circulation of the Post reached two million by the end of World War I), and as advertising revenues replaced copy price as their financial foundation, new kinds of market considerations became all-important in determining content. The new breadth of audience dictated an appeal to "middlebrow" (as opposed to both "highbrow" and "lowbrow") taste; the dependence on national advertisers dictated content not at odds with the basic values of corporate business. Publishers and editors came to think about their readers, at least in part, as potential consumers of their advertisers' goods and services. Cyrus H. K. Curtis, publisher of *Saturday Evening Post, Ladies' Home Journal,* and *Country Gentleman* (which together attracted a third of the national advertising revenue in the 1920s), initiated marketing research in 1911; under the editorship of Ben Hibbs, *Post* readers in the 1940s were polled twenty-six times a year on their reading preferences.

Successful magazines tended to develop distinctive editorial formulas; Theodore Peterson observes (p. 73) that each issue of *Collier's* in the 1930s, for example, included articles on politics, economics, sports, and a women's issue; a celebrity profile; two serials (usually with an emphasis on mystery or romance) and three short stories, one of them less than a page long; an editorial, a column of miscellany, and several cartoons. Magazines came to be distinguished less by the personality of their editors, as had been the case earlier (Richard Gilder at *Century* for twenty-eight years in the late nineteenth century, George Horace Lorimer at *Saturday Evening Post* for thirty-seven years, Edward Bok at *Ladies' Home Journal* for third years), than by these editorial formulas. Whether the fiction embedded in this new magazine environment became significantly less diverse than in the nineteenth century (when publishers, editors, and writers came overwhelmingly from similar social backgrounds) has not yet been documented. The key to a successful magazine came to lie in the publisher's ability to target an audience, devise a formula for attracting it, and sell the concept to advertisers. The "popular" in this sense, ironically, came to include the specialized: magazines such as *Popular Mechanics*, *American Rifleman*, and numerous others with large yet narrow audiences.

The typical contents of an issue of *Collier's* suggest a still-important role for fiction in popular magazines, a situation that changed dramatically after World War II. Human-interest features and celebrity profiles usurped much of fiction's place; the immensely popular confessional magazines (beginning with *True Story* in 1919), true-crime magazines (beginning with *True Detective* in 1924), movie magazines, and men's adventure magazines became other alternatives. But popular fiction flourished more widely than ever in the pulps, the cheap-fiction end of the twentieth-century magazine industry. The story papers and dime novels died in the 1880s and 1890s, but in 1896 Frank Munsey, one of the major publishers of late-nineteenth-century cheap fiction, began the pulp era when he converted his *Argosy* to an all-fiction magazine for adults, printed on rough wood-pulp paper and selling for a dime. Several other major producers of nineteenth-century cheap fiction, most notably Street and Smith, as well as a new generation of cheap publishers, soon followed Munsey into the pulp market. The story papers and dime novels, initially printed on rag paper, both turned to news-print in the 1870s. The pulps differed from their cheap-fiction predecessors in size and format: they were bound magazines with slick covers, much thicker (generally 150 to 200 pages), eventually well illustrated. They continued both the family- and male-oriented appeals of the story papers and dime novels; like the dime novels in particular, they grew more sensational over time. With perhaps ten million regular readers the pulps reached a smaller audience than nineteenth-century story papers, and considerably smaller than twentieth-century slick magazines, which by 1946 were read by 68.7 percent of Americans fifteen years old or older. Yet in the unprecedented quality of at least some of their writing, and in the particulars of their relationship to readers, the pulps represent the zenith of the age of cheap fiction.

For writers the pulps provided not only regular income (as the fiction weeklies and dime novels had done) but also, for some, an apprenticeship in literary craft. A handful of pulp authors—including Dashiell Hammett, Raymond Chandler, H. P. Lovecraft, Ray Bradbury, and Isaac Asimov—were the first writers in the cheap-fiction tradition to break through the walls of critical condescension. For readers the pulps provided a steady output of narrative fiction in immediately recognizable genres, for the publishers' offerings responded directly and immediately to readers' desires as expressed in newsstand sales. Although the first generation of pulps emphasized adventure of a general nature, specialized publications appeared as early as 1906 with *Railroad Man's Magazine.* By the late teens, as pulp publishers discovered the marketing advantages of targeting specific audiences, first *Detective Story Magazine* (1915), then *Western Story Magazine* (1919), established two of the most popular and enduring pulp genres (romance, beginning most notably with *Love Story Magazine* in 1921, was the third). *Snappy Stories* (1912), *The Thrill Book* (1919), *Black Mask* (1920), *Weird Tales* (1923), *Sport Story* (1926), and *Amazing Stories* (1926) were major innovators in the genres of sex, fantasy, hard-boiled mystery, horror, sport, and science fiction. The superhero pulps of the 1930s—magazines featuring Doc Savage, the Shadow, the Spider, and numerous others—crossed several genres while becoming a transgeneric genre in themselves.

The pulps were published weekly, bimonthly, or monthly. No individual title approached such magazines as *Saturday Evening Post* in circulation; like the dime novels and story papers, their numerical popularity was collective. Also like dime novels, the pulps were sold chiefly on newsstands and depended for their revenues on cover price rather than advertising—this last an important fact for assessing their function as popular literature in an age when aspects of the publishing business were being transformed. The myriad ads in *Saturday Evening Post* were intended to construct their readers as consumers; with few ads, for nonmainstream products, the pulps affected their readers more exclusively through their formulaic narratives.

Though tied to generic convention, the pulps were the form of cheap fiction least bound by standards of propriety (considerably less bound than the contemporary slicks). At their best the pulps challenged the too-narrow boundaries of middle-class respectability; at their worst they wallowed in extremes of violence and perversion. In matters of form as well as of content, the pulps had an unprecedented license for innovation and risk. Besides the major genres of mystery, Western, and romance, publishers tried the market with numerous others that failed to catch on: short-lived railroad pulps, gangster pulps, sea-story pulps, aviation pulps, Civil War pulps, fire-fighter pulps, and so on. With cheap production (small profits were possible even if half the copies were unsold), and with publishers carrying as many as thirty titles at a time (the unsuccessful ones quickly disappearing), the pulps thrived on an unusually close relationship between publisher and reader. By not buying certain titles readers said "no" to publishers; by buying others in abundance they said "yes." Individual writers often produced stories in a variety of pulps, adapting the same conventions of plot to only superficially different genres. But the variety as well as the sameness of the pulps must be acknowledged. Whether truly subversive or merely degenerate, the pulps were less ideologically narrow than the more respectably middle-class, mass-circulation slick magazines.

PAPERBACKS AND BEST-SELLERS. The pulps flourished between the world wars and then died quickly from a variety of causes: internal problems (a decline in quality and misguided attempts at respectability) as well as external factors (increased production costs due to paper quotas during World War II and competition from comic books and the new slick adventure magazines, beginning in 1945 with yet another metamorphosis of *Argosy*). Perhaps the chief factor was the appearance in 1939, and then proliferation through the 1940s and 1950s, of a new generation of inexpensive paperback fiction. Fiction in paper covers is at least as old as the chapbooks; the first complete paperback novels published in the United States date from 1829 and were available intermittently through the nineteenth century until the Copyright Act of 1891 put an end to cheap pirated reprints. Various attempts at paperback publishing in the 1920s and 1930s were unsuccessful for several reasons, most often problems with distribution.

The "paperback revolution" that began in 1939 with the publication of the first ten Pocket Books describes not a new kind of popular book, then, but the transformation of both the publishing industry and the reading habits of a vast popular audience. The keys to the spectacular success of the new paperback publishers were price and distribution. At twenty-five cents Pocket Books were nearly as affordable as pulp magazines; more important, the new paperbacks were sold not as books were traditionally sold (chiefly through bookshops) but as periodicals were sold (through the magazine distribution system). Paperbacks appeared on racks in department stores, chain stores, stationery stores, drugstores, and eventually newsstands, reaching out not to a relatively small book-buying readership but to an immense magazine-buying public.

The first paperbacks had none of the marks, or the stigma, of cheap fiction. Pocket Books' initial ten titles began with James Hilton's best-selling novel of 1935, *Lost Horizon*, and included a volume of five of Shakespeare's tragedies, Dorothy Parker's poems, the children's classic *Bambi*, and a self-improvement book, in addition to five more novels: both classics (*Wuthering Heights* and *The Way of All Flesh*) and popular contemporary works (Thorne Smith's *Topper*, Agatha Christie's *The Murder of Roger Ackroyd*, and Thornton Wilder's *The Bridge of San Luis Rey*). This list of ten provides a revealing case study in editorial selection and the construction of a middle-class popular audience in the mid twentieth century. Clearly, different books were meant to attract different readers, and the strategy succeeded:

The "paperback revolution" that began in 1939 with the publication of the first ten Pocket Books describes not a new kind of book but the transformation of both the publishing industry and the reading habits of a vast popular audience.

by 1941, 302,000 copies of *Wuthering Heights* had been sold (compared with 239,000 copies of *Lost Horizon*). Avon Books, created in 1941 not by a publisher but by a magazine distributor, the American News Company (after Pocket Books abandoned it for independent distributors), included in its initial twelve titles novels by Sinclair Lewis and William Faulkner, in addition to the mysteries that became one of its staples. A third early contributor to the paperbacking of America, the Armed Services Editions published between 1943 and 1947 for distribution to soldiers, was oriented even more toward "quality" fiction.

The paperback emerged, then, not as a competitor to the pulps but as the "cheap" alternative to hardcover best-sellers, whose audience was expanded by the creation of book clubs in the 1920s and by a flourishing system of public libraries. In content the best-selling novels between the wars reflect an American middle class groping to come to terms with deeply disturbing changes. The pastoral innocence of pre-World War I best-sellers by Gene Stratton Porter, Harold Bell Wright, and Booth Tarkington partially gave way in the 1920s to social criticism (Sinclair Lewis's *Main Street* and *Babbitt*) and tentative explorations of the new sexual permissiveness (the fiction of "flaming youth"). But these new voices never drowned out the old, in novels celebrating traditional values of self-reliance, religious feeling, and rural virtue. The hardcover bestseller has always been more conservative than the cheap fiction of any period. The most conspicuous best-sellers of the 1930s—*The Good Earth*, *Anthony Adverse*, and *Gone With the Wind*, each topping the lists for two years running—reaffirmed traditional values more emphatically than ever. In general, while hardcover best-sellers and the various forms of cheap fiction have equally affirmed the mainstream middle-class values of the day, cheap fiction has directly or indirectly challenged those values more daringly before ultimately affirming them. Bestsellers have more obviously functioned to accommodate change to traditional verities.

The modern paperback that appeared in 1939 was a hybrid: a book marketed as a magazine. Initially it was tied to neither the hardcover best-seller nor the formulaic genres of cheap fiction. By the end of the 1940s, however, it had acquired more and more of the characteristics of the cheap-fiction tradition. It increasingly specialized in mysteries and Westerns, the popular genres at the center of both pulp publishing and the cheap-reprint trade of the 1930s. Chiefly through their brilliantly lurid cover illustrations, paperbacks acquired the reputation for prurience and sensationalism that clung earlier to both the dime novels and the pulps. But the paperbacks also remained books, their popularity tied to individual titles, not to publishers or publications, and some titles sold as few novels had sold before. Margaret Mitchell's *Gone With the Wind* (1936) made hardcover publishing history by selling more than a million copies in its first seven months; the paperback made such extraordinary figures nearly routine. The first million-seller was Dale Carnegie's *How to Win Friends and Influence People* (1936, paperback 1940); by 1945 an additional twenty Pocket Books, including twelve works of fiction, had reached that figure (seven were mysteries, one a Western). More significant, with print runs ten times those of typical hardcover books, every paperback was a best-seller by traditional book standards.

The success of Pocket Books quickly spawned competitors: Avon in 1941, Pocket Library in 1942, Dell in 1943. It is significant that although Pocket Books was started by men from book publishing, Avon was created by a magazine distributor, Pocket Library by a pulp publisher, and Dell by a magazine publisher—clear signs of the paperback's mixed parentage. With its cheap-fiction aura, the paperback remained the somewhat embarrassing and scorned stepchild of the book trade until the 1970s, its publishers collectively, and sometimes individually, torn by the competing demands of art and the marketplace. In the 1950s, for some intellectuals the paperback embodied their hopes for democratic culture by making the classics available to millions of readers. For others the paperback threatened to debase Western culture by pandering to vulgar tastes. Congressional probes into the paperback, comic, and magazine industries in 1952, and the well-publicized obscenity trials of publishers of *Lady Chatterly's Lover*, *Tropic of Cancer*, and *Fanny Hill* focused additional attention on the morality of paperbacks generally. Within this climate of intense scrutiny, the appearance of handfuls of "highbrow" literary titles on publishers' lists, alongside truckloads of Westerns, mysteries, and sexual potboilers, points to the paperback's continuing existence in a netherworld between the traditional book and sensational cheap fiction.

Through the paperback American popular literature has been transformed since World War II. In 1939 three million paperback books were sold; in 1950 the total was 214 million, by 1960, 280 million. And in 1960 the offering of stock in Pocket Books, the acquisition of Alfred A. Knopf by Random House, and the purchase of New American Library by the Times Mirror Company signaled yet another fundamental restructuring of the publishing industry. But an event outside the literary world had a more immediate impact on readers. The emergence of television in the 1950s would have doomed the pulp magazines if other factors had not already done so; the spectacular growth of the new medium after 1960 did not kill the best-seller or the paperback, but it had profound consequences on the place of reading in American culture. Although not immediately apparent, the simultaneous rise of television and accelerated transformation of publishing from a cottage industry to a corporate business created a distinctively new era in the history of American popular literature.

The Age of the Blockbuster: The 1960s to the 1980s

In 1987, 6,298 separate works of fiction were published in the United States, 2,632 of them mass-market paperback titles (two and a half times the number in 1960). In both 1985 and 1986, five hardcover books exceeded one million copies in sales; in 1987, fifty-two works of fiction and seventy-two of nonfiction sold at least one hundred thousand copies. By 1989 there were 14.5 million paperback copies of J. R. R. Tolkien's *The Hobbit* in print, 12.8 million of George Orwell's 1984, 12.4 million of William Peter Blatty's *The Exorcist.* By virtually any measurement the growth since 1960 was impressive.

Yet these figures can mislead. The years since 1960 did not see steady growth in the publishing industry but a series of short-term booms and recessions. The 1960s began impressively. Trade paperbacks opened up bookstores to paperbacks generally; the growing use of paperbacks in classrooms created another huge market. Yet in 1969 an essay in the *New York Times Book Review* asked if the paperback revolution had ended: total sales were not much higher than in 1959, while the population had increased by 15 percent. No sooner was the question asked than the 1970s saw a new boom in which paperback titles selling eight million copies became common. A slump in the early 1980s, followed by mid-decade recovery, followed by hints of another decline as sales for 1988 and 1989 fell behind the 1987 figures, confirmed that book publishing had become a particularly volatile business.

This volatility, and the economic forces that underlay it, had important consequences for popular literature and the reading public. One more set of figures is necessary for comparative purposes: through the 1940s paperbacks cost twenty-five cents; in 1960 the average price was sixty-nine cents. In 1988 the average mass-market paperback cost $4.55, an increase since 1960 nearly double the rise in the cost of living; the age of cheap fiction had ended. Even in 1987, the industry's high point, although more books were sold than ever before, it seems almost certain that the audience for popular literature was a significantly smaller percentage of the population than during the era of the pulps and the cheap paperbacks. Television most obviously replaced cheap fiction in providing narrative entertainment for the largest popular audience (a revealing development: nonfiction best-sellers permanently passed fiction in sales during the 1950s). Magazine circulations reached astonishing figures—16.5 million for the monthly *Reader's Digest* in 1989—but fiction nearly disappeared from the large-circulation magazines. Sensational journalism—the *National Enquirer, True Story,* and so on—continued the popular tradition of the penny papers and the *Police Gazette* in which supposed fact was indistinguishable from sensational fiction; and hardcover novels, if measured simply by sales, achieved their greatest popularity ever. But the meaning of "popular" itself changed. The popular literature of this period was distinguished by a double paradox: an unprecedented quantity of books published yet a narrowing of options for readers, an unprecedented quantity of books purchased yet a decline in the importance of popular literature. This paradoxical expansion and contraction

A Police Gazette *cover, May 11, 1889. Today's supermarket tabloids continue the sensational journalistic tradition of the penny papers and the* Police Gazette *in which supposed fact was indistinguishable from sensational fiction.*

was epitomized by the overwhelming predominance of generic paperbacks and "blockbuster" novels.

Both of these developments resulted to a considerable degree from the restructuring of the book industry. Publishing houses had come and gone, as profits rose and fell, since the beginning of mass-market publishing in the mid nineteenth century, but the concentration of ownership that began in the 1960s led to major changes within the industry that had equally profound consequences for readers. Private companies went public; publishing houses emerged; publishers of hardcover books purchased paperback houses; large conglomerates acquired publishing houses that became minor assets within the corporate structure. Although it became too easy for critics to romanticize traditional publishers for their love of literature, and to vilify the new corporations for their single-minded commitment to profits, a less extreme shift of this sort did occur with incorporation. As profits became the driving force behind publishing as never before, genre fiction and blockbuster best-sellers narrowed the range of popular literature as never before.

The latest genre fiction—the mysteries, romances, Westerns, men's adventure tales, fantasies, and science fiction that closely followed a limited number of formulas—continued a tradition in popular literature that began with the story papers and dime novels of the nineteenth century and continued with the pulps and paperbacks of the twentieth. But compared with the golden age of the pulps in particular, the range of genres markedly shrank. Pulp publishers virtually created hard-boiled detective stories and science fiction; they sustained minor genres such as sports and aviation fiction; they continually experimented with new genres, most of which proved unsuccessful but all of which contributed to a breadth of possibilities for readers. Publishers of genre fiction in the 1970s and 1980s perfected the marketing of a handful of popular genres, but they neither supported less profitable minor genres nor created new ones.

In one sense, the latest genre fiction was more popular than ever, in that it probably commanded a greater share of the entire fiction market than ever before. Women's romances alone, supplanting Westerns as the dominant genre in popular fiction by the end of the 1970s, claimed 40 percent of the domestic paperback market. But in other ways the new genre fiction was less "popular." Whereas pulp publishers and pulp readers in effect collaborated in the creation of popular literature—publishers trying new lines, readers buying or not buying them—the relationship was now more one-way, despite seemingly contrary developments. Publishers polled readers of romances for their preferences and devised techniques for determining the demographics of their audience, but their intention was to develop a few formulas with the broadest appeal, not many formulas with something for everyone. And just as postal regulations and copyright laws significantly affected popular literature in earlier periods, so the 1979 ruling by the United States Supreme Court that books held in inventory could not be depreciated contributed importantly to the emphasis on fast-selling titles and a short life for all other books.

Genre fiction also was no longer cheap. Initially a hybrid, a book marketed like a magazine, the paperback became more fully a book, and the relationship between clothbound and paperbound books became increasingly complex. By the 1950s the practice of issuing paperback editions of reasonably successful hardcover books, within a year or two of initial publication, became the norm. Paperback publishers, the stepchildren of the publishing industry, purchased the rights from the original publishers for relatively small fees. The second-class status of the paperback began to change in the 1960s, however. Modest hardcover sellers like *Catch-22* sometimes became spectacular successes in paperback; fees for paperback reprint rights during a frenzied period in the late 1970s were auctioned for astounding sums (Judith Krantz's *Princess Daisy* topped all records, selling for $3,208,875 in 1979). Established book publishers consequently purchased paperback companies in order to control the price of subsidiary rights more effectively; "paperback originals" offered publishers a way to avoid reprinting fees altogether. Novels appeared simultaneously in cloth and paper; paperbacks appeared in both more expensive trade and less expensive mass-market editions. For readers all these developments meant that they now encountered popular fiction in books rather than in periodicals, and that the particular form of that book was most likely a paperback.

Readers also encountered books in an altered environment. The incorporation of book publishing was part of a larger restructuring of the book trade. The growth of huge bookstore chains (by 1983 B. Dalton and Waldenbooks were selling half of the books purchased in the United States) made them not just outlets for books but also arbiters of what kinds of books should be published and how large the printings should be. The chain stores turned the quiet bookshop into a supermarket, displaying certain books prominently in order to snare impulse buyers, turning their inventory over rapidly. Books that did not sell within a few weeks were returned to the publishers; return rates approached 50 percent. The possible "steady seller," a book that might gradually acquire a popular audience, disappeared, leaving the shelf space to instant best-sellers and quickly disappearing failures. With two hundred new paperback titles appearing each month, publishers ag-

> *The latest genre fiction—mysteries, romances, Westerns, crime and detective novels, science fiction and fantasy—continued a tradition in popular literature that began with the nineteenth century's story papers and dime novels and continued with the twentieth's pulps and paperbacks.*

gressively competed for rack space in the chain stores and other outlets, and for the displays that leaped out at potential buyers as they entered the stores. When, in 1985, publishers began distributing hardcover best-sellers in supermarkets and discount stores, the book's increasing status as a commodity was only confirmed.

The emergence of powerful literary agents, who orchestrated the astonishingly lucrative royalty agreements and reprint auctions for a handful of novelists, introduced another new force into the book world. Together with the agent came the book tour, pioneered by Jacqueline Susann in 1966 with *Valley of the Dolls*, following the earlier discovery (beginning in 1960, as the *Tonight Show* made bestsellers of books by Alexander King and Harry Golden) that appearances on television talk shows could boost sales spectacularly and transform the right authors into celebrities. Finally, the increasingly complex relationship between books and other media, particularly television and movies, made the popular novels part of a multifaceted package. The resulting "blockbuster complex" meant that a handful of popular novels sold more spectacularly than ever before but then disappeared from readers' consciousness as new blockbusters appeared. The profits from the blockbusters enabled publishers to print novels that would not succeed financially, yet the concentration of resources on the potential best-seller almost guaranteed the other novels' commercial failure. Huge advances and paperback rights drove up the prices of books beyond levels affordable for many groups that had been readers in earlier periods. Popular literature thus simultaneously expanded and contracted.

The blockbuster complex created a new cultural environment for the popular novel: certain books were now encountered as cultural phenomena rather than more simply as literary narratives for personal pleasure. Popular literature became part of a much larger network of popular entertainment, its own role diminished even as the audience reached by the varied aspects of this total network became the largest ever. Women's romance narratives, for example, became available in both brand-name lines (Harlequin, Silhouette) and best-selling novels by celebrity authors (Danielle Steel, Rosemary Rogers, Janet Dailey), as well as in daytime and primetime soap operas and television miniseries. A little-read novel called *First Blood* led to the blockbuster series of *Rambo* movies, which in turn created a new audience for the original book. A reversal of the book-to-movie norm, the "novelization" of popular movie scripts was most spectacularly successful in 1982 and 1983, when first *E.T.: The Extraterrestrial Storybook* and then *Return of the Jedi* topped the hardcover best-seller lists. The marriage of book and movie spawned many offspring: action-figure toys, board games, promotional give-aways at fast-food restaurants, Saturday-morning cartoon shows. Whether as the original narrative or as an intermediate product, the popular novel reached the smallest audience of all these cultural forms.

The most basic question about popular literature that emerges from examining the current literary situation is whether "popular literature" even continues to exist. One answer must be an emphatic "yes." The concentration of publishing in huge, diversified corporations and the increasing dominance of the bookstore chains have almost totally driven out the traditional elitism of the book trade. The distribution of books through supermarket-like stores in shopping malls and the overwhelming emphasis on genre books (the traditionally popular forms) also contribute to what would seem a thorough democratizing of literature. The popular reigns nearly unchallenged. Certainly the most passionate spokesmen for high culture today fear the disappearance of great literature under an avalanche of popular schlock. But the narrowing of the popular audience to a smaller segment of the middle class (large enough, however, for blockbuster sales), the narrowing of choices compared with what was available during the age of cheap fiction, the diminished role of print itself in an electronic age—all these factors suggest a more tentative "no." The most reasonable response is to recognize that popular literature survives, but with new meanings for both "popular" and "literature." The future may reveal that we are now in the early stages of a third print revolution, following those of the fifteenth and nineteenth centuries, a third major restructuring of popular literature's place within Western cultures.

[See also The Culture of Consumption; Intellectuals and the Intelligentsia; Journalism; Literacy; Mass Culture and Its Critics; Print and Publishing; Radio; Television.]

BIBLIOGRAPHY

Cawelti, John G. *Adventure, Mystery, and Romance: Formula Stories as Art and Popular Culture* (1976).

Davidson, Cathy N., ed. *Reading in America: Literature and Social History* (1989).

Davis, Kenneth C. *Two-Bit Culture: The Paperbacking of America* (1984).

Denning, Michael. *Mechanic Accents: Dime Novels and Working-Class Culture in America* (1987).

Fiedler, Leslie. *What Was Literature? Class Culture and Mass Society* (1982).

Gilmore, William J. *Reading Becomes a Necessity of Life: Material and Cultural Life in Rural New, England, 1780–1835* (1989).

Hart, James D. *The Popular Book: A History of America's Literary Taste* (1950; 1963).

Inge, M. Thomas, ed. *Handbook of American Popular Literature* (1988).

Isaac, Rhys. "Books and the Social Authority of Learning: The Case of Mid-Eighteenth-Century Virginia." In *Printing and Society in Early America*, edited by William L. Joyce et al. (1983).

Johannsen, Albert. *The House of Beadle and Adams and Its Dime and Nickel Novels. A Story of a Vanished Literature.* 3 vols. (1950–1962).

Joyce, William L., et al., eds. *Printing and Society in Early America* (1983).

Lehmann-Haupt, Hellmut, Lawrence C. Wroth, and Rollo G. Silver. *The Book in America: A History, of the Making and Selling of Books in the United States* (1952).

Lockridge, Kenneth A. *Literacy in Colonial New England: An Enquiry into the Social Context of Literacy in the Early Modern West* (1974).

Mott, Frank Luther. *A History of American Magazines.* 5 vols. (1938–1968).

Mott, Frank Luther. *Golden Multitudes: The Story of Best Sellers in the United States* (1947).

Noel, Mary. *Villains Galore: The Heyday of the Popular Story Weekly* (1954).

Nye, Russel. *The Unembarrassed Muse: The Popular Arts in America* (1970).

Peterson, Theodore. *Magazines in the Twentieth Century* (1956; 2d ed. 1964).

Radway, Janice A. *Reading the Romance: Women, Patriarchy, and Popular Literature* (1984).

Reynolds, David S. *Beneath the American Renaissance: The Subversive Imagination in the Age of Emerson and Melville* (1988).

Rosenberg, Bernard, and David Manning White, eds. *Mass Culture: The Popular Arts in America* (1957).

Sagendorph, Robb. *America and Her Almanacs: Wit, Wisdom, and Weather, 1636–1970* (1970).

Shera, Jesse H. *Foundations of the Public Library: The Origins of the Public Library Movement in New England, 1629–1855* (1949).

Stiverson, Cynthia Z., and Gregory A. Stiverson. "The Colonial Retail Book Trade: Availability and Affordability of Reading Material in Mid-Eighteenth-Century Virginia." In *Printing and Society in Early America*, edited by William L. Joyce et al. (1983).

Tebbel, John. *A History of Book Publishing in the United States.* 4 vols. (1972–1981).

Whiteside, Thomas. *The Blockbuster Complex: Conglomerates, Show Business, and Book Publishing* (1981).

Winans, Robert B. "The Growth of a Novel-reading Public in Late-Eighteenth-Century America." *Early American Literature* 9 (1975).

Wroth, Lawrence C. "Book Production and Distribution from the Beginning to the American Revolution." In *The Book in America: A History of the Making and Selling of Books in the United States*, edited by Hellmut Lehmann-Haupt et al. (1952).

— MICHAEL ORIARD

POPULAR MUSIC BEFORE 1950

Popular music differs from classical music in its greater simplicity and its accessibility to large sections of the population. Unlike folk music, popular music begins life as written music, and its styles are usually neither regional nor ethnic. There is an inescapable element of commerciality in popular music, which is composed for the purpose of being sold. The greater the distribution, the greater the profit, with the result that popular music can be defined, particularly in recent years, as mass-disseminated music.

The Colonial Period

The first book published in the American colonies was in this sense popular music, though it contained no printed notes, probably because no one could engrave the plates. *The Whole Booke of Psalmes Faithfully Translated into English Metre*, more commonly known as the *Bay Psalm Book* (1640), featured every psalm rendered into one of six metrical patterns and indicated to which of forty-eight tunes each should be sung. The same principle was observed in the broadside ballads hawked on the streets of England and America at this time, for they too contained lyrics only; customers were expected to know the melody.

The Pilgrims had brought the Ainsworth psalter, which included music as well as words, with them on the *Mayflower*. There was evidently a high level of musical literacy and ability among early Pilgrim singers, as Edward Winslow recalled of their Leyden sojourn: "Wee refreshed ourselves after our teares with singing of Psalmes, making joyfull melody in our hearts, as well as with the voice, there being many of the Congregation very expert in Musick." As the decades passed, however, there was a considerable falling off; later generations at Plymouth found the Ainsworth tunes too difficult, and few could read music. In addition, the Massachusetts Bay inhabitants were never as musically knowledgeable as the first Pilgrims had been. The *Bay Psalm Book* that was eventually adopted throughout the colony represented a significant impoverishment compared to the Ainsworth psalter. Whereas the Ainsworth psalter had featured fifteen types of meter, the *Bay Psalm Book* had only six. The ninth edition of the *Bay Psalm Book* (1698) included music for the first time and is the first known book with music to be printed in the colonies. It contained but thirteen tunes, one-third the number in its imported predecessor, the Ainsworth psalter.

Though the Psalmist had enjoined a joyful noise, by 1718 Puritan clergyman Cotton Mather found that the singing had become an "odd noise." Another observer in 1721 complained that the psalm tunes "are now miserably tortured, and twisted, and quavered, in some Churches, into an horrid Medly of confused and disorderly Noises." The tempos had evidently slowed down considerably, and the length of the services was effectively doubled by the practice of "lining-out," in which a deacon would speak or sing each line of the psalm and wait for the congregation to repeat it. The abler singers had to wait for the dawdlers to catch up and passed the time improvising flourishes, grace notes, and turns. One witness reported, "I myself have twice in one note paused to take breath." On one occasion, a deacon, apologizing to his flock for his failing eyesight, announced, "My eyes, indeed, are very blind." Like sheep, the congregation faithfully sang the line back, thinking it was the first line of the psalm. Trying to explain, the deacon added, "I cannot see at all." Same response. In amazement, he exclaimed, "I really believe you are bewitched!" They sang this back, too, as they did his final despairing words: "The mischief's in you all!"

In a pattern that would be repeated throughout the history of American music, gentility sought to improve upon rural backwardness. Bostonians grew embarrassed at what they perceived to be uncouth behavior, and a movement arose to replace "lining-out," which was essentially singing by ear, with "regular singing," or singing by note. Eventually the urban progressives won the day, and the practice of lining-out retreated to the remoter hinterlands, surviving to the present in isolated pockets of the Appalachians. But the A.R.S.es (a Harvard pun of the time on "Anti-Regular Singers") put up a fight, for they did enjoy the freedom and self-expression that lining-out provided. Their improvisations had the spontaneity of the jazz of a much later generation, and they resented the straitjacket their "betters" wished to impose on their singing. Ironically, those who stifled native expression, the more closely to imitate European practice by singing only what was printed on the page, were actually farther from the desired model than were the ornament-loving lining-outers. For the ability to play around with a note was at that time prized among European classical musicians as a most valuable skill. It would have been a poor performer indeed who sang a line of Handel exactly as written.

The rough democracy that lining-out encouraged emerged again in the "fuguing tunes" of William Billings (1746–1800). Fuguing tunes began with hymnlike homophony, after which a wild polyphony set in, as Billings put it, "each part striving for mastery and victory. The audience entertained and delighted, their minds surprisingly agitated and extremely fluctuated, sometimes declaring for one part and sometimes for another." Harmony was restored in the third and final part of the fuguing tune, which returned to the homophony with which it began. Though he had done his best to learn the rules of composition, autodidact Billings's naive polyphony violated strictures against parallel fifths and did not shy away from dissonance. Yet it was exhilarating and, at least for a while, popular. He did not after all invent fuguing tunes, but exploited what was already a popular pastime.

When Cotton Mather publicly complained that something had to be done about the poor quality of psalm-singing, Boston bookstore owner Samuel Gerrish, who had printed Mather's pamphlet, seized the chance to profit by publishing the first music instruction book in America, John Tufts's *Compleat Treatise of Singing* (1721). Tufts's method replaced notes with the letters F S L M (for *fa so la mi*, a simplification of the traditional solmization, or use of syllables to represent notes) to indicate the pitches and used dots to indicate the rhythm. This system had earlier appeared in the 1698 edition of the *Bay Psalm Book*, though accompanied there by notes. Tufts's book soon sold out and ultimately went through seven more editions. The fifth edition (1726) included a new song that some scholars have attributed to Tufts; thus "100 Psalm Tune New" may be the first piece of published music composed by an American. Or that honor may go to James Lyon, who included six tunes of his own composition in *Urania* (1761), a collection that also featured British tunes as well as hymn texts by Isaac Watts and John Wesley. In 1801 *The Easy Instructor*, by William Little and William Smith, introduced a shaped-note system of notating *fa so la mi* that achieved wide popularity among rural Americans.

By the second quarter of the eighteenth century, a singing-school movement was flourishing. Young people of both sexes, despite the severe disapproval of their elders, who preferred the old lining-out tradition, gathered in churches or taverns throughout New England two or three evenings a week to study Tufts's instruction manual, under the tutelage of a singing master who made sure they bought the books and sufficient manuscript paper. These were evidently mirthful occasions, as one Yale student wrote of "going to a singing meeting tonight and indulging myself a little in some of the carnal pleasures of the flesh, such as kissing & squeezing." Enthusiastic graduates of the singing schools moved to the front pew of their congregations to lead in the singing of psalms; thus were American church choirs born.

The Puritans had allowed only psalms to be sung in church, since only they were scriptural; hymns could be sung only in family and private devotions in the home. The Great Awakening of the early 1740s, which itself was made possible by the waning of Puritan fervor, changed all this. Evangelist George Whitefield introduced the hymns of Watts and Wesley to his American converts and even persuaded the fiery revivalist Jonathan Edwards to adopt them in his church. Watts's hymns enjoyed yet another surge of popularity in the Second Great Awakening of the early nineteenth century and exerted a significant influence not only on white but on black American folk hymnody as well. Gospel singer Mahalia Jackson spoke affectionately of the "old Doctor Watts songs" she heard as a child in black churches in South Carolina and Georgia, and Tony Heilbut suggested that one Watts hymn in particular, with "its mood of desolation and loss" and a metrical structure that anticipated the sixteen-bar form, "became an ancestor of the modern blues."

The Massachusetts patriot Samuel Adams was a singing master, and he organized the workmen of Boston into choruses that fomented revolution. At a banquet in 1769, 350 Sons of Liberty, sang John Dickinson's words to a popular English tune by William Boyce: "In Freedom we're born and in Freedom we'll live, / Our purses are ready. / Steady, Friends, steady. Not as slaves, but as Freemen our money we'll give." Billings's "Chester," with its opening words of defiance—"Let tyrants shake their iron rod"—was a rousing favorite with American soldiers during the Revolution. Broadsides, too, contributed to the revolutionary spirit. "Yankee Doodle" was originally sung by British redcoats, often just outside churches, to make sport of the Americans

Whereas the Puritans had allowed only psalms (not hymns) to be sung in church, the Great Awakening of the early 1740s changed all this; soon after, the hymns of such composers as Isaac Watts and John Wesley were introduced to American congregations.

and to disrupt the psalm-singing within, but the colonists adopted the song as their own and took delight in playing it at British General Charles Cornwallis's surrender at Yorktown. Sigmund Spaeth points out that "Yankee Doodle" is practically the only humorous national air in existence and "is certainly more characteristic of our people, in its comic nonchalance and quiet effrontery" than are more serious patriotic songs. Perhaps only in the confidence of extreme youth is such a healthy self-deprecation possible.

The Post-Revolutionary Period

Popular music in eighteenth-century America was based on English tunes, and English popular music in the last quarter of the century was barely distinguishable from the classical repertoire of George Frideric Handel, Thomas Arne, and Johann Christian Bach, "the London Bach." American song publishing, which really began only after the Revolution, borrowed heavily from collections of songs of the type popular in London's Vauxhall Gardens. In 1788, gentleman amateur Francis Hopkinson, a signer of the Declaration of Independence, published his *Seven Songs for the Harpsichord,* one of the earliest collections of secular music in the newly formed United States, written very much in the Arne style. Other American composers in the post-Revolutionary era were recent immigrants James Hewitt, former music director at the court of George III, Benjamin Carr, and Alexander Reinagle. The music of Hopkinson and his contemporaries was not, however, truly popular. Too pretentious, genteel, and imitative of European models, it could not reflect the American frontier and revolutionary experience.

Very little of the popular music written in the first decades of the nineteenth century has retained its popularity today. An exception is "Home, Sweet Home" (1823), with words by John Howard Payne and music by Henry R. Bishop, which was composed for the ballad opera *Clari, or The Maid of Milan.* The British style remained the predominant influence, although Irish and Scottish melodies attained great popularity with the publication of *The Scots Musical Museum* (including "The Blue Bells of Scotland") in 1787 and Irish poet Thomas Moore's *A Selection of Irish Melodies* (with "Believe Me If All Those Endearing Young Charms," "The Last Rose of Summer," and "The Minstrel Boy"), published in folios at intervals from 1808 to 1834. Irish tunes exerted a fascination on Britons and Americans for some of the same reasons that black music did in later decades. The music of these oppressed people was perceived as uncouth yet weirdly evocative. One could look down on the singer yet appropriate the song for one's own purposes, including that of expressing longings repressed in one's own culture. The poet Moore complained in a preface to his book that it was impossible to notate Irish music in an authentic manner, because the tunes rebelled against the strict rhythm that the printed notes implied they should have.

Italian bel canto opera exerted a disproportionate influence on American popular music of the first half of the nineteenth century, given the fraction of the population that was Italian. Operas by Gioacchino Rossini and Vincenzo Bellini were performed to capacity crowds, and arias from the operas were published with English texts and sung in parlors throughout the country. Singer and songwriter Henry Russell, who had studied with Rossini, made a fortune touring the East Coast from 1833 to 1841, performing his Italianate songs on such topics as motherhood ("The Old Arm Chair"), madness ("The Maniac"), and nostalgia ("Woodman Spare That Tree"). It is noteworthy that Louis Moreau Gottschalk's piano piece "Columbia, Caprice Américain" (1860), though essentially a meditation on Stephen Collins Foster's "My Old Kentucky Home" (1853), gives equal time to a ravishing melody from Charles-François Gounod's *Faust* (1859)—as if good, singable tunes from European opera (in this case French) could be immediately adopted as American. Giuseppe Verdi was "American" enough in this sense for music from *Rigoletto* to be played at Lincoln's first inaugural, and Union soldiers marched to the beat of "La Traviata Quickstep." As Lawrence Levine has pointed out, this lowbrow infatuation with Italian opera fell victim in the second half of the nineteenth century to the "sacralization of art," by which highbrows called for "standards" to stamp out popular enthusiasms, turning to northern Europe, in particular Germany, for their inspiration.

The desire to correct the musical behavior of others, already evident in the battle over how psalms should be sung, was the guiding force in the career of Bostonian Lowell Mason (1792–1872), who did well by his efforts, becoming one of the first American composers to make a fortune from his music. He may have done some good as well, through his efforts to bring musical education into the public schools and his composition of some hymns still widely sung today ("My Faith Looks Up to Thee," "When I Survey the Wondrous Cross," "Nearer, My God, to Thee"). But his contributions came at the cost of practically wiping out New England psalmody and fuguing tunes and seriously endangering the development of a native American hymnody. Fasola and shaped-note singing stayed alive on the frontier, blossoming into what came to be known as *Sacred Harp* music, after the title of an 1844 collection. It was a raw, vigorous, participatory hymnody characterized by independent three- and four-part singing, with the melody—as had been common before 1800—in the tenor. By contrast, Mason's bland hymns were part of the general trend toward the sentimentalization of Christianity. Indeed, the transfer of the melody from the tenor to the soprano not only represented a harmonic submission (with the three other parts now merely serving to accompany the top line's melody) but may also have incarnated what Ann Douglas has described as the feminization of American culture. Women in the early nineteenth century were beginning to greatly outnumber men in the churches; a revivalist hymn such as "Jesus Is Tenderly Calling" presents a maternal vision of God strikingly at variance with the wrathful judge depicted by Jonathan Edwards. Indeed, Gilbert Chase reports that in the late eighteenth century, when men still held the melody, women enjoyed screaming out the high notes to such a degree that it "may have been a compensatory means of feminine self-assertion."

In the mid 1800s, minstrel music became an important resource for the sheet music industry, although writing down the songs for the American parlor involved an inevitable loss of rhythmic subtlety.

In 1797 the tiny frontier town of Washington, Kentucky, later to be the site of the slave auction that would inspire Harriet Beecher Stowe to write *Uncle Tom's Cabin*, saw an amateur production of the British comic opera *The Padlock* (1768), featuring Mungo, a drunken character played in black-face. A sign of things to come in American popular musical entertainment, Mungo would soon be reincarnated in countless minstrel performers in circuses and stage productions in the early decades of the nineteenth century. In 1828 Thomas Dartmouth ("Daddy") Rice introduced his song *Jim Crow*, inspired by a crippled stable hand he saw singing at his work in Louisville. The genre took on an ensemble aspect with the Virginia Minstrels in 1843 and developed into an entertainment form that would retain its popularity for several decades. Minstrel music became an important resource for the sheet music industry, though writing down the songs for the American parlor involved an inevitable loss of rhythmic subtlety. The immense popularity of the "Ethiopian business" in white America must in part be explained as a way of salving bad conscience over slavery: slaves were portrayed as happy children. Yet other factors may have been at work, too: delight in seeing urban sophistication lampooned by country folk wisdom, the innate attraction of black music (much of which must have come through even when played by whites), and an increasing nostalgia among city dwellers for a lost rural past.

The songs of Stephen Collins Foster (1826–1864) play upon that evocation of loss, of homesickness for an Old Kentucky Home that never was, yet for a virgin landscape that had indeed once been—a regret for lost innocence in industrial America. The Pittsburgh of his birth was already dark with factory smoke, though its isolation from Europe protected him from the foreign influence to which Lowell Mason had pledged allegiance. His childhood there and his youth in Cincinnati gave ideal exposure to the mix of North and South, to the vanishing frontier, and to the African American music of church and levee alike. Foster's music shows the

A late portrait of Julia Ward Howe (1819–1910) whose poem "Battle Hymn of the Republic" celebrated the justice of the Union cause. Set to music, it was one of an estimated ten thousand songs inspired by the Civil War.

influence not only of black music but also of the Irish tunes and Italian opera that had been so popular earlier in the century.

At about the same time that the Virginia Minstrels rose to fame, the Hutchinson Family Singers of Milford, New Hampshire, achieved considerable success with what was in many ways a diametrically opposed approach. In 1842, when the three brothers added their sister to the act, what had been a local amateur group became an international phenomenon. The fad had begun with singing families who came from the Alpine regions of central Europe in the 1820s, and American imitators soon sprang up, particularly from New England. But none could match the success of the Hutchinsons, who performed songs with a social conscience based on a typically American faith in social progress. They lent themselves to the abolitionist cause, most spectacularly with "Get Off the Track," a controversial song that represented the emancipation of the slaves as a freedom train.

Despite the nation's optimism in the years before the Civil War, American popular songs were steeped in sadness and grief. Maudlin and morbid, they sentimentalized the death of the beautiful and young, broken families, maternal grief, and disasters such as fires and storms ("Ship of Fire" managed to combine the latter into one horrendously effective performance). Songs on the stage were valued for their drama, and songs sung in the home, for their decorous gentility. Young ladies in middle- and upper-class homes inevitably studied the piano, which became increasingly popular as the development of upright models brought prices down significantly by 1860. The demand for sheet music consequently increased, and the invention of the cylinder power press in 1850 helped disseminate the material by lowering the cost of publication. The sheet music industry came into its own during the Civil War, which inspired the composition of what has been estimated as ten thousand songs. Some celebrated the justice of the cause ("Dixie," "The Battle Hymn of the Republic"), but many, perhaps most, allowed the soldiers to express love of home and family ("Who Will Care for Mother Now?") and fear of a sudden and lonely death ("All Quiet Along the Potomac Tonight"). "Weeping, Sad, and Lonely" sold over a million copies, though Union generals banned it for fear it would lower morale.

In the wake of the originality and tragic sensibility evinced by Civil War-era songs, popular music in the Gilded Age reverted to pale imitations of European culture and shallow sentimentality. Song texts, as Spaeth observed, were based on thoughts of "mothers' graves, girls' names and tender associations with mills, lanes, gates and other possible rendezvous." And such songs as "In the Gloaming," "Silver Threads Among the Gold," and "When You and I Were Young, Maggie," reveal, as Hughson Mooney put it, "the social thinking of a nation dominated by males and built upon the sanctity of marriage, prenuptial chastity and perennial passivity of women.

But other influences were at work. Blacks now joined the minstrel stage in troupes of their own. James Bland, the first black composer to succeed in the sheet music industry, published "Oh, Dem Golden Slippers," "In the Evening by the Moonlight," and "Carry Me Back to Old Virginny." The Fisk Jubilee Singers achieved international renown with their highly polished performances of Negro spirituals. The minstrel show would eventually be replaced by vaudeville, whose roots may be traced back to Tony Pastor's Opera House, which opened in New York's Bowery in 1865. While the songs and dances and comic skits of minstrelsy drew upon rural southern culture, those of vaudeville grew out of the developing urban culture of the North. Popular songs such as "The Bowery" (1892) and "The Sidewalks of New York" (1894) began to depict life in the city. The intense nationalism of the late nineteenth century found fulfilment in the stirring marches of John Philip Sousa, who sold his music to as many as ten thousand military bands in 1889, a figure that would grow to eighteen thousand by 1900. Between 1890 and 1910 band concerts were the country's most popular musical entertainment. If Stephen Collins Foster and those who loved his music felt threatened by the coming industrialization of America and sought solace in nostalgia for a vanishing rural past, Sousa's listeners, as Wilfrid Mellers has observed, embraced the mechanized present with an adolescent bodily joy.

The American music industry mechanized itself to a significant degree in the 1880s when Thomas Harms and M. Witmark began to specialize in popular music and to treat it as an industrial product. The new firms conducted market research and commissioned songs by their in-house composers to conform to what they thought would sell. Tin Pan Alley acquired its name from the tinny-sounding pianos everywhere audible on West 28th Street, where Witmark relocated in 1893 and was soon joined by a raft of other publishers. By the late 1890s, thirteen hundred dollars was spent to launch a typical Tin Pan Alley song, including publication, advertising, and a five hundred dollar payment to a singer to perform it regularly. Less than half these songs paid back their investment, but on average one out of twenty made a considerable profit. Charles K. Harris's "After the Ball" (1892), for example, sold more than five million copies, which means that nearly one out of every thirteen Americans bought one. The Gay Nineties acquired their name partly as a consequence of the new role that marketing now played in the music business, as publishers made the conscious decision to banish sad themes and reality in general from popular music. In waltz time, Tin Pan Alley songs such as "The Band Played On" (1895), "Let Me Call You Sweetheart" (1910), and "Down by the Old Mill Stream" (1910) satisfied a perceived desire for entertainment as a respite from the rigors of daily life. The birth of Tin Pan Alley followed the passage of an 1891 copyright law that finally gave protection to European music and thereby changed the face of the American music publishing industry. Since 1790, foreign music had been free for the taking, and American publishers had always thrived on piracy; thanks to the new legislation, the proportion of published music in the United States that was of native origin rose from 10 percent in the early nineteenth century to 70 percent by its close.

Despite the false gaiety of American popular music at the turn of the century, intense commercialization did allow expression of popular sentiments. The patriotism inspired by America's imperial adventures and its sense of manifest destiny, as noted, surfaced in Sousa's marches, as well as in songs like "America, the Beautiful" (1895) and George M. Cohan's "You're a Grand Old Flag" (1906). Hughson Mooney's analysis of lyrics of the period detects, in addition to this new nationalism, an affirmation of the common man, American-style, in the way love songs replaced old European "poetical" stereotypes with language of the street in such songs as "Little Annie Rooney" (1889) and "The Bicycle Built for Two" (1892). A third wave of popular expression was an almost libertine hedonism that can be attributed not only to a revolt against elitist morality but also to the increasing freedom experienced by women as they left the restraints of home and hearth and migrated to jobs in the cities. The rise of ragtime songs, with their fairly licentious lyrics featuring aggressive women and frank descriptions of physical love, allowed white men and women to break free, at least vicariously, from culturally imposed proprieties by pretending for a moment to be black. The progress of the sexual revolution in mainstream popular song can be measured by the distance traversed from the kiss that for decades had been the farthest imaginable limit to 1894's "Their Heads Nestle Closer Together" to 1904's "Won't You Fondle Me?" and 1910's "Cuddle Up a Little Closer." The new freedom afforded by the invention of the automobile was reflected in "You May Go as Far as You Like with Me, in My Merry Oldsmobile" (1906).

Though rhythmically related to the ragtime song, ragtime piano music was a separate phenomenon—according to Rudi Blesh and Harriet Janis, "remarkably nonerotic." Whereas the former was a purely American and proletarian expression, the latter was a marriage of Victorian parlor piano music with black folk-dance forms. Scott Joplin, whose "Maple Leaf Rag" sold over a million copies within seven years of its 1899 publication by John Stark of Sedalia, Missouri, studied composition with a German-born teacher. Tin Pan Alley was astounded by the popular success of this obscure product of Middle America, especially because the music was too difficult for most amateur pianists to play. The success of ragtime piano sheet music was all the more remarkable for the fact that there were no lyrics. Buyers associated it, of course, with the ragtime songs for which there were words, but other factors in its popularity were its ubiquity on player pianos (which constituted one out of every eight pianos manufactured in 1909 and three out of five in 1921); the meticulous precision and marchlike regularity ragtime piano shared with the music of the still-popular John Philip Sousa; and music lovers' admiration for the virtuosic razzle-dazzle of black ragtime pianists such as Eubie Blake and

Luckey Roberts, easterners who did not obey Joplin's repeated stricture to "play it slow." The invention of the phonograph helped increase the popularity of instrumental music, since the first machines in the 1890s were too primitive to accurately record the human voice, and hence contributed to the wide diffusion of ragtime played by woodwind and brass ensembles. Ragtime represented a way to defuse pomposity, as the work of European masters (such as Felix Mendelssohn's "Spring Song") was subjected to syncopated "ragging" arrangements. The delightful discovery was soon made that Antonin Dvorak's "Humoresque" could be played as a countermelody to Foster's "Old Folks at Home" in ragtime.

The vast improvement in sound reproduction brought about by electric recording and the replacement of the cylinder by the disc meant that by the mid 1920s a song often sold more records than sheet music. The development of commercial radio, dating from the first commercial broadcast by Pittsburgh's KDKA in 1920, offered still more competition to the music publishing industry, since the mainstay of radio programming was popular music. When Hollywood turned to sound in 1927 and developed the musical film by the mid 1930s, millions more who could not read music could hear it. The parlor piano was being replaced by the Victrola, and the passive listener eventually came to predominate over the performing amateur among the consumers of American popular music. Even popular music itself took on a languid passivity, as the technology of radio and electrical amplification encouraged a new style of singing, impossible before, in the "crooning" style of Rudy Vallee in 1928 and Bing Crosby in 1931 (preceded by Jack Smith, the "Whispering Baritone").

Ragtime represented a way to defuse pomposity, as the work of European masters (such as Felix Mendelssohn's "Spring Song") was subjected to syncopated "ragging" arrangement.

The popular music industry developed, in the period between the two world wars, a remarkably sophisticated style, influenced by such classical European composers as Claude Debussy, Sergei Rachmaninoff, and Edvard Grieg. As the English, the Irish, the Italians, and the African Americans had made their marks on popular music in previous decades, during the war years Jewish New Yorkers made an immense contribution to American culture through the music of Irving Berlin, George Gershwin, and Jerome Kern (Cole Porter, from the American heartland of Peru, Indiana, was a significant exception). They brought European sophistication and the minor tonalities of synagogue cantors (no Stephen Collins Foster song, sad as some may have been, was ever written in a minor key). Their music has the sense of ongoing movement toward climax and release, of an underlying musical logic in which each piece contributes to the effect of the whole, that had always been characteristic of classical music but until then had not been found in popular song. The simple chords of an earlier era were enriched by lush harmonies of added sixths, sevenths, and ninths and by canny modulations to distant keys. In two examples from the early 1930s, "Body and Soul," by Johnny Green, moves from D-minor to D-flat major and Jerome Kern's "Smoke Gets in Your Eyes," though it shifts abruptly from E-flat major to B-major in the middle section, eases gently back into E-flat for the close.

The Great Depression of the 1930s left its imprint on the lyrics of popular songs, which no longer embodied the rebellious spirit of the ragtime era or the energy of the twenties but offered relaxation and solace to the battered soul. Far from the participatory and communal experience popular music had been in the nineteenth century when every home had a piano or a guitar, during the 1930s this music increasingly became not only a passive but a solitary experience, as each listener tuned into his or her private radio, drifting away to the despair-tinged words of "Stardust" or "Solitude" or "Blue Lovebirds Die Alone."

There remained, of course, millions of Americans to whom the music of the last generation of Tin Pan Alley composers did not appeal—most blacks, as well as the whites of rural America who had their own popular music traditions. The growth of radio and the recording industry, however, did encourage the development of these other forms of popular music (see *Country and Western Music* and *African American Music*). During the 1920s and 1930s recording companies targeted eastern European groups with polkas and other ethnic music as well. Yet much of blues singer Billie Holliday's repertoire was made up of songs by Gershwin, Kern, Porter, and other Tin Pan Alley composers, as was that of such black jazz bands as those led by Count Basie, Cab Calloway, and Louis Armstrong. The "swing" style of the big band era, from 1935 to 1945, represented a fresh influx of black-inspired music into the American mainstream.

The nation's entry into World War II did not greatly change the melancholy mood of popular lyrics, nor did the war inspire many patriotic songs. Even World War I had generated only a few (such as Cohan's "Over There" and Berlin's "Oh! How I Hate to Get Up in the Morning"), for in the Tin Pan Alley era songs did not usually reflect the events of the day as they had in the years before and during the Civil War.

When the big bands declined in popularity at the end of World War II, the vocalists they had always featured in a minor role—singing the slow ballads while the bands alone shone on the fast, rhythmic numbers—now took center stage. The decade from 1945 to 1955 might be called the era of the big singer. The bands played a background role to the personal styling of vocalists such as Frank Sinatra, Perry Como, Nat "King" Cole, Mel Tormé, Dinah Shore, Peggy Lee, and Ella Fitzgerald. As the nearly fifty-year hegemony of Tin Pan Alley began to fade, popular music in the forties acquired more variety, if not quality, as novelty ("Pistol Packin' Mama"), Latin ("Tico-Tico"), and country and western songs ("Deep in the Heart of Texas") took to the radio airwaves. At the same time, cynicism was beginning to be replaced by warm images of family and home. The Broadway musical *Oklahoma*! (1943), with its celebration of old-fashioned American agrarian values, set the tone. Such late 1940s and early 1950s songs as "Buttons and Bows," "Dear Hearts and Gentle People," "On Top of Old Smoky," and "Oh, My Papa" continued the strain, preparing the country for the withdrawal into conservative orthodoxy that would characterize the McCarthy years of the early 1950s. These same songs and others like them would also prepare America to welcome the sea change that rock and roll would bring.

[See Also African American Music; Concert Music; Country and Western Music; Folk Song and Folk Music; Nightlife; Rock Music.]

BIBLIOGRAPHY

Blesh, Rudi, and Harriet Janis. *They All Played Ragtime: The True Story of an American Music* (4th rev. ed. 1971).

Chase, Gilbert. *America's Music: From the Pilgrims to the Present* (3d rev. ed. 1987).

Davis, Ronald L. *A History of Music in American Life.* 3 vols. (1980–1981).

Douglas, Ann. *The Feminization of American Culture* (1977).

Gold, Edward. Liner notes to *Louis Moreau Gottschalk: Piano Music* (1973).

Hall, Roger. Liner notes to *Harp of Joy* (1979).

Hamm, Charles. *Yesterdays: Popular Song in America* (1979).

Heilbut, Anthony. *The Gospel Sound: Good News and Bad Times* (1971; rev. ed. 1985).

Levine, Lawrence W. *Highbrow/Lowbrow: The Emergence of Cultural Hierarchy in America* (1988).

Mellers, Wilfrid. *Music in a New Found Land: Themes and Developments in the History of American Music.* (1965; rev. ed. 1987).

Mooney, Hughson F. "Songs, Singers, and Society, 1890–1954." *American Quarterly* 6 (1954): 221–232.

Mooney, Hughson F. "Popular Music Since the 1920s: The Significance of Shifting Taste." *American Quarterly* 20 (1968): 67–85.

Roell, Craig H. *The Piano in America, 1890–1940* (1989).

Sanjek, Russell. *American Popular Music and Its Business: The First Four Hundred Years.* 3 vols. (1988).

Schafer, William J., and Johannes Riedel. *The Art of Ragtime: Form and Meaning of an Original Black American Art* (1973).

Scheurer, Timothy E. *Born in the U.S.A.: The Myth of America in Popular Music from Colonial Times to the Present* (1991).

Seeger, Charles. "Music and Class Structure in the United States." *American Quarterly* 9 (1957): 281–294.

Spaeth, Sigmund. *A History of Popular Music in America* (1948).

Wilder, Alec. *American Popular Song: The Great Innovators, 1900–1950* (1972).

Williams, Peter W. *America's Religions: Traditions and Cultures* (1990).

— RANDOLPH PAUL RUNYON

PRINT AND PUBLISHING

Print is a technology for communication. Like all technologies widely adopted by cultures, it has come to shape human interaction as much as it has been shaped by it. The printed word engenders particular kinds of thinking, and the presence of print in a culture supports the development of certain cultural biases: the valuing of rational, analytic, and precise thought; the decontextualization of knowledge that we have come to call "objectivity"; a separation of past from present, logic from rhetoric, academic learning from wisdom. As Walter Ong puts it, writing—and print as a special case of writing—is "a technology that restructures thought."

Print has been part of the experience of the American peoples since the European migration to the continent, but has only recently attracted the attention of historians as a force in the shaping of society. It is a truism in the history of ideas that people come to reflect self-consciously about the mental structures that make thought possible only as those structures are threatened, or as clear alternatives to them arise. The explosion of the electronic media in the twentieth century—television, radio, film and video, and sound recording—has made the role of print in contemporary America more problematic than in the past, giving rise to a historiography about its role in American culture.

That role has always been intimately tied to its position in the market economy. For if print is a vehicle for the transmission of ideas and the reproduction of culture, it has always been a business as well. As economies of scale have developed, both what people have been able to say through print and how they have been able to say it have changed.

Print in an Era of Scarcity

Perhaps not half of the early European migrants to North America were literate, yet the cultures they brought with them were not primarily oral. Whether or not particular individuals were able to read, they had come of age in a culture profoundly influenced by writing, books, and the printed word. Since its invention by the goldsmith Johannes Gutenberg in about 1440, the movable-type printing press had spread rapidly throughout western Europe, making books the first modern-style, mass-produced commodity. By the sixteenth century, Stephen Gardiner thought reading books "such as few can skill of, and not the hundredth part of the realm," with clergy, merchants, and large landowners the chief possessors of the ability to read (quoted in Cressy, p. 43). But literacy was becoming an increasingly widespread and valuable skill among the English. Those who could not read—approximately 70 percent of the English in the 1640s, according to one estimate—were frequently the beneficiaries of reading aloud by those who could. By the seventeenth century, a network of distribution had been well developed whereby printed ballads, broadsides, chapbooks (small volumes of tales and poems), and religious works reached town and countryside. In circular fashion, the availability of printed matter, some of it cheap enough to be widely affordable, spurred the rise of literacy and, in turn, growing numbers of literate people stimulated the market for print, so that literacy rose gradually during the seventeenth century and the quantity of printed materials grew. Febvre and Martin estimate that, during the seventeenth century alone, somewhere between 150,000 and 200,000 editions of books were published in Europe.

Migration to the New England colonies in British North America drew disproportionately on literate groups from East Anglia and the environs of London. In 1660, about 61 percent of men and 31 percent of women in New England could sign their names to wills, a rudimentary measure of literacy that historians have used, based on our knowledge that reading was generally taught before writing in both English and New England culture. By 1710, that figure would rise to 69 percent of men and 41 percent of women, and by 1760, to 84 percent and 46 percent. Although literacy figures for the southern colonies were somewhat lower, with about 50 percent male signature literacy in the mid seventeenth century and 67 percent in the mid eighteenth, the rates were still no worse than those for much of England and probably a bit better than those for most European rural areas. Clearly, by the eighteenth century, the largely rural British colonies on the North American continent had a literacy rate among the highest in the world, comparable to that of cosmopolitan, commercial Amsterdam.

Moreover, New Englanders committed themselves to engendering literacy skills among the young, especially among young men. The Massachusetts Bay Colony mandated basic literacy education through the school law of 1647, "it being the chief project of that could deluder, Sathan, to keepe men from the knowledge of the Scriptures" (quoted in Hall, *Worlds of Wonder*, p. 38). Children were taught rudimentary reading skills by women—frequently mothers—in households, using oral repetition of passages from the Bible, primers, and catechisms. "Dame schools," overseen by women, taught ciphering and writing skills, while male schoolmasters in "grammar schools" taught Latin grammar to boys with an expectation of progressing in the professions. Although girls were expected to read as a way of achieving piety and conformance to God's will, writing was a skill particularly valuable for those engaging in business—hence, for boys. The Puritan emphasis on direct reception of the word of God through pious reading may be one explanation for the emphasis on virtually universal literacy; equally plausible as an explanation, however, was the necessity from the beginning of the colonial experience of dealing with a variety of legal documents, including land titles and transfers. Moreover, mercantile activity demanded the ability to read. In both a religious and an economic sense, literacy was a crucial skill, particularly for men.

One colonial response to the presence and valuing of literacy was the early establishment of the printing trade in British North America. As early as 1638, at a time when authorized printing in England was restricted to a handful of printers in London, Oxford, and Cambridge, the Reverend Jose Glover brought the first printing press to the British American colonies. Although Glover died on the transatlantic voyage, his wife engaged Stephen Daye, a locksmith, to set up the press. In 1640 the press published the first book to issue from a British American printing establishment, *The Whole Booke of Psalmes Faithfully Translated into English Metre*, or the Bay Psalm Book. Printing spread slowly to other British American colonies, constrained by the expense of imported paper, type, and ink; scarce labor; and the relatively small market for printed materials in the colonies. In 1685, William Bradford, a London émigré, set up the first press in Philadelphia; by 1688 he had opened a bookstore and by 1690 (in partnership with Samuel Carpenter and William Rittenhouse) had established the first paper mill in America. (Bradford fled to New York in 1693 after printing a pamphlet for Quaker dissident George Keith, becoming the first printer in that colony as well.) By 1810, the printer and publisher Isaiah Thomas estimated that about 195 paper mills existed. These produced hand-manufactured, rag-based paper for use in the colonies. Until the invention of the papermaking machine in 1798 and the development of the technology for manufacturing paper from wood pulp in the 1850s, however, the American appetite for paper was dampened by the expense of the final product.

Throughout the first half of the eighteenth century, printing spread slowly from colony to colony. Printers usually located themselves at seats of government, since appointment as printer to the government or the reception of state-sponsored jobs usually made the difference between making a go of things financially and failing. Economically, printing remained a somewhat tenuous proposition in colonial America. In a land marked by scarcity of labor, the labor-intensive work of printing made print an expensive commodity. Typesetting and the inking of type were done by hand. The state-of-the-art "two-pull press" required two experienced pressmen to operate and at full speed could produce only about two hundred sheets per hour, printed on one side only. Although American printers produced a variety of work prior to the introduction of more efficient methods in the early nineteenth century, the common denominator among printed materials was that they were short. American presses produced blank forms, laws and other government publications, short godly books or works of religion, almanacs, ballads, broadsides, newspapers, and, by the later eighteenth century, even short works of fiction. Anything longer was imported from England, or sometimes Germany.

In the early to mid 1700s there were formed some twenty social libraries dedicated to the advancement of "useful knowledge": The most famous of these was the Library Company of Philadelphia (1731), the brainchild of printer Benjamin Franklin.

Throughout the colonial era, the book trade centered in London. Booksellers arranged with printer-publishers there to import books of interest to their clientele. Colonial booksellers were peripheral to the London trade, however, and often found themselves the dumping grounds for "remaindered" works that did not sell well in England. Like printers, booksellers in the colonial era found it impossible to specialize; they frequently carried a variety of merchandise related in some way to written and print communication, including stationery, blanks, paper, ink, quills, and sealing wax. Sometimes they branched out further, selling items such as tinware, patent medicines, cloth, and jewelry to supplement their income. It was not uncommon for printers to operate a bookstore as a side enterprise or for printers or booksellers to function as postmasters for particular locales.

Books were expensive and so were generally limited to those with some degree of wealth—clergy, lawyers, planters, merchants, and others among the professional and well-to-do. For example, Thomas Ruddiman's *Rudiments of the Latin Tongue*, a schoolbook, cost the equivalent of two pairs of shoes or half a hog in Virginia in 1760. This sum represented two days' work for a common laborer or one day's work for a more highly paid artisan such as a carpenter. Tobias Smollett's fifteen-volume history of England would have cost a common laborer half a year's earnings, and a skilled artisan three months' pay. Not surprisingly, book ownership became not only the prerogative of a gentleman, but the sign of one.

In some areas, the demand for books coupled with their expense led to the establishment of libraries, which made available a variety of printed material to subscribers at a fairly modest cost. The first libraries consisted of no more than a few hundred volumes and were generally inaccessible to the public, serving colleges such as Harvard and William and Mary. In a few locations—probably no more than ten or twelve by the end of the Seven Years' War (1754–1763)—book collections viewed as public property were established during the first two-thirds of the eighteenth century. Particularly in the South, the Society for the Propagation of the Gospel established parochial collections for the dissemination of religious literature. These relatively accessible institutions were supplemented by a number of commercial endeavors designed to moderate the cost of book use for particular groups. For example, during the half century prior to the Revolution, privately formed proprietary groups founded some twenty social libraries, jointly owned and acquired to advance the cause of "useful knowledge." The most famous of these, the Library Company of Philadelphia, was the brainchild of Philadelphia printer Benjamin Franklin in 1731. Geared mainly to the needs of men in the trades, it offered its members access to a collection comprising primarily works on history, literature, and science. A second category of restrictive collection, the commercial circulating or subscription library, charged users a modest fee to borrow books. Fueled by interest in novels, which came to form a substantial portion of these circulating collections, these dozen or so libraries catered to a new reading audience in the decade and a half prior to the Revolution: individuals, many of whom were women, who read for entertainment. Unlike the other types of libraries, subscription libraries actively encouraged women to borrow.

People of modest means often owned books of specific kinds; Bibles and testaments, psalm-books, small godly works, and schoolbooks formed a list of "steady sellers." Bibles alone accounted for 20 percent of all book importation by bulk in Philadelphia in the mid eighteenth century. Those either blessed with more considerable resources or spurred on by professional need might accumulate a more substantial personal collection. David Hall has found that in seventeenth-century New England, ministers on average owned libraries of about one hundred books each, with Cotton Mather's three-thousand-volume collection being one of the most extensive in the colonies at this time. Lawyers, physicians, and scholars might also accumulate relatively extensive holdings for use in their work.

Attitudes Toward Reading

During this early era of print scarcity, books generally embodied knowledge considered authoritative for the culture. Moreover, the oral repetition of the Bible and other religious works as a technique of literacy training established these texts as reading prototypes. As a result, certain characteristic attitudes and practices regarding reading and literacy developed. Printed matter was often shared through reading aloud; hence, reading on the whole was not yet particularly experienced as a private, solitary activity as it would later become. The scarcity of print coupled with the emphasis on the authoritative meaning of most works available led to a style of reading a number of historians have termed "intensive." A text was to be tasted slowly, its meaning to be savored for its truth value. Knowledge depended less on the accumulation of information and participation in interpretive discourse than on an explication of those authoritative sources already believed to contain the marrow of truth. For most people in the colonies prior to the mid eighteenth century at least, print served mainly to confirm their status in a revealed and well-articulated social order.

Some historians and cultural critics have argued that this situation began to change in the first half of the eighteenth century. Print began to contribute substantially to the emergence of a public sphere of discourse that encouraged individuals to define themselves as citizens to whom public institutions had particular responsibilities, rather than primarily as subjects with divinely mandated responsibilities to established authority. Beginning in England in the late seventeenth century, a coffee-house culture of discussion and debate based on printed resources—newspapers, pamphlets, and books—began to develop, according to Jürgen Habermas. In this culture, print became mainly a vehicle for questioning and reinterpreting social identity and institutions, rather than merely a way of confirming their legitimate authority. The subsequent role of print in catalyzing new notions of the public sphere and of public discourse can be seen concretely in the development of the newspaper press in the three-quarters of a century prior to the American Revolution.

Newspapers in the English colonies first appeared in 1704 with the publication of John Campbell's *Boston News-Letter*. There was no expectation that they would publish controversial opinion—or, indeed, opinion of any sort. An expansion of a commercial newsletter service offered privately to government officials and merchants, Campbell's newsletter provided little by way of either local news or controversy. Newspapers were gradually recognized by colonial printers tottering on the brink of financial insolvency (like Campbell) as relatively ephemeral, consumable commodities capable of generating consistent revenue and repeat business. By 1739, according to Ian Steele, thirteen newspapers were being printed in English America, serving mainly the commercial community—in Bridgetown (Barbados), Kingston (Jamaica), Charles Town (South Carolina), Williamsburg, Philadelphia, New York, and Boston. Boston, with its wealth of readers and its burgeoning commercial economy, was second only to London in the Atlantic empire in the number of newspapers published.

Thus the publication of newspapers was primarily an economic move for most colonial printers, with little or no sense that the circulation of information might fill any particular civic need. And with a limited clientele and with support frequently provided in part by government printing contracts, it continued for some time to be in the best interest of printers to keep controversy out of their papers. Indeed, in colonies such as Virginia, the printing trade itself had been actively excluded from the life of the young colony until 1730 for fear that printing would spread divergent opinion and lead to the creation of sects and social disorder.

There were exceptions that presaged the emergence of a new ethic. In 1721 James Franklin established his *New-England Courant* to criticize explicitly the powerful clergy of Massachusetts for advocating inoculation of the population against smallpox. Franklin was eventually imprisoned and his paper banned, but not before his younger brother Benjamin received valuable experience, both in the printing trade and the politics of controversial authorship. In 1732 a political faction in New York led by lawyers James Alexander and William Smith commissioned one of William Bradford's partners, John Peter Zenger, to publish a newspaper in opposition to the regime of Governor William Cosby. Like Franklin, Zenger threatened to undermine a social order based largely on status by taking on the legitimacy of the standing order; like Franklin, he was imprisoned for his seditious libel against the government.

Unlike Franklin's, Zenger's case became a cause célèbre when it came to trial. Under English law the truth was not considered a defense against libel. Zenger's lawyer, Andrew Hamilton, urged the jury to throw out the law on the implicit principle that (as Michael Warner puts it) "censure of an official is an exercise of virtue rather than a violation of status." The jury returned a verdict of not guilty; "freedom of the press" became the power to exert oneself in civic affairs. Print was becoming legitimized as an arena for public controversy.

Nevertheless, despite the gradual decline of raw censorship, printers still had the withdrawal of patronage or support to fear and therefore imposed a form of self-censorship. "Open to all parties, but influenced by none," as a typical masthead slogan of the time had it, printers for the most part pledged themselves to accommodate all rational public discourse without discrimination. Just as the market promoted an impersonality of exchange of goods and currency, print (as it came ideally to be conceived) grew to be a place where what was assumed to be an impersonal, rational, and impartial exchange of ideas occurred.

By the time of the Revolution, this notion of an open press as the primary locus of public discourse had become so culturally embedded that the press was seen as critical to the maintenance of good government. Rather than keeping political discourse and discussion out of the newspapers they published, printers were obliged—for reasons of civic responsibility as well as of economy—to ensure that all rationally expressed opinion had fair access to their journals. The ideology followed what was just good business sense for colonial printers, who, after all, looked to the newspapers they published to turn a profit. In a limited market, it paid to open the press to a wide variety of opinions. To adopt a particular political position oneself, however, was to run the risk of alienating precious customers.

The 1765 Stamp Act, which placed a tax on every half-sheet of newspaper, every advertisement, and every almanac, blew this world apart. Not only was it an economic blow to printers already just barely in the black, but also it virtually destroyed any room that the printer-publisher might have had to claim a neutral ground. To adhere voluntarily to its provisions conveyed the impression that the printer had adopted a Tory point of view. Not to do so, however, conveyed endorsement of the patriot position. Printers who had habitually assumed a middle ground were faced with a decision in which no middle ground was possible.

The result was a forced abandonment of any notion of "neutrality of the trade" and adoption of party identification by the press, although many printers tried to maintain a nonpartisan posture for as long as they could sustain it. Eventually twice as many newspapers exhibited patriot sympathies as Tory. One of the major legacies of the Revolution, as far as the character of print in American culture is concerned, was the large-scale transformation of the print medium into the principal vehicle for public discourse, discussion, and polemic. As printed matter, particularly newspapers took blatantly partisan political (and eventually religious) positions, the number of newspapers published increased enormously. In the dozen controversial years after 1763, for example, the number of newspapers published in the colonies seems to have about doubled, from the twenty-one published in the year of the Treaty of Paris. By 1800 more than a hundred fifty public journals were published in the United States. Isaiah Thomas, renowned printer, publisher, and historian of the trade, could write in 1810 that "there are now more newspapers published in the United States, than in the United Kingdom of Great Britain and Ireland" (quoted in *History of Printing,* p. 14).

The rise in number correlated directly with the heightened stature of the newspaper as the principal vehicle for political discourse. In 1803 the Reverend Samuel Miller marveled in his *Retrospect of the Eighteenth Century* at how greatly the station of print in general and newspapers in particular had changed. "Instead . . . of being considered now, as they once were, of small moment in society," he wrote, "they have become immense moral and political engines, closely connected with the welfare of the state, and deeply involving both its peace and prosperity" (quoted in *History of Printing,* p. 18). Prior to the Revolution, the only essential printed document in most colonial households was a Bible; for the post-Revolutionary generation, the newspaper became an indispensable connection with the outside world.

Print in the Era of Market Expansion

With the expansion of the market during the first half of the nineteenth century, the scope and reach of print grew enormously in the United States, particularly in the North and West. Although raw numbers and statistics do not adequately convey the qualitative difference that print made in people's lives, they do suggest the magnitude of the growth in some print-related endeavors.

PRINTING AND PUBLISHING. By 1859, the number of printing shops in the United States had risen to about four thousand, from about fifty in the mid eighteenth century. Additionally, about four hundred publisher/capitalists financed, coordinated, and supervised production and distribution of books and other printed matter.

NEWSPAPER PUBLISHING. By 1854, 254 dailies circulated, supplemented by a vast array of weeklies, biweeklies, and triweeklies. In 1800, only 15 dailies and 220 papers of any sort had appeared regularly. The number of papers produced per capita per year was just under 22 in 1850, up from an average of about four in 1810. The largest circulation newspapers by this time averaged sales of between 10,000 and 40,000 copies daily.

PERIODICAL PUBLISHING. In 1850, American publishers issued about six hundred different periodicals geared toward a variety of interests and audiences. During the entire first half century of American periodical publication (1741–1791), American printer/editors had produced only forty-five periodicals, with the majority of these short-lived and appearing only sporadically.

POSTAL DELIVERY. In 1845, 14,000 post offices for the transmission of written and printed communication existed, up from 75 in 1789.

This tremendous growth in the presence and availability of the printed word can be accounted for by a number of factors. First, the dynamic growth of the United States population during this period resulted in a larger pool of potential readers. Between 1790 and 1860, the population of the United States grew eightfold and the nation's geographical area more than tripled. The printing press—and its ubiquitous adjunct, the newspaper—accompanied white settlement of the Ohio and Mississippi valleys. Boosters used the press to tout the presence of prime lands and a lucrative business environment to potential settlers.

Technological development and innovation in the fields of printing and papermaking also undeniably contributed to the print explosion of the early nineteenth century. These enabled print, printed images, and reading matter to be produced relatively cheaply and disseminated widely.

As the increased demand for print became obvious from the mid eighteenth century on, entrepreneurs had incentive to develop domestic sources of the printing essentials, including paper mills, type foundries, and press and ink manufactories. By the first quarter of the nineteenth century, rapid changes in printing technology, spurred on by the increased consumer appetite for print, led to a revolution in the printing industry. The two-pull wooden press gave way to iron presses strong enough and large enough to print a newspaper page with one pull of the platen. This Stanhope press (so called after its inventor) was first imported to the United States in 1811, and Philadelphian George Clymer invented an improved iron lever press within five years of the Stanhope press's introduction. In the 1820s printers experimented first with horsepower then with steam, as ways of powering presses. At about the same time, some large, urban print shops had begun to use the recently invented process of stereotyping (and later electrotyping). These allowed the production of relatively permanent metal plates from set type that could be saved for subsequent editions. The invention of lithography, the mechanization of some aspects of the binding process, the introduction of the cylinder press (1846), the mechanization of paper-making (widespread by the 1830s), the ability to manufacture paper from wood pulp instead of rags and to produce it in continuous rolls instead of sheets (1854)—all of these contributed substantially to the growth of the print industry. Moreover, the innovations of the transportation revolution, including the development of roads, canals, steam-powered ships, and finally railroads, gave entrepreneurs both the incentive to produce for wider markets and the ability to do so.

But as significant as was the introduction of new technologies to the widespread dissemination of print, it would be a mistake to view technology as the only—or even necessarily the primary—prod to the development of print as the dominant vehicle for the transmission and reproduction of culture during this era. Indeed, expansion of print's influence had begun in substantial ways *before* the widespread introduction of the major new technologies. Literacy rates rose notably, particularly among women in the North, during the early nineteenth century. Female literacy, only about 50 percent in New England in 1790, rose to a stable rate of about 85 percent, even in rural areas, by 1830. By 1840, when the cheap penny press was still in its youth, illiteracy rates were consistently less than 10 percent in the North and about 20 percent in the South, where as recently as 1800 they had hovered between 40 and 50

The printing press accompanied white settlement of the Ohio and Mississippi valleys; boosters used the press to tout the presence of prime lands and a lucrative business environment to potential settlers.

percent. The self-reports of the 1850 census on literacy indicated that the chief gaps in literacy existed between native-born whites on the one hand and nonwhites and foreign-born whites on the other.

Ideologically, print and literacy had come to occupy a key position in the continued health and prosperity of the new nation. The ability to read, to educate oneself on public issues, and to take advantage of developments in the area of useful knowledge were regarded as vital to both citizenship and effective participation in the economy. In addition, print followed the lines of market development, encouraging people to keep track of what happened at a distance. Faraway events and processes became increasingly of interest as they were perceived as having an impact on individual lives—politically, religiously, and economically. Not surprisingly, as part of the bargain, the new abundance of print made newspapers, novels, periodicals, pamphlets, and tracts into consumable commodities good not only for providing vital information and spiritual edification, but for furnishing entertainment as well.

Literacy was now viewed as essential to full functioning in society; illiteracy, rather than being seen as a fact of life, was labeled a social problem. In the religious sphere, many Protestant evangelical leaders hoped that in a less close-knit social environment, printed religious materials would act as the glue to hold together socially diverse and geographically far-flung people in a cohesive Christian union. Organizations such as the American Education Society (1814–1815), the American Bible Society (1816), the American Tract Society (1825), and the American Sunday School Union (1824) trained ministers, provided basic literacy skills, and distributed materials designed to form Christian character and maintain piety. Methodists especially took the lead in the West. There they distributed Bibles, tracts, books, and pamphlets, acting as the major supplier of printed materials in the region. In 1784 they had founded their own publishing house, the Methodist Book Concern; by the time of the Civil War, they would be joined by the American Baptist Publication Society, the Presbyterian Board of Publication, and the Lutheran Publication Society, among others. In the East, organizations like Arthur Tappan's New York Tract Society tried to provide each citizen of the city with a new tract every month.

Moreover, during an era of increasing denominational contention, religious journalism became an important vehicle for Solidifying denominational identity. Practically nonexistent in 1800, the religious press by 1830 had become a staple of daily life. In Jacksonville, Illinois, for example, over half of all subscriptions recorded by the post office during the years 1831 and 1832 were for religious periodicals. Although the steady sellers (such as John Foxe's *Book of Martyrs* or John Bunyan's *Pilgrim's Progress*) that formed the backbone of pious colonial literature declined in importance, the amount of religious material as a percentage of total print output seems to have increased in some areas.

In the secular sphere, republican ideology spurred widespread efforts to provide common schooling for an informed citizenry. The Northwest Ordinance of 1787, for example, encouraged the establishment of common schools, although it did not formally provide for their support. In practice, the lack of a firmly established tax base, particularly in sparsely settled areas, meant that practice sometimes lagged far behind the ideal. Women, responding to the claims of the ideology of republican motherhood, took up the pursuit of literacy in order to be able to provide a proper education in republicanism for their children. Common schools increasingly began to accommodate them as students.

Many free African Americans also recognized that literacy had become key to full participation in American society. Although barred in most places from attending schools established for European Americans, and without reliable means of support for schools to meet their own needs, African Americans in the North pursued the ability to read and to write in a variety of ways. Adult literacy education took place most often in groups organized principally to serve other purposes, such as the benevolent and mutual aid societies formed to provide social and economic security, and in the black churches. Still, as late as 1840, nonwhite seamen in Philadelphia had an illiteracy rate of about 75 percent, as compared with 30 percent for white males in that group, according to Lee Soltow and Edward Stevens. Black illiteracy overall did not begin to decline dramatically until the end of the century. In the South, where gatherings of free blacks were often restricted or schools illegal, literacy education took place sporadically. Slaves for their part seem to have been almost entirely illiterate, having been prohibited access to literacy skills because of white fears of revolt and insurrection.

In the wake of this dramatic rise in emphasis upon reading, schoolbooks, particularly of an indigenous variety, were among the printed commodities most in demand. Noah Webster's textbooks, for example, were widely distributed throughout the nation. But other new genres also captured the popular imagination as some of those formerly in demand fell by the wayside. For example, the novel, feared by the clergy as the supplanter of moral and socially useful literature, replaced chap-book versions of romances and fairy tales and found an audience particularly among women. Newly popular periodicals such as *Godey's Lady's Book, Graham's,* and *Peterson's* published the work of "literary domestics" such as Mrs. E. D. E. N. Southworth, Fanny Fern, Mary Virginia Terhune, and Harriet Beecher Stowe, serializing their novels and disseminating their short stories and sketches to an eager public. By the 1850s, this "damn'd mob of scribbling women," as Nathaniel Hawthorne called them, held a powerful place in the American literary market. *The Scarlet Letter,* Hawthorne's commercial success, sold 6,800 copies in its Ticknor and Fields editions of the 1850s. In contrast, Parton sold 70,000 copies of her *Fern Leaves from Fanny's Portfolio* in about the same period of time. By 1871, three-quarters of all American novels published were written by women.

Magazines and Periodicals

This era also saw, in addition to the novel, an explosion in the number of magazines and periodicals. The two principal early genres included the religious magazine and the literary miscellany. Such periodicals as the *North American Review* (1815), *Knickerbocker Magazine* (1833), and *Graham's Magazine* (1840) published serious essays, commentaries, and reviews, often touting the work of American authors such as Washington Irving, James Fenimore Cooper, and Edgar Allan Poe. Articles on female virtue and clothing styles and, later, fiction were staples of magazines directed primarily toward women, with *Godey's Lady's Book,* edited for some forty years by Sarah Josepha Hale, the most prominent of them all. Periodicals such as *Youth's Companion* (1827) catered to younger audiences, while adjuncts of large publishing houses, such as *Harper's New Monthly Magazine* (established in 1850) and *Putnam's Monthly Magazine* (1853), covered a variety of topics from public affairs to household matters. Espousing middle-class values, their goal was to appeal to all members of the family.

In the area of newspaper publication, the single most striking event of the era was the emergence of the penny press. Some historians, such as Dan Schiller, argue that the penny press emerged out of a nascent working-class press of the 1830s. Newspapers such as the *Mechanics' Press* and the *Working Men's Advocate* showed particular sensitivity to issues of class in an era when many artisans and mechanics were losing independence and autonomy within their trades. Others, such as Michael Schudson, have seen the penny press as the result of the emergence of an egalitarian middle-class ethic of the period, a response in part to increased participation in an abstract market that did not distinguish among individuals in its operation.

Whatever the case, the penny press, enabled in part by the new technology that lent itself to mass production, was innovative in a number of respects: it refused to be financed by party patronage, as the press had been since the era of the early republic; it relied on advertising not as a subsidiary means of gaining revenue but as its major means of self-support; and it valued an ethic of objectivity and factuality, seeming thereby to deal even-handedly and impartially with the truth for all comers. Professional managing editors and reporters supplanted the printer as collector of information and the party hack as manager.

In large part, the penny press was successful because it was cheap, reaching out to working-class and immigrant audiences. Whereas an older, established paper would have sold for six cents, the penny press, as its name implies, sold for a penny. The older, established press had been distributed mainly via subscription; the penny press reached its audiences in large part through street hawkers who sold individual papers. Blessed with a persisting reputation for sensationalism, largely due to the tenor of its advertising and its extensive coverage of crime, the penny press expanded the paying audience for news dramatically. For example, the *Philadelphia Public Ledger* (1836) reached ten thousand readers after eight months in business. The largest prior circulation of a paper in that city was two thousand copies. Benjamin Day's *New York Sun* (1833), the first of the penny dailies, had a circulation of thirty-eight thousand by 1843.

Developed in the 1830s, the penny press was innovative in several respects: It refused to be financed by party patronage; it relied on advertising as its major means of support; and it valued objectivity and factuality, seeming thereby to deal even-handedly with the truth.

The penny press was most successful in the larger cities of the North—and later, the West. In the South, by the time of the Civil War, only two major penny papers existed: the New Orleans *Picayune* and the *Richmond Dispatch.* The South had fewer paper mills, less well-developed means of transportation, and fewer newspapers overall. In smaller towns and villages throughout the country, local papers responded to the competitive pressure of the large urban dailies by increasingly turning to the publication of local news.

As individuals gained access to greater amounts of printed material and wider varieties of it, their cultural preconceptions about reading changed as well. In place of the early "intensive" approach to reading—concentrated attention on a few key texts—an ethos emphasizing "extensive" reading gradually came to dominate. People now thought themselves best advantaged by reading large amounts of material relatively quickly, thereby accumulating a larger fund of information and experience from which to reason, judge, and act.

The valuing of access to large amounts of printed material during this period stimulated the growth of libraries of a variety of sorts. Circulating libraries—book-rental agencies, in effect—originated in bookstores but quickly spread to a variety of sites governed only by their accessibility to the intended clientele. These included general stores, drugstores, dry goods stores, confectionaries, taverns, and brokerage firms. Such new book outlets provided fiction to those willing to pay the required subscription fee, but also supplied increasing numbers of works on politics and belles lettres. Since women had come to constitute a very large audience of readers, circulating libraries run by women principally for women operated in places such as millinery shops.

For men, the advent of privately owned subscription reading rooms, operated for profit, provided the opportunity to read a variety of materials, particularly newspapers. The Postal Law of 1792 had provided that printers might exchange copies of newspapers with others for free. These exchange newspapers often ended up in coffeehouses, which provided reading space for their customers. Sometime in the first decade of the nineteenth century, however, particularly in the West, the need for more formal reading space gave rise to for-profit subscription reading rooms. These facilities provided clients, mainly those involved in commerce, with access to current business information. During the 1820s and 1830s, mechanics' and mercantile libraries arose to meet other needs. Mechanics' libraries grew out of the workingmen's benevolent organizations founded in large cities to provide financial aid and assistance to the families of mechanics in distress and comprised mostly works of "useful knowledge." Mercantile libraries, in contrast, catered to the needs of young clerks and merchants. Eventually, mechanics' libraries became viewed principally as a way to keep young apprentices off the street, while mercantile libraries were an institution through which young men learned the attitudes, values, manners, and behaviors appropriate to their class status. Both, however, made printed materials widely available to individuals who could not or would not otherwise have bought them. Free African Americans were by and large excluded from societies organized by whites, so they organized their own debating and literary societies, lyceums, and prose reading groups in cities such as Boston, Brooklyn, and Philadelphia.

Eventually, all of these proprietary reading establishments gave way to the tax-supported public library, first established in New York State in 1835.

The nineteenth century produced an explosion of the number of magazines and periodicals. People preferred to read large amounts of material thereby accumulating a large fund of information and experience from which to reason, judge and act.

Linked with school districts but not constituted as school libraries, these institutions supplied mainly works of nonfiction to adults (fiction still being considered of specious social value). These libraries were supplemented by a variety of philanthropic endeavors, including Sunday school libraries, which provided young people with "didactic fiction," and Young Men's Christian Associations collections. In 1852 the establishment of the Boston Public Library marked the beginning of a large-scale trend toward public support of the nation's reading habit that by 1900 provided most Americans with access to printed works.

Innovations in Marketing and Distribution

Widespread demand for printed materials was both the cause and the result of a major reorganization in book and periodical production that took place between 1790 and 1840. During that era, full-fledged publishers arose, responsible for coordinating production, distribution, and marketing and for maintaining a primary relationship with authors. Prior to this time, book production had been financed principally by the author, with the printer usually receiving either a flat fee or a percentage of the profit to cover costs. Occasionally, printers had functioned as publishers, holding final financial responsibility and oversight over the work. Often, in order to ensure that costs would be covered, books were published only after a certain number of subscriptions had been taken, indicating that there would be an adequate market for them.

The new publishers introduced innovations in marketing and distribution that quickly led to the demise of the old printer/publishers. The first American publisher worthy of the name, Irish immigrant Mathew Carey, abandoned the trade of master printer early on in his career to establish an extensive sales network of agents, contacts, correspondents, and "adjutants" (as they were called) from his headquarters in Philadelphia in the late 1790s. With the assistance of Mason Locke Weems, an itinerant bookseller and ordained Episcopal minister from Maryland, Carey was able to tap a new market in the Upper South, supplying people there with cheap, popular works. Engaging a well-developed network of distributors to take subscriptions for Carey works or sell them on consignment, Weems and agents like him helped to establish the Carey firm as a dominant national presence for almost half a century.

As large firms like J. and J. Harper—later Harper and Brothers—discovered, dealing in large volume and developing a widespread distribution network would become the keys to successful publishing in the nineteenth century. Harper's emerged as the largest publisher in America in the 1840s by experimenting with strategies to minimize risk and maximize production. Founded as a job printing firm in 1817, Harper's quickly adopted state-of-the-art technological innovations (such as stereotyping and the newly invented steam-driven press) that required a greater initial outlay of capital but that resulted in the ability to produce in volume a list of books that could be reprinted and issued in new editions if demand warranted. After the passage in New York of legislation establishing school district libraries, Harper's took advantage of the new library market by initiating "library" series designed to be purchased in toto, especially by these new public institutions. The Harper's Family Library, the Library of Select Novels, Boys' and Girls' Library, the Classical Library, and the School District Library all attempted to establish appropriate standards of reading taste and culture. The motive was not—or not only—altruism or civic responsibility. Grouping the books together into a canonical set meant that Harper's imprint would stand for desirable cultural values, an incentive to purchase for certain audiences.

Other major publishers, such as D. Appleton, Putnam's, A. S. Barnes and Company, Scribners, D. Van Nostrand, and E. P. Dutton and Company, also operated on a large scale, sometimes producing specialized lists in areas of science or educational materials. Many of the publishers of the period from about 1830 to 1870 were, like Harper's, family-owned and -run businesses that valued maintaining a certain personal quality in their relationship with authors. Most too were located in the New York—Philadelphia nexus. These cities, the endpoints of important transportation routes to the West and South, were the earliest to be able to take advantage of economies of scale. Through the 1830s, most New England publishers continued to reach only local audiences; authors who wanted to accrue a national reputation were well advised to seek New York or Philadelphia publishers for their works.

The large New York and Philadelphia publishing houses solidified their hold on national markets by acting increasingly as wholesalers, distributing to retailers rather than directly to customers. A publisher such as Harper's might send its sheets to another city for local binding or might sell or rent plates to local printers so that one work might be published under multiple imprints, thus realizing a profit while minimizing transportation costs. Although Carey-type book agents, peddling door-to-door, remained active until at least the end of the century, most of the action began to take place within the book trade itself. Trade sales, parcel sales, and book fairs funneled new books, bound or in sheets, to booksellers and jobbers.

A few black book publishers existed in the antebellum period, with most (like the AME Book Concern, formed in Philadelphia in 1817, and the African Methodist Zion Publishing House, formed in New York in 1840) affiliated with a particular religious denomination. Within the black community, publishers faced obstacles in acquiring capital and in getting their books reviewed. In addition, the small number of literate African Americans in this period, and their relative poverty, meant that the mass market that sprang up for books produced by European American publishers did not exist for African American publishers. Black periodicals fared somewhat better, but even here, only three out of eleven African American-produced periodicals in the antebellum era lasted more than five years. Many of these early periodicals encouraged self-improvement and education. Meanwhile, the infant African American press, having sprung out of the abolitionist movement with Samuel E. Cornish and John B. Russworm's *Freedom's Journal* in 1827, tended to be explicitly reformist in tone, urging the uplift and empowerment of blacks.

In 1809 the Cherokee tribesman Sequoya invented an eighty-six-character alphabet whose use spread rapidly among the Cherokee; in 1828 the Cherokee Phoenix, *a bilingual newspaper, began publication in New Echota, Georgia.*

Some European American ethnic publishers had a good deal more success than did African Americans. For example, by the 1840s a German book trade was well established, having existed in North America since the mid eighteenth century. Centered in Philadelphia, Cincinnati, Saint Louis, Boston, and New York, the trade produced books that by the 1840s were status symbols among intellectuals and students enamored of German romanticism. German and bilingual newspapers flourished after 1830, when genres roughly equivalent to those published in English proliferated wherever substantial numbers of German speakers settled. The first Hebrew press was established in the United States in New York by Henry Frank, a Jewish German immigrant, in 1849 or 1850. His firm produced prayer books and other scholarly and devotional works.

In addition, a small American Indian press addressed the needs of Native Americans. Sequoya, a member of the Cherokee tribe, recognized the need for literacy as a way for Indians to gain power with respect to white society. In 1809 he invented an eighty-six-character alphabet whose use spread rapidly among the Cherokee. In 1828 the *Cherokee Phoenix*, a bilingual newspaper, began publication in New Echota, Georgia. The Cherokee, Chickasaw, Choctaw, and Creek peoples published newspapers and periodicals by and for an Indian audience in a number of states during the nineteenth century.

As the publishing industry became well established, two important developments shaped the industry. First, the ability of printers to act as independent editor-publishers and entrepreneurs eroded as their social status declined. As the size of the average print shop increased and printing increasingly became absorbed into the larger world of publishing, tasks within the printing trade became more segmented and routinized. Wages and status plummeted. Artisans and mechanics, who before had had a claim on the work of ideological production through editing and publishing, now became industrial cogs in the larger publishing machine.

In addition, competition to produce books more cheaply and to disseminate them more widely led to the introduction of the cheap paperback book. In 1839 New York journalists Park Benjamin and Rufus Griswold produced *Brother Jonathan*, a weekly periodical that serialized pirated British fiction in a format that looked like a newspaper. If it looked like a newspaper, they reasoned, the publication might take advantage of cheap postal rates for newspapers. In 1840 *New World* followed suit. Such "story papers," as they were called, could be bound together to form a book. Yet as it became apparent that novels in their entirety might be published before serialization was complete, cutting into sales, these penny-paper publishers began to issue "extras" or "supplements" containing the entire text of a novel just off the boat. The cost of these supplements might be a little over a dime, compared with a dollar or two for clothbound editions. In 1843 Congress changed postal regulations to prohibit the practice of marketing books in the guise of newspapers, but not before competition within the book industry drove prices down.

Throughout the nineteenth century as well, property rights vested in texts were continually at issue among publishers and authors. The United States copyright law of 1790 gave the copyright holder, usually the author, the sole right to print, publish, and distribute a work for a period of fourteen years, renewable for another fourteen. As publishing firms came to dominate the book business, authors increasingly sold copyrights to their publishers in return for fixed royalties. Because the law extended only to works published domestically, however, the copyright law had important implications for American authors. Until 1891, when the United States agreed to abide by international copyright law, works of foreign publication could be—and were—pirated without compensation to the original publishing firm or author. Thus American authors were simply more expensive to publish than were European. Gradually, out-and-out piracy moderated, as a practice known as "courtesies of the trade" (or "the Harper rule") came to govern the interactions of domestic with foreign publishers. Domestic publishers made arrangements with foreign publishers to reprint material and in return provided some agreed-upon compensation for the right to do so. Other domestic publishers, in their turn, had a gentleman's agreement to respect the relationship of a domestic publisher with its foreign counterpart or with a foreign author unless either of the foreign correspondents expressed an interest in changing the agreement. The "courtesies of the trade" were effective only during periods of "business as usual," however; when competition heated up, they were largely disregarded as the market became flooded with cheap reprints.

Print in the Era of Mass Commercial Culture

In the second half of the nineteenth century, three principal forces thoroughly transformed the market for print in the United States: standardization in the production of certain kinds of printed materials; the shift to advertising and away from circulation as the major source of periodical income; and coordinated methods of print distribution. Each of these factors was meant to maximize the profit of publisher-entrepreneurs involved in a notoriously chancy business with historically low returns. However, as T. J. Jackson Lears has noted elsewhere in this encyclopedia, who pays the bill makes a difference in what gets said. Rationalized methods for production, financing, and distribution meant substantial changes in the forms and genres of printed materials available to the new mass audience—and in their overall tone and tenor.

While family-owned houses, such as Harper's, Putnam's, and Ticknor and Fields (established 1843), continued to maintain a paternalistic and noncommercial ethos and to generate genteel literature designed for family reading, a new breed of more commercially oriented publishers turned fiction writing into an assembly-line business. In 1859 the firm of Beadle and Adams adapted the format of the cheap, paperbound music books they had been publishing to the realm of fiction. The new works, bound in yellow and selling for a dime, encompassed both reprints and new stories. So successful were they that by 1865 Beadle and Company (helped by a brisk trade among Civil War soldiers) had published over four million of these "dime novels." Irwin and Erastus Beadle's effort spawned a number of imitators, nearly all of whom had begun in the printing trades but had sought out new avenues of opportunity as skilled craftwork was downgraded and routinized through industrialization. By the 1870s, firms had begun to issue whole "libraries" of sensational adventure and detective stories, sentimental romances, frontier and western fiction, and city stories.

As the appetite for cheap fiction grew, publishers discovered that generating a standard format and standard procedures would not only ensure customer loyalty to their product, but also would lower the costs of production. Beadle and Adams were the first to standardize manuscript lengths and payment rates for authors. Subsequent dime-novel publishers reserved the right to change the manuscript in any way they felt appropriate in order to fit the recognizable format of the firm's line. In addition, famous "library" characters such as Deadwood Dick, Ned Buntline, and the Old Sleuth became publishers' (not authors') property, as did the pseudonyms under which authors wrote. By the 1880s, standardization of characters, plots, and manuscript lengths had become so common that the production process has been likened to a factory system.

Even among the gentlemen publishers who clung to an older ideal, the expansion and rationalization of production led to an increasing gap between author and publisher. By the 1880s and 1890s, firms began to divide into specialized divisions, each of which had a separate budget and staff and produced a different list. Publishers in these large-scale enterprises found themselves increasingly playing the role of businessmen responsible for coordinating all facets of acquisition, production, and distribution. The bulk of the face-to-face work with authors and potential authors fell to the lot of a new middle manager, the editor. Whereas under the older system many houses prided themselves on the personal quality of their relationship with their authors, the new system dictated a more distant and businesslike relation. Literary agencies sprang up in New York in the 1870s and 1880s to handle negotiations between author and publisher. In addition, a number of writers' organizations and "unions" arose to gain leverage for authors in their dealings with publishers.

The new impetus toward mass production culminated in the printed mass product par excellence, the general-interest mass-market magazine. Although family magazines had begun to flourish in the decades before the Civil War and the number of magazines published annually had nearly quintupled between 1865 and 1885, the 1890s saw the beginning of an explosion of magazines with very large circulations. By the end of World War I, *McClure's* magazine would boast circulation figures of over half a million, *Cosmopolitan* and *Collier's* of over a million, and the *Saturday Evening Post* of over two million. What accounted for this incredible increase in the volume of circulating printed materials was neither a dramatic rise in the literacy rate nor a discernible rise in consumer affluence, although marginal increases in each of these areas may have had some effect. Some portion of it can also be explained by the increasing use of attractive illustration, made possible through chromolithography, halftone photoengraving, and electrotyping. Perhaps more instrumental in the industry's shift into overdrive, however, were the introduction of organizational rationalization into the industry and the move to advertising as the major source of revenue. And these, in turn, had their effects on the ways in which authors who published in mass-market periodicals defined themselves.

The shift came first in the newspaper industry. Joseph Pulitzer's New York *World* (revived in 1883) and William Randolph Hearst's New York *Journal* (1895) enjoyed rapid rises in circulation and posed a challenge to older, more established newspapers such as the *Times* (1851), the *Herald* (1835), and the *Tribune* (1841). Lowering their price to a penny, the World and the *Journal* turned to advertising revenue for the bulk of their financial support. Before this time, advertisements tended to be small and unobtrusive; under Pulitzer's and Hearst's regimes, advertising became bold and flashy and eventually took up nearly 50 percent of print space. Standard advertising rates were established based on circulation figures.

At the same time, the two papers concentrated on entertaining readers through sensational stories and self-promotion. Commuters on trains and omnibuses increasingly turned to attention-grabbing headlines and garish illustrations to amuse themselves on the way to work. The elite got its information (particularly business news) from information-oriented newspapers such as Adolph Ochs's *New York Times.* The rest got theirs from the new papers, whose explicit goal was to entertain the reader. Pulitzer's Sunday supplement to the *World,* first published in the 1880s, emphasized the role of newspaper reading as leisure activity. Comics, in-depth articles, and a large volume of advertisement all contributed to the sense that a newspaper was as much for lingering over with a second cup of coffee as for procuring information.

Newspaper circulation shot up. The combination of the low price and the orientation to entertainment was a formula borrowed by magazines that had to compete with this new kind of story-oriented newspaper for audiences and revenue. In the 1870s these same magazines had utilized premiums and club combinations to boost circulation. Now their strategy was to liken themselves explicitly to the new genre of newspaper in order to appeal to potential customers. "A good magazine is a good newspaper in a dress suit," George Horace Lorimer, the editor of the *Saturday Evening Post,* said of his own endeavor (quoted in Tebbell and Zuckerman, *The Magazine in America* p. 67). New muckraking magazines, such as *McClure's, Everybody's, Munsey's,* and *Collier's,* hired reporters to uncover sensational instances of corporate or government wrongdoing. Professional editors ensured that the product was delivered in a standardized format and commissioned stories to fit their need rather than merely waiting for them to be volunteered or delivered by free-lance writers. Although the genteel magazines of the Harpers and the Scribners survived, magazines sponsored by chains increasingly displaced them in popular influence. The latter aimed to entertain rather than to edify. Moreover, as part of marketing groups, they had access to large advertising revenues that lowered the cover price, raised their profit, and contributed to high circulation figures. The Curtis group (*The Ladies' Home Journal, The Saturday Evening Post, The Country Gentleman*), the Hearst chain (*Cosmopolitan, Hearst's Magazine, Good Housekeeping*), and the Crowell-Collier group (*Collier's, American Woman's Home Companion,* and *Farm and Fireside*) were the most important of these.

Before the late 1800s, newspaper advertisements tended to be small and unobtrusive; under Joseph Pulitzer's and William Randolph Hearst's regimes, however, advertising became bold and flashy and eventually took up nearly 50 percent of print space.

Along with the general interest magazines, a host of special interest magazines sprang up. Directed at women, children, farmers, and professionals of all stripes, some were more specialized than others. The "Golden Age of Magazines" temporarily destroyed the dime-novel business. (It would reemerge in the 1930s as the paperback trade.) In its stead, a hybrid product emerged that dealt with dime-novel themes and contained mainly fiction but that also contained advertisements, letters from readers, and a host of other features. These pulp magazines, invented in 1896 by dime-novel and mass-market publisher Frank Munsey, became a staple for the juvenile audience.

The new regime resulted in changes for both authors and readers. Newspaper and magazine writers sometimes seemed less like authors in the old-fashioned sense and more like employees of large, bureaucratically organized corporations. The standardized format and expectations of the industry frequently dictated more about the shape of an article or story than the author's own preferences. Yet the pretense of objectivity among these new "reporters" masked a world in which certain facts were presented and marketed in certain predictable ways to sell advertising space and magazines or newspapers. The news was not manufactured out of whole cloth, but it was cut and tailored to serve particular commercial purposes.

Audiences for their part could no longer imagine being addressed by authors as "gentle readers." Rather, they were now consumers—not only of the printed word, but also of the products whose manufacturers financed their access to the printed word. Women were particularly targeted as potential purchasers as they became identified as the chief consumers for the family. Advertisers flocked to publications such as Cyrus Curtis's the *Ladies' Home Journal*, with its formula of household hints, celebrity profiles, and short fiction, and in 1900 helped make it the first of all the million-seller magazines. Indeed, so powerful has been the link between advertisers and women's magazines that the feminist magazine *Ms.* dropped its connections with all advertisers in 1990, complaining that they demanded too much control over the magazine's content. Although radio and television later came to take the place of print as the dominant media of mass entertainment, the mode of commercial sponsorship developed in the mass-market magazines has endured.

Because it could not appeal to as large a mass market, the black periodical press suffered by comparison. Initial optimism about the advent of legal equality during the Reconstruction period gave way by the 1880s to the clear realization that social equality was nowhere on the horizon. As a result, the African American periodical press enjoyed a revival during this period, for the most part existing to combat racial stereotypes and to emphasize the importance of education to racial uplift. Literacy among blacks grew considerably between 1870 and 1910, from 20 percent to 70 percent. Along with the small urban middle classes, these new readers provided new audiences for black newspapers such as T. Thomas Fortune's *New York Age* (1887–1937) or the *Washington Bee* (1882–1922).

If white-owned magazines were sold in large numbers on newsstands, black-owned and -oriented magazines had to depend largely on subscription agents to ensure circulation. Although black commercial magazines, following the trend of the age, turned to advertising from both black businesses and white-owned corporations to support themselves, a large percentage of African American periodicals were sponsored by the black churches and other established nonprofit organizations, such as the Afro-American League (1890), the National Association of Colored Women (1896), and the National Negro Business League (1900). In contrast to the mammoth white-owned mass-market periodicals, the two largest black publications at the turn of the century were the *Colored American* (17,840 peak circulation) and the *Voice of the Negro* (about 15,000 at peak). The influential *Crisis*, affiliated with the National Association for the Advancement of Colored People and edited by W. E. B. DuBois, reached a circulation of about 35,000 in 1915.

Not everyone saw the spread of the often-sensational wares of the mass market as an unbridled good. Librarians in particular, organized professionally in 1876 as the American Library Association, fought to protect the older patrician culture from the pernicious influences of the newer, cheaper dime novels and pulp fiction. ALA founders, including individuals such as Melvil Dewey, Charles Cutter, and William F. Poole, were by and large middle-aged Protestants whose families had migrated to the New World four or more generations back. Although they were dedicated to providing (as the ALA motto had it) "the best reading for the largest numbers at the least cost," the class bias in their understanding of what the "best reading" might be was clear from the very beginning. Designed to ameliorate class friction during a period of high tension by making "good" reading materials democratically available, the style and values of the public libraries of the period often left members of the working classes cold. Nor did Andrew Carnegie's famous gifts for use in the construction and establishment of public libraries help matters much; many members of the working class saw his beneficence as part of an elitist and paternalistic scheme of social control and resisted using the new facilities. For middle-class, white women, however, the new system of public libraries provided professional opportunities heretofore unavailable. And professional librarians did have room to exercise social power as censors of inappropriate reading materials, particularly novels. The Comstock Law of 1873, designed to check the spread of pornographic and salacious printed materials, was an additional manifestation of the tendency of the middle class to fear and censor printed materials that challenged bourgeois norms.

The distribution of printed materials also underwent a revolution during the late nineteenth and the early twentieth centuries. Founded in 1864, Sinclair Tousey's American News Company (ANC) came to hold a virtual monopoly on the distribution of mass-market magazines and paperbound novels to newsstands, railway stations, and hotel lobbies through the 1930s; eventually its operation would spread to chain stores (including grocery and drug chains). Buying periodicals at discount and selling them to local dealers, the ANC operation succeeded because it provided a high-profit, no-risk situation to retailers. Retailers received a certain percentage of the cover price of each magazine sold; they were not charged for unsold magazines.

Publishers of books faced a greater challenge in coordinating marketing and distribution. Books have always been tricky commodities to sell because of their variety and because of the lack of what might be called a "general audience." In order to compete in the new mass-market environment, publishers needed to come up with new and effective strategies for distributing what would come to be called the mass-market "best-seller." The book trade began to publish information about what was selling and what was not with the founding in 1895 of the trade journal *Bookman.* Best-sellers of the early twentieth century included mainly novels. In the 1910s and 1920s such works as Eleanor H. Porter's *Pollyanna* (1913), Edgar Rice Burroughs's *Tarzan of the Apes* (1914), Sinclair Lewis's *Main Street* (1920), and Edith M. Hull's *The Sheik* (1921) began to reach large audiences. Two important innovations in sales and distribution, however, brought book sales into the age of mass marketing: the mail-order book club and the mass-market paperback trade.

Established in 1926, Harry Scherman's Book-of-the-Month Club was the first modern mail-order distributor to advertise through the mail using "bait" premiums and considerable discounts to purchasers. A staff of editors sought out "middlebrow" works and offered them on a regular basis to consumers, who presumably got into the habit of buying. Utilizing such mass-production techniques as standard packaging and direct mail, book clubs quickly captured the largest segment of United States book sales, with a hundred fifty different clubs responsible for more sales than all U.S. retail outlets in 1980 (Stevens and Garcia, p. 113). All but two of the books to make the best-seller list in the twenty years following the establishment of the Book-of-the-Month Club were book club selections.

At about the same time that the book club phenomenon was catching on, a variety of publishers began to produce a series of cheap, rack-sized books that could be sold at a variety of retail outlets. Inspired by successful German and English precedents, Robert Fair de Graff (with financing help from Simon and Schuster) began to publish the Pocket Books series in 1939. Paperbound versions of hardback best-sellers selling for a quarter a copy, these portable books could be distributed easily to newsstands, grocery stores, or other mass-market outlets. As a result of the introduction of Pocket Books, people began to buy (rather than borrow) a greater percentage of the books they read. In short order, additional paperback houses sprang up, among them Bantam, Avon, Dell, New American Library, and Popular Library. In time, not only would new material begin to be produced in paperback form; but also hardcover publishers such as Doubleday (which created its Anchor Books division in 1953), Alfred A. Knopf (Vintage Books), and E. P. Dutton (Everyman Paperbacks) would find it necessary to get into the trade paperback publishing business to continue to compete in the market.

With its headlong entry into mass-market publishing and distribution, the book trade increasingly became less the province of a well-read gentry at family-owned publishing houses willing to take a loss on good literature, and more a subsidiary enterprise of massive multinational conglomerates concerned with the bottom line. Beginning in the 1950s, a number of the older family houses either merged with others or were bought outright by larger entertainment enterprises. Although publishers of all sorts were subject to mergers, takeover attempts, and buyouts during this period, the fortunes of Macmillan (parent company of the publisher of this Compendium) illustrate the kinds of financial transformations wracking the book industry during the middle and later decades of the twentieth century.

The Macmillan Company was originally a British-owned publishing firm that opened an independent partnership in the United States in 1890. In 1960 Crowell-Collier, which had risen to prominence as a publisher of encyclopedias and mass-market magazines, took over Macmillan when the latter ran out of capital to invest in the new and lucrative textbook market. The new company, known as Crowell-Collier and Macmillan, Inc., began to buy properties in areas outside its own fields, such as music publishing. By the 1970s, the company had become simply Macmillan, Inc., a large conglomerate acquiring new properties and struggling to fight takeover attempts from nonbook conglomerates. In the heady business climate of the 1980s, Macmillan acquired the old-line house of Scribners, which had itself acquired Atheneum. In 1988, Maxwell Communication Corporation, part of British publisher Robert Maxwell's empire, acquired Macmillan, Inc., making it part of an even larger and more diverse multinational enterprise; this empire, however, collapsed after the death of founder Maxwell in 1991 and ensuing revelations of financial irregularities. Although Macmillan may be a particularly prominent example of corporate vertigo in publishing, similar changes in status have befallen a number of the family-founded houses in the latter half of the twentieth century.

In the area of retailing, the privately owned and run bookstore has also given way to new economies of scale. While many small, independent booksellers have gone out of business, the total number of bookstores in the United States has risen in the past few decades, mainly due to the dominance of shopping mall-type chain stores. Waldenbooks and B. Dalton, currently the two largest bookselling chains, focus mainly on the sale of bestsellers. Computer-controlled inventories maximize sales and minimize risk by ensuring that retailers are aware of mass-market tastes and trends at any given moment. Although the number of bookstores has multiplied, the large chains tend to stock the same few titles at stores across the country. The number of titles offered for sale on the retail book market has perhaps decreased as a result.

Since the 1980s the nation's largest bookselling chains have used computer-controlled inventories to maximize sales and minimize risk by ensuring that retailers are aware of mass-market tastes at any given moment; as a result, the large chains tend to stock the same few titles.

Print in the Electronic Age

In the twentieth century, the new audiovisual and electronic media have had as great an effect on print, literacy, and reading as has the rise of the mass market—but historians and cultural observers still disagree about the extent of those effects and their implications for the future of print. Those who see more radical changes argue that the introduction of radio, film, the phonograph, and especially television has undermined the primacy of print in American culture and is leading to a decline in literacy and in reading in general. Those who see the changes wrought by the electronic revolution as more modest in scope argue that new computer and data communications technologies have made print more important than ever as a vehicle for information transmission.

From the 1860s through the 1910s, print was the dominant source of information and entertainment for most Americans. At the beginning of the century, an estimated 90 percent of households, for example, regularly purchased and read newspapers. Literacy was nearly universal among the native-born white population. Even with the advent of radio as a source of mass entertainment in the 1920s, per capita spending on reading materials (controlled for inflation) continued to climb—except for a small decline during the Great Depression—until 1979, when it began to slip.

Different sectors of the print economy began to feel the impact of television, introduced on a national scale in 1947, at different times. The first to sustain damage were mass-market magazines, whose advertising revenues and circulations began to decline in the 1950s. There were two reasons for television's tremendous impact on the magazine industry. First, it provided an alternative vehicle for advertising. Second, it provided Americans with an alternative source of entertainment. *TV Guide* became the mass-market magazine with the largest circulation.

The magazine industry in the early 1960s fought back by trying to boost circulation figures. Cutting prices and offering special premiums and package deals to subscribers, magazine publishers hoped to lure back advertising dollars that had migrated to television. Such moves were by and large disastrous, failing to boost circulation and resulting in lost revenues. More successful magazine publishers learned to target their products to specialized audiences whose needs would not necessarily be served by the general audience programming of television. Advertisers, more concerned with who, rather than how many, got the message, returned to these specialized vehicles. New periodicals sprang up for working women, the politically radical, gay men and lesbians, foreign-language speakers, African Americans, sports fans, environmentalists, and other market segments.

Newspapers showed some of the same effects of television's ubiquitousness. As network news shows expanded to a half-hour format and increasing portions of network budgets were devoted to information programming, television became the dominant source of news for most Americans by the 1960s. In response, some newspaper entrepreneurs turned to specialization as well, with suburban and specialty newspapers an area of growth since the 1960s. Major dailies suffered, however, with newspaper buying declining following the peak year of 1960. By the 1980s many major cities were left with only one substantial newspaper of any size; mergers and buyouts meant that many metropolitan areas were left with only one major printed news source. The number of people who said that they read a newspaper regularly declined from the levels of the 1960s as well, with older people more likely than younger ones to read.

Meanwhile, the number of people who claim to be book readers has held constant over the past half century at 20 to 25 percent of the American population. Women read more than men, younger people more than older, whites more than non-whites, and the middle class more than the working class. Much of the book reading that takes place in the United States is a leisure activity, although individuals also report reading for information, for religious inspiration or self-improvement, for critical cultural commentary, or for alternatives to the dominant cultural perspective.

Have literacy levels dropped in recent years? It depends on how one defines literacy. By census self-report measures, 99.5 percent of the United States population older than fourteen years of age can read. A number of studies indicate, however, that perhaps 20 percent of that population has difficulty comprehending enough to accomplish certain basic cultural tasks—that is, about 20 percent are estimated to be functionally illiterate. Functional illiteracy is not distributed randomly across the population; it is highest (according to National Institute of Education figures) in black urban youth (47 percent) and Hispanic youth (56 percent). Several contemporary critics have also lamented another type of illiteracy that they call "cultural illiteracy," meaning an unfamiliarity with the basic knowledge necessary for informed cultural participation.

The glass that is half empty from one perspective is half full from another. Electronic publishing, photocopying, word processing, data bases, and computer software have democratized the production of information and the printed word—at least for those able to afford or have access to the necessary equipment. Indeed, far from becoming extinct as a medium for communication, printed material is increasing in quantity so rapidly that a major new cultural challenge has been the control and management of information generated through print. In many countries today, including the United States, Japan, Canada, and the nations of the European Community, information-making, -managing, and -processing industries account for about half of the gross national product. If people seem to read less for entertainment, they are likely to have to read much more in the course of their work performance. The danger is that a literacy gap based mainly on class will yawn wider between those who can manipulate printed symbols and those who cannot—between those who inhabit the ranks of the relatively well-to-do and those consigned to a low-paying service economy with few employment options. Although Americans are not in danger of becoming a nation of illiterates anytime soon, there is a danger of clear and growing class divisions based on literacy and the ability, or the lack thereof, to process printed information.

[See also The Culture of Consumption; Intellectuals and the Intelligentsia; Journalism; Mass Culture and Its Critics; Popular Literature; Radio; Technology and Social Change; Television.]

BIBLIOGRAPHY

General Works on Print and Literacy

Baumann, Gerd, ed. *The Written Word: Literacy in Transition* (1986).

Bullock, Penelope L. *The Afro-American Periodical Press, 1838–1909* (1981).

Cazden, Robert E. *A Social History of the German Book Trade in America to the Civil War* (1984).

Darnton, Robert. *The Kiss of Lamourette: Reflections in Cultural History* (1990).

Davidson, Cathy N., ed. *Reading in America: Literature and Social History* (1989).

Febvre, Lucien, and Henri-Jean Martin. *The Coming of the Book: The Impact of Printing, 1450–1800.* Translated by Geoffrey Nowell-Smith and David Wooton (1976).

Gouldner, Alvin W. *The Dialectic of Ideology and Technology: The Origins, Grammar, and Future of Ideology* (1976).

Graff, Harvey J. *The Legacies of Literacy: Continuities and Contradictions in Western Culture and Society* (1987).

Hall, David D. *On Native Ground: From the History of Printing to the History of the Book* (1984).

Harris, Michael H., ed. *Reader in American Library History* (1971).

Joyce, Donald Franklin. *Gatekeepers of Black Culture: Black-Owned Book Publishing in the United States, 1817–1981* (1983).

Kaser, David. *A Book for a Sixpense: The Circulating Library in America.* Beta Phi Mu Chapbook, no. 14 (1980).

Neufeldt, Harvey G., and Leo McGee, eds. *Education of the African American Adult: An Historical Overview* (1990).

Ong, Walter J. "Writing Is a Technology that Restructures Thought." In *The Written Word,* edited by Gerd Baumann (1986).

Resnick, Daniel P., ed. *Literacy in Historical Perspective* (1983).

Tebbel, John. *Between Covers: The Rise and Transformation of Book Publishing in America* (1987).

Tebbel, John, and Mary Ellen Waller-Zuckerman. *The Magazine in America, 1741–1990* (1991).

Print in the Era of Scarcity

Bailyn, Bernard, and John B. Hench, eds. *The Press and the American Revolution* (1980).

Botein, Stephen. " 'Meer Mechanics' and an Open Press: The Business and Political Strategies of Colonial American Printers." *Perspectives in American History* 9 (1975): 125–225.

Cressy, David. *Literacy and the Social Order: Reading and Writing in Tudor and Stuart England* (1980).

Habermas, Jürgen. *The Structural Transformation of the Public Sphere: An Inquiry into a Category of Bourgeois Society.* Translated by Thomas Burger (1989).

Hall, David D. *Worlds of Wonder, Days of Judgment: Popular Religious Belief in Early New England* (1990).
Joyce, William L., David D. Hall, Richard D. Brown, and John B. Hench, eds. *Printing and Society in Early America* (1983).
Kett, Joseph F., and Patricia A. McClung. "Book Culture in Post-Revolutionary Virginia." *Proceedings of the American Antiquarian Society* 94 (1984): 97–147.
Lockridge, Kenneth A. *Literacy in Colonial New England: An Enquiry into the Social Context of Literacy in the Early Modern West* (1974).
Spufford, Margaret. *Small Books and Pleasant Histories: Popular Fiction in Its Readership in Seventeenth-Century England* (1981).
Steele, Ian K. *The English Atlantic, 1675–1740: An Exploration of Communication and Community* (1986).
Thomas, Isaiah. *The History of Printing in America.* 2d ed., edited by Marcus A. McCorison (repr. 1970).
Warner, Michael. *The Letters of the Republic: Publication and the Public Sphere in Eighteenth-Century America* (1990).

Print in the Era of Market Expansion

Charvat, William. *Literary Publishing in America, 1790–1850* (1959).
Gilmore, William J. *Reading Becomes a Necessity of Life: Material and Cultural Life in Rural New England, 1780–1835* (1989).
Hackenberg, Michael, ed. *Getting the Books Out: Papers of the Chicago Conference on the Book in Nineteenth-Century America* (1987).
Kelley, Mary. *Private Woman, Public Stage: Literary Domesticity in Nineteenth-Century America* (1984).
Murphy, James E., and Sharon M. Murphy. *Let My People Know: American Indian Journalism, 1828–1978* (1981).
Schiller, Dan. *Objectivity and the News: The Public and the Rise of Commercial Journalism* (1981).
Schudson, Michael. *Discovering the News: A Social History of American Newspapers* (1978).
Silver, Rollo G. *The American Printer, 1787–1825* (1967).
Soltow, Lee, and Edward Stevens. *The Rise of Literacy and the Common School in the United States: A Socioeconomic Analysis to 1870* (1981).

Print in the Era of Mass Commercial Culture

Bold, Christine. *Selling the Wild West: Popular Western Fiction, 1860–1960* (1987).
Coultrap-McQuin, Susan. *Doing Literary Business: American Women Writers in the Nineteenth Century* (1990).
Denning, Michael. *Mechanic Accents: Dime Novels and Working-Class Culture in America* (1987).
Garrison, Dee. *Apostles of Culture: The Public Librarian and American Society, 1876–1920* (1979).
Wilson, Christopher P. "The Rhetoric of Consumption: Mass-Market Magazines and the Demise of the Gentle Reader, 1880–1920." In *The Culture of Consumption: Critical Essays in American History, 1880–1980,* edited by Richard W. Fox and T. J. Jackson Lears (1983).
Wilson, Christopher P. *The Labor of Words: Literary Professionalism in the Progressive Era* (1985).

Print in the Electronic Era

Beniger, James R. *The Control Revolution: Technological and Economic Origins of the Information Society* (1986).
Bonn, Thomas L. *Under Cover: An Illustrated History of American Mass Market Paperbacks* (1982).
Cole, John Y., ed. *Books in Our Future: Perspectives and Proposals* (1987).
Davis, Kenneth C. *Two-Bit Culture: The Paperbacking of America* (1984).
Graubard, Stephen, ed. *Reading in the 1980s* (1983).
Kaestle, Carl F., Helen Damon-Moore, Lawrence C. Stedman, Katherine Tinsley, and William Vance Trollinger, Jr. *Literacy in the United States: Readers and Reading Since 1880* (1991).
West, James L. W., III. *American Authors and the Literary Marketplace Since 1900* (1988).

— MARY KUPIEC CAYTON

THE PROFESSIONS

The professions are a disputed category because they are not inert or passive objects, like preserved butterflies under a lepidopterist's gaze, to be calmly classified, labeled, and considered. Rather, they are active, changing, influential social groups that energetically classify, label, and consider themselves—they take an important part in their own definition. Originally the term "profession" referred to any occupation, and this is still its primary meaning in most Romance languages. The word goes back to the practice of the Roman tax collector, who called upon taxpayers to declare publicly (to profess) their occupation so that they might be properly assessed. By the eighteenth century its primary meaning had narrowed in the Anglo-Saxon world to refer more particularly to clergymen, lawyers, and physicians (and often to military officers). These were occupations endowed with honor and authority: they were worthy of a gentleman.

In nineteenth- and twentieth-century America this definition was extended in various overlapping ways—through resemblance, differentiation, self-definition, and social designation. A driving force behind such extension was ambition. To enter a profession or to transform one's occupation into a profession was a way of rising in life. The resemblance of the professions to one another, even in the eighteenth century, when there were few, was of a loose sort. It would be difficult to isolate a single feature that essentially defined a profession. The professions were occupations of gentlemen, but there were gentlemanly pursuits—superintending one's landed estate, for example—that were not considered professions; and the lower ranks of the professions of medicine and law (surgeons and solicitors) were often not considered gentlemanly. A classical education was a common preparation for the upper ranks of most professions, though clearly less common among military officers. Subordination to exogenous requirements diminished within the professions but was much praised among the clergy of the Church of England. The similarities that helped define the professions in the eighteenth century, and more decidedly afterward, were like family resemblances, shared by many members but rarely by all.

Differentiation was also important in defining the professions. In the eighteenth century, a profession stood in contrast with a trade, something usually considered beneath the dignity of a gentleman. Mercantile pursuits for profit and handicrafts were clearly not professions. In nineteenth-century America, such disdain for working with one's hands rapidly disappeared, although as late as the end of the twentieth century even a highly skilled blue-collar worker would not be regarded as a professional. That some American craftsmen won the appellation "professional" owed much to their energetic campaigns of self-definition. Dentists and pharmacists (the latter both mechanical and mercantile) were disdained by the medical profession, and they in response mimicked the physicians with a vengeance: they too formed associations to declare themselves professionals and to lobby legislatures for such recognition. Dentists even beset the Census Bureau until it classified them as professionals.

Not all such campaigns of self-definition succeeded. If the resemblances to the traditional professions was too incongruous, social designation would often be withheld. When in the late nineteenth and early twentieth centuries librarianship and public-school teaching came to be dominated by women, and the women were placed in clearly subordinate positions, these occupations declined in status and lost much of their earlier public recognition as professions. In that era a woman was rarely granted authority over anyone except children, and her honor was defined by her chastity. A profession made up largely of women seemed to be an anomaly. The definition of the professions is a social and historical matter, shifting but still bearing some relation to the qualities of the traditional professions.

General Historiographical Trends

The first writings on the history of the professions were by the professionals themselves. These were usually commemorative works about a ministerial, medical, or bar association, extolling the leadership and the achievements of the particular group. In such works the well-being of the practitioners and the progress of their science were usually assumed to be indistinguishable. They therefore provided justification for the authority and honor that the profession had or should have achieved. However, the scholarly studies of the histories of the relevant disciplines—medicine, law, and religion—in their usually brief discussions of their organized professions sometimes provided a refreshing contrast to the apologetic works written by practitioners.

An important turning point in the historiography of the professions was the publication of a work by two Englishmen. This study, *The Professions* (1933), written by A. M. Carr-Saunders and P. A. Wilson, placed the discussion of these occupational groups into a broader social setting than had been envisioned in the earlier scholarship. Though they drew extensively upon the special histories of diverse professions, the authors tried to extract from those narratives a social role for the professions that they believed had great contemporary importance. They argued that the professions provided the social leaven that might raise society to a new era of "freedom, dignity, and responsibility."

In nineteenth-century America, earlier disdain for working with one's hands rapidly disappeared, although as late as the end of the twentieth century even a highly skilled blue-collar worker would not be regarded as a professional.

The essential characteristic of the professions, Carr-Saunders and Wilson argued, was the application to the ordinary business of life of intellectual techniques acquired through long training. Since the industrial revolution, such intellectual techniques were preeminently those of the natural sciences. This made the professions both progressive and stabilizing, for the advance of the natural sciences seemed obviously progressive and the requirements of extensive training prescribed the sustaining of institutions. This argument worked best with the scientific professions like medicine and less well with what the authors called the "institutional professions," such as law. Significantly, they omitted the ministry altogether. Modern society, they asserted, had entered an era of large-scale organizations, and this had affected the professions. But what differentiated professional organization from the rest, they thought, was that it provided for both cooperation and autonomy. It also provided the means of bringing "the expert into service of democracy." Their hope was that the modalities of professional organization would spread to society at large.

Writing early in the Great Depression, when the social order in most Western nations was badly shaken, Carr-Saunders and Wilson proposed the professions as a third way between the anarchic laissez-faire capitalism of the United States and the oppressive statism of the

Soviet Union. Such a vision was strikingly similar to pronouncements of some of the professionals themselves, but rarely had it been put forward so boldly and comprehensively. The work of Carr-Saunders and Wilson gave impulse and direction to much of the scholarly writing on the professions in the generation that followed, yet those studies were seldom as ideologically explicit as their influential predecessor.

An advantageous way of looking at some of the changes in the literature on the professions brought about by the scholars of the generation that followed would be to compare the Carr-Saunders and Wilson article on the professions in the *Encyclopaedia of the Social Sciences* (1934) with that on the same subject by Talcott Parsons in the *International Encyclopedia of the Social Sciences* (1968). While many of the ideas of Carr-Saunders and Wilson are retained in Parsons's analysis, clearly Parsons's argument is more systematic and coherent, for he casts his discussion within the framework of Max Weber's methodology, theory, and general worldview. This makes the subject of the professions even more momentous than it had been in the work of Carr-Saunders and Wilson. In Parsons's analysis, the professions become the embodiment of "cognitive rationality" and instruments in "the main historical trend" of the extension of "the range of rationally ordered organization" in the world. If Parsons seems more audacious than Carr-Saunders and Wilson, his empirical supports are much slighter. Most often he does not refer to any profession in particular, and when he does, it is usually medicine. Nonetheless, he maintains and develops many of the themes found in the earlier literature. The element of intellectual training is central to his discussion, and he places great stress upon the role of the universities in providing cognitive and technical proficiency. He also looks to the professional association as the "institutional means of putting competence to socially responsible use." In this particular, like Carr-Saunders and Wilson in others, he accepts the professionals at their own valuation.

Whatever the shortcomings of Carr-Saunders and Wilson's as well as of Parsons's work on the professions, they gave the subject a kind of excitement that made it an attractive meeting ground for sociologists and historians. Carr-Saunders and Wilson's study had notable influence upon the writing about the professions before World War II, and Parsons's idea held sway after the war, but by the 1960s and 1970s the new scholarship turned sharply critical of both. Some of this development owed much to Parsons's efforts to make available the writings of Max Weber to American audiences. For Weber not only described the "rationalization" of the world, he also gave an account of growing monopolization (with its restrictive and malefic effects) as a special rational response to market uncertainties.

The New Critical scholarship of the 1960s and 1970s emphasized the monopolistic aspects of the professions, their interest in limiting the supply of practitioners in order to increase their income. Moreover, these scholars charged that Parsons had taken the professions' "ideology of service" at face value. The new studies tried to treat the professions as one would any occupation, except that they had a remarkably successful sales talk which enabled them to win monopolistic powers from the government. The upshot was "right-wing" and "left-wing" Weberian scholarship—the former emphasizing professional expertise and granting professional privileges some legitimacy, the latter emphasizing professional monopolistic and restrictive practices and discrediting the legitimacy of those privileges. Alongside the left-wing Weberians stood some Marxist critics who also stressed the monopolistic practices of the professions and, in addition, treated "professional posturing" as false consciousness and predicted the future proletarianization of "mental labor in advanced capitalism."

More recently, the description of modernization as the spread of "cognitive rationality" and "extending the range of rationally ordered organization" has come under attack from many writers as being too one-sided. Theodor Adorno and Herbert Marcuse, for example, have argued provocatively that the advance of this kind of rationality and the advance of neurosis go hand in hand. The Weberian analysis of the professions also has come to seem one-sided in both motives and effects. Rather than portray the professions as the epitome of modernization, I have argued elsewhere that the special importance of the professions is their success in maintaining much that is precapitalist and predemocratic in the modern world. The present article is written from that perspective.

Before discussing the historical development of the professions, it will be helpful to engage in a brief survey of the major turns and events of that development.

The American professions were born in the mid eighteenth century. In this era the colonies were brought closer politically and economically to the mother country, and the rapid social differentiation in the cities and the southern colonies created an upper class that ardently mimicked British gentlemanly ways. It also provided some basis for the adoption of gentlemanly usages by those engaged in occupations that were considered professions in Britain.

By 1830 it had become evident that a powerful egalitarian impulse in America was sweeping before it many of the marks of a society that had been run by finished gentlemen. This was an ambivalent egalitarianism, combining a vague eagerness for leveling in the social order with a distinct desire to remove all restraints upon the ambitious and the capable. The professions, both in their style and in their science that seemed to support their style, came under attack. Though diminished in reputation, privileges, and self-assurance, they managed to enclose and preserve the authority and honor of the traditional gentleman in their relationships to their clients if not to society at large.

The years 1880 to 1900 were ones of economic expansion and consolidation, as well as of rapid increase in social stratification and what were considered persuasive justifications for that stratification. The professions' traditional claim of authority and honor also found new supports that helped the associations win new licensing legislation. Those laws distinguished between rightful and wrongful practitioners and ostensibly granted monopoly powers to the legitimate ones.

After the 1880s the professions increased and extended their powers and numbers. This was particularly true in the first decades of the twentieth century. If, nonetheless, the discussion of twentieth-century developments may seem somewhat abbreviated in this article, that follows from one of its principal arguments—that the last decades of the nineteenth century were the formative era of the modern professions. Their models of aspiration and achievement were fashioned in the 1880s and 1890s. Much of the professions' earlier history culminated in the late nineteenth century, and much of their later history derived from that era. However, in the 1960s and 1970s, the professions again came under attack in a manner reminiscent of the egalitarian assaults of the mid-nineteenth century. These new attacks were far less consequential, and by the 1980s the expanding professions had recovered their momentum. The professions today are prominent models for a singular kind of social position. They seem to offer an escape from vexing supervision at work as well as from some of the depersonalization and uncertainty of markets and bureaucracies.

The Rise of the Professions, 1750–1830

The first wave of professionalization consisted largely of the acquisition of the proprieties and learning of the upper ranks of the British professions by men of lower standing in the colonies who did similar work. The learning itself was a propriety, for today much of it would seem to have little immediate and practical relevance. One of the important marks of an eighteenth-century professional was a liberal arts education. Being almost exclusively a privilege of the upper classes, classical learning conferred dignity and social status upon those who acquired it. Instruction in the classical languages and authors, it was said, engendered a refinement, embellishment, and enlargement of mind that contrasted sharply with the narrowness and even coarseness of the tradesman and mechanic, who had access only to apprenticeship training. Therefore, one of the characteristic features of the professionalization of American occupations in this era was the increasing proportion of practitioners who boasted a liberal arts education. In the ministry that percentage had always been high, but in medicine and law this development was remarkable. By 1771, the Suffolk bar demanded a liberal education for admission to practice, and somewhat earlier the bar association in New York City agreed to accept only college graduates as clerks. Those with bachelor's degrees were favored in most jurisdictions. Later writers were to wonder at the many professionals in this era with such degrees. Between 1800 and 1830 more than 90 percent of Massachusetts lawyers were college graduates.

Alongside this desire to make a gentleman's education a qualification for these occupations in America, the professionals demonstrated their interest in appropriating the science cultivated by the upper ranks of their callings in England. Actually, the Americans were often more resolute and formal about this than their English counterparts. American physicians set up medical schools along the pattern of those in Scotland, where many early leaders of the profession studied. American lawyers sponsored lectures on law, borrowing from Sir William Blackstone's Vinerian Lectures, then expanded and regularized these into proto-law schools, usually attached to established colleges. (Before the Revolution, some of the foremost colonial lawyers had attended the Inns of Court and were actually called to the English bar.) By the early nineteenth century American ministers had established theological seminaries, something that had almost no parallel in England.

Other features of the English gentlemanly professions translated less well. The eminent Dr. John Morgan (1735–1789) on his return from his grand tour of the Continent, tried to establish honoraria rather than fixed fees as the proper mode of payment, but to no avail. Nor was he more successful in setting up ranks within the profession. A few of the more distinguished American physicians refused to practice surgery or to compound drugs, but most doctors ignored those punctilios of the London physician. Lawyers were somewhat more successful in setting up ranks in their profession. The rank of barrister (sometimes called counsel) in a number of colonies was separated from the attorneys, and members of the new rank were given a monopoly on practice in the superior courts. New Jersey in addition set up the rank of serjeant, and Massachusetts provided three grades: attorney, counselor, and barrister. Often a lawyer might rise through the ranks and practice in them simultaneously, thereby gaining entry to all courts.

Such laxity was characteristic of the monopoly powers granted to the professions. These powers, the professionals expected, would help secure them a suitable income—a competence. That was a favorite term. It meant both the sufficiency of means for comfortable living and the distinctive skills that those easy circumstances could advance and sustain. It was the income with which a gentleman could preserve his proper "port and carriage," his honor and authority; but the notion of maximization of income was lacking. This, in part, explains the looseness of the monopoly powers granted by the professional licensing laws and the meager force behind them. They did, however, clearly distinguish between reputable and disreputable practitioners. By 1800, three-quarters of the states had such laws governing the practice of law, and by 1830 only three states were without them for medicine. Licensed professionals flaunted the public recognition of their competence. They were authoritative and respected, and stood at the head of their professions.

While a tradesman or mechanic gave his customer what he wanted, the professional gave his client what he needed: This was a relation of authority and dependence.

The most important feature of the English gentlemanly professions adopted by their American counterparts was the special relation of professional and client. In the English setting, this was the interjection of the general relation between gentlemen and those below them into the world of occupations. While a tradesman or mechanic gave his customer what he wanted, the professional gave his client what he needed. This was a relation of authority and dependence. It had its origins in the traditions of feudal Europe as well as in the transference of feelings from parent-child relationships to class ties—a shift not uncommon in aristocratic societies. The relation of professional and client characteristic of the upper ranks of the English professions became an ideal for their American imitators.

That relation received explicit expression in the codes of medical ethics adopted by the medical societies of this era; later it appeared in the code of the American Medical Association, where it remained throughout the nineteenth century. All these codes derived from that of Dr. Thomas Percival of Manchester, England. Percival was an ardent admirer of the great eighteenth-century London physicians. But what could be taken for granted in London had to be expounded and explicated in Manchester—and even more so in America. Percival's initial purpose had been to set off the domain of the physician and to protect it from the intrusive upstart surgeons. Percival called his work a code of medical ethics, yet for the most part it dealt with etiquette. The confusion of ethics and etiquette was an important characteristic of gentlemanly culture. The salient point of the code was its description of the relationship between the physician and his patient.

Percival bade doctors "so to unite *tenderness* with *firmness,* and *condescension* with *authority,* as to inspire the minds of their patients with gratitude, respect and confidence" (Leake, ed., *Percival's Medical Ethics,* p. 27). This was the epitome of gentlemanly bearing. The virtues of the gentlemanly doctor were mastery delicately balanced by compassion; the virtues of the deferential patient were unmitigated respect for the physician and compliance with his directions. If in this formula we today bridle at the word "condescension," it is because our more egalitarian age has coarsened the meaning of what the eighteenth century took to be a subtle moral imperative. Condescension was a form of humility that could counterbalance authority (Dr. Samuel Johnson called it a "voluntary humiliation: descent from superiority") and was exercised by those of elevated mind and social station. It was the humane act of a superior who, while he condescended, remained superior, for he was performing an act of grace toward those on whose level he was placing himself.

Ministers and lawyers, without such a code, had other devices with which to strengthen the professional relationship of authority and dependence. Perhaps as important as the relationship between the professional and his client was the relationship among the professions themselves. The ministry, the preeminent profession in seventeenth-century New England played a special role in giving particularity to the concept and ideal of the professions much beyond their time and place. The years 1750–1830, however, were not only the era of the establishment of the gentlemanly professions, they were also the years in which the ministry clearly declined from preeminence in America and the lawyers rose to a paramount position. This shift owed much to developments within these professions as well as to changes in society at large. It was primarily in seventeenth-century New England that the ministry held an exalted position in society, and the effects of that prominence were felt in varying degrees in the other colonies. The decline of the ministry from that prominence has been often linked to secularization, a term perhaps somewhat indefinite but still useful in describing the diminishing importance of religious ideas and experience for the ordering of the broader society.

Protestantism's special emphasis on the inwardness of religion as well as its propensity for dissension contributed to this secularization, as did the growing economic and social diversification of the society in which Protestantism flourished. In addition, the Great Awakening in the second quarter of the eighteenth century, which fostered religion of the heart—religion at a high emotional temperature—endangered and weakened the authority of some of the most commanding ministers. In this era of relative decline, the rapidly growing body of Anglican clergy in the colonies set in motion a brief countercurrent in the mid-eighteenth century in their campaign to bring a bishop to America and to augment their priestly powers. This endeavor closely paralleled the efforts of colonial lawyers and doctors to assume professional standing. Because they backed what proved to be the losing side in the Revolution, however, the priests' hopes were dashed. By 1830 the ministry had declined in power, yet its influence was still great. At the least, the ministers were the philosophers of the multitude, supplying a foundation of moral belief and behavior as well as a scheme of general purposes and ends that helped give meaning to life. Without this, the amazing practical accomplishments of Americans would have been less likely.

Between 1830 and 1880, ambitious businessmen entered markets that had been based upon local connections, traditional restraints, and various insular forms of monopoly.

The lawyers quickly rose to preeminence among the professions. In broadest terms, this can be seen as part of a prevailing cultural shift from the world outlook of John Calvin (1509–1564) to the world outlook of John Locke (1632–1704), from the preoccupation with sin to the preoccupation with rights. The lawyer was the priest of rights. It is not at all surprising, therefore, that the lawyers played such an extraordinary role in the Revolution and in the establishment of the new government. The Constitution, which embodied the fundamental principles of American government, defined itself as law. That meant those principles could be determined in the courts through the ordinary practice of litigation. This was the lawyer's domain. William Wirt (1772–1834), son of a tavern keeper who rose to the post of attorney general of the United States, described the esteem of the profession through which he himself had been raised: "Men of talents in this country have generally been bred in the profession of law," he wrote in 1803, "and indeed throughout the United States, I have met with few persons of exalted intellect whose powers have been directed to any other pursuit. The bar in America is the road to honor" (Robert A. Ferguson, *Law and Letters in American Culture* [1984], p. 12).

The Egalitarian Interregnum, 1830–1880

Although the ideal of the profession, developed and elaborated in America between 1750 and 1830, showed surprising durability, some of its institutional fixtures constructed during this era were swiftly dismantled in the years that followed. The years from about 1830 to 1880, from the standpoint of organizational power and effectiveness, were the nadir of the professions in America; in this period a widespread and powerful egalitarian impulse that had been latent in much of American culture became manifest and demolished the underpinnings of a society that had previously been run by gentlemen. Clearly it was an equivocal egalitarianism, in that it mixed a sentiment for leveling with a distinct eagerness for rising in the world. That volatile mixture was compounded in varying proportions in different sections of the country and segments of society.

Among the principal sources of this egalitarianism were the expanding political democracy, market capitalism, and evangelical Protestantism. Each took on new force and momentum in this era, pressing against different kinds of exclusiveness for the sake of dissimilar sorts of opportunity and exhibiting distinctive styles of leveling. Suffrage extension, and the new political devices that accompanied it, to all appearances made most white males—irrespective of social standing, religious belief, merit, and even virtue—members of the ruling class. Government by gentlemen, often vociferously attacked, gave way to government by political machine, in which democrats equably acquiesced.

Market capitalism, quickened by the rapid improvement of transportation and more generally invigorated by public support for the construction of social-overhead capital, unwittingly furnished an extraordinary corrosive for the prescriptive and decorous ranks in society. Ambitious businessmen entered markets that had been based upon local connections, traditional restraints, and various insular forms of monopoly. In the world of commerce and industry, authority and honor took on new connotations. Special recognition was granted to success in the marketplace as in the past success in war, politics, and art had been given distinctive approbation. The honor granted to commercial success helped to justify the increasingly unequal distribution of wealth that characterized the major cities. However, in the rural North, where most of the American population lived, commercial agriculture and smallholdings prevailed. There markets worked with fewest restraints and the distribution of wealth was probably brought closer to some sort of equality than at any other time or place in the nation's history.

Evangelical Protestantism, the third component of the equivocal egalitarian impulse of the era, embodied an attack upon authority but could also provide a justification of existing conditions. Two principal and interrelated developments within the evangelical Protestantism of these years were the gradual erosion of the Calvinist distinction between God's predestined elect and all others, and the emergence of the seasonal revival, with its unique spiritual technology, as a central institution of Protestant piety. This turned evangelical Protestants away from church establishments, hierarchies, ritual, elevated and learned clergy, creeds, and sometimes separate denominations. It turned them toward such vagaries as perfectionism and millenarianism, latent with social disruption. Strictly speaking, evangelical Protestant egalitarianism extended to the realm of salvation and not to the scheme of creation. In nineteenth-century America, however, those categories became increasingly porous.

In this setting, the traditional distinction between gentlemen and ordinary folk dissolved rapidly. There was no clamor for the replacement of that honorific title with a more egalitarian term; rather, the bulk of the white male population, without much fuss, simply took on and was granted the designation "gentleman." This posed a threat to the distinction between professions and ordinary occupations. The classical education, the science, and even the technical education of the professional came under attack. Classical learning, once an indicium of gentlemanly status, was now widely derided as exclusive and useless. After 1830, a growing number of young men bypassed the colleges, the fortresses of classical education, on their way to the professions. The laymen's charge that the vaunted science of the professions was useless and encumbering found acceptance within the professions themselves.

In this era, the sciences of the professions—their systematized knowledge based upon theoretical understanding—were beset with difficulties. The resulting doubts weakened the professionals' resolve in response to the attacks upon their elevated standing and privileges. The science of the physician in the eighteenth and early nineteenth centuries was a humoral "system" explaining in comprehensive terms the cause and cure of disease. Benjamin Rush (1745–1813), for example, declared that there was but one disease, its cause the irregular convulsive action of blood vessels and its primary treatment bloodletting. Some doctors held fast to such systems and the heroic treatment they required (usually bleeding, mercurials, and narcotics); others, though, shaken by their melancholy experience and the unsettling findings of the French clinician Pierre Louis (1787–1872)—who through rigorous statistical studies demonstrated that venesection had few beneficial effects—were led to conclude that medicine was an uncertain science. It was not surprising, therefore, that the simple (but patented) "botanic medicine" of Samuel Thomson (1769–1843), and the recondite homeopathy of Samuel Hahnemann (1755–1843) would find acceptance—botanic medicine by the commonalty, and homeopathy by the upper classes.

The science of law in late-eighteenth- and early-nineteenth-century America derived from a long and venerable accumulation of custom, judicial decision, and legislation, most of which, to the disgust of some patriots, had been received from England. The substantive law was intricately entangled with procedure and confined within the various common-law forms of action. Ironically, William Blackstone's attempt to give a connected and rational account of the whole legal system helped lead Americans willy-nilly away from the forms and fictions that he cherished. The comprehensiveness and clarity of his work raised the hope among his American imitators that law might be freed from inherited modes in order to deal more directly with justice in a democratic society. In addition to such theoretical considerations there were some practical embarrassments. To the extent that Americans accepted the common-law rule of stare decisis, the many American courts with their many rulings threatened to confuse even the most learned lawyers. The legal profession therefore was divided and weakened by its doubts when faced with the resolute campaign of David Dudley Field (1805–1894) for the reform of law. Field contended that the law could be so simplified and codified that its basic principles might easily be grasped by all, and the number of lawyers reduced. In the Jacksonian era, the movement for legal reform often combined with a drive against the legal profession.

The theological science of the majority of American ministers in the eighteenth and early nineteenth centuries had been one of the various forms of modified Calvinism. Its basic doctrines, however, seemed to deny that man could be active in his own salvation. Yet in times of declining religious fervor some ministers brushed aside this dogma and appealed to their congregations to "make a new heart and spirit." The apparent successes of the religion of the heart, breaking forth in a series of great revivals, led some of the most renowned Calvinist theologians to becloud fundamental issues and the leading revivalists to downgrade doctrine altogether. What was the recourse of the gentlemanly ministry, guardians of orthodox doctrine, when the revivalists attacked the traditional notion that a valid ministry was an educated one? And what was it when the lowly revivalists joined the patrician statesmen of Enlightenment persuasion to disestablish the already discredited Anglican church after the Revolution as well as the Standing Order in Massachusetts and Connecticut some time later?

The disestablishment of the clergy was a foreshadowing. When the licensed doctors tried to use governmental powers against the medical sects, the latter struck back with Samuel Thomson in the lead and various Evangelicals as allies. When the dust had cleared, ten states had repealed their laws giving the medical societies the right to examine candidates and grant licenses. At the same time, bar associations that had arisen in the late eighteenth and early nineteenth centuries were deprived of their powers to admit new lawyers to practice. The Indiana state constitution went so far as to provide that "every person of good moral character who is a voter is entitled to practice law in any of the courts of the state" (Roscoe Pound, *The Lawyer from Antiquity to Modern Times* [1953], p. 233).

With the relinquishment of their classical learning and the downgrading of their science, some professionals began to place more emphasis upon their craft. After 1830, two seemingly opposite tendencies in technical education for the professions came to light: a widespread disparagement of training for the professions in favor of giving free play to natural talent-gained currency, and a booming market appeared for technical instruction, resulting from a rush of young men into the professions once they seemed accessible. The outcome was the rapid proliferation of proprietary schools for awarding professional degrees. In medicine, competition was brisk, and quite soon entry into these schools became exceedingly easy and graduation a matter of course. Between 1830 and 1845 the number of medical colleges doubled.

The legal profession was rife with propriety schools as well, but these were of less consequence. For in law such schools competed not only with apprenticeship preparation but also with do-it-yourself training, Blackstone's *Commentaries* in hand. The most reputable proprietary school, at Litchfield, Connecticut, which usually catered to young men with bachelor's degrees, closed in 1833. The small number of college-connected law schools that survived had no fixed entry requirements. Most lawyers in this era did not get their training through formal education. This seems to have been true of the ministers as well. The first theological seminaries, formed in the early nineteenth century to ensure the inculcation of Calvinist doctrine and to ward off threatening Enlightenment notions then gaining influence in the colleges, were later supplemented by seminaries with the more limited purpose of upholding denominational standards and imparting homiletic skills. The seminary catalogs often listed a bachelor's degree as prerequisite for admission, but their students more often came directly out of the revivals than out of the colleges. Among the Methodists and the Baptists, the two largest denominations by midcentury, most ministers had avoided the seminaries altogether.

In the mid 1830s, with the relinquishment of their classical learning and the downgrading of their science, some professionals began to place more emphasis upon their craft.

Yet for those ministers who attended the seminaries, the experience was one of the most important sources of camaraderie and colleagueship that their profession afforded. The seminary alumni associations were often the most vital professional associations of ministers in this era. As for the doctors, their state and local medical societies aimed to serve more diverse purposes. During the period 1830–1880, the number of those societies grew, though they were often factious and unstable. One of the leaders of the New York State society, Dr. Nathan Smith Davis (1817–1904), who had been able to enter the profession because many of the traditional requirements had been abandoned, was unwilling to see his own achievement devalued by further laxity and want of distinction. He gathered about him a band of zealous doctors whose common cause was raising the profession to its former standing. This group became the basis for the American Medical Association (founded 1847), whose chief concerns were the struggle against "irregular" medicine and the improvement of medical education. In a manner characteristic of the outlook of professionals, these doctors sought those measures that would make their duty and their interest the same. They would benefit practitioners, but in ways they believed would improve the quality of medical services. The glut of poorly trained and "irregular" doctors was harmful to the public as well as to the well-trained and proficient practitioners. "Numbers should be restricted," wrote Davis, "by adding to the standard of requirements" (*History of Medical Education and Institutions in the United States* [1851], p. 227). In this interim period the AMA accomplished little; it persisted, nonetheless, and so became the saving remnant that carried the memory and ambition of earlier days into a later, more favorable era.

Perhaps the most salutary medical organizations of this era were the nascent specialty associations. Humoral pathology held back specialization because it was based upon the belief that the causes of disease were general, and the studying of organs meant studying symptoms rather than causes. From this standpoint, only quacks who were ignorant of medical science or charlatans who pandered to popular superstition for profit would be specialists. The first ophthalmologists and laryngologists were given both these labels. But when humoral pathology was refuted, "Baconian" inductive principles were defined as the true scientific method—and the customary scorn for specialists was more difficult to maintain. A motion recognizing specialties as legitimate fields of practice was tabled at an AMA convention in 1854 and not passed until fifteen years later.

Specialization served not only to subdivide medical practice but also led to the establishment of new healing professions. The humbling of the medical profession encouraged those who had done its most menial work to aspire to equal standing with doctors. Apothecaries, traditionally the lowest rank in medicine, laid the groundwork of the new profession of pharmacy in this era. In addition, men who had combined the crudest minor surgery of the mouth with skillful cosmetic embellishments now began to call themselves dentists. These dentists, owing to their rudimentary medical training, were unwelcome at the medical society meetings and quickly set up their own associations. Soon it would no longer be a disgrace to be called a dentist, promised the first president of the American Society of Dental Surgeons, and the organization provided that each and every member "shall be entitled to a diploma, or degree of Doctor of Dental Surgery" (Charles R. E. Koch, *History of Dental Surgery*, vol. 1 [1909], p. 173). The founding of the Baltimore College of Dental Surgery in 1839 afforded a somewhat more reputable form of credentialing, and the school became one of the principal centers of the new profession.

The profession of law resisted specialization and occupational division. Moreover, compared with doctors, lawyers showed less interest in professional organization. They had less need of such devices. The work of the lawyers brought them together in the county courthouses and the appellate courts, where they could fraternize and confer on common concerns. The most spirited lawyers' organizations of this era were the law library associations, usually with headquarters and facili-

Daniel Webster, eminent attorney and cabinet member during the nineteenth century, exemplified the preeminence of the law profession. A lawyer's sphere of influence included the most fundamental issues of government during this period.

ties in the county courthouse. The leading lawyers joined these organizations to collectively purchase and own the enginery of their work—the law treatises, court reports, reference works—that enabled them to pepper their arguments with copious precedents, lofty allusions, and indisputable information. Those organizations usually provided the bases for the local bar associations formed in a later era.

Without any more elaborate organizational structures, the law in this era remained the most eminent of the professions. The most fundamental issues of government—constitutional questions, the very ends of dominion and sovereignty, as lawyers were wont to assert and many Americans to grant—were within the practitioner's ken. To the extent that lawyers could extol the law and the Constitution as a national holy of holies, to that degree they became honored Levites of that shrine. While the lawyers' authority and honor may have dimmed somewhat in this period compared with the previous era, lawyers nonetheless adapted more easily than ministers and physicians to the new deliverances and constraints of these years.

Yet all three traditional professions maintained gentlemanly authority and honor within their work setting though they surrendered some of both in society at large. They adopted a strategy of attempting to strengthen what they took to be the centers of professional distinctiveness and coherence when they found the boundaries increasingly undefendable. The central fact of this era for the professions was that they were able to maintain the distinction between the specially honored and authoritative professions and the ordinary occupations. That prodigious accomplishment invites attention to the factors that made it possible.

First of all, as has been suggested, the leveling attack upon the professions was peculiarly equivocal. While some Americans wanted to bring all barriers down and looked upon the distinctiveness of the professions as pure humbug, others wanted to make entry less restrictive but keep the dominion and esteem of the professions intact. Less obvious but still important was the local sheltered-market situation that the professions enjoyed. The client usually chose a professional through personal connections, and that meant the market for professional services was local, personal, and differentiated. Professionals, therefore, could usually avoid the sharp rivalry and price competition that might have undermined their authoritative standing with their clients. Furthermore, the professions, with all the difficulties in their sciences during this era, remained significantly the work of the intellect—which, notwithstanding the corrosive effects of revivalism, was still often intertwined with spirit and placed above the mundane. And intellect retained some of its association with elevated standing in the community.

Finally, the three traditional professions dealt with men and women who were in peril or pain, leaving them dependent and sometimes childlike. The structure of the situation brought to light the circumstantial inequality between the bestower and the recipient of the service. The professional relationship of authority and dependence echoed the reciprocal relationship of protection and subordination that pervaded earlier eras in Europe. It is not surprising, therefore, that the professional found the various usages of the traditional gentlemanly class particularly congenial.

The Reestablishment of the Professions: 1880–1900

By the 1880s important changes were apparent in the organizational momentum and direction of the professions. New professions appeared more rapidly, and both old and new professions took on a fresh spirit, moving toward legislative enactments that once again gave them public recognition and some governmental support for their efforts to raise educational standards and restrict entry into their ranks. Such legislation, it was hoped, would assure professional competence (in both senses of the word) and strengthen the authoritative relationship between the professional and his client. State legislatures passed a great variety of licensing laws, but these enactments were not secure until the Supreme Court, in *Dent* v. *West Virginia* (1888), upheld a model licensing law that enabled a board of health composed of regular doctors to deprive Dr. Marmaduke Dent, who held a diploma from the American Eclectic College of Medicine, of the right to practice. As if to make amends for past humiliations, this victory worsted a doctor trained in one of the offshoot schools of the Thomsonian movement that had led the successful campaign to set aside medical practice laws in the 1830s.

Justice Stephen Field, who just fifteen years earlier had upheld a citizen's "inalienable right to pursue his own calling," now found, along with the rest of the court, that "no one has the right to practice a profession without having the necessary qualifications" determined by "an authority competent to judge." That authority turned out to be the organized profession itself. This decision was a signal blow to the prestige of the "irregular" and unconforming practitioners. (Its practical effects in West Virginia were less drastic than might be imagined, however, because the irregulars quietly pushed an enactment through the legislature setting up licensing boards parallel to those of the regulars that would admit them to practice.)

What is striking about this new wave of legislation that reestablished the professions is how readily it was accepted by the public. This acquiescence in turn owed much to broader changes in American society. Contemporaries often called attention to the rapid expansion as well as the consolidation and new restrictions in the economy and the social order. The railroads in the 1880s became prototypes of centralization, hierarchy, rapid expansion, and new types of restriction. In this decade railway expansion astonished even some of its most sanguine promoters, adding at least a hundred thousand miles of track, a greater amount than the total previously in use. This increase was accompanied by the appearance of hierarchical and centralized bureaucracies, the growth of cartels, and nationwide railroad systems. Similar changes arose in other industries, and parallel development of expansion and restriction appeared in other areas: immigration, labor organization, urbanization, race relations, and the civil service. Those forces which had promoted the equivocal egalitarianism of an earlier era—political democracy, evangelical Protestantism, and market capitalism—now exhibited similar tendencies toward expansion as well as new kinds of constraints and restrictions of their own.

This new strengthening of social and economic hierarchies was accompanied by significant shifts in social thought. Open and self-confident attacks upon "the dogma of equality" became more acceptable. "Inequality appears to be the divine order," wrote Charles Dudley Warner ("Equality," *Atlantic* 45 [1880]: 24), and many Darwinians found it to be the natural order as well. The notion of science also shifted. In the eighteenth and early nineteenth centuries the professions spoke proudly of their science, but it usually meant simply a body of systematized knowledge. It was placed in contrast with art: "A science teaches us to know, and an art to do" (William Stanley Jevons, *Elementary Lessons in Logic* [1870], vol. 1, p. 7). But by the 1880s, "science" more often meant "natural science" (what the eighteenth century called "natural philosophy"), which was thought to be the most rigorous form of truth. Moreover, after the mid-nineteenth century, "science" was applied more extensively to technology. It taught not only to know but also to do. In addition, within natural science there was a shift of attention from the descriptive sciences like botany and geology, in which lay collectors played a role, to experimental sciences like chemistry and physics, in which amateurs had less importance.

Linked to these changes was the new preeminence of medicine among the traditional professions—it was based upon natural science, whereas law rested upon an "institutional" science—and the astonishingly rapid growth of engineering among the more recent professions. Germ theory gave the doctor a convincing explanation of the causes of disease, and advances in physiology provided some understanding of how the body and various remedies responded to such ailments. The diphtheria antitoxin seemed to be the decisive instance. What had been a frightening and horrible disease that could choke a child to death before one's eyes now yielded to the new "serum therapy." The outcome was an enormously increased self-confidence among doctors and a growing popular respect for them.

The new preeminence of medicine was part of a broader intellectual shift, a new understanding of human nature and the requisites of human happiness. The rise of law had been linked to the Enlightenment, the blurring of the sense of human sin, and the sharpening of the sense of human rights. The rise of medicine was linked to the blurring of the sense of human rights and a sharpening of the sense of human needs. The preeminence of law had reflected the decline of Calvin and the rise of Locke as guide to human affairs; the preeminence of medicine reflected the decline of Locke and the rise of Darwin as the interpreter of the human condition. Of course this outline may be helpful only in suggesting the direction of change. In 1990 Calvin was alive for Princeton Seminary at least, and Locke inhered in many Supreme Court decisions. Surely the sense of sin and the demand for rights were powerful and moving forces in the late nineteenth century; yet now they were mitigated by the insistence of the students of the rapidly advancing physiological sciences that man must also be seen as a complex biological organism, and that much of his conduct could best be understood in those terms.

The new preeminence of medicine was part of a new understanding of human nature and the requisites of happiness; the rise of law had been linked to the Enlightenment and the sharpening of the sense of human rights.

The capital of scientific medicine in this era was the Johns Hopkins Medical School (opened 1893). The school was generously endowed and therefore only loosely linked to economic considerations in forming its curriculum, hiring its faculty, and determining its very high entrance requirements. It led in American medical education for the next half-century. The brilliant pathologist William Henry Welch (1850–1934), the first dean of the school, assumed the role of evangelist of the methods and teachings of the German medical laboratory. It was in response to a call from Johns Hopkins that the Association of American Medical Colleges was formed (1890) with the purpose of reforming medical education. The association laid the groundwork for the decisive changes that followed the famous Flexner Report (1910). The outcome of that report was the closing of those schools whose facilities for training doctors capable of keeping up with new scientific discoveries were inadequate. The resulting restriction upon entry into the medical profession did not seem to be sinister.

While the physicians' authority and esteem rose more rapidly in this era than did those of the other professions, the rate of growth of the engineers in sheer numbers clearly outpaced that of their fellow professionals. Three national associations of engineers—mining, mechanical, and electrical—were established and joined the formerly less-specialized society of civil engineers to represent the profession. This specialization reflected the growth of particular markets for technical skills as well as the increasing application of science to technology. Leaders in the profession were usually the consulting engineers and educators, whose situation resembled that of the members of the older professions. But the bulk of the engineers were lesser employees in the bureaucracies of large organizations. The discrepancy between the preachments of the presidents of the engineering societies and the work experience of those engineering employees brought to the surface some signs of restiveness among the latter. They had little of the right to command and not much of the regard and approbation they had been led to believe were appropriate to professional standing. Eventually, the expanding corporations were able to alleviate such disquiet through vertical-line promotions and horizontal honorific distinctions within the firm. Nonetheless, the image of a profession among these low-ranking engineers was a much diminished one.

The neo-Weberian analysis of the professions, with its emphasis upon cognitive rationality, monopoly, and bureaucracy (the rational ordering of "social action"), can be quite helpful in the discussion of the foremost and the most rapidly growing professions of the late nineteenth century—medicine and engineering. However, these were but two of the professions that quickened, strengthened, and grew in the late nineteenth century. The ministry and law, for example, among the traditional professions, and architecture as well as college teaching, among the newer ones in America, also took on new vigor and attained new influence and stature in this era. For these professions, among others, the Weberian concepts are less illuminating. Even in medicine, the prime instance for the neo-Weberian analysis, there is an extraordinary dimension that is obscured from such a perspective. That is the presence of the past: the power of the English gentlemanly ideal to find new supports and to flourish in differing circumstances.

The epitome of that dimension in American medicine of the late nineteenth century was William Osler (1849–1919), who, along with William Henry Welch, shed luster upon Johns Hopkins's first medical school faculty. If anything, Osler was the more illustrious. He was a clinician and did scientific work, but his reputation did not rest upon any of his discoveries. Rather, he is remembered for his eloquent reassertion of English gentlemanly ways to the galaxy of his brilliant students and before the meetings of the various medical societies in which he took an active part. The doctor, taught Osler, must be the carrier of high culture, learned, affable, and humane. Osler reaffirmed the importance of the personal rapport between the physician and the patient based upon a relationship of authority and dependence. The authority of the doctor was to rest upon the new medical sciences, the physician's culture and bearing, and what seemed to be the intrinsic inequality in the relationship between the healer and the sufferer.

Gentlemanly ideals also flourished in the rapidly growing profession of college teacher, one of whose important tasks was still passing civic culture on to the coming generation. Like the engineers, these professionals increasingly found themselves working in bureaucratic settings. However, the business corporations, in which the engineers worked, pursued narrow objectives and their success could readily be measured in dollars. The objectives of the university, by contrast, were broad and diverse, and the measure of success was uncertain. The professor, unlike the engineer (but much like the physician in the hospital), helped to set the objectives and gauge the success of the organization in which he worked. Under these conditions the professor could more readily maintain authority and honor.

Among the architects and the military, the quest for authority and honor was evident as well. Both reflected and utilized the conditions of the late nineteenth century that were favorable to all professions. For the architects, the rapid growth of cities and the rise of a class of newly rich with a zest for lavish spending created a boom market for civic, commercial, and residential building. The leading American architects responded to these favorable circumstances by striving to remold their occupation into an honorable and circumscribed profession. For much of the nineteenth century most of the designing of buildings was done by carpenter-builders using architectural handbooks. Most of the men who called themselves architects had little formal architectural education. The American Institute of Architecture had been founded in 1857, and though its requirements for membership were not exacting, its membership remained small until the 1880s. The most important impetus for elevating the standing of the profession came from the Society of Beaux-Arts Architects, founded in 1894. This was truly the elite of the profession, made up of Americans who had studied at that famous Paris school. Until the 1880s, England with its craft tradition in architecture was the chief influence upon American practice. In the last decades of the century, the French tradition, which held that architecture was both a fine art and a science, became dominant. That shift brought with it the ideal image of the French architect, who combined the temperament of an artist with the authority of a scientist. That ideal image did much to help the American architect assert himself with regard to his client, and it also contributed to the drive for the educational reforms, the licensing laws, and the professional codes of ethics adopted in the years that followed.

A change of European models was also important to the American military in the last decades of the nineteenth century. Prior to the Franco-Prussian War the American army had borrowed many of its patterns and practices from the French, but by the 1880s German organization was gradually replacing them. The military attitudes and manners of American officers derived from the earlier model of the English gentleman-officer. This was the eighteenth-century version of the ancient ideal of the gentleman-warrior whose virtues were courage and courtesy, and whose honor was appropriate to his rank. Sequestered at West Point, this tradition withstood the powerful leveling assaults of the Jacksonian era. West Point at that time had been attacked as aristocratic and "wholly inconsistent with the spirit of our liberal institutions" (Stephen E. Ambrose, *Duty, Honor, Country: A History of West Point* [1966], pp. 64–65). By the 1880s, America's rapidly growing industrial might have led many to believe that the nation's era of isolationism was drawing to a close and that its military had taken on a new importance. In addition, the hierarchies that spread through American society made military organization and authority less anomalous. The junior officers entered upon a wide-ranging discussion about their professional standing and how to improve it. Raising educational standards for officers and barring entry to the incompetent were recurrent themes. In addition, they occasionally contrasted the professional ideals of the military with the commercial character of civilian life. The officer's code rejected money-making, selfish gain, and luxurious living. Oddly, the gentleman officer could easily slip into a disdainful attitude toward the society he had vowed to protect.

Although this attitude was clearly not characteristic of the professional of this era, gentlemanly authority and honor nonetheless had taken on new meaning in the polarized society of the late nineteenth century. The professional now asserted that he was neither a capitalist nor a worker; rather, he stood in some third position with an outlook arising from that standing. He was not a capitalist because his authority and honor were not derived from wealth and the dollar was not usually the best indication of his achievement. He was not a worker, though he was employed, because he worked from a position of authority and was therefore never wholly at the bidding of those who employed him. He maintained precapitalist presumptions. He was not self-denying, but his self-interest was directed and constrained by the requirements of his vocation. For him, duty guided self-interest; this duty arose from an abiding relationship between persons and entailed action that one's position required. This ideology was later reflected in Carr-Saunders and Wilson's arguments and hopes for the professions.

Since 1900

While much of the modern conception and self-understanding of the professions rapidly took shape in the last decades of the nineteenth century, many of the more remarkable organizational achievements occurred in the first decades of the twentieth. The American Medical Association, which previously had been national largely in name only, now set up a substantial organization with an able staff to coordinate and invigorate the activities of the state medical societies. The American Bar Association, which had been a gentlemen's club of eminent lawyers who cooled themselves at Saratoga every summer and, amid innocent dissipations, discussed selected legal issues, rapidly moved away from that splendorous spa; they met instead in the major cities of the nation and reached out to lawyers who had previously been ignored. Not only did the national organizations of doctors and lawyers attract an increasing proportion of practicing doctors and lawyers, but the national organizations of architects, dentists, engineers, and pharmacists absorbed a growing portion of their practitioners as well. The state organizations pushed more effective licensing laws through their legislatures. In this, the Progressive Era, when the use of legislation to regulate markets in the interests of morality, general prudence, and social beneficence was widely accepted, professional licensing laws could be seen as serving those interests. Moreover, as the catchwords "efficiency" and "uplift" became Progressive slogans, accountancy and social work put forward their claims to professional status. Pediatrics established itself as a specialty in medicine in these years, with considerable help from the crusading Children's Bureau. The first two decades of the century was an era of reform, but it was reform with few egalitarian proclivities. The professions prospered in such circumstances.

Little noticed in these years was the beginning of a shift in American economic life that was to have a far-reaching influence during the rest of the century. This was the rise of the service economy. It involved the transfer of the American labor force from agriculture, mining, and manufacturing to leisure industries, civil service, and education; and within manufacturing, from direct production to planning, allocation, and distribution. This shift produced new jobs, some better and some worse than those they replaced. Most of the new jobs were less susceptible to the rigorous work discipline characteristic of the factory. It is not surprising that many workers in such jobs reached toward the modes of professionalism. The conspicuous appetite for professional status in the service sector is one of the unmistakable elements in the growth of this important part of the American economy.

The rise in the service economy that has occurred since 1900 involved the transfer of the labor force from agriculture, mining, and manufacturing to leisure industries, civil service, and education.

One of the results of these developments was the appearance of what Amitai Etzioni called the semi-professions"—occupations whose workers adopted many of the devices of the professions but were not generally accorded the authority or honor of the traditional professions. A noteworthy characteristic of some of these semi-professions—for example, nursing, public school teaching, social work, and librarianship—was that they were composed largely of women. Some of them clung fervently to the usages of the professions, others adopted the methods of trade unions, and still others chose the instrumentalities of both. It is for these semi-professions that the Marxist discussion of the "proletarianization" of educated labor had some relevance.

However, in the period from the 1960s to the late 1970s, under the impact of a new egalitarian movement, it seemed that the traditional professions might well be leveled or at least be drastically transformed. Young doctors were setting up hospital meetings with nurses, social workers, occupational therapists, physical therapists, and even orderlies to discuss patients' progress. Young lawyers were giving up practice to write books showing how almost anyone could do her or his legal work without a lawyer. Young nuns and priests were shedding their distinctive dress and rushing out to social confrontations without attempting to say anything distinctive about the spiritual significance of those encounters. For all that, unlike the egalitarian onslaught of the mid-nineteenth century, these tumults had few lasting effects upon the professions. Reformers of the 1960s and 1970s did not provide much of a persuasive critique of the science or praxis of the professions, and most practitioners maintained their self-confidence and stood their ground. One important change of this era was the opening of the major professional associations to blacks and to increasing numbers of women. During the process of reestablishing the professions in the nineteenth century, they had been excluded, not because they posed much of an economic threat but because blacks (like women) were not granted a white man's authority and honor in society at large. Admitting them would have threatened the standing of the other members of the professional association. The civil rights movement and advancing feminism mitigated that threat.

Historically, the market economy in America has provided an impressive growth of industrial productivity as well as a notable rise in living standards. Yet this has not been achieved without cost. Intrinsic to that achievement was the development of less-gratifying work and the exclusion of a larger, more elevated purpose for economic endeavor. The leading professions in bringing ideals and predispositions of an earlier era into the modern world strove to retain what the market economy relinquished. Professions, of course, are occupations and therefore can be understood, in part, as economic interest groups. Yet they offer much more than economic betterment—they offer a way of life. This is the power of their attraction.

[See also The Aristocracy of Inherited Wealth; Business Culture; Collegiate Education; Gender Roles and Relations; The Medical Profession; Minorities and Work; The Research University; Science as a Profession; Women and Work.]

BIBLIOGRAPHY

Statistical Information

United States Bureau of the Census. *Comparative Occupation Statistics for the United States 1870–1940* (1943).

United States Bureau of the Census. *Historical Statistics of the United States, Colonial Times to 1970* (1975).

Historiographical Discussion

Abbott, Andrew. *The System of Professions: An Essay on the Division of Expert Labor* (1988). Chapter 1 examines the sociological literature; there is an extensive bibliography.

Berlant, Jeffrey. *Profession and Monopoly: A Study of Medicine in the United States and Great Britain* (1975). A Neo-Weberian perspective.

Carr-Saunders, A. M., and P. A. Wilson. *The Professions* (1933; repr. 1964).

Carr-Saunders, A. M., and P. A. Wilson. "Professions." In *Encyclopaedia of the Social Sciences.* Vol. 12 (1934).

Geison, Gerald, ed. *Professions and Professional Ideologies in America* (1983).

Haber, Samuel. *The Quest for Authority and Honor in the American Professions, 1750–1900* (1991). A full exposition of the standpoint of this article.

Larson, Magali S. *The Rise of Professionalism: A Sociological Analysis* (1977). A Neo-Marxist study.

Parsons, Talcott. "Professions." *International Encyclopedia of the Social Sciences,* Vol. 12 (1968).

The Era of Establishment, 1750–1830

Bell, Whitfield J. *The Colonial Physician and Other Essays* (1975).

Haber, Samuel. "The Professions and Higher Education in America: A Historical View." In *Higher Education and the Labor Market,* edited by Margaret S. Gordon (1974).

Hudson, Winthrop. "The Ministry in the Puritan Age." In *The Ministry in Historical Perpectives,* edited by H. Richard Niebuhr and Daniel D. Williams (1956).

Leake, Chauncey, ed. *Percival's Medical Ethics* (1927).

Murrin, John M. "The Legal Transformation: The Bench and Bar of Eighteenth-Century Massachusetts." In *Colonial America,* edited by Stanley Katz (1971; rev. ed. 1987).

Youngs, John William Theodore. *God's Messengers: Religious Leadership in Colonial New England, 1700–1750* (1976).

The Egalitarian Interregnum 1830–1880

Atack, Jeremy, and Fred Bateman. *To Their Own Soil: Agriculture in the Antebellum North* (1987). Statistical study of equality of condition.

Beck, Dorothy Fahs. "The Development of the Dental Profession in the United States." Master's thesis, University of Chicago (1932).

Bloomfield, Maxwell. *American Lawyers in a Changing Society, 1776–1876* (1976).

Ferguson, Robert A. *Law and Letters in American Culture* (1984).

Gallman, Robert E. " 'The Egalitarian Myth,' Once Again." *Social Science History* 5 (1981). One installment in the important exchange between Gallman and Edward Pessen indicating that Pessen's "hard facts" are quite impressionistic.

Kett, Joseph F. *The Formation of the American Medical Profession: The Role of Institutions, 1780–1860* (1968).

Mead, Sidney E. "The Rise of the Evangelical Conception of the Ministry in America: 1607–1850." In *The Ministry in Historical Perspectives,* edited by H. Richard Niebuhr and Daniel D. Williams (1956).

Pessen, Edward. *Riches, Class, and Power Before the Civil War* (1973). Social stratification in eastern cities.

Pound, Roscoe. *The Lawyer from Antiquity to Modern Times* (1953).

Scott, Donald M. *From Office to Profession: The New England Ministry, 1780–1850* (1978).

Warner, John Harley. *The Therapeutic Perspective: Medical Practice, Knowledge, and Identity in America, 1820–1885* (1986).

Reestablishment, 1880–1900

Bacon, Mardges. *Ernest Flagg: Beaux-Arts Architect and Urban Reformer* (1985).

Calvert, Monte. *The Mechanical Engineer in America, 1830–1910: Professional Cultures in Conflict* (1967).

Hobson, W. K. "Symbol of the New Profession: Emergence of the Large Law Firm, 1875–1915." In *The New High Priests: Lawyers in Post-Civil War America,* edited by Gerard W. Gawalt (1984).

Huntington, Samuel P. *The Soldier and the State: The Theory and Politics of Civil-Military Relations* (1957).

Matzko, John A. "The Early Years of the American Bar Association, 1878–1928." Ph.D. diss., University of Virginia (1984).

Moldow, Gloria. *Women Doctors in Gilded-Age Washington: Race, Gender, and Professionalization* (1987).

Osler, William. *Counsels and Ideals from the Writings of William Osler,* C. N. B. Camac, comp. (1906).

Rothstein, William G. *American Physicians in the Nineteenth Century: From Sects to Science* (1972).

Veysey, Laurence R. *The Emergence of the American University* (1965).

Since 1900

Etzioni, Amitai, ed. *The Semi-Professions and Their Organization: Teachers, Nurses, Social Workers* (1969).

Freidson, Eliot. *Professional Powers: A Study of the Institutionalization of Formal Knowledge* (1986).

Gerstl, Joel, and Glenn Jacobs, eds. *Professions for the People: The Politics of Skill* (1976). Reflects the spirit of the 1960s.

Ginzberg, Eli, and George J. Vojta. "The Service Sector of the U.S. Economy." *Scientific American* 244 (March 1981): 48–55.

Halpern, Sydney. "Segmental Professionalization Within Medicine: The Case of Pediatrics." Ph.D. diss., University of California-Berkeley (1982).

Lipset, Seymour Martin. "White Collar Workers and Professionals—Their Attitudes and Behavior Towards Unions." In *Readings in Industrial Society,* edited by William A. Faunce (1967).

Morais, Herbert M. *The History of the Negro in Medicine* (1967).

Morantz-Sanchez, Regina Markell. *Sympathy and Science: Women Physicians in American Medicine* (1985).

Morello, Karen Berger. *The Invisible Bar: The Woman Lawyer in America, 1638–1986* (1986).

Starr, Paul. *The Social Transformation of American Medicine* (1982).

— SAMUEL HABER

PUBLIC ARCHITECTURE

American public architecture is a physical symbol, often on a monumental scale, of the definition of government and its role in American society. It is within public buildings that the drama of a democratic government has taken place. "Public" architecture can be variously defined. In the broadest sense, any building that is open to all people or contributes to establishing the public face of a city can be considered public. However, the essence of public architecture is composed of those buildings that are built by the people to serve fundamental needs of society, particularly those of government and education. It is these two central categories of public buildings which will be examined here.

Colonial Buildings

Before the American Revolution, the goals of public architecture were quite different from what would be sought after 1776. Rather than defining a new nation, public architecture at first was a colonial extension of the imperial ambitions of European governments. The Palace of the Governors in Santa Fe, New Mexico (1610–1614; Fig. 1), was a tiny outpost on the edge of the Spanish world, which sought to provide administrative order to the Christian missionary efforts directed at the Native Americans. This building is atypical among colonial civic buildings in the New World in that the Spanish learned from Native American building techniques and utilized the Pueblo material of adobe. This is in sharp contrast to the public buildings of the English colonies, where native traditions in building were ignored in favor of transplanted European ideas and forms.

In Puritan New England, it was the meetinghouse that first emerged in the seventeenth century as the major public building in a community. These typically large, square, and very plain wooden buildings on the town's common were built primarily for religious services, but they also served as a convenient gathering point for town meetings. A less pious but more convivial setting for holding discussions about the welfare of a community was the local tavern, where government officials often chose to meet. In New Amsterdam, the City Tavern (1641–1642) was even converted in 1653 into the Stadt Huys (city hall), since it was one of the largest and most prominent buildings in the Dutch settlement on the island of Manhattan. This tradition continued into the eighteenth century as can be seen in Williamsburg, Virginia, where the Raleigh Tavern was a center of political discussions second only to the Capitol.

The emergence of a civic architecture beyond meetinghouses and taverns was rather slow and limited during the seventeenth century. Boston's first Town Hall (1657–1658, destroyed 1711) was a rough wooden building with medieval gables exhibiting little architectural pretension other than two belfries that crowned its roof, denoting that the building was a place of assembly. Continuing a medieval tradition, the open first floor of the structure was a market, which added to the importance of the building within the lives of the people of Boston. This market also suggests one of the British government's primary hopes for the colonies as a promising economic venture.

The largest buildings built in the English colonies were colleges, reflecting the importance that education held for colonial society. American colleges throughout their history were often perceived to be ideal communities providing on a small scale a model of what society could be. At first a single building, looking like an enlarged house, was built to contain all of the functions of the college, including dormitories for the students, and sometimes housing for the faculty. The earliest college buildings follow this pattern, such as the Old College at Harvard in Cambridge, Massachusetts (1638–1642, demolished 1678), and the College of William and Mary in Williamsburg, Virginia (1695–1699, rebuilt 1705–1715). A common type of college building emerged during the Georgian period of the eighteenth century and is exemplified by Nassau Hall (by Robert Smith and William Shippen, 1754–1756) of the College of New Jersey (later Princeton University). A large symmetrical block is given distinction through a central pavilion and cupola, and stands grandly on a large open, green space, in contrast to the tight, cloistered enclosures of England's Oxford and Cambridge.

When new capital cities were laid out according to a plan, such as Philadelphia (1682), Annapolis (1694), and Williamsburg (1699), care was taken to provide prominent central locations for major public buildings that would create an architectural climax at the end of central avenues. In the plan for the new capital of Virginia, Williamsburg, the College of William and Mary and the Capitol anchor opposite ends of the town's major street, the Duke of Gloucester Street. Adjoining the center of this east-west street is a secondary axis running north: the palace green terminating with the Governor's Palace. At the crossing of these two axes stands Bruton Parish Church. Williamsburg's plan diagrams a balance of the institutions of education, religion, and government with the palace of the crown governor standing at the head of this colonial capital for the British empire.

It was through the Capitol in Williamsburg (1701–1705; rebuilt 1928–1934) that the judgments of royal authority were dispensed to the people of Virginia. The towering two-story cupola asserted this building as an important landmark. The open arcade at its center provided a welcoming gesture to the public. The H plan of the building architecturally expressed the bicameral nature of colonial government, with the House of Burgesses in the east wing and the Governor's Council in the west wing. Another major chamber within the Capitol was the General Court. By colonial American standards, the Virginia Capitol was atypical in its commanding presence and its articulation of its functions.

The more common solution for a major civic building (or college building) was to design along the lines of a great house as seen in Richard Munday's Old Colony House at Newport, Rhode Island (1739–1741; Fig. 2), where only the building's size, cupola, and isolated position on a central site set the building apart from the general residential fabric of the town. The most monumental and prominent urban landmarks in colonial cities were church spires. The Old State House in Philadelphia (Independence Hall; Andrew Hamilton and Edmund Woolley, 1731–1753) is a prime example of the dilemma of definition of public architecture in colonial America. A large Georgian block, reminiscent of a house, is fronted by a churchlike tower; however, the building does not appear to be a church since the tower is placed on the broad side, rather than on the traditional narrow end. American society in the English colonies was not one of monumental institutions. The dominant architectural forms of the time were the house and the church. Public and educational buildings tended to be hybrids and transformations of these more prevalent types. Colonial public architecture suggests that it was built for a society whose ultimate political control lay elsewhere, with the crown and parliament back in England.

Building for the New Republic

With the revolutionary war and the establishment of the United States of America, the role of public architecture had suddenly and dramatically changed. New edifices needed to be conceived to house the just-created democratic institutions of the nascent country. One figure who was especially sensitive to the important role that architecture could play in the definition of a nation and its people was Thomas Jefferson, who was a gentleman-amateur architect, along with his numerous other talents. He played a key role in having the capital of Virginia moved from that symbol of the British crown, Williamsburg, to Richmond, where a fresh start further west could be made. While he was the American minister to France, he designed a new capitol with the assistance of C.-L. Clérisseau. Jefferson modeled his new State Capitol (1785–1798; Fig. 3) after an ancient Roman temple, the Maison Carrée in Nimes. Jefferson had created a truly monumental and grand structure unlike any American colonial public building. The order, scale, and nobility of a rectangular temple block provided the ideal model of a young nation desiring to establish instant monuments. Moreover, such a building was invested with romantic associations with the classical past, particularly in the mind of Jefferson: republican Rome. From this building on, the neoclassical temple would be a type repeatedly associated with public buildings and would come to symbolize authority, stability, and culture.

Jefferson's neoclassical buildings were used as models to promote an ideal architectural environment that would ennoble and improve the United States. Nowhere are his architectural ambitions better seen than in his design for the University of Virginia at Charlottesville (1817–1826). In contrast to the large, single institutional block of most colonial colleges, he broke up the university into a series of smaller units and called it his "academical village." His social aim was to create a small, ideal educational community that would encourage intellectual discourse between faculty and students. Faculty lived in two-story pavilions with their living quarters above and classrooms below; each pavilion illustrates a different example of classical architecture. One-story dormitories fronted by colonnades link the pavilions and form two ranges flanking a central quadrangular lawn. More student rooms and six "hotels" (for dining) were located in two outer ranges parallel to the two inner ranges. At the head of the lawn is the Rotunda (originally housing the library), modeled after the ancient Roman Pantheon. Jefferson had replaced the central role given to chapels in colonial college buildings and campuses by placing at the heart of his design a pantheon, dedicated not to religion or pagan gods, but to enlightened thought through books.

Since the erection of Thomas Jefferson's State Capitol in Williamsburg, Virginia, the neoclassical Roman temple would be a type repeatedly associated with America's public buildings and would come to symbolize authority, stability, and culture.

During the presidency of George Washington (1789–1797), the government decided to build a new capital city for the nation, reinforcing an often repeated theme during the first century of the United States, a theme of optimistic new beginnings on a generous and ever-enlarging land. A French engineer and architect, Pierre Charles L'Enfant, laid out the new federal city in 1791. He conceived of it on a truly monumental scale, and it was not until the twentieth century that Washington, D.C., began to approximate L'Enfant's original vision. L'Enfant's design is based upon baroque urban and garden planning, which accentuated sites for major buildings or fountains by use of radial avenues. He adapted principles that in Europe symbolized absolute power (such as in papal Rome or the gardens of Versailles) to create a democratic capital. This was a continual theme in American public architecture: appropriating architectural forms that were used in the past to represent dogmatic authority and recasting them for more republican purposes. At the end of a broad mall, two buildings were to be the centerpieces of this federal city: the President's House and the Capitol (in an arrangement not unlike Williamsburg).

The complicated history of the United States Capitol is one of multiple architects, an evolving design, political division, foreign invasion, civil war, and a key opportunity for a new nation to establish a dominant architectural symbol. A competition for the new building was held in 1792, and the surviving entries make clear the inability of most American architects and builders to think beyond the small scale of colonial examples. However, a late entry by William Thornton pleased the eyes of both Washington and Jefferson. Thornton was encouraged to continue work on a new design and during the mid 1790s the first design for the Capitol was developed. The composition was a hybrid of forms and motifs: a long palacelike block (to provide separate wings for the Senate and House of Representatives) was accentuated in the center with a low Pantheon-like dome and portico facing to the east and a much taller dome and semicircular colonnade on the west (mall) side of the building. How unified the various states wanted to be under a single federal government would be a debate that would continue throughout American society. Nonetheless, from the very start, the dominant architectural symbol for this gathering of the legislators would be the unifying containment of a circular dome (although Thornton in this early design had conceived of two domes).

After Benjamin H. Latrobe was appointed Architect of the Capitol in 1803, the competing domes were reduced to one (the tall, west dome was eliminated from the plans). During the War of 1812, the partially built Capitol and President's House were burned as the British tried to demoralize their former colonial possession by destroying its public buildings. Latrobe returned to rebuild the Capitol (1815–1817; Fig. 4). As a European-trained architect and engineer Latrobe was able to design and build monumental and dignified classical spaces with masonry vaulting of a quality that had previously been unknown in America. He even invented new American orders of columns with capitals decorated with tobacco leaves or cobs of maize, one of the first attempts to create American architectural forms beyond the European tradition.

The Boston architect Charles Bulfinch finally brought the Capitol to completion in 1826. His major addition to the design was to change the building's dome from the low, saucerlike dome of previous designs into a taller, more prominent, and awkward dome. The building was completed, but by 1851 it had grown inadequate for the rapidly growing nation. In the late eighteenth century the future dimensions of the United States were vague and unpredictable. By the mid nineteenth century it was necessary for the nation's major architectural symbol to undergo a radical alteration and expansion to stay in step with the new scale of the United States. The architect Thomas U. Walter added two large wings (1851–1859) to the ends of the original building to provide entirely new and much larger chambers for the House and Senate. To unify the sprawling breadth of the expanded Capitol, Walter built a new and much taller dome (1855–1863). Reminiscent of the domes of Renaissance-baroque churches (particularly Sir Christopher Wren's Saint Paul's Cathedral in London), it secularizes a long-used religious architectural form to symbolize the unity of many states under the single dome of the federal government. The dome was built in iron, reflecting the growing industrial capacity of the nation. Iron was certainly precious to the Union military cause during the Civil War, yet Abraham Lincoln insisted that construction of the dome continue during the war: "If people see the Capitol going on, it is a sign we intend the Union shall go on" (quoted in Hitchcock and Seale, *Temples of Democracy*, p. 141).

No other public building before the Civil War required the enormous size of the United States Capitol. The dominant image for a public building by the early nineteenth century was the classical temple, usually Greek in its inspiration. A Greek temple stimulated romantic thoughts of democracy and the beginnings of Western civilization. Greek Revival buildings were found throughout antebellum America from diminutive temples serving as county courthouses in rural Virginia to boldly scaled capitols in stone to serve the newly created states of the west, as can be seen in Columbus, Ohio, and Nashville, Tennessee. Such buildings proclaimed the arrival of an instant culture evocative of the greatest legacies of antiquity, yet could serve as the context for the workings of a grassroots democracy as exemplified by George Caleb Bingham's painting *The Verdict of the People* (1854–1855), where election results are read to a community from the steps of a classical portico. Greek temples were used in nearly every building type, as seen in Philadelphia, where William Strickland based his design for the Second Bank of the United States (1818–1824) on the Parthenon in Athens, and

Thomas U. Walter created a monumental Corinthian temple to serve as the central building at Girard College (1833–1847). Despite this compelling fashion for the Greek, a temple is a rather restrictive form, often poorly lighted because of shadowy colonnades. Both of these Philadelphia examples have interiors vaulted in the Roman manner to make them more functional.

In Washington, D.C., during the 1830s and 1840s several federal buildings were being built in the neoclassical manner by Robert Mills, who in 1836 had also designed the Washington Monument to be built at the heart of the city. This 555.5-foot (169.3-meter) monument (completed by Thomas L. Casey in 1884) in the shape of an ancient Egyptian obelisk is a prime example of the cult worship that arose around President Washington in the nineteenth century as the new nation sought to establish its own history of heroes and myths. This tribute to Washington seeks to outdo the structures of the most monumental builders of all time, the ancient Egyptian pharaohs.

In the mid nineteenth century a major exception to Washington's classical norm for federal buildings was built on a prominent location on the Mall. The architect James Renwick erected the Smithsonian Institution (1846–1855), a dark, brooding, asymmetrical pile of medieval towers and Romanesque arches, appearing like a picturesque cluster of buildings constructed over several generations. The head of the building committee, Congressman Robert Dale Owen published *Hints on Public Architecture* (1849) in which he promoted medieval revival architecture as more flexible, functional, and economical than Greek Revival temples. Other than the late-nineteenth-century Richardsonian Romanesque, classical styles with their civic and public connotations have tended to be preferred over medieval styles for major governmental buildings. Such styles as the Gothic Revival are more associated with religion, natural settings, and individuality.

An Expanding Land and the Gilded Age

In the early nineteenth century there was an explosive growth in the founding of new colleges, much of it fueled by the desire of various religious groups to have colleges established throughout an ever-growing land. In 1862, Abraham Lincoln signed the Morrill Act providing the means for all states to establish land-grant colleges. Rather than stressing a traditional curriculum of classical or theological education, these new, more democratic institutions were to be built around the pragmatic fields of agriculture, the mechanical arts, and military science. Many of these land-grant colleges would be placed in isolated, rural locations, such as State College, Pennsylvania, and Urbana-Champaign, Illinois. Along with facilitating the agricultural mission of these schools, such a location reflected an often-repeated theme in American higher education; the need to create an ideal learned community of young adults uncorrupted by the temptations of the big city. Another advantage, to the nineteenth-century romantic mind, was life close to nature, with all of its moral and aesthetic advan-

The Smithsonian Institution (1846–1855), designed by James Renwick in a medieval and Romanesque style, defied the nineteenth century tradition of neo-classical public buildings.

tages. The landscape architect Frederick Law Olmsted was a popular campus planner in the late nineteenth century. He advocated campuses designed like picturesque parks, with small buildings informally grouped. This represented a sharp break from the rigid classical arrangements of the past, which were dominated by a central, large building. Many campuses followed this more naturalistic approach, as can be seen in such diverse places as Smith College and the Kansas State Agricultural College (now Kansas State University); however, most of these colleges were still built with an Old Main dominating the grounds.

For most American children in the nineteenth century the architectural domain of education was the one-room rural schoolhouse. Although there were many variations, the archetypal rural school evoked the higher moral environments of the home and church. A houselike rectangular, gabled block often had such churchlike elements as a bell-tower, pure white color, and separate entrances for females and males. Most often, children of all ages were taught by one teacher, who encouraged the older children to help the younger. The building became a community gathering point for dispersed rural populations as they congregated for such events as a holiday pageant. To many immigrant families it represented assimilation into American society, for children met people from many backgrounds and were required to learn English. For Native Americans, though, a reservation school teaching only the knowledge, values, and language of white society represented a ruthless effort to eliminate their culture.

In the official realm, the restrictive form of a neoclassical temple often seemed too confining to the growing scale and bureaucracy of government in Victorian America. When the State, War, and Navy Building (1871–1888; now the Old Executive Office Building; Fig. 5) was built in Washington by Alfred B. Mullett (the Treasury Department's Supervising Architect, 1866–1874), it dwarfed its surroundings, including the White House to the east. The chaste, democratic Greek Revival of the early nineteenth century was replaced by the fashionable neo-baroque elegance of Napoleon III's Second Empire in France. Mullett's sprawling palacelike block is animated with pavilions, mansard roofs, and a seemingly endless succession of columns.

This enlargement in scale can also be seen in state capitols. The modest Greek Revival Illinois State Capitol in Springfield by John F. Rague, built in the 1830s, was superseded by a much more grandly scaled and ornamented capitol by J. C. Cochrane (1867–1888), reflecting changes in how the people of Illinois thought of themselves. Their state was no longer a western outpost of ill-defined opportunities, but had become a rapidly growing agricultural, commercial, and industrial center for the Midwest, with more sophisticated tastes—as their new capitol made clear. By this time a common type had emerged for state capitols (although there were many individual departures and variations), where wings accommodating the two houses of the legislature flanked a central ceremonial space, usually a domed rotunda, fronted by a portico providing public access. This formula was first suggested by the U.S. Capitol in its various forms and found its first mature expression in a state capitol in Harrisburg, Pennsylvania (Stephen Hills; 1810–1821; now destroyed).

County courthouses, state universities, and capitols often played substantial roles in the competition among cities to predominate in their particular region. The question of which city was to be the county seat or home of the state university often led to major political struggles with long-term economic impact on the winning and losing communities. State capitals often moved in the nineteenth century following changes in population growth and convenience; as a result, capitol buildings often proved to be temporary dwellings of government, echoing the nature of a transient society filling a land of changing boundaries with an unpredictable future. On the other hand, state capitols and county courthouses were monumental symbols in the nineteenth century of the systematic taking of land from the Native Americans for the primary use of white Americans of European descent.

For many citizens direct interaction with the state capitol or Washington, D.C., is minimal. The county courthouse is a more tangible presence of government that is involved in a person's legal relationship to a community, from marriage licenses to court trials. The courthouse is also the archive for the county, where such vital records as land deeds are kept. The workings of a civilized community living under laws is manifested in the county courthouse. It is a place where a community gathers on special occasions and builds memorials to its leaders and military dead. And it is occasionally the stage for landmark legal cases with implications well beyond the county, such as the courtroom struggle of William Jennings Bryan and Clarence Darrow in the 1925 Scopes trial in the Rhea County Courthouse at Dayton, Tennessee.

By the late nineteenth century the courthouse tended to be the dominant architectural landmark in its city. Often standing alone in the central square in town, a tower or dome proclaimed the building's preeminence over the local architectural environment. This pride-filled symbol of the booster spirit of a county seat was sometimes inflated in size and expense beyond what was truly appropriate for a particular county. One notorious example is the Macoupin County Courthouse (1867–1870) in Carlinville, Illinois, by Elijah E. Myers, the architect of several state capitols. Although the building was budgeted to cost $50,000, the final bill was for $1,380,000 due to graft and the extravagance of its classical design. It took over four decades for the county to pay off the debt.

With the growth of cities in the nineteenth century, the responsibilities of municipal government grew markedly. The design for Philadelphia City Hall (1871–1901) by John McArthur, Jr., reflected a combination of the growing size of local government, city pride, and the excesses of political corruption. Filling the center square of Philadelphia, this heavily ornamented Second Empire masonry pile boasts a tower 511 feet (156 meters) high, topped by a 37-foot (11-meter) statue of William Penn. During this building's lengthy construction, a seminal public building was built in Pittsburgh: the Allegheny County Courthouse and jail (1884–1888), designed by America's most prominent architect of the day, Henry Hobson Richardson. Like the Philadelphia City Hall, Richardson's courthouse is a large pavilioned block culminating in a landmark tower. However, Richardson has calmed down the exuberance and eclecticism of Victorian architecture. Unlike the Philadelphia building, ornament and picturesque effects do not dominate. Richardson concentrated on the essential masses, where the forms correspond to the functions within; the rusticated stone walls are articulated by the round arched openings of his distinctive Richardsonian Romanesque style. The Richardsonian romanesque, with its qualities of massiveness, stability, and functional clarity, made it one of the most popular architectural styles for public buildings at the end of the nineteenth century, from the Old Post Office Building in Washington, D.C. (1891–1899, by W. J. Edbrooke), to numerous courthouses built throughout Texas.

By the late nineteenth century the courthouse, often standing alone in the town or city's central square, tended to be the dominant landmark, with a dome or tower proclaiming the building's preeminence over the local architectural environment.

The American Renaissance Versus the Skyscraper

A return to classical order at the end of the Victorian era was heralded by the 1893 World's Columbian Exposition in Chicago. This was a temporary city with white plaster walls organized around a central court of honor. Its classicism, inspired by the teachings of the École des Beaux-Arts in Paris, was one of richness and magnitude suggesting Roman imperialism in contrast to the Greek reserve and severity seen at the beginning of the century. America had moved from a democratic experiment to a world power with imperial aspirations. This world's fair presented a unified ensemble of generously spaced classical buildings that was in sharp contrast to the random development of the emerging skyscraper city in the congestion of downtown Chicago. Ibis illusionary "White City" of the fair would be a compelling model for public architecture for years to come.

Sometimes called the American Renaissance, the turn of the century often saw a desire to reform the center of a city into a unified classical vision, a "City Beautiful." The construction of Washington, D.C., in the nineteenth century had departed sharply from L'Enfant's original intentions. In 1901–1902, a Senate Park Commission advised a return to a modified L'Enfant plan that would be the basis for much of monumental Washington. Many City Beautiful plans were made, but few were fully realized; nonetheless, this planning movement had a major impact upon those model cities for Americla, the college campus. Cass Gilbert's 1910 master plan for the University of Minnesota, Minneapolis, reflected a revival of interest in Jefferson's plan for the University of Virginia, now greatly monumentalized in the Beaux-Arts classical manner.

Many new state capitols were built during the American Renaissance, most reaffirming the domed, two-winged type, though now academically executed in a more knowing manner of classical and Renaissance sources (in contrast to the innocent simplicity of the Greek Revival and the free eclecticism of the Victorian era). Cass Gilbert's Minnesota State Capitol in Saint Paul (1895–1904) is one of the more refined examples, while Joseph M. Huston's Pennsylvania State Capitol in Harrisburg (1901–1909) was one of the most excessive (this building's financial scandal eventually landed the architect in jail).

The often-seen tendency of some communities to aggrandize their cities with public buildings of a scale and form associated with more important buildings is well represented by San Francisco's City Hall (1913–1915, by John Bakewell, Jr., and Arthur Brown, Jr.). Clearly mimicking the domed-palace-block form of Beaux-Arts classical state capitols, this building stands impressively at the heart of a unified civic center of buildings in the City Beautiful manner. However, many Beaux-Arts classical city halls are less dominant in their design, and appear to be just one classical block within a master plan, such as the understated Des Moines City Hall (1910–1911). This city hall was built for a progressive, commission form of city government: a large hall allowed the public to watch the city employees at work (no city bosses would be making deals behind closed doors).

The early development of modern architecture in America was not fought out in the conservative field of governmental architecture. One notable exception was the Woodbury County Courthouse (1915–1918) at Sioux City, Iowa, by the Prairie School firm of Purcell and Elmslie (for William L. Steele). It combines the abstract rectilinear geometry of Frank Lloyd Wright with the organic ornamentation of Louis H. Sullivan. Form follows function as the public offices and courtrooms are contained in the broad base. A skyscraper tower contains more private functions. Despite the radical nature of the building's aesthetic, Purcell and Elmslie did incorporate several traditional features: the series of piers across the front facade is reminiscent of a colonnade, the large lobby is capped with a dome, and the building establishes a landmark presence with its tower.

The skyscraper, that quintessential symbol of the modern American city began to have an impact upon state capitols by the 1920s and 1930s. Rather than the traditional Renaissance Revival dome, Bertram Goodhue's Nebraska State Capitol at Lincoln (1922–1932) is topped with a soaring skyscraper tower. Louisiana governor Huey Long's political ego was monumentalized in a similar skyscraper capitol at Baton Rouge (1931–1932). Even some university campuses started to go vertical: most spectacularly, Charles Z. Klauder's forty-two-story Gothic Revival Cathedral of Learning at the University of Pittsburgh (1924–1937).

In the early twentieth century, there was a renewed interest in the Gothic style for college campuses. It offered an alternative to the sometimes cold and monumental classicism of the day. Architects like Ralph Adam Cram and such educators as Woodrow Wilson at Princeton advocated the English Collegiate Gothic and its monastic quadrangles as evocative of the original ideals of college life. This introspective turning toward an elite club of the intellectually and socially select reveling in things English was especially appealing to the private universities of the Ivy League, and is well illustrated by the cloistered confines of Princeton and Yale universities. Many state universities opted for a more open approach of generously spaced buildings, often in the more economical and "American" style of the Georgian revival, as can be seen in the early-twentieth-century architecture of the University of Illinois at Urbana-Champaign.

From the 1920s to the 1950s, most one-room, single-teacher schoolhouses were abandoned in favor of consolidated schools in town, an approach facilitated by the coming of the yellow school bus. The typical urban school of the early twentieth century was a large multiple-classroom building of several stories, where students were now divided by grade level and were taught in a building with a great variety of rooms, allowing for such diverse activities as shop and theater. The nineteenth-century image of a schoolhouse evocative of home and church was replaced by an institutional building whose modular regularity sometimes suggests a factory. Nonetheless, many schools were embellished with the forms and ornament of fashionable architectural styles, making them proud cultural monuments at the center of a community, as can be seen in the neo-Gothic Evanston Township High School in Illinois by Perkins, Fellows and Hamilton (1923–1924). Elegant school architecture could also symbolize the gross inequities of American society, as was played out on the steps of Central High School in Little Rock, Arkansas, when this exclusively white public school was ordered by the federal government to desegregate in 1957.

Washington, D.C., underwent tremendous growth during the twentieth century, including a number of national shrines as American society continued to sanctify its history The primary function of Henry Bacon's Lincoln Memorial (1911–1922) and John Russell Pope's Jefferson Memorial (1935–1943) is to contain a larger-than-life statue of a revered president; these structures come much closer than most neoclassical buildings to the original use of classical temples as the abode of a cult figure to a god. While the White House and the Capitol, the quarters for the executive and legislative branches of the federal government, have always been at the core of the plan of Washington and its buildings, the third major branch of government, the judiciary, did not have a building of its own until Cass Gilbert's Supreme Court Building was built (1928–1935) to the east of the Capitol. Since the 1860s the Supreme Court had been meeting in the Old Senate Chamber of the Capitol. Gilbert's white marble temple is one of the most imperial neoclassical buildings in America; to those who pass through its immense portico the building communicates the supreme authority and judgment of the country's laws. Perhaps the greatest impression of twentieth-century Washington, D.C., is not its monuments but the endless number of buildings that have been built for the country's bureaucracy, such as the Federal Triangle, where block after classical block was built during the 1920s and 1930s to accommodate various departments of the nation's government.

From the PWA to Modernism and Beyond

Franklin D. Roosevelt's New Deal ushered in a degree of federal involvement in local affairs previously unseen. Such traditional symbols of local pride as a city hall or a public library were now being built by the federal government under New Deal programs such as the Public Works Administration (PWA; 1933–1939). A PWA building often meant a significant upgrading of a local public facility. It was a tangible symbol of governmental stability during the Great Depression, as well as a symbol that the nation was going back to work. The styles of PWA buildings exhibited great variety, sometimes reassuringly using regional traditions such as a colonial revival post office in Delaware or a Pueblo-style courthouse in New Mexico. Some buildings were more radically modern, such as John Lloyd Wright's Coolspring School in Indiana. However, the style often associated with PWA buildings is stripped classicism, as seen in Charles Z. Klauder's design for Pattee Library at Pennsylvania State University. This austere, more abstract approach to classicism was especially suitable for a nation in a depression desiring to build monumental buildings without ostentation.

In 1939, Ludwig Mies van der Rohe began to create a new plan for the Illinois Institute of Technology on the south side of Chicago. Several city blocks were replaced with a new campus consisting of glass, steel, and brick blocks that looked like carefully designed factories. In the era after World War II, modernism would triumph in American architecture creating a dilemma for public architecture. Civic architecture has often been conservative, reaffirming traditional architectural images of authority such as the portico, dome, or tower. Could a glass box convey such symbolism? Chicago's Richard J. Daley Center (1960–1966) is a steel-and-glass skyscraper containing 121 courtrooms for the city and Cook County. Nothing distinguishes its exterior from a corporate skyscraper other than its isolated location on an entire city block surrounded by an open plaza (Fig. 7).

Some architects deemed the anonymous glass box insufficient as a model for a major public building. A striking alternative was offered by Kallmann, McKinnell, and Knowles's Boston City Hall (1963–1969). Influenced by the brutal concrete forms of Le Corbusier's late buildings, Boston City Hall represents a turning toward a monumentality of heavy masses and geometric shapes. The various functions find separate expression yet all are brought together into a unified whole, appearing a bit like an abstract classical temple. While this building is clearly a monument to modern Boston, other communities have de-emphasized the symbolic role of public architecture. Any functional, no-frills office building is sufficient to house the growing administrative nature of local government. A building that makes a major architectural statement can be construed as a waste of the taxpayers' money. The changing nature of local government can also be seen in city council chambers, which in recent times have tended to emphasize dialogue by having citizens face the council members in modestly scaled rooms, in contrast to the large, formal chambers of the past, where the audience looked down on the proceedings from balconies.

The baby boom years after World War II were naturally boom years for school architecture. The multistory, revival-style educational institutions of the early twentieth century were often replaced with sprawling one-story suburban schools where generously fenestrated modern geometric blocks were distributed in wings appropriate to their functions. An important early precursor to this development is the Crow Island Elementary School in Winnetka, Illinois (1939–1940), by Eliel and Eero Saarinen, and Perkins, Wheeler, and Will. School architecture in recent times has often reflected revisionist attitudes toward curriculum, such as the flexible open plans popular during the 1960s, which allowed for such approaches as team teaching.

At the end of his life, America's most noted modern architect, Frank Lloyd Wright, finally had an opportunity to design a major governmental building, the Marin County Civic Center at San Rafael, California (1957–1972). The building sprawls across its site, addressing the natural context in a manner characteristic of Wright. However, at its center he included a low dome and a separate tower; unlike much of his earlier work, Wright chose to link this building (though in an abstract manner) with the architectural traditions of its type: the American county courthouse.

Civic architecture has often been conservative, reaffirming traditional architectural images of authority such as the portico, dome, or tower: Could a glass box convey such symbolism?

Postmodernism has brought about a renewed interest in the tradition of building types and historical styles. Michael Graves's Public Service Building in Portland, Oregon (1980–1983; Fig. 8), reflects a partial return to monumental classical forms and symbolic ornament, but with a mannerist manipulation of motifs evocative of the uneasy and disjointed links between contemporary life and the traditions of history. The growth of historic preservation has sought to save the public architecture of the past and to adapt sensitively and add on to existing landmarks. A case in point is the new Civic Center (1982–1990) that Charles Moore and the Urban Innovations Group integrated into the older complex of the 1932 Spanish baroque revival city hall in Beverly Hills, California. Old and new play off of each other as a popular new public place is created.

College architecture has been an arena for all major currents in architecture since 1945. When many new buildings went up to accommodate the explosive growth of colleges and universities from the late 1940s to the 1960s many unified Beaux-Arts classical or Gothic Revival campuses were violated by the ahistorical individuality typical of so many modern buildings. Campus planning became more open-ended where unpredictable growth was expected. Colleges and universities sometimes became the experimental grounds for innovative architects. Charles W Moore and William Turnbull radically rethought a residential college into a playful village where such communal features as the laundromat were given landmark status in their design for Kresge College (1965–1974) at the University of California, Santa Cruz. Peter Eisenman in his Wexner Center for the Visual Arts (1983–1989) entered into a deconstructionist dialogue with Ohio State University's existing buildings, the aesthetics of demolished buildings, and the conflicting grids of Columbus, Ohio.

The past few decades have been an uneasy time for American monuments. When Venturi and Rauch created Franklin Court in Philadelphia (1972–1976) as a bicentennial tribute to Benjamin Franklin, they chose not to rebuild Franklin's house but to create a ghostly outline of it in stainless steel, with hooded openings in the pavement so that one could see what was left of the foundations. Instead of reconstructing history (like twentieth-century Williamsburg) they clarified what we do and do not know. Maya Lin's Vietnam Veterans Memorial (1981–1982) is the opposite of most of Washington's monuments; it is dark and abstract and recedes into the ground. Its two granite walls (inscribed with the names of the over 58,000 Americans who died in Vietnam) align with the Washington Monument and the Lincoln Memorial as a new example of public building continues the complex symbolizing of American society.

The public architecture of America provides a monumental chronicle of society's changing attitudes toward government and education. At first, colonial public architecture reflected in a diminutive manner the distant institutions of civilization in the homeland. With the founding of a new nation, instant monuments evocative of noble aspirations were sought. As the country grew, so did the scale of government, and the size and constituency of education. Historical forms and styles have often been appropriated for their symbolic associations. The modernist disdain in the mid-twentieth century with history in favor of function and structure created the paradox of creating useful buildings devoid of traditional meanings. Many public buildings in recent years have returned to a dialogue with the past, as one sees a renewal of interest in establishing a meaningful architecture for the public realm.

[See also The City; Commercial Architecture; Landscapes; Parades, Holidays, and Public Rituals; Urban Cultural Institutions; Village and Town.]

BIBLIOGRAPHY

Allen, William C. *The United States Capitol: A Brief Architectural History* (1990).

American Bar Association and American Institute of Architects. *The American Courthouse: Planning and Design for the Judicial Process* (1973).

Craig, Lois, and Federal Architecture Project. *The Federal Presence: Architecture, Politics, and Symbols in United States Government Building* (1978).

Glazer, Nathan, and Mark Lilla, eds. *The Public Face of Architecture: Civic Culture and Public Spaces* (1987).

Gulliford, Andrew. *America's Country Schools* (1984).

Hitchcock, Henry-Russell, and William Seale. *Temples of Democracy: The State Capitols of the U.S.A.* (1976).

Hoyt, Charles King. *Public, Municipal, and Community Buildings* (1980).

Klauder, Charles Z., and Herbert C. Wise. *College Architecture in America and Its Part in the Development of the Campus* (1929).

Lebovich, William L., and Historic American Buildings Survey. *America's City Halls* (1984).

Lowry, Bates. *Building a National Image: Architectural Drawings for the American Democracy, 1789–1912* (1985).

Maddex, Diane, ed. *Built in the U.S.A.: American Buildings from Airports to Zoos* (1985).

Morrison, Hugh. *Early American Architecture: From the First Colonial Settlements to the National Period* (1952).

Owen, Robert Dale. *Hints on Public Architecture* (1849).

Pare, Richard, ed. *Court House: A Photographic Document* (1978).

Reiff, Daniel D. *Washington Architecture, 1791–1861: Problems in Development* (1971).

Roth, Leland M. *A Concise History of American Architecture* (1979).

Sexton, R. W., ed. *American Public Buildings of Today* (1931).

Short, C. W., and R. Stanley-Brown. *Public Buildings: A Survey of Architecture of Projects Constructed by Federal and Other Governmental Bodies Between the Years 1933 and 1939 with the Assistance of the Public Works Administrations* (1939; repr. 1986).

Turner, Paul Venable. *Campus: An American Planning Tradition* (1984).

U.S. Treasury Department. *A History of Public Buildings Under the Control of the Treasury Department.* Compiled by W. H. Wills and J. A. Sutherland (1901).

Zabel, Craig, and Susan S. Munshower, eds. *American Public Architecture: European Roots and Native Expressions* (1989).

— CRAIG ZABEL

PUBLIC EDUCATION

Public education has played a prominent role in the social history of the United States. In an ethnically diverse nation the public schools attempted to socialize young people by offering a common curriculum rooted in Anglo-American culture, thereby prompting debates over the content and control of public schooling. In a country with an egalitarian political tradition, people increasingly came to see education as the key to equal opportunity; and in an advanced capitalist economy, they came to see schooling as crucial to individual success and collective prosperity. To some degree, these cultural, political, and economic agendas combined to reinforce the importance of public schooling; on the other hand, they also provided the contradictory goals that have characterized the public schools.

Most Americans have a clear notion of what the phrase "public education" means in the twentieth century. "Education" means schools, and "public education" means schools that are tax-supported, tuition-free, and regulated by elected civil authorities. But there were no such schools in colonial America, and so the roots of public schooling must be sought in diverse institutions. Nor is it sufficient to limit the scope to British America or to white institutions, for the public schools of the United States today are descended also from mission schools in Spanish America, the clandestine schools of black slaves, and other educational efforts.

Education is rooted in the social structure. Although education can promote individual mobility and can disrupt the social structure at times, public education systems generally reflect and reinforce a society's prejudices, group conflicts, and hierarchical social relations. Thus, different groups have been treated differently in the public schools; in discussing the development of public schooling, we must clearly identify which clients we have in mind. After a brief look at the schooling of white children in the British colonies and the antebellum states, this article will consider public policies toward the education of nonwhites, including those in the western territories and in southern slavery.

Education in the Colonies

Earlier historians of American education looked upon seventeenth-century New England as the cradle of American public schooling. A Massachusetts law of 1647, warning that the "old deluder Satan" tried to keep men ignorant of the Scriptures, required towns of fifty households to provide instruction in reading and writing, and towns of one hundred households to establish grammar schools to prepare youths for the universities. Aside from the fact that enforcement of this law was weak, there are three important differences between the colonial New England arrangements and what came to be called public schools in the twentieth century. Schooling was not compulsory in colonial New England; attendance was a parental decision. Nor were the schools entirely tax-supported; rather, they were usually financed by a combination of general town taxes, tuition payments by parents, and donations of fuel. Third, there was no separation of church and state in education, so religion was sprinkled liberally through the curriculum. Two biases operated with regard to access. Girls were often entirely excluded from the schools, or permitted to go only a few hours each day, and they were not allowed to attend the grammar schools or the colonial colleges. Furthermore, the requirement that parents pay part of the tuition for elementary schooling meant that the children of poorer parents might not receive as much schooling as the children of the more affluent. Literacy rates reflect these circumscribed opportunities along gender and class lines, though literacy estimates based on ability to sign documents probably underestimate the number of women and poor males who could read, since reading was taught first and writing later.

Formal schooling played a smaller role in children's upbringing in the colonial period than later. In an influential 1960 work Bernard Bailyn argued that historians should think of education as the whole process by which culture is transmitted across generations; Lawrence Cremin (1970) championed a somewhat more limited but still broad definition in his comprehensive history of American education: education is all deliberate instruction. According to such a definition, education extended far beyond classrooms, especially in colonial America. The colonial mode of education emphasized parental responsibility and a limited government role. Education took place in the family, the church, the school, and the workplace. Schooling was non-compulsory, supported by a combination of funding sources, and characterized by brief terms and unequal access.

Educational arrangements in the other regions of British America were not dramatically different. Scattered population made formal schooling even more difficult and less important in the South and on the frontier. The New England mode of education—parental responsibility, education in a variety of settings, little government interference, and modest amounts of schooling—reigned across all the regions. Religious motives and religious content pervaded education, not only in the church and the family, but in schools as well. In *The New England Primer* (ca. 1690), the most popular beginning reading text in colonial British America, children learned their alphabet from a series of rhymed couplets that began "In Adam's Fall/We sinned all" and ended "Zaccheus he did climb the Tree/Our Lord to see." The first level of schooling, then, was for reading, pervaded by religious content and moral lessons, plus a bit of arithmetic. Writing in English followed later, sometimes in a separate school. Small bits of history, literature, and geography were present in the readers of the late colonial period. English grammar followed and then, for boys only, Latin grammar.

In cities such as New York, Boston, and Philadelphia, as well as Schenectady, Hartford, and other medium-sized cities, a variety of schools developed in the eighteenth century, from elite private schools, to cheap pay schools, to free charity schools for the poor.

The Early National Period

Given the importance of an intelligent citizenry in republican political thought, the American Revolution had surprisingly little immediate effect at the grass-roots level. Republican theorists like Thomas Jefferson and Benjamin Rush, motivated by the need for virtuous republican citizens and the fear of fragmentation in the new nation, offered plans for innovative state school systems. But their concerns were not widely shared, and their plans called for unprecedented government activism in an area traditionally left to the family. Most white children received some rudimentary intellectual training, and most people seem to have believed that the modest levels of schooling in late-eighteenth-century America were adequate. Thus, there was a lag of two generations between the Revolution and the creation of public school systems regulated by the states. When state intervention did occur, it was for motives similar to those expressed by Jefferson and Rush—to homogenize and discipline the population, to produce intelligent and moderate citizens, and to disseminate a common culture. By the late 1830s and early 1840s, the desire for social order and public morality became sufficiently strong to overcome other worries about state intervention. But this shift in the public mood, more favorable to the creation of public school systems, was a response to more general and alarming problems than existed in the early national period.

The predominant form of schooling in rural areas was the local district school, supported partially by property taxes and partially by parental tuition payments; in the cities, inexpensive pay schools were supplemented by an expanding number of charity schools operated by churches and nondenominational societies. Enrollments were increasing in the Northeast during the early national period, despite the lack of state intervention. Capitalism, Protestantism, and republicanism each played a background role in encouraging education. As more farmers were brought into the cash market, literacy and numeracy became more necessary; periodic Protestant revivalism emphasized Bible reading, and denominational rivalry spurred school foundings; the gradually expanding franchise also encouraged more schooling. In cities, increasingly visible poverty and immigration roused fears of social disruption and prompted the founding of more charity schools modeled on British institutions.

But the greatest part of the rise in school attendance in the early national period was occasioned by the increasing participation of girls. Town school records and literacy rates both suggest a substantial increase in access and attendance by girls. Essayists emphasized mothers' role in raising sons for republican citizenship, and town officials changed their school rules to allow more equal access to elementary education. In 1827 an unsigned letter to the editor of the *Salem* (Massachusetts) *Register* lamented that the town was so "backward" in regard to female education, while in the countryside "the public schools are open alike to males and females" because "the importance of female education is now so unanimously acknowledged." Female academies proliferated during this period, furthering the notion of women's intellectual capability. Teaching swung from being a male profession to being predominantly female at the elementary level, partly because attitudes about women's abilities were changing and partly because town officials found it attractive to save money through the lower wages paid to female teachers. Even Catharine Beecher (1800–1878), a principal architect of the female teaching profession, promoted women as "the best, as well as the cheapest guardian and teacher of childhood."

The great watershed in the political history of public schooling were in the two decades preceding the Civil War. By the 1840s, conditions were more favorable for state intervention in local schooling. Massive immigration, Protestant-Catholic tension, increasing urbanization, and the gradual acceptance of the role of government in the development of transportation and the building of institutions laid the groundwork for school reforms. Reformers in most states argued for increased state aid to local schooling, the establishment of a chief state school officer and county superintendents, licensing examinations and increased pay for teachers, required record keeping, longer school terms, and full tax support for free public schools. Horace Mann, the most famous of the common school reformers, in his *Eleventh Annual Report* (1847) as secretary of the Massachusetts Board of Education, argued that education would make the nation prosperous and "redeem the state from social vices and crimes." In addition to goals of productivity and social order, Mann often sounded democratic themes. In his *Twelfth Annual Report* (1848) he called public education "the great equalizer of the conditions of men—the balance-wheel of the social machinery," and added that schools would disseminate basic principles of republican government necessary. for citizens to remain free.

REFORM AND OPPOSITION. Despite growing support for these several arguments, the reforms elicited spirited opposition. They were generally opposed by Roman Catholic officials, who in some cities were receiving public funds for their charity schools and who viewed the public schools either as godless institutions or as bastions of Protestantism. Some conservative Protestants resisted on religious grounds because they feared the watered-down Protestantism of the reformers. They wished to protect local control, under which they could merge distinctive, doctrinal religion with public schooling. For example, in the 1830s all the school-children in some Indiana towns went to Quaker meeting at midweek. In the 1840s Mann met vigorous resistance in Massachusetts when he proposed a state-approved book list that omitted books featuring Calvinist concepts like infant damnation.

Other opposition arose from racial or political considerations and from differences between rural and urban attitudes. Black leaders in the Northeast opposed some aspects of school reform, periodically fighting to protect black curriculum, black teachers, or other black rights within the generally segregated and unequal public schooling that was offered in northern cities. In New York City, for example, blacks boycotted the public schools in the 1830s when black teachers were replaced with white teachers; the black teachers were reinstated. In the 1840s blacks formed the New York Society for the Promotion of Education Among Colored Children to promote black control of education and self-help in the black community. In Boston, black leaders fought early in the century to obtain public support for separate black schools, then continued to demand improvements and equal treatment. In the 1840s, because their efforts to attain equal treatment had failed, they fought for integration into the white public schools, which was achieved in 1855 after much struggle.

Rural areas were less enthusiastic about state intervention, property taxes to support schools, longer school years, and other reforms. They prized local control, resisted outside regulation, and disagreed on the need for longer school terms and better-trained teachers. The district school, with its short sessions and untrained local teachers, fit with the rhythms and customs of rural life, and many rural people were loath to see it reformed.

The religious and demographic lines of conflict overlapped partially with the political split between Democrats and Whigs. The school reform program was a Whig invention, supported selectively but less comfortably by some Democrats. School reformers, including Horace Mann of Massachusetts, Henry Barnard of Connecticut, Samuel Lewis of Ohio, and others, were Whigs supported by Whig majorities. Rural voters and Catholics tended to oppose school reform, especially when it meant an enhancement of state authority over education. Democratic politicians and Catholic essayists both characterized state intervention as a "Prussian" form of centralization.

Historians differ on how much class-based opposition existed; it is difficult to define and document the role of class in school reform, partly because class interests often coincided with religious or ethnic affiliation, partly because people were more likely to announce their allegiance to a religious position or an ethnic or racial group than to label their class position. Michael Katz (1968) mustered evidence that in 1860 working-class voters in Beverly, Massachusetts, voted to discontinue the high school in greater numbers than more affluent voters, but even that hard data may be interpreted in various ways. Evidence about the extent of working-class voters' support for the creation and financing of public elementary schooling is murky.

By the 1840s, conditions were more favorable for state intervention in local schooling: Massive immigration, increasing urbanization, and the gradual acceptance of government's role in developing transportation and institutions laid the groundwork for reforms.

Despite much opposition, the school reform program of the Whigs eventually prevailed in every northern state. Laws creating state and county superintendencies, consolidating rural districts, establishing property taxation for school support, and making other innovations were passed. But political intention and social effect were quite different. The political activity was focused on the state level, where reformers proposed plans for state intervention to create and regulate public schools. But the work of education—what happened to children and teachers in schools—occurred on the local level. In the early national period, there was a large gap between these two levels. Early laws often failed to pass, or were passed in a form that made local compliance voluntary, or were left without effective enforcement. Thus, local schooling continued with little or no state interference. After 1840, however, teachers' memoirs and local records reveal that communities were drawn slowly into a rudimentary set of state regulations and associations. Teachers more often went to summer institutes, belonged to teachers' associations, passed examinations administered by county superintendents, and in some states chose textbooks from state-approved lists. Much local control remained, but the social history and the political history of education had begun to intertwine.

By the time of the Civil War, free public schooling was a local reality for whites in the North. In the South the same forces of reform and opposition existed and sounded much like their counterparts in the North; but the balance was different, and the existence of slavery generated some nervousness about widespread popular education, even for poor whites. The northern middle-class program of property taxes to support free public schooling was not adopted in the South until the end of the nineteenth century, and then only within the context of separate and unequal schools for black children.

THE EDUCATION OF NONWHITES. Legally sanctioned segregation was mostly a southern phenomenon, but it was consistent with a long history of educational policy toward nonwhites, North and South. For subordinated racial groups in American history, the reality of public education policy, was that schools would be used either to exclude them or to segregate them, to impose the dominant culture and ideology on them, and to reinforce their subordinate position in the economy. Thus, while much twentieth-century education policy has moved in the direction of attempting to equalize opportunity, educators as well as students have had to struggle against traditions of inequality based on ethnic conflict and economic exploitation, traditions reaching back to the colonial period.

Colonial authorities generally ignored or prohibited the education of subject people, although occasionally they contemplated the use of schools for indoctrination or cultural conversion. Spanish authorities did little about schooling in eighteenth-century Spanish America for native inhabitants or Spanish colonists, seeing education as a matter for church and the family. The practical result was that elite families and middling-status artisans among the Spanish colonists provided education for their children through tutors or private schools, while missions made intermittent, ineffectual efforts to educate poor Spanish colonists or Indians. Periodically (for example, in 1717 and again in 1793) the royal authorities instructed missions to start schools to convert all the Indians from their native languages to Castilian. Little came of these edicts, although there are occasional reports of missions that selected a few Navajo children to be schooled at the mission and returned home in the hope that they would indoctrinate the rest.

Neglect and discrimination in the education of nonwhites were justified by stereotypes about their low level of civilization, their limited mental capacity, and their necessarily menial place in the economy.

Little changed for poor Spanish Americans or for Native Americans during the period of Mexican independence. After the Mexican War, the territorial governments in the United States, like their predecessors, did little to encourage the education of Mexican Americans or Indians. Even for the white settlers, early school laws were more exhortatory than regulatory, as was the case throughout trans-Appalachian America in the early nineteenth century. Funds were rarely appropriated for local education in significant amounts.

Neglect and discrimination in the education of nonwhites were justified by stereotypes about their low level of civilization, their limited mental capacity, and their necessarily menial place in the economy. The same stereotypes existed among American slaveholders in the eighteenth and early nineteenth centuries. Yet with so much daily contact and a shared English language, some slaveholders were inclined to teach African Americans how to read. Thus, slave narratives often mention informal reading lessons from the owner's wife. Frederick Douglass recalled being taught to read by his owner's wife in Baltimore; when the owner discovered what was happening, he rebuked his wife: "If you teach that nigger how to read, there would be no keeping him." Douglass said this was "a new and special revelation," showing him "the pathway from slavery to freedom."

Such informal efforts to teach slaves to read were supplemented in the colonial period by the efforts of the Society for the Propagation of the Gospel in Foreign Parts, the missionary arm of the Anglican church, which taught literacy and a selective view of Christianity that endorsed slavery and obedience. Somewhat more subversive were the efforts of the Quakers, who associated literacy with eventual manumission and who provided some schools for slaves until they were prevented from doing so by increasingly nervous slaveholders in the nineteenth century. As abolitionism, sectionalism, and slave rebellions increased in the nineteenth century, southern states passed laws prohibiting the teaching of slaves, and many slaveholders administered severe physical punishments to slaves caught with reading materials.

In the late nineteenth and early twentieth centuries whites took various actions to incorporate racial minorities into evolving public school systems, but on a segregated and unequal basis. There were few public schools of any kind in the Southwest before the turn of the century, but by 1920 the pattern was established in New Mexico and Texas: Mexican Americans were in segregated public schools in substantial numbers, assigned to lower grades than whites of the same age, regardless of ability, and had shorter school years and poorer facilities; there was no accommodation of Spanish culture. Said one Texas school superintendent in 1928: "It is up to the white population to keep the Mexican on his knees in an onion patch. . . . This does not mix well with education" (Weinberg, *A Chance to Learn*, p. 146).

In the case of American Indians, the federal government generally ignored promises of education it made in treaties, and so there was little active policy in education. The modest moneys available from the "Civilization Fund" passed by Congress in 1819 apparently stimulated some missionary activity, especially among the southern tribes. In these early days there was some give-and-take and some tribal control. The Creeks, for example, successfully forbade white teachers to teach their children Christianity. The Cherokees spent money from the sale of lands to create schools in their control, schools that enrolled more than five thousand students by 1880. But these aspects of tribal control ended when the government took over all Indian schooling activities between 1890 and 1910. Thereafter, there were federal boarding schools and contracts with neighboring public schools, together serving a small minority of Indian children, with no concessions to Indian culture. Within the tribes, Indian education continued in traditional, nonschool settings.

Black Americans also created their own educational institutions. Recent research has shown that even under slavery, many clandestine schools were conducted. These schools, and the literate minority they produced, laid the basis for black educational efforts during the Civil War and afterward. In Savannah and Augusta, in Natchez, Charleston, and Richmond, secret schools were conducted. Lila Grandison's school in Natchez met with a dozen students from eleven at night until two in the morning. Of Grandison's school a northern abolitionist wrote, "Every window and door was carefully closed to prevent discovery. In that little school hundreds of slaves learned to read and write a legible hand." These efforts created momentum to start schools after emancipation. Because the freed slaves were poor and had few teachers among their ranks, the efforts of northern white missionaries were important. The indigenous educational efforts of African Americans in the Reconstruction South have, however, been underestimated until recently. In New Orleans blacks organized the Louisiana Educational Relief Association in 1866, and by 1867 their sixty-five schools enrolled more children than the fifty-six schools of the Freedmen's Bureau. Similarly, the Georgia Education Association supported 96 of the state's 123 black schools in full or in part in 1866. Despite poverty, black Americans contributed heavily to the development of common schools for black children, and the tradition of self-help continued into the separate and unequal systems of public schools that followed Reconstruction.

From leaders to parents, members of non-white groups faced with discriminatory, public policies toward education had two related problems: what to do about public education that was unequal, segregated, and culturally abusive, and how to create supplementary or alternative educational arrangements. Social historians of the 1960s and 1970s tended to emphasize the power advantage of mainstream Protestant Americans, and the resulting inequalities and cultural imposition of the schools. Recent social historians have focused more on the activism of ordinary people in making decisions about the institutions they faced. Thus, there is a greater appreciation that nonelite people in the working and middle classes and members of oppressed groups were also actors in history and made a difference.

Consolidation, Expansion, Bureaucratization

In the history of public education as a system, the story in the second half of the nineteenth century is one of consolidation, expansion, and bureaucratization. By 1880, most white children attended school sometime during the year for at least a few years. In the peak common school years, ages eight to eleven, enrollment rates in the Northeast were near 90 percent, even among less privileged white groups. But the age at which children left school was sharply affected by their ethnic group and their parents' occupations. Public high schools, rare before the Civil War, were spreading rapidly; they catered to the children of middling groups: upper-status artisan families and lower-status white-collar families. By 1890, public high school students outnumbered private academy students; initially a male-dominated institution, the public high school became a predominantly female preserve by the turn of the century (59 percent female students in 1900). Women in their teens found fewer places in the industrial work force, but they also found various attractions in high schools: preparing to become a teacher, training in various new vocational programs for women, taking part in the social activities and peer friendships centered in high schools, or gaining some further education for the intelligent pursuit of the domestic roles of wife and mother. Although the percentage of high-school-age children in private and public schools more than doubled between 1890 and 1910 (from 7 percent to 15 percent), it was still the experience of only a minority of children, mostly middle-class whites. By 1920, the percentage had climbed to 32 percent, and by 1930 it was 51 percent. Children of native-born white parents attended in greater proportions than those of nonwhite and foreign-born parents, but the differences were narrowing. A child's eventual role and status in society were still strongly influenced by parents' occupations and educational backgrounds, but schools increasingly acted as arbiters in the process. Industry provided fewer jobs for teenagers; high schools, in turn, provided more vocational or general programs for youths not bound for college, further increasing the appeal of school attendance for those between the ages of fourteen and seventeen.

In addition to adding high schools, public school systems in this era of rapid urbanization and bureaucratization became larger and more structured. Two administrative roles developed, the principal and the superintendent. In the antebellum urban school the principal had been a "principal teacher" who both taught and supervised younger assistant teachers. In the late nineteenth century, principals increasingly became full-time administrators as urban schools became larger. Also, big-city school boards began to hire professional superintendents to oversee the whole system of public education.

Public education had not lost its capacity to stir controversy and to dramatize more general social conflicts. In the late nineteenth century, for example, Protestants and Catholics disagreed on many issues concerning public education. Disputes involving Bible reading in the public schools, taxation of church property, proposals to aid Catholic schools with public funds, and other matters erupted into battles around the country. Catholics argued that the King James Bible was different from their Douay version and that it symbolized the Protestant bias of the public schools. Protestants argued variously that America's public schools should reflect the Protestant origins of the nation or that reading the King James Bible without comment was a neutral practice and that opposition to it reflected Catholic hostility to lay Bible reading. Issues such as these arose following a vote by the Cincinnati school board to eliminate Bible reading from the public schools that led to a protracted controversy dubbed the "Cincinnati Bible War," one of many. Similar disputes prompted cartoons by Thomas Nast, one in 1871 showing crocodile-like bishops about to devour children before the ruins of a public school while Tammany Hall—the very image of Saint Peter's Church—dominates the background; a few years later Nast drew Bishop Richard Gilmour of Cleveland hurling lightning bolts at Catholic parents who supported public schools. Catholic essayists charged that public

In the late 1800s, disputes involving Bible reading in public schools, taxation of church property, and proposals to publicly fund Catholic schools erupted into battles between Protestants and Catholics around the country.

schools spread immorality, while Protestant writers charged Catholics with being un-American. Like minorities who were ambivalent about compromises with a hostile public school system, Catholics displayed a range of attitudes and practices. Ethnicity reinforced the religious dilemma for some. Thus, the German bishops opposed compromise because language as well as religion was at stake.

Many Catholics sent their children to public schools, however, and some Catholic leaders favored attempts at accommodation. Most prominently, Archbishop John Ireland of Minneapolis attempted to reconcile Catholics' desire for distinctive schools with the public schools' monopoly on tax money through a plan pioneered in Poughkeepsie, New York, in the 1870s. Under the Poughkeepsie Plan, the public board paid for Catholic teachers and supplies in return for the elimination of religious instruction during regular school hours; before and after school, Catholic schoolchildren attended mass and received religious instruction. Similar plans had been implemented with some success in scattered locations when Archbishop Ireland tried to make the Poughkeepsie plan a national solution, lobbying the National Education Association and Rome. Approved begrudgingly in Rome in 1892, the plan failed in the United States due to strong Protestant opposition to the two pilot programs in Minnesota. Intense Protestant-Catholic controversy over educational issues nationwide during the late 1880s and early 1890s reinforced the split between the two school systems.

PROGRESSIVE EDUCATION. By 1900, then, the public school system had expanded into secondary education, consolidated its exclusive hold on public funds, and developed a more bureaucratic structure, especially in urban schools. Two of these features helped prompt the reform movement loosely known as "Progressive education," which occurred between the 1890s and the 1920s. The schools' bureaucratic structure and the increasing proportion of students going to high schools combined to concern educators. Were the schools too uniform, too rigid? Was the same education appropriate for all students? In a series of exposés in *The Forum*, Joseph Mayer Rice complained that the typical urban school was "a hard, unsympathetic, mechanical-drudgery school, a school into which the light of science has not yet entered." Surveying a system that had not gotten the reform message by 1916, the administrative wizard Ellwood Cubberley wrote: "The most fundamental principle observed in the present conduct of the Portland school system is the maintenance unchanged of a rigidly prescribed, mechanical system, poorly adapted to the needs either of the children or of the community" (*The Portland Survey* [1916], p. 125).

These concerns combined to produce a reform devoted to the refinement of school bureaucracy. Efficiency now came to be seen as different programs for different students. Different skills meant different destinies. Often this form of efficiency ethic was governed by ethnic, racial, and gender prejudices; but it came in the guise of science, bolstered by new findings in psychology by such leaders as Edward L. Thorndike, a founder of behaviorist psychology, and it became the dominant school reform of the Progressive Era in the hands of curriculum reformers like David Snedden of Massachusetts and administrative theorists like J. Franklin Bobbitt of the University of Chicago.

Social Reform versus Efficiency

The depression of the mid-1890s brought poignancy and contrasting themes to school reform. Some reformers concluded that the schools were out of touch with the reality of urban, industrial, immigrant America. They responded not just with differentiated programs like vocational education but also with more social services from the schools, like lunch programs and home visits by teachers. Some educators saw the two motives of efficiency and compassion as compatible, and endorsed specialized curricula for different children as well as the schools' involvement in children's social needs and their individual interests. But these goals existed in tension. In practice, tracking children meant early predictions about each child's probable fate, and these predictions were often based on gender, race, ethnicity, or family income. In 1908 David Snedden endorsed a hierarchical notion of a democracy "of team players": "Equality of opportunity can only be secured by recognition of differences which theoretically individual, may nevertheless, for practical purposes, be regarded as characterizing distinguishable groups of children" (quoted in Marvin Lazerson, *Origins of the Urban School* [1971] pp. 200–201). But John Dewey, in *The New Republic*, disputed Snedden's program of vocational education, arguing against early tracking and decrying "any use of the public school system which takes for granted the perpetuity of the existing industrial régime, and whose inevitable effect is to perpetuate it" (19 December 1914). Similar issues enlivened educational controversies in Illinois, where the Chicago Federation of Teachers was particularly active, arguing against separate vocational high schools and IQ testing.

More recent works in the social history of education—for example, those by William Reese (1986) and Julia Wrigley (1982)—have shown that public schools were not the unremitting tools of a power elite; rather, they were the subject of many battles, big and small, and many compromises. The sides were usually not equal in power, but parents, teachers, immigrants, socialists, club women, people of color, and others were not powerless when they dissented. On the other hand, the powerful alliance that David Tyack analyzed in *The One Best System* (1974), between businessmen, professionals, college presidents, and school administrators, emphasized education for efficiency within the existing social and economic system. These "administrative progressives," as Tyack called them, had a greater impact on school systems through centralized management, standardized testing, and differentiation of the curriculum than those often stereotyped as "Progressive" educators—those interested in child-centered pedagogy emphasizing more creativity, choice, and activity by individual children. Some of their slogans entered mainstream public schools, but thoroughgoing experiments in child-centered pedagogy remained at the fringes. Larry Cuban's (1984) work on the history of teaching methods suggests that most classrooms have been teacher-centered throughout the twentieth century. By the 1920s, the split between the pedagogical progressives and the administrative progressives was more visible, and the relative victory of the administrative progressives was evident. Robert and Helen Lynd concluded in their study of Muncie, Indiana (*Middletown in Transition*, 1937), that "in the struggle between quantitative administrative efficiency and qualitative educational goals," the "big guns" were on the side of efficiency. Harold Rugg and Ann Shumaker wrote that the child-centered schools "constitute but a corporal's guard as compared with the great regiment of formal schools" (*The Child-centered School*, 1928).

In the South the Progressive Era saw a more basic sort of reform. Common school advocates had failed in the antebellum South. Voters rejected property taxes for free public schools. Local educational arrangements, including tutors, pay schools, partially free schools, and charity schools, prevailed. Local schooling in the postbellum South remained sparse by northern standards; both in per-pupil expenditures and in days of school attended, southern states spent money and sent children to school at rates one-fourth to one-fifth that in Massachusetts. Schooling in rural areas was especially meager. Schools for black children were doubly disadvantaged, both by region and by race. Despite some help from such philanthropic sources as the Peabody Fund and the Slater Fund, blacks were thrown largely upon their own resources for education.

REFORM IN THE SOUTH. Northern philanthropists, collaborating with reform-minded southerners, attempted to export the common school idea. After years of politicking and publicity, these "New South" forces won, but only by acquiescing in the unequally funded, segregated system of public schools for black children. The southern education campaign faced not only traditional racism but also the particular virulence of the Jim Crow period, when southern states were erecting new laws of segregation. As a result, the gap between spending on white education and black education actually increased during the early twentieth century. South Carolinians spent six times as much per pupil in white schools as in black schools in 1900, but the ratio was twelve to one by 1915. This was the reality of a system later defended as "separate but equal." But the South was not unique, and blacks were not alone. By the early twentieth century, separate and unequal schooling was the norm for nonwhite groups throughout the United States.

REFORM BETWEEN THE WARS. John Dewey, the philosopher of Progressive education, had tempered his child-centered pedagogy not only with a solid appreciation of traditional subject matter but also with a notion that democracy is an evolving form of shared government and that children need to learn to criticize and improve the society in which they live. He was intermittently critical of the existing system of industrial capitalism. This strain of socially critical Progressive educational thought became stronger in a small group of education professors in the next generation, active in the 1920s and 1930s. The movement was led by George Counts of Teachers College, Columbia University, who in 1932 presented the Progressive Education Association with the challenge "Dare the Schools Build a New Social Order?" Counts went on to lead a group known as the "reconstructionists," including Harold Rugg of Teachers College, who published a controversial series of politically progressive social studies texts, and Boyd Bode of Ohio State University, who declared Progressive education to be "at the crossroads" between social consciousness and a self-indulgent emphasis on the child.

John Dewey, Progressive philosopher, psychologist and educator, believed that children should learn to criticize and improve the society in which they live.

The activities of these men caused some commentary, and the debate makes a stirring story in the history of educational ideas; but, as David Tyack, Robert Lowe, and Elisabeth Hansot (1984) demonstrated, the reconstructionists had little effect on either the practice of education or the direction of educational administration. After a brief period of self-doubt among educationists in the early years of the Great Depression, local school officials and experts in educational administration recovered their admiration of business models and returned to efficiency and standardization as ways to face fiscal stringency, while businessmen and editors (most notably William Randolph Hearst) railed against the "red" threat to the public schools. To the extent that the New Deal included educational policies, they were implemented outside of the public schools in temporary relief agencies such as the Civilian Conservation Corps and the National Youth Administration, and ended when those agencies ended.

LIFE ADJUSTMENT AND ITS CRITICS. The version of Progressive education that survived in the public schools after 1940 was neither child-centered pedagogy nor democratic social criticism but a version of "teaching the whole child" that included not just academic learning but social roles, health, leisure pursuits, and other matters. In the 1940s this approach was known as "life adjustment" education, and it was aimed at the middle 60 percent of youth in high schools who, the life adjusters argued, were not well served by a strictly academic curriculum or by trade education. While this curriculum thinking lacked the element of active choice present in Dewey's thought and the element of social criticism present in the reconstructionists' progressivism, it put the imprimatur of the educators on many features of school life that parents and children had come to expect: guidance, extracurricular activities, and courses dealing with health, citizenship, job applications, and other practical matters. In the early 1950s it attracted critics from among traditionalists like Arthur Bestor, the author of *Educational Wastelands* (1953), who wanted a return to more academic work and tougher standards.

This critique got a tremendous boost when the Soviet Union launched the first artificial satellite, *Sputnik*, in 1957. *Sputnik* scared the public; it symbolized and dramatized the cold war situation: technology in the service of superpower competition. It seemed obvious that education was relevant. *Sputnik*, said Admiral Hyman Rickover, demonstrated that the Russian school system caused "all children to stretch their intellectual capacities to the utmost." in contrast, as *Life* magazine sneered in 1958, in the United States "a quarter century has been wasted with the squabbling over whether to make a child well adjusted or teach him something. . . . The standards of education are shockingly low." The traditionalist critics of the early 1950s had been as concerned with the humanities as with the sciences; but *Sputnik* gave a scientific and international direction to school reform. The curriculum reforms spawned by Jerome Bruner's influential conference volume, *The Process of Education* (1960), emphasized new mathematics and new science approaches; and the federal government entered the reform with the National Defense Education Act of 1958, aimed principally at promoting learning in mathematics, science, and foreign languages. One of the functions of the public school curriculum is to dramatize for children what the nation's political and educational leaders believe is important. The cold war moved science and technology to center stage. It also moved the focus from the middle 60 percent in ability to the higher-achieving students. Educational rhetoric in this period emphasized the rigorous identification and training of talent, in the national interest.

The effects of such reform pendulum swings on schools at the grass roots are less dramatic than the shifts in the themes of debate, and they are hard to estimate. Follow-up studies of the 1950s reforms suggest that curriculum reforms such as the new mathematics were widely adopted and widely abandoned, and that perhaps the most substantial effect on public schools was a modest increase in teaching of foreign languages and the availability of language laboratories.

In the 1950s most teenagers attended high school; by 1950, 77 percent of the high-school age group attended public or private high schools, and by 1960 the figure was 86 percent. With the higher-education sector expanding, especially through the growth of community colleges, more high-school graduates went on to further education (41 percent in 1950, 53 percent in 1960). High-school activities and social relations thus became more important as the modal experience of teenagers, and more important in the lives of their communities. Extracurricular activities, dating, and social cliques all loomed large in the socialization process of teenagers. If a social history of the high school includes

In the 1940s, the concept of "teaching the whole child" became known as "life adjustment" education and was aimed at the middle 60 percent of high school youths who were not well served by a strictly academic curriculum or by trade education.

issues on the minds of the students, going steady was as important in the 1950s as *Sputnik.*

Equality and Integration

Even among curriculum reformers the cold war preoccupation with talent and technology did not remain at center stage for very long. In one of the most dramatic pendulum swings in the history of American educational reform, the 1960s witnessed a change in themes and focus toward ideals of equality and racial integration, toward the educational problems of the disadvantaged, the poor, and those who faced discrimination. Like the cold war reforms, these reforms were driven by more general crises in American society—the civil rights movement and the war on poverty. On the surface it seemed that the agenda changed very quickly, because educational reform does seem to move in pendulum swings. But in the background the crises of poverty and race relations had been building for decades.

Eighty years of separate and drastically unequal public education elapsed between the end of Reconstruction and the landmark Supreme Court *Brown* decisions of 1954 and 1955, which declared legally sanctioned segregation in education to be unconstitutional. Those decades of hardship and struggle had bred many sacrifices, many protests, and much self-help. In Alton, Illinois, Scott Bibb and other working-class black parents boycotted segregated schools during the 1890s while pursuing integration in court. Black parents staged similar protests in East Orange, New Jersey, in 1906, in Springfield, Ohio, in 1922, and in Dayton, Ohio, in 1926. Even where northern courts declared segregation illegal, the decisions yielded little satisfaction; local school officials always found ways around them and enforcement was dilatory. Living in a racist society created a continual dilemma for members of minorities, whether black, Chicano, Native American, or Asian: the choice between accommodation and going a separate way, between cooperation and protest, between gradualism and urgency. These tensions played out in various ways prior to 1954.

Several developments prepared the way for the *Brown* decision. In the 1930s and 1940s the Supreme Court had begun applying the Bill of Rights to state law in cases involving free speech and free exercise of religion. The National Association for the Advancement of Colored People (NAACP) pressed in the lower courts for more equal school resources. World War II brought racial matters to a head in some regards: the war was fought against a racist Nazi regime, and it was fought with the help of nonwhite American soldiers in segregated units; some beginnings of integration in the U.S. Army followed the war. Also, the GI Bill of Rights (1944) allowed many veterans to attend college after the war, including many minority students, and they raised questions about segregation in higher education.

Some of these issues reached the Supreme Court prior to *Brown,* and decisions in these cases chipped away at the old segregationist principle of "separate but equal." In *Sweatt* v. *Painter* (1950) the Court declared that the all-black law school created by Texas officials to avoid integration could not be separate and be truly equal to the white University of Texas law school, even if it had similar resources, because its graduates would lack the prestige that went with the white school's reputation and would lack such intangibles as contacts with influential alumni. Finally, the NAACP's Legal Defense Fund, which brought the higher-education cases, had also worked hard to develop arguments and cases for elementary schooling. Until the 1940s the NAACP generally just argued for the equalization of resources between black and white schools, and sometimes they gained some redress. But after 1950 they employed a "two-stringed bow," never conceding equality without integration. And they had won some strong dissenting minority opinions, such as that of J. Waties Waring, a federal appeals judge in South Carolina, who wrote in *Briggs* v. *Elliott* (1951) that "segregation is per se inequality." This position prevailed in the unanimous decision in *Brown* four years later.

For nearly ten years, resistance to the *Brown* decision was quite effective. Local school authorities and lower courts interpreted the ruling only to mean that laws sanctioning or requiring segregated schools had to be eliminated, but that *Brown* did not actually require integration. School boards used busing patterns, school boundary changes, voluntary choice programs, and other means, coupled with intimidation, to keep schools segregated. In 1964, ten years after *Brown,* fewer than 1 percent of all black children in the South went to schools with any white children. In a series of clarifying decisions, the Supreme Court declared (especially in *Green* v. *County School Board of New Kent County,* 1968) that federal courts would insist on proof of racial integration in areas that formerly had legally sanctioned segregated schools. By 1976, 77 percent of black schoolchildren in the South were in schools that had at least 10 percent white students. In the Northeast and the Midwest only 41 percent of the black students were in schools integrated to that degree, and in the West, 56 percent. Federal intervention in segregation outside the South came after *Keyes* v. *School District No. 1, Denver, Colorado* (1972), in which the Supreme Court declared unconstitutional not just laws sanctioning segregation but school segregation resulting from education policy, such as school board decisions on district boundaries, location of new buildings, and busing patterns. School segregation that had until then often been attributed to de facto residential segregation was now seen to be the result of deliberate public policies and therefore unconstitutional. But integration did not move as swiftly in the North. The demography of big cities with a high percentage of nonwhites made busing solutions difficult, and the nation lost its political resolve to endure the difficult adjustment to integration. Division occurred both among whites and among blacks about the ultimate desirability of integrated schooling in the face of its costs.

In addition to racial issues, policymakers turned their attention to issues of income and resources in the 1960s. Although the Supreme Court ruled in *San Antonio Independent School District* v. *Rodriguez* (1973) that states were not required by the United States Constitution to equalize per-pupil expenditures between rich districts and poor districts, many states moved voluntarily toward partial equalization, and some state courts ruled that their state constitutions required some form of equalization. In addition to this reallocation of funds, the federal government passed the Elementary and Secondary Education Act of 1965, Title I of which was aimed at remedial training in basic skills for children in schools with a high percentage of low-income families. Title I programs (renamed Chapter I in 1981) became a prominent feature of public schools. It is difficult to estimate the effects of such remedial programs on student achievement; evaluations that directly studied the skills of the children in the programs, like similar evaluations of the preschool Head Start programs, ranged from claiming no lasting change to claiming modest gains. More indirect evidence came from national assessments of basic skills of all the children in the nation; these showed a partial narrowing of the skills gaps between whites and other racial groups that correlate somewhat with income groups. Whatever their educational effects, however, there is no doubt that Chapter I programs became popular locally and in Congress, and that they represented a substantial redistribution of education moneys.

World War II brought racial matters to a head in some regards: Many of the veterans who attended college under the GI Bill were minority students, and they began to raise questions about segregation in higher education.

THE AGENDAS OF GROUP RIGHTS. The assertion of civil rights and educational needs was not confined to African Americans and the poor. During the 1970s various groups argued such rights and needs strenuously. Each group's struggles had their own history and were unique to some extent; but to some extent the groups active in the late 1960s and early 1970s modeled their efforts on the civil rights movement, which had focused on discrimination against black Americans, and they drew upon common principles. The civil rights movement not only had provided some precedents in tactics and concrete legislation but also had created a congressional and a public mood that were, for a brief time, receptive to the expansion of rights.

Women's rights advocates pointed to a variety of problems of access and discrimination. Much attention was given to sex-role socialization and much was written about it. Girls were encouraged less than boys to achieve in mathematics and science, to consider professional careers, to attain leadership positions; they were treated differently in classrooms and denied access to programs such as professional schools. A start on rectifying some of these problems was made through the passage of Title IX of the Educational Amendments of 1972 and various follow-up regulations of the federal government. Although federal oversight was intermittent, some of the goals and principles were institutionalized at the local or state level; the active recruitment of women as students or faculty became a widespread feature of affirmative action programs. The percentage of women in professional schools rose, as did the percentage of women faculty members in higher education. Textbook publishers, responding to state and local scrutiny, began to balance sex roles portrayed in their books.

The educational rights of children with limited or no proficiency in English also received attention in this period of expanding civil rights activity. First, the federal government offered financial assistance to local districts for bilingual education on a voluntary basis, in Title VII of the renewed Elementary and Secondary Education Act of 1967; then the Supreme Court, in the *Lau* v. *Nichols* decision of 1974, made the schools' obligations to those not proficient in English mandatory. The resulting federal guidelines provided occasion for continuing vigorous debate, but the basic obligation has remained: schools cannot ignore the English-language problems of those with limited English proficiency.

The Conservative Reaction

In the late 1970s, popular support waned for the liberal agenda of group rights, racial integration, and equalizing resources. Courts became more cautious in identifying unconstitutional segregation; federal agencies slowed the enforcement of civil rights laws. Many Americans were weary of the disruptions brought by new rights, new requirements, and new relationships; the conservative swing was both symbolized and reinforced by the election of Ronald Reagan as president in 1980. Again attention returned to the main academic curriculum of the schools; a "back-to-basics" reform in the 1970s was followed by a campaign to increase graduation requirements in the 1980s. Declining Scholastic Aptitude Test scores and alarming results on functional literacy tests were used to dramatize the concern that the schools should concentrate harder on the academic achievement of all students.

A second premise of the 1980s conservative agenda was that the federal government should relinquish part of its activist role and encourage the states to do more. Thus, during the 1980s, the federal share of local school budgets declined from about 9 percent to about 6 percent, and some of that was in block grants that allowed local authorities great latitude in allocating funds. In turn politicians and educators in many states mounted school reform programs that focused unprecedented attention on education in statehouses and governors' offices. Higher academic standards, higher teacher salaries, improved teacher training, and new roles for teachers were among the most common goals. Concrete results were realized in many states, including legislation requiring more courses for high school graduation, as well as higher teacher salaries and experiments with new structures and roles for teachers. But whether these 1980s reforms translated into more effective schools and more learning by students was, as with all reforms of public education, in doubt. Among the questions that remained as public schools entered the 1990s were whether the reform impetus of the 1980s could be sustained, and whether the strategies of the 1980s would meet the challenges of the 1990s.

[See also Adolescence; Alternative Education; Childhood and Children; The Clergy; Collegiate Education; Literacy; Women's Organizations.]

BIBLIOGRAPHY

General Works

Bailyn, Bernard. *Education in the Forming of American Society: Needs and Opportunities for Study* (1960).

Sedlak, Michael W., and Timothy Walch. *American Educational History: A Guide to Information Sources* (1981).

Colonial Period

Cremin, Lawrence A. *American Education: The Colonial Experience, 1607–1783* (1970).

Monaghan, E. Jennifer. "Literacy Instruction and Gender in Colonial New England." *American Quarterly* 40 (Spring 1988).

Nineteenth Century

Cremin, Lawrence A. *American Education: The National Experience, 1783–1876* (1980).

Elson, Ruth Miller. *Guardians of Tradition: American Schoolbooks of the Nineteenth Century* (1964).

Kaestle, Carl F. *Pillars of the Republic: Common Schools and American Society, 1780–1860* (1983).

Kaestle, Carl F., and Maris A. Vinovskis. *Education and Social Change in Nineteenth-Century Massachusetts* (1980).

Katz, Michael B. *The Irony of Early School Reform: Educational Innovation in Mid-Nineteenth Century Massachusetts* (1968).

Vinovskis, Maris A. *The Origins of Public High Schools: A Reexamination of the Beverly High School Controversy* (1985).

Progressive Era, 1880–1920

Cremin, Lawrence A. *The Transformation of the School: Progressivism in American Education, 1876–1957* (1961).

Cuban, Larry. *How Teachers Taught: Constancy and Change in American Classrooms, 1890–1980* (1984).

Kliebard, Herbert M. *The Struggle for the American Curriculum, 1893–1958* (1986).

Krug, Edward A. *The Shaping of the American High School.* 2 vols. (1964–1972).

Reese, William J. *Power and the Promise of School Reform: Grass Roots Movements During the Progressive Era* (1986).

Tyack, David B. *The One Best System: A History of American Urban Education* (1974).

Wrigley, Julia. *Class Politics and Public Schools: Chicago, 1900–1950* (1982).

Later Twentieth Century

Bestor, Arthur. *Educational Wastelands: The Retreat from Learning in Our Public Schools* (1953).

Bruner, Jerome. *The Process of Education* (1960).

Cremin, Lawrence A. *American Education: The Metropolitan Experience, 1876–1980* (1988).

Lynd, Robert, and Helen M. Lynd. *Middletown in Transition* (1937).

Modell, John. *Into Ones Own: From Youth to Adulthood in the United States, 1920–1975* (1989).

Ravitch, Diane. *The Troubled Crusade: American Education, 1945–1980* (1983).

Salomone, Rosemary C. *Equal Education Under Law: Legal Rights and Federal Policy in the Post-"Brown" Era* (1986).

Spring, Joel H. *The Sorting Machine: National Educational Policy Since 1945* (1976).

Tyack, David, Robert Lowe, and Elisabeth Hansot. *Public Schools in Hard Times: The Great Depression and Recent Years* (1984).

Education of Particular Groups

Anderson, James D. *The Education of Blacks in the South, 1860–1935* (1988).

Gutman, Herbert. "Schools for Freedom: The Post-Emancipation Origins of Afro-American Education." In *Power and Culture: Essays on the American Working Class,* edited by Ira Berlin (1987).

Harlan, Louis R. *Separate and Unequal: Public School Campaigns and Racism in the Southern Seaboard States, 1901–1915* (1958).

Jorgenson, Lloyd P. *The State and the Non-Public School, 1825–1925* (1987).

Kluger, Richard. *Simple Justice: The History of Brown v. Board of Education and Black America's Struggle for Equality* (1976).

Rury, John. "Race and Common School Reform: The Strange Career of the NYSPECC, 1847–1860." *Urban Education* 20 (January 1986).

Rury, John. *Education and Women's Work: Female Schooling and the Division of Labor in Urban America, 1870–1930* (1991).

San Miguel, Guadalupe, Jr. *"Let All of Them Take Heed": Mexican Americans and the Campaign for Educational Equality in Texas, 1910–1981* (1987).

Szasz, Margaret. *Education and the American Indian: The Road to Self-Determination, 1928–1973* (1974).

Tyack, David, and Elisabeth Hansot. *Learning Together: A History of Coeducation in American Public Schools* (1990).

Weinberg, Meyer. *A Chance to Learn: A History of Race and Education in the United States* (1977).

— CARL F. KAESTLE

PUBLIC HEALTH

Public health, whose meaning has been redefined from time to time, essentially means community action to avoid disease and other threats to the health and welfare of individuals and the community at large. Today the definition has been broadened to include the promotion of physical and mental health rather than simply the maintenance of it. The application of public-health measures in any period is based upon the prevailing medical concepts, and for much of American history diseases, and epidemics in particular, were attributed to what is known as the miasmatic thesis. The Hippocratic physicians attributed sickness to an imbalance or corruption of one or more of the four basic bodily humors. Hippocrates himself had also suggested that climate and environment played a role in determining health or sickness. Neither of these explanations nor any of the new medical theories of the sixteenth and seventeenth centuries satisfactorily explained the mysterious appearance and disappearance of deadly epidemic diseases. Thomas Sydenham, a leading English physician, late in the seventeenth century theorized that epidemics were caused by a miasma or effluvia arising from what he termed the bowels of the earth.

Disease and Sanitary Conditions

If atmospheric conditions and effluvia contributed to fevers and sickness, then it seemed logical that the foul odors arising from filth and putrefying matter would have the same effect. Malaria, whose name literally means bad air, had long been associated with low-lying marshy land and warm weather. When yellow fever struck American colonial ports, it always appeared first in the low areas around the waterfront. These were invariably the older parts of the towns where the poor lived crowded together in squalid, filthy, foul-smelling homes. It was noted, too, that sickness was always present in ships, hospitals, jails, army camps, and wherever individuals were jammed together in dirty and unsanitary conditions. The obvious connection between filth and sickness gave credence to the miasmatic theory, one that dominated medical thinking to the end of the nineteenth century.

It was this assumption, along with aesthetic reasons, that underlay the early colonial sanitary laws and the sanitary movement of the nineteenth century. In the seventeenth century the colonial towns and villages were still too small to have major sanitary problems. Nonetheless, by the second half of the century most colonies had enacted laws with respect to privies, garbage, and dead animals, and had started to regulate the so-called nuisance industries, such as those operated by butchers, slaughterers, and tanners. The food supply also came under regulation, with ordinances setting minimum standards for the quality of bread and meat. As the major ports expanded in the eighteenth century, the health and welfare of the citizens became increasingly a function of government. Private wells gave way to public wells, and by the end of the century elementary water systems began to appear. The regulations and ordinances governing sanitation, food, and water supplies became both more specific and comprehensive.

The two most feared diseases in the colonial period were smallpox and yellow fever. The contagiousness of smallpox was all too well known, but yellow fever presented a difficult problem. It clearly affected a neighborhood, but an individual could contract the disease in one area and return to his home without infecting anyone in his family. Lacking any knowledge of the role of the *Aëdes egypti* mosquito in spreading the infection, the nature of yellow fever remained a major source of disagreement among physicians until the end of the nineteenth century. Dr. Cadwallader Colden, a Scottish physician who settled in New York, published an essay in 1720 entitled "An Account of the Climate and Diseases of New York." At that time he attributed the hot-weather fevers in the city to its poor water supply. Subsequently, two yellow-fever outbreaks in New York City in 1741 and 1742 led Dr. Colden, who was then serving as surveyor general of the province, to revise his view of fevers. He now came to the conclusion that these fevers arose from the effects of "noxious vapors from stagnating filthy water" on the "animal oeconomy." The various miasmas produced by fermentation in these waters, he wrote, resulted in "different fermentations in the animal fluids" or humors (quoted in Jarcho [1955]). Consequently, the type of fever was dependent upon the kind of miasmas produced by the filthy water or putrefying substance.

Dr. John Jones, a founder of King's College (Columbia University) Medical School, propounded a variation on this theme in a book published in 1775 as a practical guide to military surgeons. He pointed out that the "morbid effluviae" exhaled from the lungs of sick and wounded men vitiated the air and could "generate a jail or hospital fever" that could kill patients and attendants alike. In 1796, a year when yellow fever was striking up and down the East Coast, Noah Webster summarized the prevailing medical thought in a work entitled *A Collection of Papers on the Subject of Bilious Fevers . . .* Until Americans can learn that "Epidemic and Pestilential maladies may be generated by local causes," he wrote, they would continue to bring on sickness and pestilence by wallowing in filth, crowding into cities with dirty houses, neglecting bathing and washing, and "devouring in hot seasons undue quantities of animal food." Thus by 1800 the miasmatic theory was firmly established, laying the basis for the sanitary movement of the nineteenth century.

Along with the belief in miasma was a recognition that certain diseases were spread by direct contact. Dating back to the time of leprosy and the Black Death in the medieval period, the majority of people were convinced that they could protect themselves by keeping away from the victims of epidemic diseases. Applying this reasoning, the colonists quarantined infected areas and often refused any contact with the sick. Fortunately, the isolation of the colonies from Europe and each other minimized the extent of epidemic diseases; yet when smallpox, measles, and other disorders gained a foothold after an absence of fifteen or twenty years, the presence of a generation of nonimmunes guaranteed a heavy mortality.

Quarantines and Early Treatments

Public belief that diseases were spread by direct contact led very early to quarantine laws. In the majority of cases the laws were temporary emergency measures, although Charleston, South Carolina, appointed a port quarantine commissioner in 1712. Since vessels arriving from European or Caribbean ports often arrived short of food and water, some provision had to be made for isolating the sick and permitting the healthy to land. In consequence, pesthouses began appearing. Led by Massachusetts, which established a permanent pest-house on Spectacle Island in Boston Harbor in 1717, by the mid-eighteenth century almost every colony had at least one pesthouse to care for those with "pestilential diseases." In most cases the care provided was largely custodial, since pesthouses were designed primarily to safeguard the community rather than care for the sick.

Since the medical profession was convinced that pestilences, with the exception of smallpox, were generated locally, and the public was equally sure that diseases were spread by contact, whenever a dangerous fever threatened or was present, government authorities played safe by accepting both theses: infected areas were immediately quarantined and victims of the disease isolated. At the same time a general sanitary program was initiated. The city council would give orders to clean the streets, drain filthy stagnant gutters and pools, empty overflowing privies, remove the carcasses of dead animals from the streets, and spread lime in privies, gutters, and all foul-smelling places. Once the epidemic had swept through the town, the quarantine and sanitary regulations usually fell into abeyance.

The one epidemic disease for which a relatively effective preventive was discovered was smallpox, possibly the most contagious of diseases and certainly one of the most fatal. Inoculation, a folk-medicine procedure dating far back in history, consists of taking a small amount of matter from a pustule of a victim and inserting it under the skin of a healthy person. The inoculated individual ordinarily suffers a mild case of the disease but is thereafter immune from it. The practice was introduced into the colonies by the Reverend Cotton Mather of Boston in 1721, and although it spread slowly, by the time of the Revolution it had gained general acceptance. Possibly the greatest value derived from inoculation was that it paved the way for the rapid acceptance of vaccination when it was introduced by the English physician Edward Jenner in 1798.

The economic disruption and the constant movement of troops during the Revolutionary War spread disease far and wide. Yet America recovered quickly, and cities such as Boston, Philadelphia, and New York rapidly expanded. Unfortunately, sanitary problems tend to grow at a much faster rate than populations. Colonial sanitary laws placed most of the responsibility for cleaning the streets, emptying privies, and removing health nuisances upon private citizens. Water supply was also a private matter, although towns and cities were assuming more responsibility for public wells. This was the situation when a series of major yellow-fever epidemics affected the entire East Coast from Providence to Savannah in the years from 1793 to 1806. Every community responded with quarantine, isolation of the sick, and sanitary programs. The heavy casualties also forced communities to provide temporary hospitals, medical care, and nursing for the sick, and food and housing for widows and children. As the epidemics continued, civic authorities ordered the evacuation of entire sections of cities and provided housing for those in need of it. However most civic authorities failed to take action at the onset of the epidemics, and instead volunteer citizens health committees were created. These committees quickly gained official government recognition, and the first permanent health agencies came into existence.

The paternalistic spirit demonstrated by the community during these yellow-fever epidemics did not carry over into the era of the industrial revolution. The rise of city slums physically separated the poor from the well-to-do and turned them into a faceless mass, dehumanized by their deplorable living conditions. The poor drew their water from polluted shallow wells or from standpipes located one or two blocks apart, and as many as forty persons or more used a single privy. Under these filthy conditions, life expectancy was short and infant mortality high. Since the prevailing Christian doctrine preached that the virtues of thrift, hard work, and cleanliness insured economic success, it seemed apparent to the more fortunate that the dirty and intemperate poor were responsible for their own deplorable condition. The only group of professionals that evinced any concern for community health were the physicians. Motivated by their belief in the local origin of contagious diseases, individual physicians and medical societies actively promoted civic cleanliness and advocated the appointment of health boards and health officers.

In the years between 1805 and 1860 relatively little was accomplished in terms of public health, although the introduction of vaccination in 1800 led to some progress in controlling smallpox. Whenever the disease flared up in epidemic proportions, city officials, often under pressure from local physicians, would allocate funds to provide free vaccination for the poor. As vaccination became more common, the incidence of smallpox began falling. Its success, as is often true with public health measures, proved almost self-defeating. Once the memory of this terrible disease faded from public consciousness, few individuals saw the need for vaccination. As a result of this neglect, the incidence of smallpox began rising in the 1840s and did not fall until major vaccination programs were undertaken late in the century.

In addition to smallpox outbreaks, the antebellum years witnessed two major Asiatic cholera epidemics (1832–1833 and 1849–1850), and yellow fever struck with increasing intensity on the south Atlantic and Gulf coasts from Norfolk, Virginia, to Brownsville, Texas. Cholera is a filth disease, spread by discharges from the bowels of infected persons. If untreated, it can cause violent vomiting and diarrhea and bring death in a matter of hours. An endemic disorder in the Far East, it spread to the West with improvements in transportation. The crowded urban slums where the poor lived jammed together in conditions of indescribable filth proved a perfect breeding ground for this pestilence. Since neither its cause nor cure were known, popular journals, newspapers, and medical journals began campaigning for massive sanitary programs. Medical articles urged the public to avoid fresh fruit, cold water, and immoderate exercise in warm weather. They also advocated a moderate diet and personal hygiene. As was the case with yellow fever, the two cholera epidemics aroused heated debates within the medical profession, but little light was shed on the disease.

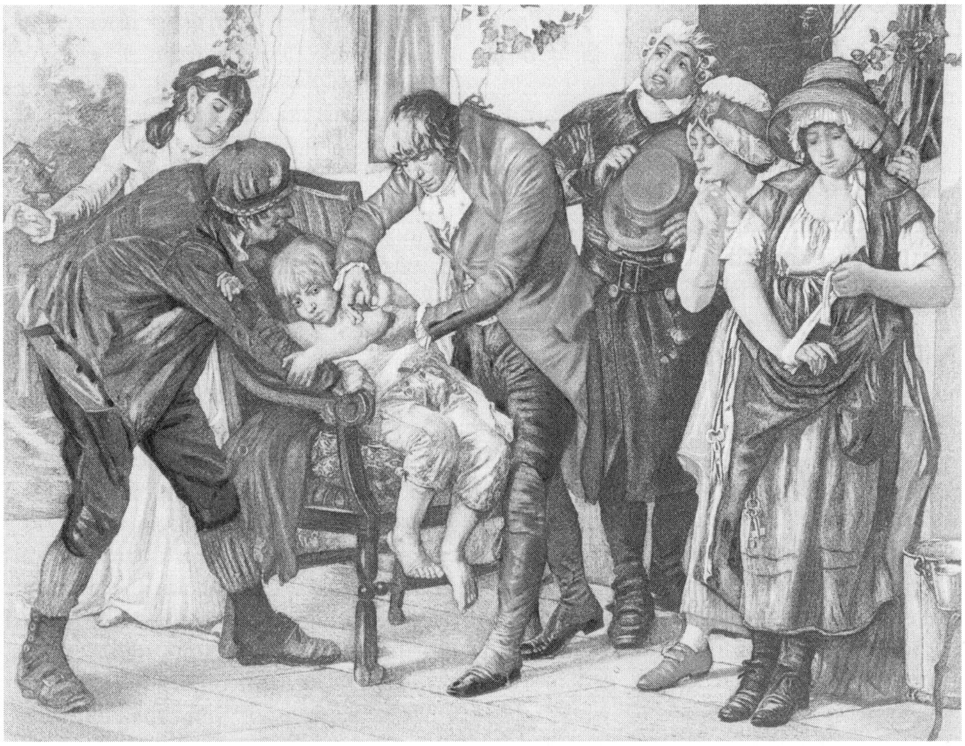

English physician Edward Jenner's first smallpox vaccination, performed on James Phipps in 1796. This program spread to the colonies and led to widespread acceptance of vaccination as a public health policy.

Following practices that had been instituted in colonial days, when confronted with the presence of an epidemic disease or its threat, city councils or temporary health boards would provide for the isolation of the sick and institute much needed sanitary programs. Once the epidemic had run its course, civic officials quickly lost all interest in community health, and sanitary conditions were oftentimes worse than before the epidemic. The few permanent health boards, whose function in any event was largely advisory, met only in summer, the season of fevers. Unfortunately, one of the immediate results of the industrial revolution was to crowd masses of workers into urban slums, with dire health consequences. The years from 1820 to 1860 saw a rise in mortality and morbidity rates. While no major gains in medical knowledge resulted from the cholera and yellow-fever epidemics, they did help to increase public awareness of community health problems and stimulate a demand for public-health reform.

As the sanitary movement gathered strength in France and England, a number of socially conscious American physicians undertook to study health conditions in the United States. In 1837 Dr. Benjamin McCready published the essay "On the influence of Trades, Professions, and Occupations in the United States in the Production of Disease" in which he listed specific occupational problems, adding that deplorable housing and living conditions were a major factor in the poor health of workers. McCready's observations were given much greater credence in 1845 when Dr. John H. Griscom published his classic study, *The Sanitary Condition of the Laboring Class of New York, With Suggestions for Its Improvement.* In it he first demonstrated the enormous sickness and mortality among the working class, and then pointed out that a sound public health program could prevent much of it. Elsewhere in the United States the reform work was carried on by leaders such as Dr. Edwin Miller Snow in Providence, Drs. Edward Barton and J. C. Simonds in New Orleans, and Dr. Wilson Jewell in Philadelphia. By the time the sectional crisis became acute in the 1850s, the appeals of health reformers were beginning to bear fruit. In 1857 Jewell issued a call for a national quarantine and sanitary convention in order to standardize state and local quarantine laws; the debates eventually centered around the subject of the contagiousness of yellow fever and Asiatic cholera. In the course of four annual meetings, the delegates agreed that these disorders were not personally contagious—blaming epidemic diseases largely on unsanitary conditions—but held that a limited quarantine was necessary to prevent their importation.

The onset of the Civil War, with its mobilization of masses of men and the constant movement of troops, spread smallpox, measles, and other diseases throughout the country. The armies on both sides were ill-prepared to care for the sick and wounded, and neither the medical corps nor the general officers showed much interest in camp sanitation. Poor food, exposure, and unsanitary conditions led to an enormous amount of sickness among the soldiers, particularly in the first two years of the war. Fortunately, volunteer citizens groups North and South stepped into the breach. The most influential of these was the United States Sanitary Commission, an outgrowth of one of these volunteer groups. Under the leadership of its executive secretary, Frederick Law Olmsted, the Sanitary Commission provided medical care, fresh food, blankets, and whatever was needed. More than this, its members agitated for reform of the archaic and underfunded army medical corps. A major success of the Commission was to win the appointment of Dr. William A. Hammond as Surgeon General of the Army. Hammond promptly moved to reorganize the entire medical system. With constant prodding from the Sanitary Commission and the emergence of general officers with an interest in the welfare of their troops, camp sanitation steadily improved.

The onset of the Civil War, with its mobilization of masses of men and the constant movement of troops, spread smallpox, measles, and other diseases throughout the country.

The war taught many officers and army surgeons the value of cleanliness, and it aroused a more general appreciation of sanitation. It also contributed to the development of the New York City Metropolitan Board of Health, the forerunner of the present city health department. In 1863 a riot in New York, started as a protest against the military draft, destroyed a major section of Broadway and killed scores of black residents. The violence awakened the upper classes to the dreadful conditions in the slums and lent credence to the demands of the reformers. Three more years of agitation, backed by a survey showing the atrocious state of the slums, led in 1866 to the establishment of the Metropolitan Board of Health. The Board was given broad authority, and it set the pattern for city health departments throughout the country. When a third Asiatic cholera outbreak occurred between 1866 and 1867, Chicago,

Cincinnati, St. Louis, and several other cities quickly established health departments modeled on that of New York.

Modern Sanitary Conditions

The post-Civil War years saw the full blossoming of the sanitary revolution. One of the more significant aspects was the tremendous expansion of water and sewer systems. In the first half of the century the introduction of cast iron pipes and steam pumps brought large quantities of water into cities, much greater than the primitive drainage and sewer systems could handle. As the water closet began to replace privies in the mid century, the need for sewers became all too apparent. By the 1870s the field of sanitary engineering emerged, and the assorted and unconnected sewer lines of earlier days were gradually standardized and brought into integrated systems. Two major developments affecting the quality of water were the introduction of filtration methods in the 1890s and the addition of chlorination beginning in 1908. These technological advances were largely responsible for reducing the high incidence of typhoid and other enteric disorders.

The federal government did little to promote health during the first one hundred years of its existence. In 1798 a federal health law created the United States Marine Hospital Service to provide care for sick or wounded seamen, and in 1813 Congress gave limited support to smallpox vaccination for a few years. Nothing further was done until the threat of a major yellow-fever epidemic in 1878 prodded Congress into passing a relatively innocuous federal quarantine law. The epidemic struck with full force during the summer and fall of 1878, and a series of laws the following spring and summer created the National Board of Health with an appropriation of $500,000. The National Board of Health was to serve as a consultant to state and local authorities and help in cases of emergency. The Board performed quite well in its allotted tasks but unfortunately ran afoul of the United States Marine Hospital Service, whose head was seeking to expand its activities, as well as Dr. Joseph Jones, the irrascible head of the Louisiana State Board of Health and a stout defender of states' rights, and other local health officials jealous of their authority. Their joint efforts cut off appropriations for the Board in 1883 and led to its official demise in 1893.

Aided by several minor yellow-fever epidemics and the threat of Asiatic cholera, the Marine Hospital Service gradually expanded in the closing years of the nineteenth century. In the 1890s it established a small laboratory for bacteriological work. Its image was greatly improved in 1901 through the work of Walter Reed and his associates in identifying the role of the Aëdes egypti mosquito in spreading yellow fever, and its prompt action to minimize two small bubonic plague outbreaks in San Francisco. As the Marine Hospital Service expanded its operations, Congress in 1902 renamed it the United States Public Health and Marine Hospital Service. In the succeeding years the outstanding work of Charles Wardell Stiles on hookworm and Joseph Goldberger on pellagra helped establish the Service, now called the United States Public Health Service, as the federal health agency.

Revolutionary discoveries in bacteriology were changing the face of medicine and shifting the emphasis in public health from sanitation to disease control. As the miasmic theory slowly died at the turn of the century, health officials began fighting specific diseases by means of vaccines and disinfection. By this date every health department of any consequence had a laboratory to perform chemical analyses of food and water and to provide diagnostic services for physicians. These years also saw an increasing emphasis on maternal and child care and school health. The school health movement grew out of vaccination programs for schoolchildren instituted by school boards and health departments shortly after the Civil War. In the 1890s school physicians began screening schoolchildren for contagious disorders, and within a few years physicians and school nurses started giving physical examinations. Simultaneously, visiting nurses, the forerunners of public-health nurses, began calling at the homes of expectant mothers and those with small children. Led by the New York City Health Department, which established a Division of Child Hygiene in 1908, children's bureaus were established in health departments throughout the country, and in 1912 the federal government organized a Children's Bureau.

The physical examinations of schoolchildren revealed an alarming number of diseases and disabilities, leading health departments to build clinics to treat those who could not afford private medical care. In so doing, they antagonized the medical profession. In the twentieth century a reorganized American Medical Association, which had been founded in the late 1840s, and its constituent societies constituted a powerful lobby, and public-health officials, dependent upon government funding, were compelled to give ground. In consequence by World War I most public-health clinics had been shut down, reducing medical care to a minimum, and health departments thereafter concentrated on educating the public about health matters, supervising food and water, and providing vaccines and diagnostic help to physicians.

Twentieth-Century Public Health

Until the twentieth century public health was primarily an urban phenomena, but the entrance of the automobile helped to inaugurate a new era for rural health. Yet it was the railways that first brought health education to small towns and rural communities. In 1910 Dr. Oscar Dowling, president of the Louisiana State Board of Health, conceived the idea of a traveling health exhibit and persuaded a local railway to lend a locomotive and cars. The success of the health train induced other states to follow suit. The automobile, however, was beginning to provide easier access to rural areas and soon replaced trains. In the meantime the Public Health Service and private foundations such as the Red Cross, Rockefeller Foundation, Commonwealth Fund, and the Milbank Memorial Fund were promoting the organization of county health units. Although progress was slow, by 1930 a growing number of county health departments were in operation. The real impetus to their development came in the 1930s as a result of the various New Deal measures.

The Great Depression shook American Society to its foundations, and the Roosevelt era brought a major shift in the role of government. Whereas health and welfare formerly had been a concern of individuals or local government, the New Deal sought to encourage government at all levels to assume responsibility for these matters. Federal grants promoted maternal and child-health programs, built clinics and health centers, provided public-health nurses, subsidized health education and health research, and supported a host of other health programs. The 1930s also saw the beginning of mass screening drives to identify cases of disease as early as possible. The first of these efforts was directed at tuberculosis and was made possible by better and cheaper X-ray film. Advances in living standards and improved technology in subsequent years made it feasible to conduct massive screenings for a wide range of disorders.

By 1940 the great killer diseases of the early years—smallpox, diphtheria, scarlet fever, whooping cough, and yellow fever—had been conquered, and the incidence of tuberculosis and malaria had been cut drastically. Little progress, however, had been made in reducing venereal diseases. This failure was due in part to the harshness and relative ineffectiveness of the only therapeutics available. Probably more significant was the refusal of the public to discuss anything related to sex. World War I temporarily lifted the veil of silence, and with federal support, venereal-disease clinics were established. At the end of the war most of the clinics were closed, and the veil again descended, not to be raised until Surgeon General Thomas Parran in the Roosevelt administration once again brought the issue out into the open. The discovery in 1943 that penicillin was remarkably effective against syphilis and other venereal diseases opened the way to conquering them. By the late 1950s antibiotics had been so successful as to convince many health leaders that syphilis and gonorrhea would soon be of little consequence. The optimism proved short-lived. The abuse of penicillin and other antibiotics quickly engendered resistant strains of both diseases, and this factor, combined with the sexual revolution of the 1960s and 1970s, once more made venereal disorders a serious public health problem.

The opening of World War II disrupted normal civilian activities and created a tremendous need for health personnel. Health departments faced heavy demands at a time when they were losing personnel to wartime agencies. Many sanitary regulations had to be eased and staff shortages made it impossible to enforce others. On the brighter side, the war ended unemployment and raised the standard of living for lower-income groups. Wartime rationing and price control ensured that the average American was probably better fed than in peacetime. For the South, the influx of troops into army camps created new economic opportunities and raised southern living standards, while the health measures instituted to protect the soldiers were responsible for eliminating malaria, reducing venereal disorders, and promoting local public-health programs.

Under the New Deal, federal grants promoted maternal and child-health programs, built clinics and health centers, provided public-health nurses, and subsidized health education and health research.

Although some basic research suffered, the war speeded up the application of existing medical knowledge. An improved vaccine for yellow fever and a more effective one for typhus were developed. Other significant developments included the mass production of sulfa drugs and penicillin. Following the war, the effect of these "miracle" drugs was to add to the prestige of scientific medicine and, in the process, help win public support for stronger health programs.

One of the functions of public health is to recognize and provide solutions to community health problems.

Once the problem has been solved, health departments spin off separate agencies to deal with them. In earlier times health boards fought for street cleaning, garbage collection, better housing, and pure water supplies. Having won the battle, health authorities, while maintaining some supervision, turned the responsibility over to separate divisions or departments. And as each successive problem has been solved, health agencies have looked for other fields to conquer. The first vaccines were produced by health departments, but once private companies assumed the task, they withdrew from the field. As the great killer diseases of the earlier days were gradually brought under control, health agencies turned their attention to those constitutional and organic disorders that had moved to the front rank as causes of mortality and morbidity. In the late 1930s, for example, cardiovascular disease and cancer began coming under the purview of public health.

Contemporary Public-Health Issues

In the post-World War II years the field of public health widened to encompass a broad range of personal and environmental concerns. One of these was mental health. Some awareness of it had been evinced in the 1930s, but the large number of individuals rejected by the armed forces for psychiatric reasons during World War II brought community mental health problems sharply into focus. Another area that received only minor consideration before the 1930s, occupational health, was given an impetus by the New Deal, one that has carried over to the 1990s. The first tentative efforts to promote occupational health began in the late nineteenth century when a number of state laws regulating the working hours of women and children were enacted, but little was done to enforce them. In part these laws reflected the maternal and child-health movement that developed at the turn of the century. By the mid-twentieth century, under pressure from unions and insurance companies, state and local regulations had removed the most flagrant occupational hazards. During the past fifty years attempts have been made to deal with the more subtle conditions resulting from chronic exposure to harmful substances such as lead poisoning, silicosis, and radiation. One of the first of these occupational diseases to be recognized was pneumoconiosis, the most common form of which is the so-called black-lung disease of coal miners. By the 1960s another form, byssinosis or brown-lung disease, was identified among textile workers who had inhaled cotton dust over long periods of time. This same period saw a rising concern about the association between lung cancer and the inhalation of asbestos particles by workers in the asbestos industry. Currently alarms have been raised about the possible dangers from repetitive actions and long hours spent in front of computer terminals.

Growing out of the studies of occupational health has come recognition that the public at large is also at hazard from long-term exposure to harmful substances. Workers involved in industries associated with the manufacturing and processing of lead have always been at risk. Some fifty years ago it was recognized that many infants in tenement and slum areas were ingesting leaded paint. Studies subsequently demonstrated that leaded gasoline polluted both the atmosphere and water supplies. Whereas technology has contributed to solving the major problems associated with lead, the myriad chemicals pouring into the earth's air and water have created new questions as to their long-term effects on the public health. More recently questions have been raised as to the possible dangers from chronic exposure to the electromagnetic radiation from high-power lines, condensers, and computer screens. Unfortunately, since most of these hazards require many years of exposure, it is exceedingly difficult to assess their impact on any individual or to determine the precise point at which exposure becomes harmful.

The latter half of the twentieth century has seen a renewed interest in a more broadly defined personal hygiene, and alcoholism, drug abuse, smoking, diet, and exercise have moved to the forefront of public-health issues. Health departments still must keep a watchful eye on some of the traditional contagious disorders such as measles, syphilis, and gonorrhea, while at the same time attempting to limit the ravages of newer ones. Of the latter, acquired immune deficiency syndrome (AIDS) presents the greatest challenge today. As with poliomyelitis in the 1940s, it is a deadly disease for which we have neither a preventive nor a cure. Presumably medical science can solve the problem within a few years, but in the meantime public-health authorities are approaching it as a personal hygiene problem—one that requires individuals to modify certain aspects of their life.

This same period has also seen a much stronger movement toward promoting sex equality and recognizing the role played by women in the past. Traditionally women were responsible for nursing and home medical care, and in the late nineteenth century they moved into the area of community health. Women's sanitary associations contributed notably to the sanitary movement, and women supplied much of the leadership in the school health movement and the drive for better maternal and child care. Among the outstanding leaders in the health field were Jane Addams, Lillian D. Wald, and Mary Brewster, who fought to improve health conditions in the tenements; Dr. Sara Josephine

Baker, whose pioneer work in New York City was largely responsible for the establishment of childrens' bureaus at all levels of government; and Dr. Alice Hamilton, who led the occupational-health movement in the twentieth century. In addition, the emergence of school and public-health nurses created new career opportunities for women.

Insofar as minorities are concerned, most notably African Americans, Native Americans, and Hispanic Americans, the record of public health has left much to be desired. Subject to discrimination by the general population and without political influence in the past, they received little attention from public-health authorities. African Americans were at least fortunate in having a measure of genetic resistance to yellow fever and malaria, but this was more than offset by their susceptibility to the much more common respiratory and enteric disorders. Native Americans were highly susceptible to all the infectious diseases of the Old World, and in addition, the breakup of their culture subjected them to alcoholism, mental illness, and other problems. Poor educational facilities and occupational discrimination have kept large numbers of these minority groups at a poverty level, thus compounding their health problems. Growing public awareness of the long history of discrimination against minority groups has led to special efforts by public-health authorities to improve their health conditions, but the problems are deep-seated.

Public-health professionals have long recognized the association between income level and health and have known, for example, that differences in morbidity and mortality rates between racial and cultural groups are largely a factor of poverty and all that it connotes. For this reason, they have always favored government action to reduce the number of needy and improve access to medical care. The American Public Health Association was a leading advocate for a national health insurance program during the period of World War I, and it has consistently supported federal legislation to make medical care available for all citizens. Since the beginning of modern public health, one of the major functions of the public-health movement has been to create an awareness of health problems and to teach the principles of personal and community health. With the renewed emphasis on personal hygiene, health education has taken on greater significance. A fine example of a successful public-health campaign was the one inaugurated in 1964 by the *Surgeon General's Report on Smoking and Health.* Pushed ahead by successive surgeons general, the result has been a sharp reduction in smoking, a significant source of cardiovascular, respiratory, and other complaints.

Conclusion

One of the difficulties in discussing current public-health issues is the problem of assessing their significance. A few years ago Legionnaires' disease was the center of public attention; today it is scarcely mentioned. Poliomyelitis aroused enormous attention from the 1930s to 1960; now it is no longer a significant health problem. Should an effective vaccination be found for AIDS within the next three to five years, it too will be supplanted by other more pressing issues. Public-health agencies in a democracy are responsive to the public, and whenever public attention is focused on a particular health concern, public-health administrators must respond. A classic example is the swine-flu vaccination program of 1976. In this instance virologists and epidemiologists were undecided as to the nature of the threatening influenza and other medical authorities raised questions about the need for a mass vaccination program. Once the federal administration placed itself firmly behind the program, however, and Congress entered the scene, the vaccination program was pushed ahead until it became obvious that it was not needed. Public-health policy must respond to changing conditions and medical developments, yet at the same time it must both educate and respond to the public.

[See also Alternative Medicine; Childhood and Children; The City; Death; Health Care; Housing; The Medical Profession; Old Age; Technology and Social Change.]

BIBLIOGRAPHY

General Histories

Duffy, John. *The Sanitarians: A History of American Public Health* (1990).

Rosen, George. *Preventive Medicine in the United States, 1900–1975: Trends and Interpretations* (1975).

State Histories

Gillson, Gordon E. *The Louisiana State Board of Health: The Formative Years.* Ph.D. diss., Louisiana State University (1967). Also published as an abstract of the Louisiana State Board of Health (n.d.).

Greenfield, Myrtle. *A History of Public Health in New Mexico* (1962).

Pfister, Harriet S. *Kansas State Board of Health* (1955).

Rosenkrantz, Barbara G. *Public Health and the State: Changing Views in Massachusetts, 1842–1936* (1972).

Municipal Studies

Blake, John B. *Public Health in the Town of Boston, 1630–1822* (1959).

Duffy, John. *A History of Public Health in New York City, 1625–1866* (1968).

Duffy, John. *A History of Public Health in New York City, 1866–1966* (1974).

Galishoff, Stuart. *Safeguarding the Public Health: Newark, 1895–1918* (1975).

Galishoff, Stuart. *Newark: The Nation's Unhealthiest City, 1832–1895* (1988).

Leavitt, Judith W. *The Healthiest City: Milwaukee and the Politics of Health Reform* (1982).

Miscellaneous Studies

Beardsley, Edward H. *A History of Neglect: Health Care for Blacks and Mill Workers in the Twentieth-Century South* (1987).

Jarcho, Saul. "Cadwallader Colden as a Student of Infectious Disease." *Bulletin of the History of Medicine* 29 (1955): 99–115.

Melosi, Martin V. *Garbage in the Cities: Refuse, Reform, and the Environment, 1880–1980* (1981).

Rosner, David, and Gerald Markowitz, eds. *Dying for Work: Essays on the History of Workers' Safety and Health in Twentieth Century America* (1987).

Webster, Noah. *Collection of Papers on the Subject of Bilious Fevers Prevalent in the United States for a Few Years Past* (1796).

— JOHN DUFFY

R

RADIO

In John Cheever's short story "The Enormous Radio" a young couple buy a new radio because they enjoy classical music. But the radio brings more than music into the Westcott home. The narrator describes the radio as "powerful and ugly" with a "mistaken sensitivity to discord" which allows Irene Westcott to eavesdrop on the arguments and troubles of the other families in her apartment building. The Westcotts get the radio repaired so that it again plays classical music, but it is too late to fix the damage done to the family's peaceful facade. Jim accuses Irene of wasting money, stealing from her dying mother, and having an abortion. At the end of the story, Irene turns to the radio:

> . . . hoping that the instrument might speak to her kindly. . . . Jim continued to shout at her from the door. The voice on the radio was suave and noncommittal. "An early-morning railroad disaster in Tokyo," the loudspeaker said, "killed twenty-nine people. A fire in a Catholic hospital near Buffalo for the care of blind children was extinguished early this morning by nuns. The temperature is forty-seven. The humidity is eighty-nine." (Cheever, p. 41)

Cheever describes how the introduction of radio changed American lives, a change which involved not only specific radio programs but also the relationships among people, and between people and the world around them.

Social historians interested in radio have tended to focus on three sites of change: radio audiences, and how they changed and were changed; the technological and organizational structure of the broadcasting industry and its profit-making operations; and particular programs. Radio has influenced how Americans interact with popular culture, with the government, with new technology, and with commercial culture. Yet only when the interactions among the three aspects of radio—programming, structure, and audiences—are considered, can we chart the importance of radio broadcasting in American life. The changes brought by and to radio need to be considered in four time periods: prebroadcast radio; prenetwork radio; the golden age of network radio; and radio in the era of television.

Prebroadcast Radio

People first used radio to communicate with other individuals. Not until around 1920 did the idea of "broadcasting," sending one message to many individuals—one transmitter, many receivers—become possible and popular. But before anyone imagined radio broadcasting, a group of skilled hobbyists used radio to talk to each other across the country. Early radio listeners thought of radio as an active, rather than as a passive, medium. The first "hams" (middle-class, urban white men and boys) experimented with radio transmission and reception in the decade before World War I. Using inexpensive crystals as detectors, oatmeal boxes wound with wire as tuning coils, and telephones as headsets, the young hobbyists learned from each other, from magazines, from the Boy Scout Manual, and from trial and error to build their own equipment. They designed receivers and transmitters to pick up distant signals and to communicate with each other, using their varying skills at Morse code. The active participation of these young men in their new hobby influenced the shape of the radio industry.

Early in radio history, these amateurs set up a national relay or network, in order to send messages across the country. Connecting the various radio clubs, the American Radio Relay League (ARRL), founded in 1914, had two hundred stations from coast to coast within four months. The ARRL network, disbanded during World War I by government order but revived in 1919, allowed amateurs to engage in their favorite activity: communicating with other operators who lived far away. From the beginning, amateur radio operators were thrilled to be part of a group, an audience, separated by long distances.

Hams held contests to see who could transmit the fastest and the farthest. Susan Douglas showed that the mostly male amateurs used their hobby to forge a concept of masculinity measured by mastery of the new technology rather than by physical prowess. In the process, they proved that middle-class Americans wanted to know what people in different cities or states were like and showed that "these Americans had a feeling that there was more information available to them than they routinely received" (*Inventing American Broadcasting*, p. 206). Even before broadcast radio was conceived, then, the amateurs used radio to communicate across long distances, to find out what was happening across the country, and to make connections with other people in this country and abroad.

The days of amateurs receiving and sending signals across the country, however, were numbered. After World War I, corporations gained control of American radio and reduced the role both of amateur radio users and of government broadcasters. Unlike Great Britain and Europe, in the United States large companies, rather than individuals or governments, developed radio technology. While some inventors, like Lee De Forest, tried to set up companies to exploit their inventions, existing electrical companies moved quickly to control all patents except those held by the British Marconi Company. In 1919, the American government, in the guise of protecting national security, forced British Marconi to turn its American operations over to an American holding company, the Radio Corporation of America. RCA, a patent pool formed with the help of the federal government by General Electric, American Telephone and Telegraph, Western Electric, and United Fruit Company (soon to be joined by Westinghouse), controlled radio receiver and transmitter manufacture. When broadcasting began, RCA scrambled to gain a place in that field of radio as well.

The end of World War I brought not only organizational changes but also technological changes to the radio industry which affected the composition of the radio audience. The development of the Audion, a new form of vacuum tube, and its availability to amateurs after World War I made the transmission of words and music possible. Listeners no longer needed to know Morse code, a skill that the young hams had enjoyed developing but which had limited the number of radio hobbyists. In addition, amateurs increasingly found transmitters more difficult to build than receivers as transmitter technology became more complex. When each radio fan did not need to be both a sender and a receiver, and when radio listeners could enjoy their hobby without learning Morse code, more people became interested in radio.

In 1919, when one of the hams, Frank Conrad, a Westinghouse engineer, began airing a regular program of recorded music from a well-made transmitter in his Pittsburgh garage, many people wanted to listen. They sent a son, or the boy next door, or the war veteran down the block who had learned about radio in the service, to buy the materials needed to build a radio receiving set. Conrad's employer, Westinghouse, noticed it sold more equipment when Conrad broadcast. In 1920, to encourage sales, Westinghouse moved Conrad's transmitter to the top of their factory, applied for a federal license, set regular transmitting hours, and named the station KDKA. Radio had changed from point-to-point communication into a potential mass medium.

In the almost seven years before the first radio network was formed in 1926, listeners and the large radio companies explored the possibilities for programming and financing radio broadcasting. These experiments illustrated interesting roads not taken in American media organization and proved that commercialized broadcasting was neither natural nor inevitable, but simply the easiest and most profitable solution for the corporations already involved in radio. By the time the first radio station went on the air in 1920, companies that manufactured radio equipment expected to profit from their radio operations, but they did not know where that profit would come from and how it would come. Options other than selling time on the air existed, as did nonprofit alternatives to commercial broadcasting. The particular commercial form American broadcasting took resulted from the interaction of several decisions and predispositions, beginning with a desire, on the part of both ordinary people and the radio industry, for national radio service.

As radio stations sprang up across the country, built by newspapers, feed stores, municipalities, colleges, and radio equipment manufacturers, many of the habits of the earlier hams carried over into radio listening. Because ready-made receivers were not yet available, new listeners to the recently established broadcasting stations needed help to assemble a receiving set. Much like the early hackers who helped spread an interest in computers, the prewar hams eagerly helped others build receiving sets and, in the process, indoctrinated new audience members into the culture of radio listening (including the thrill of receiving signals from distant places).

Prenetwork Radio

Early radio fans eagerly searched for faraway stations. In 1923, *Radio Broadcast* magazine identified one of the continuing attractions of broadcast radio as the "ability to astound our friends by tuning in a program a thousand miles away for their particular benefit" and concluded that there "is something fascinating about hearing a concert from a long way off, and the pleasure does not seem to wane with familiarity" (Morecroft, p. 361). A listener could bring distant events into the living room (or garage). In addition, the small, early radio stations programmed local "talent," and so it might be more entertaining to hear a station many miles away. A poem published in the *New Yorker*, and reprinted in the largest magazine for the new radio listeners, *Radio Broadcast* (May 1925), described long-distance listeners.

THE DISTANCE FIEND

He was a distance fiend,
A loather of anything near,
Though WOOF had a singer of opera fame,
And WOW a soprano of national name,
He passed them both up for a Kansas quartet
A thousand miles off and hence "harder to get."
New York was too easy to hear.
He was a distance fiend . . .

He was a distance fiend,
Alas, but he died one day.
Saint Peter obligingly asked would he tell
His choice of residence—Heaven or Hell?
He replied, with a show of consistency fine:
"Good sir, you have hit on a hobby of mine,
Which place is the farthest away?"
He was a distance fiend.

("The Distance Fiend," p. 35)

Eventually, long-distance listeners found themselves unable to overcome technological barriers—no amount of fiddling with the dials could banish static. By the mid-1920s, the radio audience turned away from distant broadcasts and returned to local stations, but quickly realized that local programs remained at an amateurish level and that they missed the thrill of listening in on faraway events. Listeners sought easily available and reliable radio service which featured both broadcasts from distant places and programming of sophisticated content.

Although the number of "distance fiends" dwindled, they left an important legacy. The collective memory of radio listeners contained the possibility, and the excitement, of hearing distant people and events. Rural listeners knew of more varied programming available from urban stations and sought accurate market and weather information; people from the rural South who had moved to the urban North, including African Americans, sought familiar music; sports fans wanted to follow their teams on the road. The early radio fans "fished" for faraway stations and thus demonstrated the public's interest in national radio, over which the audience could hear programs from around the country.

Three technological options existed for providers of national radio service superpower, with a few powerful transmitters serving the entire country; wired networks, with programs sent over telephone wires from a single source for rebroadcast by scattered local stations; and shortwave rebroadcasting, which connected local stations to the programming source with radio waves instead of wires. The reasons for choosing one option rather than another went beyond the technological, even at the earliest experimental stage. The radio industry decided on wired networks because they proved technologically feasible, were part of a compromise hammered out among feuding radio patent holders, and avoided the appearance of a radio monopoly by using local stations to broadcast national programs. The choice of wired networks to provide national radio service was the deciding factor in the development of the organization, economics, and form of broadcast radio.

Network radio brought expensive wire line charges and thus the need for broadcasting, as well as receiver, sales to make money. By the 1920s, radio stations in large cities sold time for commercial messages, or accepted free programs provided by commercial enterprises, in order to raise money and cut expenses. Yet ambivalence about radio advertising started early and remained. From the beginning of the 1920s, listeners, government officials, and radio magazines complained about broadcast advertising and searched for alternative methods of financing radio. The omnipresent question "Who is to pay for broadcasting?" showed that many did not immediately accept commercialized broadcasting as the best answer. College, church, union, and municipal radio stations flourished. Broadcast advertising gained rich and powerful proponents when RCA founded the National Broadcasting Company in 1926, and the Columbia Broadcasting System began in the next year, both as for-profit concerns. The high quality of programming available on the new networks and network dominance and influence overrode some concerns, but the networks still worked to sell commercialized broadcasting to the public.

From the beginning of the 1920s, listeners, government officials, and radio magazines complained about broadcast advertising and searched for alternative methods of financing radio.

Contemporary American broadcasting presents itself as the "natural," sometimes even the inevitable, application of American capitalism to communication. Yet the American commercialized broadcasting system did not evolve naturally but rather grew out of a struggle over its form and content. During the first fourteen years of radio broadcasting, listeners, broadcasters, advertisers, and educators fought for control over radio.

Listeners wanted national radio service. The provision of such service over wired networks resulted from a combination of technological, economic, cultural, and political factors. Wired networks brought with them a specific broadcasting structure and particular kinds of radio programs. The use of radio advertising to pay the expensive wire rentals brought early and continuing protests from educators and others who hoped radio would do more than sell products.

Broadcast advertising also faced other, more influential, skeptics. Potential advertisers and the advertising industry itself doubted that advertisements over the radio would be effective. Networks, and the promoters they hired, campaigned to convince doubters that broadcasting was the perfect advertising medium. The campaign to promote broadcast advertising worked to satisfy advertising industry that radio was a medium they could understand and use without difficulty. Promoters involved advertising agencies in radio broadcasting, began merchandising radio programs, and commodified radio time. They then convinced broadcasters to change radio to conform to prevailing theories and practices of advertising. Like other advertising professionals, the promoters of radio advertising changed the product they had been hired to sell in order to make their job easier. For example, because advertisers had recently come to think of consumers as middle-class women, promoters of broadcast advertising depicted radio not as a boy's toy or a male-controlled entertainment medium but as an instructional tool staffed by home economists in order to enter the home during the day and sell to women. Broadcast advertising developed as a continuation and extension of widely accepted advertising principles. The attempt to sell radio advertising to advertisers and broadcasting's resulting acceptance of basic advertising ideas had important consequences for the form of both radio programs and radio broadcasting.

Wired networks and the development of broadcast advertising shaped radio programming. Other forms of national radio service might have presented different performers, formats, and material. The particular demands of national advertising led networks to drop local musicians in favor of vaudeville artists who had long performed for audiences across the country. They also replaced regional sponsors with large companies seeking a national market, companies that had the money to hire vaudeville stars. In one of the first sponsored programs, recording artists Billy Jones and Ernie Hare performed whimsical, nostalgic numbers as the Happiness Boys for the Happiness Candy Company (a northeastern manufacturer and distributor that also owned restaurants). Jones and Hare were soon replaced by hard-hitting vaudeville comedians representing huge companies.

The increasing commercialization and monopolization of the airwaves by the networks brought new complaints about the commercialization of radio broadcasting. A poem in *Radio Revue* (March 1930) illustrated some of the concerns:

SPONSORITIS

Dame nature has a "funny" way
Of spoiling our enjoyment
For everyone who lives today
Has his or her annoyment;
And each disease beneath the sun
Has diff'rent germs to bite us
Now RADIO's developed one—
They call it "SPONSORITIS".

It's thriving like a healthy weed
Or fungus newly grafted,
And mercenaries sow the seed
Wherever sound is wafted
The artists rave then grow morose
Because of laryngitis,
And "fans" then get a stronger dose
Of this same SPONSORITIS.

No use to try to save the wreck
Or prophesy disaster,
For he who signs the mighty check
Is boss and lord and master;
When there's a program spoiled or botched,
It's money bags who fight us,
With heavy hearts we've stood and watched
The spread of SPONSORITIS. . . .

In one important challenge to commercialized broadcasting, radio stations supported by colleges and universities worked for an amendment to radio regulatory legislation to guarantee 15 percent of all radio frequencies for nonprofit stations. They lost that battle, and the war.

Commercialized broadcasters moved quickly to smash the early 1930s backlash against broadcast advertising, and they succeeded in destroying most nonprofit alternatives. Under new regulations pushed by the radio industry, many educational stations ceased to exist because they found broadcasting too expensive. The 1934 Communications Act, which was supposed to regulate the industry, failed to mention advertising or networks. Broadcasting, as presented in the Communications Act, was made up of independent local units financed in whatever way they chose, even though most stations were commercial and used network programming for the entire broadcast day. The new law gave no protection to—indeed, continued the harassment of—nonprofit and educational stations.

The results of the acceptance of networks and broadcast advertising were evident as early as the 1930s. For example, affiliation with a network emphasized, for local broadcasters, the importance of time and illustrated the changes in programming that accompanied the organizational and conceptual changes involved in broadcast advertising. Unlike earlier radio performers who were urged to fill as much time as they could, a singer on an early network show remembered that "timing was the sword of Damocles hanging over our heads. We could not be ten seconds overtime without infringing on another sponsor's territory" (Dragonette, p. 104). Radio's growing commercialism brought about part of the increasing emphasis on time. Radio existed in time only and time was the commodity sold to finance broadcasting. One observer wrote that "a statue of radio Thespis would assuredly be blind and with a stopwatch in one hand, or perhaps in each" (Goldsmith and Lescarboura, p. 98). Network affiliation and the inclusion of advertisements brought a rigid form to radio. Each programming segment was carefully timed, and sponsors, who spent enormous amounts of money buying radio time, wanted the same programming formula (a certain number of jokes, so many songs in each segment) followed each week. Some of the artists used the rigid form as a spur to creativity, like poets working within a strict sonnet form, but for most it limited program possibilities.

Entertainment programming, particularly comedy and drama, played an important part in the everyday life of most Americans in the 1930s and 1940s as radio entered what the industry liked to call its "golden age."

Commercialized radio proved more responsive to advertisers than to listeners. Uncertainty over listener response (a continuing worry for the television networks, which distrust current ratings systems and experiment with people meters) forced advertisers to rely on their own impressions of what listeners liked. Advertisers and networks worried incessantly about offending listeners. Several years after Gertrude Berg went on NBC in 1929 with *The Rise of the Goldbergs*, a program about a Jewish immigrant family, the network and the sponsor (Pepsodent) became concerned that a program about Jews might alienate listeners. The NBC statistical department did a study in 1932 and reassured network executives and the sponsor "that there is a large audience for good programs of Jewish type"; that "the success of this program should make a telling argument for Jewish programs"; and that "an analysis of their mail receipts indicates that this popularity is not restricted to any geographic region." Further, the report quoted the Pepsodent advertising manager that "although the program concerns a Jewish family, the vast majority . . . of appeals to keep it on the air came from Gentiles." Unable to clearly identify what made a program popular or unpopular, advertisers relied on their instincts about what the public wanted. Such instincts often had more to do with the prejudices and predilections of advertisers than the wishes of the radio audience.

Most importantly, radio became a way to sell products. Programs filled the time between commercials, just as many critics feel that they do in current television offerings. Programs joined with commercials in trying—sometimes successfully, sometimes not—to manipulate the audience, not to entertain or educate or uplift, unless those actions would help sell.

The Golden Age of Network Radio

Despite its drawbacks, commercialized national radio did offer its audience some benefits. If listeners missed a sense of direct human connection with the voices they heard, if they had little control over programming, the performers who flocked to radio in the 1930s nonetheless brought the audience professional entertainment, some variety, and a sense of belonging to a national community. Entertainment programming, particularly comedy and drama, played an important part in the everyday life of most Americans in the 1930s and 1940s as radio entered what the industry liked to call its "golden age."

Vaudeville performers began to form the backbone of comedy programs in the early 1930s. In 1931, Eddie Cantor became the host of *The Chase and Sanborn Hour*, and by the next year new radio shows featured Ed Wynn, Burns and Allen, Jack Benny, George Jessel, Jack Pearl, and Fred Allen. The new programs took the form of the variety show, which in the 1920s had featured musical hosts such as Wendell Hall on the *Eveready Hour, Harry Reser of the Cliquot Club Eskimos*, Rudy Vallee on *The Fleischman Hour*, and Jessica Dragonette on the *Cities Service Concerts*. Now, however, comedians served as the stars and hosts of programs which featured comedy sketches.

Performers, subject matter, advertising, and the form of the entertainment remained interwoven, so that a change in one affected the others. Cantor, for example, was clearly a participant in the "new humor" brought by immigrants to the vaudeville stage. Albert McLean describes vaudeville's urban and ethnic (mostly Jewish) humor as based on verbal misunderstandings, rooted in stories of family life and of the underdog, and with a compressed and frantic form built around the joke (a modern invention). The compression and verbal basis of this humor made it a natural for radio. The radio comedians of the 1920s, coming from different personal and professional backgrounds, had relied on music and on what McLean calls the "relaxed whimsy of the minstrel show" (p. 116).

Cantor's programs featured jokes, skits, and stories about Ida Cantor and the couple's five daughters. Cantor's scripts, written by David Freedman (many of the writers, as well as the performers, came from vaudeville), depended on a "joke factory" where young writers reworked old jokes to fit the week's subject. Programs with a midwestern, small-town flavor, including *Vic and Sade, Easy Aces, and Fibber McGee and Molly,* joined comedies which had come out of a Jewish and/or urban experience. Nevertheless, the influx of vaudevillians to radio in the early 1930s, and the good fit between the needs of radio and the form of the "new humor," determined the course of radio programming for many years.

Comedy, in a variety of formats, remained popular radio fare through the 1940s and into the 1950s. Comedians smoothly made the transition from gently spoofing the Great Depression to gently spoofing World War II, always mindful that the federal government regulated radio broadcasting and that major corporations paid the bills. By the 1940s, radio comedy, like all radio programming, featured more commercialized programs with heavy-hitting advertising, often as part of the program, produced by advertising agencies located in Hollywood. Several novels, including *The Hucksters* (1946) by Frederic Wakeman and Herman Wouk's *Inside, Outside* (1985), explained how the increasing commercialization of radio brought new pressures to bear on radio writers and performers.

Dramatic shows during radio's "golden age" grew out of the continuing comedy serials which began with *Amos 'n' Andy* and *The Rise of the Goldbergs* in 1929. By the end of the 1930s, network radio featured several dramatic anthology programs. The writers on such series, often drawing upon the left-wing political consciousness of the 1930s, experimented with radio's aural qualities and ability to deliver political messages. Plays had widely varied formats, and some featured musical montages and poetry. Norman Corwin, a writer for *Columbia Workshop* on CBS, wrote and directed twenty-six radio programs in as many weeks in 1940, in a series called *26 by Corwin.* The programs included plays about submarine crews, hillbilly harmonica players, a boy who searches for his dog in Heaven and in Curgatory, a soliloquy for one voice with a few sound effects, and a biblical trilogy. Corwin's next project, an exploration of the Bill of Rights entitled *We Hold These Truths,* took up patriotic themes which he had explored before. Broadcast just eight days after the attack on Pearl Harbor, the show illustrated how many of the radio writers of the late 1930s and early 1940s moved quite easily, both professionally and intellectually, into wartime radio.

World War II changed the nature of broadcasting. Radio made three contributions to the war effort: news programs supported American intervention, propaganda broadcast over shortwave radio targeted Nazi-occupied Europe, and broadcasts to the troops via the Armed Forces Radio Service boosted morale. Yet such extensive news reporting was quite new to radio. Newspapers saw radio as a competitor, since radio news bulletins could reach people before newspapers could. In the "press-radio war" of the mid 1930s, newspapers in 1933 refused to allow the radio networks to broadcast wire service reports. CBS and NBC countered by establishing their own news departments. But neither network wanted to spend the money necessary to compete with the wire services, since few sponsors seemed interested in news programs.

A truce allowed radio announcers to "comment" on the news rather than report it, and the wire services again made their copy available for broadcast in 1934. The "commentators," as radio reporters came to be called, did just that until the Munich crisis of 1938, when H. V. (Hans Von) Kaltenborn, a former newspaper reporter, made 102 broadcasts in 18 days. Sleeping at the CBS studio, Kaltenborn, the son of German immigrants, translated the speeches of French and German leaders as they came over the shortwave radio and broadcast them to American listeners. With the help of radio broadcasts, Americans began to seek a connection to other parts of the world.

In *News for Everyman* (1976), historian David Culbert contends that between 1938 and the attack on Pearl Harbor, "radio emerged as the principal medium for combatting isolationism in America" and that "radio commentators played a major role in creating a climate of opinion favorable to an interventionist foreign policy though they did not directly make foreign policy"

(Culbert, pp. 6, 7). Culbert describes how six radio newsmen—Kaltenborn, Boake Carter, Raymond Gram Swing, Elmer Davis, Fulton Lewis, Jr., and Edward R. Murrow—brilliantly and creatively invented broadcast journalism in the 1940s and demonstrated that such programming had commercial potential.

As the war began, the United States rushed to keep up with the Axis powers, which had begun using radio for propaganda in the 1930s. Americans knew the political power of radio, having heard President Franklin Roosevelt's effective use of radio during his Fireside Chats, but many remained fearful of the power of propaganda. Finally, in 1942, the president authorized the Overseas Branch of the Office of War Information to begin broadcasting over the Voice of America (VOA) to areas under Axis control. As Holly Cowan Shulman describes in *The Voice of America*, the broadcasts heard over the VOA changed as American foreign policy, war aims, domestic politics, and cultural climate changed over the course of the war. The first VOA broadcasts drew directly from the experimental programs of commercial radio in the 1930s. VOA programmers, including John Houseman, borrowed radio techniques from Norman Corwin to make their broadcasts appealing. As the war progressed, VOA broadcasts became more factual and detailed, and resembled news reporting more than modernist radio documentaries. In part, VOA programming responded to the progress of the war. When the VOA had no victories to report, it explained America's moral stance and described war production in imaginative terms. As Allied triumphs brought the shape of the postwar world into focus, direct reporting became more effective propaganda.

The VOA illustrated the division in broadcast programming that took place in the 1940s, a change given impetus by the war. Entertainment programming and news programming separated, and listeners came to believe that such a division was natural and preferable to the intermingling of fact and fiction that 1930s radio had featured. Contemporary critics disparage television "docudramas," which resemble Norman Corwin's and John Houseman's radio programs, for confusing television watchers about the difference between "truth" and "fiction." The VOA, at least in part to hide its propaganda aims, helped construct the broadcast convention that news programs were both objective and oppositional to entertainment programming.

Another wartime radio activity, that of the Armed Forces Radio Service (AFRS), also influenced commercial radio programming. Radio was so much a part of American life that during World War II the armed forces arranged for soldiers in both Europe and the Pacific to listen in. Samuel Brylawski, a Library of Congress archivist in charge of the huge collection of AFRS recordings, notes that by 1945 the AFRS sent fifty hours of radio programming weekly to overseas outlets—producing forty-three programs (fourteen hours) itself and distributing thirty-six hours of American commercial radio (with commercial messages deleted) each week. One program, *Command Performance*, began six months before the founding of the AFRS in August 1942 and used prerecorded programs, which made performers' lives easier and proved to the radio industry that the technology existed to edit radio programs and broadcast them from disks. The program supposedly reflected the desires of American soldiers who would receive a "command performance" from America's best-known radio and film stars. Radio producers recorded performers and edited together the best "takes," deleted off-color jokes and dated material, and sent shows out to AFRS stations on records for rebroadcast.

President Franklin D. Roosevelt delivers a radio address during one of his fireside chats. Although Americans recognized the reassuring influence of these broadcasts, they remained fearful of the power of propaganda.

Recorded programs had long been anathema to the radio networks, which had the money to provide live performances and boasted about their live entertainment in the 1930s and 1940s. Even after the technology existed to play recordings over the air electrically, the networks had blocked their use. Recorded programs could be cheaper to produce and represented competition for live broadcasts over the networks. Bing Crosby's experience on *Command Performance* may have moved him to demand a transcription clause in his new contract with the American Broadcasting Company in 1946. That clause gave Crosby the right to record his program in Los Angeles at his convenience and ship it to New York for broadcast. The use of such recorded material paved the way for the rebirth of radio as a musical medium after the introduction of television.

As an alternative programmer in an industry controlled by networks, the presence of AFRS demonstrated a wider range of possibilities for radio than most people had imagined. For example, the ambivalent relationship between AFRS and commercialized broadcasting illustrated continuing listener dissatisfaction with radio advertising. While dependent on the networks for many of its most popular programs, the AFRS deleted all commercial references and advertising. AFRS even retitled programs that carried a sponsor's name. *Camel Caravan* became *Comedy Caravan; Maxwell House Program* became *Fanny Brice—Frank Aforgan*; and *Chase and Sanborn Hour* became *Charlie McCarthy.*

The Voice of America illustrated the division in broadcast programming that took place in the 1940s, a change given impetus by war.

Brylawski notes a number of reasons for the "denaturing" of programs, including complaints by service personnel, the unfair advantages to those commercial programs used by the AFRS, and American agreements with the noncommercial British Broadcasting Corporation to use its transmitters to broadcast the programs. Most important, the advertisements seemed inappropriate for GIs in the field: "Troops fighting in the Pacific did not want to hear about 'refreshing Coca-Cola' nor did they appreciate the 'dangers of the common cold'" (Brylawski, p. 335). The radio industry had worked since the 1920s to make broadcast advertising seem natural and reassuringly American, but the contrast between wartime service and danger and the profit-making techniques of radio advertising showed that advertising was neither wholly accepted nor particularly patriotic.

Radio in the Era of Television

After the war, opposition to commercialized broadcasting resurfaced. Like the outbursts of anti-commercial sentiment when broadcasting began in the 1920s and again just before the passage of the Communications Act in 1934, the criticism of broadcasting in 1946 appeared in a number of different forums. The Federal Communications Commission (FCC), usually the servant of the radio industry, issued a study of radio programming in March 1946 entitled *Public Service Responsibility of Broadcast Licensees.* The report said that station owners had not fulfilled the provisions of their licenses which mandated public service. In April, Charles Siepmann, a former employee of both the British Broadcasting Corporation and the FCC, reiterated the charge that radio stations had failed to serve the public interest in his book *Radio's Second Chance.*

The critique of broadcasting that reached the most people, however, was Frederic Wakeman's enormously popular novel, *The Hucksters* (1946). Wakeman, a former employee of the Lord and Thomas advertising agency, wrote a fictional account of his experiences producing radio programs and working for George Washington Hill, president of the American Tobacco Company, a large radio advertiser and a Lord and Thomas client. The book, and the movie of the next year, tell the story of a young advertising agency executive who works for an eccentric and demanding client. Wakeman presents funny pictures of the subservience of advertising and broadcasting professionals to their clients. In *The Hucksters,* selling Beautee Soap meant bowing to the wishes of the president of the company to present stupidly simple radio programs and ad campaigns. Wakeman blames the sorry state of radio programming on sponsors and clearly states that they controlled radio. Nevertheless, the ongoing resistance to commercialized radio represented by Wakeman's book and other protests had little effect because of the enormous power and influence of the radio networks.

After World War II, the story of programming, commercialization, and audience response continued to unfold in television, while radio changed dramatically. During the 1950s television quickly took over radio's central place in the living room, presenting news, entertainment, and educational programs for white middle-class families watching together in the evening and broadcasting programs aimed at women and children in special time periods. Radio, with its programming usurped by television, reinvented itself after the war. Technological changes (including the development of the transistor), programming changes begun during the war (including the use of recorded shows), and new ways of thinking about the audience on the part of both broadcasters and advertisers (including the rise of demographic research) turned radio into a commercialized music box programmed for particular audience segments.

Most important, in response to television's popularity, radio stations adopted a strategy that they had previously rejected: specialization. Stations aimed at African Americans pointed to a new direction for radio. Television, taking up where radio had left off, offered programs aimed primarily at white, urban, upper-middle-class families. Many African Americans, uninterested in television and some not able to afford the new sets, turned to radio. Hoping for a new audience to replace those listeners lost to television, a few radio stations responded by playing recordings made for black audiences, so-called race records. "Negro radio" had important implications for broadcasting. The success of such stations showed that a segmented market approach could work for radio. Following up on the success of "Negro radio," broadcasters looked for other special-interest groups who had found little to interest them on television. Relying on specialized programming, radio "escaped direct competition with television and found it could profit without the evening audiences" (Fornatale and Mills, p. 17).

Equally important, the first specialized radio stations, programmed for African American listeners, attracted another audience as well. White teenagers found the music they heard on such stations so compelling in its form and content that they spent more and more time tuned in. Postwar broadcast radio had found its best audience: teenagers.

The transistor acted like a vacuum tube in conducting, modulating, and amplifying radio signals, allowing radios to be cheaper, smaller, and more durable than prewar radios.

Teenage interest in radio grew out of a technological change as well as social and cultural factors. The invention of the transistor in 1947, like the introduction of the Audion after World War I, changed the audience for radio. The transistor acted like a vacuum tube in conducting, modulating, and amplifying radio signals, allowing radios to be cheaper, smaller, and more durable than prewar radios. With transistor radios, broadcast listening became a personal and portable experience. The smaller size and lower cost of the new radios allowed teenagers and others to own their own radios and to tune in without family interference. A teenager could listen alone in her bedroom, or with her friends gathered out-of-doors, to music that her parents might not enjoy or even condone. After the introduction of television and the transistor in the 1950s, radio became the medium of those marginalized by society.

Not many historians have looked at the connection between the development of rock and roll and radio in the 1950s. Clearly, rock and radio were made for each other. Based on musical styles derived (or stolen) from African Americans, rock and roll, broadcast over millions of radios, allowed young people to temporarily cross some class and racial lines. Record companies and radio stations, both struggling for a place in the entertainment industry after World War II, found that a relationship could be mutually beneficial. Record companies provided radio stations with hit songs and got free publicity. One estimate says that record sales nearly tripled from 1954 to 1959. Radio stations kept operating costs low by hiring a single performer (the disc jockey) to play recorded music, and found a new lease on life.

This kind of interaction, overlooked in many other industries, brought a government investigation into "payola" and charges that record companies paid disc jockeys to play certain records. Critics have seen the payola scandal as a racist attempt to limit the influence of rock and roll, since those prosecuted were primarily black or promoted black artists, while government investigators largely ignored white promoters and artists. Others simply point to the hypocrisy of the persecutions. One disc jockey, Alan Freed, commented, "What they call payola in the disc jockey business, they call lobbying in Washington." The payola investigations and prosecutions led to tightened controls by stations over play lists and cut off experimental, multicultural radio programming.

The FCC's reassignment of the FM spectrum in July 1962 opened a new venue for experimentation, delighting young radio listeners who remained interested in alternative music. After the war, the government tried to get consumers and broadcasters interested in a different set of radio frequencies in order to increase the number of radio stations available. Since most radios did not receive FM audiences and advertisers remained wary of stations that required the listeners to purchase new equipment. Many of the first FM stations were completely noncommercial, and commercial FM stations found sponsors difficult to find or keep. As a result, FM radio had few interruptions and could program longer pieces of music. The 1962 FCC ruling responded to the growth in the number of FM stations by assigning frequencies to particular communities, thus allowing for the orderly growth of FM.

Again the radio and recording industries developed together in the mid 1960s as rock 'n' roll performers began to focus on albums rather than singles. As AM radio became more rigid, listeners could hear experimental rock and roll on FM radio. The new FM stations had time for the music of the counterculture and to play entire rock and roll albums. Many listeners remember the days of progressive FM, free-form radio with the same fondness their parents reserve for radio programs of the 1930s. Contributing to FM's eventual success was its technical superiority. As rock and roll music became more complex, and as record players improved so that people found out how good records could sound, the fact that FM stations broadcast with better fidelity, in stereo, brought new listeners. As Fornatale and Mills explain it:

> Progressive FM was killed by its own success: As it drew more and more advertising accounts it had to make changes in the format to retain them. As FM rockers demonstrated their hold on the 18- to 34-year-old market, advertisers fell all over themselves trying to get on the air. (p. 140)

Increasing commercialization brought more conservative programming.

Radio's experimentation with new audiences and formats coincided with a reemphasis within the advertising industry on market research. As the market for consumer goods grew after the war, advertisers worked to sell more and more services to manufacturers. Advertising professionals found demographic information critical to targeting products for particular buyers. Radio and then television became, in David Marc's memorable phrase, "demographic vistas."

The 1970s and 1980s saw a proliferation of extremely specialized stations, many with automated play lists which gave responsibility for what music went over the air to the station's marketing department. An article by Ken Barnes on Top 40 radio called it "a fragment of the imagination" and listed twenty-four different station formats, including adult contemporary, album-oriented rock, beautiful music, big band, contemporary hit radio, country, easy listening radio, gold, and music of your life. The conservatism of music radio comes from the advertising professionals' belief that people like best the music they have heard before. With the introduction of cable television stations (such as MTV) that play video versions of top rock songs, much of the newest musical experimentation happens on television rather than radio. College radio stations remain the exception to this rule. Noncommercial since the 1920s, college stations serve as a key site for disseminating new music and introducing new artists.

The period since 1970 has brought both a revival of "noncommercial" radio and a boom in "talk" radio. The Corporation for Public Broadcasting, under the Public Broadcasting Act of 1967, funded National Public Radio (NPR) as both a production center for programming and a network linking member stations. Controversial NPR membership requirements kept out the small stations that had maintained the noncommercial radio option since 1920. Also, because most NPR stations are supported by listeners, programming is aimed at those most likely to contribute, and so the stations provide less diversity than the framers of the original legislation had hoped.

However, talk radio, in several different formats, has grown wonderfully diverse. Call-in shows, with listeners offering opinions or experts giving answers to questions, take radio back to its local roots. Debates on neighborhood issues fill local radio shows, and the hosts of such programs often become influential political figures in their communities. National variations of such programs exist (Larry King interviews celebrities and invites audience questions; Rush Limbaugh rants on conservative political issues; Bruce Williams dispenses business advice; and many doctors diagnose ailments from Alaska to Rhode Island). The local programs provide the audience and stations to host their national brothers and sisters.

Conclusion

In many ways the history of radio can be seen as a series of expansions and contractions. Technological developments (the Audion, networks, the transistor), social and cultural changes (brought by wars, migrations within the country, and the increasing commercialization of everyday life), and innovative programming brought radio listeners new possibilities for entertainment and education. Yet as each possibility has appeared, various factors have worked to close it off. Network radio brought the chance to hear national programs but turned listeners into passive rather than active participants in radio. Commercialization promised to provide radio programming free to listeners but introduced rigid programming options and too many advertisements. During radio's development, listeners and critics protested several times that commercialized broadcasting blocked the development of more interesting possibilities. Rock and roll on 1950s radio allowed teenagers to explore African American music and to participate in a youth culture, but the focus on demographics and the growth of automated Top 40 stations resulted in a homogenization that cut off the diversity young listeners had sought. At the same time, as new possibilities brought conservative responses, other avenues sometimes appeared. When AM radio became uninteresting, FM became the home of musical experimentation.

John Cheever is right that radio changed the Westcotts, but he shows them as helpless, much like the accident victims they hear about on their new receiver. Within the commercial considerations of large corporations which control broadcasting, radio listeners have found ways of using the medium in their own interests. Along with the Westcotts, the family in Woody Allen's film *Radio Days* (1987) represents radio audiences. They integrate radio into their everyday lives, using it to reinforce and underline their activities. Perhaps more important, the narrator of the film shows that radio provides the shape and content of his memories. Far from being victimized by broadcasting, he uses his radio memories to create a warm picture of his family life, where different members of his extended family enjoy different programs and music over the radio. The radio brings outside tragedies (a little girl dying from a fall down a well) into the home, but instead of inspiring fear, as the daily news does in the Cheever story, in *Radio Days* such news serves as a way to connect this one family with people all over the country. Allen has his narrator say, "Now it's all gone. Except for the memories." But it's not "all gone" as people continue to listen to and to use radio in varied ways and each generation remembers a different time as radio's "golden age."

[See also African American Music; The Culture of Consumption; Humor and Comedy; Journalism; Rock Music; Technology and Social Change; Television.]

BIBLIOGRAPHY

Bannerman, R. LeRoy. *Norman Corwin and Radio: The Golden Years* (1986).

Barnes, Ken. "Top 40 Radio: A Fragment of the Imagination." In *Facing the Music*, edited by Simon Frith (1989).

Barnouw, Eric. *A Tower in Babel: A History of Broadcasting in the United States, Volume I—to 1933* (1966).

Barnouw, Eris. *The Golden Web: A History of Broadcasting in the United States.* Vol. 2 1933–1953 (1968).

Brylawski, Samuel. "Armed Forces Radio Service: The Invisible Highway Abroad." In *Wonderful Inventions: Motion Pictures, Broadcasting, and Recorded Sound at the Library of Congress*, edited by Iris Newsom (1985).

Cheever, John. *The Stories of John Cheever* (1978).

Culbert, David Holbrook. *News for Everyman: Radio and Foreign Affairs in Thirties America* (1976).

Czitrom, Daniel. *Media and the American Mind: From Morse to McLuhan* (1982).

Douglas, Susan J. *Inventing American Broadcasting, 1899–1922* (1987).

Dragonette, Jessica. *Faith Is a Song: The Odyssey of an American Artist* (1951).

Fornatale, Peter, and Joshua E. Mills. *Radio in the Television Age* (1980).

Goldsmith, Alfred N., and Austin C. Lescarboura. *This Thing Called Broadcasting* (1930).

Havig, Alan. "Frederic Wakeman's *The Hucksters* and the Postwar Debate over Commercial Radio." *Journal of Broadcasting* 28, no. 2 (Spring 1984).

MacDonald, J. Fred. *Don't Touch That Dial! Radio Programming in American Life, 1920–1960* (1979).

McLean, Albert. *American Vaudeville as Ritual* (1965).

Morecroft, J. H. "The March of Radio: Preparing for Long Distance." *Radio Broadcast* 3 (September 1923).

Page, Leslie J., Jr. "The Nature of the Broadcast Receiver and Its Market in the United States from 1922 to 1927." *Journal of Broadcasting* 4, no. 2 (Spring 1960).

Shulman, Holly Cowan. *The Voice of America: Propaganda and Democracy, 1941–1945* (1990).

Spalding, John W. "1928: Radio Becomes a Mass Advertising Medium." *Journal of Broadcasting* 8, no. 1 (Winter 1963–1964).

Sterling, Christopher, and John Kittross. *Stay Tuned: A Concise History of American Broadcasting* (1978).

Wertheim, Arthur Frank. *Radio Comedy* (1979).

— SUSAN SMULYAN

REPRODUCTION AND PARENTHOOD

Fertility Rates and Birth Control

Human fertility has varied widely across time and space, but the period covering the history of the United States has produced the most dramatic changes in fertility rates in human history. In 1800 the average woman living in the United States gave birth to 7.04 children. In 1988 that number was 1.9. The drop was gradual and steady until the period following World War II, when Americans produced the baby boom generation; births rose from 2.10 in 1940 to 3.00 in 1950 and 3.52 in 1960 before beginning to fall again. When isolated from the population as a whole, the fertility of black women shows a different pattern of change from that of whites. Their fertility rate declined later, beginning about 1880, and at a somewhat faster rate. These demographic shifts resulting in steadily fewer births represent a significant change in the patterns of women's and men's lives. The story of decreasing fertility in the United States reflects a striking shift in human perceptions and attitudes, and stands as graphic evidence of technological advances in birth control and abortion. At the same time, decreasing infant mortality rates, especially after the middle of the nineteenth century, have meant that over time each wanted pregnancy has had a greater likelihood of producing a living child.

The decline in fertility that began at the turn of the nineteenth century stemmed largely from increased reliance on birth control and abortion rather than other factors such as reduced marriage rates or marriage postponements. Residents of the United States continued to marry often throughout the nineteenth and twentieth centuries; the marriage rate was at its lowest, 90.4 percent, during the generation born between 1865 and 1875, and at its highest point of 95.2 percent during the 1960s, a period of heightened fertility control. Similarly, Americans continued to marry in their early to mid-twenties. Only since 1970 have census figures indicated a developing trend toward later marriages, particularly among the college educated. What has most interested historians is the fact that fertility rates began to decline before the advent of effective mechanical forms of contraception, indicating increased reliance on abstinence and especially abortion for the purpose of limiting family size.

In the seventeenth and eighteenth centuries, English couples' efforts at controlling their fertility were restricted to maintaining two-year birth intervals, or, late in a woman's reproductive life, postponing births. Birth intervals varied from region to region in other parts of Europe, and could be as short as sixteen to eighteen months. Methods of birth control were limited and, with the exception of periodic abstinence, largely ineffective. They ranged from coitus interruptus to reliance on various forms of barriers and pessaries (cervical covers or shields). The general absence of spermicides in medicinal recipe books of the period indicates that they had minimal value. Some women relied on intensive breastfeeding as a means of delaying pregnancy, as frequent nipple stimulation inhibits ovulation in most women for periods from six to twelve months, sometimes even longer. Among Native Americans and some African Americans, intensive breastfeeding for two to five years, and the observation of periodic sexual abstinence during that time, produced longer birth intervals. Largely as a result of breastfeeding practices, European women had a higher fertility rate in the early modern period than Native American women. It is impossible to determine with certainty the normal birth intervals of African Americans, whose lives were so disrupted by slavery, but it appears they were also longer than those of Europeans until late in the eighteenth century, due both to breastfeeding practices and their conditions of enslavement.

In the middle of the nineteenth century, social and political concern focused on the falling birthrates of middle- and upper-class whites. A combination of factors, including increased abstinence, a higher incidence of abortion, and greater reliance on mechanical forms of contraception, contributed to the falling birthrate. In 1873, concern about issues such as "race suicide" and the influence of the women's rights movement on women's social roles led Congress to enact the Comstock Law, an anti-obscenity statute designed in part to prevent the distribution of contraceptive information through the mails. Many policymakers, including leaders of the women's rights movement, feared that access to mechanical means of contraception would lead to immorality, especially an increase in prostitution. Through legislation such as the Comstock Law and statutes outlawing abortion, legislators denied women full control over their fertility. Thus as the birthrate fell and more Americans heralded the benefits of small families, pressure mounted to outlaw birth control. In the eyes of many nineteenth-century Americans, the only acceptable form of birth control was abstinence, which could produce small families without endangering public morality.

Advocates of birth control during this period frequently came from the ranks of the political Left, activists who regarded governmental efforts to control information as repressive, particularly of the poor. For them, birth control was a political movement with revolutionary implications. Their political radicalism made it difficult for them to work effectively in the mainstream, however, and it was not until a more moderate figure in the person of Margaret Sanger (1879–1966) gained prominence in the movement that it became more generally popular. Her role in opening a birth control clinic in Brooklyn, New York, to distribute information about contraceptives led to her imprisonment in 1916, but the appeal of her case resulted in increased rights for doctors to distribute birth control information to their patients. Sanger's imprisonment earned her widespread popular respect, and she was able in the late 1910s and 1920s to help broaden support for birth control among philanthropists and the medical establishment.

The Comstock Law was overturned in 1938, but despite the efforts of reformers open dissemination of birth control information remained illegal in many states through the 1950s. In the early 1960s a number of issues forced a reevaluation of national policy on birth control. Particularly important was the release in the United States of a contraceptive pill that enabled every woman to control her fertility if given access to the proper information. Scientists and physicians hailed the pill as a major breakthrough in birth control, advocating its wide dispersal while refusing to acknowledge the risks it might pose to some women. Many women accepted the pill as a convenient, safe form of contraception. It met a widespread need for reliable fertility control, for it appeared just as increasing numbers of married women were entering the wage labor force. Unmarried women also sought reliable birth control in increasing numbers. More young women postponed marriage to complete college and to enter professional schools or the labor force. The women's movement advocated greater freedom from pregnancy as a necessity for women's wider public roles. It heralded effective birth control as a boon to women's lives.

Government response to these pressures came via the judiciary. In 1965 the Supreme Court granted all women access to information about birth control when it stated in *Griswold* v. *Connecticut* that an individual's right to privacy included the decision to use contraception. Widespread belief in global overpopulation, combined with women's militant desire for greater sexual freedom as expressed in the women's movement of the 1960s, led to widespread acceptance of birth control both within and outside of marriage.

Abortion

Unmarried women and men always have made the greatest efforts to prevent pregnancy. During much of American history births outside of marriage were illegal and were considered serious moral failings. Secular and religious punishment for extramarital sexual activity, especially when it led to pregnancy, could be severe, with women suffering harsher penalties than men. Enforcement of legal codes on "illegitimate births" varied widely across time and place, but society in general frowned on unwed motherhood. Contraceptive methods were so unreliable, however, that women often became pregnant outside marriage and had to resort to abortion, or, less frequently, infanticide. Published medicinal recipe books and women's own private collections of recipes from the seventeenth century through the middle of the nineteenth century invariably contained remedies to promote menstruation or remove "stoppages" and "obstructions." The failure to identify these medicines openly as abortifacients demonstrates a widespread taboo on acknowledging sexual activity outside of marriage or the desire to abort within marriage. Sexual purity remained the ideal for unmarried women, and frequent births gave status to matrons as symbols of health, strength, and submission to God's will. Yet the frequency with which abortifacients were included in collections of medicinal recipes indicates an unspoken acknowledgment of their importance and utility. This is particularly striking in light of the fact that recipes for spermicides were uncommon in similar collections. Abortion, rather than contraception, was the primary form of birth control before it became illegal in the second half of the nineteenth century.

Abortion, rather than contraception, was the primary form of birth control before it became illegal in the second half of the nineteenth century.

American toleration of abortion as a form of fertility limitation can be understood only in the context of early modern beliefs about fetal development. In the seventeenth century, when the American legal tradition was established, western Europeans made an important distinction between the abortion of a fetus before and after quickening. Quickening, the first sensation of fetal movement felt by the mother, varies from woman to woman but occurs generally about halfway through a pregnancy, at four and a half to five months (later for a first pregnancy, earlier in subsequent ones). The distinction between an abortion conducted before or after quickening—a distinction that was both psychologically and legally significant—lasted in many areas of the United States until the second half of the nineteenth century.

According to early American medical understanding, only after quickening could a woman be sure she was pregnant. Before that time, cessation of menstrual flow might be an indication of disease. A woman might believe that her periods were unnaturally blocked and that medical intervention was necessary to remove the obstruction and restore her to health. If she knew or suspected she was pregnant, she still could feel justified in seeking an abortion because she did not regard the fetus as fully alive. In the era before complete medical understanding of fetal development, quickening marked the point at which a fetus was considered to be a separate person. It had no soul before quickening, according to some religious authorities, and it had not demonstrated its independent existence through movement, according to medical wisdom. It was a part of the pregnant woman, an extraneous part that could be removed without ethical constraint. Therefore, healers, midwives, and formally trained physicians could respond to a woman's pleas for help without qualms, even if they suspected she was pregnant rather than "obstructed."

By the middle of the nineteenth century, the longstanding American custom of secret abortion practices had changed. Abortion became socially acceptable, widely acknowledged as a means of family limitation for the married as well as a distasteful but necessary step for the unmarried. Advertisements in newspapers and magazines testified to people's greater willingness to acknowledge abortion. Similarly, in home health guides authors more blatantly discussed women's need for abortions and the means by which to procure them with drugs or instruments.

Historians believe that beginning around 1840 the incidence of abortion rose dramatically in the United States. James C. Mohr posits that by the Civil War era there was one abortion for every five or six live births, whereas at the beginning of the nineteenth century the figure was one for every twenty-five to thirty live births. While Americans always had tolerated if not condoned abortion before quickening for single women, now changing social conditions led to widespread reliance on abortion among married women. Beginning at mid-century among white, middle- and upper-class, native-born and Protestant Americans from all regions of the country, smaller families became highly desirable, even fashionable. Changing religious beliefs no longer demanded women's submission to their biological destiny; a condition of fewer births per woman was acceptable to the Protestant establishment. Urbanization made large families more expensive to maintain, and help with childcare became difficult to find. Couples with young children increasingly lived far from relatives, and young single women could find wage work that paid better than household service. Higher expectations for parenting, particularly the mothering of young children, made smaller families necessary. And finally, educated women's rising sense of self-worth led them to demand freedom from the discomforts, pain, and fear of death associated with frequent pregnancies.

Considerable evidence indicates the willingness of couples in these social groups to employ various forms of contraception to prevent pregnancy. Reliance on vaginal douches, suppositories, and condoms increased. Probably the nature of intercourse changed as well, with coitus interruptus and oral and anal intercourse gaining greater acceptance. Periodic abstinence, and the widespread Victorian belief in women's distaste for frequent sexual intercourse also helped lower the birthrate. But when all of these failed and a pregnancy occurred, women turned to abortion as a last resort.

Among other social groups, abortion occurred less frequently. New immigrants, particularly Catholics, continued to have large families, and even native-born Catholics resisted the national trend toward fewer births per woman. As demonstrated by Mohr, one exception to the pattern among new immigrants was the Germans. Advertisements for abortion services in the German-language press were common. Lower-class, native-born Americans imitated the patterns of immigrants more than those of their more prosperous native-born counterparts. They continued to raise larger-than-average families. Evidence is slim for nineteenth-century blacks, although some historical evidence indicates that enslaved African Americans did practice abortion as a form of resistance.

The nineteenth-century upsurge in abortion alarmed many Americans, both for the changing mores it indicated and the physical dangers it presented to women. Before the Civil War, however, beliefs about quickening prevented full-scale moral outrage against abortion because most married women sought abortions early in pregnancy, before quickening occurred. The first public outcries against abortion were aimed at practitioners rather than patients. Unscrupulous and ignorant abortionists who endangered womens' health by administering poisonous drugs received heavy public censure. Early legislation, enacted in the 1840s and 1850s, equated abortifacients with poisons and aimed at punishing those who prescribed the powerful drugs. During this period the quickening doctrine remained largely intact, with only a few states making the administration of drugs to women before quickening a criminal offense. Although concern for women's health seemed the impetus for early legislation, such concern was limited to women whose fetuses had developed to a recognized point. Admittedly, abortion became more dangerous as the fetus grew, but the distinction between a quickened and unquickened fetus was largely anachronistic once concern became focused on the dangers of abortifacients.

Under the leadership of the newly organized American Medical Association (1847), that anachronism was eliminated. Beginning in 1855, the AMA led a successful campaign to make all abortions illegal. "Regular physicians" (the term applied to those practitioners recognized by the organization) regarded quickening as irrelevant to the question of when a fetus began its life as a being separate from its mother. They sharply criticized "irregular physicians" and midwives for endangering women's health with harmful drugs and improperly performed instrumental abortions. Ironically, regular physicians became important in the movement to criminalize abortion during the same period when their own ability to perform instrumental abortions improved considerably, due both to rising professional standards and greater understanding of fetal development and the gravid uterus. Historians believe their campaign was directed at least in part at eliminating competition from unlicensed caregivers. Public sentiment was ripe for physicians' claims, however, and legislation enacted in the 1860s and 1870s made both abortionists and their clients criminally liable. Slowly after 1860, and intensifying in the 1870s, legislators and judges developed a consensus against abortion echoed in the public mind; convictions in cases of abortion grew easier to obtain. At the same time, anti-obscenity laws and a prohibition against advertising made it difficult for women to learn about abortion services. By the 1880s abortion rates had dropped, and once again only the most desperate women, particularly the unmarried, were seeking abortions.

The nineteenth-century shift in attitudes toward abortion reflects a number of factors. First, many Americans feared the social ramifications of abortion as it was practiced at midcentury. Nativist and racist attitudes fed fears that the nation would suffer if white, educated, prosperous, native-born citizens lowered their birthrates while immigrant, ignorant, and impoverished residents reproduced in large numbers. Restrictions on abortions represented a public policy favoring high birthrates for all Americans. Second, physicians acted to promote their own position as policymakers in campaigning against abortion. Their newly established professional status enabled them to influence public opinion in a significant way, at the same time that they solidified their position as the sole authorities on women's health. Finally, by the late nineteenth century many educated women with access to physician-controlled information on birth control had adopted methods that helped them avoid unwanted pregnancies, lowering their tolerance for those women less skilled than themselves.

The abortion policies established in the nineteenth century lasted until the 1960s, when about a third of the states revised their statutes in the direction of greater tolerance. Public opinion had shifted away from the restrictive position of the second half of the nineteenth century, returning to a standard much like that of the colonial and early national periods. Changing sexual mores meant widespread toleration for premarital intercourse, but most unmarried women remained unwilling to bear children. Wide availability of effective forms of contraception, now including the birth control pill, had given women and men so much control over their fertility that in the event of an unwanted pregnancy, they demanded access to abortion as a means of guaranteeing control. Estimates vary, but experts agree that by the late 1960s at least one million illegal abortions occurred annually in the United States. According to Alfred Kinsey (1894–1956) and associates, one out of every four American women had an abortion at some time in her life. The number was thought to be higher among poor women. Nineteenth-century fears and concerns about the safety of abortion had evaporated. When conducted by a physician in a proper facility, an abortion was significantly safer than going full-term with a pregnancy and delivery. In addition, Americans had come to fear overpopulation in general more than underpopulation by elite social groups. And significantly, most physicians had reversed their earlier ethical stand against family limitation, favoring fuller and easier access to all birth control methods, including abortion.

In response to changing attitudes, legislators in many states had begun to dismantle outdated laws restricting abortion. Against this backdrop, the United States Supreme Court handed down an opinion in 1973 that standardized abortion policy throughout the country. *Roe* v. *Wade* established a woman's right to abortion on demand through the first trimester and, with her physician's consent, through the second trimester of pregnancy. Only in the third trimester was abortion restricted to those cases in which it is necessary to save the life of the mother. At that point, the Court majority declared, the state has a legitimate interest in protecting the life of the fetus, which has become capable in most instances of sustaining itself outside the uterus. American abortion policy after 1973 was thus remarkably similar to that of the early national period, with the concept of viability being substituted for that of quickening.

Opponents of abortion were horrified by the decision of the Supreme Court in *Roe* v. *Wade*. They saw the new abortion policy of the United States as criminal, one that would result in countless deaths of "unborn children," as they termed aborted fetuses. Catholic clergymen in particular decried abortion rights for women, and immediately began a campaign to overturn the decision of the Supreme Court. The Catholic church maintained a leadership position in the anti-abortion movement, which grew slowly in the late 1970s and early 1980s. Then, in the mid 1980s, the movement gained considerable strength from Protestant radicals, fundamentalists who initiated militant anti-abortion tactics such as attempts to close abortion clinics and the harassment of physicians known to perform abortions. They regarded their activities as divinely inspired and termed themselves "pro-life." In general, opponents of abortion described themselves as frequent churchgoers and political conservatives. They advocated traditional roles for women, opposing the Equal Rights Amendment, and criticizing women for placing their own needs above those of their unborn children. Alternatively, most "pro-choice" advocates, as supporters of abortion rights were called, described themselves as infrequent churchgoers or not religious, and supported women's active public roles. They were more politically progressive than their opponents on abortion, supporting, for example, the Equal Rights Amendment.

The two groups have great difficulty communicating with each other. Each believes its position is the only morally correct one. Compromise has proved impossible, as anti-abortion activists equate abortion with murder, while pro-abortion advocates believe restrictions on abortion represent coercive repression of women's individual freedom.

Anti-abortion sentiment grew dramatically in strength under the political leadership of President Ronald Reagan (1980–1988). Leaders of the early anti-abortion movement had focused on the need to elect politicians such as Reagan who would fight to change abortion laws. In particular, they hoped to change the composition of the Supreme Court, filling it with pro-life justices, but they also worked for the appointment of lower federal court judges who would interpret *Roe*

v. *Wade* conservatively. On both fronts, they were successful. One significant result was the decision of the Supreme Court in *Webster* v. *Reproductive Health Services* (1989), which upheld the right of state governments to impose certain restrictions on abortion availability. The future of abortion rights remains unclear, as the Supreme Court prepares to hear new cases on women's right to abortion.

Birth

Until the third decade of the twentieth century, when women began as a matter of routine to deliver in hospitals, birth was a home-centered event, dominated by the female friends and relatives of the parturient woman. Even after women requested the presence of physicians—usually male—at their births, they continued to exercise significant control during labor and delivery. Women and their female attendants decided if and when to have a male physician present and what procedures he would be allowed to perform. Until late in the nineteenth century, when the birthrate dropped to less than four children per woman, the cycle of pregnancy, birth, and lactation dominated the majority of women's lives. They remained occupied on a daily basis not only with their own cycles, but with those of relatives, friends, and neighbors. To be excluded from a neighbor's childbed was a slight, inclusion an acknowledgment of close female bonds. Thus for most of American history, the nature of women's childbirth experiences has been determined according to women's desires, and birth has been a major component of women's culture.

In the seventeenth and first half of the eighteenth century in the colonies, European women prepared for childbirth in the traditions of their mothers. They arranged in advance to be attended by a local midwife, and if possible by a number of relatives, neighbors, and friends. Only in the most isolated areas would white women deliver alone or with only their husbands in attendance. Birth was a social event in women's lives, a time when women gathered together to share the burdens of their biological role. For the most part, men were excluded from the rituals of birth. While male neighbors and relatives might be responsible for helping women get to the home of a laboring woman, once the flooding roads or snowbanks were crossed the men simply turned around and went home. Even husbands found themselves largely excluded. They visited the woman in labor, but left when the pains increased or birth seemed imminent. Most husbands went about their daily chores, anxious and concerned, but separated, ignorant of the birth process. Women wanted it that way.

Parturient women in the New England and middle colonies rarely found themselves so isolated that they could not be attended by several women, at least one of whom was knowledgeable about midwifery. This was less generally the case in the colonial South (and, later, the western frontier), where families more often lived on isolated farms, miles from their nearest neighbor. Whenever possible, a female relative would come to stay with a pregnant woman as her time for delivery approached, or the midwife might come early and await the onset of labor for days or even weeks. Sometimes a woman, particularly for a first birth, might travel to her mother's or sister's home for the birth. Often, however, women faced labor with only their husbands or nearest neighbors to help them. Given Englishwomen's culture of social birth in an exclusively female setting, this must have been considered a great hardship. On the larger plantations beginning late in the colonial period, black and white women regularly attended each other in childbirth, but we can only speculate on the possibility of female bonding across the color line.

Unlike white women, and African American women living among whites, Native American women experienced childbirth with only a midwife and mother or other female relative present. In the eastern tribes, a woman generally left her home and went into an unsettled area to deliver, either in the open or in a little hut built specifically for the birth. Most new mothers returned to their homes soon, and barring injury or infection resumed their normal activities. Among some tribes, however, a period of quarantine was observed, and newly delivered women lived alone for forty days before returning to their families.

Native American women's culture demanded that they withstand the pains of childbirth silently. Their rapid resumption of normal work loads after birth testified to their health, stamina, and courage, and led

Birth was a social event in women's lives, a time when women gathered together to share the burdens of their biological role.

many early commentators to write that they experienced no pain in childbirth. In the colonial settlements, white and black women acknowledged their pain openly, and whenever possible rested for days or—in the case of wealthy women—weeks after a birth. Pregnancy and parturition were regarded as dangerous, even critical, states, and women referred to themselves as ill, sick, or in distress. They expected, and received, special treatment until their recoveries were complete. This was true even for many enslaved African Americans, whose childbearing capacity was valued by owners. Slave women's work loads generally were reduced during pregnancy, and they were given a period of time following birth to recover their strength before resuming work at a reduced pace.

Women in all cultural groups remained active during parturition, walking, standing, and sitting up rather than lying down to promote labor. Native American women often pulled on a strap hung above their heads during intense labor. White and African American women frequently sat up to give birth, pushing against a footboard or the floor, supported by two or three women attendants. Birthing stools, common in western Europe during this period, were available in more densely settled areas, but most women probably did without them. Rituals were universal among women, governing all aspects of pregnancy and birth. An African American midwife might place an ax under the bed of a parturient woman to "cut" her labor pains. Indian women of the Fox tribe observed special dietary rules to guarantee safe deliveries, such as avoiding nuts that might prevent the fetus from breaking out of the amniotic membrane, and crawfish that might cause a breech birth. Englishwomen wore lode-stones or coral to prevent spontaneous abortion, removing them during labor to speed delivery. All these techniques were psychologically comforting, giving women a sense of control in the face of their fears of injury and death.

Midwives in all cultural groups possessed knowledge about fetal development and the process of birth that were of great assistance when difficulties arose. Some midwives could turn the baby in utero to prevent breech births; others massaged and stretched perineal tissues to ease the delivery of head and shoulders without causing tears. Many knew the value of various herbs and potions: ergot strengthened contractions, mint syrup quieted nausea. And all but the most ignorant realized the importance of the full discharge of the afterbirth, and how to aid its expulsion manually or with medicines. For the most part, midwives were respected for their skill, knowledge, and dedication in easing women's suffering.

Although historians disagree about the extent to which midwives interfered unnecessarily in the process of birth, thereby causing injuries and infections, European women in the era before the founding of the American colonies uniformly sought their assistance and regarded the presence of a midwife as beneficial if not essential. Midwives generally occupied positions of respect in their communities, particularly among women. At the same time, certain negative attitudes toward midwives and female healers persisted throughout the early modern period. Particularly in the sixteenth and seventeenth centuries, midwives' powers over the process of pregnancy, birth, and recovery could lead to suspicion of criminal activity when things went wrong. Midwives were mistrusted in particular for their ability to provide abortifacients and otherwise interfere with pregnancy, birth, and sexual activity. Such suspicions occasionally led to accusations of witchcraft.

The transition from reliance on female midwives to male physicians began in urban areas in the second half of the eighteenth century. (Medical schools were closed to women in the United States until the second half of the nineteenth century.) Initially, modesty and traditional ideas about male-female interactions made it unpleasant for women to employ men as childbed assistants. But women's fears, and the evidence men gave of their skill in managing childbirth, allowed parturient women to overcome their misgivings and invite men into the birthing room. While prior to 1760 male physicians assisted only in the most life-threatening cases, after that time men attended normal births in ever increasing numbers. Nineteenth-century women were, if anything, eager to experiment with new birthing techniques. Highly experimental drugs were taken by wealthy, educated women. The first woman to give birth under ether, for example, was Frances Appleton Longfellow, wife of the poet, in 1847. Early advocates of "twilight sleep," an unconscious state induced by scopolamine and morphine, also came from prosperous and educated backgrounds. Such examples demonstrate women's active attempts to reduce the pain and trauma of childbirth.

Although women were convinced that medical science could help them avoid injury and death in childbirth, the historical evidence on the benefits of physician-attended birth in the late eighteenth and nineteenth centuries is less clear. Some physicians' techniques were dangerous—bloodletting in cases of hemorrhage, for example, or administration of laudanum to slow contractions. Forceps delivery could increase a woman's pain and lead to severe injury to the woman or her baby if used improperly. At the same time, drugs could aid a woman in relaxing enough to promote delivery, and forceps saved infants and mothers from death in instances where delivery was impossible without them. We can only conclude that physicians' interventions could be beneficial when properly employed. The question remains, much as in the case of midwives for earlier centuries: How often did caregivers make mistakes due to ignorance or errors in judgment?

Significant historical evidence indicates that male physicians intervened in the birth process more often than midwives, both because their training prepared them to, and because their patients expected intervention. Called in to assist midwives and female attendants, men did not feel comfortable in a passive role. They wanted to justify their presence by taking medical action to hasten delivery and reduce pain. For many physicians, however, inadequate medical training and hasty decisions led to accidents resulting in uterine, vaginal, or perineal tears, and fetal injuries. As a result of frequent injuries, even leaders in obstetric medicine decried unnecessary forceps delivery as dangerous for mother and child. In lectures and textbooks they wrote that the new technique could be beneficial, but that errors in judgment had led to abuse. As a result of malpractice, accusations of "meddlesome midwifery" followed physicians throughout the nineteenth century.

"Meddling" in the normal process of birth frequently led to infections as well as injuries. Physicians' greater tendency to examine women during labor, as well as their use of forceps, led to the introduction of infected material into the woman's bloodstream, either through the wound resulting from placental separation or a perineal laceration. Until the introduction of antibiotics in the twentieth century, women often died from infections, referred to generally as puerperal fever. The number of deaths probably rose in conjunction with men's increasing presence in the birthing room, as their active interventions made it more likely infection would be transmitted. Unlike midwives, moreover, physicians often went from sickbed to childbed, carrying bacterial infections with them.

The evidence is considerable that attendance by a male physician carried a risk as well as a possible benefit to a woman in childbed. On the whole, it was probably safer to employ a midwife during the nineteenth century, unless a woman had access to one of the few highly skilled urban practitioners who taught obstetrics and understood the danger as well as the value of active intervention. Despite physicians' inadequacies, however, by the turn of the twentieth century about half of the babies born in the United States were delivered by physicians. Ironically, disadvantaged women—poor, of African American and Native American descent, or newly immigrated—may have suffered fewer complications in birth due to their inability to command regular medical care. Relegated by society to traditional home births attended by midwives, they escaped the "meddlesome midwifery" more privileged women faced in their physician-attended deliveries. And again ironically, the most desperate women—poor, single, and living in urban slums—may have experienced the best of modern medical care in their confinements, as professor-obstetricians treated them in medical schools while teaching their growing number of students.

Over the course of the nineteenth century, medical training improved and knowledge expanded. Increasing numbers of medical students received practical as well as theoretical training, as poor women became more willing to deliver in the charity wards of medical school hospitals. Of particular importance was scientific discovery in the area of bacteriology, following the path-breaking work of Louis Pasteur in the 1860s. By the end of the century physicians were accepting a hypothesis that had horrified them only decades before: that they were responsible for maternal deaths due to puerperal fever. By the decade of the 1880s, most were taking steps to ensure cleanliness, of themselves, the parturient woman, and the delivery room. It was this belief in the necessity for sterile conditions that prompted many physicians to argue strongly for restricting births to hospitals. They found it impossible to enforce cleanliness in private homes, particularly the homes of the poor. Doctors also preferred hospitals because the availability of trained help and proper equipment made their jobs easier. They did not have to travel in unfamiliar neighborhoods in bad weather or after dark. And most important, they exercised more control over the patient in a hospital; it was the doctor's domain, rather than the parturient woman's.

Ironically, it was the most desperate women—poor and single—who may have experienced the best of modern medical care, as professor-obstetricians at the turn of the century treated them in medical schools while teaching their growing number of students.

The movement to hospital births marks a major shift in women's birth experiences. It occurred for the majority of women between 1910 and 1930, and according to historian Judith Leavitt two factors were important in facilitating the shift. First, after the advent of bacteriological studies, medical knowledge became less comprehensible to the common person. At the same time, physicians increasingly applied their new knowledge to the successful control of infectious disease, giving rise to greater faith in medicine generally. As a result of both this mystification of medicine and increased confidence in its benefits, people became more willing to follow doctors' advice and go to hospitals for medical care. A second factor was necessary, however, to make women forego the comfort of a home birth. Leavitt argues convincingly that twentieth-century women no longer had the support they needed from female friends and relatives for home births. Urbanization and mobility were splitting families and creating anonymous environments for many women. Women's increasing responsibility within their own homes, as husbands and older children went out to work and school, made it difficult for them to attend each other for more than short periods of time, and growing reliance on the medical profession made them less skillful as nurses. Into this void stepped the professional staff of the hospital, skillful and able to care for mother and child until they were fully recovered. Women's need for professional care in the twentieth century helped them overcome their fears about hospital deliveries, despite the fact that maternal mortality rates remained high for hospital births until the advent of antibiotics at midcentury. Only then did the hospital become in reality a safer place to deliver a baby. Women, then, turned to hospitals at least as much out of need as desire. By 1940, 55 percent of births took place in hospitals. In 1950 the figure was 88 percent, and in 1960 almost all births outside of some isolated areas occurred in hospitals.

The change from home to hospital deliveries caused women to lose control over the process of birth. As demonstrated by Leavitt, it is a popular misconception that women rapidly surrendered control over childbirth to the medical establishment once doctors began to attend home deliveries. Throughout the nineteenth and early twentieth centuries, the physician-attended home-delivery norm had allowed women to retain considerable power. At home, women were in familiar surroundings, advised and cared for by relatives and friends who could help them maintain control over their birth experiences. Physicians complained frequently about their inability to give medical care in the face of determined female opposition. In hospitals, women found themselves alone; once a woman placed herself into the hands of a physician and hospital staff, they made all decisions about her delivery: whom she could see, whether she could walk, sit, or lie down, what drugs she should have, whether she should have an episiotomy, and so on.

Women's attempts to regain control over birth is ongoing, a story of the 1970s and 1980s that continues right up to the present. The natural childbirth movement of those decades was an attempt by women to experience birth in a safe environment—a hospital or birthing center—without resorting to drugs, particularly drugs that caused unconsciousness or semiconsciousness. Women in the movement advocated medical intervention only when necessary to preserve their health and the health of their infants, but they wanted to determine when and under what conditions drugs, fetal monitors, and other intrusive procedures would be employed. The hope was that no drugs would be necessary, that women could control their responses to the pain of childbirth enough so that they could remain fully conscious and in control. In this connection the psychoprophylactic techniques of the French physician Fernand Lamaze (1890–1957) were highly important. A smaller group of women in this movement wanted home births, and they argued that the benefits of medical intervention did not outweigh the problems of the alienating hospital environment. Particularly important for these women was the presence of familiar surroundings and the emotional support of husbands, other family members, and friends. The home-birth movement has placed pressure on hospitals to create homelike birthing rooms for labor and delivery and to allow husbands and others (usually mothers, sisters, or female friends) to remain with the parturient woman.

In the early years, the natural childbirth movement was highly class-specific, begun and popularized by upper- and upper-middle-class women. It thereby followed the pattern established by women in earlier periods of change, for women of means also had led the movement for physician-attended and hospital births in the nineteenth century. Poor women have always been dependent on society's decisions regarding their birth experiences, and middle-class or less well-educated women have always been slower to accept change than their wealthier and better-educated counterparts. In the 1990s natural childbirth is still largely unavailable to the poor and uneducated, who remain dependent on public welfare for medical care. Trained to believe they have few or no options in the kind of medical care they receive, they ask few questions and therefore remain ignorant of birth options.

Parenthood

The history of parenthood received scant attention until the 1970s, when feminist and social historians began to investigate issues ranging from inheritance patterns to the nature of motherhood. Most work has focused on the nineteenth century, and the relationship between industrialization, urbanization, and changing parental roles. Historians have emphasized the need of nineteenth-century men to leave their families for most of the day in order to work at wage labor, while mothers (at least, those living above the subsistence level) remained at home where they assumed the roles of fathers in supervising children. Unfortunately, maternal roles have received greater attention than paternal ones, but in recent years historians such as Elaine May have begun to look seriously at fathers as well as mothers. Much historical work remains to be done in this area of family life, particularly for the colonial periods and the twentieth century.

NURSING. With the birth of her infant, a woman entered the third phase of her reproductive cycle: lactation. Although women in many cultural settings employed wet nurses during the early modern period, colonial women, whether African American, Native American, or European, nursed their own infants. For wealthy European women, and even some in the middling ranks, this represented a break from tradition, but the colonial population was too thin and dispersed to allow ready availability of wet nurses. Moreover, some religious groups such as the Puritans and Quakers encouraged maternal nursing as ordained by God, the duty of a responsible mother. Native Americans lived in egalitarian settings in which no woman had to provide lactation services for another, while enslaved Africans came from societies in which maternal breast-feeding was the norm.

The length of time women nursed their children varied significantly, both among cultural groups and individuals, but the lower limit for everyone was about one year. Observers reported much longer nursing periods for many Native American and African groups, ranging from two to five years. Sexual abstinence to protect the mother's milk supply was the rule during breast-feeding for many of these peoples, although lapses were common. Native Americans opposed pregnancy during breast-feeding to such a degree that nursing women observed a custom of self-induced abortion if they became pregnant. This allowed them to avoid the strain of nourishing both a fetus and an infant at the same time. Europeans gave lip service to sexual abstinence during breast-feeding, and a belief in its efficacy may have led originally to the widespread use of wet nurses among the elite, but by the seventeenth century the custom was disregarded. Only for women with a history of resumption of menstruation during breast-feeding did abstinence remain important. These women probably observed periodic abstinence in order to achieve two-year birth intervals. Most Native American women were able to maintain longer birth intervals of three to four years.

Under slavery, African patterns of infant nurture changed. Particularly in the late eighteenth and nineteenth centuries, women on farms and plantations in the Upper South were encouraged to produce as many children as possible, and some were granted incentives such as work reductions and increased rations in exchange for high fertility. Breast-feeding in those cases was reduced to the minimum needed for survival. Although most white women breast-fed their own infants, those who employed slaves as wet nurses demanded the early weaning of the nurses' infants. And finally, owners who were not as interested in infant survival as they were in the productive capacity of their workers, cut nursing time severely. African American women did not have the freedom to determine their own patterns of infant nurture.

Bottle- or spoon-feeding (called bringing an infant up "by hand") enjoyed a brief popularity at the end of the eighteenth century in England and in some areas of the United States. An increased understanding of the need for fresh milk made it slightly more healthful than in previous periods. But infants usually sickened and died under the regimen, and physicians advised strongly against it. Breast-feeding for an infant's first year remained the cultural norm in the United States until the twentieth century, when—by the decade of the 1940s—it had been replaced by an almost universal reliance on infant formula. The reasons for this shift were numerous. Improvements in the nutritional value of formula, coupled with an increased understanding of the need for boiled water and sterilized bottles and nipples, had made bottle-feeding healthier for infants. Probably of equal importance was commercial promotion of formula through advertising and the distribution of free samples in hospitals. Finally, physicians largely supported bottle-feeding over breast-feeding, heralding the "scientific" accuracy that could accompany scheduled feedings of uniform amounts of formula. They did not yet understand the important health benefits to infants of maternal antibodies. It was not until 1979 that the American Academy of Pediatrics and the Canadian Paediatric Society made a joint statement advocating breast-feeding over bottle-feeding as a matter of policy.

Among educated women, breast-feeding has enjoyed a resurgence in popularity since the 1970s, when research demonstrated the unquestionable benefits of breastmilk to infant health.

Among educated women, breast-feeding has enjoyed a resurgence in popularity since the 1970s, when research demonstrated the unquestionable benefits of breastmilk to infant health. But cultural antipathy to women's breast-feeding in public, resulting in large part from a twentieth-century emphasis on breasts as the focus of sexual desire rather than infant nurture, has made it difficult for many women to breast-feed despite the advantages for their infants.

PARENTAL ROLES. Major shifts in attitudes toward parental roles have occurred from the colonial period until the present day. In the late twentieth century, patterns of child rearing show interesting similarities to those of the colonial period, while parents in the nineteenth and first half of the twentieth century occupied roles that can no longer be sustained in modern life.

Like colonial parents, women and men today increasingly rely on the income generated by both parents to run their households. As a result of women's widening role as wage earners, men are spending more time with their children. Also like colonial parents, women and men in the late twentieth century depend on outside help to care for their children. In the colonial and early national periods, women's high fertility and the amount of physical effort and time needed to run a household made help, either that of servants or unmarried female relatives, essential rather than a luxury. Matrons at all wealth levels depended on the labor of teenaged girls, and to be deprived of such help was considered a hardship. By the middle of the nineteenth century, when birthrates were declining and modern conveniences such as bakeries and fabric stores were increasing, servant help was common only among the elite. Middle-class women ran their households themselves, or with the help of their older children. Working-class women always have had to combine wage earning with child rearing, employing strategies ranging from laboring at home on piecework to reliance on relatives, neighbors, and older children for child care.

During the nineteenth century, farm and artisan families shrank in number, and well-entrenched patterns of domestic labor shifted accordingly. Over time, increasing numbers of men and older children worked for wages outside the home, in jobs that were often unrelated to each other. Families became units of consumption rather than units of production, a shift that historian Mary Ryan posits was of great historical importance.

As the necessity of women's economic contributions declined among nineteenth-century (and later, twentieth-century) middle- and upper-class families, matrons assumed increased personal control over their children's care and education. Men, working outside the home for much of the day, became distanced from their children, playing a reduced role in discipline and education. In particular, men lost their primary role of overseeing the training of older sons. In the colonial and early national periods, many fathers trained their sons in their own occupations, or took direct responsibility for settling boys in apprenticeships. In addition, they assumed management of sons' daily activities after about the age of seven, with mothers continuing the supervision of daughters. In the nineteenth century, however, fathers relied increasingly on schools to train their children, or sent them into the work force to be supervised by others. At the same time, women assumed almost exclusive control over the religious education of their youngsters, replacing men as the primary arbiters of moral values. The rise of the "moral mother," as she was called in the early nineteenth century, left men with a sharply reduced role in children's religious development at the same time that women came to exercise increased control over the training and discipline of both daughters and sons.

These new economic and emotional relationships within the family resulted in significant changes in the structure of domestic authority. In particular, the traditional pattern of patriarchal dominance and wifely submission eroded. By midcentury, Americans were praising the gentle, persuasive governance of mothers over the rigid authority of the paterfamilias. The impetuses behind this change were numerous, but essential was the fact that the mother remained in close, daily contact with her children. They turned to her for guidance, as her domestic role expanded to cover tasks previously defined as male. From the standpoint of society, mothers alone assumed the key role previously accorded to both fathers and mothers. Their task was to produce useful, honest citizens, to mold the character of the next generation.

Middle- and upper-class women's preeminence in the home in the second half of the nineteenth century served as a substitute for their lack of political and economic power in society generally. One important control their new domestic role gave them was sexual. Women's increased power in the home gave them the ability to refuse their husband's sexual demands, and Victorian women became associated with sexual restraint. Although women undoubtedly paid a high price for their supposed distaste for frequent sexual relations, losing intimacy with their husbands, they gained control over their fertility. Throughout the nineteenth and early twentieth centuries, women's fertility declined steadily, due to a number of factors including restraint. The benefits for women were significant. Once women's childbearing role was restricted to a relatively short period of time, increased emphasis could be placed on the higher education of girls and young women, leading to careers in public service and the professions. Working class and immigrant women experienced greater difficulty in controlling their fertility, leaving them without the freedom of their wealthier counterparts. Recognition of this discrepancy led reformers to fight for poor women's access to birth control information. Once birth control became socially acceptable, women in all social classes were freer to discard the restraints of Victorian sexuality, and the modern sexual revolution was born.

In the second half of the twentieth century, increasing numbers of married women sought employment outside the home. By 1990 more than 50 percent of women with children under the age of six worked for wages. A number of factors, including both the positive—greater educational opportunities for women, and the negative—an increase in the cost of living relative to wages, resulted in married women's decisions to work outside the home. Of key importance, however, was women's declining fertility. Low fertility has meant that although child care is expensive, it is a necessity for only a relatively short period of time. For most parents, the expense of child care is offset by the advantages of a second paycheck. Many parents complain, however, about the difficulty of locating good child care close to their homes or places of work. The United States is behind other industrialized nations in providing adequate child care to working parents.

More difficult than obtaining good child care for many women is the problem of convincing husbands to assume an equal share of household tasks. In the late twentieth century, men are finding that they cannot imitate the distant roles of their fathers and grandfathers, but instead must play an active part in caring for their children and homes. Infant and child nurture is now an essential part of fatherhood as well as motherhood, but many men are resistant and women continue to bear most of the double burden of wage work and housework.

In addition, families with two wage-earning parents must cope with the problems of care of sick children and aged or invalid parents. There are few resources for overburdened families in the United States today, and recent legislative proposals for improving support services have not been successful. Without the tightly knit, interdependent families and communities of early America, and without the full-time labor of nineteenth-century matrons, American families today face serious problems in meeting the needs of dependent members. Already well embarked on a new economic course based on two-paycheck families, we have not yet found the means to replace old systems of domestic labor requiring women's full-time presence in the home.

Despite current problems in supporting the work of families, the strength of Americans' commitment to the nuclear family, is unquestioned. It remains the seat of our most vital emotional attachments, the focus of our need for love and companionship. To guarantee the stability of the family, policymakers are beginning to explore new definitions of the workplace, and the relationship of individuals to their work. Programs such as extended parental leaves in the event of family illness, job-sharing plans, and temporary part-time work options are being discussed as a means of accommodating society's need for stable, secure families. New parental roles—especially maternal ones—have solidified rapidly in recent decades, but the social changes necessary to safeguard the family are yet unrealized. Given Americans' belief in family values, this will remain a priority for business, political, and social leaders into the next century.

[See also Adolescence; Courtship, Marriage, Separation, and Divorce; Family Structures; Life Stages; Sexual Behavior and Morality.]

BIBLIOGRAPHY

General

Apple, Rima D. *Women, Health, and Medicine in America: A Historical Handbook* (1990).

Birth Control and Abortion

Gordon, Linda. *Woman's Body, Woman's Right: A Social History of Birth Control in America* (1976; rev. ed. 1990).

McLaughlin, Loretta. *The Pill, John Rock, and the Church: The Biography of a Revolution* (1982).

Mohr, James C. *Abortion in America: The Origins and Evolution of National Policy, 1800–1900.* (1978).

Tribe, Laurence, H. *Abortion: The Clash of Absolutes* (1990).

Birth

Axtell, James, ed. *The Indian Peoples of Eastern America: A Documentary History of the Sexes* (1981).

Eakins, Pamela S. *The American Way of Birth* (1986).

Hoffert, Sylvia D. *Private Matters: American Attitudes Toward Childbearing and Infant Nurture in the Urban North, 1800–1860* (1989).

Leavitt, Judith Walzer. *Brought to Bed: Childbearing in America, 1750 to 1950* (1986).

McMillen, Sally G. *Motherhood in the Old South: Pregnancy, Childbirth and Infant Rearing* (1990).

Scholten, Catherine M. *Childbearing in American Society, 1650–1850* (1985).

Ulrich, Laurel Thatcher. *Good Wives: Image and Reality in the Lives of Women in Northern New England, 1650–1750* (1982).

Ulrich, Laurel Thatcher. *A Midwife's Tale: The Life of Martha Ballard, Based on Her Diary, 1785–1812* (1990).

Wertz, Richard W., and Dorothy C. Wertz. *Lying-In: A History of Childbirth in America* (1977).

Infant Nurture and Parenthood

Bloch, Ruth H. "American Feminine Ideals in Transition: The Rise of the Moral Mother, 1785–1815." *Feminist Studies* 4, no. 2 (1978): 101–126.

Fildes, Valerie A. *Breasts, Bottles, and Babies: A History of Infant Feeding* (1986).
Jones, Jacqueline. *Labor of Love, Labor of Sorrow: Black Women, Work, and the Family from Slavery to the Present* (1985).
Tyler May, Elaine. *Homeward Bound: American Families in the Cold War Era* (1988).
Ryan, Mary P. *Cradle of the Middle Class: The Family in Oneida County, New York, 1790–1865* (1981).

— MARYLYNN SALMON

THE RESEARCH UNIVERSITY

After World War II the research university became a formidable institution in American life that acquired international distinction for its mission of combining advanced scholarship, undergraduate teaching, and public service. Leading American universities typically were large and complex, each usually having an enrollment of over twenty thousand students and an annual operating budget comparable to that of a city. A research university was a substantial part of its local economy, often hailed as a community's "largest smokeless industry." This was true not only in campus towns but also in some metropolitan areas; for example, from 1960 since Johns Hopkins University has emerged as the single largest employer in Baltimore, and Brown University played the same role in Providence.

More significant than being large employers, the major research universities became the nation's fertile source of expertise in scholarship and the learned professions. Applied research and innovations in science and technology transformed state and regional economies. What Clark Kerr called the "knowledge industry" and the "City of Intellect" in *The Uses of the University* (1963) is illustrated by Stanford's ties to the computer industry's "Silicon Valley," the University of California's part in agribusiness, the role of Harvard and Massachusetts Institute of Technology in creating Boston's "Electronics Belt," and the economic development fostered by the "Research Triangle" of Duke, North Carolina, and North Carolina State universities.

The history of the American research university is a success story leavened by criticisms and controversies. The price for its achievements was a "curse of bigness"; critics in the 1960s often spoke of the impersonality of the "multiversity." A paradox of the university's prestige was that it became the institution coveted by every state, yet it also was indicted by undergraduate students and their parents for having neglected teaching in favor of research. Herein lies a key point for working from present to past in order to reconstruct the development of the research university: its primacy in American society is relatively new. The accusation that research had usurped teaching reversed concerns about university priorities voiced in the late nineteenth century. Then the complaint would have been puzzling because the organized research effort associated with the campus was marginal.

Prelude: The "False Dawn" of the American University

The period 1780 to 1860 was the "false dawn" of the university, characterized by bold attempts to expand the classical collegiate curriculum and to make the campus a home for advanced studies. The documentary record is misleading because impressive proposals surpassed the actual operation of universities throughout the United States. A conspicuous episode was the failure to create a *national* university. Benjamin Rush's 1788 proposal for a "Federal University" foundered despite support from influential people, including two presidents: George Washington and, later, James Madison. An 1817 bill for creating a national university failed, indicating an American aversion to a central education system. College and university building was left to the initiative of states and voluntary associations.

At the state level, the creation of universities suffered an equally bleak fate. Although obtaining a charter was relatively easy, securing financial support was unlikely. For example, in Georgia, the legislature chartered the state university in 1785, without funding it. Sixteen years passed before courses were offered. When this university did open, its curriculum did not include advanced scholarship or research. Given the absence of a "true university" in the United States, over a fifty-year period, hundreds of Americans pursued post-bachelor's degree studies at European universities, especially in Germany. Upon their return, these academic "innocents abroad" told tales (often embellished and myopic) about the marvels of the German university and led disparate campaigns to introduce selected features of the continental university to American soil.

Between 1815 and 1860 there were some extraordinary innovations that tested many elements now associated with a modern university. Pioneering presidents left such established institutions as Yale and Princeton to act as educational missionaries, spreading the gospel of higher education. Horace Holley, for example, at Transylvania University in Lexington, Kentucky (one of many places to call itself the "Athens of the West"), from 1818 to 1827 led his institution beyond the classical undergraduate curriculum to modern language instruction, scientific studies, fieldwork in botany, a cosmopolitan faculty, and courses in law, commerce, and political economy. Transylvania gained local favor as Holley attracted support for its performing arts and literary groups. The result was an expansion and secularization of institutional mission that, perhaps was too effective. Eventually Transylvania's innovations offended religious denominations and most Kentucky legislators. In Tennessee, Philip Lindsley, as president of the new University of Nashville from 1825 to 1850, tried to build a single strong regional institution to counter the pattern of small, financially strapped denominations each building a college. Lindsley's extended campaign for a modern curriculum free from sectarian bickering made sense in terms of educational efficiency and regional needs, but the quarreling religious denominations never were converted to his vision.

Other presidential campaigns for a cosmopolitan university included those of Thomas Cooper at the University of South Carolina from 1820 to 1834 and of Henry Tappan at the University of Michigan from 1852 to 1863. These imaginative presidents' ideals failed to generate understanding or financial support, whether the constituency was a state legislature or a religious group. Many new institutions started in what was then known as the West were unlikely places for either wealthy or educationally sophisticated donors; as a result, they entered the ranks of forgotten experiments that were briefly exciting.

Between 1815 and 1860 pioneering presidents left such established institutions as Yale and Princeton to act as educational missionaries, spreading the gospel of higher education.

Some ideas did reach fruition. Thomas Jefferson lived to see the result of thirty years of planning when his beloved University of Virginia opened in 1819. Yet even Jefferson's "academical village" of advanced studies, modern languages, sciences, and useful arts fell short of his expectations. In New England, innovation included Francis Wayland's reform proposals to arrest declining enrollments and endowments at Brown University, where he was president from 1827 to 1855. These plans to make the campus and curriculum more useful and intellectually rigorous were ideas ahead of their time. Even though institutions went into eclipse, the experiments were resurrected by a later generation of university builders and reformers.

Institutional Roots: The "A&M" Legacy

Central to the heritage of the American university is the land-grant legacy of the Morrill Act (1862), which allocated to each state thirty thousand acres (4,800 hectares) of land for each representative and senator to which it was entitled, as an endowment for colleges that would provide instruction in agriculture, mining, mechanical arts, and military science, popularly known as "A&M." This policy ultimately would be important in developing the state universities. A distinct yet related phenomenon was the establishment of "scientific schools," either as free-standing institutions or as separate curricula grafted onto established liberal arts colleges.

The impact of the Morrill Act has often been misunderstood. Although the federal legislation was passed in 1862, its substantive role in creating comprehensive universities actually did not occur until the late nineteenth century. The policy was characterized by unexpected consequences. Even though it was intended to promote "practical arts," its terms never precluded the liberal arts. Administering land-grant monies often involved the creativity of a "bootleg curriculum": for example, a professor hired in agricultural sciences might give most attention to research in biology, with only incidental concern about crop yield. Such avoidance worked both ways, though, for farmers initially distrusted faculty experts. Furthermore, a tendency to romanticize the appeal of "useful" education in agriculture overlooked a central feature of social and geographic mobility in late-nineteenth-century American life: most students from rural areas viewed higher education as a way of moving out of farming toward law, medicine, or teaching, or into business. Thus, ironically, land-grant funding, often praised for preserving rural values, may well have had some opposite effect. Nor were the land-grant programs necessarily connected to promoting educational opportunity for low-income students, despite the A&M egalitarian lore.

Another risky claim was that the Morrill Act "created" the great state universities. Patterns in fact varied from state to state. In New Hampshire, the legislature originally opted to attach its state agricultural program to *private* Dartmouth College; only later did it decide to build a state agricultural college at Durham. A state's flagship university often was distinct from its land-grant campus (a distinction that still holds today)—for example, Indiana University and Purdue, the University of Michigan and Michigan State University.

Subsequent federal legislation supplemented the Morrill Act to flesh out the land-grant program. This included setting up agricultural experiment stations in accordance with the Hatch Act in 1887. The second Land Grant Act in 1890 provided A&M colleges for blacks and continuing federal support for college instruction. The Smith-Lever Act of 1914 created the Agricultural Extension Service. Hence, only after 1890 did the great state universities of the Midwest and West really take shape. This belated collective strength of the land-grant institutions was led by the lobbying of George Atherton, a political economy professor from Rutgers, who first saw the strategic possibilities for federal funding and resources. Later, as president of Pennsylvania State College (from 1882), he took the lead in organizing the land-grant colleges to have continuing presence in Washington, D.C.

The University Movement: 1870 to 1910

The research university experience shifted from adversity to success with the founding of new universities after 1870. The founding of the Johns Hopkins University in 1876 was the foremost example of a transplant of the scholarly ideals of the continental European university to the United States. It also was an exemplary combination of private philanthropy, civic support, and an able president, Daniel Coit Gilman (1875–1902). Elsewhere, outstanding new universities and their dynamic presidents included Andrew Dickson White at Cornell (1868–1885), William Rainey Harper at Chicago (1892–1906), G. Stanley Hall at Clark (1888–1919), Charles Van Hise at Wisconsin (1903–1918), James Angell at Michigan (1871–1909), Benjamin Ide Wheeler at California (1899–1919), and David Starr Jordan at Stanford (1885–1913).

Realizing the "truly modern American University" included innovations and expansions within historic institutions, for example, the introduction of the elective system by President Charles Eliot of Harvard (1869–1909) and President Nicholas Murray Butler's stewardship of Columbia University (1902–1945) as the "Colossus on the Hudson." Just as the great economic expansion of these decades was linked with "captains of industry," so university building was linked to "captains of erudition." At both old and new universities, a common denominator of presidential success was the ability to gain the support of such major philanthropists as John D. Rockefeller, Leland Stanford, Ezra Cornell, William H. Vanderbilt, and Andrew Carnegie, as well as donations from an institution's alumni and surrounding community.

The period from 1870 to 1910 saw the flowering of the "university movement" in which libraries, lectures, laboratories, research seminars, doctoral programs, and academic departments came to be familiar features of higher education. The movement's intellectual style was associated with the rise of *science:* rigorous inquiry, systematic study, and experimental design in disparate fields ranging from psychology to biology. Closely related was the development of the academic profession, including a proliferation of scholarly associations, conferences, and journals specific to individual disciplines. Shaping the modern university depended on an innovation that today is taken as a matter of course: incorporation of the professional schools—law, medicine, engineering, agriculture, education, and business—into the academic setting and campus structure. The professional schools gained academic and scholarly credibility by raising admissions standards and adopting the scholarly ethos of arts and sciences. In return, professional schools made interesting, often underrated, contributions to fulfilling the university ideal of research and development, including support of new scholarship. For example, in the 1880s, when the liberal arts faculty at the University of Pennsylvania rejected the fields of political economy and history, the faculty members in these new disciplines were welcomed into the Wharton School of Finance and Commerce.

The heroic events and figures of the university movement warrant careful consideration because they risk being simplistically portrayed as inevitable successes. If there was historic continuity in success and prestige in university building between 1870 and 1910, there was as much continuity in the confusion, contradictions, and complexities of the emergence of the research university. There was no imperative that it would assume its now familiar forms and functions. Nor was there consensus about what constituted a research university.

University Builders and the Great Debates

Although the founding of research universities dates only from the end of the nineteenth century, the institution has a much longer legacy of debate. Throughout the nineteenth and early twentieth centuries the American intelligentsia showed persistent fascination with the creation and definition of a distinctive university. A high point of interest was John W. Burgess's *The American University: When Shall It Be? Where Shall It Be? What Shall It Be?* (1884), whose title succinctly captures the debate. Although Burgess appeared to offer a timely, dispassionate inquiry, he was less interested in raising questions than in urging his own answers. He wrote:

> The primest function of the University is the discovery of *new* truth, the *increase* of knowledge in every direction. The fitting out of Academies and even Colleges with extensive laboratories, cabinets, museums, and libraries is a great waste of substance. These things all belong to the University, to be used not as curiosities to entertain, but as means to new discoveries. (Hofstadter and Smith, eds., *American Higher Education* [1961], vol. 2, p. 664)

His recipe for greatness called for three elements: urban location, proximity to great wealth, and control by a private board (instead of a state legislature). Not surprisingly, Burgess found university greatness close to home, for these were three characteristics of Columbia University in New York City, where he was professor and dean of graduate studies in political science.

Burgess concluded his lengthy prescription by noting that all this "is so patent and necessary that I need not expend time in attempting to give reasons." His tone showed that the campaigns for creating the great American university were neither modest nor objective, and the debates showed little concern for converting the uninitiated. Advocates were preoccupied with countering arguments raised within the circle of university enthusiasts, as each battled for minds and money.

This heroic period of university founding was neither coherent nor cooperative; rather, it is best seen as clashes among what Laurence Veysey has called "rival conceptions of learning," rivalries in which emphasis on scholarly research competed with piety and discipline, liberal culture, and utilitarian research. Debates over the purpose of the American university included, on the one hand, thoughtful commentary on the philosophy of education and curriculum coexisting with, on the other, the prosaic and often ruthless activities of fund-raising, faculty raiding, and keen competition for support that was bounded by few, if any, ground rules.

The heroic period of university founding—between 1870 and 1910—was neither coherent nor cooperative; it was a period of rivalries in which emphasis on scholarly research competed with piety and discipline, liberal culture, and utilitarian research.

Contours and Complexities of the University Movement

"The Essential difference between a college and university is in the way they look. A college looks backward and a university looks forward." So wrote Edwin Slosson, influential editor of *The Independent*, in his *Great American Universities* (1910, p. 374). Slosson concluded his profiles of fourteen "great American universities" with the confident claim that now one could identify what he called the "standard American university." On closer inspection, however, Slosson's observation fared less well as a conclusion and better as an intriguing hypothesis, because the complexities and compromises of university building were the truly interesting features of the institutional story.

The "university builders" tended to exaggerate their own achievements, while belittling the strength and innovation of colleges. As James Axtell has pointed out, announcing the "death of the liberal arts college" was premature. Contrary to the depictions advanced by the university builders, in the late nineteenth century such New England colleges as Amherst, Wesleyan, and Williams surpassed many of the midwestern state universities in library holdings, operating budgets, student enrollments, and faculty scholarship. Slosson acknowledged that even his great universities had split personalities, noting that the "university looks older as it is newer."

One key to popular acceptance of the research universityy was its physical facade. Whether this was the "academic Gothic" design at the University of Chicago in 1893 or the "Cathedral of Learning" at the University of Pittsburgh in 1929, civic boosters and donors wanted the modern institution at least to appear to be of great age. The American landscape became dotted with the monumental campuses, sources of local pride, even tourist attractions, in which research laboratories and libraries were clothed in the same pseudo-Gothic or Georgian Revival shells as were fieldhouses, football stadiums, and undergraduate dormitories. The research university was an American hybrid that was neither pure nor historically accurate, but was well suited to accommodating disparate activities.

The rush to proclaim the triumph of the university over the college needs to be questioned on other grounds. Few, if any, of the great emerging research universities were able to abandon the collegiate features of undergraduate curriculum and student life, a theme that permeated Abraham Flexner's 1930 critique, *Universities.* Before 1900 Johns Hopkins University and Clark University tried in vain to exist as sanctuaries for graduate studies and advanced scholarship. However, the need for tuition dollars and the public's interest in intercollegiate athletics and outreach programs usually brought about accommodation. Well into the 1930s the University of Chicago's football team was champion of the Western Conference (forerunner of the Big Ten) and was scolded by Abraham Flexner for its garish billboards that announced its varsity football schedule at two of the city's most prominent intersections. Robert Maynard Hutchins later decried the excesses of big-time

The lovely campus of Cornell University, designated a research university as early as 1910, is an example of the elaborate design style favored by major Universities built during the eighteenth and nineteenth centuries.

sports and eventually led the university to drop varsity football.

Defining the Research University

By 1910 articles and studies were preoccupied with defining and standardizing institutional categories within higher education. This meant ranking and measuring universities' scholarly quality and research productivity. Although these exercises appeared to be predictive and objective, they were often subjective and retrospective judgments. Slosson's slate of "great universities" had to make special allowance for Princeton and Johns Hopkins, since neither met his general size requirements for expenditures or enrollments. This was testimony to a feature of American higher education: it had no formal definition of what constituted a "real" university. The founding of the Association of American Universities in 1900 signaled the collective identity of the research university. But membership was still a shifting, imperfect indicator of stature; for example, early AAU members Clark University and Catholic University were unable to sustain national reputations in their respective models for advanced scholarship. More problematic was the fact that while AAU membership ratified one's standing as a bona fide research university, it gave few clues about institutions that were building a research emphasis. Slosson's 1910 roster of California, Chicago, Columbia, Cornell, Harvard, Illinois, Johns Hopkins, Michigan, Minnesota, Pennsylvania, Princeton, Stanford, Wisconsin, and Yale provides an intriguing cluster; and, as noted by Roger Geiger, the addition of California Institute of Technology and Massachusetts Institute of Technology in the 1930s formed an enduring core. Less clear is whether or when other institutions warranted inclusion in this company over the next half-century.

External Relations and Resources, 1910–1940

The standard American university of 1910 was a largely inanimate entity that had yet to flesh out its structure. Even the great universities were still small; Columbia, Harvard, Michigan, Cornell, and Pennsylvania were the only American universities to enroll more than five thousand students. Doctoral and master's degree programs were undersubscribed; only Columbia reported graduate students as more than 10 percent of the total student body. Resources devoted to research were minuscule, and teaching loads for all faculty were heavy. If research activities in the university were to flourish, a campus had to develop mechanisms to attract external resources. The temptation is to assume that our familiar structures were inevitable, glossing over the historical fact that in 1910 it was not at all evident that universities would prevail as the dominant sites of large-scale scientific research and advanced studies.

Philanthrophy and government funding could have been focused elsewhere. Roger Geiger's study, *To Advance Knowledge* (1986), narrates the development of foundations, government agencies, special programs, and private industry between the world wars. Whereas from 1870 to 1910, emphasis was on building the campus, from 1910 to 1940 the great universities dealt with "horizontal" structures: relations with foundations, state legislatures, industry, and the federal government. After 1910 serious university research became involved with such new entities as the Carnegie Foundation, the Social Science Research Council, the Rockefeller Foundation, the Institute for Government Research, and the National Bureau of Economic Research. This was largely an activity of a handful of universities that was over the heads and outside the purview of the American public. Whereas the emergence of the American university contributed the heroic figure of the captain of erudition, the developing relations with foundations and government agencies were less conspicuous and characterized by diplomacy and expertise. Beardsley

Ruml, for example, left the University of Chicago in 1934 and was influential for several decades as a leader and liaison among foundations, universities, and government, all with scant public recognition.

The endeavor that set the research university apart from other institutions was science. This statement needs careful explanation because "science" was a vague term whose connotations obscured rather than clarified the essence of the research university. "Science" could connote utilitarian applications ranging from agricultural extension services to animal husbandry or home economics. Or it could apply more or less to all academic disciplines, as even the humanities appealed to the "science" of systematic analysis or textual criticism. Certainly economics, sociology, government, history, and psychology made gains in stature and resources as social and behavioral sciences. On balance, these variations were peripheral to the large-scale, expensive research in the natural and physical sciences, biomedicine, and engineering. The ethos of "big science as the best science" did not necessarily mean that the largest universities were the best research sites. A critical mass of talent and resources, rather than institutional size, was the key determinant. During the 1930s foremost examples of "best science," in which a small number of talented scholars and administrators brought about institutional transformation, included the physicist Robert Millikan at Cal Tech, James Bryant Conant (chemist and president, 1933–1953) at Harvard, and the physicist Ernest Lawrence at Berkeley. Princeton's strategy to forgo professional schools of medicine and law in favor of selected doctoral programs demonstrated how a relatively small institution could develop an extraordinary research presence over several decades. Another variation was Massachusetts Institute of Technology, a relatively young institution that used industrial relations to energize its faculty research effort.

Patronage and Partnerships, 1940–1990

Prior to World War II the research universities were distinctive because research was not at center stage at most American universities. In 1940 many flagship state universities awarded few doctoral degrees and attracted meager external research grants. A university often was merely a campus that had professional schools to prepare students for entry-level positions in engineering, law, medicine, education, and business, none of which was an inherent indicator of a commitment to research.

Involvement in government projects during World War II enhanced the research universities' external research. Teams of physicists, chemists, and engineers from university faculties received federal funding for defense-related projects, including nuclear physics and development of the atomic and hydrogen bombs, along with foreign languages, international studies, and naval architecture. Indicative of changing institutional priorities was the University of Chicago, where the old locker rooms beneath the abandoned football stadium provided laboratory space for the Manhattan Project.

The success of the universities' "big science" did not stop with the end of the war. The war effort set a precedent for the federal government as contractor for university-based research and development, creating the "federal grant university" over the ensuing half-century. According to Clark Kerr's *The Uses of the University* (1963), federal support for higher education increased a hundredfold between 1940 and 1960. In 1960 two-thirds of this $1.5 billion went to university research centers and project research. Kerr estimated that the $1 billion for research represented 75 percent of all university research expenditures and 15 percent of total university budgets. Primary sources of federal research money were the National Institutes of Health, National Science Foundation, Department of Defense, National Aeronautics and Space Administration, and Department of Agriculture. The grant money was concentrated in a few institutions; twenty universities received about 80 percent of the federal funding for research centers and projects. Federal grants were not the only factor in the massive expansion of university research after 1940, though. Stanford University offers the foremost example of how academic departments collaborated with private industry in engineering and physics to transform a campus and build a potent, enduring research and development base.

After 1965 the "federal grant university" became the model that was increasingly emulated, both in form and substance.

The dynamics of federal funding changed after 1965 to spread research money to additional universities. The "federal grant university" became the model that was increasingly emulated, both in form and in substance, as some young universities such as the University of California, Los Angeles, joined the AAU. By 1990 there were fifty-six members of the AAU and probably another fifty universities that could realistically claim funded research as an important and growing part of their institutional mission. A much larger number of institutions aspired to research university stature. Between 1960 and 1980 annual federal funding for university research tripled, from one billion to three billion dollars. Despite this growth, there were worries within the university research community. After fifteen years of 13 percent annual growth (in constant dollars) between 1953 and 1968, annual increases were almost flat over the next decade. This shock to the academic research community caused concern that the partnership with the federal government had diminished. Big science now faced competition with other higher education activities for federal dollars, most notably expanded financial aid for undergraduates and entitlements in social-justice legislation. Shifting federal priorities exposed a tension between the research universities and American society: how, in a democracy, ought resources to be distributed to develop talent?

Excellence and Equity: The Distribution of Talent

Successful expansion of the research university was cited in 1968 by the sociologists Christopher Jencks and David Riesman as part of an academic revolution in twentieth-century American life. Faculty gained prestige and public deference, and the university exerted inordinate influence in the nation's culture of professionalism. Academic judgments were sought in the larger society. Many employers and professions looked to the university for instruction and certification.

The hallmark of the research university was an emphasis on talent. Early scientific schools and, later, doctoral programs stood apart from the social-class elitism associated with the undergraduate colleges. Entering a doctoral program usually involved self-selection and a prolonged scholarly apprenticeship, a commitment that held little prestige for or appeal to most American college students and seldom aroused the curiosity or affection of the general public. Graduate students existed in a world apart from the glamour and indulgence of the undergraduate campus life. Accomplishments within the international scientific community reinforced the contention that the American university was earnestly committed to rewarding merit. Accommodation of first-rate scholars continued in the 1930s as American universities provided appointments and facilities for European refugee professors. After World War II, selective undergraduate colleges and top graduate programs cooperated, a sign of mutual interest in promoting academic achievement. Despite this admirable record, imbalances in gender, geography, and race suggested that over the twentieth century the American research university embodied what Jencks and Riesman called the "partial triumph of meritocracy."

Concentration of talent promoted imbalance. Not until after 1960 do rosters of prestigious research universities include institutions in the South. This changed dramatically by the 1980s, when North Carolina, Duke, Virginia, Rice, Georgia, Vanderbilt, Tulane, and Florida had become members of the AAU. Gender was another matter. Options available to women as professors and graduate students during the university-building decades were limited even though the late-nineteenth-century women's colleges, especially in the Northeast, had strong faculty and laboratories in the sciences. Bryn Mawr College was nicknamed "Jane Hopkins" as tribute to the number of its graduates and faculty enrolled in doctoral programs and institutes at Johns Hopkins. But this was exceptional, and such alliances eroded by 1910.

Although graduate programs avoided the snobbery of social-class exclusion, they exhibited their own inaccessibility. Bernard Jaffe's longitudinal study of scientific achievement bore the apt and ironic title, *Men of Science in America* (1944), graphically conveying the tendency to screen out or ignore women in the research university. As Maresi Nerad's historical research has shown, the case of Professor Agnes Fay Morgan illustrated that overt discrimination was hardly absent from the university. Morgan earned a doctorate in chemistry from the University of Chicago and joined the Berkeley faculty in the early 1900s to chair the home economics department. Although Morgan's research brought her national stature in the sciences, her efforts to build a strong department grounded in the sciences were undercut. Women at other universities faced comparable obstacles to having their work taken seriously.

After World War II, academic tracking and gender socialization overtook overt exclusion as the cause of the underrepresentation of women in graduate programs. Efforts to recruit women to doctoral programs in the 1970s helped redress imbalance; in 1988–1989 more than one-third of the thirty-six thousand doctoral degrees conferred were earned by women. However, disaggregated data have shown that traditional gender imbalances in engineering, sciences, and mathematics remained.

Conclusion

In gauging the place of the research university in late-twentieth-century American culture, perhaps the ultimate compliment was that journalists in the national press wrote about universities in much the same way they discussed baseball teams. For example, a 1988 article in the *Washington Post* about university competition for multimillion-dollar federal research grants referred to the company of such universities as MIT, Stanford, Berkeley, Wisconsin, Cornell, and Chicago as the "big leagues of science" (22 March 1988, p. A3).

Research universities of the 1990s faced a new set of problems that may best be described as the perils of prosperity. Traditional procedures of awarding major research often shifted from academic criteria to political decisions. University officials talked about the "postindustrial pork barrel," whereby research funds were sought as earmarked projects within federal legislation, in contrast with the custom of grants awarded via scholarly peer-review competition. Also, big science had become so sufficiently established nationwide that to do research as a biologist or a physicist at a major university was no longer possible without substantial external monies. This dependency meant that even though federal dollars for basic research increased, the number of qualified applicants far surpassed funding. The research university's reliance on external funding also raised serious public and legal concerns about who set the agenda for research and development and how it was set. Finally, research universities encountered increasing tension over federal regulations. If the modern research university was, indeed, a "knowledge industry," it followed that it would be expected to comply with government regulations on affirmative-action hiring, toxic-waste disposal, and treatment of laboratory animals. It meant that by 1980 lawsuits by consumer groups convinced the courts to require a university to analyze the social as well as the economic impact of large-scale industrial and agricultural research. The new policy climate was that the prestige of research success, once considered grounds for a university to receive exemption or special treatment, increasingly called for government regulation and public accountability within a mass society.

[See also Collegiate Education; The Medical Profession; The Professions; Science as a Profession; Technology and Social Change.]

BIBLIOGRAPHY

Books

Cheit, Earl F. *The Useful Arts and the Liberal Tradition* (1975).

Finn, Chester E., Jr. *Scholars, Dollars, and Bureaucrats* (1978).

Flexner, Abraham. *Universities: American, English, German* (1930).

Geiger, Roger L. *To Advance Knowledge: The Growth of American Research Universities, 1900–1940* (1986).

Hofstadter, Richard, and Wilson Smith, eds. *American Higher Education: A Documentary History.* 2 vols. (1961).

Jarausch, Konrad H., ed. *The Transformation of Higher Learning, 1860–1930* (1983).

Jencks, Christopher, and David Riesman. *The Academic Revolution* (1968).

Kerr, Clark. *The Uses of the University* (1963).

Morison, Robert S., ed. *The Contemporary University: U.S.A.* (1967).

Nerad, Maresi. *Gender in Higher Education: The History of the Home Economics Department at the University of California at Berkeley* (1991).

Oleson, Alexandra, and John Voss, eds. *The Organization of Knowledge in Modern America, 1860–1920* (1979).

Perkins, James A. *The University in Transition* (1966).

Rosenzweig, Robert M., with Barbara Turlington, *The Research Universities and Their Patrons* (1982).

Rudolph, Frederick. *The American College and University: A History* (1962; 2d ed. 1990).

Slosson, Edwin E. *Great American Universities* (1910).

Tobias, Marilyn. *Old Dartmouth on Trial: The Transformation of the Academic Community in Nineteenth-Century America* (1982).

Veysey, Laurence R. *The Emergence of the American University* (1965).

Webster, David S. *Academic Quality Rankings of American Colleges and Universities* (1986).

Williams, Roger. *The Origins of Federal Support for Higher Education* (1991).

Wilshire, Bruce. *The Moral Collapse of the University: Professionalism, Purity, and Alienation* (1990).

Articles

Axtell, James. "The Death of the Liberal Arts College." *History of Education Quarterly* 11, no. 4 (Winter 1971): 339–356.

Borrowman, Merle, "The False Dawn of the State University." *History of Education Quarterly* 1, no. 2 (1961): 6–22.

Glazer, Nathan. "Regulating Business and the Universities: One Problem or Two?" *The Public Interest* 54, no. 56 (1979): 43–65.

Hawkins, Hugh. "The University-Builders Observe the Colleges." *History of Education Quarterly* 11, no. 4 (1971): 353–362.

Hawkins, Hugh. "University Identity: The Teaching and Research Functions." In *The Organization of Knowledge in Modern America, 1860–1920,* edited by Alexandra Oleson and John Voss (1979).

Lowen, Rebecca S. "Transforming the University: Administrators, Physicists, and Industrial and Federal Patronage at Stanford, 1935 to 1949." *History of Education Quarterly* 31 (Fall 1991).

Mattingly, Paul H. "Structures over Time: Institutional History." In *Historical Inquiry in Education: A Research Agenda,* edited by John Hardin Best (1983), pp. 34–55.

Shils, Edward. "The University: A Backward Glance." *American Scholar* 51, no. 2 (Spring 1982): 163–179.

Veysey, Laurence. "The Plural Organized Worlds of the Humanities." In *The Organization of Knowledge in Modern America, 1860–1920,* edited by Alexandra Oleson and John Voss (1979).

— JOHN R. THELIN

ROCK MUSIC

Background: The Early 1950s

Popular music of the early 1950s continued to embody trends from previous decades, incorporating Tin Pan Alley stylings, swing from the 1930s and 1940s, and tunes from Broadway and Hollywood musicals. Performed by full orchestras and vocal stylists such as Frank Sinatra, Perry Como, Nat King Cole, and Peggy Lee, most pop songs featured slow-to-moderate tempos, uncomplicated rhythms, and simple melodies and lyrics written by professional songwriters.

Pop music's homogenized sound, nonthreatening lyrics, and familiar themes appealed to middle-class listeners caught up in cold war politics and rapid social change. Good-time records like Teresa Brewer's "Music, Music, Music" (1950) and Patti Page's "[How Much Is] That Doggie in the Window?" (1953) continued pop's novelty-song tradition. Ballads such as Mario Lanza's "Be My Love" (1951) and Tony Bennett's "Because of You" (1951) focused on old-fashioned romance. Other traditional beliefs were advanced on numerous records in the early 1950s: Eddie Fisher's "Oh My Papa" idealized the patriarchal family; Arthur Godfrey's "What Is a Boy?" reinforced traditional sexual stereotypes; Tony Bennett's "Rags to Riches" continued the Horatio Alger myth; and Frankie Laine's "I Believe" plugged into traditional religious beliefs. Even the structure of the pop music industry reflected the era's conservative attitudes toward race and gender. The pop field was dominated by white males, who did most of the songwriting, performing, producing, and marketing.

The Rise of Rock and Roll: 1954–1963

By the mid 1950s, an alternate style of pop music had emerged: rock and roll. Some experts claim the roots of the music can be traced to the back-country ring shouts of African American slaves. Others maintain that rock sprang from black spirituals of the 1920s and 1930s. Still others claim that rock was an offspring of black rhythm and blues from the 1940s, noting that R&B songs such as Wild Bill Moore's "We're Gonna Rock, We're Gonna Roll" (1947) and Wynonie Harris's "Good Rockin' Tonight" (1948), with a cover by Roy Brown that same year, used the terms "rock" and "roll" as euphemisms for sexual intercourse.

Actually, rock and roll was more than just the offspring of African American music. It also descended from white country and western music and traditional white pop. By the late 1950s, three main rock styles were evident: R&B rock, country rock, and pop rock. Each was a variation of the new idiom, blending R&B and country music with pop-style lyrics that appealed to teenagers.

R&B rock had the closest ties to rhythm and blues. Black R&B rockers such as Chuck Berry, Fats Domino, Little Richard, and Lloyd Price had begun their careers in the rhythm and blues field. When they crossed over to rock, they took their musical stylings with them, retaining the rhythm and beats found in their original music, but singing lyrics that were more pop-oriented than blues-oriented. For example, Chuck Berry combined teen-oriented pop lyrics with rhythm and blues and country and western to produce hits like "School Day" (1957) and "Sweet Little Sixteen" (1958).

Rocking wildly in his trademark style, Elvis Presley did more than any artist to popularize black rhythm and blues with a country and western flavor.

The second style, country rock (also known as rockabilly), emerged from the country and western tradition of Hank Williams, Roy Acuff, and other Grand Ole Opry stars. Rockabilly artists such as Elvis Presley, Jerry Lee Lewis, Buddy Holly, and Carl Perkins used their country and western backgrounds to modify black rhythm and blues. Presley became the most successful purveyor of the new sound, which Carl Perkins described as "blues with a country beat." Legend has it that Sam Phillips, owner of Sun Records in Memphis, once remarked: "If I could only find a white man who had the Negro sound and the Negro feel I could make a million dollars." The young working-class singer from Tupelo, Mississippi, made Phillips a prophet, and in the process changed the course of American popular music. Although not the inventor of rock and roll, Elvis certainly did more than any artist to popularize it. His unique blend of country and western and rhythm and blues—evident on hits such as "Heartbreak Hotel" (1956) and "Hound Dog" (1956)—earned him 52 top thirty hits between 1956 and 1963, establishing him as the undisputed King of Rock and Roll.

The third type of rock music—pop rock—was performed mostly by young, white singers influenced by R&B rock, rockabilly, and traditional pop. At its best, when performed by pop rockers such as Ricky Nelson, Del Shannon, or Bobby Vee, pop rock authentically captured the spirit of rock and roll. Like rockabilly with its proletarian southern roots or R&B rock with its working-class black roots, this type of pop rock had its own socially based constituency. It was the music of white middle-class neighborhoods, in tune with white teenage culture. Less interpretive was the pop rock style of performers such as Frankie Avalon, Fabian, and Connie Francis, who were closer to the Tin Pan Alley stylings of 1940s and 1950s' pop singers like Perry Como.

The emergence of rock and roll was linked to social change of the post-World War II era, particularly the migration of blacks to northern and western cities; the rise of the baby boom generation; the growth of a consumer culture; and the rise of new technologies.

White America's sudden discovery of black rhythm and blues music was the result of the movement of large numbers of blacks from the South to large urban areas in the North and West during and after World War II. When blacks migrated northward to jobs in New York City, Chicago, Detroit, and other urban areas, they brought along cultural baggage, including rhythm and blues. For the first time on a large scale, whites living in cities outside the South could listen to black music in bars or record stores or on the radio.

By the early 1950s, R&B songs such as the Orioles' "Crying in the Chapel" (1953), the Crows' "Gee" (1954), Big Joe Turner's "Shake, Rattle, and Roll" (1954), and the Chords' "Sh-Boom" (1954) were attracting white audiences. Two of the first white performers to record rhythm and blues-influenced songs were Johnnie Ray ("Cry" and "The Little White Cloud That Cried," both 1951) and Bill Haley and His Comets ("We're Gonna Rock This Joint Tonight," 1952; "Crazy Man Crazy," 1953; and "Shake, Rattle, and Roll," 1954).

A white disc jockey named Alan Freed did much to popularize the new sound. In 1952, he began playing black rhythm and blues on his radio program in Cleveland, Ohio. To avoid the racial stigma associated with R&B, Freed called the music "rock and roll"—a phrase readily accepted by an unsuspecting white audience. Disc jockeys across the country followed Freed's lead, bringing the rock and roll sound to millions of white teenagers.

Public response to early rock and roll reflected racial tensions of the era. Prejudiced whites often condemned rock and roll as "African" or "race" music, fearing the allegedly lustful sound would lead to miscegenation. Several white congregations in the South even pushed for a ban on rock and roll in 1956, insisting the music was an NAACP conspiracy to corrupt white teenagers.

The practice of releasing "cover records" suggests more subtle forms of prejudice. The success of rhythm and blues artists on the pop charts by the early 1950s prompted major record companies to record white singers copying the black sound. Many times a black R&B song hit the record charts, only to be quickly covered (re-recorded) by a white performer. For example, Pat Boone had hits with cover versions of Fats Domino's "Ain't That a Shame" (1955) and Little Richard's "Tutti-Frutti" (1956). Although covers usually lacked the artistic integrity of the originals, they were often more commercially successful for several reasons. Cover records were more familiar-sounding to listeners raised on traditional pop. They also appealed to whites who wanted to avoid black culture. Some covers "cleaned up" black songs that were deemed too crude or sexually suggestive for a white middle-class audience. For example, Etta James's 1955 rhythm and blues hit "Roll with Me, Henry," became "Dance with Me, Henry" when covered by white pop star Georgia Gibbs. Cover records, distributed nationally by major companies with connections in all the big cities, also had marketing advantages over the black originals, released on small, local labels.

In 1952 a white disc jockey named Alan Freed began playing black rhythm and blues on his Cleveland radio program, calling the music "rock and roll" to avoid the racial stigma associated with R&B.

Even the black artists who were able to crack the predominantly white pop charts felt the sting of racial prejudice. Chuck Berry, perhaps the most skilled singer/songwriter of the era, never received the public acclaim or movie offers accorded white performers such as Elvis Presley or Ricky Nelson, while black songwriters such as Little Richard and Maurice Williams were cheated out of royalties when their songs were covered by white pop singers.

If the birth of rock was linked to the emergence of blacks in American society, its growth was dependent upon another major demographic change in American society and culture—the coming of the baby boom generation. The boom began after World War II and continued until 1964, producing 76.5 million babies—one third of America's population. Rock music—like the baby boomers themselves—came of age after World War II. The new sound, with its distinctive beat and adolescent themes, was perfect for a new generation that considered itself unique.

Rock and roll became the boundary marker for the youth culture (and its various subcultures) that developed in the 1950s and early 1960s. The music contributed to teenagers' collective memory and identity, allowing members of the baby boom generation to clarify who they were by listening to the type of music that appealed to their particular subculture. Rock taught adolescents how to dance, how to talk, how to dress, and how to date. It also communicated group attitudes about school, parents, and everyday life. Ricky Nelson's phenomenal success on the rock charts depended upon the bond between rock music and the teen audience. The young teen idol, who first gained television fame as the wisecracking youngster on *The Adventures of Ozzie and Harriet*, sang about young love on "A Teenager's Romance" (1957); described teen interests on "Waitin' in School" (1957); and explained how cars and curfews could cause problems on "It's Late" (1959).

The market for rock and roll expanded rapidly in the mid 1950s as teenage patrons contributed to the creation of a new culture of consumption. By 1963, young American consumers were spending $22 billion annually on rock and roll records, phonographs, transistor radios, clothes, and other products geared to the youth audience.

Technological advances further aided the growth of rock and roll. Prior to World War II, the recording industry had been limited to elaborate studios in New York City or Los Angeles. But by the 1950s, the introduction of magnetic tape and modern tape recorders (first developed in Hitler's Germany) enabled small, independent companies to record local rock and roll talent anywhere in the country. Sam Phillips and his Memphis-based Sun Records produced records by Elvis Presley, Carl Perkins, and Johnny Cash, while Norman Petty's tiny studio in Clovis, New Mexico, recorded Buddy Holly and the Crickets.

Rock and roll thrived on other technological innovations. New 45 rpm records with their wide hole in the middle gave the music a more distinct appearance, while portable record players and transistor radios allowed teenagers to carry rock and roll wherever they went. The rise of television programs such as *The Ed Sullivan Show*, *The Adventures of Ozzie and Harriet*, and Dick Clark's *American Bandstand* provided public forums for early rock and rollers. Radio stations showcased rock and roll through new formats featuring jive-talking disc jockeys. And the development of inexpensive car radios allowed teenagers to listen to all the latest hits as they cruised America's streets.

Early rock and roll demonstrates that American society was anything but monolithic in the 1950s and early 1960s. The music carried different messages for various subcultures and classes. For some, rock and roll was a form of cultural rebellion. The 1955 movie *The Blackboard Jungle*, which depicted juvenile delinquency and featured Bill Haley and His Comets' "Rock Around the Clock" in its soundtrack, helped convince many Americans that rock music and rebellion went hand-in-hand.

To an extent, rock's rebellious image was true. Rock's close ties to black music were a direct affront to segregationist views of the era. Its working-class origins threatened white middle-class society. Some songs, such as Eddie Cochran's "Summertime Blues" (1958) or the Coasters' "Yakety Yak" (1958), raised the specter of teenage rebellion. Rock and roll's implicit sexuality and uninhibited nature also challenged the straitlaced, conformist attitudes of the 1950s and early 1960s. Elvis Presley, with his long sideburns and outrageous "cat clothes," epitomized the wild rock singer, while uninhibited dances like the twist made some parents wince. Fearful adults linked rock and roll to pornography, drugs, prostitution, alcohol, juvenile delinquency, organized crime, teen pregnancies, and even Communist subversion. Local officials banned rock and roll concerts and regulated teen dances and parties. Even the United States Congress investigated the financing of rock and roll in the notorious payola hearings of 1959–1960. Viewed from the 1990s, these attacks tell more about American paranoia of the 1950s and early 1960s than they do about the music.

In many ways, early rock and roll reflected more consensus than conflict between the generations. At times, dominant groups used rock to maintain cultural hegemony. A form of social engineering took place as traditional values and acceptable patterns of behavior were stressed on Dick Clark's popular TV show, *American Bandstand*, and numerous rock idols, including Pat Boone, Ricky Nelson, and Fabian, were marketed as safe role models for teenagers. Even Elvis Presley's rebellious image was homogenized as he portrayed all-American boys in various Hollywood films.

Rock and roll songs frequently expressed the values of the dominant culture. Hit records praising religion, marriage, the family, parents, individualism, and America abounded on the rock charts. Even America's cold war against communism was waged on the rock and roll front. For example, while President John F. Kennedy was steering America through cold war crises involving Cuba and Berlin, teenagers were listening to patriotic hits such as Johnny Burnette's "God, Country, and My Baby" (1961) and Miss Toni Fisher's "West of the Wall" (1962).

Early rock promoted the American belief in equality. Elvis Presley introduced many whites to R&B-influenced music, opening the door for black rock and rollers like Jackie Wilson, Lloyd Price, and Fats Domino. Rock music became a form of cultural integration, as white teenagers cheered on black performers, purchased records previously sold only to blacks, and even sat beside blacks at integrated concerts. At a time when segregation ruled many areas of the country, rock provided a public sphere for integrated groups such as the Crests and the Impalas, and it offered opportunity not just for black singers, but for white ethnics such as the Hispanics Ritchie Valens and Trini Lopez and the Italian Americans Frankie Avalon, Frankie Valli, and Bobby Rydell. Some hit records, for example Gene Chandler's "Duke of Earl" (1962) and Jay and the Americans' "Only in America" (1963), even expressed the belief that any person regardless of color, class, or wealth could find success in the United States.

Rock and roll of the 1950s and early 1960s demonstrates that teenagers, like adults, were participating in the building of consumption communities based on the era's affluence, planned obsolescence, and conspicuous consumption. The commodification of American culture was advanced through records such as Elvis Presley's "Money Honey" (1956) or Barrett Strong's "Money (That's What I Want)" (1960). Fashions were advertised on numerous hits, including Carl Perkins's "Blue Suede Shoes" (1956) and the Royal Teens' "Short Shorts" (1958). And America's love affair with automobiles was mirrored in car songs like Chuck Berry's "No Money Down" (1956) and the Beach Boys' "Little Deuce Coupe" (1963).

Early rock and roll expressed other middle-class beliefs and stereotypes. Rock music—like American society itself—treated women as second-class citizens. Females were depicted as passive sex objects on numerous hits, including Buddy Knox's "Party Doll" (1957), Johnny Tillotson's "Poetry in Motion" (1960), and Eddie Hodges's "[Girls, Girls, Girls] Made to Love" (1962). Blacks were portrayed as comic figures on the Coasters' "Charlie Brown" (1959); they were depicted as lustful native dancers on Little Anthony and the Imperials' "Shimmy, Shimmy, Ko-Ko-Bop" (1959); and their alleged fondness for watermelon inspired Mongo Santamaria's "Watermelon Man" (1963).

Other racial and ethnic groups were similarly stereotyped by rock and roll, which, like society in general, was dominated by white males. Native Americans appeared as silly, cartoon characters on novelty hits such as Johnny Preston's "Running Bear" (1959) and Larry Verne's "Mr. Custer" (1960). Hispanics and Italians were ridiculed for their accents on Pat Boone's "Speedy Gonzales" (1962) or Lou Monte's "Pepino the Italian Mouse" (1962). And Arabs became the brunt of jokes about camels and sheiks on Ray Stevens's "Ahab, the Arab" (1962).

Rock music provides evidence that the mythic American West influenced people of all ages in the 1950s and early 1960s. While many adults watched TV Westerns like *Gunsmoke* and *Have Gun, Will Travel,* teenagers celebrated America's alleged frontier heritage through Duane Eddy's "Ramrod" (1958), Marty Robbins's "El Paso" (1959), and Johnny Cash's "Don't Take Your Guns to Town" (1959). California was frequently seen as the ultimate western paradise. The belief in the mythic West coupled with real economic opportunities convinced many Americans to move to California in the post-World War II decade. Rock music contributed to the era's glorification of the California dream. The Beach Boys' "Surfin' U.S.A." (1963) and Jan and Dean's "Surf City" (1963) plugged into images of the mythic West as a land of opportunity and happiness, focusing on the hedonistic pleasures to be found in California—the western Garden of Eden.

Early rock and roll was in harmony with the times. A product of technological change, it reflected major demographic shifts involving youths and blacks. It also mirrored the affluence and anxieties, as well as the conflict and consensus of America in the fifties and early sixties. But rock and roll—like the nation itself—was forever altered by the changes that occurred in the United States after the autumn of 1963.

Rock's Golden Decade: 1964–1974

The assassination of President Kennedy on 22 November 1963 sent shock waves throughout American society and culture. Teenagers who identified with the young president were particularly stunned by the incident. The bullets that killed Kennedy shattered the illusions of many youths, who had been taught that America was a land of freedom and opportunity and that good always triumphed over evil.

If Kennedy's death caused many baby boomers despair and disillusionment, the arrival of the Beatles (John Lennon, Paul McCartney, George Harrison, and Ringo Starr) just a few weeks later provided new hope. The English group and their music projected optimism, enthusiasm, and fun. The four rock and rollers carried on like the Marx Brothers, spoofing the establishment and refusing to take themselves too seriously. Their lighthearted approach to life contrasted sharply with the seriousness and gloom of America after Kennedy's assassination. The Beatles, with their shaggy, mop haircuts, mod clothing, and outrageous chords and musical stylings, offered American youths a new identity, at a time when they desperately needed one. Prior to the fall of 1963, American teens had dismissed foreign rock stars as mere imitators of American rock and roll. But after November 1963, American youths, perhaps realizing that American culture did not have all the answers, turned eagerly to foreign approaches. The Beatles' first American hit, "I Want to Hold Your Hand," triggered a Beatle-mania craze in January 1964. Over the next two years, the Beatles earned nine additional number-one hits, making them the first non-American superstars in the history of rock and roll.

If the November 1963 death of John F. Kennedy caused baby boomers despair and disillusionment, the arrival of the Beatles just a few weeks later provided new hope.

The Beatles' success launched a British rock invasion of the American pop charts. Some British groups, specifically the Dave Clark Five and Gerry and the Pacemakers, offered Beatle-esque pop rock that appealed to white middle-class teenagers. Others, like the Rolling Stones and the Animals, delivered less-polished, R&B-influenced music with greater working-class appeal. The British invasion altered the way American teenagers saw themselves and their world. Teenagers underwent rapid change as they adopted the British rockers' music, haircuts, and clothing styles. The foreign performers also provided the means for American teenagers to look beyond their own shores to see how others viewed the world.

British rock and pop rejuvenated American music, increasing record sales and altering styles. Initially the "new sound" from England was largely just a throwback to American rock and roll and rhythm and blues of the 1950s and 1960s. Many English performers even covered songs by Buddy Holly, Chuck Berry, and other early rockers. But eventually the British rock sound interacted with American music, as well as with social and cultural movements involving civil rights, the peace movement, and youth culture, to create a sense of experimentation in pop and rock.

One of the first new styles to emerge was folk-rock, which blended folk music's socially aware lyrics with British rock's electric guitars and drums. Two number-one records of 1965—the Byrds' "Mr. Tambourine Man" (written by Bob Dylan) and Barry McGuires "Eve of Destruction" (written by P. F. Sloan)—marked folk-rock's arrival. The Turtles, the Mamas and the Papas, Simon and Garfunkel, James Taylor, and Carly Simon also found success with the new style. Even established folksingers like Bob Dylan and Joan Baez added electric guitars and drums to their music.

Folk-rock in turn influenced the Beatles, the Rolling Stones, Donovan, and other British rockers, who began experimenting with complex musical arrangements and more meaningful lyrics about personal relationships, society, and politics. The Beatles revolutionized the pop music industry in 1967 with the release of *Sgt. Pepper's Lonely Hearts Club Band.* Instead of the ten or twelve unrelated songs normally included on pop albums, *Sgt. Pepper* wove together a series of songs telling the story of a make-believe band. The concept album broke new ground, inspiring other rock artists to experiment with complex music and lyrics.

American pop rock underwent similar changes as performers incorporated the English sound and folk-rock into their music. Pop rockers let their hair grow long, switched to mod clothing styles, and began singing message songs. Teen idol Bobby Vee typified the changes many American performers were going through. Having begun his career in the late 1950s singing rockabilly-influenced pop rock, Vee tried to capitalize on the Beatles' success in 1964 with an album entitled *The New Sound from England.* By the end of the decade, he was sporting a Beatles haircut and singing message songs such as "Come Back When You Grow Up" (1967) and "Maybe Just Today" (1968). In 1972 he recorded an entire album of original folk-rock songs under his real name, Robert Thomas Velline, completing his transformation from a 1950s teen idol to a mature singer/songwriter.

The rock and pop renaissance of the 1960s and early 1970s sparked an explosion of musical experimentation. Some groups developed an electrified blues sound, characterized by a driving rock beat and loud, power chords. This "hard rock" style produced mainstream rock classics such as the Kinks' "All Day and All of the Night" (1964) and Cream's "Sunshine of Your Love" (1968).

Other bands developed art rock or progressive rock. Building on the musical innovations of *Sgt. Pepper,* these groups blended rock with a variety of traditional music forms. The Moody Blues and Procol Harum combined rock with classical music, song cycles, and orchestras. Pink Floyd, Rick Wakeman, Keith Emerson, and Mike Oldfield experimented with synthesizers and electronic music. Oldfield's *Tubular Bells* (1973), featured in the soundtrack of *The Exorcist*, is an excellent example of the electronic music that came to be known as electro-rock or techno-rock. Jethro Tull, Chicago, and Blood, Sweat, and Tears mixed rock with jazz. Experiments in progressive rock also led to rock operas such as the Who's *Tommy* (1969) and *Quadrophenia* (1973), as well as rock musicals like *Hair* (1967) and *Godspell* (1971).

R&B rock was also influenced by musical experimentation and the changing times. The success of Berry Gordy's Motown Records was linked in part to the emergence of blacks in society. The Detroit-based company achieved phenomenal success with the Supremes, the Miracles, the Temptations, and other black groups who could deliver an appealing hybrid of rhythm and blues and pop to whites whose consciousness of black music and culture had been raised by the growing civil rights movement of the early 1960s. By the late 1960s and early 1970s, some Motown artists were blending R&B rock with socially relevant lyrics to produce Stevie Wonder's "Blowin' in the Wind" (1966) and Marvin Gaye's "Inner City Blues (Make Me Wanna Holler)" (1971).

As interest in African American culture developed in the mid 1960s, the market for more authentic-sounding black music expanded. The emergence of black pride contributed greatly to the advent of "soul music." James Brown, Wilson Pickett, Aretha Franklin, Otis Redding, and Sam and Dave found tremendous success with earthy, emotional songs that captured the spirit of black gospel and early rhythm and blues. Though less polished than the Motown sound, soul music more accurately expressed various aspects of black culture in the 1960s. The Impressions' "Keep On Pushing" (1964) mirrored the optimism of the early civil rights movement. Aretha Franklin's "Respect" (1967) became an anthem for racial equality. James Brown's "Say It Loud—I'm Black and I'm Proud" (1968) plugged into the emergence of black pride. Other songs communicated the emotional side of the African American experience: Wilson Pickett's "In the Midnight Hour" (1965), Arthur Conley's "Sweet Soul Music" (1967), and Sam and Dave's "Soul Man" (1967).

Country and western singers were also influenced by the changes occurring in rock music and American culture. Willie Nelson, Waylon Jennings, and others gained notoriety as "country music outlaws," because they adopted the longer hairstyles associated with the counterculture and incorporated rock beats and folk-rock lyrics into their music.

Even traditional pop singers were swept up by the currents of musical change. Frank Sinatra staged a comeback with the message songs "That's Life" (1966) and "Cycles" (1968). Shirley Jones and television's Partridge Family enjoyed a string of formula pop rock hits. And, in the wake of the British rock invasion, English pop stars Tom Jones, Engelbert Humperdinck, and Petula Clark found enthusiastic audiences on American shores.

Rock and pop music addressed all the major social and cultural issues of the late 1960s and early 1970s, as numerous performers became active participants in social and political movements for equality, peace, and human rights. Joan Baez emerged as one of the era's most visible advocates of justice and nonviolence. She began her career singing traditional folk songs in small clubs in Cambridge, Massachusetts, eventually moving on to New York City's Greenwich Village. By 1963, Baez was one of the nation's most popular folksingers, with three albums on the best-selling charts and a *Time* magazine cover to her credit. With national attention riveted on the civil rights movement and an escalating war in Vietnam, Baez became increasingly involved with social protest. Pointing the way for other folksingers, she began marching and singing for civil rights, peace, and student rights.

In 1965 Bob Dylan surprised his fans by switching from acoustic to electric guitar, and for the remainder of the 1960s his folk-rock compositions reflected the dissatisfaction, anger, and concerns of much of America's youth.

Joan Baez also helped introduce the public to another young folksinger who would provide a major voice for social change in the 1960s and early 1970s—Bob Dylan. The Minnesota native had begun his career in the Midwest with a brief stint as a piano player in a backup band for pop rocker Bobby Vee. After moving to New York City to meet his idol Woody Guthrie, Dylan began singing in folk clubs, where he was discovered by John Hammond, a producer for Columbia Records. His early songs reflected main currents in the protest movements of the day. In 1962 Dylan wrote and recorded "Blowin' in the Wind," which became a best-selling hit record for Peter, Paul, and Mary in 1963, as well as an unofficial anthem of the civil rights movement. Dylan was among the first to herald the arrival of the baby boom generation with his seminal "The Times They Are A-Changin'" (1964). And he gave voice to the antiwar movement through songs such as "Hard Rain" (1963) and "Talkin' World War III Blues" (1963). After the Byrds had a number one record in 1965 with a rock version of Dylan's "Mr. Tambourine Man," Dylan surprised his fans by switching to an electric guitar and folk-rock. Throughout the rest of the 1960s, Dylan songs such as "Like a Rolling Stone" (1965), "Rainy Day Women #12 & 35" (1966), and "All Along the Watchtower" (1967) reflected the dissatisfaction, anger, and concerns of many troubled youths.

Bob Dylan not only gave a voice to the concerns of the Young generation, but he pointed the way for mainstream rock artists. John Lennon of the Beatles became one of the most important rock activists. By the late 1960s and early 1970s, he had thrown himself wholeheartedly into the peace movement, joining protests, staging "love-ins," and writing and recording the best-selling songs "Give Peace a Chance" (1969), "Imagine" (1971), and "Happy Xmas (War Is Over)" (1972).

Along with social and political protest, rock music became intertwined with the era's growing counterculture. By the mid 1960s, many youths (primarily from white middle-class backgrounds) felt alienated from American culture and society: Disheartened by the Vietnam War, distressed by society's treatment of minorities, and concerned about a culture which they felt was spiritually and morally bankrupt, these "hippies" advocated alternate means to structure society. The values and characteristics of this brave new world were detailed in rock music, which became the lifeblood of the counterculture.

While concerts such as the Monterey Pop Festival and Woodstock provided public spheres for communal celebration, recorded music expressed countercultural themes involving love, peace, youth solidarity, brotherhood, mysticism, and drugs. Scott McKenzie's "San Francisco (Be Sure to Wear Flowers in Your Hair)" encouraged members of the young generation to come to San Francisco for the 1967 "Summer of Love." The Youngbloods' "Get Together" (1969) preached harmony, brotherhood, and understanding. And the 5th Dimension's "Aquarius / Let the Sunshine In" (from the rock musical *Hair*, 1969) publicized the countercultural revolution that was allegedly creating a new age.

Countercultural fashions were adopted by most rock peformers and spotlighted on various songs. Even the names of some rock groups radiated the optimism of the counterculture. There were groups like the Sunshine Company, the Yellow Balloon, Parade, and the Peppermint Rainbow.

Many rock artists followed the hippies' lead and began experimenting with LSD and other drugs. At first, songs like the Byrds' "Eight Miles High" (1966) or the Beatles "Lucy in the Sky with Diamonds" (1967) cloaked drug references in allegedly innocent lyrics. But after Timothy Leery and other counterculture enthusiasts began publicly advocating the use of LSD as a means to heightened awareness and spiritual truth, rock music began dealing more openly with drug topics. Acid rock—a musical style that emerged in San Francisco—sought to emulate or heighten the LSD psychedelic experience through blatant lyrics, extended instrumental improvisations, and loud, electronically amplified music. Light shows featuring bright colors and strobe units added to the effect, as did longhaired performers dressed in wild-colored clothes. San Francisco became the counterculture's psychedelic capital, boasting groups such as Jefferson Airplane, Quicksilver Messenger Service, and the Grateful Dead. Their brand of acid rock or psychedelic rock spread nationally through Jefferson Airplane's "White Rabbit" (1967) and albums such as the Grateful Dead's *Anthem of the Sun* (1968). The style was furthered by non-San Francisco bands like the Doors and the Jimi Hendrix Experience.

Rock music followed the counterculture's lead in rejecting middle-class values. For example, songs such as the Rolling Stones' "Let's Spend the Night Together" (1967) promoted more open attitudes toward sex. The

San Francisco became the counterculture's psychedelic capital, boasting groups such as Jefferson Airplane, Quicksilver Messenger Service, and the Grateful Dead.

Beatles showed how far the music industry had come in just four years when they released "Why Don't We Do It in the Road?" (1968), a far cry from their 1964 hit, "I Want to Hold Your Hand." The alleged hypocrisy of middle-class adults was the subject of Joe South's "Games People Play" (1969). Materialism was the target of the Beatles' "All You Need is Love" (1966). And middle-class notions involving careers and planning for the future were rejected by the Grass Roots' "Let's Live for Today" (1967).

Along with reflecting social movements involving blacks and youths, rock and pop music of the late sixties and early seventies mirrored the changing role of women in American society. Whereas early rock and roll tended to treat women as dependent, passive objects, rock of the 1960s and early 1970s contained far more complex images in keeping with the changes occurring in American culture. Rock songs that treated women as second-class citizens or mere sex objects were still common, as evidenced by Roy Orbison's "Pretty Woman" (1964), the Rolling Stones' "Stupid Girl" (1966), or the O'Kaysions' "Girl Watcher" (1968). But by the mid-sixties and early seventies, alternative images of liberated women could be found in Gale Garnett's "We'll Sing in the Sunshine (Then I'll Be on My Way)" (1964); Lesley Gore's "You Don't Own Me" (1964); Nancy Sinatra's "These Boots Are Made for Walkin'" (1966); and Helen Reddy's "I Am Woman" (1972). The persona of strong-willed female singers such as Janis Joplin or Grace Slick of the Jefferson Airplane also reflected gains being made by women.

Rock and pop music furthered the cause of other groups during the late 1960s and early 1970s. The gay liberation movement gained publicity through the rise of glitter rock (or glam rock). The highly visual and theatrical style of presentation was pioneered by David Bowie, who appeared in women's clothes on the cover photo of his 1970 album, *The Man Who Sold the World.* Male glitter rockers like Bowie, Mott the Hoople, and the New York Dolls often wore eye shadow, makeup, tight-fitting jumpsuits, and platform shoes. In addition, songs such as Mott the Hoople's "All the Young Dudes" (1972) and Lou Reed's "Walk on the Wild Side" (1973) were interpreted as possible celebrations of homosexuality.

Native American rights were also advanced by rock and pop. As the American Indian Movement (AIM) gained momentum in the 1970s, the Raiders' "Indian Reservation (The Lament of the Cherokee Reservation Indian)" (1971) and Cher's "Half-Breed" (1973) appeared on the charts, while Floyd Westerman, a full-blooded Sioux, found success with an Indian-rights album based on Vine De-Loria's best-selling book, *Custer Died for Your Sins.*

By the late 1960s and early 1970s, the American public was deeply divided over women's liberation, the Vietnam War, the civil rights movement, and the counterculture. Hit records provided ample evidence of the polarization in the country. The Buffalo Springfield's "For What It's Worth" (1967) described a violent confrontation between student demonstrators and police in riot gear. Steppenwolf's "Monster" (1970) charged that a brutal, fascist government had taken over the United States. Crosby, Stills, Nash, and Young's "Ohio" (1970) found Richard Nixon guilty of the murder of four college students by the National Guard at Kent State University.

Even the rise of "heavy metal" music could be linked to the troubled times. The new brand of rock took its name from a phrase used in Steppenwolf's hit "Born to Be Wild" (which had borrowed the line from William Burroughs's novel *Naked Lunch*). The blues-based sound, which rock writer Ken Tucker called "angry music for angry times," featured extra-loud, repetitive chords and riffs played aggressively by young rockers screaming out their lyrics. Heavy metal artists, inspired by hard rockers such as the Who, the Kinks, Eric Clapton, and Steppenwolf, cranked up their amplifiers even louder to produce high-voltage records like Iron Butterfly's "In-A-Gadda-Da-Vida" (1968), Led Zeppelin's "Whole Lotta Love" (1969), and Black Sabbath's "Paranoid" (1970).

If some songs reflected dissatisfaction with American society and culture, others mirrored public support. In 1965, the Spokesmen's "The Dawn of Correction" provided a patriotic response to Barry McGuire's "Eve of Destruction." The following year, Staff Sergeant Barry Sadler demonstrated that many Americans backed the Vietnam War with his number one hit, "The Ballad of the Green Berets." Records condemning the counterculture also appeared. Victor Lundberg's "An Open Letter to My Teenage Son" (1967) praised youths who upheld traditional American values, while Merle Haggard's "[I'm Proud to Be an] Okie from Muskogee" (1969) blasted hippies and student protesters.

By the early 1970s, rock and pop music—like the youth culture itself—seemed burned out. The Band's "The Weight"(1968), Dion's "Abraham, Martin, and John" (1968), and the Beatles' "Let It Be" (1970) showed signs of resignation. The Doors depicted the brooding, nihilistic side of the counterculture on their dark recording "The End" (1967). And Neil Young captured the somber, if not depressed, mood of the nation with his albums *Everybody Knows This Is Nowhere* (1969) and *After the Gold Rush* (1970).

Rock's Third Decade and Beyond: 1975—Present

By the mid 1970s, rock and pop were among the most successful forms of entertainment in the United States, sustained by the unprecedented level of discretionary income enjoyed by American teenagers. The Record Industry Association of America estimated total sales for 1976 at $2.7 billion. The following year, record sales increased to $3.3 billion. The expansion of the pop music field occurred during a time of rapid social change. The polarization of American society in the late 1960s and early 1970s gave way to fragmentation by the mid 1970s as public opinion splintered over myriad social, cultural, and political issues. Pop and rock also fragmented due to new subcultures with different beliefs, interests, and age groups.

Though rock and pop appeared to flow in numerous directions after 1974, most of the routes had been mapped out during the 1960s. With few exceptions, post-1975 rock and pop merely continued earlier styles such as blues-based hard rock, pop rock, traditional pop, country music, progressive rock, and R&B rock.

For example, the blues-based, hard rock style of sixties performers like the Rolling Stones, the Who, and Eric Clapton became even more popular after 1975 with the emergence of talented hard rockers Rod Stewart, Bob Seger, and Bruce Springsteen. Heavy metal also gained in popularity after 1975 through the highly amplified music of aggressive metal bands such as Led Zeppelin, Rush, Mötley Crüe, and AC/DC.

An even more outrageous offshoot of hard rock was the punk rock style developed in the mid-1970s and early 1980s by the Ramones, Iggy Pop, the New York Dolls, the Clash, and the Sex Pistols. Punk rock seemed to be rebelling against everything, including hard rock itself. Image was often more important than music, as punk rockers screamed out obscenities, stuck pins in their bodies, slashed themselves with razors, dyed their hair orange, and devised other means to shock audiences. By the early 1980s, punk rock had been transformed into a milder (and therefore more commercially viable) form known as "New Wave" by performers such as Elvis Costello, Talking Heads, the Police, and Blondie.

Another 1960s style that prospered after 1975 was pop rock—a softer sound more acceptable to middle-of-the-road listeners. Post-sixties pop rock ranged from rock-influenced performers like Elton John, Paul McCartney, and Huey Lewis and the News to folk-influenced artists such as James Taylor, Paul Simon, and Billy Joel, all three of whom continued the singer/songwriter tradition from the 1960s.

Traditional pop also flourished after 1975, as singers like Barry Manilow and Debby Boone produced slow-to-moderate-tempo pop songs, spiced with light touches of rock. Perhaps the most significant development in 1970s pop was "disco"—a blend of pop, rock, and black music characterized by a pronounced dance beat and repetitive, electronically produced rhythms. Popular disco hits included George McCrae's "Rock Your Baby" (1974), Van McCoy's "The Hustle" (1975), and Gloria Gaynor's "I Will Survive" (1979). The Bee Gees, a popular rock group from the 1960s, soared to even greater heights in 1977 with dance hits recorded for the quintessential disco movie, *Saturday Night Fever*.

Another style which made a strong showing on the pop charts after 1975 was country music. Bob Dylan, the Band, Neil Young, Rick (former teen-rocker Ricky) Nelson, and the Eagles were among the first rock artists to experiment with blends of rock and country music. Their success paved the way for the country-influenced singers Glen Campbell, Linda Ronstadt, and Kenny Rogers, and enabled Willie Nelson, Waylon Jennings, Dolly Parton, and other country artists to cross over onto the pop charts. By the late 1980s, a younger generation of country artists, including Dwight Yoakam, Randy Travis, Steve Earle, and Alabama, were reaching a wide pop audience through their well-crafted blends of country, pop, and rock.

Art rock, which had roots in the 1960s, also flourished after 1975. Sixties groups such as the Moody Blues and Procol Harum continued to mix classical music with hard rock, while newer progressive rock bands like Emerson, Lake, and Palmer; Jethro Tull; and Pink Floyd experimented with blends of rock, jazz, and classical music. Blood, Sweat, and Tears and Chicago, early jazz-rock groups, continued to record excellent jazz-influenced rock music, while Miles Davis, Chuck Mangione, and Spyro Gyra moved even closer toward a fusion of jazz and rock.

Punk rock—a style developed in the mid-1970s and early 1980s by the Ramones, Iggy Pop, the New York Dolls, the Clash, and the Sex Pistols—seemed to be rebelling against everything, including hard rock itself.

R&B rock also built on trends from the 1960s and early 1970s. Tower of Power; Earth, Wind, and Fire; and MFSB mixed rhythm and blues with jazz. Stevie Wonder, Marvin Gaye, and Prince combined socially relevant lyrics with pop, rock, jazz, and R&B. Other black singers like Michael Jackson, Lionel Richie, and Diana Ross provided smooth mixtures of pop and rhythm and blues. The most innovative development in 1970s black music was hip-hop or rap music—a postmodern, rapid-fire, musical collage of rhyming lyrics; heavy drum beats; loud, thumping bass lines; polyrhythmic sounds; and musical sampling from other styles. Beginning in the late seventies and stretching into the nineties, rappers like Run-D.M.C., Hammer, and Public Enemy attracted a wide audience, encouraging later white imitators such as Vanilla Ice and New Kids on the Block.

The music industry reinforced pop and rock's tendency to remain within familiar musical forms after 1975. By the 1970s, six major companies dominated the recording industry: CBS, Polygram, RCA, Capitol-EMI, Warner Communications, and MCA. The high costs of recording coupled with a declining and more fragmented market made the major labels reluctant to record new groups or any music that was too innovative. Specialized radio programming contributed further to the trend toward proven musical styles. The fragmentation of American culture and popular music resulted in a proliferation of radio formats aimed at particular segments of the splintered pop music audience. By the 1980s, listeners could choose among stations specializing in hard rock, soft rock, country-rock, oldies but goodies, dance music, rap, progressive rock, and heavy metal, in addition to country, classical music, rhythm and blues, jazz, big band, ethnic music, and Christian music. Musicians were constrained by these specialized formats, realizing their music would be ignored if it became too innovative.

Other market considerations made it even more difficult for new artists to be heard. By the late 1970s and 1980s, many performers were finding it unprofitable to tour due to rising costs for travel, sound equipment, stage lighting, and other tour-related items. Established acts with known box-office appeal were able to subsidize tour expenses through corporate sponsorship. Well-known performers could guarantee additional profits by marketing T-shirts, programs, and other concert souvenirs. The rise of MTV (the music television channel) in the 1980s also helped solidify the position of established stars, whose music videos guaranteed a viewing audience. Repeated exposure on MTV led to the rise of a cult of celebrity. Michael Jackson, Madonna, and George Michael, singer/dancers who could produce dynamic music videos of high visual quality, attracted huge audiences, enabling them to grab large shares of the rock and pop market.

Contemporary rock and pop have continued to address issues involving youth, race, ethnicity, class, and gender. Rock music has had much to say about the baby boom generation and youth culture. Pop and rock of the 1970s, 1980s, and 1990s recorded the passing of the baby boom into middle age. The older baby boomers' desire to hear music from their youth guaranteed the success of "oldies but goodies" radio formats, as well as middle-aged rock performers and nostalgia groups like Sha Na Na. Some songs, like the Four Seasons' "December, 1963 (Oh, What a Night)" (1976) and their lead singer Frankie Valli's solo record "Grease" (1978), looked back fondly at the past; while other hits, such as Bob Seger's "Against the Wind" (1980) and Don Henley's "The End of the Innocence" (1989), displayed more bittersweet nostalgia.

By the 1990s, rock music was no longer the sole property of the baby boom generation. As rock rolled toward the twenty-first century, it expanded its audience to include a new generation. Millions of post-baby boomers tuned in rock, as evidenced by second-generation rockers such as Nelson (the twin sons of Ricky Nelson) and Wilson Phillips (the daughters of Beach Boy Brian Wilson and John and Michelle Phillips of the Mamas and the Papas). Teenage singers like New Kids on the Block, Menudo, and Debbie Gibson aimed their music directly at this youthful audience.

Contemporary rock—like early rock and roll—has been greatly influenced by African American culture. While the problems of blacks and the civil rights movement seemed to fade from public view during the seventies, eighties, and early nineties, they remained an important subject for musicians. British rock bands such as the Clash and Sham 69 staged "Rock Against Racism" concerts in the late 1970s. Paul McCartney and Stevie Wonder's "Ebony and Ivory" (1982), U2's *The Unforgettable Fire* (1984), and Depeche Mode's "People Are People" (1983) stressed racial equality. And apartheid was the target of Peter Gabriel's "Biko" (1980) and the United Artists Against Apartheid's "Sun City" (1985).

Notions of black power and black pride have survived through Sister Sledge's "We Are Family" (1979), which became an anthem in many black communities. Rap music, which showcased inner-city African American culture, provided an even more important vehicle for young blacks to express views and concerns. Black pride surfaced on numerous rap hits in the 1980s, including Run D.M.C.'s "Proud to Be Black," Big Daddy Kane's "Young, Gifted, and Black," and Grandmaster Flash's "Freedom." Some rappers like Queen Latifah dressed in African-style clothes to demonstrate cultural pride. Others stressed black militancy. Members of the group Public Enemy expressed support for Louis Farakhan, and were accompanied on stage by uniformed guards carrying toy Uzi machine guns. Their aggressive image and enormous popularity among young, urban blacks caught the attention of the film director Spike Lee, who signed Public Enemy to record "Fight the Power" for his controversial *Do the Right Thing* (1989).

Rap music has provided a voice for specific concerns of the black community. Grandmaster Flash's "The Message" (1982) described inner-city poverty. Public Enemy's *Yo! Bum Rush the Show* (1987) explored urban violence. And N.W.A. (Niggaz with Attitude) dealt with police brutality and drugs in the late 1980s' songs "Straight Outta Compton" and "Dopeman."

Contemporary rock and pop have addressed the plight of other minorities in American society. The oppression of Native Americans was explored on Neil Young's "Cortez the Killer" (1975), Robbie Robertson's "Showdown at Big Sky" (1987), and Europe's "Trail of Tears" (1988). Hispanics gained public recognition through performers such as Los Lobos, Freddy Fender, and Gloria Estefan, and records like Los Lobos' cover of "La Bamba" (1987) and Linda Ronstadt's *Canciones de mi padre* (1987). Gay liberation was furthered in the late 1970s and early 1980s by the Village People and Boy George of Culture Club, who acknowledged their homosexuality, and by disco clubs that provided a public arena for homosexuals.

Contemporary rock continues to express the hopes, needs, and fears of working-class people. Bruce Springsteen's rise to superstardom in the mid 1970s and 1980s provided the most significant voice on the rock charts for middle- and working-class America. Capturing the sound and feel of his old neighborhood in Asbury Park, New Jersey, Springsteen sang about blue-collar life ("Factory," 1978); unfulfilled dreams ("The River," 1980); decaying cities ("My Hometown," 1984); unemployment ("Downbound Train," 1984); and other subjects of concern to ordinary Americans.

The plight of working-class Americans found expression in the music of other performers. The downturn of American industry in the seventies and eighties inspired Bob Seger's "Makin' Thunderbirds" (1982) and Billy Joel's "Allentown" (1982), while the depths to which many working-class people had fallen became the subject of John Mellencamp's "Down and Out in Paradise" (1987). The economic hard times that hit small farmers were portrayed on Mellencamp's "Rain on the Scarecrow" (1985) and Steve Earle's "The Rain Came Down" (1987). Performers led by Mellencamp and Willie Nelson even staged a benefit concert, "Farm Aid," to help farmers facing bankruptcy.

Whenever it is to her advantage, Madonna projects an innocent charm and sexuality, but at the same time she always lets her fans know that she, and not the man, is in charge.

Contemporary rock also reflects changing gender roles in the United States. The ubiquity of women in rock and pop after 1975 mirrored the emergence of liberated women in American society and culture. Independent women were featured on Mary MacGregor's "Torn Between Two Lovers" (1976), Pat Benatar's "Hit Me with Your Best Shot" (1980), and K. T. Oslin's "80s Ladies" (1987). The seventies, eighties, and nineties witnessed the growth of female rock bands such as the Bangles, the Go-Go's, and Heart; women rappers like Queen Latifah, MC Lyte, and Roxanne Shanté; and numerous women singers like Linda Ronstadt, Joan Jett, Tina Turner, Stevie Nicks, Cher, Aretha Franklin, Patti LaBelle, Janet Jackson, Rosanne Cash, Annie Lennox, and Sinéad O'Connor. But no singer better illustrates the new images of women in contemporary rock and pop than Madonna.

In many ways, Madonna is the antithesis of the women found in early rock and roll. Her many hit records, music videos, and roles in motion pictures serve as counterpoints to traditional female stereotypes. Whenever it is to her advantage, Madonna projects an innocent charm and sexuality (as in "Like a Virgin" or "Material Girl"). But, at the same time, Madonna always lets her fans know that she, and not the man, is in charge ("Papa Don't Preach" or "Who's That Girl"). En route to stardom in the eighties and early nineties, Madonna demonstrated that she could be as aggressive, dominant, and successful as any man. While her music and videos often portrayed males as sexual playthings and pushed social and cultural mores to the limits, Madonna's personal life attracted media attention because she pumped iron, used profanity in concerts, and had a brief but stormy marriage to badboy actor Sean Penn, followed by a well-publicized romantic fling with playboy Warren Beatty. Throughout it all, Madonna followed her own rules. For many female fans, she epitomized the new super-woman who could have it all: beauty, brains, career, sex, love, and freedom.

Like rock and roll of earlier decades, contemporary rock has potential for both liberation and repression. For some listeners, it remains a music of rebellion; for others, it provides a means to express traditional values or maintain cultural hegemony.

The fact that post-1975 rock music continued to be a voice for political and social protest suggests that the liberal politics of the 1960s did not die out as commonly believed. During the 1980s, numerous artists, including Talking Heads, the Ramones, Sting, R.E.M., Elvis Costello, and Midnight Oil, released records criticizing President Reagan and his policies. America's interventionist foreign policy was condemned by the Clash's "I'm So Bored with the U.S.A." (1977) and *Sandinista!* (1980); the haunting memories of the Vietnam War inspired Bruce Springsteen's "Born in the

U.S.A." (1984); and Reagan's Star Wars project was ridiculed on INXS's "Guns in the Sky," (1987).

Rock and pop musicians went on record against conservative domestic policies that seemed to ignore major problems such as urban violence, drug abuse, the savings-and-loan scandal, pollution, and poverty. One of the most thorough indictments of government's mishandling of America's social problems was Neil Young's album *Freedom* (1989). The dark, brooding LP graphically described urban problems and social injustice, while lampooning President George Bush's "thousand points of light" approach to social problems.

Some singers, like modern-day muckrakers, exposed social problems and injustice wherever they found them, focusing on a wide range of topics such as domestic violence, bigotry, and greed. For example, Suzanne Vega's "Luka" (1987) uncovered child abuse, while Dire Straits' "Money for Nothing" (1985) satirized America's consumerism and the wealth of many pop stars.

Social-activist rock artists also criticized the rise of religious fundamentalism in the 1970s and 1980s. The Crass's "Asylum" (1978) questioned Christ's divinity. The sinister musical cover of the Cramps' *Songs the Lord Taught Us* (1980) hinted that religion had a dark side. And Bruce Springsteen's "Reason to Believe" (1982) suggested religion made people meek and fatalistic.

Social awareness and an international outlook remained integral elements of rock and pop music after 1975. African music influenced the Talking Heads' *Remain in Light* (1980) and Paul Simon's *Graceland* (1986). The expanded worldview of many Americans helped create a market for "world music," featuring artists such as Jamaica's Bob Marley and the Wailers, Brazil's Uakti, and South Africa's Ladysmith Black Mambazo. Global concerns also brought musicians together for a variety of causes during the eighties and nineties. Bob Geldof of the Boomtown Rats was nominated for a Nobel Peace Prize for organizing the "Band Aid" concert of 1985. The event, featuring superstars Paul McCartney, Eric Clapton, Mick Jagger, Neil Young, and Pete Townshend, raised millions of dollars for famine relief in Ethiopia, and led to numerous other benefit concerts on behalf of the environment, human rights, and cultural understanding.

After 1975, numerous performers demonstrated that rock music was still on the cutting edge of cultural rebellion. If conservative listeners had been offended by the implicit sexuality of early rock and roll, they were shocked and appalled by the explicit sexual contents of contemporary rock. Donna Summer's "Love to Love You Baby" (1975), which featured the singer moaning and groaning in orgasmic ecstasy, led to the rise of what some critics called porno-rock. In the 1980s, Prince recorded several songs dealing with taboo topics: "Sister" explored incest; "Head" described oral sex; and "Jack U Off" focused on masturbation. Music videos on MTV during the eighties and early nineties also grew more and more daring: Madonna released videos depicting homosexuality, blasphemy, fornication, and sadomasochism; performers like Michael Jackson commonly grabbed their crotches while singing and dancing; the Divinyls' "I Touch Myself" (1991) celebrated female masturbation; and Chris Isaak's "Wicked Game" (1989) provided a soft-porn music video for home-viewing pleasure.

Contemporary rock's rebellious image was furthered in other ways. The creation of a Rock and Roll Hall of Fame in the 1980s institution-

The expanded worldview of many Americans after 1975 created a market for world music featuring artists like Jamaica's Bob Marley.

alized the "rock as rebellion" myth, canonizing rebellious figures like Elvis Presley, Jerry Lee Lewis, the Who, and the Rolling Stones. Rock grew even more outrageous as new performers—attempting to be more rebellious than the older ones—transformed protest rock into "shock rock." Heavy metal groups kept cranking up the volume, and screaming louder and louder to be noticed; hard rockers and glitter rockers appeared in a variety of bizarre costumes; punk rockers pushed the outer limits of shock rock even further, shaving their heads, gashing themselves, biting the heads off chickens, and giving themselves names like Sid Vicious, Johnny Rotten, the Dead Kennedys, the Butthole Surfers, and the Circle Jerks. Records by Alice Cooper, Kiss, and Mötley Crüe voiced anger and aggression toward parents, teachers, and other authority figures. Songs by Ozzy Osbourne, AC/DC, Blue Öyster Cult, and Metallica suggested suicide as the ultimate form of rebellion. Other records by Venom, Iron Maiden, and Megadeth sought notoriety by dabbling in satanism and the occult. Still others, like Guns N' Roses' *Appetite for Destruction* (1987) and N.W.A.'s "F_____k da Police" (1989), used profanity or violence for shock effect.

Despite the defiant image, however, contemporary rock may not be as rebellious as it appears. Some critics claim that heavy metal and shock rock merely allow teenagers to think they are outsiders, providing them with temporary escape from boring middle-class lives. By serving as safety valves for frustrated teenagers, these musical styles actually wind up defusing rebellion and inhibiting long-term change.

The rebellious image of contemporary rock should not obscure the conservative and even culturally repressive elements found in the music. Materialism, patriotism, religion, attitudes toward technology, individualism, and other traditional beliefs and values continue to be expressed in post-1975 rock and pop. For example, America's consumer culture inspired Madonna's "Material Girl" (1985) and Run-D.M.C.'s "My Adidas" (1986), and powered the growth of the disco fad and MTV. Religion was celebrated on Bob Dylan's *Slow Train Coming* (1979) and Johnny River's *Not a Through Street* (1983). The individualistic spirit of the "Me Decade" was mirrored in 1970s rock and pop. Singer/songwriters James Taylor, Carly Simon, and Carole King produced introspective records that encouraged listeners to explore personal problems rather than social issues. Disco music allowed narcissists to dance in the spotlight, displaying themselves in ostentatious clothes and jewelry. Contemporary music also facilitated the quest for self-fulfillment by providing the soundtrack for church services, aerobics classes, jogging, walking, and a variety of other personal activities.

Contemporary rock and pop reflect Americans' longstanding ambivalence toward technology. After 1975 many musicians eagerly experimented with multiple synthesizers, keyboards, and other advances in electronic technology. The dissemination of the music changed due to the introduction of the music video, the "boom box," the compact disc, the Sony Walkman, and improved home and car stereos. At the same time, the ambivalent relationship between humans and machines might explain the rise of music and dance steps that treated humans like androids. Man and machine seemed to merge in the techno-pop style of Devo's "Whip It" (1980) or Neil Young's *Trans* (1981), while disco and break dancing popularized robotic dance steps.

After 1975 certain groups continued to use rock and pop music as the means to maintain cultural hegemony. The sexism of modern America is evident in music videos such as Robert Palmer's "Addicted to Love" (1986), which spotlighted zombie-like women gyrating to a hypnotic beat; or the Fabulous Thunderbirds' "Tuff Enuff" (1986), which featured long-legged female dancers dressed in hard hats and skimpy costumes. And racism can be found in remarks made in the late 1980s by white performers such as Elvis Costello, David Bowie, and Eric Clapton. Racial animosities heated up again in the 1990s, encouraged by groups such as Public Enemy and Guns N' Roses.

Contemporary rock also provided a public forum for conservatives in the 1980s. In 1985, the U.S. Senate, in response to groups such as the Parents' Music Resource Center founded by Tipper Gore (the wife of Tennessee Senator Albert Gore) and Susan Baker (the wife of cabinet member James Baker), opened hearings to investigate the alleged obscenity of rock lyrics. Ironically, the hearings occurred at a time when many rock and rollers were actually joining the conservative cause. Neil Young, Prince, and the Beach Boys were among the many rock stars who endorsed Reagan's presidency. Other performers advanced positions associated with the political Right: Sammy Hagar, lead singer for the heavy metal band Van Halen, advocated a strong military buildup; Alice Cooper praised the capitalistic features of rock music; Guns N' Roses, by their very name, provided implicit support for the National Rifle Association; and the rise of a host of Christian rock groups can be linked to the rise of religious fundamentalism. Syndicated columnist George Will even claimed Bruce Springsteen as a disciple of conservatism, insisting (despite the singer's objections) that "Born in the U.S.A." was a patriotic anthem.

When rock and roll music first appeared in the United States in the mid 1950s, it appealed mostly to various youth subcultures. But by the 1990s, rock music had become the dominant form of popular music in the United States, if not the world, making it one of the most important cultural developments in post-World War II America. Rock music now permeates almost every aspect of American society and culture. It has influenced country music, jazz, traditional pop, and other forms of contemporary music. It has been adopted by most social and economic groups. And it has become a fixture in everyday life. Rock music can be found on television, in movies, in commercials, at weddings, at funerals, at athletic events, and in schools, churches, community centers, senior citizen homes, or anywhere else where people gather. The music's relationship to millions of Americans, its ubiquitous position in modern society, and its potential as a source of information about recent American life and thought impart rock music with significance for social historians.

[See also Adolescence; African American Music; Country and Western Music; Nightlife; Radio; Television.]

BIBLIOGRAPHY

General Works

Chapple, Steve, and Reebee Garofalo. *Rock 'n' Roll Is Here to Pay: The History and Politics of the Music Industry* (1977).
Frith, Simon. *Sound Effects: Youth, Leisure, and the Politics of Rock 'n' Roll* (1981).
Marcus, Greil. *Mystery Train: Images of America in Rock 'n' Roll Music* (1976).
Miller, Jim, ed. *The Rolling Stone Illustrated History of Rock and Roll* (rev, ed. 1980).
Stambler, Irwin. *Encyclopedia of Pop, Rock, and Soul* (1977).
Stuessy, Joe. *Rock and Roll: Its History and Stylistic Development* (1990).
Szatmary, David P. *Rockin' in Time: A Social History of Rock and Roll* (1987).
Ward, Ed, Geoffrey Stokes, and Ken Tucker. *Rock of Ages: The Rolling Stone History of Rock & Roll* (1986).
Whitcomb, Ian. *After the Ball* (1973).

The Rise of Rock and Roll (1954–1963)

Aquila, Richard. *The Old Time Rock & Roll: A Chronicle of an Era, 1954–63* (1989).
Berry, Chuck. *Chuck Berry: The Autobiography* (1987).
Gillett, Charlie. *The Sound of the City: The Rise of Rock and Roll* (rev. ed. 1983).
Goldrosen, John. *The Buddy Holly Story* (1979).
Guralnick, Peter. *Feel Like Going Home: Portraits in Blues and Rock 'n' Roll* (1971).
Hopkins, Jerry. *Elvis: A Biography* (1971).
Jackson, John A. *Big Beat Heat: Alan Freed and the Early Years of Rock & Roll* (1991).
Shaw, Arnold. *Honkers and Shouters. The Golden Years of Rhythm and Blues* (1978).

Rock's Golden Decade (1964–1974)

George, Nelson. *Where Did Our Love Go? The Rise and Fall of the Motown Sound* (1985).
Gleason, Ralph. *The Jefferson Airplane and the San Francisco Sound* (1969).
Norman, Philip. *Shout! The Beatles in Their Generation* (1981).
Norman, Philip. *Symphony for the Devil: The Rolling Stones Story* (1984).
Pichaske, David. *A Generation in Motion: Popular Music and Culture in the Sixties* (1979).
Rodnitzky, Jerome L. *Minstrels of the Dawn: The Folk-Protest Singer as a Cultural Hero* (1976).

Rock's Third Decade and Beyond (1975–1992)

Adler, Jerry, Jennifer Foote, and Ray Sawhill. "The Rap Attitude." *Newsweek*, 19 March 1990.
Cohen, Barney. *Sting: Every Breath He Takes* (1984).
George, Nelson, Sally Barnes, Susan Flinker, and Patty Romanowski. *Fresh: Hip Hop Don't Stop* (1985).
Lerner, Michael. "The Heavy-Metal Frenzy." *Newsweek*, 10 August 1987.
Marsh, Dave. *Born to Run: The Bruce Springsteen Story* (1979).
Pareles, Jon, and Patricia Romanowski, eds. *The Rolling Stone Encyclopedia of Rock and Roll* (1983).
Shelton, Robert. *No Direction Home: The Life and Music of Bob Dylan* (1986).

— RICHARD AQUILA

RURAL LIFE IN THE NORTH

Nowhere is the distance between the agricultural past and the postindustrial present greater than in "the North": the fourteen states of New England, the Middle Atlantic, and the Old Northwest, ranging from Maine to Wisconsin. Now the most urban and industrial part of the United States, this region has great ethnic and social diversity; but its rural history, although complex, can usefully be considered as a whole. It is primarily the history of men and women of European descent, who began to arrive and farm in North America in the early seventeenth century and were completing the agricultural settlement of this area by the time of the Civil War. Here, slavery was comparatively unimportant and later nonexistent, free family labor was the norm, and the ownership of land was widespread. Here too, agricultural society was first transformed and then overshadowed by the market, the city, and the factory.

The vast majority of Americans once lived on scattered farms or in small hamlets, worked according to the cycle of the seasons, and passed their lives within the compass of face-to-face communities. But with the successive transformations that have washed over American society, those ways of life now only survive in a few traditionalist enclaves, or as re-creations in museums of living history.

Completely satisfying definitions of "rural" and "urban" elude historians and social scientists. The census dividing line between places of under and over twenty-five hundred people is arbitrary, but it can be applied continuously over time. It roughly marks off the low-density settlement landscapes of open countryside and small villages from the denser concentrations of town and city life. At least up through the early twentieth century, the census line also consistently demarcated communities whose economies were primarily agricultural, or at least deeply intertwined with farming. This simple measure shows great change. In 1800 the settled area defined as the North was 91 percent rural; in 1850, after an enormous surge of westward expansion and the growth of commercial cities, it was 79 percent rural. By 1900 the rural proportion had dropped below half, to 43 percent. And in 1980 the North's rural population was holding steady at 23 percent; but only a small proportion of these country dwellers still had anything to do with agriculture.

Creating the Countryside

It is important to realize that the earliest American rural communities were not literally carved out of a trackless wilderness. Instead they were imposed on landscapes long inhabited by a diverse array of Algonkian-speaking Native American societies, whose tribal economies combined farming, fishing, hunting, and gathering in various ways. Their numbers greatly reduced and their morale weakened by previous visitations of European disease, they were dispossessed through negotiation and economic coercion, the force of arms, and the sheer accumulating numbers of the settlers with a voracious appetite for ownership of the land.

The creation of European agricultural communities in the North began with the landing at Plymouth in 1620, and the subsequent Puritan migration to Massachusetts Bay between 1630 and 1640. In those twenty years a few thousand English farmers and artisans and their families, with a sprinkling of ministers and magistrates, founded New England. Their prolific descendants soon created North America's most populous agricultural society. In the 1620s Dutch and Swedish farming settlements began in the Hudson and Delaware valleys. When in 1664 the British seized the New Netherlands and renamed it New York, they brought under the crown's authority several thousand largely Dutch settlers along the Hudson and on eastern Long Island. Swedish settlement proved impermanent, and British emigration to the Delaware Valley, dominated by Quakers from England and Wales, began with the founding of Pennsylvania in 1681. They were joined by a rapidly growing number of German settlers from the Rhineland, and later in the eighteenth century by emigrants from the north of England, Scotland, and northern Ireland. By 1720 there were over 250,000 people living along an arc from what is now southern Maine to southeastern Pennsylvania. Almost three-fifths of the total lived in New England. The first federal census, in 1790, counted two million people, the vast majority of whom were still in agricultural communities. The growth of New York and Pennsylvania, due to continuing inmigration from the British Isles and Germany, had outpaced that of New England, which now contained just under half of the North's population.

Europeans transformed the landscape of Native American settlement, where ownership was a fluid concept, boundaries were loosely defined, and cultivation was communal, by laying out permanent fields and building fences on land that had never seen either. They further appropriated the soil by reorganizing the land in familiar systems of land measurement, title, and transfer. Settlers also brought with them the cultural baggage of farming: their own local and regional specific ensembles of crops (and weeds), livestock, tools, patterns of building, and practices of cultivation. These forms of material culture and work were diverse in their details, but taken together they constituted a single vast invasion. During the seventeenth century, rye, wheat, oats, barley, garden crops, and English grasses for hay and pasture colonized the New World, along with cattle, horses, pigs, sheep, chickens, geese, and goats. With their houses and barns, their plows and carts, scythes and sickles, winnowing baskets and felling axes, settlers created material worlds that were at first outposts of rural Europe.

Juxtaposed with these agricultural inheritances was the shaping power of a new environment. North America's continental climate, untouched by the Gulf Stream that warmed western Europe, confounded the expectations of the first generations of settlers, who felt the impact of blistering summers, frigid winters, and unpredictable frosts, and painfully adapted their ways of farming. Abundances of wood and land and a scarcity of labor shaped resource-intensive patterns of farming, fencing, and building, ensuring that American farmers would be careless of natural resources and preoccupied with the felling of trees and the clearing of land for many generations.

In the seventeenth century, agricultural settlers moved gradually westward from the coastal edge, exploiting the clearings created by Native American cultivation and searching out land that appeared fertile to European eyes. The early populations were small, and the process of settlement often moved in discontinuous jumps. In New England, for example, the rich and level alluvial terraces of the lower Connecticut Valley, although many miles inland, were settled several decades before farm families moved from the coastal plain into the hilly terrain of central Massachusetts and northeastern Connecticut. Those areas were filled up during the early eighteenth century as subsequent generations reached out for land, creating a landscape of continuous rural settlement.

Northern agriculture became a synthesis of European and native crops and traditions of cultivation. Corn, beans, squash, and pumpkins, plants unknown to Europeans but which thrived in hot North American summers, were swiftly adopted by the settlers. Corn was to become the single most important American crop, and the autumn rituals of the cornhusking emerged as a distinctive harvest celebration in virtually every American rural community. However, in most respects the settlers' diet and ensemble of crops remained heavily dominated by their European inheritances: wheat and rye for breadstuffs, oats and barley, beef and pork, butter and cheese.

The land was abundant beyond anything known in Britain or western Europe for centuries. Settlers may have been in part echoing Native American agricultural practices when they adopted the long fallow as their regime of cultivation. Prodigal of abundant land rather than manure or scarce labor, American farmers would exhaust the fertility of their tillage fields in a few years and then abandon them for new ones. Increasingly scruffy and overgrown, the "old fields" lay fallow for a decade or two and then were cycled back into cultivation. In consequence, American farmsteads appeared wildly wasteful and slovenly to observers from Britain and western Europe, where land was expensive and labor relatively abundant.

The Patterns of Early Rural Society

Some of the immense particularity of British and European village life was transplanted to North America, as emigrants struggled to reenact familiar ways on unfamiliar soil. The new settlements, with their rail fences and recently built houses, could not have looked much like their ancestral communities. But dialect, the ways of family and church, the remembered patterns of customary regulation and land use, were at first traditional and wholly familiar. They changed slowly into the distinctive patterns of provincial rural America.

Many of the patterns of rural time and place changed in these emigrant societies. The two most powerfully formative streams in the North's culture, Puritanism and Quakerism, accomplished in America what they could not do in Britain: they radically simplified the traditional church and village calendars of country life. Saint's days and the elaborate observances of Christmas and Easter were abolished in many places, and their very absence became a matter of tradition. Even less radically Protestant communities, because they were new, lacked the long, place-specific histories on which customary observances and village festivals were based. With settlers mingling from many different places, local European traditions transplanted poorly. Thus the public calendars of American agricultural communities were somewhat austere and uneventful by the standards of Europe, and local landscapes had little to hallow them. The weeks were punctuated by the recurrence of the Sabbath; time was otherwise marked by yearly and quarterly civil occasions such as militia trainings, court sessions, and town meetings.

Other seasonal calendars were far more reminiscent of Europe. The rhythms of plowing, planting, cultivation, and harvest shaped intimate behavior as well as work. Most marriages in the northern countryside came in the early spring or the late fall, avoiding both the dead of winter and the months of heavy farm work from May through October. Couples married either in anticipation or in fulfillment of the cycle of planting and harvest. The seasons dictated another, more mysterious rhythm of procreation and sexuality. Births rose and fell with the seasons, peaking in the late winter and early spring, and then falling to a minimum in the later spring and summer, and sometimes rising to a second, smaller peak in the early fall. Rural couples were thus most likely to conceive in the planting season, between April and June, and least likely in the months of haying and harvest, from July through September.

Ways of gathering and drinking, courting and marrying were distinctive among America's New Englanders and Quakers, Dutch and Germans, Ulster Irish and Welsh.

The sociability of rural Northerners was structured by the household, the congregation, and the neighborhood, those little communities whose boundaries and intricate social webs encompassed most daily experience. The patterns of that world are now shrouded in contemporary nostalgia, but they were real enough: visiting and neighborly exchanges of work and goods, cooperative work rituals such as cornhuskings, house and barn raisings, logrollings, quilting parties, and spinning frolics. Ways of gathering and drinking, courting and marrying were distinctive among America's New Englanders and Quakers, Dutch and Germans, Ulster Irish and Welsh. Rooted in the social patterns of their ancestral regions, they were evolving toward a provincial American diversity.

The countryside between Maine and Pennsylvania became one of the healthiest and most prolific areas in the world. Abundant food, relatively low population densities, agricultural opportunity, and a temperate climate (contrasting sharply with the malarial South) meant that by the standards of rural Europe northern farm families produced many children—in some places averaging seven to eight per completed family—and saw more of them survive into adulthood. Natural increase combined with heavy eighteenth-century in-migration south of New England, particularly to Pennsylvania, to create an enormous surge of population. The North's population tripled between 1700 and 1750, fueling rural families' hunger for land.

Patterns of rural settlement for a time echoed and then increasingly diverged from inherited ones. Some of New England's early-seventeenth-century communities were tightly clustered villages surrounded by intricately subdivided tillage fields. They resembled those in many grain-farming regions in England, particularly the Puritan heartland of East Anglia. Village living had the sanction of tradition, made communities more defensible in conflict with the Native Americans, and was encouraged by New England's rulers because it made community life easier to supervise. But in most places it did not endure. Tradition, defense, and communal order yielded to the requirements of a more pastoral, livestock-centered agriculture and the constant pull of available land. By the early eighteenth century, a widespread pattern of dispersed settlement had emerged, with houses scattered along the roads that linked family farmsteads. In Pennsylvania there was an even swifter transition. Settlers in the first generation abandoned or ignored the village plans of the colony's proprietors to create an open rural landscape of dispersed settlement.

New Englanders continued to live more closely together than other rural Americans, and the form of the New England town, with its central meetinghouse and common, the placing of town center, and the radial roads leading to the center, remained distinctive. Most northern agricultural communities were less sharply defined in space. Churches, stores, and taverns were often strung along the roads, and families traded and socialized in country neighborhoods whose existence was clear but whose boundaries were not clearly marked.

Rural landscapes were also powerful statements of economic and social stratification. The distribution of one- and two-story, "mean" and "commodious" houses mapped out the zones of soil fertility and embodied the distribution of wealth and power. The unpainted dwellings and debris-strewn homelots of ordinary farmers contrasted sharply with the painted houses, fenced dooryards, and orderly gardens of the gentry.

Up through the end of the eighteenth century, old limits on the tools and motive powers of agriculture held fast. Virtually all work was accomplished by the muscles of men and women and draft animals, marginally assisted by the power of falling water. Oxen in New England, horses elsewhere, hauled the harvest, pulled plows and harrows, and dragged stones and timber. Waterwheels drove small-scale mills for grinding grain, sawing lumber, and fulling handwoven cloth. Almost all other tasks were performed by human effort, using the heavy, locally made implements of regional tradition.

Men's and women's tasks were intertwined and interdependent, but in space, time, tools, and authority they were generally distinct. Farmyard, garden, house, kitchen, and hearth, in diminishing concentric circles, enclosed and bounded women's daily realm. The world of men's work faced outward, from farmyard to fields and then out to neighborhood, community, and the roads leading elsewhere.

Women's work, although it had some seasonal components, was, for the most part, daily, repetitive, and constantly liable to interruption. Men's work, although it included daily chores, was far more strongly seasonal and varied more from day to day. With their edge tools, heavy implements, and care of large animals, men occupied the realm of major physical force. Cooking pots, crockery, washtubs, churns, spinning wheels, cloth, needles, and thread were counted as distinctively female. Men and boys usually handled the raw materials of farm production and undertook the first steps in processing them, after which they handed them over to women and girls to finish. Families worked as patriarchal units, governed by their male head. Men's work, and men's decisions about work, were primary.

Gender boundaries, however, were not absolute. The urgency of the harvest traditionally blurred the sexual division of labor. During the wheat harvest in eighteenth-century Pennsylvania, women worked alongside men, reaping, gathering, and binding. Haying season in New England sometimes brought women into the field to help rake and load the region's most important crop. Accepted boundaries also varied according to ethnicity. German-American women often undertook the heavy outdoor labor of preparing flax for spinning, greatly surprising observers from New England, who thought of it as men's and boys' work.

The North's abundance of both land and children meant that gaining control of land, holding on to it, and passing it along to the next generation were the crucial concerns of most rural families. Over the course of each family's span, parents struggled to acquire property and productive resources and then, as their children matured to parcel them out. Land, if possible, went to sons; other and lesser property went to daughters.

After a couple of generations of settlement, most members of the younger generation had to leave their communities to acquire land elsewhere. American farms were divisible only to a limited extent. Most rural places in the North, as they became fully settled agricultural communities, developed remarkably stable structures of landholding and the distribution of productive resources. The number of farms in most communities changed relatively little and remained virtually unchanged for a century or longer.

Contemporary travelers and some rural Northerners themselves, joined by later historians, proclaimed a roughly equal distribution of property as the defining signature of their communities. This was not strictly true; landless men and families, tenancy, and substantial inequality could be found everywhere, although in varying proportions that depended on the nature of initial settlement, the productivity of the land, and the strength of markets. Landholding was most widespread among household heads, although not universal, in New England, where farms were smaller and less productive than farther south. Tenancy was the powerful reality in the early Hudson Valley, where thousands of families lived on the immense proprietary estates of the "patroons." Pennsylvania had both a majority of independent proprietors and a substantial minority of tenants. Everywhere in northern rural America there came to be substantial numbers of families who did not own enough land for a viable, household-sustaining farm; many of them were genuinely poor. In virtually every community there were households supported by day labor; in other households, older children left to work for more prosperous families.

Nevertheless, in the broadest sense these commentators were right. When measured against the landholding systems of rural England, or the burgeoning economic inequality of the plantation South and American seaport cities, the rural North seemed egalitarian indeed. Tenancy itself did not always signal poverty or economic marginality. In areas of highly productive agriculture and expensive land it was a strategy for access to land that could sustain "middling" farm families—although family proprietorship remained the cherished goal.

Market, family, and community all shaped rural economic life. Northern farm families were unfailingly conscious of the need to sustain their lineages, but bought, sold, and mortgaged their property within a free market for land. They sought to produce their own food and raw materials, but almost never practiced household "self-sufficiency." Instead, they participated in intricate networks of neighborhood exchange of goods, labor, and the use of tools and livestock. They reckoned up their accounts with monetary values for prices and wages—but did not charge interest, settled up irregularly, and often carried debit balances for years. Depending on their location and their resources, they pursued markets for surplus grain, hay, livestock, butter, and cheese. Yet their drives to pass land to their children, to maintain linkages of kinship and community, clearly informed their search for such opportunities.

Also enmeshed in the exchange networks of country neighborhoods were the artisans, whose largely British-descended skills created most of the physical fabric of rural life. Blacksmiths, housewrights, cabinetmakers, shoemakers, potters, and coopers combined their crafts with farming and transmitted their skills and tools, as precious resources, to their sons or nephews. Rural American artisans usually practiced a much wider range of skills than their European counterparts, early establishing a distinctive pattern of occupational fluidity and versatility. Northern woodworkers might combine coopering, cabinetmaking, and housewrighting, while other "mechanics" undertook both blacksmithing and pottery, or combined clockmaking and cabinetwork. Their shaping of houses, furniture, tools, and other everyday objects began with European models but gradually and subtly developed into regional and local traditions.

Northern farm families sought to produce their own food and raw materials but almost never practiced household "self-sufficiency"; instead they participated in neighborhood exchange of goods, labor, and the use of tools and livestock.

Economic and Social Transition in the Northeast

Beginning late in the eighteenth century two powerful and unsettling processes of change took shape in northern rural society. One was a transformation—the reshaping of society and economy in long-settled communities. The other was an expansion—an immense surge of movement that multiplied farm families and rural communities across a thousand-mile stretch of territory.

Stimulated by a long-term upswing in European population and food consumption, the pattern of northern agricultural production began to intensify. Adopting some of the precepts of England's earlier "agricultural revolution," farmers gave up the long fallow for continuous cropping production on their fields, adopting crop rotation, the intensive use of manures, and the planting of root crops to maintain fertility. They cleared and planted increasingly larger portions of their farms, creating a more open agricultural landscape with unobstructed views.

Between the Revolution and the Civil War, northeastern farm families were drawn deeper into the market economy than before. Small streams of trade became torrents, moving over greatly improved and expanded roads. They increasingly turned toward more specialized and market-driven forms of agriculture, impelled both by competition from western farms and the emergence of city and village markets close at hand. As grain production lost its profitability, sometimes even for domestic use, farmers modified their patterns of diversified farming to concentrate on marketable crops. Zones of production emerged, determined principally by distance and transportation costs. Farms continued to produce goods for the household's use, but specialized in cheese or butter, wool for textile factories, livestock, hay for horse fodder, or, for those closest to city markets, whole milk, vegetables, and fresh meat. By midcentury, most New England farm families abandoned the cultivation of bread grains entirely; like city folk, they were eating bread made from New York and Ohio flour.

In those years, too, the rural Northeast became the site of America's first industrial revolution. In the countryside from Pennsylvania to southern New Hampshire, small manufacturing villages grew up along hundreds of small- and medium-sized streams. Adapting British technology and organization, most of these rural factories harnessed water-power to drive machinery for spinning and later weaving cotton and wool; others turned chair legs, gun barrels, or clock parts. Marginal rural families left their meager holdings to cluster around the mills; their children and unmarried daughters became the nation's first factory workers.

Outside the mills, a variety of other forms of rural production for distant markets emerged. Working in small shops or their own houses, rural "mechanics" made shoes, assembled chairs and clocks, forged farm implements, printed books, and built wagons. Women and girls braided straw, made palm-leaf hats, finished shoe uppers, or painted furniture, clock dials, and tinware. As late as 1850, the northeastern countryside accounted for a major share of American industrial production. In terms of total output and employment, rural mill villages kept pace with the great factory cities such as Lowell, Massachusetts, and Manchester, New Hampshire, until the 1840s. Villagers and market-oriented artisans, who did not produce much of their own food, became major consumers of agricultural produce.

Clustered settlements reappeared in the rural Northeast in the early nineteenth century, but as outposts of commerce and industry. Commercial villages emerged at the nodes of a swiftly improving road system. In New England they were called "center villages" and arose at the traditional town centers. All of them were settled primarily by shopkeepers and artisans; they were places where farm families came to trade and find services and where small-shop production became concentrated. In most places they became the focal points of social life, economic organization, and political leadership in the countryside.

A revolution in rural childbearing also began in the same years. The age of marriage rose in many places, and married couples began to limit their fertility—lengthening the interval between children or having their last child earlier. These changes happened first in the earliest settled, most densely populated parts of the countryside. They were places where family limitation would seem economically rational: land was increasingly expensive and the cost of settling children in agricultural security was becoming substantial. They were also communities, with high literacy and widespread schooling, where new attitudes toward procreation would logically take shape. Between the 1760s and the 1840s, average completed family size in some communities dropped from nearly eight children per couple to five and a half.

In the process of industrial and commercial transformation, many traditional ways were altered or abandoned. Cash transactions began to supplant long-term local exchange. Agricultural reformers denounced huskings, frolics, and customary labor exchanges as wasteful and inefficient and persuaded many farmers to give them up. A highly successful temperance movement, coming to power in the 1820s, successfully attacked another rural tradition, heavy drinking in the course of work and sociability.

The Westward Expansion of Rural Society

At the end of the eighteenth century, an enormous number of families responded to what by American standards was crowding on the land as their ancestors had done, by moving dramatically outward in search of new farms. In a great migration far swifter than the generations-long progress inland of the colonial period, hundreds of thousands of northerners filled up the western and northern margins of the established states and went on to settle five more east of the Mississippi. Migrants from southern New England pushed north to take up lands in Vermont, Maine, and northern New Hampshire. Michigan and Wisconsin were settled primarily from the northeastern states. With some exceptions, like the substantial New England presence in southeastern Ohio around Marietta, the northern and central sections of those states were claimed by New Englanders, Pennsylvanians, and New Yorkers. Many of the paths of migration roughly paralleled the lines of latitude. Western New York, northern Ohio, Indiana and Illinois, and southern Michigan and Wisconsin all bore the heavy imprint of New England settlement. In the central and southern sections, Pennsylvanians were joined by large numbers of emigrants from Kentucky, Tennessee, western Virginia and North Carolina, mostly poorer families who were leaving the slave economy behind. Indiana, with the highest proportion of upland southerners and the fewest New Englanders, was the most clearly "southern" state in the North.

Migration was not a single wave but an immense succession of overlapping movements. In 1860 in the westernmost states of Illinois and Wisconsin, the largest proportions of adult residents had been born not on the eastern seaboard but in western New York, Vermont, and Ohio; they were the children and grandchildren of original emigrants.

This expansion of northern rural society in the years between 1780 and 1860 was in many ways deeply destructive; it involved many deaths in battle and massacre and the violent displacement of tens of thousands of Native Americans and the obliteration of their camps and villages, fields and hunting grounds. From the victorious settlers' point of view, their invasion was also enormously creative, leading to the building of hundreds of thousands of new farms and the founding of thousands of new communities. In the process of penetrating to the backcountry, emigrant families gave up much in the way of material comfort and settled society, even risking early death. Adult life expectancy was lower and infant and child mortality were substantially greater in new communities than in the settled Northeast. They undertook the enormous physical challenge of clearing new land and endured often debilitating isolation—expecting not short-term benefits but agricultural opportunity for themselves and their children.

Travel times and the cost of moving goods declined rapidly in the process of America's nineteenth-century revolution in transportation, which had a dramatic impact on the North's rural economy. The expansion and improvement of roads and vehicles, the building of canals, the development of the river steamboat, and the appearance of the railroad meant that the new rural settlements, although much farther away in miles from the eastern seaboard than their colonial counterparts, decade by decade became effectively far closer in time and cost of travel. The completion of the Erie Canal in 1825, providing low-cost transportation between New York City and the farms of western New York, was only the most dramatic of these developments. Connections with wider markets followed the advancing edge of settlement with increased speed.

The rural economies of newly settled areas, like those in the East generations earlier, were sustained by semi-subsistence farming, elaborate networks of local exchange, and a trickle of outside trade. But when their communities came within reach of efficient transportation to markets, farm families found themselves responding to a changing structure of prices and opportunities by adapting and reshaping their patterns of labor, production, and marketing. As the relative costs of production and transportation changed, the geography of wheat cultivation, for example, altered dramatically. In 1800 the area of heaviest wheat production was still centered in eastern Pennsylvania. It then shifted westward across the northern states to western New York, then to northern Ohio, and by 1860 to northern Indiana and Illinois, the center of the wheat belt at the time of the Civil War. Farmers in each successive "old" wheat growing area adjusted by gradually moving away from the crop and shifting to a variety of production patterns depending on soil and location: hay and dairy, cattle, wool, corn, and hogs.

As late as 1860, mechanization played a minor role in increasing agricultural productivity. Northern farmers had widely adopted improved farm implements—cast iron and then steel plows; more effective mass-produced scythes, hoes, axes, and shovels; better farm vehicles. These made work more efficient and, along with changes in land use and cropping, allowed for the Northeast's expansion of production on long-used land. But the burgeoning output of western farms was simply based on the opening of new and highly fertile land to cultivation.

Changes in technology, some advance in productivity, and the expansion of markets allowed for a long-term increase in rural standards of living. After 1830, mass-produced implements, utensils, cloth, and furniture began to fill the households of the countryside as well as those of the city. Country cabinetmakers gave way to chair factories; rural blacksmiths early lost their roles as fabricators of tools and became repairmen. Even carpenter-builders, whose trade necessarily remained part of the local economy, moved away from traditional styles and house-framing systems. The shapes of farmhouses, plows, and chairs became far less distinctive identifiers of locality. In the Northeast this transition was long and complex. Later on and farther west, communities could go from pioneer privation to mass-produced goods, acquired via the railroad, in a couple of decades.

The great surveys of the territory north of the Ohio and east of the Mississippi, carried out under the Land Ordinance of 1785, comprised the most massive project of mapping, recording, and ordering the land undertaken up to that time. From northwestern Ohio onward they created a rectilinear rural landscape of square-cornered fields and gridded roads. For the first decade or two some settlers tried to lay out farms and houses in the more irregular patterns of the East, but all eventually conformed to the logic of the survey. This new landscape of habitation, with its 640-acre (256-hectare) sections and 160-acre (64-hectare) quarter sections, was laid out on terrain far more rolling and open than that of the East. These lines of demarcation differentiated the new rural communities of the North even more from those of rural Europe. The survey system, with its widely separated, right-angled roads, was subsequently blamed for imposing scattered settlement on nineteenth-century rural America and diminishing the cohesion of community life. But the vast majority of arriving emigrants came from places that had had dispersed farmsteads for generations. The grid system simply strengthened their existing ways of settlement. Settling groups could easily have created small hamlets of three or four dwellings where farm boundaries cornered at road intersections, but rarely chose to do so.

The new communities did not develop as the egalitarian frontier societies of American myth. In their economic structure they came to resemble the communities that the settlers had left. Substantial inequalities in wealth emerged; early-arriving families with substantial land claims were often able to gain control of the best land. Tenant farmers and marginal laboring families became as common in settled Illinois communities as in Pennsylvania.

The Noontide of Rural Society

By 1860, ten million Americans were living in thousands of rural communities from Maine to Wisconsin. This population was still most heavily concentrated in the eastern core—southern New England, the lower Hudson Valley, and eastern Pennsylvania and New Jersey—but aside from the northern reaches of Maine, Wisconsin, and Michigan, rural life everywhere was at least into its second or third generation. The daily texture of community life had in most places become relatively dense. Women and children were much less likely to lead isolated lives on their farmsteads, extensive networks of visiting and organized voluntary societies were appearing, schools and churches were more numerous and closer at hand.

Across this great expanse from the Atlantic shore to the Mississippi there was still considerable variation in material standards and the risks to health. Although considerably less isolated and gradually becoming healthier, many of the newer settlements were still difficult and dangerous environments. Malaria, for example, had not yet been banished from the river valleys of Indiana and Illinois. But overall, no large rural population in history had ever been as healthy, as materially prosperous, and as widely literate and numerate. The expansion of markets for farm production had also brought an increasing array of manufactured goods to farm households.

During the eighteenth century, New England's tax-supported district school systems had been the first to put elementary literacy within the grasp of the great majority. By the mid-nineteenth century, schooling was widely accessible, although not everywhere free, across the North. Schoolhouses became focal points of neighborhood life—and neighborhood conflict. In many settlements, the oral ways of upland southerners mingled, and sometimes collided, with the print-oriented culture of New Englanders; Yankee account keeping, for example, often offended migrants from the South, who relied on their memories and took the ledger book as a sign of mistrust. In most places, the arrangements for schooling, and often the teachers themselves, bore the Yankee cultural stamp. On the whole, however, the country people of the mid-nineteenth-century North had become far better connected with the world—through books, newspapers, periodicals, and the expanding postal system—than previous generations had been.

As the revolution in childbearing moved across the North in the nineteenth century, there were sharp east-west variations in family size and marital fertility. Families were largest—echoing the high birthrates of the colonial period—in new communities just behind

After 1830 country cabinetmakers gave way to chair factories, rural blacksmiths had to become repairmen, and even carpenter-builders moved away from traditional styles and house-framing systems.

the edge of settlement. Here land was most available and disincentives to fertility the fewest. Families grew smaller in each successive generation after settlement, as communities approximated the conditions—expensive land, high literacy, and widespread information—that triggered the transformation. Over the decades, the maximum birthrates of new settlements started to decline as well; communities with the highest fertility in 1860 were still substantially lower than their counterparts had been in 1800. The east-west gradient of rural fertility narrowed greatly over the nineteenth century. By 1900 rural families across the North were averaging no more than four or five children; their birthrate continued to decline, moving toward urban levels, but it was always somewhat higher.

Living in a sea of white faces, rural African American families held on to the lowest rungs of the occupational ladder as laborers and marginal tenant farmers, much more rarely as landowners or skilled craftsmen.

Although rarely acknowledged, and pushed to the social margin, African Americans and Native Americans were enduring presences in the settled countryside. Throughout the nineteenth century blacks could be found widely, if thinly, scattered across the rural North: most sparsely settled in northern New England with about 0.5 percent of the population, most densely in New Jersey with 3 percent, and in most other places between 1 and 2 percent. Most northern blacks had lived in the region for generations, the descendants of farm and household slaves, while some had come more recently from the South. Living in a sea of white faces, rural African American families held on to the lowest rungs of the occupational ladder as laborers and marginal tenant farmers, much more rarely as landowners or skilled craftsmen. Usually too scattered to form cohesive black communities but obviously distinct, they lived as hybridized "Afro-Yankees." Everywhere they faced racial hostility; it was most powerful, both in law and practice, in Ohio, Indiana, and Illinois, where southern emigrants were most numerous.

There were long stretches of the countryside in which few Native Americans remained; yet sizeable remnant groups still lived in many eastern communities. Farming on dwindling ancestral lands or leading a semi-itinerant existence, they traded traditional crafts or doctoring skills with their neighbors. They intermarried with African Americans and whites to create a complex, sometimes ambiguous social and cultural identity; it was one they often protected by concealment, taking on many of their white neighbors' most visible ways as a protective social front.

The great tides of foreign immigration in the nineteenth century flowed disproportionately to the cities of the North; the majority of immigrants gave up both agriculture and their ancestral soil at the same time. The northern countryside received relatively small, but visible, numbers of newcomers. By 1880 the agricultural work force had significant numbers (5 percent or more) of the Irish in southern New England, New York, and New Jersey; of French-Canadians in Maine and Vermont; of British Canadians and Dutch in Michigan; and of immigrant Germans, the largest foreign-born group in rural America, more evenly spread from New York westward through Ohio, Indiana, Michigan, and Illinois. But in each of these states, immigrants remained significantly underrepresented in agricultural work; Americans of long-settled British stock continued to dominate farming. Substantial next to the uniformly African American and Anglo-American complexion of the southern countryside, this sprinkling of ethnic diversity was relatively meager compared to the polyglot complexity of the region's cities. Only in Wisconsin was there a different balance. There Scandinavian and German immigrants were primarily rural, taking up the North's newest lands in equal numbers with the native-born.

During the nineteenth century, many kinds of production once central to the work of northern farm households moved outside its sphere. The most significant and symbolically important was the manufacture of woolen and linen cloth. In early America the vast majority of textiles for domestic use was produced in the household, although not all families spun and wove and there was substantial local exchange of cloth and yarn. Loom and wheel were the preeminent implements of female labor. But when cheap, factory-made cotton and woolen fabric became widely available to rural families, they reduced and finally abandoned household production. In southern New England wheels and looms had vanished almost completely by the 1840s. By 1860 they were disappearing across the North as the railroad penetrated the countryside and the "homespun frontier" receded across the Mississippi. Although seen by some observers as a calamitous abandonment of female industry, the disappearance of textile production created little leisure for rural women. They turned to more intensive dairying and gardening, outwork, or ever-expanding sewing.

The traditional division of work between the sexes—the oppositions of field and household, large animals and small, edge tools and needles, seasonal swings and daily repetitions—altered gradually. Probably fewer northern farm women performed fieldwork than in the eighteenth century. And there were significant changes in dairying. As grain production, primarily men's work, lost its economic importance on northeastern farms, dairying, traditionally women's work, became more widely shared between the sexes. Many farmers started to milk along with the women and some began to manage the dairy, churning butter and making cheese as well. In part, at least, men were moving to take greater control of what was now their farms' most important production process. In prosperous farm households from Massachusetts to Illinois, wives moved toward the "genteel" urban pattern, leaving garden and dairy entirely to husbands and hired help in order to concentrate on cooking, housekeeping, and childrearing. But by the second half of the nineteenth century, there seemed to be an even wider range of possibilities; in at least a few households wives moved in the opposite direction to share more traditionally male tasks like plowing and haying.

Starting around 1850, rural industrialization in the Northeast began to stagnate and then to reverse itself. A few of the bucolic manufacturing villages—those with major locational advantages—became cities. The others gradually succumbed to the economies of scale offered by urban factories, whose increasingly steam-driven technologies were independent of waterpower sites. The small production shops, once widely distributed in the countryside, and the extensive networks of outwork manufacturing in rural households yielded as well to centralization.

The great seasonal cycles of marriage and conception, so unmistakably the signature of rural society up through the early nineteenth century, began to attenuate. Births and marriages in the countryside, starting with communities closest to the cities, lost their connections with the rhythms of farm work and approximated the far less seasonal urban pattern.

The Overshadowing of Rural Society

The countryside had grown faster than the cities in colonial America, but after the Revolution this was no longer true. Starting from a very small base, urban centers developed rapidly, outpacing the still high population growth of rural communities. After 1800 rural communities in the Northeast began to lose ground in relative terms. As urbanization and industrialization developed a powerful momentum from the mid nineteenth century onward, rural predominance declined in the newer states of the North as well. In 1860, three of every four northerners lived in rural communities—a proportion that varied from one out of two in southern New England to nearly nine out of ten in Indiana and Illinois. By 1900, fewer than half of the region's people lived in the countryside.

In absolute numbers, rural population continued to grow through the end of the nineteenth century—simply much more slowly than the burgeoning cities. Although their birthrates continued to decline, rural families still produced sizeable numbers of children. As they usually had in the past, most of them left the localities of their birth—an increasing number moving farther west or to the cities, whose growth had always been fueled by rural out-migration. But their numbers were much less often replaced by in-migrants than in the past. Settled rural communities ceased to grow and their populations became increasingly older. The most marginal places—hill communities with poor soil, hardscrabble settlements isolated by geography—lost population, but most maintained a rough equilibrium. With much justification, local chroniclers and orators began to lament the loss of their best and brightest to out-migration.

Northern agricultural society faced inescapable constraints and powerful forces of transformation. The long-established land and labor patterns of American agriculture and the expectations of rural families—exemplified in the striking stability of the number of farms and the scale of farming—did not allow for the continuing subdivision and ever more intensive cultivation of the land. In the early nineteenth century, New England regional spokesmen and agricultural reformers who wanted to stem emigration and see the rural population increase had already proposed precisely this "English solution" to their countrymen, but in vain.

The enduring structures of northern agricultural society thus put a ceiling on the size of the farming population settled rural society could sustain. Other forces would drive it down. In the years after the Civil War, mechanization began to have a powerful impact on the operation of northern farms. Horse-powered reapers and threshers, mowers and cultivators, binders and hayrakes, were widely adopted by ordinary farmers. They transformed fieldwork and vastly increased the productivity of agricultural labor. Fewer hands could raise and harvest ever larger crops. Agricultural wages, and the rate of return on investment in agriculture, remained lower than those in the urban-industrial sectors of the economy. Farmland remained relatively expensive to acquire. Economic forces pulled sons out of the region to farms farther west, or pushed them out of farming entirely. Daughters found rural marriage and employment opportunities even less promising and left in larger proportions.

Added to this was the continuing cultural marginalization of rural life. In the early nineteenth century, many rural families had begun to shed much of the material slovenliness of the early American agricultural world. With painted houses and more orderly yards they strove for a gentility that beckoned from village centers and more distantly from cities. But it was not enough. They confronted a powerful sense, shaped by the now-dominant standards of the urban middle class, that the ways of the countryside were no longer normative, but painfully ungenteel, rustic, and backward. The persisting images of the "country bumpkin" or the "hick" also did their share to pull more migrants from farm to city.

Between 1880 and 1910, depending on the place, agricultural society in the North began a long and uneven absolute decline. Farm population—families living and working on farms—peaked at about 9,000,000 people in 1900 and then started a precipitous fall, with an accelerating decline in the demand for agricultural labor. The number of farms and the total acreage in cultivation declined as well. The least productive lands were abandoned; other farms were swallowed up by the expansion of cities and towns. As some fields went back to forest, the northern rural landscape reversed a three-hundred-year process of clearing and increasing openness.

After the Civil War, mechanization began to affect the operation of the northern farms. Horse-powered combine harvester and threshers like this transformed fieldwork and vastly increased productivity of agricultural labor.

The Problem of Rural Life

As early as the middle of the nineteenth century some influential northerners had begun to look at the countryside with a mixture of nostalgia, concern, and condescension. They saw agriculture and the rural landscape as a world of the past that was gradually slipping away. Men often no more than a generation removed from the farm cherished rural life—from afar—as a reservoir of physical vitality and moral virtue. But this was coupled with a growing disdain for what else they saw in rural life: narrow horizons, drudgery, and physical coarseness.

By the early twentieth century, these concerns had crystallized in the work of the Country Life movement. Social analysis and engineering emerged as a response to the enormously complex problems faced by the United States as it became a nation of cities, immigrants, and large-scale industry. Most of the Progressive Era's experts concerned themselves with slum housing, immigrant assimilation, industrial labor, or economic regulation; a few turned to the "problem" of rural life. The investigations of the Country Life Commission of 1912, and the broader work of the Country Life movement, assumed that American society was weakened by rural depopulation, social stagnation, and cultural decline. Only the countryside, in their view, could supply the cities with a sturdy "Anglo-Saxon" stock to revitalize an enervated urban population and counter the threat to native Protestant cultural and racial dominance posed by the immigrants. They feared the depletion of the rural population reservoir, and sought to reverse it by making the countryside a better place to live. But their solutions—revitalized churches, improved schools, programs of recreation and social activity—were not sought by country people themselves. When rural folk were surveyed, they wanted not social reconstruction but higher incomes.

The Country Life movement could not reverse a half century of technological change or redistribute American incomes; its aims, in fact, were rooted in professional and urban needs and realities, not rural ones.

The loss of agricultural population did not mean that the countryside was in desperate economic decline. Northern farm families continued to live well by the standards of other societies, and between 1900 and 1920 real farm incomes were rising. But they probably felt some relative deprivation. The differences between the ways in which farm families and middle-class urban households lived, although quantitatively no greater than they had been fifty years earlier, were increasingly visible and dramatic. Indoor plumbing, gas light, and easy availability of popular entertainment and a wide range of consumer goods, readily available public transportation for shopping and visiting, and even the future prospect of telephone service, electric lighting, and appliances were alluring standards not easily attained.

The Country Life movement could not reverse a half century of technological change or redistribute American incomes. Its aims in fact were rooted in professional and urban needs and realities, not rural ones. Most of its major figures were men born in the rural North who had themselves left the countryside for higher education and professional careers. They aimed at revitalizing a countryside that would be a bulwark of social stability as the United States lurched toward modernity. Their work helped to create both the discipline of rural sociology and the widespread network of Agricultural Extension agents and services rarely familiar in the countryside; but they did not massively alter rural life or put an end to population decline.

The Countryside Empties and Fills

From 1900 to 1950 the agricultural population of the New England and Middle Atlantic states and the number of farms decreased by half, while farm acreage dropped by one-third. On the more productive lands from Ohio to Wisconsin, change was substantial but less dramatic. The farming population fell by one-third, the number of farms decreased by one-fifth, but total acreage held roughly steady.

The meanings of "agricultural" and "rural" began to diverge in the twentieth century. As measured by the census, rural population actually increased during these years, while the number of farms and farm families fell. An increasing number of rural places lost all or most of their agriculture and became outer suburbs, residential communities of usually well-to-do urban commuters. In other communities people moved within the rural landscape, leaving farms to live and work in villages. High agricultural productivity meant that a declining farm population could sustain a substantial service and transportation infrastructure. Over the long term, the villages and small towns that functioned as centers of trade, service, and sociability for farming neighborhoods would lose customers, prosperity, and finally population. But this happened more gradually than the exodus from the farm.

The technological development of horse-powered equipment continued into the twentieth century, but a different kind of mechanization began to transform the work of farming again, beginning after 1920 and continuing into the 1950s. A proliferation of power equipment of all kinds—gasoline-powered tractors, harvesters, and giant combines; electric milking parlors and refrigerators—continued to reduce the role of agricultural labor. During roughly the same years, rural electrification, the expansion of the telephone system, and the widespread use of the automobile connected the communities of the northern countryside with the emerging national systems of power, communications, and transportation. These changes surely made rural life more attractive, but did not alter the long-term decline of farm population.

The Great Depression years saw the only reversal of these trends in the twentieth century. Between 1930 and 1940, farm population, total acreage, and the number of farms in the North increased slightly. The virtual disappearance of economic opportunity in the cities reduced the flow of population from the countryside and prompted a powerful counterstream of returning rural emigrants seeking security and lower living expenses on the farm.

In the 1940s, however, farm depopulation accelerated again. During World War II, the largest stream of rural emigration in American history left the countryside to serve in the armed forces or to take city jobs in wartime factories. In the climate of postwar prosperity relatively few of them returned. By 1950, only 8 percent of the North's people were living on farms.

Farming today is pursued by a minuscule fraction of the North's population; the immediate postwar figure of 8 percent dropped to less than 3 percent in 1980. There are productive farms in every state, but agriculture is dwindling in the Northeast. A "back to the land" movement among some well-educated urbanites, stressing organic farming and the conservation ethic, began in the 1970s. It has had some cultural impact, but has not been of great economic or demographic significance. Dairy farming is under severe economic stress, and much of the Northeast's best farmland has been converted to other, more profitable uses. So many less valuable fields have gone back to forest that the percentage of wooded land in the New England states is returning to levels below those of the late eighteenth century.

Farms in Illinois, Indiana, Wisconsin, and parts of Michigan and Ohio are still part of America's agricultural heartland. Fertilizers, pesticides, and genetically engineered crop varieties, the products of biological and chemical engineering applied to agriculture, have created immense harvests. Along with them ecological damage has appeared from toxic materials and repetitive monoculture. Although corporate farming, or agribusiness, is expanding in some highly productive areas, the great majority of Northern farms remain family operations. But the successful ones are very different from the farms of earlier times; they are highly mechanized and even computerized. Average farm size has nearly doubled since the early twentieth century, and the capital costs, for land and equipment, of farm operation have become enormous. Beginning in farming is now as expensive as starting up a small factory; even the most costly college education is now far cheaper than settling a child on the land.

Since 1950, changes in transportation, communications, and work have made possible an ex-urban pattern of rural life for an increasing number of American families. Now that rural distances have yielded to high-speed highways and houses can be built or rebuilt with superior domestic technology virtually anywhere, many families have pushed well past the suburbs in their search for affordable housing and open space. In the process, many Americans have accepted long commutes to work. Others can travel to workplaces in the countryside; in many of the new service and knowledge industries, telecommunications and networked computers have nullified the old economic advantages of urban concentration.

The new patterns of rural life in the North have nothing to do with actual agriculture, but they are ironically intertwined with its history. Seeking an uncluttered landscape and low-density settlement, urban and suburban American families are returning to lands that their predecessors once took up—just as hopefully, but with far different purposes in mind.

[See also Agriculture; The Frontier; Geographic Mobility; Household Labor; Landscapes; The Natural Environment: The North; Technology and Social Change.]

BIBLIOGRAPHY

Barron, Hal S. *Those Who Stayed Behind: Rural Society in Nineteenth-Century New England* (1984).

Bidwell, Percy Wells, and John I. Falconer. *History of Agriculture in the Northern United States, 1620–1860* (1941).

Bowers, William L. *The Country Life Movement in America, 1900–1920* (1974).

Cronon, William. *Changes in the Land: Indians, Colonists, and the Ecology of New England* (1983).

Danhof, Clarence. *Change in Agriculture: The Northern United States, 1820–1870* (1969).

Faragher, John Mack. *Sugar Creek: Life on the Illinois Prairie* (1986).

Fletcher, Stevenson W. *Pennsylvania Agriculture and Country Life, 1640 to 1940.* 2 vols. (1950–1955).

Garkovich, Lorraine. *Population and Community in Rural America* (1989).

Gates, Paul Wallace. *The Farmer's Age: Agriculture, 1815–1860* (1960).

Gross, Robert A. *The Minutemen and Their World* (1976).

Hahn, Steven, and Jonathan Prude, eds. *The Countryside in the Age of Capitalist Transformation: Essays in the Social History of Rural America* (1985).

Hart, John Fraser. *The Look of the Land* (1975).

Jensen, Joan M. *Loosening the Bonds: Mid-Atlantic Farm Women, 1750–1850* (1986).

Lemon, James T. *The Best Poor Man's Country: A Geographical Study of Early Southeastern Pennsylvania* (1972).

Osterud, Nancy Grey. *Bonds of Community: The Lives of Farm Women in Nineteenth-Century New York* (1991).

Prude, Jonathan. *The Coming of Industrial Order: Town and Factory Life in Rural Massachusetts, 1810–1860* (1983).

Rutman, Darrett B. *Husbandmen of Plymouth: Farms and Villages in the Old Colony, 1629–1692* (1967).

Shannon, Fred A. *The Farmer's Last Frontier. Agriculture, 1860–1897* (1945).

Thornton, Tamara Plakins. *Cultivating Gentlemen: The Meaning of Country Life Among the Boston Elite, 1785–1860* (1989).
Underwood, Francis H. *Quabbin: The Story of a Small Town with Outlooks upon Puritan Life.* New foreword by Robert A. Gross (1893; repr. 1986).

— JACK LARKIN

RURAL LIFE IN THE SOUTH

The American South, by my definition, encompasses some 700,000 square miles (1,820,000 square kilometers), nearly one-fourth of the land area of the coterminous United States. It stretches some 900 miles (1,440 kilometers) from the banks of the Ohio River to the Gulf of Mexico and some 1,200 miles (1,900 kilometers) from the Outer Banks of North Carolina to the edge of the semiarid grasslands of Texas and Oklahoma. In these spans, the region cuts across a myriad of environments, ranging from the sandy lowlands of the Gulf-Atlantic coastal plains to the highlands of the Appalachians and the Ozarks, from the cooler continental climates on the north to the steamy subtropics on the south, and from the humid and rainy biomes on the east coast to the margins of the dryland plains on the west. Amid this spacious diversity, however, southerners have forged an abiding and almost unique attachment to region and to place, an attachment that binds them together even as the winds of change transform the social and economic bases of regional consciousness.

Rurality lies at the heart of southern identity. In this most rural of American regions, the overwhelming majority of southerners during the past four centuries have been born and bred in rural communities, on plantations and farms, quarters and tenements, dispersed in open-country neighborhoods. As late as 1860, when the rest of the nation experienced an industrial and urban revolution, the countryside was home for nine out of every ten southerners. A century later, nearly half of all southerners reported a rural residence. Rurality thus has served as a powerful force shaping the South's distinctive regional identity, an identity that has not been lost despite the region's extraordinary environmental, economic, racial, ethnic, and ideological diversity.

To understand the South is to come to grips with the region's rural history and its derivatives: material derivatives such as the plantation and staple crops, slavery, race, and juxtapositions of poverty and concentrated wealth; and nonmaterial derivatives of gentility and violence, of evangelical religion, of an acutely refined sense of history (and of defeat), of bravery and courage, and of provincialism and orthodoxy. What was life like in this vast regional sea of rurality? How did it differ from life elsewhere in the nation? How have southern lives and landscapes changed over the past four centuries? These are questions that in one way or another return us to the origins of the South some four centuries ago.

The First South: Chesapeake Origins

The story of the rural South properly begins on the dawn of the seventeenth century, with the death of Queen Elizabeth (1603) and the establishment of an English colony named in her honor. The Chesapeake colony of Virginia, established in 1607 by the Virginia Company of London, would become a model for southern society, economy, and culture. By 1700, that model presented a place that was resoundingly rural, that was animated by planters and bond laborers who scattered widely across the tidewater landscape in pursuit of profits from a plantation staple crop, in this case, tobacco. The society that evolved in the Chesapeake, however, was hardly the one envisioned by the company on the outset of colonization. The directors in London envisioned instead an urban society of highly skilled artisans and craftsmen engaged in producing commodities that were in short supply in England—potash from the forests, grapes and wine, spices, silk from imported worms and native mulberry leaves, citrus fruit, and the like.

The chief flaw in the company's plan was its reliance upon a geographical theory that ascribed climate to latitudinal position. The directors believed, quite wrongly, that Virginia's location in Mediterranean latitudes would duplicate the environs and the commodities of France, Portugal, and Spain. American realities proved quite different. Dispensing with outlandish theory, colonists on the scene rapidly adapted their economy to this robust land. Within a decade of settlement, Virginians abandoned the quest for exotic Mediterranean commodities and turned instead to the bounty of native crops—to Indian corn and what King James regarded as "the stinking weed," tobacco.

Tobacco changed everything. The "weed's" adoption by Chesapeake colonists was truly ineluctable since prices were outrageously high, a pound (45 kilograms) of tobacco leaf bringing as much as three shillings before the mid-1620s. Capitalizing on the European demand for pipe tobacco, Virginians of modest means enjoyed huge profits, earning seven times or more what they could have earned as common laborers in England. Wealth and its accoutrements were instantly acquired. Within a decade of initial settlement, Virginians planted tobacco everywhere, even in the streets of the capital at Jamestown. In time, these Virginians styled themselves as "planters," their settlements "plantations"—terms which meant nothing more than an agrarian commitment to a *planted* row crop such as tobacco—in contradistinction to "farms" and farmers committed to sown or broadcast (farmed) crops such as wheat and other small grains.

Ignoring the company's continuing insistence on the production of Mediterranean crops, Virginians sought to secure the land and labor required for growing tobacco on dispersed plantations. Land was cheap and readily available; labor was neither. To solve the problem of labor scarcity, the planters turned to the bond labor of servants and slaves. Although a score of African slaves came into the colony in 1619, the institution of chattel slavery made little headway until very late in the century. Planters initially preferred the labor of English indentured servants. The indenture or contract obligated the servant's labor for four to seven years in exchange for the planter's provision of transportation and, at term's end, a small amount of land, tools, and clothes. With the gearing up of the servant trade, Virginians secured regular supplies of labor (several thousand bonded servants and slaves each year) and expanded the region of settlement from its initial nucleus in the James River valley across the sandy coastal plain and along the estuarine valleys of the York, the Rappahannock, and the Potomac.

The Chesapeake frontier at first expanded at a modest pace. Following the dissolution of the Virginia Company of London in 1624 and the decline in tobacco prices at the end of that decade and into the 1630s, settlement remained concentrated in the James Valley and the peninsula between the James and York rivers. The establishment of Maryland in 1632 brought a new wave of settlers to the Chesapeake. Following a decade or so of experimentation with feudal systems of land tenure, Marylanders also turned to tobacco and dispersed plantation settlement. The pace of frontier expansion quickened noticeably after 1650 (aided by the productivity-improving innovations of tobacco topping and house curing); indeed the rate of expansion in the next quarter century (over 3 percent per annum) ranks among the largest in the history of the American frontier.

The results, however, dismayed visitors to the Chesapeake in the 1670s and 1680s who lamented the recklessness and disorder of expansion. They were horrified by a landscape of small, slovenly maintained clearings punctuated by hilled rows of tobacco and corn, animals running freely about the landscape, isolated ramshackle dwellings and crude barns (the early tobacco houses), and the utter absence of towns—all of which in their view jeopardized a civilized English way of life. Nor was life entirely agreeable for settlers themselves, faced as they were with a short life (on average, about forty years for those who survived to twenty years of age), high infant mortality, the debilitations of malaria and assorted waterborne diseases, and in consequence, an unusual number of the widowed and orphaned. In all this bleakness, however, there was the beacon of modest opportunities for achieving a rude and egalitarian sufficiency. Not a few servants became free, moved up into the ranks of the small planter, married, and had children. Somehow, this disordered, disheveled, and dispersed way of life seemed to be working. But all of that was about to change.

The rough egalitarianism of Chesapeake life in 1680 gave way by 1730 to a class-structured society, stratified in descending order of wealth and status. Among the freemen, planter elites stood at the top, ordinary planters in the middle, and white tenants at the bottom; slaves were, of course, lower still. This massive transformation of Chesapeake society was set in motion by the wholesale importation of slaves, mostly off-loaded from West Indian sugar plantations strapped with huge debts accumulated during the economic crisis of the 1680s. Chesapeake blacks, who accounted for scarcely 5 percent of the population in 1675, contributed 25 percent by 1710. In the most productive tobacco counties, slave proportions occasionally exceeded 50 or 60 percent by the time of the American Revolution. Simultaneously, the indentured servant virtually disappeared from Chesapeake probate inventories.

The rough egalitarianism of Chesapeake life in 1680 gave way by 1730 to a class-structured society, stratified in descending order of wealth and status.

Although the reasons for this sudden labor transformation in the Chesapeake are in dispute—was it purely a market response, on the one hand, or planter dissatisfaction with the unruly and rebellious behavior of servants, on the other—scholars do not disagree about slavery's structural effects on Chesapeake society. The mass importation of slaves at once narrowed the ordinary planter's opportunities for economic mobility and concentrated wealth and income in the hands of those with the capital sufficient for slave purchase. Given the tenfold (and often more) differential between a solitary planter's annual income from tobacco and the costs of a slave, slave ownership—and productive power and wealth—soon became concentrated in the hands of half or fewer of the white households. Low tobacco prices in the 1680s and 1690s exacerbated the problems of the poorer planters, such that in some tobacco districts as many as a third of the white households in 1710 owned neither slaves nor land. The revival of tobacco prices offered little solace; tenancy continued to grow, encompassing half or more of all households in some areas by the Revolution. For many in the Chesapeake, tenancy had become a permanent status. Simultaneously, the planter elite solidified its wealth and power. Between 1720 and 1750, the largest planters—those owning thousands of acres and a hundred or more slaves—differentiated themselves from the lesser sorts through the refinements of conspicuous consumption, formal education, Anglicanism, provincial politics, and local patronage and philanthropy.

In this ossifying social system, exit offered the principal option for poor white planters and tenants. Accordingly, the outflow of tidewater migrants to the piedmont and the backcountry became a flood as the century progressed. Frontier expansion lurched forward. (It had previously been slowed to a trickle by the depression of the 1680s and 1690s, increasing at a rate of barely 1 percent per annum.) In the back parts of Maryland and Virginia, the tidewater's refugees mingled with others from Pennsylvania who came in search of land or freedom from religious and political persecution. Out of this curious mélange of tidewater creoles, pietist Germans, Scots, and Scotch-Irish emerged a new rural ethos, one that was disposed toward freedom, egalitarianism, religious enthusiasm, and the appeals of the Great Awakening. Evangelical preachers on the circuit found their most receptive audiences among these isolated, often aggrieved, and oddly cosmopolitan peoples.

The Second South: Carolina

As Chesapeake planters made the turn toward slave labor and poised for expansion into the back-country, the Carolina proprietors were giving birth to a second South some 500 miles (800 kilometers) away. Having secured a colonial charter following the restoration of the Stuart monarchy in return for their loyalty to royalist causes, the Carolina proprietors envisioned a colonial refuge for nobility, lordly ideals, and feudal baronial tenures. After a series of false starts, settlement was launched at Charleston in 1680 and the town's progress exceeded all expectations. Charleston grew rapidly as it attracted the well-to-do dispossessed—the West Indian sugar planters escaping hard times and the French Huguenots (Protestants) fleeing the Counter-Reformation—as well as English traders seeking profits from the deerskin trade with the dense Indian populations of the interior.

As the town grew and settlement spread into the surrounding lowlands, the feudal dreams of the proprietors quickly slipped by the wayside. Carolinians sought a more enduring and practical economic base for their colony. The Indian trade and provisions exports to the sugar islands in the West Indies proved serviceable for the pioneer economy, but these trades gradually gave way to productions of rice and, at a later date, indigo. Rice—and its corollary, slavery—swiftly assumed hegemony over the Carolina economy. Between the successful introduction of rice in the late 1690s and 1730, wealthy Carolinians and their slaves installed one of the most sophisticated agrarian systems in American rural history. They deployed an irrigation system that relied upon the technology of tidal hydraulics for raising and lowering water levels in the freshwater back-swamps where rice was grown. The intricate system of embankments, canals, channels, sluiceways, and subtle gradients required by rice demanded an enormous investment in the preparation and maintenance of irrigation's infrastructure. This system was unthinkable in the absence of massive labor inputs. The minimum cost of entry, by most accounts, was ownership of fifty slaves per rice plantation. With initial investment running at £3,000 (and often more), Carolina's agrarian economy precluded all but the wealthiest men. But for those who could afford it, the investment paid enormous dividends. By the early eighteenth century consumers in southern Europe and in England were more than willing to pay a premium for the moist, full-bodied rice of the Carolina low country.

Carolina's prosperity soon shaped a distinctive social geography unlike any other along the Atlantic seaboard of North America. The wealthiest men in America, and perhaps the world, merely sojourned on their vast rice plantations. Most of them and their families spent only a few months of the year in the humid back-swamps of coastal Carolina and among their slaves (many directly from Africa) who constituted anywhere from 70 to 90 percent of the population, depending on the season. Plantation overseers conducted most of the daily business, especially in the summer and early fall when planters and their families fled the fetid air, malaria, and dysentery in favor of their town houses in Charleston or the healthier climes such as Newport, Rhode Island. As one observer, Johann David Schöpf, remarked about this region, it was in the spring a paradise, in the summer a hell, and in the fall a hospital. Rich planters and their families simply evacuated the region when conditions grew hellish; slaves and overseers meanwhile endured the insects, the muck, the sickness, and the death in anticipation of October's glorious relief.

Although the Carolinas and the Chesapeake by 1730 shared the institution of slavery, the two regions in other respects could not have been more unlike. Only the very elite among the Chesapeake planters could compare in wealth with Carolina rice planters. In the Chesapeake, ownership of fifty or one hundred slaves was exceptional; in Carolina, these were the minimal costs of entry. Consider too the contrasting meaning of rurality in these two regions. In the Chesapeake, except for an occasional trip to the capital or the rare trip to Europe, planters and their families spent their days in the countryside. Middling and small planters were even more isolated, their travels limited to the county court, country stores, local inns, and tobacco inspection stations. Oddly enough, owing to the numerous tidal tributaries of the Chesapeake Bay, news from England was often more readily available than news of one's neighbors several estuaries away. In the Carolina low country, by contrast, rurality for the rich was seasonal. When the planters left the swamps in late spring, the social scene shifted to their town houses in Charleston. Their flight, in turn, enabled the black majority in the rural districts to preserve and to nurture a distinctive way of life that accented African cultural traits and values—a way of life that was denied to slaves in the Chesapeake, divided up as they were into small groups and scattered among the far-flung plantations.

The Upland South

If coastal Carolina was a world apart, so too was its backcountry. Superficially, South Carolina's backcountry seemed merely an extension of migrant streams that had flowed along the Appalachian flanks in Virginia and North Carolina; but in fact, the differences in these two frontiers were profound. To the South Carolina frontier goes the distinction of having served as the seedbed for a new American, what we have come to know variously as the upland southerner or, less kindly, as the "cracker" and the "redneck." This type traces its origins to the interior's sociogeographic insularity. The upland South was insulated, in the first instance, by its geographical distance from the coastal life of South Carolina—the linear distance of some 100 miles (160 kilometers) or more and the social distance between the arrogance of great wealth and the humility of rude sufficiency—and, in the second instance, by the frontier's unusual ethnocultural homogeneity—mostly migrants originating from the margins of the British Isles, from Scotland, Wales, and northern Ireland—and its reinforcement by the dense distribution of these groups. Unleavened by coastal Anglicanism or the German pietism that was so widespread in the Virginia and North Carolina backcountry, the upland southerners of South Carolina and Georgia adhered to a more austere Presbyterianism that was nonetheless well suited to an economy of subsistence and, as applied by the privileged coastal elite, a provincial polity that neglected the backcountry.

As the American Revolution unfolded, the British military sought to take advantage of the geopolitical tensions that divided South Carolina's upland from its low country. Following their humiliating defeat at Saratoga in 1777, the British shifted the theater of action south from New England to the West Indies, South Carolina, and Georgia. On the mainland, they quickly won control of Charleston. Soon after the city was secure, they thrust units into the interior hoping to capitalize on the upland's disaffection. The British strategy was foiled by the military genius of General Nathanael Greene. Although winning few battles in the upland and the backcountry, Greene succeeded in extending British supply lines, forcing the invading army to commandeer provisions and materials from the residents of the interior, and shifting the upland's allegiance from the British to the American cause. More important for the rural South, there emerged from this maelstrom a new southerner—devout and evangelical, intensely rural, tough, and, when necessary, violent—poised for the headlong expansion that was to come.

The Cotton South

The rural South stood at the crossroads in the years immediately following American independence. The path taken led to the region that we know today; the path not taken led in an entirely different direction, into the American mainstream. The latter path for the South, in fact, seemed more probable as late as 1790. At that point, the future of the institution of slavery was clouded; many tobacco planters, faced with unusually soft markets for their crop, abandoned the "weed" in favor of wheat and corn. These crops lent themselves to seasonal wage labor rather than slave labor. Most Americans in the 1780s seem to have envisioned a withering away of slavery to a residual nucleus confined to the coastal swamps of South Carolina and Georgia—all of which may explain the constitutional abolition of slave importation by 1808.

This vision, however, did not allow for the invention of the cotton gin in 1794 nor for the spectacular profitability of short-staple upland cotton, nor even for the concatenation of gin, cotton, slavery, and the evangelistic farmers of the upland South. Wedding themselves to this new and revitalized plantation economy, upland southerners swept southwestward and around the tip of the Appalachians, planting slavery and cotton in the Georgia piedmont, the fertile black belt of central Alabama and Mississippi, and the rich alluvial soils in the valleys of the Alabama, Tombigbee, Pearl, and Mississippi rivers. In the flush times of high cotton prices between 1800 and 1830, the rate of expansion on the southern cotton frontier was astonishing, tripling or quadrupling rates of expansion elsewhere in the nation. Many of these settlers, especially those from the Upper South, brought slaves with them, but most upland southerners, having no prior experience with slavery, brought only their families, acquiring slaves as their ensuing prosperity and the domestic slave trade allowed. Although opportunities for economic advance were vastly improved through slave ownership, the lack of slaves did not preclude small planters from engaging in cotton production; indeed, many white households in the cotton belt relied exclusively on family labor, women included.

Cotton output, aided by the muscular economic recovery of the 1850s, increased to over five million bales per annum by 1860: Cotton was king, commanding the economy of the Lower South.

The breakneck pace of southern frontier expansion effectively came to an end with the long depression that began in the late 1830s. During the next two decades, frontier expansion gave way to intensification, to the concentration of people and cotton production in regions of fertile soil. Cotton output, aided by the muscular economic recovery of the 1850s, increased to over five million bales per annum by 1860. Cotton was king, commanding the economy of the Lower South and, with 52 percent of the value of all American exports, influencing the economy of the nation at large.

The cotton belt and rurality were synonymous on the eve of the Civil War. The rural economy offered little scope for cities and towns since the marketing of cotton created very modest demands for transportation and handling services. The usual marketing margin (the proportion of the market price allotted to mercantile services and transportation) for cotton of 7 or 8 percent was half to a fifth the margin charged for Northern grains and livestock. Moreover, the exceptionally high level of wages in Southern cities—a reflection of the returns one could make in the countryside—further blunted the urban impetus. Cities and towns accordingly were few in number, and those that did exist served as mere adjuncts to the cotton trade—coastal entrepôts, for example, or the tiny steamboat landings that lined the riverways. Most of the rural population of the South, 90 percent or more, worked cotton plantations; roughly half of their plantations used slave labor, supervised in the case of large plantations by white overseers; those who did not own slaves hoped to do so, by first acquiring land and then a mule or two. Although wealth was highly concentrated among the larger planters, small planters were rarely poor. So long as cotton prices remained high, the economy offered tangible opportunities for social advancement; the dramatic increase in cotton demand and slave prices during the 1850s was worrisome to their prospects however.

The mentality of cotton planters is much debated among historians. Some historians see a mentality of quasi-feudal paternalism embedded within a two-tiered society of planter elites and poor whites; others describe a rational, market (capitalist) mentality operating within a continuously differentiated social structure. More recently, proponents of the dual-society hypothesis have argued that evidence of high levels of subsistence production (corn and hogs) among the lesser planters at once warrants seeing them as peasant-like yeomen and confirms the more general hypothesis. Conversely, critics of this hypothesis point out that subsistence production was in fact a rationally efficient strategy of crop management in which planters rotated cotton with corn intercropped with soil-renovating cowpeas. That strategy enabled planters to maintain profits while reducing the costs of soil erosion (declining productivity and out-migration expenses). The success of this sophisticated system of crop rotation explains, according to the proponents of a capitalist mentality, the cotton belt's self-sufficiency in food as well as its increasing disregard for frontier expansion. One thing seems clear after the dust has settled around this debate—nonslaveholding planters in the cotton belt were not poor by standards elsewhere in the South or in the nation.

The Other Antebellum South

A case in point is the sad fate of the first South and its planters who lived alongside the tidal estuaries of the Chesapeake Bay. Their woes were several: the post-Revolutionary introduction of a series of unwise agrarian reforms, including the substitution of plowing for hoe-hilling (the practices of hoe-tillage and planting crops in tiny mounds or "hills"); the ensuing erosion and exhaustion of once-fertile soils; the migration of tobacco production into the piedmont; and the incessant fluctuations in tobacco markets and prices. Devolution of the coastal economy was manifested in a series of regional pathologies—a dual economy of poor whites and threadbare elite planters; a fiercely competitive labor force mottled by poor whites, recently manumitted blacks, and hired slaves; and a boiling mix of class and racial enmity.

Here in the first South was a hothouse for extremist ideology. And each class found its standard-bearer; for the threadbare elite, the Virginia planter George Fitzhugh (1806–1881) called for order through the paternalist enslavement of all men, poor whites as well as blacks; for the poor whites, the North Carolinian Hinton Rowan Helper (1829–1909) called (in virulently racist language) for the emancipation of poor whites through the African repatriation of American blacks; and for blacks, the Virginian Nat Turner (1800–1831) called for the emancipation of slaves through his example of violent rebellion. Reactions varied. Northern abolitionists, papering over the extremism of ideologies nurtured in the decay of the Old South, rather too eagerly projected these insensibilities to the South as a whole. In truth, planters in the cotton belt, or for that matter in the tobacco belt of the Virginia and North Carolina piedmont, had little sympathy for any ideology other than the one which justified their continuing pursuit of profit in a slave society.

The South in 1860, then, was not a monolith. More correctly, it consisted of a curious patchwork of disparate rural regions and conflicting ideologies bound together only by slavery's thin strand. Regional ideologies, ranging from the cotton belt's capitalist boosterism trumpeted in *De Bow's Review* to the mid South's pragmatic accommodationism voiced by the legatees of Henry Clay in Kentucky and Tennessee to the tidewater extremism of Fitzhugh, Helper, and Turner, were as varied as the South itself. Secession joined the first and the third of these in an uneasy and sometimes contradictory coalition, which nonetheless fought valiantly and at great cost in behalf of the preservation of slavery and the various meanings that were attached to a "southern way of life."

The Postbellum South

The grisly costs of the Civil War were especially high in the rural South. In just four years of war, over a quarter of a million Southerners died; hundreds of thousands of others were injured. Physical destruction decimated parts of the South, especially the war-torn valleys of the Mississippi and the Tennessee rivers, the corridor from Chattanooga to Atlanta to Charleston, and tidewater Virginia. Other parts escaped relatively unscathed. But the outcome of the war reached into every corner of the region. Slavery was abolished once and for all, and Southerners set about reconstructing a new way of life.

Perhaps the hardest adjustment for the postwar South involved piecing together a rural economy that had been smashed apart by emancipation. The task amounted to a reunification of the property rights in labor which henceforth were vested in black freemen with the property rights in land which remained in the hands of planters—some desultory attempts at land reform notwithstanding. The reunification occurred through a series of private negotiations, later reinforced in law, between the white owners of land and the black owners of labor. Planters assumed the initiative, introducing a bewildering array of contractual agreements for the right to use their lands. These tenancy agreements ranged from straightforward cash rentals of land to highly ornate contracts specifying the freeman's share of the crop in return for the planter's provision of land, implements, seed, and capital.

These agreements achieved their highest refinement in the cotton belt. The share or cropper contracts provided poor blacks and poor whites with an annual lease on land, equipment, mules, seed, fertilizer, and provisions in return for delivering to landowners some negotiated fraction of the crop output at harvest. The share of the crop delivered in these agreements usually ranged from one-third to three-quarters, the amount depending on such factors as labor scarcity and the inputs contributed by the cropper and the landowner. These agreements soon fragmented the orderly geography of the antebellum plantation landscape into a myriad of small tenantries of twenty to forty acres (eight to sixteen hectares) dotted by the frame cabins of the freemen. By 1880, tenant farms constituted over half of all farms in the cotton South; of these, three-fifths were worked on sharecropping agreements.

The restructuring of postbellum land tenure and plantation settlement was accompanied by dramatic changes in crop combinations and land management. Planters and tenants soon abandoned antebellum crop diversification with its rotation of cotton, corn, and cowpeas in favor of cotton monoculture and commercial fertilizers. The availability of cheap fertilizers—using phosphate rock mined from the South Carolina coast after 1868—ignited a "guano craze" in the eastern cotton belt in the 1870s. Persuaded of fertilizer's low costs and high yields by the promotional efforts of the industry and state agricultural experts, planters and their tenants eagerly switched to a system of cotton monoculture. Henceforth, on credit accounts with country stores and local merchants, they purchased corn, pork, and other provisions as well as fertilizers.

Initially, the returns from the new agrarian system were promising, but yields soon declined owing to nitrogen deficiencies in the commercial manures. Seeking to counter declining yields, planters and tenants applied even more fertilizer. Debts for the additional fertilizer and provisions mounted, and crop liens ensued. As debts accumulated, claims on the cotton crop were projected two, three, or more years into the future, all of which has been summarized under the label of "debt peonage." Flight was one of the few ways of escaping out from under this mounting debt burden—and many did just that; state legislatures, in response, attempted to check debt flight by enacting laws that restricted mobility.

As the adversities associated with cotton monoculture, fertilizers, and debt peonage diffused ever westward into the cotton belt between 1870 and 1910, it collided with an equally devastating pathology that was working its way east. The boll weevil came east from Texas in the 1890s, to Louisiana and central Mississippi by 1910 and to South Carolina and Georgia by 1920. In the wake of this destructive insect, cotton acreage and yields fell by 27 and 31 percent, respectively. In Georgia, yields declined by half.

The boll weevil's advance constituted an "economic black death" for the cotton belt; the invader set in motion a sharp reduction in cotton acreage, calls for diversification, and a glut of excess labor. Croppers and tenants, mainly black, left the South in growing numbers. Between 1900 and 1930, 712,000 blacks left the region, a fivefold increase over the 1890s. Although black population in the South continued to grow, outmigrants from the region exceeded net additions by 70 percent. In some parts of the South, black evacuation reached such proportions that labor shortages ensued. Planters in the rich plantation districts along the Mississippi River, for example, looked increasingly toward mechanization as a solution to the heavy losses incurred by the black exodus.

Elsewhere in the South, the Civil War and slave emancipation resulted in similar restructurings of rural life and landscape. In the postbellum tobacco economy of Virginia and North Carolina, plantations were fragmented into scores of small cropper and cash tenements. Two differences were noteworthy, however. First was the spectacular rise in the world demand for tobacco. Unlike southern cotton production which peaked in 1930 at nearly fourteen million bales and then fell to eight million bales, tobacco output increased rapidly between 1890 and 1930 and has maintained that position since. Second was the need for quality control in tobacco production and the advantage that need conferred upon tenancies based on rentals rather than shares. In the case of sharecropping agreements, responsibility for quality control rested with the landowner; in cash rentals, the incentives for quality were shifted to the tenant. Black as well as white tenants thus acquired increasing responsibility for the wider range of entrepreneurial decisions that are usually associated with a market economy. The market's penetration into the tobacco belts of Virginia, North Carolina, and central Kentucky received an added fillip by the taking off of the cigarette industry after World War I with its even more exacting demands for high-quality leaf and quality differentiation.

Much more might be said about postbellum restructurings in other parts of the South—for example, among the vast and highly capital-

Most of the Southern tenant farmers were sharecroppers, providing a percentage of their crop to a landlord in return for an annual lease of land and equipment. A twentieth century sharecropper stands next to his tobacco barn in South Carolina.

ized plantations that lingered on in the old coastal rice districts of South Carolina and Georgia and in the riverine sugar plantations in southern Louisiana. The scale of operation in these regions precluded the profusion of tenancy and devolved instead toward a production system reliant principally upon wage labor, bound by various devices to the production units. Least affected by emancipation perhaps were the many small and diversified farms that fringed the great staple regions of cotton, tobacco, sugar, and rice. Corn, hogs, and assorted other crops continued to provide subsistence and small market surpluses for farmers in the Appalachians, the sandy Gulf Coast, and Kentucky and Tennessee distant from the rich alluvial soils or the productive basins around Nashville and Lexington.

The New South: Restructuring Agrarian Economy and Society

The most recent changes in the history of the rural South have been the most sweeping in their scope. An Old South has given gave way to a New South. Originating in the calamities that beset the region earlier in this century—the boll weevil, failing cotton yields and acreages, massive out-migration, and finally the Great Depression—the New South presented by the 1960s a stripped-down, mechanized, and diversified version of the traditional rural economy. In the process, cotton moved from the center to the margin of southern rural life. The core regions of cotton production shifted westward into Texas and, eventually, the irrigated fields of Arizona and California. Southern cotton output fell from fourteen million bales in 1930 to about eight million bales by 1970. Tenants and croppers, white and black, left the countryside en masse; constituting 40 to 50 percent of farm operators as late as 1950, their proportion had fallen to 12 percent by 1974. Black farm population declined from 536,000 in 1950 to 56,000 in 1978. Concurrently, rural population fell from some 70 percent in 1930 to about 40 percent by 1970. The painful human consequences associated with these dislocations is not hard to imagine.

A new way of life filled the void left by the evacuees. Farm machinery, often subsidized by federal crop-support payments, quickly replaced the croppers, tenants, and mules. Over one-fifth of all southern farms in 1950 used tractors for cultivation. Mechanized cotton pickers, developed in the 1940s, harvested a quarter of the cotton in the Delta counties of Mississippi by the early 1950s. The peanut harvest was increasingly mechanized. Tobacco planters introduced the riding primer for harvesting the leaf in the 1950s followed by the bulk curing barn and the tobacco combine. Chemical weed killers were added to this technological arsenal during the 1950s. These technologies set in motion what one historian has called the "great enclosure." Southern landowners reassembled the fragmented southern landscape. Reconstituting the miniholdings of departed or displaced croppers and tenants, farmers and planters created a neoplantation that bore a striking resemblance to its antebellum precursor. Southern farm size increased steadily; abandoned cropper cabins were bulldozed under, monoculture was abandoned in favor of diversified production—livestock (facilitated by pasture improvements and veterinary medicine), fruit, peanuts, soybeans, wheat, poultry, forestry products; machines replaced the labor of men and mules; agrarian decision making was returned into the hands of a relatively small number of landowners. Rural residents declined from 60 to 70 percent of the population in the 1930s to 30 to 40 percent by the 1970s.

The invasions of electrification, industrialization, urbanization, and the state into the countryside contributed also to the transformation of the rural South. Federal and state policies promoted rural economic development; subsidized electrification, mass communications, and agricultural mechanization; and encouraged diversification of the agrarian economy. Rural industrialization, though dating to the 1880s and the rise of textile factories in the Carolina piedmont and steel mills in central Alabama, accelerated dramatically after World War II. Attracted by cheaper labor, anti-unionism, and state subsidies, industrial firms have flocked into the rural South. In the 1990s automobile assembly plants and parts suppliers have transformed the rural landscape of Tennessee much as petrochemical plants previously reconfigured riverine and coastal Louisiana and Mississippi in the first half of the twentieth century. Mobile, Alabama, once a great cotton entrepôt second only to New Orleans, claimed fame as the world's leading port for the export of pulp and paper manufactured in interior mills. A string of cities, an incipient southern megalopolis, tied together the country from Winston-Salem in North Carolina to Birmingham, Alabama. Many other cites experienced rapid growth, pulling to them non-southerners and rural

Originating in the calamities that beset the region earlier in the century, the New South of the 1960s presented a stripped-down, mechanized, and diversified version of the traditional rural economy.

southerners alike and increasing the religious and ethnic diversity of the region.

The paradox of the rural South is that its values and mentalities endure even as its material substrate evanesces. Consider the continuing impress of rurality in southern culture, in matters of faith, race, honor, and history. The Baptist faith, as any map of American religion plainly shows, remains the rock of southern religious life for blacks and whites. The evangelicalism, the revivals, and the awakenings first nurtured by backcountry settlers in the eighteenth century and later syncretized into slave society during the nineteenth century persist into the present. In the matter of race, the rural South is unique among American regions. Although the nearly four centuries of southern race relations have been unusually difficult for both races, that history has on occasions such as the civil rights movement produced moments of extraordinary heroism and creativity.

The rural South's refined sense of personal honor similarly endures in its tradition of military service, as casualty maps from the Civil War to the Vietnam War readily attest. It endures too, less felicitously perhaps, in the region's historical propensity for extralegal violence and vigilantism—from colonial duels to slave insurrections, from secession to lynching. And last there is the burden of southern history, the reality that the South alone among American regions has suffered the crushing defeat of war. Could it be, paradoxically, that in the troubles that the rural South has seen—in matters of faith, race, honor, and defeat—lie the seeds of the unusual loyalty and allegiance of its diverse peoples.

The continuing vibrance of southern ruralism is no mere cultural lag, as the sociologist John Shelton Reed is at pains to point out. Regional consciousness in the South, he observes, transcends ethnicity, race, gender, class, and the transformations imposed by the New South. Its origins lie in a uniquely rural geography, a distinctively troubled history, and the heightened sensitivity that ensues from relentless external critique. It is one thing for one southerner to call another a "redneck," a "cracker," a racist, or the like; it is quite another for the outlander who tries to follow suit.

[See also Agriculture; The Frontier; Geographic Mobility; Household Labor; Minorities and Work; The Natural Environment: The South; The Plantation; Slavery; Technology and Social Change.]

BIBLIOGRAPHY

General Works

Cooper, William J., and Thomas E. Terrill. *The American South: A History* (1991).

Gray, Lewis C. *History of Agriculture in the Southern United States to 1860.* 2 vols. (1933).

McCusker, John J., and Russell R. Menard. *The Economy of British America, 1607–1789* (1985).

Reed, John Shelton. *One South: An Ethnic Approach to Regional Culture* (1982).

The First South

Earle, Carville. *The Evolution of a Tidewater Settlement System: All Hallow's Parish, Maryland, 1650–1783* (1975).

Isaac, Rhys. *The Transformation of Virginia, 1740–1790* (1982).

Morgan, Edmund S. *American Slavery, American Freedom: The Ordeal of Colonial Virginia* (1975).

The Second South and the Upland South

Clowse, Converse D. *Economic Beginnings in Colonial South Carolina, 1670–1730* (1971).

Coclanis, Peter A. *The Shadow of a Dream: Economic Life and Death in the South Carolina Low Country, 1670–1920* (1989).

Fischer, David H. *Albion's Seed: Four British Folkways in America* (1989).

The Cotton South and the Other Antebellum South

Fogel, Robert W., and Stanley L. Engerman. *Time on the Cross.* 2 vols. (1974).

Genovese, Eugene D. *The Political Economy of Slavery: Studies in the Economy and Society of the Slave South* (1965).

Moore, John H. *The Emergence of the Cotton Kingdom in the Old Southwest: Mississippi, 1770–1860* (1988).

Woodman, Harold D. *King Cotton and His Retainers: Financing and Marketing the Cotton Crop of the South, 1800–1925* (1968).

Wright, Gavin. *The Political Economy of the Cotton South: Households, Markets, and Wealth in the Nineteenth Century* (1978).

The Postbellum South

DeCanio, Stephen. *Agriculture in the Postbellum South: The Economics of Production and Supply* (1974).

Earle, Carville. "The Myth of the Southern Soil Miner: Macrohistory, Agricultural Innovation, and Environmental History." In *The Ends of the Earth: Perspectives on Modern Environmental History*, edited by Donald Worster (1988), pp. 175–210.

Ransom, Roger L., and Richard Sutch. *One Kind of Freedom: The Economic Consequences of Emancipation* (1977).

The New South

Daniel, Pete. *Breaking the Land: The Transformation of Cotton, Tobacco, and Rice Cultures Since 1880* (1985).

Fite, Gilbert C. *Cotton Fields No More: Southern Agriculture 1865–1980* (1984).

Wright, Gavin. *Old South, New South: Revolutions in the Southern Economy Since the Civil War* (1986).

— CARVILLE EARLE

RURAL LIFE IN THE WEST

Native Americans

Among the Native Americans, the first farmers in the American West, the women primarily controlled the use of the land and planted, cultivated, and harvested the crops. As early as 1300 B.C., Indian farmers in the Southwest had adopted agricultural practices from

Mexico. By about the beginning of the Christian era, the Hohokam, who lived along the Gila and Salt rivers in present-day Arizona, had developed an extensive irrigation system. These canals, built by both men and women, extended across the land in a veinlike fashion for at least 150 miles (240 kilometers), earning these people the sobriquet "Canal Builders." This culture not only established the only true irrigation culture on the North American continent before white settlement, but also made an agricultural life possible where farming would have been nearly impossible without it. At the beginning of the Christian era, the Indian farmers in the Southwest had made the seed selections necessary to develop the plant varieties best suited to the climatic conditions of that region.

On the fringe of the Great Plains the Native Americans began agriculture about 1500 B.C., by farming the river floodplains. Probably they had learned agriculture from the Hopewell and Woodland peoples in the Mississippi Valley. At the time of European contact, the Caddo, who lived on the eastern fringe of the Great Plains in present-day Texas, tilled the soil. They may have created the "hearth" from which Indian agriculture spread onto the Great Plains.

The Mandan and Hidatsa were the most skilled agriculturists on the fringe of the Great Plains at European contact. They occupied permanent villages along the tributaries of the upper Missouri, where the women raised corn, beans, and squash in the rich alluvial soil. The Indian women of the West became skilled plant breeders whose ability to select the best seeds for plant improvement remained unsurpassed until the creation of the agricultural experiment station system during the late nineteenth century. Mandan and Hidatsa villages in present-day North Dakota became important trading centers. The hunting tribes of the High Plains, such as the Sioux and Cheyenne, craved vegetables, particularly corn, and the Mandans and Hidatsas traveled to the High Plains annually to trade for buffalo meat and antelope hides. This trade was beneficial and hazardous. The Sioux, who were good customers of these farming tribes, were temperamentally unpredictable, and any trade with them had to be conducted with extreme caution. When white settlers moved into the trans-Mississippi West, they adopted many of the seed varieties and agricultural methods, including the use of old irrigation canals, of the Native American farmers.

The Indian women not only tilled the soil but also controlled the use of the land. Most tribes or cultural groups adopted two forms of land tenure. Ultimate land tenure depended upon village sovereignty over a particular area, while individual control of a field depended on the actual occupation and use of the land. Usually the individual farmer controlled the use of the land as long as she or he cultivated it. Generally the Indians in the West did not think of private property as an absolute personal right or consider land a commodity that could be bought, sold, or permanently alienated. Among the Native Americans, the community owned the land, while the individual claimed a portion by cultivating it. Moreover, land tenure or control was vested with the lineage or household, not the individual. This control unit could be either patrilineal or matrilineal, depending on the particular culture. Among the Plains tribes, land usually passed from mother to daughter. Among the Yuman-speaking tribes in the Southwest, men inherited the land, whereas a matrilineal land inheritance system prevailed among the Pueblos.

By the mid-nineteenth century, white settlement began to encroach on the lands of the Native Americans in the West. White settlers considered the lands of the agricultural and hunting tribes underutilized. Although the federal government removed many tribes to reservations, the rapid settlement of the West created great demand for Indian lands. By 1887, the federal government could no longer resist white pressure for unused tribal lands, and Congress passed the Dawes General Allotment (also called the Severalty) Act to enable the transfer of reservation land to white farmers. This legislation gave each head of a tribal household 160 acres (64 hectares) of reservation land, but Indians who received allotments could not take full title for twenty-five years. After that trust period, they had the same rights to their lands as any white farmer because they could sell, lease, or cultivate it. The federal government intended this act to help force the Indians to become small-scale farmers who would not rely on the government for support. Without experience in landownership as white culture understood it, most Indians who had received allotments lost their lands. By 1932 more than 90 million acres (36 million hectares) had been lost by the Native Americans. Without land, credit, capital, technology, or scientific aid, the Native Americans did not have any chance to become small-scale, independent farmers, as federal Indian policy had intended, to ensure acculturation and assimilation.

Although the Indian New Deal attempted to restore tribal culture and stopped the sale of Indian lands, the Native Americans remained too poverty-stricken and without adequate educational and financial support to develop into small-scale, family farmers in the white tradition. With the exception of the Navajo, most tribal groups did not have the land base or the financial means to support either self-sufficient or commercial agriculture. By the late twentieth century, only several thousand Indian farmers remained on the land. Most Native

Americans continued to live in the rural West, but they were not agricultural. Although the Native Americans were once the most skilled farmers in the American West, their considerable agricultural achievements had been relegated to the distant past.

The Colonial Period

When the Spanish began establishing settlements north of Mexico during the late seventeenth century, they adopted the crop varieties of the Native Americans and, in time, taught them to raise wheat and sheep among other Spanish agricultural endeavors. At first, however, the Spanish primarily were interested in cattle ranching. As early as 1690, the Spanish brought cattle to their newly established mission of San Francisco de los Tejos in East Texas. In 1718, they established the presidio and settlement of San Antonio, where cattle raising became the most important economic activity. By 1746, the diamond tip of Texas (an area bounded by San Antonio on the north and the Gulf Coast on the south, with the sides of the diamond formed by lines drawn west from San Antonio to Laredo on the Rio Grande and to the Gulf Coast on the east) had been settled by large-scale ranchers, and thousands of cattle and sheep grazed the land. As the herds grew, the ranchers needed markets for their cattle because they could not make enough money from slaughtering their livestock for tallow and hides. By the mid eighteenth century, Spanish ranchers had developed an important cattle trade with New Orleans.

Although cattlemen had driven herds to Ohio in 1846, to California in the 1850s, and to Chicago in 1856, major expansion of the livestock industry did not occur until the late 1860s.

Farther to the west, in present-day California, the Spanish based their colonial expansion on military power, the Catholic church, and agriculture. In many respects, the agricultural and rural history of the American West began along the Pacific Coast during the late eighteenth century. In 1769, Spanish soldiers established the first presidio at San Diego; and in 1777, Spain established the first pueblo or town in California, San Jose. The Spanish pueblo grants favored private citizens and groups that promised to establish communities. After four years of cultivation, the government provided full title for individual ownership. The Spanish based their colonial policy in California on the philosophy that land should be used to support subsistence agriculture and that farming would strengthen Spanish authority over an increasingly large empire. Spain continued to make other land grants for the creation of presidios, pueblos, and missions until the Mexican Revolution in 1822.

Although Spanish supply columns brought seeds of all kinds to the newly established presidios, missions, and pueblos, cattle raising became the most important economic endeavor in California. The early ranchers in California, like those in Texas, slaughtered their livestock primarily for the hides and tallow because they did not have a market for fresh meat and could not adequately preserve their beef for shipment to foreign markets. By rendering the fat for soap and the tallow for candles, and preparing the hides for leather, these early agriculturists capitalized on distant foreign markets. The export markets, especially the New England trade, became particularly important after 1810. As cattle raising and the ranches expanded, the roundup became the major annual activity.

Despite these agricultural introductions and improvements, profit was not the overriding motive for agricultural development among the Spanish in California and the Southwest. Rather, the Spanish intended subsistence agriculture to enable colonization, religious conversion of the Indians, and military defense of the frontier. With the exception of the large-scale landowners, who grazed cattle, most settlers cultivated small plots of land and lived in poverty. They did not develop a market economy for commercial gain.

The Open-Range Cattle Industry

Between 1820 and 1840, the Spanish cattle industry merged with the Anglo-American cattle culture on the humid coastal prairies of Texas. The settlers who emigrated from the southern United States brought a different cattle-raising tradition with them that they established in northeastern Texas. The Spanish, however, were responsible for establishing the open-range livestock industry that spread into the central and northern Great Plains after the Civil War.

Although cattlemen had driven herds to Ohio in 1846, to California in the 1850s, and to Chicago in 1856, major expansion of the livestock industry did not occur until the late 1860s. With buyers in Chicago offering ten times the price that ranchers received in Texas, cattlemen began trailing their herds to northern markets. In 1867, Joseph G. McCoy founded Abilene, Kansas, as a railroad shipping point; more cattle from Texas were moved north than ever before, destined primarily for stockyards in Chicago. During the late

1870s, the open-range cattle industry expanded into the northern Great Plains. Eastern and foreign investors often financed large-scale cattle companies that controlled several thousand acres and operated with a multi-million-dollar capitalization. The Swan Land and Cattle Company, for example, controlled more than 500,000 acres (200,000 hectares) in Wyoming and Nebraska, grazed 120,000 head, and operated with a capitalization of 3.7 million dollars. In 1885 the XIT Ranch, controlled by the Capitol Freehold Land and Investment Company in Chicago, exceeded all other ranches in size. Capitalized with $15 million, it covered more than 3 million acres (1.2 million hectares); its headquarters was at Buffalo Springs, Texas. The cattle companies competed with small-scale ranchers for the use of the public domain, that is, for the free grass on the federal lands.

Few ranchers or cattle companies actually owned their grazing land. Rather, they occupied specific ranges by custom and consent. In time, they viewed their grazing lands as private property. Whenever they purchased land, they usually selected grasslands that bordered streams or surrounded water holes to prevent the use of that rangeland by other cattlemen or farmers. In order to protect themselves from the large-scale cattle companies, small-scale ranchers organized stock growers' associations, such as the Wyoming Stock Growers' Association, the Colorado Stock Growers' Association, and the Montana Stock Growers' Association. These organizations regulated roundups, prevented rustling, registered brands, and aided in the shipping and marketing processes. The stock growers' associations improved breeding practices and promoted better range management with the use of barbed wire fencing and windmills to pump water.

The open-range cattlemen did not provide adequate care for their livestock. Ranchers left their cattle to fend for themselves, and they did not provide feed or shelter. During the mid-1880s, recurring drought and hard winters culminated in disastrous blizzards and bitter temperatures during the winter of 1886–1887 and destroyed the open-range livestock industry. Many cattlemen sold their herds. Those who remained improved their range management practices, pared their herds, and emphasized winter feeding and sheltering.

The Farmer's Frontier

With the collapse of the open-range cattle industry, farmers claimed the grasslands and moved west of the 100th meridian onto the High Plains. By 1860 many farmers had moved onto the fringe of the Great Plains from the humid prairie lands of Iowa, Missouri, and Minnesota. They did not, however, know about the harsh environmental limitations of the semiarid Great Plains. During the late 1860s and early 1870s, settlers moved onto the Great Plains in a rush. They acquired land from the federal government under the Homestead Act of 1862, or they purchased it from the railroads that had been granted public domain to help finance construction, or from the states that had received land grants from the federal government.

Prior to passage of the Homestead Act in 1862, settlers in the trans-Mississippi West acquired land in two major ways—purchase from the federal government or preemption. Between 1820 and 1862, many people acquired farms under the Land Act of 1820. This statute enabled a settler to purchase a minimum of 80 acres (32 hectares) for $1.25 per acre after the land had been surveyed. Many settlers, however, squatted or claimed public domain prior to survey and sale, and they pressured the federal government for a preemption act that would permit them to purchase the land that they had settled and improved before it could be sold to another settler or a speculator. Although Congress provided a limited preemption act in 1830, it legalized squatting with the Preemption Act of 1841. This act enabled squatters to purchase 160 acres (64 hectares) at $1.25 per acre. Settlers purchased much of the land in Iowa and Missouri under the Land Act of 1820 and the Preemption Act of 1841.

Many settlers could not afford two hundred dollars for 160 acres, and westerners continued to advocate cheap or free land to encourage settlement and the development of a strong agricultural economy that would benefit the nation. Others advocated expensive public lands to help provide operating revenue for the federal government. Both positions received extensive discussion in Congress. Although public land policy became entangled with abolitionism because southerners believed northerners wanted to block the expansion of slavery in the territories, westerners continued to advocate free public land and state legislatures passed resolutions that supported those demands. Finally, after the secession of the South, Congress passed the Homestead Act and President Abraham Lincoln signed it into law on 20 May 1862. This act provided 160 acres of public domain free to settlers who lived on the land and improved it for five years. Or, after six months' residence, a settler could purchase the land for $1.25 per acre. Both men and women twenty-one years of age or older could claim a homestead, provided they were citizens or had filed a declaration to become a citizen. The Homestead Act finally realized the demand of westerners for free public land.

Although the first homestead was claimed near Beatrice, Nebraska, on 1 January 1863, a homesteading boom did not occur until the early 1870s on the Minnesota, Dakota, Nebraska, and Kansas frontiers. By 1900 more than 400,000 settlers had applied for homesteads. Not all western lands were open for homesteading, however, because the transcontinental railroads, state governments, and Indian tribes claimed millions of acres. Still, approximately 605 million acres (242 million hectares) of public domain were available for acquisition under the Homestead Act. Much of this land, however, was in the desert Southwest and the arid intermontane region, where agriculture was impossible without irrigation or because of the mountainous terrain. Moreover, the environmental and geographical limitations of the West, as well as economic depression, insufficient financial reserves, and inadequate agricultural knowledge, caused two-thirds of the homesteaders to fail by 1890.

The Homestead Act remains one of the most important laws in American history because it provided free land and, along with other federal legislation, stimulated the settlement of the West. However, homestead land often was distant from transportation and markets because the railroads controlled the best lands. Those settlers who bought railroad lands paid higher prices, but they had relatively easy access to market. The transcontinental railroads, which controlled 110 million acres (44 million hectares) of land, lured settlers to the West with massive publicity campaigns. Settlers often preferred to purchase railroad land because they could pay over a ten-year period with only one-fourth of the purchase price down. Easy terms such as these were more important than the price, which often reached ten dollars per acre, and the railroads became the most important creditors in the West. Still, the Homestead Act enabled settlers to gain a propertied stake in society and economic independence, provided they had adequate financial reserves and access to a railroad, and withstood the harsh climate of the Great Plains.

The early settlers on the Great Plains first built sod houses because there was little timber for constructing the traditional log cabin of the forested East. Then they turned their attention to breaking the prairie for cropland. This was hard work, because the grassland did not plow easily, and they were lucky to turn 10 to 15 acres (4 to 6 hectares) for corn, wheat, and potatoes during their first year. Those who arrived too late to plant and harvest a crop suffered if they did not have adequate money for supplies to carry them through their first winter. If homesteaders could survive for two or three years, their chances for success improved substantially, although they always had to contend with the possibilities of drought, grasshoppers, and low prices that could bring bankruptcy and failure. Often the homesteaders took outside employment on nearby railroad construction crews or left the farm during the winter for jobs in town, either near or far away. Often wives and children remained on the land, enduring the hardships of isolation and the environment, until the men returned with money to help meet their needs during the next crop year.

The settlers in the West never were completely self-sufficient, and subsistence agriculture was not their primary goal. Rather, they sought economic gain by producing a cash crop. At first this crop was corn because of their cultural heritage—that is, they raised corn because they had been taught to do so by family and friends on farms in the humid East. In time, they learned that the Great Plains had inadequate precipitation for corn, and they converted to wheat production during the mid 1870s.

During the late 1870s, settlers had expanded onto the central plains, and above-normal precipitation enabled them to settle far west of the 100th meridian, where farming based on traditional methods was impossible in times of average or below-normal rainfall. In the 1880s, a boom psychology prevailed among settlers who moved onto the northern Great Plains. When drought came in 1889, the agricultural boom collapsed and a sharp decline occurred in the farm and rural population. Those farmers who remained on the land adjusted by adopting new farming techniques, such as summer fallowing, and by planting wheat, raising drought-resistant grain sorghum, and diversifying with more cattle. But drought, crop failure, and economic hard times kept the farm and rural population from expanding, and also caused the agrarian revolt and the formation of the People's party. With the return of normal precipitation during the late 1890s, agricultural expansion boomed again, particularly after 1900 in South Dakota west of the Missouri River.

The Agrarian Revolt

By the last quarter of the nineteenth century, most of the farmers in the West no longer were engaged primarily in self-sufficient, subsistence agriculture. They had become commercial farmers who concentrated on the production of wheat and corn. Because of this specialization, their fortunes were closely tied to the banking, railroading, and manufacturing interests. They no longer were masters of their own destiny. They sold their grain on an unprotected international market but bought most of the items needed for daily living at high prices because of the protective tariff. Overproduction at home and abroad drove prices down, while an insufficient currency supply kept farmers in need of cash and credit.

The western farmer was caught in a vicious cycle: by using new farm implements, he could increase production and ease his labors; greater production forced agricultural prices still lower; and he tried to recover lost income by producing still more. Eastern land companies often held western mortgages, and the interest rates reached usurious levels. Monopoly in the form of barbed wire, farm machinery, and fertilizer trusts kept prices high, and the railroads discriminated and overcharged for their services. Grain elevator companies unfairly graded the farmer's crops and offered prices below the fair value.

Confronted with these problems, the western farmer first attempted to gain economic reform through the organization of the Patrons of Husbandry (the Grange) and the National Farmers' Alliance and Industrial Union. Both organizations championed collective action to reduce operating costs and provided a social organization to help eliminate the isolation and monotony of rural life in the American West. The Grange was most active and successful during the mid 1870s, and the Farmers' Alliance spread rapidly during the late 1880s. In addition to supporting cooperative buying and selling, the Farmers' Alliance advocated nonpartisan political activity. Although the organization was not a political party, the Alliance men and women believed it should support any politician who advocated its reform program. Although the Patrons of Husbandry and the Farmers' Alliance failed to improve the economic position of western farmers and miners, both organizations provided the experience farmers needed to organize the People's (Populist) party in 1892. The People's party was a vociferous advocate of major economic change through the political process until its defeat in the presidential election of 1896.

In the 1880s a boom psychology prevailed among the settlers who moved onto the northern Great Plains, but when drought came in 1889, the agricultural boom collapsed, and a sharp decline occurred in the farm and rural population.

Westerners who supported the People's party advocated government ownership of the railroads to ensure fair competition and rates. The party also demanded reduction of interest rates on mortgages, expansion of the currency supply, and government credit through a subtreasury system that would enable farmers to obtain loans at a low interest rate from the federal government with their crops pledged as security. The party also favored an eight-hour day, woman suffrage, the initiative and referendum, and the direct election of senators.

The Populists advocated paternalism by the federal government and a mild dose of socialism to ensure economic and social equity. Mary Elizabeth Lease, a Populist leader in Kansas, typified the party leadership and gained national attention with her strong party loyalty and her forceful public speaking, the latter trait earning her the nickname "Mary Yellin" from her enemies. To her friends, she clearly described the problems of the western farmer and worker, and she told the public that only the People's party could remedy the ills of American society. These views earned her the sobriquet among her friends of "Patrick Henry in Petticoats." Ultimately the Populists failed to achieve major economic and social reform through the political process because the Democratic party stole their platform and the Republican party remained too entrenched in certain areas to enable a political victory at the polls. In 1896, William McKinley, the Republican nominee, defeated William Jennings Bryan, the Democratic (and Populist) candidate for the presidency, and the People's party quickly disintegrated. Before it did, however, the party had enabled western farmers, miners, and townspeople to express their dissatisfaction with the economic system through political means. It also had established an agenda for progressive reform that, with the exception of federal ownership of the railroads and telegraph systems, would be achieved by the end of the New Deal.

Technological Change

The prairie sod in the trans-Mississippi West was too tough for the wooden moldboard and cast-iron plows that farmers used in the East. These plows bucked out of the ground or became clogged with the sticky prairie soil. In 1837, John Deere developed a "singing plow" with a steel shear and a highly polished wrought-iron moldboard that easily cut through the prairie grasses and scoured the sticky soils of Iowa, Missouri, and Minnesota. Deere's plow and others like it soon became popular on the prairie of the trans-Mississippi West. Western farmers also used seed drills to plant their small-grain crops, such as wheat and oats. They seeded their corn crop with check-row planters, lister seeders, or one-row, horse-drawn planters; and they weeded their crops with a variety of walking and sulky cultivators.

Farmers used the header in the prairie/plains regions and in California to harvest their small grain crops. During the 1860s, the header became the most important harvesting machine in California, and a decade later it gained popularity in Kansas and Nebraska. In contrast with the reapers which became popular in the Midwest by the 1850s, headers eliminated binding, shocking, and hauling the sheaves to the threshing site and reduced the number of workers required at harvest time.

During the mid 1870s, the self-binder achieved popularity. This implement cut and bound the grain into sheaves ready for shocking. Binders further reduced the manpower required to harvest grain because only one man, the driver, was required to operate it. In 1880, implement companies began manufacturing twine binders to replace the original wire binders. After the grain had been harvested, farmers threshed it with a horse- or steam-powered machine. Although the gasoline tractor replaced the steam tractor during the 1920s, the threshing machine remained a necessary implement for the grain farmer until tractor-powered combines became readily available during the 1930s.

In California, grain farmers began using combines during the early 1880s. These giant machines often required at least thirty horses or mules for draft power, and they were suitable only for flat lands. During the 1890s, steam- and horse-powered combines almost completely replaced the header on the bonanza wheat farms in California. The combines that farmers used east of the Rocky Mountains prior to World War I operated on the Great Plains, where the dry climate made the wheat suitable for machine harvesting.

Technological change during the late nineteenth and early twentieth centuries had an important effect on rural women besides saving the household time and money. As manufacturers developed and improved various grain harvesters and threshing machines, fewer hired hands were needed at harvest and threshing time. As a result, technological change lightened the cooking burden for farm women who had the responsibility of preparing three hearty meals, and frequently an afternoon lunch, at harvest and threshing time.

During the twentieth century, tractors with internal-combustion engines and mechanical cotton pickers became the most important mechanical developments for the agriculture of the American West. The gasoline tractor helped reduce the drudgery of plowing, planting, cultivating, and harvesting cereal grains and other crops, while the cotton picker eliminated the bottleneck at harvest time. Combines also became practical for the small-scale wheat farms of the Great Plains. Center-pivot irrigation systems, which rely on deep wells and powerful pumps to deliver the water to the surface, made arid and submarginal lands agriculturally productive. In West Texas, irrigation technology helped extend the cotton kingdom far onto the semiarid High Plains. Irrigation from deep wells also enabled corn production on the High Plains, where this crop would have been impossible without it, and feedlots and meat packers moved into the region to capitalize on this new form of agriculture. At the same time, however, the water table dropped rapidly and water mining threatened the future of irrigation agriculture on the Great Plains. After the mid-twentieth century, biotechnological change influenced agricultural and rural life more than did changes in hardware. Farmers increased production and reduced costs with the adoption of hybrid seeds, commercial fertilizers, herbicides, pesticides, and drugs to prevent and cure animal diseases.

These technological changes increased the farmers' dependence on bankers for capital, necessitated the improvement of their management skills, and encouraged the consolidation of farms. Technological change during the twentieth century had other negative effects. Tractors encouraged the cultivation of submarginal lands subject to erosion, and the cotton, tomato, and sugar beet harvesters replaced thousands of workers in the fields. The tractor also increased operating costs because it is expensive, and it contributed to one-crop agriculture. Farmers increased their application of pesticides and fertilizers to boost production and profit from their lands to pay for their new implements. The result was environmental damage, overproduction, low prices, and depopulation as many farmers fled the land for jobs in the towns and cities. As the agricultural population declined, the farms decreased in number and became larger as more prosperous farmers bought out the less successful agriculturists.

The Twentieth Century

The economy of the West remained agricultural during the early twentieth century. Adequate precipitation, new crop varieties, and international demand helped increase production and boost prices. On the Great Plains farmers expanded west of the 100th meridian to the slopes of the Rocky Mountains and beyond. In 1909, Congress encouraged this settlement process by enacting the Enlarged Homestead Act, which provided land grants of 320 acres (128 hectares) in some semiarid western states, with full title granted after five years of residency. In 1916, Congress passed the Stock Raising Homestead Act, which enabled settlers to receive 640 acres (240 hectares) of land that was unsuitable for crop production but that could support cattle and sheep raising. Between 1902 and 1910, more than ninety-eight thousand homesteaders claimed 18 million acres (7.2 million hectares). The rate of settlement became so great during the first two decades of the twentieth century that farmers homesteaded more land than during the nineteenth century following the Homestead Act.

In the arid West, the federal government entered the irrigation business with the Newlands (or Reclamation) Act of 1902. This legislation enabled the federal government to develop irrigation projects on arid public lands prior to their sale in order to encourage settlement. Congress created the Reclamation Service, which became the Bureau of Reclamation in 1923, to supervise this work. The Reclamation Service constructed many reservoirs for irrigation purposes, such as those formed by Roosevelt Dam on Arizona's Salt River, Arrowrock Dam near Boise, Idaho, and Imperial Dam in California. Much of the impounded water, however, benefited the large-scale, capital-intensive growers rather than small-scale farmers. By the late twentieth century, increasing competition for water between the urban and rural West had generated considerable litigation and bitter debate about who had the legal right to use the water. Despite a policy that favored large-scale growers, the Bureau of Reclamation helped create an oasis environment in the West, where irrigated valleys enabled the production of vegetables, fruits, and grains.

By the late twentieth century, increasing competition for water between the urban and rural West had generated considerable litigation and bitter debate about who had the legal right to use the water.

The number of farmers and ranchers in the West peaked during World War I, when high prices encouraged maximum production and investment in new technology. In 1920, European readjustment and surplus production caused agricultural prices to fall precipitously, and the region plunged into an economic depression that lasted until World War II, when wartime demands increased prices and boosted production. In the meantime, many farmers lost their farms in bankruptcy and the rural population diminished. Farmers now had to become better businessmen, use the best technology, reduce unit costs, increase productivity, and manage efficiently in order to survive.

Faced with economic difficulties beyond their control, farmers in the West turned to economic and political associations to resolve their problems. In 1915, the Nonpartisan League organized in North Dakota and remained a strong political force until 1922. It advocated state ownership of banks, mills, and terminal elevators to ensure equitable treatment. The National Farmers Union (1902) and the American Farm Bureau Federation (1920) advocated cooperative marketing, and western congressmen formed an ad hoc "farm bloc" during the 1920s to gain federal aid for agriculture. With declining numbers, however, western agriculturists no longer had significant political power, and the conservative Republican presidential administrations during the 1920s did not favor direct economic aid to farmers. The federal government's unwillingness to aid agriculture helped provide the stimulus for the creation of the radical, violent Farmers' Holiday Association, which was active in Iowa, Nebraska, Minnesota, and Wisconsin from 1932 to 1937. The Farmers' Holiday Association blockaded roads to prevent the sale of agricultural commodities and to force price increases. The penny auction sales—in which friends and neighbors bid only a few cents for the property of bankrupt farmers, frequently returning it to them and leaving the creditor with a pittance—also grew out of this movement.

The rural West did not receive agricultural support until the "First Hundred Days" Congress that followed Franklin Delano Roosevelt's presidential inauguration on 4 March 1933. With Roosevelt's support, the federal government began to provide economic aid to help western farmers remain on the land and regain sound agricultural operations. During the Great Depression, Roosevelt's New Deal policies initiated a revolutionary role for the federal government in western agriculture. Economic depression, combined with drought and dust storms on the Great Plains, brought unprecedented federal intervention in agriculture.

Congress passed the Agricultural Adjustment Act (AAA, 1933), which authorized the federal government to pay farmers to reduce production in order to increase prices, particularly for wheat, cotton, and hogs in the trans-Mississippi West. On the Great Plains the federal government sponsored the Emergency Cattle Purchase Program (1934) to enable the removal of surplus cattle from the open market. Under this program the federal government bought thousands of cattle for slaughter and distribution to needy families. The federal government also created the Soil Conservation Service (1935) to help farmers practice the best soil conservation methods. The Resettlement Administration (1935) and the Farm Security Administration (1937) sponsored a land purchase program that returned submarginal, wind-eroded land to grassland. In 1960 these land utilization projects became national grasslands, twenty-two of which are located in the West. The Soil Conservation and Domestic Allotment Act of 1936, which Congress expanded with the Agricultural Adjustment Act (Pope-

McGill Farm Act) of 1938, enabled farmers to reduce surplus production by planting soil-conserving crops while receiving monetary support from the federal government for their cooperation.

In the Far West, the Taylor Grazing Act (1934) opened federal rangelands to stockmen who obtained grazing permits. This act also closed federal lands to public entry—that is, to claim and purchase—and ensured better range management practices. The Rural Electrification Administration (REA, 1935) was the most popular New Deal agency in the West. Although farmers along the Pacific Coast had easier access to electricity because of hydroelectric development, most farmers did not have the advantage of such favorable locations. The REA loaned money to cooperatives to build power plants, string electric lines, and wire homes. With electricity, farm men and women could use laborsaving implements such as stoves, irons, feed mills, and cream separators. Electricity also enabled indoor plumbing, hot water heaters, and leisure activities at night.

The New Deal programs of the federal government played an instrumental role in helping western farmers remain on the land until normal precipitation returned and until World War II increased prices and eliminated agricultural surpluses. But the New Deal did not have a beneficial effect on everyone. The AAA drove many tenant farmers from the land. Landlords in Oklahoma and Texas released their tenants in order to collect AAA checks for reducing cotton production. They often used these funds to purchase tractors and additional equipment for the production of other crops. Forced from the land, many tenants moved west to California. Their plight was portrayed by John Steinbeck in *The Grapes of Wrath* (1939).

Ethnic Diversity

Many ethnic groups contributed to the agricultural development of the American West, particularly the Mexicans, Chinese, and Japanese. During the late nineteenth century, the bonanza wheat farmers in California employed contract Asian laborers. After completion of the transcontinental railroads, many Chinese sought work on these large-scale farms, but the panic of 1893 caused Anglos to complain that the Chinese deprived white Americans of jobs. After violence drove the Chinese from the farms and into the cities, the landowners sought docile, reliable, and industrious workers in the Japanese community. Racial hostility toward Asians reemerged during the early twentieth century, and the growers increasingly turned to Mexican workers to meet their labor needs.

During the twentieth century, the Hispano-Americans became the most important ethnic group in the West. Millions of Mexicans entered Arizona, California, and Texas to find employment, usually as stoop labor in the fields. The growers exploited them with low wages, abysmal living conditions, and arbitrary authority. The large-scale growers and the federal government particularly exploited migrant workers with the bracero program from 1942 through 1964. Under that program, growers could hire workers temporarily from Mexico to prevent labor shortages. This policy kept labor plentiful and wages low, both of which contributed to the abject poverty of these people.

On several occasions the migrant workers in California attempted to organize and bargain collectively in order to improve their wages and working conditions. They achieved some success with the Cannery and Agricultural Workers' Industrial Union (1931), the National Farm Labor Union (1946), and the Agricultural Workers Organizing Committee (1959). The United Farm Workers Union (1965), led by Cesar Chávez, had the greatest success representing the migrant workers. Most migrant workers, however, are not union members. The large-scale growers responded to the unionization efforts of the migrant workers by adopting laborsaving implements such as the cotton, tomato, and sugar beet harvesters.

Other ethnic groups have played important roles in the development of the rural West. On the Great Plains, the Germans have been the largest non-English-speaking ethnic group. By 1900, approximately one-third of the white population in Texas claimed German heritage. Large groups of Scandinavians settled in the Dakotas, and Czechs became an important ethnic group in Nebraska. In Kansas, Swedish and Volga German communities enriched the cultural milieu. Although the people of west European descent quickly assimilated, the dark-skinned Hispanos suffered racial discrimination and social segregation.

The Mormons, while not an ethnic group, are a religious group whose original support of polygamy made it a distinctive and unwanted sect in established settlements. Fleeing persecution, Brigham Young led the first Mormons to present-day Utah, where they settled near the Great Salt Lake in 1847. The Mormons developed an irrigation agricultural system in which each head of a household received a plot of land to permit subsistence farming and enough water to make it productive. The strong sense of group identity and cohesiveness helped the Mormons establish a successful community based on agriculture which expanded into Arizona, Nevada, Idaho, and Oregon. The Mormons became the most important cultural group to colonize the intermontane West.

Women in the West

The women in the rural West were closely tied to the soil during the nineteenth century. Although many single young women acquired land under the Homestead Act, particularly in the Dakotas, most did not farm but only established claims for the purpose of selling for high capital gains when land prices increased. Usually the women who migrated to the American West did not have primary responsibility for cultivating the soil. Instead, these women of Euro-American cultural heritage attended to a host of domestic tasks that were determined by gender, because farming with a plow generally was considered "man's work." Frontier women contributed to the survival of the family farm even though they often were not included in the decision-making process. Many women, however, considered their work to be cooperation with their husbands, and they did not believe themselves to be second-class partners. Frontier women adapted to the physical and psychological realities of western rural life with a realistic understanding, particularly in regard to the harsh environment, isolation, and loneliness.

In the frontier West women pursued a host of domestic tasks, such as cooking, cleaning, raising children, tending gardens, and helping with the farm and ranch work. They preserved the family's historical record, often in the Bible, and maintained cultural or ethnic traditions. In the towns, they often occupied gender-determined positions, serving as schoolteachers, shop clerks, milliners, nurses, and domestic servants. These positions were closely linked to the jobs women performed in the home and were, therefore, socially acceptable.

Socially, women participated actively in community life. They organized clubs and church socials and attended dances and picnics, and they sought anti-prostitution, anti-gambling, and temperance reforms. Nevertheless, the primary focus for most women, whether single or married, was their household world. For the most part, gender determined their place and work in the West far more than did ethnicity, social class, marital status, race, education, or religion. When women deviated from societal expectations, they often met with criticism and social rejection. In general, women usually experienced greater similarities than differences in their lives because of gender and generally agreed-upon concepts of women's work, which invariably centered on domestic service. This service was wide-ranging, from hoeing the garden to bearing and caring for children to cooking for the threshing crew. Women were not less important than men; their social roles differed. Homogeneity, not heterogeneity, governed their lives.

Technological change affected the lives of women more slowly and less dramatically than the lives of men in the nineteenth century. Not until the twentieth century, particularly with the increasing availability of electricity after the creation of the Rural Electrification Administration, did women have access to technology in the form of electric irons, refrigerators, washing machines, lights, and water pumps, all of which made their daily tasks easier.

During the twentieth century, the domestic world remained the focus of women in the rural West. Whether they lived and worked in small towns or on farms and ranches, whether they married or lived with family or alone, gender—rather than ability and opportunity to excel or to exhibit independence in the social, economic, and political world relegated to men—governed household and social responsibilities. Still, near the mid twentieth century, western women, compared with northern and southern women, were better educated, held more varied jobs, adhered less to traditional religious beliefs and denominations, maintained optimism, accepted change with greater flexibility, and approved of equality between the sexes. In all of these areas, the values of western women continued to be influenced by the frontier past.

Frontier women adapted to the physical and psychological realities of western rural life with a realistic understanding, particularly in regard to the harsh environment, isolation, and loneliness.

Since the Great Depression of the 1930s, women as well as men have left the rural West. Many of those who remained could not support themselves on their land, and were forced to take jobs in the nearby towns and cities. Others left the farm because of the lure of better-paying jobs, with less drudgery and isolation, in urban America, although there, too, gender both limited and defined the lives of women. Many who can neither leave the land nor earn an adequate living from it are Hispanic women whose lives remain tied to the vegetable fields in California and the Southwest. Bound by both family—that is, domestic responsibilities—and a migratory way of life, they continue to suffer from inadequate education, nutrition, and health care.

Hispanic and other women who worked in the fields and canneries for low wages joined unionization activities; took part in confrontations with growers, strikebreakers, and thugs; and sometimes lost their lives in these struggles. Usually the growers relegated Hispanic women to the lowest-paying jobs. Although most Hispanic women now live in the urban barrios of Los Angeles, Phoenix, and San Antonio, many remain in rural areas. For them, the West is a rural ghetto from which there is no escape. Across the West, poor rural women work in low-paying service, clerical, and light industrial jobs. Although these women do not rely on agriculture for their livelihood, many continue to live in rural areas and commute to their jobs.

In the late twentieth century, gender continued to determine the life of middle-class women who remained on the farm. But rural women had assumed responsibility for many farm-related tasks that previously had been considered the province of men, such as keeping farm accounts, driving trucks and tractors, and providing general farm management, particularly if their husbands held off-the-farm jobs. The most rural of all women in the late-twentieth-century West, however, were the Native Americans. Approximately three of every four Native American women lived in rural areas, where they suffered from poverty, discrimination, and high mortality.

The Late Twentieth Century

By the last half of the twentieth century, agriculture in the American West was more productive than ever before. The federal government attempted to curb the production levels of farmers through various programs in order to maintain prices. But science and technology, in the form of hybrid seeds, fertilizer, pesticides, herbicides, improved tractors, grain drills, and combines, made farmers more efficient and productive. As productivity increased, however, low prices kept many farm families from earning an adequate income and many left the rural West for better jobs in the towns and cities.

As farmers left the countryside, corporations or more prosperous farmers bought their land. As a result, farms decreased in number but increased in size. With the decline of farms, the social structure of the rural West changed significantly. With a decline in the farm population, merchants in the towns often suffered severe financial hardship. Tax revenues declined and local governments reduced services in both towns and countryside. Until the late twentieth century many people had considered the family farm a symbol of democratic government. The decline in the rural population, however, decreased the political power of the rural West, which shifted to the urban areas of the region. With the economic and political position of the family farm in jeopardy, many westerners began to defend the family farm on moral grounds. For them, farming represented independence, ensured democratic government, and preserved a good life. By the late twentieth century, however, farming had become more than a way of life; it was a business, and little room remained for small-scale, undercapitalized, and inefficient farmers. Government programs favored the large-scale, capital-intensive farmers. With little economic and political power, and a declining social position, many farmers left the land.

Near the end of the twentieth century, west-

Ranches and farms still dominate the economy of the West, despite the problems of surplus production and declining population. A rancher and his son round up cattle at a family run ranch in Montana.

ern farmers continued to advocate higher commodity prices while the public pressed political leaders to maintain relatively low food prices through tariff adjustments, reduced price support programs, and restrictions on exports. Farmers also confronted a public that increasingly demanded accountability for the use of chemical fertilizers, herbicides, and pesticides to prevent the pollution of drinking water and to ensure safe, healthy foods. Bad weather, inflation, and foreign markets, production and exchange rates, and international events remained beyond the control of farmers and affected the lives of all residents in the rural West. There were no easy solutions to the economic, social, political, moral, or ethical problems of the region. Yet while uncertainty often prevailed, the people of the rural West generally preferred their way of life, because they believed it to be much safer, more peaceful, and more fulfilling than any alternative. Their tenacious, independent spirit enabled many to remain in the rural West even during hard times. Nevertheless, the transformation of the West from a rural to an urban society reflects a major change in American society in general. No one can say what effects that change will have on rural life during the twenty-first century.

Conclusion

The harsh arid and semi-arid environment of the American West has shaped the agricultural and rural life of the people from the frontier period to the present. Although environment determines the parameters for life in the region, culture, social relationships, technology, and institutions, particularly legal institutions, enabled westerners to gain increased control over the environmental limitations of the region. Western agriculture remains an extractive industry. The people have little control over markets and prices, and they depend on others for capital and policy, both domestic and foreign. Since the New Deal, however, the federal government has dominated western agriculture and rural life with a host of programs to help cushion the effects of domestic and international economic problems. By the late twentieth century, much of the agricultural income in the West was dependent upon government subsidies.

Since the 1920s, western farmers and ranchers have confronted the problems of surplus production and declining population. Technological and scientific developments have increased efficiency and reduced the need for a large number of farmers. The chemical and biotechnological revolutions enabled farmers to improve production but required improved business expertise for the best management of land and capital. With low prices and high operating costs, urban employment lured many men and women from the land. As residents left the farms for better jobs, more money, and a higher standard of living, many small towns suffered severe economic decline. Stores closed, schools and churches consolidated, and the rural population decreased further.

By the late twentieth century, however, agriculture still dominated the economy of the West; the Dakotas had the highest percentage of residents engaged in agriculture. North and South Dakota remained the most rural states in the West, with more than 50 percent of the population living outside cities of more than 2,500 people. California was the most important agricultural state, primarily because of the high productivity in the Central and Imperial valleys, and the marketing centers of Fresno, Bakersfield, and Sacramento supplied the nation with much of its food and fiber. The Great Plains, including Texas, remained the primary cattle- and wheat-producing region. The corn belt extended west of the Mississippi into Iowa, Minnesota, Missouri, and the Great Plains.

Agriculture remained important in the West during the late twentieth century, and farmers and ranchers continued to be affected by influences beyond their control. As the population of the West continued to grow, urban demands for water affected agricultural activities. The continued use of chemical fertilizers, pesticides, and herbicides threatened to pollute drinking water supplies, and irrigation from the underground supply endangered the water table. The environment influenced the settlement of the West during the nineteenth century; the federal government dominated rural life during most of the twentieth century; and the availability of water increasingly affected agricultural and rural life during the late twentieth century. No one could say what effects these influences and the trends toward consolidation and flight from the land would have on rural life in the West and on American society during the twenty-first century.

[See also Agriculture; The Frontier; Geographic Mobility; National Parks and Preservation; The Natural Environment: The West; Technology and Social Change.]

BIBLIOGRAPHY

General Works

Briggs, Charles L., and John R. Van Ness. *Land, Water and Culture: New Perspectives on Hispanic Land Grants* (1987).

Fite, Gilbert C. *The Farmers' Frontier, 1865–1900* (1966). An excellent topical introduction to western agricultural history in the late nineteenth century.

Paul, Rodman W. *The Far West and the Great Plains in Transition, 1859–1900* (1988).

Shannon, Fred A. *The Farmer's Last Frontier: Agriculture, 1860–1897* (1945; repr. 1975).

Westphall, Victor. *Mercedes Reales: Hispanic Land Grants of the Upper Rio Grande Region* (1983).

The Great Plains

Blouet, Brian W., and Frederick C. Luebke, eds. *The Great Plains: Environment and Culture* (1979).

Hurt, R. Douglas. *The Dust Bowl: An Agricultural and Social History* (1981).

Kraenzel, Carl Frederick. *The Great Plains in Transition* (1955).

Miner, Craig. *West of Wichita: Settling the High Plains of Kansas, 1865–1890* (1986). A good introduction to agricultural and rural life in a Great Plains state that has application to the general region.

Nelson, Paula M. *After the West Was Won: Homesteaders and Town-builders in Western South Dakota, 1900–1917* (1986). An excellent social history of rural life in western South Dakota during the early twentieth century.

Webb, Walter Prescott. *The Great Plains* (1931). The standard rural history of the Great Plains during the nineteenth century by an environmental determinist. Webb does not discuss political affairs, such as the Farmers' Alliance or the People's party.

The Cattle Industry

Atherton, Lewis. *The Cattle Kings* (1961). An important social history of the cattle industry.

Dale, Edward Everett. *The Range Cattle Industry: Ranching on the Great Plains from 1865 to 1925* (1930; new ed. 1960). A standard introduction to the range-cattle industry.

Osgood, Ernest Staples. *The Day of the Cattleman* (1929).

Schlebecker, John T. *Cattle Raising on the Plains, 1900–1961* (1963). The best history of the cattle industry on the Great Plains during the first half of the twentieth century.

The Far West

Gibson, James R. *Farming the Frontier: The Agricultural Opening of the Oregon Country, 1786–1846* (1985).

Jelinek, Lawrence. *Harvest Empire: A History of California Agriculture.* 2d ed. (1982). A brief but useful survey.

Lowitt, Richard. *The New Deal and the West* (1984). An essential source for an overview of the New Deal in the West.

Malone, Michael P., and Richard W Etulain. *The American West: A Twentieth-Century History* (1989). The best survey of the twentieth-century West; includes a useful introduction to agriculture and rural life.

Agricultural Labor

Craig, Richard B. *The Bracero Program: Interest Groups and Foreign Policy* (1971).

Daniel, Cletus E. *Bitter Harvest. A History of California Farmworkers, 1870–1941* (1981). A comprehensive study of agricultural organization in California.

Jenkins, J. Craig. *The Politics of Insurgency: The Farm Worker Movement in the 1960s* (1985).

McWilliams, Carey. *Factories in the Field: The Story of Migratory Farm Labor in California* (1935).

Meister, Dick, and Anne Loftis. *A Long Time Coming: The Struggle to Unionize America's Farm Workers* (1977). A good general survey of the efforts to organize California's farm workers.

Ethnicity

Luebke, Frederick C., ed. *Ethnicity on the Great Plains* (1980).

McQuillan, D. Aidan. *Prevailing over Time: Ethnic Adjustment in the Kansas Prairies, 1875–1925* (1990).

Agrarian Revolt

Clanton, Gene. *Populism: The Humane Preference in America, 1890–1900* (1991).

Hicks, John D. *The Populist Revolt* (1931). The standard introductory work on populism in the Great Plains. It is particularly good for economic causation.

Larson, Robert W. *Populism in the Mountain West* (1986).

McMath, Robert C., Jr. *Populist Vanguard. A History of the Southern Farmers' Alliance* (1975).

Morlan, Robert L. *Political Prairie Fire: The Nonpartisan League, 1915–1922* (1985).

Saloutos, Theodore, and John D. Hicks. *Agricultural Discontent in the Middle West, 1900–1939* (1951). A standard overview of the major agricultural organizations, with emphasis on the Great Plains.

Native Americans

Castetter, Edward F., and Willis H. Bell. *Pima and Papago Indian Agriculture* (1942; repr. 1980).

Hurt, R. Douglas. *Indian Agriculture in America: Prehistory to the Present* (1987). A survey of Indian agriculture with emphasis on the trans-Mississippi West.

Parman, Donald L. *The Navajos and the New Deal* (1976).

White, Richard. *The Roots of Dependency: Subsistence, Environment, and Social Change Among the Choctaws, Pawnees and Navajos* (1983).

Technology

Hurt, R. Douglas. *American Farm Tools: From Hand Power to Steam Power* (1982).

Rogin, Leo. *The Introduction of Farm Machinery in Its Relation to the Productivity of Labor in the Agriculture of the United States During the Nineteenth Century* (1931).

Wik, Reynold M. *Steam Power on the American Farm* (1953).

Women in the West

Jeffrey, Julie Roy. *Frontier Women: The Trans-Mississippi West, 1840–1880* (1979).

Myres, Sandra L. *Westering Women and the Frontier Experience, 1800–1915* (1982). An excellent topical introduction to women in the West.

Riley, Glenda. *The Female Frontier: A Comparative View of Women on the Prairie and the Plains* (1988). The standard source on the rural experiences of women on the midwestern prairie and Great Plains.

Schlissel, Lillian, Vicki L. Ruiz, and Janice Monk, eds. *Western Women: Their Land, Their Lives* (1988). A wide-ranging topical study of women in the West, with an emphasis on the rural West.

— R. DOUGLAS HURT

S

SCIENCE AS A PROFESSION

When Captain John Smith and his fellow adventurers sailed for Virginia in 1607, they left behind a culture more medieval than modern. Although more than six decades had passed since Copernicus sent the Earth circling the Sun and Vesalius challenged the authority of ancient anatomists, most Europeans still clung to the old ways. While the Virginians were struggling to establish a permanent settlement on the banks of the James River, Galileo was lecturing in obscurity at the University of Padua and young Dr. William Harvey was quietly practicing medicine in London. Yet less than 170 years later, when the American colonists declared their political independence, a scientific revolution had propelled the Western world into the modern era, bringing with it new ideas, new expectations, and new institutions.

Colonial Science

Scientific activity in the New World began long before the arrival of the English at Jamestown. Ever since the voyages of Columbus in the 1490s Spanish observers had been describing the plants, animals, and terrain of the New World for eager audiences in Europe, and since the 1530s French explorers of present-day Canada had been returning to Europe with accounts of the flora and fauna of that region. The English joined the reconnaissance in 1585, when the mathematician and astronomer Thomas Hariot accompanied Sir Walter Raleigh's ill-fated expedition to found a colony on Roanoke Island, off the coast of what is now North Carolina.

Early scientific explorers like Hariot traveled to the New World to increase their wealth, convert Native Americans to Christianity, or discover a passage to the Orient. Similarly, the early English settlers—whether Anglican planter, Puritan divine, or Quaker merchant—crossed the Atlantic for economic and religious reasons. They risked their lives and suffered privation to create a new society, not a new science. The initial task of transplanting European society to a "howling wilderness" left little time for the pleasures of science. As John Winthrop the Younger, the first governor of Connecticut, explained: "Plantations in their beginnings have work yough, & find difficulties sufficient to settle a comfortable way of subsistence, there beinge buildings, fencings, cleeringe and breakinge up of ground, lands to be attended, orchards to be planted, highways & bridges & fortifications to be made, & all thinges to doe, as in the beginninge of the world" (quoted in Stearns, *Science in the British Colonies*, p. 133). Even for a man like Winthrop, who counted some of England's leading scientists among his friends, survival necessarily took precedence over science.

The first scientific stirrings in the English colonies of North America appeared in the 1660s in response to appeals from the fledgling Royal Society of London. Learned societies, not universities, were then the premier institutions of the scientific revolution. First created in Italy in the late sixteenth century, these organizations spread through western Europe; within a century such giants as the Royal Society of London (founded 1660) and the Paris Academy of Sciences (1666) were orchestrating much of the scientific activity of the age. The fellows of the Royal Society aspired to become a universal clearinghouse, a "general Banck," for all scientific and technical knowledge. In their Repository of Rarities they aimed to collect plant, animal, and mineral specimens from around the world, including America. To this end the society sought to identify scientifically inclined persons in the New World, such as Winthrop in Connecticut and the Anglican minister and naturalist John Banister in Virginia, to serve as agents. In return for their services these agents obtained the patronage of the society. Banister, for example, expected his English patrons to provide such items as scientific books, brown paper for drying plants, and "a good microscope." At one point he suggested that "4 or 6 young negroes" would be appreciated, because they would give him the financial security to carry out his scientific work (Ewan and Ewan, pp. 74, 82).

Before 1700 the Royal Society elected only two resident Americans to fellowship. In the eighteenth century the society honored thirty-one more Americans, although only a dozen or so became fellows on their scientific merit. Few colonial Americans, except for a handful of college teachers, itinerant lecturers, and specimen collectors, earned a living by means of science. No more than seven of the nine colonial colleges employed science professors, and the two pre-revolutionary war medical schools, at the College of Philadelphia and King's College in New York City, offered only part-time appointments in the sciences.

In 1711 the College of William and Mary in Virginia hired the first science teacher in the British colonies, an immigrant identified only as Le Fevre. Regrettably, his habitual drunkenness and fondness for disreputable women soon cost him his job. Le Fevre's most notable successor, the brilliant Scottish physician William Small, is remembered today primarily as one of Thomas Jefferson's favorite teachers. Harvard College created its first position in science, the Hollis Professorship of Mathematics and Natural Philosophy, in 1727. The initial occupant of this chair, Isaac Greenwood, proved to be an effective and uncommonly popular lecturer but was also, like Le Fevre, a heavy drinker. After issuing repeated warnings to Greenwood to reform his ways, the disappointed college trustees in 1738 relieved him of his duties. His professorship then passed to one of his former students, John Winthrop IV, scion of a distinguished colonial family. Winthrop, who lived a more temperate and circumspect life than his mentor, brought international glory to the college during his long tenure as Hollis Professor.

Most Americans with scientific interests studied nature only part-time. For example, John Bartram, a self-taught farmer who lived along the Schuylkill River near Philadelphia, enjoyed unparalleled success as a collector of botanical specimens. When word of his exploits reached London in the early 1730s, the Quaker merchant Peter Collison surmised that this colonial farmer-botanist might be ideal for collecting new plants and seeds to supply eager English horticulturalists. To finance Bartram's activities Collinson lined up several gentlemen gardeners willing to subscribe to Bartram's services, generally at an annual cost of five pounds per person. Through Collinson's patronage and encouragement Bartram acquired a reputation as "the greatest natural botanist in the world," an encomium reportedly bestowed by the eminent Swedish naturalist Carl von Linnaeus.

Although Bartram was unsurpassed as a collector, he lacked the requisite training to classify and publish what he discovered. Thus, when he won the coveted title of King's Botanist in America, at least one scientific acquaintance greeted the news with disbelief and embarrassment. "Surely John is a worthy man," wrote Alexander Garden of South Carolina, "but to give the title of King's Botanist to a man who can scarcely spell, much less make out the characters of any one genus of plants, appears rather hyperbolical" (Berkeley and Berkeley, p. 203).

Collinson also served as the scientific agent for the Philadelphia printer Benjamin Franklin, who began conducting electrical experiments in the 1740s using apparatus sent by Collinson. Franklin kept Collinson abreast of his research through letters, which the latter collected and published in book form as *Experiments and Observations on Electricity, Made at Philadelphia in America, by Mr. Benjamin Franklin* (1751), a volume long recognized as colonial America's most valuable contribution to modern science. Prior to his death in 1768 Collinson aided dozens of Americans like Bartram and Franklin and served as the colonies' major conduit to the scientific centers of the world.

Americans' reliance on British patrons during the years before independence gave American science a distinctly colonial orientation. However, during the eighteenth century local scientific communities came to play an increasingly vital role in the scientific life of the colonies until by the eve of the Revolution these groups rivaled Old World institutions in providing direction for scientific pursuits. By the close of the colonial period Americans enjoyed sufficient wealth and leisure to support strong scientific communities in Philadelphia and Boston and moderately active ones in Charleston and New York. The most enterprising members of these communities continued to work closely with the major scientific centers of the Old World while at the same time developing intercolonial ties. For instance, the cultivators of natural history established an informal network of correspondents, later known as the Natural History Circle, and the American Philosophical Society, though essentially a Philadelphia institution, reached out to scientists in every colony.

Because of the blurry boundaries between dilettantes and scientists—the term "scientist" did not come into use until the 1840s—it is impossible even to enumerate the number of colonial Americans who might be called scientists. Scores of persons contributed actively to the discovery and dissemination of scientific knowledge. They came from all walks of life: medicine, law, commerce, the skilled trades, farming, and the ministry. But as we have seen, only a very few earned a living doing science.

Virtually all of the colonials who engaged in scientific activity were white males. Blacks came to the colonies primarily as chattel, and it was not until after the revolutionary war that Benjamin Banneker, a Maryland tobacco planter, earned his reputation as America's first black man of science. Although most women lacked the educational opportunity, the leisure, and the encouragement to cultivate science, several contributed modestly to botany and agriculture. Peter Collinson, for example, corresponded with a Mrs. Thomas Lamboll of Charleston, a woman locally famous for her flower and kitchen gardens, and traded specimens with the most acclaimed woman botanist in America, Jane Colden. Tutored by her naturalist father, Colden mastered the

Linnaean system of classification and began corresponding with botanists on both sides of the Atlantic. Male scientists marveled at the lady Linnaean, although they sometimes admired her more for her skill in the kitchen than in the field. Despite Colden's undisputed scientific ability, the evidence suggests that her fame derived in large part from the novelty of her accomplishment.

Colonial Americans excelled in those areas of science for which their unique location gave them an advantage: botany, zoology, geology, geography, and astronomy. Living in the New World offered access to unexplored mountains and valleys, a host of novel plants and animals, and a distinctive window on the heavens. As one visitor noted during the American Revolution, "The extent of her empire offers for her observation a large portion of heaven and earth. What observations may not be made from Penobscot to Savannah? From the lakes to the sea? Natural History and Astronomy are her particular provinces, and the first of these sciences at least is still susceptible of great improvement" (de Chastellux, *Travels*, p. 546). However, the advantages Americans enjoyed while tracking planets and collecting plants disappeared when they turned to the nonobservational sciences. Franklin stood virtually alone as a colonial contributor to scientific theory.

The scientific achievements of the British colonists are best measured against those of the French to the north and the Spanish to the south. The Spanish, who had settled Central and South America more than a century before the founding of Jamestown, were operating educational and scientific institutions as early as 1553, when the Royal and Pontifical University of Mexico opened. During the colonial period the universities of New Spain, New Granada, and Peru trained thousands of students, but because these schools modeled themselves after the still-medieval universities of Spain their graduates received scant exposure to modern science. Throughout the seventeenth and early eighteenth centuries Catholic Spain remained in the backwaters of the scientific revolution and thus provided little leadership for its colonies. It was not until the reign of Charles III (1759–1788) that the Spanish undertook scientific explorations of their American kingdoms. Although these practically oriented explorations brought few direct benefits to science, they did stimulate other scientific endeavors. After visiting the Americas in 1803, the German naturalist Alexander von Humboldt ranked Mexico City first among the metropolitan settlements of the New World for scientific institutions.

The French also preceded the British in creating institutions of higher learning in America—Jesuit missionaries opened a school in Quebec in 1635, a year before the founding of Harvard—but the priests who came to New France did little to encourage the cultivation of modern science. Unlike the Spanish, however, the French participated actively in the scientific revolution, and the Paris Academy of Sciences created a network of correspondents similar to that of the Royal Society of London. Scientific activity in New France peaked in the mid eighteenth century during the brief governorship of the Marquis de la Galissonière, a Free Associate of the Paris Academy. One European visitor during his tenure reported that the citizens of New France "had a much greater taste for natural history and other parts of literature than in the *English* colonies, where it was every body's sole care and employment to scrape a fortune together, and where the sciences were held in universal contempt" (Kalm, p. 362). Unfortunately for science, the French government soon recalled La Galissonière, and the British conquest in 1759 left only a sprinkling of physicians and preachers to till the field of science.

Notwithstanding their relatively late start in pursuing science, by the 1770s the English colonies clearly led Canada scientifically and trailed Mexico, if at all, only slightly. Yet much remained to be done. As Jeremy Belknap of New England wrote shortly after independence, "Nature is not half explored; and in what is partly known there are many mysteries, which time, observation and experience must unfold" (*The History of New-Hampshire*, p. 329).

Science in the New Nation

Between the American Revolution and the Civil War the number of persons earning a living by doing science ballooned from fewer than two dozen to an estimated fifteen hundred or more. In this period scientific leadership shifted from a diffuse group of men like Franklin, who cultivated science as a leisure-time activity, to an elite of career-oriented professionals. George H. Daniels has described the emergence of this community of professionals as "the most significant development in nineteenth-century American science" ("Process of Professionalization," p. 151).

Before 1860 American men of science (as they most commonly called themselves) rarely, if ever, talked of professionalization. The very name "scientist" did not come into currency until after mid century, and in the absence of licensing or credentialing by means of graduate degrees the boundary between professionals and nonprofessionals remained indistinct. In an attempt to bring order to a confusing situation, as well as to avoid the pejorative term "amateur" and the anachronistic term "professional," Nathan Reingold has divided the antebellum scientific community into three groups: researchers, who contributed to the growth of science knowledge; practitioners, who earned their livings in science-related occupations; and cultivators, who joined and supported scientific organizations but for whom science remained an avocational interest. Reingold estimates that between 1800 and 1860 there were some two hundred researchers, three thousand practitioners, and eleven thousand cultivators ("Definitions and Speculations," p. 62).

Contemporary scientific leaders such as Alexander Dallas Bache of the U.S. Coast Survey and Joseph Henry of the Smithsonian Institution often contrasted "men of science" with "quacks." As Hugh R. Slotten has observed, the former were distinguished by such characteristics as their moral values, contributions to knowledge, avoidance of wild theorizing, and training, which often included travel to Europe. To eliminate the quacks and promote the true men of science, Bache and Henry sought to restructure American science in such a way "that the 'best' men of science would retain control and that support for original research, especially from the government, would be maximized" ("Patronage, Politics, and Practice," pp. 56–57). Talented persons from the lower classes, like Henry himself, would not be excluded from the community of science, but their entry into it would not be made easy.

The very name "scientist" did not come into currency until after the mid nineteenth century, and in the absence of licensing or credentialing by means of graduate degrees, the boundary between professionals and nonprofessionals remained indistinct.

In the absence of a wealthy aristocracy such as existed in some European countries, Bache and Henry and their coterie, known collectively as the Lazzaroni (a name borrowed from Neopolitan beggars), stressed the necessity of federal funding for science. No one proved more successful at this than Bache himself. After capturing the superintendency of the Coast Survey in 1843, he transformed that lethargic organization into the largest and best-funded scientific institution in the United States. By the late 1850s the Survey was supporting more than 750 employees and spending over half a million dollars annually. Bache used this money not only to survey the coastline but to support scientific friends in fields ranging from astronomy to zoology and to train a generation of young men to become proper scientists. Under Bache the Survey became, in Slotten's words, "the single most important institution supporting the advancement of science in the United States" ("Patronage, Politics, and Practice," p. 278).

Although no other single institution rivaled the Coast Survey for the quantity of scientists it employed, American colleges together hired the greatest number of scientists. As institutions of higher education mushroomed across America and as science grew increasingly complex and fractured into distinct disciplines, academic jobs for scientists proliferated. At the time of the Revolution one person, typically the professor of mathematics and natural philosophy, taught all the science in the curriculum. By the eve of the Civil War the better colleges were hiring four or five science professors to teach courses in mathematics, astronomy, physics, chemistry, geology, botany, and zoology.

Scientific jobs outside of government and academia remained scarce throughout the antebellum period. A few geologists worked as consultants, and after 1850 some chemists found employment in industry. Self-supported gentlemen scientists were rapidly becoming extinct. In 1846, according to Robert V. Bruce, "15 per cent of the leading scientists . . . were simon-pure amateurs, drawing no income at all from science-related work, but by 1861 the proportion had fallen to 9 per cent" and was dropping quickly (*The Launching of Modern American Science*, p. 135).

The acceptance of an authoritarian and autonomous scientific elite in a self-consciously democratic culture was not easily attained—especially in view of the scientists' expectation that society should foot the bill for their ambitious schemes. George H. Daniels has helpfully broken down the process of achieving professional autonomy into three overlapping stages: preemption, institutionalization, and legitimation. The first stage occurred when the professionalizing elite used the growing complexity of science to eliminate nonexperts from participating in what had previously been an undifferentiated effort. For example, as chemistry moved from the relatively simple system of Lavoisier, in which each element had a characteristic function, to a complicated study of metals and gases, the cultivators found themselves left behind. The promoters of this new chemistry, complained one Boston physician, "have made it less captivating to the general scholar; they have lessened the interest with which it is viewed by those not immediately engaged in its pursuits, by rendering it more complicated and more difficult to be understood, and less applicable as a whole to the explication of those phenomena of the natural world with which we are most familiar" (quoted in Daniels, *American Science in the Age of Jackson*, p. 36).

A similar development took place in geology, as specialists in reconstructing the history of the earth adopted a new nomenclature and difficult new methods. Elite geologists sought especially to drive the meddlesome "scriptural geologists" from the field, arguing that only persons trained in science should attempt to interpret the book of nature. This imperious move sometimes produced complaints and controversy, but it found support among professionalizing biblical scholars, who were happy to give up the study of nature in return for autonomy in studying the Bible. Thus, as James R. Moore discovered, conflicts typically found professionalizing geologists and biblical scholars allied in their opposition to the amateurs who persisted in dabbling in both areas ("Geologists and Interpreters of Genesis," pp. 322–350).

Daniels's second stage saw the creation of institutions, such as journals and societies, designed specifically to further the interests of professionals. Few contributed more to this process than Yale professor of natural history and chemistry Benjamin Silliman who, according to Robert V. Bruce, "did more than any other man in the first half of the nineteenth century to establish science in America as a profession" (quoted in *The Launching of Modern American Science*, p. 15). Silliman not only trained many of the leading scientists in the United States but established, in 1818, the *American Journal of Science and Arts*, a landmark in the institutionalization of American science. Although he was sometimes criticized for allowing inferior papers to appear in his journal, Silliman for decades led the drive toward professionalization.

In 1840 Silliman and a small group of fellow geologists, who represented the most rapidly professionalizing scientific discipline, created the Association of American Geologists. The organizers pointedly excluded any person "not devoted to Geological research with scientific views and objects." Eight years later the society expanded its mission and metamorphosed into the American Association for the Advancement of Science. "As initiator of and agent for the emerging professional aspirations of men of science," observes Sally Gregory Kohlstedt, "the AAAS became the arena for a debate over the amateur tradition versus professionalism" (Kohlstedt, pp. 67, 138).

Although membership in the AAAS was open to all interested persons, the professionals maintained control of it by monitoring the articles that appeared in its annual *Proceedings* and refereeing oral presentations. Not all amateurs appreciated their newly subordinate status. For example, in 1853 a scientific enthusiast from Cleveland named Jehu Brainerd read an unsophisticated paper on pebble-making that the AAAS leaders refused to publish in the official *Proceedings*. When Brainerd protested, a committee of elite scientists adjudicating his case ruled that his paper contained "erroneous reasoning and unsound views, which, if sanctioned by this body would injure the cause of science and bring the Association into disrepute" (quoted in Kohlstedt, p. 141). Brainerd's complaints of censorship fell on professionally deaf ears.

In legitimizing their professional claims, the third and final stage Daniels recognizes on the road to autonomy, scientists stressed the utility of their work—even when its practical payoff was remote—and emphasized their contribution to, rather than conflict with, traditional values. Their investigations, they argued, aided religion by showing God's power, wisdom, and goodness in nature. They also attempted to reconcile their overtly elitist aims with the democratic values of American society by stressing their commitment to free inquiry and their willingness (in theory, at least) to embrace any person of talent, regardless of class.

Although the astronomer Maria Mitchell won professional praise for discovering a comet in 1847, she remained on the margins of the scientific community because of her gender.

Gender, however, was another matter. Although the astronomer Maria Mitchell won professional praise for discovering a comet in 1847, she remained on the margins of the scientific community. In redefining and restructuring American science the male professional elite carefully kept the comparatively few scientific women, who were often educators and illustrators, on the periphery. Of the twenty-two hundred persons who joined or participated in the AAAS before the Civil War, only four were women. None held a position of leadership, and only one presented a paper.

By the outbreak of the Civil War the American scientific community may not have achieved the autonomy and support it desired, but it had made considerable progress. Symbolic of its newfound status was Congress's creation of the National Academy of Sciences in 1863, during a period of national emergency. Bache and the Lazzaroni used the occasion to push for the establishment of a highly selective national body that would provide scientific assistance to the federal government. This self-perpetuating group of fifty of the country's "best" scientists, headed by Bache, contributed little to the war effort but audaciously demonstrated the growing self-confidence of America's scientific elite.

Science in Industrial America

Between the Civil War and World War I the American scientific community took advantage of new positions and new patronage to elevate itself to a position of scientific parity with its European counterparts. According to Nathan Reingold, the "great trend" of American science in this period was "not the growth in accomplishment, considerable as that was, but the near extinction of cultivators and the tremendous expansion of the number of practitioners." The number of persons earning a living in science-related occupations, not including medicine and engineering, jumped from an estimated 1,500 in 1860 to 14,200 in 1900. More than 60 percent of the latter found employment as chemists, assayers, and metallurgists ("Definitions and Speculations," pp. 47, 57–59). Collecting rocks and flowers and gazing through telescopes and microscopes remained popular activities with many Americans, but such hobbyists had less and less interaction with professional scientists.

The four hundred or so scientific researchers, who represented the professional elite, most often found employment within the federal government, in colleges and universities and, toward the end of the period, in industrial laboratories. During and after the Civil War, Congress, setting aside its earlier concerns about the constitutional correctness of supporting science, established permanent scientific institutions. These included most notably the Department of Agriculture (1862), the U.S. Geological Survey (1879), the Hygienic Laboratory (1887), the National Bureau of Standards (1901), and the Bureau of Mines (1910). During its first half century the Department of Agriculture alone spawned bureaus of entomology, animal industry, plant industry, meteorology, chemistry, and soils. "By 1916," writes A. Hunter Dupree, "no other great economic interest in the United States could boast such a research establishment for the application of science either in or out of the government" (*Science in the Federal Government*, p. 183).

While government scientists were spending most of their time applying knowledge of the natural world to the solution of practical problems, basic researchers were finding a home in the new American universities. U.S. colleges had long provided scientists with a place of employment—but primarily to teach, not conduct research. The first major academic commitment to basic scientific research came with the creation of the Johns Hopkins University in Baltimore in 1876, followed shortly thereafter by the appearance of Clark University in Worcester, Massachusetts, and the University of Chicago. Meanwhile, older universities such as Harvard, Columbia, and Wisconsin also began to create positions for scientific researchers. Original research came to play an increasingly important role in hiring and promoting science faculty, but throughout the nineteenth century teaching remained the primary responsibility of the college professor. As late as 1889 the president of the Massachusetts Institute of Technology declared that "*the mind of the student*, not scientific discovery, not professional accomplishment," should be the primary aim of undergraduate education (quoted in Kevles, *The Physicists*, p. 34).

During the late nineteenth and early twentieth centuries more and more American scientists found a home in industrial settings, especially ones associated with chemistry and electricity. At first, industry-based scientists stuck mostly to applied and consulting work, but in late 1900 General Electric created what one historian has called "a new role for professional scientists," as industrial researchers seeking to discover new knowledge. Within a few years such industrial giants as Du Pont, American Telephone and Telegraph, and Eastman Kodak had followed suit, and by the mid 1920s the number of industrial research laboratories was approaching a thousand.

Whether scientists worked for the government, higher education, or industry they increasingly distinguished themselves from persons they considered to be nonscientists by possessing graduate degrees in science, acquired either abroad or in the new American graduate schools. A Ph.D. not only certified that the holder had contributed to the knowledge base of a particular discipline but separated the professional scientist from uncredentialed amateurs as well as from such practitioners as physicians and engineers. In touting original research as the epitome of scientific activity, writes Nathan Reingold, "scientists were often animated . . . as much by the desire to avoid a lower place on the occupational totem pole as by any intellectual stimuli" ("Definitions and Speculations," p. 47).

American scientists of this period tended, as described by Kevles, "to come from a narrow, upper-crust fragment of society. Most were the sons—or married the daughters—of well-to-do merchants, gentry, lawyers, ministers, or teachers. Almost all were white Anglo-Saxon Protestants. Almost all were male" (Kevles, "American Science," p. 113). The more professionalized the scientific community grew, the less hospitable it became to women, who as Margaret W.

George Washington Carver, who was Director of Agricultural Research at the racially segregated Tuskegee Institute, was an exception. In reality, blacks rarely pursued scientific careers in the nineteenth century.

Rossiter has shown were generally segregated either hierarchically (e.g., as subordinate assistants in large astronomical observatories) or territorially (say, as chemists in departments of home economics), a pattern that persisted well into the twentieth century. And despite the growing fame of the agricultural scientist George Washington Carver, who remained professionally segregated at the Tuskegee Institute in Alabama, blacks rarely pursued scientific careers. When they did, they often encountered racial discrimination. Furthermore, widespread anti-Semitism blocked the ascent of many Jews, although a few, such as the University of Chicago physicist Albert A. Michelson and the Rockefeller Institute pathologist Simon Flexner, made it to the top. For a variety of religious and cultural reasons, Catholics received little encouragement to become scientists.

During the post-Civil War years the rhetoric of elite science often clashed with the language of democracy, especially when scientists began advocating the pursuit of science for its own sake. In the antebellum period professionalizing scientists had stressed their utilitarian and religious contributions to society. After the war, however, as their numbers and authority soared, they grew increasingly resentful of the need to legitimize their activities externally. They wanted society to support them, but not to control them or even to expect immediate benefits from their work. The advocates of pure science purposely distanced themselves from those whom they considered mere inventors. The Johns Hopkins physicist Henry Rowland, for example, in an 1883 address pleading for support for "pure science" protested the common practice of calling "telegraphs, electric lights, and such conveniences by the name of science." He noted that "the cook who invents a new and palatable dish for the table benefits the world to a certain degree, yet we do not dignify him by the name of chemist" (quoted in Kevles, *The Physicists*, p. 43). Nevertheless, despite their desire to win support for science on nonutilitarian grounds, the leaders of American science recognized that their professional interests required at least the promise of vague returns in the future. Thus their "standard formula," as expressed by the historian George H. Daniels, took the following form: "Utility is not to be a test of scientific work, but all knowledge will ultimately prove useful" ("The Pure-Science Ideal," p. 1705).

In return for status and autonomy, scientists also promised to live exemplary lives. "The more detached from their fellow citizens that scientists became," notes David A. Hollinger, "the more necessary did it become for the Victorian moralists—including those who were scientists—to trust that scientists were subject to an ethical code intrinsic to their practice" ("Inquiry and Uplife," p. 147). As humble, incorruptible seekers of truth, scientists assumed the role of latter-day saints living in a climate of moral decay, and science itself took on the trappings of a quasi-religious vocation. Ministers, being committed to dogma rather than to truth, began to suffer by comparison. Among educated Americans, observed Harvard president Charles W. Eliot in the 1880s, the scientific method of inquiry had come to set a new standard for sincerity and truth to which "Protestant theologians and ministers must rise . . . if they would continue to command the respect of mankind" (quoted in Hofstadter and Metzger, p. 351).

By the early twentieth century the United States was finally reaching a position of scientific equality with the major European powers. Support from government, industry, and higher education made this possible, as did contributions from such philanthropists as Andrew Carnegie and John D. Rockefeller. The great natural laboratories of the American West and the willingness of the federal government to support extensive surveys gave an early advantage to geology and paleontology. Americans also did well in certain of the biological sciences such as genetics, which benefited from its connection with agriculture, and physiology, which carved out a space for itself in American medical schools. Turn-of-the-century astronomers in the United States possessed more observatories than they could profitably use, and even physicists and chemists enjoyed considerable prosperity. American scientists may not have been content with their status on the eve of World War I, but compared with their peers in other countries they had little reason for complaint.

Science in Twentieth-Century America

If American scientists needed additional demonstrations of their social worth to solidify their professional authority, they received them in dramatic fashion in the two world wars. By giving scientists—especially chemists—a chance to prove their usefulness to the military and to industry, World War I helped elevate science to the status of a valuable national resource. The successes of wartime science also led to increased philanthropic support for basic research, which usually flowed into the coffers of a handful of major research universities.

World War II, in which physicists contributed both radar and the atomic bomb to the Allied victory, raised scientists to even greater professional heights. The war also "marked the beginning of a new era in the relations of the federal government and science" (Dupree, *Science in the Federal Government*, p. 369). Before 1940, support for science from the government, industry, and higher education remained relatively separate, if not quite equal. During the war, however, the federal government attempted, through the Office of Scientific Research and Development, to centralize scientific research, in part by awarding research contracts to university and industrial laboratories. The government continued this policy in peacetime, channeling huge sums of money to university and industry researchers through such new agencies as the National Institute of Health (established in 1930), the Atomic Energy Commission (1946), the Office of Naval Research (1946), the National Science Foundation (1950), and the National Aeronautics and Space Administration (1958). By the mid 1960s the federal government was pouring $15 billion annually into scientific research and development, conducted in government, university, and especially industry laboratories. Within two decades this figure had multiplied fourfold as educational and industrial budgets grew increasingly dependent on government largess.

The number of professional scientists soared as jobs proliferated. The production of Ph.D.s in the natural sciences rose from less than three hundred in 1916 to more than three thousand annually in the 1950s and to a high of over nine thousand in 1971. Scientific careers became a vehicle for upward social mobility, especially for lower- and middle-class white Protestant males, but increasingly for Jews, Catholics, blacks, and women as well. By the second half of the century scientists—especially nuclear physicists—ranked among the most admired professionals in the country.

By the mid twentieth century American scientists had translated their status and authority into financial support scarcely dreamed of just a generation earlier. To protect their privileged position they carefully guarded their boundaries against incursion from "pseudoscientists" and shunned responsibility for unwelcome applications of science. When charged with contributing to the death of humans and the destruction of the environment, scientists carefully distinguished between the production and consumption of scientific knowledge. In seeking public funds they claimed credit for making the world a better place through science; yet in disbursing the monies they obtained scientists often ruled out engineers and other technologists as eligible recipients because they were nonscientists.

By the mid 1960s the federal government was pouring $15 billion annually into scientific research and development conducted in both the public and private sectors; within two decades this figure had multiplied fourfold.

The protracted debate between evolutionists and creationists over the issue of human origins nicely illustrates how the established scientific community sought to discredit the scientific claims of groups challenging its monopoly. In an attempt to squeeze creationism into science classrooms by stripping it of its explicitly biblical content, creationists in the late 1960s began attaching the labels "creation science" and "scientific creationism" to their belief in the recent special creation of the world and the deposition of fossil-bearing rocks during the brief period of Noah's flood. "Creationism is on the way back," announced one prominent creationist, "this time not primarily as a religious belief, but as an alternative scientific explanation of the world in which we live" (quoted in Numbers, p. 244).

The creationists' attempt to sell their beliefs as science proved extremely effective, at least initially. Two state legislatures, in Arkansas and Louisiana, and various school boards endorsed the teaching of creation science. In 1982, however, a federal judge convinced by the testimony of scientific experts declared that creationism lay outside the domain of science and within the realm of religion. Thus, its teaching in public schools was unconstitutional. (Merely showing creation science to be "bad science" would have been insufficient in this case, because the Constitution does not ban the teaching of bad science in public schools.) Three years later a court in Louisiana reached a similar judgment. The United States Supreme Court upheld these decisions in 1987.

Not surprisingly, the American scientific establishment refused to share its hard-won position of privilege and power with what it regarded as a disreputable band of scientific pretenders and religious zealots. Just as creationists pushed to expand the limits of science to accommodate their religiously inspired agenda, so their opponents invoked a narrow definition of science to maintain what the sociologist Thomas E Gieryn has described as the "professional scientists' monopoly over the market for 'scientific' knowledge in Arkansas schoolrooms" (Gieryn et al., p. 403). By discrediting the creationists as mere pseudo-scientists unworthy of public patronage, the professional elite hoped to eliminate a politically powerful competitor for scarce resources.

The outspoken opposition of the scientific establishment to such widely held views as creationism (believed by nearly half of all Americans and tolerated by millions more), together with suspicions of scientists' self-interest and possible complicity in many of society's ills, began by the late 1960s to erode public confidence in the then much vaunted morality of science. Scientists had won immense sums of money for their research and gained virtual autonomy to control their own affairs—in exchange for implicitly promising to maintain impartiality and probity and to punish those who failed to do so. Nonetheless, when problems arose the scientific community all too often chose to deny or minimize the wrongs, thus violating the public trust.

The 1970s and 1980s saw the appearance of story after story alleging scientific misconduct: from the supposed misusing of funds and plagiarizing of prose to the "improving" and even falsifying of data. Such charges led to an unprecedented congressional hearing on the subject in 1981 and the publication of books with such provocative and disturbing titles as *Betrayers of the Truth* and *False Prophets.* According to the authors of the former exposé, William Broad and Nicholas Wade, the mechanisms established to prevent fraud and deceit, such as peer-reviewing grant applications and refereeing manuscripts, had failed to accomplish their goals. The professionalization of science had brought many rewards to its practitioners, but it had not eradicated the human element in science.

[See also Collegiate Education; The Professions; The Research University; Technology and Social Change.]

BIBLIOGRAPHY

General Works

Daniels, George H. "The Process of Professionalization in American Science: The Emergent Period, 1820–1860." *Isis* 58 (1967).

Daniels, George H. "The Pure-Science Ideal and Democratic Culture." *Science* 156 (30 June 1967).

Gieryn, Thomas F. "Boundary-Work and the Demarcation of Science from Non-Science: Strains and Interests in Professional Ideologies of Scientists." *American Sociological Review* 48 (1983).

Gieryn, Thomas F. "Boundary-Work and the Demarcation of Science from Non-Science: Strains and Interests in Professional Ideologies of Scientists, et al. "Professionalization of American Scientists: Public Science in the Creation/Evolution Trials." *American Sociological Review* 50 (1985).

Kevles, Daniel J. "American Science." In *The Professions in American History,* edited by Nathan O. Hatch (1987).

Topical Histories

Berkeley, Edmund, and Dorothy Smith Berkeley. *Dr. Alexander Garden of Charles Town* (1969).

Broad, William, and Nicholas Wade. *Betrayers of the Truth* (1983).

Dupree, A. Hunter. *Science in the Federal Government: A History of Policies and Activities to 1940* (1957).

Ewan, Joseph, and Nesta Ewan. *John Banister and His Natural History of Virginia, 1678–1692* (1970).

Geiger, Roger L. *To Advance Knowledge: The Growth of American Research Universities, 1900–1940* (1986).

Guralnick, Stanley M. "The American Scientist in Higher Education, 1820–1910." In *The Sciences in the American Context: New Perspectives,* edited by Nathan Reingold (1979).

Hofstadter, Richard, and Walter P. Metzger. *The Development of Academic Freedom in the United States* (1955).

Hollinger, David A. "Inquiry and Uplift: Late-Nineteenth-Century American Academics and the Moral Efficacy of Scientific Practice." In *The Authority of Experts: Studies in History and Theory,* edited by Thomas L. Haskell (1984).

Reingold, Nathan. "Definitions and Speculations: The Professionalization of Science in America in the Nineteenth Century." In *The Pursuit of Knowledge in the Early American Republic: American Scientific and Learned Societies from Colonial Times to the Civil War,* edited by Alexandra Oleson and Sanborn C. Brown (1976).

Chronological Histories

Bruce, Robert V. *The Launching of Modern American Science, 1846–1876* (1987).

Daniels, George H. *American Science in the Age of Jackson* (1968).

Greene, John C. *American Science in the Age of Jefferson* (1984).

Hindle, Brooke. *The Pursuit of Science in Revolutionary America, 1735–1789* (1956).

Keeney, Elizabeth Barnaby. *The Botanizers: Amateur Scientists in Nineteenth-Century America* (1992).

Kevles, Daniel J. *The Physicists: The History of a Scientific Community in Modern America* (1978).

Kohler, Robert E. *Partners in Science: Foundations and Natural Scientists, 1900–1945* (1991).
Kohlstedt, Sally Gregory. *The Formation of the American Scientific Community: The American Association for the Advancement of Science, 1848–60* (1976).
Miller, Howard S. *Dollars for Research: Science and Its Patrons in Nineteenth-Century America* (1970).
Moore, James R. "Geologists and Interpreters of Genesis in the Nineteenth
Century. " In *God and Nature: Historical Essays on the Encounter Between Christianity and Science*, edited by David C. Lindberg and Ronald L. Numbers (1986).
Numbers, Ronald L. *The Creationists* (1992).
Rossiter, Margaret W. *Women Scientists in America: Struggles and Strategies to 1940* (1982).
Slotten, Hugh Richard. "Patronage, Politics, and Practice in Nineteenth-Century American Science: Alexander Dallas Bache and the United States Coast Survey." Ph.D. diss., University of Wisconsin-Madison, 1991.
Stearns, Raymond Phineas. *Science in the British Colonies of America* (1970).
Thackray, Arnold, et al. *Chemistry in America, 1876–1976* (1985).
Wise, George. "A New Role for Professional Scientists in Industry: Industrial Research at General Electric, 1900–1916." *Technology and Culture* 21 (July 1980).

Contemporary Accounts

Belknap, Jeremy. *The History of New-Hampshire* (1792).
de Chastellux, François Jean. *Travels in North America in the Years 1780, 1781, and 1782.* Translated by Howard C. Rice, Jr. (1963).
Kalm, Peter. *Travels into North America.* Translated by John Reinhold Forster (1972).

— RONALD L. NUMBERS

SEXUAL BEHAVIOR AND MORALITY

Colonial America

Patterns of sexual life in the British colonies were shaped both by the social customs settlers brought with them and by conditions of migration and settlement in the New World. In the agrarian villages from which most colonists came, sexuality was linked closely to marriage and reproduction. Family survival in such preindustrial economies depended on the labor of children, which encouraged high birthrates. In the patriarchal household, which was the dominant family form in England at the time, the father controlled the labor and sexual lives of his wife, children, and servants in ways that best supported the family economy. Sons could be forced to delay marriage until fathers parceled out land or the homestead to them. The stability of the household demanded even greater control of the sexuality of wives and daughters. Children born out of wedlock threatened the limited economic resources of families and the need to ensure "legitimate" male heirs.

The agrarian communities of preindustrial England tolerated premarital sexual activity between betrothed men and women, however, because it was understood that marriage would follow. The religious beliefs of the colonists reinforced an ideal of marital, reproductive sexuality. Protestant churches placed strong prohibitions on sex outside of marriage and urged sexual moderation within marriage. Religious authorities considered sexual intercourse a marital duty of husbands and wives for the purposes of both procreation and pleasure.

English colonists in New England and in the Chesapeake colonies of Virginia and Maryland brought similar sexual customs and beliefs with them to America, but differing patterns of settlement, motives for migration, and economic and labor systems in the two regions created marked variations in family and sexual life during the seventeenth century. The Puritans, who settled the New England colonies in the 1620s and 1630s, successfully reestablished English patriarchal family structures and marital sexual relations there. They arrived in family groups and came from similar social backgrounds, primarily middling farm and artisanal families. They left England in search of land but were also motivated by a strong religious purpose. Dissatisfied with the Church of England, Puritans migrated to the New World to establish religious communities, modeled on their moral principles, for the rest of the world to imitate. Driven by this mission and aided by an abundance of land, they created orderly communities, a productive economy based on subsistence agriculture, and large, stable families.

For both religious and economic reasons Puritans emphasized the necessity of sexual relations and reproduction in marriage. Failure to fulfill this conjugal duty could result in serious punishment. James Mattock, for instance, was expelled from the First Church of Boston because, among other offenses, "he denyed Coniugall fellowship vnto his wife for the space of 2 years together vpon pretense of taking Revenge upon himself for his abusing of her before marryage." Most couples upheld the ideal of marital, reproductive sex. Families had an average of seven or eight children. This large family size, along with a relatively low mortality rate, led to rapid population growth. While they considered reproduction the central aim of marital sex, Puritans also believed that sexual relations should provide pleasure for husbands and wives. According to popular medical opinion of the period, orgasm by both partners was necessary in order for conception to take place.

Families, church, and civic authorities worked together to monitor the sexual behavior of young people and to channel sexuality into marriage and reproduction. Puritan fathers retained authority over their children's labor and sexual lives. Though parents did not arrange marriages, they had a strong voice in determining the choice of a partner and the timing of marriage for their children. Traditional English courtship customs continued in New England. Through the practice of "bundling," couples were permitted to sleep in the same bed together as long as they remained clothed or kept a "bundling" board between them. Courting couples had little privacy and were seldom out of sight of family members in the small, crowded houses in which all members of the household often slept in the same room. If pregnancy did occur, family, community, and religious authorities made sure that marriage took place. The low rate of premarital pregnancy and illegitimacy indicates the effectiveness of moral regulation of youth in Puritan New England. In seventeenth-century New England less than one-tenth of all brides were pregnant at the time of marriage, and only between 1 and 3 percent of all births took place outside of marriage.

Very different patterns of family and sexual life developed among the European colonists who settled in the Chesapeake after 1607. Demographic, economic, and environmental conditions in this region inhibited the establishment of patriarchal family structures and marital sexual relations, at least for the first century of colonial development. Unlike the Puritans, the colonists who settled in the South came from varied social backgrounds, ranging from servant to nobleman, and did not migrate in family groups. The desire for profit from tobacco production, rather than a strong religious mission, motivated settlers in the Chesapeake. With this goal in mind, the colonial authorities recruited primarily young single men as indentured servants to provide cheap labor for tobacco plantations. As many as three-quarters of the early inhabitants were indentured servants. The focus on male labor resulted in a high sex imbalance in Virginia and Maryland, with men outnumbering women by four to one. The sex ratio, along with a high mortality rate, slowed population growth and inhibited the formation of families. Parents often died before their children reached adulthood and thus could not exert much control over their marital choices and sexual lives. Conditions of servitude further prevented stable family life, for servants were prohibited from marrying until they completed their period of service. The dispersed patterns of settlement, particularly in frontier regions, led many couples to live together and have children without civil or religious marriage.

The weak family ties and the skewed sex ratio in the Chesapeake contributed to a much higher incidence of premarital and extramarital sexual activity than in New England. Up to one-third of all brides were pregnant at the time of marriage among the immigrant population in the southern colonies. This situation presented both risks and advantages to women. The lack of family connections made them more vulnerable to sexual exploitation by masters and male laborers. Because of the shortage of women, however, premarital sexual relations and illegitimate births did not carry the same social stigma for southern women as they did in England or New England. As long as they were not bound in servitude, women with out-of-wedlock children could find husbands with relative ease in the Chesapeake colonies.

By the early eighteenth century, family and sexual patterns in New England and the Chesapeake were more similar, the result of changing demographic and economic conditions. The strict moral order maintained in seventeenth-century New England eroded somewhat with the growth of towns, the migration of children from their parents' homes to new settlements, and the decline of religious fervor that initially had bound community members together. As a result of these conditions, the premarital pregnancy rate in New England rose steadily throughout the eighteenth century. At the same time, family life became more stable in Virginia and Maryland, as the native-born population increased and the sex imbalance declined. By 1700, the sex ratio was three men to two women, which encouraged earlier marriages and thus increased marital reproduction. As in New England, white women in the Chesapeake now bore an average of eight live children and sometimes had ten or more pregnancies. With improved life expectancy, marriages lasted longer and more children reached maturity under their parents' care. Fathers were able to exercise greater control over their children's sexual lives and choice of marriage partners. The relative sexual and social autonomy young women had experienced in the early decades of settlement gave way to more traditional forms of regulation, leading to a significant decline in the rates of illegitimacy and premarital pregnancy.

Further hindrances to marriage and family formation among southern white colonists were removed by 1700 when slaves began to replace indentured servants as the dominant form of labor in the Chesapeake. At the same time, the introduction of slavery created new sexual patterns among the growing number of Africans imported to labor for white masters. As they had done with white servants, planters initially imported male slaves to work in the fields. This resulted in a high sex imbalance and seriously impeded the development of family life among slaves. The formation of families was made even more difficult by the fact that many Africans lived on small farms with a few slaves spread over a vast territory. Fertility rates remained low among African immigrant women due to high infant mortality rates, the trauma caused by forced migration and enslavement, and the African custom of long nursing periods, which delayed subsequent conception. By 1750 slave family and sexual patterns had become more stable as the native-born black population began to reproduce itself. The sex ratio had evened out, which allowed most slaves to marry, have children, and develop families and kinship networks. Birthrates increased steadily, so that by the late eighteenth century African American women bore an average of six children. In spite of these developments, the conditions of enslavement posed a constant threat to the family and sexual lives of African Americans. Masters frequently separated family members by selling them for profit or bequeathing them to married sons and daughters. Furthermore, slave women were subjected to sexual advances, rape, and impregnation by white planters and their sons.

Although colonial society attempted to channel sexuality into marriage and reproduction, illicit sex remained a constant problem. Communities regularly were confronted with cases of fornication, adultery, sodomy, bestiality, bastardy, rape, and interracial sex. Religious and civil authorities subjected sexual transgressors to a range of punishments including fines, whipping, branding, sitting in the stocks, and banishment. Certain offenses—sodomy, rape, bestiality, and adultery—were punishable by death, but in practice the courts only rarely resorted to execution. A central component of colonial punishment was public humiliation, which both chastised the offender and set an example for the rest of the community.

Religious and civil authorities in colonial society subjected sexual transgressors to a range of punishments, including fines, whipping, branding, sitting in the stocks, and banishment, with certain offenses even punishable by death.

Colonial society punished women more harshly than men for engaging in premarital or extramarital sex. In the early years of settlement, the New England courts had attempted to treat men and women equally for the crimes of fornication and bastardy. Typically the offending couple was brought before the court, admonished for their sinful behavior, and persuaded to marry or punished with a whipping or a fine. By the early eighteenth century, however, the New England courts were prosecuting primarily single women and not their male partners in fornication proceedings. Southern courts also punished women more diligently than men for premarital sex. Female servants in the Chesapeake paid a great cost for an unmarried pregnancy. They could not marry to make the birth legitimate unless someone paid their masters for the time they had left to serve. They were fined heavily or whipped and had to serve an extra twelve to twenty-four months in order to repay masters for lost labor during pregnancy and childbirth. The severe sanctions unmarried mothers faced in colonial society led some to resort to abortion or infanticide. Although the extent of infanticide is unknown, the practice may have become more common in the eighteenth century: every colony enacted legislation to punish the unmarried mothers of dead infants as murderers, unless a witness would testify that the child had been stillborn.

In part, colonial authorities prosecuted women more diligently for fornication and bastardy because pregnancy made the woman's guilt in the affair far easier to prove than the man's. More important, harsher treatment of female offenders stemmed from a double standard of morality that placed far greater value on female chastity because of the need to ensure the legitimacy of heirs in the patriarchal household. By custom and law a woman's chastity was not her own property but that of her father, if she were single, and of her husband, if she were married.

Colonial authorities considered sodomy, in contrast to fornication and bastardy, primarily a man's offense. It was punishable by execution, but as with other capital offenses, courts seldom resorted to the death penalty. Still, many received severe punishments for sodomitic acts. In 1636, when John Alexander and Thomas Roberts were "found guilty of lude behavior and uncleane carriage one [with] another, by often spendinge their seede one upon another," Alexander was whipped, burned with a hot iron, and banished from the colony, while Roberts, a servant, was whipped, sent back to his master, and forbidden to own land in the colony. The seventeenth-century concept of sodomy differs in important ways from the modern notion of homosexuality. Sodomy referred to nonprocreative sexual acts between two men, between a man and a woman, or between a man and an animal. It did not define a particular category of persons or an identity, in the way that the term "homosexuality" does. Typically, those convicted of sodomy did not become permanent social outcasts. If they acknowledged wrongdoing and accepted punishment, they could be reintegrated into the community just like other moral offenders.

In policing moral boundaries, colonial authorities also attempted to prohibit interracial sex. In the first half of the seventeenth century, interracial couples guilty of fornication, bastardy, or adultery faced the same sorts of penalties as white couples. As slavery became entrenched in the southern colonies, colonial governments began to enact more stringent laws against interracial unions, in an effort to strengthen control over the slave labor force and to maintain a fixed boundary between the races. In 1662 the Virginia legislature doubled the fines for interracial sex, and by the mid-eighteenth century all southern colonies, along with Pennsylvania and Massachusetts, had passed strict laws prohibiting interracial marriages and sexual unions. Ministers who presided over such unions were subject to punishment, and the guilty parties faced double fines and whippings as well as possible servitude and banishment from the colonies or both.

Another aspect of Native American sexual life that aroused the hostility of colonists was the existence of berdache, *men who dressed and acted as women and in some cultures had sexual relations with and married other men.*

White masters, however, because of their social position and power, regularly violated the law with impunity by having sexual relations with female slaves. Planters' interracial liaisons did not threaten racial boundaries because mulatto children were generally confined to the status of slaves. This system contrasted sharply with that of the Spanish and Portuguese colonies, where planters often freed the children of their interracial unions. Far more threatening to the social order in the British colonies were sexual unions between black men and white women. This less common type of interracial union was punishable by castration. English colonists justified their sexual abuse and domination of slave men and women by constructing a stereotype of blacks as lewd, lascivious, and beastlike. According to the colonists' distorted reasoning, black women were always desirous of sexual relations, which absolved white men of blame; and black men lusted after white women and therefore required severe measures of control.

The colonists also constructed stereotypes of sexual depravity and immorality in response to Native American cultures. The many tribes that inhabited North America had varied marriage and sexual customs differing markedly from the colonists' ideal of marital, reproductive sex. In contrast with European cultures, many tribes did not have strict prohibitions against sex outside of marriage. They permitted sexual experimentation, including masturbation, among youth, and premarital sexual activity between opposite-sex or same-sex partners. Various Indian societies allowed trial marriages, practiced polygamy, and did not enforce strict monogamy within marriage. Among the Iroquois, Delaware, Montagnais, and numerous other groups, marriages were not contracted for life, as they were in European cultures. Married couples separated when either spouse desired to do so. Although divorce was common and easy to obtain, couples tended to stay together once they had children.

In contrast with Europeans, many Native American tribes granted women considerable sexual autonomy, both before and after marriage. They did not conceive of female sexuality as man's property and therefore did not stigmatize out-of-wedlock births or women's extramarital affairs, a degree of permissiveness that greatly disturbed European colonists. Another aspect of Native American sexual life that aroused the hostility of colonists was the existence of *berdache* (from the French term for sodomite), men who dressed and acted as women and in some cultures had sexual relations with and married other men. Although they were not as common as cross-dressing men, some Indian women, too, primarily in the tribes of western North America and the Great Plains, lived as men and performed traditionally male tasks of hunting, trapping, and fighting. What particularly disturbed colonists was the acceptance and respect the *berdache* enjoyed within their tribal societies. Cross-gender men and women had a clearly recognized social status and often performed special ceremonial roles and economic functions for their people.

Using their own cultural and religious standards, the colonists condemned Native American divorce, polygamy, cross-gender identities, and extramarital sex as savage and barbaric. Throughout the colonial period European missionaries engaged in vigorous, often violent, but largely unsuccessful efforts to convert Indians to the Christian ideals of monogamous heterosexual marriage and female chastity.

The Nineteenth Century

VICTORIAN AMERICA. The social, economic, and demographic transformations accompanying the rise of industrial capitalism in the late eighteenth and early nineteenth centuries led to significant changes in sexual patterns, ideologies, and methods of regulation. The shift from an economy based on agriculture and artisanal labor to one based on commerce and manufacturing created a new and more stratified class structure with a middle class of businessmen, factory owners, and professionals and a class of wage laborers made up of both displaced artisans and farm laborers and newly arrived immigrants from England, Ireland, and Germany. The subsistence farms of the colonial period were increasingly replaced by commercial farming enterprises, a development fueled by an expanding transportation network of canals and railroads. Cities grew rapidly in the period after 1820, especially in areas where commerce and manufacturing created new jobs and economic opportunities. Industrialization and urban growth took place over a long period of time and occurred at different paces in the various regions of the country. By mid century industrial capitalism was most advanced in the Northeast, while the South remained tied to a system of plantation agriculture and slave labor, and western frontier communities were based on family farm economies.

The shift to an industrial economy generated new family and sexual patterns. Within the emerging middle class, a nuclear family structure and an ideal of sexual restraint took hold. Different patterns and ideologies developed among working-class people, a topic that will be covered later. Among middle-class Americans, the patriarchal household of the colonial era was replaced by the nuclear family with its separate spheres of activity for women and men. Economic production increasingly shifted from household to factory, a development that sharpened the sexual division of labor within middle-class families. In the new capitalist order, husbands worked in offices and factories to earn the income that supported the family, while wives remained at home to take care of children and household duties. A doctrine of separate spheres was elaborated within the middle class during this period that posited distinctly different roles and characteristics for women and men. Women, characterized as gentle, selfless, pious, and pure, were to be the moral guardians of the home. Men, on the other hand, were defined as bold, aggressive, and competitive, best suited for the public world of politics, business, and war.

The role of children within the middle-class family also changed significantly. An economic asset as farm laborers in an agrarian economy, they became an economic liability in an industrial economy. Not only was middle-class children's labor power irrelevant, but their parents found it more difficult to secure their economic future. Instead of land, middle-class parents provided their children with education and character-building to enable them to succeed in the world. This demanded a much greater investment of parents' time, money, and attention, and encouraged families to have fewer children. Marital fertility rates show a marked decline over the course of the nineteenth century. By the end of the century, the average number of children in a family had fallen to four. Considering that high birthrates persisted among working-class, immigrant, and rural families, the decline among the urban middle class was even sharper than this figure indicates.

A new ideology of sexual restraint prevalent among middle-class Americans both facilitated the desire for fertility control and became a marker of class status. Disseminated by physicians, ministers, and health reformers in medical texts and advice literature, this ideology promoted male continence and female purity. Physicians and reformers urged men to avoid all sexual stimulation before marriage and to practice sexual control within marriage. They warned that excessive sexual indulgence destroyed a man's physical and mental powers and undermined his ability to rule his family and compete successfully in the business world. Some advice manuals recommended that married couples limit coitus to once a month and then only for the purpose of procreation.

The "master vice" of masturbation was chief among the sexual indulgences warned against in men's advice literature. Although religious and medical authorities in earlier periods had written about the supposed harmful effects of masturbation, the early nineteenth century witnessed an intensification of anxieties and a voluminous production of antimasturbation literature. Lay and medical writers ascribed to this practice a host of ills from acne to insanity. According to the physician William Acton, the masturbator "cannot look anyone in the face, and becomes careless in dress and uncleanly in person. His intellect has become sluggish and enfeebled, and if his habits are persisted in, he may end in becoming a drivelling idiot or a peevish valetudinarian" (quoted in Marcus, p. 19). To guard against these adverse effects, health reformers Sylvester Graham, Reverend John Todd, and others recommended preventive measures such as cold baths and bland diets. Some also promoted more extreme measures, including surgery and mechanical restraining devices.

While men were encouraged to exert sexual control to uphold their role as breadwinner and head of the family, women faced an even more restrictive code of morality. Nineteenth-century sexual advice literature overturned an earlier image of women as passionate by claiming that women were inherently chaste and pure. They were expected to be the moral guardians of the home, to stem the lustful natures of husbands and sons. Many health and medical writers went so far as to deny that women experienced sexual passion at all. Dr. William Acton, a British physician whose work on female sexuality was widely read in the United States wrote that "The majority of women (happily for society) are not very much troubled with sexual feelings of any kind." According to Acton, "Love of home, of children, and of domestic duties are the only passions they feel" (quoted in Hellerstein et al., pp. 177–179).

Though other physicians expressed dissenting opinions about the nature of women's sexuality, female passionlessness became a dominant ideal within middle-class culture. Although promoted by male physicians and health reformers, the ideal of female purity was embraced by many middle-class women for their own uses. It granted women a position of moral authority within the family and society, and gave them a certain element of control in sexual relations by providing grounds for rejecting unwanted sexual activity and limiting reproduction. Given the dangers of childbirth and venereal disease, many women may have welcomed sexual restraint.

The notion of female purity may have offered some advantages to middle-class women, but it also served to intensify social censure of those women who did not adhere to the bourgeois conception of female respectability. Because women supposedly occupied a higher moral plane than men, their fall from virtue was seen as far more serious. Victorian society condemned, yet tolerated, illicit sexual activity on the part of men. Women who engaged in sex outside of marriage, however, were considered permanently "ruined."

Along with an ideology of sexual restraint, the middle class adopted a romantic ideal of courtship and marriage. While economic considerations remained important, middle-class Americans began to consider romantic love essential for a happy marriage. Unlike colonial couples, who expected to grow to love one another, middle-class couples expected to experience "true love" before they decided to marry. Middle-class courtship also became more private than it had been in rural settings. Courting couples usually met and exchanged intimacies in the parlors of middle-class homes, where they were expected to behave in a respectable manner.

The sexual practices of middle-class Americans did not always conform to the ideals of male continence and female purity promoted in sermons and medical literature. The letters and diaries of Victorian men and women sometimes describe the sensual pleasures they experienced in courtship and marriage. Other evidence, however, suggests that the proponents of sexual restraint had a decisive impact on their middle-class audience. The significant decline in the rate of premarital pregnancy suggests that young middle-class men and women had internalized norms of sexual continence and control. The rate dropped from 20 percent of all marriages in the 1830s to 10 percent in the 1850s. A survey of married women conducted by Dr. Clelia D. Mosher in the 1890s reveals the strong influence of, if not strict adherence to, Victorian sexual ideology. While many of the women interviewed acknowledged experiencing sexual desire, they also expressed feelings of guilt and confusion about their sexual lives. For the most part, they thought that sexual relations should be confined to marriage, and the vast majority believed that reproduction was the primary aim of sexual activity. The point is not that middle-class Americans invariably followed Victorian sexual standards in their daily lives, but that they often tried, and felt guilty when they failed.

The changing social and economic order required new methods of sexual regulation for middle-class Americans. Traditional forms of control were no longer effective in a rapidly growing, industrializing society. The community surveillance of individuals characteristic of the colonial era was difficult to maintain in expanding urban areas with highly mobile populations. In an increasingly secularized society, church leaders no longer had the authority to intervene in the moral lives of their congregations, although they continued to preach about moral issues. State involvement in the regulation of morals also eroded during this period. By the nineteenth century, legislatures and courts had backed away from the rigorous regulation of private morality they had practiced in the colonial period.

With the decline of traditional moral authorities, American society placed increasing emphasis on self-control and the internalization of sexual restraint. The characteristic feature of the new system of sexual regulation was the reliance on individuals, rather than external authorities, to police their sexual desires and behavior. The task of instilling sexual self-control rested primarily with the family, particularly mothers, who were held responsible for the proper moral upbringing of their children. Physicians also assumed a position as sexual authorities in the nineteenth century, publishing tracts, books, and pamphlets instructing people how to manage and control their sexual lives.

Victorian sexual ideals did face opposition. Some middle-class Americans experimented with alternative sexual systems and methods of regulation. Mormons, Shakers, Oneidans, and free-love advocates formed communities that departed from the dominant social order based on the nuclear family and marital, reproductive sex. Shakers, who lived in communal villages in New England, upstate New York, and the Old Northwest, practiced celibacy and tried to overcome physical desire by living a spiritual life. Instead of individual self-control, Shakers relied on close community surveillance to enforce sexual restraint among men, women, and children. The Mormon religion, founded by Joseph Smith in 1830, challenged Victorian sexual codes by permitting polygamy. Mormons formed cohesive patriarchal communities in the Great Salt Lake Valley in which men took multiple wives to enhance opportunities for reproduction, while women were bound by a strict code of chastity. John Humphrey Noyes and his followers explored other alternative sexual arrangements in the utopian community they formed at Oneida, New York, in 1848. Noyes urged Oneidan members to explore sexual pleasures outside of the confines of marriage and to practice "amative" over reproductive sex through coitus reservatus, a procedure in which the man withdrew without ejaculating.

Free lovers directly challenged the sanctity of monogamous marriage by arguing that love and attraction, rather than marriage, should be the basis for a sexual union. Frances Wright, one of the earliest and most outspoken advocates of free love, organized an interracial utopian community in Nashoba, Tennessee. Her radical positions on marriage and race sparked vehement opposition and sometimes violent riots. One writer accused her of trying to turn the world "into one vast immeasurable brothel." In the 1850s sexual anarchists established two short-lived communities—Modern Times on Long Island, and Berlin Heights, near Cleveland, Ohio. The free-love movement reached a broader audience after the Civil War, when Victoria Woodhull began voicing her radical sexual theories in public lectures and writings. Woodhull encouraged open sexual unions, not restricted by church or law. She rejected marriage as an institution that oppressed women and stifled love and sexual pleasure. Woodhull was joined by free lovers Ezra Heywood and Moses Harman, who wrote frankly about sexuality and protested women's sexual slavery in their respective journals, *The Word* and *Lucifer, the Light Bearer.*

The growth of industrial capitalism altered family life, sexual patterns, and methods of regulation among the expanding class of wage laborers, but in ways different from those experienced by the middle class. Laboring men and women did not experience the sharp separation between domestic and work spheres that characterized middle-class family life. Because of the instability of men's employment in a wage-labor economy and the meagerness of wages, working-class families often depended on the economic contributions of all members of the household. In addition to caring for the home and children, working-class wives earned income through activities such as doing laundry, dressmaking, and piece work. Children continued to be an economic asset in working-class families, and consequently birthrates remained high. Parents sent children into the labor force as early as possible; those too young to be wage earners contributed to the family economy through street peddling, scavenging, and assisting mothers with income-producing work done in the home. In this context, working-class marriages were practical arrangements characterized by strong bonds of mutual support and sometimes fierce sexual antagonisms between husbands and wives. In contrast with middle-class marriages, an ideal of romantic love did not become an important aspect of conjugal relations among laboring men and women.

Some Victorian-era Americans experimented with alternative sexual systems: Mormons, Shakers, Oneidans, and free-love advocates formed communities that departed from the dominant social order based on marital, reproductive sex.

The experience of wage earning gave working-class youth greater social and sexual autonomy than they had known in preindustrial economies, where sons and daughters labored under the close supervision of parents in rural households or artisanal shops. Young working men and women met and courted openly in parks and city streets, often away from the watchful eyes of family and neighbors. It was not uncommon for working-class courtship to include premarital sexual activity. This stemmed from the rural practice of permitting sexual relations between betrothed couples in the expectation that marriage would take place if pregnancy resulted. In an urban industrial setting, however, this practice made unmarried women increasingly vulnerable to pregnancy and abandonment. In rural communities, young women could depend on family, neighbors, and church authorities to compel young men to marry them in the case of pregnancy. In large cities with highly mobile populations, the policing of male sexual behavior proved much more difficult. Most of the unwed mothers in the New York Anchorage, a nineteenth-century home for "wayward and erring girls," explained their situation as the result of broken promises of marriage by young men with whom they had become intimately involved.

Traditional forms of moral regulation had weakened significantly in working-class and immigrant communities, but they had not disappeared completely. Families and neighbors continued to monitor sexual behavior and to punish individuals who had violated community moral standards. But despite the existence of both distinct moral codes and the means of enforcing them, to middle-class observers the working-class communities appeared to be teeming with vice and sin. According to public officials and bourgeois reformers, working-class home life in crowded tenements encouraged overbreeding, promiscuity, and vicious habits among family members. Children who, according to middle-class standards, should have been carefully sheltered in the domestic sphere were sent out to labor in the streets, where, according to one moral reformer, "they graduate in every kind of vice known." Reformers expressed particular concern about the impact of industrialization and wage work on women's moral behavior. In a study of prostitution, William Sanger warned that "the employment of females in various trades in this city, in the pursuit of which they are forced into constant communication with male operatives has a disastrous effect upon their characters" (quoted in Stansell, p. 266). Inspired by evangelical Protestantism and a new ideology of sexual continence, middle-class men and women launched numerous efforts to reform the morals of laboring people. They established Bible societies and Sunday schools and organized temperance and antiprostitution campaigns, but in the end they had little success in converting working people to their standards of morality.

THE ANTEBELLUM SOUTH. The institution of slavery produced a distinct sexual system in the antebellum South for both white slaveholders and black slaves. Southern society, rooted in plantation agriculture and slave labor, did not experience the economic changes that generated new sexual patterns in northern cities and towns. The patriarchal household in which fathers exercised authority over wives, children, and slaves persisted in the South until the Civil War. Although most southern households did not have slaves, the patriarchal ideal served as a model for smaller farms as well. The household remained the central unit of economic production, in which all members had specific tasks and duties. Slaves performed domestic chores and backbreaking field work; wives oversaw the garden, dairy, and manufacture of clothing; husbands managed the plantation and conducted business and commercial transactions; and sons and daughters assisted parents with their respective tasks. White birthrates remained high in the agrarian South—up to seven children per family—for large families brought prestige and provided security for parents in old age. Planter parents continued to have a strong voice in the selection of mates for daughters and sons because the protection and consolidation of property and status rested on a wise union. In areas of the South not based on slave labor, families engaged in subsistence agriculture. Far less is known of the sexual lives of these groups, but traditional rural patterns of sexuality and marriage probably persisted, including high fertility rates, tolerance of premarital sex among the betrothed, and common-law marriages.

In the social context of the plantation South, Victorian sexual ideology developed only shallow roots. The southern moral code placed great value on female chastity both to ensure legitimate heirs and to protect family honor, but it neither denied female sexual desire nor promoted an ideal of women's passionlessness. Southern custom dictated that unmarried women remain virginal and that wives uphold moral decorum, but unlike the northern middle class, southerners thought that women, as well as men, were subject to sexual feelings. Women, in fact, were considered more prone to moral weakness due to their childlike, emotional natures. They were thought to be easily seduced and manipulated by scheming men.

The belief in women's moral vulnerability led families to watch their daughters carefully during the courtship period. Chaperons were present whenever daughters met with suitors, attended parties and balls, or visited friends and neighbors. Married women, too, were chaperoned to protect their reputations. Those accused of marital infidelity could face divorce, loss of their children, and physical abuse by their husbands.

While southern white women were hemmed in by strict moral codes, southern white men were permitted great sexual privilege, both before and after marriage. The qualities of male continence and self-control promoted among the northern middle class never became ideals for men in the antebellum South. Society tolerated, even expected, young men to engage in sexual affairs before marriage. Sexual experience was a point of honor for single men; male virginity aroused suspicion and ridicule. Married men could take mistresses or engage in casual affairs without damaging their reputations or family name. Such behavior could even enhance a man's prestige in the eyes of his companions.

Both single and married white men expected to have sexual access to enslaved women. Young men's sexual initiation often was with female slaves, and married men frequently took black mistresses and concubines. Southern men defended this practice by arguing that sex with female slaves protected the purity of southern white women. Because of their subordinate position within southern society, planters' wives did not openly acknowledge or oppose their husbands' interracial relations, but these affairs sometimes caused considerable strain in the marriages. According to one slave, her mistress "don't never have no more children, and she ain't so cordial with the Massa" after she learned of his relations with female slaves. Other planters' wives took out their frustration and rage on slave women, who were even more powerless to challenge white men's sexual demands.

When white Americans looked at slave family and social life, they saw only immorality and licentiousness. Slavery advocates claimed that African Americans were inherently depraved, while northern abolitionists argued that the institution of slavery had destroyed any semblance of family life and morality among black men and women. Contrary to the stereotypes perpetuated by whites, however, the slave community lived by distinct codes governing marriage, courtship, and sexual relations shaped by both African American cultural traditions and the institution of slavery. Historian Herbert Gutman has argued that slave sexual and marital norms closely resembled practices of preindustrial cultures in the acceptance of premarital sex among the young, high fertility rates, and the tendency toward settled unions between men and women, often without legal marriage. One crucial difference is that African Americans had to adjust their sexual customs to the dictates of the slave system. Through various means, masters had extensive, though never complete, authority over the sexuality and family lives of slave men and women.

Contrary to the stereotypes perpetuated by whites, the slave community lived by distinct codes governing marriage, courtship, and sexual relations—codes that were shaped by both African American cultural traditions and the institution of slavery.

The courtship and marriage patterns of slaves demonstrate the combined influence of white masters and African American culture. Despite demanding work loads, young men and women found time for courting at church services, holiday celebrations, and plantation parties on Friday and Saturday nights. Courtships often lasted over an extended period of time, sometimes as long as a year, and were supervised by family and community members. Slaves accepted premarital sex among youth as part of the courtship process. In case of pregnancy, it was generally expected that marriage would take place. As an elderly male former slave explained, "If you fooled up a girl with a arm full of you, you had to take care of her." Although marriage followed most prenuptial pregnancies, slaves did not ostracize unmarried mothers but accepted and cared for them and their children as members of the community. Most of the women who had "outside" children eventually settled into long-term relationships with one man.

Despite the constant threat of separation posed by the slave system, slave men and women expected to form long-term, monogamous unions. Some couples had trial marriages, in which they lived together to determine if they were suitable for one another. Although legal marriage was prohibited under slavery, African Americans legitimized and celebrated their marriages in a variety of ways. Both black and white ministers or respected elders of the community conducted wedding ceremonies. Other couples cemented their union by jumping over a broomstick in the presence of friends and neighbors. Spouses did not always live together. Many had "abroad marriages" in which husbands lived on separate plantations and visited their families when they could, usually on holidays and weekend nights.

Once married, spouses were expected to be faithful to one another. Strong church and community sanctions existed to enforce marital and sexual norms. Black churches punished people guilty of sexual transgressions. The Beaufort Baptist Church in South Carolina suspended those who committed adultery for three months; a second offense resulted in a six-month suspension. Acceptance of the sinner back into the church required the approval of church members. Slaves in Darien, Georgia, adopted a West African custom of "putting on the banjo," singing about a young woman's inappropriate sexual behavior in order to warn her to reform.

The demands of the slave system shaped marriage, courtship, and sexual patterns within the slave community in a number of ways. Masters interfered with slave family life through the control of reproduction, sexual assault of women, and separation of family members. In addition to the production of commodities, slavery demanded the reproduction of the slave labor force, particularly after the slave trade was abolished in 1808. Thus, owners placed a premium on slave women's reproductive capacities and expected them to bear children often and as early as possible. Slave women usually began bearing children at around age nineteen, two years earlier than southern white women, and maintained high fertility rates. Plantation owners used a variety of means to ensure reproduction, both by offering inducements, such as lighter work loads or additional rations for pregnant slaves, and by compelling women to mate with men against their will.

In addition to forced unions with male slaves, women were sexually exploited by white owners and their sons. When resisted by slave women or their husbands, owners often resorted to force to satisfy their sexual desires and assert their dominance. Ruth Allen, the daughter of a white master and a female slave, stated, "My mammy didn' have any more to say about what they did with her than the rest of the slaves in them days" (quoted in Jennings, p. 62). Some women fiercely resisted their master's advances, but often at great cost. A cook named Sukie, who punched her master and pushed him in a tub of water when he tore off her dress and attempted to rape her, avoided the assault but was sold to slave traders for her rebellious behavior.

Although reproduction did not require the existence of families, most owners encouraged settled unions among slave men and women for both moral and economic reasons. Southern ministers urged masters to do their Christian duty by promoting slave marriages and family life. The existence of families not only satisfied religious obligations but also facilitated owners' management and control of slaves. Masters could command obedience from slave men and women by threatening to whip or sell their children or spouses. Familial bonds also discouraged slaves from running away and leaving their loved ones behind.

The exploitation of family ties and women's reproduction made motherhood an ambivalent experience for slave women, who produced an additional source of profit for their owners each time they gave birth, and whose children might be whipped, assaulted, or sold to new masters. Some slave mothers responded by practicing birth control or abortion. Most women, however, did not resort to such measures. Whatever its dangers, they placed great value on motherhood, for it offered them a source of personal fulfillment that was denied in other areas of their lives.

SEXUAL CONFLICTS IN VICTORIAN AMERICA. The late nineteenth century saw intense conflicts over sexuality and its regulation in Victorian America. With urban and industrial development, opportunities for sexual expression outside of marriage gradually expanded. This was most evident in the growing market for pornography and prostitution in cities and towns throughout the country. Social purity crusaders responded with aggressive campaigns to restore sex to a marital, reproductive framework.

The mass production of pornographic literature began in the United States in the 1840s and grew rapidly after the Civil War with the dissemination of novels like *The Confessions of a Lady's Waiting Maid*, and prints and photographs of women in various erotic scenes and poses. Prostitution, which had developed on a small scale in seaport cities of the late eighteenth century, also expanded throughout the nineteenth century. The economic disruptions caused by industrial capitalism increased both the demand for and the supply of prostitutes, as cities and towns filled with young women in search of employment and single men living apart from families. By the end of the century an extensive market in prostitution catered to men of all economic backgrounds. Male customers could choose from fifty-cent "crib houses," one-and two-dollar brothels, and expensive parlor houses. A thriving prostitution trade also took root in western cattle and mining towns, where a severe shortage of women and an abundance of single men produced a great demand for sexual commerce. It is estimated that 20 percent of all women in California were prostitutes in the decade after the gold rush. A particularly exploitative system involving Asian prostitutes developed in some West Coast cities. Asian women who had been sold by their poor families or kidnapped were contracted to perform sexual services for a specified period of time, usually four to six years.

The growth of sexual commerce inspired many middle-class women and men to organize social purity campaigns aimed at cleansing cities of vice and immorality. The earliest purity reform efforts began in Boston and New York in the 1820s, when Protestant clergy and businessmen conducted missionary work in poor neighborhoods to convert prostitutes to a moral way of life. Evangelical women, who formed the American Female Moral Reform Society, came to the forefront of the antiprostitution movement in the 1830s and 1840s. They aimed not only to reform prostitutes but also to change male sexual behavior and eliminate the double standard of morality. Inspired by these goals, women campaigned for criminal sanctions against male seducers. They had little success, however, and by the 1850s the original fervor of the movement had dissipated.

A second wave of purity reform that took shape in the 1870s attracted a national following and developed a more ambitious political agenda. Composed of temperance reformers, women's rights advocates, and Protestant clergy, the movement originally formed in opposition to the efforts of police and medical authorities to prevent the spread of venereal disease by licensing prostitutes. Arguing that such a system promoted vice and the double standard, reformers successfully defeated licensing attempts in Chicago, New York, and other cities.

After this victory; the purity movement expanded the scope of its activities and developed into a broad social crusade to abolish prostitution and to establish a single standard of morality for both sexes. Reformers used both educational and legislative methods to achieve these goals. They organized societies and clubs for young working women to provide wholesome amusements and prevent them from being lured into prostitution. Moral reformers in the Woman's Christian Temperance Union established White Cross societies to convert young men to the single standard.

Even as they used educational means, reformers increasingly called on the state to monitor and reform illicit sexual behavior. As a result of their activities, numerous vice and sex codes were enacted during this period. In an effort to shield young women from male vice, purity activists waged an effective campaign in the 1880s and 1890s to raise the age at which females could consent to sexual relations. Men who had sex with young women under this age would face criminal penalties, whether the women had agreed to have sex or not. By 1915, almost every state had raised the age of consent to sixteen or eighteen years. Other moral crusaders, under the leadership of Anthony Comstock, called on the state to prohibit the publication and dissemination of obscene literature. They achieved a major victory in 1873 when Congress passed the Comstock Law, forbidding the mailing of obscene and indecent materials, including articles that discussed contraception or abortion.

With the growth of Progressive reform after 1900, the antiprostitution movement became a powerful political force that encompassed a wide range of social groups with varying agendas.

State regulation of sexuality was further expanded with the criminalization of abortion in the late nineteenth century. Prior to this time, the legal system did not consider the termination of a pregnancy before quickening (which occurs in the fourth or fifth month) a crime. In response to a vigorous campaign organized by American physicians, state legislatures throughout the country passed laws that outlawed abortion at any stage of pregnancy and subjected both the abortionist and the patient to criminal penalties.

After 1900 the antiprostitution movement secured major legislative changes that seriously undermined the system of commercialized prostitution in American cities. With the growth of Progressive reform, the movement became a powerful political force that encompassed a wide range of social groups with varying agendas. Vice crusaders sought to rid the nation of immorality; municipal reformers aimed to rid cities of corrupt politicians who profited from the prostitution trade; physicians and social hygienists wanted to control the spread of venereal disease; and feminists saw the end of prostitution as central to women's emancipation. Much of the campaign focused on dismantling red-light districts through the enactment of red-light abatement laws, which enabled private individuals to file complaints against suspected places of prostitution. This law was first enacted in Iowa in 1909 and by 1917 had passed in thirty-one other states.

The Progressive campaign reached its peak during World War I, when the federal government enlisted the support of reformers in a major effort to eradicate prostitution and venereal disease among the armed forces. In order to "protect" soldiers from vice and disease, federal officials shut down red-light districts and ordered the arrest, compulsory testing, and quarantine of women suspected of infection. In the end, the Progressive campaign did not abolish prostitution but merely changed its structure in a way that made the profession more dangerous and precarious for women. The removal of brothels and red-light districts forced more prostitutes to turn to streetwalking and strengthened the control of pimps in the trade.

The Rise and Fall of Sexual Liberalism

Even as moral crusaders mounted an impressive campaign against prostitution, enormous social and economic changes were eroding the foundations of the Victorian sexual order they sought to uphold. In the period from 1870 to 1920, the pace of industrialization and urbanization accelerated rapidly, spread to new regions of the country, and changed basic patterns of life ever more drastically. The tremendous growth of the manufacturing and retail sectors of the economy created a great demand for labor filled by American men and women leaving the countryside and by millions of immigrants who entered the country, mostly from southern and eastern Europe. In the face of these developments, Victorian standards of sexual restraint and marital, reproductive sex began to break down. The production of a wide array of new consumer goods and the increased standard of living of many Americans led to a major reorientation of values within middle-class culture. A new ethic of consumption and self-gratification replaced the Victorian emphasis on thrift, sobriety, and self-denial. An industrialized consumer society increased opportunities for sexual commerce and erotic expression outside of marriage. The doctrine of separate spheres, and the ideal of female purity that it embodied, crumbled as middle-class daughters left home for college and professional careers and working-class daughters moved into jobs in factories, department stores, and offices. Black and white rural migrants and the immigrants who flocked to American cities challenged Victorian sexual conventions by participating in an urban world of commercialized leisure that promoted sexual pleasure and romance.

New forms of work and recreation in early-twentieth-century cities provided young people, particularly women, with greater freedom from family and community constraints. As women moved beyond the domestic sphere, they explored sexual experiences outside of marriage and procreation. Many middle-class daughters rejected marriage and domesticity altogether in order to attend college, pursue professional careers, and engage in social reform. Unable to combine careers with traditional family life, women professionals and reformers such as Jane Addams, Sophinisba Breckinridge, and Vida Scudder created alternative family arrangements by forming close and often lifelong relationships with other women. The nature of these relationships varied widely, but at least some involved sexual intimacy. One college-educated woman said that her female partner was "as much a real mate as a husband would be. I have come to think that certain women, many in fact, possibly most of those who are unmarried, are more attracted to women than to men."

Working-class and immigrant daughters also challenged Victorian sexual codes as they explored heterosexual pleasures in early-twentieth-century cities. The expansion and commercialization of leisure at the turn of the century created a youth-oriented, two-sex world of amusement that weakened traditional social controls and encouraged sexual and romantic relations. Instead of the sex-segregated, family-based entertainments of the past, young women and men attended dance halls, amusement parks, and movie theaters. These provided social spaces for flirtation and intimate encounters with members of the opposite sex, away from the watchful eyes of parents and neighbors. Within this world of urban amusements, young women dressed in the latest finery, attended dance halls and amusement parks unescorted, and often picked up young men to pay their way once they arrived. Dancing styles emphasized the heightened sexuality of urban youth culture. "Tough dances" such as the grizzly bear, the Charlie Chaplin wiggle, and the dip encouraged bodily contact and the shaking of the hips and shoulders. The sexual code of working-class female youth tolerated premarital sexual intercourse in certain social contexts. Some were willing to engage in sex with their "steadies." Others had sexual relations with male partners in exchange for gifts, dinner, or a night's entertainment, a custom known as "treating." Clearly among some young women, particularly Catholic immigrants, traditional codes of female chastity prevailed. Even so, the increased rate of premarital pregnancy—which rose from 10 percent in the mid nineteenth century to 23 percent in the period between 1880 to 1910—suggests a growing incidence of sexual experimentation.

The new sexual mores first evident among urban working-class

Instead of the sex-segregated, family-based entertainments of the past, social spaces like dance halls provided opportunities for flirtation and intimate encounters with members of the opposite sex during the Victorian era.

youth had spread to middle-class youth in a tamer form by the 1920s. In dress, mannerisms, and behavior, middle-class female youth of the 1920s adopted a freer and more provocative sexual style. Their shorter skirts, bobbed hair, rouge, and silk stockings defied the nineteenth-century image of female purity and innocence. New rituals of courtship among middle-class youth further undermined Victorian conventions. Instead of receiving male admirers in the parlor at home, young women went out on "dates" with their partners to parties, movies, or cabarets. By the 1920s a central component of the new practice of dating was the automobile, which one juvenile court judge called "a house of prostitution on wheels." Free of adult supervision, dating gave youth greater autonomy in their romantic encounters. Linked to dating was the practice of "petting," in which youth experimented with a range of erotic contacts short of intercourse, from casual kisses to physical fondling. Sexual studies by Alfred Kinsey and others indicate that middle-class women born after 1900 were more willing to engage in premarital petting and intercourse than those born in the nineteenth century.

In addition to new patterns of heterosexual interaction, the early twentieth century witnessed the growth of homosexual subcultures in American cities. Urbanization and the spread of a wage-labor economy enabled an increasing number of individuals to live independently of their families and to explore sexual desires that departed from the heterosexual norm. In large, anonymous cities, men and women pursued same-sex relations and forged the beginnings of an underground homosexual community. They came to identify their erotic interest in the same sex as a characteristic that set them apart from the majority of people. Bars, cafes, and boardinghouse neighborhoods provided meeting places for gay men and lesbians. According to one commentator in 1908, in cities like Boston, Saint Louis, and New Orleans, "certain smart clubs are well-known for their homosexual atmospheres."

In the years before World War I, political radicals and bohemians in Greenwich Village launched an attack on Victorian codes of respectability through both their political writings and their personal lives. Influenced by the studies of Sigmund Freud and British sex theorists Edward Carpenter and Havelock Ellis, they rejected monogamous marriage and sexual self-restraint. Sex radicals experimented with open sexual unions based on emotional compatibility and attraction, rather than on legal marriage.

Radical women in Greenwich Village and elsewhere further assaulted middle-class sexual conventions in their fight for reproductive freedom. The first organized efforts for women's reproductive rights had occurred in the late nineteenth century, when reformers called for voluntary motherhood and women's right to abstain from sexual relations. Radical women made a decisive break with their nineteenth-century predecessors by demanding artificial methods of birth control for the purposes of both fertility control and sexual pleasure. The anarchist Emma Goldman defied the Comstock Law by smuggling contraceptive devices into the country and disseminating pamphlets on birth control methods. Margaret Sanger, a socialist and public-health nurse, called for women's reproductive freedom in the journal Woman Rebel, which she edited and distributed at political meetings and labor union events. As a result, many working-class people wrote to Sanger seeking contraceptive information. After publishing several issues of the journal, Sanger was indicted under the Comstock Law. Rather than face jail, she left the country for England.

Sanger's writings and the subsequent arrest and conviction of her husband for distributing them gained widespread support and publicity for the birth control cause. Many middle- and upper-class liberals added their voices to the movement and organized to repeal the laws prohibiting the free distribution of contraceptive information. When Sanger returned to the United States after several months, the federal government dropped the charges against her to avoid further publicity.

During the next few years Sanger and other activists spoke widely on the issue of birth control, developed national support, and helped to establish birth control leagues and clinics staffed by women reformers. By the 1920s, however, the movement had shifted in a conservative direction. In response to political repression and the decline of feminism, Sanger and her followers distanced themselves from left-wing causes and increasingly sought the support of the medical profession. As physicians assumed a larger role, the movement advocated birth control as a matter of family planning and population control, rather than as a key element in the struggle for women's liberation. Nevertheless, birth control advocates made important gains during this period. By 1930 more than three hundred clinics throughout the country were providing contraceptive information and devices to American women. A major legislative victory came in 1936 when a federal appeals court overturned the anticontraception provisions of the Comstock Law.

In response to the radical changes in sexual mores and attitudes in the early twentieth century, social experts, including physicians, psychologists, educators, and social scientists, attempted to explain and direct the new patterns of behavior. Unlike fundamentalists, Catholics, and other moral conservatives, they did not call for a return to the morality of the past. Instead, they constructed an ideology of sexual liberalism (the term used by historians John D'Emilio and Estelle B. Freedman in *Intimate Matters*) that viewed sexual desire as positive but attempted to channel it into heterosexual relations and marriage. Liberal sex reformers popularized an American version of the writings of Freud and Havelock Ellis. Although they rejected the Victorian ideal of sexual continence, they established new guidelines for acceptable male and female behavior and defined new categories of sexual deviance.

Sexual liberals of the 1920s decried the notion of sexual restraint. Ben Lindsey, one of the authorities on modern marriage, criticized moralists who thought of sex as "ugliness, original sin, and fig leaves." Sexual repression, he and others argued, threatened to undermine marriage, the very institution it was designed to uphold, by causing frustration, anxiety, and illicit affairs. As one commentator warned, "Futile repression ends in volcanic upheaval and a fresh outbreak of license." Sex modernists proposed to deal with this crisis by "sexualizing" marriage. They promoted an ideal of companionate marriage that emphasized the importance of sexual pleasure for husbands and wives. Spouses were encouraged to be both amiable companions and pleasing sexual partners. Proponents advocated early marriage and the use of birth control to enhance sexual pleasure for couples without the fear of unwanted pregnancy.

Although liberal sex reformers rejected the Victorian ideal of sexual continence, they established new guidelines for acceptable male and female behavior and defined new categories of sexual deviance.

The new ideal of marriage required new attitudes and behaviors from both sexes. Men were expected to demonstrate a vigorous sex drive; those who did not, appeared feeble and unmanly, and raised suspicions of homosexuality. Women were called on to keep the thrill in marriage by carefully maintaining their appearance. Films and advertisements, new shapers of sexual mores in the twentieth century, bombarded women with the message that "The first duty of woman is to attract." Sexual liberalism was intricately linked to consumer capitalism. To enhance their sex appeal, women were told they needed to buy cosmetics, mouthwash, stylish clothes, and a wide array of other consumer products. Even as modern sex reformers departed from an ideology of sexual restraint, they established rigid boundaries between "normal" and "deviant" behavior. Clear limits were placed on women's sexual behavior. They were expected to be sexually alluring but not promiscuous; to arouse male desire but not to initiate or control romantic relations; and, most important, to channel their sexual desires into marriage. Those who transgressed these boundaries faced serious consequences.

Even more than female promiscuity, sexual liberalism targeted homosexuality as a particularly deviant form of behavior. Drawing on the work of late-nineteenth-century physicians, modern sex theorists rejected the earlier view of homosexuality as sinful behavior of which anyone was capable, and instead characterized it as an abnormal or diseased condition associated with a particular type of individual. Initially medical authorities scrutinized the traits and life-styles of male homosexuals only, but with the new awareness of women's sexuality in the 1920s, they also identified lesbianism as a serious social problem. Women's intimate friendships became increasingly suspect to those eager to channel female sexuality into heterosexual marriage. Physicians and psychologists debated whether homosexuality was an acquired form of mental illness or a congenital defect; in either case, they called for strict regulation and methods of correction. Homosexual men and women were subjected to a range of medical procedures designed to "cure" their condition, from psychotherapy and hypnosis to castration, hysterectomy, and lobotomy.

Blacks, too, were defined as sexual deviants who required careful monitoring and control. The stereotype of the black man as lustful aggressor continued to have great cultural force in white America even after slavery and was used to justify the murder and torture of blacks. Defenders of white supremacy continually raised the specter of the black male rapist assaulting the southern white woman. This became the most common defense for the widespread lynching of black men in the late nineteenth and twentieth centuries. Between 1889 and 1941 at least 3,811 blacks were lynched in the South. South Carolina senator Benjamin Tillman defended the practice before his colleagues in Washington in a typical fashion: "When stern and sad-faced white men put to death a creature in human form who has deflowered a white woman, they have avenged the greatest wrong, the blackest crime." In reality, few lynchings were associated with sexual assault. A 1931 study revealed that only one-sixth of the lynch victims between 1889 and 1929 were even accused of rape. The primary purpose of this brutal act was to instill terror in blacks and to maintain the system of white supremacy.

The stereotype of black female promiscuity also persisted into the twentieth century and shaped public policy in numerous ways. Birth control and family planning experts persistently portrayed black women as careless breeders and promoted contraception as a way to limit the reproduction of blacks and other "defective" groups. As Sanger argued at one point, birth control would produce "more children from the fit, less from the unfit." Many southern states, usually conservative on sexual issues, encouraged birth control in the 1930s to stem the tide of black population growth. Reproduction abuse of nonwhite women continued in the post-World War II era, when physicians and public health officials targeted poor black, Hispanic, and Native American women for sterilization, often without obtaining their informed consent. Contrary to the racist views that informed such policies, black fertility rates declined steadily after the turn of the century; by 1945, black women bore an average of 2.5 children.

Clearly, the sexual behavior of Americans did not always conform to dominant liberal values. Alfred Kinsey's studies of male and female sexual behavior, published in 1948 and 1953, indicated a sharp conflict between sexual practices and publicly espoused ideals. Ninety percent of the men and 50 percent of the women surveyed had engaged in premarital intercourse, and half of the men and a quarter of the women had had extramarital relations. Kinsey's findings about homosexuality proved even more shocking to conventional values. Fifty percent of the men acknowledged feeling homosexual desire, and more than a third had engaged in homosexual activity as adults.

Despite the conflict between behavior and ideals revealed in the Kinsey reports, most Americans did not publicly question established sexual values and institutions. It was not until the 1960s, with the rise of the youth, feminist, and gay liberation movements, that many began to challenge the ideological dominance of sexual liberalism—acknowledgment of the importance of sexuality, as long as sex remained heterosexual, noninterracial, and largely confined to marriage—in the United States. Stirred by the civil rights struggle, middle-class college students engaged in protest movements to demand free speech on college campuses and to oppose the draft and the war in Vietnam. The student movement included a cultural as well as a political critique of American society. Youth in the 1960s rejected the mores of capitalist society to explore alternative life-styles and values. A hippie counterculture took shape in cities and university towns as young people experimented with new forms of dress and hairstyles, freer sexual behavior, rock music, and hallucinatory drugs. San Francisco's Haight-Ashbury district became a hippie mecca where thousands of "flower children" flocked during the "Summer of Love" of 1967. Some young men and women rejected traditional family arrangements by forming communes where they practiced open sexual unions and raised children in common.

Through their participation in civil rights and student protests, college women gained political skills and a radical ideology that led them to question established gender roles and sexual relations. As they applied the principles of democracy and egalitarianism to their own lives, women activists became increasingly dissatisfied with their marginal role within the student movement and society in general, and broke away to organize a movement for their own liberation. From the beginning, issues of sexuality lay at the heart of the women's liberation movement. Feminists called for a fundamental restructuring of marriage, family, and sexuality—those aspects of life which previously had been defined as private and personal. "The personal is political" became a rallying cry of the movement.

Feminists mounted a sharp critique of the widespread sexual objectification of women in American culture. In one of the first political acts of women's liberation, radical women protested the 1968 Miss America pageant in Atlantic City by crowning a live sheep as queen and throwing girdles, bras, high-heeled shoes, and curlers into a "freedom trashcan." Others challenged confining sexual images and roles by protesting bridal fairs and the distribution of *Playboy* on college campuses. Feminists redefined rape and sexual harassment as political problems that contributed to gender oppression. They ran seminars and established rape crisis centers to provide women with the resources and support to deal with sexual violence and abuse.

While they addressed sexual dangers, activists also called for enhancement of women's sexual pleasure. In a famous article, "The Myth of the Vaginal Orgasm," published in *Radical Feminism* (1973), Anne Koedt charged that women's pleasure had been defined in terms of men's needs and desires. She and other feminists drew on studies by Kinsey and Masters and Johnson that disputed Freudian theory by locating the source of the female orgasm in the clitoris rather than the vagina. Knowledge of the clitoral orgasm, Koedt contended, demanded greater attention to women's desires in heterosexual relations. More significant still, it challenged the very institutions of heterosexuality and marriage by indicating "that sexual pleasure was obtainable from either men or women, thus making heterosexuality not an absolute, but an option" (p. 206).

One of the central battles over sexuality was feminists' fight for reproductive freedom. The growing availability of birth control pills in the 1960s greatly facilitated women's ability to control their fertility, but the nineteenth-century criminal abortion laws remained a major barrier. In the early 1960s physicians and public-health officials organized to reform existing abortion statutes by broadening the conditions under which doctors could recommend abortion. In the late 1960s feminists decisively altered the terms of the debate by arguing that abortion was a woman's right and demanding the repeal of all restrictions on abortion. To build support for the cause, activists staged teach-ins, conducted petition drives, and engaged in civil disobedience by referring women to abortionists. An important legislative landmark was the Supreme Court decision in *Roe* v. *Wade* in 1973, which invalidated state laws that prohibited abortions in the first trimester and made abortions in the second trimester easier to obtain.

The central tenets of sexual liberalism were further challenged by the gay liberation movement, which flowered in the 1970s after several decades of change within gay communities. The gay subcultures and networks that had emerged in the early twentieth century expanded greatly during World War II, when millions of men and women left families, small towns, and farms to serve in the armed forces or to seek jobs in large cities. Living in sex-segregated environments outside of family contexts allowed many men and women to explore same-sex relationships for the first time in their lives. This period of discovery was followed by one of fierce repression during the McCarthy era. According to anticommunist crusaders, homosexuals posed a serious threat to both national security and the preservation of the traditional family. As a result of cold war politics, gay men and lesbians were purged from the armed forces and government jobs and subjected to increased criminal prosecution and police harassment. The severe repression disrupted and destroyed many lives, but it also forged a minority group consciousness among gays. With the founding of the Mattachine Society and the Daughters of Bilitis in the 1950s, a small political movement took root that aimed to secure better treatment and a more positive image of homosexuals in American society.

The growing availability of birth control pills in the 1960s greatly facilitated women's ability to control their fertility, but the nineteenth-century criminal abortion laws remained a major barrier.

The Stonewall Riot in June 1969 led to a radical change in the nature of gay politics. When police conducted a routine raid of the Stonewall Inn, a gay bar in Greenwich Village, customers and bystanders did not respond in a routine fashion. Instead of tolerating the arrests, they fought back by throwing beer cans and bottles, and rioting throughout the night. The Gay Liberation Front, formed in the wake of the Stonewall, dispensed with respectable politics and polite demands for equal treatment. Influenced by the tactics and ideology of feminism and the black power movement, activists made a bold call for "gay power" and the revolutionary transformation of existing social institutions, specifically the system of heterosexuality and the nuclear family structure that upheld it. Gay activists repudiated the pervasive conception of homosexuality as disease and declared that same-sex desire was a normal, human capacity that had been repressed by family and society. The gay liberation movement grew rapidly throughout the 1970s and led millions of men and women across the country to "come out," to publicly acknowledge and take pride in their gay identity. The movement also had a decisive impact on public policies and attitudes. By the end of the 1970s, half of the states had repealed their sodomy laws and numerous cities, including Houston, Los Angeles, Detroit, and Washington, D.C., amended their civil rights statutes to include provisions that prohibited discrimination on the basis of sexual orientation. In 1974 the American Psychiatric Association reversed a long-held position by removing homosexuality from its list of mental disorders.

The feminist and gay liberation movements did not bring about a radical transformation of American society, but they did contribute to decisive shifts in sexual attitudes and behavior. After the 1960s, there was much greater tolerance for and incidence of nonmarital sexual activity. Youth were far more likely to have premarital intercourse than those of earlier decades, often with partners they did not expect to marry. The rate of premarital sex increased most sharply among women, due in part to the easier access to birth control and abortion. Compared with the 1950s, couples married later and had fewer children. Numerous couples chose to remain childless, and many others lived together openly without being married, an arrangement that earlier would have aroused great social condemnation, especially for women. Declining fertility and marriage rates meant that motherhood did not occupy the central part of women's lives that it once had. The gay movement encouraged millions of men and women to live outside of the institution of heterosexuality altogether and to establish same-sex relationships. These various developments contributed to a marked decline in traditional nuclear family arrangements. By the 1980s, only about 10 percent of all American households adhered to the traditional model of two parents with two or more children at home and the husband as the sole breadwinner.

The vast changes in sexual mores and family life since the 1960s provoked a conservative political movement that aimed to restore traditional moral values and turn back the gains of feminism and gay liberation. The religious-based New Right organized a powerful political coalition around a "pro-family" ideology that defended traditional family and gender roles and opposed sexual expression outside of the marital, reproductive framework. New Right activists opposed sex education in the school, teenage sexuality, women's access to abortion, and gay rights. They enlisted the support of groups such as the fundamentalist Moral Majority and the National Right to Life Committee and called on television preachers Jerry Falwell, Pat Robertson, and Jim Bakker to mobilize the millions of evangelical Protestants behind their cause. In the 1980 election, presidential candidate Ronald Reagan actively courted the support of the New Right by endorsing its position on abortion and other "pro-family" policies. With Reagan's landslide victory, moral conservatives found strong support from the federal government.

New Right leaders specifically targeted abortion and gay rights as areas for enforcing their moral agenda. "Right-to-life" committees organized a national campaign for a "human life amendment" to the Constitution that would declare the fetus to be a human person and thus make abortion equivalent to murder. Although this amendment was never enacted, the antiabortion activists did secure the passage of the Hyde Amendment in 1977, which prohibited the use of federal funds to pay for or promote abortions, thereby sharply curtailing poor women's access to abortion services. At the state level, many legislatures began to require parental or spousal consent before abortions were performed on unmarried minors or on wives.

The New Right also succeeded in restricting gay rights. Former beauty queen Anita Bryant led a successful campaign to repeal the gay rights ordinance in Dade County, Florida, in 1977. Encouraged by Bryant's victory, conservatives successfully defeated similar ordinances in other cities, including Saint Paul, Minnesota, Wichita, Kansas, and Eugene, Oregon. New Right activists also called on the federal government to prohibit the employment of gays in any "public sector" or "high visibility public jobs," and to prohibit federal funding of any organization which "suggests" that homosexuality "can be an acceptable lifestyle." They had less success in securing federal legislation, but they influenced President Reagan to appoint moral conservatives to the federal judiciary. In 1986 the Supreme Court expressed its New Right leanings by affirming the constitutionality of sodomy laws that prohibit homosexuality in the *Bowers* v. *Hardwick* decision.

The AIDS epidemic struck a further blow to gay communities in the United States. In 1981 physicians identified a deadly new disease among gay men who were dying from rare forms of cancer and pneumonia. Acquired Immune Deficiency Syndrome, or AIDS, as it is called, is the destruction of the body's immune system making the victim susceptible to life-threatening opportunistic infections. In 1983 medical researchers discovered and most medical professionals believed that the disease was caused by a virus transmitted through the exchange of blood and semen. With no cure in sight, the case-load grew at an alarming pace: from 225 in 1981 to 40,000 in 1987. Although gay men have constituted the great majority of AIDS sufferers, they are not the only ones at risk for the disease. Researchers have learned that the virus is also transmitted through heterosexual intercourse, blood transfusions, and the sharing of unsterilized needles by intravenous-drug users. The AIDS crisis has greatly curtailed sexual experimentation and casual encounters among both heterosexuals and gays.

American society has been sharply divided over how to respond to the epidemic. New Right leaders, claiming that AIDS is a divine retribution for homosexuals, supported proposals for the quarantine of those infected with the virus, the reenactment of sodomy laws in states where they have been overturned, and the removal of people with AIDS from schools, jobs, and housing. Strengthened by decades of activism, gay people vigorously protested such discriminatory policies and the inaction of the federal government in face of the crisis. Drawing on the resources of their own communities, gays have raised funds for AIDS education and research; recruited thousands of volunteers to provide services, counseling, and information for the sick; and organized effective "safe sex" educational campaigns. Even members of the conservative Reagan administration had conflicting ideas about how to deal with AIDS. Secretary of Education William Bennett called for educational materials that promoted sexual abstinence as the only effective means of preventing AIDS, while Surgeon General C. Everett Koop urged comprehensive sex education in the schools that informed youth about the effectiveness of condoms. The continuation of the AIDS epidemic ensures that sexuality will remain a divisive issue at the center of American politics for years to come.

The very notion of a history of sexuality challenges a long-held understanding of sexuality as a fixed biological instinct present in all individuals. Such a conception cannot account for the wide variety of sexual patterns and meanings found within different historical periods and among different cultures. In American society, sexual behavior, ideologies, and methods of regulation have undergone major transformations from the seventeenth century to the present, a result of social, economic, and political developments. Patterns of sexual life have also varied in important ways according to class, race, ethnicity, and region. Throughout American history sexuality has been a site of struggle and conflict. Dominant groups in society have asserted political power and cultural authority over blacks, ethnic minorities, women, and gays through the control and organization of sexuality. These efforts have, in turn, met with resistance by subordinate groups and positive assertions of alternative sexual identities.

[See also Adolescence; Courtship; Marriage, Separation, and Divorce; Family Structures; Gender Roles and Relations; Reproduction and Parenthood.]

BIBLIOGRAPHY

General Works

D'Emilio, John, and Estelle B. Freedman. *Intimate Matters: A History of Sexuality in America* (1988). Excellent survey of the subject from the colonial era to the present.

Gordon, Linda. *Woman's Body, Woman's Right: A Social History of Birth Control in America* (1976).

Peiss, Kathy, and Christina Simmons, eds. *Passion and Power: Sexuality in History* (1989). Collection of essays on sexuality in the United States in the nineteenth and twentieth centuries.

Rothman, Ellen K. *Hands and Hearts: A History of Courtship in America* (1984).

The Colonial Period

Axtell, James, ed. *The Indian Peoples of Eastern America: A Documentary History of the Sexes* (1981). Contains informative documents on marriage and sexual mores in Indian cultures.

Gutierrez, Ramon A. *When Jesus Came, the Corn Mothers Went Away: Marriage, Sexuality, and Power in New Mexico* (1991).

Kulikoff, Allan. "A 'Prolifick' People: Black Population Growth in the Chesapeake Colonies, 1700–1790." *Southern Studies* 16 (Winter 1977).

Morgan, Edmund S. "The Puritans and Sex." *New England Quarterly* 15 (December 1942).

Oaks, Robert. " 'Things Fearful to Name': Sodomy and Buggery in Seventeenth-Century New England." *Journal of Social History* 12 (Winter 1978).

Thompson, Roger. *Sex in Middlesex: Popular Mores in a Massachusetts County, 1649–1699* (1986).

Verduin, Kathleen. " 'Our Cursed Natures': Sexuality and the Puritan Conscience." *New England Quarterly* 56 (June 1983).

Walsh, Lorena S. " 'Till Death Do Us Part': Marriage and Family in Seventeenth-Century Maryland." In *The Chesapeake in the Seventeenth Century: Essays in Anglo-American Society*, edited by Thad W. Tate and David L. Ammerman (1979).

Wells, Robert V. "Illegitimacy and Bridal Pregnancy in Colonial America." In *Bastardy and Its Comparative History*, edited by Peter Laslett, Karla Oosterveen, and Richard M. Smith (1980).

Williams, Walter L. *The Spirit and the Flesh: Sexual Diversity in American Indian Culture* (1986).

The Victorian Period

Barker-Benfield, G. J. *The Horrors of the Half-Known Life: Male Attitudes Toward Women and Sexuality in Nineteenth-Century America* (1976).

Cott, Nancy F. "Passionlessness: An Interpretation of Victorian Sexual Ideology, 1790–1850." In *A Heritage of Her Own*, edited by Nancy F. Cott and Elizabeth H. Pleck (1979).

Degler, Carl N. "What Ought to Be and What Was: Women's Sexuality in the Nineteenth Century." *American Historical Review* 79 (December 1974).

Hellerstein, Erna Olafson, Leslie Parker Hume, and Karen M. Offen, eds. *Victorian Women: A Documentary Account of Women's Lives in Nineteenth-Century England, France, and the United States* (1981).

Hobson, Barbara Meil. *Uneasy Virtue: The Politics of Prostitution and the American Reform Tradition* (1987).

Kern, Louis J. *An Ordered Love: Sex Roles and Sexuality in Victorian Utopias—The Shakers, the Mormons, and the Oneida Community* (1981).

Marcus, Steven. *The Other Victorians: A Study of Sexuality and Pornography in Mid-Nineteenth Century England* (1964).

Mohr, James C. *Abortion in America: The Origins and Evolution of National Policy, 1800–1900* (1978).

Pivar, David J. *Purity Crusade: Sexual Morality and Social Control, 1868–1900* (1973).

Rosenberg, Charles E. "Sexuality, Class and Role in 19th-Century America." *American Quarterly* 25 (May 1973).

Sears, Hal D. *The Sex Radicals: Free Love in High Victorian America* (1977).

Smith-Rosenberg, Carroll. *Disorderly Conduct: Visions of Gender in Victorian America* (1985).

Stansell, Christine. *City of Women: Sex and Class in New York, 1789–1860* (1986). Best treatment of marriage and sexuality in nineteenth-century working-class communities.

The Antebellum South

Clinton, Catherine. *The Plantation Mistress: Woman's World in the Old South* (1982).

Fox-Genovese, Elizabeth. *Within the Plantation Household. Black and White Women of the Old South* (1988).

Gutman, Herbert. *The Black Family in Slavery and Freedom, 1750–1925* (1976).

Jennings, Thelma. " 'Us Colored Women Had to Go Through a Plenty': Sexual Exploitation of African-American Slave Women." *Journal of Women's History* 1 (Winter 1990).

White, Deborah Gray. *Ar'n't I a Woman? Female Slaves in the Plantation South* (1985).

Wyatt-Brown, Bertram. *Southern Honor: Ethics and Behavior in the Old South* (1982).

Sexual Liberalism

Altman, Dennis. *AIDS in the Mind of America* (1986).

Davis, Angela Y. "Rape, Racism and the Myth of the Black Rapist." In her *Women, Race and Class* (1981).

D'Emilio, John. *Sexual Politics, Sexual Communities: The Making of a Homosexual Minority in the United States, 1940–1970* (1983).

Fass, Paula S. *The Damned and the Beautiful: American Youth in the 1920's* (1977).
Kennedy, David M. *Birth Control in America: The Career of Margaret Sanger* (1970).
Koedt, Anne, Ellen Levine, and Anita Rapone, eds. *Radical Feminism* (1973).
Peiss, Kathy *Cheap Amusements: Working Women and Leisure in Turn-of-the-Century New York* (1986).
Petchesky, Rosalind P. *Abortion and Woman's Choice: The State, Sexuality, and the Conditions of Reproductive Freedom* (1984).
Robinson, Paul A. *The Modernization of Sex: Havelock Ellis, Alfred Kinsey, William Masters, and Virginia Johnson* (1976; repr. 1989).
Snitow, Ann, Christine Stansell, and Sharon Thompson, eds. *Powers of Desire: The Politics of Sexuality* (1983).

— MARY E. ODEM

SLAVERY

Take away all someone's freedom and you have a slave. It is that simple: slavery is the complete denial of freedom. Unlike the feudal serf, the indentured servant, the battered wife, or the imprisoned thief, the slave is completely unfree, totally subordinate to the authority of the master. This means that the slave cannot enter into any of the commonly recognized social relationships that define people as human beings—marriage, work, citizenship, even parenthood—except to the extent that the master allows it. Because marriage involves formal rights and responsibilities between husbands and wives, for example, a legally married slave is something of an anomaly, since the spouse would have obligations to someone other than the master, thus undermining the essence of slavery. The slave, in short, is "socially dead," formally barred from participation in any social relationships that might interfere with his or her total subordination to the master. And since participation in society defines people as human beings, slavery is the most thoroughly dehumanizing of all forms of subordination.

To dehumanize a human being is not only to perpetrate an abomination—it is also to construct an inherent contradiction. It has often been said, at least since Hegel, that the contradictions arising from the dehumanization of the slave virtually define the system of bondage. Much of the history of American slavery can be reviewed by tracing these contradictions through the day-to-day interactions of master and slave. But concentrating on the contradictions means that a good deal that is historically specific to slavery in the American South will be lost. After all, slave systems have appeared in all parts of the globe, from antiquity onward. If to be human is to participate in society, the meaning of dehumanization must vary with the form of society within which slavery appears. To distinguish the slavery of ancient Rome from that of the Old South, therefore, is to appreciate not only the contradictions intrinsic to slavery itself but also the specific tensions arising from slavery's relationship to a liberal political structure, a capitalist world system, and a racist cultural framework. Above all, we need to understand the implications of the fact that in the modern world, the histories of slave labor and free labor are inextricably intertwined.

The South as a Slave Society

The wealth of the Old South derived not from the corn and pork it produced in abundance to feed itself but from the "surplus" commodities—tobacco, rice, sugar, and especially cotton—generated by the slaves and sold largely outside the South. We may therefore speak of the Old South as a slave economy or, more generally, as a slave society. In so doing, however, we are making a distinction of tremendous historical importance. For although dozens of societies have had slaves, by some counts there have been only five genuine slave societies in all of human history: Greece, Rome, Brazil, the Caribbean, and the American South. Where slaves in most times and places counted for little more than 5 or 10 percent of the population, full-scale slave societies were perhaps one-fourth to one-half slaves. But these numbers are misleading insofar as they divert our attention from the more important qualitative characteristics of a true slave society. For in slave societies slaves were not merely present in large numbers; their presence dominated the economic, social, and political history of their age.

One way to envision a slave society is to construct what economic historians call a counter-factual. Imagine the Old South without slaves. Everything is different. The social pyramid—slaveholders on top, nonslaveholders in the middle, slaves on the bottom—does not simply change with the hypothetical removal of slaves; it collapses altogether. However oversimplified the pyramid undoubtedly is, its mere plausibility demonstrates how thoroughly slavery defined the entire structure of southern society before the Civil War. Do the same thing with the northern colonies of British North America in the middle of the eighteenth century, and the results are very different. In every colony slavery was legal, and in places like New York City slaves were at times surprisingly numerous. In colonial New England a substantial proportion of the most prominent leaders were slaveholders. Yet if all the slaves had been removed from the northern colonies, the structure of society would not have been fundamentally altered. The basis of the economy, the organization of politics, and the social hierarchy might have changed somewhat, but they would not have been radically transformed. The difference between the northern and southern colonies in the eighteenth century was the difference between a society with slaves and a slave society.

In the antebellum South social standing was determined by whether one was slave or free and, if free, whether one owned or did not own slaves. "It is in truth the slave labour in Virginia which gives value to her soil and habitations," Thomas R. Dew explained in 1832; "take away this and you pull down the atlas that upholds the whole system" (Drew Gilpin Faust, ed., *The Ideology of Slavery*, p. 30). So overwhelming was slavery's presence in the economy and society that the preservation of the slaveholders' power became, directly or indirectly, the guiding force of the most significant political activities.

The Origins of Southern Slavery

The origins of plantation slavery can be traced to a dramatic social transformation that radically increased the purchasing power of western Europeans on both sides of the Atlantic. The first phase of the Atlantic slave trade, from roughly 1450 to 1650, preceded this consumer revolution; it therefore appears in retrospect to have been a mere expansion of slavery's geographic scope. After about 1650, however, commercial expansion became substantive economic change. Slaves were no longer merely present in European outposts; rather, European colonies became slave societies—the first in Western history since the decline of Rome. Early attempts to exploit the labor of indigenous Indian populations or to encourage the migration of a European work force were largely abandoned as one New World colony after another switched to the labor of imported Africans. Around the mid-seventeenth century the slave trade expanded dramatically, and it did so largely in response to an equally dramatic increase in the demand for consumer goods.

Throughout the seventeenth century a rapidly growing proportion of English working people sold their labor for wages and purchased the basic commodities they needed to survive. Above the wage laborers there grew a prosperous new middle class of men and women who began to purchase items once deemed luxuries, items that far surpassed their subsistence needs. But consumer demand mostly grew out of more pressing concerns. For quick comfort and inexpensive calories, for relaxation and for warmth, the new wage-earning classes of London and elsewhere, together with prosperous farmers in Old and New England, generated an unprecedented demand for tobacco, sugar, cocoa, coffee, rice, and cotton. New World slave societies came into existence to serve the needs of this exploding population of consumers stretched along the rim of the North Atlantic basin.

The colonial South was inescapably swept up in all these changes. By 1620 Virginians had discovered that Europeans could afford to develop an addiction for tobacco. All the colonists had to do was to get the land and labor to cultivate it. As part of the headright system Virginia planters were rewarded with a fifty-acre tract for each indentured servant brought to America. (Indentured servants were those who promised to work for five to seven years in return for all or part of the cost of their passage to America.) This system facilitated the growth of a tobacco economy in the seventeenth century by allowing settlers to build up large plantations and at the same time providing them with the necessary workers. Thus the colonial South's dependence on the growing demand for tobacco was established at a time when the bulk of the labor was performed by British servants.

But indentured servitude could only be a short-term solution to the labor problem of the seventeenth century. Over the long run the system put itself out of business—in general because laborers were released from their indentures after completing their years of service and, in Maryland and Virginia in particular, because so many servants died before their service was completed. In these circumstances the labor shortage would never disappear and could actually intensify over time. There was, however, an alternative.

Even as tobacco plantations developed with an indentured labor force, free Virginians steadily acquainted themselves with the resources of the Atlantic slave trade. Slowly they established the legal distinction between slave and free, reconstructing absolute bondage in their own world. The first Africans had arrived in Virginia in 1619, but their numbers were small and grew only erratically until the closing decades of the seventeenth century. After 1680, when the flow of British indentured servants slowed down, Virginians began the changeover that would transform their colony from a society with slaves into a slave society in about a generation. Slave imports to Virginia and Maryland skyrocketed; South Carolina quickly followed suit; and by 1750 even Georgia—whose founders had initially prohibited slavery—was fully dependent on the plantation system that by then characterized the North American slave economy.

If southern slavery was linked at birth to a developing capitalist society with a seemingly insatiable demand for slave-produced goods, it does not follow that slavery itself was "capitalist." For all the slave system's affinities with the consumer revolution and private property, master and slave confronted one another in ways that differed profoundly from the social relations of a free labor system. The results for the southern economy as a whole were, in the long run, devastating. Slavery's short-term profitability is now widely acknowledged, and for some scholars the mere fact that southern planters drew a healthy return on their investment is all that needs to be said. But critics of the Old South, beginning with the abolitionists, were not entirely mistaken in their conclusion that slavery was responsible for the increasing economic backwardness of the region's economy. Slavery encouraged the exhaustion of the soil, discouraged savings, and retarded technological development. Without a free market in labor power, the slave South lacked not only capitalism's incentives to industrious labor but also the capacity to develop a robust home market in consumer goods. So while slavery was shaped by capitalism, it nonetheless lacked many of capitalism's salient features.

The letters and diaries of antebellum slaveholders reveal the distinctive fusion of slavery and capitalism that characterized daily life in the Old South. If double-entry bookkeeping had yet to reach the antebellum plantations, the irrational pursuit of quick riches that nearly destroyed the earliest settlement at Jamestown had long since given way to a more calculating ethic that alone could ensure the survival of a slave economy in a capitalist world. Every tedious journal entry recording the weather, the condition and whereabouts of the field hands, or the numbers of rows planted, weeds dug, or bales packed was sparked by the capitalist world's demand for cotton. Behind every task assigned to every slave every day stood the mill owners and factory hands of Old and New England. At the root of every systematic attempt to sustain the slaves' productivity—including the bribes, the whippings, and the crude efforts to encourage breeding—was the growing consumer demand of the free laborers, dependent and independent, on farms and in cities on both sides of the Atlantic. Thus was the rationalizing force of capitalism fused with the nonrational substance of slavery.

The hybrid nature of the Old South—its combination of slavery and capitalism—presents special problems. Slavery is what distinguished southern society; its particular economic tendencies separated the South from the North, pushing southern history along its own path of development. Yet capitalism is what set New World slave societies apart from their predecessors in antiquity. American masters were among the first in history whose power depended on commercial relations with a capitalist world that was ultimately more powerful than all the slave societies put together.

The Politics of Slavery

If slavery was the denial of freedom, in liberal societies that meant, primarily, the denial of rights. Difficult as it is to define liberalism, the best shorthand definition must acknowledge the primacy of rights. Whereas medieval society recognized the rights of certain groups within a hierarchical social order, liberalism made rights universal; rights were the primary device by which the social order was established. A liberal political structure is dedicated to the preservation of rights. Thus, if liberalism defines social life as a series of rights, it defines social death—slavery—as the denial of rights.

In the simplest cases this appeared in the law as the mere "exception" of the slave from the rights of free citizens. A 1638 "act for the liberties of the people" of Maryland located the slaves, literally, in parentheses: "[A]ll Christian inhabitants (slaves excepted) to have and enjoy all such rights, liberties, immunities, privileges and free customs, within this province, as any natural born subject of England hath or ought to have or enjoy in the realm of England" (John Codman Hurd, *The Law of Freedom and Bondage in the United States* [1858; repr. 1968], vol. 1, p. 248). By the nineteenth century the statutes regulating slavery had become far more specific. The Louisiana slave code of 1824 was a quite detailed list of the rights that, in their explicit denial, defined the essence of slavery. Much of the statute reads as a series of negations. The slave was "incapable" of making contracts, owned no possessions, could bequeath nothing, could not hold public office or engage in any civil procedures, could neither sue nor be sued, and could marry only with the consent of the master (slave marriages "could not produce any of the civil effects which result from such contract"). Alabama's slave code of 1852 did much the same thing when it defined slavery, in effect, by turning the Bill of Rights upside down.

There was a curious irony in this, for slavery actually revealed the boundaries of freedom by specifying what it meant to be unfree. Southerners could define slavery only in the terms they used to define freedom. That is what Thomas R. R. Cobb, one of the antebellum South's best legal scholars, did when he declared: "Of the three great absolute rights guaranteed to every citizen by the common law, viz., the right of personal security, the right of personal liberty, and the right of private property, the slave, in a state of pure or absolute slavery, is totally deprived" (*An Inquiry into the Law of Negro Slavery in the United States of America* [1858], p. 83). Only in a society where freedom was understood as the primacy of rights could "absolute or pure slavery" be defined in simple Lockean terms as "the condition of that individual, over whose life, liberty, and property another has the unlimited control" (*An Inquiry*, p. 3). This is how southern law put the slave outside of society. Without rights, the slave could form none of the basic economic, political, or personal relationships that together bring society into existence.

Liberalism had a robust variety of linguistic devices for imagining the slave's place outside of society. The first was the "state of nature," where no one's rights were secure and where life degenerated into a Hobbesian nightmare, a perpetual state of war. The "social compact" invoked by state constitutions all across the South presumed the existence of a world where no compact had been made prior to man's entrance into society. Where there was no compact there was no society, and without society no one's rights were secure. Here was the perfect place for the slave—outside society, banished forever to a state of nature that had degenerated into the chaos of perpetual war. Locke defined slavery as "the state of war continued" (*Two Treatises of Government*).

More commonly, liberalism recognized the master-slave relationship by retaining a language of property rights stripped of its origins in the state of nature. Notwithstanding the enormous moral and political difficulties raised by the definition of humans as property, southern states fell into the habit of such definition from their earliest slave codes. Virginia's 1705 statute declared that all slaves "shall be held to be real estate and not chattels and shall descend unto heirs and widows according to the custom of land inheritance" (A. Leon Higginbotham, Jr., *In the Matter of Color*, p. 52). Other colonies followed Virginia's lead by defining slaves as either real or personal property. Once this was done, the way was clear for a defense of slavery on the grounds of property rights. The "right of property is before and higher than any constitutional sanction," one southern state constitution declared in 1850, adding quickly that "the right of the owner of a slave to such slave and its increase is the same and as inviolable as the right of the owner of any property whatever" (Hurd, *Law of Freedom and Bondage*, vol. 2, p. 18). In such ways the language of liberalism provided masters with a justification for slavery that was compatible with liberal political culture.

By defining slaves as property, masters facilitated the reduction of their labor force to the status of a commodity—items to be bought and sold on the open market as freely and profitably as the cotton and tobacco and sugar the slaves labored to produce. This degree of commodification helps explain why the South could simultaneously embrace the practice of human slavery and the principle of human equality. For it is in the nature of commodity exchange that it *appears* to be equitable. It was no accident that the secular ideal of human equality emerged in Western history at the moment when consumer society was born. For with the spread of the commodity form based on the "universal equivalent" of money, it was possible for the first time to imagine that the most important relationships among men and women were grounded on the principle of equal exchange. The fact that modern slavery not only arose in this setting but also extended the commodification of society by defining human beings as salable goods, goes a long way toward explaining the paradox of slavery and freedom in American history.

But there were problems in defining slavery in terms of property and commodity. It was easy enough to invoke the right of property in defense of slavery or to demonstrate that the Bible and historical precedent sanctioned slavery. What the master class had to do, however, was to justify the specific enslavement of one particular group of human beings—dark-skinned Africans and their descendants. Here the liberal distinction between "natural" and "artificial" inequality proved crucial, for it provided slaveholders with a powerful justification for distributing or withholding rights differentially throughout society. Racism—the proposition that blacks are by nature, and not by law, a distinct and inferior race of people—merged in the late eighteenth century almost as a counter-weight to the developing doctrine of human equality. Drawing on a host of European prejudices against blackness, heathenism, cultural difference in general, and the lower classes in particular, racism distinguished itself by unifying these prejudices under the framework of a pseudoscientific geneticism specific to the Enlightenment. In short, the eighteenth century invented the modern concept of "race," and with it a relentlessly deterministic dogma that justified the enslavement of an inherently, and so perpetually, inferior "Negro."

Drawing on European prejudices against blackness, heathenism, cultural difference in general, and the lower classes in particular, racism distinguished itself by unifying these prejudices under the framework of a pseudoscientific geneticism specific to the Enlightenment.

By the late eighteenth century the state's awesome power to define who should and should not be enslaved occasioned almost no comment, given the consensus within which white Americans operated: slaves should be Negroes and Negroes should be slaves. "White per-

TO BE SOLD,

A Likely negro Man, his Wife and Child; the negro Man capable of doing all ſorts of Plantation Work, and a good Miller: The Woman exceeding fit for a Farmer, being capable of doing any Work, belonging to a Houſe in the Country, at reaſonable Rates, inquire of the Printer hereof.

Undated newspaper advertisement offering slaves for sale. Slavery is the complete denial of freedom. Dehumanized, a slave is totally subordinate to the authority of the master.

sons may not be enslaved," one southern legal scholar explained. "The presumption of freedom arises from the color," just as "the black color of the race raises the presumption of slavery" (Thomas R. R. Cobb, *An Inquiry*, pp. 66–67). By 1860 racism had become the single most important means by which masters attempted to reconcile the contradiction between slavery and freedom in their society.

The Ruling Race

Racism served also to mask the powerful divisions slavery had created among free southerners. At any given time the majority of free men in the South did not own even a single slave. Within the slaveholding class itself the majority of masters owned a relatively small fraction of the slaves. The richest 10 percent of the owners—2 or 3 percent of the South's free men—held 50 percent of the slaves. Half the masters owned no more than five slaves each; only one in four owned more than ten. And since landownership and slave ownership patterns tended to coincide, those with the most slaves had the best lands with the highest proportions of improved acreage.

By participating in the invention of a category called race, and by employing that category as a way of distinguishing slave from free, the slaveholders sought to define themselves as something other than the ruling class they were. In the words of one southern politician, "we are the governing race." Although nearly universal among slaveholders, the idea of a ruling race falsely suggested that membership in the South's dominant class depended on biology rather than the more prosaic processes of social reproduction. In fact, the social hierarchy of the Old South had to be re-created with each new generation. The answer to the question of how a slave society reproduced itself in a liberal capitalist world must come from somewhere other than racist ideology.

The great challenge for slaveholding parents was to raise their children to the exercise of despotic rule and, at the same time, to a world of individual freedom and political equality. The source of this ambiguity is easy enough to trace: slaveholding families were strongly influenced by new Anglo-American ideas about how to order domestic life properly, as well as by the presence of slaves within the household. The result was a master class whose culture was at once recognizably American and yet distinctively southern. Standing at the intersection of slavery and liberal capitalism, planter families were a paradigm in miniature of the larger history of the antebellum South.

At first glance there is nothing distinctively southern about the "enlightened" attitudes toward marriage and child rearing that made their appearance among planter families sometime in the middle-to-late eighteenth century. As early as 1750 Virginia planters began to express unprecedented concern for privacy, to idealize the affectionate companionship of husband and wife, and to sentimentalize children. With the elevation of her role as nurturing mother, the plantation mistress increasingly nursed her own children, abandoning the aristocratic tradition of wet-nursing that still prevailed on the European continent. Plantation homes were constructed with a newfound concern for the solitude of the individual. The evocative symbolism of southern family portraiture was transformed: the father, no longer aloof and above his family, instead assumed a loving pose beside his wife and among his children. Gone, or at least substantially diminished, was the image of the family as the domestic reflection of patriarchal government, with its emphasis on hierarchy and subordination, obedience, and intergenerational continuity. The new understanding demanded that children be nourished on love more than on filiopietism, reared to individual autonomy rather than hierarchical interdependence. In this emerging image of the family, the world was remade with each generation.

Certainly the Old South was no stronghold of sexual equality. Male-dominated families prevailed throughout nineteenth-century America, and perhaps more firmly in the South than elsewhere. Property laws continued to disadvantage women. Given the dangers of childbirth, large families continued to place southern women's lives and health in jeopardy. And, of course, to be a slaveowner was to be, nine times out of ten, a male. Nevertheless, relatively egalitarian inheritance patterns, female literacy, property rights for women, and the legal recognition of the distinctive interests of wives and children represented major inroads of liberal political culture among slaveholding families.

Without entailed estates, with no tradition of primogeniture, and with none of the elaborate legal mechanisms that preserved the integrity of noble privilege in Europe, the slaveholders developed child-rearing and inheritance patterns that reflected the powerful force of liberalism. In the late eighteenth century every southern state abolished primogeniture, long after it had been abandoned in practice. Planters broke up their estates with each passing generation, distributing their property differentially but broadly among their children. Eldest sons could expect to take possession of the family home, but land and slaves were distributed among sons and daughters. The diaries and letters of slaveholders make it clear that by the nineteenth century the advantages of the well-born, although considerable, were by themselves insufficient to ensure that the child would live in the same degree of comfort as the parents. Every young man was expected to make his own contribution to the social reproduction of the slaveholding class. Self-discipline, hard work, and the systematic acquisition of wealth became central ideals passed down from father to son in slaveholding families.

Given the prevalence of the bourgeois ideals of equal opportunity and individual achievement, each new generation of slaveholders faced the challenge of reconstructing a society that distributed its wealth very unevenly. For this pattern of inequality to remain constant in a society in which estates were divided up every generation, at least some of the children of wealthy planters had to rebuild their parents' fortunes, and many others had to fail in that endeavor. Because the children of small slaveholders usually began their adult lives as slaveless farmers, most of them had to reenter the slaveholding class on their own, and some had to remain outside the master class throughout their productive lives. The statistical evidence bears this out. Upward—and downward—mobility were, almost by definition, characteristic of the life cycle within the master class. Because slave ownership was something that came later in life, upward mobility was a normal experience for successful masters. Nor was this a rare experience in the Old South, for in 1860 one out of every four free families owned at least one slave, and the proportion had usually been higher than that. Most often, slave ownership rates ranged from 30 to 35 percent, and in many parts of the South they were higher still, even in 1860. Over the course of a free man's lifetime there was probably a fifty-fifty chance of becoming a slaveholder for some period of time.

Yet it would be a mistake to conclude from all of this that the history of the slaveholding class was a mere variation on a larger liberal theme. The South was, at bottom, a slave society, and the significance of slavery extended well beyond the relationship of master and slave. The ownership of even a single slave affected all the other relationships that made up the master's world. Slavery reshaped the ties between farmers and merchants; it transformed the relationship between slaveholders and their neighbors; and it profoundly influenced the bonds of marriage and the patterns of child rearing within the master's family. For all liberalism's influence, slavery nevertheless reproduced itself in distinctive ways, beginning with the organization of family life.

Consider what could happen to the rhythm of daily life when a free farmer acquired a slave. We know that slaveless farmers relied extensively on the labor of their own families, that they divided work in patterns based on age and gender, and that these patterns changed over time as the family grew and matured. The ownership of only a few slaves, perhaps even one, could subtly but profoundly alter these patterns. No doubt the effects multiplied as the number of slaves in the household increased. But the consequences appeared, and were perhaps most pronounced, with the ownership of the first few.

With a slave on the farm, particularly a male, a father could more easily afford the labor lost by sending his son to school or by having his daughters tutored. Not surprisingly, the slaveholders' children were absent from school less frequently than were the children of slaveless yeomen farmers. Despite the fact that public education in the South advanced more slowly than in the North, the children of slaveholders, girls as well as boys, were almost always educated. So widespread was literacy within the slaveholding class that the overall literacy rate among free southerners was one of the highest in the Western world.

Slavery reshaped the ties between farmers and merchants; it transformed the relationship between slave-holders and their neighbors; and it profoundly influenced the bonds of marriage and the patterns of child rearing within the master's family.

A female slave, perhaps only one, could relieve the mistress of some of the most onerous chores of housekeeping, from cooking and cleaning to gathering wood and tending the family's vegetable garden. Whereas nine out of ten women on slaveless farms did their own chores at home, less than a third of small slaveholders' wives did. And only 7.7 percent of the mistresses on large plantations performed their own household chores, for as the number of slave laborers grew, the mistress was transformed into a domestic manager.

As free children reached adulthood, slave labor could make it easier for parents to subsist and prosper without the help of their own offspring. Bound labor often replaced child labor in the life cycle of the slaveholding family. Free men were most likely to own slaves when they were in their forties and fifties, when their children came of age and moved out on their own. Thus slavery loosened the bonds of intergenerational dependency that made older parents traditionally reliant on their grown children. In turn, children benefited from the age structure of the slaveholding class. The average number of slaves a master owned peaked in middle age but declined among those who reached their sixties. Slavery thus allowed the most prosperous parents to transfer some of their wealth to their grown children in the critical years of early adulthood.

As with relationships within the family, the ties between family and society began to change with the purchase of a single slave. Most masters were farmers for whom the cost of a slave was a significant expense, in fact a major investment. Whether farmers borrowed the money to buy a slave or saved the cash, they naturally expected the fruits of slave labor to repay the initial expense. Property taxes on slaves added to the burden. Since slaveholders monopolized the most productive soils, the taxes on their lands were often higher than those of yeomen farmers. To own even a single slave, therefore, was to be subject to periodic payments and yearly taxes that slaveless farmers did not have to meet.

Simply put, slavery required production for the market. In most cases this meant that the slave's labor would be devoted primarily to producing crops for which there was a relatively predictable consumer demand in the market. Statistical evidence shows a fairly clear correlation between slave ownership and production of staples such as cotton, tobacco, sugar, and rice. The more slaves a master owned, the more land he was likely to devote to marketable crops.

But slavery also made market production easier. By some estimates the average slave produced at least twice as much as was necessary for his or her subsistence, thus making slave ownership a source of considerable profit to masters for as long as the market in staples was flourishing. It was not that slave labor was intrinsically more productive than free labor—evidence of slavery's efficiency is subject to tremendous dispute. But it is clear that a slave was normally expected to work longer and harder than were any members of the master's family. Slave children went to work in the fields at a younger age than did free children; slave women were expected to do fieldwork, which few free women did except at harvest time. Slave men worked longer hours and had fewer holidays than did free men. In the slave quarters of large plantations, cooking and baby-sitting were frequently communal chores, often reserved for elderly slaves, and this, too, increased the labor power available in the work force. Slaves usually produced most of their own food, provided much of the diet for the master's family as well, and at the same time increased the farm's production of marketable staples.

For all the economic obligations slave ownership entailed, it also liberated masters from the heavy reliance on neighbors that was essential to successful yeoman communities. Slave ownership eased the settlement process by fulfilling at least some of the demands for labor that all farmers experienced. Slaves could clear the fields, build the barns, perfect the crafts, and perform the labors that normally impelled yeomen farmers into cooperation with their neighbors. At the same time, superior access to markets made it easier to purchase inexpensive goods from distant manufacturers than from a local class of artisans, craftsmen, and merchants. Just as slave labor eased settlers' reliance on neighbors, so did the combination of plantation self-sufficiency and dependence on international markets effectively limit the slaveholders' economic links to their own communities. The larger the plantation, the more removed it was likely to be from the commercial activities of the locality.

Slavery undermined community attachments in many ways that contemporary observers could scarcely fail to notice. Neighbors complained about the social isolation of local planters. Slaveholders' wives were tortured by their husbands' incessant readiness to uproot their families and abandon their communities. Travelers were astonished by the high rates of turnover of plantation ownership. And they had good reason to be. Only a small minority of planter families, as few as 20 percent, lived in the same place for more than two decades. The reasons for the relentless migration of the slaveholding class lie in the social consequences of slavery itself.

Take away a master's land and he was still a master; take away his slaves and his entire social identity was transformed. By definition, slavery gave the master the power not simply to dispose of the slave but to transport the slave to and fro at will. This meant that the slaveholder's power, unlike the feudal lord's, was not tied to a specific landed estate. Slavery required relatively few ties to place and community. As a class the masters had a far greater interest in protecting their slaves than in protecting their soils—which the slaveholders in fact exhausted far more than was necessary. Thus slavery not only facilitated migration; it also encouraged farming methods that spurred movement.

In the end physical expansion was the only way the slave economy could grow enough to sustain the social reproduction of the master class. It was possible to introduce more efficient farming techniques that might enhance the productivity of the slave plantations. But given the masters' paramount interest in slaves rather than in land, the advantage of reforming agriculture was never as clear to the masters as it was to their critics. Even with such techniques, the productive potential intrinsic to slave labor was probably limited. The indisputable growth of the southern economy before the Civil War, in particular the rise in per capita incomes, depended almost entirely on the expansion of slavery onto new western lands. It was no accident that the issue which, more than any other, precipitated the sectional crisis was the expansion of slavery.

The Master-Slave Relationship

Slavery in the United States "was above all a labor system," as Kenneth Stampp pointed out in *The Peculiar Institution* (p. 34), and the bulk of the slaves' labor was performed on rural plantations. To be sure, slaves in southern society served in many other capacities that were common to slavery elsewhere. They were a source of prestige and an indication of wealth; they worked as domestic servants on family farms, in plantation houses, and in urban residences. They were skilled craftsmen, factory operatives, nurses, and sometimes plantation managers. On the other hand, they did not serve in the military, they were not teachers, and they did not staff the government bureaucracy as slaves did in other times and places. Rather, slaves in North America were primarily field hands on farms and plantations.

The unparalleled level of consumer demand for slave-produced goods emanating from the capitalist world sustained a competitive environment in which masters had little choice but to impose some system of labor management, however ineffective or informal, on their slaves. Seventy-five percent of the slave population was concentrated on farms with ten or more slaves, and for most of them systematic management of some sort was all but impossible to avoid. By 1860—with four million slaves, almost four hundred thousand masters, and commodity prices that guaranteed few quick fortunes—the most successful farms were those that sustained the highest levels of productivity over the long term.

Nevertheless, slavery actually provided little room for significant improvement in productivity. As laborers, the slaves had little incentive to care very much or to work very hard. They had nothing like the feudal serf's powerful claim to rights in the land. Slaves also lacked the incentives built into a wage-labor economy: the sheer need to go to work to survive, the promise of more pay for more work, and the added enticement of upward mobility in the future. They had nothing to gain from working hard on cash crops that did not add to their basic subsistence. The limited hierarchy within the slave community offered no real possibility of social advancement. Slave parents could work neither for their own nor for their children's eventual independence. No institutionalized promise of future freedom provided an incentive for slaves to work hard. So, while countless slaves took justifiable pride in their skills as nurses, managers, cooks, or artisans, the vast majority of slave laborers, the field hands, had no motivation to care very much about the success of the master's efforts to produce a good crop.

Thus southern masters tried to rationalize the labor of slaves who had every reason to resent such efforts, and this proved a major source of tension within the master-slave relationship. Work was what the slaves did all day, and so work was what provoked many of the conflicts between master and slave. The rules of the workplace set the daily, seasonal, and yearly rhythms of life on farms throughout the slave economy. Yet the very effort to impose a system that would increase worker output appeared to slaves as a direct reminder of the master's arbitrary power.

While countless slaves took pride in their skills as nurses, managers, cooks, or artisans, the vast majority of slave laborers—the field hands—had no motivation to care about the master's success with his crop.

On the well-managed plantation order was ideally maintained by a hierarchy of the work force—extending from field hands to drivers to overseers to the master—and an often elaborate set of rules and regulations. There were general rules of the plantation and special rules for field hands, children, and women, particularly "breeders" and "sucklers." There were different rules for winter and summer, and rules for different days of the week. There were even rules requiring that rules be enforced uniformly. Slaves were to wake up and go to sleep according to the rules, and rules determined when they ate, how much they ate, and how their meals were prepared. Rules governed the slaves' intercourse with other slaves as well as with whites, on and off the plantation. Additional instructions described in detail how each job was to be performed, how far apart rows should be planted, how many bales should be picked by each hand, and how quickly slave songs should be sung in the field. By 1860 the accumulated list of suggested rules published in dozens of articles on plantation management could have filled volumes.

As the existence of such rules suggests, the subordination of the slaves to the master's authority extended well beyond the control of labor. Because slaves were a source of wealth separate from the crops they produced, their care and feeding, and ultimately their sexual reproduction, were as important to masters as the productive cultivation of crops and soil. Many owners therefore distinguished the management of slaves from the rational organization of their labor, and they often insisted that slaves were at least as important as what they produced. No comparable interest in serf management appears in the manorial documents that survive from medieval Europe, nor can this aspect of slave management be equated with the problem of labor control in capitalist enterprises. When the masters contemplated the management of slaves, they were reflecting on the appropriate exercise of powers that extended far beyond those of a factory owner or a feudal lord.

Just as masters boasted of their success in improving the productivity of slave labor, so did they emphasize the material rewards of maintaining a healthy slave population. Yet the very detail with which masters explored the subject of slave management inadvertently reveals that the essence of slavery was not treatment at all but, rather, the master's power over the intimate details of slave life. The masters cared about the treatment of slaves not simply because they had an interest in them but because they had the power to control the slaves' private lives. Masters could decide whether slaves would get married, where they would live, what they would eat, when they would wake up and go to bed, and how they would dress. What the masters exposed in their detailed examinations of slave treatment was not that they were uniquely humane but that they were extraordinarily powerful.

They exposed more than that. Owners addressed the treatment question by trading suggestions about how best to arrange the most mundane aspects of slave life, things free men and women assumed were private affairs. It seemed perfectly ordinary for one master to require that slaves not overcook their vegetables, for another to insist that slave women "have a change of *drawers* for the winter," and for still others to set rules determining at what time and in what manner the slaves could eat their supper. This was not the language of uninhibited greed but of rational calculation.

Nevertheless, it was a rationalism that exposed the distinctive character of slavery. That distinctiveness derived in large part from the fact that the slave family subsisted within the master's household. The family remained the procreative unit, but the economic functions of the household were under the control of the masters, giving them power to make many of the domestic decisions denied to the slave family. Every time the masters extended their control over another aspect of the slave's daily life, they demonstrated in precise and highly personal terms what it meant to be unfree. For slaves there was no such thing as a right of privacy. To be a slave could mean filing past the master for receipt of weekly rations or to be examined for cleanliness or torn clothing. Slave cabins were not simply built to the masters' specifications; they were open to periodic inspections.

If total subordination meant that masters could demand much more than hard work and obedience from their slaves, the denial of rights had similarly practical consequences for day-to-day treatment of slaves. Masters took it for granted that they had every right to choose which ministers the slaves would hear, when slaves could attend church services, and which sermons were appropriate. Slave-holders enforced the laws restricting the slaves' freedom of movement by prohibiting them from "strolling about" or leaving the plantation without permission. Others denied slaves permission to trade commodities they cultivated on their own. Some were so intent on restricting trade that they did not allow slaves to plant their own gardens.

The slaveholders' power was nowhere more evident than in slave families. Masters often reserved the right to veto a proposed marriage. On large units they sometimes prevented slaves from marrying anyone off the plantation. Masters set the rules about how much work pregnant women could perform, when nursing mothers should return to the fields, how small children were to be cared for while the parents were at work, and the age at which slave children should begin labor. Even the personal relations of husband and wife were subject to the owner's arbitration. And masters never relinquished their power to break up a marriage.

Hence the fatal paradox: what masters defined as issues of treatment, as problems of management, appeared to slaves as extreme assertions of the master's power. The most trivial rules—making sure slaves got to bed on time, for example—were among the most palpable symbols of unfreedom. For, unlike the periodic shock of family breakup or the brutal beating of a particularly unruly field hand, the day-to-day treatment of slaves was a relentless and perpetual reminder of how far the master's power extended and how completely the freedom of the slaves was denied. This was, with labor control, the second of the two great sources of conflict between masters and slaves.

The Slave Family

The tensions intrinsic to the master-slave relationship arose most commonly out of a contradiction perhaps distinctive to slavery in the Old South: the same families that had no recognition under the law had nonetheless become essential to slavery's survival. The "peculiar institution" could not reproduce itself without slave families. As early as 1750 southern slavery was becoming uniquely dependent upon the physical reproduction of the slave population, and with the withdrawal of the United States from the Atlantic slave trade in 1808, the masters no longer had a dependable alternative source of slaves. The system could survive only with slave families. And yet these families lacked all legal standing; they were neither the primary units of economic productivity nor the chief mechanism for the redistribution of power in society.

Without the civil recognition that distributes legal and property rights among husbands, wives, and children, the slave family was neither patriarchal nor matriarchal—for neither spouse had the formal powers that normally justify the use of such terms. If all slaves had no legal rights, then husbands could have no more rights than wives. If slaves could own no property, the family could not be the vehicle for the transmission of estates. If slavery was perpetual, slaves could not rear their children for the eventual assumption of power or independence. The family structure that emerged from such conditions was unique in American social history.

Gender distinctions that prevailed in free families, for example, were undermined by the slave labor system. The work each slave was expected to perform was limited primarily by physical capacity, and women could do most of the jobs men could do. From early childhood all slaves—boys and girls, men and women—mostly did the same kinds of tasks. If men concentrated on plowing and digging where women focused on hoeing and weeding, what distinguished slavery was the fact that the majority of slaves, men and women, spent their days doing field work. Thus, while certain gender differences were maintained, there was no sense that the labor of slave women was primarily domestic, or that their work should be confined to meeting the subsistence needs of their families.

Nevertheless, many of the distinctions associated with family life did emerge within the slave community. Masters assigned communal cooking and child-rearing tasks to women, while traditional artisanal crafts were reserved for male slaves. Domestic service in the master's house was largely restricted to females. Above all, as bearers of children, as nursing mothers, slave women assumed roles and obligations different from those of slave men. This made women uniquely vulnerable to their masters' interest in sexual reproduction, but it also gave them a kind of leverage unavailable to slave men. In the master's dependence upon her fertility the slave woman found and exercised a degree of influence—a bargaining chip—in her dealings not only with her master but also within her own family. Slave women thereby assumed a degree of influence within their families that helped to counteract the formal powerlessness of both husbands and wives.

With the modicum of influence they recovered through their reproductive capacities, slave women protected the integrity and emotional life of their families as best they could, and with surprising success. The slave family was notoriously subject to the disruptive intrusions of the master and at the same time profoundly important to the cultural stability of the slave community. Above all, the slave family was a creative adaptation to the anarchic realities of slavery. Although it was a legal nonentity, the slave family's existence was tolerated by masters who could respect or destroy it as their interests and inclinations determined. But as a cultural anchor within the slave community, the family developed in ways that compensated for its intrinsic vulnerability.

Kinship, for example, radiated outward from the slave family, embracing cousins and nieces, nephews and in-laws, as close rather than distant relatives. Fictive kin—"aunts" and "uncles" with no blood ties—further extended the lines of family outward until they blended smoothly and indistinguishably into the slave community as a whole. In a world where nuclear families were intrinsically vulnerable to the master's power to break them apart, the extended relations of the slave community preserved a sense of family stability in the wake of otherwise wrenching dislocations. One of the largest forced migrations in history, the slave trade within the antebellum South was so widespread that the average slave could expect to be sold at least once in a lifetime and would likely witness the sale of half a dozen close relatives. Yet the family provided an anchor for the larger community of slaves, and the slave community in turn nourished a sense of self-worth and solidarity that helped sustain each member of the family.

At the same time, the slave family gave masters a potent weapon in the perpetual struggle with their slaves. Owners clearly recognized that the strength of slavery rested in large measure on the strength of the slave family. The stronger the family attachments, the less likely a slave was to run away. Thus most escapees were young men who had grown beyond the protective umbrella of their childhood families and had not yet established new families of their own. A wife and child were powerful restraints on a slave who yearned to escape but who could not face the prospect of leaving his family behind. The slaves had taken full advantage of the contradictions of the system to create a family life, a community, and a culture that could generate, support, and justify the acts of resistance that the master's demands provoked. But the more successfully the slaves protected their families, the more fully they realized their community life, the more effectively their culture explained their circumstances—the more bearable, and peaceful, slavery became.

Slave Resistance

But life was not always peaceful on antebellum plantations. Overt tensions between master and slave repeatedly erupted in the workplace. Slave-holders complained that their bondsmen were impudent because they very often *were* impudent; masters complained that their slaves were lazy because they rarely exhibited any zest for their labors. By deliberate lassitude, by running away, by sabotage, slaves withheld their labor from the master. By planning their individual and collective acts of day-to-day resistance as deliberate responses to particular grievances, the slaves made known their objections to mistreatment, neglect, and overwork.

The field hand who had been pushed too hard by an overseer or whipped once too often by the master did not decide whether or not to strike back impulsively but in consultation with family members and in consideration of their welfare.

If forced labor inevitably generated resistance, it was often the strength of family ties that determined the strength of a slave's militancy. Pushed too hard by an overseer, whipped once too often by the master, a field hand's decision to strike back or not was most often made in consultation with family members and in consideration of family attachments. In more direct ways resistance was commonly tied to family life. Women ran away with their children to prevent their families from being broken up; husbands fled to find relatives from whom they had been separated. Acts of resistance were often provoked by the master's abuse of a slave's spouse or child, or by a particularly galling intrusion into the slave's personal affairs.

It was, then, a precarious peace that rested on the security of the slave community and the vibrancy of African American culture. The slaveholders saw the advantages of family stability, but there was no way for the master class to maintain itself without disrupting and destroying slave families on a massive scale. To "manage negroes" was to interfere inevitably in the personal lives of slave families and thereby to provoke hostility. To discipline a slave was to anger and horrify that slave's husband, wife, parent, or child. To own slaves was to enjoy the right to break up a family, but to exercise that right was to rekindle within the slave community a passionate hatred of bondage. Family life made slavery bearable, it held slaves to their plantations, it gave slaves something whose integrity was not worth risking. But children gave parents a powerful incentive to struggle for freedom, while the family in general gave all slaves something worth protecting. In the end the legal kinlessness of the slaves made slavery the inveterate enemy of the very families it created. And so the slaves resisted.

[See also African American Music; Agriculture; The Clergy; Family Structures; Household Labor; Minorities and Work; The Natural Environment: The South; The Plantation; Rural Life in the South.]

BIBLIOGRAPHY

Censer, Jane Turner. *North Carolina Planters and Their Children: 1800–1860* (1984).

Clinton, Catherine. *The Plantation Mistress: Woman's World in the Old South* (1982).

Davis, David Brion. *The Problem of Slavery in Western Culture* (1966).

Davis, David Brion. *The Problem or Slavery in the Age of Revolution, 1770–1823* (1975).

Faust, Drew Gilpin, ed. *The Ideology of Slavery: Proslavery Thought in the Antebellum South, 1830–1860* (1981).

Finley, M. I. *Ancient Slavery and Modern Ideology* (1980).

Fox-Genovese, Elizabeth. *Within the Plantation Household* (1988).

Franklin, John Hope. *The Militant South, 1800–1861* (1956).

Freehling, William. *The Road to Disunion. Vol. 1, Secessionists at Bay 1776–1854* (1990).

Genovese, Eugene D. *The Political Economy of Slavery: Studies in the Economy and Society of the Slave South* (1965).

Genovese, Eugene D. *Roll, Jordan, Roll: The World the Slaves Made* (1974).

Higginbotham, A. Leon, Jr. *In the Matter of Color: Race and the American Legal Process, The Colonial Period* (1978).

Isaac, Rhys. *The Transformation of Virginia, 1740–1790* (1982).

Kulikoff, Allan. *Tobacco and Slaves: The Development of Southern Cultures in the Chesapeake, 1680–1800* (1986).

Lewis, Jan. *The Pursuit of Happiness: Family and Values in Jefferson's Virginia* (1983).

Miller, Joseph C. *Way of Death: Merchant Capitalism and the Angolan Slave Trade, 1730–1830* (1988).
Morgan, Edmund S. *American Slavery, American Freedom: The Ordeal of Colonial Virginia* (1975).
Oakes, James. *The Ruling Race: A History of American Slaveholders* (1982).
Oakes, James. *Slavery and Freedom: An Interpretation of the Old South* (1990).
Patterson, Orlando. *Slavery and Social Death: A Comparative Study* (1982).
Smith, Daniel Blake. *Inside the Great House: Planter Family Life in Eighteenth-Century Chesapeake Society* (1980).
Stampp, Kenneth M. *The Peculiar Institution: Slavery in the Ante-bellum South* (1956).
Thornton, J. Mills, III. *Politics and Power in a Slave Society: Alabama, 1800–1860* (1978).
Wright, Gavin. *The Political Economy of the Cotton South: Households, Markets and Wealth in the Nineteenth Century* (1978).
Wyatt-Brown, Bertram. *Southern Honor: Ethics and Behavior in the Old South* (1982).

— JAMES OAKES

SPORTS THROUGH THE NINETEENTH CENTURY

Sports as we know them are a very recent phenomenon. Not until the end of the nineteenth century did many of the features we take for granted become part of sports. Indeed, our usage of the word is rather new. In the eighteenth century, "sport" would more likely have been used in a phrase like "sporting man," or an individual might have been called a "sport." Both terms were less than flattering, for an individual so designated was likely a rake, a gambler, a man who lived by his wits. By 1900, however, "sports" connoted athletic games played by professionals or highly trained amateurs under clearly spelled out rules with masses of paying spectators cheering their favorites in specially built stadia. Events themselves were now supported by businesses or institutions (the National League, the sporting goods firm of A. G. Spalding and Brothers, Yale University, the National Collegiate Athletic Association, for examples), reported in mass-circulation newspapers, and evaluated with statistics. So severed from their folk origins had sports become that one game—basketball—had no past at all; it was simply made up in 1891 by one James Naismith, who worked at the Young Men's Christian Association Training School in Springfield, Massachusetts, as a way to keep athletes in shape between the baseball and football seasons. This essay will trace the transformation of sports from folk games to modern spectacles.

The British Heritage

British colonists seem to have played mainly the games they remembered from their ancestral homeland. Of course North America was not "virgin land"; hundreds of thousands of Indians inhabited the continent. Eastern woodland tribes, for example, played a game colonists called stickball ("lacrosse" for the French), yet the British seem not to have adopted this or other Indian games. Perhaps they felt a need to keep intact all of their folk-ways in this strange land; and perhaps the Indian game was too alien to them, surrounded as it was by the various tribes' customs and observances. After all, Indians often played stickball and other games within a context of sacred dancing, chanting and drumming, shamanism, dietary restrictions, body painting, pipe-smoking, and other ritual practices, all part of a distinct religious worldview.

The English played various games on the eve of colonization, and they held a range of opinions as to the proper place of recreation. No single game was typical, but Richard Carew's description of "hurling" in Cornwall at the beginning of the seventeenth century gives us a sense of what was possible. The countryside for miles around could be the playing field, and the teams consisted of entire parishes:

> Some two or more Gentlemen doe commonly make this match, appointing that on such a holyday, they will bring to such an indifferent place, two, three, or more parishes of the East or South quarter, to hurle against so many other, of the West or North. Their goales are either those Gentlemens houses, or some townes or villags, three or four miles asunder, of which either side maketh choice after the neernesse to their dwellings. When they meet, there is neyther comparing of numbers, nor matching of men: but a silver ball is cast up, and that company, which can catch, and cary it by force, or sleight, to their place assigned, gaineth the ball and victory.

To gain the victory, however, men subjected themselves to brutal competition:

> Whosoever getteth seizure of this ball, findeth himself generally pursued by the adverse party; neither will they leave, till . . . he be laid flat on Gods deare earth. . . . The Hurlers take their next way over hilles, dales, hedges, ditches; yea, and thorow bushes, briers, mires, plashes and rivers whatsoever; so as you shall sometimes see 20 or 30 lie tugging together in the water, scrambling and scratching for the ball. . . . (*The Quest for Excitement: Sport and Leisure in the Civilizing Process.* Edited by Norbert Elias and Eric Dunning [1986]).

Whichever team carried the ball to their goal—a church, a manor, a parish seat–won the game.

Note that no restrictions on team size existed, that the playing field was the entire countryside for miles around, and that parish membership determined who played on each team. As Carew described it, the game was singularly violent, and such contests no doubt became ready opportunities to settle old personal grudges or larger community rivalries. Gentlemen arranged the matches, and they undoubtedly offered prizes for the winners, along with a feast for all after the game. These were great men, local nobility or gentry, patrons in the community, whose largesse helped secure the loyalty of their baseborn neighbors. Such games were a social glue, binding men together despite an intensely hierarchical social system. Carew added that hurling helped prepare men for war, for the game required that players know the terrain and anticipate their opponents' movements in order to ambush them. He concluded that hurling "put courage into their hearts, to meete an enemie in the face"; but while the game gave men fortitude, it also left them with bloody heads, broken bones, and injuries that might shorten their days. Though Carew did not mention it, hurling left them with something else–a sense of manhood. Sports like this one seem to have been primarily part of male culture. Implicitly, they defined masculinity–aggressiveness, courage, competitiveness–against femininity. This elemental conception of maleness characterized most sports through the nineteenth century.

Carew wrote his description just as popular recreations were becoming a controversial topic. On the one hand, there was the Renaissance tradition, which celebrated England's national love of play. But on the other, there was the rising tide of Puritanism, a theology suspicious of all worldly pleasures that threatened to divert people from their personal confrontation with God. Just when Jamestown, Plymouth, and Boston were settled the controversy boiled over. King James I issued his "Book of Sports" (1618) to reassure his subjects that the crown still approved their old entertainments:

> Our pleasure likewise is, Our good people be not disturbed, letted, or discouraged from any lawful recreation, Such as dancing, either of men or women, Archery for men, leaping, vaulting, or any other such harmlesse, Recreation, nor from having of May Games, Whitson Ales, and Morris-dances, and the setting up of Maypoles, and other sports. . . . (quoted in *Popular Recreations,* p. 7)

The "Book of Sports" was a rebuke to the Puritans who insisted that the Sabbath must be spent solely in prayer and quiet introspection. Puritans responded that the very recreations the king praised led away from God to superstition and idolatry, to sin and wickedness. So powerful were the Puritans in many parishes that they refused to promulgate the king's decree. They enforced their pious Sabbath, and also banned as "corrupt" and "pagan" the festivals and saints days of the Catholic and Anglican calendars.

The middle decades of the seventeenth century saw the triumph of Puritanism under Oliver Cromwell, then its demise during the Restoration of the monarchy. The ideological battles fought in England were part of the heritage of those who initially settled the British colonies. Some who migrated were champions of Puritan piety, but others bore the tradition of country recreations, of feast days, cockfights, and ball games.

Early American Sports

In the Old World and the New, Puritans (or Calvinists) were suspicious of excessive worldly joys. Those who envisioned godly communities in the wilderness found human nature inherently untrustworthy, too much leisure dangerous, and work a holy endeavor. Sober religious folk were determined to keep amusements hedged within useful and moderate bounds, which threatened to constrict until they contained nothing at all. Yet others shaped their visions of the New World by the age-old ideal of a leisured paradise. These individuals dreamed of a toilless and bountiful life, and the English heritage of fairs, feast days, and sports became the palpable expression of the leisure ethic. The seeming boundlessness of the New World stirred their imaginations.

Puritans took King James's "Book of Sports" (1618) as a rebuke, believing that the very recreations that the king praised led away from God to superstition and idolatry, to sin and wickedness.

All of England's North American colonies inherited the dual-leisure tradition. Many colonial Virginians held Calvinist beliefs in original sin, predestination, and election; many came from pious middle-class stock. On the other hand, the Massachusetts Bay Colony was plagued by people who rejected Puritan hegemony, and by individuals who would rather play than work. But as a general rule, austerity was stronger in the North, while leisure found fuller expression in the South.

Early Virginia was disproportionately settled by men, and a boom in tobacco growing in the 1620s gave the colony the raucous tone of a mining camp. Drinking, gambling, and many of the pastimes of Old England flourished; with social status unclear and land abundant and unfenced, hunting, fishing and fowling, sports of the privileged back home, could be enjoyed by all. Within a generation, however, a gentry elite had established itself. Often from well-off families, these men controlled the labor of others through a system of indentured servitude, followed by black chattel slavery. By 1700, the southern colonies constituted a highly stratified society, with a planter elite that styled itself after the English country gentry, a middling group of white farmers, and a large body of black slaves.

The early boom economy, with its lack of settled domestic life, encouraged men's willingness to follow bouts of hard moneymaking with interludes of abandon. Later, the rhythms of the plantation, of sowing, tending, and harvesting, encouraged alternating periods of work and idleness rather than regular sustained labor. As the colony settled into a stable, highly stratified pattern late in the seventeenth century, the old English leisure ideal well served Virginia's social alignments. Men in this environment worked hard, but not with the Puritan's regularity, diligence, or sense of the transcendent godliness of labor. For the gentry on both sides of the Atlantic, to celebrate leisure, especially to do so with enormous wagers, was a way to identify themselves as members of a distinct ruling class, regardless of the poverty or ruthless competitiveness of their ancestors.

So several factors came together by the beginning of the eighteenth century to help make play a dominant southern value: the English leisure heritage, the erosion of the Calvinist notion of calling among the most influential men in the South, and the rise of the rural gentry to ruling-class status. But one more element was crucial. Black chattel slavery drove the final wedge between labor and leisure. How could men value hard work unequivocally once labor was inextricably associated with degraded, servile blacks? How pretend that work was ennobling, character forming, even sanctified in a society whose hardest workers were seen as dangerous, half-civilized heathens, capable of nothing but brutish tasks?

For all of these reasons, sports and games became a major preoccupation in Virginia and the other southern colonies. Games and amusements were important to all classes, but by the end of the seventeenth century, the gentry had the time, motivation, and means for great displays of consumption and conviviality. As class lines became distinct during the new century, roughly two or three hundred tidewater families comprised Virginia's aristocracy. Knit together by kinship ties, they shared a gracious life in which leisure lay at the heart of their class style and identity. Horse racing, cockfighting, and hunting were the great gentry passions. Men also eagerly participated in boating, wrestling, fencing, quoits (something like horseshoes), bowling, and cudgeling (fighting with long sticks).

Educated in England like so many young colonial men, the rich and accomplished William Byrd II (1674–1744), for example, participated in the whole panoply of English sporting customs on his enormous family estate at Westover, early in the eighteenth century. He played billiards, laid out a bowling green, competed in cricket, ninepins, and skittles. Wealthy Virginians like Byrd seized every opportunity for merrymaking, including dancing, partying, or gambling over a sociable bottle. Religion and law now buttressed rather than assailed these practices. Ministers of the Anglican church, whose congregations often depended on the patronage of local gentry, offered little resistance to the ethic of leisure, while county courts recognized gambling debts as legally enforceable.

Timothy H. Breen has demonstrated how a horse race among the Virginia gentry facilitated great displays of wealth, personal honor, and patriarchal prestige. The "merry-dispos'd gentlemen" of Hanover County who celebrated Saint Andrews Day in the 1730s with quarter-horse races did so to cultivate social solidarity, vent their competitiveness, and enjoy each others' company. Spectators could observe their betters, provided they "behave themselves with Decency and Sobriety, the Subscribers being resolved to discountenance all Immorality with the utmost Rigour." As Breen points out, however, what made horse races so central to southern culture was the dramatic tension between control and abandon. On the one hand, events should be orderly, reflecting the good harmony of the new society; they should be moderate, not leading men to licentiousness or excess; and they should not become too distracting from productive endeavors. But on the other hand, sport as a vehicle for displays of prowess, wealth, and status encouraged men to compete recklessly, to drink, gamble, and assert themselves as if their very social position, even their masculinity, were in question. Time and again, governors and legislators inveighed against the disorderliness that accompanied horse races, but this failed to stop men from impulsively betting entire fortunes on a single race.

Before long, the southern gentry was building English-style circular tracks; importing thoroughbred horses; retaining breeders, trainers, jockeys, and stablemen (often blacks); and generally making racing a central symbol of upper-class life. The gentry, however, did not monopolize popular recreations. Various groups might mingle at a single event. Just as in the example of hurling by Richard Carew, great men would initiate contests, and lesser ones would receive their largesse. Thus, Elkanah Watson described a raucous cockfight in Southampton County, Virginia, at which there were "many genteel people, promiscuously mingled with the vulgar and debased" (*Men and Times of the Revolution; or, Memoirs of Elkanab Watson,* edited by Winslow C. Watson, 2d ed. [1856], pp. 300–301).

Yet on other occasions, events were more segregated. Observed Phillip Vickers Fithian one Easter, "Negroes now are all disbanded till Wednesday morning and are at Cock Fights through the County"; a week later he noticed "a ring of Negroes at the Stable, fighting cocks" (*Journal and Letters of Philip Vickers Fithian, 1773–1774,* edited by Hunter Dickinson Farish, new ed. [1957], pp. 91, 96). Blacks even continued some of the games of Africa in the slave quarters. Moreover, poor and middling whites claimed leisure space for themselves. They held their own races, cockfights, and bear baits; they hunted and fished for pleasure as well as game; they even staged their own ferocious eye-gouging battles. Nonregular working rhythms of plantations, farms, and market towns enabled individuals to find time for such activities. The hours taken in the middle of work could expand to days for annual events such as the "Public Times," held every spring and fall for court and assembly sessions at the county seats. Mid-eighteenth-century Williamsburg, for example, grew to three times its normal population during these events, as individuals watched or participated in horse races, plays, dancing, fiddling, acrobatics, wrestling, and other pleasures.

Whether describing them as leisure-loving or lazy, many commentators have declared that southerners developed a distinct regional ethic, one which rejected labor as the all-consuming goal of life. When they esteemed commerce and enterprise at all, it was less because piling up wealth contained religious or moral value than because productivity facilitated the good life. While gentlemen-planters were not a hereditary aristocracy, they took their cue from great landed Englishmen, embracing sociability, gracious living, and personal polish as core values. Conspicuous consumption rather than rational saving was the hallmark of the region, because displays of luxury and fine living were markers of a man's status in society. Above all, we must not view the southern ethic as aberrant or unique. Nonregular working rhythms, conspicuous display, love of finery, and games and sports, all had deep roots in Western cultures. The compulsion to work steadily and regularly, to make leisure a subordinate value accepted only for its ability to increase one's capacity for labor, and to divide work and play into separate compartmentalized realms were the novel ideas.

The settlers of New England and the middle colonies were also heirs to the dual-leisure tradition. Yet the North proved a more austere climate for traditional recreations. About 1627, Thomas Morton, a renegade from Puritan society, led a hand of like-minded settlers to the edge of Plymouth Colony, and there defied his pious neighbors. William Bradford (1590–1657), governor of Plymouth, accused Morton of atheism and paganism—categories that Puritans tended to conflate. Bradford described the renegades' revels: "They also set up a maypole, drinking and dancing about it many days together, inviting the Indian women for their consorts, dancing and frisking together like so many fairies, or furies, rather . . . as if they had anew revived and celebrated the feasts of the Roman goddess Flora, or the beastly practices of the mad Baccanalians" (*Of Plymouth Plantation: 1620–1647,* edited by Samuel Eliot Morison [1952], pp. 205–206). Morton taunted his Pilgrim neighbors, and they finally responded; in 1628 they cut down the maypole, arrested Morton for selling arms to the Indians, and shipped him back to England in irons.

Generally, however, conflicts over popular recreations took less dramatic forms. In 1621, Bradford had to deal with some new settlers who objected to working on Christmas Day (the Pilgrims of Plymouth, indeed, the Puritans in general, considered Christmas celebrations part of the pagan hangover of the Catholic church). The governor decided not to force these people to work against their consciences, but when he and the others returned from their labors that day, they found the newcomers "in the street at play, openly; some pitching the bar, and some at stool-ball, and such like sports." Bradford took away their sporting toys, not because they played, but because they did so openly: "If they made the keeping of it (Christmas) matter of devotion, let them keep their houses; but there should be no gaming or revelling in the streets" (p. 97). At least the appearance of a godly community would remain, and the diligent not be tempted from their labor.

Dissenting Protestants, Puritans among them, did not object to all recreations. They allowed innocent amusements like simple ball games, played in moderation; hunting and fishing provided food; martial sports like cudgeling or swordplay taught skills useful to the defense of the settlements; sociable activities like cornhuskings, or spinning or quilting bees were encouraged. But they drew the line at recreations that violated the Sabbath, encouraged passion, or smacked of the old pagan excesses. The true test of recreations was their usefulness; proper leisure helped people live righteously by serving useful ends, ends which included refreshing them for work. Thus, even as he condemned profane or promiscuous dancing, Increase Mather observed, "The Prince of Philosophers has observed truly, that Dancing and Leaping, is a natural expression of joy: So that there is no more Sin in it, than in laughter, or any outward expression of inward Rejoycing" ("An Arrow Against Profane and Promiscuous Dancing," [1684] excerpted in Perry Miller and Thomas Johnson, *The Puritans: A Sourcebook of Their Writings,* vol. 2 [1938] p. 411).

This spirit of moderation grew out of the Puritans' dominant theology, Calvinism. After the fall from Eden, they believed, all humankind was tainted with sin. In his mercy, God, through Christ, saved a small number from eternal damnation. In other words, the Lord had predetermined the fate of all people, saving a few for reasons only He understood, damning the rest. Since their fates were predestined, it followed that earthly efforts had no impact on people's futures. Nor could one know for sure whether one was among the elect. Still, through constant self-scrutiny, an individual might discover evidence of Christ's grace. Leading an upright life according to God's laws was a sign—albeit, a tenuous one—of salvation.

The Puritans' idea of "calling"—that laboring diligently in one's worldly occupation was a religious observation—infused daily business life with religious significance.

For the Puritans, an upright life meant far more than merely observing ritual forms. Their idea of "calling"—that laboring diligently in one's worldly occupation was a religious observation—infused daily business life with religious significance. The hardworking farmer or tradesman did the Lord's bidding as surely as the writer of sermons. Work was pleasing to God and it followed that success in one's earthly endeavors might just be a sign of inner grace. But even while individuals strove to succeed in the world, they must never overvalue the material fruits of success. Signs of salvation, not the good life, were what one sought in pursuing one's calling. Even as men's labor bore fruit, they must never overvalue the comforts of life, their eyes must always be on the Lord. Above all, the bond between piety and labor meant that play could never be unequivocally valued in its own right. Whereas southern life turned men away from seeing work as a transcendent value, northerners eyed leisure with suspicion.

It would be a mistake, however, to interpret northern ideas about sports, play, and leisure purely from the Puritan viewpoint. A more accurate depiction would see this cluster of Protestant ideas as a presence that sometimes dominated the northern colonies, sometimes was challenged by less than pious groups, but always made itself felt. In Massachusetts and New England, but also among the Dutch Calvinists of New York and the Quakers of Pennsylvania, ideas like calling and worldly asceticism tempered people's commitment to play. Moreover, the Protestant ethic did not simply fade with the seventeenth century, but rather it washed over communities in successive waves. The various religious awakenings that swept through people's lives from the mid-eighteenth through the early nineteenth centuries always contained a powerful element of Protestant self-control, an austerity that cast suspicious glances at those too immersed in the passions of the world. Indeed, even a deist and man of the world like Benjamin Franklin could not escape the earnest spirit of improvement, the suspicion of frivolity, that was his Protestant heritage.

Nonetheless, the English leisure tradition survived in the North: neither harsh frontier conditions nor Puritan hegemony obviated pleasures of the flesh. Crossroads taverns, community gatherings like elections or muste days, and marketing times tied to rural life were all loci of traditional games. What failed to emerge out of the old folkways was an ethos of leisure conferring social rewards, a cultural challenge to the Puritan work ethic, a way of life like that of the southern gentry which assumed that humans worked to play rather than played so they might work.

One exception to this rule emerged in the eighteenth century in cities like Boston, New York, and Philadelphia. Here an urban gentry began to form, consisting partly of British colonial officials and military officers, partly of newly prosperous merchants, and partly of men of landed wealth who lived and governed from the city. In Philadelphia, for example, such a group rivaled the pious Quakers in political clout. The Philadelphia gentry forged group identity through common membership in such organizations as the Mount Regal Fishing Club, the Dancing Assembly, the Gloucester Hunting Club, and the Jockey Club. In New York, too, balls, plays, dances, horse races, and cockfights were important venues where the new urban elite came to identify with each other. But not only the elites of growing cities were active in leisure pursuits. Tavern keepers, to attract customers, tradesmen and laborers among them, became pioneer promoters of recreations. They provided dart boards and bowling greens; they brought bulls and bears to confront pit bulls; they built rings for cockfights; and they held the stakes for various forms of gambling. By the mid eighteenth century, then, cities were becoming the focus of a whole new realm of leisure. Here, where individuals were most oriented to the marketplace, recreations took their first steps toward commercialization.

Perhaps it is best to speak of various sporting heritages during the colonial era. By the last quarter of the eighteenth century, sporting events at their most organized might attract a few thousand spectators, rich and poor, mostly white, mostly male, watching thoroughbreds, for example, race for high stakes. Such an event would likely pit two local elites against each other, would be held on a track with grandstands built by a rich jockey club, would even be an annual occasion. But

By the last quarter of the eighteenth century, sporting events at their most organized might attract a few thousand spectators, rich and poor, mostly white, mostly male, watching thoroughbreds, for example, race for high stakes.

at the other extreme, and certainly more common, would be events centered in the countryside and small towns, where the vast bulk of the population lived. Most common were activities like hunting and fishing, where leisure and labor cannot even be distinguished from each other. The most likely form of "sport" might be simple ball games, played according to uncodified rules with available equipment in pastures or clearings. Folk games and recreations were part of communal preindustrial life; they grew out of face-to-face relationships, and expressed the tensions and cohesiveness of particular localities.

The Antebellum Era

In June 1802, the grand jury sitting in Philadelphia received a petition against Hart's racecourse, a local institution: "This English dissipation of horseracing may be agreeable to a few idle landed gentlemen, who bestow more care in training their horses than educating their children, and it may be amusing to British merchantile agents, and a few landed characters in Philadelphia; but it is in the greatest degree injurious to the mechanical and manufacturing interest, and will tend to our ruin if the nuisance is not removed by your patriotic exertions" (quoted in John Thomas Scharf and Thompson Westcott, *History of Philadelphia 1609–1884* [1884] p. 940). The petition was signed by fifteen hundred mechanics and twelve hundred manufacturers, which in that era generally meant craftsmen who worked in their homes or shops with the aid of families and perhaps an apprentice or journeyman.

The petition was filled with code words: Dissipated idle gentlemen who train horses rather than educate their children will ruin manufacturers without the jury's patriotic exertions. Here is a classic example of republican ideology, that set of ideas that helped drive the colonies to rebel against England, and to form a virtuous commonwealth. On one side, the idleness and dissipation of merchants and landed characters; on the other side, producers motivated by the spirit of hard work. Selfishness, luxury, corruption, in the republican lexicon, versus self-restraint, virtue, communal improvement. The racetrack became a symbol of a serious social and ideological schism.

Sports and leisure, as we have seen, had always had a conflicted history. During the revolutionary era, the Continental Congress outlawed games, sports, the theater, all of the usual amusements, as unfit for a virtuous people embarking on independence. Horse racing returned after the war, but the problem of proper versus improper amusement sharpened during the nineteenth century. The old republican tradition that had emphasized individual self-restraint in the name of communal welfare lived on long after the revolution. But as American society increasingly came under the sway of capitalism and the liberal ideology that accompanied it, sports and leisure were not immediately liberated from old prejudices. On the contrary, the newfound freedom of Americans to transact business during the antebellum era was accompanied by singularly stern cultural strictures that demanded rigid adherence to tough rules of personal conduct.

Historians have documented a transformation in the American economy that occurred largely during the first half of the nineteenth century. Agricultural production shifted from an orientation toward semi-subsistence and local consumption to market production. Especially with the opening of new lands, the development of inland waterways, and the building of new transportation systems, increasing numbers of farmers produced staples that they sold in national and international markets. Even more important for our purposes, cities burgeoned as centers of trade and manufacturing, while the methods of making goods were transformed. Machine production was part of this process, as was the increasing concentration of productive property in fewer hands, and the growing pull of the marketplace.

The Philadelphia petitioners against Hart's racecourse represented the old, preindustrial economy, in which apprentices learned a trade, and with luck, finally became skilled master craftsmen, and proprietors of their own shops. This system was part of a household economy that produced goods for local markets. Work and family were often contiguous: apprentices lived in the master's house, family members labored alongside the head of the household, and this patriarchal extended family was seen as the font of public order.

The new system was much more recognizably part of the modern capitalist order. Old words like apprentice and journeyman hung on, but working relationships were transformed: employers paid wages or piece rates (as low as they could get away with) to individuals who sold their labor for as much as they could command. Trades were rationalized, the size of firms expanded, and the possibilities of workers ever becoming independent property owners diminished. One tendency that accompanied these changes was the destruction of old craft skills; it was to owners' advantage to break down the production process into simple tasks that required cheap, easily replaceable workers. Moreover, entrepreneurs now found themselves much less burdened with fellow feeling for their employees; young workers lived in boardinghouses until they married and started their own families. The new order was based far less on customary or paternalistic relationships, much more on contractual ones.

This new organization of society—of productive relationships—had ideological implications. The old Protestant ethic was very serviceable in the new order. Protestantism's emphasis on stable, sober, dependable behavior was useful to a society whose organization of work increasingly demanded time, thrift, and intense specialization of tasks. Sheer productivity for its own sake had religious sanction, while landlords, speculators, and merchants were sometimes seen as manipuiators of markets, accumulators who produced nothing while living extravagantly. For the new middle class, delayed gratification and moral certitude were the cornerstones of society. The economies and social relationships in different parts of the country were not all transformed at once; but the total result, certainly by the middle of the nineteenth century, was a thoroughly changed society. By then, national markets, mass print media, telegraphy, steamships, railroads, voluntary associations, and above all, a powerful consensus of values bound most white, northern Protestant middle-class Americans together. For want of a better term, we can label the ascendant national culture that accompanied social and economic change Victorian.

Like the Puritans, Victorians would never argue that wealth was a sure sign of moral worth, but they did believe in a connection, or in the sociologist Max Weber's term, an "elective affinity", between prosperity and good morals. Capitalists and Evangelicals—often the same people—feared idleness, craved regularity, practiced self-control, and idealized usefulness. The millennial hopes of preachers, the belief in eternal life, in spiritual perfectibility, were as real to the saints as the profits that accrued from temperance, thrift, and hard work. Choosing Christ and controlling social stress were part of a single process; converting employees saved souls and secured a reliable labor force; establishing urban missions helped prepare for the millennium and assured a stable business climate. Business and religion were bound together with an earnest tone of moral certitude.

Victorianism, again like Puritanism, contained seeds of repression for popular recreations. Whereas for the Puritans a sociable dram or a local lottery for a good cause were acceptable, the new Evangelicals often condemned such practices as sinful, insisting on an unprecedented level of asceticism. Virtually every recreational outlet was condemned at one time or another, from cockfighting to checkers, from horse racing to croquet. All leisure activities potentially fostered the evils of drinking, gambling, swearing, idleness, and Sabbath breaking. Declared a Congregational magazine, the *New, Englander,* in 1851, "Let our readers, one and all, remember that we were sent into the world, not for sport and amusement, but for labor; not to enjoy and please ourselves, but to serve and glorify God, and be useful to our fellow men." In a similar vein, William A. Alcott warned youthful readers in his *Young Man's Guide* (1833), "Everyman who enjoys the privilege of civilized society, owes it to that society to earn as much as he can, or in other words, to improve every minute of his time. He who loses an hour or a minute, is the price of that hour debtor to the community. Moreover, it is a debt which he can never repay." Even in the West, where the constraints of civilization supposedly were left behind, and the South, where the slave system encouraged an ethic of leisure, Victorianism found staunch adherents, and the wilder the sports, the more strenuous reformers were in suppressing all that stood in the way of the City of God and the progress of man.

Yet there were powerful countertrends. The same transformations that gave rise to the Victorian ethic of hard work and sober self-control also created an environment potentially conducive to popular recreations. By divorcing work from the extended family of shop and farm, the new capitalist order freed men and women not only to labor as best they could, but also to spend their leisure time according to their own lights. One of the constant refrains heard from antebellum reformers regarded the dangers of young people roaming the streets, free to go to theaters, gambling houses, dance halls, bars, and other places of recreation.

By mid century a distinct working-class subculture had emerged in American cities, especially New York, and for young unmarried men, sports were an important part of that subculture. A cluster of images captures the scene: the volunteer fire companies where men gathered to drink, play cards, and occasionally display their heroics as fire fighters; ward-bosses in city politics who knew how to distribute largesse and secure elections with the aid of ballot-box stuffers and strong-arm enforcers; the Bowery in New York (and little Bowerys in other cities) where theaters packed in the crowds for melodramas, and working-class men donned the distinctive dress of the "Bowery B'hoy"; taverns where men treated each other to round after round of drinks, and where sporting events like cockfights, bare-knuckle boxing matches, or bull-baits were arranged or staged.

Beyond the working class and immigrant sporting underground, there were other factors contributing to the rise of sports. Steam-power printing, telegraphy, and the penny press all could be used to disseminate sporting news. America's first sporting magazine appeared in the second decade of the nineteenth century, and there were three new magazines in each of the next three decades, four in the 1850s, and nine in the 1860s. The *Spirit of the Times* became a main source of sporting news beginning in the 1830s, but before long, cheap working-class daily newspapers like the *New York Herald* covered sports with depth and regularity. Steamboats and railroads carried runners, or boxers, or thoroughbreds to matches; manufacturers marketed cricket bats, billiard tables, and archery equipment; telegraph lines flashed news of important contests. Perhaps most important, cities grew at an unprecedented pace during the antebellum era—nine had populations over one hundred thousand by 1860—creating a new potential market for popular entertainment like sports. Although America remained predominantly rural, cities, as nodes of production and distribution, had growing cultural influence.

Increasingly, recreation was transformed into entertainment, a sort of cultural goods to be purchased with earnings. Minstrel shows, melodramas, popular museums like P. T. Barnum's in New York (1842), circuses, pleasure gardens, and sporting events all became cultural commodities. Control of thoroughbred racing in this era passed from the hands of landed gentlemen to promoters who organized yearly meetings and standardized rules; boxing came into its own, as fight organizers coined money chartering trains and boats to transport fans to the scenes of battle; and by the 1850s the old folk game of baseball developed clubs and leagues which began charging admission to games and paying players. Pedestrianism, as foot racing was called, came as close as any sport to the modern athletic events of today. Wealthy socialite John Cox Stevens initiated the commercialization with a challenge in 1835 to pay $1,000 to the first man to run ten miles in under an hour. Roughly thirty thousand spectators showed up at the Union Race Course on Long Island to watch a field of runners take up the challenge. Over the next twenty-five years, crowds up to fifty thousand would cheer as runners competed for purses as large as $4,000. In an era when the average laborer earned something around $200 a year, the contests were irresistible to young athletic men, some of whom made a living traveling from race to race.

But athletics on this scale remained rare. Some sports, harness racing prime among them, displayed important "modern" characteristics—standardized rules, the keeping of statistics, regular schedules, and so forth—and some events attracted massive newspaper coverage and paid athletes handsomely. The $10,000 championship prizefight between Yankee Sullivan and Tom Hyer in 1849 is a good example. But mass spectator events remained rare. Professionalism was still unusual, profits secondary, organizations informal, and scheduling irregular. Sports as a commodity were in their infancy, far from the regular, profitable, well-managed, repeatable spectacles of the twentieth century.

Voluntary association more than money motivated this early stage of sports development. This was certainly true of most events in which working-class men watched or participated. Often their contests played out ethnic rivalries, especially Irish versus native-born. Similarly, young Germans who migrated to America after the abortive revolution of 1848 brought their Turner societies over from the old country. These organizations (the name comes from *Turnerbund*, literally "gymnastic society") blended nationalism, anticlericalism, and utopian socialism. As part of their program of universal education to prepare men for political and social democracy, the Turner groups placed great emphasis on gymnastic training and sponsored competitions of athletic skill. Similarly, Scottish immigrants in the 1850s replicated their track-and-field events in the Caledonian games. In these and other cases, ethnic groups helped perpetuate their identity through sports, even as outsiders sometimes attended competitions as spectators. Sports, then, could become a point of solidarity for foreign groups in an alien environment.

Men of the upper class, too, organized new sporting institutions. Metropolitan, university, and union clubs both symbolized and buttressed class prerogatives, reinforcing elite styles of dress, speech, and values, while creating new social and business networks. In the two decades before the Civil War, cricket, racquet, yacht, and rowing clubs began to spring up as exclusive men's organizations. The ubiquitous John Cox Stevens, for example, founded the New York Yacht Club in 1844, which attracted some of the city's leading men. When Stevens's yacht, *America*, defeated eighteen British rivals in the first America's Cup Race (1851), other cities quickly organized their own yacht clubs, and these spun out webs of social activities including balls and cruises. Boat clubs, crew teams, and regattas arose at prestigious Ivy League colleges, and in 1852, Harvard and Yale oarsmen competed in the nation's first—albeit informal—intercollegiate athletic contest. The embryonic alliance between sport and capitalism is especially clear in this example, because the Boston, Concord, and Montreal Railroad sponsored the regatta and paid all of the expenses as a business promotion.

Baseball also first became organized around the club ideal, and we still refer to multimillion dollar businesses as "ball clubs." Folk versions of baseball had been around for centuries, but in 1845, the New York Knickerbocker Baseball Club became America's first organized team. Merchants, professionals, clerks, and a handful of tradesmen were members of the club during its first fifteen years. By 1858, sixty teams affiliated together as the National Association of Base Ball Players. In part their goal was to prevent the sport from becoming a vulgar commercial spectacle. Early on, clubs tried to assure the social status of the game by excluding men lower down on the pecking order, by keeping the game open mainly to society's upper half. Certainly every mechanic and laborer could not take off whole afternoons for practice as the National Association clubs did, nor could they afford the elaborate banquets that followed games. But a ball, a bat, and an empty lot were easily procured, and before long, fire fighters, policemen, teachers, bartenders, and others organized their own clubs all over America. Some of the working-class teams were so good they began charging admission to their games and paying players. Betting, drinking, and boisterous cheering often accompanied these games. Distasteful as the low-caste game was, amateur clubs quietly conceded to professionalization when they purchased the services of "ringers."

Boat clubs, crew teams, and regattas arose at prestigious Ivy League colleges, and in 1852, Harvard and Yale oarsmen competed in the nation's first—albeit informal—intercollegiate athletic contest.

By the Civil War sports had grown more prominent than ever in American life. Some of the games we recognize in the twentieth century—baseball, boxing, track and field prime among them—were no longer purely folk events. An occasional horse race, especially one pitting a thoroughbred from the North against one from the South, might even attract as many as fifty thousand people and dominate the news for a few days. But if sports proliferated in this era, they were neither highly organized nor well integrated into the larger society. The permanent arenas, regular schedules, massive coverage, compulsive record keeping, and high salaries we associate with modern sports were largely missing. Above all, still absent was an ideology of sports appropriate for a modern, capitalist, bourgeois society.

As the antebellum era came to a close, however, the outline of such an ideology was beginning to appear. The same nationalism that encouraged some to define American's mission as virtuous hard work caused others to wish for a nation of vigorous, physically fit men. Oliver Wendell Holmes, Sr., was one who sounded the alarm: "I am satisfied that such a set of black-coated, stiff-jointed, soft-muscled, paste-complexioned youth as we can boast in our Atlantic cities never before sprang from loins of Anglo-Saxon lineage. . . . " ("The Autocrat of the Breakfast-Table," *Atlantic Monthly* 1, no. 6 [1858], 881). Like many others of the northern intellectual and social elite—Thomas Wentworth Higginson, Catherine Beecher, Horace Mann, Ralph Waldo Emerson, Walt Whitman among them—Holmes began calling for vigorous exercise for American youth. But these early sports advocates were careful to denounce raucous dissipations. The spirit of improvement, the progress of the race, the innocence of play were their ideals.

An avant-garde of clergymen, journalists, and reformers began the chant. Henry David Thoreau believed that "the body existed for the highest development of the soul" (Bradford Torrey and Francis H. Allen, eds. *The Journal of Henry David Thoreau*, vol. 1 [1962] p. 176), so he advocated not stuffy exercises like calisthenics, nor artificial games like baseball, but activities that immersed one in nature, such as walking, swimming, and rowing. Drawing on romantic faith in human perfectibility, men like Walt Whitman began to view the body as divine, and reformers like the Unitarian minister William Ellery Channing advocated wholesome recreations as part of the larger reform agenda.

These early "muscular Christians," as they were sometimes called on both sides of the Atlantic, could advocate recreations with missionary zeal. Declared Frederic W. Sawyer in his influential *Plea for Amusements* (1847): "The moral, social, and religious advancement of the people of this country, for the next half century, depends more upon the principles that are adopted with regard to amusements generally, and how those principles are carried out, than to a great many other things of apparently greater moment" (p. 291). Sawyer argued that moral amusements could displace immoral ones, gymnasiums, for example, supplanting smoke-filled billiard halls. While more orthodox individuals scoffed at such suggestions, the tide seemed to be running in favor of liberal reformers and religionists. In colleges, the sons of America's elites began to participate in the earliest intercollegiate athletic competitions. Amherst, Brown, Yale, and Williams led the way. But in the popular imagination, too, bodily health took on new importance. The Cincinnati *Star in the West*, 6 December 1856, for example declared it equally sinful to neglect the body as the spirit or intellect: "God made man to develop all his faculties to the highest possible degree—to stand erect with broad shoulders and expanding lungs, a picture of physical and moral perfection."

These first glimmerings of modern sports were highly gendered—broad shoulders and expanding lungs were "manly" ideals—and while some reformers like Catherine Beecher recommended athletics for young women, the overwhelming emphasis of these early years was on sports for men. In important ways, the language of the new athletic advocates was infused with the rigid gender definitions of bourgeois culture. Sports, it was said, taught independence, self-reliance, courage, discipline—qualities valued in the rough-and-tumble world of business. In domestic ideology, so prominent in the popular culture of this era, women were to domesticate men, but this civilizing process, some feared, threatened to blunt masculine assertiveness in the social, political, and economic spheres. The same society that produced unprecedented quantities of consumer goods associated consumption with femininity and self-denial with manliness. Commercial success, love of luxury, soft living threatened to overwhelm masculine virtues in a sea of goods; spartan and manly sports, a few advanced thinkers seemed to be suggesting, might offer a way out of this trap. Advocating sports in the schools, the New York *Spirit of the Times* declared on 20 June 1857: "The object of education is to make men out of boys. Real live men, not bookworms, not smart fellows, but manly fellows."

So the antebellum era wove several strands of sporting life. In rural areas, gentry sports and country amusements continued. The growing cities witnessed the flowering of a working-class culture that highly valued athletic prowess especially when expressed in the form of ethnic rivalry. While the dominant chord of middle-class Victorianism, especially among Evangelicals, was in opposition to leisure and play, new voices were just beginning to be heard that advocated sports in the name of bourgeois ideals, and as a way to reform the unwashed masses. In the middle decades of the nineteenth century; then, the very structure of society, with its emerging classes, strict division of labor, glimmerings of a consumption ethic, and sharp separation of work time from nonwork time, opened up new opportunities for sports. And a justification for sports began to emerge, clustered around virtuous, bourgeois manliness: gymnastics gave men endurance, baseball promoted discipline, cricket taught self-control. In coming decades, such ideas would flood the nation.

Sports in the Gilded Age

In 1810, a free black American, Tom Molineaux, fought for the boxing championship of all England. Britons feared the prowess of this foreigner, yet were reassured by, the skill of their champion, Thomas Cribb. The fight proved a great one, and the English press covered the event in minute detail. In America, on the other hand, the bout was scarcely noted. While boxing was the "national sport of England", few people on these shores had ever even heard of prizefighting; there simply was no interest in such an event here. Yet half a century later, when an American of Irish extraction, John C. Heenan, ventured to England to fight for the title against Tom Sayers, the American press exploded with coverage. Newspapers might condemn the illegal match (all prizefighting was illegal in this era), but they covered it round by round.

The interest in sports that characterized the antebellum era—an efflorescence of working-class events like boxing matches that at once expressed a class sensibility and ethnic divisions; the rise of baseball initially as a genteel middle- and upper-middle-class game; the very first intercollegiate athletic competitions between boys from elite schools; and harness races, which Oliver Wendell Holmes, Sr., praised for their democratic virtues, and which were distinctly modern in their emphasis on fixed rules, record keeping, and equality of entry—grew at an unprecedented pace during the Gilded Age By the last decade of the nineteenth century, sports as we know them today had been born. And that birth was attended by the whole range of modern institutions we associate with urban-industrial America, bureaucratic structures, corporate organizations, capitalist ideologies, urban development.

By bringing men together in enormous numbers, the Civil War afforded unprecedented opportunities for sports. Between battles, men boxed, played baseball, and raced horses, often for the first time in their lives. More important, the war speeded the transformation of American society. The nation's capacity for manufacturing and distributing goods expanded, communication and transportation networks thickened, the organizational structure of society grew more sophisticated. As American capitalism matured with the century—as the division between those who owned the means of production and those who labored for wages grew deeper—images of stern competition, of winning the race of life, of survival of the fittest, took on enhanced ideological meaning. Athletics were readily enlisted in the cause of new social alignments.

The problem of moral sports in a Christian land did not go away. Some commentators maintained a hard line against all forms of frivolous amusements. More commonly, ministers and urban reformers gave renewed support to wholesome recreations. Thus, Henry Bergh (1811–1888) called for healthful and invigorating sports to replace cock mains, dogfights, bear baits, and boxing matches. Bergh substituted for the singular "sport"—a rowdy, one who defied social custom—the plural "sports", meaning rational and useful athletic activities. Dogfights and cock mains still found large and enthusiastic audiences, especially in the tradition-bound rural South and in polyglot cities like New York and New Orleans. The reformers never fully had their way with rural or working-class people. Nonetheless, new sports like baseball—not exactly a deacon's first choice, but better than prizefighting—grew extremely popular in working-class communities, as men organized countless teams and leagues.

The most important institutional form of the new physicality was the Young Men's Christian Association (YMCA). Originally founded in England, the "Y" gave youths a refuge against the temptations of the metropolis. Here Christian fellowship, intellectual stimulation, and wholesome physical exercise supplanted the loneliness of boardinghouses and the evils of commercial amusements. Where urban life threatened good morals and communal order, YMCAs' and similar organizations upheld these old ideals. The "Y" represented a rejuvenated, muscular, middle-class ethos. By 1869, San Francisco, Washington, and New York City all had "Y" gymnasia; within twenty-five years, there were 261 YMCA gyms scattered across America. Religious leaders like Washington Gladden and Henry Ward Beecher praised the "Y" for offering sports like baseball, football, swimming, calisthenics, bowling, and weight lifting in a wholesome and clean atmosphere. The underlying assumption of "Y" programs was that supervised athletics promoted religious and moral goals. Simply put, it made more sense to teach physical training under Christian auspices, imparting the values of fair play, cooperation, and good sportsmanship, than to have young men roam the streets. Gymnasia countered the licentiousness of pool halls; men who did calisthenics did not bet on horse races; clean sports engendered leadership, discipline, and toughmindedness for capitalist society.

The "Y" movement was an early and prominent example of a widespread rehabilitation of sports that took place after the Civil War. Yet the proliferation of such urban institutions was testimony to the resiliency of the working-class ways that the reformers wished to change. No doubt, some laboring men were persuaded that the Christian athlete was on the road to bourgeois respectability and social mobility. Others probably participated in "wholesome" athletics some of the time, but also patronized beer gardens, dance halls, gambling parlors, saloons, burlesque houses, and the disreputable sports which were part of that culture. The public parks movement which swept the cities late in the nineteenth century provides a fine example of how men found their own paths. As antidotes to moral anarchy, vice, and corruption, city planners developed landscaped parks for public leisure. Clear brooks, lush trees, and blue skies were moral agents, they believed, which would improve the temperament of workers and elevate their thoughts. Parks could mollify class antagonism, planners argued, for here rich and poor came together in harmonious communion with nature. Unfortunately, rather than passively soaking up virtue, the urban multitudes came with beer, bats, and balls, ignored the "keep off the grass" signs, and had a rollicking good time.

The underlying assumption of YMCA programs was that it made more sense to teach physical training under Christian auspices, imparting the values of fair play, cooperation, and good sportsmanship, than to have young men roam the streets.

But the efforts of neither the moral reformers nor their opponents ultimately were decisive in the rise of sports. More important was the commercialization of culture. Between the Civil War and the turn of the century, baseball became the acknowledged "national pastime," boxing under new rules exploded in popularity, football grew into a college mania, and basketball took firm root in urban athletic clubs. In addition, tennis, golf, and bicycling swept over the upper middle class in waves of popularity, while laborers started their own semiprofessional and amateur leagues in various team sports. Organizational and business structures arose to regulate and rationalize new activities. If sports in that era were rudimentary compared to today, the games themselves and the structures that supported them were in place by the end of the nineteenth century.

Despite a vertiginous boom-and-bust cycle, this era left many workers with a little more disposable time and money than previously, especially those in the burgeoning white-collar sector. The old work ethic was in part a victim of its own success. As the economy slowly solved the age-old problem of insufficient productive capacity, and as work increasingly came to be thought of as a distinct realm of life, Americans were left with gaps of time to fill. Put another way, America's exploding productive capacity was changing people's perceptions of time. The dawning economy of potential abundance—where supply of aggregate goods and services might exceed demand—necessitated the stimulation of new wants and desires. The emergent ethos of play, of having fun, of "letting go" made a virtue of necessity.

New social conditions, then, transformed consciousness as well as material life. Production had shifted away from individuals' making objects for themselves and their communities, toward nameless workers' making goods for unseen others in return for cash. Now leisure more than ever revolved around the abstract concept of monetary exchange. Although Americans continued to create their own entertainment, the emergent national culture idealized the purchase of mass-produced commodities as a great human privilege and goal. Homegrown recreations competed for attention with mass entertainment, and the latter increasingly dominated and structured the former. To purchase leisure—to be a spectator at a ball game, or buy a bicycle or a baseball mitt—was to partake of a new cultural hallmark, the consumption of leisure. Entrepreneurs were quick to come in: A. J. Spalding began mass-producing sporting goods; newspaper tycoons like William Randolph Hearst for the first time printed entire sports sections; and authors like Gilbert Patten (creator of Frank Merriwell) coined money for himself and his publishers by churning out formula fiction.

Sports were integrally tied to the transformation of life in a mature capitalist economy. Cities became the foci of new activities not just because overcrowding militated against old traditional amusements, but because the city was where the commodification of life was most

A striking likeness of heavyweight boxing champion John L. Sullivan. Symbolically, Sullivan espoused both Irish Nationalism and American patriotism.

pervasive; in cities, people were already learning the cycle of desire, pleasure, and more desire that came with the ethic of consumption. Moreover, new technologies opened up recreational possibilities: pneumatic tires facilitated the bicycle craze of the 1880s and 1890s, motion pictures allowed countless fans to see prizefights, electric lightbulbs illuminated grand new downtown arenas. And sports were becoming firmly entrenched in American business culture. By the 1870s, for example, baseball had already been hit with strikes, blacklistings, and combinations to restrain trade. The team owners who founded the National League in 1876 soon wrested control of the game from the players, destroyed rival clubs, took over the apprenticeship system (the minor leagues), and instituted the reserve clause, which denied players the right to sell their labor to other franchises. Owners had, in short, attained what businessmen elsewhere strove for with varying degrees of success—controlled markets that minimized risk.

Both professional and amateur sports were part of the larger organizational revolution. League schedules were established, national rules promulgated, and regulatory bodies like the National Collegiate Athletic Association and Amateur Athletic Union formed. By the 1880s, professional baseball generated millions of dollars each year in revenue, and a prosperous franchise could draw five thousand spectators per game. Moreover, sports became interlocked with the larger world of business. A successful local team brought trade to hotels, restaurants, and bars; a new stadium meant jobs in construction, maintenance, and concessions. And sports replicated the structures of modernity. The keeping of statistics, the rational measurement of means and ends, bureaucratic organizations, all permeated American life, including sports. Sports also articulated the dominant ideologies of an advanced democratic capitalist society—meritocracy, scientific worldview, equal competition, victory through brains, pluck, and hard work. Sports were a metaphor for life: that is, for the life of males in a modern capitalist country.

Still, it would be a mistake to view sports as simply one more manifestation of a modernizing juggernaut. Older, more traditional sports, such as boxing and cockfighting thrived in the late nineteenth century and appealed to ancient ideals of honor. Despite the structure of new professional and amateur sports, a subculture of raucous old pastimes continued to thrive. Modernization theory does capture the most striking trend in sports development—toward bureaucratic structures, rationalized play, quantifiable results. The problem is that these trends were often so mixed with seemingly antimodern ones. Richard Kyle Fox, for example, owner of the *National Police Gazette* during its heyday in the 1880s and 1890s used the most modern business techniques to promote traditional sport; his publication, brilliantly rationalized in production and distribution, was filled with misogyny and racism, hardly the stuff of an egalitarian society.

Indeed, while reformers argued that sports taught the ideal of equal opportunity, the fact is that the playing fields of athletics, like those of life, were never level. Exclusive organizations like the New York Athletic Club—and every major city had exclusive athletic clubs by the end of the century—allowed only the most wealthy and powerful men to join. While workers might become interested in the outcome of a Harvard-Yale football game, indeed, while those schools might even employ a "ringer" or two to assure victory, colleges remained elite institutions, effectively closed to the majority of Americans. To the extent that prestigious colleges did open up in this era, sports were part of the process by which the children of an industrial elite that was pushing its way into the most powerful positions in American life dispelled the boredom of the rigid old classical curriculum. Finally, the late nineteenth century saw the proliferation of exclusive country clubs and elite watering places like Newport, Rhode Island, and Saratoga, New York, that brought wealthy people together in play while excluding all lesser folk.

At high-amateur and professional levels, sports did admit whole new groups of people as spectators and participants. Yet a majority of Americans were largely left out. First, while there were some important gestures toward women's sports during this era, domestic ideology, notions of female delicacy, and lingering Victorian prudishness kept most women from active interest in things athletic. Gender roles still defined men as active, women as passive, and the operative metaphors of sports all tended toward patriarchy. Tough competition, physical violence, the importance of winning, teamwork—sports as metaphor did not just reflect masculine ideals, they helped constitute and define those ideals. Competing, achieving, and winning were at the very core of late Victorian notions of manhood, so sports not only excluded women, they helped define and give shape to a masculine world that feared, or devalued, or mystified all that it regarded as feminine.

Ethnically too, athletics in this era contained a strong streak of exclusivity While sports had become an important symbol of American culture, most men of the immigrant generation probably were not terribly interested as spectators, and if they played sports at all, it was more likely to be games from their homelands. The children of immigrants, however, found in athletics a powerful sense of belonging to the only culture they knew at firsthand. Symbolically, sports provided a sense of dual identity. Thus, heavyweight boxing champion John L. Sullivan espoused both Irish nationalism and American patriotism, and he literally cloaked himself in both the Stars and Stripes and the emerald green when he entered the ring. For Irish Americans who had long suffered severe discrimination, Sullivan represented not

Symbolically, sports provided a sense of dual identity: Heavyweight boxing champion John L. Sullivan espoused both Irish nationalism and American patriotism, literally cloaking himself in both the Stars and Stripes and the emerald green when he entered the ring.

only glittering success, but also the possibility of identifying with both America and Ireland. In the twentieth century, baseball players like Joe DiMaggio and Hank Greenberg repeated this pattern for new immigrant groups.

The situation for blacks, however, was different. Despite the rhetoric of "may the best man win," by late in the nineteenth century, the openings that had existed in early professional sports closed down almost entirely. During the 1890s, African Americans were systematically barred from major league baseball, resulting in the formation of the all-black Negro leagues until Jackie Robinson reintegrated baseball after World War II. Moreover, heavyweight boxing champion John L. Sullivan simply refused to fight black opponents, though the strongest contender during the late 1880's was an Australian black named Peter Jackson. Even in the now obscure, but then quite popular, sport of bicycle racing, African American Marshall W. "Major" Taylor was the best cyclist in the world during the 1890s, vet he was systematically barred from major races. So in the late nineteenth century—an era of lynching and Jim Crow legislation, of the most virulent racism since Reconstruction—the sporting meritocracy proved meretricious at best. Access to organized sports, then, was generally restricted by race and gender, and often by class.

Nevertheless, the sporting ideology that had become a commonplace of the late Victorian era was a powerful cement in American culture. Those excluded from the mainstream still created a sporting space with games and leagues of their own. Equally important, the ideas associated with sports—universal rules, fair play, utter seriousness in a frivolous cause, measurable performance, the joy of physical excellence, the tension of keen competition, the expertise of spectators—were constantly spreading into the larger national culture. Not for all Americans, but for increasing numbers of them, sometimes even crossing deep social chasms, sports were becoming a kind of national language or currency, a set of shared practices, values, and experiences so common as to become invisible as air.

In 1892, roughly a century after the illegal sport of boxing first appeared in America, William Lyon Phelps, professor of English at Yale, was reading the daily newspaper to his blind father, a Baptist minister. The old outlaw prizefighting was in the news, and Phelps read the headline "Corbett Defeats Sullivan," then turned the page, assuming the elderly Victorian gentleman would not be interested. Phelps Senior leaned forward and said to his son, "Read it by rounds."

[See also Business Culture; The Culture of Consumption; Mass Culture and Its Critics; Popular Entertainment before the Civil War.]

BIBLIOGRAPHY

The *Journal of Sport History* (19-), published by The North American Society for Sport History, is the single most important source for the history of American sports

Adelman, Melvin. *A Sporting Time: New York City and the Rise of Modern Athletics, 1820–70* (1986).

Betts, John Rickards. *America's Sporting Heritage, 1850–1950* (1974).

Breen, Timothy H. "Horses and Gentlemen: The Cultural Significance of Gambling Among the Gentry of Virginia." *William and Mary Quarterly* 40, no. 2 (1977):239–257.

Carson, Jane. *Colonial Virginians at Play* (1965).

Dulles, Foster Rae. *America Learns to Play: A History of Popular Recreation, 1607–1940* (1940).

Goldstein, Warren. *Playing for Keeps: A History of Early Baseball* (1989).

Gorn, Elliott J. " 'Gouge and Bite, Pull Hair, and Scratch': The Social Significance of Fighting in the Southern Backcountry." *American Historical Review* 90, no. 1 (1985):18–43.

Gorn, Elliott J. *The Manly Art: Bare-Knuckle Prize Fighting in America* (1986).

Gorn, Elliott J. " 'Good-Bye Boys, I Die a True American': Homicide, Nativism, and Working-Class Culture in Antebellum New York City." *Journal of American History* 74, no. 2 (1987): 388–410.

Green, Harvey. *Fit for America: Health, Fitness, Sport, and American Society,* (1986).

Grover, Kathryn, ed. *Fitness in American Culture: Images of Health, Sport, and the Body, 1830–1940* (1989).

Guttmann, Allen. *From Ritual to Record: The Nature of Modern Sports* (1978).

Guttmann, Allen. *Sports Spectators* (1986).

Guttmann, Allen. *A Whole New Ballgame: An Interpretation of American Sports* (1988).

Hardy, Stephen. *How Boston Played: Sport, Recreation, and Community, 1865–1915* (1982).

Higham, John. "The Reorientation of American Culture in the 1890's." In *The Origins of Modern Consciousness, edited by John Weiss* (1965).

Holliman, Jennie. *American Sports (1785–1835)* (1931).

Kirsch, George B. *The Creation of American Team Sports: Baseball and Cricket, 1838–1872* (1989).

Levine, Peter. *A. G. Spalding and the Rise of Baseball: The Promise of American Sport* (1985).

Lucas, John A., and Ronald A. *Smith. Saga of American Sport* (1978).

Malcolmson, Robert W. *Popular Recreations in English Society, 1700–1850* (1973).

Messenger, Christian Karl. *Sport and the Spirit of Play in American Fiction: Hawthorne to Faulkner* (1981).

Mrozek, Donald. *Sport and American Mentality, 1880–1910* (1983).

Oriard, Michael. *Dreaming of Heroes: American Sports Fiction, 1868–1980* (1982).

Oriard, Michael. *Sporting with the Gods: The Rhetoric of Play and Game in American Culture* (1991).

Rader, Benjamin G. *American Sports: From the Age of Folk Games to the Age of Spectators* (1983).

Riess, Steven A. *City Games: The Evolution of American Urban Society and the Rise of Sports* (1989).

Rosenzweig, Roy. *Eight Hours for What We Will: Workers and Leisure in an Industrial City, 1870–1920* (1983).

Seymour, Harold. *Baseball.* Vol. 1, *The Early Years* (1960).

Smith, Ronald A. *Sports and Freedom: The Rise of Bigtime College Athletics* (1988).
Somers, Dale A. *The Rise of Sports in New Orleans: 1850–1900* (1972).

— ELLIOTT J. GORN

SPORTS IN THE TWENTIETH CENTURY

During the 1890s, American sports were important experiences for two large groups of people: athletes and spectators. Millions of boys and men played baseball and football formally and informally, while girls and women practiced gymnastics, rode horses and bicycles, and played basketball. Millions of men, women, and children watched professional, college, and informal sports, from boxing to horse racing, college football to sandlot baseball games.

A hundred years later, sports had come to influence and shape central institutions of American life: secondary and higher education; print and electronic media; the economic life of cities and suburbs. From a perch on the sidelines of American culture, sports began to structure the experience of culture in new ways signaling new patterns in the relations between sexes and races; the use and pursuit of leisure time; the networks by which social classes cohere and recreate themselves over time; even the language in which political leaders speak of politics, foreign policy, and war.

Consider these manifestations of modern sports:

—The best-known human being in the world during the 1970s and 1980s was an African American boxer and world heavyweight champion who joined the Nation of Islam, changed his name, and successfully defied the United States government's attempt to jail him for refusing to submit to the Vietnam-era draft.

—A commercially successful national cable television network broadcasts sports news and events twenty-four hours a day. In the words of a founder, "We believe that the appetite for sports in this country is insatiable."

—Major league teams in basketball, football, and baseball frequently field teams made up mostly of African American or Hispanic players.

—A major league baseball player signed a multiyear contract prior to the 1992 season worth twenty-nine million dollars.

—An upset in the women's 1991 Wimbledon singles championship match received front-page coverage in the *New York Times* and drew tens of millions of television viewers.

—"He was stiff-armed," announced the United States president in late 1990 when his secretary of state returned from the Middle East having failed to persuade Iraq to withdraw its troops from Kuwait. No reporter objected to the metaphor; instead, men nodded to themselves, remembering what it was like to feel the heel of a charging ball-carrier's palm at the end of a stiff, outstretched arm come thudding into one's chin, snapping back the head and momentarily scrambling neurons.

In 1890 these developments were inconceivable. Although organized sport could occasionally captivate the nation, it lacked the wherewithal to frame public discourse. One of many influential social and cultural institutions—political parties, organized religion, business corporations—sports had yet to reach its potential power at the center of American life, whether urban or rural, Protestant or Catholic; black or white; rich, poor, or middling.

Before the administration of Theodore Roosevelt, no president would have used a football metaphor to describe a great matter of state. Such usage would have been met with confusion. It took both the conversion of the upper class to sporting ideology and the machinery of the mass media to popularize such concepts.

Nor is it only in talk of war that sports language dominates common discourse. It may be that the only common language of the public realm is now that of sports. A century ago people talked of Almighty God, of the help and intervention of Divine Providence. Today they: speak of aggressive coaches and celebrity athletes nailing slam dunks, hitting home runs, and taking hits.

These images and developments represent enormous changes in the past century. First, sports have become a pervasive fact of American life; sport grips hundreds of millions of people at the level of spectatorship. Second, sports comprise a multibillion-dollar business industry, driven by a logic that has little to do with the "play of the game." Third, with teams largely integrated along racial lines (though important exceptions remain) organized sport functions as a cultural icon of equal opportunity. Fourth, women athletes and coaches have achieved major significance in the competitive arena although gender segregation remains active. Finally, sports and television, consummating a marriage between media and athletics begun when sporting newspapers covered local events and pursued during the heyday of radio, may soon cease to be distinctly separate institutions.

During the past hundred years competitive participation and spectator attention have grown in many sports: the racing sports—horse, automobile, and bicycle; in team sports—hockey, volleyball, lacrosse, soccer; in individual sports—swimming, golf, bowling, track and field, skiing, ice skating; and many others. But nothing has captured the American imagination more than baseball. Since baseball has been the most popular and therefore most significant sport during the period, most of this essay focuses on the development of "the national pastime," while football, boxing, basketball, and tennis receive secondary attention.

The Sporting Landscape in 1890

The modern sports landscape dates from the 1890s. We begin with the national pastime. In the forty-five years since its formal "invention" in New York City, baseball had become the most widely played and most watched American sport. Two professional major leagues (three in 1890) distributed franchises in large and medium-sized cities east of the Mississippi and north of the Ohio rivers. Minor leagues (eight in 1884, nineteen in 1903), usually in smaller cities and towns spread throughout the country, included dozens of professional teams. Attendance of major league games probably totaled one to two million spectators per year, while another million or so attended minor league games. Hundreds, if not thousands, of organized and barely organized semiprofessional teams accounted for many more thousands of players and millions of active spectators.

Originally baseball culture perched at the border between respectability and low life, and still straddles that line somewhat to this day. In the past its two major leagues enforced policies at games designed to appeal to different segments of the urban population. National League teams charged fifty cents for admission, played no Sunday ball, and banned the sale of alcohol. The rival American Association sought poorer, working-class immigrant spectators by charging a quarter, playing on Sundays, and allowing the sale of liquor.

The popularity of the game received two blows in the 1890s. Long restive over the insertion of a "reserve clause" in player contracts (which effectively wiped out players' market bargaining power over salaries), the Brotherhood of Professional Base Ball Players convinced most of its members to break their contracts with National League clubs and join the new Players' League. The latter's management was to be shared between representatives of the players and the clubs' financial backers. A three-way battle erupted between the Players' League, the American Association, and the National League—whose "war committee" chose to schedule games directly opposite those of the upstart league. Disaster nearly resulted for organized baseball. Despite purposely inflated figures, attendance at major league games, the lifeblood of professional sports, decreased from 1889 to 1890. Modern fans who lament that there's too much business news in the sports pages are part of a long tradition. That year, despite efforts of the Knights of Labor and the American Federation of Labor to promote the Players' League and boycott the National League, too many fans chose to avoid the ballparks altogether. The few remaining solid teams in the National League bought out the Players' League's financial backers and buried the most radical experiment in the history of American professional sports. Thereafter, the "reserve rule" was enshrined as the centerpiece of baseball's labor relations, and owners exercised virtually undisputed control over the baseball business until the mid 1970s.

While the "national game" remained overwhelmingly popular in the late nineteenth century, baseball's business side—battles between labor and management, labor discipline and blacklists and Pinkertons, franchise shifts, booms and busts, cartel agreements made and broken—rocked with the instability of much of Gilded Age business culture. Not until the rival American League, under the leadership of Ban Johnson, schemed and muscled its way into major league status and hammered out an agreement with the National League in 1901 did organized baseball settle down into a half-century of stable franchises and nearly uninterrupted growth.

Although baseball dominated the late-nineteenth-century sporting world, it was not the only pastime. By the 1890s football—college football—had moved beyond its Ivy League origins to public and private colleges and universities across the nation. The spread of this absorbing, extraordinarily violent game, however, carried controversy in its wake. While faculties worried that the competitiveness, violence, and hoopla of college football misdirected undergraduate energies, alumni sensed the game's potential publicity value and took control of its organization and administration. Collegiate football soon became a huge spectacle, and the main instrument of public relations for institutions of higher education. The annual Thanksgiving Day game in New York City between the two best college teams (usually Yale and Princeton during the 1890s) drew up to forty thousand spectators and served to kick off the winter social season. Paralleling and assisting the rise of the extracurriculum in American education, football became the principal means by which alumni, public relations, professionals, and fund-raisers gained control of American college life. For Theodore Roosevelt and like-minded men (such as Henry Cabot Lodge, Brooks Adams, and Alfred Thayer Mahan), football served as a key demonstration of the "strenuous life." Football as both experience and metaphor was used by these men in their campaign to reinvigorate the American elite. The game, they felt, would toughen and prepare children to exercise national power and wrest world leadership from effete old-world corruption.

If football was born in the heart of elite male culture, and baseball blossomed in the no-man's-land between urban working-class and middle-class sporting culture, basketball, which first appeared in this same decade, owed its creation to one of the principal institutions of middle-class evangelical reform: the Young Men's Christian Association (YMCA). Three pious young men, who wanted to do God's work but also enjoyed the somewhat less respectable (and apparently less godly) rough-and-tumble of physical sports, gathered at the YMCA training school (now Springfield College) in Massachusetts in the early 1890s. James Naismith, Amos Alonzo Stagg, and Luther Halsey Gulick soon saw themselves as missionaries come to preach the gospel of bodily health and exercise as well as the gospel of Jesus Christ. Gulick even created the YMCA symbol, the inverted triangle of "mind-body-spirit."

While the "national game" remained overwhelmingly popular in the late nineteenth century, baseball's business side rocked with the instability of much of Gilded Age business culture.

Leading the effort to "reform" urban immigrant children, the YMCA wanted a vigorous sport that could be played indoors during the winter. Naismith invented the game in the winter of 1891, and basketball quickly took off, spreading first through the YMCA networks, then much more widely. Before the game had celebrated its first birthday, Luther Gulick exulted:

> It is doubtful whether a gymnastic game has ever spread so rapidly over the continent as has "basket ball." It is played from New York to San Francisco and from Maine to Texas by hundreds of teams in associations, athletic clubs and schools. (Bernice Larson Webb, *The Basketball Man: James Naismith* [1973], p. 72)

Women, too, particularly college women, took up basketball, and before the end of the century special rules had been developed for the women's game.

Racial segregation in American sports had found its voice by the 1890s. In 1887 Adrian "Cap" Anson, the Hall of Fame first baseman and later manager of the Chicago White Stockings, one of the most talented and popular of nineteenth-century ball players, threatened not to play a match as long as the black player George Stovey remained on the opposing team. Anson had tried the same gambit four years earlier against a Toledo team and failed. This time he succeeded and Stovey withdrew. Over the next few years what became known as "organized baseball" became white baseball and stayed that way until 1946.

From its origins, organized sports in America depended on the press for publicity, for legitimation, and for communication with the mass of potential participants and spectators. Nineteenth-century reporters pretended to no ideology of objectivity and participated actively in the sporting worlds they chronicled. By the 1890s, however, the New York press was facing the competition of the popular "yellow" press of William Randolph Hearst and Joseph Pulitzer. Seeking massive working-class readership, these entrepreneurs introduced the modern tabloid sports pages. Increasingly, then, a pattern began that would be repeated with radio and television—spectator sports were reported and packaged as a way of selling newspapers.

Progressives, Reformed Play, and World War I

Psychologists' "discovery" of children's play and adolescence in the late nineteenth century invested urban reformers with a theory by which to approach the hordes of immigrant children swarming American cities during these years. Settlement houses made vigorous use of the new game of basketball, and gymnasia became important parts of their physical plants.

Luther Gulick organized the Playground Association of America (PAA) in 1906, a group of middle-class reformers, YMCA advocates, and socialites (Theodore Roosevelt was the group's first honorary president) dedicated to providing spaces for urban children to play. At least partly because of the PAA's prodding, the number of playgrounds in major American cities grew dramatically in the years before World War I. Between 1911 and 1917, PAA statistics for a large group of reporting cities showed that playgrounds had more than doubled, from 1,543 to 3,940.

While the PAA social workers had little influence on the course of spectator sports, they did provide an avenue along which middle-class Protestants adapted more and more to the idea and practice of play in American culture. Previously, sporting culture's least ambivalent adherents were either upper-class sportsmen like Theodore Roosevelt and the football players at elite colleges or the much less established working classes—primarily men who sought display of skill and the experience of excitement in sporting events. The middle class joined America's sporting culture principally through basketball and the play movement—what might be called the domestication of sports. Sports were promoted and justified as character building, as uplifting, even as Americanizing. These qualified as no small virtues to native-born, middle-class Protestants, many of whom believed the national character was being drowned in a flood of foreign-looking, dirt-poor, and frequently incomprehensible immigrants who produced children at astonishingly high birthrates.

Progressives did help change American sports, though obliquely, at this moment. Pioneering the growth of bureaucracies in the administration of play, they developed science as a governing language to deal with the large number of children in urban settlements, and they helped organize America for World War I. For it was in the American effort in the Great War that the two streams in sports history—represented by college football and YMCA basketball—converged. Walter Camp, the former Yale football star who had become the czar of Yale's powerful football machine, joined the U.S. Navy Commission on Training Camp Activities as its athletic director. James Naismith joined the war effort as a "hygiene" lecturer, supporting YMCA efforts to look after the morals of the American Expeditionary Force.

World War I bureaucratized American culture as no event since the Civil War. It absorbed much of the progressive cultural agenda (scientific planning, rational social engineering, Americanization of immigrants) to oil the machinery of organized violence. Football always had been promoted at least partly because it appeared to strengthen the martial abilities of young, upper-class men, and World War I made use of that training and toughening. The military employed massive physical education and sports programs to condition recruits, in the process further legitimizing the mass ideology of sports. Ironically, World War I cemented the importance of organized play in the national consciousness. Public schools' adoption of physical education and athletic programs throughout the country followed on the heels of the war.

But the experience of sports themselves during this period was contradictory. Boxing, for instance, produced one of its great controversial champions in the decade before World War I—the African American heavyweight Jack Johnson. First, Johnson had to pursue the White title-holder around the world until he got a chance to fight for the championship. When he defeated Tommy Burns in Australia in 1908, the stunned white boxing establishment went on a desperate search for a "Great White Hope" to take back the title. At last, in 1910, undefeated but retired former heavyweight champion Jim Jeffries announced he would take up the cause of the "portion of the white race that has been looking to me to defend its athletic superiority." Johnson crushed Jeffries, however, and that night racial violence claimed eight lives. Johnson's victory stuck in the craw of white America, and Johnson himself did nothing to make it easier to swallow.

Ty Cobb built his unremarkable physical skills and average means into exceptional baseball ability, an extraordinary career, and a good sized fortune.

In and out of the ring, Johnson thumbed his nose at white opponents and social conventions. He lived in the public eye, spending money on flashy clothes, fast cars, and the high life, including his three white wives and numerous white mistresses. Authorities pursued him on morals charges, finally securing a conviction in 1913. Johnson jumped bail and fled to Europe, then lost his title to Jess Willard in Cuba in 1915 (in a match that some, including Johnson, have claimed was fixed), and returned to the United States to serve his prison term in 1920.

The completely white game of organized baseball grew in popularity until 1909, when attendance reached more than seven million, doubling the 1901 total. Though attendance declined somewhat before World War I, these first two decades of the twentieth century were the golden era of pitching, strategy, and what became known as "scientific" and "inside" baseball. Dominated by such pitchers as Christy Matthewson, Cy Young, and Mordecai "Three-Finger" Brown, and hitters such as Nap Lajoie, Honus Wager, and Ty Cobb, these years, some of the finest in the history of the game, only now are receiving their due from baseball historians.

If one player in particular expresses fully the social and cultural history of the period, he is Tyrus Raymond Cobb. In his long and extraordinary baseball career (1905–1928) Cobb set records which have stood for more than half a century, retaining the highest lifetime batting average to 1998 and beyond. Cobb's calculating, penetrating shrewdness made the most of any game situation. A proponent and the finest practitioner of "scientific baseball," Cobb analyzed, strategized, and bullied his way around the diamond. Consequently, Cobb was feared and disliked as much for his manner as his skill. An aggressive, vicious, racist brawler, on the field and off, Cobb also exemplified the character traits of the nineteenth-century American hero of production: acquisitive, self-reliant, normally under tight self-control, prepared for violence. A stingy, introverted loner who felt the world was against him, Cobb built his unremarkable physical skills and average means into exceptional baseball ability and a good-sized fortune. Cobb died a lonely millionaire after a long, bitter life, his funeral attended by just three people from organized baseball.

Cobb had no monopoly on mean-spirited acquisitiveness. The notorious penny pinching of Chicago White Sox owner Charles Comiskey helped lay the groundwork for the biggest scandal in American sports history—the fixed 1919 World Series. Even today, controversy swirls around the exceptionally complicated affair, as historians, novelists, and filmmakers promote competing versions of the fix, rearranging and reassigning varying levels of guilt, innocence, and blame. As many as eight players on the heavily favored White Sox were involved in a scheme to lose the Series to the Cincinnati Reds, in exchange for large sums of money from gamblers. The scandal, which did not even come to light until well into the following season, shook up baseball so terribly that owners surrendered much of their power over the game to a commissioner who promised to "clean up" the mess. Though the players were acquitted, Commissioner Kenesaw Mountain Landis banned the eight "Black Sox" from baseball for life. The fix itself provided baseball with a powerful myth of lost innocence. As the famous, and probably apocryphal, story goes, a distraught boy approached "Shoeless" Joe Jackson as the star outfielder came out of the grand jury room, and pleaded with his hero, "Say it ain't so, Joe." What helped baseball regain its popularity, and some of its ingenuousness, was a curious and riveting new phenomenon named George Herman "Babe" Ruth.

Sports and the Culture of Consumption

If Ty Cobb exemplified the character traits of the culture of production, Babe Ruth helped promote the newer economy and culture founded on consumption. A talented young pitcher and slugger with the Boston Red Sox, Ruth was purchased by the New York Yankees for the 1920 season and soon began hitting home runs at a faster pace than any previous player.

Ruth's contributions to twentieth-century sports, to the history of baseball, and to the culture of consumption were all enormous. First, though not single-handedly, he deflected a good bit of public attention away from the unfolding World Series scandal and into the ballparks themselves, where the shape of the game was changing dramatically. At the same time, Ruth showed what home run power could do to the game's offensive strategy. In fact, the home run hitting of Ruth and fellow players on the Yankees transformed the baseball strategy of the previous thirty years: one run at a time, base stealing, bunting, what Bill James has called "long sequence" offense. (For example: walk, hit and run, sacrifice fly—three successful at-bats to produce one run.)

Ruth's personality both fit and helped shape the period. Unlike Cobb, he appeared to play baseball "naturally," without calculation, almost (as the nicknames "the Babe" and "the Bambino" captured) with the manner of an overgrown child.

Like a child, Babe Ruth spent liberally—everything he had, in all senses of the term. A prodigious consumer of food, drink, clothing, and women, Ruth was himself an advertisement for consumption. He bought silk shirts dozens at a time, discarding them after a single wearing; he slept with hundreds, perhaps thousands, of women; he ate several dozen hot dogs at a sitting while gulping down beer by the quart. At ease surrounded by children, he had a notoriously bad memory for other people's names (even his own teammates), which he made up for by calling them "Kid."

Ruth became that most modern of sports heroes, a celebrity. Created by the pioneering press agent Christy Walsh and sought after for public appearances, Ruth's persona became as important as the man, and Walsh sold it to endorse a myriad of products. Babe Ruth's life both helped bring about the culture of consumption and served as one of its most impressive creations.

But beyond individual players was the game itself. Perhaps more than any other institution in American society, baseball in the twentieth century brought together large numbers of people in one place for several hours at a time, thousands of times during a six-month period from April to October. Today, Major League teams play one hundred sixty-two games per season; the most successful franchises draw as many as two million paying spectators over the course of a season. (Professional and college football and basketball teams now rival baseball as audience creators, but only since the advent of television.) As a result, advertisers are as drawn to the ballpark as fans are to the game.

To all media—newspapers, radio, and television—sports spectacles are crucial providers of an essential element in a consumption economy: potential customers. That is why sporting events played such a huge role in the growth of media, first of the popular press, and then in the subsequent development of radio and television.

In the 1920s, Babe Ruth shared the cultural limelight with boxers Jack Dempsey and Gene Tunney, college and professional football player Harold Edward "Red" Grange, golfer Bobby Jones, and tennis player Big Bill Tilden.

As the American economy exploded into consumer goods—and the need to sell them—after World War I, baseball, radio, and sports pages helped turn the cultural and economic trick. Radio carried Babe Ruth's stunning achievements to baseball fans across the country, and multi-station hookups carried many of the decade's big sports events: heavyweight boxing championships, baseball's annual World Series, football's Rose Bowl. Newspapers remained a key connection through which advertising was married to sports. But whereas a combination of society and sports pages had covered Ivy League football in the 1890s, the biggest fights or bowl games of the twenties got remarkable publicity, commercial sponsorship, and national attention. Sports pages themselves grew to enormous size at this time, while publishers and reporters frequently promoted organized sports.

The experience of sports became truly nationalized in the 1920s. That decade is known as, alternately, the Golden Age of Sport, and the Golden Age of Heroes. As disposable income climbed and working hours declined somewhat, people spent more time and money on sports events, while the media created and promoted sports heroes into an elite galaxy of celebrities.

Babe Ruth shared the cultural limelight with boxers Jack Dempsey and Gene Tunney, college and professional football player Harold Edward "Red" Grange, golfer Bobby Jones, and tennis player Big Bill Tilden. All of these figures received a degree of public attention, publicity, and adulation inconceivable in the culture of thirty years before. Much of America's new mass culture focused on such people. More than one hundred thousand attended the second Dempsey-Tunney fight in Chicago's Soldier's Field; an estimated fifty million listened to the seventy-three stations on the NBC-radio hookup. Before this time it was literally impossible for so many people to give such intense, detailed, and simultaneous attention to a sporting event.

Leo Lowenthal's study of popular biographies in the early twentieth century noted a profound shift in the type of American hero that journalists held up for public adulation. At the beginning of the century magazine heroes tended to be men who had achieved recognition through productive work: businessmen, financiers, scientists, writers, artists, politicians or statesmen—what Lowenthal called "idols of production." Later, beginning in the 1920s, national heroes derived more from the world of entertainment: boxers, stars and starlets, baseball players, and the like—in Lowenthal's term, "idols of consumption." In the 1920s the distinctively modern convergence of sports and the entertainment business began. People, like Babe Ruth, Rudolph Valentino, and occasionally men like Charles Lindbergh, merged in the public mind; in the newsreels, in newspapers, on radio, and in advertisements, they all seemed to take part in the great national culture of fame and celebrity. The parties created by F. Scott Fitzgerald in *The Great Gatsby*, (1925) capture this facet of the Roaring Twenties perfectly: as department store magnates rubbed shoulders with Broadway performers and polo players, symphony conductors and athletes and movie actresses, the kaleidoscopic whirl of celebrity enfolded them all in its ephemeral embrace.

Sensitively attuned to the currents reshaping American culture then, Fitzgerald noted the New Woman's role in entertainment culture. Women, too, moved into the sporting world during the 1920s, particularly the individual sports of tennis, golf, and swimming. Because of the demands of this new publicity machine, they were taken up as celebrities as much as athletes: Mildred "Babe" Didrikson in golf, Gertrude Ederle in swimming, Suzanne Lenglen in tennis. That Fitzgerald makes his golfer Jordan Baker into a cheat suggests his discomfort both with the New Woman and with the hucksterism and dishonesty pervading the culture of entertainment—including sports. One of the men who fixed the 1919 World Series—the gambler Arnold Rothstein—appears in *The Great Gatsby*, metamorphosed into Meyer Wolfsheim, Gatsby's partner in business "gonnegtions." For Fitzgerald the surrounding culture of sports was omnipresent: Tom Buchanan's polo playing, Baker's tournaments, Wolfsheim's gambling, even Gatsby's odd term of endearment, "old sport." The sporting world's public hucksterism emerged full-blown in this decade, and we are able to glimpse the patterns of modern sports in the lives of Babe Ruth, Red Grange, and Babe Didrikson.

Professional football had a halting beginning in 1920, with the formation of the American professional Football Association, soon to be known as the National Football League (NFL). Populated mostly by working-class ethnics in grimy factory towns, the professional game boasted little of the glamour and respectability of the college game. In fact, professional football received most attention during this decade when the nation's most famous college player, Red Grange, sometimes called the "Galloping Ghost," finished his final season at Illinois and promptly joined the professional Chicago Bears. Managed brilliantly by the sports promoter Charles C. "Cash and Carry" Pyle, Grange became a phenomenal celebrity, barnstorming the country and collecting huge sums in product endorsements. But Grange was a rare exception. Not until the 1950s and especially the 1960s (under the skilled leadership of NFL Commissioner Pete Rozelle) would pro football shed its old image and begin to share the television and celebrity limelight with college ball.

The preeminence of collegiate football, however, was due mainly to the fact that it was a thoroughly professionalized operation run under the banner of amateurism. The amateur sporting ideal has always existed more in imagination than in reality in this country. Once players, spectators, managers, owners, or athletic directors got a taste of victory and its rewards—fame, publicity, money—they found it difficult to uphold principles which make winning less likely. But college football (for most of the twentieth century) and basketball (in the past few decades) claim allegiance to amateurism only as a matter of pious public relations. Between the efforts of alumni boosters, athletic departments, and the promotion-oriented intercollegiate governing bodies like the National Collegiate Athletic Association (NCAA), colleges have managed to create essentially professional programs which serve, frankly, as a farm system for professional leagues. They produce topflight athletes, exciting entertainment (in which television networks invest heavily), and occasional—and soon forgotten—scandals which suggest the genuinely professional nature of college sports (eligibility violations, gambling, recreational and performance enhancing drug use). The American sports public apparently prefers to believe in an ideal of amateur sports, despite overwhelming evidence that the reality has hardly, if ever, existed.

Baseball, Black and White

Barred from the white organized game, African American players and entrepreneurs nevertheless made baseball their "national pastime" as well. Professional clubs formed in the late nineteenth and early twentieth centuries as independent barnstorming (traveling) businesses. The star pitcher Rube Foster first put together the Chicago American Giants in 1911, and then, in 1920 founded the Negro National League composed of eight similar teams. The economics of black baseball worked against the league: spectators were poor and there were few sources of the capital required to back a professional team. With the onset of the Depression the league collapsed in 1931.

Then in 1933, W. A. "Gus" Greenlee, Pittsburgh's black numbers boss, reassembled the Negro National League around his heavily funded Pittsburgh Crawfords. Four years later a Negro American League joined the fray; both leagues lasted into the postwar years. While the Negro Leagues never provided much organizational or financial stability for players or owners, during their heyday in the 1930s and 1940s they did field some of the game's greatest players. During the Depression Greenlee's Crawfords included a remarkable cast of future Hall of Fame players: pitcher Satchel Paige, catcher Leroy "Josh" Gibson, third baseman Judy Johnson, first baseman Oscar Charleston, and center fielder James Thomas "Cool Papa" Bell.

While the Negro Leagues never provided much stability for players and owners, during their heyday in the 1930s and 1940s they fielded some of the game's greatest players—Satchel Paige, Leroy "Josh" Gibson, Judy Johnson, Oscar Charleston, James Thomas "Cool Papa" Bell.

Black clubs continued to barnstorm the entire country since intra-league play could never make them enough money. They played white major leaguers frequently enough so that ballplayers and spectators could compare the best of both worlds. Although the overall level of Negro League play was probably below that of the white major leagues, the best black players were clearly at least the equals of their white counterparts. Negro League play differed somewhat from white baseball during these years. Major league baseball strategy had become more conservative, revolving principally around the home run. Black baseball, on the other hand, was not only more inventive and daring in organizational terms (opportunistic scheduling, pre-game entertainment, players excelling at more than one position), but also put a premium on speed, cunning, and risk-taking—what was known at the time as "tricky baseball."

Negro League baseball was central to African American culture throughout the United States. Ballplayers were well-known heroes, and baseball stories were staples of black newspapers' society pages. Opening-day celebrations could be extraordinarily elaborate, as in a 1937 Kansas City parade that included five hundred decorated cars, two marching bands, civil groups, politicians, and celebrities. Still, African American players and audiences knew that organized black baseball was the result of segregation, and they struggled to eliminate the very color barrier that had created the Negro Leagues.

Organized white baseball had achieved some real business stability by 1920. Attendance boomed to more than ninety million during the 1920s, as compared with fifty-six million the previous decade. These heights did not survive the Depression or World War II, when attendance averaged roughly a million spectators less per year. But in 1946, attendance surged to a record high, and the figure for the decade is nearly half again higher than it had ever been. Coinciding with this phenomenal growth in attendance was one of the most dramatic stories in the history of American sports, the racial integration of organized baseball.

The story begins with two characters: Jack Roosevelt Robinson and Wesley Branch Rickey. A California-raised African American, Robinson was one of the finest athletes in the country during his college years (the first UCLA athlete ever to letter in four sports: football, baseball, basketball, and track). He fought segregation and racism from his earliest years. The army court-martialed him for defying the illegal segregation on a Fort Hood bus, but Robinson was acquitted. Branch Rickey was a shrewd, farsighted cigar chewing showman, occasional Methodist moralist, and general manager of the Brooklyn Dodgers. Rickey developed the farm system, fully integrating minor league teams into the major league club's player development strategies. He determined in 1945 to break baseball's unwritten but absolute color line by bringing a black player into the Dodger organization. After a nationwide search for the right combination of baseball talent and self-disciplined character, Rickey decided on Jackie Robinson, then a player with the Negro League Kansas City Monarchs.

Robinson accepted Rickey's offer to integrate organized baseball, promising not to retaliate against what both men expected to be torrents of racist abuse. After spending the 1946 season with the Dodgers' AAA Montreal farm club and leading his team to the championship of the minor league World Series, Robinson was promoted to the Brooklyn Dodgers in 1947. That season he became a national phenomenon, combining first-rate, exciting, aggressive diamond play with a dignified restraint in the face of vicious racism ranging from insults and catcalls to beanballs, hate mail, and death threats.

Robinson's obvious courage, pride, and determination drew the admiration of whites as well as blacks, and may very well have inspired fellow African Americans as they developed the theory and practice of nonviolence in the following decade. Also restrained and dignified, the African American response to Robinson demonstrated the black rejection of "separate but equal" strategies in favor of racial integration. Even before the Montgomery bus boycott began in late 1955, for example, black baseball fans in Shreveport and New Orleans, Louisiana, had organized boycotts of minor league teams that refused to hire black players.

Robinson's style of play combined the daring opportunism known as "tricky baseball" in the Negro Leagues, with an intimidating aggressiveness on the base paths. According to his manager Leo Durocher, "This guy didn't just come to play. He come to beat ya. He come to stuff the goddamn bat right up your ass." Named Rookie of the Year in 1947 and Most Valuable Player in 1949, Robinson established himself as perhaps the single most exciting player in the game.

African American sportswriters focused attention on Robinson's achievements and the black players who followed him, thus encouraging the integration of professional football, tennis, and basketball. Consequently, the Negro Leagues, one of the most important institutions of twentieth-century, African American cultural life during segregation, quickly began to lose players, spectators, and media coverage. Despite the relatively slow pace of racial integration in baseball—the New York Yankees and Boston Red Sox did not add a single black player until 1955 and 1959, respectively—the Negro Leagues had been reduced to four teams by the mid-1950s, and were dead by 1960. The paradoxical result was that there were actually fewer opportunities for African Americans to make a living from professional baseball, a stark reality that may still prevail today.

This history of baseball's segregation and integration calls into question the simplistic idea that professional sport embodies the democratic promise of a meritocratic society. For over half a century the color line simply excluded hundreds, if not thousands, of players who could have performed creditably in professional baseball. Even when the color line began to be crossed, baseball talent and skill alone did not make the difference. Rickey's choice of Jackie Robinson, as opposed to any one of several dozen first-rate pros in the Negro Leagues, was political, commercial, and psychological. Rickey wanted a particular kind of ballplayer to be the pioneer. And because he held extraordinary power in the baseball world, he got his way. In sports as in other areas of American endeavor, background, education, class, and the ability to "fit in" counted quite as much as so-called pure talent. This is not to say that mediocre talent with the right connections could survive the world of topflight sports, but that topflight ability alone has never been sufficient for an athlete to reach the highest echelons. At least through the 1970s, black major leaguers, taken together, had consistently higher batting averages than comparable groups of white players. To make it in the big leagues and stay there, African American players had to be better than their white counterparts. And despite more than forty years of baseball integration, African Americans remain disproportionately scarce in management and front-office positions, and no major league sports franchise is owned by a nonwhite.

The 1950s: Portents of Change

Modern cultural folklore, including that of organized sports, has settled on the 1950s as the decade of romantic inertia. If there was a certain glacierlike quality to international politics and the postwar revival of the cult of domesticity, there were also currents swirling underneath the surface that would crack the cultural monolith of the Eisenhower administration and the *Donna Reed Show* wide open.

Because spectator sports depend on a demographic base, the profound population shifts which began in the 1950s changed the shape of American sports. As suburbs mushroomed after World War II, drawing middle- and working-class families out of the older northeastern cities, the hometowns of some of the country's most venerable sporting franchises began a steady process of decay. The gathering momentum of this self-feeding cycle—the more inner cities are abandoned, the less desirable they become as places to live and do business, so more people leave—had serious consequences for sports teams, many of whose facilities dated from the early part of the century. The African American migration out of the South, a trickle beginning during World War I, became a flood in the years following World War II. To white suburbanites, who now made fewer trips into the cities they had abandoned, old stomping grounds began to look like unfamiliar territory, as poorer African and Hispanic Americans took their place. The combination of factors seriously reduced attendance at older ballparks located in central cities.

At the same time, Americans began a substantial internal migration to the Sunbelt cities of the South and West, a trend which continued well into the 1980s. Between 1940 and 1980 the population of the Sunbelt increased more than two and a half times as fast as that of the Midwest and Northeast, or frostbelt.

Television, a curiosity at the end of World War II, was fast becoming a dominant presence in American entertainment. In 1949 just under a million families owned a TV set; by 1951 the number had climbed to ten million, and two years later it doubled again. In 1955, two-thirds of American households owned a television, and by decade's end only 12 percent of households in the United States did not boast at least one.

Although TV networks neither invested heavily in sports programming in the 1950s nor claimed the kind of immense power in the sporting world they achieved two decades later, the new medium already began to influence patterns of sporting display and spectatorship. When fans could watch nationally televised, big-league baseball games, they stopped going to the hundreds of minor league parks in the country. Minor league attendance dropped precipitously, from forty-two million in 1949 to fifteen million in 1957.

Television changed boxing and other arena sports by first promoting them into new prominence, but then reshaping them in ways that contributed to their demise. During the brief "Golden Age" of boxing, for example, Gilette sponsored regular telecasts of Friday night bouts at Madison Square Garden. But in a development that foreshadowed TV's effect on other sports, boxing aficionados discovered that TV audiences, according to sponsors who presumed to speak for them, wanted a different kind of sport. They wanted offense—in this case slugging—and a lot of it. Boxing strategy deteriorated, and local gyms and clubs found they couldn't compete with televised boxing. By the late 1950s half the nation's fight clubs had closed and only nominal audiences actually showed up for the broadcasts at Madison Square Garden.

The growth of TV, suburbanization, and the Sunbelt demographic shift helped to produce a decade of tremendous franchise movement in major league baseball. After fifty years of geographical stability, the Boston Braves moved to Milwaukee in 1953 and reversed its sorry fortunes. Two years later the Saint Louis Browns relocated to Baltimore, and the year after the Philadelphia Athletics moved to Kansas City. Then in 1958 the Brooklyn Dodgers, long a beloved symbol of working-class ethnic pride and home of baseball's "great experiment" with integration, departed their cramped and decaying quarters in Brooklyn for the suburban freeways of southern California. That same year the New York Giants accompanied their rivals west, to San Francisco.

It is a matter of some note that the Dodgers' relocation to Los Angeles still lives in sports mythology as an act of betrayal, second only to the fixing of the 1919 World Series. And yet owner Walter O'Malley's move was a thoroughly rational business decision: he was offered three hundred (120 hectares) acres of land near downtown, good access to highways, and the media market of the nation's third largest metropolitan area, factors which compared more than favorably with the thirty-five-thousand-seat Ebbets Field and attendance which had declined steadily for ten years despite excellent teams. Very little in the history of American capitalism suggests stability, and yet fans still felt that "their" team would stay put forever. This set of anomalies suggests the way that professional sport, unquestionably an entertainment business for almost a century, still occasionally offers a vision of relationships not wholly defined by the marketplace. There is, necessarily, a constant tension in professional sport in which business decisions frequently eclipse competing moral or emotional claims. Rational calculation of dollars and cents leaves little room for loyalty to neighborhood and peers.

Modern Times

The last generation of American sports history has been governed by five developments: TV's maturation into the single most powerful force in the sports business; the ascendancy of football; the fantastic growth of the financial stakes in professional sports; the rebellion of black and female athletes against condescension, segregation, and racial and sexual discrimination; and the changing power relations between owners and players. All of these were closely connected.

Roone Arledge, the most influential figure in televised sports in the past thirty years, through his productions *Wide World of Sports* (beginning in 1961) and ABC *Monday Night Football* (1970), transformed the way Americans thought about and watched sports on television. By using multiple camera angles, directional microphones, and striking close-ups, instant slow-motion replays, human interest crowd shots, and employing outspoken announcers with distinct personalities, Arledge repackaged football into an innovative sporting entertainment that crossed class, race, and gender boundaries. This novel program was meant to be comprehensible even to people who didn't know anything about football. As a result, professional football was able to shed its older image as a violent working-class sport perfectly suited to the grim realities of factory towns, and join—in fact, help create—a homogenous national culture of the managerial middle class. By the early 1970s professional football had surpassed baseball in TV, popularity, and had become the preferred sport of politicians. (Baseball's declining fortunes led owners to create divisions within leagues, to change rules in favor of the offense, and in the American League, to create a new position, the designated hitter.)

Monday Night Football, and Arledge's inspired broadcasts of the Olympics in the 1960s and 1970s, brought new groups of spectators to sports, audiences that advertisers were willing to pay for. More than ever before, the middle class, including women, watched the games and the ads. Until the 1980s, when networks faced intense competition from cable stations, the profitable partnership between sports and TV seemed to have no limit.

Television money has completed the transformation of college sports programs, particularly in football and basketball, into professional farm teams for the National Basketball Association and the National Football League. Colleges stand to earn so much money and publicity from topflight winning teams—one million dollars for each of the final four teams in the 1980 NCAA basketball tournament—that any remnant of an amateur ethos has little chance against the effort to subvert regulations against professionalism. Increasingly, heavily recruited high school athletes are being integrated into the same pyramid, with money and goods being supplied (on top of college scholarships) by advertisers like beer and sneaker companies.

Television also helped to create the careers, the financial base for, and, therefore, the symbolic power of black and female athletes in the 1960s, 1970s, and 1980s. The boxer Muhammad Ali, who first came to prominence as Cassius Clay, winning Golden Glove and Olympic championships in 1959 and 1960, had become the best known athlete in the world by the end of that decade. Combining unusual skill and energy in the ring ("float like a butterfly, sting like a bee," he characterized his style) with a quick outrageous wit and an extraordinary flair for self-promotion ("I am the greatest"), Ali outraged the sports world, after he won the heavyweight crown in 1964, by renouncing his "slave name" in favor of his new Muslim name.

Ali's vocal, unapologetic involvement with the separatist black nationalist Nation of Islam, and his 1967 refusal to be drafted into the army (on religious grounds) attracted enormous hostility from the white sporting and press establishment, but also gained him the adulation of more militant African Americans who admired his firm stance in the face of white disapproval. Ali evoked the memory of the first black champion, Jack Johnson, perhaps even more when he was indicted for refusing induction and the boxing authorities took his title away. Unlike Johnson, Ali fought his conviction until the Supreme Court overturned it in 1970. Then he won back the heavyweight title four years later.

Like Tommy Smith and John Carlos—American track stars who gave the black power salute on the victory stand at the 1968 Olympics and were summarily thrown out of the Games—Ali became a symbol for black athletes who struggled during the sixties and seventies to redress a history of unequal treatment in schools, sports programs, and on playing fields. Ali's success and power also owed much to TV, the medium which made him into a celebrity far beyond his ring exploits.

The boxer Muhammad Ali, who first came to prominence as Cassius Clay, outraged the sports world when he renounced his "slave name" in favor of his new Muslim name after winning the heavyweight crown in 1964.

If the black revolt in sports saw some important gains—better salaries, more professional players, less public insistence that blacks conform to white cultural styles—significant discrimination remains to the present. African Americans are still overrepresented in certain sports (basketball, football) and positions within sports (outfielder, lineman) and underrepresented in other areas (tennis, swimming, quarterback, catcher), and there remain very few blacks in ownership, management, or front-office positions.

Women's sports, too, underwent massive transformations in the past thirty years. Under the leadership of Billie Jean King, women's tennis vaulted to unprecedented levels of popularity, with purses to match. Through her outstanding tennis skills and articulate determination, King brought greater gender equality to women's tennis and also made the game of tennis more democratic, less dominated by the upper-class gentility of its origins. She brokered the successful marriage of women's tennis and television that brought money into her sport, and made her into a feminist heroine.

There have been other attempts to organize women's professional sports leagues—most notably in basketball and fast-pitch softball—but these have not yet found the financial backing necessary to survive in the world of televised professional sports. Although professional tennis remains the glamour sport for women, the women's movement of the late 1960s and 1970s had far-reaching impact on less visible sports. With the assistance of Title IX of the Educational Amendments Act of 1972 (passed through the efforts of women), females in school sports began to receive more funding.

The political controversies of the 1960s and 1970s—the civil rights and black power movements, the women's movement, even the anti-war movement—had important impact on the world of organized sports. While most of these were unsettling to the white men who continued to make up the largest part of the audience for professional and college sports, the one that perhaps provoked the most outcry was the changed relationship between players and owners in professional sports.

In the late 1960s and 1970s players in professional baseball, basketball, and football all organized newly aggressive unions and hired professional organizers. In 1975 a baseball arbitrator ruled that the game's "reserve clause" only held for a single year following the end of a player's contract, and that players could become "free agents" after that year. In one stroke players' market negotiating power was restored to a level not seen for a century. In the meantime, with TV contracts and new stadiums, the game had become much more lucrative. Players suddenly commanded extraordinary salaries.

Baseball salaries soared in the next fifteen years from an average of $46,000 annually in 1975 to $433,000 in 1988 to more than $850,000 in 1991. By the late 1980s the game's stars could command two and three million dollars per year, and Bobby Bonilla stunned the sports world when the New York Mets gave him a $29 million multiyear contract in the winter of 1991. Baseball owners fought back against the laws of supply and demand in ways reminiscent of more traditional industries. They stalled contract negotiations, staged lockouts, and—secretly and illegally—agreed among themselves to cap salaries. All of these strategies failed, as players shrewdly stuck together and outmaneuvered the owners. All the while, despite owners' periodic warnings of bankruptcy, the baseball business continued to prosper. Into the 1990s, franchises continued to mushroom in value, and after-tax balance sheets remained profitable.

Conclusion

Without television, neither Muhammad Ali nor Billie Jean King would have become powerful symbols or celebrities. Without TV, professional football probably would have remained a relatively class-bound, defensively oriented, unglamorous sport. Without the electronic media, beer and sporting goods companies would not have a pipeline through which they could pump hundreds of millions of dollars into the coffers of professional sports organizations and the pockets of athletes. And without the peculiar marriage of TV, sneaker companies, and the National Basketball Association, Chicago Bulls star Michael Jordan would not have become such a cultural and commercial icon in the black community.

As an entertainment business, modern sport seems to have inexhaustible potential. One of the central components of mass culture, sporting spectacles now appeal to nearly all demographic "markets." Even as late as the last quarter of the nineteenth century the sports audience was much more limited to working-class men and a significant minority from the middle and upper classes. TV's restless search for larger audiences with money to spend continues to domesticate and homogenize individual sports. And now the sports "seasons" that television created overlap and blend into each other almost without ceremonial pause—but not without pauses for commercials. With the assistance of sponsors, athletes have completed their transformation into celebrities, and now they are barely distinguishable from personalities on TV sitcoms or morning news/entertainment shows.

Ironically, the very nature of sport as business—the dream of riches it holds out to young athletes and hungry producers alike—guarantees it will remain intimately connected to the seedier side of culture and society: gambling, alcohol, drugs, and sexual promiscuity. The extraordinary pressures on athletes to succeed—to have a chance at the big money, or once having achieved it, to keep earning it—frequently lead them to the consolations of alcohol and other recreational drugs. Where so much depends on the proper functioning of a superbly trained body, performance enhancing drugs (painkillers and steroids, for example) seem to offer crucial assistance. And for men who have been emotionally coddled since adolescence the lure of sexual opportunism is hard to resist.

If Michael Jordan, known as "Air" Jordan (after the name of the shoes he sells for Nike) represents one image of modern sports, Pete Rose may stand for the other. For more than two decades Rose played baseball single-mindedly, passionately, and exceptionally well, fully earning the nickname Charlie Hustle. But Rose's gambling activities (which got him banished from the game in 1989) placed him firmly inside baseball's 150-year-old relationship with the culture and society of urban low-life.

By virtue of its inherent vitality, the modern sports business is drawn in competing directions, toward greater blandness and homogeneity in an effort to further broaden its televised appeal, while the promises it makes to potential participants encourage Faustian bargains. Along with the lottery and with about the same odds—the sports arena remains one of the last places in America where a person can strike it rich.

[See also Business Culture; The Culture of Consumption; Mass Culture and Its Critics; Radio; Technology and Social Change; Television.]

BIBLIOGRAPHY

General Works

Ashe, Arthur. *A Hard Road to Glory: The History of the African-American Athlete 1946–1986.* 3 vols. (1988).

Covallo, Dominick. Muscles, *Muscles and Morals Organized Playgrounds and Urban Reform, 1880–1920* (1981).

Guttman, Allen. *From Ritual to Record: The Nature of Modern Sports* (1978).

Guttman, Allen. *A Whole New Ball Game: An Interpretation of American Sports* (1988).

Higham, John. "The Reorientation of American Culture in the 1890s." In his *Writing American History: Essays on Modern Scholarship* (1970).

Lasch, Christopher. "The Moral and intellectual Rehabilitation of the Ruling Class." In his *The World of Nations: Reflections on American History, Politics, and Culture* (1973).

Messna, Michael A. *Power at Play: Sports and the Problem of Masculinity* (1992).

Rader, Benjamin G. *In Its Own Image: How Television Has Transformed Sports* (1984).

Rader, Benjamin G. *American Sports: From the Age of Folk Games to the Age of Televised Sports.* 2d ed. (1990).

Riess, Steven A. *City Games: The Evolution of American Urban Society, and the Rise of Sports* (1989).

Roberts, Randy, and James Olson. *Winning Is the Only Thing: Sports in America Since 1945* (1989).

Ruck, Rob. *Sandlot Seasons: Sport in Black Pittsburgh* (1987).

Smith, Ronald A. *Sports and Freedom: The Rise of Big-Time College Athletics* (1988).

Vincent, Ted. *Mudville's Revenge: The Rise and Fall of American Sport* (1981).

Individual Sports and Biographies

Axthelm, Pete. *The City Game: Basketball in New York from the World Champion Knicks to the World of the Playgrounds* (1970).

Isaacs, Neil D. *All the Moves: A History of College Basketball* (1975).

James, Bill. *The Bill James Historical Baseball Abstract* (1988).

King, Billie Jean, and Kim Chapin. *Billie Jean* (1974).

Peterson, Robert W. *Cages to Jump Shots: Pro Basketball's Early Years* (1990).

Roberts, Randy. *Jack Dempsey, the Manassa Mauler* (1979).

Roberts, Randy. *Papa Jack: Jack Johnson and the Era of White Hopes* (1983).
Rogosin, Donn. *Invisible, Men: Life in Baseball's Negro Leagues* (1983).
Seymour, Harold. *Baseball.* 2 vols. (1960, 1971).
Seymour, Harold. *Baseball: The People's Game* (1990).
Smith, Leverett T. *The American Dream and the National Game* (1975).
Tygiel, Jules. *Baseball's Great Experiment: Jackie Robinson and His Legacy* (1983).

— WARREN GOLDSTEIN

THE SUBURBS

Images of suburbs underlie much of American culture today. Television sitcoms from *The Dick Van Dyke Show* to *Roseanne* have made a suburban setting familiar, funny, and resonant with their American audiences. A 1962 Malvina Reynolds song, "Little Boxes," characterized suburbs where

> And the people in the houses
> All went to the university,
> Where they were put in boxes
> And they came out all the same.

In the early 1990s David Byrne sang of a suburban landscape full of Taco Bells and parking lots. Erma Bombeck's *The Grass Is Always Greener over the Septic Tank* (1976) is only one of many imaginatively titled volumes on suburban living that have been published since the 1950s.

American culture is suffused with suburban images because today it is overwhelmingly suburban. Kenneth T. Jackson, in his path-breaking synthesis of American suburban history, *Crabgrass Frontier* (1985), describes how the decades after World War II brought "the suburbanization of the United States." The evidence for such a process is manifold. Suburbs became the predominant home for Americans, with more than 40 percent of the population living in the suburbs, according to the 1980 census. Between 1950 and 1970, more than three-quarters of all new manufacturing and retail jobs were located in suburban areas. Overall between 1950 and 1970, 83 percent of the nation's total growth took place in suburbs. The overwhelming extent of this postwar suburbanization, with its trademark shopping malls, express highways, and industrial parks, leads many to assume that it *began* in 1945—which is not the case. Indeed, settlements on the fringes of cities are as old as the oldest American cities.

Early Suburbs

The earliest suburbs bore little resemblance to the ideal described by the famous landscape architect and planner Frederick Law Olmsted (1822–1903): "the most attractive, the most refined, and the most soundly wholesome forms of domestic life, and the best application of the arts of civilization to which mankind has yet attained" (quoted in Fishman, *Bourgeois Utopias*, p. 198). Before improvements in urban transportation transformed the "walking city," the most highly prized residential locations were close to the center of town. In Europe this was a centuries-old tradition: those with wealth and influence lived in town, while the poor and other outcasts lived outside city walls. In the United States similar forces were at work, and the word "suburb" had definite pejorative connotations. Early-nineteenth-century Philadelphians, for instance, forced unwanted businesses, such as slaughterhouses, and people of lower status to the outskirts of the city.

The suburban villa was an important exception to low-status outlying settlements. It was in many respects the antecedent of the modern suburb. From ancient Greece to eighteenth-century England, the wealthy elites of many societies have had country estates and houses. Such houses were located on the outskirts of cities—far enough away to avoid city problems but close enough for easy travel to and from town. These estates had many of the amenities available in city homes because large retinues of servants ensured the provision of basic comforts such as heated rooms, baths, and lighting. Elite families with many servants operated as self-contained islands—regardless of whether they were in the city or the country. It was not until the development of mechanical systems to provide services and amenities—and all of the socioeconomic changes the elite relied upon—that proximity to neighbors and a community became important to the comfort of a household.

Robert Fishman places the birth of suburbia in late-eighteenth-century London. The tremendous growth of London during that century led to an urban crisis. Some called for reforms such as urban squares and wide streets to alleviate congestion and disorder. However, a growing repulsion toward the city, especially by middle-class merchants, led many to establish weekend villas where their families could escape London's turmoil. These merchants prized "picturesque," naturalistic landscapes. By concentrating villas while still employing picturesque landscaping, they created the first romantic suburbs. As Fishman describes an early suburb at Clapham, outside London, "each property is private, but each contributes to the total landscape of *houses in a park*" (p. 55). Manchester's Victoria Park and Liverpool's Rock Park, both designed in the 1830s, are other examples of early British romantic suburbs.

A similar process took hold in the United States within decades. In antebellum Chicago, the word "suburb" often described an outlying community that was a small agricultural town or an industrial site. There were no commuters in these areas, but the residents were tied more closely to cities than were their more distant counterparts by farming for the city and by coexisting with noxious industries that city dwellers gave rise to but would not tolerate. Frequently, newspaper accounts used the term as an adjective—a "suburban" villa or "suburban" home. For instance, "suburban" served to describe the second home of a wealthy Chicagoan whose family spent summers and holidays away from the congestion and disease of the city. It also characterized the home of a Chicagoan who had retired from an active life in the city to become a gentleman farmer. As time went on, real estate developers planned romantic suburbs such as Chicago's Riverside and Lake Forest; these places combined rural living with urban amenities.

The Suburb in the Industrial Era

In the nineteenth century, suburban communities developed across the United States as the demands of their residents—often newly transplanted from cities—for services and amenities came to resemble those of urbanites more than those of rural dwellers. Suburbs emerged from new communities as well as older rural settlements. Only after the emergence of uniquely urban services and amenities—which is to say, those unavailable in the countryside—did people feel a need for suburban governments, associations, or developers. Initially, transitional areas between the city and country contained some urban-oriented activities but had no special services to distinguish them from the adjacent countryside. As cities grew, though, they physically impinged upon these formerly outlying communities, causing many to take on the features of a suburb—that is, a place that sought to combine the services and amenities of the city with country living.

The solitary country estate with an army of servants gradually gave way to suburban communities with mechanical service improvements. This transition from human to mechanical supports extended the option of suburban living, formerly reserved for the wealthy, to the middle classes. Lewis Mumford argued that the widening economic base of the suburban movement in Britain in the early nineteenth century, and in the United States later in the century, was the result of transportation innovations. While transportation advances were certainly important in making suburban living possible and affordable for more people, it was the extension of urban amenities to outlying communities that permitted the modern suburb. This is not to say that they negated disparities in wealth, though; transportation improvements did remain essential to the suburban option for all but the wealthiest. Until the 1830s, settlement in and around American cities was largely circumscribed by the distance a person could walk in an hour or so. However, the introduction of the steam ferry (1811) and the omnibus (1830s), the railroad and the horsecar (from the 1840s), the cable car (1870s), and the electric streetcar (1880s) transformed the pattern of settlement within cities. For the first time people could live at some distance from their place of work and commute by means of public transportation.

This separation of work and home was integral to the modernization process in nineteenth-century cities. Facilitated by improving intracity transportation, it gave rise to urban residential areas based on class, ethnicity, or race. These residential areas no longer needed to contain a wide range of economic functions and types of people. Suburbs became an archetype of this segregation into residential areas homogeneous with regard to class. Sam Bass Warner, Jr., has ably explored the agglomeration of Boston's population by class in late-nineteenth-century streetcar suburbs. At the base of this segregation was a community, not an individual home. As Carol O'Connor explains in "The Suburban Mosaic," "early observers [of suburbs] note the existence of relatively homogeneous local units within heterogeneous suburban regions" (p. 245).

Suburban dwellers were the first to take advantage of ferryboat services. A ferry connection between Manhattan and Brooklyn in 1814 made Brooklyn one of the first commuter suburbs in the United States. Commuters on ferries became a familiar sight by the late nineteenth century. And compact, built-up communities in New York and Philadelphia allowed horse-drawn omnibuses to proliferate in the early nineteenth century. By the second half of the nineteenth century, the railroad, too, had an important impact on suburbs by tying outlying areas more closely to the city center. Thus, the range of areas considered suburban expanded dramatically to include larger towns that served as trading centers for agricultural areas close to the city.

In 1888 the perfection of the electrified street railway (first tested in Richmond, Virginia) led to even more changes in suburban commutation patterns. By 1895, 85 percent of all street railways in the United States had been electrified. The electric streetcar revolutionized mass transit and opened up hundreds of locations for suburban development. No longer restricted to the radial patterns of commuter stops, suburban developers began to fill in the territory between stops.

The automobile took this filling-in process one step further. First visible in cities at the turn of the century, automobiles began to predominate by the 1920s. In 1920 there were over nine million cars in the United States; by 1930 this number had more than tripled to twenty-six million.

It is important to remember that the railroads, streetcars, and automobiles did not *create* these settlements on the outskirts of American cities. Rather, they expanded the area in which suburbs could appear and, as noted earlier, made suburban living affordable for more people. These transportation advances also worked to concentrate suburban settlement along their lines, particularly near railroad and streetcar stations.

Increasingly the term "suburb" was used to designate the settlement surrounding a railroad station. By the 1870s, the frequency and fares of trains to outlying areas were important factors in defining an area as suburban. The availability of relatively inexpensive commuter tickets was crucial for suburban development.

By the 1880s, many of these early suburbs tried to provide urban amenities. Suburbanites did not wish to forsake the society and comforts of the city, so parks, schools, cultural associations, and services like running water and sewer connections became part of the ideal suburban community. These improvements, of course, did not take place overnight. In 1873 the existence of a waterworks in Irving Park, a community outside Chicago, was noted in advertisements for suburban homes. It was an amenity not available in many other suburban communities and was thus cause for special mention. By the 1890s the "model" suburban home was found in a community with paved streets, schools, good transportation, and other services usually available only in the city. This was a far cry from the antebellum picture of a "model" suburban home: an isolated country house to which a wealthy family retired.

The suburban character of many former agricultural towns that could be seen developing after the 1880s can be traced in commuter schedules, inclusion of their residents in society registers, and the growing demands for urban services.

This evolution was also evident in changes taking place in established rural towns, as the railroad and population growth pressed suburban expansion further from the city. The increasingly suburban character of many former agricultural towns can be traced in commuter schedules, inclusion of their residents in society registers, and the growing demands for urban services. These demands were met in part by community associations (or real estate developers in new areas), but more and more residents turned to local government for their provision.

In addition to residential development, industry and commerce had been a part of the suburban scene from the beginning. The hinterland was already home to market towns and noxious industries, and suburbanization simply engulfed many of these functions. Also, by the turn of the century, the owners of manufacturing establishments took advantage of relatively inexpensive land along railroad lines to establish suburban plants. For instance, George Pullman established his Pullman car works—and the model town Pullman—in south suburban Chicago in 1882. Glendale, near Cincinnati, was another such planned suburb.

The general trends outlined here were the result of thousands of individual decisions. In his study of Boston's nineteenth-century streetcar suburbs, Sam Bass Warner, Jr., notes "a building process which rested in the hands of thousands of small agents" (p. 117). One set of actors is particularly important to this process: the real estate developers who planned, built, and marketed suburban communities.

The most visible developers were those who created planned suburbs. In the nineteenth century Frederick Law Olmsted was among the most notable designers. He was joined in the twentieth century by developers such as Jessie Clyde Nichols, William Levitt, and James Rouse. Olmsted and his partner, Calvert Vaux, planned sixteen suburbs in the decades after the Civil War, among them Brookline and Chestnut Hill in Massachusetts, Sudbrook and Roland Park in Maryland, Yonkers and Tarrytown Heights in New York, and Riverside in Illinois.

Backed by the Riverside Improvement Company, Olmsted and Vaux sought in designing a suburb in 1868 to "unite at once the beauties and healthy properties of a park with the conveniences and improvements of the city" (Keating, *Building Chicago*, p. 73). Water and sewer mains, individual gas hookups, streetlamps, paved roads, parks, sidewalks, and a railroad depot were just some of the amenities offered. Deeds for lots sold in Riverside included restrictions on building lines, minimum prices for homes and the prohibition of fences; community parkland adjoined all lots. A contemporary account reminded potential residents that "parties buying at Riverside will have the satisfaction of avoiding the demand upon their resources for taxation in the way of improvements, so constant in all towns."

In the nineteenth and twentieth centuries real estate syndicates, land companies, and improvement associations opened thousands of subdivisions in suburban areas across the United States. Through these improvement companies, speculators sought to direct urban growth into the hinterland. Improvements to heighten marketability and attract settlement to particular subdivisions fell into two basic categories: those outside the subdivision and those within it. In the first category were extensions of streetcar and commuter rail lines, the construction of connecting highways, and the development of neighboring parks and boulevards. Among the improvements within subdivisions were commuter rail stations, industries and/or businesses, home construction, and infrastructure such as sidewalks, paved roads, electricity, and water and sewer lines.

While much suburbanization has been unplanned, there are notable exceptions; their influence, however, is debatable. In 1927 Clarence Stein and Henry Wright, under the financial sponsorship of Alexander Bing, planned Radburn, New Jersey, the first garden city in the United States.

During the New Deal the federal government directed the construction of three model suburban communities: Greenbelt, Maryland, near Washington; Greenhills, Ohio, near Cincinnati; and Greendale, Wisconsin, outside Milwaukee. Rexford Tugwell supervised these projects under the Resettlement Administration. Planning began in 1935, and construction was under way for the following three years. The three projects contained housing for 2,267 families. Tugwell believed there should have been not three but three thousand of these projects.

One of the purposes of the program was to demonstrate the advantages of resettling both urban and rural residents in a suburban environment where homes and jobs were located. There was to be plenty of light and many gardens and parks. Urban amenities such as good schools, public utilities, and job opportunities were included in the original plans for each town. But the greenbelt towns never worked out economically, and Congress authorized their sale in 1949 at just over $18 million, half of their $36 million total cost to the federal government.

Origins of Suburban Government

In the same way that the concept of a suburb evolved over the course of the nineteenth century, its government developed and changed. Early in the century a move to an outlying area was seen as a way of avoiding much of the intrusion of local government on one's life. By the 1870s this changed for many suburban areas, whose residents clamored for more government involvement in the provision of services.

Such demands, though, were not calls for the replication of urban forms. By the mid-nineteenth century, city government had acquired an unenviable reputation. An 1869 *Chicago Times* editorial (7 April) commented: "Municipal government in this country is a system of machinery to collect and consume taxes without returning anything like an adequate compensation. It has been refined, and expanded, and compounded to an extent that renders it next to unbearable." Outlying residents sought to obtain and to avoid city government; they needed a form of government somewhere between the urban and the rural.

The contrast between urban and rural government was strong from colonial settlement through the antebellum period. The chartered municipal form, drawn from British antecedents, gave special rights and privileges to urban governments that other local governments did not receive. While the early nineteenth century saw the erosion of the special powers held by chartered cities, their governments were still easily distinguishable from those of rural areas. Suburban government emerged as a new form by the end of the nineteenth century, providing many of the services of chartered urban governments while being shaped by rural governments.

Robert C. Wood examined suburbs and their governments in *Suburbia: Its People and Their Politics* (1958). He felt that while suburbs were home for modern Americans, their governments were decidedly archaic: "They join the other suburban political units around our large cities in clinging persistently to the independence they received when they were isolated villages and hamlets in a rustic countryside" (p. 9). According to Wood and others, suburban government has hindered the development of metropolitan governments that could better serve urban areas. Such an indictment of suburban government goes back to the early years of the twentieth century, when political scientists began to criticize metropolitan governments, often in conjunction with reformers (or as reformers) advocating metropolitan consolidation.

Consolidation and Annexation

Annexation to the core city was a significant issue for suburbs until the early twentieth century; in some areas, notably those where development and increasing population have been more recent, it remains important. Core cities generally provided superior services and drew many early suburbs within their boundaries as suburbanites sought improvements. In addition, some suburban governments were successful while others were short-lived and soon abandoned; annexation often involved unsuccessful suburban forms.

Studies have identified several important factors in explaining the halt to annexations around the turn of the century. Jon C. Teaford and Kenneth Jackson have provided the most succinct discussions on this subject. Teaford explains:

> By 1910 suburban America was a segregated collection of divergent interests, industrial and residential, Protestant and Catholic, truck farmer and commuter, saloon habitué and abstainer. . . . Each of these segments sought to escape from others and to achieve its goals by taking advantage of the state's willingness to abdicate its control over the creation of municipalities. (*City and Suburb*, p. 12)

Jackson notes that this fragmentation heightened racial, ethnic, and class distinctions. Coupled with these divisions was the fact that by the end of the nineteenth century, incorporation as a suburban municipality was an easy process. Suburban municipalities, as well as special districts, dramatically improved the services available outside the city, thus eliminating what had been the strongest drawing card of annexation to the center city—better and less expensive services.

For instance, Brooklyn was incorporated as a city in 1834, and it later annexed two neighboring entities in 1855 and more territory in 1896. This process was spurred on by the introduction of a street railway network and the opening of the Brooklyn Bridge in 1883, both of which encouraged suburban settlement in its nearby rural townships. These townships, like those around Chicago, were composed of multiple settlements that competed for limited town funds. The fledgling suburban communities turned first to the rural townships with their demands for improvements, but they received only limited satisfaction. It was to receive better services and representation that the citizens of these townships agreed to annexation.

In New York the incorporated township and the incorporated village emerged in the closing decades of the nineteenth century to serve an increasing number of suburban communities. The forms were not unlike those found in Chicago: the contiguous townships that were providing suburban services were eventually annexed to the center city. At the same time that the adjacent townships were being absorbed by the city, a number of outlying suburbs began to incorporate as villages. Mount Vernon, just outside the Bronx towns that were annexed to New York City, incorporated in 1892 and avoided annexation. Nearby Bronxville was developed as an exclusive suburb after 1890; it incorporated as a distinct village in 1898, in order to facilitate the orderly development of the area. The end result of these annexations and incorporations was a metropolitan area composed of a central city surrounded by incorporated suburbs.

To the north, as Boston grew to metropolitan status, a similar process was taking place. The major difference was that village incorporation was not an option in Massachusetts. Many of these outlying townships possessed a unique, independent history until the mid-nineteenth century, when commuter railroads and streetcar lines drew them into a suburban orbit. Massachusetts's Chariestown, Cambridge, and Roxbury were among the towns that incorporated during the 1840s. Like the towns surrounding Chicago, they were composed of multiple settlements that were joined in a single incorporated government. The town of Cambridge, for instance, was composed of at least three settlements: Old Cambridge, Cambridgeport, and East Cambridge. Some of these modified rural governments became successful suburban forms, and Boston annexed others. As noted earlier, suburbanites created new townships that could more easily provide suburban services and representation. In contrast to New York City, Brooklyn, and Chicago, incorporated townships in Massachusetts became the most familiar suburban type as well as the form of government involved in annexations.

While the township was an important form for suburban governance in the nineteenth century (and beyond for Boston), it played virtually no role in metropolitan areas in the South and the West. For instance, California did not use the township except as a judicial unit. Townships did not serve as intermediate forms while cities like Los Angeles and San Francisco grew. Instead, the county was the basic unit of local government in California. There, as in some other western and southern states, a chartered county form evolved, which was employed in urban areas where more functions were demanded of local government.

The city and county of San Francisco were made coterminous in 1856, after the first spurt of urban growth; but no significant area has subsequently been annexed to San Francisco. Surrounding the city were chartered counties that absorbed further metropolitan growth. Within these counties, however, were incorporated villages and cities similar in scope to those in midwestern and Middle Atlantic metropolitan areas. In the Los Angeles metropolitan area today, numerous chartered counties form the basis of government, with incorporated suburbs and cities—including Los Angeles proper—serving parts of the counties.

Students of Suburbs

Late-nineteenth-century observers heralded the suburban community as the great hope for an industrializing world. One of the first to describe the suburb was Adna Ferrin Weber, in his 1899 study of urban growth, *Growth of Cities in the Nineteenth Century.* According to Weber, a suburb combined the healthfulness of the country with urban improvements. Weber's suburb had a lower population density than the center city and was distinguished from the surrounding countryside by its city improvements, comforts, and society. Weber saw that the continued deconcentration of urban populations, even in an unplanned fashion, would greatly improve the daily lives of metropolitan residents.

In New York the incorporated township and the incorporated village emerged in the closing decades of the nineteenth century to serve an increasing number of suburban communities.

Suburbs were seen by many early social scientists and reformers as a means of humanizing city life. Henry George, the popular nineteenth-century economist and social critic, promoted the benefits of the single tax, arguing that such a government levy on all land rents would make suburban living possible for more of the nation's population. George's 1879 *Progress and Poverty* argued that this would be a dramatic improvement for residents of metropolitan areas:

> The destruction of speculative land values would tend to diffuse population where it is too dense and to concentrate it where it is too sparse; to substitute for the tenement house, homes surrounded by gardens, and to fully settle agricultural districts before people were driven far from neighbors to look for land. The people of the cities would thus get more of the pure air and sunshine of the country, the people of the country more of the economics and social life of the city. (p. 147)

Visionary planners such as Ebenezer Howard of London sought to create garden suburbs that would allow as many people as possible to enjoy the benefits of suburban living. In his 1898 study *Garden Cities of Tomorrow* (1902; repr. 1945), Howard argued that "town and country *must be married*, and out of this joyous union will spring a new hope, a new life, a new civilization" (p. 48).

Howard's garden-city idea was essentially a plan for moving individuals, as well as industry, out from the city center to provide a more healthful environment. He proposed construction of a town-country magnet that would draw people from cities and rural areas alike. Natural beauty, social opportunities, high wages, and low rents would draw residents to new garden cities. The garden city would be economically self-sufficient yet be at one with nature. Population would be restricted, and all residents would be provided with jobs within the bounds of the community.

Like Weber and George, Howard called for further suburbanization (deconcentration) so that more metropolitan residents could take advantage of the benefits of suburban living. Also in agreement was the urban reformer Frederic C. Howe. In *The City: The Hope of Democracy* (1905), a study of the future of the city in American society, he argued that suburbanization represented the democratic hope of the future.

As the first generation of academic social scientists began to examine and evaluate life in American metropolitan areas, they were struck with the improvements that suburbs brought to metropolitan life. During the 1920s political scientist Harlan Paul Douglass admired suburbs that combined the virtues of city and country: "It [the suburb] is the city trying to escape the consequences of being a city while still remaining a city. It is urban society trying to eat its cake and keep it, too" (*The Suburban Trend,* p. 4).

This is not to say that suburban living was idyllic. It was often lonely—especially for women—and the challenge of maintaining city standards in suburban areas was often overwhelming. William Dean Howells wrote of many of the pitfalls of suburban living in his 1875 *Suburban Sketches*: "In town your fancy would turn to the theaters; in the country you would occupy yourself with cares of poultry or of stock: in the suburb you can but sit upon your threshold, and fight the predatory mosquito."

Other critics of suburbs focused much of their attention on its governance. In 1933 Roderick McKenzie viewed suburban government as "little short of disastrous" and noted that "every great city now has around it a metropolitan area, one with it economically and socially but without political unity" (*The Metropolitan Community,* p. 303). Many critics followed in his footsteps.

More recent historians have added a great deal to our knowledge of suburbs in the late nineteenth and early twentieth centuries. Many case studies have been completed. Warner's *Streetcar Suburbs* stands as a seminal work in the burgeoning subfield of suburban history. As Michael Ebner noted, it was "the first book by an urban historian to examine systematically the suburban tradition" ("Re-Reading Suburban America," p. 228). It served as an important model for subsequent studies.

Several of Warner's arguments were particularly important in setting an agenda for research in suburban history. First, Warner widened the scope of suburban research to include urban neighborhoods that were once suburban. He also felt that nineteenth-century Bostonians' desire for suburban homes was rooted in a rural ideal. In most basic terms, according to this ideal, the country is home to what is good about America, while the city harbors much that is bad. Second, Warner argued that the first suburbs in the United States emerged in the late nineteenth century, with the outward reach of streetcars that enabled the middle class to move from the city center. He argued that the streetcar suburbs were organized along class lines—not by the ethnic enclaves found within neighborhoods closer to the city center. Warner also found that these suburban communities were the result of thousands of individual decisions—not some large-scale plan—to build and settle within the distinct areas of Dorchester, West Roxbury, and Roxbury. Finally, Warner lamented the passing of annexation movements and the rise of politically fragmented metropolitan areas.

Later studies, responding to Warner's arguments, often refined, and sometimes disagreed with, his interpretations. Some found patterns similar to those in Roxbury, Dorchester, and West Roxbury with the arrival of the streetcar and subsequent suburban development. Henry D. Shapiro and Zane L. Miller found that Clifton, a Cincinnati suburb, resembled Warner's suburbs, with growth tied to transportation advances and a subsequent annexation to the city. Joel A. Tarr traced the growing segregation of work and residence in nineteenth-century Pittsburgh, tying this closely to transportation improvements.

By looking at two Boston suburbs, Cambridge and Somerville, Henry C. Binford found that suburban growth took place decades before the arrival of the streetcar. Thus suburbanization there had not depended on the evolution of transportation. While Warner proclaimed the late nineteenth century "the first suburban era," Binford has shown quite convincingly that Cambridge and Somerville were suburbs and commuter havens in the decades before the Civil War.

Another study that focuses on Boston suburbs is *Shaky Palaces* (1984) by Matthew Edel, Elliott Sclar, and Daniel Luria. Taking issue with Warner's view that the building process was the result of thousands of individual decisions, these authors argue that "the building of homes is not the only phase of the building of suburbs. Providing transport access and utilities, and subdividing the farms and woods for small-scale builders to purchase, are also a part of the suburban process."

The United States has become overwhelmingly suburban. Between 1950 and 1970, 83% of the nation's total growth took place in suburbs.

Ronald Dale Karr examined yet another Boston suburb, Brookline, which contrasts strongly with Warner's suburbs. Its residents were wealthier and supported an activist government that rejected annexation. Karr found that the suburban government guided development by selectively withholding services, and that developers used restrictive covenants to shape the communities they were founding. These forces were not apparent in Dorchester, Roxbury, and West Roxbury.

Carol A. O'Connor, in her study of Scarsdale, New York, found that the village government was engaged in actively shaping the community through construction regulations. Zane Miller's study of Forest Park, a twentieth-century Cincinnati suburb, explored the important interaction between developers, local government, and residents in shaping the community.

Post-World War II Suburbs

Although suburbs do have a long history in the context of metropolitan areas across the United States, the explosion in suburban growth after World War II eclipsed much of the earlier growth. Between 1950 and 1970 the suburban population more than doubled, from thirty-six million to seventy-four million. In the fifteen largest metropolitan areas in 1980, the majority of the population lived in suburbs (with the exception of Houston, where only 45 percent of the population lived in suburbs).

There are many reasons for this tremendous growth. As in the earlier periods of suburban growth, transportation innovations spurred new outward expansion from city centers. The automobile and, more important, the superhighway transformed local transportation and settlement patterns across metropolitan areas. Although the federal highway program, including its capstone 1956 Interstate Highway Act, was aimed not at cities, but at connecting them with one another and with rural areas, subsequent highway development transformed the suburban landscape. Public transit went into a permanent decline as the ratio of citizens to registered passenger automobiles dropped from 1,078:1 in 1905 to 4:1 in 1950 to 2:1 in 1970.

Between 1950 and 1970 America's suburban population more than doubled, going from thirty-six million to seventy-four million.

Another important reason for the post-World War II suburban boom was the predominance of Federal Housing Administration (FHA) and Veterans Administration (VA) insured-loan programs, which made it less expensive to own a home than to rent in many metropolitan areas. Before the FHA began operation, individuals generally had to put down between one-third and one-half of the property cost. With FHA the down payment necessary for most homes dropped to under 10 percent, lowering a tremendous barrier to home ownership. Between 1934 and 1972 the percentage of American families owning homes jumped from 44 percent to 63 percent. In addition, although the FHA and VA did not lend money to developers, their loan assurances for home buyers allowed developers to borrow the extremely large sums of money necessary to construct large suburban tracts such as those of Levitt and Sons. The FHA also established minimum standards for home construction. Most homes built to FHA and VA standards had central heating, indoor plumbing, telephones, and several major appliances.

Both the FHA and VA insured-loan programs fueled new building in suburban areas. FHA insurance went to new residential developments, primarily in suburban areas (or outlying districts within some cities). In establishing criteria for underwriting home loans, the FHA made it virtually impossible to receive their insurance within older city neighborhoods. Jackson notes that in a sample of 241 new homes insured by the FHA in metropolitan Saint Louis (1935–1939), 91 percent were located in the suburbs.

This dramatic shift from city to suburb in metropolitan areas across the country affected many social and cultural trends. Young white people, through the VA and FHA insured-loan programs, were able to purchase homes far away from their families in city neighborhoods. Women, however, were particularly isolated from the world of work and employment opportunities, as Gwendolyn Wright notes, and this led to many frustrations and problems. Perhaps no one has set out those frustrations more clearly than Betty Friedan in her 1963 book, *The Feminine Mystique*.

Another striking characteristic of suburban growth in the post-World War II period has been its racial segregation. That is, suburbs in metropolitan areas across the United States have been inhabited largely by whites. For instance, during the 1960s in Chicago, 287,000 white families moved to suburban areas; only 13,261 black families obtained residences in a six-county area outside the city. This segregation persisted despite growing numbers of black families in suburban areas during the 1970s and 1980s. In 1980 the proportion of suburban blacks in the United States reached 23.3 percent.

This continuing segregation may stem in part from actions of the federal government. Jackson uncovered important connections between the FHA and VA insured-loan programs and residential segregation in the decades since 1930. He found that FHA underwriters "supported the income and racial segregation of suburbia" (*Crabgrass Frontier*, p. 13). Before racial covenants were outlawed by the U.S. Supreme Court in the 1948 *Shelley v. Kraemer* decision, the FHA openly recommended them. The FHA insurers also shied away from any neighborhoods that lacked "economic stability" or "protection from adverse conditions." These were means of redlining whole areas of center cities, many of which were minority occupied.

Compounding this residential segregation has been the shifting nature of occupational structure in metropolitan areas across the United States. While suburbs have been home to industry and business from their beginnings, there was a remarkable shift in manufacturing activity in the years after World War II. Between 1947 and 1967, 293,307 manufacturing jobs (4 percent) were lost by central cities in Standard Metropolitan Statistical Areas (SMSAs—areas with populations greater than one hundred thousand in 1960). At the same time, manufacturing employment in the suburbs increased by 3,902,326 (a 94 percent increase). The suburban share of SMSA manufacturing employment increased from 36 percent in 1947 to 53 percent in 1967. This suburbanization of certain job opportunities has been particularly disadvantageous for the minority groups, who have limited access to suburban residential areas.

A Postsuburban Era?

Does "suburb" remain a usable word in the 1990s? Many historians and journalists think not. "Exurbia," "outer city," edge city," and "technoburb" are among recently coined terms to describe recent varieties of suburbs and/or their predominant trends. The suburb, once a hallmark of modernity, may have become an anachronism.

No one better explores this question than Robert Fishman in *Bourgeois Utopias* (1987). He argues that "suburb" is no longer a useful description of contemporary America: "To me the massive rebuilding that began in 1945 represents not the culmination of the 200 year history of suburbia but rather its end. Indeed, this massive change is not suburbanization at all but the creation of a new kind of city, with principles that are directly opposed to the true suburb" (p. 183). In contrast with suburbs, which were closely tied to central cities, Fishman finds "technoburbs." A technoburb is a peripheral zone, possibly as large as a county, that operates as a viable socioeconomic unit. The boundaries of a technoburb are defined by the locations that can be accessed easily by car:

> Spread out along its highway growth corridors are shopping malls, industrial parks, campuslike office complexes, hospitals, schools, and a full range of housing types. Its residents look to their immediate surroundings rather than to the city for their jobs and other needs; and its industries find not only the employees they need but also the specialized services. (p. 184)

While less definitive about the end of a "suburban era," Jackson also sees fundamental changes ahead, perhaps a postsuburban age. With urban gentrification and a rural renaissance, Jackson posits in *Crabgrass Frontier*, "that the long process of suburbanization, which has been operative in the United States since about 1815, will slow over the next two decades" (p. 297).

Whatever the future, the fact remains that the physical shell of suburbanization—including housing, schools, commercial centers, transportation, and other infrastructure improvements—will remain with us for years to come. Suburbanization as a process may come to an end, but we will continue to live with what past generations have built.

In addition, one of the most dramatic characteristics of suburbanization—its ability to create relatively homogeneous local units within larger heterogeneous regions—does not appear to be loosing its hold. The technoburbs that Fishman identifies no longer look to central cities, but they still purposefully exclude those enterprises, peoples, and activities deemed inappropriate by law and custom. Continued political fragmentation further strengthens the power of these relatively homogeneous local units, just as it did in the past. In short, while suburbs have changed dramatically, we will not soon be rid of their physical manifestations; nor has new outlying development abandoned all suburban characteristics.

[See also The Culture of Consumption; Geographic Mobility; Landscapes; Mass Culture and Its Critics; Technology and Social Change; Transportation and Mobility.]

BIBLIOGRAPHY

General Works

Blumin, Stuart M. "The Center Cannot Hold: Historians and the City." *Journal of Policy History* 2, no. 1 (1990).

Dolce, Philip C., ed. *Suburbia: The American Dream and Dilemma* (1976).

Douglass, Harlan Paul. *The Suburban Trend* (1925).

Ebner, Michael H. "Re-reading Suburban America: Urban Population Deconcentration, 1810–1980." In *American Urbanism: A Historiographical Review*, edited by Howard Gillette, Jr., and Zane L. Miller (1987).

Fishman, Robert. *Bourgeois Utopias: The Rise and Fall of Suburbia* (1987).

Goldfield, David R., and Blaine A. Brownell. *Urban America: From Downtown to No Town* (1979).

Jackson, Kenneth T. *Crabgrass Frontier: The Suburbanization of the United States* (1985).

Mohl, Raymond A. *The New City: Urban America in the Industrial Age, 1860–1920* (1985).

Muller, Peter O. *Contemporary Suburban America* (1981).

O'Connor, Carol A. "The Suburban Mosaic: Patterns of Land Use, Class, and Culture." In *American Urbanism: A Historiographical Review*, edited by Howard Gillette, Jr., and Zane L. Miller (1987).

Stilgoe, John R. *Borderland: Origins of the American Suburb, 1820–1939* (1988).

Tarr, Joel. "From City to Suburb: The 'Moral' Influence of Transportation Technology." In *American Urban History: An Interpretative Reader with Commentaries*, edited by Alexander B. Callow, Jr. 2d. ed. (1973).

Teaford, Jon C. *City and Suburb: The Political Fragmentation of Metropolitan America, 1850–1970* (1979).

Case Studies

Arnold, Joseph L. *The New Deal in the Suburbs: A History of the Greenbelt Town Program, 1935–1954* (1971).

Berry, Brian J. L., Carole A. Goodwin, Robert W. Lake, and Katherine B. Smith. "Attitudes Toward Integration: The Role of Status in Community Response to Racial Change." In *The Changing Face of the Suburbs*, edited by Barry Schwartz (1976).

Binford, Henry C. *The First Suburbs: Residential Communities on the Boston Periphery, 1815–1860* (1985).

Ebner, Michael H. *Creating Chicago's North Shore: A Suburban History* (1988).

Edel, Matthew, Elliott D. Sclar, and Daniel Luria. *Shaky Palaces: Homeownership and Social Mobility in Boston's Suburbanization* (1984).

Gans, Herbert. *The Levittowners: Ways of Life and Politics in a New Suburban Community* (1967).

Karr, Ronald Dale. "Brookline and the Making of an Elite Suburb." *Chicago History* 13, no. 2 (1984).

Kasarda, John D. "The Changing Occupational Structure of the American Metropolis: Apropos the Urban Problem." In *The Changing Face of the Suburbs*, edited by Barry Schwartz (1976).

Keating, Ann Durkin. *Building Chicago: Suburban Developers and the Creation of a Divided Metropolis* (1988).

Miller, Zane L. *Suburb: Neighborhood and Community in Forest Park, Ohio, 1935–1976* (1981).

O'Connor, Carol A. *A Sort of Utopia: Scarsdale, 1891–1981* (1983).

Shapiro, Henry A., and Zane L. Miller. *Clifton: Neighborhood and Community in an Urban Setting* (1976).

Warner, Sam Bass, Jr. *Streetcar Suburbs: The Process of Growth in Boston, 1870–1900* (1962).

— ANN DURKIN KEATING

T

TECHNOLOGY AND SOCIAL CHANGE

Manufacturing America: The Seventeenth Century

Modern vessels brought the first European settlers to the New World. Brightly colored and round-sterned, these caravel-built ships were among the most sophisticated products of European technology. Though the early colonists traveled to North America in relative comfort on seaworthy ships, they faced very different circumstances once they landed. Inclement weather, death, and disease were now their constant companions. Relations with Indians often were poor, and European shipping was frequently disrupted by shipwrecks and pirates. The first British colonists had to rely on their Old World technical skills to stay alive.

An abundance of fertile land, much of it forest, was cleared and cultivated. Trees furnished the primary building material and fuel, and were a source of naval stores. The continent's rivers and streams provided water for drinking—and waste disposal—facilitated transportation inland by pole boats, barges, and ships, and supplied an important source of power.

Colonization was understood by the European nation-states that invested in expeditions and by the explorers themselves as a business relationship. A primary goal of the mercantilism that led to the business relationship was to accumulate wealth (which was thought to be finite), and a primary means of doing this was discovering natural resources and converting them—by means of the technologies involved in shipping (as in spices), processing (fabrics), and mining (gems), for example—into products that could be exported at a profit. Imports were discouraged because the payments for them left the nation-state's jurisdiction. Obviously, then, the nation-states that invested in colonization expected to benefit financially, as did the colonists themselves (though not necessarily equally). Investor nation-states issued colonists a charter granting them exclusive privilege to settle or trade in an area, and expected in return to secure a percentage of the profits or to collect taxes in the settled area. As the colonies evolved from tenuous settlements governed locally by closed commercial corporations into financial powers in their own right, the balance of power implicit in these early agreements became a source of conflict that in many ways shaped the course of technological development.

THE MILL. Mills were crucial for large-scale production, and on a smaller scale they were among the first structures erected in pioneering settlements and served as the foci of rural communities. Because the New World possessed an abundance of land and minerals but a shortage of labor, success in attracting colonists to unsettled regions improved markedly when mills were established to ease work burdens.

Mills harnessed continuous motion in useful form. Animals or humans turned the simplest mills by walking in a circle or on a treadmill. Windmills were especially common in the early 1600s. Neither type of mill proved ideal, however: the former demanded investment in human labor or in beasts of burden, while the wind's capriciousness limited the latter. Water mills were more reliable and powerful, and settlers capitalized on the New World's plentiful streams and rivers.

An extraordinary variety and number of mills dotted the colonial landscape. Gristmills appeared on plantations as early as 1617, in Jamestown in 1621, in Massachusetts in 1628, and in virtually every community soon thereafter. They were highly prized for the time and labor saved, as well as for the improved quality of flour or meal produced. Rural sawmills proved nearly as desirable: clearing land provided colonists a ready supply of logs for fuel and shelter, and sawmills speeded and eased the cutting of logs for firewood and timbers.

Mills' importance in the life and economy of the colonies marked those who built and repaired them, the millwrights, as the New World's most valued artisans. Like most colonial artisans, many millwrights learned their trade through the Old World master-apprentice system, which colonists adapted to the New World's abundant resources and critical shortages of artisans and labor. They blurred the lines among apprentices, journeymen, and masters, and generally accelerated and informalized the apprenticeship process.

THE TECHNOLOGY OF NECESSITIES. The overwhelming majority of colonists lived on their own land or rented it, grew their own food, and made their own cloth and tools. The virgin New World soil was forgiving and seemed to require neither regular fertilization nor careful rotation of crops. Thus plantations dominated the southern agricultural scene by 1700, while small farms, usually from ten to two hundred acres (four to eighty hectares) were typical of the Middle Atlantic and New England colonies. Agricultural practices and implements of both areas were fundamentally similar. Blacksmiths, the most numerous colonial metalworkers, used charcoal-fired hearths, bellows, tongs, anvils, and hammers to fashion a wide assortment of agricultural implements. The earliest settlers used pickaxes, hoes, and spades to break the soil. Plows appeared regularly from the 1640s on, but many northern farmers could not afford them. Their lands often were tilled by other farmers who had purchased a plow made in the colonies or in England.

Colonists transformed plants and animal skins into cloth and leather by means of processes that, until the late eighteenth century, remained virtually identical to those employed by rural Europeans. Both men and women participated in the time-consuming processes of making clothing: men sheared sheep, skinned animals, and gathered fibrous material from flax; women cleaned wool and flax, and spun yarn and thread. Both sexes operated the family's hand loom, which because of its size, often stood in a barn or shed. Like spinning wheels, these locally built looms remained similar in design to those built for centuries in Europe.

Fulling was the only cloth-making operation done outside the home; woolen fabric was sent to a fulling mill for finishing. These mills, known in Europe since the Middle Ages, became almost as widespread as gristmills and sawmills. Unlike the latter, they were not essential to survival or easing daily burdens, so their rapid proliferation indicates that rural communities desired and could sustain enterprises not directly linked to their immediate survival.

New Englanders favored woolen clothing to protect them from the elements, while Southerners opted for cool linen (cotton did not become important until the late eighteenth century); neither group used one fabric exclusively, though. Use of both materials required colonials to master two quite different technologies.

Unlike cloth, leather goods were made entirely by artisans. Leather's durability and suppleness were prized for harnesses, aprons, breeches, saddles, and especially shoes and boots, and its manufacture was well established in New World settlements by the mid seventeenth century. Unlike textile industries, however, tanning produced terrible smells, so tanneries were situated only on the fringes of settlements, far from population concentrations.

Most seventeenth-century technical activities were small enough that they could be established even in sparsely inhabited rural settlements. The largest of colonial enterprises, iron manufacture and shipbuilding, deviated from that pattern: both were pursued in limited areas, involved a range of craftsmen, and served distant communities. Both took advantage of raw materials abundant in the New World but scarce in England, and thereby reduced colonial and English imports. They were manifestations of the mercantile philosophy in action.

Beyond Subsistence: The Eighteenth Century

As the English had hoped, the colonial economy moved from subsistence to surplus in the eighteenth century: colonists began to export surpluses of several commodities in short supply in the Old World (including beer, flour, and shoes). Agricultural surpluses helped support the populations necessary for increased colonial iron production and shipbuilding, and for the expanding mercantile centers of the New World.

PRINTING. The export-generated interest in nonlocal affairs produced local markets for information about other settlements and areas that were fed by the mid-eighteenth-century rise of colonial presses and newspapers. By 1763 colonial master printers operated some forty presses, published at least a dozen newspapers, and issued thousands of pamphlets. This communications boom was furthered by the end of colonial printers' dependence on European raw materials. Benjamin Franklin provided financial support for several journeymen printers to establish their own print shops and, more important, reigned from the mid 1730s as the largest supplier of white linen rags, the essential ingredient in paper. He proved equally adept at ensuring the availability of ink.

The significance of communication to the mid-eighteenth-century colonial mind is evident in the colonists' resistance to three acts that the British Parliament passed. The Sugar Act of 1764, which levied taxes on sugar, coffee, molasses, and wine, posed a potent challenge to public drinking establishments. The Stamp Act of 1765 taxed colonial newspapers, pamphlets, almanacs, and playing cards. The Townshend Acts of 1767 endangered the colonial papermaking industry and teahouses. These acts seemed to be an effort to transform the colonies from full, if unequal, partners into serfs, and the colonists' vehement response opened a new chapter in the imperial relationship: a boycott of English products, which fortified many extant colonial industries and spawned new ones.

MANUFACTURE OF ARMS. After 4 July 1776, each newly emancipated state initially pursued its own course against the common foe: their contributions to the Continental Congress and Continental Army were secondary to each state's efforts to ensure its own defense and to encourage production of a full range of war supplies within its borders. Most offered inducements—bounties, land, freedom from taxation—for the manufacture of gunpowder, cannons, and guns; and all exempted from military service gunsmiths, cannon makers, shot and shell casters, papermakers, and gunpowder manufacturers. Only with the ratification of the Articles of Confederation (1781) did the states concede that in war their interests were virtually indistinguishable, and only then did they begin actively to provide for the common defense. Congress's creation of armories and factories for ordnance at Carlisle, Pennsylvania, Springfield, Massachusetts, West Point, New York, and New London, Virginia, was a product of that concession.

Of the necessary war ordnance, colonists were most familiar with firearms manufacture. Gunsmithing had been an established colonial trade, and its practitioners quickly geared up for the conflict. Colonists also had extensive experience producing gunpowder, but only two of its ingredients, charcoal and sulfur, were plentiful in America; the third, saltpeter, was in short supply (most was purchased from France). By contrast, Americans were relatively unacquainted with cannons. They seized British armaments and (especially after 1777) purchased French cannons. These two sources proved sufficient to provide Americans with a supply of mobile artillery.

TECHNOLOGY AFTER THE REVOLUTION. Not until 1790 was technology defined as a common concern by the colonies-turned-states. In that year Congress created a patent board (which ruled on priority of inventions and granted inventors monopolistic rights for specified periods); a few years later it established the United States Mint, and sought to develop a standard of weights and measures.

That Congress should regulate commerce and manufacturing was without question, according to mercantile theory. What this meant in practical terms sparked great debate. Secretary of the Treasury Alexander Hamilton emerged as the most notable advocate of large-scale, direct federal intervention. In his "Report on Manufactures," submitted to Congress in December 1791, Hamilton compared manufactures to agriculture, arguing that both remained critical to the public weal, but that manufacturing held some wealth-accruing advantages. Hamilton maintained that manufacturing increased workers' skills, expanded the number of producers (by including women and children), allowed machinery to reduce the drudgery of heavy labor, fostered recognition of talent and enhanced productivity, encouraged wealth-producing immigration, and enlarged and stabilized demand for the nation's agricultural products, thus ensuring farmers consistent, fair prices. Although most of Hamilton's recommendations were in line with established mercantile theory, much of his report horrified many Americans. Among them was Thomas Jefferson, who was not opposed to manufacturing per se but detested the huge European factories and the teeming industrial cities they bred—and feared that Hamilton's scheme would reproduce the corrupt European System in America.

Although the anti-Hamiltonians offered no formal alternative to his report, they prevailed in Congress and effectively impeded any active federal role in fostering manufacturing. Initiative rested on private citizens' shoulders, in particular several local associations to promote manufacturing (which predated Hamilton's report).

The United States had emerged as a serious economic rival to Europe less than two hundred years after the first permanent English settlement. North American inhabitants had combined New World abundances and Old World technologies to go beyond subsistence, to enter the export trade, and, by the late eighteenth century, to begin to frame larger (albeit still modest) commercial and manufacturing objectives.

Young America and Individual Opportunity: 1800 to the 1830s

BEYOND MERCANTILISM. After about 1800, Americans surveyed their abundant lands and natural resources and increasingly emphasized progress, development, and growth—which technology would be instrumental in fulfilling. Put simply, where eighteenth-century Americans focused on the whole in these efforts, their nineteenth-century counterparts concentrated on the parts—of which the individual was the fundamental unit. This social calculation is evident in the organization, conduct, and explanation of technological enterprises—in particular the emergence of a new kind of business entity, the corporation, which (with family partnerships) became the predominant form of large-scale manufacturing and commerce. (Unlike the previous centuries' joint-stock companies, plantations, and town governments, early-nineteenth-century corporations functioned as individuals.)

BUILDING THE NATION'S INFRASTRUCTURE: TRANSPORTATION. A building boom swept early-nineteenth-century America, resulting in a spate of turnpikes, canals, bridges, and railroads that, taken together, linked the West more securely to the East and seaboard cities with those inland, joined producers and markets, and generally facilitated travel, commerce, and communications. Although this boom stemmed in part from the recognition that individual opportunity and economic development went hand in hand, the federal government played a crucial role in the infrastructural revolution. As part of its constitutionally mandated responsibility to provide for the national defense, it improved harbors and seacoast fortifications, built the

National Road, and provided numerous topographical surveys. The Army Corps of Engineers, stationed at West Point, planned and executed these works.

Most colonial roadways had been unimproved pathways kept clear of underbrush only by traffic, so the adaptation of the turnpike, a type of roadway common in Europe, constituted a major commercial innovation. By the mid 1810s, Americans had built several hundred-mile or longer stretches of these for-profit tollways. Because early-nineteenth-century American commercial vehicles had no standardized form, turnpikes needed to accommodate different kinds of traffic traveling at different speeds. A wide turnpike with plenty of room for passing was the American solution.

Improved river travel, which formerly had been limited to poled and rowed vessels, required neither large construction expenditures nor laborers and materials but inventors and inventions. By 1807 Robert Fulton's *North River* (often incorrectly called the *Clermont*) was steaming on the Hudson River between New York City and Albany. Elsewhere, the Louisiana Purchase of 1803 had opened the port of New Orleans to Americans, and the Mississippi, Missouri, and Ohio rivers seemed to provide natural routes to tap and settle the nation's interior. With the exception of the Orleans territory, however, western states and territories favored competition for their trade and refused to grant Fulton and his partner, Robert Livingston, monopolistic privileges. Due to technical problems—notably the inability to move upstream against western rivers' swift currents—his "atmospheric" Steamboats were soon superseded by the lighter and vastly more powerful high-pressure steamboats, the first of which was introduced in 1816 by Henry M. Shreve. In less than a decade more than two-thirds of the western steamboats used high-pressure steam engines; by 1830 some two hundred steamboats were in operation in the West.

A building boom swept early nineteenth-century America, resulting in a spate of turnpikes, canals, bridges, and railroads that, taken together, linked the West more securely to the East.

Canals were perhaps the most spectacular of the early-nineteenth-century internal improvements. America's first canals, built in New England in the 1780s, were patterned after the English canals of the 1760s. They traversed short, straight, level distances, and (like those of the nineteenth century) were bordered by towpaths from which horse or mule teams could pull special flat-bottomed canal boats.

New York's decision to build the Erie Canal joining Albany to Buffalo on Lake Erie sparked the canal boom. Constructed between 1817 and 1825 (at a cost of more than seven million dollars) as a means for New York to counter New Orleans's growing commercial influence, it dwarfed all preceding American canals with its 363-mile-long and four-foot-deep channel and 84 locks. Although the towage speed averaged less than two miles per hour, freight charges on the canal were reduced to one-twentieth of the overland price.

Canals began to proliferate across the nation. Prior to 1815 Americans had built fewer than 100 canal miles; during the next twenty-five years more than $125 million was spent on nearly 3,100 canal miles.

Railways were the last of the early-nineteenth-century transportation initiatives. The first American railways—in Massachusetts (1826) and the Mauch Chunk Road in Pennsylvania (1827)—were (like earlier British railroads) horse-drawn, single-purpose railways used to transport large granite blocks from quarries. Not until 1827 did the Maryland legislature charter the general-purpose railway, the Baltimore and the Ohio. These first general-purpose railways, much like canals and turnpikes in their purpose, organization, and design, were treated as common roads, open to anyone who paid tolls and used proper cars. Their advocates—for example, the states and municipalities that sponsored them—boasted that they were faster than canal travel, were not subject to freezing in winter, and were flood- and drought-resistant.

With the advent of the steam-powered locomotive (also of British origin), railway lines began to proliferate across America: from twenty-eight operating miles in 1830 to more than twenty-three hundred in 1839. Construction techniques used to build canals and turnpikes facilitated this growth to a certain extent, but the new locomotives, whose power was generated in high-pressure boilers, gave rise to a new set of problems. Although the British had discovered in 1810 that the wheels of their earliest locomotives slipped continuously because of excessive power (not from the contact of frictionless surfaces), the new technology was still malleable enough that American designers experimented, for example, with rails made of stone, wood, and iron-plated wood before finally settling on iron. These problems, though, paled before the advance represented by the steam locomotive: in 1836 William Norris (1802–1867), the owner of a Philadelphia engine factory, demonstrated that a locomotive could easily run up a grade as steep as 363 feet per mile. For the first time mechanized transportation seemed able to overcome even difficult terrain.

CHANGES IN MANUFACTURING AND LABOR. Early-nineteenth-century manufacturers continued to borrow heavily from European technology. Immigrants and industrial espionage brought European practices and techniques, especially machinery, to America. For the most part, though, Americans used waterwheels, not steam engines, to power their manufacturing machines.

The explosive growth of mills testifies to the proliferation of manufacturing in the early nineteenth century, while their relatively small power output—generally less than one hundred horsepower—indicates the modest size of most manufacturing establishments. Demand for millwrights far exceeded that in the colonial period, but machinery-dependent production also required a new type of craftsman/manufacturer—one who worked in a machine shop, fashioning devices from wood and metal to fit individual specifications and repairing broken machines. Because completed machinery was often unwieldy to transport, machine shops were usually located near manufacturing complexes and on transportation routes. The number of machine shops increased markedly through 1830, but their form remained essentially unchanged. These single-room operations rarely employed more than fifteen men and were equipped with hand- or foot-powered lathes, workbenches with vises and grindstones, and assorted hammers, chisels, and files. Larger establishments, often called "works," combined a machine shop and foundry (for castings, rods, and sheet metal), a drafting room, a pattern storeroom, a blacksmith shop, and an assembly room. They sometimes employed as many as fifty men in their machine shops and produced larger items, such as steam engines.

Although most Americans continued to sew their own clothing, fewer wove their own cloth. They no longer needed to because textile manufacturing was the most significant consumer industry to mechanize: carding engines, spinning jennies, water frames, mules, throttles, and power looms became integral parts of the early-nineteenth-century American textile industry.

As textile manufacturers shifted to machine production, they reduced labor costs by hiring less skilled or unskilled workers, or even children. Adult American textile workers' wages were from 30 to 50 percent higher than those of their European counterparts.

As with other technological advances, the development of textile machine shops was made possible by the introduction of British textile machines, which had been invented some decades earlier. Americans had sought to pirate these machines almost as soon as they were created, but Samuel Slater (1768–1835), an English cotton-spinning mill manager who emigrated in 1789, was the first to produce workable devices in America.

Early spinning and weaving mills were dwarfed by the textile venture undertaken by Francis Cabot Lowell (1775–1817) and other Boston merchants. They erected a huge textile factory on the lower Merrimack River—which provided ten thousand horsepower by means of dams and races of unprecedented size and scope—that was connected to Boston, twenty miles away, by the Middlesex Canal. This venture also provided an opportunity for an experiment in social technology. Lowell's visits to Robert Owen's (1771–1858) New Lanark cotton mills in Scotland suggested to him that, in addition to sizable profits, large manufacturing ventures could provide character-building opportunities for workers. Lowell Mills opened in 1823 and employed mostly rural New England women between the ages of seventeen and twenty-four. The mills were founded on a belief that individual success rested on mental discipline and moral management—character—which repetition and regimentation would inculcate, and which workers' dormitories supervised by matrons would guarantee. Although the unprofitable Lowell social experiment was abandoned soon after 1835—it continued to operate with immigrant labor—larger mills (without democratic, utopian pretensions) became common in the mid nineteenth century along rivers in Massachusetts, New Hampshire, and Maine.

REDUCING LABOR COSTS; WORKERS' RESPONSES. Extensive machine use, however, was hardly the only method early-nineteenth-century entrepreneurs adopted to trim labor costs of large-scale production. Machines made no inroads into shoe manufacture, for example, but replacing well-paid artisans with lower-paid semiskilled labor, much of it female, reduced costs drastically and made American shoes highly competitive in the world market. Early nineteenth-century American artisans in various trades vehemently protested employers' attempts to replace artisans with less skilled laborers in order to keep wages low and to lengthen workdays. These workers' parties never managed to dominate the American political scene and disappeared almost as suddenly as they began, due in great part to their internal battles for control. More traditional parties co-opted many of their proposals, and by 1840 they ceased to exist.

Mechanics' Institutes were another, more moderate response to the social effects of America's industrialization. Although these institutes—which functioned as de facto vocational schools—were based on earlier British institutions, they scarcely resembled them. Americans identified as "mechanics" almost all urban workingmen except merchants and bankers. The institutes' motto—"knowledge to all seeking it"—reflected a commitment to a large segment of the population, dissatisfaction with colleges as bastions of the privileged, and an attack on guilds as well as other restrictive societies.

Americans expressed much less anxiety over the rapid mechanization of industry than did the English, for example. In Britain, "Luddite" protesters broke machines and others decried machinery's effects.

America as a Social Unit: The 1830s to the 1870s

By the 1840s many Americans, especially the middle class, celebrated the symbols of progress. They embraced technology as a means to further unify America. Improved transportation and communication technologies—expanded railroads coupled with telegraphy—bound city with country, state with nation. Clipper ships joined ports, steam railroads connected cities and suburbs, and omnibuses and horse-drawn street railways linked various districts within each city. Mid-century technologies also permitted Americans to tap the nation's natural resources in new ways, at new locations, and on a grander scale. Water remained the dominant source of power, but coal- and wood-fueled steampower began to make inroads, which freed enterprising manufacturers from their dependence on rivers and streams. Factories began to spread into previously impractical areas and soon blanketed the nation. Some entrepreneurs recognized that the idea of a unified, homogenized America implied a nationwide market—a common material experience—and they geared their establishments to supply that demand. They introduced new production techniques, established the factory as the quintessential industrial locus, and distributed their products nationwide over the new transportation routes. They also devised new promotional strategies to demonstrate to a sometimes skeptical public the intrinsically American quality of themselves, their products, and their production methods.

Early nineteenth-century artisans in various trades vehemently protested employers' attempts to replace artisans with less skilled laborers using machinery in order to keep wages low and to lengthen workdays.

PROVIDING A COMMON MATERIAL EXPERIENCE. Demand for a common material experience understood as "American" proved so compelling that consumers welcomed nationally distributed goods even as local factories suffered. National distribution is especially evident in mid-nineteenth-century food industries: Buffalo and Rochester became national flour-milling centers, and Baltimore, then Cincinnati, and finally Chicago dominated the pork trade. This demand was likewise evident in manufactured products: New England emerged as the nation's textile center, and Cyrus McCormick (1809–1884) and Isaac Singer (1811–1875) successfully marketed reapers and sewing machines, respectively, nationwide. Yet it would be mistaken to assume that each firm with national aspirations adopted an identical approach to marketing, or that identical goods were distributed throughout the nation. Production techniques and sales strategies differed drastically among manufacturers, as generally did the quality—and sometimes even the style—of goods produced by a single firm and distributed nationally under a single name. Indeed, furnishing a common material experience required industrialists only to *convince* purchasers of the uniformity of goods or interchangeability of parts, whether or not this was the case. Uniformity could be accomplished in several ways: brand names (a company's reputation as guarantor of similarity) and identification of product type (familiarity of nomenclature as guarantor of similarity) were two common means. Perhaps the least characteristic mid-century way to provide a common material experience was through production of truly identical items.

This dream was realized at the army's Springfield Armory. Interchangeability generally depended on drop- or die-forging, but it also demanded special-purpose milling and/or planing machines, rationally designed jigs and fixtures, precision gauges, and employees both able and willing to apply the most exact standards. Interchangeability found its initial grand-scale application in the fully interchangeable Model 1841 percussion rifle and the Model 1842 percussion musket, both produced by the armory in 1847. Interchangeability required an exceedingly large capital investment and strict quality control. And if it originated from a governmental agency—the army—that was neither profitable nor accountable, this should come as no surprise. For the overwhelming majority of manufacturers uniformity, not interchangeability, ruled the day.

RAILROADS AND THE TELEGRAPH. Railroads quickly outstripped canals as the nation's primary overland transportation mode. In the two decades after 1840, Americans laid track totaling twenty-six thousand miles, while they abandoned as many canal miles as they built. Railroad construction focused in the Northeast and Old Northwest, often parallel to—and supplanting—established canal routes.

Railroads offered entrepreneurs the virtues of speed, all-weather dependability, and flexible as well as larger cargo capacities; their drawbacks were huge capital and maintenance costs for rails, locomotives, and rolling stock. Despite these expenses, the overwhelming majority of prewar railroads were built and maintained with little or no governmental assistance. But the massive sums of money required investment arrangements more substantial than ad hoc consortia of local citizens.

Railroad expansion was facilitated by telegraphy, which offered almost instantaneous communication over long distances, permitting railroads to synchronize operations and thereby to prevent minor problems (like traffic jams) from becoming major ones. This telegraph-railroad nexus flowered after 1850, more than a decade after Samuel F. B. Morse (1791–1872) adapted electrical telegraphy, an older European invention, to American conditions-notably the country's great size (which made European multiple-circuit transmission prohibitively expensive). His high-speed single-circuit telegraph worked effectively and cheaply over long distances by transmitting signals in short relays.

The first experimental telegraph line was completed in 1844 along the Baltimore and the Ohio Railroad, which connected Baltimore and Washington. Only after 1852 did a railroad line—the Erie—employ telegraphy extensively, setting a precedent that led railroads and telegraphy to develop hand in hand for the remainder of the decade. Between 1852 and 1860, twenty-three thousand miles of telegraph lines were built. Most early telegraph companies failed; the survivors pooled resources in 1866 to create Western Union.

In 1869 the Central Pacific and Union Pacific railroads were joined at Promontory Point in the Utah territory to form the nation's first transcontinental railway. (A telegraph line had first joined the coasts in 1861.) This event both symbolized national unification and linked the East Coast commercial center of New York City with its West Coast counterpart, San Francisco.

THE FACTORY. The factory came to be identified around the mid nineteenth century as the characteristically American locus of large-scale production. Generally located on cities' fringes near railroad terminals, mid-century factories took on a form and function that differed from artisans' shops and from European manufacturing establishments. These large industrial facilities contained batteries of machines, foundries, or furnaces, employed large numbers of operators, and were driven by central power sources (either waterwheels or steam engines). Power was transmitted from such a source to upright iron shafts, then throughout a building by iron horizontal line shafts.

Mid-century factories produced more than uniform goods: routine factory life, which accompanied uniform production, made American factory workers more uniform than their predecessors. A common work experience was "manufactured" by employee-regulating work codes, which stressed responsibility, morality, and cleanliness. Those most adept at demonstrating their adaptation to these codes rose from the ranks to assume supervisory positions as foremen.

AGRICULTURE. Although mid-nineteenth-century Americans viewed factories as new to America, and felt free to define and orient these manufacturing facilities without regard to the past, farming had been a traditional enterprise, and any modification had to overcome centuries of tradition. Contemporaries advocated a new kind of farming—a machine-based agriculture that would emulate machine-based manufacturing—to make farming more rational and efficient. Mid-century agricultural societies sponsored thousands of farm implement competitions, and agricultural publications were awash with advertisements for advanced machines. These plows, drills, cultivators, and harvesters generally required animal or steam power and were constructed of iron or steel rather than of wood. Use of these implements, as well as neat, clean farms with rowed fields and soils prepared to a proper, nearly uniform texture, began to define the American farmer.

Generally located on the fringes of cities near railroad terminals, mid-century factories contained batteries of machines, foundries, or furnaces; employed a large number of operators; and were driven by central power sources.

INTERNATIONALIZATION. In the 1850s American business began to capitalize on the British-inspired international industrial exhibition to penetrate world markets. The first international exhibition was held in London in May 1851, in a remarkable building constructed for the event: a structure consisting of a modular iron frame covered with glass, named the Crystal Palace. American manufacturers entered about 500 exhibits—less than 3 percent of the total—and received roughly 3 percent of the 170 Council Awards (the exhibition's highest honor) and about 3.5 percent of the

2,918 prize medals. The McCormick reaper, Colt revolver, Robbins and Lawrence rifle, and Day and Newell safe were singled out for public acclaim. Other American prizewinners indicate the diversity of the entries: Charles Goodyear's vulcanized rubber products, Gail Borden's nutritious dried-meat biscuit, David Dick's antifriction punch press, and William C. Bond's astronomical clock. The country's exhibition showing reaffirmed that the nation had become, at least with respect to manufacturing, a full-fledged member of the industrial world. Its success encouraged a similar industrial contest in New York City in 1853.

America's prominence also led the British to establish in 1853 a special commission to investigate American arms manufacture. Committee members coined the term "the American System" to describe armory practice. To the British, the American System of manufacturing came to define the distinctly American civilization, though only a handful of American firms practiced it.

TRANSOCEANIC TELEGRAPHY. Acknowledgment that America operated in a world economy placed a premium on up-to-date international information. Prior to the mid 1860s, transoceanic crossings by ship were the sole source of this intelligence, and they began to seem much too slow.

Several Americans in the early 1850s proposed laying underwater telegraph cables to transmit information instantaneously between continents, but Cyrus W. Field (1819–1892) deserves the most credit. Field put together a consortium of Anglo-American investors to run a cable across the ocean floor from Newfoundland to Ireland. After several failures, the 1866 voyage proved successful, and on 27 July the telegraph linked the continents. The crews also managed to follow the previous year's cable and splice more on to finish the crossing. The second line opened on 1 September.

THE CIVIL WAR: A MASS EXPERIENCE. America's Civil War was striking for how little permanent change it brought about in northern industry and agriculture. The case was somewhat different in the South, which during the Civil War began to implement established northern practices: it built armories and powder mills to manufacture weapons, erected textile factories to make uniforms, laid railroad tracks to facilitate transportation, employed horse-drawn agricultural machines to increase food production, and started to tap Alabama's abundant iron ore and coal assets to produce iron.

The war itself provided a homogenizing material experience: Northern soldiers wore similar uniforms, used similar weapons, ate similar foods, and slept in similar facilities, as did their Southern counterparts. Civilian populations, Northern and Southern, also suffered roughly the same shortages and dislocations. The most significant technological effect of the war was the commonality it reinforced: it was the archetypical mass experience in an era distinguished by attempts to provide common experience.

Systematizing America: The 1870s to the 1920s

"System" was the touchstone of late-nineteenth- and early-twentieth-century America, and it influenced virtually every aspect of American life. Electrical and telephone systems dotted the nation's landscape, and electric traction systems coursed through cities. Mining and metalworking were systematized, as were factory production, agriculture, and even the professions.

THE ELECTRIFICATION OF AMERICA. The first practical, cost-efficient electric generators—dynamos—were produced in the 1870s by Europeans who applied principles discovered earlier in the century. Dynamos offered prospects for developing new commercial uses for inexpensive electricity. In the mid 1870s Charles Brush (1849–1929) realized that the brilliance of arc lights made them unsuitable for homes or businesses: their future would be outdoors, replacing gas street lamps. In 1879 he erected the nation's first central electric station to power twenty-two electric arc lamps in San Francisco. Within a year he had stations in New York, Philadelphia, and Boston, and more than five thousand arc lights in operation. Brush's success bred competition and yielded improvements.

Another significant innovation in the late nineteenth century was incandescent lighting, much of the credit for devising and manufacturing of which goes to Thomas Edison (1847–1931). Edison had acquired a reputation as an inventor par excellence before he produced his first incandescent lamp. His youthful experience as a telegraph operator provided rudimentary understanding of electrical principles and also introduced him to telegraph investors. Edison parlayed their backing and his prominence to assemble an impressive staff of technical associates and to stock extensive facilities. Rather than exploring the possibility of incandescence or developing a lamp, he simply assumed that incandescence was possible and focused on marketability and practicality. He saw that success depended on the ability of incandescence to supplant gas lighting indoors, and sought to create a direct-current (DC) system with as much illumination (about sixteen-candlepower) as gaslights, at a lower or equivalent price. By late 1881 Edison was ready to construct his first commercial central station on Pearl Street, in the heart of New York City's financial community. It began operation on 4 September 1882, and Edison distributed electricity free for the remainder of the year to induce reluctant New Yorkers to tap into the system.

Edison assumed that Pearl Street would be the first of hundreds of stations throughout America. He helped create a system of corporations to control future developments, with the Edison Electric Light Company, chartered in 1878, at the apex. No company could seriously challenge the Edison organization's preeminence in DC incandescent lighting. The competition came from another quarter: in 1886 George Westinghouse's (1846–1914) Westinghouse Lighting Company devised an alternating-current (AC) incandescent lighting system. By 1892, more than one thousand AC central stations were in operation.

Alternating current's advantage over direct current was the lower cost of transmission over distance; the difficulty of insulating wires and the public's fear of its high voltages were its disadvantages. Because DC worked well for heavily populated areas, whereas AC was best suited for thinly settled regions, Westinghouse and Edison tapped different markets. Early customers had been forced to choose which system to employ, but by 1900 there were devices to free them from that decision: rotary converters could change between AC and DC, for example, and motor-generator couplers could run on one type of electricity while supplying the other. This and the standardization of the electric systems allowed customers to select from a wide range those devices best suited to their particular needs.

The number of electric streetcars in America increased from 130 in 1888 to 8,000 in 1892; the electrification of street railway mileage increased from 16 percent in 1890 to 98 percent in 1903.

In the later nineteenth century, proponents of electric traction capitalized on the increasing population density of cities, and the division of urban space into distinct commercial, industrial, and residential neighborhoods, to push their new service. To be sure, they were not the first to profit from a desire to flee urban congestion, but electric traction overcame the disadvantages of steam commuter railroads, omnibus lines, and horse-drawn street railways. In 1888, 130 electric streetcars transported American urbanites; four years later, more than 8,000 provided that service. By 1890, 16 percent of American street railway mileage was electrified; by 1903, 98 percent.

DEVELOPMENT OF THE TELEPHONE. As with electric lighting, the development of the telephone in America graphically demonstrates both the centrality of systems in late-nineteenth-century thought and practice, and the debt that many late-century inventors and entrepreneurs owed to telegraphy. Alexander Graham Bell (1847–1922) proposed telephonic central stations and had labored to redesign telegraphic devices. Also like electric lighting, much of the telephone's early funding came from men experienced with telegraphy; unlike it, the telephone system competed directly with the telegraph and ultimately led to its demise.

Bell was passionately involved with speech, not with destroying telegraphy. In 1874 he developed a phonautograph, which converted sounds into written markings. In June 1875 came the breakthrough—the harmonic telegraph—for which Bell submitted a patent application on 14 February 1876. As an afterthought he scribbled notes about a battery telephone in the margin. Bell's patent was approved in March, and some Western Union customers replaced telegraphs with telephones. The giant company immediately recognized the telephone as a threat to its business preeminence and challenged the Bell patent, maintaining that a competitor had priority, and converted its subsidiary Western Electric, hitherto the nation's largest electrical supplier, into a telephone manufacturer. Bell countered by filing a patent-infringement suit.

Western Union's interest in the telephone guaranteed its success. By the time the two parties reached accord in late 1879, and Western Union had withdrawn from the telephone business and sold its phones to Bell, the telegraph company's telephones numbered nearly fifty-six thousand. Six hundred other groups contested the Bell patent, but it stood until the early 1890s.

Western Union's exit was shortsighted. A year earlier Bell had conceived of the telephone in a new way—linked to a central exchange system. At the time telephone lines ran above ground from place to place, and only a handful of rudimentary exchanges existed; many feared that expansion would result in a Byzantine maze of wires. The switchbox and adaptation of telegraph switchboards, however, enabled those connected to an exchange to converse with each other; the introduction of multiple switchboards in the mid 1880s allowed for far more complex interexchange systems. Bell Telephone began to bury cables underground in New York City and then in other cities during the early 1880s.

Long-distance service was vital to Bell Telephone's fortunes after Alexander Bell's patents expired and it faced competition from numerous independent phone companies. Bell lowered prices and improved service to counter them. However, the fact that Bell was the sole

As the sole competent provider, long distance service was critical to the success of Bell Telephone. This engraving shows Alexander Graham Bell opening the telephone line from New York to Chicago in 1892.

competent long-distance company made it indispensable to consumers. This situation led Bell to favor government telephone regulation after 1906, which would preserve its entrenched position and guarantee its investors a dependable, substantial return; Bell would become America's telephone company.

In 1907 Lee De Forest (1873–1961) formed a company to contest Bell Telephone's long-distance supremacy. Unlike earlier competitors, De Forest planned to send messages through the air, not wires. Bell Telephone initially discounted the radio threat and concentrated on developing coast-to-coast service; on 25 January 1915, it inaugurated its first transcontinental line.

SYSTEMATIZING THE TECHNOLOGISTS. Not until 1867 was the nation's first exclusive engineering organization, the American Society of Civil Engineers (ASCE), established. The diversity of American engineering, however, led to more specialized organizations, such as the American Institute of Mining Engineers (1871), the American Society of Mechanical Engineers (1880), the American Institute of Electrical Engineers (1884), the American Institute of Chemical Engineers (1908), and the Institute of Radio Engineers (1912).

The formation of these organizations signaled the emergence of self-consciousness among America's engineers which was part of a general late-nineteenth-century rise in American society of "expertise" (replacing "character") as the sine qua non for evaluating competence. Engineers began to see themselves as a discrete group, and their societies from their inception sought public sanction. Political participation was one avenue they explored, but they devoted more effort to internal affairs, gradually developing rules to guarantee that their present and future membership's expertise would match the social responsibility they proclaimed. They held regular meetings, published periodicals whose content was subject to peer review, and established standards of practice and codes of ethics to govern professional and private behavior. The societies also recommended curricula for engineering schools, thereby systematizing entrance into the profession. These varied devices helped convince an often skeptical public that engineers met their self-announced criteria, and therefore deserved the authority they sought. Through these societies' efforts, a formal collegiate engineering education became de rigueur by 1910, and nearly all engineers accepting their first position after that date held engineering degrees.

SYSTEMATIZING TECHNICAL RESEARCH. As with the formation of college curricula and professional organizations, the engineers' self-consciousness of the last third of the nineteenth century spawned questions about the relationship among engineers, research, and industry. To be sure, American technologists always had tried to improve established processes or discover new ones, and had had a long, profitable relationship with American industry; but these efforts were primarily ad hoc problem-solving inquiries. After about 1870, research became inextricably linked to a kind of expertise in a particular subject and—more important—the techniques of systematic, rational inquiry.

Not until around the turn of the century, when engineering colleges began to treat research as essential, did industry find new employment for corporate engineers. They were to work in industrial research laboratories, a new type of institution that was clearly derived from laboratories *and* academe. Industrial research laboratories were not responsible to production facilities. Companies generally located laboratories away from manufacturing sites to insulate them from the most pressing demands of business.

SYSTEMATIZING THE URBAN ENVIRONMENT. The urban landscape was redesigned in the late nineteenth and early twentieth centuries. Residential neighborhoods became characterized by their inhabitants' class, religion, nationality, race, and occupation. Mercantile transactions were the focus of the central business district, while heavy industry was relegated to other city sections.

The changing nature and increasing size of the new city created a persistent call for massive new construction, and hence for building materials. Through the 1870s brick, cut stone, concrete, cast and wrought iron, and wood were standard building materials. In that decade Americans began to use iron and steel supports, and the introduction of reinforced concrete in the mid 1880s gave rise to a new municipal building form, the skyscraper, a symbol of corporate wealth and success that quickly transformed the city skyline.

SYSTEMATIZING NATURE. Americans expressed an abiding love of and reverence for nature, even though they increasingly inhabited cities. Most sought to combine nature with the industrial urban present in order to civilize the future. The wilderness was not inviolable, but nature was; nature was a cornerstone of the future.

As the source of materials necessary for modern American life, nature was cherished for the bounty it furnished. The commercial mining and logging industries were among the most prominent natural-resource-based operations; faced with unprecedented demands for their products, they increased productivity and profits by systematizing procedures and operating on economies of scale.

From the 1870s federal administrators in the West argued that nature was public property requiring federal regulation. The evolution of this group in many ways paralleled that of the engineers. They contended that America needed rational planning to promote an orderly development that would yield raw materials now and protect nature for posterity—and that only they, backed by national legislation, could effectively plan and implement the necessary program. They frequently portrayed mining and lumber concerns as ravaging nature without regard to the future (although both mining and lumber interests generally favored national management policy).

SYSTEMATIZING LEISURE. In the late nineteenth century, Americans made as rigid a distinction between work and leisure as they did between city and farm. The idea that citizens ought to pursue leisure activities was new, as was the notion that work and leisure constituted radically different but essential elements of the human developmental system. On one aspect of leisure Americans agreed: systematization and rationalization of leisure endeavors would yield the most efficient, and therefore the most satisfactory, leisure. In that sense, the precepts surrounding leisure were virtually indistinguishable from those of work.

The rise of spectator and participant sports created a corresponding demand for sports equipment. Albert G. Spalding (1850–1915) parlayed careers as a star baseball player, a promoter, and a founder of the National League to achieve a dominant position in the sports equipment industry.

The 1876 Centennial Exhibition first brought bicycles to America's attention. These expensive English imports with large front and small rear wheels were popular among the upper class; the introduction of cheaper, chain-driven safety bicycles about a decade later touched off a middle-class boom, and rubber pneumatic tires a few years later continued it. In 1895 an estimated four million Americans owned cycles and several million more rented them.

The bicycle boom collapsed once the nation discovered the automobile—a European invention in which Americans expressed an interest during the late nineteenth century. Buyers initially had difficulty deciding among machines powered by steam, electric, or internal-combustion engines; each was an improved version of a long-familiar engine, and each had its good and bad points. Clearly, the internal-combustion engine won out.

Wealthy Americans constituted the initial market for early auto manufacturers, who sought to build fast, large, luxurious, and dependable cars. Ransom E. Olds (1864–1950) was probably most successful in tapping the middle class: he led the nation's largest automobile producer, which manufactured five thousand vehicles a year as early as 1904. Henry Ford's yearly sales did not surpass Olds's until Ford permanently left the luxury car field some years later.

The motion picture industry also was rationalized in the early twentieth century, as several large consortia came to dominate picture production and distribution. This predominantly urban leisure form, however, became increasingly accessible to all social classes before the close of the century. A new recreational institution, the movie house, was born: there were five thousand in 1907 and twice as many three years later.

The early motion picture industry profited by establishing a technologically based leisure activity designed to attract diverse social groups. In that sense, it differed from automobiles, bicycles, and spectator sports, which produced profits by serving the desires for leisure of more circumscribed markets. But the manner in which these several leisure forms were shaped and shaped themselves was fundamentally the same: those who viewed them recognized each as constituting an element in a system of discrete yet interdependent, hierarchically arranged parts, or as the system itself.

SYSTEMATIZING WORKERS AND THE WORKPLACE. Americans accorded production machinery new prominence in the half century after 1870, but the nature of the factory engendered early concern. Critics, many of whom called themselves "mechanical engineers," maintained that factory administration was outmoded, chaotic, or wasteful, and therefore a detriment to productivity. By 1920, few factories resembled their 1870 predecessors: factories and factory work had been reconceptualized and rearranged. Mass production techniques and scientific management methods were the result of that reconceptualization.

The central office stood at the apex of this new factory system. Until the 1870s manufacturing establishments often consigned paperwork to small "cages" on factory floors, industrialists' offices resembled parlors, and clerks were more nearly apprentice businessmen—virtually all were males—than office help (the term "secretary" referred to either a rolltop desk or to the manager of a business). "Letterpresses" (file folders) and ledgers had constituted the mainstays of record keeping. These ad hoc, undifferentiated office practices gave way in the decades after 1870. Offices became the brains of businesses, where material was gathered and analyzed for future needs and strategies. Their significance was reflected in spatial arrangements: post-1870 offices grew larger, more populous, and (in the case of manufacturing) physically distinct. Each specialist, many of whom were now women, was counted on to standardize the appropriate record forms and establish precise record-keeping systems. Standardized desks, filing cabinets, ledgers, paper and envelopes, carbon paper, and typewriters rationalized the office.

After about 1900 factories usually were significantly larger than they had been earlier. Most consisted of several buildings, not single massive structures, and suburban locations often replaced more expensive city sites. Structural steel and reinforced concrete were predominant construction materials, which encouraged new structural forms, larger windows, and flexibility of design.

Only after 1920 did electricity surpass steam and water as the predominant power source, and come to play a significant role in factory design. By 1929, 78 percent of industrial power was electric. The union of motor and machine in a single device permitted factory owners to remove shafting, belts, and pulleys, leaving overhead space for traveling cranes. Motor failure disabled only a single tool. Machines became truly portable, and factory design and expansion knew no restraints. Most manufacturers chose to minimize handling and emphasize production flow; they organized factories by the natural sequence of manufacturing operations.

Ford began to rationalize factory operations and prepare for high-volume automobile manufacture as early as 1906. His advisers included gifted machinists and mechanics steeped in European production techniques. Together these men emphasized interchangeable parts, special-purpose machine tools, rational jigs, fixtures, and gauges, and sequential machine-tool arrangement.

Demand soon exceeded production capacity, and in 1910 Ford opened an extensively planned plant in Highland Park, Michigan, which would make only the Model T. Ford's staff designed special-purpose—often single-purpose—machine tools for Model T manufacture, rather than adapting tools from earlier sites. They seized every opportunity to replace men with machines and to eliminate skilled labor by dividing tasks into constituent actions, building new machines, and adjusting processes so as to speed output.

WORLD WAR I. The war effort dwarfed other concerns as the nation was thrust into a situation it had never before encountered. It needed to raise, equip, and send an army across the ocean, and to provide support as well as furnish matériel for its allies. That America remained undaunted by these requirements stemmed from a belief in the morality of its cause and from nearly half a century of experience rationalizing and systematizing virtually every facet of life. The new demands that World War I placed on the country were different only in scale: Americans treated the war in a characteristically late-nineteenth- or early-twentieth-century way—as the culmination of previous efforts, not the inauguration of a new agenda. The nation would manufacture what it needed to fight "a war to end all wars."

When Henry Ford's Highland Park, Michigan, plant was opened in 1910, the staff seized every opportunity to replace men with machines and to eliminate skilled labor by dividing tasks into constituent actions, building new machines, and adjusting processes so as to speed output.

American manufacture of machine guns both changed the nature of land warfare and was a response to that change. These killing machines made traditional military advances foolhardy, and impossible without massive loss of life. Rifles, bayonets, and hand-to-hand combat no longer carried the day, and horse cavalry was relegated to history's scrap heap; warfare ceased to be considered glorious and became impersonal.

Torpedo-armed German submarines transformed traditional sea warfare practices as drastically as the machine gun changed land war. Rather than engaging in conventional naval bombardments, submarines killed quietly. They also disrupted war matériel shipments and blockaded ports. Convoys—systematic assemblages of sub-chasers, destroyers, cruisers, and other ships—were the most effective antisubmarine measures: they negated submarines so completely that by war's end Germans refrained from assaulting them. Allied shipping losses had become minimal.

World War I was the first major conflict to see the air as a sphere of warfare. The American military was especially unprepared for this type of fighting: it possessed a scant 109 airplanes, mostly trainers, and had only 83 pilots when Congress declared war. European combatants operated far larger air forces and had highly refined the art of aerial warfare. Air duels, strafing, and bombing runs, as well as aerial reconnaissance and photography, were commonplace. That air power would assume such prominence was surprising, because the first manned flight of a powered, heavier-than-air craft had occurred only thirteen years earlier. And that Americans would lag so far behind Europeans was equally surprising—the airplane was an American invention.

Although the French had pioneered hot-air balloon flight in the late eighteenth century, and gas and hot-air balloons had been popular nineteenth-century entertainment, it was Orville and Wilbur Wright (1871–1948, 1867–1912) who made the first successful airplane flight on 17 December 1903, at Kitty Hawk, North Carolina. Samuel Pierpont Langley (1834–1906), the Smithsonian Institution's third secretary, had also helped to galvanize American interest in flight. He made several fruitless attempts to launch his gasoline-engine-driven *Aerodrome*—the last only nine days before the Wrights' flight.

The United States had amassed an air force on Old World soil of more than 5,500 planes by Armistice Day. Its pilots had shot down an estimated 850 enemy aircraft.

The armistice received an enthusiastic welcome, but there was no return to "normalcy." America's pursuit of the war had been conducted according to an organizational idea that had begun to be implemented some five decades earlier. Land, air, and sea warfare were separate types of combat; mobilization, production of ordnance, and manufacture of aircraft were distinct activities, united only in their contribution to the war effort. World War I marked the culmination of that mode of thought: The concept of components as rigid and encapsulated gave way in the 1920s, and with it went the post-1870 view of the nature of systems. The technologies of the 1920s and after were built upon or explained according to different premises.

Technology as a Social Solution: The 1920s to the 1950s

The notion of system, a crucial aspect of late-nineteenth- and early-twentieth-century thought, underwent drastic revision around the 1920s. Whereas systems in the earlier period were static entities composed of diverse, fixed, and limited parts hierarchically arranged—the system equaled the sum of its different parts—the new systems of the 1920s and after were dynamic, predicated on a more complex relationship among the parts: each part seemed to acquire a share of its definition from its interrelationships with the other parts.

This idea of systems as complicated dynamic processes opened new technological possibilities and solutions—to virtually every problem, including social problems. This unabashedly optimistic assessment of technology's influence began to wane in the 1950s (and continued to dwindle during the next several decades). The interwar period's notion of system remained in place, but the individuation of American society, coupled with a perception that the nation's (and the world's) resources were limited, contributed to a disillusionment with traditional decision-making apparatus. Technology as a product of experts became a subject of immense concern and after mid century was increasingly seen as both a cause of and a cure for social problems; it was a social question.

THE GOVERNMENT AND SOCIAL ENGINEERING. Government involvement in technological activities rose exponentially as Americans increasingly looked to technologies as a means to solve social problems. Government participation in this social-engineering movement was characteristically managerial: particularly in the 1920s and early 1930s, government served as coordinator, gathering together diverse teams of experts to consider multifaceted problems and to design a technological solution that took into account social, cultural, economic, and political factors. Governmental authority was informal, limited to convening teams; it relied on its power of persuasion to implement recommendations.

This governmental role was favored by Herbert Hoover (1874–1964), whose presidency epitomized America's love affair with social engineering. A former mining engineer, director of the World War I food-relief effort, and secretary of commerce, Hoover viewed the resolution of modern life's complexities as an engineering task. Systematic planning characterized his agenda, yet he recognized that technical solutions had profound social and cultural implications. These views—and a preference for cooperation between public and private sectors of the economy over direct governmental intervention—guided Hoover's attempts to regulate key emerging industries such as aviation, radio, electric power, and highway construction.

The Great Depression discredited Hoover's approach to government involvement in social engineering: Franklin D. Roosevelt (1882–1945) and his "brain trust" dismissed Hoover's political, noninterventionist stance, but they remained committed to social engineering.

Roosevelt's New Deal exemplified another vision of the government's role in social engineering. It too was managerial, relied on the wisdom of specialists, and depended on government-inspired coordination, but it accorded government the responsibility of active participation and of counterbalancing various disruptive forces—one of which seemed often to be the greed of the private sector.

A central aspect of Roosevelt's prescription for America's ills was public-works engineering projects of unprecedented scale and complexity. Numerous federal bureaus such as the Forest Service, Geological Survey, National Weather Service, Wildlife Service, and Bureau of Reclamation lent their expertise to these endeavors, as did state and local entities. Among the most frequently involved was the Army Corps of Engineers. Until the New Deal the corps had been restricted to improving navigation by building dams, levees, piers, and other facilities, and removing obstacles from rivers and harbors. Congress, however, granted the corps power to engage in other forms of river development, but mandated that each new project was to have multiple purposes: flood-control measures, for example, were also to aid navigation and to generate hydroelectric capacity. Thus the corps received primary responsibility for flood control along all American rivers and the authority to construct major hydroelectric plants.

Other New Deal efforts were even more ambitious. The Tennessee Valley Authority (TVA), established in 1933, was a conscious attempt to use government power and funds to make over a poor, predominantly rural seven-state region traversed by the Tennessee River. Technology—in this case the introduction of cheap, plentiful electricity—was to generate new government-regulated industries and thereby improve the lives of the region's inhabitants.

Dissent among supporters, as well as opposition from other sectors, prohibited the TVA from implementing its broad political, social, and cultural reforms. Although it did not result in cooperative communitarianism, the TVA did produce numerous technical and economic achievements: dams, flood-control measures, improved navigation, land reclamation, diversified crops, and above all, cheap electricity. The TVA also effected some social change with employee hiring and training programs, homes, schools, libraries, small local cooperative industries, recreational areas, and the model town of Norris, Tennessee.

The TVA model was popular among New Dealers, who sought in vain to export it to other regions. Yet the inability, for political and economic reasons, to create new TVAs did not stop New Deal power engineers, who gained crucial federal assistance in implementing various proposals in 1935. Roosevelt's Rural Electrification Administration helped many farmers form cooperative power pools and build electric lines themselves.

Although electricity and regionally planned projects such as the TVA remade much of rural America, New Dealers were less successful in the redesign of urban America. This was not due to lack of effort, however, for they created numerous model communities across the nation to demonstrate what American city life could become. Their "garden cities" program was among the most clearly articulated and sustained: New Dealers hoped to dot America with comprehensively planned communities of approximately thirty thousand people (relocated from older, decaying industrial cities), with balanced industrial and agricultural economies, and circumscribed by fields and forests, or greenbelts. Modern technologies—automobiles and electricity—would eliminate urban overcrowding and poverty. The economically, religiously, and racially diverse populations of these cities were to be linked by rapid-transit systems and superhighways to other nearby garden cities, and joined in turn to regional centers with populations of some sixty thousand apiece.

Although electricity and regionally planned projects such as the Tennessee Valley Authority remade much of rural America, New Dealers were less successful in the redesign of urban America.

The Roosevelt administration managed to construct only three garden cities, none of which proved popular. The wave of suburbanization, which began about 1920, contributed to their failure: formerly suburbs had expanded along mass-transit lines, but automobiles had enabled urbanites to flee inner cities and settle wherever there were roads. This resulted in an unprecedented commitment to building roadways for automobiles and to new public expenditures that would make cities suitable for cars: from new traffic arrangements and equipment such as one-way streets, automatic traffic signals, and garages to freeways and parkways. These latter offered fast, safe driving conditions, thanks to controlled-access roads, wide median strips, strong dividers, and cloverleaf intersections. The standardized travel of urban mass transit lost ground to the individualized travel that fed out to the suburbs.

CHANGES IN AGRICULTURE. The repeated inability of social engineers to foster the precise modifications they sought did not mean that traditional American modes of production were unchanged. On the contrary: no single aspect of farming was more indicative of this shift than the tractor boom that began in the mid-1920s. Early tractors were single-purpose machines that could pull or power machinery, but could not do both simultaneously. Manufacturers' development of the "power takeoff" in the 1920s transformed and popularized the tractor: this mechanism permitted a variety of farm implements to operate on the tractor's power while it was moving (or not). The result was the general-purpose tractor, which—with the later combine—was so successful that by about 1950 horses had virtually disappeared as sources of power.

Combination corn-pickers/huskers, which were also products of the 1920s, sold poorly because they performed miserably. Not until the late 1940s did these machines gain popularity. (Their acceptance stemmed not from improved machine design but from "design" of a machine-compatible corn, bred for the machine's needs and the limitations of the environment in which it was grown.)

After 1920 farmers not only bred animals and plants for specific traits but also modified the environment. Use of manufactured chemicals enabled agriculturists to create more productive environments. Freeing environments of weeds, an early objective, was achieved only after World War II. Synthetic growth hormones (auxins), which caused weeds to grow at uncontrolled rates—and, ironically, to starve to death—were the most effective mid-century herbicides.

The insecticide DDT (dichloro-diphenyl-trichloroethane) offered more potential and seemed an even greater panacea. Discovered in 1939 by the Swiss scientist Paul Muller, it became available in America three years later and quickly gained fame when the U.S. Army used it as an insecticide. After World War II, Americans employed it extensively against many parasites. Like herbicides, DDT appeared to increase productivity without harming desirable plants, animals, or humans. It spawned an entire generation of related insecticides, which also were used massively and unselectively. Average farm size increased markedly, but the number of farmers declined precipitously: by 1960 only 3 percent of the nation's population engaged in agricultural pursuits. Each farmer could tend a larger area or more stock—and needed to do so in order to reduce unit production costs and thus justify the expense of the new methods.

CHANGES IN MANUFACTURING. American manufacturing underwent changes comparable with those of agriculture as industrialists reconceptualized industry, industrial processes and organization, and marketing strategies. Rarely were these new developments trumpeted by the individuals directly responsible. The self-aggrandizement of Isaac Singer, Cyrus McCormick, or Henry Ford seemed out of place in this new, highly integrated industrial system.

The dramatic rise of General Motors (GM) and the decline of the Ford Motor Company in the mid-1920s is a compelling example of the new industrial system. Ford had conceived of his Model T as the car for the masses, but increasingly the masses wanted more stylish vehicles. GM's Alfred P. Sloan, Jr. (1875–1966), capitalized on this desire to effect a revolution in automobile manufacture and sales: he argued that because a corporation's primary responsibility is to provide a high return to investors, it must determine market demand rather than merely produce supplies. Demand, he asserted, is plastic, so it can be created, modified, or stimulated; added volume alone spawns profits and comes from carefully planned, superbly marketed products—that is, effective management.

The five lines of vehicles that GM developed had a price range that ran from the poorest to the wealthiest car buyers. Sloan's pricing and product-line strategy was reflected in his reorganization of GM in 1924: the corporation was split into autonomous divisions mediated by interdivisional groups that harmonized activities and provided the corporation's chief executive with ultimate authority. GM's "federal" structure facilitated Sloan's greatest car-selling coup, the annual model change, implemented around 1925: Sloan decreed that there should be a single basic GM style each year, but left it to each division's designers to modify that form to suit its targeted buyers.

Although different divisions often used the same parts, annual models made change the normal state of affairs. Because refitting facilities yearly with new single-purpose machines would be prohibitively expensive, GM introduced flexible mass production: it outfitted its plants with movable, adjustable-speed, independently powered general-purpose machines.

These initiatives captured the largest share of the American automobile market for GM. Ford responded by abandoning his beloved Model T in 1927 and replacing it with the sportier but almost as static Model A. By 1933 Ford had stopped selling the Model A, adopted the annual model change, switched to flexible mass production, and offered a product line aimed at a wide spectrum of buyers.

TRANSPORTATION. From the 1920s on, railroads concentrated on becoming bigger, faster, and more efficient. Rails were strengthened to absorb heavier loads, signals and traffic-control systems were made almost automatic, and air brakes were vastly improved to function under even the greatest burdens. Steam locomotives such as the Union Pacific 4000 class (1941) attained a weight of more than six hundred tons and could travel at seventy miles per hour. They began to be replaced in the 1940s by diesel locomotives, which were faster and lighter but more powerful and capable of transporting larger loads. Yet mid-century railroads lacked the flexibility demanded by an America consciously attempting to decentralize manufacturing facilities and markets; they were in effect single-purpose carriers. Aside from the question of exceedingly high capital costs, huge locomotives maximized economies only when pulling a very large number of cars or very heavy cargo over considerable distance.

Trucks and buses capitalized on the railroads' drawbacks and also served to convey goods to areas inaccessible to railroads. Pneumatic tires, developed by the Goodyear Tire and Rubber Company in 1916, prevented these heavy vehicles from damaging roadways, cargo, and themselves through constant pounding. In 1927 the Fageol brothers of Kent, Ohio, introduced the twin-coach bus; its engines were placed underneath the passenger compartment to make the vehicle's whole body suitable for heavier loads (earlier bus bodies were simply placed on truck chassis). Larger trucks later separated their power unit from the cargo units, which became semitrailers that could be attached or detached as needed.

Numerous small bus companies sprinkled throughout the nation consolidated into the Greyhound system, which in 1929 became America's largest bus line, delivering goods and passengers nationwide. These smaller, flexible carriers were able to capture a profitable share of the freight and passenger trade in an era of poor roadways and, until 1956, no interstate highway system.

Even had the railroad industry been more vigilant, it is unlikely that it could have stemmed its inevitable losses to commercial airlines. The latter specialized in longer-distance haulage than many truck and bus concerns, and competed directly with railroads in that sector; but like railroads, the speedier airlines had huge capital costs.

Commercial aviation's roots go back to early airmail service, which began in 1918 when the U.S. Post Office used army aircraft and young World War I veterans for the initial New York-Philadelphia-Washington route. Despite considerable loss of life, by 1924 the Post Office had established regular transcontinental mail flights. A year later, however, the federal government transferred mail service to commercial airlines, which invariably were eager for the contracts, given their generally precarious financial conditions.

Those airmail routes eventually became parts of the first major airlines, including American, Delta, and United, in the 1920s and 1930s. In the latter decade, flimsy cloth-covered biplanes gave way to all-metal craft, beginning with the Ford Trimotor. The Douglas Commercial, or DC-3, inaugurated in 1935, promptly became the principal civilian airliner. (The American military also used it in World War II.)

Two events in the 1920s helped solidify the aviation industry's legitimacy. Charles Lindbergh's solo transatlantic flight in 1927 drew attention to the airplane's potential, and the establishment of the Daniel Guggenheim Fund for the Promotion of Aeronautics in 1926 fostered aviation achievement. The fund enabled eight universities to form aeronautical engineering programs to train students and undertake research. Offshoots of Guggenheim-sponsored research included instrument-only flight, short-takeoff-and-landing (STOL) aircraft, and weather reporting services. As air traffic increased, so did the need for support facilities, navigation and communications equipment, and airport controllers, ground crews, and other technical personnel. The New Deal's Works Progress Administration provided funds for building and enlarging terminals and runways.

Two events that helped to solidify the aviation industry's legitimacy were Charles Lindbergh's solo transatlantic flight in 1927 and the establishment of the Daniel Guggenheim Fund for the Promotion of Aeronautics in 1926.

What fortified early commercial aviation and entitled it to this unusual level of governmental support was its modern character. A "winged gospel" permeated America as the new technology's exciting, liberating potential captured public imagination. Commentators repeatedly maintained that airplanes would eliminate urban congestion, poverty, industrial competition, and even war. Aviation was to resolve almost all social questions. In that sense, the role of aviation was comparable with the New Deal insistence that electricity and automobiles would pave the way for a new America "fit for life and the living."

TECHNOLOGY IN WORLD WAR II. World War II shattered the peace that had reigned since 1918 and placed dramatic new strains on the nation, which responded in a characteristically mid-century way. The war certainly did not disrupt America's optimistic assessment of technology's possibilities. This war was "total war"—"everybody's war"—and the country's technological capabilities promised to win battles at home and abroad. The new Office of Scientific Research and Development (OSRD, created 1941) was charged with overseeing and coordinating all wartime research and development.

The OSRD stimulated and funded production and development of numerous new armaments, but most significantly it sponsored research on what would become the atomic bomb. It did not, however, start this research: the earliest, most compelling work was done in Nazi Germany.

In December 1942, Enrico Fermi (1901–1954), an immigrant from fascist Italy, achieved with backing from the OSRD the first controlled release of nuclear energy, under the University of Chicago's football stadium. Fermi's demonstration and the OSRD's strong recommendation helped convince Franklin Roosevelt of the bomb's immediacy. He authorized the Manhattan Project to keep bomb research secret, and charged it with building an atomic device within three years. General Leslie Groves (1896–1970) headed the project, which involved a gigantic research team composed of scientists from numerous disciplines and the Army Corps of Engineers. Project members secretly constructed plutonium-generating reactors at Hanford, Washington, a gas-diffusion facility at Oak Ridge, Tennessee, and a physics research laboratory at Los Alamos, New Mexico. Under their director, Berkeley physicist J. Robert Oppenheimer (1904–1967), Los Alamos scientists and engineers designed and built bombs from the materials produced at Hanford and Oak Ridge.

The OSRD then devoted all its efforts to conventional weaponry. The nexus between the OSRD and universities became especially pronounced as several interdisciplinary research centers were established to focus on particular types of weapons development. Investigators from across the nation, for example, were brought to the MIT Radiation Laboratory for radar research. Harvard's Radio Research Laboratory spearheaded antiradar measures, and Johns Hopkins University's Applied Physics Laboratory became America's proximity fuse center.

Airplanes played a far larger role in World War II than in World War I and were integral parts of most military operations. They provided cover for ground and naval assaults, protected land and sea convoys, diverted enemy fire, and transported troops, munitions, and supplies. The B-17 "Flying Fortress," B-24 "Liberator," and B-29 "Superfortress" bombers had been designed before America entered the war, but wartime production and performance needs prompted repeated modifications, from leakproof fuel tanks to aluminum airframes. In total, the nation produced more than 296,000 aircraft during the war.

Superior airpower and weaponry as well as America's material resources helped decide the outcome of war, but the use of the atomic bomb marked its formal conclusion. The first atomic weapon was tested at Alamogordo, New Mexico, on 16 July 1945. Its core of plutonium-239 was triggered by implosion. Buoyed by the test's success, President Harry Truman (1884–1972) issued Japan an unconditional surrender ultimatum—the war with Germany had ended—that hinted at a new aerial weapon of unprecedented power. Japan's silence led to the dropping of "Little Boy" (an enriched uranium-235 bomb triggered by firing one subcritical mass into another) on Hiroshima on 6 August 1945. The blast killed eighty thousand people and destroyed or heavily damaged 96 percent of the city's buildings. Japan's continued silence brought about the Nagasaki bombing (using "Fatman," which was similar in design to the Alamagordo bomb), which took thirty-nine thousand lives and leveled 40 percent of the city's structures. Each bomb contained more explosive power than twenty thousand tons of TNT. Japan surrendered on 15 August.

In December 1942, Enrico Fermi, an immigrant from fascist Italy, achieved with backing from America's new Office of Scientific Research and Development the first controlled release of nuclear energy, under the University of Chicago's football stadium.

THE DEVELOPMENT OF COMPUTERS AND TRANSISTORS. The mid-century classification of airplanes, electricity, and automobiles as modern, high-technology initiatives was ironic, for none was truly on the cutting edge: heavier-than-air powered flight had first occurred in 1903, and automobiles and the generation and distribution of electricity dated from the previous century. Mid-century America did in fact have genuinely modern technologies, but they remained virtually unknown to the public until later in the century. Generally developed by physicists or electrical engineers laboring in universities or industry, they concentrated not on human-scale system/part relationships but on *much* smaller (often atomic) manifestations, in the contemporary physics of indeterminacy, quantum mechanics, or electronics. Other technologists focused on the macroatomic level and strove to integrate several functions within single machines. From these undertakings came photoduplication, television, transistors, a new class of servomechanisms, and computers.

The early history of the computer demonstrates how mid-century organizational notions were reflected in that machine's conception and design. Computers were not merely calculating, measuring, or tabulating machines, which late-nineteenth- and early-twentieth-century Americans patented and built in great numbers. Rather, they were electronic, digital, integrated, multipurpose systems that harmoniously combined various tasks—gathering, storing, and processing data—within a single device. The ENIAC (Electronic Numerical Integrator and Computer), designed in the mid-1940s by J. Presper Eckert, Jr., and John Mauchly at the University of Pennsylvania's Moore School of Electrical Engineering, was the first machine that met all the criteria and had general applicability.

The ENIAC went into operation in 1946. It had eighteen thousand vacuum tubes, was as large as a boxcar, and weighed thirty tons. The ENIAC was programmed by plugging cables from one of its parts to another, much like a telephone switchboard. Punch cards carried data. A million cards were needed for its initial project, a simulation for the then-untested hydrogen bomb.

The Universal Automatic Computer (UNIVAC) was private enterprise's initial computer. Designed by Eckert and Mauchly, it gained priceless publicity by predicting Dwight Eisenhower's election as president in 1952, one hour after the polls closed. A few years later IBM entered the computer field with its Model 701, which computed at about the same speed as UNIVAC but was smaller and cheaper—and soon outsold (or, more precisely, outrented) its rivals. Yet total rentals were modest; computers seemed useful only for large-scale scientific, military, and industrial projects.

The transistors of the early 1950s seemed even less practical than did computers. These tiny metallic devices were the product of a quest, beginning in the 1930s, to find adequate substitutes for amplifying vacuum tubes (which, beyond being bulky, fragile, and short-lived, consumed large amounts of energy). While other solutions were explored, researchers produced solid-state replacements for another type of vacuum tube, the rectifying diode. Of particular importance was the notion that electrons occupied and were restricted to energy levels (bands) in solids, and that they could jump bands. This notion overthrew traditional conductor-insulator distinctions and established a continuum between them. From these assumptions came the concept of semiconductors, which made the idea of amplifying transistors appear logical and their developments seem possible.

TECHNOLOGY IN THE POSTWAR WORLD. Although World War II reaffirmed America's technological strength, the nation faced many foreign as well as domestic challenges soon after its conclusion. One response was the establishment in 1950 of the National Science Foundation to support basic research, some of which had military implications.

America's technological might also held out hope of nonmilitary solutions to the spread of communism. The nation's industrial prowess could inaugurate a worldwide era of plenty; it could stop and isolate communism by remaking the world in the American image. The Marshall Plan, the reformation of Japan, foreign aid, and the establishment of the United Nations were attempts by the United States to engineer a different world. Technical development emerged as a vital component of foreign policy, much as it had formed a crucial aspect of New Deal domestic policy.

Atomic power grew in prominence after the Soviet Union exploded an atomic bomb in September 1949. Truman ordered a crash program to develop the hydrogen bomb. Several physicists active in the Manhattan Project, including Fermi and Oppenheimer, opposed Truman's initiative. Their advice was rejected, particularly once Edward Teller (b. 1908) and others devised practical means to control fusion reactions. The first American H-bomb was tested in 1954: with the explosive power of fifteen million tons of TNT, it was more than 750 times as powerful as the A-bomb. A year later, the Soviet Union exploded a less powerful but similar device.

Technology as a Social Question: The 1950s to the Present

To some, technology was still a social benison, while to others it had become a monster and those who unleashed it, villains. Few post-1950 Americans adopted

Astronaut Edwin "Buzz" Aldrin, Jr. walking near the lunar module during the Apollo 11 moonlanding on July 20, 1969.

either position outright; they saw technology as a force but not as monolithic, regarding it instead as a social question. Some technologies seemed harmful and others beneficial, but most appeared to be a little of both.

THE NUCLEAR AGE. No technology provided a more compelling example of the relationship between technology and society than nuclear power, both military and civilian. The 1946 Atomic Energy Act, America's first important legislation concerning nuclear technology, established the Atomic Energy Commission, which monopolized nuclear materials and thus stymied private initiatives while taking formal control of atomic energy out of the military's hands. President Dwight Eisenhower reversed this trend in 1953 by beginning an "Atoms for Peace" program, which encouraged civilian construction of nuclear power plants. The first of these plants, at Shippingport, Pennsylvania, opened in 1957.

Although nuclear weapons were essential to the nation's defense, disarmament demonstrations began in 1955, soon after the Soviet Union exploded its hydrogen bomb, and persisted into the early 1960s. A thriving bomb-shelter industry emerged, and citizens' groups reacted passionately to the disclosure that atmospheric nuclear tests had released radioactive debris. The Soviet Union and the United States agreed in 1963 to end atmospheric tests, but continued testing bombs of ever-increasing size. This expansion continued until the Strategic Arms Limitation Talks (SALT) accords with the Soviet Union. Salt I (1972) established temporary offensive-weapons limits and prohibited sea-and space-based antiballistic-missile development, testing, and deployment. SALT II (1979), which controls the number and type of nuclear weapons and limits development and testing, was never ratified by the U.S. Senate, although both nations have roughly abided by its provisions.

The social concern that began in the mid 1950s intensified from the mid 1970s on, as rapid increases in the power of nuclear weapons and methods of protecting them from preemptive enemy strikes called into question the basic assumptions of earlier arms-control agreements. The larger debate about nuclear technologies, both military and civilian, was further fueled in 1979 when an accident at Pennsylvania's Three Mile Island nuclear power plant vividly demonstrated both the potential dangers of nuclear power and the shortcomings of the institutions that maintained and oversaw the industry; construction of power plants virtually ceased in the ensuing years. It was against this backdrop that President Ronald Reagan (b. 1911) accelerated the arms buildup and announced the Strategic Defensive Initiative (SDI), or "Star Wars"—an extraordinarily (and to some, absurdly) complex and costly antiballistic-missile program. This trend, however, was dealt setbacks in the late 1980s as U.S.-Soviet relations improved and as information about the environmental problems caused by nuclear-weapons production facilities was made public.

SPACEFLIGHT. The history of spaceflight in many ways parallels that of the uses of nuclear energy: both emerged from research begun during World War II, and both became the subject of superpower competition. Initially accorded overwhelming public support, both eventually lost much of their luster as various groups questioned their proponents' abilities, objectivity, and ambitions.

The "Space Age" formally began on 4 October 1957, when the supposedly backward Soviet Union successfully launched the first artificial satellite, *Sputnik I.* Americans were shocked: within a year President Eisenhower established the National Aeronautics and Space Administration (NASA), and on 31 January 1958, America's first successful satellite, *Explorer I,* was launched, followed by *Vanguard I* on 17 March 1958. Thus began the "space race" between the United States and the Soviet Union, which continues today.

The space race was invigorated on 12 April 1961, when Soviet cosmonaut Yuri Gagarin (1934–1968) in

Vostok I became the first person to orbit the earth and return safely. On 25 May 1961 President John F. Kennedy (1917–1963) stirred the nation with a pledge to land a man on the moon by 1970.

The seven original *Mercury* astronauts became national heroes as they ventured into space. Their most memorable flights were those of Alan Shepard, the first American in space (on 5 May 1961, aboard *Mercury* 3), and John Glenn, the first American to orbit the earth (on 20 February 1962, aboard *Mercury* 6). Following the Mercury program (1958–1963) came the Gemini program (1962–1966), which included the world's first successful orbital rendezvous and manned flights of record length. It was succeeded by the Apollo moon program (1961–1972), which competed with superior Soviet rocket thrusters by developing more powerful booster rockets and lunar landing vehicles. This program culminated with the *Apollo 11* moon landing of 20 July 1969. As millions around the world watched, Neil Armstrong and Edwin Aldrin conducted experiments on the lunar surface, collected rock and soil samples, and returned safely to Earth.

NASA's moon program (1961-1972) culminated on 20 July 1969 with the landing of Neil Armstrong and Edwin Aldrin, who conducted experiments on the lunar surface, collected rock and soil samples, and safely returned to Earth as they were watched by millions around the world.

Public and congressional support for the space program declined sharply after the moon landing, which seemed the climax of, rather than a stage in, ongoing "spacefaring" activities. In 1972 NASA began the space-shuttle program in order to provide practical means for further scientific exploration, future colonization, and commercial activities (especially carrying private communications satellites, including foreign ones, into space). The shuttle promised to be even more practical than any of its predecessors: a reusable spacecraft that would save millions of dollars which otherwise would have been spent on new vehicles.

The initial twenty-four shuttle missions, beginning with *Columbia* on 12 April 1981, were generally so successful—notable was America's first female astronaut, Sally Ride, in 1983—that public interest in the space program had, ironically, faded once again by the time the *Challenger* exploded on 28 January 1986. That tragedy not only claimed seven lives but also postponed for several years further shuttle launches, as well as future NASA projects like space stations. The inability or refusal of key NASA officials to explain the situation to the public until forced to do so by government investigation, along with their extreme reluctance to take responsibility for their decisions, damaged public confidence.

TELEVISION AND THE FABRIC OF AMERICA. In recent decades a similar questioning has characterized the nation's relationship to television, a technology that has granted Americans unprecedented visual access to a wide range of events. In the late 1940s and early 1950s, television seemed a technical marvel. Americans rushed to purchase huge vacuum-tube-based sets. Small screens, the need for frequent repair, poor reception, and long waits for the set to warm up did not detract from television's initial popularity. Radio and movie audiences plummeted in size. During the next several decades solid-state electronics, improved sound and picture quality, and color were added. Yet television's programming reputation failed to keep pace with the hardware. By 1961, many Americans agreed with Federal Communications Commission Chairman Newton Minow's characterization of the medium as "a vast wasteland," a critique that persists to the present.

Although most commentators saw television as a purveyor of mass culture—much of it lowbrow or explicitly harmful—a handful reversed the indictment and attacked television for fostering isolation and alienation. More advanced television-related technologies did little to mollify television's critics. Communications satellites in stationary orbits paved the way for "superstations," cable television, and receiving dishes, which provided a smorgasbord of options able to placate even the most fragmented of societies. The videocassette recorder (VCR) of the 1970s proved enormously popular and was followed in the 1980s by the "camcorder," a miniaturized lightweight camera for making home videotapes. Laser videodisc, giant-screen TV, and video games expanded the "home entertainment centers" with which Americans further isolated themselves and relied more heavily on visual images.

THE ADVENT OF HIGH-TECH ELECTRONICS. The pervasive individuation of post-1950 American society formed the context for the introduction of high-tech consumer electronics. Pocket radios, cheap enough for almost everyone, were the first major transistor-based consumer product. Patrick Haggerty, president of Texas Instruments (TI), deserves credit for understanding this potential market.

Working independently in the late 1950s, Jack Kilby (b. 1923), a TI engineer, and Robert Noyce (1927–1990), a physicist at Fairchild Semiconductor, devised the "monolithic idea" that eventually became the silicon microchip. That these important inventors remained virtually anonymous in an age of celebrity is ironic. Both of these men envisioned a complete circuit that would consist of a single block of semiconducting silicon containing all the components and connections of even the most complex circuit designs, with the wiring printed onto the chip during production; the individual part and the system became coterminous. Hence the "monolithic integrated circuit," which became the core not only of computers and calculators but also of cameras, clocks, pacemakers, toasters, typewriters, and countless other electronic devices.

Noyce left Fairchild in 1968 to help found Intel, and within a year one of his engineers, Ted Hoff, developed an advanced "superchip" integrated circuit, which brought together electronics and information processing. By 1971 he had devised a one-chip central processor unit known as the "microprocessor," which combined data storage and logic functions into one element: the component is the computer, and the computer is a single component. Whereas custom-made chips were limited to the specific product for which they were designed (and thus posed financial and technological problems for their manufacturers), these general-purpose chips could be manufactured in huge quantities and then programmed for specific applications. Microprocessors inserted intelligence and self-regulation into such now "smart" devices as elevators, engines, gasoline pumps, traffic lights, typewriters, supermarket checkout stands, and clothes dryers.

This technology assisted in making computers a fact of life for nearly all Americans without requiring that they know even simple mathematics or physics to operate these "user-friendly" computers. The replacement of vacuum tubes with transistors and then microchip-based integrated electronic circuits was only one facet of the miniaturization and individualization of computers. Magnetic storage tapes, and then hard and floppy disks and diskettes, replaced plugboards and paper tapes; high-speed line printers, plotters, and video terminals replaced electric typewriters and punch cards.

These developments enabled Americans to enter, store, manipulate, and retrieve information in unprecedented amounts and at unprecedented speed. Nevertheless, these activities, and the use of computers in general, gave rise to critics who voiced concern about computer-generated unemployment and underemployment; psychological (alienation, boredom) and perhaps physical (excessive sedentary posture, eyestrain, exposure to electrical fields) maladies; invasions of privacy; transfer, scrambling, or destruction of military, financial, legal, medical, and other confidential records; and above all, computer dependence or domination.

THE NEW AMERICAN MANUFACTURING. Computer manufacturers, as well as producers of other new technologies, rarely set up shop in America's traditional urban industrial heartland, which had begun to decline following World War II. The South and West had steadily attracted new businesses through tax incentives, lower living costs, and opposition to organized labor. The nation's new labor field was not manufacturing but service: banking, government, teaching, fast foods, and the like. America was becoming "deindustrialized." The inner-city riots of the middle and late 1960s, the Vietnam War, and the oil crisis of 1973 exacerbated the decline of the "frostbelt." These three events also challenged the long-standing assumption about the limitlessness of American material and human resources.

Hard-hit states, such as Massachusetts and Michigan, soon counterattacked by moving aggressively toward "high-tech" industries, such as office and personal computers, fiber optics, lasers, video equipment, robotics, machine vision, and genetic engineering. But it is unlikely that high-tech industries will prove a permanent solution to long-term economic problems. The history of Silicon Valley in California, America's earliest locus of high-tech industries, presents a very different picture.

Silicon Valley is the popular name for the center of the nation's semiconductor industry, located in Santa Clara County, south of San Francisco, which until 1940 was a quiet, productive farming area. Silicon Valley owes its spectacular rise to many factors, foremost among them the efforts and vision of Frederick Terman, a Stanford University electrical engineering professor and administrator. Terman pioneered new ties between the university, business, and government that have since been wisely imitated. By 1970 Santa Clara had become one of America's wealthiest counties through its concentration of high-tech enterprises; in the 1980s, however, it was confronted with saturated markets and fierce competition both domestically and abroad. High-tech's vaunted ability to set up shop almost anywhere had, ironically, sent Silicon Valley into a decline as fast as its rise.

THE CONSEQUENCES OF HIGH-TECH. Robotic technologies, which early on were used primarily for manipulating and manufacturing large, heavy objects, were found to be equally adept—far more so than humans—at the fine assembly work essential to high-tech miniaturization. Moreover, robots need no time off and do not criticize management. The obvious implication, which commentators have predicted, is the "workerless factory" operated by centralized computer systems and incorporating computer-aided design, computer-aided manufacturing, and completely automated processes. Many displaced workers would be compelled to seek lower-paying service jobs. Critics have contended that robots are designed not merely to replace some workers but also to control those who remain by dictating the pace of operations.

Manufacturers in the period after 1950 also increasingly scorned railroads, such that their percentage of the nation's freight haulage dipped well below 30 percent by 1980. The Federal Highway Act, passed in 1956, was instrumental. It specified that funds collected from taxes on gasoline and tire sales, as well as on truck use, would go into the Highway Trust Fund, which would pay for the largest building program in American history: forty-one thousand miles of interstate highways connecting 90 percent of America's cities with populations more than fifty thousand, including five thousand miles in urban areas, with 90 percent of the cost to be paid by the federal government and the states paying the rest.

Air transport also contributed to the railroads' demise, becoming the foremost carrier of mail and passengers over long distances. This was true even before Boeing introduced the first successful commercial jet, the 707, in 1958. This and later jets added to air's advantages: their engines were easily maintained, and they had greater passenger and cargo capacity as well as speed.

HIGH-TECH AGRICULTURE. Rachel Carson (1907–1964), a fish and wildlife biologist, wrote *Silent Spring* (1962), which showed that pesticide overuse and misuse had led to the depletion of natural predators of pests, pesticide resistance in pests, the transformation of helpful species into pests, the extinction or near-extinction of many species, and the rise of cancer, leukemia, hypertension, and liver-cirrhosis rates among persons exposed to large amounts of pesticides. A biochemical dream had become a nightmare. Carson's initiative and others' protests, lawsuits, and legislation resulted in a virtual ban on DDT and the subsequent regulation of safer pesticides and herbicides.

Critics of agricultural mechanization have had less success. A U.S. Department of Agriculture pronouncement in 1968 that "machines are not made to harvest crops; in reality, crops must be designed to be harvested by machines" has become a standard dictum (R. E. Webb and W. M. Bruce, "Redesigning the Tomato for Mechanized Production," *U.S. Department of Agriculture Yearbook* [1968], p. 104). The tomato is a case in point. In 1961 two University of California at Davis staff members, Gordie C. (Jack) Hanna and Coby Lorenson, Jr., marketed both a mechanical tomato harvester and a strain of tomato plant whose fruit would ripen on schedule, remain on the vine for thirty days without deteriorating, survive mechanical harvesting, and withstand shipment—and would be hard and tasteless. Nevertheless, by 1967 the hard tomato and the mechanical harvester were used in combination on 90 percent of California's tomato acreage, easily a majority of the nation's crop. An estimated thirty-two thousand migrant tomato pickers lost their jobs. Although California tomato acreage actually increased, three-quarters of the state's farmers left the business, selling their land to larger growers. Similar harvester-producer combinations are now employed for lettuce, grapes, and other crops, resulting in similar "technological unemployment."

THE GROWTH OF BIOTECHNOLOGY. Hybridization, pesticides, and herbicides were pre-1950 technologies that became social questions in the 1950s and after. Biotechnology was born after mid century and immediately became a social question. In the early 1950s, scientists discovered the genetic code by which deoxyribonucleic acid (DNA) controls cell reproduction in living organisms and passes hereditary information from generation to generation. By the early 1970s, researchers could alter that code by recombination—cutting a piece of DNA and splicing it with another piece—and thus alter the specific qualities of an organism, whether a bacterium, fungus, protozoan, plant, or mammal. This overall process is called genetic engineering.

By the early 1970s, researchers could alter the genetic code by which DNA controls cell production and passes hereditary information from generation to generation; thus they could alter the specific qualities of an organism, whether a bacterium or a mammal.

Biotechnology is at least as revolutionary a phenomenon as computers. It represents a new conception of nature and of life itself as programmed matter. There is enormous potential for genetic engineering not only for agricultural and pharmaceutical companies but also for chemical and energy firms: fragrances, paints, plastics, resins, and solvents, for example, can all be produced by genetic engineering. Toward this and other ends manufacturers of scientific instruments have produced sophisticated computerized machines that make artificial strands of DNA and others that decode genetic instructions.

In 1986, President Reagan signed a comprehensive package of rules, guidelines, and definitions that established America's regulatory policies regarding biotechnology.

THE ENVIRONMENT AND ENGINEERS. Attempts to regulate biotechnology, pesticides, and herbicides were manifestations of a more generalized concern about the quality of American life, which led to creation of numerous national and state regulatory agencies in the 1960s and 1970s. The Environmental Protection Agency (1970) and the Occupational Safety and Health Administration (1973) were among the most powerful and active. This regulation of technology vis-à-vis quality of life was a repudiation of technical expertise as the sole criterion of evaluation, and a rejection of engineers and scientists as the most appropriate decision makers.

Engineers and planners modifying the urban environment also received criticism. Until the late 1960s a "bulldozer mentality," epitomized by Robert Moses, who spent more than $25 billion refurbishing New York City and its environs, characterized urban renewal efforts. Beginning in the 1960s, though, those living in or near razed neighborhoods—generally poor people—publicly objected to destruction of their neighborhoods and formed associations to combat it. These associations got a boost following the 1973 oil embargo, when former suburbanites and young suburbanbred professionals reversed a century-old trend and began to settle in increasing numbers inside city limits. The result was "gentrified" neighborhoods in which shells of old buildings were restored and preserved, while the insides were refitted for new uses. However, this process was sometimes accompanied by concerted drives to force longstanding "undesirable" residents out of their neighborhoods. Infatuated with urban life, "yuppies," or young urban professionals, led a resurgence of inner cities and demanded urban mass transit to meet their needs.

The Technology of Policy

Attempts to analyze, plan, or predict in an era of individual prerogative may seem hopeless, but several methods and establishments have sprung up to undertake these tasks. They explicitly acknowledge relationships between technology and society, and hope their determinations will shape opinion and serve as the basis for public policy. Rarely are they as successful in this last endeavor as they would like.

SYSTEMS ANALYSIS. Systems analysis (SA) originated during World War II as a British military technique to incorporate radar and other unconventional equipment into the air defenses, and is the grandparent of the modern technology of policy. It remains an influential and popular technique for "solving"—and, sometimes, anticipating and even preventing—problems of modern technological societies. Far from being limited to strictly technical or material problems, SA is frequently applied broadly to social problems as well.

SA presumes that all problems are fundamentally technical in nature and thus are quantifiable. Moreover, even if problems are defined in non-technical ways, this theory states that they can be reduced to terms subject to SA. Problems that are supposedly not reducible—philosophical or moral problems—are, by definition, not genuine problems: they must be reformulated or abandoned. SA also presumes group efforts, usually teams of experts from various disciplines who work together to devise the best solutions, or range of alternative solutions, to the problems at hand.

In recent years SA has been criticized as not only elitist, self-justifying, self-perpetuating, and narrowly conceived but also as inefficient, inadequate, and unscientific. Providing a range of alternative solutions to problems is one thing, but providing the solution is quite another matter. Nor does SA have a particularly stellar record in the field in which it originated: the military. There, a seemingly endless progression of poorly made weapons and vehicles, and enormous cost overruns, have led many Americans to equate military expenditures with waste and greed.

TECHNOLOGY ASSESSMENT. Technology assessment (TA), another form of the technology of policy, is the systematic study of the possible impact on a society of a particular form of technology. It is especially concerned with effects that are unintended, indirect, or delayed. The term was coined in the late 1960s by Connecticut Congressman Emilio Daddario. His efforts led to passage of the Technology Assessment Act of 1972 and to the creation that same year of the federal Office of Technology Assessment (OTA).

Closely related to TA and the OTA is the environmental impact statement (EIS), the mandatory use of which since 1969 (when the National Environmental Policy Act became law), has been widespread and significant. Though in some cases such statements may limit or even halt technological developments like dams and power plants, in others they may speed the project's completion.

SEARCHING FOR THE GOOD LIFE. A great many Americans have become concerned with the harmful effects on their health of chemical and synthetic fertilizers, pesticides, and food additives. They have sought to replace chemical methods of food growth, processing, and preparation with "natural" biological ones. Some "natural" food enthusiasts have become severe critics of giant agribusiness corporations, and proponents of conservationist practices such as recycling. Their practices are usually not alternatives to affluence but its by-products. Growing up in a highly technological society, these people wish not to abandon technology but to reform it.

AMERICANS AND THEIR TECHNOLOGIES. Concern about specific technologies functions as a way of providing individuals a group identity in an individual society, and enables them to renounce responsibility for future technological developments even as they make a show of exercising that "responsibility." This paradox stems directly from post-1950 American notions—as does the assumption that technology is both a social solution and a cause of social problems, and its corollary, that technology is the progenitor of society and culture. An examination of the history of technology in America, however, reveals the flaws in that assumption and corollary. Technologies and their applications in America's past have been the consequence of cultural notions and, within that context, social desires, needs, and ambitions. Rather than a progenitor of society and culture, technology has stood as a manifestation or reflection of cultural and social perceptions; it is a human product. And as these notions and desires have differed from one period to another in the nation's past, technologies also have changed as Americans have understood and employed them in a manner consonant with their contemporary ideas. This has led to an abandonment of some technologies as no longer viable, a reinterpretation (often subtle) of other existing technologies, and the creation of new technologies. Indeed, technology has been an integral facet of American experience, but as a mechanism through which cultural notions and social desires were expressed or achieved. It remains so.

[See also The Business Culture; The Culture of Consumption; Film; Mass Culture and Its Critics; Radio; Television; Transportation and Mobility.]

BIBLIOGRAPHY

Barnouw, Erik. *Tube of Plenty: The Evolution of American Television* (1975).

Bilstein, Roger E. *Flight in America, 1900–1983: From the Wrights to the Astronauts* (1984).

Bruce, Robert V. *Bell: Alexander Graham Bell and the Conquest of Solitude* (1973).

Calhoun, Daniel H. *The American Civil Engineer: Origins and Conflicts* (1960).

Chandler, Alfred D., Jr. *The Visible Hand: The Managerial Revolution in American Business* (1977).

Condit, Carl W. *The Rise of the Skyscraper* (1952).

Corn, Joseph J., ed. *Imagining Tomorrow: History, Technology, and the American Future* (1986).

Cowan, Ruth S. *More Work for Mother: The Ironies of Household Technology from the Open Hearth to the Microwave* (1983).

Ellis, John. *The Social History of the Machine Gun* (1975).

Flink, James J. *The Car Culture* (1975).

Graham, Otis L., Jr. *Toward a Planned Society: From Roosevelt to Nixon* (1976).

Haber, Samuel. *Efficiency and Uplift: Scientific Management in the Progressive Era, 1890–1920* (1964).

Hays, Samuel P. *Conservation and the Gospel of Efficiency: The Progressive Conservation Movement, 1890–1920* (1959).

Hounshell, David A. *From the American System to Mass Production, 1800–1932: The Development of Manufacturing Technology in the United States* (1984).

Howard, Robert. *Brave New Workplace* (1985).

Hughes, Thomas P. *Networks of Power: Electrification in Western Society, 1880–1930* (1983).

Hughes, Thomas P. *American Genesis: A Century of Invention and Technological Enthusiasm, 1870–1970* (1989).

Josephson, Matthew. *Edison: A Biography* (1959).

Kasson, John F. *Civilizing the Machine: Technology and Republican Values in America, 1776–1900* (1976).

Lewis, Walter David. *Iron and Steel in America* (1976).

McDougall, Walter A. *The Heavens and the Earth: A Political History of the Space Age* (1985).

Marcus, Alan I. *Agricultural Science and the Quest for Legitimacy: Farmers, Agricultural Colleges, and Experiment Stations, 1870–1890* (1985).

Marcus, Alan I., and Howard P. Segal. *Technology in America: A Brief History* (1989).

Noble, David E. *America by Design: Science, Technology, and the Rise of Corporate Capitalism* (1977).

Passer, Harold C. *The Electrical Manufacturers, 1875–1900* (1953).

Schlebecker, John T. *Whereby We Thrive: A History of American Farming, 1607–1972* (1975).

Scott, Mel. *American City Planning Since 1890* (1969).

Segal, Howard P. *Technological Utopianism in American Culture* (1985).

Smith, Merritt Roe. *Harpers Ferry Armory and the New Technology: The Challenge of Change* (1977).

Teaford, Jon G. *The Municipal Revolution in America: Origins of Modern Urban Government, 1650–1825* (1975).

Tunis, Edwin. *Colonial Craftsmen and the Beginnings of American Industry* (1965).

Turkle, Sherry. *The Second Self: Computers and the Human Spirit* (1984).

White, John H., Jr. *American Locomotives: An Engineering History, 1830–1880* (1968).

— HOWARD P. SEGAL

TELEVISION

No means of communication has equaled the capacity of television to reach large masses of people. With the launching of communications satellites in the 1960s, television could instantly transmit both sound and moving pictures to millions of people from anywhere on earth as well as from outer space. In 1969, for example, an estimated 723 million people, more than triple the population of the United States, saw a human first set foot on the moon. Subsequent improvements in transmission and the widespread ownership of receivers soon made it possible to reach more than half the world's peoples simultaneously.

Within less than a generation after its introduction in the late 1930s, television had woven itself completely into the fabric of all modern societies. By the 1990s, Americans spent about one-quarter of their lives watching television, and on average, American households had at least one set turned on for seven hours each day. For many people the rhythms of daily, weekly, and seasonal programming measured the passage of time as much as watches or calendars. Viewers frequently "knew" the actors, comedians, politicians, and news commentators on television better than their neighbors, friends, or co-workers. For most Americans, television replaced friends, the print media, radio, and the movies as their primary source of both entertainment and news. The "mediated" world of television, one framed by the technical limits of the medium and by what its controllers presented, also offered abundant cues for daily living. In particular, television programming and advertising suggested consumption as a therapy for feelings of impotency, loneliness, sexual deprivation, and meaningless work.

In the United States, program content was the product of varied social influences, government regulations, and, above all, the medium's economic character. Social influences included the experiences, aesthetic judgments, values, creativity, and artistic skills of those involved in program production; the industry's internal codes; the influence of media critics; and the varied pressures exerted by the television audience on programming. Government regulations arose from television's dependence upon the airwaves for transmission. The Communications Act of 1934 mandated that, in exchange for receiving exclusive use of the airwaves, commercial television stations, along with radio stations, "operate in the public interest, convenience, and necessity." The degree to which the Federal Communications Commission (FCC), the federal agency assigned responsibility for enforcing the act and its subsequent modifications, exercised authority over program content and regulated other facets of the industry varied over time. (In the late 1970s and in the 1980s Congress and the FCC removed most of the accumulated government-imposed restrictions and guidelines.)

Except for public television, nothing ultimately determined program content as much as the industry's dependence upon receipts from advertising. Vigorous competition for advertising revenues among the local stations and their program suppliers (until the 1980s almost exclusively three national networks), as well as competition between television and other media, drove the industry to seek mass audiences. To obtain larger audiences, the program producers turned to entertainment. Entertainment, the use of virtually any technique to keep the viewer riveted to the receiver, thus became a salient characteristic of nearly all programming. The requirements of entertainment invaded even what were officially labeled as newscasts, sportscasts, and educational programming.

Television in the United States, in contrast with television in nearly all other nations, has been almost entirely a private rather than a public enterprise. In most nations, if there is a system dependent upon advertising, it must compete with a strong system subsidized by the public. In the United States, on the other hand, public television has received meager state support and has never drawn more than 5 percent of the total viewers. Of some 1,400 American television stations in operation in 1990, only 335 were public or educational stations. Until the 1980s nearly 90 percent of the privately owned stations were affiliated with one of the three giant commercial networks—the American Broadcasting Company (ABC), the Columbia Broadcasting System (CBS), and the National Broadcasting Company (NBC), which provided them with about two-thirds of their programming.

The Evolution of the Television Industry

In the 1920s and 1930s, the Radio Corporation of America (RCA), a giant company that manufactured radio equipment and owned NBC, was at the forefront in the development of American television. Hoping to profit from the sale of television cameras, transmission equipment, and receivers, RCA, under the direction of hard-driving David Sarnoff, spent an estimated fifty million dollars financing the continuing research of Vladimir K. Zworykin, a Russian-born American scientist, who in 1929 had demonstrated the first practical electronic system for both transmission and reception of images. Sarnoff also purchased valuable licensing agreements and patent rights from Philo T. Farnsworth, an American inventor. As early as 1936, RCA conducted tests of its all-electronic television system from atop the Empire State Building, broadcasting pictures at a rate of thirty complete pictures (frames) per second. In the same year, CBS purchased a system from RCA and installed it in the Chrysler Building, near its radio studios in the Grand Central Terminal Building.

The year 1939 marked a series of firsts: NBC began regular telecasts in New York City with the opening ceremonies at the World's Fair and the network beamed the first televised baseball game, from Baker Field at

Columbia University. In 1941, the FCC approved limited commercial broadcasting and accepted the television industry's recommendations for 525 lines per frame and 30 pictures per second as transmission standards, standards that are still in use today. During World War II, however, as engineers and their sponsors turned their energies elsewhere, improvements in television's technology came to an abrupt halt. Only six stations remained on the air, and they broadcast only locally, irregularly, and a few hours a day to fewer than ten thousand receivers.

After the war, a striking improvement in the television camera stimulated the industry's growth. To obtain what at best was a mediocre picture, Zworykin's iconoscope camera required great quantities of light. In response to the poor picture quality, Zworykin invented, and in 1945 RCA introduced, the image orthicon camera tube, which was even more sensitive to nuances in light and dark than most of the motion picture cameras of the day. "All of a sudden, we had an instrument that reproduced a quality, picture with the atmosphere and mood that [Alfred] Hitchcock or [Ingmar] Bergman might require," recalled Worthington Minor, who at the time was CBS's manager of program development.

The year 1939 marked a series of firsts: NBC began regular telecasts in New York City with the opening ceremonies at the World's Fair, and the network beamed the first televised baseball game, from Baker Field at Columbia University.

Abetted by the orthicon camera, by the FCC's decision to resume the licensing of new stations in 1945, by the resumption of the production of transmitters and receivers at the end of the war, by American Telephone and Telegraph's (AT&T) rapid construction of intercity coaxial cable links, by corporations eager to advertise their goods, and by consumers with accumulated savings, commercial television prospered, Taverns in particular rushed to acquire sets; groups made up mostly of men gathered around them nightly to watch wrestling, boxing, and other sports. In 1948, an estimated one million sets were in use, forty-eight television stations were in operation, and about seventy stations were under construction. Although an FCC freeze that had been imposed in order to bring some order to the chaotic industry halted the licensing of new stations between 1948 and 1952, the completion by AT&T of a transcontinental coaxial cable trunk in 1951 allowed the networks to inaugurate nationwide telecasts. Families owning sets skyrocketed from 50 percent of all families in 1953 to 90 percent in 1960.

Other technical improvements aided the industry's growth. The perfection of magnetic videotape in the late 1950s eliminated the contingencies of live programming and permitted endless reruns. In 1953 the FCC finally approved a color system compatible with black-and-white sets, but because of the additional costs in production, transmission, and receiving, color television grew slowly. Until 1965 only NBC, whose parent company, RCA, was the major manufacturer of color sets, showed more than a few programs in color. In 1965 a little-noted poll indicated that viewers had a decided preference for color, which led CBS to introduce a full array of color shows that fall; ABC announced that it would begin to transmit mainly in color in the fall of 1966. Within two years, monochrome network shows disappeared, the prices of color sets fell by about half, and color picture quality improved substantially. (The old black-and-white sets continued to receive broadcasts but still reproduced programs in monocolor.)

Apart from technical limitations, television operated within constraints imposed by the FCC, pressure groups, and advertisers. The Communications Act of 1934 guaranteed access to commercial television by those holding views not shared by the station ownership. In 1949, the FCC formalized the access concept with a set of procedures called the Fairness Doctrine. Although modified several times by the FCC, the courts, and Congress, in essence the doctrine required broadcasters to devote a reasonable amount of time to controversial issues of public importance and to give those with opposing viewpoints a reasonable amount of air time to express their positions. In practice, the doctrine may have been counterproductive. Neither the networks nor the stations relished giving "free" time and possibly reducing their audiences by the presentation of contentious issues, so they chose simply to reduce their coverage of controversial topics, thereby avoiding the need to give air time to unpopular subjects or personalities.

Self-regulation was a far more important restraint than FCC policies. Fearing the loss of sponsor support and alienation of a share of the audience, each network established a standards-and-practices department. These "network censors" acted as gatekeepers between program producers and the audience. They reviewed program concepts, story lines, scripts, and proposed footage in terms of what might give offense to sponsors or the audience. During the early cold war years of the late 1940s and the 1950s, the networks also blacklisted many performers and writers who had been charged by self-appointed investigators with being Communists or Communist sympathizers. Threatened by the withdrawal of sponsors, the media shamelessly fired or refused to hire persons found on such lists; they even employed their own "security checkers" and required employees to sign loyalty oaths. Blacklisting continued until the late 1950s, when the domestic anticommunist movement lost some of its momentum.

Sponsors, particularly in the early days of network television, exercised an exceptionally large and direct influence over program content. Until the late 1950s, a single advertiser frequently sponsored an entire program (as had been the practice in radio), which was typically produced by the sponsor's advertising agency. Sponsors could be explicit about what they wanted in a show. For example, writers for *Man Against Crime*, a show sponsored by Camel cigarettes, received mimeographed instructions to delete all scenes of "disreputable persons" smoking cigarettes; neither could cigarette smokers be shown coughing. But with rapidly escalating costs in the late 1950s, few advertisers could afford to purchase the time for an entire program. Multiple advertisers gave the networks far greater control over program content, though networks continued to remain sensitive to the responses of sponsors.

In the 1980s the near-monopoly once enjoyed by the "big three" commercial networks on the delivery of programs abruptly ended. In the 1970s and 1980s new competition arising from the rapid growth of independent stations, the appearance of "superstations"—stations that employed communications satellites to beam programs nationwide—the growth of cable television systems, and the mass marketing of videocassette recorders (VCRs) sharply reduced the proportional audience share and advertising revenues of the "big three" networks. The networks' audience share dropped from more than 90 percent in the 1970s to about 70 percent in 1990, and their proportion of total television advertising revenues fell by about one-fourth. Deregulation added to the television industry's instability. Beginning in the late 1970s and continuing through the 1980s, the FCC dropped many of its regulations, including the Fairness Doctrine (1987). In the 1980s, marketplace forces almost completely determined the industry's direction.

Effects on American Life

Although not easily isolable from other forces, television quickly, directly, and in some instances drastically affected American life. One of its most readily observable effects was on leisure. In the first half of the twentieth century, urbanites had usually looked to the inner city for entertainment; those residing in the suburbs used street railways to make their way downtown to shop or go to restaurants, movies, indoor arenas, saloons, concert halls, and the theater. Baseball parks, football fields, and amusement parks, though often located outside the central business district, could be reached cheaply by mass transit.

As millions moved to the sprawling suburbs after World War II and purchased their first television sets, they took their leisure activities with them. They made home repairs and worked in their yards, listened to music on high-fidelity phonograph records, and watched television. With television, each family had at its fingertips entertainment previously available only by going out to the theater, vaudeville, or the movies. "More than a year passed before we again visited a movie theater, recalled one man after the purchase of the family's first television set in 1950. "Money which previously would have been spent on books was saved for TV payments. Social evenings with friends became fewer and fewer still." Families went out less, slept less, and read less, and the children played outside less than before. That by 1970 comic book sales had plummeted to half the 1950 totals suggested the medium's power over children.

Novelty alone did not account for the medium's magnetism. With each subsequent decade, viewing time increased. People did not necessarily watch closely; studies indicated that family members frequently did other things while "watching" television, although they could often recall substantial amounts of program content. Viewing was consistently greater among children of elementary school age or younger than among high school or college-age youth; older people watched more than younger adults, blacks and Hispanics more than whites, and the less educated more than the better educated. Yet the discrepancy among these groups in viewing time typically averaged less than forty-five minutes a day, thus revealing the truly mass character of the new medium.

The shift of spare-time activities from public places to the privacy of the home nearly destroyed inner-city commercial leisure. In the 1950s and 1960s, movie theaters, bars, restaurants, dance pavilions, nightclubs, and amusement parks closed in great numbers. The large dance bands that had been so popular in the 1930s and 1940s all but disappeared. Attendance at inner-city high school sports events and at wrestling and boxing matches fell; none ever regained the prosperity that they had once enjoyed at the local level. In the 1950s both major-league and minor-league baseball attendance fell; the minor leagues never recovered, and even the big leagues never caught up proportionally with the population growth of the cities they served.

With the advent of television, the fans at home rather than those in the stands increasingly became the ultimate arbiters of which sports thrived and which ones failed. College and professional football fared much better on television than baseball. Baseball, with its multiple perspectives and wide vistas, did not translate well onto the small screen, whereas the more concentrated action and recurring drama in each series of downs made football an ideal sport for the new medium. The perfection in the 1960s of the instant replay and the slow-motion shot allowed fans at home to experience football in an entirely different way from those in the stands. The televised Super Bowl, a product of the merger of competing professional football leagues in 1966, eventually became an unofficial national holiday and a spectacle regularly watched by more than half of the nation's population. The exciting telecast from Munich of the 1972 Olympic Games, which included monumental blunders, sparkling heroes, and the tragedy resulting from the invasion of the Israeli compound by Palestinian terrorists, transformed the games into a worldwide quadrennial spectacle.

Television quickly altered the character of competing forms of entertainment. Network radio programming gave way almost completely to television; by the early 1960s few network entertainment programs remained on radio, and less than a third of the radio stations had a national affiliation. In the age of television, radio became a largely local medium, with each station aiming at a special audience. Confronted with competition from television, the movie industry either adjusted by making films for the new medium or aiming its fare at teenagers and young adults (those who watched television the least), a strategy that encouraged film content to become more experimental, violent, and sexually provocative.

Within a decade, *Life, Look, Collier's,* and *The Saturday Evening Post* had ceased to exist as mass-circulation weekly magazines. On the other hand, television, with its emphasis upon capturing a mass audience, left ample room for periodicals that appealed in depth to specialized tastes; in the 1970s and 1980s these magazines proliferated and prospered.

Television induced changes in the content of print media. Newspapers soon began to set aside regular allotments of space for columns on television and the listing of upcoming programs. *TV Guide,* founded in 1953 and completely devoted to television, became the largest circulation periodical in the United States; by 1976, it sold 20 million copies weekly. Blatantly copying formulas successfully employed by television, in the 1970s and 1980s the popular magazines *People, Us,* and several imitators featured short articles—nothing requiring more than a minute-and-a-half to read, ordered one editor—and abundant illustrations, all laced with titillating accounts of the activities of celebrities. *USA Today,* a national daily newspaper that imitated television news and talk shows, completed the cycle in 1980 when it syndicated its own television program, *USA Today: The Television Show.* By the 1990s newspapers throughout the country were beginning to ban stories that continued on another page, feature more celebrity stories, and employ more eye-catching graphics.

Television exerted a large, perhaps equal influence on politics. In 1952, Richard M. Nixon's "Checkers speech" on television aided the senator in salvaging his shaky vice-presidential candidacy. In 1960, viewers and journalists alike proclaimed the handsome and relaxed John F. Kennedy the "winner" over a swarthy and wary Richard M. Nixon in the first televised debates between presidential nominees, but several studies agreed that the debates affected the final decisions of only a few voters. Nonetheless, because of the popular belief that the debates of 1960 had damaged Nixon, the better-known candidate and the front runner in the polls at the time of the first debate, no debates were held in 1964, 1968, or 1972. In 1976, both Jimmy Carter, a relative unknown, and Gerald Ford, an incumbent president who had been tied to Nixon's presidency and initially trailed badly in the polls, had reason to engage in televised debates. The decisions by Ford in 1976 and Carter again in 1980 to debate apparently set a precedent that made it difficult for any future incumbent to avoid a televised debate. Television debates among candidates for lesser posts also became commonplace.

Television quickly began to exert a large influence on politics: In 1960, viewers and journalists alike proclaimed the handsome and relaxed John F. Kennedy the "winner" over a swarthy- and wary-appearing Richard M. Nixon in the first televised debates between presidential nominees.

Television, along with computers and public opinion polls, introduced what has been described as "the new politics." Candidates employed professional pollsters to gather the opinions of various constituencies, computers sorted the data, and finally media consultants plotted a strategy based upon the results of the polls. The media experts approached campaigns in terms of "selling a candidate," which entailed the same strategy as selling consumer goods to the public. Thus media people considered the management of images or impressions to be far more important to success than where the candidate stood on the issues. Richard M. Nixon's presidential campaign of 1968 was a classic example. Nixon's campaign staff put together a series of clever television advertisements that projected a "new Nixon," one who was more unflappable, relaxed, and skillful in dealing with controversy than he had been in the past. "Reason pushes the viewer back, it assaults him, it demands that he agree or disagree," explained one of Nixon's media consultants, while "impressions can envelop him, invite him, without making an intellectual demand."

The media consultants frequently resorted to images that appealed to primitive fears. During the 1964 election, President Lyndon Johnson's media people aired the "daisy" commercial aimed at his opponent, Barry Goldwater, who was accused of being too aggressive in relations with the Soviet Union. The commercial showed a little girl in white pulling the petals off a daisy. As she counted down to zero, the scene dissolved into an atomic explosion, and then a voice—by implication Johnson's—came on: "These are the stakes. To make a world in which all God's children can live, or go into the dark." Although political scientists repeatedly expressed skepticism about the efficacy of image manipulation, either their reservations were not shared by the candidates or the candidates were unwilling to take any chances. In the 1980s, appeals to raw emotions through image advertising became even more common.

Television refashioned politics in other ways. Candidates sought to say and do things that would maximize their coverage on television news programs. Presenting elections in terms of sporting contests, the medium increased the importance of the presidential primaries, especially the earlier ones, in the nominating process. Rather than serving as meetings to choose candidates, the national party conventions became carefully orchestrated television shows for acclaiming decisions already made. With television becoming the largest single item in campaign budgets, the costs of running for public office escalated to undreamed-of heights. Astronomical campaign costs generated a rising concern in the 1980s about the influence of large campaign contributors on the political process.

Early Programming

Even though nearly all commercial television programs were designed simply to entertain, they simultaneously disseminated information and suggested models for daily living. Apart from the news, the endless commercials, the tales of outlawry in the old West, of urban crime, and of international intrigue, the miniseries and the docudramas, and the antic tensions in situation comedies (sitcoms) all furnished viewers with implicit or explicit interpretations of the past and the present. With its enormous power to evoke images and fantasies, television also offered viewers visions of and strategies for achieving personal fulfillment.

Although changes in technology enlarged the medium's capabilities and the nation experienced great social upheavals during network television's first four decades, most program forms remained remarkably constant. The early morning news shows, soap operas, the late-night and midday talk shows, Saturday morning children's cartoons, evening news programs, game shows, sitcoms, and even the commercials all had their origins in the late 1940s and early 1950s. Only drama altered its essential character. In the early years, television presented drama live and, rather than weekly shows based upon the same set of characters and situations, viewers could see dozens of completely new productions each week.

Nothing that viewers saw on television was more pervasive or constant than commercials. In the late nineteenth century, advertisers had begun to sense the effectiveness of suggesting a causal relationship between consuming a particular brand of a product and being youthful, desirable, rich, powerful, or successful. Television gave advertisers the opportunity to convey the linkage between consumption and the satisfaction of personal needs in far more compelling, but at the same time more subtle, ways than had earlier media. The ads did not need to be explicit: in the 1950s viewers saw scores of cleaning products used in fifteen-thousand-dollar kitchens, and in the 1960s they saw countless soft-drink ads with the young engaged in exuberant play. Smoking a certain brand of cigarette seemed to promise excitement, romance, and ultimately sexual satisfaction. Ads not only appropriated lifestyles and held out consumption as a solution for personal needs, they also sold visions of America itself. Nothing distinguished the United States from other nations—not even democracy or respect for individual liberties—as much as its capacity to provide consumer goods. The ads depicted the United States as a consumer paradise.

Entertainment program content also reflected television's close ties to the consumer culture. During its first full season in 1949, television explicitly conjoined consumption and entertainment in such programs as *Kelvinator Kitchen* and *Missus Goes A-Shopping*, the latter a supermarket customer participation show. Debates over the purchases of goods for the home furnished the main story line for innumerable postwar sitcoms, and before FCC rules eventually prohibited the practice, news, quiz, and variety shows usually displayed the sponsor's name conspicuously on podiums, clocks, or walls so that it would be visible to viewers throughout the program. Shows in the 1940s and 1950s took the name of their sponsors: *The Kraft Television Theater, Camel News Caravan,* and *The Bell Telephone Hour,* for example. Variety show host Milton Berle's program was called *The Texaco Star Theater* and opened with service station attendants, outfitted in Texaco uniforms, singing "Tonight we may be showmen, but . . . tomorrow we'll be servicing your car!"

The variety show, a format that could be cheaply and easily produced, was a favorite of early television. Rooted in earlier vaudeville, circuses, and radio, the variety shows filled the screens with singers, dancers, magicians, jugglers, and animal acts. Comedians, including Sid Caesar, George Gobel, and Milton Berle, usually hosted the shows. Between 1948 and 1956, Milton Berle, a Catskills resort comedian and a child of vaudeville, earned the title of Mr. Television or, more informally, Uncle Miltie. Berle, who had not been a top performer in radio, found in television a perfect medium for the employment of his sight gags, outrageous costumes, and general buffoonery. A noncomedian, Broadway gossip columnist Ed Sullivan, hosted a far more enduring variety show. With a keen sense for presenting acts when they were of the most topical interest, he premiered both Elvis Presley (1956) and the Beatles (1964) on network television.

No other show exceeded the popularity of I Love Lucy, *featuring the zany and always scheming Lucille Ball; her shows ran almost continuously on CBS from 1951 to the actress's retirement in 1974.*

Variety shows soon lost their central place on prime-time television, however. Although Ed Sullivan, Jack Benny, and Red Skelton survived for more than a decade by employing a traditional format, competition with filmed series either ended variety shows or forced them to offer something distinctive. *The Smothers Brothers* succeeded in the late 1960s by offering comedy that was irreverent and antiestablishment, and *Rowan & Martin's Laugh-in* for a time (1967–1973) captivated audiences by fast-paced cutting from one scene to another and its more candid handling of sexual and political materials. But by the mid 1970s, except in non-prime-time hours, the variety show disappeared almost entirely from network television.

Sitcoms, a direct transplant from radio, were a far more enduring staple of prime-time television. Week after week the same basic cast of characters played in the same format. In the 1950s Jackie Gleason as Ralph Kramden, Phil Silvers as Sergeant Bilko, and Lucille Ball as Lucy Arnaz were all inclined to concoct elaborate schemes to advance their fortunes that in the end invariably miscarried. No other show exceeded the popularity of *I Love Lucy.* Featuring the beautiful, zany, and always scheming Ball, her shows ran almost continuously, with only short interruptions, on CBS from 1951 until Ball's retirement (with her ratings still high) in 1974. Even in the 1990s, viewers could find Ball reruns on stations throughout the world.

The family sitcoms of the 1950s communicated no simple, monolithic message. True, no shows equaled the sitcoms in their emphases upon the benefits of traditional family life, the suburbs, and the consumer culture. The lives depicted in the typical 1950s sitcoms mirrored the fantasies of a generation who sought to escape and forget the deprivations and turmoil that they had experienced in the Great Depression and World War II. Yet the dramatic tension required to attract viewers often revolved around the dissonance between the past and the present, between inner-city, ethnic, working-class family origins and the transformation of the family into homogeneous, middle-class suburbanites devoted to consumption. Ethnic working-class sitcoms, such as *The Goldbergs, Mama, The Honeymooners,* and *The Life of Riley,* presented families in inner-city neighborhoods and explored value conflicts that revolved around family identity, consumer spending, gender roles, ethnicity, and the nature of work and leisure.

Shows designed for children quickly became an integral part of network programming. Although children spent many hours watching whatever was shown, as early as 1947 NBC's *Howdy Doody* captivated them with its frenzied action. While Howdy Doody regularly promoted good behavior, Clarabell, the show's androgynous clown, regularly flouted adult authority. *Kukla, Fran, and Ollie* and *Captain Kangaroo,* both of which originated in the 1950s, had much more relaxed paces. By the mid-1960s, the three networks set aside Saturday morning entirely for children; then children could see made-for-television cartoons, all of which incorporated fast-paced action and most of them unending violence. The Saturday morning format remained in place for the next two decades.

Nothing about television programming caused as much widespread concern as its possible effects on children. In 1952 Senator Estes Kefauver held the first of many congressional hearings on the subject, and by 1990 more than 250 separate studies had been conducted on children's television. A consensus of the studies indicated that television watching encouraged short-term aggressive behavior and insensitivity to violence. Less debatable was the patent abuse of the child market by advertisers. The sponsors unrelentingly assaulted children with alluring advertisements for toys and non-nutritious foods. A 1991 study, for example, counted 222 junk food ads in one Saturday morning's set of cartoon shows. Critics also blamed the medium for a decline in College Entrance Examination Board scores (beginning in 1964), a decline in ability to think sequentially, encouragement of sensual gratification, and a general distrust of authority. All of the charges were plausible, but inventing a research design that could pinpoint the precise influence of television on such behaviors was impossible.

The 1950s achieved its vaunted and exaggerated reputation as the "golden age" of television through its live Broadway-like drama and public affairs programming rather than through variety shows, sitcoms, or children's shows. For a brief interlude, mainly from 1952 to 1955, live drama, with completely new shows ranging from thirty minutes to a hour and a half each week, was part of the regular nightly fare of network television. The shows offered opportunities for scores of talented young playwrights, producers, directors, actors, and actresses. The writers included Rod Serling, Gore Vidal, and Paddy Chayefsky. Chayefsky's *Marty*, later made into a movie, became a television classic.

Television's brief experimentation in the 1950s with live theater and large quantities of public affairs programming arose more from special circumstances than from audience preferences. Inadequate technology limited the possibilities of taped shows, and Hollywood, fearing competition from the new medium, initially refused to provide television with first-run movies. With CBS's near-monopoly on the stars in the 1950s, NBC had little choice but to experiment with live shows, even when they were expensive and their costs were not necessarily covered by advertising revenues. In addition, the longer live shows offered the networks an opportunity to gain greater control over programming. By 1960, packagers—companies that combined talent, production facilities, and program ideas—produced about 60 percent of television network programming, the networks about 20 percent, sponsors only about 14 percent, and individuals—like Lucille Ball—the rest.

Walter Cronkite in CBS Studio, 1967. The personality of the anchorperson has almost always influenced the ratings in television news.

In some instances, the absence of sponsorship fostered experimental programming. Several of the public affairs programs, including Edward R. Murrow's *See It Now* on CBS and *Today*, which was introduced in 1952 by NBC to fill a morning scheduling gap, initially had no sponsors. With Dave Garroway in Chicago as host, *Today* included an innovative magazine format, a combination of news, informational features, and light banter. Neither ABC nor DuMont (a short-lived fourth network) had many sponsors for daytime programming; hence they beamed the Army-McCarthy hearings of 1954 in full while NBC and CBS, with more sponsored daytime programming, carried only limited parts of the hearings.

The high-stakes, prime-time quiz shows contributed to the demise of the golden age. At the height of the fad, five shows were shown in a single day. In order to guarantee that popular contestants remained on the air, producers began providing them with answers prior to the show. When this practice was exposed in 1959, network executives denied knowing anything about the rigging, but they quickly canceled almost all of the shows. The scandal led to a congressional inquiry, the adoption of internal controls against deceit, steps by the networks to gain greater control over their programming, and the growing use of filmed series from Hollywood.

By the late 1950s, network competition had settled into a pattern that encouraged program standardization. CBS had demonstrated that, on the whole, the regular showing of familiar series was more popular than dramatic anthologies. NBC fired its chairman (and effectively, director of programming), Sylvester (Pat) Weaver, in 1956, the same year that CBS overtook NBC in the ratings, and named Robert Kintner, a past president of ABC, as its president; he had broken the Hollywood boycott by persuading Walt Disney in 1954 and Warner Brothers in 1955 to become makers of television programs. Kintner preferred the more predictable filmed series over live shows, and he inaugurated a new era in which Hollywood films became a staple of network programming.

Television News

Copying the format used in radio and without the resources to provide extensive film footage, the first television newscasts consisted of little more than a camera focused on a journalist reading from a script. In one of the few instances of clear-cut "advocacy" news in the history of television, Edward R. Murrow in 1954 exposed the methods of Senator Joseph McCarthy, though the live telecasts of the Army-McCarthy hearings in the same year contributed even more to the senator's rapid fall from power. Even in the 1950s there were signs that obtaining high ratings depended more on the personality of the person who delivered the news and the way the news was packaged—how entertaining it was—than on the network's effectiveness in presenting or analyzing events. Chet Huntley and David Brinkley's conversational and lighthearted treatment of the national political conventions in 1956 transformed those newsmen into stars for NBC; that fall they became the hosts of NBC's evening news show. In 1962, Walter Cronkite, who conveyed an image of avuncular omniscience, began his tenure as anchorman and star of CBS's evening news program.

Television news came of age in the 1960s. With the expansion of nightly news from fifteen to thirty minutes in 1962 by both CBS and NBC, more exciting drama could frequently be found on the news programs than on prime-time entertainment shows. Television's reporting of the space race with the Soviet Union, beginning with John Glenn's orbital flight in 1962 and culminating with the moon landing in 1969, captivated millions worldwide. The assassination of President John F. Kennedy and subsequent events in November 1963 led the networks to cancel their regular schedules completely. For four days, as many as 93 percent of American homes watched television's intimate coverage of the events. In such times of crisis, the electronic media seemed to allay panic and ease the transition of power.

While nearly all Americans applauded television's handling of the space race and Kennedy's assassination, television's treatment of the divisive social issues of the 1960s soon embroiled the news media in controversy. Whether because of the "liberal" or "modern" values of television newscasters or because of the compulsion to make the news more entertaining—as critics charged—or simply by showing the savagery of white responses to peaceful demonstrations by blacks, televised newscasts added momentum to the civil rights movement. Simply by giving it coverage and by magnifying its size, television also abetted and shaped the character of the youth revolt of the 1960s. On the other hand, by its coverage of the burning and looting of urban ghettos during the "long, hot summer" of 1965 and the more violent and radical side of the youth rebellion in the late 1960s, the medium encouraged a widespread backlash against both movements.

For fifteen years (1961–1975), television news-casts brought to American homes the "living room war" in Vietnam. Although initially the networks stressed the value and the successes of the American military effort, no previous war had been so accessible to reporters. Reporters could cover and film almost anything they wished. While military press briefings consisted mainly of dry, "factual" material, including daily "body counts" of the enemy allegedly killed, the television reporters sent back vivid images—of body bags containing corpses, of angry, frustrated soldiers, of troops setting fire to a village with their cigarette lighters, of Vietnamese orphans, of Buddhist monks setting themselves on fire with gasoline. With the Tet offensive that was mounted by the enemy in 1968, journalists began to abandon remaining pretenses of neutrality. A decisive turning point in public support for the war came when, according to President Lyndon Johnson, Walter Cronkite urged on his evening newscast that the United States pull out.

Entertainment Programming in the 1960s and 1970s

Throughout the 1960s entertainment programming reflected none of the great social upheavals found on the network news shows. Rather than family life in the suburbs or urban-oriented variety shows, rural, small-town, and western settings characterized much of the prime-time television fare from the late 1950s to the early 1970s. The Westerns entered their heyday; an astonishing thirty-two Western series were shown in the 1959–1960 season alone. Two of them—*Gunsmoke* (1955–1975) and *Bonanza* (1959–1973)—were among the longest-running shows in television history; their romanticization of the American West won them a worldwide audience as well. Dozens of family sitcoms, including *The Andy Griffith Show, Mister Ed, The Beverly Hillbillies, Green Acres, Petticoat Junction,* and *The Real McCoys,* reflected the appeal of non-urban settings.

Although frequently dismissed by television critics as trivial entertainment, Paul Henning's CBS sitcoms, *The Beverly Hillbillies, Green Acres,* and *Petticoat Junction,* satirized modern, urban America, especially its preoccupation with technology and consumption. *The Beverly Hillbillies,* a show rivaled in popularity only by *Bonanza,* returned to an ancient theme in American and European literature: the physical and moral superiority of pastoral or rural life over urban life. Although transplanted from the Ozarks to the decadence and splendor of California's Beverly Hills, Jed Clampett, the male lead played by Buddy Ebsen, remained selfless, honest, fair, and incorruptible. He was, in the words of media critic David Marc, "a yeoman beyond the fantasies of Jefferson. Henning's *Green Acres,* a mirror reversal of *The Beverly Hillbillies* in that it placed city slickers amid rural people, brought into even sharper relief the fundamental conflict between America's past and its present.

While the Westerns did not frontally assault modernity, they were part of a wide-ranging and flourishing culture of compensation. In the 1955–1956 season, the "adult Westerns," such as *Cheyenne, Gunsmoke,* and *Tales of the Texas Rangers,* with their more complex plots and vivid renderings of violence, rode into prime time. Amid the daily network news programs depicting bitter internal divisions and the continuing perils of the cold war, the Westerns affirmed the continuing potency of the individual. The heroes came in different guises. Some were strong and brave, others dashing and romantic, and still others shrewd and comic, but in the end they all relied mainly upon their own resources to conquer villains. An urban counterpart to the adult Westerns was *The Untouchables,* an exceptionally violent show that starred Robert Stack as Eliot Ness, an incorruptible government agent who relentlessly and successfully pursued mobsters in the 1920s. Women may have found some compensation for their special plight in *I Dream of Jeannie, Bewitched,* or *The Flying Nun,* shows that portrayed women with magical powers. By implicitly drawing attention to the subordinate position of women, such shows may even have contributed to the coming of the women's liberation movement of the 1960s and 1970s.

The televised version of the bone-crunching game of college and professional football also furnished forceful images and fantasies of individual power. Television triggered a literal "takeoff" in football's popularity in the 1960s. While networks marketed the game as an endless array of spectacular collisions between padded giants, the perfection of slow motion, instant replay, and color increased audience appreciation of the sport's intricate plays, and the long completed pass and the breakaway run suggested the possibilities—at least on occasion—of the lone individual transcending the vast odds arrayed against him. Professional football even invaded prime-time television; in 1970 ABC inaugurated *Monday Night Football,* a program that almost at once absorbed the attention of millions of American men (and a number of American women) every Monday night in the fall.

The 1969–1970 season represented something of a watershed in television's programming history; not a single holdover from the 1968–1969 "top ten" series retained its position five years later. Westerns and rural sitcoms all but disappeared from regularly scheduled network programming. The programs looked different: blacks and ethnics suddenly became prominent, and hippielike hairstyles and clothing became common. The programs sounded different: a wave of greater permissiveness in language swept through the medium, and programs began treating previously taboo subjects such as interracial marriage, sexual impotence, and ethnic conflicts.

"Demographics," the industry's term for describing potential viewers in terms of such marketing characteristics as age, sex, and income level, rather than general audience ratings, dictated the sweeping program changes. The prevailing rural sitcoms and Westerns appealed to a broad constituency, but more to the young and the old than to the especially hard-to-reach young adults, those eighteen to thirty-four years old, who purchased the most goods and services. Under Robert D. Wood, CBS, the leader in network prime-time overall audience ratings, startled the industry by dropping a large number of still-popular shows—Jackie Gleason, Red Skelton, Andy Griffith, Ed Sullivan, *The Beverly Hillbillies, Green Acres, Hee-Haw,* and *Petticoat Junction*—and replacing them with urban-oriented shows that purported to have more "contemporary relevance."

Norman Lear's *All in the Family,* a sitcom based upon a popular show in Great Britain, led the way. Premiering in 1971, *All in the Family* not only leaped to the top of ratings charts but also revealed, for the first time on prime-time television, fundamental clashes between the young and the old, whites and blacks, men and women, as well as ethnic and religious divisions, and may have introduced a new synonym for "bigot"—"Archie Bunker"—into the language. The success of *All in the Family* led Lear to produce such spinoffs as *Maude,* whose heroine had an abortion and went through a long separation from her husband, and *The Jeffersons*, a show based on an upwardly mobile black family. "Relevancy," "realism," and "timeliness" became watchwords of sitcom producers in the 1970s.

In a fundamental sense, the new sitcoms were far less radical than they seemed. They incorporated and institutionalized the stresses and styles of the 1960s, thereby taming them and bringing them into the mainstream of popular culture. In the shows, family ties if not the family itself remained essentially conventional. Even *All in the Family* presented traditional marriages, an extended family living for most of the show's duration under the same roof, and the irascible Archie as an emotionally vulnerable person devoted in his own way to his wife and daughter. And sitcoms without fathers, mothers, or children invariably depicted the family as a critical source of strength and values. In *M*A*S*H, The Mary Tyler Moore Show, Barney Miller,* and *Cheers,* among other shows, family-like relationships with workmates served as effective surrogates for those of the more traditional family.

In M*A*S*H, The Mary Tyler Moore Show, Barney Miller, Taxi, Cheers, *and numerous other sitcoms of the 1970s and 1980s, family-like relationships with workmates served as effective surrogates for those of the more traditional family.*

Only public television offered some kinds of programming not available on the commercial networks. In 1952 the FCC set aside channels for noncommercial television, but growth was slow until the late 1960s, when improved funding from foundations, federal and state governments, and viewer contributions encouraged the establishment of national programming services. No program established public television's visibility more than *Sesame Street,* a show introduced in 1969 to teach preschool-age children their numbers and letters. Using techniques employed by commercials, the show was an instant success and soon was shown in language-adapted forms in all the major countries of the world. In the 1970s and 1930s original series such as *The Adams Chronicles,* in-depth documentaries, and several series from Britain won the raves of critics and occasionally audiences equal to those of network programs in some cities.

The Effects of Deregulation and Increased Competition

The advent of deregulation of the networks and the fierce competition offered by cable systems and VCRs in the 1980s failed to produce dramatic changes in programming. True, cable provided viewers with around-the-clock news, weather, sports, music videos, religion, reruns, movies, and shopping programs, but none of the cable networks had the resources or promise of a big enough audience to justify spending large amounts of money on new programming. Except for quantity, cable entertainment shows looked much like their network counterparts. Influenced in part by the programming successes of public television, the networks presented more made-for-television movies, docudramas, dramatic specials, and miniseries. Television drama, with such shows as *Hill Street Blues, Miami Vice,* and *St. Elsewhere,* incorporated a more explicitly gritty realism, both visual and verbal, than had ever been shown before on network television. On the other hand, prime-time soap operas such as *Dallas* and *Dynasty* not only stoked desires for ostentatious consumption but also eclipsed in popularity. or drove off the air such urban, working-class shows as *All in the Family, Kojak,* and *Good Times. The Cosby Show,* which featured a black family of five children headed by a father and mother who were both professionals, proved that the traditional family sitcom could still command a huge audience.

In the last decade of the twentieth century television continued to be a defining characteristic of modern life. It affected leisure and political behavior, encouraged consumption, paradoxically both fostered and eroded traditional values, and created new galaxies of celebrities who were better known for their mere presence on television than for their actual deeds. Television, as Marshall McLuhan observed in 1964, increased the visual at the expense of the aural; it increased the importance of the vicarious at the expense of direct experience. With its own "language" it entertained, provided information, and served as a source of values while, as a secondary form of experience, it pared life of some of its poignancy, urgency, individuality, and subtlety.

[See also The Culture of Consumption; Film; Humor and Comedy; Journalism; Mass Culture and Its Critics; Radio; Sports in the Twentieth Century; Technology and Social Change; Theater and Musical Theater.]

BIBLIOGRAPHY

Barnouw, Erik. *Tube of Plenty: The Evolution of American Television* (1975; 2d rev. ed. 1990). Remains the standard history.

Baughman, James L. "Television in the 'Golden Age': An Entrepreneurial Experiment." *The Historian* 47, no. 2 (1985).

Bogart, Leo. *The Age of Television: A Study of Viewing Habits and the Impact of Television on American Life.* 3rd ed. (1972).

Brown, Les. *The New York Times Encyclopedia of Television* (1977).

Cassata, Mary, and Thomas Skill. *Television: A Guide to the Literature* (1985).

Cole, Barry, and Mal Oettinger. *Reluctant Regulators: The FCC and the Broadcast Audience* (1978).

Comstock, George. *The Evolution of American Television* (1989). Good survey of the results of social science research.

Greenberg, Bradley. *Life on Television* (1980).

Greenfield, Jeff. *Television: The First Fifty Years* (1977).

McLuhan, Marshall. *Understanding Media: The Extensions of Man* (1964).

Marc, David. *Demographic Vistas: Television in American Culture* (1984).

Marc, David. *Comic Visions: Television Comedy and American Culture* (1989).

Newcomb, Horace. *TV: The Most Popular Art* (1974).

O'Connor, John E., ed. *American History, American Television: Interpreting the Video Past* (1983).

Rader, Benjamin G. *In Its Own Image: How Television Has Transformed Sports* (1984).

Sterling, Christopher H., and John M. Kittross. *Stay Tuned: A Concise History of American Broadcasting.* 2d ed. (1990).

Wright, Charles R. *Mass Communication: A Sociological Perspective.* 3d ed. (1986).

— BENJAMIN G. RADER

THEATER AND MUSICAL THEATER

The social history of the American theater is an absorbing chronicle that has played against a dynamic backdrop of aesthetic, technological, economic, sociological, and political forces. The interactive and separate energies of these forces have informed a vibrant and galvanizing dialectic between audiences and theatrical practitioners—play-wrights, producers, directors, actors, designers, composers, and critics.

In American theater history, as well as in the chronicles of most other American arts, several significant motifs recur. First is the struggle between artistic aspirations and commercial realities. With few exceptions, the American theater has had to earn its own way at the box office. Therefore, the bulk of American theater productions have been carefully tailored to appeal to audiences willing to pay the price of admission for being entertained, edified, or uplifted, or some combination thereof.

A second theme involves technology. The development of the transcontinental rail system after the Civil War, for example, helped establish New York City as the nation's preeminent theatrical center. No less significant was the introduction of industrially based entertainment media, such as the motion picture. Within the theater itself, the appearance of technologies such as dependable electrical systems drastically changed the aesthetic impact of theatrical lighting.

Another motif that has threaded through discussions of American arts and letters, including theater, can be described as a national artistic inferiority complex. Indeed, the debate between those who have argued for the cultural superiority of things European, especially British, and those who have insisted on the need for works of a distinctive American identity continues to rage. This dialectic has taken a variety of bipolar forms under such euphemisms as "elite" (European) versus "mass" (American) culture; high culture versus folk culture; high art versus popular art; and, especially in the twentieth century, art versus entertainment.

Theater, like the other arts, has tended to reinforce the ideology of the dominant ruling class. Composer Irving Berlin, in two extreme examples, used all-soldier casts to beat the drum of American patriotism for World War I in *Yip, Yip, Yapbank* (1918) and then again in World War II with *This Is the Army,* (1942). The hegemony of white males in these two popular shows, both staged during the traumas of global conflict, reflects the racial-gender equation found, until only recently, in virtually all genres of American theater, and in American society itself. Since 1945, however, the American theater has opened itself up as never before to women, and to nonwhites and other minorities.

Tied to ideology is the question of politics and a manifest of issues relating to censorship. Here, the struggle has been joined by those advocating the freedoms of speech and expression enumerated in the First Amendment of the Bill of Rights and, on the other side, by those who believe that government has a legal right, indeed, an obligation, to define and enforce moral standards, a position reflecting the still potent puritanical heritage bequeathed by the early colonial settlers. Specific topics that continue to embroil the theater in controversy are the use of nudity and profanity and the depiction of characters seen by some as deviant, such as political radicals, hedonistic freethinkers, homosexuals, prostitutes, and wantonly violent criminals; similarly problematic are those dramatic situations, such as miscegenation, that have been deemed beyond the bounds of contemporary standards of propriety.

This, then, is the matrix against which the social history of theater in the United States has developed.

Colonial and Early National Periods

It should not be surprising that the earliest New World dramas reflected the national backgrounds of the various Europeans who came to conquer, subjugate, and settle. Some of the earliest dramas, in addition to providing a "touch of home" for transplanted Europeans, also served a proselytizing function. Spanish missionaries, for example, came with the Spanish conquistadores, and translated short, didactic religious plays into various Native American languages. In 1538 such playlets were presented in what is now Corpus Christi, Texas, as a prelude to baptisms of the newly converted. The Spanish influence, however, was most significant in Mexico and is therefore usually treated in histories of Latin American theater. In Quebec, the antecedents of a French tradition included a 1640 Jesuit school drama which in part provided religious instruction for indigenous Native Americans.

In the British settlements, London's influence was pervasive. In what would become the United States, the earliest theatrical productions reflected the substance and manner of the English Restoration and Georgian periods, but the formidable distances between population centers inhibited the development of any economically viable or sustained theatrical enterprises.

The greatest barrier to establishing a dynamic theater in the American colonies, however, was a persistent prejudice against the stage, an enmity associated with the Puritans of New England and the Quakers of Pennsylvania. In England, the Puritan bias against the theater's alleged immorality and frivolity reached a climax in the mid seventeenth century. Then, civil unrest between Royalists and Puritans led to the establishment of Oliver Cromwell's Commonwealth and a Puritan-dominated Parliament which attempted to supress dramatic activity. In 1649, Cromwell's Parliament even allowed the prosecution of actors as "rogues." In 1660, two year's after Cromwell's death, the Royalists finally prevailed, the English monarchy was restored and so, too, was theater. During the decades preceding and following the Cromwellian era, the Puritans were themselves persecuted, leading them to seek religious freedom in America. The Puritans and their political leaders like William Penn regarded theater as a threat to the kind of moral sobriety essential to maintain a well-run and conservative society. Given their own quest for liberty, the Puritans' unwillingness to sanction the rights of others to free expression demonstrates their paradoxical frame of mind, as well as the ideological basis for the still-contentious struggles between artistic freedom and censorship today.

The bias against theater was hardly limited to these regions. In Virginia, for example, the first known production of an English-language play in America, William Darby's *Ye Bare and Ye Cubb* (1665), resulted in charges against the actor-playwright and his cohorts. Although, after the cast gave a courtroom reenactment in costume, they were found "not guilty of fault," the incident marked the beginning of a pattern of judicial-legal interventions based on morality and taste; such issues of probity have continued to spur contentious debates on censorship that still clog court dockets and cloud the creative process.

Virginia and Maryland were the only two colonies that never formally prohibited theater, by either legislative or judicial fiat. Nonetheless, in 1752, when William Hallam sent his respected family troupe from London to Williamsburg, Virginia, it was necessary to secure Governor Robert Dinwiddie's permission to perform after assurances as to the propriety of their offerings had been made. After a successful stay of eleven months in Williamsburg, the Hallams and their troupe moved on to New York armed with a certificate of good behavior. This formality was necessary in order to counter the bad impressions created by another theatrical company's "roystering young men" with their "tricks and mischief." The early incident points up yet another source of the lingering prejudice against theater: "proper folks" were concerned about the moral fiber and behavior of actors and those who worked in the theater, a concern distinct from and yet linked to the plays and entertainments on which they labored.

The first American play published in the colonies was *Androboros* (1714), a three-act "biographical farce" authored by no less a figure than the governor of New York, Robert Hunter, whose intent was to pillory his obstructionist lieutenant governor. Fifty years passed before the next American play, *The Paxton Boys* (1764), was published. It, too, was a satire, but since it targeted Presbyterians, its author opted for anonymity. There is no evidence that either play was ever produced, underscoring the fact that much colonial drama was "produced" in the theater of the mind, rather than on stage. Another sanctuary from the period's censorious and economic prohibitions was the university. *Gustavus Vasa*, written by undergraduate student Benjamin Coleman, was given one performance at Harvard College in 1690; in 1702, students recited a "pastoral colloquy" at William and Mary College.

As the American colonies approached the revolutionary war, an increasing number of plays by American authors, often writing on American subjects, appeared. Thomas Godfrey's five-act heroic tragedy in verse, *The Prince of Parthia*, first produced in 1767, is generally regarded as the first play by an American to be professionally produced in America. There was also a sympathetic portrayal of a tragic-heroic Native American, *Ponteach; or, The Savages America* (1766), by Major Robert Rogers, a veteran of the Seven Years' War (1754–63); in addition to its topical appeal, *Ponteach* (pronounced Pontiac) was significant in anticipating the wave of dramas on Indian themes that appeared over the next century.

Still, it was the British who largely set the pace. Restoration plays such as George Farquhar's *The Recruiting Officer* (1706) were favored by professionals and amateurs alike; in 1732, for example, Farquhar's comedy was the first play of record to be mounted in New York, which in less than a century would become the center of American theater activity. Several years later in Williamsburg, *The Recruiting Officer* was performed by amateurs attuned to the fashions of the London stage.

The first musical divertissement staged in America was the English ballad opera *Flora; or, The Hob in the Well*, which was mounted in Charleston, South Carolina, in 1735. The ballad opera form proved popular, particularly in less costly and abridged versions that served as "ballad after-pieces" to an evening's featured production.

It was Shakespeare, however, whose plays were most often produced in the colonies during the last half of the eighteenth century, accounting for a larger share of the American repertoire than that of Britain. But given the censorious pressures in the colonies, even Shakespeare, on occasion, had to be "sold." For example, when Hallam's Company of Comedians of London moved into New England in 1763 after a successful run in New York, the troupe was accused of trading in "vice, impiety, and immorality." To counter the claim, Hallam's Company hit upon the strategy of promoting its plays as "moral dialogues"; *Othello* was transformed and touted as "a Series of Moral Dialogues in five parts/ Depicting the evil effects of Jealousy and Other Bad Passions, and Proving that Happiness can only Spring from the Pursuit of Virtue." In the mid-1770s, however, the tensions between England and its American colonies exploded in armed hostilities, bringing to an end, by governmental decree, virtually all live theater in what would soon be the United States.

When the Second Continental Congress was summoned to Philadelphia in 1775 to make preparations for war with England, it passed a resolution recommending the suspension of "every species of extravagance and dissipation, especially all horse-racing, and all kinds of gaming, cock-fighting, exhibitions of shows, plays, and other expensive diversions and entertainments" in order to encourage frugality and industry. In 1778, in the midst of the War for Independence, Congress greatly strengthened the earlier edict. Therefore, live theatrical entertainment, with the exception of amateur productions by British soldiers who occupied the majority of existing theaters, came to a virtual standstill.

During this period, patriots who espoused the cause of nationhood formally articulated in the Declaration of Independence of 1776 wrote "pamphlet plays" intended for publication rather than performance. Though the genre was dominated by satire, John Leacock's *The Fall of British Tyranny; or, America Triumphant, the First Campaign* (1776) was a highly popular "tragicomedy of five acts" tracing the causes of the Revolution; it also enjoyed the distinction of becoming America's first chronicle play and the first of many patriotic-historic dramas to feature George Washington as a character. Hugh Henry Brackenridge's *The Battle of Bunker's Hill* (1776) and *The Death of General Montgomery* (1777), as Felicia Hardison Londre observes in her masterful *History of World Theater* (p. 168), were unusual in that seriousness of tone and historical accuracy took precedence over satiric and propagandistic values.

With the formal signing of the Peace of Paris in 1783, the new nation and its theater embarked on what would prove to be a period of unprecedented growth and vitality. At first, however, the war's economic hardships discouraged most city and state governments from repealing their wartime anti-theater laws. But the lifting of such prohibitions by Pennsylvania, the bastion of Quakerdom, in 1789 led to the legalization of theater everywhere. And though the process encountered pockets of resistance, it was clear that expressing the variegated saga of the American experience was a deeply felt need.

Royall Tyler's comedy *The Contrast* (1787), the first American comedy to be professionally staged, introduced "Jonathan," the prototype for a long line of theatrical Yankees. Imbued with honesty, common sense, plain talk, and, significantly, a passionate sense of himself as "a true blue son of liberty," Tyler's Jonathan captured a sense of the optimistic confidence coursing through the new nation. Yet, despite *The Contrast*'s success, and lingering animosities from the long war with Britain, the bulk of the repertoire of America's professional theaters was English.

Still, the unique enticements of the stage attracted aspiring American authors. William Dunlap, lured by the stage while studying painting in London in 1784 with Benjamin West, returned to New York and a sustained and influential career as both a playwright and a theater manager. Of Dunlap's approximately sixty plays, his most influential was *Andre* (1798), based on an actual event concerning a British spy in the revolutionary war. Dunlap, by dint of his translations of thirteen of the plays of the German playwright August Friedrich Ferdinand von Kotzebue, is also credited with initiating the turn-of-the-century American vogue for Kotzebue, then hailed across the Western world as "the German Shakespeare." Dunlap also wrote the significant *History of the American Theatre* (1832), the first attempt to chronicle the new nation's quixotic affair with live drama.

In the 1790s, opportunities for American playwrights writing on American themes increased. Susanna Rowson, one of America's first female playwrights, contributed *Slaves in Algiers; or, A Struggle for Freedom* (1794), a musical melodrama about American prisoners in Algiers, and *The Female Patriot* (1795); in treating the horrors of slavery and privileging the role of women in American history, Rowson focused on topics whose significance to American drama and culture would only continue to grow. John Daly Burk's patriotic *Bunker Hill; or, The Death of General Warren* (1797) anticipated the growing role of spectacle with an elaborately staged fifteen-minute battle scene without dialogue. These—as well as many of the plays by Margaretta Bleeker Faugeres, John Murdock, and David Everett—anticipated such staples of nineteenth-century American melodrama as an emphasis on action and spectacle, a nationalistic spirit, and exotic locales.

This period also saw substantial growth in the American theater's infrastructure. During the 1790s, Philadelphia's Chestnut Street and New York's Park theaters vied for supremacy; even in Boston, the last bastion of Puritan values, sustained dramatic enterprise finally took hold with the opening of the Federal Street Theatre in 1794, while Charleston continued its preeminence in the South. With the construction of permanent theaters came the establishment of permanent theatrical companies and the emergence of strong-willed managers who attempted to balance commercial imperatives against artistic aspirations.

While British and Continental influences continued to be potent forces in the American theater, the melodrama soon became the most popular and culturally significant theatrical form. William Dunlap helped pave the way with Americanized adaptations of Kotzebue, including *False Shame; or, The American Orphan in Germany* (1799); inserting the word "American" in Kotzebue's *Falsche Scham* (1796) appealed to national pride, while the play's romanticism capitalized on the audience's appetite for drama made larger than life. During the first decades of the new century, the popularity of the American "Yankee" grew to the point that actors such as James Henry Hackett could forge successful careers by specializing in variations of the role. Other popular topics included the American Revolution, the Native American, and the expanding western frontier. James Nelson Barker was the first to tackle another popular subject, the War of 1812; the propagandistic slant of his play *Marmion; or, The Battle of Flodden Field,* written in the midst of the conflict, helped focus Americans' anti-British sentiment.

John Howard Payne, best remembered as the lyricist of the still-popular ballad "Home Sweet Home," was smitten by the theater at an early age; when just fourteen, he published the critical journal *The Thespian Mirror* (1805–1806). His first play, the comedic melodrama *Julia* (1806), was produced at the prestigious Park Theatre in New York. Hailed as "a child prodigy" upon his 1809 acting debut in New York, Payne pursued a productive acting career for several years. But in the face of waning popularity he departed for London, where his plays attained popular and critical success. Payne wrote approximately sixty plays; the most significant—*Brutus* (1818), in which Edmund Kean acted the lead, and *Charles II* (1824), starring Charles Kemble—reflected European influences and won initial acclaim in London, thus making Payne America's first notable international playwright.

Expansion and Diversification, 1812–1865

The successful conclusion of the War of 1812, while securing America's access to the world's great international sea-lanes, also opened the way for an unprecedented period of westward expansion and settlement. In 1803, President Thomas Jefferson concluded the purchase of the vast Louisiana Territory from Napoleon, thus adding France's lands west of the Mississippi River to the existing United States. Florida was added in 1819, and Texas, the Southwest, and California were annexed in the 1840s, so that by 1850, the United States, tripling its original size, now stretched from the Atlantic to the Pacific. Many kinds of people were attracted to the new territories—adventurers, settlers, soldiers, merchants, and actors.

The first significant touring company on the frontier was that of Samuel Drake, whose production of *Pizarro,* Richard Brinsley Sheridan's adaptation of a play by Kotzebue, was the troupe's most popular offering. Conditions on the road were rigorous. When Drake's company made a six-month tour that took it from Albany to Kentucky in 1815, its modes of travel included horse-drawn wagon, flatboat, and foot. Its scenery was designed to meet all possible venues, and the plays were altered to meet the particular circumstances of a given location. The capacity to improvise was a definite asset. Drake established one of the first regional circuits; though based around the Kentucky towns of Lexington, Louisville, and Frankfort, his troupe often made forays into Ohio, Indiana, Tennessee, and Missouri.

Drake's success encouraged competitors, including Noah Ludlow, a member of Drake's company who formed his own troupe in 1817. Ludlow toured regions of the South and Midwest (then the west) and is credited with establishing the first English-language theater in predominantly French-speaking New Orleans. After alternating between sundry management and acting engagements, including a failed tenure as manager of the Chatham Theatre in New York, Ludlow joined forces with Solomon Smith in 1835. Their successful partnership dominated the theater scene in the cities along the Mississippi, including Saint Louis. In 1853 Ludlow opted to retire; his highly regarded autobiography, *Dramatic Life as I Found It* (1880), written when he was in his eighties, provides a historically important portrait of America's frontier theater at the middle of the nineteenth century.

The move into the West was abetted by improvements in transportation. Canals and toll roads were built in the early decades of the nineteenth century. The first railroad appeared in 1830; others were soon constructed. The standard mode of travel, though, was water; thus it is not surprising that most frontier towns—and theaters—were located along the banks of the continent's interior river system. Small itinerant companies were found virtually everywhere, though few were located north of the Ohio River. Chicago, for example, did not host a professional production until 1833; its first professional theater was not established until 1847. The traveling companies set up makeshift stages in each town they visited. In 1831, however, the showboat was devised by William Chapman, an English actor who had come to America in 1827. Chapman's Floating Theatre made its maiden voyage in the form of a flatboat that docked for nightly presentations of Shakespeare or Kotzebue as it drifted downriver from Pittsburgh to New Orleans; at the end of voyage, Chapman would sell the boat for firewood, build another flatboat upriver, and start the cycle again. In 1836, after amassing enough savings to buy a steamboat with a twenty-foot-wide stage, Chapman was able to play the river in both directions. Though showboats continued regular runs (except during the Civil War years) until about 1925, the heyday of the genre was between 1875 and 1900.

With the construction of permanent theaters in the late 1700s came the establishment of permanent theatrical companies and the emergence of strong-willed managers who attempted to balance commercial imperatives against artistic aspirations.

With industrialization becoming a major force along the Atlantic seaboard after 1820, eastern cities and their theaters continued to grow. During the first decade of the nineteenth century, established theaters like the Chestnut Street in Philadelphia and the Park in New York were each enlarged to seat over two thousand spectators. Though Philadelphia and New York had vied for the honor of being the new nation's theatrical center since the end of the revolutionary war, by 1830, New York, by virtue of its four permanent and prosperous theaters, had become the dominant force. The largest of these, the three-thousand-seat Bowery, opened in 1826; at the same time, the number of shows per week was increased to six. With new theaters came new companies, so that by 1850 there were over fifty resident troupes nationwide performing on a regular basis. And with rapid expansion came competition, a battle for patronage that led to various strategies.

The most prominent stratagem, at least from the public's point of view, was the introduction of the star system. Impressed by the great success of British actor Edmund Kean's American tour of 1820–1821, entrepreneurs like Stephen Price made frequent trips to London to recruit performers. Among the growing number of stars to traverse the Atlantic were Charles Mathews the Elder in 1822 and 1833–1835; William C. Macready in 1826–1827, 1843–1845, and 1849; and Charles and Fanny Kemble in 1832–1834. Initially, tours were confined to the eastern states, but stars soon ventured to New Orleans and up the Mississippi. Eventually, the high salaries demanded by stars squeezed profits for those who organized their tours, but managers were reluctant to abandon the system because of high public demand.

The struggle to gain a competitive edge also influenced repertoire. Entr'actes increased in number and kind, as did novelties such as the employment of child actors and specialty actors and the use of animals. And though "quality" fare such as productions of Shakespeare continued to win favor among upper-class audiences, it was melodrama that captured the fancy of the middle and lower classes. Its suspenseful plots, theatrical effects, didactic moralizing, and the convention of the happy ending made it particularly appealing to unsophisticated audiences who supported live theater in ever-increasing numbers. It also was a form congenial to the insertion of commentaries on such contemporary issues as slavery, the rights of workers, and slum life. As a rule, better-educated and more sophisticated audiences looked to Europe for their standards; they also tended to give only condescending attention to native-born talent. As a result, American playwrights and actors usually won acceptance from the mass audience before winning approval from America's self-styled cultural elite. After 1830, this trend was ameliorated somewhat by the phenomenon of Jacksonian democracy, which increased pride in things American, and by the time the century was half over the number of American plays produced on the American stage had increased from 2 percent to 15 percent.

American melodrama flourished in the work of a growing cadre of native writers. Capitalizing on the public's continuing fascination with the War of 1812, Mordecai M. Noah's *She Would Be a Soldier; or, The Plains of Chippewa* (1819) was a tightly plotted spectacle featuring a spunky heroine who disguises herself as a soldier, a noble Indian chief, and caricatures of a Frenchman, a foppish Englishman, and an American yokel; songs, dances, a military display, and a last-minute rescue enlivened the production. Noah prefaced this and his other patriotic spectacles with fascinating accounts of the American theater and with pleas for reducing "prejudices against native productions."

By by virtue of its four permanent and prosperous theaters, the largest of which was the three-thousand-seat Bowery (opened in 1826), New York had become the dominant force in American theater by 1830.

Actor Edwin Forrest, the first great tragedian of the American stage, encouraged American playwrights by sponsoring a series of nine playwriting contests. The first winner was John Augustus Stone whose *Metamora; or, The Last of the Wampanoags* (1829) provided Forrest, in the title role of the "noble savage" who lives and dies free of the "White man's bondage," one of the great roles of his illustrious career. Between 1825 and 1860, more than fifty Indian plays were produced for the American stage, many performed by Forrest. John Brougham's burlesque, *Po-ca-hon-tas* (1855), dealt a decisive blow to the genre through parody and satire which undermined the seriousness of the form's basic premises and conventions. Still, the character of the "noble savage" persisted until about 1870 before being abandoned.

The stock character of the American Yankee, though first introduced in Royall Tyler's *The Contrast* in 1787, did not flourish until 1824 with Charles Mathews's *A Trip to America.* Between 1830 and 1850 the Yankee had become such an important type that actors such as James Henry Hackett and George Handel Hill appeared regularly as common men who, though superficially simple and naive, eschewed pretense and deceit and embodied democratic values.

James K. Pauling's 1831 comic melodrama, *The Lion of the West; or, A Trip to Washington,* introduced the character of the backwoodsman, who became another important melodramatic type. The adventures of Pauling's central character, Colonel Nimrod Wildfire, were based on the exploits of Davy Crockett, the period's archetypal model for the practical, resourceful, self-taught American individualist. The mythologizing of Crockett reached its nineteenth-century apex with Frank Murdock's *Davy Crockett; or, Be Sure You're Right, Then Go Ahead* (1873), a melodramatic spectacle given over two thousand performances, with Frank Mayo in the title role.

The unprecedented success of a stage version of *Uncle Tom's Cabin* epitomized melodrama's ascendency as the dominant genre in nineteenth-century American theater. Indeed, the popularity of Harriet Beecher Stowe's novel, with its heartfelt aim "to awaken sympathy and feeling for the African race," inspired dozens of adaptations. These, though, had been opposed by Stowe, who feared abasement of her novel's moral intent—an indication of the low regard in which theater was held by the nation's literary and political Brahmins. Initially, Stowe's reservation seemed well-founded; the first stage version of *Uncle Tom's Cabin,* which opened in New York in 1852, was dismissed for its "bad taste" and "overdrawn characters." But George L. Aiken's six-act adaptation, which opened at Purdy's National Theatre on 18 July 1853, was hailed as "an agent for the cause of abolition" as well as a force for gaining new respectability for theater itself.

Although Aiken's version of Stowe's novel was regarded as a sensitive shaping of Stowe's characters and moral concerns, it also epitomized the basic elements of the melodramatic format with its archvillain, the viciously cruel Simon Legree; the suffering innocent, embodied by both Uncle Tom and Little Eva; thrilling spectacle, the chase across the ice floes on the Ohio River; comic relief, through the character of Topsy; and poetic justice, with the shooting death of Legree and the apotheosis of Uncle Tom. In keeping with the conventions of the day, the black characters were performed by whites in blackface. However, in many touring post-Civil War companies, *Uncle Tom's Cabin* employed blacks as chorus members for the plantation songs; therefore, the play is regarded as one of the first important vehicles for allowing black performers an entree into the mainstream of American theater.

The most popular American play of its era, Aiken's staging of *Uncle Tom's Cabin* is significant for the unique role it and Stowe's original novel played in raising the issue of abolition in the years immediately prior to the Civil War. Also, Aiken's production is regarded as the first play to have been offered on Broadway without an afterpiece or any other entr'acte or divertissement. The play's enduring popularity was similarly unprecedented. Indeed, *Uncle Tom's Cabin* enjoyed a continuous stage life of some ninety, years. There were forty-nine companies performing the play in 1879, and no fewer than a dozen touring troupes as late as 1927.

The Octoroon (1859), by Irish-born Dion Boucicault, also dealt with slavery. Based on Mayne Reid's novel *The Quadroon*, and incorporating events surrounding the murder of a slave from Albany Fonblanque's novel *The Filibuster*, Boucicault's play ridiculed southern racial laws by making Zoe an octoroon instead of a quadroon (that is, one-eighth instead of one-quarter black). Boucicault, though, attempted to balance sectional interests; while the characters and dialogue tilted sympathies to the South, the action was unmistakenly abolitionist. Boucicault, who lived in the United States between 1853 and 1860 and who thereafter divided his time between London and New York, was the most successful master of melodrama during the middle decades of the century. Boucicault's fondness for lavish special effects and his practice of borrowing freely from a variety of sources, including French melodrama (he had lived in France for a time), as well as his incorporation of the latest scientific devices into his plots, were all important influences on theatrical production.

From Melodrama to Realism, From Commercialism to Competition, 1865–1929

The end of the American Civil War brought new challenges and new opportunities. As a result of the issuance of Lincoln's Emancipation Proclamation and of the successful prosecution of the war by the North, slavery, as well as the influence of the rural South, had come to an end. Consolidated as never before, the United States embarked on a period of unprecedented territorial, economic, and political growth. The first transcontinental railroad was finished in 1869; by 1880 there were several more. Progress through discovery, invention, individual initiative, and uninhibited capitalistic exploitation were among the basic elements galvanizing the national psyche, as well as the country's political agenda and its policy of laissez-faire economics. These same elements also helped define the American theater as a clearly entrepreneurial, commercially based enterprise.

Vaudeville evolved due to the popular trend toward mass entertainment in the decades following the Civil War. Elaborate dramatic sketches like this shared the stage with standard musical and novelty acts.

Immediately following the Civil War, one of the most significant theatrical forms to make its debut was the forerunner of what would eventually become the musical. In the United States, music—in forms such as the interpolated song, the entr'acte, and the afterpiece—had been a popular theatrical component since the colonial period. The American musical drama, though, came into its own in Charles M. Barras's *The Black Crook; An Original Magical and Spectacular Drama in Four Acts* (1866). Produced at the unprecedented cost of fifty thousand dollars, *The Black Crook*, was a melodramatic musical spectacular that played at Niblo's Garden in New York City for 475 performances. It was the first play to run for over a year, and with gross receipts totaling more than one million dollars, the most successful Broadway play up to that time. Though details are sketchy, the production was apparently made possible when a large French ballet troupe was deprived of a stage because of a fire that destroyed the New York

Academy of Music, its scheduled venue. Though Barras was wary of having his metaphysical melodrama transformed into a musical spectacle, the penniless playwright agreed to the changes; some six months later he had already earned over sixty thousand dollars. The visual spectacles included transformations, phantasmagorias, displays of fire and water, and an eighty-strong bevy of chorines displaying much more of the female leg than had customarily been seen on stage. Excoriations from the pulpit and other bastions of moral rectitude only heightened interest in the "indecent and demoralizing exhibition." Revived regularly in New York during the rest of the century, *The Black Crook* spawned a host of traveling companies and such spin-offs as *The Black Crook Burlesque* and *The Black Crook Song Book.*

The success of *The Black Crook* inspired similar enterprises, including the 1869 appearance of Lydia Thompson and her "British Blondes," whose burlesques emphasized feminine attributes. Thompson and her imitators helped establish burlesque as a program of variety acts interspersed with musical production numbers featuring the allures of lovely young women. With its obvious sexual appeal, it is not surprising that burlesque attracted a primarily male audience. Though the form remained popular until the late 1920s, burlesque quickly degenerated in the face of competition from the then-new mass-mediated entertainments made possible by synchronized sound film and by network radio. Though the introduction of the striptease kept burlesque alive during the years of the Depression and World War II, burlesque had a tawdry existence mostly at the fringes of bourgeois middle-class values.

Modern vaudeville developed from the same movement toward popular mass entertainment. But in contrast to burlesque, which played primarily in concert saloons during the decades following the Civil War, vaudeville (or variety, as it was first called) found a home in regular theaters. This acceptance was due largely to the efforts of New York entrepreneur Tony Pastor, who attracted family audiences by promoting his Saturday matinees as occasions "when Ladies and Children can safely attend without escort" and by boasting of "selling no drink stronger than ice water." Pastor had additional influence through his practice of including elaborate dramatic sketches as well as the standard musical and novelty acts. Comedic parodies such as *The White Crook* (1867) and *Hamlet the Second* (1870), a send-up of Edwin Booth's then-current and acclaimed Shakespearean production, were representative of the "dramas" Pastor created. Through the years, Pastor continued to move his base of operations, always opening his latest theater further uptown. By 1881, when Tony Pastor's New 14th Street Theatre opened, the performer-turned-entrepreneur had at last succeeded in attracting women to evening performances and the term "variety" was being replaced by the more genteel-sounding "vaudeville."

Pastor's success was emulated with even more spectacular results by the theater-management team of Edward Franklin Albee and Benjamin Franklin Keith. In 1885, Albee helped reverse the declining fortunes of a run-down variety house managed by Keith in Boston. From this modest beginning, the combination of Albee's shrewd showmanship and Keith's sharp business practices resulted in the building of a theater chain that by the turn of the century dominated the East Coast.

Among the vaudeville headlines who played New York's Palace Theatre and eventually went on to bigger success were such ethnically and racially varied entertainers as the Marx Brothers, George Burns and Gracie Allen, W. C. Fields, Will Rogers, and Bill "Bojangles" Robinson.

Similarly powerful chains included the extensive West Coast-based Orpheum circuit, as well as the Loew's and Pantages groups. There were also hundreds of "small-time" and independent vaudeville houses. "Small-time" performers dreamed of breaking into the "two-a-day" performance schedule of the "big time"; another dream was to play New York's Palace Theatre, the Carnegie Hall of vaudeville until 1932, when it was converted into a movie house. Among vaudeville headliners who played the Palace and eventually went on to even bigger success as movie and radio stars were such ethnically and racially varied entertainers as the Marx Brothers, George Burns and Gracie Allen, W. C. Fields, Eddie Cantor, Ray Bolger, Will Rogers, Ed Wynn, and the black tap dancer Bill "Bojangles" Robinson. In contrast to mainstream society, show business offered opportunities for fame and fortune to Jewish and African American minorities.

The minstrel show, another uniquely American genre, also flourished in the decades following the Civil War. A paradoxical entertainment that exploited black musical and dance forms while creating opportunities for black performers, the minstrel show first appeared about 1830 when Thomas D. Rice, a white entertainer, performed various Negro tunes in blackface. The success of Rice's "Jim Crow" song and dance led to a number of imitators, including Dan Emmett, who in 1843 organized the Virginia Minstrels, a blackface ensemble whose fame took them as far as London; Emmett also composed a number of popular songs that remain standards in the American folk repertoire, including "Dixie," "The Blue Tail Fly," and "Early in the Morning." The minstrel show's definitive two-part form was established in 1846 by Edwin P. Christy's Christy Minstrels. In the first part, the entertainers formed a semicircle, with a tambourine player, "Mr. Tambo," at one end and a "bones" player, "Mr. Bones," at the other. The "Interlocutor," or middleman, hosted the proceedings and joked with the end men between musical selections. The second part, the "olio" as it was called, was given over to specialty routines performed in a freely improvised manner responsive to the tastes of individual audiences. In the decade before the Civil War, the minstrel show's widespread popularity exceeded even that of the legitimate theater.

After the Civil War, Charles B. Hicks, a black showman, established the Georgia Minstrels. This pioneering group opened the door for a number of "Simon Pure" or "genuine" minstrel companies that successfully toured throughout the northern United States. Billy Kersands, an alumnus of Hicks's troupe, later headlined with Haverly's Genuine Colored Minstrels in England during the 1870s. With the growing popularity of burlesque and vaudeville, however, the minstrel show declined steadily. In 1896, only ten companies survived, and by 1919 there were only three, mere curiosities from a bygone era.

Several black performers from the nineteenth century deserve mention. William Henry Lane, who performed as Master Juba, was known as the "father of American tap dancing." Sam Lucas helped open up other areas to black performers by dint of his extraordinary talents as a singer, composer, and actor. In 1878 he became the first black to play Uncle Tom in *Uncle Tom's Cabin*; he was also the first black to star in a motion picture, the 1915 version of Stowe's novel.

George Walker and Bert Williams, a popular turn-of-the-century, black song-and-dance team, were engaged by the top vaudeville houses and also produced their own musicals, including *A Lucky Coon* (1899) and the Broadway hit *In Dahomey* (1903), the first evening-length black musical to play a regular New York legitimate theater. In spite of mostly favorable reviews and many raves for Williams, *In Dahomey* was boycotted by many white New York theatergoers; in London, where prejudices against blacks were not so prevalent, *In Dahomey* ran for seven months.

In the years following the Civil War, as rail transportation became increasingly reliable and extensive, new modes of organizing the logistics of touring units appeared. In the immediate postwar period, the resident stock company was at its apogee; while an individual star often toured from one town to the next to perform a particularly well-known and celebrated role—as did Joseph Jefferson III, who portrayed Dion Boucicault's *Rip Van Winkle* (1865) more than 2,500 times—it was always with support from the local resident stock company. However, with the innovation of the "combination company"—a traveling unit complete with star, supporting players, and backstage personnel, as well as sets, costumes, and props—the fortunes of the resident stock company began to decline. In 1877, there were nearly one hundred combination companies traveling with full casts, scenery, and properties; by 1886, there were 282. The combination company, then, was a continuation of the nineteenth-century practice of the star system; now, however, the stars traveled with full companies. Between 1883 and 1902, English leading man Henry Irving made eight tours of America; Benoit Constant Coquelin, a star of the Parisian Comédie Française, toured three times between 1889 and 1900, and French diva Sarah Bernhardt, nine times between 1880 and 1918.

In the mid eighteenth century Edwin Booth, who began his theatrical career with his actor father, Junius Brutus Booth, became one of America's greatest stars, with a reputation as a masterful interpreter of the classics, especially Shakespeare's Hamlet.

New York City, with its affluent and cosmopolitan audiences, became the nation's theatrical center, the city where the majority of the combination companies were booked and assembled. Edwin Booth, who began his theatrical career with his father, the noted actor Junius Brutus Booth, became one of America's greatest stars, with a reputation as a masterful interpreter of the classics. His production of *Hamlet*, in which he starred, ran for one hundred performances, the longest continuous run that Shakespeare's play had yet enjoyed. But after his brother, John Wilkes Booth, assassinated President Abraham Lincoln, Edwin retired for several years.

When he returned to active production at his own Booth's Theatre, which he had built to his personal specifications, he introduced a number of innovations, including a level stage, hydraulic elevators, flying machinery (used to raise scenery from the stage into overhead space), and "free plantation," a system that allowed the placement of scenery anywhere on stage. Booth also eliminated the stage apron and used box settings, where the actors and action were enclosed for interior scenes by a semblance of three walls and often even a ceiling, to enhance the illusion of reality, an increasingly important theatrical trend at the time.

Augustin Daly was a New York drama critic who later gained recognition as a playwright, producer, and director. Although his many plays were largely derived from German and French sources, he is credited with nudging the theater toward a more realistic approach and with making the theater worthy of the support of the day's most refined citizens. Like Booth, he established a repertory company of talented performers whose youth made them amenable to Daly's then-unique concept of direction. For example, he discarded the practice of casting according to "lines of business," the traditional, four-tier system whose ranks included players of leading roles, players of secondary roles, players of third-line or "walking" parts, and general utility players. Daly also assumed the right to help shape his actors' interpretations, blocking, and stage business.

Playwright-manager Steele MacKave was also concerned with a realistic approach to drama, as exemplified by his production of *Hazel Kirke* (1880), a melodrama that featured sympathetic characters who spoke with natural dialogue. MacKaye's most lasting influence, however, was as an educator. After training in Paris with François Delsarte, who had developed a "scientific" approach to acting in which the laws of stage expression were schematized like the laws of physics, MacKaye taught Delsarte's system in a variety of pioneering acting schools. His most significant training program, offered in 1884 at the Lyceum Theatre, established a curriculum that grew into the American Academy of Dramatic Art.

The trend toward realism continued in other arenas. Inspired by the popularity of "realist" novelists like Bret Harte and Mark Twain, dramas such as Bartley Campbell's *My Partner* (1879) exploited the details of frontier life. In contrast, Edward Harrigan examined urban life in a series of plays such as *Cordelia's Aspirations* (1883), which presented working-class life in relatively realistic, if comic, terms. These plays were an extension of the Bowery Boy tradition with its Dickensian focus on the adventures and tribulations of adolescent youngsters growing up in hostile and impoverished urban ghettoes.

Actor-playwright William Gillette, who wrote the Civil War dramas *Held by the Enemy* (1886) and *Secret Service* (1895), attempted to create the "illusion of the first time" at each performance by focusing on the moment-to-moment development of the action. In 1890 James A. Herne offered *Margaret Fleming*, often regarded as the outstanding realistic American drama of the nineteenth century. No New York producer would touch it, however, since its themes include infidelity and illegitimate pregnancy. Without a commercial backer, Herne had to produce *Margaret Fleming* with his own resources in relatively obscure venues. However, he recouped his financial losses with *Shore Acres* (1892), a successful play about an endearing New England character. A pattern had been set, or perhaps more accurately, reasserted. Realism was readily assimilated into the American theater as an element of scenography, or design. However, when realism implied adult themes and issues, it was often considered at best problematic and at worst subversive and downright un-American.

By 1900, commercial considerations had clearly come to dominate the American stage. Actors, for example, had become secondary to both directors and producers. With the ascendancy of the traveling combination company, they had to journey to New York, the home base of many of the companies, to secure employment. Actors were hired for the run of the play rather than by the season, and because there was no union to protect their interests, they received no salaries for rehearsals and might find themselves stranded far from home if a production suddenly closed on the road.

Another change involved the appearance of a new class of theatrical workers, the booking agents. The need for such middlemen arose because of difficulties experienced by theater managers outside of New York in arranging their seasons. The introduction of bookers was a matter of simple economics and of convenience; it was easier for local managers to engage touring productions of long-running New York hits for several nights than it was for a stock company to add a new play to its repertoire each week in order to draw area audiences. Nonetheless, the complexity of the combination system, even with the addition of booking agents, was still daunting. For example, when local managers met in New York each summer prior to the new season, managers had to negotiate with as many as forty different production representatives, each of whom was trying to configure the most closely plotted and lucrative schedule for their troupes as possible; double bookings and other devious practices abounded. One solution devised by theaters located along a single rail line was to hire one agent to represent them all;

producers used a similar solution involving the hiring of a booking agent to represent a group of shows.

Such chaos paved the way for what became known as the Theatrical Syndicate. Emulating the monopolistic oligarchs in the steel, railroad, and oil industries, six theater owners—Marc Klaw, Abraham Erlanger, Sam Nixon, J. Fred Zimmerman, Al Hayman, and Charles Frohman—joined to form the Syndicate in 1896. These men sought nothing less than total control of the American theater. At first, the Syndicate was welcomed. It did, indeed, create a new degree of order and stability for local managers. The only catch was that each manager had to sign an exclusive contract and take only those shows sent by the Syndicate, a monopolistic practice later imitated by the early movie moguls, who called the system "block booking." So powerful was the Syndicate that when a local manager refused to sign, the group simply built a rival theater, sent it star attractions, and charged artificially low prices until the competition withered and died. The Syndicate also took control of advertising, thus giving it a weapon to use against those artists who attempted to chart independent courses. *The New York Dramatic Mirror*, under the defiant editorship of Harrison Grey Fiske, opposed the Syndicate even though opposition meant the loss of advertising revenue; the Syndicate even tried to forbid its performers from reading the renegade newspaper.

In 1900, after being in existence for only four years, the Theatrical Syndicate controlled over 5,000 theaters, including virtually every first-class stage across the United States. Greed, however, led to severe cost-cutting, which in turn undermined the quality of the Syndicate's product. Audience complaints provoked managers to complain in turn to the Syndicate. *The New York World* openly accused the Syndicate of deceit and fraud for sending out "inferior companies, falsely representing them as the original casts of New York successes." Charles Frohman, though an original Syndicate member, was an honest showman; disgusted with the Syndicate's duplicity and increasingly shabby offerings, Frohman disavowed his participation in the association.

The Syndicate also faced competition from ambitious new rivals like the Shubert brothers, who in 1905 began to build their own chain of theaters. The Shuberts profited from the favorable publicity and boffo box office take generated by Sarah Bernhardt's 1906 American tour. The Syndicate's stranglehold was finally broken in 1915. Ironically, the Shuberts, the big winners, proved every bit as autocratic as the Syndicate; in 1956, after decades of controlling "the road" and years of litigation, the Shubert organization was declared a monopoly in restraint of trade under the provisions of the Sherman Antitrust Act of 1885. However, because of the Syndicate's domination and its emphasis on profits in the early years of the century, the American theater became, and has remained, an extremely conservative commercial enterprise.

Other opponents of the Syndicate included David Belasco, a flamboyant playwright-manager who came into his own when he opened the Belasco Theatre in 1902. In addition to achieving realistic effects through his virtuosity with electric lighting, Belasco sought realism in stage design, even including the duplication of an actual Child's Restaurant for the concluding scene of his production of Alice Bradley's *The Governor's Lady* (1912). Belasco's singular productions were in such great demand that in 1909, the Syndicate agreed to a nonexclusive contract for Belasco's road-show bookings, a concession regarded as one of the first important breaks in the monopoly's power.

Actress Minnie Maddern Fiske, along with her husband, Harrison Fiske of the *New York Dramatic Mirror*, also opposed the Syndicate's stifling practices. Like other stars such as Sarah Bernhardt, who had resisted the monopoly, Fiske was subjected to negative reviews bought for and placed by the Syndicate in newspapers beholden to it because of its steady stream of advertising. In 1903, after being blacklisted and forced to play only secondary venues, Mrs. Fiske and her husband acquired the Manhattan Theatre. Here, they helped chart the course of modern theater by presenting a number of outstanding works with an emphasis on ensemble rather than star effects.

By 1915, the American theater, whatever its form or genre, was in decline. Many theater historians put a large measure of blame on the theater itself, particularly the Syndicate and the Shuberts, whose basic interests were commercial rather than artistic. Each organization's commitment to standardizing product for maximum public appeal and, therefore, profitability squeezed out most innovations except those of a technical nature. Similarly, the practices of blacklisting and block booking tended to squelch and marginalize alternative voices.

At the same time, the American theater faced increasingly potent competition from spectator sports, particularly baseball and boxing, and "the galloping tintypes," or motion pictures. Movies, which had started out as penny arcade "peep show" attractions in the form of Edison's hand-cranked kinetoscope in 1893, by 1915 had become big business. In that year, D. W. Griffith released the two-hour *Birth of a Nation*, his controversial—some believed racist—film drama about the American Civil War and Reconstruction. The work, described by President Woodrow Wilson as "history writ with lightning," attracted a huge audience willing to pay road-show, legitimate-theater admission fees and helped standardize the one- to two-hour feature film as the industry's basic unit. The 1914 opening of the first large-scale movie house, the 3,300-seat Strand Theatre in New York, inaugurated the era of the palatial "cathedral of the motion picture." Just before and after World War I, and throughout the 1920s, these trends continued unabated. Indeed, even the quintessential American show-business dream began to shift. Geographically, along with New York, there was now Hollywood; and with the immediate excitements of live theater, there was now the larger-than-life stardom offered by the movies. It would soon become clear, however, that Broadway and Hollywood also had much to share.

From Modernism to Postmodernism, 1915 to the Present

By 1915, the relative isolation of the American theater from European innovations—largely the result of the conservative and monopolistic business practices of America's principal theatrical entrepreneurs—was further exacerbated by the hostilities of World War I, then raging in Europe. Anti-German sentiment, for example, brought a quick end to the production of the Viennese operas that had dominated the American musical stage during the previous decade.

The United States entered the conflict in 1917, and the next year the long-stalemated struggle came to an end. With victory, America was on the verge of an unprecedented period of economic expansion and speculation. And in spite of the passage in 1919 of the Eighteenth Amendment prohibiting the manufacture, sale, or transportation of liquor, good times were about to roll. The syncopated rhythms of jazz provided the 1920s with a signature sound and spirit; indeed, the "jazz age" evoked an attitude of individual liberation and assertiveness, a turn of mind especially significant for women who had just won the right to vote with the passage of the Nineteenth Amendment in 1920.

Theatrically, the period's hedonistic yet stylish self-indulgence was probably best represented in the lavish entertainments produced by Florenz Ziegfeld. After a string of successful melodramas, such as *A Parisian Model* (1906), featuring his first wife, Anna Held, Ziegfeld presented *Follies* of 1907, the first of his famous series of revues featuring beautiful showgirls in sumptuous yet revealing costumes. With the addition of his name to the title and of even more lavish production values in 1911, the *Ziegfeld Follies* became the most fabled and longest-lived series of extravagant revues in show business history. Annual editions were mounted through 1925, with irregular stagings thereafter; even after Ziegfeld's death in 1932, the *Ziegfeld Follies* continued, since the name had been acquired by the Shuberts. Ziegfeld's idealization of feminine allures was underscored in 1922 when the revue acquired the subtitle "Glorifying the American Girl." Critic George Jean Nathan observed that Ziegfeld had transformed the vulgar leg show into "a thing of grace and beauty, and symmetry, and bloom." The public agreed. Among the stars presented by Ziegfeld were Fanny Brice, Eddie Cantor, W. C. Fields, Marilyn Miller, Will Rogers, and Bert Williams.

Throughout the 1920s, the revue was Broadway's most dependable staple. Imitators of Ziegfeld's formula included the Shuberts' more daring *The Passing Show* (1912–1924) and the even more risque *Artists and Models*, of which five editions appeared between 1923 and 1930. In 1919, George White, a former hoofer and musical-comedy juvenile, initiated his series of *Scandals*, and in 1923, the Earl Carroll Vanities began. The public's mania for revues led to late-night roof-garden shows such as Ziegfeld's *Midnight Frolic*, an adjunct to the Follies, atop the New Amsterdam, and the *Morris Gest Midnight Whirl* on the Century, Roof. The vogue for after-show entertainments proved strong enough to justify moving such programs to all-season, ground-level and basement locations; thus nightclubs supplanted the more elegant roof-garden cabarets. In addition to a gaudy array of singers, comics, dancers, skits, and novelty acts, revues featured the latest works of beguiling tunesmiths such as Irving Berlin, George and Ira Gershwin, Jerome Kern, Cole Porter, Richard Rodgers, and Lorenz Hart, all on their way to even more notable accomplishments in the 1930s.

There were also Harlem-bred revues. The most significant, since it was the first all-black potpourri to appear on Broadway since the turn-of-the-century, collaborations of Bert Williams and George Walker, was *Shuffle Along* (1921), the Noble Sissle—Eubie Blake success that yielded "I'm Just Wild About Harry." However, Lew Leslie's *Blackbirds* series beginning in 1928, earned the distinction of being the most successful of the Harlem-to-Broadway ventures. With their jazz-age syncopations and spirited tap dancing and their introduction of performers such as Bill "Bojangles" Robinson and Ethel Waters, Leslie's revues attracted both white and black theatergoers, itself a major breakthrough. The last edition appeared in 1939.

In Harlem during the 1920s, black writers and artists gathered in what became known as the Harlem Renaissance. In music, the lavish "sepia" revues at Harlem venues such as the Cotton Club attracted white socialites and intellectuals who helped tout the exuberant talents of the dancing Nicholas Brothers and composer-performers Duke Ellington, Cab Calloway, and Louis Armstrong. Thomas "Fats" Waller, another storied jazz composer-player, penned the American classic "Honeysuckle Rose" for the all-black Broadway revue *Keep Shufflin'* (1928); for the Broadway-bound *Hot Chocolates* (1929), Waller and lyricist Andy Razaf produced "Ain't Misbehavin'." But by the mid-1930s, the Harlem-Broadway connection had withered, a victim of exacerbated racial tensions, and other forces unleased by the Depression.

Though the operetta with its middle-European antecedents had suffered during the war years, it had a final fling during the 1920s. More important, *Show Boat* (1927), although in the tradition of the operetta, had special significance as the forerunner of the integrated musical in which song, dance, dialogue, and settings cohere to tell an essentially serious story. Based on the best-selling novel by Edna Ferber, it had a book by Oscar Hammerstein II and a catalog of indelible songs by Jerome Kern, including "Ol' Man River," "Can't Help Lovin' Dat Man," and "Make Believe." As the precursor of the modern American musical drama that reached maturity. with *Oklahoma!* (1943), *Show Boat* was perhaps most significant for having so effectively mined the American past and for Kern's adroit use of native American musical idioms.

In the 1920s revues at Harlem venues such as the Cotton Club attracted white socialites and intellectuals who helped tout the exuberant talents of the dancing Nicholas Brothers and composer-performers Duke Ellington, Cab Calloway, and Louis Armstrong.

In the post-World War I period, the most important alternative to the commercial theater of musical revues, operettas, and smart satirical burlesques was the so-called little theater movement. Inspired by Europe's independent theaters, Boston's Toy Theatre and the Chicago Little Theatre opened in 1912. They were soon joined by the Neighborhood Playhouse and the Washington Square Players in New York and the Provincetown Players of Provincetown, Massachusetts, all in 1915. By 1917, the number of such groups had reached fifty Though reflecting the passionate and idiosyncratic views of their respective founders, each theater group shared a common set of goals and methods. Dedicated to exploring advanced ideas and works from Europe, each company relied on unpaid volunteers for its personnel and upon subscribers for financial underwriting. In part, the impetus for the movement came from theater people disenchanted with the circumscribed conventions of the commercial theater; other supporters came from such newly established university drama programs as those founded by George Pierce Baker at Radcliffe and Harvard and Thomas Wood Stevens at the Carnegie Institute of Technology.

One of the little theater's greatest contributions was its encouragement of what became known as the "new stagecraft." Though reflecting a variety of influences, including the expressionistic approach popularized by the German Max Reinhardt, the American version of the new stagecraft eventually distilled itself into what might be called a simplified yet heightened realism. Instead of a literal reproduction of reality like that sought by Belasco, the new aesthetic of design simplicity tried to capture the spirit rather than the photographic detail of the script.

In 1916 Sheldon Cheyney of the Detroit Arts and Crafts Theatre launched *Theatre Arts Magazine*, until 1948 the most important American forum for new ideas concerning the theater. Foremost among these were the new theories of acting advanced by Richard Boleslavsky and Maria Ouspenskaya, veterans of the famed Moscow Art Theatre who in 1925 established the American Laboratory Theatre. There, they taught Konstantin Stanislavsky's "method," with its emphasis on enhancing the actor's imagination and memory.

The little theater movement is also significant for having supported a number of young American playwrights, including Eugene O'Neill. In 1914, five of his one-act plays were published with the support of his father, the legendary actor James O'Neill. At the same time, he began attending Baker's play-writing class at Harvard. The next year, he began his association with the Provincetown Players, who produced his first short plays and encouraged him to go to New York City, where the group itself moved in 1916. In 1921 the Players split, with O'Neill, producer-historian Kenneth Macgowan, and designer Robert Edmond Jones presiding over a branch committed to quality foreign and period plays as well as to the noncommercial works of O'Neill and others. In the meantime, O'Neill's first full-length play, *Beyond the Horizon* (1920), debuted on Broadway and won that year's Pulitzer Prize for the best play of the year. Not incidentally, the establishment of the Pulitzer Prize in 1918 for the best new American drama performed in New York, along with the initiation of the Drama Critics Circle Awards in 1936, were important factors in encouraging American playwrights as well as the American theater itself.

O'Neill, bucking the hegemony of the commercial theater's lighter musical and comic fare, scored an unprecedented string of critical successes with plays that continue to live in revivals around the world. *The Emperor Jones* (1920), *The Hairy Ape* (1922), *Desire Under the Elms* (1924), *The Great God Brown* (1926), *Strange Interlude* (1928), and *Mourning Becomes Electra* (1931) established O'Neill as a master of an essentially realistic and tragic approach probing the dark, convoluted aspects of human nature. After 1934, O'Neill withheld his works from production, although he continued to write prolifically. In 1936 O'Neill became the first and only American playwright to win the Nobel Prize for literature. He died in 1953. Though his reputation suffered during the 1940s, the successful 1956 mountings of *The Iceman Cometh* (1946) and *Long Day's Journey into Night* (1941) reestablished O'Neill's standing as America's foremost dramatist.

Although it disbanded in 1941, the Group Theatre remained an important force owing to the efforts of former members Lee Strasberg and Stella Adler, who disseminated the system of Moscow's Konstantin Stanislavsky throughout America.

By 1930, although the energies and resources of companies like the Provincetown Players had dissipated due to the Depression and Broadway's commercialism, other independent groups had taken their place. The Group Theatre was formed in 1931 by Lee Strasberg, Harold Clurman, and Cheryl Crawford on the model of Stanislavsky's Moscow Art Theatre, with its ensemble approach. With a troupe that included Stella Adler, Morris Carnovsky, and Elia Kazan, it staged works by Paul Green, Maxwell Anderson, William Saroyan, Clifford Odets, and other promising young writers. Although it disbanded in 1941, the Group Theatre remained an important force due to the efforts of former members such as Strasberg and Adler, who disseminated Stanislavsky's system throughout the United States.

One of the most innovative responses to the Depression came in the mid 1930s with the establishment by Congress of the Federal Theatre Project (1935–1939). Designed to combat unemployment among theater workers, it put some five thousand professionals to work in New York City alone. It offered free and often quality performances of imaginative restagings of classics, as well as new works, including children's and foreign language plays.

Though pledged to provide adult and uncensored drama, the Federal Theatre ran into problems with *Ethiopia* (1936), the first production of its notable Living Newspaper series. A "theatrical documentary" probing Italy's attack on the African country, *Ethiopia* was deemed too volatile by the United States State Department which, despite Mussolini's aggression, did not want to offend the dictator. Indeed, the show's powerful multimedia mix of clips from motion picture newsreels, sound bites from topical radio speeches, projected headlines from the daily newspapers, and live and rhetorically charged dramatic vignettes was judged inimical to American foreign policy objectives.

Domestic issues tackled by the Living Newspaper series were at first less problematic. *One Third of a Nation* (1938), for example, took its title from President Franklin Delano Roosevelt's claim that one-third of the nation was ill-fed, ill-clad, and ill-housed. Like other editions of the Living Newspaper, the production used as its protagonist an "everyman" who, after raising the basic issue, was led through the background of the problem and its possible solutions. In 1939 congressional ire with the Federal Theatre's obvious pro—New Deal leanings led to a cutoff of appropriations.

In spite of its brief life, the Federal Theatre had a significant impact. In addition to the innovative multimedia experiments of the Living Newspaper and other richly varied enterprises that sprang up across the country, the Federal Theatre gave a boost to black drama through the Negro People's Theatre, a unit of the Federal Theatre headquartered at the Lafayette Theatre in Harlem and led by John Houseman. Among its successes were a seven-month run of Orson Welles's all-black, voodoo *Macbeth* (1935–1936), set in Haiti, and an ambitious *Doctor Faustus* (1937) with Welles in the title role. Also impressive was the Chicago production of *The Swing Mikado* (1938), which transformed the Gilbert and Sullivan operetta into a celebratory display of dancing and singing set in the Caribbean. When the production moved to New York in 1939, its raves inspired showman Michael Todd to mount a hastily thrown together and Harlemized imitation, *The Hot Mikado* (1939), with Bill Robinson.

Also notable was the infamous nonstaging of composer Marc Blitzstein's *The Cradle Will Rock* (1938), a biting musical probe into the inherent conflicts in labor-management relations in a steel factory. When the Works Project Administration, the Federal Theatre's parent agency, ordered the play's postponement because of its perceived political volatility, an ad hoc, unsanctioned "rehearsal" performance was quickly arranged.

Provoked by the specter of federal censorship, Welles and Houseman, Blitzstein's producers, formed their own company, the Mercury Theatre, in 1937. In its short yet illustrious life, the Mercury presented vivacious updatings of plays by Georg Büchner, Thomas Dekker, George Bernard Shaw, and Shakespeare. Its greatest and most provocative stage success was a modern-dress rendition of Shakespeare's *Julius Caesar* (1938), fashioned as a sharp commentary on fascism with the conspirators garbed in uniforms resembling those of the German and Italian military Welles and Houseman also took their dramatic acumen to the airwaves with the Mercury Radio Theatre, which produced the harrowing and historic Halloween night broadcast of *The War of the Worlds* (1938), which convinced a sizable portion of the population that Martians had landed in New Jersey. The troupe was soon lured to Hollywood where it scored its greatest triumphs, the watershed motion pictures *Citizen Kane* (1941) and *The Magnificent Ambersons* (1942).

The years between the two world wars were marked by an ongoing struggle between the stage's commercial productions and its more highbrow ambitions. Along with the era's frothy revues, there were musical comedies like *Of Thee I Sing* (1931), with a book by George S. Kaufman and Morrie Ryskind and music by George and Ira Gershwin, that pilloried presidential politics; like the satiric works of Gilbert and Sullivan, this American musical persuasively argued public issues by means of laughter. There were more self-consciously "serious" works by such talents as Clifford Odets, Elmer Rice, Maxwell Anderson, Robert E. Sherwood, John Howard Lawson, Paul Green, and Lillian Hellman. There were also sophisticated comedies such as Philip Barry's *The Philadelphia Story* (1939), the George S. Kaufman-Moss Hart collaborations *You Can't Take It with You* (1936) and *The Man Who Came to Dinner* (1939), and the whimsical meditations on the human condition offered by Thornton Wilder in *Our Town* (1938) and *The Merchant of Yonkers* (1938), rewritten in 1954 as *The Matchmaker* and adapted for the musical *Hello, Dolly!* in 1964. Ironically, one of the 1930s' towering theatrical and musical achievements, George Gershwin's American folk opera *Porgy and Bess* (1935), based on Dubose Heyward's book with lyrics by Heyward and Ira Gershwin, was not a commercial success.

The Second World War, like the first, ruptured the theater's normal patterns. Theater people, like their counterparts in the other entertainment arts, discovered that their talents had a unique value in helping to keep morale up. They toured army camps and visited stage-door canteens. Broadway developed a new élan and, in so doing, attracted an audience expanded by curious soldiers and civilians newly affluent from the prosperity generated by the all-out war effort.

Irving Berlin's *This Is the Army* (1942) represented the zenith of wartime revues. Opening with an all-soldier cast on the patriotic date of July 4, just seven months after Pearl Harbor, the show evoked fervent, red-white-and-blue support for United States troops everywhere. GIs identified with the sentiments expressed in "This Is the Army, Mr. Jones." But the show-stopper came when three hundred soldiers trooped across the Broadway Theatre's stage to the insistent beat of their own feet marching in precisely choreographed close-order drills. The show was adapted successfully by Hollywood in 1944 and included a scene with heavyweight boxing champion Joe Louis in an obvious but no less sincere attempt to "include" American blacks in the patriotic pageantry.

The euphoria of victory was short-lived, for after World War II the United States entered into an era of international militarization and domestic conformity. The American theater responded with a sharp increase in the number of plays that explored the convoluted labyrinths of the human mind. In treating such basic and universal themes, many of America's most prominent and socially aware dramatists added poignancy and power to their works by the use of regional settings. Arthur Miller's *Death of a Salesman* (1949) and *A View from the Bridge* (1955), for example, reflected the playwright's blue-collar, working-class Brooklyn background; and Tennessee Williams's *A Streetcar Named Desire* (1947) and *Cat on a Hot Tin Roof* (1955) simmered with southern idioms.

Though an extension of the Group Theatre's approach first taught in the 1920s, it was the Actors Studio that became the postwar period's primary influence on acting. Established in 1947, the Actors Studio achieved its greatest impact with Lee Strasberg, who taught a performance approach based on the actor's individual psyche and emotional memory. The "method" attained its greatest notoriety with Marlon Brando's controversial characterization of Stanley Kowalski in Williams's *A Streetcar Named Desire.* As directed by Actors Studio co-founder Elia Kazan, Brando's Kowalski inflamed debate by popularizing an acting style that for some seemed to trade on boorish street talk, brutish behavior, and slovenly attire. While the novelty of the method's departure from tradition has mostly dissipated, it remains one of the touchstones of the contemporary theater both in America and abroad.

With the increasing postwar emphasis on cultural diversity, the American theater, like other national institutions, was opened to participants of all backgrounds, working in virtually all sections of the country. In part, such activity has been a reaction to Broadway's ever-increasing conservatism and the tendency of Broadway producers, reacting to multimillion dollar production budgets and escalating ticket prices, to try to lure mass audiences by relying on well-known and therefore pre-sold stories and stars, many of them, ironically, from such competing media as movies, television, and popular music.

Women, though traditionally well represented as performers, did not begin to break into the front rank of playwrights until the 1930s. Among the first women to achieve celebrity as a writer was Clare Boothe, whose *The Women* (1936), with an all-female cast, and *Kiss the Boys Good-Bye* (1938) were among the decade's biggest hits. Even more prominent was Lillian Hellman, whose distinguished career included *The Children's Hour* (1934), *The Little Foxes* (1939), and *Toys in the Attic* (1960). More recently, contemporary playwright Beth Henley tapped into her southern roots for searing yet humorous explorations of family life with *Crimes of the Heart* (1979; Pulitzer Prize, 1981) and *The Miss Firecracker Contest* (1984). Wendy Wasserstein, who first attracted attention with *Uncommon Women and Others* (1977) and *Isn't It Romantic?* (1981), won the 1989 Pulitzer Prize for *The Heidi Chronicles* (1988), the story of art historian Heidi Holland's twenty-five-year-long struggle to attain personal happiness and professional fulfillment and her development of a feminist perspective. Along with the rise of female writing talent, the 1980s witnessed a thriving feminist theater movement that included the Women's Experimental Theatre in New York, At the Foot of the Mountain in Minneapolis, and the Omaha Magic Theatre.

The first black female writer to have a play produced on Broadway was Lorraine Hansberry, whose *A Raisin in the Sun* (1959) won the New York Drama Critics Circle Award. It also featured Sidney Poitier, Claudia McNeil, Ruby Dee, and Diana Sands, a group of talented black players who would achieve further success in films and television, as well as on the stage. Though conventional in form, *A Raisin in the Sun* introduced a number of themes of continuing significance, such as the need for blacks to define their own aspirations, the importance of eliminating discrimination, and the place of African culture within the black American experience. A montage of excerpts from Hansberry's letters, notes, and plays was posthumously produced as *To Be Young, Gifted, and Black* (1971).

The first African American playwright to win the Pulitzer Prize was Charles Gordone for *No Place to Be Somebody* (1969), a tragic story of an illiterate black who attempts to emulate the Mafia as a means of vengeance against the repressive white world. Black anger against "the system" was perhaps most tellingly articulated by Imamu Baraka (LeRoi Jones) who, in arguing for racial separation, spurned New York's white cultural establishment to set up his Spirit House in the midst of the black ghetto of Newark, New Jersey. Baraka's militancy was most forcefully expressed in *Slave Ship* (1967), an epic collage of scenes depicting the black American experience. Charles Fuller's *A Soldier's Play* (1981), produced by the Negro Ensemble Company, is a poignant examination of racism in the army during World War II. Its successful Broadway run and a Pulitzer Prize took Fuller to Hollywood where his adaptation, *A Soldier's Story* (1984), proved one of the decade's best black-oriented films.

Inspired by the examples of Hansberry, Baraka, and Bullins, members of other minorities began to see the arts as uniquely effective forms for expressing their own cultural and political concerns. In 1965, for example, Luis Valdez, in cooperation with the National Farm Workers Association, founded El Teatro Campesino (Fieldworker's Theater), to dramatize the need for the unionization of farm laborers. After successfully achieving that objective, Valdez drew attention to the problem of discrimination against Americans of Mexican descent in *Zoot Suit* (1976) and *I Don't Have to Show You No Stinking Badge* (1987). The growth in Hispanic theater was documented in a 1985 survey that found over one hundred active regional troupes with specific ties to Chicano, Cuban, Puerto Rican, and other Spanish-speaking groups.

Lorraine Hansberry's Raisin in the Sun *(1959) introduced a number of themes of continuing significance, such as the need for blacks to define their own aspirations, the importance of eliminating discrimination, and the place of African culture within the black American experience.*

The increasing visibility of Asian Americans has most recently been reflected in the successful career of David Henry Hwang, whose concerns for East-West cross-cultural interactions are central to *FOB* (1979) and *The Dance and the Railroad* (1981). Hwang's most celebrated work, *M. Butterfly* (1988), is based on the actual case of a French diplomat who claimed that he did not know that the Chinese star of the Beijing Opera with whom he had lived for two decades was actually a man. In Hwang's absorbing recounting, the tale becomes a metaphor for the West's inability to see through its stereotypes of the East as exotic, feminine, and passive. Asian American theatrical efforts have received significant encouragement from institutions such as the Pan Asian Repertory Theatre in New York and the East-West Players in Los Angeles.

In addition to a dramatic increase in minority involvement in the theater throughout the 1960s, the decade also saw a strong movement toward decentralization of the theater. Fueled by growing disenchantment with the rampant commercialization of Broadway and its ever-escalating production and ticket costs, as well as by the foment provoked by the civil rights and women's movements and the protests against America's involvement in the Vietnam War, theatrical enterprises seemed to pop up everywhere.

On the streets, there were groups like the San Francisco Mime Troupe, created in 1959 by R. G. Davis. Combining a commedia dell'arte approach with the techniques of Soviet agitprop plays, the troupe systematically ridiculed everything and everyone in authority. In *A Minstrel Show, or, Civil Rights in a Cracker Barrel* (1966), the troupe savaged both racism and naive integration. One of the few radical theater groups born in the 1960s to have survived while sustaining its anti-establishment focus, the San Francisco Mime Troupe has kept its political drive alive in works such as *Steeltown* (1985), an examination of the marginalization of the labor movement and political left. The Bread and Puppet Theater, founded in 1961 by Peter Schumann, literally used puppets or "living sculptures," some twelve feet tall, and bread given to the audience at each performance as part of a communionlike ritual. In parables such as *The Cry of the People for Meat* (1969), Schumann's ensemble depicted the imperialistic evils of the Vietnam War as a consequence of capitalism's proclivity, for violence.

Some of the most exciting experiments of the period were carried out by the Living Theatre Company. Though founded in 1947 by Judith Malina and Julian Beck to explore poetic drama and nonrealistic production strategies, it gradually began to incorporate the advanced techniques of theorists Antonin Artaud and Bertolt Brecht. By the 1960s, the Living Theatre traveled throughout the United States and Europe espousing revolution, anarchy, and freedom from the restraints of government and bourgeois convention. In works such as *Paradise Now* (1968), the traditional barriers between performers and audience were broken down in order to smash the heritage of theatrical illusionism and to establish a performer-audience solidarity for the revolutionary political tasks at hand. Despite its decline in the 1980s, the Living Theatre left a legacy that lives on in such strategies as the decentering of dialogue in favor of Artaudian and Brechtian techniques, the confrontational blitzing of audiences, and the whipping up of impassioned exhortations.

Though less politically radical, the Off-Broadway and Off-Off-Broadway movements provided a more varied but no less significant influence. Founded in 1951 by Jose Quintero and Theodore Mann, the Circle in the Square helped establish the careers of the actors Geraldine Page, Jason Robards, Jr., George C. Scott, and Colleen Dewhurst. Quintero had spectacular success with revivals of Tennessee Williams's *Summer and Smoke* in 1952, and Eugene O'Neill's *The Iceman Cometh* in 1956. During the 1950s, Off-Broadway theaters focused on repertory rather than experimentation; the goal was to attain a level of artistry more serious than that offered by Broadway.

At the start of the 1960s, Off-Broadway venues started feeling economic pressures similar to those affecting Broadway, including increased labor and overhead costs. Inspired by the opportunity created by Off Broadway's diminished offerings and growing caution, various bootstrap entrepreneurs began to offer plays wherever a room could be found. Joe Cino, who started using his Caffé Cino as an art center in 1958, is credited with initiating the Off-Off-Broadway phenomenon that by 1965 had produced some four hundred plays by approximately two hundred different playwrights. The most significant Off-Off-Broadway producer was Ellen Stewart, who began offering plays in 1961 under the banner of the Café La Mama (later renamed La Mama Experimental Theatre Club). In the 1969–1970 season, La Mama alone presented more original plays than did Broadway.

Outside New York, yet paralleling the Off- and Off-Off-Broadway movements, a significant array of regional theaters developed. In 1947 Margo Jones established her Theatre 47 (the name changed with the coming of each new year) in Dallas. The Alley Theatre, also founded in 1947, was set up in Houston by Nina Vance, while the Arena Stage of Washington, D.C., was put into operation in 1949 by Zelda Fichandler. Women, indeed, were at the forefront of the regional theater movement. The establishment of the Missouri Repertory Theatre in Kansas City by Patricia McIlrath in 1964 and Jo Ann Schmidman's Omaha Magic Theatre in 1969 were also significant.

A trend toward stabilizing such operations with resident companies was bolstered by the example of Tyrone Guthrie, who opened the formidable Guthrie Theater in Minneapolis in 1963. Substantial Ford Foundation grants available to those companies deemed likely to grow had also been a stabilizing force. Then, in 1965, the creation of the National Endowment for the Arts provided additional support. However, the challenge of financing American arts in general and American theater in particular has remained problematic, especially in view of the 1990 congressional debates on whether to continue funding for the arts endowment in view of controversies over tax-supported work that some have considered morally objectionable.

Still, regional theaters have remained strong. In 1990, there were more than two hundred such nonprofit professional operations collectively offering more than three thousand productions. Employment figures for actors were similarly striking. In 1966, for example, a survey revealed that for the first time in the twentieth century, more stage actors were employed outside New York than in it. By 1990, for every actor working on Broadway, there were four being paid by nonprofit regional theaters.

In many ways, regional theaters have functioned like subsidized European theaters, offering repertoires composed mainly of popular classic and contemporary titles. By 1990, however, some regional theaters had also become important supporters of new works. The Goodman Theatre of Chicago, founded in 1925 during the heyday of the little theater movement, took on this function in the 1980s by producing the American premieres of David Mamet's Pulitzer Prize-winning examination of real estate swindlers, *Glengarry Glen Ross* (1984), and David Rabe's excoriating probe of Hollywood, *Hurlyburly* (1984), both of which enjoyed successful Broadway runs. A number of theaters also established working relationships with playwrights; an example is the productive alliance between the Yale Repertory Theatre and August Wilson, whose insightful *Fences* (1985) and *The Piano Lesson* (1990) each earned a Pulitzer for the black playwright.

Theatrical entrepreneur Joseph Papp established the New York Shakespeare Festival which in 1957 began offering free, city-supported performances in Central Park. This photograph of Shakespeare in the Park was taken on July 6, 1961.

Entrepreneur Joseph Papp offered yet another alternative through his ability to forge successful links between the commercial, nonprofit, and educational theater worlds. In 1954 Papp established the New York Shakespeare Festival, which in 1957 began offering free, city-supported performances in Central Park; in 1962 the outdoor Delacorte Theatre was built to house the productions. Like jazz musician Billy

Taylor and his Jazzmobile, Papp took productions as well as workshops into New York's ethnic neighborhoods. This was an important part of his lifelong ambition to "liberate" theater from its essentially bourgeois and intellectual middle-class orientation.

In 1966 Papp enlarged his operation with the acquisition of the Astor Library in downtown New York. Born again under the banner of the Public Theatre with five auditoriums, the old Astor Library got off to a rousing start with its inaugural event, Papp's production of the bellwether rock musical *Hair* (1967), with music by Galt MacDermott and book by Gerome Ragni and James Rado. It was the perfect vehicle for capitalizing on Papp's concern for expanding theater's demographic boundaries. Its characters were archetypal, youthful 1960s outsiders wrestling with racism, sexism, public attitudes toward homosexuality, the responsibilities of parenthood, drugs, poverty, and the Vietnam War. Significantly, and in contrast to the book musicals of the period like *Hello, Dolly!* (1964) and *Fiddler on the Roof* (1964), *Hair* features the pounding rhythms and amplified guitar licks of rock and roll, as well as the period's obscenity-laced, anti-establishment argot. Embraced by young people, the general public, and the critics, and widely publicized because of a nude scene, *Hair* moved to Broadway in expanded form to become the season's runaway hit. Catching the Zeitgeist of the period, it also caught the public's ear with such pop music hits as "Aquarius." Papp's comfortable embrace of everything from Shakespeare to rock music, as well as his openness to both conceptual and technical innovation, made him one of the American theater's most influential entrepreneurs.

A Postmodern Postscript

The breaking down of traditional assumptions and boundaries, though itself a long-standing tradition in the arts and human affairs, has in recent decades accelerated at unprecedented rates. Indeed, the speed and degree of change have been so great that the term "postmodern" is now commonly used in discussions of contemporary arts and culture to bracket the works of the late 1980s on from those of the immediately preceding "modern" era. Though a multitude of widely different styles prospered under the aegis of "modernism," each tended to adhere to a general set of characteristics that gave every work a signature relating it to such categories as surrealism or absurdism. In contrast, postmodern art has come to be characterized by a singular lack of consistency, either external or internal. In fact, the willful mixing and confusing of seemingly contradictory style, generic, and narrative elements has become a hallmark of the postmodern approach. Various manifestations of contemporary "performance art," with roots in European dadaism and surrealism of the 1920s as well as in the "happenings" and multimedia events of the 1960s, embody important aspects of the post-modern aesthetic. So, too, do the large-scale works of such contemporary artists as Robert Wilson, Richard Foreman, and the Wooster Group.

Related to postmodern production practice but focused on the role played in the artistic transaction by the spectator or reader is a group of theories grouped under the rubrics of poststructuralism and deconstruction. Based largely on the works of authors Jacques Derrida, Roland Barthes, and Jacques Lacan, poststructuralism calls into question the basic assumption of structuralism—and, implicitly, all Western culture—that statements about truth and reality are independent of language. Poststructuralism argues that language profoundly influences its users to see and understand the world in very particular, language-inflected ways, invalidating or at least seriously compromising any claim to ultimate truth or objectivity. This destabilization of meaning has resulted in a condition, at least for postmodern critics and artists, that posits that, at best, truth is relative.

The critical-analytic process necessary to uncover the ideologic-linguistic values percolating just beneath a language's or work's surface structure has come to be known as deconstruction. The most ardent deconstructionists have been feminists, whose analysis of language has revealed various ways in which the values of white American and European men have tended to be privileged over those of women and people of color.

Today, the American theater is a richly variegated and lively enterprise. Like the other arts, it embodies and reflects the concerns and controversies of contemporary society. And though it is fashionable to declare Broadway a vast wasteland, itself a debatable proposition given the stylish and appealing successes of talents such as Neil Simon and Stephen Sondheim, it is far more accurate and revealing to conceive of the American theater as being in a dynamic steady state in which a dazzling array of forms, formats, and activities coexist. Furthermore, it should be recalled that in addition to Broadway, live theater abounds in regional, community, university, and even public school productions. Also, American movies and television might be considered in part as technological extensions of the American theater. Indeed, given the free and frequent movement of actors, directors, writers, producers, and composers among dramatic media, it may be overly restrictive to confine "theater" only to its live, stagebound manifestations.

As the twenty-first century nears, the American theater will continue to evolve. And as it confronts society's and its own political, ideological, and technological upheavals, as well as its ever-increasing symbiosis with cinema and video, it may well be that part of its strategy for ensuring its capacity for adaptation and survival will revolve around attempts to deal with the pivotal question, "What is theater?"

[See also African American Music; Concert Music; Film; Humor and Comedy; Popular Entertainment before the Civil War; Radio; Television; Urban Cultural Institutions.]

BIBLIOGRAPHY

General Works

Abramson, Doris E. *Negro Playwrights in the American Theatre, 1925–1959* (1969).

Atkinson, Brooks. *Broadway Scrapbook* (1947).

Atkinson, Brooks. *Broadway, 1900–1970* (1974).

Bentley, Eric. *In Search of Theatre* (1954).

Bentley, Eric. *The Life of the Drama* (1964).

Bigsby, C. W. E. *A Critical Introduction to Twentieth-Century American Drama.* 3 vols. (1983; 1984; 1985).

Bond, Frederick W. *The Negro and the Drama* (1940).

Bordman, Gerald. *The American Musical Theatre* (1978; rev. 1986).

Bordman, Gerald. *The Concise Oxford Companion to American Theatre* (1987).

Brockett, Oscar G. *History of the Theatre.* 6th ed. (1991).

Brockett, Oscar G., and Robert R. Findlay. *Century of Innovation: A History of European and American Theatre and Drama Since the Late Nineteenth Century.* 2d ed. (1991).

Brustein, Robert. *Revolution as Theatre: Notes on the New Radical Style* (1971).

Carlson, Marvin. *Theories of the Theatre: A Historical and Critical Survey, from the Greeks to the Present* (1984).

Chinoy, Helen K., and Linda W. Jenkins. *Women in American Theatre* (1981; rev. 1987).

Cooper, Roberta Krensky. *The American Shakespeare Theatre: Stratford, 1955–1985* (1986).

Flanagan, Hallie. *Arena: The Story of the Federal Theatre* (1988).

Gard, Robert E., Marston Balch, and Pauline B. Temkin. *Theater in America* (1968).

Gardner, R. H. *The Splintered Stage: The Decline of the American Theatre* (1965).

Gilbert, Douglas. *American Vaudeville: Its Life and Times* (1940).

Gorelik, Mordecai. *New Theatres for Old* (1940).

Green, Stanley. *The World of Musical Comedy.* 4th ed. (1980).

Green, Stanley. *Broadway Musicals: Show by Show.* 3d ed. (1990).

Gronbeck-Tedesco, John L. *Acting Through Exercises* (1992).

Hill, Errol, ed. *The Theatre of Black Americans.* 2 vols. (1980).

Hirsch, Foster. *A Method to Their Madness: The History of the Actors Studio* (1984).

Jenkins, Ron. *Acrobats of the Soul: Comedy and Virtuosity in Contemporary American Theatre* (1988).

Kernan, Alvin B., ed. *The Modern American Theater: A Collection of Critical Essays* (1967).

Kirby, Michael. *Happenings* (1965).

Kline, Herbert, ed. *New Theatre and Film, 1934–1937* (1985).

Krutch, Joseph W. *The American Drama Since 1918.* Rev. ed. (1957).

Levine, Lawrence W. *Highbrow/Lowbrow: The Emergence of Cultural Hierarchy in America* (1988).

Lewis, Philip C. *Trouping: How the Show Came to Town* (1973).

Londre, Felicia Hardison. *The History of World Theater: From the English Restoration to the Present* (1991).

McConachie, Bruce A., and Daniel Friedman, eds. *Theatre for Working-Class Audiences in the United States, 1830–1980* (1985).

MacGowan, Kenneth. *The Theatre of Tomorrow* (1921).

MacGowan, Kenneth. *Footlights Across America, Towards a National Theater* (1929).

McLean, Albert F., Jr. *American Vaudeville as Ritual* (1965).

Mersand, Joseph. *The American Drama Since 1930: Essays on Playwrights and Plays* (1949).

Mitchell, Loften. *Black Drama: The Story of the American Negro in the Theatre* (1967).

Nagler, A. M. *A Source Book in Theatrical History* (1959).

Nicoll, Allardyce. *Film and Theatre* (1936).

O'Connor, John, and Lorraine Brown, eds. *Free, Adult, Uncensored. The Living History of the Federal Theatre Project* (1978).

Patterson, Lindsay, ed. *Anthology of the American Negro in the Theatre: A Critical Approach* (1967).

Pottlitzer, Joanne. *Hispanic Theatre in the United States and Puerto Rico* (1988).

Rabkin, Gerald. *Drama and Commitment: Politics in the American Theatre of the Thirties* (1964).

Sanders, Leslie Catherine. *The Development of Black Theatre in America: From Shadows to Selves* (1988).

Saylor, Oliver M. *Our American Theatre* (1970).

Schechner, Richard. *Environmental Theater* (1973).

Schechner, Richard. *The End of Humanism: Writings on Performance* (1982).

Sellner, Maxine S., ed. *Ethnic Theatre in the United States* (1983).

Shank, Theodore. *American Alternative Theatre* (1982).

Smith, Cecil M., and Glenn Litton. *Musical Comedy in America* (1981).

Taylor, John Russell. *Anger and After: A Guide to the New British Drama* (1963).

Vardac, A. Nicholas. *Stage to Screen: Theatrical Method from Garrick to Griffith* (1949).

Weales, Gerald. *American Drama Since World War II* (1962).

Weales, Gerald. *The Jumping Off Place: American Drama in the 1960s* (1969).

Wilson, Garff B. *Three Hundred Years of American Drama and Theatre* (1973; 2d ed. 1982).

Ziegler, Joseph Wesley. *Regional Theatre: The Revolutionary Stage* (1977).

Journals

American Theatre (1984–).

Journal of Dramatic Theory and Criticism (1986–).

TDR (The Drama Review) (1955–).

Theatre History Studies

Theatre Journal (1941–).

— CHARLES MERRELL BERG

THEME PARKS

See AMUSEMENT AND THEME PARKS

TOWN

See VILLAGE AND TOWN

TRANSPORTATION AND MOBILITY

Mobility practically defines American social history. The march of Europeans and their descendants across the North American landscape, from 1607 to the present day, transforming the face of the land, reordering time and space, restlessly moving in search of wealth, freedom, and satisfaction—this story embraces the whole of American history. Immigration to America marks a common beginning for the earliest voyagers and the most recent arrivals. The potential for movement in America shaped and guided the lives of all who dared to take make the trip. In turn, the restless energies of these mobile voyagers fostered innovations that revolutionized the world in which Americans lived and worked—and moved.

There is nothing uniquely American about these habits of mobility and innovation, but their relentless influence placed a distinctive mark on the history of American society. For generations, Americans measured "progress" in terms of mobility, innovation, and technological "improvement." Most Americans have understood the exploitation of fossil fuels, and the assault on space and time, as natural, unambiguous triumphs. Critical assessment, on the other hand, may undermine our confidence in the virtue of these changes. Throughout this essay such value-laden terms as "progress" and "improvement" are meant to convey sentiments held in the past, whose merits, like all history, deserve scrutiny today.

Voyagers to the West

Fifteenth-century breakthroughs in navigation and ship design inaugurated Europe's conquest of the Americas. Beginning with the 1492 voyage of Columbus, square-rigged caravels and heavy galleons mastered the Atlantic waters, landing white adventurers (and their diseases) on New World shores, hauling treasure to the vaults of Europe, shuttling Africans into American slavery, and forging networks of commerce and communication that revolutionized the early modern world. Ranging in size from Columbus's *Santa María* (probably about 78 by 26 feet, drawing about 6 feet of water) to George III's three-decked men-of-war (up to 150 by 51 feet), these wooden ships with canvas sails serviced the world's first global empires. An age of restlessness had begun.

Atlantic crossings marked all immigrants to British America as voyagers, although individual experiences varied and the shock of transplantation differed according to one's expectations. Most early white settlers came from the restless classes of seventeenth-century England. Displaced agricultural laborers, unemployed urban workers, the "wandering poor" of Stuart England swelled the ranks of indentured servants who filled the Chesapeake colonies. West Country Puritans—spiritual voyagers before they became geographical pioneers—poured into New England. Younger sons of English gentlemen, uprooted by primogeniture from their ancestral lands, seized great estates in the new plantations. Restless entrepreneurs came to exploit a field for investment more open than Europe's markets ever would be.

The voyage itself often proved more grueling than adventurous. Crowded below decks with their livestock and luggage, immigrants suffered bad food, disease, and every discomfort for six to eight weeks or more—the longest trip on record lasted twenty-six weeks. Africans, of course, did not share even the bleakest hopes of the westering whites because they did not choose to move to America. Sold to Dutch, English, or Portuguese traders on the African coast, black slaves experienced a cruel deportation rendered positively demonic by conditions on the dreaded Middle Passage. Chained in tightly packed rows in dark, filthy holds, poisoned by the stench of wastes and death, hungry and terrified, black captives grieved for home and family, wondering what ghastly fate awaited them.

At the end of these immigrant voyages lay the North American coast. Mainland shores boasted ancient forests, sometimes rendered parklike by the Indians' annual burnings, but vastly deeper and more wild than the English had known. Because diseases that preceded the colonists—especially smallpox and influenza—had destroyed up to nine-tenths of the native population, the English saw what they were inclined to believe God and their sovereign had granted them: a bountiful paradise practically uninhabited.

Of course the North American coast actually sheltered thousands of native people. Dependent on hunting, gathering, and agriculture for subsistence, most Eastern Woodlands Indians pursued mobility patterns that inadvertently contributed to European myths about Indian life. Whereas Englishmen fixed their fortunes to the ground, moving people and things to suit their needs, Indians moved their communities to capture seasonal bounties within the natural environment. Their transience and lack of fixtures appeared to the English as simple indolence. Europeans who defined themselves by attachments to property and place could only condemn as savages women and men who acquired little and roamed about in the wild forests.

The habits of the Indians nevertheless served the early colonists well. Indian trails marked overland paths for Europeans through the "trackless" New World forests. Indian canoes, dug out of logs or sewn together from white birchbark, extended navigation into much smaller streams than English ships could pass. Much of what white settlers learned of survival on North America's frontier they gleaned from Indian ways, and yet they never overcame their dread of these rootless, mobile natives. Even while they perfected their own penchant for moving around, the English viewed with suspicion any drift toward "savagery."

Colonial settlements first clustered near convenient landings, and the sea remained the primary highway for all transplanted Europeans. Gradually, as their numbers rose and they grew more familiar with the environment (and with native transportation), they spread along shorelines and up navigable streams, mastering the land as they came, fixing their claims to the ground in the form of clearings, buildings, fences, roads, docks, churches, and towns. Seventeenth-century colonists perfected their conquest of the coastal regions with little more for transportation than the natural waterways assisted by common roads. The latter were built, as in England, by local taxpayers, and the quality of these paths varied according to the ambitions of their users. In this primitive world most travelers walked or rode horseback, and goods moved in wagons or carts to town—or to the nearest waterway for more distant destinations.

In the eighteenth century the British plantations grew more prosperous and complex. Their populations expanded at unprecedented rates, from both natural increase and continued immigration, and the area of settlement quickly doubled. Eager to continue their successful assaults on the frontier, Anglo-Americans soon found development constrained by the limits of transportation over so large a field: if the fringes of colonial settlement were not to languish in wretched isolation, they must find ready communication with the centers of trade and culture. From this developmental necessity sprang the urge to improve transportation.

The Beginnings of Improvement

Improved transportation documented the triumph of English over Indian ways. Pioneers may have traveled light and borrowed Indian survival and farming techniques, but they never intended to detach themselves from the lifelines of European empire. Settlers roamed the Shenandoah Valley, pushed through the Cumberland Gap into the valley of the Ohio, explored upstream along all the major rivers of the Atlantic seaboard, venturing however far, then crying out for improvement of the routes back to metropolitan centers. British policy in the Proclamation of 1763 discouraged this accelerating movement into Indian lands, but the American rebellion seemed to raise expectations even higher. With independence in 1783 came policies that encouraged the westward movement, and the formation of political union stimulated Atlantic communities to improve connections with each other and with the backcountry.

Internal improvements appeared almost everywhere in the first years of American nationhood. Coastal cities such as Boston, Providence, Philadelphia, and Baltimore chartered corporations to build turnpike roads, extending their trading networks deep into their hinterlands. Cleared of stumps (the largest were cut off at a foot or so), sometimes ditched and dressed with broken stone, turnpikes in the 1790s provided more or less all-weather roadways on which wagons and coaches transported goods, people, and information to bustling port cities. Improved post roads, especially north and east of New York, speeded the flow of newspapers and letters in the care of the new federal post office. Enterprising people and corporations erected bridges where fords and ferries had delayed or endangered the traveling public. Bowing to the sensitivities of local citizens, turnpike charters sometimes exempted common farmers from paying the tolls imposed on commercial carriers; however, the customary rights of ferrymen and others who benefited from the lay of the land fell quickly to the ambitions of improvers.

Water transportation received equal attention as local enterprisers schemed to perfect the system of routes already laid down by nature. Certain canal projects immediately recommended themselves: across Cape Cod at Barnstable Harbor; from Boston to the Merrimack River; across the isthmus separating the Delaware River from Chesapeake Bay; through the Dismal Swamp of southern Virginia to North Carolina's Albemarle Sound. Gentlemen of grander vision dreamed of interregional canals from New York's Hudson River to Lakes Ontario and Champlain; from Philadelphia via the Schuylkill and Susquehanna rivers to Lake Erie; or the centerpiece of new American nationalism, a Potomac Canal linking the waters of the Ohio River system with the new national capital. American funds and engineering expertise could not sustain this first generation's designs, but canal fever persisted and the breakthrough was close at hand.

New York's Erie Canal, built between 1817 and 1825, repaid the frustrations of early improvers with spectacular success. Taking advantage of a "water-level" route (rising some six hundred feet [180 meters]) as well as the fastest-growing city in the postwar United States, New York's DeWitt Clinton gambled the credit of the state against the hope of control over commerce with the American interior. After 1825, in part because the canal captured westering traffic and in part because fair prospects energized the metropolis's enterprising merchants, New York City brokered American commerce the way London had served the British Empire.

Much of the work of improving transportation involved making special vehicles. Pennsylvania wagon builders, for example, attached a boat-shaped box (which naturally centered its cargo) to a rugged undercarriage, producing a Conestoga wagon capable of traversing the punishing roads of the trans-Appalachian frontier. Interior merchants and farmers fashioned crude "arks" and flatboats on which they rafted lumber, whiskey, and surplus grain down the rivers to New Orleans. Long, narrow keelboats, when poled or pulled upstream, offered laborious (and expensive) returns for early pioneers of the Old Northwest. Canal transport via New York soon became so cheap that interior farmers often walked home empty-handed and bought supplies from the continuous downstream flow. Specially designed sailing packets linked New Orleans and other coastal ports with New York, rendering the selection of goods in the markets on Manhattan Island inevitably richer and fresher than almost anywhere else in the network.

Much of the work of improving transportation in the early 1800s involved making special vehicles: Pennsylvania wagon builders attached a boat-shaped box to a rugged undercarriage, producing a Conestoga wagon able to cross the punishing roads of the trans-Appalachian frontier.

Another important improvement required no hardware change whatever. Beginning in 1818, the Black Ball Line placed square-rigged ships on a regular schedule, sailing monthly between Liverpool and New York. Guaranteeing fixed departures, scheduled packets allowed American buyers and sellers to make a market predictably in England. Some scoffed as the first ships sailed with partial cargoes, but within a decade much long-haul business with the mother country was conducted on schedule. America's major export, cotton, found its best market in New York, far from southern fields, largely because scheduled shippers hustled to attract Liverpool buyers in order to fill their ships.

The cumulative effect of these and dozens of other specific improvements in the early American transportation environment produced a genuine revolution in commerce and mobility. Long-distance freight rates between New York City and the agricultural interior fell dramatically (often 95 percent or better). Exports of surplus food and fiber grew apace. Interior cities suddenly boomed. Rochester, New York, for example, grew in a decade from a village of fifteen hundred to a city of ten thousand. The farming frontier quickly pushed across the entire Old Northwest, and cotton planters seized fertile lands from Georgia to Texas. Responding to the excitement, settlers poured into Ohio, Indiana, Illinois, Michigan, Kentucky, Tennessee, Alabama, and Mississippi—all demanding more roads, canals, and transportation services in order to bring new wilderness lands into profitable communication with burgeoning American markets.

The social impact of this revolution in mobility proved no less dramatic. Boom towns like Rochester experienced unbelievable social disruption as thousands of transients came and went each year. The circulation of information increased astonishingly: New York news, which in 1790 took three weeks to reach Ohio, arrived in 1830 in six days or less. With the decline of frontier isolation, more Americans turned to pioneering with rising expectations. The operations of civil courts, the circulation of money and credit, the promises of campaigning politicians—all were transformed by this communications revolution. American habits by the 1830s appeared so hectic that foreign visitors experienced vertigo. Religious mission and reform societies reached out from New York and New England expressly to stir the fires of civilization among western residents, who seemed in danger of reverting to "savagery."

Far Western Frontiers

While American families consolidated their hold on eastern woodlands, frontiersmen scouted the sprawling continental wilderness beyond the Mississippi River. Here scarce water, harsh landscapes, and the rising hostility of displaced Indians rendered transportation both more difficult and more important to survival. Once again voyagers studied the ways of the Indians in order to master this new field for human mobility.

Forced by scant vegetation to range over much longer distances than their woodland neighbors, Indians of the dry plains stretched their patterns of movement over a grand terrain. At first dogs shared the burdens of nomadic life, but the spread of horses in the seventeenth and eighteenth centuries lent new speed, range, and power to migratory systems. Water, weather, and the habits of the bison set the boundaries of native life into the nineteenth century, when the relocation of eastern Indians and the approach of white traders crowded Indian lands and distorted these rhythms. As earlier in coastal forests, traffic in furs broached the cultural barrier separating Indians and whites, redirecting Indian patterns and initiating whites into the mysteries of this difficult land.

Like the adventurers at Jamestown two centuries before, explorers in the Far West received important assistance from a sponsoring "metropolis"—this time the infant United States. In 1803 President Thomas Jefferson sent Meriwether Lewis and William Clark on the first of many official expeditions, this one to open the Louisiana Purchase. The army officers Zebulon Pike and Stephen H. Long charted routes to the southern Rockies, and dozens of less famous individuals probed the mountains for passes. After 1820 private fur companies recruited mountain men—characters like Jim Bridger, Jedediah Smith, and Bill Sublette—who worked in the shadows between enterprise and expatriation, living among the Indians and gathering information on physical and cultural geography that would make American advances possible. The great trails that later carried emigrants to Santa Fe, California, and Oregon were blazed by these vagrant traders, and at mid century wagon trains still found refuge and succor among them.

When overland migrations to Oregon and California quickened in the 1840s, emigrants organized themselves into trains that followed regular, tested procedures. Outfits consisted of sturdy covered wagons, two or three teams of oxen or horses, clothing, cooking equipment, food and water, perhaps a milk cow, and what tools and furniture could be wedged in beside the children. Starting after the worst spring floods, armed with one of many popular emigrants' handbooks or hand-drawn maps, or guided by a hired wagonmaster, several families bound for the same destination adopted rules of association and set out from Independence, Missouri. If equipment, animals, and weather held; if Indians did not attack; if maps and guides proved faithful; if men did not turn quarrelsome or illness become epidemic—if nothing delayed such travelers, they struggled through the mountains by late summer, descending toward the Pacific before September snows closed the high passes. For many, things did not go well: for the famous Donner Party of 1846–1847, small mistakes compounded into fatal disaster. Trapped by early snows in the high Sierras, most of these emigrants starved to death, and some were reduced to cannibalism. On the overland trails, the margin for error proved very small.

Overland wagon trains delivered thousands of Americans to California and Oregon, but integration of the Pacific Coast into the United States depended on regular commercial transportation. Stimulated by California gold rush traffic after 1848, the United States Post Office; private contractors such as George Giddings and John Butterfield; and express companies like Wells Fargo, Adams Express, American Express, and National Express struggled to carry regular mail and passengers through the wastelands. Threatened with the loss of their final domain, mounted Indians in the three decades after 1850 preyed mercilessly on way stations where coaches stopped for water and fresh mules. To protect commercial carriers the U.S. Army took steps to "pacify" the Plains Indians, which in turn lured more travelers, traders, and settlers into the region. Ranchers assembled huge herds of longhorn cattle that, like the bison and the Indians before them, found water and grass where they could until they were driven to Kansas, the railhead, and the markets of the East.

Horse-powered transportation thus opened even the most forbidding American environments to the restless people of the United States. By the era of the Civil War they had planted settlers across a continent that their grandfathers believed would lie empty for ten generations. Three thousand miles (4,800 kilometers) between Jamestown and San Francisco had been subdued with the same transport technology that first brought Englishmen to Virginia: sailing ships, boats, and barges; wheeled wagons; mules, oxen, and horses. No celebration marked the achievement, though, because a more dramatic transportation revolution had captured center stage. On 10 May 1869, at Promontory Point, Utah, a justly proud assembly of capitalists witnessed the driving of the golden spike. The first transcontinental steam railroad was complete. The age of speed and power had begun.

The Impact of Steam Power

Steam power brought a new order of magnitude to changes in American mobility. Steam engines harnessed the energy of burning fuels to machinery that could overcome the natural forces of wind, water, and gravity; speed up the movement of vehicles; and sustain exertions for hours without rest or refreshment. Steam introduced dimensions of speed and power unimaginable ever before.

Successful steamboat navigation in the United States began in August 1807, when Robert Fulton's *Clermont* steamed up the Hudson River from New York to Albany. Quickly, side-wheel steamers appeared on the Atlantic coastal waters wherever contrary winds, downstream currents, or traffic congestion rendered sailing difficult. After 1817, specially designed shallow-draft steamboats (Henry M. Shreve's *Washington* was the first) revolutionized travel on the Mississippi and Ohio rivers. Over the next fifty years improvements in engine technology and boat design steadily increased speed (to over thirty miles [forty-eight kilometers] per hour), safety, and efficiency. Boats drawing little more than a foot of water probed the secondary rivers of the interior, and "floating palaces" adorned the lower Mississippi River. Steam engines' voracious appetites for fuel slowed their adoption on long-distance sailing ships, but by the 1840s transatlantic steam packets offered scheduled liners a measure of protection against delays in calm weather.

Improved water transportation facilitated interior settlement and economic growth, which in turn stimulated demand for even better transportation. Encouraged by England's first successful railway, the Stockton and Darlington (1825), American innovators quickly mated the steam locomotive with the flange-wheeled tramcar system used in mining operations. By the 1830s experimental railroads served Boston, Providence, New York, Baltimore, and Charleston, and chartered corporations projected routes all over the eastern United States. Still imperfect in hardware and operating procedures, early railways struggled for another decade, often bankrupting the promoters who hoped to harness this complex new technology. By 1845, however, the recognizably modern steam train, running on heavy iron "T" rails fixed to wooden cross-ties on raised, improved roadways, stood ready to "annihilate" space and time.

Unlike canals, which were public or mixed enterprises, American railroads were built by private profit-seeking corporations. This organizational difference restricted their access to public money, but it freed railroaders from the control of the local voting taxpayers whose demands often frustrated public-works projects. Railroad developers found that economies of scale favored carload lots, regular schedules, discrimination of freight by weight and value, discrimination of places by competition and traffic potential, integrated operations over long distances, and coordinated interchange with connecting roads. As hardware evolved and construction costs skyrocketed, outside capitalists displaced local investors. In the early 1850s, eastern railroad builders manipulated many short roads into operating trunk lines between New York and Chicago. By the time of the Civil War, American railroaders thought of themselves not as servants but as creators of interior markets.

High fixed costs for construction, equipment, expansion, and debt forced railroads to seek revenue more aggressively than any earlier carriers. They worked tirelessly to build up their territories and capture new ones to the west. Speed and all-weather service gave railroads some advantage over water and wagon competition, but their real transforming power lay in rate discrimination. Low rates for long hauls brought interior places artificially near the coasts, encouraging farming where there was no market. Special rates built up key towns as collection centers. Cutthroat competition drove prices below the normal profit margin on major routes; but much higher local rates recouped the losses incurred on service from points where competition was strongest. Pursuing their own strategies, interstate companies manipulated rates with apparent disregard for the traditional laws of trade.

This new power in the hands of absentee capitalists struck interior farmers and merchants as undemocratic and unfair: "If rates were a guide," quipped an Iowan in 1890, "Omaha was situated between Chicago and Iowa, Denver was on the Mississippi, and San Francisco on the Missouri, while the interior towns of Iowa and Nebraska were located on Behring [*sic*] Strait" (Larson, *Bonds of Enterprise*, p. 178). This capacity to redraw maps produced both regional benefits and local injuries that bewildered a generation. From the 1870s through the 1890s the popular Grange and other farmers' organizations protested this dilemma with demands for government regulation. State and federal laws mandating fairness in pricing brought some relief; but the struggle for control of the railroads produced more heat than light, and subsequent American transportation policies have been distorted by that bitter experience.

Speed and all-weather service gave railroads some advantage over wagon competition, but their real transforming power lay in cost: Low rates for long hauls brought interior places artificially near the coasts, encouraging farming where no market had existed.

While producers and shippers wrestled with the new steam railroad network, American consumers enjoyed unimagined benefits. Cheap transportation may have injured the local shopkeeper, but it placed in his customers' hands quality goods at lower prices. In the two decades after 1880 urban wholesalers, followed by retailers, penetrated the country trade. Drummers showed buyers their catalogs and samples, then relayed orders to cities like Chicago (often by electric telegraph), where jobbers and manufacturers shipped out the goods by railway. Giant department stores such as Marshall Field seized economies of scale by ordering large lots from manufacturers, limiting markups, and guaranteeing customer satisfaction; and mail-order houses such as Sears, Roebuck and Company, and Montgomery Ward eliminated the drummer and storekeeper alike, placing the contents of their warehouses within everyone's easy reach.

By the start of the twentieth century the railroads had established a comprehensive nationwide transportation network that bound Americans together in unprecedented ways. Railroads pioneered national advertising by promoting their crack passenger trains and by pulling private billboard cars that touted consumer goods by name. Railroads delivered the nation's mail in hours and days instead of weeks. The mail sacks bulged with newspapers and magazines advertising uniform, brand-name merchandise to the households of New York, Indiana, and Oregon. After 1886, when southern railroads changed their five-foot tracks to the northern standard gauge, passengers could travel on a through ticket to just about anywhere in the Union. In 1883 Congress adopted the four standard time zones, eliminating almost one hundred different local times and imposing artificial demarcations that symbolized the powerful integrative forces behind this transportation system. In the new century electric interurban cars offered clean, quick, inexpensive rides to a generation more affluent, restless, and rootless than any that came before.

Work itself changed in the railway age. Hundreds of employees worked for each large railroad firm, spread over many miles, some moving, some stationary, performing a wide variety of tasks. Impossible to supervise from a single venue, this army of workers coordinated a daily schedule of trains with sufficient precision to avoid delay, confusion, or accidental death. Early railroad managers invented bureaucratic procedures and systems of classification. Section gangs tended fifty-mile (eighty-kilometer) units of track. Train crews operated the moving trains. Stationmasters coordinated the interface between moving and stationary workplaces. Dozens of conductors, freight agents, and passenger agents sold the product of the firm, quoting rates from printed schedules (and deviating from those schedules according to corporate strategies). Auditors and statisticians devised recordkeeping systems that kept all these variables in constant check.

Individuals hired by the railroads inevitably joined a bureaucratic class paid according to scale for type, rank, and perhaps time in service. For most workers, the boss was not their employer but another paid employee. At first, railway workers responded to these new conditions of employment by forming protective brotherhoods of engineers (1863), conductors (1868), and firemen and enginemen (1873); by 1900 specialized craft unions enrolled most of the individuals eligible to join. However, many classes of employees—track gangs, Pullman porters, baggage handlers (often black workers)—enjoyed no collective bargaining power. Railroad managers attacked all efforts at comprehensive labor organization, such as Eugene V. Debs's American Railway Union (1893), by blacklisting suspected labor radicals and calling in state or federal authorities to protect property from "communistic" strikers. Although everything about the railroad business assumed the character of class action, owners clung to the "free labor" fiction that every American deserved to negotiate for his own wage.

White-collar work found an early articulation on the railroads as well. Hundreds of men worked for wages by handling railroad money and information, with no stake in the ownership or profits of the firm. Some individuals found lucrative careers in the middle ranks of railroad management; but just as quickly as experienced professionals rose to positions of authority, ownership slipped into the hands of bankers and passive investors. "Heroic" entrepreneurs built nineteenth-century railroads, but the mature twentieth-century systems were controlled by salaried professionals—the first of their kind.

In the twentieth century, America's railroads paid for two generations of cutthroat capitalism. Government regulations limited railroad profits just when the industry most needed fresh capital to expand and refurbish the network. New competition from automobiles, trucks, buses, and airplanes cut into the railroads' monopoly on high-speed transportation, each new rival enjoying greater flexibility of operation (no fixed roadway) and generous public subsidies besides. Dieselization, streamlining, reorganization, and retrenchment kept the trains alive, though in steady decline, after World War II.

Urban Public Transportation

The rise and decline of the railroads can be seen compressed and intensified in the story of urban public transportation. Horse-drawn streetcars, first introduced in Manhattan in 1832 and in common use by the 1850s, exploded the integrated structure of the preindustrial "walking city." Relatively easy transportation allowed middle- and upper-class residents to live in parklike suburban neighborhoods away from the noise and filth of industry, the poverty of workers, and the ethnic cacophony that characterized post-Civil War inner cities. Tied to the freight lines of steam railroads, commerce and manufacturing remained tightly packed in downtown areas, creating a pattern of residential suburbs surrounding a business core that inverted the typical layout of colonial and European cities. The new structure inevitably concentrated problems of crowding, poverty, sanitation, crime, and disorder in a central district which could not easily expand or adjust. Industrial growth usually escaped these city cores along the lines of the major railways. Streetcar companies then extended lines to carry laborers out to the factories—or new working-class neighborhoods sprang up to rival the genteel suburbs.

Running below ten miles (sixteen kilometers) per hour and fouling the city streets with tons of waste each year, horsecars could not long keep up with the extraordinary rise of American cities. In 1888 Frank Sprague's electric trolley system in Richmond, Virginia, provided a model of quick and clean transportation capable of integrating much larger cities within easy commuting networks. During the surge of growth that followed the 1893 depression, Boston, New York, and Chicago tried to relieve street congestion by elevating main trolley lines on stilts, creating hierarchical systems with rapid-transit service on the "elevateds" (or "els") and local feeder service at street level. Subways, pioneered in London in the 1860s, provided even faster high-volume transportation in Boston (1898) and New York (1904); however, the high costs and extraordinary disruption attending subways' construction limited their appeal.

Like steam railroads, most American street railways were built by private profit-seeking companies. City governments awarded franchises to developers who then installed tracks and electrical lines at corporate expense and operated the cars with a primary concern for revenue. This practice spared urban taxpayers the burden of paying for their streetcars directly, but it left them utterly dependent on private monopolies that frequently delivered poor service at rates many riders thought too high. Corrupt deals between traction magnates and city leaders further convinced early-twentieth-century riders that streetcars existed more to line the pockets of investors than to facilitate transportation in the city. Huge, consolidated steam railroad companies often purchased these traction franchises, cementing in the public mind a link between disappointing local service and the crimes of interstate "octopus" corporations such as the Southern Pacific Railroad.

By the 1920s, as their growth continued to choke the cities with more traffic than streets could handle, Americans looked for new solutions to the problems created by their escalating habits of mobility. Two paths to a better future seemed imaginable. One path required planning that would regulate land use, industrial and commercial growth, and residential patterns of mobility. Hierarchically coordinated, fixed-rail rapid-transit systems fit nicely into the drawings of new professional urban planners who dreamed of laying down pathways before the people swarmed in to use them. The siren call of the private automobile marked the other path to the future. Freedom was the promise of a Ford: freedom from fixed-rail routes, schedules and timetables, inelastic fares, corrupt franchises, rude conductors, crowded cars, long waits—not to mention freedom from the planners of such sys-

In order to relieve street congestion, New York built elevated train tracks called "els" in the late nineteenth century. This is the "el" platform at 6th Avenue and 34th Street.

tems, who would place new limits on enterprise, property rights, residential liberty, and personal freedom of movement. Since 1920, Americans have endured the interference of urban planners and traffic engineers—but they have fallen in love with their cars.

The All-American Auto

No people on earth took to the motorcar so quickly or so passionately as the Americans. Inventors such as Charles and (James) Frank Duryea (1893) and Elwood Haynes (1894) pioneered the American horseless carriage. By the turn of the century, dozens of small firms across the country designed and manufactured experimental cars. Gradually acquiring familiar features such as steering wheels, pneumatic tires, brakes, lights, electric starters, windshields, and closed bodies, modern automobiles took shape in the 1910s. Most early automobiles catered to a luxury buyer with a sporting sense of adventure; the real revolution in mobility came with the cheap, popular car.

In 1901 Ransom E. Olds produced the first successful cheap car, the Merry Oldsmobile. It fell to Henry Ford, however, to place the motorcar in the hands of ordinary working people. The first Model T sold in 1908 for $850. Sales nearly doubled every year, rising from twelve thousand in 1909 to a half million in 1916, while the price fell to $360. Ford's secret lay in the innovative moving assembly line that by 1914 cut assembly time from around twelve hours to just over two. Workers performed the same simple task on each unit as it passed—an efficient (and monotonous) use of labor that required less skill as machines became more automated. To lure and keep good workers, Ford advertised an astonishing five-dollar daily wage, but his terms included conformity to personal and moral habits so exacting that few workers actually qualified.

Ford consolidated his revolution in mass production with a parallel system of mass marketing. He located branch assembly plants in two dozen cities across the country and established dealerships (with parts and service) in almost every town. Aggressive marketing of this quality, low-cost automobile produced results: soon very ordinary, middle- and working-class families aspired to car ownership. By 1927 Americans had purchased fifteen million Model T cars and a like number of other models, and many cities reported automobile registrations nearly equal to the number of households.

Of course, the popular car stimulated urgent demands for better roads. Before the twentieth century, the United States had almost no hard-surfaced highways. Everywhere dirt roads choked travelers with dust or mired them in mud. If people were going to drive cars, they needed paved roads, but who should build and pay for them? Tradition laid the burden squarely on local authorities, who by the same tradition showed no initiative. In 1912 Carl Fisher, who owned the Indianapolis Motor Speedway, campaigned for a "Coast-to-Coast Rock Highway" (the Lincoln Highway) to be funded by private and corporate subscriptions. Henry Ford preferred tax-supported highways and threw his considerable influence against Fisher's proprietary road: "As long as private interests are willing to build good roads for the general public, the general public will not be very much interested in building good roads for itself" (Hokanson, *The Lincoln Highway*, p. 8).

Ford's commitment to public roads rekindled a jurisdictional debate that once had plagued canal-era internal improvements. Local authorities, indifferent to the plight of the motoring public, could interrupt any network of good roads by refusing to improve their own segments. On the other hand, national mandates for integrated systems offended local interests and state government sovereignty. Congress cautiously addressed this

All around the country, travelers in their Model Ts were choked with dust or mired in mud, and the question arose as to who was going to build and pay for the paved roads that the nation's new motorists demanded.

dilemma in the 1916 Federal-Aid Road Act, which placed seventy-five million dollars over five years at the disposal of the secretary of agriculture to improve rural post roads, the money to be disbursed through state highway departments. Many states created their highway departments in response to this measure, and subsequent federal initiatives encouraged construction of primary highways with offers of matching funds. Competition for scarce tax dollars, however, especially during the Great Depression, often thwarted the hopes of highway reformers.

The democratic promise of the private automobile lay in the freedom it allowed owner-operators to pick their routes and travel times according to personal convenience. Traffic jams, however, easily frustrated this potential. Railroads regulated traffic flow by rigidly adhering to closely timed schedules, but motorists insisted on freeing themselves from precisely that kind of control. Better roads eased congestion for a short time, but nicely paved routes simply encouraged motorists to use them more often. City streets, already crowded with carts, wagons, and streetcars, approached gridlock with the introduction of moving and parked cars. In 1926 Connecticut began planning the Merritt Parkway, one of the nation's first high-speed, limited-access roads designed to separate local and through traffic coming out of New York City. Similar expressways reduced congestion in Boston, Philadelphia, Chicago, and Los Angeles, imposing on the private motorist's universe concepts of hierarchy and discrimination typical of fixed-rail operations. Initially cheaper and more popular than subways or trains, expressways since 1945 have cut great scars through most American cities without really solving rush-hour crowding.

Trucks and buses made special contributions to the automotive revolution. Capable of moving freight from door to door on virtually any route, trucks combined the economies of rail transportation with the flexibility of automobiles. Quickly after 1910, trucks filled urban delivery networks, displacing handcarts and horse-drawn vehicles. Trucks made it possible for industries to locate farther away from fixed-rail services. Both trucks and buses brought motor transportation to rural places too small to support branch-line rail service. Gradually, as highways and vehicles both improved, buses and semitrailer trucks entered intercity and interstate markets wherever small lots, flexible scheduling, multiple deliveries, or other special needs rendered them advantageous.

As intercity traffic grew denser, rural expressways like the Pennsylvania Turnpike (1940) were created to eliminate conflicts between over-the-road vehicles and local folk. Built with public credit (bonds were serviced by tolls paid by the highway users), such long-distance, limited-access highways combined some of the benefits of a specialized railway with freedom for private motorists who could drive on these "tubes" if they chose. This integration of traffic-control principles into automotive transportation reached its logical culmination in the interstate highway system, launched in 1956 to provide a nationwide network of free expressways. Concerns over national defense gave Congress an excuse finally to seize the initiative in national highway planning, and the Highway Trust Fund, filled by user fees and taxes on fuels, tires, and vehicles, promised pay-as-you-go funding.

Automobile travel drove American mobility to even higher orders of magnitude. While cars, trucks, and buses stole some business from existing modes of transportation, the vast majority of car trips never would have been made by train, boat, or wagon. Americans of every class and occupation changed their lives to adjust to the car culture. Cars became a necessity, not a luxury, in the American household: even during the Great Depression, when new car sales plummeted, car use did not decline. Female motorists discovered behind the wheel a new measure of personal and geographical liberty (to the consternation of male commentators, who never tired of poking fun at "women drivers"). Young people—especially the college-age sons and daughters of the middle and upper classes—found in the automobile an instrument of escape, independence, and privacy particularly adapted to courting couples. Spontaneous, unscheduled movement made it easier than ever before for youngsters (or bootleggers, or bank robbers) to flout authority, elude capture, and undermine the conventions of society.

The car culture changed the face of cities and towns. Businesses deserted downtown, centered on its elegant railroad station, for the suburbs and shopping centers with plenty of parking. Hotels lost customers to new roadside motels. Diners sprang up along the highways, some resembling gleaming railroad dining cars, others wacky reproductions of giant coffee pots, milk bottles, or Dutch windmills. Billboards moved from the boxcar to the roadside. And gasoline filling stations took over prime corner lots in almost every American town.

In the 1950s, buoyed (and alienated) by postwar affluence, American teenagers constructed an entire youth culture around souped-up hot rods. Late-1950s-model Chevys with engines and suspensions customized for speed, painted with vivid colors, stripes, and flames, tuck-and-roll interiors, fuzzy dice suspended from the mirror, rock-and-roll on the radio, loaded with teens drinking Cokes and smoking cigarettes, cruised down evening streets in California, Iowa, and New Jersey, stopping at the drive-in, looking for girls, looking for challengers, ducking the cops, looking for trouble. Black, Chicano, and regional variations fed a youth car cult that remained fresh, immediate, and compelling to young people across the country. For a generation protected by the Salk vaccine and penicillin, late-night drag races and drunk driving kept death alive in the youth culture. Hit songs such as "Teen Angel" sentimentalized the fatal car crash, and James Dean and the young Marlon Brando modeled cool behavior on film. Later nostalgic films such as George Lucas's *American Graffiti* (1973) captured the bittersweet interior of a popular culture based on movement—going nowhere.

The Aviation Age

While American youth cruised summer streets in the 1950s and 1960s, the more affluent of their parents learned to "fly the friendly skies" on commercial airliners. Invented before World War I, the airplane found little acceptance for its risky and expensive services in early-twentieth-century popular markets. As a way of fostering an aviation industry, the federal government in 1918 initiated airmail service, first through the post office and then through subsidized private contractors. Scheduled passenger service began in California in 1925, and rising demand quickly overwhelmed the small planes in operation. Aircraft manufacturers scrambled to meet this small, high-value market, developing by 1935 excellent planes such as Douglas's twenty-one-passenger, 200-mile-per-hour DC-3.

Aviation development responded less to mass-market demands than to technological competition and government stimulation, always closely related to national defense. Almost all aviation services began with contracts to carry the mail. The federal government also assumed, in 1926, responsibility for navigational aids and safety systems, which spared the carriers enormous expense for ground facilities and traffic control. New Deal public-works programs funded airport, runway, and terminal construction in many cities and towns. Charges of collusion in the post office brought new regulatory reforms, culminating in a 1938 act that placed both safety regulation and economic control in the hands of the Civil Aeronautics Board (CAB). In 1958 the Federal Aviation Administration (FAA) assumed responsibility for airspace, navigation, and traffic control.

The strategies of the CAB and FAA fostered competition within a comprehensive regulatory framework. Clearly, the government wanted aviation to grow while still allowing the marketplace to determine service quality and price. After World War II, large reliable carriers received protection from the kind of cutthroat competition that once had deranged the railroad marketplace. Union labor enjoyed a measure of protection from regulators intent on keeping peace through arbitration. At the same time new carriers equipped with war-surplus DC-3s were allowed to extend passenger service into new markets. Major airlines responded with innovations, including jet service, which often enjoyed subsidies through government spending on research and development in the defense aerospace industry. Early jets consumed fuel so extravagantly nobody could afford to fly them; however, by 1958 practical jetliners such as the Boeing 707 and the Douglas DC-8 entered the fleets of international and interstate carriers.

Jet service required a new round of public investments in longer runways and huge private outlays for the planes. First associated in the early 1960s with jet-setter life-styles—skiing in Aspen, lunch in Las Vegas, dinner in Los Angeles—air travel soon became more affordable as the airlines targeted mass markets. Aggressive promotion and discount fares sold middle-class Americans on the comfort and convenience of flying. The successful democratization of flight called forth still more public investment in traffic control and passenger terminals.

In 1978, responding to public dissatisfaction with prices and service as well as a political revulsion against centralized regulation, Congress ordered deregulation of the airline industry. Over the next five years the CAB systematically dismantled the framework that shaped the industry, giving carriers their first experience in a relatively free market. Fares on some flights fell dramatically, and popular deep discounts ("super savers") have made certain preplanned trips cheaper than ever. Traffic patterns quickly changed from the trunk-line systems that resembled railroads into hub-and-spoke networks that concentrated passengers and planes in regional centers such as Chicago, Atlanta, and Dallas. Labor lost the fostering hand of government as aggressive operators, such as Texas Air's Frank Lorenzo, sought complete freedom over the wage bill. Union busting culminated in President Ronald Reagan's 1981 dismissal of striking air-traffic controllers, whose complaints included fear that deregulated airways were becoming unsafe. Even under deregulation, aviation remains uniquely privileged among American transportation industries: governments at various levels supply airport facilities, safety inspections, and navigation and traffic control, freeing airlines to fly planes.

Early jets consumed fuel so extravagantly that nobody could afford to fly them; however, by 1958 practical jetliners such as the Boeing 707 and the Douglas DC-8 entered the fleets of international and interstate carriers.

Intersections with the Present

Mobility is part of the American self-definition. Personal liberty on a continental scale has required ready access to easy transportation, and Americans have come to assume that their right to unrestricted movement is as basic as the Constitution. Car ownership in America is more nearly universal than employment or adequate income. Most Americans equate automobility with independence. During the Arab oil embargoes of the 1970s, Americans exhibited an irrational preoccupation with keeping their gas tanks filled. Not just mobility but the potential for spontaneous flight seems almost as important as life, liberty, and the pursuit of happiness. Transportation has become an essential servant of the culture.

Because of this close association between liberty and movement, Americans favor the automobile over more structured or inflexible systems of transportation. Neither air pollution nor oil crises have seriously eroded the car culture, and much of the response to both problems has focused on making cars cleaner and more economical in order to keep driving them freely. Urban crowding continues to spawn expressway improvements far more often than developments in bus or fixed-rail transit. Only three new subway systems graced American cities since the 1970s: San Francisco's BART, Washington, D.C.'s METRO and Atlanta's MARTA. (The BART system barely survived a political opposition that condemned fixed-rail transit as undemocratic.) Buffalo's foray into rapid transit went broke. Chicago adopted an integrated, multimodal regional transit authority, coordinating rapid transit, commuter rail, and bus systems throughout the greater metropolitan area. Still, traffic on the Windy City's expressways congeals each morning and evening with hundreds of thousands of cars.

Why do Americans move so much? Primarily in response to perceived opportunities in social structures and economic markets. For early white Americans, mobility yielded enrichment and liberatation. Their descendants wove the connection into a culture dominated by markets forces and people on the move. African Americans, Native Americans, immigrants from every land gradually adjusted traditional, more sedentary values to find a niche in American life. Eventually mobility became not just a means to liberation but something of an end in itself.

Has all this "progress" in transportation improved American life? Certainly each reduction in the barriers to movement opened up new opportunities for personal and economic achievement. Just as certainly, each new "annihilation" of space and time has destroyed the virtues of original environments, small-scale communities, low-energy ways of life. Native American populations taught the first colonists how to get around in North America, but they were displaced relentlessly by successive waves of mobile newcomers. Africans became Americans against their will due to white mobility, but because of racial discrimination they have never received a fair share of the fruits of transportation improvements. All kinds of immigrants found homes in American communities, in part because Americans moved too much to defend effectively against intruders. In the generation of the 1990s, affluent white suburbanites race about so madly they cannot feel attachment to communities at all. The record clearly is mixed, but mobility remains at the center of American social history, propelling the story through time and shaping for good or ill the diverse narratives of a complex people.

[See also The Culture of Consumption; Geographic Mobility; Landscapes; The Natural Environment: The North; The Natural Environment: The South; The Natural Environment: The West; The Suburbs; Technology and Social Change.]

BIBLIOGRAPHY

General Works

Daniels, Roger. *Coming to America: A History of Immigration and Ethnicity in America* (1990).

Colonial Period

Bailyn, Bernard. *Voyagers to the West: A Passage in the Peopling of America on the Eve of the Revolution* (1986).
Cronon, William. *Changes in the Land. Indians, Colonists, and the Ecology of New England* (1983).
Landström, Björn. *The Ship: An Illustrated History* (1961).
Meining, D. W. *The Shaping of America: A Geographical Perspective on 500 Years of History, Atlantic America, 1492–1800* (1986).

The Nineteenth Century

Albion, Robert G. *The Rise of New York Port, 1815–1860* (1939).
Austerman, Wayne R. *Sharps Rifles and Spanish Mules: The San Antonio—El Paso Mail, 1851–1881* (1985).
Chandler, Alfred D., Jr. *The Visible Hand: The Managerial Revolution in American Business* (1977).
Goetzmann, William H. *Exploration and Empire: The Explorer and the Scientist in the Winning of the American West* (1966).
Haites, Eric F., James Mak, and Gary M. Walton. *Western River Transportation: The Era of Early Internal Development, 1810–1860* (1975).
Larson, John Lauritz. *Bonds of Enterprise: John Murray Forbes and Western Development in America's Railway Age* (1984).
Licht, Walter. *Working for the Railroad. The Organization of Work in the Nineteenth Century* (1983).
Shaw, Ronald E. *Canals for a Nation: The Canal Era in the United States, 1790–1860* (1990).
Stover, John F. *Iron Road to the West: American Railroads in the 1850s* (1978).
Taylor, George Rogers. *The Transportation Revolution, 1815–1860* (1951).
Unruh, John D., Jr. *The Plains Across: The Overland Immigrants and the Trans-Mississippi West, 1840–60* (1979).

The Twentieth Century

Bailey, Elizabeth E., David R. Graham, and Daniel P. Kaplan. *Deregulating the Airlines* (1985).
Bottles, Scott L. *Los Angeles and the Automobile: The Making of the Modern City* (1987).
Flink, James J. *The Car Culture* (1975).
Hokanson, Drake. *The Lincoln Highway: Main Street Across America* (1988).
Jackson, Kenneth T. *Crabgrass Frontier: The Suburbanization of the United States* (1985).
Kelly, Charles J., Jr. *The Sky's the Limit: The History of the Airlines* (1963).

Martin, Albro. *Enterprise Denied. Origins of the Decline of American Railroads, 1897–1917* (1971).
Rae, John B. *The Road and the Car in American Life* (1971).
Rose, Mark H. *Interstate: Express Highway Politics, 1941–1956* (1979). Rev. ed., *Interstate: Express Highway Politics, 1939–1989* (1990).

— JOHN LAURITZ LARSON

TRAVEL AND VACATIONS

Americans spend a substantial proportion of their time in leisure activities, including the taking of vacations and associated travel. Travel away from the place of permanent residence is the critical factor distinguishing tourist or holiday vacation activity from other leisure pursuits. Vacations are clearly important in and of themselves to those taking them; thus the impetus behind them and the rewards of vacationing are examined here. In addition, the total flow of tourists is so great that it results in an economic sector, the tourism industry, that is of major importance to all states and innumerable localities. On an international level, tourism is projected to be the single leading economic sector by the year 2000. Holiday travel by Americans both within and outside the United States is a chief component of this emerging reality. Finally, tourism has consequences that include substantial social, cultural, and environmental effects, along with those that are purely economic.

Central to all of these concerns is how the notion of vacations has evolved and historically been practiced by Americans. First, however, it is necessary to delimit the subject of vacations and tourism. Precise definitions continue to be debated among researchers and organizations concerned with tourism. The efforts to standardize terminology and data collection are centered at the international level in the World Tourism Organization and within this country by such agencies as the United States Travel Data Center, the Bureau of the Census, and the United States Travel and Tourism Administration. The basic question is what makes a traveler a tourist, which is to say someone who is taking a vacation. Most define a person traveling away from home for pleasure as a tourist if the trip exceeds twenty-four hours in duration. Domestic tourism is usually thought of as travel that also exceeds some minimum distance from the normal place of residence, which is commonly set as fifty or one hundred miles.

The European Background

Travel for pleasure is usually thought to have begun in the sixteenth century, restricted to a small, privileged group. Prior to that time are recorded wanderings of early Greeks and Romans, along with larger numbers of people engaged in pilgrimages to the Holy Land or other sacred places. The latter part of the Renaissance was an era of great exploration and increasing knowledge about the world in which the affluent and the nobility, especially the English, engaged in travel to various preferred locales on the Continent. This flow soon resulted in the concept of the Grand Tour, a circuitous journey through a number of European cultural and social centers that became part of the background of the well-bred young Englishman. In addition, scholars and diplomats were frequent travelers along the same route. The Grand Tour initially had an educational focus, but it eventually shifted to a search for pleasure.

The notion of taking a respite from work or other obligations also has a long history. The term "holiday" derives from "holy days," days established as times of worship and ritual, free of daily toil and allowing for recreation time. Originally, such days were devoted primarily to making offerings and performing various rites and ceremonies; some of these days were based on world religions such as Christianity, whereas others had pre-Christian beginnings. In any case it seems probable that holy days had a strong linkage to natural events; that is, to the predictable, regular changes that occur in nature such as the daily and annual courses of the sun and the phases of the moon. Particular days having a natural origin thus might relate to the annual harvest periods and the beginning of the new year. Governments around the world have frequently formalized a number of these special days and, in effect, made them into national holidays. The latter effort has resulted in some arbitrary shifts of dates to make certain holidays fall on Mondays, thus establishing periodic long weekends.

Many observers have identified health concerns as another factor in the establishment of vacation practices. As early as the seventeenth century, medical people in England and the Low Countries were recommending to wealthy patients that they "take the waters" at some spa. For nearly two hundred years more, communities possessing the appropriate resources flourished for this purpose, one of the most notable being Bath, England, which was used as a spa as early as the Roman period. Similarly, some people were steered to sea bathing as a curative for various ills. Brighton, some fifty miles (80 kilometers) to the south of London, became in 1754 the first seaside resort catering to this demand. It then became the model for numerous other seaside resort communities later. In the nineteenth century the English, clearly the first significant group of holidaymakers, reduced their travels to Continental locations as wars and other disturbances affected the attractiveness of their intended destinations. This resulted in the substantial growth of England's domestic resort industry at locations much as Margate in Kent and Scarborough in Yorkshire, and later at Blackpool, near Liverpool. More recently, in the late nineteenth and twentieth centuries the British have again returned to many Continental destinations in their search for desirable vacation settings.

The present-day desire for vacations among citizens of the more developed countries has evolved over the past two hundred years. The modern concept of taking periodic holidays is a product of the industrial revolution. Numerous economic and social changes resulted from its dramatic altering of the means and nature of production. Special days like Christmas, Easter, and Whitsuntide became recognized as days of nonwork in England, to which was added the August national bank holiday, observed on a Monday (thus creating a long weekend). These and other holidays often became formalized by agreements between employers and their employees. Through such processes a disassociation of holidays from their original religious roots took place. It also became increasingly recognized that, given the climatic regimen in western Europe, summer was to be preferred for vacations, because of the probability then of better weather. This factor has lost some of its importance in more recent times as mobility and affluence increased, permitting people to look farther afield for their vacation sites.

As countries' economies developed, an increasing share of their population moved into middle-income categories and the taking of vacations changed from being the nearly exclusive prerogative of the privileged to one being available now to the middle class. In time, with additional changes in society in the more developed countries, the taking of vacations has become available to a large part of national populations, and the notion of mass vacations and tourism has become common. For example, excursion trains for day trippers from large urban centers to reasonably nearby vacation centers went into operation in the 1840s. Resorts, both at the seaside and elsewhere, became very popular between 1870 and 1914. However, it was not until after World War II and the postwar recovery period that true mass tourism became the norm. At this time a great diversity of types of holidays and tourist facilities and systems emerged.

The Evolution of Vacation Travel

Several stages can be identified in the evolution of holiday-making by Americans since the Civil War. These steps, developed by scholar Carlton S. Van Doren, are based on such ever-changing variables as demographic, social, cultural, technological, income, time availability, and organizational and other realities and constraints. These stages may be described first as a period when only the privileged traveled for pleasure (the high society era, from 1860 to 1920), then a period when great numbers became participants (high participation, 1920–1958), followed by an extension of the previous period when travel became far faster and easier (high mobility, 1958–1973), and finally a period of change and adaptation after the energy crisis of 1973. The last period not only saw adjustments as a result of changing energy realities but also witnessed notable changes as a function of recessions in the early 1980s and 1990s and social factors such as the changing composition of the household. Let us examine first, however, the earlier period in which American leisure travel had its beginnings. In these descriptions of the evolution of vacation travel, I am indebted to Carlton S. Van Doren.

The Beginnings of American Leisure Travel

The roots of American holiday travel go back to the latter half of the eighteenth century and the first half of the nineteenth. This period saw the complete filling in of the lands east of the Appalachians and major movements into the interior lowlands to the west of that highland system. It also saw independence established and confirmed. These two events resulted in quite different stimuli for leisure travel. On the one hand, Americans tended to emulate Europeans, especially the British, while at the same time strongly identifying with and appreciating the land itself. In addition, technological developments contributed to fundamental changes in, for example, the developing national economy and transportation. However, conditions were still such that only the privileged could take advantage of the new options available for their leisure time.

Americans quickly copied the English practice of taking the waters for health purposes. A variety of locations possessing springs that offered presumed health benefits saw early resort development. Saratoga Springs, New York, may have been used by frontiersmen by the middle 1700s, and George Washington identified the possibilities of Berkeley Springs (later renamed Bath), on the eastern edge of the Alleghenies in 1748. Other spas developed, with those having the maximum accessibility by stagecoach routes to major population centers having the greatest importance. Bristol, Pennsylvania, was often described as the most attractive spa for the privileged of the time, because of its location on the main route from Philadelphia to New York City. These spas initially offered quite rudimentary facilities but responded rapidly to the desire for comfort by the rich. Simultaneously, coastal resorts with refreshing summer sea breezes and comfortable waters to attract the privileged had their beginnings in places such as Newport, Rhode Island, and Cape May, New Jersey. The practice of emulating the English also took the form of having young adults from wealthy families pay visits to European centers of culture in a direct copying of the Grand Tour concept.

The other influence upon early Americans' travel was their close link to the land. Most were rural or small-town dwellers who depended either directly or indirectly upon agriculture for their livelihoods. To these people the notion of a frontier beyond them was a factor that also steered their thinking toward the land and its attributes. Their knowledge of and appreciation for the land were also furthered by the reports of those to first penetrate beyond the Appalachians into the interior and later by the reports of early explorers and adventurers such as the mountain men who traveled through large areas of the mountain and plateau country of the West. These and other considerations have led historians to suggest that at an early stage Americans developed a meaningful part of their identity as a result of their relationship to the land and that a large measure of pride in the land and landscape of the United States is rooted in these early experiences and attitudes. An extension of this perspective is the idea that the land became a means of defining America as a place. Thus, in the years before 1860 Americans started to journey to and take holidays at various points in the Hudson and Connecticut River valleys and at inns in highland areas such as the Catskills, the Berkshires, and the White Mountains. The greatest landscape feature accessible to the affluent in these early days was Niagara Falls, New York, which had become the single most important tourist location by as early as the 1830s. As the Falls became progressively more important as a landscape feature, with its unusually great beauty and distinctive uniqueness, special holiday associations developed. Most prominently, by the late 1830s Niagara Falls had become a honeymoon destination, the result simply of newlyweds' going where everyone else was going.

In the century before 1860 Americans became awed by the rough-and-tumble American West through the explorations of Lewis and Clark and a rapidly increasing body of travel writing; thus the notion of distant places came to strongly fascinate the average mind.

This period also saw the rapid extension of benefits from scientific and technological advances, particularly as transportation was revolutionized. In the period from 1790 to 1820 a significant network of turnpikes and toll roads was developed throughout the settled East, followed by steamboats and railroads in the 1820s. Complementing the region's naturally navigable waterways was a rapidly expanded set of canals. Steamboats improved coastal and transatlantic transportation, aided in the early years, commencing in 1825, by the opening of a number of canals. The era of canals and rivers and lakes had only a brief life as a major mover of people, though, given the rapid growth of the faster and more spatially comprehensive railroad system. By 1860 a well-developed railroad net covered the eastern half of what was not yet a continentwide United States, with the West soon to be served by transcontinental links. In addition, the base for economic change was expanding as the rate of urbanization increased, the middle class began steady growth, and more comforts became available in accommodations catering to travelers. All these developments contributed over time toward a larger and larger part of the population having the attributes permitting holiday travel: adequate money, the time to pursue leisure activities, available transportation to reach the places of interest, and higher quality facilities and accommodations than previously available.

The century prior to 1860 saw only a small part of the American people engage in travel for leisure purposes. Those who did were primarily the handful of the affluent or those suffering from ailments for which mineral-spring spas or seaside resorts offered hoped-for cures to those able to afford them. More importantly, this period saw a number of fundamental attitudes about the land implanted in many Americans, which ultimately resulted in a great deal of vacation travel linked to appreciating the country's landscape. This trend can be seen in the awe Americans developed for the rough-and-tumble American West created by the explorations of Lewis and Clark and by the rapidly increasing body of travel writing. Thus, although those actually traveling during these times were few, the notion of distant places came to hold a strong fascination for the average mind.

The High Society Period: 1860–1920

The high society period provides an American parallel to the leisure-time practices of the privileged in England and elsewhere in Europe then. The vast majority of the population at this time were members of large families, had very long workweeks, continued to be rural or small-town residents except in the growing industrial centers of the Northeast, received hourly wages or were self-employed, and had little discretionary income and only limited mobility. They were typically imbued with a puritanical work ethic; for many, self-denial was implicit in their life-styles. These characteristics changed slowly for many groups in society, and it is only relatively recently that these deeply rooted attributes have altered to permit more and more people to have different perspectives on their time budgets.

Conversely, during this same era a rich group of industrialists, financiers, railroad magnates, and related professionals emerged, a group that engaged in acquiring summer and winter homes in pleasant locales, had family members who traveled to Europe, and developed various resorts and related facilities. During this period the communities that had already gotten a start, such as Newport and Saratoga Springs, took on even greater importance. Equally notable is the growth of innumerable new seashore and mountain resort communities in locations relatively accessible to East Coast population centers. The practice of taking regular vacations now became increasingly the norm. Destination preferences were divided into the return to some familiar holiday retreat as the most common, but with increasing interest in visiting new and different places.

This period saw the affluent come to appreciate the virtues of Florida's winter weather, which led to the emergence of a significant development of vacation locales in the central part of the Florida peninsula. High society eventually focused on the Palm Beach area on Florida's east coast. It was not long before the dreams of Henry M. Flagler and others led to southward penetration of railroads, with the erection of resort hotels at strategic locations. In the ten years following the end of World War I many of these developments came to fruition and the great tourist flow to Florida took off. Ultimately, Flagler's dream was to create an American Riviera along the East Coast south of Palm Beach. Similar kinds of railroad-hotel-linked developments occurred elsewhere, especially along the main lines that crossed the American West, making accessible a new set of environments. The Coronado Hotel in San Diego is often cited as an example of the accommodations available to a traveler having crossed the entire breadth of the United States in the new Pullman sleeping cars.

Numerous developments in the 1860 to 1920 period made travel simpler and less uncertain. The first telephone exchange in the United States went into use in New Haven, Connecticut, in 1878, making communications far more rapid both in dealing with travel needs and in maintaining contact with home and work. In 1865, Thomas Cook of Britain opened the first travel agency in this country, which was eventually followed fourteen years later by the first such agency opened by Americans. Then American Express Company employee Marcellus Berry, broadened the company's functions by introducing traveler's checks, in 1891. The American Automobile Association was established in 1902. And picture postcards became available, providing a strong impetus to those back home to visit places their friends or relatives had experienced.

Although the greater part of the population was not able to become actively involved in pleasure travel and vacations during this period, it was a time when many of the developments that would affect the whole population and its leisure activities in the future had their beginnings, as for instance the means of providing mass transportation, communication, and entertainment. While these developments were occurring, Henry Ford and other industrialists began implementing work-limiting procedures such as the five-day workweek and a shortening of the workday, so that discretionary time became far more widely available in periods of potential leisure. In this same period, government at all levels started to preserve open as well as recreational space, including the first national parks and forests. Of special importance were the identification and setting aside of the spectacularly beautiful Yosemite as first a state park (1864) then a national park (1890), the establishment of Yellowstone as the first formally created national park in 1872, and the increasing recognition of places of great natural beauty to be maintained for the general enjoyment of the people through time.

Various special forms of holiday-making evolved during this period. One example is the phenomenon of summer camps for young people that developed offering several-week outings for the young, providing training in a variety of sports and handicraft activities. Children from affluent families were served by a wide array of private camps, but the poor also were often able to participate, at church-related and YMCA facilities. Such camps, at first concentrated primarily in New England, were by the start of World War I attracting many thousands of girls and boys. Church-sponsored summer camps sprang up with many different denominations as sponsors, such as the Methodist facility at Ocean Grove on the New Jersey coast. By the 1880s, prominent New Yorkers led by Whitelaw Reid had developed a program to fund camp stays for children from the poorer neighborhoods of New York City, an idea that in slightly modified form continues to the present day. Summer camp holidays for the young received a further boost in the first decade of the 1900s with the 1910 incorporation of the Boy Scouts of America, and other youth groups with similar summer programs soon emerged.

Increasingly, young people were exposed to places other than their immediate area of residence and became imbued with the practice of diverse leisure-time activities and travel.

The high society period thus saw an evolution in the vacationing tendencies of the American people. The scale of tourism had clearly changed, by 1885 more Americans were enjoying holidays. The long-established Niagara Falls became the ultimate symbol of a tourist attraction, with something of a golden age in the late 1800s and early 1900s, although other attractions were also becoming prominent. Simultaneously and inevitably, holiday taking was becoming more commercialized, the places visited becoming centers of mass consumption. All these developments were further intensified by the expansion of communications with photography, the wireless, and the broader dissemination of newspapers, magazines, books, and eventually silent movies. Complementing these forms of information diffusion were such spectacular events as the Chicago fair of 1893 (formally called the World's Columbian Exposition), which assisted in bringing a new consciousness about places and things to far more people. This fair also saw the introduction of the midway concept, a feature included in many future developments.

Spectacular events such as the Chicago fair of 1893 (formally called the World's Columbian Exposition) assisted in bringing a new consciousness about places and things to far more Americans.

The High Participation Period: 1920–1958

The high participation period witnessed continued expansion in the total population, increasing urbanization and, because of greatly improved communications, much greater public awareness of the whole country, especially the West. Changing attitudes toward free time encouraged leisure activities. Workweeks continued gradually to shorten (to the dismay of other industrialists, Henry Ford began closing his factories on Saturdays in 1926), paid holidays became more common, incomes rose, families grew smaller, and a much improved variety of recreational equipment became available. The Diner's Club became the first credit card designed for leisure-time use, appearing in 1949. Car ownership became far more widespread. Where the bulk of holiday travel had formerly been to a specific place, auto touring came into its own after 1920, resulting in a rapid expansion of facilities serving the motoring public.

Paralleling these changes was a surge in the number of attractions and facilities to entice and accommodate tourists. Seaside resorts, cottage communities on lakes and rivers, resort complexes near national parks, and specialized recreational communities developed into more common features of the tourist landscape. As services facilitating tourism expanded, previously introduced travel aids, including credit cards, traveler's checks, travel agents, and automobile clubs grew far more important. A flood of information about places to see and things to do was one product of the universal exposure to the mass media outlets that developed in this period. A gradual growth of holiday-making in all seasons occurred as people sought to escape the northern winter, enjoy the autumn foliage, open the spring fishing season, or hunt game during specified times. Paralleling participation in all these outdoor-oriented activities was a major flow of travelers to cities and other places where historic, cultural, spectator sport, shopping, dining, and other entertainments abounded.

Thus, tourism emerged across the country. Florida became more and more of a mecca for those seeking a respite from cold northern winters. The population of Miami and its neighboring communities exploded with the completion of rail connections to the north in the 1890s and 1900s. Towns based on tourism that were located at strategic points grew in importance, such as Gatlinburg, Tennessee, and Jackson, Wyoming. Readily accessible beach resorts, such as Hampton Beach north of Boston and Virginia Beach, near Norfolk, became crowded. Cities developed the infrastructure and accommodations needed to satisfy the increasing numbers of tourists seeking urban amenities. Resorts serving religious and educational purposes, such as that at Chautauqua, New York, continued to be important, and the lake districts of northern New England and the Upper Great Lakes states became popular summer vacation areas. Motels, amusement parks, roadside restaurants, and the like grew and changed rapidly. For example, in the early 1920s tourist cabins phased out camping areas and were in turn gradually replaced by the forerunners of modern motels, from the late 1920s on. Each progression in the type of facility was marked by the provision of greater comfort and additional features. The accommodation industry eventually created its own trade journal, *Tourist Trade*, which appeared in 1932. Franchising contributed to the development of huge chains of motels, fast-food restaurants, and other kinds of facilities. By the end of this high participation period in

1958 an intricate array of facilities and tourist attractions existed across the country. Serving the leisure-time needs of the growing population had become a major economic activity as measured by the number of jobs created, the amount of income generated, and the alterations to the travel landscape. The now-familiar Holiday Inn logo appeared in 1958 in Memphis, Tennessee. Howard Johnson's opened its first ice cream parlor in Quincy, Massachusetts, in 1925, and entered the motel business in 1954 with an inn in Savannah, Georgia. Hertz Rental Cars opened in 1918. Disneyland, in Anaheim, California, introduced the theme park concept in 1955 and became a popular family destination. Club Méditerraneé (now known as Club Med) opened its first resort complex in 1950.

This second period in the development of tourism was a tumultuous era in American history, with the Great Depression, World War II, and the recovery periods following both world wars. It was a time when Americans were learning more about their own country as the media extended through talking movies to television and a deluge of information occurred. The late 1940s and the 1950s saw a satisfying of the material wants of a large part of the American people and newly available time and discretionary income that allowed increasing choices to be made in how leisure time was spent. Family vacations were now common, typically involving visits to relatives, touring part of the United States, or staying at a cottage or campground set up for recreational purposes. Holiday-making in the United States became both more common and more diverse in the activities undertaken and places visited as this period approached its end.

In addition to domestic travel, the 1920s and 1950s both saw many Americans travel abroad. Most of that travel was to Europe or to neighboring Canada and Mexico. For this international movement the earlier decade was still dominated by the privileged, while the post-World War II decade saw a far larger mass movement. The Depression and World War II had contrasting impacts on foreign travel. During these periods domestic as well as foreign travel was very limited, either because of economic or war-related conditions. Conversely, the events of these two stressful periods may be considered to have furthered a desire by the population in general to travel once conditions eventually permitted.

The closing date of this high participation period, 1958, was not chosen arbitrarily but rather because it reflected a convergence of events. In that year transportation was revolutionized by the opening of the first stretch of interstate highway, and the first commercial jet airliner flew then. At the same time, the postwar "baby boom" ended as the birth-rate peaked and started to decline. Many Americans had by then completed updating their personal household goods and automobiles, and many had moved out of the central cities into the rapidly growing suburbs. Nearly universal automobile ownership helped overcome one fundamental geographic fact about the United States: its sheer size. Amid increasing concern about the resources available to serve the American people, in 1958 President Eisenhower appointed the Outdoor Recreation Resources Review Commission, whose landmark report (released in 1962–1963) marked a new recognition of the importance of leisure time to Americans and helped stimulate a major expansion in the facilities and outdoor recreational lands available to the public.

The High Mobility Period: 1958–1973

The brief high mobility era was marked by continued growth in the volume and in the variety of vacation taking by the American public. Several technical developments in transportation profoundly affected where and how fast people could travel and communicate. By the end of this period, the interstate highway system, which saw its first segment open in 1958, offered access to much of the country. Americans started making lengthy tours of large sections of the United States, Canada, and Mexico, as they suddenly were able to complete five hundred or more miles per day comfortably in their own cars. The introduction of the commercial jet airliner in 1958 made distant points readily available, and widespread access to rental cars permitted freedom of movement at one's destination. The development of the modern international air route system led to an enormous increase in the flow of Americans abroad, both to traditional destinations in Europe and to other continents, at seasons other than summer.

Widespread new travel services and amenities made vacation trips more attractive. Artificial control of local environments became far more common with the spread of air conditioning. Camping took on a new look as the number of tent campers was for the first time exceeded by those using a remarkable variety of recreational vehicles. Tollfree reservation systems came into widespread use, and the nature and variety of tourist attractions and accommodations expanded enormously. The federal government followed up on the recommendations of several important studies about the recreational needs of Americans by both expanding and diversifying the kinds of lands administered for the public's use. Existing national parks and monuments were now complemented by additional national lakeshores and seashores; scenic and wild rivers were identified and protected. In the service area, real estate practices became more diverse as the concepts of time-sharing, condominiums, and retirement communities became common. A great growth in the amount of travel literature and publicity accorded to vacation spots made an ever-growing part of the public aware of their vacation opportunities. Simultaneously, the travel industry began catering increasingly to all segments of society. Budget motels and fast-food restaurants contributed to a broadening of the potential travel market.

In the period of high mobility the destinations sought by holiday-makers became more and more diverse. Urban tourism continued to grow as the attractions of individual cities became more widely known. Every big city, had its own substantial amount of tourism, but tourist facilities of New York City, San Francisco, Los Angeles, Miami, New Orleans, and Washington, D.C., were especially notable. Cities and places with special resources or facilities became more important as better transportation made them more accessible, as for instance Reno and Las Vegas, which led in nightlife and gambling. Mountain communities that had once been important for mining were reborn as popular winter sport centers or meeting places, as was the case with Aspen and Vail. Special groups in the population came to identify their own favorite resort areas: college students descended upon such Florida beach cities as Fort Lauderdale and Daytona Beach; the retired and elderly sought a more friendly winter environment in Florida or Arizona. Specialized group tours became readily available to a vast array of places and areas. Cruise liners became more popular.

Between 1958 and 1973 the spread of air-conditioning allowed artificial control of local environments, and camping took on a new look as the number of tent campers was for the first time exceeded by those using a wide variety of recreational vehicles.

In effect, a revolution was occurring in the tourism and travel industry. Numerous entrepreneurs started to serve what they perceived as an immense market. Package tours became much more common. And the factors permitting holiday taking—the income needed, the time, and the desire—were increasingly being enjoyed by more and more of the population. All these new dimensions to the tourist industry were superimposed upon the traditional holiday-making activities, which continued unabated.

The high mobility era ended abruptly in 1973–1974 when an energy crisis swept the world as the major oil-producing countries established controls on their production and prices. Not only was the price of a gallon of gasoline or oil now much greater, but supplies became a problem, which intensified in a second stage of the energy crisis, in the late 1970s. The adjustments to travel practices that became essential for most individuals and families commonly resulted in greatly reduced holiday travel in the short run, then the making of conscious decisions to overcome the difficulties raised by the energy situation. These constraints upon mobility formed the basis for a fourth stage.

Change and Adaptation

After the new energy realities of the 1970s came into effect, numerous other forces also were at work. The federal government deregulated a number of major industries, including the airlines. Families continued to become smaller, more and more wives went to work outside the home, and the two-income family became common. More and more households were now headed by single parents, and the population as a whole was aging. Americans were seeking an incredibly diverse range of leisure-time activities. For example, visiting distant places and participating in high-risk recreational activities, such as white-water rafting and hang gliding, became far more common. Vacation attractions and facilities expanded to meet this changing, growing demand. Such negative factors as high energy costs were offset by fuel-efficient smaller cars, and the two-income household helped meet rising costs.

Recent years have seen greater attention being paid to tourism by blacks and other minority groups. African Americans had rarely entered into the mainstream types of holiday-making and travel described previously. Continuing forces of segregation and discrimination along with their resultant low incomes, comparatively low levels of educational attainment, limited mobility, and the like help explain this phenomenon. Various studies suggest that blacks involved themselves in leisure activities that were the most likely to be relatively free of discrimination and were in familiar settings, meaning in effect that urban and near-to-home visits were the most usual. Such an urban orientation continues to this day, although an increase in the number of middle-income blacks is resulting in a level of holiday-making comparable to that of equivalent groups in the white population. Blacks have in the past not been frequent visitors to the national parks, a function of the factors previously noted and the fact that until recently there were few accommodations available along the routes to the west. Today, as can be seen in two issues of a popular magazine (*Ebony*, January and May 1991), blacks are seeking the sun in the winter and making other holiday journeys that suggest a convergence of their travel plans with white patterns. There is also a tendency among African Americans to take holidays that examine their black heritage. Festivals celebrating black culture are now common in the United States, but many also visit similar events in the U.S. Virgin Islands, the Bahamas, and Jamaica. Similarly, visits by blacks to museums, libraries, and historic places identified with the South and the civil rights movement have been common and are becoming increasingly so. The drive to discover one's roots is clearly an important one.

Since the start of the 1970s energy crisis we have been in a time of continuing adjustments. The energy situation has been augmented by other difficulties, including inflation, changes in the family and household structure, increasing withdrawal of the federal government from regulatory activity and social-service delivery functions, concern over the political stability of destination areas abroad, and a fluctuating value of the dollar relative to other currencies. Whether we are still in the postmobility phase is uncertain, although it seems increasingly clear that we are now less constrained in our mobility when compared to the late 1970s and early 1980s and are in a period when abundant choices and mass movements of people are quite common.

The Recent Past and the Present

In 1988, residents of the United States spent $318 billion traveling away from home. The great bulk of that sum, $294 billion, was spent on domestic travel. The total travel spending, both resident and foreign, within the United States represented 6.4 percent of the gross national product in 1988, enough to position those businesses serving tourists among the leading commercial economic sectors. Data collected by the U.S. Travel Data Center indicate that most travel was for vacations, visiting friends and relatives, entertainment and outdoor recreation, and weekend pleasure travel. Only a relatively small part of the total travel reported was for business and conventions. The primary destinations of Americans traveling within their own country, according to the U.S. Travel Data Center, in 1988 had the South Atlantic region clearly in the lead, with 231.9 million person-trips. It was followed by the Pacific Coast states, with 183.1 million person-trips; the Great Lakes region, with 165.3 million person-trips; the West South Central, with 138.4 million person-trips; and the Middle Atlantic states, with 125.4 million person-trips. It should be understood that these total figures do not indicate the relative role tourism plays in a particular region's economy. For example, the Rocky Mountain region ranks sixth in total person-trips, but of the six regions it is also the area with the smallest amount of other economic activity. In a relative sense, tourism is more important to that region than to any of

By the 1960s, recreational vehicle use exceeded the number of tent campers. Trailers like this made camping more convenient and comfortable.

the other eight regions. California, Florida, Texas, and New York, in that order, have the largest travel-generated employment among the states.

The major destinations of American tourists obviously indicate their vacation preferences. In 1986 Disney World, in Orlando, Florida, was the leading theme park in terms of attendance, which was nearly double that of its sister facility, Disneyland, and more than five times that of the third most popular park. Based on total sales, the Las Vegas Hilton was the leading resort hotel, followed by a number of comparable facilities in coastal, gambling, and special resource (e.g., theme park) settings. The leading ski resort in 1986 was Mammoth Mountain, California, with all but one of the next eleven ski resorts in popularity being in California, Colorado, or Utah. Only two of the top twenty skiing centers were east of the Rocky Mountains. The greatest number of nonresident fishing license sales were in Wisconsin, followed by Michigan, Montana, Colorado, and Minnesota. Montana, South Dakota, Colorado, and Pennsylvania had the most nonresident hunting license sales. This sampling reflects the diversity of America's tourism resources and helps explain the problems inherent in describing the landscape of tourism.

Americans seek many different things from their vacation travels. The most important single reason for such travel is likely being to visit friends and relatives. Such travel is difficult to measure and is not fully reflected in the available statistics. It is interesting that a substantial part of the volume of family and friend visits runs counter to the patterns of internal migration of Americans in the past few decades. That is, those who move away from an area frequently visit those who remain there. Equally difficult to obtain an accurate assessment of is vacation travel centered on cities. This is certainly a major sector of pleasure travel, but again it is often merged with the other indicators of economic activity for each metropolitan area. Nevertheless, when one thinks of vacation travel, visits to San Francisco, with its cable cars, Chinatown, Fisherman's Wharf, and so on; New Orleans, with its Bourbon Street and various residential districts; and New York, with Times Square, Central Park, museums, the Statue of Liberty, and the Empire State Building definitely symbolize the travel desires of a large proportion of Americans. By now a family visit to Washington, D.C., has become a must. Typically, thoughts on vacation destinations also center on national parks like Yellowstone, Great Smoky Mountain, and Yosemite or on favored Florida beach centers like Miami, Palm Beach, Daytona, and Fort Myers. The list is endless. When there is such a vast set of alternative destinations in a population where many can choose what suits them best, a remarkably intricate pattern of vacation travel destinations arises. It is also evident that, with the substantial changes that have occurred in the American economy in recent years, tourism looms ever larger in the thinking of local economic planners. The United States has now reached a point where nearly every locality has begun competing for the tourist dollar.

A few examples may illustrate the complexity of contemporary vacation tendencies in an American society that has become more and more diverse. Some of the characteristics of this society have been pointed out earlier. For one thing, an increasing number of people, usually couples, find that their work schedules and other obligations make it ever more difficult for two people to get away at the same time for an extended holiday. The result is a strong tendency to take a number of short two- to five-day holidays scattered throughout the year. Many of these may be close to their residence and focus on participation in favored recreational activities.

Typical American thoughts on vacation destinations center on national parks like Yellowstone, Great Smoky Mountain, and Yosemite or on favored Florida beach centers like Miami, Palm Beach, Daytona, and Fort Myers: The list is endless.

Other trips might involve a flight to a city or resort within or beyond the United States. A recognition of this evolving pattern is causing state development agencies as well as the private sector to push particular local attractions in competing for this sizable market. The increase in the number of single-parent households, single-person households, households containing a retired couple or widow or widower, and other combinations present still other kinds of needs for leisure-related travel.

The merchandising of vacation packages is now quite common, with the public being inundated with advertisements typically offering seven nights in a first-class hotel plus air fare plus excursions at a quite reasonable price in some population resort area like Cancun or Waikiki, or several days on a cruise ship, or a stay at a self-contained resort hotel complex such as the Greenbriar in West Virginia or the Broadmoor in Colorado. Similar kinds of attractions are offered to encourage the purchase of a second home, whether it be a condo, time-share units, or some other plan, in a resort community containing a remarkably broad array of facilities and services. The latter is particularly attractive to those who are retired; the Sun City, Arizona, image has become a major draw to many retired individuals and couples.

Resort developments cater not only to the elderly and retired, the sun worshiper and skier, but also to black Americans and other identifiable groups in the total society. In fact, the increasing ability to identify market segments has led to extremely focused targeting of publicity campaigns for the seemingly endless series of groups found within the larger society. Places attractive to each of these groups have been identified, to serve as symbols of what that specific element of the population may be seeking. Thus, the facilities for holiday-making run the gamut from very upscale to rudimentary.

Most recently, increasing attention is being paid to minimizing the impact of tourism on the environment. Ecotourism, a form of sustainable economic activity, has been one result. It represents an effort to encourage people to be ultrasensitive to their environment and to engage in activities to preserve the integrity of natural systems. These low-impact activities are frequently experienced in a natural setting and have their primary appeal to the allocentric tourist. Unfortunately, it has yet to be demonstrated that ecotourism can both satisfy its commendable environmental goals and simultaneously create sufficient economic benefits in the host area.

International tourism is important today both for Americans traveling abroad and for foreigners visiting this country. One estimate suggests that 1990 was the first year when the United States had a favorable tourism trade balance, with more spent in this country by visitors than was expended by Americans abroad. This major development is a consequence of a long-standing interest on the part of many foreigners in visiting this country, but it has been especially stimulated by the financial bargain the United States has come to offer to Europeans and the Japanese in the context both of actual costs and of exchange rates favoring foreign currencies. Most foreign tourist destinations are on the east and west coasts, with a few "islands" of particular interest in the interior, including certain national parks and New Orleans. The presence of foreign tourists is increasingly obvious to the casual observer of crowds at the Grand Canyon, in San Francisco, and in other favored spots. The United States is not yet the most convenient tourist destination for foreigners, as we are only beginning to develop more abundant currency exchange locations, tourist industry workers competent in foreign languages, travel guides and menus available in the languages of other countries, and the like. The continued growth in air connections, packaged vacations, and the attractiveness of American holidays to affluent foreigners suggest that their volume here will continue to grow. Foreign interests are also major investors in an increasing number of the facilities serving the tourist; for example, many large American hotel chains are currently owned by the Japanese. Japanese investors have also purchased the largest development and management company on California's Monterey Peninsula, an area extremely popular with tourists that contains several renowned golf courses, a sport for which Japan has a desperate shortage of facilities.

Americans also travel abroad in large numbers. Estimates for the late 1980s suggest that over 41 million Americans go out of the country for pleasure purposes each year. The total flow can be roughly divided into three streams, going to Canada, Mexico, and elsewhere in the world. Of the 14 million or more Americans who go overseas, about one-half visit Europe. The American tourist has long been characterized in often-unflattering terms, especially there. Nevertheless, U.S. travelers are vital to the economic well-being of many countries, and their business is pursued vigorously. In the early 1990s, travel to destinations other than Europe is increasing, as the number of Americans seeking new experiences expands. Many have already followed their own personal version of the Grand Tour or been on one or more package tours duplicating part of that itinerary. The growth in the flow to the Pacific Rim countries, Latin America, and elsewhere reflects this developing trend.

Two additional themes emerge from a consideration of pleasure travel by Americans. The first centers on the belief that many Americans may now be working largely to support their leisure rather than, as was historically true, placing primary emphasis on their work. This perception is for the most part based on the notion that increasing numbers of people seem ultimately to receive little real satisfaction from their work and that their fulfillment is to be sought in other directions. Given that premise, many people appear to be seeking meaning from their leisure-time activities, very frequently from their travels. This perspective is partly based on appreciating that more and more people may be overeducated and overtrained for the work they do, that the role of the individual in producing a product is becoming less and less visible given the nature of modern production and management methods, and that a growing dissatisfaction with contemporary bigness, particularly in business, may be taking place. Such perceptions are contributing to newer, riskier forms of recreational activity on the one hand and to looking at our American heritage on the other. Both reactions contribute to significant tourist activity.

The second theme is also related to how very common an undertaking tourism is for the majority of the American people. It provides today, as it did for smaller groups in the past, common popular cultural experiences that help form our identity as a people. Where tourism was once the prerogative of the privileged, it is now shared in by members of all economic classes. As a result, travel has become a mass-consumption activity participated in by all the groups in the society. The development of a resulting "culture of consumption" is reflected in the remarkably diverse array of commercial outlets that surround and attach themselves to nearly all tourist attractions. Shopping malls have themselves become legitimate tourist attractions in some instances. Thus, we create distinctive manmade landscapes that may range from highway strip developments in many communities to the extremes typified by Reno and Las Vegas or Gatlinburg and the Outer Banks of North Carolina or the immense array of service outlets surrounding Disney World. Modern tourist attractions have come to symbolize major points of consumption. Thus, leisure is not only likely to attract more and more participation but is likely to have an ever-greater impact on our landscapes and habits, as well as being more significant as an economic activity.

[See also Amusement and Theme Parks; Geographical Mobility; National Parks and Preservation; Technology and Social Change; Transportation and Mobility.]

BIBLIOGRAPHY

Amory, Cleveland. *The Last Resorts* (1952).

Baydo, Gerald R., ed. *The Evolution of Mass Culture in America: 1877 to the Present* (1982).

Belasco, Warren James. *Americans on the Road. From Autocamp to Motel, 1910–1945* (1979).

Dulles, Foster Rhea. *America Learns to Play. A History of Popular Recreation, 1607–1940* (1940).

Elliott, Michael. "The Pleasure Principle." *The Economist* 318, no. 7699 (1991).

Feifer, Maxine. *Tourism in History: From Imperial Rome to the Present* (1986).

Furnas, J. C. *The Americans: A Social History of the United States, 1587–1914* (1969).

Furnas, J. C. *Great Times: An Informal Social History of the United States, 1914–1929* (1974).

Jakle, John A. *The Tourist: Travel in Twentieth-Century North America* (1985).

Kagle, Steven E., ed. *America: Exploration and Travel* (1979).

Pearce, P. L. *The Ulysses Factor: Evaluating Visitors in Tourist Settings* (1990).

Pomeroy, Earl. *In Search of the Golden West: The Tourist in Western America* (1957).

Robinson, Harry. *A Geography of Tourism* (1979).

Rybczynski, Witold. *Waiting for the Weekend* (1991).

Sears, John F. *Sacred Places: American Tourist Attractions in the Nineteenth Century* (1989).

Turner, Louis, and John Ash. *The Golden Hordes: International Tourism and the Pleasure Periphery* (1975).

United States Travel Data Center. *The 1988–1989 Economic Review of Travel in America* (1989).

Van Doren, Carlton S. "Outdoor Recreation Trends in the 1980s: Implications for Society." *Journal of Travel Research* (Winter 1981).

Van Doren, Carlton S. "Chronology of Travel and Tourism Changes in the United States: 1946–1973." *Annals of Tourism Research* 12, no. 3 (1985).

— RICHARD V. SMITH

U

URBAN CULTURAL INSTITUTIONS

In his suggestive study *City People*, Gunther Barth argues that in America the "current of urban life stirred people into constant activity. It also left little opportunity for unrestrained adulation of traditional cultural expressions," which were challenged in the nineteenth century by exciting new forms like baseball, the metropolitan newspaper, the department store, and vaudeville. Whereas Europeans deemed it "a timeless affair . . . culture [the composer Jacques Offenbach noted] 'lives in America from day to day' " (p. 24). Still, the fine arts found permanent homes in American cities. The lyceum, the museum, the library, the theater, and the symphony orchestra were among the salient cultural institutions that appeared.

Urban cultural institutions began to take shape in colonial America, and by the end of the nineteenth century, most of the important, enduring ones were established. Their evolution reflected mixed purposes that included the stimulation and satisfaction of the curiosities of urban audiences, the conservation of the arts and ideas considered important, the making accessible to appreciative taste groups the pleasures offered by cultural activities, the affirmation of the status of patrons, and the effort to educate, tame, and uplift the minds and sensibilities of the uninitiated. First created because elites sought to replicate European cultural activities, American cultural institutions developed in response to native forces, experience, and needs. With the successful culmination of the Revolution, they continued to evolve in great part through the efforts of private promoters who offered the arts as entertainments to paying customers. Then, during the late nineteenth and early twentieth centuries, urban cultural institutions again fell under the control of elites and became important weapons of status definition, legitimizing of taste, and attempts at social control. By the mid-twentieth century, however, cultural institutions as well as artists ironically became co-conspirators in the mass marketing of art and the mind—an activity quite consonant with America's consumer, media reality.

What follows is a selective overview of the history of urban cultural organizations and spaces that Americans created to house, exhibit, and promote the expressive arts and ideas. Discussion touches upon a variety of activities and of necessity treats changing definitions of art as well as evolving notions of the purposes of art and the nature of artistic patronage and production.

Culture: Verb to Noun

During the nineteenth century, art and thought in its elite forms became identified with the term "culture." Prior to that, "culture" was a verb, associated with "growth or nourishment" and linked with a wide variety of things, including taste in the fine arts. Culture was associated with cultivation ("to cultivate"). Of course, the evolving European definition of the fine arts had elite connotations well before the nineteenth century, both because of the social structure of patronage (particularly in the fields of painting and music) and because of the establishment of institutions like Cardinal Richelieu's *Académie Française*, created in 1735, and the Royal Academy of Art founded by Sir Joshua Reynolds (1723–1792) in 1762. From the Renaissance onward, patronage initially came from the church and the aristocracy, though members of the mercantile classes eventually began to support artists, and as commerce and modern capitalism developed, the wealthy bourgeoisie emerged as major sponsors of the arts and intellect. Academies, in turn, were created for the purpose of controlling the definition of, and standards surrounding, fine art and intellectual production, establishing a support community of artists, teaching art and promoting connoisseurship, and facilitating the distribution of works and ideas. The standards and conventions codified became what has been termed the "cultivated tradition."

During the nineteenth century, the word culture evolved into a noun—culture became a thing itself and represented a body of works (usually drawn from painting, music, architecture, and belles lettres) that was believed to represent the best that had been created in the history of Western civilization. Raymond Williams explores the evolution of that concept in *Culture and Society, 1780–1950,* tracing its origins in the thought of Edmund Burke (1729–1797), Samuel Taylor Coleridge (1772–1834), and William Cobbett (1763–1835) through its first clear formulation in the writings of John Ruskin (1819–1900), John Stuart Mill (1806–1873), Newman, and Matthew Arnold (1822–1888) to its modern elaborations by T. S. Eliot (1888–1965), Ivor Armstrong Richards (1893–1979), Frank Raymond Leavis (1895–1978), and George Orwell (1903–

1950). Starting with Burke's generalized notions on the matter and Coleridge's particular idea of the need for a "clerisy"—a class of educated, thinking individuals who could apply their learning and tastes to evaluating and bettering society—culture took shape as an entity embodying a mission, an uplifting enterprise. It refined and civilized one. Signaling the possession of knowledge and taste of the proper kinds, culture became a legitimizing process, and its possessors, a distinctive and proud status group.

In *Democracy in America* (1835, 1840) Alexis de Tocqueville (1805–1859) considered the question of the state of the arts in the new republic. This was one among many aspects he explored during his 1831–1832 trip to the United States. He concluded that the arts would always be subject to the marketplace demand of a people who had no tradition of, and little time for, connoisseurship. Because of capitalism and a deeply held belief in equality, no cultivated leisure class would arise in America. Money and superficial taste would rule, pride in craft would disappear, and art would lack quality, substance, sentiment, and thought. Being quickly and easily made for profit, shallow in content, sensationalized, and transitory, American art would invariably be a diminished product. Tocqueville's observations were translated into English almost immediately and entered the discourse over the arts that was taking place. American artists, writers, intellectuals, and connoisseurs responded in a variety of ways to such charges and have been responding ever since.

Culture did indeed have to compete for attention in an increasingly egalitarian and materialistic atmosphere. American cultural forms could never be confined for long to the categories that elite arts producers, promoters, and taste groups sought to identify, delimit, and control, nor would the cultural institutions they established, supported, and worked through remain untouched by democracy and capitalism.

Cultural Growth

In *Cultural Excursions*, social historian Neil Harris identifies "four stages of cultural growth" that American cities have gone through: the colonial period; the national period from the end of the Revolution in 1870 or so; the period of rapid industrial growth between the 1870s and the Great Depression; and the 1930s through the present. His model offers a useful framework for a meaningful discussion of the types of cultural institutions that emerged, the changes in their shape, and the various purposes they espoused as well as practiced. Yet, because history is a kind of ebb and flow in which ideas and behavioral patterns appear and then seem to disappear only to reappear again in slightly different form, my discussion sometimes violates the boundaries of Harris's stages.

During the colonial era the city was only of modest size, ten to fifteen thousand people. For most of the urban elite the city was an environment that, in keeping with the age of enlightenment, was culturally sophisticated: its institutions, formed through cosmopolitan thinking, tended to replicate those of the old world. Social organizations existed in surprising numbers before 1750 in cities like Boston, New York, Philadelphia, Baltimore, and Charleston, and in most instances they were privately supported. Typical institutions included an odd variety—coffeehouses, dancing assemblies, and fishing and hunting clubs as well as theaters, libraries, and galleries. The tavern or coffeehouse was especially important, for that was where much of the colonists' social life went on. Men's clubs met in taverns, and entertainments, exhibits of oddities and curiosities, and even book auctions took place there. Boston had its Physical Club, and Newport its Philosophical Society, but the best known of the clubs is Franklin's Junto, formed in Philadelphia in 1727. Its members met to discuss politics, science, morals, and other intellectual and civic issues of the day. Given their interest in books, too, it is not Surprising that the Junto founded the famous Library Company of Philadelphia in 1731, an idea soon replicated in other colonial cities.

Because reading was so important to colonials, bookstores emerged as another prominent urban cultural institution, complementing the subscription library societies that had begun to be established.

The well-to-do, of course, kept private libraries housing books on subjects that ranged from gardening and architecture to literature, history, science, and philosophy. Because reading was so important to colonials, bookstores emerged as another prominent urban cultural institution, complementing the subscription library societies that had begun to be established. Cities like Boston, Philadelphia, and Charleston often had more than one bookseller who stocked local publications as well as the latest imported editions and magazines like the *Guardian* and the *Spectator*.

Music and the visual arts, though not as widely pursued as literature and ideas, were also of growing interest to colonists. Architecture and decorative gardens were important and enhanced the city by their presence.

More public in intention were the picture sellers who set up shop. A notable example was William Price, whose "Picture Store" did business in Boston from about 1720 onwards. Such places enabled aspiring artists and connoisseurs to see and buy reproductions of European works and develop a taste for the visual arts. Indeed, the first American art exhibit occurred in such a store in 1730. Painter John Smibert (1688–1751), recently moved from Newport, set up a color-and-paint shop and studio in Boston, where he exhibited original paintings by himself and other Americans as well as copies he had made of works by Van Dyke and Reubens. Smibert's studio became an art center for the colonies.

Urban culture during this period was dependent upon personal wealth, and the homes of the rich became places where cultural events were frequently staged. Both the visual arts and music benefited from private patronage. On the one hand, when artists like Robert Feke (c. 1705–c. 1750) visited a town to paint portraits of important persons and families, their presence provided the opportunity for private social events to be hosted by local patrons. However, social disapproval contributed to the fact that musical performances were more often held in private than in public. An annual subscription concert, for instance, was offered at Philadelphia's "Concert Room" in 1740, but after being attacked by Reverend George Whitefield (1714–1770), it had to be held privately as the "Musick Club." Still, successful public musical performances took place. The first public "Concert of Musick on Sundry Instruments" was given in Boston in 1729, and the "New Concert Room" there offered several instrumental and vocal performances during the early 1730s.

By mid century, cultural institutions were playing an increasingly important role in town life. Greater sophistication was resulting from increased wealth and leisure time, further enhancing secular urban life and culture. Clubs continued to flourish at taverns. Coffeehouses also continued to provide space for an odd variety of entertainments—from the display of exotic animals, "A White Negro Girl," and the "Philosophical Optical Machine" to a highly popular show, the "Elaborate and Matchless Pile of Art, called the Microcosm, or the World in Miniature." Yet, despite the presence of such a mix of curiosities and entertainments, city people were taking seriously Joseph Addison's dictum, "A man that has a taste of musick, painting or architecture, is like one that has another sense" (quoted in *Cities in Revolt*, p. 192), and they pursued those and other arts with increasing vigor.

Theater, in particular, became established. Professional plays had been performed earlier (prior to 1737 in Charleston) and they were popular; but Reverend Whitefield had successfully put a damper on public play performances, too. Pious Quakers had also sought to do the same in Philadelphia, but the theater began to take root in spite of religious opposition. As it became more popular among the gentry during the 1750s, buildings were built or remodeled specifically for theater performances. Lewis Hallam, an actor and head of the "London Company of Comedians," built the Nassau Street Theater in New York; Charleston constructed a "new theater" on Queen Street; and Philadelphia put one up on Society Hill. The performances offered in these and other theaters by traveling companies included works such as Shakespeare's *Richard III*, Thomas Otway's *The Orphan* (1680), and John Gay's *The Beggar's Opera* (1728).

Music was a popular cultural pastime as well. More and more music sellers opened shops in cities, offering instruments, instruction, books, and music scores. Despite Whitefield's efforts to suppress them, concerts continued to occur in many cities with varying frequency. While these were still usually private, amateur affairs, the number of public concerts increased. As with the theater, music performances were an important part of the social life of an urban aristocracy after 1750. The American Company toured colonial towns, giving instrumental concerts and staging operas. Boston's Concert Hall housed subscription performances. New Yorkers could also attend subscription concerts as well as be entertained by touring companies, and some citizens successfully organized an amateur group in 1767 called the Harmonic Society. In Charleston, the Saint Cecilia Society was formed in 1762 to revive the interest in music that had been condemned by Whitefield, and it was successful in building a vital public music scene. Philadelphia could boast of holding an annual winter subscription series at the Assembly Room and of being the home of one of America's foremost colonial composers and music directors, Giovanni Gualdo, who ran a music shop and gave concerts that included the works of Bach and others as well as his own.

Museums emerged more slowly. No art schools or museums existed anywhere in the colonies before the Revolution. Harvard College began collecting curiosities in 1750, and they eventually built a display room for their artifacts but no artworks were among them. The first public museum, established by the Library Society of Charleston in 1773, had the purpose of gathering and exhibiting only natural history artifacts. The public would have to wait until after 1780 to see paintings displayed in public. Collecting was just beginning among the wealthy who could afford to have portraits painted by artists like Smibert, Feke, John Singleton

Copley (1738–1815), Benjamin West (1738–1820), and Gustavus Hesselius (1682–1755). The wealthy also had opportunity to travel and acquire work done in Europe. A few notable private collections were put together. A Newport collector may have had a Van Dyke, and Charleston's Judge Egerton Leigh possessed some Italian masters like Veronese, Giordano, and Correggio. Two Philadelphia collectors owned copies of works by Correggio and Titian. The graphic arts, available at the picture shops, were collected, too; so were originals and copies of antiquities.

John Singleton Copley once lamented, "A taste of painting is too much Wanting to affoard any kinds of helps" for American painters. Partly for that reason, the most gifted of colonial America's artists, Boston's Copley and Philadelphia's Benjamin West, went to Europe before the Revolution and remained there. Yet, there was a climate of hope in the minds of some regarding the future of art. The painter and art promoter Charles Willson Peale noted in a 1771 letter to Benjamin Franklin, (1741–1827): "The people here have a growing taste for the arts, and are becoming more and more fond of encouraging their progress amongst them." Franklin agreed: "The Arts have always travelled westward, and there is no doubt of their flourishing hereafter on our side of the Atlantic, as the number of wealthy inhabitants shall increase . . . it appears that our people are not deficient in genius" (quoted in *Cities in Revolt*, p. 398). In important ways, the optimism of both Peale and Franklin was borne out. The arts and intellectual life continued to develop and expand in interesting and unexpected ways after America became a new republic.

The earliest American art museum appeared in 1782, when Charles Wilson Peale opened a "gallery of famous men," showing his own painted portraits; in 1875 he opened a small public space in an annex to his Philadelphia home and exhibited his collection of natural history specimens.

Art in a Democracy

At the time America entered its early national period, art was distrusted by many because it was thought to reflect sensuality and luxury, traits associated with Europe and the danger of corruption. Of course, America's first order of business was to find an identity as well as solve the day-to-day problems posed by independence. The ideologies of republicanism, nationalism, and democracy conjoined in that effort and influenced the response to the question of the proper place of art in the new society. If the republican ideology helped create a fear of art, nationalism succeeded in undermining that fear. Not surprisingly, America's act of declaring its independence soon had an impact in the cultural realm.

The period between the end of the Revolution and 1870 witnessed an extraordinary expansion in the type and number of public cultural institutions as well as a change in the types of audiences that supported them. And, it must be reemphasized, the city was the natural place for this growth to happen, since art could only thrive where there was a community of creative minds and patrons. Indeed, cultural institutions were established in cities located in all regions, and they often had the effect of popularizing the arts and intellect. "Libraries, historical societies, art unions, art academies, lyceums, theaters, and opera companies appear, not only in eastern cities," writes Harris, "but in the newer western towns such as Lexington, Cincinnati, Pittsburgh, Buffalo, and Indianapolis" (*Cultural Excursions*, p. 17). These institutions were still mainly in private individual hands, and though some, like Boston's Athenaeum, continued to be the preserve of local elites keeping alive the link between the wealthy leisured class and the fine arts, most were open to the public. And, in keeping with the newly emerging democratic ethos and the entrepreneurial spirit, their offerings—still a broad mix of things—were increasingly calculated to appeal to larger, more socially diverse audiences.

The museum—a place Dr. Samuel Johnson (1709–1784) called, in his 1775 *Dictionary*, a repository "of learned curiosities"—began to appear in America following the Revolution. The institution was first established in Europe after 1750. The British Museum (1751) and the Louvre (1793) established significant cultural precedents, the former because it offered treasures of science, literature, and art for the study of scholars, and the latter because it opened up the impressive private collections of the French kings to the public. While America, too, had witnessed the founding of Charleston's Museum in 1773 and Philadelphia's American Museum of Pierre Eugène Du Simitière (c. 1736–1784) in 1782, the earliest art museum appeared when Charles Willson Peale opened his "gallery of famous men" in 1782, showing portraits he had painted. Soon after, he opened a small public space in the annex of his Philadelphia home in 1785 and exhibited his collection of natural history specimens, Indian and South Seas island artifacts, as well as paintings (mostly his own).

His collection grew so large that he moved it first to Philosophical Hall in 1794 and then in 1802 to Independence Hall. Though Peale's museum did not survive long after his death in 1827, it helped establish the museum as a popular urban cultural institution and was the first serious American effort to educate the public in history, science, and the arts, thereby promoting nationalism and republican values through the dispensing of knowledge. Peale's act also set a precedent for the philanthropic habit of giving private collections to public museums.

Museums began to spring up in cities like Boston, Salem, New York, Albany, Providence, Pittsburgh, Cincinnati, Lexington, and Saint Louis, and they usually followed the pattern of showing a variety of things. Daniel Bowen founded an early museum at Boston's American Coffee House in 1791, though it was moved and renamed the Columbian Museum four years later. It initially displayed wax figures of American political notables and then exhibited paintings and a living natural history collection until its collection was sold to the New England Museum in 1825. In New York the Saint Tammany Society began exhibiting some Indian relics in a room at the City Hall in 1790; Baker's American Museum, as the collection was soon named, wound up in the hands of John Scudder in 1802, who continued to expand its holdings. After he died in 1821, the American Museum remained in possession of his family and thrived for several years until, becoming troubled financially, it was bought by P. T. Barnum in 1841. Meanwhile in 1814, Peale's son Rembrandt (1778–1860) established a museum in Baltimore and displayed portraits along with other things until it closed several years later. Boston's Museum and Gallery of Fine Art was opened in 1841. Privately owned and charging admission, it mingled art and entertainment that included concerts and plays but survived only as a theater. Most of these museums were open to the public on at least a part-time basis.

Specialized collections were also made available to the public during this period. Because history was very important to the national identity, some fifty historical societies were formed between 1823 and the Civil War. Science, too, was highly valued. America's first museum in Charleston displayed natural history objects, and scientific collections made up a large part of the eclectic displays in other early museums. Soon institutions like Philadelphia's Academy of the Natural Sciences (1812) were established and usually focused on a single branch of science; for example, geology. What would become one of America's most significant museums was founded in 1816 in Washington, D.C. First named the Columbian Institute, it soon became the National Museum. A bequest of over a half-million dollars to the United States by Englishman James Smithson (1765–1829) enabled Congress to turn it into the Smithsonian Institution in 1846.

During this period, artists and collectors were very concerned about the role of art in a democracy. Besides creating museums that exhibited art, they formed arts organizations. The founding of an "American Academy of Painting, Sculpture, Architecture Etc."—the Columbianum—by Peale in 1795 was an early valiant but ill-fated attempt to bring artists together and exhibit only art objects. More successful was the creation of the Pennsylvania Academy of Fine Arts in 1805—Peale was again among its founders. In 1810 the Society of Artists of the United States was created, also in Philadelphia. Similar efforts occurred elsewhere. In New York prominent citizens formed the New York Academy of the Fine Arts in 1802. It became the American Academy of the Arts in 1808 and eventually constructed a building in 1831 for showing art. And in 1825 a group of New York artists founded a teaching and exhibiting organization that, the next year, was renamed the National Academy of Design. It functioned as a major force in the American art world until 1908. Boston's Atheneum, though founded as a library in 1807, began holding an annual, two-month-long art exhibition in 1826, charging twenty-five cents admission. The Atheneum subsequently installed a permanent picture gallery in its new building in 1845, though its art collection would eventually be loaned permanently to the Boston Museum of Fine Arts. Yale built the Trumbull Gallery in 1832, a space devoted solely to exhibiting art (they would acquire the James Jackson Jarves [1818–1888] collection in 1871). Finally, the National Institute opened an art exhibition space at the Washington Patent Office in the 1840s.

Still, the eclectic museum, housing a mixed collection of amusing objects and activities, persisted during the first half of the nineteenth century, and P. T. Barnum (1810–1891) was the quintessential figure who perfected its shape as a place of spectacle and pure entertainment. Beginning in 1841, Barnum's American Museums hawked a bizarre mixture of things: a copy of "the great picture of CHRIST HEALING THE SICK IN THE TEMPLE, by Benjamin West, Esq., THE ALBINO LADY; and 500,000 curiosities (quoted in *The Tastemakers*, p. 17). His fare delighted New Yorkers and frustrated early cultural custodians for nearly three decades before he abandoned his enterprise after his building burned a second time in 1868. Henry Tappan disdained Barnum's museum as "a place for some stuffed birds and animals, for the exhibition of monsters, and for vulgar dramatic performances—a mere place of popular amusement, and George Templeton Strong called it "an eyesore, with its huge pictures" as well as its "horrible little brass band . . . tooting in its balcony" (quoted in *Humbug*, p. 33, 17). But in *A Small Boy and Others*, Henry James fondly remembered the charm and fascination that the American Museum held for an impressionable child of the 1850s. Barnum, of course, was not the only promoter who vulgarly mingled art and enterprise. Perhaps the most shameless was Dr. Collyer. He described his New York establishment, "Palmo's Opera House," as "a new movement in the fine arts." Displayed was a *tableau vivant* advertised as "living men and women in almost the same state in which Gabriel saw them in the Garden of Eden on the first morning of creation" (Humbug, p. 19). Immensely popular, it drew people from all classes.

Of course, bread and circuses were not the only fare available to urban Americans. A loftier enterprise was the art union idea, launched by painter James Herring in 1838. First opening the Apollo Gallery in New York, and charging admission, he settled upon a scheme whereby he invited people to buy a five dollar annual subscription to the Gallery, renamed the Apollo Association in 1839. In return each "patron" got "a large and costly Original Engraving from an American painting" and a numbered ticket. At the year's end, a drawing was held and original paintings were given away to the holders of winning numbers. The lottery grew in popularity, and in 1844 it changed its name to the American Art Union. It became so successful that the union idea was copied by others; and it was so highly respected that it could make William Cullen Bryant one of its presidents. The Union continued to "give away" increasing numbers of paintings to subscribers; and, of course, those members who did not win paintings still had the consolation of collecting the engravings sent to them during the year. By the late 1840s, the Union had about 10,000 members and it was virtually in control of the art market, distributing more than 450 paintings a year worth $40,907, including Thomas Cole's (1801–1848) *Youth* (from *The Voyage of Life* series) and George Caleb Bingham's (1811–1879) *The Jolly Flatboatman.* It finally closed down only because it was declared illegal in 1851 as a lottery by the New York Supreme Court. During its entire life span, the Union estimated that it had "given away" about 150,000 engravings and 2,400 paintings. Ironically, the final sale in 1853 of the Union's remaining collection was a failure.

The joining of democracy and education is perhaps best illustrated by another urban cultural institution that emerged in the 1820s—the American lyceum movement, founded by Josiah Holbrook (1788–1854) in 1826. Originated in England, the lyceum was purported to offer practical scientific knowledge to skilled workers through lectures and demonstrations. By 1846 it became a vehicle for offering lectures and lecture series on a variety of topics to a broadly based audience of townspeople. Its first chapter was established in Millbury, Massachusetts, but the Boston branch, founded in 1828, quickly became the center for what was soon to be a widespread national phenomenon. The American Lyceum, formed in 1831, caught on quickly in a political climate that had already allowed a widening of the franchise and favored the development of public schools and libraries. Lyceum branches were most prevalent in New England but also existed in cities such as Buffalo, Saint Louis, Richmond, Nashville, Mobile, Natchez, New Orleans, Little Rock, Louisville, Indianapolis, and Cincinnati. Of course, some chapters disappeared and new ones emerged; still, though the movement suffered some decline during periods like the panic of 1837, it continued to grow until the 1860s.

From the beginning, the lyceum movement attracted the attention of well-known Americans like Daniel Webster (1782–1852), Caroline Beecher (1800–1878), Theodore Dwight (1822–1892), and Albert Gallatin (1761–1849), and its lecturers included intellectuals of the stature of Ralph Waldo Emerson (1803–1882), Henry David Thoreau (1817–1862), and Oliver Wendell Holmes (1809–1894). Support for it also came from those who participated in the public school and library movements. The lyceum offered programs ranging from adult education to pure entertainment. Theodore Parker (1810–1860) lectured on "The Political Destiny of America," Edgar Allan Poe (1809–1849) on "Selections from English Poetry with Critical Remarks," and Louis Agassiz (1807–1873) on "Glaciers," and E. P. Whipple (1819–1896) amused audiences with comments on "The Ludicrous Side of Life." Starr King (1824–1864) delighted them with his facile views on "Substance and Show," and Henry Ward Beecher (1813–1887) edified them with lectures like "Six Warnings" and "Popular Amusements." "The lyceum is my pulpit," Emerson once said; Starr King responded to the query about what he got from it with the answer, "FAME—fifty And My Expenses"; and Holmes ironically remarked, "a lecturer was a literary strumpet."

The lyceum movement did not survive long after the Civil War, though its traces reemerged in the Chautauqua movement that began in the 1870s as well as in certain urban institutions like New York's Ethical Culture School, the Educational Alliance, the People's Institute at Cooper Union, and the William Morris Club—all aimed at educating immigrants during the late nineteenth and early twentieth centuries. The popularity of the lyceum movement for nearly a forty-year period—and its rebirth under other names—suggests that Americans were starved for knowledge, even if they were not always discriminating regarding its content. The lyceum, moreover, bore an important relation to literature and the growing publication industry, for its lecturers were often literary men, and the platform it provided frequently gave birth to published work, Emerson's essays for example. And the growing literacy that the organization reflected and probably stimulated contributed to the development of the library movement then beginning to surface.

The museum and the lyceum were, of course, not the only urban cultural institutions reflecting the influences and pressures of democracy. Opera and theater did, too. The latter, a well-established institution in cities before the Revolution, suffered when the Continental Congress criticized "Plays" as well as "Cock Fighting" and "Horse Racing" in 1774 and when buildings were subsequently closed during the war. Still, theater survived this brief attack, and once again began to thrive in the cities after the Revolution. According to Lawrence Levine in *Highbrow/Lowbrow*, Shakespeare eventually "dominated the theater" in both the northeastern and southeastern regions (16). Tocqueville had noted the existence of Shakespeare in "the recesses of the forests of the New World," and the fact that Twain could include a delightful parody of Hamlet's soliloquy in *Adventures of Huckleberry Finn* suggests just how well-known Shakespeare was among common Americans. Of course, the bowdlerization of his plays indicated the types of performances insisted upon by appreciative but unruly audiences—bombastically acted lines, for example, interspersed with the singing of popular songs like "The Swiss Drover Boy." Theater's widespread popularity is further suggested by the fact that many traveling companies found it profitable to tour cities and towns throughout America during the nineteenth century—often playing in buildings that townspeople had built especially for such performances. Whether put on in New York or Natchez, plays were attended by people from all classes, though audiences were often segregated in terms of their seating—"the dandies, and people of the first respectability and fashion" sat in the boxes, noted a contemporary spectator, while the "middling classes" were seated in the pit, and the working poor, prostitutes, and blacks in the gallery (24). Audiences continued to see a theater bill that mixed Shakespeare with plays like *Ten Nights in a Bar-Room* and multiple versions of *Uncle Tom's Cabin.*

The fact that Mark Twain could include a delightful parody of Hamlet's soliloquy in Adventures of Huckleberry Finn *suggests just how well-known Shakespeare was among common Americans of the mid nineteenth century.*

Operatic, instrumental, and play performances were often given in places like the Chicago Museum, and the New York museums like the American and Peale's. In many cities, particularly in western towns, a distinct building was used for musical performances and plays. Sometimes, as in Beaver Dam, Wisconsin, it was called the Concert Hall; other times, as in Central City, Colorado, it was the Opera House or, in Portland, Oregon, the Casino Theater. Music was as popular among a broad social cross-section of the American people as theater. Opera had a wide following. Comic opera especially tended to be favored although grand opera gained a foothold among audiences by the 1840s. Italian operas like Vincenzo Bellini's (1801–1835) *La Sonnambula* became particularly popular, so much so that in 1851 George Templeton Strong exclaimed, "people are *Sonnambula*-mad. Everybody goes, and nob and snob . . . sit side by side fraternally on the hard benches" (25). As in theater, traveling companies put on performances all over America. Levine explains that opera, especially English translations of arias, remained part of popular culture until it began to be wrested from the people by elites during the late nineteenth century.

Culture: High and Low

American society and its economy changed radically during the 1800s. Industrial growth dominated the scene and contributed to an unprecedented urban population growth. A few cities reached over one million people by 1900, several others had one hundred thousand or more. By 1921 the majority of Americans lived in urban areas. The increase in population reflected not only a change in size but also a dramatic alteration in the ethnic mix of the people. The explosion of knowledge, vast increases in wealth, and sense of discontinuity that modernity was stimulating helped mold the new shape of the city, too. It was in this environment that popular cultural forms like the department store, baseball, vaudeville, and the movies were born. Of course, the old cultural institutions—theater, concerts, and museums among them—continued to persist.

Despite the fact that during the first two-thirds of the nineteenth century many cultural institutions were patronized by audiences that cut across class lines, Levine argues that after 1870, culture became sacralized and segregated in terms of taste groups, and the gap between the fine and the popular arts widened. During the third stage in the evolution of American urban cultural institutions, "highbrow" culture became distinct from "lowbrow" culture. Profit-seeking entrepreneurs moved in the direction of creating entertainments that were put in the lowbrow category (vaudeville, burlesque, musical theater, and movies); elites established the highbrow. The cultivated tradition had its moment of triumph because it was implanted in institutions created by a whole generation of sons of old elites (men like Charles Eliot Norton [1827–1908]) and scions of new elites (individuals like Andrew Carnegie [1835–1919]), who began to exercise power and influence outside politics through organizations like the nationally based Sanitary Commission and Union League Clubs, founded during the Civil War, and the great cultural institutions formed afterwards. Such men worried about the course American civilization was taking. They believed that Americans suffered from degraded taste, that artists were unappreciated and unsupported, and that the spiritual and moral realms were threatened by materialism. They acted through the best means available to them: philanthropy replaced politics, and art and intellect were seized upon to correct wayward sensibilities. Given the seriousness of this mission, art and mind could neither be amusement nor decoration, only moral and aesthetic uplift.

The age of great new museums, opera houses, and symphonies was at hand. Of the museums established, most housed art, and these included: Washington's Corcoran Gallery (founded in 1859), Boston's Museum of Fine Arts and New York's Metropolitan Museum of Art (both 1870), the Philadelphia Museum of Art (1876), Chicago's Art Institute (1879), Saint Louis's Museum of Fine Arts (1879), Minneapolis's Institute of Art (1883) and Walker Art Gallery (1876), Cleveland's Museum of Art (1916), New York's Museum of Modern Art (1929) and Whitney Museum (1932), and Washington's National Gallery of Art (1941). The music organizations included the Boston Symphony Orchestra (1881), Boston Pops (1885), Chicago Symphony Orchestra (1891), and the Philadelphia Orchestra (1900). New York already had a Philharmonic Society (1842), a musician-run orchestra, but another, the New York Symphony Orchestra, was founded in 1878; they would merge in 1928. New York's Metropolitan Opera appeared in 1883, and Chicago's Opera Society in 1910, though most resident opera companies appeared later than did symphonies and museums. They proliferated after 1900 in cities like Santa Fe, San Francisco, Kansas City, and Houston.

Libraries also began to be founded in great numbers during this period. Of course, private subscription libraries had been established in cities like Philadelphia and Charleston as early as the eighteenth century, and the Library of Congress (for the use of its members) had been in existence since 1800. However, the idea of a free library available to everyone was relatively new, and the establishment of the tax-supported Boston Public Library (1852) marked the beginning of the public library movement in America. Other cities quickly followed Boston's lead—Cincinnati in 1856, Saint Louis and Detroit in 1865, Cleveland in 1869, Louisville in 1871, and Chicago in 1873. The Enoch Pratt Free Library was founded in Baltimore in 1882, and Chicago's Newberry (a research collection whose public use was limited) appeared in 1887. The New York Public Library came along later in 1895. As was true of art museums and music organizations, wealthy individuals were important to the library's creation. The most famous library patron, Andrew Carnegie, donated forty-one million dollars between 1890 and 1917 to construct sixteen hundred library buildings in cities and towns throughout America.

In theory, these institutions were open to the public, but many were in fact closed to the majority by the price of admission, the elitist tone permeating the activity, or restrictions placed on their use. Together, opera and symphony societies, art museums, and many libraries took on a daunting aura. The art museum, a good example of the contradiction between the democratic ideal and exclusive reality, was made into a hallowed chamber into which all were invited—provided they came only at certain times, behaved properly, and either contemplated knowingly or struggled seriously to have their taste elevated and their sensibilities refined. Consider the Boston Museum of Fine Arts, incorporated in 1870 by the state legislature and opened in 1876. Though the rhetoric surrounding its creation and early administration insisted that it was "to be a popular institution," its practice sanctified art instead of welcoming people. The museum secretary summed up its elitism early in the twentieth century: "A collection of science is gathered primarily in the interest of the real; a collection of art primarily in the interest of the ideal. . . . A museum of science is in essence a school; a museum of art is in essence a temple." For many years, Bostonians could only gain free admittance on Sundays. And though education eventually became more than a rhetorical mission at museums like Boston's, it was guided by docents carefully explaining the displayed works to viewers who were, in turn, watched by museum guards to ensure that they kept a proper distance from the art they were learning to worship.

At first the art museum's function seemed to parallel that of the modern public library movement: it appeared to be moving from being a "storehouse" to a "workshop," where anyone could pursue knowledge through the study of extensive collections of copies as well as a few original works. But those who wished museums to be storehouses for masterpieces won out. Museums increasingly benefited from gifts by wealthy collectors like Thomas J. Bryan (d. 1870), William W. Corcoran (1798–1888), James Jackson Jarves, Thomas B. Clarke (1848–1931), J. P. Morgan (1837–1913), Henry Clay Frick (1849–1919), and Henry Marquand (1819–1902). The gifts included art from China and Japan as well as Europe—and, eventually, America and Africa. The collections were housed in new buildings constructed in the "palace style" that clothed the artworks in a grand and hallowed aura and provided the city with an example of civilized urban space.

Of course, there were also museums featuring artifacts besides art, Washington's Smithsonian Institution and Chicago's Field Museum of Natural History being early examples. The latter grew out of the collections gathered for the 1893 Chicago Columbian Exposition; the Smithsonian had existed in one form or another since the early nineteenth century, but by 1870, it had given up its library and art collection, essentially concentrating on being a natural history museum but later adding cultural history to its purview (one historian has termed it America's "national attic"). Like the Field Museum, it was the beneficiary of gifts from a world's fair—the Philadelphia Centennial Exposition of 1876. As both institutions verify, world's fairs (which began in 1851 in London and continued through the nineteenth and twentieth centuries) were important in the development of the museum idea. In America, between 1876 and World War I, fairs took place every four or five years in cities like New Orleans, Chicago, Atlanta, Saint Louis, Nashville, San Francisco, Omaha, and San Diego. Attended by huge audiences (twenty-five million people visited the 1893 Columbian Exposition), fairs introduced Americans to modern innovations like electricity and telephones and exposed them to art, often for the first time. Museums of "progress" (the exhibition of Western achievements), of "exotica" (the imperialist display of artifacts of subject nations), and of fine art (traditional Western masterpieces brought together under one roof), they exposed audiences to the wondrousness of the present, appealed to consumers, expressed national pride, and linked science, commerce, and high culture. Their buildings, mostly beaux-arts, renaissance, or neoclassical, also helped establish the architectural style believed appropriate for cultural institutions as well as necessary to bringing order to America's chaotic urban environment.

The New York Public Library at 5th Avenue and 42nd Street was built in 1895.

Unlike museums, libraries moved away from the storehouse to the workshop function. The shape of their collections and the mission they identified reflect a struggle that never ceased to take place during the nineteenth and twentieth centuries: the struggle over taste and the selection of works to be admitted into the realm of high culture. The motives for starting public libraries included a wish to collect and preserve important writings, a genuine commitment to educate people, and a desire to use books as a means of social control. Books, it was asserted, improved minds and taste. A debate emerged, however, regarding the issue of accumulation as opposed to use, and the motive of improving people took precedence over the "quality" of the collection. Tellingly, it was stimulated partly by the question of whether or not to collect popular fiction—a form that had become very important in the publishing industry. Uplift of the masses could only occur if the collections were used, it was argued, so the conclusion was drawn that libraries ought to house popular books to entice readers. Those favoring the inclusion of popular fiction won out, and recreation became one of the purposes of public library use.

Clearly, democracy was a phenomenon not wholly absent from the cultural scene between 1870 and the 1920s. The masses might be kept out of symphony halls and operatic performances by high ticket prices, an exclusive repertoire, and socially enforced etiquette. Hierarchy in the arts might separate classical from popular music and fine art from modern forms like photography, movies, commercial art, and industrial design. But the economic, political, and social landscapes were changing so dramatically by the turn of the century that elite cultural institutions could not remain untouched.

The shape of libraries' collections and their identified mission reflect a struggle that never ceased to take place during the nineteenth and twentieth centuries—the struggle over taste and the selection of works to be admitted into the realm of high culture.

As already indicated, the quality of the works collected was increasingly a crucial consideration for art museums. They were abetted in their efforts to canonize artists by groups such as the National Academy of Design (1825) and the Society of American Artists (1877), which virtually controlled the exhibition of contemporary works and defined artistic standards. Like their European counterparts, American academies were conservative in taste and exclusive in the admission of artists to their ranks, and during their heyday, they were quite successful in promoting the work and status of their members. For the most part, academic artists were solidly bourgeois, widely recognized, highly respected, well supported, and sometimes wealthy and powerful (like their patrons). But the hegemony of the monied class and the fine-art academies was challenged during the first decade of the twentieth century by artists who exhibited independently. One of the most notable of these challenges occurred when "The Eight" made a rude disturbance by withdrawing their entries to the annual National Academy's exhibition and showed their works at New York's Macbeth Gallery in 1908.

The concept "culture," Raymond Williams reminds us, had undergone a revolution during the nineteenth century that made the artist into "a specially endowed person" at a time when he or she was in danger of becoming "just one more producer of a commodity for the market" and art was drawn into the cultural struggle to soften the jagged edges of a successful materialism. By the time of The Eight's show, however, culture had rejoined the class struggle, for a significant number of young artists and writers were beginning to see themselves as workers and social democrats. The Eight included Robert Henri (1865–1928) and several members of his group—John Sloan (1871–1951), George Luks (1866–1933), William Glackens (1870–1938), and Everett Shinn (1873–1958)—painters who, with the second generation of Henri students such as George Bellows (1882–1925) and Stuart Davis (1892–1964), were dubbed the "Ash Cans" in 1913.

What repulsed academicians were the Ashcans' subjects, which seemed to celebrate "lowlife" and immorality—urban scenes of slums and the tenderloin districts, portraits of working-class people and prostitutes. Their politics—democratic, in Walt Whitman's (1819–1892) sense, and socialist—were threatening, too. Sloan, for instance, not only lived in a New York City working-class neighborhood, but also ran for the state legislature as the Socialist candidate and, for a time, was art director of the radical *Masses* magazine. The Eight also repudiated the academic jury system that rigidly selected and rejected works on the basis of conventional taste, the prize system that accorded honors to a few, and the hierarchical hanging order that placed the most favored works at eye level and the rest above or below. Their show had no jury, no prizes, and democratically hung every work at eye level.

The Eight's revolt signaled the end of the academy as a power in the art world, yet it by no means put an end to that world's elitism and exclusiveness. While most artists remained poor, few held on to a working-class commitment for long. Class-based warfare disappeared from the art scene by 1920, replaced by a bohemianism symbolized by New York's Greenwich Village. After a brief hiatus, political consciousness and engagement on the part of cultural producers reappeared with the creation of institutions like The New Playwright's Theater (1926) and the protest against the execution of Sacco and Vanzetti (1927). Artists and writers began to redraw their workers' banners, and they proceeded to wave them in public for over a decade. The Artist's Union was formed in 1933; the League of American Writers grew out of the American Writers' Congress of 1935; and in 1936, the American Artists' Congress was founded. Through such organizations, artists and writers became, in Max Eastman's phrase, "artists in uniform." Just as influential in politicizing the fine arts were governmental agencies such as the Works Progress Administration (1935–1943) which, through programs like the Federal Art Project, Federal Theater Project, and Federal Writers' Project, hired thousands of artists at hourly wages to create works that would enhance the urban public sphere. These ranged from state travel guides and murals painted in public buildings to theater and dance performances. By the beginning of World War II, however, the issue of radical social change ceased to be important to artists, and they involved themselves in direct political action only sporadically thereafter.

During the first half of the twentieth century, museums rarely engaged in political activities. Indeed, a radical political viewpoint did not substantially affect most fine arts institutions until the 1960s, when museum workers began to organize, the Civil Rights and anti-Vietnam movements threatened the establishment, and feminism turned a mirror on the institutions' exhibiting practices. Then, the consciences of many arts community members were once again jarred, and individuals like the Metropolitan Museum's director, Thomas Hoving, the New York Public Theater's head, Joseph Papp, and the New York Philharmonic's conductor, Leonard Bernstein, entered the battle taking sides on causes, often bringing their institutions with them into the fray.

Modernity and Specialization

After the turn of the century, the fine arts community was increasingly challenged by modernity: complex, difficult science and technology, rampant industrialism, pervasive consumerism and mass media, disturbing new cultural forms and ideas, and a growing social-democratic thrust. That community also encountered unprecedented upheavals that included war, depression, and holocaust. And it collided with the phenomenon of modernism. Rather than hide, most artists, patrons, and cultural institutions faced the brave new world of the twentieth century and tried to deal with its realities as best they could. If arts institutions were able to resist for nearly six decades the pressures of the age's social and political upheavals, they were less successful at keeping modernism and modernity's component parts at bay.

The modern phenomenon of specialization really took hold in the museum world after 1920, and by the end of the first third of the twentieth century, fields such as art, history, and science were seldom mixed. Specialized museums included those devoted to an explicit category of art (modern or American or folk) and those that might be called living history museums. The latter, in which whole towns made up the exhibit, were begun in the 1920s: Old Deerfield Village, Massachusetts, was restored; Colonial Williamsburg, Virginia, was reconstructed; and Greenfield Village, Michigan, was fabricated entirely from old buildings brought together to create an ersatz place. Similar to the museums of living history were the botanical gardens, zoological parks, and aquariums featuring plants, birds, animals, and fish in simulated environments. Botanical gardens, originating with John Bartram's (1699–1777) 1728 garden near Philadelphia, began to appear in greater numbers. Living zoos, related to the stuffed-animal exhibits that had also been common since the eighteenth century, were established, too. One, the San Diego Zoological Park, grew out of the World's Fair of 1915–1916. Large aquariums were founded later: Boston's, built during the 1960s, is perhaps the most famous of them.

The modern phenomenon of specialization really took hold in the museum world after 1920, and by the end of the first third of the twentieth century, fields such as art, history, and science were seldom mixed for public display.

Specialized art museums featuring contemporary styles and/or media, or American art, or folk art are especially significant, for they either rejected or affirmed modernity. American art and folk museums complemented the efforts of history museums by their nostalgic attempt to recover and legitimize cultural roots, while galleries like the Museum of Modern Art countered such efforts by privileging modernity over the past. The latter museum, MOMA, became one of the most powerful cultural institutions in twentieth-century America. Established in 1929, it was the first of several contemporary art museums to be established. Under the inspired directorship of Alfred Barr, MOMA not only highlighted a style of art that had been challenging the Academy since the 1870s but also featured the "arts" not traditionally associated with the word "fine." Besides departments of painting, sculpture, and architecture, MOMA also had departments of film, photography, and industrial design.

Through aggressively innovative exhibitions of modernist painting as well as topical shows like the *International Exhibition of Modern Architecture* (1932) and *Machine Art* (1934), MOMA argued that art, on the one hand, and modern science and technology, on the other, were not antithetical. Alfred Stieglitz (1864–1946) had already successfully convinced Buffalo's Albright Gallery to exhibit and purchase art photographs in 1910; the 1913 Armory Show had introduced modern art to audiences in New York, Boston, and Chicago; and Weimar Germany's Bauhaus had pioneered the merging of technology and art, beginning in 1919. But established museums were still wary of showing modern works. New York's Metropolitan, for example, did put on an exhibition of Postimpressionist art in 1921 but did so only under extreme pressure from patrons like John Quinn, Mrs. Havermeyer, and Lillie P. Bliss. The Met was so openly opposed to modern art that Quinn decided to sell his brilliant collection of paintings rather than bequeath it to a museum he believed would disdain it. Quinn was probably correct, since the Met on one occasion refused Gertrude Vanderbilt Whitney's offer of a gift of her extraordinary American art collection. Barr and MOMA benefactors Bliss, Abby Rockefeller, and Mrs. Cornelius Sullivan were challenging established definitions of fine art and taste, and their courage was amply rewarded. MOMA succeeded in changing the definition of art and became the most famous and respected contemporary art museum in the world. Moreover, it established a practice whereby museums functioned as active participants and patrons in the creation of contemporary art-works and movements. Eventually such established museums as New York's Metropolitan, Minneapolis's Institute of Art, and Chicago's Art Institute would follow suit.

Institutions devoted strictly to ethnic and national collections have been a fairly recent phenomenon, and have taken on new resonance of late. A few ethnic cultural institutions have already been noted—New York's Ethical Culture Society, for example. Others include the rich Yiddish theater that thrived in New York during the late nineteenth and early twentieth centuries. Jazz must be added to this list for, although a lowbrow form, it was eventually admitted to elite concert halls. The first such instance was African American bandleader James Reese Europe's (1881–1919) Clef Club "Concert of Negro Music," held in Carnegie Hall in 1912. Carnegie Hall also hosted musical performances by W. C. Handy (1924), by Paul Whiteman and George Gershwin (1928), and by Benny Goodman (1938). The Whiteman/Gershwin concert, "Experiment in Modern Music," premiered *Rhapsody in Blue* (1924). America's indigenous music had earlier been stimulated by New York's National Conservatory of Music when they invited Antonin Dvořák to become director in 1892. During his three-year stay in America, the great Czech composer wrote several pieces like the *New World* (1893) symphony that drew upon American folk music, including the African American tradition. By the 1950s, that tradition, by then called jazz, was established as one of the significant fine arts, and groups like the "Modern Jazz Quartet" appeared as guest performers with symphony orchestras. What was occurring, of course, was just the reverse of the nineteenth-century practice, exemplified by John Philip Sousa's band as well as orchestras like the Boston Pops, of mingling popular songs, marches, and "classical" excerpts at popular concerts.

MULTICULTURALISM. Other salient examples of the phenomenon that would later be termed multiculturalism occurred in the 1920s at the Harlem branches of the New York Public Library and the YMCA, both on 135th Street. At the former, librarian Ernestine Rose held poetry readings and discussions on books and culture. She also exhibited African sculpture. These cultural events were attended by individuals who became major African American artists, figures such as Countee Cullen (1903–1946), Langston Hughes (1902–1967), and Jacob Lawrence. Rose also accumulated a major collection of African American studies materials with the help of the Carnegie Foundation, and this collection and library itself was later renamed the Arthur Schomberg Collection. As David Levering Lewis puts it, "the intellectual pulse of Harlem throbbed at the 135th Street library" (p. 105). Complementing the activities of the Library, the "Y" gave theater performances. There was also a Harlem Symphony. Though European arts were often featured at these places, African and African American culture was of central concern. Harlem cultural institutions set a precedent that would be followed by museums like MOMA and the Metropolitan as well as specialized museums that eventually took African and African American artifacts and cultural expression seriously by presenting them as art forms.

ETHNOLOGY. The interest in national, ethnic, and folk forms was first reflected in ethnology collections displayed in early museums like Peale's. World's fairs often included such artifacts, too. One of the earliest museums to departmentalize its ethnology collection was the Brooklyn Museum, in 1903. The idea of housing such collections in specialized exhibits was eventually adapted to entire museums, as exemplified by the establishment of Santa Fe's Museum of Navaho Ceremonial Art, and New York's Museum of Primitive Art and Museum of Early American Folk Art. A similar pattern occurred with regard to collections of national art and artifacts. Museums founded to highlight distinct national traditions included New York's Whitney Museum of American Art, Tulsa's Thomas Gilcrease Institute of American History and Art, Fort Worth's Amon Carter Museum of Western Art (featuring art and artifacts of the American West), Brooklyn's Jewish Museum, and Chicago's Polish Museum of America.

DISPLAY SPACES. The important shifts that occurred regarding collection emphases and practices clearly reflect the influence of modernity, with its machine and commercial landscape and its altered demographic patterns. These forces also effected changes in audiences and the way museums responded to them. Commerce and "mass media changed standards of receptivity," Neil Harris has argued, because they offered "images and information on a daily basis, fresh and immediate, easily available;" they made the museum, in particular, seem "stodgy and fatiguing" by comparison (*Cultural Excursions*, p. 144). Consider the influence of a popular modern urban institution, the department store. Harris correctly notes that the museum and the department store have shared several things: the time of their birth (the 1870s), their function (displaying artifacts), and techniques (the art of display). They even shared the same architectural style. Harris asserts that museums, fairs, and department stores served the ideal that valued continuity with the past. Each put art and beauty in a high position. But by the 1920s, museums were threatened by commerce: the department store was replacing the museum as an attraction and an arbiter of taste. While museums were dull, poorly lit, daunting, and uncomfortable, department stores had become innovators in the techniques of display and comfort as well as in the development of educational exhibits and demonstrations of various kinds, all to attract customers. Critic Forest H. Cooke, in a 1926 issue of *Century Magazine*, revealed the extent to which department stores had begun to set a standard for judging museums when he wrote, museum "rooms open to the public should be of great beauty as rooms, well ventilated, restful, and inviting leisure." Metropolitan Museum of Art president, Robert W. deForest, acknowledged the museum's failure when he admitted to a group of department store executives in 1930: "You are the most fruitful source of art in America." This competition pushed museums to move from being mere storehouses to becoming appealing display spaces.

As museums moved into the mid-twentieth century and beyond, they became part of the modern popular consumer reality through the use of modern display ideas and techniques borrowed from marketing and media. They created simplified spaces and backdrops for art, highlighted particular works, used dramatic lighting, emphasized advertising, promotion, and education, designed logos, and held blockbuster shows. Collections and exhibitions were made accessible to the public through special catalogues, tape-recorded tours, and slide-shows screened in special media rooms. Museums, theaters, and libraries became retailers of products linked to their collections and exhibitions. Most cultural institutions now contain stores that sell posters, reproductions, postcards, slides, books, T-shirts, and artifacts like earrings that reflect "good" design and the particular specialty of the organization. All these activities have reflected the increased pressure to draw mass audiences.

By the same token, businesses became more involved in culture. Corporations began to collect and display art at their home offices. Some, like the Philip Morris Company and Container Corporation of America, advertised themselves in magazines using works of art. Corporate sponsorship of increasingly expensive special exhibitions became common, too. During the early 1970s, Dayton's Department Store, in downtown Minneapolis, donated space on its top floor so that Walker Art Center could continue to exhibit while its new building was being completed. Such patronage not only advertised businesses but made them appear as good cultural citizens. The most dubious instance of this kind of collaboration occurred when several "historical" costume shows were put on during the 1980s at New York's Metropolitan Museum of Art, all curated by museum consultant Diana Vreeland, former fashion editor at *Vogue* and *Harper's Bazaar*. These exhibits were curiously linked with commercial activities occurring outside the museum. One pairing was the Met's "Chinese Imperial Robes" show and Bloomingdale's sales venture that featured "Imperial" Chinese artifacts and crafts. Others conjoined the Met with fashion entrepreneurs: "Twenty-five Years of Yves Saint Laurent" (1983), one of Mrs. Ronald Reagan's favorite designers, and "Man and the Horse" (1984), sponsored by Polo/Ralph Lauren. Such examples reflect blatantly what Debora Silverman has termed, a "movement of aristocratic invocation in 1980s American culture, whose participants combined representation from the worlds of the museum, the department store, fashion design, and media."

SUPPORT. American cultural institutions have been unique in the sense that most have been private organizations controlled and supported by private philanthropy. By contrast, Europe's great cultural institutions have been governmentally owned and supported. A few

American cultural institutions like the Smithsonian, most public libraries, and more recently, urban arts complexes like New York's Lincoln Center and Washington's Kennedy Center (both created after 1960) provide an exception to this rule, though some—like Washington's National Gallery and Hirshorn Museum—have benefited greatly from private money. Government involvement in American art did not occur in any systematic way until the 1930s with the WPA's Federal Projects for Art, Writers, Theater, and Music; the Treasury Department's Arts Program; and the Farm Security Administration's History Section with its film and photography division. As already noted, the governmental arts projects of the 1930s stimulated the urban arts by putting artists to work, and making their productions available to the public; but this died at the start of World War II. Government support for the arts did not again occur until the 1960s, when the National Endowments for the Arts and the Humanities were created in 1966. These agencies have been extremely valuable in helping urban cultural institutions meet the increasing costs of putting on exhibitions and programs. Indeed, without the Endowments, some arts organizations would have had to cut back or might have failed completely.

Postmodernism, Popular Culture, and Politics

Since the end of World War II, many new museums, repertory theaters, and opera companies have been established—institutions such as New York's Guggenheim Museum, the Los Angeles Museum of Contemporary Art, Atlanta's High Museum, the J. Paul Getty Center near Los Angeles, Minneapolis's Tyrone Guthrie Theater, the Vivian Beaumont Theater at New York's Lincoln Center, New York's Public Theater (its Shakespeare in the Park productions have been of unique importance in repopularizing the Stratford Bard), the Sante Fe Opera, and Montgomery, Alabama's Carolyn Blount Theater (home of the Alabama Shakespeare Festival). The number of orchestras continued to increase, too, as did ballet and dance companies. George Balanchine's New York City Ballet became the resident company at Lincoln Center; the Dance Theatre of Harlem appeared, as did other private companies like those of Merce Cunningham, Alvin Ailey, and Twyla Tharp. Performance art, in particular, evolved new forms like "Happenings," and museums around the country began to expand their offerings to include live presentations of all kinds as well as film programs and poetry readings.

Most twentieth-century cultural institutions, with the exception of the theater, have tended to perpetuate a high-culture canon, but they have also striven to educate large audiences by courting popularity. Museums and theaters have been more receptive than symphony orchestras and opera companies to featuring modernist works. Concert-goers and opera lovers have been very conservative regarding the repertoire they support, though a few organizations such as the Saint Paul Chamber Orchestra have emphasized modern music. Theater, however, is more difficult to discuss in terms of the types of works offered and levels of taste.

Recall that the theater had been one of the most democratic art forms during the 1800s, and that Shakespeare was wrenched by elites from the popular domain during the second half of the nineteenth century. A further segregating of theater audiences occurred when avant-garde production companies were founded in the 1910s. Chicago's Little Theater appeared in 1912, and the Province-town Players was begun in Provincetown, Massachusetts, in the summer of 1916, and moved to New York that fall. The picture was further complicated by the fact that "little theaters" cropped up in small cities all over America, but instead of offering an experimental fare, these "civic" theaters brought popular plays as well as serious "classics" to townspeople. Popular commercial theaters were thriving also, offering vaudeville, burlesque, conventional melodrama and farce, and a newly developing genre, the musical. Theaters with widely differing purposes continued to exist into the present; they range from New York's commercial Broadway houses, summer-stock playhouses, and dinner theaters to urban public theaters, amateur production companies, university groups, and experimental theaters (such as New York's Off-Off-Broadway houses and companies like New York's La Mama Experimental Theatre Club and Chicago's Steppenwolf Theatre Company).

A further segregation of theater audiences occurred when avant-garde companies arose in the 1910s: Chicago's Little Theater appeared in 1912, and the Provincetown Players began in Massachusetts in 1916 and moved to New York later that same year.

The urban cultural scene of the past forty years has shown great flexibility with its variety of forms and styles and its openness to change. Postmodernism—the mode of pastiche, surface, and eclectic style—became the apt characterization for the creative output of much of the period. Highbrow art and low, popular culture and elite remained the categories around which discussions of art often centered, but they hardened *and* became increasingly slippery in their application. Beginning in the 1920s with the Frankfurt School thinkers, intellectuals sought to keep them theoretically separate and pure, but practically, they continued to be as amorphous as ever. Throughout the century, defining art and judging quality were complicated by the persistent challenges of the avant-garde artists like Alfred Stieglitz, Marcel Duchamp, John Cage, and Merce Cunningham; events like the Armory Show; and institutions like the Museum of Modern Art. New materials like welded steel, found objects, and neon light, and technologies like video, laser, computers, and synthesizers mixed things up. So did the appropriation (intact or in combination or through caricature) of discarded styles and motifs. And the fact that popular forms like the movies and jazz and pop music performances became thought of as art added to the confusion. By the 1960s, even rock and roll began to be taken seriously by cultural commentators like the critic Susan Sontag and composer Ned Rorem, and exhibitions touching upon popular culture were more frequently sponsored by museums—for example the Metropolitan Museum's "Harlem on My Mind" (1969) and MOMA's "High and Low (1990–1991)."

The art and literary worlds were also made to face certain absences that were inbred in their exhibition and publishing practices. Feminism, in particular, forced cultural institutions to admit that the work of women artists had been grossly neglected. Women had played significant roles in the American art world during the nineteenth century. The Women's Pavillion at the 1893 Chicago Columbian Exposition was a notable reminder of that fact. Women, moreover, were a prominent part of the avant-garde during the first third of the twentieth century. Harriet Monroe was the founder and editor of *Poetry* and Margaret Anderson headed *The Little Review.* Mabel Dodge presided over a salon that drew together some of the best artists and minds of the second decade of the twentieth century. Mary Cassatt, Gertrude Stein, Isadora Duncan, Amy Lowell, and Georgia O'Keeffe were well-regarded artists. Katherine Dreier, Lillie P. Bliss, Gertrude Vanderbilt Whitney, and Abby Rockefeller were patrons who were instrumental in the founding of distinguished museums. And the 1917 Independents' show in New York was an art exhibition where "women took center stage"—of the 1,235 artists exhibited, 414 were women.

Yet, though women continued thereafter to be distinguished in the American cultural world, they did not effectively challenge the essentially male power structure until the late 1960s. It would be another decade before the hard questions feminists were asking confronted the museum world in the guise of an exhibition: Judy Chicago's *The Dinner Party* (1973–1979) opened in March 1979 at the San Francisco Museum of Modern Art. The work, a large installation piece—a triangular-shaped table with embroidered tablecloths, porcelain plates, cups, and dinnerwear—was a collaborative effort that embodied the history and mythology of women through images, language (the names of famous women), and sculpture. Though the expensive production received about $40,000 in support from the National Endowment for the Arts, the only major museums that exhibited it were San Francisco's Modern and New York's Brooklyn Museum. Still, serious issues were raised and remain as an important part of the art discourse of the late twentieth century.

Once again, culture was politicized. By 1990, the battle lines were clearly drawn between a new set of custodians of elite culture like Allan Bloom and Hilton Kramer (supported by politicians such as Republican Senator Jesse Helms of North Carolina) and the new cultural radicals who were challenging the traditional (white, male) canon of artworks and fighting for feminist as well as gay rights and multicultural agendas. The conflict reached its most vocal level when the National Endowment for the Arts suddenly struck a cultural nerve by funding, among other things, a traveling exhibition of the work of Robert Mapplethorpe (1946–1989). Because Mapplethorpe was gay and his nude photographs were considered by some people to be obscene, the participating museums and the Endowment came under fire from the cultural and political Right. This time, major cultural institutions could not ignore the struggle. Some openly fought against the conservatives by refusing grants from a newly politicized NEA. Others capitulated by bowing to censorship. Funds for the Endowment were reduced by Congress, and so the agency ceased to underwrite proposals that might be controversial. The cultural war soon faded, but the fires that it generated still smolder.

Conclusion

In 1839 Alexis de Tocqueville could not predict the particulars of the course that the arts would take during the following century and a half. Yet, he was uncannily correct in his observations regarding the socio-economic forces and conditions that would influence the production and appreciation of art. Whether he was right in assuming that art would be degraded and appreciation shallow is still hotly debated. Of course, he could in no way have imagined the half-tone revolution and the invention of the movies that occurred in the 1890s, nor could he have had an inkling of the twentieth-century phenomena of radio, recorded sound, television, and the computer. Technological innovations as well as social changes have had an extraordinary impact on the arts and, thus, on the institutions that have promoted them. Regrettably, there has been too little space here to do more than survey broadly the development of urban cultural institutions and their influences. Missing, for example, is discussion of the moviehouse and the university, both of which have been important agencies in bringing culture to urban audiences. Still, I hope that the reader has at least a sense of the richness and complexity that is part and parcel of the evolution of American cultural life. Art has been alive and well in the United States for over two hundred years. Culture in the sense that Matthew Arnold defined it now touches more lives than ever before, and urban cultural institutions have contributed immensely to that result.

[See also Business Culture; The City; Commercial Architecture; The Culture of Consumption; Gender Roles and Relations; Intellectuals and the Intelligentsia; Literacy; Mass Culture and Its Critics; Public Architecture; Public Education; Theater and Musical Theater; Urban Parks.]

BIBLIOGRAPHY

The following sources offer valuable starting points for those interested in pursuing more deeply the subject of urban cultural institutions. Most of the works listed below contain excellent bibliographies that provide students and scholars with rich sources for further study. The task of writing this essay was made easier by the help given me by my graduate research assistant, Matthew Murray, who is currently doing doctoral work at the University of Wisconsin, Madison. Thanks are also due to Margaret Vines, whose several readings of this piece were invaluable.

Alloway, Lawrence. "Museums and Unionization." *Artforum* 8, no. 6 (February 1975): 46–48.

Badger, Reid. "James Reese Europe and the Pre-history of Jazz." *American Music* 7 (1989): 48–68.

Barth, Gunther. *City People: The Rise of Modern City Culture in Nineteenth-Century America* (1980).

Bode, Carl. *The American Lyceum: Town Meeting of the Mind* (1956).

Bridenbaugh, Carl. *Cities in Revolt: Urban Life in America, 1743–1776* (1955).

Bridenbaugh, Carl. *Cities in the Wilderness: The First Century of Urban Life in America, 1625–1742* (1938; repr. 1968).

Bronner, Simon J. "Object Lessons: The Work of Ethnological Museums and Collections." In *Consuming Visions: Accumulation and Display of Goods in America, 1880–1920*, edited by Simon J. Bronner (1989).

Brown, Milton W. *American Painting from the Armory Show to the Depression* (1955).

Cole, John Y. "Storehouses and Workshops: American Libraries and the Uses of Knowledge." In *The Organization of Knowledge in Modern America, 1860–1920*, edited by Alexandra Oleson and John Voss (1979).

Davis, Douglas. *Art and the Future: A History/Prophecy of the Collaboration Between Science, Technology, and Art* (1973).

De Veaux, Scott. "The Emergence of the Jazz Concert, 1935–45." *American Music* 7 (1989): 6–25.

Egbert, Donald Drew. *Socialism and American Art in the Light of European Utopianism, Marxism, and Anarchism* (1967).

Fisher, Philip. *Making and Effacing Art: Modern Art in a Culture of Museums* (1991).

Fox, Daniel M. *Engines of Culture: Philanthropy and Art Museums* (1963).

Fredrickson, George M. *The Inner Civil War: Northern Intellectuals and the Crisis of the Union* (1965).

Greenhalgh, Paul. *Ephemeral Vistas: The Expositions Universelles, Great Exhibitions, and World's Fairs, 1851–1939* (1988).

Harris, Neil. *The Artist in American Society: The Formative Years, 1790–1860* (1966).

Harris, Neil. *Humbug: The Art of P. T. Barnum* (1973).

Harris, Neil. *Cultural Excursions: Marketing Appetites and Cultural Tastes in Modern America* (1990).

Homer, William Innes. *Alfred Stieglitz and the Photo-Secession* (1983).

Horowitz, Helen Lefkowitz. *Culture and the City: Cultural Philanthropy in Chicago from the 1880s to 1917* (1976; repr. 1989).

Howe, Irving. *World of Our Fathers: The Journey of the East European Jews to America and the Life They Found and Made* (1975).

Hughes, Robert. "The Decline of the City of Mahagonny." *New Republic*, 25 June 1990, pp. 27–38.

Katz, Herbert and Marjorie Katz. *Museums, U.S.A.: A History and Guide* (1965).

Levine, Lawrence W. *Highbrow/Lowbrow: The Emergence of Cultural Hierarchy in America* (1988).

Lewis, David Levering. *When Harlem Was in Vogue* (1981).

Lippard, Lucy. "Judy Chicago's 'Dinner Party'." *Art in America* 68, no. 4 (April 1980): 114–126.

Lynes, Russell. *The Tastemakers* (1954).

Mates, Julian. *America's Musical Stage: Two Hundred Years of Musical Theatre* (1985).

Mathews, Tom. "Fine Art or Foul." *Newsweek*, 2 July 1990: 47–53.

Miller, Lillian B. *Patrons and Patriotism: The Encouragement of the Fine Arts in the United States, 1790–1860* (1966).

Mueller, John H. *The American Symphony Orchestra: A Social History of Musical Taste* (1951).

O'Doherty, Brian, ed. *Museums in Crisis* (1972).

Ross, Andrew. *No Respect: Intellectuals and Popular Culture* (1989).

Rothstein, Edward. "Roll Over Beethoven." *New Republic*, 4 February 1991, pp. 29–34.

Russell, John. "The Royal Academy." *Horizon* 4 (May 1962): 56–79.

Saarinen, Aline B. *The Proud Possessors* (1958).

Silverman, Debora. *Selling Culture: Bloomingdale's, Diana Vreeland, and the New Aristocracy of Taste in Reagan's America* (1986).

Simpson, Lewis P. *The Man of Letters in New England and the South: Essays on the History of the Literary Vocation in America* (1973).

Susman, Warren I. *Culture as History: The Transformation of American Society in the Twentieth Century* (1984).

Taylor, Joshua C. *The Fine Arts in America* (1979).

Toll, Robert C. *On with the Show: The First Century of Show Business in America* (1976).

Tomkins, Calvin. *Merchants and Masterpieces: The Story of the Metropolitan Museum of Art* (1970).

Trachtenberg, Alan. *The Incorporation of America: Culture and Society in the Gilded Age* (1982).

Watson, Steven. *Strange Bedfellows: The First American Avant-Garde* (1991).

Whisnant, David E. *All That Is Native and Fine: The Politics of Culture in an American Region* (1983).

Ziff, Larzer. *Literary Democracy: The Declaration of Cultural Independence in America* (1981).

— RALPH F. BOGARDUS

URBAN PARKS

The word "park" originally had little connection with towns or cities. In medieval and early modern England, "park" described "an enclosed tract of land held by royal grant or prescription for keeping beasts of the chase." Such parks—often called deer parks in reference to the animals gathered in them—grew in number in the sixteenth century as English aristocrats and gentry families cleared and enclosed large tracts of land around their country estates, sometimes taking over entire villages and common fields. Eighteenth-century landlords continued the "imposition and theft" that characterized the English enclosure movement, the cultural critic Raymond Williams tells us. In the process the meaning of "park" shifted from a hunting woodland to an artificially constructed scenic landscape. With the help of landscape gardeners like Humphrey Repton and Lancelot ("Capability") Brown, these landlords created, as Williams writes, "the view, the ordered proprietary repose, the prospect"—"a rural landscape emptied of rural labour and labourers; a sylvan and watery prospect, with a hundred analogies in neo-pastoral painting and poetry, from which the facts of production had been banished" (The Country and the City, pp. 122–125).

The English gardeners' carefully crafted landscapes were intended to mimic or improve upon nature while making it appear as though no human hands had intervened. And since their work "was centered upon the great expanse of land and woods that in the typical large country place was simply called the Park," historian Norman Newton points out, their artificially natural landscapes became closely associated with the term "park" (*Design on the Land*, p. 20). English travelers readily extended this usage to the royal and aristocratic grounds of the Continent, where landscape gardeners initially adhered to a more formal style in arranging nature for human edification and enjoyment.

Only in the late eighteenth and early nineteenth centuries did parks become identified with cities. German towns, for example, turned old fortifications into public gardens. The London public had been conditionally admitted to royal grounds like Hyde Park from the seventeenth century, and gradually other royal lands were opened to public use. By the early nineteenth century, municipal and national governments in England and on the Continent had begun to establish and landscape new public parks that represented the romantic ideal of *rus in urbe*—country in the city.

Although this history closely linked the term "park" with designed natural landscapes, there has long existed an alternative, but more difficult to document, vernacular tradition associated with the concept of public open space, if not always the specific word "park." The cultural geographer J. B. Jackson contrasts "two types of park land": the " 'designed' parks" produced by landscape gardeners and " 'unstructured' playgrounds," where at least until the late nineteenth century "the common people and particularly adolescents, could exercise and play and enjoy themselves, and at the same time participate in community life." Jackson finds evidence of these unstructured areas in the churchyards of medieval Europe, in the stretches of undeveloped land outside the city walls or along riverbanks (what the French call *terrains vagues*), and in the "grove out in the country near the river" (*American Space*, pp. 127–130).

This same dual heritage of vernacular and designed public spaces marks the development of urban parks in the United States. One strand of the vernacular tradition stretches back to the New England commons—spaces held by the community for shared utilitarian purposes (for example, grazing cattle or gathering fuel) as well as for public assemblies, particularly militia drills. Another strand included the eighteenth-century commercial proprietors who opened private parks, modeled on London's pleasure gardens, for outdoor entertainments. More elusive to historical recovery, though, are the innumerable open spaces appropriated by youths and adults for sports and games. In late-eighteenth- and early-nineteenth-century Baltimore, for example, boys played in a "public square," and Colonel John Eager Howard opened his private estate—"Howard Park"—as a recreational space for city residents. The city's springs provided another popular recreational spot. Early-nineteenth-century Brooklynites similarly turned the privately owned land along the bluffs of Brooklyn Heights into a popular setting for public promenades and socializing.

The growth of cities and the urban real estate market placed increasing pressure on these informal "common" spaces. In Baltimore, donations of land from the Howard estate for Lexington Market, the Baltimore Cathedral, and the Washington Monument gradually ate away at Howard Park until it had disappeared by the 1840s. As early as the 1820s, Brooklyn landowners "infected with the rage for improvement" eroded the "elegant walk" along Brooklyn Heights by tearing down trees and fencing their lands ("Promenade to Park," p. 532). In response, city officials increasingly marked out more formal, specialized, and publicly owned spaces and designated them as parks. New York's Common, for example, had served a diverse set of purposes in the seventeenth and eighteenth centuries—pasture ground for cattle, the setting for executions, the home of the almshouse and jail, and the site of public festivals and protests. But only in 1797—five years after it was enclosed for the first time—was it labeled "The Park" (rather than The Fields or The Common) on a city map. And the designations "City Hall Park" or "The Park" only became widely used in the first decade of the nineteenth century, when the area was landscaped during the construction of City Hall.

Other American cities also set aside open spaces—sometimes called parks but more often commons or squares. Drawing on English models, for example, William Penn's 1683 Philadelphia plan and James Ogelthorpe's 1733 Savannah plan reserved squares that were later surrounded by residences and institutions. Similarly, the 1811 street plan that established New York's famous grid street system set aside seven open spaces, most less than twenty-five acres (ten hectares). And in the next three decades, local real estate developers won city officials' sanctions to create private squares—Gramercy and St. John's parks, in particular—as the center of elite residential neighborhoods and promenades.

In the late 1830s and 1840s, wealthy and middle-class families also satisfied their desires for a public venue in which to see and be seen by resorting to "rural" cemeteries landscaped in the English romantic style. Cambridge's Mount Auburn, Philadelphia's Laurel Hill, and Brooklyn's Greenwood cemeteries helped to foster a taste for pastoral landscapes and a habit of urban picnickers and excursionists seeking "country," within the city. Urban gentry families also took up horticulture and hired landscape gardeners like Andrew Jackson Downing to improve their country estates.

Yet elite families still complained that their cities lacked proper parks, by which they meant large landscaped public grounds in the European tradition. Gentlemen merchants and their wives, who visited Europe for business and pleasure, bemoaned the contrast between European and American public spaces. *The New York Times* was "mortified" by the contrast between the grand parks of London, Paris, and Brussels and New York's "penurious" 145 acres (48 hectares) of public spaces (23 June 1853).

Nowhere was the pressure to imitate landscaped European public parks greater than in the nation's largest city, New York. Starting around 1850, the city's leading merchants and bankers-seconded by many of its newspaper editors—campaigned to create a grand, public park as a way of establishing New York's credentials as an international capital. Such a park, moreover, would provide appealing scenic vistas through which members of their class could ride their carriages.

As would be true in other cities, the movement for a large public park won support beyond the merchant class. Owners of land surrounding the proposed sites realized that such an amenity would greatly enhance the value of their property by attracting wealthy families to live near the park. And some social reformers believed that a park would improve the health and morals of the city's poorer citizens; it would serve as the "lungs of the city" and as an instrument of social improvement. Yet not all reformers agreed: leaders of the public health movement, for example, argued that removing land for a large public park would only exacerbate the city's housing problems—the source of the most serious health ills. Moreover, many working-class New Yorkers argued that smaller, dispersed downtown parks would be less aristocratic and more democratic.

After two years of debate, in 1853 the state legislature authorized New York City to use powers of eminent domain to acquire more than seven hundred acres in upper Manhattan for Central Park. After a design competition in which politics figured prominently in the outcome, the park commissioners selected the Greensward Plan of the English-immigrant architect Calvert Vaux (who had also worked as a junior partner to Andrew Jackson Downing) and Frederick Law Olmsted, Sr., the park's superintendent. Vaux and Olmsted crafted their design largely according to the English pastoral tradition. The designers proposed open meadows and picturesque woodlands that would offer a refreshing antidote to the bustle and aesthetic monotony of city streets. They further separated the park from the city by sinking the four commercial roads that crossed the park beneath the surface so ordinary traffic would not interfere with the continuous movement of parkgoers' views.

After two years of debate, in 1853 the state legislature authorized New York City to use powers of eminent domain to acquire more than seven hundred acres in upper Manhattan for Central Park.

In selecting the Greensward Plan for what would become the nation's most influential public park, the commissioners narrowed the definition of a park. They rejected those plans that worked within the more classical, continental design tradition with formal avenues and

This 1961 photo of Central Park, the nation's most influential public park, illustrates the remarkable pastoral beauty within an urban setting achieved by designers Frederick Law Olmsted and Calvert Vaux.

gardens. And they even more firmly ruled out the possibility that the park would be organized within the more eclectic, vernacular tradition of commercial pleasure gardens, which liberally mixed all styles of art and decoration to create recreational spaces answering popular desires for novelty and diversion.

As soon as Central Park opened to ice skaters in December 1858, it spawned imitators. The following year, according to David Schuyler, *The Horticulturalist* observed that parks were becoming "the great features in all cities of any importance" and credited "the great Central Park" for providing the "initiative" and the "conviction of their importance" (quoted in *The New Urban Landscape*, p. 101). By 1861, Philadelphia, Baltimore, Brooklyn, Hartford, and Detroit had begun to plan for their own landscaped urban parks. In 1865, Olmsted and Vaux designed Brooklyn's Prospect Park.

Philadelphia's Fairmount Park had been laid out earlier in the century to "ornament" the city's waterworks on the banks of the Schuylkill River; and in the mid 1850s, Philadelphia greatly expanded the park's area. In 1859—following the precedent set in New York—the park's designers (James C. Sidney and Andrew Adams) were selected in a competition. But the coming of the Civil War as well as further piecemeal additions meant that Fairmount Park was not entirely completed until the Centennial Exposition was held there in 1876.

Developments moved much more swiftly in Baltimore, which purchased a five-hundred-acre estate for Druid Hill Park in 1860. The landscape gardener Howard Daniels, who had won fourth prize in the Central Park competition, designed a romantic landscape. But design was not the only lesson that park-makers learned from Central Park: they also grasped the close and enduring connection between park development and real estate profits. Schuyler quotes the *Baltimore American*, noting the rise in property values around Central Park, and forecasting that the "cost of the entire park would be materially reduced by taking into consideration the probable enhanced value of the city property contiguous to its borders" (p. 109). One final lesson that Baltimore learned from New York was regulation: Druid Hill opened in 1860 with twenty-six carefully worded rules and regulations prohibiting everything from abusive language and gambling to the fast driving of carriages and picnicking without permission.

Despite the pervasive adoption of the pastoral landscape model for the nation's urban parks in the late nineteenth century, it would be a mistake to assume that the impulse to create these parks represented an equally pervasive antiurbanisrn—a Jeffersonian retreat from the city. As Daniel Bluestone points out in his history of Chicago's park system, energetic park advocates were also the strongest boosters of the city itself. But in some cities park referenda revealed resistance to this pro-growth vision. In Saint Louis and Minneapolis, for example, working-class voters initially opposed proposals for large parks located far from their neighborhoods.

Still, in these cities as well as in Chicago the New York model proved influential. Illinois Lieutenant Governor William Bross credited his own interest in a grand landscaped space to a long discussion about Central Park that he had with Olmstead atop the Sierra Nevada. And in 1869, Chicago turned to Olmsted, Vaux & Company (which was simultaneously designing the nearby suburb of Riverside) to draw up the plans for the city's South Parks. What set Chicago apart from New York—but made it typical of cities from Buffalo to Boston—was that the 1869 bills establishing its parks created a citywide system, with six large parks connected by landscaped boulevards. Landscape architects like Horace W. S. Cleveland, who outlined a regional park system for Minneapolis and Saint Paul in 1883, anticipated the comprehensive city planning movements of the twentieth century.

As the park movement took hold in small as well as large cities, city residents continued to debate the definition of a public park. In 1870 Edward Winslow Lincoln became chairman of the Commission on Shade Trees and Public Grounds in Worcester, Massachusetts—an industrial city with about forty thousand residents. The city's parklands consisted of an eight-acre Common and a twenty-eight acre tract known as Elm Park. Imbued with the naturalistic aesthetic, Lincoln transformed the unsightly Elm Park into a mini-Central Park with broad stretches of lawn and artistically arranged trees and shrubs. He also sought to banish active and eclectic uses of Elm Park. Circuses, which had earlier lost their home on the Common, were banned in 1875. Three years later, the soon-to-be-familiar "keep off the grass" signs were given legal sanction. Baseball playing continued, but Lincoln hoped that this "dreary," amusement would soon be removed from his cherished Elm Park to specially designated playing fields in "different sections" of the city. The rowdy, exuberant, collective style of socializing that characterized many immigrant working-class communities in this era was the antithesis of what Lincoln wanted for Elm Park.

This clash between what J. B. Jackson calls "two distinct and conflicting definitions of the park"—"the upper-class definition with its emphasis on cultural enlightenment and greater refinement of manners, and a lower-class definition emphasizing fun and games"—continued throughout Lincoln's park regime (1972, pp. 214–215). When wealthy residents petitioned to triple the size of Elm Park, which was located adjacent to city's most affluent neighborhood, working-class Worcesterites objected. If Elm Park were to be expanded, they insisted, then the city must provide space for "the less favored children" in the city's working-class neighborhoods. Through their political mobilization they not only gained two parks for the working-class East Side but also won the designation of those parks as "playgrounds" rather than landscaped parks."

In some cities, class divisions over park use were less readily visible. For example, Saint Louis's Forest Park (opened in 1876) included numerous baseball and soccer fields as well as a racetrack for trotting matches, a feature deliberately excluded from many northern parks for fear of attracting mixed-class crowds of gamblers and sports. And unlike Central Park and other eastern parks, Forest Park regularly accommodated the large picnics of German and other ethnic fraternal associations. But Saint Louis park officials, like those in other border and southern cities, promoted racial segregation by defining the smaller Tandy Park as a "black park."

In the late nineteenth century, political contests over the definition of a park intensified alongside skirmishes over patterns of day-to-day use. In Boston, for example, Stephen Hardy notes that many working-class residents and their representatives regarded much of the city's "Emerald Necklace" park system as "rich man's parks" accessible only to those who owned "elegant equipages" ("Parks for the People," p. 17). But residents of poorer neighborhoods traded their support for these landscaped parks in return for receiving playgrounds and small parks in their own districts. Their political pressure also won changes in restrictive park rules to allow active sports, merry-go-rounds, and refreshment stands within the city's parks.

A similar process reshaped New York's Central Park. In the 1860s, the park's first decade of operation, the city's wealthiest citizens, riding in their carriages, dominated the park, which was tightly regulated under rules set down by Olmsted and the park board president, Andrew Haswell Green. But as political changes after 1870 made the park's administration more susceptible to the rough and tumble of city politics, rules were gradually loosened, and the park's design became increasingly eclectic. Rules prohibiting walking on the grass, the use of the carriage drives by commercial vehicles, ball playing by boys over sixteen, and Sunday concerts were modified or less rigorously enforced. At the same time, restaurants, commercial amusements (goat and pony rides and a carousel), and statues honoring cultural heroes of the city's immigrant communities appeared within the pastoral landscape. An extremely popular zoo brought Barnumesque amusements and boisterous crowds to the previously genteel park.

Many working-class Boston residents regarded much of that city's "Emerald Necklace" park system—the brainchild of Frederick Law Olmstead—as "rich men's parks" accessible only to those who owned "elegant equipages."

An equally powerful force for change came from growing numbers of immigrant, working-class New Yorkers who now found the park more accessible and more to their liking. As immigrant and working-class New Yorkers spread out across the landscape, they animated its natural scenery. On Sunday, "every seat, every, arbor, every, nook was occupied, and the music of human voices and laughter drowned and silenced the precocious chirping and whistling of insects and birds," a newspaper reported. "In these crowded centres the illusion of country was completely lost" (*New York Herald*, 20 August 1877). By early next century, enormous crowds turned out to see flower displays in the park's conservatory, flycasting exhibitions on the park's lake, and elaborate sound-and-light shows in the meadows.

Thus, the nineteenth-century ideal of *rus in urbe* gave way to "urb in rus" spectacles.

Late-nineteenth-century parks also accommodated middle-class Americans' growing enthusiasm for active sports. In the 1880s and 1890s, tennis courts were laid out on former meadows; by World War I most courts had been paved. In the 1890s, the bicycling boom erupted on park drives. By the first decade of the twentieth century, golf courses in city parks offered a new mode of communing with nature.

Some of these new sports altered patterns of socializing in parks. In the mid nineteenth century, park officials had regarded women as a special class of parkgoers who required protection. By the 1890s, the visibility of women cycling and playing tennis in city parks established the image of the "new woman" freely playing outdoors and socializing with men. But new recreational facilities also sharpened other lines of social segregation. Although black and white groups were allowed to picnic in Forest Park, its tennis courts, golf course, and playgrounds were more rigidly segregated. When black residents of Saint Louis challenged this "separate but equal" policy in court, they won small concessions—for example, the right to use the Forest Park golf course before noon on Mondays.

New park uses and users in the early twentieth century stirred other debates about what constituted a proper park. One position, marked out by progressives and their working-class allies, defined parks as utilitarian recreational spaces rather than as pastoral landscapes. This impulse found its clearest expression in the playground movement that spread across the country in the early twentieth century, but it was also reflected in earlier movements to create small parks in the poorer districts of the city. The advocates of small parks and playgrounds—most often middle-class social reformers—argued that organized and supervised play would "Americanize" new immigrants and remedy many of the ills of the city, particularly crime and juvenile delinquency. Playground movement leaflets luridly asked: "Shall We Provide a Playground? Or Enlarge the Jail?" Reformers stressed the need for structured and directed play. "On the vacant lot we can do as we please," one playground advocate noted disapprovingly, but "when we have a fenced playground it becomes an institution" (quoted in *The Park and the People*, pp. 146–147).

As was true of the intentions of nineteenth-century landscape architects, the dreams of playground advocates were often frustrated by the social realities of the city. Playgrounds probably had little impact on juvenile delinquency. And although reformers had promised to turn playgrounds into melting pots, playground use seems to have followed existing ethnic lines. Some city children viewed the playground supervisors cynically: "They get on me nerves with so many men and women around telling you what to do," complained one eleven-year-old about the playground workers in his city (quoted in *The Park and the People*, p. 151).

But if working-class children sometimes found the playground supervisors annoying and their rules restrictive, they (and their parents) nevertheless appreciated the increased recreational facilities and programs. After all, working-class families had long been fighting for more recreational space. Thus, while these city dwellers and their political representatives did not always share the reform goals of the playground movement, they often enthusiastically backed proposals to increase the number and availability, of swings, ballfields, swimming pools, and similar facilities.

At the same time that some early-twentieth-century progressives sought to remake public space in a recreational mold, others threw their support behind efforts to create monumental public spaces and institutions in line with the City Beautiful movement. City Beautiful advocates wanted to bring order to a seemingly chaotic city by designing wide tree-lined boulevards and grand civic centers. Unlike Olmsted and Vaux and the first generation of park designers, the adherents of City Beautiful wanted to visually integrate parks with the city. San Francisco, for example, acquired Sutro Heights and the top of Telegraph Hill as parklands primarily because they offered superb views of the city. The City Beautiful aesthetic both influenced the design of particular park systems—for example, those in Kansas City and Seattle—and accelerated the trend to place important civic and cultural institutions, particularly museums, within parks.

While playground proponents and City Beautiful advocates argued for transforming the "rural" park in order to accommodate new urban realities (whether new immigrants, automobiles, or the new scenic vista of skylines), preservationists and landscape architects reasserted a mid-nineteenth-century vision of the pastoral landscapes that resisted rather than embraced the city. They organized societies to protect aging parks from the encroachment of playgrounds and museums. In the 1920s, they started preserving and publishing the papers and writings of the founders of the urban park movement, such as Olmsted and Vaux.

The result of these countervailing forces is difficult to map on a national level. Nevertheless, most urban parks became increasingly eclectic as they added recreation features that appealed to new constituencies. Moreover, other forces of change proved as powerful as the ideological agenda of either progressive reformers or preservationists. The new urban immigrants who took possession of city parks infused them with their own distinctive modes of socializing—collective picnics, for example. Parks competed with other centers of commercial entertainment—amusement rides, spectator sports, and the movies. But public parks were free, and as administrators permitted new sports and pageants, parks took on some of the attractions of the commercial city.

The automobile, which had such a profound impact on the structure of American cities, also reshaped urban parks. Between 1900 and 1930, the number of Americans who owned cars went from eight thousand to twenty-three million. By the 1910s and 1920s, cars whizzed along the formerly sedate carriage roads of the large urban parks. And the parks themselves were reconfigured to accommodate cars: drives were straightened and asphalted, and parking lots displaced pastures. Still, between 1910 and 1930, as park systems dramatically expanded with suburban growth and annexation, urban planners promoted parks as antidotes to traffic and congestion. Park-makers like George E. Kessler, who designed park systems in Kansas City, Dallas, Salt Lake City, and Toledo, gained national reputations within the new professions of urban planning and park administration. Probably the most influential figure in adapting open spaces to the automobile was Robert Moses. Beginning in the 1920s Moses laid out an enormous park system in New York State that was accessible only by car.

In 1934 Moses became commissioner of New York City's park system and brought his car-centered and recreation-oriented approach to park-making directly within the city. With the assistance of huge appropriations of New Deal funds, Moses transformed the city's park system, adding three hundred playgrounds, fifteen swimming pools, seven golf courses, and eight thousand acres of parkland. Despite his autocratic management style, Moses dramatically democratized the city's park system by bringing recreational facilities within the reach of most city residents. (Most, but not quite, all: black neighborhoods remained underserved even after his massive expansion of the park system.) The West Side Improvement, a $200-million transformation of Manhattan's Riverside Park and the nearby railroad tracks, was a typical Moses project. It gave priority to the automobile (the most spectacular views were reserved for the car driver rather than the parkgoer); it reversed the pastoral emphasis of Olmsted's original Riverside Park plan by introducing playgrounds and tennis courts; and, notably, it failed to cover the railroad tracks where they ran through Harlem.

Despite the limitations of Moses and his vision, by the end of the 1930s Americans had come to view access to open urban space and recreational facilities almost as a fundamental right. The words "basic," "universal," and "essential" were now frequently coupled with "public parks"—an indication that they were accepted as necessary public services. Parks and playgrounds were now also routinely linked with other institutions like schools and housing. In 1941, for example, San Francisco began coordinating the work of its Housing Authority with the recreation and park departments. By the late 1940s in cities like Saint Louis, black residents had also successfully begun to challenge the segregation of such public recreation facilities as golf courses and tennis courts. As the civil rights struggle gained momentum in the South in the late 1950s and early 1960s, its targets included segregated public parks, beaches, and pools.

In the post-World War II era, the nation's urban parks increasingly suffered some of the woes of the cities themselves. In the 1950s and 1960s, cities underwent a dramatic social transformation as millions of white middle-class residents retreated to the suburbs and new migrants from the rural South and from Puerto Rico and Central and South America took their places. Some of the social tensions that resulted from that shift were manifest in a heightened concern about urban crime. Although parks generally had a lower crime rate than other parts of the city, they were often perceived as especially threatening environments, particularly at night. One-liners on late-night TV shows—"It was so quiet in Central Park last night, you could have heard a knife drop"—encapsulated and fostered the association of parks and crime.

With huge appropriations of New Deal funds, Parks Commissioner Robert Moses transformed New York City's park system by adding three hundred playgrounds, fifteen swimming pools, seven golf courses, and eight thousand acres of parkland.

Despite the crime scares, city dwellers never abandoned their parks. Indeed, in the late 1960s urban park use seems to have increased. Youthful adherents of the counterculture and the antiwar movement claimed public parks as their assembly points. At times—for example, in the fight over Berkeley's People's Park—they even waged struggles to secure and increase public open space within the city. In addition, growing interest in the environment and in physical fitness—particularly the jogging craze that began in the 1970s—brought new groups of regular users into parks. Finally, many park officials embraced a broader agenda for the spaces under their command. They much more willingly tolerated the use of parks for active recreation, rock concerts, ethnic festivals, and even political protests.

But if urban parks retained a vital social constituency in the 1960s, 1970s, and 1980s, their political constituency substantially eroded. As cities lost important portions of their tax base to the suburbs, they faced recurring fiscal crises in the 1970s and 1980s. When faced with difficult choices, city officials usually opted to cut park facilities and maintenance rather than police, fire, or welfare services. Moreover, as white middle-class families abandoned cities, various governmental policies and corporate practices encouraged private solutions to public problems. In the late twentieth century, the distinction between designed and vernacular public parks has taken on a new connotation. For example, private organizations have raised money to restore and maintain what had come to be seen as landmarks, such as Central Park—supplying more than half its budget in 1990. But the majority, of urban parks, like public schools and housing, are increasingly viewed, at least within mainstream discourse, as unsafe, poorly maintained, and second-rate. Such views foster inadequate public funding, which make such perceptions into realities.

The neglect of urban public parks has been most dramatic when they are in poor and especially in black neighborhoods. Boston's Franklin Park, designed by Olmsted and his stepson as the "jewel" in the Emerald Necklace, was allowed to deteriorate in the 1960s and 1970s as its surrounding neighborhoods turned largely black. In the early 1980s, city officials virtually abandoned the park, assigning no full-time workers to the maintenance of this five-hundred-acre park.

Despite uneven and inadequate public funding, urban parks retained a vitality, and excitement that reflected the cities in which they were located. Even in the worst times, black residents of Roxbury took advantage of the space afforded by Franklin Park, and interracial groups like the Franklin Park Coalition fought to win improved maintenance. At times, urban parks became the setting for clashes between warring ethnic and racial groups, which sought to defend their "turf." But parks could also serve as one of the few peaceful meeting grounds for diverse sets of urban residents. While acknowledging the "patterns of caste and class stratification and polarization throughout society as a whole," New York City Park Commissioner Gordon Davis argued in 1981 that Central Park reflected a profound form of social democracy, a degree of social and racial integration not found elsewhere in the city. In the face of the urban fiscal crisis, the recession of the 1990s, and the movement of more Americans to the suburbs, emerging coalitions of park activists and environmentalists have suggested new models for creating and administering open public spaces. They have suggested, for example, converting abandoned canal and railroad routes into parks and organizing regional park districts to overcome the political barriers between the suburbs and the city. Yet, in the 1990s and beyond, Americans—beset by profound social divisions and faced by daunting urban fiscal problems—would have to struggle with whether they could manage to maintain and expand the degree of social democracy that they had won in their most important urban public spaces over the past two centuries.

[See also The City; Landscapes; Mass Culture and Its Critics; Parades, Holidays, and Public Rituals; Popular Entertainment before the Civil War; Public Architecture; Urban Cultural Institutions.]

BIBLIOGRAPHY

Bluestone, Daniel. "From Promenade to Park: The Gregarious Origins of Brooklyn's Park Movement. "*American Quarterly* 39, no. 4 (1987).

Bluestone, Daniel. *Constructing Chicago* (1991).

Chadwick, George F: *The Park and the Town: Public Landscape in the 19th and 20th Centuries* (1966).

Cranz, Galen. *The Politics of Park Design: A History of Urban Parks in America* (1982).

Delano, Lewis A. "A Great Moral and Sanitary Agency: Baltimore's Druid Hill Park in 1860." Senior Seminar Paper, University of Maryland, Baltimore County (1984).

Hardy, Stephen. "'Parks for People': Reforming the Boston Park System, 1870–1915." *Journal of Sport History* 7, no. 3 (1980).

Jackson, John Brinckerhoff. *American Space: The Centennial Years, 1865–1876* (1972).

Jackson, John Brinckerhoff. *Discovering the Vernacular Landscape* (1984).

Kowsky, Frank, ed. *The Best Planned City: The Olmsted Legacy in Buffalo* (1992).

Loughlin, Caroline, and Catherine Anderson. *Forest Park* 1986).

McLaughlin, Charles C., and Charles E. Beveridge, eds. *The Papers of Frederick Law Olmsted.* Five vols. to date. (1977–).

Newton, Norman T. *Design on the Land: The Development of Landscape Architecture* (1971).

Rosenzweig, Roy. *Eight Hours for What We Will: Workers and Leisure in an Industrial City, 1870–1920* (1983).

Rosenzweig, Roy, and Elizabeth Blackmar. *The Park and the People: A History of New York's Central Park* (1992).

Schuyler, David. *The New Urban Landscape: The Redefinition of City Form in Nineteenth-Century America* (1986).

Van Hoffman, Alexander. "'Of Greater Lasting Consequence': Frederick Law Olmsted and the Fate of Franklin Park, Boston." *Journal of the Society, of Architectural Historians* 47, no. 4 (1988).

Williams, Raymond. *The Country, and the City* (1973).

Wilson, William H. *The City Beautiful Movement* (1989).

— ROY ROSENZWEIGELIZABETH BLACKMAR

V

VACATIONS

See TRAVEL AND VACATIONS

VILLAGE AND TOWN

The history of America can be traced through its towns and villages and hamlets. These have served as the primary cells of the body politic, outposts of a migrant, westward-moving people, embryos of cities, and repositories of the dream of community. The small town has engraved a durable image upon the American collective unconscious—in social myth, literature, historical memory, ideals. Perhaps in no other national culture do the words "small town" pulsate with such strong positive and negative emotional currents—especially among those who grew up in such places. They elicit a deep ambivalence: attraction and repulsion, affection and repugnance, nostalgia and frustration. In a mobile, individualistic, ever-urbanizing (and sub-urbanizing) society the small town (a nonmetropolitan place of as few as two or three hundred up to twenty-five to thirty thousand people) has shown a remarkable durability, despite the social and economic forces impinging upon it, and it continues to be a symbol of deeply held American values of roots and community.

The Colonial Era

European immigrants, mainly from England in the early seventeenth century, planted the precursors of the modern American town. When the tide of transoceanic migration reached these shores, it divided into two streams, one originating on the land of the Massachusetts Bay Colony and the other on the territory of the Virginia Company. These disparate environments further influenced the patterns of early urbanization.

The first settlers of both regions were adjured to form towns. The obvious reason for such instructions was to provide mutual protection against the "hideous howling wilderness." But the principals in England also saw commercial advantages in settling groups of people with complementary skills on a single site, thus providing a division of labor capable, it was hoped, of exploiting the putative riches of the New World. The owners also regarded collective settlement as a means of ensuring social control, to prevent these good English men and women from reverting to savagery.

VIRGINIA. The Virginia Company ordered the teams of "planters" it backed to found "handsome towns," later modified to "compact and orderly villages." But the investors' vision of rows of brick houses along cobbled streets quickly shattered on the reefs of reality. The first settlement, Jamestown, founded in 1607, was a collection of huts surrounded by a wooden palisade. It was sited in a marshy area, and malaria wiped out large numbers of its inhabitants; fires and Indian raids finished the job.

Subsequent colonizing efforts similarly failed, until the settlers found their salvation in the profitable cultivation of tobacco (*Nicotiana tabacum*). This single-crop economy favored a plantation system of agriculture rather than one centered in the agricultural villages of Europe that provided the model in Massachusetts. Under the dominance of the landed proprietor, plantations became self-sufficient communities with their own stores and artisans—and a labor force of indentured servants and later slaves. A sprinkling of small farmers and freed bond servants formed a loose society of neighborhoods—networks of people who lived close enough to one another that each might practice some specialized trade useful to the others as well as cultivate a crop for private profit.

The primary governing institution of planter society, aside from the colonial legislature, was the county court; in the courthouse the records of all-important land transactions were kept, property disputes were settled, and justice was dispensed. Those with legal business journeyed many miles and put up at nearby taverns. Court sessions were social as well as civic events; the planters clattered in astride their fine horses and wearing colorful coats and high boots, seeking diversion from isolated plantation life. Churches were similarly situated in open countryside; the parish was the basic unit of religious governance.

The first settlements in Virginia were ports to which planters brought their crops for shipment to England and where they purchased a wide range of supplies. These entrepôts, comprising a few houses and stores, their docks piled with bales of tobacco at harvest time, were located at the heads of the numerous inlets, bays, and estuaries that formed natural harbors along the coastline of tidewater Virginia and neighboring Maryland's Chesapeake Bay.

And so Thomas Jefferson wrote in his *Notes on the State of Virginia* (1781): "We have no townships. Our country being much intersected with navigable waters, and trade brought generally to our doors . . . has probably been one of the causes why we have no towns of any consequence." The result was a scattered society that to visitors from England seemed primitive and anarchic. The writer John Aubrey (1626–1697) described some squatters he happened upon as "mean people who live lawless, nobody to govern them, they care for nobody, having no dependence on anybody."

Another inhibition to urban development in the South was the tendency of new groups of settlers to split up and claim individual tracts of the fertile bottomland rather than to band together to found a town. Periodically, the British authorities complained about the slow pace of urbanization, and they sent detailed plans with each new contingent of emigrants. But nearly one hundred years after the settling of Jamestown, the historian Robert Beverly (1673–1722) wrote that the people of Virginia "have not any place of cohabitation among them that may reasonably bear the name of town."

MASSACHUSETTS BAY. In contrast, by 1717 the Massachusetts Bay Colony claimed more than one hundred towns. The people in the northern stream of settlement were largely Puritan dissenters organized into homogeneous congregations. The first civic act of these groups was to draw up a covenant, setting forth the rights and obligations of each inhabitant, which all the original grantees (proprietors) had to sign. Town and church were coterminous, and congregations were self-governing. That unique New England institution, the town meeting, evolved from a church body into a political assembly open to all property holders and dealing with secular matters. Town meetings were the first independent political units of colonial America. As Alexis de Tocqueville wrote, "the doctrine of the sovereignty of the people came out of the townships and took possession of the states."

The system of town-founding by congregations was codified in colonial law. A group of people wishing to "plant" a town was required to draw up a covenant and apply to the legislature for a land grant. The proprietors then apportioned their tract among themselves according to need and rank. They laid out their habitats in the immemorial pattern of the English agricultural village—a parallel row of houses along a single street with long, narrow strips of fields extending perpendicularly behind the houses. Common land was set aside for the church and for pastures and meadows—thus the New England village green, site of the square wooden meetinghouse with its cupola and bell (later replaced by a tall-spired church). Initially, plots of land were worked communally, with families living in the village. But gradually communal farming gave way to individual ownership and control, and the more independent souls moved farther out. They were disapprovingly called "out-livers," and it was feared that, deprived of daily surveillance by pious neighbors, their morals would degenerate. They were required to live within a day's travel so they could at least attend church on the Sabbath.

Under the tight lid of religious conformity, enforced by the minister and church elders, the Puritan towns were small theocracies. Beneath a surface harmony, they bubbled with tensions and spites. The religious authorities sought to mediate the resulting disputes, lawyers being anathema to the Puritans. There were also incessant theological arguments, and the bacteria of dissenters might fester and poison the Christian ideals of love, harmony, and cooperation. Eventually the infection came to a head, and the dissenters were excommunicated or won control of the town meeting or seceded in a body—"hiving off," it was called—to found a new church elsewhere.

Collective agriculture was soon abandoned, as the harder-working, more proficient farmers accumulated additional tracts of land. Disparities in landed wealth formed the basis of class divisions between rich and poor. At death, the father's property was divided among all the sons and daughters (as dowries). In an era when families of ten or twelve children were common, the third generation found its portions too small to provide a living. As a result, the young and ambitious looked north and west, where virgin land abounded. Also eyeing this territory were speculators in town plots—a new breed of entrepreneurs who bought up a tract and sold it off in parcels, setting aside church and school lots, to groups or individuals. Thus the covenant gradually gave way to the cash nexus.

The Midwest in the Nineteenth Century

After the war of 1812, the vast public domain west of the Appalachians, known as the Old Northwest Territory, was opened to settlement. Communal groups from New England founded towns much like the ones they had left, but Puritan-style theocracy did not take hold; there were too many competing sects on the frontier. Nor did the town meeting prosper in the villages founded by New Englanders. The states carved out of the Northwest Territory adopted the township-county system as a compromise between New England and Virginia. If the architectural emblem of the New England town was the church spire, in the Midwest it was the courthouse cupola, symbolizing a society governed by secular, legal norms rather than religious precepts.

Many southern pioneers retained their aversion to town life and cleared small farms in the vast forests. Although some scions of the landed gentry brought slaves with them, the plantation system itself did not take root for a variety of reasons, political, moral, and economic. Instead, wealthy speculators became the largest landholders, buying up huge tracts of the best soil and selling portions to settlers or hiring tenants to farm them.

The pioneer villages of the Midwest sprouted around crossroads taverns, along wilderness trails, at ferry landings, on the sites of forts built during the Indian wars. A few sprang up near deposits of coal and iron ore and carried on elementary manufacturing. Many a town grew up around a gristmill to which farmers brought their corn to be ground, or a general store where they bartered pork and cornmeal for supplies.

Economic rivalry among the embryonic pioneer towns was endemic. Competition for designation as a county seat, which guaranteed an economic base of courthouse business, touched off the fiercest battles.

The pioneer villages of the Midwest sprouted around crossroads taverns, along wilderness trails, at ferry landings, on the sites of forts built during the Indian wars.

New settlements energetically vied for the prize, using bribery, trickery, and sometimes violence to advance their claims. Communities also competed for the farmers' trade. Inevitably, the economic interests of farmers and town merchants began to diverge as the latter charged what the traffic would bear. Farmers complained that dealers' grain prices were too low, storekeepers' prices too high, and bankers' interest rates too dear.

The typical midwestern country town of the nineteenth century had been founded as a real estate proposition by a speculator. Streets and town lots were laid out in the ubiquitous gridiron or checkerboard pattern, which was best adapted to the sale of individual lots. The boomers'cries of a glorious future were taken to heart by those who settled there, and they became an article of faith of the gospel of growth. Civic pride was perverted into the admonition "Boost, don't knock," and ever-rising property values became the central goal.

Yet in those towns which survived the vicissitudes of pioneer days, people put down roots and acquired a sense of belonging; in the nineteenth century it was said that people were "born into" a town much as they were born into a church. Memories of pioneer days, when people helped each other out of necessity and when birth and status counted for little, were still alive, contributing to a spirit of community. In the postpioneer period, a rudimentary civic spirit veneered the raw acquisitive energy and survival drive that had dominated the early days. Women, in their traditional role as nurturers and promoters of domesticity and culture, became vocal, demanding the introduction of amenities. One of the first gestures to posterity in western towns was to plant trees along the unpaved streets.

Pioneer towns were little more than log cabins strewn helter-skelter along a single street. Gradually they metamorphosed into rows of frame houses with porches and lawns and backyards, along shaded streets down which clopped the spring wagons of merchants. The bell of the trolley car might be heard as it meandered along its appointed route, stopping whenever anyone hailed it. In the business district office blocks of beef-red brick rose two or three stories, a modest but dignified vernacular architecture. New, more elaborate courthouses rose in the central squares—edifices of brick or limestone with an imposing tower, elaborate masonry trim, a statue of a Union or Confederate soldier nearby, and benches for the old men who whiled away their days talking and whittling.

Still, the typical midwestern town was on the whole an ugly place of slatternly false-fronted buildings and unpaved streets that were rutted or muddy in winter and dusty and reeking of garbage and horse dung under the summer sun. Nearly every town had been laid out with a main street, often officially called that, which became the main business and social artery. Through it flowed the lifeblood of the town—its strollers and shoppers, its parades and celebrations, its political rallies.

Every Saturday farmers parked their buggies along it and embarked on their weekly shopping trip. To them the country town was a Rome, a Paris, an urban oasis at which to refresh grim, isolated lives. Country folk chatted in the courthouse square, purchased necessities and a few simple luxuries in dimly lit general stores redolent of harness leather and kerosene, and blinked sleepily at the new electric streetlights before heading home.

Meanwhile, the townspeople created their own recreational and cultural life: band concerts, baseball teams, cotillions and at homes, reading clubs, lectures by itinerant savants, shows by traveling theatrical troupes at the new opera house, circuses, revival meetings. The public schools were a boon to the farmers' sons and daughters who could attend them. High schools encouraged social mobility; they were stepping-stones to college and the cities. Human capital became one of the chief exports of the small towns. Surveys showed a disproportionately high percentage of scientists, business executives, and writers came from small towns. But rural areas battered by the ups and downs of farm prices also shipped their surplus sons and daughters to factories in the cities.

So to many, the hometown became the place you were from, a focal point of nostalgia. To its residents, it provided status, identity, and support. It also encouraged an insular civic pride, partly based on rivalry with other places; people felt *their* town was somehow superior to the next one, though an outsider might see little to choose between them. Small towns also declared their superiority to the cities. Preachers and editorialists promulgated the official gospel of small-town goodness and neighborliness, and inveighed against metropolitan alienation, immorality, and corruption.

Another type of town indigenous to the West with an exaggerated reputation for bumptiousness was the cattle town—Dodge City, Abilene, and Wichita being the most famous.

After the turn of the twentieth century, rising prosperity on the farms, the economic lifeblood of the country town, contributed to a smug sense that here was the good life. Trains arrived eight or ten times a day, wreathed in smoke, noise, and commotion, bringing news and goods and travelers from the city. The station was a favorite meeting place for locals, who watched the trains whizzing by "with the languid scorn a permanent fixture always has for a transient and the pity an American feels for a fellow-being who does not live in his town," as Booth Tarkington wrote in his novel *The Gentleman from Indiana.*

Blacksmith shops, livery stables, drugstores, and saloons were male bastions of somewhat shady repute. Women's lives centered on their homes; their labors were dawn to dusk, sweating over coal-burning stoves, pumping water, heating water for baths or laundry. The days of their weeks were structured by well-worn ritual: Monday, washing; Tuesday, ironing; and so on through Sunday, reserved for church and the heavy noon meal that followed. Women traditionally held the family together and dominated their homes; outside the home they specialized in religious, charitable, and cultural activities and watched over the morality of their husbands and children. Their husbands pursued their small-business dreams, though many found only a precarious living and sank into a dependent role of "diminished potency and power," in the words of historian Page Smith. A kind of small-town matriarchy prevailed, except in the male preserves of politics and commerce.

Every town had its rich families that dominated civic and economic affairs. They set the social tone and encouraged class distinctions; newcomers aspiring to acceptance found they must undergo a long vetting process. Even small villages had two rudimentary classes: those who worked and saved and went to church, and the rest, who were "no-accounts." The poor were blamed for their plight and formed a separate caste.

Such divisions clashed with the egalitarian ethos small towns still professed. There were invidious racial and ethnic distinctions as well, with blacks and foreigners segregated into "Bucktowns" and "Polish Towns," the poor to their shantytowns. Gossip was a potent weapon of social control, enforcing loosely articulated norms of morality and respectability. Yet the grapevine also carried news of sickness or a death in the family, bringing help from neighbors. Although there was a certain latitude for eccentricity, woe to those who willfully defied public opinion. The tyranny of the majority, which Alexis de Tocqueville identified as the drawback of democracy in America, was most pronounced in small towns, imposing a stifling dullness and provincialism. This, and the lack of economic opportunity for young people, save those who had a family business waiting for them, drove the best and the brightest to seek city lights.

Prairie Junctions: Mining Camps and Cow Towns

During the 1870s and 1880s, covered-wagon loads—later trainloads—of immigrants, many of them communal groups from Europe, poured into the Great Plains. The foreign immigrants had been recruited by agents for the railroad companies, which needed to populate the huge land grants along their rights-of-way. Railroads became the leading town promoters in the Far West. They laid out villages along their tracks at regular intervals, and named them in alphabetical order after railroad employees. Existing towns were told that they must pay a subsidy or be bypassed. Impelled by economic imperatives, town officials paid up, raising the money by bond subscriptions. They knew farmers must ship their produce to the cities and would take their trade to the town that had a grain elevator and a depot.

Farmers led lives of unrelieved toil and hardship. Agriculture was a precarious venture on the Great Plains because of the ferocious storms, low rainfall, and plagues of grasshoppers, and this retarded the growth of country towns. Railroads that gained a monopoly in their area added to the struggling farmers' costs by charging exorbitant freight rates, a cause of the Populist revolt of the 1880s and 1890s.

"Precarious" was the word for towns in the gold and silver country of California, Arizona, and the Rocky Mountains. Here, the mining camp was the primary form of settlement; it appeared wherever the precious ore was found. These disposable towns, dubbed "rag cities" because they consisted mainly of tents, plus a store or two and a shack that served as saloon, lasted only as long as the gold or silver held out. Nevertheless, they developed a legal system administered by ad hoc miners' courts which awarded claims, resolved disputes, and held criminal proceedings not far removed from lynch law. Still, the miners kept order, belying the reputation for rowdiness that mining camps acquired in romantic fiction.

Another type of town indigenous to the West with an exaggerated reputation for bumptiousness was the cattle town. Dodge City, Abilene, Wichita, and other Kansas towns served in turn as shipping points for beef on the hoof that had been driven in great herds from Texas to be transported to the abattoirs of Chicago. With the cattle came hordes of dusty, rowdy drovers eager for recreation after months on the trail.

The city officials' way of dealing with the free-spending cowboys was to quarantine them: all the saloons, bordellos, and gambling halls were confined to one side of the railroad tracks that ran down the main street, while the respectable folk lived on the other, insulated from the hell-raising and leading humdrum lives. The cattle towns took a perverse civic pride in their lurid reputations, inflated by eastern reporters in search of "color." Even in their heyday, the cow towns had schools, elections, churches, reform movements, economic conflicts; and after the cattle trade departed, officials repented their wickedness in an effort to attract the once-scorned farmers, who had "stood in the way of progress" by fencing the open range.

In California, the miners who had opened up the state were followed by farmers and town-boomers. Some of the old Spanish pueblos, presidios, and missions grew into towns and cities. A few mining camps acquired stability when industrial mining operations sank shafts to systematically extract ore-veined rock deep beneath the surface. Others were resurrected as agricultural centers.

The Revolt from the Village

By the early twentieth century, the fortunes of country towns were closely tied to national markets. A long-term exodus from the farms, hastened by the agricultural depression after the boom of World War I, and sustained by the mechanization of farming, gradually eroded the traditional economic base of the country towns. The larger towns diversified by attracting industries, but industrialization brought with it city-style problems—pollution, hardening class divisions, the decline of craftsmanship and the advent of mass production, and the replacement of local owners by distant corporate control. Labor unions were banned and local politics was dominated by business elites bent on keeping wages low and "agitators" out.

Attracting industry had other drawbacks. Many growth-obsessed towns offered excessive subsidies in the form of tax concessions and infrastructure improve-

Nineteenth century gold mining towns of the West and Northwest were precarious settlements held together as long as the gold or silver held out.

ments to attract new factories. Small-town businesses became dependent on large corporate suppliers that served national markets. In his classic 1923 essay "The Country Town," the iconoclastic economist Thorstein Veblen described small-town shopkeepers as mere "toll-gate keepers for the distribution of goods and collection of customs for the large absentee owners of business."

Standardization, industrialization, and the rise of mass culture through radio, movies, and nationally distributed periodicals exposed provincial towns that prided themselves on their self-reliance and resistance to urban ways. The 1920 census was a watershed; it revealed that for the first time in American history more than half of the population dwelled in urban places of 2,500 people and above. And in an increasingly urbanized society, small towns were damned by urban intellectuals (most of them escapees) as backward and provincial.

The reaction was particularly visible in fiction. At the turn of the century, when the influx from the country to the city was accelerating, writers such as Booth Tarkington and Zona Gale celebrated the friendliness and folksiness of small towns; but in the 1910s and 1920s, a new critical realism focused a pitiless gaze on the emotional and cultural aridity of small-town life, giving rise to a literary movement called "the revolt from the village." In 1915, Edgar Lee Masters's *Spoon River Anthology* removed the facade of hypocrisy from small-town lives in terse epigrammatic poems. Sherwood Anderson's *Winesburg, Ohio* (1919), a series of linked, plotless stories tinged by Freudianism, displayed villagers as sexually repressed grotesques. The most stinging indictment was Sinclair Lewis's satirical *Main Street* (1920), which caustically evoked the social and cultural ugliness of Gopher Prairie, Minnesota.

Lewis wrote of his fictional town, "This is America—a town of a few thousand. . . . [I]ts Main Street is the continuation of Main Streets everywhere." To the village rebels, the small town was a metaphor for American culture—its provincialism, fundamentalism, anti-intellectualism, materialism, Fordism. Indeed, in 1922 an anthology edited by Harold E. Stearns appeared under the bland but ironically intended title *Civilization in the United States.* Louis Raymond Reed, the contributor of the essay "The Small Town" wrote: "The civilization of America is predominantly the civilization of the small town" (p. 286).

The intellectuals and urbanites regarded prohibition as small-town morality writ large. The temperance movement had grown from frontier beginnings into a national crusade, culminating in the moral fervor of World War I and the passage of the Eighteenth Amendment. Prohibition pitted rural America against urban America. Walter Lippmann saw it as "a test of strength between social orders. When the Eighteenth Amendment goes down, the cities will be dominant politically and socially as they now are economically." From the ramparts of his *American Mercury,* H. L. Mencken hurled thunderbolts of invective against small-town morality and hypocrisy. To progressive urban intellectuals, small towns stood for nativist opposition to labor unions, foreigners, and radicalism. And there was truth to the indictment, for small-town businessmen embraced the big-business—Republican party credo of laissez-faire and low taxes.

After the village rebels had raked over small-town America, a wave of probing sociologists descended on it. One of the first such studies was Robert and Helen Lynd's *Middletown* (1929), which found in Muncie, Indiana, the conformity and conservatism that the novelists had shown. It was followed by *Middletown in Transition* (1937), analyzing the impact of the Great Depression on Muncie. Other prominent studies included W. Lloyd Warner and associates' five-volume "Yankee City" series about industrialization in Newburyport, Massachusetts, and his *Democracy in Jonesville* (1949), Hollingshead's *Elmtown's Youth* (1949), Blumenthal's *Small-Town Stuff* (1932), and James West's *Plainville USA* (1955). As late as the 1960s, Arthur Vidich and Joseph Bensman, in their *Small Town in Mass Society* (1968), could proclaim that an upstate New York town was "a backwash" and "the last link in America to the nineteenth century and its values." The inhabitants of "Springdale" still proclaimed the old values of individualism, self-help, and autonomy, even though their town had become dependent on state and federal aid. Its politics were dominated by a self-perpetuating elite skilled at extracting subsidies from the state, and its small businessmen were at the mercy of their big corporate suppliers.

Towns in the Industrial Era

The Great Depression was a watershed, undermining the traditional rural values of self-help and individualism. The 1930s saw an unprecedented intrusion of the federal government into local government. Small-town and rural people had traditionally relied on charity and neighborliness to cope with troubles too big for the individual to handle; poverty was considered a disgrace, and ending one's days at the county poor farm was a fate to be dreaded. And so when unemployment struck, its victims sought to hide their disgrace. A common saying during the Depression was "if I have to be poor I want to be poor in a city where everybody doesn't know I'm broke."

Even in industrial towns the old individualism retained its hold. In Middletown, the Lynds noted, the factory workers were mainly farm boys and "thus close to the network of habits of thought engendered by the isolated, self-contained enterprise of farming." Consequently, they clung to the dream of going into business for themselves and achieving financial success, rather than joining together to assert their economic interests. Similarly, business-dominated, small-town governments, chronically resistant to change and "rocking the boat," averted their eyes from the rising tide of misery among their constituents and chanted the mantra of "Boost, don't knock." But they could not forever ignore the fact that their miserly poor-relief budgets were inadequate to deal with the misery lapping at their doorstep. Eventually, they swallowed their principles and accepted Uncle Sam's helping hand. Federal largess financed a host of public-works projects, from post offices to bridges to new roads. These improvements would never have been made by traditionally parsimonious town fathers.

The Depression brought many people from the cities back to the land, even as the wave of bankruptcies drove others off it. But the countryside was the net loser in this exchange. The rural exodus was temporarily stalled by the agricultural boom of World War II, but it resumed at an even faster pace after the war. More than 8.6 million people departed for cities in the 1940s; the flight continued at the rate of a million per year in the 1950s, and three-quarters of a million annually in the 1960s. The flight of southern blacks from the land was a major component of this human tide, as the mechanization of cotton picking made their labor unnecessary. In 1940 the rural population made up 40 percent of the national population; by 1970 it was only 26.5 percent. In 1975 only 4 percent of the total population was engaged in farming.

Small towns suffered, perforce, from the loss of farmers. A favorite statistic of rural sociologists is the 1:5 ratio—for every five farmers who move away, one business in town goes under. The proof of this theorem was visible in the boarded-up stores along every Main Street. In the 1960s small-town businesses were decimated by a new invader—the shopping mall, often a gallery of stores set down in a former cornfield. The automobile had long been choking Main Street; shopping malls with acres of parking lots and "stripvilles" of establishments catering to the car culture "solved" that problem—at the expense of downtown merchants. Revitalization of central business districts became the challenge of the 1970s. One strategy was restoration of old buildings and the introduction of pedestrian malls and more ample parking facilities.

The "rural Renaissance"

During the 1970s, there was a modest turnaround in the fortunes of rural America. Countering a trend of country-to-city migration nearly as old as the republic, rural counties showed a 15.4 percent gain in population—around four million people in all. The counties with the lowest population densities had the largest increases.

The rush to the countryside sparked a flurry of stories in the press about a "rural renaissance," and demographers scrambled to understand what had happened. Their main conclusions: First, many of the migrants were acting out of the long-standing preference among Americans, consistently shown in opinion polls, for small-town or country living—more for the latter. Second, and a seeming corollary to this, many of the rural immigrants cited "quality of life" as their primary reason for moving. Dissatisfaction with decaying, crime-ridden cities (and overgrown suburbs) was possibly an impetus, but the pull of areas affording natural beauty, space, and privacy was even more decisive. Third, although the usual incentive for moving, economic betterment, was not often cited, the availability of nonfarming jobs—professional, white-collar, and blue-collar—in rural areas made the move feasible for many. This development resulted from diverse causes, including decentralization of industry facilitated by improved communications; the relocation of governmental facilities to low-density areas; the energy boom in the Appalachians, the West, and the "oil patch" states; cheap gasoline; the aging of the general population and a growing number of longer-lived, more affluent retired people who preferred small-town life; the proliferation of community colleges, which alleviated cultural isolation; and the growth of the recreation and nursing-home industries. As commuters to city jobs moved farther out, a new postsuburbia proliferated in the rural fringes of metropolitan areas. The result was clusters of homes that were neither urban nor rural; sociologists christened them "countrified cities" or "linear suburbs" or "plug-in towns."

The migration to rural areas brought problems: environmental degradation, pollution, and the loss of irreplaceable farmland. Some developers did not provide adequate roads or sewage lines; many unincorporated villages tapped groundwater, which was insufficient for their population and polluted by agricultural pesticides. Newcomers roiled the stagnant waters of local politics by demanding urban-style services. The aging machinery of county government creaked under the strain of the demands for services—sewage, paved roads, water.

All this raised a larger question: Would the immigrants seeking quality of life end up degrading that same quality of life? And what of the impact on democratic participation of a diffuse population living in "plug-in cities"? Would the inhabitants shun involvement in local government? Would they take part in community activities in nearby towns? Would they form communities of their own? Or would the open land spawn an alienated population of latter-day outlivers, with no ties to place other than the financial nexus of real estate values?

The Future of the Small Town

By the mid-1980s, the rural renaissance stalled and the movement to urban areas resumed. Mining regions, hit by falling energy prices, suffered a net loss of 1.7 percent in population; nearly half of all rural counties declined in population. Counties in which manufacturing was the dominant economic activity were shaken by deindustrialization—the restructuring of the national economy from one dominated by manufacturing to one primarily geared to providing services. In Ohio, the heart of the Rustbelt, eighty of eighty-four counties showed a net loss of people.

The economic malaise in the rural areas was starkly etched in unemployment figures. Between May 1985 and May 1986, agricultural employment fell by nearly 4 percent, mining employment by more than 16 percent, and manufacturing employment by 0.6 percent. The rural poor increased by 43 percent between 1978 and 1983, according to the Census Bureau. A Senate subcommittee reported that during the 1980s, net farm income averaged nearly 40 percent less than in the 1970s. More than one thousand rural counties had unemployment rates above 9 percent, compared with the national average of 5.2 percent. Some towns became "rural ghettos."

> *The farm crisis of the 1980s delivered a devastating blow to agriculturally based towns: More than 270,000 family farms disappeared in a wave of bankruptcies, and the land was gobbled up by agribusiness and consolidated into larger spreads.*

The farm crisis of the 1980s delivered a devastating blow to agriculturally based towns. More than 270,000 family farms disappeared in a wave of bankruptcies; the land was gobbled up by agribusinesses and consolidated into larger spreads. These corporate farming operations bypassed town merchants and made their bulk purchases in urban centers. They also imported hired laborers who, with no community ties and little hope of acquiring land of their own, formed a permanent underclass.

As town businesses closed their doors, the young and the able fled, leaving behind the poor and the nonaffluent elderly. In some small towns in the farm belt, the median age was over fifty, and many counties showed an excess of deaths over births. The fewer young workers who remained shouldered a heavier tax burden because of the need to provide health care for the oldsters, as well as to maintain schools and basic services.

Manufacturing towns that watched local industries go under to foreign competition or be bought out by conglomerates which cut the work force or shut the plants, found it harder to attract traditionally good-paying factory jobs. In the 1970s and 1980s, the phenomenon of "footloose" industries became more prevalent—establishments that were not tied to any site and left with little concern for the impact on the places they abandoned. Some towns sought to attract service industries, but the jobs often paid less than factory work. And the new factories that did relocate often hired outside workers rather than locals.

All this shuttered stores along Main Street. One study reported that in each decade since 1950 an average of 76 percent of towns of less than 2,500 population suffered a net loss of retail and service establishments—gas stations, grocery stores, lumberyards, hardware, farm implement, and furniture stores. This erosion was not due solely to loss of population; increased competition came from large chains, which offered goods and supplies more cheaply (and were not averse to monopolistic price-cutting). People drove to shopping malls to make their big-ticket purchases rather than buying at home. As a result, some towns could survive only as bedroom communities for cities some 50 miles (80 kilometers) away. Between 1983 and 1986, places outside a Standard Metropolitan Statistical Area (a densely populated area contiguous to a city of fifty thousand or more) suffered the greatest population declines.

Cutbacks in federal aid under the Reagan administration added to the woes of small towns already confronted by a dwindling tax base. They were starved for money to repair bridges and roads, and had to worry about city-style problems like crime, drugs, inadequate schools, air and soil pollution, toxic waste, AIDS, and polluted water tables. Federal crop-support payments to farmers continued, but much of the money went to large operators and the rest did not always help a town's economy, since it was used to pay off the big mortgages assumed during the 1970s rather than to make consumer purchases.

To be sure, many larger towns survived on a solid base of industry and farming and maintained basic services. But even they were hit by the loss of important amenities—a hospital, say, because Medicaid payments are lower for rural areas. The local bank might be taken over by a remote financial conglomerate that was less sensitive to local needs. Deregulation enabled air, rail, and bus lines to halt unprofitable local service, meaning that many towns were cut off from urban centers.

Town and Community

Yet, the crisis of the small town is not new; as we have seen, many of the trends are of long standing. The harsh judgment of history is that some small towns are doomed and others will survive only if they adapt to new circumstances. But self-help is often not enough. Governmental policies properly tailored to the needs of the one-quarter of the population in rural areas are needed. Measures designed to shore up the family farm, for example, would slow the small-town death rate in states like Iowa. The festering problem of rural poverty, which has been on the national agenda since at least the 1960s, must be addressed more decisively by the federal government in areas such as health care, housing, and small business assistance, instead of placing the entire burden on the states.

The picture is by no means uniformly bleak. Many towns are showing adaptability and planning moderate growth strategies. These municipalities, which sociologists call "entrepreneurial towns"—those with newspapers that air local issues, an activist political leadership, schools that emphasize academics rather than sports, and a citizenry willing to spend tax money on infrastructure improvements—have been able to revive fading local businesses or attract new ones to offset their losses.

A contemporary school of "neotraditionalist" city planners draws upon the classic small-town model in laying out new towns with low-traffic streets, local gathering places, sidewalks, pedestrian scale. Even shopping malls—those ravagers of so many small-town businesses—are being torn down and rebuilt as imitation Main Streets with small stores, community centers, and residential areas.

With enlightened leadership and planning, many towns can survive. But survival should not be judged by purely economic criteria or in terms of growth at any price; it should also include invigoration of the town's cultural life and preservation of its history and intangible values of community, smallness and human scale, face-to-face relationships over time, and a sense of place.

So we return to the ideal of community first declared by the early Puritans. John Winthrop described it eloquently in a sermon aboard the *Arbella*: "We must delight in each other, make others' conditions our own, rejoice together, always having before our eyes our commission and community in the work, our community as members of the same bond." New constellations of this old dream must be discovered that are appropriate for a heterogeneous, secular society.

[See also The City; The Frontier; Geographic Mobility; Landscapes; Rural Life in the North; Rural Life in the South; Rural Life in the West; The Suburbs; Technology and Social Change; Transportation and Mobility.]

BIBLIOGRAPHY

Atherton, Lewis E. *Main Street on the Middle Border* (1954).
Blumenthal, Albert. *Small-Town Stuff* (1932).
Brownell, Blaine A., and David R. Goldfield, eds. *The City in Southern History: The Growth of Urban Civilization in the South* (1977).
Bushman, Richard L. *From Puritan to Yankee: Character and the Social Order in Connecticut, 1690–1765* (1967).
Critchfield, Richard. *Villages* (1981).
Davidson, Osha Gray. *Broken Heartland: The Rise of America's Rural Ghetto* (1990).
Debo, Angie. *Prairie City: The Story of an American Community* (1944).
Demos, John. *A Little Commonwealth: Family Life in Plymouth Colony* (1970).
Dollard, John. *Caste and Class in a Southern Town.* 3d ed. (1957).
Dykstra, Robert R. *The Cattle Towns* (1968).Goist, Park Dixon. *From Main Street to State Street: Town, City, and Community in America* (1977).
Greven, Philip J., Jr. *Four Generations: Population, Land, and Family in Colonial Andover, Massachusetts* (1970).
Hilfer, Anthony Channell. *The Revolt from the Village, 1915–1930* (1969).
Hollingshead, August de Belmont. *Elmtown's Youth: The Impact of Social Classes on Adolescents* (1949).
Lesy, Michael. *Wisconsin Death Trip* (1973).
Lingeman, Richard. *Small-Town America: A Narrative History, 1620-the Present* (1980).
Lockridge, Kenneth A. *A New England Town: The First Hundred Years, Dedham, Massachusetts, 1636–1736* (1970).
Lynd, Robert S., and Helen M. Lynd. *Middletown: A Study in Contemporary American Culture* (1929).
Lynd, Robert S., and Helen M. Lynd. *Middletown in Transition: A Study of Cultural Conflicts* (1937).
Parker, Tony. *Bird, Kansas* (1989).
Powers, Ron. *Far from Home: Life and Loss of Two American Towns* (1991).
Redfield, Robert. *The Little Community, and Peasant Society and Culture* (1962).
Rifkind, Carole. *Main Street: The Face of Urban America* (1977).
Schwab, Jim. *Raising Less Corn and More Hell: Midwestern Farmers Speak Out* (1988).
Shinn, Charles Howard. *Mining Camps: A Study in American Frontier Government.* Edited by Rodman W. Paul (1965).
Smith, Page. *As a City upon a Hill: The Town in American History* (1966).
Varenne, Hervé. *Americans Together: Structured Diversity in a Midwestern Town* (1977).
Vidich, Arthur, and Joseph Bensman. *Small Town in Mass Society: Class, Power, and Religion in a Rural Community* (1968).
West, James. *Plainville USA* (1955).

— RICHARD LINGEMAN

W

WOMEN AND WORK

The history of women and work in the United States is woven of change and continuity. The shift from an agrarian to a commercial and industrial economy in turn transferred the location of much of women's work from the domestic to the public sphere. The demography of the female labor force changed, too, as the working girl of the nineteenth century gave way to the working mother of the mid to late twentieth century. The class composition of the female labor force also diversified, especially as the tertiary sector expanded. Despite the sometimes dramatic evidence of change, long threads of continuity reach back into the seventeenth century and forward to the present. Women remain principally responsible for work in the home despite their ever-growing presence in jobs outside the home. The gender division of labor also endures in the public sphere. Gender distinctions and gender hierarchies have always defined occupations, wages, and working conditions and have shaped women's employment opportunities.

The history of women and work in the United States has grown apace with the larger field of women's history. Like much early women's history, women's labor history was "contributory" in character. As the title of one notable survey of working women in America announced, historians sought to prove that "we were there" in the labor force and the labor movement from the beginning. In time the goals and purposes of historians became more interesting and sophisticated. Historians of women and work, for example, have emphasized the importance of defining work broadly to include unpaid labor as well as the more conventional remunerated work outside the home. Based on a male model of behavior, an emphasis on paid involvement in the public sphere overlooks or undervalues women's many contributions to family survival. Whether they produced goods in their homes, took in and cared for boarders or other women's children, engaged in the unpaid work of family nurture, or took jobs outside the home, women have always worked. Challenging the tendency to accept at face value the division of spheres, scholars have evaluated both the significance of, and public attitudes toward, all these activities. Historians also have moved from narrative descriptions to analyses of the indirect, uneven, and complex impact of industrialization on women. The consequences of work for women have provoked lively debate among historians, who ask to what extent it reduced the differences between the sexes or advanced the cause of gender equality. Other questions raised by historians of women and work concern the significance of class, race, and ethnicity for women's labor experience, the role of the state in regulating and defining women's work, and the individual and collective efforts of women workers to direct their own lives.

This essay draws on the growing secondary literature to examine the history of women and work from the seventeenth century to the present. Describing the varied character of women's work and assessing the extent and sources of change and continuity, it is organized chronologically in four sections. The first examines the preindustrial era in colonial America. The second describes the relationship of women to the commercialization of agriculture and the beginning of industrialism in the years between the Revolution and the Civil War. The third part focuses on the Gilded Age and the Progressive Era, a period when women's place in the economy grew as the economy itself expanded significantly. The last section explores the changes and continuities of the modern era from World War I to the present.

The Preindustrial Era, 1600–1800

In the seventeenth and eighteenth centuries, the vast majority of women lived on farms. Although tasks were divided on the basis of gender, men's and women's spheres were both complementary and overlapping. Men were responsible for work in the fields and the outbuildings; women were responsible for work inside the house and for dairying and gardening. Women's work was skilled, complex, and arduous; with the exception of the cultivation of grain and supervision of livestock, they were responsible for the production of nearly all food and clothing. The colonial American housewife was expected to possess the knowledge of a flax spinster, wool spinster, weaver, dyer, fuller, tailor, knitter, miller, brewer, baker, gardener, dairy maid, chandler, and soapmaker. Dependence defined women's place in the colonial economy and society. But although married women themselves owned no property and had no legal right to their own earnings, they engaged in barter or trade of the goods they produced to obtain other items. Scholars debate the extent and significance of this economic activity, but there is evidence that colonial families supplemented homegrown products with textiles, flour, butter, and meat bought from tradesmen, peddlers, and neighboring producers, often with women's income. Women also traded or bought such household necessities as soap, candles, and herbal medicine. Moreover, just as men hired hands to assist in the production of grain, women sought assistance with their own work, partly by relying on craftspeople for various steps in the production process. Even before the Revolution there was a primitive putting-out system in New England in which women sold yarn to storekeepers who then put it out to knitters or weavers; women also might have paid to have the fabric whitened or fulled. Not only did some women in this way buy themselves freedom from the most onerous work, but the women with whom the merchant contracted for the work gained a means of support as well. The system was sufficiently developed that by the 1770s many women, especially those in towns, did not themselves produce cloth.

Despite the power of patriarchy in colonial America, women occasionally assumed male responsibilities and engaged in the public sphere as economic actors. If a husband was absent or incapacitated, a wife might assume the role of "deputy husband" and act as farmer, weaver, or merchant, all male-defined roles. As long as such behavior was only temporary, it was tolerated by colonial society. Denied access to formal apprenticeship and unable to sign contracts or own property, women were excluded from the skilled trades. But women were not entirely without their own resources. There is evidence from the eighteenth century of women engaged in business, although usually on a partnership basis with their husbands or as an auxilliary job to housewifery. Women customarily operated taverns and boarding houses; others had small shops selling pastries, dry goods, hardware, or liquor; some women opened schools. Many more, especially single women, hired themselves out as domestic servants. Midwifery was another employment engaged in by women; payment came in the form of goods or cash. A very few exceptional women were lawyers, landowners, and merchants.

Not all women in colonial America, of course, were free. In New England, white women usually arrived with their families, but in the middle and southern colonies, they more often came alone as indentured servants or prospective wives for male settlers. Although most indentured servants were male, women also bound themselves for a period of time, usually several years, in return for transportation and room and board. Some did agricultural work, but most performed the domestic work expected of white women. Indentured servants had little freedom; they could not marry or bear children, they—or, more properly stated, their terms of service—could be bought, traded, or sold, and they had limited rights to redress of grievances against their masters. But indentured servants, who were white, had something that slaves, who were black, did not: the promise of freedom after the contract expired. The only difference between female servants when their indentures ended and white women who never served an indenture was later age at marriage and first birth. Race, however, mattered. Beginning in the late seventeenth century, African men and women were bought and sold in the colonies. Slavery spread in the southern colonies, where landowners engaged in the production of labor-intensive cash crops. It is indicative of the racist dimension of white gender ideology that slave women were expected to perform not only domestic but also agricultural work.

The work of Native American women also differed in several important respects from that of free white women in colonial America. The tribes were unified by a subsistence economy that generally assigned to women the work of gathering and processing food and caring for children and to men the tasks of hunting and warfare. There were, however, many tribes with diverse ways of organizing labor. Indian societies differed in both the definition of appropriate tasks for women and men and the degree of flexibility or rigidity in applying each definition. The Iroquois Confederacy, for example, provided women with considerably more economic and political power than Europeans considered possible or preferable. Indifferent to the dynamics of gender politics among the Indians, European observers saw only a division of labor that assigned to women tasks that their culture assigned to men. They therefore perceived Indian women as mere drudges or slaves of Indian men. The irony was that as they chopped wood, built houses, carried heavy loads, and engaged in agriculture and trade, native American women actually enjoyed much greater freedom and autonomy than did European women. Although a few colonists considered or hailed the Indian alternatives, the counterexamples of gender-role definitions and gender relations offered by Indian societies were overlooked by most Europeans.

The American Revolution marked something of a turning point for women and work. During the war, women's work acquired a new political value. Whether they boycotted British tea, spun yarn and wove cloth to avoid purchasing British goods, or performed the work of men who were in the military, patriot women endowed their prosaic production with great importance. The spur that the Revolution gave to domestic manufacturing of consumer goods formerly purchased from

British producers also expanded economic and employment opportunities for American women, particularly the growing number of poorer women—notably widows with children—responsible for their own and their families' support. The ideology of republican motherhood, the political philosophy that defined women's place in the new nation, expanded women's traditional role to include the training of children for citizenship. The legacy of the Revolution for women and work, however, was ambiguous. The higher esteem in which American women were held during the Revolution was not translated into equality or independence after the war. The social changes demanded by war were regarded as temporary, and women's dependent and inferior status was codified in the new Constitution and in state regulations. Republican motherhood reconfirmed rather than challenged the gender division of labor. And in asserting women's distance from the public sphere, it also suggested a new gendered definition of labor that would make equivocal the women's place in the economy of the early national period.

Early Industrialism and National Expansion, 1790–1860

The period between the Revolution and the Civil War has always attracted the interest of historians of women in the United States. The growth of commerce and industry as the nation emerged from colonial status irrevocably changed people's lives. Much attention has been paid to the putative separation of home from work and the rise of a middle class. For their part, historians of women's role in labor have shifted attention from middle-class women to those who could not afford to emulate the bourgeois ideal of the leisured woman. Although much scholarship has focused on women and the textile industry, the story recently has grown more complex. Historians have uncovered the continued importance of domestic manufacturing throughout the nineteenth century. They also have emphasized the extent to which race and ethnicity as much as gender shaped women's relationship to work.

Even as the nation's economy changed and diversified, agriculture continued to be the principal occupation of most Americans. For women who continued to live in rural and agricultural settings in all regions, the daily content and rhythms of life varied remarkably little from that of their foremothers in colonial America. The westward movement uprooted people but not values; by and large, behavior, not attitudes, changed as Americans crossed the Allegheny and Appalachian mountains to homestead on the westward-moving frontier. But despite the continuity in gender roles, farm families, particularly those in New England, experienced change. Population growth, urbanization, and the rapidly developing transportation system promoted the commercialization of agriculture. In the hinterlands of larger towns and cities, farm women increased their involvement with the marketplace by expanding their butter-making enterprises. But only larger farms close to urban markets could take advantage of the demand for dairy products. As land prices in New England skyrocketed and people contemplated the high cost of moving westward, many farm families sought other sources of cash. Additionally, there were more consumer goods available for purchase, which enhanced the quality of life not only aesthetically but practically, as it cost less to buy than to produce cloth, furniture, and other items.

Outwork was one answer to the cash needs of farm families in the antebellum period. Some goods were manufactured in homes. Beginning in the 1820s, for example, Boston merchants imported palm leaf from the Caribbean and distributed it to country storekeepers in central Massachusetts and southern New Hampshire. The storekeepers split the leaf and put it out to local people, mostly women, who braided hats for sale in the South and Midwest. Payment often took the form of credit on store accounts. Tens of thousands of people earned money this way from the 1820s to the 1850s.

The social changes demanded by the Revolutionary War were regarded as temporary, and women's dependent and inferior status was codified in the new Constitution and in state regulations.

In several industries some steps in the production process remained hand operations while others were mechanized. Women in their homes would perform one or two steps in the process of production, while others working in shops or factories did the rest, often using machinery. Home manufacture thus complemented and indeed facilitated factory manufacture.

The boot and shoe industry developed in this way in the nineteenth century. Men in cities such as Lynn, Massachusetts, cut the leather, using hand tools early in the century and later operating machines. The pieces were shipped to the countryside, where women working in their homes sewed together the uppers of the shoe; their work was not mechanized and shifted from homes to factories until the 1870s. Once sewn together, the pieces were shipped back to Lynn, where men and women working in shops and factories completed the process. In its early stages, the textile industry also integrated home work with mill work. Beginning in the 1790s, spinning was the first step to move from the home into mills. Rather than drive textile production out of the household, spinning mills actually created greater demand for household labor as women were sought to weave on consignment for local mill merchants.

Despite the significance of the so-called Rhode Island system for the production of cloth and the sustenance of the rural family economy, its days were numbered as a method of organizing textile production. Power looms were introduced in textile mills in the 1820s. Once weaving was mechanized, all the principal steps in the production of cloth were integrated under one roof. The scale of operation increased dramatically. In contrast to the relatively small-scale spinning mills employing just several hundred people, by the 1830s the eight major textile firms in Lowell, Massachusetts, together employed six thousand workers. And in contrast to the composition of the spinning-mill labor force, which consisted largely of children and adult men, the people who worked in the new textile factories were the daughters, usually between fifteen and twenty-five years old, of farm families. The commercialization of agriculture and the increasing reliance by farm families on goods produced off their own farms, therefore, not only increased the need for cash but also created the free, mobile labor supply required by American industry. As the need for their labor in maintaining the home diminished, they followed their work out of the home into the factory, leaving rural communities too small or too remote to sustain much cottage industry.

The hiring policies of textile manufacturers beginning in the 1820s made women the first factory work force in the United States.

The hiring policies of textile manufacturers beginning in the 1820s made women the first factory work force in the United States. Two decades later, in 1840, 37 percent of American workers earned their living outside agriculture. Of these half-million people, 9 percent were in manufacturing; women still made up half of all workers in manufacturing. In some factories, women comprised 90 to 95 percent of the work force. The labor-recruitment strategy was novel enough but not completely unfamiliar or unexpected. In the early republic, advocates of industrialism urged the employment of women as a means to ensure the survival and dominance of American agriculture. Alexander Hamilton (1755–1804) argued that factory work would provide the farmer with a new source of profit and support "from the increased industry of his wife and daughters," while women and children would be "rendered more useful, and the latter more early useful, by manufacturing establishments, than they would otherwise be." Tench Coxe (1755–1824) was even more explicit. "Female aid in manufactures," he remarked, "prevents the diversion of men and boys from agriculture." The decision to hire young, native-born women thus met the labor requirements of textile manufacturers, but it also satisfied the interest of farm daughters in employment and addressed the concerns of farm families particularly and society generally about the future of agriculture in the new nation.

The parallel and overlapping intents and purposes of the various participants make it impossible to frame a simple analysis of the impact of economic change on women in the antebellum period. The Yankee farm girls who entered the textile factories confounded conventional attitudes about proper female behavior. Many were impelled not by poverty but by the desire for independence, the chance to enjoy urban amenities, and the opportunity to earn money for their own purposes. They evidently sought and appreciated the independence and freedom of living and working away from home. At least at the outset, they were not viewed and did not view themselves as an inferior or lower class. Indeed their sense of class equality with their employers as well as the importance of their employment prompted their collective resistance to what they perceived as the degradation of their labor. As manufacturers responded to increased competition by speeding up the pace of work, reducing wages, and intensifying discipline, women workers reacted by striking against wage cuts in the 1830s and mobilizing a movement for ten-hour laws in the 1840s.

There is also evidence that this group of American women experienced as much exploitation as liberation. The jobs generally were an interlude before marriage to a farmer rather than a long-term route to female independence. Most women took their first factory jobs in their late teens; most stayed less than five years, returning home to marry and become farm wives. The paternalistic labor-relations policies of the mill owners replicated and reinforced patriarchal family relations. Work itself was hierarchically gendered. All supervision in the factory was male; the occupational structure was organized according to a strict sexual division of labor; there was no upward mobility for women within the factory.

Although factory jobs paid more than any other form of female employment in the antebellum period, women received lower wages than men, even if they performed the same work. The rationale for women's low wages drew on old ideas, such as the notion that without employment, women might otherwise be idle; therefore, the public service performed by the factory owners for the community justified low wages.

The women working in the textile factories also were regarded not as heads of households but rather as supplementary wage earners not requiring more than the soon-to-be proverbial "pin money." Women's work, moreover, always had been regarded as intrinsically less valuable than men's, if only because women were not perceived as producing for the market. Despite the fallacious reasoning, the devaluation of women's work sustained the wage-determination policies of factory owners. The potential of factory work to liberate women from parental or male control was further blunted when it became stigmatized as unsuitable employment for middle-class women. Unwilling to redress the grievances of the Yankee farm girls, manufacturers replaced the departing and dwindling supply of native-born workers with Irish women and men in the late 1840s and 1850s. Once the factory labor force was predominantly foreign-born, the work was no longer acceptable for native-born women with certain class aspirations.

Descriptions of other women's work in the antebellum period further indicate the limited and ambiguous impact of economic change on women. The situation of female garment makers illuminates the persistent vulnerability of women. Before the advent of the sewing machine in the 1850s, the garment industry emphasized the outwork system in such cities as New York. After the sewing machine was invented, the location of production began to move "inside" to a factory setting, but outwork persisted, especially for such finishing steps as button-holing and button-sewing. As was the case in the boot and shoe industry during this period, inside garment workers were unmarried women and out workers were married women, often heads of households. The garment industry became one of the most important sources of employment for urban women. By 1860, one-quarter of the 100,000 employed women in New York City worked in manufacturing, and two-thirds of these worked in the garment trades alone. The work, however, was extremely low paid, required constant effort, and involved children as well as adults. As early as 1830, labor reformer Mathew Carey called out workers' wages and working conditions "harrowing truths." By the 1850s, the exploitation of these women had become firmly entrenched as contractors forced already low wages lower by unscrupulously cutting rates and withholding wages for allegedly inferior work. That the starving seamstress became something of a Victorian sentimentality indicates both growing class divisions in the United States and the class-specific character of female employment.

By the 1850s, most forms of female employment were considered inappropriate for middle-class women and girls. Not only did this Victorian gender ideology differentiate experience by sex, but it defined each sphere, domestic and public, by virtue of its separation from the other. Woman was defined as the embodiment of all that was contrary to the values and behavior of men in the marketplace, and thus, to the marketplace itself. The "pastoralization of housework," as Jeanne Boydston terms it, rendered invisible the economic dimension of women's work. Women performed their labor for reasons other than profit. For middle-class women, the ideology of separate spheres, therefore, proscribed their paid employment and reinforced their dependence on men. The exigencies of working-class life, however, meant that working-class women actually violated ideological injunctions. Unable or unwilling to remain in their homes, women ventured into the public sphere as seamstresses, vendors, washerwomen, servants, and prostitutes. In so doing, they encountered reformers, the majority of whom were female, who declared them poor mothers. Those who worked at home were even more vulnerable. Responsible for their own and their children's survival, desperate, and isolated, they developed neither the gender-consciousness nor class-consciousness that might have served as a resource against economic exploitation. As Mary Blewett has shown, divisions among working-class women were just as, if not more, important than divisions between working-class women and men. Unmarried inside workers often had a very different perspective on industry than did married out workers, and their clashes, such as during the 1860 shoemakers' strike, demonstrated another of the diverse and insidious consequences of economic development and ideological changes in antebellum America.

The experience of black women before the Civil War offers additional insight into the difficulty of assessing the subject of women and work in the antebellum period. The vast majority lived as slaves in the South. Although they lived on farms of varying size, they all generally did agricultural work as well as domestic work in their own quarters and in the Big House. In this regard, white masters did not respect any gender division of labor in African societies or in African American society. They also denied to their slaves the right or privilege of equal treatment: black women were expected to do work that white women were not. Black women as a result regarded their work differently depending on whether it benefited their masters or their own families and the slave community. The willingness and eagerness of black people before and after emancipation to act according to the precepts of Victorian gender ideology must not be understood (or dismissed) as mere mimicking of elite whites. Black women's attitudes toward domesticity actually did not indicate capitulation as much as resistance.

At the other end of the occupational spectrum from women in manufacturing and domestic service were women who taught, wrote, or sought entry into the male professions. The common-school reform movement created job opportunities for women with some education. Taking advantage of gender notions of appropriate wages, boards of education consistently paid women teachers one-third to one-half less than men. As new job opportunities opened for men and as teachers earned less money, women increasingly filled the gap. Comprising 25 percent of all teachers in 1860, women represented 60 percent of the labor force in 1880. The development of publishing offered some women work as writers in the middle period. Sarah Josepha Hale (1788–1879) edited *Godey's Lady's Book*; Catharine Beecher (1800–1878) and others wrote domestic-management treatises; and a host of novelists, including Harriet Beecher Stowe (1811–1896) and Catherine Sedgwick (1789–1867), gained a popular audience. The professionalization of medicine gradually diminished the role played by women as healers; male doctors took over areas of medicine customarily practiced by women, most notably obstetrics, and erected institutional barriers to women's efforts to continue the practice of medicine. Although all these occupations were generally closed to working-class women and thus were deemed acceptable for unmarried middle-class women, they, too, were shaped in significant ways by the mid nineteenth century's gender definition of labor.

Women's Work in the Gilded Age and the Progressive Era

The changes that occurred in the history of women and work between the Civil War and World War I are evident in statistics. In 1860, nearly all black women worked and approximately 10 percent of all white women held paying jobs. By 1880, 16 percent of all women were in the labor force. Twenty years later, the figure was 21 percent, and by 1920, 23 percent of all women were employed. The rising trend is clear, but there were important differences in women's labor force participation rates with respect to race and nativity. Black women's labor force activity was much greater than that of either native- or foreign-born white women until well into the twentieth century; 40 percent of black women in 1890 and 44 percent by 1920 were employed. In comparison, 15 percent of native-born white women and 20 percent of foreign-born white women held paying jobs in 1890. By 1920, white women's labor force participation had changed, too, although it is important to recognize that the work performed by many immigrant wives inside the home as well as the work of women on farms may not have been fully recorded by census enumerators. The proportion of foreign-born white women in the labor force remained about the same as in 1890, but the figure for native-born white women jumped to 23 percent, an increase that reflects the growth of white-collar and professional employment for women.

Several factors account for the increased extent of female labor force participation between 1860 and 1920. The increasing mechanization of the labor process in manufacturing created new and more job opportunities for women. The growth of business also increased the demand for women to fill clerical, retail, and other service jobs. Immigration increased dramatically between 1880 and 1915, while the birthrate among native-born whites decreased, enlarging the size of a working class dependent on female as well as male wage earning. The emergence of the women's professions created vocational space for middle- and upper-class women and further diversified, and divided, the female labor force along class lines.

In the late nineteenth and early twentieth centuries, the American working class was a large and diverse group. Millions of native-born whites, the majority of whom were female, migrated from farms and rural communities to towns and cities in search of work. Living largely in the South until World War I and denied access to manufacturing jobs on account of racism and the structure of the economy, blacks constituted another important component of the working class; black women generally worked as agricultural laborers or as domestic servants. First- and second-generation immigrants swelled the ranks of the working class in these decades, dominating the population of major northern cities and holding a variety of cultural attitudes toward female employment. Regardless of race, nativity, and geography, however, the American working-class family formed a wage-earning unit because the wages paid adult men were wholly inadequate to support a family. Low wages, unstable and seasonal employment, illness, and accidents all made more than one wage earner absolutely necessary to the survival of the working-class family in the Gilded Age and the Progressive Era. The importance of wage work for working-class women in this period is reflected in women's increasing share of the labor force. In 1820, women represented a mere 6 percent of all workers; in 1870, the proportion was nearly 14 percent; and by 1910, the figure had grown to 25 percent.

Working-class women worked in a variety of jobs. In manufacturing, the mechanization and subdivision of the labor process created jobs for women in such male-dominated trades as printing; in the growing industries of food processing and paper box making, which already employed women; and in wholly new industries like electrical-goods production. The service sector also expanded in this period. The growth of business required larger clerical staffs. At the same time, a technological revolution in office equipment and procedures introduced machines into the labor process, subdividing the work of the all-around clerk, reducing wages, and undermining the status of the job as a route to upward mobility in a firm. As men left clerical work, women filled the gap. Representing just 2.6 percent of all office workers in 1870, women increased their share of the clerical labor force to 19.4 percent in 1890 and 37.7 percent in 1910. The feminization of clerical work was paralleled by a similar process in retail trade. The growth of cities and the development of the department store created new space for women; women's share of the sales work force grew from barely 4 percent in 1870 to 25 percent in 1910. The growth in telephone communications mirrored developments in manufacturing, clerical work, and sales. By World War I, the feminization of work in the industry was so complete that women had come to account for almost 99 percent of the nation's more than 140,000 switchboard operators.

As men left clerical work, women filled the gap: Representing just 2.6 percent of all office workers in 1870, women increased their share of the clerical labor force to 19.4 percent in 1890 and 37.7 percent in 1910.

The new job opportunities in the manufacturing and service sectors of the economy prompted the decline of the relative importance of domestic and personal service for women. In 1870, three of every five employed women in the United States were domestic servants. By 1910, just one in four was so employed. The higher wages and greater freedom of nonservice jobs were important factors in the reorganization of the female labor force. Also significant were new living arrangements in the growing cities and new household technology that simplified housekeeping. Apartments were smaller than single-family homes, and well-off urban residents benefited most immediately from such improvements as gas lines, electricity, running water, and heated water, which reduced the need for servants. Ironically, because washing machines required steam heat and huge facilities until the 1910s, middle-class urban households commonly made use of commercial laundries; female employment in laundries multiplied several times over between 1870 and 1910, even as the demand for domestic servants to do such work declined.

Despite the increasing opportunities for employment, occupational segregation by sex continued to define and delimit the place of women in the American economy. A very high degree of job concentration in the female labor force characterized this period. In 1900, five million women worked in 294 of 303 occupations, but only 43 of these jobs had more than 5,000 women. By contrast, an impressive 90 percent of all working women were in jobs in which women predominated. Women were concentrated in low-paid unskilled or semi-skilled jobs in textile mills, garment centers, food-processing plants, tobacco factories, and commercial laundries; men were concentrated in mining, construction, transportation, and heavy industrial production. Even the jobs newly available to women in offices and department stores were soon feminized. Within industries, too, male and female jobs were differentiated. In the garment industry, women sewed, and men cut and pressed. In canneries, men processed the food, shipped the goods, and managed the operations; women washed bottles, scrubbed floors, sorted food, and labeled and filled jars. The gender division of labor defined women's work not only as fundamentally different than men's but also as less skilled or less difficult or less valuable. For these reasons, as well as the intense competition among women for a small number of jobs, women's wages always were lower than men's.

Although the dual labor market denied women access to jobs in all but a few occupational categories, there were in absolute terms more opportunities than ever before. The diversity within the female labor force has prompted debate about the kinds of choices women made about employment and how they made them. For example, although the proportion of married women in the labor force increased in these years, from 4.6 percent in 1890 to 10.7 percent in 1910, married women generally did not work for wages outside the home. The force of circumstances, however, could send married women out to work. Because of black men's limited employment opportunities, persistent poverty, and racism, black married women had high rates of labor force activity. In seven southern cities in 1880, 35 percent of married black women but only 7 percent of married white women were employed outside the home. Similarly, in cotton-textile towns, where male wage rates were very low and there was a tradition of female hiring, many married white women worked, comprising as much as one-third of the female labor force in the mills. Large urban areas with mixed economies offered women a variety of options. Married women could take in boarders or do piecework without leaving the home to work. The importance of the structure of opportunity makes it difficult to weigh or determine precisely the role of ethnic traditions. The behavior of single and married Italian women, whose labor force participation rates were lower than those of other immigrant women, suggests the power of cultural conventions. Irish women's expectations of late marriage and economic independence help explain their seeming preference for domestic work.

The impact of work on women themselves also has been the souce of much debate among historians of women and work in this period. The power and authority of occupational segregation by sex, some argue, meant that employment was not at all liberating for women and was actually a conservative experience that confirmed rather than challenged gender inequality. It was difficult for women to regard wage work as a route to independence and equality: wages generally were too low to support a woman living by herself, let alone a family; there was little if any upward mobility in the female labor market; and marriage and childrearing became an escape from onerous and unappealing work rather than a form of female oppression. Not disputing or minimizing the low wage and occupational status of working women, other scholars criticize the model of female victimization implicit in such interpretations. They emphasize instead the extent to which women's culture in and out of the workplace served as a resource rather than a trap for working women, enabling them to engage in many forms of resistance that ranged from individual and small group actions to union organizing, strike activity, and collective bargaining.

Generalizations about the impact of economic change and employment on middle-class women are also difficult to make or sustain. Because clerical jobs required a level of education that poorer women, particularly those who were foreign-born or black, likely did not have, they were deemed especially suitable for native-born or middle-class white women in the years between high school and marriage. Also significant was the development of the women's professions: teaching, nursing, library work, and social work. Either older vocations already feminized and now elevated to the status of professions, such as teaching, or new vocations shaped and staffed by educated women, like social work, the women's professions emerged in part because the male professions of law, religion, and medicine resisted the entrance of women. Women made some gains in medicine, but the male bastions of the ministry and the law remained relatively secure. In 1920, only 3 percent of American attorneys were female. By contrast, in 1900, women comprised 10 percent of the medical profession, although that was a peak figure that soon declined. The women's professions, however, also developed as an outlet for women who by talent, training, and inclination wanted to do something outside the domestic sphere. This was especially true for the first generation of college-educated women, who dominated the ranks of professional women in this period.

Although middle-class women were more fully integrated into the labor force in the late nineteenth and early twentieth centuries, they also felt the restrictions of occupational segregation by sex and gender hierarchy. Marriage and vocation, for example, were still regarded as incompatible and mutually exclusive for middle-class women. The women's professions defined themselves by extending women's sphere, "by suggesting that women were naturally inclined and equipped to care for the young, sick, or poor, or to serve as guardians of culture, or to guide young women on the path to adulthood." The women's professions usually were practiced in places that were homelike: hospitals, schoolrooms, libraries, colleges, and settlement houses. Described and justified as extensions of conventional notions of femininity, the women's professions were defined as the helping professions. For women, vocation meant service, not profit. Women professionals, therefore, received less pay, had limited upward occupational mobility, and their work was accorded less prestige than that of men professionals. By creating a lower-level professional caste, the women's professions helped by contrast to define the distinctive qualities of men's professions: high status, profit, and expertise.

The growing interest of the state in female employment indicates the persistence of Victorian gender ideology as a factor shaping the relationship of women to work. The positions taken by legislators and judges on the subject of state regulation of female employment illuminate attitudes toward gender, work, and politics—central concerns in the Gilded Age and the Progressive Era. Two Supreme Court decisions illustrate the political economy of gender in this period. The Illinois State Supreme Court rejected an appeal by Myra Bradwell of her exclusion from the Illinois bar in 1869 on the grounds that she was a married woman and therefore not a fully free agent capable of acting in the interest of clients in courts of law. The court, moreover, declared that the "hot strife of the bar, in the presence of the public," would destroy her femininity. The United States Supreme Court upheld the lower-court ruling in 1873, agreeing that the timidity and delicacy of the female sex "unfit it for many of the occupations of civil life." *Bradwell* v. *Illinois* was widely used thereafter to defend the exclusion of women from professional careers. In *Muller* v. *Oregon* in 1908, the Supreme Court ruled that an Oregon law limiting the number of hours women could be employed was constitutional because "the physical well-being of women becomes an object of public interest and care in order to preserve the strength and vigor of the race." In contrast to *Bradwell*, *Muller* could not reasonably call for the exclusion of women from wage labor. But like the earlier decision, the court's 1908 ruling affirmed the fundamental inequality of the sexes. Grounded in a gender conception of labor, both decisions rejected similar regulations of men's employment.

Protective legislation for women had complex consequences. In an era when organized labor was weak and not particularly friendly toward women workers, the state appeared to be the only ally in the effort to challenge their exploitation by employers. Working women themselves endorsed and sought female-labor laws as a means of improving the conditions of employment. Some women, however, were hurt by protective legislation: their income decreased or their work was speeded up; they were dismissed from jobs requiring night work or overtime; and employers (and unions) used the laws to deny women access to better-paying men's jobs. Once codified, the notion of female weakness and dependence embedded in the laws and the court decisions was difficult to extirpate.

The experience of working women during World War I revealed both how far they had come since the Civil War and how far they had yet to go. Women did gain access to men's jobs, although not on the scale that they would during World War II. The concept of equal pay for equal work gained some legitimacy as the National War Labor Board stipulated its incorporation into some agreements. The creation of the wartime Women in Industry Service of the Department of Labor, which was granted permanent status in 1920 as the Women's Bureau of the Department of Labor, institutionalized an advocate for women wage earners inside the federal government. And insofar as women's efforts during the war secured for them the elective franchise, then the period marked an advance. But the war also accelerated long-term trends in occupational segregation by sex and exacerbated tensions and conflict between women and men in workplaces. The limits of change during World War I indicate the power of tradition and continuity.

1920 to the Present

Despite its uneven rhythms, change rather than continuity appears most significant in the period since 1920. Broken up by the Great Depression and World War II, the trend toward greater female labor force participation by married women seems inevitable in light of social and demographic changes on the one hand and long-term developments in the structure of the economy on the other. The greater presence of women in professional jobs, another hallmark of the modern era, seems a less foregone conclusion and due as much to the politics of feminism as to objective factors and structural forces.

Historians debate the timing and causes of married women's massive entrance into the paid labor force. Some highlight the years between World War I and World War II, and especially the 1920s, offering evidence of the rising standard of living among middle-class Americans and their now-greater need for additional income. Others emphasize the impact of women's employment experience during World War II in changing attitudes about married women's work outside the home. Still other scholars stress post-1945 developments, particularly the tremendous expansion of the service sector, in explaining the transition from the working girl to the working mother. The preoccupation of historians with middle-class women has prompted recent efforts to examine diversity within the female labor force and to generate a specifically working-class history of women and work. In general, however, scholarship on women and work in the post-World War I period does not yet look much beyond 1950. Even the secondary literature on the period from 1920 to 1950 is less extensive quantitatively and qualitatively than for earlier historical periods. There is much room for new work on the modern era.

The image of the flapper dominates our view of the 1920s. The public's flirtation with her reveals a great deal about perceptions of and attitudes toward women and work at the onset of the modern era. Glamorous, economically independent, sexually free, and single, the flapper reflected the wide approval of employment for young, single women regardless of class. Indeed the flapper was typically represented as a middle-class office worker. But the reality of clerical work with its low wages and limited horizons meant that the flapper also reflected the widespread lack of support for female independence and married women's employment. The class-specific character of the flapper denied the extent to which working-class women had initiated the same behavior before World War I and then drew on the motifs of youth, consumption, and independence to mobilize labor militancy in southern textile towns during the 1920s. The middle-class orientation of the flapper also masked the exigencies of wage earning for working-class females in the 1920s. The atmosphere of consumerism and optimism that pervaded the seemingly prosperous 1920s obscured continuing realities of economic hardship for rural women and working-class families. The 1920s, then, consolidated prewar trends such as the feminization and expansion of clerical work and updated the image of the working woman rather than introducing any significant changes.

The Great Depression reversed, if only temporarily, whatever change might have been underway by 1930 in social attitudes toward women jobholders. Although women as well as men lost jobs, they remained nearly invisible. Public attention instead focused on men and the psychological consequences for them of the inability to fulfill the expected male role of provider. The extent of concern for the battered male ego meant that wives who worked felt responsible for their own husbands' trauma. Women also became society's scapegoat for unemployment. This view found expression in the popular opinion that women should not work and deprive men of jobs. "There are approximately ten million people out of work in the United States today," wrote Norman Cousins in 1939. "There are also ten million or more women, married and single, who are jobholders. Simply fire the women, who shouldn't be working anyway, and hire the men. Presto! No unemployment. No relief rolls. No depression." A few leaders and policy makers challenged these views, pointing out that men would not want the jobs held by women, that most married women who worked were supporting families as heads of households or members of two-income families, and that if the right to work was to be based on need, then single men should be fired, too. But their counterarguments were ineffective.

The view of women as illegitimate competitors in the labor market sustained campaigns throughout the 1930s to eliminate married women from the work force. The 1932 Federal Economy Act decreed that in the event of layoffs, married employees should be fired first if the spouse also held a job with the federal government. Although written in gender-neutral terms, in practice the act penalized women; some 1,600 married female employees were dismissed within a year of implementation of the act. Federal employees were not the only women vulnerable to discriminatory treatment. State and municipal governments pressed married women to leave civil-service jobs beginning in 1930 and 1931. Three-quarters of the school systems in the United States refused to hire married women as teachers during the 1930s; half the systems fired female teachers who married. Employers in the private sector fired women who married or introduced a means test for women workers seeking to obtain or retain jobs. As late as 1939, twenty-six state legislatures were considering bills that would explicitly bar married women from state jobs.

Yet whatever society did or tried to do, women did not give up their jobs or stop searching for work. Despite private and public policy and notwithstanding the persistent unemployment problem, women's proportion of the work force inched up slightly to 25.1 percent in 1940 rather than declined from their 24.3 percent share in 1930. Three factors account for this seeming anomaly, First, women were largely absent from industries that suffered most from the Depression. Construction, transportation, autos, and steel lost heavily and only slowly recovered, but light industry, where female manufacturing workers were concentrated, recovered more rapidly than heavy industry. Similarly, clerical and social-service jobs, in which women predominated, not only recovered more rapidly but actually expanded during the decade. Finally, jobs in domestic service, another female-dominated category, started to become available again as early as 1932 and 1933. Women like men lost their jobs and found it difficult to obtain reemployment, but the gender division of labor created different experiences for women and men.

In the early 1900s—an era when organized labor was weak and not particularly friendly toward women workers—that state appeared to be women's only ally in the effort to challenge their exploitation by employers.

No assessment of the 1930s is complete without consideration of the New Deal. On balance, New Deal legislation improved working conditions and labor standards and advanced the idea of gender equality but at the same time offered new official sanction to gender discrimination. The New Deal's relief efforts generally ignored women because they focused on the notion of a principal—male—breadwinner. Also, the public-works projects that generally characterized work relief benefited men to a much greater extent than women. The labor-standards provisions of the National Recovery Administration's industry codes codified sex-differentiated wage rates. After the National Industrial Recovery Act (1933) was declared unconstitutional in 1935, the principle of federal labor-standards was incorporated into the Fair Labor Standards Act (FLSA, 1938). Although the act's wage and hour provisions were gender neutral, it exempted groups, including farm workers, domestic servants, and food-service workers, that contained many women. The FLSA's prohibition of homework sought to eliminate exploitation and raise the wages of factory workers, but it also disadvantaged married women who sought to contribute to the family income while staying at home with their children. These and other New Deal policies demonstrate the invisibility of women workers generally and married women workers particularly in the 1930s. The Depression and its unemployment may have given new official sanction to married women's work outside the home if the family needed their wages. But women were still defined in relation to the family, not as individuals.

Made to feel guilty about their labor force activity during the Great Depression, women were encouraged, indeed exhorted, to enter the labor force and were made to feel guilty for not working outside the home during World War II. The dramatic change from blame to praise prompted many at the time to assert that the war would be a turning point in women's history, marking the beginning of a new era of female independence and gender equality. The significance of World War II for American women remains a central question in analyses of the female experience in this century. With one eye on the entrance of married women into the paid labor force and another on the resurgence of feminism in the 1960s, historians have evaluated the short- and long-term impact of the war, debating the extent of change and continuity in social, political, and economic terms. There is much grist for the mill. Nearly half of the eleven million women employed in the United States in 1940 worked in low-paid, low-status clerical, sales, and service jobs. Similarly, the 20 percent who worked in manufacturing were concentrated in a few low-paid industries, such as textiles and clothing. The demand for labor to meet the nation's wartime needs led to the greater employment of women in all areas of the economy. At the peak of women's wartime employment in 1944, the percentage of the female labor force in clerical, sales, and service jobs had declined to 36 percent, while the proportion employed in manufacturing had increased to 34 percent. Although the entrance of over 3 million women into manufacturing represented a significant 140 percent increase over the figure for 1940, perhaps the most striking change occurred in male-dominated basic industries, where the number of women increased by 640 percent. Other notable developments involved the entrance of married women, particularly those with young children, into the labor force and the upward occupational mobility of black women, who moved out of domestic work and into manufacturing jobs for the first time. Although many of these changes were only temporary, their impact on the attitudes and behavior of women and men, unionists and employers, and policy makers and political activists has been hotly contested.

The treatment accorded women workers during the war conveyed a double message. Women were supposed to work but only temporarily. The war was not supposed to institute any revolutionary or long-term changes in ideology and practice. Stressing patriotism as the sole motive for taking jobs, the War Manpower Commission and the Office of War Information glamorized war work to suggest that women would not lose femininity even if they took male jobs. The federal government for the first time assumed responsibility for constructing and operating facilities for the care of children of women working in defense industries, but programs were inefficiently administered, too few centers were constructed, and funds were canceled at the end of the war. Employers only reluctantly recruited women for jobs that were not traditional women's work. Faced with the inevitable, they tried to feminize the work, redrawing rather than subverting the boundaries of the gender division of labor and justifying lower wage rates as well. Employers, moreover, had no plans to retain wartime women employees after the war, as seniority provisions denying women rights to wartime jobs after reconversion to domestic production made clear.

At the peak of women's wartime employment in 1944, 36 percent of the female labor force held clerical, sales, and service jobs (down from about 50 percent in 1940), while 34 percent were employed in manufacturing (up from 20 percent in 1940).

The federal government's policy on equal pay reinforced the limited character of change during World War II. In November 1942, the National War Labor Board (NWLB) declared that women were to receive pay equal to men's if placed in the same or substantially similar jobs. In disputed cases, the board demanded the elimination of sex labels on jobs to more fairly deter-

A World War II poster encourages American women to join the workforce to fill in for men in uniform. The number of working women declined after war especially in the manufacturing sector.

mine wage rates. Many women received wage increases as a result of the order and the vigilance of unions in seeking its application. But the NWLB also allowed loopholes by which employers evaded the more radical implications of the government's equal-pay policy: the terms "heavy" and "light" were permitted as substitutes for "male" and "female" in job classifications; equal work was defined narrowly to avoid a general equalization of men's and women's wage rates and inevitable conflict over the idea of comparable worth. Although there were important exceptions, unions generally shared the view that women would be—or should be—only temporarily employed "for the duration."

Reconversion confirmed the temporary character of most wartime gains for working women. Voluntarily and involuntarily, many women left the labor force in 1945. Nationally, the proportion of women among all workers employed in basic industries fell from a wartime high of 25 percent in October 1944 to 13 percent in April 1947, a figure only four percentage points higher than that for 1939. Although the number of women in the labor force never fell to prewar levels and eventually exceeded wartime figures, the occupational distribution of women resembled that before 1941. Of the 17 million women working outside the home in 1950, 58 percent were employed in the clerical, retail, and service sectors; and the majority of the 19 percent employed in manufacturing worked in the textile and clothing industries. The war years left some indelible marks. The movement for pay equity survived and the wartime women's movement in unions regrouped and began pressing for the elimination of all forms of gender discrimination in employment. Although it had no singular or uniform impact, wartime employment also affected the attitudes and behavior of women and their families. The resurgence in the immediate postwar period of domesticity and conventional ideas about the proper place of women and men, however, all but overwhelmed the few challenges that survived the ravages of reconversion.

Economic and demographic forces, however, undermined all efforts to prevent change. After World War II, the size of the female labor force increased dramatically, the woman who did not work for wages became the exception rather than the rule, and the working wife became a standard feature of American life. Statistics illustrate the trends. In 1940, 25 percent of women over the age of sixteen worked outside the home. In 1960, 40 percent of women were working. By 1980, 51.5 percent of all adult women held jobs outside the home. Women's share of the labor force grew as well. Women were 29 percent of the work force in 1950, 35 percent in 1965, and 40 percent by 1975; in the 1980s, more than half of all workers were female. Equally significant was the growing importance of employment for married women. In 1940, just 15 percent of all married women worked for wages outside the home. In 1950, when married women represented half of all women in the labor force for the first time since the Census Bureau recorded such information, 21 percent of wives were employed. The percentage of married women at work increased another 10 percent in each of the next three decades; by 1980, 50 percent of all married women were employed outside the home. At first, most of the new married women workers were over the age of forty or forty-five, past the years when they would normally have children living at home. But the proportion of women with school-age children who held jobs also increased. Of women with children between the ages of six and seventeen, 25 percent in 1948, 40 percent in 1960, and 60 percent by 1980 were employed outside the home. In the past twenty years, women with preschool-age children also have established a significant presence in the labor force. At the end of the 1960s, one-third of women with preschool-age children worked outside the home. In 1980, 45 percent of women with children under the age of six were employed. By 1985, the figure already had increased to 53.4 percent, and it continued to rise.

Supply and demand explain the post-World War II trends. On the one hand, the greatest growth in the economy after World War II occurred in the service sector, creating ever-increasing numbers of white- and pink-collar jobs that were already defined as women's work. On the other hand, postwar inflationary trends increasingly made a second income necessary for families to achieve and, eventually, to maintain a middle-class life-style. These factors also account for the ideological shift that justified women's new role. As long as married women's labor-force activity could be considered supplementary and dispensable and in familial rather than individual terms, then it was deemed compatible with traditional notions of female dependence and domesticity. Many women considered themselves only temporarily employed until specific items were paid for—a home, a second car, a vacation, a child's college education. The gender division of labor reinforced the view of married women's wage earning as marginal and episodic. The traditionally low-paid, dead-end jobs available to women not only kept their contribution to family income low but were unlikely to inspire confidence as routes to independence.

As women realized that their lives would be shaped by a permanent relationship to work, however, they began to reevaluate their status in the labor market. Their interest in higher wages, upward occupational mobility, and greater job satisfaction was addressed in legislation forbidding discrimination on the basis of sex. Women's entrance into the skilled trades at one end of the occupational spectrum and their increasing share of the professions of law, medicine, and business at the other end illustrate the significance of the changes that have occurred in women's relationship to work since World War II. Having acquired identities as workers, women began to assess critically the obstacles to their achievement in the labor market. Their confrontation with gender inequality in the workplace occurred at the same time as gender relations came under scrutiny. For all these reasons, the extent of change in the past fifty years appears far greater than that which occurred over the course of the preceding century.

Yet the fundamental changes coexist with seemingly intractable dilemmas. The idea that women belong in the home has lost much of its material base, but women still are principally responsible for housework. The passage of antidiscriminatory legislation and the massive entrance of women into the labor force has not eliminated gender segregation in the labor market. Most women still work in female-dominated, low-paid jobs. Acknowledging occupational segregation by sex but rejecting the principle of gender hierarchy on which the division of labor is based, advocates of working women advance comparable worth as a strategy for redressing the persistent disparity between the wages of women and men. Pay equity, however, remains a distant goal for the mass of women in clerical and service jobs because the cost of closing the gap between men's and women's wages is great. Comparable worth also seems to offer little relief to women employed in industries characterized by intense competition, low profits, and low capital investment. Women in business and the professions complain that there is a "glass ceiling" that limits their access to the highest ranks. As the very term suggests, it will be difficult to break that invisible barrier until it has become visible, until women's complaints are recognized as legitimate. The final chapter in the history of women and work in America has not yet been written.

[See also Family Structures; Gender Roles and Relations; Household Labor; Labor: Colonial Times through 1820; Labor: The Jacksonian Era through Reconstruction; Labor: The Gilded Age through the 1920s; Labor: The Depression to the 1990s; Literacy; Minorities and Work; The Professions; Public Education; Women's Organizations.]

BIBLIOGRAPHY

Surveys and Overviews

Evans, Sara M. *Born for Liberty: A History of Women in America* (1989).

Kessler-Harris, Alice. *Out to Work: A History of Wage-earning Women in the United States* (1982).

Kleinberg, S. Jay. "Women in the Economy of the United States from the American Revolution to 1920." In *Retrieving Women's History: Changing Perceptions of the Role of Women in Politics and Society*, edited by S. Jay Kleinberg (1988).

Matthaei, Julie A. *An Economic History of Women in America: Women's Work, the Sexual Division of Labor, and the Development of Capitalism* (1982).

Weiner, Lynn Y. *From Working Girl to Working Mother. The Female Labor Force in the United States, 1820–1980* (1985).

Wertheimer, Barbara Mayer. *We Were There: The Story of Working Women in America* (1977).

Monographs and Essay Collections

Baron, Ava, ed. *Work Engendered: Toward a New History of American Labor* (1991).

Benson, Susan Porter. *Counter Cultures: Saleswonwn, Managers, and Customers in American Department Stores, 1890–1940* (1986).

Blewett, Mary H. *Men, Women, and Work: Class, Gender, and Protest in the New England Shoe Industry, 1780–1910* (1988).

Boydston, Jeanne, *Home and Work: Housework, Wages, and the Ideology of Labor in the Early Republic* (1990).

Cantor, Milton, and Bruce Laurie, eds. Class, *Sex, and the Woman Worker* (1977).

Cowan, Ruth Schwartz. *More Work for Mother: The Ironies of Household Technology from the Open Hearth to the Microwave* (1983).
Davies, Margery W. *Woman's Place Is at the Typewriter: Office Work and Office Workers, 1870–1930* (1982).
Diner, Hasia R. *Erin's Daughters in America: Irish Immigrant Women in the Nineteenth Century* (1983).
Dublin, Thomas. *Women at Work: The Transformation of Work and Community in Lowell, Massachusetts, 1826–1860* (1979).
Dudden, Faye E. *Serving Women: Household Service in Nineteenth-Century America* (1983).
Gabin, Nancy F. *Feminism in the Labor Movement: Women and the United Auto Workers, 1935–1975* (1990).
Greenwald, Maurine W. *Women, War, and Work: The Impact of World War I on Women Workers in the United States* (1980).
Groneman, Carol, and Mary Beth Norton, eds. *"To Toil the Livelong Day": America's Women at Work, 1780–1980* (1987).
Hall, Jacquelyn Dowd, et al. *Like a Family: The Making of a Southern Cotton Mill World* (1987).
Harris, Barbara J. *Beyond Her Sphere: Women and the Professions in American History* (1978).
Jensen, Joan M. *Loosening the Bonds: Mid-Atlantic Farm Women, 1750–1850* (1986).
Jensen, Joan M. *With These Hands: Women Working on the Land* (1981).
Jensen, Joan M., and Sue Davidson, eds. *A Needle, a Bobbin, a Strike: Women Needleworkers in America* (1984).
Jones, Jacqueline. *Labor of Love, Labor of Sorrow: Black women, Work, and the Family from Slavery to the Present* (1985).
Kessler-Harris, Alice. *A Woman's Wage: Historical Meanings and Social Consequences* (1990).
Melosh, Barbara. *"The Physician's Hand": Work Culture and Conflict in American Nursing* (1982).
Milkman, Ruth. *Gender at Work: The Dynamics of Job Segregation by Sex During World War II* (1987).
Milkman, Ruth, ed. *Women, Work, and Protest: A Century of Women's Labor History* (1985).
Morantz-Sanchez, Regina M. *Sympathy and Science: Women Physicians in American Medicine* (1985).
Stansell, Christine. *City of Women: Sex and Class in New York, 1798–1860* (1986).
Tentler, Leslie, Woodcock. *Wage-earning Women: Industrial Work and Family Life in the United States, 1900–1930* (1979).
Ulrich, Laurel Thatcher. *Good Wives: Image and Reality in the Lives of Women in Northern New England, 1650–1750* (1982).
Walsh, Mary Roth. *'Doctors Wanted: No Women Need Apply': Sexual Barriers in the Medical Profession, 1835–1975 (1977).*

— NANCY F. GABIN

WOMEN'S ORGANIZATIONS

Social reform has always played a major role in American history, and women contributed to this activity by building a vast array of voluntary organizations. During the nineteenth century, female reformers laid the groundwork for various organizations as they entered the public sphere, formed single-sex institutions, and gained the power to provide women with social and cultural resources. Initially these voluntary societies emerged as extensions of local charities and churches. As women changed their relationship to the state, these organizations set new goals. Even as "voluntary," associations, most organizations expanded their formal connections to government on municipal, state, and federal levels. Because of their persistent role as welfare agencies, women's organizations necessarily confronted a wide range of social problems; as class, ethnic, gender, and racial dimensions of the larger society changed, these groups modified how they defined their constituencies, reform practices, and policies. Women's organizations have always provided services to the community, but in significant ways these institutions also transformed the role and status of women in the American polity.

Women's Societies, 1800–1837

When women first organized benevolent societies after the revolutionary war, they were guided by a philosophy drawn from the eighteenth century. "Society" meant "polite intercourse" and "friendly visits" among the English well-to-do classes; it defined a special enclave that protected elites from the contamination of the world—or, the temptations of "the flesh, and the devil" (Spacks, p. 1). By adapting this view to a republican nation, reformers argued that societies could serve a civic and moral function in the public sphere. "Carnal talk," idleness, and fleshy indulgences could be mitigated through benevolent assistance and moral supervision. At the same time, the "love of society" instilled citizens with a sense of duty, trust, and discipline, all the essential virtues necessary for a young Christian republic.

In their most basic form, the early societies represented an extension of the moral functions of the church. In 1818, when the Colored Female Religious and Moral Society organized in Salem, Massachusetts, its constitution made moral guidance a paramount concern, resolving "to be charitably watchful over each other, to advise, caution and admonish" (Scott, p. 14). In addition to rigid rules of moral discipline, societies also encouraged self-control as another useful virtue for their female constituency. Economic duties also defined the link between the church and most local women's societies. Disestablishment made most congregations dependent upon the proceedings of these organizations to maintain church facilities. Cent, mite, and sewing circles all engaged in raising money for various church projects. In Virginia, both black and white societies retained strong ties to particular churches and their biblical heritage, identifying themselves as the "Dorcas Society" and the "Good Samaritan Sisters" (Lebsock, pp. 216–217, 223).

Female charitable societies directed most of their finances toward subsidizing the welfare needs of women in the community: They not only knitted for the poor but they also solicited money and goods to organize

Sunday schools, orphanages, workrooms, and asylum houses for training young girls as domestic servants. Programs often addressed the specific economic needs of women; for example, Mary Webb of Boston worked to establish a Fragment Society (1812) to clothe poor women and children, a Fatherless and Widows Society for indigent widows and abandoned women, and a Children's Friends' Society (1833) for caring for the babies of working women. In a practical way, these societies filled a gap in the available community services, especially when towns and cities reduced aid to the poor. These institutions also offered an alternative to the almshouses that benevolent workers felt represented the worst aspects of the "world."

One of the earliest societies in New York City was the Society for the Relief of Poor Widows with Small Children organized in 1797 by Isabella Graham (1742–1814) and her daughter, Joanna Bethune (1770–1860). This mother and daughter team laid the foundation for a series of organizations, such as the Orphan Asylum, which was incorporated in 1807 and given state funding as early as 1811. Following the War of 1812, they also established a House of Industry for women, and later they organized the Female Union Society for the Promotion of Sabbath Schools. Through her family and class connections, Bethune secured patronage from city officials. Through incorporation, these societies granted female directors legal powers not usually afforded women; they could own property, invest, sue, and manage institutions without the direct supervision of men. Most societies adopted standard business practices, assigning "managers" to visit people and "providential committees" to allocate goods and money (Scott, p. 14).

Benevolent women never actually claimed rights to political powers. Instead, they claimed the duty to protect women, especially such "respectable women" as widows, orphans, and deserving daughters of the middling classes. Much of the early charity work was aimed at widows, a group that symbolized the precarious nature of married women's economic dependency on men. Implicitly, then, benevolent women realized that the "protection" of women could not be left in the hands of men alone. Prodigal husbands or greedy fathers could destroy a family, leaving even virtuous women destitute. Benevolent women valued and protected women and they learned to utilize the available community resources for moral and material purposes.

Women's Societies, 1837–1860

During the 1830s women shifted the scope and purpose of their organizations from local benevolence to collective campaigns for the moral regeneration of the nation. In response to the message of evangelical religion, female reformers replaced the older philosophy of guardianship with a new focus on transforming human behavior and attitudes. Conversion became the goal of most antebellum societies; members were called upon to spread the gospel of reform while they battled "sin" in all segments of society. Through the distribution of tracts and petitions, female reformers shaped "moral opinion" in a more visible and public way than their benevolent predecessors. At the same time, the eradication of sin called for more radical measures: the passage of more stringent laws, the holding of public events such as rallies and fairs, and the aggressive condemnation of a new enemy—immoral and unrepentant men.

What made this new generation of reformers "militant" was their explicit attack on male authority. When the New York Female Moral Reform Society formed in 1834, the organizers sought to eliminate prostitution through old and new measures: they would protect and "reclaim" their "fallen sisters" and they would "create a public sentiment" against the sexual double standard. Moral reformers called for the public humiliation of men who seduced "innocent" female victims, advocating criminal prosecution or exclusion from the company of "all virtuous female society" (Smith-Rosenberg, p. 201).

This new zeal reflected changes in the class composition of female reformers. Unlike the benevolent matrons with ties to elite members of the government, these moral reformers came from the artisan and middling ranks of society. Such class tensions emerged in their literature, which often portrayed the villains as powerful and influential men and their victims as women from poor but respectable families. Hostility toward aristocratic privileges emerged as a theme of other reforms, like temperance, in part because it reflected the social upheaval wrought by economic dislocation. One catalyst for the Daughters of Temperance was the depression of 1839–1843 that left many families destitute. For women, intemperate behavior came to symbolize male seduction, which changed "a kind and affectionate father" into a "terror" who abused his wife and children and left them impoverished (Tyrell, p. 139).

Like moral reform and temperance, the slavery issue aroused female reformers' sense of moral outrage, and, as in other causes, the unrepentant male slave-owner, driven by avarice, lust, and selfishness, was cast as the principal villain. Called to pray, write, and speak against this national sin, antislavery women aimed to battle slavery through education. By spreading the gospel of reform, they would reach the hearts and minds of American women. Indeed, they believed that the power of women's sympathies for the "oppressed female slave" could move the entire nation toward emancipation.

If salvation from sin was the end, then education provided the means for saving the American masses. Consequently, education loomed large as another major concern of antebellum female reformers.

Teaching became a sacred vocation, and women as well as men were needed for this redemptive work. In 1837, Mary Lyon (1797–1849) established Mount Holyoke Female Seminary on principles that differed from the previous female academies. Lyon's fund-raising strategies reflected her evangelical roots; she went door-to-door distributing circulars and recruiting pledges for her school. Lyon also believed that not only the state but also the "Christian public" should finance her institution. That same public should supply students and converts from the "daughters of the church." By making Mount Holyoke a "school for Christ," Lyon also felt its goal was to "cultivate the missionary spirit among its pupils" (Sklar, pp. 198–199). As a result, her graduates would spread the gospel of moral reform while building new schools and forming a national network of female reformers.

The antebellum period, then, saw the rise of women's public activism as the basis for their organizations. Female reformers combined the evangelical quest for moral perfectionism with the democratic ethos of nation building. Whereas women shared many of the same techniques as their male peers, especially in their use of the media, they also surpassed men in such endeavors as raising money through fairs and collecting subscriptions. Antislavery women transformed the meaning of collecting petitions by organizing the first national political campaign that included the signatures of both men and women. Women not only contributed their "works" to these various reform causes, but their "words" in identifying how gender constructed power relations. Within this new climate, middle- and working-class women claimed reform as their arena for public service and political change.

Women's Associations, 1860–1890

WOMEN'S WAR RELIEF. The Civil War brought a new generation of women reformers into the field of benevolent work. These women were less concerned with moral reform than with coordinating a quasi-military organization for the relief of soldiers. In the North, the Woman's Central Association of Relief (WCAR) in New York organized in 1861; it recruited women of the urban elite with professional and business rather than evangelical aspirations. Unlike their antebellum counterparts, this new cohort of women sought a "partnership" with the government and they established close working relations with men involved in the United States Sanitary Commission.

Confederate women, like Union supporters, organized a variety of local sewing circles (Thimble Brigades in the South), Soldier's Friends Associations, and societies for relief. In 1862, Georgia women founded the Ladies Gunboat Association to collect funds for dwindling military supplies. In the North, civilian aid assumed a rigid and hierarchical structure. Local societies sewed, canned goods, and prepared packages; the regional offices collected the supplies and sent them to railroad stations; and the central office distributed the items to agents and hospitals on the front. In 1863, the WCAR adopted the Boston Plan for Sectional Divisions, which called for associate managers to serve as intermediaries between the national and local branches. Managers kept the central office abreast of "the state of affairs in her neighborhood" (Ginzberg, p. 152). Success depended on the distribution of information as well as supplies, which required managers to keep detailed records and to maintain constant correspondence with their Washington supervisors. Such efficiency assumed a corporate model; good business management characterized women's war work.

After the war, northern women sought formal access to state governments through appointments to the charity boards. In 1872, Louisa Lee Schuyler (1837–1926) organized the State Charities Aid Association, which recruited city professionals and elites, promoted expert supervision of charity services, employed associate managers and visiting committees, and kept detailed records of recipients and resources. Clearly, the climate had changed in the postwar era, yielding both positive and negative results. Although these women paved the way for a more bureaucratic charity system, they also advocated a rather narrow vision of moral reform. Middle-class leaders of the New York Charities Association and state boards had little sympathy with alternative methods of reform, such as the Catholic Sisters organizations, which vied with Protestant groups for limited state resources. By imitating men so well, charity reformers often placed efficiency above the particular welfare needs of women, a strategy that aided the vast growth of the corporate state in the aftermath of the Civil War.

WOMEN'S MISSIONS AND THE CHRISTIAN TEMPERANCE UNION. The missionary zeal of evangelical reform had not died by the postwar years. In 1861, Sarah Doremus (1802–1877) a leader in the Dutch Reformed Church, organized an ecumenical Woman's Union Missionary Society, which survived the war and laid the groundwork for the various denominational societies. Congregational, Methodist, Presbyterian, and Baptist women all formed foreign missions between 1869 and 1871. Combining local meetings with a national newspaper, the mission societies resembled their antebellum models. What had changed was a new sense of American exceptionalism and expansion that mission women both embraced and critiqued. Although they advocated the spread of Christianity in distant lands, they noted the harsh consequences of imperialism unmediated by women's religious influence. Mission women evoked a woman's point of view when evaluating foreign cultures; they focused on the troubling similarities between male authority afar and at home. Yet they did not escape their own cultural heritage, producing a literary and political message that combined exoticism with feminine empathy for their "heathen sisters."

The very same organizational techniques and gospel message would emerge in the Women's Christian Temperance Union (WCTU), one of the most influential religious and political movements of the nineteenth century. Although temperance was not new, the WCTU made the campaign a woman's enterprise. Organized in 1873–1874, the initial crusaders adopted a militant style; they visited hotels and saloons, praying and singing, while asking the owners to stop selling alcoholic beverages. What began as revival quickly changed into a well-coordinated national campaign that drew women from different regions and denominations. The WCTU adopted the women's mission pattern for mobilizing a large, but locally based, network of female laborers. Early programs gained grass-roots support by signing pledges and calling for members to hold mass meetings. At an early stage, however, the WCTU functioned as both a "praying society" and an "activist organization" (Bordin, p. 13). It retained a stable and professional corps of national leaders and adopted a broad-based policy of "Do Everything" that gave autonomy to local unions. Like the mission movement, the WCTU relied on an extensive communication network and published its own newspaper, the *Union Signal*, whose circulation grew to 14,000 by 1884.

By imitating men so well, charity reformers often placed efficiency above the particular welfare needs of women, a strategy that aided the vast growth of the corporate state in the aftermath of the Civil War.

Frances Willard (1837–1898), serving as president of the national movement from 1879 until her death, gained prominence as a traveling ambassador and lecturer. In advance of most local union members, Willard combined the goals of temperance and suffrage under the rubric of "Home Protection." By praying and working for legislation, Willard argued that temperance women could preserve the tranquillity of the home. By adopting the theme of "maternal love," Willard assigned to women a special destiny as the divinely chosen guardians of human morality. Ultimately, the WCTU attempted to transform the state and civil society according to their vision of maternal virtue. To protect the home, women had to instill certain feminine ideals into the very fabric of all local, state, and national institutions.

YOUNG WOMEN'S CHRISTIAN ASSOCIATION. Another kind of home mission work emerged in the cities during the nineteenth century. The Young Women's Christian Association (YWCA) started as a prayer society and blossomed into clubs, boardinghouses, and classes for working women. In 1858, the New York Ladies' Christian Association held prayer meetings in a Manhattan skirt factory and soon established a residence for twenty-one young women. Similar organizations formed in other cities, as founders embarked on city missionary work that aimed to provide "the influence and protection of a Christian home" for single laboring women (Scott, p. 104). Grace Hoadley Dodge (1856–1914), one of the leaders of the movement, established the 38th St. Working Girls' Society in 1884; by the following year, clubs in other cities joined forces to form the Working Girls' Association of Clubs. During the next ten years, nineteen clubs existed in New York City alone.

At first the clubs provided inexpensive housing for working women, but the goals of the association expanded to include cheap amusements, libraries, and gymnastic facilities. The YWCA sharply distinguished itself from charity facilities that provided welfare for the poor and instead it advocated self-support and self-improvement among working women. Instruction in vocational training was combined in most working girls' clubs with more traditional classes in home economics.

Although the organizers of the YWCA sought to cross class barriers, they did not always succeed. A gulf existed between working women and their middle-class benefactors, especially by the 1890s when factory women attempted to push the clubs toward labor activism. Too much supervision over working women's behavior also became a point of contention. Even the domestic ideology offered by YWCA leaders had little appeal for working women, in part because it suited middle-class and non-working-class households. And despite their appeals to diversity, the YWCA focused on American-born workers and rarely extended its services to foreign-born women. As a result, the YWCA may not have achieved all of its goals, but it did create an organization that recognized working women as actors and not simply as passive recipients of charity assistance.

WOMEN'S CLUB MOVEMENT. Working girls' clubs differed from the more prominent branch of the Club movement that began with the New England Women's Club and Sorosis in 1868. Through the initiative of Jane Croly (1829–1901), Sorosis aimed to provide an all-women environment that encouraged "self-culture" among its membership. A place for educated women "hungry for the society of women," Sorosis established four committees on literature, art, drama, and music. Although Croly believed that women shared a special appreciation for "culture for culture's sake," she believed that club women should study culture's effects upon the welfare of women. At first, Sorosis functioned as an elite "think tank," recruiting the most talented professional women from the city. As a "kind of freemasonry among women," Croly hoped to establish a neutral gathering place for different reformers, making the club a forum for unity and discussion (Blair, pp. 20, 23, 25, 28, 31).

Sorosis meant "aggregation," and the New York club attracted women already involved in other reform activities. The New England Women's Club (NEWC) was active from its inception in political causes, nor did the group limit its membership to women alone. Ednah Dow Cheney (1824–1904), one of the founders, had been active in a variety of campaigns before the club's formation: she started the Boston School of Design (1851); served as secretary and president of the New England Hospital for Women and Children (1862); and she organized a teacher's program for the Freedmen's Bureau from 1867 to 1875. Perhaps the major advance of the NEWC was the organization of the Women's Education and Industrial Union in 1877, under the direction of Dr. Harriet Clisby. "Industriousness," not merely self-culture, served as their motto. They produced several reform experiments, including a women's store, lunchroom, health clinic, job registry, and legal assistance service (Blair, p. 80).

From the beginning, Croly sought to nationalize and centralize the club movement, calling a Woman's Parliament in 1869, forming the Woman's Congress and Association for the Advancement for Women in 1873, and organizing the General Federation of Women's Clubs in 1890. At the same time, black middle-class women organized the National Association of Colored Women (NACW) in 1896, the first national organization of black club women, which combined two older groups: the National Federation of Afro-American Women (organized under the aegis of the New Era Club of Boston) and the National League of Colored Women. Although Josephine St. Pierre Ruffin (1842–1924) was the guiding force of the Boston black women's club, Mary Church Terrell (1863–1954) would inherit the leadership of the national organization. Like Sorosis, the NACW served as an informational clearinghouse of ideas from the "talented tenth" of the black community. The NACW also shared the domestic philosophy of the WCTU and the white women's club movement. Terrell advocated specific reforms that recognized the economic needs of black working women. Kindergartens, day nurseries, and mother's clubs became the principle items of their agenda. Their demand for "Homes, more homes, better homes, purer homes" reflected a specific urgency not found in the white women's club movement (Jones, p. 26). It indicated that black club women had to contend with racism as a force that permeated all aspects of the black community.

Through the end of the nineteenth century, clubs served a variety of purposes for their members. On the local level, women used the clubs for cultural activities, such as reading and study groups. Class status, religion, and even professional affiliation separated the membership of clubs in most communities and cities. Within each region or municipality, the clubs assumed a wider role in supporting community projects, such as the funding of memorials, playgrounds, and libraries. Black club women often focused their efforts on establishing health facilities, including hospitals and health clinics. Yet the clubs also served a third and decidedly political function: they provided a female training ground in "civics" for future political activists. By the 1890s, most clubs had joined forces with other organizations for the promotion of legislative and political reforms. Like the WCTU, club members claimed that society was an extension of the home and women had a special vocation for "Home Protection" and "Municipal Housekeeping."

Women's Associations, 1889–1930

SETTLEMENT HOUSES. While the clubs gained national prominence in the 1890s, another reform experiment emerged on the urban landscape, the Settlement House. The best-known settlement was Hull-House, organized by Jane Addams (1860–1935) and Ellen Gates Starr (1859–1940) in 1889, which was modeled on Toynbee Hall, a settlement formed by male university students in East London. By creating a distinctive "colony" of female reformers, the settlement house served both "objective" and "subjective needs," in the words of Addams: it offered social services to the urban poor, mainly the foreign-born population, while it created a unique retreat for educated women with professional aspirations (Rousmaniere, p. 47). Most settlements duplicated the unique female culture offered in the women's seminaries and colleges. As a female community, Hull-House provided its members with an alternative to a more traditional family life. Equally important, as a separate female institution, the settlement offered women a supportive base within the larger community of Progressive reformers. Here women could establish networks with male activists, business leaders, and government officials without losing their influence as female activists.

Initially, the settlements resembled the urban clubs, offering literary and cultural activities. Soon the settlement became a more complex kind of reform agency that provided services for working women, day care for their children, rooms for social and political gatherings, and a training ground for educated women interested in the scientific study of urban problems. By 1910, Hull-House had expanded into a vast array of buildings filling an entire city block. Soliciting funds was part of Addams's duties as an administrator, and she served as a link between the settlement's workers and its financial backers. Similarly, but for different ends, the settlement mediated between the urban population and city institutions. It worked to bring needed services into the community while protecting the neighborhood from the encroachment of the ward bosses. Addams believed that Hull-House, as a model social democracy, integrated the political, economic, and cultural life of the city. In a unique way, the settlements placed a premium on human solidarity and diversity, recognizing that together the residents and reformers created a multicultural experiment in political democracy.

As a female community, Hull-House, a Settlement House organized by Jane Addams and Ellen Gates Starr in 1899, offered women a supportive base within the larger community of Progressive reformers.

WOMEN'S LEAGUES. Interest in the problems facing working women led reformers in new directions during the late nineteenth and early twentieth century. Middle-class women recognized their prominent role as consumers and they mobilized their concerns into a new organization that would improve working conditions for women and children. Under the guidance of Maud Nathan (1862–1946) and Josephine Lowell (1843–1905) the Consumers' League was formed in 1890 in New York City. Its primary goal was to convince consumers to patronize those department stores that adhered to the "Standards of a Fair House," a guideline published by the League that promulgated fair wages, hours, and safe working conditions. As a pressure group, the League created a "White list" that identified those stores that met the League's standards. In 1899, the National Consumers' League was organized and spawned the formation of branch groups across the United States and abroad.

The National Consumers' League was not always successful in gaining the support of the labor unions. In 1904, the use of product labels triggered a clash with the International Ladies Garment Workers' Union. Yet another organization, the New York Women's Trade Union League (WTUL), made a more concerted effort to work with unions. Organized in 1903, the WTUL promoted the advantages of unions for female workers, supported the formation of several women's trade unions, and worked to convince male labor organizers to support their efforts. What made the WTUL different from other middle-class organizations was its commitment to unionization. Its other unique feature was the prominence of working-class women in leadership positions. By 1907, as the initial constitution had stipulated, three of the five board officers were working-class activists. One key member of the board was Leonora O'Reilly (1870–1927), a settlement worker and an early labor organizer for the Knights of Labor. The WTUL did not achieve a perfect alliance between working- and middle-class members. Nor did the leadership secure a harmonious relationship with male unionists. But the WTUL did gain publicity for a large number of strikes, such as the New York garment strike of 1909–1910. Similar to other women's organizations, the WTUL generated public opinion, offering a "radically" different perspective from "the accepted opinions and ideals of men" (Dye, p. 285).

Similarly, the Women's International League for Peace and Freedom (WILPF), formed from the membership of the Woman's Peace Party in 1915, followed this tradition and extended its influence into the arena of world politics and foreign policy. One of its principal organizers was Jane Addams, whose devotion to peace and international tolerance had its roots in her theories of social democracy. In 1899, Addams began lecturing against American imperialism, and in 1907 she published her lectures as *Newer Ideals of Peace.* Addams sought to change the meaning of heroism from a masculine and destructive principle to one based on harmony and justice, a shift she claimed was "the moral equivalent of war" (Degen, p. 20). The League symbolized the integral relationship between women's values and political action, demonstrating the view shared by most nineteenth-century reformers that women's influence could transform the world. The WILPF assumed that if women held more influence in the state, both domestic and foreign policy would change. Ultimately, the goal of the WILPF was to replace military conflicts with arbitration. Although this call for peace had little sway at the time, Addams's philosophy would reappear in later organizations and platforms, such as the United Nations and the Universal Declaration of Human Rights (1948).

ALUMNAE ASSOCIATIONS AND BLACK SORORITIES. The women's college associations and black women's sororities represented the last major advance in middle-class women's organizations during this period. Regional college associations first appeared in the Northeast and West in the 1880s, and eventually spread to the South in 1903. A national alliance organized in 1921 when the American Association of University Women formed. Both regional and national associations worked for educational legislation, to promote state teachers' pensions, uniform school attendance, and child labor laws. Conscious of their status as women and professionals, the college association advocated equal wages for women, calling for a "living wage" for college-educated employees (Talbot and Rosenberry, p. 229). One of its founders, Marion Talbot (1858–1948), represented a new generation of modern professional women. Rejecting the conventional assumptions about women's nature, Talbot believed that women could not lay claim to any unique moral capacities. Rather than segregating the sexes, Talbot believed in coeducation and equal opportunities for women. Based on their educational experiences, the college association members hoped to create a new identity for professional women.

White and black sororities sought to supplement the college curriculum by educating women for their future roles as citizens. As a training ground for civic leadership, sororities advocated social responsibility and self-government. The first white sororities appeared in the late nineteenth century, and they established scholarship programs, funds for the creative arts, and social welfare projects. Typically, the female Greek societies followed the pattern of male fraternities: they built chapter houses, secured an endowment fund, published an official magazine, and organized alumnae chapters in major cities. In 1902, Alpha Phi summoned the Intersorority Conference that subsequently reorganized as the National Panhellenic Conference (Baird, p. 393).

Black women's sororities combined professionalism with their continued support for "racial uplift" and political activism against racism. Alpha Kappa Alpha Sorority, founded in 1908 at Howard University, provided funding and trained personnel for the campaign against lynching in 1934, followed by a summer school for rural teachers and a nutrition

The Young Women's Christian Association begun as a prayer society, blossomed into clubs, boardinghouses, and classes for working women. Here a group of young women eat together at a weekly YWCA girls club supper in the 1950s.

clinic in 1940. The Black Public Health Movement gained much of its support from sororities, since many of the public health nurses used this organization as a communication and recruitment network.

These professional associations defined the trends in women's organizations. In the coming decades, women active in the leagues, clubs, and professions paved the way for both white and black women to play a significant role in state and even federal government during the New Deal era. Certain traditions continued as women's organizations focused on civic education, business policies, social welfare, issues of foreign relations, and the status of women. As middle-class women moved to the suburbs following World War II, local, municipal, and educational issues again became the preserve of women's reform efforts. Both environmentalism and antinuclear war sentiments drew on earlier peace efforts and conservation campaigns as well as the intellectual contributions of academic women like biologist Rachel Carson (1907–1964; author of *Silent Spring,* 1962).

Although the National Organization for Women, a public pressure group mobilized in 1966, focused on securing women's civil rights, it also endorsed broader grass-roots activities for women's liberation.

A new wave of women's organization-building reemerged during the 1960s and 1970s. Sparked by the civil rights movement, female members of Students for a Democratic Society (SDS) participated in the foundation of Economic and Research Action Projects (ERAP) in order to build ties to the "urban poverty sector" (Sealander and Smith, p. 332). Organizing around two women's issues—welfare and schools—female activists helped mobilize Mothers for Adequate Welfare (MAW) and Citizens for Adequate Welfare (CUFAW), both of which contributed to the success of the National Welfare Rights Organization (NWRO) (Evans, pp. 142–143). Welfare mothers demonstrated a new militancy as active members of these groups; between 1967 and 1969, they staged sit-ins, demonstrations, and regular disruptions at welfare offices.

Middle-class women later applied the same techniques in protesting sexual discrimination against white-collar workers. By 1977, the National Women's Employment Project (NWEP) linked together a network of urban organizations that investigated businesses, produced case studies, and publicized violations of antidiscrimination laws (Sealander and Smith, pp. 325–327). Initially, the NWEP gained support from the federal government. The Presidential Commission on the Status of Women, for example, supported the passage of the 1963 Equal Pay Act. Public-pressure groups were needed to enforce the new federal legislation. One such group was the National Organization for Women (NOW), which mobilized in 1966 "to bring American women into full participation in the mainstream of American society *now*" (Woloch, p. 513). Although NOW focused on securing women's civil rights, it endorsed the broader grass-roots activities for women's liberation. In addition to establishing consciousness-raising groups, feminists turned to the federal government to fund a variety of women's centers. Often providing "a smorgasbord of services," centers like the one started in Dayton, Ohio, provided self-help classes, advocacy and referral services, political and personal counseling, a day-care cooperative, and a meeting place for a rape task force and a lesbian organization, Sappho's Army (Sealander and Smith, pp. 325–327).

Building on well-established traditions of women's organization-building, feminists also increased their dependence on federal funding, often curtailing the growth of a viable grass-roots base of community support. While the Dayton women's center used federal Model City monies, it relied less on dues and local funding from churches and other private institutions. Resistance to the tradition of women's "volunteerism" surfaced in NOW; in the 1970s, it challenged the pattern as "an extension of unpaid housework and women's traditional roles in the home" (Gittell and Shtob, p. 577). This philosophy, coupled with the decline in federal resources, eclipsed some of the more ambitious programs and goals of the women's movement. Even with these setbacks, women demonstrated their commitment toward building organizations, such as abortion clinics, rape-counseling centers, and abused-women's shelters, thus continuing the tradition of mobilizing women to solve women's welfare, economic, and political problems.

[See also Fraternal Organizations; Gender Roles and Relations; Nightlife; Women and Work.]

BIBLIOGRAPHY

General Works

Blair, Karen J. *The History of American Women's Voluntary Organizations, 1810–1960* (1989).

James, Edward T., Janet Wilson James, and Paul S. Boyer, eds. *Notable American Women, 1607–1950.* 3 vols. (1971).

Scott, Anne Firor. *Natural Allies: Women's Associations in American History* (1991).

Trattner, Walter I., ed. *Biographical Dictionary of Social Welfare in America* (1986).

Woloch, Nancy. *Women and the American Experience* (1984).

Antebellum Societies, 1800–1860

Boylan, Anne M. "Women and Politics in the Era Before Seneca Falls." *Journal of the Early Republic* 10 (1990): 363–382.
Hewitt, Nancy A. *Women's Activism and Social Change: Rochester, New York, 1822–1872* (1984).
Hobson, Barbara Meil. *Uneasy Virtue: The Politics of Prostitution and the American Reform Tradition* (1987; repr. 1990).
Lebsock, Suzanne. *The Free Women of Petersburg: Status and Culture in a Southern Town, 1784–1860* (1984).
Sklar, Kathryn Kish. "The Founding of Mount Holyoke College." In *Women of America: A History*, edited by Carol Ruth Berkin and Mary Beth Norton (1979).
Smith-Rosenberg, Carroll. "Beauty, the Beast, and the Militant Woman: A Case Study in Sex Roles and Social Stress in Jacksonian America." In *A Heritage of Her Own: Toward a New Social History of American Women*, edited by Nancy F. Cott and Elizabeth H. Pleck (1979).
Spacks, Patricia M. "The Talents of Ready Utterance: Eighteenth-Century Female Gossip." In *Women and Society in the Eighteenth Century*, edited by Ian P. H. Duffy (1983).
Tyrrell, Ian R. "Women and Temperance in Antebellum America, 1830–1860." *Civil War History* 28, no. 2 (1982): 128–152.
Vail, Albert L. *Mary Webb and the Mother Society* (1914).
Walters, Ronald G. *American Reformers, 1815–1860* (1978).
Wellman, Judith. "Women and Radical Reform in Antebellum Upstate New York: A Profile of Grassroots Female Abolitionists." In *Clio Was a Woman: Studies in the History of American Women*, edited by Mabel E. Deutrich and Virginia C. Purdy (1980).

Women's Associations

Blair, Karen J. *The Clubwoman as Feminist: True Womanhood Redefined, 1868–1914* (1980).
Bordin, Ruth. *Woman and Temperance: The Quest for Power and Liberty, 1873–1900* (1981).
Brumberg, Joan Jacobs. "The Ethnological Mirror: Evangelical Women and Their Heathen Sisters, 1870–1910." In *Women and the Structure of Society*, edited by Barbara J. Harris and JoAnn D. McNamara (1984).
Bussey, Gertrude, and Margaret Tims. *Pioneers for Peace: Women's International League for Peace and Freedom, 1915–1965* (1965).
Davis, Allen F. "The Women's Trade Union League: Origins and Organization." *Labor History* 5, no. 1 (1964).
Degen, Marie. *The History of the Woman's Peace Party*. The Johns Hopkins University Studies in Historical and Political Science, 57, no. 3 (1939).
Dye, Nancy Schrom. "Creating a Feminist Alliance: Sisterhood and Class Conflict in the New York Women's Trade Union League, 1903–1914." In *Our Sisters: Women in American Life and Thought*. 2d ed. (1976).
Ginzberg, Lori D. *Women and the Work of Benevolence: Morality, Politics, and Class in the Nineteenth-Century United States* (1990).
Gittell, Marilyn, and Teresa Shtob. "Changing Women's Roles in Political Volunteerism and Reform of the City." *Signs* (Supp.) 5 (1980): 567–578.
Green, Fletcher M. "Women of the Confederacy in War Times." *Southern Magazine* 2 (1935): 16–20, 47–48.
Hill, Patricia R. *The World Their Household: The American Woman's Foreign Mission Movement and Cultural Transformation, 1870–1920* (1985).
Jones, Beverly W. "Mary Church Terrell and the National Association of Colored Women, 1896–1901." *Journal of Negro History* 67 (1982): 20–33.
Nathan, Maud. *The Story of an Epoch-making Movement* (1926).
Parker, Marjorie H. *Alpha Kappa Alpha Sorority, 1908–1958* (1958).
Peiss, Kathy. *Cheap Amusements: Working Women and Leisure in Turn-of-the-Century New York* (1986).
Robson, John, ed., *Baird's Manual of American College Fraternities*. 17th ed. (1963).
Rosenberg, Rosalind. "The Academic Prism: The New View of American Woman." In *Women of America: A History*, edited by Carol Ruth Berkin and Mary Beth Norton (1979).
Rousmaniere, John P. "Cultural Hybrid in the Slums: The College Woman and the Settlement House, 1889–1894." *American Quarterly* 22 (Spring 1970): 45–66.
Rudnick, Lois. "A Feminist American Success Myth: Jane Addams's Twenty Years at Hull-House." In *Tradition and the Talents of Women*, edited by Florence Howe (1991).
Sealander, Judith, and Dorothy Smith. "The Rise and Fall of Feminist Organizations in the 1970s: Dayton as a Case Study." *Feminist Studies* 12 (Summer 1986): 320–341.
Sklar, Kathryn Kish. "Hull-House in the 1890s: A Community of Women Reformers." In *Unequal Sisters: A Multicultural Reader in U.S. Women's History*, edited by Ellen Carol DuBois and Vicki L. Ruiz (1990).
Talbot, Marion, and Lois Kimball Mathews Rosenberry. *The History of the American Association of University Women, 1881–1931* (1931).
Wolfe, Allis Rosenberg. "Women, Consumerism, and the National Consumer's League in the Progressive Era, 1900–1923." *Labor History* 16 (1975).
Worrell, Dorothy. *The Women's Municipal League of Boston: A History of Thirty-five Years of Civic Endeavor, 1908–1943* (1943).

— NANCY G. ISENBERG

WORK AND MINORITIES

See MINORITIES AND WORK

Photo Credits

Page Number	*Description*	*Credit*
8	Boy Scouts, 1925	Minnesota Historical Society/Corbis
17	Spiritual Singer	Corbis-Bettmann
25	Duke Ellington	Underwood & Underwood/Corbis-Bettmann
32	Girls on Farm	Minnesota Historical/Corbis
40	FSA Client	Library of Congress/Corbis
49	Catholic School	Library of Congress/Corbis
61	Acupuncture Points	Library of Congress/Corbis
63	Colombian Exposition	Library of Congress/Corbis
73	J.P. Morgan	Corbis-Bettmann
82	Steamship	Library of Congress/Corbis
89	Breakers, Newport	Neil Rabinowitz/Corbis
102	Newspaper Boy	Library of Congress/Corbis
111	Old South Church	Library of Congress/Corbis
121	Los Angeles Skyline	Philip James Corwin/Corbis
126	Cotton Mather	Library of Congress/Corbis
138	Nineteenth Century Dress	Hulton-Deutsch Collection/Corbis
146	Harvard College	Corbis-Bettmann
162	Chrysler Building	Library of Congress/Corbis
173	Samuel Morse	Library of Congress/Corbis
181	Leonard Bernstein	Library of Congress/Corbis
190	Bill Monroe	UPI/Corbis-Bettmann
202	1950s Family	Corbis-Bettmann
209	Model T Ford	Corbis-Bettmann
222	Civil War Cemetery	U.S. Army Military History Institute/Corbis
235	Mormon Family	Corbis-Bettmann
241	Daycare	Annie Griffiths Belt/Corbis
247	United Artists Board	UPI/Corbis-Bettmann
255	Walt Disney	UPI/Corbis-Bettmann
268	Leadbelly	UPI/Corbis-Bettmann
279	Ray Kroc	Corbis-Bettmann
287	Black Masons	Library of Congress/Corbis
295	Joseph Brant	Corbis-Bettmann
313	Negro Laundress	Corbis-Bettmann
325	Homestead	UPI/Corbis-Bettmann
333	Operation at Bellevue	Corbis-Bettmann
345	African-American Maid	Corbis-Bettmann
354	Family in Tenement	Corbis-Bettmann
368	Laurel and Hardy	Corbis-Bettmann
380	Henry Wadsworth Longfellow	Hulton-Deutsch Collection/Corbis
387	William Dean Howells	Library of Congress/Corbis
394	Common Sense	Corbis-Bettmann
406	Kennedy Funeral	UPI/Corbis-Bettmann
414	Packing Tobacco	Library of Congress/Corbis
427	Textile Mill	Lee Snider/Corbis
438	Women in Factory, W.W.I	The National Archives/Corbis
454	Cesar Chavez	UPI/Corbis-Bettmann

Page Number	*Description*	*Credit*
465	Railroad Vista	Hulton-Deutsch Collection/Corbis
474	Couple on Beach	Tony Arruza/Corbis
490	Reading, 1949	Library of Congress/Corbis
502	Nineteenth Century Couple	Corbis-Bettmann
504	Walden	Corbis-Bettmann
515	Marshall McLuhan	UPI/Corbis-Bettmann
529	John Halsted, X-Ray	Corbis-Bettmann
538	Slaves Picking Cotton	Corbis-Bettmann
551	Teddy Roosevelt, John Muir	Corbis-Bettmann
559	Riverfront Pittsburgh	E.O. Hoppé/Corbis
567	Mississippi Flood Victim	Library of Congress/Corbis
571	Mammoth Springs, Yellowstone	Library of Congress/Corbis
578	Men in Saloon	Corbis-Bettmann
593	Duck & Cover Drill	UPI/Corbis-Bettmann
603	Retirement Home	Charles E. Rotkin/Corbis
616	White Robed Angels	UPI/Corbis-Bettmann
624	Plantation House	Corbis-Bettmann
638	Minstrel Entertainer	Hulton-Deutsch Collection/Corbis
644	Banneker's Almanack	Corbis-Bettmann
654	Police Gazette	Corbis-Bettmann
661	Julia Ward Howe	Library of Congress/Corbis
672	Magazines	Library of Congress/Corbis
689	Daniel Webster	Gleason's Pictorial Drawing Room Companion/Corbis
699	Smithsonian	G.E. Kidder Smith/Corbis
712	John Dewey	Library of Congress/Corbis
719	Smallpox Vaccine	Corbis-Bettmann
733	FDR Radio Address	Corbis-Bettmann
753	Cornell University	UPI/Corbis-Bettmann
757	Elvis Presley	The National Archives/Corbis
768	Bob Marley	Library of Congress/Corbis
780	Horsedrawn Thresher	Library of Congress/Corbis
789	Sharecropper	USDA Forest Service/Corbis
801	Cattle Ranch	Kevin R. Morris/Corbis
811	George Washington Carver	The National Archives/Corbis
825	Dance Hall	Library of Congress/Corbis
836	Slaves for Sale	Corbis-Bettmann
854	John L. Sullivan	Corbis-Bettmann
860	Ty Cobb	Corbis-Bettmann
875	Suburban Houses	Franklin McMahon/Corbis
888	Alexander Graham-Bell	Corbis-Bettmann
897	Moonlanding	Corbis-Bettmann
909	Walter Cronkite	UPI/Corbis-Bettmann
919	Early Vaudeville	Corbis-Bettmann
930	Shakespeare in the Park	UPI/Corbis-Bettmann
939	Elevated Train	Library of Congress/Corbis
951	Camping 1950s	Corbis-Bettmann
963	New York Public Library	Corbis-Bettmann
973	Central Park	UPI/Corbis-Bettmann
983	Goldmining Town	Leonard de Silva/Corbis
1000	Rosie the Riveter	The National Archives/Corbis
1008	YWCA Supper	Corbis-Bettmann

Index

C

D

F

J

O

Q

R

U